THE COMPLETE

Chicago Cubs

THE TOTAL ENCYCLOPEDIA OF THE TEAM

THE COMPLETE
Chicago
Cubs

THE TOTAL ENCYCLOPEDIA OF THE TEAM

With text by Derek Gentile

STATISTICAL INFORMATION PROVIDED BY STATS INC.

BLACK DOG
& LEVENTHAL
PUBLISHERS
NEW YORK

PUBLISHED BY

Black Dog & Leventhal Publishers, Inc.
151 West 19th Street
New York, NY 10011

DISTRIBUTED BY

Workman Publishing Company
708 Broadway
New York, NY 10003

Statistics provided by Stats Inc.

Manufactured in The United States of America

Cover design by 27.12 Design, Ltd.

Interior design by Martin Lubin Graphic Design

Cover photographs © AP / Wide World Photos and Transcendental Graphics

ISBN 1-57912-241-8

h g f e d c b a

Library of Congress Cataloging-in-Publication Data

Gentile, Derek.
   The complete Chicago Cubs : the total encyclopedia of the team / by Derek Gentile.
       p.   cm.
    ISBN 1-57912-241-8
1.   Chicago Cubs (Baseball team)—History.   2. Chicago Cubs (Baseball team)—Statistics.   3. Baseball players—United States—Biography. I. Title.
GV875.C6 G46 2002
796.357'64'0977311—dc21
                                    2001056630

Acknowledgments

This book, as was my previous tome on the New York Yankees, was a total team effort. It sounds corny but it is true.

I'd like to thank my mother and father for their support in this, and my four sisters and their families: Mary Beth and Ed Chapman and Nicholas; Melanie Gelaznik and Kane and Kyle; Hilary Gentile and Johnny Babeau and Karla and Doug Ball. Your support means so much to me.

Thanks too, to my tireless researchers, Brian Sullivan, sports editor of the Berkshire Eagle and Jack Passetto of radio station WSBS. A tip of the hat to the indefatigable librarians in the Baseball Hall of Fame who met our every need cheerfully and quickly.

Supportive friends and co-workers included IBM honcho Donna Mattoon, former Eagle reporter Tim Cebula, Lisi De Bourbon of New York City, Eric Malinowski at WSBS and the boys at Tune Street. Mention must be made of Erik Bruun, a fellow author at Black Dog, who got me out of a couple manuscript-related jams during this time. He is the best of people.

Thanks also to Susan Strong of Lenox, who provided technical and spiritual assistance when my first computer bit the dust. Thanks also go to the fellows at Practical Solutions and David Long at Zenn New Media, whose suggestions were helpful.

Three editors were key in the creation of this book: Michael Driscoll, now a big shot newspaper editor in West Virginia, the soft-spoken but hard-as-nails Will Kiester, who was kind enough to work with me on the book for a time, and the extremely patient and understanding Becky Koh, who did an excellent job turning my hardscrabble meanderings into something meaningful. All three are pros.

Finally, my deepest thanks to J.P. Leventhal for actually agreeing to pay me to do something I love so well. He is a gentleman of the highest order.

Contents

The Story of the Chicago Cubs

The History of the Chicago Cubs

1 THE DYNASTY OF CAP AND ALBERT

The Chicago franchise of the National League (NL) has been in one location longer than any other operation in big-league history, and since 1876, there has been a Chicago team visible in the senior circuit standings. As well as geographic stability, the team was also one of the most successful franchises of the 19th century.

Chicago continued that success into the early part of the 20th century; however, bad luck and, perhaps more tellingly, questionable management policies have caused the franchise to struggle mightily for most of the past 60 years. It has only been recently that the team seems back on a track that might give their loyal but hardened fans what they so deeply desire: a world championship.

The Chicago team has its roots in the old National Association, which might be called the first major professional league. The National Association began in 1871, and the Chicago White Stockings, as they were called then, fielded a very competitive team that first year, finishing second.

It was a feat all the more remarkable for the White Stockings had to play most of their games on the road. Midway through the season, the Great Fire of 1871 destroyed their Chicago ballpark and their equipment. It took the White Stockings two years to recover financially, and the city didn't field a team until the 1874 season. Chicago finished fifth and sixth in the league in 1874 and 1875, respectively.

But events were conspiring in another city to bring Chicago to the top rung of the baseball ladder. Albert Goodwill Spalding had been the greatest pitcher of the National Association, having led his Boston Red Stockings to the National Association title from 1872 through 1875. Spald-ing himself led the circuit in victories for five consecutive years.

The National Association was national in name only. The truth is, it consisted of only a few franchises located in small cities such as Fort Wayne, Indiana, Hartford, Connecticut, and Keokuk, Iowa. Between 1871 and 1875, the number of franchises in the National Association was 9, 11, 9, 8 and 13. Teams folded almost without notice and players were not afraid to jump from team to team.

The league itself had a bad reputation. Although the majority of the players behaved themselves, many were drunken rowdies who berated and at times fought with the umpires and each other. The ballpark for many years was not deemed an acceptable place to take women and children.

Spalding, though, was sort of the Cal Ripken Jr. of his day. He was very aware of his status as a star player in the league and felt he had a responsibility to that status. He did not smoke and refused to enter a saloon. He was a stickler for physical fitness and urged his fellow players to stay in shape during the off-season.

Spalding was also a pragmatic businessman. He knew professional baseball as it was being run at that point did not look like a candidate for longevity. Newspapers across the country were already calling for its dissolution. Changes—major changes—needed to be made. Spalding envisioned a league of franchises in larger cities with players under contract, stable management and high-quality umpiring.

That was clearly not going to happen in the National Association, so Spalding decided to start over. In 1875 he secretly signed a contract to play with the White Stockings the following year. In addition, to ensure that his team would be successful, Spalding lured three Red Stockings stars to go with him: catcher Jim "Deacon" White, second baseman Cal McVey and outfielder Ross Barnes, a childhood friend.

Albert Goodwill Spalding

Soon after Spalding enticed the three to come with him, the whole scheme became public. Although he was clearly going against every principle he had espoused by signing with one team while under contract to another, he wasn't at all repentant. Spalding coldly told Boston manager Harry Wright that if Wright and the rest of the league didn't like it, then he would simply start another league.

Of course, that was what he'd been plotting all along. Spalding had had conversations with several potential team owners for his new league, and pretty much had his ducks in order when news of the signings came out. By the end of the 1875 season, the writing was on the scoreboard: the National Association would be dissolved, and in its place would be the National League of Professional Baseball Clubs.

Spalding's co-conspirator was William Hulbert, a successful Chicago businessman whom Spalding recruited to take over the presidency of the Chicago franchise. In Hulbert, Spalding had a kindred spirit, a baseball fanatic who wanted to clean up the game and put a better product on the field.

On February 2, 1876, Hulbert met with a number of potential franchise owners in New York City. To ensure that the plan would have the support of the eastern ball clubs, Hulbert moved that Morgan Bulkeley of the Hartford club be named president, with Nick Young of the Washington franchise named secretary. The nominations were accepted, and the National League announced that play would begin in April. The NL absorbed many of the Association's old players.

Meanwhile, Spalding and J. Walter Spalding, his younger brother, moved to Chicago. In addition to pitching for the White Stockings, Spalding and his brother planned to open a "sports emporium" that sold baseball equipment and other "goods of a sporting nature." It was the beginning of the Spalding sporting-goods empire.

Along with Barnes, White and McVey, Albert Spalding also recruited another ballplayer, Adrian "Cap" Anson from the Philadelphia franchise, to play in Chicago. Anson was not as well known as the other players, but Spalding loved his athleticism and versatility. Originally, Anson played mostly third base and caught, but over the course of his 22-year National League career, he would go on to play virtually every position on the field.

The 1876 Chicago White Stockings dominated the inaugural National League season. Barnes hit .429 that season, which remains a team record 125 years later. He also scored 126 runs, 54 more runs than the second-highest scorer in the league;

Cap Anson in action
at 1st base *c*. 1892

additionally, he had 138 hits, 27 more than the runner-up. White led the league in RBIs with 60; Anson was third in batting average with a .359 mark; McVey was fifth in batting average at .347. On July 22 and then on the 25th, he made six hits in seven at-bats, a remarkable back-to-back feat that remains a Cub record for most hits in consecutive games.

Anson, clearly a star in his first big-league season with Chicago, was called "Baby" Anson and "Infant" Anson, even though he was over 6' and a bulky 202 pounds. Meanwhile, Spalding led all pitchers with 47 wins and was second in the league in shutouts with eight. The White Stockings won the pennant with a 52-14 mark, six games ahead of St. Louis and Hartford, who tied for second place. The White Stockings' first season in the National League was judged a resounding success.

The next year, the team struggled, finishing fifth in a six-team league with a 26-33 mark. But for Spalding, the season was terrific. His pitching arm, worn out from six years of hard throwing in the big leagues, was nearly burned out in 1877 and he pitched infrequently. But he played a lot of first base that year, and early in the season, he wore a black leather glove with the fingers cut out and some padding in the palm. Other players had worn gloves, but such a practice was generally considered "sissified." Virtually everyone in the bigs opted to go bare-handed.

This was different, however. The great Albert Spalding was now wearing a glove, and he clearly did not consider it emasculating. Moreover, he could just as clearly catch a hard-thrown ball much better with a glove than with his bare hand. As other players began asking him where and how they could get such equipment, Spalding was happy to direct them to his Chicago store, where the gloves were selling between $1 and $3. Almost immediately, the sporting-goods business took off.

In addition, Spalding also outbid his friend Al Reach that year to publish the official *National League Guide*. The book sold fairly well, but Spalding had an ulterior motive. For the first time that year, the *Guide* published an official rule book. And, as part of the "official rules of base ball," Spalding, through the *Guide,* declared that only Spalding balls could be used in games.

As self-serving as this sounds, Spalding had a good reason to order teams to supply his balls for official games: consistency. Prior to the installation of this rule, the home team supplied all the balls for games. This led to wildly differing standards in the quality of the balls. Some clubs made an effort to provide new balls for games. Many clubs did not, leading to pitchers throwing balls that were often soft, lopsided or badly damaged. In fact, the term "he tore the cover off the ball" was not hyperbolic in the early years of the National League. It often happened when a batter hit a damaged ball exceptionally hard. This practice drove Spalding and his fellow pitchers throughout the league up a wall. Although it clearly put money in Al Spalding's pocket, the new rule was hailed by virtually everyone as a good idea.

Chicago continued to struggle in 1878 and 1879, even with the enigmatic but talented Terry Larkin on the mound. Spalding and Anson, who had been named to the manager's post after the 1879 season, were looking for a pitcher. The White Stockings' everyday lineup was solid during this period, with standouts Edward "Ned" Williamson at third base, hard-hitting George Gore and Abner Dalrymple in the outfield and canny catcher Frank "Silver" Flint manning the backstopping chores.

Prior to the 1880 season, Anson and Spalding secured the services of not one but two stellar "twirlers": Larry Corcoran and Fred Goldsmith. Corcoran was a terrific all-around athlete who had an excellent fastball and legendary endurance. Goldsmith, meanwhile, was one of the first practitioners of the "curver," or curveball, a ball that

seemed to curve downward just as it reached the plate. The pitch was a devastating weapon in its own right, and Goldsmith added to that a pretty good fastball and a change-of-pace pitch. But the key pickup that year turned out to be a brawny, cocky Irish kid from Troy, New York, who had been playing for the Cincinnati franchise in 1878 and 1879.

Anson had already recognized that Mike "King" Kelly was one of the best players in the game. Acquiring him would be a coup for Chicago. After several weeks of haggling (Kelly was young, but he knew he was good), Kelly came aboard, ostensibly as the team's starting right fielder. But such was his versatility, he also played both other outfield positions, as well as third base, second base, shortstop and catcher. He even pitched a few games.

Kelly's athletic ability was at a higher level than most of his peers, but what really separated him from others was his innovative play. That prowess endeared him to the fans. In those days of only one umpire, who would call balls and strikes from behind the pitcher, Kelly would routinely cut across the infield from first to third base or from second to home as the umpire was trying to follow a ball hit into the outfield. The Chicago fans roared at his audacity; opposing fans and players howled at his cheating ways.

He was not primarily a catcher until his later career, but while with Chicago, he worked with Corcoran and Goldsmith on a series of signals that would enable him to determine from behind the plate what his pitchers would be throwing to him.

In addition to cutting dramatically into the number of broken fingers and smashed joints, it also enabled Kelly to work out a strategy for pitching to individual batters. It was clearly nothing like the sophisticated hitting charts pitchers and catchers have today, but it gave Chicago a leg up on their opponents, who did not employ such strategies.

He knew the rule book inside out. The late Robert Smith, a baseball historian and author of the first comprehensive history of baseball, noted that Kelly once took advantage of a rule that allowed for substitution "at any time" in a game.

Kelly was on the bench in a game in the late 1880s when a fly ball drifted his way, too far for either his catcher or third baseman to handle. Kelly leaped off the bench, shouted, "Kelly in as catcher!" and made the catch. The umpire ruled it no catch. Kelly whipped out a copy of the rules, which he had in his back pocket, and pointed to the applicable statute. The umpire reversed his call. Kelly simply knew how to win games in more ways than anyone of his time.

The pieces were all in place for a strong White Stockings team in 1880, and the squad surpassed all expectations. On July 8, Chicago defeated Providence 5-4 to win its 21st game in a row. This was a streak that would be surpassed only by the 1916 New York Giants, who would win 26 games in succession.

That win gave Chicago a 35-3 record, which essentially ended the pennant race for the year. Anson's White Stockings finished the year at 67-17, 15 games ahead of second-place Providence. The team's .798 winning percentage remains an unofficial National League record, because the NL didn't officially begin tallying such percentages until 1884.

Chicago dominated the league. It scored 538 runs, 119 more than runner-up Providence. The team's .279 batting average was 26 points higher than the second-best average, which belonged to Boston.

Dalrymple led the league in runs scored with 91, Kelly was third with 72. Anson, Kelly and Gore were the top RBI men with 74, 60 and 47, respectively. Gore led the league in batting average with a .360 mark, Anson was second at .362, Dalrymple was fourth at .335 and shortstop Tom Burns was fifth with a .333 mark.

Goldsmith and Corcoran were 1-2 in winning percentage, while Corcoran and Goldsmith were first and second, respectively, in strikeouts per game. On August 19, Corcoran threw a no-hitter against Boston. It was the first of three no-hitters Corcoran would toss, which is still a team record.

It was the first year of a decision by Anson to "rotate" his pitching staff by allowing the two to pitch on alternate days, with a day of rest. It was a radical theory at the time, as teams generally went with one pitcher throughout the season, giving him only sporadic days off. It was a hugely successful innovation. That success was not lost on the rest of the league, who soon began to emulate Anson's practice.

The 1881 season was more of the same. The White Stockings shot out to a big lead early in the season and won the pennant with a 56-36 mark, nine games ahead of Providence.

Once again, the NL statistics bore the names of a lot of Chicago ballplayers. Gore, Kelly and Dalrymple were 1-2-3 in runs scored with 86, 84 and 72, respectively. Anson and Dalrymple were 1-2 in hits with 137 and 117, respectively. Anson and Kelly were first and third in RBIs with 82 and 55, respectively. Kelly led the league in doubles with 27, while Anson won the batting championship with a .399 average. Tom Burns hit four home runs, which put him fourth in the league.

Corcoran and Goldsmith were again two of the league's best pitchers. Corcoran won 31 games, Goldsmith 24 (Kelly won the other game, in relief). Corcoran was fifth in the league in strikeouts with 130, Goldsmith was third in the league with five shutouts. Significantly, although both men pitched more than 300 innings, Corcoran was seventh in the league in that category, Goldsmith 10th. Although every team in the NL now had at least two pitchers on the roster, none rotated their staffs as consistently as Anson. And, of course, none had as much consistent success.

On April 10, 1882, just as the season was about to start, Chicago owner Will Hulbert died of heart failure. Spalding mourned Hulbert's loss as one of the innovative founders of the National League. As the majority stockholder at that point, Spalding quickly secured financing and took over control of the team.

The 1882 National League season finally featured a pennant race. Providence, featuring pitcher Charles "Old Hoss" Radbourne, held the league lead until late in the season. Chicago, trailing by 8 games at one point, went on to win 17 of their last 18 games to capture their third consecutive championship.

The White Stockings faced Providence in the last month of the season in a key three-game set in Chicago. Not surprisingly, it was Kelly who made the key play in the key game that pushed the White Stockings to victory.

Trailing 4-3 with one out in the bottom of the ninth, Kelly slapped a single up the middle. The next batter, Tom Burns, hit a slow roller to Providence shortstop George Wright. Wright rushed toward the second-base bag to touch it and start a double play that would have won the game for Providence. But Kelly got to the bag first.

In his autobiography, Kelly claimed his right arm "inadvertently" came up as he was stepping on the base. That was fortunate because Kelly's inadvertent arm movement jostled Wright, who threw the ball over his first baseman's head. Kelly raced around third to score, and Burns was right behind him as befuddled Providence players searched in vain for the ball in the stands.

Chicago went on to win the next two games with Providence, and as the White Stockings were going 9-1 the rest of the way, Providence went 2-8. One of those games, on September 20, was Corcoran's second career no-hitter, a 5-0 win over Worcester.

Providence manager Harry Wright (George's older brother) was furious and declared (after he had gotten out of Chicago, of course) that Kelly and his "infernal tricks" had won the game for the White Stockings.

Kelly heard about Wright's comments and after the season sought him out.

"I have never played this game to hurt another player," he told Wright. "But I always play to win."

Wright could probably have argued that, but he was impressed that Kelly went out of his way to present his side of the story.

The Chicago squad was again well represented in major league statistics, as Gore led the league in runs scored with 99 and walks with 29, Kelly was once again the best in doubles with 37,

Anson topped the circuit in RBIs with 83 and Corcoran led in winning percentage with a .692 mark and ERA with a 1.95 figure.

This was also the first year a second professional league, the American Association, had sprung up. The Cincinnati team of the American Association, winners of that pennant, agitated for a championship series between the two squads. Cincinnati had been kicked out of the National League a few years before for violating the National League's ban against selling liquor at the ballpark. The club joined the American Association and won the pennant by 11½ games.

Neither Anson nor Spalding saw any advantage for Chicago, as both considered the American Association to be little more than a pretty good minor league. But eventually, the White Stockings agreed to a two-game series, with both games to be played in Cincinnati. Cincinnati won the first game, 4-0. But the next day, a well-rested Corcoran tossed a three-hitter, and Chicago won the second contest, 2-0. There were not enough games played in the series for this to be dubbed a championship playoff, but as it was technically the first postseason in baseball history, it deserves note.

Although the White Stockings had to battle their way to a third pennant that year, Chicago dominated the National League from 1880 to 1882. Kelly believed that his White Stockings, many times, had the opposition beaten before they took the field. That may have been true. The Chicago team was a squad of physical giants, at least for that era. Anson, Kelly, Gore, Dalrymple, Goldsmith and Flint all stood over 6'. Kelly in particular was a tremendous physical specimen who undoubtedly oozed confidence as soon as he stepped onto the field.

In 1883 Boston, led by pitcher James "Grasshopper Jim" Whitney and a strong supporting cast, won the National League pennant with a 63-35 mark, four games better than Chicago. The Boston-Chicago rivalry was a hot one and Kelly admitted years later that virtually every time the two teams played, he was approached by gamblers who would offer to pay him to throw a contest.

The basic reason Chicago lost the pennant that year was that injuries had taken their toll. Kelly played the last two months with a broken finger, as did Flint. Corcoran and Goldsmith had arm trouble. Boston was healthier, and it showed.

Prior to the 1884 season, Spalding rewrote the ground rules at Lakefront Park. Before the 1884 season, balls that sailed into the park's extremely close (196 feet) right- or left-field (180 feet) fences were ground-rule doubles. In 1884 they would be designated as home runs. On May 29, fans got a glimpse of what was to come when five Chicago players hit balls over the right-field fence for home runs in a 10-4 win over Detroit. The next day, White Stockings third baseman Ned Williamson became the first player in National League history to hit three home runs in a game as Chicago routed Detroit again, 12-2.

The White Stockings went on to hit a record 142 home runs that year (Boston was second with 38), as Williamson led the league with 27, including 25 at home. Williamson's record would not be broken until Babe Ruth of the Boston Red Sox hit 29 in 1919. And the team record would not be cracked until the 1927 Yankees came along and struck 158.

All the home runs, though, didn't help. Chicago finished fifth, with a 62-50 mark, as their pitching once again faltered. The White Stockings could still hit, but Goldsmith was burning out. He would start only 21 games that year, and post a 9-11 record. Corcoran was still pretty good, but he had to do the lion's share of the work, with a whopping 60 starts, which produced a 35-23 mark.

That season turned out to be Corcoran's final full season in Chicago. He was traded to the Giants early in the 1885 season and was out of baseball by 1887, his arm shot. Four years later, he would be dead of Bright's disease, a degenerative liver ailment.

Following the 1884 season, the team had some hope for the future. The extremely graceful Fred Pfeffer made his debut at second base for Chicago, and that year led second basemen in putouts,

assists, double plays and total chances per game at his position. And Anson had found a pitcher, although John Clarkson would not emerge as a star until the next season.

Clarkson was the youngest son of a ballplaying family: his father and older brother both played in the major leagues. Anson discovered him pitching for a minor league team in 1884 in Saginaw, Michigan. When that league folded in midseason, Anson quickly snapped up Clarkson for Chicago. He pitched in only 14 games in 1884, but struck out 102 batters.

Clarkson was possibly the smartest pitcher of his era. He possessed a deadly curveball, and could throw his fastball at various speeds to confuse hitters. He was one of the first pitchers to study a batter's strengths and weaknesses and use that knowledge while on the mound. He also would polish his belt buckle and shine it in batters' eyes as he wound up to pitch.

Chicago moved into a new stadium, West Side Park, in 1885, and the players' home run totals fell back to normal levels, as the park sported deeper right- and left-field fencing (both were 216 feet)

As the 1885 season opened, Anson had planned to use Clarkson and Corcoran in his rotation, starting the veteran Corcoran in the first game. But Corcoran looked shaky in a 3-1 loss to St. Louis. Clarkson pitched well in a 9-4 win over St. Louis the next day, allowing only two earned runs. For the next few weeks, Anson alternated the two. Clarkson went 7-2, Corcoran 5-2 during this span, but Corcoran was clearly struggling and began sitting out starts with arm troubles.

Anson, the man who had espoused alternating pitchers to ensure success, had to throw that plan out the window. Clarkson started 17 of 24 games in June, and went 15-1 in that span. The other starts were alternated between rookie pitcher Ted Kennedy (hurriedly signed at the beginning of June when Corcoran went down), Pfeffer and Williamson.

When sportswriters began pressing Anson on whether Clarkson could function as the White Stockings' sole starter, Anson breezily replied that

Chicago's
West Side Park

Clarkson's "drop curve" (what we would call a sinker ball these days) didn't take that much out of Clarkson's arm, and he could easily start several games in a row.

Meanwhile, with Clarkson having one of the great pitching seasons of all time, Chicago was battling the Giants for first place. Offensively, Anson, Kelly, Gore and Dalrymple, the usual suspects, were having great years at the plate. Pfeffer was once again playing second base like he owned it, and Burns and Williamson were solid at shortstop and third base, respectively. In truth, Anson didn't really believe he could win the pennant with one man on the mound. He scoured the country for another pitcher. He finally found one in July, signing Jim McCormick for the rest of the year.

But Clarkson was doing fine. He won his 30th game in late July, and was 41-12 at the end of August. He improved that record to 44-12 by beating Buffalo three times in four days to open

the month of September. Clarkson kept winning (he was 12-1 in September), and the Giants couldn't keep up. The White Stockings won their fourth National League crown in six years, clinching first place when McCormick beat Philadelphia on October 6.

Clarkson had gone an improbable 53-16 with an exceptional 1.86 ERA. He won nine more games than the second-place finisher, struck out 60 more batters and pitched 68 complete games, 13 more than New York's Michael "Mickey" Welch. Had there been an MVP award, Clarkson would have been the unanimous choice.

Meanwhile, as the season wound down, St. Louis, the champions of the American Association, were negotiating to play a world's championship of baseball series with the winners of the National League. Neither Anson nor Spalding had much interest. A three-game exhibition series in 1884 between National League champ Providence and American Association winner New York had drawn an average of about 1,200 fans, including an embarrassing 500 for the third contest. St. Louis persisted, though. So Spalding agreed to play one game in Chicago, three in St. Louis and several other games in Pittsburgh and Cincinnati. All would be dubbed exhibitions, not championship tilts.

Few of the White Stockings players had any interest, either. Kelly and Gore believed their contracts did not include postseason games. Clarkson was exhausted and wanted to return to his home town of Cambridge, Massachusetts. In addition, the total winning share was $1,000, less than $100 per man for the series. Spalding finally convinced the White Stockings to play the series for pride. Later Kelly wryly noted that pride was almost all there was to play for—the money was so bad.

Clarkson struggled in the first game, which was called on account of darkness after eight innings. The two teams had tied, 5-5.

In the second contest the next day, McCormick didn't pitch much better, but Chicago led the game, 5-4, in the sixth, when the St. Louis players walked off the field, protesting several calls by the umpire. At that point, Anson, deeply embarrassed, was ready to throw in the towel. But St. Louis owner Chris Von der Ahe promised his team would practice no more high jinks, and the White Stockings continued.

They probably should not have. Gore had already gotten himself tossed out of the series by Anson for coming to the park drunk before the first game. Kelly, Burns and several others were staying out till all hours prior to the contests and it showed in their play. St. Louis won the next two games, 7-4 and 3-2. But Chicago bounced back with a pair of wins by identical 9-2 scores.

Von der Ahe then declared that the second game should not count because the umpiring was so bad. Thus, the seventh and final game, to be played in Cincinnati, would be for the championship of the two leagues. Anson, and probably Spalding, were basically just trying to end the thing, so they agreed.

Bad decision. Clarkson was scheduled to start and had no interest in doing so. He got to the park so drunk that day he was sent home. McCormick, who had pitched the day before and thought he was done for the year, was sent out there. He was shelled, and the Brown Stockings won the game, 13-4.

At the end of the series, St. Louis fans celebrated. That is, until Von der Ahe declared, in the interest of fairness, that the second game should count after all. This left the series with each team having three wins and a tie. Although it was never conclusively proven, many St. Louis players later complained that Von der Ahe agreed to the tie to withhold the winner's share from his players. For what it's worth, Spalding arranged for the Chicago players to get their $500, or about $40 per man. The whole thing was, in the words of Kelly years later, "a terrible mess."

The 1886 Chicago White Stockings won their fifth National League championship in seven years, sporting a 90-34 record, which placed them 2½ games above the second-place Detroit Wolverines. Kelly was the best player in the league, winning the batting title with a .388 mark, scored a league-leading 155 runs and was second in walks with 83 and third in doubles with 32.

The defense was solid. Burns at third, Williamson at shortstop, Pfeffer at second base and Anson at first were dubbed by sportswriters the "Stone Wall Infield" because baseballs rarely trickled through that quartet for base hits.

Kelly, Gore, Dalrymple and Jimmy Ryan alternated in the outfield, and Kelly also alternated the catching chores with Silver Flint. In fact, Kelly also played all four infield positions that season in another display of his amazing versatility.

Clarkson won 35 games, McCormick won 31 and newcomer John "Jocko" Flynn won 24 as Anson expanded his rotation to three pitchers. Although the Wolverines were in first place for much of the season, Chicago swept a key three-game series late in the year to clinch the pennant.

Once again, the White Stockings and American Association champ St. Louis would meet in a winner-take-all series. Anson wanted a nine-game series, but St. Louis lobbied for a seven-game set. Seven games it would be, with the first three in Chicago and the final four in St. Louis. This year, the money was better, as Von der Ahe and Spalding each put up $7,000 for the winner-take-all series.

The White Stockings won two of the first three games in Chicago, as Clarkson tossed a five-hitter for a 5-0 Chicago win in the first contest. But the Browns' Bob Caruthers tossed a two-hitter in the next game, a 12-0 St. Louis rout that featured 12 White Stockings errors.

Maybe it was playoff jitters, but Anson in particular knew better. Kelly, Gore, Ryan, Dalrymple, Burns and Williamson were all staying up late. Worse, McCormick, the starter in the second game, appeared to some reporters covering the game to be drunk on the mound.

It is difficult to tell how much boosterism comes to play in many of these old-time reports of the games. The Chicago newsmen were quick to point out McCormick's apparent difficulty that day. The problem is, these were some of the same sportswriters who were leading the crowd in cheers for the White Stockings and directing obscene chants at St. Louis players.

For whatever reason, Anson sent McCormick home. In the third game, in St. Louis, Clarkson scattered nine hits in an 11-4 Chicago win. But with McCormick out and Flynn with a sore arm, Clarkson pitched the next day as well. He was effective, allowing only six hits, but St. Louis turned four Chicago errors into runs in an 8-5 Brown Stockings win.

St. Louis won the next game, 10-3, as Anson was forced to start Ned Williamson and come in with Ryan in relief. Game 6 saw Clarkson return to the mound and fire a five-hitter, but the Browns won the game in the 10th when Curt Welch stole home to break a 3-3 tie to give St. Louis a 4-3 victory. The series went to the Brown Stockings, four games to two.

Spalding was embarrassed and furious. In addition to the late-night action on the part of his stars, there were rumors that the two teams planned to split the prize money regardless of who

won. Arlie Latham, a member of the winning team, years later admitted to baseball historian Robert Smith that his team had indeed split the proceeds with the Chicagoans.

Spalding knew at the time and didn't care. All he knew was that Kelly in particular was leading a team of drunkards onto the field. Changes, he felt, would have to be made.

So it was that prior to the 1887 season, Albert Spalding sold Mike "King" Kelly to the Boston franchise for $10,000, the most money ever spent on a baseball player up to that time. Outfielder George Gore, another drinker, was sold to the New York Giants.

It was a crossroads of sorts for the franchise. For Spalding and Anson, both disciples and practitioners of clean living, it was something that had to be done. The carousers, or at least the ringleaders, were out.

The White Stockings finished in third place in 1887, eight games behind Detroit. Kelly and Gore were missed, but Chicago's biggest problem was its pitching staff. McCormick's arm was shot from overuse and he was traded. Jocko Flynn tried to pitch through his pain in the last month of the previous season and ended up damaging his shoulder for good. He was released. McCormick, traded to Pittsburgh, was out of baseball by the end of the year, and Flynn never won another game in the majors.

That left Clarkson to put up another amazing performance, and that he did: earning 38 of Chicago's 71 wins, and leading the league in innings pitched, strikeouts, complete games and games started. Spalding quickly picked up a pair of rookies, 21-year-old lefty George Van Haltren and 22-year-old righty Mark Baldwin, to fill in when Clarkson needed a break.

But both were just barely average. Baldwin was 18-17 that year, one of only two times in his seven-year career he would be over .500 for a season. Van Haltren was 11-7, which would turn out to be easily the best mark of his nine-year career. With Clarkson pitching in virtually every big game, the White Stockings hung around until August before falling out of the race.

Clarkson turned in another superior performance in Chicago in 1888, winning 33 games. But he wasn't happy in Chicago and asked Anson to allow him to return to the Boston area, which was his home. Anson assented and then sold Clarkson to the Boston team for another $10,000. Clarkson was, of course, another individual who enjoyed a drink or two, or three, so Anson was antsy to get rid of him. He also believed that after pitching more than 1,700 innings in the past four years, Clarkson's arm was ready to fall off. It wasn't. Clarkson pitched for Boston for almost five years, helping them to a pair of National League crowns. He pitched for seven more years in all in the majors.

That 1888 season saw Anson's team in another close race. Ryan was now a star in the outfield, leading the league in home runs, hits and doubles. The Stone Wall Infield was as consistent as ever, anchored by the amazing Pfeffer, who led the league's second basemen in every defensive category imaginable. And Anson, at 36, in his 13th big league season, was terrific: he won his fourth, and final, batting championship with a .344 mark, his seventh RBI crown with 84, was second to Detroit's Dan Brouthers in runs scored with 115 and second to Ryan in hits with 177.

But the pitching was mediocre: sixth in the league in ERA, eight and last in complete games and tied for last in walks issued. The White Stockings could score runs, but too often that year their pitching failed them. Chicago finished second, nine games behind New York.

The White Stockings' last gasp of the 19th century was in 1890 and 1891. That was ironic because the White Stockings lost a number of players, including Pfeffer, Williamson and Ryan, to the newly created Players' League in 1890. The Players' League was a response by the players in the National League to the so-called reserve clause, enacted in 1879 in the National League.

The reserve clause bound players to their teams for life, or until a ball club opted to sell or release the player. The good news was that the agreement banned owners (like Spalding) from stealing players from other teams. But in addition, the owners decided what the salaries of their players would be. Superstars like Mike Kelly could often negotiate high contracts, but the majority of players' annual salaries were $2,500 or less.

Thus, prior to the 1890 season, former pitching star John Montgomery "Monte" Ward solicited backing from several wealthy entrepreneurs who agreed to form an eight-team Players' League. The league offered higher salaries and better playing conditions than the National League, and a stunning 53 percent of the men in the National League jumped to the rival league.

Anson found his team essentially gutted in 1890, except for Tom Burns, who had opted to stay. But despite losing his entire pitching staff to the Players' League, Anson had an ace in the hole: William "Wild Bill" Hutchison, a former Yale grad with a blazing fastball who would emerge that season as the best pitcher in the National League in just his second season in the majors.

Hutchison had toiled for Chicago the year before, where he had been nothing special, but he blossomed in 1890, winning 42 games and saving two more. Chicago went 84-53 and finished just behind the Brooklyn Bridegrooms for the National League championship. In 1891 Hutchison had an even better year, winning 43 games as Chicago finished 3½ games out. The Players' League had fizzled after one season, and Anson welcomed back Pfeffer—at his old salary, of course—in 1891.

But Boston, and later John McGraw's Baltimore Orioles, would dominate the National League in the 1890s. The first great dynasty in baseball had run its course.

2 TINK TO THE CRAB TO HUSK

By the mid-1890s, the White Stockings, now called by some sportswriters the Colts, were in decline. In 1891 Spalding had appointed a business acquaintance, James A. Hart, to run the day-by-day operations of the team. Spalding was becoming more involved in his sporting-goods business and it was taking up much of his time.

After naming Hart president of the team, Spalding went to Anson and took pains to assure Cap that he would continue to make managerial and personnel decisions.

But Anson didn't like it. After one season, he was openly feuding with Hart, who, in turn, criticized Anson's personnel moves to Spalding. And indeed, although Anson had signed talented outfielder Bill Lange, shortstop Bill Dahlen, third baseman Billy Everitt and pitcher Clark Griffith, Chicago finished in the middle or near the bottom of the standings from 1892 to 1897.

The 1897 season had begun with high expectations. Griffith was now the anchor of a solid staff, Dahlen and Everitt now moored the infield and Ryan continued to be a star in the outfield. But the team started slow and never really got rolling. Anson—who would *not* be the first manager to do so—blamed his players for not playing hard. Hart, meanwhile, soberly pointed out to Spalding that it might be time to replace Anson.

Hart spoke freely to the newsmen covering the team, and so it was that in the winter of 1897 Anson read in the papers that he was probably going to be released. Annoyed but unperturbed, he approached Spalding about buying the team himself. Spalding declined.

When Anson returned from a trip to Europe in February 1898, he learned that Hart had named former White Stocking star Tom Burns to manage the team. Anson was out.

Spalding clearly had mixed feelings about the deal. Anson was a longtime friend and had been one of the greatest competitors in baseball. However, he was now 45, more than a decade past the retirement age of most players of the time. A guilty Spalding arranged for a testimonial dinner for Anson and announced that the money raised, about $50,000, would go to Anson "in appreciation of what he has meant to the game."

Anson would have none of it.

"The public owes me nothing," he said, and publicly asked Spalding to call off the dinner. Soon after, he announced plans to manage the New York Giants, Chicago's longtime rival.

But he lasted only 28 games in New York, and early in the 1898 season, he retired for good.

Anson tried a number of things after leaving the game, but he found, like many players, that he was really only good at one thing: playing ball. He starred in a vaudeville show for a while and then began a number of businesses, none of which turned out very well. He stayed in the theater until his death in 1922 at age 70. His funeral in Chicago attracted one of the largest crowds in sports history.

Chicago under Burns wasn't much of an improvement. Ironically, with Griffith, Jack Taylor and James Joseph "Nixey" Callahan, Chicago's pitching staff was as good as any in the league. But the team, now professionally renamed the Orphans, because of Anson's leave-taking, had major problems scoring runs, and finished 17½ games out in 1898 and 26 games out of first in 1899.

Hart fired Burns after the 1899 season and replaced him with the utterly mediocre Tom Loftus, who led the squad to a pair of sixth-place finishes in 1900 and 1901. He was clearly not the answer, either.

Meanwhile, early in 1902, Spalding sold his interest in the team to Hart and retired as a baseball man, although he continued to run his sporting-goods operation with enormous success until his death in 1915 in San Diego. In the space of just four years, the face of the Chicago franchise had changed dramatically, and prior to the beginning of the 1902 season, it didn't look as though the changes were to the good.

But Hart's luck was about to change. After firing Loftus at the end of the 1901 campaign, Hart began a serious and studied attempt to find a manager who could turn his franchise around. His choice, Frank Selee, turned out to be perfect.

It was not, however, an easy choice. In fact, on the face of it, hiring Selee at that point in his career was a bad decision.

Selee, a New Hampshire native who never played a day in the major leagues, was nonetheless one of the most successful managers in baseball in the 1890s. He took a struggling

Frank Selee

Boston franchise and won five pennants in the decade. He was a shrewd judge of talent and a no-nonsense manager who treated his players with respect and, nonetheless, expected to be obeyed.

But he was also suffering from tuberculosis, which is why he was available in the first place, having stepped down from the Boston job at the end of the 1891 season when he believed he was too ill to continue.

But Hart visited with Selee, who didn't really want to retire, and convinced Selee to take the Chicago job. Selee's illness had flared alarmingly

midway through the 1891 season, but several months off had enabled Selee to recover. With Hart prodding him, Selee eventually believed he was fit enough to continue.

Selee's principal strength was as a judge of talent. His second-best attribute was deciding where that talent should play. In fact, were it not for Frank Selee, there would have been no Tinker to Evers to Chance, because none of those stalwart Chicagoans played those positions when they started out.

For example, the muscular Frank Chance was languishing on Chicago's bench as a catcher or outfielder when Selee came aboard. To Selee, this was foolishness. Chance was not a particularly good catcher and wasn't really fast enough to be an outfielder, but he could hit like blazes.

Selee went to Chance and told him that as of the 1902 season he would be a first baseman.

"I don't know how to play the position," Chance reportedly said.

"You'll learn" was Selee's response.

And, of course, the competitive Chance, faced now with the opportunity to be an everyday player, worked diligently to learn how to field his position, as the shrewd Selee had anticipated.

This, in turn, freed up catcher Johnny Kling to play the position full-time. Kling turned out to be, when he wasn't winning pool tournaments, one of the best catchers in the business in the decade of the 1900s.

Selee then secured the much-traveled Joe "Tink" Tinker from a minor league team in Portland, Oregon. Tinker had been a good third baseman in Oregon. Selee, after seeing him a handful of times, decided that Tinker, with his range and arm, would be a better shortstop. Tinker had played the position briefly in the minors and did not particularly think he was accomplished enough to play it in the big leagues. Selee told him he would learn. Also acquired by Selee was sweet-hitting outfielder Jimmy Slagle, who would lead the team in hitting in 1902 with a .315 average.

The Cubs, as they were now being called by sportswriters because of their youth, didn't scare anyone in 1902, finishing 68-69 that year. But late in the season, second baseman Bobby Lowe was injured. Selee sent to Troy, New York, for diminutive Johnny "the Crab" Evers. Evers was a shortstop, and at 5'9" 125 pounds, not a very big one. Selee wanted to move Evers from his regular position at shortstop to second base.

Evers's new teammates thought Selee was crazy, believing Evers was too small to play in the major leagues. Pitcher Jack Taylor taunted Evers the first day he reported to the Cubs, warning Evers he "would go home in a box."

Evers didn't disagree. He just wasn't too sure he would be as effective at second base as he was as a shortstop, and he communicated those thoughts to Selee. Selee told him not to worry, he would learn.

And Evers did, quickly. He played the last 22 games of the 1902 season at second base and did not make an error. On September 1 of that year, shortstop Joe Tinker, second baseman Johnny Evers and first baseman Frank Chance made their first appearance together. The next day, they turned their first double play.

The team improved in the win column in 1903, winning 82 games and finishing third and winning 93 games in 1904 and finishing second to the Giants. Prior to the 1903 season, Chance lobbied owner Hart and manager Selee to pick up a handicapped pitcher from St. Louis named Mordecai Brown, derisively called "Three Finger" Brown in the press. Neither Hart nor Selee was particularly interested, but Chance believed Brown, whose pitching hand had been injured in a farming accident as a youth, was slated to be a good one. Despite his injury, or perhaps because of it, Brown threw a blistering fastball, a good curve and the best screwball in the majors.

Chance was wrong. Brown was slated to be a great one.

The Giants repeated as National League champions in 1905, but Chicago added more good players, picking up outfielder and solid hitter Frank "Wildfire" Schulte, superb utilityman Arthur "Solly" Hofman and pitchers Ed Reulbach and Carl Lundgren.

The irony was that Selee, who had authored much of this superb rebuilding job, was finally breaking down physically. His tuberculosis was literally killing him, and midway through the 1905 season, Selee knew he needed to step aside as manager. In an unprecedented move, he allowed his players to vote for their new manager. Chance won easily. In August 1905, Selee retired to Colorado and left the club in Chance's hands. Selee actually continued to manage a minor league team in Denver, but died in 1909 of his disease. He was 49.

Prior to the 1906 season, Hart wanted out. He sold the team to businessman Charles Murphy for $105,000. Murphy, eager to win, asked Chance what the team needed to get by the Giants.

"Harry Steinfeldt," replied Chance, referring to the athletic third baseman for the Cincinnati Reds. Murphy traded for Steinfeldt and also picked up pitchers Orval Overall and Jack Pfiester. Pfiester would later be known as "Jack the Giant Killer" for his stunning success against the New Yorkers.

Prior to the season, Chance told reporters that the team "had a fair chance to succeed this year." They succeeded beyond anyone's expectations, winning 116 games and losing just 36, a .763 winning percentage that remains a modern baseball record. The Seattle Mariners also won 116 games in 2001, but lost 46.

Their pitching, led by the amazing Brown, was overpowering, with a 1.76 ERA that was almost a half run lower than the next best mark, and a margin that was the widest in history. The Cubs on the year allowed only 381 runs, the lowest mark in modern history. The Giants came in second in this category, allowing 484.

What is amazing about these numbers in particular is not that the Cubs were first, but that the Cubs were first by such wide margins. They simply overpowered the rest of the National League with pitching and defense.

The team also led the league in batting with a .262 average and in fielding with a .969 percentage. The Cubs finished 20 games ahead of the 96-56 Giants.

As amazing as those numbers were, the most amazing streak in baseball came to an end that year when the Cubs' tough-as-nails pitching ace Taylor was knocked out in the third inning of a game played against Brooklyn on August 13. That ended a stunning streak of 187 complete games, a record that began in 1901. Taylor would finish 278 of 286 starts in his career.

Chicago was the hub of the baseball universe that year, as the Chicago White Sox (who had stolen the White Stockings name a few years earlier) won the championship of the three-year-old American League .This set up the first World Series between two teams in the same city, a scenario the Yankees, Giants and Brooklyn Dodgers would make famous a few decades later.

The Cubs, however, didn't learn much from their unsuccessful forays against St. Louis of the American Association in the 1880s. They were almost unbearably cocky, believing they would finish off the American League champs in five or, at most, six games.

The games were, for the most part, close and well pitched. But the White Sox may have set the tone for the series in the first game when their ace Nick Altrock edged Brown 2-1 in a tense pitchers' duel. Both teams played well, but the White Sox caught a break when Brown's error in the top of the sixth led to the American League champions' second, and game-winning, run of the day.

The Cubs came back in Game 2 with a 7-1 win as Reulbach tossed the first one-hitter in World Series history, but the White Sox regained the Series lead with a 3-0 shutout by big Ed Walsh. So after three games, Cub pitching had allowed nine hits—and the team trailed in the World Series, two games to one. They were being beaten by solid pitching, timely hitting and great defense, factors the Cubs themselves had used to dominate their league.

Brown's excellent two-hitter in Game 4 tied the Series at two games each, but Game 5 saw the American League champs finally break open a game, scoring four runs in the fourth inning to snap a 3-3 tie and give the Sox an eventual 8-6 win.

Suddenly, the momentum had shifted—for good—to the White Sox. The heretofore near-invincible Cubs were clearly very vincible and very rattled. Chance pulled Brown aside before Game 6 and told his pitcher that he needed to come up with a big game to square the World Series. Brown must have wondered what more Chance wanted: he'd thrown a four-hitter in Game 1 and a two-hitter in Game 4.

But by now, the Sox were rolling. They thumped Brown early, with seven runs in the first two innings, and the game was over by the sixth as the American League champions cruised, 8-3. The White Sox had stunned the Cubs in what is still considered one of the great upsets in professional sports.

The Cubs dugout was as silent as a morgue after the final game. The players were, to be sure, deeply disappointed at the loss. But worse, many had bet their expected winning World Series shares on themselves to win. Now they had to figure out how to pay their bookies.

As spring training convened the next year, Chance gathered his players around him before the start of practice that first day. It was clear he'd spent a lot of winter evenings thinking about the previous season.

"Maybe now," he said tensely, "you sons of bitches have learned your lesson as to what happens when you underrate the other sons of bitches."

The 1907 Chicago Cubs continued to dominate the National League, winning 107 games, losing 45 and finishing 16 games ahead of the second-place Pittsburgh Pirates. Once again, led by Brown, Overall, Lundgren, Pfiester and Reulbach, the pitching was overpowering. The Cubs' team ERA of 1.73 was again more than a half run lower than number two Pittsburgh's team ERA of 2.30.

The Pirates, with Honus Wagner having an amazing year, had slightly better hitting statistics and the Cubs' team fielding was not as overpowering as the previous year, but no one could hit Cubs' pitching.

Perhaps the most telling statistic that year was that Lundgren, Pfiester, Overall and Brown were

1-2-3-5 in the category of pitchers who allowed the fewest hits per game.

The regular season wasn't much of a race as the Cubs established themselves in first place early in the season and didn't let up the rest of the year. Three Cubs—Chance, Steinfeldt and catcher Johnny Kling—led the league in fielding at their respective positions, while Tinker topped second basemen in assists.

Their opponents in the World Series were the Detroit Tigers, led by 22-year-old star Ty Cobb. Cobb was a one-man army. He had led the American League in batting average (.350), slugging percentage (.473), total bases (265), RBIs (116), stolen bases (49) and hits (212). He was third in home runs with five and runs scored with 97.

Defensively, Cobb led all American League right fielders in double plays (12), assists (30), total chances per game (1.9) and was second in the league in putouts (238). He was simply the best player in the league by a country mile.

But the 1907 World Series showcased the brilliance of team play over individual performance. After the first game ended in a 3-3 tie, which was called on account of darkness, the Cubs swept the Series. Their pitching was overwhelming, their fielding superb and their hitting timely and telling.

After the 3-3 tie, Chicago won the next four games by shutting down the Tigers as completely as a team can be stopped, winning their games by counts of 3-1, 5-1, 6-1 and 2-0. Cobb made four hits in 20 at-bats for a .200 average, stole no bases, scored one run, had one RBI and one extra-base hit, a triple.

Kling was a key performer for Chicago in the series. The Tigers attempted to steal 14 bases, and were successful only seven times, with Kling gunning down the other seven base runners. With their two principal weapons, Ty Cobb and the stolen base, taken away from them, the Tigers were effectively declawed.

After Mordecai Brown shut his team out in the fifth game, Cobb glumly declared that Brown's screwball was "the most devastating pitch I've ever seen."

After the series, Chance gave an interview to a reporter for an Eastern paper. The reporter praised Chance's 1907 squad. Chance, apparently still a little miffed over the 1906 Series, muttered, "We should have had two [championships]."

The Cubs won their third consecutive pennant in 1908, but it wasn't as easy as the first two. In fact, the Cubs triumph that year capped what many still feel was the greatest pennant race of all time.

In 1906 and 1907, the Cubs wrapped up the National League championship by the end of July. In 1908 the Giants and Pirates swapped the lead with Chicago until the last day of the season.

The Cubs started out very well and were in first place from Opening Day until July 6; then the Pirates overtook them to take a half-game lead. The Giants, who had been at .500 for most of the first two months, were starting to heat up and were in third place at that point.

Chicago and Pittsburgh traded the league lead until August 27, when the Giants surged forward, beating the Pirates two out of three times to take the lead over Chicago by a half game. Throughout September the Giants held on to the league lead by a paper-thin margin of a game to a game and a half. Then, on September 23, with New York ahead by 1½ games, the most controversial game in baseball history took place.

It was a Wednesday afternoon, a pretty nice day in New York. Giants ace Christy Mathewson was on the mound for New York, with Fred Pfiester pitching for the Cubs. Chicago scored first, as Tinker drilled a shot to right field for a sure hit. Giants outfielder "Turkey Mike" Donlin charged the ball and tried to make a spectacular catch. The ball skittered past Donlin and Tinker swiftly rounded the bases for an inside-the-park home run. Donlin made up for that gaffe in the next inning when his single scored Charles Lincoln "Buck" Herzog.

That's how it stayed until the ninth. With Harry "Moose" McCormick on first, Giants rookie Fred Merkle was up. Merkle singled sharply off Pfiester and suddenly, with two outs, there were men on first and third.

Up came Giants pinch hitter Al Bridwell. Pfiester, who already had a sore arm, was now pitching with a painful charley horse on his upper arm. His curveball came in way too soft, and Bridwell ripped it up the middle.

The fans roared. McCormick clapped his hands and trotted home. Merkle headed toward second base and saw joyous Giants fans pouring onto the field. He veered off the base path and headed toward the Giants dugout, afraid of being mobbed.

Evers, standing on the base paths, saw Merkle leaving. He whirled and saw outfielder Solly Hofman trudging in mournfully, baseball in hand.

"The ball!" screamed Evers to Hofman. "The ball!"

With a man on first base, and two outs, the base runner must touch second base because, according to baseball rules, if a game ends on a force play, any runs that score do not count. Evers, a student of the rule book, knew his team still had a chance to keep the game tied if he could get the baseball back and touch second base.

Hofman, startled, fired the ball toward third base. Giants third base coach Joe McGinnity had heard Evers. In an instant, McGinnity, a canny veteran himself, knew what Evers was up to. He beat Steinfeldt to the baseball and hurled it into the outfield. Evers screamed at Steinfeldt to get the ball back. Harry ran out, and he and rookie pitcher Floyd "Rube" Kroh wrestled the ball from a spectator. Steinfeldt threw it in to Evers, who caught it and touched second base. Chance, meanwhile, had grabbed umpire Hank O'Day to make the call. O'Day pulled away from Chance and, maybe, called Merkle out. But if he did (and news accounts of the time differ as to whether or not he did), O'Day made the call while rushing off the field. His ruling wouldn't be known until well after the game had been declared over.

Meanwhile, a lot of very drunk Giants fans were milling around the base, and Evers and Chance realized that it was time to go. They and the rest of the Cubs on the field formed a flying wedge and bulled their way into the visiting dugout. But there, they made a dismal discovery.

With virtually no security in those days, each team designated a player, usually a benchwarmer, to keep track of their cash and jewelry, all of which was dumped into a canvas bag for safekeeping. In this case, that player had been, you guessed it, Rube Kroh. Kroh had seen the controversy on the field and had rushed out of the dugout to help out, leaving the bag of valuables on the bench. When the Cubs got back to their dugout, the bag, with about $5,000 in cash and jewelry, was gone.

The controversy literally caught the attention of the entire country. In the umpire's dressing room after the game, O'Day had finally declared the game a tie. If need be, it would be replayed at the end of the season.

Giants manager John McGraw made his case in the New York papers. The call was a travesty, he said over and over. The game was won. Merkle, McGraw noted, could have easily stepped on the bag and did not do so only because he feared injury from being mobbed by the fans.

The papers called the baserunning gaffe "Merkle's Boner," a tag Merkle would live with until the day he died. But McGraw never blamed Merkle for the situation; he blamed O'Day for making a poor call.

Chance, meanwhile, made his case in the Chicago publications. Rules were rules. In fact, he noted, the Cubs should have been given the game via forfeit when the Giants failed to take the field for the top of the 10th inning. That observation didn't go over too well in New York.

Of course, the two teams ended up in a tie at the end of the season, and a replay was ordered. Chicago would have to return to the Polo Grounds to win the pennant on October 8.

It was a case of 25 Daniels strolling into a lion's den filled with thousands of the beasts that afternoon. Chance, Evers, Steinfeldt, Brown and Pfiester all later admitted to getting letters stating that if they played, they would be shot on the field.

They played. Pfiester started and ran out of gas early, allowing a first-inning run. Chance, in the key decision of the game, went to Brown in that first inning. Mathewson, exhausted by a long pennant race, admitted after the game that he had had nothing.

The Cubs exploded for four runs in the third: Tinker tripled over Giants outfielder James Bentley "Cy" Seymour's head, and Kling singled him home. Brown sacrificed Kling to second base. Wildfire Schulte crushed a double to give the Cubs a 3-1 lead and then Chance strode to the plate.

The crowd had booed and hissed him all through warm-ups and into the game. Throughout the contest, he had had to duck beer bottles, thrown programs, rocks and coins while stationed at first base. With a 1-1 count and a man on second base, Chance blasted a double up the middle. As Schulte crossed home plate with Chicago's fourth and final run, Chance slid into second. He got up, dusted himself off and adjusted his cap. No one understood the concept of "in your face" in 1908, but that's exactly what it was.

The Giants could do little with Brown. They scratched together a run in the seventh, but that was it. The Cubs had won the game, and the National League pennant, 4-2.

The World Series was almost an anticlimax. No one on the Cubs had any fear of the Tigers or Ty Cobb. The Cubs won the first game with a five-run ninth. Hofman and Kling each had key hits; Brown got the win in relief. In the second game, Overall tossed a four-hitter and Tinker hit a two-run homer in a 6-1 win.

The Tigers picked up their only win, in the third game, as Cobb amassed four of his seven Series hits in an 8-3 win, but that was it. Brown just dominated the Tigers with a four-hit shutout in Game 4 and Overall did his teammate one better with a three-hit blanking the next day as the Cubs won the Series.

It was the last time the Cubs would win a World Series—ever, but there was still success in the cards for this unit. In 1909 the Cubs won 104 games, five more than the pennant-winning squad of 1908. But Pittsburgh, with the amazing Honus Wagner, was not to be denied this year. The Pirates set a torrid pace that the Cubs matched until about Labor Day, then went on to win a total 110 games and the National League champi-

onship. Like the Cubs, they defeated the Tigers in the 1909 World Series.

But Chicago returned to form the next year when Chance snagged rookie phenom Leonard Leslie "King" Cole, who would win 20 games for the Cubs that year, to complement Brown, Overall, Reulbach and the aging Fred Pfiester. The Cubs won 104 games again and secured the pennant by 13 games over the Giants.

Following the 1908 championship, the Cubs canny infield of third baseman Steinfeldt, shortstop Tinker, second baseman Evers and first sacker Chance was now conceded to be the best defensive infield in the majors. They were perhaps not the most talented, but to most observers, it was a foursome who did not make mistakes and who maximized their abilities.

In 1910 New York writer Franklin Pierce Adams, a big Giants fan, had apparently been aggravated by yet another loss to the hated Cubs. He penned what was easily the most famous poem about real major leaguers in baseball history. He called it "Baseball's Sad Lexicon." The *New York Globe* eventually published it.

These are the saddest of possible words:
"Tinker to Evers to Chance."
Trio of Bear-cubs, fleeter than birds,
Tinker to Evers to Chance.
Ruthlessly pricking our gonfalon bubble,
Making a Giant hit into a double—
Words that are weighty with nothing but trouble:
"Tinker to Evers to Chance."

"Gonfalon" is an antique word for "flag" or "pennant," and thus refers to the hopes of Giants fans for a National League championship. The double in question in line six refers to a double play.

The ironic thing is, this eight-line poem that Adams once conceded was "a bit of doggerel" caught on. It was short, it was memorable and people liked it. In this modern day, every Cubs fan past his teens can recite it by heart. In 1946, Tinker, Evers and Chance were enshrined in the

Tinker and Evers turning two

for the Cubs' poetic infield crew. And, amazingly, their pitching was better, too. Jack Coombs, a 31-game winner and Charles Albert "Chief" Bender, who was 23-5 that year, were the only two pitchers A's manager Connie Mack used in the Series. Coombs pitched three complete-game wins, and Bender finished both games he started, going 1-1.

The Athletics won the first three games of the Series fairly easily, 4-1, 9-3 and 12-5, before the Cubs salvaged a 4-3 win in Game 4. But the A's finished the team off, 7-2, the next day.

There were no turning points that might have given Chicago a victory in this Series, no key moments that may have turned things around. The A's, who would dominate with World Series championships in 1910, 1911 and 1913 and American League flags in 1914 and 1915, were on the upswing. The Cubs were now officially on the downswing.

3 REBUILDING AND THE WRIGLEYS

The 1910 season was a clear turning point for the franchise. It was the last time Tinker, Evers and Chance would be regulars. The superb pitching staff was breaking up and Cole, the hope for the future, contracted malaria in the off-season and was never the same. He would die a few years later.

Chance was wearing down and began to manage from the bench more and more. He was also feuding with owner Charles Murphy, who, after admittedly spending money to get such players as Harry Steinfeldt and Orval Overall, was now pinching pennies just as energetically.

The Cubs won 92 games in 1911 and 93 games in 1912, but finished out of the money both years. Suddenly, according to Murphy, Frank Chance was no longer "the Peerless Leader" of men, but a bumbler. After the 1912 season, Murphy fired Chance and named Evers manager.

But before the 1913 season, Murphy began a fire sale of his stars, trading Tinker to the Reds and Ed Reulbach to the Brooklyn Dodgers. He also sent Mordecai Brown to the minors. The Cubs

Baseball Hall of Fame together, linked forever by a piece of poetry.

The Cubs were heavy favorites over the Philadelphia Athletics in the 1910 World Series. A few weeks before the series was to begin, though, Johnny Evers broke his leg and was out for the duration.

This clearly hurt the Cubs, as Evers was a defensive cornerstone at second base and a key leadoff man in the offense.

But the fact was, the A's were just better. With their "$100,000 infield" of third baseman John Franklin "Home Run" Baker, shortstop Jack Barry, second baseman Eddie Collins and first baseman Harry Davis, the Athletics were more than a match won 88 games that season, not a bad effort considering most of their best players were now no longer on the roster.

Murphy, not surprisingly, was now feuding with Evers, who had not been consulted about most of the roster moves before the season began. Evers was openly critical of Murphy, who decided to fire him when the season ended.

In a stunning little bit of irony, Murphy then hired former umpire Hank O'Day, the man who had made the crucial call in Chicago's favor in the tie game with the Giants in 1908, as the Cubs' manager for the 1914 season. In fairness to O'Day, he did have previous experience as a manager after he got out of umpiring in 1910. O'Day was a better umpire than manager. The Cubs finished 16½ games out that year. Outfielder Fred "Cy" Williams was one of the team's few bright spots. Meanwhile, Evers, declared incompetent by Murphy, signed with the Boston Braves and led them to the 1914 world championship.

National League owners were becoming fed up with Murphy, who, in addition to firing a manager every year, was now notorious for paying his players peanuts. The other owners (who, in reality, weren't paying their players much better) finally prevailed upon Murphy to sell his majority ownership of the team to businessman Charles Taft at the end of the 1914 season.

But other things were happening that season. A third professional league, the Federal League, had begun operations in 1913. The league did not pretend to be a big-league operation that first year, but by 1914 the Federal League had established franchises in eight cities, including five cities in which they were in direct competition with American or National League clubs.

Of these teams, the Chicago franchise of the Federal League was among the most successful. The owner was Charles Weeghman, a businessman who had made millions by owning and operating more than a dozen restaurants around the city. Weeghman, unlike most of the other Federal League owners, played hardball. Rather than trying to find a place for his team to play, Weeghman realized that to compete in a city with two other

big-league franchises he needed to give the fans a reason to come to see his team rather than the White Sox or Cubs.

Thus, Weeghman bought some land from the Chicago Lutheran Theological Seminary and hired architect Zachary Taylor Davis to design a ballpark that would be the envy of the rest of professional baseball.

Davis did not disappoint. When Weeghman Park opened in 1914, it had 14,000 seats, beautiful sight lines and a handsome edifice. The cost of construction was $250,000. Fans didn't know much about the Chicago Feds, as they were called, but they knew that they liked sitting in a more spacious and cleaner ballpark.

Weeghman also went after players with a vengeance. When Murphy released Joe Tinker after 1913, Weeghman signed him as a player-manager. Former White Sox pitcher Edward Harrison "Dutch" Zwilling was also signed, as was Pittsburgh's star pitcher Claude Hendrix. In 1915 Weeghman signed Three Finger Brown, who had been sent to the minor leagues in 1913.

So, while the Cubs were struggling to stay above the .500 mark in 1914, and the White Sox languished in sixth place, the Feds were in a thrilling pennant race with Indianapolis, falling short by 1½ games. In 1915, the Whales, as they were now called, won the Federal League pennant, led by Zwilling, Hendrix and, much to the chagrin of the Cubs organization, Three Finger Brown, who won 17 games and was third in the league in ERA. The White Sox finished third in the American League. In the National League, the Cubs were fourth, 17 games out of first place.

By the end of the 1915 season, however, the Federal League, with the exception of Chicago and perhaps one or two other franchises, was faltering badly. Lawsuits filed by both the American and National Leagues were wearing the Federal League owners down. And too many of the operations were being run on a shoestring.

Finally, in December 1915, the three leagues settled. The Federal League owners got some compensation money, and the league allowed Weeghman to purchase controlling interest in the

Cubs. Taft had lost enough money. The Charles Weeghman era had begun.

Weeghman merged the two franchises, giving Tinker the managerial reins and bringing Brown back to the National League with great fanfare in 1916. It turned out to be Brown's last year, and it was not a very productive year for the man his teammates called "Brownie," but it was a happy ending of sorts for the future Hall of Famer.

The team struggled in 1916 and 1917, finishing well below the .500 mark both seasons. But Weeghman was building for the future. James "Hippo" Vaughn, a hulking 6'4" lefthander, was establishing himself as one of the top pitchers in the league, as was former Whale Claude Hendrix, a savvy righthander. Right fielder Max Flack, another former Federal League star, was also making his mark.

The 1917 season was the year Vaughn and the Reds' Fred Toney locked up in the famous "double no-hitter," won by Toney when former Olympian Jim Thorpe beat out a single that scored Larry Kopf, who had made the first hit of the game in the 10th inning.

In 1918 the Cubs put it all together. Tinker had retired the previous year, giving the managerial reins to Fred Mitchell. Mitchell had no previous managerial experience and had been an undistinguished pitcher in the 1900s for several clubs, but he was a genius in 1918.

It also didn't hurt that many big-league stars had been drafted into the service to fight World War I. Still, Vaughn was nearly unhittable that year, and Hendrix and George Albert "Lefty" Tyler were nearly as tough. The infield was anchored by rookie Charlie Hollocher, a player who had a "can't miss" tag stamped on his head as soon as he stepped onto a major league diamond.

And at first base, amazingly, was a veteran National Leaguer named—Fred Merkle. This was the same Fred Merkle who had cost the Giants a pennant in 1908. He had been picked up by the Cubs in 1917, and gave the team three solid years before being released. In 1918 Merkle hit .297 and led National League first basemen with 1,388 putouts.

The Cubs won the National League pennant by 13 games over the Giants. But in the World Series, they were heavy underdogs to American League champion Boston, which had the deepest pitching staff in the majors in George Herman "Babe" Ruth, Carl Mays, "Bullet Joe" Bush, "Sad Sam" Jones and Hubert Benjamin "Dutch" Leonard.

Vaughn and Ruth locked up in the first game, and the Babe came away with a 1-0 win, pushing his streak of scoreless innings to 22. Lefty Tyler evened the series for the Cubs with a 3-1 win, but Mays beat Vaughn, pitching on only two days' rest, in Game 3, 2-1.

Ruth picked up his second win of the Series in Game 4, earning a 3-2 decision as the Babe ran his then-record scoreless streak to 29⅓ innings. The Cubs managed a win in Game 5 behind the tireless Vaughn's five-hit shutout, but the Red Sox closed out Chicago the next day, 2-1 behind Mays.

The Chicago pitching had been impressive. Boston had hit only .182 for the six games, the worst team batting average for a Series winner in history. But the Red Sox pitching had been more consistent. It was the fifth world championship in five tries for Boston. It would also be their last.

Weeghman had enjoyed the team's success in 1918, but he was hurting financially. The stock market crash of 1918 put him in deep trouble. He was looking to get out. One of his minority investors seemed interested and the two men began talking.

William Wrigley was the son of a soap maker. He worked in his father's factory but disliked it, and soon became a salesman as a teen. A savvy businessman, he made his fortune by rarely taking no for an answer and working harder and longer than anyone else. In 1919 he bought out Weeghman and began the Wrigley family's ownership in the franchise. Weeghman Park became known as Cubs Park in time for Opening Day, 1920.

Conceding he did not know how to run a baseball franchise, Wrigley hired William Veeck Sr., a former sportswriter, to run his baseball club in June 1919.

Wrigley was a heck of salesman, a great owner and a fair man. When the Cubs traded for pitcher Grover Cleveland "Pete" Alexander in 1918, Wrigley paid his wife a stipend while Alexander was in the armed service that year. Wrigley did not believe in haggling over contracts and usually made generous offers to his ballplayers.

Wrigley and Veeck were innovators. They would pioneer radio broadcasts in 1925, and in 1929 the team would begin the tradition of "Ladies Day," in which women got in free to the ballpark.

Vaughn, Alexander and Hendrix made up a solid staff in 1919, but the Cubs finished third. And for most of the early 1920s, the Cubs struggled as Wrigley and Veeck reconstructed the franchise. Pete Alexander, when he returned from the war, was a force for several years. Hollocher played well but was beset by internal ailments that limited his service.

The Cubs languished in the middle of the pack from 1920 to 1924 and fell to last place in 1925. Through it all, Alexander performed like an all-star, even though he had begun drinking heavily. He won a league-leading 27 games in 1920, led the league in shutouts in 1921 and won 22 games in 1923.

In 1922 Alexander broke in a young catcher named Charles Leo Hartnett. Hartnett was a big, strong kid, but in those early days, he didn't tend to say much. The veterans dubbed him "Gabby"; the name stuck.

Cubs manager Billy Killefer wasn't a bad guy, but he didn't have a lot with which to work. The irony is that the Cubs were pretty good up the middle, with Hartnett catching, a healthy Hollocher at shortstop and Arnold "Jigger" Statz at center field. Everybody else, however, was pretty mediocre.

Wrigley needed a change. In 1925 he fired manager Killefer and hired, first, Walter James "Rabbit" Maranville, who managed and played shortstop for 53 games, and then George Gibson. Neither replacement worked out, as the Cubs finished dead last despite picking up another solid player, first baseman Charlie Grimm of the Pirates.

Wrigley was getting desperate. Veeck, the former sportswriter, had worked in Louisville for the *Louisville Courier-Journal.* He recalled that Joe McCarthy, the coach of the minor league team there, had done a pretty good job. He began pushing McCarthy's name during the dark days of the 1925 season. Wrigley didn't actually need much pushing. As Veeck pointed out years later: "When you're in last place, you can do just about anything." So McCarthy it was.

McCarthy was born in Germantown, Pennsylvania. His father died when he was a youngster, forcing him to work during his teens to support his family. He never attended high school, but it is a measure of McCarthy's determination that he somehow won a scholarship to Niagara University in 1904. Two years later, however, he quit college to play professional baseball. He spent 15 years in the minors and never made a big-league club. He retired in 1919 and began his managerial career in Louisville. In 1925 Louisville won the championship of its league, which elevated McCarthy in Wrigley's eyes.

He was a tough man who did not suffer fools well, and he was an excellent baseball tactician. His lack of big-league experience caused problems for him early on. Alexander, in particular, simply refused to listen to McCarthy.

"No bush leaguer," said Alexander that spring, "is going to tell me how to pitch."

McCarthy realized he couldn't afford to allow Alexander to flout his leadership. Early in the 1926 season, Alexander was released. The St. Louis Cardinals picked him up, and the next year, they won a world championship over the New York Yankees. Alexander won Game 6 and saved Game 7 of that Series. When asked about Alexander in 1927, McCarthy merely shrugged. "When he pitched for us in 1925, we finished last," said McCarthy. "So if we were going to finish last in 1926, I'd rather it be without him."

The Cubs didn't finish last in 1926. McCarthy drafted Lewis Robert "Hack" Wilson away from the Giants and signed Jackson Riggs Stephenson and pitchers Charlie Root and Guy Bush. The latter three would begin their careers in Chicago that

Cuyler, Grimm, English, Hartnett singing on the dugout steps

year. Along with holdovers Grimm, Hartnett and second baseman Earl John "Sparky" Adams, the Cubs had the makings of a solid team. Chicago finished 82-72 that year, seven games out of first place. Also in 1926, the Cubs home field was renamed Wrigley Field in honor of William Wrigley.

The Cubs continued to improve over the next two years. Shortstop Woody English came aboard in 1927, and in 1928 outfielder Hazen "Kiki" Cuyler and pitcher Perce Leigh "Pat" Malone were added. Chicago's win total improved from 82 in 1926 to 85 in 1927 and 92 in 1928.

Meanwhile, Wrigley's radio experiment was clearly a success, much to the surprise of the rest of the league's owners, who were sure that broadcasting games would drain the Cubs gate.

In reality, the opposite happened. One day in 1927, Veeck was in the parking lot of Wrigley Field and noticed hundreds of out-of-state license plates. He realized that the radio broadcasts, rather than hindering attendance, were expanding it, since people listened to the broadcasts and got the urge to see the team in person.

The Cubs also drew a huge listening audience of shut-ins and elderly residents too old or infirm to get to a game. The radio idea was terrific and contributed greatly to the popularity of the Cubs throughout the Midwest. The play of the team didn't hurt things, either. In 1929 McCarthy put together a champion. The Cubs won 98 games and easily won the pennant over the Pirates.

The 1929 Cubs were solid everywhere. Malone won 22 games, Root 19 and Bush 18, with 7 saves. The infield was bolstered by future Hall of Famer second baseman Rogers Hornsby, who was acquired that season. Grimm was at first, English at second and Norm McMillan was at third base.

The outfield was all-star caliber. Wilson, who resembled either Tweedledee or Tweedledum, was an RBI machine, making a league-leading 159 that year. Stephenson was not too far behind, with 110, and Cuyler had 102. Ironically, the lone weak spot was at catcher, as Hartnett was out for most of the year with an injury. James Wren "Zack" Taylor filled in fairly well, hitting .274.

Hornsby proved to be a tremendous acquisition. He was, without question, the greatest righthanded hitter in baseball. He was also, without question, one of the biggest pains in the neck in the league. Hornsby didn't mince words, was blunt, outspoken and combative. Veeck, aware of Hornsby's reputation, didn't want the aggravation; Wrigley, convinced that the addition of Hornsby would mean the pennant, signed him.

Wrigley was absolutely correct. Hornsby had one of the great years in team history in 1929, hitting .380, with 39 homers and 149 RBIs. He also led National League second basemen in assists with 547 and double plays with 106. He clearly put the team over the top and was recognized as the league MVP.

And perhaps more gratifying to Wrigley, the Cubs broke the record for major league attendance that year, with more than 1.4 million fans pouring into the park. This didn't even count the women who were getting in free because of Wrigley's Ladies Day. The Cubs would top 1 million in attendance five years in a row, from 1927 to 1931.

But if the regular season was a resounding success, the World Series was less so. The Cubs faced the Philadelphia Athletics that year, and Connie Mack's squad was top-heavy with future Hall of Famers: first baseman Jimmie Foxx, catcher Gordon Stanley "Mickey" Cochrane, outfielder Al Simmons and all-time All-Star pitcher Robert Moses "Lefty" Grove.

Mack was no slouch in the managing department, either. Knowing the Cubs had been killing lefthanded pitching all year at Wrigley Field, Mack started righthanders Howard Ehmke and George Earnshaw in the first two games there. Both won, and the Cubs were in a 0-2 hole going to Philadelphia.

Guy Bush scattered nine hits in a 3-1 Cub win the next day in Philadelphia, but the roof fell in in Game 4. The Cubs were leading the contest, 8-0, going into the bottom of the seventh inning, and seemed poised to tie the Series at two games each. But Simmons led off with a home run off Cub starter Root, and five of the next six Athletics'

batters stroked singles as the Philly crowd, dead all afternoon, began to roar their approval.

McCarthy pulled Root and inserted Art Nehf, a veteran in his 15th and last season as a player. Nehf delivered a pitch to the Athletics' George William "Mule" Haas, who popped a lazy fly ball in Wilson's direction. But Hack lost the ball in the sun, and it rolled all the way to the outfield wall. Haas collected a three-run inside-the-park home run to cut the Cubs lead to 8-7. The shaken Nehf walked Cochrane, and McCarthy replaced him with John "Sheriff" Blake, who allowed two more singles, which plated the tying run in Cochrane.

McCarthy replaced Blake with Pat Malone, who promptly hit a batter to load the bases. The next batter, Jimmy Dykes, drilled a double to score two more runs. Malone struck the final two batters out, but the damage had been done.

It was hideous. Hartnett recalls McCarthy, standing in the dugout as Athletic after Athletic stroked hits and saying to no one in particular, "What can I do? What the hell can I do?"

As English pointed out years later, the Athletics scored all their runs on base hits. There were no errors. And no one blamed Wilson, except Wilson himself. "People forget," said Hornsby years later, "that [Wilson] led both teams with a .471 average." The A's closed the Series out the next day, 3-2. Wilson sobbed on the train all the way back to Chicago.

There were repercussions to that loss. Wrigley believed that, with Hornsby, the Cubs had enough to win a World Series. The defeat stung him and he blamed McCarthy. Late in the 1930 season, McCarthy, who could see the writing on the wall, resigned. Wrigley immediately named Hornsby as the new manager.

The Cubs fell just short of the 1930 National League crown, but that didn't prevent Wilson from having a career year. He socked 56 home runs, then a National League record, and made 190 RBIs, still a major league mark that has yet to be touched.

Wilson, dubbed by sportswriters as the "hardest-hitting hydrant in the league," was the most unlikely power hitter in baseball. He was 5'6" but weighed

190 pounds, with tremendous upper-body strength. His bat literally hummed as he whipped it around to hit a pitch. In 1930 he was the toughest out in baseball.

The Hacker liked his beer and he loved company. He and Malone were drinking buddies on the road, but when Hack hit the streets, everyone was welcome to come along. Veeck would shake his head as Wilson came to him again and again for advances on his salary. Wilson didn't gamble or drink it away; he basically gave it away, buying drinks all night.

The Cubs offensive machine stumbled somewhat in 1931 as Wilson, in particular, had an off year. Many speculated that his stellar 1930 campaign caused him to press at the plate. Also, many players believed that the ball had been slightly deadened per order of the team owners, an allegation that was never proved. For whatever reason, Wilson slumped, hitting only .261 with 13 home runs and 61 RBIs.

Hornsby the manager wasn't setting the world afire, either. He had some favorites on the team, such as English, but for the most part, he was indifferent to the ballplayers. He was also not the strategist McCarthy was, especially when it came to handling pitchers. Many Cubs on the 1931 team believed Hornsby's managerial ineffectiveness cost them games. The Cubs finished third, 15 games out.

Changes were once more in the offing. Wilson was traded to St. Louis. Pitcher Lon Warneke, signed in 1930, blossomed, as did youngsters Billy Herman at second base and Billy Jurges at shortstop. In fact, the Cubs infield was so good that Stan Hack, a future All-Star, was relegated to the bench. Hartnett was now the best catcher in the league, and the outfield, with Stephenson, Cuyler and Johnny Moore, was also of championship caliber.

But the biggest change happened off the field. On January 26, 1932, William Wrigley died at age 69. It was announced that Philip Knight Wrigley, his son, would take over the team. In the years to come, the death of William Wrigley would prove to be another turning point in Cubs history. And the turning would be mostly downward.

4   THE DOWNWARD SPIRAL

The descent didn't happen right away. The 1932 Cubs began the season playing well, despite an ankle injury to Hornsby early in the season. Unable to play, Hornsby became even crankier. But more ominously, he began gambling heavily. Hornsby had always had a fondness for the ponies; though by his own admission, he wasn't much of a horseplayer. What that meant was that Rogers lost at the track ... a lot. So Hornsby would hit up his players for loans, and many of the younger players were afraid not to lend the money. And, of course, they were also afraid to press their manager to pay it back.

It was a potentially explosive situation. By the time Veeck got wind of it, Hornsby reportedly owed his players a total of $10,000. On August 2, Veeck fired Hornsby. Even the players to whom Hornsby owed money were relieved. At least he wouldn't be after them again. Veeck opted to replace Hornsby with first baseman Grimm. It was an inspired choice. The affable Grimm encouraged his players to have fun, and unlike Hornsby, he was generous with both praise and friendly advice. The Cubs blossomed under Grimm and annexed the National League pennant.

There was another scandal that season, perhaps more sensational than the Hornsby episode. On July 6, Jurges was accidentally shot by his girlfriend, Violet Valli, a showgirl who believed she and Jurges were to be married. Valli had gone up to Jurges's hotel room to confront him, and if he refused to marry her, she would kill herself. In the ensuing struggle, Jurges was wounded in the hand and side. Contrary to popular stories, the injury did not sideline Jurges for the season, and in fact, he played 115 games that year.

The Cubs acquired former Yankee Mark Koenig to fill in for Jurges, and Koenig played well as Chicago moved past the Pirates for the National League championship.

But once again, they went up against an American League meat grinder. This time, it was the 1932 Yankees, with an astonishing eight future Hall of Famers in the lineup: Babe Ruth and Earle Combs in the outfield, Lou Gehrig at first base, Tony Lazzeri at second base, Bill Dickey at catcher and pitchers Herb Pennock, Vernon Louis "Lefty" Gomez and Charles Herbert "Red" Ruffing. Not to mention that Joe McCarthy, the Yankees manager, was a familiar face to Chicago fans, certainly.

It wasn't pretty for Cubs fans. Ruffing and Gomez picked up wins in the first two games, played in Yankee Stadium, 12-6 and 5-2. Returning to Chicago, Grimm felt his man, Charlie Root, could get the best of the Yankees' George Pipgras. And that might have happened, had not the Cubs foolishly tugged on Superman's cape by taunting Ruth throughout the third game. The most printable of the epithets was "apeface."

Ruth and Root got into it in the fifth, with the game tied at 5-5. After taking two strikes, Ruth pointed his finger at Root and warned that "it only takes one to hit it, busher!" Years later, Root conceded he probably should have fed Ruth an outside pitch in hopes the Babe would have swung. Instead, he sent a fastball spinning home.

Ruth's bat whipped around and he lashed a home run to center field. Sportswriters, particularly New York sportswriters, caught up in the moment, recalled that Ruth had pointed prior to the pitch. At something. Well, maybe he pointed to the center-field stands! No one actually asked Ruth afterward until months and years later.

Had Ruth fouled that pitch off, the myth of the "called-shot home run" might never have evolved. But he didn't foul it off. He sent the pitch into the center-field bleachers, exactly where he seemingly had indicated it would go.

The Yankees won the game, 7-5. (Gehrig stepped up and hit another homer off Root in the next at-bat, but absolutely no one remembers that.) New York closed the Cubs out the next day, 13-6.

The story livened up a pretty dull World Series. And Ruth, no fool, rarely denied that he had called the home run in later years. But Hartnett, the Cubs' catcher, made the most salient point. A huge majority of Ruth's homers were hit to right field. If Ruth had intended to hit one out, said Gabby, he almost certainly wouldn't have pointed to center field.

The Cubs finished third in 1933, but the team was struck a blow when Veeck died in the fall of that year from a blood disease. It was another key hit to the organization, as Philip Knight Wrigley was evincing no real interest in running the team. The franchise still had resources, though. Stan Hack, 24, began to blossom as an exceptional third sacker. Bill Lee was brought up in 1934 and won 13 games, and slugging outfielder Chuck Klein was picked up from the Phillies. The Cubs finished third again, behind the Cardinals.

In 1935 the Cubs dealt pitchers Guy Bush and Pat Malone, who had begun to show their age, and in midseason also moved Cuyler. The outfield had been completely made over with Augie Galan, Frank Demaree and Klein. Grimm, following a frustrating spring training, handed the first baseman's job to 18-year-old Phil Cavarretta. Larry French was added to the rotation and Lee became the league's best pitcher.

The result was another pennant in 1935. But it wasn't easy. The Cubs stood at 40-32 at the All-Star break, 9½ games behind the Giants. But then the Cubbies got hot. Hot? Actually, they were meteoric. Chicago won its last 21 games in a row to clinch the National League crown ahead of the Cardinals.

It was a combination of things. The pitching staff was outstanding, throwing 18 complete games in the 21-game streak. In 20 of 21 games, Chicago held the opposition to three runs or fewer. Six regulars topped the .340 mark in that span, led by Billy Herman's .400 average and Galan's .384.

The winning streak tied a team record set by the 1880 White Stockings. The 21st victory gave Chicago its 100th win of the year. The team hasn't won 100 since. The major league record for most wins in a row is 26, set by the 1916 New York Giants.

In contrast to the previous World Series in which the Cubs participated, Chicago's chances against the American League champion Tigers were believed to be pretty good. Most experts believed the Cubs pitching staff of Lon "the Arkansas Hummingbird" Warneke, Lee, Charlie Root and Larry French was superior to the Tigers' Lynwood Thomas "Schoolboy" Rowe, Tommy Bridges, Alvin "General" Crowder and Eldon Auker. That was probably true, but the Tigers had a fearsome hitting corps in future Hall of Famers Hank Greenberg at first base, Charlie Gehringer at second base and Mickey Cochrane behind the plate. Cavarretta, now 19 years old and in his first World Series, watched in awe as slugger Greenberg drilled ball after ball out of the park in batting practice before that first game.

But as in 1932, some ill-advised bench jockeying was also a factor that once again sank the hopes of Cubs fans.

The Cubs rode their 21-game winning streak into the first game of the Series that year, as Warneke shut the Tigers out on four hits, 3-0, in Detroit. For the first time in six World Series, since back in 1908, Chicago took the lead.

That lasted one day. Fueled by a two-run homer by Greenberg, the Tigers chased Root with four consecutive hits and led, 4-0, after the first inning. Bridges, who threw one of the best curveballs in the game, held the Cubs to six hits in an 8-3 win.

Still, the Cubs looked to have an advantage, heading back to Chicago for the next three games. But it wasn't to be. Detroit scored an unearned run in the 11th inning to win the third game, 6-5, and Crowder scattered five hits in a 2-1 Tiger win.

Hartnett's two-run homer in the third inning and Warneke's seven-hitter gave Chicago a 3-1 win in the fifth game, setting up the sixth contest in Detroit. French and Bridges dueled throughout the afternoon, and the game was tied 3-3 going into the top of the ninth. Hack led off the inning with a triple, but Bridges struck out Jurges, who batted eighth in the lineup, for the first out.

Grimm would have liked to have had a pinch hitter for the light-hitting French, but he had no one on the bench. Umpire George Moriarty, reacting to some extreme criticism of his calls, tossed most of the players in the Cubs dugout. French, a career .188 hitter, had to bat for himself and Bridges easily got him out. Galan flied out to end the inning. In the bottom of the inning, Leon Allen "Goose" Goslin's bloop single scored Cochrane with the game-winning run. The Tigers had gotten their revenge, winning the Series four games to two.

The Cubs finished second two years in a row to the New York Giants in 1936 and 1937, winning 87 and 92 games, respectively. The Giants had a solid team, led by pitcher Carl Hubbell and first baseman Mel Ott, and won the two pennants by narrow margins.

In 1938 Grimm seemed to be burned out. He went to Phil Wrigley and asked to be replaced. Grimm wanted Jurges to manage, but Jurges turned it down. Instead, Wrigley named Hartnett the new manager on July 20. The Cubs struggled for a little more than a month, then got hot again, winning 21 of their final 25 games, and edging the Pittsburgh Pirates by three games.

Late in the season, the Cubs and Pirates were neck and neck. The Pirates came to town for a four-game series late in September. It was a series that would clearly decide the pennant. With Chicago trailing the Pirates by 1½ games, the Cubs won the first contest. The game the next day would be for first place. In that tilt, the two teams were tied, 5-5, going into the bottom of the ninth. Wrigley Field, of course, had no lights. Umpire Jocko Conlon warned both teams that this inning would be the last, and he would call the game because of darkness if there was no score.

The Pirates' Mace Brown was pitching, and he quickly got two outs. Hartnett stepped to the plate and everyone was having a hard time seeing. Mace blew two quick strikes past Hartnett, and just about everyone was thinking the game would be over.

But the third pitch by Brown was a little up and Hartnett swung. Most players admitted later that they had difficulty seeing where the ball went. But Conlon saw the fans in the outfield bleachers diving for the ball and signaled a home run. The Cubs had won, 6-5, on Hartnett's legendary "Homer in the Gloamin'." The demoralized Pirates then lost the next two games.

The Cubs were back in the World Series but once again, it would be no picnic. This time, it was the Yankees of "Joltin' Joe" DiMaggio. This 1938 squad was one of the more overpowering teams in the history of the game, featuring DiMaggio, Gehrig, Dickey, Ruffing and Gomez, Hall of Famers every one.

The Cubs were swept in four games. Ruffing pitched two complete-game victories, while the Yankees' Monte Pearson pitched a third. Gomez won the other game, going seven innings for the win, with Yankees reliever Johnny Murphy picking up the save. Chicago was simply outclassed by a superior team.

Although the Cubs had not won any of the four World Series in which they had participated, it had been a heck of a run from 1929 to 1938: four National League pennants, three second-place finishes and three third-place finishes. Except for a victory in World Series competition, no other National League team could claim such success. The Giants and Cardinals had both won three pennants each in that span. Up until this point, the Cubs could truly claim legitimate status as one of the elite franchises in major league baseball.

Which is why the downward curve of their fortunes over the next 30 years was so frustrating. The Cubs clearly had the resources to continue this success in some manner. That the team did not reflects a change in philosophy of ownership, not incompetence or even indifference.

Since the death of his father, William Wrigley, Philip Knight Wrigley had tried to run the Cubs franchise in a successful manner. But as one of the best businessmen in the country in the mid-20th century, Wrigley was concerned about ways to ensure that the franchise would be profitable even if the team itself were not successful on the field.

To that end, he spent lavishly on Wrigley Field: the now-famous ivy was planted and the park itself was flush with amenities for its patrons: comfortable seats that were closer to the field than probably any other ballpark and a beautiful, easy-to-read scoreboard with pennants fluttering gaily. Philip Knight Wrigley's philosophy, and one which he required his employees to emphasize, was that the experience of seeing a baseball game should be fun, pleasant, easy and inexpensive. And under his watch, all those things were true. A day at Wrigley Field was almost always pleasant and positive in and of itself.

Wrigley's point was, if the team itself was not successful, fans would continue coming to the ballpark because the experience of watching the Cubs would be fun. In a sense, what Wrigley hoped to do was take winning and losing out of the formula for fan satisfaction. He was half successful: he took winning out of the formula.

The other half of the strategy was to reduce the team's budget for scouting and minor league teams. This was the foundation of the team's problems throughout the next three decades. The Cubs were trying to play blackjack with no aces. Their tiny scouting staff would at times bag a prospect, but they were few and far between. And many times, the Cubs scout would be authorized to pay only a certain sum as a bonus, a sum that was often easily bested by another team with deeper pockets. It was a terrible business practice. There was no investment, and with no investment, there could be very little return.

Under Hartnett, the Cubs finished fourth in 1939 and fifth in 1940. Jurges was traded in 1939. The pitching staff, although bolstered by crafty Claude Passeau, was beginning to get older, and there were no acceptable prospects coming up. At the end of the 1940 season, Hartnett, one of the mainstays of the team, was fired, and Jimmie Wilson, a nice enough guy and former ballplayer, was hired as manager.

Wrigley also passed over William Veeck's son, Bill Veeck, for the general manager's slot. Veeck, like his father, was a heck of a baseball man. But he was outspoken and brash, two traits Philip

Knight Wrigley abhorred. The new general manger was Jim Gallagher, another pretty nice guy who was in over his head.

From 1940 to 1944, the Cubs floated closer to the bottom of the National League standings than the top. This is not to say that the team did not have players of above-average professional caliber. Hack was probably the best third baseman in the league in that span, and Cavarretta was nearing his peak as well.

The Cubs picked up right fielder Bill Nicholson from the Athletics in 1939, and he would be an All-Star throughout the early 1940s, but there weren't enough good players. Wrigley didn't really care about that, but he was getting pounded in the newspapers because his team had become a perennial loser. It was time to do something.

Charlie Grimm was managing in the minors. Wrigley fired Wilson late in the 1944 season and brought back Grimm to start the 1945 season. Grimm, called "Jolly Cholly" by ballplayers and the media, was a refreshing change from Wilson. For

one thing, he encouraged the players to have fun. For another, he was a veteran manager who never panicked.

World War II didn't hurt, either. Most of the Cubs regulars were too old for the service. The St. Louis Cardinals, the dominant team in the 1940s, lost Stan Musial and several other players to the armed forces.

At the start of the season, the team was playing well. Cavarretta was having an exceptional year and would go on to win the MVP award. The infield of Hack at third, Lennie Merullo at shortstop, Don Johnson at second base and Cavarretta at first was as good as any in the league. In the outfield, second-year man Andy Pafko was clearly going to be a great one, newcomer Harry Lee "Peanuts" Lowrey was playing well and Nicholson was hitting the heck out of the ball. Pitchers Passeau, Hank Wyse and Paul Derringer anchored the staff through much of the year.

The Cubs of 1945 would have never won the pennant without Hank Borowy, though. Borowy

1945 World Series Cubs sluggers from left: Nicholson, Pafko, Cavarretta, Cowrey, Johnson and Hack

Hank Borowy after his 9-0
win over the Tigers

was a member of the Yankees' deep pitching staff in the early 1940s, where he had been a solid performer, going 56-30. But Borowy had developed blisters on the fingers of his pitching hand and had already missed several starts at the beginning of the 1945 season. So when the Cubs called, the Yankees were happy to put Borowy on waivers and allow the Cubs to pick him up for $97,000.

It was a stunning coup and a rare misjudgment by New York. After a week of rest, the blisters receded, although Borowy did have some trouble with them on one finger the rest of the year. Borowy went 11-2 for Chicago the last month of the season and enabled the Cubs to hold off St. Louis and win the 1945 National League championship.

The Detroit Tigers, the American League champions, had edged the Washington Senators for the pennant by one game. The Tigers had solid pitching and were a good defensive team, but many thought the Cubs had a slight advantage overall.

Because of wartime travel restrictions, the first three games would be played in Detroit, and the last four in Chicago. And the Tigers got a boost when Virgil Trucks, their best pitcher, came home from the service. Trucks pitched the last games of the regular season and then was slated to start Game 2 of the World Series.

By then, the Cubs had taken a 1-0 lead in games. The Borowy magic continued as he shut down the Tigers on six hits in a 9-0 rout. Cavarretta had blasted a home run and the Cubs had jumped out to a 7-0 lead after three innings.

The next day, Trucks, showing no signs of wear, scattered seven hits in a 7-1 Tiger win, but the Cubs came back behind Passeau's one-hit shutout the next day, a 3-0 Cub win.

The Cubs were excited, as were their fans. They had a 2-1 lead in games, and the next four games would be in Chicago. It was the best position they had been in since their World Series win in 1908.

But Tiger pitcher Paul Howard "Dizzy" Trout shut down the Cubs on five hits for a 4-1 Detroit win the next day. And in Game 5, "Prince Hal" Newhouser beat Borowy, 8-4, to give Detroit the lead in the Series, 3-2, for the first time.

Facing elimination, the Cubs battled back. Both Passeau and Trucks were chased in a high-scoring contest that was tied 7-7 after nine innings. Grimm, needing the win desperately, sent Borowy in to pitch in the top of the ninth. The two teams were scoreless until the bottom of the 12th, when Hack drilled an RBI double to win the game.

Two days later, the Cubs were faced with their first World Series seventh game in franchise history. And Grimm had a major problem. Passeau had gone seven innings the day before. Wyse had had a start and two relief efforts in four days. Neither Paul Derringer nor Ray Prim, 39- and 38-year-old veterans, respectively, had looked good when they had had a chance to pitch in the series. Facing the biggest game in franchise history, Charlie Grimm had essentially run out of pitchers.

Before the game, Borowy volunteered to pitch, his third appearance in four days. It was a gutsy but foolish request. No one, probably not even Grimm, thought it was a good idea, but everyone—including Grimm—hoped for the best.

It was a disaster. Borowy gave up three consecutive singles and was pulled. Derringer did little better as the Tigers scored five runs in the first inning before 41,590 stunned Cubs fans. The final was 9-3. The Cubs never got closer than four runs all day.

"There is no way," said Merullo afterward, "that Borowy should have pitched, although you have to admire his guts."

So there it was. The 10th and final World Series for the Cubs in the 20th century. Exciting and tight throughout, but ultimately heartbreaking, as most of the rest of the century would be, unfortunately.

5 BAD DAYS AND LEO

In 1946 the St. Louis Cardinals got Stan Musial back from the army, and the National League standings looked as they had in the early 1940s: St. Louis on top and the Cubs among many teams looking up. Derringer had retired, and Wyse, Passeau and Borowy struggled. The Cubs started out slowly and ended up 16 games back in third place with an 82-71 record.

That was the best season the Cubs would have for the next 20 years. Wrigley's decision to underfund the minor league system was now haunting the Cubs. Prospects were few and far between. In 1948 the Cubs finished in eighth place, 27½ games out of first place. It was only the second time in the 20th century that the Cubs had fallen so far. It would not be the last. In fact, they would do so again in 1949. Grimm was fired midway through the 1949 season and replaced by former big-league star Frankie Frisch. It didn't help.

For the Cubs, the decade of the 1950s was one of the most disheartening periods for any professional franchise in major league history. The Cubs never finished closer than 13 games out of first place or higher than fifth place. Three times, they finished more than 30 games out and once finished 40 games out.

Frisch spent 2½ years there and was fired late in the 1951 season. He was replaced by Cavarretta. In 1952 Cavarretta had the team hustling and outfielder Hank Sauer led the league in home runs and RBIs, which earned him the MVP award. Chicago had a few other good players in outfielder Frankie Baumholtz and pitcher Bob Rush. The Cubs finished 77-77, 19 games out of first. It was the only time Chicago would hit the .500 mark in the decade.

Stan Hack took over the managerial reins in 1954, the season after Ernie Banks made his big-league debut on September 17, 1953. Banks was one of two black players on the Cubs that season; the other was second baseman Gene Baker. In those days, many big-league clubs would sign two black ballplayers so that they could room together.

The team still stank, but the Cubs had a legitimate star in Banks. He could hit, run and field. More important perhaps, he played hard and clearly enjoyed himself. Chicago was still very much a racist town in the 1950s, as were many metropolises, but Cubs fans, by and large white, could easily root for the hardworking Banks. In many ways, Ernie Banks was one of the keys to integration in Chicago.

Banks was also an inspiration to the rest of the team. In 1958 Banks led the league in home runs with 47, RBIs with 129 and slugging percentage

Williams, Santo and Hickman

with a .414 mark. He was clearly the best player in the league and won the MVP award. But as a team, the Cubs finished 72-82, in sixth place, 20 games behind league leader Milwaukee. Banks became the first player from a losing team to be named most valuable player. That generated a minor ruckus as baseball fans in Milwaukee, in particular, questioned how a player, even one who had had as good a year as Banks, could be an MVP when his team was so bad.

This was also the season lefty Dale Long appeared behind the plate for Chicago. Lefthanded catchers are generally a bad idea because throwing to third base becomes awkward, if not impossible. But manager Bob Scheffing had run out of catchers that day, and Long was drafted. He became the first lefthanded player to be a catcher since 1906. The next day, Long returned to first base. He would play catcher one more time in the '58 season.

Banks repeated his MVP feat in 1959, hitting 45 homers and a league-leading 143 RBIs, as the Cubs finished sixth, this time 13 games out.

But as the 1960s opened, the Cubs were still terrible. They had a couple of solid pitchers in Glen Hobbie and Don Elston. Banks was clearly a superb player, and veteran Don "Popeye" Zimmer bolstered the infield along with newcomer Ron Santo. But in 1960 the team slipped to 60-94, leaving them in seventh place, 35 games out; in 1961 Chicago's record was 64-90, leaving them 29 games out.

In 1961 outfielder Billy Williams, perhaps the best pure hitter to ever play in Chicago, came aboard. Williams easily won the league's Rookie of the Year award. That was the good news. The 1961 season was also the first year of the "College of Coaches" experiment. That was the bad news.

The plan was to hire a number of coaches and rotate them through the Cubs major league and minor league systems. Had all the coaches been exactly tuned in to the plan, it might, and the emphasis is on *might,* have worked.

But the coaches who were hired all had different philosophies and beliefs, as would any coaches coming from varied environments. Thus, every two weeks or six weeks, or whenever the rotation was changed, the Cubs players would have a new coach with different things he wanted to emphasize. "It was absolutely ridiculous," recalled Zimmer years later. "No ball club can be expected to win under those circumstances."

The Cubs had been bad before. From 1961 through 1965, they were even worse. The Cubs finished 29, 42, 17, 17 and 25 games out of first place in that span under the College of Coaches. Dick Ellsworth won 22 games in 1963, and he probably should have gotten the Cy Young award for that effort. Larry Jackson won 24 games the next year, and he probably should have gotten the key to the city.

There were, to be honest, not a lot of rays of hope. Banks, Santo and Williams were consummate professionals. A youngster named Ken Hubbs seemed as though he would help at second base, winning the Rookie of the Year award in 1962. But he died tragically in a plane crash in 1964, just before the start of his third year.

With the Cubs at the lowest point in their history, Phil Wrigley finally reached out and hired someone who could make a difference: Leo Durocher. Durocher, a former teammate of Babe Ruth's, was known for his crafty play while in the major leagues. He became a manager soon after his retirement and became known as a tough, win-at-all-costs skipper. Durocher had been managing since 1940 when he signed a contract with the Cubs. He was a known quantity, a clever baseball man who knew how to build franchises. And if ever a franchise needed to be rebuilt, it was this one.

Wrigley hired Durocher because he was tired of being hammered in the media about being the architect of the Cubs' downfall. So, after 20 or so years of abject futility, he opted to try to turn the team around. When Durocher came aboard, just before the 1966 season, he declared that the Cubs were not an eighth-place team. He was right. That year, Chicago finished 10th, losing 103 games. Two second-year expansion teams, the Houston Colt 45s (later the Astros) and the New York Mets, finished ahead of the Cubs. It was starting to be too much to bear for Cubs fans.

Durocher, though, was already turning things around. There was no secret to it: one of the caveats under which he was hired by Wrigley was the ability to spend money to sign and pay good players. The previous coaches had not had nearly as free a hand.

Durocher almost immediately began making trades and buying ballplayers who would help the franchise. He brought up Glenn Beckert and Don Kessinger from the minor leagues and thrust them both into the starting lineup in 1965. The next year, he brought up lefty phenom Ken Holtzman.

In 1965 Durocher traded for catcher Randy Hundley and pitcher Bill Hands. In 1966 he traded for pitcher Ferguson (Fergie) Jenkins and in 1968 Durocher traded for pitcher Phil Regan and first baseman-outfielder Jim Hickman.

Slowly but surely, the Cubs were improving. Jenkins won 20 in 1967, and the Cubs finished third, with 87 wins. The 1968 season brought another third-place finish as Santo at third base, Kessinger at shortstop, Beckert at second base and Banks at first matured into a solid defensive unit. Jenkins won 20 again and anchored an improving pitching staff. Jenkins would win 20 games or more for six consecutive years for Chicago, from 1967 to 1972. In that span, no pitcher was more consistent. Williams was now one of the best outfielders in the league, and Hundley was a rock at catcher.

This improvement set the stage for the exciting, heartbreaking 1969 season. The Cubs shot out of the gate, going 11-1. The pitching was great and the everyday lineup was loaded with good hitters. The Cubs were in first place for 155 days in 1969. It was the longest any team has been in first place without winning the pennant.

On August 19, Holtzman no-hit the Atlanta Braves, winning 3-0. That put the Cubs on top by 7½ games over the surprising Mets. But that was the high point of the season. The Cubs stopped hitting and stopped winning after that, going 15-25 the rest of the way. The Mets, with a superior pitching staff, passed them and went on to win the

National League East championship, the National League championship and the World Series over the Baltimore Orioles. (In 1969 the American and National Leagues each split into Eastern and Western Divisions.)

The Cubs finished second, eight games back.

There were a lot of theories about why the Cubs fell short, but many believed that Durocher simply wore his players down. Leo was not one to use his bench much anyway, and players such as Hundley, Beckert and Kessinger, in particular, just never got a rest and ended up struggling at the end of 1969.

The Cubs would not get any closer under Leo. They may have been better in 1970, adding pitcher Milt Pappas and first baseman Joe Pepitone in 1970, but the Pirates, with Roberto Clemente, Bill Mazeroski and Willie Stargell, won the division as the Cubs finished second again.

Chicago was third in 1971, with Jenkins winning the Cy Young award, and second in 1972, when Durocher was fired midway through the season in favor of former Cubs coach Whitey Lockman.

To most other franchises, this five-year stretch would have been a hugely disappointing span. To Cubs fans, almost numbed by decades of frustration, the Leo Durocher years had brought back hope. Santo, in his autobiography, recalled that fans who followed the Cubs in that era still come up to him and thank him for the memories. "People weren't talking politics or war or economics in Chicago in the summer of 1969," said Santo. "They were talking about the Cubs."

The 1971 season was Banks's last. After an All-Star season in 1969, his playing time had been reduced in 1970 and 1971. He had played 19 years for the Cubs, taking the field as a member of some of the most abysmal teams in the history of the major leagues. Yet his professionalism never wavered, his optimism never faltered. "The only thing better than playing one ball game today," he often said, "is playing two. Let's play two!"

In later years, former teammates would be critical of him or would wonder aloud how this superior athlete could play year after year without a

"Mr. Cub," Ernie Banks

trace of frustration. But Banks many times explained that were it not for baseball, his lot in life would have been much more pedestrian; he always knew how fortunate a man he was. "Compared to Ernie Banks," the late sportswriter Jim Murray once wrote, "Rebecca of Sunnybrook Farm was a grouch." Banks left the Cubs as the franchise leader in games, at-bats, total bases, home runs, extra-base hits and optimism.

The Cubs picked up speedy outfielder Jose Cardenal and slugging outfielder Rick Monday, as well as pitcher Burt Hooton in 1972, but the Pirates were once again the better team, edging Chicago by nine games. Monday had been picked up from Oakland, and the player the Cubs sent to the Athletics was Holtzman, who was blossoming into a superior pitcher. With no one really replacing Holtzman, the Cubs began to slide again, finishing fifth in 1973.

There was a housecleaning at the end of the season. Jenkins went to the Texas Rangers for third baseman Bill Madlock and second baseman Vic Harris. Hundley was traded to Minnesota, Beckert to the Padres, the steady Hickman to the Cardinals; Billy Williams was benched.

But the changes seemed to be for change's sake, not necessarily to improve the club. The Cubs finished sixth, fifth, fourth and fourth (in a six-team division) from 1974 through 1977. After the brief euphoria of "Leo Ball," the Cubs were floundering again. And in 1974 Billy Williams, the soft-spoken hitting machine, hung up his spikes. He had tallied more than 2,500 hits and almost 400 home runs, all in Chicago. Only Banks had more homers and only Cap Anson and Ernie had more hits. But like Banks, Williams had little to show for his efforts in terms of championships. Williams had striven mightily for a franchise that simply never had enough good players.

The team, however, still had a handful of individual stars. Madlock won back-to-back batting championships in 1975 and 1976. Manny Trillo was an All-Star at second base and Bruce Sutter was learning how to pitch.

On April 12, 1977, Philip Knight Wrigley died, and William Wrigley, his son, took over ownership of the club. It was just around this time that baseball's reserve clause had been overturned, meaning players were now no longer bound to their clubs for life. The era of free agency had begun, and the tightfisted Cubs would have trouble adjusting.

Just prior to his death, Philip Wrigley traded Monday to the Dodgers for first baseman Bill Buckner and second baseman Ivan DeJesus. In 1978 the Cubs picked up slugger Dave Kingman.

But Sutter was the key, although he could not carry the club by himself. His split-fingered fastball dazzled hitters and from 1977 through 1980 he saved 31, 27, 37 and 28 games. In 1979 he won the Cy Young award, even though the Cubs finished 80-82.

On the management front, Bill Wrigley was struggling. Free agency was spiraling salaries through the ceiling. In 1976 Sutter made $19,000. In 1980, after he became a free agent, he made $700,000. Soon after, Sutter was traded to St. Louis. It was a purely financial deal to rid the team of Sutter's salary, and it essentially gave the Cardinals the 1982 World Championship, as Sutter was a key contributor to that Cardinals team.

In 1981, just four years after the death of his father, Wrigley sold the Cubs to the Chicago Tribune Company, owners of the *Chicago Tribune* newspaper, for $20.5 million. Corporate ownership did not initially sit well with many fans after 105 years of an individual or family owning the team, but at least the Tribune Company, in the 21 years they have run the Cubs, have been able to keep the team reasonably more competitive than it has been in many a year. The Wrigleys simply cannot make that claim.

6 RYNO AND, LATER, SAMMY

Just prior to the 1982 season, the Tribune Corp. hired Dallas Green to serve as the Cubs' general manager. Green was a no-nonsense guy, a shrewd judge of talent and a man who expected his players to give 100 percent on the field. Like Durocher before him, Green was given a mandate to improve the ball club.

And almost as soon as he was hired, he began cleaning house. He sent DeJesus to Philadelphia for shortstop Larry Bowa and a young second baseman named Ryne Sandberg in probably one of the best trades ever for the Cubs. Green also fired a number of Cubs scouts and administrators.

Chicago finished fifth in both 1982 and 1983, and the team still seemed to be struggling. The infield was solid with veteran ex-Dodger Bill Buckner at first base, Bowa at shortstop and another ex-Dodger, Ron Cey, at third, along with All-Star Sandberg at second. By 1984 the outfield of Gary Matthews, Bob Dernier and Keith Moreland was gelling and Jody Davis was doing an excellent job at the catcher's slot.

The pitching staff was solid, with Steve Trout, Dennis Eckersley and Scott Sanderson and reliever Lee Smith, but it was thin. Green realized he needed another starter. On June 13, 1984, he sent surefire outfield prospect Joe Carter, as well as veteran Mel Hall and Don Schultze, to Cleveland for Rick Sutcliffe and two other players.

Sutcliffe was a consistent, savvy pitcher for the Indians, and Green and new Cubs manager Jim Frey hoped he would solidify the staff and pick up a few wins in the second half of the season.

Sutcliffe did that, and more. In a scenario eerily reminiscent of the 1945 season, Sutcliffe went 16-1 the rest of the way, and, not unlike Hank Borowy almost 40 years earlier, pitched Chicago to the National League East championship.

To be sure, Sutcliffe wasn't the only player who came up big that year. Sandberg came into his own as well. On June 26, 1984, in a nationally televised game against St. Louis, Sandberg went five-for-seven, with two home runs and seven RBIs to almost single-handedly win the game and announce his entry onto the national stage. He would lead the league in several categories that year and would easily win the MVP award.

In addition, Cey was fifth in the league with 25 homers, and fourth in RBIs with 97, and Durham was fifth in slugging percentage with a .505 mark. "The Intimidator," 6'6" relief ace Smith, was second in the league in saves.

Once again, Chicago had pennant fever. And this time, unlike 1969, the team came through. Sandberg recalled in his autobiography that as the 1984 season went on, there was a lot of ink in the local newspapers about how the Cubs, in the wake of the disaster of 1969, were destined to blow the pennant in 1984.

"We didn't know anything about the history," he recalled. "All we knew was that we had the horses."

The Cubs clinched the National League East flag in Pittsburgh. It was the first time since 1945 that a Chicago team was in the postseason, and Cubs fans were delirious. When the team returned home and played its next game against the Cardinals, the fans would not leave after the game was over. So Frey gathered up the squad and led them back out of the dugout where they went into the stands and shook hands and hugged fans for a long time after.

The Cubs were slight favorites over the National League West champion San Diego Padres. And the Cubs won the first two games of the best three-of-five series, 13-0 and 4-2 behind Sutcliffe and Trout. A sweep looked likely, but the Padres had won the National League West with a combination of talented young players like Tony Gwynn and Alan Wiggins and savvy veterans like ex-Yankees Graig Nettles and Richard "Goose" Gossage and ex-Dodger Steve Garvey. With their back to the wall, the Padres didn't panic.

They won Game 3 by a score of 7-1 and tied the series with a 7-5 win the next day. Still, the Cubs were confident with the still-hot Sutcliffe going in the fifth and final contest.

But even when the Cubs jumped out to a 3-0 lead after two innings, the Padres didn't quit. They chipped away at Sutcliffe and several Cub relievers. Then, trailing 3-2 in the bottom of the seventh inning, they exploded for four runs to clinch the game and the series.

This was one of the more demoralizing losses in team history. The Padres were a good team, but man for man, the Cubs believed they were better. There was nothing to do but wait, again, until next year.

But next year was a huge disappointment. Sutcliffe pulled a hamstring muscle and went on and off the disabled list all year. The entire pitching staff soon followed him. At one point in August, all five starters were on the disabled list.

"We were calling up guys I'd never heard of from towns I never knew about," said Sandberg glumly.

The Cubs finished 77-84, 23½ games out.

Green kept trying to improve the club, but he couldn't seem to regain whatever the 1984 team had possessed. The Cubs finished 37 games out in 1986, although newcomer Shawon Dunston was already showing fine form at shortstop, and

18½ games out in 1987, despite an MVP year from outfielder Andre Dawson, who had been picked up from Montreal that year.

With only one winning season in seven years, the Dallas Green years were clearly coming to an end. The Tribune Company wanted results. Plus, the brash Green was not a fan favorite, although his players, for the most part, liked him. Following the 1987 season, Green was fired and Frey elevated to general manager. Frey then hired Don Zimmer to manage the club in 1988. This was also the first year the Cubs introduced the use of lights at the ballpark. One footnote: in 1932, the Cubs pondered installing lights for night games. Philip Wrigley was appalled at the idea.

"A passing fad" was his description of lights at the ballpark.

When the names of great managers are bandied about, "Zim" is rarely included. Yet there is no doubt he did an excellent job managing the team to the 1989 National League East championship, the Cubs' second in six years. Zimmer had been in major league baseball as either a player or a coach or a manager since 1954. His management of game situations was excellent, and he treated his players like men. They, in turn, loved the guy.

With Sandberg leading the league in runs scored with 104, and finishing fifth in home runs (30) and hits (176), first baseman Mark Grace finishing fourth overall in batting average (.314) and pitcher Greg Maddux second in the league in wins with 19, the Cubs won 93 games to finish 6 games ahead of the Mets in the National League East.

The Cubs, however, were no match for the San Francisco Giants in the National League championship series. Grace was nearly impossible to stop in the series, making 11 hits in 17 appearances for a .647 average. And Sandberg was almost as tough, hitting .400. But Cubs pitching struggled, and the Giants won the series, four games to one.

In what has become a pattern for the Cubs over the past four decades, the team once again fell back in the standings in 1990, going 77-85 and

finishing 18 games out of first place. The pitching, despite another strong year from Maddux, faltered and the hitting, despite good years from Grace, Sandberg and Dawson, was inconsistent.

What this revealed is that the Cubs had just enough talent to win if everyone had a strong year. The team had little quality depth, and when a few regulars struggled, the team's fortunes dropped.

The Tribune Company had improved the Cubs' fortunes to some extent; the team was not as horrible as in the darkest years of the Wrigley stewardship, but the winning seasons were not coming at a regular pace.

This continued into the 1990s. From 1990 to 1997, there was but one winning season, a fourth-place finish in 1993, with an 84-73 mark. A frustrated Sandberg retired in 1994, came back in 1996 and reretired in 1997. Dawson was traded to the Red Sox in 1992. Maddux, the best pitcher in the 1990s after Roger Clemens, won the Cy Young award for the Cubs in 1992, then signed as a free agent with the Braves. There, Maddux has been a driving force in the Braves' tremendous consistency in the playoffs for the past nine years.

The 1998 season was certainly a year to remember. Outfielder Sammy Sosa and Cardinals' first baseman Mark McGwire engaged in a thrilling duel for the home run championship. In the course of the year, both men broke the major league record for most homers in a season, set by the Yankees' Roger Maris, who hit 61 in 1961. They also broke Hack Wilson's National League record for homers, which was 56, set in 1930.

Sosa popped onto the home-run radar screen with an amazing performance in June, hitting 20 home runs and a stunning 40 RBIs in 27 games. After that, he and McGwire were neck and neck through most of the season. McGwire eventually won the "race," socking 72 round-trippers to Sosa's 66.

In addition to Sosa's work, rookie pitcher Kerry Wood recorded one of the most dominant pitching performances ever, striking out 20 and allowing only one hit in a 2-0 win over the Astros on May 6. The 20 strikeouts were a National League record, tying the major league record set by Roger

Sammy Sosa slamming another one home against the Marlins, 1996

Clemens when he pitched for the Red Sox. Wood finished 13-6 on the year.

But Sosa, Wood and Chicago had other concerns. The Cubs were chasing a playoff berth. The Cubs eventually finished second, with a record of 89-73. This put them in a tie with the San Francisco Giants for the final playoff berth in the league. In 1994 each league in baseball had expanded from two to three divisions. This created another tier of playoffs. The three divisional winners, plus the "wild card" team—that is, the best second-place team in the league—would play. The Giants had finished second in the National League's Western Division. The Cubs were now in the National League's Central Division. Both ended up with 89 wins.

This necessitated a one-game playoff between the two squads. Ninety years after the famed "Merkle Boner" with the New York Giants, the Cubs defeated the relocated San Francisco Giants, 5-2. Pinch hitter Matt Mieske drilled a two-run single in the sixth to give Chicago a 4-0 lead, and the Cubs hung on from there. It was the first time in 90 years that a Chicago team had won a playoff of any kind against another team.

The Cubs, worn down by the pennant race and playoff game, were swept by the Atlanta Braves in the National League divisional series. In what might be regarded as a cruel twist of fate, Maddux scattered eight hits in the final game to give the Braves a 6-2 win.

The Cubs struggled in 1999 and 2000, but Sosa did not. He came back in 1999 to hit 63 home runs, finishing second again to McGwire's 65 in that category. In 2000 Sosa "fell" to 50 homers.

The 2001 season has given rise to more optimism in Chicago. The Cubs hired a new manager, Don Baylor, in 2000; in 2001 Chicago was in the thick of the National League Central Division race until the latter part of the season, when injuries to several players took their toll. Chicago finished 88-74, the fifth best record in the National League and just out of the playoffs.

Sosa had his best all-around season ever, with 64 home runs, 160 RBIs, a .328 batting average, a .737 slugging average, 116 walks and 146 runs scored. He became the first player in major league history to hit 60 or more home runs three times, an amazing accomplishment.

Wood, after arm problems in 1999 that carried over to 2000, went 12-6 in 2001 and showed flashes of his former potential.

Pitcher Jon Lieber, after a pair of years near the .500 mark, had his best season as a pro in 2001, posting a 20-6 record and a 3.80 ERA. Outfielder Rondell White hit .307 and Fred McGriff, obtained in midseason, hit .280. Just prior to the 2002 season, the Cubs made a major deal to shore up their infield by signing former Blue Jay Alex Gonzalez, one of the best shortstops in the majors.

THE STORY OF WRIGLEY FIELD

Wrigley Field, in addition to being the oldest ballpark in the National League, is also the last remaining monument to a simpler time. Charming and intimate, Wrigley Field is, in the words of the man who built it, "an edifice of beauty."

Interestingly, the man who built Wrigley Field, Charles Weeghman, initially tried to destroy the Chicago Cubs. Weeghman was the owner of the Chicago Whales of the old Federal League, a third major professional league that ran from 1914 to 1915.

Weeghman, who had made his money operating a spate of successful luncheonettes in the Chicago area, was the best of the Federal League owners. He understood that to compete in Chicago with the White Sox and Cubs he needed a first-rate facility.

He hired famed architect Zachary Taylor Davis to design Weeghman Park.

Weeghman purchased a vacant lot from the Chicago Lutheran Theological Seminary. The lot was smack in the middle of a residential neighborhood, bounded by West Waveland Avenue, Seminary Avenue, North Clark Street, 1060 West Addison Street and North Sheffield Avenue. Davis, who had designed Comiskey Park a few years before, did a heck of a job, and much of his work remains relatively untouched.

The park was intentionally fan-friendly, with concession stands at the rear of the facility (so that hawkers wouldn't be constantly moving back and forth in front of fans). Weeghman also allowed fans to keep balls hit into the stands. Prior to this, most clubs sent ushers after fans who refused to throw batted balls back out onto the field.

By the end of 1915, there was no doubt which team was the king of Chicago. The Federal Leaguers were averaging more than 10,000 fans per

Wrigley Field

game, while the Cubs and Sox combined were lucky if they hit half that number. However, events were conspiring against the Federal League. After the 1915 season, the Federal League folded, with just about every club but Chicago losing money. Part of the settlement by the American and National Leagues with the Federals was to allow Weeghman, along with a 10-man consortium, to purchase the flagging Cubs, merge them with the Whales and play their home games in Weeghman Park. This was done, and in 1916 the Cubs opened play in Weeghman Park.

After William Wrigley purchased the team in 1919, keeping the park, now known as Cubs Park, in tip-top condition was a principal focus. Wrigley oversaw several renovations to the park, including moving the grandstand and playing field 60 feet to the southwest between the 1922 and 1923 seasons.

In 1926 Wrigley removed the left-field bleachers and added a second deck to the grandstand, increasing the capacity to 38,143. The park was also renamed Wrigley Field, in honor of William Wrigley. The expanded facility drew over 1 million fans, making Chicago the first team to reach that milestone.

The famed ivy was planted against the red brick walls in 1937. Bill Veeck, then the head of promotions for the Cubs, initially planted bittersweet, which was tougher than ivy and grew faster. In time, real ivy pushed out the bittersweet.

Also in 1937, the Wrigley Field bleachers and scoreboard were constructed when the outfield area was renovated to provide improved and expanded seating.

The original scoreboard remains intact to this day. The score by innings and pitchers' numbers are changed by hand. One of the traditions of the field is flying a flag bearing a "W" or an "L" after a Cubs win or loss, respectively. The bleacher wall is 11.5 feet high; the basket attached to the wall was built in 1970. Ernie Banks's uniform number (14) is imprinted on the flag that flies from the left-field

pole. Billy Williams's number (26) flies from the right field foul pole.

In 1988, over the objections of neighbors, fans and some city administrators, the Cubs installed lights at the field. The first night game took place on August 8 against Philadelphia, but was rained out after 3½ innings. This led to speculation (some wry, but some very serious) that the gods of baseball were also against night games at the field. However, the next evening, the Cubs defeated the Mets, 6-4, and the gods of baseball were mentioned no more, at least not in the context of denying night games in Wrigley Field. The Cubs had, in fact, been prepared to install lights once before, back in 1941, but following the attack on Pearl Harbor, the lights were donated to the war effort.

The field has been renovated several more times since the Tribune Company purchased the Cubs in 1981. These renovations included completion of a new home clubhouse in 1984 and renovation of the visitors' clubhouse in 1990. Following renovation work in 1994 and 1995, there are now 63 private boxes.

Built in the Windy City, that particular atmospheric condition has always been a factor in Wrigley Field. When the wind is blowing out, the park is a pitcher's worst enemy. When it is blowing in, home runs are almost an impossibility.

The wind notwithstanding, the foul lines are fairly deep (355 in left, 353 in right), but the power alleys are only a little deeper, 10 to 15 feet. Home runs often fly out of the park onto either Waveland or Sheffield Avenue. But the longest home run ever hit at Wrigley didn't land on either street. On April 14, 1976, Dave Kingman, playing for the Mets, hit a shot that traveled 550 feet and hit a house on the east side of Kenmore Avenue. Had the ball landed about three feet higher, it would have crashed through a window and struck the television set of Mrs. Naomi Wright, who at the time was watching Kingman trot around the bases on the tube.

OTHER FIELDS OF DREAMS

In addition to Wrigley Field, the Chicago franchise of the National League played in five other ball-parks.

THE 23RD ST. GROUNDS

Location: 23rd and State streets

Years Chicago played there: 1876–77

Chicago's record there: 42-18

Of note: Chicago went 52-14 in 1876, including a 25-6 mark at 23rd Street, to win the inaugural National League pennant.

On July 22, 1876, Chicago belted 31 hits off Louisville's John Ryan en route to a 30-7 win. Veteran first baseman Cal McVey smacked six hits.

And, in case anyone thought it was a fluke, McVey made six more hits in Chicago's next game, a 23-3 whipping of the Reds on July 25. McVey's 12 hits in two games remains a major league record.

LAKEFRONT PARK

Location: South of Randolph Street, between Michigan Ave. and Illinois Central Railroad tracks.

Years Chicago played there: 1878–84

Chicago's record there: 225-86

Of note: This was the first park to have luxury boxes. The 18 boxes were located above the grandstand on the third-base side.

Owner Albert Spalding's private box was equipped with a telephone and a gong to summon waiters.

This was the home of the first major league "dynasty," as Chicago won pennants here in 1880, 1881 and 1882.

In 1884 the league ruled that balls hit into the stands on the fly at the park would be home runs, not ground-rule doubles as had been the case in the past. Given that left field was about 180 feet

from home plate and right field about 196, Chicago set a major league record with 142 homers that year, a number not topped until 1927 when the Yankees socked 158. The four top home-run hitters in 1884 were from Chicago: Ned Williamson with 27, Fred Pfeffer with 25, Abner Dalrymple with 22 and Cap Anson with 21.

WEST SIDE PARK

Location: Congress and Throop streets

Years Chicago played there: 1885–91

Chicago's record there: 288-131

Of note: In 1891 West Side Park was used only for Monday, Wednesday and Friday home games.

Jimmy Ryan becomes the first Chicago player to hit for the cycle as Chicago outscores the Detroit Wolverines, 21-17, in 1888.

On August 16, 1890, Tom Burns and Malachi Kittridge both sock grand slams in the fifth inning as Chicago beats Pittsburgh, 18-5. It is the first time two players hit grand slams in one inning. Chicago scored 13 runs in that wild fifth, by the way.

SOUTH SIDE PARK

Location: 35th and Wentworth streets

Years Chicago played there: 1891–93

Chicago's record there: 85-75

Of note: In 1891 the park was used for Tuesday, Thursday and Saturday home games. In other words, Chicago split its 1891 home games between here and West Side. There was no Sunday baseball at the time.

South Side Park had been the home of the Chicago Pirates of the Players' League, which only lasted one season.

The park was located across the street from where Comiskey Park would eventually be constructed.

WEST SIDE GROUNDS

Location: Polk and Lincoln (now Wolcott) streets

Years Chicago played there: 1893–1915

Chicago's record there: 1,018-639

Of note: In 1893 Chicago played only Sunday ball games here.

A small balcony of box seats above the infield grandstand made this probably the first double-decker park in the major leagues.

In 1897 Chicago buries Louisville, 36-7, scoring the most runs in major league history. Chicago pitcher Jimmy Callahan has five hits to help his cause.

On August 5, 1894, a game with the Reds was suspended when the wooden bleachers caught fire.

In 1898 the Cleveland Spiders played their home games here after their ballpark burned down.

On April 30 of that year, a new major league record for attendance is set as 27,000 fans pack the park, which had a capacity of about half that. Chicago beats St. Louis, 4-0. The crowd spills out into the outfield, causing the umpire to declare that any ball hit into the spectators is worth only one base.

On September 1, 1902, Joe Tinker, Johnny Evers and Frank Chance make their Chicago debut, although not all at the positions for which they would be famous. Tinker was at third, Evers at shortstop and Chance was at first base. Bobby Lowe was at second base.

BEFORE THEY WERE THE CUBS

The Chicago franchise of the National League had several nicknames, some official, some unofficial, bestowed upon it before it became the Cubs in 1902. The first was the White Stockings, which was the original official nickname of the franchise when it entered the National League in 1876. This name came about because the team wore white stockings as part of its uniform. (The Cincinnati team was named the Red Stockings in their earliest days, before the name was shortened to the Reds.)

From 1898 through 1901, after longtime manager "Cap" Anson retired, the franchise took on the nickname "the Orphans" because Anson was no longer the team's player-manager-mentor.

From 1888 through 1889, the team was known as the "Black Stockings" because they switched to black socks those two seasons.

A number of nicknames ran concurrently for no other reason than sportswriters enjoyed dreaming them up. From 1887 to 1904, for example, the team had lost a number of veterans through retirements and trades and had acquired younger players, so many sportswriters called them "the Colts." But the team was also called the "ex-Colts" by some writers in 1898 because some of the young players had become old players.

The 1898 season was also the year the team was called by some sportswriters "the Rainmakers" because the team was involved in so many rainouts.

In 1899 the Cubs traveled to New Mexico for spring training and earned the nicknames "Cowboys" and "Rough Riders."

Two more nicknames popped up in 1901 and 1902 when, after a number of their players jumped to the American League, the Cubs were called either "the Remnants" or "the Recruits." In 1903 several players wore Panama hats to spring training, which moved some writers to call them "the Panamas." In 1905, in a tribute to Chicago as the Windy City, the team was called "the Zephyrs." In 1906 the squad was nicknamed "the Spuds" by some writers, referring to team owner Charles Murphy's Irish heritage.

The team was referred to as "the Nationals" from 1905 through 1906, which was a nod to their membership in the National League, and in 1913 the team was sometimes referred to as "the Trojans" because manager Johnny Evers was from Troy, New York.

The Cubs came into being in 1902, a year when the team was believed to be young and inexperienced. Editors liked the name even more than reporters because "Cubs" could be fit into any size headline, from one column up. Thus, "Cubs" had more staying power than the other nicknames because it was the shortest.

THE WORLD SERIES TEAMS

Yes, there haven't been a lot, but those squads that have reached the Fall Classic were all notable in some way. Here is the complete list.

1885

Record: 87-25

Manager: Cap Anson

Opponent: St. Louis (American Association)

Result: 3-3 tie

What happened: The Chicago team, called at the time the White Stockings, agreed to meet with the St. Louis Browns, the champions of the American Association, in a seven-game series for what was billed as "the professional Base-Ball championship of the United States." But, since baseball was all but unknown everywhere else, many newspapers called this series a "world championship series." The term "World Series" was not in use at the time.

At any rate, the White Stockings—with Anson, George Gore, King Kelly, pitcher extraordinaire John Clarkson, Abner Dalrymple and a host of other skilled baseballers—were heavily favored. And had they taken the whole thing a little more seriously, they might have won the championship. But the games were billed as exhibitions, with only one game played in Chicago, three in St. Louis, one in Pittsburgh and two in Cincinnati. And while the members of the upstart Browns were pumped up for the series, many Chicago players had little interest in playing for stakes of roughly $70 per man.

As it was, outfielder Gore, whom Anson believed had been drinking before the first game, was sus-

pended for the series after that initial tilt. Clarkson was so drunk prior to the final game that Anson benched him and Kelly and several other players stayed out late every night during the series.

The first game ended in a 5-5 tie when it was called due to darkness after eight innings. The White Stockings won the second game, 5-4, after the Browns walked off the field, protesting several umpires' calls. St. Louis won the next two games, 7-4 and 3-2, before Chicago took the fifth contest, 9-2. Game 6 went to St. Louis, 13-4, and the Browns claimed the championship, three games to two, saying the forfeited game shouldn't count.

Chicago fans insisted it should count and declared the whole thing a tie. Eventually, the leagues agreed. As for the Chicago players, Kelly probably spoke for all concerned when he declared years later that the whole thing was "a terrible mess."

Key Fact: The series was a miserable failure at the gate, drawing a total of about 14,000 for all seven games.

What You Probably Didn't Know: Most sports historians believe that St. Louis owner Chris Von der Ahe agreed to call the series a tie a little too easily. The reason that happened was because Von der Ahe could then withhold the prize money from his players, which he then, in fact, did.

1886

Record: 90-34

Manager: Cap Anson

Opponent: St. Louis (American Association)

Result: Lost, 4-2

What Happened: This year, three games were played in Chicago, three in St. Louis, and the attendance pushed the final purse to $15,000 for the winners, which was about seven times what the money was the previous year.

The White Stockings won the first game as John Clarkson threw a five-hit shutout. But St. Louis captured Game 2, 12-0, behind Bob Caruthers. Clarkson scattered nine hits in an 11-4 Chicago win in Game 3, but now the series shifted to St.

Louis. There, the Browns took all three contests, 8-5, 10-3 and 4-3 to clinch the series. The final game was the best one as Clarkson took a 3-0 lead into the bottom of the eighth, only to see the home side tie the game with three runs in the ninth.

In the 10th, Curt Welch singled for St. Louis (only the fourth hit allowed by Clarkson), went to second on an infield hit and to third on a sacrifice. With the next batter at the plate, he sprinted toward home. Clarkson spotted him out of the corner of his eye. Perhaps being distracted, he threw the ball high and away, far over Kelly's glove. Welch sprinted home and slid into the plate. The slide became known as the $15,000 slide, given the amount of the prize. A disgusted Kelly threw his mask over the backstop.

Key Fact: St. Louis outfielder James "Tip" O'Neill became the first player to hit two home runs in a game in the postseason when he socked a pair in Game 2.

What You Probably Didn't Know: And what the owners of the respective clubs probably didn't know, either, was that, according to Browns third baseman Arlie Latham, the players on both teams agreed before the series began to split the prize money down the middle, regardless of who won. Reportedly, that's exactly what they did.

1906

Record: 116-36

Manager: Frank Chance

Opponent: Chicago White Sox

Result: Lost, 4-2

What Happened: Needless to say, the 116-36 Cubs of "Tinker to Evers to Chance" were heavily favored over the White Sox, a squad with a team batting average of .230 and thus dubbed "the Hitless Wonders" by scribes of the time.

But the White Sox had great pitching in starters Nick Altrock, Guy Harris "Doc" White and Ed Walsh. They had a terrific defensive club, and they had hitters who could make contact in the clutch. The first four games were the big ones. Cubs pitching had allowed only 11 White Sox hits, but

had still lost two of the four games. Altrock's four-hitter had won Game 1, 2-1, for the Sox, and spitballer Walsh's two-hitter earned a White Sox Game 3 win, 3-0. Meanwhile, when the Cubs won their two games, the scores were 7-1 and 1-0.

Emboldened, the White Sox swept the next two tilts, 8-6 and 8-3. Although the Series was an upset, the White Sox won the way all champions win, with pitching, defense and key hitting.

Key Fact: The best-hitting Cub was pitcher Mordecai Brown, with a .333 average in three games.

What You Probably Didn't Know: A number of Cubs, hugely confident of the outcome, had bet their anticipated winners' share on themselves. This means they lost their losers' share and a few hundred dollars of their own money after the Series was over, adding insult to injury.

1907

Record: 107-45

Manager: Frank Chance

Opponent: Detroit Tigers

Result: Won, 4-0, with one tie

What Happened: Not much, even if you were a Cubs fan. The Tigers hit an anemic .209, with their all-time all-star, Ty Cobb, slapping four hits in 20 at-bats. Cobb did not steal a base, thanks to the rifle arm of Chicago catcher Johnny Kling. In fact, Kling threw out six of 12 Tiger base runners and essentially took away the Tigers' most intimidating weapon: their speed on the bases.

The first game ended in a 3-3 tie, and that was exactly half the number of runs the Tigers would score the entire Series. The Cubs then swept the Series, 3-1, 5-1, 6-1 and 2-0, as Mordecai Brown, Orval Overall, Jack Pfiester and Ed Reulbach all turned in complete game wins. The hitting star for Chicago was third baseman Harry Steinfeldt, with eight hits in 17 at-bats, including a double and triple, for a .471 mark.

Key Fact: The Cubs' team ERA of 0.75 was the lowest ERA in the World Series until 1950, when the Yankees swept the Phillies and posted a 0.73 ERA.

What You Probably Didn't Know: The World Series didn't have quite the cachet in 1907 that it would have in later years. The Tigers averaged a hair over 9,300 people in attendance for their pair of home games.

1908

Record: 99-55

Manager: Frank Chance

Opponent: Detroit Tigers

Result: Won, 4-1

What Happened: The Tigers vowed that this year would be different, and it was, a little. Detroit won Game 3, 8-3. But the Cubbies won the rest of the contests, 10-6, 6-1, 3-0 and 2-0, respectively. Brown and Overall were the pitching stars for the Cubs, each earning a pair of victories. Player-manager Frank Chance was the best hitter for the Cubs, making eight hits in 19 at-bats.

Key Fact: Joe Tinker's home run in the second game was the first home run in a World Series game since 1903.

What You Probably Didn't Know: Orval Overall's three-hitter to close out the Tigers in Game 5 included a four-strikeout first inning. Overall managed to strike out two of the first three Tigers and seemed to get Claude Rossman. But Johnny Kling dropped the ball and Rossman sprinted to first base. Still, Overall punched out Herman "Germany" Schaefer to finish up the inning.

1910

Record: 104-50

Manager: Frank Chance

Opponent: Philadelphia Athletics

Result: Lost, 4-1

What Happened: Chicago's pitching was good, but the Athletics' was simply better. The Cubs' two aces, Overall and Brown, were beaten in the first two games in Philadelphia by Connie Mack's own stars, Chief Bender and Jack Coombs. A five-run third inning cooked the Cubs in Game 3

as they absorbed a 12-5 shellacking. Chicago earned its only win of the Series the next day, a 4-3 triumph in 10 innings. But they were closed out in game 5, 7-2.

Key Fact: Mack used only two pitchers the entire series, the only time a manager pulled it off in the 20th century.

What You Probably Didn't Know: Not only did Bender and Coombs pitch very well, but they also hit the heck out of the ball. Coombs was 5-13 for a .385 average, while Bender was 2-6 for a .333 mark.

1918

Record: 84-45

Manager: Fred Mitchell

Opponent: Boston Red Sox

Result: Lost, 4-2.

What Happened: Babe Ruth. The pitcher, that is. Ruth spun a six-hit shutout in Game 1 as the Sox prevailed, 1-0. He also won Game 4, 3-2. In addition, Ruth "led" the Sox with two RBIs. Carl Mays picked up two other wins for the Sox, both 2-1 scores, in Games 3 and 6. The Red Sox had an absolutely overpowering staff that year, although the Cubs were no slouches, either, with James "Hippo" Vaughn, Lefty Tyler and Claude Hendrix.

Key Fact: This, of course, was the last time the Red Sox won a world championship, and they did it in Fenway Park with pitching and defense.

What You Probably Didn't Know: The .186 team batting average of the Sox was the lowest of the 20th century for a World Series winner.

1929

Record: 98-54

Manager: Joe McCarthy

Opponent: Philadelphia Athletics

Result: Lost, 4-1

What Happened: Cubs fans are inclined to say that the catastrophic seventh inning in Game 4, when the A's scored 10 runs to turn an 8-0 Cubs laugher into a 10-8 Athletics stunner, was Chicago's Waterloo. But what hurt Chicago even more was losing the first two games of the Series at home, 3-1 to the A's Howard Ehmke and 9-3 to George Earnshaw.

Never mind Game 4. A sweep or split of those first two games would have changed the Series dramatically, especially since Chicago had won Game 3, 3-1. The thing that seventh inning in Game 4 did do was basically shut the door on the Cubs. The A's would take the final game, 3-2.

Key Fact: Veteran second baseman Rogers Hornsby had probably the greatest all-round individual season in team history, Hack Wilson and Sammy Sosa notwithstanding. "The Rajah" led the team in batting average (.380), hits (229) and runs scored (156), each all-time Cubs records. He also tied Wilson for the home-run lead with 39, and led the team in doubles and triples. To top it off, Hornsby led the National League's second basemen in assists with 547 and double plays with 106. He was justifiably the MVP of the league, but it was an absolute hell of a year for a 33-year-old guy.

What You Probably Didn't Know: Howard Ehmke, the surprise starter for Game 1 of the World Series, wasn't *that* bad. Ehmke was 7-2 with a 3.29 ERA, his best in 10 years, in 1929.

1932

Record: 90-64

Manager: Rogers Hornsby/Charlie Grimm

Opponent: New York Yankees

Result: Lost, 4-0

What Happened: Babe Ruth. The hitter, that is. Ruth hit .333, teammate Lou Gehrig hit .529 and Yankee catcher Bill Dickey hit .438. All four games were high scoring, and the Yankees won 'em all, 12-6, 5-2, 7-5 and 13-6. The Cubs had several guys who hit well, including Riggs Stephenson, who hit .444, and Billy Jurges, who hit .364. But the Cubs couldn't keep up.

Key Fact: And this is a fact. Ruth did not call his shot, as legend has it, in the fifth inning of Game 3. In fact, in several postseason accounts, Ruth admitted that had he tried to show up Cubs pitcher Charlie Root, he would have been knocked on his back, which everyone, including Root, acknowledges. What happened was that Ruth pointed to Root and told him that it only took one swing to hit the ball. And it does, and he did.

What You Probably Didn't Know: The Cubs' 9.26 team ERA was the worst in World Series history.

Programs for the 1929, 1938 and 1945 World Series

1935

Record: 100-54

Manager: Charlie Grimm

Opponent: Detroit Tigers

Result: Lost, 4-2

What Happened: This was one the Cubs figured to win. Coming off a red-hot September in which they won 21 games in a row, the Cubbies took the lead in the Series by whipping the Tigers, 3-0, behind Lon Warneke in Game 1. The Tigers took Game 2, 8-3, but the Series switched back to Chicago for the next three games, where the National League champions figured to have an edge. Instead, Detroit squeezed out a 6-5 win in 11 innings on an unearned run in Game 3 and then edged Chicago, 2-1, in Game 4. The Cubs won the fifth game, 3-1, behind Warneke, but Detroit took another one-run game on an RBI single by Goose Goslin.

Key Fact: The Cubs won 100 games for the last time in their history.

What You Probably Didn't Know: Cubs righty Fabian Kowalik's real name was Fabian.

1938

Record: 89-63

Manager: Charlie Grimm/Gabby Hartnett

Opponent: New York Yankees

Result: Lost, 4-0

What Happened: Lefty, Monte and Red. That's Lefty Gomez, Monte Pearson and Red Ruffing, who were the winning pitchers in the Yanks' four-game sweep. Ruffing picked up two wins, the others one each. The Cubs held their own at the plate, with New York outhitting them, 37-33. But the Cubs did far less damage, scoring only nine runs to the Yankees' 21. The games were fairly close, but New York won them, 3-1, 6-3, 5-2 and 8-3, respectively. Outfielder Joe Marty (.500), third baseman Stan Hack (.471) and first baseman Phil Cavarretta (.462) all hit the heck out of the ball for the Cubs. But Cubs pitchers struggled.

Key Fact: The Cubs' 89 wins was four victories fewer than in 1937 when they finished second.

What You Probably Didn't Know: Cubs righty James Otto "Tex" Carleton allowed two earned runs in no innings, thus conferring upon himself the unforgettable infinite ERA for the Series. To be fair, in 1935, his World Series ERA was 1.29.

1945

Record: 98-56

Manager: Charlie Grimm

Opponent: Detroit Tigers

Result: Lost, 4-3

What Happened: The Cubs twice took leads in this Series. In Game 1, Hank Borowy fired a six-hit shutout for a 9-0 Cubs win. After the Tigers tied the series in Game 2, Claude Passeau put the Cubs back on top, two games to one, with a one-hitter, 3-0. Once again, the Cubs were sitting pretty as they now had the next four games in Chicago (due to wartime travel restrictions), but they could not take advantage.

The Tigers' Dizzy Trout evened the series with a five-hitter, 4-1, and Hal Newhouser gave the Tigers the lead in the Series in Game 5, outpitching Borowy, 8-4. Chicago won a wild one, 8-7, in 12 innings, on Stan Hack's RBI double. Borowy, clearly the pitching star for the Cubs, got the win with four strong innings of relief. But manager Grimm opted to start Borowy after that stint, and Borowy wasn't ready. The Tigers pounded him and scored five runs in the first, coasting to a frustrating 9-3 win in the Cubs' last World Series game of the 20th century.

Key Fact: The Cubs topped 1 million in paid attendance for the first time in 14 years. This span, of course, included the three National League championship teams.

What You Probably Didn't Know: Virgil Trucks got out of the navy just in time to pitch the Tigers' last game of the year and then two more games in the World Series.

THE 10 MOST DRAMATIC MOMENTS IN CUBS HISTORY

There are a lot of jokes about futility and defeat connected to the Cubs, but it will not surprise Cubs fans to hear that throughout the team's history there have been some deeply dramatic and key events that have become part of baseball lore. Herewith are the top 10. Warning: do not look for August 8, 1988, in this list. Turning on a bank of lights is decidedly not dramatic, even if it was a first for the Cubs, and, what the heck, the darn game was eventually rained out anyway.

1 September 23, 1908: The Merkle Game. Of course, this didn't become a dramatic moment until October 7, and it didn't become the Most Dramatic Moment ever until about 5:00 P.M. on October 8, but we'll get to all that.

Jack Pfiester was pitching for the Cubs against the Giants' Christy Mathewson at the Polo Grounds. The score was tied at 1-1 in the bottom of the ninth. There were two outs, and New York's Moose McCormick was on third base. Rookie Fred Merkle, who had singled, was on first base. Merkle was replacing veteran first baseman Fred Tenney in the game. This was the only game that Tenney would sit out all year (He had a bad ankle. Giants manager John McGraw decided to start Merkle because Pfiester was a lefty and Merkle had better luck against lefties than Tenney.)

Al Bridwell drilled a single off Pfiester, and McCormick easily trotted home. Happy Giants fans began to swarm onto the field. Merkle, not wanting to be stampeded, had rounded first but then veered off the base path toward the Giants clubhouse.

Immediately, Johnny Evers realized that if Merkle didn't touch second base and if he could get there with the ball in his hand and touch it instead, it would be a force out (because Merkle had left the base path). Even now, if a force out is the third out of an inning, no run scored on the play would count.

There was a little struggle for the ball. When Merkle had initially made the hit, the ball trickled into the outfield. Cubs center fielder Solly Hofman picked it up and disconsolately started walking in toward the Cubs dugout. But Evers knew the Cubs still had a chance. He screamed at Hofman to throw him the ball. Hofman threw it, and it sailed over Evers's head and onto the infield grass. Giants pitcher Joe "Iron Man" McGinnity, who was the third-base coach, quickly figured out what Evers was trying to do. McGinnity got to the ball first and, as Evers and Joe Tinker tried to grab it, threw the ball into the crowd in center field.

McGinnity guessed quite correctly that a Giants fan would pick up the ball. That is exactly what happened. But the unsung hero of this story, Cubs pitcher Rube Kroh, who was also in center field heading toward the Cubs dugout, reportedly saw who picked up the ball. (We say reportedly because McGinnity swore until the day he died that the ball Kroh found was the wrong one.)

Anyway, Kroh and third baseman Harry Steinfeldt wrestled the ball away from the fan and relayed it to Evers, who stepped on second base, first making sure that umpire Hank O'Day was there to see it. O'Day did see it and ruled Merkle out. Evers, in his memoirs, recalled that O'Day told him Merkle was out, but that these words were coming out of his mouth as he raced for the umpires' dressing room. He clearly had no intention of continuing the contest. O'Day later said he called the game on account of darkness.

Later that day, Cubs manager Frank Chance told a sportswriter that the Giants should have been required to forfeit the game because they did not return to the field after the ninth inning. Eventually, the game was ruled a tie. On October 7, with the Cubs watching anxiously, the Giants completed a sweep of the Braves, and the National League board of directors ordered the September 23 game replayed. Which leads us to:

2 October 8, 1908: Cubs 4, Giants 2. With all due respect to Bobby Thompson, beating the Dodgers at the Polo Grounds was certainly not easy, and Thompson's home run in the 1951 playoff game remains the most dramatic single event in baseball. But in 1908, the Cubs returned to the "Belly of the Beast" to earn the pennant, going into New York on the day after the regular season ended, to defeat the Giants and Christy Mathewson on the Polo Grounds before an overflow crowd estimated at 30,000, five thousand over capacity. This was one of the great games in the history of baseball.

Mordecai Brown, on two days' rest, came into the game in the first inning to relieve Pfiester and held the Giants to one run over 8⅓ innings. He set the home side down on four pitches in the ninth inning.

But the game was the easy part. Chance, who had made three hits on the day, was punched in the neck by a fan as he was leaving the field after the contest, which stunned him and robbed him of his voice for a day. Tinker was punched by fans swarming the field on two separate occasions as he tried to get to the dugout after the game. Pfiester was slashed on the arm with a knife, while utility outfielder George Elmer "Del" Howard, trying to urge Giants fans to calm down, was punched in the stomach and had his cap stolen for good measure.

"It was," recalled Brown fervently a few years later, "as near a lunatic asylum as I ever saw."

3 September 28, 1938: "Homer in the Gloamin'": It was an overcast day in Chicago, and the Cubs and Pirates were tied at 5-5. Chicago was a half game behind Pittsburgh at that point. As the ninth inning began, the umpires met to consider how to deal with the onset of dusk. They relayed their decision to both teams: one more inning and the game will be called. Charlie Root set the Pirates down in order in the top of the inning, and Pittsburgh's Mace Brown got the first two batters in the bottom of the inning. Up stepped player-manager Gabby Hartnett. Hartnett swung at Brown's first pitch and missed. He swung at the second one and fouled it off. Brown, instead of wasting a pitch, came in with a fastball. Hartnett connected.

"Maybe nobody else knew it was in the bleachers, but I did," said Hartnett, referring to the diffi-

culty of tracking the ball in the darkened field. "I knew it was gone when I hit it."

The Cubs never relinquished first place and won their fourth pennant in 10 years.

4 May 12, 1970: Ernie Banks hits home run number 500. "Mr. Cub" only played 72 games that year, but he still had some pop in his bat. His 500th homer was one of the most written-about, anticipated events in Chicago Cubs history.

5 October 10, 1908: Five in the ninth. The Tigers were eager to avenge their 1907 World Series defeat. In this, the first game of the 1908 Fall Classic, Detroit had a 6-5 lead at home going into the ninth inning. But the Cubs pulled it out, scoring five times in the top of the inning. Solly Hofman's bases-loaded single was the killer, and Three Finger Brown closed the door in the bottom of the inning for a complete-game win. The demoralized Tigers were never really in the Series after that.

6 September 13, 1998: Sammy hits number 61 and 62. Okay, Mark McGwire won the home run title that year with 70 to Sammy Sosa's 66 but on September 13 at Wrigley, it was Sammy's night. Sosa tied Roger Maris's 1961 home run total with a two-run blast off Brewers pitcher Bronswell Patrick in the fifth inning. In the ninth, he passed Maris with a solo shot off Eric Plunk.

7 May 6, 1998: Kerry Wood punches out 20. At that point, 20-year-old Kerry Wood was 2-2 with a 5.89 ERA, not exactly Hall of Fame material. But Wood put himself in the record books that day, allowing one scratch hit by Ricky "Trivia Answer" Gutierrez and getting a major league–tying 20 strikeouts. Woods struck out the side four times and struck out five batters in a row twice and seven in a row once. He is also the only major league pitcher to strike out his age.

8 October 8, 1945: The last hurrah. Game 6, extra innings, the home team is behind three games to two in the World Series when one of their stars steps to the plate. But this isn't the

1975 World Series between the Red Sox and the Reds, but the 1945 Fall Classic between the Tigers and the Cubs. And Chicago's Stan Hack, like Boston's Carlton Fisk, smacks the big hit—in this case an RBI double—to win the game in 12 innings, 8-7. And Chicago, like Boston, loses the seventh and deciding game.

9 **June 23, 1984:** "The Sandberg Game." That's what Cubs fans call one of the great clutch performances in Cubs history as second baseman Ryne Sandberg goes five for six with two dramatic late-inning homers and 7 RBIs in Chicago's 11-inning, 12-11 win over St. Louis. Sandberg hit a solo shot off the Cardinals' Bruce Sutter to tie the game at 9-9 in the bottom of the ninth inning. Then, after the Cubs fell behind 11-9 in the top of the 10th, Sandberg blasted a two-run shot off Sutter—one of the best closers in the game—to tie the contest again. Chicago won the game in the next inning on an RBI single by Dave Owens. Oh and by the way, the Cardinals' Willie McGee hit for the cycle in the game. Just an amazing game.

10 **September 27, 1935:** Putting it all together. The Cubs put together the greatest September pennant drive in baseball history, winning 21 games in a row to overtake the St. Louis Cardinals for the National League pennant. On September 27, in the first game of a doubleheader, pitcher Bill Lee scattered six Cardinals hits in a 6-2 win that clinched the pennant for the Cubs. In the second game, Chicago won its 21st tilt in a row, 5-3 over St. Louis. It was Chicago's 100th win, the last time in the 20th century Chicago would make 100 wins.

THE NEAR MISSES

One of the most erroneous perceptions about the Cubs (mostly by those who aren't Cubs fans) is that Chicago's history is sprinkled with a host of close-but-no-cigar finishes. The truth is, for much of the team's history, they weren't good enough to just miss. In 126 years, the Chicago franchise of the National League has won 16 National League pennants, 2 World Series, 2 National League East crowns and earned 1 wild-card playoff berth in 1998.

In addition to that 1998 finish, the Cubs, or their previous incarnations, have finished in second place by five games or fewer just eight times: in 1883, 1891, 1928, 1930, 1936, 1937, 1970 and 1973.

In contrast, Chicago has finished 10 games or more out of first a total of 86 times in 126 years. The Cubs have finished 30 or more games out 18 times and 40 or more games out twice. So, there haven't been a lot of close finishes, but those that were have been memorable in their own way.

1930: The Cubs had a frightening team offensively, with five regulars (Riggs Stephenson, .367, Hack Wilson, .356, Kiki Cuyler, .355, Gabby Hartnett, .339 and Woody English, .335) hitting well over .300. In addition, first baseman Charlie Grimm hit .289. This was Wilson's career year. Hack hit 56 home runs, which was the National League record until 1998 and his 190 RBIs are still a major league record.

But the pitching wasn't as top-shelf. The Cubs were fourth in team ERA and only the doormat Phillies issued more walks. Their ferocious hitting had the Cubs in first place on September 1 by five games. But they went 7-13 in their first 20 games that month, and the hot-hitting Cardinals passed them into first place. In fact, all eight of the Cardinals regulars hit better than .300 by the end of the year. An ankle injury also limited Rogers Hornsby, who had had a career year in 1929, to only 42 games in 1930. It was just enough to ensure the Cubs would fall short.

1969: No team spent more time in first place (155 of 162 games) than the 1969 Chicago Cubs with nothing to show for it. The team started out 11-1 and by the end of June were seven games in first and by mid-August, 7½ games up.

But the Mets, heretofore a second-division team, simply kept playing well. Their pitching was outstanding, with a major league–leading 28 shutouts, not to mention a devastating relief combination in lefty Tug McGraw and righty Ron Taylor. While the Cubs hit a slump in September, the Mets never really did.

Cubs manager Leo Durocher never shirked his responsibility for the 1969 disaster. In his autobiography, he admitted his team should have won. In fact, Leo admitted that he should have found a way for them to win. However, he also disagreed with critics who said he burned out the regulars, insisting that his philosophy had always been to play his best players as often as possible. Saving a good pitcher for tomorrow, he argued, was self-defeating because "tomorrow it may rain." Many years later, just before his death, Leo publicly apologized to the team and fans.

There are a lot of theories as to the Cubs' demise; in the end, the Mets won 100 games, which is almost always a ticket into the playoffs.

1984: This doesn't quite qualify as a near miss because the Cubs, after 39 years of frustration, did make the playoffs. And when they took a 2-0 lead in the National League championship series against the San Diego Padres, everybody was jumping on the Cubs bandwagon. But that was as close as the Cubs would get.

The Padres' Ed Whitson threw a five-hitter in the third game of the series to give his team a 7-1 win. In the fourth game, the Padres' Steve Garvey hit a dramatic two-run homer in the bottom of the ninth to win the contest, 7-5.

Even then, the Cubs felt they could win the series, since their best pitcher, Rick Sutcliffe, was on the mound for the final contest. But first baseman Leon Durham committed a key error in the seventh when a ground ball skittered through his legs, which allowed the eventual winning run to score. Two innings later, the Padres advanced to the World Series.

FUN WITH NUMBERS

The Chicago Cubs have retired only three numbers in their 126-year history, and one of those, number 42, was retired by Chicago and the rest of Major League baseball to honor the contributions of Jackie Robinson. The other two numbers retired by the Cubs were 14 and 26, worn, of course, by Ernie Banks and Billy Williams, respectively. Interestingly, Cubs utility outfielder Lou "the Mad Russian" Novikoff wore both 14 and 26 during his brief four-year stint in Chicago from 1941 to 1944. Novikoff wore 26 in 1941 when he played in 62 games and hit .241. He switched over to 14 in 1942 and hit .300. But that wasn't the end of the Mad Russian's number switching. In 1943 he switched numbers again, taking number 19; then in 1944, he took number 45.

In fact, Novikoff probably deserves his own chapter. Novikoff was one of the great minor leaguers of all time, for any team. He won four consecutive batting championships in the minors: hitting .376 for Moline of the Three-I League in 1938, .368 for Tulsa of the Texas League in 1939, .363 for Los Angeles of the Pacific Coast League and .370 for Milwaukee of the American Association in 1941 before he was called up by the Cubs.

Part of the reason Novikoff switched numbers was to try to change his luck, which, when it came to hitting, was not usually very good. The Cubs' brass expected big things of Novikoff, and he struggled to meet their expectations, finishing his career with a .282 lifetime average.

Novikoff was an outfielder, but he hated to touch the ivy vines in Wrigley Field. He retired in 1946, took up softball and made it to the Hall of Fame—the Softball Hall of Fame.

As we have seen, players in the early part of the 20th century were not wedded to their uniform numbers. Williams himself wore number 4 and then 41 early in his career before switching to 26 in 1961. But the champion numerologist of the Chicago Cubs was Stanley Hack, who wore eight different numbers in his 16-year career. Those numbers were (according to the Cubs media guide) 6, 20, 25, 31, 34, 39, 49 and 54. It didn't hurt his performance any. Hack was a five-time All-Star who played in four World Series for Chicago.

Also on uniform numbers, four Cubs have worn the number 13: Steven "Turk" Wendell from 1993 to 1997, Bill Faul from 1965 to 1966, Hal Manders in 1946 and Claude Passeau from 1939 to 1947.

The lowest number ever worn by a Cub was the number 1. Woody English first wore it in 1932 because he was the leadoff hitter. (The 1932 season was the first year ballplayers wore uniform numbers. Starters wore the number of their position in the batting order. Thus, English was 1, Billy Herman, who hit second, wore number 2, third hitter Kiki Cuyler wore 3; and so on.)

The highest number ever worn by a Cub was 96, worn by Bill Voiselle in 1950. Voiselle came from a town called, believe it or not, Ninety-Six, South Carolina, and thus wore that number his whole career.

As far as can be determined, it is the highest number ever worn by any major leaguer in the regular season. Voiselle had a nine-year big-league career that included being named to the All-Star team in 1944 while with the Giants. But the Cubs were his last stop, and he went 0-4 in 1950. The next year, he was eighty-sixed from the league.

ALL IN THE FAMILY

According to the *Baseball Encyclopedia,* the Cubs have had nine brother combinations on their all-time roster. These included five combinations who played together: Danny and Hal Breeden in 1971; Lew and Winfield Scott "Kid" Camp in 1894, Larry and Mike Corcoran in 1884, Walter Edward "Jiggs" and Tom Parrot in 1893 and Rick and Paul Reuschel from 1975 to 1978.

Of these combos the Reuschels had the most success. Rick Reuschel was the best pitcher the Cubs had in the late 1970s and Paul, a righthander like his brother Rick, was a Cubs reliever. Paul amassed 12 saves in his four years as a Cub. The most notable effort with his brother was when the two combined to shut out the Dodgers in August 1975.

The Breeden brothers were both journeymen, Danny for two years as a catcher, Hal for five years as a first baseman. Lew Camp (whose name was shortened from Llewellyn) was a utilityman who played three years in the National League and was used at second, third, shortstop and in the outfield and never hit better than .263. Brother Winfield Scott played two years in the bigs with Pittsburgh and the Cubs and was 0-2 in that span.

Paul Reuschel (far left)
and Rick Reuschel (left)

Larry Corcoran, a canny righthander, was one of the pitching mainstays of the Cubs in the early 1880s, winning 170 games for Chicago. Brother Mike flubbed his one chance with the team in 1884, starting one game, giving up 16 hits and walking seven in a complete-game loss.

Tom Parrot was the ultimate utilityman during his four years in the National League, both pitching and playing either third base or the outfield for Chicago, Cincinnati and St. Louis. Brother Jiggs was built from a similar mold, as he played the infield and the outfield for the Cubs for his entire four-year career. He was the regular second baseman in 1894.

The other brother combinations on Chicago's rosters included Mort Cooper, who played a year for the Cubs in 1949, five years before younger brother Walker joined the team in 1954; Solly Drake, who played for Chicago in 1956, four years before younger brother Sammy came to Chicago in 1960; Eddie Sauer, who played for Chicago from 1943 to 1945, getting to Chicago four years before older sibling Hank Sauer came to the Cubs in 1949; Jim Tyrone, who played in Chicago in 1972 and in 1974 to 1975, then exited the team a year before younger brother Wayne got there in 1976.

An aside with this group is that slugger Hank Sauer was a two-time All-Star for Chicago in 1950 and 1952, and had a long, solid career. But it was journeyman Ed who made it to the World Series in 1945 with the Cubs, making appearances in two games as a pinch hitter, albeit going hitless.

The brothers Cooper made their mark in St. Louis, where they were an All-Star battery for the Cardinals from 1942 to 1944, leading the squad to three consecutive World Series, including world championships in 1942 and 1944.

There have also been five father-son combinations in Cub history. None were even close to pulling off the Ken Griffey Sr. / Ken Griffey Jr. trick of playing on the same squad.

Infielder Bobby Adams capped a 14-year career with a three-year stint in Chicago from 1957 to 1959. Son Mike's five-year career as a big-league outfielder included two years in Chicago

from 1976 to 1977. Shortstop Jimmy Cooney spent most of his three-year major league career from 1890 to 1892 in Chicago. His son Jimmy, also a shortstop, played two of his seven big-league seasons in Chicago from 1926 to 1927. In 1879 third baseman Herm Doscher played three games with the Cubs at third base, hitting .182. Twenty-four years later, son Jack started one game for Chicago in 1903, with an equally unmemorable result, getting knocked out of the box in the fourth inning

In 1966, outfielder Marty Keough finished his 11-year career in Chicago, hitting .231 in 26 at-bats. Twenty years later, son Matt, a righthanded pitcher, capped his nine-year big-league career in Chicago and Houston, going 5-4 for the two teams in 1986. Interestingly, Matt then played a few years in Japan, where his father had migrated 20 years before after his own major league career ended.

All-Star shortstop Chris Speier spent two years, 1985 and 1986, of his stellar 19-year career in Chicago. Son Justin, a strapping (6'4", 200 pounds) righthander, made one unsuccessful relief appearance with Chicago in 1998.

10 PLAYERS YOU DIDN'T KNOW WERE CUBS

Okay, we all know that Jimmie Foxx spent two years (1942 and 1944) with the Cubbies during the war years, and that Monte Irvin finished up his career in Chicago in 1956, but here are 10 names that may surprise you.

1 Tony La Russa: Finding a picture of the present manager of the Cardinals in a Cubs uniform might be tough. La Russa appeared in one game as a Cub, as a pinch runner in 1973. He scored the run.

2 Johnny Vander Meer: Mr. "Double No-Hitter" came to the Cubs after his stellar career with the Reds, going 3-4 in Chicago in 1950.

3 Elrod (Ellie) Hendricks: The longtime backstop for the Baltimore Orioles was traded to the Cubs in 1972, released, and picked up again by the Orioles in 1973. Ellie played 17 games for Chicago, hitting .116.

4 Don Larsen: The architect of the only perfect game in World Series history, in 1955, ended his career in Chicago in 1967. And not very well, unfortunately. Larsen appeared in three games, pitched four innings and earned no decisions.

5 Rico Carty: Three years after this Atlanta Braves' All-Star won the batting title, he played for three different teams, the Cubs being one of them. Carty hit .214 for Chicago, striking out 10 times in 22 at-bats.

6 Hoyt Wilhelm: "The Knuckleball King" had several stops in his amazing 21-year career, including a brief stopover in Chicago in 1970. Wilhelm appeared in only three games, going 0-1 for Chicago.

7 Chuck Connors: Prior to his stint in "The Rifleman" on television (but a few years after he broke a backboard in Boston Garden playing for the Celtics), Connors played 66 games at first base for the Cubs, hitting .239 in 1951.

8 Dick Radatz: "The Monster" terrorized batters when he was a reliever for the Red Sox from 1962 to 1966. He wound up in Chicago in 1967 and amassed five saves in his next-to-last year in the big leagues.

9 Joe Carter: The 1981 College Player of the Year was a promising rookie for the Cubs in 1983. But his slow start (he hit .176 in 23 games that year) probably precipitated his inclusion in the blockbuster trade for Rick Sutcliffe the next year.

10 Bobby Bonds: The father of Barry ended his 14-year major league career in Chicago in 1981, hitting .215 in 45 games with the Cubs.

CUBS BAD BOYS

The Chicago franchise of the National League may not have always been successful, but these boys sure partied like they were. Drink, gambling and well-armed women were among their vices. There are a million stories in the City of Big Shoulders. Here are the most conspicuous tales.

Rogers Hornsby was the greatest righthanded hitter of the 20th century, and also a major league gambler. In fact, not only did Hornsby blow a lot of money, mostly on the ponies, but he was also in the habit of borrowing money from his teammates. Later, when he became player-manager, he hit up his players. Heck, how can you refuse your manager when he comes up to you with his hand out?

Unfortunately, Rog admitted that he never really learned how to read a racing form and he relied on "hunches" and tips from other horseplayers. Great. As he got older, Hornsby also got more interested in betting. And the Cubs ownership was none too happy. Eventually, The Rajah got the heave-ho.

When Hornsby was fired, there was more than a little consternation on the part of his players that they wouldn't get back all the money he owed them; by some accounts, this was several thousand dollars. And, in fact, quite a few Cubs were left hanging after Hornsby's departure.

Pitcher Claude Hendrix also gambled. Problem was, he didn't bet on horses; he bet on baseball games. In 1921 he was released by the Cubs after allegedly betting against his team the previous August.

It's actually a little unfair to call Billy Jurges, a shortstop for the Cubs in the 1930s, a "bad boy." But perhaps the rule of thumb is, if you get shot by a jealous girlfriend, no matter how unstable she may be, or how innocent you may be, you will qualify for inclusion in this particular sidebar.

Jurges was a ladies' man, to be sure. On July 6, 1932 Miss Violet Valli, a showgirl and Jurges's girlfriend, came up to his hotel room. Valli wanted to be married. Billy wasn't wild about the idea. Valli intended to shoot herself in front of Jurges, but when she drew the pistol, Jurges jumped up to take it from her. There was a struggle, and Jurges was shot. Billy recovered after a few weeks from a wound to his hand and side (not his butt), and went on to play in the World Series that year.

Bill Faul was a curveballing righthander for the Cubs in the 1965 and 1966 season. He was a bodybuilder who believed in the power of self-hypnosis. He was also an ordained minister who reportedly talked to his arm while he was pitching. (As odd as this seems, an awful lot of pitchers in their autobiographies, including Jim Bouton in *Ball Four* mention having conversations with their pitching arms. Mostly to beg the arm to stay intact. So Faul wasn't too far off the mark there.)

In his irreverent biography *The Wrong Stuff,* pitcher Bill Lee, who faced Faul in the minors, also claimed that Faul bit the heads off live parakeets prior to a start. (Is that where Ozzy Osbourne got this trick?) That claim was never substantiated anywhere else, however.

The self-hypnosis therapy evidently worked for a while because Faul went 6-6 with three shutouts in 1965. But once ballplayers from other teams got word of the self-hypnosis regimen, players took to hopping on the top steps of the dugout when Faul was pitching, and would swing a pocket watch and declare to Faul "You are getting sleepy, sleepy." The next year, Faul was 1-4 and was released.

Hack Wilson and Pat Malone were brawling buddies during the 1930s. Both had a fondness for the bottle, and both also enjoyed taking a poke or two at anyone who had the audacity to say anything to them. Almost all this mayhem was done on the road because when the two men played home games, their wives often went right into the locker room after a contest to get them. Wilson, by the way, spent at least one off-season as a boxer. His ring name was "Battling Stouts."

Pete Alexander claims he never pitched drunk, a claim many teammates insist was true. But he often pitched hung over, a fact many of his teammates did not dispute, either. But as Joe McCarthy, one of his former managers, once pointed out, "Maybe he drank. But how much better could he have been?" True. Alexander was, when he retired, the fourth most successful pitcher in the history of baseball.

It's worth noting that the championship teams in the 1880s, managed by temperance champion Cap Anson, were, for the most part, hard-drinking, hard-living wild men. King Kelly, perhaps the best player of the 19th century, wrote the book on living large almost 30 years before anyone had ever heard of Babe Ruth. He died of pneumonia at age 36, but had to retire from the game several years earlier because his drinking had nearly overpowered him.

Kelly was not the only member of those storied teams to live hard and die young. Catcher Silver Flint, pitcher Larry Corcoran and outfielder Ned Williamson were all dead of alcohol-related diseases by their 30s. Terry Larkin, who pitched for Chicago in the 1870s, was a drinking man, too, who battled depression and alcoholism until his early death in the 1890s.

Heinie Zimmerman was a talented performer for the Cubs who, unfortunately, thought he knew all the angles. He was a sarcastic man who more than once took his lumps after criticizing a teammate. He was also unafraid to criticize umpires, which also got him tossed. But it was his decision, allegedly, to try to fix ball games in which he played that got him in trouble. In 1919 he was one of several players, along with several members of the Chicago White Sox, who were banned from baseball for life for trying to throw games.

CUBS TRAGEDIES

Certainly, every team has a long shelf of sad stories in its history. Chicago is no different, but the Cubbies seemed to have an awful lot more than many squads.

Start with pitcher King Cole, a rookie phenom with Chicago in 1910. Cole went 20-4 that year. Midway through the 1911 season, he contracted malaria and was never the same. By 1915 he was out of the league. By 1916 he was dead. In 1911 rookie shortstop Jim Doyle hit .282 and led the National Leaguers at that position in total fielding chances per game. He gave every indication that he would be a solid, if not spectacular, player at that position. But in February of the next year, Doyle's appendix burst, killing him.

The story of Bill Lange isn't exactly a tragedy, except in hindsight. Lange was a big, strapping outfielder who could hit like the devil and run like a deer. He played for seven years in the major leagues (1893–99) and never hit below .319 after his rookie year. But Lange's sweetheart was the daughter of a wealthy San Francisco real estate magnate. San Francisco society in the late–19th century frowned on ballplayers in much the same way they frowned on show business people. Both groups were believed to be abusers of strong drink, fornicators and individuals of poor breeding.

So Lange had to make a choice: his sweetheart or his game. He chose the former and eventually regretted it: the marriage ended in divorce. For Chicago's part, Lange probably had another 10 years' worth of a career. With the veteran Lange on the squad, the Cubs might not have lost more than a handful of games.

One of the saddest Cubs stories of modern times was that of second baseman Ken Hubbs, who came to the Cubs in 1961. In 1962 he won a Gold Glove and set a National League record for errorless games by a rookie, 77 games and 416 chances. This also won him the league's Rookie of the Year award. Hubbs was afraid of flying, so he decided to conquer his fear by obtaining his pilot's license. Prior to the 1964 season, a plane he was flying crashed in Utah. He was, in the words of his friend and roommate Ron Santo, "a gifted athlete who was taken from all of us way too soon."

SUPERSTITIONS AND ODD HABITS

Cap Anson was obsessed with bats, probably more than even the players of today. Every time he saw a slab of wood or a railroad tie or any chunk of wood longer than it was wide, he would appropriate it and have it sent over to a Chicago woodworker to make a bat. A sportswriter once estimated that Anson had more than 275 bats in his basement, hung from the ceiling like hams. Anson himself once estimated the total to be closer to 500. Anson also never allowed a teammate to use one of his bats.

Anson also believed, long before it was fashionable, that the best way to stay in shape was to keep his legs strong. Thus, he would run several miles a day regularly during the off-season. When he became manager of Chicago, much to the consternation of his players, Anson would lead them on long runs several times every spring. However, rather than realize that the 40-plus Anson, who was still playing, may have had a point, the players instead contrived various ways to avoid the run.

Catcher King Kelly liked to take baths while smoking a cigar. This was not a stylish affectation. Kelly reportedly didn't like baths much, so he smoked a cigar so he could get something positive out of the experience.

Pitcher Clark "the Old Fox" Griffith believed it was bad luck to throw a shutout.

Frank Chance believed that ballplayers who played cards were, on the whole, smarter than those who did not. Cardplaying, Chance believed, gave a fellow constant practice in the art of quick thinking and decision-making under pressure. Chance also thought betting on horses stimulated a player's thought processes.

As a manager, Chance liked to see his players drink after a game. In fact, to encourage this, Chance would go out to a bar with his ballplayers and buy the first round. During rainouts, Chance reportedly sometimes took the whole club to a bar and bought all the drinks until midnight. Then he would herd them all out of the bar and home.

When he was scheduled to start, Pete Alexander would wait until exactly 20 minutes before a game before applying a special liniment to his pitching arm. This was probably to ensure the liniment lasted through the entire start. Still, teammates with the Cubs and Cardinals recall Cleveland watching the clock religiously prior to a game before applying the salve.

During the Great Depression, Cubs owner Philip Knight Wrigley hired—for $5,000—a man to put the evil eye on opposing teams when the Cubs were playing at home. William Veeck, Wrigley's general manager at the time, was sure it was a gimmick to pull people into the ballpark, but Wrigley was dead serious. Veeck believed that Wrigley, who didn't know a lot about sports, got the idea from watching professional wrestling, which Wrigley did not understand was not real. A certain wrestler of the 1930s was known to place hexes on opponents to defeat them. Wrigley appeared to believe that such a man could help his team by hexing opponents.

He positioned the man behind home plate, where he could be seen gesticulating at the opposing pitchers, none of whom seemed too bothered by the man.

Unfortunately, the evil-eye caster could not stand cold weather, so on cold days, he would go up to Wrigley's office and attempt to cast his spell on the ticker tape machine, which relayed the results of the game. That didn't work too well, either. He lasted but one year.

Cubs player-manager Rogers Hornsby did not read books or go to the movies during the season, believing that it would weaken his batting eye. He also tried to stay away from newspapers. Often, if there was a story he wanted to read, he would ask someone else to read it to him.

Shortstop and manager Rabbit Maranville kept a metal flask in his pocket during games "for emergencies." Maranville never said what was in the flask, but he was a notorious alcoholic, so it's not hard to guess.

While waiting in the on-deck circle, Phil Cavarretta would spit into the air and try to hit the gob of spittle with his bat. If he missed, he would spit again until his bat made contact.

10 BEST TRADES IN CUBS HISTORY

No, it is not true that the Cubs never made a good trade. What is true is that they haven't made enough of them over, say, the past 50 or so years. Here are the 10 best trades in team history.

1 1903: Jack Taylor and Larry McLean to the Cardinals for Three Finger Brown. Taylor was a solid, durable righty for the Cubs from 1898 to 1903, with a record of 90-82 during that span. He would win 62 more games and lose 57 over the rest of his career. McLean was a rookie throw-in at the time who would go on to have a solid catching career with the Reds and Giants. So why does this trade rank as the best? Because Chicago got the best pitcher in their history, an eventual Hall of Famer whose odd nickname didn't confer upon him the respect given his rival, Christy Mathewson. But Brown was every bit as good as Mathewson and loved to pitch in big games; more important, he won those big games.

2 1917: Mike Prendergast, William "Pickles" Dillhoefer and $55,000 to the Phillies for Pete Alexander and Billy Killefer. Pitcher Prendergast was a mediocre 41-53 lifetime, while Dillhoefer was a backup catcher who hit .223 in five big-league seasons. Neither of these men was the key to this trade; the 55 large was what cash-strapped Phillies owner Bill Baker was after. This trade might deserve an asterisk because Baker had just learned that Alexander, at that time one of the top pitchers in baseball, was to go into the service. Realizing this, he dumped Alexander on the Cubs for a couple of live bodies and the cash. The veteran Killefer was a throw-in. He had caught an average of 105 games for the Phillies since 1912 and was figured, at 30, to be on the downside of his career.

Alexander pitched in only three games in 1918 for the Cubs, but he went on to eventually win 128 games for Chicago over the next eight years, eventually ascending into the Hall of Fame, while Killefer played four solid years for the Cubs.

3 1966: Larry Jackson and Bob Buhl to the Phillies for Ferguson Jenkins, Adolfo Phillips and John Herrnstein. Statistically, a huge steal for Chicago. Both Jackson (52-50 with the Cubs) and Buhl (51-55) were solid veterans, but Jackson was 35 and Buhl 37. Phillips was a decent outfielder for three years with Chicago and Herrnstein a promising lefty who didn't really pan out for Chicago or the other two teams for whom he played in 1966. But Fergie Jenkins was another story entirely, cranking out six consecutive 20-win seasons for the Cubs and entering the Hall of Fame in 1991.

4 1906: Bob Wicker and $2,000 to the Reds for Orval Overall. A huge midseason trade that sent the struggling Wicker to Cincinnati for second-year hurler Overall. Orvie had lost 22 games for the Reds in 1905 and didn't seem to have the concentration for the big leagues. But Overall went 15-8, including a 12-3 mark for the Cubs in 1906, and went on to win 70 games for Chicago from 1906 to 1910, becoming the Cubs' second-best playoff pitcher ever.

5 1928: Harry "Socks" Seibold, Percy Jones, Lou Legett, Fred Maguire, Bruce Cunningham and $200,000 to the Boston Braves for Rogers Hornsby. Basically, five fair-to-middling guys and a pile of money for the aging Hornsby, and it paid off handsomely for the Cubs. In 1929 Hornsby was a key component to the Cubs' National League championship, with 39 homers and a .380 batting average while winning the MVP award.

6 1982: Ivan DeJesus to the Philadelphia Phillies for Larry Bowa and Ryne Sandberg. Initially, this looked like a pretty bad trade for Chicago: DeJesus was in his prime and Bowa was well past his. But what turned it around for the Cubs was "throw-in" Sandberg, who went on to be one of the great second basemen in baseball history.

7 1927: Sparky Adams and Pete Scott to the Pittsburgh Pirates for Kiki Cuyler. Cuyler, a talented loner, was in Pirates manager Donie Bush's dog-house for allegedly failing to slide into second base during a key game in the 1927 pennant race, which was won by the Pirates anyway. Thus, the hard-hitting outfielder with a world of speed was suddenly available in the off-season, and the Cubs snatched him up for aging veteran Adams and Scott, a reserve outfielder. Kiki played for two National League championships while with Chicago.

8 1949: Harry Walker and Peanuts Lowrey to the Reds for Hank Sauer and Frankie Baumholtz. The Cubs were criticized in some corners for shipping Walker, the 1947 batting champion for the Cubs, and contact hitter Lowrey for Sauer, who seemed past his prime at 32 and Baumholtz, a reserve outfielder. But Sauer had five very productive years in Chicago, including his MVP season in 1952. Baumholtz also blossomed in Chicago, turning in five good years.

9 1992: George Bell to the Chicago White Sox for Sammy Sosa and Ken Patterson. Bell, a three-time All-Star, was a terrific player for several teams, including the Cubs in 1991. But Sosa, a free-swinging strikeout artist then, has blossomed into one of the great players of the 1990s and 2000s, with a club-record 66 homers in 1998 to go with his MVP award that year.

10 1983: Vance Lovelace and Dan Cataline to the Dodgers for Ron Cey. Lovelace, a 6'5" lefty, never won a game in the majors while Cataline never made it to "the Show." Cey was no Ron Santo, but he was a winner, a solid fielder and a hitter who averaged 115 hits, 21 homers and 71 RBIs in his four years in Chicago, contributing mightily to the NL East title in 1984.

10 WORST TRADES IN CUBS HISTORY

It's no news flash to Cubs fans that Cubs management has had some bad days. These are the 10 worst moments.

1 1964: Lou Brock, Jack Spring and Paul Toth to the Cardinals for Ernie Broglio, Bobby Shantz and Doug Clemens. This, alas, is still referred to by many as one of the worst trades in baseball history. And there is no use disputing that point, unfortunately. The Cubs were mainly trying to unload the 25-year-old Brock, a promising outfield prospect who simply wasn't playing well. Broglio, a veteran pitcher for the Cardinals, was Chicago's principal focus. He would go 7-19 over the next three years for Chicago. Clemens was a reserve outfielder and Shantz, a canny veteran, never won a game in a Cubs uniform.

The transaction came in mid-1964, and it galvanized the Cardinals, who went on to win the National League crown and the World Series. Brock would become a Hall of Fame outfielder who would also contribute heavily to the Cardinals' 1967 World Series win and 1968 National League championship. He would amass 3,091 hits, the 3,000th of which would be on August 13, 1979—against the Cubs.

2 1987: Dennis Eckersley to the Oakland Athletics for David Wilder, Brian Guinn and Mark Leonette. To be fair, it's certain that in 1987 no one realized that the trade to Oakland would resurrect Eckersley as a reliever. In fact, that first year with the A's, he was still a starter, winning only six of 14 decisions. But he *did* turn his career around, becoming the most dominant closer of the late 1980s and early 1990s, saving 387 games in that span. None of the three men Eckersley was traded for ever played a game in the bigs.

3 1981: Bill Caudill and Jay Howell to the New York Yankees for Pat Tabler. Tabler was a journeyman for the Cubs who lasted two years. Caudill, traded to Seattle by New York, saved 104 games

for the Mariners and later Toronto. Howell, another reliever, had a so-so three seasons in New York, but he was a three-time All-Star for the Athletics and Dodgers.

4 1987: Lee Smith to the Boston Red Sox for Al Nipper and Calvin Schiraldi. Smith became the all-time save leader over the next decade after the trade, racking up almost 300 saves with several teams. Nipper won four games and saved one before retiring two years later, while Schiraldi was 12-19 with five saves in his two years in Chicago.

5 1934: Dolf Camilli to the Phillies for Don Hurst. Camilli had 1½ desultory seasons at first base in Chicago on his résumé when he was sent to Philadelphia for Don Hurst, who had turned in six solid seasons for the Phillies up until then. Camilli played well for the Phillies and was traded to Brooklyn, where he was a three-time All-Star and MVP, helping Brooklyn to the 1941 World Series. Hurst hit .199 for the Cubs and retired that year.

6 1972: Billy North to the Oakland Athletics for Bob Locker. This was one of those true puzzlers because North, at 24, was a prospect with speed and proven hitting ability, and Bob Locker was a 34-year-old veteran who had had a good career but who was, well, 34. So it was no real surprise when North became the leadoff man for the three-time champion A's. And it was no real surprise when Locker played only two more years for the Cubs, going 10-7 with 18 saves.

7 1983: Willie Hernandez to the Phillies for Dick Ruthven. Another hideous misjudgment of a reliever's skills, as Hernandez would be one of the best closers in baseball for the Tigers in the mid-1980s, a three-time All-Star and a winner of the Cy Young award in 1984. Ruthven was 32 when he came to the Cubs and went 22-29 in his four seasons there.

8 1973: Larry Gura to the Texas Rangers for Mike Paul. Gura spent four years languishing in the Cubs' bull pen before being traded to the Rangers. Gura was traded to the Yankees soon after, where he went 12-9. But it was at his next stop, Kansas City, where he really blossomed, going 101-79 over the next nine years, and winning several key playoff games. Mike Paul was 0-2 with Chicago.

9 1980: Bruce Sutter to the Cardinals for Leon Durham, Ken Reitz and Ty Waller. Sutter was one of the top relievers in baseball when he was dealt by the Cubs for prospect Durham and two utility players. Durham had a solid career in Chicago and was a two-time All-Star, but Sutter would lead the National League in saves three of the four years he was in St. Louis and be a major component in their World Series championship on 1982, winning two games and saving three more of their seven play-off wins over Atlanta and the Milwaukee Brewers.

10 1917: Cy Williams to the Phillies for Dode Paskert. This trade is long forgotten by most Cubs fans, but it was a bad one. The lanky (6'2", 180 pounds) Williams was a hard-hitting outfielder for the Cubs for six years. At 30, he was six years younger than Paskert, a light-hitting but solid defensive outfielder for Philly. Not surprisingly, Paskert played only four more years for the Cubs, although he was a key performer on the 1918 World Series team. Williams, however, played 13 more years in Philadelphia, leading the league in home runs three times and in slugging percentage once.

THE MANAGERS

It's safe to say that the Cubs' better bench commanders were generally the ones who managed in the 19th century and early in the 20th, although there were a handful of later skippers, like Leo Durocher, who had their day in the sun. Following is a list of all of them in chronological order, with comments about the most notable.

Albert Spalding (1876–77) W-78, L-47

Bob Ferguson (1878) W-30, L-30

Cap Anson (1879, 1880–97) W-1,282, L-932

Silver Flint (1879) W-5, L-12

Tom Burns (1898–99) W-160, L-138

Tom Loftus (1900–01) W-118, L-161

Frank Selee (1902–05) W-280, L-213

Frank Chance (1905–1912) W-768, L-389

Johnny Evers (1913, 1921) W-129, L-120

Hank O'Day (1914), W-78, L-76

Roger Bresnahan (1915) W-73, L-80

Joe Tinker (1916) W-67, L-86

Fred Mitchell (1917–20) W-308, L-269

Bill Killefer (1921–25) W-300, L-293

Rabbit Maranville (1925) W-23, L-30

George Gibson (1925) W-12, L-14

Joe McCarthy (1926–30) W-442, L-321

Rogers Hornsby (1930–32), W-141, L-116

Charlie Grimm (1932–38, 1944–49, 1960) W-946, L-782

Gabby Hartnett (1938–40) W-203, L-176

Jimmy Wilson (1941–44) W-215, L-258

Roy Johnson (interim) (1944) W-0, L-1

Frankie Frisch (1949–51) W-141, L-196

Phil Cavarretta (1951–53) W-169, L-213

Stan Hack (1954–56) W-196, L-265

Bob Scheffing (1957–59) W-208, L-254

Lou Boudreau (1960) W-54, L-83

College of Coaches (1961–62) W-123, L-193

Bob Kennedy (1963–65) W-182, L-198

Leo Durocher (1966–72) W-535, L-526

Whitey Lockman (1972–74) W-157, L-162

Jim Marshall (1974–76) W-175, L-218

Herman Franks (1977–79) W-238, L-241

Joe Amalfitano (1979, 1980–81) W-66, L-116

Preston Gomez (1980) W-38, L-52

Lee Elia (1982–83) W-127, L-158

Charlie Fox (interim) (1983) W-17, L-22

Jim Frey (1984–86) W-196, L-182

John Vukovich (interim) (1986) W-1, L-1

Gene Michael (1986–87) W-114, L-124

Frank Lucchesi (interim) (1987) W-8, L-17

Don Zimmer (1988–91) W-265, L-258

Joe Altobelli (interim) (1991) W-0, L-1

Jim Essian (1991) W-59, L-63

Jim Lefebvre (1992–93) W-162, L-162

Tom Trebelhorn (1994) W-49, L-64

Jim Riggleman (1995–1999) W-374, L-419

Don Baylor (2000–present) W-153, L-171 (Stats through 2001)

Most Successful: Cap Anson was the only Chicago coach to win more than 1,000 games. Anson was a true pioneer, a man who popularized platooning, the hit-and-run play, base coaches and pitching rotations. He was also a stickler for discipline and frowned on players drinking, which was ironic because the Chicago franchise of the late–19th century was as rowdy as any in the history of the game. Anson's teams won five National League pennants in 1880, 1881, 1882, 1885 and 1886. The 1885 and 1886 teams were considered at the time the greatest club in major league history.

The other hugely successful Chicago coach was Frank Chance, the Peerless Leader. Chance, like Anson, was an intense student of the game. He believed games were won on pitching and defense more than hitting. Chance, one of the best amateur boxers in the country, was also a tough man to cross. He fined his players for shaking hands with the opposition. And if any of his men sassed him, Chance had no problem punching them out.

Conversely, the Peerless Leader also believed that the team that drank together, won together, and Chance was not above taking the team to the nearest bar after a game and buying rounds until midnight. His .664 winning percentage is the highest all-time with the Cubs. Chance was also the only player-manager to win two World Series.

Least Successful: in 1979 and then in 1980 and 1981, Joey Amalfitano won only 66 of 182 games, a .363 mark. Several other Cub coaches who served in an interim capacity didn't even fare that

well, but of the full-timers, Amalfitano stands out. Amalfitano was a 10-year veteran infielder. He was an interim manager in 1979 and returned to coaching in 1980. But Preston Gomez, the man the Cubs hired to take over in 1980, was fired in mid-season and Amalfitano was rehired as manager. The next year, he was named the team's regular manager. But the uncertainty of the front office had everyone skittish, and Amalfitano never really had a chance. He was fired after the 1981 season.

Most times hired: Charlie Grimm managed the Cubs three separate times, and in 1932, 1936 and 1945, he managed the team into the World Series. He also managed the Cubs in 1938, but he was fired in midseason when the front office opined that the Cubs weren't playing very well. The Cubs went to the Series with Gabby Hartnett at the helm.

Grimm was laid-back, easygoing, and a mentor to the younger players, as well as a pal to the older ones. He was nicknamed "Jolly Cholly" by the press for his affable ways.

Grimm didn't win any pennants in 1960, his third go-round, but his exit was notable: he agreed to switch places with Cubs radio announcer Lou Boudreau in 1960. Thus, Boudreau became Cubs manager and Grimm got behind the mike.

Best Manager Who Never Played a Big-League Game: Joe McCarthy took over the Cubs in 1926 and had them playing in the World Series in three years. An astute judge of talent, McCarthy was a teetotaler who nevertheless understood the dynamics of a team. He tried many times to reform the hard-drinking Hack Wilson, for instance. The most memorable was when he dropped a worm into a glass of whiskey. The worm convulsed and died. What, asked McCarthy, did that illustrate to Wilson? "That I'll never get worms," concluded Wilson. McCarthy reportedly threw up his hands at that point.

Most Sarcastic Manager: When he was hired by Chicago, Leo Durocher recalled that he was the only manager in baseball who was hired to replace nobody. That was partly true: Durocher was the immediate successor to the infamous College of

Coaches, which "featured" a rotating system of coaches. "Leo the Lip" was a sharp-tongued manager who demanded the best effort from his players. He once told a reporter he'd trip his mother if she was rounding third and he was coaching there. As he had at other big-league stops, Leo had a love-hate relationship with most of the Cubs players throughout his tenure, but he pulled them up to a pair of second-place finishes in 1969 and again in 1970. Unfortunately, his team never grabbed the brass ring. Two years later, he was gone.

Best Manager With Screws in his Head: Don Zimmer managed the Cubs to the 1989 National League East championship by the seat of his pants. Zim made a lot of moves based more on intuition than "by the book," and just about every one of them worked out that year. Honest and straightforward, he was almost universally loved by his men, as he has been, in fact, just about everywhere he's worked. As to the screws, Zimmer was hit in the head by a pitch while playing in the minors in 1953. Four small screws were inserted into his skull to relieve the pressure on his brain. Somewhere along the line, the story changed into a plate in his skull. The affable Zimmer has never bothered to correct the story.

THE INFAMOUS COLLEGE OF COACHES

Following the 1960 season, the Cubs' front office decided to try something that no other franchise in major league (or, to anyone's knowledge, minor league) history had ever attempted: coaching by committee.

The theory was that coaches at all levels of the Cubs organization would rotate up and down through the Chicago major and minor leagues. The "Cubs way" would be presented by this "faculty" to the ballplayers in a consistent, orderly fashion.

Initially, eight coaches were hired: Bobby Adams, Harry Warren "Rip" Collins, Harry Craft,

Charlie Grimm, Vedie Himsl, Gordie Holt, Elvin Tappe and Verlon Walker. Later, Lou Klein, Fred Martin and Charlie Metro were hired.

Only Craft and Grimm had previous managerial experience, although Holt had coached with the Pirates and Tappe had worked in the Chicago organization previously.

But perhaps no amount of experience could have facilitated this plan. The "Cubs way" might have been a consistent concept, but as each coach rotated up to the "Big Club," their individual vision of how to attain results was very different.

As third baseman Ron Santo noted in his autobiography, "It was a very difficult situation for everyone. One head coach would come aboard and tell me what was expected of me; two weeks later, the next coach would tell me something different. I would listen to everyone. If it didn't make sense, it would go in one ear and out the other. I wasn't insubordinate, I just tried to get along and not get messed up at the plate and in the field."

Virtually everyone connected with the Cubs in that era concurred about this experiment: Chicago lost 90 games in 1961 and 103 in 1962. Bob Kennedy was named manager of the team from 1963 to 1965, and this stabilized the ship somewhat, although the other coaches were still rotated. The Cubs actually went 82-80 in 1963, but the team returned to its losing ways in 1964 and 1965.

Beyond a losing record, the College was one of the big reasons the Cubs lost outfielder Lou Brock. Brock came up to the Cubs in 1961. As Santo noted, "As confusing as the system was for veterans, it was downright perplexing for rookies."

Brock, who could run like the wind, had a good arm and hit for power, but he was often pressing at the plate and in the field. Eventually, he was traded to the Cardinals in 1964 for pitcher Ernie Broglio. It went down as the worst trade in team history.

In 1965 the experiment was discontinued, and the Cubs hired Leo Durocher. Leo might have been abrasive and downright nasty, but he deserved a lot of credit for his efforts in rebuilding the franchise after the College of Coaches debacle.

THE CHICAGO CUBS BROADCASTERS

The Chicago franchise of the National League may not have been as successful as some others, but no one can quibble about the quality of the individuals who have broadcast the games over the past several decades.

Four of the men who have broadcast Cubs games have been honored by the Baseball Hall of Fame: Bob Elson, Jack Brickhouse, Milo Hamilton and Harry Caray. A fifth, Ronald "Dutch" Reagan followed up his career as a radio personality by eventually becoming the president of the United States.

Elson, also known as "the Old Commander," was one of the Cubs' first radio voices, along with Johnny O'Hara. In 1925 Cubs owner William Wrigley Jr. announced to the rest of the National League owners that he planned to broadcast a few home games. Wrigley gave the broadcast rights to several local radio stations. The other National League owners predicted doom. They believed that with games accessible on the radio, no one would come to see the games in person.

But the opposite was true. William Veeck Sr., the Cubs general manager at the time, began to notice more and more out-of-state license plates in the Wrigley Field parking lots. Veeck assumed correctly that these fans were coming to the games because they had heard the radio broadcasts.

Reagan broadcast Cubs games in the 1930s for radio station WHO in Des Moines. Reagan's actual job was re-creating Cubs games in the studio; he rarely covered the contests in person. Reagan left WHO after a few years to pursue an acting career.

On April 16, 1948, WGN-TV broadcast a Cubs game on television for the first time. The very erudite Jack Brickhouse was the play-by-play man. Once again, the Cubs' decision to broadcast their games on television was excoriated by many of the other owners in the game. Once again, the Cubs organization was vindicated, as the television broadcasts served only to spike interest.

Caray, a former Cardinals broadcaster, replaced Brickhouse in 1982. Hamilton, for many years, was his coannouncer.

The flamboyant Caray was a sharp contrast to Brickhouse, and it took many Cubs fans a long time to really embrace him. Caray pioneered the "Take Me Out to the Ball Game" sing-along during the seventh-inning stretch. He was an unrepentant homer, but Caray was also unafraid to tell his viewers when a Cub made a bad play. Many Chicago players were not thrilled by Caray's style, but many more fans loved it. Caray died in 1998.

Caray's other baseball legacy is his very involved family. Son Skip Caray broadcasts games for the Atlanta Braves TBS Network, and grandson Chip Caray is now in his fourth season broadcasting television games for the Cubs.

The
Players

COMPLETE CUBS PLAYER CAREER STATISTICS

WITH BIOGRAPHIES OF THE 100 BEST CUBS

Key to Statistics

A NOTE ABOUT THE STATISTICS

Statisticians have yet to find a perfect system for quantifying a player's performance through numbers, and they probably never will.

Of course, that hasn't stopped generations of baseball fans from poring over numbers.

Though interpretation is subjective, numbers *in themselves* do not lie or exaggerate, and they are the best method we have in comparing a pitcher who played in 1900 with one who played in 2000.

The statistics included here are presented for that purpose and for one very specific other: to compare how a player performed during his career with his performance while a member of the Chicago Cubs. To that end, we've calculated two sets of totals and averages, one

looking at a player's performance across his career, and the other looking at his results with the Cubs.

But numbers are not perfect. Some categories (*Sacrifice Hits*, for example) aren't available for every year for every player. We've provided them where available. And while averages can help gauge a player's overall performance across many years, they can also muddy the picture by placing equal weight on each season—whether an individual appeared in 1 game or 100.

We present these statistics, therefore, not as the definitive measure of a player's worth but as a numerical standard upon which to build an interpretation, one way of looking at things. From there, readers are free to decide for themselves.

TEAM ABBREVIATIONS

Atl	Atlanta
Ari	Arizona
Bal	Baltimore
Bos	Boston
Bro	Brooklyn
Buf	Buffalo
Cal	California
Chi	Chicago
Cin	Cincinnati
Cle	Cleveland
Col	Colorado
Clm	Columbus
Det	Detroit
Fla	Florida
Hou	Houston
Ind	Indianapolis
KC	Kansas City
LA	Los Angeles
Lou	Louisville
Mil	Milwaukee
Min	Minnesota
Mon	Montreal
NY	New York
Oak	Oakland
Phi	Philadelphia
Pit	Pittsburgh
Roc	Rochester
SD	San Diego
Sea	Seattle
SF	San Francisco
StL	St. Louis
Tex	Texas
Tor	Toronto
Was	Washington

LEAGUE ABBREVIATIONS

N	National League
A	American League
F	Federal League (1914-15)
AA	American Association (1882–91)

Dunston, Shawon Donnell

HEIGHT: 6'1"   THROWS: RIGHT   BATS: RIGHT   BORN: 3/21/1963 BROOKLYN, NEW YORK   POSITIONS PLAYED: 1B, 2B, 3B, SS, OF

YEAR	TEAM	GAMES	AB	RUNS	HITS	2B	3B	HR	RBI	BB	IBB	SO	HBP	SH	SF	SB	CS	BA	OBA	SA	FA
1985	ChC-N	74	250	40	65	12	4	4	18	19	3	42	0	1	2	11	3	.260	.310	.388	.958
1986	ChC-N	150	581	66	145	37	3	17	68	21	5	114	3	4	2	13	11	.250	.278	.411	.961
1987	ChC-N	95	346	40	85	18	3	5	22	10	1	68	1	0	2	12	3	.246	.267	.358	.969
1988	ChC-N	155	575	69	143	23	6	9	56	16	8	108	2	4	2	30	9	.249	.271	.357	.973
1989	ChC-N	138	471	52	131	20	6	9	60	30	15	86	1	6	4	19	11	.278	.320	.403	.972
1990	ChC-N	146	545	73	143	22	8	17	66	15	1	87	3	4	6	25	5	.262	.283	.426	.970
1991	ChC-N	142	492	59	128	22	7	12	50	23	5	64	4	4	11	21	6	.260	.292	.407	.968
1992	ChC-N	18	73	8	23	3	1	0	2	3	0	13	0	0	0	2	3	.315	.342	.384	.986
1993	ChC-N	7	10	3	4	2	0	0	2	0	0	1	0	0	0	0	0	.400	.400	.600	1.000
1994	ChC-N	88	331	38	92	19	0	11	35	16	3	48	2	5	2	3	8	.278	.313	.435	.966
1995	ChC-N	127	477	58	141	30	6	14	69	10	3	75	6	7	3	10	5	.296	.317	.472	.969
1996	SF-N	82	287	27	86	12	2	5	25	13	0	40	1	5	1	8	0	.300	.331	.408	.957
1997	ChC-N	114	419	57	119	18	4	9	41	8	0	64	3	3	4	29	7	.284	.300	.411	.971
1997	Pit-N	18	71	14	28	4	1	5	16	0	0	11	0	2	1	3	1	.394	.389	.690	.965
1998	Cle-A	62	156	26	37	11	3	3	12	6	0	18	1	0	3	9	2	.237	.265	.404	.972
1998	SF-N	36	51	10	9	2	0	3	8	0	0	10	3	1	0	0	2	.176	.222	.392	.926
1999	StL-N	62	150	23	46	5	2	5	25	2	0	23	3	2	1	6	3	.307	.327	.467	.981
1999	NYM-N	42	93	12	32	6	1	0	16	0	0	16	2	1	1	4	1	.344	.354	.430	.979
2000	StL-N	98	216	28	54	11	2	12	43	6	0	47	3	4	2	3	1	.250	.278	.486	.984
2001	SF-N	88	186	26	52	10	3	9	25	2	0	32	2	2	1	3	1	.280	.293	.511	.966
Career average		102	340	43	92	17	4	9	39	12	3	57	2	3	3	12	5	.270	.297	.419	.968
Cubs average		**105**	**381**	**47**	**102**	**19**	**4**	**9**	**41**	**14**	**4**	**64**	**2**	**3**	**3**	**15**	**6**	**.267**	**.295**	**.407**	**.968**
Career total		1742	5780	729	1563	287	62	149	659	200	44	967	40	55	48	211	82	.270	.297	.419	.968
Cubs total		**1254**	**4570**	**563**	**1219**	**226**	**48**	**107**	**489**	**171**	**44**	**770**	**25**	**38**	**38**	**175**	**71**	**.267**	**.295**	**.407**	**.968**

Sample position player entry

STATISTICAL ABBREVIATIONS (POSITION PLAYERS)

YEAR	Year	**HBP**	Hit by Pitch
TEAM	Team	**SH**	Sacrifice Hits
GAMES	Games played	**SF**	Sacrifice Flies
AB	At-bats	**SB**	Stolen Bases
RUNS	Runs	**CS**	Caught Stealing
HITS	Hits	**BA**	Batting Average (Hits / At-bats)
2B	Doubles	**OBA**	On-Base Average ((Hits + Total Bases-on-Balls +Hit-by-Pitch) / (At-bats + Total Bases-on-Balls + Hit-by-Pitch + Sacrifice Flies))
3B	Triples		
HR	Home Runs		
RBI	Runs Batted In	**SA**	Slugging Average (Total Bases / At-bats)
BB	Bases-on-Balls	**FA**	Fielding Average ((Put-Outs + Assists) / (Put-Outs + Assists + Errors))
IBB	Intentional Bases-on-Balls		
SO	Strikeouts		

Position Players

Aberson, Clifford Alexander (Cliff or Kif)
HEIGHT: 6'0"   THROWS: RIGHT   BATS: RIGHT   BORN: 8/28/1921 CHICAGO, ILLINOIS   DIED: 6/23/1973 VALLEJO, CALIFORNIA   POSITIONS PLAYED: OF

YEAR	TEAM	GAMES	AB	RUNS	HITS	2B	3B	HR	RBI	BB	IBB	SO	HBP	SH	SF	SB	CS	BA	OBA	SA	FA
1947	ChC-N	47	140	24	39	6	3	4	20	20	—	32	0	0	—	0	—	.279	.369	.450	.920
1948	ChC-N	12	32	1	6	1	0	1	6	5	—	10	0	0	—	0	—	.188	.297	.313	.867
1949	ChC-N	4	7	0	0	0	0	0	0	0	—	2	0	0	—	0	—	.000	.000	.000	1.000
Career average		21	60	8	15	2	1	2	9	8	—	15	0	0	—	0	—	.251	.343	.408	.913
Cubs average		21	60	8	15	2	1	2	9	8	—	15	0	0	—	0	—	.251	.343	.408	.913
Career total		63	179	25	45	7	3	5	26	25	—	44	0	0	—	0	—	.251	.343	.408	.913
Cubs total		63	179	25	45	7	3	5	26	25	—	44	0	0	—	0	—	.251	.343	.408	.913

Adair, James Audrey (Jimmy or Choppy)
HEIGHT: 5'10"   THROWS: RIGHT   BATS: RIGHT   BORN: 1/25/1907 WAXAHACHIE, TEXAS   DIED: 12/9/1982 DALLAS, TEXAS   POSITIONS PLAYED: SS

YEAR	TEAM	GAMES	AB	RUNS	HITS	2B	3B	HR	RBI	BB	IBB	SO	HBP	SH	SF	SB	CS	BA	OBA	SA	FA
1931	ChC-N	18	76	9	21	3	1	0	3	1	—	8	0	2	—	1	—	.276	.286	.342	.948
Career average		18	76	9	21	3	1	0	3	1	—	8	0	2	—	1	—	.276	.286	.342	.948
Cubs average		18	76	9	21	3	1	0	3	1	—	8	0	2	—	1	—	.276	.286	.342	.948
Career total		18	76	9	21	3	1	0	3	1	—	8	0	2	—	1	—	.276	.286	.342	.948
Cubs total		18	76	9	21	3	1	0	3	1	—	8	0	2	—	1	—	.276	.286	.342	.948

Adams, Earl John (Sparky)
HEIGHT: 5'5"   THROWS: RIGHT   BATS: RIGHT   BORN: 8/26/1894 ZERBE, PENNSYLVANIA   DIED: 2/24/1989 POTTSVILLE, PENNSYLVANIA
POSITIONS PLAYED: 2B, 3B, SS, OF

YEAR	TEAM	GAMES	AB	RUNS	HITS	2B	3B	HR	RBI	BB	IBB	SO	HBP	SH	SF	SB	CS	BA	OBA	SA	FA
1922	ChC-N	11	44	5	11	0	1	0	3	4	—	3	0	1	—	1	2	.250	.313	.295	.914
1923	ChC-N	95	311	40	90	12	0	4	35	26	—	10	1	14	—	20	19	.289	.346	.367	.935
1924	ChC-N	117	418	66	117	11	5	1	27	40	—	20	1	14	—	15	17	.280	.344	.337	.948
1925	ChC-N	149	627	95	180	29	8	2	48	44	—	15	7	9	—	26	12	.287	.341	.368	.983
1926	ChC-N	154	624	95	193	35	3	0	39	52	—	27	5	19	—	27	—	.309	.367	.375	.965
1927	ChC-N	146	647	100	189	17	7	0	49	42	—	26	0	16	—	26	—	.292	.335	.340	.976
1928	Pit-N	135	539	91	149	14	6	0	38	64	—	18	4	21	—	8	—	.276	.357	.325	.976
1929	Pit-N	74	196	37	51	8	1	0	11	15	—	5	1	5	—	3	—	.260	.316	.311	.923
1930	StL-N	137	570	98	179	36	9	0	55	45	—	27	1	15	—	7	—	.314	.365	.409	.962
1931	StL-N	143	608	97	178	46	5	1	40	42	—	24	2	6	—	16	—	.293	.340	.390	.953
1932	StL-N	31	127	22	35	3	1	0	13	14	—	5	1	0	—	0	—	.276	.352	.315	.931
1933	StL-N	8	30	1	5	1	0	0	0	1	—	3	1	0	—	0	—	.167	.219	.200	.900
1933	Cin-N	137	538	59	141	21	1	1	22	44	—	30	2	15	—	3	—	.262	.320	.310	.965
1934	Cin-N	87	278	38	70	16	1	0	14	20	—	10	2	1	—	2	—	.252	.307	.317	.969
Career average		110	427	65	122	19	4	1	30	35	—	17	2	10	—	12	4	.286	.343	.353	.963
Cubs average		112	445	67	130	17	4	1	34	35	—	17	2	12	—	19	8	.292	.346	.357	.965
Career total		1424	5557	844	1588	249	48	9	394	453	—	223	28	136	—	154	50	.286	.343	.353	.963
Cubs total		672	2671	401	780	104	24	7	201	208	—	101	14	73	—	115	50	.292	.346	.357	.965

Earl John "Sparky" Adams, 2-3-ss-of, 1922–34

The diminutive (5'5", 151 pounds), lightning-quick Adams was a key utilityman for the Cubs from 1922 until 1924, then came into his own in 1925 when he became Chicago's full-time second baseman for several years.

Born August 26, 1894, in Zerbe, Pennsylvania, Adams spent several years in the minors before coming up to Chicago at age 28. He played 11 games in 1922 before becoming a semiregular the next year and for several years afterward.

But in 1925 the Cubs traded second baseman George Grantham to the Pirates for Rabbit Maranville, and Adams was inserted into the lineup at second base.

He found his niche that season, leading the team in runs scored (95), hits (180) and stolen bases (26) and tying Charlie Grimm for the team lead in doubles with 33. A speedy leadoff hitter, Adams would lead Chicago in stolen bases three consecutive years from 1925 to 1927.

His 165 singles in 1927 is the all-time third best for a Cub and his 647 at-bats that same year is 10th-best all-time one-season mark on the team.

Adams was also an excellent fielder, leading all second basemen in fielding percentage in 1925 with a .983 mark.

In 1927 manager Joe McCarthy was not afraid to use the versatile Adams at virtually every infield position but first base. Adams responded by scoring a career-high 100 runs, stealing 26 bases and hitting .292.

McCarthy sent Adams to the Pirates in 1928, where he had two more good seasons. In 1930 Sparky, so nicknamed because of his electric effect on the offense, then went to the Cardinals, where he played in two World Series and won a world championship in 1931. He retired in 1934 with the Reds. He died in 1989 in Pottstown, Pennsylvania.

Adams, Robert Henry (Bobby)
HEIGHT: 5'10"   THROWS: RIGHT   BATS: RIGHT   BORN: 12/14/1921 TUOLUMNE, CALIFORNIA   DIED: 2/13/1997 GIG HARBOR, WASHINGTON
POSITIONS PLAYED: 1B, 2B, 3B, OF

YEAR	TEAM	GAMES	AB	RUNS	HITS	2B	3B	HR	RBI	BB	IBB	SO	HBP	SH	SF	SB	CS	BA	OBA	SA	FA
1946	Cin-N	94	311	35	76	13	3	4	24	18	—	32	3	14	—	16	—	.244	.292	.344	.967
1947	Cin-N	81	217	39	59	11	2	4	20	25	—	23	4	7	—	9	—	.272	.358	.396	.967
1948	Cin-N	87	262	33	78	20	3	1	21	25	—	23	1	7	—	6	—	.298	.361	.408	.967
1949	Cin-N	107	277	32	70	16	2	0	25	26	—	36	0	5	—	4	—	.253	.317	.325	.980
1950	Cin-N	115	348	57	98	21	8	3	25	43	—	29	0	3	—	7	—	.282	.361	.414	.964
1951	Cin-N	125	403	57	107	12	5	5	24	43	—	40	1	3	—	4	10	.266	.338	.357	.957
1952	Cin-N	154	637	85	180	25	4	6	48	49	—	67	0	8	—	11	9	.283	.334	.363	.962
1953	Cin-N	150	607	99	167	14	6	8	49	58	—	67	0	12	—	3	2	.275	.338	.357	.951
1954	Cin-N	110	390	69	105	25	6	3	23	55	—	46	3	4	2	2	5	.269	.362	.387	.953
1955	Cin-N	64	150	23	41	11	2	2	20	20	1	21	3	2	1	2	0	.273	.368	.413	.970
1955	CWS-A	28	21	8	2	0	1	0	3	4	0	4	0	0	0	0	0	.095	.240	.190	.955
1956	Bal-A	41	111	19	25	6	1	0	7	25	0	15	0	5	2	1	1	.225	.362	.297	.962
1957	**ChC-N**	**60**	**187**	**21**	**47**	**10**	**2**	**1**	**10**	**17**	**0**	**28**	**2**	**5**	**0**	**0**	**3**	**.251**	**.320**	**.342**	**.949**
1958	**ChC-N**	**62**	**96**	**14**	**27**	**4**	**4**	**0**	**4**	**6**	**0**	**15**	**0**	**3**	**0**	**2**	**0**	**.281**	**.324**	**.406**	**.967**
1959	**ChC-N**	**3**	**2**	**0**	**0**	**0**	**0**	**0**	**0**	**0**	**0**	**1**	**0**	**0**	**0**	**0**	**0**	**.000**	**.000**	**.000**	**.667**
Career average		92	287	42	77	13	4	3	22	30	0	32	1	6	0	5	2	.269	.340	.368	.962
Cubs average		**42**	**95**	**12**	**25**	**5**	**2**	**0**	**5**	**8**	**0**	**15**	**1**	**3**	**0**	**1**	**1**	**.260**	**.319**	**.361**	**.953**
Career total		1281	4019	591	1082	188	49	37	303	414	1	447	17	78	5	67	30	.269	.340	.368	.962
Cubs total		**125**	**285**	**35**	**74**	**14**	**6**	**1**	**14**	**23**	**0**	**44**	**2**	**8**	**0**	**2**	**3**	**.260**	**.319**	**.361**	**.953**

Adams, Robert Michael (Mike)
HEIGHT: 5'9"   THROWS: RIGHT   BATS: RIGHT   BORN: 7/24/1948 CINCINNATI, OHIO   POSITIONS PLAYED: 2B, 3B, OF

YEAR	TEAM	GAMES	AB	RUNS	HITS	2B	3B	HR	RBI	BB	IBB	SO	HBP	SH	SF	SB	CS	BA	OBA	SA	FA
1972	Min-A	3	6	0	2	0	0	0	0	0	0	1	0	0	0	0	0	.333	.333	.333	1.000
1973	Min-A	55	66	21	14	2	0	3	6	17	0	18	1	0	0	2	1	.212	.381	.379	.978
1976	**ChC-N**	**25**	**29**	**1**	**4**	**2**	**0**	**0**	**2**	**8**	**0**	**7**	**1**	**0**	**0**	**0**	**0**	**.138**	**.342**	**.207**	**1.000**
1977	**ChC-N**	**2**	**2**	**0**	**0**	**0**	**0**	**0**	**0**	**0**	**0**	**1**	**0**	**0**	**0**	**0**	**0**	**.000**	**.000**	**.000**	**—**
1978	Oak-A	15	15	5	3	1	0	0	1	7	0	2	0	0	0	0	0	.200	.455	.267	1.000
Career average		20	24	5	5	1	0	1	2	6	0	6	0	0	0	0	0	.195	.375	.314	.985
Cubs average		**14**	**16**	**1**	**2**	**1**	**0**	**0**	**1**	**4**	**0**	**4**	**1**	**0**	**0**	**0**	**0**	**.129**	**.325**	**.194**	**1.000**
Career total		100	118	27	23	5	0	3	9	32	0	29	2	0	0	2	1	.195	.375	.314	.985
Cubs total		**27**	**31**	**1**	**4**	**2**	**0**	**0**	**2**	**8**	**0**	**8**	**1**	**0**	**0**	**0**	**0**	**.129**	**.325**	**.194**	**1.000**

Addis, Robert Gordon (Bob)
HEIGHT: 6'0"   THROWS: RIGHT   BATS: LEFT   BORN: 11/6/1925 MINERAL, OHIO   POSITIONS PLAYED: OF

YEAR	TEAM	GAMES	AB	RUNS	HITS	2B	3B	HR	RBI	BB	IBB	SO	HBP	SH	SF	SB	CS	BA	OBA	SA	FA
1950	Bos-N	16	28	7	7	1	0	0	2	3	—	5	0	0	—	1	—	.250	.323	.286	1.000
1951	Bos-N	85	199	23	55	7	0	1	24	9	—	10	0	3	—	3	2	.276	.308	.327	.982
1952	**ChC-N**	**93**	**292**	**38**	**86**	**13**	**2**	**1**	**20**	**23**	**—**	**30**	**0**	**2**	**—**	**4**	**4**	**.295**	**.346**	**.363**	**.988**
1953	**ChC-N**	**10**	**12**	**2**	**2**	**1**	**0**	**0**	**1**	**2**	**—**	**0**	**0**	**0**	**—**	**0**	**0**	**.167**	**.286**	**.250**	**1.000**
1953	Pit-N	4	3	0	0	0	0	0	0	0	—	2	0	0	—	0	0	.000	.000	.000	—
Career average		52	134	18	38	6	1	1	12	9	—	12	0	1	—	2	2	.281	.327	.341	.986
Cubs average		**52**	**152**	**20**	**44**	**7**	**1**	**1**	**11**	**13**	**—**	**15**	**0**	**1**	**—**	**2**	**2**	**.289**	**.343**	**.359**	**.989**
Career total		208	534	70	150	22	2	2	47	37	—	47	0	5	—	8	6	.281	.327	.341	.986
Cubs total		**103**	**304**	**40**	**88**	**14**	**2**	**1**	**21**	**25**	**—**	**30**	**0**	**2**	**—**	**4**	**4**	**.289**	**.343**	**.359**	**.989**

Addy, Robert Edward (Bob *or* Magnet)
HEIGHT: 5'8"   THROWS: LEFT   BATS: LEFT   BORN: 2/18/1845 ROCHESTER, NEW YORK   DIED: 4/9/1910 POCATELLO, IDAHO   POSITIONS PLAYED: OF

YEAR	TEAM	GAMES	AB	RUNS	HITS	2B	3B	HR	RBI	BB	IBB	SO	HBP	SH	SF	SB	CS	BA	OBA	SA	FA
1876	**ChN-N**	**32**	**147**	**36**	**40**	**4**	**1**	**0**	**16**	**5**	**—**	**0**	**—**	**—**	**—**	**—**	**—**	**.272**	**.296**	**.313**	**.800**
1877	Cin-N	57	245	27	68	2	3	0	31	6	—	5	—	—	—	—	—	.278	.295	.310	.805
Career average		45	196	32	54	3	2	0	24	6	—	3	—	—	—	—	—	.276	.295	.311	.803
Cubs average		**32**	**147**	**36**	**40**	**4**	**1**	**0**	**16**	**5**	**—**	**0**	**—**	**—**	**—**	**—**	**—**	**.272**	**.296**	**.313**	**.800**
Career total		89	392	63	108	6	4	0	47	11	—	5	—	—	—	—	—	.276	.295	.311	.803
Cubs total		**32**	**147**	**36**	**40**	**4**	**1**	**0**	**16**	**5**	**—**	**0**	**—**	**—**	**—**	**—**	**—**	**.272**	**.296**	**.313**	**.800**

Alexander, Manuel (Manny)
HEIGHT: 5'10"   THROWS: RIGHT   BATS: RIGHT   BORN: 3/20/1971 SAN PEDRO DE MACORIS, DOMINICAN REPUBLIC   POSITIONS PLAYED: P, 2B, 3B, SS, OF

YEAR	TEAM	GAMES	AB	RUNS	HITS	2B	3B	HR	RBI	BB	IBB	SO	HBP	SH	SF	SB	CS	BA	OBA	SA	FA
1992	Bal-A	4	5	1	1	0	0	0	0	0	0	3	0	0	0	0	0	.200	.200	.200	1.000
1993	Bal-A	3	0	1	0	0	0	0	0	0	0	0	0	0	0	0	0	—	—	—	—
1995	Bal-A	94	242	35	57	9	1	3	23	20	0	30	2	4	0	11	4	.236	.299	.318	.969
1996	Bal-A	54	68	6	7	0	0	0	4	3	0	27	0	2	0	3	3	.103	.141	.103	.936
1997	NYM-N	54	149	26	37	9	3	2	15	9	1	38	1	1	1	11	0	.248	.294	.389	.979
1997	**ChC-N**	**33**	**99**	**11**	**29**	**3**	**1**	**1**	**7**	**8**	**2**	**16**	**2**	**2**	**0**	**2**	**1**	**.293**	**.358**	**.374**	**.949**
1998	**ChC-N**	**108**	**264**	**34**	**60**	**10**	**1**	**5**	**25**	**18**	**1**	**66**	**1**	**5**	**1**	**4**	**1**	**.227**	**.278**	**.330**	**.970**
1999	**ChC-N**	**90**	**177**	**17**	**48**	**11**	**2**	**0**	**15**	**10**	**0**	**38**	**0**	**1**	**1**	**4**	**0**	**.271**	**.309**	**.356**	**.954**
2000	Bos-A	101	194	30	41	4	3	4	19	13	0	41	0	2	0	2	0	.211	.261	.325	.962
Career average		68	150	20	35	6	1	2	14	10	1	32	1	2	0	5	1	.234	.285	.328	.964
Cubs average		**77**	**180**	**21**	**46**	**8**	**1**	**2**	**16**	**12**	**1**	**40**	**1**	**3**	**1**	**3**	**1**	**.254**	**.303**	**.346**	**.960**
Career total		541	1198	161	280	46	11	15	108	81	4	259	6	17	3	37	9	.234	.285	.328	.964
Cubs total		**231**	**540**	**62**	**137**	**24**	**4**	**6**	**47**	**36**	**3**	**120**	**3**	**8**	**2**	**10**	**2**	**.254**	**.303**	**.346**	**.960**

Alexander, Matthew (Matt)

HEIGHT: 5'11" THROWS: RIGHT BATS: BOTH BORN: 1/30/1947 SHREVEPORT, LOUISIANA POSITIONS PLAYED: 2B, 3B, SS, OF

YEAR	TEAM	GAMES	AB	RUNS	HITS	2B	3B	HR	RBI	BB	IBB	SO	HBP	SH	SF	SB	CS	BA	OBA	SA	FA
1973	ChC-N	12	5	4	1	0	0	0	1	1	0	1	0	0	0	2	0	.200	.333	.200	1.000
1974	ChC-N	45	54	15	11	2	1	0	0	12	1	12	1	7	0	8	4	.204	.358	.278	.925
1975	Oak-A	63	10	16	1	0	0	0	0	1	0	1	0	0	0	17	10	.100	.182	.100	.900
1976	Oak-A	61	30	16	1	0	0	0	0	0	0	5	0	0	0	20	7	.033	.033	.033	1.000
1977	Oak-A	90	42	24	10	1	0	0	2	4	0	6	0	1	0	26	14	.238	.304	.262	1.000
1978	Pit-N	7	0	2	0	0	0	0	0	0	0	0	0	0	0	4	1	—	—	—	—
1979	Pit-N	44	13	16	7	0	1	0	1	0	0	0	0	0	0	13	1	.538	.538	.692	1.000
1980	Pit-N	37	3	13	1	1	0	0	0	0	0	0	0	0	0	10	3	.333	.333	.667	1.000
1981	Pit-N	15	11	5	4	0	0	0	0	0	0	1	0	0	0	3	2	.364	.364	.364	1.000
Career average		42	19	12	4	0	0	0	0	2	0	3	0	1	0	11	5	.214	.294	.262	.967
Cubs average		**29**	**30**	**10**	**6**	**1**	**1**	**0**	**1**	**7**	**1**	**7**	**1**	**4**	**0**	**5**	**2**	**.203**	**.356**	**.271**	**.929**
Career total		374	168	111	36	4	2	0	4	18	1	26	1	8	0	103	42	.214	.294	.262	.967
Cubs total		**57**	**59**	**19**	**12**	**2**	**1**	**0**	**1**	**13**	**1**	**13**	**1**	**7**	**0**	**10**	**4**	**.203**	**.356**	**.271**	**.929**

Allen, Ethan Nathan

HEIGHT: 6'1" THROWS: RIGHT BATS: RIGHT BORN: 1/1/1904 CINCINNATI, OHIO DIED: 9/15/1993 BROOKINGS, OREGON POSITIONS PLAYED: OF

YEAR	TEAM	GAMES	AB	RUNS	HITS	2B	3B	HR	RBI	BB	IBB	SO	HBP	SH	SF	SB	CS	BA	OBA	SA	FA
1926	Cin-N	18	13	3	4	1	0	0	0	0	—	3	0	0	—	0	—	.308	.308	.385	1.000
1927	Cin-N	111	359	54	106	26	4	2	20	14	—	23	2	13	—	12	—	.295	.325	.407	.988
1928	Cin-N	129	485	55	148	30	7	1	62	27	—	29	1	14	—	6	—	.305	.343	.402	.981
1929	Cin-N	143	538	69	157	27	11	6	64	20	—	21	0	10	—	21	—	.292	.317	.416	.988
1930	Cin-N	21	46	10	10	1	0	3	7	5	—	2	0	2	—	1	—	.217	.294	.435	.969
1930	NYG-N	76	238	48	73	9	2	7	31	12	—	23	0	8	—	5	—	.307	.340	.450	.985
1931	NYG-N	94	298	58	98	18	2	5	43	15	—	15	1	7	—	6	—	.329	.363	.453	.975
1932	NYG-N	54	103	13	18	6	2	1	7	1	—	12	2	1	—	0	—	.175	.198	.301	.957
1933	StL-N	91	261	25	63	7	3	0	36	13	—	22	1	6	—	3	—	.241	.280	.291	.984
1934	Phi-N	145	581	87	192	42	4	10	85	33	—	47	3	16	—	6	—	.330	.370	.468	.978
1935	Phi-N	156	645	90	198	46	1	8	63	43	—	54	1	11	—	5	—	.307	.351	.419	.980
1936	Phi-N	30	125	21	37	3	1	1	9	4	—	8	0	3	—	4	—	.296	.318	.360	.954
1936	**ChC-N**	**91**	**373**	**47**	**110**	**18**	**6**	**3**	**39**	**13**	**—**	**30**	**2**	**11**	**—**	**12**	**—**	**.295**	**.322**	**.399**	**.980**
1937	StL-A	103	320	39	101	18	1	0	31	21	—	17	1	7	—	3	4	.316	.360	.378	.980
1938	StL-A	19	33	4	10	3	1	0	4	2	—	4	0	1	—	0	0	.303	.343	.455	1.000
Career average		99	340	48	102	20	3	4	39	17	—	24	1	8	—	6	0	.300	.336	.410	.981
Cubs average		**91**	**373**	**47**	**110**	**18**	**6**	**3**	**39**	**13**	**—**	**30**	**2**	**11**	**—**	**12**	**—**	**.295**	**.322**	**.399**	**.980**
Career total		1281	4418	623	1325	255	45	47	501	223	—	310	14	110	—	84	4	.300	.336	.410	.981
Cubs total		**91**	**373**	**47**	**110**	**18**	**6**	**3**	**39**	**13**	**—**	**30**	**2**	**11**	**—**	**12**	**—**	**.295**	**.322**	**.399**	**.980**

Allen, Artemus Ward (Nick)

HEIGHT: 6'0" THROWS: RIGHT BATS: RIGHT BORN: 9/14/1888 NORTON, KANSAS DIED: 10/16/1939 HINES, ILLINOIS POSITIONS PLAYED: C

YEAR	TEAM	GAMES	AB	RUNS	HITS	2B	3B	HR	RBI	BB	IBB	SO	HBP	SH	SF	SB	CS	BA	OBA	SA	FA
1914	Buf-F	32	63	3	15	1	0	0	4	3	—	12	0	1	—	4	—	.238	.273	.254	.969
1915	Buf-F	84	215	14	44	7	1	0	17	18	—	34	1	4	—	4	—	.205	.269	.247	.956
1916	**ChC-N**	**5**	**16**	**1**	**1**	**0**	**0**	**0**	**1**	**0**	**—**	**3**	**0**	**0**	**—**	**0**	**—**	**.063**	**.063**	**.063**	**.958**
1918	Cin-N	37	96	6	25	2	2	0	5	4	—	7	1	0	—	0	—	.260	.297	.323	.950
1919	Cin-N	15	25	7	8	0	1	0	5	2	—	6	1	0	—	0	—	.320	.393	.400	.958
1920	Cin-N	43	85	10	23	3	1	0	4	6	—	11	3	5	—	0	0	.271	.340	.329	.961
Career average		36	83	7	19	2	1	0	6	6	—	12	1	2	—	1	0	.232	.288	.278	.958
Cubs average		**5**	**16**	**1**	**1**	**0**	**0**	**0**	**1**	**0**	**—**	**3**	**0**	**0**	**—**	**0**	**—**	**.063**	**.063**	**.063**	**.958**
Career total		216	500	41	116	13	5	0	36	33	—	73	6	10	—	8	0	.232	.288	.278	.958
Cubs total		**5**	**16**	**1**	**1**	**0**	**0**	**0**	**1**	**0**	**—**	**3**	**0**	**0**	**—**	**0**	**—**	**.063**	**.063**	**.063**	**.958**

Allison, Milo Henry (Pete)

HEIGHT: 6'0" THROWS: RIGHT BATS: LEFT BORN: 10/16/1890 ELK RAPIDS, MICHIGAN DIED: 6/18/1957 KENOSHA, WISCONSIN POSITIONS PLAYED: OF

YEAR	TEAM	GAMES	AB	RUNS	HITS	2B	3B	HR	RBI	BB	IBB	SO	HBP	SH	SF	SB	CS	BA	OBA	SA	FA
1913	ChC-N	2	6	1	2	0	0	0	0	0	—	1	0	0	—	1	—	.333	.333	.333	1.000
1914	ChC-N	1	1	0	1	0	0	0	0	0	—	0	0	0	—	0	—	1.000	1.000	1.000	—
1916	Cle-A	14	18	10	5	0	0	0	0	6	—	1	0	1	—	0	—	.278	.458	.278	1.000
1917	Cle-A	32	35	4	5	0	0	0	0	9	—	7	0	2	—	3	—	.143	.318	.143	1.000
Career average		12	15	4	3	0	0	0	0	4	—	2	0	1	—	1	—	.217	.373	.217	1.000
Cubs average		**2**	**4**	**1**	**2**	**0**	**0**	**0**	**0**	**0**	**—**	**1**	**0**	**0**	**—**	**1**	**—**	**.429**	**.429**	**.429**	**1.000**
Career total		49	60	15	13	0	0	0	0	15	—	9	0	3	—	4	—	.217	.373	.217	1.000
Cubs total		**3**	**7**	**1**	**3**	**0**	**0**	**0**	**0**	**0**	**—**	**1**	**0**	**0**	**—**	**1**	**—**	**.429**	**.429**	**.429**	**1.000**

Altman, George Lee

HEIGHT: 6'4" THROWS: RIGHT BATS: LEFT BORN: 3/20/1933 GOLDSBORO, NORTH CAROLINA POSITIONS PLAYED: 1B, OF

YEAR	TEAM	GAMES	AB	RUNS	HITS	2B	3B	HR	RBI	BB	IBB	SO	HBP	SH	SF	SB	CS	BA	OBA	SA	FA
1959	ChC-N	135	420	54	103	14	4	12	47	34	4	80	7	6	1	1	0	.245	.312	.383	.990
1960	ChC-N	119	334	50	89	16	4	13	51	32	6	67	1	2	3	4	3	.266	.330	.455	.994
1961	ChC-N	138	518	77	157	28	12	27	96	40	3	92	4	4	7	6	2	.303	.353	.560	.980
1962	ChC-N	147	534	74	170	27	5	22	74	62	14	89	5	0	2	19	7	.318	.393	.511	.981
1963	StL-N	135	464	62	127	18	7	9	47	47	2	93	2	2	6	13	4	.274	.339	.401	.979
1964	NYM-N	124	422	48	97	14	1	9	47	18	4	70	1	2	2	4	2	.230	.262	.332	.968
1965	ChC-N	90	196	24	46	7	1	4	23	19	2	36	0	1	0	3	2	.235	.302	.342	.951
1966	ChC-N	88	185	19	41	6	0	5	17	14	3	37	0	2	0	2	2	.222	.276	.335	.974
1967	ChC-N	15	18	1	2	2	0	0	1	2	0	8	0	0	0	0	0	.111	.200	.222	1.000
Career average		110	343	45	92	15	4	11	45	30	4	64	2	2	2	6	2	.269	.329	.432	.981
Cubs average		**105**	**315**	**43**	**87**	**14**	**4**	**12**	**44**	**29**	**5**	**58**	**2**	**2**	**2**	**5**	**2**	**.276**	**.340**	**.458**	**.983**
Career total		991	3091	409	832	132	34	101	403	268	38	572	20	19	21	52	22	.269	.329	.432	.981
Cubs total		**732**	**2205**	**299**	**608**	**100**	**26**	**83**	**309**	**203**	**32**	**409**	**17**	**15**	**13**	**35**	**16**	**.276**	**.340**	**.458**	**.983**

Amalfitano, John Joseph (Joey)

HEIGHT: 5'11" THROWS: RIGHT BATS: RIGHT BORN: 1/23/1934 SAN PEDRO, CALIFORNIA POSITIONS PLAYED: 1B, 2B, 3B, SS, OF

YEAR	TEAM	GAMES	AB	RUNS	HITS	2B	3B	HR	RBI	BB	IBB	SO	HBP	SH	SF	SB	CS	BA	OBA	SA	FA
1954	NYG-N	9	5	2	0	0	0	0	0	0	—	4	0	0	0	0	0	.000	.000	.000	1.000
1955	NYG-N	36	22	8	5	1	1	0	1	2	0	2	0	0	0	0	0	.227	.292	.364	.912
1960	SF-N	106	328	47	91	15	3	1	27	26	1	31	3	3	1	2	3	.277	.335	.351	.954
1961	SF-N	109	384	64	98	11	4	2	23	44	2	59	0	4	1	7	4	.255	.331	.320	.971
1962	Hou-N	117	380	44	90	12	5	1	27	45	5	43	1	5	3	4	4	.237	.317	.303	.965
1963	SF-N	54	137	11	24	3	0	1	7	12	0	18	1	2	1	2	6	.175	.245	.219	.981
1964	ChC-N	100	324	51	78	19	6	4	27	40	1	42	5	3	0	2	7	.241	.333	.373	.964
1965	ChC-N	67	96	13	26	4	0	0	8	12	0	14	2	0	0	2	2	.271	.364	.313	.980
1966	ChC-N	41	38	8	6	2	0	0	3	4	0	10	0	0	2	0	0	.158	.227	.211	.977
1967	ChC-N	4	1	0	0	0	0	0	0	0	0	1	0	0	0	0	0	.000	.000	.000	—
Career average		64	172	25	42	7	2	1	12	19	1	22	1	2	1	2	3	.244	.320	.321	.966
Cubs average		**53**	**115**	**18**	**28**	**6**	**2**	**1**	**10**	**14**	**0**	**17**	**2**	**1**	**1**	**1**	**2**	**.240**	**.330**	**.346**	**.967**
Career total		643	1715	248	418	67	19	9	123	185	9	224	12	17	8	19	26	.244	.320	.321	.966
Cubs total		**212**	**459**	**72**	**110**	**25**	**6**	**4**	**38**	**56**	**1**	**67**	**7**	**3**	**2**	**4**	**9**	**.240**	**.330**	**.346**	**.967**

Andrews, James Pratt (Jim)

HEIGHT: — THROWS: — BATS: — BORN: 6/5/1865 SHELBURNE FALLS, MASSACHUSETTS DIED: 12/27/1907 CHICAGO, ILLINOIS POSITIONS PLAYED: OF

YEAR	TEAM	GAMES	AB	RUNS	HITS	2B	3B	HR	RBI	BB	IBB	SO	HBP	SH	SF	SB	CS	BA	OBA	SA	FA
1890	ChN-N	53	202	32	38	4	2	3	17	23	—	41	2	—	—	11	—	.188	.278	.272	.900
Career average		53	202	32	38	4	2	3	17	23	—	41	2	—	—	11	—	.188	.278	.272	.900
Cubs average		**53**	**202**	**32**	**38**	**4**	**2**	**3**	**17**	**23**	**—**	**41**	**2**	**—**	**—**	**11**	**—**	**.188**	**.278**	**.272**	**.900**
Career total		53	202	32	38	4	2	3	17	23	—	41	2	—	—	11	—	.188	.278	.272	.900
Cubs total		**53**	**202**	**32**	**38**	**4**	**2**	**3**	**17**	**23**	**—**	**41**	**2**	**—**	**—**	**11**	**—**	**.188**	**.278**	**.272**	**.900**

Andrews, Darrell Shane (Shane *or* Mongo *or* Caveman)
HEIGHT: 6'1" THROWS: RIGHT BATS: RIGHT BORN: 8/28/1971 DALLAS, TEXAS POSITIONS PLAYED: 1B, 3B

YEAR	TEAM	GAMES	AB	RUNS	HITS	2B	3B	HR	RBI	BB	IBB	SO	HBP	SH	SF	SB	CS	BA	OBA	SA	FA
1995	Mon-N	84	220	27	47	10	1	8	31	17	2	68	1	1	2	1	1	.214	.271	.377	.976
1996	Mon-N	127	375	43	85	15	2	19	64	35	8	119	2	0	2	3	1	.227	.295	.429	.955
1997	Mon-N	18	64	10	13	3	0	4	9	3	0	20	0	0	2	0	0	.203	.232	.438	.895
1998	Mon-N	150	492	48	117	30	1	25	69	58	3	137	0	2	7	1	6	.238	.314	.455	.954
1999	Mon-N	98	281	28	51	8	0	11	37	43	2	88	0	0	4	1	0	.181	.287	.327	.954
1999	**ChC-N**	**19**	**67**	**13**	**17**	**4**	**0**	**5**	**14**	**7**	**1**	**21**	**1**	**0**	**1**	**0**	**1**	**.254**	**.329**	**.537**	**.955**
2000	**ChC-N**	**66**	**192**	**25**	**44**	**5**	**0**	**14**	**39**	**27**	**1**	**59**	**2**	**0**	**1**	**1**	**1**	**.229**	**.329**	**.474**	**.930**
Career average		94	282	32	62	13	1	14	44	32	3	85	1	1	3	1	2	.221	.299	.423	.954
Cubs average		**43**	**130**	**19**	**31**	**5**	**0**	**10**	**27**	**17**	**1**	**40**	**2**	**0**	**1**	**1**	**1**	**.236**	**.329**	**.490**	**.935**
Career total		562	1691	194	374	75	4	86	263	190	17	512	6	3	19	7	10	.221	.299	.423	.954
Cubs total		**85**	**259**	**38**	**61**	**9**	**0**	**19**	**53**	**34**	**2**	**80**	**3**	**0**	**2**	**1**	**2**	**.236**	**.329**	**.490**	**.935**

Andrus, Frederick Hotham (Fred)
HEIGHT: 6'2" THROWS: RIGHT BATS: RIGHT BORN: 8/23/1850 WASHINGTON, MICHIGAN DIED: 11/10/1937 DETROIT, MICHIGAN POSITIONS PLAYED: P, OF

YEAR	TEAM	GAMES	AB	RUNS	HITS	2B	3B	HR	RBI	BB	IBB	SO	HBP	SH	SF	SB	CS	BA	OBA	SA	FA
1876	**ChN-N**	**8**	**36**	**6**	**11**	**3**	**0**	**0**	**2**	**0**	—	**5**	—	—	—	—	—	**.306**	**.306**	**.389**	**.714**
1884	**ChN-N**	**1**	**5**	**3**	**1**	**0**	**0**	**0**	**0**	**1**	—	**0**	—	—	—	—	—	**.200**	**.333**	**.200**	**1.000**
Career average		5	21	5	6	2	0	0	1	1	—	3	—	—	—	—	—	.293	.310	.366	.800
Cubs average		**5**	**21**	**5**	**6**	**2**	**0**	**0**	**1**	**1**	—	**3**	—	—	—	—	—	**.293**	**.310**	**.366**	**.800**
Career total		9	41	9	12	3	0	0	2	1	—	5	—	—	—	—	—	.293	.310	.366	.800
Cubs total		**9**	**41**	**9**	**12**	**3**	**0**	**0**	**2**	**1**	—	**5**	—	—	—	—	—	**.293**	**.310**	**.366**	**.800**

Angley, Thomas Samuel (Tom)
HEIGHT: 5'8" THROWS: RIGHT BATS: LEFT BORN: 10/2/1904 BALTIMORE, MARYLAND DIED: 10/26/1952 WICHITA, KANSAS POSITIONS PLAYED: C

YEAR	TEAM	GAMES	AB	RUNS	HITS	2B	3B	HR	RBI	BB	IBB	SO	HBP	SH	SF	SB	CS	BA	OBA	SA	FA
1929	**ChC-N**	**5**	**16**	**1**	**4**	**1**	**0**	**0**	**6**	**2**	—	**2**	**0**	**3**	—	**0**	—	**.250**	**.333**	**.313**	**.968**
Career average		5	16	1	4	1	0	0	6	2	—	2	0	3	—	0	—	.250	.333	.313	.968
Cubs average		**5**	**16**	**1**	**4**	**1**	**0**	**0**	**6**	**2**	—	**2**	**0**	**3**	—	**0**	—	**.250**	**.333**	**.313**	**.968**
Career total		5	16	1	4	1	0	0	6	2	—	2	0	3	—	0	—	.250	.333	.313	.968
Cubs total		**5**	**16**	**1**	**4**	**1**	**0**	**0**	**6**	**2**	—	**2**	**0**	**3**	—	**0**	—	**.250**	**.333**	**.313**	**.968**

Anson, Adrian Constantine (Cap *or* Pop)
HEIGHT: 6'0" THROWS: RIGHT BATS: RIGHT BORN: 4/11/1852 MARSHALLTOWN, IOWA DIED: 4/14/1922 CHICAGO, ILLINOIS
POSITIONS PLAYED: P, C, 1B, 2B, 3B, SS, OF

YEAR	TEAM	GAMES	AB	RUNS	HITS	2B	3B	HR	RBI	BB	IBB	SO	HBP	SH	SF	SB	CS	BA	OBA	SA	FA
1876	ChN-N	66	321	63	110	9	7	2	59	12	—	8	—	—	—	—	—	.343	.366	.433	.850
1877	ChN-N	59	255	52	86	19	1	0	32	9	—	3	—	—	—	—	—	.337	.360	.420	.875
1878	ChN-N	60	261	55	89	12	2	0	40	13	—	1	—	—	—	—	—	.341	.372	.402	.846
1879	ChN-N	51	227	40	72	20	1	0	34	2	—	2	—	—	—	—	—	.317	.323	.414	.975
1880	ChN-N	86	356	54	120	24	1	1	74	14	—	12	—	—	—	—	—	.337	.362	.419	.973
1881	ChN-N	84	343	67	137	21	7	1	82	26	—	4	—	—	—	—	—	.399	.442	.510	.975
1882	ChN-N	82	348	69	126	29	8	1	83	20	—	7	—	—	—	—	—	.362	.397	.500	.948
1883	ChN-N	98	413	70	127	36	5	0	68	18	—	9	—	—	—	—	—	.308	.336	.419	.962
1884	ChN-N	112	475	108	159	30	3	21	102	29	—	13	—	—	—	—	—	.335	.373	.543	.953
1885	ChN-N	112	464	100	144	35	7	7	108	34	—	13	—	—	—	—	—	.310	.357	.461	.958
1886	ChN-N	125	504	117	187	35	11	10	147	55	—	19	—	—	—	29	—	.371	.433	.544	.961
1887	ChN-N	122	532	107	224	33	13	6	102	60	—	18	1	—	—	27	—	.421	.481	.566	.972
1888	ChN-N	134	515	101	177	20	12	12	84	47	—	24	1	—	—	28	—	.344	.400	.499	.986
1889	ChN-N	134	518	100	161	32	7	7	117	86	—	19	5	—	—	27	—	.311	.414	.440	.982
1890	ChN-N	139	504	95	157	14	5	7	107	113	—	23	6	—	—	29	—	.312	.443	.401	.978
1891	ChN-N	136	540	81	157	24	8	8	120	75	—	29	1	—	—	17	—	.291	.378	.409	.981
1892	ChN-N	146	559	62	152	25	9	1	74	67	—	30	4	—	—	13	—	.272	.354	.354	.973
1893	ChN-N	103	398	70	125	24	2	0	91	68	—	12	1	—	—	13	—	.314	.415	.384	.981
1894	ChN-N	83	340	82	132	28	4	5	99	40	—	15	3	7	—	17	—	.388	.457	.538	.990
1895	ChN-N	122	474	87	159	23	6	2	91	55	—	23	3	13	—	12	—	.335	.408	.422	.985

(continued)

Adrian Constantine "Cap" Anson, 1b-2b-3b-of-c-rhp, 1871–97

ADRIAN C. ANSON.
ALLEN & GINTER'S
Cigarettes
RICHMOND. VIRGINIA.

Cap Anson may not have been the best player in the 19th century, but there is no doubt that he was that era's greatest star. He played an amazing 27 years of major league baseball and is the man most credited with popularizing the sport in the game's early days.

Anson was born on April 11, 1852, in Marshalltown, Iowa. He was an excellent athlete as a young man and was an early enthusiast of the game. Anson attended Notre Dame for a year before deciding to turn to professional baseball as a career.

He signed with the Rockford Forest Citys of the old National Association, the forerunner of the National League. The Forest Citys were not a very good club, finishing dead last in the NA, but Anson, playing third base, hit .325 and led the league in doubles in his first full year.

Anson jumped to the Philadelphia Athletics the next year, where he continued his stellar play at both first and third base. In five years in the National Association, Anson hit better than .300 four times.

In 1876, when the National League was officially launched, Anson was one of the first players signed by the new league, playing for the Chicago team. At that time, they were called the White Stockings. Anson and second baseman Ross Barnes dominated the league's hitting statistics to lead Chicago to the city's first baseball championship.

In 1879 Anson, now an eight-year pro, was named to manage the Chicago team. He played virtually any position on the field, but after donning his manger's cap, Anson stayed mainly at first base for the rest of his career.

At 6'2" and about 227 pounds, Anson was the biggest man in baseball almost from the day he stepped on the diamond. He was not a gentle giant; he was prone to fisticuffs, some-times with opponents, but sometimes with players from his own team if he did not believe they were working hard or had made a foolish error or mental mistake.

But he was a smart field general. He may not have invented these strategies, but the Chicago team used the hit-and-run and base-stealing plays more often than most other NL clubs. Anson also pioneered the use of signals from a coach to a player and began thinking about rotating pitchers. Prior to that concept, teams had a regular starting pitcher who started about three-quarters of a teams' games and a backup who would start the rest. Anson gave his backup pitchers more work and found that it benefited both hurlers. In short, Anson took managing up a notch.

He was also one of the first managers to begin preseason workouts for his players (what is now called spring training), and he advocated a strict training regimen with his players that included no alcohol, a very unpopular stance in that era.

But he won pennants, a total of five from 1880 to 1886. He was also, by now, one of the best hitters in the league, leading the NL in RBIs eight times and in batting average four times from 1879 to 1887, with a high of .399 in 1881. In fact, he hit over .300 for 20 consecutive years in the National Association and National League, and was over that mark for 24 of his 27 years. He led Chicago in RBIs for 14 consecutive years, from 1881 to 1894.

He was a man of integrity in an era where throwing games was more common than not. But he was also a midwesterner who was strongly against integration in any form. Looking back on his career, many baseball historians feel than Anson was principally responsible for the banning of blacks from the National League in the 19th century. Anson once refused to take the field in an exhibition

(continued)

(continued)

game unless a black player on the other team was not allowed to play.

While Anson was certainly not shy about voicing his opinions, it is difficult to determine how influential he was. Certainly, few, if any, National League owners were comfortable with black players on their roster, believing that white fans would not tolerate them. Anson's refusal to play against black players was at least an easy way for the National League powers-that-were to throw up their collective hands and stay away from the black ballplayer for the next six decades.

In 1888 Anson became a part owner of the White Stockings and celebrated his 18th year in pro baseball by leading the National League in batting average (.345), RBIs (84) and on-base percentage (.400). He had slowed some afield, but he could still hit like blazes.

Chicago won no pennants in the 1890s under Anson, but they finished second twice. On July 18, 1897, Anson became the first major league player to make 3,000 hits. His feat went unremarked upon in the papers the next day.

He was an enormously popular player by that time, so much so that when he left Chicago the next year (he was actually fired over a contract dispute), sportswriters began calling the Chicago team "the Orphans." He moved over to New York, where he managed the Giants for 22 games before retiring for good.

Anson struggled after his baseball years, dealing with financial difficulties. The league, as a sign of gratitude, tried to award him a pension, but he turned it down. He died in 1922.

In 1939 Anson was named to the Baseball Hall of Fame. He remains the Cubs' all-time leader in may categories, including hits (3,081), batting average (.339), runs (1,711), singles (2,330), doubles (530) and RBIs (1,879).

(Anson, continued)

YEAR	TEAM																				
1896	ChN-N	108	402	72	133	18	2	2	90	49	—	10	3	5	—	24	—	.331	.407	.400	.980
1897	ChN-N	114	424	67	121	17	3	3	75	60	—	—	4	9	—	11	—	.285	.379	.361	.975
Career average		103	417	78	139	24	6	4	85	43	—	13	1	2	—	11	—	.333	.398	.449	.969
Cubs average		**103**	**417**	**78**	**139**	**24**	**6**	**4**	**85**	**43**	**—**	**13**	**1**	**2**	**—**	**11**	**—**	**.333**	**.398**	**.449**	**.969**
Career total		2276	9173	1719	3055	528	124	96	1879	952	—	294	32	34	—	247	—	.333	.398	.449	.969
Cubs total		**2276**	**9173**	**1719**	**3055**	**528**	**124**	**96**	**1879**	**952**	**—**	**294**	**32**	**34**	**—**	**247**	**—**	**.333**	**.398**	**.449**	**.969**

Archer, James Patrick (Jimmy)

HEIGHT: 5'10" THROWS: RIGHT BATS: RIGHT BORN: 5/13/1883 DUBLIN, IRELAND DIED: 3/29/1958 MILWAUKEE, WISCONSIN
POSITIONS PLAYED: C, 1B, 2B, 3B, OF

YEAR	TEAM	GAMES	AB	RUNS	HITS	2B	3B	HR	RBI	BB	IBB	SO	HBP	SH	SF	SB	CS	BA	OBA	SA	FA
1904	Pit-N	7	20	1	3	0	0	0	1	0	—	—	0	0	—	0	—	.150	.150	.150	.919
1907	Det-A	18	42	6	5	0	0	0	0	4	—	—	0	2	—	0	—	.119	.196	.119	.966
1909	ChC-N	80	261	31	60	9	2	1	30	12	—	—	1	12	—	5	—	.230	.266	.291	.960
1910	ChC-N	98	313	36	81	17	6	2	41	14	—	49	1	16	—	6	—	.259	.293	.371	.973
1911	ChC-N	116	387	41	98	18	5	4	41	18	—	43	1	13	—	5	—	.253	.288	.357	.979
1912	ChC-N	120	385	35	109	20	2	5	58	22	—	36	5	14	—	7	—	.283	.330	.384	.966
1913	ChC-N	111	368	38	98	14	7	2	44	19	—	27	5	11	—	4	—	.266	.311	.359	.969
1914	ChC-N	79	248	17	64	9	2	0	19	9	—	9	0	5	—	1	—	.258	.284	.310	.973
1915	ChC-N	97	309	21	75	11	5	1	27	11	—	38	2	9	—	5	6	.243	.273	.320	.978
1916	ChC-N	77	205	11	45	6	2	1	30	12	—	24	2	9	—	3	—	.220	.269	.283	.979
1917	ChC-N	2	2	0	0	0	0	0	0	0	—	1	0	0	—	0	—	.000	.000	.000	—
1918	Pit-N	24	58	4	9	1	2	0	3	1	—	6	2	2	—	0	—	.155	.197	.241	.990
1918	Bro-N	9	22	3	6	0	1	0	0	1	—	5	0	0	—	0	—	.273	.304	.364	.968
1918	Cin-N	9	26	2	7	1	0	0	2	1	—	3	0	0	—	0	—	.269	.296	.308	.978
Career average		71	221	21	55	9	3	1	25	10	—	20	2	8	—	3	1	.249	.288	.333	.972
Cubs average		**87**	**275**	**26**	**70**	**12**	**3**	**2**	**32**	**13**	**—**	**25**	**2**	**10**	**—**	**4**	**1**	**.254**	**.292**	**.341**	**.972**
Career total		847	2646	246	660	106	34	16	296	124	—	241	19	93	—	36	6	.249	.288	.333	.972
Cubs total		**780**	**2478**	**230**	**630**	**104**	**31**	**16**	**290**	**117**	**—**	**227**	**17**	**89**	**—**	**36**	**6**	**.254**	**.292**	**.341**	**.972**

Arcia, Jose Raimundo (Flaco)
HEIGHT: 6'3" THROWS: RIGHT BATS: RIGHT BORN: 8/22/1943 HAVANA, CUBA POSITIONS PLAYED: 1B, 2B, 3B, SS, OF

YEAR	TEAM	GAMES	AB	RUNS	HITS	2B	3B	HR	RBI	BB	IBB	SO	HBP	SH	SF	SB	CS	BA	OBA	SA	FA
1968	**ChC-N**	**59**	**84**	**15**	**16**	**4**	**0**	**1**	**8**	**3**	**0**	**24**	**0**	**2**	**0**	**0**	**0**	**.190**	**.218**	**.274**	**.976**
1969	SD-N	120	302	35	65	11	3	0	10	14	0	47	2	3	0	14	7	.215	.255	.272	.966
1970	SD-N	114	229	28	51	9	3	0	17	12	1	36	7	4	0	3	6	.223	.282	.288	.956
Career average		98	205	26	44	8	2	0	12	10	0	36	3	3	0	6	4	.215	.260	.278	.963
Cubs average		**59**	**84**	**15**	**16**	**4**	**0**	**1**	**8**	**3**	**0**	**24**	**0**	**2**	**0**	**0**	**0**	**.190**	**.218**	**.274**	**.976**
Career total		293	615	78	132	24	6	1	35	29	1	107	9	9	0	17	13	.215	.260	.278	.963
Cubs total		**59**	**84**	**15**	**16**	**4**	**0**	**1**	**8**	**3**	**0**	**24**	**0**	**2**	**0**	**0**	**0**	**.190**	**.218**	**.274**	**.976**

Arias, Alejandro (Alex)
HEIGHT: 6'3" THROWS: RIGHT BATS: RIGHT BORN: 11/20/1967 NEW YORK, NEW YORK POSITIONS PLAYED: 1B, 2B, 3B, SS

YEAR	TEAM	GAMES	AB	RUNS	HITS	2B	3B	HR	RBI	BB	IBB	SO	HBP	SH	SF	SB	CS	BA	OBA	SA	FA
1992	**ChC-N**	**32**	**99**	**14**	**29**	**6**	**0**	**0**	**7**	**11**	**0**	**13**	**2**	**1**	**0**	**0**	**0**	**.293**	**.375**	**.354**	**.967**
1993	Fla-N	96	249	27	67	5	1	2	20	27	0	18	3	1	3	1	1	.269	.344	.321	.975
1994	Fla-N	59	113	4	27	5	0	0	15	9	0	19	1	1	1	0	1	.239	.298	.283	.978
1995	Fla-N	94	216	22	58	9	2	3	26	22	1	20	2	3	3	1	0	.269	.337	.370	.953
1996	Fla-N	100	224	27	62	11	2	3	26	17	1	28	3	1	1	2	0	.277	.335	.384	.962
1997	Fla-N	74	93	13	23	2	0	1	11	12	0	12	3	4	0	0	1	.247	.352	.301	.970
1998	Phi-N	56	133	17	39	8	0	1	16	13	3	18	1	1	1	2	0	.293	.358	.376	.985
1999	Phi-N	118	347	43	105	20	1	4	48	36	6	31	4	1	2	2	2	.303	.373	.401	.988
2000	Phi-N	70	155	17	29	9	0	2	15	16	2	28	3	3	3	1	0	.187	.271	.284	.966
2001	SD-N	70	137	19	31	9	0	2	12	17	1	22	1	1	2	1	0	.226	.312	.336	.975
Career average		77	177	20	47	8	1	2	20	18	1	21	2	2	2	1	1	.266	.339	.351	.973
Cubs average		**32**	**99**	**14**	**29**	**6**	**0**	**0**	**7**	**11**	**0**	**13**	**2**	**1**	**0**	**0**	**0**	**.293**	**.375**	**.354**	**.967**
Career total		769	1766	203	470	84	6	18	196	180	14	209	23	17	16	10	5	.266	.339	.351	.973
Cubs total		**32**	**99**	**14**	**29**	**6**	**0**	**0**	**7**	**11**	**0**	**13**	**2**	**1**	**0**	**0**	**0**	**.293**	**.375**	**.354**	**.967**

Asbell, James Marion (Jim *or* Big Train)
HEIGHT: 6'0" THROWS: RIGHT BATS: RIGHT BORN: 6/22/1914 DALLAS, TEXAS DIED: 7/6/1967 SAN MATEO, CALIFORNIA POSITIONS PLAYED: OF

YEAR	TEAM	GAMES	AB	RUNS	HITS	2B	3B	HR	RBI	BB	IBB	SO	HBP	SH	SF	SB	CS	BA	OBA	SA	FA
1938	**ChC-N**	**17**	**33**	**6**	**6**	**2**	**0**	**0**	**3**	**3**	**—**	**9**	**0**	**0**	**—**	**0**	**—**	**.182**	**.250**	**.242**	**1.000**
Career average		17	33	6	6	2	0	0	3	3	—	9	0	0	—	0	—	.182	.250	.242	1.000
Cubs average		**17**	**33**	**6**	**6**	**2**	**0**	**0**	**3**	**3**	**—**	**9**	**0**	**0**	**—**	**0**	**—**	**.182**	**.250**	**.242**	**1.000**
Career total		17	33	6	6	2	0	0	3	3	—	9	0	0	—	0	—	.182	.250	.242	1.000
Cubs total		**17**	**33**	**6**	**6**	**2**	**0**	**0**	**3**	**3**	**—**	**9**	**0**	**0**	**—**	**0**	**—**	**.182**	**.250**	**.242**	**1.000**

Ashburn, Don Richard (Richie *or* Whitey *or* Put Put *or* Cornhusker Express)
HEIGHT: 5'10" THROWS: RIGHT BATS: LEFT BORN: 3/19/1927 TILDEN, NEBRASKA DIED: 9/9/1997 NEW YORK, NEW YORK POSITIONS PLAYED: 2B, OF

YEAR	TEAM	GAMES	AB	RUNS	HITS	2B	3B	HR	RBI	BB	IBB	SO	HBP	SH	SF	SB	CS	BA	OBA	SA	FA
1948	Phi-N	117	463	78	154	17	4	2	40	60	—	22	1	6	—	32	—	.333	.410	.400	.981
1949	Phi-N	154	662	84	188	18	11	1	37	58	—	38	1	7	—	9	—	.284	.343	.349	.980
1950	Phi-N	151	594	84	180	25	14	2	41	63	—	32	2	11	—	14	—	.303	.372	.402	.988
1951	Phi-N	154	643	92	221	31	5	4	63	50	—	37	2	17	—	29	6	.344	.393	.426	.988
1952	Phi-N	154	613	93	173	31	6	1	42	75	—	30	2	11	—	16	11	.282	.362	.357	.980
1953	Phi-N	156	622	110	205	25	9	2	57	61	—	35	5	14	—	14	6	.330	.394	.408	.990
1954	Phi-N	153	559	111	175	16	8	1	41	125	—	46	4	14	1	11	8	.313	.441	.376	.984
1955	Phi-N	140	533	91	180	32	9	3	42	105	5	36	3	2	1	12	10	.338	.449	.448	.983
1956	Phi-N	154	628	94	190	26	8	3	50	79	3	45	5	6	1	10	1	.303	.384	.384	.983
1957	Phi-N	156	626	93	186	26	8	0	33	94	1	44	4	1	4	13	10	.297	.390	.364	.987
1958	Phi-N	152	615	98	215	24	13	2	33	97	7	48	4	7	2	30	12	.350	.440	.441	.984
1959	Phi-N	153	564	86	150	16	2	1	20	79	4	42	6	7	4	9	11	.266	.360	.307	.971
1960	**ChC-N**	**151**	**547**	**99**	**159**	**16**	**5**	**0**	**40**	**116**	**1**	**50**	**1**	**7**	**1**	**16**	**4**	**.291**	**.415**	**.338**	**.976**
1961	**ChC-N**	**109**	**307**	**49**	**79**	**7**	**4**	**0**	**19**	**55**	**2**	**27**	**3**	**1**	**2**	**7**	**6**	**.257**	**.373**	**.306**	**.978**
1962	NYM-N	135	389	60	119	7	3	7	28	81	2	39	0	1	2	12	7	.306	.424	.393	.972
Career average		146	558	88	172	21	7	2	39	80	2	38	3	7	1	16	6	.308	.396	.382	.983
Cubs average		**130**	**427**	**74**	**119**	**12**	**5**	**0**	**30**	**86**	**2**	**39**	**2**	**4**	**2**	**12**	**5**	**.279**	**.400**	**.327**	**.977**
Career total		2189	8365	1322	2574	317	109	29	586	1198	25	571	43	112	18	234	92	.308	.396	.382	.983
Cubs total		**260**	**854**	**148**	**238**	**23**	**9**	**0**	**59**	**171**	**3**	**77**	**4**	**8**	**3**	**23**	**10**	**.279**	**.400**	**.327**	**.977**

Aspromonte, Kenneth Joseph (Ken *or* Chip)
HEIGHT: 6'0" THROWS: RIGHT BATS: RIGHT BORN: 9/22/1931 BROOKLYN, NEW YORK POSITIONS PLAYED: 1B, 2B, 3B, SS, OF

YEAR	TEAM	GAMES	AB	RUNS	HITS	2B	3B	HR	RBI	BB	IBB	SO	HBP	SH	SF	SB	CS	BA	OBA	SA	FA
1957	Bos-A	24	78	9	21	5	0	0	4	17	0	10	0	0	1	0	1	.269	.396	.333	.965
1958	Bos-A	6	16	0	2	0	0	0	0	3	0	1	0	0	0	0	0	.125	.263	.125	.952
1958	Was-A	92	253	15	57	9	1	5	27	25	1	28	1	2	1	1	1	.225	.296	.328	.966
1959	Was-A	70	225	31	55	12	0	2	14	26	0	39	0	3	1	2	1	.244	.321	.324	.957
1960	Was-A	4	3	0	0	0	0	0	0	0	0	1	0	0	0	0	0	.000	.000	.000	—
1960	Cle-A	117	459	65	133	20	1	10	48	53	0	32	2	4	3	4	1	.290	.364	.403	.958
1961	LAA-A	66	238	29	53	10	0	2	14	33	1	21	2	3	0	0	0	.223	.322	.290	.970
1961	Cle-A	22	70	5	16	6	1	0	5	6	0	3	0	1	1	0	0	.229	.286	.343	.963
1962	Cle-A	20	28	4	4	2	0	0	1	6	1	5	0	0	1	0	0	.143	.286	.214	.960
1962	Mil-N	34	79	11	23	2	0	0	7	6	0	5	1	0	2	0	1	.291	.341	.316	.987
1963	**ChC-N**	**20**	**34**	**2**	**5**	**3**	**0**	**0**	**4**	**4**	**1**	**4**	**0**	**0**	**0**	**0**	**0**	**.147**	**.237**	**.235**	**.957**
Career average		68	212	24	53	10	0	3	18	26	1	21	1	2	1	1	1	.249	.330	.338	.963
Cubs average		**20**	**34**	**2**	**5**	**3**	**0**	**0**	**4**	**4**	**1**	**4**	**0**	**0**	**0**	**0**	**0**	**.147**	**.237**	**.235**	**.957**
Career total		475	1483	171	369	69	3	19	124	179	4	149	6	13	10	7	5	.249	.330	.338	.963
Cubs total		**20**	**34**	**2**	**5**	**3**	**0**	**0**	**4**	**4**	**1**	**4**	**0**	**0**	**0**	**0**	**0**	**.147**	**.237**	**.235**	**.957**

Atwell, Maurice Dailey (Toby)
HEIGHT: 5'9" THROWS: RIGHT BATS: LEFT BORN: 3/8/1924 LEESBURG, VIRGINIA POSITIONS PLAYED: C

YEAR	TEAM	GAMES	AB	RUNS	HITS	2B	3B	HR	RBI	BB	IBB	SO	HBP	SH	SF	SB	CS	BA	OBA	SA	FA
1952	**ChC-N**	**107**	**362**	**36**	**105**	**16**	**3**	**2**	**31**	**40**	**—**	**22**	**1**	**2**	**—**	**2**	**1**	**.290**	**.362**	**.367**	**.977**
1953	**ChC-N**	**24**	**74**	**10**	**17**	**2**	**0**	**1**	**8**	**13**	**—**	**7**	**0**	**1**	**—**	**0**	**0**	**.230**	**.345**	**.297**	**.940**
1953	Pit-N	53	139	11	34	6	0	0	17	20	—	12	3	2	—	0	0	.245	.352	.288	.967
1954	Pit-N	96	287	36	83	8	4	3	26	43	—	21	3	4	3	2	3	.289	.384	.376	.990
1955	Pit-N	71	207	21	44	8	0	1	18	40	9	16	1	1	4	0	1	.213	.337	.266	.992
1956	Pit-N	12	18	0	2	0	0	0	3	1	0	5	0	1	0	0	0	.111	.158	.111	1.000
1956	Mil-N	15	30	2	5	1	0	2	7	4	1	1	0	0	0	0	0	.167	.265	.400	1.000
Career average		76	223	23	58	8	1	2	22	32	2	17	2	2	1	1	1	.260	.355	.333	.980
Cubs average		**66**	**218**	**23**	**61**	**9**	**2**	**2**	**20**	**27**	**—**	**15**	**1**	**2**	**—**	**1**	**1**	**.280**	**.359**	**.356**	**.969**
Career total		378	1117	116	290	41	7	9	110	161	10	84	8	11	7	4	5	.260	.355	.333	.980
Cubs total		**131**	**436**	**46**	**122**	**18**	**3**	**3**	**39**	**53**	**—**	**29**	**1**	**3**	**—**	**2**	**1**	**.280**	**.359**	**.356**	**.969**

Averill, Earl Douglas
HEIGHT: 5'10" THROWS: RIGHT BATS: RIGHT BORN: 9/9/1931 CLEVELAND, OHIO POSITIONS PLAYED: C, 1B, 2B, 3B, OF

YEAR	TEAM	GAMES	AB	RUNS	HITS	2B	3B	HR	RBI	BB	IBB	SO	HBP	SH	SF	SB	CS	BA	OBA	SA	FA
1956	Cle-A	42	93	12	22	6	0	3	14	14	1	25	1	2	0	0	1	.237	.343	.398	.994
1958	Cle-A	17	55	2	10	1	0	2	7	4	0	7	1	0	0	1	0	.182	.250	.309	.863
1959	**ChC-N**	**74**	**186**	**22**	**44**	**10**	**0**	**10**	**34**	**15**	**1**	**39**	**2**	**0**	**2**	**0**	**1**	**.237**	**.298**	**.452**	**.950**
1960	**ChC-N**	**52**	**102**	**14**	**24**	**4**	**0**	**1**	**13**	**11**	**1**	**16**	**1**	**1**	**2**	**1**	**1**	**.235**	**.310**	**.304**	**.979**
1960	CWS-A	10	14	2	3	0	0	0	2	4	0	2	0	0	0	0	0	.214	.389	.214	1.000
1961	LAA-A	115	323	56	86	9	0	21	59	62	1	70	2	1	4	1	0	.266	.384	.489	.992
1962	LAA-A	92	187	21	41	9	0	4	22	43	3	47	1	0	1	0	0	.219	.366	.332	1.000
1963	Phi-N	47	71	8	19	2	0	3	8	9	1	14	0	1	2	0	0	.268	.341	.423	.953
Career average		64	147	20	36	6	0	6	23	23	1	31	1	1	2	0	0	.242	.346	.409	.976
Cubs average		**63**	**144**	**18**	**34**	**7**	**0**	**6**	**24**	**13**	**1**	**28**	**2**	**1**	**2**	**1**	**1**	**.236**	**.302**	**.399**	**.960**
Career total		449	1031	137	249	41	0	44	159	162	8	220	8	5	11	3	3	.242	.346	.409	.976
Cubs total		**126**	**288**	**36**	**68**	**14**	**0**	**11**	**47**	**26**	**2**	**55**	**3**	**1**	**4**	**1**	**2**	**.236**	**.302**	**.399**	**.960**

Bailey, Lonas Edgar (Ed *or* Gar)
HEIGHT: 6'2" THROWS: RIGHT BATS: LEFT BORN: 4/15/1931 STRAWBERRY PLAINS, TENNESSEE POSITIONS PLAYED: C, 1B, OF

YEAR	TEAM	GAMES	AB	RUNS	HITS	2B	3B	HR	RBI	BB	IBB	SO	HBP	SH	SF	SB	CS	BA	OBA	SA	FA
1953	Cin-N	2	8	1	3	1	0	0	1	1	—	3	0	0	—	0	0	.375	.444	.500	1.000
1954	Cin-N	73	183	21	36	2	3	9	20	35	—	34	0	3	1	1	0	.197	.324	.388	.973
1955	Cin-N	21	39	3	8	1	1	1	4	4	0	10	3	0	0	0	0	.205	.326	.359	.962
1956	Cin-N	118	383	59	115	8	2	28	75	52	11	50	3	4	4	2	0	.300	.385	.551	.984

(continued)

(continued)

YEAR	TEAM	GAMES	AB	RUNS	HITS	2B	3B	HR	RBI	BB	IBB	SO	HBP	SH	SF	SB	CS	BA	OBA	SA	FA
1957	Cin-N	122	391	54	102	15	2	20	48	73	9	69	2	2	4	5	3	.261	.377	.463	.991
1958	Cin-N	112	360	39	90	23	1	11	59	47	10	61	1	4	2	2	2	.250	.337	.411	.988
1959	Cin-N	121	379	43	100	13	0	12	40	62	6	53	2	4	0	2	0	.264	.370	.393	.990
1960	Cin-N	133	441	52	115	19	3	13	67	59	9	70	2	1	7	1	0	.261	.346	.406	.990
1961	Cin-N	12	43	4	13	4	0	0	2	3	1	5	0	0	0	0	0	.302	.348	.395	.967
1961	SF-N	107	340	39	81	9	1	13	51	42	6	41	4	1	6	1	5	.238	.324	.385	.985
1962	SF-N	96	254	32	59	9	1	17	45	42	5	42	6	0	3	1	1	.232	.351	.476	.987
1963	SF-N	105	308	41	81	8	0	21	68	50	11	64	1	0	2	0	6	.263	.366	.494	.987
1964	Mil-N	95	271	30	71	10	1	5	34	34	2	39	1	0	3	2	0	.262	.343	.362	.982
1965	SF-N	24	28	1	3	0	0	0	3	6	1	7	0	1	2	0	0	.107	.250	.107	.985
1965	**ChC-N**	**66**	**150**	**13**	**38**	**6**	**0**	**5**	**23**	**34**	**6**	**28**	**0**	**0**	**3**	**0**	**1**	**.253**	**.385**	**.393**	**.981**
1966	Cal-A	5	3	0	0	0	0	0	0	1	0	1	0	0	0	0	0	.000	.250	.000	—
Career average		87	256	31	65	9	1	11	39	39	6	41	2	1	3	1	1	.256	.355	.429	.986
Cubs average		**66**	**150**	**13**	**38**	**6**	**0**	**5**	**23**	**34**	**6**	**28**	**0**	**0**	**3**	**0**	**1**	**.253**	**.385**	**.393**	**.981**
Career total		1212	3581	432	915	128	15	155	540	545	77	577	25	20	37	17	18	.256	.355	.429	.986
Cubs total		**66**	**150**	**13**	**38**	**6**	**0**	**5**	**23**	**34**	**6**	**28**	**0**	**0**	**3**	**0**	**1**	**.253**	**.385**	**.393**	**.981**

Baker, Eugene Walter (Gene *or* Sharp Top)

HEIGHT: 6'1"   THROWS: RIGHT   BATS: RIGHT   BORN: 6/15/1925 DAVENPORT, IOWA   DIED: 12/1/1999 DAVENPORT, IOWA   POSITIONS PLAYED: 2B, 3B, SS

YEAR	TEAM	GAMES	AB	RUNS	HITS	2B	3B	HR	RBI	BB	IBB	SO	HBP	SH	SF	SB	CS	BA	OBA	SA	FA
1953	ChC-N	7	22	1	5	1	0	0	0	1	—	4	0	1	—	1	0	.227	.261	.273	.917
1954	ChC-N	135	541	68	149	32	5	13	61	47	—	55	2	9	4	4	5	.275	.333	.425	.967
1955	ChC-N	154	609	82	163	29	7	11	52	49	1	57	2	18	3	9	7	.268	.323	.392	.967
1956	ChC-N	140	546	65	141	23	3	12	57	39	2	54	3	13	5	4	3	.258	.309	.377	.969
1957	ChC-N	12	44	4	11	3	1	1	10	6	0	3	1	0	0	0	0	.250	.353	.432	.867
1957	Pit-N	111	365	36	97	19	4	2	36	29	5	29	1	8	4	3	2	.266	.318	.356	.946
1958	Pit-N	29	56	3	14	2	1	0	7	8	0	6	0	1	1	0	0	.250	.338	.321	1.000
1960	Pit-N	33	37	5	9	0	0	0	4	2	0	9	0	0	1	0	0	.243	.275	.243	1.000
1961	Pit-N	9	10	1	1	0	0	0	0	3	1	2	0	0	0	0	0	.100	.308	.100	1.000
Career average		79	279	33	74	14	3	5	28	23	1	27	1	6	2	3	2	.265	.321	.385	.964
Cubs average		**90**	**352**	**44**	**94**	**18**	**3**	**7**	**36**	**28**	**1**	**35**	**2**	**8**	**2**	**4**	**3**	**.266**	**.322**	**.397**	**.966**
Career total		630	2230	265	590	109	21	39	227	184	9	219	9	50	18	21	17	.265	.321	.385	.964
Cubs total		**448**	**1762**	**220**	**469**	**88**	**16**	**37**	**180**	**142**	**3**	**173**	**8**	**41**	**12**	**18**	**15**	**.266**	**.322**	**.397**	**.966**

Banks, Ernest (Ernie *or* Mr. Cub)

HEIGHT: 6'1"   THROWS: RIGHT   BATS: RIGHT   BORN: 1/31/1931 DALLAS, TEXAS   POSITIONS PLAYED: 1B, 3B, SS, OF

YEAR	TEAM	GAMES	AB	RUNS	HITS	2B	3B	HR	RBI	BB	IBB	SO	HBP	SH	SF	SB	CS	BA	OBA	SA	FA
1953	ChC-N	10	35	3	11	1	1	2	6	4	—	5	0	0	—	0	0	.314	.385	.571	.981
1954	ChC-N	154	593	70	163	19	7	19	79	40	—	50	7	5	4	6	10	.275	.326	.427	.959
1955	ChC-N	154	596	98	176	29	9	44	117	45	6	72	2	0	3	9	3	.295	.345	.596	.972
1956	ChC-N	139	538	82	160	25	8	28	85	52	18	62	0	0	3	6	9	.297	.358	.530	.962
1957	ChC-N	156	594	113	169	34	6	43	102	70	11	85	3	2	5	8	4	.285	.360	.579	.977
1958	ChC-N	154	617	119	193	23	11	47	129	52	12	87	4	1	8	4	4	.313	.366	.614	.960
1959	ChC-N	155	589	97	179	25	6	45	143	64	20	72	7	2	9	2	4	.304	.374	.596	.985
1960	ChC-N	156	597	94	162	32	7	41	117	71	28	69	4	0	6	1	3	.271	.350	.554	.977
1961	ChC-N	138	511	75	142	22	4	29	80	54	21	75	2	0	6	1	2	.278	.346	.507	.968
1962	ChC-N	154	610	87	164	20	6	37	104	30	3	71	7	0	10	5	1	.269	.306	.503	.993
1963	ChC-N	130	432	41	98	20	1	18	64	39	16	73	4	1	8	0	3	.227	.292	.403	.993
1964	ChC-N	157	591	67	156	29	6	23	95	36	11	84	3	1	6	1	2	.264	.307	.450	.994
1965	ChC-N	163	612	79	162	25	3	28	106	55	19	64	6	0	7	3	5	.265	.328	.453	.992
1966	ChC-N	141	511	52	139	23	7	15	75	29	10	59	5	4	5	0	1	.272	.315	.432	.990
1967	ChC-N	151	573	68	158	26	4	23	95	27	8	93	3	8	4	2	2	.276	.310	.455	.993
1968	ChC-N	150	552	71	136	27	0	32	83	27	4	67	5	9	2	2	0	.246	.287	.469	.996
1969	ChC-N	155	565	60	143	19	2	23	106	42	7	101	7	8	7	0	0	.253	.309	.416	.997
1970	ChC-N	72	222	25	56	6	2	12	44	20	3	33	1	1	3	0	0	.252	.313	.459	.993
1971	ChC-N	39	83	4	16	2	0	3	6	6	1	14	0	3	0	0	0	.193	.247	.325	1.000
Career average		133	496	69	136	21	5	27	86	40	10	65	4	2	5	3	3	.274	.330	.500	.986
Cubs average		**133**	**496**	**69**	**136**	**21**	**5**	**27**	**86**	**40**	**10**	**65**	**4**	**2**	**5**	**3**	**3**	**.274**	**.330**	**.500**	**.986**
Career total		2528	9421	1305	2583	407	90	512	1636	763	198	1236	70	45	96	50	53	.274	.330	.500	.986
Cubs total		**2528**	**9421**	**1305**	**2583**	**407**	**90**	**512**	**1636**	**763**	**198**	**1236**	**70**	**45**	**96**	**50**	**53**	**.274**	**.330**	**.500**	**.986**

Ernest (Ernie) "Mr. Cub" Banks, 1b-ss-3b-of, 1953–71

Revered as much for his boundless optimism as for his prodigious talent, Hall of Famer Banks is almost universally acclaimed as the best player ever to don a Cubs uniform.

Banks was born on January 31, 1931, in Dallas, Texas. His father, Eddie Banks, a semi-pro baseball star around the sandlots of Dallas, dearly wanted his son to follow in his footsteps.

Ernie did, eventually. He was a high school star in basketball, track and football, good enough in the former sport to be offered a contract with the Harlem Globetrotters. But initially, Banks wasn't terribly interested in baseball. Rather, he played softball and barnstormed with a group of black softball all-stars. There was clearly money in baseball and Banks, at 19, was signed by the Kansas City Monarchs of the Negro National League as a shortstop. His initial salary was $300 per month, which to both Banks and his family in 1950 seemed like a fortune, especially since Eddie, a field hand and sometime warehouse worker, was taking in only about $200 a month.

Suddenly, a young man who had fretted about overnight trips away from Dallas was traveling with one of the best teams in the Negro Leagues, and playing in New York, Philadelphia and Kansas City. Banks's playing career was interrupted by two years of military service, but he returned to the Monarchs in 1953, hitting a robust .380.

Since 1947, when Dodger great Jackie Robinson had pushed the door open for black players, major league teams had begun evincing interest in black ballplayers. Banks was on the radar screen of a number of teams, including the Yankees and the Dodgers, but the Cubs got him first, under odd circumstances.

Chicago paid the Monarchs $15,000 for Banks's contract and then offered Ernie a major league contract for $10,000 annually, a considerable hike from his Negro League pact of $3,000. Banks, of course, jumped at it. He called his family and relayed the information to his dad. When Eddie

heard that his son was going to play in the bigs, he burst into tears.

Banks was not the first black player to be signed by the Cubs. Journeyman infielder Gene Baker actually put pen to paper long before Banks. The Cubs organization, however, was nervous about bringing up a black player, so Baker, who had actually signed with Chicago in 1950, played four years in the Pacific Coast League.

Finally, the Cubs were ready to bring up Baker. In a city, though, where segregation was still a very real institution, the Cubs had a problem: they needed someone to room with their black infielder. When the Cubs became aware of Banks, they moved quickly to sign him.

The irony was that both Banks and Baker were shortstops. Ernie was 5 1/2 years younger, so the Cubs opted to move Baker to second base, believing he could handle the transition to a new position better.

Banks signed with the Cubs on September 13, 1953, and on September 14 he was in Chicago. A few days later, on September 17, he was playing for the Cubs. Baker, nursing a rib injury, didn't actually get to play for Chicago until a few days later.

So it was that Ernie Banks integrated the Chicago Cubs. It is well to remember that Chicago in 1953 was still very much a segregated city. The Cubs and White Sox had an overwhelmingly white fan base. Cubs owner Philip Knight Wrigley was concerned that the introduction of a black player would eat into that fan base. But the opposite happened.

Banks was ebullient, delighted to be in the major leagues and a man who understood very well that at that point, fair or unfair, he was one of a very few fortunate black men to be in the major leagues. There would certainly be more and more as the years went on, but in 1953 Banks was clearly a pioneer.

And the fans loved him. He played hard, was clearly happy to be on the roster and exploded many racist whites' perceptions of black men as lazy and unintelligent. Banks was a fan favorite in Chicago because he was having so much fun, but also because he was so damn good.

He was, in fact, a much better player than a vast majority of his teammates. By 1955 Banks was one of the best players in baseball. He hit .295 with a stunning 44 home runs and 117 RBIs that year, big numbers for any shortstop, particularly pre–Cal Ripken, Jr. And he was fielding his position well: tops among league shortstops in fielding average with a .972 mark, second in putouts with 290, third in assists with 482.

He was tall and thin, with none of the bulkiness of a Jimmie Foxx or Hank Greenberg. Banks's wrists were terrifically powerful, and his bat speed was almost otherworldly. Teammates swore he could wait until a pitched ball was almost in the catcher's glove before making a decision to hit it or let it go by.

The Cubs, in the first 10 years of the Banks era, were brutally bad, never getting a whiff of .500 ball from 1953 to 1962. It was not until the late 1960s that Chicago put together more than one winning season in a row.

Yet through it all, Banks was not merely optimistic, he was positively giddy. His signature cry of "Let's play two!" was never muted by frustration, even if his team languished near the bottom of the standings, and it often did. He loved playing, as he put it, "in the bee-yoo-tee-ful confines of Wrigley Field!"

Banks was clearly a bright spot in a succession of otherwise dreary summers for a vast majority of Cubs fans, but he did have his detractors. Many were his teammates who were unable to understand that to a man who toiled in cotton fields as a youth, being paid to play a child's game, even for losing teams, was still a win-win proposition.

In 1958 Banks blasted a league-leading 47 home runs and added a league-best 129 RBIs to go with a .313 batting average. He was named MVP of the league, even though he played for a fifth-place team that ended up 10 games below .500.

There was some controversy to his selection as sportswriters wondered how a ballplayer who toiled for a fifth-place team could be a most valuable player. The next year, Banks put up similar numbers and won the award again. It was difficult to deny Banks's intensity, ability and consistency.

"If Ernie Banks had played in the 1990s, with the media exposure we have now," said former Cubs star Ron Santo, "he would have been Michael Jordan."

That's possible. From 1955 to 1960, Banks hit more home runs than anyone in the majors, including Mickey Mantle, Henry Aaron and Willie Mays. And in 1960, Banks, long criticized as a fair to middling infielder, had improved that part of his game to the point where he led all National League shortstops in hitting and fielding. He won a Gold Glove in the former season.

Injuries to Banks's legs slowed him down to the point where he accepted a move to first base in 1962. While his mobility was limited, he was still an excellent athlete, who led the National League five times in assists at first base. In 1969 he led all first basemen in fielding percentage.

At the end of the 1959 season, Cubs fans were so enamored with Banks that they wanted to give him a day. He affably declined, noting that he hadn't really accomplished anything. But by 1964 he finally agreed and the day was held.

His home run totals escalated, and in 1970 Cubs fans were eagerly awaiting Banks's 500th home run. Finally it came on May 12, off Pat Jarvis of the Atlanta Braves. Ironically, it had been raining that day in Chicago and only 5,264 Cubs fans saw the historic blast live. Banks noted wryly that the day was Tuesday, which had been traditionally Senior Citizens Day at Wrigley Field.

"Old Ern," said the 39-year-old Banks, "hit this one for his people."

Banks retired in 1971, and the Cubs immediately retired his number 14, the first such number to be retired in Chicago. Banks continued to work for the Cubs as a coach for many years. He was elected to the Hall of Fame in 1977.

Banks is at or near the top of many Chicago Cubs career lists. He is first all-time in games played (2,528), at-bats (9,421), total bases (4,706), home runs (512) and extra-base hits (1,009). Banks is second all-time in hits with 2,583 and RBIs with 1,636.

Interestingly, Banks is also the single-season leader in home runs for the Cubs at both first base (37 in 1962) and shortstop (47 in 1958). He is also the team's record holder at both positions for RBIs.

Barber, Tyrus Turner (Turner)
HEIGHT: 5'11" THROWS: RIGHT BATS: LEFT BORN: 7/9/1893 LAVINIA, TENNESSEE DIED: 10/20/1968 MILAN, TENNESSEE POSITIONS PLAYED: 1B, 2B, OF

YEAR	TEAM	GAMES	AB	RUNS	HITS	2B	3B	HR	RBI	BB	IBB	SO	HBP	SH	SF	SB	CS	BA	OBA	SA	FA
1915	Was-A	20	53	9	16	1	1	0	6	6	—	7	1	3	—	0	3	.302	.383	.358	.952
1916	Was-A	15	33	3	7	0	1	1	5	2	—	3	0	0	—	0	—	.212	.257	.364	.833
1917	ChC-N	7	28	2	6	1	0	0	2	2	—	8	0	0	—	1	—	.214	.267	.250	1.000
1918	ChC-N	55	123	11	29	3	2	0	10	9	—	16	1	2	—	3	—	.236	.293	.293	.956
1919	ChC-N	76	230	26	72	9	4	0	21	14	—	17	1	10	—	7	—	.313	.355	.387	.949
1920	ChC-N	94	340	27	90	10	5	0	50	9	—	26	3	17	—	5	6	.265	.290	.324	.988
1921	ChC-N	127	452	73	142	14	4	1	54	41	—	24	6	14	—	5	9	.314	.379	.369	.970
1922	ChC-N	84	226	35	70	7	4	0	29	30	—	9	0	6	—	7	4	.310	.391	.376	.984
1923	Bro-N	13	46	3	10	2	0	0	8	2	—	2	0	1	—	0	1	.217	.250	.261	1.000
Career average		55	170	21	49	5	2	0	21	13	—	12	1	6	—	3	3	.289	.343	.351	.978
Cubs average		74	233	29	68	7	3	0	28	18	—	17	2	8	—	5	3	.292	.347	.353	.979
Career total		491	1531	189	442	47	21	2	185	115	—	112	12	53	—	28	23	.289	.343	.351	.978
Cubs total		443	1399	174	409	44	19	1	166	105	—	100	11	49	—	28	19	.292	.347	.353	.979

Barberie, Bret Edward
HEIGHT: 5'11" THROWS: RIGHT BATS: BOTH BORN: 8/16/1967 LONG BEACH, CALIFORNIA POSITIONS PLAYED: 1B, 2B, 3B, SS

YEAR	TEAM	GAMES	AB	RUNS	HITS	2B	3B	HR	RBI	BB	IBB	SO	HBP	SH	SF	SB	CS	BA	OBA	SA	FA
1991	Mon-N	57	136	16	48	12	2	2	18	20	2	22	2	1	3	0	0	.353	.435	.515	.966
1992	Mon-N	111	285	26	66	11	0	1	24	47	3	62	8	1	2	9	5	.232	.354	.281	.951
1993	Fla-N	99	375	45	104	16	2	5	33	33	2	58	7	5	3	2	4	.277	.344	.371	.982
1994	Fla-N	107	372	40	112	20	2	5	31	23	3	65	9	2	0	2	0	.301	.356	.406	.975
1995	Bal-A	90	237	32	57	14	0	2	25	36	0	50	6	6	3	3	3	.241	.351	.325	.977
1996	ChC-N	15	29	4	1	0	0	1	2	5	0	11	0	3	0	0	1	.034	.176	.138	1.000
Career average		80	239	27	65	12	1	3	22	27	2	45	5	3	2	3	2	.271	.356	.363	.974
Cubs average		15	29	4	1	0	0	1	2	5	0	11	0	3	0	0	1	.034	.176	.138	1.000
Career total		479	1434	163	388	73	6	16	133	164	10	268	32	18	11	16	13	.271	.356	.363	.974
Cubs total		15	29	4	1	0	0	1	2	5	0	11	0	3	0	0	1	.034	.176	.138	1.000

Barnes, Roscoe Charles (Ross)
HEIGHT: 5'8" THROWS: RIGHT BATS: RIGHT BORN: 5/8/1850 MOUNT MORRIS, ILLINOIS DIED: 2/5/1915 CHICAGO, ILLINOIS POSITIONS PLAYED: P, 2B, SS

YEAR	TEAM	GAMES	AB	RUNS	HITS	2B	3B	HR	RBI	BB	IBB	SO	HBP	SH	SF	SB	CS	BA	OBA	SA	FA
1876	ChN-N	66	342	126	138	21	14	1	59	20	—	8	—	—	—	—	—	.404	.436	.556	.910
1877	ChN-N	22	92	16	25	1	0	0	5	7	—	4	—	—	—	—	—	.272	.323	.283	.838
1879	Cin-N	77	323	55	86	9	2	1	30	16	—	25	—	—	—	—	—	.266	.301	.316	.849
1881	Bos-N	69	295	42	80	14	1	0	17	16	—	16	—	—	—	—	—	.271	.309	.325	.854
Career average		59	263	60	82	11	4	1	28	15	—	13	—	—	—	—	—	.313	.349	.394	.867
Cubs average		44	217	71	82	11	7	1	32	14	—	6	—	—	—	—	—	.376	.412	.498	.892
Career total		234	1052	239	329	45	17	2	111	59	—	53	—	—	—	—	—	.313	.349	.394	.867
Cubs total		88	434	142	163	22	14	1	64	27	—	12	—	—	—	—	—	.376	.412	.498	.892

Barragan, Facundo Anthony (Cuno)
HEIGHT: 5'11" THROWS: RIGHT BATS: RIGHT BORN: 6/20/1932 SACRAMENTO, CALIFORNIA POSITIONS PLAYED: C

YEAR	TEAM	GAMES	AB	RUNS	HITS	2B	3B	HR	RBI	BB	IBB	SO	HBP	SH	SF	SB	CS	BA	OBA	SA	FA
1961	ChC-N	10	28	3	6	0	0	1	2	2	0	7	0	1	0	0	0	.214	.267	.321	1.000
1962	ChC-N	58	134	11	27	6	1	0	12	21	1	28	0	1	2	0	2	.201	.306	.261	.971
1963	ChC-N	1	1	0	0	0	0	0	0	0	0	1	0	0	0	0	0	.000	.000	.000	1.000
Career average		23	54	5	11	2	0	0	5	8	0	12	0	1	1	0	1	.202	.298	.270	.975
Cubs average		23	54	5	11	2	0	0	5	8	0	12	0	1	1	0	1	.202	.298	.270	.975
Career total		69	163	14	33	6	1	1	14	23	1	36	0	2	2	0	2	.202	.298	.270	.975
Cubs total		69	163	14	33	6	1	1	14	23	1	36	0	2	2	0	2	.202	.298	.270	.975

Barrett, Robert Schley (Bob *or* Jumbo)
HEIGHT: 5'11" THROWS: RIGHT BATS: RIGHT BORN: 1/27/1899 ATLANTA, GEORGIA DIED: 1/18/1982 ATLANTA, GEORGIA POSITIONS PLAYED: 1B, 2B, 3B, OF

YEAR	TEAM	GAMES	AB	RUNS	HITS	2B	3B	HR	RBI	BB	IBB	SO	HBP	SH	SF	SB	CS	BA	OBA	SA	FA
1923	**ChC-N**	**3**	**3**	**0**	**1**	**0**	**0**	**0**	**0**	**0**	—	**0**	**0**	**0**	—	**0**	**0**	**.333**	**.333**	**.333**	—
1924	**ChC-N**	**54**	**133**	**12**	**32**	**2**	**3**	**5**	**21**	**7**	—	**29**	**0**	**4**	—	**1**	**0**	**.241**	**.279**	**.414**	**.945**
1925	**ChC-N**	**14**	**32**	**1**	**10**	**1**	**0**	**0**	**7**	**1**	—	**4**	**0**	**2**	—	**1**	**2**	**.313**	**.333**	**.344**	**1.000**
1925	Bro-N	1	1	0	0	0	0	0	1	0	—	0	0	0	—	0	0	.000	.000	.000	—
1927	Bro-N	99	355	29	92	10	2	5	38	14	—	22	1	12	—	1	—	.259	.289	.341	.920
1929	Bos-A	68	126	15	34	10	0	0	19	10	—	6	0	4	—	3	1	.270	.324	.349	.951
Career average		48	130	11	34	5	1	2	17	6	—	12	0	4	—	1	1	.260	.296	.357	.938
Cubs average		**24**	**56**	**4**	**14**	**1**	**1**	**2**	**9**	**3**	—	**11**	**0**	**2**	—	**1**	**1**	**.256**	**.290**	**.399**	**.951**
Career total		239	650	57	169	23	5	10	86	32	—	61	1	22	—	6	3	.260	.296	.357	.938
Cubs total		**71**	**168**	**13**	**43**	**3**	**3**	**5**	**28**	**8**	—	**33**	**0**	**6**	—	**2**	**2**	**.256**	**.290**	**.399**	**.951**

Barry, John C. (Shad)
HEIGHT: — THROWS: RIGHT BATS: RIGHT BORN: 10/27/1878 NEWBURGH, NEW YORK DIED: 11/27/1936 LOS ANGELES, CALIFORNIA
POSITIONS PLAYED: 1B, 2B, 3B, SS, OF

YEAR	TEAM	GAMES	AB	RUNS	HITS	2B	3B	HR	RBI	BB	IBB	SO	HBP	SH	SF	SB	CS	BA	OBA	SA	FA
1899	Was-N	78	247	31	71	7	5	1	33	12	—	—	3	4	—	11	—	.287	.328	.368	.944
1900	Bos-N	81	254	40	66	10	7	1	37	13	—	—	2	8	—	9	—	.260	.301	.366	.924
1901	Bos-N	11	40	3	7	2	0	0	6	2	—	—	1	0	—	1	—	.175	.233	.225	.926
1901	Phi-N	67	252	35	62	10	0	1	22	15	—	—	2	12	—	13	—	.246	.294	.298	.888
1902	Phi-N	138	543	65	156	20	6	3	58	44	—	—	2	17	—	14	—	.287	.343	.363	.941
1903	Phi-N	138	550	75	152	24	5	1	60	30	—	—	6	14	—	26	—	.276	.321	.344	.971
1904	Phi-N	35	122	15	25	2	0	0	3	11	—	—	2	3	—	2	—	.205	.281	.221	.960
1904	**ChC-N**	**73**	**263**	**29**	**69**	**7**	**2**	**1**	**26**	**17**	—	—	**1**	**9**	—	**12**	—	**.262**	**.310**	**.316**	**.942**
1905	**ChC-N**	**27**	**104**	**10**	**22**	**2**	**0**	**0**	**10**	**5**	—	—	**1**	**1**	—	**5**	—	**.212**	**.255**	**.231**	**.982**
1905	Cin-N	125	494	90	160	11	12	1	56	33	—	—	5	24	—	16	—	.324	.372	.401	.982
1906	Cin-N	73	279	38	80	10	5	1	33	26	—	—	3	11	—	11	—	.287	.354	.369	.985
1906	StL-N	62	237	26	59	9	1	0	12	15	—	—	2	5	—	6	—	.249	.299	.295	.961
1907	StL-N	81	294	30	73	5	2	0	19	28	—	—	3	15	—	4	—	.248	.320	.279	.963
1908	StL-N	74	268	24	61	8	1	0	11	19	—	—	3	8	—	9	—	.228	.286	.265	.947
1908	NYG-N	37	67	5	10	1	1	0	5	9	—	—	1	4	—	1	—	.149	.260	.194	.971
Career average		110	401	52	107	13	5	1	39	28	—	—	4	14	—	14	—	.267	.321	.330	.961
Cubs average		**50**	**184**	**20**	**46**	**5**	**1**	**1**	**18**	**11**	—	—	**1**	**5**	—	**9**	—	**.248**	**.294**	**.292**	**.960**
Career total		1100	4014	516	1073	128	47	10	391	279	—	—	37	135	—	140	—	.267	.321	.330	.961
Cubs total		**100**	**367**	**39**	**91**	**9**	**2**	**1**	**36**	**22**	—	—	**2**	**10**	—	**17**	—	**.248**	**.294**	**.292**	**.960**

Bartell, Richard William (Dick *or* Rowdy Richard *or* Shortwave *or* Pepper Pot)
HEIGHT: 5'9" THROWS: RIGHT BATS: RIGHT BORN: 11/22/1907 CHICAGO, ILLINOIS DIED: 8/4/1995 ALAMEDA, CALIFORNIA POSITIONS PLAYED: 2B, 3B, SS

YEAR	TEAM	GAMES	AB	RUNS	HITS	2B	3B	HR	RBI	BB	IBB	SO	HBP	SH	SF	SB	CS	BA	OBA	SA	FA
1927	Pit-N	1	2	0	0	0	0	0	0	2	—	0	0	0	—	0	—	.000	.500	.000	1.000
1928	Pit-N	72	233	27	71	8	4	1	36	21	—	18	6	11	—	4	—	.305	.377	.386	.957
1929	Pit-N	143	610	101	184	40	13	2	57	40	—	29	2	22	—	11	—	.302	.347	.420	.963
1930	Pit-N	129	475	69	152	32	13	4	75	39	—	34	5	22	—	8	—	.320	.378	.467	.941
1931	Phi-N	135	554	88	160	43	7	0	34	27	—	38	3	30	—	6	—	.289	.325	.392	.948
1932	Phi-N	154	614	118	189	48	7	1	53	64	—	47	6	35	—	8	—	.308	.379	.414	.963
1933	Phi-N	152	587	78	159	25	5	1	37	56	—	46	5	37	—	6	—	.271	.340	.336	.951
1934	Phi-N	146	604	102	187	30	4	0	37	64	—	59	9	9	—	13	—	.310	.384	.373	.954
1935	NYG-N	137	539	60	141	28	4	14	53	37	—	52	6	21	—	5	—	.262	.316	.406	.954
1936	NYG-N	145	510	71	152	31	3	8	42	40	—	36	5	18	—	6	—	.298	.355	.418	.956
1937	NYG-N	128	516	91	158	38	2	14	62	40	—	38	10	14	—	5	—	.306	.367	.469	.958
1938	NYG-N	127	481	67	126	26	1	9	49	55	—	60	8	9	—	4	—	.262	.347	.376	.952
1939	**ChC-N**	**105**	**336**	**37**	**80**	**24**	**2**	**3**	**34**	**42**	—	**25**	**7**	**10**	—	**6**	—	**.238**	**.335**	**.348**	**.943**
1940	Det-A	139	528	76	123	24	3	7	53	76	—	53	5	11	—	12	2	.233	.335	.330	.953
1941	Det-A	5	12	0	2	1	0	0	1	2	—	2	1	1	—	0	1	.167	.333	.250	.920
1941	NYG-N	104	373	44	113	20	0	5	35	52	—	29	4	9	—	6	—	.303	.394	.397	.963
1942	NYG-N	90	316	53	77	10	3	5	24	44	—	34	8	5	—	4	—	.244	.351	.342	.959
1943	NYG-N	99	337	48	91	14	0	5	28	47	—	27	7	5	—	5	4	.270	.371	.356	.972
1946	NYG-N	5	2	0	0	0	0	0	0	0	—	0	0	0	—	0	0	.000	.000	.000	1.000
Career average		112	424	63	120	25	4	4	39	42	—	35	5	15	—	6	0	.284	.355	.391	.955
Cubs average		**105**	**336**	**37**	**80**	**24**	**2**	**3**	**34**	**42**	—	**25**	**7**	**10**	—	**6**	—	**.238**	**.335**	**.348**	**.943**
Career total		2016	7629	1130	2165	442	71	79	710	748	—	627	97	269	—	109	7	.284	.355	.391	.955
Cubs total		**105**	**336**	**37**	**80**	**24**	**2**	**3**	**34**	**42**	—	**25**	**7**	**10**	—	**6**	—	**.238**	**.335**	**.348**	**.943**

Barton, Vincent David (Vince)

HEIGHT: 6'0"   THROWS: RIGHT   BATS: LEFT   BORN: 2/1/1908 EDMONTON, ALBERTA, CANADA   DIED: 9/13/1973 TORONTO, ONTARIO, CANADA
POSITIONS PLAYED: OF

YEAR	TEAM	GAMES	AB	RUNS	HITS	2B	3B	HR	RBI	BB	IBB	SO	HBP	SH	SF	SB	CS	BA	OBA	SA	FA
1931	ChC-N	66	239	45	57	10	1	13	50	21	—	40	9	1	—	1	—	.238	.323	.452	.964
1932	ChC-N	36	134	19	30	2	3	3	15	8	—	22	1	1	—	0	—	.224	.273	.351	1.000
Career average		51	187	32	44	6	2	8	33	15	—	31	5	1	—	1	—	.233	.306	.416	.976
Cubs average		**51**	**187**	**32**	**44**	**6**	**2**	**8**	**33**	**15**	**—**	**31**	**5**	**1**	**—**	**1**	**—**	**.233**	**.306**	**.416**	**.976**
Career total		102	373	64	87	12	4	16	65	29	—	62	10	2	—	1	—	.233	.306	.416	.976
Cubs total		**102**	**373**	**64**	**87**	**12**	**4**	**16**	**65**	**29**	**—**	**62**	**10**	**2**	**—**	**1**	**—**	**.233**	**.306**	**.416**	**.976**

Bastian, Charles J. (Charlie)

HEIGHT: 5'6"   THROWS: RIGHT   BATS: RIGHT   BORN: 7/4/1860 PHILADELPHIA, PENNSYLVANIA   DIED: 1/18/1932 PENNSAUKEN, NEW JERSEY
POSITIONS PLAYED: P, 2B, 3B, SS

YEAR	TEAM	GAMES	AB	RUNS	HITS	2B	3B	HR	RBI	BB	IBB	SO	HBP	SH	SF	SB	CS	BA	OBA	SA	FA
1884	Wil-U	17	60	6	12	1	3	2	—	3	—	—	—	—	—	—	—	.200	.238	.417	.905
1884	KC-U	11	46	6	9	3	0	1	—	4	—	—	—	—	—	—	—	.196	.260	.326	.950
1885	Phi-N	103	389	63	65	11	5	4	29	35	—	82	—	—	—	—	—	.167	.236	.252	.890
1886	Phi-N	105	373	46	81	9	11	2	38	33	—	73	—	—	—	29	—	.217	.281	.316	.936
1887	Phi-N	60	240	33	66	11	1	1	21	19	—	29	3	—	—	11	—	.275	.336	.342	.918
1888	Phi-N	80	275	30	53	4	1	1	17	27	—	41	7	—	—	12	—	.193	.282	.225	.942
1889	**ChN-N**	**46**	**155**	**19**	**21**	**0**	**0**	**0**	**10**	**25**	**—**	**46**	**0**	**—**	**—**	**1**	**—**	**.135**	**.256**	**.135**	**.924**
1890	Chi-P	80	283	38	54	10	5	0	29	33	—	37	5	—	—	4	—	.191	.287	.261	.891
1891	Cin-AA	1	4	0	0	0	0	0	0	0	—	0	0	—	—	0	—	.000	.000	.000	1.000
1891	Phi-N	1	0	0	0	0	0	0	0	0	—	0	0	—	—	0	—	—	—	—	1.000
Career average		63	228	30	45	6	3	1	18	22	—	39	2	—	—	7	—	.198	.275	.271	.917
Cubs average		**46**	**155**	**19**	**21**	**0**	**0**	**0**	**10**	**25**	**—**	**46**	**0**	**—**	**—**	**1**	**—**	**.135**	**.256**	**.135**	**.924**
Career total		504	1825	241	361	49	26	11	144	179	—	308	15	—	—	57	—	.198	.275	.271	.917
Cubs total		**46**	**155**	**19**	**21**	**0**	**0**	**0**	**10**	**25**	**—**	**46**	**0**	**—**	**—**	**1**	**—**	**.135**	**.256**	**.135**	**.924**

Bates, John William (Johnny)

HEIGHT: 5'7"   THROWS: RIGHT   BATS: LEFT   BORN: 8/21/1882 STEUBENVILLE, OHIO   DIED: 2/10/1949 STEUBENVILLE, OHIO   POSITIONS PLAYED: OF

YEAR	TEAM	GAMES	AB	RUNS	HITS	2B	3B	HR	RBI	BB	IBB	SO	HBP	SH	SF	SB	CS	BA	OBA	SA	FA
1906	Bos-N	140	504	52	127	21	5	6	54	36	—	—	10	9	—	9	—	.252	.315	.349	.958
1907	Bos-N	126	447	52	116	18	12	2	49	39	—	—	7	11	—	11	—	.260	.329	.367	.979
1908	Bos-N	127	445	48	115	14	6	1	29	35	—	—	2	13	—	25	—	.258	.315	.324	.948
1909	Bos-N	63	236	27	68	15	3	1	23	20	—	—	4	6	—	15	—	.288	.354	.390	.945
1909	Phi-N	77	266	43	78	11	1	1	15	28	—	—	2	18	—	22	—	.293	.365	.353	.959
1910	Phi-N	135	498	91	152	26	11	3	61	61	—	49	4	19	—	31	—	.305	.385	.420	.954
1911	Cin-N	148	518	89	151	24	13	1	61	103	—	59	6	19	—	33	—	.292	.415	.394	.966
1912	Cin-N	81	239	45	69	12	7	1	29	47	—	16	0	11	—	10	—	.289	.406	.410	.950
1913	Cin-N	131	407	63	113	13	7	6	51	67	—	30	6	12	—	21	—	.278	.388	.388	.946
1914	Cin-N	58	155	29	39	7	5	2	15	28	—	17	4	6	—	4	—	.252	.380	.400	.913
1914	**ChC-N**	**9**	**8**	**2**	**1**	**0**	**0**	**0**	**1**	**1**	**—**	**1**	**1**	**0**	**—**	**0**	**—**	**.125**	**.300**	**.125**	**1.000**
1914	Bal-F	59	190	24	58	6	3	1	29	38	—	18	3	8	—	6	—	.305	.429	.384	.950
Career average		128	435	63	121	19	8	3	46	56	—	21	5	15	—	21	—	.278	.367	.377	.955
Cubs average		**9**	**8**	**2**	**1**	**0**	**0**	**0**	**1**	**1**	**—**	**1**	**1**	**0**	**—**	**0**	**—**	**.125**	**.300**	**.125**	**1.000**
Career total		1154	3913	565	1087	167	73	25	417	503	—	190	49	132	—	187	—	.278	.367	.377	.955
Cubs total		**9**	**8**	**2**	**1**	**0**	**0**	**0**	**1**	**1**	**—**	**1**	**1**	**0**	**—**	**0**	**—**	**.125**	**.300**	**.125**	**1.000**

Baumholtz, Frank Conrad (Frankie)

HEIGHT: 5'10"   THROWS: LEFT   BATS: LEFT   BORN: 10/7/1918 MIDVALE, OHIO   DIED: 12/14/1997 WINTER SPRINGS, FLORIDA   POSITIONS PLAYED: OF

YEAR	TEAM	GAMES	AB	RUNS	HITS	2B	3B	HR	RBI	BB	IBB	SO	HBP	SH	SF	SB	CS	BA	OBA	SA	FA
1947	Cin-N	151	643	96	182	32	9	5	45	56	—	53	1	11	—	6	—	.283	.341	.384	.977
1948	Cin-N	128	415	57	123	19	5	4	30	27	—	32	3	4	—	8	—	.296	.344	.395	.987
1949	Cin-N	27	81	12	19	5	3	1	8	6	—	8	1	3	—	0	—	.235	.295	.407	.964
1949	**ChC-N**	**58**	**164**	**15**	**37**	**4**	**2**	**1**	**15**	**9**	**—**	**21**	**1**	**4**	**—**	**2**	**—**	**.226**	**.270**	**.293**	**.986**

(continued)

Frank (Frankie) Conrad Baumholtz, of, 1947–57

Frankie Baumholtz was a fan favorite for the Cubs in the early 1950s, a solid-hitting center fielder who later became a key pinch hitter for the "Baby Bears."

Baumholtz was born on October 7, 1918, in Midvale, Ohio. He was a multisport athlete in high school and his initial foray into professional sports was as a member of the National Basketball League in 1945 to 1946 and then the NBA in 1946 to 1947. A 5'10" guard, Baumholtz averaged 14 points per game in 1946 and 1947, which placed him among the top scorers in the league, averagewise.

Baumholtz was signed by the Reds and had an auspicious rookie year, with 182 hits, 32 doubles and a career-high 96 runs scored in 1947. He hit .296 the next year, but in 1949 his numbers fell. He was traded to Chicago with Hank Sauer for Peanuts Lowrey and Harry Walker midway through the season. But he hit only .226 for the Cubs the rest of that year and was relegated to the minors in 1950.

He made it back to the Cubs' regular roster the next year, and his numbers showed a significant jump. He led the team with a .284 average that year, along with 28 doubles and 10 triples. In 1952 he had a career season, leading the club with a .325 average despite a broken hand that had sidelined him for several weeks.

The 1952 season was Baumholtz's last as a regular. He hit .302, with 36 doubles. After that year, he was used mainly by the Cubs as a pinch hitter, but he was very good at that particular discipline. In 1954 he led the league in pinch hits with 15 in 37 at-bats. He was sold to the Phillies the next season, where he played two years before retiring.

Baumholtz didn't play for the Cubs long enough to hold any all-time records, but his .325 average with the team in 1952 was the highest of any Cubs regular in the 1950s. Baumholtz died in Winter Springs, Florida, in 1997.

(continued)

Year	Team	G	AB	R	H	2B	3B	HR	RBI	BB	IBB	SO	HBP	SH	SF	SB	CS	BA	OBA	SA	FA
1951	ChC-N	146	560	62	159	28	10	2	50	49	—	36	4	2	—	5	4	.284	.346	.380	.975
1952	ChC-N	103	409	59	133	17	4	4	35	27	—	27	3	7	—	5	7	.325	.371	.416	.974
1953	ChC-N	133	520	75	159	36	7	3	25	42	—	36	1	4	—	3	3	.306	.359	.419	.980
1954	ChC-N	90	303	38	90	12	6	4	28	20	—	15	1	1	2	1	3	.297	.340	.416	.988
1955	ChC-N	105	280	23	81	12	5	1	27	16	2	24	1	7	5	0	1	.289	.325	.379	.993
1956	Phi-N	76	100	13	27	0	0	0	9	6	0	6	1	2	3	0	2	.270	.309	.270	.962
1957	Phi-N	2	2	0	0	0	0	0	0	0	0	0	0	0	0	0	0	.000	.000	.000	—
Career average		102	348	45	101	17	5	3	27	26	0	26	2	5	1	3	2	.290	.342	.389	.980
Cubs average		**106**	**373**	**45**	**110**	**18**	**6**	**3**	**30**	**27**	**0**	**27**	**2**	**4**	**1**	**3**	**3**	**.295**	**.345**	**.394**	**.980**
Career total		1019	3477	450	1010	165	51	25	272	258	2	258	17	45	10	30	20	.290	.342	.389	.980
Cubs total		**635**	**2236**	**272**	**659**	**109**	**34**	**15**	**180**	**163**	**2**	**159**	**11**	**25**	**7**	**16**	**18**	**.295**	**.345**	**.394**	**.980**

Beals, Thomas L. (Tommy)
HEIGHT: 5'5" THROWS: — BATS: RIGHT BORN: — NEW YORK DIED: 10/2/1915 SAN FRANCISCO, CALIFORNIA POSITIONS PLAYED: 2B, OF

YEAR	TEAM	GAMES	AB	RUNS	HITS	2B	3B	HR	RBI	BB	IBB	SO	HBP	SH	SF	SB	CS	BA	OBA	SA	FA
1880	ChN-N	13	46	4	7	0	0	0	3	1	—	6	—	—	—	—	—	.152	.170	.152	.773
Career average		13	46	4	7	0	0	0	3	1	—	6	—	—	—	—	—	.152	.170	.152	.773
Cubs average		**13**	**46**	**4**	**7**	**0**	**0**	**0**	**3**	**1**	**—**	**6**	**—**	**—**	**—**	**—**	**—**	**.152**	**.170**	**.152**	**.773**
Career total		13	46	4	7	0	0	0	3	1	—	6	—	—	—	—	—	.152	.170	.152	.773
Cubs total		**13**	**46**	**4**	**7**	**0**	**0**	**0**	**3**	**1**	**—**	**6**	**—**	**—**	**—**	**—**	**—**	**.152**	**.170**	**.152**	**.773**

Beaumont, Clarence Howeth (Ginger)

HEIGHT: 5'8"   THROWS: RIGHT   BATS: LEFT   BORN: 7/23/1876 ROCHESTER, WISCONSIN   DIED: 4/10/1956 BURLINGTON, WISCONSIN
POSITIONS PLAYED: 1B, OF

YEAR	TEAM	GAMES	AB	RUNS	HITS	2B	3B	HR	RBI	BB	IBB	SO	HBP	SH	SF	SB	CS	BA	OBA	SA	FA
1899	Pit-N	111	437	90	154	15	8	3	38	41	—	—	7	4	—	31	—	.352	.416	.444	.922
1900	Pit-N	138	567	105	158	14	9	5	50	40	—	—	4	21	—	27	—	.279	.331	.362	.944
1901	Pit-N	133	558	120	185	14	5	8	72	44	—	—	2	12	—	36	—	.332	.382	.418	.943
1902	Pit-N	130	541	100	193	21	6	0	67	39	—	—	4	15	—	33	—	.357	.404	.418	.975
1903	Pit-N	141	613	137	209	30	6	7	68	44	—	—	5	12	—	23	—	.341	.390	.444	.948
1904	Pit-N	153	615	97	185	12	12	3	54	34	—	—	1	23	—	28	—	.301	.338	.374	.968
1905	Pit-N	103	384	60	126	12	8	3	40	22	—	—	0	14	—	21	—	.328	.365	.424	.972
1906	Pit-N	80	310	48	82	9	3	2	32	19	—	—	2	18	—	1	—	.265	.311	.332	.945
1907	Bos-N	150	580	67	187	19	14	4	62	37	—	—	3	12	—	25	—	.322	.366	.424	.962
1908	Bos-N	125	476	66	127	20	6	2	52	42	—	—	1	13	—	13	—	.267	.328	.347	.965
1909	Bos-N	123	407	35	107	11	4	0	60	35	—	—	0	14	—	12	—	.263	.321	.310	.969
1910	**ChC-N**	**76**	**172**	**30**	**46**	**5**	**1**	**2**	**22**	**28**	**—**	**14**	**1**	**8**	**—**	**4**	**—**	**.267**	**.373**	**.343**	**.957**
Career average		122	472	80	147	15	7	3	51	35	—	1	3	14	—	21	—	.311	.362	.393	.956
Cubs average		**76**	**172**	**30**	**46**	**5**	**1**	**2**	**22**	**28**	**—**	**14**	**1**	**8**	**—**	**4**	**—**	**.267**	**.373**	**.343**	**.957**
Career total		1463	5660	955	1759	182	82	39	617	425	—	14	30	166	—	254	—	.311	.362	.393	.956
Cubs total		**76**	**172**	**30**	**46**	**5**	**1**	**2**	**22**	**28**	**—**	**14**	**1**	**8**	**—**	**4**	**—**	**.267**	**.373**	**.343**	**.957**

Beck, Clyde Eugene (Jersey)

HEIGHT: 5'10"   THROWS: RIGHT   BATS: RIGHT   BORN: 1/6/1900 BASSETT, CALIFORNIA   DIED: 7/15/1988 TEMPLE CITY, CALIFORNIA
POSITIONS PLAYED: 2B, 3B, SS

YEAR	TEAM	GAMES	AB	RUNS	HITS	2B	3B	HR	RBI	BB	IBB	SO	HBP	SH	SF	SB	CS	BA	OBA	SA	FA
1926	**ChC-N**	**30**	**81**	**10**	**16**	**0**	**0**	**1**	**4**	**7**	**—**	**15**	**0**	**3**	**—**	**0**	**—**	**.198**	**.261**	**.235**	**.993**
1927	**ChC-N**	**117**	**391**	**44**	**101**	**20**	**5**	**2**	**44**	**43**	**—**	**37**	**0**	**16**	**—**	**0**	**—**	**.258**	**.332**	**.350**	**.965**
1928	**ChC-N**	**131**	**483**	**72**	**124**	**18**	**4**	**3**	**52**	**58**	**—**	**58**	**4**	**7**	**—**	**3**	**—**	**.257**	**.341**	**.329**	**.963**
1929	**ChC-N**	**54**	**190**	**28**	**40**	**7**	**0**	**0**	**9**	**19**	**—**	**24**	**0**	**4**	**—**	**3**	**—**	**.211**	**.282**	**.247**	**.964**
1930	**ChC-N**	**83**	**244**	**32**	**52**	**7**	**0**	**6**	**34**	**36**	**—**	**32**	**0**	**9**	**—**	**2**	**—**	**.213**	**.314**	**.316**	**.951**
1931	Cin-N	53	136	17	21	4	2	0	19	21	—	14	1	5	—	1	—	.154	.272	.213	.960
Career average		78	254	34	59	9	2	2	27	31	—	30	1	7	—	2	—	.232	.317	.307	.963
Cubs average		**83**	**278**	**37**	**67**	**10**	**2**	**2**	**29**	**33**	**—**	**33**	**1**	**8**	**—**	**2**	**—**	**.240**	**.321**	**.316**	**.964**
Career total		468	1525	203	354	56	11	12	162	184	—	180	5	44	—	9	—	.232	.317	.307	.963
Cubs total		**415**	**1389**	**186**	**333**	**52**	**9**	**12**	**143**	**163**	**—**	**166**	**4**	**39**	**—**	**8**	**—**	**.240**	**.321**	**.316**	**.964**

Becker, Heinz Reinhard (Dutch *or* Bunions)

HEIGHT: 6'2"   THROWS: RIGHT   BATS: BOTH   BORN: 8/26/1915 BERLIN, GERMANY   DIED: 11/11/1991 DALLAS, TEXAS   POSITIONS PLAYED: 1B

YEAR	TEAM	GAMES	AB	RUNS	HITS	2B	3B	HR	RBI	BB	IBB	SO	HBP	SH	SF	SB	CS	BA	OBA	SA	FA
1943	**ChC-N**	**24**	**69**	**5**	**10**	**0**	**0**	**0**	**2**	**9**	**—**	**6**	**0**	**0**	**—**	**0**	**—**	**.145**	**.244**	**.145**	**.983**
1945	**ChC-N**	**67**	**133**	**25**	**38**	**8**	**2**	**2**	**27**	**17**	**—**	**16**	**2**	**0**	**—**	**0**	**—**	**.286**	**.375**	**.421**	**1.000**
1946	**ChC-N**	**9**	**7**	**0**	**2**	**0**	**0**	**0**	**1**	**1**	**—**	**1**	**0**	**0**	**—**	**0**	**—**	**.286**	**.375**	**.286**	**—**
1946	Cle-A	50	147	15	44	10	1	0	17	23	—	18	2	0	—	1	0	.299	.401	.381	.995
1947	Cle-A	2	2	0	0	0	0	0	0	0	—	1	0	0	—	0	0	.000	.000	.000	—
Career average		38	90	11	24	5	1	1	12	13	—	11	1	0	—	0	0	.263	.359	.346	.994
Cubs average		**33**	**70**	**10**	**17**	**3**	**1**	**1**	**10**	**9**	**—**	**8**	**1**	**0**	**—**	**0**	**—**	**.239**	**.332**	**.325**	**.993**
Career total		152	358	45	94	18	3	2	47	50	—	42	4	0	—	1	0	.263	.359	.346	.994
Cubs total		**100**	**209**	**30**	**50**	**8**	**2**	**2**	**30**	**27**	**—**	**23**	**2**	**0**	**—**	**0**	**—**	**.239**	**.332**	**.325**	**.993**

Beckert, Glenn Alfred

HEIGHT: 6'1"   THROWS: RIGHT   BATS: RIGHT   BORN: 10/12/1940 PITTSBURGH, PENNSYLVANIA   POSITIONS PLAYED: 2B, 3B, SS, OF

YEAR	TEAM	GAMES	AB	RUNS	HITS	2B	3B	HR	RBI	BB	IBB	SO	HBP	SH	SF	SB	CS	BA	OBA	SA	FA
1965	**ChC-N**	**154**	**614**	**73**	**147**	**21**	**3**	**3**	**30**	**28**	**0**	**52**	**3**	**6**	**2**	**6**	**8**	**.239**	**.275**	**.298**	**.973**
1966	**ChC-N**	**153**	**656**	**73**	**188**	**23**	**7**	**1**	**59**	**26**	**0**	**36**	**4**	**5**	**2**	**10**	**4**	**.287**	**.317**	**.348**	**.970**
1967	**ChC-N**	**146**	**597**	**91**	**167**	**32**	**3**	**5**	**40**	**30**	**1**	**25**	**0**	**8**	**1**	**10**	**3**	**.280**	**.314**	**.369**	**.968**
1968	**ChC-N**	**155**	**643**	**98**	**189**	**28**	**4**	**4**	**37**	**31**	**0**	**20**	**2**	**5**	**4**	**8**	**4**	**.294**	**.326**	**.369**	**.977**
1969	**ChC-N**	**131**	**543**	**69**	**158**	**22**	**1**	**1**	**37**	**24**	**0**	**24**	**6**	**4**	**5**	**6**	**0**	**.291**	**.325**	**.341**	**.965**

(continued)

Glenn Alfred "Bruno" Beckert, 1b-of-2b, 1965–75

Glenn Beckert was a four-time All-Star who was one of the most consistent players the Cubs had in the late 1960s and early 1970s.

Beckert was born on October 12, 1940, in Pittsburgh, Pennsylvania. He was a shortstop in the minor leagues, but was switched to second base in the Cubs organization upon the death of incumbent Ken Hubbs. Hubbs, a budding star in the Cubs organization, was killed in 1964 when a private plane he was piloting crashed.

Beckert became the starting second baseman for the Cubs in 1965, and initially he was not overpowering at the plate, hitting only .239 that year. But his average jumped to .287 in 1966, and for the next seven years with Chicago, he hit in the high .200s or better, topping out with a .342 average in 1971.

He was also very tough to strike out. From 1967 to 1973, Beckert whiffed an average of

only 21 times from 1967 t0 1973, while getting more than 535 at-bats per season. Conversely, Beckert didn't walk a lot, either. In that same span, he earned only about 22 walks per year.

Beckert, throughout his Cubs career, batted second behind his fellow infielder, second baseman Don Kessinger. He and Kessinger gave Chicago one of the strongest double-play combinations in the league for several years.

Beckert's nickname of "Bruno" was in honor of professional wrestler Bruno Sammartino because he sometimes bowled over other infielders as he chased pop flies.

Beckert was second in the National League in assists from 1966 to 1969, and won a Gold Glove in 1968. He was named to the National League All-Star team four years in a row, from 1969 to 1972.

In 1974 Beckert was traded to the San Diego Padres, where he was limited to part-time and pinch-hitting duty by knee and foot injuries. Beckert retired after the 1975 season.

(continued)

YEAR	TEAM	GAMES	AB	RUNS	HITS	2B	3B	HR	RBI	BB	IBB	SO	HBP	SH	SF	SB	CS	BA	OBA	SA	FA
1970	ChC-N	143	591	99	170	15	6	3	36	32	0	22	0	6	3	4	1	.288	.323	.349	.970
1971	ChC-N	131	530	80	181	18	5	2	42	24	0	24	0	12	4	3	2	.342	.367	.406	.986
1972	ChC-N	120	474	51	128	22	2	3	43	23	1	17	2	7	4	2	1	.270	.304	.344	.976
1973	ChC-N	114	372	38	95	13	0	0	29	30	1	15	2	4	2	0	2	.255	.313	.290	.984
1974	SD-N	64	172	11	44	1	0	0	7	11	0	8	0	1	0	0	2	.256	.301	.262	.938
1975	SD-N	9	16	2	6	1	0	0	0	1	0	0	0	0	0	0	0	.375	.412	.438	1.000
Career average		120	473	62	134	18	3	2	33	24	0	22	2	5	2	4	2	.283	.318	.345	.973
Cubs average		**139**	**558**	**75**	**158**	**22**	**3**	**2**	**39**	**28**	**0**	**26**	**2**	**6**	**3**	**5**	**3**	**.283**	**.318**	**.348**	**.974**
Career total		1320	5208	685	1473	196	31	22	360	260	3	243	19	58	27	49	25	.283	.318	.345	.973
Cubs total		**1247**	**5020**	**672**	**1423**	**194**	**31**	**22**	**353**	**248**	**3**	**235**	**19**	**57**	**27**	**49**	**25**	**.283**	**.318**	**.348**	**.974**

Bell, Jorge Antonio (George)

HEIGHT: 6'1"   THROWS: RIGHT   BATS: RIGHT   BORN: 10/21/1959 SAN PEDRO DE MACORIS, DOMINICAN REPUBLIC   POSITIONS PLAYED: 2B, 3B, OF

YEAR	TEAM	GAMES	AB	RUNS	HITS	2B	3B	HR	RBI	BB	IBB	SO	HBP	SH	SF	SB	CS	BA	OBA	SA	FA
1981	Tor-A	60	163	19	38	2	1	5	12	5	1	27	0	0	0	3	2	.233	.256	.350	.969
1983	Tor-A	39	112	5	30	5	4	2	17	4	1	17	2	0	0	1	1	.268	.305	.438	.954
1984	Tor-A	159	606	85	177	39	4	26	87	24	2	86	8	0	3	11	2	.292	.326	.498	.971
1985	Tor-A	157	607	87	167	28	6	28	95	43	6	90	8	0	8	21	6	.275	.327	.479	.968
1986	Tor-A	159	641	101	198	38	6	31	108	41	3	62	2	0	6	7	8	.309	.349	.532	.966
1987	Tor-A	156	610	111	188	32	4	47	134	39	9	75	7	0	9	5	1	.308	.352	.605	.960
1988	Tor-A	156	614	78	165	27	5	24	97	34	5	66	1	0	8	4	2	.269	.304	.446	.946
1989	Tor-A	153	613	88	182	41	2	18	104	33	3	60	4	0	14	4	3	.297	.330	.458	.963
1990	Tor-A	142	562	67	149	25	0	21	86	32	7	80	3	0	11	3	2	.265	.303	.422	.979
1991	**ChC-N**	**149**	**558**	**63**	**159**	**27**	**0**	**25**	**86**	**32**	**6**	**62**	**4**	**0**	**9**	**2**	**6**	**.285**	**.323**	**.468**	**.962**
1992	CWS-A	155	627	74	160	27	0	25	112	31	8	97	6	0	6	5	2	.255	.294	.418	.964
1993	CWS-A	102	410	36	89	17	2	13	64	13	2	49	4	0	9	1	1	.217	.243	.363	—
Career average		132	510	68	142	26	3	22	84	28	4	64	4	0	7	6	3	.278	.316	.469	.964
Cubs average		**149**	**558**	**63**	**159**	**27**	**0**	**25**	**86**	**32**	**6**	**62**	**4**	**0**	**9**	**2**	**6**	**.285**	**.323**	**.468**	**.962**
Career total		1587	6123	814	1702	308	34	265	1002	331	53	771	49	0	83	67	36	.278	.316	.469	.964
Cubs total		**149**	**558**	**63**	**159**	**27**	**0**	**25**	**86**	**32**	**6**	**62**	**4**	**0**	**9**	**2**	**6**	**.285**	**.323**	**.468**	**.962**

Bell, Lester Rowland (Les)

HEIGHT: 5'11" THROWS: RIGHT BATS: RIGHT BORN: 12/14/1901 HARRISBURG, PENNSYLVANIA DIED: 12/26/1985 HERSHEY, PENNSYLVANIA
POSITIONS PLAYED: 1B, 2B, 3B, SS

YEAR	TEAM	GAMES	AB	RUNS	HITS	2B	3B	HR	RBI	BB	IBB	SO	HBP	SH	SF	SB	CS	BA	OBA	SA	FA
1923	StL-N	15	51	5	19	2	1	0	9	9	—	7	0	0	—	1	0	.373	.467	.451	.917
1924	StL-N	17	57	5	14	3	2	1	5	3	—	7	1	1	—	0	0	.246	.295	.421	.905
1925	StL-N	153	586	80	167	29	9	11	88	43	—	47	0	10	—	4	5	.285	.334	.422	.924
1926	StL-N	155	581	85	189	33	14	17	100	54	—	62	0	31	—	9	—	.325	.383	.518	.950
1927	StL-N	115	390	48	101	26	6	9	65	34	—	63	1	13	—	5	—	.259	.320	.426	.904
1928	Bos-N	153	591	58	164	36	7	10	91	40	—	45	0	25	—	1	—	.277	.323	.413	.948
1929	Bos-N	139	483	58	144	23	5	9	72	50	—	42	0	20	—	4	—	.298	.364	.422	.944
1930	**ChC-N**	74	248	35	69	15	4	5	47	24	—	27	0	9	—	1	—	.278	.342	.431	.954
1931	**ChC-N**	75	252	30	71	17	1	4	32	19	—	22	0	1	—	0	—	.282	.332	.405	.944
Career average		100	360	45	104	20	5	7	57	31	—	36	0	12	—	3	1	.290	.346	.438	.936
Cubs average		**75**	**250**	**33**	**70**	**16**	**3**	**5**	**40**	**22**	**—**	**25**	**0**	**5**	**—**	**1**	**0**	**.280**	**.337**	**.418**	**.949**
Career total		896	3239	404	938	184	49	66	509	276	—	322	2	110	—	25	5	.290	.346	.438	.936
Cubs total		**149**	**500**	**65**	**140**	**32**	**5**	**9**	**79**	**43**	**—**	**49**	**0**	**10**	**—**	**1**	**0**	**.280**	**.337**	**.418**	**.949**

Benton, Alfred Lee (Butch)

HEIGHT: 6'1" THROWS: RIGHT BATS: RIGHT BORN: 8/24/1957 TAMPA, FLORIDA POSITIONS PLAYED: C

YEAR	TEAM	GAMES	AB	RUNS	HITS	2B	3B	HR	RBI	BB	IBB	SO	HBP	SH	SF	SB	CS	BA	OBA	SA	FA
1978	NYM-N	4	4	1	2	0	0	0	2	0	—	0	1	0	0	0	0	.500	.600	.500	1.000
1980	NYM-N	12	21	0	1	0	0	0	0	2	0	4	1	0	0	0	0	.048	.167	.048	.935
1982	**ChC-N**	4	7	0	1	0	0	0	1	0	0	1	0	0	0	0	0	.143	.143	.143	1.000
1985	Cle-A	31	67	5	12	4	0	0	7	3	2	9	0	1	2	0	0	.179	.208	.239	.957
Career average		13	25	2	4	1	0	0	3	1	1	4	1	0	1	0	0	.162	.213	.202	.959
Cubs average		**4**	**7**	**0**	**1**	**0**	**0**	**0**	**1**	**0**	**0**	**1**	**0**	**0**	**0**	**0**	**0**	**.143**	**.143**	**.143**	**1.000**
Career total		51	99	6	16	4	0	0	10	5	2	14	2	1	2	0	0	.162	.213	.202	.959
Cubs total		**4**	**7**	**0**	**1**	**0**	**0**	**0**	**1**	**0**	**0**	**1**	**0**	**0**	**0**	**0**	**0**	**.143**	**.143**	**.143**	**1.000**

Berryhill, Damon Scott

HEIGHT: 6'0" THROWS: RIGHT BATS: BOTH BORN: 12/3/1963 SOUTH LAGUNA, CALIFORNIA POSITIONS PLAYED: C, 1B

YEAR	TEAM	GAMES	AB	RUNS	HITS	2B	3B	HR	RBI	BB	IBB	SO	HBP	SH	SF	SB	CS	BA	OBA	SA	FA
1987	**ChC-N**	12	28	2	5	1	0	0	1	3	0	5	0	0	0	0	1	.179	.258	.214	.909
1988	**ChC-N**	95	309	19	80	19	1	7	38	17	5	56	0	3	3	1	0	.259	.295	.395	.982
1989	**ChC-N**	91	334	37	86	13	0	5	41	16	4	54	2	4	5	1	0	.257	.291	.341	.978
1990	**ChC-N**	17	53	6	10	4	0	1	9	5	1	14	0	0	1	0	0	.189	.254	.321	.978
1991	**ChC-N**	62	159	13	30	7	0	5	14	11	1	41	1	0	1	1	2	.189	.244	.327	.967
1991	Atl-N	1	1	0	0	0	0	0	0	0	0	1	0	0	0	0	0	.000	.000	.000	1.000
1992	Atl-N	101	307	21	70	16	1	10	43	17	4	67	1	0	3	0	2	.228	.268	.384	.998
1993	Atl-N	115	335	24	82	18	2	8	43	21	1	64	2	2	3	0	0	.245	.291	.382	.990
1994	Bos-A	82	255	30	67	17	2	6	34	19	0	59	0	0	2	0	1	.263	.312	.416	.995
1995	Cin-N	34	82	6	15	3	0	2	11	10	2	19	0	1	4	0	0	.183	.260	.293	.988
1997	SF-N	73	167	17	43	8	0	3	23	20	5	29	0	0	1	0	0	.257	.335	.359	.991
Career average		68	203	18	49	11	1	5	26	14	2	41	1	1	2	0	1	.240	.288	.368	.988
Cubs average		**55**	**177**	**15**	**42**	**9**	**0**	**4**	**21**	**10**	**2**	**34**	**1**	**1**	**2**	**1**	**1**	**.239**	**.281**	**.352**	**.981**
Career total		683	2030	175	488	106	6	47	257	139	23	409	6	10	23	3	6	.240	.288	.368	.988
Cubs total		**277**	**883**	**77**	**211**	**44**	**1**	**18**	**103**	**52**	**11**	**170**	**3**	**7**	**10**	**3**	**3**	**.239**	**.281**	**.352**	**.981**

Bertell, Richard George (Dick)

HEIGHT: 6'0" THROWS: RIGHT BATS: RIGHT BORN: 11/21/1935 OAK PARK, ILLINOIS DIED: 12/20/1999 MISSION VIEJO, CALIFORNIA POSITIONS PLAYED: C

YEAR	TEAM	GAMES	AB	RUNS	HITS	2B	3B	HR	RBI	BB	IBB	SO	HBP	SH	SF	SB	CS	BA	OBA	SA	FA
1960	**ChC-N**	5	15	0	2	0	0	0	2	3	0	1	0	0	1	0	0	.133	.263	.133	1.000
1961	**ChC-N**	92	267	20	73	7	1	2	33	15	3	33	0	1	4	0	0	.273	.308	.330	.982
1962	**ChC-N**	77	215	19	65	6	2	2	18	13	5	30	1	5	1	0	1	.302	.343	.377	.986
1963	**ChC-N**	100	322	15	75	7	2	2	14	24	6	41	0	2	2	0	2	.233	.284	.286	.988
1964	**ChC-N**	112	353	29	84	11	3	4	35	33	8	67	2	5	2	2	1	.238	.305	.320	.981
1965	**ChC-N**	34	84	6	18	2	0	0	7	11	2	10	0	2	1	0	0	.214	.302	.238	.981

(continued)

(continued)

YEAR	TEAM	GAMES	AB	RUNS	HITS	2B	3B	HR	RBI	BB	IBB	SO	HBP	SH	SF	SB	CS	BA	OBA	SA	FA
1965	SF-N	22	48	1	9	1	0	0	3	7	3	5	0	1	0	0	0	.188	.291	.208	.992
1967	**ChC-N**	**2**	**6**	**1**	**1**	**0**	**1**	**0**	**0**	**0**	**0**	**1**	**0**	**1**	**0**	**0**	**0**	**.167**	**.167**	**.500**	**1.000**
Career average		63	187	13	47	5	1	1	16	15	4	27	0	2	2	0	1	.250	.305	.312	.985
Cubs average		**60**	**180**	**13**	**45**	**5**	**1**	**1**	**16**	**14**	**3**	**26**	**0**	**2**	**2**	**0**	**1**	**.252**	**.305**	**.316**	**.984**
Career total		444	1310	91	327	34	9	10	112	106	27	188	3	17	11	2	4	.250	.305	.312	.985
Cubs total		**422**	**1262**	**90**	**318**	**33**	**9**	**10**	**109**	**99**	**24**	**183**	**3**	**16**	**11**	**2**	**4**	**.252**	**.305**	**.316**	**.984**

Bielaski, Oscar

HEIGHT: 5'10" THROWS: RIGHT BATS: RIGHT BORN: 3/21/1847 WASHINGTON, DISTRICT OF COLUMBIA DIED: 11/8/1911 WASHINGTON, DISTRICT OF COLUMBIA POSITIONS PLAYED: OF

YEAR	TEAM	GAMES	AB	RUNS	HITS	2B	3B	HR	RBI	BB	IBB	SO	HBP	SH	SF	SB	CS	BA	OBA	SA	FA
1876	**ChN-N**	**32**	**141**	**24**	**29**	**3**	**0**	**0**	**10**	**2**	**—**	**3**	**—**	**—**	**—**	**—**	**—**	**.206**	**.217**	**.227**	**.763**
Career average		32	141	24	29	3	0	0	10	2	—	3	—	—	—	—	—	.206	.217	.227	.763
Cubs average		**32**	**141**	**24**	**29**	**3**	**0**	**0**	**10**	**2**	**—**	**3**	**—**	**—**	**—**	**—**	**—**	**.206**	**.217**	**.227**	**.763**
Career total		32	141	24	29	3	0	0	10	2	—	3	—	—	—	—	—	.206	.217	.227	.763
Cubs total		**32**	**141**	**24**	**29**	**3**	**0**	**0**	**10**	**2**	**—**	**3**	**—**	**—**	**—**	**—**	**—**	**.206**	**.217**	**.227**	**.763**

Biittner, Lawrence David (Larry)

HEIGHT: 6'2" THROWS: LEFT BATS: LEFT BORN: 7/27/1945 POCAHONTAS, IOWA POSITIONS PLAYED: P, 1B, OF

YEAR	TEAM	GAMES	AB	RUNS	HITS	2B	3B	HR	RBI	BB	IBB	SO	HBP	SH	SF	SB	CS	BA	OBA	SA	FA
1970	Was-A	2	2	0	0	0	0	0	0	0	0	0	0	0	0	0	0	.000	.000	.000	—
1971	Was-A	66	171	12	44	4	1	0	16	16	3	20	1	0	1	1	0	.257	.323	.292	.938
1972	Tex-A	137	382	34	99	18	1	3	31	29	5	37	2	6	3	1	3	.259	.313	.335	.986
1973	Tex-A	83	258	19	65	8	2	1	12	20	0	21	1	1	1	1	0	.252	.307	.310	.992
1974	Mon-N	18	26	2	7	1	0	0	3	0	0	2	0	1	0	0	0	.269	.269	.308	1.000
1975	Mon-N	121	346	34	109	13	5	3	28	34	8	33	0	4	0	2	1	.315	.376	.408	.972
1976	Mon-N	11	32	2	6	1	0	0	1	0	0	3	0	0	0	0	0	.188	.188	.219	.947
1976	**ChC-N**	**78**	**192**	**21**	**47**	**13**	**1**	**0**	**17**	**10**	**3**	**6**	**1**	**2**	**0**	**0**	**2**	**.245**	**.286**	**.323**	**.987**
1977	**ChC-N**	**138**	**493**	**74**	**147**	**28**	**1**	**12**	**62**	**35**	**2**	**36**	**1**	**1**	**2**	**2**	**1**	**.298**	**.345**	**.432**	**.987**
1978	**ChC-N**	**120**	**343**	**32**	**88**	**15**	**1**	**4**	**50**	**23**	**4**	**37**	**1**	**1**	**6**	**0**	**1**	**.257**	**.300**	**.341**	**.986**
1979	**ChC-N**	**111**	**272**	**35**	**79**	**13**	**3**	**3**	**50**	**21**	**1**	**23**	**0**	**0**	**2**	**1**	**1**	**.290**	**.339**	**.393**	**.981**
1980	**ChC-N**	**127**	**273**	**21**	**68**	**12**	**2**	**1**	**34**	**18**	**2**	**33**	**2**	**0**	**6**	**1**	**3**	**.249**	**.294**	**.319**	**.994**
1981	Cin-N	42	61	1	13	4	0	0	8	4	1	4	0	0	1	0	0	.213	.258	.279	1.000
1982	Cin-N	97	184	18	57	9	2	2	24	17	2	16	2	2	3	1	0	.310	.369	.413	.989
1983	Tex-A	66	116	5	32	5	1	0	18	9	5	16	0	0	2	0	0	.276	.323	.336	.987
Career average		87	225	22	62	10	1	2	25	17	3	21	1	1	2	1	1	.273	.324	.359	.985
Cubs average		**115**	**315**	**37**	**86**	**16**	**2**	**4**	**43**	**21**	**2**	**27**	**1**	**1**	**3**	**1**	**2**	**.273**	**.318**	**.373**	**.987**
Career total		1217	3151	310	861	144	20	29	354	236	36	287	11	18	27	10	12	.273	.324	.359	.985
Cubs total		**574**	**1573**	**183**	**429**	**81**	**8**	**20**	**213**	**107**	**12**	**135**	**5**	**4**	**16**	**4**	**8**	**.273**	**.318**	**.373**	**.987**

Bilko, Stephen Thomas (Steve *or* Humphrey)

HEIGHT: 6'1" THROWS: RIGHT BATS: RIGHT BORN: 11/13/1928 NANTICOKE, PENNSYLVANIA DIED: 3/7/1978 WILKES-BARRE, PENNSYLVANIA POSITIONS PLAYED: 1B, OF

YEAR	TEAM	GAMES	AB	RUNS	HITS	2B	3B	HR	RBI	BB	IBB	SO	HBP	SH	SF	SB	CS	BA	OBA	SA	FA
1949	StL-N	6	17	3	5	2	0	0	2	5	—	6	0	0	—	0	—	.294	.455	.412	1.000
1950	StL-N	10	33	1	6	1	0	0	2	4	—	10	0	0	—	0	0	.182	.270	.212	.989
1951	StL-N	21	72	5	16	4	0	2	12	9	—	10	0	1	—	0	0	.222	.309	.361	.984
1952	StL-N	20	72	7	19	6	1	1	6	4	—	15	0	2	—	0	0	.264	.303	.417	.995
1953	StL-N	154	570	72	143	23	3	21	84	70	—	125	1	0	—	0	1	.251	.334	.412	.991
1954	StL-N	8	14	1	2	0	0	0	1	3	—	1	0	0	0	0	1	.143	.294	.143	1.000
1954	**ChC-N**	**47**	**92**	**11**	**22**	**8**	**1**	**4**	**12**	**11**	**—**	**24**	**0**	**0**	**0**	**0**	**0**	**.239**	**.320**	**.478**	**1.000**
1958	Cin-N	31	87	12	23	4	2	4	17	10	0	20	0	0	3	0	0	.264	.330	.494	.995
1958	LA-N	47	101	13	21	1	2	7	18	8	0	37	0	0	1	0	0	.208	.264	.465	.995
1960	Det-A	78	222	20	46	11	2	9	25	27	0	31	0	0	1	0	1	.207	.292	.396	.991
1961	LAA-A	114	294	49	82	16	1	20	59	58	2	81	0	0	2	1	1	.279	.395	.544	.989
1962	LAA-A	64	164	26	47	9	1	8	38	25	0	35	2	0	7	1	1	.287	.374	.500	.995
Career average		60	174	22	43	9	1	8	28	23	0	40	0	0	1	0	0	.249	.336	.444	.992
Cubs average		**47**	**92**	**11**	**22**	**8**	**1**	**4**	**12**	**11**	**—**	**24**	**0**	**0**	**0**	**0**	**0**	**.239**	**.320**	**.478**	**1.000**
Career total		600	1738	220	432	85	13	76	276	234	2	395	3	3	14	2	4	.249	.336	.444	.992
Cubs total		**47**	**92**	**11**	**22**	**8**	**1**	**4**	**12**	**11**	**—**	**24**	**0**	**0**	**0**	**0**	**0**	**.239**	**.320**	**.478**	**1.000**

Blackburn, Earl Stuart

HEIGHT: 5'11" THROWS: RIGHT BATS: RIGHT BORN: 11/1/1892 LEESVILLE, OHIO DIED: 8/3/1966 MANSFIELD, OHIO POSITIONS PLAYED: C

YEAR	TEAM	GAMES	AB	RUNS	HITS	2B	3B	HR	RBI	BB	IBB	SO	HBP	SH	SF	SB	CS	BA	OBA	SA	FA
1912	Pit-N	1	0	0	0	0	0	0	0	0	—	0	0	0	—	0	—	—	—	—	1.000
1912	Cin-N	1	0	0	0	0	0	0	0	1	—	0	0	0	—	0	—	—	1.000	—	1.000
1913	Cin-N	17	27	1	7	0	0	0	3	2	—	5	0	0	—	2	0	.259	.310	.259	.848
1915	Bos-N	3	6	0	1	0	0	0	0	2	—	1	0	0	—	0	—	.167	.375	.167	1.000
1916	Bos-N	47	110	12	30	4	4	0	7	9	—	21	0	4	—	2	—	.273	.328	.382	.972
1917	**ChC-N**	**2**	**2**	**0**	**0**	**0**	**0**	**0**	**0**	**0**	**—**	**0**	**0**	**0**	**—**	**0**	**—**	**.000**	**.000**	**.000**	**—**
Career average		14	29	3	8	1	1	0	2	3	—	5	0	1	—	1	0	.262	.327	.345	.954
Cubs average		**2**	**2**	**0**	**0**	**0**	**0**	**0**	**0**	**0**	**—**	**0**	**0**	**0**	**—**	**0**	**0**	**.000**	**.000**	**.000**	**—**
Career total		71	145	13	38	4	4	0	10	14	—	27	0	4	—	4	0	.262	.327	.345	.954
Cubs total		**2**	**2**	**0**	**0**	**0**	**0**	**0**	**0**	**0**	**—**	**0**	**0**	**0**	**—**	**0**	**0**	**.000**	**.000**	**.000**	**—**

Blackwell, Timothy P. (Tim)

HEIGHT: 5'11" THROWS: RIGHT BATS: BOTH BORN: 8/19/1952 SAN DIEGO, CALIFORNIA POSITIONS PLAYED: C

YEAR	TEAM	GAMES	AB	RUNS	HITS	2B	3B	HR	RBI	BB	IBB	SO	HBP	SH	SF	SB	CS	BA	OBA	SA	FA
1974	Bos-A	44	122	9	30	1	1	0	8	10	1	21	1	2	0	1	1	.246	.308	.270	.971
1975	Bos-A	59	132	15	26	3	2	0	6	19	1	13	1	5	0	0	0	.197	.303	.250	.984
1976	Phi-N	4	8	0	2	0	0	0	1	0	0	1	0	0	0	0	0	.250	.250	.250	1.000
1977	Phi-N	1	0	1	0	0	0	0	0	0	0	0	0	0	0	0	—	—	—	—	1.000
1977	Mon-N	16	22	3	2	1	0	0	0	2	1	7	0	1	0	0	0	.091	.167	.136	.925
1978	**ChC-N**	**49**	**103**	**8**	**23**	**3**	**0**	**0**	**7**	**23**	**1**	**17**	**1**	**4**	**1**	**0**	**0**	**.223**	**.367**	**.252**	**.987**
1979	**ChC-N**	**63**	**122**	**8**	**20**	**3**	**1**	**0**	**12**	**32**	**1**	**25**	**1**	**2**	**2**	**0**	**0**	**.164**	**.338**	**.205**	**.975**
1980	**ChC-N**	**103**	**320**	**24**	**87**	**16**	**4**	**5**	**30**	**41**	**6**	**62**	**0**	**2**	**3**	**0**	**1**	**.272**	**.352**	**.394**	**.982**
1981	**ChC-N**	**58**	**158**	**21**	**37**	**10**	**2**	**1**	**11**	**23**	**4**	**23**	**0**	**1**	**0**	**2**	**1**	**.234**	**.331**	**.342**	**.993**
1982	Mon-N	23	42	2	8	2	1	0	3	3	0	11	0	0	0	0	0	.190	.244	.286	.985
1983	Mon-N	6	15	0	3	1	0	0	2	1	0	3	0	0	0	0	0	.200	.250	.267	.935
Career average		43	104	9	24	4	1	1	8	15	1	18	0	2	1	0	0	.228	.328	.305	.981
Cubs average		**68**	**176**	**15**	**42**	**8**	**2**	**2**	**15**	**30**	**3**	**32**	**1**	**2**	**2**	**1**	**1**	**.238**	**.347**	**.329**	**.984**
Career total		426	1044	91	238	40	11	6	80	154	14	183	4	17	6	3	3	.228	.328	.305	.981
Cubs total		**273**	**703**	**61**	**167**	**32**	**7**	**6**	**60**	**119**	**12**	**127**	**2**	**9**	**6**	**2**	**2**	**.238**	**.347**	**.329**	**.984**

Bladt, Richard Alan (Rick)

HEIGHT: 6'1" THROWS: RIGHT BATS: RIGHT BORN: 12/9/1946 SANTA CRUZ, CALIFORNIA POSITIONS PLAYED: OF

YEAR	TEAM	GAMES	AB	RUNS	HITS	2B	3B	HR	RBI	BB	IBB	SO	HBP	SH	SF	SB	CS	BA	OBA	SA	FA
1969	**ChC-N**	**10**	**13**	**1**	**2**	**0**	**0**	**0**	**1**	**0**	**0**	**5**	**0**	**0**	**0**	**0**	**0**	**.154**	**.154**	**.154**	**1.000**
1975	NYY-A	52	117	13	26	3	1	1	11	11	0	8	1	3	1	6	2	.222	.292	.291	.973
Career average		31	65	7	14	2	1	1	6	6	0	7	1	2	1	3	1	.215	.280	.277	.976
Cubs average		**10**	**13**	**1**	**2**	**0**	**0**	**0**	**1**	**0**	**0**	**5**	**0**	**0**	**0**	**0**	**0**	**.154**	**.154**	**.154**	**1.000**
Career total		62	130	14	28	3	1	1	12	11	0	13	1	3	1	6	2	.215	.280	.277	.976
Cubs total		**10**	**13**	**1**	**2**	**0**	**0**	**0**	**1**	**0**	**0**	**5**	**0**	**0**	**0**	**0**	**0**	**.154**	**.154**	**.154**	**1.000**

Blair, Clarence Vick (Footsie)

HEIGHT: 6'1" THROWS: RIGHT BATS: LEFT BORN: 7/13/1900 INTERPRISE, OKLAHOMA DIED: 7/1/1982 TEXARKANA, TEXAS POSITIONS PLAYED: 1B, 2B, 3B

YEAR	TEAM	GAMES	AB	RUNS	HITS	2B	3B	HR	RBI	BB	IBB	SO	HBP	SH	SF	SB	CS	BA	OBA	SA	FA
1929	**ChC-N**	**26**	**72**	**10**	**23**	**5**	**0**	**1**	**8**	**3**	**—**	**4**	**0**	**2**	**—**	**1**	**—**	**.319**	**.347**	**.431**	**.972**
1930	**ChC-N**	**134**	**578**	**97**	**158**	**24**	**12**	**6**	**59**	**20**	**—**	**58**	**7**	**5**	**—**	**9**	**—**	**.273**	**.306**	**.388**	**.955**
1931	**ChC-N**	**86**	**240**	**31**	**62**	**19**	**4**	**3**	**29**	**14**	**—**	**26**	**1**	**3**	**—**	**1**	**—**	**.258**	**.302**	**.408**	**.966**
Career average		82	297	46	81	16	5	3	32	12	—	29	3	3	—	4	—	.273	.308	.397	.960
Cubs average		**82**	**297**	**46**	**81**	**16**	**5**	**3**	**32**	**12**	**—**	**29**	**3**	**3**	**—**	**4**	**—**	**.273**	**.308**	**.397**	**.960**
Career total		246	890	138	243	48	16	10	96	37	—	88	8	10	—	11	—	.273	.308	.397	.960
Cubs total		**246**	**890**	**138**	**243**	**48**	**16**	**10**	**96**	**37**	**—**	**88**	**8**	**10**	**—**	**11**	**—**	**.273**	**.308**	**.397**	**.960**

Blauser, Jeffrey Michael (Jeff)
HEIGHT: 6'1" THROWS: RIGHT BATS: RIGHT BORN: 11/8/1965 LOS GATOS, CALIFORNIA POSITIONS PLAYED: 2B, 3B, SS, OF

YEAR	TEAM	GAMES	AB	RUNS	HITS	2B	3B	HR	RBI	BB	IBB	SO	HBP	SH	SF	SB	CS	BA	OBA	SA	FA
1987	Atl-N	51	165	11	40	6	3	2	15	18	1	34	3	1	0	7	3	.242	.328	.352	.963
1988	Atl-N	18	67	7	16	3	1	2	7	2	0	11	1	3	1	0	1	.239	.268	.403	.959
1989	Atl-N	142	456	63	123	24	2	12	46	38	2	101	1	8	4	5	2	.270	.325	.410	.949
1990	Atl-N	115	386	46	104	24	3	8	39	35	1	70	5	3	0	3	5	.269	.338	.409	.966
1991	Atl-N	129	352	49	91	14	3	11	54	54	4	59	2	4	3	5	6	.259	.358	.409	.954
1992	Atl-N	123	343	61	90	19	3	14	46	46	2	82	4	7	3	5	5	.262	.354	.458	.961
1993	Atl-N	161	597	110	182	29	2	15	73	85	0	109	16	5	7	16	6	.305	.401	.436	.970
1994	Atl-N	96	380	56	98	21	4	6	45	38	0	64	5	5	6	1	3	.258	.329	.382	.970
1995	Atl-N	115	431	60	91	16	2	12	31	57	2	107	12	2	2	8	5	.211	.319	.341	.970
1996	Atl-N	83	265	48	65	14	1	10	35	40	3	54	6	0	1	6	0	.245	.356	.419	.926
1997	Atl-N	151	519	90	160	31	4	17	70	70	6	101	20	5	9	5	1	.308	.405	.482	.973
1998	**ChC-N**	**119**	**361**	**49**	**79**	**11**	**3**	**4**	**26**	**60**	**1**	**93**	**8**	**3**	**3**	**2**	**2**	**.219**	**.340**	**.299**	**.965**
1999	**ChC-N**	**104**	**200**	**41**	**48**	**5**	**2**	**9**	**26**	**26**	**0**	**52**	**8**	**2**	**2**	**2**	**2**	**.240**	**.347**	**.420**	**.959**
Career average		108	348	53	91	17	3	9	39	44	2	72	7	4	3	5	3	.262	.354	.406	.962
Cubs average		**112**	**281**	**45**	**64**	**8**	**3**	**7**	**26**	**43**	**1**	**73**	**8**	**3**	**3**	**2**	**2**	**.226**	**.343**	**.342**	**.963**
Career total		1407	4522	691	1187	217	33	122	513	569	22	937	91	48	41	65	41	.262	.354	.406	.962
Cubs total		**223**	**561**	**90**	**127**	**16**	**5**	**13**	**52**	**86**	**1**	**145**	**16**	**5**	**5**	**4**	**4**	**.226**	**.343**	**.342**	**.963**

Block, Seymour (Cy)
HEIGHT: 6'0" THROWS: RIGHT BATS: RIGHT BORN: 5/4/1919 BROOKLYN, NEW YORK POSITIONS PLAYED: 2B, 3B

YEAR	TEAM	GAMES	AB	RUNS	HITS	2B	3B	HR	RBI	BB	IBB	SO	HBP	SH	SF	SB	CS	BA	OBA	SA	FA
1942	**ChC-N**	**9**	**33**	**6**	**12**	**1**	**1**	**0**	**4**	**3**	**—**	**3**	**0**	**0**	**—**	**2**	**—**	**.364**	**.417**	**.455**	**.931**
1945	**ChC-N**	**2**	**7**	**1**	**1**	**0**	**0**	**0**	**1**	**0**	**—**	**0**	**0**	**0**	**—**	**0**	**—**	**.143**	**.143**	**.143**	**1.000**
1946	**ChC-N**	**6**	**13**	**2**	**3**	**0**	**0**	**0**	**0**	**4**	**—**	**0**	**0**	**0**	**—**	**0**	**—**	**.231**	**.412**	**.231**	**1.000**
Career average		6	18	3	5	0	0	0	2	2	—	1	0	0	—	1	—	.302	.383	.358	.960
Cubs average		**6**	**18**	**3**	**5**	**0**	**0**	**0**	**2**	**2**	**—**	**1**	**0**	**0**	**—**	**1**	**—**	**.302**	**.383**	**.358**	**.960**
Career total		17	53	9	16	1	1	0	5	7	—	3	0	0	—	2	—	.302	.383	.358	.960
Cubs total		**17**	**53**	**9**	**16**	**1**	**1**	**0**	**5**	**7**	**—**	**3**	**0**	**0**	**—**	**2**	**—**	**.302**	**.383**	**.358**	**.960**

Bobb, Mark Randall (Randy)
HEIGHT: 6'1" THROWS: RIGHT BATS: RIGHT BORN: 1/1/1948 LOS ANGELES, CALIFORNIA DIED: 6/13/1982 CARNELIAN BAY, CALIFORNIA
POSITIONS PLAYED: C

YEAR	TEAM	GAMES	AB	RUNS	HITS	2B	3B	HR	RBI	BB	IBB	SO	HBP	SH	SF	SB	CS	BA	OBA	SA	FA
1968	**ChC-N**	**7**	**8**	**0**	**1**	**0**	**0**	**0**	**0**	**1**	**0**	**2**	**0**	**0**	**0**	**0**	**0**	**.125**	**.222**	**.125**	**1.000**
1969	**ChC-N**	**3**	**2**	**0**	**0**	**0**	**0**	**0**	**0**	**0**	**0**	**1**	**0**	**0**	**0**	**0**	**0**	**.000**	**.000**	**.000**	**1.000**
Career average		5	5	0	1	0	0	0	0	1	0	2	0	0	0	0	0	.100	.182	.100	1.000
Cubs average		**5**	**5**	**0**	**1**	**0**	**0**	**0**	**0**	**1**	**0**	**2**	**0**	**0**	**0**	**0**	**0**	**.100**	**.182**	**.100**	**1.000**
Career total		10	10	0	1	0	0	0	0	1	0	3	0	0	0	0	0	.100	.182	.100	1.000
Cubs total		**10**	**10**	**0**	**1**	**0**	**0**	**0**	**0**	**1**	**0**	**3**	**0**	**0**	**0**	**0**	**0**	**.100**	**.182**	**.100**	**1.000**

Boccabella, John Dominic
HEIGHT: 6'1" THROWS: RIGHT BATS: RIGHT BORN: 6/29/1941 SAN FRANCISCO, CALIFORNIA POSITIONS PLAYED: C, 1B, 3B, OF

YEAR	TEAM	GAMES	AB	RUNS	HITS	2B	3B	HR	RBI	BB	IBB	SO	HBP	SH	SF	SB	CS	BA	OBA	SA	FA
1963	**ChC-N**	**24**	**74**	**7**	**14**	**4**	**1**	**1**	**5**	**6**	**0**	**21**	**0**	**0**	**1**	**0**	**1**	**.189**	**.247**	**.311**	**.996**
1964	**ChC-N**	**9**	**23**	**4**	**9**	**2**	**1**	**0**	**6**	**0**	**0**	**3**	**0**	**0**	**0**	**0**	**0**	**.391**	**.391**	**.565**	**1.000**
1965	**ChC-N**	**6**	**12**	**2**	**4**	**0**	**0**	**2**	**4**	**1**	**0**	**2**	**0**	**0**	**0**	**0**	**0**	**.333**	**.385**	**.833**	**.929**
1966	**ChC-N**	**75**	**206**	**22**	**47**	**9**	**0**	**6**	**25**	**14**	**1**	**39**	**0**	**6**	**3**	**0**	**1**	**.228**	**.274**	**.359**	**.996**
1967	**ChC-N**	**25**	**35**	**0**	**6**	**1**	**1**	**0**	**8**	**3**	**1**	**7**	**1**	**0**	**1**	**0**	**0**	**.171**	**.250**	**.257**	**1.000**
1968	**ChC-N**	**7**	**14**	**0**	**1**	**0**	**0**	**0**	**1**	**2**	**0**	**2**	**0**	**0**	**1**	**0**	**0**	**.071**	**.176**	**.071**	**1.000**
1969	Mon-N	40	86	4	9	2	0	1	6	6	1	30	1	0	1	1	0	.105	.170	.163	1.000
1970	Mon-N	61	145	18	39	3	1	5	17	11	2	24	0	0	0	0	1	.269	.321	.407	.992
1971	Mon-N	74	177	15	39	11	0	3	15	14	2	26	1	1	2	0	1	.220	.278	.333	.989
1972	Mon-N	83	207	14	47	8	1	1	10	9	3	29	1	2	3	1	2	.227	.259	.290	.985
1973	Mon-N	118	403	25	94	13	0	7	46	26	8	57	1	7	3	1	1	.233	.279	.318	.980
1974	SF-N	29	80	6	11	3	0	0	5	4	2	6	0	0	1	0	0	.138	.176	.175	.991

(continued)

(Boccabella, continued)

	GAMES	AB	RUNS	HITS	2B	3B	HR	RBI	BB	IBB	SO	HBP	SH	SF	SB	CS	BA	OBA	SA	FA
Career average	46	122	10	27	5	0	2	12	8	2	21	0	1	1	0	1	.219	.267	.317	.989
Cubs average	**24**	**61**	**6**	**14**	**3**	**1**	**2**	**8**	**4**	**0**	**12**	**0**	**1**	**1**	**0**	**0**	**.223**	**.272**	**.357**	**.995**
Career total	551	1462	117	320	56	5	26	148	96	20	246	5	16	16	3	7	.219	.267	.317	.989
Cubs total	**146**	**364**	**35**	**81**	**16**	**3**	**9**	**49**	**26**	**2**	**74**	**1**	**6**	**6**	**0**	**2**	**.223**	**.272**	**.357**	**.995**

Bolger, James Cyril (Jim *or* Dutch)

HEIGHT: 6'2"   THROWS: RIGHT   BATS: RIGHT   BORN: 2/23/1932 CINCINNATI, OHIO   POSITIONS PLAYED: 3B, OF

YEAR	TEAM	GAMES	AB	RUNS	HITS	2B	3B	HR	RBI	BB	IBB	SO	HBP	SH	SF	SB	CS	BA	OBA	SA	FA
1950	Cin-N	2	1	0	0	0	0	0	0	0	—	0	0	0	—	0	—	.000	.000	.000	—
1951	Cin-N	2	0	1	0	0	0	0	0	0	—	0	0	0	—	1	0	—	—	—	—
1954	Cin-N	5	3	1	1	0	0	0	0	0	—	1	0	0	0	0	0	.333	.333	.333	—
1955	**ChC-N**	64	160	19	33	5	4	0	7	9	1	17	2	2	0	2	2	.206	.257	.288	.955
1957	**ChC-N**	112	273	28	75	4	1	5	29	10	1	36	3	1	4	0	1	.275	.303	.352	.976
1958	**ChC-N**	84	120	15	27	4	1	1	11	9	0	20	1	1	0	0	1	.225	.285	.300	.940
1959	Cle-A	8	7	0	0	0	0	0	0	1	1	1	0	0	0	0	0	.000	.125	.000	—
1959	Phi-N	35	48	1	4	1	0	0	1	3	1	8	0	0	1	0	0	.083	.135	.104	.938
Career average	45	87	9	20	2	1	1	7	5	0	12	1	1	1	0	1	.229	.272	.301	.961
Cubs average	**87**	**184**	**21**	**45**	**4**	**2**	**2**	**16**	**9**	**1**	**24**	**2**	**1**	**1**	**1**	**1**	**.244**	**.286**	**.322**	**.963**
Career total	312	612	65	140	14	6	6	48	32	3	83	6	4	5	3	4	.229	.272	.301	.961
Cubs total	**260**	**553**	**62**	**135**	**13**	**6**	**6**	**47**	**28**	**2**	**73**	**6**	**4**	**4**	**2**	**4**	**.244**	**.286**	**.322**	**.963**

Bonds, Bobby Lee

HEIGHT: 6'1"   THROWS: RIGHT   BATS: RIGHT   BORN: 3/15/1946 RIVERSIDE, CALIFORNIA   POSITIONS PLAYED: OF

YEAR	TEAM	GAMES	AB	RUNS	HITS	2B	3B	HR	RBI	BB	IBB	SO	HBP	SH	SF	SB	CS	BA	OBA	SA	FA
1968	SF-N	81	307	55	78	10	5	9	35	38	0	84	1	1	2	16	7	.254	.336	.407	.978
1969	SF-N	158	622	120	161	25	6	32	90	81	3	187	10	3	4	45	4	.259	.351	.473	.978
1970	SF-N	157	663	134	200	36	10	26	78	77	7	189	2	1	2	48	10	.302	.375	.504	.969
1971	SF-N	155	619	110	178	32	4	33	102	62	6	137	5	0	5	26	8	.288	.355	.512	.994
1972	SF-N	153	626	118	162	29	5	26	80	60	4	137	5	1	5	44	6	.259	.326	.446	.978
1973	SF-N	160	643	131	182	34	4	39	96	87	9	148	4	0	4	43	17	.283	.370	.530	.970
1974	SF-N	150	567	97	145	22	8	21	71	95	8	134	4	0	4	41	11	.256	.364	.434	.966
1975	NYY-A	145	529	93	143	26	3	32	85	89	8	137	3	0	5	30	17	.270	.375	.512	.987
1976	Cal-A	99	378	48	100	10	3	10	54	41	6	90	3	0	5	30	15	.265	.337	.386	.977
1977	Cal-A	158	592	103	156	23	9	37	115	74	5	141	2	1	10	41	18	.264	.342	.520	.956
1978	CWS-A	26	90	8	19	4	0	2	8	10	1	10	0	1	1	6	2	.278	.347	.389	.956
1978	Tex-A	130	475	85	126	15	4	29	82	69	6	110	2	2	7	37	20	.265	.356	.497	.970
1979	Cle-A	146	538	93	148	24	1	25	85	74	4	135	8	4	7	34	23	.275	.367	.463	.979
1980	StL-N	86	231	37	47	5	3	5	24	33	3	74	2	1	3	15	5	.203	.305	.316	.967
1981	**ChC-N**	45	163	26	35	7	1	6	19	24	5	44	2	1	0	5	6	.215	.323	.380	.982
Career average	132	503	90	135	22	5	24	73	65	5	126	4	1	5	33	12	.268	.353	.471	.977
Cubs average	**45**	**163**	**26**	**35**	**7**	**1**	**6**	**19**	**24**	**5**	**44**	**2**	**1**	**0**	**5**	**6**	**.215**	**.323**	**.380**	**.982**
Career total	1849	7043	1258	1886	302	66	332	1024	914	75	1757	53	16	64	461	169	.268	.353	.471	.977
Cubs total	**45**	**163**	**26**	**35**	**7**	**1**	**6**	**19**	**24**	**5**	**44**	**2**	**1**	**0**	**5**	**6**	**.215**	**.323**	**.380**	**.982**

Bonura, Henry John (Zeke *or* Bananas)

HEIGHT: 6'0"   THROWS: RIGHT   BATS: RIGHT   BORN: 9/20/1908 NEW ORLEANS, LOUISIANA   DIED: 3/9/1987 NEW ORLEANS, LOUISIANA
POSITIONS PLAYED: 1B

YEAR	TEAM	GAMES	AB	RUNS	HITS	2B	3B	HR	RBI	BB	IBB	SO	HBP	SH	SF	SB	CS	BA	OBA	SA	FA
1934	CWS-A	127	510	86	154	35	4	27	110	64	—	31	0	1	—	0	2	.302	.380	.545	.996
1935	CWS-A	138	550	107	162	34	4	21	92	57	—	28	3	1	—	4	0	.295	.364	.485	.994
1936	CWS-A	148	587	120	194	39	7	12	138	94	—	29	4	2	—	4	2	.330	.426	.482	.996
1937	CWS-A	116	447	79	154	41	2	19	100	49	—	24	2	4	—	5	1	.345	.412	.573	.989
1938	Was-A	137	540	72	156	27	3	22	114	44	—	29	3	2	—	2	2	.289	.346	.472	.993
1939	NYG-N	123	455	75	146	26	6	11	85	46	—	22	4	12	—	1	—	.321	.388	.477	.992
1940	Was-A	79	311	41	85	16	3	3	45	40	—	13	1	0	—	2	0	.273	.358	.373	.982
1940	**ChC-N**	49	182	20	48	14	0	4	20	10	—	4	0	1	—	1	—	.264	.302	.407	.991
Career average	131	512	86	157	33	4	17	101	58	—	26	2	3	—	3	1	.307	.380	.487	.992
Cubs average	**49**	**182**	**20**	**48**	**14**	**0**	**4**	**20**	**10**	**—**	**4**	**0**	**1**	**—**	**1**	**0**	**.264**	**.302**	**.407**	**.991**
Career total	917	3582	600	1099	232	29	119	704	404	—	180	17	23	—	19	7	.307	.380	.487	.992
Cubs total	**49**	**182**	**20**	**48**	**14**	**0**	**4**	**20**	**10**	**—**	**4**	**0**	**1**	**—**	**1**	**0**	**.264**	**.302**	**.407**	**.991**

Borkowski, Robert Vilarian (Bob)
HEIGHT: 6'0" THROWS: RIGHT BATS: RIGHT BORN: 1/27/1926 DAYTON, OHIO POSITIONS PLAYED: 1B, OF

YEAR	TEAM	GAMES	AB	RUNS	HITS	2B	3B	HR	RBI	BB	IBB	SO	HBP	SH	SF	SB	CS	BA	OBA	SA	FA
1950	ChC-N	85	256	27	70	7	4	4	29	16	—	30	1	2	—	1	—	.273	.319	.379	.975
1951	ChC-N	58	89	9	14	1	0	0	10	3	—	16	0	1	—	0	0	.157	.185	.169	.933
1952	Cin-N	126	377	42	95	11	4	4	24	26	—	53	0	1	—	1	3	.252	.300	.334	.989
1953	Cin-N	94	249	32	67	11	1	7	29	21	—	41	1	2	—	0	1	.269	.328	.406	.975
1954	Cin-N	73	162	13	43	12	1	1	19	8	—	18	1	1	3	0	2	.265	.299	.370	1.000
1955	Cin-N	25	18	1	3	1	0	0	1	1	0	2	0	1	0	0	0	.167	.211	.222	.923
1955	Bro-N	9	19	2	2	0	0	0	0	1	0	6	0	0	0	0	0	.105	.150	.105	1.000
Career average		78	195	21	49	7	2	3	19	13	0	28	1	1	1	0	1	.251	.298	.346	.980
Cubs average		72	173	18	42	4	2	2	20	10	—	23	1	2	—	1	0	.243	.285	.325	.966
Career total		470	1170	126	294	43	10	16	112	76	0	166	3	8	3	2	6	.251	.298	.346	.980
Cubs total		143	345	36	84	8	4	4	39	19	—	46	1	3	—	1	0	.243	.285	.325	.966

Boros, Stephen (Steve)
HEIGHT: 6'0" THROWS: RIGHT BATS: RIGHT BORN: 9/3/1936 FLINT, MICHIGAN POSITIONS PLAYED: 1B, 2B, 3B, SS, OF

YEAR	TEAM	GAMES	AB	RUNS	HITS	2B	3B	HR	RBI	BB	IBB	SO	HBP	SH	SF	SB	CS	BA	OBA	SA	FA
1957	Det-A	24	41	4	6	1	0	0	2	1	0	8	0	0	0	0	0	.146	.167	.171	.921
1958	Det-A	6	2	0	0	0	0	0	0	0	0	0	0	0	0	0	0	.000	.000	.000	1.000
1961	Det-A	116	396	51	107	18	2	5	62	68	2	42	8	6	7	4	2	.270	.382	.364	.953
1962	Det-A	116	356	46	81	14	1	16	47	53	3	62	3	3	2	3	1	.228	.331	.407	.930
1963	ChC-N	41	90	9	19	5	1	3	7	12	0	19	0	2	0	0	2	.211	.304	.389	.971
1964	Cin-N	117	370	31	95	12	3	2	31	47	14	43	2	2	2	4	1	.257	.342	.322	.961
1965	Cin-N	2	0	0	0	0	0	0	0	0	0	0	0	0	0	0	0	—	—	—	1.000
Career average		60	179	20	44	7	1	4	21	26	3	25	2	2	2	2	1	.245	.344	.359	.951
Cubs average		41	90	9	19	5	1	3	7	12	0	19	0	2	0	0	2	.211	.304	.389	.971
Career total		422	1255	141	308	50	7	26	149	181	19	174	13	13	11	11	6	.245	.344	.359	.951
Cubs total		41	90	9	19	5	1	3	7	12	0	19	0	2	0	0	2	.211	.304	.389	.971

Bosley, Thaddis (Thad)
HEIGHT: 6'3" THROWS: LEFT BATS: LEFT BORN: 9/17/1956 OCEANSIDE, CALIFORNIA POSITIONS PLAYED: OF

YEAR	TEAM	GAMES	AB	RUNS	HITS	2B	3B	HR	RBI	BB	IBB	SO	HBP	SH	SF	SB	CS	BA	OBA	SA	FA
1977	Cal-A	58	212	19	63	10	2	0	19	16	0	32	1	4	2	5	4	.297	.346	.363	.963
1978	CWS-A	66	219	25	59	5	1	2	13	13	1	32	0	2	2	12	11	.269	.308	.329	.975
1979	CWS-A	36	77	13	24	1	1	1	8	9	0	14	0	0	0	4	1	.312	.384	.390	.967
1980	CWS-A	70	147	12	33	2	0	2	14	10	3	27	0	4	1	3	2	.224	.272	.279	.958
1981	Mil-A	42	105	11	24	2	0	0	3	6	0	13	0	1	0	2	1	.229	.270	.248	.966
1982	Sea-A	22	46	3	8	1	0	0	2	4	0	8	0	0	0	3	1	.174	.240	.196	1.000
1983	ChC-N	43	72	12	21	4	1	2	12	10	1	12	0	0	1	1	1	.292	.373	.458	1.000
1984	ChC-N	55	98	17	29	2	2	2	14	13	2	22	0	0	1	5	1	.296	.375	.418	.976
1985	ChC-N	108	180	25	59	6	3	7	27	20	1	29	0	0	2	5	1	.328	.391	.511	.988
1986	ChC-N	87	120	15	33	4	1	1	9	18	3	24	0	1	0	3	0	.275	.370	.350	.969
1987	KC-A	80	140	13	39	6	1	1	16	9	2	26	0	1	2	0	0	.279	.318	.357	.966
1988	KC-A	15	21	1	4	0	0	0	2	2	1	6	0	1	1	0	0	.190	.250	.190	1.000
1988	Cal-A	35	75	9	21	5	0	0	7	6	0	12	0	1	3	1	1	.280	.321	.347	.965
1989	Tex-A	37	40	5	9	2	0	1	9	3	0	11	0	0	1	2	0	.225	.273	.350	1.000
1990	Tex-A	30	29	3	4	0	0	1	3	4	1	7	0	0	0	1	0	.138	.242	.241	1.000
Career average		56	113	13	31	4	1	1	11	10	1	20	0	1	1	3	2	.272	.330	.357	.972
Cubs average		73	118	17	36	4	2	3	16	15	2	22	0	0	1	4	1	.302	.379	.443	.984
Career total		784	1581	183	430	50	12	20	158	143	15	275	1	14	16	47	24	.272	.330	.357	.972
Cubs total		293	470	69	142	16	7	12	62	61	7	87	0	1	4	14	3	.302	.379	.443	.984

Bottarini, John Charles

HEIGHT: 6'0" THROWS: RIGHT BATS: RIGHT BORN: 9/14/1908 CROCKETT, CALIFORNIA DIED: 10/8/1976 JEMEZ SPRINGS, NEW MEXICO
POSITIONS PLAYED: C, OF

YEAR	TEAM	GAMES	AB	RUNS	HITS	2B	3B	HR	RBI	BB	IBB	SO	HBP	SH	SF	SB	CS	BA	OBA	SA	FA
1937	ChC-N	26	40	3	11	3	0	1	7	5	—	10	1	0	—	0	—	.275	.370	.425	1.000
Career average		26	40	3	11	3	0	1	7	5	—	10	1	0	—	0	—	.275	.370	.425	1.000
Cubs average		**26**	**40**	**3**	**11**	**3**	**0**	**1**	**7**	**5**	**—**	**10**	**1**	**0**	**—**	**0**	**—**	**.275**	**.370**	**.425**	**1.000**
Career total		26	40	3	11	3	0	1	7	5	—	10	1	0	—	0	—	.275	.370	.425	1.000
Cubs total		**26**	**40**	**3**	**11**	**3**	**0**	**1**	**7**	**5**	**—**	**10**	**1**	**0**	**—**	**0**	**—**	**.275**	**.370**	**.425**	**1.000**

Bouchee, Edward Francis (Ed)

HEIGHT: 6'0" THROWS: LEFT BATS: LEFT BORN: 3/7/1933 LIVINGSTON, MONTANA POSITIONS PLAYED: 1B

YEAR	TEAM	GAMES	AB	RUNS	HITS	2B	3B	HR	RBI	BB	IBB	SO	HBP	SH	SF	SB	CS	BA	OBA	SA	FA
1956	Phi-N	9	22	0	6	2	0	0	1	5	0	6	0	0	0	0	0	.273	.407	.364	1.000
1957	Phi-N	154	574	78	168	35	8	17	76	84	6	91	14	0	3	1	0	.293	.394	.470	.988
1958	Phi-N	89	334	55	86	19	5	9	39	51	4	74	0	3	1	1	0	.257	.355	.425	.993
1959	Phi-N	136	499	75	142	29	4	15	74	70	4	74	5	2	5	0	4	.285	.375	.449	.986
1960	Phi-N	22	65	1	17	4	0	0	8	9	2	11	1	0	1	0	0	.262	.355	.323	.994
1960	**ChC-N**	98	299	33	71	11	1	5	44	45	4	51	2	0	6	2	0	.237	.335	.331	.991
1961	**ChC-N**	112	319	49	79	12	3	12	38	58	7	77	5	4	1	1	4	.248	.371	.417	.983
1962	NYM-N	50	87	7	14	2	0	3	10	18	2	17	0	0	1	0	0	.161	.302	.287	.976
Career average		96	314	43	83	16	3	9	41	49	4	57	4	1	3	1	1	.265	.368	.419	.988
Cubs average		**105**	**309**	**41**	**75**	**12**	**2**	**9**	**41**	**52**	**6**	**64**	**4**	**2**	**4**	**2**	**2**	**.243**	**.354**	**.375**	**.987**
Career total		670	2199	298	583	114	21	61	290	340	29	401	27	9	18	5	8	.265	.368	.419	.988
Cubs total		**210**	**618**	**82**	**150**	**23**	**4**	**17**	**82**	**103**	**11**	**128**	**7**	**4**	**7**	**3**	**4**	**.243**	**.354**	**.375**	**.987**

Bourque, Patrick Daniel (Pat)

HEIGHT: 6'0" THROWS: LEFT BATS: LEFT BORN: 3/23/1947 WORCESTER, MASSACHUSETTS POSITIONS PLAYED: 1B

YEAR	TEAM	GAMES	AB	RUNS	HITS	2B	3B	HR	RBI	BB	IBB	SO	HBP	SH	SF	SB	CS	BA	OBA	SA	FA
1971	**ChC-N**	14	37	3	7	0	1	1	3	3	0	9	0	1	0	0	0	.189	.250	.324	.957
1972	**ChC-N**	11	27	3	7	1	0	0	5	2	0	2	0	0	0	0	0	.259	.310	.296	1.000
1973	**ChC-N**	57	139	11	29	6	0	7	20	16	1	21	2	0	1	1	1	.209	.297	.403	.986
1973	Oak-A	23	42	8	8	4	1	2	9	15	2	10	0	0	2	0	0	.190	.390	.476	1.000
1974	Oak-A	73	96	6	22	4	0	1	16	15	1	20	0	0	2	0	2	.229	.327	.302	.988
1974	Min-A	23	64	5	14	2	0	1	8	7	0	11	0	0	0	0	0	.219	.296	.297	.987
Career average		50	101	9	22	4	1	3	15	15	1	18	1	0	1	0	1	.215	.313	.356	.985
Cubs average		**27**	**68**	**6**	**14**	**2**	**0**	**3**	**9**	**7**	**0**	**11**	**1**	**0**	**0**	**0**	**0**	**.212**	**.291**	**.374**	**.983**
Career total		201	405	36	87	17	2	12	61	58	4	73	2	1	5	1	3	.215	.313	.356	.985
Cubs total		**82**	**203**	**17**	**43**	**7**	**1**	**8**	**28**	**21**	**1**	**32**	**2**	**1**	**1**	**1**	**1**	**.212**	**.291**	**.374**	**.983**

Bowa, Lawrence Robert (Larry)

HEIGHT: 5'10" THROWS: RIGHT BATS: BOTH BORN: 12/6/1945 SACRAMENTO, CALIFORNIA POSITIONS PLAYED: 2B, SS

YEAR	TEAM	GAMES	AB	RUNS	HITS	2B	3B	HR	RBI	BB	IBB	SO	HBP	SH	SF	SB	CS	BA	OBA	SA	FA
1970	Phi-N	145	547	50	137	17	6	0	34	21	1	48	0	6	3	24	13	.250	.277	.303	.979
1971	Phi-N	159	650	74	162	18	5	0	25	36	2	61	5	4	1	28	11	.249	.293	.292	.987
1972	Phi-N	152	579	67	145	11	13	1	31	32	1	51	2	18	2	17	9	.250	.291	.320	.987
1973	Phi-N	122	446	42	94	11	3	0	23	24	8	31	1	4	1	10	6	.211	.252	.249	.979
1974	Phi-N	162	669	97	184	19	10	1	36	23	0	52	1	20	4	39	11	.275	.298	.338	.984
1975	Phi-N	136	583	79	178	18	9	2	38	24	0	32	2	17	2	24	6	.305	.334	.377	.962
1976	Phi-N	156	624	71	155	15	9	0	49	32	3	31	0	11	5	30	8	.248	.283	.301	.975
1977	Phi-N	154	624	93	175	19	3	4	41	32	2	32	0	13	6	32	3	.280	.313	.340	.983
1978	Phi-N	156	654	78	192	31	5	3	43	24	1	40	1	11	2	27	5	.294	.319	.370	.986
1979	Phi-N	147	539	74	130	17	11	0	31	61	5	32	1	12	6	20	9	.241	.316	.314	.991
1980	Phi-N	147	540	57	144	16	4	2	39	24	7	28	3	7	3	21	6	.267	.300	.322	.975
1981	Phi-N	103	360	34	102	14	3	0	31	26	2	17	0	4	1	16	7	.283	.331	.339	.975
1982	**ChC-N**	142	499	50	123	15	7	0	29	39	5	38	1	9	1	8	3	.246	.302	.305	.973
1983	**ChC-N**	147	499	73	133	20	5	2	43	35	1	30	0	6	4	7	3	.267	.312	.339	.984

(continued)

(continued)

YEAR	TEAM	GAMES	AB	RUNS	HITS	2B	3B	HR	RBI	BB	IBB	SO	HBP	SH	SF	SB	CS	BA	OBA	SA	FA
1984	ChC-N	133	391	33	87	14	2	0	17	28	5	24	0	3	1	10	4	.223	.274	.269	.974
1985	ChC-N	72	195	13	48	6	4	0	13	11	2	20	0	5	1	5	1	.246	.285	.318	.970
1985	NYM-N	14	19	2	2	1	0	0	2	2	0	2	0	1	0	0	0	.105	.190	.158	.939
Career average		140	526	62	137	16	6	1	33	30	3	36	1	9	3	20	7	.260	.300	.320	.980
Cubs average		**124**	**396**	**42**	**98**	**14**	**5**	**1**	**26**	**28**	**3**	**28**	**0**	**6**	**2**	**8**	**3**	**.247**	**.296**	**.308**	**.976**
Career total		2247	8418	987	2191	262	99	15	525	474	45	569	17	151	43	318	105	.260	.300	.320	.980
Cubs total		**494**	**1584**	**169**	**391**	**55**	**18**	**2**	**102**	**113**	**13**	**112**	**1**	**23**	**7**	**30**	**11**	**.247**	**.296**	**.308**	**.976**

Bowman, William G. (Bill)

HEIGHT: 5'11" THROWS: — BATS: — BORN: 1869 CHICAGO, ILLINOIS DIED: 4/1918 POSITIONS PLAYED: C

YEAR	TEAM	GAMES	AB	RUNS	HITS	2B	3B	HR	RBI	BB	IBB	SO	HBP	SH	SF	SB	CS	BA	OBA	SA	FA
1891	ChN-N	15	45	2	4	1	0	0	5	5	—	9	1	—	—	0	—	.089	.196	.111	.915
Career average		15	45	2	4	1	0	0	5	5	—	9	1	—	—	0	—	.089	.196	.111	.915
Cubs average		**15**	**45**	**2**	**4**	**1**	**0**	**0**	**5**	**5**	**—**	**9**	**1**	**—**	**—**	**0**	**—**	**.089**	**.196**	**.111**	**.915**
Career total		15	45	2	4	1	0	0	5	5	—	9	1	—	—	0	—	.089	.196	.111	.915
Cubs total		**15**	**45**	**2**	**4**	**1**	**0**	**0**	**5**	**5**	**—**	**9**	**1**	**—**	**—**	**0**	**—**	**.089**	**.196**	**.111**	**.915**

Bradley, William Joseph (Bill)

HEIGHT: 6'0" THROWS: RIGHT BATS: RIGHT BORN: 2/13/1878 CLEVELAND, OHIO DIED: 3/11/1954 CLEVELAND, OHIO POSITIONS PLAYED: P, 1B, 2B, 3B, SS

YEAR	TEAM	GAMES	AB	RUNS	HITS	2B	3B	HR	RBI	BB	IBB	SO	HBP	SH	SF	SB	CS	BA	OBA	SA	FA
1899	ChN-N	35	129	26	40	6	1	2	18	12	—	—	2	1	—	4	—	.310	.378	.419	.861
1900	ChN-N	122	444	63	125	21	8	5	49	27	—	—	5	7	—	14	—	.282	.330	.399	.904
1901	Cle-A	133	516	95	151	28	13	1	55	26	—	—	8	1	—	15	—	.293	.336	.403	.930
1902	Cle-A	137	550	104	187	39	12	11	77	27	—	—	4	16	—	11	—	.340	.375	.515	.923
1903	Cle-A	136	536	101	168	36	22	6	68	25	—	—	3	23	—	21	—	.313	.348	.496	.924
1904	Cle-A	154	609	94	183	32	8	6	83	26	—	—	5	27	—	23	—	.300	.334	.409	.955
1905	Cle-A	146	541	63	145	34	6	0	51	27	—	—	15	21	—	22	—	.268	.321	.353	.945
1906	Cle-A	82	302	32	83	16	2	2	25	18	—	—	4	16	—	13	—	.275	.324	.361	.966
1907	Cle-A	139	498	48	111	20	1	0	34	35	—	—	9	46	—	20	—	.223	.286	.267	.938
1908	Cle-A	148	548	70	133	24	7	1	46	29	—	—	13	60	—	18	—	.243	.297	.318	.942
1909	Cle-A	95	334	30	62	6	3	0	22	19	—	—	3	20	—	8	—	.186	.236	.222	.957
1910	Cle-A	61	214	12	42	3	0	0	12	10	—	—	1	8	—	6	—	.196	.236	.210	.956
1914	Bro-F	7	6	1	3	1	0	0	3	0	—	—	0	0	—	0	—	.500	.500	.667	—
1915	KC-F	66	203	15	38	9	1	0	9	9	—	18	1	7	—	6	—	.187	.225	.241	.949
Career average		104	388	54	105	20	6	2	39	21	—	1	5	18	—	13	—	.271	.317	.371	.934
Cubs average		**79**	**287**	**45**	**83**	**14**	**5**	**4**	**34**	**20**	**—**	**—**	**4**	**4**	**—**	**9**	**—**	**.288**	**.341**	**.403**	**.896**
Career total		1461	5430	754	1471	275	84	34	552	290	—	18	73	253	—	181	—	.271	.317	.371	.934
Cubs total		**157**	**573**	**89**	**165**	**27**	**9**	**7**	**67**	**39**	**—**	**—**	**7**	**8**	**—**	**18**	**—**	**.288**	**.341**	**.403**	**.896**

Bransfield, William Edward (Kitty)

HEIGHT: 5'11" THROWS: RIGHT BATS: RIGHT BORN: 1/7/1875 WORCESTER, MASSACHUSETTS DIED: 5/1/1947 WORCESTER, MASSACHUSETTS POSITIONS PLAYED: C, 1B

YEAR	TEAM	GAMES	AB	RUNS	HITS	2B	3B	HR	RBI	BB	IBB	SO	HBP	SH	SF	SB	CS	BA	OBA	SA	FA
1898	Bos-N	5	9	2	2	0	1	0	1	0	—	—	0	0	—	0	—	.222	.222	.444	.923
1901	Pit-N	139	566	92	167	26	16	0	91	29	—	—	5	9	—	23	—	.295	.335	.398	.981
1902	Pit-N	102	413	49	126	21	8	0	69	17	—	—	2	10	—	23	—	.305	.336	.395	.984
1903	Pit-N	127	505	69	134	23	7	2	57	33	—	—	3	12	—	13	—	.265	.314	.350	.981
1904	Pit-N	139	520	47	116	17	9	0	60	22	—	—	3	19	—	11	—	.223	.259	.290	.981
1905	Phi-N	151	580	55	150	23	9	3	76	27	—	—	2	18	—	27	—	.259	.294	.345	.985
1906	Phi-N	140	524	47	144	28	5	1	60	16	—	—	3	13	—	12	—	.275	.300	.353	.980
1907	Phi-N	94	348	25	81	15	2	0	38	14	—	—	0	9	—	8	—	.233	.262	.287	.978
1908	Phi-N	144	527	53	160	25	7	3	71	23	—	—	2	16	—	30	—	.304	.335	.395	.986
1909	Phi-N	140	527	47	154	27	6	1	59	18	—	—	3	22	—	17	—	.292	.319	.372	.989
1910	Phi-N	123	427	39	102	17	4	3	52	20	—	34	1	13	—	10	—	.239	.275	.319	.982
1911	Phi-N	23	43	4	11	1	1	0	3	0	—	5	0	1	—	1	—	.256	.256	.326	.987
1911	ChC-N	3	10	0	4	2	0	0	0	2	—	2	0	0	—	0	—	.400	.500	.600	1.000
Career average		111	417	44	113	19	6	1	53	18	—	3	2	12	—	15	—	.270	.304	.353	.983
Cubs average		**3**	**10**	**0**	**4**	**2**	**0**	**0**	**0**	**2**	**—**	**2**	**0**	**0**	**—**	**0**	**—**	**.400**	**.500**	**.600**	**1.000**
Career total		1330	4999	529	1351	225	75	13	637	221	—	41	24	142	—	175	—	.270	.304	.353	.983
Cubs total		**3**	**10**	**0**	**4**	**2**	**0**	**0**	**0**	**2**	**—**	**2**	**0**	**0**	**—**	**0**	**—**	**.400**	**.500**	**.600**	**1.000**

Breeden, Danny Richard
HEIGHT: 5'11"   THROWS: RIGHT   BATS: RIGHT   BORN: 6/27/1942 ALBANY, GEORGIA   POSITIONS PLAYED: C

YEAR	TEAM	GAMES	AB	RUNS	HITS	2B	3B	HR	RBI	BB	IBB	SO	HBP	SH	SF	SB	CS	BA	OBA	SA	FA
1969	Cin-N	3	8	0	1	0	0	0	1	0	0	3	0	3	0	0	0	.125	.125	.125	.941
1971	**ChC-N**	**25**	**65**	**3**	**10**	**1**	**0**	**0**	**4**	**9**	**0**	**18**	**1**	**3**	**1**	**0**	**0**	**.154**	**.263**	**.169**	**.975**
Career average		14	37	2	6	1	0	0	3	5	0	11	1	3	1	0	0	.151	.250	.164	.972
Cubs average		**25**	**65**	**3**	**10**	**1**	**0**	**0**	**4**	**9**	**0**	**18**	**1**	**3**	**1**	**0**	**0**	**.154**	**.263**	**.169**	**.975**
Career total		28	73	3	11	1	0	0	5	9	0	21	1	6	1	0	0	.151	.250	.164	.972
Cubs total		**25**	**65**	**3**	**10**	**1**	**0**	**0**	**4**	**9**	**0**	**18**	**1**	**3**	**1**	**0**	**0**	**.154**	**.263**	**.169**	**.975**

Breeden, Harold Noel (Hal)
HEIGHT: 6'2"   THROWS: LEFT   BATS: RIGHT   BORN: 6/28/1944 ALBANY, GEORGIA   POSITIONS PLAYED: 1B, OF

YEAR	TEAM	GAMES	AB	RUNS	HITS	2B	3B	HR	RBI	BB	IBB	SO	HBP	SH	SF	SB	CS	BA	OBA	SA	FA
1971	**ChC-N**	**23**	**36**	**1**	**5**	**1**	**0**	**1**	**2**	**2**	**0**	**7**	**0**	**1**	**0**	**0**	**0**	**.139**	**.184**	**.250**	**.982**
1972	Mon-N	42	87	6	20	2	0	3	10	7	1	15	0	0	2	0	0	.230	.281	.356	.994
1973	Mon-N	105	258	36	71	10	6	15	43	29	3	45	2	1	0	0	1	.275	.353	.535	.991
1974	Mon-N	79	190	14	47	13	0	2	20	24	0	35	0	0	1	0	1	.247	.330	.347	.987
1975	Mon-N	24	37	4	5	2	0	0	1	7	3	5	0	0	0	0	0	.135	.273	.189	.989
Career average		55	122	12	30	6	1	4	15	14	1	21	0	0	1	0	0	.243	.321	.413	.990
Cubs average		**23**	**36**	**1**	**5**	**1**	**0**	**1**	**2**	**2**	**0**	**7**	**0**	**1**	**0**	**0**	**0**	**.139**	**.184**	**.250**	**.982**
Career total		273	608	61	148	28	6	21	76	69	7	107	2	2	3	0	2	.243	.321	.413	.990
Cubs total		**23**	**36**	**1**	**5**	**1**	**0**	**1**	**2**	**2**	**0**	**7**	**0**	**1**	**0**	**0**	**0**	**.139**	**.184**	**.250**	**.982**

Bresnahan, Roger Philip (The Duke of Tralee)
HEIGHT: 5'9"   THROWS: RIGHT   BATS: RIGHT   BORN: 6/11/1879 TOLEDO, OHIO   DIED: 12/4/1944 TOLEDO, OHIO   POSITIONS PLAYED: P, C, 1B, 2B, 3B, SS, OF

YEAR	TEAM	GAMES	AB	RUNS	HITS	2B	3B	HR	RBI	BB	IBB	SO	HBP	SH	SF	SB	CS	BA	OBA	SA	FA
1897	Was-N	6	16	1	6	0	0	0	3	1	—	—	0	0	—	0	—	.375	.412	.375	1.000
1900	**ChN-N**	**2**	**2**	**0**	**0**	**0**	**0**	**0**	**0**	**0**	**—**	**—**	**0**	**0**	**—**	**0**	**—**	**.000**	**.000**	**.000**	**—**
1901	Bal-A	86	295	40	79	9	9	1	32	23	—	—	1	4	—	10	—	.268	.323	.369	.915
1902	Bal-A	65	235	30	64	8	6	4	34	21	—	—	2	4	—	12	—	.272	.337	.409	.904
1902	NYG-N	51	178	16	51	9	3	1	22	16	—	—	2	6	—	6	—	.287	.352	.388	.940
1903	NYG-N	113	406	87	142	30	8	4	55	61	—	—	7	12	—	34	—	.350	.443	.493	.943
1904	NYG-N	109	402	81	114	22	7	5	33	58	—	—	5	3	—	13	—	.284	.381	.410	.948
1905	NYG-N	104	331	58	100	18	3	0	46	50	—	—	11	7	—	11	—	.302	.411	.375	.970
1906	NYG-N	124	405	69	114	22	4	0	43	81	—	—	14	5	—	25	—	.281	.418	.356	.973
1907	NYG-N	110	328	57	83	9	7	4	38	61	—	—	6	6	—	15	—	.253	.380	.360	.980
1908	NYG-N	140	449	70	127	25	3	1	54	83	—	—	6	24	—	14	—	.283	.401	.359	.985
1909	StL-N	72	234	27	57	4	1	0	23	46	—	—	1	7	—	11	—	.244	.370	.269	.954
1910	StL-N	88	234	35	65	15	3	0	27	55	—	17	2	8	—	13	—	.278	.419	.368	.961
1911	StL-N	81	227	22	63	17	8	3	41	45	—	19	3	6	—	4	—	.278	.404	.463	.966
1912	StL-N	48	108	8	36	7	2	1	15	14	—	9	2	0	—	4	—	.333	.419	.463	.974
1913	**ChC-N**	**69**	**162**	**20**	**37**	**5**	**2**	**1**	**21**	**21**	**—**	**11**	**2**	**4**	**—**	**7**	**—**	**.228**	**.324**	**.302**	**.963**
1914	**ChC-N**	**101**	**248**	**42**	**69**	**10**	**4**	**0**	**24**	**49**	**—**	**20**	**2**	**12**	**—**	**14**	**—**	**.278**	**.401**	**.351**	**.977**
1915	**ChC-N**	**77**	**221**	**19**	**45**	**8**	**1**	**1**	**19**	**29**	**—**	**23**	**0**	**4**	**—**	**19**	**3**	**.204**	**.296**	**.262**	**.982**
Career average		85	264	40	74	13	4	2	31	42	—	6	4	7	—	12	0	.279	.386	.377	.965
Cubs average		**62**	**158**	**20**	**38**	**6**	**2**	**1**	**16**	**25**	**—**	**14**	**1**	**5**	**—**	**10**	**1**	**.239**	**.345**	**.306**	**.976**
Career total		1446	4481	682	1252	218	71	26	530	714	—	99	66	112	—	212	3	.279	.386	.377	.965
Cubs total		**249**	**633**	**81**	**151**	**23**	**7**	**2**	**64**	**99**	**—**	**54**	**4**	**20**	**—**	**40**	**3**	**.239**	**.345**	**.306**	**.976**

Brewster, Charles Lawrence (Charlie)
HEIGHT: 5'8"   THROWS: RIGHT   BATS: RIGHT   BORN: 12/27/1916 MARTHAVILLE, LOUISIANA   DIED: 10/1/2000 ALMA, GEORGIA   POSITIONS PLAYED: 2B, SS

YEAR	TEAM	GAMES	AB	RUNS	HITS	2B	3B	HR	RBI	BB	IBB	SO	HBP	SH	SF	SB	CS	BA	OBA	SA	FA
1943	Cin-N	7	8	0	1	0	0	0	0	0	—	1	0	1	—	0	—	.125	.125	.125	1.000
1943	Phi-N	49	159	13	35	2	0	0	12	10	—	19	2	4	—	1	—	.220	.275	.233	.901
1944	**ChC-N**	**10**	**44**	**4**	**11**	**2**	**0**	**0**	**2**	**5**	**—**	**7**	**0**	**0**	**—**	**0**	**—**	**.250**	**.327**	**.295**	**.903**
1946	Cle-A	3	2	0	0	0	0	0	0	1	—	1	0	0	—	0	0	.000	.333	.000	1.000

(continued)

(continued)

	GAMES	AB	RUNS	HITS	2B	3B	HR	RBI	BB	IBB	SO	HBP	SH	SF	SB	CS	BA	OBA	SA	FA
Career average	23	71	6	16	1	0	0	5	5	—	9	1	2	—	0	0	.221	.281	.239	.904
Cubs average	**10**	**44**	**4**	**11**	**2**	**0**	**0**	**2**	**5**	**—**	**7**	**0**	**0**	**—**	**0**	**—**	**.250**	**.327**	**.295**	**.903**
Career total	69	213	17	47	4	0	0	14	16	—	28	2	5	—	1	0	.221	.281	.239	.904
Cubs total	**10**	**44**	**4**	**11**	**2**	**0**	**0**	**2**	**5**	**—**	**7**	**0**	**0**	**—**	**0**	**—**	**.250**	**.327**	**.295**	**.903**

Bridwell, Albert Henry (Al)

HEIGHT: 5'9" THROWS: RIGHT BATS: LEFT BORN: 1/4/1884 FRIENDSHIP, OHIO DIED: 1/23/1969 PORTSMOUTH, OHIO POSITIONS PLAYED: 1B, 2B, 3B, SS, OF

YEAR	TEAM	GAMES	AB	RUNS	HITS	2B	3B	HR	RBI	BB	IBB	SO	HBP	SH	SF	SB	CS	BA	OBA	SA	FA
1905	Cin-N	82	254	17	64	3	1	0	17	19	—	—	2	15	—	8	—	.252	.309	.272	.929
1906	Bos-N	120	459	41	104	9	1	0	22	44	—	—	2	13	—	6	—	.227	.297	.251	.930
1907	Bos-N	140	509	49	111	8	2	0	26	61	—	—	6	10	—	17	—	.218	.309	.242	.942
1908	NYG-N	147	467	53	133	14	1	0	46	52	—	—	6	20	—	20	—	.285	.364	.319	.933
1909	NYG-N	145	476	59	140	11	5	0	55	67	—	—	4	19	—	32	—	.294	.386	.338	.940
1910	NYG-N	142	492	74	136	15	7	0	48	73	—	23	4	20	—	14	—	.276	.374	.335	.946
1911	NYG-N	76	263	28	71	10	1	0	31	33	—	10	3	11	—	8	—	.270	.358	.316	.917
1911	Bos-N	51	182	29	53	5	0	0	10	33	—	8	1	9	—	2	—	.291	.403	.319	.950
1912	Bos-N	31	106	6	25	5	1	0	14	5	—	5	0	5	—	2	—	.236	.270	.302	.936
1913	**ChC-N**	**136**	**405**	**35**	**97**	**6**	**6**	**1**	**37**	**74**	**—**	**28**	**1**	**15**	**—**	**12**	**—**	**.240**	**.358**	**.291**	**.948**
1914	STL-F	117	381	46	90	6	5	1	33	71	—	18	2	24	—	9	—	.236	.359	.286	.947
1915	STL-F	65	175	20	40	3	2	0	9	25	—	6	1	9	—	6	—	.229	.328	.269	.945
Career average	114	379	42	97	9	3	0	32	51	—	9	3	15	—	12	—	.255	.347	.295	.939
Cubs average	**136**	**405**	**35**	**97**	**6**	**6**	**1**	**37**	**74**	**—**	**28**	**1**	**15**	**—**	**12**	**—**	**.240**	**.358**	**.291**	**.948**
Career total	1252	4169	457	1064	95	32	2	348	557	—	98	32	170	—	136	—	.255	.347	.295	.939
Cubs total	**136**	**405**	**35**	**97**	**6**	**6**	**1**	**37**	**74**	**—**	**28**	**1**	**15**	**—**	**12**	**—**	**.240**	**.358**	**.291**	**.948**

Briggs, Dan Lee

HEIGHT: 6'0" THROWS: LEFT BATS: LEFT BORN: 11/18/1952 SCOTIA, CALIFORNIA POSITIONS PLAYED: 1B, OF

YEAR	TEAM	GAMES	AB	RUNS	HITS	2B	3B	HR	RBI	BB	IBB	SO	HBP	SH	SF	SB	CS	BA	OBA	SA	FA
1975	Cal-A	13	31	3	7	1	0	1	3	2	0	6	0	1	0	0	2	.226	.273	.355	.962
1976	Cal-A	77	248	19	53	13	2	1	14	13	3	47	1	2	2	0	3	.214	.254	.294	.987
1977	Cal-A	59	74	6	12	2	0	1	4	8	1	14	0	0	1	0	0	.162	.241	.230	.988
1978	Cle-A	15	49	4	8	0	1	1	1	4	0	9	0	0	0	0	0	.163	.226	.265	1.000
1979	SD-N	104	227	34	47	4	3	8	30	18	5	45	5	1	3	2	1	.207	.277	.357	.984
1981	Mon-N	9	11	0	1	0	0	0	0	0	0	3	0	0	0	0	1	.091	.091	.091	1.000
1982	**ChC-N**	**48**	**48**	**1**	**6**	**0**	**0**	**0**	**1**	**0**	**0**	**9**	**1**	**1**	**0**	**0**	**0**	**.125**	**.143**	**.125**	**.941**
Career average	46	98	10	19	3	1	2	8	6	1	19	1	1	1	0	1	.195	.249	.294	.985
Cubs average	**48**	**48**	**1**	**6**	**0**	**0**	**0**	**1**	**0**	**0**	**9**	**1**	**1**	**0**	**0**	**0**	**.125**	**.143**	**.125**	**.941**
Career total	325	688	67	134	20	6	12	53	45	9	133	7	5	6	2	7	.195	.249	.294	.985
Cubs total	**48**	**48**	**1**	**6**	**0**	**0**	**0**	**1**	**0**	**0**	**9**	**1**	**1**	**0**	**0**	**0**	**.125**	**.143**	**.125**	**.941**

Bright, Harry James

HEIGHT: 6'0" THROWS: RIGHT BATS: RIGHT BORN: 9/22/1929 KANSAS CITY, MISSOURI DIED: 3/13/2000 SACRAMENTO, CALIFORNIA
POSITIONS PLAYED: C, 1B, 2B, 3B, OF

YEAR	TEAM	GAMES	AB	RUNS	HITS	2B	3B	HR	RBI	BB	IBB	SO	HBP	SH	SF	SB	CS	BA	OBA	SA	FA
1958	Pit-N	15	24	4	6	1	0	1	3	1	0	6	0	0	1	0	0	.250	.269	.417	1.000
1959	Pit-N	40	48	4	12	1	0	3	8	5	0	10	0	1	0	0	0	.250	.321	.458	1.000
1960	Pit-N	4	4	0	0	0	0	0	0	0	0	2	0	0	0	0	0	.000	.000	.000	—
1961	Was-A	72	183	20	44	6	0	4	21	19	1	23	0	1	1	0	2	.240	.310	.339	.940
1962	Was-A	113	392	55	107	15	4	17	67	26	0	51	2	2	3	2	1	.273	.319	.462	.988
1963	Cin-N	1	1	0	0	0	0	0	0	0	0	1	0	0	0	0	0	.000	.000	.000	1.000
1963	NYY-A	60	157	15	37	7	0	7	23	13	1	31	1	1	1	0	0	.236	.297	.414	.981
1964	NYY-A	4	5	0	1	0	0	0	0	1	0	1	0	0	0	0	0	.200	.333	.200	1.000
1965	**ChC-N**	**27**	**25**	**1**	**7**	**1**	**0**	**0**	**4**	**0**	**0**	**8**	**0**	**0**	**1**	**0**	**0**	**.280**	**.269**	**.320**	**—**
Career average	42	105	12	27	4	1	4	16	8	0	17	0	1	1	0	0	.255	.309	.416	.980
Cubs average	**27**	**25**	**1**	**7**	**1**	**0**	**0**	**4**	**0**	**0**	**8**	**0**	**0**	**1**	**0**	**0**	**.280**	**.269**	**.320**	**—**
Career total	336	839	99	214	31	4	32	126	65	2	133	3	5	7	2	3	.255	.309	.416	.980
Cubs total	**27**	**25**	**1**	**7**	**1**	**0**	**0**	**4**	**0**	**0**	**8**	**0**	**0**	**1**	**0**	**0**	**.280**	**.269**	**.320**	**—**

Brinkopf, Leon Clarence

HEIGHT: 5'11" THROWS: RIGHT BATS: RIGHT BORN: 10/20/1926 CAPE GIRARDEAU, MISSOURI DIED: 7/2/1998 CAPE GIRARDEAU, MISSOURI
POSITIONS PLAYED: SS

YEAR	TEAM	GAMES	AB	RUNS	HITS	2B	3B	HR	RBI	BB	IBB	SO	HBP	SH	SF	SB	CS	BA	OBA	SA	FA
1952	ChC-N	9	22	1	4	0	0	0	2	4	—	5	0	0	—	0	0	.182	.308	.182	.955
Career average		9	22	1	4	0	0	0	2	4	—	5	0	0	—	0	0	.182	.308	.182	.955
Cubs average		**9**	**22**	**1**	**4**	**0**	**0**	**0**	**2**	**4**	**—**	**5**	**0**	**0**	**—**	**0**	**0**	**.182**	**.308**	**.182**	**.955**
Career total		9	22	1	4	0	0	0	2	4	—	5	0	0	—	0	0	.182	.308	.182	.955
Cubs total		**9**	**22**	**1**	**4**	**0**	**0**	**0**	**2**	**4**	**—**	**5**	**0**	**0**	**—**	**0**	**0**	**.182**	**.308**	**.182**	**.955**

Brock, Louis Clark (Lou)

HEIGHT: 5'11" THROWS: LEFT BATS: LEFT BORN: 6/18/1939 EL DORADO, ARKANSAS POSITIONS PLAYED: OF

YEAR	TEAM	GAMES	AB	RUNS	HITS	2B	3B	HR	RBI	BB	IBB	SO	HBP	SH	SF	SB	CS	BA	OBA	SA	FA
1961	ChC-N	4	11	1	1	0	0	0	0	1	0	3	0	0	0	0	0	.091	.167	.091	.750
1962	ChC-N	123	434	73	114	24	7	9	35	35	4	96	3	0	5	16	7	.263	.319	.412	.965
1963	ChC-N	148	547	79	141	19	11	9	37	31	2	122	4	2	4	24	12	.258	.300	.382	.973
1964	ChC-N	52	215	30	54	9	2	2	14	13	0	40	2	1	0	10	3	.251	.300	.340	.959
1964	StL-N	103	419	81	146	21	9	12	44	27	0	87	2	12	4	33	15	.348	.387	.527	.949
1965	StL-N	155	631	107	182	35	8	16	69	45	6	116	10	11	0	63	27	.288	.345	.445	.959
1966	StL-N	156	643	94	183	24	12	15	46	31	6	134	3	0	1	74	18	.285	.320	.429	.936
1967	StL-N	159	689	113	206	32	12	21	76	24	6	109	6	2	3	52	18	.299	.327	.472	.956
1968	StL-N	159	660	92	184	46	14	6	51	46	7	124	3	1	2	62	12	.279	.328	.418	.952
1969	StL-N	157	655	97	195	33	10	12	47	50	15	115	2	2	1	53	14	.298	.349	.434	.949
1970	StL-N	155	664	114	202	29	5	13	57	60	12	99	1	1	3	51	15	.304	.361	.422	.962
1971	StL-N	157	640	126	200	37	7	7	61	76	5	107	1	1	2	64	19	.313	.385	.425	.951
1972	StL-N	153	621	81	193	26	8	3	42	47	12	93	1	3	3	63	18	.311	.359	.393	.952
1973	StL-N	160	650	110	193	29	8	7	63	71	15	112	0	1	5	70	20	.297	.364	.398	.963
1974	StL-N	153	635	105	194	25	7	3	48	61	16	88	2	2	1	118	33	.306	.368	.381	.967
1975	StL-N	136	528	78	163	27	6	3	47	38	6	64	3	3	0	56	16	.309	.359	.400	.966
1976	StL-N	133	498	73	150	24	5	4	67	35	7	75	1	4	6	56	19	.301	.344	.394	.983
1977	StL-N	141	489	69	133	22	6	2	46	30	2	74	2	0	0	35	24	.272	.317	.354	.954
1978	StL-N	92	298	31	66	9	0	0	12	17	2	29	0	1	1	17	5	.221	.263	.252	.975
1979	StL-N	120	405	56	123	15	4	5	38	23	1	43	3	0	5	21	12	.304	.342	.398	.958
Career average		138	544	85	159	26	7	8	47	40	7	91	3	2	2	49	16	.293	.343	.410	.959
Cubs average		**82**	**302**	**46**	**78**	**13**	**5**	**5**	**22**	**20**	**2**	**65**	**2**	**1**	**2**	**13**	**6**	**.257**	**.306**	**.383**	**.965**
Career total		2616	10332	1610	3023	486	141	149	900	761	124	1730	49	47	46	938	307	.293	.343	.410	.959
Cubs total		**327**	**1207**	**183**	**310**	**52**	**20**	**20**	**86**	**80**	**6**	**261**	**9**	**3**	**9**	**50**	**22**	**.257**	**.306**	**.383**	**.965**

Brock, Tarrik Jumaan

HEIGHT: 6'2" THROWS: LEFT BATS: LEFT BORN: 12/25/1973 GOLETA, CALIFORNIA POSITIONS PLAYED: OF

YEAR	TEAM	GAMES	AB	RUNS	HITS	2B	3B	HR	RBI	BB	IBB	SO	HBP	SH	SF	SB	CS	BA	OBA	SA	FA
2000	ChC-N	13	12	1	2	0	0	0	0	4	0	4	0	0	0	1	1	.167	.375	.167	.889
Career average		13	12	1	2	0	0	0	0	4	0	4	0	0	0	1	1	.167	.375	.167	.889
Cubs average		**13**	**12**	**1**	**2**	**0**	**0**	**0**	**0**	**4**	**0**	**4**	**0**	**0**	**0**	**1**	**1**	**.167**	**.375**	**.167**	**.889**
Career total		13	12	1	2	0	0	0	0	4	0	4	0	0	0	1	1	.167	.375	.167	.889
Cubs total		**13**	**12**	**1**	**2**	**0**	**0**	**0**	**0**	**4**	**0**	**4**	**0**	**0**	**0**	**1**	**1**	**.167**	**.375**	**.167**	**.889**

Bronkie, Herman Charles (Dutch)

HEIGHT: 5'9" THROWS: RIGHT BATS: RIGHT BORN: 3/30/1885 SOUTH MANCHESTER, CONNECTICUT DIED: 5/27/1968 SOMERS, CONNECTICUT
POSITIONS PLAYED: 1B, 2B, 3B, SS

YEAR	TEAM	GAMES	AB	RUNS	HITS	2B	3B	HR	RBI	BB	IBB	SO	HBP	SH	SF	SB	CS	BA	OBA	SA	FA
1910	Cle-A	4	9	1	2	0	0	0	0	1	—	—	0	0	—	1	—	.222	.300	.222	.667
1911	Cle-A	2	6	0	1	0	0	0	0	0	—	—	0	0	—	0	—	.167	.167	.167	1.000
1912	Cle-A	6	16	1	0	0	0	0	0	1	—	—	0	2	—	0	—	.000	.059	.000	.917
1914	**ChC-N**	**1**	**1**	**1**	**1**	**1**	**0**	**0**	**1**	**0**	**—**	**0**	**0**	**0**	**—**	**0**	**—**	**1.000**	**1.000**	**2.000**	**.000**
1918	StL-N	18	68	7	15	3	0	1	7	2	—	4	0	4	—	0	—	.221	.243	.309	.984
1919	StL-A	67	196	23	50	6	4	0	14	23	—	23	1	6	—	2	—	.255	.336	.327	.945
1922	StL-A	23	64	7	18	4	1	0	2	6	—	7	0	4	—	0	2	.281	.343	.375	.917

(continued)

(continued)

Career average	17	51	6	12	2	1	0	3	5	—	5	0	2	—	0	0	.242	.307	.317	.934
Cubs average	**1**	**1**	**1**	**1**	**1**	**0**	**0**	**1**	**0**	—	**0**	**0**	**0**	—	**0**	—	**1.000**	**1.000**	**2.000**	**.000**
Career total	121	360	40	87	14	5	1	24	33	—	34	1	16	—	3	2	.242	.307	.317	.934
Cubs total	**1**	**1**	**1**	**1**	**1**	**0**	**0**	**1**	**0**	—	**0**	**0**	**0**	—	**0**	—	**1.000**	**1.000**	**2.000**	**.000**

Brooks, Jonathan Joseph (Mandy)

HEIGHT: 5'9" THROWS: RIGHT BATS: RIGHT BORN: 8/18/1897 MILWAUKEE, WISCONSIN   DIED: 6/17/1962 KIRKWOOD, MISSOURI   POSITIONS PLAYED: OF

YEAR	TEAM	GAMES	AB	RUNS	HITS	2B	3B	HR	RBI	BB	IBB	SO	HBP	SH	SF	SB	CS	BA	OBA	SA	FA
1925	ChC-N	90	349	55	98	25	7	14	72	19	—	28	2	7	—	10	3	.281	.322	.513	.977
1926	ChC-N	26	48	7	9	1	0	1	6	5	—	5	1	3	—	0	—	.188	.278	.271	1.000
Career average		58	199	31	54	13	4	8	39	12	—	17	2	5	—	5	2	.270	.316	.484	.979
Cubs average		**58**	**199**	**31**	**54**	**13**	**4**	**8**	**39**	**12**	—	**17**	**2**	**5**	—	**5**	**2**	**.270**	**.316**	**.484**	**.979**
Career total		116	397	62	107	26	7	15	78	24	—	33	3	10	—	10	3	.270	.316	.484	.979
Cubs total		**116**	**397**	**62**	**107**	**26**	**7**	**15**	**78**	**24**	—	**33**	**3**	**10**	—	**10**	**3**	**.270**	**.316**	**.484**	**.979**

Brown, Brant Michael

HEIGHT: 6'3" THROWS: LEFT BATS: LEFT BORN: 6/22/1971 PORTERVILLE, CALIFORNIA   POSITIONS PLAYED: 1B, OF

YEAR	TEAM	GAMES	AB	RUNS	HITS	2B	3B	HR	RBI	BB	IBB	SO	HBP	SH	SF	SB	CS	BA	OBA	SA	FA
1996	ChC-N	29	69	11	21	1	0	5	9	2	1	17	1	0	1	3	3	.304	.329	.536	1.000
1997	ChC-N	46	137	15	32	7	1	5	15	7	0	28	3	1	0	2	1	.234	.286	.485	.985
1998	ChC-N	124	347	56	101	17	7	14	48	30	2	95	1	1	1	4	5	.291	.348	.501	.968
1999	Pit-N	130	341	49	79	20	3	16	58	22	3	114	4	0	4	3	4	.232	.283	.449	.985
2000	Fla-N	41	73	4	14	6	0	2	6	3	0	33	0	0	0	1	0	.192	.224	.356	.978
2000	**ChC-N**	**54**	**89**	**7**	**14**	**1**	**0**	**3**	**10**	**10**	**0**	**29**	**1**	**1**	**1**	**2**	**1**	**.157**	**.248**	**.270**	**.984**
Career average		85	211	28	52	10	2	9	29	15	1	63	2	1	1	3	3	.247	.301	.445	.983
Cubs average		**63**	**161**	**22**	**42**	**7**	**2**	**7**	**21**	**12**	**1**	**42**	**2**	**1**	**1**	**3**	**3**	**.262**	**.319**	**.453**	**.982**
Career total		424	1056	142	261	52	11	45	146	74	6	316	10	3	7	15	14	.247	.301	.445	.983
Cubs total		**253**	**642**	**89**	**168**	**26**	**8**	**27**	**82**	**49**	**3**	**169**	**6**	**3**	**3**	**11**	**10**	**.262**	**.319**	**.453**	**.982**

Brown, Lewis J. (Lew *or* Blower)

HEIGHT: 5'10" THROWS: RIGHT BATS: RIGHT BORN: 2/1/1858 LEOMINSTER, MASSACHUSETTS   DIED: 1/15/1889 BOSTON, MASSACHUSETTS
POSITIONS PLAYED: P, C, 1B, OF

YEAR	TEAM	GAMES	AB	RUNS	HITS	2B	3B	HR	RBI	BB	IBB	SO	HBP	SH	SF	SB	CS	BA	OBA	SA	FA
1876	Bos-N	45	198	23	41	6	6	2	21	3	—	22	—	—	—	—	—	.207	.219	.328	.856
1877	Bos-N	58	221	27	56	12	8	1	31	6	—	33	—	—	—	—	—	.253	.273	.394	.903
1878	Prv-N	58	243	44	74	21	6	1	43	7	—	37	—	—	—	—	—	.305	.324	.453	.902
1879	Prv-N	53	229	23	59	13	4	2	38	4	—	24	—	—	—	—	—	.258	.270	.376	.843
1879	**ChN-N**	**6**	**21**	**2**	**6**	**1**	**0**	**0**	**3**	**1**	—	**4**	—	—	—	—	—	**.286**	**.318**	**.333**	**.974**
1881	Det-N	27	108	16	26	3	1	3	14	3	—	16	—	—	—	—	—	.241	.261	.370	.959
1881	Prv-N	18	75	9	18	3	1	0	10	4	—	13	—	—	—	—	—	.240	.278	.307	.940
1883	Bos-N	14	54	5	13	4	1	0	9	3	—	6	—	—	—	—	—	.241	.281	.352	.943
1883	Lou-AA	14	60	6	11	2	1	0	—	1	—	—	—	—	—	—	—	.183	.197	.250	.892
1884	Bos-U	85	325	50	75	18	3	1	—	13	—	—	—	—	—	—	—	.231	.260	.314	.923
Career average		54	219	29	54	12	4	1	24	6	—	22	—	—	—	—	—	.247	.269	.361	.905
Cubs average		**6**	**21**	**2**	**6**	**1**	**0**	**0**	**3**	**1**	—	**4**	—	—	—	—	—	**.286**	**.318**	**.333**	**.974**
Career total		378	1534	205	379	83	31	10	169	45	—	155	—	—	—	—	—	.247	.269	.361	.905
Cubs total		**6**	**21**	**2**	**6**	**1**	**0**	**0**	**3**	**1**	—	**4**	—	—	—	—	—	**.286**	**.318**	**.333**	**.974**

Brown, Roosevelt Lawayne
HEIGHT: 5'10" THROWS: RIGHT BATS: LEFT BORN: 8/3/1975 VICKSBURG, MISSISSIPPI POSITIONS PLAYED: OF

YEAR	TEAM	GAMES	AB	RUNS	HITS	2B	3B	HR	RBI	BB	IBB	SO	HBP	SH	SF	SB	CS	BA	OBA	SA	FA
1999	ChC-N	33	64	6	14	6	1	1	10	2	0	14	0	3	1	1	0	.219	.239	.391	.955
2000	ChC-N	45	91	11	32	8	0	3	14	4	0	22	1	0	2	0	1	.352	.378	.538	1.000
2001	ChC-N	39	83	13	22	6	1	4	22	7	0	12	1	0	1	0	0	.265	.326	.506	.952
Career average		39	79	10	23	7	1	3	15	4	0	16	1	1	1	0	0	.286	.323	.487	.976
Cubs average		**39**	**79**	**10**	**23**	**7**	**1**	**3**	**15**	**4**	**0**	**16**	**1**	**1**	**1**	**0**	**0**	**.286**	**.323**	**.487**	**.976**
Career total		117	238	30	68	20	2	8	46	13	0	48	2	3	4	1	1	.286	.323	.487	.976
Cubs total		**117**	**238**	**30**	**68**	**20**	**2**	**8**	**46**	**13**	**0**	**48**	**2**	**3**	**4**	**1**	**1**	**.286**	**.323**	**.487**	**.976**

Brown, Thomas Michael (Tommy *or* Buckshot)
HEIGHT: 6'1" THROWS: RIGHT BATS: RIGHT BORN: 12/6/1927 BROOKLYN, NEW YORK POSITIONS PLAYED: 1B, 2B, 3B, SS, OF

YEAR	TEAM	GAMES	AB	RUNS	HITS	2B	3B	HR	RBI	BB	IBB	SO	HBP	SH	SF	SB	CS	BA	OBA	SA	FA
1944	Bro-N	46	146	17	24	4	0	0	8	8	—	17	0	6	—	0	0	.164	.208	.192	.925
1945	Bro-N	57	196	13	48	3	4	2	19	6	—	16	0	2	—	3	—	.245	.267	.332	.918
1947	Bro-N	15	34	3	8	1	0	0	2	1	—	6	0	0	—	0	0	.235	.257	.265	.931
1948	Bro-N	54	145	18	35	4	0	2	20	7	—	17	1	3	—	1	—	.241	.281	.310	.937
1949	Bro-N	41	89	14	27	2	0	3	18	6	—	8	0	0	—	0	0	.303	.347	.427	.931
1950	Bro-N	48	86	15	25	2	1	8	20	11	—	9	1	0	—	0	—	.291	.378	.616	.917
1951	Bro-N	11	25	2	4	2	0	0	1	2	—	4	0	0	—	0	0	.160	.222	.240	.909
1951	Phi-N	78	196	24	43	2	1	10	32	15	—	21	1	1	—	1	2	.219	.278	.393	.963
1952	Phi-N	18	25	2	4	1	0	1	2	4	—	3	0	0	—	0	0	.160	.276	.320	1.000
1952	ChC-N	61	200	24	64	11	0	3	24	12	—	24	0	1	—	1	2	.320	.358	.420	.931
1953	ChC-N	65	138	19	27	7	1	2	13	13	—	17	3	0	—	1	0	.196	.279	.304	.901
Career average		55	142	17	34	4	1	3	18	9	—	16	1	1	—	1	0	.241	.292	.355	.931
Cubs average		**63**	**169**	**22**	**46**	**9**	**1**	**3**	**19**	**13**	**—**	**21**	**2**	**1**	**—**	**1**	**1**	**.269**	**.325**	**.373**	**.921**
Career total		494	1280	151	309	39	7	31	159	85	—	142	6	13	—	7	4	.241	.292	.355	.931
Cubs total		**126**	**338**	**43**	**91**	**18**	**1**	**5**	**37**	**25**	**—**	**41**	**3**	**1**	**—**	**2**	**2**	**.269**	**.325**	**.373**	**.921**

Browne, Byron Ellis
HEIGHT: 6'2" THROWS: RIGHT BATS: RIGHT BORN: 12/27/1942 ST. JOSEPH, MISSOURI POSITIONS PLAYED: OF

YEAR	TEAM	GAMES	AB	RUNS	HITS	2B	3B	HR	RBI	BB	IBB	SO	HBP	SH	SF	SB	CS	BA	OBA	SA	FA
1965	ChC-N	4	6	0	0	0	0	0	0	0	0	2	0	0	0	0	0	.000	.000	.000	.667
1966	ChC-N	120	419	46	102	15	7	16	51	40	1	143	5	1	1	3	3	.243	.316	.427	.967
1967	ChC-N	10	19	3	3	2	0	0	2	4	1	5	0	1	0	1	1	.158	.304	.263	1.000
1968	Hou-N	10	13	0	3	0	0	0	1	4	0	6	0	0	0	0	0	.231	.412	.231	1.000
1969	StL-N	22	53	9	12	0	1	1	7	11	1	14	0	0	0	0	0	.226	.359	.321	1.000
1970	Phi-N	104	270	29	67	17	2	10	36	33	5	72	0	1	3	1	2	.248	.327	.437	.975
1971	Phi-N	58	68	5	14	3	0	3	5	8	0	23	0	0	0	0	0	.206	.289	.382	1.000
1972	Phi-N	21	21	2	4	0	0	0	0	1	0	8	0	0	0	0	0	.190	.227	.190	1.000
Career average		44	109	12	26	5	1	4	13	13	1	34	1	0	1	1	1	.236	.318	.405	.973
Cubs average		**45**	**148**	**16**	**35**	**6**	**2**	**5**	**18**	**15**	**1**	**50**	**2**	**1**	**0**	**1**	**1**	**.236**	**.312**	**.414**	**.964**
Career total		349	869	94	205	37	10	30	102	101	8	273	5	3	4	5	6	.236	.318	.405	.973
Cubs total		**134**	**444**	**49**	**105**	**17**	**7**	**16**	**53**	**44**	**2**	**150**	**5**	**2**	**1**	**4**	**4**	**.236**	**.312**	**.414**	**.964**

Browne, George Edward
HEIGHT: 5'10" THROWS: RIGHT BATS: LEFT BORN: 1/12/1876 RICHMOND, VIRGINIA DIED: 12/9/1920 HYDE PARK, NEW YORK POSITIONS PLAYED: 3B, OF

YEAR	TEAM	GAMES	AB	RUNS	HITS	2B	3B	HR	RBI	BB	IBB	SO	HBP	SH	SF	SB	CS	BA	OBA	SA	FA
1901	Phi-N	8	26	2	5	1	0	0	4	1	—	—	1	0	—	2	—	.192	.250	.231	1.000
1902	Phi-N	70	281	41	73	7	1	0	26	16	—	—	2	6	—	11	—	.260	.304	.292	.910
1902	NYG-N	53	216	30	69	9	5	0	14	9	—	—	3	1	—	13	—	.319	.355	.407	.895
1903	NYG-N	141	591	105	185	20	3	3	45	43	—	—	4	14	—	27	—	.313	.364	.372	.918
1904	NYG-N	150	596	99	169	16	5	4	39	39	—	—	4	22	—	24	—	.284	.332	.347	.925
1905	NYG-N	127	536	95	157	16	14	4	43	20	—	—	2	11	—	26	—	.293	.321	.397	.915
1906	NYG-N	122	477	61	126	10	4	0	38	27	—	—	0	25	—	32	—	.264	.304	.302	.934
1907	NYG-N	127	458	54	119	11	10	5	37	31	—	—	1	24	—	15	—	.260	.308	.360	.941

(continued)

(continued)

YEAR	TEAM	GAMES	AB	RUNS	HITS	2B	3B	HR	RBI	BB	IBB	SO	HBP	SH	SF	SB	CS	BA	OBA	SA	FA
1908	Bos-N	138	536	61	122	10	6	1	34	36	—	—	0	18	—	17	—	.228	.276	.274	.950
1909	**ChC-N**	**12**	**39**	**7**	**8**	**0**	**1**	**0**	**1**	**5**	**—**	**—**	**0**	**1**	**—**	**3**	**—**	**.205**	**.295**	**.256**	**.944**
1909	Was-A	103	393	40	107	15	5	1	16	17	—	—	3	8	—	13	—	.272	.308	.344	.935
1910	Was-A	7	22	1	4	0	0	0	0	1	—	—	0	0	—	0	—	.182	.217	.182	.667
1910	CWS-A	30	112	17	27	4	1	0	4	12	—	—	0	3	—	5	—	.241	.315	.295	.952
1911	Bro-N	8	12	1	4	0	0	0	2	1	—	1	0	0	—	2	—	.333	.385	.333	1.000
1912	Phi-N	6	5	0	1	0	0	0	0	1	—	0	0	0	—	0	—	.200	.333	.200	
Career average		92	358	51	98	10	5	2	25	22	—	0	2	11	—	16	—	.273	.318	.339	.927
Cubs average		**12**	**39**	**7**	**8**	**0**	**1**	**0**	**1**	**5**	**—**	**—**	**0**	**1**	**—**	**3**	**—**	**.205**	**.295**	**.256**	**.944**
Career total		1102	4300	614	1176	119	55	18	303	259	—	1	20	133	—	190	—	.273	.318	.339	.927
Cubs total		**12**	**39**	**7**	**8**	**0**	**1**	**0**	**1**	**5**	**—**	**—**	**0**	**1**	**—**	**3**	**—**	**.205**	**.295**	**.256**	**.944**

Brumley, Anthony Michael (Mike)

HEIGHT: 5'10"   THROWS: RIGHT   BATS: BOTH   BORN: 4/9/1963 OKLAHOMA CITY, OKLAHOMA   POSITIONS PLAYED: 1B, 2B, 3B, SS, OF

YEAR	TEAM	GAMES	AB	RUNS	HITS	2B	3B	HR	RBI	BB	IBB	SO	HBP	SH	SF	SB	CS	BA	OBA	SA	FA
1987	**ChC-N**	**39**	**104**	**8**	**21**	**2**	**2**	**1**	**9**	**10**	**1**	**30**	**1**	**1**	**1**	**7**	**1**	**.202**	**.276**	**.288**	**.965**
1989	Det-A	92	212	33	42	5	2	1	11	14	0	45	1	3	0	8	4	.198	.251	.255	.952
1990	Sea-A	62	147	19	33	5	4	0	7	10	0	22	0	4	1	2	0	.224	.272	.313	.974
1991	Bos-A	63	118	16	25	5	0	0	5	10	0	22	0	4	0	2	0	.212	.273	.254	.959
1992	Bos-A	2	1	0	0	0	0	0	0	0	0	0	0	0	0	0	0	.000	.000	.000	—
1993	Hou-N	8	10	1	3	0	0	0	2	1	0	3	0	0	0	0	1	.300	.364	.300	1.000
1994	Oak-A	11	25	0	6	0	0	0	2	1	0	8	0	0	0	0	0	.240	.269	.240	.905
1995	Hou-N	18	18	1	1	0	0	1	2	0	0	6	0	0	0	1	0	.056	.056	.222	.833
Career average		37	79	10	16	2	1	0	5	6	0	17	0	2	0	3	1	.206	.261	.272	.959
Cubs average		**39**	**104**	**8**	**21**	**2**	**2**	**1**	**9**	**10**	**1**	**30**	**1**	**1**	**1**	**7**	**1**	**.202**	**.276**	**.288**	**.965**
Career total		295	635	78	131	17	8	3	38	46	1	136	2	12	2	20	6	.206	.261	.272	.959
Cubs total		**39**	**104**	**8**	**21**	**2**	**2**	**1**	**9**	**10**	**1**	**30**	**1**	**1**	**1**	**7**	**1**	**.202**	**.276**	**.288**	**.965**

Bryant, Donald Ray (Don)

HEIGHT: 6'5"   THROWS: RIGHT   BATS: RIGHT   BORN: 7/13/1941 JASPER, FLORIDA   POSITIONS PLAYED: C

YEAR	TEAM	GAMES	AB	RUNS	HITS	2B	3B	HR	RBI	BB	IBB	SO	HBP	SH	SF	SB	CS	BA	OBA	SA	FA
1966	**ChC-N**	**13**	**26**	**2**	**8**	**2**	**0**	**0**	**4**	**1**	**0**	**4**	**1**	**0**	**0**	**1**	**0**	**.308**	**.357**	**.385**	**.978**
1969	Hou-N	31	59	2	11	1	0	1	6	4	1	13	1	1	0	0	0	.186	.250	.254	.993
1970	Hou-N	15	24	2	5	0	0	0	3	1	0	8	0	0	1	0	0	.208	.231	.208	.957
Career average		20	36	2	8	1	0	0	4	2	0	8	1	0	0	0	0	.220	.271	.275	.983
Cubs average		**13**	**26**	**2**	**8**	**2**	**0**	**0**	**4**	**1**	**0**	**4**	**1**	**0**	**0**	**1**	**0**	**.308**	**.357**	**.385**	**.978**
Career total		59	109	6	24	3	0	1	13	6	1	25	2	1	1	1	0	.220	.271	.275	.983
Cubs total		**13**	**26**	**2**	**8**	**2**	**0**	**0**	**4**	**1**	**0**	**4**	**1**	**0**	**0**	**1**	**0**	**.308**	**.357**	**.385**	**.978**

Buckner, William Joseph (Bill)

HEIGHT: 6'0"   THROWS: LEFT   BATS: LEFT   BORN: 12/14/1949 VALLEJO, CALIFORNIA   POSITIONS PLAYED: 1B, OF

YEAR	TEAM	GAMES	AB	RUNS	HITS	2B	3B	HR	RBI	BB	IBB	SO	HBP	SH	SF	SB	CS	BA	OBA	SA	FA
1969	LA-N	1	1	0	0	0	0	0	0	0	0	0	0	0	0	0	0	.000	.000	.000	—
1970	LA-N	28	68	6	13	3	1	0	4	3	1	7	0	0	0	0	1	.191	.225	.265	1.000
1971	LA-N	108	358	37	99	15	1	5	41	11	4	18	5	7	2	4	1	.277	.306	.366	.996
1972	LA-N	105	383	47	122	14	3	5	37	17	2	13	1	3	1	10	3	.319	.348	.410	.991
1973	LA-N	140	575	68	158	20	0	8	46	17	5	34	3	6	5	12	2	.275	.297	.351	.997
1974	LA-N	145	580	83	182	30	3	7	58	30	10	24	4	4	2	31	13	.314	.351	.412	.976
1975	LA-N	92	288	30	70	11	2	6	31	17	7	15	2	4	4	8	3	.243	.286	.358	.986
1976	LA-N	154	642	76	193	28	4	7	60	26	6	26	1	6	5	28	9	.301	.326	.389	.985
1977	**ChC-N**	**122**	**426**	**40**	**121**	**27**	**0**	**11**	**60**	**21**	**2**	**23**	**1**	**2**	**7**	**7**	**5**	**.284**	**.314**	**.425**	**.990**
1978	**ChC-N**	**117**	**446**	**47**	**144**	**26**	**1**	**5**	**74**	**18**	**5**	**17**	**0**	**1**	**5**	**7**	**5**	**.323**	**.345**	**.419**	**.995**
1979	**ChC-N**	**149**	**591**	**72**	**168**	**34**	**7**	**14**	**66**	**30**	**6**	**28**	**2**	**1**	**4**	**9**	**4**	**.284**	**.319**	**.437**	**.995**
1980	**ChC-N**	**145**	**578**	**69**	**187**	**41**	**3**	**10**	**68**	**30**	**11**	**18**	**0**	**0**	**6**	**1**	**2**	**.324**	**.353**	**.457**	**.992**
1981	**ChC-N**	**106**	**421**	**45**	**131**	**35**	**3**	**10**	**75**	**26**	**9**	**16**	**1**	**0**	**5**	**5**	**2**	**.311**	**.349**	**.480**	**.984**
1982	**ChC-N**	**161**	**657**	**93**	**201**	**34**	**5**	**15**	**105**	**36**	**7**	**26**	**5**	**1**	**10**	**15**	**5**	**.306**	**.342**	**.441**	**.993**
1983	**ChC-N**	**153**	**626**	**79**	**175**	**38**	**6**	**16**	**66**	**25**	**5**	**30**	**5**	**4**	**5**	**12**	**4**	**.280**	**.310**	**.436**	**.992**
1984	**ChC-N**	**21**	**43**	**3**	**9**	**0**	**0**	**0**	**2**	**1**	**1**	**1**	**1**	**0**	**1**	**0**	**0**	**.209**	**.239**	**.209**	**1.000**
1984	Bos-A	114	439	51	122	21	2	11	67	24	5	38	5	0	3	2	2	.278	.321	.410	.986
1985	Bos-A	162	673	89	201	46	3	16	110	30	5	36	2	2	11	18	4	.299	.325	.447	.992

(continued)

William (Bill) Joseph Buckner, 1b-of-dh, 1969–90

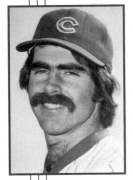

Bill Buckner will be remembered eternally for the ground ball he let slip between his legs in the 1986 World Series, which sent the Boston Red Sox to ignominious defeat.

But Chicago fans, at least, remember "Billy Buck," as he was called, for his timely hitting and gritty toughness.

Buckner, born on December 14, 1949, in Vallejo, California, was originally signed by the Dodgers and came up for a one-game cup of coffee in 1969. He was primarily an outfielder for Los Angeles from 1970 to 1976. His best year was 1974, the year Los Angeles went to the World Series, when he hit .314 with 182 hits and 83 runs scored.

But in 1977 he was traded to the Cubs along with Ivan DeJesus for Rick Monday. Cubs manager Herman Franks put Buckner at first base, and Buckner responded by hitting over .300 during his time in Chicago. He led the National League in doubles twice and won the batting title in 1980 with a .324 average.

He was elected to the All-Star team in 1981. That year, he led the Cubs in hits, doubles, batting average, home runs and RBIs.

Buckner was a model of consistency at the plate. He was nearly impossible to strike out, although he wasn't one to walk much, either.

Early in his career, Cubs star second baseman Ryne Sandberg admitted that he watched Buckner a lot, seeing how Buckner moved when he swung the bat and watching the way Buckner used to hit line drives.

In 1984 Buckner was picked up by the Red Sox and proved to be a valuable addition, helping the team make it to the World Series two years later. But foot and ankle injuries were slowing him down, and after brief stints with California, Kansas City and one more go-round with Boston, Buckner retired in 1990.

Buckner's 201 hits in 1982 remain the club record for most hits by a first baseman. That year, he also became the 12th Cub in team history to make 200 or more hits.

(Buckner, continued)

1986	Bos-A	153	629	73	168	39	2	18	102	40	9	25	4	0	8	6	4	.267	.311	.421	.989
1987	Bos-A	75	286	23	78	6	1	2	42	13	1	19	0	0	5	1	3	.273	.299	.322	.991
1987	Cal-A	57	183	16	56	12	1	3	32	9	1	7	0	1	1	1	0	.306	.337	.432	1.000
1988	Cal-A	19	43	1	9	0	0	0	9	4	0	0	0	0	1	2	0	.209	.271	.209	1.000
1988	KC-A	89	242	18	62	14	0	3	34	13	5	19	0	4	4	3	1	.256	.290	.351	.994
1989	KC-A	79	176	7	38	4	1	1	16	6	2	11	0	0	1	1	0	.216	.240	.267	.985
1990	Bos-A	22	43	4	8	0	0	1	3	3	2	2	0	1	1	0	0	.186	.234	.256	1.000
Career average		114	427	49	123	23	2	8	55	20	5	21	2	2	4	8	3	.289	.321	.408	.991
Cubs average		**122**	**474**	**56**	**142**	**29**	**3**	**10**	**65**	**23**	**6**	**20**	**2**	**1**	**5**	**7**	**3**	**.300**	**.332**	**.439**	**.992**
Career total		2517	9397	1077	2715	498	49	174	1208	450	111	453	42	47	97	183	73	.289	.321	.408	.991
Cubs total		**974**	**3788**	**448**	**1136**	**235**	**25**	**81**	**516**	**187**	**46**	**159**	**15**	**9**	**43**	**56**	**27**	**.300**	**.332**	**.439**	**.992**

Buechele, Steven Bernard (Steve)

HEIGHT: 6'2" THROWS: RIGHT BATS: RIGHT BORN: 9/26/1961 LANCASTER, CALIFORNIA POSITIONS PLAYED: 1B, 2B, 3B, SS, OF

YEAR	TEAM	GAMES	AB	RUNS	HITS	2B	3B	HR	RBI	BB	IBB	SO	HBP	SH	SF	SB	CS	BA	OBA	SA	FA
1985	Tex-A	69	219	22	48	6	3	6	21	14	2	38	2	0	1	3	2	.219	.271	.356	.969
1986	Tex-A	153	461	54	112	19	2	18	54	35	1	98	5	9	3	5	8	.243	.302	.410	.975
1987	Tex-A	136	363	45	86	20	0	13	50	28	3	66	1	4	4	2	2	.237	.290	.399	.971
1988	Tex-A	155	503	68	126	21	4	16	58	65	6	79	5	6	0	2	4	.250	.342	.404	.963
1989	Tex-A	155	486	60	114	22	2	16	59	36	0	107	5	2	1	1	3	.235	.294	.387	.972
1990	Tex-A	91	251	30	54	10	0	7	30	27	1	63	2	7	2	1	0	.215	.294	.339	.967
1991	Tex-A	121	416	58	111	17	2	18	66	39	4	69	5	10	2	0	4	.267	.335	.447	.992
1991	Pit-N	31	114	16	28	5	1	4	19	10	0	28	2	1	1	0	1	.246	.315	.412	.956
1992	Pit-N	80	285	27	71	14	1	8	43	34	4	61	2	2	2	0	2	.249	.331	.389	.957
1992	**ChC-N**	**65**	**239**	**25**	**66**	**9**	**3**	**1**	**21**	**18**	**2**	**44**	**5**	**2**	**1**	**1**	**1**	**.276**	**.338**	**.351**	**.961**
1993	**ChC-N**	**133**	**460**	**53**	**125**	**27**	**2**	**15**	**65**	**48**	**5**	**87**	**5**	**4**	**3**	**1**	**1**	**.272**	**.345**	**.437**	**.976**
1994	**ChC-N**	**104**	**339**	**33**	**82**	**11**	**1**	**14**	**52**	**39**	**2**	**80**	**4**	**2**	**3**	**1**	**0**	**.242**	**.325**	**.404**	**.980**
1995	**ChC-N**	**32**	**106**	**10**	**20**	**2**	**0**	**1**	**9**	**11**	**0**	**19**	**0**	**1**	**0**	**0**	**0**	**.189**	**.265**	**.236**	**.942**
1995	Tex-A	9	24	0	3	0	0	0	0	4	1	3	0	0	0	0	0	.125	.250	.125	1.000

(continued)

(continued)

	GAMES	AB	RUNS	HITS	2B	3B	HR	RBI	BB	IBB	SO	HBP	SH	SF	SB	CS	BA	OBA	SA	FA
Career average	121	388	46	95	17	2	12	50	37	3	77	4	5	2	2	3	.245	.316	.394	.971
Cubs average	**84**	**286**	**30**	**73**	**12**	**2**	**8**	**37**	**29**	**2**	**58**	**4**	**2**	**2**	**1**	**1**	**.256**	**.330**	**.391**	**.971**
Career total	1334	4266	501	1046	183	21	137	547	408	31	842	43	50	23	17	28	.245	.316	.394	.971
Cubs total	**334**	**1144**	**121**	**293**	**49**	**6**	**31**	**147**	**116**	**9**	**230**	**14**	**9**	**7**	**3**	**2**	**.256**	**.330**	**.391**	**.971**

Bues, Arthur Frederick (Art)
HEIGHT: 5'11" THROWS: RIGHT BATS: RIGHT BORN: 3/3/1888 MILWAUKEE, WISCONSIN DIED: 11/7/1954 WHITEFISH BAY, WISCONSIN
POSITIONS PLAYED: 2B, 3B

YEAR	TEAM	GAMES	AB	RUNS	HITS	2B	3B	HR	RBI	BB	IBB	SO	HBP	SH	SF	SB	CS	BA	OBA	SA	FA
1913	Bos-N	2	1	0	0	0	0	0	0	0	—	1	0	0	—	0	—	.000	.000	.000	—
1914	ChC-N	14	45	3	10	1	1	0	4	5	—	6	0	0	—	1	—	.222	.300	.289	.968
Career average		8	23	2	5	1	1	0	2	3	—	4	0	0	—	1	—	.217	.294	.283	.968
Cubs average		**14**	**45**	**3**	**10**	**1**	**1**	**0**	**4**	**5**	**—**	**6**	**0**	**0**	**—**	**1**	**—**	**.222**	**.300**	**.289**	**.968**
Career total		16	46	3	10	1	1	0	4	5	—	7	0	0	—	1	—	.217	.294	.283	.968
Cubs total		**14**	**45**	**3**	**10**	**1**	**1**	**0**	**4**	**5**	**—**	**6**	**0**	**0**	**—**	**1**	**—**	**.222**	**.300**	**.289**	**.968**

Buford, Damon Jackson
HEIGHT: 5'10" THROWS: RIGHT BATS: RIGHT BORN: 6/12/1970 BALTIMORE, MARYLAND POSITIONS PLAYED: 2B, 3B, OF

YEAR	TEAM	GAMES	AB	RUNS	HITS	2B	3B	HR	RBI	BB	IBB	SO	HBP	SH	SF	SB	CS	BA	OBA	SA	FA
1993	Bal-A	53	79	18	18	5	0	2	9	9	0	19	1	1	0	2	2	.228	.315	.367	.984
1994	Bal-A	4	2	2	1	0	0	0	0	0	0	1	0	0	0	0	0	.500	.500	.500	—
1995	Bal-A	24	32	6	2	0	0	0	2	6	0	7	0	3	1	3	1	.063	.205	.063	1.000
1995	NYM-N	44	136	24	32	5	0	4	12	19	0	28	5	0	2	7	7	.235	.346	.360	1.000
1996	Tex-A	90	145	30	41	9	0	6	20	15	0	34	0	1	1	8	5	.283	.348	.469	1.000
1997	Tex-A	122	366	49	82	18	0	8	39	30	0	83	3	3	2	18	7	.224	.287	.339	.990
1998	Bos-A	86	216	37	61	14	4	10	42	22	1	43	1	0	2	5	5	.282	.349	.523	1.000
1999	Bos-A	91	297	39	72	15	2	6	38	21	0	74	2	1	3	9	2	.242	.294	.367	.985
2000	**ChC-N**	150	495	64	124	18	3	15	48	47	3	118	8	4	2	4	6	.251	.324	.390	.986
2001	**ChC-N**	35	85	11	15	2	0	3	8	4	0	23	0	0	0	0	0	.176	.213	.306	1.000
Career average		78	206	31	50	10	1	6	24	19	0	48	2	1	1	6	4	.242	.311	.385	.989
Cubs average		**93**	**290**	**38**	**70**	**10**	**2**	**9**	**28**	**26**	**2**	**71**	**4**	**2**	**1**	**2**	**3**	**.240**	**.309**	**.378**	**.987**
Career total		699	1853	280	448	86	9	54	218	173	4	430	20	13	13	56	35	.242	.311	.385	.989
Cubs total		**185**	**580**	**75**	**139**	**20**	**3**	**18**	**56**	**51**	**3**	**141**	**8**	**4**	**2**	**4**	**6**	**.240**	**.309**	**.378**	**.987**

Bullett, Scott Douglas
HEIGHT: 6'2" THROWS: LEFT BATS: LEFT BORN: 12/25/1968 MARTINSBURG, WEST VIRGINIA POSITIONS PLAYED: OF

YEAR	TEAM	GAMES	AB	RUNS	HITS	2B	3B	HR	RBI	BB	IBB	SO	HBP	SH	SF	SB	CS	BA	OBA	SA	FA
1991	Pit-N	11	4	2	0	0	0	0	0	0	0	3	1	0	0	1	1	.000	.200	.000	1.000
1993	Pit-N	23	55	2	11	0	2	0	4	3	0	15	0	0	1	3	2	.200	.237	.273	1.000
1995	**ChC-N**	104	150	19	41	5	7	3	22	12	2	30	1	1	0	8	3	.273	.331	.460	.968
1996	**ChC-N**	109	165	26	35	5	0	3	16	10	0	54	0	1	1	7	3	.212	.256	.297	.986
Career average		62	94	12	22	3	2	2	11	6	1	26	1	1	1	5	2	.233	.283	.356	.983
Cubs average		**107**	**158**	**23**	**38**	**5**	**4**	**3**	**19**	**11**	**1**	**42**	**1**	**1**	**1**	**8**	**3**	**.241**	**.292**	**.375**	**.978**
Career total		247	374	49	87	10	9	6	42	25	2	102	2	2	2	19	9	.233	.283	.356	.983
Cubs total		**213**	**315**	**45**	**76**	**10**	**7**	**6**	**38**	**22**	**2**	**84**	**1**	**2**	**1**	**15**	**6**	**.241**	**.292**	**.375**	**.978**

Burgess, Forrest Harrill (Smoky)
HEIGHT: 5'8" THROWS: RIGHT BATS: LEFT BORN: 2/6/1927 CAROLEEN, NORTH CAROLINA DIED: 9/15/1991 ASHEVILLE, NORTH CAROLINA
POSITIONS PLAYED: C

YEAR	TEAM	GAMES	AB	RUNS	HITS	2B	3B	HR	RBI	BB	IBB	SO	HBP	SH	SF	SB	CS	BA	OBA	SA	FA
1949	**ChC-N**	**46**	**56**	**4**	**15**	**0**	**0**	**1**	**12**	**4**	**—**	**4**	**0**	**0**	**—**	**0**	**—**	**.268**	**.317**	**.321**	**1.000**
1951	**ChC-N**	**94**	**219**	**21**	**55**	**4**	**2**	**2**	**20**	**21**	**—**	**12**	**0**	**0**	**—**	**2**	**0**	**.251**	**.317**	**.315**	**.980**
1952	Phi-N	110	371	49	110	27	2	6	56	49	—	21	1	3	—	3	1	.296	.380	.429	.978
1953	Phi-N	102	312	31	91	17	5	4	36	37	—	17	2	0	—	3	2	.292	.370	.417	.993
1954	Phi-N	108	345	41	127	27	5	4	46	42	—	11	0	1	4	1	5	.368	.432	.510	.975

(continued)

(Burgess, continued)

YEAR	TEAM	GAMES	AB	RUNS	HITS	2B	3B	HR	RBI	BB	IBB	SO	HBP	SH	SF	SB	CS	BA	OBA	SA	FA
1955	Phi-N	7	21	4	4	2	0	1	1	3	1	1	0	0	0	0	0	.190	.292	.429	1.000
1955	Cin-N	116	421	67	129	15	3	20	77	47	4	35	1	2	6	1	1	.306	.373	.499	.986
1956	Cin-N	90	229	28	63	10	0	12	39	26	4	18	0	1	2	0	1	.275	.346	.476	1.000
1957	Cin-N	90	205	29	58	14	1	14	39	24	5	16	0	0	3	0	0	.283	.353	.566	.988
1958	Cin-N	99	251	28	71	12	1	6	31	22	3	20	1	0	0	0	0	.283	.343	.410	.988
1959	Pit-N	114	377	41	112	28	5	11	59	31	9	16	2	2	6	0	0	.297	.349	.485	.984
1960	Pit-N	110	337	33	99	15	2	7	39	35	12	13	0	0	4	0	1	.294	.356	.412	.994
1961	Pit-N	100	323	37	98	17	3	12	52	30	8	16	2	0	1	1	0	.303	.365	.486	.991
1962	Pit-N	103	360	38	118	19	2	13	61	31	9	19	0	2	6	0	1	.328	.375	.500	.988
1963	Pit-N	91	264	20	74	10	1	6	37	24	8	14	1	0	4	0	1	.280	.338	.394	.990
1964	Pit-N	68	171	9	42	3	1	2	17	13	3	14	1	2	0	2	1	.246	.303	.310	.992
1964	CWS-A	7	5	1	1	0	0	1	1	2	2	0	0	0	0	0	0	.200	.429	.800	—
1965	CWS-A	80	77	2	22	4	0	2	24	11	4	7	0	0	1	0	0	.286	.371	.416	1.000
1966	CWS-A	79	67	0	21	5	0	0	15	11	2	8	1	0	1	0	0	.313	.413	.388	1.000
1967	CWS-A	77	60	2	8	1	0	2	11	14	6	8	1	0	1	0	0	.133	.303	.250	—
Career average		94	248	27	73	13	2	7	37	27	4	15	1	1	2	1	1	.295	.362	.446	.988
Cubs average		**70**	**138**	**13**	**35**	**2**	**1**	**2**	**16**	**13**	**—**	**8**	**0**	**0**	**—**	**1**	**0**	**.255**	**.317**	**.316**	**.982**
Career total		1691	4471	485	1318	230	33	126	673	477	80	270	13	13	39	13	14	.295	.362	.446	.988
Cubs total		**140**	**275**	**25**	**70**	**4**	**2**	**3**	**32**	**25**	**—**	**16**	**0**	**0**	**—**	**2**	**0**	**.255**	**.317**	**.316**	**.982**

Burke, Leo Patrick

HEIGHT: 5'11"　THROWS: RIGHT　BATS: RIGHT　BORN: 5/6/1934 HAGERSTOWN, MARYLAND　POSITIONS PLAYED: C, 1B, 2B, 3B, SS, OF

YEAR	TEAM	GAMES	AB	RUNS	HITS	2B	3B	HR	RBI	BB	IBB	SO	HBP	SH	SF	SB	CS	BA	OBA	SA	FA
1958	Bal-A	7	11	4	5	1	0	1	4	1	0	2	0	0	0	0	0	.455	.500	.818	.667
1959	Bal-A	5	10	0	2	0	0	0	1	0	0	5	1	0	0	0	0	.200	.273	.200	1.000
1961	LAA-A	6	5	0	0	0	0	0	0	0	0	1	0	0	0	0	0	.000	.000	.000	—
1962	LAA-A	19	64	8	17	1	0	4	14	5	1	11	1	0	0	0	0	.266	.329	.469	.897
1963	StL-N	30	49	6	10	2	1	1	5	4	0	12	0	0	0	0	0	.204	.264	.347	.926
1963	**ChC-N**	**27**	**49**	**4**	**9**	**0**	**0**	**2**	**7**	**4**	**1**	**13**	**0**	**0**	**1**	**0**	**1**	**.184**	**.241**	**.306**	**.943**
1964	**ChC-N**	**59**	**103**	**11**	**27**	**3**	**1**	**1**	**14**	**7**	**1**	**31**	**1**	**0**	**0**	**0**	**0**	**.262**	**.315**	**.340**	**.966**
1965	**ChC-N**	**12**	**10**	**0**	**2**	**0**	**0**	**0**	**0**	**0**	**0**	**4**	**0**	**0**	**0**	**0**	**0**	**.200**	**.200**	**.200**	**1.000**
Career average		24	43	5	10	1	0	1	6	3	0	11	0	0	0	0	0	.239	.294	.365	.938
Cubs average		**33**	**54**	**5**	**13**	**1**	**0**	**1**	**7**	**4**	**1**	**16**	**0**	**0**	**0**	**0**	**0**	**.235**	**.286**	**.321**	**.953**
Career total		165	301	33	72	7	2	9	45	21	3	79	3	0	1	0	1	.239	.294	.365	.938
Cubs total		**98**	**162**	**15**	**38**	**3**	**1**	**3**	**21**	**11**	**2**	**48**	**1**	**0**	**1**	**0**	**1**	**.235**	**.286**	**.321**	**.953**

Burns, Thomas Everett (Tom)

HEIGHT: 5'7"　THROWS: RIGHT　BATS: RIGHT　BORN: 3/30/1857 HONESDALE, PENNSYLVANIA　DIED: 3/19/1902 JERSEY CITY, NEW JERSEY
POSITIONS PLAYED: P, C, 2B, 3B, SS, OF

YEAR	TEAM	GAMES	AB	RUNS	HITS	2B	3B	HR	RBI	BB	IBB	SO	HBP	SH	SF	SB	CS	BA	OBA	SA	FA
1880	ChN-N	85	333	47	103	17	3	0	43	12	—	23	—	—	—	—	—	.309	.333	.378	.857
1881	ChN-N	84	342	41	95	20	3	4	42	14	—	22	—	—	—	—	—	.278	.306	.389	.871
1882	ChN-N	84	355	55	88	23	6	0	48	15	—	28	—	—	—	—	—	.248	.278	.346	.873
1883	ChN-N	97	405	69	119	37	7	2	67	13	—	31	—	—	—	—	—	.294	.316	.435	.855
1884	ChN-N	83	343	54	84	14	2	7	44	13	—	50	—	—	—	—	—	.245	.272	.359	.840
1885	ChN-N	111	445	82	121	23	9	7	71	16	—	48	—	—	—	—	—	.272	.297	.411	.844
1886	ChN-N	112	445	64	123	18	10	3	65	14	—	40	—	—	—	15	—	.276	.298	.382	.890
1887	ChN-N	115	458	57	146	20	10	3	60	34	—	32	1	—	—	32	—	.319	.367	.426	.876
1888	ChN-N	134	483	60	115	12	6	3	70	26	—	49	3	—	—	34	—	.238	.281	.306	.905
1889	ChN-N	136	525	64	127	27	6	4	66	32	—	57	2	—	—	18	—	.242	.288	.339	.880
1890	ChN-N	139	538	86	149	17	6	5	86	57	—	45	2	—	—	44	—	.277	.348	.359	.898
1891	ChN-N	59	243	36	55	8	1	1	17	21	—	21	0	—	—	18	—	.226	.288	.280	.889
1892	Pit-N	12	39	7	8	0	0	0	4	3	—	8	0	—	—	1	—	.205	.262	.205	.688
Career average		96	381	56	103	18	5	3	53	21	—	35	1	—	—	12	—	.269	.308	.368	.872
Cubs average		**103**	**410**	**60**	**110**	**20**	**6**	**3**	**57**	**22**	**—**	**37**	**1**	**—**	**—**	**13**	**—**	**.270**	**.308**	**.369**	**.873**
Career total		1251	4954	722	1333	236	69	39	683	270	—	454	8	—	—	162	—	.269	.308	.368	.872
Cubs total		**1239**	**4915**	**715**	**1325**	**236**	**69**	**39**	**679**	**267**	**—**	**446**	**8**	**—**	**—**	**161**	**—**	**.270**	**.308**	**.369**	**.873**

Thomas (Tom) Everett "Tommy" Burns, ss-3b-2b-of-c, 1880–92

Tom Burns was a versatile and talented member of Chicago's superb "Stonewall Infield" during the glory years of the 1880s.

Born on March 30, 1857, in Honesdale, Pennsylvania, Burns had starred in the minor leagues with Albany of the New York State League in the late 1870s. He came to Chicago in 1880 and was an immediate star, with a .309 batting average that was fifth in the league and a .333 on-base percentage that also ranked him fifth as Chicago easily won the National League crown.

Burns was a smart player and an aggressive base runner, one of the few ballplayers in the league to slide headfirst into a base in those days.

Manager–first baseman Cap Anson loved Burns because he eschewed alcohol entirely, even in the off-season. But the impish Burns was also the master of the practical joke, and even Anson himself was not spared. One of Burns's most well-known tricks on Anson was stealing parts of Cap's uniform, usually his baseball shoes, and watching as the big manager tore apart the clubhouse trying to find them.

For the first six years of his career in Chicago, Burns played shortstop. But in 1886 Anson moved him to third and switched third baseman Ned Williamson to shortstop. Anson's theory was that Williamson could cover more ground at shortstop while Burns had a stronger arm that would be more effective at third base.

Although such a move might have been seen to be disruptive, there are no reports of either man criticizing Anson's decision. And indeed, it was tough to do so, when Chicago, which had finished fifth in 1884, bounced back to win the National League pennant in 1885 and 1886. Anson believed that the 1885 and 1886 units comprised the greatest professional baseball teams of all time to that point.

Burns was a full-time player for Chicago until 1890, almost never missing a game. But the next year, injuries limited him to playing only 59 games. He finished his career in 1892 as a part-time player with Pittsburgh.

Burns later came back to manage Chicago for two years after his friend and mentor Anson was forced out. He later became a respected National League umpire. Burns died in Jersey City, New Jersey, in 1902.

Burton, Ellis Narrington (Bones)
HEIGHT: 5'11"   THROWS: RIGHT   BATS: BOTH   BORN: 8/12/1936 LOS ANGELES, CALIFORNIA   POSITIONS PLAYED: OF

YEAR	TEAM	GAMES	AB	RUNS	HITS	2B	3B	HR	RBI	BB	IBB	SO	HBP	SH	SF	SB	CS	BA	OBA	SA	FA
1958	StL-N	8	30	5	7	0	1	2	4	3	0	8	1	0	0	0	1	.233	.324	.500	1.000
1960	StL-N	29	28	5	6	1	0	0	2	4	0	14	0	2	0	0	2	.214	.313	.250	1.000
1963	Cle-A	26	31	6	6	3	0	1	1	4	0	4	0	0	0	0	0	.194	.286	.387	1.000
1963	**ChC-N**	**93**	**322**	**45**	**74**	**16**	**1**	**12**	**41**	**36**	**1**	**59**	**4**	**6**	**5**	**6**	**3**	**.230**	**.311**	**.398**	**.975**
1964	**ChC-N**	**42**	**105**	**12**	**20**	**3**	**2**	**2**	**7**	**17**	**0**	**22**	**0**	**3**	**0**	**4**	**0**	**.190**	**.303**	**.314**	**.981**
1965	**ChC-N**	**17**	**40**	**6**	**7**	**1**	**0**	**0**	**4**	**1**	**0**	**10**	**0**	**1**	**2**	**1**	**0**	**.175**	**.186**	**.200**	**1.000**
Career average		43	111	16	24	5	1	3	12	13	0	23	1	2	1	2	1	.216	.300	.365	.981
Cubs average		**51**	**156**	**21**	**34**	**7**	**1**	**5**	**17**	**18**	**0**	**30**	**1**	**3**	**2**	**4**	**1**	**.216**	**.299**	**.362**	**.979**
Career total		215	556	79	120	24	4	17	59	65	1	117	5	12	7	11	6	.216	.300	.365	.981
Cubs total		**152**	**467**	**63**	**101**	**20**	**3**	**14**	**52**	**54**	**1**	**91**	**4**	**10**	**7**	**11**	**3**	**.216**	**.299**	**.362**	**.979**

Butler, John Stephen (Johnny *or* Trolley Line)
HEIGHT: 6'0" THROWS: RIGHT BATS: RIGHT BORN: 3/20/1893 FALL RIVER, KANSAS   DIED: 4/29/1967 SEAL BEACH, CALIFORNIA
POSITIONS PLAYED: 2B, 3B, SS

YEAR	TEAM	GAMES	AB	RUNS	HITS	2B	3B	HR	RBI	BB	IBB	SO	HBP	SH	SF	SB	CS	BA	OBA	SA	FA
1926	Bro-N	147	501	54	135	27	5	1	68	54	—	44	5	17	—	6	—	.269	.346	.349	.954
1927	Bro-N	149	521	39	124	13	6	2	57	34	—	33	6	16	—	9	—	.238	.292	.298	.959
1928	**ChC-N**	**62**	**174**	**17**	**47**	**7**	**0**	**0**	**16**	**19**	**—**	**7**	**3**	**6**	**—**	**2**	**—**	**.270**	**.352**	**.310**	**.947**
1929	StL-N	17	55	5	9	1	1	0	5	4	—	5	0	0	—	0	—	.164	.220	.218	.969
Career average		94	313	29	79	12	3	1	37	28	—	22	4	10	—	4	—	.252	.320	.317	.956
Cubs average		**62**	**174**	**17**	**47**	**7**	**0**	**0**	**16**	**19**	**—**	**7**	**3**	**6**	**—**	**2**	**—**	**.270**	**.352**	**.310**	**.947**
Career total		375	1251	115	315	48	12	3	146	111	—	89	14	39	—	17	—	.252	.320	.317	.956
Cubs total		**62**	**174**	**17**	**47**	**7**	**0**	**0**	**16**	**19**	**—**	**7**	**3**	**6**	**—**	**2**	**—**	**.270**	**.352**	**.310**	**.947**

Cairo, Miguel Jesus
HEIGHT: 6'1" THROWS: RIGHT BATS: RIGHT BORN: 5/4/1974 ANACO, VENEZUELA   POSITIONS PLAYED: 1B, 2B, 3B, SS, OF

YEAR	TEAM	GAMES	AB	RUNS	HITS	2B	3B	HR	RBI	BB	IBB	SO	HBP	SH	SF	SB	CS	BA	OBA	SA	FA
1996	Tor-A	9	27	5	6	2	0	0	1	2	0	9	1	0	0	0	0	.222	.300	.296	1.000
1997	**ChC-N**	**16**	**29**	**7**	**7**	**1**	**0**	**0**	**1**	**2**	**0**	**3**	**1**	**0**	**0**	**0**	**0**	**.241**	**.313**	**.276**	**1.000**
1998	TB-A	150	515	49	138	26	5	5	46	24	0	44	6	11	2	19	8	.268	.307	.367	.978
1999	TB-A	120	465	61	137	15	5	3	36	24	0	46	7	7	5	22	7	.295	.335	.368	.986
2000	TB-A	119	375	49	98	18	2	1	34	29	0	34	2	6	5	28	7	.261	.314	.328	.983
2001	**ChC-N**	**66**	**123**	**20**	**35**	**3**	**1**	**2**	**9**	**16**	**1**	**21**	**0**	**7**	**1**	**2**	**1**	**.285**	**.364**	**.374**	**.917**
2001	StL-N	27	33	5	11	5	0	1	7	2	0	2	0	0	0	0	0	.333	.371	.576	.929
Career average		85	261	33	72	12	2	2	22	17	0	27	3	5	2	12	4	.276	.323	.360	.980
Cubs average		**41**	**76**	**14**	**21**	**2**	**1**	**1**	**5**	**9**	**1**	**12**	**1**	**4**	**1**	**1**	**1**	**.276**	**.355**	**.355**	**.941**
Career total		507	1567	196	432	70	13	12	134	99	1	159	17	31	13	71	23	.276	.323	.360	.980
Cubs total		**82**	**152**	**27**	**42**	**4**	**1**	**2**	**10**	**18**	**1**	**24**	**1**	**7**	**1**	**2**	**1**	**.276**	**.355**	**.355**	**.941**

Callaghan, Martin Francis (Marty)
HEIGHT: 5'10" THROWS: LEFT BATS: LEFT BORN: 6/9/1900 NORWOOD, MASSACHUSETTS   DIED: 6/23/1975 NORFOLK, MASSACHUSETTS
POSITIONS PLAYED: OF

YEAR	TEAM	GAMES	AB	RUNS	HITS	2B	3B	HR	RBI	BB	IBB	SO	HBP	SH	SF	SB	CS	BA	OBA	SA	FA
1922	**ChC-N**	**74**	**175**	**31**	**45**	**7**	**4**	**0**	**20**	**17**	**—**	**17**	**1**	**2**	**—**	**2**	**3**	**.257**	**.326**	**.343**	**.946**
1923	**ChC-N**	**61**	**129**	**18**	**29**	**1**	**3**	**0**	**14**	**8**	**—**	**18**	**1**	**0**	**—**	**2**	**5**	**.225**	**.275**	**.279**	**.969**
1928	Cin-N	81	238	29	69	11	4	0	24	27	—	10	0	19	—	5	—	.290	.362	.370	.980
1930	Cin-N	79	225	28	62	9	2	0	16	19	—	25	1	12	—	1	—	.276	.335	.333	.986
Career average		74	192	27	51	7	3	0	19	18	—	18	1	8	—	3	2	.267	.332	.338	.973
Cubs average		**68**	**152**	**25**	**37**	**4**	**4**	**0**	**17**	**13**	**—**	**18**	**1**	**1**	**—**	**2**	**4**	**.243**	**.305**	**.316**	**.955**
Career total		295	767	106	205	28	13	0	74	71	—	70	3	33	—	10	8	.267	.332	.338	.973
Cubs total		**135**	**304**	**49**	**74**	**8**	**7**	**0**	**34**	**25**	**—**	**35**	**2**	**2**	**—**	**4**	**8**	**.243**	**.305**	**.316**	**.955**

Callahan, James Joseph (Nixey)
HEIGHT: 5'10" THROWS: RIGHT BATS: RIGHT BORN: 3/18/1874 FITCHBURG, MASSACHUSETTS   DIED: 10/4/1934 BOSTON, MASSACHUSETTS
POSITIONS PLAYED: P, 1B, 2B, 3B, SS, OF

YEAR	TEAM	GAMES	AB	RUNS	HITS	2B	3B	HR	RBI	BB	IBB	SO	HBP	SH	SF	SB	CS	BA	OBA	SA	FA
1894	Phi-N	9	21	4	5	0	0	0	0	0	—	7	0	0	—	0	—	.238	.238	.238	.923
1897	**ChN-N**	**94**	**360**	**60**	**105**	**18**	**6**	**3**	**47**	**10**	**—**	**—**	**5**	**8**	**—**	**12**	**—**	**.292**	**.320**	**.400**	**.892**
1898	**ChN-N**	**43**	**164**	**27**	**43**	**7**	**5**	**0**	**22**	**4**	**—**	**—**	**0**	**4**	**—**	**3**	**—**	**.262**	**.280**	**.366**	**.908**
1899	**ChN-N**	**47**	**150**	**21**	**39**	**4**	**3**	**0**	**18**	**8**	**—**	**—**	**2**	**5**	**—**	**9**	**—**	**.260**	**.306**	**.327**	**.911**
1900	**ChN-N**	**32**	**115**	**16**	**27**	**3**	**2**	**0**	**9**	**6**	**—**	**—**	**0**	**5**	**—**	**5**	**—**	**.235**	**.273**	**.296**	**.975**
1901	CWS-A	45	118	15	39	7	3	1	19	10	—	—	0	4	—	10	—	.331	.383	.466	.923
1902	CWS-A	70	218	27	51	7	2	0	13	6	—	—	2	13	—	4	—	.234	.261	.284	.948
1903	CWS-A	118	439	47	128	26	5	2	56	20	—	—	1	11	—	24	—	.292	.324	.387	.901
1904	CWS-A	132	482	66	126	23	2	0	54	39	—	—	1	33	—	29	—	.261	.318	.317	.953
1905	CWS-A	96	345	50	94	18	6	1	43	29	—	—	4	10	—	26	—	.272	.336	.368	.956
1911	CWS-A	120	466	64	131	13	5	3	60	15	—	—	2	21	—	45	—	.281	.306	.350	.963
1912	CWS-A	111	408	45	111	9	7	1	52	12	—	—	3	22	—	19	—	.272	.298	.336	.939
1913	CWS-A	6	9	0	2	0	0	0	1	0	—	2	0	0	—	0	—	.222	.222	.222	1.000

(continued)

(continued)

	GAMES	AB	RUNS	HITS	2B	3B	HR	RBI	BB	IBB	SO	HBP	SH	SF	SB	CS	BA	OBA	SA	FA
Career average	71	253	34	69	10	4	1	30	12	—	1	2	10	—	14	—	.273	.311	.352	.928
Cubs average	**54**	**197**	**31**	**54**	**8**	**4**	**1**	**24**	**7**	**—**	**0**	**2**	**6**	**—**	**7**	**—**	**.271**	**.302**	**.364**	**.911**
Career total	923	3295	442	901	135	46	11	394	159	—	9	20	136	—	186	—	.273	.311	.352	.928
Cubs total	**216**	**789**	**124**	**214**	**32**	**16**	**3**	**96**	**28**	**—**	**0**	**7**	**22**	**—**	**29**	**—**	**.271**	**.302**	**.364**	**.911**

Callison, John Wesley (Johnny)

HEIGHT: 5'10" THROWS: RIGHT BATS: LEFT BORN: 3/12/1939 QUALLS, OKLAHOMA POSITIONS PLAYED: OF

YEAR	TEAM	GAMES	AB	RUNS	HITS	2B	3B	HR	RBI	BB	IBB	SO	HBP	SH	SF	SB	CS	BA	OBA	SA	FA
1958	CWS-A	18	64	10	19	4	2	1	12	6	0	14	0	0	1	1	0	.297	.352	.469	.976
1959	CWS-A	49	104	12	18	3	0	3	12	13	0	20	1	0	0	0	1	.173	.271	.288	.983
1960	Phi-N	99	288	36	75	11	5	9	30	45	2	70	0	2	0	0	4	.260	.360	.427	.989
1961	Phi-N	138	455	74	121	20	11	9	47	69	5	76	3	6	5	10	4	.266	.363	.418	.967
1962	Phi-N	157	603	107	181	26	10	23	83	54	1	96	6	8	1	10	3	.300	.363	.491	.980
1963	Phi-N	157	626	96	178	36	11	26	78	50	4	111	2	13	1	8	3	.284	.339	.502	.994
1964	Phi-N	162	654	101	179	30	10	31	104	36	3	95	6	6	3	6	3	.274	.316	.492	.988
1965	Phi-N	160	619	93	162	25	16	32	101	57	2	117	6	4	5	6	5	.262	.328	.509	.982
1966	Phi-N	155	612	93	169	40	7	11	55	56	4	83	3	2	4	8	8	.276	.338	.418	.990
1967	Phi-N	149	556	62	145	30	5	14	64	55	17	63	3	3	3	6	12	.261	.329	.408	.977
1968	Phi-N	121	398	46	97	18	4	14	40	42	4	70	3	3	2	4	3	.244	.319	.415	1.000
1969	Phi-N	134	495	66	131	29	5	16	64	49	11	73	3	1	4	2	1	.265	.332	.440	.990
1970	**ChC-N**	**147**	**477**	**65**	**126**	**23**	**2**	**19**	**68**	**60**	**11**	**63**	**3**	**0**	**3**	**7**	**2**	**.264**	**.348**	**.440**	**.973**
1971	**ChC-N**	**103**	**290**	**27**	**61**	**12**	**1**	**8**	**38**	**36**	**8**	**55**	**2**	**1**	**4**	**2**	**1**	**.210**	**.298**	**.341**	**.982**
1972	NYY-A	92	275	28	71	10	0	9	34	18	1	34	0	2	5	3	0	.258	.299	.393	.992
1973	NYY-A	45	136	10	24	4	0	1	10	4	0	24	0	0	2	1	1	.176	.197	.228	.960
Career average		118	416	58	110	20	6	14	53	41	5	67	3	3	3	5	3	.264	.331	.441	.984
Cubs average		**125**	**384**	**46**	**94**	**18**	**2**	**14**	**53**	**48**	**10**	**59**	**3**	**1**	**4**	**5**	**2**	**.244**	**.329**	**.403**	**.976**
Career total		1886	6652	926	1757	321	89	226	840	650	73	1064	41	51	43	74	51	.264	.331	.441	.984
Cubs total		**250**	**767**	**92**	**187**	**35**	**3**	**27**	**106**	**96**	**19**	**118**	**5**	**1**	**7**	**9**	**3**	**.244**	**.329**	**.403**	**.976**

Camilli, Adolph Louis (Dolph)

HEIGHT: 5'10" THROWS: LEFT BATS: LEFT BORN: 4/23/1907 SAN FRANCISCO, CALIFORNIA DIED: 10/21/1997 SAN MATEO, CALIFORNIA
POSITIONS PLAYED: 1B

YEAR	TEAM	GAMES	AB	RUNS	HITS	2B	3B	HR	RBI	BB	IBB	SO	HBP	SH	SF	SB	CS	BA	OBA	SA	FA
1933	**ChC-N**	**16**	**58**	**8**	**13**	**2**	**1**	**2**	**7**	**4**	**—**	**11**	**0**	**1**	**—**	**3**	**—**	**.224**	**.274**	**.397**	**.994**
1934	**ChC-N**	**32**	**120**	**17**	**33**	**8**	**0**	**4**	**19**	**5**	**—**	**25**	**2**	**1**	**—**	**1**	**—**	**.275**	**.315**	**.442**	**.988**
1934	Phi-N	102	378	52	100	20	3	12	68	48	—	69	2	1	—	3	—	.265	.350	.429	.985
1935	Phi-N	156	602	88	157	23	5	25	83	65	—	113	3	2	—	9	—	.261	.336	.440	.987
1936	Phi-N	151	530	106	167	29	13	28	102	116	—	84	3	2	—	5	—	.315	.441	.577	.988
1937	Phi-N	131	475	101	161	23	7	27	80	90	—	82	2	3	—	6	—	.339	.446	.587	.994
1938	Bro-N	146	509	106	128	25	11	24	100	119	—	101	0	1	—	6	—	.251	.393	.485	.995
1939	Bro-N	157	565	105	164	30	12	26	104	110	—	107	4	5	—	1	—	.290	.409	.524	.990
1940	Bro-N	142	512	92	147	29	13	23	96	89	—	83	4	1	—	9	—	.287	.397	.529	.992
1941	Bro-N	149	529	92	151	29	6	34	120	104	—	115	4	4	—	3	—	.285	.407	.556	.989
1942	Bro-N	150	524	89	132	23	7	26	109	97	—	85	3	1	—	10	—	.252	.372	.471	.992
1943	Bro-N	95	353	56	87	15	6	6	43	65	—	48	1	1	—	2	1	.246	.365	.374	.992
1945	Bos-A	63	198	24	42	5	2	2	19	35	—	38	0	1	—	2	0	.212	.330	.288	.991
Career average		124	446	78	124	22	7	20	79	79	—	80	2	2	—	5	0	.277	.388	.492	.990
Cubs average		**24**	**89**	**13**	**23**	**5**	**1**	**3**	**13**	**5**	**—**	**18**	**1**	**1**	**—**	**2**	**—**	**.258**	**.302**	**.427**	**.990**
Career total		1490	5353	936	1482	261	86	239	950	947	—	961	28	24	—	60	1	.277	.388	.492	.990
Cubs total		**48**	**178**	**25**	**46**	**10**	**1**	**6**	**26**	**9**	**—**	**36**	**2**	**2**	**—**	**4**	**—**	**.258**	**.302**	**.427**	**.990**

Camp, Robert Plantagenet (Lew)

HEIGHT: 6'0" THROWS: RIGHT BATS: LEFT BORN: 2/23/1868 COLUMBUS, OHIO DIED: 10/1/1948 OMAHA, NEBRASKA POSITIONS PLAYED: 2B, 3B, SS, OF

YEAR	TEAM	GAMES	AB	RUNS	HITS	2B	3B	HR	RBI	BB	IBB	SO	HBP	SH	SF	SB	CS	BA	OBA	SA	FA
1892	StL-N	42	145	19	30	3	1	2	13	17	—	27	1	—	—	12	—	.207	.294	.283	.776
1893	**ChN-N**	**38**	**156**	**37**	**41**	**7**	**7**	**2**	**17**	**19**	**—**	**19**	**1**	**—**	**—**	**30**	**—**	**.263**	**.347**	**.436**	**.871**
1894	**ChN-N**	**8**	**33**	**1**	**6**	**2**	**0**	**0**	**1**	**1**	**—**	**6**	**0**	**1**	**—**	**0**	**—**	**.182**	**.206**	**.242**	**.830**
Career average		29	111	19	26	4	3	1	10	12	—	17	1	0	—	14	—	.231	.311	.350	.825
Cubs average		**23**	**95**	**19**	**24**	**5**	**4**	**1**	**9**	**10**	**—**	**13**	**1**	**1**	**—**	**15**	**—**	**.249**	**.324**	**.402**	**.859**
Career total		88	334	57	77	12	8	4	31	37	—	52	2	1	—	42	—	.231	.311	.350	.825
Cubs total		**46**	**189**	**38**	**47**	**9**	**7**	**2**	**18**	**20**	**—**	**25**	**1**	**1**	**—**	**30**	**—**	**.249**	**.324**	**.402**	**.859**

Campbell, Arthur Vincent (Vin)

HEIGHT: 6'0" THROWS: RIGHT BATS: LEFT BORN: 1/30/1888 ST. LOUIS, MISSOURI DIED: 11/16/1969 TOWSON, MARYLAND POSITIONS PLAYED: OF

YEAR	TEAM	GAMES	AB	RUNS	HITS	2B	3B	HR	RBI	BB	IBB	SO	HBP	SH	SF	SB	CS	BA	OBA	SA	FA
1908	ChC-N	1	1	0	0	0	0	0	0	0	—	—	0	0	—	0	—	.000	.000	.000	—
1910	Pit-N	97	282	42	92	9	5	4	21	26	—	23	4	12	—	17	—	.326	.391	.436	.895
1911	Pit-N	42	93	12	29	3	1	0	10	8	—	7	0	2	—	6	—	.312	.366	.366	.923
1912	Bos-N	145	624	102	185	32	9	3	48	32	—	44	3	22	—	19	—	.296	.334	.391	.938
1914	Ind-F	134	544	92	173	23	11	7	44	37	—	47	6	10	—	26	—	.318	.368	.439	.925
1915	New-F	127	525	78	163	18	10	1	44	29	—	35	5	7	—	24	—	.310	.352	.389	.947
Career average		91	345	54	107	14	6	3	28	22	—	26	3	9	—	15	—	.310	.357	.408	.929
Cubs average		1	1	0	0	0	0	0	0	0	—	—	0	0	—	0	—	.000	.000	.000	—
Career total		546	2069	326	642	85	36	15	167	132	—	156	18	53	—	92	—	.310	.357	.408	.929
Cubs total		1	1	0	0	0	0	0	0	0	—	—	0	0	—	0	—	.000	.000	.000	—

Campbell, Joseph Earl (Joe)

HEIGHT: 6'1" THROWS: RIGHT BATS: RIGHT BORN: 3/10/1944 LOUISVILLE, KENTUCKY POSITIONS PLAYED: OF

YEAR	TEAM	GAMES	AB	RUNS	HITS	2B	3B	HR	RBI	BB	IBB	SO	HBP	SH	SF	SB	CS	BA	OBA	SA	FA
1967	ChC-N	1	3	0	0	0	0	0	0	0	0	3	0	0	0	0	0	.000	.000	.000	—
Career average		1	3	0	0	0	0	0	0	0	0	3	0	0	0	0	0	.000	.000	.000	—
Cubs average		1	3	0	0	0	0	0	0	0	0	3	0	0	0	0	0	.000	.000	.000	—
Career total		1	3	0	0	0	0	0	0	0	0	3	0	0	0	0	0	.000	.000	.000	—
Cubs total		1	3	0	0	0	0	0	0	0	0	3	0	0	0	0	0	.000	.000	.000	—

Campbell, Ronald Thomas (Ron)

HEIGHT: 6'1" THROWS: RIGHT BATS: RIGHT BORN: 4/5/1940 CHATTANOOGA, TENNESSEE POSITIONS PLAYED: 2B, 3B, SS

YEAR	TEAM	GAMES	AB	RUNS	HITS	2B	3B	HR	RBI	BB	IBB	SO	HBP	SH	SF	SB	CS	BA	OBA	SA	FA
1964	ChC-N	26	92	7	25	6	1	1	10	1	0	21	0	1	1	0	1	.272	.277	.391	.941
1965	ChC-N	2	2	0	0	0	0	0	0	0	0	0	0	0	0	0	0	.000	.000	.000	—
1966	ChC-N	24	60	4	13	1	0	0	4	6	2	5	0	0	1	1	1	.217	.284	.233	.972
Career average		17	51	4	13	2	0	0	5	2	1	9	0	0	1	0	1	.247	.276	.325	.950
Cubs average		17	51	4	13	2	0	0	5	2	1	9	0	0	1	0	1	.247	.276	.325	.950
Career total		52	154	11	38	7	1	1	14	7	2	26	0	1	2	1	2	.247	.276	.325	.950
Cubs total		52	154	11	38	7	1	1	14	7	2	26	0	1	2	1	2	.247	.276	.325	.950

Campbell, William Gilthorpe (Gilly)

HEIGHT: 5'7" THROWS: RIGHT BATS: LEFT BORN: 2/13/1908 KANSAS CITY, KANSAS DIED: 2/21/1973 LOS ANGELES, CALIFORNIA
POSITIONS PLAYED: C, 1B, OF

YEAR	TEAM	GAMES	AB	RUNS	HITS	2B	3B	HR	RBI	BB	IBB	SO	HBP	SH	SF	SB	CS	BA	OBA	SA	FA
1933	ChC-N	46	89	11	25	3	1	1	10	7	—	4	2	1	—	0	—	.281	.347	.371	.949
1935	Cin-N	88	218	26	56	7	0	3	30	42	—	7	1	0	—	3	—	.257	.379	.330	.987
1936	Cin-N	89	235	28	63	13	1	1	40	43	—	14	1	0	—	2	—	.268	.384	.345	.984
1937	Cin-N	18	40	3	11	2	0	0	2	5	—	1	0	0	—	0	—	.275	.356	.325	.967
1938	Bro-N	54	126	10	31	5	0	0	11	19	—	9	2	0	—	0	—	.246	.354	.286	.958
Career average		59	142	16	37	6	0	1	19	23	—	7	1	0	—	1	—	.263	.371	.332	.949
Cubs average		46	89	11	25	3	1	1	10	7	—	4	2	1	—	0	—	.281	.347	.371	.949
Career total		295	708	78	186	30	2	5	93	116	—	35	6	1	—	5	—	.263	.371	.332	.977
Cubs total		46	89	11	25	3	1	1	10	7	—	4	2	1	—	0	—	.281	.347	.371	.949

Canavan, James Edward (Jim)

HEIGHT: 5'8"   THROWS: RIGHT   BATS: RIGHT   BORN: 11/26/1866 NEW BEDFORD, MASSACHUSETTS   DIED: 5/27/1949 NEW BEDFORD, MASSACHUSETTS
POSITIONS PLAYED: 1B, 2B, 3B, SS, OF

YEAR	TEAM	GAMES	AB	RUNS	HITS	2B	3B	HR	RBI	BB	IBB	SO	HBP	SH	SF	SB	CS	BA	OBA	SA	FA
1891	Cin-AA	101	426	74	97	13	14	7	66	27	—	44	5	—	—	21	—	.228	.282	.373	.860
1891	Mil-AA	35	142	33	38	2	4	3	21	16	—	10	0	—	—	7	—	.268	.342	.401	.863
1892	**ChN-N**	**118**	**439**	**48**	**73**	**10**	**11**	**0**	**32**	**48**	**—**	**48**	**0**	**—**	**—**	**33**	**—**	**.166**	**.248**	**.239**	**.923**
1893	Cin-N	121	461	65	104	13	7	5	64	51	—	20	2	—	—	31	—	.226	.305	.317	.932
1894	Cin-N	101	356	77	97	16	9	13	70	62	—	25	0	5	—	13	—	.272	.380	.478	.897
1897	Bro-N	63	240	25	52	9	3	2	34	26	—	—	2	1	—	9	—	.217	.299	.304	.909
Career average		108	413	64	92	13	10	6	57	46	—	29	2	1	—	23	—	.223	.304	.344	.899
Cubs average		**118**	**439**	**48**	**73**	**10**	**11**	**0**	**32**	**48**	**—**	**48**	**0**	**—**	**—**	**33**	**—**	**.166**	**.248**	**.239**	**.923**
Career total		539	2064	322	461	63	48	30	287	230	—	147	9	6	—	114	—	.223	.304	.344	.899
Cubs total		**118**	**439**	**48**	**73**	**10**	**11**	**0**	**32**	**48**	**—**	**48**	**0**	**—**	**—**	**33**	**—**	**.166**	**.248**	**.239**	**.923**

Cannizzaro, Christopher John (Chris)

HEIGHT: 6'0"   THROWS: RIGHT   BATS: RIGHT   BORN: 5/3/1938 OAKLAND, CALIFORNIA   POSITIONS PLAYED: C, OF

YEAR	TEAM	GAMES	AB	RUNS	HITS	2B	3B	HR	RBI	BB	IBB	SO	HBP	SH	SF	SB	CS	BA	OBA	SA	FA
1960	StL-N	7	9	0	2	0	0	0	1	1	0	3	0	0	1	0	0	.222	.273	.222	1.000
1961	StL-N	6	2	0	1	0	0	0	0	0	0	0	0	0	0	0	0	.500	.500	.500	1.000
1962	NYM-N	59	133	9	32	2	1	0	9	19	1	26	1	1	2	1	1	.241	.335	.271	.973
1963	NYM-N	16	33	4	8	1	0	0	4	1	0	8	0	1	0	0	0	.242	.257	.273	1.000
1964	NYM-N	60	164	11	51	10	0	0	10	14	2	28	1	2	1	0	0	.311	.367	.372	.988
1965	NYM-N	114	251	17	46	8	2	0	7	28	4	60	2	3	0	0	5	.183	.270	.231	.977
1968	Pit-N	25	58	5	14	2	2	1	7	9	4	13	0	3	0	0	2	.241	.343	.397	.976
1969	SD-N	134	418	23	92	14	3	4	33	42	8	81	1	4	2	0	1	.220	.290	.297	.988
1970	SD-N	111	341	27	95	13	3	5	42	48	8	49	1	7	3	2	7	.279	.366	.378	.980
1971	SD-N	21	63	2	12	1	0	1	8	11	0	10	1	0	0	0	0	.190	.320	.254	.992
1971	**ChC-N**	**71**	**197**	**18**	**42**	**8**	**1**	**5**	**23**	**28**	**2**	**24**	**1**	**6**	**2**	**0**	**0**	**.213**	**.311**	**.340**	**.983**
1972	LA-N	73	200	14	48	6	0	2	18	31	5	38	0	1	1	0	1	.240	.341	.300	.983
1973	LA-N	17	21	0	4	0	0	0	3	3	1	3	0	1	1	0	0	.190	.280	.190	1.000
1974	SD-N	26	60	2	11	1	0	0	4	6	0	11	0	1	0	0	0	.183	.258	.200	.979
Career average		57	150	10	35	5	1	1	13	19	3	27	1	2	1	0	1	.235	.319	.309	.983
Cubs average		**71**	**197**	**18**	**42**	**8**	**1**	**5**	**23**	**28**	**2**	**24**	**1**	**6**	**2**	**0**	**0**	**.213**	**.311**	**.340**	**.983**
Career total		740	1950	132	458	66	12	18	169	241	35	354	7	28	14	3	17	.235	.319	.309	.983
Cubs total		**71**	**197**	**18**	**42**	**8**	**1**	**5**	**23**	**28**	**2**	**24**	**1**	**6**	**2**	**0**	**0**	**.213**	**.311**	**.340**	**.983**

Cardenal, Jose Rosario

HEIGHT: 5'10"   THROWS: RIGHT   BATS: RIGHT   BORN: 10/7/1943 MATANZAS, CUBA   POSITIONS PLAYED: 1B, 2B, 3B, SS, OF

YEAR	TEAM	GAMES	AB	RUNS	HITS	2B	3B	HR	RBI	BB	IBB	SO	HBP	SH	SF	SB	CS	BA	OBA	SA	FA
1963	SF-N	9	5	1	1	0	0	0	2	1	0	1	0	0	0	0	1	.200	.333	.200	—
1964	SF-N	20	15	3	0	0	0	0	0	2	0	3	0	0	0	2	0	.000	.118	.000	.909
1965	Cal-A	134	512	58	128	23	2	11	57	27	1	72	2	3	6	37	17	.250	.287	.367	.965
1966	Cal-A	154	561	67	155	15	3	16	48	34	5	69	4	3	4	24	11	.276	.320	.399	.992
1967	Cal-A	108	381	40	90	13	5	6	27	15	0	63	2	6	1	10	5	.236	.268	.344	.986
1968	Cle-A	157	583	78	150	21	7	7	44	39	3	74	2	2	3	40	18	.257	.305	.353	.974
1969	Cle-A	146	557	75	143	26	3	11	45	49	3	58	0	4	6	36	6	* .257	.314	.373	.983
1970	StL-N	148	552	73	162	32	6	10	74	45	0	70	1	1	0	26	9	.293	.348	.428	.969
1971	StL-N	89	301	37	73	12	4	7	48	29	1	35	0	2	7	12	3	.243	.303	.379	.969
1971	Mil-A	53	198	20	51	10	0	3	32	13	0	20	1	0	7	9	5	.258	.297	.354	.979
1972	**ChC-N**	**143**	**533**	**96**	**155**	**24**	**6**	**17**	**70**	**55**	**3**	**58**	**1**	**1**	**3**	**25**	**14**	**.291**	**.356**	**.454**	**.971**
1973	**ChC-N**	**145**	**522**	**80**	**158**	**33**	**2**	**11**	**68**	**58**	**9**	**62**	**5**	**4**	**4**	**19**	**7**	**.303**	**.375**	**.437**	**.980**
1974	**ChC-N**	**143**	**542**	**75**	**159**	**35**	**3**	**13**	**72**	**56**	**3**	**67**	**1**	**2**	**3**	**23**	**9**	**.293**	**.359**	**.441**	**.965**
1975	**ChC-N**	**154**	**574**	**85**	**182**	**30**	**2**	**9**	**68**	**77**	**5**	**50**	**4**	**4**	**7**	**34**	**12**	**.317**	**.397**	**.423**	**.976**
1976	**ChC-N**	**136**	**521**	**64**	**156**	**25**	**2**	**8**	**47**	**32**	**0**	**39**	**1**	**3**	**3**	**23**	**14**	**.299**	**.339**	**.401**	**.981**
1977	**ChC-N**	**100**	**226**	**33**	**54**	**12**	**1**	**3**	**18**	**28**	**2**	**30**	**1**	**2**	**1**	**5**	**4**	**.239**	**.324**	**.341**	**.977**
1978	Phi-N	87	201	27	50	12	0	4	33	23	2	16	0	0	2	2	3	.249	.323	.368	.987
1979	Phi-N	29	48	4	10	3	0	0	9	8	1	8	0	0	0	1	0	.208	.321	.271	1.000
1979	NYM-N	11	37	8	11	4	0	2	4	6	0	3	1	0	0	1	0	.297	.409	.568	1.000
1980	NYM-N	26	42	4	7	1	0	0	4	6	0	4	0	0	1	0	0	.167	.265	.190	1.000
1980	KC-A	25	53	8	18	2	0	0	5	5	0	5	0	0	3	0	0	.340	.377	.377	.970

(continued)

Jose Rosario Domec Cardenal, of-1b, 1963–80

The speedy Cardenal played for nine teams in 18 major league seasons, but the Cubs were his longest layover.

Born in Matanzas, Cuba, on October 7, 1943, Cardenal's first big-league stop was with the San Francisco Giants in 1963. He couldn't break into the starting lineup there and was shipped to California in 1965, where he came into his own, stealing 37 bases, second in the American League.

Cardenal's speed also showed up in center field, where he showed excellent range. He also had a strong throwing arm, but he often quarreled with his coaches, so stints in Cleveland, St. Louis and Milwaukee followed his term with the Angels.

In 1971 Cardenal was traded to Chicago, where he had some of his most productive years. From 1972 to 1976, Cardenal hit .301 with Chicago and led the team in stolen bases every year. In 1973 he led Chicago in batting average with a .303 mark, and doubles with 33.

Cardenal was colorful as well as talented. He sported a huge afro during his Cubs years, perching his cap atop it like a beanie.

After a subpar season in Chicago in 1977, Cardenal was traded to the Phillies, which he helped win the National League Eastern Division. But he was traded to the Mets in 1979 and wound up his career in Kansas City, where he started two games in right field in the 1980 World Series. He retired after that year.

Cardenal has remained in the game, working as a coach for several organizations, including the Reds, Cardinals and Yankees.

(Cardenal, continued)

Career average	112	387	52	106	19	3	8	43	34	2	45	1	2	3	18	8	.275	.333	.395	.978
Cubs average	**137**	**486**	**72**	**144**	**27**	**3**	**10**	**57**	**51**	**4**	**51**	**2**	**3**	**4**	**22**	**10**	**.296**	**.363**	**.424**	**.975**
Career total	2017	6964	936	1913	333	46	138	775	608	38	807	26	37	61	329	139	.275	.333	.395	.978
Cubs total	**821**	**2918**	**433**	**864**	**159**	**16**	**61**	**343**	**306**	**22**	**306**	**13**	**16**	**21**	**129**	**60**	**.296**	**.363**	**.424**	**.975**

Carney, William John (Bill)

HEIGHT: 5'10" THROWS: RIGHT BATS: BOTH BORN: 3/25/1874 ST. PAUL, MINNESOTA DIED: 7/31/1938 HOPKINS, MINNESOTA POSITIONS PLAYED: OF

YEAR	TEAM	GAMES	AB	RUNS	HITS	2B	3B	HR	RBI	BB	IBB	SO	HBP	SH	SF	SB	CS	BA	OBA	SA	FA
1904	ChC-N	2	7	0	0	0	0	0	0	1	—	—	0	0	—	0	—	.000	.125	.000	1.000
Career average		2	7	0	0	0	0	0	0	1	—	—	0	0	—	0	—	.000	.125	.000	1.000
Cubs average		**2**	**7**	**0**	**0**	**0**	**0**	**0**	**0**	**1**	**—**	**—**	**0**	**0**	**—**	**0**	**—**	**.000**	**.125**	**.000**	**1.000**
Career total		2	7	0	0	0	0	0	0	1	—	—	0	0	—	0	—	.000	.125	.000	1.000
Cubs total		**2**	**7**	**0**	**0**	**0**	**0**	**0**	**0**	**1**	**—**	**—**	**0**	**0**	**—**	**0**	**—**	**.000**	**.125**	**.000**	**1.000**

Carroll, Samuel Clifford (Cliff)

HEIGHT: 5'8" THROWS: RIGHT BATS: BOTH BORN: 10/18/1859 CLAY GROVE, IOWA DIED: 6/12/1923 PORTLAND, OREGON POSITIONS PLAYED: OF

YEAR	TEAM	GAMES	AB	RUNS	HITS	2B	3B	HR	RBI	BB	IBB	SO	HBP	SH	SF	SB	CS	BA	OBA	SA	FA
1882	Prv-N	10	41	4	5	0	0	0	2	0	—	4	—	—	—	—	—	.122	.122	.122	1.000
1883	Prv-N	58	238	37	63	12	3	1	20	4	—	28	—	—	—	—	—	.265	.277	.353	.902
1884	Prv-N	113	452	90	118	16	4	3	54	29	—	39	—	—	—	—	—	.261	.306	.334	.904

(continued)

(continued)

YEAR	TEAM	GAMES	AB	RUNS	HITS	2B	3B	HR	RBI	BB	IBB	SO	HBP	SH	SF	SB	CS	BA	OBA	SA	FA
1885	Prv-N	104	426	62	99	12	3	1	40	29	—	29	—	—	—	—	—	.232	.281	.282	.886
1886	WaN-N	111	433	73	99	11	6	2	22	44	—	26	—	—	—	31	—	.229	.300	.296	.862
1887	WaN-N	103	437	79	121	17	4	4	37	17	—	30	9	—	—	40	—	.277	.317	.362	.902
1888	Pit-N	5	20	1	0	0	0	0	0	0	—	8	0	—	—	2	—	.000	.000	.000	.667
1890	**ChN-N**	**136**	**582**	**134**	**166**	**16**	**6**	**7**	**65**	**53**	**—**	**34**	**7**	**—**	**—**	**34**	**—**	**.285**	**.352**	**.369**	**.936**
1891	**ChN-N**	**130**	**515**	**87**	**132**	**20**	**8**	**7**	**80**	**50**	**—**	**42**	**15**	**—**	**—**	**31**	**—**	**.256**	**.340**	**.367**	**.920**
1892	StL-N	101	407	82	111	14	8	4	49	47	—	22	11	—	—	30	—	.273	.363	.376	.901
1893	Bos-N	120	438	80	98	7	5	2	54	88	—	28	5	—	—	29	—	.224	.360	.276	.917
Career average		90	363	66	92	11	4	3	38	33	—	26	4	—	—	18	—	.254	.323	.332	.905
Cubs average		**133**	**549**	**111**	**149**	**18**	**7**	**7**	**73**	**52**	**—**	**38**	**11**	**—**	**—**	**33**	**—**	**.272**	**.346**	**.368**	**.930**
Career total		991	3989	729	1012	125	47	31	423	361	—	290	47	—	—	197	—	.254	.323	.332	.905
Cubs total		**266**	**1097**	**221**	**298**	**36**	**14**	**14**	**145**	**103**	**—**	**76**	**22**	**—**	**—**	**65**	**—**	**.272**	**.346**	**.368**	**.930**

Carter, Joseph Chris (Joe)

HEIGHT: 6'3" THROWS: RIGHT BATS: RIGHT BORN: 3/7/1960 OKLAHOMA CITY, OKLAHOMA POSITIONS PLAYED: 1B, 2B, 3B, OF

YEAR	TEAM	GAMES	AB	RUNS	HITS	2B	3B	HR	RBI	BB	IBB	SO	HBP	SH	SF	SB	CS	BA	OBA	SA	FA
1983	**ChC-N**	**23**	**51**	**6**	**9**	**1**	**1**	**0**	**1**	**0**	**0**	**21**	**0**	**1**	**0**	**1**	**0**	**.176**	**.176**	**.235**	**1.000**
1984	Cle-A	66	244	32	67	6	1	13	41	11	0	48	1	0	1	2	4	.275	.307	.467	.968
1985	Cle-A	143	489	64	128	27	0	15	59	25	2	74	2	3	4	24	6	.262	.298	.409	.982
1986	Cle-A	162	663	108	200	36	9	29	121	32	3	95	5	1	8	29	7	.302	.335	.514	.988
1987	Cle-A	149	588	83	155	27	2	32	106	27	6	105	9	1	4	31	6	.264	.304	.480	.980
1988	Cle-A	157	621	85	168	36	6	27	98	35	6	82	7	1	6	27	5	.271	.314	.478	.985
1989	Cle-A	162	651	84	158	32	4	35	105	39	8	112	8	2	5	13	5	.243	.292	.465	.981
1990	SD-N	162	634	79	147	27	1	24	115	48	18	93	7	0	8	22	6	.232	.290	.391	.979
1991	Tor-A	162	638	89	174	42	3	33	108	49	12	112	10	0	9	20	9	.273	.330	.503	.974
1992	Tor-A	158	622	97	164	30	7	34	119	36	4	109	11	0	13	12	5	.264	.309	.498	.971
1993	Tor-A	155	603	92	153	33	5	33	121	47	5	113	9	0	10	8	3	.254	.312	.489	.974
1994	Tor-A	111	435	70	118	25	2	27	103	33	6	64	2	0	13	11	0	.271	.317	.524	.991
1995	Tor-A	139	558	70	141	23	0	25	76	37	5	87	3	0	5	12	1	.253	.300	.428	.979
1996	Tor-A	157	625	84	158	35	7	30	107	44	2	106	7	0	6	7	6	.253	.306	.475	.980
1997	Tor-A	157	612	76	143	30	4	21	102	40	5	105	7	0	9	8	2	.234	.284	.399	.991
1998	Bal-A	85	283	36	70	15	1	11	34	18	4	48	2	0	0	3	1	.247	.297	.424	.963
1998	SF-N	41	105	15	31	7	0	7	29	6	0	13	0	0	4	1	0	.295	.322	.562	.991
Career average		137	526	73	137	27	3	25	90	33	5	87	6	1	7	14	4	.259	.306	.464	.981
Cubs average		**23**	**51**	**6**	**9**	**1**	**1**	**0**	**1**	**0**	**0**	**21**	**0**	**1**	**0**	**1**	**0**	**.176**	**.176**	**.235**	**1.000**
Career total		2189	8422	1170	2184	432	53	396	1445	527	86	1387	90	10	105	231	66	.259	.306	.464	.981
Cubs total		**23**	**51**	**6**	**9**	**1**	**1**	**0**	**1**	**0**	**0**	**21**	**0**	**1**	**0**	**1**	**0**	**.176**	**.176**	**.235**	**1.000**

Carty, Ricardo Adolfo (Rico)

HEIGHT: 6'3" THROWS: RIGHT BATS: RIGHT BORN: 9/1/1939 SAN PEDRO DE MACORIS, DOMINICAN REPUBLIC POSITIONS PLAYED: C, 1B, 3B, OF

YEAR	TEAM	GAMES	AB	RUNS	HITS	2B	3B	HR	RBI	BB	IBB	SO	HBP	SH	SF	SB	CS	BA	OBA	SA	FA
1963	Mil-N	2	2	0	0	0	0	0	0	0	0	2	0	0	0	0	0	.000	.000	.000	—
1964	Mil-N	133	455	72	150	28	4	22	88	43	4	78	3	0	4	1	2	.330	.388	.554	.978
1965	Mil-N	83	271	37	84	18	1	10	35	17	0	44	3	0	2	1	4	.310	.355	.494	.958
1966	Atl-N	151	521	73	170	25	2	15	76	60	7	74	0	0	7	4	4	.326	.391	.468	.971
1967	Atl-N	134	444	41	113	16	2	15	64	49	10	70	1	1	1	4	3	.255	.329	.401	.962
1969	Atl-N	104	304	47	104	15	0	16	58	32	3	28	0	0	3	0	2	.342	.401	.549	.952
1970	Atl-N	136	478	84	175	23	3	25	101	77	6	46	2	0	3	1	2	.366	.454	.584	.974
1972	Atl-N	86	271	31	75	12	2	6	29	44	4	33	0	0	0	0	0	.277	.378	.402	.979
1973	Tex-A	86	306	24	71	12	0	3	33	36	2	39	1	0	4	2	0	.232	.311	.301	—
1973	**ChC-N**	**22**	**70**	**4**	**15**	**0**	**0**	**1**	**8**	**6**	**0**	**10**	**0**	**1**	**0**	**0**	**0**	**.214**	**.276**	**.257**	**.947**
1973	Oak-A	7	8	1	2	1	0	1	1	2	0	1	0	0	0	0	0	.250	.400	.750	—
1974	Cle-A	33	91	6	33	5	0	1	16	5	0	9	0	0	0	0	0	.363	.396	.451	.985
1975	Cle-A	118	383	57	118	19	1	18	64	45	3	31	2	0	6	2	2	.308	.378	.504	.987
1976	Cle-A	152	552	67	171	34	0	13	83	67	9	45	0	0	9	1	1	.310	.379	.442	1.000
1977	Cle-A	127	461	50	129	23	1	15	80	56	6	51	0	0	4	1	2	.280	.355	.432	1.000
1978	Tor-A	104	387	51	110	16	0	20	68	36	5	41	0	1	6	1	1	.284	.340	.481	—
1978	Oak-A	41	141	19	39	5	1	11	31	21	2	16	0	0	1	0	0	.277	.368	.560	—
1979	Tor-A	132	461	48	118	26	0	12	55	46	4	45	1	0	4	3	1	.256	.322	.390	—
Career average		110	374	47	112	19	1	14	59	43	4	44	1	0	4	1	2	.299	.369	.464	.974
Cubs average		**22**	**70**	**4**	**15**	**0**	**0**	**1**	**8**	**6**	**0**	**10**	**0**	**1**	**0**	**0**	**0**	**.214**	**.276**	**.257**	**.947**
Career total		1651	5606	712	1677	278	17	204	890	642	65	663	13	3	54	21	26	.299	.369	.464	.974
Cubs total		**22**	**70**	**4**	**15**	**0**	**0**	**1**	**8**	**6**	**0**	**10**	**0**	**1**	**0**	**0**	**0**	**.214**	**.276**	**.257**	**.947**

Casey, James Patrick (Doc)

HEIGHT: 5'6"   THROWS: RIGHT   BATS: BOTH   BORN: 3/15/1870 LAWRENCE, MASSACHUSETTS   DIED: 12/31/1936 DETROIT, MICHIGAN
POSITIONS PLAYED: C, 3B, SS

YEAR	TEAM	GAMES	AB	RUNS	HITS	2B	3B	HR	RBI	BB	IBB	SO	HBP	SH	SF	SB	CS	BA	OBA	SA	FA
1898	Was-N	28	112	13	31	2	0	0	15	3	—	—	1	1	—	15	—	.277	.302	.295	.877
1899	Was-N	9	34	3	4	2	0	0	2	2	—	—	0	1	—	1	—	.118	.167	.176	.853
1899	Bro-N	134	525	75	141	14	8	1	43	25	—	—	9	6	—	27	—	.269	.313	.331	.892
1900	Bro-N	1	3	0	1	0	0	0	1	0	—	—	1	0	—	0	—	.333	.500	.333	1.000
1901	Det-A	128	540	105	153	16	9	2	46	32	—	—	10	12	—	34	—	.283	.335	.357	.887
1902	Det-A	132	520	69	142	18	7	3	55	44	—	—	7	9	—	22	—	.273	.338	.352	.904
1903	**ChC-N**	**112**	**435**	**56**	**126**	**8**	**3**	**1**	**40**	**19**	**—**	**—**	**3**	**20**	**—**	**11**	**—**	**.290**	**.324**	**.329**	**.915**
1904	**ChC-N**	**136**	**548**	**71**	**147**	**20**	**4**	**1**	**43**	**18**	**—**	**—**	**7**	**20**	**—**	**21**	**—**	**.268**	**.300**	**.325**	**.913**
1905	**ChC-N**	**144**	**526**	**66**	**122**	**21**	**10**	**1**	**56**	**41**	**—**	**—**	**6**	**21**	**—**	**22**	**—**	**.232**	**.295**	**.316**	**.950**
1906	Bro-N	149	571	71	133	17	8	0	34	52	—	—	8	17	—	22	—	.233	.306	.291	.919
1907	Bro-N	141	527	55	122	19	3	0	19	34	—	—	3	32	—	16	—	.231	.282	.279	.955
Career average		111	434	58	112	14	5	1	35	27	—	—	6	14	—	19	—	.258	.310	.320	.915
Cubs average		**131**	**503**	**64**	**132**	**16**	**6**	**1**	**46**	**26**	**—**	**—**	**5**	**20**	**—**	**18**	**—**	**.262**	**.305**	**.323**	**.926**
Career total		1114	4341	584	1122	137	52	9	354	270	—	—	55	139	—	191	—	.258	.310	.320	.915
Cubs total		**392**	**1509**	**193**	**395**	**49**	**17**	**3**	**139**	**78**	**—**	**—**	**16**	**61**	**—**	**54**	**—**	**.262**	**.305**	**.323**	**.926**

Cassidy, John P.

HEIGHT: 5'8"   THROWS: LEFT   BATS: RIGHT   BORN: 1857 BROOKLYN, NEW YORK   DIED: 7/3/1891 BROOKLYN, NEW YORK
POSITIONS PLAYED: P, C, 1B, 2B, 3B, SS, OF

YEAR	TEAM	GAMES	AB	RUNS	HITS	2B	3B	HR	RBI	BB	IBB	SO	HBP	SH	SF	SB	CS	BA	OBA	SA	FA
1876	Har-N	12	48	6	13	2	0	0	8	1	—	0	—	—	—	—	—	.271	.286	.313	.957
1877	Har-N	60	251	43	95	10	5	0	27	3	—	3	—	—	—	—	—	.378	.386	.458	.723
1878	**ChN-N**	**60**	**256**	**33**	**68**	**7**	**1**	**0**	**29**	**9**	**—**	**11**	**—**	**—**	**—**	**—**	**—**	**.266**	**.291**	**.301**	**.813**
1879	Try-N	9	37	4	7	1	0	0	1	2	—	4	—	—	—	—	—	.189	.231	.216	.867
1880	Try-N	83	352	40	89	14	8	0	29	12	—	34	—	—	—	—	—	.253	.277	.338	.871
1881	Try-N	85	370	57	82	13	3	1	11	18	—	21	—	—	—	—	—	.222	.258	.281	.870
1882	Try-N	29	121	14	21	3	1	0	9	3	—	16	—	—	—	—	—	.174	.194	.215	.699
1883	Prv-N	89	366	46	87	16	5	0	42	19	—	38	—	—	—	—	—	.238	.256	.309	.861
1884	Bro-AA	106	433	57	109	11	6	2	—	19	—	—	2	—	—	—	—	.252	.286	.319	.827
1885	Bro-AA	54	221	36	47	6	2	1	28	8	—	—	3	—	—	—	—	.213	.250	.271	.852
Career average		59	246	34	62	8	3	0	18	8	—	13	1	—	—	—	—	.252	.278	.316	.835
Cubs average		**60**	**256**	**33**	**68**	**7**	**1**	**0**	**29**	**9**	**—**	**11**	**—**	**—**	**—**	**—**	**—**	**.266**	**.291**	**.301**	**.813**
Career total		587	2455	336	618	83	31	4	184	84	—	127	5	—	—	—	—	.252	.278	.316	.835
Cubs total		**60**	**256**	**33**	**68**	**7**	**1**	**0**	**29**	**9**	**—**	**11**	**—**	**—**	**—**	**—**	**—**	**.266**	**.291**	**.301**	**.813**

Cavarretta, Philip Joseph (Phil *or* Philabuck)

HEIGHT: 5'11"   THROWS: LEFT   BATS: LEFT   BORN: 7/19/1916 CHICAGO, ILLINOIS   POSITIONS PLAYED: 1B, OF

YEAR	TEAM	GAMES	AB	RUNS	HITS	2B	3B	HR	RBI	BB	IBB	SO	HBP	SH	SF	SB	CS	BA	OBA	SA	FA
1934	ChC-N	7	21	5	8	0	1	1	6	2	—	3	0	0	—	1	—	.381	.435	.619	1.000
1935	ChC-N	146	589	85	162	28	12	8	82	39	—	61	2	6	—	4	—	.275	.322	.404	.986
1936	ChC-N	124	458	55	125	18	1	9	56	17	—	36	5	6	—	8	—	.273	.306	.376	.987
1937	ChC-N	106	329	43	94	18	7	5	56	32	—	35	0	5	—	7	—	.286	.349	.429	.980
1938	ChC-N	92	268	29	64	11	4	1	28	14	—	27	4	4	—	4	—	.239	.287	.321	.987
1939	ChC-N	22	55	4	15	3	1	0	0	4	—	3	0	0	—	2	—	.273	.322	.364	.991
1940	ChC-N	65	193	34	54	11	4	2	22	31	—	18	3	4	—	3	—	.280	.388	.409	.991
1941	ChC-N	107	346	46	99	18	4	6	40	53	—	28	2	6	—	2	—	.286	.384	.413	.990
1942	ChC-N	136	482	59	130	28	4	3	54	71	—	42	1	12	—	7	—	.270	.365	.363	.991
1943	ChC-N	143	530	93	154	27	9	8	73	75	—	42	3	12	—	3	—	.291	.382	.421	.987
1944	ChC-N	152	614	106	197	35	15	5	82	67	—	34	4	3	—	5	—	.321	.389	.451	.993
1945	ChC-N	132	498	94	177	34	10	6	97	81	—	34	4	3	—	2	—	.355	.449	.500	.984
1946	ChC-N	139	510	89	150	28	10	8	78	88	—	54	3	1	—	2	—	.294	.401	.435	.982
1947	ChC-N	127	459	56	144	22	5	2	63	58	—	35	0	5	—	2	—	.314	.391	.397	.994
1948	ChC-N	111	334	41	93	16	5	3	40	35	—	29	1	3	—	4	—	.278	.349	.383	.994
1949	ChC-N	105	360	46	106	22	4	8	49	45	—	31	1	8	—	2	—	.294	.374	.444	.994
1950	ChC-N	82	256	49	70	11	1	10	31	40	—	31	2	2	—	1	—	.273	.376	.441	.986
1951	ChC-N	89	206	24	64	7	1	6	28	27	—	28	1	3	—	0	0	.311	.393	.442	.994
1952	ChC-N	41	63	7	15	1	1	1	8	9	—	3	0	0	—	0	0	.238	.333	.333	.991
1953	ChC-N	27	21	3	6	3	0	0	3	6	—	3	0	0	—	0	0	.286	.444	.429	—

(continued)

Philip (Phil) Joseph "Philabuck" Cavarretta, 1b-of, 1934–55

Phil Cavarretta came to Chicago during the depths of the Great Depression and made himself into one of the fiercest hitters in team history.

Born in Chicago on July 19, 1916, Cavarretta was the son of Italian immigrants. His father, in particular, became suspicious when young Philip spent much of his time playing hardball, but Cavarretta quickly became a schoolboy star as a pitcher and first baseman. A few weeks before he was to graduate, Cavarretta dropped out of high school to sign a professional contract with the Cubs. Within a year, Cavarretta, at 18, was the starting first baseman for the National League champions.

He was a line-drive hitter whose infrequent home runs always seemed to make a difference in a game. Although Cavarretta himself admitted that his fielding at the major league level was at least initially not great, he eventually made himself into a strong glove man by sheer hard work.

Cavarretta was a hustler and the darling of the fans because he always tried to give 110 percent on the field. He was a terrific all-around athlete and a very competitive player.

In his first eight years with Chicago, Cavarretta hit in between .270 and .285. But during the war years and late 1940s, he hit his stride. (He was exempted from the service because of an inner-ear problem.)

Cavarretta was named to the All-Star team four consecutive years, from 1944 to 1947, and hit over .300 in 1944, 1945 and 1948. In 1945 his .355 average led the league and he was named the National League MVP as he led the Cubs to their last World Series.

He was, for the most part, a tough out in the postseason. After a shaky 1935 World Series, where he made only three hits against the Tigers, Cavarretta shone in the 1938 Fall Classic, even if most of his teammates did not. Cavarretta hit .462 in a losing effort as the Cubs were swept by the Yankees.

He showed a similar side in the 1945 Series, hitting .423 to lead both teams in the last World Series for Chicago in the 20th century.

Things began going south for the Cubs soon after that October swan song, but not necessarily for Cavarretta. He continued to be the Cubs leader on and off the field despite the team's struggles. Cavarretta hit .294 in 1949 and .311 in 1950.

In 1951 he was made player-manager, but the team was beginning its long slide into mediocrity. In spring 1954 Cavarretta wanted Cubs owner Phil Wrigley to do something about it. Following a meeting with Cavarretta, the eccentric Wrigley did do something: he fired a stunned Cavarretta.

Cavarretta caught on with the White Sox for two more years as a part-time player before retiring for good in 1955. Following his playing career, Cavarretta coached in the Tigers organization and was an excellent batting coach for the Mets for many years.

Cavarretta is ninth all-time with the Cubs in runs scored with 968, hits with 1,927, singles with 1,395, extra-base hits with 532 and RBIs with 896. He is also 10th all-time with the Cubs in total bases with 2,742.

(Cavarretta, continued)																				
1954 CWS-A	71	158	21	50	6	0	3	24	26	—	12	2	1	1	4	0	.316	.417	.411	.990
1955 CWS-A	6	4	1	0	0	0	0	0	0	0	1	0	0	0	0	0	.000	.000	.000	1.000
Career average	92	307	45	90	16	5	4	42	37	0	27	2	4	0	3	0	.293	.372	.416	.989
Cubs average	**98**	**330**	**48**	**96**	**17**	**5**	**5**	**45**	**40**	—	**29**	**2**	**4**	—	**3**	**0**	**.292**	**.371**	**.416**	**.989**
Career total	2030	6754	990	1977	347	99	95	920	820	0	598	37	89	1	65	0	.293	.372	.416	.989
Cubs total	**1953**	**6592**	**968**	**1927**	**341**	**99**	**92**	**896**	**794**	—	**585**	**35**	**88**	—	**61**	**0**	**.292**	**.371**	**.416**	**.989**

Cey, Ronald Charles (Ron *or* The Penguin)

HEIGHT: 5'10"   THROWS: RIGHT   BATS: RIGHT   BORN: 2/15/1948 TACOMA, WASHINGTON   POSITIONS PLAYED: 1B, 3B

YEAR	TEAM	GAMES	AB	RUNS	HITS	2B	3B	HR	RBI	BB	IBB	SO	HBP	SH	SF	SB	CS	BA	OBA	SA	FA
1971	LA-N	2	2	0	0	0	0	0	0	0	0	2	0	0	0	0	0	.000	.000	.000	—
1972	LA-N	11	37	3	10	1	0	1	3	7	0	10	1	0	0	0	0	.270	.400	.378	.900
1973	LA-N	152	507	60	124	18	4	15	80	74	7	77	2	4	8	1	1	.245	.338	.385	.961
1974	LA-N	159	577	88	151	20	2	18	97	76	13	68	7	3	10	1	1	.262	.349	.397	.959
1975	LA-N	158	566	72	160	29	2	25	101	78	15	74	7	3	8	5	4	.283	.372	.473	.960
1976	LA-N	145	502	69	139	18	3	23	80	89	13	74	3	2	4	0	4	.277	.386	.462	.965
1977	LA-N	153	564	77	136	22	3	30	110	93	6	106	2	3	7	3	4	.241	.347	.450	.964
1978	LA-N	159	555	84	150	32	0	23	84	96	9	96	7	2	7	2	5	.270	.380	.452	.966
1979	LA-N	150	487	77	137	20	1	28	81	86	8	85	2	0	4	3	3	.281	.389	.499	.977
1980	LA-N	157	551	81	140	25	0	28	77	69	5	92	5	4	1	2	2	.254	.342	.452	.972
1981	LA-N	85	312	42	90	15	2	13	50	40	3	55	3	1	3	0	2	.288	.372	.474	.941
1982	LA-N	150	556	62	141	23	1	24	79	57	6	99	4	2	8	3	2	.254	.323	.460	.963
1983	**ChC-N**	**159**	**581**	**73**	**160**	**33**	**1**	**24**	**90**	**62**	**11**	**85**	**5**	**1**	**9**	**0**	**0**	**.275**	**.346**	**.460**	**.955**
1984	**ChC-N**	**146**	**505**	**71**	**121**	**27**	**0**	**25**	**97**	**61**	**10**	**108**	**6**	**0**	**8**	**3**	**2**	**.240**	**.324**	**.442**	**.967**

(continued)

Ronald (Ron) Charles, "the Penguin" Cey, 3b-dh-1b, 1971–87

Ron Cey wasn't with the Cubs long, but during his four years there, he provided Chicago with a consistent third baseman the Cubs hadn't had since Ron Santo.

Born on February 15, 1948, in Tacoma, Washington, Cey spent the first 12 years of his career with the Dodgers. The 5'10" 185-pound Cey looked ungainly, particularly when he ran, earning him the nickname "the Penguin."

But there was nothing ungainly about him at the plate or afield. A six-time All-Star with the Dodgers, Cey drilled more than 100 RBIs twice and hit 20 or more home runs and 20 or more doubles seven times in that span. He led National League third basemen in fielding in 1979.

In 1983 Cubs general manager Dallas Green sent two minor league players to Los Angeles for Cey. Chicago sportswriters grumbled that the 35-year-old Cey would be little more than a backup at his age.

But the Penguin fooled everyone. He took over third base immediately in 1984, hitting .275 with 33 doubles, 24 home runs and 90 RBIs. In 1984 his offensive numbers dropped slightly, but he led all National League third sackers in fielding percentage with a .967 mark, was third in the league in assists and fourth in double plays as the Cubs won the division title in 1984. It was the team's first first-place finish since 1945.

Cey led the team in home runs and RBIs in 1983 and 1984, but he began to tail off in 1985, hitting only .232 with 63 RBIs. After one more season in Chicago, where he hit .273, he moved over to Oakland, where he played one year before retiring.

Cey didn't crack any all-time lists for the Cubs, but he did hit 84 home runs for Chicago in that four-year span, tops on the team during that time.

(continued)

YEAR	TEAM	GAMES	AB	RUNS	HITS	2B	3B	HR	RBI	BB	IBB	SO	HBP	SH	SF	SB	CS	BA	OBA	SA	FA
1985	ChC-N	145	500	64	116	18	2	22	63	58	9	106	4	0	2	1	1	.232	.316	.408	.943
1986	ChC-N	97	256	42	70	21	0	13	36	44	1	66	3	1	2	0	0	.273	.384	.508	.952
1987	Oak-A	45	104	12	23	6	0	4	11	22	1	32	1	0	1	0	0	.221	.359	.394	.984
Career average		122	421	57	110	19	1	19	67	60	7	73	4	2	5	1	2	.261	.354	.445	.961
Cubs average		**137**	**461**	**63**	**117**	**25**	**1**	**21**	**72**	**56**	**8**	**91**	**5**	**1**	**5**	**1**	**1**	**.254**	**.337**	**.447**	**.954**
Career total		2073	7162	977	1868	328	21	316	1139	1012	117	1235	62	26	82	24	29	.261	.354	.445	.961
Cubs total		**547**	**1842**	**250**	**467**	**99**	**3**	**84**	**286**	**225**	**31**	**365**	**18**	**2**	**21**	**4**	**3**	**.254**	**.337**	**.447**	**.954**

Chance, Frank Leroy (Husk *or* The Peerless Leader)

HEIGHT: 6'0"   THROWS: RIGHT   BATS: RIGHT   BORN: 9/9/1877 FRESNO, CALIFORNIA   DIED: 9/15/1924 LOS ANGELES, CALIFORNIA
POSITIONS PLAYED: C, 1B, OF

YEAR	TEAM	GAMES	AB	RUNS	HITS	2B	3B	HR	RBI	BB	IBB	SO	HBP	SH	SF	SB	CS	BA	OBA	SA	FA
1898	ChN-N	53	147	32	41	4	3	1	14	7	—	—	6	2	—	7	—	.279	.338	.367	.904
1899	ChN-N	64	192	37	55	6	2	1	22	15	—	—	4	2	—	10	—	.286	.351	.354	.951
1900	ChN-N	56	149	26	44	9	3	0	13	15	—	—	15	8	—	8	—	.295	.413	.396	.930
1901	ChN-N	69	241	38	67	12	4	0	36	29	—	—	9	4	—	27	—	.278	.376	.361	.945
1902	ChC-N	75	240	39	69	9	4	1	31	35	—	—	8	2	—	27	—	.288	.396	.371	.970
1903	ChC-N	125	441	83	144	24	10	2	81	78	—	—	10	2	—	67	—	.327	.439	.440	.972
1904	ChC-N	124	451	89	140	16	10	6	49	36	—	—	16	11	—	42	—	.310	.382	.430	.990
1905	ChC-N	118	392	92	124	16	12	2	70	78	—	—	17	15	—	38	—	.316	.450	.434	.990
1906	ChC-N	136	474	103	151	24	10	3	71	70	—	—	12	18	—	57	—	.319	.419	.430	.989
1907	ChC-N	111	382	58	112	19	2	1	49	51	—	—	13	5	—	35	—	.293	.395	.361	.992

(continued)

Frank Leroy "the Peerless Leader," "Husk" Chance, 1b-c-of, 1898–1914

It would be a great argument to debate whether Frank Chance won more games with his tactics than his talent. The Cubs benefited from both facets of this remarkable player for 15 years.

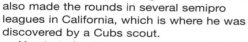

Born on September 9, 1877, in Fresno, California, Chance was a schoolboy star at Fresno High School and later played two years at Washington University at Irvington, California. He also made the rounds in several semipro leagues in California, which is where he was discovered by a Cubs scout.

He started out as a catcher in high school and college, and originally believed that he did belong behind the plate.

Chance came to the Cubs in 1898 and was a part-time player as a catcher, first baseman and outfielder for his first four years. His first two Chicago managers, Tom Burns and Tom Loftus, were content to keep Chance, for the most part, behind the plate in that span.

But in 1902 new Cubs manager Frank Selee thought that Chance was more effective at first base. Chicago also had the very capable Johnny Kling at catcher by this time, so Selee had no worries about the backstop position.

But Chance wasn't convinced. He had been a catcher for virtually all of his career and was not happy about a switch. At one point, he threatened to retire if Selee insisted on moving him to first. It didn't work, for Selee called his player's bluff. Chance became the Cubs' regular first baseman in 1903.

Showing no ill effects from the switch (as Selee had anticipated), Chance hit a team-high .327 and led the National League with 67 stolen bases, still a team record. That began a stretch of six consecutive years in which Chance had more than 110 hits per season.

Chance was a tough son of a gun. When at bat, he crowded the plate. This did not endear

(continued)

(continued)

him to pitchers of the day, who often hit Chance when attempting to "back him off" the dish. In one doubleheader, he was hit by a pitch three times in the first game and twice more in the second contest, a major league record. Chance estimated he had been hit in the head more than 30 times and well over 150 times overall.

He was a very shrewd judge of ballplayers. He lobbied heavily, for example, for the team to acquire pitcher Mordecai "Three Finger" Brown despite objections by some Cubs scouts that Brown, due to his handicap, would have difficulty pitching in the major leagues.

The Cubs picked up catcher Jack O'Neill in the Brown trade, another Chance choice. Chance also convinced Selee not to trade the notoriously prickly but talented Johnny Evers, even though most players on the team would not have minded seeing Evers go.

By 1905 the tuberculosis that had gripped Selee for a number of years was beginning to take its toll. At midseason Selee was too ill to continue in the dugout. He asked the players who should manage in his place. Chance was the overwhelming favorite. That year, the Cubs, on the verge of a breakout, won 92 games and finished third behind the New York Giants, who would win the World Series that year.

In 1906 the Chicago Cubs of player-manager Frank Chance had the greatest regular season in the 20th century, winning 116 games and losing 36. Chance hit .319 and scored 103 runs, stole 57 bases and had an on-base percentage of .419, all league highs.

The Cubs lost that World Series to the White Sox in six games, but the 1906 season ushered in an era of still-unmatched success for Chicago and Chance, with four World Series appearances and two world championships during 1906 to 1910.

Chance was the master of Dead Ball Era managing. He played the game one run at a time, hated to waste base runners and was adept at manufacturing runs. He loved to order a player to pretend to bunt on the first pitch and miss deliberately. Then, with the third baseman moving in to defend the bunt, Chance would have the player punch the ball over his head.

His players, for the most part, loved him. He treated them as adults and, in fact, regularly led them all to a bar for a couple of rounds on him when a game was rained out.

The alternative to being on Chance's good side was not particularly fun. He was a big man for his time, 6' and 190 pounds. His players nicknamed him "Husk" on account of his husky build. Chance was also a terrific amateur boxer who had no qualms about laying low a recalcitrant ballplayer. And his men knew it.

In addition to being a very tough out, Chance made himself into a very good defensive first baseman. He worked at digging balls out of the dirt on errant throws until he became as good as any first baseman in the league.

From 1905 to 1910, Chance was one of the best offensive players Chicago had. And, of course, he was the cornerstone of the famed Joe Tinker to Johnny Evers to Frank Chance double-play combination. Injuries limited his play dramatically in 1911 and 1912, and new Cubs owner Charles Murphy didn't think he could play anymore.

Murphy was probably right, but Chance's inelegant departure from Chicago was messy. He and Murphy traded insults, and Chance jumped to the New York Highlanders of the fledgling American League.

But the Highlander management had little interest in improving the team, and after two seasons, Chance retired. Managerial stints in the minor leagues and with the Red Sox in 1923 and the White Sox in 1924 followed. During that year, he became ill and died in September. In 1946 he, Tinker and Evers were elected to the Hall of Fame.

Chance remains the Cubs all-time stolen-base leader with an even 400.

(Chance, continued)

YEAR	TEAM	GAMES	AB	RUNS	HITS	2B	3B	HR	RBI	BB	IBB	SO	HBP	SH	SF	SB	CS	BA	OBA	SA	FA
1908	ChC-N	129	452	65	123	27	4	2	55	37	—	—	8	16	—	27	—	.272	.338	.363	.989
1909	ChC-N	93	324	53	88	16	4	0	46	30	—	—	4	12	—	29	—	.272	.341	.346	.994
1910	ChC-N	88	295	54	88	12	8	0	36	37	—	15	10	6	—	16	—	.298	.395	.393	.996
1911	ChC-N	31	88	23	21	6	3	1	17	25	—	13	5	6	—	9	—	.239	.432	.409	.990
1912	ChC-N	2	5	2	1	0	0	0	0	3	—	0	0	1	—	1	—	.200	.500	.200	1.000
1913	NYY-A	11	24	3	5	0	0	0	6	8	—	1	0	1	—	1	—	.208	.406	.208	1.000
1914	NYY-A	1	0	0	0	0	0	0	0	0	—	0	0	0	—	0	0	—	—	—	1.000
Career average		76	253	47	75	12	5	1	35	33	—	2	8	7	—	24	0	.296	.394	.394	.984
Cubs average		**85**	**285**	**53**	**85**	**13**	**5**	**1**	**39**	**36**	**—**	**2**	**9**	**7**	**—**	**27**	**—**	**.297**	**.394**	**.395**	**.984**
Career total		1286	4297	797	1273	200	79	20	596	554	—	29	137	111	—	401	0	.296	.394	.394	.984
Cubs total		**1274**	**4273**	**794**	**1268**	**200**	**79**	**20**	**590**	**546**	**—**	**28**	**137**	**110**	**—**	**400**	**—**	**.297**	**.394**	**.395**	**.984**

Chapman, Harry E.

HEIGHT: 5'11" THROWS: RIGHT BATS: RIGHT   BORN: 10/26/1887 SEVERENCE, KANSAS   DIED: 10/21/1918 NEVADA, MISSOURI
POSITIONS PLAYED: C, 1B, 2B, OF

YEAR	TEAM	GAMES	AB	RUNS	HITS	2B	3B	HR	RBI	BB	IBB	SO	HBP	SH	SF	SB	CS	BA	OBA	SA	FA
1912	**ChC-N**	**1**	**4**	**1**	**1**	**0**	**1**	**0**	**1**	**0**	**—**	**0**	**0**	**0**	**—**	**1**	**—**	**.250**	**.250**	**.750**	**1.000**
1913	Cin-N	2	2	0	1	0	0	0	0	0	—	1	0	0	—	0	—	.500	.500	.500	—
1914	StL-F	64	181	16	38	2	1	0	14	13	—	27	2	4	—	2	—	.210	.270	.232	.973
1915	StL-F	62	186	19	37	6	3	1	29	22	—	24	0	9	—	4	—	.199	.284	.280	.989
1916	StL-A	18	31	2	3	0	0	0	0	2	—	5	0	2	—	0	—	.097	.152	.097	.981
Career average		29	81	8	16	2	1	0	9	7	—	11	0	3	—	1	—	.198	.269	.250	.982
Cubs average		**1**	**4**	**1**	**1**	**0**	**1**	**0**	**1**	**0**	**—**	**0**	**0**	**0**	**—**	**1**	**—**	**.250**	**.250**	**.750**	**1.000**
Career total		147	404	38	80	8	5	1	44	37	—	57	2	15	—	7	—	.198	.269	.250	.982
Cubs total		**1**	**4**	**1**	**1**	**0**	**1**	**0**	**1**	**0**	**—**	**0**	**0**	**0**	**—**	**1**	**—**	**.250**	**.250**	**.750**	**1.000**

Childs, Clarence Algernon (Cupid)

HEIGHT: 5'8" THROWS: RIGHT BATS: LEFT   BORN: 8/8/1867 CALVERT COUNTY, MARYLAND   DIED: 11/8/1912 BALTIMORE, MARYLAND
POSITIONS PLAYED: 2B, SS

YEAR	TEAM	GAMES	AB	RUNS	HITS	2B	3B	HR	RBI	BB	IBB	SO	HBP	SH	SF	SB	CS	BA	OBA	SA	FA
1888	Phi-N	2	4	0	0	0	0	0	0	0	—	0	0	—	—	0	—	.000	.000	.000	.857
1890	Syr-AA	126	493	109	170	33	14	2	89	72	—	—	6	—	—	56	—	.345	.434	.481	.928
1891	Cle-N	141	551	120	155	21	12	2	83	97	—	32	7	—	—	39	—	.281	.395	.374	.910
1892	Cle-N	145	558	136	177	14	11	3	53	117	—	20	9	—	—	26	—	.317	.443	.398	.938
1893	Cle-N	124	485	145	158	19	10	3	65	120	—	12	4	—	—	23	—	.326	.463	.425	.926
1894	Cle-N	118	479	143	169	21	12	2	52	107	—	11	5	4	—	17	—	.353	.475	.459	.916
1895	Cle-N	119	462	96	133	15	3	4	90	74	—	24	6	8	—	20	—	.288	.393	.359	.921
1896	Cle-N	132	498	106	177	24	9	1	106	100	—	18	4	13	—	25	—	.355	.467	.446	.942
1897	Cle-N	114	444	105	150	15	9	1	61	74	—	—	2	17	—	25	—	.338	.435	.419	.944
1898	Cle-N	110	413	90	119	9	4	1	31	69	—	—	4	14	—	9	—	.288	.395	.337	.931
1899	StL-N	125	464	73	123	11	11	1	48	74	—	—	2	13	—	11	—	.265	.369	.343	.934
1900	**ChN-N**	**137**	**531**	**67**	**128**	**14**	**5**	**0**	**44**	**57**	**—**	**—**	**7**	**20**	**—**	**15**	**—**	**.241**	**.323**	**.286**	**.935**
1901	**ChN-N**	**63**	**236**	**24**	**61**	**9**	**0**	**0**	**21**	**30**	**—**	**—**	**7**	**1**	**—**	**3**	**—**	**.258**	**.359**	**.297**	**.939**
Career average		112	432	93	132	16	8	2	57	76	—	9	5	7	—	21	—	.306	.416	.389	.930
Cubs average		**100**	**384**	**46**	**95**	**12**	**3**	**0**	**33**	**44**	**—**	**0**	**7**	**11**	**—**	**9**	**—**	**.246**	**.334**	**.289**	**.937**
Career total		1456	5618	1214	1720	205	100	20	743	991	—	117	63	90	—	269	—	.306	.416	.389	.930
Cubs total		**200**	**767**	**91**	**189**	**23**	**5**	**0**	**65**	**87**	**—**	**0**	**14**	**21**	**—**	**18**	**—**	**.246**	**.334**	**.289**	**.937**

Childs, Peter Pierre (Pete)

HEIGHT: — THROWS: RIGHT BATS: —   BORN: 11/15/1871 PHILADELPHIA, PENNSYLVANIA   DIED: 2/15/1922 PHILADELPHIA, PENNSYLVANIA
POSITIONS PLAYED: 2B, SS, OF

YEAR	TEAM	GAMES	AB	RUNS	HITS	2B	3B	HR	RBI	BB	IBB	SO	HBP	SH	SF	SB	CS	BA	OBA	SA	FA
1901	StL-N	29	79	12	21	1	0	0	8	14	—	—	2	0	—	0	—	.266	.389	.278	.892
1901	**ChN-N**	**61**	**213**	**23**	**48**	**5**	**1**	**0**	**14**	**26**	**—**	**—**	**2**	**3**	**—**	**4**	**—**	**.225**	**.315**	**.258**	**.959**
1902	Phi-N	123	403	25	78	5	0	0	25	34	—	—	0	10	—	6	—	.194	.256	.206	.945
Career average		107	348	30	74	6	1	0	24	37	—	—	2	7	—	5	—	.212	.291	.230	.944
Cubs average		**61**	**213**	**23**	**48**	**5**	**1**	**0**	**14**	**26**	**—**	**—**	**2**	**3**	**—**	**4**	**—**	**.225**	**.315**	**.258**	**.959**
Career total		213	695	60	147	11	1	0	47	74	—	—	4	13	—	10	—	.212	.291	.230	.944
Cubs total		**61**	**213**	**23**	**48**	**5**	**1**	**0**	**14**	**26**	**—**	**—**	**2**	**3**	**—**	**4**	**—**	**.225**	**.315**	**.258**	**.959**

Chiti, Harry

HEIGHT: 6'2" THROWS: RIGHT BATS: RIGHT BORN: 11/16/1932 KINCAID, ILLINOIS POSITIONS PLAYED: C

YEAR	TEAM	GAMES	AB	RUNS	HITS	2B	3B	HR	RBI	BB	IBB	SO	HBP	SH	SF	SB	CS	BA	OBA	SA	FA
1950	ChC-N	3	6	0	2	0	0	0	0	0	—	0	0	0	—	0	—	.333	.333	.333	1.000
1951	ChC-N	9	31	1	11	2	0	0	5	2	—	2	0	1	—	0	0	.355	.394	.419	.913
1952	ChC-N	32	113	14	31	5	0	5	13	5	—	8	0	0	—	0	1	.274	.305	.451	.984
1955	ChC-N	113	338	24	78	6	1	11	41	25	8	68	1	3	5	0	0	.231	.282	.352	.984
1956	ChC-N	72	203	17	43	6	4	4	18	19	3	35	1	3	1	0	0	.212	.281	.340	.981
1958	KCA-A	103	295	32	79	11	3	9	44	18	4	48	3	5	6	3	2	.268	.311	.417	.987
1959	KCA-A	55	162	20	44	11	1	5	25	17	1	26	1	0	0	0	1	.272	.344	.444	.988
1960	KCA-A	58	190	16	42	7	0	5	28	17	0	33	1	5	0	1	0	.221	.288	.337	.983
1960	Det-A	37	104	9	17	0	0	2	5	10	1	12	0	1	1	0	3	.163	.235	.221	.984
1961	Det-A	5	12	0	1	0	0	0	0	1	0	2	0	0	0	0	0	.083	.154	.083	1.000
1962	NYM-N	15	41	2	8	1	0	0	0	1	0	8	1	0	0	0	0	.195	.233	.220	.971
Career average		50	150	14	36	5	1	4	18	12	2	24	1	2	1	0	1	.238	.294	.365	.983
Cubs average		**46**	**138**	**11**	**33**	**4**	**1**	**4**	**15**	**10**	**2**	**23**	**0**	**1**	**1**	**0**	**0**	**.239**	**.291**	**.368**	**.980**
Career total		502	1495	135	356	49	9	41	179	115	17	242	8	18	13	4	7	.238	.294	.365	.983
Cubs total		**229**	**691**	**56**	**165**	**19**	**5**	**20**	**77**	**51**	**11**	**113**	**2**	**7**	**6**	**0**	**1**	**.239**	**.291**	**.368**	**.980**

Christmas, Stephen Randall (Steve)

HEIGHT: 6'0" THROWS: RIGHT BATS: LEFT BORN: 12/9/1957 ORLANDO, FLORIDA POSITIONS PLAYED: C, 1B

YEAR	TEAM	GAMES	AB	RUNS	HITS	2B	3B	HR	RBI	BB	IBB	SO	HBP	SH	SF	SB	CS	BA	OBA	SA	FA
1983	Cin-N	9	17	0	1	0	0	0	1	1	0	3	0	0	1	0	0	.059	.105	.059	1.000
1984	CWS-A	12	11	1	4	1	0	1	4	0	0	2	0	0	0	0	0	.364	.364	.727	1.000
1986	ChC-N	3	9	0	1	1	0	0	2	0	0	1	0	0	0	0	0	.111	.111	.222	1.000
Career average		8	12	0	2	1	0	0	2	0	0	2	0	0	0	0	0	.162	.179	.297	1.000
Cubs average		**3**	**9**	**0**	**1**	**1**	**0**	**0**	**2**	**0**	**0**	**1**	**0**	**0**	**0**	**0**	**0**	**.111**	**.111**	**.222**	**1.000**
Career total		24	37	1	6	2	0	1	7	1	0	6	0	0	1	0	0	.162	.179	.297	1.000
Cubs total		**3**	**9**	**0**	**1**	**1**	**0**	**0**	**2**	**0**	**0**	**1**	**0**	**0**	**0**	**0**	**0**	**.111**	**.111**	**.222**	**1.000**

Christopher, Lloyd Eugene (Loyd *or* Feather)

HEIGHT: 6'2" THROWS: RIGHT BATS: RIGHT BORN: 12/31/1919 RICHMOND, CALIFORNIA DIED: 9/5/1991 RICHMOND, CALIFORNIA POSITIONS PLAYED: OF

YEAR	TEAM	GAMES	AB	RUNS	HITS	2B	3B	HR	RBI	BB	IBB	SO	HBP	SH	SF	SB	CS	BA	OBA	SA	FA
1945	Bos-A	8	14	4	4	0	0	0	4	3	—	2	0	0	—	0	0	.286	.412	.286	1.000
1945	ChC-N	1	0	0	0	0	0	0	0	0	—	0	0	0	—	0	—	—	—	—	—
1947	CWS-A	7	23	1	5	0	1	0	0	2	—	4	0	0	—	0	1	.217	.280	.304	1.000
Career average		8	19	3	5	0	1	0	2	3	—	3	0	0	—	0	1	.243	.333	.297	1.000
Cubs average		**1**	**0**	**0**	**0**	**0**	**0**	**0**	**0**	**0**	**—**	**0**	**0**	**0**	**—**	**0**	**0**	**—**	**—**	**—**	**—**
Career total		16	37	5	9	0	1	0	4	5	—	6	0	0	—	0	1	.243	.333	.297	1.000
Cubs total		**1**	**0**	**0**	**0**	**0**	**0**	**0**	**0**	**0**	**—**	**0**	**0**	**0**	**—**	**0**	**0**	**—**	**—**	**—**	**—**

Churry, John

HEIGHT: 5'9" THROWS: RIGHT BATS: RIGHT BORN: 11/26/1900 JOHNSTOWN, PENNSYLVANIA DIED: 2/8/1970 ZANESVILLE, OHIO POSITIONS PLAYED: C

YEAR	TEAM	GAMES	AB	RUNS	HITS	2B	3B	HR	RBI	BB	IBB	SO	HBP	SH	SF	SB	CS	BA	OBA	SA	FA
1924	ChC-N	6	7	0	1	1	0	0	0	2	—	0	0	0	—	0	0	.143	.333	.286	1.000
1925	ChC-N	3	6	1	3	0	0	0	1	0	—	0	0	0	—	0	0	.500	.500	.500	1.000
1926	ChC-N	2	4	0	0	0	0	0	0	1	—	2	0	0	—	0	—	.000	.200	.000	1.000
1927	ChC-N	1	1	0	1	0	0	0	0	0	—	0	0	0	—	0	—	1.000	1.000	1.000	1.000
Career average		3	5	0	1	0	0	0	0	1	—	1	0	0	—	0	0	.278	.381	.333	1.000
Cubs average		**3**	**5**	**0**	**1**	**0**	**0**	**0**	**0**	**1**	**—**	**1**	**0**	**0**	**—**	**0**	**0**	**.278**	**.381**	**.333**	**1.000**
Career total		12	18	1	5	1	0	0	1	3	—	2	0	0	—	0	0	.278	.381	.333	1.000
Cubs total		**12**	**18**	**1**	**5**	**1**	**0**	**0**	**1**	**3**	**—**	**2**	**0**	**0**	**—**	**0**	**0**	**.278**	**.381**	**.333**	**1.000**

Clark, Alfred Robert (Dad *or* Fred)
HEIGHT: 5'11"   THROWS: LEFT   BATS: LEFT   BORN: 7/16/1873 SAN FRANCISCO, CALIFORNIA   DIED: 7/26/1956 OGDEN, UTAH   POSITIONS PLAYED: 1B

YEAR	TEAM	GAMES	AB	RUNS	HITS	2B	3B	HR	RBI	BB	IBB	SO	HBP	SH	SF	SB	CS	BA	OBA	SA	FA
1902	ChC-N	12	43	1	8	1	0	0	2	4	—	—	0	1	—	1	—	.186	.255	.209	.938
Career average		12	43	1	8	1	0	0	2	4	—	—	0	1	—	1	—	.186	.255	.209	.938
Cubs average		**12**	**43**	**1**	**8**	**1**	**0**	**0**	**2**	**4**	**—**	**—**	**0**	**1**	**—**	**1**	**—**	**.186**	**.255**	**.209**	**.938**
Career total		12	43	1	8	1	0	0	2	4	—	—	0	1	—	1	—	.186	.255	.209	.938
Cubs total		**12**	**43**	**1**	**8**	**1**	**0**	**0**	**2**	**4**	**—**	**—**	**0**	**1**	**—**	**1**	**—**	**.186**	**.255**	**.209**	**.938**

Clark, David Earl (Dave)
HEIGHT: 6'2"   THROWS: RIGHT   BATS: LEFT   BORN: 9/3/1962 TUPELO, MISSISSIPPI   POSITIONS PLAYED: OF

YEAR	TEAM	GAMES	AB	RUNS	HITS	2B	3B	HR	RBI	BB	IBB	SO	HBP	SH	SF	SB	CS	BA	OBA	SA	FA
1986	Cle-A	18	58	10	16	1	0	3	9	7	0	11	0	2	1	1	0	.276	.348	.448	1.000
1987	Cle-A	29	87	11	18	5	0	3	12	2	0	24	0	0	0	1	0	.207	.225	.368	1.000
1988	Cle-A	63	156	11	41	4	1	3	18	17	2	28	0	0	1	0	0	.263	.333	.359	.947
1989	Cle-A	102	253	21	60	12	0	8	29	30	5	63	0	1	1	0	2	.237	.317	.379	.964
1990	**ChC-N**	**84**	**171**	**22**	**47**	**4**	**2**	**5**	**20**	**8**	**1**	**40**	**0**	**0**	**2**	**7**	**1**	**.275**	**.304**	**.409**	**1.000**
1991	KC-A	11	10	1	2	0	0	0	1	1	0	1	0	0	0	0	0	.200	.273	.200	—
1992	Pit-N	23	33	3	7	0	0	2	7	6	0	8	0	0	0	0	0	.212	.325	.394	1.000
1993	Pit-N	110	277	43	75	11	2	11	46	38	5	58	1	0	2	1	0	.271	.358	.444	.957
1994	Pit-N	86	223	37	66	11	1	10	46	22	0	48	0	1	3	2	2	.296	.355	.489	.974
1995	Pit-N	77	196	30	55	6	0	4	24	24	1	38	1	0	2	3	3	.281	.359	.372	.961
1996	Pit-N	92	211	28	58	12	2	8	35	31	3	51	0	0	1	2	1	.275	.366	.464	.988
1996	LA-N	15	15	0	3	0	0	0	1	3	0	2	0	0	0	0	0	.200	.333	.200	—
1997	**ChC-N**	**102**	**143**	**19**	**43**	**8**	**0**	**5**	**32**	**19**	**3**	**34**	**2**	**0**	**2**	**1**	**0**	**.301**	**.386**	**.462**	**.953**
1998	Hou-N	93	131	12	27	7	0	0	4	14	1	45	1	0	0	1	1	.206	.288	.260	.885
Career average		70	151	19	40	6	1	5	22	17	2	35	0	0	1	1	1	.264	.338	.408	.969
Cubs average		**93**	**157**	**21**	**45**	**6**	**1**	**5**	**26**	**14**	**2**	**37**	**1**	**0**	**2**	**4**	**1**	**.287**	**.343**	**.433**	**.981**
Career total		905	1964	248	518	81	8	62	284	222	21	451	5	4	16	19	12	.264	.338	.408	.969
Cubs total		**186**	**314**	**41**	**90**	**12**	**2**	**10**	**52**	**27**	**4**	**74**	**2**	**0**	**4**	**8**	**1**	**.287**	**.343**	**.433**	**.981**

Clarke, Sumpter Mills
HEIGHT: 5'11"   THROWS: RIGHT   BATS: RIGHT   BORN: 10/18/1897 SAVANNAH, GEORGIA   DIED: 3/16/1962 KNOXVILLE, TENNESSEE   POSITIONS PLAYED: 3B, OF

YEAR	TEAM	GAMES	AB	RUNS	HITS	2B	3B	HR	RBI	BB	IBB	SO	HBP	SH	SF	SB	CS	BA	OBA	SA	FA
1920	**ChC-N**	**1**	**3**	**0**	**1**	**0**	**0**	**0**	**0**	**0**	**—**	**1**	**0**	**0**	**—**	**0**	**0**	**.333**	**.333**	**.333**	**1.000**
1923	Cle-A	1	3	0	0	0	0	0	0	0	—	0	0	0	—	0	0	.000	.000	.000	1.000
1924	Cle-A	45	104	17	24	6	1	0	11	6	—	12	0	3	—	0	0	.231	.273	.308	1.000
Career average		16	37	6	8	2	0	0	4	2	—	4	0	1	—	0	0	.227	.267	.300	1.000
Cubs average		**1**	**3**	**0**	**1**	**0**	**0**	**0**	**0**	**0**	**—**	**1**	**0**	**0**	**—**	**0**	**0**	**.333**	**.333**	**.333**	**1.000**
Career total		47	110	17	25	6	1	0	11	6	—	13	0	3	—	0	0	.227	.267	.300	1.000
Cubs total		**1**	**3**	**0**	**1**	**0**	**0**	**0**	**0**	**0**	**—**	**1**	**0**	**0**	**—**	**0**	**0**	**.333**	**.333**	**.333**	**1.000**

Clarke, Thomas Aloysius (Tommy)
HEIGHT: 5'11"   THROWS: RIGHT   BATS: RIGHT   BORN: 5/9/1888 NEW YORK, NEW YORK   DIED: 8/14/1945 CONORA, NEW YORK   POSITIONS PLAYED: C, 1B

YEAR	TEAM	GAMES	AB	RUNS	HITS	2B	3B	HR	RBI	BB	IBB	SO	HBP	SH	SF	SB	CS	BA	OBA	SA	FA
1909	Cin-N	18	52	8	13	3	2	0	10	6	—	—	0	5	—	3	—	.250	.328	.385	.965
1910	Cin-N	64	151	19	42	6	5	1	20	19	—	17	3	7	—	1	—	.278	.370	.404	.971
1911	Cin-N	86	203	20	49	6	7	1	25	25	—	22	1	14	—	4	—	.241	.328	.355	.968
1912	Cin-N	72	146	19	41	7	2	0	22	28	—	14	1	5	—	9	—	.281	.400	.356	.983
1913	Cin-N	114	330	29	87	11	8	1	38	39	—	40	2	3	—	2	—	.264	.345	.355	.979
1914	Cin-N	113	313	30	82	13	7	2	25	31	—	30	2	5	—	6	—	.262	.332	.367	.973
1915	Cin-N	96	226	23	65	7	2	0	21	33	—	22	1	8	—	7	3	.288	.381	.336	.981
1916	Cin-N	78	177	10	42	10	1	0	17	24	—	20	0	3	—	8	—	.237	.328	.305	.965
1917	Cin-N	58	110	11	32	3	3	1	13	11	—	12	1	0	—	2	—	.291	.361	.400	.991
1918	**ChC-N**	**1**	**0**	**0**	**0**	**0**	**0**	**0**	**0**	**0**	**—**	**0**	**0**	**0**	**—**	**0**		**—**	**—**	**—**	**—**
Career average		70	171	17	45	7	4	1	19	22	—	18	1	5	—	4	0	.265	.351	.358	.975
Cubs average		**1**	**0**	**0**	**0**	**0**	**0**	**0**	**0**	**0**	**—**	**0**	**0**	**0**	**—**	**0**	**0**	**—**	**—**	**—**	**—**
Career total		700	1708	169	453	66	37	6	191	216	—	177	11	50	—	42	3	.265	.351	.358	.975
Cubs total		**1**	**0**	**0**	**0**	**0**	**0**	**0**	**0**	**0**	**—**	**0**	**0**	**0**	**—**	**0**	**0**	**—**	**—**	**—**	**—**

Clemens, Clement Lambert (Clem *or* Count)
HEIGHT: 5'11"   THROWS: RIGHT   BATS: RIGHT   BORN: 11/2/1886 CHICAGO, ILLINOIS   DIED: 11/2/1967 ST. PETERSBURG, FLORIDA   POSITIONS PLAYED: C, 2B

YEAR	TEAM	GAMES	AB	RUNS	HITS	2B	3B	HR	RBI	BB	IBB	SO	HBP	SH	SF	SB	CS	BA	OBA	SA	FA
1914	Chi-F	13	27	4	4	0	0	0	2	3	—	—	0	1	—	0	—	.148	.233	.148	.950
1915	Chi-F	11	22	3	3	1	0	0	3	1	—	—	0	0	—	0	—	.136	.174	.182	1.000
1916	**ChC-N**	**10**	**15**	**0**	**0**	**0**	**0**	**0**	**0**	**1**	**—**	**6**	**0**	**0**	**—**	**0**	**—**	**.000**	**.063**	**.000**	**.941**
Career average		11	21	2	2	0	0	0	2	2	—	2	0	0	—	0	—	.109	.174	.125	.963
Cubs average		**10**	**15**	**0**	**0**	**0**	**0**	**0**	**0**	**1**	**—**	**6**	**0**	**0**	**—**	**0**	**—**	**.000**	**.063**	**.000**	**.941**
Career total		34	64	7	7	1	0	0	5	5	—	6	0	1	—	0	—	.109	.174	.125	.963
Cubs total		**10**	**15**	**0**	**0**	**0**	**0**	**0**	**0**	**1**	**—**	**6**	**0**	**0**	**—**	**0**	**—**	**.000**	**.063**	**.000**	**.941**

Clemens, Douglas Horace (Doug)
HEIGHT: 6'0"   THROWS: RIGHT   BATS: LEFT   BORN: 6/9/1939 LEESPORT, PENNSYLVANIA   POSITIONS PLAYED: 1B, OF

YEAR	TEAM	GAMES	AB	RUNS	HITS	2B	3B	HR	RBI	BB	IBB	SO	HBP	SH	SF	SB	CS	BA	OBA	SA	FA
1960	StL-N	1	0	0	0	0	0	0	0	0	0	0	0	0	0	0	0	—	—	—	1.000
1961	StL-N	6	12	1	2	1	0	0	0	3	0	1	0	0	0	0	0	.167	.333	.250	.667
1962	StL-N	48	93	12	22	1	1	1	12	17	1	19	0	1	0	0	0	.237	.355	.301	.974
1963	StL-N	5	6	1	1	0	0	1	2	1	0	2	0	1	0	0	0	.167	.286	.667	1.000
1964	StL-N	33	78	8	16	4	3	1	9	6	0	16	1	4	0	0	0	.205	.271	.372	.970
1964	**ChC-N**	**54**	**140**	**23**	**39**	**10**	**2**	**2**	**12**	**18**	**2**	**22**	**1**	**0**	**1**	**0**	**0**	**.279**	**.363**	**.421**	**.923**
1965	**ChC-N**	**128**	**340**	**36**	**75**	**11**	**0**	**4**	**26**	**38**	**4**	**53**	**2**	**3**	**3**	**5**	**8**	**.221**	**.300**	**.288**	**.981**
1966	Phi-N	79	121	10	31	1	0	1	15	16	0	25	2	0	0	1	0	.256	.353	.289	1.000
1967	Phi-N	69	73	2	13	5	0	0	4	8	0	15	1	0	2	0	0	.178	.262	.247	1.000
1968	Phi-N	29	57	6	12	1	1	2	8	7	1	13	0	0	1	0	0	.211	.292	.368	.969
Career average		50	102	11	23	4	1	1	10	13	1	18	1	1	1	1	1	.229	.317	.321	.969
Cubs average		**91**	**240**	**30**	**57**	**11**	**1**	**3**	**19**	**28**	**3**	**38**	**2**	**2**	**2**	**3**	**4**	**.238**	**.319**	**.327**	**.961**
Career total		452	920	99	211	34	7	12	88	114	8	166	7	9	7	6	8	.229	.317	.321	.969
Cubs total		**182**	**480**	**59**	**114**	**21**	**2**	**6**	**38**	**56**	**6**	**75**	**3**	**3**	**4**	**5**	**8**	**.238**	**.319**	**.327**	**.961**

Cline, Tyrone Alexander (Ty)
HEIGHT: 6'0"   THROWS: LEFT   BATS: LEFT   BORN: 6/15/1939 HAMPTON, SOUTH CAROLINA   POSITIONS PLAYED: 1B, OF

YEAR	TEAM	GAMES	AB	RUNS	HITS	2B	3B	HR	RBI	BB	IBB	SO	HBP	SH	SF	SB	CS	BA	OBA	SA	FA
1960	Cle-A	7	26	2	8	1	1	0	2	0	0	4	0	1	0	0	0	.308	.308	.423	1.000
1961	Cle-A	12	43	9	9	2	1	0	1	6	0	1	2	0	0	1	0	.209	.333	.302	1.000
1962	Cle-A	118	375	53	93	15	5	2	28	28	0	50	5	2	1	5	4	.248	.308	.331	.992
1963	Mil-N	72	174	17	41	2	1	0	10	10	0	31	2	3	1	2	1	.236	.283	.259	.992
1964	Mil-N	101	116	22	35	4	2	1	13	8	0	22	3	4	1	0	1	.302	.359	.397	.989
1965	Mil-N	123	220	27	42	5	3	0	10	16	2	50	0	4	0	2	2	.191	.246	.241	.974
1966	**ChC-N**	**7**	**17**	**3**	**6**	**0**	**0**	**0**	**2**	**0**	**0**	**2**	**0**	**0**	**0**	**1**	**0**	**.353**	**.353**	**.353**	**1.000**
1966	Atl-N	42	71	12	18	0	0	0	6	3	0	11	2	1	0	2	1	.254	.303	.254	.988
1967	Atl-N	10	8	0	0	0	0	0	0	0	0	3	1	0	0	0	0	.000	.111	.000	1.000
1967	SF-N	64	122	18	33	5	5	0	4	9	0	13	1	1	0	2	1	.270	.326	.393	1.000
1968	SF-N	116	291	37	65	6	3	1	28	11	1	26	1	6	1	0	2	.223	.253	.275	.986
1969	Mon-N	101	209	26	50	5	3	2	12	32	1	22	2	1	0	4	3	.239	.346	.321	.989
1970	Mon-N	2	2	0	1	0	0	0	0	0	0	0	0	0	0	0	0	.500	.500	.500	—
1970	Cin-N	48	63	13	17	7	1	0	8	12	1	11	0	3	0	1	2	.270	.387	.413	.971
1971	Cin-N	69	97	12	19	1	0	0	1	18	0	16	2	1	0	2	2	.196	.333	.206	1.000
Career average		74	153	21	36	4	2	1	10	13	0	22	2	2	0	2	2	.238	.304	.304	.988
Cubs average		**7**	**17**	**3**	**6**	**0**	**0**	**0**	**2**	**0**	**0**	**2**	**0**	**0**	**0**	**1**	**0**	**.353**	**.353**	**.353**	**1.000**
Career total		892	1834	251	437	53	25	6	125	153	5	262	21	27	4	22	19	.238	.304	.304	.988
Cubs total		**7**	**17**	**3**	**6**	**0**	**0**	**0**	**2**	**0**	**0**	**2**	**0**	**0**	**0**	**1**	**0**	**.353**	**.353**	**.353**	**1.000**

Clines, Eugene Anthony (Gene *or* Road Runner)
HEIGHT: 5'9"   THROWS: RIGHT   BATS: RIGHT   BORN: 10/6/1946 SAN PABLO, CALIFORNIA   POSITIONS PLAYED: OF

YEAR	TEAM	GAMES	AB	RUNS	HITS	2B	3B	HR	RBI	BB	IBB	SO	HBP	SH	SF	SB	CS	BA	OBA	SA	FA
1970	Pit-N	31	37	4	15	2	0	0	3	2	0	5	0	0	0	2	1	.405	.436	.459	1.000
1971	Pit-N	97	273	52	84	12	4	1	24	22	0	36	3	2	0	15	6	.308	.366	.392	.981
1972	Pit-N	107	311	52	104	15	6	0	17	16	1	47	2	3	2	12	6	.334	.369	.421	.958
1973	Pit-N	110	304	42	80	11	3	1	23	26	0	36	3	4	0	8	7	.263	.327	.329	.968
1974	Pit-N	107	276	29	62	5	1	0	14	30	2	40	4	4	3	14	2	.225	.307	.250	.989
1975	NYM-N	82	203	25	46	6	3	0	10	11	1	21	1	0	1	4	4	.227	.269	.286	.982
1976	Tex-A	116	446	52	123	12	3	0	38	16	0	52	4	10	4	11	9	.276	.304	.316	.987
1977	**ChC-N**	**101**	**239**	**27**	**70**	**12**	**2**	**3**	**41**	**25**	**2**	**25**	**1**	**1**	**3**	**1**	**2**	**.293**	**.358**	**.397**	**.986**
1978	**ChC-N**	**109**	**229**	**31**	**59**	**10**	**2**	**0**	**17**	**21**	**1**	**28**	**1**	**2**	**1**	**4**	**3**	**.258**	**.321**	**.319**	**.978**
1979	**ChC-N**	**10**	**10**	**0**	**2**	**0**	**0**	**0**	**0**	**0**	**0**	**1**	**0**	**0**	**0**	**0**	**0**	**.200**	**.200**	**.200**	**—**
Career average		87	233	31	65	9	2	1	19	17	1	29	2	3	1	7	4	.277	.329	.341	.979
Cubs average		**73**	**159**	**19**	**44**	**7**	**1**	**1**	**19**	**15**	**1**	**18**	**1**	**1**	**1**	**2**	**2**	**.274**	**.338**	**.356**	**.982**
Career total		870	2328	314	645	85	24	5	187	169	7	291	19	26	14	71	40	.277	.329	.341	.979
Cubs total		**220**	**478**	**58**	**131**	**22**	**4**	**3**	**58**	**46**	**3**	**54**	**2**	**3**	**4**	**5**	**5**	**.274**	**.338**	**.356**	**.982**

Clingman, William Frederick (Billy)
HEIGHT: 5'11"   THROWS: RIGHT   BATS: BOTH   BORN: 11/21/1869 CINCINNATI, OHIO   DIED: 5/14/1958 CINCINNATI, OHIO   POSITIONS PLAYED: 2B, 3B, SS, OF

YEAR	TEAM	GAMES	AB	RUNS	HITS	2B	3B	HR	RBI	BB	IBB	SO	HBP	SH	SF	SB	CS	BA	OBA	SA	FA
1890	Cin-N	7	27	2	7	1	0	0	5	1	—	0	0	—	—	0	—	.259	.286	.296	.895
1891	Cin-AA	1	5	0	1	1	0	0	0	0	—	0	0	—	—	0	—	.200	.200	.400	.667
1895	Pit-N	106	382	69	99	16	4	0	45	41	—	43	2	10	—	19	—	.259	.334	.322	.887
1896	Lou-N	121	423	57	99	10	2	2	37	57	—	51	3	4	—	19	—	.234	.329	.281	.925
1897	Lou-N	113	395	59	90	14	7	2	47	37	—	—	5	8	—	14	—	.228	.302	.314	.947
1898	Lou-N	154	538	65	138	12	6	0	50	51	—	—	5	15	—	15	—	.257	.327	.301	.915
1899	Lou-N	109	366	67	96	15	4	2	44	46	—	—	3	9	—	13	—	.262	.349	.342	.916
1900	**ChN-N**	**47**	**159**	**15**	**33**	**6**	**0**	**0**	**11**	**17**	**—**	**—**	**2**	**1**	**—**	**6**	**—**	**.208**	**.292**	**.245**	**.872**
1901	Was-A	137	480	66	116	10	7	2	55	42	—	—	4	11	—	10	—	.242	.308	.304	.932
1903	Cle-A	21	64	10	18	1	1	0	7	11	—	—	0	1	—	2	—	.281	.387	.328	.922
Career average		82	284	41	70	9	3	1	30	30	—	9	2	6	—	10	—	.246	.323	.306	.917
Cubs average		**47**	**159**	**15**	**33**	**6**	**0**	**0**	**11**	**17**	**—**	**0**	**2**	**1**	**—**	**6**	**—**	**.208**	**.292**	**.245**	**.872**
Career total		816	2839	410	697	86	31	8	301	303	—	94	24	59	—	98	—	.246	.323	.306	.917
Cubs total		**47**	**159**	**15**	**33**	**6**	**0**	**0**	**11**	**17**	**—**	**0**	**2**	**1**	**—**	**6**	**—**	**.208**	**.292**	**.245**	**.872**

Clymer, Otis Edgar
HEIGHT: 5'11"   THROWS: RIGHT   BATS: BOTH   BORN: 1/27/1876 PINE GROVE, PENNSYLVANIA   DIED: 2/27/1926 ST. PAUL, MINNESOTA
POSITIONS PLAYED: 1B, 2B, 3B, OF

YEAR	TEAM	GAMES	AB	RUNS	HITS	2B	3B	HR	RBI	BB	IBB	SO	HBP	SH	SF	SB	CS	BA	OBA	SA	FA
1905	Pit-N	96	365	74	108	11	5	0	23	19	—	—	1	4	—	23	—	.296	.332	.353	.987
1906	Pit-N	11	45	7	11	0	1	0	1	3	—	—	0	0	—	1	—	.244	.292	.289	.900
1907	Pit-N	22	66	8	15	2	0	0	4	5	—	—	3	2	—	4	—	.227	.311	.258	.881
1907	Was-A	57	206	30	65	5	5	1	16	18	—	—	4	4	—	18	—	.316	.382	.403	.912
1908	Was-A	110	368	32	93	11	4	1	35	20	—	—	0	9	—	19	—	.253	.291	.313	.929
1909	Was-A	45	138	11	27	5	2	0	6	17	—	—	0	4	—	7	—	.196	.284	.261	.922
1913	**ChC-N**	**30**	**105**	**16**	**24**	**5**	**1**	**0**	**7**	**14**	**—**	**18**	**0**	**1**	**—**	**9**	**—**	**.229**	**.319**	**.295**	**.933**
1913	Bos-N	14	37	4	12	3	1	0	6	3	—	3	0	1	—	2	—	.324	.375	.459	.880
Career average		64	222	30	59	7	3	0	16	17	—	4	1	4	—	14	—	.267	.322	.332	.934
Cubs average		**30**	**105**	**16**	**24**	**5**	**1**	**0**	**7**	**14**	**—**	**18**	**0**	**1**	**—**	**9**	**—**	**.229**	**.319**	**.295**	**.933**
Career total		385	1330	182	355	42	19	2	98	99	—	21	8	25	—	83	—	.267	.322	.332	.934
Cubs total		**30**	**105**	**16**	**24**	**5**	**1**	**0**	**7**	**14**	**—**	**18**	**0**	**1**	**—**	**9**	**—**	**.229**	**.319**	**.295**	**.933**

Coggins, Franklin (Frank *or* Swish)
HEIGHT: 6'2"　THROWS: RIGHT　BATS: BOTH　BORN: 5/22/1944 GRIFFIN, GEORGIA　POSITIONS PLAYED: 2B

YEAR	TEAM	GAMES	AB	RUNS	HITS	2B	3B	HR	RBI	BB	IBB	SO	HBP	SH	SF	SB	CS	BA	OBA	SA	FA
1967	Was-A	19	75	9	23	3	0	1	8	2	0	17	0	0	1	1	0	.307	.321	.387	.964
1968	Was-A	62	171	15	30	6	1	0	7	9	2	33	0	2	1	1	1	.175	.215	.222	.953
1972	**ChC-N**	**6**	**1**	**1**	**0**	**0**	**0**	**0**	**0**	**1**	**0**	**0**	**0**	**0**	**0**	**0**	**0**	**.000**	**.500**	**.000**	**—**
Career average		29	82	8	18	3	0	0	5	4	1	17	0	1	1	1	0	.215	.249	.271	.957
Cubs average		**6**	**1**	**1**	**0**	**0**	**0**	**0**	**0**	**1**	**0**	**0**	**0**	**0**	**0**	**0**	**0**	**.000**	**.500**	**.000**	**—**
Career total		87	247	25	53	9	1	1	15	12	2	50	0	2	2	2	1	.215	.249	.271	.957
Cubs total		**6**	**1**	**1**	**0**	**0**	**0**	**0**	**0**	**1**	**0**	**0**	**0**	**0**	**0**	**0**	**0**	**.000**	**.500**	**.000**	**—**

Collins, James Anthony (Ripper)
HEIGHT: 5'9"　THROWS: LEFT　BATS: BOTH　BORN: 3/30/1904 ALTOONA, PENNSYLVANIA　DIED: 4/15/1970 NEW HAVEN, NEW YORK
POSITIONS PLAYED: 1B, OF

YEAR	TEAM	GAMES	AB	RUNS	HITS	2B	3B	HR	RBI	BB	IBB	SO	HBP	SH	SF	SB	CS	BA	OBA	SA	FA
1931	StL-N	89	279	34	84	20	10	4	59	18	—	24	3	1	—	1	—	.301	.350	.487	.995
1932	StL-N	149	549	82	153	28	8	21	91	38	—	67	3	8	—	4	—	.279	.329	.474	.993
1933	StL-N	132	493	66	153	26	7	10	68	38	—	49	3	8	—	7	—	.310	.363	.452	.994
1934	StL-N	154	600	116	200	40	12	35	128	57	—	50	2	3	—	2	—	.333	.393	.615	.991
1935	StL-N	150	578	109	181	36	10	23	122	65	—	45	3	1	—	0	—	.313	.385	.529	.987
1936	StL-N	103	277	48	81	15	3	13	48	48	—	30	1	1	—	1	—	.292	.399	.509	.989
1937	**ChC-N**	**115**	**456**	**77**	**125**	**16**	**5**	**16**	**71**	**32**	**—**	**46**	**5**	**10**	**—**	**2**	**—**	**.274**	**.329**	**.436**	**.991**
1938	**ChC-N**	**143**	**490**	**78**	**131**	**22**	**8**	**13**	**61**	**54**	**—**	**48**	**3**	**8**	**—**	**1**	**—**	**.267**	**.344**	**.424**	**.996**
1941	Pit-N	49	62	5	13	2	2	0	11	6	—	14	0	2	—	0	—	.210	.279	.306	.949
Career average		120	420	68	125	23	7	15	73	40	—	41	3	5	—	2	—	.296	.360	.492	.991
Cubs average		**129**	**473**	**78**	**128**	**19**	**7**	**15**	**66**	**43**	**—**	**47**	**4**	**9**	**—**	**2**	**—**	**.271**	**.337**	**.430**	**.993**
Career total		1084	3784	615	1121	205	65	135	659	356	—	373	23	42	—	18	—	.296	.360	.492	.991
Cubs total		**258**	**946**	**155**	**256**	**38**	**13**	**29**	**132**	**86**	**—**	**94**	**8**	**18**	**—**	**3**	**—**	**.271**	**.337**	**.430**	**.993**

Collins, Robert Joseph (Rip)
HEIGHT: 5'11"　THROWS: RIGHT　BATS: RIGHT　BORN: 9/18/1909 PITTSBURGH, PENNSYLVANIA　DIED: 4/19/1969 PITTSBURGH, PENNSYLVANIA
POSITIONS PLAYED: C

YEAR	TEAM	GAMES	AB	RUNS	HITS	2B	3B	HR	RBI	BB	IBB	SO	HBP	SH	SF	SB	CS	BA	OBA	SA	FA
1940	**ChC-N**	**47**	**120**	**11**	**25**	**3**	**0**	**1**	**14**	**14**	**—**	**18**	**1**	**1**	**—**	**4**	**—**	**.208**	**.296**	**.258**	**.951**
1944	NYY-A	3	3	0	1	0	0	0	0	1	—	0	0	0	—	0	0	.333	.500	.333	1.000
Career average		25	62	6	13	2	0	1	7	8	—	9	1	1	—	2	0	.211	.302	.260	.953
Cubs average		**47**	**120**	**11**	**25**	**3**	**0**	**1**	**14**	**14**	**—**	**18**	**1**	**1**	**—**	**4**	**—**	**.208**	**.296**	**.258**	**.951**
Career total		50	123	11	26	3	0	1	14	15	—	18	1	1	—	4	0	.211	.302	.260	.953
Cubs total		**47**	**120**	**11**	**25**	**3**	**0**	**1**	**14**	**14**	**—**	**18**	**1**	**1**	**—**	**4**	**—**	**.208**	**.296**	**.258**	**.951**

Collins, William Shirley (Bill)
HEIGHT: 6'0"　THROWS: RIGHT　BATS: BOTH　BORN: 3/27/1882 CHESTERTON, INDIANA　DIED: 6/26/1961 SAN BERARDINO, CALIFORNIA
POSITIONS PLAYED: 3B, OF

YEAR	TEAM	GAMES	AB	RUNS	HITS	2B	3B	HR	RBI	BB	IBB	SO	HBP	SH	SF	SB	CS	BA	OBA	SA	FA
1910	Bos-N	151	584	67	141	6	7	3	40	43	—	48	13	16	—	36	—	.241	.308	.291	.977
1911	Bos-N	17	44	8	6	1	1	0	8	1	—	8	0	3	—	4	—	.136	.156	.205	1.000
1911	**ChC-N**	**7**	**3**	**2**	**1**	**1**	**0**	**0**	**0**	**1**	**—**	**3**	**0**	**0**	**—**	**0**	**—**	**.333**	**.500**	**.667**	**1.000**
1913	Bro-N	32	95	8	18	1	0	0	4	8	—	11	2	2	—	2	—	.189	.267	.200	.921
1914	Buf-F	21	47	6	7	2	2	0	2	1	—	8	0	2	—	0	—	.149	.167	.277	.864
Career average		57	193	23	43	3	3	1	14	14	—	20	4	6	—	11	—	.224	.287	.276	.967
Cubs average		**7**	**3**	**2**	**1**	**1**	**0**	**0**	**0**	**1**	**—**	**3**	**0**	**0**	**—**	**0**	**—**	**.333**	**.500**	**.667**	**1.000**
Career total		228	773	91	173	11	10	3	54	54	—	78	15	23	—	42	—	.224	.287	.276	.967
Cubs total		**7**	**3**	**2**	**1**	**1**	**0**	**0**	**0**	**1**	**—**	**3**	**0**	**0**	**—**	**0**	**—**	**.333**	**.500**	**.667**	**1.000**

Congalton, William Millar (Bunk)
HEIGHT: 5'11" THROWS: LEFT BATS: LEFT BORN: 1/24/1875 GUELPH, ONTARIO, CANADA DIED: 8/19/1937 CLEVELAND, OHIO POSITIONS PLAYED: OF

YEAR	TEAM	GAMES	AB	RUNS	HITS	2B	3B	HR	RBI	BB	IBB	SO	HBP	SH	SF	SB	CS	BA	OBA	SA	FA
1902	ChC-N	45	179	14	40	3	0	1	24	7	—	—	0	4	—	3	—	.223	.253	.257	.987
1905	Cle-A	12	47	4	17	0	0	0	5	2	—	—	0	0	—	3	—	.362	.388	.362	.923
1906	Cle-A	117	419	51	134	13	5	3	50	24	—	—	3	24	—	12	—	.320	.361	.396	.957
1907	Cle-A	9	22	2	4	0	0	0	2	4	—	—	0	0	—	0	—	.182	.308	.182	1.000
1907	Bos-A	127	496	44	142	11	8	2	47	20	—	—	3	13	—	13	—	.286	.318	.353	.969
Career average		78	291	29	84	7	3	2	32	14	—	—	2	10	—	8	—	.290	.326	.351	.967
Cubs average		**45**	**179**	**14**	**40**	**3**	**0**	**1**	**24**	**7**	**—**	**—**	**0**	**4**	**—**	**3**	**—**	**.223**	**.253**	**.257**	**.987**
Career total		310	1163	115	337	27	13	6	128	57	—	—	6	41	—	31	—	.290	.326	.351	.967
Cubs total		**45**	**179**	**14**	**40**	**3**	**0**	**1**	**24**	**7**	**—**	**—**	**0**	**4**	**—**	**3**	**—**	**.223**	**.253**	**.257**	**.987**

Connally, Fritzie Lee (Fritz)
HEIGHT: 6'3" THROWS: RIGHT BATS: RIGHT BORN: 5/19/1958 BRYAN, TEXAS POSITIONS PLAYED: 1B, 3B

YEAR	TEAM	GAMES	AB	RUNS	HITS	2B	3B	HR	RBI	BB	IBB	SO	HBP	SH	SF	SB	CS	BA	OBA	SA	FA
1983	ChC-N	8	10	0	1	0	0	0	0	0	0	5	0	0	0	0	0	.100	.100	.100	1.000
1985	Bal-A	50	112	16	26	4	0	3	15	19	0	21	1	2	1	0	0	.232	.346	.348	.980
Career average		29	61	8	14	2	0	2	8	10	0	13	1	1	1	0	0	.221	.329	.328	.980
Cubs average		**8**	**10**	**0**	**1**	**0**	**0**	**0**	**0**	**0**	**0**	**5**	**0**	**0**	**0**	**0**	**0**	**.100**	**.100**	**.100**	**1.000**
Career total		58	122	16	27	4	0	3	15	19	0	26	1	2	1	0	0	.221	.329	.328	.980
Cubs total		**8**	**10**	**0**	**1**	**0**	**0**	**0**	**0**	**0**	**0**	**5**	**0**	**0**	**0**	**0**	**0**	**.100**	**.100**	**.100**	**1.000**

Connor, James Matthew (Jim)
HEIGHT: 5'11" THROWS: RIGHT BATS: RIGHT BORN: 5/11/1863 PORT JERVIS, NEW YORK DIED: 9/3/1950 PROVIDENCE, RHODE ISLAND
POSITIONS PLAYED: 2B, 3B

YEAR	TEAM	GAMES	AB	RUNS	HITS	2B	3B	HR	RBI	BB	IBB	SO	HBP	SH	SF	SB	CS	BA	OBA	SA	FA
1892	ChN-N	9	34	0	2	0	0	0	0	1	—	7	1	—	—	0	—	.059	.111	.059	.917
1897	ChN-N	77	285	40	83	10	5	3	38	24	—	—	4	5	—	10	—	.291	.355	.393	.936
1898	ChN-N	138	505	51	114	9	9	0	67	42	—	—	3	13	—	11	—	.226	.289	.279	.946
1899	ChN-N	69	234	26	48	7	1	0	24	18	—	—	1	10	—	6	—	.205	.265	.244	.923
Career average		73	265	29	62	7	4	1	32	21	—	2	2	7	—	7	—	.233	.296	.295	.938
Cubs average		**73**	**265**	**29**	**62**	**7**	**4**	**1**	**32**	**21**	**—**	**2**	**2**	**7**	**—**	**7**	**—**	**.233**	**.296**	**.295**	**.938**
Career total		293	1058	117	247	26	15	3	129	85	—	7	9	28	—	27	—	.233	.296	.295	.938
Cubs total		**293**	**1058**	**117**	**247**	**26**	**15**	**3**	**129**	**85**	**—**	**7**	**9**	**28**	**—**	**27**	**—**	**.233**	**.296**	**.295**	**.938**

Connors, Kevin Joseph Aloysius (Chuck)
HEIGHT: 6'5" THROWS: LEFT BATS: LEFT BORN: 4/10/1921 BROOKLYN, NEW YORK DIED: 11/10/1992 LOS ANGELES, CALIFORNIA POSITIONS PLAYED: 1B

YEAR	TEAM	GAMES	AB	RUNS	HITS	2B	3B	HR	RBI	BB	IBB	SO	HBP	SH	SF	SB	CS	BA	OBA	SA	FA
1949	Bro-N	1	1	0	0	0	0	0	0	0	—	0	0	0	—	0	0	.000	.000	.000	—
1951	ChC-N	66	201	16	48	5	1	2	18	12	—	25	0	1	—	4	0	.239	.282	.303	.984
Career average		34	101	8	24	3	1	1	9	6	—	13	0	1	—	2	0	.238	.280	.302	.984
Cubs average		**66**	**201**	**16**	**48**	**5**	**1**	**2**	**18**	**12**	**—**	**25**	**0**	**1**	**—**	**4**	**0**	**.239**	**.282**	**.303**	**.984**
Career total		67	202	16	48	5	1	2	18	12	—	25	0	1	—	4	0	.238	.280	.302	.984
Cubs total		**66**	**201**	**16**	**48**	**5**	**1**	**2**	**18**	**12**	**—**	**25**	**0**	**1**	**—**	**4**	**0**	**.239**	**.282**	**.303**	**.984**

Cook, James Fitchie (Jim)
HEIGHT: 5'9" THROWS: RIGHT BATS: RIGHT BORN: 11/10/1879 DUNDEE, ILLINOIS DIED: 6/17/1949 ST. LOUIS, MISSOURI POSITIONS PLAYED: 1B, 2B, OF

YEAR	TEAM	GAMES	AB	RUNS	HITS	2B	3B	HR	RBI	BB	IBB	SO	HBP	SH	SF	SB	CS	BA	OBA	SA	FA
1903	ChC-N	8	26	3	4	1	0	0	2	2	—	—	1	0	—	1	—	.154	.241	.192	.909
Career average		8	26	3	4	1	0	0	2	2	—	—	1	0	—	1	—	.154	.241	.192	.909
Cubs average		**8**	**26**	**3**	**4**	**1**	**0**	**0**	**2**	**2**	**—**	**—**	**1**	**0**	**—**	**1**	**—**	**.154**	**.241**	**.192**	**.909**
Career total		8	26	3	4	1	0	0	2	2	—	—	1	0	—	1	—	.154	.241	.192	.909
Cubs total		**8**	**26**	**3**	**4**	**1**	**0**	**0**	**2**	**2**	**—**	**—**	**1**	**0**	**—**	**1**	**—**	**.154**	**.241**	**.192**	**.909**

Coomer, Ronald Bryan (Ron)
HEIGHT: 6'0" THROWS: RIGHT BATS: RIGHT BORN: 11/18/1966 CHICAGO, ILLINOIS POSITIONS PLAYED: 1B, 3B, OF

YEAR	TEAM	GAMES	AB	RUNS	HITS	2B	3B	HR	RBI	BB	IBB	SO	HBP	SH	SF	SB	CS	BA	OBA	SA	FA
1995	Min-A	37	101	15	26	3	1	5	19	9	0	11	1	0	0	0	1	.257	.324	.455	.988
1996	Min-A	95	233	34	69	12	1	12	41	17	1	24	0	0	3	3	0	.296	.340	.511	.988
1997	Min-A	140	523	63	156	30	2	13	85	22	5	91	0	0	5	4	3	.298	.324	.438	.969
1998	Min-A	137	529	54	146	22	1	15	72	18	1	72	0	0	8	2	2	.276	.295	.406	.990
1999	Min-A	127	467	53	123	25	1	16	65	30	1	69	1	0	3	2	1	.263	.307	.424	.991
2000	Min-A	140	544	64	147	29	1	16	82	36	2	50	4	0	5	2	0	.270	.317	.415	.995
2001	**ChC-N**	**111**	**349**	**25**	**91**	**19**	**1**	**8**	**53**	**29**	**1**	**70**	**2**	**0**	**6**	**0**	**0**	**.261**	**.316**	**.390**	**.977**
Career average		112	392	44	108	20	1	12	60	23	2	55	1	0	4	2	1	.276	.315	.426	.988
Cubs average		**111**	**349**	**25**	**91**	**19**	**1**	**8**	**53**	**29**	**1**	**70**	**2**	**0**	**6**	**0**	**0**	**.261**	**.316**	**.390**	**.977**
Career total		787	2746	308	758	140	8	85	417	161	11	387	8	0	30	13	7	.276	.315	.426	.988
Cubs total		**111**	**349**	**25**	**91**	**19**	**1**	**8**	**53**	**29**	**1**	**70**	**2**	**0**	**6**	**0**	**0**	**.261**	**.316**	**.390**	**.977**

Cooney, James Edward (Jimmy *or* Scoops)
HEIGHT: 5'11" THROWS: RIGHT BATS: RIGHT BORN: 8/24/1894 CRANSTON, RHODE ISLAND DIED: 8/7/1991 WARWICK, RHODE ISLAND
POSITIONS PLAYED: 2B, 3B, SS, OF

YEAR	TEAM	GAMES	AB	RUNS	HITS	2B	3B	HR	RBI	BB	IBB	SO	HBP	SH	SF	SB	CS	BA	OBA	SA	FA
1917	Bos-A	11	36	4	8	1	0	0	3	6	—	2	0	6	—	0	—	.222	.333	.250	1.000
1919	NYG-N	5	14	3	3	0	0	0	1	0	—	0	0	1	—	0	—	.214	.214	.214	1.000
1924	StL-N	110	383	44	113	20	8	1	57	20	—	20	0	11	—	12	10	.295	.330	.397	.970
1925	StL-N	54	187	27	51	11	2	0	18	4	—	5	1	10	—	1	3	.273	.292	.353	.975
1926	**ChC-N**	**141**	**513**	**52**	**129**	**18**	**5**	**1**	**47**	**23**	**—**	**10**	**3**	**20**	**—**	**11**	**—**	**.251**	**.288**	**.312**	**.972**
1927	**ChC-N**	**33**	**132**	**16**	**32**	**2**	**0**	**0**	**6**	**8**	**—**	**7**	**0**	**9**	**—**	**1**	**—**	**.242**	**.286**	**.258**	**.973**
1927	Phi-N	76	259	33	70	12	1	0	15	13	—	9	0	10	—	4	—	.270	.305	.324	.980
1928	Bos-N	18	51	2	7	0	0	0	3	2	—	5	0	0	—	1	—	.137	.170	.137	.972
Career average		64	225	26	59	9	2	0	21	11	—	8	1	10	—	4	2	.262	.298	.327	.974
Cubs average		**87**	**323**	**34**	**81**	**10**	**3**	**1**	**27**	**16**	**—**	**9**	**2**	**15**	**—**	**6**	**0**	**.250**	**.287**	**.301**	**.972**
Career total		448	1575	181	413	64	16	2	150	76	—	58	4	67	—	30	13	.262	.298	.327	.974
Cubs total		**174**	**645**	**68**	**161**	**20**	**5**	**1**	**53**	**31**	**—**	**17**	**3**	**29**	**—**	**12**	**0**	**.250**	**.287**	**.301**	**.972**

Cooney, James Joseph (Jimmy)
HEIGHT: 5'9" THROWS: RIGHT BATS: BOTH BORN: 7/9/1865 CRANSTON, RHODE ISLAND DIED: 7/1/1903 CRANSTON, RHODE ISLAND
POSITIONS PLAYED: C, SS

YEAR	TEAM	GAMES	AB	RUNS	HITS	2B	3B	HR	RBI	BB	IBB	SO	HBP	SH	SF	SB	CS	BA	OBA	SA	FA
1890	**ChN-N**	**135**	**574**	**114**	**156**	**19**	**10**	**4**	**52**	**73**	**—**	**23**	**6**	**—**	**—**	**45**	**—**	**.272**	**.360**	**.361**	**.936**
1891	**ChN-N**	**118**	**465**	**84**	**114**	**15**	**3**	**0**	**42**	**48**	**—**	**17**	**2**	**—**	**—**	**21**	**—**	**.245**	**.318**	**.290**	**.917**
1892	**ChN-N**	**65**	**238**	**18**	**41**	**1**	**0**	**0**	**20**	**23**	**—**	**5**	**1**	**—**	**—**	**10**	**—**	**.172**	**.248**	**.176**	**.912**
1892	Was-N	6	25	5	4	0	1	0	4	4	—	3	0	—	—	1	—	.160	.276	.240	.862
Career average		108	434	74	105	12	5	1	39	49	—	16	3	—	—	26	—	.242	.324	.300	.923
Cubs average		**106**	**426**	**72**	**104**	**12**	**4**	**1**	**38**	**48**	**—**	**15**	**3**	**—**	**—**	**25**	**—**	**.244**	**.324**	**.301**	**.925**
Career total		324	1302	221	315	35	14	4	118	148	—	48	9	—	—	77	—	.242	.324	.300	.923
Cubs total		**318**	**1277**	**216**	**311**	**35**	**13**	**4**	**114**	**144**	**—**	**45**	**9**	**—**	**—**	**76**	**—**	**.244**	**.324**	**.301**	**.925**

Cooper, William Walker (Walker *or* Walk)
HEIGHT: 6'3" THROWS: RIGHT BATS: RIGHT BORN: 1/8/1915 ATHERTON, MISSOURI DIED: 4/11/1991 SCOTTSDALE, ARIZONA POSITIONS PLAYED: C

YEAR	TEAM	GAMES	AB	RUNS	HITS	2B	3B	HR	RBI	BB	IBB	SO	HBP	SH	SF	SB	CS	BA	OBA	SA	FA
1940	StL-N	6	19	3	6	1	0	0	2	2	—	2	0	0	—	1	—	.316	.381	.368	1.000
1941	StL-N	68	200	19	49	9	1	1	20	13	—	14	0	2	—	1	—	.245	.291	.315	.966
1942	StL-N	125	438	58	123	32	7	7	65	29	—	29	1	6	—	4	—	.281	.327	.434	.972
1943	StL-N	122	449	52	143	30	4	9	81	19	—	19	2	6	—	1	—	.318	.349	.463	.975
1944	StL-N	112	397	56	126	25	5	13	72	20	—	19	1	8	—	4	—	.317	.352	.504	.980
1945	StL-N	4	18	3	7	0	0	0	1	0	—	1	0	0	—	0	—	.389	.389	.389	.966
1946	NYG-N	87	280	29	75	10	1	8	46	17	—	12	0	3	—	0	2	.268	.310	.396	.972
1947	NYG-N	140	515	79	157	24	8	35	122	24	—	43	3	4	—	2	1	.305	.339	.586	.979
1948	NYG-N	91	290	40	77	12	0	16	54	28	—	29	1	3	—	1	—	.266	.332	.472	.979

(continued)

(continued)

YEAR	TEAM	GAMES	AB	RUNS	HITS	2B	3B	HR	RBI	BB	IBB	SO	HBP	SH	SF	SB	CS	BA	OBA	SA	FA
1949	NYG-N	42	147	14	31	4	2	4	21	7	—	8	3	0	—	0	1	.211	.261	.347	.982
1949	Cin-N	82	307	34	86	9	2	16	62	21	—	24	2	1	—	0	—	.280	.330	.479	.978
1950	Cin-N	15	47	3	9	3	0	0	4	0	—	5	0	0	—	0	—	.191	.191	.255	.972
1950	Bos-N	102	337	52	111	19	3	14	60	30	—	26	3	3	—	1	—	.329	.389	.528	.973
1951	Bos-N	109	342	42	107	14	1	18	59	28	—	18	1	1	—	1	1	.313	.367	.518	.981
1952	Bos-N	102	349	33	82	12	1	10	55	22	—	32	1	3	—	1	0	.235	.282	.361	.983
1953	Mil-N	53	137	12	30	6	0	3	16	12	—	15	1	1	—	1	0	.219	.287	.328	.983
1954	Pit-N	14	15	0	3	2	0	0	1	2	—	1	0	0	0	0	0	.200	.294	.333	1.000
1954	**ChC-N**	**57**	**158**	**21**	**49**	**10**	**2**	**7**	**32**	**21**	—	**23**	**2**	**0**	**0**	**0**	**0**	**.310**	**.398**	**.532**	**.978**
1955	**ChC-N**	**54**	**111**	**11**	**31**	**8**	**1**	**7**	**15**	**6**	**1**	**19**	**1**	**1**	**0**	**0**	**0**	**.279**	**.322**	**.559**	**.961**
1956	StL-N	40	68	5	18	5	1	2	14	3	1	8	0	1	0	0	0	.265	.296	.456	.984
1957	StL-N	48	78	7	21	5	1	3	10	5	1	10	0	1	1	0	0	.269	.310	.474	.957
Career average		82	261	32	75	13	2	10	45	17	0	20	1	2	0	1	0	.285	.332	.464	.977
Cubs average		**56**	**135**	**16**	**40**	**9**	**2**	**7**	**24**	**14**	**1**	**21**	**2**	**1**	**0**	**0**	**0**	**.297**	**.368**	**.543**	**.973**
Career total		1473	4702	573	1341	240	40	173	812	309	3	357	22	44	1	18	5	.285	.332	.464	.977
Cubs total		**111**	**269**	**32**	**80**	**18**	**3**	**14**	**47**	**27**	**1**	**42**	**3**	**1**	**0**	**0**	**0**	**.297**	**.368**	**.543**	**.973**

Corriden, John Michael (Red)

HEIGHT: 5'9" THROWS: RIGHT BATS: RIGHT BORN: 9/4/1887 LOGANSPORT, INDIANA DIED: 9/28/1959 INDIANAPOLIS, INDIANA
POSITIONS PLAYED: 2B, 3B, SS, OF

YEAR	TEAM	GAMES	AB	RUNS	HITS	2B	3B	HR	RBI	BB	IBB	SO	HBP	SH	SF	SB	CS	BA	OBA	SA	FA
1910	StL-A	26	84	19	13	3	0	1	4	13	—	—	4	9	—	5	—	.155	.297	.226	.916
1912	Det-A	38	138	22	28	6	0	0	5	15	—	—	1	3	—	4	—	.203	.286	.246	.903
1913	**ChC-N**	**46**	**97**	**13**	**17**	**3**	**0**	**2**	**9**	**10**	—	**14**	**0**	**2**	—	**4**	—	**.175**	**.252**	**.268**	**.905**
1914	**ChC-N**	**107**	**318**	**42**	**73**	**9**	**5**	**3**	**29**	**35**	—	**33**	**9**	**17**	—	**13**	—	**.230**	**.323**	**.318**	**.893**
1915	**ChC-N**	**6**	**3**	**1**	**0**	**0**	**0**	**0**	**0**	**2**	—	**1**	**2**	**0**	—	**0**	**0**	**.000**	**.571**	**.000**	**.667**
Career average		45	128	19	26	4	1	1	9	15	—	10	3	6	—	5	0	.205	.304	.281	.900
Cubs average		**53**	**139**	**19**	**30**	**4**	**2**	**2**	**13**	**16**	—	**16**	**4**	**6**	—	**6**	**0**	**.215**	**.311**	**.304**	**.895**
Career total		223	640	97	131	21	5	6	47	75	—	48	16	31	—	26	0	.205	.304	.281	.900
Cubs total		**159**	**418**	**56**	**90**	**12**	**5**	**5**	**38**	**47**	—	**48**	**11**	**19**	—	**17**	**0**	**.215**	**.311**	**.304**	**.895**

Cotter, Richard Raphael (Dick)

HEIGHT: 5'11" THROWS: RIGHT BATS: RIGHT BORN: 10/12/1889 MANCHESTER, NEW HAMPSHIRE DIED: 4/4/1945 BROOKLYN, NEW YORK
POSITIONS PLAYED: C

YEAR	TEAM	GAMES	AB	RUNS	HITS	2B	3B	HR	RBI	BB	IBB	SO	HBP	SH	SF	SB	CS	BA	OBA	SA	FA
1911	Phi-N	20	46	2	13	0	0	0	5	5	—	7	0	1	—	1	—	.283	.353	.283	.975
1912	**ChC-N**	**26**	**54**	**6**	**15**	**0**	**2**	**0**	**10**	**6**	—	**13**	**1**	**0**	—	**1**	—	**.278**	**.361**	**.352**	**.954**
Career average		23	50	4	14	0	1	0	8	6	—	10	1	1	—	1	—	.280	.357	.320	.964
Cubs average		**26**	**54**	**6**	**15**	**0**	**2**	**0**	**10**	**6**	—	**13**	**1**	**0**	—	**1**	—	**.278**	**.361**	**.352**	**.954**
Career total		46	100	8	28	0	2	0	15	11	—	20	1	1	—	2	—	.280	.357	.320	.964
Cubs total		**26**	**54**	**6**	**15**	**0**	**2**	**0**	**10**	**6**	—	**13**	**1**	**0**	—	**1**	—	**.278**	**.361**	**.352**	**.954**

Cotter, Harvey Louis (Hooks)

HEIGHT: 5'10" THROWS: LEFT BATS: LEFT BORN: 5/22/1900 HOLDEN, MISSOURI DIED: 8/6/1955 LOS ANGELES, CALIFORNIA POSITIONS PLAYED: 1B

YEAR	TEAM	GAMES	AB	RUNS	HITS	2B	3B	HR	RBI	BB	IBB	SO	HBP	SH	SF	SB	CS	BA	OBA	SA	FA
1922	**ChC-N**	**1**	**1**	**0**	**1**	**1**	**0**	**0**	**0**	**0**	—	**0**	**0**	**0**	—	**0**	**0**	**1.000**	**1.000**	**2.000**	—
1924	**ChC-N**	**98**	**310**	**39**	**81**	**16**	**4**	**4**	**33**	**36**	—	**31**	**0**	**7**	—	**3**	**5**	**.261**	**.338**	**.377**	**.989**
Career average		50	156	20	41	9	2	2	17	18	—	16	0	4	—	2	3	.264	.340	.383	.989
Cubs average		**50**	**156**	**20**	**41**	**9**	**2**	**2**	**17**	**18**	—	**16**	**0**	**4**	—	**2**	**3**	**.264**	**.340**	**.383**	**.989**
Career total		99	311	39	82	17	4	4	33	36	—	31	0	7	—	3	5	.264	.340	.383	.989
Cubs total		**99**	**311**	**39**	**82**	**17**	**4**	**4**	**33**	**36**	—	**31**	**0**	**7**	—	**3**	**5**	**.264**	**.340**	**.383**	**.989**

Cotto, Henry
HEIGHT: 6'2" THROWS: RIGHT BATS: RIGHT BORN: 1/5/1961 NEW YORK, NEW YORK POSITIONS PLAYED: OF

YEAR	TEAM	GAMES	AB	RUNS	HITS	2B	3B	HR	RBI	BB	IBB	SO	HBP	SH	SF	SB	CS	BA	OBA	SA	FA
1984	**ChC-N**	**105**	**146**	**24**	**40**	**5**	**0**	**0**	**8**	**10**	**2**	**23**	**1**	**3**	**0**	**9**	**3**	**.274**	**.325**	**.308**	**.984**
1985	NYY-A	34	56	4	17	1	0	1	6	3	0	12	0	1	0	1	1	.304	.339	.375	.977
1986	NYY-A	35	80	11	17	3	0	1	6	2	0	17	0	0	1	3	0	.213	.229	.288	1.000
1987	NYY-A	68	149	21	35	10	0	5	20	6	0	35	1	0	0	4	2	.235	.269	.403	.989
1988	Sea-A	133	386	50	100	18	1	8	33	23	0	53	2	4	3	27	3	.259	.302	.373	.992
1989	Sea-A	100	295	44	78	11	2	9	33	12	3	44	3	0	0	10	4	.264	.300	.407	.988
1990	Sea-A	127	355	40	92	14	3	4	33	22	2	52	4	6	3	21	3	.259	.307	.349	.990
1991	Sea-A	66	177	35	54	6	2	6	23	10	0	27	2	2	1	16	3	.305	.347	.463	.981
1992	Sea-A	108	294	42	76	11	1	5	27	14	3	49	1	3	1	23	2	.259	.294	.354	1.000
1993	Sea-A	54	105	10	20	1	0	2	7	2	0	22	1	1	0	5	4	.190	.213	.257	.983
1993	Fla-N	54	135	15	40	7	0	3	14	3	0	18	1	1	2	11	1	.296	.312	.415	.977
Career average		88	218	30	57	9	1	4	21	11	1	35	2	2	1	13	3	.261	.299	.370	.989
Cubs average		**105**	**146**	**24**	**40**	**5**	**0**	**0**	**8**	**10**	**2**	**23**	**1**	**3**	**0**	**9**	**3**	**.274**	**.325**	**.308**	**.984**
Career total		884	2178	296	569	87	9	44	210	107	10	352	16	21	11	130	26	.261	.299	.370	.989
Cubs total		**105**	**146**	**24**	**40**	**5**	**0**	**0**	**8**	**10**	**2**	**23**	**1**	**3**	**0**	**9**	**3**	**.274**	**.325**	**.308**	**.984**

Covington, John Wesley (Wes)
HEIGHT: 6'1" THROWS: RIGHT BATS: LEFT BORN: 3/27/1932 LAURINBURG, NORTH CAROLINA POSITIONS PLAYED: OF

YEAR	TEAM	GAMES	AB	RUNS	HITS	2B	3B	HR	RBI	BB	IBB	SO	HBP	SH	SF	SB	CS	BA	OBA	SA	FA
1956	Mil-N	75	138	17	39	4	0	2	16	16	3	20	1	2	0	1	0	.283	.361	.355	.979
1957	Mil-N	96	328	51	93	4	8	21	65	29	7	44	2	5	7	4	1	.284	.339	.537	.981
1958	Mil-N	90	294	43	97	12	1	24	74	20	7	35	5	3	2	0	0	.330	.380	.622	.953
1959	Mil-N	103	373	38	104	17	3	7	45	26	8	41	3	1	2	0	1	.279	.329	.397	.963
1960	Mil-N	95	281	25	70	16	1	10	35	15	1	37	1	0	2	1	2	.249	.288	.420	.964
1961	Mil-N	9	21	3	4	1	0	0	0	2	0	4	0	0	0	0	0	.190	.261	.238	1.000
1961	CWS-A	22	59	5	17	1	0	4	15	4	1	5	0	2	0	0	0	.288	.333	.508	.900
1961	KCA-A	17	44	3	7	0	0	1	6	4	0	7	2	0	0	0	0	.159	.260	.227	1.000
1961	Phi-N	57	165	23	50	9	0	7	26	15	1	17	0	0	3	0	0	.303	.355	.485	.950
1962	Phi-N	116	304	36	86	12	1	9	44	19	1	44	2	1	5	0	0	.283	.324	.418	.944
1963	Phi-N	119	353	46	107	24	1	17	64	26	7	56	2	2	0	1	0	.303	.354	.521	.937
1964	Phi-N	129	339	37	95	18	0	13	58	38	6	50	3	0	3	0	0	.280	.355	.448	.972
1965	Phi-N	101	235	27	58	10	1	15	45	26	8	47	1	0	2	0	0	.247	.322	.489	.968
1966	**ChC-N**	**9**	**11**	**0**	**1**	**0**	**0**	**0**	**0**	**1**	**1**	**2**	**0**	**0**	**0**	**0**	**0**	**.091**	**.167**	**.091**	**1.000**
1966	LA-N	37	33	1	4	0	1	1	6	6	0	5	2	0	0	0	0	.121	.293	.273	1.000
Career average		98	271	32	76	12	2	12	45	22	5	38	2	1	2	1	0	.279	.337	.466	.961
Cubs average		**9**	**11**	**0**	**1**	**0**	**0**	**0**	**0**	**1**	**1**	**2**	**0**	**0**	**0**	**0**	**0**	**.091**	**.167**	**.091**	**1.000**
Career total		1075	2978	355	832	128	17	131	499	247	51	414	24	16	26	7	4	.279	.337	.466	.961
Cubs total		**9**	**11**	**0**	**1**	**0**	**0**	**0**	**0**	**1**	**1**	**2**	**0**	**0**	**0**	**0**	**0**	**.091**	**.167**	**.091**	**1.000**

Cowan, Billy Rolland
HEIGHT: 6'0" THROWS: RIGHT BATS: RIGHT BORN: 8/28/1938 CALHOUN CITY, MISSISSIPPI POSITIONS PLAYED: 1B, 2B, 3B, SS, OF

YEAR	TEAM	GAMES	AB	RUNS	HITS	2B	3B	HR	RBI	BB	IBB	SO	HBP	SH	SF	SB	CS	BA	OBA	SA	FA
1963	**ChC-N**	**14**	**36**	**1**	**9**	**1**	**1**	**1**	**2**	**0**	**0**	**11**	**0**	**0**	**0**	**0**	**1**	**.250**	**.250**	**.417**	**.917**
1964	**ChC-N**	**139**	**497**	**52**	**120**	**16**	**4**	**19**	**50**	**18**	**5**	**128**	**1**	**2**	**2**	**12**	**3**	**.241**	**.268**	**.404**	**.968**
1965	NYM-N	82	156	16	28	8	2	3	9	4	1	45	1	1	0	3	2	.179	.205	.314	1.000
1965	Mil-N	19	27	4	5	1	0	0	0	0	0	9	0	0	0	0	0	.185	.185	.222	1.000
1967	Phi-N	34	59	11	9	0	0	3	6	4	0	14	0	2	1	1	0	.153	.203	.305	1.000
1969	NYY-A	32	48	5	8	0	0	1	3	3	0	9	0	0	0	0	0	.167	.216	.229	1.000
1969	Cal-A	28	56	10	17	1	0	4	10	3	1	9	1	0	0	0	0	.304	.350	.536	1.000
1970	Cal-A	68	134	20	37	9	1	5	25	11	2	29	1	0	0	0	1	.276	.336	.470	.981
1971	Cal-A	74	174	12	48	8	0	4	20	7	1	41	0	1	0	1	1	.276	.304	.391	.990
1972	Cal-A	3	3	0	0	0	0	0	0	0	0	2	0	0	0	0	0	.000	.000	.000	—
Career average		62	149	16	35	6	1	5	16	6	1	37	1	1	0	2	1	.236	.269	.387	.980
Cubs average		**77**	**267**	**27**	**65**	**9**	**3**	**10**	**26**	**9**	**3**	**70**	**1**	**1**	**1**	**6**	**2**	**.242**	**.267**	**.405**	**.966**
Career total		493	1190	131	281	44	8	40	125	50	10	297	4	6	3	17	8	.236	.269	.387	.980
Cubs total		**153**	**533**	**53**	**129**	**17**	**5**	**20**	**52**	**18**	**5**	**139**	**1**	**2**	**2**	**12**	**4**	**.242**	**.267**	**.405**	**.966**

Cox, Larry Eugene
HEIGHT: 5'10"   THROWS: RIGHT   BATS: RIGHT   BORN: 9/11/1947 BLUFFTON, OHIO   DIED: 2/17/1990 BELLEFONTAINE, OHIO   POSITIONS PLAYED: C

YEAR	TEAM	GAMES	AB	RUNS	HITS	2B	3B	HR	RBI	BB	IBB	SO	HBP	SH	SF	SB	CS	BA	OBA	SA	FA
1973	Phi-N	1	0	0	0	0	0	0	0	0	0	0	0	0	0	0	0	—	—	—	1.000
1974	Phi-N	30	53	5	9	2	0	0	4	4	0	9	1	0	0	0	0	.170	.241	.208	.990
1975	Phi-N	11	5	0	1	0	0	0	1	1	0	0	0	0	1	1	0	.200	.286	.200	1.000
1977	Sea-A	35	93	6	23	6	0	2	6	10	0	12	0	1	0	1	1	.247	.320	.376	.970
1978	**ChC-N**	**59**	**121**	**10**	**34**	**5**	**0**	**2**	**18**	**12**	**0**	**16**	**0**	**0**	**0**	**0**	**0**	**.281**	**.346**	**.372**	**.967**
1979	Sea-A	100	293	32	63	11	3	4	36	22	0	39	0	3	5	2	1	.215	.266	.314	.981
1980	Sea-A	105	243	18	49	6	2	4	20	19	0	36	0	9	0	1	2	.202	.260	.292	.993
1981	Tex-A	5	13	0	3	1	0	0	0	0	0	4	0	0	0	0	0	.231	.231	.308	1.000
1982	**ChC-N**	**2**	**4**	**1**	**0**	**0**	**0**	**0**	**0**	**2**	**1**	**1**	**0**	**0**	**0**	**0**	**0**	**.000**	**.333**	**.000**	**1.000**
Career average		39	92	8	20	3	1	1	9	8	0	13	0	1	1	1	0	.221	.280	.314	.983
Cubs average		**31**	**63**	**6**	**17**	**3**	**0**	**1**	**9**	**7**	**1**	**9**	**0**	**0**	**0**	**0**	**0**	**.272**	**.345**	**.360**	**.968**
Career total		348	825	72	182	31	5	12	85	70	1	117	1	13	6	5	4	.221	.280	.314	.983
Cubs total		**61**	**125**	**11**	**34**	**5**	**0**	**2**	**18**	**14**	**1**	**17**	**0**	**0**	**0**	**0**	**0**	**.272**	**.345**	**.360**	**.968**

Croft, Henry T. (Harry)
HEIGHT: —   THROWS: —   BATS: —   BORN: 8/1/1875 CHICAGO, ILLINOIS   DIED: 12/11/1933 OAK PARK, ILLINOIS   POSITIONS PLAYED: 2B, OF

YEAR	TEAM	GAMES	AB	RUNS	HITS	2B	3B	HR	RBI	BB	IBB	SO	HBP	SH	SF	SB	CS	BA	OBA	SA	FA
1899	Lou-N	2	2	0	0	0	0	0	0	0	—	—	0	0	—	0	—	.000	.000	.000	—
1899	Phi-N	2	7	0	1	0	0	0	0	1	—	—	0	0	—	0	—	.143	.250	.143	1.000
1901	**ChN-N**	**3**	**12**	**1**	**4**	**0**	**0**	**0**	**4**	**0**	**—**	**—**	**0**	**0**	**—**	**0**	**—**	**.333**	**.333**	**.333**	**1.000**
Career average		4	11	1	3	0	0	0	2	1	—	—	0	0	—	0	—	.238	.273	.238	1.000
Cubs average		**3**	**12**	**1**	**4**	**0**	**0**	**0**	**4**	**0**	**—**	**—**	**0**	**0**	**—**	**0**	**—**	**.333**	**.333**	**.333**	**1.000**
Career total		7	21	1	5	0	0	0	4	1	—	—	0	0	—	0	—	.238	.273	.238	1.000
Cubs total		**3**	**12**	**1**	**4**	**0**	**0**	**0**	**4**	**0**	**—**	**—**	**0**	**0**	**—**	**0**	**—**	**.333**	**.333**	**.333**	**1.000**

Cross, Joffre James (Jeff)
HEIGHT: 5'11"   THROWS: RIGHT   BATS: RIGHT   BORN: 8/28/1918 TULSA, OKLAHOMA   DIED: 7/23/1997 HUNTSVILLE, TEXAS   POSITIONS PLAYED: 2B, 3B, SS

YEAR	TEAM	GAMES	AB	RUNS	HITS	2B	3B	HR	RBI	BB	IBB	SO	HBP	SH	SF	SB	CS	BA	OBA	SA	FA
1942	StL-N	1	4	0	1	0	0	0	1	0	—	0	0	0	—	0	—	.250	.250	.250	1.000
1946	StL-N	49	69	17	15	3	0	0	6	10	—	8	0	1	—	4	—	.217	.316	.261	.958
1947	StL-N	51	49	4	5	1	0	0	3	10	—	6	0	0	—	0	—	.102	.254	.122	.934
1948	StL-N	2	0	0	0	0	0	0	0	0	—	0	0	0	—	0	—	—	—	—	.934
1948	**ChC-N**	**16**	**20**	**1**	**2**	**0**	**0**	**0**	**0**	**0**	**—**	**4**	**0**	**0**	**—**	**0**	**—**	**.100**	**.100**	**.100**	**.786**
Career average		30	36	6	6	1	0	0	3	5	—	5	0	0	—	1	—	.162	.265	.190	.936
Cubs average		**16**	**20**	**1**	**2**	**0**	**0**	**0**	**0**	**0**	**—**	**4**	**0**	**0**	**—**	**0**	**—**	**.100**	**.100**	**.100**	**.786**
Career total		119	142	22	23	4	0	0	10	20	—	18	0	1	—	4	—	.162	.265	.190	.936
Cubs total		**16**	**20**	**1**	**2**	**0**	**0**	**0**	**0**	**0**	**—**	**4**	**0**	**0**	**—**	**0**	**—**	**.100**	**.100**	**.100**	**.786**

Cruz, Hector Louis (Heity)
HEIGHT: 5'11"   THROWS: RIGHT   BATS: RIGHT   BORN: 4/2/1953 ARROYO, PUERTO RICO   POSITIONS PLAYED: 3B, OF

YEAR	TEAM	GAMES	AB	RUNS	HITS	2B	3B	HR	RBI	BB	IBB	SO	HBP	SH	SF	SB	CS	BA	OBA	SA	FA
1973	StL-N	11	11	1	0	0	0	0	0	1	0	3	0	0	0	0	0	.000	.083	.000	1.000
1975	StL-N	23	48	7	7	2	2	0	6	2	0	4	0	1	1	0	0	.146	.176	.271	.889
1976	StL-N	151	526	54	120	17	1	13	71	42	7	119	2	4	3	1	0	.228	.286	.338	.934
1977	StL-N	118	339	50	80	19	2	6	42	46	1	56	1	2	3	4	3	.236	.326	.357	.959
1978	**ChC-N**	**30**	**76**	**8**	**18**	**5**	**0**	**2**	**9**	**3**	**1**	**6**	**0**	**1**	**0**	**0**	**0**	**.237**	**.266**	**.382**	**1.000**
1978	SF-N	79	197	19	44	8	1	6	24	21	2	39	1	1	0	0	2	.223	.301	.365	.981
1979	SF-N	16	25	2	3	0	0	0	1	3	0	7	0	0	0	0	0	.120	.214	.120	.909
1979	Cin-N	74	182	24	44	10	2	4	27	31	3	39	0	1	1	0	1	.242	.350	.385	.984
1980	Cin-N	52	75	5	16	4	1	1	5	8	1	16	0	0	0	0	0	.213	.289	.333	.955
1981	**ChC-N**	**53**	**109**	**15**	**25**	**5**	**0**	**7**	**15**	**17**	**0**	**24**	**0**	**0**	**1**	**2**	**2**	**.229**	**.331**	**.468**	**.952**
1982	**ChC-N**	**17**	**19**	**1**	**4**	**1**	**0**	**0**	**0**	**2**	**0**	**4**	**0**	**0**	**0**	**0**	**0**	**.211**	**.286**	**.263**	**1.000**
Career average		69	179	21	40	8	1	4	22	20	2	35	0	1	1	1	1	.225	.301	.353	.954
Cubs average		**33**	**68**	**8**	**16**	**4**	**0**	**3**	**8**	**7**	**0**	**11**	**0**	**0**	**0**	**1**	**1**	**.230**	**.304**	**.417**	**.972**
Career total		624	1607	186	361	71	9	39	200	176	15	317	4	10	9	7	8	.225	.301	.353	.954
Cubs total		**100**	**204**	**24**	**47**	**11**	**0**	**9**	**24**	**22**	**1**	**34**	**0**	**1**	**1**	**2**	**2**	**.230**	**.304**	**.417**	**.972**

Culler, Richard Broadus (Dick)

HEIGHT: 5'9" THROWS: RIGHT BATS: RIGHT BORN: 1/15/1915 HIGH POINT, NORTH CAROLINA DIED: 6/16/1964 CHAPEL HILL, NORTH CAROLINA
POSITIONS PLAYED: 2B, 3B, SS

YEAR	TEAM	GAMES	AB	RUNS	HITS	2B	3B	HR	RBI	BB	IBB	SO	HBP	SH	SF	SB	CS	BA	OBA	SA	FA
1936	Phi-A	9	38	3	9	0	0	0	1	1	—	3	0	1	—	0	0	.237	.256	.237	.951
1943	CWS-A	53	148	9	32	5	1	0	11	16	—	11	1	2	—	4	5	.216	.297	.264	.960
1944	Bos-N	8	28	2	2	0	0	0	0	4	—	2	0	0	—	0	—	.071	.188	.071	.904
1945	Bos-N	136	527	87	138	12	1	2	30	50	—	35	2	8	—	7	—	.262	.328	.300	.951
1946	Bos-N	134	482	70	123	15	3	0	33	62	—	18	2	7	—	7	—	.255	.342	.299	.948
1947	Bos-N	77	214	20	53	5	1	0	19	19	—	15	0	8	—	1	—	.248	.309	.280	.967
1948	**ChC-N**	**48**	**89**	**4**	**15**	**2**	**0**	**0**	**5**	**13**	**—**	**3**	**0**	**3**	**—**	**0**	**—**	**.169**	**.275**	**.191**	**.968**
1949	NYG-N	7	1	0	0	0	0	0	0	1	—	0	0	0	—	0	0	.000	.500	.000	.889
Career average		59	191	24	47	5	1	0	12	21	—	11	1	4	—	2	1	.244	.320	.281	.953
Cubs average		**48**	**89**	**4**	**15**	**2**	**0**	**0**	**5**	**13**	**—**	**3**	**0**	**3**	**—**	**0**	**0**	**.169**	**.275**	**.191**	**.968**
Career total		472	1527	195	372	39	6	2	99	166	—	87	5	29	—	19	5	.244	.320	.281	.953
Cubs total		**48**	**89**	**4**	**15**	**2**	**0**	**0**	**5**	**13**	**—**	**3**	**0**	**3**	**—**	**0**	**0**	**.169**	**.275**	**.191**	**.968**

Curley, Walter James (Doc)

HEIGHT: — THROWS: RIGHT BATS: RIGHT BORN: 3/12/1874 UPTON, MASSACHUSETTS DIED: 9/23/1920 WORCESTER, MASSACHUSETTS
POSITIONS PLAYED: 2B

YEAR	TEAM	GAMES	AB	RUNS	HITS	2B	3B	HR	RBI	BB	IBB	SO	HBP	SH	SF	SB	CS	BA	OBA	SA	FA
1899	**ChN-N**	**10**	**37**	**7**	**4**	**0**	**1**	**0**	**2**	**3**	**—**	**—**	**3**	**1**	**—**	**0**	**—**	**.108**	**.233**	**.162**	**.907**
Career average		10	37	7	4	0	1	0	2	3	—	—	3	1	—	0	—	.108	.233	.162	.907
Cubs average		**10**	**37**	**7**	**4**	**0**	**1**	**0**	**2**	**3**	**—**	**—**	**3**	**1**	**—**	**0**	**—**	**.108**	**.233**	**.162**	**.907**
Career total		10	37	7	4	0	1	0	2	3	—	—	3	1	—	0	—	.108	.233	.162	.907
Cubs total		**10**	**37**	**7**	**4**	**0**	**1**	**0**	**2**	**3**	**—**	**—**	**3**	**1**	**—**	**0**	**—**	**.108**	**.233**	**.162**	**.907**

Cusick, John Peter (Jack)

HEIGHT: 6'0" THROWS: RIGHT BATS: RIGHT BORN: 6/12/1928 WEEHAWKEN, NEW JERSEY DIED: 11/17/1989 EDGEWOOD, NEW JERSEY
POSITIONS PLAYED: 3B, SS

YEAR	TEAM	GAMES	AB	RUNS	HITS	2B	3B	HR	RBI	BB	IBB	SO	HBP	SH	SF	SB	CS	BA	OBA	SA	FA
1951	**ChC-N**	**65**	**164**	**16**	**29**	**3**	**2**	**2**	**16**	**17**	**—**	**29**	**0**	**4**	**—**	**2**	**1**	**.177**	**.254**	**.256**	**.953**
1952	Bos-N	49	78	5	13	1	0	0	6	6	—	9	0	0	—	0	1	.167	.226	.179	.970
Career average		57	121	11	21	2	1	1	11	12	—	19	0	2	—	1	1	.174	.245	.231	.958
Cubs average		**65**	**164**	**16**	**29**	**3**	**2**	**2**	**16**	**17**	**—**	**29**	**0**	**4**	**—**	**2**	**1**	**.177**	**.254**	**.256**	**.953**
Career total		114	242	21	42	4	2	2	22	23	—	38	0	4	—	2	2	.174	.245	.231	.958
Cubs total		**65**	**164**	**16**	**29**	**3**	**2**	**2**	**16**	**17**	**—**	**29**	**0**	**4**	**—**	**2**	**1**	**.177**	**.254**	**.256**	**.953**

Cuyler, Hazen Shirley (Kiki)

HEIGHT: 5'10" THROWS: RIGHT BATS: RIGHT BORN: 8/30/1898 HARRISVILLE, MICHIGAN DIED: 2/11/1950 ANN ARBOR, MICHIGAN POSITIONS PLAYED: OF

YEAR	TEAM	GAMES	AB	RUNS	HITS	2B	3B	HR	RBI	BB	IBB	SO	HBP	SH	SF	SB	CS	BA	OBA	SA	FA
1921	Pit-N	1	3	0	0	0	0	0	0	0	—	1	0	0	—	0	0	.000	.000	.000	1.000
1922	Pit-N	1	0	0	0	0	0	0	0	0	—	0	0	0	—	0	0	—	—	—	—
1923	Pit-N	11	40	4	10	1	1	0	2	5	—	3	1	0	—	2	3	.250	.348	.325	.931
1924	Pit-N	117	466	94	165	27	16	9	85	30	—	62	7	12	—	32	11	.354	.402	.539	.943
1925	Pit-N	153	617	144	220	43	26	18	102	58	—	56	13	12	—	41	13	.357	.423	.598	.967
1926	Pit-N	157	614	113	197	31	15	8	92	50	—	66	9	21	—	35	—	.321	.380	.459	.968
1927	Pit-N	85	285	60	88	13	7	3	31	37	—	36	3	5	—	20	—	.309	.394	.435	.980
1928	**ChC-N**	**133**	**499**	**92**	**142**	**25**	**9**	**17**	**79**	**51**	**—**	**61**	**7**	**24**	**—**	**37**	**—**	**.285**	**.359**	**.473**	**.982**
1929	**ChC-N**	**139**	**509**	**111**	**183**	**29**	**7**	**15**	**102**	**66**	**—**	**56**	**5**	**16**	**—**	**43**	**—**	**.360**	**.438**	**.532**	**.974**
1930	**ChC-N**	**156**	**642**	**155**	**228**	**50**	**17**	**13**	**134**	**72**	**—**	**49**	**10**	**17**	**—**	**37**	**—**	**.355**	**.428**	**.547**	**.980**
1931	**ChC-N**	**154**	**613**	**110**	**202**	**37**	**12**	**9**	**88**	**72**	**—**	**54**	**5**	**20**	**—**	**13**	**—**	**.330**	**.404**	**.473**	**.970**
1932	**ChC-N**	**110**	**446**	**58**	**130**	**19**	**9**	**10**	**77**	**29**	**—**	**43**	**4**	**10**	**—**	**9**	**—**	**.291**	**.340**	**.442**	**.969**
1933	**ChC-N**	**70**	**262**	**37**	**83**	**13**	**3**	**5**	**35**	**21**	**—**	**29**	**4**	**7**	**—**	**4**	**—**	**.317**	**.376**	**.447**	**.978**
1934	**ChC-N**	**142**	**559**	**80**	**189**	**42**	**8**	**6**	**69**	**31**	**—**	**62**	**4**	**13**	**—**	**15**	**—**	**.338**	**.377**	**.474**	**.971**
1935	**ChC-N**	**45**	**157**	**22**	**42**	**5**	**1**	**4**	**18**	**10**	**—**	**16**	**5**	**5**	**—**	**3**	**—**	**.268**	**.331**	**.389**	**.981**
1935	Cin-N	62	223	36	56	8	3	2	22	27	—	18	2	1	—	5	—	.251	.337	.341	.985

(continued)

Hazen Shirley "Kiki" Cuyler, of, 1921–38

The gentlemanly Cuyler was one of the Cubs' best post-season performers in the 1920s and 1930s and one-third of a devastating outfield in that span.

Cuyler was born on August 30, 1898, in Harrisville, Michigan, and was a schoolboy and minor league star. As a teen, he was known as "Cuy" by his friends and teammates. While toiling for the Southern League, his fellow outfielders would call out "Cuy, Cuy," when a ball was headed Cuyler's way. Sportswriters heard it and nicknamed him "Kiki," pronouncing it with a long *i*. Over the years, however, the spelling has pushed the pronounciation to "keekee."

Cuyler was signed by the Pirates and came up for one game in both the 1921 and 1922 seasons, getting no hits either year.

He got a longer look in 1923, 11 games, and was brought up for good by Pittsburgh in 1924. He hit the ground running that year, leading Pittsburgh in batting average (.354), slugging percentage (.539), stolen bases (32) and home runs (9).

He was a star for the Pirates from 1924 to 1927, hitting over .300 every year. But he was traded to the Cubs before the 1928 season after an incident in 1927 when Cuyler went into second base standing up in an attempt to prevent a double play. Cuyler was tagged out, and Pittsburgh manager Donie Bush believed Kiki could have avoided the tag had he slid.

Cuyler had also not endeared himself with Pirates owner Barney Dreyfuss by winning a salary dispute prior to the start of that year. Thus, when the Pirates brought up Lloyd Waner in 1928 to star in the outfield with brother Paul, Cuyler was deemed expendable and traded to Chicago.

Dreyfuss solemnly declared that Cuyler was washed up after the trade, and Kiki delighted in proving him wrong again and again over the years. Cuyler hit over .300 five of the next seven years and led the league in stolen bases from 1928 to 1930.

Cuyler was something of a loner throughout his career. He was also a bit of a man-about-town in Chicago but was rarely seen with other Cubs. This did not generate any real animosity on the squad, but few Cubs players could say they knew Cuyler.

In 1929 Cuyler was a member of a potent offensive outfield with Riggs Stephenson and Hack Wilson that cruised to the pennant. The three hit .350 as a unit with 371 RBIs and 71 home runs. This trio was one of the most prolific outfields of all time.

Cuyler hit .300 in the Cubs' 1929 loss to the Athletics. Chicago returned to the World Series in 1932 as Cuyler hit .291 in the regular season and .278 in a losing effort in the Series against the Yankees. His .289 batting average in World Series play is ninth all-time for Chicago, and his .474 slugging average is second all-time only to Charlie Grimm's .515.

A broken foot in 1932 slowed the speedy Cuyler over the next few years, and his batting average began to drop. He was eventually traded to the Reds in 1935 and played there for three years before ending his career with the Dodgers in 1938.

Cuyler was a player-coach with both teams, respectively, as his career wound down. When he retired, he returned to the Southern League to manage. In the 1940s, he was hired by the Cubs to coach and in 1950 was working as a coach for the Red Sox when he died of heart failure.

He was elected to the Hall of Fame in 1968.

Cuyler did not play long enough in Chicago to crack any Cubs' all-time lists, but his 228 hits in 1930 is the second-highest season total in Cubs history behind Rogers Hornsby's 229 in 1929.

Cuyler also holds the Cubs record for right fielders for batting average (.360 in 1929), runs scored (155 in 1930), hits (228 in 1930) and doubles (50 in 1930). Cuyler is also the holder of the Cubs record for most doubles by a center fielder, 42 in 1934.

(Cuyler,continued)

YEAR	TEAM	GAMES	AB	RUNS	HITS	2B	3B	HR	RBI	BB	IBB	SO	HBP	SH	SF	SB	CS	BA	OBA	SA	FA
1936	Cin-N	144	567	96	185	29	11	7	74	47	—	67	2	7	—	16	—	.326	.380	.453	.974
1937	Cin-N	117	406	48	110	12	4	0	32	36	—	50	2	5	—	10	—	.271	.333	.320	.973
1938	Bro-N	82	253	45	69	10	8	2	23	34	—	23	2	1	—	6	—	.273	.363	.399	.993
Career average		104	398	73	128	22	9	7	59	38	—	42	5	10	—	18	2	.321	.386	.474	.972
Cubs average		**119**	**461**	**83**	**150**	**28**	**8**	**10**	**75**	**44**	—	**46**	**6**	**14**	—	**20**	**0**	**.325**	**.391**	**.485**	**.975**
Career total		1879	7161	1305	2299	394	157	128	1065	676	—	752	85	176	—	328	27	.321	.386	.474	.972
Cubs total		**949**	**3687**	**665**	**1199**	**220**	**66**	**79**	**602**	**352**	—	**370**	**44**	**112**	—	**161**	**0**	**.325**	**.391**	**.485**	**.975**

Dahlen, William Frederick (Bill *or* Bad Bill)

HEIGHT: 5'9"   THROWS: RIGHT   BATS: RIGHT   BORN: 1/5/1870 NELLISTON, NEW YORK   DIED: 12/5/1950 BROOKLYN, NEW YORK
POSITIONS PLAYED: 2B, 3B, SS, OF

YEAR	TEAM	GAMES	AB	RUNS	HITS	2B	3B	HR	RBI	BB	IBB	SO	HBP	SH	SF	SB	CS	BA	OBA	SA	FA
1891	ChN-N	135	549	114	143	18	13	9	76	67	—	60	7	—	—	21	—	.260	.348	.390	.881
1892	ChN-N	143	581	114	169	23	19	5	58	45	—	56	5	—	—	60	—	.291	.347	.422	.922
1893	ChN-N	116	485	113	146	28	15	5	64	58	—	30	5	—	—	31	—	.301	.381	.452	.896
1894	ChN-N	121	502	149	179	32	14	15	107	76	—	33	3	10	—	42	—	.357	.444	.566	.899
1895	ChN-N	129	516	106	131	19	10	7	62	61	—	51	10	5	—	38	—	.254	.344	.370	.904
1896	ChN-N	125	474	137	167	30	19	9	74	64	—	36	8	27	—	51	—	.352	.438	.553	.915
1897	ChN-N	75	276	67	80	18	8	6	40	43	—	—	7	13	—	15	—	.290	.399	.478	.930
1898	ChN-N	142	521	96	151	35	8	1	79	58	—	—	23	17	—	27	—	.290	.385	.393	.921
1899	Bro-N	121	428	87	121	22	7	4	76	67	—	—	15	4	—	29	—	.283	.398	.395	.943
1900	Bro-N	133	483	87	125	16	11	1	69	73	—	—	7	2	—	31	—	.259	.364	.344	.938
1901	Bro-N	131	511	69	136	17	9	4	82	30	—	—	5	7	—	23	—	.266	.313	.358	.930

(continued)

WILLIAM F. DAHLEN, Shortstop, CHICAGO N.L. 1895

William (Bill) Francis "Bad Bill" Dahlen, ss-2b-3b, 1891–1911

Long before Ernie Banks starred for Chicago as a heavy-hitting shortstop, there was "Bad Bill" Dahlen.

Born on January 5, 1870, in Nelliston, NewYork, Dahlen spent most of his rookie year in Chicago in 1891 as a third baseman and outfielder. By the next year, he was splitting time at shortstop with Jim Cooney. By 1895, however, his hitting and fielding won him the starting shortstop's job.

Dahlen played a National League–record 20 years at the shortstop position and thus finished second all-time in putouts for a shortstop with 4,850 and third all-time in assists with 7,500.

But Dahlen was better known in his time as a formidable hitter in the Dead Ball Era. In six of his eight years in Chicago, he hit better than .290, with a high of .352 in 1896.

In 1884 he hit in 42 consecutive games, a record until "Wee Willie" Keeler broke that

mark three years later. Interestingly, Dahlen hit safely from June 20 to August 6 to establish the streak. After going 0-6 in 10 innings against the Reds the next day, he hit in 28 consecutive games after that, thus hitting safely in 70 of 71 games in that span.

Dahlen was an excellent base runner as well, swiping 60 bases for Chicago in 1892 and 51 in 1896. Twice Dahlen hit three triples in one game, in 1896 and then in 1898. He finished his career with 163 three-baggers, 33rd all-time in the major leagues.

After eight solid years in Chicago, Dahlen was traded to Brooklyn in 1899 and later to the Giants in 1904. He finished his stellar career with short stints in Boston and again with Brooklyn.

Dahlen led Chicago in runs scored five times during his years there and led the team in triples five times as well. He is fourth all-time on the team in triples with 106 and 10th in runs scored with 896. Dahlen died in Brooklyn in 1950.

(continued)

YEAR	TEAM	GAMES	AB	RUNS	HITS	2B	3B	HR	RBI	BB	IBB	SO	HBP	SH	SF	SB	CS	BA	OBA	SA	FA
1902	Bro-N	138	527	67	139	25	8	2	74	43	—	—	8	9	—	20	—	.264	.329	.353	.916
1903	Bro-N	138	474	71	124	17	9	1	64	82	—	—	2	8	—	34	—	.262	.373	.342	.948
1904	NYG-N	145	523	70	140	26	2	2	80	44	—	—	1	11	—	47	—	.268	.326	.337	.930
1905	NYG-N	148	520	67	126	20	4	7	81	62	—	—	12	7	—	37	—	.242	.337	.337	.948
1906	NYG-N	143	471	63	113	18	3	1	49	76	—	—	10	8	—	16	—	.240	.357	.297	.938
1907	NYG-N	143	464	40	96	20	1	0	34	51	—	—	4	10	—	11	—	.207	.291	.254	.941
1908	Bos-N	144	524	50	125	23	2	3	48	35	—	—	8	21	—	10	—	.239	.296	.307	.952
1909	Bos-N	69	197	22	46	6	1	2	16	29	—	—	0	5	—	4	—	.234	.332	.305	.909
1910	Bro-N	3	2	0	0	0	0	0	0	0	—	0	0	1	—	0	—	.000	.000	.000	
1911	Bro-N	1	3	0	0	0	0	0	0	0	—	3	0	0	—	0	—	.000	.000	.000	1.000
Career average		116	430	76	117	20	8	4	59	51	—	13	7	8	—	26	—	.272	.358	.382	.926
Cubs average		**123**	**488**	**112**	**146**	**25**	**13**	**7**	**70**	**59**	**—**	**33**	**9**	**9**	**—**	**36**	**—**	**.299**	**.384**	**.382**	**.926**
Career total		2443	9031	1589	2457	413	163	84	1233	1064	—	269	140	165	—	547	—	.272	.358	.382	.926
Cubs total		**986**	**3904**	**896**	**1166**	**203**	**106**	**57**	**560**	**472**	**—**	**266**	**68**	**72**	**—**	**285**	**—**	**.299**	**.384**	**.449**	**.909**

Dahlgren, Ellsworth Tenney (Babe)

HEIGHT: 6'0" THROWS: RIGHT BATS: RIGHT BORN: 6/15/1912 SAN FRANCISCO, CALIFORNIA DIED: 9/4/1996 ARCADIA, CALIFORNIA
POSITIONS PLAYED: C, 1B, 3B, SS

YEAR	TEAM	GAMES	AB	RUNS	HITS	2B	3B	HR	RBI	BB	IBB	SO	HBP	SH	SF	SB	CS	BA	OBA	SA	FA
1935	Bos-A	149	525	77	138	27	7	9	63	56	—	67	3	12	—	6	5	.263	.337	.392	.988
1936	Bos-A	16	57	6	16	3	1	1	7	7	—	1	0	1	—	2	1	.281	.359	.421	.980
1937	NYY-A	1	1	0	0	0	0	0	0	0	—	0	0	0	—	0	0	.000	.000	.000	—
1938	NYY-A	27	43	8	8	1	0	0	1	1	—	7	0	0	—	0	0	.186	.205	.209	.922
1939	NYY-A	144	531	71	125	18	6	15	89	57	—	54	2	13	—	2	3	.235	.312	.377	.991
1940	NYY-A	155	568	51	150	24	4	12	73	46	—	54	5	3	—	1	1	.264	.325	.384	.990
1941	Bos-N	44	166	20	39	8	1	7	30	16	—	13	1	0	—	0	—	.235	.306	.422	.991
1941	**ChC-N**	**99**	**359**	**50**	**101**	**20**	**1**	**16**	**59**	**43**	**—**	**39**	**1**	**0**	**—**	**2**	**—**	**.281**	**.360**	**.476**	**.991**
1942	**ChC-N**	**17**	**56**	**4**	**12**	**1**	**0**	**0**	**6**	**4**	**—**	**2**	**0**	**0**	**—**	**0**	**—**	**.214**	**.267**	**.232**	**.986**
1942	StL-A	2	2	0	0	0	0	0	0	0	—	0	0	0	—	0	0	.000	.000	.000	—
1942	Bro-N	17	19	2	1	0	0	0	0	4	—	5	0	0	—	0	0	.053	.217	.053	1.000
1943	Phi-N	136	508	55	146	19	2	5	56	50	—	39	2	5	—	2	—	.287	.354	.362	.975
1944	Pit-N	158	599	67	173	28	7	12	101	47	—	56	6	7	—	2	—	.289	.347	.419	.987
1945	Pit-N	144	531	57	133	24	8	5	75	51	—	51	2	7	—	1	—	.250	.318	.354	.996
1946	StL-A	28	80	2	14	1	0	0	9	8	—	13	0	1	—	0	1	.175	.250	.188	.981
Career average		95	337	39	88	15	3	7	47	33	—	33	2	4	—	2	1	.261	.329	.383	.988
Cubs average		**58**	**208**	**27**	**57**	**11**	**1**	**8**	**33**	**24**	**—**	**21**	**1**	**0**	**—**	**1**	**0**	**.272**	**.348**	**.443**	**.990**
Career total		1137	4045	470	1056	174	37	82	569	390	—	401	22	49	—	18	11	.261	.329	.383	.988
Cubs total		**116**	**415**	**54**	**113**	**21**	**1**	**16**	**65**	**47**	**—**	**41**	**1**	**0**	**—**	**2**	**0**	**.272**	**.348**	**.443**	**.990**

Daily, Cornelius F. (Con)

HEIGHT: 6'0" THROWS: — BATS: LEFT BORN: 9/11/1864 BLACKSTONE, MASSACHUSETTS DIED: 6/14/1928 BROOKLYN, NEW YORK
POSITIONS PLAYED: C, 1B, 2B, 3B, SS, OF

YEAR	TEAM	GAMES	AB	RUNS	HITS	2B	3B	HR	RBI	BB	IBB	SO	HBP	SH	SF	SB	CS	BA	OBA	SA	FA
1884	Phi-U	2	8	0	0	0	0	0	—	0	—	—	—	—	—	—	—	.000	.000	.000	.857
1885	Prv-N	60	223	20	58	6	1	0	19	12	—	20	—	—	—	—	—	.260	.298	.296	.894
1886	Bos-N	50	180	25	43	4	2	0	21	19	—	29	—	—	—	2	—	.239	.312	.283	.912
1887	Bos-N	36	129	12	28	5	0	0	13	9	—	8	2	—	—	7	—	.217	.279	.256	.912
1888	Ind-N	57	202	14	44	6	1	0	14	10	—	28	0	—	—	15	—	.218	.255	.257	.899
1889	Ind-N	62	219	35	55	6	2	0	26	28	—	21	4	—	—	14	—	.251	.347	.297	.893
1890	Bro-P	46	168	20	42	6	3	0	35	15	—	14	1	—	—	6	—	.250	.315	.321	.903
1891	Bro-N	60	206	25	66	10	1	0	30	15	—	13	4	—	—	7	—	.320	.378	.379	.922
1892	Bro-N	80	278	38	65	10	1	0	28	38	—	21	1	—	—	18	—	.234	.328	.277	.943
1893	Bro-N	61	215	33	57	4	2	1	32	20	—	12	5	—	—	13	—	.265	.342	.316	.929
1894	Bro-N	67	234	40	60	14	7	0	32	31	—	22	3	6	—	8	—	.256	.351	.376	.933
1895	Bro-N	40	142	17	30	3	2	1	11	10	—	18	1	3	—	3	—	.211	.268	.282	.957
1896	**ChN-N**	**9**	**27**	**1**	**2**	**0**	**0**	**0**	**1**	**1**	**—**	**2**	**0**	**1**	**—**	**1**	**—**	**.074**	**.107**	**.074**	**.969**
Career average		48	172	22	42	6	2	0	20	16	—	16	2	1	—	7	—	.247	.317	.302	.915
Cubs average		**9**	**27**	**1**	**2**	**0**	**0**	**0**	**1**	**1**	**—**	**2**	**0**	**1**	**—**	**1**	**—**	**.074**	**.107**	**.074**	**.969**
Career total		630	2231	280	550	74	22	2	262	208	—	208	21	10	—	94	—	.247	.317	.302	.915
Cubs total		**9**	**27**	**1**	**2**	**0**	**0**	**0**	**1**	**1**	**—**	**2**	**0**	**1**	**—**	**1**	**—**	**.074**	**.107**	**.074**	**.969**

Dallessandro, Nicholas Dominic (Dom *or* Dim Dom)

HEIGHT: 5'6" THROWS: LEFT BATS: LEFT BORN: 10/3/1913 READING, PENNSYLVANIA DIED: 4/29/1988 INDIANAPOLIS, INDIANA POSITIONS PLAYED: OF

YEAR	TEAM	GAMES	AB	RUNS	HITS	2B	3B	HR	RBI	BB	IBB	SO	HBP	SH	SF	SB	CS	BA	OBA	SA	FA
1937	Bos-A	68	147	18	34	7	1	0	11	27	—	16	0	1	—	2	1	.231	.351	.293	.965
1940	ChC-N	107	287	33	77	19	6	1	36	34	—	13	1	1	—	4	—	.268	.348	.387	.969
1941	ChC-N	140	486	73	132	36	2	6	85	68	—	37	1	4	—	3	—	.272	.362	.391	.987
1942	ChC-N	96	264	30	69	12	4	4	43	36	—	18	0	2	—	4	—	.261	.350	.383	.986
1943	ChC-N	87	176	13	39	8	3	1	31	40	—	14	1	1	—	1	—	.222	.369	.318	.967
1944	ChC-N	117	381	53	116	19	4	8	74	61	—	29	0	2	—	1	—	.304	.400	.438	.982
1946	ChC-N	65	89	4	20	2	2	1	9	23	—	12	0	0	—	1	—	.225	.384	.326	.971
1947	ChC-N	66	115	18	33	7	1	1	14	21	—	11	0	0	—	0	—	.287	.397	.391	1.000
Career average		93	243	30	65	14	3	3	38	39	—	19	0	1	—	2	0	.267	.369	.381	.980
Cubs average		**97**	**257**	**32**	**69**	**15**	**3**	**3**	**42**	**40**	**—**	**19**	**0**	**1**	**—**	**2**	**0**	**.270**	**.370**	**.389**	**.981**
Career total		746	1945	242	520	110	23	22	303	310	—	150	3	11	—	16	1	.267	.369	.381	.980
Cubs total		**678**	**1798**	**224**	**486**	**103**	**22**	**22**	**292**	**283**	**—**	**134**	**3**	**10**	**—**	**14**	**0**	**.270**	**.370**	**.389**	**.981**

Dalrymple, Abner Frank

HEIGHT: 5'10" THROWS: RIGHT BATS: LEFT BORN: 9/9/1857 WARREN, ILLINOIS DIED: 1/25/1939 WARREN, ILLINOIS POSITIONS PLAYED: OF

YEAR	TEAM	GAMES	AB	RUNS	HITS	2B	3B	HR	RBI	BB	IBB	SO	HBP	SH	SF	SB	CS	BA	OBA	SA	FA
1878	Mil-N	61	271	52	96	10	4	0	15	6	—	29	—	—	—	—	—	.354	.368	.421	.832
1879	ChN-N	71	333	47	97	25	1	0	23	4	—	29	—	—	—	—	—	.291	.300	.372	.728
1880	ChN-N	86	382	91	126	25	12	0	36	3	—	18	—	—	—	—	—	.330	.335	.458	.859
1881	ChN-N	82	362	72	117	22	4	1	37	15	—	22	—	—	—	—	—	.323	.350	.414	.835
1882	ChN-N	84	397	96	117	25	11	1	36	14	—	18	—	—	—	—	—	.295	.319	.421	.877
1883	ChN-N	80	363	78	108	24	4	2	37	11	—	29	—	—	—	—	—	.298	.318	.402	.826
1884	ChN-N	111	521	111	161	18	9	22	69	14	—	39	—	—	—	—	—	.309	.327	.505	.882
1885	ChN-N	113	492	109	135	27	12	11	61	46	—	42	—	—	—	—	—	.274	.336	.445	.879
1886	ChN-N	82	331	62	77	7	12	3	26	33	—	44	—	—	—	16	—	.233	.302	.353	.952
1887	Pit-N	92	403	45	121	18	5	2	31	45	—	43	6	—	—	29	—	.300	.379	.385	.900
1888	Pit-N	57	227	19	50	9	2	0	14	6	—	28	2	—	—	7	—	.220	.247	.278	.909
1891	Mil-AA	32	135	31	42	7	5	1	22	7	—	18	0	—	—	6	—	.311	.345	.459	.909
Career average		79	351	68	104	18	7	4	34	17	—	30	1	—	—	5	—	.296	.329	.416	.863
Cubs average		**89**	**398**	**83**	**117**	**22**	**8**	**5**	**41**	**18**	**—**	**30**	**—**	**—**	**—**	**2**	**—**	**.295**	**.325**	**.428**	**.857**
Career total		951	4217	813	1247	217	81	43	407	204	—	359	8	—	—	58	—	.296	.329	.416	.863
Cubs total		**709**	**3181**	**666**	**938**	**173**	**65**	**40**	**325**	**140**	**—**	**241**	**—**	**—**	**—**	**16**	**—**	**.295**	**.325**	**.428**	**.857**

Daly, Thomas Daniel (Tom)

HEIGHT: 5'11" THROWS: RIGHT BATS: RIGHT BORN: 12/12/1891 ST. JOHN, NEW BRUNSWICK, CANADA DIED: 11/7/1946 MEDFORD, MASSACHUSETTS
POSITIONS PLAYED: C, 1B, 3B, OF

YEAR	TEAM	GAMES	AB	RUNS	HITS	2B	3B	HR	RBI	BB	IBB	SO	HBP	SH	SF	SB	CS	BA	OBA	SA	FA
1913	CWS-A	1	3	0	0	0	0	0	0	0	—	0	0	0	—	0	—	.000	.000	.000	1.000
1914	CWS-A	61	133	13	31	2	0	0	8	7	—	13	0	2	—	3	4	.233	.271	.248	.943
1915	CWS-A	29	47	5	9	1	0	0	3	5	—	9	0	1	—	0	0	.191	.269	.213	.959
1916	Cle-A	31	73	3	16	1	1	0	8	1	—	2	0	1	—	0	—	.219	.230	.260	.982
1918	ChC-N	1	1	0	0	0	0	0	0	0	—	0	0	0	—	0	—	.000	.000	.000	.667
1919	ChC-N	25	50	4	11	0	1	0	1	2	—	5	0	1	—	0	—	.220	.250	.260	.956
1920	ChC-N	44	90	12	28	6	0	0	13	2	—	6	1	1	—	1	1	.311	.333	.378	.981
1921	ChC-N	51	143	12	34	7	1	0	22	8	—	8	0	2	—	1	2	.238	.278	.301	.973
Career average		30	68	6	16	2	0	0	7	3	—	5	0	1	—	1	1	.239	.274	.281	.968
Cubs average		**30**	**71**	**7**	**18**	**3**	**1**	**0**	**9**	**3**	**—**	**5**	**0**	**1**	**—**	**1**	**1**	**.257**	**.290**	**.317**	**.970**
Career total		243	540	49	129	17	3	0	55	25	—	43	1	8	—	5	7	.239	.274	.281	.968
Cubs total		**121**	**284**	**28**	**73**	**13**	**2**	**0**	**36**	**12**	**—**	**19**	**1**	**4**	**—**	**2**	**3**	**.257**	**.290**	**.317**	**.970**

Abner Frank Dalrymple, of, 1878–91

According to Chicago star Cap Anson, Abner Dalrymple was a "terrific wielder of the ash." In other words, Big Al could hit.

Dalrymple was born on September 9, 1857, in Warren, Illinois. He broke into the major leagues with the Milwaukee entry of the National League in 1878. Dalrymple hit the ground running, smacking 96 hits to take the batting crown with a .354 average. (Research in the 1960s gave 1878 runner-up Paul Hines of Providence enough extra hits to amass a .358 average, thus taking the crown from Dalrymple. But neither man was alive to find that out by then.)

Meanwhile, back in 1879, the Milwaukee franchise went bankrupt, and Dalrymple signed with Chicago. Anson put him in left field and made him the leadoff hitter. Chicago struggled that year, but beginning in 1880, Anson's squad would win five pennants in seven years. Dalrymple was a key component of those squads. He led the majors in runs scored in 1880, and he was in the top five in that cate-

gory for four of those seven years. He also was in the top four in hits three of those seven years, and he led the majors in home runs (11) in 1885.

In 1883 the speedy Dalrymple hit four doubles in one game, tying a major league record with many other players. He also led Chicago in triples three different years.

Dalrymple was an average fielder in the outfield, and Anson admitted that were it not for his hitting, Dalrymple would not have been a regular. But as much as Anson liked Dalrymple, Cap disapproved of his left fielder's drinking, which got heavier as his career continued.

Finally, with Anson's tacit approval, Chicago owner A.J. Spalding sold Dalrymple to Pittsburgh, claiming he was washed up. It was probably true; Dalrymple barely cracked .200 in his two-year stint in the Steel City.

But after two years in the minor leagues, Dalrymple signed with Milwaukee of the American Association and hit .314 in a part-time role. He retired for good from the majors after that year.

Dalrymple died January 25, 1939, in his hometown.

Daly, Thomas Peter (Tom *or* Tido)

HEIGHT: 5'7"   THROWS: RIGHT   BATS: BOTH   BORN: 2/7/1866 PHILADELPHIA, PENNSYLVANIA   DIED: 10/29/1938 BROOKLYN, NEW YORK
POSITIONS PLAYED: C, 1B, 2B, 3B, SS, OF

YEAR	TEAM	GAMES	AB	RUNS	HITS	2B	3B	HR	RBI	BB	IBB	SO	HBP	SH	SF	SB	CS	BA	OBA	SA	FA
1887	**ChN-N**	**74**	**278**	**45**	**75**	**10**	**4**	**2**	**17**	**22**	—	**25**	**0**	—	—	**29**	—	**.270**	**.323**	**.356**	**.934**
1888	**ChN-N**	**65**	**219**	**34**	**42**	**2**	**6**	**0**	**29**	**10**	—	**26**	**1**	—	—	**10**	—	**.192**	**.230**	**.256**	**.938**
1889	WaN-N	71	250	39	75	13	5	1	40	38	—	28	1	—	—	18	—	.300	.394	.404	.914
1890	Bro-N	82	292	55	71	9	4	5	43	32	—	43	4	—	—	20	—	.243	.326	.353	.964
1891	Bro-N	58	200	29	50	11	5	2	27	21	—	34	2	—	—	7	—	.250	.327	.385	.901
1892	Bro-N	124	446	76	114	15	6	4	51	64	—	61	5	—	—	34	—	.256	.355	.343	.929
1893	Bro-N	126	470	94	136	21	14	8	70	76	—	65	0	—	—	32	—	.289	.388	.445	.892
1894	Bro-N	123	492	135	168	22	10	8	82	77	—	42	5	4	—	51	—	.341	.436	.476	.908
1895	Bro-N	120	455	89	128	17	8	2	68	52	—	52	3	10	—	28	—	.281	.359	.367	.930
1896	Bro-N	67	224	43	63	13	6	3	29	33	—	25	5	0	—	19	—	.281	.385	.433	.907
1898	Bro-N	23	73	11	24	3	1	0	11	14	—	1	1	0	—	6	—	.329	.443	.397	.993
1899	Bro-N	141	498	95	156	24	9	5	88	69	—	—	12	8	—	43	—	.313	.409	.428	.929
1900	Bro-N	97	343	72	107	17	3	4	55	46	—	—	6	5	—	27	—	.312	.403	.414	.926
1901	Bro-N	133	520	88	164	38	10	3	90	42	—	—	4	10	—	31	—	.315	.371	.444	.944
1902	CWS-A	137	489	57	110	22	3	1	54	55	—	—	0	15	—	19	—	.225	.303	.288	.957
1903	CWS-A	43	150	20	31	11	0	0	19	20	—	—	1	5	—	6	—	.207	.304	.280	.948
1903	Cin-N	80	307	42	90	14	9	1	38	16	—	—	2	7	—	5	—	.293	.332	.407	.937
Career average		98	357	64	100	16	6	3	51	43	—	25	3	4	—	24	—	.281	.364	.389	.930
Cubs average		**70**	**249**	**40**	**59**	**6**	**5**	**1**	**23**	**16**	—	**26**	**1**	—	—	**20**	—	**.235**	**.283**	**.312**	**.936**
Career total		1564	5706	1024	1604	262	103	49	811	687	—	401	52	64	—	385	—	.281	.364	.389	.930
Cubs total		**139**	**497**	**79**	**117**	**12**	**10**	**2**	**46**	**32**	—	**51**	**1**	—	—	**39**	—	**.235**	**.283**	**.312**	**.936**

Daniels, Kalvoski (Kal)

HEIGHT: 5'11" THROWS: RIGHT BATS: LEFT BORN: 8/20/1963 VIENNA, GEORGIA POSITIONS PLAYED: 1B, OF

YEAR	TEAM	GAMES	AB	RUNS	HITS	2B	3B	HR	RBI	BB	IBB	SO	HBP	SH	SF	SB	CS	BA	OBA	SA	FA
1986	Cin-N	74	181	34	58	10	4	6	23	22	1	30	2	1	1	15	2	.320	.398	.519	.967
1987	Cin-N	108	368	73	123	24	1	26	64	60	11	62	1	1	0	26	8	.334	.429	.617	.968
1988	Cin-N	140	495	95	144	29	1	18	64	87	10	94	3	0	4	27	6	.291	.397	.463	.982
1989	Cin-N	44	133	26	29	11	0	2	9	36	1	28	2	0	1	6	4	.218	.390	.346	1.000
1989	LA-N	11	38	7	13	2	0	2	8	7	0	5	0	0	1	3	0	.342	.435	.553	1.000
1990	LA-N	130	450	81	133	23	1	27	94	68	1	104	3	2	3	4	3	.296	.389	.531	.987
1991	LA-N	137	461	54	115	15	1	17	73	63	4	116	1	0	6	6	1	.249	.337	.397	.979
1992	LA-N	35	104	9	24	5	0	2	8	10	0	30	1	0	1	0	0	.231	.302	.337	.979
1992	**ChC-N**	**48**	**108**	**12**	**27**	**6**	**0**	**4**	**17**	**12**	**0**	**24**	**1**	**0**	**1**	**0**	**2**	**.250**	**.328**	**.417**	**1.000**
Career average		104	334	56	95	18	1	15	51	52	4	70	2	1	3	12	4	.285	.382	.479	.980
Cubs average		**48**	**108**	**12**	**27**	**6**	**0**	**4**	**17**	**12**	**0**	**24**	**1**	**0**	**1**	**0**	**2**	**.250**	**.328**	**.417**	**1.000**
Career total		727	2338	391	666	125	8	104	360	365	28	493	14	4	18	87	26	.285	.382	.479	.980
Cubs total		**48**	**108**	**12**	**27**	**6**	**0**	**4**	**17**	**12**	**0**	**24**	**1**	**0**	**1**	**0**	**2**	**.250**	**.328**	**.417**	**1.000**

Dark, Alvin Ralph (Al or Blackie or The Swamp Fox)

HEIGHT: 5'11" THROWS: RIGHT BATS: RIGHT BORN: 1/7/1922 COMANCHE, OKLAHOMA POSITIONS PLAYED: P, 1B, 2B, 3B, SS, OF

YEAR	TEAM	GAMES	AB	RUNS	HITS	2B	3B	HR	RBI	BB	IBB	SO	HBP	SH	SF	SB	CS	BA	OBA	SA	FA
1946	Bos-N	15	13	0	3	3	0	0	1	0	—	3	0	0	—	0	—	.231	.231	.462	.909
1948	Bos-N	137	543	85	175	39	6	3	48	24	—	36	2	10	—	4	—	.322	.353	.433	.963
1949	Bos-N	130	529	74	146	23	5	3	53	31	—	43	1	11	—	5	—	.276	.317	.355	.960
1950	NYG-N	154	587	79	164	36	5	16	67	39	—	60	6	11	—	9	—	.279	.331	.440	.962
1951	NYG-N	156	646	114	196	41	7	14	69	42	—	39	6	6	—	12	7	.303	.352	.454	.944
1952	NYG-N	151	589	92	177	29	3	14	73	47	—	39	5	8	—	6	6	.301	.357	.431	.965
1953	NYG-N	155	647	126	194	41	6	23	88	28	—	34	6	12	—	7	2	.300	.335	.488	.969
1954	NYG-N	154	644	98	189	26	6	20	70	27	—	40	5	12	5	5	3	.293	.325	.446	.956
1955	NYG-N	115	475	77	134	20	3	9	45	22	2	32	5	4	2	2	1	.282	.319	.394	.962
1956	NYG-N	48	206	19	52	12	0	2	17	8	0	13	1	3	4	0	0	.252	.279	.340	.961
1956	StL-N	100	413	54	118	14	7	4	37	21	0	33	2	2	4	3	1	.286	.320	.383	.959
1957	StL-N	140	583	80	169	25	8	4	64	29	4	56	4	5	4	3	4	.290	.326	.381	.965
1958	StL-N	18	64	7	19	0	0	1	5	2	0	6	0	0	0	0	0	.297	.318	.344	.942
1958	**ChC-N**	**114**	**464**	**54**	**137**	**16**	**4**	**3**	**43**	**29**	**1**	**23**	**5**	**2**	**6**	**1**	**1**	**.295**	**.339**	**.366**	**.949**
1959	**ChC-N**	**136**	**477**	**60**	**126**	**22**	**9**	**6**	**45**	**55**	**9**	**50**	**3**	**7**	**3**	**1**	**1**	**.264**	**.342**	**.386**	**.950**
1960	Phi-N	55	198	29	48	5	1	3	14	19	2	14	2	2	0	1	1	.242	.315	.323	.953
1960	Mil-N	50	141	16	42	6	2	1	18	7	2	13	1	0	3	0	0	.298	.329	.390	.969
Career average		131	516	76	149	26	5	9	54	31	1	38	4	7	2	4	2	.289	.333	.411	.959
Cubs average		**125**	**471**	**57**	**132**	**19**	**7**	**5**	**44**	**42**	**5**	**37**	**4**	**5**	**5**	**1**	**1**	**.279**	**.341**	**.376**	**.949**
Career total		1828	7219	1064	2089	358	72	126	757	430	20	534	54	95	31	59	27	.289	.333	.411	.959
Cubs total		**250**	**941**	**114**	**263**	**38**	**13**	**9**	**88**	**84**	**10**	**73**	**8**	**9**	**9**	**2**	**2**	**.279**	**.341**	**.376**	**.949**

Darling, Conrad (Dell)

HEIGHT: 5'8" THROWS: RIGHT BATS: RIGHT BORN: 12/21/1861 ERIE, PENNSYLVANIA DIED: 11/20/1904 ERIE, PENNSYLVANIA
POSITIONS PLAYED: C, 1B, 2B, 3B, SS, OF

YEAR	TEAM	GAMES	AB	RUNS	HITS	2B	3B	HR	RBI	BB	IBB	SO	HBP	SH	SF	SB	CS	BA	OBA	SA	FA
1883	Buf-N	6	18	1	3	0	0	0	1	2	—	5	—	—	—	—	—	.167	.250	.167	.875
1887	**ChN-N**	**38**	**163**	**28**	**67**	**7**	**4**	**3**	**20**	**22**	**—**	**18**	**0**	**—**	**—**	**19**	**—**	**.411**	**.481**	**.558**	**.885**
1888	**ChN-N**	**20**	**75**	**12**	**16**	**3**	**1**	**2**	**7**	**3**	**—**	**12**	**1**	**—**	**—**	**0**	**—**	**.213**	**.253**	**.360**	**.932**
1889	**ChN-N**	**36**	**120**	**14**	**23**	**1**	**1**	**0**	**7**	**25**	**—**	**22**	**0**	**—**	**—**	**5**	**—**	**.192**	**.331**	**.217**	**.960**
1890	Chi-P	58	221	45	57	12	4	2	39	29	—	28	3	—	—	5	—	.258	.352	.376	.909
1891	StL-AA	17	53	9	7	1	3	0	9	10	—	11	0	—	—	0	—	.132	.270	.264	.885
Career average		29	108	18	29	4	2	1	14	15	—	16	1	—	—	5	—	.266	.360	.375	.915
Cubs average		**31**	**119**	**18**	**35**	**4**	**2**	**2**	**11**	**17**	**—**	**17**	**0**	**—**	**—**	**8**	**—**	**.296**	**.384**	**.402**	**.927**
Career total		175	650	109	173	24	13	7	83	91	—	96	4	—	—	29	—	.266	.360	.375	.915
Cubs total		**94**	**358**	**54**	**106**	**11**	**6**	**5**	**34**	**50**	**—**	**52**	**1**	**—**	**—**	**24**	**—**	**.296**	**.384**	**.402**	**.927**

Darwin, Arthur Bobby Lee (Bobby)
HEIGHT: 6'2"   THROWS: RIGHT   BATS: RIGHT   BORN: 2/16/1943 LOS ANGELES, CALIFORNIA   POSITIONS PLAYED: P, OF

YEAR	TEAM	GAMES	AB	RUNS	HITS	2B	3B	HR	RBI	BB	IBB	SO	HBP	SH	SF	SB	CS	BA	OBA	SA	FA
1962	LAA-A	1	1	0	0	0	0	0	0	0	0	1	0	0	0	0	0	.000	.000	.000	.000
1969	LA-N	6	0	1	0	0	0	0	0	0	0	0	0	0	0	0	0	—	—	—	—
1971	LA-N	11	20	2	5	1	0	1	4	2	0	9	0	0	0	0	0	.250	.318	.450	1.000
1972	Min-A	145	513	48	137	20	2	22	80	38	4	145	8	1	0	2	3	.267	.326	.442	.980
1973	Min-A	145	560	69	141	20	2	18	90	46	5	137	3	0	5	5	2	.252	.309	.391	.980
1974	Min-A	152	575	67	152	13	7	25	94	37	2	127	14	0	4	1	3	.264	.322	.442	.970
1975	Min-A	48	169	26	37	6	0	5	18	18	1	44	4	0	1	2	0	.219	.307	.343	.969
1975	Mil-A	55	186	19	46	6	2	8	23	11	0	54	3	1	0	4	1	.247	.300	.430	.978
1976	Mil-A	25	73	6	18	3	1	1	5	6	1	16	2	0	0	0	0	.247	.321	.356	.977
1976	Bos-A	43	106	9	19	5	2	3	13	2	0	35	3	1	0	0	0	.179	.216	.349	.964
1977	Bos-A	4	9	1	2	1	0	0	1	0	0	4	0	0	0	1	0	.222	.222	.333	.500
1977	**ChC-N**	**11**	**12**	**2**	**2**	**1**	**0**	**0**	**0**	**0**	**0**	**5**	**0**	**0**	**0**	**0**	**0**	**.167**	**.167**	**.250**	
Career average		72	247	28	62	8	2	9	36	18	1	64	4	0	1	2	1	.251	.311	.412	.975
Cubs average		**11**	**12**	**2**	**2**	**1**	**0**	**0**	**0**	**0**	**0**	**5**	**0**	**0**	**0**	**0**	**0**	**.167**	**.167**	**.250**	**—**
Career total		646	2224	250	559	76	16	83	328	160	13	577	37	3	12	15	9	.251	.311	.412	.975
Cubs total		**11**	**12**	**2**	**2**	**1**	**0**	**0**	**0**	**0**	**0**	**5**	**0**	**0**	**0**	**0**	**0**	**.167**	**.167**	**.250**	**—**

Dascenzo, Douglas Craig (Doug)
HEIGHT: 5'8"   THROWS: LEFT   BATS: BOTH   BORN: 6/30/1964 CLEVELAND, OHIO   POSITIONS PLAYED: P, OF

YEAR	TEAM	GAMES	AB	RUNS	HITS	2B	3B	HR	RBI	BB	IBB	SO	HBP	SH	SF	SB	CS	BA	OBA	SA	FA
1988	ChC-N	26	75	9	16	3	0	0	4	9	1	4	0	1	0	6	1	.213	.298	.253	1.000
1989	ChC-N	47	139	20	23	1	0	1	12	13	0	13	0	3	2	6	3	.165	.234	.194	1.000
1990	ChC-N	113	241	27	61	9	5	1	26	21	2	18	1	5	3	15	6	.253	.312	.344	1.000
1991	ChC-N	118	239	40	61	11	0	1	18	24	2	26	2	6	1	14	7	.255	.327	.314	.985
1992	ChC-N	139	376	37	96	13	4	0	20	27	2	32	0	4	2	6	8	.255	.304	.311	.978
1993	Tex-A	76	146	20	29	5	1	2	10	8	0	22	0	3	1	2	0	.199	.239	.288	.990
1996	SD-N	21	9	3	1	0	0	0	0	1	0	2	0	0	0	0	1	.111	.200	.111	1.000
Career average		77	175	22	41	6	1	1	13	15	1	17	0	3	1	7	4	.234	.293	.297	.990
Cubs average		**89**	**214**	**27**	**51**	**7**	**2**	**1**	**16**	**19**	**1**	**19**	**1**	**4**	**2**	**9**	**5**	**.240**	**.301**	**.300**	**.990**
Career total		540	1225	156	287	42	10	5	90	103	7	117	3	22	9	49	26	.234	.293	.297	.990
Cubs total		**443**	**1070**	**133**	**257**	**37**	**9**	**3**	**80**	**94**	**7**	**93**	**3**	**19**	**8**	**47**	**25**	**.240**	**.301**	**.300**	**.990**

Davidson, William Simpson (Bill)
HEIGHT: 5'10"   THROWS: RIGHT   BATS: RIGHT   BORN: 5/10/1887 LAFAYETTE, INDIANA   DIED: 5/23/1954 LINCOLN, NEBRASKA   POSITIONS PLAYED: OF

YEAR	TEAM	GAMES	AB	RUNS	HITS	2B	3B	HR	RBI	BB	IBB	SO	HBP	SH	SF	SB	CS	BA	OBA	SA	FA
1909	**ChC-N**	**2**	**7**	**2**	**1**	**0**	**0**	**0**	**0**	**1**	**—**	**—**	**0**	**0**	**—**	**1**	**—**	**.143**	**.250**	**.143**	**1.000**
1910	Bro-N	136	509	48	121	13	7	0	34	24	—	54	4	12	—	27	—	.238	.277	.291	.961
1911	Bro-N	87	292	33	68	3	4	1	26	16	—	21	1	8	—	18	—	.233	.275	.281	.956
Career average		75	269	28	63	5	4	0	20	14	—	25	2	7	—	15	—	.235	.276	.286	.959
Cubs average		**2**	**7**	**2**	**1**	**0**	**0**	**0**	**0**	**1**	**—**	**—**	**0**	**0**	**—**	**1**	**—**	**.143**	**.250**	**.143**	**1.000**
Career total		225	808	83	190	16	11	1	60	41	—	75	5	20	—	46	—	.235	.276	.286	.959
Cubs total		**2**	**7**	**2**	**1**	**0**	**0**	**0**	**0**	**1**	**—**	**—**	**0**	**0**	**—**	**1**	**—**	**.143**	**.250**	**.143**	**1.000**

Davis, Bryshear Bennett (Brock)
HEIGHT: 5'10"   THROWS: LEFT   BATS: LEFT   BORN: 10/19/1943 OAKLAND, CALIFORNIA   POSITIONS PLAYED: OF

YEAR	TEAM	GAMES	AB	RUNS	HITS	2B	3B	HR	RBI	BB	IBB	SO	HBP	SH	SF	SB	CS	BA	OBA	SA	FA
1963	Hou-N	34	55	7	11	2	0	1	2	4	1	10	0	1	0	0	0	.200	.254	.291	.864
1964	Hou-N	1	3	0	0	0	0	0	0	1	0	1	0	0	0	0	0	.000	.250	.000	1.000
1966	Hou-N	10	27	2	4	1	0	0	1	5	0	4	0	0	0	1	0	.148	.281	.185	1.000
1970	**ChC-N**	**6**	**3**	**0**	**0**	**0**	**0**	**0**	**0**	**0**	**0**	**1**	**0**	**0**	**0**	**0**	**0**	**.000**	**.000**	**.000**	
1971	**ChC-N**	**106**	**301**	**22**	**77**	**7**	**5**	**0**	**28**	**35**	**0**	**34**	**2**	**4**	**2**	**0**	**6**	**.256**	**.335**	**.312**	**.982**
1972	Mil-A	85	154	17	49	2	0	0	12	12	0	23	0	1	1	6	4	.318	.365	.331	.970
Career average		40	91	8	24	2	1	0	7	10	0	12	0	1	1	1	2	.260	.331	.306	.973
Cubs average		**56**	**152**	**11**	**39**	**4**	**3**	**0**	**14**	**18**	**0**	**18**	**1**	**2**	**1**	**0**	**3**	**.253**	**.332**	**.309**	**.982**
Career total		242	543	48	141	12	5	1	43	57	1	73	2	6	3	7	10	.260	.331	.306	.973
Cubs total		**112**	**304**	**22**	**77**	**7**	**5**	**0**	**28**	**35**	**0**	**35**	**2**	**4**	**2**	**0**	**6**	**.253**	**.332**	**.309**	**.982**

Davis, Herman Thomas (Tommy)
HEIGHT: 6'2" THROWS: RIGHT BATS: RIGHT BORN: 3/21/1939 BROOKLYN, NEW YORK POSITIONS PLAYED: 1B, 2B, 3B, OF

YEAR	TEAM	GAMES	AB	RUNS	HITS	2B	3B	HR	RBI	BB	IBB	SO	HBP	SH	SF	SB	CS	BA	OBA	SA	FA
1959	LA-N	1	1	0	0	0	0	0	0	0	0	1	0	0	0	0	0	.000	.000	.000	—
1960	LA-N	110	352	43	97	18	1	11	44	13	2	35	2	3	4	6	2	.276	.302	.426	.977
1961	LA-N	132	460	60	128	13	2	15	58	32	4	53	2	9	5	10	4	.278	.325	.413	.940
1962	LA-N	163	665	120	230	27	9	27	153	33	6	65	2	3	8	18	6	.346	.374	.535	.943
1963	LA-N	146	556	69	181	19	3	16	88	29	5	59	4	1	7	15	10	.326	.359	.457	.948
1964	LA-N	152	592	70	163	20	5	14	86	29	6	68	4	1	5	11	8	.275	.311	.397	.982
1965	LA-N	17	60	3	15	1	1	0	9	2	1	4	0	1	1	2	1	.250	.270	.300	1.000
1966	LA-N	100	313	27	98	11	1	3	27	16	4	36	0	1	1	3	3	.313	.345	.383	.973
1967	NYM-N	154	577	72	174	32	0	16	73	31	10	71	7	1	5	9	3	.302	.342	.440	.972
1968	CWS-A	132	456	30	122	5	3	8	50	16	3	48	0	4	6	4	2	.268	.289	.344	.965
1969	Sea-A	123	454	52	123	29	1	6	80	30	5	46	4	1	5	19	4	.271	.318	.379	.964
1969	Hou-N	24	79	2	19	3	0	1	9	8	0	9	1	0	0	1	1	.241	.318	.316	1.000
1970	Hou-N	57	213	24	60	12	2	3	30	7	1	25	0	0	0	8	3	.282	.305	.399	.949
1970	Oak-A	66	200	17	58	9	1	1	27	8	1	18	1	2	2	2	4	.290	.318	.360	.966
1970	**ChC-N**	**11**	**42**	**4**	**11**	**2**	**0**	**2**	**8**	**1**	**0**	**1**	**0**	**0**	**0**	**0**	**0**	**.262**	**.279**	**.452**	**.938**
1971	Oak-A	79	219	26	71	8	1	3	42	15	1	19	0	1	3	7	1	.324	.363	.411	.984
1972	**ChC-N**	**15**	**26**	**3**	**7**	**1**	**0**	**0**	**6**	**2**	**0**	**3**	**0**	**0**	**0**	**0**	**1**	**.269**	**.321**	**.308**	**.970**
1972	Bal-A	26	82	9	21	3	0	0	6	6	0	18	0	0	0	2	0	.256	.307	.293	1.000
1973	Bal-A	137	552	53	169	20	3	7	89	30	3	56	1	3	4	11	3	.306	.341	.391	.971
1974	Bal-A	158	626	67	181	20	1	11	84	34	9	49	3	3	7	6	2	.289	.325	.377	—
1975	Bal-A	116	460	43	130	14	1	6	57	23	2	52	0	2	3	2	0	.283	.315	.357	—
1976	Cal-A	72	219	16	58	5	0	3	26	15	3	18	1	0	2	0	1	.265	.312	.329	1.000
1976	KC-A	8	19	1	5	0	0	0	0	1	0	0	0	0	0	0	0	.263	.300	.263	—
Career average		111	401	45	118	15	2	9	58	21	4	42	2	2	4	8	3	.294	.329	.405	.964
Cubs average		**13**	**34**	**4**	**9**	**2**	**0**	**1**	**7**	**2**	**0**	**2**	**0**	**0**	**0**	**0**	**1**	**.265**	**.296**	**.397**	**.959**
Career total		1999	7223	811	2121	272	35	153	1052	381	66	754	32	35	68	136	59	.294	.329	.405	.964
Cubs total		**26**	**68**	**7**	**18**	**3**	**0**	**2**	**14**	**3**	**0**	**4**	**0**	**0**	**0**	**0**	**1**	**.265**	**.296**	**.397**	**.959**

Davis, Jody Richard
HEIGHT: 6'4" THROWS: RIGHT BATS: RIGHT BORN: 11/12/1956 GAINESVILLE, GEORGIA POSITIONS PLAYED: C, 1B

YEAR	TEAM	GAMES	AB	RUNS	HITS	2B	3B	HR	RBI	BB	IBB	SO	HBP	SH	SF	SB	CS	BA	OBA	SA	FA
1981	ChC-N	56	180	14	46	5	1	4	21	21	3	28	1	3	2	0	1	.256	.333	.361	.972
1982	ChC-N	130	418	41	109	20	2	12	52	36	4	92	1	4	7	0	1	.261	.316	.404	.984
1983	ChC-N	151	510	56	138	31	2	24	84	33	5	93	2	0	5	0	2	.271	.315	.480	.984
1984	ChC-N	150	523	55	134	25	2	19	94	47	15	99	1	1	7	5	6	.256	.315	.421	.984
1985	ChC-N	142	482	47	112	30	0	17	58	48	5	83	0	2	4	1	0	.232	.300	.400	.990
1986	ChC-N	148	528	61	132	27	2	21	74	41	4	110	0	4	8	0	1	.250	.300	.428	.992
1987	ChC-N	125	428	57	106	12	2	19	51	52	2	91	2	1	2	1	2	.248	.331	.418	.989
1988	ChC-N	88	249	19	57	9	0	6	33	29	3	51	1	2	3	0	3	.229	.309	.337	.995
1988	Atl-N	2	8	2	2	0	0	1	3	0	0	1	0	0	0	0	0	.250	.250	.625	1.000
1989	Atl-N	78	231	12	39	5	0	4	19	23	3	61	1	1	1	0	0	.169	.246	.242	.986
1990	Atl-N	12	28	0	2	0	0	0	1	3	0	3	0	0	0	0	0	.071	.161	.071	1.000
Career average		108	359	36	88	16	1	13	49	33	4	71	1	2	4	1	2	.245	.307	.403	.987
Cubs average		**124**	**415**	**44**	**104**	**20**	**1**	**15**	**58**	**38**	**5**	**81**	**1**	**2**	**5**	**1**	**2**	**.251**	**.313**	**.416**	**.987**
Career total		1082	3585	364	877	164	11	127	490	333	44	712	9	18	39	7	16	.245	.307	.403	.987
Cubs total		**990**	**3318**	**350**	**834**	**159**	**11**	**122**	**467**	**307**	**41**	**647**	**8**	**17**	**38**	**7**	**16**	**.251**	**.313**	**.416**	**.987**

Davis, Steven Michael (Steve)
HEIGHT: 6'1" THROWS: RIGHT BATS: RIGHT BORN: 12/30/1953 OAKLAND, CALIFORNIA POSITIONS PLAYED: 2B, 3B

YEAR	TEAM	GAMES	AB	RUNS	HITS	2B	3B	HR	RBI	BB	IBB	SO	HBP	SH	SF	SB	CS	BA	OBA	SA	FA
1979	ChC-N	3	4	0	0	0	0	0	1	0	0	0	0	0	0	0	0	.000	.000	.000	1.000
Career average		3	4	0	0	0	0	0	1	0	0	0	0	0	0	0	0	.000	.000	.000	1.000
Cubs average		**3**	**4**	**0**	**0**	**0**	**0**	**0**	**1**	**0**	**0**	**0**	**0**	**0**	**0**	**0**	**0**	**.000**	**.000**	**.000**	**1.000**
Career total		3	4	0	0	0	0	0	1	0	0	0	0	0	0	0	0	.000	.000	.000	1.000
Cubs total		**3**	**4**	**0**	**0**	**0**	**0**	**0**	**1**	**0**	**0**	**0**	**0**	**0**	**0**	**0**	**0**	**.000**	**.000**	**.000**	**1.000**

Jody Richard Davis, c-1b, 1981–90

Jody Davis was a stabilizing force behind the plate and a clutch performer for Chicago for most of the 1980s.

Davis was born on November 12, 1956, in Gainesville, Georgia. He was originally drafted by the Mets and was traded to the Cardinals before ultimately ending up in the Chicago organization.

Davis broke in with Chicago in 1981 and eventually earned the starting spot that year, hitting .256 in limited action. The next year, he started 130 games at catcher and remained the starter for Chicago until 1987.

In 1984 Davis hit .256 and was second on the team in RBIs with 94. He made the All-Star team and turned in a huge performance against San Diego in the National League

Championship Series with seven hits, six RBIs and a .359 average in a losing cause.

Davis's .245 career average belied his reputation as a clutch hitter. In addition to the 1984 NLCS, Davis had a number of big games or series, always seeming to get a big hit when needed.

Davis was an All-Star again in 1986, winning a Gold Glove and throwing out 17 base stealers. He also led the team in home runs that year with 21.

Davis was durable, catching over 138 games for the Cubs from 1982 to 1986. In 1987 he caught 125 games. But in 1988, a stint on the disabled list forced the Cubs to bring up Damon Berryhill, the player who eventually replaced Davis.

That year, 1988, Davis was traded to Atlanta; he finished out his major league career there, retiring in 1990.

Dawson, Andre Nolan (Hawk)

HEIGHT: 6'3"   THROWS: RIGHT   BATS: RIGHT   BORN: 7/10/1954 MIAMI, FLORIDA   POSITIONS PLAYED: OF

YEAR	TEAM	GAMES	AB	RUNS	HITS	2B	3B	HR	RBI	BB	IBB	SO	HBP	SH	SF	SB	CS	BA	OBA	SA	FA
1976	Mon-N	24	85	9	20	4	1	0	7	5	1	13	0	2	0	1	2	.235	.278	.306	.969
1977	Mon-N	139	525	64	148	26	9	19	65	34	4	93	2	1	4	21	7	.282	.326	.474	.989
1978	Mon-N	157	609	84	154	24	8	25	72	30	3	128	12	4	5	28	11	.253	.299	.442	.988
1979	Mon-N	155	639	90	176	24	12	25	92	27	5	115	6	8	4	35	10	.275	.309	.468	.988
1980	Mon-N	151	577	96	178	41	7	17	87	44	7	69	6	1	10	34	9	.308	.358	.492	.986
1981	Mon-N	103	394	71	119	21	3	24	64	35	14	50	7	0	5	26	4	.302	.365	.553	.980
1982	Mon-N	148	608	107	183	37	7	23	83	34	4	96	8	4	6	39	10	.301	.343	.498	.982
1983	Mon-N	159	633	104	189	36	10	32	113	38	12	81	9	0	18	25	11	.299	.338	.539	.980
1984	Mon-N	138	533	73	132	23	6	17	86	41	2	80	2	1	6	13	5	.248	.301	.409	.975
1985	Mon-N	139	529	65	135	27	2	23	91	29	8	92	4	1	7	13	4	.255	.295	.444	.973
1986	Mon-N	130	496	65	141	32	2	20	78	37	11	79	6	1	6	18	12	.284	.338	.478	.986
1987	**ChC-N**	**153**	**621**	**90**	**178**	**24**	**2**	**49**	**137**	**32**	**7**	**103**	**7**	**0**	**2**	**11**	**3**	**.287**	**.328**	**.568**	**.986**
1988	**ChC-N**	**157**	**591**	**78**	**179**	**31**	**8**	**24**	**79**	**37**	**12**	**73**	**4**	**1**	**7**	**12**	**4**	**.303**	**.344**	**.504**	**.989**
1989	**ChC-N**	**118**	**416**	**62**	**105**	**18**	**6**	**21**	**77**	**35**	**13**	**62**	**1**	**0**	**7**	**8**	**5**	**.252**	**.307**	**.476**	**.987**
1990	**ChC-N**	**147**	**529**	**72**	**164**	**28**	**5**	**27**	**100**	**42**	**21**	**65**	**2**	**0**	**8**	**16**	**2**	**.310**	**.358**	**.535**	**.981**
1991	**ChC-N**	**149**	**563**	**69**	**153**	**21**	**4**	**31**	**104**	**22**	**3**	**80**	**5**	**0**	**6**	**4**	**5**	**.272**	**.302**	**.488**	**.988**
1992	**ChC-N**	**143**	**542**	**60**	**150**	**27**	**2**	**22**	**90**	**30**	**8**	**70**	**4**	**0**	**6**	**6**	**2**	**.277**	**.316**	**.456**	**.992**
1993	Bos-A	121	461	44	126	29	1	13	67	17	4	49	13	0	7	2	1	.273	.313	.425	1.000
1994	Bos-A	75	292	34	70	18	0	16	48	9	3	53	4	0	1	2	2	.240	.271	.466	—
1995	Fla-N	79	226	30	58	10	3	8	37	9	1	45	8	0	3	0	0	.257	.305	.434	.908
1996	Fla-N	42	58	6	16	2	0	2	14	2	0	13	1	0	0	0	0	.276	.311	.414	.833
Career average		125	473	65	132	24	5	21	76	28	7	72	5	1	6	15	5	.279	.323	.482	.983
Cubs average		**145**	**544**	**72**	**155**	**25**	**5**	**29**	**98**	**33**	**11**	**76**	**4**	**0**	**6**	**10**	**4**	**.285**	**.327**	**.507**	**.987**
Career total		2627	9927	1373	2774	503	98	438	1591	589	143	1509	111	24	118	314	109	.279	.323	.482	.983
Cubs total		**867**	**3262**	**431**	**929**	**149**	**27**	**174**	**587**	**198**	**64**	**453**	**23**	**1**	**36**	**57**	**21**	**.285**	**.327**	**.507**	**.987**

Andre Nolan "The Hawk," "Awesome" Dawson, of-dh, 1978–96

Who could have imagined that after a very good decade with the Montreal Expos, Andre Dawson would reach even greater heights with the Cubs?

Dawson was born on July 10, 1954, in Miami, Florida. He began his major league career with the Expos with a September call-up in 1976. The next year, Dawson was a regular, and for 10 consecutive years with Montreal, he had at least 119 hits, 17 home runs and 21 doubles, as well as averaging 17 stolen bases a year.

He was also one of the best defensive outfielders in the National League in that span. Between 1981 and 1983, he led all major league outfielders in total chances. He earned six Gold Gloves from 1980 to 1985.

Dawson was, for most of his time in Montreal, somewhat overshadowed by catcher Gary Carter. But more important, at least to Dawson, was the toll Montreal's artificial turf was taking on his knees.

He wanted out and became a free agent in 1986. He signed a blank contract with the Cubs. Chicago filled in $500,000, a stunningly low figure, considering the Expos had offered him $2 million over two years.

The move was a financial disaster for Dawson, but it took his career to another level. The man known to fellow ballplayers as "the Hawk" simply exploded in Chicago. He hit .287, with 49 home runs and 137 RBIs, the latter two numbers tops in the league. The Cubs were dismal, finishing dead last in the National League's Eastern Division, but Dawson came to play every day and was the league's most valuable player, the only man to earn that award playing for a last-place team. On April 29, he hit for the cycle against the Giants.

Dawson also won his seventh Gold Glove that year. In 1988 Dawson became the only Cubs outfielder to win two Gold Gloves.

Within two years, the Cubs and Dawson would be on top of the heap, winning the NL Eastern pennant and facing the San Francisco Giants in the National League Championship Series. But the Giants' pitching was too much, and Chicago fell in five games.

Dawson had a strong season in 1990, but injuries spiked the Cubs' playoff chances. At one point, Dawson and the Cubs' two other starting outfielders, Dwight Smith and Jerome Walton, were all on the disabled list at the same time.

In 1992 Dawson had, for him, a relatively off year—although 150 hits, 27 doubles, 22 home runs and 90 RBIs is a terrific year for just about anyone else. After five consecutive years as an All-Star with the Cubs, he was not named to the team that season.

But he was a free agent again and there were no blank contracts this time. Dawson signed with the Red Sox and had one good year and one not-so-good year. He finished his career with the Florida Marlins before retiring in 1996.

Dawson still holds several club records. Twice in 1987 he hit five home runs over three consecutive games, a Cubs record. He also walked five times in one game on May 22, 1990, a modern Cubs record. Dawson is also 10th all-time in home runs with the Cubs with 174.

Day, Charles Frederick (Boots)
HEIGHT: 5'9"   THROWS: LEFT   BATS: LEFT   BORN: 8/31/1947 ILION, NEW YORK   POSITIONS PLAYED: OF

YEAR	TEAM	GAMES	AB	RUNS	HITS	2B	3B	HR	RBI	BB	IBB	SO	HBP	SH	SF	SB	CS	BA	OBA	SA	FA
1969	StL-N	11	6	1	0	0	0	0	0	1	0	1	0	0	0	0	0	.000	.143	.000	—
1970	**ChC-N**	**11**	**8**	**2**	**2**	**0**	**0**	**0**	**0**	**0**	**0**	**3**	**0**	**0**	**0**	**0**	**0**	**.250**	**.250**	**.250**	**.875**
1970	Mon-N	41	108	14	29	4	0	0	5	6	2	18	0	4	0	3	2	.269	.307	.306	.987
1971	Mon-N	127	371	53	105	10	2	4	33	33	5	39	1	16	1	9	4	.283	.342	.353	.982
1972	Mon-N	128	386	32	90	7	4	0	30	29	3	44	1	12	0	3	6	.233	.288	.272	.979
1973	Mon-N	101	207	36	57	7	0	4	28	21	1	28	0	6	0	0	3	.275	.342	.367	1.000
1974	Mon-N	52	65	8	12	0	0	0	2	5	0	8	0	1	1	0	0	.185	.239	.185	1.000
Career average		79	192	24	49	5	1	1	16	16	2	24	0	7	0	3	3	.256	.314	.312	.983
Cubs average		**11**	**8**	**2**	**2**	**0**	**0**	**0**	**0**	**0**	**0**	**3**	**0**	**0**	**0**	**0**	**0**	**.250**	**.250**	**.250**	**.875**
Career total		471	1151	146	295	28	6	8	98	95	11	141	2	39	2	15	15	.256	.314	.312	.983
Cubs total		**11**	**8**	**2**	**2**	**0**	**0**	**0**	**0**	**0**	**0**	**3**	**0**	**0**	**0**	**0**	**0**	**.250**	**.250**	**.250**	**.875**

Dayett, Brian Kelly
HEIGHT: 5'10"   THROWS: RIGHT   BATS: RIGHT   BORN: 1/22/1957 NEW LONDON, CONNECTICUT   POSITIONS PLAYED: OF

YEAR	TEAM	GAMES	AB	RUNS	HITS	2B	3B	HR	RBI	BB	IBB	SO	HBP	SH	SF	SB	CS	BA	OBA	SA	FA
1983	NYY-A	11	29	3	6	0	1	0	5	2	0	4	0	1	0	0	0	.207	.258	.276	1.000
1984	NYY-A	64	127	14	31	8	0	4	23	9	0	14	1	0	2	0	0	.244	.295	.402	.988
1985	**ChC-N**	**22**	**26**	**1**	**6**	**0**	**0**	**1**	**4**	**0**	**0**	**6**	**1**	**0**	**0**	**0**	**0**	**.231**	**.259**	**.346**	**1.000**
1986	**ChC-N**	**24**	**67**	**7**	**18**	**4**	**0**	**4**	**11**	**6**	**0**	**10**	**0**	**0**	**0**	**0**	**1**	**.269**	**.316**	**.507**	**1.000**
1987	**ChC-N**	**97**	**177**	**20**	**49**	**14**	**1**	**5**	**25**	**20**	**0**	**37**	**0**	**0**	**1**	**0**	**0**	**.277**	**.348**	**.452**	**1.000**
Career average		44	85	9	22	5	0	3	14	7	0	14	0	0	1	0	0	.258	.316	.427	.995
Cubs average		**48**	**90**	**9**	**24**	**6**	**0**	**3**	**13**	**9**	**0**	**18**	**0**	**0**	**1**	**0**	**0**	**.270**	**.332**	**.456**	**1.000**
Career total		218	426	45	110	26	2	14	68	37	0	71	2	1	6	0	1	.258	.316	.427	.995
Cubs total		**143**	**270**	**28**	**73**	**18**	**1**	**10**	**40**	**26**	**0**	**53**	**1**	**0**	**4**	**0**	**1**	**.270**	**.332**	**.456**	**1.000**

Deal, Charles Albert (Charlie)
HEIGHT: 6'0"   THROWS: RIGHT   BATS: RIGHT   BORN: 10/30/1891 WILKINSBURG, PENNSYLVANIA   DIED: 9/16/1979 COVINA, CALIFORNIA
POSITIONS PLAYED: 2B, 3B, SS

YEAR	TEAM	GAMES	AB	RUNS	HITS	2B	3B	HR	RBI	BB	IBB	SO	HBP	SH	SF	SB	CS	BA	OBA	SA	FA
1912	Det-A	42	142	13	32	4	2	0	11	9	—	—	0	7	—	4	—	.225	.272	.282	.942
1913	Det-A	16	50	3	11	0	2	0	3	1	—	7	0	2	—	2	—	.220	.235	.300	.862
1913	Bos-N	10	36	6	11	1	0	0	3	2	—	1	1	2	—	1	—	.306	.359	.333	.935
1914	Bos-N	79	257	17	54	13	2	0	23	20	—	23	1	15	—	4	—	.210	.270	.276	.944
1915	STL-F	65	223	21	72	12	4	1	27	12	—	16	0	15	—	10	—	.323	.357	.426	.951
1916	STL-A	23	74	7	10	1	0	0	10	6	—	8	0	1	—	4	—	.135	.200	.149	.970
1916	**ChC-N**	**2**	**8**	**2**	**2**	**1**	**0**	**0**	**3**	**0**	**—**	**0**	**0**	**0**	**—**	**0**	**—**	**.250**	**.250**	**.375**	**1.000**
1917	**ChC-N**	**135**	**449**	**46**	**114**	**11**	**3**	**0**	**47**	**19**	**—**	**18**	**0**	**29**	**—**	**10**	**—**	**.254**	**.284**	**.292**	**.957**
1918	**ChC-N**	**119**	**414**	**43**	**99**	**9**	**3**	**2**	**34**	**21**	**—**	**13**	**2**	**22**	**—**	**11**	**—**	**.239**	**.279**	**.290**	**.942**
1919	**ChC-N**	**116**	**405**	**37**	**117**	**23**	**5**	**2**	**52**	**12**	**—**	**12**	**4**	**22**	**—**	**11**	**—**	**.289**	**.316**	**.385**	**.973**
1920	**ChC-N**	**129**	**450**	**48**	**108**	**10**	**5**	**3**	**39**	**20**	**—**	**14**	**8**	**34**	**—**	**5**	**8**	**.240**	**.285**	**.304**	**.973**
1921	**ChC-N**	**115**	**422**	**52**	**122**	**19**	**8**	**3**	**66**	**13**	**—**	**9**	**0**	**19**	**—**	**3**	**5**	**.289**	**.310**	**.393**	**.973**
Career average		85	293	30	75	10	3	1	32	14	—	12	2	17	—	7	1	.257	.293	.327	.957
Cubs average		**103**	**358**	**38**	**94**	**12**	**4**	**2**	**40**	**14**	**—**	**11**	**2**	**21**	**—**	**7**	**2**	**.262**	**.294**	**.332**	**.964**
Career total		851	2930	295	752	104	34	11	318	135	—	121	16	168	—	65	13	.257	.293	.327	.957
Cubs total		**616**	**2148**	**228**	**562**	**73**	**24**	**10**	**241**	**85**	**—**	**66**	**14**	**126**	**—**	**40**	**13**	**.262**	**.294**	**.332**	**.964**

Decker, George A. (Gentleman George)
HEIGHT: 6'1"   THROWS: LEFT   BATS: LEFT   BORN: 6/1/1869 YORK, PENNSYLVANIA   DIED: 6/7/1909 PATTON, CALIFORNIA
POSITIONS PLAYED: 1B, 2B, 3B, SS, OF

YEAR	TEAM	GAMES	AB	RUNS	HITS	2B	3B	HR	RBI	BB	IBB	SO	HBP	SH	SF	SB	CS	BA	OBA	SA	FA
1892	**ChN-N**	**78**	**291**	**32**	**66**	**6**	**7**	**1**	**28**	**20**	**—**	**49**	**0**	**—**	**—**	**9**	**—**	**.227**	**.277**	**.306**	**.867**
1893	**ChN-N**	**81**	**328**	**57**	**89**	**9**	**8**	**2**	**48**	**24**	**—**	**22**	**2**	**—**	**—**	**22**	**—**	**.271**	**.325**	**.366**	**.926**
1894	**ChN-N**	**91**	**384**	**74**	**120**	**17**	**6**	**8**	**92**	**24**	**—**	**17**	**5**	**2**	**—**	**23**	**—**	**.313**	**.361**	**.451**	**.944**
1895	**ChN-N**	**73**	**297**	**51**	**82**	**9**	**7**	**2**	**41**	**17**	**—**	**22**	**4**	**3**	**—**	**11**	**—**	**.276**	**.324**	**.374**	**.950**

(continued)

		GAMES	AB	RUNS	HITS	2B	3B	HR	RBI	BB	IBB	SO	HBP	SH	SF	SB	CS	BA	OBA	SA	FA
(Decker, continued)																					
1896	ChN-N	107	421	68	118	23	11	5	61	23	—	14	0	8	—	20	—	.280	.318	.423	.968
1897	ChN-N	111	428	72	124	12	7	5	63	24	—	—	4	9	—	11	—	.290	.333	.386	.971
1898	StL-N	76	286	26	74	10	0	1	45	20	—	—	3	5	—	4	—	.259	.314	.304	.980
1898	Lou-N	42	148	27	44	4	3	0	19	9	—	—	1	3	—	9	—	.297	.342	.365	.990
1899	Lou-N	38	135	13	36	8	0	1	18	12	—	—	2	12	—	3	—	.267	.336	.348	.968
1899	Was-N	4	9	0	0	0	0	0	0	0	—	—	0	0	—	0	—	.000	.000	.000	.955
Career average		88	341	53	94	12	6	3	52	22	—	16	3	5	—	14	—	.276	.324	.376	.959
Cubs average		**90**	**358**	**59**	**100**	**13**	**8**	**4**	**56**	**22**	**—**	**21**	**3**	**4**	**—**	**16**	**—**	**.279**	**.325**	**.389**	**.947**
Career total		701	2727	420	753	98	49	25	415	173	—	124	21	42	—	112	—	.276	.324	.376	.959
Cubs total		**541**	**2149**	**354**	**599**	**76**	**46**	**23**	**333**	**132**	**—**	**124**	**15**	**22**	**—**	**96**	**—**	**.279**	**.325**	**.389**	**.947**

DeJesus, Ivan
HEIGHT: 5'11"   THROWS: RIGHT   BATS: RIGHT   BORN: 1/9/1953 SANTURCE, PUERTO RICO   POSITIONS PLAYED: 3B, SS

YEAR	TEAM	GAMES	AB	RUNS	HITS	2B	3B	HR	RBI	BB	IBB	SO	HBP	SH	SF	SB	CS	BA	OBA	SA	FA
1974	LA-N	3	3	1	1	0	0	0	0	0	0	2	0	0	0	0	0	.333	.333	.333	1.000
1975	LA-N	63	87	10	16	2	1	0	2	11	0	15	0	1	0	1	2	.184	.276	.230	.974
1976	LA-N	22	41	4	7	2	1	0	2	4	0	9	0	2	0	0	1	.171	.244	.268	.957
1977	ChC-N	155	624	91	166	31	7	3	40	56	4	90	4	7	4	24	12	.266	.328	.353	.962
1978	ChC-N	160	619	104	172	24	7	3	35	74	5	78	2	15	2	41	12	.278	.356	.354	.967
1979	ChC-N	160	636	92	180	26	10	5	52	59	1	82	2	17	2	24	20	.283	.345	.379	.959
1980	ChC-N	157	618	78	160	26	3	3	33	60	2	81	4	8	2	44	16	.259	.327	.325	.969
1981	ChC-N	106	403	49	78	8	4	0	13	46	2	61	0	10	1	21	9	.194	.276	.233	.971
1982	Phi-N	161	536	53	128	21	5	3	59	54	9	70	2	11	3	14	4	.239	.309	.313	.966
1983	Phi-N	158	497	60	126	15	7	4	45	53	18	77	0	11	4	11	4	.254	.323	.336	.966
1984	Phi-N	144	435	40	112	15	3	0	35	43	7	76	2	1	3	12	5	.257	.325	.306	.951

(continued)

Ivan DeJesus, ss-3b, 1974–84

Ivan DeJesus, a brilliant shortstop for the Cubs in the late 1970s and early 1980s, was also one of the team's most durable ballplayers.

DeJesus, born in Santurce, Puerto Rico, on January 9, 1953, was signed by the Dodgers out of high school in 1969. He made it to the majors in 1974 and was a part-time player in Los Angeles for all of his three years there.

In 1977 he came to Chicago with first baseman Bill Buckner in a trade for Rick Monday and Mike Garman. The trade was beneficial to DeJesus, who led the Cubs in stolen bases from 1977 to 1980, in both hits and triples from 1977 to 1979 and in runs scored from 1977 to 1978 and 1980 to 1981.

His 104 runs scored led the National League in 1978 and his 44 stolen bases in 1980 set a record for Cubs shortstops.

DeJesus was also an excellent fielder. His 595 assists in 1977 are still a Cubs record. He was a player whom teammates respected because he played the game hard all the time. He was also durable, playing in a record 160 games at shortstop twice for the Cubs, in 1978 and 1979.

In 1980, against the Cardinals, the light-hitting DeJesus became the 11th, and unlikeliest, Cub to hit for the cycle.

In 1981 DeJesus struggled, hitting only .194, and the Cubs moved him to Philadelphia for aging veteran Larry Bowa and a rookie. The press howled at trading DeJesus for a man seven years older than he; a few years later, however, the Cubs looked like geniuses because the rookie was Ryne Sandberg.

DeJesus spent three years in Philadelphia, playing for the Phillies in their World Series loss to Baltimore in 1983, before moving on. He played a year each with the Cardinals, Yankees, Giants and Tigers before retiring in 1988.

(continued)

YEAR	TEAM	GAMES	AB	RUNS	HITS	2B	3B	HR	RBI	BB	IBB	SO	HBP	SH	SF	SB	CS	BA	OBA	SA	FA
1985	StL-N	59	72	11	16	5	0	0	7	4	0	16	0	1	1	2	2	.222	.260	.292	.965
1986	NYY-A	7	4	1	0	0	0	0	0	1	0	1	0	0	0	0	0	.000	.200	.000	.900
1987	SF-N	9	10	0	2	0	0	0	1	0	0	2	0	0	0	0	0	.200	.200	.200	.840
1988	Det-A	7	17	0	3	0	0	0	0	1	0	4	0	3	0	0	1	.176	.222	.176	.893
Career average		91	307	40	78	12	3	1	22	31	3	44	1	6	1	13	6	.254	.323	.326	.963
Cubs average		**148**	**580**	**83**	**151**	**23**	**6**	**3**	**35**	**59**	**3**	**78**	**2**	**11**	**2**	**13**	**6**	**.261**	**.330**	**.336**	**.963**
Career total		1371	4602	595	1167	175	48	21	324	466	48	664	16	87	22	194	88	.254	.323	.326	.963
Cubs total		**738**	**2900**	**414**	**756**	**115**	**31**	**14**	**173**	**295**	**14**	**392**	**12**	**57**	**11**	**154**	**69**	**.261**	**.330**	**.336**	**.963**

Del Greco, Robert George (Bobby *or* The Greek)

HEIGHT: 5'10"   THROWS: RIGHT   BATS: RIGHT   BORN: 4/7/1933 PITTSBURGH, PENNSYLVANIA   POSITIONS PLAYED: 2B, 3B, OF

YEAR	TEAM	GAMES	AB	RUNS	HITS	2B	3B	HR	RBI	BB	IBB	SO	HBP	SH	SF	SB	CS	BA	OBA	SA	FA
1952	Pit-N	99	341	34	74	14	2	1	20	38	—	70	3	3	—	6	5	.217	.301	.279	.977
1956	Pit-N	14	20	4	4	0	0	2	3	3	0	3	0	1	0	0	0	.200	.304	.500	1.000
1956	StL-N	102	270	29	58	16	2	5	18	32	3	50	6	3	4	1	1	.215	.308	.344	.987
1957	**ChC-N**	**20**	**40**	**2**	**8**	**2**	**0**	**0**	**3**	**10**	**0**	**17**	**0**	**1**	**0**	**1**	**0**	**.200**	**.360**	**.250**	**.967**
1957	NYY-A	8	7	3	3	0	0	0	0	2	0	2	0	0	0	1	0	.429	.556	.429	1.000
1958	NYY-A	12	5	1	1	0	0	0	0	1	0	1	0	0	0	1	0	.200	.333	.200	1.000
1960	Phi-N	100	300	48	71	16	4	10	26	54	0	64	1	8	0	1	5	.237	.355	.417	.970
1961	Phi-N	41	112	14	29	5	0	2	11	12	1	17	3	1	1	0	5	.259	.344	.357	1.000
1961	KCA-A	74	239	34	55	14	1	5	21	30	2	31	1	5	1	1	0	.230	.317	.360	.983
1962	KCA-A	132	338	61	86	21	1	9	38	49	0	62	13	3	0	4	1	.254	.370	.402	.984
1963	KCA-A	121	306	40	65	7	1	8	29	40	1	52	5	4	3	1	2	.212	.311	.320	.982
1965	Phi-N	8	4	1	0	0	0	0	0	0	0	3	0	0	0	0	0	.000	.000	.000	—
Career average		81	220	30	50	11	1	5	19	30	1	41	4	3	1	2	2	.229	.330	.352	.981
Cubs average		**20**	**40**	**2**	**8**	**2**	**0**	**0**	**3**	**10**	**0**	**17**	**0**	**1**	**0**	**1**	**0**	**.200**	**.360**	**.250**	**.967**
Career total		731	1982	271	454	95	11	42	169	271	7	372	32	29	9	16	15	.229	.330	.352	.981
Cubs total		**20**	**40**	**2**	**8**	**2**	**0**	**0**	**3**	**10**	**0**	**17**	**0**	**1**	**0**	**1**	**0**	**.200**	**.360**	**.250**	**.967**

Delahanty, James Christopher (Jim)

HEIGHT: 5'10"   THROWS: RIGHT   BATS: RIGHT   BORN: 6/20/1879 CLEVELAND, OHIO   DIED: 10/17/1953 CLEVELAND, OHIO
POSITIONS PLAYED: P, 1B, 2B, 3B, SS, OF

YEAR	TEAM	GAMES	AB	RUNS	HITS	2B	3B	HR	RBI	BB	IBB	SO	HBP	SH	SF	SB	CS	BA	OBA	SA	FA
1901	**ChN-N**	**17**	**63**	**4**	**12**	**2**	**0**	**0**	**4**	**3**	**—**	**—**	**1**	**3**	**—**	**5**	**—**	**.190**	**.239**	**.222**	**.877**
1902	NYG-N	7	26	3	6	1	0	0	3	1	—	—	0	1	—	0	—	.231	.259	.269	.917
1904	Bos-N	142	499	56	142	27	8	3	60	27	—	—	9	6	—	16	—	.285	.333	.389	.894
1905	Bos-N	125	461	50	119	11	8	5	55	28	—	—	10	7	—	12	—	.258	.315	.349	.962
1906	Cin-N	115	379	63	106	21	4	1	39	45	—	—	10	12	—	21	—	.280	.371	.364	.903
1907	StL-A	33	95	8	21	3	0	0	6	5	—	—	2	4	—	6	—	.221	.275	.253	.908
1907	Was-A	109	404	44	118	18	7	2	54	36	—	—	12	10	—	18	—	.292	.367	.386	.937
1908	Was-A	83	287	33	91	11	4	1	30	24	—	—	3	9	—	16	—	.317	.376	.394	.963
1909	Was-A	90	302	18	67	13	5	1	21	23	—	—	6	12	—	4	—	.222	.290	.308	.956
1909	Det-A	46	150	29	38	10	1	0	20	17	—	—	9	9	—	9	—	.253	.364	.333	.943
1910	Det-A	106	378	67	111	16	2	3	45	43	—	—	9	13	—	15	—	.294	.379	.370	.940
1911	Det-A	144	542	83	184	30	14	3	94	56	—	—	10	20	—	15	—	.339	.411	.463	.960
1912	Det-A	78	266	34	76	14	1	0	41	42	—	—	7	8	—	9	—	.286	.397	.346	.921
1914	Bro-F	74	214	28	62	13	5	0	15	25	—	21	3	13	—	4	—	.290	.372	.397	.955
1915	Bro-F	17	25	0	6	1	0	0	2	3	—	3	1	0	—	1	—	.240	.345	.280	.857
Career average		91	315	40	89	15	5	1	38	29	—	2	7	10	—	12	—	.283	.357	.373	.939
Cubs average		**17**	**63**	**4**	**12**	**2**	**0**	**0**	**4**	**3**	**—**	**—**	**1**	**3**	**—**	**5**	**—**	**.190**	**.239**	**.222**	**.877**
Career total		1186	4091	520	1159	191	59	19	489	378	—	24	92	127	—	151	—	.283	.357	.373	.939
Cubs total		**17**	**63**	**4**	**12**	**2**	**0**	**0**	**4**	**3**	**—**	**—**	**1**	**3**	**—**	**5**	**—**	**.190**	**.239**	**.222**	**.877**

Joseph Franklin (Frank) Demaree, of, 1932–33, 1935–44

Frank Demaree was a potent hitter for the Cubs in the early-to-late 1930s, playing on three pennant winners.

Demaree was born on June 10, 1910, in Winters, California. He made his major league debut in Chicago, coming up in August 1932 and playing fairly well in a part-time role. In 1933 he won the center fielder's job when Kiki Cuyler injured his knee. Demaree hit .272 with 24 doubles and 51 RBIs.

Cuyler came back in 1934 and Demaree was sent down to Los Angeles of the Pacific Coast League. He tore up the circuit down there, winning the MVP award by hitting .383 with 190 RBIs and 45 stolen bases.

Demaree was brought back up to Chicago the following year and began the first of three excellent seasons, hitting .325, .350 and

.324. He made 212 hits in 1936 and 199 in 1937.

His 212 hits is the sixth-best single-season performance by a Cub all-time, and Demaree's 159 singles that same year is fourth best on the Cubs' all-time list.

The 1936 and 1937 seasons were the two years he was on the All-Star team. Demaree was the starting center fielder for the National League both years.

Demaree did pretty well in two out of the three World Series in which he participated, hitting .286 in the 1932 classic and leading both teams in home runs in 1935 with two. His three World Series home runs are still a Cubs record.

Demaree was traded to the Giants along with Billy Jurges and Ken O'Dea in 1939, and he had two good years in New York, averaging .302, 155 hits and 22 doubles. He was traded to the Braves in 1942 and retired a few years later. He died in 1958 in Los Angeles.

Demaree, Joseph Franklin (Frank)

HEIGHT: 5'11" THROWS: RIGHT BATS: RIGHT BORN: 6/10/1910 WINTERS, CALIFORNIA DIED: 8/30/1958 LOS ANGELES, CALIFORNIA POSITIONS PLAYED: OF

YEAR	TEAM	GAMES	AB	RUNS	HITS	2B	3B	HR	RBI	BB	IBB	SO	HBP	SH	SF	SB	CS	BA	OBA	SA	FA
1932	ChC-N	23	56	4	14	3	0	0	6	2	—	7	1	2	—	0	—	.250	.288	.304	1.000
1933	ChC-N	134	515	68	140	24	6	6	51	22	—	42	2	11	—	4	—	.272	.304	.377	.965
1935	ChC-N	107	385	60	125	19	4	2	66	26	—	23	1	8	—	6	—	.325	.369	.410	.973
1936	ChC-N	154	605	93	212	34	3	16	96	49	—	30	1	17	—	4	—	.350	.400	.496	.968
1937	ChC-N	154	615	104	199	36	6	17	115	57	—	31	1	14	—	6	—	.324	.382	.485	.980
1938	ChC-N	129	476	63	130	15	7	8	62	45	—	34	4	7	—	1	—	.273	.341	.384	.972
1939	NYG-N	150	560	68	170	27	2	11	79	66	—	40	4	13	—	2	—	.304	.381	.418	.986
1940	NYG-N	121	460	68	139	18	6	7	61	45	—	39	0	16	—	5	—	.302	.364	.413	.980
1941	NYG-N	16	35	3	6	0	0	0	1	4	—	1	0	1	—	0	—	.171	.256	.171	1.000
1941	Bos-N	48	113	20	26	5	2	2	15	12	—	5	0	2	—	2	—	.230	.304	.363	1.000
1942	Bos-N	64	187	18	42	5	0	3	24	17	—	10	0	4	—	2	—	.225	.289	.299	1.000
1943	StL-N	39	86	5	25	2	0	0	9	8	—	4	0	3	—	1	—	.291	.351	.314	1.000
1944	StL-A	16	51	4	13	2	0	0	6	6	—	3	0	1	—	0	0	.255	.333	.294	.969
Career average		96	345	48	103	16	3	6	49	30	—	22	1	8	—	3	0	.299	.357	.415	.978
Cubs average		**117**	**442**	**65**	**137**	**22**	**4**	**8**	**66**	**34**	**—**	**28**	**2**	**10**	**—**	**4**	**—**	**.309**	**.360**	**.434**	**.972**
Career total		1155	4144	578	1241	190	36	72	591	359	—	269	14	99	—	33	0	.299	.357	.415	.978
Cubs total		**701**	**2652**	**392**	**820**	**131**	**26**	**49**	**396**	**201**	**—**	**167**	**10**	**59**	**—**	**21**	**—**	**.309**	**.360**	**.434**	**.972**

DeMontreville, Eugene Napoleon (Gene)
HEIGHT: 5'8"   THROWS: RIGHT   BATS: RIGHT   BORN: 3/26/1874 ST. PAUL, MINNESOTA   DIED: 2/18/1935 MEMPHIS, TENNESSEE
POSITIONS PLAYED: 1B, 2B, 3B, SS, OF

YEAR	TEAM	GAMES	AB	RUNS	HITS	2B	3B	HR	RBI	BB	IBB	SO	HBP	SH	SF	SB	CS	BA	OBA	SA	FA
1894	Pit-N	2	8	0	2	0	0	0	0	1	—	4	0	0	—	0	—	.250	.333	.250	.889
1895	Was-N	12	46	7	10	1	3	0	9	3	—	4	0	0	—	5	—	.217	.265	.370	.929
1896	Was-N	133	533	94	183	24	5	8	77	29	—	27	3	16	—	28	—	.343	.381	.452	.890
1897	Was-N	133	566	92	193	27	8	3	93	21	—	—	1	14	—	30	—	.341	.366	.433	.897
1898	Bal-N	151	567	93	186	19	2	0	86	52	—	—	10	12	—	49	—	.328	.394	.369	.934
1899	**ChN-N**	**82**	**310**	**43**	**87**	**6**	**3**	**0**	**40**	**17**	**—**	**—**	**5**	**14**	**—**	**26**	**—**	**.281**	**.328**	**.319**	**.902**
1899	Bal-N	60	240	40	67	13	4	1	36	10	—	—	2	5	—	21	—	.279	.313	.379	.961
1900	Bro-N	69	234	34	57	8	1	0	28	10	—	—	3	6	—	21	—	.244	.283	.286	.931
1901	Bos-N	140	577	83	173	14	4	5	72	17	—	—	1	24	—	25	—	.300	.321	.364	.942
1902	Bos-N	124	481	51	125	16	5	0	53	12	—	—	1	26	—	23	—	.260	.279	.314	.936
1903	Was-A	12	44	0	12	2	0	0	3	0	—	—	0	1	—	0	—	.273	.273	.318	.933
1904	StL-A	4	9	0	1	0	0	0	0	2	—	—	0	0	—	0	—	.111	.273	.111	1.000
Career average		84	329	49	100	12	3	2	45	16	—	3	2	11	—	21	—	.303	.340	.373	.921
Cubs average		**82**	**310**	**43**	**87**	**6**	**3**	**0**	**40**	**17**	**—**	**0**	**5**	**14**	**—**	**26**	**—**	**.281**	**.328**	**.319**	**.902**
Career total		922	3615	537	1096	130	35	17	497	174	—	35	26	118	—	228	—	.303	.340	.373	.921
Cubs total		**82**	**310**	**43**	**87**	**6**	**3**	**0**	**40**	**17**	**—**	**0**	**5**	**14**	**—**	**26**	**—**	**.281**	**.328**	**.319**	**.902**

Dernier, Robert Eugene (Bob)
HEIGHT: 6'0"   THROWS: RIGHT   BATS: RIGHT   BORN: 1/5/1957 KANSAS CITY, MISSOURI   POSITIONS PLAYED: OF

YEAR	TEAM	GAMES	AB	RUNS	HITS	2B	3B	HR	RBI	BB	IBB	SO	HBP	SH	SF	SB	CS	BA	OBA	SA	FA
1980	Phi-N	10	7	5	4	0	0	0	1	1	0	0	0	0	0	3	0	.571	.625	.571	1.000
1981	Phi-N	10	4	0	3	0	0	0	0	0	0	0	0	0	0	2	1	.750	.750	.750	1.000
1982	Phi-N	122	370	56	92	10	2	4	21	36	0	69	1	3	2	42	12	.249	.315	.319	.981
1983	Phi-N	122	221	41	51	10	0	1	15	18	0	21	0	5	1	35	7	.231	.288	.290	.988
1984	**ChC-N**	**143**	**536**	**94**	**149**	**26**	**5**	**3**	**32**	**63**	**0**	**60**	**2**	**11**	**0**	**45**	**17**	**.278**	**.356**	**.362**	**.986**
1985	**ChC-N**	**121**	**469**	**63**	**119**	**20**	**3**	**1**	**21**	**40**	**1**	**44**	**3**	**7**	**2**	**31**	**8**	**.254**	**.315**	**.316**	**.972**
1986	**ChC-N**	**108**	**324**	**32**	**73**	**14**	**1**	**4**	**18**	**22**	**1**	**41**	**0**	**5**	**0**	**27**	**2**	**.225**	**.275**	**.312**	**.987**
1987	**ChC-N**	**93**	**199**	**38**	**63**	**4**	**4**	**8**	**21**	**19**	**0**	**19**	**1**	**1**	**0**	**16**	**7**	**.317**	**.379**	**.497**	**.989**
1988	Phi-N	68	166	19	48	3	1	1	10	9	0	19	1	3	0	13	6	.289	.330	.337	.980
1989	Phi-N	107	187	26	32	5	0	1	13	14	0	28	0	1	3	4	3	.171	.225	.214	.970
Career average		90	248	37	63	9	2	2	15	22	0	30	1	4	1	22	6	.255	.318	.333	.982
Cubs average		**116**	**382**	**57**	**101**	**16**	**3**	**4**	**23**	**36**	**1**	**41**	**2**	**6**	**1**	**30**	**9**	**.264**	**.330**	**.355**	**.982**
Career total		904	2483	374	634	92	16	23	152	222	2	301	8	36	8	218	63	.255	.318	.333	.982
Cubs total		**465**	**1528**	**227**	**404**	**64**	**13**	**16**	**92**	**144**	**2**	**164**	**6**	**24**	**2**	**119**	**34**	**.264**	**.330**	**.355**	**.982**

Derrick, Claud Lester (Deek)
HEIGHT: 6'0"   THROWS: RIGHT   BATS: RIGHT   BORN: 6/11/1886 BURTON, GEORGIA   DIED: 7/15/1974 CLAYTON, GEORGIA   POSITIONS PLAYED: 1B, 2B, 3B, SS

YEAR	TEAM	GAMES	AB	RUNS	HITS	2B	3B	HR	RBI	BB	IBB	SO	HBP	SH	SF	SB	CS	BA	OBA	SA	FA
1910	Phi-A	2	1	0	0	0	0	0	0	0	—	—	0	0	—	0	—	.000	.000	.000	.500
1911	Phi-A	36	100	14	23	1	2	0	5	7	—	—	2	7	—	7	—	.230	.294	.280	.972
1912	Phi-A	21	58	7	14	0	1	0	7	5	—	—	1	3	—	1	—	.241	.313	.276	.884
1913	NYY-A	22	65	7	19	1	0	1	7	5	—	8	1	0	—	2	—	.292	.352	.354	.872
1914	Cin-N	3	6	2	2	1	0	0	1	0	—	0	0	0	—	1	—	.333	.333	.500	.889
1914	**ChC-N**	**28**	**96**	**5**	**21**	**3**	**1**	**0**	**13**	**5**	**—**	**13**	**0**	**3**	**—**	**2**	**—**	**.219**	**.257**	**.271**	**.895**
Career average		22	65	7	16	1	1	0	7	4	—	4	1	3	—	3	—	.242	.298	.294	.908
Cubs average		**28**	**96**	**5**	**21**	**3**	**1**	**0**	**13**	**5**	**—**	**13**	**0**	**3**	**—**	**2**	**—**	**.219**	**.257**	**.271**	**.895**
Career total		112	326	35	79	6	4	1	33	22	—	21	4	13	—	13	—	.242	.298	.294	.908
Cubs total		**28**	**96**	**5**	**21**	**3**	**1**	**0**	**13**	**5**	**—**	**13**	**0**	**3**	**—**	**2**	**—**	**.219**	**.257**	**.271**	**.895**

DeShields, Delino Lamont
HEIGHT: 6'1" THROWS: RIGHT BATS: LEFT BORN: 1/15/1969 SEAFORD, DELAWARE POSITIONS PLAYED: 1B, 2B, 3B, SS, OF

YEAR	TEAM	GAMES	AB	RUNS	HITS	2B	3B	HR	RBI	BB	IBB	SO	HBP	SH	SF	SB	CS	BA	OBA	SA	FA
1990	Mon-N	129	499	69	144	28	6	4	45	66	3	96	4	1	2	42	22	.289	.375	.393	.981
1991	Mon-N	151	563	83	134	15	4	10	51	95	2	151	2	8	5	56	23	.238	.347	.332	.962
1992	Mon-N	135	530	82	155	19	8	7	56	54	4	108	3	9	3	46	15	.292	.359	.398	.976
1993	Mon-N	123	481	75	142	17	7	2	29	72	3	64	3	4	2	43	10	.295	.389	.372	.983
1994	LA-N	89	320	51	80	11	3	2	33	54	0	53	0	1	1	27	7	.250	.357	.322	.984
1995	LA-N	127	425	66	109	18	3	8	37	63	4	83	1	3	1	39	14	.256	.353	.369	.980
1996	LA-N	154	581	75	130	12	8	5	41	53	7	124	1	2	5	48	11	.224	.288	.298	.975
1997	StL-N	150	572	92	169	26	14	11	58	55	1	72	3	7	6	55	14	.295	.357	.448	.972
1998	StL-N	117	420	74	122	21	8	7	44	56	2	61	0	4	4	26	10	.290	.371	.429	.983
1999	Bal-A	96	330	46	87	11	2	6	34	37	0	52	1	5	1	11	8	.264	.339	.364	.977
2000	Bal-A	151	561	84	166	43	5	10	86	69	2	82	1	3	9	37	10	.296	.369	.444	.975
2001	Bal-A	58	188	29	37	8	2	3	21	31	1	42	1	1	1	11	1	.197	.312	.309	.967
2001	**ChC-N**	**68**	**163**	**26**	**45**	**9**	**3**	**2**	**16**	**28**	**0**	**35**	**0**	**3**	**1**	**12**	**1**	**.276**	**.380**	**.405**	**.969**
Career average		129	469	71	127	20	6	6	46	61	2	85	2	4	3	38	12	.270	.354	.379	.976
Cubs average		**68**	**163**	**26**	**45**	**9**	**3**	**2**	**16**	**28**	**0**	**35**	**0**	**3**	**1**	**12**	**1**	**.276**	**.380**	**.405**	**.969**
Career total		1548	5633	852	1520	238	73	77	551	733	29	1023	20	51	41	453	146	.270	.354	.379	.976
Cubs total		**68**	**163**	**26**	**45**	**9**	**3**	**2**	**16**	**28**	**0**	**35**	**0**	**3**	**1**	**12**	**1**	**.276**	**.380**	**.405**	**.969**

Dexter, Charles Dana (Charlie)
HEIGHT: 5'7" THROWS: RIGHT BATS: RIGHT BORN: 6/15/1876 EVANSVILLE, INDIANA DIED: 6/9/1934 CEDAR RAPIDS, IOWA
POSITIONS PLAYED: C, 1B, 2B, 3B, SS, OF

YEAR	TEAM	GAMES	AB	RUNS	HITS	2B	3B	HR	RBI	BB	IBB	SO	HBP	SH	SF	SB	CS	BA	OBA	SA	FA
1896	Lou-N	107	402	65	112	18	7	3	37	17	—	34	6	2	—	21	—	.279	.318	.381	.901
1897	Lou-N	76	257	43	72	12	5	2	46	21	—	—	3	2	—	12	—	.280	.342	.389	.881
1898	Lou-N	112	421	76	132	13	5	1	66	26	—	—	7	13	—	44	—	.314	.363	.375	.954
1899	Lou-N	80	295	47	76	7	1	1	33	21	—	—	5	20	—	21	—	.258	.318	.298	.915
1900	**ChN-N**	**40**	**125**	**7**	**25**	**5**	**0**	**2**	**20**	**1**	**—**	**—**	**1**	**3**	**—**	**2**	**—**	**.200**	**.213**	**.288**	**.957**
1901	**ChN-N**	**116**	**460**	**46**	**123**	**9**	**5**	**1**	**66**	**16**	**—**	**—**	**7**	**5**	**—**	**22**	**—**	**.267**	**.302**	**.315**	**.965**
1902	**ChC-N**	**69**	**266**	**30**	**60**	**12**	**0**	**2**	**26**	**19**	**—**	**—**	**5**	**15**	**—**	**13**	**—**	**.226**	**.290**	**.293**	**.933**
1902	Bos-N	48	183	33	47	3	0	1	18	16	—	—	2	6	—	16	—	.257	.323	.290	.922
1903	Bos-N	123	457	82	102	15	1	3	34	61	—	—	6	12	—	32	—	.223	.323	.280	.927
Career average		96	358	54	94	12	3	2	43	25	—	4	5	10	—	23	—	.261	.318	.328	.934
Cubs average		**75**	**284**	**28**	**69**	**9**	**2**	**2**	**37**	**12**	**—**	**0**	**4**	**8**	**—**	**12**	**—**	**.244**	**.286**	**.304**	**.954**
Career total		771	2866	429	749	94	24	16	346	198	—	34	42	78	—	183	—	.261	.318	.328	.934
Cubs total		**225**	**851**	**83**	**208**	**26**	**5**	**5**	**112**	**36**	**—**	**0**	**13**	**23**	**—**	**37**	**—**	**.244**	**.286**	**.304**	**.954**

Diaz, Michael Anthony (Mike or Rambo)
HEIGHT: 6'2" THROWS: RIGHT BATS: RIGHT BORN: 4/15/1960 SAN FRANCISCO, CALIFORNIA POSITIONS PLAYED: C, 1B, 3B, OF

YEAR	TEAM	GAMES	AB	RUNS	HITS	2B	3B	HR	RBI	BB	IBB	SO	HBP	SH	SF	SB	CS	BA	OBA	SA	FA
1983	**ChC-N**	**6**	**7**	**2**	**2**	**1**	**0**	**0**	**1**	**0**	**0**	**0**	**0**	**0**	**0**	**0**	**0**	**.286**	**.286**	**.429**	**1.000**
1986	Pit-N	97	209	22	56	9	0	12	36	19	0	43	2	0	3	0	1	.268	.330	.483	.986
1987	Pit-N	103	241	28	58	8	2	16	48	31	3	42	3	0	7	1	0	.241	.326	.490	.982
1988	Pit-N	47	74	6	17	3	0	0	5	16	1	13	0	0	0	0	0	.230	.367	.270	1.000
1988	CWS-A	40	152	12	36	6	0	3	12	5	0	30	1	0	0	0	1	.237	.266	.336	.987
Career average		73	171	18	42	7	1	8	26	18	1	32	2	0	3	0	1	.247	.319	.429	.986
Cubs average		**6**	**7**	**2**	**2**	**1**	**0**	**0**	**1**	**0**	**0**	**0**	**0**	**0**	**0**	**0**	**0**	**.286**	**.286**	**.429**	**1.000**
Career total		293	683	70	169	27	2	31	102	71	4	128	6	0	10	1	2	.247	.319	.429	.986
Cubs total		**6**	**7**	**2**	**2**	**1**	**0**	**0**	**1**	**0**	**0**	**0**	**0**	**0**	**0**	**0**	**0**	**.286**	**.286**	**.429**	**1.000**

Dillard, Stephen Bradley (Steve)
HEIGHT: 6'1" THROWS: RIGHT BATS: RIGHT BORN: 2/8/1951 MEMPHIS, TENNESSEE POSITIONS PLAYED: 2B, 3B, SS

YEAR	TEAM	GAMES	AB	RUNS	HITS	2B	3B	HR	RBI	BB	IBB	SO	HBP	SH	SF	SB	CS	BA	OBA	SA	FA
1975	Bos-A	1	5	2	2	0	0	0	0	0	0	0	0	0	0	0	0	.400	.400	.400	1.000
1976	Bos-A	57	167	22	46	14	0	1	15	17	1	20	0	2	1	6	4	.275	.341	.377	.936
1977	Bos-A	66	141	22	34	7	0	1	13	7	0	13	0	2	4	4	3	.241	.270	.312	.972
1978	Det-A	56	130	21	29	5	2	0	7	6	0	11	0	7	0	1	2	.223	.257	.422	.984
1979	**ChC-N**	**89**	**166**	**31**	**47**	**6**	**1**	**5**	**24**	**17**	**4**	**24**	**1**	**5**	**1**	**1**	**0**	**.283**	**.351**		

(continued)

(continued)

YEAR	TEAM	GAMES	AB	RUNS	HITS	2B	3B	HR	RBI	BB	IBB	SO	HBP	SH	SF	SB	CS	BA	OBA	SA	FA
1980	ChC-N	100	244	31	55	8	1	4	27	20	2	54	1	0	2	2	2	.225	.285	.316	.949
1981	ChC-N	53	119	18	26	7	1	2	11	8	0	20	0	0	0	0	0	.218	.268	.345	.963
1982	CWS-A	16	41	1	7	3	1	0	5	1	0	5	0	0	0	0	1	.171	.190	.293	.959
Career average		55	127	19	31	6	1	2	13	10	1	18	0	2	1	2	2	.243	.295	.343	.962
Cubs average		81	176	27	43	7	1	4	21	15	2	33	1	2	1	1	1	.242	.302	.355	.965
Career total		438	1013	148	246	50	6	13	102	76	7	147	2	16	8	15	12	.243	.295	.343	.962
Cubs total		242	529	80	128	21	3	11	62	45	6	98	2	5	3	3	2	.242	.302	.355	.965

Dillhoefer, William Martin (Pickles)

HEIGHT: 5'7" THROWS: RIGHT BATS: RIGHT BORN: 10/13/1894 CLEVELAND, OHIO DIED: 2/23/1922 ST. LOUIS, MISSOURI POSITIONS PLAYED: C

YEAR	TEAM	GAMES	AB	RUNS	HITS	2B	3B	HR	RBI	BB	IBB	SO	HBP	SH	SF	SB	CS	BA	OBA	SA	FA
1917	ChC-N	42	95	3	12	1	1	0	8	2	—	9	0	7	—	1	—	.126	.144	.158	.985
1918	Phi-N	8	11	0	1	0	0	0	0	1	—	1	0	0	—	2	—	.091	.167	.091	.923
1919	StL-N	45	108	11	23	3	2	0	12	8	—	6	0	3	—	5	—	.213	.267	.278	.969
1920	StL-N	76	224	26	59	8	3	0	13	13	—	7	0	3	—	2	1	.263	.304	.326	.953
1921	StL-N	76	162	19	39	4	4	0	15	11	—	7	0	2	—	2	1	.241	.289	.315	.953
Career average		49	120	12	27	3	2	0	10	7	—	6	0	3	—	2	0	.223	.266	.283	.962
Cubs average		42	95	3	12	1	1	0	8	2	—	9	0	7	—	1	—	.126	.144	.158	.985
Career total		247	600	59	134	16	10	0	48	35	—	30	0	15	—	12	2	.223	.266	.283	.962
Cubs total		42	95	3	12	1	1	0	8	2	—	9	0	7	—	1	—	.126	.144	.158	.985

Dilone, Miguel Angel

HEIGHT: 6'0" THROWS: RIGHT BATS: BOTH BORN: 11/1/1954 SANTIAGO, DOMINICAN REPUBLIC POSITIONS PLAYED: 3B, OF

YEAR	TEAM	GAMES	AB	RUNS	HITS	2B	3B	HR	RBI	BB	IBB	SO	HBP	SH	SF	SB	CS	BA	OBA	SA	FA
1974	Pit-N	12	2	3	0	0	0	0	0	1	0	0	0	0	0	2	0	.000	.333	.000	1.000
1975	Pit-N	18	6	8	0	0	0	0	0	0	0	1	0	0	0	2	2	.000	.000	.000	1.000
1976	Pit-N	16	17	7	4	0	0	0	0	0	0	0	0	0	0	5	1	.235	.235	.235	1.000
1977	Pit-N	29	44	5	6	0	0	0	0	2	0	3	0	3	0	12	0	.136	.174	.136	1.000
1978	Oak-A	135	258	34	59	8	0	1	14	23	0	30	1	10	0	50	23	.229	.294	.271	.976
1979	Oak-A	30	91	15	17	1	2	1	6	6	0	7	0	2	0	6	5	.187	.237	.275	.959
1979	**ChC-N**	43	36	14	11	0	0	0	1	2	0	5	0	0	0	15	5	.306	.342	.306	1.000
1980	Cle-A	132	528	82	180	30	9	0	40	28	1	45	2	6	2	61	18	.341	.375	.432	.973
1981	Cle-A	72	269	33	78	5	5	0	19	18	1	28	0	2	0	29	10	.290	.334	.346	.971
1982	Cle-A	104	379	50	89	12	3	3	25	25	1	36	2	6	0	33	5	.235	.286	.306	.964
1983	Cle-A	32	68	15	13	3	1	0	7	10	0	5	0	0	0	5	1	.191	.295	.265	1.000
1983	CWS-A	4	3	1	0	0	0	0	0	0	0	0	0	0	0	1	0	.000	.000	.000	1.000
1983	Pit-N	7	0	1	0	0	0	0	0	0	0	0	0	0	0	2	0	—	—	—	—
1984	Mon-N	88	169	28	47	8	2	1	10	17	0	18	1	1	1	27	2	.278	.346	.367	.987
1985	Mon-N	51	84	10	16	0	2	0	6	6	0	11	0	0	1	7	3	.190	.242	.238	.974
1985	SD-N	27	46	8	10	0	1	0	1	4	0	8	0	0	1	10	3	.217	.280	.261	.917
Career average		67	167	26	44	6	2	1	11	12	0	16	1	3	0	22	7	.265	.315	.333	.974
Cubs average		43	36	14	11	0	0	0	1	2	0	5	0	0	0	15	5	.306	.342	.306	1.000
Career total		800	2000	314	530	67	25	6	129	142	2	197	6	30	4	267	78	.265	.315	.333	.974
Cubs total		43	36	14	11	0	0	0	1	2	0	5	0	0	0	15	5	.306	.342	.306	1.000

Dobbs, John Gordon

HEIGHT: 5'9" THROWS: RIGHT BATS: LEFT BORN: 6/3/1875 CHATTANOOGA, TENNESSEE DIED: 9/9/1934 CHARLOTTE, NORTH CAROLINA
POSITIONS PLAYED: 2B, 3B, SS, OF

YEAR	TEAM	GAMES	AB	RUNS	HITS	2B	3B	HR	RBI	BB	IBB	SO	HBP	SH	SF	SB	CS	BA	OBA	SA	FA
1901	Cin-N	109	435	71	119	17	4	2	27	36	—	—	6	11	—	19	—	.274	.338	.345	.928
1902	Cin-N	63	256	39	76	7	3	1	16	19	—	—	1	16	—	7	—	.297	.348	.359	.963
1902	**ChC-N**	59	235	31	71	8	2	0	35	18	—	—	0	10	—	3	—	.302	.352	.353	.977
1903	**ChC-N**	16	61	8	14	1	1	0	4	7	—	—	2	3	—	0	—	.230	.329	.279	1.000
1903	Bro-N	111	414	61	98	15	7	2	59	48	—	—	5	13	—	23	—	.237	.323	.321	.966
1904	Bro-N	101	363	36	90	16	2	0	30	28	—	—	1	11	—	11	—	.248	.304	.303	.934
1905	Bro-N	123	460	59	117	21	4	2	36	31	—	—	2	14	—	15	—	.254	.304	.330	.938
Career average		116	445	61	117	17	5	1	41	37	—	—	3	16	—	16	—	.263	.325	.331	.949
Cubs average		38	148	20	43	5	2	0	20	13	—	—	1	7	—	2	—	.287	.347	.338	.982
Career total		582	2224	305	585	85	23	7	207	187	—	—	17	78	—	78	—	.263	.325	.331	.949
Cubs total		75	296	39	85	9	3	0	39	25	—	—	2	13	—	3	—	.287	.347	.338	.982

Dolan, Patrick Henry (Cozy)

HEIGHT: 5'10" THROWS: LEFT BATS: LEFT BORN: 12/3/1872 CAMBRIDGE, MASSACHUSETTS DIED: 3/29/1907 LOUISVILLE, KENTUCKY
POSITIONS PLAYED: P, 1B, 2B, OF

YEAR	TEAM	GAMES	AB	RUNS	HITS	2B	3B	HR	RBI	BB	IBB	SO	HBP	SH	SF	SB	CS	BA	OBA	SA	FA
1892	Was-N	5	13	1	3	0	0	0	1	2	—	5	0	—	—	0	—	.231	.333	.231	1.000
1895	Bos-N	26	83	12	20	4	1	0	7	6	—	7	1	1	—	3	—	.241	.300	.313	.938
1896	Bos-N	6	14	4	2	0	0	0	0	0	—	1	0	2	—	0	—	.143	.143	.143	.765
1900	**ChN-N**	**13**	**48**	**5**	**13**	**1**	**0**	**0**	**2**	**2**	—	—	**0**	**0**	—	**2**	—	**.271**	**.300**	**.292**	**.826**
1901	**ChN-N**	**43**	**171**	**29**	**45**	**1**	**2**	**0**	**16**	**7**	—	—	**1**	**1**	—	**3**	—	**.263**	**.296**	**.292**	**.878**
1901	Bro-N	66	253	33	66	11	1	0	29	17	—	—	2	4	—	7	—	.261	.313	.312	.967
1902	Bro-N	141	592	72	166	16	7	1	54	33	—	—	5	10	—	24	—	.280	.324	.336	.936
1903	CWS-A	27	104	16	27	5	1	0	7	6	—	—	2	0	—	5	—	.260	.313	.327	.969
1903	Cin-N	93	385	64	111	20	3	0	58	28	—	—	2	7	—	11	—	.288	.340	.356	.937
1904	Cin-N	129	465	88	132	8	10	6	51	39	—	—	2	16	—	19	—	.284	.342	.383	.960
1905	Cin-N	22	77	7	18	2	1	0	4	7	—	—	1	2	—	2	—	.234	.306	.286	.942
1905	Bos-N	112	433	44	119	11	7	3	48	27	—	—	3	9	—	21	—	.275	.322	.353	.945
1906	Bos-N	152	549	54	136	20	4	0	39	55	—	—	2	13	—	17	—	.248	.318	.299	.923
Career average		84	319	43	86	10	4	1	32	23	—	1	2	7	—	11	—	.269	.322	.333	.942
Cubs average		**28**	**110**	**17**	**29**	**1**	**1**	**0**	**9**	**5**	—	**0**	**1**	**1**	—	**3**	—	**.265**	**.297**	**.292**	**.867**
Career total		835	3187	429	858	99	37	10	316	229	—	13	21	65	—	114	—	.269	.322	.333	.942
Cubs total		**56**	**219**	**34**	**58**	**2**	**2**	**0**	**18**	**9**	—	**0**	**1**	**1**	—	**5**	—	**.265**	**.297**	**.292**	**.867**

Dolan, Thomas J. (Tom)

HEIGHT: 5'11" THROWS: RIGHT BATS: RIGHT BORN: 1/10/1859 NEW YORK, NEW YORK DIED: 1/16/1913 ST. LOUIS, MISSOURI
POSITIONS PLAYED: P, C, 3B, OF

YEAR	TEAM	GAMES	AB	RUNS	HITS	2B	3B	HR	RBI	BB	IBB	SO	HBP	SH	SF	SB	CS	BA	OBA	SA	FA
1879	**ChN-N**	**1**	**4**	**0**	**0**	**0**	**0**	**0**	**0**	**0**	—	**2**	—	—	—	—	—	**.000**	**.000**	**.000**	**1.000**
1882	Buf-N	22	89	12	14	0	1	0	8	2	—	11	—	—	—	—	—	.157	.176	.180	.926
1883	StL-AA	81	295	32	63	9	2	1	18	9	—	—	—	—	—	—	—	.214	.237	.268	.935
1884	StL-AA	35	137	19	36	6	2	0	—	6	—	—	1	—	—	—	—	.263	.299	.336	.871
1884	StL-U	19	69	9	13	3	0	0	—	4	—	—	—	—	—	—	—	.188	.233	.232	.883
1885	StL-N	3	9	1	2	0	0	0	0	2	—	1	—	—	—	—	—	.222	.364	.222	.810
1886	StL-N	15	44	8	11	3	0	0	1	7	—	9	—	—	—	2	—	.250	.353	.318	.928
1886	Bal-AA	38	125	13	19	3	2	0	12	8	—	—	0	—	—	8	—	.152	.203	.208	.918
1888	StL-AA	11	36	1	7	1	0	0	1	1	—	—	0	—	—	1	—	.194	.216	.222	.914
Career average		32	115	14	24	4	1	0	6	6	—	3	0	—	—	2	—	.204	.242	.256	.909
Cubs average		**1**	**4**	**0**	**0**	**0**	**0**	**0**	**0**	**0**	—	**2**	—	—	—	—	—	**.000**	**.000**	**.000**	**1.000**
Career total		225	808	95	165	25	7	1	40	39	—	23	1	—	—	11	—	.204	.242	.256	.909
Cubs total		**1**	**4**	**0**	**0**	**0**	**0**	**0**	**0**	**0**	—	**2**	—	—	—	—	—	**.000**	**.000**	**.000**	**1.000**

Donahue, Timothy Cornelius (Tim *or* Bridget)

HEIGHT: 5'11" THROWS: RIGHT BATS: LEFT BORN: 6/8/1870 RAYNHAM, MASSACHUSETTS DIED: 6/12/1902 TAUNTON, MASSACHUSETTS
POSITIONS PLAYED: C, 1B, 2B, SS

YEAR	TEAM	GAMES	AB	RUNS	HITS	2B	3B	HR	RBI	BB	IBB	SO	HBP	SH	SF	SB	CS	BA	OBA	SA	FA
1891	Bos-AA	4	7	0	0	0	0	0	0	0	—	5	0	—	—	0	—	.000	.000	.000	.833
1895	**ChN-N**	**63**	**219**	**29**	**59**	**9**	**1**	**2**	**36**	**20**	—	**25**	**3**	**3**	—	**5**	—	**.269**	**.339**	**.347**	**.915**
1896	**ChN-N**	**57**	**188**	**27**	**41**	**10**	**1**	**0**	**20**	**11**	—	**15**	**4**	**4**	—	**11**	—	**.218**	**.276**	**.282**	**.937**
1897	**ChN-N**	**58**	**188**	**28**	**45**	**7**	**3**	**0**	**21**	**9**	—	—	**2**	**4**	—	**3**	—	**.239**	**.281**	**.309**	**.945**
1898	**ChN-N**	**122**	**396**	**52**	**87**	**12**	**3**	**0**	**39**	**49**	—	—	**8**	**12**	—	**17**	—	**.220**	**.318**	**.265**	**.962**
1899	**ChN-N**	**92**	**278**	**39**	**69**	**9**	**3**	**0**	**29**	**34**	—	—	**7**	**15**	—	**10**	—	**.248**	**.345**	**.302**	**.951**
1900	**ChN-N**	**67**	**216**	**21**	**51**	**10**	**1**	**0**	**17**	**19**	—	—	**5**	**6**	—	**8**	—	**.236**	**.313**	**.292**	**.925**
1902	Was-A	3	8	0	2	0	0	0	1	0	—	—	0	0	—	0	—	.250	.250	.250	1.000
Career average		58	188	25	44	7	2	0	20	18	—	6	4	6	—	7	—	.236	.314	.294	.942
Cubs average		**77**	**248**	**33**	**59**	**10**	**2**	**0**	**27**	**24**	—	**7**	**5**	**7**	—	**9**	—	**.237**	**.316**	**.296**	**.942**
Career total		466	1500	196	354	57	12	2	163	142	—	45	29	44	—	54	—	.236	.314	.294	.942
Cubs total		**459**	**1485**	**196**	**352**	**57**	**12**	**2**	**162**	**142**	—	**40**	**29**	**44**	—	**54**	—	**.237**	**.316**	**.296**	**.942**

Doolan, Michael Joseph (Mickey *or* Doc)
HEIGHT: 5'10"   THROWS: RIGHT   BATS: RIGHT   BORN: 5/7/1880 ASHLAND, PENNSYLVANIA   DIED: 11/1/1951 ORLANDO, FLORIDA   POSITIONS PLAYED: 2B, SS

YEAR	TEAM	GAMES	AB	RUNS	HITS	2B	3B	HR	RBI	BB	IBB	SO	HBP	SH	SF	SB	CS	BA	OBA	SA	FA
1905	Phi-N	136	492	53	125	27	11	1	48	24	—	—	2	6	—	17	—	.254	.292	.360	.935
1906	Phi-N	154	535	41	123	19	7	1	55	27	—	—	2	22	—	16	—	.230	.270	.297	.930
1907	Phi-N	145	509	33	104	19	7	1	47	25	—	—	1	9	—	18	—	.204	.243	.275	.929
1908	Phi-N	129	445	29	104	25	4	2	49	17	—	—	3	19	—	5	—	.234	.267	.321	.939
1909	Phi-N	147	493	39	108	12	10	1	35	37	—	—	2	24	—	10	—	.219	.276	.290	.939
1910	Phi-N	148	536	58	141	31	6	2	57	35	—	56	6	12	—	16	—	.263	.315	.354	.948
1911	Phi-N	146	512	51	122	23	6	1	49	44	—	65	2	16	—	14	—	.238	.301	.313	.936
1912	Phi-N	146	532	47	137	26	6	1	62	34	—	59	0	21	—	6	—	.258	.302	.335	.950
1913	Phi-N	151	518	32	113	12	6	1	43	29	—	68	2	19	—	17	—	.218	.262	.270	.942
1914	Bal-F	145	486	58	119	23	6	1	53	40	—	47	7	26	—	30	—	.245	.311	.323	.949
1915	Bal-F	119	404	41	75	13	7	2	21	24	—	39	4	21	—	10	—	.186	.238	.267	.946
1915	Chi-F	24	86	9	23	1	1	.0	9	2	—	7	1	2	—	5	—	.267	.292	.302	.914
1916	**ChC-N**	**28**	**70**	**4**	**15**	**2**	**1**	**0**	**5**	**8**	**—**	**7**	**0**	**4**	**—**	**0**	**—**	**.214**	**.295**	**.271**	**.918**
1916	NYG-N	18	51	4	12	3	1	1	3	2	—	4	0	3	—	1	—	.235	.264	.392	.963
1918	Bro-N	92	308	14	55	8	2	0	18	22	—	24	0	13	—	8	—	.179	.233	.218	.968
Career average		133	460	39	106	19	6	1	43	28	—	29	2	17	—	13	—	.230	.279	.306	.941
Cubs average		**28**	**70**	**4**	**15**	**2**	**1**	**0**	**5**	**8**	**—**	**7**	**0**	**4**	**—**	**0**	**—**	**.214**	**.295**	**.271**	**.918**
Career total		1728	5977	513	1376	244	81	15	554	370	—	376	32	217	—	173	—	.230	.279	.306	.941
Cubs total		**28**	**70**	**4**	**15**	**2**	**1**	**0**	**5**	**8**	**—**	**7**	**0**	**4**	**—**	**0**	**—**	**.214**	**.295**	**.271**	**.918**

Dorsett, Brian Richard
HEIGHT: 6'4"   THROWS: RIGHT   BATS: RIGHT   BORN: 4/9/1961 TERRE HAUTE, INDIANA   POSITIONS PLAYED: C, 1B

YEAR	TEAM	GAMES	AB	RUNS	HITS	2B	3B	HR	RBI	BB	IBB	SO	HBP	SH	SF	SB	CS	BA	OBA	SA	FA
1987	Cle-A	5	11	2	3	0	0	1	3	0	0	3	1	0	0	0	0	.273	.333	.545	1.000
1988	Cal-A	7	11	0	1	0	0	0	2	1	0	5	0	0	0	0	0	.091	.167	.091	1.000
1989	NYY-A	8	22	3	8	1	0	0	4	1	0	3	0	0	0	0	0	.364	.391	.409	1.000
1990	NYY-A	14	35	2	5	2	0	0	0	2	0	4	0	0	0	0	0	.143	.189	.200	1.000
1991	SD-N	11	12	0	1	0	0	0	1	0	0	3	0	0	0	0	0	.083	.083	.083	1.000
1993	Cin-N	25	63	7	16	4	0	2	12	3	0	14	0	0	0	0	0	.254	.288	.413	1.000
1994	Cin-N	76	216	21	53	8	0	5	26	21	7	33	1	1	2	0	0	.245	.313	.352	.991
1996	**ChC-N**	**17**	**41**	**3**	**5**	**0**	**0**	**1**	**3**	**4**	**0**	**8**	**0**	**0**	**1**	**0**	**0**	**.122**	**.196**	**.195**	**1.000**
Career average		20	51	5	12	2	0	1	6	4	1	9	0	0	0	0	0	.224	.281	.326	.995
Cubs average		**17**	**41**	**3**	**5**	**0**	**0**	**1**	**3**	**4**	**0**	**8**	**0**	**0**	**1**	**0**	**0**	**.122**	**.196**	**.195**	**1.000**
Career total		163	411	38	92	15	0	9	51	32	7	73	2	1	3	0	0	.224	.281	.326	.995
Cubs total		**17**	**41**	**3**	**5**	**0**	**0**	**1**	**3**	**4**	**0**	**8**	**0**	**0**	**1**	**0**	**0**	**.122**	**.196**	**.195**	**1.000**

Doscher, John Henry (Herm)
HEIGHT: 5'10"   THROWS: RIGHT   BATS: RIGHT   BORN: 12/20/1852 NEW YORK, NEW YORK   DIED: 3/20/1934 BUFFALO, NEW YORK
POSITIONS PLAYED: 3B, SS, OF

YEAR	TEAM	GAMES	AB	RUNS	HITS	2B	3B	HR	RBI	BB	IBB	SO	HBP	SH	SF	SB	CS	BA	OBA	SA	FA
1879	Try-N	47	191	16	42	8	0	0	18	2	—	10	—	—	—	—	—	.220	.228	.262	.806
1879	**ChN-N**	**3**	**11**	**1**	**2**	**0**	**0**	**0**	**1**	**0**	**—**	**3**	**—**	**—**	**—**	**—**	**—**	**.182**	**.182**	**.182**	**.700**
1881	Cle-N	5	19	2	4	0	0	0	0	0	—	2	—	—	—	—	—	.211	.211	.211	.895
1882	Cle-N	25	104	7	25	2	0	0	10	0	—	11	—	—	—	—	—	.240	.240	.260	.865
Career average		27	108	9	24	3	0	0	10	1	—	9	—	—	—	—	—	.225	.229	.255	.826
Cubs average		**3**	**11**	**1**	**2**	**0**	**0**	**0**	**1**	**0**	**—**	**3**	**—**	**—**	**—**	**—**	**—**	**.182**	**.182**	**.182**	**.700**
Career total		80	325	26	73	10	0	0	29	2	—	26	—	—	—	—	—	.225	.229	.255	.826
Cubs total		**3**	**11**	**1**	**2**	**0**	**0**	**0**	**1**	**0**	**—**	**3**	**—**	**—**	**—**	**—**	**—**	**.182**	**.182**	**.182**	**.700**

Douthit, Taylor Lee (Ball Hawk)
HEIGHT: 5'11"   THROWS: RIGHT   BATS: RIGHT   BORN: 4/22/1901 LITTLE ROCK, ARKANSAS   DIED: 5/28/1986 FREMONT, CALIFORNIA   POSITIONS PLAYED: OF

YEAR	TEAM	GAMES	AB	RUNS	HITS	2B	3B	HR	RBI	BB	IBB	SO	HBP	SH	SF	SB	CS	BA	OBA	SA	FA
1923	StL-N	9	27	3	5	0	2	0	0	0	—	4	0	0	—	1	0	.185	.185	.333	1.000
1924	StL-N	53	173	24	48	13	1	0	13	16	—	19	3	9	—	4	3	.277	.349	.364	.976
1925	StL-N	30	73	13	20	3	1	1	8	2	—	6	2	3	—	0	0	.274	.312	.384	.981
1926	StL-N	139	530	96	163	20	4	3	52	55	—	46	2	37	—	23	—	.308	.375	.377	.958
1927	StL-N	130	488	81	128	29	6	5	50	52	—	45	2	13	—	6	—	.262	.336	.377	.964

(continued)

(Douthit, continued)

YEAR	TEAM	GAMES	AB	RUNS	HITS	2B	3B	HR	RBI	BB	IBB	SO	HBP	SH	SF	SB	CS	BA	OBA	SA	FA
1928	StL-N	154	648	111	191	35	3	3	43	84	—	36	10	10	—	11	—	.295	.384	.372	.984
1929	StL-N	150	613	128	206	42	7	9	62	79	—	49	5	11	—	8	—	.336	.416	.471	.974
1930	StL-N	154	664	109	201	41	10	7	93	60	—	38	4	20	—	4	—	.303	.364	.426	.964
1931	StL-N	36	133	21	44	11	2	1	21	11	—	9	1	4	—	1	—	.331	.386	.466	.972
1931	Cin-N	95	374	42	98	9	1	0	24	42	—	24	2	5	—	4	—	.262	.340	.291	.983
1932	Cin-N	96	333	28	81	12	1	0	25	31	—	29	2	9	—	3	—	.243	.311	.285	.985
1933	Cin-N	1	0	1	0	0	0	0	0	0	—	0	0	0	—	0	—	—	—	—	—
1933	**ChC-N**	**27**	**71**	**8**	**16**	**5**	**0**	**0**	**5**	**11**	**—**	**7**	**0**	**3**	**—**	**2**	**—**	**.225**	**.329**	**.296**	**.930**
Career average		98	375	60	109	20	3	3	36	40	—	28	3	11	—	6	0	.291	.364	.384	.972
Cubs average		**27**	**71**	**8**	**16**	**5**	**0**	**0**	**5**	**11**	**—**	**7**	**0**	**3**	**—**	**2**	**0**	**.225**	**.329**	**.296**	**.930**
Career total		1074	4127	665	1201	220	38	29	396	443	—	312	33	124	—	67	3	.291	.364	.384	.972
Cubs total		**27**	**71**	**8**	**16**	**5**	**0**	**0**	**5**	**11**	**—**	**7**	**0**	**3**	**—**	**2**	**0**	**.225**	**.329**	**.296**	**.930**

Downey, Thomas Edward (Tom)
HEIGHT: 5'10" THROWS: RIGHT BATS: RIGHT BORN: 1/1/1884 LEWISTON, MAINE DIED: 8/3/1961 PASSAIC, NEW JERSEY
POSITIONS PLAYED: C, 1B, 2B, 3B, SS, OF

YEAR	TEAM	GAMES	AB	RUNS	HITS	2B	3B	HR	RBI	BB	IBB	SO	HBP	SH	SF	SB	CS	BA	OBA	SA	FA
1909	Cin-N	119	416	39	96	9	6	1	32	32	—	—	1	19	—	16	—	.231	.287	.288	.909
1910	Cin-N	111	378	43	102	9	3	2	32	34	—	28	3	17	—	12	—	.270	.335	.325	.889
1911	Cin-N	111	360	50	94	16	7	0	36	44	—	38	2	10	—	10	—	.261	.345	.344	.907
1912	Phi-N	54	171	27	50	6	3	1	23	21	—	20	0	15	—	3	—	.292	.370	.380	.886
1912	**ChC-N**	**13**	**22**	**4**	**4**	**0**	**2**	**0**	**4**	**1**	**—**	**5**	**0**	**1**	**—**	**0**	**—**	**.182**	**.217**	**.364**	**.829**
1914	Buf-F	151	541	69	118	20	3	2	42	40	—	55	1	23	—	35	—	.218	.273	.277	.962
1915	Buf-F	92	282	24	56	9	1	1	19	26	—	26	1	7	—	11	—	.199	.269	.248	.940
Career average		109	362	43	87	12	4	1	31	33	—	29	1	15	—	15	—	.240	.306	.304	.920
Cubs average		**13**	**22**	**4**	**4**	**0**	**2**	**0**	**4**	**1**	**—**	**5**	**0**	**1**	**—**	**0**	**—**	**.182**	**.217**	**.364**	**.829**
Career total		651	2170	256	520	69	25	7	188	198	—	172	8	92	—	87	—	.240	.306	.304	.920
Cubs total		**13**	**22**	**4**	**4**	**0**	**2**	**0**	**4**	**1**	**—**	**5**	**0**	**1**	**—**	**0**	**—**	**.182**	**.217**	**.364**	**.829**

Downs, Jerome Willis (Red)
HEIGHT: 5'11" THROWS: RIGHT BATS: RIGHT BORN: 8/22/1883 NEOLA, IOWA DIED: 10/19/1939 COUNCIL BLUFFS, IOWA POSITIONS PLAYED: 2B, 3B, SS, OF

YEAR	TEAM	GAMES	AB	RUNS	HITS	2B	3B	HR	RBI	BB	IBB	SO	HBP	SH	SF	SB	CS	BA	OBA	SA	FA
1907	Det-A	105	374	28	82	13	5	1	42	13	—	—	2	14	—	3	—	.219	.249	.289	.930
1908	Det-A	84	289	29	64	10	3	1	35	5	—	—	1	8	—	2	—	.221	.237	.287	.925
1912	Bro-N	9	32	2	8	3	0	0	3	1	—	5	0	1	—	3	—	.250	.273	.344	.881
1912	**ChC-N**	**43**	**95**	**9**	**25**	**4**	**3**	**1**	**14**	**9**	**—**	**17**	**0**	**2**	**—**	**5**	**—**	**.263**	**.327**	**.400**	**.916**
Career average		80	263	23	60	10	4	1	31	9	—	7	1	8	—	4	—	.227	.256	.304	.924
Cubs average		**43**	**95**	**9**	**25**	**4**	**3**	**1**	**14**	**9**	**—**	**17**	**0**	**2**	**—**	**5**	**—**	**.263**	**.327**	**.400**	**.916**
Career total		241	790	68	179	30	11	3	94	28	—	22	3	25	—	13	—	.227	.256	.304	.924
Cubs total		**43**	**95**	**9**	**25**	**4**	**3**	**1**	**14**	**9**	**—**	**17**	**0**	**2**	**—**	**5**	**—**	**.263**	**.327**	**.400**	**.916**

Doyle, James Francis (Jim)
HEIGHT: 5'10" THROWS: RIGHT BATS: RIGHT BORN: 12/25/1881 DETROIT, MICHIGAN DIED: 2/1/1912 SYRACUSE, NEW YORK POSITIONS PLAYED: 3B, OF

YEAR	TEAM	GAMES	AB	RUNS	HITS	2B	3B	HR	RBI	BB	IBB	SO	HBP	SH	SF	SB	CS	BA	OBA	SA	FA
1910	Cin-N	7	13	1	2	2	0	0	1	0	—	2	0	2	—	0	—	.154	.154	.308	.875
1911	**ChC-N**	**130**	**472**	**69**	**133**	**23**	**12**	**5**	**62**	**40**	**—**	**54**	**2**	**19**	**—**	**19**	**—**	**.282**	**.340**	**.413**	**.922**
Career average		69	243	35	68	13	6	3	32	20	—	28	1	11	—	10	—	.278	.336	.410	.921
Cubs average		**130**	**472**	**69**	**133**	**23**	**12**	**5**	**62**	**40**	**—**	**54**	**2**	**19**	**—**	**19**	**—**	**.282**	**.340**	**.413**	**.922**
Career total		137	485	70	135	25	12	5	63	40	—	56	2	21	—	19	—	.278	.336	.410	.921
Cubs total		**130**	**472**	**69**	**133**	**23**	**12**	**5**	**62**	**40**	**—**	**54**	**2**	**19**	**—**	**19**	**—**	**.282**	**.340**	**.413**	**.922**

Doyle, John Joseph (Jack *or* Dirty Jack)

HEIGHT: 5'9"   THROWS: RIGHT   BATS: RIGHT   BORN: 10/25/1869 KILLORGIN, IRELAND   DIED: 12/31/1958 HOLYOKE, MASSACHUSETTS
POSITIONS PLAYED: C, 1B, 2B, 3B, SS, OF

YEAR	TEAM	GAMES	AB	RUNS	HITS	2B	3B	HR	RBI	BB	IBB	SO	HBP	SH	SF	SB	CS	BA	OBA	SA	FA
1889	CoC-AA	11	36	6	10	1	1	0	3	6	—	6	0	—	—	9	—	.278	.381	.361	.902
1890	CoC-AA	77	298	47	80	17	7	2	44	13	—	—	0	—	—	27	—	.268	.299	.393	.877
1891	Cle-N	69	250	43	69	14	4	0	43	26	—	44	3	—	—	24	—	.276	.351	.364	.869
1892	Cle-N	24	88	17	26	4	1	1	14	6	—	10	0	—	—	5	—	.295	.340	.398	.871
1892	NYG-N	90	366	61	109	22	1	5	55	18	—	30	3	—	—	42	—	.298	.336	.404	.865
1893	NYG-N	82	318	56	102	17	5	1	51	27	—	12	5	—	—	40	—	.321	.383	.415	.913
1894	NYG-N	105	422	90	155	30	8	3	100	35	—	3	3	4	—	42	—	.367	.420	.498	.962
1895	NYG-N	82	319	52	100	21	3	1	66	24	—	12	2	0	—	35	—	.313	.365	.408	.951
1896	Bal-N	118	487	116	165	29	4	1	101	42	—	15	8	9	—	73	—	.339	.400	.421	.974
1897	Bal-N	114	460	91	163	29	4	2	87	29	—	—	1	2	—	62	—	.354	.394	.448	.979
1898	Was-N	43	177	26	54	2	2	2	26	7	—	—	1	0	—	9	—	.305	.335	.373	.963
1898	NYG-N	82	297	42	84	15	3	1	43	12	—	—	3	4	—	14	—	.283	.317	.364	.948
1899	NYG-N	118	448	55	134	15	7	3	76	33	—	—	4	3	—	35	—	.299	.353	.384	.976
1900	NYG-N	133	505	69	135	24	1	1	66	34	—	—	3	2	—	34	—	.267	.317	.325	.971
1901	**ChN-N**	**75**	**285**	**21**	**66**	**9**	**2**	**0**	**39**	**7**	**—**	**—**	**5**	**2**	**—**	**8**	**—**	**.232**	**.263**	**.277**	**.973**
1902	NYG-N	49	186	21	56	13	0	0	19	10	—	—	1	2	—	12	—	.301	.340	.371	.991
1902	Was-A	78	312	52	77	15	2	1	20	29	—	—	0	5	—	6	—	.247	.311	.317	.941
1903	Bro-N	139	524	84	164	27	6	0	91	54	—	—	5	9	—	34	—	.313	.383	.387	.981
1904	Bro-N	8	22	2	5	1	0	0	2	6	—	—	1	0	—	1	—	.227	.414	.273	1.000
1904	Phi-N	66	236	20	52	10	3	1	22	19	—	—	1	3	—	4	—	.220	.281	.301	.977
1905	NYA-A	1	3	0	0	0	0	0	0	0	—	—	0	1	—	0	—	.000	.000	.000	.833
Career average		92	355	57	106	19	4	1	57	26	—	8	3	3	—	30	—	.299	.351	.385	.960
Cubs average		**75**	**285**	**21**	**66**	**9**	**2**	**0**	**39**	**7**	**—**	**0**	**5**	**2**	**—**	**8**	**—**	**.232**	**.263**	**.277**	**.973**
Career total		1564	6039	971	1806	315	64	25	968	437	—	132	49	46	—	516	—	.299	.351	.385	.960
Cubs total		**75**	**285**	**21**	**66**	**9**	**2**	**0**	**39**	**7**	**—**	**0**	**5**	**2**	**—**	**8**	**—**	**.232**	**.263**	**.277**	**.973**

Doyle, Lawrence Joseph (Larry *or* Laughing Larry)

HEIGHT: 5'10"   THROWS: RIGHT   BATS: LEFT   BORN: 7/31/1886 CASEYVILLE, ILLINOIS   DIED: 3/1/1974 SARANAC LAKE, NEW YORK   POSITIONS PLAYED: 2B

YEAR	TEAM	GAMES	AB	RUNS	HITS	2B	3B	HR	RBI	BB	IBB	SO	HBP	SH	SF	SB	CS	BA	OBA	SA	FA
1907	NYG-N	69	227	16	59	3	0	0	16	20	—	—	0	4	—	3	—	.260	.320	.273	.917
1908	NYG-N	104	377	65	116	16	9	0	33	22	—	—	5	25	—	17	—	.308	.354	.398	.935
1909	NYG-N	147	570	86	172	27	11	6	49	45	—	—	7	12	—	31	—	.302	.360	.419	.940
1910	NYG-N	151	575	97	164	21	14	8	69	71	—	26	5	19	—	39	—	.285	.369	.412	.930
1911	NYG-N	143	526	102	163	25	25	13	77	71	—	39	5	20	—	38	—	.310	.397	.527	.944
1912	NYG-N	143	558	98	184	33	8	10	90	56	—	20	2	13	—	36	—	.330	.393	.471	.948
1913	NYG-N	132	482	67	135	25	6	5	73	59	—	29	5	12	—	38	—	.280	.364	.388	.955
1914	NYG-N	145	539	87	140	19	8	5	63	58	—	25	10	16	—	17	—	.260	.343	.353	.959
1915	NYG-N	150	591	86	189	40	10	4	70	32	—	28	3	15	—	22	18	.320	.358	.442	.947
1916	NYG-N	113	441	55	118	24	10	2	47	27	—	23	4	16	—	17	—	.268	.316	.381	.960
1916	**ChC-N**	**9**	**38**	**6**	**15**	**5**	**1**	**1**	**7**	**1**	**—**	**1**	**0**	**0**	**—**	**2**	**—**	**.395**	**.410**	**.658**	**.982**
1917	**ChC-N**	**135**	**476**	**48**	**121**	**19**	**5**	**6**	**61**	**48**	**—**	**28**	**0**	**26**	**—**	**5**	**—**	**.254**	**.323**	**.353**	**.952**
1918	NYG-N	75	257	38	67	7	4	3	36	37	—	10	0	4	—	10	—	.261	.354	.354	.969
1919	NYG-N	113	381	61	110	14	10	7	52	31	—	17	5	3	—	12	—	.289	.350	.433	.956
1920	NYG-N	137	471	48	134	21	2	4	50	47	—	28	2	10	—	11	9	.285	.352	.363	.967
Career average		126	465	69	135	21	9	5	57	45	—	20	4	14	—	21	2	.290	.357	.408	.949
Cubs average		**72**	**257**	**27**	**68**	**12**	**3**	**4**	**34**	**25**	**—**	**15**	**0**	**13**	**—**	**4**	**0**	**.265**	**.329**	**.375**	**.954**
Career total		1766	6509	960	1887	299	123	74	793	625	—	274	53	195	—	298	27	.290	.357	.408	.949
Cubs total		**144**	**514**	**54**	**136**	**24**	**6**	**7**	**68**	**49**	**—**	**29**	**0**	**26**	**—**	**7**	**0**	**.265**	**.329**	**.375**	**.954**

Drake, Samuel Harrison (Sammy)

HEIGHT: 5'11"   THROWS: RIGHT   BATS: BOTH   BORN: 10/7/1934 LITTLE ROCK, ARKANSAS   POSITIONS PLAYED: 2B, 3B, OF

YEAR	TEAM	GAMES	AB	RUNS	HITS	2B	3B	HR	RBI	BB	IBB	SO	HBP	SH	SF	SB	CS	BA	OBA	SA	FA
1960	**ChC-N**	**15**	**15**	**5**	**1**	**0**	**0**	**0**	**0**	**1**	**0**	**4**	**0**	**0**	**0**	**0**	**0**	**.067**	**.125**	**.067**	**1.000**
1961	**ChC-N**	**13**	**5**	**1**	**0**	**0**	**0**	**0**	**0**	**1**	**0**	**1**	**0**	**0**	**0**	**0**	**0**	**.000**	**.167**	**.000**	**1.000**
1962	NYM-N	25	52	2	10	0	0	0	7	6	1	12	0	1	0	0	0	.192	.276	.192	.962
Career average		18	24	3	4	0	0	0	2	3	0	6	0	0	0	0	0	.153	.238	.153	.966
Cubs average		**14**	**10**	**3**	**1**	**0**	**0**	**0**	**0**	**1**	**0**	**3**	**0**	**0**	**0**	**0**	**0**	**.050**	**.136**	**.050**	**1.000**
Career total		53	72	8	11	0	0	0	7	8	1	17	0	1	0	0	0	.153	.238	.153	.966
Cubs total		**28**	**20**	**6**	**1**	**0**	**0**	**0**	**0**	**2**	**0**	**5**	**0**	**0**	**0**	**0**	**0**	**.050**	**.136**	**.050**	**1.000**

Drake, Solomon Louis (Solly)

HEIGHT: 6'0" THROWS: RIGHT BATS: BOTH BORN: 10/23/1930 LITTLE ROCK, ARKANSAS POSITIONS PLAYED: OF

YEAR	TEAM	GAMES	AB	RUNS	HITS	2B	3B	HR	RBI	BB	IBB	SO	HBP	SH	SF	SB	CS	BA	OBA	SA	FA
1956	ChC-N	65	215	29	55	9	1	2	15	23	0	35	1	3	0	9	5	.256	.331	.335	.993
1959	LA-N	9	8	2	2	0	0	0	0	1	0	3	0	0	0	1	0	.250	.333	.250	.667
1959	Phi-N	67	62	10	9	1	0	0	3	8	0	15	0	0	0	5	5	.145	.243	.161	1.000
Career average		71	143	21	33	5	1	1	9	16	0	27	1	2	0	8	5	.232	.311	.295	.989
Cubs average		65	215	29	55	9	1	2	15	23	0	35	1	3	0	9	5	.256	.331	.335	.993
Career total		141	285	41	66	10	1	2	18	32	0	53	1	3	0	15	10	.232	.311	.295	.989
Cubs total		65	215	29	55	9	1	2	15	23	0	35	1	3	0	9	5	.256	.331	.335	.993

Driscoll, John Leo (Paddy)

HEIGHT: 5'8" THROWS: RIGHT BATS: RIGHT BORN: 1/11/1895 EVANSTON, ILLINOIS DIED: 6/28/1968 CHICAGO, ILLINOIS
POSITIONS PLAYED: 2B, 3B, SS

YEAR	TEAM	GAMES	AB	RUNS	HITS	2B	3B	HR	RBI	BB	IBB	SO	HBP	SH	SF	SB	CS	BA	OBA	SA	FA
1917	ChC-N	13	28	2	3	1	0	0	3	2	—	6	0	2	—	2	—	.107	.167	.143	.848
Career average		13	28	2	3	1	0	0	3	2	—	6	0	2	—	2	—	.107	.167	.143	.848
Cubs average		13	28	2	3	1	0	0	3	2	—	6	0	2	—	2	—	.107	.167	.143	.848
Career total		13	28	2	3	1	0	0	3	2	—	6	0	2	—	2	—	.107	.167	.143	.848
Cubs total		13	28	2	3	1	0	0	3	2	—	6	0	2	—	2	—	.107	.167	.143	.848

Duffy, Hugh

HEIGHT: 5'7" THROWS: RIGHT BATS: RIGHT BORN: 11/26/1866 CRANSTON, RHODE ISLAND DIED: 10/19/1954 BOSTON, MASSACHUSETTS
POSITIONS PLAYED: C, 1B, 2B, 3B, SS, OF

YEAR	TEAM	GAMES	AB	RUNS	HITS	2B	3B	HR	RBI	BB	IBB	SO	HBP	SH	SF	SB	CS	BA	OBA	SA	FA
1888	ChN-N	71	298	60	84	10	4	7	41	9	—	32	1	—	—	13	—	.282	.305	.413	.890
1889	ChN-N	136	584	144	172	21	7	12	89	46	—	30	2	—	—	52	—	.295	.348	.416	.879
1890	Chi-P	138	596	161	191	36	16	7	82	59	—	20	2	—	—	78	—	.320	.384	.470	.917
1891	Bos-AA	127	536	134	180	20	8	9	110	61	—	29	4	—	—	85	—	.336	.408	.453	.923
1892	Bos-N	147	612	125	184	28	12	5	81	60	—	37	1	—	—	51	—	.301	.364	.410	.933
1893	Bos-N	131	560	147	203	23	7	6	118	50	—	13	1	—	—	44	—	.363	.416	.461	.953
1894	Bos-N	125	539	160	237	51	16	18	145	66	—	15	1	10	—	48	—	.440	.502	.694	.919
1895	Bos-N	130	531	110	187	30	6	9	100	63	—	16	4	16	—	42	—	.352	.425	.482	.945
1896	Bos-N	131	527	97	158	16	8	5	113	52	—	19	2	20	—	39	—	.300	.365	.389	.947
1897	Bos-N	134	550	130	187	25	10	11	129	52	—	—	6	13	—	41	—	.340	.403	.482	.974
1898	Bos-N	152	568	97	169	13	3	8	108	59	—	—	1	17	—	29	—	.298	.365	.373	.957
1899	Bos-N	147	588	103	164	29	7	5	102	39	—	—	3	11	—	26	—	.279	.327	.378	.970
1900	Bos-N	55	181	27	55	5	4	2	31	16	—	—	0	5	—	11	—	.304	.360	.409	.959
1901	Mil-A	79	285	40	86	15	9	2	45	16	—	—	1	12	—	12	—	.302	.341	.439	.967
1904	Phi-N	18	46	10	13	1	1	0	5	13	—	—	0	1	—	3	—	.283	.441	.348	.850
1905	Phi-N	15	40	7	12	2	1	0	3	1	—	—	0	0	—	0	—	.300	.317	.400	.909
1906	Phi-N	1	1	0	0	0	0	0	0	0	—	—	0	0	—	0	—	.000	.000	.000	—
Career average		102	414	91	134	19	7	6	77	39	—	12	2	6	—	34	—	.324	.384	.449	.939
Cubs average		104	441	102	128	16	6	10	65	28	—	31	2	—	—	33	—	.290	.334	.415	.883
Career total		1737	7042	1552	2282	325	119	106	1302	662	—	211	29	105	—	574	—	.324	.384	.449	.939
Cubs total		207	882	204	256	31	11	19	130	55	—	62	3	—	—	65	—	.290	.334	.415	.883

Dungan, Samuel Morrison (Sam)

HEIGHT: 5'11" THROWS: — BATS: RIGHT BORN: 7/29/1866 FERNDALE, CALIFORNIA DIED: 3/16/1939 SANTA ANA, CALIFORNIA POSITIONS PLAYED: 1B, OF

YEAR	TEAM	GAMES	AB	RUNS	HITS	2B	3B	HR	RBI	BB	IBB	SO	HBP	SH	SF	SB	CS	BA	OBA	SA	FA
1892	ChN-N	113	433	46	123	19	7	0	53	35	—	19	6	—	—	15	—	.284	.346	.360	.905
1893	ChN-N	107	465	86	138	23	7	2	64	29	—	8	9	—	—	11	—	.297	.350	.389	.920
1894	ChN-N	10	39	5	9	2	0	0	3	7	—	1	0	0	—	1	—	.231	.348	.282	1.000
1894	Lou-N	8	32	6	11	1	0	0	3	4	—	1	0	1	—	2	—	.344	.417	.375	.941
1900	ChN-N	6	15	1	4	0	0	0	1	1	—	—	0	0	—	0	—	.267	.313	.267	.800
1901	Was-A	138	559	70	179	26	12	1	73	40	—	—	2	9	—	9	—	.320	.368	.415	.970
Career average		76	309	43	93	14	5	1	39	23	—	6	3	2	—	8	—	.301	.356	.386	.945
Cubs average		59	238	35	69	11	4	1	30	18	—	7	4	0	—	7	—	.288	.347	.370	.915
Career total		382	1543	214	464	71	26	3	197	116	—	29	17	10	—	38	—	.301	.356	.386	.945
Cubs total		236	952	138	274	44	14	2	121	72	—	28	15	0	—	27	—	.288	.347	.370	.915

Dunn, Ronald Ray (Ron)
HEIGHT: 5'11" THROWS: RIGHT BATS: RIGHT BORN: 1/24/1950 OKLAHOMA CITY, OKLAHOMA POSITIONS PLAYED: 2B, 3B, OF

YEAR	TEAM	GAMES	AB	RUNS	HITS	2B	3B	HR	RBI	BB	IBB	SO	HBP	SH	SF	SB	CS	BA	OBA	SA	FA
1974	ChC-N	23	68	6	20	7	0	2	15	12	3	8	0	0	0	0	0	.294	.400	.485	.917
1975	ChC-N	32	44	2	7	3	0	1	6	6	0	17	0	0	2	0	0	.159	.250	.295	.958
Career average		28	56	4	14	5	0	2	11	9	2	13	0	0	1	0	0	.241	.341	.411	.926
Cubs average		**28**	**56**	**4**	**14**	**5**	**0**	**2**	**11**	**9**	**2**	**13**	**0**	**0**	**1**	**0**	**0**	**.241**	**.341**	**.411**	**.926**
Career total		55	112	8	27	10	0	3	21	18	3	25	0	0	2	0	0	.241	.341	.411	.926
Cubs total		**55**	**112**	**8**	**27**	**10**	**0**	**3**	**21**	**18**	**3**	**25**	**0**	**0**	**2**	**0**	**0**	**.241**	**.341**	**.411**	**.926**

Dunston, Shawon Donnell
HEIGHT: 6'1" THROWS: RIGHT BATS: RIGHT BORN: 3/21/1963 BROOKLYN, NEW YORK POSITIONS PLAYED: 1B, 2B, 3B, SS, OF

YEAR	TEAM	GAMES	AB	RUNS	HITS	2B	3B	HR	RBI	BB	IBB	SO	HBP	SH	SF	SB	CS	BA	OBA	SA	FA
1985	ChC-N	74	250	40	65	12	4	4	18	19	3	42	0	1	2	11	3	.260	.310	.388	.958
1986	ChC-N	150	581	66	145	37	3	17	68	21	5	114	3	4	2	13	11	.250	.278	.411	.961
1987	ChC-N	95	346	40	85	18	3	5	22	10	1	68	1	0	2	12	3	.246	.267	.358	.969
1988	ChC-N	155	575	69	143	23	6	9	56	16	8	108	2	4	2	30	9	.249	.271	.357	.973
1989	ChC-N	138	471	52	131	20	6	9	60	30	15	86	1	6	4	19	11	.278	.320	.403	.970
1990	ChC-N	146	545	73	143	22	8	17	66	15	1	87	3	4	6	25	5	.262	.283	.426	.970

(continued)

Shawon Donnell Dunston, ss-1b-2b-3b-of-dh, 1985–present

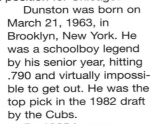

Shawon Dunston had a strong arm and good power for a shortstop; along with Joe Tinker, Ernie Banks and Don Kessinger, he was another all-time great at that position for Chicago.

Dunston was born on March 21, 1963, in Brooklyn, New York. He was a schoolboy legend by his senior year, hitting .790 and virtually impossible to get out. He was the top pick in the 1982 draft by the Cubs.

By 1985 he was named the Cubs' Opening Day shortstop; he struggled a bit, eventually spending some time in the minor leagues that season. He ended up hitting .260 on the year.

In 1986 Dunston came up to stay and turned in a strong season, with 145 hits, 37 doubles, 17 home runs and 68 RBIs. He also led National League shortstops in putouts, assists, double plays—and errors.

Dunston had the unique distinction of being the first everyday player to be produced by the Cubs' relatively anemic farm system since Don Kessinger in 1966. Dunston was an All-Star in 1988 and 1990, and he was a key performer in the Cubs' 1989 annexation of the National League East title. He hit over .400 in September as the Cubs pulled away from the rest of the pack.

For three years in a row, from 1989 to 1991, Dunston led the team in triples.

He was also a notoriously slow starter, a player who apparently got better as the temperature got warmer. This led Cubs fans in 1989 to come up with the "Shawon-O-Meter," which measured his batting average as the season went on. The "Shawon-O-Meter" was displayed in the bleachers during Dunston's career in Chicago.

Dunston missed parts of three seasons from 1992 to 1994, but in 1995, he had the best year of his career, hitting .296 with 30 doubles and 69 RBIs, all career highs.

After a stint in San Francisco in 1996, Dunston returned to Chicago in 1997, where he hit .284. He then went on to play for Pittsburgh, Cleveland, San Francisco, St. Louis and the New York Mets. In 2000 he played again for St. Louis and then moved to San Francisco in 2001.

Dunston is third all-time on the Cubs in games played by a shortstop with 1,228.

(Dunston, continued)

YEAR	TEAM	GAMES	AB	RUNS	HITS	2B	3B	HR	RBI	BB	IBB	SO	HBP	SH	SF	SB	CS	BA	OBA	SA	FA
1991	**ChC-N**	**142**	**492**	**59**	**128**	**22**	**7**	**12**	**50**	**23**	**5**	**64**	**4**	**4**	**11**	**21**	**6**	**.260**	**.292**	**.407**	**.968**
1992	**ChC-N**	**18**	**73**	**8**	**23**	**3**	**1**	**0**	**2**	**3**	**0**	**13**	**0**	**0**	**0**	**2**	**3**	**.315**	**.342**	**.384**	**.986**
1993	**ChC-N**	**7**	**10**	**3**	**4**	**2**	**0**	**0**	**2**	**0**	**0**	**1**	**0**	**0**	**0**	**0**	**0**	**.400**	**.400**	**.600**	**1.000**
1994	**ChC-N**	**88**	**331**	**38**	**92**	**19**	**0**	**11**	**35**	**16**	**3**	**48**	**2**	**5**	**2**	**3**	**8**	**.278**	**.313**	**.435**	**.966**
1995	**ChC-N**	**127**	**477**	**58**	**141**	**30**	**6**	**14**	**69**	**10**	**3**	**75**	**6**	**7**	**3**	**10**	**5**	**.296**	**.317**	**.472**	**.969**
1996	SF-N	82	287	27	86	12	2	5	25	13	0	40	1	5	1	8	0	.300	.331	.408	.957
1997	**ChC-N**	**114**	**419**	**57**	**119**	**18**	**4**	**9**	**41**	**8**	**0**	**64**	**3**	**3**	**4**	**29**	**7**	**.284**	**.300**	**.411**	**.971**
1997	Pit-N	18	71	14	28	4	1	5	16	0	0	11	0	2	1	3	1	.394	.389	.690	.965
1998	Cle-N	62	156	26	37	11	3	3	12	6	0	18	1	0	3	9	2	.237	.265	.404	.972
1998	SF-N	36	51	10	9	2	0	3	8	0	0	10	3	1	0	0	2	.176	.222	.392	.926
1999	StL-N	62	150	23	46	5	2	5	25	2	0	23	3	2	1	6	3	.307	.327	.467	.981
1999	NYM-N	42	93	12	32	6	1	0	16	0	0	16	2	1	1	4	1	.344	.354	.430	.979
2000	StL-N	98	216	28	54	11	2	12	43	6	0	47	3	4	2	3	1	.250	.278	.486	.984
2001	SF-N	88	186	26	52	10	3	9	25	2	0	32	2	2	1	3	1	.280	.293	.511	.966
Career average		102	340	43	92	17	4	9	39	12	3	57	2	3	3	12	5	.270	.297	.419	.968
Cubs average		**105**	**381**	**47**	**102**	**19**	**4**	**9**	**41**	**14**	**4**	**64**	**2**	**3**	**3**	**15**	**6**	**.267**	**.295**	**.407**	**.968**
Career total		1742	5780	729	1563	287	62	149	659	200	44	967	40	55	48	211	82	.270	.297	.419	.968
Cubs total		**1254**	**4570**	**563**	**1219**	**226**	**48**	**107**	**489**	**171**	**44**	**770**	**25**	**38**	**38**	**175**	**71**	**.267**	**.295**	**.407**	**.968**

Dunwoody, Todd Franklin
HEIGHT: 6'1" THROWS: LEFT BATS: LEFT BORN: 4/11/1975 LAFAYETTE, INDIANA POSITIONS PLAYED: OF

YEAR	TEAM	GAMES	AB	RUNS	HITS	2B	3B	HR	RBI	BB	IBB	SO	HBP	SH	SF	SB	CS	BA	OBA	SA	FA
1997	Fla-N	19	50	7	13	2	2	2	7	7	0	21	1	0	0	2	0	.260	.362	.500	.929
1998	Fla-N	116	434	53	109	27	7	5	28	21	0	113	4	3	0	5	1	.251	.292	.380	.989
1999	Fla-N	64	186	20	41	6	3	2	20	12	0	41	1	0	1	3	4	.220	.270	.317	.981
2000	KC-A	61	178	12	37	9	0	1	23	8	0	42	1	2	6	3	0	.208	.238	.275	.976
2001	**ChC-N**	**33**	**61**	**6**	**13**	**4**	**0**	**1**	**3**	**3**	**0**	**14**	**0**	**0**	**0**	**0**	**1**	**.213**	**.250**	**.328**	**.973**
Career average		59	182	20	43	10	2	2	16	10	0	46	1	1	1	3	1	.234	.278	.350	.981
Cubs average		**33**	**61**	**6**	**13**	**4**	**0**	**1**	**3**	**3**	**0**	**14**	**0**	**0**	**0**	**0**	**1**	**.213**	**.250**	**.328**	**.973**
Career total		293	909	98	213	48	12	11	81	51	0	231	7	5	7	13	6	.234	.278	.350	.981
Cubs total		**33**	**61**	**6**	**13**	**4**	**0**	**1**	**3**	**3**	**0**	**14**	**0**	**0**	**0**	**0**	**1**	**.213**	**.250**	**.328**	**.973**

Durbin, Blaine Alphonsus (Kid)
HEIGHT: 5'8" THROWS: LEFT BATS: LEFT BORN: 9/10/1886 LAMAR, MISSOURI DIED: 9/11/1943 KIRKWOOD, MISSOURI POSITIONS PLAYED: P, OF

YEAR	TEAM	GAMES	AB	RUNS	HITS	2B	3B	HR	RBI	BB	IBB	SO	HBP	SH	SF	SB	CS	BA	OBA	SA	FA
1907	**ChC-N**	**11**	**18**	**2**	**6**	**0**	**0**	**0**	**0**	**1**	**—**	**—**	**0**	**0**	**—**	**0**	**—**	**.333**	**.368**	**.333**	**1.000**
1908	**ChC-N**	**14**	**28**	**3**	**7**	**1**	**0**	**0**	**0**	**2**	**—**	**—**	**1**	**1**	**—**	**0**	**—**	**.250**	**.323**	**.286**	**1.000**
1909	Cin-N	6	5	1	1	0	0	0	0	1	—	—	0	0	—	0	—	.200	.333	.200	—
1909	Pit-N	1	0	0	0	0	0	0	0	0	—	0	0	0	—	0	—	—	—	—	—
Career average		11	17	2	5	0	0	0	0	1	—	0	0	0	—	0	—	.275	.339	.294	1.000
Cubs average		**13**	**23**	**3**	**7**	**1**	**0**	**0**	**0**	**2**	**—**	**—**	**1**	**1**	**—**	**0**	**—**	**.283**	**.340**	**.304**	**1.000**
Career total		32	51	6	14	1	0	0	0	4	—	0	1	1	—	0	—	.275	.339	.294	1.000
Cubs total		**25**	**46**	**5**	**13**	**1**	**0**	**0**	**0**	**3**	**—**	**—**	**1**	**1**	**—**	**0**	**—**	**.283**	**.340**	**.304**	**1.000**

Durham, Leon (Bull)
HEIGHT: 6'1" THROWS: LEFT BATS: LEFT BORN: 7/31/1957 CINCINNATI, OHIO POSITIONS PLAYED: 1B, OF

YEAR	TEAM	GAMES	AB	RUNS	HITS	2B	3B	HR	RBI	BB	IBB	SO	HBP	SH	SF	SB	CS	BA	OBA	SA	FA
1980	StL-N	96	303	42	82	15	4	8	42	18	1	55	1	3	5	8	5	.271	.309	.426	.985
1981	**ChC-N**	**87**	**328**	**42**	**95**	**14**	**6**	**10**	**35**	**27**	**6**	**53**	**0**	**0**	**0**	**25**	**11**	**.290**	**.344**	**.460**	**.973**
1982	**ChC-N**	**148**	**539**	**84**	**168**	**33**	**7**	**22**	**90**	**66**	**14**	**77**	**2**	**0**	**2**	**28**	**14**	**.312**	**.388**	**.521**	**.964**
1983	**ChC-N**	**100**	**337**	**58**	**87**	**18**	**8**	**12**	**55**	**66**	**12**	**83**	**3**	**0**	**3**	**12**	**6**	**.258**	**.381**	**.466**	**.972**
1984	**ChC-N**	**137**	**473**	**86**	**132**	**30**	**4**	**23**	**96**	**69**	**11**	**86**	**1**	**0**	**5**	**16**	**8**	**.279**	**.369**	**.505**	**.994**
1985	**ChC-N**	**153**	**542**	**58**	**153**	**32**	**2**	**21**	**75**	**64**	**24**	**99**	**0**	**0**	**1**	**7**	**6**	**.282**	**.357**	**.465**	**.995**
1986	**ChC-N**	**141**	**484**	**66**	**127**	**18**	**7**	**20**	**65**	**67**	**16**	**98**	**1**	**0**	**5**	**8**	**7**	**.262**	**.350**	**.452**	**.995**
1987	**ChC-N**	**131**	**439**	**70**	**120**	**22**	**1**	**27**	**63**	**51**	**9**	**92**	**0**	**0**	**2**	**2**	**2**	**.273**	**.348**	**.513**	**.990**
1988	**ChC-N**	**24**	**73**	**10**	**16**	**6**	**1**	**3**	**6**	**9**	**2**	**20**	**0**	**0**	**0**	**0**	**1**	**.219**	**.305**	**.452**	**.995**
1988	Cin-N	21	51	4	11	3	0	1	2	5	1	12	0	0	0	0	0	.216	.286	.333	.993
1989	StL-N	29	18	2	1	1	0	0	1	2	0	4	1	0	1	0	1	.056	.182	.111	.961

(continued)

Leon "Bull" Durham, 1b-of, 1980–89

Leon Durham was the Cubs' slugging outfielder–first baseman who helped Chicago in 1984 to its first postseason series in 40 years.

Born in Cincinnati on July 31, 1957, Durham appeared in the big leagues in 1980 as an outfielder for the Cardinals. He played well in St. Louis, with 82 hits in 96 games for an average of .271.

In 1981 he and Ken Reitz and Ty Waller were sent to Chicago for Bruce Sutter—an infamously bad trade for the Cubs, because Sutter would go on to be one of the decade's greatest closers.

But of the three new Cubbies, Durham at least could play. He hit .290 in 1981 and finished third in the National League batting race in 1982 with a .312 average. He also hit 22 home runs and stole 28 bases, becoming the first player to accomplish the "20 homer, 20 steals" double since Frank "Wildfire" Schulte did it in 1911.

Durham also led the Cubs in triples three years in a row, from 1981 to 1983, the only time a Cubs first baseman has done so.

He was an All-Star in 1982 and again in 1983. In 1984 Durham hit .279 and his 96 RBIs was one behind team leader Ron Cey's 97, while his 28 home runs were also second on the team. He was second in the National League in assists by a first baseman as the Cubs won the National League East title.

At the plate, Durham hit pretty well, drilling two home runs in the series against the West champion Padres. But in the seventh inning of the fifth and deciding game of the best-three-of-five series, Durham let a sharp grounder roll between his legs. His team was ahead 4-3 at that point, and Durham's error enabled the Padres to tie the game. The Padres added three more runs in that inning to win 6-3 and knock Chicago out of the playoffs.

After another strong year in 1985, Durham's production began to drop. He was eventually traded to his hometown Reds in 1988 but missed most of the season due to drug problems. Durham came back to Major League Baseball in 1989 with the Cardinals, but he was again suspended for drug use.

Durham's 10 multiple home run games is 11th all-time on the Cubs.

(continued)

Career average	107	359	52	99	19	4	15	53	44	10	68	1	0	2	11	6	.277	.356	.475	.991
Cubs average	**115**	**402**	**59**	**112**	**22**	**5**	**17**	**61**	**52**	**12**	**76**	**1**	**0**	**2**	**12**	**7**	**.279**	**.362**	**.484**	**.991**
Career total	1067	3587	522	992	192	40	147	530	444	96	679	9	3	24	106	61	.277	.356	.475	.991
Cubs total	**921**	**3215**	**474**	**898**	**173**	**36**	**138**	**485**	**419**	**94**	**608**	**7**	**0**	**18**	**98**	**55**	**.279**	**.362**	**.484**	**.991**

Eaddy, Donald Johnson (Don)

HEIGHT: 5'11" THROWS: RIGHT BATS: RIGHT BORN: 2/16/1934 GRAND RAPIDS, MICHIGAN POSITIONS PLAYED: 3B

YEAR	TEAM	GAMES	AB	RUNS	HITS	2B	3B	HR	RBI	BB	IBB	SO	HBP	SH	SF	SB	CS	BA	OBA	SA	FA
1959	ChC-N	15	1	3	0	0	0	0	0	0	0	1	0	0	0	0	0	.000	.000	.000	.500
Career average		15	1	3	0	0	0	0	0	0	0	1	0	0	0	0	0	.000	.000	.000	.500
Cubs average		**15**	**1**	**3**	**0**	**0**	**0**	**0**	**0**	**0**	**0**	**1**	**0**	**0**	**0**	**0**	**0**	**.000**	**.000**	**.000**	**.500**
Career total		15	1	3	0	0	0	0	0	0	0	1	0	0	0	0	0	.000	.000	.000	.500
Cubs total		**15**	**1**	**3**	**0**	**0**	**0**	**0**	**0**	**0**	**0**	**1**	**0**	**0**	**0**	**0**	**0**	**.000**	**.000**	**.000**	**.500**

Eagan, William (Bill *or* Bad Bill)
HEIGHT: — THROWS: — BATS: — BORN: 6/1/1869 CAMDEN, NEW JERSEY DIED: 2/13/1905 DENVER, COLORADO POSITIONS PLAYED: 2B

YEAR	TEAM	GAMES	AB	RUNS	HITS	2B	3B	HR	RBI	BB	IBB	SO	HBP	SH	SF	SB	CS	BA	OBA	SA	FA
1891	StL-AA	83	302	49	65	11	4	4	43	44	—	54	3	—	—	21	—	.215	.321	.318	.929
1893	**ChN-N**	6	19	3	5	0	0	0	2	5	—	5	0	—	—	4	—	.263	.417	.263	.912
1898	Pit-N	19	61	14	20	2	3	0	5	8	—	—	6	1	—	1	—	.328	.453	.459	.914
Career average		36	127	22	30	4	2	1	17	19	—	20	3	0	—	9	—	.236	.348	.338	.925
Cubs average		**6**	**19**	**3**	**5**	**0**	**0**	**0**	**2**	**5**	**—**	**5**	**0**	**—**	**—**	**4**	**—**	**.263**	**.417**	**.263**	**.912**
Career total		108	382	66	90	13	7	4	50	57	—	59	9	1	—	26	—	.236	.348	.338	.925
Cubs total		**6**	**19**	**3**	**5**	**0**	**0**	**0**	**2**	**5**	**—**	**5**	**0**	**—**	**—**	**4**	**—**	**.263**	**.417**	**.263**	**.912**

Earl, Howard J. (Slim Jim)
HEIGHT: 6'2" THROWS: — BATS: — BORN: 2/25/1867 PALMYRA, NEW YORK DIED: 12/23/1916 NORTH BAY, NEW YORK POSITIONS PLAYED: 1B, 2B, SS, OF

YEAR	TEAM	GAMES	AB	RUNS	HITS	2B	3B	HR	RBI	BB	IBB	SO	HBP	SH	SF	SB	CS	BA	OBA	SA	FA
1890	**ChN-N**	92	384	57	95	10	3	7	51	18	—	47	2	—	—	17	—	.247	.285	.344	.880
1891	Mil-AA	31	129	21	32	5	2	1	17	5	—	13	1	—	—	3	—	.248	.281	.341	.955
Career average		62	257	39	64	8	3	4	34	12	—	30	2	—	—	10	—	.248	.284	.343	.891
Cubs average		**92**	**384**	**57**	**95**	**10**	**3**	**7**	**51**	**18**	**—**	**47**	**2**	**—**	**—**	**17**	**—**	**.247**	**.285**	**.344**	**.880**
Career total		123	513	78	127	15	5	8	68	23	—	60	3	—	—	20	—	.248	.284	.343	.891
Cubs total		**92**	**384**	**57**	**95**	**10**	**3**	**7**	**51**	**18**	**—**	**47**	**2**	**—**	**—**	**17**	**—**	**.247**	**.285**	**.344**	**.880**

Easterwood, Roy Charles (Shag)
HEIGHT: 6'0" THROWS: RIGHT BATS: RIGHT BORN: 1/12/1915 WAXAHACHIE, TEXAS DIED: 8/24/1984 GRAHAM, TEXAS POSITIONS PLAYED: C

YEAR	TEAM	GAMES	AB	RUNS	HITS	2B	3B	HR	RBI	BB	IBB	SO	HBP	SH	SF	SB	CS	BA	OBA	SA	FA
1944	**ChC-N**	17	33	1	7	2	0	1	2	1	—	11	0	0	—	0	—	.212	.235	.364	1.000
Career average		17	33	1	7	2	0	1	2	1	—	11	0	0	—	0	—	.212	.235	.364	1.000
Cubs average		**17**	**33**	**1**	**7**	**2**	**0**	**1**	**2**	**1**	**—**	**11**	**0**	**0**	**—**	**0**	**—**	**.212**	**.235**	**.364**	**1.000**
Career total		17	33	1	7	2	0	1	2	1	—	11	0	0	—	0	—	.212	.235	.364	1.000
Cubs total		**17**	**33**	**1**	**7**	**2**	**0**	**1**	**2**	**1**	**—**	**11**	**0**	**0**	**—**	**0**	**—**	**.212**	**.235**	**.364**	**1.000**

Eden, Charles M. (Charlie)
HEIGHT: — THROWS: LEFT BATS: LEFT BORN: 1/18/1855 LEXINGTON, KENTUCKY DIED: 9/17/1920 CINCINNATI, OHIO POSITIONS PLAYED: P, C, 1B, 3B, OF

YEAR	TEAM	GAMES	AB	RUNS	HITS	2B	3B	HR	RBI	BB	IBB	SO	HBP	SH	SF	SB	CS	BA	OBA	SA	FA
1877	**ChN-N**	15	55	9	12	0	1	0	5	3	—	6	—	—	—	—	—	.218	.259	.255	.679
1879	Cle-N	81	353	40	96	31	7	3	34	6	—	20	—	—	—	—	—	.272	.284	.425	.810
1884	Pit-AA	32	122	12	33	7	4	1	—	7	—	—	6	—	—	—	—	.270	.341	.418	.759
1885	Pit-AA	98	405	57	103	18	6	0	38	17	—	—	8	—	—	—	—	.254	.298	.328	.794
Career average		57	234	30	61	14	5	1	19	8	—	7	4	—	—	—	—	.261	.296	.372	.787
Cubs average		**15**	**55**	**9**	**12**	**0**	**1**	**0**	**5**	**3**	**—**	**6**	**—**	**—**	**—**	**—**	**—**	**.218**	**.259**	**.255**	**.679**
Career total		226	935	118	244	56	18	4	77	33	—	26	14	—	—	—	—	.261	.296	.372	.787
Cubs total		**15**	**55**	**9**	**12**	**0**	**1**	**0**	**5**	**3**	**—**	**6**	**—**	**—**	**—**	**—**	**—**	**.218**	**.259**	**.255**	**.679**

Edwards, Charles Bruce (Bruce *or* Bull)
HEIGHT: 5'8" THROWS: RIGHT BATS: RIGHT BORN: 7/15/1923 QUINCY, ILLINOIS DIED: 4/25/1975 SACRAMENTO, CALIFORNIA
POSITIONS PLAYED: C, 1B, 2B, 3B, OF

YEAR	TEAM	GAMES	AB	RUNS	HITS	2B	3B	HR	RBI	BB	IBB	SO	HBP	SH	SF	SB	CS	BA	OBA	SA	FA
1946	Bro-N	92	292	24	78	13	5	1	25	34	—	20	2	10	—	1	1	.267	.348	.356	.982
1947	Bro-N	130	471	53	139	15	8	9	80	49	—	55	2	6	—	2	4	.295	.364	.418	.983
1948	Bro-N	96	286	36	79	17	2	8	54	26	—	28	2	4	—	4	—	.276	.341	.434	.962
1949	Bro-N	64	148	24	31	3	0	8	25	25	—	15	0	0	—	0	0	.209	.324	.392	.985
1950	Bro-N	50	142	16	26	4	1	8	16	13	—	22	1	0	—	1	—	.183	.256	.394	1.000
1951	Bro-N	17	36	6	9	2	0	1	8	1	—	3	0	0	—	0	0	.250	.270	.389	

(continued)

(continued)

YEAR	TEAM	GAMES	AB	RUNS	HITS	2B	3B	HR	RBI	BB	IBB	SO	HBP	SH	SF	SB	CS	BA	OBA	SA	FA
1951	ChC-N	51	141	19	33	9	2	3	17	16	—	14	1	0	—	1	2	.234	.316	.390	.958
1952	ChC-N	50	94	7	23	2	2	1	12	8	—	12	0	1	—	0	0	.245	.304	.340	.989
1954	ChC-N	4	3	1	0	0	0	0	1	2	—	2	0	1	—	0	0	.000	.400	.000	—
1955	Was-A	30	57	5	10	2	0	0	3	16	0	6	0	0	0	0	0	.175	.400	.000	—
1956	Cin-N	7	5	0	1	0	0	0	0	0	0	2	0	0	0	0	1	.200	.356	.211	.974
Career average		59	168	19	43	7	2	4	24	19	0	18	1	2	0	1	1	.256	.335	.390	.978
Cubs average		**35**	**79**	**9**	**19**	**4**	**1**	**1**	**10**	**9**	**—**	**9**	**0**	**0**	**0**	**0**	**1**	**.235**	**.313**	**.366**	**.967**
Career total		591	1675	191	429	67	20	39	241	190	0	179	8	21	0	9	8	.256	.335	.390	.978
Cubs total		**105**	**238**	**27**	**56**	**11**	**4**	**4**	**30**	**26**	**—**	**28**	**1**	**1**	**0**	**1**	**2**	**.235**	**.313**	**.366**	**.967**

Edwards, Henry Albert (Hank)

HEIGHT: 6'0"   THROWS: LEFT   BATS: LEFT   BORN: 1/29/1919 ELMWOOD PLACE, OHIO   DIED: 6/22/1988 SANTA ANA, CALIFORNIA   POSITIONS PLAYED: OF

YEAR	TEAM	GAMES	AB	RUNS	HITS	2B	3B	HR	RBI	BB	IBB	SO	HBP	SH	SF	SB	CS	BA	OBA	SA	FA
1941	Cle-A	16	68	10	15	1	1	1	6	2	—	4	0	2	—	0	0	.221	.243	.309	.929
1942	Cle-A	13	48	6	12	2	1	0	7	5	—	8	0	0	—	2	1	.250	.321	.333	.968
1943	Cle-A	92	297	38	82	18	6	3	28	30	—	34	0	2	—	4	8	.276	.343	.407	.983
1946	Cle-A	124	458	62	138	33	16	10	54	43	—	48	0	1	—	1	3	.301	.361	.509	.968
1947	Cle-A	108	393	54	102	12	3	15	59	31	—	55	1	2	—	1	3	.260	.315	.420	.990
1948	Cle-A	55	160	27	43	9	2	3	18	18	—	18	1	0	—	1	1	.269	.346	.406	.987
1949	Cle-A	5	15	3	4	0	0	1	1	1	—	2	0	0	—	0	0	.267	.313	.467	1.000
1949	**ChC-N**	**58**	**176**	**25**	**51**	**8**	**4**	**7**	**21**	**19**	**—**	**22**	**0**	**1**	**—**	**0**	**—**	**.290**	**.359**	**.500**	**.988**
1950	**ChC-N**	**41**	**110**	**13**	**40**	**11**	**1**	**2**	**21**	**10**	**—**	**13**	**0**	**0**	**—**	**0**	**—**	**.364**	**.417**	**.536**	**.976**
1951	Bro-N	35	31	1	7	3	0	0	3	4	—	9	0	0	—	0	0	.226	.314	.323	
1951	Cin-N	41	127	14	40	9	1	3	20	13	—	17	0	0	—	0	2	.315	.379	.472	.985
1952	Cin-N	74	184	24	52	7	6	6	28	19	—	22	0	0	—	0	3	.283	.350	.484	.988
1952	CWS-A	8	18	2	6	0	0	0	1	0	—	2	0	0	—	0	0	.333	.333	.333	1.000
1953	StL-A	65	106	6	21	3	0	0	9	13	—	10	0	0	—	0	1	.198	.286	.226	1.000
Career average		67	199	26	56	11	4	5	25	19	—	24	0	1	—	1	2	.280	.343	.440	.981
Cubs average		**50**	**143**	**19**	**46**	**10**	**3**	**5**	**21**	**15**	**—**	**18**	**0**	**1**	**—**	**0**	**0**	**.318**	**.381**	**.514**	**.984**
Career total		735	2191	285	613	116	41	51	276	208	—	264	2	8	—	9	22	.280	.343	.440	.981
Cubs total		**99**	**286**	**38**	**91**	**19**	**5**	**9**	**42**	**29**	**—**	**35**	**0**	**1**	**—**	**0**	**0**	**.318**	**.381**	**.514**	**.984**

Eggler, David Daniel (Dave)

HEIGHT: 5'9"   THROWS: RIGHT   BATS: RIGHT   BORN: 4/30/1851 BROOKLYN, NEW YORK   DIED: 4/5/1902 BUFFALO, NEW YORK   POSITIONS PLAYED: OF

YEAR	TEAM	GAMES	AB	RUNS	HITS	2B	3B	HR	RBI	BB	IBB	SO	HBP	SH	SF	SB	CS	BA	OBA	SA	FA
1876	PhN-N	39	176	28	52	4	0	0	19	2	—	4	—	—	—	—	—	.295	.303	.318	.913
1877	**ChN-N**	**33**	**136**	**20**	**36**	**3**	**0**	**0**	**20**	**1**	**—**	**5**	**—**	**—**	**—**	**—**	**—**	**.265**	**.270**	**.287**	**.861**
1879	Buf-N	78	317	41	66	5	7	0	27	11	—	41	—	—	—	—	—	.208	.235	.268	.919
1883	Bal-AA	53	202	15	38	2	0	0	7	1	—	—	—	—	—	—	—	.188	.192	.198	.916
1883	Buf-N	38	153	13	38	2	1	0	13	2	—	29	—	—	—	—	—	.248	.258	.275	.845
1884	Buf-N	63	241	25	47	3	1	0	20	6	—	54	—	—	—	—	—	.195	.215	.216	.887
1885	Buf-N	6	24	0	2	0	0	0	0	2	—	4	—	—	—	—	—	.083	.154	.083	.938
Career average		52	208	24	47	3	2	0	18	4	—	23	—	—	—	—	—	.223	.239	.253	.894
Cubs average		**33**	**136**	**20**	**36**	**3**	**0**	**0**	**20**	**1**	**—**	**5**	**—**	**—**	**—**	**—**	**—**	**.265**	**.270**	**.287**	**.861**
Career total		310	1249	142	279	19	9	0	106	25	—	137	—	—	—	—	—	.223	.239	.253	.894
Cubs total		**33**	**136**	**20**	**36**	**3**	**0**	**0**	**20**	**1**	**—**	**5**	**—**	**—**	**—**	**—**	**—**	**.265**	**.270**	**.287**	**.861**

Elia, Lee Constantine

HEIGHT: 5'11"   THROWS: RIGHT   BATS: RIGHT   BORN: 7/16/1937 PHILADELPHIA, PENNSYLVANIA   POSITIONS PLAYED: 2B, 3B, SS

YEAR	TEAM	GAMES	AB	RUNS	HITS	2B	3B	HR	RBI	BB	IBB	SO	HBP	SH	SF	SB	CS	BA	OBA	SA	FA
1966	CWS-A	80	195	16	40	5	2	3	22	15	3	39	2	1	3	0	1	.205	.265	.297	.954
1968	**ChC-N**	**15**	**17**	**1**	**3**	**0**	**0**	**0**	**3**	**0**	**0**	**6**	**1**	**0**	**0**	**0**	**0**	**.176**	**.222**	**.176**	**1.000**
Career average		48	106	9	22	3	1	2	13	8	2	23	2	1	2	0	1	.203	.262	.288	.955
Cubs average		**15**	**17**	**1**	**3**	**0**	**0**	**0**	**3**	**0**	**0**	**6**	**1**	**0**	**0**	**0**	**0**	**.176**	**.222**	**.176**	**1.000**
Career total		95	212	17	43	5	2	3	25	15	3	45	3	1	3	0	1	.203	.262	.288	.955
Cubs total		**15**	**17**	**1**	**3**	**0**	**0**	**0**	**3**	**0**	**0**	**6**	**1**	**0**	**0**	**0**	**0**	**.176**	**.222**	**.176**	**1.000**

Elko, Peter (Pete *or* Piccolo Pete)
HEIGHT: 5'11" THROWS: RIGHT BATS: RIGHT BORN: 6/17/1918 WILKES-BARRE, PENNSYLVANIA DIED: 9/17/1993 WILKE-BARRE, PENNSYLVANIA
POSITIONS PLAYED: 3B

YEAR	TEAM	GAMES	AB	RUNS	HITS	2B	3B	HR	RBI	BB	IBB	SO	HBP	SH	SF	SB	CS	BA	OBA	SA	FA
1943	ChC-N	9	30	1	4	0	0	0	0	4	—	5	0	0	—	0	—	.133	.235	.133	.852
1944	ChC-N	7	22	2	5	1	0	0	0	0	—	1	0	0	—	0	—	.227	.227	.273	1.000
Career average		8	26	2	5	1	0	0	0	2	—	3	0	0	—	0	—	.173	.232	.192	.902
Cubs average		**8**	**26**	**2**	**5**	**1**	**0**	**0**	**0**	**2**	**—**	**3**	**0**	**0**	**—**	**0**	**—**	**.173**	**.232**	**.192**	**.902**
Career total		16	52	3	9	1	0	0	0	4	—	6	0	0	—	0	—	.173	.232	.192	.902
Cubs total		**16**	**52**	**3**	**9**	**1**	**0**	**0**	**0**	**4**	**—**	**6**	**0**	**0**	**—**	**0**	**—**	**.173**	**.232**	**.192**	**.902**

Elliott, Allen Clifford (Ace)
HEIGHT: 6'0" THROWS: RIGHT BATS: LEFT BORN: 12/25/1897 ST. LOUIS, MISSOURI DIED: 5/6/1979 ST. LOUIS, MISSOURI POSITIONS PLAYED: 1B

YEAR	TEAM	GAMES	AB	RUNS	HITS	2B	3B	HR	RBI	BB	IBB	SO	HBP	SH	SF	SB	CS	BA	OBA	SA	FA
1923	ChC-N	53	168	21	42	8	2	2	29	2	—	12	2	9	—	3	3	.250	.267	.357	.992
1924	ChC-N	10	14	0	2	0	0	0	0	0	—	1	0	1	—	0	0	.143	.143	.143	1.000
Career average		32	91	11	22	4	1	1	15	1	—	7	1	5	—	2	2	.242	.258	.341	.992
Cubs average		**32**	**91**	**11**	**22**	**4**	**1**	**1**	**15**	**1**	**—**	**7**	**1**	**5**	**—**	**2**	**2**	**.242**	**.258**	**.341**	**.992**
Career total		63	182	21	44	8	2	2	29	2	—	13	2	10	—	3	3	.242	.258	.341	.992
Cubs total		**63**	**182**	**21**	**44**	**8**	**2**	**2**	**29**	**2**	**—**	**13**	**2**	**10**	**—**	**3**	**3**	**.242**	**.258**	**.341**	**.992**

Elliott, Carter Ward
HEIGHT: 5'11" THROWS: RIGHT BATS: LEFT BORN: 11/29/1893 ATCHISON, KANSAS DIED: 5/21/1959 PALM SPRINGS, CALIFORNIA POSITIONS PLAYED: SS

YEAR	TEAM	GAMES	AB	RUNS	HITS	2B	3B	HR	RBI	BB	IBB	SO	HBP	SH	SF	SB	CS	BA	OBA	SA	FA
1921	ChC-N	12	28	5	7	2	0	0	0	5	—	3	0	2	—	0	0	.250	.364	.321	.964
Career average		12	28	5	7	2	0	0	0	5	—	3	0	2	—	0	0	.250	.364	.321	.964
Cubs average		**12**	**28**	**5**	**7**	**2**	**0**	**0**	**0**	**5**	**—**	**3**	**0**	**2**	**—**	**0**	**0**	**.250**	**.364**	**.321**	**.964**
Career total		12	28	5	7	2	0	0	0	5	—	3	0	2	—	0	0	.250	.364	.321	.964
Cubs total		**12**	**28**	**5**	**7**	**2**	**0**	**0**	**0**	**5**	**—**	**3**	**0**	**2**	**—**	**0**	**0**	**.250**	**.364**	**.321**	**.964**

Elliott, Harold B. (Rowdy)
HEIGHT: 5'9" THROWS: RIGHT BATS: RIGHT BORN: 7/8/1890 KOKOMO, INDIANA DIED: 2/12/1934 SAN FRANCISCO, CALIFORNIA POSITIONS PLAYED: C

YEAR	TEAM	GAMES	AB	RUNS	HITS	2B	3B	HR	RBI	BB	IBB	SO	HBP	SH	SF	SB	CS	BA	OBA	SA	FA
1910	Bos-N	3	2	0	0	0	0	0	0	0	—	0	0	0	—	0	—	.000	.000	.000	1.000
1916	ChC-N	23	55	5	14	3	0	0	3	3	—	5	0	4	—	1	—	.255	.293	.309	.969
1917	ChC-N	85	223	18	56	8	5	0	28	11	—	11	2	8	—	4	—	.251	.292	.332	.969
1918	ChC-N	5	10	0	0	0	0	0	0	2	—	1	0	0	—	0	—	.000	.167	.000	.952
1920	Bro-N	41	112	13	27	4	0	1	13	3	—	6	1	4	—	0	0	.241	.267	.304	.964
Career average		31	80	7	19	3	1	0	9	4	—	5	1	3	—	1	0	.241	.281	.311	.967
Cubs average		**38**	**96**	**8**	**23**	**4**	**2**	**0**	**10**	**5**	**—**	**6**	**1**	**4**	**—**	**2**	**—**	**.243**	**.288**	**.316**	**.968**
Career total		157	402	36	97	15	5	1	44	19	—	23	3	16	—	5	0	.241	.281	.311	.967
Cubs total		**113**	**288**	**23**	**70**	**11**	**5**	**0**	**31**	**16**	**—**	**17**	**2**	**12**	**—**	**5**	**—**	**.243**	**.288**	**.316**	**.968**

English, Elwood George (Woody)
HEIGHT: 5'10" THROWS: RIGHT BATS: RIGHT BORN: 3/2/1907 FREDONIA, OHIO DIED: 9/26/1997 NEWARK, OHIO POSITIONS PLAYED: 2B, 3B, SS

YEAR	TEAM	GAMES	AB	RUNS	HITS	2B	3B	HR	RBI	BB	IBB	SO	HBP	SH	SF	SB	CS	BA	OBA	SA	FA
1927	ChC-N	87	334	46	97	14	4	1	28	16	—	26	1	23	—	1	—	.290	.325	.365	.941
1928	ChC-N	116	475	68	142	22	4	2	34	30	—	28	2	15	—	4	—	.299	.343	.375	.946
1929	ChC-N	144	608	131	168	29	3	1	52	68	—	50	3	21	—	13	—	.276	.352	.339	.955
1930	ChC-N	156	638	152	214	36	17	14	59	100	—	72	6	11	—	3	—	.335	.430	.511	.967
1931	ChC-N	156	634	117	202	38	8	2	53	68	—	80	7	18	—	12	—	.319	.391	.413	.966
1932	ChC-N	127	522	70	142	23	7	3	47	55	—	73	2	12	—	5	—	.272	.344	.360	.956

(continued)

Elwood (Woody) George English, ss-3b-2b, 1927-38

Woody English was a model of consistency for the Cubs infield from the late 1920s into the early 1930s.

Born on March 2, 1907, in Fredonia, Ohio, English was purchased by the Cubs from the New York Giants' Toledo, Ohio, minor league team for $5,000 and two prospects. The Toledo squad actually had several offers for English, but he lobbied for the Cubs because two former Toledo teammates, Lewis Robert "Hack" Wilson and Earl Webb, were already there.

Thus, at age 20, English became a Cub. He hit .290 in a part-time role in 1927. In 1928 he took over the shortstop position from journeyman Jimmy Cooney and spent seven solid years there.

English hit over .300 twice in his career with the Cubs, and he hit .299 another season. In 1930 he became only the fifth Cub to make 200 hits, and in 1931 he did it again. He could also be patient at the plate, walking 100 times in 1930.

English was a versatile performer defensively. In 1929 he played shortstop and was third in the league in assists. In 1930 he was switched to third base, where he committed a league-low nine errors.

In 1931 manager Rogers Hornsby, who had taken over for Joe McCarthy in midseason the previous year, moved English back to shortstop, where he led the league in putouts. But in 1932, English was manning third again, where he once again committed a league-low 14 errors and led the league in fielding percentage in 1933.

That was the year English, along with catcher Gabby Hartnett and pitcher Lon Warneke, played in the first-ever All-Star Game, at Comiskey Park across town.

In 1934 English split his time between shortstop and third base as Cubs manager Charlie Grimm tried to work in newcomer Stan Hack at third. Woody still managed to get more at-bats than either Hack or shortstop Billy Jurges, and he hit .279.

In 1935 and 1936, English's playing time dropped dramatically, and he was eventually traded to the Dodgers, where he played two more years before retiring. He died in Ohio in 1997 at the age of 90.

Although English isn't a leader in any of the Cubs' career offensive categories, he is ninth all-time in number of games played at shortstop with 707 and 10th all-time in number of games played at third in a Chicago uniform with 379.

(continued)

YEAR	TEAM	G	AB	R	H	2B	3B	HR	RBI	BB	IBB	SO	HBP	SH	SF	SB	CS	BA	OBA	SA	FA
1933	ChC-N	105	398	54	104	19	2	3	41	53	—	44	0	6	—	5	—	.261	.348	.342	.973
1934	ChC-N	109	421	65	117	26	5	3	31	48	—	65	1	5	—	6	—	.278	.353	.385	.967
1935	ChC-N	34	84	11	17	2	0	2	8	20	—	4	2	3	—	1	—	.202	.368	.298	.933
1936	ChC-N	64	182	33	45	9	0	0	20	40	—	28	4	6	—	1	—	.247	.394	.297	.980
1937	Bro-N	129	378	45	90	16	2	1	42	65	—	55	0	3	—	4	—	.238	.350	.299	.956
1938	Bro-N	34	72	9	18	2	0	0	7	8	—	11	1	0	—	2	—	.250	.333	.278	.968
Career average		105	396	67	113	20	4	3	35	48	—	45	2	10	—	5	—	.286	.366	.378	.959
Cubs average		110	430	75	125	22	5	3	37	50	—	47	3	12	—	5	—	.291	.368	.386	.959
Career total		1261	4746	801	1356	236	52	32	422	571	—	536	29	123	—	57	—	.286	.366	.378	.959
Cubs total		1098	4296	747	1248	218	50	31	373	498	—	470	28	120	—	51	—	.291	.368	.386	.959

Ernaga, Frank John

HEIGHT: 6'1" THROWS: RIGHT BATS: RIGHT BORN: 8/22/1930 SUSANVILLE, CALIFORNIA POSITIONS PLAYED: OF

YEAR	TEAM	GAMES	AB	RUNS	HITS	2B	3B	HR	RBI	BB	IBB	SO	HBP	SH	SF	SB	CS	BA	OBA	SA	FA
1957	ChC-N	20	35	9	11	3	2	2	7	9	0	14	0	0	0	0	0	.314	.455	.686	.950
1958	ChC-N	9	8	0	1	0	0	0	0	0	0	2	0	0	0	0	0	.125	.125	.125	—
Career average		15	22	5	6	2	1	1	4	5	0	8	0	0	0	0	0	.279	.404	.581	.950
Cubs average		15	22	5	6	2	1	1	4	5	0	8	0	0	0	0	0	.279	.404	.581	.950
Career total		29	43	9	12	3	2	2	7	9	0	16	0	0	0	0	0	.279	.404	.581	.950
Cubs total		29	43	9	12	3	2	2	7	9	0	16	0	0	0	0	0	.279	.404	.581	.950

William (Bill) Lee "Wild Bill" Everitt, 1b-2b-3b-of, 1895–1901

Bill Everitt was an accomplished and consistent hitter for Chicago in the late 1890s.

Everitt was born on December 13, 1868, in Fort Wayne, Indiana. After a few years in the minors, Chicago purchased his contract, and Everitt was elevated to the big club in 1895. Manager Cap Anson stuck the rookie third baseman in the sixth slot on Opening Day, but by the beginning of the next season, the speedy Everitt was leading off.

He was at once the best hitting and second-worst fielding third baseman in his rookie year, with a .358 batting average and a hefty 75 errors. Only Bill Joyce of Washington, with 77 fielding miscues, was worse.

By the next season, Everitt was still hitting well (.320) and had improved his fielding considerably, cutting down on his errors, although Chicago newspapermen still described his work in the field as "always honest," if not always very good.

But he was the perfect leadoff man: no power to speak of, but a player who always made contact with the ball and who could run the bases.

In 1898, after several disappointing seasons, Anson was out as manager and former Chicago shortstop-third baseman Tom Burns was elevated to the managerial slot. Burns loved Everitt's hitting, but like a lot of people, he winced at his fielding.

He convinced Everitt to try first base, which wouldn't be as demanding in the field. Everitt responded well, leading the team in hits and finishing second in the league in putouts from his new position. In 1899 he topped 100 hits for the fifth consecutive year.

Everitt tailed off dramatically in Chicago in 1900, playing in only 23 games and hitting .264. He was traded to the Washington franchise in the American League, where he played one more year before retiring. He died in 1938 in Denver.

Everitt still holds the Cubs record for most singles in a season with 169 in 1899. He is also second all-time on that list with 165 singles in 1895. He is also sixth all-time on the Cubs' career batting average list, at .323.

Everitt, William Lee (Bill *or* Wild Bill)

HEIGHT: 6'0" THROWS: RIGHT BATS: LEFT BORN: 12/13/1868 FORT WAYNE, INDIANA DIED: 1/19/1938 DENVER, COLORADO
POSITIONS PLAYED: 1B, 2B, 3B, OF

YEAR	TEAM	GAMES	AB	RUNS	HITS	2B	3B	HR	RBI	BB	IBB	SO	HBP	SH	SF	SB	CS	BA	OBA	SA	FA
1895	ChN-N	133	550	129	197	16	10	3	88	33	—	42	4	9	—	47	—	.358	.399	.440	.856
1896	ChN-N	132	575	130	184	16	13	2	46	41	—	43	2	7	—	46	—	.320	.367	.403	.882
1897	ChN-N	92	379	63	119	14	7	5	39	36	—	—	0	11	—	26	—	.314	.373	.427	.869
1898	ChN-N	149	596	102	190	15	6	0	69	53	—	—	3	9	—	28	—	.319	.377	.364	.974
1899	ChN-N	136	536	87	166	17	5	1	74	31	—	—	3	14	—	30	—	.310	.351	.366	.971
1900	ChN-N	23	91	10	24	4	0	0	17	3	—	—	0	1	—	2	—	.264	.287	.308	.979
1901	Was-A	33	115	14	22	3	2	0	8	15	—	—	3	4	—	7	—	.191	.301	.252	.967
Career average		100	406	76	129	12	6	2	49	30	—	12	2	8	—	27	—	.317	.368	.389	.946
Cubs average		**111**	**455**	**87**	**147**	**14**	**7**	**2**	**56**	**33**	—	**14**	**2**	**9**	—	**30**	—	**.323**	**.371**	**.395**	**.945**
Career total		698	2842	535	902	85	43	11	341	212	—	85	15	55	—	186	—	.317	.368	.389	.946
Cubs total		**665**	**2727**	**521**	**880**	**82**	**41**	**11**	**333**	**197**	—	**85**	**12**	**51**	—	**179**	—	**.323**	**.371**	**.395**	**.945**

Evers, John Joseph (Johnny *or* Crab *or* Trojan)

HEIGHT: 5'9"   THROWS: RIGHT   BATS: LEFT   BORN: 7/21/1881 TROY, NEW YORK   DIED: 3/28/1947 ALBANY, NEW YORK   POSITIONS PLAYED: 2B, 3B, SS, OF

YEAR	TEAM	GAMES	AB	RUNS	HITS	2B	3B	HR	RBI	BB	IBB	SO	HBP	SH	SF	SB	CS	BA	OBA	SA	FA
1902	ChC-N	26	90	7	20	0	0	0	2	3	—	—	2	3	—	1	—	.222	.263	.222	.964
1903	ChC-N	124	464	70	136	27	7	0	52	19	—	—	3	11	—	25	—	.293	.325	.381	.922
1904	ChC-N	152	532	49	141	14	7	0	47	28	—	—	4	23	—	26	—	.265	.307	.318	.943
1905	ChC-N	99	340	44	94	11	2	1	37	27	—	—	2	20	—	19	—	.276	.333	.329	.937
1906	ChC-N	154	533	65	136	17	6	1	51	36	—	—	2	24	—	49	—	.255	.305	.315	.947
1907	ChC-N	151	508	66	127	18	4	2	51	38	—	—	5	14	—	46	—	.250	.309	.313	.964
1908	ChC-N	126	416	83	125	19	6	0	37	66	—	—	5	22	—	36	—	.300	.402	.375	.964
1909	ChC-N	127	463	88	122	19	6	1	24	73	—	—	4	12	—	28	—	.263	.369	.337	.960
1910	ChC-N	125	433	87	114	11	7	0	28	108	—	18	2	13	—	28	—	.263	.413	.321	.942
1911	ChC-N	46	155	29	35	4	3	0	7	34	—	10	2	4	—	6	—	.226	.372	.290	.950
1912	ChC-N	143	478	73	163	23	11	1	63	74	—	18	2	14	—	16	—	.341	.431	.441	.963
1913	ChC-N	136	446	81	127	20	5	3	49	50	—	14	3	24	—	11	—	.285	.361	.372	.959
1914	Bos-N	139	491	81	137	20	3	1	40	87	—	26	2	31	—	12	—	.279	.390	.338	.960
1915	Bos-N	83	278	38	73	4	1	1	22	50	—	16	0	21	—	7	8	.263	.375	.295	.976
1916	Bos-N	71	241	33	52	4	1	0	15	40	—	19	1	12	—	5	—	.216	.330	.241	.959
1917	Bos-N	24	83	5	16	0	0	0	0	13	—	8	0	2	—	1	—	.193	.302	.193	.951
1917	Phi-N	56	183	20	41	5	1	1	12	30	—	13	0	6	—	8	—	.224	.333	.279	.950
1922	CWS-A	1	3	0	0	0	0	0	1	2	—	0	0	0	—	0	—	.000	.400	.000	.972
1929	Bos-N	1	0	0	0	0	0	0	0	0	—	0	0	0	—	0	0	.000	—	—	1.000
Career average		99	341	51	92	12	4	1	30	43	—	8	2	14	—	18	0	.270	.356	.334	.953
Cubs average		117	405	62	112	15	5	1	37	46	—	5	3	15	—	24	—	.276	.354	.334	.950
Career total		1784	6137	919	1659	216	70	12	538	778	—	142	39	256	—	324	8	.270	.356	.334	.953
Cubs total		1409	4858	742	1340	183	64	9	448	556	—	60	36	184	—	291	—	.276	.354	.345	.950

John (Johnny) Joseph "the Crab," "the Trojan" Evers, 2b-3b-ss-of, 1902–17, 1922, 1929

The diminutive, clever Evers was the lynchpin of the most famous double-play combination of all time, along with shortstop Joe Tinker and first sacker Frank Chance.

Evers (which rhymes with "weavers," not "nevers") was born on July 21, 1881, in Troy, New York. He was a minor league star in that city when he was called up on Labor Day by the Cubs in 1902. Some of his teammates took one look at the 5'5" 125-pound Evers and declared that he would be eaten alive at second base.

But they greatly underestimated Evers's gritty toughness. He played 26 games that year and got 20 hits. In 1903 Evers played in 124 games, hitting .293, which led all National League second basemen. He was also third in fielding percentage for National League second basemen.

That was also the year the famed Tinker to Evers to Chance double-play combination was born. Surprisingly, Chicago never led the league in double plays during the eight years the three men manned their respective positions.

But, as many have pointed out, the Cubs pitching, particularly from 1906 to 1910, was so overpowering that opposing base runners were in relatively short supply. From 1903 to 1910, Cubs pitchers were first in National League team ERAs five times, second twice and third once. It has been fashionable to portray the three as only average defensive players, but average players don't win four pennants in five years.

Besides, the Dead Ball Era of the late–19th and early–20th century simply precluded a lot of hits and base runners anyway by modern standards.

The fact is, the Cubs won their championships behind great pitching and great defense and Tinker, Evers and Chance were

(continued)

(continued)

the core of that defense. The three, as well as third baseman Harry Steinfeldt, worked exceptionally well together and were, in the eyes of many, the best defensive unit of the era.

Evers was nicknamed "the Trojan" for his city of birth and "the Crab" because of the way he sidled up to ground balls in the infield. The latter moniker could also describe his prickly disposition.

Evers was wound pretty tight throughout his career, and, in fact, he missed much of the 1911 season after suffering a nervous breakdown. Despite being a little guy, he was not afraid to castigate fellow players if they made an error, and at one point in 1908, Chance, by then the team's manager, seriously considered putting him in the outfield just to get him out of earshot.

He and Tinker weren't exactly pals off the field, either. Evers said it was because Tinker gunned a ball over to him from his shortstop position and laughed when Evers jammed his finger. Other Cubs report that the two got into an argument over cab fare. For whatever reason, it didn't take much to set either man off against the other, and the stories about fistfights in the Cubs clubhouse between the two were not made up. For many years, the two men did not speak, until they had a tearful reunion during the Cubs' 1938 World Series appearance.

It was also rumored that Evers was so "full of electricity" that he couldn't wear a watch because his highly-charged body would stop it.

Well, let's remember that most watches of the 1910s were spring-wound, not electric, so maybe Evers was just so nerved up that he'd forget to wind the darn thing from time to time.

Between 1906 and 1910, Evers averaged more than 120 hits and 32 stolen bases a season. He also led the Cubs in runs scored in 1908 and 1909. In 1908 Evers made the most famous defensive play in baseball history, touching second base in a September game against the Giants that

Fanning, William James (Jim)

HEIGHT: 5'11" THROWS: RIGHT BATS: RIGHT BORN: 9/14/1927 CHICAGO, ILLINOIS POSITIONS PLAYED: C

YEAR	TEAM	GAMES	AB	RUNS	HITS	2B	3B	HR	RBI	BB	IBB	SO	HBP	SH	SF	SB	CS	BA	OBA	SA	FA
1954	ChC-N	11	38	2	7	0	0	0	1	1	—	7	0	0	0	0	0	.184	.205	.184	1.000
1955	ChC-N	5	10	0	0	0	0	0	0	1	0	2	0	0	0	0	0	.000	.091	.000	1.000
1956	ChC-N	1	4	0	1	0	0	0	0	0	0	0	0	0	0	0	0	.250	.250	.250	.800
1957	ChC-N	47	89	3	16	2	0	0	4	4	1	17	1	1	0	0	0	.180	.223	.202	.981
Career average		16	35	1	6	1	0	0	1	2	0	7	0	0	0	0	0	.170	.209	.184	.979
Cubs average		16	35	1	6	1	0	0	1	2	0	7	0	0	0	0	0	.170	.209	.184	.979
Career total		64	141	5	24	2	0	0	5	6	1	26	1	1	0	0	0	.170	.209	.184	.979
Cubs total		64	141	5	24	2	0	0	5	6	1	26	1	1	0	0	0	.170	.209	.184	.979

Fanzone, Carmen Donald

HEIGHT: 6'0" THROWS: RIGHT BATS: RIGHT BORN: 8/30/1943 DETROIT, MICHIGAN POSITIONS PLAYED: 1B, 2B, 3B, SS, OF

YEAR	TEAM	GAMES	AB	RUNS	HITS	2B	3B	HR	RBI	BB	IBB	SO	HBP	SH	SF	SB	CS	BA	OBA	SA	FA
1970	Bos-A	10	15	0	3	1	0	0	3	2	0	2	1	0	1	0	0	.200	.316	.267	.750
1971	ChC-N	12	43	5	8	2	0	2	5	2	0	7	0	0	0	0	0	.186	.222	.372	.939
1972	ChC-N	86	222	26	50	11	0	8	42	35	6	45	3	0	4	2	3	.225	.333	.383	.975
1973	ChC-N	64	150	22	41	7	0	6	22	20	1	38	0	1	1	1	2	.273	.357	.440	.967
1974	ChC-N	65	158	13	30	6	0	4	22	15	1	27	2	2	3	0	1	.190	.264	.304	.918
Career average		47	118	13	26	5	0	4	19	15	2	24	1	1	2	1	1	.224	.313	.372	.955
Cubs average		57	143	17	32	7	0	5	23	18	2	29	1	1	2	1	2	.225	.313	.375	.959
Career total		237	588	66	132	27	0	20	94	74	8	119	6	3	9	3	6	.224	.313	.372	.955
Cubs total		227	573	66	129	26	0	20	91	72	8	117	5	3	8	3	6	.225	.313	.375	.959

resulted in a force out in the ninth inning after New York base runner Fred Merkle, perched on first base, had left the base path to celebrate the win before touching second.

That tie game resulted in a replay game at the Polo Grounds that the Cubs won, 4-2. Chicago went on to win its final World Series of the century against the Tigers.

After his unexpected 1911 Sabbath, Evers bounced back with strong seasons in 1912 and 1913. That was the year he replaced Chance as manager of the Cubs. Chance and Cubs owner Charles Murphy didn't get along, so Murphy canned the Peerless Leader during the 1913 spring season and elevated Evers. But Murphy soon found the prickly Evers was no prize, either, and canned him at the end of the year.

Evers was thought to be washed up, but he signed with the Braves, and Boston, a doormat for several years, surged to the National League flag

as Evers won the most valuable player award. With Evers dominating the World Series with a .438 average, the "Miracle Braves" went on to win the World Championship that year.

Evers was a part-time player with the Braves and the Phillies for three more years before retiring in 1917. Coaching stints in several towns followed, including a year with John McGraw and the Giants. He also managed the White Sox briefly. He, Tinker and Chance were named to the Hall of Fame in 1946. Evers got to enjoy that nomination for just six months, dying in March 1947.

Evers is sixth all-time with the Cubs in stolen bases with 291, and he also ranks very well in a host of Cubs' World Series categories, including sixth in most hits with 17, fourth in runs scored with nine, 10th in batting average with a .283 mark and ninth in at-bats with 60.

Farrell, Charles Andrew (Duke)

HEIGHT: 6'1"   THROWS: RIGHT   BATS: BOTH   BORN: 8/31/1866 OAKDALE, MASSACHUSETTS   DIED: 2/15/1925 BOSTON, MASSACHUSETTS   POSITIONS PLAYED: C, 1B, 3B, SS, OF

YEAR	TEAM	GAMES	AB	RUNS	HITS	2B	3B	HR	RBI	BB	IBB	SO	HBP	SH	SF	SB	CS	BA	OBA	SA	FA
1888	ChN-N	64	241	34	56	6	3	3	19	4	—	41	0	—	—	8	—	.232	.245	.320	.879
1889	ChN-N	101	407	66	101	19	7	11	75	41	—	21	1	—	—	13	—	.248	.318	.410	.908
1890	Chi-P	117	451	79	131	21	12	2	84	42	—	28	1	—	—	8	—	.290	.352	.404	.937
1891	Bos-AA	122	473	108	143	19	13	12	110	59	—	48	4	—	—	21	—	.302	.384	.474	.923
1892	Pit-N	152	605	96	130	10	13	8	77	46	—	53	5	—	—	20	—	.215	.276	.314	.877
1893	Was-N	124	511	84	144	13	13	4	75	47	—	12	5	—	—	11	—	.282	.348	.382	.919
1894	NYG-N	114	401	47	114	20	12	4	66	35	—	15	3	3	—	9	—	.284	.346	.424	.927
1895	NYG-N	90	312	38	90	16	9	1	58	38	—	18	3	4	—	11	—	.288	.371	.407	.929
1896	NYG-N	58	191	23	54	7	3	1	37	19	—	7	1	7	—	2	—	.283	.351	.366	.897
1896	Was-N	37	130	18	39	7	3	1	30	7	—	3	2	5	—	2	—	.300	.345	.423	.961
1897	Was-N	78	261	41	84	9	6	0	53	17	—	—	9	5	—	8	—	.322	.383	.402	.944
1898	Was-N	99	338	47	106	12	6	1	53	34	—	—	4	3	—	12	—	.314	.383	.393	.952
1899	Was-N	5	12	2	4	1	0	0	1	2	—	—	0	0	—	1	—	.333	.429	.417	1.000
1899	Bro-N	80	254	40	76	10	7	2	55	35	—	—	7	1	—	6	—	.299	.399	.417	.948
1900	Bro-N	76	273	33	75	11	5	0	39	11	—	—	3	4	—	3	—	.275	.310	.352	.944
1901	Bro-N	80	284	38	84	10	6	1	31	7	—	—	3	2	—	7	—	.296	.320	.384	.973
1902	Bro-N	74	264	14	64	5	2	0	24	12	—	—	2	7	—	6	—	.242	.281	.277	.979
1903	Bos-A	17	52	5	21	5	1	0	8	5	—	—	1	4	—	1	—	.404	.466	.538	.960
1904	Bos-A	68	198	11	42	9	2	0	15	15	—	—	4	6	—	1	—	.212	.281	.278	.958
1905	Bos-A	7	21	2	6	1	0	0	2	1	—	—	0	0	—	0	—	.286	.318	.333	1.000
Career average		87	316	46	87	12	7	3	51	27	—	14	3	3	—	8	—	.275	.338	.383	.933
Cubs average		**83**	**324**	**50**	**79**	**13**	**5**	**7**	**47**	**23**	—	**31**	**1**	—	—	**11**	—	**.242**	**.293**	**.377**	**.897**
Career total		1563	5679	826	1564	211	123	51	912	477	—	246	58	51	—	150	—	.275	.338	.383	.933
Cubs total		**165**	**648**	**100**	**157**	**25**	**10**	**14**	**94**	**45**	—	**62**	**1**	—	—	**21**	—	**.242**	**.293**	**.377**	**.897**

Farrell, Edward Stephen (Doc)
HEIGHT: 5'8" THROWS: RIGHT BATS: RIGHT BORN: 12/26/1901 JOHNSON CITY, NEW YORK DIED: 12/20/1966 LIVINGSTON, NEW JERSEY POSITIONS PLAYED: 1B, 2B, 3B, SS

YEAR	TEAM	GAMES	AB	RUNS	HITS	2B	3B	HR	RBI	BB	IBB	SO	HBP	SH	SF	SB	CS	BA	OBA	SA	FA
1925	NYG-N	27	56	6	12	1	0	0	4	4	—	6	0	2	—	0	1	.214	.267	.232	.938
1926	NYG-N	67	171	19	49	10	1	2	23	12	—	17	2	5	—	4	—	.287	.341	.392	.953
1927	NYG-N	42	142	13	55	10	1	3	34	12	—	11	2	3	—	0	—	.387	.442	.535	.904
1927	Bos-N	110	424	44	124	13	2	1	58	14	—	21	0	19	—	4	—	.292	.315	.340	.941
1928	Bos-N	134	483	36	104	14	2	3	43	26	—	26	5	19	—	3	—	.215	.263	.271	.933
1929	Bos-N	5	8	0	1	0	0	0	2	0	—	1	0	0	—	0	—	.125	.125	.125	1.000
1929	NYG-N	63	178	18	38	6	0	0	16	9	—	17	0	5	—	2	—	.213	.251	.247	.936
1930	StL-N	23	61	3	13	1	1	0	6	4	—	2	0	1	—	1	—	.213	.262	.262	.960
1930	StL-N	23	61	3	13	1	1	0	6	4	—	2	0	1	—	0	—	.292	.344	.372	.925
1930	**ChC-N**	**46**	**113**	**21**	**33**	**6**	**0**	**1**	**16**	**9**	**—**	**5**	**0**	**3**	**—**	**0**	**0**	**.175**	**.212**	**.222**	**.963**
1932	NYY-A	26	63	4	11	1	1	0	4	2	—	8	1	1	—	0	0	.269	.376	.269	.941
1933	NYY-A	44	93	16	25	0	0	0	6	16	—	6	0	3	—	0	0	.286	.375	.429	.917
1935	Bos-A	4	7	1	2	1	0	0	1	1	—	0	0	0	—	0	0				
Career average		66	200	20	52	7	1	1	24	12	—	13	1	7	—	2	0	.260	.306	.320	.937
Cubs average		**46**	**113**	**21**	**33**	**6**	**0**	**1**	**16**	**9**	**—**	**5**	**0**	**3**	**—**	**0**	**0**	**.292**	**.344**	**.372**	**.925**
Career total		591	1799	181	467	63	8	10	213	109	—	120	10	61	—	14	1	.260	.306	.320	.937
Cubs total		**46**	**113**	**21**	**33**	**6**	**0**	**1**	**16**	**9**	**—**	**5**	**0**	**3**	**—**	**0**	**0**	**.292**	**.344**	**.372**	**.925**

Felderman, Marvin Wilfred (Marv *or* Coonie)
HEIGHT: 6'1" THROWS: RIGHT BATS: RIGHT BORN: 12/20/1915 BELLEVUE, IOWA DIED: 8/6/2000 RIVERSIDE, CALIFORNIA POSITIONS PLAYED: C

YEAR	TEAM	GAMES	AB	RUNS	HITS	2B	3B	HR	RBI	BB	IBB	SO	HBP	SH	SF	SB	CS	BA	OBA	SA	FA
1942	**ChC-N**	**3**	**6**	**0**	**1**	**0**	**0**	**0**	**0**	**1**	**—**	**4**	**0**	**0**	**—**	**0**	**—**	**.167**	**.286**	**.167**	**1.000**
Career average		3	6	0	1	0	0	0	0	1	—	4	0	0	—	0	—	.167	.286	.167	1.000
Cubs average		**3**	**6**	**0**	**1**	**0**	**0**	**0**	**0**	**1**	**—**	**4**	**0**	**0**	**—**	**0**	**—**	**.167**	**.286**	**.167**	**1.000**
Career total		3	6	0	1	0	0	0	0	1	—	4	0	0	—	0	—	.167	.286	.167	1.000
Cubs total		**3**	**6**	**0**	**1**	**0**	**0**	**0**	**0**	**1**	**—**	**4**	**0**	**0**	**—**	**0**	**—**	**.167**	**.286**	**.167**	**1.000**

Felske, John Frederick
HEIGHT: 6'3" THROWS: RIGHT BATS: RIGHT BORN: 5/30/1942 CHICAGO, ILLINOIS POSITIONS PLAYED: C, 1B

YEAR	TEAM	GAMES	AB	RUNS	HITS	2B	3B	HR	RBI	BB	IBB	SO	HBP	SH	SF	SB	CS	BA	OBA	SA	FA
1968	**ChC-N**	**4**	**2**	**0**	**0**	**0**	**0**	**0**	**0**	**0**	**0**	**1**	**0**	**0**	**0**	**0**	**0**	**.000**	**.000**	**.000**	**.833**
1972	Mil-A	37	80	6	11	3	0	1	5	8	0	23	0	1	0	0	0	.138	.216	.213	.978
1973	Mil-A	13	22	1	3	0	1	0	4	1	0	11	0	0	1	0	0	.136	.167	.227	1.000
Career average		18	35	2	5	1	0	0	3	3	0	12	0	0	0	0	0	.135	.202	.212	.979
Cubs average		**4**	**2**	**0**	**0**	**0**	**0**	**0**	**0**	**0**	**0**	**1**	**0**	**0**	**0**	**0**	**0**	**.000**	**.000**	**.000**	**.833**
Career total		54	104	7	14	3	1	1	9	9	0	35	0	1	1	0	0	.135	.202	.212	.979
Cubs total		**4**	**2**	**0**	**0**	**0**	**0**	**0**	**0**	**0**	**0**	**1**	**0**	**0**	**0**	**0**	**0**	**.000**	**.000**	**.000**	**.833**

Ferguson, Robert Vavasour (Bob *or* Death to Flying Things)
HEIGHT: 5'9" THROWS: RIGHT BATS: BOTH BORN: 1/31/1845 BROOKLYN, NEW YORK DIED: 5/3/1894 BROOKLYN, NEW YORK
POSITIONS PLAYED: P, C, 1B, 2B, 3B, SS, OF

YEAR	TEAM	GAMES	AB	RUNS	HITS	2B	3B	HR	RBI	BB	IBB	SO	HBP	SH	SF	SB	CS	BA	OBA	SA	FA
1876	Har-N	69	312	48	82	8	5	0	32	2	—	11	—	—	—	—	—	.263	.268	.321	.826
1877	Har-N	58	254	40	65	7	2	0	35	3	—	10	—	—	—	—	—	.256	.265	.299	.842
1878	**ChN-N**	**61**	**259**	**44**	**91**	**10**	**2**	**0**	**39**	**10**	**—**	**12**	**—**	**—**	**—**	**—**	**—**	**.351**	**.375**	**.405**	**.877**
1879	Try-N	30	123	18	31	5	2	0	4	4	—	3	—	—	—	—	—	.252	.276	.325	.843
1880	Try-N	82	332	55	87	9	0	0	22	24	—	24	—	—	—	—	—	.262	.312	.289	.904
1881	Try-N	85	339	56	96	13	5	1	35	29	—	12	—	—	—	—	—	.283	.340	.360	.904
1882	Try-N	81	319	44	82	15	2	0	32	23	—	21	—	—	—	—	—	.257	.307	.317	.905
1883	Phi-N	86	329	39	85	9	2	0	27	18	—	21	—	—	—	—	—	.258	.297	.298	.862
1884	Pit-AA	10	41	2	6	0	0	0	—	0	—	—	0	—	—	—	—	.146	.146	.146	.872
Career average		62	256	38	69	8	2	0	25	13	—	13	0	—	—	—	—	.271	.305	.322	.878
Cubs average		**61**	**259**	**44**	**91**	**10**	**2**	**0**	**39**	**10**	**—**	**12**	**—**	**—**	**—**	**—**	**—**	**.351**	**.375**	**.405**	**.877**
Career total		562	2308	346	625	76	20	1	226	113	—	114	0	—	—	—	—	.271	.305	.322	.878
Cubs total		**61**	**259**	**44**	**91**	**10**	**2**	**0**	**39**	**10**	**—**	**12**	**—**	**—**	**—**	**—**	**—**	**.351**	**.375**	**.405**	**.877**

Fermin, Felix Jose (Gato)
HEIGHT: 5'11"   THROWS: RIGHT   BATS: RIGHT   BORN: 10/9/1963 MAO VALVERDE, DOMINICAN REPUBLIC   POSITIONS PLAYED: 1B, 2B, 3B, SS

YEAR	TEAM	GAMES	AB	RUNS	HITS	2B	3B	HR	RBI	BB	IBB	SO	HBP	SH	SF	SB	CS	BA	OBA	SA	FA
1987	Pit-N	23	68	6	17	0	0	0	4	4	1	9	1	2	0	0	0	.250	.301	.250	.980
1988	Pit-N	43	87	9	24	0	2	0	2	8	1	10	3	1	1	3	1	.276	.354	.322	.955
1989	Cle-A	156	484	50	115	9	1	0	21	41	0	27	4	32	1	6	4	.238	.302	.260	.967
1990	Cle-A	148	414	47	106	13	2	1	40	26	0	22	0	13	5	3	3	.256	.297	.304	.975
1991	Cle-A	129	424	30	111	13	2	0	31	26	0	27	3	13	3	5	4	.262	.307	.302	.980
1992	Cle-A	79	215	27	58	7	2	0	13	18	1	10	1	9	2	0	0	.270	.326	.321	.969
1993	Cle-A	140	480	48	126	16	2	2	45	24	1	14	4	5	1	4	5	.263	.303	.317	.960
1994	Sea-A	101	379	52	120	21	0	1	35	11	0	22	4	12	5	4	4	.317	.338	.380	.977
1995	Sea-A	73	200	21	39	6	0	0	15	6	0	6	4	8	1	2	0	.195	.232	.225	.979
1996	**ChC-N**	**11**	**16**	**4**	**2**	**1**	**0**	**0**	**1**	**2**	**0**	**0**	**0**	**1**	**0**	**0**	**1**	**.125**	**.222**	**.188**	**.923**
Career average		90	277	29	72	9	1	0	21	17	0	15	2	10	2	3	2	.259	.305	.303	.971
Cubs average		**11**	**16**	**4**	**2**	**1**	**0**	**0**	**1**	**2**	**0**	**0**	**0**	**1**	**0**	**0**	**0**	**.125**	**.222**	**.188**	**.923**
Career total		903	2767	294	718	86	11	4	207	166	4	147	24	96	19	27	21	.259	.305	.303	.971
Cubs total		**11**	**16**	**4**	**2**	**1**	**0**	**0**	**1**	**2**	**0**	**0**	**0**	**1**	**0**	**0**	**0**	**.125**	**.222**	**.188**	**.923**

Fernandez, Frank
HEIGHT: 6'0"   THROWS: RIGHT   BATS: RIGHT   BORN: 4/16/1943 STATEN ISLAND, NEW YORK   POSITIONS PLAYED: C, OF

YEAR	TEAM	GAMES	AB	RUNS	HITS	2B	3B	HR	RBI	BB	IBB	SO	HBP	SH	SF	SB	CS	BA	OBA	SA	FA
1967	NYY-A	9	28	1	6	2	0	1	4	2	0	7	1	0	1	1	1	.214	.281	.393	1.000
1968	NYY-A	51	135	15	23	6	1	7	30	35	2	50	0	0	0	1	0	.170	.341	.385	.989
1969	NYY-A	89	229	34	51	6	1	12	29	65	3	68	0	0	1	1	3	.223	.399	.415	.992
1970	Oak-A	94	252	30	54	5	0	15	44	40	4	76	3	0	1	1	0	.214	.327	.413	.993
1971	Oak-A	4	9	1	1	1	0	0	1	1	0	3	0	0	0	0	0	.111	.200	.222	1.000
1971	Was-A	18	30	0	3	0	0	0	4	4	0	10	0	0	0	0	0	.100	.194	.100	1.000
1971	**ChC-N**	**17**	**41**	**11**	**7**	**1**	**0**	**4**	**4**	**17**	**0**	**10**	**0**	**1**	**2**	**0**	**0**	**.171**	**.414**	**.488**	**.980**
1972	**ChC-N**	**3**	**3**	**0**	**0**	**0**	**0**	**0**	**0**	**0**	**0**	**2**	**0**	**0**	**0**	**0**	**0**	**.000**	**.000**	**.000**	**1.000**
Career average		48	121	15	24	4	0	7	19	27	2	39	1	0	1	1	1	.199	.350	.395	.991
Cubs average		**10**	**22**	**6**	**4**	**1**	**0**	**2**	**2**	**9**	**0**	**9**	**0**	**0**	**0**	**0**	**0**	**.159**	**.393**	**.455**	**.980**
Career total		285	727	92	145	21	2	39	116	164	9	231	6	1	4	4	4	.199	.350	.395	.980
Cubs total		**20**	**44**	**11**	**7**	**1**	**0**	**4**	**4**	**17**	**0**	**17**	**0**	**0**	**0**	**0**	**0**	**.159**	**.393**	**.455**	**.980**

Figueroa, Jesus Maria
HEIGHT: 5'10"   THROWS: LEFT   BATS: LEFT   BORN: 2/20/1957 SANTO DOMINGO, DOMINICAN REPUBLIC   POSITIONS PLAYED: OF

YEAR	TEAM	GAMES	AB	RUNS	HITS	2B	3B	HR	RBI	BB	IBB	SO	HBP	SH	SF	SB	CS	BA	OBA	SA	FA
1980	**ChC-N**	**115**	**198**	**20**	**50**	**5**	**0**	**1**	**11**	**14**	**0**	**16**	**2**	**2**	**0**	**2**	**1**	**.253**	**.308**	**.293**	**.979**
Career average		115	198	20	50	5	0	1	11	14	0	16	2	2	0	2	1	.253	.308	.293	.979
Cubs average		**115**	**198**	**20**	**50**	**5**	**0**	**1**	**11**	**14**	**0**	**16**	**2**	**2**	**0**	**2**	**1**	**.253**	**.308**	**.293**	**.979**
Career total		115	198	20	50	5	0	1	11	14	0	16	2	2	0	2	1	.253	.308	.293	.979
Cubs total		**115**	**198**	**20**	**50**	**5**	**0**	**1**	**11**	**14**	**0**	**16**	**2**	**2**	**0**	**2**	**1**	**.253**	**.308**	**.293**	**.979**

Fischer, William Charles
HEIGHT: 6'0"   THROWS: RIGHT   BATS: LEFT   BORN: 3/2/1891 NEW YORK, NEW YORK   DIED: 9/4/1945 RICHMOND, VIRGINIA   POSITIONS PLAYED: C, 1B

YEAR	TEAM	GAMES	AB	RUNS	HITS	2B	3B	HR	RBI	BB	IBB	SO	HBP	SH	SF	SB	CS	BA	OBA	SA	FA
1913	Bro-N	62	165	16	44	9	4	1	12	10	—	5	1	2	—	0	—	.267	.313	.388	.974
1914	Bro-N	43	105	12	27	1	2	0	8	8	—	12	0	3	—	1	—	.257	.310	.305	.958
1915	Chi-F	105	292	30	96	15	4	4	50	24	—	19	2	11	—	5	—	.329	.384	.449	.972
1916	**ChC-N**	**65**	**179**	**15**	**35**	**9**	**2**	**1**	**14**	**11**	**—**	**8**	**1**	**5**	**—**	**2**	**—**	**.196**	**.246**	**.285**	**.973**
1916	Pit-N	42	113	11	29	7	1	1	6	10	—	3	1	4	—	1	—	.257	.323	.363	.974
1917	Pit-N	95	245	25	70	9	2	3	25	27	—	19	1	4	—	11	—	.286	.359	.376	.962
Career average		82	220	22	60	10	3	2	23	18	—	13	1	6	—	4	—	.274	.332	.374	.969
Cubs average		**65**	**179**	**15**	**35**	**9**	**2**	**1**	**14**	**11**	**—**	**8**	**1**	**5**	**—**	**2**	**—**	**.196**	**.246**	**.285**	**.973**
Career total		412	1099	109	301	50	15	10	115	90	—	66	6	29	—	20	—	.274	.332	.374	.969
Cubs total		**65**	**179**	**15**	**35**	**9**	**2**	**1**	**14**	**11**	**—**	**8**	**1**	**5**	**—**	**2**	**—**	**.196**	**.246**	**.285**	**.973**

Fisher, Robert Taylor (Tom)

HEIGHT: 5'9"   THROWS: RIGHT   BATS: RIGHT   BORN: 11/3/1886 NASHVILLE, TENNESSEE   DIED: 8/4/1963 JACKSONVILLE, FLORIDA
POSITIONS PLAYED: 2B, 3B, SS, OF

YEAR	TEAM	GAMES	AB	RUNS	HITS	2B	3B	HR	RBI	BB	IBB	SO	HBP	SH	SF	SB	CS	BA	OBA	SA	FA
1912	Bro-N	82	257	27	60	10	3	0	26	14	—	32	0	13	—	7	—	.233	.273	.296	.915
1913	Bro-N	132	474	42	124	11	10	4	54	10	—	43	1	16	—	16	—	.262	.278	.352	.923
1914	**ChC-N**	**15**	**50**	**5**	**15**	**2**	**2**	**0**	**5**	**3**	**—**	**4**	**0**	**3**	**—**	**2**	**—**	**.300**	**.340**	**.420**	**.943**
1915	**ChC-N**	**147**	**568**	**70**	**163**	**22**	**5**	**5**	**53**	**30**	**—**	**51**	**3**	**42**	**—**	**9**	**20**	**.287**	**.326**	**.370**	**.933**
1916	Cin-N	61	136	9	37	4	3	0	11	8	—	14	0	2	—	7	—	.272	.313	.346	.905
1918	StL-N	63	246	36	78	11	3	2	20	15	—	11	0	5	—	7	—	.317	.356	.411	.979
1919	StL-N	3	11	0	3	1	0	0	1	0	—	2	0	1	—	0	—	.273	.273	.364	.900
Career average		72	249	27	69	9	4	2	24	11	—	22	1	12	—	7	3	.276	.309	.359	.933
Cubs average		**81**	**309**	**38**	**89**	**12**	**4**	**3**	**29**	**17**	**—**	**28**	**2**	**23**	**—**	**6**	**10**	**.288**	**.327**	**.374**	**.934**
Career total		503	1742	189	480	61	26	11	170	80	—	157	4	82	—	48	20	.276	.309	.359	.933
Cubs total		**162**	**618**	**75**	**178**	**24**	**7**	**5**	**58**	**33**	**—**	**55**	**3**	**45**	**—**	**11**	**20**	**.288**	**.327**	**.374**	**.934**

Fitzgerald, Howard Chumney (Howie *or* Lefty)

HEIGHT: 5'11"   THROWS: LEFT   BATS: LEFT   BORN: 5/16/1902 EAGLE LAKE, TEXAS   DIED: 2/27/1959 MATHEWS, TEXAS   POSITIONS PLAYED: OF

YEAR	TEAM	GAMES	AB	RUNS	HITS	2B	3B	HR	RBI	BB	IBB	SO	HBP	SH	SF	SB	CS	BA	OBA	SA	FA
1922	**ChC-N**	**10**	**24**	**3**	**8**	**1**	**0**	**0**	**4**	**3**	**—**	**2**	**0**	**1**	**—**	**1**	**0**	**.333**	**.407**	**.375**	**.818**
1924	**ChC-N**	**7**	**19**	**1**	**3**	**0**	**0**	**0**	**2**	**0**	**—**	**2**	**0**	**0**	**—**	**0**	**0**	**.158**	**.158**	**.158**	**1.000**
1926	Bos-A	31	97	11	25	2	0	0	8	5	—	7	0	1	—	1	4	.258	.294	.278	.882
Career average		16	47	5	12	1	0	0	5	3	—	4	0	1	—	1	1	.257	.297	.279	.878
Cubs average		**9**	**22**	**2**	**6**	**1**	**0**	**0**	**3**	**2**	**—**	**2**	**0**	**1**	**—**	**1**	**0**	**.256**	**.304**	**.279**	**.867**
Career total		48	140	15	36	3	0	0	14	8	—	11	0	2	—	2	4	.257	.297	.279	.878
Cubs total		**17**	**43**	**4**	**11**	**1**	**0**	**0**	**6**	**3**	**—**	**4**	**0**	**1**	**—**	**1**	**0**	**.256**	**.304**	**.279**	**.867**

Flack, Max John

HEIGHT: 5'7"   THROWS: LEFT   BATS: LEFT   BORN: 2/5/1890 BELLEVILLE, ILLINOIS   DIED: 7/31/1975 BELLEVILLE, ILLINOIS   POSITIONS PLAYED: OF

YEAR	TEAM	GAMES	AB	RUNS	HITS	2B	3B	HR	RBI	BB	IBB	SO	HBP	SH	SF	SB	CS	BA	OBA	SA	FA
1914	Chi-F	134	502	66	124	15	3	2	39	51	—	48	6	10	—	37	—	.247	.324	.301	.973
1915	Chi-F	141	523	88	164	20	14	3	45	40	—	21	2	18	—	37	—	.314	.365	.423	.969
1916	**ChC-N**	**141**	**465**	**65**	**120**	**14**	**3**	**3**	**20**	**42**	**—**	**43**	**0**	**39**	**—**	**24**	**19**	**.258**	**.320**	**.320**	**.991**
1917	**ChC-N**	**131**	**447**	**65**	**111**	**18**	**7**	**0**	**21**	**51**	**—**	**34**	**0**	**12**	**—**	**17**	**—**	**.248**	**.325**	**.320**	**.947**
1918	**ChC-N**	**123**	**478**	**74**	**123**	**17**	**10**	**4**	**41**	**56**	**—**	**19**	**6**	**12**	**—**	**17**	**—**	**.257**	**.343**	**.360**	**.978**
1919	**ChC-N**	**116**	**469**	**71**	**138**	**20**	**4**	**6**	**35**	**34**	**—**	**13**	**3**	**11**	**—**	**18**	**—**	**.294**	**.346**	**.392**	**.986**
1920	**ChC-N**	**135**	**520**	**85**	**157**	**30**	**6**	**4**	**49**	**52**	**—**	**15**	**7**	**13**	**—**	**13**	**19**	**.302**	**.373**	**.406**	**.967**
1921	**ChC-N**	**133**	**572**	**80**	**172**	**31**	**4**	**6**	**37**	**32**	**—**	**15**	**4**	**7**	**—**	**17**	**11**	**.301**	**.342**	**.400**	**.989**
1922	**ChC-N**	**17**	**54**	**7**	**12**	**1**	**0**	**0**	**6**	**2**	**—**	**4**	**0**	**1**	**—**	**2**	**1**	**.222**	**.250**	**.241**	**.933**
1922	StL-N	66	267	46	78	12	1	2	21	31	—	11	1	3	—	3	5	.292	.368	.367	.968
1923	StL-N	128	505	82	147	16	9	3	28	41	—	16	3	13	—	7	8	.291	.348	.376	.951
1924	StL-N	67	209	31	55	11	3	2	21	21	—	5	0	4	—	3	5	.263	.330	.373	.971
1925	StL-N	79	241	23	60	7	8	0	28	21	—	9	0	4	—	5	3	.249	.309	.344	.991
Career average		118	438	65	122	18	6	3	33	40	—	21	3	12	—	17	6	.278	.342	.366	.972
Cubs average		**114**	**429**	**64**	**119**	**19**	**5**	**3**	**30**	**38**	**—**	**20**	**3**	**14**	**—**	**15**	**7**	**.277**	**.341**	**.366**	**.975**
Career total		1411	5252	783	1461	212	72	35	391	474	—	253	32	147	—	200	71	.278	.342	.366	.972
Cubs total		**796**	**3005**	**447**	**833**	**131**	**34**	**23**	**209**	**269**	**—**	**143**	**20**	**95**	**—**	**108**	**50**	**.277**	**.341**	**.366**	**.975**

Fletcher, Scott Brian

HEIGHT: 5'11"   THROWS: RIGHT   BATS: RIGHT   BORN: 7/30/1958 FORT WALTON BEACH, FLORIDA   POSITIONS PLAYED: 1B, 2B, 3B, SS

YEAR	TEAM	GAMES	AB	RUNS	HITS	2B	3B	HR	RBI	BB	IBB	SO	HBP	SH	SF	SB	CS	BA	OBA	SA	FA
1981	**ChC-N**	**19**	**46**	**6**	**10**	**4**	**0**	**0**	**1**	**2**	**0**	**4**	**0**	**0**	**0**	**0**	**0**	**.217**	**.250**	**.304**	**.963**
1982	**ChC-N**	**11**	**24**	**4**	**4**	**0**	**0**	**0**	**1**	**4**	**0**	**5**	**0**	**0**	**0**	**1**	**0**	**.167**	**.286**	**.167**	**1.000**
1983	CWS-A	114	262	42	62	16	5	3	31	29	0	22	2	7	2	5	1	.237	.315	.370	.964
1984	CWS-A	149	456	46	114	13	3	3	35	46	2	46	8	9	2	10	4	.250	.328	.311	.973
1985	CWS-A	119	301	38	77	8	1	2	31	35	0	47	0	11	1	5	5	.256	.332	.309	.976
1986	Tex-A	147	530	82	159	34	5	3	50	47	0	59	4	10	3	12	11	.300	.360	.400	.974

(continued)

Max John Flack, of, 1914–25

Max Flack was a talented defensive outfielder whose most memorable play—unfortunately—was an outfield error that cost the Cubs the 1918 World Series.

Flack was born on February 5, 1890, in Belleville, Illinois. He started his major league career with the Chicago Whales of the Federal League, hitting .247 in his rookie year of 1914 with the Whales and socking .314 in 1915, which was third in the league.

Flack's offensive and defensive skills made him one of the better players in the Federal League, and when the Cubs bought out the Whales after the 1915 season, Flack became an immediate starter in the Cubs outfield.

Flack wasn't as strong a hitter with the Cubs, but he was one of the best defensive right fielders in baseball when he came to the National League. He twice led National League outfielders in fielding, in 1916 with a .991 mark and again in 1921 with a .989 fielding percentage. He was second in the league in 1918 and 1919.

As a leadoff man, Flack did his job, however. He led the Cubs in runs scored five years in a row, from 1916 to 1920, with a career high of 85 in 1920. He also led the team in hits three times, in doubles once, in triples once and in home runs three times. Of course, in the Dead Ball Era, this meant his long-ball totals were four in 1918, six in 1919 and six in 1921.

But his worst day as a Cubs came in Game 6 of the 1918 World Series. The Cubs were leading the Red Sox, 1-0, in the third inning when Flack dropped a line drive by Sox hitter George Whitman for what should have been the third out. Instead, two Red Sox scored, and a fine outing by George Albert "Lefty" Tyler went by the boards as the Sox won the game, 2-1, and the World Series in six games.

Although he was still playing well, Flack got off to a slow start in 1922, hitting only .222 for the Cubs. Manager Joe McCarthy, fearing he was washed up, traded Flack in between games of a doubleheader with the Cardinals for St. Louis outfielder Cliff Heathcote. The trade worked out immediately for both teams as Flack and Heathcote, both hitless in the first game, each got a hit in the second.

Flack played three more years in St. Louis and was fairly productive until his retirement in 1925. Flack died in his hometown of Belleville in 1975.

(continued)

Year	Team																			
1987	Tex-A	156	588	82	169	28	4	5	63	61	3	66	5	12	2	13	12	.287	.358	.374	.966
1988	Tex-A	140	515	59	142	19	4	0	47	62	1	34	12	15	5	8	5	.276	.364	.328	.983
1989	Tex-A	83	314	47	75	14	1	0	22	38	1	41	2	2	2	1	0	.239	.323	.290	.960
1989	CWS-A	59	232	30	63	11	1	1	21	26	0	19	1	9	3	1	1	.272	.344	.341	.993
1990	CWS-A	151	509	54	123	18	3	4	56	45	3	63	3	11	5	1	3	.242	.304	.312	.988
1991	CWS-A	90	248	14	51	10	1	1	28	17	0	26	3	6	3	0	2	.206	.262	.266	.992
1992	Mil-A	123	386	53	106	18	3	3	51	30	1	33	7	6	4	17	10	.275	.335	.360	.986
1993	Bos-A	121	480	81	137	31	5	5	45	37	1	35	5	6	3	16	3	.285	.341	.402	.982
1994	Bos-A	63	185	31	42	9	1	3	11	16	1	14	2	3	0	8	1	.227	.296	.335	.996
1995	Det-A	67	182	19	42	10	1	1	17	19	0	27	3	4	1	1	0	.231	.312	.313	1.000
Career average		107	351	46	92	16	3	2	34	34	1	36	4	7	2	7	4	.262	.332	.342	.980
Cubs average		**15**	**35**	**5**	**7**	**2**	**0**	**0**	**1**	**3**	**0**	**5**	**0**	**0**	**0**	**1**	**0**	**.200**	**.263**	**.257**	**.974**
Career total		1612	5258	688	1376	243	38	34	510	514	13	541	57	111	36	99	58	.262	.332	.342	.980
Cubs total		**30**	**70**	**10**	**14**	**4**	**0**	**0**	**2**	**6**	**0**	**9**	**0**	**0**	**0**	**1**	**0**	**.200**	**.263**	**.257**	**.974**

Flint, Frank Sylvester (Silver)

HEIGHT: 6'0" THROWS: RIGHT BATS: RIGHT BORN: 8/3/1855 PHILADELPHIA, PENNSYLVANIA DIED: 1/14/1892 CHICAGO, ILLINOIS
POSITIONS PLAYED: C, 1B, OF

YEAR	TEAM	GAMES	AB	RUNS	HITS	2B	3B	HR	RBI	BB	IBB	SO	HBP	SH	SF	SB	CS	BA	OBA	SA	FA
1878	Ind-N	63	254	23	57	7	0	0	18	2	—	15	—	—	—	—	—	.224	.230	.252	.900
1879	ChN-N	79	324	46	92	22	6	1	41	6	—	44	—	—	—	—	—	.284	.297	.398	.915
1880	ChN-N	74	284	30	46	10	4	0	17	5	—	32	—	—	—	—	—	.162	.176	.225	.932
1881	ChN-N	80	306	46	95	18	0	1	34	6	—	39	—	—	—	—	—	.310	.324	.379	.939
1882	ChN-N	81	331	48	83	18	8	4	44	2	—	50	—	—	—	—	—	.251	.255	.390	.934
1883	ChN-N	85	332	57	88	23	4	0	32	3	—	69	—	—	—	—	—	.265	.272	.358	.872
1884	ChN-N	73	279	35	57	5	2	9	45	7	—	57	—	—	—	—	—	.204	.224	.333	.884
1885	ChN-N	68	249	27	52	8	2	1	17	2	—	52	—	—	—	—	—	.209	.215	.269	.927
1886	ChN-N	54	173	30	35	6	2	1	13	12	—	36	—	—	—	1	—	.202	.254	.277	.896
1887	ChN-N	49	191	22	54	8	6	3	21	4	—	28	0	—	—	7	—	.283	.297	.435	.912
1888	ChN-N	22	77	6	14	3	0	0	3	1	—	21	1	—	—	1	—	.182	.203	.221	.926
1889	ChN-N	15	56	6	13	1	0	1	9	3	—	18	0	—	—	1	—	.232	.271	.304	.903
Career average		62	238	31	57	11	3	2	25	4	—	38	0	—	—	1	—	.240	.254	.331	.912
Cubs average		62	237	32	57	11	3	2	25	5	—	41	0	—	—	1	—	.242	.257	.339	.913
Career total		743	2856	376	686	129	34	21	294	53	—	461	1	—	—	10	—	.240	.254	.331	.912
Cubs total		680	2602	353	629	122	34	21	276	51	—	446	1	—	—	10	—	.242	.257	.339	.913

Fluhrer, John Lister

HEIGHT: 5'9" THROWS: RIGHT BATS: RIGHT BORN: 1/3/1894 ADRIAN, MICHIGAN DIED: 7/17/1946 COLUMBUS, OHIO POSITIONS PLAYED: OF

YEAR	TEAM	GAMES	AB	RUNS	HITS	2B	3B	HR	RBI	BB	IBB	SO	HBP	SH	SF	SB	CS	BA	OBA	SA	FA
1915	ChC-N	6	6	0	2	0	0	0	0	1	—	0	0	0	—	1	0	.333	.429	.333	.500
Career average		6	6	0	2	0	0	0	0	1	—	0	0	0	—	1	0	.333	.429	.333	.500
Cubs average		6	6	0	2	0	0	0	0	1	—	0	0	0	—	1	0	.333	.429	.333	.500
Career total		6	6	0	2	0	0	0	0	1	—	0	0	0	—	1	0	.333	.429	.333	.500
Cubs total		6	6	0	2	0	0	0	0	1	—	0	0	0	—	1	0	.333	.429	.333	.500

Flynn, George A. (Dibby)

HEIGHT: 5'9" THROWS: — BATS: — BORN: 5/24/1871 CHICAGO, ILLINOIS DIED: 12/28/1901 CHICAGO, ILLINOIS POSITIONS PLAYED: OF

YEAR	TEAM	GAMES	AB	RUNS	HITS	2B	3B	HR	RBI	BB	IBB	SO	HBP	SH	SF	SB	CS	BA	OBA	SA	FA
1896	ChN-N	29	106	15	27	1	2	0	4	11	—	9	2	3	—	12	—	.255	.336	.302	.878
Career average		29	106	15	27	1	2	0	4	11	—	9	2	3	—	12	—	.255	.336	.302	.878
Cubs average		29	106	15	27	1	2	0	4	11	—	9	2	3	—	12	—	.255	.336	.302	.878
Career total		29	106	15	27	1	2	0	4	11	—	9	2	3	—	12	—	.255	.336	.302	.878
Cubs total		29	106	15	27	1	2	0	4	11	—	9	2	3	—	12	—	.255	.336	.302	.878

Fondy, Dee Virgil

HEIGHT: 6'3" THROWS: LEFT BATS: LEFT BORN: 10/13/1924 SLATON, TEXAS DIED: 8/19/1999 REDLANDS, CALIFORNIA POSITIONS PLAYED: 1B, OF

YEAR	TEAM	GAMES	AB	RUNS	HITS	2B	3B	HR	RBI	BB	IBB	SO	HBP	SH	SF	SB	CS	BA	OBA	SA	FA
1951	ChC-N	49	170	23	46	7	2	3	20	11	—	20	1	2	—	5	6	.271	.319	.388	.976
1952	ChC-N	145	554	69	166	21	9	10	67	28	—	60	1	4	—	13	11	.300	.334	.424	.990
1953	ChC-N	150	595	79	184	11	11	18	78	44	—	106	1	1	—	10	7	.309	.358	.477	.987
1954	ChC-N	141	568	77	162	30	4	9	49	35	—	84	1	2	4	20	5	.285	.326	.400	.993
1955	ChC-N	150	574	69	152	23	8	17	65	35	6	87	2	3	4	8	9	.265	.307	.422	.991
1956	ChC-N	137	543	52	146	22	9	9	46	20	5	74	0	7	10	9	7	.269	.296	.392	.985
1957	ChC-N	11	51	3	16	3	1	0	2	0	0	9	0	0	0	1	2	.314	.314	.412	.991
1957	Pit-N	95	323	42	101	13	2	2	35	25	0	59	1	4	4	11	5	.313	.360	.384	.982
1958	Cin-N	89	124	23	27	1	1	1	11	5	0	27	0	1	1	7	1	.218	.246	.266	.989
Career average		121	438	55	125	18	6	9	47	25	1	66	1	3	3	11	7	.286	.324	.413	.988
Cubs average		112	436	53	125	19	6	9	47	25	2	63	1	3	3	9	7	.285	.323	.422	.989
Career total		967	3502	437	1000	144	47	69	373	203	11	526	7	24	23	84	53	.286	.324	.413	.988
Cubs total		783	3055	372	872	130	44	66	327	173	11	440	6	19	18	66	47	.285	.323	.422	.989

Foote, Barry Clifton
HEIGHT: 6'3" THROWS: RIGHT BATS: RIGHT BORN: 2/16/1952 SMITHFIELD, NORTH CAROLINA POSITIONS PLAYED: C, 1B, 3B

YEAR	TEAM	GAMES	AB	RUNS	HITS	2B	3B	HR	RBI	BB	IBB	SO	HBP	SH	SF	SB	CS	BA	OBA	SA	FA
1973	Mon-N	6	6	0	4	0	1	0	1	0	0	0	0	0	0	0	0	.667	.667	1.000	—
1974	Mon-N	125	420	44	110	23	4	11	60	35	11	74	3	2	12	2	1	.262	.315	.414	.984
1975	Mon-N	118	387	25	75	16	1	7	30	17	6	48	1	4	1	0	1	.194	.229	.295	.985
1976	Mon-N	105	350	32	82	12	2	7	27	17	3	32	1	0	0	2	1	.234	.272	.340	.989
1977	Mon-N	15	49	4	12	3	1	2	8	4	0	10	0	0	0	0	0	.245	.302	.469	.988
1977	Phi-N	18	32	3	7	1	0	1	3	3	0	6	0	0	0	0	0	.219	.286	.344	.980
1978	Phi-N	29	57	4	9	0	0	1	4	1	0	11	0	0	0	0	0	.158	.172	.211	1.000
1979	**ChC-N**	**132**	**429**	**47**	**109**	**26**	**0**	**16**	**56**	**34**	**7**	**49**	**5**	**0**	**1**	**0**	**0**	**.254**	**.316**	**.427**	**.979**
1980	**ChC-N**	**63**	**202**	**16**	**48**	**13**	**1**	**6**	**28**	**13**	**2**	**18**	**0**	**0**	**1**	**5**	**2**	**.238**	**.282**	**.401**	**.992**
1981	**ChC-N**	**9**	**22**	**0**	**0**	**0**	**0**	**0**	**1**	**3**	**0**	**7**	**0**	**0**	**1**	**1**	**1**	**.000**	**.115**	**.000**	**1.000**
1981	NYY-A	40	125	12	26	4	0	6	10	8	0	21	0	4	1	0	0	.208	.256	.384	.996
1982	NYY-A	17	48	4	7	5	0	0	2	1	0	11	0	0	1	0	0	.146	.160	.250	.973
Career average		69	213	19	49	10	1	6	23	14	3	29	1	1	2	1	1	.230	.277	.368	.986
Cubs average		**68**	**218**	**21**	**52**	**13**	**0**	**7**	**28**	**17**	**3**	**25**	**2**	**0**	**1**	**2**	**1**	**.240**	**.298**	**.404**	**.983**
Career total		687	2127	191	489	103	10	57	230	136	29	287	10	10	17	10	6	.230	.277	.368	.986
Cubs total		**204**	**653**	**63**	**157**	**39**	**1**	**22**	**85**	**50**	**9**	**74**	**5**	**0**	**3**	**6**	**3**	**.240**	**.298**	**.404**	**.983**

Foster, Elmer Ellsworth
HEIGHT: 5'10" THROWS: LEFT BATS: RIGHT BORN: 8/15/1861 MINNEAPOLIS, MINNESOTA DIED: 7/22/1946 DEEPHAVEN, MINNESOTA
POSITIONS PLAYED: C, 2B, 3B, OF

YEAR	TEAM	GAMES	AB	RUNS	HITS	2B	3B	HR	RBI	BB	IBB	SO	HBP	SH	SF	SB	CS	BA	OBA	SA	FA
1884	Phi-AA	4	11	4	2	0	0	0	—	3	—	—	0	—	—	—	—	.182	.357	.182	.885
1884	Phi-U	1	3	0	1	0	1	0	—	0	—	—	—	—	—	—	—	.333	.333	1.000	.625
1886	NY-AA	35	125	16	23	0	1	0	7	7	—	—	2	—	—	3	—	.184	.239	.200	.828
1888	NYG-N	37	136	15	20	3	2	0	10	9	—	20	3	—	—	13	—	.147	.216	.199	.831
1889	NYG-N	2	4	2	0	0	0	0	0	3	—	1	0	—	—	2	—	.000	.429	.000	1.000
1890	**ChN-N**	**27**	**105**	**20**	**26**	**4**	**2**	**5**	**23**	**9**	**—**	**21**	**3**	**—**	**—**	**18**	**—**	**.248**	**.325**	**.467**	**.986**
1891	**ChN-N**	**4**	**16**	**3**	**3**	**0**	**0**	**1**	**1**	**1**	**—**	**2**	**0**	**—**	**—**	**1**	**—**	**.188**	**.235**	**.375**	**.875**
Career average		18	67	10	13	1	1	1	7	5	—	7	1	—	—	6	—	.188	.261	.280	.861
Cubs average		**16**	**61**	**12**	**15**	**2**	**1**	**3**	**12**	**5**	**—**	**12**	**2**	**—**	**—**	**6**	**—**	**.240**	**.313**	**.455**	**.975**
Career total		110	400	60	75	7	6	6	41	32	—	44	8	—	—	37	—	.188	.261	.280	.861
Cubs total		**31**	**121**	**23**	**29**	**4**	**2**	**6**	**24**	**10**	**—**	**23**	**3**	**—**	**—**	**19**	**—**	**.240**	**.313**	**.455**	**.975**

Foxx, James Emory (Jimmie *or* Beast *or* Double X)
HEIGHT: 6'0" THROWS: RIGHT BATS: RIGHT BORN: 10/22/1907 SUDLERSVILLE, MARYLAND DIED: 7/21/1967 MIAMI, FLORIDA
POSITIONS PLAYED: P, C, 1B, 3B, SS, OF

YEAR	TEAM	GAMES	AB	RUNS	HITS	2B	3B	HR	RBI	BB	IBB	SO	HBP	SH	SF	SB	CS	BA	OBA	SA	FA
1925	Phi-A	10	9	2	6	1	0	0	0	0	—	1	0	0	—	0	0	.667	.667	.778	—
1926	Phi-A	26	32	8	10	2	1	0	5	1	—	6	0	2	—	1	0	.313	.333	.438	1.000
1927	Phi-A	61	130	23	42	6	5	3	20	14	—	11	1	1	—	2	0	.323	.393	.515	.977
1928	Phi-A	118	400	85	131	29	10	13	79	60	—	43	1	12	—	3	8	.328	.416	.548	.971
1929	Phi-A	149	517	123	183	23	9	33	118	103	—	70	2	16	—	9	7	.354	.463	.625	.995
1930	Phi-A	153	562	127	188	33	13	37	156	93	—	66	1	18	—	7	7	.335	.429	.637	.990
1931	Phi-A	139	515	93	150	32	10	30	120	73	—	84	1	4	—	4	3	.291	.380	.567	.986
1932	Phi-A	154	585	151	213	33	9	58	169	116	—	96	0	0	—	3	7	.364	.469	.749	.992
1933	Phi-A	149	573	125	204	37	9	48	163	96	—	93	1	0	—	2	7	.356	.449	.703	.990
1934	Phi-A	150	539	120	180	28	6	44	130	111	—	75	1	1	—	11	2	.334	.449	.653	.993
1935	Phi-A	147	535	118	185	33	7	36	115	114	—	99	0	0	—	6	4	.346	.461	.636	.997
1936	Bos-A	155	585	130	198	32	8	41	143	105	—	119	1	2	—	13	4	.338	.440	.631	.990
1937	Bos-A	150	569	111	162	24	6	36	127	99	—	96	1	4	—	10	8	.285	.392	.538	.994
1938	Bos-A	149	565	139	197	33	9	50	175	119	—	76	0	1	—	5	4	.349	.462	.704	.987
1939	Bos-A	124	467	130	168	31	10	35	105	89	—	72	2	5	—	4	3	.360	.464	.694	.992
1940	Bos-A	144	515	106	153	30	4	36	119	101	—	87	0	2	—	4	7	.297	.412	.581	.991
1941	Bos-A	135	487	87	146	27	8	19	105	93	—	103	0	2	—	2	5	.300	.412	.505	.989
1942	Bos-A	30	100	18	27	4	0	5	14	18	—	15	2	0	—	0	0	.270	.392	.460	.996
1942	**ChC-N**	**70**	**205**	**25**	**42**	**8**	**0**	**3**	**19**	**22**	**—**	**55**	**0**	**0**	**—**	**1**	**—**	**.205**	**.282**	**.288**	**.983**
1944	**ChC-N**	**15**	**20**	**0**	**1**	**1**	**0**	**0**	**2**	**2**	**—**	**5**	**0**	**0**	**—**	**0**	**—**	**.050**	**.136**	**.100**	**1.000**
1945	Phi-N	89	224	30	60	11	1	7	38	23	—	39	0	1	—	0	—	.268	.336	.420	.978

(continued)

(Foxx, continued)

	GAMES	AB	RUNS	HITS	2B	3B	HR	RBI	BB	IBB	SO	HBP	SH	SF	SB	CS	BA	OBA	SA	FA
Career average	116	407	88	132	23	6	27	96	73	—	66	1	4	—	4	4	.325	.428	.609	.990
Cubs average	**43**	**113**	**13**	**22**	**5**	**0**	**2**	**11**	**12**	**—**	**30**	**0**	**0**	**—**	**1**	**0**	**.191**	**.269**	**.271**	**.983**
Career total	2317	8134	1751	2646	458	125	534	1922	1452	—	1311	13	71	—	87	72	.325	.428	.609	.990
Cubs total	**85**	**225**	**25**	**43**	**9**	**0**	**3**	**21**	**24**	**—**	**60**	**0**	**0**	**—**	**1**	**0**	**.191**	**.269**	**.271**	**.983**

Franco, Matthew Neil (Matt)
HEIGHT: 6'1" THROWS: RIGHT BATS: LEFT BORN: 8/19/1969 SANTA MONICA, CALIFORNIA POSITIONS PLAYED: P, 1B, 2B, 3B, OF

YEAR	TEAM	GAMES	AB	RUNS	HITS	2B	3B	HR	RBI	BB	IBB	SO	HBP	SH	SF	SB	CS	BA	OBA	SA	FA
1995	**ChC-N**	**16**	**17**	**3**	**5**	**1**	**0**	**0**	**1**	**0**	**0**	**4**	**0**	**0**	**0**	**0**	**0**	**.294**	**.294**	**.353**	**1.000**
1996	NYM-N	14	31	3	6	1	0	1	2	1	0	5	1	0	1	0	0	.194	.235	.323	.900
1997	NYM-N	112	163	21	45	5	0	5	21	13	4	23	0	0	1	0	1	.276	.330	.399	.966
1998	NYM-N	103	161	20	44	7	2	1	13	23	6	26	1	1	1	0	0	.273	.366	.360	.991
1999	NYM-N	122	132	18	31	5	0	4	21	28	3	21	0	0	1	0	0	.235	.366	.364	.987
2000	NYM-N	101	134	9	32	4	0	2	14	21	3	22	0	1	1	0	0	.239	.340	.313	.969
Career average		78	106	12	27	4	0	2	12	14	3	17	0	0	1	0	0	.255	.344	.359	.972
Cubs average		**16**	**17**	**3**	**5**	**1**	**0**	**0**	**1**	**0**	**0**	**4**	**0**	**0**	**0**	**0**	**0**	**.294**	**.294**	**.353**	**1.000**
Career total		468	638	74	163	23	2	13	72	86	16	101	2	2	4	1	1	.255	.344	.359	.972
Cubs total		**16**	**17**	**3**	**5**	**1**	**0**	**0**	**1**	**0**	**0**	**4**	**0**	**0**	**0**	**0**	**0**	**.294**	**.294**	**.353**	**1.000**

Francona, Terry Jon
HEIGHT: 6'1" THROWS: LEFT BATS: LEFT BORN: 4/22/1959 ABERDEEN, SOUTH DAKOTA POSITIONS PLAYED: P, 1B, 3B, OF

YEAR	TEAM	GAMES	AB	RUNS	HITS	2B	3B	HR	RBI	BB	IBB	SO	HBP	SH	SF	SB	CS	BA	OBA	SA	FA
1981	Mon-N	34	95	11	26	0	1	1	8	5	1	6	1	3	0	1	0	.274	.317	.326	1.000
1982	Mon-N	46	131	14	42	3	0	0	9	8	0	11	0	5	0	2	3	.321	.360	.344	.956
1983	Mon-N	120	230	21	59	11	1	3	22	6	2	20	0	0	2	0	2	.257	.273	.352	.984
1984	Mon-N	58	214	18	74	19	2	1	18	5	3	12	1	1	2	0	0	.346	.360	.467	.994
1985	Mon-N	107	281	19	75	15	1	2	31	12	4	12	1	2	0	5	5	.267	.299	.349	.987
1986	**ChC-N**	**86**	**124**	**13**	**31**	**3**	**0**	**2**	**8**	**6**	**0**	**8**	**1**	**0**	**2**	**0**	**1**	**.250**	**.286**	**.323**	**.995**
1987	Cin-N	102	207	16	47	5	0	3	12	10	1	12	1	1	0	2	0	.227	.266	.295	.981
1988	Cle-A	62	212	24	66	8	0	1	12	5	1	18	0	2	2	0	0	.311	.324	.363	.989
1989	Mil-A	90	233	26	54	10	1	3	23	8	3	20	0	1	2	2	1	.232	.255	.322	1.000
1990	Mil-A	3	4	1	0	0	0	0	0	0	0	0	0	0	0	0	0	.000	.000	.000	1.000
Career average		71	173	16	47	7	1	2	14	7	2	12	1	2	1	1	1	.274	.300	.351	.990
Cubs average		**86**	**124**	**13**	**31**	**3**	**0**	**2**	**8**	**6**	**0**	**8**	**1**	**0**	**2**	**0**	**1**	**.250**	**.286**	**.323**	**1.000**
Career total		708	1731	163	474	74	6	16	143	65	15	119	5	15	10	12	12	.274	.300	.351	.990
Cubs total		**86**	**124**	**13**	**31**	**3**	**0**	**2**	**8**	**6**	**0**	**8**	**1**	**0**	**2**	**0**	**1**	**.250**	**.286**	**.323**	**1.000**

Freese, George Walter (Bud)
HEIGHT: 6'0" THROWS: RIGHT BATS: RIGHT BORN: 9/12/1926 WHEELING, WEST VIRGINIA POSITIONS PLAYED: 3B

YEAR	TEAM	GAMES	AB	RUNS	HITS	2B	3B	HR	RBI	BB	IBB	SO	HBP	SH	SF	SB	CS	BA	OBA	SA	FA
1953	Det-A	1	1	0	0	0	0	0	0	0	—	0	0	0	—	0	0	.000	.000	.000	—
1955	Pit-N	51	179	17	46	8	2	3	22	17	2	18	2	3	1	1	1	.257	.327	.374	.936
1961	**ChC-N**	**9**	**7**	**0**	**2**	**0**	**0**	**0**	**1**	**1**	**0**	**4**	**0**	**0**	**0**	**0**	**0**	**.286**	**.375**	**.286**	**—**
Career average		20	62	6	16	3	1	1	8	6	1	7	1	1	0	0	0	.257	.327	.369	.936
Cubs average		**9**	**7**	**0**	**2**	**0**	**0**	**0**	**1**	**1**	**0**	**4**	**0**	**0**	**0**	**0**	**0**	**.286**	**.375**	**.286**	**—**
Career total		61	187	17	48	8	2	3	23	18	2	22	2	3	1	1	1	.257	.327	.369	.936
Cubs total		**9**	**7**	**0**	**2**	**0**	**0**	**0**	**1**	**1**	**0**	**4**	**0**	**0**	**0**	**0**	**0**	**.286**	**.375**	**.286**	**—**

Freigau, Howard Earl (Ty)

HEIGHT: 5'10"   THROWS: RIGHT   BATS: RIGHT   BORN: 8/1/1902 DAYTON, OHIO   DIED: 7/18/1932 CHATTANOOGA, TENNESSEE
POSITIONS PLAYED: 1B, 2B, 3B, SS, OF

YEAR	TEAM	GAMES	AB	RUNS	HITS	2B	3B	HR	RBI	BB	IBB	SO	HBP	SH	SF	SB	CS	BA	OBA	SA	FA
1922	StL-N	3	1	0	0	0	0	0	0	0	—	0	0	0	—	0	0	.000	.000	.000	1.000
1923	StL-N	113	358	30	94	18	1	1	35	25	—	36	2	7	—	5	4	.263	.314	.327	.930
1924	StL-N	98	376	35	101	17	6	2	39	19	—	24	1	10	—	10	3	.269	.306	.362	.958
1925	StL-N	9	26	2	4	0	0	0	0	2	—	1	0	0	—	0	0	.154	.214	.154	.940
1925	**ChC-N**	**117**	**476**	**77**	**146**	**22**	**10**	**8**	**71**	**30**	**—**	**31**	**1**	**16**	**—**	**10**	**6**	**.307**	**.349**	**.445**	**.921**
1926	**ChC-N**	**140**	**508**	**51**	**137**	**27**	**7**	**3**	**51**	**43**	**—**	**42**	**0**	**18**	**—**	**6**	**—**	**.270**	**.327**	**.368**	**.967**
1927	**ChC-N**	**30**	**86**	**12**	**20**	**5**	**0**	**0**	**10**	**9**	**—**	**10**	**1**	**0**	**—**	**0**	**—**	**.233**	**.313**	**.291**	**.883**
1928	Bro-N	17	34	6	7	2	0	0	3	1	—	3	0	3	—	0	—	.206	.229	.265	.810
1928	Bos-N	52	109	11	28	8	1	1	17	9	—	14	1	4	—	1	—	.257	.319	.376	.931
Career average		83	282	32	77	14	4	2	32	20	—	23	1	8	—	5	2	.272	.322	.370	.937
Cubs average		**96**	**357**	**47**	**101**	**18**	**6**	**4**	**44**	**27**	**—**	**28**	**1**	**11**	**—**	**5**	**2**	**.283**	**.335**	**.396**	**.937**
Career total		579	1974	224	537	99	25	15	226	138	—	161	6	58	—	32	13	.272	.322	.370	.937
Cubs total		**287**	**1070**	**140**	**303**	**54**	**17**	**11**	**132**	**82**	**—**	**83**	**2**	**34**	**—**	**16**	**6**	**.283**	**.335**	**.396**	**.937**

Frey, Linus Reinhard (Lonny *or* Junior)

HEIGHT: 5'10"   THROWS: RIGHT   BATS: LEFT   BORN: 8/23/1910 ST. LOUIS, MISSOURI   POSITIONS PLAYED: 2B, 3B, SS, OF

YEAR	TEAM	GAMES	AB	RUNS	HITS	2B	3B	HR	RBI	BB	IBB	SO	HBP	SH	SF	SB	CS	BA	OBA	SA	FA
1933	Bro-N	34	135	25	43	5	3	0	12	13	—	13	0	2	—	4	—	.319	.378	.400	.896
1934	Bro-N	125	490	77	139	24	5	8	57	52	—	54	5	9	—	11	—	.284	.358	.402	.942
1935	Bro-N	131	515	88	135	35	11	11	77	66	—	68	5	2	—	6	—	.262	.352	.437	.939
1936	Bro-N	148	524	63	146	29	4	4	60	71	—	56	4	8	—	7	—	.279	.369	.372	.919
1937	**ChC-N**	**78**	**198**	**33**	**55**	**9**	**3**	**1**	**22**	**33**	**—**	**15**	**0**	**7**	**—**	**6**	**—**	**.278**	**.381**	**.369**	**.950**
1938	Cin-N	124	501	76	133	26	6	4	36	49	—	50	0	7	—	4	—	.265	.331	.365	.962
1939	Cin-N	125	484	95	141	27	9	11	55	72	—	46	4	25	—	5	—	.291	.388	.452	.976
1940	Cin-N	150	563	102	150	23	6	8	54	80	—	48	3	17	—	22	—	.266	.361	.371	.977
1941	Cin-N	146	543	78	138	29	5	6	59	72	—	37	3	11	—	16	—	.254	.345	.359	.970
1942	Cin-N	141	523	66	139	23	6	2	39	87	—	38	2	8	—	9	—	.266	.373	.344	.977
1943	Cin-N	144	586	78	154	20	8	2	43	76	—	56	0	5	—	7	—	.263	.347	.334	.985
1946	Cin-N	111	333	46	82	10	3	3	24	63	—	31	1	3	—	5	—	.246	.368	.321	.963
1947	**ChC-N**	**24**	**43**	**4**	**9**	**0**	**0**	**0**	**3**	**4**	**—**	**6**	**0**	**0**	**—**	**0**	**—**	**.209**	**.277**	**.209**	**1.000**
1947	NYY-A	24	28	10	5	2	0	0	2	10	—	1	1	1	—	3	0	.179	.410	.250	.923
1948	NYY-A	1	0	1	0	0	0	0	0	0	—	0	0	0	—	0	0	—	—	—	—
1948	NYG-N	29	51	6	13	1	0	1	6	4	—	6	0	0	—	0	—	.255	.309	.333	.920
Career average		110	394	61	106	19	5	4	39	54	—	38	2	8	—	8	0	.269	.359	.374	.960
Cubs average		**51**	**121**	**19**	**32**	**5**	**2**	**1**	**13**	**19**	**—**	**11**	**0**	**4**	**—**	**3**	**—**	**.266**	**.363**	**.340**	**.958**
Career total		1535	5517	848	1482	263	69	61	549	752	—	525	28	105	—	105	0	.269	.359	.374	.960
Cubs total		**102**	**241**	**37**	**64**	**9**	**3**	**1**	**25**	**37**	**—**	**21**	**0**	**7**	**—**	**6**	**—**	**.266**	**.363**	**.340**	**.958**

Friberg, Bernard Albert (Bernie)

HEIGHT: 5'11"   THROWS: RIGHT   BATS: RIGHT   BORN: 8/18/1899 MANCHESTER, NEW HAMPSHIRE   DIED: 12/8/1958 LYNN, MASSACHUSETTS
POSITIONS PLAYED: P, 1B, 2B, 3B, SS, OF

YEAR	TEAM	GAMES	AB	RUNS	HITS	2B	3B	HR	RBI	BB	IBB	SO	HBP	SH	SF	SB	CS	BA	OBA	SA	FA
1919	**ChC-N**	**8**	**20**	**0**	**4**	**1**	**0**	**0**	**1**	**0**	**—**	**2**	**0**	**0**	**—**	**0**	**—**	**.200**	**.200**	**.250**	**1.000**
1920	**ChC-N**	**50**	**114**	**11**	**24**	**5**	**1**	**0**	**7**	**6**	**—**	**20**	**0**	**4**	**—**	**2**	**2**	**.211**	**.250**	**.272**	**.964**
1922	**ChC-N**	**97**	**296**	**51**	**92**	**8**	**2**	**0**	**23**	**37**	**—**	**37**	**2**	**8**	**—**	**8**	**10**	**.311**	**.391**	**.351**	**.980**
1923	**ChC-N**	**146**	**547**	**91**	**174**	**27**	**11**	**12**	**88**	**45**	**—**	**49**	**2**	**23**	**—**	**13**	**19**	**.318**	**.372**	**.473**	**.955**
1924	**ChC-N**	**142**	**495**	**67**	**138**	**19**	**3**	**5**	**82**	**66**	**—**	**53**	**5**	**21**	**—**	**19**	**27**	**.279**	**.369**	**.360**	**.954**
1925	**ChC-N**	**44**	**152**	**12**	**39**	**5**	**3**	**1**	**16**	**14**	**—**	**22**	**2**	**3**	**—**	**0**	**1**	**.257**	**.327**	**.349**	**.936**
1925	Phi-N	91	304	41	82	12	1	5	22	39	—	35	0	5	—	1	1	.270	.353	.365	.967
1926	Phi-N	144	478	38	128	21	3	1	51	57	—	77	0	18	—	2	—	.268	.346	.331	.976
1927	Phi-N	111	335	31	78	8	2	1	28	41	—	49	3	17	—	3	—	.233	.322	.278	.961
1928	Phi-N	52	94	11	19	3	0	1	7	12	—	16	0	7	—	0	—	.202	.292	.266	.928
1929	Phi-N	128	455	74	137	21	10	7	55	49	—	54	1	13	—	1	—	.301	.370	.437	.943
1930	Phi-N	105	331	62	113	21	1	4	42	47	—	35	1	8	—	1	—	.341	.425	.447	.945
1931	Phi-N	103	353	33	92	19	5	1	26	33	—	25	0	6	—	1	—	.261	.324	.351	.959
1932	Phi-N	61	154	17	37	8	2	0	14	19	—	23	0	5	—	0	—	.240	.324	.318	.957
1933	Bos-A	17	41	5	13	3	0	0	9	6	—	1	0	1	—	0	0	.317	.404	.390	.942
Career average		93	298	39	84	13	3	3	34	34	—	36	1	10	—	4	4	.281	.356	.373	.959
Cubs average		**81**	**271**	**39**	**79**	**11**	**3**	**3**	**36**	**28**	**—**	**31**	**2**	**10**	**—**	**7**	**10**	**.290**	**.361**	**.388**	**.957**
Career total		1299	4169	544	1170	181	44	38	471	471	—	498	16	139	—	51	60	.281	.356	.373	.959
Cubs total		**487**	**1624**	**232**	**471**	**65**	**20**	**18**	**217**	**168**	**—**	**183**	**11**	**59**	**—**	**42**	**59**	**.290**	**.361**	**.388**	**.957**

Friend, Owen Lacey (Red)
HEIGHT: 6'1"   THROWS: RIGHT   BATS: RIGHT   BORN: 3/21/1927 GRANITE CITY, ILLINOIS   POSITIONS PLAYED: 2B, 3B, SS

YEAR	TEAM	GAMES	AB	RUNS	HITS	2B	3B	HR	RBI	BB	IBB	SO	HBP	SH	SF	SB	CS	BA	OBA	SA	FA
1949	StL-A	2	8	1	3	0	0	0	1	0	—	0	0	0	—	0	0	.375	.375	.375	1.000
1950	StL-A	119	372	48	88	15	2	8	50	40	—	68	1	14	—	2	1	.237	.312	.352	.953
1953	Det-A	31	96	10	17	4	0	3	10	6	—	9	1	1	—	0	0	.177	.233	.313	.947
1953	Cle-A	34	68	7	16	2	0	2	13	5	—	16	0	0	—	0	0	.235	.288	.353	1.000
1955	Bos-A	14	42	3	11	3	0	0	2	4	0	11	0	0	0	0	0	.262	.326	.333	.951
1955	**ChC-N**	**6**	**10**	**0**	**1**	**0**	**0**	**0**	**0**	**0**	**0**	**3**	**0**	**0**	**0**	**0**	**0**	**.100**	**.100**	**.100**	**1.000**
1956	**ChC-N**	**2**	**2**	**0**	**0**	**0**	**0**	**0**	**0**	**0**	**0**	**2**	**0**	**0**	**0**	**0**	**0**	**.000**	**.000**	**.000**	**—**
Career average		42	120	14	27	5	0	3	15	11	0	22	0	3	0	0	0	.227	.295	.339	.958
Cubs average		**4**	**6**	**0**	**1**	**0**	**0**	**0**	**0**	**0**	**0**	**3**	**0**	**0**	**0**	**0**	**0**	**.083**	**.083**	**.083**	**1.000**
Career total		208	598	69	136	24	2	13	76	55	0	109	2	15	0	2	2	.227	.295	.339	.958
Cubs total		**8**	**12**	**0**	**1**	**0**	**0**	**0**	**0**	**0**	**0**	**5**	**0**	**0**	**0**	**0**	**0**	**.083**	**.083**	**.083**	**1.000**

Gabler, William Louis (Gabe)
HEIGHT: 6'1"   THROWS: RIGHT   BATS: LEFT   BORN: 8/4/1930 ST. LOUIS, MISSOURI

YEAR	TEAM	GAMES	AB	RUNS	HITS	2B	3B	HR	RBI	BB	IBB	SO	HBP	SH	SF	SB	CS	BA	OBA	SA	FA
1958	**ChC-N**	**3**	**3**	**0**	**0**	**0**	**0**	**0**	**0**	**0**	**0**	**3**	**0**	**0**	**0**	**0**	**0**	**.000**	**.000**	**.000**	**—**
Career average		3	3	0	0	0	0	0	0	0	0	3	0	0	0	0	0	.000	.000	.000	—
Cubs average		**3**	**3**	**0**	**0**	**0**	**0**	**0**	**0**	**0**	**0**	**3**	**0**	**0**	**0**	**0**	**0**	**.000**	**.000**	**.000**	**—**
Career total		3	3	0	0	0	0	0	0	0	0	3	0	0	0	0	0	.000	.000	.000	—
Cubs total		**3**	**3**	**0**	**0**	**0**	**0**	**0**	**0**	**0**	**0**	**3**	**0**	**0**	**0**	**0**	**0**	**.000**	**.000**	**.000**	**—**

Gabrielson, Leonard Gary (Len)
HEIGHT: 6'4"   THROWS: RIGHT   BATS: LEFT   BORN: 2/14/1940 OAKLAND, CALIFORNIA   POSITIONS PLAYED: 1B, 3B, OF

YEAR	TEAM	GAMES	AB	RUNS	HITS	2B	3B	HR	RBI	BB	IBB	SO	HBP	SH	SF	SB	CS	BA	OBA	SA	FA
1960	Mil-N	4	3	1	0	0	0	0	0	1	0	0	0	0	0	0	0	.000	.250	.000	—
1963	Mil-N	46	120	14	26	5	0	3	15	8	1	23	0	0	1	1	1	.217	.264	.333	.974
1964	Mil-N	24	38	0	7	2	0	0	1	1	0	8	0	0	0	1	0	.184	.205	.237	1.000
1964	**ChC-N**	**89**	**272**	**22**	**67**	**11**	**2**	**5**	**23**	**19**	**1**	**37**	**1**	**1**	**0**	**9**	**4**	**.246**	**.298**	**.357**	**.990**
1965	**ChC-N**	**28**	**48**	**4**	**12**	**0**	**0**	**3**	**5**	**7**	**2**	**16**	**0**	**0**	**0**	**0**	**2**	**.250**	**.345**	**.438**	**1.000**
1965	SF-N	88	269	36	81	6	5	4	26	26	5	48	2	2	2	4	0	.301	.365	.405	.981
1966	SF-N	94	240	27	52	7	0	4	16	21	3	51	0	4	2	0	1	.217	.278	.296	.968
1967	Cal-A	11	12	2	1	0	0	0	2	2	0	4	0	0	0	0	0	.083	.214	.083	—
1967	LA-N	90	238	20	62	10	3	7	29	15	3	41	1	3	0	3	1	.261	.307	.416	.980
1968	LA-N	108	304	38	82	16	1	10	35	32	3	47	0	5	2	1	1	.270	.337	.428	.976
1969	LA-N	83	178	13	48	5	1	1	18	12	1	25	0	2	2	1	2	.270	.313	.326	.984
1970	LA-N	43	42	1	8	2	0	0	6	1	0	15	0	0	1	0	0	.190	.205	.238	1.000
Career average		79	196	20	50	7	1	4	20	16	2	35	0	2	1	2	1	.253	.309	.366	.981
Cubs average		**59**	**160**	**13**	**40**	**6**	**1**	**4**	**14**	**13**	**2**	**27**	**1**	**1**	**0**	**5**	**3**	**.247**	**.305**	**.369**	**.990**
Career total		708	1764	178	446	64	12	37	176	145	20	315	4	17	10	20	12	.253	.309	.366	.981
Cubs total		**117**	**320**	**26**	**79**	**11**	**2**	**8**	**28**	**26**	**3**	**53**	**1**	**1**	**0**	**9**	**6**	**.247**	**.305**	**.369**	**.990**

Gaetti, Gary Joseph
HEIGHT: 6'0"   THROWS: RIGHT   BATS: RIGHT   BORN: 8/19/1958 CENTRALIA, ILLINOIS   POSITIONS PLAYED: P, 1B, 2B, 3B, SS, OF

YEAR	TEAM	GAMES	AB	RUNS	HITS	2B	3B	HR	RBI	BB	IBB	SO	HBP	SH	SF	SB	CS	BA	OBA	SA	FA
1981	Min-A	9	26	4	5	0	0	2	3	0	0	6	0	0	0	0	0	.192	.192	.423	1.000
1982	Min-A	145	508	59	117	25	4	25	84	37	2	107	3	4	13	0	4	.230	.280	.443	.959
1983	Min-A	157	584	81	143	30	3	21	78	54	2	121	4	0	8	7	1	.245	.309	.414	.967
1984	Min-A	162	588	55	154	29	4	5	65	44	1	81	4	3	5	11	5	.262	.315	.350	.960
1985	Min-A	160	560	71	138	31	0	20	63	37	3	89	7	3	1	13	5	.246	.301	.409	.964
1986	Min-A	157	596	91	171	34	1	34	108	52	4	108	6	1	6	14	15	.287	.347	.518	.956
1987	Min-A	154	584	95	150	36	2	31	109	37	7	92	3	1	3	10	7	.257	.303	.485	.973
1988	Min-A	133	468	66	141	29	2	28	88	36	5	85	5	1	6	7	4	.301	.353	.551	.977
1989	Min-A	130	498	63	125	11	4	19	75	25	5	87	3	1	9	6	2	.251	.286	.404	.974
1990	Min-A	154	577	61	132	27	5	16	85	36	1	101	3	1	8	6	1	.229	.274	.376	.961

(continued)

(continued)

Year	Team																				
1991	Cal-A	152	586	58	144	22	1	18	66	33	3	104	8	2	5	5	5	.246	.293	.379	.965
1992	Cal-A	130	456	41	103	13	2	12	48	21	4	79	6	0	3	3	1	.226	.267	.342	.966
1993	Cal-A	20	50	3	9	2	0	0	4	5	0	12	0	0	1	1	0	.180	.250	.220	.978
1993	KC-A	82	281	37	72	18	1	14	46	16	0	75	8	2	6	0	3	.256	.309	.477	.980
1994	KC-A	90	327	53	94	15	3	12	57	19	3	63	2	1	3	0	2	.287	.328	.462	.985
1995	KC-A	137	514	76	134	27	0	35	96	47	6	91	8	3	6	3	3	.261	.329	.518	.962
1996	StL-N	141	522	71	143	27	4	23	80	35	6	97	8	4	5	2	2	.274	.326	.473	.974
1997	StL-N	148	502	63	126	24	1	17	69	36	3	88	6	4	6	7	3	.251	.305	.404	.982
1998	StL-N	91	306	39	81	23	1	11	43	31	1	39	6	0	3	1	1	.265	.339	.454	.986
1998	**ChC-N**	**37**	**128**	**21**	**41**	**11**	**0**	**8**	**27**	**12**	**1**	**23**	**5**	**1**	**1**	**0**	**0**	**.320**	**.397**	**.594**	**.979**
1999	**ChC-N**	**113**	**280**	**22**	**57**	**9**	**1**	**9**	**46**	**21**	**0**	**51**	**2**	**0**	**5**	**0**	**1**	**.204**	**.260**	**.339**	**.961**
2000	Bos-A	5	10	0	0	0	0	0	1	0	0	3	0	0	1	0	0	.000	.000	.000	—
Career average		125	448	57	114	22	2	18	67	32	3	80	5	2	5	5	3	.255	.308	.434	.968
Cubs average		**75**	**204**	**22**	**49**	**10**	**1**	**9**	**37**	**17**	**1**	**37**	**4**	**1**	**3**	**0**	**1**	**.240**	**.304**	**.419**	**.966**
Career total		2507	8951	1130	2280	443	39	360	1341	634	57	1602	96	32	104	96	65	.255	.308	.434	.968
Cubs total		**150**	**408**	**43**	**98**	**20**	**1**	**17**	**73**	**33**	**1**	**74**	**7**	**1**	**6**	**0**	**1**	**.240**	**.304**	**.419**	**.966**

Gagliano, Philip Joseph (Phil)

HEIGHT: 6'1"   THROWS: RIGHT   BATS: RIGHT   BORN: 12/27/1941 MEMPHIS, TENNESSEE   POSITIONS PLAYED: 1B, 2B, 3B, SS, OF

YEAR	TEAM	GAMES	AB	RUNS	HITS	2B	3B	HR	RBI	BB	IBB	SO	HBP	SH	SF	SB	CS	BA	OBA	SA	FA
1963	StL-N	10	5	1	2	0	0	0	1	1	0	1	0	0	0	0	0	.400	.500	.400	1.000
1964	StL-N	40	58	5	15	4	0	1	9	3	0	10	0	0	1	0	1	.259	.290	.379	.931
1965	StL-N	122	363	46	87	14	2	8	53	40	0	45	1	1	6	2	1	.240	.312	.355	.959
1966	StL-N	90	213	23	54	8	2	2	15	24	1	29	1	2	2	2	1	.254	.329	.338	.989
1967	StL-N	73	217	20	48	7	0	2	21	19	3	26	1	3	3	0	0	.221	.283	.281	.964
1968	StL-N	53	105	13	24	4	2	0	13	7	0	12	1	1	1	0	0	.229	.281	.305	.988
1969	StL-N	62	128	7	29	2	0	1	10	14	0	12	0	1	0	0	0	.227	.303	.266	.988
1970	StL-N	18	32	0	6	0	0	0	2	1	0	3	0	0	0	0	1	.188	.212	.188	.970
1970	**ChC-N**	**26**	**40**	**5**	**6**	**0**	**0**	**0**	**5**	**5**	**0**	**5**	**0**	**1**	**0**	**0**	**0**	**.150**	**.244**	**.150**	**.980**
1971	Bos-A	47	68	11	22	5	0	0	13	11	0	5	0	1	1	0	0	.324	.413	.397	1.000
1972	Bos-A	52	82	9	21	4	1	0	10	10	0	13	0	1	1	0	0	.256	.333	.329	.958
1973	Cin-N	63	69	8	20	2	0	0	7	13	2	16	0	1	0	0	0	.290	.402	.319	.885
1974	Cin-N	46	31	2	2	0	0	0	0	15	1	7	0	0	0	0	0	.065	.370	.065	1.000
Career average		59	118	13	28	4	1	1	13	14	1	15	0	1	1	0	0	.238	.316	.313	.969
Cubs average		**26**	**40**	**5**	**6**	**0**	**0**	**0**	**5**	**5**	**0**	**5**	**0**	**1**	**0**	**0**	**0**	**.150**	**.244**	**.150**	**.980**
Career total		702	1411	150	336	50	7	14	159	163	7	184	4	12	15	5	4	.238	.316	.313	.969
Cubs total		**26**	**40**	**5**	**6**	**0**	**0**	**0**	**5**	**5**	**0**	**5**	**0**	**1**	**0**	**0**	**0**	**.150**	**.244**	**.150**	**.980**

Galan, August John (Augie *or* Goo Goo)

HEIGHT: 6'0"   THROWS: RIGHT   BATS: BOTH   BORN: 5/23/1912 BERKELEY, CALIFORNIA   DIED: 12/28/1993 FAIRFIELD, CALIFORNIA
POSITIONS PLAYED: 1B, 2B, 3B, SS, OF

YEAR	TEAM	GAMES	AB	RUNS	HITS	2B	3B	HR	RBI	BB	IBB	SO	HBP	SH	SF	SB	CS	BA	OBA	SA	FA
1934	**ChC-N**	**66**	**192**	**31**	**50**	**6**	**2**	**5**	**22**	**16**	**—**	**15**	**0**	**0**	**—**	**4**	**—**	**.260**	**.317**	**.391**	**.963**
1935	**ChC-N**	**154**	**646**	**133**	**203**	**41**	**11**	**12**	**79**	**87**	**—**	**53**	**4**	**11**	**—**	**22**	**—**	**.314**	**.399**	**.467**	**.978**
1936	**ChC-N**	**145**	**575**	**74**	**152**	**26**	**4**	**8**	**81**	**67**	**—**	**50**	**3**	**4**	**—**	**16**	**—**	**.264**	**.344**	**.365**	**.987**
1937	**ChC-N**	**147**	**611**	**104**	**154**	**24**	**10**	**18**	**78**	**79**	**—**	**48**	**1**	**4**	**—**	**23**	**—**	**.252**	**.339**	**.412**	**.977**
1938	**ChC-N**	**110**	**395**	**52**	**113**	**16**	**9**	**6**	**69**	**49**	**—**	**17**	**2**	**3**	**—**	**8**	**—**	**.286**	**.368**	**.418**	**.987**
1939	**ChC-N**	**148**	**549**	**104**	**167**	**36**	**8**	**6**	**71**	**75**	**—**	**26**	**4**	**13**	**—**	**8**	**—**	**.304**	**.392**	**.432**	**.970**
1940	**ChC-N**	**68**	**209**	**33**	**48**	**14**	**2**	**3**	**22**	**37**	**—**	**23**	**0**	**2**	**—**	**9**	**—**	**.230**	**.346**	**.359**	**.970**
1941	**ChC-N**	**65**	**120**	**18**	**25**	**3**	**0**	**1**	**13**	**22**	**—**	**10**	**0**	**1**	**—**	**0**	**—**	**.208**	**.331**	**.258**	**.959**
1941	Bro-N	17	27	3	7	3	0	0	4	3	—	1	0	1	—	0	—	.259	.333	.370	1.000
1942	Bro-N	69	209	24	55	16	0	0	22	24	—	12	0	1	—	2	—	.263	.339	.340	.993
1943	Bro-N	139	495	83	142	26	3	9	67	103	—	39	2	4	—	6	5	.287	.412	.406	.986
1944	Bro-N	151	547	96	174	43	9	12	93	101	—	23	2	4	—	4	1	.318	.426	.495	.988
1945	Bro-N	152	576	114	177	36	7	9	92	114	—	27	2	4	—	13	—	.307	.423	.441	.979
1946	Bro-N	99	274	53	85	22	5	3	38	68	—	21	2	4	—	8	2	.310	.451	.460	.941
1947	Cin-N	124	392	60	123	18	2	6	61	94	—	19	2	3	—	0	—	.314	.449	.416	.988
1948	Cin-N	54	77	18	22	3	2	2	16	26	—	4	1	2	—	0	—	.286	.471	.455	.967
1949	NYG-N	22	17	0	1	1	0	0	2	5	—	3	0	0	—	0	—	.059	.273	.118	1.000
1949	Phi-A	12	26	4	8	2	0	0	0	9	—	2	0	1	—	0	0	.308	.486	.385	1.000
Career average		109	371	63	107	21	5	6	52	61	—	25	2	4	—	8	1	.287	.390	.419	.978
Cubs average		**113**	**412**	**69**	**114**	**21**	**6**	**7**	**54**	**54**	**—**	**30**	**2**	**5**	**—**	**11**	**—**	**.277**	**.363**	**.409**	**.977**
Career total		1742	5937	1004	1706	336	74	100	830	979	—	393	25	62	—	123	8	.287	.390	.419	.978
Cubs total		**903**	**3297**	**549**	**912**	**166**	**46**	**59**	**435**	**432**	**—**	**242**	**14**	**38**	**—**	**90**	**—**	**.277**	**.363**	**.409**	**.977**

August (Augie) John "Goo Goo" Galan, of-1b-2b-ss-3b, 1934—49

Augie Galan was a talented but injury-prone utilityman who still managed to have a very good major league career despite his physical problems.

Galan was born on May 25, 1912, in Berkeley, California. As a child, he injured his right elbow in a sandlot baseball game. The injury left Galan with a "bend" in his arm that made it hang unnaturally. Galan overcame that handicap to become an excellent second baseman in the minor leagues, a switch-hitter who could run and throw.

In 1934 Galan was brought up to the big club for most of the season. He hit .260 that year and showed great promise. But Cubs manager Charlie Grimm already had the very capable Billy Herman at second base, so Galan was moved to left field in 1935.

He thrived at the position, hitting .314 and leading the National League with 133 runs scored and 22 stolen bases. The Cubs surged to the National League pennant that year, riding a 21-game winning streak in September. Galan hit .384 over the course of the streak.

Galan also set a record that still stands today: in 646 at-bats, he didn't hit into a double play all year—although he did hit into a triple play.

With Galan as Chicago's leadoff man, and Herman batting second, the Cubs also had a formidable hit-and-run team for several years.

In 1936 Galan made the All-Star team, and his home run off the Tigers' Lynwood Thomas "Schoolboy" Rowe with teammate Herman on base gave the National League a 4-0 lead. The Nationals eventually held on for a 4-3 win, their first in four All-Star Games. Galan was also the first Cub to hit a homer in an All-Star Game.

The switch-hitting Galan also set another home run record in 1937 when he became the first major leaguer to hit a home run from both sides of the plate.

Galan had several more strong seasons for the Cubs, but in 1940 he broke his right knee. The Cubs, believing him to be finished, traded him to Brooklyn. Galan recovered nicely from his injuries, made two more appearances in the All-Star Game for the Dodgers and hit over .300 for four consecutive seasons for Brooklyn and later the Reds.

Galan finally retired in 1949 after a stint with the New York Giants and the Philadelphia A's, for whom he hit .308. He later returned to the A's in 1954 as a coach. Galan died in California in 1993.

Galan's name is not on any of the Cubs' all-time hitting lists, but his 351 putouts in 1935 are still a record for a Cubs left fielder.

Gamble, Oscar Charles

HEIGHT: 5'11" THROWS: RIGHT BATS: LEFT BORN: 12/20/1949 RAMER, ALABAMA POSITIONS PLAYED: 1B, OF

YEAR	TEAM	GAMES	AB	RUNS	HITS	2B	3B	HR	RBI	BB	IBB	SO	HBP	SH	SF	SB	CS	BA	OBA	SA	FA
1969	**ChC-N**	**24**	**71**	**6**	**16**	**1**	**1**	**1**	**5**	**10**	**1**	**12**	**0**	**0**	**0**	**0**	**2**	**.225**	**.321**	**.310**	**.913**
1970	Phi-N	88	275	31	72	12	4	1	19	27	3	37	1	2	0	5	4	.262	.330	.345	.956
1971	Phi-N	92	280	24	62	11	1	6	23	21	2	35	1	3	4	5	2	.221	.275	.332	.970
1972	Phi-N	74	135	17	32	5	2	1	13	19	0	16	1	0	2	0	1	.237	.331	.326	1.000
1973	Cle-A	113	390	56	104	11	3	20	44	34	1	37	3	3	2	3	4	.267	.329	.464	.971
1974	Cle-A	135	454	74	132	16	4	19	59	48	10	51	5	0	2	5	6	.291	.363	.469	1.000
1975	Cle-A	121	348	60	91	16	3	15	45	53	4	39	2	1	1	11	5	.261	.361	.454	.987
1976	NYY-A	110	340	43	79	13	1	17	57	38	4	38	4	2	0	5	3	.232	.317	.426	.981
1977	CWS-A	137	408	75	121	22	2	31	83	54	2	54	6	1	1	1	2	.297	.386	.588	.987
1978	SD-N	126	375	46	103	15	3	7	47	51	11	45	6	0	5	1	2	.275	.366	.387	.979
1979	Tex-A	64	161	27	54	6	0	8	32	37	11	15	1	0	2	2	1	.335	.458	.522	1.000
1979	NYY-A	36	113	21	44	4	1	11	32	13	1	13	0	0	0	0	0	.389	.452	.735	.943
1980	NYY-A	78	194	40	54	10	2	14	50	28	4	21	4	0	3	2	0	.278	.376	.567	1.000
1981	NYY-A	80	189	24	45	8	0	10	27	35	2	23	1	0	2	0	2	.238	.357	.439	1.000
1982	NYY-A	108	316	49	86	21	2	18	57	58	2	47	4	0	4	6	3	.272	.387	.522	1.000
1983	NYY-A	74	180	26	47	10	2	7	26	25	1	23	3	0	0	0	0	.261	.361	.456	.942
1984	NYY-A	54	125	17	23	2	0	10	27	25	0	18	0	0	1	1	0	.184	.318	.440	1.000
1985	CWS-A	70	148	20	30	5	0	4	20	34	3	22	1	0	1	0	0	.203	.353	.318	—
Career average		93	265	39	70	11	2	12	39	36	4	32	3	1	2	3	2	.265	.356	.454	.977
Cubs average		**24**	**71**	**6**	**16**	**1**	**1**	**1**	**5**	**10**	**1**	**12**	**0**	**0**	**0**	**0**	**2**	**.225**	**.321**	**.310**	**.913**
Career total		1584	4502	656	1195	188	31	200	666	610	62	546	43	12	30	47	37	.265	.356	.454	.977
Cubs total		**24**	**71**	**6**	**16**	**1**	**1**	**1**	**5**	**10**	**1**	**12**	**0**	**0**	**0**	**0**	**2**	**.225**	**.321**	**.310**	**.913**

Gannon, William G. (Bill)
HEIGHT: 5'9"   THROWS: —   BATS: —   BORN: 1876 NEW HAVEN, CONNECTICUT   DIED: 4/26/1927 FORT WORTH, TEXAS   POSITIONS PLAYED: OF

YEAR	TEAM	GAMES	AB	RUNS	HITS	2B	3B	HR	RBI	BB	IBB	SO	HBP	SH	SF	SB	CS	BA	OBA	SA	FA
1901	ChN-N	15	61	2	9	0	0	0	0	1	—	—	0	1	—	5	—	.148	.161	.148	1.000
Career average		15	61	2	9	0	0	0	0	1	—	—	0	1	—	5	—	.148	.161	.148	1.000
Cubs average		15	61	2	9	0	0	0	0	1	—	—	0	1	—	5	—	.148	.161	.148	1.000
Career total		15	61	2	9	0	0	0	0	1	—	—	0	1	—	5	—	.148	.161	.148	1.000
Cubs total		15	61	2	9	0	0	0	0	1	—	—	0	1	—	5	—	.148	.161	.148	1.000

Ganzel, John Henry
HEIGHT: 6'0"   THROWS: RIGHT   BATS: RIGHT   BORN: 4/7/1874 KALAMAZOO, MICHIGAN   DIED: 1/14/1959 ORLANDO, FLORIDA   POSITIONS PLAYED: 1B, 2B, SS

YEAR	TEAM	GAMES	AB	RUNS	HITS	2B	3B	HR	RBI	BB	IBB	SO	HBP	SH	SF	SB	CS	BA	OBA	SA	FA
1898	Pit-N	15	45	5	6	0	0	0	2	4	—	—	1	0	—	0	—	.133	.220	.133	.963
1900	ChN-N	78	284	29	78	14	4	4	32	10	—	—	7	7	—	5	—	.275	.316	.394	.980
1901	NYG-N	138	526	42	113	13	3	2	66	20	—	—	8	7	—	6	—	.215	.255	.262	.986
1903	NYA-A	129	476	62	132	25	7	3	71	30	—	—	12	15	—	9	—	.277	.336	.378	.988
1904	NYA-A	130	465	50	121	16	10	6	48	24	—	—	9	4	—	13	—	.260	.309	.376	.987
1907	Cin-N	145	531	61	135	20	16	2	64	29	—	—	3	12	—	9	—	.254	.297	.363	.990
1908	Cin-N	112	388	32	97	16	10	1	53	19	—	—	2	18	—	6	—	.250	.289	.351	.990
Career average		107	388	40	97	15	7	3	48	19	—	—	6	9	—	7	—	.251	.297	.346	.987
Cubs average		78	284	29	78	14	4	4	32	10	—	—	7	7	—	5	—	.275	.316	.394	.980
Career total		747	2715	281	682	104	50	18	336	136	—	—	42	63	—	48	—	.251	.297	.346	.987
Cubs total		78	284	29	78	14	4	4	32	10	—	—	7	7	—	5	—	.275	.316	.394	.980

Garagiola, Joseph Henry (Joe)
HEIGHT: 6'0"   THROWS: RIGHT   BATS: LEFT   BORN: 2/12/1926 ST. LOUIS, MISSOURI   POSITIONS PLAYED: C

YEAR	TEAM	GAMES	AB	RUNS	HITS	2B	3B	HR	RBI	BB	IBB	SO	HBP	SH	SF	SB	CS	BA	OBA	SA	FA
1946	StL-N	74	211	21	50	4	1	3	22	23	—	25	0	1	—	0	—	.237	.312	.308	.990
1947	StL-N	77	183	20	47	10	2	5	25	40	—	14	3	2	—	0	—	.257	.398	.415	.987
1948	StL-N	24	56	9	6	1	0	2	7	12	—	9	1	0	—	0	—	.107	.275	.232	.990
1949	StL-N	81	241	25	63	14	0	3	26	31	—	19	1	2	—	0	—	.261	.348	.357	.984
1950	StL-N	34	88	8	28	6	1	2	20	10	—	7	1	0	—	0	—	.318	.388	.477	1.000
1951	StL-N	27	72	9	14	3	2	2	9	9	—	7	0	1	—	0	0	.194	.284	.375	1.000
1951	Pit-N	72	212	24	54	8	2	9	35	32	—	20	2	3	—	4	1	.255	.358	.439	.986
1952	Pit-N	118	344	35	94	15	4	8	54	50	—	24	2	0	—	0	1	.273	.369	.410	.978
1953	Pit-N	27	73	9	17	5	0	2	14	10	—	11	2	1	—	1	0	.233	.341	.384	.989
1953	ChC-N	74	228	21	62	9	4	1	21	21	—	23	1	1	—	0	0	.272	.336	.360	.988
1954	ChC-N	63	153	16	43	5	0	5	21	28	—	12	4	1	1	0	0	.281	.403	.412	.982
1954	NYG-N	5	11	1	3	2	0	0	1	1	—	2	0	0	1	0	0	.273	.308	.455	1.000
Career average		75	208	22	53	9	2	5	28	30	—	19	2	1	0	1	0	.257	.354	.385	.986
Cubs average		69	191	19	53	7	2	3	21	25	—	18	3	1	1	0	0	.276	.365	.381	.986
Career total		676	1872	198	481	82	16	42	255	267	—	173	16	12	2	5	2	.257	.354	.385	.986
Cubs total		137	381	37	105	14	4	6	42	49	—	35	5	2	1	0	0	.276	.365	.381	.986

Garbark, Robert Michael (Bob)
HEIGHT: 5'11"   THROWS: RIGHT   BATS: RIGHT   BORN: 11/13/1909 HOUSTON, TEXAS   DIED: 8/15/1990 MEADVILLE, PENNSYLVANIA   POSITIONS PLAYED: C, 1B

YEAR	TEAM	GAMES	AB	RUNS	HITS	2B	3B	HR	RBI	BB	IBB	SO	HBP	SH	SF	SB	CS	BA	OBA	SA	FA
1934	Cle-A	5	11	1	0	0	0	0	0	1	—	3	0	0	—	0	0	.000	.083	.000	1.000
1935	Cle-A	6	18	4	6	1	0	0	4	5	—	1	0	0	—	0	0	.333	.478	.389	1.000
1937	ChC-N	1	1	0	0	0	0	0	0	0	—	0	0	0	—	0	—	.000	.000	.000	—
1938	ChC-N	23	54	2	14	0	0	0	5	1	—	0	0	0	—	0	—	.259	.273	.259	1.000
1939	ChC-N	24	21	1	3	0	0	0	0	0	—	3	0	1	—	0	—	.143	.143	.143	1.000
1944	Phi-A	18	23	2	6	2	0	0	2	1	—	0	0	1	—	0	0	.261	.292	.348	1.000
1945	Bos-A	68	199	21	52	6	0	0	17	18	—	10	2	6	—	0	1	.261	.329	.291	.993
Career average		21	47	4	12	1	0	0	4	4	—	2	0	1	—	0	0	.248	.307	.275	.996
Cubs average		16	25	1	6	0	0	0	2	0	—	1	0	0	—	0	0	.224	.234	.224	1.000
Career total		145	327	31	81	9	0	0	28	26	—	17	2	8	—	0	1	.248	.307	.275	.996
Cubs total		48	76	3	17	0	0	0	5	1	—	3	0	1	—	0	0	.224	.234	.224	1.000

Garrett, Henry Adrian (Adrian *or* Pat)
HEIGHT: 6'3" THROWS: RIGHT BATS: LEFT BORN: 1/3/1943 BROOKSVILLE, FLORIDA POSITIONS PLAYED: C, 1B, OF

YEAR	TEAM	GAMES	AB	RUNS	HITS	2B	3B	HR	RBI	BB	IBB	SO	HBP	SH	SF	SB	CS	BA	OBA	SA	FA
1966	Atl-N	4	3	0	0	0	0	0	0	0	0	2	0	0	0	0	0	.000	.000	.000	—
1970	ChC-N	3	3	0	0	0	0	0	0	0	0	3	0	0	0	0	0	.000	.000	.000	—
1971	Oak-A	14	21	1	3	0	0	1	2	5	1	7	0	0	0	0	0	.143	.308	.286	1.000
1972	Oak-A	14	11	0	0	0	0	0	0	1	0	4	0	0	0	0	0	.000	.083	.000	1.000
1973	ChC-N	36	54	7	12	0	0	3	8	4	1	18	0	0	2	1	0	.222	.267	.389	.953
1974	ChC-N	10	8	0	0	0	0	0	0	1	0	1	0	0	0	0	0	.000	.111	.000	1.000
1975	ChC-N	16	21	1	2	0	0	1	6	1	0	8	0	0	1	0	0	.095	.130	.238	1.000
1975	Cal-A	37	107	17	28	5	0	6	18	14	0	28	0	1	1	3	0	.262	.344	.477	.989
1976	Cal-A	29	48	4	6	3	0	0	3	5	0	16	0	0	1	0	0	.125	.204	.188	.978
Career average		20	35	4	6	1	0	1	5	4	0	11	0	0	1	1	0	.185	.263	.333	.981
Cubs average		**16**	**22**	**2**	**4**	**0**	**0**	**1**	**4**	**2**	**0**	**8**	**0**	**0**	**1**	**0**	**0**	**.163**	**.211**	**.302**	**.973**
Career total		163	276	30	51	8	0	11	37	31	2	87	0	1	5	4	0	.185	.263	.333	.981
Cubs total		**65**	**86**	**8**	**14**	**0**	**0**	**4**	**14**	**6**	**1**	**30**	**0**	**0**	**3**	**1**	**0**	**.163**	**.211**	**.302**	**.973**

Garriott, Virgil Cecil (Cecil *or* Rabbit)
HEIGHT: 5'8" THROWS: RIGHT BATS: LEFT BORN: 8/15/1916 HARRISTOWN, ILLINOIS DIED: 2/20/1990 LAKE ELSINORE, CALIFORNIA

YEAR	TEAM	GAMES	AB	RUNS	HITS	2B	3B	HR	RBI	BB	IBB	SO	HBP	SH	SF	SB	CS	BA	OBA	SA	FA
1946	ChC-N	6	5	1	0	0	0	0	0	0	—	2	1	0	—	0	—	.000	.167	.000	—
Career average		6	5	1	0	0	0	0	0	0	—	2	1	0	—	0	—	.000	.167	.000	—
Cubs average		**6**	**5**	**1**	**0**	**0**	**0**	**0**	**0**	**0**	**—**	**2**	**1**	**0**	**—**	**0**	**—**	**.000**	**.167**	**.000**	**—**
Career total		6	5	1	0	0	0	0	0	0	—	2	1	0	—	0	—	.000	.167	.000	—
Cubs total		**6**	**5**	**1**	**0**	**0**	**0**	**0**	**0**	**0**	**—**	**2**	**1**	**0**	**—**	**0**	**—**	**.000**	**.167**	**.000**	**—**

Gastfield, Edward (Ed)
HEIGHT: 5'10" THROWS: — BATS: RIGHT BORN: 8/1/1865 CHICAGO, ILLINOIS DIED: 12/1/1899 CHICAGO, ILLINOIS POSITIONS PLAYED: C, 1B, OF

YEAR	TEAM	GAMES	AB	RUNS	HITS	2B	3B	HR	RBI	BB	IBB	SO	HBP	SH	SF	SB	CS	BA	OBA	SA	FA
1884	Det-N	23	82	6	6	1	0	0	2	2	—	34	—	—	—	—	—	.073	.095	.085	.844
1885	Det-N	1	3	0	0	0	0	0	0	0	—	2	—	—	—	—	—	.000	.000	.000	.714
1885	ChN-N	1	3	0	0	0	0	0	0	0	—	1	—	—	—	—	—	.000	.000	.000	1.000
Career average		13	44	3	3	1	0	0	1	1	—	19	—	—	—	—	—	.068	.089	.080	.847
Cubs average		**1**	**3**	**0**	**0**	**0**	**0**	**0**	**0**	**0**	**—**	**1**	**—**	**—**	**—**	**—**	**—**	**.000**	**.000**	**.000**	**1.000**
Career total		25	88	6	6	1	0	0	2	2	—	37	—	—	—	—	—	.068	.089	.080	.847
Cubs total		**1**	**3**	**0**	**0**	**0**	**0**	**0**	**0**	**0**	**—**	**1**	**—**	**—**	**—**	**—**	**—**	**.000**	**.000**	**.000**	**1.000**

Geiss, Emil August
HEIGHT: 5'11" THROWS: RIGHT BATS: RIGHT BORN: 3/20/1867 CHICAGO, ILLINOIS DIED: 10/4/1911 CHICAGO, ILLINOIS POSITIONS PLAYED: P, 1B, 2B

YEAR	TEAM	GAMES	AB	RUNS	HITS	2B	3B	HR	RBI	BB	IBB	SO	HBP	SH	SF	SB	CS	BA	OBA	SA	FA
1887	ChN-N	3	12	0	1	0	0	0	0	0	—	7	0	—	—	0	—	.083	.083	.083	.850
Career average		3	12	0	1	0	0	0	0	0	—	7	0	—	—	0	—	.083	.083	.083	.850
Cubs average		**3**	**12**	**0**	**1**	**0**	**0**	**0**	**0**	**0**	**—**	**7**	**0**	**—**	**—**	**0**	**—**	**.083**	**.083**	**.083**	**.850**
Career total		3	12	0	1	0	0	0	0	0	—	7	0	—	—	0	—	.083	.083	.083	.850
Cubs total		**3**	**12**	**0**	**1**	**0**	**0**	**0**	**0**	**0**	**—**	**7**	**0**	**—**	**—**	**0**	**—**	**.083**	**.083**	**.083**	**.850**

George, Charles Peter (Greek)
HEIGHT: 6'2" THROWS: RIGHT BATS: RIGHT BORN: 12/25/1912 WAYCROSS, GEORGIA DIED: 8/15/1999 METAIRIE, LOUISIANA POSITIONS PLAYED: C

YEAR	TEAM	GAMES	AB	RUNS	HITS	2B	3B	HR	RBI	BB	IBB	SO	HBP	SH	SF	SB	CS	BA	OBA	SA	FA
1935	Cle-A	2	0	0	0	0	0	0	0	0	—	0	0	0	—	0	0	—	—	—	1.000
1936	Cle-A	23	77	3	15	3	0	0	5	9	—	16	0	0	—	0	0	.195	.279	.234	.994
1938	Bro-N	7	20	0	4	0	1	0	2	0	—	4	0	0	—	0	—	.200	.200	.300	1.000
1941	ChC-N	35	64	4	10	2	0	0	6	2	—	10	0	1	—	0	—	.156	.182	.188	.973
1945	Phi-A	51	138	8	24	4	1	0	11	17	—	29	0	4	—	0	0	.174	.265	.217	.972

(continued)

(continued)

Career average	24	60	3	11	2	0	0	5	6	—	12	0	1	—	0	0	.177	.248	.221	.983
Cubs average	**35**	**64**	**4**	**10**	**2**	**0**	**0**	**6**	**2**	**—**	**10**	**0**	**1**	**—**	**0**	**0**	**.156**	**.182**	**.188**	**.973**
Career total	118	299	15	53	9	2	0	24	28	—	59	0	5	—	0	0	.177	.248	.221	.983
Cubs total	**35**	**64**	**4**	**10**	**2**	**0**	**0**	**6**	**2**	**—**	**10**	**0**	**1**	**—**	**0**	**0**	**.156**	**.182**	**.188**	**.973**

Gernert, Richard Edward (Dick)
HEIGHT: 6'3" THROWS: RIGHT BATS: RIGHT BORN: 9/28/1928 READING, PENNSYLVANIA POSITIONS PLAYED: 1B, OF

YEAR	TEAM	GAMES	AB	RUNS	HITS	2B	3B	HR	RBI	BB	IBB	SO	HBP	SH	SF	SB	CS	BA	OBA	SA	FA
1952	Bos-A	102	367	58	89	20	2	19	67	35	—	83	5	0	—	4	1	.243	.317	.463	.987
1953	Bos-A	139	494	73	125	15	1	21	71	88	—	82	5	3	—	0	7	.253	.371	.415	.986
1954	Bos-A	14	23	2	6	2	0	0	1	6	—	4	0	1	0	0	0	.261	.414	.348	1.000
1955	Bos-A	7	20	6	4	2	0	0	1	1	0	5	0	0	0	0	0	.200	.238	.300	.974
1956	Bos-A	106	306	53	89	11	0	16	68	56	1	57	2	2	4	1	0	.291	.399	.484	.990
1957	Bos-A	99	316	45	75	13	3	14	58	39	3	62	3	1	3	1	1	.237	.324	.430	.987
1958	Bos-A	122	431	59	102	19	1	20	69	59	4	78	2	2	2	2	0	.237	.330	.425	.991
1959	Bos-A	117	298	41	78	14	1	11	42	52	3	49	0	0	2	1	2	.262	.369	.426	.994
1960	**ChC-N**	**52**	**96**	**8**	**24**	**3**	**0**	**0**	**11**	**10**	**0**	**19**	**0**	**1**	**0**	**1**	**0**	**.250**	**.321**	**.281**	**.988**
1960	Det-A	21	50	6	15	4	0	1	5	4	0	5	0	0	0	0	0	.300	.352	.440	.990
1961	Det-A	6	5	1	1	0	0	1	1	1	0	2	0	0	0	0	0	.200	.333	.800	—
1961	Cin-N	40	63	4	19	1	0	0	7	7	1	9	0	0	2	0	0	.302	.361	.317	.993
1962	Hou-N	10	24	1	5	0	0	0	1	5	0	7	0	0	0	0	0	.208	.345	.208	1.000
Career average	76	227	32	57	9	1	9	37	33	1	42	2	1	1	1	1	.254	.351	.426	.989
Cubs average	**52**	**96**	**8**	**24**	**3**	**0**	**0**	**11**	**10**	**0**	**19**	**0**	**1**	**0**	**1**	**0**	**.250**	**.321**	**.281**	**.988**
Career total	835	2493	357	632	104	8	103	402	363	12	462	17	10	13	10	11	.254	.351	.426	.989
Cubs total	**52**	**96**	**8**	**24**	**3**	**0**	**0**	**11**	**10**	**0**	**19**	**0**	**1**	**0**	**1**	**0**	**.250**	**.321**	**.281**	**.988**

Gessler, Harry Homer (Doc *or* Brownie)
HEIGHT: 5'10" THROWS: LEFT BATS: LEFT BORN: 12/23/1880 GREENSBURG, PENNSYLVANIA DIED: 12/24/1924 GREENSBURG, PENNSYLVANIA
POSITIONS PLAYED: 1B, 2B, OF

YEAR	TEAM	GAMES	AB	RUNS	HITS	2B	3B	HR	RBI	BB	IBB	SO	HBP	SH	SF	SB	CS	BA	OBA	SA	FA
1903	Det-A	29	105	9	25	5	4	0	12	3	—	—	2	4	—	1	—	.238	.273	.362	.974
1903	Bro-N	49	154	20	38	8	3	0	18	17	—	—	12	9	—	9	—	.247	.366	.338	.984
1904	Bro-N	104	341	41	99	18	4	2	28	30	—	—	4	6	—	13	—	.290	.355	.384	.921
1905	Bro-N	126	431	44	125	17	4	3	46	38	—	—	14	3	—	26	—	.290	.366	.369	.971
1906	Bro-N	9	33	3	8	1	2	0	4	3	—	—	1	3	—	3	—	.242	.324	.394	.946
1906	**ChC-N**	**34**	**83**	**8**	**21**	**3**	**0**	**0**	**10**	**12**	**—**	**—**	**1**	**0**	**—**	**4**	**—**	**.253**	**.354**	**.289**	**1.000**
1908	Bos-A	128	435	55	134	13	14	3	63	51	—	—	11	10	—	19	—	.308	.394	.423	.950
1909	Bos-A	111	396	57	115	24	1	0	46	31	—	—	8	5	—	16	—	.290	.354	.356	.933
1909	Was-A	17	54	10	13	2	1	0	8	12	—	—	3	1	—	4	—	.241	.406	.315	1.000
1910	Was-A	145	487	58	126	17	12	2	50	62	—	—	16	12	—	18	—	.259	.361	.355	.953
1911	Was-A	128	450	65	127	19	5	4	78	74	—	—	20	9	—	29	—	.282	.406	.373	.945
Career average	110	371	46	104	16	6	2	45	42	—	—	12	8	—	18	—	.280	.370	.370	.959
Cubs average	**34**	**83**	**8**	**21**	**3**	**0**	**0**	**10**	**12**	**—**	**—**	**1**	**0**	**—**	**4**	**—**	**.253**	**.354**	**.289**	**1.000**
Career total	880	2969	370	831	127	50	14	363	333	—	—	92	62	—	142	—	.280	.370	.370	.959
Cubs total	**34**	**83**	**8**	**21**	**3**	**0**	**0**	**10**	**12**	**—**	**—**	**1**	**0**	**—**	**4**	**—**	**.253**	**.354**	**.289**	**1.000**

Gigon, Norman Phillip (Norm)
HEIGHT: 6'0" THROWS: RIGHT BATS: RIGHT BORN: 5/12/1938 TEANECK, NEW JERSEY POSITIONS PLAYED: 2B, 3B, OF

YEAR	TEAM	GAMES	AB	RUNS	HITS	2B	3B	HR	RBI	BB	IBB	SO	HBP	SH	SF	SB	CS	BA	OBA	SA	FA
1967	ChC-N	34	70	8	12	3	1	1	6	4	0	14	2	0	1	0	0	.171	.234	.286	.983
Career average	34	70	8	12	3	1	1	6	4	0	14	2	0	1	0	0	.171	.234	.286	.983
Cubs average	**34**	**70**	**8**	**12**	**3**	**1**	**1**	**6**	**4**	**0**	**14**	**2**	**0**	**1**	**0**	**0**	**.171**	**.234**	**.286**	**.983**
Career total	34	70	8	12	3	1	1	6	4	0	14	2	0	1	0	0	.171	.234	.286	.983
Cubs total	**34**	**70**	**8**	**12**	**3**	**1**	**1**	**6**	**4**	**0**	**14**	**2**	**0**	**1**	**0**	**0**	**.171**	**.234**	**.286**	**.983**

Gilbert, Charles Mader (Charlie)
HEIGHT: 5'9"   THROWS: LEFT   BATS: LEFT   BORN: 7/8/1919 NEW ORLEANS, LOUISIANA   DIED: 8/13/1983 NEW ORLEANS, LOUISIANA   POSITIONS PLAYED: OF

YEAR	TEAM	GAMES	AB	RUNS	HITS	2B	3B	HR	RBI	BB	IBB	SO	HBP	SH	SF	SB	CS	BA	OBA	SA	FA
1940	Bro-N	57	142	23	35	9	1	2	8	8	—	13	0	1	—	0	—	.246	.287	.366	.960
1941	ChC-N	39	86	11	24	2	1	0	12	11	—	6	0	2	—	1	—	.279	.361	.326	1.000
1942	ChC-N	74	179	18	33	6	3	0	7	25	—	24	0	2	—	1	—	.184	.284	.251	.981
1943	ChC-N	8	20	1	3	0	0	0	0	3	—	3	0	0	—	1	—	.150	.261	.150	1.000
1946	ChC-N	15	13	2	1	0	0	0	1	1	—	4	0	0	—	0	—	.077	.143	.077	1.000
1946	Phi-N	88	260	34	63	5	2	1	17	25	—	18	2	6	—	3	—	.242	.314	.288	1.000
1947	Phi-N	83	152	20	36	5	2	2	10	13	—	14	1	0	—	1	—	.237	.301	.336	.961
Career average		61	142	18	33	5	2	1	9	14	—	14	1	2	—	1	—	.229	.302	.299	.982
Cubs average		**34**	**75**	**8**	**15**	**2**	**1**	**0**	**5**	**10**	**—**	**9**	**0**	**1**	**—**	**1**	**—**	**.205**	**.299**	**.258**	**.988**
Career total		364	852	109	195	27	9	5	55	86	—	82	3	11	—	7	—	.229	.302	.299	.982
Cubs total		**136**	**298**	**32**	**61**	**8**	**4**	**0**	**20**	**40**	**—**	**37**	**0**	**4**	**—**	**3**	**—**	**.205**	**.299**	**.258**	**.988**

Gill, John Wesley (Johnny *or* Patcheye)
HEIGHT: 6'2"   THROWS: RIGHT   BATS: LEFT   BORN: 3/27/1905 NASHVILLE, TENNESSEE   DIED: 12/26/1984 NASHVILLE, TENNESSEE   POSITIONS PLAYED: OF

YEAR	TEAM	GAMES	AB	RUNS	HITS	2B	3B	HR	RBI	BB	IBB	SO	HBP	SH	SF	SB	CS	BA	OBA	SA	FA
1927	Cle-A	21	60	8	13	3	0	1	4	7	—	13	2	0	—	1	1	.217	.319	.317	1.000
1928	Cle-A	2	2	0	0	0	0	0	0	0	—	1	0	0	—	0	0	.000	.000	.000	—
1931	Was-A	8	30	2	8	2	1	0	5	1	—	6	1	3	—	0	1	.267	.313	.400	1.000
1934	Was-A	13	53	7	13	3	0	2	7	2	—	3	1	0	—	0	0	.245	.286	.415	1.000
1935	ChC-N	3	3	2	1	1	0	0	1	0	—	1	0	0	—	0	—	.333	.333	.667	—
1936	ChC-N	71	174	20	44	8	0	7	28	13	—	19	1	1	—	0	—	.253	.309	.420	.938
Career average		20	54	7	13	3	0	2	8	4	—	7	1	1	—	0	0	.245	.306	.398	.968
Cubs average		**37**	**89**	**11**	**23**	**5**	**0**	**4**	**15**	**7**	**—**	**10**	**1**	**1**	**—**	**0**	**0**	**.254**	**.309**	**.424**	**.938**
Career total		118	322	39	79	17	1	10	45	23	—	43	5	4	—	1	2	.245	.306	.398	.968
Cubs total		**74**	**177**	**22**	**45**	**9**	**0**	**7**	**29**	**13**	**—**	**20**	**1**	**1**	**—**	**0**	**0**	**.254**	**.309**	**.424**	**.938**

Gillespie, Paul Allen
HEIGHT: 6'3"   THROWS: RIGHT   BATS: LEFT   BORN: 9/18/1920 CARTERSVILLE, GEORGIA   DIED: 8/11/1970 ANNISTON, ALABAMA   POSITIONS PLAYED: C, OF

YEAR	TEAM	GAMES	AB	RUNS	HITS	2B	3B	HR	RBI	BB	IBB	SO	HBP	SH	SF	SB	CS	BA	OBA	SA	FA
1942	ChC-N	5	16	3	4	0	0	2	4	1	—	2	0	0	—	0	—	.250	.294	.625	1.000
1944	ChC-N	9	26	2	7	1	0	1	2	3	—	3	0	0	—	0	—	.269	.345	.423	.903
1945	ChC-N	75	163	12	47	6	0	3	25	18	—	9	2	0	—	2	—	.288	.366	.380	.989
Career average		30	68	6	19	2	0	2	10	7	—	5	1	0	—	1	—	.283	.358	.405	.978
Cubs average		**30**	**68**	**6**	**19**	**2**	**0**	**2**	**10**	**7**	**—**	**5**	**1**	**0**	**—**	**1**	**—**	**.283**	**.358**	**.405**	**.978**
Career total		89	205	17	58	7	0	6	31	22	—	14	2	0	—	2	—	.283	.358	.405	.978
Cubs total		**89**	**205**	**17**	**58**	**7**	**0**	**6**	**31**	**22**	**—**	**14**	**2**	**0**	**—**	**2**	**—**	**.283**	**.358**	**.405**	**.978**

Girardi, Joseph Elliott (Joe)
HEIGHT: 5'11"   THROWS: RIGHT   BATS: RIGHT   BORN: 10/14/1964 PEORIA, ILLINOIS   POSITIONS PLAYED: C

YEAR	TEAM	GAMES	AB	RUNS	HITS	2B	3B	HR	RBI	BB	IBB	SO	HBP	SH	SF	SB	CS	BA	OBA	SA	FA
1989	ChC-N	59	157	15	39	10	0	1	14	11	5	26	2	1	1	2	1	.248	.304	.331	.981
1990	ChC-N	133	419	36	113	24	2	1	38	17	11	50	3	4	4	8	3	.270	.300	.344	.985
1991	ChC-N	21	47	3	9	2	0	0	6	6	1	6	0	1	0	0	0	.191	.283	.234	.972
1992	ChC-N	91	270	19	73	3	1	1	12	19	3	38	1	0	1	0	2	.270	.320	.300	.991
1993	Col-N	86	310	35	90	14	5	3	31	24	0	41	3	12	1	6	6	.290	.346	.397	.989
1994	Col-N	93	330	47	91	9	4	4	34	21	1	48	2	6	2	3	3	.276	.321	.364	.992
1995	Col-N	125	462	63	121	17	2	8	55	29	0	76	2	12	1	3	3	.262	.308	.359	.988
1996	NYY-A	124	422	55	124	22	3	2	45	30	1	55	5	11	3	13	4	.294	.346	.374	.996
1997	NYY-A	112	398	38	105	23	1	1	50	26	1	53	2	5	2	2	3	.264	.311	.334	.994
1998	NYY-A	78	254	31	70	11	4	3	31	14	1	38	2	8	1	2	4	.276	.317	.386	.995
1999	NYY-A	65	209	23	50	16	1	2	27	10	0	26	0	8	2	3	1	.239	.271	.354	.984
2000	ChC-N	106	363	47	101	15	1	6	40	32	3	61	3	6	3	1	0	.278	.339	.375	.993
2001	ChC-N	78	229	22	58	10	1	3	25	21	4	50	0	2	1	0	1	.253	.315	.345	1.000
Career average		90	298	33	80	14	2	3	31	20	2	44	2	6	2	3	2	.270	.318	.355	.991
Cubs average		**81**	**248**	**24**	**66**	**11**	**1**	**2**	**23**	**18**	**5**	**39**	**2**	**2**	**2**	**2**	**1**	**.265**	**.316**	**.339**	**.990**
Career total		1171	3870	434	1044	176	25	35	408	260	31	568	25	76	22	43	31	.270	.318	.355	.991
Cubs total		**488**	**1485**	**142**	**393**	**64**	**5**	**12**	**135**	**106**	**27**	**231**	**9**	**14**	**10**	**11**	**7**	**.265**	**.316**	**.339**	**.990**

Glanville, Douglas Metunwa (Doug)
HEIGHT: 6'2"   THROWS: RIGHT   BATS: RIGHT   BORN: 8/25/1970 HACKENSACK, NEW JERSEY   POSITIONS PLAYED: OF

YEAR	TEAM	GAMES	AB	RUNS	HITS	2B	3B	HR	RBI	BB	IBB	SO	HBP	SH	SF	SB	CS	BA	OBA	SA	FA
1996	ChC-N	49	83	10	20	5	1	1	10	3	0	11	0	2	1	2	0	.241	.264	.361	.973
1997	ChC-N	146	474	79	142	22	5	4	35	24	0	46	1	9	2	19	11	.300	.333	.392	.989
1998	Phi-N	158	678	106	189	28	7	8	49	42	1	89	6	5	4	23	6	.279	.325	.376	.995
1999	Phi-N	150	628	101	204	38	6	11	73	48	1	82	6	5	5	34	2	.325	.376	.457	.980
2000	Phi-N	154	637	89	175	27	6	8	52	31	1	76	2	12	7	31	8	.275	.307	.374	.990
2001	Phi-N	153	634	74	166	24	3	14	55	19	1	91	4	10	7	28	6	.262	.285	.375	.991
Career average		135	522	77	149	24	5	8	46	28	1	66	3	7	4	23	6	.286	.323	.394	.988
Cubs average		98	279	45	81	14	3	3	23	14	0	29	1	6	2	11	6	.291	.323	.388	.987
Career total		810	3134	459	896	144	28	46	274	167	4	395	19	43	26	137	33	.286	.323	.394	.988
Cubs total		195	557	89	162	27	6	5	45	27	0	57	1	11	3	21	11	.291	.323	.388	.987

Gleeson, James Joseph (Jim *or* Gee Gee)
HEIGHT: 6'1"   THROWS: RIGHT   BATS: BOTH   BORN: 3/5/1912 KANSAS CITY, MISSOURI   DIED: 5/1/1996 KANSAS CITY, MISSOURI   POSITIONS PLAYED: OF

YEAR	TEAM	GAMES	AB	RUNS	HITS	2B	3B	HR	RBI	BB	IBB	SO	HBP	SH	SF	SB	CS	BA	OBA	SA	FA
1936	Cle-A	41	139	26	36	9	2	4	12	18	—	17	0	1	—	2	1	.259	.344	.439	.958
1939	ChC-N	111	332	43	74	19	6	4	45	39	—	46	2	10	—	7	—	.223	.308	.352	.957
1940	ChC-N	129	485	76	152	39	11	5	61	54	—	52	6	6	—	4	—	.313	.389	.470	.983
1941	Cin-N	102	301	47	70	10	0	3	34	45	—	30	4	5	—	7	—	.233	.340	.296	.981
1942	Cin-N	9	20	3	4	0	0	0	2	2	—	2	1	1	—	0	—	.200	.304	.200	.889
Career average		78	255	39	67	15	4	3	31	32	—	29	3	5	—	4	0	.263	.350	.391	.972
Cubs average		120	409	60	113	29	9	5	53	47	—	49	4	8	—	6	0	.277	.356	.422	.973
Career total		392	1277	195	336	77	19	16	154	158	—	147	13	23	—	20	1	.263	.350	.391	.972
Cubs total		240	817	119	226	58	17	9	106	93	—	98	8	16	—	11	0	.277	.356	.422	.973

Glenalvin, Robert J. (Bob)
HEIGHT: 5'9"   THROWS: RIGHT   BATS: —   BORN: 1/17/1867 INDIANAPOLIS, INDIANA   DIED: 3/24/1944 DETROIT, MICHIGAN   POSITIONS PLAYED: 2B

YEAR	TEAM	GAMES	AB	RUNS	HITS	2B	3B	HR	RBI	BB	IBB	SO	HBP	SH	SF	SB	CS	BA	OBA	SA	FA
1890	ChN-N	66	250	43	67	10	3	4	26	19	—	31	7	—	—	30	—	.268	.337	.380	.928
1893	ChN-N	16	61	11	21	3	1	0	12	7	—	3	0	—	—	7	—	.344	.412	.426	.928
Career average		41	156	27	44	7	2	2	19	13	—	17	4	—	—	19	—	.283	.352	.389	.928
Cubs average		41	156	27	44	7	2	2	19	13	—	17	4	—	—	19	—	.283	.352	.389	.928
Career total		82	311	54	88	13	4	4	38	26	—	34	7	—	—	37	—	.283	.352	.389	.928
Cubs total		82	311	54	88	13	4	4	38	26	—	34	7	—	—	37	—	.283	.352	.389	.928

Glenn, Edward D. (Ed)
HEIGHT: —   THROWS: RIGHT   BATS: RIGHT   BORN: 10/1875 OHIO   DIED: 12/6/1911 LUDLOW, KENTUCKY   POSITIONS PLAYED: SS

YEAR	TEAM	GAMES	AB	RUNS	HITS	2B	3B	HR	RBI	BB	IBB	SO	HBP	SH	SF	SB	CS	BA	OBA	SA	FA
1898	Was-N	1	4	0	0	0	0	0	0	0	—	—	0	0	—	0	—	.000	.000	.000	1.000
1898	NYG-N	2	4	1	1	0	0	0	0	3	—	—	0	4	—	1	—	.250	.571	.250	.750
1902	ChC-N	2	7	0	0	0	0	0	0	1	—	—	0	0	—	0	—	.000	.125	.000	1.000
Career average		3	8	1	1	0	0	0	0	2	—	—	0	2	—	1	—	.067	.263	.067	.923
Cubs average		2	7	0	0	0	0	0	0	1	—	—	0	0	—	0	—	.000	.125	.000	1.000
Career total		5	15	1	1	0	0	0	0	4	—	—	0	4	—	1	—	.067	.263	.067	.923
Cubs total		2	7	0	0	0	0	0	0	1	—	—	0	0	—	0	—	.000	.125	.000	1.000

Glenn, John W.
HEIGHT: 5'8"   THROWS: RIGHT   BATS: RIGHT   BORN: 1849 ROCHESTER, NEW YORK   DIED: 11/10/1888 SANDY HILL, NEW YORK   POSITIONS PLAYED: 1B, OF

YEAR	TEAM	GAMES	AB	RUNS	HITS	2B	3B	HR	RBI	BB	IBB	SO	HBP	SH	SF	SB	CS	BA	OBA	SA	FA
1876	ChN-N	66	288	55	84	9	2	0	32	12	—	6	—	—	—	—	—	.292	.320	.337	.904
1877	ChN-N	50	202	31	46	6	1	0	20	8	—	16	—	—	—	—	—	.228	.257	.267	.933
Career average		58	245	43	65	8	2	0	26	10	—	11	—	—	—	—	—	.265	.294	.308	.918
Cubs average		58	245	43	65	8	2	0	26	10	—	11	—	—	—	—	—	.265	.294	.308	.918
Career total		116	490	86	130	15	3	0	52	20	—	22	—	—	—	—	—	.265	.294	.308	.918
Cubs total		116	490	86	130	15	3	0	52	20	—	22	—	—	—	—	—	.265	.294	.308	.918

Gload, Ross P.
HEIGHT: 6'0"   THROWS: LEFT   BATS: LEFT   BORN: 4/5/1976 BROOKLYN, NEW YORK   POSITIONS PLAYED: 1B, OF

YEAR	TEAM	GAMES	AB	RUNS	HITS	2B	3B	HR	RBI	BB	IBB	SO	HBP	SH	SF	SB	CS	BA	OBA	SA	FA
2000	ChC-N	18	31	4	6	0	1	1	3	3	0	10	0	0	1	0	0	.194	.257	.355	1.000
Career average		18	31	4	6	0	1	1	3	3	0	10	0	0	1	0	0	.194	.257	.355	1.000
Cubs average		18	31	4	6	0	1	1	3	3	0	10	0	0	1	0	0	.194	.257	.355	1.000
Career total		18	31	4	6	0	1	1	3	3	0	10	0	0	1	0	0	.194	.257	.355	1.000
Cubs total		18	31	4	6	0	1	1	3	3	0	10	0	0	1	0	0	.194	.257	.355	1.000

Glossop, Alban (Al)
HEIGHT: 6'0"   THROWS: RIGHT   BATS: BOTH   BORN: 7/22/1914 CHRISTOPHER, ILLINOIS   DIED: 7/2/1991 WALNUT CREEK, CALIFORNIA
POSITIONS PLAYED: 2B, 3B, SS, OF

YEAR	TEAM	GAMES	AB	RUNS	HITS	2B	3B	HR	RBI	BB	IBB	SO	HBP	SH	SF	SB	CS	BA	OBA	SA	FA
1939	NYG-N	10	32	3	6	0	0	1	3	4	—	2	0	1	—	0	—	.188	.278	.281	.980
1940	NYG-N	27	91	16	19	3	0	4	8	10	—	16	1	0	—	1	—	.209	.294	.374	.952
1940	Bos-N	60	148	17	35	2	1	3	14	17	—	22	0	0	—	1	—	.236	.315	.324	.944
1942	Phi-N	121	454	33	102	15	1	4	40	29	—	35	1	6	—	3	—	.225	.273	.289	.961
1943	Bro-N	87	217	28	37	9	0	3	21	28	—	27	1	4	—	0	1	.171	.268	.253	.916
1946	ChC-N	4	10	2	0	0	0	0	0	1	—	3	2	1	—	0	—	.000	.231	.000	.941
Career average		62	190	20	40	6	0	3	17	18	—	21	1	2	—	1	0	.209	.280	.291	.949
Cubs average		4	10	2	0	0	0	0	0	1	—	3	2	1	—	0	0	.000	.231	.000	.941
Career total		309	952	99	199	29	2	15	86	89	—	105	5	12	—	5	1	.209	.280	.291	.949
Cubs total		4	10	2	0	0	0	0	0	1	—	3	2	1	—	0	0	.000	.231	.000	.941

Golvin, Walter George (Walt)
HEIGHT: 6'0"   THROWS: LEFT   BATS: LEFT   BORN: 2/1/1894 HERSHEY, NEBRASKA   DIED: 6/11/1973 GARDENA, CALIFORNIA   POSITIONS PLAYED: 1B

YEAR	TEAM	GAMES	AB	RUNS	HITS	2B	3B	HR	RBI	BB	IBB	SO	HBP	SH	SF	SB	CS	BA	OBA	SA	FA
1922	ChC-N	2	2	0	0	0	0	0	1	0	—	0	0	0	—	0	0	.000	.000	.000	1.000
Career average		2	2	0	0	0	0	0	1	0	—	0	0	0	—	0	0	.000	.000	.000	1.000
Cubs average		2	2	0	0	0	0	0	1	0	—	0	0	0	—	0	0	.000	.000	.000	1.000
Career total		2	2	0	0	0	0	0	1	0	—	0	0	0	—	0	0	.000	.000	.000	1.000
Cubs total		2	2	0	0	0	0	0	1	0	—	0	0	0	—	0	0	.000	.000	.000	1.000

Gomez, Leonardo (Leo)
HEIGHT: 6'0"   THROWS: RIGHT   BATS: RIGHT   BORN: 3/2/1966 CANOVANAS, PUERTO RICO   POSITIONS PLAYED: 1B, 3B, SS

YEAR	TEAM	GAMES	AB	RUNS	HITS	2B	3B	HR	RBI	BB	IBB	SO	HBP	SH	SF	SB	CS	BA	OBA	SA	FA
1990	Bal-A	12	39	3	9	0	0	0	1	8	0	7	0	1	0	0	0	.231	.362	.231	.886
1991	Bal-A	118	391	40	91	17	2	16	45	40	0	82	2	5	7	1	1	.233	.302	.409	.974
1992	Bal-A	137	468	62	124	24	0	17	64	63	4	78	8	5	8	2	3	.265	.356	.425	.951
1993	Bal-A	71	244	30	48	7	0	10	25	32	1	60	3	3	2	0	1	.197	.295	.348	.951
1994	Bal-A	84	285	46	78	20	0	15	56	41	0	55	3	0	4	0	0	.274	.366	.502	.975
1995	Bal-A	53	127	16	30	5	0	4	12	18	1	23	2	0	2	0	1	.236	.336	.370	.980
1996	ChC-N	136	362	44	86	19	0	17	56	53	0	94	7	3	2	1	4	.238	.344	.431	.977
Career average		87	274	34	67	13	0	11	37	36	1	57	4	2	4	1	1	.243	.336	.417	.964
Cubs average		136	362	44	86	19	0	17	56	53	0	94	7	3	2	1	4	.238	.344	.431	.977
Career total		611	1916	241	466	92	2	79	259	255	6	399	25	17	25	4	10	.243	.336	.417	.964
Cubs total		136	362	44	86	19	0	17	56	53	0	94	7	3	2	1	4	.238	.344	.431	.977

Gonzalez, Luis Emilio
HEIGHT: 6'2"   THROWS: RIGHT   BATS: LEFT   BORN: 9/3/1967 TAMPA, FLORIDA   POSITIONS PLAYED: 1B, 3B, OF

YEAR	TEAM	GAMES	AB	RUNS	HITS	2B	3B	HR	RBI	BB	IBB	SO	HBP	SH	SF	SB	CS	BA	OBA	SA	FA
1990	Hou-N	12	21	1	4	2	0	0	0	2	1	5	0	0	0	0	0	.190	.261	.286	1.000
1991	Hou-N	137	473	51	120	28	9	13	69	40	4	101	8	1	4	10	7	.254	.320	.433	.984
1992	Hou-N	122	387	40	94	19	3	10	55	24	3	52	2	1	2	7	7	.243	.289	.385	.993
1993	Hou-N	154	540	82	162	34	3	15	72	47	7	83	10	3	10	20	9	.300	.361	.457	.978
1994	Hou-N	112	392	57	107	29	4	8	67	49	6	57	3	0	6	15	13	.273	.353	.429	.991

(continued)

(continued)

YEAR	TEAM	GAMES	AB	RUNS	HITS	2B	3B	HR	RBI	BB	IBB	SO	HBP	SH	SF	SB	CS	BA	OBA	SA	FA
1995	Hou-N	56	209	35	54	10	4	6	35	18	3	30	3	1	3	1	3	.258	.322	.431	.980
1995	**ChC-N**	**77**	**262**	**34**	**76**	**19**	**4**	**7**	**34**	**39**	**5**	**33**	**3**	**0**	**3**	**5**	**5**	**.290**	**.384**	**.473**	**.978**
1996	**ChC-N**	**146**	**483**	**70**	**131**	**30**	**4**	**15**	**79**	**61**	**8**	**49**	**4**	**1**	**6**	**9**	**6**	**.290**	**.384**	**.473**	**.978**
1997	Hou-N	152	550	78	142	31	2	10	68	71	7	67	5	0	5	10	6	.271	.354	.443	.988
1998	Det-A	154	547	84	146	35	5	23	71	57	7	62	8	0	8	10	7	.258	.345	.376	.982
1999	Ari-N	153	614	112	206	45	4	26	111	66	6	63	7	1	5	12	7	.267	.340	.475	.988
2000	Ari-N	162	618	106	192	47	2	31	114	78	6	85	12	2	12	9	5	.336	.403	.549	.983
2001	Ari-N	162	609	128	198	36	7	57	142	100	24	83	14	0	5	2	4	.311	.392	.544	.990
																1	1	.325	.429	.688	1.000
Career average		133	475	73	136	30	4	18	76	54	7	64	7	1	6	8	6	.286	.363	.484	.987
Cubs average		**112**	**373**	**52**	**104**	**25**	**4**	**11**	**57**	**50**	**7**	**41**	**4**	**1**	**5**	**7**	**6**	**.278**	**.365**	**.484**	**.984**
Career total		1599	5705	878	1632	365	51	221	917	652	87	770	79	10	69	101	74	.286	.363	.454	.987
Cubs total		**223**	**745**	**104**	**207**	**49**	**8**	**22**	**113**	**100**	**13**	**82**	**7**	**1**	**9**	**14**	**11**	**.278**	**.365**	**.454**	**.984**

Gonzalez, Miguel Angel (Mike)

HEIGHT: 6'1"   THROWS: RIGHT   BATS: RIGHT   BORN: 9/24/1890 HAVANA, CUBA   DIED: 2/19/1977 HAVANA, CUBA   POSITIONS PLAYED: C, 1B, 2B, OF

YEAR	TEAM	GAMES	AB	RUNS	HITS	2B	3B	HR	RBI	BB	IBB	SO	HBP	SH	SF	SB	CS	BA	OBA	SA	FA
1912	Bos-N	1	2	0	0	0	0	0	0	1	—	1	0	0	—	0	—	.000	.333	.000	.875
1914	Cin-N	95	176	19	41	6	0	0	10	13	—	16	2	5	—	2	—	.233	.293	.267	.954
1915	StL-N	51	97	12	22	2	2	0	10	8	—	9	3	3	—	4	2	.227	.306	.289	.990
1916	StL-N	118	331	33	79	15	4	0	29	28	—	18	3	8	—	5	—	.239	.304	.308	.984
1917	StL-N	106	290	28	76	8	1	1	28	22	—	24	1	9	—	12	—	.262	.316	.307	.979
1918	StL-N	117	349	33	88	13	4	3	20	39	—	30	0	4	—	14	—	.252	.327	.338	.978
1919	NYG-N	58	158	18	30	6	0	0	8	20	—	9	3	4	—	3	—	.190	.293	.228	.963
1920	NYG-N	11	13	1	3	0	0	0	0	3	—	1	0	0	—	1	0	.231	.375	.231	1.000
1921	NYG-N	13	24	3	9	1	0	0	0	1	—	0	0	2	—	0	0	.375	.400	.417	.983
1924	StL-N	120	402	34	119	27	1	3	53	24	—	22	1	7	—	1	5	.296	.337	.391	.986
1925	StL-N	22	71	9	22	3	0	0	4	6	—	2	2	1	—	1	2	.310	.380	.352	.982
1925	**ChC-N**	**70**	**197**	**26**	**52**	**13**	**1**	**3**	**18**	**13**	**—**	**15**	**2**	**6**	**—**	**2**	**1**	**.264**	**.316**	**.386**	**.993**
1926	**ChC-N**	**80**	**253**	**24**	**63**	**13**	**3**	**1**	**23**	**13**	**—**	**17**	**1**	**8**	**—**	**3**	**—**	**.249**	**.288**	**.336**	**.989**
1927	**ChC-N**	**39**	**108**	**15**	**26**	**4**	**1**	**1**	**15**	**10**	**—**	**8**	**1**	**4**	**—**	**1**	**—**	**.241**	**.311**	**.324**	**.994**
1928	**ChC-N**	**49**	**158**	**12**	**43**	**9**	**2**	**1**	**21**	**12**	**—**	**7**	**0**	**5**	**—**	**2**	**—**	**.272**	**.324**	**.373**	**.983**
1929	**ChC-N**	**60**	**167**	**15**	**40**	**3**	**0**	**0**	**18**	**18**	**—**	**14**	**1**	**3**	**—**	**1**	**—**	**.240**	**.317**	**.257**	**.992**
1931	StL-N	15	19	1	2	0	0	0	3	0	—	3	0	0	—	0	—	.105	.105	.105	1.000
1932	StL-N	17	14	0	2	0	0	0	3	0	—	2	0	0	—	0	—	.143	.143	.143	1.000
Career average		61	166	17	42	7	1	1	15	14	—	12	1	4	—	3	1	.253	.314	.324	.981
Cubs average		**60**	**177**	**18**	**45**	**8**	**1**	**1**	**19**	**13**	**—**	**12**	**1**	**5**	**—**	**2**	**0**	**.254**	**.309**	**.337**	**.990**
Career total		1042	2829	283	717	123	19	13	263	231	—	198	20	69	—	52	10	.253	.314	.324	.981
Cubs total		**298**	**883**	**92**	**224**	**42**	**7**	**6**	**95**	**66**	**—**	**61**	**5**	**26**	**—**	**9**	**1**	**.254**	**.309**	**.337**	**.990**

Gonzalez, Victor Raul (Raul)

HEIGHT: 5'9"   THROWS: RIGHT   BATS: RIGHT   BORN: 12/27/1973 SANTURCE, PUERTO RICO   POSITIONS PLAYED: OF

YEAR	TEAM	GAMES	AB	RUNS	HITS	2B	3B	HR	RBI	BB	IBB	SO	HBP	SH	SF	SB	CS	BA	OBA	SA	FA
2000	**ChC-N**	**3**	**2**	**0**	**0**	**0**	**0**	**0**	**0**	**0**	**0**	**2**	**0**	**0**	**0**	**0**	**0**	**.000**	**.000**	**.000**	**—**
2001	Cin-N	11	14	0	3	0	0	0	0	1	0	3	0	0	0	0	0	.214	.267	.214	1.000
Career average		7	8	0	2	0	0	0	0	1	0	3	0	0	0	0	0	.188	.235	.188	1.000
Cubs average		**3**	**2**	**0**	**0**	**0**	**0**	**0**	**0**	**0**	**0**	**2**	**0**	**0**	**0**	**0**	**0**	**.000**	**.000**	**.000**	**—**
Career total		14	16	0	3	0	0	0	0	1	0	5	0	0	0	0	0	.188	.235	.188	—
Cubs total		**3**	**2**	**0**	**0**	**0**	**0**	**0**	**0**	**0**	**0**	**2**	**0**	**0**	**0**	**0**	**0**	**.000**	**.000**	**.000**	**—**

Good, Wilbur David (Lefty)

HEIGHT: 5'6"   THROWS: LEFT   BATS: LEFT   BORN: 9/28/1885 PUNXSUTAWNEY, PENNSYLVANIA   DIED: 12/30/1963 BROOKSVILLE, FLORIDA
POSITIONS PLAYED: P, OF

YEAR	TEAM	GAMES	AB	RUNS	HITS	2B	3B	HR	RBI	BB	IBB	SO	HBP	SH	SF	SB	CS	BA	OBA	SA	FA
1905	NYA-A	6	8	2	3	0	0	0	0	0	—	—	0	0	—	0	—	.375	.375	.375	.889
1908	Cle-A	46	154	23	43	1	3	1	14	13	—	—	4	4	—	7	—	.279	.351	.344	.845
1909	Cle-A	94	318	33	68	6	5	0	17	28	—	—	9	5	—	13	—	.214	.296	.264	.953
1910	Bos-N	23	86	15	29	5	4	0	11	6	—	13	0	4	—	5	—	.337	.380	.488	.969
1911	Bos-N	43	165	21	44	9	3	0	15	12	—	22	0	4	—	3	—	.267	.316	.358	.945
1911	**ChC-N**	**58**	**145**	**27**	**39**	**5**	**4**	**2**	**21**	**11**	**—**	**17**	**2**	**5**	**—**	**10**	**—**	**.269**	**.329**	**.400**	**.928**
1912	**ChC-N**	**39**	**35**	**7**	**5**	**0**	**0**	**0**	**1**	**3**	**—**	**7**	**0**	**0**	**—**	**3**	**—**	**.143**	**.211**	**.143**	**1.000**
1913	**ChC-N**	**49**	**91**	**11**	**23**	**3**	**2**	**1**	**12**	**11**	**—**	**16**	**1**	**0**	**—**	**5**	**—**	**.253**	**.340**	**.363**	**.974**
1914	**ChC-N**	**154**	**580**	**70**	**158**	**24**	**7**	**2**	**43**	**53**	**—**	**74**	**7**	**24**	**—**	**31**	**—**	**.272**	**.341**	**.348**	**.930**

(continued)

(Good, continued)

YEAR	TEAM	GAMES	AB	RUNS	HITS	2B	3B	HR	RBI	BB	IBB	SO	HBP	SH	SF	SB	CS	BA	OBA	SA	FA
1915	ChC-N	128	498	66	126	18	9	2	27	34	—	65	5	8	—	19	17	.253	.307	.337	.936
1916	Phi-N	75	136	25	34	4	3	1	15	8	—	13	3	5	—	7	—	.250	.306	.346	.983
1918	CWS-A	35	148	24	37	9	4	0	11	11	—	16	3	1	—	1	—	.250	.315	.365	.982
Career average		68	215	29	55	8	4	1	17	17	—	22	3	5	—	9	2	.258	.322	.342	.941
Cubs average		86	270	36	70	10	4	1	21	22	—	36	3	7	—	14	3	.260	.324	.345	.936
Career total		750	2364	324	609	84	44	9	187	190	—	243	34	60	—	104	17	.258	.322	.342	.941
Cubs total		428	1349	181	351	50	22	7	104	112	—	179	15	37	—	68	17	.260	.324	.345	.936

Goodman, Ival Richard (Goodie)

HEIGHT: 5'11" THROWS: RIGHT BATS: LEFT BORN: 7/23/1908 NORTHVIEW, MISSOURI DIED: 11/25/1984 CINCINNATI, OHIO POSITIONS PLAYED: OF

YEAR	TEAM	GAMES	AB	RUNS	HITS	2B	3B	HR	RBI	BB	IBB	SO	HBP	SH	SF	SB	CS	BA	OBA	SA	FA
1935	Cin-N	148	592	86	159	23	18	12	72	35	—	50	4	6	—	14	—	.269	.314	.429	.960
1936	Cin-N	136	489	81	139	15	14	17	71	38	—	53	9	9	—	6	—	.284	.347	.476	.972
1937	Cin-N	147	549	86	150	25	12	12	55	55	—	58	7	7	—	10	—	.273	.347	.428	.974
1938	Cin-N	145	568	103	166	27	10	30	92	53	—	51	15	12	—	3	—	.292	.368	.533	.988
1939	Cin-N	124	470	85	152	37	16	7	84	54	—	32	7	22	—	2	—	.323	.401	.515	.981
1940	Cin-N	136	519	78	134	20	6	12	63	60	—	54	0	15	—	9	—	.258	.335	.389	.970
1941	Cin-N	42	149	14	40	5	2	1	12	16	—	15	1	2	—	1	—	.268	.343	.349	.966
1942	Cin-N	87	226	21	55	18	1	0	15	24	—	32	1	6	—	0	—	.243	.319	.332	.991
1943	**ChC-N**	**80**	**225**	**31**	**72**	**10**	**5**	**3**	**45**	**24**	—	**20**	**2**	**1**	—	**4**	—	**.320**	**.390**	**.449**	**.968**
1944	**ChC-N**	**62**	**141**	**24**	**37**	**8**	**1**	**1**	**16**	**23**	—	**15**	**3**	**1**	—	**0**	—	**.262**	**.377**	**.355**	**1.000**
Career average		111	393	61	110	19	9	10	53	38	—	38	5	8	—	5	—	.281	.352	.445	.975
Cubs average		71	183	28	55	9	3	2	31	24	—	18	3	1	—	2	—	.298	.385	.413	.979
Career total		1107	3928	609	1104	188	85	95	525	382	—	380	49	81	—	49	—	.281	.352	.445	.975
Cubs total		142	366	55	109	18	6	4	61	47	—	35	5	2	—	4	—	.298	.385	.413	.979

Goodwin, Curtis Lamar

HEIGHT: 5'11" THROWS: LEFT BATS: LEFT BORN: 9/30/1972 OAKLAND, CALIFORNIA POSITIONS PLAYED: OF

YEAR	TEAM	GAMES	AB	RUNS	HITS	2B	3B	HR	RBI	BB	IBB	SO	HBP	SH	SF	SB	CS	BA	OBA	SA	FA
1995	Bal-A	87	289	40	76	11	3	1	24	15	0	53	2	7	3	22	4	.263	.301	.332	.990
1996	Cin-N	49	136	20	31	3	0	0	5	19	0	34	0	1	0	15	6	.228	.323	.250	.970
1997	Cin-N	85	265	27	67	11	0	1	12	24	0	53	1	6	1	22	13	.253	.316	.306	1.000
1998	Col-N	119	159	27	39	7	0	1	6	16	0	40	0	10	1	5	1	.245	.313	.308	.983
1999	**ChC-N**	**89**	**157**	**15**	**38**	**6**	**1**	**0**	**9**	**13**	**1**	**38**	**0**	**4**	**1**	**2**	**4**	**.242**	**.298**	**.293**	**1.000**
1999	Tor-A	2	8	0	0	0	0	0	0	0	0	3	0	0	0	0	0	.000	.000	.000	.983
Career average		86	203	26	50	8	1	1	11	17	0	44	1	6	1	13	6	.248	.307	.302	.988
Cubs average		89	157	15	38	6	1	0	9	13	1	38	0	4	1	2	4	.242	.298	.293	.983
Career total		431	1014	129	251	38	4	3	56	87	1	221	3	28	6	66	28	.248	.307	.302	.988
Cubs total		89	157	15	38	6	1	0	9	13	1	38	0	4	1	2	4	.242	.298	.293	.983

Gordon, Michael William (Mike)

HEIGHT: 6'3" THROWS: RIGHT BATS: BOTH BORN: 9/11/1953 LEOMINSTER, MASSACHUSETTS POSITIONS PLAYED: C

YEAR	TEAM	GAMES	AB	RUNS	HITS	2B	3B	HR	RBI	BB	IBB	SO	HBP	SH	SF	SB	CS	BA	OBA	SA	FA
1977	ChC-N	8	23	0	1	0	0	0	2	2	0	8	0	1	0	0	0	.043	.120	.043	.970
1978	ChC-N	4	5	0	1	0	0	0	0	3	1	2	1	0	0	0	0	.200	.556	.200	1.000
Career average		6	14	0	1	0	0	0	1	3	1	5	1	1	0	0	0	.071	.235	.071	.979
Cubs average		6	14	0	1	0	0	0	1	3	1	5	1	1	0	0	0	.071	.235	.071	.979
Career total		12	28	0	2	0	0	0	2	5	1	10	1	1	0	0	0	.071	.235	.071	.979
Cubs total		12	28	0	2	0	0	0	2	5	1	10	1	1	0	0	0	.071	.235	.071	.979

George F. "Piano Legs" Gore, of-1b-3b, 1879-92

George Gore was a sweet-hitting, hard-drinking righthander who roamed the outfield for Chicago during the team's glory years of the 1880s.

Gore was born on May 3, 1857, in Saccarappa, Maine. He played for a number of local teams in his late teens and his early 20s. A Chicago manager discovered Gore playing for a local New England all-star team and signed him soon after. He was called "piano legs" because of his powerful upper thighs.

Gore was a good player in 1879. By 1880 he was one of the best players in the league, leading the National League in batting average (.360), slugging percentage (.463) and on-base percentage (.399), while also being third in hits (116), walks (21) and RBIs (67), fourth in doubles (23) and fifth in runs scored (70).

Gore was an offensive machine, leading the league in runs scored in 1881 and 1882, in walks in 1882, 1884 and 1886 and always being near the top of the National League in on-base percentage.

In 1885 Gore hit two doubles and three triples to set a since-tied mark of five extra-base hits in one game. He also set a National League record in 1881, which has also been tied, by stealing seven bases in one game.

He was one of several hard-drinking players on the Chicago squad. He hated preseason conditioning drills.

Anson could usually control Gore during the regular season, but preseason exhibitions were another story. In addition, Chicago twice played postseason series with the winner of the fledgling American Association, in 1885 and 1886. Gore was among several Chicago players who played at least one of the games drunk. Chicago lost both series.

The aftermath of the disappointing 1886 series saw Anson trading Gore to the New York team, where he played well two of the three seasons he was there. In 1890 Gore jumped to the New York entry in the Players' League. He wound up his career back with the New York entry in the National League and later in St. Louis.

Gore remains ninth on the Cubs' all-time list with a batting average of .315. He is also one of only three players with more than 4,000 at-bats with more runs scored (1,327) than games played (1,310). Billy Hamilton and Harry Stovey, both 19th-century stars, are the other two. Gore died in Utica, New York, in 1933.

Gore, George F. (Piano Legs)

HEIGHT: 5'11"   THROWS: RIGHT   BATS: LEFT   BORN: 5/3/1857 SACCARAPPA, MAINE   DIED: 9/16/1933 UTICA, NEW YORK   POSITIONS PLAYED: 1B, 3B, OF

YEAR	TEAM	GAMES	AB	RUNS	HITS	2B	3B	HR	RBI	BB	IBB	SO	HBP	SH	SF	SB	CS	BA	OBA	SA	FA
1879	ChN-N	63	266	43	70	17	4	0	32	8	—	30	—	—	—	—	—	.263	.285	.357	.914
1880	ChN-N	77	322	70	116	23	2	2	47	21	—	10	—	—	—	—	—	.360	.399	.463	.905
1881	ChN-N	73	309	86	92	18	9	1	44	27	—	23	—	—	—	—	—	.298	.354	.463	.876
1882	ChN-N	84	367	99	117	15	7	3	51	29	—	19	—	—	—	—	—	.319	.369	.422	.842
1883	ChN-N	92	392	105	131	30	9	2	52	27	—	13	—	—	—	—	—	.334	.377	.472	.867
1884	ChN-N	103	422	104	134	18	4	5	34	61	—	26	—	—	—	—	—	.318	.404	.472	.867
1885	ChN-N	109	441	115	138	21	13	5	57	68	—	25	—	—	—	—	—	.313	.405	.454	.884
1886	ChN-N	118	444	150	135	20	12	6	63	102	—	30	—	—	—	—	—	.304	.434	.444	.876
1887	NYG-N	111	501	95	175	16	5	1	49	42	—	18	7	—	—	23	—	.349	.407	.407	.889
1888	NYG-N	64	254	37	56	4	4	2	17	30	—	31	2	—	—	39	—	.220	.308	.291	.836
1889	NYG-N	120	488	132	149	21	7	7	54	84	—	28	8	—	—	11	—	.305	.416	.420	.864
1890	NY-P	93	399	132	127	26	8	10	55	77	—	23	3	—	—	28	—	.318	.432	.499	.877
1891	NYG-N	130	528	103	150	22	7	2	48	74	—	34	7	—	—	28	—	.284	.379	.364	.909
1892	NYG-N	53	193	47	49	11	2	0	11	49	—	16	3	—	—	19	—	.254	.412	.332	.932
1892	StL-N	20	73	9	15	0	1	0	4	18	—	6	0	—	—	20	—	.205	.363	.233	.844
Career average		94	386	95	118	19	7	3	44	51	—	24	2	—	—	12	—	.306	.391	.415	.881
Cubs average		**90**	**370**	**97**	**117**	**20**	**8**	**3**	**48**	**43**	**—**	**22**	**—**	**—**	**—**	**3**	**—**	**.315**	**.386**	**.434**	**.879**
Career total		1310	5399	1327	1654	262	94	46	618	717	—	332	30	—	—	170	—	.306	.391	.415	.881
Cubs total		**719**	**2963**	**772**	**933**	**162**	**60**	**24**	**380**	**343**	**—**	**176**	**—**	**—**	**—**	**23**	**—**	**.315**	**.386**	**.434**	**.879**

Goryl, John Albert (Johnny)
HEIGHT: 5'10" THROWS: RIGHT BATS: RIGHT BORN: 10/21/1933 CUMBERLAND, RHODE ISLAND POSITIONS PLAYED: 2B, 3B, SS

YEAR	TEAM	GAMES	AB	RUNS	HITS	2B	3B	HR	RBI	BB	IBB	SO	HBP	SH	SF	SB	CS	BA	OBA	SA	FA
1957	ChC-N	9	38	7	8	2	0	0	1	5	0	9	1	0	0	0	1	.211	.318	.263	.952
1958	ChC-N	83	219	27	53	9	3	4	14	27	2	34	2	2	0	0	1	.242	.331	.365	.938
1959	ChC-N	25	48	1	9	3	1	1	6	5	0	3	0	0	0	1	1	.188	.264	.354	.977
1962	Min-A	37	26	6	5	0	1	2	2	2	0	6	0	1	0	0	0	.192	.250	.500	.923
1963	Min-A	64	150	29	43	5	3	9	24	15	4	29	1	7	1	0	0	.287	.353	.540	.960
1964	Min-A	58	114	9	16	0	2	0	1	10	2	25	1	3	0	1	0	.140	.216	.175	.979
Career average		46	99	13	22	3	2	3	8	11	1	18	1	2	0	0	1	.225	.305	.371	.956
Cubs average		**39**	**102**	**12**	**23**	**5**	**1**	**2**	**7**	**12**	**1**	**15**	**1**	**1**	**0**	**0**	**1**	**.230**	**.319**	**.351**	**.944**
Career total		276	595	79	134	19	10	16	48	64	8	106	5	13	1	2	3	.225	.305	.371	.956
Cubs total		**117**	**305**	**35**	**70**	**14**	**4**	**5**	**21**	**37**	**2**	**46**	**3**	**2**	**0**	**1**	**3**	**.230**	**.319**	**.351**	**.944**

Grabarkewitz, Billy Cordell
HEIGHT: 5'10" THROWS: RIGHT BATS: RIGHT BORN: 1/18/1946 LOCKHART, TEXAS POSITIONS PLAYED: 2B, 3B, SS, OF

YEAR	TEAM	GAMES	AB	RUNS	HITS	2B	3B	HR	RBI	BB	IBB	SO	HBP	SH	SF	SB	CS	BA	OBA	SA	FA
1969	LA-N	34	65	4	6	1	1	0	5	4	1	19	0	1	0	1	0	.092	.145	.138	.959
1970	LA-N	156	529	92	153	20	8	17	84	95	8	149	6	3	7	19	9	.289	.399	.454	.963
1971	LA-N	44	71	9	16	5	0	0	6	19	0	16	0	0	0	1	2	.225	.389	.296	1.000
1972	LA-N	53	144	17	24	4	0	4	16	18	1	53	2	0	2	3	0	.167	.265	.278	.929
1973	Cal-A	61	129	27	21	6	1	3	9	28	0	27	1	1	0	2	2	.163	.316	.295	.955
1973	Phi-N	25	66	12	19	2	0	2	7	12	0	18	0	1	0	3	1	.288	.397	.409	.960
1974	Phi-N	34	30	7	4	0	0	1	2	5	0	10	0	0	0	3	1	.133	.257	.233	1.000
1974	**ChC-N**	53	125	21	31	3	2	1	12	21	2	28	1	1	1	1	2	.248	.358	.328	.961
1975	Oak-A	6	2	0	0	0	0	0	0	0	0	1	0	0	0	0	0	.000	.000	.000	.833
Career average		67	166	27	39	6	2	4	20	29	2	46	1	1	1	5	2	.236	.351	.364	.960
Cubs average		**53**	**125**	**21**	**31**	**3**	**2**	**1**	**12**	**21**	**2**	**28**	**1**	**1**	**1**	**1**	**2**	**.248**	**.358**	**.328**	**.961**
Career total		466	1161	189	274	41	12	28	141	202	12	321	10	7	10	33	17	.236	.351	.364	.960
Cubs total		**53**	**125**	**21**	**31**	**3**	**2**	**1**	**12**	**21**	**2**	**28**	**1**	**1**	**1**	**1**	**2**	**.248**	**.358**	**.328**	**.961**

Grace, Robert Earl (Earl)
HEIGHT: 6'0" THROWS: RIGHT BATS: LEFT BORN: 2/24/1907 BARLOW, KENTUCKY DIED: 12/22/1980 PHOENIX, ARIZONA POSITIONS PLAYED: C, 1B

YEAR	TEAM	GAMES	AB	RUNS	HITS	2B	3B	HR	RBI	BB	IBB	SO	HBP	SH	SF	SB	CS	BA	OBA	SA	FA
1929	ChC-N	27	80	7	20	1	0	2	17	9	—	7	1	4	—	0	—	.250	.333	.338	1.000
1931	ChC-N	7	9	2	1	0	0	0	1	4	—	1	0	1	—	0	—	.111	.385	.111	1.000
1931	Pit-N	47	150	8	42	6	1	1	20	13	—	5	0	4	—	0	—	.280	.337	.353	.974
1932	Pit-N	115	390	41	107	17	5	8	55	14	—	23	3	4	—	0	—	.274	.305	.405	.998
1933	Pit-N	93	291	22	84	13	1	3	44	26	—	23	1	0	—	0	—	.289	.349	.371	.980
1934	Pit-N	95	289	27	78	17	1	4	24	20	—	19	0	0	—	0	—	.270	.317	.377	.983
1935	Pit-N	77	224	19	59	8	1	3	29	32	—	17	0	1	—	1	—	.263	.355	.348	.990
1936	Phi-N	86	221	24	55	11	0	4	32	34	—	20	1	1	—	0	—	.249	.352	.353	.976
1937	Phi-N	80	223	19	47	10	1	6	29	33	—	15	0	2	—	0	—	.211	.313	.345	.990
Career average		78	235	21	62	10	1	4	31	23	—	16	1	2	—	0	—	.263	.331	.367	.987
Cubs average		**17**	**45**	**5**	**11**	**1**	**0**	**1**	**9**	**7**	**—**	**4**	**1**	**3**	**—**	**0**	**—**	**.236**	**.340**	**.315**	**1.000**
Career total		627	1877	169	493	83	10	31	251	185	—	130	6	17	—	1	—	.263	.331	.367	.987
Cubs total		**34**	**89**	**9**	**21**	**1**	**0**	**2**	**18**	**13**	**—**	**8**	**1**	**5**	**—**	**0**	**—**	**.236**	**.340**	**.315**	**1.000**

Grace, Mark Eugene
HEIGHT: 6'2" THROWS: LEFT BATS: LEFT BORN: 6/28/1964 WINSTON-SALEM, NORTH CAROLINA POSITIONS PLAYED: 1B

YEAR	TEAM	GAMES	AB	RUNS	HITS	2B	3B	HR	RBI	BB	IBB	SO	HBP	SH	SF	SB	CS	BA	OBA	SA	FA
1988	ChC-N	134	486	65	144	23	4	7	57	60	5	43	0	0	4	3	3	.296	.371	.403	.987
1989	ChC-N	142	510	74	160	28	3	13	79	80	13	42	0	3	3	14	7	.314	.405	.457	.996
1990	ChC-N	157	589	72	182	32	1	9	82	59	5	54	5	1	8	15	6	.309	.372	.413	.992
1991	ChC-N	160	619	87	169	28	5	8	58	70	7	53	3	4	7	3	4	.273	.346	.373	.995
1992	ChC-N	158	603	72	185	37	5	9	79	72	8	36	4	2	8	6	1	.307	.380	.430	.998
1993	ChC-N	155	594	86	193	39	4	14	98	71	14	32	1	1	9	8	4	.325	.393	.475	.997

(continued)

Mark Eugene "Amazing" Grace, 1b, 1988–present

One of the great first basemen in Chicago Cubs history and one of the best players in all of baseball in the 1990s, Mark Grace has been a model of consistency and durability his entire career.

Grace was born on June 28, 1964, in Winston-Salem, North Carolina. After a little more than two years in the minors, Grace was elevated to the Cubs and made his major league debut on May 2, 1988. He hit .296 for the Cubs and was named the Rookie of the Year by the *Sporting News*.

In 1989 Grace led the Cubs in RBIs with 79 and was fourth in hitting in the league with a .314 batting average as Chicago won their second National League East title in five years. The Cubs lost to the Giants in five games, but Grace was virtually impossible to get out, hitting .647 in the series with three doubles, a triple, a home run, eight RBIs and a slugging percentage of 1.118.

In the 1990s, it was difficult to find a player more consistent than Grace. His 1,754 hits in the decade rank first among all major leaguers. He is also first in doubles with 364 and second to Tony Gwynn in singles with 1,238.

He has hit over .300 in nine of his 13 big-league seasons. He has been in the top 10 in hitting in the National League eight times in his career.

Grace is also the best fielding first baseman in Cubs history. His .995 fielding percentage at first base for Chicago includes the 1992 season, in which Grace made only four errors and led the league with a fielding percentage of .998, a record for Chicago first basemen.

That was the year he won the first of four Gold Gloves. The other three Gold Gloves came in 1993, 1995 and 1996. In 1990 he set a National League record for assists with 180, which included a major league–tying three assists in one inning against the Dodgers.

In 1998, while teammate Sammy Sosa was justifiably garnering headlines for his pursuit of the major league home-run record, Grace quietly hit .309 with 39 doubles and career highs in both home runs (17) and walks (93). He struggled in his second postseason appearance, however, hitting .083 as the Cubs lost to the Braves.

As the 2001 season opened, Grace signed with the Arizona Diamondbacks. Although Cubs fans rued his departure, many were happy that Grace was at last a world champion, as Arizona won the World Series, beating the Yankees in seven inspiring games.

Grace has his name all over the Cubs record books. He is 8th all-time in games played with 1,810, 10th in batting average with a .308 mark, 7th in at-bats with 7,156, 7th in runs scored with 1,057, 5th in hits with 2,206, 7th in RBIs with 1,004, 3rd in walks with 935, 2nd all-time in doubles with 456 and 6th in singles with 1,554.

(continued)

Year	Team	G	AB	R	H	2B	3B	HR	RBI									AVG	OBP	SLG	FLD%
1994	ChC-N	106	403	55	120	23	3	6	44	48	5	41	0	0	3	0	1	.298	.370	.414	.993
1995	ChC-N	143	552	97	180	51	3	16	92	65	9	46	2	1	7	6	2	.326	.395	.516	.995
1996	ChC-N	142	547	88	181	39	1	9	75	62	8	41	1	0	6	2	3	.331	.396	.455	.995
1997	ChC-N	151	555	87	177	32	5	13	78	88	3	45	2	1	8	2	4	.319	.409	.465	.997
1998	ChC-N	158	595	92	184	39	3	17	89	93	8	56	3	0	7	4	7	.319	.409	.465	.995
1999	ChC-N	161	593	107	183	44	5	16	91	83	4	44	2	0	7	4	7	.309	.401	.471	.994
2000	ChC-N	143	510	75	143	41	1	11	82	95	11	28	6	2	10	3	4	.309	.390	.481	.994
2001	Ari-N	145	476	66	142	31	2	15	78	67	6	36	4	1	8	1	2	.280	.394	.429	.997
															5	1	0	.298	.386	.466	.995
Career average		147	545	80	167	35	3	12	77	72	8	43	2	1	7	5	3	.307	.386	.447	.995
Cubs average		147	550	81	169	35	3	11	77	73	8	43	2	1	7	5	4	.308	.386	.445	.995
Career total		2055	7632	1123	2343	487	45	163	1082	1013	106	597	33	16	93	68	48	.307	.386	.447	.995
Cubs total		1910	7156	1057	2201	456	43	148	1004	946	100	561	29	15	88	67	48	.308	.386	.445	.995

Graham, George Frederick (Peaches)

HEIGHT: 5'9" THROWS: RIGHT BATS: RIGHT BORN: 3/23/1877 ALEDO, ILLINOIS DIED: 7/25/1939 LONG BEACH, CALIFORNIA
POSITIONS PLAYED: P, C, 1B, 2B, 3B, SS, OF

YEAR	TEAM	GAMES	AB	RUNS	HITS	2B	3B	HR	RBI	BB	IBB	SO	HBP	SH	SF	SB	CS	BA	OBA	SA	FA
1902	Cle-A	2	6	0	2	0	0	0	1	1	—	—	0	0	—	0	—	.333	.429	.333	1.000
1903	**ChC-N**	**1**	**2**	**0**	**0**	**0**	**0**	**0**	**0**	**0**	**—**	**—**	**0**	**0**	**—**	**0**	**—**	**.000**	**.000**	**.000**	**1.000**
1908	Bos-N	75	215	22	59	5	0	0	22	23	—	—	6	6	—	4	—	.274	.361	.298	.952
1909	Bos-N	92	267	27	64	6	3	0	17	24	—	—	0	15	—	7	—	.240	.302	.285	.948
1910	Bos-N	110	291	31	82	13	2	0	21	33	—	15	2	9	—	5	—	.282	.359	.340	.964
1911	Bos-N	33	88	7	24	6	1	0	12	14	—	5	0	1	—	2	—	.273	.373	.364	.912
1911	**ChC-N**	**36**	**71**	**6**	**17**	**3**	**0**	**0**	**8**	**11**	**—**	**8**	**3**	**4**	**—**	**2**	**—**	**.239**	**.365**	**.282**	**.972**
1912	Phi-N	24	59	6	17	1	0	1	4	8	—	5	0	0	—	1	—	.288	.373	.356	.944
Career average		53	143	14	38	5	1	0	12	16	—	5	2	5	—	3	—	.265	.347	.314	.952
Cubs average		**19**	**37**	**3**	**9**	**2**	**0**	**0**	**4**	**6**	**—**	**4**	**2**	**2**	**—**	**1**	**—**	**.233**	**.356**	**.274**	**.972**
Career total		373	999	99	265	34	6	1	85	114	—	33	11	35	—	21	—	.265	.347	.314	.952
Cubs total		**37**	**73**	**6**	**17**	**3**	**0**	**0**	**8**	**11**	**—**	**8**	**3**	**4**	**—**	**2**	**—**	**.233**	**.356**	**.274**	**.972**

Grammas, Alexander Peter (Alex)

HEIGHT: 6'0" THROWS: RIGHT BATS: RIGHT BORN: 4/3/1926 BIRMINGHAM, ALABAMA POSITIONS PLAYED: 2B, 3B, SS

YEAR	TEAM	GAMES	AB	RUNS	HITS	2B	3B	HR	RBI	BB	IBB	SO	HBP	SH	SF	SB	CS	BA	OBA	SA	FA
1954	StL-N	142	401	57	106	17	4	2	29	40	—	29	5	4	5	6	1	.264	.335	.342	.966
1955	StL-N	128	366	32	88	19	2	3	25	33	9	36	3	5	1	4	1	.240	.308	.328	.968
1956	StL-N	6	12	1	3	0	0	0	1	1	0	2	0	0	0	0	0	.250	.308	.250	1.000
1956	Cin-N	77	140	17	34	11	0	0	16	16	1	18	1	10	1	0	1	.243	.323	.321	.968
1957	Cin-N	73	99	14	30	4	0	0	8	10	0	6	0	1	1	1	3	.303	.364	.343	.978
1958	Cin-N	105	216	25	47	8	0	0	12	34	1	24	2	7	0	2	2	.218	.329	.255	.980
1959	StL-N	131	368	43	99	14	2	3	30	38	6	26	1	5	3	3	3	.269	.337	.342	.964
1960	StL-N	102	196	20	48	4	1	4	17	12	1	15	1	3	1	0	1	.245	.290	.337	.968
1961	StL-N	89	170	23	36	10	1	0	21	19	3	21	1	6	1	0	1	.212	.293	.282	.967
1962	StL-N	21	18	0	2	0	0	0	1	1	1	6	0	0	0	0	0	.111	.158	.111	.933
1962	**ChC-N**	**23**	**60**	**3**	**14**	**3**	**0**	**0**	**3**	**2**	**0**	**7**	**1**	**0**	**0**	**1**	**1**	**.233**	**.270**	**.283**	**1.000**
1963	**ChC-N**	**16**	**27**	**1**	**5**	**0**	**0**	**0**	**0**	**0**	**0**	**3**	**0**	**0**	**0**	**0**	**0**	**.185**	**.185**	**.185**	**.955**
Career average		91	207	24	51	9	1	1	16	21	2	19	2	4	1	2	1	.247	.318	.317	.969
Cubs average		**20**	**44**	**2**	**10**	**2**	**0**	**0**	**2**	**1**	**0**	**5**	**1**	**0**	**0**	**1**	**1**	**.218**	**.244**	**.253**	**.989**
Career total		913	2073	236	512	90	10	12	163	206	22	193	15	41	13	17	14	.247	.318	.317	.969
Cubs total		**39**	**87**	**4**	**19**	**3**	**0**	**0**	**3**	**2**	**0**	**10**	**1**	**0**	**0**	**1**	**1**	**.218**	**.244**	**.253**	**.989**

Grant, Thomas Raymond (Tom)

HEIGHT: 6'2" THROWS: RIGHT BATS: LEFT BORN: 5/28/1957 WORCESTER, MASSACHUSETTS POSITIONS PLAYED: OF

YEAR	TEAM	GAMES	AB	RUNS	HITS	2B	3B	HR	RBI	BB	IBB	SO	HBP	SH	SF	SB	CS	BA	OBA	SA	FA
1983	ChC-N	16	20	2	3	1	0	0	2	3	0	4	0	0	0	0	0	.150	.261	.200	1.000
Career average		16	20	2	3	1	0	0	2	3	0	4	0	0	0	0	0	.150	.261	.200	1.000
Cubs average		**16**	**20**	**2**	**3**	**1**	**0**	**0**	**2**	**3**	**0**	**4**	**0**	**0**	**0**	**0**	**0**	**.150**	**.261**	**.200**	**1.000**
Career total		16	20	2	3	1	0	0	2	3	0	4	0	0	0	0	0	.150	.261	.200	1.000
Cubs total		**16**	**20**	**2**	**3**	**1**	**0**	**0**	**2**	**3**	**0**	**4**	**0**	**0**	**0**	**0**	**0**	**.150**	**.261**	**.200**	**1.000**

Grantham, George Farley (Boots)

HEIGHT: 5'10" THROWS: RIGHT BATS: LEFT BORN: 5/20/1900 GALENA, KANSAS DIED: 3/16/1954 KINGMAN, ARIZONA POSITIONS PLAYED: 1B, 2B, 3B, OF

YEAR	TEAM	GAMES	AB	RUNS	HITS	2B	3B	HR	RBI	BB	IBB	SO	HBP	SH	SF	SB	CS	BA	OBA	SA	FA
1922	**ChC-N**	**7**	**23**	**3**	**4**	**1**	**1**	**0**	**3**	**1**	**—**	**3**	**0**	**0**	**—**	**2**	**0**	**.174**	**.208**	**.304**	**1.000**
1923	**ChC-N**	**152**	**570**	**81**	**160**	**36**	**8**	**8**	**70**	**71**	**—**	**92**	**0**	**24**	**—**	**43**	**28**	**.281**	**.360**	**.414**	**.942**
1924	**ChC-N**	**127**	**469**	**85**	**148**	**19**	**6**	**12**	**60**	**55**	**—**	**63**	**2**	**13**	**—**	**21**	**21**	**.316**	**.390**	**.458**	**.937**
1925	Pit-N	114	359	74	117	24	6	8	52	50	—	29	3	11	—	14	4	.326	.413	.493	.989
1926	Pit-N	141	449	66	143	27	13	8	70	60	—	42	1	12	—	6	—	.318	.400	.490	.990
1927	Pit-N	151	531	96	162	33	11	8	66	74	—	39	6	23	—	9	—	.305	.396	.454	.963
1928	Pit-N	124	440	93	142	24	9	10	85	59	—	37	4	19	—	9	—	.323	.408	.486	.986
1929	Pit-N	110	349	85	107	23	10	12	90	93	—	38	1	14	—	10	—	.307	.454	.533	.970

(continued)

(continued)

YEAR	TEAM	GAMES	AB	RUNS	HITS	2B	3B	HR	RBI	BB	IBB	SO	HBP	SH	SF	SB	CS	BA	OBA	SA	FA
1930	Pit-N	146	552	120	179	34	14	18	99	81	—	66	2	17	—	5	—	.324	.413	.534	.959
1931	Pit-N	127	465	91	142	26	6	10	46	71	—	50	2	17	—	5	—	.305	.400	.452	.967
1932	Cin-N	126	493	81	144	29	6	6	39	56	—	40	0	11	—	4	—	.292	.364	.412	.963
1933	Cin-N	87	260	32	53	14	3	4	28	38	—	21	2	7	—	4	—	.204	.310	.327	.961
1934	NYG-N	32	29	5	7	2	0	1	4	8	—	6	0	0	—	0	—	.241	.405	.414	1.000
Career average		111	384	70	116	22	7	8	55	55	—	40	2	13	—	10	4	.302	.392	.461	.968
Cubs average		**95**	**354**	**56**	**104**	**19**	**5**	**7**	**44**	**42**	—	**53**	**1**	**12**	—	**22**	**16**	**.294**	**.370**	**.431**	**.940**
Career total		1444	4989	912	1508	292	93	105	712	717	—	526	23	168	—	132	53	.302	.392	.461	.968
Cubs total		**286**	**1062**	**169**	**312**	**56**	**15**	**20**	**133**	**127**	—	**158**	**2**	**37**	—	**66**	**49**	**.294**	**.370**	**.431**	**.940**

Graves, Joseph Ebenezer (Joe)

HEIGHT: 5'10"   THROWS: RIGHT   BATS: RIGHT   BORN: 2/26/1906 MARBLEHEAD, MASSACHUSETTS   DIED: 12/22/1980 SALEM, MASSACHUSETTS
POSITIONS PLAYED: 3B

YEAR	TEAM	GAMES	AB	RUNS	HITS	2B	3B	HR	RBI	BB	IBB	SO	HBP	SH	SF	SB	CS	BA	OBA	SA	FA
1926	ChC-N	2	5	0	0	0	0	0	0	0	—	1	0	0	—	0	—	.000	.000	.000	.250
Career average		2	5	0	0	0	0	0	0	0	—	1	0	0	—	0	—	.000	.000	.000	.250
Cubs average		**2**	**5**	**0**	**0**	**0**	**0**	**0**	**0**	**0**	—	**1**	**0**	**0**	—	**0**	—	**.000**	**.000**	**.000**	**.250**
Career total		2	5	0	0	0	0	0	0	0	—	1	0	0	—	0	—	.000	.000	.000	.250
Cubs total		**2**	**5**	**0**	**0**	**0**	**0**	**0**	**0**	**0**	—	**1**	**0**	**0**	—	**0**	—	**.000**	**.000**	**.000**	**.250**

Green, Edward (Danny)

HEIGHT: —   THROWS: RIGHT   BATS: LEFT   BORN: 11/6/1876 BURLINGTON, NEW JERSEY   DIED: 11/9/1914 CAMDEN, NEW JERSEY   POSITIONS PLAYED: OF

YEAR	TEAM	GAMES	AB	RUNS	HITS	2B	3B	HR	RBI	BB	IBB	SO	HBP	SH	SF	SB	CS	BA	OBA	SA	FA
1898	ChN-N	47	188	26	59	4	3	4	27	7	—	—	1	3	—	12	—	.314	.342	.431	.970
1899	ChN-N	117	475	90	140	12	11	6	56	35	—	—	7	8	—	18	—	.295	.352	.404	.947
1900	ChN-N	103	389	63	116	21	5	5	49	17	—	—	7	6	—	28	—	.298	.339	.416	.938
1901	ChN-N	133	537	82	168	16	12	6	61	40	—	—	3	6	—	31	—	.313	.364	.421	.932
1902	CWS-A	129	481	77	150	16	11	0	62	53	—	—	7	24	—	35	—	.312	.388	.391	.942
1903	CWS-A	135	499	75	154	26	7	6	62	47	—	—	6	16	—	29	—	.309	.375	.425	.933
1904	CWS-A	147	536	83	142	16	10	2	62	63	—	—	9	14	—	28	—	.265	.352	.343	.964
1905	CWS-A	112	379	56	92	13	6	0	44	53	—	—	6	16	—	11	—	.243	.345	.309	.914
Career average		115	436	69	128	16	8	4	53	39	—	—	6	12	—	24	—	.293	.359	.391	.941
Cubs average		**100**	**397**	**65**	**121**	**13**	**8**	**5**	**48**	**25**	—	—	**5**	**6**	—	**22**	—	**.304**	**.352**	**.416**	**.941**
Career total		923	3484	552	1021	124	65	29	423	315	—	—	46	93	—	192	—	.293	.359	.391	.941
Cubs total		**400**	**1589**	**261**	**483**	**53**	**31**	**21**	**193**	**99**	—	—	**18**	**23**	—	**89**	—	**.304**	**.352**	**.416**	**.941**

Greene, Willie Louis

HEIGHT: 5'11"   THROWS: RIGHT   BATS: LEFT   BORN: 9/23/1971 MILLEDGEVILLE, GEORGIA   POSITIONS PLAYED: 1B, 3B, SS, OF

YEAR	TEAM	GAMES	AB	RUNS	HITS	2B	3B	HR	RBI	BB	IBB	SO	HBP	SH	SF	SB	CS	BA	OBA	SA	FA
1992	Cin-N	29	93	10	25	5	2	2	13	10	0	23	0	0	1	0	2	.269	.337	.430	.948
1993	Cin-N	15	50	7	8	1	1	2	5	2	0	19	0	0	1	0	0	.160	.189	.340	.982
1994	Cin-N	16	37	5	8	2	0	0	3	6	1	14	0	0	1	0	0	.216	.318	.270	.958
1995	Cin-N	8	19	1	2	0	0	0	0	3	0	7	0	0	0	0	0	.105	.227	.105	1.000
1996	Cin-N	115	287	48	70	5	5	19	63	36	6	88	0	1	1	0	1	.244	.327	.495	.927
1997	Cin-N	151	495	62	125	22	1	26	91	78	5	111	1	1	3	6	0	.253	.354	.459	.954
1998	Cin-N	111	356	57	96	18	1	14	49	56	2	80	3	0	2	6	3	.270	.372	.444	.945
1998	Bal-A	24	40	8	6	1	0	1	5	13	0	10	0	0	0	1	0	.150	.358	.250	.941
1999	Tor-A	81	226	22	46	7	0	12	41	20	0	56	0	0	2	0	0	.204	.266	.394	.933
2000	ChC-N	105	299	34	60	15	2	10	37	36	2	69	2	0	2	4	0	.201	.289	.365	.967
Career average		73	211	28	50	8	1	10	34	29	2	53	1	0	1	2	1	.234	.326	.423	.951
Cubs average		**105**	**299**	**34**	**60**	**15**	**2**	**10**	**37**	**36**	**2**	**69**	**2**	**0**	**2**	**4**	**0**	**.201**	**.289**	**.365**	**.967**
Career total		655	1902	254	446	76	12	86	307	260	16	477	6	2	13	17	6	.234	.326	.423	.951
Cubs total		**105**	**299**	**34**	**60**	**15**	**2**	**10**	**37**	**36**	**2**	**69**	**2**	**0**	**2**	**4**	**0**	**.201**	**.289**	**.365**	**.967**

Griffith, Thomas Herman (Tommy)
HEIGHT: 5'10" THROWS: RIGHT BATS: LEFT BORN: 10/26/1889 PROSPECT, OHIO DIED: 4/13/1967 CINCINNATI, OHIO POSITIONS PLAYED: OF

YEAR	TEAM	GAMES	AB	RUNS	HITS	2B	3B	HR	RBI	BB	IBB	SO	HBP	SH	SF	SB	CS	BA	OBA	SA	FA
1913	Bos-N	37	127	16	32	4	1	1	12	9	—	8	0	3	—	1	—	.252	.301	.323	.886
1914	Bos-N	16	48	3	5	0	0	0	1	2	—	6	0	0	—	0	—	.104	.140	.104	.931
1915	Cin-N	160	583	59	179	31	16	4	85	41	—	34	2	23	—	6	24	.307	.355	.436	.952
1916	Cin-N	155	595	50	158	28	7	2	61	36	—	37	2	8	—	16	—	.266	.310	.346	.967
1917	Cin-N	115	363	45	98	18	7	1	45	19	—	23	1	10	—	5	—	.270	.308	.366	.974
1918	Cin-N	118	427	47	113	10	4	2	48	39	—	30	1	12	—	10	—	.265	.326	.321	.969
1919	Bro-N	125	484	65	136	18	4	6	57	23	—	32	1	11	—	8	—	.281	.315	.372	.954
1920	Bro-N	93	334	41	87	9	4	2	30	15	—	18	0	14	—	3	3	.260	.292	.329	.972
1921	Bro-N	129	455	66	142	21	6	12	71	36	—	13	0	17	—	3	3	.312	.364	.464	.972
1922	Bro-N	99	329	44	104	17	8	4	49	23	—	10	0	12	—	7	1	.316	.361	.453	.952
1923	Bro-N	131	481	70	141	21	9	8	66	50	—	19	1	14	—	8	2	.293	.361	.424	.927
1924	Bro-N	140	482	43	121	19	5	3	67	34	—	19	0	15	—	0	5	.251	.300	.330	.965
1925	Bro-N	7	4	2	0	0	0	0	0	3	—	2	0	0	—	1	0	.000	.429	.000	1.000
1925	**ChC-N**	**76**	**235**	**38**	**67**	**12**	**1**	**7**	**27**	**21**	**—**	**11**	**1**	**5**	**—**	**2**	**4**	**.285**	**.346**	**.434**	**.937**
Career average		108	381	45	106	16	6	4	48	27	—	20	1	11	—	5	3	.280	.328	.382	.956
Cubs average		**76**	**235**	**38**	**67**	**12**	**1**	**7**	**27**	**21**	**—**	**11**	**1**	**5**	**—**	**2**	**4**	**.285**	**.346**	**.434**	**.937**
Career total		1401	4947	589	1383	208	72	52	619	351	—	262	9	144	—	70	42	.280	.328	.382	.956
Cubs total		**76**	**235**	**38**	**67**	**12**	**1**	**7**	**27**	**21**	**—**	**11**	**1**	**5**	**—**	**2**	**4**	**.285**	**.346**	**.434**	**.937**

Grigsby, Denver Clarence
HEIGHT: 5'9" THROWS: RIGHT BATS: LEFT BORN: 3/25/1901 JACKSON, KENTUCKY DIED: 11/10/1973 SAPULPA, OKLAHOMA POSITIONS PLAYED: OF

YEAR	TEAM	GAMES	AB	RUNS	HITS	2B	3B	HR	RBI	BB	IBB	SO	HBP	SH	SF	SB	CS	BA	OBA	SA	FA
1923	**ChC-N**	**24**	**72**	**8**	**21**	**5**	**2**	**0**	**5**	**7**	**—**	**5**	**1**	**3**	**—**	**1**	**3**	**.292**	**.363**	**.417**	**1.000**
1924	**ChC-N**	**124**	**411**	**58**	**123**	**18**	**2**	**3**	**48**	**31**	**—**	**47**	**6**	**12**	**—**	**10**	**19**	**.299**	**.357**	**.375**	**.974**
1925	**ChC-N**	**51**	**137**	**20**	**35**	**5**	**0**	**0**	**20**	**19**	**—**	**12**	**0**	**12**	**—**	**1**	**1**	**.255**	**.346**	**.292**	**.966**
Career average		66	207	29	60	9	1	1	24	19	—	21	2	9	—	4	8	.289	.355	.361	.975
Cubs average		**66**	**207**	**29**	**60**	**9**	**1**	**1**	**24**	**19**	**—**	**21**	**2**	**9**	**—**	**4**	**8**	**.289**	**.355**	**.361**	**.975**
Career total		199	620	86	179	28	4	3	73	57	—	64	7	27	—	12	23	.289	.355	.361	.975
Cubs total		**199**	**620**	**86**	**179**	**28**	**4**	**3**	**73**	**57**	**—**	**64**	**7**	**27**	**—**	**12**	**23**	**.289**	**.355**	**.361**	**.975**

Grimes, Oscar Ray (Ray)
HEIGHT: 5'11" THROWS: RIGHT BATS: RIGHT BORN: 9/11/1893 BERGHOLZ, OHIO DIED: 5/25/1953 MINERVA, OHIO POSITIONS PLAYED: 1B

YEAR	TEAM	GAMES	AB	RUNS	HITS	2B	3B	HR	RBI	BB	IBB	SO	HBP	SH	SF	SB	CS	BA	OBA	SA	FA
1920	Bos-A	1	4	1	1	0	0	0	0	1	—	0	0	0	—	0	0	.250	.400	.250	1.000
1921	**ChC-N**	**147**	**530**	**91**	**170**	**38**	**6**	**6**	**79**	**70**	**—**	**55**	**6**	**16**	**—**	**5**	**8**	**.321**	**.406**	**.449**	**.993**
1922	**ChC-N**	**138**	**509**	**99**	**180**	**45**	**12**	**14**	**99**	**75**	**—**	**33**	**6**	**6**	**—**	**7**	**7**	**.354**	**.442**	**.572**	**.987**
1923	**ChC-N**	**64**	**216**	**32**	**71**	**7**	**2**	**2**	**36**	**24**	**—**	**17**	**2**	**3**	**—**	**5**	**0**	**.329**	**.401**	**.407**	**.991**
1924	**ChC-N**	**51**	**177**	**33**	**53**	**6**	**5**	**5**	**34**	**28**	**—**	**15**	**2**	**4**	**—**	**4**	**2**	**.299**	**.401**	**.475**	**.982**
1926	Phi-N	32	101	13	30	5	0	0	15	6	—	13	1	1	—	0	—	.297	.343	.347	.981
Career average		72	256	45	84	17	4	5	44	34	—	22	3	5	—	4	3	.329	.413	.480	.989
Cubs average		**100**	**358**	**64**	**119**	**24**	**6**	**7**	**62**	**49**	**—**	**30**	**4**	**7**	**—**	**5**	**4**	**.331**	**.418**	**.490**	**.989**
Career total		433	1537	269	505	101	25	27	263	204	—	133	17	30	—	21	17	.329	.413	.480	.989
Cubs total		**400**	**1432**	**255**	**474**	**96**	**25**	**27**	**248**	**197**	**—**	**120**	**16**	**29**	**—**	**21**	**17**	**.331**	**.418**	**.490**	**.989**

Grimm, Charles John (Charlie *or* Jolly Cholly)
HEIGHT: 5'11" THROWS: LEFT BATS: LEFT BORN: 8/28/1898 ST. LOUIS, MISSOURI DIED: 11/15/1983 SCOTTSDALE, ARIZONA POSITIONS PLAYED: 1B, 3B, OF

YEAR	TEAM	GAMES	AB	RUNS	HITS	2B	3B	HR	RBI	BB	IBB	SO	HBP	SH	SF	SB	CS	BA	OBA	SA	FA
1916	Phi-A	12	22	0	2	0	0	0	0	2	—	4	0	0	—	0	—	.091	.167	.091	.875
1918	StL-N	50	141	11	31	7	0	0	12	6	—	15	2	6	—	2	—	.220	.262	.270	.971
1919	Pit-N	14	44	6	14	1	3	0	6	2	—	4	0	1	—	1	—	.318	.348	.477	.968
1920	Pit-N	148	533	38	121	13	7	2	54	30	—	40	4	14	—	7	8	.227	.273	.289	.995
1921	Pit-N	151	562	62	154	21	17	7	71	31	—	38	2	16	—	6	8	.274	.314	.409	.994
1922	Pit-N	154	593	64	173	28	13	0	76	43	—	15	3	10	—	6	10	.292	.343	.383	.994
1923	Pit-N	152	563	78	194	29	13	7	99	41	—	43	0	10	—	6	9	.345	.389	.480	.995

(continued)

Charles (Charlie) John "Jolly Cholly" Grimm, 1b-3b-of, 1916–26

Charlie Grimm was a fun-loving, affable first baseman for the Cubs whose easygoing style belied a man who was one of the best all-around first basemen in either league.

Grimm was born on August 28, 1898, in St. Louis, Missouri. He broke in with the Philadelphia Athletics in 1916 in midseason and played a dozen games in the outfield for A's manager Connie Mack.

Grimm resurfaced in 1918 with St. Louis, this time as a first baseman, with mediocre results, playing in 50 games and hitting .220.

His third home in three big-league seasons was Pittsburgh in 1919, and after a so-so first year there, he came into his own in 1920. Grimm still wasn't much of a hitter, but he was a graceful, very sure-handed first sacker who led the league in fielding percentage in 1920 with a .995 mark, with only eight errors all year.

Grimm, in fact, was the best defensive first baseman in the league with the Pirates from 1920 to 1924, leading first basemen in fielding three of the five years he started for the Bucs.

At the end of the 1924 season, Grimm and shortstop Walter James "Rabbit" Maranville were traded to Chicago. Maranville was only in Chicago a year, but Grimm became a fixture there, hitting .306 and leading the Cubs with 29 doubles and 76 RBIs in the "Friendly Confines" of Wrigley Field in his first season.

Grimm would hit between .294 and .311 seven times in his next 10 years as a Cub. He would also lead the league in fielding percentage four times and finish second twice more.

He was also a clubhouse favorite, a laughing banjo player dubbed "Jolly Cholly" by sportswriters.

In midseason in 1932, the easygoing Grimm was hired to be the manager of the Cubs. Grimm's decidedly low-key management style was a sharp contrast to the no-nonsense style of outgoing Cubs manager Rogers Hornsby. The Cubs went on to win the 1932 pennant, before losing the World Series to the Yankees.

Grimm may have been a joker in the clubhouse, but he was a terror in the postseason.

Although neither World Series team with which Grimm played was a winner, Jolly Cholly got the job done. In both 1929 and 1932, he led the Cubs in hits, average, slugging average and RBIs.

Grimm remains the Cubs' all-time career slugging-average leader in World Series games with a .515 mark. He is second to Riggs Stephenson for the Cubs in World Series batting with a .364 average.

Grimm managed the Cubs three separate times. After he helped manage the squad to the National League pennant in 1932, Grimm repeated that accomplishment in 1935. But midway through the 1938 season, he resigned, believing he could no longer relate to his players. Gabby Hartnett replaced him and Grimm went into the broadcast booth.

Grimm returned to the Cubs as a coach in 1941, and the next year, he managed in the minors, leading Milwaukee to the American Association championship. In 1945 he returned to Chicago and was the manager when the Cubs won their final pennant of the century that season.

He was replaced in 1949, but after stints in the minor leagues and in Boston and later with the Milwaukee Braves, Grimm returned to manage the Cubs in 1960. But it wasn't as much fun as before, and he stepped down after 17 games.

The amazing part of this story is that the Cubs opted to hire former star Lou Boudreau, who was at that time broadcasting Cubs games. And of course, when Boudreau resigned as a broadcaster, well, somebody had to step in, and Grimm had experience. So in one of the more, let's say, unusual trades in major league history, manager Grimm was "swapped" for broadcaster Boudreau. Only in Chicago.

It must be noted that during his three stints as manager, Grimm won a total of 942 games, second only to Adrian "Cap" Anson.

Grimm stayed with the Cubs for several years, holding a variety of front-office positions. When he died in 1983, his widow, at his dying request, scattered his ashes over Wrigley Field.

(Grimm, continued)

YEAR	TEAM	GAMES	AB	RUNS	HITS	2B	3B	HR	RBI	BB	IBB	SO	HBP	SH	SF	SB	CS	BA	OBA	SA	FA
1924	Pit-N	151	542	53	156	25	12	2	63	37	—	22	2	18	—	3	6	.288	.336	.389	.995
1925	ChC-N	141	519	73	159	29	5	10	76	38	—	25	0	10	—	4	3	.306	.354	.439	.989
1926	ChC-N	147	524	58	145	30	6	8	82	49	—	25	3	26	—	3	—	.277	.342	.403	.988
1927	ChC-N	147	543	68	169	29	6	2	74	45	—	21	3	26	—	3	—	.311	.367	.398	.990
1928	ChC-N	147	547	67	161	25	5	5	62	39	—	20	1	28	—	7	—	.294	.342	.386	.993
1929	ChC-N	120	463	66	138	28	3	10	91	42	—	25	1	10	—	3	—	.298	.358	.436	.992
1930	ChC-N	114	429	58	124	27	2	6	65	41	—	26	6	14	—	1	—	.289	.359	.403	.995
1931	ChC-N	146	531	65	176	33	11	4	66	53	—	29	1	11	—	1	—	.331	.393	.458	.993
1932	ChC-N	149	570	66	175	42	2	7	80	35	—	22	2	9	—	2	—	.307	.349	.425	.993
1933	ChC-N	107	384	38	95	15	2	3	37	23	—	15	0	6	—	1	—	.247	.290	.320	.996
1934	ChC-N	75	267	24	79	8	1	5	47	16	—	12	1	2	—	1	—	.296	.338	.390	.995
1935	ChC-N	2	8	0	0	0	0	0	0	0	—	1	0	0	—	0	—	.000	.000	.000	1.000
1936	ChC-N	39	132	13	33	4	0	1	16	5	—	8	0	2	—	0	—	.250	.277	.303	1.000
Career average		108	396	45	115	20	5	4	54	29	—	21	2	11	—	3	2	.290	.341	.397	.993
Cubs average		**111**	**410**	**50**	**121**	**23**	**4**	**5**	**58**	**32**	**—**	**19**	**2**	**12**	**—**	**2**	**0**	**.296**	**.349**	**.405**	**.992**
Career total		2166	7917	908	2299	394	108	79	1077	578	—	410	31	219	—	57	44	.290	.341	.397	.993
Cubs total		**1334**	**4917**	**596**	**1454**	**270**	**43**	**61**	**696**	**386**	**—**	**229**	**18**	**144**	**—**	**26**	**3**	**.296**	**.349**	**.405**	**.992**

Gross, Gregory Eugene (Greg)

HEIGHT: 5'11" THROWS: LEFT BATS: LEFT BORN: 8/1/1952 YORK, PENNSYLVANIA POSITIONS PLAYED: P, 1B, OF

YEAR	TEAM	GAMES	AB	RUNS	HITS	2B	3B	HR	RBI	BB	IBB	SO	HBP	SH	SF	SB	CS	BA	OBA	SA	FA
1973	Hou-N	14	39	5	9	2	1	0	1	4	0	4	0	0	0	2	1	.231	.302	.333	1.000
1974	Hou-N	156	589	78	185	21	8	0	36	76	4	39	1	9	1	12	20	.314	.393	.377	.994
1975	Hou-N	132	483	67	142	14	10	0	41	63	1	37	0	9	3	2	2	.294	.373	.364	.958
1976	Hou-N	128	426	52	122	12	3	0	27	64	3	39	0	5	6	2	6	.286	.375	.329	.978
1977	ChC-N	115	239	43	77	10	4	5	32	33	4	19	0	3	5	0	1	.322	.397	.460	.991
1978	ChC-N	124	347	34	92	12	7	1	39	33	5	19	0	3	7	3	1	.265	.323	.349	.979
1979	Phi-N	111	174	21	58	6	3	0	15	29	4	5	0	0	3	5	1	.333	.422	.402	.978
1980	Phi-N	127	154	19	37	7	2	0	12	24	1	7	1	3	0	1	1	.240	.346	.312	.974
1981	Phi-N	83	102	14	23	6	1	0	7	15	4	5	0	0	2	2	2	.225	.319	.304	.982
1982	Phi-N	119	134	14	40	4	0	0	10	19	3	8	0	2	0	4	3	.299	.386	.328	.983
1983	Phi-N	136	245	25	74	12	3	0	29	34	4	16	1	1	3	3	5	.302	.385	.376	.991
1984	Phi-N	112	202	19	65	9	1	0	16	24	3	11	1	0	2	1	0	.322	.393	.376	.990
1985	Phi-N	93	169	21	44	5	2	0	14	32	1	9	0	2	2	1	0	.260	.374	.314	1.000
1986	Phi-N	87	101	11	25	5	0	0	8	21	7	11	1	1	1	1	0	.248	.379	.297	1.000
1987	Phi-N	114	133	14	38	4	1	1	12	25	4	12	1	1	3	0	0	.286	.395	.353	1.000
1988	Phi-N	98	133	10	27	1	0	0	5	16	1	3	1	1	1	0	0	.203	.291	.211	.991
1989	Hou-N	60	75	2	15	0	0	0	4	11	2	6	1	1	1	0	0	.200	.310	.200	.974
Career average		106	220	26	63	8	3	0	18	31	3	15	0	2	2	2	3	.287	.372	.351	.984
Cubs average		**120**	**293**	**39**	**85**	**11**	**6**	**3**	**36**	**33**	**5**	**19**	**0**	**3**	**6**	**2**	**1**	**.288**	**.354**	**.394**	**.984**
Career total		1809	3745	449	1073	130	46	7	308	523	51	250	8	40	39	39	44	.287	.372	.351	.984
Cubs total		**239**	**586**	**77**	**169**	**22**	**11**	**6**	**71**	**66**	**9**	**38**	**0**	**6**	**12**	**3**	**2**	**.288**	**.354**	**.394**	**.984**

Gudat, Marvin John (Marv)

HEIGHT: 5'11" THROWS: LEFT BATS: LEFT BORN: 8/27/1905 GOLIAD, TEXAS DIED: 3/1/1954 LOS ANGELES, CALIFORNIA POSITIONS PLAYED: P, 1B, OF

YEAR	TEAM	GAMES	AB	RUNS	HITS	2B	3B	HR	RBI	BB	IBB	SO	HBP	SH	SF	SB	CS	BA	OBA	SA	FA
1929	Cin-N	9	10	0	2	0	0	0	0	0	—	0	0	0	—	0	—	.200	.200	.200	.800
1932	ChC-N	60	94	15	24	4	1	1	15	16	—	10	1	1	—	0	—	.255	.369	.351	.976
Career average		35	52	8	13	2	1	1	8	8	—	5	1	1	—	0	—	.250	.355	.337	.966
Cubs average		**60**	**94**	**15**	**24**	**4**	**1**	**1**	**15**	**16**	**—**	**10**	**1**	**1**	**—**	**0**	**—**	**.255**	**.369**	**.351**	**.976**
Career total		69	104	15	26	4	1	1	15	16	—	10	1	1	—	0	—	.250	.355	.337	.966
Cubs total		**60**	**94**	**15**	**24**	**4**	**1**	**1**	**15**	**16**	**—**	**10**	**1**	**1**	**—**	**0**	**—**	**.255**	**.369**	**.351**	**.976**

Gustine, Frank William (Frankie)
HEIGHT: 6'0" THROWS: RIGHT BATS: RIGHT BORN: 2/20/1920 HOOPESTON, ILLINOIS DIED: 4/1/1991 DAVENPORT, IOWA
POSITIONS PLAYED: C, 1B, 2B, 3B, SS

YEAR	TEAM	GAMES	AB	RUNS	HITS	2B	3B	HR	RBI	BB	IBB	SO	HBP	SH	SF	SB	CS	BA	OBA	SA	FA
1939	Pit-N	22	70	5	13	3	0	0	3	9	—	4	0	5	—	0	—	.186	.278	.229	.896
1940	Pit-N	133	524	59	147	32	7	1	55	35	—	39	2	4	—	7	—	.281	.328	.374	.941
1941	Pit-N	121	463	46	125	24	7	1	46	28	—	38	1	5	—	5	—	.270	.313	.359	.947
1942	Pit-N	115	388	34	89	11	4	2	35	29	—	27	2	3	—	5	—	.229	.286	.294	.953
1943	Pit-N	112	414	40	120	21	3	0	43	32	—	36	0	8	—	5	—	.290	.341	.355	.944
1944	Pit-N	127	405	42	93	18	3	2	42	33	—	41	0	8	—	12	—	.230	.288	.304	.939
1945	Pit-N	128	478	67	134	27	5	2	66	37	—	33	2	6	—	8	—	.280	.335	.370	.937
1946	Pit-N	131	495	60	128	23	6	8	52	40	—	52	3	10	—	8	—	.259	.318	.378	.967
1947	Pit-N	156	616	102	183	30	6	9	67	63	—	65	2	10	—	2	—	.297	.364	.409	.945
1948	Pit-N	131	449	68	120	19	2	9	42	42	—	62	2	6	—	5	—	.267	.333	.379	.947
1949	**ChC-N**	**76**	**261**	**29**	**59**	**13**	**4**	**4**	**27**	**18**	—	**22**	**1**	**5**	—	**3**	—	**.226**	**.279**	**.352**	**.942**
1950	StL-A	9	19	1	3	1	0	0	2	3	—	8	0	1	—	0	1	.158	.273	.211	.857
Career average		105	382	46	101	19	4	3	40	31	—	36	1	6	—	5	0	.265	.322	.359	.946
Cubs average		**76**	**261**	**29**	**59**	**13**	**4**	**4**	**27**	**18**	—	**22**	**1**	**5**	—	**3**	—	**.226**	**.279**	**.352**	**.942**
Career total		1261	4582	553	1214	222	47	38	480	369	—	427	15	71	—	60	1	.265	.322	.359	.946
Cubs total		**76**	**261**	**29**	**59**	**13**	**4**	**4**	**27**	**18**	—	**22**	**1**	**5**	—	**3**	—	**.226**	**.279**	**.352**	**.942**

Gutierrez, Ricardo (Ricky)
HEIGHT: 6'1" THROWS: RIGHT BATS: RIGHT BORN: 5/23/1970 MIAMI, FLORIDA POSITIONS PLAYED: 2B, 3B, SS, OF

YEAR	TEAM	GAMES	AB	RUNS	HITS	2B	3B	HR	RBI	BB	IBB	SO	HBP	SH	SF	SB	CS	BA	OBA	SA	FA
1993	SD-N	133	438	76	110	10	5	5	26	50	2	97	5	1	1	4	3	.251	.334	.331	.973
1994	SD-N	90	275	27	66	11	2	1	28	32	1	54	2	2	3	2	6	.240	.321	.305	.931
1995	Hou-N	52	156	22	43	6	0	0	12	10	3	33	1	1	1	5	0	.276	.321	.314	.956
1996	Hou-N	89	218	28	62	8	1	1	15	23	3	42	3	4	1	6	1	.284	.359	.344	.951
1997	Hou-N	102	303	33	79	14	4	3	34	21	2	50	3	0	1	6	1	.261	.315	.363	.974
1998	Hou-N	141	491	55	128	24	3	2	46	54	5	84	6	3	7	13	7	.261	.337	.334	.976
1999	Hou-N	85	268	33	70	7	5	1	25	37	4	45	2	3	1	2	5	.261	.354	.334	.971
2000	**ChC-N**	**125**	**449**	**73**	**124**	**19**	**2**	**11**	**56**	**66**	**0**	**58**	**7**	**16**	**4**	**8**	**2**	**.276**	**.375**	**.401**	**.986**
2001	**ChC-N**	**147**	**528**	**76**	**153**	**23**	**3**	**10**	**66**	**40**	**0**	**56**	**10**	**17**	**11**	**4**	**3**	**.290**	**.345**	**.402**	**.971**
Career average		107	347	47	93	14	3	4	34	37	2	58	4	5	3	5	3	.267	.342	.355	.969
Cubs average		**136**	**489**	**75**	**139**	**21**	**3**	**11**	**61**	**53**	**0**	**57**	**9**	**17**	**8**	**6**	**3**	**.284**	**.359**	**.401**	**.978**
Career total		964	3126	423	835	122	25	34	308	333	20	519	39	47	29	49	29	.267	.342	.355	.969
Cubs total		**272**	**977**	**149**	**277**	**42**	**5**	**21**	**122**	**106**	**0**	**114**	**17**	**33**	**15**	**12**	**5**	**.284**	**.359**	**.401**	**.978**

Haas, George Edwin (Eddie)
HEIGHT: 5'11" THROWS: RIGHT BATS: LEFT BORN: 5/26/1935 PADUCAH, KENTUCKY POSITIONS PLAYED: OF

YEAR	TEAM	GAMES	AB	RUNS	HITS	2B	3B	HR	RBI	BB	IBB	SO	HBP	SH	SF	SB	CS	BA	OBA	SA	FA
1957	**ChC-N**	**14**	**24**	**1**	**5**	**1**	**0**	**0**	**4**	**1**	**0**	**5**	**0**	**0**	**1**	**0**	**0**	**.208**	**.231**	**.250**	**1.000**
1958	Mil-N	9	14	2	5	1	0	0	1	2	0	1	0	0	0	0	0	.357	.438	.357	1.000
1960	Mil-N	32	32	4	7	2	0	1	5	5	0	14	0	0	0	0	0	.219	.324	.375	1.000
Career average		18	23	2	6	1	0	0	3	3	0	7	0	0	0	0	0	.243	.316	.329	1.000
Cubs average		**14**	**24**	**1**	**5**	**1**	**0**	**0**	**4**	**1**	**0**	**5**	**0**	**0**	**1**	**0**	**0**	**.208**	**.231**	**.250**	**1.000**
Career total		55	70	7	17	3	0	1	10	8	0	20	0	0	1	0	0	.243	.316	.329	1.000
Cubs total		**14**	**24**	**1**	**5**	**1**	**0**	**0**	**4**	**1**	**0**	**5**	**0**	**0**	**1**	**0**	**0**	**.208**	**.231**	**.250**	**1.000**

Hack, Stanley Camfield (Stan *or* Smiling Stan)
HEIGHT: 6'0" THROWS: RIGHT BATS: LEFT BORN: 12/6/1909 SACRAMENTO, CALIFORNIA DIED: 12/15/1979 DIXON, ILLINOIS POSITIONS PLAYED: 1B, 3B

YEAR	TEAM	GAMES	AB	RUNS	HITS	2B	3B	HR	RBI	BB	IBB	SO	HBP	SH	SF	SB	CS	BA	OBA	SA	FA
1932	ChC-N	72	178	32	42	5	6	2	19	17	—	16	1	2	—	5	—	.236	.306	.365	.913
1933	ChC-N	20	60	10	21	3	1	1	2	8	—	3	3	0	—	4	—	.350	.451	.483	.983
1934	ChC-N	111	402	54	116	16	6	0	21	45	—	42	2	9	—	11	—	.289	.363	.366	.949
1935	ChC-N	124	427	75	133	23	9	4	64	65	—	17	3	9	—	14	—	.311	.406	.436	.950
1936	ChC-N	149	561	102	167	27	4	6	78	89	—	39	2	14	—	17	—	.298	.396	.392	.962

(continued)

Stanley Camfield "Smiling Stan" Hack, 3b-1b, 1932–47

A player of reliability and durability, Stan Hack was also one of the Cubs' best players in the postseason, hitting .348 in four World Series.

Hack was born on December 6, 1909, in Sacramento, California. He was a minor league star in his hometown by the time the Cubs signed him in 1932. Hack played in 72 games in his first year, hitting .236. He played only briefly in 1933, before returning to the minors, but he was brought up to the Cubs for good the next year. He won the starting job in 1934, hitting .289 and finishing third in putouts and second in assists among National League third basemen.

Hack was a popular player with both the fans and his teammates. He was an ebullient man who seemed to enjoy his work. Writers dubbed him "Smiling Stan."

Hack wasn't graceful. Often, when he had to drop down to field a hot grounder, his knees would buckle inward inelegantly. He didn't have a powerful arm. But his work ethic, combined with his athleticism, made Hack among the best third basemen of his generation.

He led the National League in putouts five times, twice in fielding percentage and twice in assists. In 1942 he went 54 games without committing an error at third base, which was then a record.

On offense, Hack twice led the league in stolen bases in 1938 and 1939, and twice he led the league in hits in 1940 and 1941. He scored 100 or more runs seven times, including six consecutive times from 1936 to 1941. He led the Cubs in batting average four times, including three years in a row, from 1940 to 1942.

He was a line-drive hitter who could spray balls to all fields and who ended his career with a .301 average. Hack didn't have much power, but he could hit and run; he was one of the best leadoff men in the business.

He played in four World Series for Chicago and always performed well, except in the 1932 classic, where he made only one unsuccessful appearance at the plate as a pinch hitter. In the 1935 World Series, he had five hits, including a double and a triple. In the 1938 Series, he led all players with a .471 batting average and eight hits. He smacked 11 hits in the 1945 World Series.

Strangely enough, Hack had actually retired from the Cubs in 1943, at least in part because he wasn't getting along with Cubs manager Jimmie Wilson. But when Wilson was fired in 1944, the new Cubs manager, Charlie Grimm, convinced Hack to come out of retirement and return to the team.

Where Wilson was often critical of his star veteran, Grimm would often sit down with Hack and have a beer with him after the game. The message of both managers might have been the same, but Grimm's delivery was, in Hack's mind, presented in a more positive vein. For whatever reason, Grimm's gamble to get Hack back paid off magnificently. Hack hit .323 in 1945, fourth in the league, and scored 110 runs, fifth in the league, as the Cubs won the 1945 pennant.

Hack hung on until 1947, and even then, at 38, he hit .271 in part-time work for Chicago. After retirement, he managed the Cubs for a few years, but his teams never finished higher than sixth. He also worked as a coach for the Cardinals and also managed in the minor leagues into the 1960s. He died in Dixon, Illinois, in 1979.

Hack is in several categories in the Cubs record books. He is the all-time leader for the Cubs in walks with 1,092, seventh in games played with 1,938, sixth in at-bats with 7,278, sixth in runs scored with 1,239, fifth in hits with 2,193, ninth in total bases with 2,889, second all-time in singles with 1,692, seventh in doubles with 363, and ninth in triples with 81.

(Hack, continued)

YEAR	TEAM	GAMES	AB	RUNS	HITS	2B	3B	HR	RBI	BB	IBB	SO	HBP	SH	SF	SB	CS	BA	OBA	SA	FA
1937	ChC-N	154	582	106	173	27	6	2	63	83	—	42	3	10	—	16	—	.297	.388	.375	.968
1938	ChC-N	152	609	109	195	34	11	4	67	94	—	39	0	4	—	16	—	.320	.411	.432	.954
1939	ChC-N	156	641	112	191	28	6	8	56	65	—	35	2	15	—	17	—	.298	.364	.398	.956
1940	ChC-N	149	603	101	191	38	6	8	40	75	—	24	3	5	—	21	—	.317	.395	.439	.955
1941	ChC-N	151	586	111	186	33	5	7	45	99	—	40	1	8	—	10	—	.317	.417	.427	.954
1942	ChC-N	140	553	91	166	36	3	6	39	94	—	40	0	10	—	9	—	.300	.402	.409	.965
1943	ChC-N	144	533	78	154	24	4	3	35	82	—	27	0	15	—	5	—	.289	.384	.366	.960
1944	ChC-N	98	383	65	108	16	1	3	32	53	—	21	0	4	—	5	—	.282	.369	.352	.955
1945	ChC-N	150	597	110	193	29	7	2	43	99	—	30	1	5	—	12	—	.323	.420	.405	.975
1946	ChC-N	92	323	55	92	13	4	0	26	83	—	32	0	3	—	3	—	.285	.431	.350	.968
1947	ChC-N	76	240	28	65	11	2	0	12	41	—	19	0	2	—	0	—	.271	.377	.333	.962
Career average		121	455	77	137	23	5	4	40	68	—	29	1	7	—	10	—	.301	.394	.397	
Cubs average		**121**	**455**	**77**	**137**	**23**	**5**	**4**	**40**	**68**	—	**29**	**1**	**7**	—	**10**	—	**.301**	**.394**	**.397**	**.959**
Career total		1938	7278	1239	2193	363	81	57	642	1092	—	466	21	115	—	165	—	.301	.394	.397	.959
Cubs total		**1938**	**7278**	**1239**	**2193**	**363**	**81**	**57**	**642**	**1092**	—	**466**	**21**	**115**	—	**165**	—	**.301**	**.394**	**.397**	**.959**

Hairston, John Louis (Johnny)

HEIGHT: 6'2" THROWS: RIGHT BATS: RIGHT BORN: 8/29/1944 BIRMINGHAM, ALABAMA POSITIONS PLAYED: C, OF

YEAR	TEAM	GAMES	AB	RUNS	HITS	2B	3B	HR	RBI	BB	IBB	SO	HBP	SH	SF	SB	CS	BA	OBA	SA	FA
1969	ChC-N	3	4	0	1	0	0	0	0	0	0	2	0	0	0	0	0	.250	.250	.250	1.000
Career average		3	4	0	1	0	0	0	0	0	0	2	0	0	0	0	0	.250	.250	.250	1.000
Cubs average		**3**	**4**	**0**	**1**	**0**	**0**	**0**	**0**	**0**	**0**	**2**	**0**	**0**	**0**	**0**	**0**	**.250**	**.250**	**.250**	**1.000**
Career total		3	4	0	1	0	0	0	0	0	0	2	0	0	0	0	0	.250	.250	.250	1.000
Cubs total		**3**	**4**	**0**	**1**	**0**	**0**	**0**	**0**	**0**	**0**	**2**	**0**	**0**	**0**	**0**	**0**	**.250**	**.250**	**.250**	**1.000**

Hall, Jimmie Randolph

HEIGHT: 6'0" THROWS: RIGHT BATS: LEFT BORN: 3/17/1938 MOUNT HOLLY, NORTH CAROLINA POSITIONS PLAYED: 1B, OF

YEAR	TEAM	GAMES	AB	RUNS	HITS	2B	3B	HR	RBI	BB	IBB	SO	HBP	SH	SF	SB	CS	BA	OBA	SA	FA
1963	Min-A	156	497	88	129	21	5	33	80	63	4	101	0	9	2	3	3	.260	.342	.521	.982
1964	Min-A	149	510	61	144	20	3	25	75	44	3	112	1	2	5	5	2	.282	.338	.480	.985
1965	Min-A	148	522	81	149	25	4	20	86	51	6	79	1	0	6	14	7	.285	.347	.464	.976
1966	Min-A	120	356	52	85	7	4	20	47	33	5	66	0	0	2	1	2	.239	.302	.449	.978
1967	Cal-A	129	401	54	100	8	3	16	55	42	7	65	0	1	3	4	1	.249	.318	.404	.990
1968	Cal-A	46	126	15	27	3	0	1	8	16	3	19	0	0	0	1	0	.214	.303	.262	.981
1968	Cle-A	53	111	4	22	4	0	1	8	10	3	19	0	0	0	1	0	.198	.264	.261	.983
1969	Cle-A	4	10	1	0	0	0	0	0	2	1	3	0	0	0	1	0	.000	.167	.000	1.000
1969	NYY-A	80	212	21	50	8	5	3	26	19	1	34	0	0	2	8	3	.236	.296	.363	.966
1969	**ChC-N**	**11**	**24**	**1**	**5**	**1**	**0**	**0**	**1**	**1**	**0**	**5**	**0**	**0**	**0**	**0**	**0**	**.208**	**.240**	**.250**	**1.000**
1970	**ChC-N**	**28**	**32**	**2**	**3**	**1**	**0**	**0**	**1**	**4**	**1**	**12**	**0**	**0**	**0**	**0**	**0**	**.094**	**.194**	**.125**	**1.000**
1970	Atl-N	39	47	7	10	2	0	2	4	2	1	14	0	0	0	0	0	.213	.245	.383	1.000
Career average		120	356	48	91	13	3	15	49	36	4	66	0	2	3	5	2	.254	.321	.434	.981
Cubs average		**20**	**28**	**2**	**4**	**1**	**0**	**0**	**1**	**3**	**1**	**9**	**0**	**0**	**0**	**0**	**0**	**.143**	**.213**	**.179**	**1.000**
Career total		963	2848	387	724	100	24	121	391	287	35	529	2	12	20	38	18	.254	.321	.434	.981
Cubs total		**39**	**56**	**3**	**8**	**2**	**0**	**0**	**2**	**5**	**1**	**17**	**0**	**0**	**0**	**0**	**0**	**.143**	**.213**	**.179**	**1.000**

Hall, Melvin (Mel)

HEIGHT: 6'1" THROWS: LEFT BATS: LEFT BORN: 9/16/1960 LYONS, NEW YORK POSITIONS PLAYED: OF

YEAR	TEAM	GAMES	AB	RUNS	HITS	2B	3B	HR	RBI	BB	IBB	SO	HBP	SH	SF	SB	CS	BA	OBA	SA	FA
1981	ChC-N	10	11	1	1	0	0	1	2	1	0	4	0	0	0	0	0	.091	.167	.364	—
1982	ChC-N	24	80	6	21	3	2	0	4	5	1	17	2	0	1	0	1	.263	.318	.350	.939
1983	ChC-N	112	410	60	116	23	5	17	56	42	6	101	3	1	2	6	6	.283	.352	.488	.988
1984	ChC-N	48	150	25	42	11	3	4	22	12	3	23	0	0	2	2	1	.280	.329	.473	.961
1984	Cle-A	83	257	43	66	13	1	7	30	35	5	55	2	0	5	1	1	.257	.344	.397	.993
1985	Cle-A	23	66	7	21	6	0	0	12	8	0	12	0	0	1	0	1	.318	.387	.409	1.000
1986	Cle-A	140	442	68	131	29	2	18	77	33	8	65	2	0	3	6	2	.296	.346	.493	.972
1987	Cle-A	142	485	57	136	21	1	18	76	20	6	68	1	0	2	5	4	.280	.309	.439	.989
1988	Cle-A	150	515	69	144	32	4	6	71	28	12	50	0	2	8	7	3	.280	.312	.439	.989
1989	NYY-A	113	361	54	94	9	0	17	58	21	4	37	0	1	8	0	0	.260	.295	.427	.967
1990	NYY-A	113	360	41	93	23	2	12	46	6	2	46	2	0	3	0	0	.258	.272	.433	.993
1991	NYY-A	141	492	67	140	23	2	19	80	26	6	40	3	0	6	0	1	.285	.321	.455	.987

(continued)

(Hall, continued)

YEAR	TEAM	GAMES	AB	RUNS	HITS	2B	3B	HR	RBI	BB	IBB	SO	HBP	SH	SF	SB	CS	BA	OBA	SA	FA
1992	NYY-A	152	583	67	163	36	3	15	81	29	4	53	1	0	9	4	2	.280	.310	.429	.990
1996	SF-N	25	25	3	3	0	0	0	5	1	0	4	0	0	1	0	0	.120	.148	.120	—
Career average		98	326	44	90	18	2	10	48	21	4	44	1	0	4	2	2	.276	.318	.437	.981
Cubs average		**49**	**163**	**23**	**45**	**9**	**3**	**6**	**21**	**15**	**3**	**36**	**1**	**0**	**1**	**2**	**2**	**.276**	**.340**	**.465**	**.976**
Career total		1276	4237	568	1171	229	25	134	620	267	57	575	16	4	51	31	22	.276	.318	.437	.981
Cubs total		**194**	**651**	**92**	**180**	**37**	**10**	**22**	**84**	**60**	**10**	**145**	**5**	**1**	**5**	**8**	**8**	**.276**	**.340**	**.465**	**.976**

Hallinan, James H. (Jimmy)
HEIGHT: 5'9" THROWS: LEFT BATS: LEFT BORN: 5/27/1849 IRELAND DIED: 10/28/1879 CHICAGO, ILLINOIS POSITIONS PLAYED: 2B, SS, OF

YEAR	TEAM	GAMES	AB	RUNS	HITS	2B	3B	HR	RBI	BB	IBB	SO	HBP	SH	SF	SB	CS	BA	OBA	SA	FA
																		.277	.283	.380	.757
1876	NYM-N	54	242	45	67	7	6	2	36	2	—	4	—	—	—	—	—	.370	.378	.411	.854
1877	Cin-N	16	73	18	27	1	1	0	7	1	—	1	—	—	—	—	—	.281	.312	.348	.800
1877	**ChN-N**	**19**	**89**	**17**	**25**	**4**	**1**	**0**	**11**	**4**	**—**	**2**	**—**	**—**	**—**	**—**	**—**	**.284**	**.333**	**.328**	**.765**
1878	**ChN-N**	**16**	**67**	**14**	**19**	**3**	**0**	**0**	**2**	**5**	**—**	**6**	**—**	**—**	**—**	**—**	**—**	**.250**	**.250**	**.417**	**.667**
1878	Ind-N	3	12	0	3	2	0	0	1	0	—	2	—	—	—	—	—				
Career average		36	161	31	47	6	3	1	19	4	—	5	—	—	—	—	—	.292	.309	.373	.780
Cubs average		**18**	**78**	**16**	**22**	**4**	**1**	**0**	**7**	**5**	**—**	**4**	**—**	**—**	**—**	**—**	**—**	**.282**	**.321**	**.340**	**.779**
Career total		108	483	94	141	17	8	2	57	12	—	15	—	—	—	—	—	.292	.309	.373	.780
Cubs total		**35**	**156**	**31**	**44**	**7**	**1**	**0**	**13**	**9**	**—**	**8**	**—**	**—**	**—**	**—**	**—**	**.282**	**.321**	**.340**	**.779**

Haney, Fred Girard (Pudge)
HEIGHT: 5'6" THROWS: RIGHT BATS: RIGHT BORN: 4/25/1898 ALBUQUERQUE, NEW MEXICO DIED: 11/9/1977 BEVERLY HILLS, CALIFORNIA
POSITIONS PLAYED: 1B, 2B, 3B, SS, OF

YEAR	TEAM	GAMES	AB	RUNS	HITS	2B	3B	HR	RBI	BB	IBB	SO	HBP	SH	SF	SB	CS	BA	OBA	SA	FA
1922	Det-A	81	213	41	75	7	4	0	25	32	—	14	1	12	—	3	7	.352	.439	.423	.957
1923	Det-A	142	503	85	142	13	4	4	67	45	—	23	5	27	—	13	5	.282	.347	.348	.957
1924	Det-A	86	256	54	79	11	1	1	30	39	—	13	0	11	—	7	4	.309	.400	.371	.924
1925	Det-A	114	398	84	111	15	3	0	40	66	—	29	2	17	—	11	1	.279	.384	.332	.953
1926	Bos-A	138	462	47	102	15	7	0	52	74	—	28	1	28	—	13	6	.221	.330	.284	.957
1927	Bos-A	47	116	23	32	4	1	3	12	25	—	14	0	8	—	4	1	.276	.404	.405	.936
1927	**ChC-N**	**4**	**3**	**0**	**0**	**0**	**0**	**0**	**0**	**0**	**—**	**0**	**0**	**0**	**—**	**0**	**—**	**.000**	**.000**	**.000**	
1929	StL-N	10	26	4	3	1	1	0	2	1	—	2	1	0	—	0	—	.115	.179	.231	.958
Career average		89	282	48	78	9	3	1	33	40	—	18	1	15	—	7	3	.275	.368	.342	.951
Cubs average		**4**	**3**	**0**	**0**	**0**	**0**	**0**	**0**	**0**	**—**	**0**	**0**	**0**	**—**	**0**	**0**	**.000**	**.000**	**.000**	**—**
Career total		622	1977	338	544	66	21	8	228	282	—	123	10	103	—	51	24	.275	.368	.342	.951
Cubs total		**4**	**3**	**0**	**0**	**0**	**0**	**0**	**0**	**0**	**—**	**0**	**0**	**0**	**—**	**0**	**0**	**.000**	**.000**	**.000**	**—**

Haney, Todd Michael
HEIGHT: 5'9" THROWS: RIGHT BATS: RIGHT BORN: 7/30/1965 GALVESTON, TEXAS POSITIONS PLAYED: 2B, 3B, SS, OF

YEAR	TEAM	GAMES	AB	RUNS	HITS	2B	3B	HR	RBI	BB	IBB	SO	HBP	SH	SF	SB	CS	BA	OBA	SA	FA
1992	Mon-N	7	10	0	3	1	0	0	1	0	0	0	0	1	0	0	0	.300	.300	.400	1.000
1994	**ChC-N**	**17**	**37**	**6**	**6**	**0**	**0**	**1**	**2**	**3**	**0**	**3**	**1**	**1**	**1**	**2**	**1**	**.162**	**.238**	**.243**	**.980**
1995	**ChC-N**	**25**	**73**	**11**	**30**	**8**	**0**	**2**	**6**	**7**	**0**	**11**	**0**	**1**	**0**	**0**	**0**	**.411**	**.463**	**.603**	**.979**
1996	**ChC-N**	**49**	**82**	**11**	**11**	**1**	**0**	**0**	**3**	**7**	**0**	**15**	**0**	**2**	**1**	**1**	**0**	**.134**	**.200**	**.146**	**.970**
1998	NYM-N	3	3	0	0	0	0	0	0	1	0	0	0	0	0	1	0	.000	.250	.000	—
Career average		20	41	6	10	2	0	1	2	4	0	6	0	1	0	1	0	.244	.305	.337	.976
Cubs average		**30**	**64**	**9**	**16**	**3**	**0**	**1**	**4**	**6**	**0**	**10**	**0**	**1**	**1**	**1**	**0**	**.245**	**.307**	**.339**	**.976**
Career total		101	205	28	50	10	0	3	12	18	0	29	1	5	2	3	1	.244	.305	.337	.976
Cubs total		**91**	**192**	**28**	**47**	**9**	**0**	**3**	**11**	**17**	**0**	**29**	**1**	**4**	**2**	**3**	**1**	**.245**	**.307**	**.339**	**.976**

Hankinson, Frank Edward
HEIGHT: 5'11"   THROWS: RIGHT   BATS: RIGHT   BORN: 4/29/1856 NEW YORK, NEW YORK   DIED: 4/5/1911 PALISADES PARK, NEW JERSEY
POSITIONS PLAYED: P, 1B, 2B, 3B, SS, OF

YEAR	TEAM	GAMES	AB	RUNS	HITS	2B	3B	HR	RBI	BB	IBB	SO	HBP	SH	SF	SB	CS	BA	OBA	SA	FA
1878	**ChN-N**	**58**	**240**	**38**	**64**	**8**	**3**	**1**	**27**	**5**	**—**	**36**	**—**	**—**	**—**	**—**	**—**	**.267**	**.282**	**.338**	**.876**
1879	**ChN-N**	**44**	**171**	**14**	**31**	**4**	**0**	**0**	**8**	**2**	**—**	**14**	**—**	**—**	**—**	**—**	**—**	**.181**	**.191**	**.205**	**.902**
1880	Cle-N	69	263	32	55	7	4	1	19	1	—	23	—	—	—	—	—	.209	.212	.278	.860
1881	Try-N	85	321	34	62	15	0	1	19	10	—	41	—	—	—	—	—	.193	.218	.249	.904
1883	NYG-N	94	337	40	74	13	6	2	30	19	—	38	—	—	—	—	—	.220	.261	.312	.868
1884	NYG-N	105	389	44	90	16	7	2	43	23	—	59	—	—	—	—	—	.231	.274	.324	.871
1885	NY-AA	94	362	43	81	12	2	2	44	12	—	—	1	—	—	—	—	.224	.251	.285	.906
1886	NY-AA	136	522	66	126	14	5	2	63	49	—	—	0	—	—	—	—	.241	.306	.299	.873
1887	NY-AA	127	550	79	175	29	11	1	71	38	—	—	0	—	—	10	—	.318	.362	.416	.861
1888	KC-AA	37	155	20	27	4	1	1	20	11	—	—	0	—	—	19	—	.174	.229	.232	.897
Career average		85	331	41	79	12	4	1	34	17	—	21	0	—	—	3	—	.237	.275	.309	.879
Cubs average		**51**	**206**	**26**	**48**	**6**	**2**	**1**	**18**	**4**	**—**	**25**	**—**	**—**	**—**	**—**	**—**	**.231**	**.244**	**.282**	**.885**
Career total		849	3310	410	785	122	39	13	344	170	—	211	1	—	—	31	—	.237	.275	.309	.879
Cubs total		**102**	**411**	**52**	**95**	**12**	**3**	**1**	**35**	**7**	**—**	**50**	**—**	**—**	**—**	**—**	**—**	**.231**	**.244**	**.282**	**.885**

Hanlon, William Joseph (Bill *or* Big Bill)
HEIGHT: 6'0"   THROWS: —   BATS: —   BORN: 6/24/1876 LOS ANGELES, CALIFORNIA   DIED: 11/23/1905 LOS ANGELES, CALIFORNIA   POSITIONS PLAYED: 1B

YEAR	TEAM	GAMES	AB	RUNS	HITS	2B	3B	HR	RBI	BB	IBB	SO	HBP	SH	SF	SB	CS	BA	OBA	SA	FA
1903	ChC-N	8	21	4	2	0	0	0	2	6	—	—	0	3	—	1	—	.095	.296	.095	.980
Career average		8	21	4	2	0	0	0	2	6	—	—	0	3	—	1	—	.095	.296	.095	.980
Cubs average		**8**	**21**	**4**	**2**	**0**	**0**	**0**	**2**	**6**	**—**	**—**	**0**	**3**	**—**	**1**	**—**	**.095**	**.296**	**.095**	**.980**
Career total		8	21	4	2	0	0	0	2	6	—	—	0	3	—	1	—	.095	.296	.095	.980
Cubs total		**8**	**21**	**4**	**2**	**0**	**0**	**0**	**2**	**6**	**—**	**—**	**0**	**3**	**—**	**1**	**—**	**.095**	**.296**	**.095**	**.980**

Hansen, David Andrew (Dave)
HEIGHT: 6'0"   THROWS: RIGHT   BATS: LEFT   BORN: 11/24/1968 LONG BEACH, CALIFORNIA   POSITIONS PLAYED: 1B, 2B, 3B, SS, OF

YEAR	TEAM	GAMES	AB	RUNS	HITS	2B	3B	HR	RBI	BB	IBB	SO	HBP	SH	SF	SB	CS	BA	OBA	SA	FA
1990	LA-N	5	7	0	1	0	0	0	1	0	0	3	0	0	0	0	0	.143	.143	.143	.500
1991	LA-N	53	56	3	15	4	0	1	5	2	0	12	0	0	0	1	0	.268	.293	.393	1.000
1992	LA-N	132	341	30	73	11	0	6	22	34	3	49	1	0	2	0	2	.214	.286	.299	.968
1993	LA-N	84	105	13	38	3	0	4	30	21	3	13	0	0	1	0	1	.362	.465	.505	.927
1994	LA-N	40	44	3	15	3	0	0	5	5	0	5	0	0	0	0	0	.341	.408	.409	.857
1995	LA-N	100	181	19	52	10	0	1	14	28	4	28	1	0	1	0	0	.287	.384	.359	.933
1996	LA-N	80	104	7	23	1	0	0	6	11	1	22	0	0	1	0	0	.221	.293	.231	.988
1997	**ChC-N**	**90**	**151**	**19**	**47**	**8**	**2**	**3**	**21**	**31**	**1**	**32**	**1**	**2**	**1**	**1**	**2**	**.311**	**.429**	**.450**	**.929**
1999	LA-N	100	107	14	27	8	1	2	17	26	0	20	2	0	1	0	0	.252	.404	.402	.962
2000	LA-N	102	121	18	35	6	2	8	26	26	0	32	0	0	0	0	1	.289	.415	.570	.973
2001	LA-N	92	140	13	33	10	0	2	20	32	5	29	0	0	3	0	1	.236	.371	.350	.973
Career average		80	123	13	33	6	0	2	15	20	2	22	0	0	1	0	1	.265	.365	.379	.961
Cubs average		**90**	**151**	**19**	**47**	**8**	**2**	**3**	**21**	**31**	**1**	**32**	**1**	**2**	**1**	**1**	**2**	**.311**	**.429**	**.450**	**.929**
Career total		878	1357	139	359	64	5	27	167	216	17	245	5	2	10	2	7	.265	.365	.379	.961
Cubs total		**90**	**151**	**19**	**47**	**8**	**2**	**3**	**21**	**31**	**1**	**32**	**1**	**2**	**1**	**1**	**2**	**.311**	**.429**	**.450**	**.929**

Harbridge, William Arthur (Bill *or* Yaller Bill)
HEIGHT: —   THROWS: LEFT   BATS: LEFT   BORN: 3/29/1855 PHILADELPHIA, PENNSYLVANIA   DIED: 3/17/1924 PHILADELPHIA, PENNSYLVANIA
POSITIONS PLAYED: C, 1B, 2B, 3B, SS, OF

YEAR	TEAM	GAMES	AB	RUNS	HITS	2B	3B	HR	RBI	BB	IBB	SO	HBP	SH	SF	SB	CS	BA	OBA	SA	FA
1876	Har-N	30	109	11	23	2	1	0	6	3	—	2	—	—	—	—	—	.211	.232	.248	.798
1877	Har-N	41	167	18	37	5	2	0	8	3	—	6	—	—	—	—	—	.222	.235	.275	.861
1878	**ChN-N**	**54**	**240**	**32**	**71**	**12**	**0**	**0**	**37**	**6**	**—**	**13**	**—**	**—**	**—**	**—**	**—**	**.296**	**.313**	**.346**	**.878**
1879	**ChN-N**	**4**	**18**	**2**	**2**	**0**	**0**	**0**	**1**	**0**	**—**	**5**	**—**	**—**	**—**	**—**	**—**	**.111**	**.111**	**.111**	**.571**
1880	Try-N	9	27	3	10	0	1	0	2	0	—	3	—	—	—	—	—	.370	.370	.444	.873
1882	Try-N	32	123	11	23	1	1	0	13	10	—	17	—	—	—	—	—	.187	.248	.211	.868

(continued)

(Harbridge, continued)

YEAR	TEAM	GAMES	AB	RUNS	HITS	2B	3B	HR	RBI	BB	IBB	SO	HBP	SH	SF	SB	CS	BA	OBA	SA	FA
1883	Phi-N	73	280	32	62	12	3	0	21	24	—	20	—	—	—	—	—	.221	.283	.286	.778
1884	Cin-U	82	341	59	95	12	5	2	—	25	—	—	—	—	—	—	—	.279	.328	.361	.899
Career average		41	163	21	40	6	2	0	11	9	—	8	—	—	—	—	—	.248	.286	.306	.846
Cubs average		**29**	**129**	**17**	**37**	**6**	**0**	**0**	**19**	**3**	—	**9**	—	—	—	—	—	**.283**	**.299**	**.329**	**.872**
Career total		325	1305	168	323	44	13	2	88	71	—	66	—	—	—	—	—	.248	.286	.306	.846
Cubs total		**58**	**258**	**34**	**73**	**12**	**0**	**0**	**38**	**6**	—	**18**	—	—	—	—	—	**.283**	**.299**	**.329**	**.872**

Hardie, Lewis W. (Lou)

HEIGHT: 5'11" THROWS: — BATS: RIGHT BORN: 8/24/1864 NEW YORK, NEW YORK DIED: 3/5/1929 OAKLAND, CALIFORNIA
POSITIONS PLAYED: C, 1B, 3B, SS, OF

YEAR	TEAM	GAMES	AB	RUNS	HITS	2B	3B	HR	RBI	BB	IBB	SO	HBP	SH	SF	SB	CS	BA	OBA	SA	FA
1884	Phi-N	3	8	0	3	2	0	0	0	0	—	2	—	—	—	—	—	.375	.375	.625	.857
1886	**ChN-N**	**16**	**51**	**4**	**9**	**0**	**0**	**0**	**3**	**4**	—	**10**	—	—	—	**1**	—	**.176**	**.236**	**.176**	**.966**
1890	Bos-N	47	185	17	42	8	0	3	17	18	—	36	0	—	—	4	—	.227	.296	.319	.887
1891	Bal-AA	15	56	7	13	0	3	0	1	8	—	8	0	—	—	3	—	.232	.328	.339	1.000
Career average		20	75	7	17	3	1	1	5	8	—	14	0	—	—	2	—	.223	.294	.307	.915
Cubs average		**16**	**51**	**4**	**9**	**0**	**0**	**0**	**3**	**4**	—	**10**	—	—	—	**1**	—	**.176**	**.236**	**.176**	**.966**
Career total		81	300	28	67	10	3	3	21	30	—	56	0	—	—	8	—	.223	.294	.307	.915
Cubs total		**16**	**51**	**4**	**9**	**0**	**0**	**0**	**3**	**4**	—	**10**	—	—	—	**1**	—	**.176**	**.236**	**.176**	**.966**

Hardin, William Edgar (Bud)

HEIGHT: 5'10" THROWS: RIGHT BATS: RIGHT BORN: 6/14/1922 SHELBY, NORTH CAROLINA DIED: 9/28/1997 RANCHO SANTE FE, CALIFORNIA
POSITIONS PLAYED: 2B, SS

YEAR	TEAM	GAMES	AB	RUNS	HITS	2B	3B	HR	RBI	BB	IBB	SO	HBP	SH	SF	SB	CS	BA	OBA	SA	FA
1952	ChC-N	3	7	1	1	0	0	0	0	0	—	0	0	0	—	0	0	.143	.143	.143	1.000
Career average		3	7	1	1	0	0	0	0	0	—	0	0	0	—	0	0	.143	.143	.143	1.000
Cubs average		**3**	**7**	**1**	**1**	**0**	**0**	**0**	**0**	**0**	—	**0**	**0**	**0**	—	**0**	**0**	**.143**	**.143**	**.143**	**1.000**
Career total		3	7	1	1	0	0	0	0	0	—	0	0	0	—	0	0	.143	.143	.143	1.000
Cubs total		**3**	**7**	**1**	**1**	**0**	**0**	**0**	**0**	**0**	—	**0**	**0**	**0**	—	**0**	**0**	**.143**	**.143**	**.143**	**1.000**

Hardtke, Jason Robert

HEIGHT: 5'10" THROWS: RIGHT BATS: BOTH BORN: 9/15/1971 MILWAUKEE, WISCONSIN POSITIONS PLAYED: 2B, 3B, OF

YEAR	TEAM	GAMES	AB	RUNS	HITS	2B	3B	HR	RBI	BB	IBB	SO	HBP	SH	SF	SB	CS	BA	OBA	SA	FA
1996	NYM-N	19	57	3	11	5	0	0	6	2	0	12	1	0	0	0	0	.193	.233	.281	1.000
1997	NYM-N	30	56	9	15	2	0	2	8	4	1	6	1	0	1	1	1	.268	.323	.411	.981
1998	**ChC-N**	**18**	**21**	**2**	**5**	**0**	**0**	**0**	**2**	**2**	**0**	**6**	**0**	**0**	**0**	**0**	**0**	**.238**	**.304**	**.238**	**1.000**
Career average		22	45	5	10	2	0	1	5	3	0	8	1	0	0	0	0	.231	.283	.328	.991
Cubs average		**18**	**21**	**2**	**5**	**0**	**0**	**0**	**2**	**2**	**0**	**6**	**0**	**0**	**0**	**0**	**0**	**.238**	**.304**	**.238**	**1.000**
Career total		67	134	14	31	7	0	2	16	8	1	24	2	0	1	1	1	.231	.283	.328	.991
Cubs total		**18**	**21**	**2**	**5**	**0**	**0**	**0**	**2**	**2**	**0**	**6**	**0**	**0**	**0**	**0**	**0**	**.238**	**.304**	**.238**	**1.000**

Hardy, John Doolittle (Jack)

HEIGHT: 6'0" THROWS: RIGHT BATS: RIGHT BORN: 6/23/1877 CLEVELAND, OHIO DIED: 10/20/1921 CLEVELAND, OHIO POSITIONS PLAYED: C, 2B, OF

YEAR	TEAM	GAMES	AB	RUNS	HITS	2B	3B	HR	RBI	BB	IBB	SO	HBP	SH	SF	SB	CS	BA	OBA	SA	FA
1903	Cle-A	5	19	1	3	1	0	0	1	1	—	—	0	0	—	1	—	.158	.200	.211	1.000
1907	**ChC-N**	**1**	**4**	**0**	**1**	**0**	**0**	**0**	**0**	**0**	—	—	**0**	**0**	—	**0**	—	**.250**	**.250**	**.250**	**.909**
1909	Was-A	10	24	3	4	0	0	0	4	1	—	—	0	0	—	0	—	.167	.200	.167	.977
1910	Was-A	7	8	1	2	0	0	0	0	0	—	—	0	0	—	0	—	.250	.250	.250	.875
Career average		6	14	1	3	0	0	0	1	1	—	—	0	0	—	0	—	.182	.211	.200	.947
Cubs average		**1**	**4**	**0**	**1**	**0**	**0**	**0**	**0**	**0**	—	—	**0**	**0**	—	**0**	—	**.250**	**.250**	**.250**	**.909**
Career total		23	55	5	10	1	0	0	5	2	—	—	0	0	—	1	—	.182	.211	.200	.947
Cubs total		**1**	**4**	**0**	**1**	**0**	**0**	**0**	**0**	**0**	—	—	**0**	**0**	—	**0**	—	**.250**	**.250**	**.250**	**.909**

Hargrave, Eugene Franklin (Bubbles)

HEIGHT: 5'10" THROWS: RIGHT BATS: RIGHT BORN: 7/15/1892 NEW HAVEN, INDIANA DIED: 2/23/1969 CINCINNATI, OHIO POSITIONS PLAYED: C

YEAR	TEAM	GAMES	AB	RUNS	HITS	2B	3B	HR	RBI	BB	IBB	SO	HBP	SH	SF	SB	CS	BA	OBA	SA	FA
1913	ChC-N	3	3	0	1	0	0	0	1	0	—	0	0	0	—	0	—	.333	.333	.333	1.000
1914	ChC-N	23	36	3	8	2	0	0	2	0	—	4	0	1	—	2	—	.222	.222	.278	.930
1915	ChC-N	15	19	2	3	0	1	0	2	1	—	5	0	0	—	0	—	.158	.200	.263	1.000
1921	Cin-N	93	263	28	76	17	8	1	38	12	—	15	3	6	—	4	2	.289	.327	.426	.973
1922	Cin-N	98	320	49	101	22	10	7	57	26	—	18	2	10	—	7	4	.316	.371	.513	.982
1923	Cin-N	118	378	54	126	23	9	10	78	44	—	22	12	10	—	4	5	.333	.419	.521	.988
1924	Cin-N	98	312	42	94	19	10	3	33	30	—	20	4	8	—	2	2	.301	.370	.455	.983
1925	Cin-N	87	273	28	82	13	6	2	33	25	—	23	1	3	—	4	3	.300	.361	.414	.979
1926	Cin-N	105	326	42	115	22	8	6	62	25	—	17	4	10	—	2	—	.353	.406	.525	.988
1927	Cin-N	102	305	36	94	18	3	0	35	31	—	18	2	11	—	0	—	.308	.376	.387	.988
1928	Cin-N	65	190	19	56	12	3	0	23	13	—	14	4	8	—	4	—	.295	.353	.389	.991
1930	NYY-A	45	108	11	30	7	0	0	12	10	—	9	0	3	—	0	0	.278	.339	.343	.992
Career average		71	211	26	66	13	5	2	31	18	—	14	3	6	—	2	1	.310	.372	.452	.983
Cubs average		**14**	**19**	**2**	**4**	**1**	**0**	**0**	**2**	**0**	**—**	**3**	**0**	**0**	**—**	**1**	**0**	**.207**	**.220**	**.276**	**.955**
Career total		852	2533	314	786	155	58	29	376	217	—	165	32	70	—	29	16	.310	.372	.452	.983
Cubs total		**41**	**58**	**5**	**12**	**2**	**1**	**0**	**5**	**1**	**—**	**9**	**0**	**1**	**—**	**2**	**0**	**.207**	**.220**	**.276**	**.955**

Harley, Richard Joseph (Dick)

HEIGHT: 5'10" THROWS: RIGHT BATS: LEFT BORN: 9/25/1872 PHILADELPHIA, PENNSYLVANIA DIED: 4/3/1952 PHILADELPHIA, PENNSYLVANIA
POSITIONS PLAYED: OF

YEAR	TEAM	GAMES	AB	RUNS	HITS	2B	3B	HR	RBI	BB	IBB	SO	HBP	SH	SF	SB	CS	BA	OBA	SA	FA
1897	StL-N	89	330	43	96	6	4	3	35	36	—	—	11	6	—	23	—	.291	.379	.361	.899
1898	StL-N	142	549	74	135	6	5	0	42	34	—	—	22	6	—	13	—	.246	.316	.275	.926
1899	Cle-N	142	567	70	142	15	7	1	50	40	—	—	13	4	—	15	—	.250	.315	.307	.924
1900	Cin-N	5	21	2	9	1	0	0	5	1	—	—	0	2	—	4	—	.429	.455	.476	1.000
1901	Cin-N	133	535	69	146	13	2	4	27	31	—	—	9	21	—	37	—	.273	.323	.327	.898
1902	Det-A	125	491	59	138	9	8	2	44	36	—	—	12	10	—	20	—	.281	.345	.344	.930
1903	ChC-N	104	386	72	89	9	1	0	33	45	—	—	11	15	—	27	—	.231	.328	.259	.923
Career average		106	411	56	108	8	4	1	34	32	—	—	11	9	—	20	—	.262	.332	.312	.918
Cubs average		**104**	**386**	**72**	**89**	**9**	**1**	**0**	**33**	**45**	**—**	**—**	**11**	**15**	**—**	**27**	**—**	**.231**	**.328**	**.259**	**.923**
Career total		740	2879	389	755	59	27	10	236	223	—	—	78	64	—	139	—	.262	.332	.312	.918
Cubs total		**104**	**386**	**72**	**89**	**9**	**1**	**0**	**33**	**45**	**—**	**—**	**11**	**15**	**—**	**27**	**—**	**.231**	**.328**	**.259**	**.923**

Harris, Victor Lanier (Vic)

HEIGHT: 5'11" THROWS: RIGHT BATS: BOTH BORN: 3/27/1950 LOS ANGELES, CALIFORNIA POSITIONS PLAYED: 2B, 3B, SS, OF

YEAR	TEAM	GAMES	AB	RUNS	HITS	2B	3B	HR	RBI	BB	IBB	SO	HBP	SH	SF	SB	CS	BA	OBA	SA	FA
1972	Tex-A	61	186	8	26	5	1	0	10	12	1	39	0	0	0	7	3	.140	.192	.177	.961
1973	Tex-A	152	555	71	138	14	7	8	44	55	1	81	2	2	4	13	12	.249	.317	.342	.954
1974	**ChC-N**	**62**	**200**	**18**	**39**	**6**	**3**	**0**	**11**	**29**	**3**	**26**	**0**	**4**	**2**	**9**	**3**	**.195**	**.294**	**.255**	**.943**
1975	**ChC-N**	**51**	**56**	**6**	**10**	**0**	**0**	**0**	**5**	**6**	**0**	**7**	**0**	**1**	**1**	**0**	**0**	**.179**	**.254**	**.179**	**.935**
1976	StL-N	97	259	21	59	12	3	1	19	16	0	55	1	6	0	1	2	.228	.275	.309	.952
1977	SF-N	69	165	28	43	12	0	2	14	19	1	36	0	2	3	2	1	.261	.332	.370	.954
1978	SF-N	53	100	8	15	4	0	1	11	11	1	24	0	3	2	0	0	.150	.230	.220	.951
1980	Mil-A	34	89	8	19	4	1	1	7	12	0	13	0	1	1	4	1	.213	.304	.315	.969
Career average		72	201	21	44	7	2	2	15	20	1	35	0	2	2	5	3	.217	.287	.295	.953
Cubs average		**57**	**128**	**12**	**25**	**3**	**2**	**0**	**8**	**18**	**2**	**17**	**0**	**3**	**2**	**5**	**2**	**.191**	**.286**	**.238**	**.942**
Career total		579	1610	168	349	57	15	13	121	160	7	281	3	19	13	36	22	.217	.287	.295	.953
Cubs total		**113**	**256**	**24**	**49**	**6**	**3**	**0**	**16**	**35**	**3**	**33**	**0**	**5**	**3**	**9**	**3**	**.191**	**.286**	**.238**	**.942**

Hartnett, Charles Leo (Gabby)

HEIGHT: 6'1" THROWS: RIGHT BATS: RIGHT BORN: 12/20/1900 WOONSOCKET, RHODE ISLAND DIED: 12/20/1972 PARK RIDGE, ILLINOIS
POSITIONS PLAYED: C, 1B

YEAR	TEAM	GAMES	AB	RUNS	HITS	2B	3B	HR	RBI	BB	IBB	SO	HBP	SH	SF	SB	CS	BA	OBA	SA	FA
1922	ChC-N	31	72	4	14	1	1	0	4	6	—	8	0	4	—	1	0	.194	.256	.236	.982
1923	ChC-N	85	231	28	62	12	2	8	39	25	—	22	3	4	—	4	0	.268	.347	.442	.989
1924	ChC-N	111	354	56	106	17	7	16	67	39	—	37	5	9	—	10	2	.299	.377	.523	.963
1925	ChC-N	117	398	61	115	28	3	24	67	36	—	77	2	7	—	1	5	.289	.351	.555	.958
1926	ChC-N	93	284	35	78	25	3	8	41	32	—	37	2	7	—	0	—	.275	.352	.468	.978
1927	ChC-N	127	449	56	132	32	5	10	80	44	—	42	3	13	—	2	—	.294	.361	.454	.973
1928	ChC-N	120	388	61	117	26	9	14	57	65	—	32	2	9	—	3	—	.302	.404	.523	.989
1929	ChC-N	25	22	2	6	2	1	1	9	5	—	5	0	1	—	1	—	.273	.407	.591	1.000
1930	ChC-N	141	508	84	172	31	3	37	122	55	—	62	1	14	—	0	—	.339	.404	.630	.989
1931	ChC-N	116	380	53	107	32	1	8	70	52	—	48	1	5	—	3	—	.282	.370	.434	.981
1932	ChC-N	121	406	52	110	25	3	12	52	51	—	59	1	4	—	0	—	.271	.354	.436	.983
1933	ChC-N	140	490	55	135	21	4	16	88	37	—	51	0	8	—	1	—	.276	.326	.433	.989
1934	ChC-N	130	438	58	131	21	1	22	90	37	—	46	3	9	—	0	—	.299	.358	.502	.996
1935	ChC-N	116	413	67	142	32	6	13	91	41	—	46	1	6	—	1	—	.344	.404	.545	.984
1936	ChC-N	121	424	49	130	25	6	7	64	30	—	36	6	8	—	0	—	.307	.361	.443	.991
1937	ChC-N	110	356	47	126	21	6	12	82	43	—	19	0	6	—	0	—	.354	.424	.548	.996
1938	ChC-N	88	299	40	82	19	1	10	59	48	—	17	3	3	—	1	—	.274	.380	.445	.995

(continued)

Charles Leo "Gabby" Hartnett, c-1b, 1922–41

While baseball fans argue the merits of Yogi Berra, Johnny Bench and Mickey Cochrane, Cubs fans have long insisted that Hartnett is also in that upper pantheon of great catching stars.

Hartnett was born on December 20, 1900, in Woonsocket, Rhode Island. He came from a family of ballplayers, as his father and several older brothers had played in town teams and semipro leagues throughout the East.

Hartnett was signed to a professional contract at age 20 by Worcester of the Eastern League. He hit .264 and was signed the next year by the Cubs for $2,500.

In 1922 and 1923, Hartnett was a part-time backstopper, playing a total of only 66 games behind the plate in that span. But in 1924, Hartnett became a regular, hitting .299 with 67 RBIs.

Veteran pitcher Grover Cleveland "Pete" Alexander recognized Hartnett's abilities as a catcher early on. When Hartnett came up in 1922, Alexander requested that Hartnett catch him. That began a relationship that lasted until Alexander was traded in 1926.

Hartnett was a shy man, which of course was why Cubs veterans tagged him with his nickname.

His talent, though, spoke volumes. He was simply "the perfect catcher," according to Joe McCarthy, who managed Hartnett in the 1920s. He could hit for average and power, was durable and was the greatest fielding catcher of his era. He was a great clutch performer, and he gave the Cubs a huge advantage at that position throughout his career.

Seven times, he led the National League in fielding percentage. In 1925, 1927, 1930 and 1934, Hartnett led all National League catchers in putouts, assists, double plays and total fielding chances per game. Leading the league in two such categories four times is the mark of a solid player. Doing so in all four defensive columns reveals Hartnett to be a dominating defensive performer. Consider that Cochrane, Bench and Berra combined only led their respective leagues in all those categories as many times.

In 1929 an arm injury limited Hartnett to only 25 games, but in 1930 he came back with a career year, hitting .339, with 122 RBIs and 37 home runs to go along with his stellar work behind the plate. That year remains one of the best two-way performances by a catcher in league history as Hartnett went on to become the first catcher in major league history to top 30 home runs, 100 RBIs and a .300 batting average that season.

(continued)

YEAR	TEAM	GAMES	AB	RUNS	HITS	2B	3B	HR	RBI	BB	IBB	SO	HBP	SH	SF	SB	CS	BA	OBA	SA	FA
1939	ChC-N	97	306	36	85	18	2	12	59	37	—	32	1	7	—	0	—	.278	.358	.467	.992
1940	ChC-N	37	64	3	17	3	0	1	12	8	—	7	0	1	—	0	—	.266	.347	.359	.952
1941	NYG-N	64	150	20	45	5	0	5	26	12	—	14	1	2	—	0	—	.300	.356	.433	.994
Career average		100	322	43	96	20	3	12	59	35	—	35	2	6	—	1	0	.297	.370	.489	.984
Cubs average		101	331	45	98	21	3	12	61	36	—	36	2	7	—	1	0	.297	.370	.490	.984
Career total		1990	6432	867	1912	396	64	236	1179	703	—	697	35	127	—	28	7	.297	.370	.489	.984
Cubs total		1926	6282	847	1867	391	64	231	1153	691	—	683	34	125	—	28	7	.297	.370	.490	.984

Hartsel, Tully Frederick (Topsy)

HEIGHT: 5'5" THROWS: LEFT BATS: LEFT BORN: 6/26/1874 POLK, OHIO DIED: 10/14/1944 TOLEDO, OHIO POSITIONS PLAYED: OF

YEAR	TEAM	GAMES	AB	RUNS	HITS	2B	3B	HR	RBI	BB	IBB	SO	HBP	SH	SF	SB	CS	BA	OBA	SA	FA
1898	Lou-N	22	71	11	23	0	0	0	9	11	—	—	1	2	—	2	—	.324	.422	.324	.931
1899	Lou-N	30	75	8	18	1	1	1	7	11	—	—	1	2	—	1	—	.240	.345	.320	.927
1900	Cin-N	18	64	10	21	2	1	2	5	8	—	—	0	6	—	7	—	.328	.403	.484	.957
1901	**ChN-N**	140	558	111	187	25	16	7	54	74	—	—	1	3	—	41	—	.335	.414	.475	.951
1902	Phi-A	137	545	109	154	20	12	5	58	87	—	—	2	3	—	47	—	.283	.383	.391	.955
1903	Phi-A	98	373	65	116	19	14	5	26	49	—	—	0	6	—	13	—	.311	.391	.477	.968
1904	Phi-A	147	534	79	135	17	12	2	25	75	—	—	2	13	—	19	—	.253	.347	.341	.959

(continued)

In 1935 Hartnett was once again an overpowering two-way player, hitting .344 (third in the league), with 32 homers and 91 RBIs. He also topped National League catchers in fielding percentage, assists, double plays and total fielding chances per game, plus he was second in putouts. He led the Cubs to the National League crown and won the MVP for his efforts.

Hartnett was an All-Star six consecutive years. His most memorable moment in the All-Star Game was in 1934. Hartnett was the catcher for the National League when the Giants' Carl Hubbell fanned, in order, Babe Ruth, Lou Gehrig, Jimmie Foxx, Al Simmons and Mickey Cochrane over a two-inning span.

"We have to look at that guy all season," shouted Hartnett to the American League bench after Cochrane went down.

But his most famous moment was yet to come. In 1938, with the Cubs battling the Pirates for the NL crown, Hartnett blasted an 0-2 pitch to break a 5-5 tie with Pittsburgh in a late-September game. The home run sailed into the stands as dusk was falling. The so-called "Homer in the Gloamin'" put the Cubs in first place to stay.

He performed well in two of the four World Series in which he played. In 1929 his arm injury limited him to three hitless at-bats. In 1932, however, he hit .313 with a .625 slugging average with two doubles and a home run against the Yankees. He hit .292 in the 1935 Series, but in 1938 he hit .091 in three games.

Hartnett had been named to manage the Cubs in 1938, and he continued in that role until 1940 when he was fired. Hartnett's principal problem was that he expected his players to be as good as he was. When they were not, he got impatient. As much as Cubs players respected Hartnett the All-Star catcher, they didn't much appreciate Hartnett the constantly annoyed manager. Hartnett signed with the Giants and hit .300 as a pinch hitter and backup in 1941 before retiring.

Hartnett managed in the minor leagues for six years, and he later took a position as a coach in Kansas City for a few years, beginning in 1964. Hartnett died in 1972.

Hartnett's name is all over the Cubs record books. He is 10th in hits all-time with Chicago with 1,867, 6th in total bases with 3,079, 6th in doubles with 391, 6th in home runs with 231, 6th in extra-base hits with 686, 5th in RBIs with 1,153 and 10th in walks with 691.

He also holds the Cubs career record for most putouts with 7,154, most total chances with 8,531 and most double plays with 162. His 24-game hitting streak in 1937 is tied for 10th best with Stan Hack.

Hartnett was elected to the Hall of Fame in 1955.

(Hartsel, continued)

YEAR	TEAM	GAMES	AB	RUNS	HITS	2B	3B	HR	RBI	BB	IBB	SO	HBP	SH	SF	SB	CS	BA	OBA	SA	FA
1905	Phi-A	150	538	88	148	22	8	0	28	121	—	—	1	14	—	37	—	.275	.409	.346	.939
1906	Phi-A	144	533	96	136	21	9	1	30	88	—	—	2	9	—	31	—	.255	.363	.334	.969
1907	Phi-A	143	507	93	142	23	6	3	29	106	—	—	0	11	—	20	—	.280	.405	.367	.967
1908	Phi-A	129	460	73	112	16	6	4	29	93	—	—	0	8	—	15	—	.243	.371	.330	.960
1909	Phi-A	83	267	30	72	4	4	1	18	48	—	—	0	8	—	3	—	.270	.381	.326	.966
1910	Phi-A	90	285	45	63	10	3	0	22	58	—	—	0	8	—	11	—	.221	.353	.277	.945
1911	Phi-A	25	38	8	9	2	0	0	1	8	—	—	2	3	—	0	—	.237	.396	.289	.941
Career average		97	346	59	95	13	7	2	24	60	—	—	1	7	—	18	—	.276	.384	.370	.956
Cubs average		**140**	**558**	**111**	**187**	**25**	**16**	**7**	**54**	**74**	**—**	**—**	**1**	**3**	**—**	**41**	**—**	**.335**	**.414**	**.475**	**.951**
Career total		1356	4848	826	1336	182	92	31	341	837	—	—	12	96	—	247	—	.276	.384	.370	.956
Cubs total		**140**	**558**	**111**	**187**	**25**	**16**	**7**	**54**	**74**	**—**	**—**	**1**	**3**	**—**	**41**	**—**	**.335**	**.414**	**.475**	**.951**

Harvey, Ervin King (Erwin *or* ZaZa)

HEIGHT: 6'0" THROWS: LEFT BATS: LEFT BORN: 1/5/1879 SARATOGA, CALIFORNIA DIED: 6/3/1954 SANTA MONICA, CALIFORNIA POSITIONS PLAYED: P, OF

YEAR	TEAM	GAMES	AB	RUNS	HITS	2B	3B	HR	RBI	BB	IBB	SO	HBP	SH	SF	SB	CS	BA	OBA	SA	FA
1900	**ChN-N**	**2**	**3**	**0**	**0**	**0**	**0**	**0**	**0**	**0**		**—**	**0**	**0**	**—**	**0**	**—**	**.000**	**.000**	**.000**	**1.000**
1901	CWS-A	17	40	11	10	3	1	0	3	2	—	—	1	2	—	1	—	.250	.302	.375	.930
1901	Cle-A	45	170	21	60	5	5	1	24	9	—	—	2	1	—	15	—	.353	.392	.459	.890
1902	Cle-A	12	46	5	16	2	0	0	5	3	—	—	0	1	—	1	—	.348	.388	.391	1.000
Career average		25	86	12	29	3	2	0	11	5	—	—	1	1	—	6	—	.332	.373	.429	.914
Cubs average		**2**	**3**	**0**	**0**	**0**	**0**	**0**	**0**	**0**	**—**	**—**	**0**	**0**	**—**	**0**	**—**	**.000**	**.000**	**.000**	**1.000**
Career total		76	259	37	86	10	6	1	32	14	—	—	3	4	—	17	—	.332	.373	.429	.914
Cubs total		**2**	**3**	**0**	**0**	**0**	**0**	**0**	**0**	**0**	**—**	**—**	**0**	**0**	**—**	**0**	**—**	**.000**	**.000**	**.000**	**1.000**

Hassey, Ronald William (Ron)

HEIGHT: 6'2" THROWS: RIGHT BATS: LEFT BORN: 2/27/1953 TUCSON, ARIZONA POSITIONS PLAYED: C, 1B

YEAR	TEAM	GAMES	AB	RUNS	HITS	2B	3B	HR	RBI	BB	IBB	SO	HBP	SH	SF	SB	CS	BA	OBA	SA	FA
1978	Cle-A	25	74	5	15	0	0	2	9	5	0	7	1	1	2	2	0	.203	.256	.284	.993
1979	Cle-A	75	223	20	64	14	0	4	32	19	2	19	0	4	3	1	0	.287	.339	.404	.993
1980	Cle-A	130	390	43	124	18	4	8	65	49	3	51	1	1	6	0	2	.318	.390	.446	.994
1981	Cle-A	61	190	8	44	4	0	1	25	17	0	11	2	3	3	0	1	.232	.297	.268	.992
1982	Cle-A	113	323	33	81	18	0	5	34	53	5	32	1	3	2	3	2	.251	.356	.353	.993
1983	Cle-A	117	341	48	92	21	0	6	42	38	2	35	2	2	5	2	2	.270	.342	.384	.995
1984	Cle-A	48	149	11	38	5	1	0	19	15	2	26	0	0	1	1	0	.255	.321	.302	.996
1984	**ChC-N**	**19**	**33**	**5**	**11**	**0**	**0**	**2**	**5**	**4**	**1**	**6**	**0**	**0**	**0**	**0**	**1**	**.333**	**.405**	**.515**	**.982**
1985	NYY-A	92	267	31	79	16	1	13	42	28	4	21	3	0	0	0	0	.296	.369	.509	.984
1986	NYY-A	64	191	23	57	14	0	6	29	24	1	16	2	1	1	1	1	.298	.381	.466	.985
1986	CWS-A	49	150	22	53	11	1	3	20	22	2	11	1	0	1	0	0	.353	.437	.500	1.000
1987	CWS-A	49	145	15	31	9	0	3	12	17	2	11	2	0	1	0	0	.214	.303	.338	1.000
1988	Oak-A	107	323	32	83	15	0	7	45	30	1	42	4	3	5	2	0	.257	.323	.368	.994
1989	Oak-A	97	268	29	61	12	0	5	23	24	2	45	1	1	4	1	0	.228	.290	.328	.991
1990	Oak-A	94	254	18	54	7	0	5	22	27	3	29	1	1	3	0	0	.213	.288	.299	.997
1991	Mon-N	52	119	5	27	8	0	1	14	13	1	16	0	2	1	1	1	.227	.301	.319	.989
Career average		85	246	25	65	12	1	5	31	28	2	27	2	2	3	1	1	.266	.340	.382	.992
Cubs average		**19**	**33**	**5**	**·11**	**0**	**0**	**2**	**5**	**4**	**1**	**6**	**0**	**0**	**0**	**0**	**1**	**.333**	**.405**	**.515**	**.982**
Career total		1192	3440	348	914	172	7	71	438	385	31	378	21	22	38	14	10	.266	.340	.382	.992
Cubs total		**19**	**33**	**5**	**11**	**0**	**0**	**2**	**5**	**4**	**1**	**6**	**0**	**0**	**0**	**0**	**1**	**.333**	**.405**	**.515**	**.982**

Hatcher, William Augustus (Billy)

HEIGHT: 5'10" THROWS: RIGHT BATS: RIGHT BORN: 10/4/1960 WILLIAMS, ARIZONA POSITIONS PLAYED: 2B, OF

YEAR	TEAM	GAMES	AB	RUNS	HITS	2B	3B	HR	RBI	BB	IBB	SO	HBP	SH	SF	SB	CS	BA	OBA	SA	FA
1984	**ChC-N**	**8**	**9**	**1**	**1**	**0**	**0**	**0**	**0**	**1**	**1**	**0**	**0**	**0**	**0**	**2**	**0**	**.111**	**.200**	**.111**	**1.000**
1985	**ChC-N**	**53**	**163**	**24**	**40**	**12**	**1**	**2**	**10**	**8**	**0**	**12**	**3**	**2**	**2**	**2**	**4**	**.245**	**.290**	**.368**	**.988**
1986	Hou-N	127	419	55	108	15	4	6	36	22	1	52	5	6	1	38	14	.258	.302	.356	.983
1987	Hou-N	141	564	96	167	28	3	11	63	42	1	70	9	7	5	53	9	.296	.352	.415	.986
1988	Hou-N	145	530	79	142	25	4	7	52	37	4	56	8	8	8	32	13	.268	.321	.370	.983
1989	Hou-N	108	395	49	90	15	3	3	44	30	2	53	1	3	4	22	6	.228	.281	.304	.991
1989	Pit-N	27	86	10	21	4	0	1	7	0	0	9	1	0	0	2	1	.244	.253	.326	1.000
1990	Cin-N	139	504	68	139	28	5	5	25	33	5	42	6	1	1	30	10	.276	.327	.381	.997
1991	Cin-N	138	442	45	116	25	3	4	41	26	4	55	7	4	3	11	9	.262	.312	.360	.981

(continued)

(continued)

YEAR	TEAM	GAMES	AB	RUNS	HITS	2B	3B	HR	RBI	BB	IBB	SO	HBP	SH	SF	SB	CS	BA	OBA	SA	FA
1992	Cin-N	43	94	10	27	3	0	2	10	5	0	11	0	0	3	0	2	.287	.314	.383	.967
1992	Bos-A	75	315	37	75	16	2	1	23	17	1	41	3	6	1	4	6	.238	.283	.311	.968
1993	Bos-A	136	508	71	146	24	3	9	57	28	4	46	11	11	4	14	7	.287	.336	.400	.993
1994	Bos-A	44	164	24	40	9	1	1	18	11	0	14	1	3	2	4	7	.287	.336	.400	.993
1994	Phi-N	43	134	15	33	5	1	2	13	6	0	14	1	3	2	4	5	.244	.292	.329	.968
1995	Tex-A	6	12	2	1	1	0	0	0	1	0	1	0	0	0	0	0	.083	.154	.167	1.000
Career average		103	362	49	96	18	3	5	33	22	2	40	5	4	3	18	7	.264	.312	.364	.986
Cubs average		**31**	**86**	**13**	**21**	**6**	**1**	**1**	**5**	**5**	**1**	**6**	**2**	**1**	**1**	**2**	**2**	**.238**	**.285**	**.355**	**.988**
Career total		1233	4339	586	1146	210	30	54	399	267	23	476	55	53	38	218	87	.264	.312	.364	.986
Cubs total		**61**	**172**	**25**	**41**	**12**	**1**	**2**	**10**	**9**	**1**	**12**	**3**	**2**	**2**	**4**	**4**	**.238**	**.285**	**.355**	**.988**

Hatton, Grady Edgebert

HEIGHT: 5'8"   THROWS: RIGHT   BATS: LEFT   BORN: 10/7/1922 BEAUMONT, TEXAS   POSITIONS PLAYED: 1B, 2B, 3B, SS, OF

YEAR	TEAM	GAMES	AB	RUNS	HITS	2B	3B	HR	RBI	BB	IBB	SO	HBP	SH	SF	SB	CS	BA	OBA	SA	FA
1946	Cin-N	116	436	56	118	18	3	14	69	66	—	53	2	3	—	6	—	.271	.369	.422	.938
1947	Cin-N	146	524	91	147	24	8	16	77	81	—	50	0	5	—	7	—	.281	.377	.448	.938
1948	Cin-N	133	458	58	110	17	2	9	44	72	—	50	0	3	—	7	—	.240	.343	.345	.933
1949	Cin-N	137	537	71	141	38	5	11	69	62	—	48	3	3	—	4	—	.263	.342	.413	.975
1950	Cin-N	130	438	67	114	17	1	11	54	70	—	39	3	3	—	6	—	.260	.366	.379	.954
1951	Cin-N	96	331	41	84	9	3	4	37	33	—	32	0	2	—	4	—	.254	.321	.335	.972
1952	Cin-N	128	433	48	92	14	1	9	57	66	—	60	2	5	—	4	2	.212	.319	.312	.990
1953	Cin-N	83	159	22	37	3	1	7	22	29	—	24	0	3	—	5	4	.233	.351	.396	.995
1954	Cin-N	1	1	0	0	0	0	0	0	0	—	0	0	0	0	0	0	.000	.000	.000	—
1954	CWS-A	13	30	3	5	1	0	0	3	5	—	3	0	0	1	1	0	.167	.278	.200	1.000
1954	Bos-A	99	302	40	85	12	3	5	33	58	—	25	2	3	1	1	1	.281	.399	.391	.966
1955	Bos-A	126	380	48	93	11	4	4	49	76	3	28	0	4	5	0	1	.245	.367	.326	.976
1956	Bos-A	5	5	0	2	0	0	0	2	0	0	0	0	0	0	0	0	.400	.400	.400	—
1956	StL-N	44	73	10	18	1	2	0	7	13	0	7	0	3	0	1	0	.247	.360	.315	.951
1956	Bal-A	27	61	4	9	1	0	1	3	13	1	6	0	1	0	0	0	.148	.297	.213	.985
1960	**ChC-N**	**28**	**38**	**3**	**13**	**0**	**0**	**0**	**7**	**2**	**1**	**5**	**1**	**1**	**1**	**0**	**0**	**.342**	**.381**	**.342**	**.931**
Career average		109	351	47	89	14	3	8	44	54	0	36	1	3	1	4	1	.254	.354	.374	.964
Cubs average		**28**	**38**	**3**	**13**	**0**	**0**	**0**	**7**	**2**	**1**	**5**	**1**	**1**	**1**	**0**	**0**	**.342**	**.381**	**.342**	**.931**
Career total		1312	4206	562	1068	166	33	91	533	646	5	430	13	39	8	42	9	.254	.354	.374	.964
Cubs total		**28**	**38**	**3**	**13**	**0**	**0**	**0**	**7**	**2**	**1**	**5**	**1**	**1**	**1**	**0**	**0**	**.342**	**.381**	**.342**	**.931**

Hayden, John Francis (Jack)

HEIGHT: 5'9"   THROWS: LEFT   BATS: LEFT   BORN: 10/21/1880 BRYN MAWR, PENNSYLVANIA   DIED: 8/3/1942 HAVERFORD, PENNSYLVANIA
POSITIONS PLAYED: OF

YEAR	TEAM	GAMES	AB	RUNS	HITS	2B	3B	HR	RBI	BB	IBB	SO	HBP	SH	SF	SB	CS	BA	OBA	SA	FA
1901	Phi-A	51	211	35	56	6	4	0	17	18	—	—	0	6	—	4	—	.265	.323	.332	.841
1906	Bos-A	85	322	22	80	6	4	1	14	17	—	—	3	10	—	6	—	.248	.292	.301	.973
1908	**ChC-N**	**11**	**45**	**3**	**9**	**2**	**0**	**0**	**2**	**1**	**—**	**—**	**0**	**2**	**—**	**1**	**—**	**.200**	**.217**	**.244**	**1.000**
Career average		49	193	20	48	5	3	0	11	12	—	—	1	6	—	4	—	.251	.298	.308	.929
Cubs average		**11**	**45**	**3**	**9**	**2**	**0**	**0**	**2**	**1**	**—**	**—**	**0**	**2**	**—**	**1**	**—**	**.200**	**.217**	**.244**	**1.000**
Career total		147	578	60	145	14	8	1	33	36	—	—	3	18	—	11	—	.251	.298	.308	.929
Cubs total		**11**	**45**	**3**	**9**	**2**	**0**	**0**	**2**	**1**	**—**	**—**	**0**	**2**	**—**	**1**	**—**	**.200**	**.217**	**.244**	**1.000**

Hayes, William Ernest (Bill)

HEIGHT: 6'0"   THROWS: RIGHT   BATS: RIGHT   BORN: 10/24/1957 CHEVERLY, MARYLAND   POSITIONS PLAYED: C

YEAR	TEAM	GAMES	AB	RUNS	HITS	2B	3B	HR	RBI	BB	IBB	SO	HBP	SH	SF	SB	CS	BA	OBA	SA	FA
1980	**ChC-N**	**4**	**9**	**0**	**2**	**1**	**0**	**0**	**0**	**0**	**0**	**3**	**0**	**0**	**0**	**0**	**0**	**.222**	**.222**	**.333**	**1.000**
1981	**ChC-N**	**1**	**0**	**0**	**0**	**0**	**0**	**0**	**0**	**0**	**0**	**0**	**0**	**0**	**0**	**0**	**0**	**—**	**—**	**—**	**—**
Career average		3	5	0	1	1	0	0	0	0	0	2	0	0	0	0	0	.222	.222	.333	1.000
Cubs average		**3**	**5**	**0**	**1**	**1**	**0**	**0**	**0**	**0**	**0**	**2**	**0**	**0**	**0**	**0**	**0**	**.222**	**.222**	**.333**	**1.000**
Career total		5	9	0	2	1	0	0	0	0	0	3	0	0	0	0	0	.222	.222	.333	1.000
Cubs total		**5**	**9**	**0**	**2**	**1**	**0**	**0**	**0**	**0**	**0**	**3**	**0**	**0**	**0**	**0**	**0**	**.222**	**.222**	**.333**	**1.000**

Heath, William Chris (Bill)
HEIGHT: 5'8" THROWS: RIGHT BATS: LEFT BORN: 3/10/1939 YUBA CITY, CALIFORNIA POSITIONS PLAYED: C

YEAR	TEAM	GAMES	AB	RUNS	HITS	2B	3B	HR	RBI	BB	IBB	SO	HBP	SH	SF	SB	CS	BA	OBA	SA	FA
1965	CWS-A	1	1	0	0	0	0	0	0	0	0	0	0	0	0	0	0	.000	.000	.000	—
1966	Hou-N	55	123	12	37	6	0	0	8	9	1	11	1	0	0	1	0	.301	.353	.350	.995
1967	Hou-N	9	11	0	1	0	0	0	0	4	0	3	0	0	0	0	0	.091	.333	.091	1.000
1967	Det-A	20	32	0	4	0	0	0	4	1	0	4	0	0	0	0	0	.125	.152	.125	1.000
1969	**ChC-N**	**27**	**32**	**1**	**5**	**0**	**1**	**0**	**1**	**12**	**2**	**4**	**0**	**0**	**1**	**0**	**0**	**.156**	**.378**	**.219**	**.979**
Career average		28	50	3	12	2	0	0	3	7	1	6	0	0	1	0	0	.236	.326	.276	.993
Cubs average		**27**	**32**	**1**	**5**	**0**	**1**	**0**	**1**	**12**	**2**	**4**	**0**	**0**	**1**	**0**	**0**	**.156**	**.378**	**.219**	**.979**
Career total		112	199	13	47	6	1	0	13	26	3	22	1	0	1	1	0	.236	.326	.276	.993
Cubs total		**27**	**32**	**1**	**5**	**0**	**1**	**0**	**1**	**12**	**2**	**4**	**0**	**0**	**1**	**0**	**0**	**.156**	**.378**	**.219**	**.979**

Heathcote, Clifton Earl (Cliff *or* Rubberhead)
HEIGHT: 5'10" THROWS: LEFT BATS: LEFT BORN: 1/24/1898 GLEN ROCK, PENNSYLVANIA DIED: 1/18/1939 YORK, PENNSYLVANIA
POSITIONS PLAYED: 1B, OF

YEAR	TEAM	GAMES	AB	RUNS	HITS	2B	3B	HR	RBI	BB	IBB	SO	HBP	SH	SF	SB	CS	BA	OBA	SA	FA
1918	StL-N	88	348	37	90	12	3	4	32	20	—	40	1	6	—	12	—	.259	.301	.345	.934
1919	StL-N	114	401	53	112	13	4	1	29	20	—	41	1	11	—	27	—	.279	.315	.339	.970
1920	StL-N	133	489	55	139	18	8	3	56	25	—	31	1	16	—	21	14	.284	.320	.372	.964
1921	StL-N	62	156	18	38	6	2	0	9	10	—	9	1	10	—	7	5	.244	.293	.308	.926
1922	StL-N	34	98	11	24	5	2	0	14	9	—	4	1	4	—	0	2	.245	.315	.337	.950
1922	**ChC-N**	**76**	**243**	**37**	**68**	**8**	**7**	**1**	**34**	**18**	**—**	**15**	**0**	**8**	**—**	**5**	**2**	**.280**	**.330**	**.383**	**.986**
1923	**ChC-N**	**117**	**393**	**48**	**98**	**14**	**3**	**1**	**27**	**25**	**—**	**22**	**2**	**11**	**—**	**32**	**17**	**.249**	**.298**	**.308**	**.980**
1924	**ChC-N**	**113**	**392**	**66**	**121**	**19**	**7**	**0**	**30**	**28**	**—**	**28**	**1**	**12**	**—**	**26**	**24**	**.309**	**.356**	**.393**	**.979**
1925	**ChC-N**	**109**	**380**	**57**	**100**	**14**	**5**	**5**	**39**	**39**	**—**	**26**	**7**	**12**	**—**	**15**	**11**	**.263**	**.343**	**.366**	**.970**

(continued)

Clifton "Cliff," "Rubberhead" Earl Heathcote, of-1b, 1918–32

Cliff Heathcote was a veteran left-handed hitter who led off for the Cubs and manned the outfield for several years, as well as being a valuable utilityman off the bench in the pennant-winning year of 1929.

Born on January 24, 1898, in Glen Rock, Pennsylvania, Heathcote broke into the major leagues with the St. Louis Cardinals in 1918. He became a full-time player the next season, hitting .279.

The Cubs acquired Heathcote in one of the odder trades in baseball history. Heathcote was traded for Max Flack between games of a doubleheader between the Cubs and St. Louis. Neither player had had a hit in the first game, but in the second, they both connected for safeties. The Cubs won both games.

The slim (5'10", 160 pounds) Heathcote was never a power hitter for the Cubs. He only hit 42 homers in his career, but he was adept at getting on base and was also a smart base runner. Heathcote cracked the .300 mark in 1924 and 1929 and hit .294 in 1927.

In 1922 Heathcote was five for five, with five runs scored in a wild 26-23 Cubs win over the Phillies in the highest scoring game in major league history.

He also honed his base-stealing skills. Although leading the team in base swipes only once, when he stole 26 bases in 1924, Heathcote stole 117 bases as a Cub, the most of any Chicago player in the 1920s.

Heathcote became a utility player and pinch hitter for Chicago from 1927 to 1930. In 1931 he was traded to the Reds. He played one more year before retiring with the Phillies in 1932. He died in York, Pennsylvania, in 1939.

(continued)																					
1926	ChC-N	139	510	98	141	33	3	10	53	58	—	30	2	19	—	18	—	.276	.353	.412	.985
1927	ChC-N	83	228	28	67	12	4	2	25	20	—	16	3	7	—	6	—	.294	.359	.408	.987
1928	ChC-N	67	137	26	39	8	0	3	18	17	—	12	0	5	—	6	—	.285	.364	.409	.973
1929	ChC-N	82	224	45	70	17	0	2	31	25	—	17	1	7	—	9	—	.313	.384	.415	.985
1930	ChC-N	70	150	30	39	10	1	9	18	18	—	15	1	2	—	4	—	.260	.343	.520	.986
1931	Cin-N	90	252	24	65	15	6	0	28	32	—	16	0	2	—	3	—	.258	.342	.365	.989
1932	Cin-N	8	3	3	0	0	0	0	0	0	—	0	0	0	—	0	—	.000	.000	.000	—
1932	Phi-N	30	39	7	11	2	0	1	5	3	—	3	0	2	—	0	—	.282	.333	.410	.962
Career average		94	296	43	81	14	4	3	30	24	—	22	1	9	—	13	5	.275	.333	.375	.971
Cubs average		**95**	**295**	**48**	**83**	**15**	**3**	**4**	**31**	**28**	**—**	**20**	**2**	**9**	**—**	**13**	**6**	**.280**	**.345**	**.390**	**.981**
Career total		1415	4443	643	1222	206	55	42	448	367	—	325	22	134	—	191	75	.275	.333	.375	.971
Cubs total		**856**	**2657**	**435**	**743**	**135**	**30**	**33**	**275**	**248**	**—**	**181**	**17**	**83**	**—**	**121**	**54**	**.280**	**.345**	**.390**	**.981**

Hebner, Richard Joseph (Richie)
HEIGHT: 6'1"   THROWS: RIGHT   BATS: LEFT   BORN: 11/26/1947 BOSTON, MASSACHUSETTS   POSITIONS PLAYED: 1B, 2B, 3B, OF

YEAR	TEAM	GAMES	AB	RUNS	HITS	2B	3B	HR	RBI	BB	IBB	SO	HBP	SH	SF	SB	CS	BA	OBA	SA	FA
1968	Pit-N	2	1	0	0	0	0	0	0	0	0	0	0	0	0	0	0	.000	.000	.000	—
1969	Pit-N	129	459	72	138	23	4	8	47	53	10	53	8	9	3	4	1	.301	.380	.420	.944
1970	Pit-N	120	420	60	122	24	8	11	46	42	5	48	7	3	3	2	3	.290	.362	.464	.940
1971	Pit-N	112	388	50	105	17	8	17	67	32	1	68	3	5	6	2	2	.271	.326	.487	.949
1972	Pit-N	124	427	63	128	24	4	19	72	52	7	54	6	0	7	0	0	.300	.378	.508	.969
1973	Pit-N	144	509	73	138	28	1	25	74	56	12	60	4	3	4	0	1	.271	.346	.477	.939
1974	Pit-N	146	550	97	160	21	6	18	68	60	5	53	6	5	7	0	3	.291	.363	.449	.937
1975	Pit-N	128	472	65	116	16	4	15	57	43	6	48	10	3	5	0	1	.246	.319	.392	.946
1976	Pit-N	132	434	60	108	21	3	8	51	47	2	39	4	4	4	1	3	.249	.325	.366	.953
1977	Phi-N	118	397	67	113	17	4	18	62	61	8	46	3	1	4	7	8	.285	.381	.484	.989
1978	Phi-N	137	435	61	123	22	3	17	71	53	16	58	9	4	4	4	7	.283	.369	.464	.993
1979	NYM-N	136	473	54	127	25	2	10	79	59	6	59	8	1	8	3	1	.268	.354	.393	.942
1980	Det-A	104	341	48	99	10	7	12	82	38	3	45	2	2	5	0	3	.290	.360	.466	.993
1981	Det-A	78	226	19	51	8	2	5	28	27	5	28	2	1	2	1	2	.226	.311	.345	.995
1982	Det-A	68	179	25	49	6	0	8	18	25	2	21	0	0	1	1	1	.274	.361	.441	.990
1982	Pit-N	25	70	6	21	2	0	2	12	5	0	3	0	1	0	4	0	.300	.347	.414	.982
1983	Pit-N	78	162	23	43	4	1	5	26	17	4	28	1	2	4	8	3	.265	.332	.395	.982
1984	**ChC-N**	**44**	**81**	**12**	**27**	**3**	**0**	**2**	**8**	**10**	**2**	**15**	**0**	**0**	**0**	**1**	**0**	**.333**	**.407**	**.444**	**.985**
1985	**ChC-N**	**83**	**120**	**10**	**26**	**2**	**0**	**3**	**22**	**7**	**1**	**15**	**1**	**0**	**0**	**0**	**1**	**.217**	**.266**	**.308**	**.971**
Career average		106	341	48	94	15	3	11	49	38	5	41	4	2	4	2	2	.276	.352	.438	.971
Cubs average		**64**	**101**	**11**	**27**	**3**	**0**	**3**	**15**	**9**	**2**	**15**	**1**	**0**	**0**	**1**	**1**	**.264**	**.324**	**.363**	**.975**
Career total		1908	6144	865	1694	273	57	203	890	687	95	741	74	44	67	38	40	.276	.352	.438	.971
Cubs total		**127**	**201**	**22**	**53**	**5**	**0**	**5**	**30**	**17**	**3**	**30**	**1**	**0**	**0**	**1**	**1**	**.264**	**.324**	**.363**	**.975**

Hechinger, Michael Vincent (Mike)
HEIGHT: 6'0"   THROWS: RIGHT   BATS: RIGHT   BORN: 2/14/1890 CHICAGO, ILLINOIS   DIED: 8/13/1967 CHICAGO, ILLINOIS   POSITIONS PLAYED: C

YEAR	TEAM	GAMES	AB	RUNS	HITS	2B	3B	HR	RBI	BB	IBB	SO	HBP	SH	SF	SB	CS	BA	OBA	SA	FA
1912	**ChC-N**	**2**	**3**	**0**	**0**	**0**	**0**	**0**	**0**	**2**	**—**	**0**	**0**	**0**	**—**	**0**	**—**	**.000**	**.400**	**.000**	**1.000**
1913	**ChC-N**	**2**	**2**	**0**	**0**	**0**	**0**	**0**	**0**	**0**	**—**	**0**	**0**	**0**	**—**	**0**	**—**	**.000**	**.000**	**.000**	**—**
1913	Bro-N	9	11	1	2	1	0	0	0	0	—	2	0	0	—	0	—	.182	.182	.273	1.000
Career average		7	8	1	1	1	0	0	0	1	—	1	0	0	—	0	—	.125	.222	.188	1.000
Cubs average		**2**	**3**	**0**	**0**	**0**	**0**	**0**	**0**	**1**	**—**	**1**	**0**	**0**	**—**	**0**	**—**	**.125**	**.222**	**.188**	**1.000**
Career total		13	16	1	2	1	0	0	0	2	—	2	0	0	—	0	—	.000	.286	.000	1.000
Cubs total		**4**	**5**	**0**	**0**	**0**	**0**	**0**	**0**	**2**	**—**	**0**	**0**	**0**	**—**	**0**	**—**	**.000**	**.286**	**.000**	**1.000**

Hegan, James Edward (Jim)
HEIGHT: 6'2"   THROWS: RIGHT   BATS: RIGHT   BORN: 8/3/1920 LYNN, MASSACHUSETTS   DIED: 6/17/1984 SWAMPSCOTT, MASSACHUSETTS
POSITIONS PLAYED: C

YEAR	TEAM	GAMES	AB	RUNS	HITS	2B	3B	HR	RBI	BB	IBB	SO	HBP	SH	SF	SB	CS	BA	OBA	SA	FA
1941	Cle-A	16	47	4	15	2	0	1	5	4	—	7	0	2	—	0	0	.319	.373	.426	.973
1942	Cle-A	68	170	10	33	5	0	0	11	11	—	31	0	3	—	1	3	.194	.243	.224	.977
1946	Cle-A	88	271	29	64	11	5	0	17	17	—	44	1	3	—	1	4	.236	.284	.314	.991
1947	Cle-A	135	378	38	94	14	5	4	42	41	—	49	1	6	—	3	1	.249	.324	.344	.989
1948	Cle-A	144	472	60	117	21	6	14	61	48	—	74	0	4	—	6	3	.248	.317	.407	.990

(continued)

(Hegan, continued)

YEAR	TEAM	GAMES	AB	RUNS	HITS	2B	3B	HR	RBI	BB	IBB	SO	HBP	SH	SF	SB	CS	BA	OBA	SA	FA
1949	Cle-A	152	468	54	105	19	5	8	55	49	—	89	0	12	—	1	0	.224	.298	.338	.990
1950	Cle-A	131	415	53	91	16	5	14	58	42	—	52	0	12	—	1	0	.219	.291	.383	.993
1951	Cle-A	133	416	60	99	17	5	6	43	38	—	72	0	3	—	0	3	.238	.302	.346	.991
1952	Cle-A	112	333	39	75	17	2	4	41	29	—	47	0	2	—	0	2	.225	.287	.324	.987
1953	Cle-A	112	299	37	65	10	1	9	37	25	—	41	1	4	—	1	2	.217	.280	.348	.976
1954	Cle-A	139	423	56	99	12	7	11	40	34	—	48	0	7	4	0	1	.234	.289	.374	.994
1955	Cle-A	116	304	30	67	5	2	9	40	34	5	33	0	7	7	0	1	.220	.293	.339	.997
1956	Cle-A	122	315	42	70	15	2	6	34	49	6	54	0	4	0	1	1	.222	.327	.340	.985
1957	Cle-A	58	148	14	32	7	0	4	15	16	1	23	0	2	1	0	1	.216	.291	.345	1.000
1958	Det-A	45	130	14	25	6	0	1	7	10	1	32	0	0	0	0	0	.192	.250	.262	.996
1958	Phi-N	25	59	5	13	6	0	0	6	4	0	16	0	0	0	0	0	.220	.270	.322	.991
1959	Phi-N	25	51	1	10	1	0	0	8	3	1	10	0	1	2	0	1	.196	.232	.216	.990
1959	SF-N	21	30	0	4	1	0	0	0	1	0	10	0	0	0	0	1	.133	.161	.167	.975
1960	**ChC-N**	**24**	**43**	**4**	**9**	**2**	**1**	**1**	**5**	**1**	**0**	**10**	**1**	**0**	**0**	**0**	**0**	**.209**	**.244**	**.372**	**.977**
Career average		98	281	32	64	11	3	5	31	27	1	44	0	4	1	0	1	.228	.295	.344	.990
Cubs average		**24**	**43**	**4**	**9**	**2**	**1**	**1**	**5**	**1**	**0**	**10**	**1**	**0**	**0**	**0**	**0**	**.209**	**.244**	**.372**	**.977**
Career total		1666	4772	550	1087	187	46	92	525	456	14	742	4	72	14	15	24	.228	.295	.344	.990
Cubs total		**24**	**43**	**4**	**9**	**2**	**1**	**1**	**5**	**1**	**0**	**10**	**1**	**0**	**0**	**0**	**0**	**.209**	**.244**	**.372**	**.977**

Heist, Alfred Michael (Al)

HEIGHT: 6'2" THROWS: RIGHT BATS: RIGHT BORN: 10/5/1927 BROOKLYN, NEW YORK POSITIONS PLAYED: OF

YEAR	TEAM	GAMES	AB	RUNS	HITS	2B	3B	HR	RBI	BB	IBB	SO	HBP	SH	SF	SB	CS	BA	OBA	SA	FA
1960	**ChC-N**	**41**	**102**	**11**	**28**	**5**	**3**	**1**	**6**	**10**	**0**	**12**	**0**	**1**	**0**	**3**	**1**	**.275**	**.339**	**.412**	**.985**
1961	**ChC-N**	**109**	**321**	**48**	**82**	**14**	**3**	**7**	**37**	**39**	**0**	**51**	**1**	**4**	**1**	**3**	**3**	**.255**	**.337**	**.383**	**.978**
1962	Hou-N	27	72	4	16	1	0	0	3	3	0	9	1	0	0	0	0	.222	.263	.236	.974
Career average		59	165	21	42	7	2	3	15	17	0	24	1	2	0	2	1	.255	.327	.368	.979
Cubs average		**75**	**212**	**30**	**55**	**10**	**3**	**4**	**22**	**25**	**0**	**32**	**1**	**3**	**1**	**3**	**2**	**.260**	**.338**	**.390**	**.980**
Career total		177	495	63	126	20	6	8	46	52	0	72	2	5	1	6	4	.255	.327	.368	.979
Cubs total		**150**	**423**	**59**	**110**	**19**	**6**	**8**	**43**	**49**	**0**	**63**	**1**	**5**	**1**	**6**	**4**	**.260**	**.338**	**.390**	**.980**

Hemsley, Ralston Burdett (Rollie)

HEIGHT: 5'10" THROWS: RIGHT BATS: RIGHT BORN: 6/24/1907 SYRACUSE, OHIO DIED: 7/31/1972 WASHINGTON, DISTRICT OF COLUMBIA
POSITIONS PLAYED: C, 1B, OF

YEAR	TEAM	GAMES	AB	RUNS	HITS	2B	3B	HR	RBI	BB	IBB	SO	HBP	SH	SF	SB	CS	BA	OBA	SA	FA
1928	Pit-N	50	133	14	36	2	3	0	18	4	—	10	0	3	—	1	—	.271	.292	.331	.962
1929	Pit-N	88	235	31	68	13	7	0	37	11	—	22	0	9	—	3	—	.289	.321	.404	.954
1930	Pit-N	104	324	45	82	19	6	2	45	22	—	21	0	10	—	3	—	.253	.301	.367	.979
1931	Pit-N	10	35	3	6	3	0	0	1	3	—	3	0	0	—	0	—	.171	.237	.257	1.000
1931	**ChC-N**	**66**	**204**	**28**	**63**	**17**	**4**	**3**	**31**	**17**	**—**	**30**	**0**	**3**	**—**	**4**	**—**	**.309**	**.362**	**.475**	**.975**
1932	**ChC-N**	**60**	**151**	**27**	**36**	**10**	**3**	**4**	**20**	**10**	**—**	**16**	**0**	**4**	**—**	**2**	**—**	**.238**	**.286**	**.424**	**.975**
1933	Cin-N	49	116	9	22	8	0	0	7	6	—	8	0	0	—	0	—	.190	.230	.259	.970
1933	StL-A	32	95	7	23	2	1	1	15	11	—	12	0	1	—	0	0	.242	.321	.316	.965
1934	StL-A	123	431	47	133	31	7	2	52	29	—	37	2	11	—	6	2	.309	.355	.427	.974
1935	StL-A	144	504	57	146	32	7	0	48	44	—	41	2	10	—	3	2	.290	.349	.381	.979
1936	StL-A	116	377	43	99	24	2	2	39	46	—	30	0	4	—	2	3	.263	.343	.353	.969
1937	StL-A	100	334	30	74	12	3	3	28	25	—	29	0	5	—	0	0	.222	.276	.302	.969
1938	Cle-A	66	203	27	60	11	3	2	28	23	—	14	0	4	—	1	1	.296	.367	.409	.980
1939	Cle-A	107	395	58	104	17	4	2	36	26	—	26	0	11	—	2	4	.263	.309	.342	.984
1940	Cle-A	119	416	46	111	20	5	4	42	22	—	25	0	5	—	1	3	.267	.304	.368	.994
1941	Cle-A	98	288	29	69	10	5	2	24	18	—	19	0	3	—	2	0	.240	.284	.330	.980
1942	Cin-N	36	115	7	13	1	2	0	7	4	—	11	0	0	—	0	—	.113	.143	.157	.982
1942	NYY-A	31	85	12	25	3	1	0	15	5	—	9	0	2	—	1	0	.294	.333	.353	.991
1943	NYY-A	62	180	12	43	6	3	0	24	13	—	9	0	6	—	0	1	.239	.290	.339	.981
1944	NYY-A	81	284	23	76	12	5	2	26	9	—	13	0	6	—	0	2	.268	.290	.366	.983
1946	Phi-N	49	139	7	31	4	1	0	11	9	—	10	0	4	—	0	—	.223	.270	.266	.977
1947	Phi-N	2	3	0	1	0	0	0	1	0	—	0	0	0	—	0	—	.333	.333	.333	1.000
Career average		84	266	30	70	14	4	2	29	19	—	21	0	5	—	2	1	.262	.311	.360	.978
Cubs average		**63**	**178**	**28**	**50**	**14**	**4**	**4**	**26**	**14**	**—**	**23**	**0**	**4**	**—**	**3**	**—**	**.279**	**.330**	**.454**	**.975**
Career total		1593	5047	562	1321	257	72	31	555	357	—	395	4	101	—	29	18	.262	.311	.360	.978
Cubs total		**126**	**355**	**55**	**99**	**27**	**7**	**7**	**51**	**27**	**—**	**46**	**0**	**7**	**—**	**6**	**—**	**.279**	**.330**	**.454**	**.975**

Henderson, Kenneth Joseph (Ken)

HEIGHT: 6'2"   THROWS: RIGHT   BATS: BOTH   BORN: 6/15/1946 CARROLL, IOWA   POSITIONS PLAYED: 1B, 3B, OF

YEAR	TEAM	GAMES	AB	RUNS	HITS	2B	3B	HR	RBI	BB	IBB	SO	HBP	SH	SF	SB	CS	BA	OBA	SA	FA
1965	SF-N	63	73	10	14	1	1	0	7	9	4	19	0	0	1	1	1	.192	.277	.233	.980
1966	SF-N	11	29	4	9	1	1	1	1	2	0	3	1	0	0	0	1	.310	.375	.517	.917
1967	SF-N	65	179	15	34	3	0	4	14	19	0	52	2	2	1	0	1	.190	.274	.274	.947
1968	SF-N	3	3	1	1	0	0	0	0	2	0	1	0	0	0	0	0	.333	.600	.333	1.000
1969	SF-N	113	374	42	84	14	4	6	44	42	2	64	5	0	0	0	0	.225	.308	.332	.969
1970	SF-N	148	554	104	163	35	3	17	88	87	9	78	5	4	4	6	4	.294	.394	.460	.966
1971	SF-N	141	504	80	133	26	6	15	65	84	12	76	5	1	2	20	3	.264	.370	.429	.966
1972	SF-N	130	439	60	113	21	2	18	51	38	6	66	3	3	4	18	3	.257	.317	.437	.974
1973	CWS-A	73	262	32	68	13	0	6	32	27	2	49	1	0	1	3	4	.260	.330	.378	.972
1974	CWS-A	162	602	76	176	35	5	20	95	66	9	112	2	2	8	12	7	.292	.360	.467	.987
1975	CWS-A	140	513	65	129	20	3	9	53	74	14	65	4	1	5	5	3	.251	.347	.355	.990
1976	Atl-N	133	435	52	114	19	0	13	61	62	7	68	1	2	5	5	7	.262	.352	.395	.987
1977	Tex-A	75	244	23	63	14	0	5	23	18	4	37	3	2	0	2	1	.258	.317	.377	.983
1978	NYM-N	7	22	2	5	2	0	1	4	4	1	4	0	0	2	0	1	.227	.346	.455	1.000
1978	Cin-N	64	144	10	24	6	1	3	19	23	3	32	0	0	0	0	1	.167	.278	.285	1.000
1979	Cin-N	10	13	1	3	1	0	0	2	0	0	2	0	0	0	0	0	.231	.231	.308	1.000
1979	**ChC-N**	**62**	**81**	**11**	**19**	**2**	**0**	**2**	**8**	**15**	**1**	**16**	**1**	**0**	**0**	**0**	**0**	**.235**	**.361**	**.333**	**.950**
1980	**ChC-N**	**44**	**82**	**7**	**16**	**3**	**0**	**2**	**9**	**17**	**3**	**19**	**0**	**0**	**0**	**0**	**0**	**.195**	**.333**	**.305**	**.944**
Career average		90	285	37	73	14	2	8	36	37	5	48	2	1	2	5	3	.257	.343	.396	.977
Cubs average		**53**	**82**	**9**	**18**	**3**	**0**	**2**	**9**	**16**	**2**	**18**	**1**	**0**	**0**	**0**		**.215**	**.347**	**.319**	**.946**
Career total		1444	4553	595	1168	216	26	122	576	589	77	763	30	19	36	86	42	.257	.343	.396	.977
Cubs total		**106**	**163**	**18**	**35**	**5**	**0**	**4**	**17**	**32**	**4**	**35**	**1**	**0**	**0**	**0**	**0**	**.215**	**.347**	**.319**	**.946**

Henderson, Steven Curtis (Steve)

HEIGHT: 6'2"   THROWS: RIGHT   BATS: RIGHT   BORN: 11/18/1952 HOUSTON, TEXAS   POSITIONS PLAYED: 1B, OF

YEAR	TEAM	GAMES	AB	RUNS	HITS	2B	3B	HR	RBI	BB	IBB	SO	HBP	SH	SF	SB	CS	BA	OBA	SA	FA
1977	NYM-N	99	350	67	104	16	6	12	65	43	2	79	1	0	4	6	3	.297	.372	.480	.980
1978	NYM-N	157	587	83	156	30	9	10	65	60	3	109	2	0	5	13	7	.266	.333	.399	.968
1979	NYM-N	98	350	42	107	16	8	5	39	38	6	58	4	1	0	13	5	.306	.380	.440	.990
1980	NYM-N	143	513	75	149	17	8	8	58	62	3	90	3	3	3	23	12	.290	.368	.402	.981
1981	**ChC-N**	**82**	**287**	**32**	**84**	**9**	**5**	**5**	**35**	**42**	**7**	**61**	**2**	**3**	**4**	**5**	**7**	**.293**	**.382**	**.411**	**.951**
1982	**ChC-N**	**92**	**257**	**23**	**60**	**12**	**4**	**2**	**29**	**22**	**3**	**64**	**0**	**3**	**1**	**6**	**5**	**.233**	**.293**	**.335**	**.956**
1983	Sea-A	121	436	50	128	32	3	10	54	44	2	82	0	1	3	10	14	.294	.356	.450	.970
1984	Sea-A	109	325	42	85	12	3	10	35	38	4	62	1	0	0	2	4	.262	.341	.409	.936
1985	Oak-A	85	193	25	58	8	3	3	31	18	0	34	0	1	1	0	0	.301	.358	.420	.953
1986	Oak-A	11	26	2	2	1	0	0	3	0	0	5	0	0	1	0	0	.077	.074	.115	.800
1987	Oak-A	46	114	14	33	7	0	3	9	12	1	19	0	0	1	0	0	.289	.357	.430	.943
1988	Hou-N	42	46	4	10	2	0	0	5	7	1	14	0	0	0	1	1	.217	.321	.261	1.000
Career average		90	290	38	81	14	4	6	36	32	3	56	1	1	2	7	5	.280	.352	.413	.968
Cubs average		**87**	**272**	**28**	**72**	**11**	**5**	**4**	**32**	**32**	**5**	**63**	**1**	**3**	**3**	**6**	**6**	**.265**	**.341**	**.375**	**.953**
Career total		1085	3484	459	976	162	49	68	428	386	32	677	13	11	22	79	58	.280	.352	.413	.968
Cubs total		**174**	**544**	**55**	**144**	**21**	**9**	**7**	**64**	**64**	**10**	**125**	**2**	**5**	**5**	**11**	**12**	**.265**	**.341**	**.375**	**.953**

Hendrick, Harvey (Gink)

HEIGHT: 6'2"   THROWS: RIGHT   BATS: LEFT   BORN: 11/9/1897 MASON, TENNESSEE   DIED: 10/29/1941 COVINGTON, TENNESSEE
POSITIONS PLAYED: 1B, 2B, 3B, SS, OF

YEAR	TEAM	GAMES	AB	RUNS	HITS	2B	3B	HR	RBI	BB	IBB	SO	HBP	SH	SF	SB	CS	BA	OBA	SA	FA
1923	NYY-A	37	66	9	18	3	1	3	12	2	—	8	0	1	—	3	0	.273	.294	.485	.947
1924	NYY-A	40	76	7	20	0	0	1	11	2	—	7	1	1	—	1	0	.263	.291	.303	.975
1925	Cle-A	25	28	2	8	1	2	0	9	3	—	5	0	2	—	0	0	.286	.355	.464	1.000
1927	Bro-N	128	458	55	142	18	11	4	50	24	—	40	4	9	—	29	—	.310	.350	.424	.982
1928	Bro-N	126	425	83	135	15	10	11	59	54	—	34	2	12	—	16	—	.318	.397	.478	.923
1929	Bro-N	110	384	69	136	25	6	14	82	31	—	20	1	8	—	14	—	.354	.404	.560	.971
1930	Bro-N	68	167	29	43	10	1	5	28	20	—	19	2	3	—	2	—	.257	.344	.419	.960
1931	Bro-N	1	1	0	0	0	0	0	0	0	—	0	0	0	—	0	—	.000	.000	.000	—
1931	Cin-N	137	530	74	167	32	9	1	75	53	—	40	2	8	—	3	—	.315	.379	.415	.987
1932	StL-N	28	72	8	18	2	0	0	5	5	—	9	0	0	—	0	—	.250	.299	.319	.889
1932	Cin-N	94	398	56	120	30	3	4	40	23	—	29	1	6	—	3	—	.302	.341	.422	.986
1933	**ChC-N**	**69**	**189**	**30**	**55**	**13**	**3**	**4**	**23**	**13**	**—**	**17**	**3**	**3**	**—**	**4**	**—**	**.291**	**.346**	**.455**	**.979**
1934	Phi-N	59	116	12	34	8	0	0	19	9	—	15	0	2	—	0	—	.293	.344	.362	.951

(continued)

(Hendrick, continued)

	GAMES	AB	RUNS	HITS	2B	3B	HR	RBI	BB	IBB	SO	HBP	SH	SF	SB	CS	BA	OBA	SA	FA
Career average	84	265	39	81	14	4	4	38	22	—	22	1	5	—	7	0	.308	.364	.443	.977
Cubs average	**69**	**189**	**30**	**55**	**13**	**3**	**4**	**23**	**13**	**—**	**17**	**3**	**3**	**—**	**4**	**0**	**.291**	**.346**	**.455**	**.979**
Career total	922	2910	434	896	157	46	48	413	239	—	243	16	55	—	75	0	.308	.364	.443	.977
Cubs total	**69**	**189**	**30**	**55**	**13**	**3**	**4**	**23**	**13**	**—**	**17**	**3**	**3**	**—**	**4**	**0**	**.291**	**.346**	**.455**	**.979**

Hendricks, Elrod Jerome (Ellie)
HEIGHT: 6'1"   THROWS: RIGHT   BATS: LEFT   BORN: 12/22/1940 CHARLOTTE AMALIE, VIRGIN ISLANDS   POSITIONS PLAYED: P, C, 1B

YEAR	TEAM	GAMES	AB	RUNS	HITS	2B	3B	HR	RBI	BB	IBB	SO	HBP	SH	SF	SB	CS	BA	OBA	SA	FA
1968	Bal-A	79	183	19	37	8	1	7	23	19	2	51	1	0	1	0	0	.202	.279	.372	.991
1969	Bal-A	105	295	36	72	5	0	12	38	39	5	44	2	0	3	0	1	.244	.333	.383	.998
1970	Bal-A	106	322	32	78	9	0	12	41	33	4	44	4	2	4	1	0	.242	.317	.382	.986
1971	Bal-A	101	316	33	79	14	1	9	42	39	5	38	2	2	2	0	1	.250	.334	.386	.986
1972	Bal-A	33	84	6	13	4	0	0	4	12	2	19	0	1	1	0	1	.155	.258	.202	.986
1972	**ChC-N**	**17**	**43**	**7**	**5**	**1**	**0**	**2**	**6**	**13**	**6**	**8**	**0**	**0**	**0**	**0**	**1**	**.116**	**.321**	**.279**	**.978**
1973	Bal-A	41	101	9	18	5	1	3	15	10	4	22	1	1	1	0	0	.178	.257	.337	.994
1974	Bal-A	66	159	18	33	8	2	3	8	17	4	25	1	0	3	0	0	.208	.283	.340	1.000
1975	Bal-A	85	223	32	48	8	2	8	38	34	5	40	1	2	2	0	1	.215	.319	.377	.995
1976	Bal-A	28	79	2	11	1	0	1	4	7	1	13	0	0	1	0	0	.139	.209	.190	.971
1976	NYY-A	26	53	6	12	1	0	3	5	3	0	10	0	0	0	0	0	.226	.263	.415	1.000
1977	NYY-A	10	11	1	3	1	0	1	5	0	0	2	0	0	0	0	0	.273	.273	.636	1.000
1978	Bal-A	13	18	4	6	1	0	1	1	3	2	3	0	0	0	0	0	.333	.429	.556	.955
1979	Bal-A	1	1	0	0	0	0	0	0	0	0	0	0	0	0	0	0	.000	.000	.000	.500
Career average	59	157	17	35	6	1	5	19	19	3	27	1	1	2	0	0	.220	.306	.361	.990
Cubs average	**17**	**43**	**7**	**5**	**1**	**0**	**2**	**6**	**13**	**6**	**8**	**0**	**0**	**0**	**0**	**1**	**.116**	**.321**	**.279**	**.978**
Career total	711	1888	205	415	66	7	62	230	229	40	319	12	8	18	1	5	.220	.306	.361	.990
Cubs total	**17**	**43**	**7**	**5**	**1**	**0**	**2**	**6**	**13**	**6**	**8**	**0**	**0**	**0**	**0**	**1**	**.116**	**.321**	**.279**	**.978**

Hendricks, John Charles (Jack)
HEIGHT: 5'11"   THROWS: LEFT   BATS: LEFT   BORN: 4/9/1875 JOLIET, ILLINOIS   DIED: 5/13/1943 CHICAGO, ILLINOIS   POSITIONS PLAYED: OF

YEAR	TEAM	GAMES	AB	RUNS	HITS	2B	3B	HR	RBI	BB	IBB	SO	HBP	SH	SF	SB	CS	BA	OBA	SA	FA
1902	NYG-N	8	26	1	6	2	0	0	0	2	—	—	0	3	—	2	—	.231	.286	.308	.929
1902	**ChC-N**	**2**	**7**	**0**	**4**	**0**	**1**	**0**	**0**	**0**	**—**	**—**	**0**	**1**	**—**	**0**	**—**	**.571**	**.571**	**.857**	**1.000**
1903	Was-A	32	112	10	20	1	3	0	4	13	—	—	0	8	—	3	—	.179	.264	.241	.891
Career average	21	73	6	15	2	2	0	2	8	—	—	0	6	—	3	—	.207	.281	.283	.909
Cubs average	**2**	**7**	**0**	**4**	**0**	**1**	**0**	**0**	**0**	**—**	**—**	**0**	**1**	**—**	**0**	**—**	**.571**	**.571**	**.857**	**1.000**
Career total	42	145	11	30	3	4	0	4	15	—	—	0	12	—	5	—	.207	.281	.283	.909
Cubs total	**2**	**7**	**0**	**4**	**0**	**1**	**0**	**0**	**0**	**—**	**—**	**0**	**1**	**—**	**0**	**—**	**.571**	**.571**	**.857**	**1.000**

Herman, Floyd Caves (Babe)
HEIGHT: 6'4"   THROWS: LEFT   BATS: LEFT   BORN: 6/26/1903 BUFFALO, NEW YORK   DIED: 11/27/1987 GLENDALE, CALIFORNIA   POSITIONS PLAYED: 1B, OF

YEAR	TEAM	GAMES	AB	RUNS	HITS	2B	3B	HR	RBI	BB	IBB	SO	HBP	SH	SF	SB	CS	BA	OBA	SA	FA
1926	Bro-N	137	496	64	158	35	11	11	81	44	—	53	1	13	—	8	—	.319	.375	.500	.984
1927	Bro-N	130	412	65	112	26	9	14	73	39	—	41	1	14	—	4	—	.272	.336	.481	.980
1928	Bro-N	134	486	64	165	37	6	12	91	38	—	36	2	16	—	1	—	.340	.390	.514	.937
1929	Bro-N	146	569	105	217	42	13	21	113	55	—	45	0	13	—	21	—	.381	.436	.612	.941
1930	Bro-N	153	614	143	241	48	11	35	130	66	—	56	4	15	—	18	—	.393	.455	.678	.978
1931	Bro-N	151	610	93	191	43	16	18	97	50	—	65	0	1	—	17	—	.313	.365	.525	.960
1932	Cin-N	148	577	87	188	38	19	16	87	60	—	45	0	5	—	7	—	.326	.389	.541	.969
1933	**ChC-N**	**137**	**508**	**77**	**147**	**36**	**12**	**16**	**93**	**50**	**—**	**57**	**0**	**7**	**—**	**6**	**—**	**.289**	**.353**	**.502**	**.957**
1934	**ChC-N**	**125**	**467**	**65**	**142**	**34**	**5**	**14**	**84**	**35**	**—**	**71**	**0**	**5**	**—**	**1**	**—**	**.304**	**.353**	**.488**	**.974**
1935	Pit-N	26	81	8	19	8	1	0	7	3	—	10	1	0	—	0	—	.235	.271	.358	.932
1935	Cin-N	92	349	44	117	23	5	10	58	35	—	25	0	2	—	5	—	.335	.396	.516	.980
1936	Cin-N	119	380	59	106	25	2	13	71	39	—	36	1	1	—	4	—	.279	.348	.458	.969
1937	Det-A	17	20	2	6	3	0	1	3	1	—	6	0	0	—	2	0	.300	.364	.450	1.000
1945	Bro-N	37	34	6	9	1	0	1	9	5	—	7	1	0	—	0	—	.265	.359	.382	—
Career average	119	431	68	140	31	8	14	77	40	—	43	1	7	—	7	0	.324	.383	.532	.971
Cubs average	**131**	**488**	**71**	**145**	**35**	**9**	**15**	**89**	**43**	**—**	**64**	**0**	**6**	**—**	**4**	**—**	**.296**	**.353**	**.495**	**.965**
Career total	1552	5603	882	1818	399	110	181	997	520	—	553	11	92	—	94	0	.324	.383	.532	.971
Cubs total	**262**	**975**	**142**	**289**	**70**	**17**	**30**	**177**	**85**	**—**	**128**	**0**	**12**	**—**	**7**	**—**	**.296**	**.353**	**.495**	**.965**

Herman, William Jennings Bryan (Billy)

HEIGHT: 5'11"   THROWS: RIGHT   BATS: RIGHT   BORN: 7/7/1909 NEW ALBANY, INDIANA   DIED: 9/5/1992 WEST PALM BEACH, FLORIDA
POSITIONS PLAYED: 1B, 2B, 3B

YEAR	TEAM	GAMES	AB	RUNS	HITS	2B	3B	HR	RBI	BB	IBB	SO	HBP	SH	SF	SB	CS	BA	OBA	SA	FA
1931	ChC-N	25	98	14	32	7	0	0	16	13	—	6	0	4	—	2	—	.327	.405	.398	.939
1932	ChC-N	154	656	102	206	42	7	1	51	40	—	33	5	22	—	14	—	.314	.358	.404	.961
1933	ChC-N	153	619	82	173	35	2	0	44	45	—	34	4	13	—	5	—	.279	.332	.342	.956
1934	ChC-N	113	456	79	138	21	6	3	42	34	—	31	3	8	—	6	—	.303	.355	.395	.975
1935	ChC-N	154	666	113	227	57	6	7	83	42	—	29	3	24	—	6	—	.341	.383	.476	.964
1936	ChC-N	153	632	101	211	57	7	5	93	59	—	30	1	17	—	5	—	.334	.392	.470	.975
1937	ChC-N	138	564	106	189	35	11	8	65	56	—	22	1	11	—	2	—	.335	.396	.479	.954
1938	ChC-N	152	624	86	173	34	7	1	56	59	—	31	2	11	—	3	—	.277	.342	.359	.981
1939	ChC-N	156	623	111	191	34	18	7	70	66	—	31	5	19	—	9	—	.307	.378	.453	.967
1940	ChC-N	135	558	77	163	24	4	5	57	47	—	30	0	11	—	1	—	.292	.347	.376	.974
1941	ChC-N	11	36	4	7	0	1	0	0	9	—	5	0	0	—	0	—	.194	.356	.250	.898
1941	Bro-N	133	536	77	156	30	4	3	41	58	—	38	1	9	—	1	—	.291	.361	.379	.970
1942	Bro-N	155	571	76	146	34	2	2	65	72	—	52	0	4	—	6	—	.256	.339	.333	.973
1943	Bro-N	153	585	76	193	41	2	2	100	66	—	26	0	12	—	4	6	.330	.398	.417	.972
1946	Bro-N	47	184	24	53	8	4	0	28	26	—	10	0	1	—	2	0	.288	.376	.375	.970
1946	Bos-N	75	252	32	77	23	1	3	22	43	—	13	1	5	—	1	—	.306	.409	.440	.973
1947	Pit-N	15	47	3	10	4	0	0	6	2	—	7	0	0	—	0	—	.213	.245	.298	1.000
Career average		128	514	78	156	32	5	3	56	49	—	29	2	11	—	4	0	.304	.367	.407	.968
Cubs average		**122**	**503**	**80**	**155**	**31**	**6**	**3**	**52**	**43**	**—**	**26**	**2**	**13**	**—**	**5**	**—**	**.309**	**.366**	**.417**	**.968**
Career total		1922	7707	1163	2345	486	82	47	839	737	—	428	26	171	—	67	6	.304	.367	.407	.968
Cubs total		**1344**	**5532**	**875**	**1710**	**346**	**69**	**37**	**577**	**470**	**—**	**282**	**24**	**140**	**—**	**53**	**—**	**.309**	**.366**	**.417**	**.966**

William (Billy) Jennings Bryan Herman, 1b-2b-3b, 1931–41

One of a long line of excellent Cubs second basemen, Billy Herman, in the eyes of many, was the best second baseman of the 1930s and one of the best at the hit-and-run play in the history of baseball.

Herman was born on July 7, 1909, in New Albany, Indiana. He was signed by the Cubs as a 20-year-old while playing for Louisville. In 1931 he was brought up at the end of the season and looked very good, hitting .327 in just 25 games.

Although Herman was clearly his replacement at second base, Cubs manager Rogers Hornsby saw the writing on the wall. Hornsby inserted Herman at second base at the end of 1931 and moved himself to the bench. The competitive Hornsby was clearly not very happy with the arrangement, and Herman found himself looking over his shoulder at his manager when he made a mistake.

In 1932 any problems with replacing Hornsby at second base were removed when the taciturn Hornsby was fired and the more affable Charlie Grimm took his place as manager.

Herman admitted many years later that the tough-as-nails Hornsby had intimidated him during his first year on the squad. Grimm, nicknamed "Jolly Cholly" by sportswriters, set a more relaxed tone that younger players like Herman found more conducive to playing well.

Whether it was Grimm's good-natured presence on the bench or sheer talent, Herman made the most of his chance at second base in 1932. He hit .314 and led the team in hits with 206, runs scored with 102 and stolen bases with 14. Defensively, he led National League second basemen in assists with 527 and total fielding chances per game with an average of 6.3.

He and the Cubs ended up in the World Series that year, and the 23-year-old second baseman had four hits, including a double, and led the Cubs in runs scored with five, although Chicago was swept by the Yankees.

From 1932 to 1940, Billy Herman was the Cubs second baseman. For most of that span,

(continued)

(continued)

he was the best second sacker in the National League. He was a great defensive player, leading the National League in putouts six times while with the Cubs (seven times in his career overall), in assists three times and fielding percentage three times in that span.

In 1933 Herman tied the major league record for most putouts by a second baseman in a doubleheader with 16 and tied the record for most putouts in a game with 11. That season, Herman set the NL season record for most putouts by a second baseman with 466.

On offense, he hit over .300 seven times for the Cubs and made more than 200 hits three times for Chicago. He hit 30 or more doubles seven times, including a league-leading 57 in 1935.

But Herman was more than numbers. Former teammate Billy Jurges recalled that Herman was the master of studying hitters. Former opponent and future coach Leo Durocher flatly stated that Herman was the best at the hit-and-run play he had ever seen.

He played in 10 All-Star Games and was one of the best players there, too, hitting .433 in those contests.

But despite that amazing run, the Cubs got jittery as the 32-year-old Herman struggled to begin the 1941 season, hitting only .194 in his first 11 games. In addition, Cubs manager Jimmie Wilson realized that if anyone was in line to take his place, it was the smart and savvy Herman.

Wilson was among several Cubs executives who believed the All-Star second baseman was losing it, so the Cubs shipped Herman to Brooklyn for $65,000 and two journeymen players.

It was a huge mistake. Herman snapped out of it, hit .291 for the Dodgers and helped Brooklyn to the 1941 National League pennant. He played superbly for Brooklyn for two more years, then finished up his career with the Boston Braves and later as a player-manager with the Pirates.

After retiring as a player, Herman managed for several years in the minors, and he later took over the helm of the Boston Red Sox in the mid-1960s but never finished higher than eighth in Boston. He was also a coach for a number of organizations before his death in 1993 in Florida.

Herman is 10th all-time for the Cubs with 346 doubles. In 1975 he was named to the Hall of Fame.

Hermanski, Eugene Victor (Gene)

HEIGHT: 5'11" THROWS: RIGHT BATS: LEFT BORN: 5/11/1920 PITTSFIELD, MASSACHUSETTS POSITIONS PLAYED: OF

YEAR	TEAM	GAMES	AB	RUNS	HITS	2B	3B	HR	RBI	BB	IBB	SO	HBP	SH	SF	SB	CS	BA	OBA	SA	FA
1943	Bro-N	18	60	6	18	2	1	0	12	11	—	7	1	0	—	1	1	.300	.417	.367	.976
1946	Bro-N	64	110	15	22	2	2	0	8	17	—	10	1	0	—	2	2	.200	.313	.255	.938
1947	Bro-N	79	189	36	52	7	1	7	39	28	—	7	3	5	—	5	2	.275	.377	.434	.982
1948	Bro-N	133	400	63	116	22	7	15	60	64	—	46	2	4	—	15	—	.290	.391	.493	.971
1949	Bro-N	87	224	48	67	12	3	8	42	47	—	21	5	6	—	12	4	.299	.431	.487	.980
1950	Bro-N	94	289	36	86	17	3	7	34	36	—	26	3	4	—	2	—	.298	.381	.450	.989
1951	Bro-N	31	80	8	20	4	0	1	5	10	—	12	0	0	—	3	0	.250	.333	.338	.977
1951	**ChC-N**	**75**	**231**	**28**	**65**	**12**	**1**	**3**	**20**	**35**	—	**30**	**4**	**1**	—	**2**	**0**	**.255**	**.330**	**.320**	**.981**
1952	**ChC-N**	**99**	**275**	**28**	**70**	**6**	**0**	**4**	**34**	**29**	—	**32**	**2**	**4**	—	**1**	**0**	**.150**	**.227**	**.175**	**1.000**
1953	**ChC-N**	**18**	**40**	**1**	**6**	**1**	**0**	**0**	**1**	**4**	—	**7**	**0**	**0**	—	**0**	**0**	**.177**	**.282**	**.226**	**1.000**
1953	Pit-N	41	62	7	11	0	0	1	4	8	—	14	1	0	—	0	0	.281	.385	.381	.966
Career average		82	218	31	59	9	2	5	29	32	—	24	2	3	—	5	1	.272	.372	.404	.977
Cubs average		**64**	**182**	**19**	**47**	**6**	**0**	**2**	**18**	**23**	—	**23**	**2**	**2**	—	**2**	**0**	**.258**	**.347**	**.335**	**.975**
Career total		739	1960	276	533	85	18	46	259	289	—	212	22	24	—	43	11	.272	.372	.404	.977
Cubs total		**192**	**546**	**57**	**141**	**19**	**1**	**7**	**55**	**68**	—	**69**	**6**	**5**	—	**6**	**0**	**.258**	**.347**	**.335**	**.975**

Hernandez, Jose Antonio
HEIGHT: 6'1"   THROWS: RIGHT   BATS: RIGHT   BORN: 7/14/1969 VEGA ALTA, PUERTO RICO   POSITIONS PLAYED: 1B, 2B, 3B, SS, OF

YEAR	TEAM	GAMES	AB	RUNS	HITS	2B	3B	HR	RBI	BB	IBB	SO	HBP	SH	SF	SB	CS	BA	OBA	SA	FA
1991	Tex-A	45	98	8	18	2	1	0	4	3	0	31	0	6	0	0	1	.184	.208	.224	.976
1992	Cle-A	3	4	0	0	0	0	0	0	0	0	2	0	0	0	0	0	.000	.000	.000	.857
1994	**ChC-N**	56	132	18	32	2	3	1	9	8	0	29	1	5	0	0	0	.242	.291	.326	.971
1995	**ChC-N**	93	245	37	60	11	4	13	40	13	3	69	0	8	2	2	2	.245	.281	.482	.971
1996	**ChC-N**	131	331	52	80	14	1	10	41	24	4	97	1	5	2	1	0	.242	.293	.381	.952
1997	**ChC-N**	121	183	33	50	8	5	7	26	14	2	42	0	1	1	4	0	.273	.323	.486	.955
1998	**ChC-N**	149	488	76	124	23	7	23	75	40	3	140	1	2	2	5	5	.254	.311	.471	.970
1999	**ChC-N**	99	342	57	93	12	2	15	43	40	3	101	5	1	0	8	8	.272	.357	.450	.973
1999	Atl-N	48	166	22	42	8	0	4	19	12	3	44	0	1	1	4	1	.253	.302	.373	.966
2000	Mil-N	124	446	51	109	22	1	11	59	41	3	125	6	2	3	4	4	.244	.315	.372	.955
2001	Mil-N	152	542	67	135	26	2	25	78	39	8	185	2	3	4	4	7	.249	.300	.443	.972
Career average		102	298	42	74	13	3	11	39	23	3	87	2	3	2	3	3	.250	.306	.420	.966
Cubs average		**108**	**287**	**46**	**73**	**12**	**4**	**12**	**39**	**23**	**3**	**80**	**1**	**4**	**1**	**3**	**3**	**.255**	**.313**	**.442**	**.966**
Career total		1021	2977	421	743	128	26	109	394	234	29	865	16	34	15	32	28	.250	.306	.420	.966
Cubs total		**649**	**1721**	**273**	**439**	**70**	**22**	**69**	**234**	**139**	**15**	**478**	**8**	**22**	**7**	**20**	**15**	**.255**	**.313**	**.442**	**.965**

Hernandez, Salvador Jose (Chico)
HEIGHT: 6'0"   THROWS: RIGHT   BATS: RIGHT   BORN: 1/3/1916 HAVANA, CUBA   DIED: 1/3/1986 HAVANA, CUBA   POSITIONS PLAYED: C

YEAR	TEAM	GAMES	AB	RUNS	HITS	2B	3B	HR	RBI	BB	IBB	SO	HBP	SH	SF	SB	CS	BA	OBA	SA	FA
1942	**ChC-N**	47	118	6	27	5	0	0	7	11	—	13	0	1	—	0	—	.229	.295	.271	.975
1943	**ChC-N**	43	126	10	34	4	0	0	9	9	—	9	1	1	—	0	—	.270	.324	.302	.981
Career average		45	122	8	31	5	0	0	8	10	—	11	1	1	—	0	—	.250	.309	.287	.978
Cubs average		**45**	**122**	**8**	**31**	**5**	**0**	**0**	**8**	**10**	**—**	**11**	**1**	**1**	**—**	**0**	**—**	**.250**	**.309**	**.287**	**.978**
Career total		90	244	16	61	9	0	0	16	20	—	22	1	2	—	0	—	.250	.309	.287	.978
Cubs total		**90**	**244**	**16**	**61**	**9**	**0**	**0**	**16**	**20**	**—**	**22**	**1**	**2**	**—**	**0**	**—**	**.250**	**.309**	**.287**	**.978**

Hernon, Thomas H. (Tom)
HEIGHT: 5'8"   THROWS: RIGHT   BATS: RIGHT   BORN: 11/4/1866 EAST BRIDGEWATER, MASSACHUSETTS   DIED: 2/4/1902 NEW BEDFORD, MASSACHUSETTS
POSITIONS PLAYED: OF

YEAR	TEAM	GAMES	AB	RUNS	HITS	2B	3B	HR	RBI	BB	IBB	SO	HBP	SH	SF	SB	CS	BA	OBA	SA	FA
1897	ChN-N	4	16	2	1	0	0	0	2	0	—	—	0	1	—	1	—	.063	.063	.063	1.000
Career average		4	16	2	1	0	0	0	2	0	—	—	0	1	—	1	—	.063	.063	.063	1.000
Cubs average		**4**	**16**	**2**	**1**	**0**	**0**	**0**	**2**	**0**	**—**	**—**	**0**	**1**	**—**	**1**	**—**	**.063**	**.063**	**.063**	**1.000**
Career total		4	16	2	1	0	0	0	2	0	—	—	0	1	—	1	—	.063	.063	.063	1.000
Cubs total		**4**	**16**	**2**	**1**	**0**	**0**	**0**	**2**	**0**	**—**	**—**	**0**	**1**	**—**	**1**	**—**	**.063**	**.063**	**.063**	**1.000**

Herrnstein, John Ellett
HEIGHT: 6'3"   THROWS: LEFT   BATS: LEFT   BORN: 3/31/1938 HAMPTON, VIRGINIA   POSITIONS PLAYED: 1B, OF

YEAR	TEAM	GAMES	AB	RUNS	HITS	2B	3B	HR	RBI	BB	IBB	SO	HBP	SH	SF	SB	CS	BA	OBA	SA	FA
1962	Phi-N	6	5	0	1	0	0	0	1	1	0	3	0	0	0	0	0	.200	.333	.200	—
1963	Phi-N	15	12	1	2	0	0	1	1	1	0	5	0	0	0	0	0	.167	.231	.417	1.000
1964	Phi-N	125	303	38	71	12	4	6	25	22	0	67	2	8	3	1	2	.234	.288	.360	.989
1965	Phi-N	63	85	8	17	2	0	1	5	2	1	18	1	3	0	0	0	.200	.227	.259	.985
1966	Phi-N	4	10	0	1	0	0	0	1	0	0	7	0	0	0	0	0	.100	.100	.100	1.000
1966	**ChC-N**	9	17	3	3	0	0	0	0	3	0	8	0	0	0	0	0	.176	.300	.176	.975
1966	Atl-N	17	18	2	4	0	0	0	1	0	0	7	0	0	0	0	0	.222	.222	.222	1.000
Career average		48	90	10	20	3	1	2	7	6	0	23	1	2	1	0	0	.220	.270	.322	.988
Cubs average		**9**	**17**	**3**	**3**	**0**	**0**	**0**	**0**	**3**	**0**	**8**	**0**	**0**	**0**	**0**	**0**	**.176**	**.300**	**.176**	**.975**
Career total		239	450	52	99	14	4	8	34	29	1	115	3	11	3	1	2	.220	.270	.322	.988
Cubs total		**9**	**17**	**3**	**3**	**0**	**0**	**0**	**0**	**3**	**0**	**8**	**0**	**0**	**0**	**0**	**0**	**.176**	**.300**	**.176**	**.975**

Herzog, Charles Lincoln (Buck)

HEIGHT: 5'11" THROWS: RIGHT BATS: RIGHT BORN: 7/9/1885 BALTIMORE, MARYLAND DIED: 9/4/1953 BALTIMORE, MARYLAND POSITIONS PLAYED: 1B, 2B, 3B, SS, OF

YEAR	TEAM	GAMES	AB	RUNS	HITS	2B	3B	HR	RBI	BB	IBB	SO	HBP	SH	SF	SB	CS	BA	OBA	SA	FA
1908	NYG-N	64	160	38	48	6	2	0	11	36	—	—	7	10	—	16	—	.300	.448	.363	.917
1909	NYG-N	42	130	16	24	2	0	0	8	13	—	—	1	2	—	10	—	.185	.264	.200	.912
1910	Bos-N	106	380	51	95	20	3	3	32	30	—	34	15	20	—	13	—	.250	.329	.342	.915
1911	Bos-N	79	294	53	91	19	5	5	41	33	—	21	10	19	—	26	—	.310	.398	.459	.937
1911	NYG-N	69	247	37	66	14	4	1	26	14	—	19	7	11	—	22	—	.267	.325	.368	.930
1912	NYG-N	140	482	72	127	20	9	2	47	57	—	34	7	17	—	37	—	.263	.350	.355	.942
1913	NYG-N	96	290	46	83	15	3	3	31	22	—	12	6	6	—	23	—	.286	.349	.390	.948
1914	Cin-N	138	498	54	140	14	8	1	40	42	—	27	9	15	—	46	—	.281	.348	.347	.939
1915	Cin-N	155	579	61	153	14	10	1	42	34	—	21	8	20	—	35	16	.264	.314	.328	.945
1916	Cin-N	79	281	30	75	14	2	1	24	21	—	12	5	12	—	15	12	.267	.329	.342	.937
1916	NYG-N	77	280	40	73	10	4	0	25	22	—	24	5	12	—	19	16	.261	.326	.325	.957
1917	NYG-N	114	417	69	98	10	8	2	31	31	—	36	13	16	—	12	—	.235	.308	.312	.948
1918	Bos-N	118	473	57	108	12	6	0	26	29	—	28	5	19	—	10	—	.228	.280	.279	.960
1919	Bos-N	73	275	27	77	8	5	1	25	13	—	11	6	13	—	16	—	.280	.327	.356	.953
1919	**ChC-N**	**52**	**193**	**15**	**53**	**4**	**4**	**0**	**17**	**10**	**—**	**7**	**8**	**7**	**—**	**12**	**—**	**.275**	**.336**	**.337**	**.987**
1920	**ChC-N**	**91**	**305**	**39**	**59**	**9**	**2**	**0**	**19**	**20**	**—**	**21**	**8**	**17**	**—**	**8**	**9**	**.193**	**.261**	**.236**	**.932**
Career average		115	406	54	105	15	6	2	34	33	—	24	9	17	—	25	4	.259	.329	.335	.943
Cubs average		**72**	**249**	**27**	**56**	**7**	**3**	**0**	**18**	**15**	**—**	**14**	**8**	**12**	**—**	**10**	**5**	**.225**	**.290**	**.275**	**.951**
Career total		1493	5284	705	1370	191	75	20	445	427	—	307	120	216	—	320	53	.259	.329	.335	.943
Cubs total		**143**	**498**	**54**	**112**	**13**	**6**	**0**	**36**	**30**	**—**	**28**	**16**	**24**	**—**	**20**	**9**	**.225**	**.290**	**.275**	**.951**

Hiatt, Jack E.

HEIGHT: 6'2" THROWS: RIGHT BATS: RIGHT BORN: 7/27/1942 BAKERSFIELD, CALIFORNIA POSITIONS PLAYED: C, 1B, OF

YEAR	TEAM	GAMES	AB	RUNS	HITS	2B	3B	HR	RBI	BB	IBB	SO	HBP	SH	SF	SB	CS	BA	OBA	SA	FA
1964	LAA-A	9	16	2	6	0	0	0	2	2	0	3	0	0	0	0	0	.375	.444	.375	.950
1965	SF-N	40	67	5	19	4	0	1	7	12	2	14	0	1	0	0	0	.284	.392	.388	.977
1966	SF-N	18	23	2	7	2	0	0	1	4	0	5	0	1	0	0	0	.304	.407	.391	.982
1967	SF-N	73	153	24	42	6	0	6	26	27	1	37	1	1	0	0	0	.275	.387	.431	.988
1968	SF-N	90	224	14	52	10	2	4	34	41	4	61	1	0	2	0	0	.232	.351	.348	.995
1969	SF-N	69	194	18	38	4	0	7	34	48	5	58	0	1	2	0	0	.196	.352	.325	.992
1970	Mon-N	17	43	4	14	2	0	0	7	14	0	14	0	0	0	0	0	.326	.491	.372	.964
1970	**ChC-N**	**66**	**178**	**19**	**43**	**12**	**1**	**2**	**22**	**31**	**2**	**48**	**0**	**5**	**1**	**0**	**0**	**.242**	**.352**	**.354**	**.990**
1971	Hou-N	69	174	16	48	8	1	1	16	35	2	39	2	2	1	0	1	.276	.401	.351	.991
1972	Hou-N	10	25	2	5	3	0	0	0	5	2	5	0	0	0	0	0	.200	.333	.320	1.000
1972	Cal-A	22	45	4	13	0	1	1	5	5	0	11	0	0	0	0	0	.289	.360	.400	1.000
Career average		54	127	12	32	6	1	2	17	25	2	33	0	1	1	0	0	.251	.374	.363	.990
Cubs average		**66**	**178**	**19**	**43**	**12**	**1**	**2**	**22**	**31**	**2**	**48**	**0**	**5**	**1**	**0**	**0**	**.242**	**.352**	**.354**	**.990**
Career total		483	1142	110	287	51	5	22	154	224	18	295	4	11	6	0	1	.251	.374	.363	.990
Cubs total		**66**	**178**	**19**	**43**	**12**	**1**	**2**	**22**	**31**	**2**	**48**	**0**	**5**	**1**	**0**	**0**	**.242**	**.352**	**.354**	**.990**

Hickey, Edward A. (Eddie)

HEIGHT: — THROWS: — BATS: — BORN: 8/18/1872 CLEVELAND, OHIO DIED: 3/25/1941 TACOMA, WASHINGTON POSITIONS PLAYED: 3B

YEAR	TEAM	GAMES	AB	RUNS	HITS	2B	3B	HR	RBI	BB	IBB	SO	HBP	SH	SF	SB	CS	BA	OBA	SA	FA
1901	ChN-N	10	37	4	6	0	0	0	3	2	—	—	1	0	—	1	—	.162	.225	.162	.743
Career average		10	37	4	6	0	0	0	3	2	—	—	1	0	—	1	—	.162	.225	.162	.743
Cubs average		**10**	**37**	**4**	**6**	**0**	**0**	**0**	**3**	**2**	**—**	**—**	**1**	**0**	**—**	**1**	**—**	**.162**	**.225**	**.162**	**.743**
Career total		10	37	4	6	0	0	0	3	2	—	—	1	0	—	1	—	.162	.225	.162	.743
Cubs total		**10**	**37**	**4**	**6**	**0**	**0**	**0**	**3**	**2**	**—**	**—**	**1**	**0**	**—**	**1**	**—**	**.162**	**.225**	**.162**	**.743**

Hickman, James Lucius (Jim)

HEIGHT: 6'3" THROWS: RIGHT BATS: RIGHT BORN: 5/10/1937 HENNING, TENNESSEE POSITIONS PLAYED: P, 1B, 3B, OF

YEAR	TEAM	GAMES	AB	RUNS	HITS	2B	3B	HR	RBI	BB	IBB	SO	HBP	SH	SF	SB	CS	BA	OBA	SA	FA
1962	NYM-N	140	392	54	96	18	2	13	46	47	2	96	3	7	3	4	4	.245	.328	.401	.971
1963	NYM-N	146	494	53	113	21	6	17	51	44	1	120	1	3	4	0	5	.229	.291	.399	.938
1964	NYM-N	139	409	48	105	14	1	11	57	36	4	90	2	0	1	0	1	.257	.319	.377	.976
1965	NYM-N	141	369	32	87	18	0	15	40	27	3	76	2	1	1	3	1	.236	.291	.407	.979
1966	NYM-N	58	160	15	38	7	0	4	16	13	0	34	1	0	0	2	1	.238	.299	.356	.990
1967	LA-N	65	98	7	16	6	1	0	10	14	1	28	0	2	0	1	1	.163	.268	.245	1.000
1968	**ChC-N**	**75**	**188**	**22**	**42**	**6**	**3**	**5**	**23**	**18**	**2**	**38**	**1**	**3**	**3**	**1**	**1**	**.223**	**.290**	**.367**	**.975**
1969	**ChC-N**	**134**	**338**	**38**	**80**	**11**	**2**	**21**	**54**	**47**	**3**	**74**	**0**	**0**	**4**	**2**	**1**	**.237**	**.326**	**.467**	**.981**

(continued)

James (Jim) Lucius Hickman, of-1b-3b, 1962–74

Remembered mostly for a clutch late-season hitting spree in the "dark year" (1969), Jim Hickman was a slugging outfielder-first baseman for the Cubs in the late 1960s and early 1970s.

Hickman was born on May 10, 1937, in Henning, Tennessee. He was a member of the first New York Mets team in 1962. Hickman spent five so-so seasons patrolling center field for the Mets, never hitting better than .257, in 1964.

Hickman did, however, squeeze into the Mets record books, becoming the first Met to hit for the cycle in 1963 and the first to hit three home runs in one game in 1965.

After a one-season stint with the Dodgers in 1967, he was traded to the Cubs just before the 1968 season. He didn't hit for average, and Hickman didn't hit very many home runs initially. But in 1969, he began coming around. After a slow start, he ended the season with 21 homers.

Hickman's play for the first few months of the 1969 season was solid but unspectacular. In August, when the rest of the Cubs were reeling as the Mets crept up on them, Hickman hit .301 with 10 home runs and 25 RBIs. In September only Hickman and fellow outfielder Billy Williams hit better than their averages to that point.

"He hit 21 home runs, and it seemed like just about every one of them won a game for us that year," recalled Glenn Beckert.

Hickman also had a powerful outfield arm. In 1970, he once threw out two base runners at the plate in one inning, but it was a similar play he didn't make the year before that still haunts Cubs fans. With the score tied, 2-2, in a September 8 game against the Mets at Shea Stadium, Hickman fielded the ball in right field and appeared to gun down the Mets' Tommie Agee at the plate. Much to the astonishment of the Cubs dugout, home plate umpire Satch Davidson called Agee safe. Cubs catcher Randy Hundley later swore he tagged Agee out about six feet up the line. That turned out to be the winning run—and continued the Cubs' slide that year.

Hickman had a career year in 1970, hitting .315 with 115 RBIs and 32 home runs. It was the first of three consecutive seasons in which Hickman would average 120 hits and 23 home runs per season. He was named to the All-Star team in 1970, and his single in the bottom of the 12th inning scored Pete Rose with the game-winning run.

Hickman's production dropped off in 1973, and he retired in 1974 after playing part-time for the Cardinals.

(continued)

YEAR	TEAM	GAMES	AB	RUNS	HITS	2B	3B	HR	RBI	BB	IBB	SO	HBP	SH	SF	SB	CS	BA	OBA	SA	FA
1970	ChC-N	149	514	102	162	33	4	32	115	93	8	99	1	2	3	0	1	.315	.419	.582	.987
1971	ChC-N	117	383	50	98	13	2	19	60	50	7	61	3	3	5	0	1	.256	.342	.449	.994
1972	ChC-N	115	368	65	100	15	2	17	64	52	3	64	2	2	1	3	1	.272	.364	.462	.992
1973	ChC-N	92	201	27	49	1	2	3	20	42	2	42	0	2	4	1	1	.244	.368	.313	.989
1974	StL-N	50	60	5	16	0	0	2	4	8	0	10	0	0	0	0	0	.267	.353	.367	.986
Career average		109	306	40	77	13	2	12	43	38	3	64	1	2	2	1	1	.252	.335	.426	.983
Cubs average		**114**	**332**	**51**	**89**	**13**	**3**	**16**	**56**	**50**	**4**	**63**	**1**	**2**	**3**	**1**	**1**	**.267**	**.362**	**.467**	**.989**
Career total		1421	3974	518	1002	163	25	159	560	491	36	832	16	25	29	17	19	.252	.335	.426	.983
Cubs total		**682**	**1992**	**304**	**531**	**79**	**15**	**97**	**336**	**302**	**25**	**378**	**7**	**12**	**20**	**7**	**6**	**.267**	**.362**	**.467**	**.989**

Hildebrand, R.E.

HEIGHT: — THROWS: — BATS: — BORN: — POSITIONS PLAYED: OF

YEAR	TEAM	GAMES	AB	RUNS	HITS	2B	3B	HR	RBI	BB	IBB	SO	HBP	SH	SF	SB	CS	BA	OBA	SA	FA
1902	ChC-N	1	4	1	0	0	0	0	0	1	—	—	0	0	—	0	—	.000	.200	.000	1.000
Career average		1	4	1	0	0	0	0	0	1	—	—	0	0	—	0	—	.000	.200	.000	1.000
Cubs average		**1**	**4**	**1**	**0**	**0**	**0**	**0**	**0**	**1**	**—**	**—**	**0**	**0**	**—**	**0**	**—**	**.000**	**.200**	**.000**	**1.000**
Career total		1	4	1	0	0	0	0	0	1	—	—	0	0	—	0	—	.000	.200	.000	1.000
Cubs total		**1**	**4**	**1**	**0**	**0**	**0**	**0**	**0**	**1**	**—**	**—**	**0**	**0**	**—**	**0**	**—**	**.000**	**.200**	**.000**	**1.000**

Hill, Glenallen
HEIGHT: 6'3"   THROWS: RIGHT   BATS: RIGHT   BORN: 3/22/1965 SANTA CRUZ, CALIFORNIA   POSITIONS PLAYED: OF

YEAR	TEAM	GAMES	AB	RUNS	HITS	2B	3B	HR	RBI	BB	IBB	SO	HBP	SH	SF	SB	CS	BA	OBA	SA	FA
1989	Tor-A	19	52	4	15	0	0	1	7	3	0	12	0	0	0	2	1	.288	.327	.346	.964
1990	Tor-A	84	260	47	60	11	3	12	32	18	0	62	0	0	0	8	3	.231	.281	.435	.983
1991	Tor-A	35	99	14	25	5	2	3	11	7	0	24	0	1	1	2	2	.253	.296	.434	.967
1991	Cle-A	37	122	15	32	3	0	5	14	16	0	30	0	1	1	4	2	.262	.345	.410	.978
1992	Cle-A	102	369	38	89	16	1	18	49	20	0	73	4	0	4	9	6	.241	.287	.436	.956
1993	Cle-A	66	174	19	39	7	2	5	25	11	1	50	1	1	4	7	3	.224	.268	.374	.940
1993	**ChC-N**	**31**	**87**	**14**	**30**	**7**	**0**	**10**	**22**	**6**	**0**	**21**	**0**	**0**	**0**	**1**	**0**	**.345**	**.387**	**.770**	**.957**
1993	**ChC-N**	**31**	**87**	**14**	**30**	**7**	**0**	**10**	**22**	**6**	**0**	**21**	**0**	**0**	**1**	**19**	**6**	**.297**	**.365**	**.461**	**.987**
1994	**ChC-N**	**89**	**269**	**48**	**80**	**12**	**1**	**10**	**38**	**29**	**0**	**57**	**0**	**0**	**2**	**25**	**5**	**.264**	**.317**	**.483**	**.959**
1995	SF-N	132	497	71	131	29	4	24	86	39	4	98	1	0	3	6	3	.280	.344	.499	.960
1996	SF-N	98	379	56	106	26	0	19	67	33	3	95	6	0	6	7	4	.261	.297	.435	.947
1997	SF-N	128	398	47	104	28	4	11	64	19	0	87	4	0	7	1	1	.290	.332	.521	.965
1998	Sea-A	74	259	37	75	20	2	12	33	14	1	45	3	0	1	1	0	.351	.414	.573	.984
1998	**ChC-N**	**48**	**131**	**26**	**46**	**5**	**0**	**8**	**23**	**14**	**1**	**34**	**0**	**0**	**0**	**0**	**0**	**.300**	**.353**	**.581**	**.955**
1999	**ChC-N**	**99**	**253**	**43**	**76**	**9**	**1**	**20**	**55**	**22**	**1**	**61**	**0**	**0**	**3**	**5**	**1**	**.262**	**.303**	**.494**	**.955**
2000	**ChC-N**	**64**	**168**	**23**	**44**	**4**	**1**	**11**	**29**	**10**	**2**	**43**	**0**	**0**	**0**	**0**	**1**	**.333**	**.378**	**.735**	**1.000**
2000	NYY-A	40	132	22	44	5	0	16	29	9	0	33	1	0	1	0	0	.136	.136	.182	—
2001	Ana-A	16	66	4	9	0	0	1	2	0	0	20	0	0	0	0	0	.271	.321	.482	.964
Career average		89	286	41	77	14	2	14	45	21	1	65	2	0	2	7	3	.271	.321	.482	.964
Cubs average		**66**	**182**	**31**	**55**	**7**	**1**	**12**	**33**	**16**	**1**	**43**	**0**	**0**	**1**	**5**	**2**	**.304**	**.360**	**.546**	**.972**
Career total		1162	3715	528	1005	187	21	186	586	270	13	845	20	2	26	96	38	.271	.321	.482	.964
Cubs total		**331**	**908**	**154**	**276**	**37**	**3**	**59**	**167**	**81**	**4**	**216**	**0**	**0**	**4**	**25**	**8**	**.304**	**.360**	**.546**	**.972**

Hines, Paul A.
HEIGHT: 5'9"   THROWS: RIGHT   BATS: RIGHT   BORN: 3/1/1852 WASHINGTON, DISTRICT OF COLUMBIA   DIED: 7/10/1935 HYATTSVILLE, MARYLAND
POSITIONS PLAYED: P, 1B, 2B, 3B, SS, OF

YEAR	TEAM	GAMES	AB	RUNS	HITS	2B	3B	HR	RBI	BB	IBB	SO	HBP	SH	SF	SB	CS	BA	OBA	SA	FA
1876	**ChN-N**	**64**	**306**	**62**	**101**	**21**	**3**	**2**	**59**	**1**	**—**	**3**	**—**	**—**	**—**	**—**	**—**	**.330**	**.332**	**.438**	**.923**
1877	**ChN-N**	**60**	**261**	**44**	**73**	**11**	**7**	**0**	**23**	**1**	**—**	**8**	**—**	**—**	**—**	**—**	**—**	**.280**	**.282**	**.375**	**.798**
1878	Prv-N	62	257	42	92	13	4	4	50	2	—	10	—	—	—	—	—	.358	.363	.486	.843
1879	Prv-N	85	409	81	146	25	10	2	52	8	—	16	—	—	—	—	—	.357	.369	.482	.867
1880	Prv-N	85	374	64	115	20	2	3	35	13	—	17	—	—	—	—	—	.307	.331	.396	.942
1881	Prv-N	80	361	65	103	27	5	2	31	13	—	12	—	—	—	—	—	.285	.310	.404	.881
1882	Prv-N	84	379	73	117	28	10	4	34	10	—	14	—	—	—	—	—	.309	.326	.467	.868
1883	Prv-N	97	442	94	132	32	4	4	45	18	—	23	—	—	—	—	—	.299	.326	.416	.925
1884	Prv-N	114	490	94	148	36	10	3	41	44	—	28	—	—	—	—	—	.302	.360	.435	.908
1885	Prv-N	98	411	63	111	20	4	1	35	19	—	18	—	—	—	—	—	.270	.302	.345	.879
1886	WaN-N	121	487	80	152	30	8	9	56	35	—	21	—	—	—	21	—	.312	.358	.462	.889
1887	WaN-N	123	526	83	195	32	5	10	72	48	—	24	8	—	—	46	—	.371	.431	.508	.898
1888	Ind-N	133	513	84	144	26	3	4	58	41	—	45	8	—	—	31	—	.281	.343	.366	.917
1889	Ind-N	121	486	77	148	27	1	6	72	49	—	22	5	—	—	34	—	.305	.374	.401	.965
1890	Pit-N	31	121	11	22	1	0	0	9	11	—	7	1	—	—	6	—	.182	.256	.190	.950
1890	Bos-N	69	273	41	72	12	3	2	48	32	—	20	4	—	—	9	—	.264	.350	.352	.888
1891	Was-AA	54	206	25	58	7	5	0	31	21	—	16	10	—	—	6	—	.282	.376	.364	.900
Career average		93	394	68	121	23	5	4	47	23	—	19	2	—	—	10	—	.306	.348	.418	.912
Cubs average		**62**	**284**	**53**	**87**	**16**	**5**	**1**	**41**	**1**	**—**	**6**	**—**	**—**	**—**	**—**	**—**	**.307**	**.309**	**.409**	**.861**
Career total		1481	6302	1083	1929	368	84	56	751	366	—	304	36	—	—	153	—	.306	.348	.418	.912
Cubs total		**124**	**567**	**106**	**174**	**32**	**10**	**2**	**82**	**2**	**—**	**11**	**—**	**—**	**—**	**—**	**—**	**.307**	**.309**	**.409**	**.861**

Hiser, Gene Taylor
HEIGHT: 5'11"   THROWS: LEFT   BATS: LEFT   BORN: 12/11/1948 BALTIMORE, MARYLAND   POSITIONS PLAYED: 1B, OF

YEAR	TEAM	GAMES	AB	RUNS	HITS	2B	3B	HR	RBI	BB	IBB	SO	HBP	SH	SF	SB	CS	BA	OBA	SA	FA
1971	**ChC-N**	**17**	**29**	**4**	**6**	**0**	**0**	**0**	**1**	**4**	**0**	**8**	**0**	**1**	**0**	**1**	**0**	**.207**	**.303**	**.207**	**1.000**
1972	**ChC-N**	**32**	**46**	**2**	**9**	**0**	**0**	**0**	**4**	**6**	**0**	**8**	**0**	**1**	**0**	**1**	**0**	**.196**	**.288**	**.196**	**1.000**
1973	**ChC-N**	**100**	**109**	**15**	**19**	**3**	**0**	**1**	**6**	**11**	**1**	**17**	**1**	**5**	**1**	**4**	**5**	**.174**	**.254**	**.229**	**.980**
1974	**ChC-N**	**12**	**17**	**2**	**4**	**1**	**0**	**0**	**1**	**0**	**0**	**3**	**0**	**0**	**0**	**0**	**0**	**.235**	**.235**	**.294**	**1.000**
1975	**ChC-N**	**45**	**62**	**11**	**15**	**3**	**0**	**0**	**6**	**11**	**1**	**7**	**0**	**2**	**1**	**0**	**1**	**.242**	**.351**	**.290**	**1.000**
Career average		41	53	7	11	1	0	0	4	6	0	9	0	2	0	1	1	.202	.289	.240	.992
Cubs average		**41**	**53**	**7**	**11**	**1**	**0**	**0**	**4**	**6**	**0**	**9**	**0**	**2**	**0**	**1**	**1**	**.202**	**.289**	**.240**	**.992**
Career total		206	263	34	53	7	0	1	18	32	2	43	1	9	2	6	6	.202	.289	.240	.992
Cubs total		**206**	**263**	**34**	**53**	**7**	**0**	**1**	**18**	**32**	**2**	**43**	**1**	**9**	**2**	**6**	**6**	**.202**	**.289**	**.240**	**.992**

Hoak, Donald Albert (Don *or* Tiger)
HEIGHT: 6'1"   THROWS: RIGHT   BATS: RIGHT   BORN: 2/5/1928 ROULETTE, PENNSYLVANIA   DIED: 10/9/1969 PITTSBURGH, PENNSYLVANIA
POSITIONS PLAYED: 2B, 3B, SS

YEAR	TEAM	GAMES	AB	RUNS	HITS	2B	3B	HR	RBI	BB	IBB	SO	HBP	SH	SF	SB	CS	BA	OBA	SA	FA
1954	Bro-N	88	261	41	64	9	5	7	26	25	—	39	4	4	2	8	3	.245	.318	.398	.950
1955	Bro-N	94	279	50	67	13	3	5	19	46	0	50	1	6	0	9	5	.240	.350	.362	.960
1956	**ChC-N**	**121**	**424**	**51**	**91**	**18**	**4**	**5**	**37**	**41**	**0**	**46**	**1**	**8**	**4**	**8**	**3**	**.215**	**.283**	**.311**	**.949**
1957	Cin-N	149	529	78	155	39	2	19	89	74	5	54	4	5	4	8	15	.293	.381	.482	.971
1958	Cin-N	114	417	51	109	30	0	6	50	43	4	36	2	3	1	6	8	.261	.333	.376	.964
1959	Pit-N	155	564	60	166	29	3	8	65	71	4	75	4	6	6	9	2	.294	.374	.399	.961
1960	Pit-N	155	553	97	156	24	9	16	79	74	9	74	1	4	4	3	2	.282	.366	.445	.948
1961	Pit-N	145	503	72	150	27	7	12	61	73	8	53	3	3	4	4	2	.298	.388	.451	.953
1962	Pit-N	121	411	63	99	14	8	5	48	49	5	49	1	1	5	4	2	.241	.320	.350	.969
1963	Phi-N	115	377	35	87	11	3	6	24	27	1	52	1	3	3	5	5	.231	.282	.324	.958
1964	Phi-N	6	4	0	0	0	0	0	0	0	0	2	0	2	0	0	0	.000	.000	.000	—
Career average		115	393	54	104	19	4	8	45	48	3	48	2	4	3	6	4	.265	.345	.396	.959
Cubs average		**121**	**424**	**51**	**91**	**18**	**4**	**5**	**37**	**41**	**0**	**46**	**1**	**8**	**4**	**8**	**3**	**.215**	**.283**	**.311**	**.949**
Career total		1263	4322	598	1144	214	44	89	498	523	36	530	22	45	33	64	47	.265	.345	.396	.959
Cubs total		**121**	**424**	**51**	**91**	**18**	**4**	**5**	**37**	**41**	**0**	**46**	**1**	**8**	**4**	**8**	**3**	**.215**	**.283**	**.311**	**.949**

Hoffman, Lawrence Charles (Larry)
HEIGHT: —   THROWS: RIGHT   BATS: RIGHT   BORN: 7/18/1882 CHICAGO, ILLINOIS   DIED: 12/29/1948 CHICAGO, ILLINOIS   POSITIONS PLAYED: 2B, 3B

YEAR	TEAM	GAMES	AB	RUNS	HITS	2B	3B	HR	RBI	BB	IBB	SO	HBP	SH	SF	SB	CS	BA	OBA	SA	FA
1901	ChN-N	6	22	2	7	1	0	0	6	0	—	—	1	1	—	1	—	.318	.348	.364	.824
Career average		6	22	2	7	1	0	0	6	0	—	—	1	1	—	1	—	.318	.348	.364	.824
Cubs average		**6**	**22**	**2**	**7**	**1**	**0**	**0**	**6**	**0**	**—**	**—**	**1**	**1**	**—**	**1**	**—**	**.318**	**.348**	**.364**	**.824**
Career total		6	22	2	7	1	0	0	6	0	—	—	1	1	—	1	—	.318	.348	.364	.824
Cubs total		**6**	**22**	**2**	**7**	**1**	**0**	**0**	**6**	**0**	**—**	**—**	**1**	**1**	**—**	**1**	**—**	**.318**	**.348**	**.364**	**.824**

Hofman, Arthur Frederick (Solly or Circus Solly)
HEIGHT: 6'0"   THROWS: RIGHT   BATS: RIGHT   BORN: 10/29/1882 ST. LOUIS, MISSOURI   DIED: 3/10/1956 ST. LOUIS, MISSOURI
POSITIONS PLAYED: 1B, 2B, 3B, SS, OF

YEAR	TEAM	GAMES	AB	RUNS	HITS	2B	3B	HR	RBI	BB	IBB	SO	HBP	SH	SF	SB	CS	BA	OBA	SA	FA
1903	Pit-N	3	2	1	0	0	0	0	0	0	—	—	0	0	—	0	—	.000	.000	.000	—
1904	**ChC-N**	**7**	**26**	**7**	**7**	**0**	**0**	**1**	**4**	**1**	**—**	**—**	**0**	**1**	**—**	**2**	**—**	**.269**	**.296**	**.385**	**.923**
1905	**ChC-N**	**86**	**287**	**43**	**68**	**14**	**4**	**1**	**38**	**20**	**—**	**—**	**1**	**8**	**—**	**15**	**—**	**.237**	**.289**	**.324**	**.952**
1906	**ChC-N**	**64**	**195**	**30**	**50**	**2**	**3**	**2**	**20**	**20**	**—**	**—**	**0**	**6**	**—**	**13**	**—**	**.256**	**.326**	**.328**	**.978**
1907	**ChC-N**	**134**	**470**	**67**	**126**	**11**	**3**	**1**	**36**	**41**	**—**	**—**	**1**	**24**	**—**	**29**	**—**	**.268**	**.328**	**.311**	**.949**
1908	**ChC-N**	**120**	**411**	**55**	**100**	**15**	**5**	**2**	**42**	**33**	**—**	**—**	**6**	**28**	**—**	**15**	**—**	**.243**	**.309**	**.319**	**.965**
1909	**ChC-N**	**153**	**527**	**60**	**150**	**21**	**4**	**2**	**58**	**53**	**—**	**—**	**1**	**32**	**—**	**20**	**—**	**.285**	**.351**	**.351**	**.965**
1910	**ChC-N**	**136**	**477**	**83**	**155**	**24**	**16**	**3**	**86**	**65**	**—**	**34**	**0**	**30**	**—**	**29**	**—**	**.325**	**.406**	**.461**	**.976**
1911	**ChC-N**	**143**	**512**	**66**	**129**	**17**	**2**	**2**	**70**	**66**	**—**	**40**	**3**	**24**	**—**	**30**	**—**	**.252**	**.341**	**.305**	**.978**
1912	**ChC-N**	**36**	**125**	**28**	**34**	**11**	**0**	**0**	**18**	**22**	**—**	**13**	**1**	**2**	**—**	**5**	**—**	**.272**	**.385**	**.360**	**.981**
1912	Pit-N	17	53	7	15	4	1	0	2	5	—	6	0	2	—	0	—	.283	.345	.396	1.000
1913	Pit-N	28	83	11	19	5	2	0	7	8	—	6	0	4	—	3	—	.229	.297	.337	.964
1914	Bro-F	147	515	65	148	25	12	5	83	54	—	41	2	12	—	34	—	.287	.357	.412	.959
1915	Buf-F	109	346	29	81	10	6	0	27	30	—	28	0	10	—	12	—	.234	.295	.298	.970
1916	NYY-A	6	27	0	8	1	1	0	2	1	—	1	0	1	—	1	—	.296	.321	.407	1.000
1916	**ChC-N**	**5**	**16**	**2**	**5**	**2**	**1**	**0**	**2**	**2**	**—**	**2**	**0**	**0**	**—**	**0**	**—**	**.313**	**.389**	**.563**	**1.000**
Career average		85	291	40	78	12	4	1	35	30	—	12	1	13	—	15	—	.269	.340	.352	.966
Cubs average		**88**	**305**	**44**	**82**	**12**	**4**	**1**	**37**	**32**	**—**	**9**	**1**	**16**	**—**	**16**	**—**	**.271**	**.343**	**.348**	**.966**
Career total		1194	4072	554	1095	162	60	19	495	421	—	171	15	184	—	208	—	.269	.340	.352	.966
Cubs total		**884**	**3046**	**441**	**824**	**117**	**38**	**14**	**374**	**323**	**—**	**89**	**13**	**155**	**—**	**158**	**—**	**.271**	**.343**	**.348**	**.966**

Hollocher, Charles Jacob (Charlie)
HEIGHT: 5'7"   THROWS: RIGHT   BATS: LEFT   BORN: 6/11/1896 ST. LOUIS, MISSOURI   DIED: 8/14/1940 FRONTENAC, MISSOURI   POSITIONS PLAYED: SS

YEAR	TEAM	GAMES	AB	RUNS	HITS	2B	3B	HR	RBI	BB	IBB	SO	HBP	SH	SF	SB	CS	BA	OBA	SA	FA
1918	ChC-N	131	509	72	161	23	6	2	38	47	—	30	4	26	—	26	—	.316	.379	.397	.929
1919	ChC-N	115	430	51	116	14	5	3	26	44	—	19	7	21	—	16	—	.270	.347	.347	.941
1920	ChC-N	80	301	53	96	17	2	0	22	41	—	15	3	24	—	20	14	.319	.406	.389	.954
1921	ChC-N	140	558	71	161	28	8	3	37	43	—	13	2	26	—	5	16	.289	.342	.384	.963

(continued)

Arthur Frederick "Solly," "Circus Solly" Hofman, of-2b-ss-3b-1b, 1903—16

Solly Hofman was a key utility player for the 1906 to 1910 Cubs dynasty, a man so versatile that manager Frank Chance hated to make him a starter, so useful were his talents off the bench.

Hofman was born on October 29, 1882, in St. Louis, Missouri. He began his big-league career in Pittsburgh, playing a handful of games with the Pirates in the outfield before being traded to the Cubs in 1904.

Hofman had played in the outfield for Pittsburgh, but while playing semipro ball in St. Louis, he had been judged as the best shortstop in the country in the minors. Cubs manager Frank Chance used Hofman as an outfielder and shortstop in 1904 and was so impressed with Hofman's athletic ability, he used him at every infield position except catcher in 1905, and as a replacement outfielder as well.

By 1906 Chance had no qualms about playing Hofman everywhere but pitcher and catcher. In addition to hitting fairly well, Hofman was a terrific defensive player wherever Chance happened to station him. He was called "Circus

Solly" because of the acrobatic catches he would make afield.

In 1907 Hofman played in 134 games, hit .268, stole 29 bases and scored 67 runs without having a regular position. In one week in 1908, Hofman played six different positions in six games.

In 1909 Chance finally had to start Hofman in center field. Solly responded by making a team-high 150 hits for a team-high .285 average. The next year, he hit a career-high .325 and led the Cubs in triples with 16, RBIs with 86 and stolen bases with 29 as Chicago won the National League pennant.

After a so-so season for the Cubs in 1911, Hofman was sold to the Pittsburgh Pirates, where he spent most of his year and a half there on the bench. Hofman then signed with the Brooklyn franchise of the Federal League. Hofman had two productive seasons with Brooklyn and later Buffalo before the Federal League folded.

Hofman, at 34, signed with the New York Highlanders in 1916. New York released him, and he returned to Chicago briefly that year before retiring. Hofman died in St. Louis, Missouri, in 1956.

(Hollocher, continued)

YEAR	TEAM	GAMES	AB	RUNS	HITS	2B	3B	HR	RBI	BB	IBB	SO	HBP	SH	SF	SB	CS	BA	OBA	SA	FA
1922	ChC-N	152	592	90	201	37	8	3	69	58	—	5	5	37	—	19	29	.340	.403	.444	.965
1923	ChC-N	66	260	46	89	14	2	1	28	26	—	5	4	9	—	9	10	.342	.410	.423	.963
1924	ChC-N	76	286	28	70	12	4	2	21	18	—	7	1	8	—	4	11	.245	.292	.336	.969
Career average		109	419	59	128	21	5	2	34	40	—	13	4	22	—	14	11	.304	.370	.392	.954
Cubs average		**109**	**419**	**59**	**128**	**21**	**5**	**2**	**34**	**40**	**—**	**13**	**4**	**22**	**—**	**14**	**11**	**.304**	**.370**	**.392**	**.954**
Career total		760	2936	411	894	145	35	14	241	277	—	94	26	151	—	99	80	.304	.370	.392	.954
Cubs total		**760**	**2936**	**411**	**894**	**145**	**35**	**14**	**241**	**277**	**—**	**94**	**26**	**151**	**—**	**99**	**80**	**.304**	**.370**	**.392**	**.954**

Holm, William Frederick (Billy)
HEIGHT: 5'10" THROWS: RIGHT BATS: RIGHT BORN: 7/21/1912 CHICAGO, ILLINOIS DIED: 7/27/1977 EAST CHICAGO, INDIANA POSITIONS PLAYED: C

YEAR	TEAM	GAMES	AB	RUNS	HITS	2B	3B	HR	RBI	BB	IBB	SO	HBP	SH	SF	SB	CS	BA	OBA	SA	FA
1943	ChC-N	7	15	0	1	0	0	0	0	2	—	4	0	0	—	0	—	.067	.176	.067	1.000
1944	ChC-N	54	132	10	18	2	0	0	6	16	—	19	1	5	—	1	—	.136	.235	.152	.979
1945	Bos-A	58	135	12	25	2	1	0	9	23	—	17	3	5	—	1	1	.185	.317	.215	.980
Career average		40	94	7	15	1	0	0	5	14	—	13	1	3	—	1	0	.156	.272	.177	.981
Cubs average		**31**	**74**	**5**	**10**	**1**	**0**	**0**	**3**	**9**	**—**	**12**	**1**	**3**	**—**	**1**	**—**	**.129**	**.229**	**.143**	**.981**
Career total		119	282	22	44	4	1	0	15	41	—	40	4	10	—	2	1	.156	.272	.177	.981
Cubs total		**61**	**147**	**10**	**19**	**2**	**0**	**0**	**6**	**18**	**—**	**23**	**1**	**5**	**—**	**1**	**—**	**.129**	**.229**	**.143**	**.981**

Charles (Charlie) Jacob Hollocher, ss, 1918–24

One of Chicago's rising stars of the 1920s, Charlie Hollocher's bright story eventually turned into a sad tragedy.

Hollocher was born on June 11, 1896, in St. Louis, Missouri. He was an exceptional player at both the semipro and minor league level, and the Cubs signed him before the 1918 season.

It was a great decision. Hollocher led the National League with 161 hits, 509 at-bats and 202 total bases. Defensively, he was third in the league in putouts and assists by shortstops. The Cubs went from fifth in 1917 to first in 1918, and there was no doubt that the dynamic Hollocher was the key. It is not hyperbole to suggest that while teammate and pitcher James "Hippo" Vaughn was probably the most valuable player in the league that year, Hollocher was one of the best everyday players in the league.

The intense Hollocher was at that time already beset by what the newspapers cited as "mysterious internal ailments," which modern fans and writers speculate may have been

ulcers. In 1919 he played 115 games at shortstop, but his production dropped significantly as he continued to struggle with his illness.

Hollocher played well in 1920, just not often. His .319 batting average would have easily led the Cubs, but he only played 80 games that year. As it was, his 20 stolen bases tied him for the team lead.

Hollocher's condition seemed to improve in 1921, and his play began to draw comparisons to that of former Pirates shortstop Honus Wagner. He made 201 hits in 1922, which translated into a .340 batting average, still a Cubs record for a shortstop. It was also the highest average for a shortstop since Wagner's .358 in 1908.

In 1921 and 1922, he also led all National League shortstops in fielding percentage. But the next two years saw Hollocher continue unsuccessfully to try to control his illness, and while he hit well when in the lineup, he only started 136 games in the two seasons. He retired after the 1924 season at the age of 28.

Hollocher never completely overcame his internal agonies, which appeared to worsen as he got older. In 1940 he took his own life by shooting himself.

Holmes, Frederick C. (Fred)

HEIGHT: — THROWS: RIGHT BATS: RIGHT BORN: 7/1/1878 CHICAGO, ILLINOIS DIED: 2/13/1956 NORWOOD PARK, ILLINOIS POSITIONS PLAYED: C, 1B

YEAR	TEAM	GAMES	AB	RUNS	HITS	2B	3B	HR	RBI	BB	IBB	SO	HBP	SH	SF	SB	CS	BA	OBA	SA	FA
1903	NYA-A	1	0	0	0	0	0	0	0	1	—	0	0	0	—	0	—	—	1.000	—	.833
1904	ChC-N	1	3	1	1	1	0	0	0	0	—	—	0	0	—	0	—	.333	.333	.667	1.000
Career average		1	2	1	1	1	0	0	0	1	—	0	0	0	—	0	—	.333	.500	.667	.909
Cubs average		1	3	1	1	1	0	0	0	0	—	—	0	0	—	0	—	.333	.333	.667	1.000
Career total		2	3	1	1	1	0	0	0	1	—	0	0	0	—	0	—	.333	.500	.667	.909
Cubs total		1	3	1	1	1	0	0	0	0	—	0	0	0	—	0	—	.333	.333	.667	1.000

Honan, Martin Weldon (Marty)

HEIGHT: — THROWS: — BATS: — BORN: 1870 CHICAGO, ILLINOIS DIED: 8/20/1908 CHICAGO, ILLINOIS POSITIONS PLAYED: C

YEAR	TEAM	GAMES	AB	RUNS	HITS	2B	3B	HR	RBI	BB	IBB	SO	HBP	SH	SF	SB	CS	BA	OBA	SA	FA
1890	ChN-N	1	3	0	0	0	0	0	1	0	—	2	0	—	—	0	—	.000	.000	.000	.857
1891	ChN-N	5	12	1	2	0	1	0	3	1	—	3	0	—	—	0	—	.167	.231	.333	.963
Career average		3	8	1	1	0	1	0	2	1	—	3	0	—	—	0	—	.133	.188	.267	.941
Cubs average		3	8	1	1	0	1	0	2	1	—	3	0	—	—	0	—	.133	.188	.267	.941
Career total		6	15	1	2	0	1	0	4	1	—	5	0	—	—	0	—	.133	.188	.267	.941
Cubs total		6	15	1	2	0	1	0	4	1	—	5	0	—	—	0	—	.133	.188	.267	.941

Hornsby, Rogers (Rajah)

HEIGHT: 5'11"   THROWS: RIGHT   BATS: RIGHT   BORN: 4/27/1896 WINTERS, TEXAS   DIED: 1/5/1963 CHICAGO, ILLINOIS   POSITIONS PLAYED: 1B, 2B, 3B, SS, OF

YEAR	TEAM	GAMES	AB	RUNS	HITS	2B	3B	HR	RBI	BB	IBB	SO	HBP	SH	SF	SB	CS	BA	OBA	SA	FA
1915	StL-N	18	57	5	14	2	0	0	4	2	—	6	0	2	—	0	2	.246	.271	.281	.922
1916	StL-N	139	495	63	155	17	15	6	65	40	—	63	4	11	—	17	—	.313	.369	.444	.934
1917	StL-N	145	523	86	171	24	17	8	66	45	—	34	4	17	—	17	—	.327	.385	.484	.939
1918	StL-N	115	416	51	117	19	11	5	60	40	—	43	3	7	—	8	—	.281	.349	.416	.933
1919	StL-N	138	512	68	163	15	9	8	71	48	—	41	7	10	—	17	—	.318	.384	.430	.946
1920	StL-N	149	589	96	218	44	20	9	94	60	—	50	3	8	—	12	15	.370	.431	.559	.962
1921	StL-N	154	592	131	235	44	18	21	126	60	—	48	7	15	—	13	13	.397	.458	.639	.968
1922	StL-N	154	623	141	250	46	14	42	152	65	—	50	1	15	—	17	12	.401	.459	.722	.967
1923	StL-N	107	424	89	163	32	10	17	83	55	—	29	3	5	—	3	7	.384	.459	.627	.967
1924	StL-N	143	536	121	227	43	14	25	94	89	—	32	2	13	—	5	12	.424	.507	.696	.965
1925	StL-N	138	504	133	203	41	10	39	143	83	—	39	2	16	—	5	3	.403	.489	.756	.954
1926	StL-N	134	527	96	167	34	5	11	93	61	—	39	0	16	—	3	—	.317	.388	.463	.962

(continued)

Rogers "the Rajah" Hornsby, 1b-2b-3b-ss-of, 1915–37

The nickname was accurate because Rogers Hornsby was a truly majestic righthand hitter, even if he had seen his better days before he became a Cub.

He was born on April 27, 1896, in the tiny town of Winters, Texas. His mother, Mary Rogers Hornsby, gave her son her maiden name.

Hornsby was an exceptional athlete growing up. By 15 he was playing baseball with grown men; by 17 he was a minor league star and by 19 was signed to a major league contract to play for the St. Louis Cardinals in the National League.

Hornsby was brought up to St. Louis in the latter part of the 1915 season, and didn't show a lot: he hit .246 in 18 games. At 5'11", 135 pounds, he was a skinny question mark for St. Louis manager Miller Huggins. Huggins saw a degree of potential in Hornsby but admitted many years later that he would never have predicted such a career from that shaky first season.

But Hornsby built himself up, working on a farm during the off-season, and eating four and sometimes five meals a day. He increased his weight to 175 pounds. He also worked on his batting stance, moving back into the far corner of the batter's box and using a lighter bat.

The transformation the next year was dramatic. Hornsby's new stance, coupled with his extraordinary quickness, gave him a hair more time to react to a pitch. His level swing, which St. Louis sportswriters crowed could be measured on a pane of glass, sprayed hits to all parts of the field. He was on his way.

During his St. Louis years, from 1915 to 1926, Hornsby hit the living bejesus out of the baseball. He cracked the .400 mark an astonishing three times, including a stunning .424 in 1924 that remains the highest average of the 20th century. He led the league in batting six times while in St. Louis, in on-base percentage six times and in slugging average seven times.

Although his hitting prowess was always exalted above his fielding, Hornsby was a hardworking fielder who led the league in fielding percentage in 1922 as a second baseman.

In 1926 Hornsby, by then a player-manager, led the Cardinals past the New York Yankees in one of the more improbable upsets in baseball's World Series history and also won the league's MVP award.

Hornsby was also a piece of work. He was supremely confident in everything he did on the ball field and was never afraid to remind teammates, coaches and sportswriters of that. He believed his batting prowess was due in part because of his exceptional eyesight and refused to watch motion pictures or even read newspapers or books. He would ask teammates or even passing strangers to read him menus, racing forms and marquees. He eschewed alcohol and tobacco and ate copiously. He trained on huge slabs of steak, believing it gave him energy.

(continued)

Year	Team																			
1927	NYG-N	155	568	133	205	32	9	26	125	86	—	38	4	26	—	9	—	.361	.448	.586	.972
1928	Bos-N	140	486	99	188	42	7	21	94	107	—	41	1	25	—	5	—	.387	.498	.632	.973
1929	**ChC-N**	**156**	**602**	**156**	**229**	**47**	**8**	**39**	**149**	**87**	—	**65**	**1**	**22**	—	**2**	—	**.380**	**.459**	**.679**	**.973**
1930	**ChC-N**	**42**	**104**	**15**	**32**	**5**	**1**	**2**	**18**	**12**	—	**12**	**1**	**3**	—	**0**	—	**.308**	**.385**	**.433**	**.916**
1931	**ChC-N**	**100**	**357**	**64**	**118**	**37**	**1**	**16**	**90**	**56**	—	**23**	**0**	**5**	—	**1**	—	**.331**	**.421**	**.574**	**.946**
1932	**ChC-N**	**19**	**58**	**10**	**13**	**2**	**0**	**1**	**7**	**10**	—	**4**	**2**	**0**	—	**0**	—	**.224**	**.357**	**.310**	**.871**
1933	StL-N	46	83	9	27	6	0	2	21	12	—	6	2	0	—	1	—	.325	.423	.470	.967
1933	StL-A	11	9	2	3	1	0	1	2	2	—	1	0	0	—	0	0	.333	.455	.778	—
1934	StL-A	24	23	2	7	2	0	1	11	7	—	4	1	0	—	0	0	.304	.484	.522	1.000
1935	StL-A	10	24	1	5	3	0	0	3	3	—	6	0	0	—	0	0	.208	.296	.333	1.000
1936	StL-A	2	5	1	2	0	0	0	2	1	—	0	0	0	—	0	0	.400	.500	.400	1.000
1937	StL-A	20	56	7	18	3	0	1	11	7	—	5	0	0	—	0	0	.321	.397	.429	.947
Career average		98	355	69	127	24	7	13	69	45	—	30	2	9	—	6	3	.358	.434	.577	.958
Cubs average		**79**	**280**	**61**	**98**	**23**	**3**	**15**	**66**	**41**	—	**26**	**1**	**8**	—	**1**	**0**	**.350**	**.435**	**.604**	**.958**
Career total		2259	8173	1579	2930	541	169	301	1584	1038	—	679	48	216	—	135	64	.358	.434	.577	.958
Cubs total		**317**	**1121**	**245**	**392**	**91**	**10**	**58**	**264**	**165**	—	**104**	**4**	**30**	—	**3**	**0**	**.350**	**.435**	**.604**	**.958**

He suffered fools not at all and was brusque with coaches and managers, who he believed were incompetent, and with owners who he believed were meddlers.

That was his undoing over the next few years. Hornsby was traded three times—from St. Louis to the New York Giants to the Boston Braves and finally to the Cubs in 1929. At each stop, he had squabbled with ownership. When he finally came to the Cubs, Hornsby was, at 33, believed to be over the hill and a detriment to an organization because of his eccentric ways.

But Hornsby redeemed himself magnificently in Chicago. He scored 156 runs, had 409 total bases and slugged .679 in 1929, all league bests. He also made 229 hits, had 149 RBIs and batted .380, all third in the National League. His 47 doubles were second in the league; his 39 homers fourth. For his efforts, Hornsby was the runaway MVP of the league.

In short, Hornsby was the missing piece for William Wrigley's 1929 Cubs, who already had star batsmen Hazen "Kiki" Cuyler, Lewis "Hack" Wilson, Riggs Stephenson and Charlie Grimm. Chicago swept to the National League pennant. Many years later, Hornsby himself would admit that "the 1929 Cubs had the best individual talent of any team I ever played on."

Hornsby, who also admitted that the 1929 season was one of the most enjoyable of his life, played every inning of every game that year. Such a strategy didn't pay off in the World Series against the Philadelphia Athletics. A foot injury suffered during the 1928 regular season and aggravated in 1929 limited him in the World Series. Hornsby would hit only .238, and the Cubs would lose.

Still, there was no reason to believe that the Cubs couldn't return to the top in 1930. But after an operation, Hornsby's foot did not improve and the Cubs could not hold off the hard-charging St. Louis Cardinals for the pennant.

Late in the season, with the Cubs still largely in contention, manager Joe McCarthy was fired and Hornsby elevated to the post, with owner William Wrigley hoping the change would jump-start the team. It didn't.

The next two years, the aging Hornsby was a part-time player, and his brusque demeanor was off-putting for many Cubs. So was his gambling, which had been excessive for years. Now Hornsby, who admitted he was no genius when it came to playing the ponies, began hitting up his players for loans.

The whole thing was something of a mess, and in 1932 Hornsby was fired and replaced by Grimm in midseason. The Cubs responded by winning the National League championship. Hornsby was signed by the Cardinals in 1933 and from there went to the Browns until his retirement in 1937.

He managed several teams after his retirement, including stints with the Browns and Cincinnati Reds, as well as stints in the minor leagues. He also worked as a scout for the Mets.

Hornsby was elected to the Hall of Fame in 1942. He died in 1963.

Hornsby did not play for the Cubs long enough to crack any all-time lists, but his .380 in 1929 is a Cubs record for the 20th century, and his 156 runs scored and 229 hits that year are all-time Cubs records.

Hosley, Timothy Kenneth (Tim)
HEIGHT: 5'11" THROWS: RIGHT BATS: RIGHT BORN: 5/10/1947 SPARTANBURG, SOUTH CAROLINA POSITIONS PLAYED: C, 1B

YEAR	TEAM	GAMES	AB	RUNS	HITS	2B	3B	HR	RBI	BB	IBB	SO	HBP	SH	SF	SB	CS	BA	OBA	SA	FA
1970	Det-A	7	12	1	2	0	0	1	2	0	0	6	0	0	1	0	0	.167	.154	.417	1.000
1971	Det-A	7	16	2	3	0	0	2	6	0	0	1	0	0	0	0	0	.188	.188	.563	1.000
1973	Oak-A	13	14	3	3	0	0	0	2	2	0	3	0	0	0	0	0	.214	.313	.214	.952
1974	Oak-A	11	7	3	2	0	0	0	1	1	0	2	0	1	1	0	0	.286	.333	.286	1.000
1975	**ChC-N**	62	141	22	36	7	0	6	20	27	3	25	2	1	0	1	1	.255	.382	.433	.968
1976	**ChC-N**	1	1	0	0	0	0	0	0	0	0	0	0	0	0	0	0	.000	.000	.000	—
1976	Oak-A	37	55	4	9	2	0	1	4	8	0	12	0	0	0	0	0	.164	.270	.255	.968
1977	Oak-A	39	78	5	15	0	0	1	10	16	0	13	1	0	1	0	0	.192	.333	.231	.949
1978	Oak-A	13	23	1	7	2	0	0	3	1	0	6	1	0	0	0	0	.304	.360	.391	.962
1981	Oak-A	18	21	2	2	0	0	1	5	2	0	5	0	0	0	0	0	.095	.174	.238	.750
Career average		23	41	5	9	1	0	1	6	6	0	8	0	0	0	0	0	.215	.324	.342	.966
Cubs average		**32**	**71**	**11**	**18**	**4**	**0**	**3**	**10**	**14**	**2**	**13**	**1**	**1**	**0**	**1**	**1**	**.254**	**.380**	**.430**	**.968**
Career total		208	368	43	79	11	0	12	53	57	3	73	4	2	3	1	1	.215	.324	.342	.966
Cubs total		**63**	**142**	**22**	**36**	**7**	**0**	**6**	**20**	**27**	**3**	**25**	**2**	**1**	**0**	**1**	**1**	**.254**	**.380**	**.430**	**.968**

Houseman, John Franklin
HEIGHT: — THROWS: — BATS: — BORN: 1/10/1870 NETHERLANDS DIED: 11/4/1922 CHICAGO, ILLINOIS POSITIONS PLAYED: 2B, 3B, SS, OF

YEAR	TEAM	GAMES	AB	RUNS	HITS	2B	3B	HR	RBI	BB	IBB	SO	HBP	SH	SF	SB	CS	BA	OBA	SA	FA
1894	**ChN-N**	4	15	5	6	3	1	0	4	5	—	3	1	0	—	2	—	.400	.571	.733	.923
1897	StL-N	80	278	34	68	6	6	0	21	28	—	—	7	4	—	16	—	.245	.329	.309	.923
Career average		42	147	20	37	5	4	0	13	17	—	2	4	2	—	9	—	.253	.344	.331	.923
Cubs average		**4**	**15**	**5**	**6**	**3**	**1**	**0**	**4**	**5**	**—**	**3**	**1**	**0**	**—**	**2**	**—**	**.400**	**.571**	**.733**	**.923**
Career total		84	293	39	74	9	7	0	25	33	—	3	8	4	—	18	—	.253	.344	.331	.923
Cubs total		**4**	**15**	**5**	**6**	**3**	**1**	**0**	**4**	**5**	**—**	**3**	**1**	**0**	**—**	**2**	**—**	**.400**	**.571**	**.733**	**.923**

Houston, Tyler Sam
HEIGHT: 6'1" THROWS: RIGHT BATS: LEFT BORN: 1/17/1971 LONG BEACH, CALIFORNIA POSITIONS PLAYED: C, 1B, 2B, 3B, SS, OF

YEAR	TEAM	GAMES	AB	RUNS	HITS	2B	3B	HR	RBI	BB	IBB	SO	HBP	SH	SF	SB	CS	BA	OBA	SA	FA
1996	Atl-N	33	27	3	6	2	1	1	8	1	0	9	0	0	0	0	0	.222	.250	.481	1.000
1996	**ChC-N**	46	115	18	39	7	0	2	19	8	1	18	0	0	0	3	2	.339	.382	.452	.982
1997	**ChC-N**	72	196	15	51	10	0	2	28	9	1	35	0	0	2	1	2	.260	.290	.342	.984
1998	**ChC-N**	95	255	26	65	7	1	9	33	13	1	53	0	1	1	2	2	.255	.290	.396	.990
1999	**ChC-N**	100	249	26	58	9	1	9	27	28	4	67	0	1	1	1	1	.233	.309	.386	.921
1999	Cle-A	13	27	2	4	1	0	1	3	3	0	11	0	0	0	0	0	.148	.233	.296	1.000
2000	Mil-N	101	284	30	71	15	0	18	43	17	3	72	0	4	0	2	1	.250	.292	.493	.974
2001	Mil-N	75	235	36	68	7	0	12	38	18	1	62	1	2	0	0	0	.289	.343	.472	.934
Career average		89	231	26	60	10	1	9	33	16	2	55	0	1	1	2	1	.261	.309	.424	.972
Cubs average		**78**	**204**	**21**	**53**	**8**	**1**	**6**	**27**	**15**	**2**	**43**	**0**	**1**	**1**	**2**	**1**	**.261**	**.309**	**.388**	**.975**
Career total		535	1388	156	362	58	3	54	199	97	11	327	1	8	4	9	6	.261	.309	.424	.972
Cubs total		**313**	**815**	**85**	**213**	**33**	**2**	**22**	**107**	**58**	**7**	**173**	**0**	**2**	**4**	**7**	**5**	**.261**	**.309**	**.388**	**.975**

Howard, George Elmer (Del)
HEIGHT: 6'0" THROWS: RIGHT BATS: LEFT BORN: 12/24/1877 KENNEY, ILLINOIS DIED: 12/24/1956 SEATTLE, WASHINGTON
POSITIONS PLAYED: P, 1B, 2B, SS, OF

YEAR	TEAM	GAMES	AB	RUNS	HITS	2B	3B	HR	RBI	BB	IBB	SO	HBP	SH	SF	SB	CS	BA	OBA	SA	FA
1905	Pit-N	123	435	56	127	18	5	2	63	27	—	—	8	14	—	19	—	.292	.345	.370	.978
1906	Bos-N	147	545	46	142	19	8	1	54	26	—	—	10	10	—	17	—	.261	.306	.330	.917
1907	Bos-N	50	187	20	51	4	2	1	13	11	—	—	5	6	—	11	—	.273	.330	.332	.964
1907	**ChC-N**	51	148	10	34	2	2	0	13	6	—	—	2	1	—	3	—	.230	.269	.270	.970
1908	**ChC-N**	96	315	42	88	7	3	1	26	23	—	—	5	11	—	11	—	.279	.338	.330	.965
1909	**ChC-N**	69	203	25	40	4	2	1	24	18	—	—	6	14	—	6	—	.197	.282	.251	.980
Career average		107	367	40	96	11	4	1	39	22	—	—	7	11	—	13	—	.263	.318	.326	.965
Cubs average		**72**	**222**	**26**	**54**	**4**	**2**	**1**	**21**	**16**	**—**	**—**	**4**	**9**	**—**	**7**	**—**	**.243**	**.306**	**.293**	**.975**
Career total		536	1833	199	482	54	22	6	193	111	—	—	36	56	—	67	—	.263	.318	.326	.965
Cubs total		**216**	**666**	**77**	**162**	**13**	**7**	**2**	**63**	**47**	**—**	**—**	**13**	**26**	**—**	**20**	**—**	**.243**	**.306**	**.293**	**.975**

Hubbard, Michael Wayne (Mike)
HEIGHT: 6'1" THROWS: RIGHT BATS: RIGHT BORN: 2/16/1971 LYNCHBURG, VIRGINIA POSITIONS PLAYED: C, 2B, 3B

YEAR	TEAM	GAMES	AB	RUNS	HITS	2B	3B	HR	RBI	BB	IBB	SO	HBP	SH	SF	SB	CS	BA	OBA	SA	FA
1995	ChC-N	15	23	2	4	0	0	0	1	2	0	2	0	0	0	0	0	.174	.240	.174	.971
1996	ChC-N	21	38	1	4	0	0	1	4	0	0	15	0	0	1	0	0	.105	.103	.184	1.000
1997	ChC-N	29	64	4	13	0	0	1	2	2	1	21	0	0	0	0	0	.203	.227	.250	.992
1998	Mon-N	32	55	3	8	1	0	1	3	0	0	17	1	0	0	0	0	.145	.161	.218	1.000
2000	Atl-N	2	1	0	0	0	0	0	0	0	0	1	0	0	0	0	0	.000	.000	.000	1.000
2001	Tex-A	5	11	1	3	1	0	1	1	0	0	4	0	0	0	0	0	.273	.273	.636	1.000
Career average		17	32	2	5	0	0	1	2	1	0	10	0	0	0	0	0	.167	.187	.240	.994
Cubs average		**22**	**42**	**2**	**7**	**0**	**0**	**1**	**2**	**1**	**0**	**13**	**0**	**0**	**0**	**0**	**0**	**.168**	**.192**	**.216**	**.994**
Career total		104	192	11	32	2	0	4	11	4	1	60	1	0	1	0	0	.167	.187	.240	.994
Cubs total		**65**	**125**	**7**	**21**	**0**	**0**	**2**	**7**	**4**	**1**	**38**	**0**	**0**	**1**	**0**	**0**	**.168**	**.192**	**.216**	**.991**

Hubbs, Kenneth Douglass (Ken)
HEIGHT: 6'2" THROWS: RIGHT BATS: RIGHT BORN: 12/23/1941 RIVERSIDE, CALIFORNIA DIED: 2/15/1964 PROVO, UTAH POSITIONS PLAYED: 2B

YEAR	TEAM	GAMES	AB	RUNS	HITS	2B	3B	HR	RBI	BB	IBB	SO	HBP	SH	SF	SB	CS	BA	OBA	SA	FA
1961	ChC-N	10	28	4	5	1	1	1	2	0	0	8	0	0	0	0	0	.179	.179	.393	1.000
1962	ChC-N	160	661	90	172	24	9	5	49	35	0	129	3	13	3	3	7	.260	.299	.346	.983
1963	ChC-N	154	566	54	133	19	3	8	47	39	2	93	2	3	4	8	9	.235	.285	.322	.974
Career average		108	418	49	103	15	4	5	33	25	1	77	2	5	2	4	5	.247	.290	.336	.979
Cubs average		**108**	**418**	**49**	**103**	**15**	**4**	**5**	**33**	**25**	**1**	**77**	**2**	**5**	**2**	**4**	**5**	**.247**	**.290**	**.336**	**.979**
Career total		324	1255	148	310	44	13	14	98	74	2	230	5	16	7	11	16	.247	.290	.336	.979
Cubs total		**324**	**1255**	**148**	**310**	**44**	**13**	**14**	**98**	**74**	**2**	**230**	**5**	**16**	**7**	**11**	**16**	**.247**	**.290**	**.336**	**.979**

Hudson, John Wilson (Johnny or Mr. Chips)
HEIGHT: 5'10" THROWS: RIGHT BATS: RIGHT BORN: 6/30/1912 BRYAN, TEXAS DIED: 11/7/1970 BRYAN, TEXAS POSITIONS PLAYED: 2B, 3B, SS

YEAR	TEAM	GAMES	AB	RUNS	HITS	2B	3B	HR	RBI	BB	IBB	SO	HBP	SH	SF	SB	CS	BA	OBA	SA	FA
1936	Bro-N	6	12	1	2	0	0	0	0	2	—	1	0	1	—	0	—	.167	.286	.167	.857
1937	Bro-N	13	27	3	5	4	0	0	2	3	—	9	0	0	—	0	—	.185	.267	.333	.875
1938	Bro-N	135	498	59	130	21	5	2	37	39	—	76	0	9	—	7	—	.261	.315	.335	.963
1939	Bro-N	109	343	46	87	17	3	2	32	30	—	36	2	4	—	5	—	.254	.317	.338	.960
1940	Bro-N	85	179	13	39	4	3	0	19	9	—	26	0	1	—	2	—	.218	.255	.274	.941
1941	ChC-N	50	99	8	20	4	0	0	6	3	—	15	0	4	—	3	—	.202	.225	.242	.924
1945	NYG-N	28	11	8	0	0	0	0	0	1	—	1	0	0	—	0	—	.000	.083	.000	.900
Career average		61	167	20	40	7	2	1	14	12	—	23	0	3	—	2	—	.242	.296	.314	.952
Cubs average		**50**	**99**	**8**	**20**	**4**	**0**	**0**	**6**	**3**	**—**	**15**	**0**	**4**	**—**	**3**	**—**	**.202**	**.225**	**.242**	**.924**
Career total		426	1169	138	283	50	11	4	96	87	—	164	2	19	—	17	—	.242	.296	.314	.952
Cubs total		**50**	**99**	**8**	**20**	**4**	**0**	**0**	**6**	**3**	**—**	**15**	**0**	**4**	**—**	**3**	**—**	**.202**	**.225**	**.242**	**.924**

Hughes, Joseph Thompson (Joe)
HEIGHT: 5'10" THROWS: RIGHT BATS: RIGHT BORN: 2/21/1880 PARDO, PENNSYLVANIA DIED: 3/13/1951 CLEVELAND, OHIO POSITIONS PLAYED: OF

YEAR	TEAM	GAMES	AB	RUNS	HITS	2B	3B	HR	RBI	BB	IBB	SO	HBP	SH	SF	SB	CS	BA	OBA	SA	FA
1902	ChC-N	1	3	0	0	0	0	0	0	0	—	—	0	0	—	0	—	.000	.000	.000	—
Career average		1	3	0	0	0	0	0	0	0	—	—	0	0	—	0	—	.000	.000	.000	—
Cubs average		**1**	**3**	**0**	**0**	**0**	**0**	**0**	**0**	**0**	**—**	**—**	**0**	**0**	**—**	**0**	**—**	**.000**	**.000**	**.000**	**—**
Career total		1	3	0	0	0	0	0	0	0	—	—	0	0	—	0	—	.000	.000	.000	—
Cubs total		**1**	**3**	**0**	**0**	**0**	**0**	**0**	**0**	**0**	**—**	**—**	**0**	**0**	**—**	**0**	**—**	**.000**	**.000**	**.000**	**—**

Hughes, Roy John (Jeep *or* Sage)
HEIGHT: 5'10" THROWS: RIGHT BATS: RIGHT BORN: 1/11/1911 CINCINNATI, OHIO DIED: 3/5/1995 ASHEVILLE, NORTH CAROLINA POSITIONS PLAYED: 1B, 2B, 3B, SS

YEAR	TEAM	GAMES	AB	RUNS	HITS	2B	3B	HR	RBI	BB	IBB	SO	HBP	SH	SF	SB	CS	BA	OBA	SA	FA
1935	Cle-A	82	266	40	78	15	3	0	14	18	—	17	1	8	—	13	3	.293	.340	.372	.956
1936	Cle-A	152	638	112	188	35	9	0	63	57	—	40	4	9	—	20	9	.295	.356	.378	.973
1937	Cle-A	104	346	57	96	12	6	1	40	40	—	22	0	9	—	11	6	.277	.352	.355	.968
1938	StL-A	58	96	16	27	3	0	2	13	12	—	11	0	1	—	3	—	.281	.361	.375	.963
1939	StL-A	17	23	6	2	0	0	0	1	4	—	4	0	1	—	0	0	.087	.222	.087	1.000
1939	Phi-N	65	237	22	54	5	1	1	16	21	—	18	0	8	—	4	—	.228	.291	.270	.984
1940	Phi-N	1	0	0	0	0	0	0	0	0	—	0	0	0	—	0	—	—	—	—	1.000
1944	**ChC-N**	126	478	86	137	16	6	1	28	35	—	30	1	17	—	16	—	.287	.337	.351	.963
1945	**ChC-N**	69	222	34	58	8	1	0	8	16	—	18	0	8	—	6	—	.261	.311	.306	.955
1946	Phi-N	89	276	23	65	11	1	0	22	19	—	15	1	5	—	7	—	.236	.287	.283	.960
Career average		85	287	44	78	12	3	1	23	25	—	19	1	7	—	9	2	.273	.332	.340	.967
Cubs average		98	350	60	98	12	4	1	18	26	—	24	1	13	—	11	0	.279	.328	.337	.960
Career total		763	2582	396	705	105	27	5	205	222	—	175	7	66	—	80	18	.273	.332	.340	.967
Cubs total		195	700	120	195	24	7	1	36	51	—	48	1	25	—	22	0	.279	.328	.337	.960

Hughes, Terry Wayne
HEIGHT: 6'1" THROWS: RIGHT BATS: RIGHT BORN: 5/13/1949 SPARTANBURG, SOUTH CAROLINA POSITIONS PLAYED: 1B, 3B, OF

YEAR	TEAM	GAMES	AB	RUNS	HITS	2B	3B	HR	RBI	BB	IBB	SO	HBP	SH	SF	SB	CS	BA	OBA	SA	FA
1970	ChC-N	2	3	0	1	0	0	0	0	0	0	0	0	0	0	0	0	.333	.333	.333	—
1973	StL-N	11	14	1	3	1	0	0	1	1	0	4	0	0	0	0	0	.214	.267	.286	1.000
1974	Bos-A	41	69	5	14	2	0	1	6	6	0	18	2	1	1	0	0	.203	.282	.275	.958
Career average		18	29	2	6	1	0	0	2	2	0	7	1	0	0	0	0	.209	.281	.279	.965
Cubs average		2	3	0	1	0	0	0	0	0	0	0	0	0	0	0	0	.333	.333	.333	—
Career total		54	86	6	18	3	0	1	7	7	0	22	2	1	1	0	0	.209	.281	.279	.965
Cubs total		2	3	0	1	0	0	0	0	0	0	0	0	0	0	0	0	.333	.333	.333	—

Hundley, Cecil Randolph (Randy *or* The Rebel)
HEIGHT: 5'11" THROWS: RIGHT BATS: RIGHT BORN: 6/1/1942 MARTINSVILLE, VIRGINIA POSITIONS PLAYED: C

YEAR	TEAM	GAMES	AB	RUNS	HITS	2B	3B	HR	RBI	BB	IBB	SO	HBP	SH	SF	SB	CS	BA	OBA	SA	FA
1964	SF-N	2	1	1	0	0	0	0	0	0	0	1	0	0	0	0	0	.000	.000	.000	—
1965	SF-N	6	15	0	1	0	0	0	0	0	0	4	0	1	0	0	0	.067	.067	.067	1.000
1966	**ChC-N**	149	526	50	124	22	3	19	63	35	3	113	3	10	5	1	3	.236	.285	.397	.986
1967	**ChC-N**	152	539	68	144	25	3	14	60	44	6	75	2	7	5	2	4	.267	.322	.403	.996
1968	**ChC-N**	160	553	41	125	18	4	7	65	39	6	69	4	5	5	1	0	.226	.280	.311	.995
1969	**ChC-N**	151	522	67	133	15	1	18	64	61	7	90	3	6	3	2	3	.255	.334	.391	.992
1970	**ChC-N**	73	250	13	61	5	0	7	36	16	0	52	0	4	1	0	1	.244	.288	.348	.990
1971	**ChC-N**	9	21	1	7	1	0	0	2	0	0	2	0	0	0	0	0	.333	.333	.381	.979
1972	**ChC-N**	114	357	23	78	12	0	5	30	22	10	62	0	4	4	1	0	.218	.261	.294	.995
1973	**ChC-N**	124	368	35	83	11	1	10	43	30	8	51	0	6	2	5	6	.226	.283	.342	.993
1974	Min-A	32	88	2	17	2	0	0	3	4	0	12	0	1	0	0	0	.193	.228	.216	.965
1975	SD-N	74	180	7	37	5	1	2	14	19	1	29	1	0	1	0	0	.206	.284	.278	.970
1976	**ChC-N**	13	18	3	3	2	0	0	1	1	0	4	0	0	1	0	0	.167	.200	.278	.923
1977	**ChC-N**	2	4	0	0	0	0	0	0	0	0	1	0	0	0	0	0	.000	.000	.000	1.000
Career average		76	246	22	58	8	1	6	27	19	3	40	1	3	2	1	1	.236	.292	.350	.990
Cubs average		95	316	30	76	11	1	8	36	25	4	52	1	4	3	1	2	.240	.296	.359	.992
Career total		1061	3442	311	813	118	13	82	381	271	41	565	13	44	27	12	17	.236	.292	.350	.990
Cubs total		947	3158	301	758	111	12	80	364	248	40	519	12	42	26	12	17	.240	.296	.359	.992

Hundley, Todd Randolph
HEIGHT: 5'11" THROWS: RIGHT BATS: BOTH BORN: 5/27/1969 MARTINSVILLE, VIRGINIA POSITIONS PLAYED: C, OF

YEAR	TEAM	GAMES	AB	RUNS	HITS	2B	3B	HR	RBI	BB	IBB	SO	HBP	SH	SF	SB	CS	BA	OBA	SA	FA
1990	NYM-N	36	67	8	14	6	0	0	2	6	0	18	0	1	0	0	0	.209	.274	.299	.988
1991	NYM-N	21	60	5	8	0	1	1	7	6	0	14	1	1	1	0	0	.133	.221	.217	1.000
1992	NYM-N	123	358	32	75	17	0	7	32	19	4	76	4	7	2	3	0	.209	.256	.316	.996
1993	NYM-N	130	417	40	95	17	2	11	53	23	7	62	2	2	4	1	1	.228	.269	.357	.988

(continued)

Cecil Randolph (Randy) "the Rebel" Hundley, c, 1964–77

A solid performer for the Cubs in the late 1960s, the hard-hitting Randy Hundley was the best catcher the Cubs had since Gabby Hartnett.

Hundley was born on June 1, 1942, in Martinsville, Virginia. He signed with the San Francisco Giants farm system as a precocious 17-year-old in 1959. He worked his way up the minor league ladder to the big club for a cup of coffee in 1964.

He made the team in 1965 but languished again on the bench. Hundley asked to be traded and got his wish; the Giants sent him to Chicago before the start of the 1966 season.

It was a key pickup for the Cubs. Hundley immediately took over behind the plate and was extremely effective, hitting 19 home runs, third among National League catchers, with 63 RBIs. He was first in the National League in assists for a catcher that year with 85.

From that season until 1969, Hundley was the most durable catcher in the National League. In 1968 he set a major league record for catchers by appearing in 160 games and also became the first player in major league history to catch 150 or more games three consecutive years (1967–69). Hundley was usually second or third in the league in both home runs and RBIs for a catcher in that span, and he also was among the league leaders in fielding at his position.

Hundley was an intense competitor and a team leader as the Cubs began to improve under manager Leo Durocher. He was one of the first catchers to popularize the "hinged glove," a catcher's mitt that enabled him to catch one-handed and protect his throwing hand. An excellent defensive backstop, his lifetime .992 fielding percentage for the Cubs is one of the highest in major league history.

Like many of Durocher's players, Hundley both admired and despised his manager; Durocher loved Hundley's combativeness. Maybe too much. Durocher hated to sit Hundley down, and Hundley himself didn't enjoy taking too many days off. As a result, he began to break down in 1970 after an All-Star season in 1969.

Hundley missed much of the 1970 and 1971 seasons with injuries to both knees. He played more regularly for Chicago the next two years, but he had clearly lost a step. In 1974 he was traded to Minnesota and then moved on to San Diego the next year. He returned to Chicago for the 1976 and 1977 seasons as a part-timer before his retirement.

Hundley worked as a coach for the Cubs for several years; then in 1983 he got the very smart idea to operate a baseball fantasy camp. The Hundley fantasy camp is the oldest of what is now a cottage industry.

Although his career as a Cub was relatively brief, Hundley holds many of the Cubs fielding records for a catcher, including highest fielding percentage in one season (.996 in 1967, tying him with three others), putouts in a season (978 in 1969), games played (160 in 1968) and total chances (1,065 in 1969).

(continued)

Year	Team																			
1994	NYM-N	91	291	45	69	10	1	16	42	25	4	73	3	3	1	2	1	.237	.303	.443	.990
1995	NYM-N	90	275	39	77	11	0	15	51	42	5	64	5	1	3	1	0	.280	.382	.484	.987
1996	NYM-N	153	540	85	140	32	1	41	112	79	15	146	3	0	2	1	3	.259	.356	.550	.992
1997	NYM-N	132	417	78	114	21	2	30	86	83	16	116	3	0	5	2	3	.273	.394	.549	.987
1998	NYM-N	53	124	8	20	4	0	3	12	16	0	55	1	0	1	1	1	.161	.261	.266	.928
1999	LA-N	114	376	49	78	14	0	24	55	44	3	113	4	1	3	3	0	.207	.295	.436	.979
2000	LA-N	90	299	49	85	16	0	24	70	45	6	69	2	1	6	0	1	.284	.375	.579	.979
2001	**ChC-N**	**79**	**246**	**23**	**46**	**10**	**0**	**12**	**31**	**25**	**0**	**89**	**3**	**0**	**2**	**0**	**0**	**.187**	**.268**	**.374**	**.993**
Career average		93	289	38	68	13	1	15	46	34	5	75	3	1	3	1	1	.237	.321	.445	.987
Cubs average		**79**	**246**	**23**	**46**	**10**	**0**	**12**	**31**	**25**	**0**	**89**	**3**	**0**	**2**	**0**	**0**	**.187**	**.268**	**.374**	**.993**
Career total		1112	3470	461	821	158	7	184	553	413	60	895	31	17	30	14	10	.237	.321	.445	.987
Cubs total		**79**	**246**	**23**	**46**	**10**	**0**	**12**	**31**	**25**	**0**	**89**	**3**	**0**	**2**	**0**	**0**	**.187**	**.268**	**.374**	**.993**

Hunter, Herbert Harrison (Herb)

HEIGHT: 6'0" THROWS: RIGHT BATS: LEFT BORN: 12/25/1896 BOSTON, MASSACHUSETTS DIED: 7/25/1970 ORLANDO, FLORIDA
POSITIONS PLAYED: 1B, 2B, 3B, OF

YEAR	TEAM	GAMES	AB	RUNS	HITS	2B	3B	HR	RBI	BB	IBB	SO	HBP	SH	SF	SB	CS	BA	OBA	SA	FA
1916	NYG-N	21	28	3	7	0	0	1	4	0	—	5	0	0	—	0	—	.250	.250	.357	1.000
1916	**ChC-N**	**2**	**4**	**0**	**0**	**0**	**0**	**0**	**0**	**0**	**—**	**0**	**0**	**0**	**—**	**0**	**—**	**.000**	**.000**	**.000**	**.750**
1917	ChC-N	3	3	0	0	0	0	0	0	0	—	0	0	0	—	0	—	.000	.000	.000	.833
1920	Bos-A	4	12	2	1	0	0	0	0	1	—	1	0	1	—	0	0	.083	.154	.083	.857
1921	StL-N	9	2	3	0	0	0	0	0	1	—	0	0	0	—	0	3	.000	.333	.000	1.000
Career average		10	12	2	2	0	0	0	1	1	—	2	0	0	—	0	1	.163	.196	.224	.935
Cubs average		**3**	**4**	**0**	**0**	**0**	**0**	**0**	**0**	**0**	**—**	**0**	**0**	**0**	**—**	**0**	**—**	**.000**	**.000**	**.000**	**.800**
Career total		39	49	8	8	0	0	1	4	2	—	6	0	1	—	0	3	.163	.196	.224	.935
Cubs total		**5**	**7**	**0**	**0**	**0**	**0**	**0**	**0**	**0**	**—**	**0**	**0**	**0**	**—**	**0**	**—**	**.000**	**.000**	**.000**	**.800**

Hurst, Frank O'Donnell (Don)

HEIGHT: 6'0" THROWS: LEFT BATS: LEFT BORN: 8/12/1905 MAYSVILLE, KENTUCKY DIED: 12/6/1952 LOS ANGELES, CALIFORNIA
POSITIONS PLAYED: 1B, OF

YEAR	TEAM	GAMES	AB	RUNS	HITS	2B	3B	HR	RBI	BB	IBB	SO	HBP	SH	SF	SB	CS	BA	OBA	SA	FA
1928	Phi-N	107	396	73	113	23	4	19	64	68	—	40	1	10	—	3	—	.285	.391	.508	.989
1929	Phi-N	154	589	100	179	29	4	31	125	80	—	36	3	20	—	10	—	.304	.390	.525	.985
1930	Phi-N	119	391	78	128	19	3	17	78	46	—	22	2	12	—	6	—	.327	.401	.522	.982
1931	Phi-N	137	489	63	149	37	5	11	91	64	—	28	1	13	—	8	—	.305	.386	.468	.986
1932	Phi-N	150	579	109	196	41	4	24	143	65	—	27	7	14	—	10	—	.339	.412	.547	.993
1933	Phi-N	147	550	58	147	27	8	8	76	48	—	32	1	11	—	3	—	.267	.327	.389	.985
1934	Phi-N	40	130	16	34	9	0	2	21	12	—	7	0	1	—	1	—	.262	.324	.377	.994
1934	**ChC-N**	**51**	**151**	**13**	**30**	**5**	**0**	**3**	**12**	**8**	**—**	**18**	**0**	**0**	**—**	**0**	**—**	**.199**	**.239**	**.291**	**.986**
Career average		129	468	73	139	27	4	16	87	56	—	30	2	12	—	6	—	.298	.375	.478	.987
Cubs average		**51**	**151**	**13**	**30**	**5**	**0**	**3**	**12**	**8**	**—**	**18**	**0**	**0**	**—**	**0**	**—**	**.199**	**.239**	**.291**	**.986**
Career total		905	3275	510	976	190	28	115	610	391	—	210	15	81	—	41	—	.298	.375	.478	.987
Cubs total		**51**	**151**	**13**	**30**	**5**	**0**	**3**	**12**	**8**	**—**	**18**	**0**	**0**	**—**	**0**	**—**	**.199**	**.239**	**.291**	**.986**

Huson, Jeffrey Kent (Jeff)

HEIGHT: 6'3" THROWS: RIGHT BATS: LEFT BORN: 8/15/1964 SCOTTSDALE, ARIZONA POSITIONS PLAYED: 1B, 2B, 3B, SS, OF

YEAR	TEAM	GAMES	AB	RUNS	HITS	2B	3B	HR	RBI	BB	IBB	SO	HBP	SH	SF	SB	CS	BA	OBA	SA	FA
1988	Mon-N	20	42	7	13	2	0	0	3	4	2	3	0	0	0	2	1	.310	.370	.357	.937
1989	Mon-N	32	74	1	12	5	0	0	2	6	3	6	0	3	0	3	0	.162	.225	.230	.929
1990	Tex-A	145	396	57	95	12	2	0	28	46	0	54	2	7	3	12	4	.240	.320	.280	.962
1991	Tex-A	119	268	36	57	8	3	2	26	39	0	32	0	9	1	8	3	.213	.312	.287	.965
1992	Tex-A	123	318	49	83	14	3	4	24	41	2	43	1	8	6	18	6	.261	.342	.362	.979
1993	Tex-A	23	45	3	6	1	1	0	2	0	0	10	0	1	0	0	0	.133	.133	.200	.918
1995	Bal-A	66	161	24	40	4	2	1	19	15	1	20	1	2	1	5	4	.248	.315	.317	.993
1996	Bal-A	17	28	5	9	1	0	0	2	1	0	3	0	0	1	0	0	.321	.333	.357	.974
1997	Mil-A	84	143	12	29	3	0	0	11	5	0	15	2	2	1	3	0	.203	.238	.224	.994
1998	Sea-A	31	49	8	8	1	0	1	4	5	0	6	0	0	0	1	1	.163	.241	.245	.957
1999	Ana-A	97	225	21	59	7	1	0	18	16	0	27	0	1	3	10	1	.262	.307	.302	.980
2000	**ChC-N**	**70**	**130**	**19**	**28**	**7**	**1**	**0**	**11**	**13**	**1**	**9**	**0**	**1**	**0**	**2**	**1**	**.215**	**.287**	**.285**	**.976**
Career average		69	157	20	37	5	1	1	13	16	1	19	1	3	1	5	2	.234	.304	.295	.969
Cubs average		**70**	**130**	**19**	**28**	**7**	**1**	**0**	**11**	**13**	**1**	**9**	**0**	**1**	**0**	**2**	**1**	**.215**	**.287**	**.285**	**.976**
Career total		827	1879	242	439	65	13	8	150	191	9	228	6	34	16	64	21	.234	.304	.295	.969
Cubs total		**70**	**130**	**19**	**28**	**7**	**1**	**0**	**11**	**13**	**1**	**9**	**0**	**1**	**0**	**2**	**1**	**.215**	**.287**	**.285**	**.976**

Hutchinson, Edwin Forrest (Ed)

HEIGHT: 5'11" THROWS: RIGHT BATS: LEFT BORN: 5/19/1867 PITTSBURGH, PENNSYLVANIA DIED: 7/19/1934 COLFAX, CALIFORNIA POSITIONS PLAYED: 2B

YEAR	TEAM	GAMES	AB	RUNS	HITS	2B	3B	HR	RBI	BB	IBB	SO	HBP	SH	SF	SB	CS	BA	OBA	SA	FA
1890	ChN-N	4	17	0	1	1	0	0	0	0	—	0	0	—	—	0	—	.059	.059	.118	1.000
Career average		4	17	0	1	1	0	0	0	0	—	0	0	—	—	0	—	.059	.059	.118	1.000
Cubs average		**4**	**17**	**0**	**1**	**1**	**0**	**0**	**0**	**0**	**—**	**0**	**0**	**—**	**—**	**0**	**—**	**.059**	**.059**	**.118**	**1.000**
Career total		4	17	0	1	1	0	0	0	0	—	0	0	—	—	0	—	.059	.059	.118	1.000
Cubs total		**4**	**17**	**0**	**1**	**1**	**0**	**0**	**0**	**0**	**—**	**0**	**0**	**—**	**—**	**0**	**—**	**.059**	**.059**	**.118**	**1.000**

Irvin, Montford Merrill (Monte)
HEIGHT: 6'1"   THROWS: RIGHT   BATS: RIGHT   BORN: 2/25/1919 COLUMBUS, ALABAMA   POSITIONS PLAYED: 1B, 3B, OF

YEAR	TEAM	GAMES	AB	RUNS	HITS	2B	3B	HR	RBI	BB	IBB	SO	HBP	SH	SF	SB	CS	BA	OBA	SA	FA
1949	NYG-N	36	76	7	17	3	2	0	7	17	—	11	0	0	—	0	1	.224	.366	.316	.986
1950	NYG-N	110	374	61	112	19	5	15	66	52	—	41	5	1	—	3	—	.299	.392	.497	.981
1951	NYG-N	151	558	94	174	19	11	24	121	89	—	44	9	1	—	12	2	.312	.415	.514	.986
1952	NYG-N	46	126	10	39	2	1	4	21	10	—	11	1	0	—	0	1	.310	.365	.437	1.000
1953	NYG-N	124	444	72	146	21	5	21	97	55	—	34	3	0	—	2	0	.329	.406	.541	.973
1954	NYG-N	135	432	62	113	13	3	19	64	70	—	23	2	3	5	7	4	.262	.363	.438	.973
1955	NYG-N	51	150	16	38	7	1	1	17	17	0	15	3	1	2	3	0	.253	.337	.333	.961
1956	**ChC-N**	**111**	**339**	**44**	**92**	**13**	**3**	**15**	**50**	**41**	**5**	**41**	**0**	**3**	**4**	**1**	**0**	**.271**	**.346**	**.460**	**.991**
Career average		96	312	46	91	12	4	12	55	44	1	28	3	1	1	4	1	.293	.383	.475	.981
Cubs average		**111**	**339**	**44**	**92**	**13**	**3**	**15**	**50**	**41**	**5**	**41**	**0**	**3**	**4**	**1**	**0**	**.271**	**.346**	**.460**	**.991**
Career total		764	2499	366	731	97	31	99	443	351	5	220	23	9	11	28	8	.293	.383	.475	.981
Cubs total		**111**	**339**	**44**	**92**	**13**	**3**	**15**	**50**	**41**	**5**	**41**	**0**	**3**	**4**	**1**	**0**	**.271**	**.346**	**.460**	**.991**

Irwin, Charles Edwin (Charlie)
HEIGHT: 5'10"   THROWS: RIGHT   BATS: LEFT   BORN: 2/15/1869 CLINTON, ILLINOIS   DIED: 9/21/1925 CHICAGO, ILLINOIS
POSITIONS PLAYED: 1B, 2B, 3B, SS, OF

YEAR	TEAM	GAMES	AB	RUNS	HITS	2B	3B	HR	RBI	BB	IBB	SO	HBP	SH	SF	SB	CS	BA	OBA	SA	FA
1893	**ChN-N**	**21**	**82**	**14**	**25**	**6**	**2**	**0**	**13**	**10**	**—**	**1**	**2**	**—**	**—**	**4**	**—**	**.305**	**.394**	**.427**	**.910**
1894	**ChN-N**	**128**	**498**	**84**	**144**	**24**	**9**	**8**	**95**	**63**	**—**	**23**	**9**	**4**	**—**	**35**	**—**	**.289**	**.379**	**.422**	**.860**
1895	**ChN-N**	**3**	**10**	**4**	**2**	**0**	**0**	**0**	**0**	**2**	**—**	**1**	**0**	**0**	**—**	**0**	**—**	**.200**	**.333**	**.200**	**.900**
1896	Cin-N	127	476	77	141	16	6	1	67	26	—	17	4	10	—	31	—	.296	.338	.361	.931
1897	Cin-N	134	505	89	146	26	6	0	74	47	—	—	9	10	—	27	—	.289	.360	.364	.940
1898	Cin-N	136	501	77	120	14	5	3	55	31	—	—	10	14	—	18	—	.240	.297	.305	.940
1899	Cin-N	90	314	42	73	4	8	1	52	26	—	—	2	7	—	26	—	.232	.295	.306	.915
1900	Cin-N	87	333	59	91	15	6	1	44	14	—	—	6	9	—	9	—	.273	.314	.363	.927
1901	Cin-N	67	260	25	62	12	2	0	25	14	—	—	3	4	—	13	—	.238	.285	.300	.893
1901	Bro-N	65	242	25	52	13	2	0	20	14	—	—	4	4	—	4	—	.215	.269	.285	.956
1902	Bro-N	131	458	59	125	14	0	2	43	39	—	—	11	11	—	13	—	.273	.344	.317	.925
Career average		99	368	56	98	14	5	2	49	29	—	4	6	7	—	18	—	.267	.330	.344	.917
Cubs average		**51**	**197**	**34**	**57**	**10**	**4**	**3**	**36**	**25**	**—**	**8**	**4**	**1**	**—**	**13**	**—**	**.290**	**.380**	**.419**	**.869**
Career total		989	3679	555	981	144	46	16	488	286	—	42	60	73	—	180	—	.267	.330	.344	.917
Cubs total		**152**	**590**	**102**	**171**	**30**	**11**	**8**	**108**	**75**	**—**	**25**	**11**	**4**	**—**	**39**	**—**	**.290**	**.380**	**.419**	**.869**

Isbell, William Frank (Frank or Bald Eagle)
HEIGHT: 5'11"   THROWS: RIGHT   BATS: LEFT   BORN: 8/21/1875 DELEVAN, NEW YORK   DIED: 7/15/1941 WICHITA, KANSAS
POSITIONS PLAYED: P, C, 1B, 2B, 3B, SS, OF

YEAR	TEAM	GAMES	AB	RUNS	HITS	2B	3B	HR	RBI	BB	IBB	SO	HBP	SH	SF	SB	CS	BA	OBA	SA	FA
1898	**ChN-N**	**45**	**159**	**17**	**37**	**4**	**0**	**0**	**8**	**3**	**—**	**—**	**1**	**6**	**—**	**3**	**—**	**.233**	**.252**	**.258**	**.836**
1901	CWS-A	137	556	93	143	15	8	3	70	36	—	—	7	13	—	52	—	.257	.311	.329	.979
1902	CWS-A	137	515	62	130	14	4	4	59	14	—	—	3	23	—	38	—	.252	.276	.318	.986
1903	CWS-A	138	546	52	132	25	9	2	59	12	—	—	6	22	—	26	—	.242	.266	.332	.975
1904	CWS-A	96	314	27	66	10	3	1	34	16	—	—	3	18	—	19	—	.210	.255	.271	.970
1905	CWS-A	94	341	55	101	21	11	2	45	15	—	—	5	28	—	15	—	.296	.335	.440	.965
1906	CWS-A	143	549	71	153	18	11	0	57	30	—	—	7	31	—	37	—	.279	.324	.352	.950
1907	CWS-A	125	486	60	118	19	7	0	41	22	—	—	4	24	—	22	—	.243	.281	.311	.957
1908	CWS-A	84	320	31	79	15	3	1	49	19	—	—	4	17	—	18	—	.247	.297	.322	.982
1909	CWS-A	120	433	33	97	17	6	0	33	23	—	—	1	20	—	23	—	.224	.265	.291	.991
Career average		112	422	50	106	16	6	1	46	19	—	—	4	20	—	25	—	.250	.289	.326	.974
Cubs average		**45**	**159**	**17**	**37**	**4**	**0**	**0**	**8**	**3**	**—**	**—**	**1**	**6**	**—**	**3**	**—**	**.233**	**.252**	**.258**	**.836**
Career total		1119	4219	501	1056	158	62	13	455	190	—	—	41	202	—	253	—	.250	.289	.326	.974
Cubs total		**45**	**159**	**17**	**37**	**4**	**0**	**0**	**8**	**3**	**—**	**—**	**1**	**6**	**—**	**3**	**—**	**.233**	**.252**	**.258**	**.836**

Jackson, Darrin Jay

HEIGHT: 6'0" THROWS: RIGHT BATS: RIGHT BORN: 8/22/1963 LOS ANGELES, CALIFORNIA POSITIONS PLAYED: P, OF

YEAR	TEAM	GAMES	AB	RUNS	HITS	2B	3B	HR	RBI	BB	IBB	SO	HBP	SH	SF	SB	CS	BA	OBA	SA	FA
1985	ChC-N	5	11	0	1	0	0	0	0	0	0	3	0	0	0	0	0	.091	.091	.091	1.000
1987	ChC-N	7	5	2	4	1	0	0	0	0	0	0	0	0	0	0	0	.800	.800	1.000	1.000
1988	ChC-N	100	188	29	50	11	3	6	20	5	1	28	1	2	1	4	1	.266	.287	.452	.983
1989	ChC-N	45	83	7	19	4	0	1	8	6	1	17	0	0	0	1	2	.229	.281	.313	.970
1989	SD-N	25	87	10	18	3	0	3	12	7	4	17	0	0	2	0	2	.207	.260	.345	.954
1990	SD-N	58	113	10	29	3	0	3	9	5	1	24	0	1	1	3	0	.257	.286	.363	.985
1991	SD-N	122	359	51	94	12	1	21	49	27	2	66	2	3	3	5	3	.262	.315	.476	.992
1992	SD-N	155	587	72	146	23	5	17	70	26	4	106	4	6	5	14	3	.249	.283	.392	.996
1993	Tor-A	46	176	15	38	8	0	5	19	8	0	53	0	5	0	0	2	.216	.250	.347	.989
1993	NYM-N	31	87	4	17	1	0	1	7	2	0	22	0	1	1	0	0	.195	.211	.241	1.000
1994	CWS-A	104	369	43	115	17	3	10	51	27	3	56	3	2	2	7	1	.312	.362	.455	.996
1997	Min-A	49	130	19	33	2	1	3	21	4	0	21	0	3	2	2	0	.254	.272	.354	.990
1997	Mil-A	26	81	7	22	7	0	2	15	2	0	10	0	2	0	2	1	.272	.289	.432	1.000
1998	Mil-N	114	204	20	49	13	1	4	20	9	0	37	1	0	0	1	1	.240	.276	.373	.982
1999	CWS-A	73	149	22	41	9	1	4	16	3	0	20	0	2	1	4	1	.275	.288	.430	.972
Career average		80	219	26	56	10	1	7	26	11	1	40	1	2	2	4	1	.257	.293	.403	.989
Cubs average		39	72	10	19	4	1	2	7	3	1	12	0	1	0	1	1	.258	.287	.408	.979
Career total		960	2629	311	676	114	15	80	317	131	16	480	11	27	18	43	17	.257	.293	.403	.989
Cubs total		157	287	38	74	16	3	7	28	11	2	48	1	2	1	5	3	.258	.287	.408	.979

Jackson, Louis Clarence (Lou)

HEIGHT: 5'10" THROWS: RIGHT BATS: LEFT BORN: 7/26/1935 RIVERTON, LOUISIANA DIED: 5/27/1969 TOKYO, JAPAN POSITIONS PLAYED: OF

YEAR	TEAM	GAMES	AB	RUNS	HITS	2B	3B	HR	RBI	BB	IBB	SO	HBP	SH	SF	SB	CS	BA	OBA	SA	FA
1958	ChC-N	24	35	5	6	2	1	1	6	1	0	9	0	0	0	0	1	.171	.194	.371	1.000
1959	ChC-N	6	4	2	1	0	0	0	1	0	0	2	0	0	0	0	0	.250	.250	.250	—
1964	Bal-A	4	8	0	3	0	0	0	0	0	0	2	0	0	0	0	0	.375	.375	.375	1.000
Career average		11	16	2	3	1	0	0	2	0	0	4	0	0	0	0	1	.213	.229	.362	1.000
Cubs average		15	20	4	4	1	1	1	4	1	0	6	0	0	0	0	1	.179	.200	.359	1.000
Career total		34	47	7	10	2	1	1	7	1	0	13	0	0	0	0	1	.213	.229	.362	1.000
Cubs total		30	39	7	7	2	1	1	7	1	0	11	0	0	0	0	1	.179	.200	.359	1.000

Jackson, Ransom Joseph (Randy *or* Handsom Ransom)

HEIGHT: 6'1" THROWS: RIGHT BATS: RIGHT BORN: 2/10/1926 LITTLE ROCK, ARKANSAS POSITIONS PLAYED: 3B, OF

YEAR	TEAM	GAMES	AB	RUNS	HITS	2B	3B	HR	RBI	BB	IBB	SO	HBP	SH	SF	SB	CS	BA	OBA	SA	FA
1950	ChC-N	34	111	13	25	4	3	3	6	7	—	25	0	2	—	4	—	.225	.271	.396	.911
1951	ChC-N	145	557	78	153	24	6	16	76	47	—	44	1	4	—	14	3	.275	.332	.425	.956
1952	ChC-N	116	379	44	88	8	5	9	34	27	—	42	1	2	—	6	5	.232	.285	.351	.958
1953	ChC-N	139	498	61	142	22	8	19	66	42	—	61	0	9	—	8	4	.285	.341	.476	.949
1954	ChC-N	126	484	77	132	17	6	19	67	44	—	55	2	9	4	2	1	.273	.333	.450	.955
1955	ChC-N	138	499	73	132	13	7	21	70	58	6	58	1	3	4	0	2	.265	.340	.445	.949
1956	Bro-N	101	307	37	84	15	7	8	53	28	3	38	2	4	5	2	1	.274	.333	.446	.993
1957	Bro-N	48	131	7	26	1	0	2	16	9	0	20	0	3	2	0	0	.198	.246	.252	.976
1958	LA-N	35	65	8	12	3	0	1	4	5	1	10	0	0	0	0	0	.185	.243	.277	.964
1958	Cle-A	29	91	7	22	3	1	4	13	3	0	18	0	0	0	0	0	.242	.266	.429	.901
1959	Cle-A	3	7	0	1	0	0	0	0	0	0	1	0	0	0	0	0	.143	.143	.143	1.000
1959	ChC-N	41	74	7	18	5	1	1	10	11	1	10	0	6	0	0	0	.243	.341	.378	.941
Career average		96	320	41	84	12	4	10	42	28	1	38	1	4	2	4	2	.261	.320	.421	.955
Cubs average		106	372	50	99	13	5	13	47	34	1	42	1	5	1	5	2	.265	.327	.430	.951
Career total		955	3203	412	835	115	44	103	415	281	11	382	7	42	15	36	16	.261	.320	.421	.955
Cubs total		739	2602	353	690	93	36	88	329	236	7	295	5	35	8	34	15	.265	.327	.430	.951

Jacobs, Morris Elmore (Mike)

HEIGHT: — THROWS: — BATS: — BORN: 1877 LOUISVILLE, KENTUCKY DIED: 3/21/1949 LOUISVILLE, KENTUCKY POSITIONS PLAYED: SS

YEAR	TEAM	GAMES	AB	RUNS	HITS	2B	3B	HR	RBI	BB	IBB	SO	HBP	SH	SF	SB	CS	BA	OBA	SA	FA
1902	ChC-N	5	19	1	4	0	0	0	2	0	—	—	0	0	—	0	—	.211	.211	.211	.880
Career average		5	19	1	4	0	0	0	2	0	—	—	0	0	—	0	—	.211	.211	.211	.880
Cubs average		5	19	1	4	0	0	0	2	0	—	—	0	0	—	0	—	.211	.211	.211	.880
Career total		5	19	1	4	0	0	0	2	0	—	—	0	0	—	0	—	.211	.211	.211	.880
Cubs total		5	19	1	4	0	0	0	2	0	—	—	0	0	—	0	—	.211	.211	.211	.880

Ransom (Randy) Joseph "Handsome Ransom" Jackson, 3b-of, 1950–59

Randy Jackson was a power-hitting third baseman for the Cubs in the early 1950s, a big, strong former football player who quietly got the job done.

Jackson was born on February 10, 1926, in Little Rock, Arkansas. He was a tremendous athlete, and in addition to being a very good baseball player, he was heavily recruited in football as well. He ended up attending Texas Christian University and playing in the 1946 Cotton Bowl.

After college, though, Jackson became a baseball player full-time. He broke into the big leagues with the Cubs in 1950.

He became the team's starter in 1951 and had a great year, hitting .275 with 16 home runs and 76 RBIs. He also led all National League third basemen in putouts, assists, total fielding chances per game—and errors. He was fast, too, for a big guy, leading the Cubs in stolen bases wth 14.

From 1953 to 1955, Jackson averaged almost 20 home runs a season and led the National League in double plays started in 1955 with 26. He was named to the All-Star team in 1954 and 1955.

In 1956 the Cubs sent him to the Dodgers, who hoped he could succeed Jackie Robinson at third base. But a knee injury in 1957 severely diminished his effectiveness. Two years later, after returning in midseason to the Cubs, Jackson retired.

Jackson's 198 putouts in 1951 remain a single-season Cubs record for third basemen.

Jacobs, Raymond Frederick (Ray)

HEIGHT: 6'0"   THROWS: RIGHT   BATS: RIGHT   BORN: 1/2/1902 SALT LAKE CITY, UTAH   DIED: 4/5/1952 LOS ANGELES, CALIFORNIA

YEAR	TEAM	GAMES	AB	RUNS	HITS	2B	3B	HR	RBI	BB	IBB	SO	HBP	SH	SF	SB	CS	BA	OBA	SA	FA
1928	ChC-N	2	2	0	0	0	0	0	0	0	—	1	0	0	—	0	—	.000	.000	.000	—
Career average		2	2	0	0	0	0	0	0	0	—	1	0	0	—	0	—	.000	.000	.000	—
Cubs average		**2**	**2**	**0**	**0**	**0**	**0**	**0**	**0**	**0**	**—**	**1**	**0**	**0**	**—**	**0**	**—**	**.000**	**.000**	**.000**	**—**
Career total		2	2	0	0	0	0	0	0	0	—	1	0	0	—	0	—	.000	.000	.000	—
Cubs total		**2**	**2**	**0**	**0**	**0**	**0**	**0**	**0**	**0**	**—**	**1**	**0**	**0**	**—**	**0**	**—**	**.000**	**.000**	**.000**	**—**

Jacobson, Merwin John William

HEIGHT: 5'11"   THROWS: LEFT   BATS: LEFT   BORN: 3/7/1894 NEW BRITAIN, CONNECTICUT   DIED: 1/13/1978 BALTIMORE, MARYLAND   POSITIONS PLAYED: OF

YEAR	TEAM	GAMES	AB	RUNS	HITS	2B	3B	HR	RBI	BB	IBB	SO	HBP	SH	SF	SB	CS	BA	OBA	SA	FA
1915	NYG-N	8	24	0	2	0	0	0	0	1	—	5	0	0	—	0	0	.083	.120	.083	.909
1916	ChC-N	4	13	2	3	0	0	0	0	1	—	4	0	0	—	2	0	.231	.286	.231	1.000
1926	Bro-N	110	288	41	71	9	2	0	23	36	—	24	0	7	—	5	—	.247	.330	.292	.975
1927	Bro-N	11	6	4	0	0	0	0	1	0	—	1	0	1	—	0	—	.000	.000	.000	1.000
Career average		33	83	12	19	2	1	0	6	10	—	9	0	2	—	2	0	.230	.309	.269	.973
Cubs average		**4**	**13**	**2**	**3**	**0**	**0**	**0**	**0**	**1**	**—**	**4**	**0**	**0**	**—**	**2**	**0**	**.231**	**.286**	**.231**	**1.000**
Career total		133	331	47	76	9	2	0	24	38	—	34	0	8	—	7	0	.230	.309	.269	.973
Cubs total		**4**	**13**	**2**	**3**	**0**	**0**	**0**	**0**	**1**	**—**	**4**	**0**	**0**	**—**	**2**	**0**	**.231**	**.286**	**.231**	**1.000**

Jahn, Arthur Charles (Art)
HEIGHT: 6'0"　THROWS: RIGHT　BATS: RIGHT　BORN: 12/2/1895 STRUBLE, IOWA　DIED: 1/9/1948 LITTLE ROCK, ARKANSAS　POSITIONS PLAYED: OF

YEAR	TEAM	GAMES	AB	RUNS	HITS	2B	3B	HR	RBI	BB	IBB	SO	HBP	SH	SF	SB	CS	BA	OBA	SA	FA
1925	ChC-N	58	226	30	68	10	8	0	37	11	—	20	1	5	—	2	2	.301	.336	.416	.985
1928	NYG-N	10	29	7	8	1	0	1	7	2	—	5	0	1	—	0	—	.276	.323	.414	1.000
1928	Phi-N	36	94	8	21	4	0	0	11	4	—	11	2	0	—	0	—	.223	.270	.266	.978
Career average		52	175	23	49	8	4	1	28	9	—	18	2	3	—	1	1	.278	.317	.375	.985
Cubs average		**58**	**226**	**30**	**68**	**10**	**8**	**0**	**37**	**11**	**—**	**20**	**1**	**5**	**—**	**2**	**2**	**.301**	**.336**	**.416**	**.985**
Career total		104	349	45	97	15	8	1	55	17	—	36	3	6	—	2	2	.278	.317	.375	.985
Cubs total		**58**	**226**	**30**	**68**	**10**	**8**	**0**	**37**	**11**	**—**	**20**	**1**	**5**	**—**	**2**	**2**	**.301**	**.336**	**.416**	**.985**

James, Cleo Joel
HEIGHT: 5'10"　THROWS: RIGHT　BATS: RIGHT　BORN: 8/31/1940 CLARKSDALE, MISSISSIPPI　POSITIONS PLAYED: 3B, OF

YEAR	TEAM	GAMES	AB	RUNS	HITS	2B	3B	HR	RBI	BB	IBB	SO	HBP	SH	SF	SB	CS	BA	OBA	SA	FA
1968	LA-N	10	10	2	2	1	0	0	0	0	0	6	0	0	0	0	0	.200	.200	.300	1.000
1970	ChC-N	100	176	33	37	7	2	3	14	17	5	24	5	2	0	5	0	.210	.298	.324	1.000
1971	ChC-N	54	150	25	43	7	0	2	13	10	0	16	6	5	1	6	2	.287	.353	.373	.979
1973	ChC-N	44	45	9	5	0	0	0	0	1	0	6	0	1	0	5	0	.111	.130	.111	.960
Career average		52	95	17	22	4	1	1	7	7	1	13	3	2	0	4	1	.228	.299	.318	.988
Cubs average		**66**	**124**	**22**	**28**	**5**	**1**	**2**	**9**	**9**	**2**	**15**	**4**	**3**	**0**	**5**	**1**	**.229**	**.302**	**.318**	**.988**
Career total		208	381	69	87	15	2	5	27	28	5	52	11	8	1	16	2	.228	.299	.318	.988
Cubs total		**198**	**371**	**67**	**85**	**14**	**2**	**5**	**27**	**28**	**5**	**46**	**11**	**8**	**1**	**16**	**2**	**.229**	**.302**	**.318**	**.988**

Jeffcoat, Harold Bentley (Hal)
HEIGHT: 5'10"　THROWS: RIGHT　BATS: RIGHT　BORN: 9/6/1924 WEST COLUMBIA, SOUTH CAROLINA　POSITIONS PLAYED: P, OF

YEAR	TEAM	GAMES	AB	RUNS	HITS	2B	3B	HR	RBI	BB	IBB	SO	HBP	SH	SF	SB	CS	BA	OBA	SA	FA
1948	ChC-N	134	473	53	132	16	4	4	42	24	—	68	1	14	—	8	—	.279	.315	.355	.976
1949	ChC-N	108	363	43	89	18	6	2	26	20	—	48	1	4	—	12	—	.245	.286	.344	.963
1950	ChC-N	66	179	21	42	13	1	2	18	6	—	23	0	2	—	7	—	.235	.259	.352	.967
1951	ChC-N	113	278	44	76	20	2	4	27	16	—	23	1	4	—	8	4	.273	.315	.403	.989
1952	ChC-N	102	297	29	65	17	2	4	30	15	—	40	1	7	—	7	2	.219	.259	.330	.996
1953	ChC-N	106	183	22	43	3	1	4	22	21	—	26	0	3	—	5	0	.235	.314	.328	.973
1954	ChC-N	56	31	13	8	2	1	1	6	1	—	7	0	0	2	2	0	.258	.265	.484	.892
1955	ChC-N	52	23	3	4	0	0	1	1	2	0	9	0	2	0	0	0	.174	.240	.304	.903
1956	Cin-N	49	54	5	8	2	0	0	5	3	0	20	0	3	0	0	1	.148	.193	.185	.969
1957	Cin-N	53	69	13	14	3	1	4	11	5	0	20	1	8	0	0	0	.203	.267	.449	.958
1958	Cin-N	50	9	2	5	0	0	0	0	1	0	2	0	0	0	0	0	.556	.600	.556	1.000
1959	Cin-N	17	1	1	1	1	0	0	0	0	0	0	0	0	0	0	0	1.000	1.000	2.000	1.000
1959	StL-N	12	3	0	0	0	0	0	0	0	0	3	0	0	0	0	0	.000	.000	.000	1.000
Career average		77	164	21	41	8	2	2	16	10	0	24	0	4	0	4	1	.248	.291	.355	.974
Cubs average		**92**	**228**	**29**	**57**	**11**	**2**	**3**	**22**	**13**	**0**	**31**	**1**	**5**	**0**	**6**	**1**	**.251**	**.293**	**.355**	**.974**
Career total		918	1963	249	487	95	18	26	188	114	0	289	5	47	2	49	7	.248	.291	.355	.974
Cubs total		**737**	**1827**	**228**	**459**	**89**	**17**	**22**	**172**	**105**	**0**	**244**	**4**	**36**	**2**	**49**	**6**	**.251**	**.293**	**.355**	**.974**

Jelinich, Frank Anthony (Jelly)
HEIGHT: 6'2"　THROWS: RIGHT　BATS: RIGHT　BORN: 9/3/1919 SAN JOSE, CALIFORNIA　DIED: 6/27/1992 ROCHESTER, MINNESOTA　POSITIONS PLAYED: OF

YEAR	TEAM	GAMES	AB	RUNS	HITS	2B	3B	HR	RBI	BB	IBB	SO	HBP	SH	SF	SB	CS	BA	OBA	SA	FA
1941	ChC-N	4	8	0	1	0	0	0	2	1	—	2	0	0	—	0	—	.125	.222	.125	1.000
Career average		4	8	0	1	0	0	0	2	1	—	2	0	0	—	0	—	.125	.222	.125	1.000
Cubs average		**4**	**8**	**0**	**1**	**0**	**0**	**0**	**2**	**1**	**—**	**2**	**0**	**0**	**—**	**0**	**—**	**.125**	**.222**	**.125**	**1.000**
Career total		4	8	0	1	0	0	0	2	1	—	2	0	0	—	0	—	.125	.222	.125	1.000
Cubs total		**4**	**8**	**0**	**1**	**0**	**0**	**0**	**2**	**1**	**—**	**2**	**0**	**0**	**—**	**0**	**—**	**.125**	**.222**	**.125**	**1.000**

Jennings, James Douglas (Doug)
HEIGHT: 5'10" THROWS: LEFT BATS: LEFT BORN: 9/30/1964 ATLANTA, GEORGIA POSITIONS PLAYED: 1B, OF

YEAR	TEAM	GAMES	AB	RUNS	HITS	2B	3B	HR	RBI	BB	IBB	SO	HBP	SH	SF	SB	CS	BA	OBA	SA	FA
1988	Oak-A	71	101	9	21	6	0	1	15	21	1	28	2	1	3	0	1	.208	.346	.297	.989
1989	Oak-A	4	4	0	0	0	0	0	0	0	0	2	0	0	0	0	0	.000	.000	.000	1.000
1990	Oak-A	64	156	19	30	7	2	2	14	17	0	48	2	2	3	0	3	.192	.275	.301	.989
1991	Oak-A	8	9	0	1	0	0	0	0	2	0	2	0	0	0	0	1	.111	.273	.111	1.000
1993	**ChC-N**	**42**	**52**	**8**	**13**	**3**	**1**	**2**	**8**	**3**	**0**	**10**	**2**	**0**	**0**	**0**	**0**	**.250**	**.316**	**.462**	**1.000**
Career average		38	64	7	13	3	1	1	7	9	0	18	1	1	1	0	1	.202	.302	.317	.993
Cubs average		**42**	**52**	**8**	**13**	**3**	**1**	**2**	**8**	**3**	**0**	**10**	**2**	**0**	**0**	**0**	**0**	**.250**	**.316**	**.462**	**1.000**
Career total		189	322	36	65	16	3	5	37	43	1	90	6	3	6	0	5	.202	.302	.317	.993
Cubs total		**42**	**52**	**8**	**13**	**3**	**1**	**2**	**8**	**3**	**0**	**10**	**2**	**0**	**0**	**0**	**0**	**.250**	**.316**	**.462**	**1.000**

Jennings, Robin Christopher
HEIGHT: 6'2" THROWS: LEFT BATS: LEFT BORN: 4/11/1972 SINGAPORE, SINGAPORE POSITIONS PLAYED: 1B, OF

YEAR	TEAM	GAMES	AB	RUNS	HITS	2B	3B	HR	RBI	BB	IBB	SO	HBP	SH	SF	SB	CS	BA	OBA	SA	FA
1996	**ChC-N**	**31**	**58**	**7**	**13**	**5**	**0**	**0**	**4**	**3**	**0**	**9**	**1**	**0**	**0**	**1**	**0**	**.224**	**.274**	**.310**	**1.000**
1997	**ChC-N**	**9**	**18**	**1**	**3**	**1**	**0**	**0**	**2**	**0**	**0**	**2**	**0**	**0**	**1**	**0**	**0**	**.167**	**.158**	**.222**	**1.000**
1999	**ChC-N**	**5**	**5**	**0**	**1**	**0**	**0**	**0**	**0**	**0**	**0**	**2**	**0**	**0**	**0**	**0**	**0**	**.200**	**.200**	**.200**	**—**
2001	Oak-A	20	52	4	13	3	0	0	4	2	0	6	0	0	1	0	0	.250	.273	.308	1.000
2001	Col-N	1	3	0	0	0	0	0	0	0	0	1	0	0	0	0	0	.000	.000	.000	.000
2001	Cin-N	27	77	10	22	5	2	3	14	5	1	11	0	0	0	0	0	.286	.329	.519	.965
Career average		23	53	6	13	4	1	1	6	3	0	8	0	0	1	0	0	.244	.279	.371	.976
Cubs average		**15**	**27**	**3**	**6**	**2**	**0**	**0**	**2**	**1**	**0**	**4**	**0**	**0**	**0**	**0**	**0**	**.210**	**.244**	**.284**	**1.000**
Career total		93	213	22	52	14	2	3	24	10	1	31	1	0	2	1	0	.244	.279	.371	.976
Cubs total		**45**	**81**	**8**	**17**	**6**	**0**	**0**	**6**	**3**	**0**	**13**	**1**	**0**	**1**	**1**	**0**	**.210**	**.244**	**.284**	**1.000**

Jestadt, Garry Arthur
HEIGHT: 6'2" THROWS: RIGHT BATS: RIGHT BORN: 3/19/1947 CHICAGO, ILLINOIS POSITIONS PLAYED: 2B, 3B, SS

YEAR	TEAM	GAMES	AB	RUNS	HITS	2B	3B	HR	RBI	BB	IBB	SO	HBP	SH	SF	SB	CS	BA	OBA	SA	FA
1969	Mon-N	6	6	1	0	0	0	0	1	0	0	0	0	0	0	0	0	.000	.000	.000	.667
1971	**ChC-N**	**3**	**3**	**0**	**0**	**0**	**0**	**0**	**0**	**0**	**0**	**0**	**0**	**0**	**0**	**0**	**0**	**.000**	**.000**	**.000**	**—**
1971	SD-N	75	189	17	55	13	0	0	13	11	0	24	0	3	1	1	3	.291	.328	.360	.941
1972	SD-N	92	256	15	63	5	1	6	22	13	2	21	0	10	1	0	0	.246	.281	.344	.949
Career average		59	151	11	39	6	0	2	12	8	1	15	0	4	1	0	1	.260	.296	.344	.943
Cubs average		**3**	**3**	**0**	**0**	**0**	**0**	**0**	**0**	**0**	**0**	**0**	**0**	**0**	**0**	**0**	**0**	**.000**	**.000**	**.000**	**—**
Career total		176	454	33	118	18	1	6	36	24	2	45	0	13	2	1	3	.260	.296	.344	.943
Cubs total		**3**	**3**	**0**	**0**	**0**	**0**	**0**	**0**	**0**	**0**	**0**	**0**	**0**	**0**	**0**	**0**	**.000**	**.000**	**.000**	**—**

Jimenez, Manuel Emilio (Manny)
HEIGHT: 6'1" THROWS: RIGHT BATS: LEFT BORN: 11/19/1938 SAN PEDRO DE MACORIS, DOMINICAN REPUBLIC POSITIONS PLAYED: OF

YEAR	TEAM	GAMES	AB	RUNS	HITS	2B	3B	HR	RBI	BB	IBB	SO	HBP	SH	SF	SB	CS	BA	OBA	SA	FA
1962	KCA-A	139	479	48	144	24	2	11	69	31	3	34	11	2	5	0	1	.301	.354	.428	.985
1963	KCA-A	60	157	12	44	9	0	0	15	16	2	14	5	1	2	0	1	.280	.361	.338	.960
1964	KCA-A	95	204	19	46	7	0	12	38	15	1	24	5	0	1	0	0	.225	.293	.436	.939
1966	KCA-A	13	35	1	4	0	1	0	1	6	0	4	0	0	0	0	0	.114	.244	.171	.909
1967	Pit-N	50	56	3	14	2	0	2	10	1	0	4	1	0	0	0	0	.250	.276	.393	1.000
1968	Pit-N	66	66	7	20	1	1	1	11	6	0	15	5	0	0	0	0	.303	.403	.394	.857
1969	**ChC-N**	**6**	**6**	**0**	**1**	**0**	**0**	**0**	**0**	**0**	**0**	**2**	**0**	**0**	**0**	**0**	**0**	**.167**	**.167**	**.167**	**—**
Career average		61	143	13	39	6	1	4	21	11	1	14	4	0	1	0	0	.272	.337	.401	.966
Cubs average		**6**	**6**	**0**	**1**	**0**	**0**	**0**	**0**	**0**	**0**	**2**	**0**	**0**	**0**	**0**	**0**	**.167**	**.167**	**.167**	**—**
Career total		429	1003	90	273	43	4	26	144	75	6	97	27	3	8	0	2	.272	.337	.401	.966
Cubs total		**6**	**6**	**0**	**1**	**0**	**0**	**0**	**0**	**0**	**0**	**2**	**0**	**0**	**0**	**0**	**0**	**.167**	**.167**	**.167**	**—**

Johnson, Clifford (Cliff)

HEIGHT: 6'4" THROWS: RIGHT BATS: RIGHT BORN: 7/22/1947 SAN ANTONIO, TEXAS POSITIONS PLAYED: C, 1B, OF

YEAR	TEAM	GAMES	AB	RUNS	HITS	2B	3B	HR	RBI	BB	IBB	SO	HBP	SH	SF	SB	CS	BA	OBA	SA	FA
1972	Hou-N	5	4	0	1	0	0	0	0	2	0	0	0	0	0	0	0	.250	.500	.250	1.000
1973	Hou-N	7	20	6	6	2	0	2	6	1	0	7	1	0	0	0	0	.300	.364	.700	1.000
1974	Hou-N	83	171	26	39	4	1	10	29	33	1	45	3	0	3	0	1	.228	.357	.439	.986
1975	Hou-N	122	340	52	94	16	1	20	65	46	5	64	5	1	1	1	0	.276	.370	.506	.982
1976	Hou-N	108	318	36	72	21	2	10	49	62	6	59	4	0	0	0	0	.226	.359	.399	.982
1977	Hou-N	51	144	22	43	8	0	10	23	23	2	30	4	0	0	0	1	.299	.409	.563	.976
1977	NYY-A	56	142	24	42	8	0	12	31	20	0	23	6	0	0	0	1	.296	.405	.606	.994
1978	NYY-A	76	174	20	32	9	1	6	19	30	5	32	1	0	0	0	0	.184	.307	.351	.976
1979	NYY-A	28	64	11	17	6	0	2	6	10	4	7	0	1	1	0	0	.266	.360	.453	1.000
1979	Cle-A	72	240	37	65	10	0	18	61	24	1	39	5	0	5	2	0	.271	.343	.538	—
1980	Cle-A	54	174	25	40	3	1	6	28	25	5	30	1	0	4	0	1	.230	.320	.362	—
1980	**ChC-N**	**68**	**196**	**28**	**46**	**8**	**0**	**10**	**34**	**29**	**5**	**35**	**1**	**0**	**1**	**0**	**0**	**.235**	**.335**	**.429**	**.990**
1981	Oak-A	84	273	40	71	8	0	17	59	28	2	60	3	0	6	5	3	.260	.329	.476	1.000
1982	Oak-A	73	214	19	51	10	0	7	31	26	2	41	2	0	2	1	2	.238	.324	.383	.987
1983	Tor-A	142	407	59	108	23	1	22	76	67	8	69	5	1	4	0	1	.265	.373	.489	1.000
1984	Tor-A	127	359	51	109	23	1	16	61	50	4	62	3	0	3	0	1	.304	.390	.507	1.000
1985	Tex-A	82	296	31	76	17	1	12	56	31	2	44	3	1	3	0	0	.257	.330	.443	—
1985	Tor-A	24	73	4	20	0	0	1	10	9	0	15	0	0	1	0	0	.274	.349	.315	.947
1986	Tor-A	107	336	48	84	12	1	15	55	52	1	57	4	0	2	0	1	.250	.355	.426	1.000
Career average		91	263	36	68	13	1	13	47	38	4	48	3	0	2	1	1	.258	.355	.459	.985
Cubs average		**68**	**196**	**28**	**46**	**8**	**0**	**10**	**34**	**29**	**5**	**35**	**1**	**0**	**1**	**0**	**0**	**.235**	**.335**	**.429**	**.990**
Career total		1369	3945	539	1016	188	10	196	699	568	53	719	50	4	36	9	12	.258	.355	.459	.985
Cubs total		**68**	**196**	**28**	**46**	**8**	**0**	**10**	**34**	**29**	**5**	**35**	**1**	**0**	**1**	**0**	**0**	**.235**	**.335**	**.429**	**.990**

Johnson, David Allen (Dave)

HEIGHT: 6'1" THROWS: RIGHT BATS: RIGHT BORN: 1/30/1943 ORLANDO, FLORIDA POSITIONS PLAYED: 1B, 2B, 3B, SS

YEAR	TEAM	GAMES	AB	RUNS	HITS	2B	3B	HR	RBI	BB	IBB	SO	HBP	SH	SF	SB	CS	BA	OBA	SA	FA
1965	Bal-A	20	47	5	8	3	0	0	1	5	0	6	0	0	1	3	0	.170	.245	.234	.941
1966	Bal-A	131	501	47	129	20	3	7	56	31	3	64	1	1	7	3	4	.257	.298	.351	.970
1967	Bal-A	148	510	62	126	30	3	10	64	59	10	82	4	5	8	4	5	.247	.325	.376	.980
1968	Bal-A	145	504	50	122	24	4	9	56	44	5	80	5	3	3	7	3	.242	.308	.359	.978
1969	Bal-A	142	511	52	143	34	1	7	57	57	2	52	3	2	7	3	4	.280	.351	.391	.984
1970	Bal-A	149	530	68	149	27	1	10	53	66	8	68	0	3	1	2	1	.281	.360	.392	.990
1971	Bal-A	142	510	67	144	26	1	18	72	51	5	55	5	4	4	3	1	.282	.351	.443	.984
1972	Bal-A	118	376	31	83	22	3	5	32	52	5	68	4	2	2	1	1	.221	.320	.335	.990
1973	Atl-N	157	559	84	151	25	0	43	99	81	9	93	9	0	2	5	3	.270	.370	.546	.966
1974	Atl-N	136	454	56	114	18	0	15	62	75	6	59	3	4	4	1	2	.251	.358	.390	.989
1975	Atl-N	1	1	0	1	1	0	0	1	0	0	0	0	0	0	0	0	1.000	1.000	2.000	—
1977	Phi-N	78	156	23	50	9	1	8	36	23	1	20	2	2	3	1	1	.321	.408	.545	1.000
1978	Phi-N	44	89	14	17	2	0	2	14	10	0	19	2	0	1	0	0	.191	.284	.281	.942
1978	**ChC-N**	**24**	**49**	**5**	**15**	**1**	**1**	**2**	**6**	**5**	**0**	**9**	**2**	**0**	**0**	**0**	**0**	**.306**	**.393**	**.490**	**.839**
Career average		110	369	43	96	19	1	10	47	43	4	52	3	2	3	3	2	.261	.340	.404	.981
Cubs average		**24**	**49**	**5**	**15**	**1**	**1**	**2**	**6**	**5**	**0**	**9**	**2**	**0**	**0**	**0**	**0**	**.306**	**.393**	**.490**	**.839**
Career total		1435	4797	564	1252	242	18	136	609	559	57	675	40	26	43	33	25	.261	.340	.404	.981
Cubs total		**24**	**49**	**5**	**15**	**1**	**1**	**2**	**6**	**5**	**0**	**9**	**2**	**0**	**0**	**0**	**0**	**.306**	**.393**	**.490**	**.839**

Johnson, Donald Spore (Don *or* Pop)

HEIGHT: 6'0" THROWS: RIGHT BATS: RIGHT BORN: 12/7/1911 CHICAGO, ILLINOIS DIED: 4/6/2000 LAGUNA BEACH, CALIFORNIA POSITIONS PLAYED: 2B, 3B

YEAR	TEAM	GAMES	AB	RUNS	HITS	2B	3B	HR	RBI	BB	IBB	SO	HBP	SH	SF	SB	CS	BA	OBA	SA	FA
1943	ChC-N	10	42	5	8	2	0	0	1	2	—	4	0	1	—	0	—	.190	.227	.238	.957
1944	ChC-N	154	608	50	169	37	1	2	71	28	—	48	1	7	—	8	—	.278	.311	.352	.947
1945	ChC-N	138	557	94	168	23	2	2	58	32	—	34	3	22	—	9	—	.302	.343	.361	.975
1946	ChC-N	83	314	37	76	10	1	1	19	26	—	39	3	10	—	6	—	.242	.306	.290	.981
1947	ChC-N	120	402	33	104	17	2	3	26	24	—	45	1	7	—	2	—	.259	.302	.333	.971
1948	ChC-N	6	12	0	3	0	0	0	0	0	—	1	0	0	—	1	—	.250	.250	.250	.750
Career average		85	323	37	88	15	1	1	29	19	—	29	1	8	—	4	—	.273	.315	.337	.965
Cubs average		**85**	**323**	**37**	**88**	**15**	**1**	**1**	**29**	**19**	**—**	**29**	**1**	**8**	**—**	**4**	**—**	**.273**	**.315**	**.337**	**.965**
Career total		511	1935	219	528	89	6	8	175	112	—	171	8	47	—	26	—	.273	.315	.337	.965
Cubs total		**511**	**1935**	**219**	**528**	**89**	**6**	**8**	**175**	**112**	**—**	**171**	**8**	**47**	**—**	**26**	**—**	**.273**	**.315**	**.337**	**.965**

Johnson, Howard Michael (HoJo)

HEIGHT: 5'10" THROWS: RIGHT BATS: BOTH BORN: 11/29/1960 CLEARWATER, FLORIDA POSITIONS PLAYED: 1B, 2B, 3B, SS, OF

YEAR	TEAM	GAMES	AB	RUNS	HITS	2B	3B	HR	RBI	BB	IBB	SO	HBP	SH	SF	SB	CS	BA	OBA	SA	FA
1982	Det-A	54	155	23	49	5	0	4	14	16	1	30	1	1	0	7	4	.316	.384	.426	.916
1983	Det-A	27	66	11	14	0	0	3	5	7	0	10	1	0	0	0	0	.212	.297	.348	.851
1984	Det-A	116	355	43	88	14	1	12	50	40	1	67	1	4	2	10	6	.248	.324	.394	.938
1985	NYM-N	126	389	38	94	18	4	11	46	34	10	78	0	1	4	6	4	.242	.300	.393	.937
1986	NYM-N	88	220	30	54	14	0	10	39	31	8	64	1	1	0	8	1	.245	.341	.445	.904
1987	NYM-N	157	554	93	147	22	1	36	99	83	18	113	1	0	3	32	10	.265	.364	.504	.942
1988	NYM-N	148	495	85	114	21	1	24	68	86	25	104	5	2	8	23	7	.230	.343	.422	.955
1989	NYM-N	153	571	104	164	41	3	36	101	77	8	126	3	0	6	41	8	.287	.369	.559	.929
1990	NYM-N	154	590	89	144	37	3	23	90	69	12	100	1	0	9	34	8	.244	.319	.434	.945
1991	NYM-N	156	564	108	146	34	4	38	117	78	12	120	0	0	15	30	16	.259	.342	.535	.932
1992	NYM-N	100	350	48	78	19	0	7	43	55	5	79	1	0	3	22	5	.223	.329	.337	.981
1993	NYM-N	72	235	32	56	8	2	7	26	43	3	43	2	0	2	6	4	.238	.354	.379	.944
1994	Col-N	93	227	30	48	10	2	10	40	39	2	73	0	0	2	6	4	.238	.354	.379	.944
1995	**ChC-N**	**87**	**169**	**26**	**33**	**4**	**1**	**7**	**22**	**34**	**0**	**46**	**1**	**0**	**2**	**1**	**1**	**.195**	**.330**	**.405**	**.981**
Career average		109	353	54	88	18	2	16	54	49	8	75	1	1	4	17	6	.249	.340	.446	.940
Cubs average		**87**	**169**	**26**	**33**	**4**	**1**	**7**	**22**	**34**	**0**	**46**	**1**	**0**	**2**	**1**	**1**	**.195**	**.330**	**.355**	**.940**
Career total		1531	4940	760	1229	247	22	228	760	692	105	1053	17	9	57	231	77	.249	.340	.446	.940
Cubs total		**87**	**169**	**26**	**33**	**4**	**1**	**7**	**22**	**34**	**0**	**46**	**1**	**0**	**2**	**1**	**1**	**.195**	**.330**	**.355**	**.940**

Johnson, Kenneth Lance (Lance)

HEIGHT: 5'11" THROWS: LEFT BATS: LEFT BORN: 7/6/1963 LINCOLN HEIGHTS, OHIO POSITIONS PLAYED: OF

YEAR	TEAM	GAMES	AB	RUNS	HITS	2B	3B	HR	RBI	BB	IBB	SO	HBP	SH	SF	SB	CS	BA	OBA	SA	FA
1987	StL-N	33	59	4	13	2	1	0	7	4	1	6	0	0	0	6	1	.220	.270	.288	.931
1988	CWS-A	33	124	11	23	4	1	0	6	6	0	11	0	2	0	6	2	.185	.223	.234	.970
1989	CWS-A	50	180	28	54	8	2	0	16	17	0	24	0	2	0	16	3	.300	.360	.367	.983
1990	CWS-A	151	541	76	154	18	9	1	51	33	2	45	1	8	4	36	22	.285	.325	.357	.973
1991	CWS-A	160	588	72	161	14	13	0	49	26	2	58	1	6	3	26	11	.274	.304	.342	.995
1992	CWS-A	157	567	67	158	15	12	3	47	34	4	33	1	4	5	41	14	.279	.318	.363	.987
1993	CWS-A	147	540	75	168	18	14	0	47	36	1	33	1	4	5	41	14	.279	.318	.363	.987
1994	CWS-A	106	412	56	114	11	14	3	54	26	5	23	0	3	0	35	7	.311	.354	.396	.980
1995	CWS-A	142	607	98	186	18	12	10	57	32	2	31	2	0	3	26	6	.277	.321	.393	1.000
1996	NYM-N	160	682	117	227	31	21	9	69	33	8	40	1	2	3	40	6	.306	.341	.425	.991
1997	NYM-N	72	265	43	82	10	6	1	24	33	2	21	1	3	5	50	12	.333	.362	.479	.971
1997	**ChC-N**	**39**	**145**	**17**	**44**	**6**	**2**	**4**	**15**	**9**	**1**	**10**	**1**	**0**	**1**	**15**	**10**	**.309**	**.385**	**.404**	**.975**
1998	**ChC-N**	**85**	**304**	**51**	**85**	**8**	**4**	**2**	**21**	**26**	**1**	**22**	**0**	**0**	**1**	**5**	**2**	**.303**	**.342**	**.455**	**.963**
1999	**ChC-N**	**95**	**335**	**46**	**87**	**11**	**6**	**1**	**21**	**37**	**0**	**20**	**0**	**1**	**1**	**10**	**6**	**.280**	**.335**	**.352**	**.975**
2000	NYY-A	18	30	6	9	1	0	0	2	0	0	7	0	4	1	13	3	.260	.332	.337	.988
Career average		103	384	55	112	13	8	2	35	25	2	27	1	3	2	23	8	.291	.334	.386	.983
Cubs average		**73**	**261**	**38**	**72**	**8**	**4**	**2**	**19**	**24**	**1**	**17**	**0**	**2**	**1**	**9**	**4**	**.276**	**.335**	**.386**	**.983**
Career total		1448	5379	767	1565	175	117	34	486	352	29	384	7	35	27	327	105	.291	.334	.386	.980
Cubs total		**219**	**784**	**114**	**216**	**25**	**12**	**7**	**57**	**72**	**2**	**52**	**0**	**5**	**3**	**28**	**11**	**.276**	**.335**	**.365**	**.980**

Johnson, Louis Brown (Lou *or* Slick)

HEIGHT: 5'11" THROWS: RIGHT BATS: RIGHT BORN: 9/22/1934 LEXINGTON, KENTUCKY POSITIONS PLAYED: OF

YEAR	TEAM	GAMES	AB	RUNS	HITS	2B	3B	HR	RBI	BB	IBB	SO	HBP	SH	SF	SB	CS	BA	OBA	SA	FA
1960	**ChC-N**	**34**	**68**	**6**	**14**	**2**	**1**	**0**	**1**	**5**	**1**	**19**	**1**	**1**	**0**	**3**	**1**	**.206**	**.270**	**.265**	**1.000**
1961	LAA-A	1	0	0	0	0	0	0	0	0	0	0	0	0	0	0	0	—	—	—	—
1962	Mil-N	61	117	22	33	4	5	2	13	11	0	27	1	0	0	6	1	.282	.349	.453	1.000
1965	LA-N	131	468	57	121	24	1	12	58	24	8	81	16	7	3	15	6	.259	.315	.391	.985
1966	LA-N	152	526	71	143	20	2	17	73	21	4	75	14	9	2	8	10	.272	.316	.414	.985
1967	LA-N	104	330	39	89	14	1	11	41	24	5	52	7	7	3	4	3	.270	.330	.418	.976
1968	**ChC-N**	**62**	**205**	**14**	**50**	**14**	**3**	**1**	**14**	**6**	**2**	**23**	**7**	**2**	**0**	**3**	**1**	**.244**	**.289**	**.356**	**.970**
1968	Cle-A	65	202	25	52	11	1	5	23	9	2	24	4	0	3	6	1	.257	.298	.396	.989
1969	Cal-A	67	133	10	27	8	0	0	9	10	1	19	3	1	1	5	1	.203	.272	.263	.935
Career average		85	256	31	66	12	2	6	29	14	3	40	7	3	2	6	3	.258	.311	.389	.981
Cubs average		**48**	**137**	**10**	**32**	**8**	**2**	**1**	**8**	**6**	**2**	**21**	**4**	**2**	**0**	**3**	**1**	**.234**	**.284**	**.333**	**.981**
Career total		677	2049	244	529	97	14	48	232	110	23	320	53	27	12	50	24	.258	.311	.389	.981
Cubs total		**96**	**273**	**20**	**64**	**16**	**4**	**1**	**15**	**11**	**3**	**42**	**8**	**3**	**0**	**6**	**2**	**.234**	**.284**	**.333**	**.980**

Johnson, Richard Allan (Footer *or* Treads)
HEIGHT: 5'11" THROWS: LEFT BATS: LEFT BORN: 2/15/1932 DAYTON, OHIO

YEAR	TEAM	GAMES	AB	RUNS	HITS	2B	3B	HR	RBI	BB	IBB	SO	HBP	SH	SF	SB	CS	BA	OBA	SA	FA
1958	ChC-N	8	5	1	0	0	0	0	0	0	0	1	0	0	0	0	0	.000	.000	.000	—
Career average		8	5	1	0	0	0	0	0	0	0	1	0	0	0	0	0	.000	.000	.000	—
Cubs average		8	5	1	0	0	0	0	0	0	0	1	0	0	0	0	0	.000	.000	.000	—
Career total		8	5	1	0	0	0	0	0	0	0	1	0	0	0	0	0	.000	.000	.000	—
Cubs total		8	5	1	0	0	0	0	0	0	0	1	0	0	0	0	0	.000	.000	.000	—

Johnston, James Harle (Jimmy)
HEIGHT: 5'10" THROWS: RIGHT BATS: RIGHT BORN: 12/10/1889 CLEVELAND, TENNESSEE DIED: 2/14/1967 CHATTANOOGA, TENNESSEE
POSITIONS PLAYED: 1B, 2B, 3B, SS, OF

YEAR	TEAM	GAMES	AB	RUNS	HITS	2B	3B	HR	RBI	BB	IBB	SO	HBP	SH	SF	SB	CS	BA	OBA	SA	FA
1911	CWS-A	1	2	0	0	0	0	0	2	0	—	—	0	0	—	0	—	.000	.000	.000	1.000
1914	ChC-N	50	101	9	23	3	2	1	8	4	—	9	1	5	—	3	—	.228	.264	.327	.914
1916	Bro-N	118	425	58	107	13	8	1	26	35	—	38	3	9	—	22	19	.252	.313	.327	.964
1917	Bro-N	103	330	33	89	10	4	0	25	23	—	28	2	14	—	16	—	.270	.321	.324	.948
1918	Bro-N	123	484	54	136	16	8	0	27	33	—	31	1	10	—	22	—	.281	.328	.347	.971
1919	Bro-N	117	405	56	114	11	4	1	23	29	—	26	3	16	—	11	—	.281	.334	.336	.962
1920	Bro-N	155	635	87	185	17	12	1	52	43	—	23	2	28	—	19	15	.291	.338	.361	.935
1921	Bro-N	152	624	104	203	41	14	5	56	45	—	26	1	19	—	28	16	.325	.372	.460	.933
1922	Bro-N	138	567	110	181	20	7	4	49	38	—	17	2	10	—	18	9	.319	.364	.400	.946
1923	Bro-N	151	625	111	203	29	11	4	60	53	—	15	0	15	—	16	13	.325	.378	.426	.946
1924	Bro-N	86	315	51	94	11	2	2	29	27	—	10	1	11	—	5	6	.298	.356	.365	.942
1925	Bro-N	123	431	63	128	13	3	2	43	45	—	15	4	10	—	7	5	.297	.369	.355	.901
1926	Bos-N	23	57	7	14	1	0	1	5	10	—	3	0	0	—	2	—	.246	.358	.316	1.000
1926	NYG-N	37	69	11	16	0	0	0	5	6	—	5	0	0	—	0	—	.232	.293	.232	1.000
Career average		106	390	58	115	14	6	2	32	30	—	19	2	11	—	13	6	.294	.347	.374	.944
Cubs average		50	101	9	23	3	2	1	8	4	—	9	1	5	—	3	—	.228	.264	.327	.914
Career total		1377	5070	754	1493	185	75	22	410	391	—	246	20	147	—	169	83	.294	.347	.374	.944
Cubs total		50	101	9	23	3	2	1	8	4	—	9	1	5	—	3	—	.228	.264	.327	.914

Johnstone, John William (Jay)
HEIGHT: 6'1" THROWS: RIGHT BATS: LEFT BORN: 11/20/1945 MANCHESTER, CONNECTICUT POSITIONS PLAYED: 1B, 2B, OF

YEAR	TEAM	GAMES	AB	RUNS	HITS	2B	3B	HR	RBI	BB	IBB	SO	HBP	SH	SF	SB	CS	BA	OBA	SA	FA
1966	Cal-A	61	254	35	67	12	4	3	17	11	1	36	1	2	0	3	3	.264	.297	.378	.975
1967	Cal-A	79	230	18	48	7	1	2	10	5	0	37	0	2	0	3	2	.209	.226	.274	.973
1968	Cal-A	41	115	11	30	4	1	0	3	7	0	15	0	2	0	2	1	.261	.303	.313	.984
1969	Cal-A	148	540	64	146	20	5	10	59	38	5	75	5	8	6	3	9	.270	.321	.381	.983
1970	Cal-A	119	320	34	76	10	5	11	39	24	6	53	1	3	3	1	0	.238	.290	.403	.981
1971	CWS-A	124	388	53	101	14	1	16	40	38	4	50	3	5	2	10	5	.260	.329	.425	.968
1972	CWS-A	113	261	27	49	9	4	4	17	25	2	42	0	4	0	0	1	.188	.259	.268	.988
1973	Oak-A	23	28	1	3	1	0	0	3	2	0	4	0	0	0	0	1	.107	.167	.143	1.000
1974	Phi-N	64	200	30	59	10	4	6	30	24	4	28	0	0	0	5	5	.295	.371	.475	.968
1975	Phi-N	122	350	50	115	19	2	7	54	42	7	39	0	3	3	7	3	.329	.397	.454	.976
1976	Phi-N	129	440	62	140	38	4	5	53	41	5	39	2	1	7	5	5	.318	.373	.457	.974
1977	Phi-N	112	363	64	103	18	4	15	59	38	3	38	2	1	7	3	7	.284	.349	.479	.997
1978	Phi-N	35	56	3	10	2	0	0	4	6	0	9	0	0	0	0	2	.179	.258	.214	.988
1978	NYY-A	36	65	6	17	0	0	1	6	4	0	10	3	0	1	0	1	.262	.329	.308	1.000
1979	NYY-A	23	48	7	10	1	0	1	7	2	0	7	0	0	1	1	0	.208	.240	.292	1.000
1979	SD-N	75	201	10	59	8	2	0	32	18	3	21	0	4	2	1	3	.294	.348	.353	.981
1980	LA-N	109	251	31	77	15	2	2	20	24	1	29	2	2	0	3	2	.307	.372	.406	.965
1981	LA-N	61	83	8	17	3	0	3	6	7	0	13	0	0	0	1	1	.205	.267	.349	.974
1982	LA-N	21	13	1	1	1	0	0	2	5	1	2	0	0	1	0	0	.077	.316	.154	—
1982	ChC-N	98	269	39	67	13	1	10	43	40	8	41	0	1	3	0	1	.249	.343	.416	.982
1983	ChC-N	86	140	16	36	7	0	6	22	20	6	24	3	2	0	1	1	.257	.362	.436	.935
1984	ChC-N	52	73	8	21	2	2	0	3	7	4	18	0	0	0	0	0	.288	.350	.370	1.000
1985	LA-N	17	15	0	2	1	0	0	2	1	1	2	0	0	0	0	0	.133	.188	.200	—
Career average		87	235	29	63	11	2	5	27	21	3	32	1	2	2	3	3	.267	.329	.394	.979
Cubs average		79	161	21	41	7	1	5	23	22	6	28	1	1	1	0	1	.257	.350	.415	.971
Career total		1748	4703	578	1254	215	38	102	531	429	61	632	22	40	35	50	54	.267	.329	.394	.979
Cubs total		236	482	63	124	22	3	16	68	67	18	83	3	3	3	1	3	.257	.350	.415	.971

(continued)

(continued)

Jones, Charles Wesley (Charley *or* Baby)
HEIGHT: 5'11"   THROWS: RIGHT   BATS: RIGHT   BORN: 4/30/1850 ALAMANCE COUNTY, NORTH CAROLINA   POSITIONS PLAYED: P, 1B, OF

YEAR	TEAM	GAMES	AB	RUNS	HITS	2B	3B	HR	RBI	BB	IBB	SO	HBP	SH	SF	SB	CS	BA	OBA	SA	FA
1876	Cin-N	64	283	40	79	17	4	4	38	7	—	17	—	—	—	—	—	.279	.297	.410	.857
1877	Cin-N	55	232	52	72	11	10	2	36	14	—	25	—	—	—	—	—	.310	.350	.470	.871
1877	**ChN-N**	**2**	**8**	**1**	**3**	**1**	**0**	**0**	**2**	**1**	**—**	**0**	**—**	**—**	**—**	**—**	**—**	**.375**	**.444**	**.500**	**1.000**
1878	Cin-N	61	261	50	81	11	7	3	39	4	—	17	—	—	—	—	—	.310	.321	.441	.896
1879	Bos-N	83	355	85	112	22	10	9	62	29	—	38	—	—	—	—	—	.315	.367	.510	.933
1880	Bos-N	66	280	44	84	15	3	5	37	11	—	27	—	—	—	—	—	.300	.326	.429	.826
1883	Cin-AA	90	391	84	115	15	12	10	80	20	—	—	—	—	—	—	—	.294	.328	.471	.876
1884	Cin-AA	112	472	117	148	19	17	7	71	37	—	—	10	—	—	—	—	.314	.376	.470	.887
1885	Cin-AA	112	487	108	157	19	17	5	35	21	—	—	9	—	—	—	—	.322	.362	.462	.891
1886	Cin-AA	127	500	87	135	22	10	6	68	61	—	—	6	—	—	3	—	.270	.356	.390	.879
1887	Cin-AA	41	172	28	67	7	4	2	40	19	—	—	3	—	—	7	—	.390	.459	.512	.900
1887	NY-AA	62	259	30	75	11	3	3	29	12	—	—	6	—	—	8	—	.290	.336	.390	.904
1888	KC-AA	6	25	2	4	0	1	0	5	1	—	—	0	—	—	1	—	.160	.192	.240	.750
Career average		80	339	66	103	15	9	5	49	22	—	11	3	—	—	2	—	.304	.351	.447	.883
Cubs average		**2**	**8**	**1**	**3**	**1**	**0**	**0**	**2**	**1**	**—**	**0**	**—**	**—**	**—**	**—**	**—**	**.375**	**.444**	**.500**	**1.000**
Career total		881	3725	728	1132	170	98	56	542	237	—	124	34	—	—	19	—	.304	.351	.447	.883
Cubs total		**2**	**8**	**1**	**3**	**1**	**0**	**0**	**2**	**1**	**—**	**0**	**—**	**—**	**—**	**—**	**—**	**.375**	**.444**	**.500**	**1.000**

Jones, Clarence Woodrow
HEIGHT: 6'2"   THROWS: LEFT   BATS: LEFT   BORN: 11/7/1941 ZANESVILLE, OHIO   POSITIONS PLAYED: 1B, OF

YEAR	TEAM	GAMES	AB	RUNS	HITS	2B	3B	HR	RBI	BB	IBB	SO	HBP	SH	SF	SB	CS	BA	OBA	SA	FA
1967	**ChC-N**	**53**	**135**	**13**	**34**	**7**	**0**	**2**	**16**	**14**	**3**	**33**	**0**	**2**	**4**	**0**	**0**	**.252**	**.314**	**.348**	**.979**
1968	**ChC-N**	**5**	**2**	**0**	**0**	**0**	**0**	**0**	**0**	**2**	**0**	**1**	**0**	**0**	**0**	**0**	**0**	**.000**	**.500**	**.000**	**1.000**
Career average		29	69	7	17	4	0	1	8	8	2	17	0	1	2	0	0	.248	.318	.343	.979
Cubs average		**29**	**69**	**7**	**17**	**4**	**0**	**1**	**8**	**8**	**2**	**17**	**0**	**1**	**2**	**0**	**0**	**.248**	**.318**	**.343**	**.979**
Career total		58	137	13	34	7	0	2	16	16	3	34	0	2	4	0	0	.248	.318	.343	.979
Cubs total		**58**	**137**	**13**	**34**	**7**	**0**	**2**	**16**	**16**	**3**	**34**	**0**	**2**	**4**	**0**	**0**	**.248**	**.318**	**.343**	**.979**

Jones, David Jefferson (Davy *or* Kangaroo)
HEIGHT: 5'10"   THROWS: RIGHT   BATS: LEFT   BORN: 6/30/1880 CAMBRIA, WISCONSIN   DIED: 3/31/1972 MANKATO, MINNESOTA   POSITIONS PLAYED: OF

YEAR	TEAM	GAMES	AB	RUNS	HITS	2B	3B	HR	RBI	BB	IBB	SO	HBP	SH	SF	SB	CS	BA	OBA	SA	FA
1901	Mil-A	14	52	12	9	0	0	3	5	11	—	—	1	0	—	4	—	.173	.328	.346	.911
1902	StL-A	15	49	4	11	1	1	0	3	6	—	—	0	1	—	5	—	.224	.309	.286	.973
1902	**ChC-N**	**64**	**243**	**41**	**74**	**12**	**3**	**0**	**14**	**38**	**—**	**—**	**0**	**14**	**—**	**12**	**—**	**.305**	**.399**	**.379**	**.955**
1903	**ChC-N**	**130**	**497**	**64**	**140**	**18**	**3**	**1**	**62**	**53**	**—**	**—**	**1**	**8**	**—**	**15**	**—**	**.282**	**.352**	**.336**	**.970**
1904	**ChC-N**	**98**	**336**	**44**	**82**	**11**	**5**	**3**	**39**	**41**	**—**	**—**	**2**	**4**	**—**	**14**	**—**	**.244**	**.330**	**.333**	**.932**
1906	Det-A	84	323	41	84	12	2	0	24	41	—	—	2	2	—	21	—	.260	.347	.310	.981
1907	Det-A	126	491	101	134	10	6	0	27	60	—	—	4	11	—	30	—	.273	.357	.318	.971
1908	Det-A	56	121	17	25	2	1	0	10	13	—	—	0	4	—	11	—	.207	.284	.240	.960
1909	Det-A	69	204	44	57	2	2	0	10	28	—	—	1	6	—	12	—	.279	.369	.309	.982
1910	Det-A	113	377	77	100	6	6	0	24	51	—	—	6	9	—	25	—	.265	.362	.313	.956
1911	Det-A	98	341	78	93	10	0	0	19	41	—	—	2	7	—	25	—	.273	.354	.302	.950
1912	Det-A	97	316	54	93	5	2	0	24	38	—	—	0	12	—	16	—	.294	.370	.323	.963
1913	CWS-A	10	21	2	6	0	0	0	0	9	—	0	0	1	—	1	—	.286	.500	.286	.867
1914	Pit-F	97	352	58	96	9	8	2	24	42	—	16	3	15	—	15	—	.273	.355	.361	.970
1915	Pit-F	14	49	6	16	0	1	0	4	6	—	0	0	0	—	1	—	.327	.400	.367	.926
Career average		78	269	46	73	7	3	1	21	34	—	1	2	7	—	15	—	.270	.356	.325	.962
Cubs average		**97**	**359**	**50**	**99**	**14**	**4**	**1**	**38**	**44**	**—**	**—**	**1**	**9**	**—**	**14**	**—**	**.275**	**.356**	**.345**	**.956**
Career total		1085	3772	643	1020	98	40	9	289	478	—	16	22	94	—	207	—	.270	.356	.325	.962
Cubs total		**292**	**1076**	**149**	**296**	**41**	**11**	**4**	**115**	**132**	**—**	**—**	**3**	**26**	**—**	**41**	**—**	**.275**	**.356**	**.345**	**.956**

Jurges, William Frederick (Billy)
HEIGHT: 5'11"   THROWS: RIGHT   BATS: RIGHT   BORN: 5/9/1908 BRONX, NEW YORK   DIED: 3/3/1997 CLEARWATER, FLORIDA   POSITIONS PLAYED: 2B, 3B, SS

YEAR	TEAM	GAMES	AB	RUNS	HITS	2B	3B	HR	RBI	BB	IBB	SO	HBP	SH	SF	SB	CS	BA	OBA	SA	FA
1931	ChC-N	88	293	34	59	15	5	0	23	25	—	41	0	17	—	2	—	.201	.264	.287	.966
1932	ChC-N	115	396	40	100	24	4	2	52	19	—	26	1	10	—	1	—	.253	.288	.348	.965
1933	ChC-N	143	487	49	131	17	6	5	50	26	—	39	5	8	—	3	—	.269	.313	.359	.958
1934	ChC-N	100	358	43	88	15	2	8	33	19	—	34	3	5	—	1	—	.246	.289	.366	.966
1935	ChC-N	146	519	69	125	33	1	1	59	42	—	39	5	18	—	3	—	.241	.304	.314	.964
1936	ChC-N	118	429	51	120	25	1	1	42	23	—	25	3	4	—	4	—	.280	.321	.350	.960
1937	ChC-N	129	450	53	134	18	10	1	65	42	—	41	6	8	—	2	—	.298	.365	.389	.975
1938	ChC-N	137	465	53	114	18	3	1	47	58	—	53	5	12	—	3	—	.245	.335	.303	.953
1939	NYG-N	138	543	84	155	21	11	6	63	47	—	34	6	15	—	3	—	.285	.349	.398	.965
1940	NYG-N	63	214	23	54	3	3	2	36	25	—	14	6	3	—	2	—	.252	.347	.322	.967
1941	NYG-N	134	471	50	138	25	2	5	61	47	—	36	3	7	—	0	—	.293	.361	.386	.957
1942	NYG-N	127	464	45	119	7	1	2	30	43	—	42	3	10	—	1	—	.256	.324	.289	.978
1943	NYG-N	136	481	46	110	8	2	4	29	53	—	38	4	6	—	2	3	.229	.310	.279	.960
1944	NYG-N	85	246	28	52	2	1	1	23	23	—	20	0	12	—	4	1	.211	.279	.240	.964
1945	NYG-N	61	176	22	57	3	1	3	24	24	—	11	0	1	—	2	—	.324	.405	.403	.945
1946	ChC-N	82	221	26	49	9	2	0	17	43	—	28	1	5	—	3	—	.222	.351	.281	.977
1947	ChC-N	14	40	5	8	2	0	1	2	9	—	9	0	0	—	0	—	.200	.347	.325	.925
Career average		107	368	42	95	14	3	3	39	33	—	31	3	8	—	2	0	.258	.325	.335	.964
Cubs average		**107**	**366**	**42**	**93**	**18**	**3**	**2**	**39**	**31**	**—**	**34**	**3**	**9**	**—**	**2**	**0**	**.254**	**.316**	**.337**	**.963**
Career total		1816	6253	721	1613	245	55	43	656	568	—	530	51	141	—	36	4	.258	.325	.335	.964
Cubs total		**1072**	**3658**	**423**	**928**	**176**	**34**	**20**	**390**	**306**	**—**	**335**	**29**	**87**	**—**	**22**	**0**	**.254**	**.316**	**.337**	**.963**

Kahoe, Michael Joseph (Mike)
HEIGHT: 6'0"   THROWS: RIGHT   BATS: RIGHT   BORN: 9/3/1873 YELLOW SPRINGS, OHIO   DIED: 5/14/1949 AKRON, OHIO   POSITIONS PLAYED: C, 1B, 3B, SS

YEAR	TEAM	GAMES	AB	RUNS	HITS	2B	3B	HR	RBI	BB	IBB	SO	HBP	SH	SF	SB	CS	BA	OBA	SA	FA
1895	Cin-N	3	4	0	0	0	0	0	0	0	—	0	0	0	—	0	—	.000	.000	.000	1.000
1899	Cin-N	14	42	2	7	1	1	0	4	0	—	—	0	2	—	1	—	.167	.167	.238	.957
1900	Cin-N	52	175	18	33	3	3	1	9	4	—	—	2	3	—	3	—	.189	.215	.257	.950
1901	Cin-N	4	13	0	4	0	0	0	0	1	—	—	0	0	—	0	—	.308	.357	.308	1.000
1901	ChN-N	67	237	21	53	12	2	1	21	8	—	—	0	6	—	5	—	.224	.249	.304	.966
1902	ChC-N	7	18	0	4	1	0	0	2	0	—	—	0	1	—	0	—	.222	.222	.278	.857
1902	StL-A	55	197	21	48	9	2	2	28	6	—	—	1	5	—	4	—	.244	.270	.340	.967
1903	StL-A	77	244	26	46	7	5	0	23	11	—	—	1	6	—	1	—	.189	.227	.258	.971
1904	StL-A	72	236	9	51	6	1	0	12	8	—	—	0	8	—	4	—	.216	.242	.250	.968
1905	Phi-N	16	51	2	13	2	0	0	4	1	—	—	0	1	—	1	—	.255	.269	.294	.975
1907	ChC-N	5	10	0	4	0	0	0	1	0	—	—	0	0	—	0	—	.400	.400	.400	1.000
1907	Was-A	17	47	3	9	1	0	0	1	0	—	—	0	0	—	0	—	.191	.191	.213	.976
1908	Was-A	17	27	1	5	1	0	0	0	0	—	—	0	3	—	0	—	.185	.185	.222	.983
1909	Was-A	4	8	0	1	0	0	0	0	0	—	—	0	0	—	2	—	.125	.125	.125	.867
Career average		37	119	9	25	4	1	0	10	4	—	0	0	3	—	2	—	.212	.237	.276	.965
Cubs average		**26**	**88**	**7**	**20**	**4**	**1**	**0**	**8**	**3**	**—**	**0**	**0**	**2**	**—**	**2**	**—**	**.230**	**.253**	**.306**	**.961**
Career total		410	1309	103	278	43	14	4	105	39	—	0	4	35	—	21	—	.212	.237	.276	.965
Cubs total		**79**	**265**	**21**	**61**	**13**	**2**	**1**	**24**	**8**	**—**	**0**	**0**	**7**	**—**	**5**	**—**	**.230**	**.253**	**.306**	**.961**

Kaiser, Alfred Edward (Al *or* Deerfoot)
HEIGHT: 5'9"   THROWS: RIGHT   BATS: RIGHT   BORN: 8/3/1886 CINCINNATI, OHIO   DIED: 4/11/1969 CINCINNATI, OHIO   POSITIONS PLAYED: 1B, OF

YEAR	TEAM	GAMES	AB	RUNS	HITS	2B	3B	HR	RBI	BB	IBB	SO	HBP	SH	SF	SB	CS	BA	OBA	SA	FA
1911	ChC-N	26	84	16	21	0	5	0	7	7	—	12	0	3	—	6	—	.250	.308	.369	.905
1911	Bos-N	66	197	20	40	5	2	2	15	10	—	26	2	8	—	4	—	.203	.249	.279	.922
1912	Bos-N	4	13	0	0	0	0	0	0	0	—	3	0	1	—	0	—	.000	.000	.000	.900
1914	Ind-F	59	187	22	43	10	0	1	16	17	—	41	2	9	—	6	—	.230	.301	.299	.895
Career average		52	160	19	35	5	2	1	13	11	—	27	1	7	—	5	—	.216	.274	.295	.908
Cubs average		**26**	**84**	**16**	**21**	**0**	**5**	**0**	**7**	**7**	**—**	**12**	**0**	**3**	**—**	**6**	**—**	**.250**	**.308**	**.369**	**.905**
Career total		155	481	58	104	15	7	3	38	34	—	82	4	21	—	16	—	.216	.274	.295	.908
Cubs total		**26**	**84**	**16**	**21**	**0**	**5**	**0**	**7**	**7**	**—**	**12**	**0**	**3**	**—**	**6**	**—**	**.250**	**.308**	**.369**	**.905**

William (Billy) Frederick Jurges, ss, 1931–47

Billy Jurges is better known for being shot by a jealous girlfriend, but Billy from the Bronx was also a heck of a shortstop, even with a bullet hole in his hand.

Jurges was born on May 9, 1908, in the Bronx, New York. After a great high school and minor league career, he was called up to the Cubs in 1931. His terrific defensive play prompted the Cubs to move the very capable Woody English to second base.

In 1932 Jurges was hitting well and leading the league in fielding. He was a handsome guy and, at 24, enjoyed a good time. Jurges was staying at the Carliss Hotel in Chicago, where most of the single Cubs ballplayers were living during the season.

On July 6, Violet Valli, apparently one of Jurges's girlfriends, called the young shortstop on the telephone and then went up to his room. Although the tale has changed somewhat over the years, news reports of the time indicate that while Miss Valli did indeed have a gun, she did not intend to shoot Jurges—at least not initially.

Valli was reportedly upset that Jurges did not want to marry her and threatened to commit suicide in his hotel room. The two argued and soon were struggling with the gun. The weapon went off, striking Jurges in the hand and the side.

Interestingly, many former teammates of Jurges's, when retelling the tale, indicate that he was shot either in the buttocks or directly in the stomach. He was not shot in the rear, and had he been shot in the stomach, he would have missed much more than the 37 games he did sit out. In fact, Jurges came back for the Cubs in the World Series that year, played three of the four games and hit .364.

Jurges himself didn't often stop to correct the record, especially when teammate Billy Herman would kid him about having two, um, holes in his butt.

When he wasn't being shot at, Jurges was a pretty good player. He led the National League in fielding by a shortstop in 1932 with a .964 mark, one of four times in his 17-year career he would do so. Three of those times were with the Cubs, in 1932, 1935 and 1937. He was second in the league in 1933, 1934 and 1936 and third in 1938. He teamed up with Herman to give Chicago a formidable double-play combination in the 1930s.

The fiery Jurges was not a great hitter, although as teammate Phil Cavarretta once said wryly, "He thought he was." Still, Jurges made 100 hits or more six of his first eight years in Chicago. His best year at the plate was 1937, hitting .298 with 10 triples. He made the All-Star team for the first time that year.

Following the 1938 season, Cubs manager Gabby Hartnett believed that Jurges was losing a step. He sent the shortstop to the Giants. Jurges promptly proved he hadn't lost a heck of a lot, hitting .285, leading the league in fielding with a .965 mark and again making the All-Star team.

Jurges would play in New York for seven years before returning for a final hurrah with the Cubs in the 1946 and 1947 seasons.

Jurges also served as a coach for the Cubs during that span. He went to manage the Red Sox in the 1949 and 1950 seasons. He also coached briefly in Washington with the Senators. Jurges died in Clearwater, Florida on March 3, 1997.

Kane, John Francis
HEIGHT: 5'6" THROWS: RIGHT BATS: RIGHT BORN: 9/24/1882 CHICAGO, ILLINOIS DIED: 1/28/1934 ST. ANTHONY, IDAHO POSITIONS PLAYED: 2B, 3B, SS, OF

YEAR	TEAM	GAMES	AB	RUNS	HITS	2B	3B	HR	RBI	BB	IBB	SO	HBP	SH	SF	SB	CS	BA	OBA	SA	FA
1907	Cin-N	79	262	40	65	9	4	3	19	22	—	—	8	19	—	20	—	.248	.325	.347	.913
1908	Cin-N	130	455	61	97	11	7	3	23	43	—	—	12	26	—	30	—	.213	.298	.288	.981
1909	**ChC-N**	**20**	**45**	**6**	**4**	**1**	**0**	**0**	**5**	**2**	**—**	**—**	**1**	**5**	**—**	**1**	**—**	**.089**	**.146**	**.111**	**.943**
1910	**ChC-N**	**32**	**62**	**11**	**15**	**0**	**0**	**1**	**12**	**9**	**—**	**10**	**0**	**3**	**—**	**2**	**—**	**.242**	**.338**	**.290**	**.938**
Career average		65	206	30	45	5	3	2	15	19	—	3	5	13	—	13	—	.220	.302	.297	.952
Cubs average		**26**	**54**	**9**	**10**	**1**	**0**	**1**	**9**	**6**	**—**	**5**	**1**	**4**	**—**	**2**	**—**	**.178**	**.261**	**.215**	**.941**
Career total		261	824	118	181	21	11	7	59	76	—	10	21	53	—	53	—	.220	.302	.297	.952
Cubs total		**52**	**107**	**17**	**19**	**1**	**0**	**1**	**17**	**11**	**—**	**10**	**1**	**8**	**—**	**3**	**—**	**.178**	**.261**	**.215**	**.941**

Kearns, Edward Joseph (Teddy)
HEIGHT: 5'11" THROWS: RIGHT BATS: RIGHT BORN: 1/1/1900 TRENTON, NEW JERSEY DIED: 12/21/1949 TRENTON, NEW JERSEY POSITIONS PLAYED: 1B

YEAR	TEAM	GAMES	AB	RUNS	HITS	2B	3B	HR	RBI	BB	IBB	SO	HBP	SH	SF	SB	CS	BA	OBA	SA	FA
1920	Phi-A	1	1	0	0	0	0	0	0	0	—	0	0	0	—	0	0	.000	.000	.000	—
1924	**ChC-N**	**4**	**16**	**0**	**4**	**0**	**1**	**0**	**1**	**1**	**—**	**1**	**0**	**0**	**—**	**0**	**0**	**.250**	**.294**	**.375**	**1.000**
1925	**ChC-N**	**3**	**2**	**0**	**1**	**0**	**0**	**0**	**0**	**0**	**—**	**0**	**0**	**0**	**—**	**0**	**0**	**.500**	**.500**	**.500**	**1.000**
Career average		3	6	0	2	0	0	0	0	0	—	0	0	0	—	0	0	.263	.300	.368	1.000
Cubs average		**4**	**9**	**0**	**3**	**0**	**1**	**0**	**1**	**1**	**—**	**1**	**0**	**0**	**—**	**0**	**0**	**.278**	**.316**	**.389**	**1.000**
Career total		8	19	0	5	0	1	0	1	1	—	1	0	0	—	0	0	.263	.300	.368	1.000
Cubs total		**7**	**18**	**0**	**5**	**0**	**1**	**0**	**1**	**1**	**—**	**1**	**0**	**0**	**—**	**0**	**0**	**.278**	**.316**	**.389**	**1.000**

Keating, Walter Francis (Chick)
HEIGHT: 5'9" THROWS: RIGHT BATS: RIGHT BORN: 8/8/1891 PHILADELPHIA, PENNSYLVANIA DIED: 7/13/1959 PHILADELPHIA, PENNSYLVANIA
POSITIONS PLAYED: 2B, 3B, SS

YEAR	TEAM	GAMES	AB	RUNS	HITS	2B	3B	HR	RBI	BB	IBB	SO	HBP	SH	SF	SB	CS	BA	OBA	SA	FA
1913	**ChC-N**	**2**	**5**	**0**	**1**	**1**	**0**	**0**	**0**	**0**	**—**	**1**	**0**	**0**	**—**	**0**	**—**	**.200**	**.200**	**.400**	**1.000**
1914	**ChC-N**	**20**	**30**	**3**	**3**	**0**	**1**	**0**	**0**	**6**	**—**	**9**	**0**	**0**	**—**	**0**	**—**	**.100**	**.250**	**.167**	**.951**
1915	**ChC-N**	**4**	**8**	**1**	**0**	**0**	**0**	**0**	**0**	**0**	**—**	**3**	**0**	**0**	**—**	**1**	**0**	**.000**	**.000**	**.000**	**.750**
1926	Phi-N	4	2	0	0	0	0	0	0	0	—	0	0	0	—	0	—	.000	.000	.000	.750
Career average		8	11	1	1	0	0	0	0	2	—	3	0	0	—	0	0	.089	.196	.156	.906
Cubs average		**9**	**14**	**1**	**1**	**0**	**0**	**0**	**0**	**2**	**—**	**4**	**0**	**0**	**—**	**0**	**0**	**.093**	**.204**	**.163**	**.917**
Career total		30	45	4	4	1	1	0	0	6	—	13	0	0	—	1	0	.089	.196	.156	.906
Cubs total		**26**	**43**	**4**	**4**	**1**	**1**	**0**	**0**	**6**	**—**	**13**	**0**	**0**	**—**	**1**	**0**	**.093**	**.204**	**.163**	**.917**

Kelleher, John Patrick
HEIGHT: 5'11" THROWS: RIGHT BATS: RIGHT BORN: 9/13/1893 BROOKLINE, MASSACHUSETTS DIED: 8/21/1960 BRIGHTON, MASSACHUSETTS
POSITIONS PLAYED: 1B, 2B, 3B, SS, OF

YEAR	TEAM	GAMES	AB	RUNS	HITS	2B	3B	HR	RBI	BB	IBB	SO	HBP	SH	SF	SB	CS	BA	OBA	SA	FA
1912	StL-N	8	12	0	4	1	0	0	1	0	—	2	0	0	—	0	—	.333	.333	.417	1.000
1916	Bro-N	2	3	0	0	0	0	0	0	0	—	0	0	0	—	0	—	.000	.000	.000	1.000
1921	**ChC-N**	**95**	**301**	**31**	**93**	**11**	**7**	**4**	**47**	**16**	**—**	**16**	**1**	**23**	**—**	**2**	**5**	**.309**	**.346**	**.432**	**.963**
1922	**ChC-N**	**63**	**193**	**23**	**50**	**7**	**1**	**0**	**20**	**15**	**—**	**14**	**1**	**13**	**—**	**5**	**7**	**.259**	**.316**	**.306**	**.945**
1923	**ChC-N**	**66**	**193**	**27**	**59**	**10**	**0**	**6**	**21**	**14**	**—**	**9**	**0**	**6**	**—**	**2**	**4**	**.306**	**.353**	**.451**	**.934**
1924	Bos-N	1	1	0	0	0	0	0	0	0	—	1	0	0	—	0	0	.000	.000	.000	—
Career average		39	117	14	34	5	1	2	15	8	—	7	0	7	—	2	3	.293	.337	.400	.949
Cubs average		**75**	**229**	**27**	**67**	**9**	**3**	**3**	**29**	**15**	**—**	**13**	**1**	**14**	**—**	**3**	**5**	**.294**	**.339**	**.402**	**.949**
Career total		235	703	81	206	29	8	10	89	45	—	42	2	42	—	9	16	.293	.337	.400	.949
Cubs total		**224**	**687**	**81**	**202**	**28**	**8**	**10**	**88**	**45**	**—**	**39**	**2**	**42**	**—**	**9**	**16**	**.294**	**.339**	**.402**	**.949**

Kelleher, Michael Dennis (Mick)

HEIGHT: 5'9"   THROWS: RIGHT   BATS: RIGHT   BORN: 7/25/1947 SEATTLE, WASHINGTON   POSITIONS PLAYED: 2B, 3B, SS

YEAR	TEAM	GAMES	AB	RUNS	HITS	2B	3B	HR	RBI	BB	IBB	SO	HBP	SH	SF	SB	CS	BA	OBA	SA	FA
1972	StL-N	23	63	5	10	2	1	0	1	6	0	15	0	2	0	0	0	.159	.232	.222	.984
1973	StL-N	43	38	4	7	2	0	0	2	4	1	11	1	1	0	0	0	.184	.279	.237	.955
1974	Hou-N	19	57	4	9	0	0	0	2	5	0	10	0	0	0	0	0	.158	.226	.158	.944
1975	StL-N	7	4	0	0	0	0	0	0	0	0	1	0	0	0	1	1	.000	.000	.000	.909
1976	**ChC-N**	**124**	**337**	**28**	**77**	**12**	**1**	**0**	**22**	**15**	**3**	**32**	**0**	**4**	**0**	**0**	**0**	**.228**	**.264**	**.270**	**.976**
1977	**ChC-N**	**63**	**122**	**14**	**28**	**5**	**2**	**0**	**11**	**9**	**2**	**12**	**2**	**7**	**2**	**0**	**4**	**.230**	**.288**	**.303**	**.981**
1978	**ChC-N**	**68**	**95**	**8**	**24**	**1**	**0**	**0**	**6**	**7**	**0**	**11**	**1**	**1**	**0**	**0**	**0**	**.230**	**.288**	**.303**	**.981**
1979	**ChC-N**	**73**	**142**	**14**	**36**	**4**	**1**	**0**	**10**	**7**	**0**	**9**	**2**	**8**	**1**	**4**	**1**	**.253**	**.304**	**.263**	**1.000**
1980	**ChC-N**	**105**	**96**	**12**	**14**	**1**	**1**	**0**	**4**	**9**	**1**	**17**	**0**	**1**	**1**	**1**	**0**	**.254**	**.296**	**.296**	**.974**
1981	Det-A	61	77	10	17	4	0	0	6	7	0	10	0	8	1	1	3	.146	.217	.177	.968
1982	Det-A	2	1	0	0	0	0	0	0	0	0	0	0	8	1	0	0	.221	.282	.273	.963
1982	Cal-A	34	49	9	8	1	0	0	1	5	0	5	1	3	0	1	1	.163	.255	.184	.969
Career average		57	98	10	21	3	1	0	6	7	1	12	1	3	0	1	1	.213	.266	.253	.974
Cubs average		**87**	**158**	**15**	**36**	**5**	**1**	**0**	**11**	**9**	**1**	**16**	**1**	**4**	**1**	**1**	**2**	**.226**	**.272**	**.268**	**.978**
Career total		622	1081	108	230	32	6	0	65	74	7	133	7	35	5	9	10	.213	.266	.253	.974
Cubs total		**433**	**792**	**76**	**179**	**23**	**5**	**0**	**53**	**47**	**6**	**81**	**5**	**21**	**4**	**7**	**8**	**.226**	**.272**	**.268**	**.978**

Kellert, Frank William

HEIGHT: 6'2"   THROWS: RIGHT   BATS: RIGHT   BORN: 7/6/1924 OKLAHOMA CITY, OKLAHOMA   DIED: 11/19/1976 OKLAHOMA CITY, OKLAHOMA
POSITIONS PLAYED: 1B

YEAR	TEAM	GAMES	AB	RUNS	HITS	2B	3B	HR	RBI	BB	IBB	SO	HBP	SH	SF	SB	CS	BA	OBA	SA	FA
1953	StL-A	2	4	0	0	0	0	0	0	0	—	0	0	0	—	0	0	.000	.000	.000	1.000
1954	Bal-A	10	34	3	7	2	0	0	1	5	—	4	0	0	0	0	0	.206	.308	.265	1.000
1955	Bro-N	39	80	12	26	4	2	4	19	9	0	10	0	0	2	0	1	.325	.385	.575	.983
1956	**ChC-N**	**71**	**129**	**10**	**24**	**3**	**1**	**4**	**17**	**12**	**1**	**22**	**0**	**1**	**1**	**0**	**0**	**.186**	**.254**	**.318**	**.990**
Career average		31	62	6	14	2	1	2	9	7	0	9	0	0	1	0	0	.231	.301	.389	.991
Cubs average		**71**	**129**	**10**	**24**	**3**	**1**	**4**	**17**	**12**	**1**	**22**	**0**	**1**	**1**	**0**	**0**	**.186**	**.254**	**.318**	**.990**
Career total		122	247	25	57	9	3	8	37	26	1	36	0	1	3	0	1	.231	.301	.389	.991
Cubs total		**71**	**129**	**10**	**24**	**3**	**1**	**4**	**17**	**12**	**1**	**22**	**0**	**1**	**1**	**0**	**0**	**.186**	**.254**	**.318**	**.990**

Kelly, George Lange (High Pockets)

HEIGHT: 6'4"   THROWS: RIGHT   BATS: RIGHT   BORN: 9/10/1895 SAN FRANCISCO, CALIFORNIA   DIED: 10/13/1984 BURLINGAME, CALIFORNIA
POSITIONS PLAYED: P, 1B, 2B, 3B, OF

YEAR	TEAM	GAMES	AB	RUNS	HITS	2B	3B	HR	RBI	BB	IBB	SO	HBP	SH	SF	SB	CS	BA	OBA	SA	FA
1915	NYG-N	17	38	2	6	0	0	1	4	1	—	9	0	1	—	0	1	.158	.179	.237	.971
1916	NYG-N	49	76	4	12	2	1	0	3	6	—	24	0	2	—	1	—	.158	.220	.211	.982
1917	NYG-N	11	7	0	0	0	0	0	0	0	—	3	0	0	—	0	—	.000	.000	.000	1.000
1917	Pit-N	8	23	2	2	0	1	0	0	0	—	9	0	0	—	0	—	.087	.125	.174	1.000
1919	NYG-N	32	107	12	31	6	2	1	14	3	—	15	1	0	—	0	—	.290	.315	.411	.971
1920	NYG-N	155	590	69	157	22	11	11	94	41	—	92	1	5	—	1	—	.266	.320	.397	.994
1921	NYG-N	149	587	95	181	42	9	23	122	40	—	73	6	14	—	6	16	.308	.356	.528	.994
1922	NYG-N	151	592	96	194	33	8	17	107	30	—	65	3	17	—	4	12	.328	.356	.528	.990
1923	NYG-N	145	560	82	172	23	7	16	103	47	—	64	1	15	—	12	3	.307	.363	.497	.993
1924	NYG-N	144	571	91	185	37	9	21	136	38	—	52	5	13	—	14	7	.324	.362	.452	.993
1925	NYG-N	147	586	87	181	29	3	20	99	35	—	54	2	10	—	7	2	.309	.371	.531	.991
1926	NYG-N	136	499	70	151	24	4	13	80	36	—	52	2	15	—	5	2	.303	.350	.471	.982
1927	Cin-N	61	222	27	60	16	4	5	21	11	—	23	1	2	—	4	—	.270	.352	.445	.989
1928	Cin-N	116	402	46	119	33	7	3	58	28	—	35	2	17	—	1	—	.296	.308	.446	.985
1929	Cin-N	147	577	73	169	45	9	5	103	33	—	61	1	21	—	2	—	.293	.345	.435	.989
1930	Cin-N	51	188	18	54	10	1	5	35	7	—	20	0	11	—	7	—	.287	.332	.428	.993
1930	**ChC-N**	**39**	**166**	**22**	**55**	**6**	**1**	**3**	**19**	**7**	**—**	**16**	**1**	**4**	**—**	**0**	**—**	**.331**	**.313**	**.431**	**.993**
1932	Bro-N	64	202	23	49	9	1	4	22	22	—	27	0	2	—	0	—	.243	.362	.434	.998
Career average		101	375	51	111	21	5	9	64	24	—	43	2	10	—	4	3	.297	.317	.356	.984
Cubs average		**39**	**166**	**22**	**55**	**6**	**1**	**3**	**19**	**7**	**—**	**16**	**1**	**4**	**—**	**0**	**0**	**.331**	**.342**	**.452**	**.991**
Career total		1622	5993	819	1778	337	76	148	1020	386	—	694	28	158	—	65	43	.297	.362	.434	.998
Cubs total		**39**	**166**	**22**	**55**	**6**	**1**	**3**	**19**	**7**	**—**	**16**	**1**	**4**	**—**	**0**	**0**	**.331**	**.342**	**.452**	**.991**

Kelly, Joseph Henry (Joe)

HEIGHT: 5'10" THROWS: RIGHT BATS: RIGHT BORN: 9/23/1886 WEIR CITY, KANSAS DIED: 8/16/1977 ST. JOSEPH, MISSOURI POSITIONS PLAYED: OF

YEAR	TEAM	GAMES	AB	RUNS	HITS	2B	3B	HR	RBI	BB	IBB	SO	HBP	SH	SF	SB	CS	BA	OBA	SA	FA
1914	Pit-N	141	508	47	113	19	9	1	48	39	—	59	0	19	—	21	15	.222	.278	.301	.946
1916	**ChC-N**	**54**	**169**	**18**	**43**	**7**	**1**	**2**	**15**	**9**	**—**	**16**	**1**	**0**	**—**	**10**	**—**	**.254**	**.296**	**.343**	**.953**
1917	Bos-N	116	445	41	99	9	8	3	36	26	—	45	2	16	—	21	—	.222	.268	.299	.933
1918	Bos-N	47	155	20	36	2	4	0	15	6	—	12	1	4	—	12	—	.232	.265	.297	.943
1919	Bos-N	18	64	3	9	1	0	0	3	0	—	11	1	1	—	2	—	.141	.154	.156	.945
Career average		75	268	26	60	8	4	1	23	16	—	29	1	8	—	13	3	.224	.270	.298	.945
Cubs average		**54**	**169**	**18**	**43**	**7**	**1**	**2**	**15**	**9**	**—**	**16**	**1**	**0**	**—**	**10**	**0**	**.254**	**.296**	**.343**	**.953**
Career total		376	1341	129	300	38	22	6	117	80	—	143	5	40	—	66	15	.224	.270	.298	.945
Cubs total		**54**	**169**	**18**	**43**	**7**	**1**	**2**	**15**	**9**	**—**	**16**	**1**	**0**	**—**	**10**	**0**	**.254**	**.296**	**.343**	**.953**

Kelly, Joseph James (Joe)

HEIGHT: 6'0" THROWS: LEFT BATS: LEFT BORN: 4/23/1900 NEW YORK, NEW YORK DIED: 11/24/1967 LYNNBROOK, NEW YORK POSITIONS PLAYED: 1B, OF

YEAR	TEAM	GAMES	AB	RUNS	HITS	2B	3B	HR	RBI	BB	IBB	SO	HBP	SH	SF	SB	CS	BA	OBA	SA	FA
1926	**ChC-N**	**65**	**176**	**16**	**59**	**15**	**3**	**0**	**32**	**7**	**—**	**11**	**0**	**6**	**—**	**0**	**—**	**.335**	**.361**	**.455**	**.953**
1928	**ChC-N**	**32**	**52**	**3**	**11**	**1**	**0**	**1**	**7**	**1**	**—**	**3**	**2**	**2**	**—**	**0**	**—**	**.212**	**.255**	**.288**	**.974**
Career average		49	114	10	35	8	2	1	20	4	—	7	1	4	—	0	—	.307	.336	.417	.966
Cubs average		**49**	**114**	**10**	**35**	**8**	**2**	**1**	**20**	**4**	**—**	**7**	**1**	**4**	**—**	**0**	**—**	**.307**	**.336**	**.417**	**.966**
Career total		97	228	19	70	16	3	1	39	8	—	14	2	8	—	0	—	.307	.336	.417	.966
Cubs total		**97**	**228**	**19**	**70**	**16**	**3**	**1**	**39**	**8**	**—**	**14**	**2**	**8**	**—**	**0**	**—**	**.307**	**.336**	**.417**	**.966**

Kelly, Michael Joseph (King)

HEIGHT: 5'10" THROWS: RIGHT BATS: RIGHT BORN: 12/31/1857 TROY, NEW YORK DIED: 11/8/1894 BOSTON, MASSACHUSETTS
POSITIONS PLAYED: P, C, 1B, 2B, 3B, SS, OF

YEAR	TEAM	GAMES	AB	RUNS	HITS	2B	3B	HR	RBI	BB	IBB	SO	HBP	SH	SF	SB	CS	BA	OBA	SA	FA
1878	Cin-N	60	237	29	67	7	1	0	27	7	—	7	—	—	—	—	—	.283	.303	.321	.833
1879	Cin-N	77	345	78	120	20	12	2	47	8	—	14	—	—	—	—	—	.348	.363	.493	.839
1880	**ChN-N**	**84**	**344**	**72**	**100**	**17**	**9**	**1**	**60**	**12**	**—**	**22**	**—**	**—**	**—**	**—**	**—**	**.291**	**.315**	**.401**	**.810**
1881	**ChN-N**	**82**	**353**	**84**	**114**	**27**	**3**	**2**	**55**	**16**	**—**	**14**	**—**	**—**	**—**	**—**	**—**	**.323**	**.352**	**.433**	**.840**
1882	**ChN-N**	**84**	**377**	**81**	**115**	**37**	**4**	**1**	**55**	**10**	**—**	**27**	**—**	**—**	**—**	**—**	**—**	**.305**	**.323**	**.432**	**.827**
1883	**ChN-N**	**98**	**428**	**92**	**109**	**28**	**10**	**3**	**61**	**16**	**—**	**35**	**—**	**—**	**—**	**—**	**—**	**.255**	**.282**	**.388**	**.813**
1884	**ChN-N**	**108**	**452**	**120**	**160**	**28**	**5**	**13**	**95**	**46**	**—**	**24**	**—**	**—**	**—**	**—**	**—**	**.354**	**.414**	**.524**	**.799**
1885	**ChN-N**	**107**	**438**	**124**	**126**	**24**	**7**	**9**	**75**	**46**	**—**	**24**	**—**	**—**	**—**	**—**	**—**	**.288**	**.355**	**.436**	**.865**
1886	**ChN-N**	**118**	**451**	**155**	**175**	**32**	**11**	**4**	**79**	**83**	**—**	**33**	**—**	**—**	**—**	**53**	**—**	**.388**	**.483**	**.534**	**.899**
1887	Bos-N	116	539	120	211	34	11	8	63	55	—	40	1	—	—	84	—	.391	.449	.540	.852
1888	Bos-N	107	440	85	140	22	11	9	71	31	—	39	4	—	—	56	—	.318	.368	.480	.892
1889	Bos-N	125	507	120	149	41	5	9	78	65	—	40	2	—	—	68	—	.294	.376	.448	.857
1890	Bos-P	89	340	83	111	18	6	4	66	52	—	22	2	—	—	51	—	.326	.419	.450	.884
1891	Bos-N	16	52	7	12	1	0	0	5	6	—	10	1	—	—	6	—	.231	.322	.250	.824
1891	Cin-AA	82	283	56	84	15	7	1	53	51	—	28	2	—	—	22	—	.297	.408	.410	.907
1891	Bos-AA	4	15	2	4	0	0	1	4	0	—	2	0	—	—	1	—	.267	.267	.467	.950
1892	Bos-N	78	281	40	53	7	0	2	41	39	—	32	0	—	—	24	—	.189	.288	.235	.904
1893	NYG-N	20	67	9	18	1	0	0	15	6	—	5	1	—	—	3	—	.269	.329	.284	.885
Career average		91	372	85	117	22	6	4	59	34	—	26	1	—	—	23	—	.314	.373	.453	.862
Cubs average		**97**	**406**	**104**	**128**	**28**	**7**	**5**	**69**	**33**	**—**	**26**	**—**	**—**	**—**	**8**	**—**	**.316**	**.367**	**.453**	**.843**
Career total		1455	5949	1357	1868	359	102	69	950	549	—	418	12	—	—	368	—	.314	.373	.453	.862
Cubs total		**681**	**2843**	**728**	**899**	**193**	**49**	**33**	**480**	**229**	**—**	**179**	**—**	**—**	**—**	**53**	**—**	**.316**	**.367**	**.453**	**.843**

Michael Joseph "King" Kelly, of-c-3b-ss-2b-1b-p, 1878–93

Colorful, versatile, immensely talented, the best player of his era and perhaps the century. Babe Ruth? Nope. Not in the 19th century, anyway. That accolade goes to Mike "King" Kelly, a 19th-century star who was the cornerstone of several championship Chicago teams of the 1800s.

Kelly was born on New Year's Eve, 1857, in Troy, New York. He began playing semiprofessional baseball as a teenager and was as good or better than most of the veterans in the various leagues in which he played. In 1878 he played for the Cincinnati Buckeyes of the fledgling National League, propelling the club from last place to second that year. At that point, Kelly was the Buckeyes' jack-of-all-trades, playing 47 games in the outfield, 17 as a catcher and 2 at third base.

The next year, Kelly became one of the best players in the league, hitting .348, fourth best in the NL. Again, Kelly was playing just about everywhere, including 33 games at third base, 29 in the outfield, 21 as a catcher and even 1 game at second base.

After two years of seeing Kelly play, Chicago player-coach Adrian "Cap" Anson wanted him desperately. He went out to California that winter and spent a week trying to sign Kelly, who was playing for an all-star team out there. Anson finally succeeded, thus cementing the cornerstone for the greatest baseball dynasty in history to that point.

With Kelly in right field, hitting .291 and coming in second behind Anson with 60 RBIs, Chicago made a shambles of the National League race, winning the flag with a 67-17 mark, 15 games ahead of second-place Providence. At one point, Chicago reeled off a 21-game winning streak to go 35-3, essentially ending the race by July.

Chicago, with a strong pitching staff, great infield and the versatile Kelly, won the National League championship in 1880, 1881, 1882, 1885 and 1886.

Kelly was a great hitter, hitting over .300 eight times in his career. He led the league with a .388 average in 1886. He also had a tremendous arm, whether it was from behind the plate or from the outfield.

It was his baserunning, however, that left fans gasping and applauding. He was both fast and cunning. Many players who had seen both believed Kelly was a better base runner than Ty Cobb. Kelly was the foremost practitioner of the "hook slide," in which a base runner deliberately slides away from the bag and touches the base with his hand to avoid being tagged.

He was a sensational base stealer, swiping 50 or more bases five consecutive years, a record that many claim should be extended, as stolen bases were only counted beginning in 1886, or halfway into Kelly's career. He once stole six bases in one game.

His audacity was legendary. Once, with the game tied in the ninth inning, Kelly stood on third and a teammate was at second. As part of a prearranged plan, Kelly took off to steal home while teammate Ned Williamson began sprinting to third from second base. Kelly hesitated halfway down the line, as if confused, then continued his sprint toward home plate. Williamson, meanwhile, had rounded third base. Kelly, reaching home plate standing up, was tagged out by the catcher. But Williamson, now right behind him, slid through Kelly's legs to touch home and win the game.

Another, more frequently used trick in this era of only one umpire was to simply cut the corner when running from second base. That is, on a fly ball, Kelly would watch the umpire to see when he turned his head to follow the ball. As soon as the ump was occupied else-

(continued)

(continued)

where, Kelly would veer off the base path and sprint through the infield to home plate.

His antics moved Chicago fans to shout, "Slide, Kelly, slide!" as he neared a base. Several years later, when Kelly was playing for the Boston Braves, an enterprising songwriter made a tune out of the phrase.

Kelly was an early student of the game. He is said to have invented the hit-and-run play, and while that point is disputed, there is no doubt that he was a master of it, both as a base runner and as a batter. Most also believe that Kelly was one of the first, if not the first, catcher to call pitches with hand signals.

He was a handsome guy, popular with the fans. In addition to his ballplayer's salary of around $3,000 annually, Kelly endorsed a dozen or more products. His beaming face with its handlebar mustache could be seen on billboards across the country hawking various items.

He was also a man who liked the nightlife and, unfortunately, the taste of whiskey. Anson admired Kelly's talents greatly, but the manager abhorred his drinking. Kelly reveled in it. Asked if he ever played a game while drunk, he replied, "It depends on how many innings it goes."

This devil-may-care attitude only increased his popularity. Fans and sportswriters referred to him as King Kelly, and opponents didn't dis-agree. But at the end of the 1886 season, Anson had had enough. Kelly, he believed, thought he was bigger than the team. Anson sold him to Boston for a then-unheard-of sum of $10,000.

Chicago fans were outraged, and many boycotted the team, except when Kelly came to town. After three years with the Boston Braves, Kelly jumped to the Players' League and led his team to the championship of that circuit in 1890. In 1891 Kelly caught, played every infield position, pitched in relief and played in the outfield. None of this was a gimmick—the guy could play anywhere.

When that league broke up, Kelly played in the American Association before negotiating a contract with the Braves midway through the 1891 season. He helped the team with two titles in 1891 and 1892, mostly as a catcher.

He finished his professional career with the Giants in 1893. By this time, the drinking had taken hold. He managed in the minor leagues in 1894, opened a saloon and appeared onstage. But on November 8 of that year, after an extended bout with pneumonia, Kelly died.

Kelly is not on any of Chicago's all-time leader lists, but his 155 runs scored in 1886 is the second-best one-season total in Chicago history to Rogers Hornsby's 156 in 1929. Kelly was elected to the Hall of Fame in 1945.

Kennedy, Junior Raymond

HEIGHT: 5'11" THROWS: RIGHT BATS: RIGHT BORN: 8/9/1950 FORT GIBSON, OKLAHOMA POSITIONS PLAYED: 2B, 3B, SS

YEAR	TEAM	GAMES	AB	RUNS	HITS	2B	3B	HR	RBI	BB	IBB	SO	HBP	SH	SF	SB	CS	BA	OBA	SA	FA
1974	Cin-N	22	19	2	3	0	0	0	0	6	1	4	0	0	0	0	0	.158	.360	.158	.933
1978	Cin-N	89	157	22	40	2	2	0	11	31	2	28	1	1	0	4	1	.255	.381	.293	.979
1979	Cin-N	83	220	29	60	7	0	1	17	28	0	31	0	2	0	4	3	.273	.355	.318	.982
1980	Cin-N	104	337	31	88	16	3	1	34	36	6	34	0	4	8	3	1	.261	.325	.335	.988
1981	Cin-N	27	44	5	11	1	0	0	5	1	0	5	0	0	2	0	0	.250	.255	.273	.982
1982	ChC-N	105	242	22	53	3	1	2	25	21	1	34	0	5	3	1	4	.219	.278	.264	.968
1983	ChC-N	17	22	3	3	0	0	0	3	1	0	6	0	0	1	0	0	.136	.167	.136	1.000
Career average		64	149	16	37	4	1	1	14	18	1	20	0	2	2	1	2	.248	.325	.299	.980
Cubs average		61	132	13	28	2	1	1	14	11	1	20	0	3	2	1	2	.212	.269	.254	.971
Career total		447	1041	114	258	29	6	4	95	124	10	142	1	12	14	12	9	.248	.325	.299	.980
Cubs total		122	264	25	56	3	1	2	28	22	1	40	0	5	4	1	4	.212	.269	.254	.971

Kennedy, Sherman Montgomery (Snapper)
HEIGHT: 5'10" THROWS: RIGHT BATS: BOTH BORN: 11/1/1878 CONNEAUT, OHIO DIED: 8/15/1945 PASADENA, TEXAS POSITIONS PLAYED: OF

YEAR	TEAM	GAMES	AB	RUNS	HITS	2B	3B	HR	RBI	BB	IBB	SO	HBP	SH	SF	SB	CS	BA	OBA	SA	FA
1902	ChC-N	1	5	0	0	0	0	0	0	0	—	—	0	0	—	0	—	.000	.000	.000	1.000
Career average		1	5	0	0	0	0	0	0	0	—	—	0	0	—	0	—	.000	.000	.000	1.000
Cubs average		**1**	**5**	**0**	**0**	**0**	**0**	**0**	**0**	**0**	**—**	**—**	**0**	**0**	**—**	**0**	**—**	**.000**	**.000**	**.000**	**1.000**
Career total		1	5	0	0	0	0	0	0	0	—	—	0	0	—	0	—	.000	.000	.000	1.000
Cubs total		**1**	**5**	**0**	**0**	**0**	**0**	**0**	**0**	**0**	**—**	**—**	**0**	**0**	**—**	**0**	**—**	**.000**	**.000**	**.000**	**1.000**

Keough, Richard Martin (Marty)
HEIGHT: 6'0" THROWS: LEFT BATS: LEFT BORN: 4/14/1934 OAKLAND, CALIFORNIA POSITIONS PLAYED: 1B, OF

YEAR	TEAM	GAMES	AB	RUNS	HITS	2B	3B	HR	RBI	BB	IBB	SO	HBP	SH	SF	SB	CS	BA	OBA	SA	FA
1956	Bos-A	3	2	1	0	0	0	0	1	1	0	0	0	0	0	0	0	.000	.333	.000	—
1957	Bos-A	9	17	1	1	0	0	0	0	4	0	3	0	0	0	0	0	.059	.238	.059	1.000
1958	Bos-A	68	118	21	26	3	3	1	9	7	0	29	0	0	1	1	1	.220	.262	.322	.964
1959	Bos-A	96	251	40	61	13	5	7	27	26	0	40	3	4	1	3	1	.243	.320	.418	.994
1960	Bos-A	38	105	15	26	6	1	1	9	8	1	8	0	1	2	2	2	.248	.296	.352	1.000
1960	Cle-A	65	149	19	37	5	0	3	11	9	0	23	1	4	1	2	3	.248	.294	.342	.986
1961	Was-A	135	390	57	97	18	9	9	34	32	1	60	2	4	3	12	5	.249	.307	.410	.982
1962	Cin-N	111	230	34	64	8	2	7	27	21	4	31	4	3	2	3	1	.278	.346	.422	.981
1963	Cin-N	95	172	21	39	8	2	6	21	25	4	37	4	3	1	1	4	.227	.337	.401	.993
1964	Cin-N	109	276	29	71	9	1	9	28	22	1	58	1	1	0	1	2	.257	.314	.395	.992
1965	Cin-N	62	43	14	5	0	0	0	3	3	0	14	1	1	0	1	2	.116	.191	.116	.988
1966	Atl-N	17	17	1	1	0	0	0	1	1	0	6	1	0	0	0	0	.059	.111	.059	.964
1966	**ChC-N**	**33**	**26**	**3**	**6**	**1**	**0**	**0**	**5**	**5**	**0**	**9**	**1**	**0**	**0**	**1**	**0**	**.231**	**.375**	**.269**	**1.000**
Career average		76	163	23	39	6	2	4	16	15	1	29	2	2	1	2	2	.242	.309	.379	.986
Cubs average		**33**	**26**	**3**	**6**	**1**	**0**	**0**	**5**	**5**	**0**	**9**	**1**	**0**	**0**	**1**	**0**	**.231**	**.375**	**.269**	**1.000**
Career total		841	1796	256	434	71	23	43	176	164	11	318	17	20	11	26	19	.242	.309	.379	.986
Cubs total		**33**	**26**	**3**	**6**	**1**	**0**	**0**	**5**	**5**	**0**	**9**	**1**	**0**	**0**	**1**	**0**	**.231**	**.375**	**.269**	**1.000**

Kerr, John Melville (Mel)
HEIGHT: 5'11" THROWS: LEFT BATS: LEFT BORN: 5/22/1903 SOURIS, MANITOBA, CANADA DIED: 8/9/1980 VERO BEACH, FLORIDA

YEAR	TEAM	GAMES	AB	RUNS	HITS	2B	3B	HR	RBI	BB	IBB	SO	HBP	SH	SF	SB	CS	BA	OBA	SA	FA
1925	ChC-N	1	0	1	0	0	0	0	0	0	—	0	0	0	—	0	0	—	—	—	—
Career average		1	0	1	0	0	0	0	0	0	—	0	0	0	—	0	0	—	—	—	—
Cubs average		**1**	**0**	**1**	**0**	**0**	**0**	**0**	**0**	**0**	**—**	**0**	**0**	**0**	**—**	**0**	**0**	**—**	**—**	**—**	**—**
Career total		1	0	1	0	0	0	0	0	0	—	0	0	0	—	0	0	—	—	—	—
Cubs total		**1**	**0**	**1**	**0**	**0**	**0**	**0**	**0**	**0**	**—**	**0**	**0**	**0**	**—**	**0**	**0**	**—**	**—**	**—**	**—**

Kessinger, Donald Eulon (Don)
HEIGHT: 6'1" THROWS: RIGHT BATS: BOTH BORN: 7/17/1942 FORREST CITY, ARKANSAS POSITIONS PLAYED: 1B, 2B, 3B, SS

YEAR	TEAM	GAMES	AB	RUNS	HITS	2B	3B	HR	RBI	BB	IBB	SO	HBP	SH	SF	SB	CS	BA	OBA	SA	FA
1964	ChC-N	4	12	1	2	0	0	0	0	0	0	1	0	0	0	0	0	.167	.167	.167	1.000
1965	ChC-N	106	309	19	62	4	3	0	14	20	1	44	2	3	2	1	2	.201	.252	.233	.948
1966	ChC-N	150	533	50	146	8	2	1	43	26	5	46	0	15	4	13	7	.274	.306	.302	.951
1967	ChC-N	145	580	61	134	10	7	0	42	33	1	80	4	7	4	6	13	.231	.275	.272	.973
1968	ChC-N	160	655	63	157	14	7	1	32	38	1	86	2	11	1	9	9	.240	.283	.287	.962
1969	ChC-N	158	664	109	181	38	6	4	53	61	4	70	1	6	5	11	8	.273	.332	.366	.976
1970	ChC-N	154	631	100	168	21	14	1	39	66	6	59	2	10	2	12	6	.266	.337	.349	.972
1971	ChC-N	155	617	77	159	18	6	2	38	52	6	54	3	14	1	15	8	.258	.318	.316	.966
1972	ChC-N	149	577	77	158	20	6	1	39	67	8	44	2	13	1	8	7	.274	.351	.334	.965
1973	ChC-N	160	577	52	151	22	3	0	43	57	18	44	0	7	2	6	6	.262	.327	.310	.964
1974	ChC-N	153	599	83	155	20	7	1	42	62	7	54	4	7	1	7	7	.259	.332	.321	.958
1975	ChC-N	154	601	77	146	26	10	0	46	68	2	47	1	14	9	4	7	.243	.317	.319	.966
1976	StL-N	145	502	55	120	22	6	1	40	61	5	51	1	9	4	3	0	.239	.320	.313	.967
1977	StL-N	59	134	14	32	4	0	0	7	14	1	26	0	0	1	0	0	.239	.309	.269	.959
1977	CWS-A	39	119	12	28	3	2	0	11	13	2	7	0	1	1	2	1	.235	.308	.294	.967

(continued)

Donald (Don) Eulon Kessinger, ss-1b-2b-3b, 1964–79

The soft-spoken Kessinger manned the shortstop position for the Cubs for 11 years and played more games at that position than any other Chicago player.

Kessinger was born on July 17, 1942, in Forrest City, Arkansas. He was signed by the Cubs and brought up to the big team briefly in 1964. In 1965, on the strength of his potential more than anything else, he became the team's regular shortstop.

After a shaky rookie season (a league-leading 28 errors at shortstop and a .201 batting average) in 1965, "Kess" picked things up. In 1966 his .274 batting average was third best among National League shortstops and he led all players at his position in assists with 474. The Cubs were hideous that year, finishing 10th and last. But with Kessinger, third baseman Ron Santo, second baseman Glenn Beckert and Ernie Banks at first, the infield was gelling into a strong unit.

Kessinger was extremely religious and played a very economical game. With no frills or theatrics, he made difficult plays look easy. Kessinger led National League shortstops in assists four times, in putouts three times, in double plays four times and in overall fielding percentage once.

At bat, he made himself into a solid hitter, learning to switch-hit and training himself to be patient at the plate. During his All-Star years with the Cubs, he hit in the mid to high .200s. He was an excellent base runner, leading the Cubs in stolen bases four times and in triples five times.

In 1938 he set a Cubs record for shortstops with 38 doubles. He was a six-time All-Star with the Cubs, and one year, 1969, the entire Cubs infield played in the All-Star Game.

His two best years were in 1969 and 1970, and not coincidentally, those were the two best years the Cubs had during that time. Kessinger hit .273 and .266, respectively, and won both his Gold Gloves in those years.

After the 1975 season, Kessinger was traded to the St. Louis Cardinals. Midway through the 1977 season, he was sent back to Chicago, only it was the White Sox, not the Cubs, to whom he returned. In 1979 he became a player-manager for the White Sox before retiring for good.

Kessinger is 10th on the Cubs' all-time list in at-bats with 6,355 and 10th all-time for Chicago with 1,336 singles. He is the record holder for most games played at shortstop for the Cubs with 1,618, and he is also tops all-time in assists for Chicago with 5,346 and double plays with 982.

(Kessinger, continued)

YEAR	TEAM	GAMES	AB	RUNS	HITS	2B	3B	HR	RBI	BB	IBB	SO	HBP	SH	SF	SB	CS	BA	OBA	SA	FA
1978	CWS-A	131	431	35	110	18	1	1	31	36	1	34	0	12	1	2	4	.255	.312	.309	.976
1979	CWS-A	56	110	14	22	6	0	1	7	10	1	12	0	3	1	1	0	.200	.264	.282	.988
Career average		130	478	56	121	16	5	1	33	43	4	47	1	8	3	6	5	.252	.314	.312	.965
Cubs average		**137**	**530**	**64**	**135**	**17**	**6**	**1**	**36**	**46**	**5**	**52**	**2**	**9**	**3**	**8**	**7**	**.255**	**.315**	**.314**	**.964**
Career total		2078	7651	899	1931	254	80	14	527	684	69	759	22	132	40	100	85	.252	.314	.312	.965
Cubs total		**1648**	**6355**	**769**	**1619**	**201**	**71**	**11**	**431**	**550**	**59**	**629**	**21**	**107**	**32**	**92**	**80**	**.255**	**.315**	**.314**	**.964**

Kieschnick, Michael Brooks (Brooks)

HEIGHT: 6'4"   THROWS: RIGHT   BATS: LEFT   BORN: 6/6/1972 ROBSTOWN, TEXAS   POSITIONS PLAYED: 1B, OF

YEAR	TEAM	GAMES	AB	RUNS	HITS	2B	3B	HR	RBI	BB	IBB	SO	HBP	SH	SF	SB	CS	BA	OBA	SA	FA
1996	ChC-N	25	29	6	10	2	0	1	6	3	0	8	0	0	0	0	0	.345	.406	.517	.833
1997	ChC-N	39	90	9	18	2	0	4	12	12	0	21	0	0	0	1	0	.200	.294	.356	.952
2000	Cin-N	14	12	0	0	0	0	0	0	1	0	5	0	0	0	0	0	.000	.077	.000	1.000
2001	Col-N	35	42	5	10	2	1	3	9	3	0	13	0	0	0	0	0	.238	.289	.548	.833
Career average		28	43	5	10	2	0	2	7	5	0	12	0	0	0	0	0	.220	.297	.405	.918
Cubs average		**32**	**60**	**8**	**14**	**2**	**0**	**3**	**9**	**8**	**0**	**15**	**0**	**0**	**0**	**1**	**0**	**.235**	**.321**	**.395**	**.938**
Career total		113	173	20	38	6	1	8	27	19	0	47	0	0	0	1	0	.220	.297	.405	.918
Cubs total		**64**	**119**	**15**	**28**	**4**	**0**	**5**	**18**	**15**	**0**	**29**	**0**	**0**	**0**	**1**	**0**	**.235**	**.321**	**.395**	**.938**

Kilduff, Peter John (Pete)

HEIGHT: 5'7" THROWS: RIGHT BATS: RIGHT BORN: 4/4/1893 WEIR CITY, KANSAS DIED: 2/14/1930 PITTSBURG, KANSAS POSITIONS PLAYED: 2B, 3B, SS

YEAR	TEAM	GAMES	AB	RUNS	HITS	2B	3B	HR	RBI	BB	IBB	SO	HBP	SH	SF	SB	CS	BA	OBA	SA	FA
1917	NYG-N	31	78	12	16	3	0	1	12	4	—	11	1	2	—	2	—	.205	.253	.282	.942
1917	**ChC-N**	**56**	**202**	**23**	**56**	**9**	**5**	**0**	**15**	**12**	**—**	**19**	**2**	**9**	**—**	**11**	**—**	**.277**	**.324**	**.371**	**.929**
1918	**ChC-N**	**30**	**93**	**7**	**19**	**2**	**2**	**0**	**13**	**7**	**—**	**7**	**1**	**8**	**—**	**1**	**—**	**.204**	**.267**	**.269**	**.935**
1919	**ChC-N**	**31**	**88**	**5**	**24**	**4**	**2**	**0**	**8**	**10**	**—**	**5**	**2**	**3**	**—**	**1**	**—**	**.273**	**.360**	**.364**	**.923**
1919	Bro-N	32	73	9	22	3	1	0	8	12	—	11	1	3	—	1	—	.301	.407	.370	.866
1920	Bro-N	141	478	62	130	26	8	0	58	58	—	43	0	22	—	5	—	.272	.351	.360	.966
1921	Bro-N	107	372	45	107	15	10	3	45	31	—	36	1	16	—	6	6	.288	.344	.406	.963
Career average		86	277	33	75	12	6	1	32	27	—	26	2	13	—	6	3	.270	.338	.364	.952
Cubs average		**39**	**128**	**12**	**33**	**5**	**3**	**0**	**12**	**10**	**—**	**10**	**2**	**7**	**—**	**4**	**—**	**.258**	**.319**	**.345**	**.929**
Career total		428	1384	163	374	62	28	4	159	134	—	132	8	63	—	28	15	.270	.338	.364	.952
Cubs total		**117**	**383**	**35**	**99**	**15**	**9**	**0**	**36**	**29**	**—**	**31**	**5**	**20**	**—**	**13**	**—**	**.258**	**.319**	**.345**	**.929**

Killefer, William Lavier (Bill *or* Reindeer Bill)

HEIGHT: 5'10" THROWS: RIGHT BATS: RIGHT BORN: 10/10/1887 BLOOMINGDALE, MICHIGAN DIED: 7/3/1960 ELSMERE, DELAWARE
POSITIONS PLAYED: C, 1B, OF

YEAR	TEAM	GAMES	AB	RUNS	HITS	2B	3B	HR	RBI	BB	IBB	SO	HBP	SH	SF	SB	CS	BA	OBA	SA	FA
1909	StL-A	11	29	0	4	0	0	0	1	0	—	—	0	0	—	2	—	.138	.138	.138	.905
1910	StL-A	74	193	14	24	2	2	0	7	12	—	—	2	8	—	0	—	.124	.184	.155	.938
1911	Phi-N	6	16	3	3	0	0	0	2	0	—	2	0	2	—	0	—	.188	.188	.188	.975
1912	Phi-N	85	268	18	60	6	3	1	21	4	—	14	2	15	—	6	—	.224	.241	.280	.973
1913	Phi-N	120	360	25	88	14	3	0	24	4	—	17	1	10	—	2	—	.244	.255	.280	.988
1914	Phi-N	98	299	27	70	10	1	0	27	8	—	17	3	10	—	3	—	.234	.261	.274	.978
1915	Phi-N	105	320	26	76	9	2	0	24	18	—	14	4	3	—	5	3	.238	.287	.278	.972
1916	Phi-N	97	286	22	62	5	4	3	27	8	—	14	3	10	—	2	—	.217	.246	.294	.985
1917	Phi-N	125	409	28	112	12	0	0	31	15	—	21	4	9	—	4	—	.274	.306	.303	.984
1918	**ChC-N**	**104**	**331**	**30**	**77**	**10**	**3**	**0**	**22**	**17**	**—**	**10**	**3**	**13**	**—**	**5**	**—**	**.233**	**.276**	**.281**	**.982**
1919	**ChC-N**	**103**	**315**	**17**	**90**	**10**	**2**	**0**	**22**	**15**	**—**	**8**	**2**	**13**	**—**	**5**	**—**	**.286**	**.322**	**.330**	**.987**
1920	**ChC-N**	**62**	**191**	**16**	**42**	**7**	**1**	**0**	**16**	**8**	**—**	**5**	**8**	**5**	**—**	**2**	**2**	**.220**	**.280**	**.267**	**.977**
1921	**ChC-N**	**45**	**133**	**11**	**43**	**1**	**0**	**0**	**16**	**4**	**—**	**4**	**3**	**4**	**—**	**3**	**3**	**.323**	**.357**	**.331**	**.964**
Career average		80	242	18	58	7	2	0	18	9	—	10	3	8	—	3	1	.238	.273	.283	.977
Cubs average		**79**	**243**	**19**	**63**	**7**	**2**	**0**	**19**	**11**	**—**	**7**	**4**	**9**	**—**	**4**	**1**	**.260**	**.303**	**.301**	**.981**
Career total		1035	3150	237	751	86	21	4	240	113	—	126	35	102	—	39	8	.238	.273	.283	.977
Cubs total		**314**	**970**	**74**	**252**	**28**	**6**	**0**	**76**	**44**	**—**	**27**	**16**	**35**	**—**	**15**	**5**	**.260**	**.303**	**.301**	**.981**

Kimm, Bruce Edward

HEIGHT: 5'11" THROWS: RIGHT BATS: RIGHT BORN: 6/29/1951 CEDAR RAPIDS, IOWA POSITIONS PLAYED: C

YEAR	TEAM	GAMES	AB	RUNS	HITS	2B	3B	HR	RBI	BB	IBB	SO	HBP	SH	SF	SB	CS	BA	OBA	SA	FA
1976	Det-A	63	152	13	40	8	0	1	6	15	0	20	0	7	0	4	3	.263	.329	.336	.970
1977	Det-A	14	25	2	2	1	0	0	1	0	0	4	1	0	0	0	1	.080	.115	.120	.958
1979	**ChC-N**	**9**	**11**	**0**	**1**	**0**	**0**	**0**	**0**	**0**	**0**	**0**	**0**	**0**	**0**	**0**	**1**	**.091**	**.091**	**.091**	**.969**
1980	CWS-A	100	251	20	61	10	1	0	19	17	0	26	0	4	1	1	3	.243	.290	.291	.985
Career average		47	110	9	26	5	0	0	7	8	0	13	0	3	0	1	2	.237	.290	.292	.977
Cubs average		**9**	**11**	**0**	**1**	**0**	**0**	**0**	**0**	**0**	**0**	**0**	**0**	**0**	**0**	**0**	**1**	**.091**	**.091**	**.091**	**.969**
Career total		186	439	35	104	19	1	1	26	32	0	50	1	11	1	5	8	.237	.290	.292	.977
Cubs total		**9**	**11**	**0**	**1**	**0**	**0**	**0**	**0**	**0**	**0**	**0**	**0**	**0**	**0**	**0**	**1**	**.091**	**.091**	**.091**	**.969**

Kindall, Gerald Donald (Jerry *or* Slim)

HEIGHT: 6'2" THROWS: RIGHT BATS: RIGHT BORN: 5/27/1935 ST. PAUL, MINNESOTA POSITIONS PLAYED: 1B, 2B, 3B, SS

YEAR	TEAM	GAMES	AB	RUNS	HITS	2B	3B	HR	RBI	BB	IBB	SO	HBP	SH	SF	SB	CS	BA	OBA	SA	FA
1956	**ChC-N**	**32**	**55**	**7**	**9**	**1**	**1**	**0**	**0**	**6**	**1**	**17**	**0**	**1**	**0**	**1**	**0**	**.164**	**.246**	**.218**	**.956**
1957	**ChC-N**	**72**	**181**	**18**	**29**	**3**	**0**	**6**	**12**	**8**	**0**	**48**	**0**	**1**	**0**	**1**	**0**	**.160**	**.196**	**.276**	**.924**
1958	**ChC-N**	**3**	**6**	**0**	**1**	**1**	**0**	**0**	**0**	**0**	**0**	**3**	**0**	**3**	**0**	**1**	**0**	**.167**	**.167**	**.333**	**1.000**
1960	**ChC-N**	**89**	**246**	**17**	**59**	**16**	**2**	**5**	**23**	**5**	**3**	**52**	**0**	**0**	**2**	**4**	**3**	**.240**	**.253**	**.346**	**.966**
1961	**ChC-N**	**96**	**310**	**37**	**75**	**22**	**3**	**9**	**44**	**18**	**0**	**89**	**2**	**3**	**2**	**2**	**2**	**.242**	**.288**	**.419**	**.944**
1962	Cle-A	154	530	51	123	21	1	13	55	45	9	107	0	8	5	4	3	.232	.290	.349	.978
1963	Cle-A	86	234	27	48	4	1	5	20	18	0	71	2	7	2	3	1	.205	.266	.295	.972

(continued)

(Kindall, continued)

		GAMES	AB	RUNS	HITS	2B	3B	HR	RBI	BB	IBB	SO	HBP	SH	SF	SB	CS	BA	OBA	SA	FA
1964	Cle-A	23	25	5	9	1	0	2	2	2	0	7	0	0	0	0	0	.360	.407	.640	.989
1964	Min-A	62	128	8	19	2	0	1	6	7	1	44	1	3	0	0	0	.148	.199	.188	.969
1965	Min-A	125	342	41	67	12	1	6	36	36	3	97	3	8	6	2	2	.196	.274	.289	.957
Career average		82	229	23	49	9	1	5	22	16	2	59	1	4	2	2	1	.213	.266	.327	.963
Cubs average		**58**	**160**	**16**	**35**	**9**	**1**	**3**	**16**	**7**	**1**	**42**	**0**	**2**	**0**	**2**	**1**	**.217**	**.253**	**.350**	**.949**
Career total		742	2057	211	439	83	9	44	198	145	17	535	8	36	15	17	11	.213	.266	.327	.963
Cubs total		**292**	**798**	**79**	**173**	**43**	**6**	**17**	**79**	**37**	**4**	**209**	**2**	**10**	**2**	**8**	**5**	**.217**	**.253**	**.350**	**.949**

Kiner, Ralph McPherran
HEIGHT: 6'2"   THROWS: RIGHT   BATS: RIGHT   BORN: 10/27/1922 SANTA RITA, NEW MEXICO   POSITIONS PLAYED: 1B, OF

YEAR	TEAM	GAMES	AB	RUNS	HITS	2B	3B	HR	RBI	BB	IBB	SO	HBP	SH	SF	SB	CS	BA	OBA	SA	FA
1946	Pit-N	144	502	63	124	17	3	23	81	74	—	109	1	2	—	3	—	.247	.345	.430	.969
1947	Pit-N	152	565	118	177	23	4	51	127	98	—	81	2	1	—	1	—	.313	.417	.639	.983
1948	Pit-N	156	555	104	147	19	5	40	123	112	—	61	3	0	—	1	—	.265	.391	.533	.975
1949	Pit-N	152	549	116	170	19	5	54	127	117	—	61	1	0	—	6	—	.310	.432	.658	.979
1950	Pit-N	150	547	112	149	21	6	47	118	122	—	79	3	0	—	2	—	.272	.408	.590	.965
1951	Pit-N	151	531	124	164	31	6	42	109	137	—	57	2	0	—	2	1	.309	.452	.627	.978
1952	Pit-N	149	516	90	126	17	2	37	87	110	—	77	7	0	—	3	0	.244	.384	.500	.970
1953	Pit-N	41	148	27	40	6	1	7	29	25	—	21	2	0	—	1	0	.270	.383	.466	1.000
1953	**ChC-N**	**117**	**414**	**73**	**117**	**14**	**2**	**28**	**87**	**75**	**—**	**67**	**1**	**1**	**—**	**1**	**1**	**.283**	**.394**	**.529**	**.964**
1954	**ChC-N**	**147**	**557**	**88**	**159**	**36**	**5**	**22**	**73**	**76**	**—**	**90**	**2**	**5**	**3**	**2**	**0**	**.243**	**.367**	**.452**	**.986**
1955	Cle-A	113	321	56	78	13	0	18	54	65	1	46	0	0	4	0	0	.279	.398	.548	.975
Career average		147	521	97	145	22	4	37	102	101	0	75	2	1	1	2	0	.279	.398	.548	.975
Cubs average		**132**	**486**	**81**	**138**	**25**	**4**	**25**	**80**	**76**	**—**	**79**	**2**	**3**	**2**	**2**	**1**	**.284**	**.381**	**.505**	**.968**
Career total		1472	5205	971	1451	216	39	369	1015	1011	1	749	24	9	7	22	2	.279	.398	.548	.975
Cubs total		**264**	**971**	**161**	**276**	**50**	**7**	**50**	**160**	**151**	**—**	**157**	**3**	**6**	**3**	**3**	**1**	**.284**	**.381**	**.505**	**.968**

King, Charles Gilbert (Chick)
HEIGHT: 6'2"   THROWS: RIGHT   BATS: RIGHT   BORN: 11/10/1930 PARIS, TENNESSEE   POSITIONS PLAYED: OF

YEAR	TEAM	GAMES	AB	RUNS	HITS	2B	3B	HR	RBI	BB	IBB	SO	HBP	SH	SF	SB	CS	BA	OBA	SA	FA
1954	Det-A	11	28	4	6	0	1	0	3	3	—	8	0	0	0	0	0	.214	.290	.286	.958
1955	Det-A	7	21	3	5	0	0	0	0	1	0	2	0	0	0	0	0	.238	.273	.238	.923
1956	Det-A	7	9	0	2	0	0	0	0	1	0	4	0	0	0	0	0	.222	.300	.222	.800
1958	**ChC-N**	**8**	**8**	**1**	**2**	**0**	**0**	**0**	**1**	**3**	**1**	**1**	**0**	**0**	**0**	**0**	**0**	**.250**	**.455**	**.250**	**1.000**
1959	**ChC-N**	**7**	**3**	**3**	**0**	**0**	**0**	**0**	**0**	**0**	**0**	**1**	**0**	**0**	**0**	**0**	**0**	**.000**	**.000**	**.000**	**1.000**
1959	StL-N	5	7	0	3	0	0	0	1	0	0	2	0	0	1	0	0	.429	.375	.429	1.000
Career average		9	15	2	4	0	0	0	1	2	0	4	0	0	0	0	0	.237	.306	.263	.947
Cubs average		**8**	**6**	**2**	**1**	**0**	**0**	**0**	**1**	**2**	**1**	**1**	**0**	**0**	**0**	**0**	**0**	**.182**	**.357**	**.182**	**1.000**
Career total		45	76	11	18	0	1	0	5	8	1	18	0	0	1	0	0	.237	.306	.263	.947
Cubs total		**15**	**11**	**4**	**2**	**0**	**0**	**0**	**1**	**3**	**1**	**2**	**0**	**0**	**0**	**0**	**0**	**.182**	**.357**	**.182**	**1.000**

King, James Hubert (Jim)
HEIGHT: 6'0"   THROWS: RIGHT   BATS: LEFT   BORN: 8/27/1932 ELKINS, ARKANSAS   POSITIONS PLAYED: C, OF

YEAR	TEAM	GAMES	AB	RUNS	HITS	2B	3B	HR	RBI	BB	IBB	SO	HBP	SH	SF	SB	CS	BA	OBA	SA	FA
1955	**ChC-N**	**113**	**301**	**43**	**77**	**12**	**3**	**11**	**45**	**24**	**1**	**39**	**2**	**3**	**3**	**2**	**1**	**.256**	**.312**	**.425**	**.990**
1956	**ChC-N**	**118**	**317**	**32**	**79**	**13**	**2**	**15**	**54**	**30**	**5**	**40**	**1**	**2**	**4**	**1**	**2**	**.249**	**.313**	**.445**	**1.000**
1957	StL-N	22	35	1	11	0	0	0	2	4	2	2	0	0	0	0	1	.314	.385	.314	1.000
1958	SF-N	34	56	8	12	2	1	2	8	10	1	8	1	0	0	0	1	.214	.343	.393	1.000
1961	Was-A	110	263	43	71	12	1	11	46	38	3	45	2	0	3	4	0	.270	.363	.449	.980
1962	Was-A	132	333	39	81	15	0	11	35	55	9	37	3	2	3	3	2	.243	.353	.387	.979
1963	Was-A	136	459	61	106	16	5	24	62	45	3	43	1	3	2	3	0	.231	.300	.444	.987
1964	Was-A	134	415	46	100	15	1	18	56	55	7	65	5	0	3	3	1	.241	.335	.412	.973
1965	Was-A	120	258	46	55	10	2	14	49	44	2	50	5	0	2	1	0	.213	.337	.430	.993
1966	Was-A	117	310	41	77	14	2	10	30	38	2	41	0	1	1	4	0	.248	.330	.403	.987
1967	Was-A	47	100	10	21	2	2	1	12	15	0	13	3	0	1	0	1	.210	.328	.300	.962
1967	CWS-A	23	50	2	6	1	0	0	2	4	0	16	0	0	0	0	0	.120	.185	.140	1.000
1967	Cle-A	19	21	2	3	0	0	0	0	1	0	2	0	0	0	0	0	.143	.182	.143	1.000
Career average		102	265	34	64	10	2	11	36	33	3	36	2	1	2	2	1	.240	.326	.411	.984
Cubs average		**116**	**309**	**38**	**78**	**13**	**3**	**13**	**50**	**27**	**3**	**40**	**2**	**3**	**4**	**2**	**2**	**.252**	**.312**	**.435**	**.990**
Career total		1125	2918	374	699	112	19	117	401	363	35	401	23	11	22	23	8	.240	.326	.411	.984
Cubs total		**231**	**618**	**75**	**156**	**25**	**5**	**26**	**99**	**54**	**6**	**79**	**3**	**5**	**7**	**3**	**3**	**.252**	**.312**	**.435**	**.990**

David (Dave) Arthur "Kong" Kingman, of-1b-3b-dh-p, 1971–86

Dave Kingman's career as a Cub was relatively short, but few will argue that it was also memorable, for both him and the Cubs.

Kingman, born on December 21, 1948, in Pendleton, Oregon, was initially a pitcher for the University of Southern California before he was converted to the outfield. He was eventually signed by the Giants and played first and third base, the outfield and even pitched a few games from 1971 to 1974.

He was traded to the Mets the following year, and his powerful uppercut swing brought him many home runs and even more strikeouts. He hit 36 and 37 home runs in 1975 and 1976, making the All-Star team in 1976.

But Kingman's equally prodigious strikeout totals moved the Mets to trade him to San Diego in 1977. In a rather busy season, "Kong" played for the Mets, Padres, Angels and Yankees.

He became a Cub in 1978, and enjoyed three fine seasons, making the All-Star team twice in that span. In 1979 he hit a league-leading 48 home runs and also led the National League in slugging percentage with a .613 mark. He also hit a career-high .288 that year.

And, although his defense was much maligned, Kingman was fourth in National League right fielders in assists that year. He also tied a major league record for most home runs in two consecutive games (five), and he tied another mark by twice hitting three home runs in one game.

Kingman was beset with injuries in 1980, but he still hit 18 home runs and had 57 RBIs in about half a season. But that was the year he began to openly clash with management, going AWOL at one point and then refusing to travel with the team while injured. Kingman probably knew his days as a Cub were numbered when he was booed by Cubs fans on Dave Kingman T-shirt Day.

Sure enough, he was traded back to the Mets for three years and then shipped to Oakland for three more. Kingman was still blasting home runs, but his strikeout totals were escalating, and despite popping 35 homers during the 1986 season, Kingman found no takers at the end of the year as he entered free agency.

Kingman still holds the Cubs record for home runs by a left fielder with 48 and his career slugging average of .569 is still third all-time for Chicago.

Kingman, David Arthur (Dave *or* Kong)
HEIGHT: 6'6"   THROWS: RIGHT   BATS: RIGHT   BORN: 12/21/1948 PENDLETON, OREGON   POSITIONS PLAYED: P, 1B, 3B, OF

YEAR	TEAM	GAMES	AB	RUNS	HITS	2B	3B	HR	RBI	BB	IBB	SO	HBP	SH	SF	SB	CS	BA	OBA	SA	FA
1971	SF-N	41	115	17	32	10	2	6	24	9	0	35	1	0	3	5	0	.278	.328	.557	.978
1972	SF-N	135	472	65	106	17	4	29	83	51	2	140	4	0	4	16	6	.225	.303	.462	.968
1973	SF-N	112	305	54	62	10	1	24	55	41	3	122	2	1	2	8	5	.203	.300	.479	.954
1974	SF-N	121	350	41	78	18	2	18	55	37	2	125	3	2	1	8	8	.223	.302	.440	.969
1975	NYM-N	134	502	65	116	22	1	36	88	34	5	153	4	1	2	7	5	.231	.284	.494	.977
1976	NYM-N	123	474	70	113	14	1	37	86	28	4	135	5	0	3	7	4	.238	.286	.506	.972
1977	NYM-N	58	211	22	44	7	0	9	28	13	3	66	3	0	1	3	2	.209	.263	.370	.985
1977	SD-N	56	168	16	40	9	0	11	39	12	1	48	2	2	3	2	3	.238	.292	.488	.976
1977	Cal-A	10	36	4	7	2	0	2	4	1	0	16	1	1	0	0	0	.194	.237	.417	.975
1977	NYY-A	8	24	5	6	2	0	4	7	2	0	13	1	0	0	0	1	.250	.333	.833	—
1978	**ChC-N**	**119**	**395**	**65**	**105**	**17**	**4**	**28**	**79**	**39**	**8**	**111**	**6**	**2**	**6**	**3**	**4**	**.266**	**.336**	**.542**	**.975**
1979	**ChC-N**	**145**	**532**	**97**	**153**	**19**	**5**	**48**	**115**	**45**	**7**	**131**	**4**	**0**	**8**	**4**	**2**	**.288**	**.343**	**.613**	**.954**
1980	**ChC-N**	**81**	**255**	**31**	**71**	**8**	**0**	**18**	**57**	**21**	**3**	**44**	**0**	**0**	**4**	**2**	**2**	**.278**	**.329**	**.522**	**.942**
1981	NYM-N	100	353	40	78	11	3	22	59	55	7	105	1	1	2	6	0	.221	.326	.456	.967
1982	NYM-N	149	535	80	109	9	1	37	99	59	9	156	4	3	6	4	0	.204	.285	.432	.986

(continued)

(Kingman, continued)

YEAR	TEAM	GAMES	AB	RUNS	HITS	2B	3B	HR	RBI	BB	IBB	SO	HBP	SH	SF	SB	CS	BA	OBA	SA	FA
1983	NYM-N	100	248	25	49	7	0	13	29	22	1	57	1	1	1	2	1	.198	.265	.383	.994
1984	Oak-A	147	549	68	147	23	1	35	118	44	8	119	6	0	14	2	1	.268	.321	.505	1.000
1985	Oak-A	158	592	66	141	16	0	30	91	62	6	114	2	2	8	3	2	.238	.309	.417	1.000
1986	Oak-A	144	561	70	118	19	0	35	94	33	3	126	3	0	7	3	3	.210	.255	.431	.895
Career average		121	417	56	98	15	2	28	76	38	5	114	3	1	5	5	3	.236	.302	.478	.974
Cubs average		**115**	**394**	**64**	**110**	**15**	**3**	**31**	**84**	**35**	**6**	**95**	**3**	**1**	**6**	**3**	**3**	**.278**	**.338**	**.569**	**.960**
Career total		1941	6677	901	1575	240	25	442	1210	608	72	1816	53	16	75	85	49	.236	.302	.478	.974
Cubs total		**345**	**1182**	**193**	**329**	**44**	**9**	**94**	**251**	**105**	**18**	**286**	**10**	**2**	**18**	**9**	**8**	**.278**	**.338**	**.569**	**.960**

Kinzie, Walter Harris (Walt)

HEIGHT: 5'10" THROWS: RIGHT BATS: RIGHT BORN: 3/16/1857 CHICAGO, ILLINOIS DIED: 11/5/1909 CHICAGO, ILLINOIS POSITIONS PLAYED: 2B, 3B, SS

YEAR	TEAM	GAMES	AB	RUNS	HITS	2B	3B	HR	RBI	BB	IBB	SO	HBP	SH	SF	SB	CS	BA	OBA	SA	FA
1882	Det-N	13	53	5	5	0	1	0	2	0	—	8	—	—	—	—	—	.094	.094	.132	.852
1884	**ChN-N**	**19**	**82**	**4**	**13**	**3**	**0**	**2**	**8**	**0**	**—**	**13**	**—**	**—**	**—**	**—**	**—**	**.159**	**.159**	**.268**	**.839**
1884	StL-AA	2	9	0	1	0	0	0	—	0	—	—	0	—	—	—	—	.111	.111	.111	.727
Career average		17	72	5	10	2	1	1	5	0	—	11	0	—	—	—	—	.132	.132	.208	.836
Cubs average		**19**	**82**	**4**	**13**	**3**	**0**	**2**	**8**	**0**	**—**	**13**	**—**	**—**	**—**	**—**	**—**	**.159**	**.159**	**.268**	**.839**
Career total		34	144	9	19	3	1	2	10	0	—	21	0	—	—	—	—	.132	.132	.208	.836
Cubs total		**19**	**82**	**4**	**13**	**3**	**0**	**2**	**8**	**0**	**—**	**13**	**—**	**—**	**—**	**—**	**—**	**.159**	**.159**	**.268**	**.839**

Kirby, James Herschel (Jim)

HEIGHT: 5'11" THROWS: RIGHT BATS: RIGHT BORN: 5/5/1923 NASHVILLE, TENNESSEE

YEAR	TEAM	GAMES	AB	RUNS	HITS	2B	3B	HR	RBI	BB	IBB	SO	HBP	SH	SF	SB	CS	BA	OBA	SA	FA
1949	ChC-N	3	2	0	1	0	0	0	0	0	—	0	0	0	—	0	—	.500	.500	.500	—
Career average		3	2	0	1	0	0	0	0	0	—	0	0	0	—	0	—	.500	.500	.500	—
Cubs average		**3**	**2**	**0**	**1**	**0**	**0**	**0**	**0**	**0**	**—**	**0**	**0**	**0**	**—**	**0**	**—**	**.500**	**.500**	**.500**	**—**
Career total		3	2	0	1	0	0	0	0	0	—	0	0	0	—	0	—	.500	.500	.500	—
Cubs total		**3**	**2**	**0**	**1**	**0**	**0**	**0**	**0**	**0**	**—**	**0**	**0**	**0**	**—**	**0**	**—**	**.500**	**.500**	**.500**	**—**

Kitsos, Christopher Anestos (Chris)

HEIGHT: 5'9" THROWS: RIGHT BATS: BOTH BORN: 2/11/1928 NEW YORK, NEW YORK POSITIONS PLAYED: SS

YEAR	TEAM	GAMES	AB	RUNS	HITS	2B	3B	HR	RBI	BB	IBB	SO	HBP	SH	SF	SB	CS	BA	OBA	SA	FA
1954	ChC-N	1	0	0	0	0	0	0	0	0	—	0	0	0	0	0	0	—	—	—	1.000
Career average		1	0	0	0	0	0	0	0	0	—	0	0	0	0	0	0	—	—	—	1.000
Cubs average		**1**	**0**	**0**	**0**	**0**	**0**	**0**	**0**	**0**	**—**	**0**	**0**	**0**	**0**	**0**	**0**	**—**	**—**	**—**	**1.000**
Career total		1	0	0	0	0	0	0	0	0	—	0	0	0	0	0	0	—	—	—	1.000
Cubs total		**1**	**0**	**0**	**0**	**0**	**0**	**0**	**0**	**0**	**—**	**0**	**0**	**0**	**0**	**0**	**0**	**—**	**—**	**—**	**1.000**

Kittridge, Malachi Jeddidah (Jedediah)

HEIGHT: 5'7" THROWS: RIGHT BATS: RIGHT BORN: 10/12/1869 CLINTON, MASSACHUSETTS DIED: 6/23/1928 GARY, INDIANA POSITIONS PLAYED: P, C

YEAR	TEAM	GAMES	AB	RUNS	HITS	2B	3B	HR	RBI	BB	IBB	SO	HBP	SH	SF	SB	CS	BA	OBA	SA	FA
1890	**ChN-N**	**96**	**333**	**46**	**67**	**8**	**3**	**3**	**35**	**39**	**—**	**53**	**1**	**—**	**—**	**7**	**—**	**.201**	**.287**	**.270**	**.944**
1891	**ChN-N**	**79**	**296**	**26**	**62**	**8**	**5**	**2**	**27**	**17**	**—**	**28**	**0**	**—**	**—**	**4**	**—**	**.209**	**.252**	**.291**	**.940**
1892	**ChN-N**	**69**	**229**	**19**	**41**	**5**	**0**	**0**	**10**	**11**	**—**	**27**	**0**	**—**	**—**	**2**	**—**	**.179**	**.217**	**.201**	**.946**
1893	**ChN-N**	**70**	**255**	**32**	**59**	**9**	**5**	**2**	**30**	**17**	**—**	**15**	**0**	**—**	**—**	**3**	**—**	**.231**	**.279**	**.329**	**.939**
1894	**ChN-N**	**51**	**168**	**36**	**53**	**8**	**2**	**0**	**23**	**26**	**—**	**20**	**0**	**5**	**—**	**2**	**—**	**.315**	**.407**	**.387**	**.925**
1895	**ChN-N**	**60**	**212**	**30**	**48**	**6**	**3**	**3**	**29**	**16**	**—**	**9**	**1**	**6**	**—**	**6**	**—**	**.226**	**.284**	**.325**	**.976**
1896	**ChN-N**	**65**	**215**	**17**	**48**	**4**	**1**	**1**	**19**	**14**	**—**	**14**	**1**	**5**	**—**	**6**	**—**	**.223**	**.274**	**.265**	**.962**
1897	**ChN-N**	**79**	**262**	**25**	**53**	**5**	**5**	**1**	**30**	**22**	**—**	**—**	**0**	**7**	**—**	**9**	**—**	**.202**	**.264**	**.271**	**.952**
1898	Lou-N	86	287	27	70	8	5	1	31	15	—	—	0	10	—	9	—	.244	.281	.317	.944
1899	Lou-N	45	129	11	26	2	1	0	12	26	—	—	1	13	—	3	—	.202	.340	.233	.974
1899	Was-N	44	133	14	20	3	0	0	11	10	—	—	1	4	—	2	—	.150	.215	.173	.949
1901	Bos-N	114	381	24	96	14	0	2	40	32	—	—	1	13	—	2	—	.252	.312	.304	.984
1902	Bos-N	80	255	18	60	7	0	2	30	24	—	—	1	6	—	4	—	.235	.304	.286	.981

(continued)

(continued)

YEAR	TEAM	GAMES	AB	RUNS	HITS	2B	3B	HR	RBI	BB	IBB	SO	HBP	SH	SF	SB	CS	BA	OBA	SA	FA
1903	Bos-N	32	99	10	21	2	0	0	6	11	—	—	0	6	—	1	—	.212	.291	.232	.981
1903	Was-A	60	192	8	41	4	1	0	16	10	—	—	0	6	—	1	—	.214	.252	.245	.978
1904	Was-A	81	265	11	64	7	0	0	24	8	—	—	1	9	—	2	—	.242	.266	.268	.982
1905	Was-A	76	238	16	39	8	0	0	14	15	—	—	0	10	—	1	—	.164	.213	.197	.978
1906	Was-A	22	68	5	13	0	0	0	3	1	—	—	0	2	—	0	—	.191	.203	.191	.946
1906	Cle-A	5	10	0	1	0	0	0	0	0	—	—	0	0	—	0	—	.100	.100	.100	.938
Career average		76	252	23	55	7	2	1	24	20	—	10	1	6	—	4	—	.219	.277	.274	.961
Cubs average		**71**	**246**	**29**	**54**	**7**	**3**	**2**	**25**	**20**	—	**21**	**0**	**3**	—	**5**	—	**.219**	**.279**	**.288**	**.947**
Career total		1214	4027	375	882	108	31	17	390	314	—	166	8	102	—	64	—	.219	.277	.274	.961
Cubs total		**569**	**1970**	**231**	**431**	**53**	**24**	**12**	**203**	**162**	—	**166**	**3**	**23**	—	**39**	—	**.219**	**.279**	**.288**	**.947**

Klein, Charles Herbert (Chuck)

HEIGHT: 6'0" THROWS: RIGHT BATS: LEFT BORN: 10/7/1904 INDIANAPOLIS, INDIANA DIED: 3/28/1958 INDIANAPOLIS, INDIANA POSITIONS PLAYED: 1B, OF

YEAR	TEAM	GAMES	AB	RUNS	HITS	2B	3B	HR	RBI	BB	IBB	SO	HBP	SH	SF	SB	CS	BA	OBA	SA	FA
1928	Phi-N	64	253	41	91	14	4	11	34	14	—	22	1	7	—	0	—	.360	.396	.577	.978
1929	Phi-N	149	616	126	219	45	6	43	145	54	—	61	0	9	—	5	—	.356	.407	.657	.966
1930	Phi-N	156	648	158	250	59	8	40	170	54	—	50	4	13	—	4	—	.386	.436	.687	.960
1931	Phi-N	148	594	121	200	34	10	31	121	59	—	49	1	2	—	7	—	.337	.398	.584	.971
1932	Phi-N	154	650	152	226	50	15	38	137	60	—	49	1	0	—	20	—	.348	.404	.646	.960
1933	Phi-N	152	606	101	223	44	7	28	120	56	—	36	1	4	—	15	—	.368	.422	.602	.986
1934	**ChC-N**	**115**	**435**	**78**	**131**	**27**	**2**	**20**	**80**	**47**	—	**38**	**2**	**1**	—	**3**	—	**.301**	**.372**	**.510**	**.962**
1935	**ChC-N**	**119**	**434**	**71**	**127**	**14**	**4**	**21**	**73**	**41**	—	**42**	**1**	**9**	—	**4**	—	**.293**	**.355**	**.488**	**.958**
1936	**ChC-N**	**29**	**109**	**19**	**32**	**5**	**0**	**5**	**18**	**16**	—	**14**	**0**	**1**	—	**0**	—	**.294**	**.384**	**.477**	**.917**
1936	Phi-N	117	492	83	152	30	7	20	86	33	—	45	0	5	—	6	—	.309	.352	.520	.930
1937	Phi-N	115	406	74	132	20	2	15	57	39	—	21	1	3	—	3	—	.325	.386	.495	.949
1938	Phi-N	129	458	53	113	22	2	8	61	38	—	30	0	4	—	7	—	.247	.304	.356	.960
1939	Phi-N	25	47	8	9	2	1	1	9	10	—	4	0	2	—	1	—	.191	.333	.340	1.000
1939	Pit-N	85	270	37	81	16	4	11	47	26	—	17	0	6	—	1	—	.300	.361	.511	.951
1940	Phi-N	116	354	39	77	16	2	7	37	44	—	30	0	2	—	2	—	.218	.304	.333	.984
1941	Phi-N	50	73	6	9	0	0	1	3	10	—	6	0	1	—	0	—	.123	.229	.164	.958
1942	Phi-N	14	14	0	1	0	0	0	0	0	—	2	0	0	—	0	—	.071	.071	.071	—
1943	Phi-N	12	20	0	2	0	0	0	3	0	—	3	0	0	—	1	—	.100	.100	.100	1.000
1944	Phi-N	4	7	1	1	0	0	0	0	0	—	2	0	0	—	0	—	.143	.143	.143	1.000
Career average		103	382	69	122	23	4	18	71	35	—	31	1	4	—	5	—	.320	.379	.543	.962
Cubs average		**88**	**326**	**56**	**97**	**15**	**2**	**15**	**57**	**35**	—	**31**	**1**	**4**	—	**2**	—	**.297**	**.366**	**.497**	**.954**
Career total		1753	6486	1168	2076	398	74	300	1201	601	—	521	12	69	—	79	—	.320	.379	.543	.962
Cubs total		**263**	**978**	**168**	**290**	**46**	**6**	**46**	**171**	**104**	—	**94**	**3**	**11**	—	**7**	—	**.297**	**.366**	**.497**	**.954**

Kling, John (Johnny *or* Noisy)

HEIGHT: 5'9" THROWS: RIGHT BATS: RIGHT BORN: 2/25/1875 KANSAS CITY, MISSOURI DIED: 1/31/1947 KANSAS CITY, MISSOURI
POSITIONS PLAYED: C, 1B, 3B, SS, OF

YEAR	TEAM	GAMES	AB	RUNS	HITS	2B	3B	HR	RBI	BB	IBB	SO	HBP	SH	SF	SB	CS	BA	OBA	SA	FA
1900	ChN-N	15	51	8	15	3	1	0	7	2	—	—	0	1	—	0	—	.294	.321	.392	.901
1901	ChN-N	74	253	26	70	6	3	0	21	9	—	—	1	3	—	8	—	.277	.304	.324	.950
1902	ChC-N	114	431	49	123	19	3	0	57	29	—	—	0	12	—	24	—	.285	.330	.343	.971
1903	ChC-N	132	491	67	146	29	13	3	68	22	—	—	2	9	—	23	—	.297	.330	.428	.969
1904	ChC-N	123	452	41	110	18	0	2	46	16	—	—	1	14	—	7	—	.243	.271	.296	.972
1905	ChC-N	111	380	26	83	8	6	1	52	28	—	—	0	17	—	13	—	.218	.272	.279	.966
1906	ChC-N	107	343	45	107	15	8	2	46	23	—	—	1	8	—	14	—	.312	.357	.420	.982
1907	ChC-N	104	334	44	95	15	8	1	43	27	—	—	2	4	—	9	—	.284	.342	.386	.987
1908	ChC-N	126	424	51	117	23	5	4	59	21	—	—	3	13	—	16	—	.276	.315	.382	.978
1910	ChC-N	91	297	31	80	17	2	2	32	37	—	27	2	7	—	3	—	.269	.354	.360	.979
1911	ChC-N	27	80	8	14	3	2	1	5	8	—	14	0	1	—	1	—	.175	.250	.300	.969
1911	Bos-N	75	241	32	54	8	1	2	24	30	—	29	0	7	—	0	—	.224	.310	.290	.951
1912	Bos-N	81	252	26	80	10	3	2	30	15	—	30	0	7	—	3	—	.317	.356	.405	.958
1913	Cin-N	80	209	20	57	7	6	0	23	14	—	14	0	3	—	2	—	.273	.318	.364	.975
Career average		97	326	36	89	14	5	2	39	22	—	9	1	8	—	9	—	.272	.319	.357	.970
Cubs average		**93**	**321**	**36**	**87**	**14**	**5**	**1**	**40**	**20**	—	**4**	**1**	**8**	—	**11**	—	**.271**	**.317**	**.358**	**.973**
Career total		1260	4238	474	1151	181	61	20	513	281	—	114	12	106	—	123	—	.272	.319	.357	.970
Cubs total		**1024**	**3536**	**396**	**960**	**156**	**51**	**16**	**436**	**222**	—	**41**	**12**	**89**	—	**118**	—	**.271**	**.317**	**.358**	**.973**

John (Johnny) "Noisy" Kling, c-of-1b-ss-3b, 1900—13

One of the more underrated stars of the "Tinker to Evers to Chance" Cubs, Johnny Kling was a superb defensive catcher who also potted key hits for the Cubbies during his tenure.

Kling was born on February 25, 1875, in Kansas City, Missouri. Teammate Johnny Evers, in his autobiography *Touching Second,* reported admiringly that Kling "was born knowing baseball." That wasn't quite true, but Kling began playing semipro ball as a teenager and became the manager of a local Kansas City nine at age 18. He was a star of several Midwestern minor league squads for several years.

The Cubs signed him to a major league contract in 1900; Kling was 25. He hit .294 in limited action that year, but by 1901 he was the Cubs' starting catcher.

He was immediately the best backstopper in the league. In 1902 he led all National League catchers in putouts, assists and double plays. He would go on to lead the league in putouts by a catcher for six consecutive years. He would also be the top fielding catcher in the league four times.

Kling had a rifle arm and a steel-trap mind. In the early 1900s, when bunting was a huge weapon used by every team, Kling had a club-record 189 assists in 1903. He also developed the "snap throw," which is a throw to second base from a crouching position. This skill he reportedly learned from the great Negro League catcher, Bruce "Buddy" Petway.

Kling was also a crafty cuss. He regularly stole signs from other catchers and he, along with Giants pitcher Roger Bresnahan, in those days of only one umpire, were expert at throwing their mask in front of a base runner as he exited the box after making a hit.

Kling was an excellent base runner himself. He stole 24 bases in 1902 and 23 in 1903, one of the few catchers to swipe more than 20 bases in a season. He also twice led the Cubs in triples.

The Cubs won the National League pennant in 1906, 1907, 1908 and 1910. The year they faltered was the year Kling took a year off to play professional billiards. An accomplished pool shark, Kling initially believed that he could make more money at billiards than baseball. In fact, he won the world pro championship in the 1908 to 1909 billiards season. He was defeated in his attempt to retain the crown and returned to baseball in 1910.

Kling was a key performer in both the 1907 and 1908 World Series, in which the Cubs defeated Ty Cobb's Detroit Tigers. The Tigers, led by the speedy Cobb, were a running squad. But in 1907, Kling gunned down seven of 13 Tiger base runners. Cobb didn't steal one base. In 1908 the wary Tigers were much less aggressive, and the Cubs were victorious again.

In 1911 the Cubs traded the 36-year-old Kling to Boston, where he performed creditably for two years and acted as manager for the Braves in 1912. Kling finished his career in Cincinnati in 1913. He died in 1947, in his hometown.

Kling is third all-time for the Cubs in most games played by a catcher. His 1,244 career assists is tops for a Cubs catcher and his 1903 record of 189 assists is still a team mark.

Klugmann, Josie (Joe)

HEIGHT: 5'11"   THROWS: RIGHT   BATS: RIGHT   BORN: 3/26/1895 ST. LOUIS, MISSOURI   DIED: 7/18/1951 MOBERLY, MISSOURI
POSITIONS PLAYED: 1B, 2B, 3B, SS

YEAR	TEAM	GAMES	AB	RUNS	HITS	2B	3B	HR	RBI	BB	IBB	SO	HBP	SH	SF	SB	CS	BA	OBA	SA	FA
1921	ChC-N	6	21	3	6	0	0	0	2	1	—	2	1	1	—	0	1	.286	.348	.286	.969
1922	ChC-N	2	2	0	0	0	0	0	0	0	—	0	0	0	—	0	0	.000	.000	.000	1.000
1924	Bro-N	31	79	7	13	2	1	0	3	2	—	9	0	1	—	0	0	.165	.185	.215	.929
1925	Cle-A	38	85	12	28	9	2	0	12	8	—	4	0	3	—	3	1	.329	.387	.482	.949
Career average		19	47	6	12	3	1	0	4	3	—	4	0	1	—	1	1	.251	.296	.342	.944
Cubs average		**4**	**12**	**2**	**3**	**0**	**0**	**0**	**1**	**1**	**—**	**1**	**1**	**1**	**—**	**0**	**1**	**.261**	**.320**	**.261**	**.973**
Career total		77	187	22	47	11	3	0	17	11	—	15	1	5	—	3	2	.251	.296	.342	.944
Cubs total		**8**	**23**	**3**	**6**	**0**	**0**	**0**	**2**	**1**	**—**	**2**	**1**	**1**	**—**	**0**	**1**	**.261**	**.320**	**.261**	**.973**

Kmak, Joseph Robert (Joe)
HEIGHT: 6'0" THROWS: RIGHT BATS: RIGHT BORN: 5/3/1963 NAPA, CALIFORNIA POSITIONS PLAYED: C, 3B

YEAR	TEAM	GAMES	AB	RUNS	HITS	2B	3B	HR	RBI	BB	IBB	SO	HBP	SH	SF	SB	CS	BA	OBA	SA	FA
1993	Mil-A	51	110	9	24	5	0	0	7	14	0	13	2	1	0	6	2	.218	.317	.264	1.000
1995	**ChC-N**	**19**	**53**	**7**	**13**	**3**	**0**	**1**	**6**	**6**	**0**	**12**	**1**	**0**	**1**	**0**	**0**	**.245**	**.328**	**.358**	**1.000**
Career average		35	82	8	19	4	0	1	7	10	0	13	2	1	1	3	1	.227	.321	.294	1.000
Cubs average		**19**	**53**	**7**	**13**	**3**	**0**	**1**	**6**	**6**	**0**	**12**	**1**	**0**	**1**	**0**	**0**	**.245**	**.328**	**.358**	**1.000**
Career total		70	163	16	37	8	0	1	13	20	0	25	3	1	1	6	2	.227	.321	.294	1.000
Cubs total		**19**	**53**	**7**	**13**	**3**	**0**	**1**	**6**	**6**	**0**	**12**	**1**	**0**	**1**	**0**	**0**	**.245**	**.328**	**.358**	**1.000**

Knabe, Franz Otto (Otto *or* Dutch)
HEIGHT: 5'8" THROWS: RIGHT BATS: RIGHT BORN: 6/12/1884 CARRICK, PENNSYLVANIA DIED: 5/17/1961 PHILADELPHIA, PENNSYLVANIA
POSITIONS PLAYED: 2B, 3B, SS, OF

YEAR	TEAM	GAMES	AB	RUNS	HITS	2B	3B	HR	RBI	BB	IBB	SO	HBP	SH	SF	SB	CS	BA	OBA	SA	FA
1905	Pit-N	3	10	0	3	1	0	0	2	3	—	—	0	0	—	0	—	.300	.462	.400	.786
1907	Phi-N	129	444	67	113	16	9	1	34	52	—	—	5	40	—	18	—	.255	.339	.338	.961
1908	Phi-N	151	555	63	121	26	8	0	27	49	—	—	7	42	—	27	—	.218	.290	.294	.969
1909	Phi-N	114	402	40	94	13	3	0	34	35	—	—	8	24	—	9	—	.234	.308	.281	.938
1910	Phi-N	137	510	73	133	18	6	1	44	47	—	42	3	37	—	15	—	.261	.327	.325	.954
1911	Phi-N	142	528	99	125	15	6	1	42	94	—	35	0	21	—	23	—	.237	.352	.294	.950
1912	Phi-N	126	426	56	120	11	4	0	46	55	—	20	2	11	—	16	—	.282	.366	.326	.952
1913	Phi-N	148	571	70	150	25	7	2	53	45	—	26	3	41	—	14	—	.263	.320	.342	.959
1914	Bal-F	147	469	45	106	26	2	2	42	53	—	28	2	27	—	10	—	.226	.307	.303	.956
1915	Bal-F	103	320	38	81	16	2	1	25	37	—	16	2	13	—	7	—	.253	.334	.325	.975
1916	Pit-N	28	89	4	17	3	1	0	9	6	—	6	2	6	—	1	—	.191	.258	.247	.962
1916	**ChC-N**	**51**	**145**	**17**	**40**	**8**	**0**	**0**	**7**	**9**	**—**	**18**	**2**	**3**	**—**	**3**	**—**	**.276**	**.327**	**.331**	**.940**
Career average		116	406	52	100	16	4	1	33	44	—	17	3	24	—	13	—	.247	.325	.313	.956
Cubs average		**51**	**145**	**17**	**40**	**8**	**0**	**0**	**7**	**9**	**—**	**18**	**2**	**3**	**—**	**3**	**—**	**.276**	**.327**	**.331**	**.940**
Career total		1279	4469	572	1103	178	48	8	365	485	—	191	36	265	—	143	—	.247	.325	.313	.956
Cubs total		**51**	**145**	**17**	**40**	**8**	**0**	**0**	**7**	**9**	**—**	**18**	**2**	**3**	**—**	**3**	**—**	**.276**	**.327**	**.331**	**.940**

Knisely, Peter Cole (Pete)
HEIGHT: 5'9" THROWS: RIGHT BATS: RIGHT BORN: 8/11/1887 WAYNESBURG, PENNSYLVANIA DIED: 7/1/1948 BROWNSVILLE, PENNSYLVANIA
POSITIONS PLAYED: 2B, SS, OF

YEAR	TEAM	GAMES	AB	RUNS	HITS	2B	3B	HR	RBI	BB	IBB	SO	HBP	SH	SF	SB	CS	BA	OBA	SA	FA
1912	Cin-N	21	67	10	22	7	3	0	7	4	—	5	1	1	—	3	—	.328	.375	.522	.933
1913	**ChC-N**	**2**	**2**	**0**	**0**	**0**	**0**	**0**	**0**	**0**	**—**	**1**	**0**	**0**	**—**	**0**	**—**	**.000**	**.000**	**.000**	**—**
1914	**ChC-N**	**37**	**69**	**5**	**9**	**0**	**1**	**0**	**5**	**5**	**—**	**6**	**1**	**1**	**—**	**0**	**—**	**.130**	**.200**	**.159**	**.975**
1915	**ChC-N**	**64**	**134**	**12**	**33**	**9**	**0**	**0**	**17**	**15**	**—**	**18**	**2**	**4**	**—**	**1**	**2**	**.246**	**.331**	**.313**	**.904**
Career average		31	68	7	16	4	1	0	7	6	—	8	1	2	—	1	1	.235	.307	.324	.929
Cubs average		**34**	**68**	**6**	**14**	**3**	**0**	**0**	**7**	**7**	**—**	**8**	**1**	**2**	**—**	**0**	**1**	**.205**	**.285**	**.259**	**.927**
Career total		124	272	27	64	16	4	0	29	24	—	30	4	6	—	4	2	.235	.307	.324	.929
Cubs total		**103**	**205**	**17**	**42**	**9**	**1**	**0**	**22**	**20**	**—**	**25**	**3**	**5**	**—**	**1**	**2**	**.205**	**.285**	**.259**	**.927**

Koenig, Mark Anthony
HEIGHT: 6'0" THROWS: RIGHT BATS: BOTH BORN: 7/19/1904 SAN FRANCISCO, CALIFORNIA DIED: 4/22/1993 WILLOWS, CALIFORNIA
POSITIONS PLAYED: P, 1B, 2B, 3B, SS, OF

YEAR	TEAM	GAMES	AB	RUNS	HITS	2B	3B	HR	RBI	BB	IBB	SO	HBP	SH	SF	SB	CS	BA	OBA	SA	FA
1925	NYY-A	28	110	14	23	6	1	0	4	5	—	4	0	2	—	0	1	.209	.243	.282	.944
1926	NYY-A	147	617	93	167	26	8	5	62	43	—	37	1	17	—	4	3	.271	.319	.363	.931
1927	NYY-A	123	526	99	150	20	11	3	62	25	—	21	2	15	—	3	2	.285	.320	.382	.936
1928	NYY-A	132	533	89	170	19	10	4	63	32	—	19	2	11	—	3	2	.319	.360	.415	.923
1929	NYY-A	116	373	44	109	27	5	3	41	23	—	17	1	3	—	1	1	.292	.335	.416	.912
1930	NYY-A	21	74	9	17	5	0	0	9	6	—	5	1	5	—	0	0	.230	.296	.297	.909
1930	Det-A	76	267	37	64	9	2	1	16	20	—	15	1	13	—	2	0	.240	.295	.300	.922
1931	Det-A	106	364	33	92	24	4	1	39	14	—	12	1	2	—	8	2	.253	.282	.349	.939
1932	**ChC-N**	**33**	**102**	**15**	**36**	**5**	**1**	**3**	**11**	**3**	**—**	**5**	**1**	**0**	**—**	**0**	**—**	**.353**	**.377**	**.510**	**.932**
1933	**ChC-N**	**80**	**218**	**32**	**62**	**12**	**1**	**3**	**25**	**15**	**—**	**9**	**0**	**6**	**—**	**5**	**—**	**.284**	**.330**	**.390**	**.936**
1934	Cin-N	151	633	60	172	26	6	1	67	15	—	24	0	13	—	5	—	.272	.289	.336	.938

(continued)

(Koenig, continued)

YEAR	TEAM	GAMES	AB	RUNS	HITS	2B	3B	HR	RBI	BB	IBB	SO	HBP	SH	SF	SB	CS	BA	OBA	SA	FA
1935	NYG-N	107	396	40	112	12	0	3	37	13	—	18	0	11	—	0	—	.283	.306	.336	.963
1936	NYG-N	42	58	7	16	4	0	1	7	8	—	4	1	1	—	0	—	.276	.373	.397	.894
Career average		97	356	48	99	16	4	2	37	19	—	16	1	8	—	3	1	.279	.316	.367	.933
Cubs average		**57**	**160**	**24**	**49**	**9**	**1**	**3**	**18**	**9**	—	**7**	**1**	**3**	—	**3**	**0**	**.306**	**.345**	**.428**	**.934**
Career total		1162	4271	572	1190	195	49	28	443	222	—	190	11	99	—	31	14	.279	.316	.367	.933
Cubs total		**113**	**320**	**47**	**98**	**17**	**2**	**6**	**36**	**18**	—	**14**	**1**	**6**	—	**5**	**0**	**.306**	**.345**	**.428**	**.934**

Kreevich, Michael Andreas (Mike)
HEIGHT: 5'7" THROWS: RIGHT BATS: RIGHT BORN: 6/10/1908 MOUNT OLIVE, ILLINOIS DIED: 4/25/1994 PANA, ILLINOIS POSITIONS PLAYED: 3B, OF

YEAR	TEAM	GAMES	AB	RUNS	HITS	2B	3B	HR	RBI	BB	IBB	SO	HBP	SH	SF	SB	CS	BA	OBA	SA	FA
1931	**ChC-N**	**5**	**12**	**0**	**2**	**0**	**0**	**0**	**0**	**0**	—	**6**	**0**	**0**	—	**1**		**.167**	**.167**	**.167**	**1.000**
1935	CWS-A	6	23	3	10	2	0	0	2	1	—	0	0	0	—	1	1	.435	.458	.522	1.000
1936	CWS-A	137	550	99	169	32	11	5	69	61	—	46	2	15	—	10	5	.307	.378	.433	.964
1937	CWS-A	144	583	94	176	29	16	12	73	43	—	45	0	16	—	13	1	.302	.350	.468	.988
1938	CWS-A	129	489	73	145	26	12	6	73	55	—	23	3	4	—	23	10	.297	.371	.436	.975
1939	CWS-A	145	541	85	175	30	8	5	77	59	—	40	0	22	—	15	7	.323	.390	.436	.974
1940	CWS-A	144	582	86	154	27	10	8	55	34	—	49	0	21	—	17	5	.265	.305	.387	.982
1941	CWS-A	121	436	44	101	16	8	0	37	35	—	26	0	13	—	7	9	.232	.289	.305	.994
1942	Phi-A	116	444	57	113	19	1	1	30	47	—	31	0	6	—	4	1	.255	.326	.309	.993
1943	StL-A	60	161	24	41	6	0	0	10	26	—	13	0	10	—	3	3	.255	.358	.292	.986
1944	StL-A	105	402	55	121	15	6	5	44	27	—	24	2	7	—	4	1	.301	.348	.405	.991
1945	StL-A	84	295	34	70	11	1	2	21	37	—	27	0	2	—	7	5	.237	.322	.302	.971
1945	Was-A	45	158	22	44	8	2	1	23	21	—	9	0		—			.278	.363	.373	
Career average		103	390	56	110	18	6	4	43	37	—	28	1	10	—	10	4	.283	.346	.391	.981
Cubs average		**5**	**12**	**0**	**2**	**0**	**0**	**0**	**0**	**0**	—	**6**	**0**	**0**	—	**1**	—	**.167**	**.167**	**.167**	**1.000**
Career total		1241	4676	676	1321	221	75	45	514	446	—	339	7	119	—	115	53	.283	.346	.391	.981
Cubs total		**5**	**12**	**0**	**2**	**0**	**0**	**0**	**0**	**0**	—	**6**	**0**	**0**	—	**1**	—	**.167**	**.167**	**.167**	**1.000**

Kreitner, Albert Joseph (Mickey)
HEIGHT: 6'3" THROWS: RIGHT BATS: RIGHT BORN: 10/10/1922 NASHVILLE, TENNESSEE POSITIONS PLAYED: C

YEAR	TEAM	GAMES	AB	RUNS	HITS	2B	3B	HR	RBI	BB	IBB	SO	HBP	SH	SF	SB	CS	BA	OBA	SA	FA
1943	**ChC-N**	**3**	**8**	**0**	**3**	**0**	**0**	**0**	**2**	**1**	—	**2**	**0**	**0**	—	**0**	—	**.375**	**.444**	**.375**	**1.000**
1944	**ChC-N**	**39**	**85**	**3**	**13**	**2**	**0**	**0**	**1**	**8**	—	**16**	**1**	**3**	—	**0**	—	**.153**	**.234**	**.176**	**.992**
Career average		21	47	2	8	1	0	0	2	5	—	9	1	2	—	0	—	.172	.252	.194	.992
Cubs average		**21**	**47**	**2**	**8**	**1**	**0**	**0**	**2**	**5**	—	**9**	**1**	**2**	—	**0**	—	**.172**	**.252**	**.194**	**.992**
Career total		42	93	3	16	2	0	0	3	9	—	18	1	3	—	0	—	.172	.252	.194	.992
Cubs total		**42**	**93**	**3**	**16**	**2**	**0**	**0**	**3**	**9**	—	**18**	**1**	**3**	—	**0**	—	**.172**	**.252**	**.194**	**.992**

Krieg, William Frederick (Bill)
HEIGHT: 5'8" THROWS: RIGHT BATS: RIGHT BORN: 1/29/1859 PETERSBURG, ILLINOIS DIED: 3/25/1930 CHILLICOTHE, ILLINOIS
POSITIONS PLAYED: C, 1B, SS, OF

YEAR	TEAM	GAMES	AB	RUNS	HITS	2B	3B	HR	RBI	BB	IBB	SO	HBP	SH	SF	SB	CS	BA	OBA	SA	FA
1884	Chi-U	61	240	27	55	10	3	0	—	10	—	—	—	—	—	—	—	.229	.260	.296	.909
1884	Pit-U	10	39	8	14	5	1	0	—	1	—	—	—	—	—	—	—	.359	.375	.538	.934
1885	**ChN-N**	**1**	**3**	**0**	**0**	**0**	**0**	**0**	**0**	**0**	—	**2**	—	—	—	—	—	**.000**	**.000**	**.000**	**.800**
1885	Bro-AA	17	60	7	9	4	0	1	5	2	—		0	—	—	—	—	.150	.177	.267	.917
1886	WaN-N	27	98	11	25	6	3	1	15	3	—	12	—	—	—	2	—	.255	.277	.408	.975
1887	WaN-N	25	102	9	31	4	1	2	17	7	—	5	1	—	—	2	—	.304	.355	.422	.968
Career average		35	136	16	34	7	2	1	9	6	—	5	0	—	—	1	—	.247	.279	.352	.932
Cubs average		**1**	**3**	**0**	**0**	**0**	**0**	**0**	**0**	**0**	—	**2**	—	—	—	—	—	**.000**	**.000**	**.000**	**.800**
Career total		141	542	62	134	29	8	4	37	23	—	19	1	—	—	4	—	.247	.279	.352	.932
Cubs total		**1**	**3**	**0**	**0**	**0**	**0**	**0**	**0**	**0**	—	**2**	—	—	—	—	—	**.000**	**.000**	**.000**	**.800**

Krug, Everett Ben (Chris)

HEIGHT: 6'4" THROWS: RIGHT BATS: RIGHT BORN: 12/25/1939 LOS ANGELES, CALIFORNIA POSITIONS PLAYED: C

YEAR	TEAM	GAMES	AB	RUNS	HITS	2B	3B	HR	RBI	BB	IBB	SO	HBP	SH	SF	SB	CS	BA	OBA	SA	FA
1965	ChC-N	60	169	16	34	5	0	5	24	13	2	52	1	0	3	0	1	.201	.258	.320	.980
1966	ChC-N	11	28	1	6	1	0	0	1	1	0	8	0	0	0	0	0	.214	.241	.250	1.000
1969	SD-N	8	17	0	1	0	0	0	0	1	0	6	0	1	0	0	0	.059	.111	.059	.938
Career average		26	71	6	14	2	0	2	8	5	1	22	0	0	1	0	0	.192	.245	.290	.980
Cubs average		**36**	**99**	**9**	**20**	**3**	**0**	**3**	**13**	**7**	**1**	**30**	**0**	**0**	**2**	**0**	**1**	**.203**	**.256**	**.310**	**.984**
Career total		79	214	17	41	6	0	5	25	15	2	66	1	1	3	0	1	.192	.245	.290	.980
Cubs total		**71**	**197**	**17**	**40**	**6**	**0**	**5**	**25**	**14**	**2**	**60**	**1**	**0**	**3**	**0**	**1**	**.203**	**.256**	**.310**	**.984**

Krug, Gary Eugene

HEIGHT: 6'4" THROWS: LEFT BATS: LEFT BORN: 2/12/1955 GARDEN CITY, KANSAS

YEAR	TEAM	GAMES	AB	RUNS	HITS	2B	3B	HR	RBI	BB	IBB	SO	HBP	SH	SF	SB	CS	BA	OBA	SA	FA
1981	ChC-N	7	5	0	2	0	0	0	0	1	0	1	0	0	0	0	0	.400	.500	.400	—
Career average		7	5	0	2	0	0	0	0	1	0	1	0	0	0	0	0	.400	.500	.400	—
Cubs average		**7**	**5**	**0**	**2**	**0**	**0**	**0**	**0**	**1**	**0**	**1**	**0**	**0**	**0**	**0**	**0**	**.400**	**.500**	**.400**	**—**
Career total		7	5	0	2	0	0	0	0	1	0	1	0	0	0	0	0	.400	.500	.400	—
Cubs total		**7**	**5**	**0**	**2**	**0**	**0**	**0**	**0**	**1**	**0**	**1**	**0**	**0**	**0**	**0**	**0**	**.400**	**.500**	**.400**	**—**

Krug, Martin John (Marty)

HEIGHT: 5'9" THROWS: RIGHT BATS: RIGHT BORN: 9/10/1888 KOBLENZ, GERMANY DIED: 6/27/1966 GLENDALE, CALIFORNIA
POSITIONS PLAYED: 2B, 3B, SS

YEAR	TEAM	GAMES	AB	RUNS	HITS	2B	3B	HR	RBI	BB	IBB	SO	HBP	SH	SF	SB	CS	BA	OBA	SA	FA
1912	Bos-A	16	39	6	12	2	1	0	7	5	—	—	0	3	—	2	—	.308	.386	.410	.900
1922	ChC-N	127	450	67	124	23	4	4	60	43	—	43	3	28	—	7	9	.276	.343	.371	.931
Career average		72	245	37	68	13	3	2	34	24	—	22	2	16	—	5	5	.278	.346	.374	.928
Cubs average		**127**	**450**	**67**	**124**	**23**	**4**	**4**	**60**	**43**	**—**	**43**	**3**	**28**	**—**	**5**	**5**	**.276**	**.343**	**.371**	**.931**
Career total		143	489	73	136	25	5	4	67	48	—	43	3	31	—	9	9	.278	.346	.374	.928
Cubs total		**127**	**450**	**67**	**124**	**23**	**4**	**4**	**60**	**43**	**—**	**43**	**3**	**28**	**—**	**7**	**9**	**.276**	**.343**	**.371**	**.931**

Kuenn, Harvey Edward

HEIGHT: 6'2" THROWS: RIGHT BATS: RIGHT BORN: 12/4/1930 WEST ALLIS, WISCONSIN DIED: 2/28/1988 PEORIA, ARIZONA
POSITIONS PLAYED: 1B, 3B, SS, OF

YEAR	TEAM	GAMES	AB	RUNS	HITS	2B	3B	HR	RBI	BB	IBB	SO	HBP	SH	SF	SB	CS	BA	OBA	SA	FA
1952	Det-A	19	80	2	26	2	2	0	8	2	—	1	1	2	—	2	1	.325	.349	.400	.962
1953	Det-A	155	679	94	209	33	7	2	48	50	—	31	1	1	—	6	5	.308	.356	.386	.973
1954	Det-A	155	656	81	201	28	6	5	48	29	—	13	1	6	4	9	9	.306	.335	.390	.966
1955	Det-A	145	620	101	190	38	5	8	62	40	3	27	1	0	5	8	3	.306	.347	.423	.956
1956	Det-A	146	591	96	196	32	7	12	88	55	3	34	3	0	8	9	5	.332	.387	.470	.968
1957	Det-A	151	624	74	173	30	6	9	44	47	4	28	0	6	2	5	8	.277	.327	.388	.955
1958	Det-A	139	561	73	179	39	3	8	54	51	8	34	0	3	4	5	10	.319	.373	.442	.984
1959	Det-A	139	561	99	198	42	7	9	71	48	1	37	1	3	4	7	2	.353	.402	.501	.988
1960	Cle-A	126	474	65	146	24	0	9	54	55	6	25	1	4	3	3	4	.308	.379	.416	.963
1961	SF-N	131	471	60	125	22	4	5	46	47	2	34	1	4	7	5	4	.265	.329	.361	.959
1962	SF-N	130	487	73	148	23	5	10	68	49	3	37	1	6	5	3	6	.304	.365	.433	.966
1963	SF-N	120	417	61	121	13	2	6	31	44	3	38	2	2	4	2	1	.290	.358	.374	.931
1964	SF-N	111	351	42	92	16	2	4	22	35	4	32	1	1	2	0	1	.262	.329	.353	.960
1965	SF-N	23	59	4	14	0	0	0	6	10	0	3	1	2	1	3	1	.237	.352	.237	1.000
1965	ChC-N	54	120	11	26	5	0	0	6	22	1	13	0	0	1	1	0	.217	.336	.258	.935
1966	ChC-N	3	3	0	1	0	0	0	0	0	0	1	0	0	0	0	0	.333	.333	.333	—
1966	Phi-N	86	159	15	47	9	0	0	15	10	1	16	0	5	2	0	0	.296	.333	.352	.993
Career average		122	461	63	139	24	4	6	45	40	3	27	1	3	3	5	4	.303	.357	.408	.966
Cubs average		**29**	**62**	**6**	**14**	**3**	**0**	**0**	**3**	**11**	**1**	**7**	**0**	**0**	**1**	**1**	**0**	**.220**	**.336**	**.260**	**.935**
Career total		1833	6913	951	2092	356	56	87	671	594	39	404	15	44	52	68	56	.303	.357	.408	.966
Cubs total		**57**	**123**	**11**	**27**	**5**	**0**	**0**	**6**	**22**	**1**	**14**	**0**	**0**	**1**	**1**	**0**	**.220**	**.336**	**.260**	**.935**

Kunkel, Jeffrey William (Jeff)
HEIGHT: 6'2"   THROWS: RIGHT   BATS: RIGHT   BORN: 3/25/1962 WEST PALM BEACH, FLORIDA   POSITIONS PLAYED: P, 1B, 2B, 3B, SS, OF

YEAR	TEAM	GAMES	AB	RUNS	HITS	2B	3B	HR	RBI	BB	IBB	SO	HBP	SH	SF	SB	CS	BA	OBA	SA	FA
1984	Tex-A	50	142	13	29	2	3	3	7	2	0	35	1	3	2	4	3	.204	.218	.324	.922
1985	Tex-A	2	4	1	1	0	0	0	0	0	0	3	0	0	0	0	0	.250	.250	.250	1.000
1986	Tex-A	8	13	3	3	0	0	1	2	0	0	2	0	0	0	0	0	.231	.231	.462	.769
1987	Tex-A	15	32	1	7	0	0	1	2	0	0	10	1	1	0	0	1	.227	.250	.357	.961
1988	Tex-A	55	154	14	35	8	3	2	15	4	1	35	1	1	1	0	1	.270	.323	.437	.934
1989	Tex-A	108	293	39	79	21	2	8	29	20	0	75	3	10	0	3	2	.170	.221	.280	.961
1990	Tex-A	99	200	17	34	11	1	3	17	11	0	66	2	5	0	2	1	.138	.138	.207	.970
1992	**ChC-N**	**20**	**29**	**0**	**4**	**2**	**0**	**0**	**1**	**0**	**0**	**8**	**0**	**0**	**0**	**0**	**0**	**.138**	**.138**	**.207**	**.970**
Career average		45	108	11	24	6	1	2	9	5	0	29	1	3	0	1	1	.221	.259	.355	.943
Cubs average		**20**	**29**	**0**	**4**	**2**	**0**	**0**	**1**	**0**	**0**	**8**	**0**	**0**	**0**	**0**	**0**	**.138**	**.138**	**.207**	**.970**
Career total		357	867	88	192	44	9	18	73	37	1	234	8	20	3	9	8	.221	.259	.355	.943
Cubs total		**20**	**29**	**0**	**4**	**2**	**0**	**0**	**1**	**0**	**0**	**8**	**0**	**0**	**0**	**0**	**0**	**.138**	**.138**	**.207**	**.970**

La Russa, Anthony (Tony)
HEIGHT: 6'0"   THROWS: RIGHT   BATS: RIGHT   BORN: 10/4/1944 TAMPA, FLORIDA   POSITIONS PLAYED: 2B, 3B, SS

YEAR	TEAM	GAMES	AB	RUNS	HITS	2B	3B	HR	RBI	BB	IBB	SO	HBP	SH	SF	SB	CS	BA	OBA	SA	FA
1963	KCA-A	34	44	4	11	1	1	0	1	7	0	12	0	1	1	0	0	.250	.346	.318	.964
1968	Oak-A	5	3	0	1	0	0	0	0	0	0	0	0	0	0	0	0	.333	.333	.333	—
1969	Oak-A	8	8	0	0	0	0	0	0	0	0	1	0	0	0	0	0	.000	.000	.000	—
1970	Oak-A	52	106	6	21	4	1	0	6	15	1	19	1	0	1	0	0	.198	.301	.255	.969
1971	Oak-A	23	8	3	0	0	0	0	0	0	0	4	0	0	0	0	0	.000	.000	.000	.882
1971	Atl-N	9	7	1	2	0	0	0	0	1	0	1	0	0	0	0	0	.286	.375	.286	.933
1973	**ChC-N**	**1**	**0**	**1**	**0**	**0**	**0**	**0**	**0**	**0**	**0**	**0**	**0**	**0**	**0**	**0**	**0**	**—**	**—**	**—**	**—**
Career average		22	29	3	6	1	0	0	1	4	0	6	0	0	0	0	0	.199	.292	.250	.960
Cubs average		**1**	**0**	**1**	**0**	**0**	**0**	**0**	**0**	**0**	**0**	**0**	**0**	**0**	**0**	**0**	**0**	**—**	**—**	**—**	**—**
Career total		132	176	15	35	5	2	0	7	23	1	37	1	1	2	0	0	.199	.292	.250	.960
Cubs total		**1**	**0**	**1**	**0**	**0**	**0**	**0**	**0**	**0**	**0**	**0**	**0**	**0**	**0**	**0**	**0**	**—**	**—**	**—**	**—**

LaCock, Ralph Pierre (Pete)
HEIGHT: 6'2"   THROWS: LEFT   BATS: LEFT   BORN: 1/17/1952 BURBANK, CALIFORNIA   POSITIONS PLAYED: 1B, OF

YEAR	TEAM	GAMES	AB	RUNS	HITS	2B	3B	HR	RBI	BB	IBB	SO	HBP	SH	SF	SB	CS	BA	OBA	SA	FA
1972	**ChC-N**	**5**	**6**	**3**	**3**	**0**	**0**	**0**	**4**	**0**	**0**	**1**	**0**	**0**	**1**	**1**	**0**	**.500**	**.429**	**.500**	**1.000**
1973	**ChC-N**	**11**	**16**	**1**	**4**	**1**	**0**	**0**	**3**	**1**	**0**	**2**	**0**	**0**	**0**	**0**	**0**	**.250**	**.294**	**.313**	**1.000**
1974	**ChC-N**	**35**	**110**	**9**	**20**	**4**	**1**	**1**	**8**	**12**	**2**	**16**	**1**	**2**	**0**	**0**	**0**	**.182**	**.268**	**.264**	**.986**
1975	**ChC-N**	**106**	**249**	**30**	**57**	**8**	**1**	**6**	**30**	**37**	**7**	**27**	**0**	**2**	**4**	**0**	**2**	**.229**	**.324**	**.341**	**.989**
1976	**ChC-N**	**106**	**244**	**34**	**54**	**9**	**2**	**8**	**28**	**42**	**6**	**37**	**1**	**2**	**1**	**1**	**4**	**.221**	**.337**	**.373**	**.974**
1977	KC-A	88	218	25	66	12	1	3	29	15	1	25	1	0	4	2	1	.303	.345	.419	.991
1978	KC-A	118	322	44	95	21	2	5	48	21	2	27	0	1	3	1	0	.295	.335	.380	.993
1979	KC-A	132	408	54	113	25	4	3	56	37	7	26	1	1	6	2	1	.277	.334	.380	.997
1980	KC-A	114	156	14	32	6	0	1	18	17	1	10	1	0	2	1	0	.205	.284	.263	.994
Career average		79	192	24	49	10	1	3	25	20	3	19	1	1	2	1	1	.257	.326	.366	.990
Cubs average		**53**	**125**	**15**	**28**	**4**	**1**	**3**	**15**	**18**	**3**	**17**	**0**	**1**	**1**	**0**	**1**	**.221**	**.320**	**.341**	**.982**
Career total		715	1729	214	444	86	11	27	224	182	26	171	5	8	21	8	8	.257	.326	.366	.990
Cubs total		**263**	**625**	**77**	**138**	**22**	**4**	**15**	**73**	**92**	**15**	**83**	**2**	**6**	**6**	**2**	**6**	**.221**	**.320**	**.341**	**.982**

Lake, Steven Michael (Steve)
HEIGHT: 6'1"   THROWS: RIGHT   BATS: RIGHT   BORN: 3/14/1957 INGLEWOOD, CALIFORNIA   POSITIONS PLAYED: C

YEAR	TEAM	GAMES	AB	RUNS	HITS	2B	3B	HR	RBI	BB	IBB	SO	HBP	SH	SF	SB	CS	BA	OBA	SA	FA
1983	**ChC-N**	**38**	**85**	**9**	**22**	**4**	**1**	**1**	**7**	**2**	**2**	**6**	**1**	**0**	**0**	**0**	**0**	**.259**	**.284**	**.365**	**1.000**
1984	**ChC-N**	**25**	**54**	**4**	**12**	**4**	**0**	**2**	**7**	**0**	**0**	**7**	**1**	**1**	**1**	**0**	**0**	**.222**	**.232**	**.407**	**.955**
1985	**ChC-N**	**58**	**119**	**5**	**18**	**2**	**0**	**1**	**11**	**3**	**1**	**21**	**1**	**4**	**1**	**1**	**0**	**.151**	**.177**	**.193**	**.995**
1986	**ChC-N**	**10**	**19**	**4**	**8**	**1**	**0**	**0**	**4**	**1**	**1**	**2**	**0**	**1**	**0**	**0**	**0**	**.421**	**.450**	**.474**	**1.000**
1986	StL-N	26	49	4	12	1	0	2	10	2	0	5	0	0	0	0	0	.245	.275	.388	.976
1987	StL-N	74	179	19	45	7	2	2	19	10	4	18	0	5	1	0	0	.251	.289	.346	.996
1988	StL-N	36	54	5	15	3	0	1	4	3	0	15	2	0	0	0	0	.278	.339	.389	.983

YEAR	TEAM	GAMES	AB	RUNS	HITS	2B	3B	HR	RBI	BB	IBB	SO	HBP	SH	SF	SB	CS	BA	OBA	SA	FA
1989	Phi-N	58	155	9	39	5	1	2	14	12	4	20	0	1	1	0	0	.252	.304	.335	.990
1990	Phi-N	29	80	4	20	2	0	0	6	3	1	12	1	0	0	0	0	.250	.286	.275	.993
1991	Phi-N	58	158	12	36	4	1	1	11	2	1	26	0	4	0	0	0	.228	.238	.285	.993
1992	Phi-N	20	53	3	13	2	0	1	2	1	0	8	0	0	1	0	0	.228	.238	.285	.993
1993	**ChC-N**	**44**	**120**	**11**	**27**	**6**	**0**	**5**	**13**	**4**	**3**	**19**	**0**	**2**	**0**	**0**	**0**	**.245**	**.255**	**.340**	**.975**
Career average		43	102	8	24	4	0	2	10	4	2	14	1	2	0	0	0	.225	.250	.400	.985
Cubs average		**35**	**79**	**7**	**17**	**3**	**0**	**2**	**8**	**2**	**1**	**11**	**1**	**2**	**0**	**0**	**0**	**.237**	**.268**	**.331**	**.989**
Career total		476	1125	89	267	41	5	18	108	43	17	159	6	18	5	1	0	.219	.243	.335	.988
Cubs total		**175**	**397**	**33**	**87**	**17**	**1**	**9**	**42**	**10**	**7**	**55**	**3**	**8**	**2**	**1**	**0**	**.237**	**.268**	**.331**	**.989**

Lamers, Pierre (Pete)
HEIGHT: 5'10" THROWS: RIGHT BATS: — BORN: 12/1873 NEW YORK, NEW YORK DIED: 10/24/1931 BROOKLYN, NEW YORK POSITIONS PLAYED: C

YEAR	TEAM	GAMES	AB	RUNS	HITS	2B	3B	HR	RBI	BB	IBB	SO	HBP	SH	SF	SB	CS	BA	OBA	SA	FA
1902	**ChC-N**	**2**	**9**	**2**	**2**	**0**	**0**	**0**	**0**	**0**	**—**	**—**	**0**	**0**	**—**	**0**	**—**	**.222**	**.222**	**.222**	**.857**
1907	Cin-N	1	2	0	0	0	0	0	0	0	—	—	0	0	—	0	—	.000	.000	.000	1.000
Career average		2	6	1	1	0	0	0	0	0	—	—	0	0	—	0	—	.182	.182	.182	.867
Cubs average		**2**	**9**	**2**	**2**	**0**	**0**	**0**	**0**	**0**	**—**	**—**	**0**	**0**	**—**	**0**	**—**	**.222**	**.222**	**.222**	**.857**
Career total		3	11	2	2	0	0	0	0	0	—	—	0	0	—	0	—	.182	.182	.182	.867
Cubs total		**2**	**9**	**2**	**2**	**0**	**0**	**0**	**0**	**0**	**—**	**—**	**0**	**0**	**—**	**0**	**—**	**.222**	**.222**	**.222**	**.857**

Landrith, Hobart Neal (Hobie)
HEIGHT: 5'10" THROWS: RIGHT BATS: LEFT BORN: 3/16/1930 DECATUR, ILLINOIS POSITIONS PLAYED: C

YEAR	TEAM	GAMES	AB	RUNS	HITS	2B	3B	HR	RBI	BB	IBB	SO	HBP	SH	SF	SB	CS	BA	OBA	SA	FA
1950	Cin-N	4	14	1	3	0	0	0	1	2	—	1	0	0	—	0	—	.214	.313	.214	1.000
1951	Cin-N	4	13	3	5	1	0	0	0	1	—	1	0	0	—	0	—	.385	.429	.462	1.000
1952	Cin-N	15	50	1	13	4	0	0	4	0	—	4	0	0	—	0	0	.260	.260	.340	1.000
1953	Cin-N	52	154	15	37	3	1	3	16	12	—	8	1	0	—	0	1	.240	.299	.331	.985
1954	Cin-N	48	81	12	16	1	0	5	14	18	—	9	0	2	1	0	0	.198	.340	.383	.986
1955	Cin-N	43	87	9	22	3	0	4	7	10	1	14	0	1	0	1	0	.253	.330	.425	1.000
1956	**ChC-N**	**111**	**312**	**22**	**69**	**10**	**3**	**4**	**32**	**39**	**15**	**38**	**1**	**7**	**3**	**0**	**2**	**.221**	**.307**	**.311**	**.975**
1957	StL-N	75	214	18	52	6	0	3	26	25	1	27	0	1	3	1	2	.243	.318	.313	.987
1958	StL-N	70	144	9	31	4	0	3	13	26	4	21	0	1	0	0	1	.215	.335	.306	.992
1959	SF-N	109	283	30	71	14	0	3	29	43	7	23	0	5	4	0	4	.251	.345	.332	.992
1960	SF-N	71	190	18	46	10	0	1	20	23	2	11	0	3	2	1	1	.242	.321	.332	.992
1961	SF-N	43	71	11	17	4	0	2	10	12	3	7	0	2	3	0	0	.239	.337	.380	.966
1962	NYM-N	23	45	6	13	3	0	1	7	8	0	3	0	0	1	0	0	.289	.389	.422	.985
1962	Bal-A	60	167	18	37	4	1	4	17	19	1	9	1	0	2	0	0	.222	.302	.329	.982
1963	Bal-A	2	1	0	0	0	0	0	0	0	0	0	0	0	0	0	0	.000	.000	.000	1.000
1963	Was-A	42	103	6	18	3	0	1	7	15	1	12	0	1	0	0	0	.175	.280	.233	.978
Career average		55	138	13	32	5	0	2	15	18	3	13	0	2	1	0	1	.233	.320	.327	.983
Cubs average		**111**	**312**	**22**	**69**	**10**	**3**	**4**	**32**	**39**	**15**	**38**	**1**	**7**	**3**	**0**	**2**	**.221**	**.307**	**.311**	**.975**
Career total		772	1929	179	450	69	5	34	203	253	35	188	3	23	19	5	12	.233	.320	.327	.983
Cubs total		**111**	**312**	**22**	**69**	**10**	**3**	**4**	**32**	**39**	**15**	**38**	**1**	**7**	**3**	**0**	**2**	**.221**	**.307**	**.311**	**.975**

Landrum, Cedric Bernard (Ced)
HEIGHT: 5'9" THROWS: RIGHT BATS: LEFT BORN: 9/3/1963 BUTLER, ALABAMA POSITIONS PLAYED: OF

YEAR	TEAM	GAMES	AB	RUNS	HITS	2B	3B	HR	RBI	BB	IBB	SO	HBP	SH	SF	SB	CS	BA	OBA	SA	FA
1991	**ChC-N**	**56**	**86**	**28**	**20**	**2**	**1**	**0**	**6**	**10**	**0**	**18**	**0**	**3**	**0**	**27**	**5**	**.233**	**.313**	**.279**	**.968**
1993	NYM-N	22	19	2	5	1	0	0	1	0	0	5	0	1	0	0	0	.263	.263	.316	—
Career average		39	53	15	13	2	1	0	4	5	0	12	0	2	0	14	3	.238	.304	.286	.968
Cubs average		**56**	**86**	**28**	**20**	**2**	**1**	**0**	**6**	**10**	**0**	**18**	**0**	**3**	**0**	**27**	**5**	**.233**	**.313**	**.279**	**.968**
Career total		78	105	30	25	3	1	0	7	10	0	23	0	4	0	27	5	.238	.304	.286	.968
Cubs total		**56**	**86**	**28**	**20**	**2**	**1**	**0**	**6**	**10**	**0**	**18**	**0**	**3**	**0**	**27**	**5**	**.233**	**.313**	**.279**	**.968**

Landrum, Donald Leroy (Don)
HEIGHT: 6'0"   THROWS: RIGHT   BATS: LEFT   BORN: 2/16/1936 SANTA ROSA, CALIFORNIA   POSITIONS PLAYED: 2B, OF

YEAR	TEAM	GAMES	AB	RUNS	HITS	2B	3B	HR	RBI	BB	IBB	SO	HBP	SH	SF	SB	CS	BA	OBA	SA	FA
1957	Phi-N	2	7	1	1	1	0	0	0	2	0	1	0	0	0	0	0	.143	.333	.286	1.000
1960	StL-N	13	49	7	12	0	1	2	3	4	0	6	1	1	0	3	0	.245	.315	.408	1.000
1961	StL-N	28	66	5	11	2	0	1	3	5	0	14	0	3	0	1	0	.167	.225	.242	1.000
1962	StL-N	32	35	11	11	0	0	0	3	4	1	2	0	2	1	2	0	.314	.375	.314	1.000
1962	**ChC-N**	**83**	**238**	**29**	**67**	**5**	**2**	**1**	**15**	**30**	**0**	**31**	**3**	**1**	**0**	**9**	**2**	.282	.369	.332	.969
1963	**ChC-N**	**84**	**227**	**27**	**55**	**4**	**1**	**1**	**10**	**13**	**1**	**42**	**4**	**2**	**1**	**6**	**3**	.242	.294	.282	.972
1964	**ChC-N**	**11**	**11**	**2**	**0**	**0**	**0**	**0**	**0**	**1**	**0**	**2**	**0**	**0**	**0**	**0**	**0**	.000	.083	.000	1.000
1965	**ChC-N**	**131**	**425**	**60**	**96**	**20**	**4**	**6**	**34**	**36**	**3**	**84**	**10**	**4**	**2**	**14**	**8**	.226	.300	.334	.988
1966	SF-N	72	102	9	19	4	0	1	7	9	0	18	1	0	0	1	1	.186	.259	.255	.968
Career average		57	145	19	34	5	1	2	9	13	1	25	2	2	1	5	2	.234	.307	.310	.982
Cubs average		**77**	**225**	**30**	**55**	**7**	**2**	**2**	**15**	**20**	**1**	**40**	**4**	**2**	**1**	**7**	**3**	.242	.315	.316	.979
Career total		456	1160	151	272	36	8	12	75	104	5	200	19	13	4	36	14	.234	.307	.310	.982
Cubs total		**309**	**901**	**118**	**218**	**29**	**7**	**8**	**59**	**80**	**4**	**159**	**17**	**7**	**3**	**29**	**13**	.242	.315	.316	.979

Lange, William Alexander (Bill *or* Little Eva)
HEIGHT: 6'1"   THROWS: RIGHT   BATS: RIGHT   BORN: 6/6/1871 SAN FRANCISCO, CALIFORNIA   DIED: 7/23/1950 SAN FRANCISCO, CALIFORNIA
POSITIONS PLAYED: C, 1B, 2B, 3B, SS, OF

YEAR	TEAM	GAMES	AB	RUNS	HITS	2B	3B	HR	RBI	BB	IBB	SO	HBP	SH	SF	SB	CS	BA	OBA	SA	FA
1893	ChN-N	117	469	92	132	8	7	8	88	52	—	20	4	—	—	47	—	.281	.358	.380	.902
1894	ChN-N	111	442	84	145	16	9	6	90	56	—	18	1	4	—	65	—	.328	.405	.446	.893
1895	ChN-N	123	478	120	186	27	16	10	98	55	—	24	4	9	—	67	—	.389	.456	.575	.924
1896	ChN-N	122	469	114	153	21	16	4	92	65	—	24	5	6	—	84	—	.326	.414	.465	.933
1897	ChN-N	118	479	119	163	24	14	5	83	48	—	—	5	9	—	73	—	.340	.406	.480	.946
1898	ChN-N	113	442	79	141	16	11	5	69	36	—	—	5	7	—	22	—	.319	.377	.439	.971
1899	ChN-N	107	416	81	135	21	7	1	58	38	—	—	1	8	—	41	—	.325	.382	.416	.973
Career average		116	456	98	151	19	11	6	83	50	—	12	4	6	—	57	—	.330	.401	.459	.932
Cubs average		**116**	**456**	**98**	**151**	**19**	**11**	**6**	**83**	**50**	—	**12**	**4**	**6**	—	**57**	—	.330	.401	.459	.932
Career total		811	3195	689	1055	133	80	39	578	350	—	86	25	43	—	399	—	.330	.401	.459	.932
Cubs total		**811**	**3195**	**689**	**1055**	**133**	**80**	**39**	**578**	**350**	—	**86**	**25**	**43**	—	**399**	—	.330	.401	.459	.932

LaRose, Victor Raymond (Vic)
HEIGHT: 5'11"   THROWS: RIGHT   BATS: RIGHT   BORN: 12/23/1944 LOS ANGELES, CALIFORNIA   POSITIONS PLAYED: 2B, SS

YEAR	TEAM	GAMES	AB	RUNS	HITS	2B	3B	HR	RBI	BB	IBB	SO	HBP	SH	SF	SB	CS	BA	OBA	SA	FA
1968	**ChC-N**	**4**	**2**	**0**	**0**	**0**	**0**	**0**	**0**	**0**	**0**	**1**	**1**	**0**	**0**	**0**	**0**	.000	.333	.000	.857
Career average		4	2	0	0	0	0	0	0	0	0	1	1	0	0	0	0	.000	.333	.000	.857
Cubs average		**4**	**2**	**0**	**0**	**0**	**0**	**0**	**0**	**0**	**0**	**1**	**1**	**0**	**0**	**0**	**0**	.000	.333	.000	.857
Career total		4	2	0	0	0	0	0	0	0	0	1	1	0	0	0	0	.000	.333	.000	.857
Cubs total		**4**	**2**	**0**	**0**	**0**	**0**	**0**	**0**	**0**	**0**	**1**	**1**	**0**	**0**	**0**	**0**	.000	.333	.000	.857

Lauer, John Charles (Chuck)
HEIGHT: —   THROWS: RIGHT   BATS: —   BORN: 4/5/1865 PITTSBURGH, PENNSYLVANIA   POSITIONS PLAYED: P, C, 1B, OF

YEAR	TEAM	GAMES	AB	RUNS	HITS	2B	3B	HR	RBI	BB	IBB	SO	HBP	SH	SF	SB	CS	BA	OBA	SA	FA
1884	Pit-AA	13	44	5	5	0	0	0	—	0	—	—	0	—	—	—	—	.114	.114	.114	.864
1889	Pit-N	4	16	2	3	0	0	0	1	0	—	5	0	—	—	0	—	.188	.188	.188	.828
1890	**ChN-N**	**2**	**8**	**1**	**2**	**1**	**0**	**0**	**2**	**0**	—	**0**	**0**	—	—	**0**	—	.250	.250	.375	.833
Career average		6	23	3	3	0	0	0	1	0	—	2	0	—	—	0	—	.147	.147	.162	.841
Cubs average		**2**	**8**	**1**	**2**	**1**	**0**	**0**	**2**	**0**	—	**0**	**0**	—	—	**0**	—	.250	.250	.375	.833
Career total		19	68	8	10	1	0	0	3	0	—	5	0	—	—	0	—	.147	.147	.162	.841
Cubs total		**2**	**8**	**1**	**2**	**1**	**0**	**0**	**2**	**0**	—	**0**	**0**	—	—	**0**	—	.250	.250	.375	.833

William (Bill) Alexander "Little Eva" Lange, of-2b, 1893–99

The legend of Billy Lange has out-stripped reality over the last century, but his is a compelling story nonetheless.

Lange was born on June 6, 1871, in San Francisco. He was a semipro star in California, a big man (6'1" 190 pounds) who could also run well for his size. He was signed by Chicago and won a starting job at second base immediately.

Lange was very light on his feet for such a big man, and was called "Little Eva" by his teammates. His first year in Chicago, he hit .281 and led the team in home runs with eight, and stolen bases with 47.

The next year, manager Cap Anson moved Lange out to center field and Lange responded by hitting .328 with 90 RBIs. It was the first of six consecutive years that Lange would hit .300. He also scored more than 110 runs three times and had at least 132 hits every year he played.

He was a terror on the base paths, although his feats over the years were sometimes exaggerated. In 1896, he reportedly stole 103 bases, which would have made him (and not Maury Wills) the first man to steal more than 100 bases in a season.

But a firm criteria for stolen bases was not developed until decades later. In the 19th century, players were credited for "stealing" a base if they took an extra base on a long single, or stretched a double into a triple. Later research showed that Lange stole "only" 84 bases in 1896. But he came back the next year and stole a league-leading 73.

He was also said to have walked away from the game at age 28 because of a woman, and that is true. Lange was engaged to the daughter of a wealthy San Francisco real estate baron, who would not let his daughter marry a ballplayer. Forced to choose between his bride-to-be and the game, he opted out of baseball.

It was a decision he later regretted. Although he became a wealthy businessman and part-time scout for the Cubs, Lange's marraige ended in divorce.

Lange is the Cubs' number two all-time base stealer with 399. He is also fourth all-time on the Cubs' batting average list with a .330 mark and 10th all-time on the Cubs' list of triples with 80. Lange died in San Francisco in 1950.

Law, Vance Aaron

HEIGHT: 6'2"   THROWS: RIGHT   BATS: RIGHT   BORN: 10/1/1956 BOISE, IDAHO   POSITIONS PLAYED: P, 1B, 2B, 3B, SS, OF

YEAR	TEAM	GAMES	AB	RUNS	HITS	2B	3B	HR	RBI	BB	IBB	SO	HBP	SH	SF	SB	CS	BA	OBA	SA	FA
1980	Pit-N	25	74	11	17	2	2	0	3	3	0	7	0	1	0	2	0	.230	.260	.311	.966
1981	Pit-N	30	67	1	9	0	1	0	3	2	0	15	0	1	1	1	1	.134	.157	.164	1.000
1982	CWS-A	114	359	40	101	20	1	5	54	26	1	46	1	7	5	4	2	.281	.327	.384	.947
1983	CWS-A	145	408	55	99	21	5	4	42	51	1	56	1	6	5	3	1	.243	.325	.348	.967
1984	CWS-A	151	481	60	121	18	2	17	59	41	2	75	1	6	4	4	1	.252	.309	.403	.958
1985	Mon-N	147	519	75	138	30	6	10	52	86	0	96	2	8	6	6	5	.266	.369	.405	.986
1986	Mon-N	112	360	37	81	17	2	5	44	37	1	66	1	2	2	3	5	.225	.298	.325	.993
1987	Mon-N	133	436	52	119	27	1	12	56	51	5	62	0	2	3	8	5	.273	.347	.422	.981
1988	**ChC-N**	**151**	**556**	**73**	**163**	**29**	**2**	**11**	**78**	**55**	**4**	**79**	**3**	**4**	**3**	**1**	**4**	**.293**	**.358**	**.412**	**.953**
1989	**ChC-N**	**130**	**408**	**38**	**96**	**22**	**3**	**7**	**42**	**38**	**0**	**73**	**0**	**1**	**7**	**2**	**2**	**.235**	**.296**	**.355**	**.949**
1991	Oak-A	74	134	11	28	7	1	0	9	18	0	27	0	5	0	0	0	.209	.303	.276	.955
Career average		110	346	41	88	18	2	6	40	37	1	55	1	4	3	3	2	.256	.326	.376	.971
Cubs average		**141**	**482**	**56**	**130**	**26**	**3**	**9**	**60**	**47**	**2**	**76**	**2**	**3**	**5**	**2**	**3**	**.269**	**.332**	**.388**	**.952**
Career total		1212	3802	453	972	193	26	71	442	408	14	602	9	43	36	34	26	.256	.326	.376	.971
Cubs total		**281**	**964**	**111**	**259**	**51**	**5**	**18**	**120**	**93**	**4**	**152**	**3**	**5**	**10**	**3**	**6**	**.269**	**.332**	**.388**	**.952**

Lazzeri, Anthony Michael (Tony or Poosh 'Em Up Tony)

HEIGHT: 5'11"   THROWS: RIGHT   BATS: RIGHT   BORN: 12/6/1903 SAN FRANCISCO, CALIFORNIA   DIED: 8/6/1946 SAN FRANCISCO, CALIFORNIA
POSITIONS PLAYED: 1B, 2B, 3B, SS, OF

YEAR	TEAM	GAMES	AB	RUNS	HITS	2B	3B	HR	RBI	BB	IBB	SO	HBP	SH	SF	SB	CS	BA	OBA	SA	FA
1926	NYY-A	155	589	79	162	28	14	18	114	54	—	96	2	20	—	16	7	.275	.338	.462	.958
1927	NYY-A	153	570	92	176	29	8	18	102	69	—	82	0	21	—	22	14	.309	.383	.482	.965
1928	NYY-A	116	404	62	134	30	11	10	82	43	—	50	1	15	—	15	5	.332	.397	.535	.956
1929	NYY-A	147	545	101	193	37	11	18	106	68	—	45	4	18	—	9	10	.354	.429	.561	.969
1930	NYY-A	143	571	109	173	34	15	9	121	60	—	62	3	16	—	4	4	.303	.372	.462	.963
1931	NYY-A	135	484	67	129	27	7	8	83	79	—	80	1	4	—	18	9	.267	.371	.401	.974

(continued)

(Lazzeri, continued)

YEAR	TEAM	GAMES	AB	RUNS	HITS	2B	3B	HR	RBI	BB	IBB	SO	HBP	SH	SF	SB	CS	BA	OBA	SA	FA
1932	NYY-A	142	510	79	153	28	16	15	113	82	—	64	2	7	—	11	11	.300	.399	.506	.979
1933	NYY-A	139	523	94	154	22	12	18	104	73	—	62	2	4	—	15	7	.294	.383	.486	.968
1934	NYY-A	123	438	59	117	24	6	14	67	71	—	64	0	5	—	11	1	.267	.369	.445	.969
1935	NYY-A	130	477	72	130	18	6	13	83	63	—	75	3	1	—	11	5	.273	.361	.417	.968
1936	NYY-A	150	537	82	154	29	6	14	109	97	—	65	1	3	—	8	5	.287	.397	.441	.968
1937	NYY-A	126	446	56	109	21	3	14	70	71	—	76	0	1	—	7	1	.244	.348	.399	.966
1938	**ChC-N**	**54**	**120**	**21**	**32**	**5**	**0**	**5**	**23**	**22**	**—**	**30**	**0**	**1**	**—**	**0**	**—**	**.267**	**.380**	**.433**	**.947**
1939	Bro-N	14	39	6	11	2	0	3	6	10	—	7	2	0	—	1	—	.282	.451	.564	.918
1939	NYG-N	13	44	7	13	0	0	1	8	7	—	6	0	0	—	0	—	.295	.392	.364	.889
Career average		124	450	70	131	24	8	13	85	62	—	62	2	8	—	11	6	.292	.380	.467	.966
Cubs average		**54**	**120**	**21**	**32**	**5**	**0**	**5**	**23**	**22**	**—**	**30**	**0**	**1**	**—**	**0**	**0**	**.267**	**.380**	**.433**	**.947**
Career total		1740	6297	986	1840	334	115	178	1191	869	—	864	21	116	—	148	79	.292	.380	.467	.966
Cubs total		**54**	**120**	**21**	**32**	**5**	**0**	**5**	**23**	**22**	**—**	**30**	**0**	**1**	**—**	**0**	**0**	**.267**	**.380**	**.433**	**.947**

Leach, Thomas William (Tommy *or* The Wee)

HEIGHT: 5'6" THROWS: RIGHT BATS: RIGHT BORN: 11/4/1877 FRENCH CREEK, NEW YORK DIED: 9/29/1969 HAINES CITY, FLORIDA
POSITIONS PLAYED: 2B, 3B, SS, OF

YEAR	TEAM	GAMES	AB	RUNS	HITS	2B	3B	HR	RBI	BB	IBB	SO	HBP	SH	SF	SB	CS	BA	OBA	SA	FA
1898	Lou-N	3	10	0	1	0	0	0	0	0	—	—	0	0	—	0	—	.100	.100	.100	.750
1899	Lou-N	106	406	75	117	10	6	5	57	37	—	—	1	10	—	19	—	.288	.349	.379	.886
1900	Pit-N	51	160	20	34	1	2	1	16	21	—	—	0	5	—	8	—	.213	.304	.263	.888
1901	Pit-N	98	374	64	114	12	13	2	44	20	—	—	4	10	—	16	—	.305	.347	.422	.906
1902	Pit-N	135	514	97	143	14	22	6	85	45	—	—	4	13	—	25	—	.278	.341	.426	.926
1903	Pit-N	127	507	97	151	16	17	7	87	40	—	—	2	12	—	22	—	.298	.352	.438	.879
1904	Pit-N	146	579	92	149	15	12	2	56	45	—	—	5	4	—	23	—	.257	.316	.335	.907
1905	Pit-N	131	499	71	128	10	14	2	53	37	—	—	1	17	—	17	—	.257	.309	.345	.960
1906	Pit-N	133	476	66	136	10	7	1	39	33	—	—	1	16	—	21	—	.286	.333	.342	.946
1907	Pit-N	149	547	102	166	19	12	4	43	40	—	—	1	29	—	43	—	.303	.352	.404	.947
1908	Pit-N	152	583	93	151	24	16	5	41	54	—	—	2	27	—	24	—	.259	.324	.381	.938
1909	Pit-N	151	587	126	153	29	8	6	43	66	—	—	2	27	—	27	—	.261	.337	.368	.968
1910	Pit-N	135	529	83	143	24	5	4	52	38	—	62	0	20	—	18	—	.270	.319	.357	.964
1911	Pit-N	108	386	60	92	12	6	3	43	46	—	50	2	12	—	19	—	.238	.323	.324	.975
1912	Pit-N	28	97	24	29	4	2	0	19	12	—	9	0	1	—	6	—	.299	.376	.381	.986
1912	**ChC-N**	**82**	**265**	**50**	**64**	**10**	**3**	**2**	**32**	**55**	**—**	**20**	**3**	**6**	**—**	**14**	**—**	**.242**	**.378**	**.325**	**.972**
1913	**ChC-N**	**131**	**456**	**99**	**131**	**23**	**10**	**6**	**32**	**77**	**—**	**44**	**1**	**6**	**—**	**21**	**—**	**.287**	**.391**	**.421**	**.980**
1914	**ChC-N**	**153**	**577**	**80**	**152**	**24**	**9**	**7**	**46**	**79**	**—**	**50**	**1**	**19**	**—**	**16**	**—**	**.263**	**.353**	**.373**	**.956**
1915	Cin-N	107	335	42	75	7	5	0	17	56	—	38	2	3	—	20	14	.224	.338	.275	.959
1918	Pit-N	30	72	14	14	2	3	0	5	19	—	5	0	3	—	2	—	.194	.363	.306	.909
Career average		113	419	71	113	14	9	3	43	43	—	15	2	13	—	19	1	.269	.340	.370	.934
Cubs average		**122**	**433**	**76**	**116**	**19**	**7**	**5**	**37**	**70**	**—**	**38**	**2**	**10**	**—**	**17**	**—**	**.267**	**.372**	**.380**	**.967**
Career total		2156	7959	1355	2143	266	172	63	810	820	—	278	32	240	—	361	14	.269	.340	.370	.934
Cubs total		**366**	**1298**	**229**	**347**	**57**	**22**	**15**	**110**	**211**	**—**	**114**	**5**	**31**	**—**	**51**	**—**	**.267**	**.372**	**.380**	**.967**

Lear, Frederick Francis (Fred *or* King)

HEIGHT: 6'0" THROWS: RIGHT BATS: RIGHT BORN: 4/7/1894 NEW YORK, NEW YORK DIED: 10/13/1955 EAST ORANGE, NEW JERSEY
POSITIONS PLAYED: 1B, 2B, 3B, SS

YEAR	TEAM	GAMES	AB	RUNS	HITS	2B	3B	HR	RBI	BB	IBB	SO	HBP	SH	SF	SB	CS	BA	OBA	SA	FA
1915	Phi-A	2	2	0	0	0	0	0	0	0	—	2	0	0	—	0	0	.000	.000	.000	.600
1918	**ChC-N**	**2**	**1**	**0**	**0**	**0**	**0**	**0**	**0**	**1**	**—**	**0**	**0**	**0**	**—**	**0**	**—**	**.000**	**.500**	**.000**	**—**
1919	**ChC-N**	**40**	**76**	**8**	**17**	**3**	**1**	**1**	**11**	**8**	**—**	**11**	**1**	**3**	**—**	**2**	**—**	**.224**	**.306**	**.329**	**.967**
1920	NYG-N	31	87	12	22	0	1	1	7	8	—	15	1	1	—	0	2	.253	.323	.310	.952
Career average		19	42	5	10	1	1	1	5	4	—	7	1	1	—	1	1	.235	.314	.313	.955
Cubs average		**21**	**39**	**4**	**9**	**2**	**1**	**1**	**6**	**5**	**—**	**6**	**1**	**2**	**—**	**1**	**0**	**.221**	**.310**	**.325**	**.967**
Career total		75	166	20	39	3	2	2	18	17	—	28	2	4	—	2	2	.235	.314	.313	.955
Cubs total		**42**	**77**	**8**	**17**	**3**	**1**	**1**	**11**	**9**	**—**	**11**	**1**	**3**	**—**	**2**	**0**	**.221**	**.310**	**.325**	**.967**

Leathers, Harold Langford (Hal *or* Chuck)

HEIGHT: 5'8" THROWS: RIGHT BATS: LEFT BORN: 12/2/1898 SELMA, CALIFORNIA DIED: 4/12/1977 MODESTO, CALIFORNIA POSITIONS PLAYED: 2B, SS

YEAR	TEAM	GAMES	AB	RUNS	HITS	2B	3B	HR	RBI	BB	IBB	SO	HBP	SH	SF	SB	CS	BA	OBA	SA	FA
1920	ChC-N	9	23	3	7	1	0	1	1	1	—	1	0	1	—	1	0	.304	.333	.478	.837
Career average		9	23	3	7	1	0	1	1	1	—	1	0	1	—	1	0	.304	.333	.478	.837
Cubs average		**9**	**23**	**3**	**7**	**1**	**0**	**1**	**1**	**1**	**—**	**1**	**0**	**1**	**—**	**1**	**0**	**.304**	**.333**	**.478**	**.837**
Career total		9	23	3	7	1	0	1	1	1	—	1	0	1	—	1	0	.304	.333	.478	.837
Cubs total		**9**	**23**	**3**	**7**	**1**	**0**	**1**	**1**	**1**	**—**	**1**	**0**	**1**	**—**	**1**	**0**	**.304**	**.333**	**.478**	**.837**

Leiber, Henry Edward (Hank *or* Goldilocks)
HEIGHT: 6'1" THROWS: RIGHT BATS: RIGHT BORN: 1/17/1911 PHOENIX, ARIZONA DIED: 11/8/1993 TUCSON, ARIZONA POSITIONS PLAYED: P, 1B, OF

YEAR	TEAM	GAMES	AB	RUNS	HITS	2B	3B	HR	RBI	BB	IBB	SO	HBP	SH	SF	SB	CS	BA	OBA	SA	FA
1933	NYG-N	6	10	1	2	0	0	0	0	0	—	2	0	0	—	0	—	.200	.200	.200	1.000
1934	NYG-N	63	187	17	45	5	3	2	25	4	—	13	0	4	—	1	—	.241	.257	.332	.971
1935	NYG-N	154	613	110	203	37	4	22	107	48	—	29	10	9	—	0	—	.331	.389	.512	.965
1936	NYG-N	101	337	44	94	19	7	9	67	37	—	41	1	9	—	1	—	.279	.352	.457	.961
1937	NYG-N	51	184	24	54	7	3	4	32	15	—	27	0	3	—	1	—	.293	.347	.429	.988
1938	NYG-N	98	360	50	97	18	4	12	65	31	—	45	0	3	—	0	—	.269	.327	.442	.974
1939	**ChC-N**	**112**	**365**	**65**	**113**	**16**	**1**	**24**	**88**	**59**	—	**42**	**4**	**3**	—	**1**	—	**.310**	**.411**	**.556**	**.977**
1940	**ChC-N**	**117**	**440**	**68**	**133**	**24**	**2**	**17**	**86**	**45**	—	**68**	**3**	**3**	—	**1**	—	**.302**	**.371**	**.482**	**.985**
1941	**ChC-N**	**53**	**162**	**20**	**35**	**5**	**0**	**7**	**25**	**16**	—	**25**	**1**	**5**	—	**0**	—	**.216**	**.291**	**.377**	**.976**
1942	NYG-N	58	147	11	32	6	0	4	23	19	—	27	2	1	—	0	—	.218	.315	.340	.980
Career average		81	281	41	81	14	2	10	52	27	—	32	2	4	—	1	—	.288	.356	.462	.974
Cubs average		**94**	**322**	**51**	**94**	**15**	**1**	**16**	**66**	**40**	—	**45**	**3**	**4**	—	**1**	—	**.291**	**.374**	**.492**	**.980**
Career total		813	2805	410	808	137	24	101	518	274	—	319	21	40	—	5	—	.288	.356	.462	.974
Cubs total		**282**	**967**	**153**	**281**	**45**	**3**	**48**	**199**	**120**	—	**135**	**8**	**11**	—	**2**	—	**.291**	**.374**	**.492**	**.980**

Lennon, Robert Albert (Bob *or* Arch)
HEIGHT: 6'0" THROWS: LEFT BATS: LEFT BORN: 9/15/1928 BROOKLYN, NEW YORK POSITIONS PLAYED: OF

YEAR	TEAM	GAMES	AB	RUNS	HITS	2B	3B	HR	RBI	BB	IBB	SO	HBP	SH	SF	SB	CS	BA	OBA	SA	FA
1954	NYG-N	3	3	0	0	0	0	0	0	0	—	0	0	0	0	0	0	.000	.000	.000	—
1956	NYG-N	26	55	3	10	1	0	0	1	4	1	17	0	0	1	0	0	.182	.233	.200	.885
1957	**ChC-N**	**9**	**21**	**2**	**3**	**1**	**0**	**1**	**3**	**1**	**0**	**9**	**0**	**0**	**0**	**0**	**0**	**.143**	**.182**	**.333**	**1.000**
Career average		13	26	2	4	1	0	0	1	2	0	9	0	0	0	0	0	.165	.212	.228	.900
Cubs average		**9**	**21**	**2**	**3**	**1**	**0**	**1**	**3**	**1**	**0**	**9**	**0**	**0**	**0**	**0**	**0**	**.143**	**.182**	**.333**	**1.000**
Career total		38	79	5	13	2	0	1	4	5	1	26	0	0	1	0	0	.165	.212	.228	.900
Cubs total		**9**	**21**	**2**	**3**	**1**	**0**	**1**	**3**	**1**	**0**	**9**	**0**	**0**	**0**	**0**	**0**	**.143**	**.182**	**.333**	**1.000**

Lennox, James Edgar (Ed *or* Eggie)
HEIGHT: 5'10" THROWS: RIGHT BATS: RIGHT BORN: 11/3/1885 CAMDEN, NEW JERSEY DIED: 10/26/1939 CAMDEN, NEW JERSEY POSITIONS PLAYED: 3B

YEAR	TEAM	GAMES	AB	RUNS	HITS	2B	3B	HR	RBI	BB	IBB	SO	HBP	SH	SF	SB	CS	BA	OBA	SA	FA
1906	Phi-A	6	17	1	1	1	0	0	0	1	—	—	0	0	—	0	—	.059	.111	.118	.909
1909	Bro-N	126	435	33	114	18	9	2	44	47	—	—	2	13	—	11	—	.262	.337	.359	.959
1910	Bro-N	110	367	19	95	19	4	3	32	36	—	39	5	10	—	7	—	.259	.333	.357	.950
1912	**ChC-N**	**27**	**81**	**13**	**19**	**4**	**1**	**1**	**16**	**12**	—	**10**	**2**	**6**	—	**1**	—	**.235**	**.347**	**.346**	**.934**
1914	Pit-F	124	430	71	134	25	10	11	84	71	—	38	4	14	—	19	—	.312	.414	.493	.954
1915	Pit-F	55	53	1	16	3	1	1	9	7	—	12	0	1	—	0	—	.302	.383	.453	1.000
Career average		75	231	23	63	12	4	3	31	29	—	17	2	7	—	6	—	.274	.361	.400	.953
Cubs average		**27**	**81**	**13**	**19**	**4**	**1**	**1**	**16**	**12**	—	**10**	**2**	**6**	—	**1**	—	**.235**	**.347**	**.346**	**.934**
Career total		448	1383	138	379	70	25	18	185	174	—	99	13	44	—	38	—	.274	.361	.400	.953
Cubs total		**27**	**81**	**13**	**19**	**4**	**1**	**1**	**16**	**12**	—	**10**	**2**	**6**	—	**1**	—	**.235**	**.347**	**.346**	**.934**

Leslie, Roy Reid
HEIGHT: 6'1" THROWS: RIGHT BATS: RIGHT BORN: 8/23/1894 BAILEY, TEXAS DIED: 4/9/1972 SHERMAN, TEXAS POSITIONS PLAYED: 1B

YEAR	TEAM	GAMES	AB	RUNS	HITS	2B	3B	HR	RBI	BB	IBB	SO	HBP	SH	SF	SB	CS	BA	OBA	SA	FA
1917	**ChC-N**	**7**	**19**	**1**	**4**	**0**	**0**	**0**	**1**	**1**	—	**5**	**0**	**0**	—	**1**	—	**.211**	**.250**	**.211**	**.969**
1919	StL-N	12	24	2	5	1	0	0	4	4	—	3	0	0	—	0	—	.208	.321	.250	.957
1922	Phi-N	141	513	44	139	23	2	6	50	37	—	49	0	17	—	3	7	.271	.320	.359	.990
Career average		53	185	16	49	8	1	2	18	14	—	19	0	6	—	1	2	.266	.318	.349	.988
Cubs average		**7**	**19**	**1**	**4**	**0**	**0**	**0**	**1**	**1**	—	**5**	**0**	**0**	—	**1**	—	**.211**	**.250**	**.211**	**.969**
Career total		160	556	47	148	24	2	6	55	42	—	57	0	17	—	4	7	.266	.318	.349	.988
Cubs total		**7**	**19**	**1**	**4**	**0**	**0**	**0**	**1**	**1**	—	**5**	**0**	**0**	—	**1**	—	**.211**	**.250**	**.211**	**.969**

Lezcano, Carlos Manuel
HEIGHT: 6'2" THROWS: RIGHT BATS: RIGHT BORN: 9/30/1955 ARECIBO, PUERTO RICO POSITIONS PLAYED: OF

YEAR	TEAM	GAMES	AB	RUNS	HITS	2B	3B	HR	RBI	BB	IBB	SO	HBP	SH	SF	SB	CS	BA	OBA	SA	FA
1980	ChC-N	42	88	15	18	4	1	3	12	11	0	29	1	2	2	1	2	.205	.294	.375	.948
1981	ChC-N	7	14	1	1	0	0	0	2	0	0	4	0	0	0	0	0	.071	.071	.071	1.000
Career average		25	51	8	10	2	1	2	7	6	0	17	1	1	1	1	1	.186	.267	.333	.952
Cubs average		25	51	8	10	2	1	2	7	6	0	17	1	1	1	1	1	.186	.267	.333	.952
Career total		49	102	16	19	4	1	3	14	11	0	33	1	2	2	1	2	.186	.267	.333	.952
Cubs total		49	102	16	19	4	1	3	14	11	0	33	1	2	2	1	2	.186	.267	.333	.952

Lindstrom, Frederick Charles (Freddy *or* Lindy)
HEIGHT: 5'11" THROWS: RIGHT BATS: RIGHT BORN: 11/21/1905 CHICAGO, ILLINOIS DIED: 10/4/1981 CHICAGO, ILLINOIS
POSITIONS PLAYED: 2B, 3B, SS, OF

YEAR	TEAM	GAMES	AB	RUNS	HITS	2B	3B	HR	RBI	BB	IBB	SO	HBP	SH	SF	SB	CS	BA	OBA	SA	FA
1924	NYG-N	52	79	19	20	3	1	0	4	6	—	10	1	2	—	3	1	.253	.314	.316	.935
1925	NYG-N	104	356	43	102	15	12	4	33	22	—	20	2	5	—	5	9	.287	.332	.430	.953
1926	NYG-N	140	543	90	164	19	9	9	76	39	—	21	2	28	—	11	—	.302	.351	.420	.962
1927	NYG-N	138	562	107	172	36	8	7	58	40	—	40	2	15	—	10	—	.306	.354	.436	.968
1928	NYG-N	153	646	99	231	39	9	14	107	25	—	21	2	14	—	15	—	.358	.383	.511	.958
1929	NYG-N	130	549	99	175	23	6	15	91	30	—	28	0	21	—	10	—	.319	.354	.464	.966
1930	NYG-N	148	609	127	231	39	7	22	106	48	—	33	0	14	—	15	—	.379	.425	.575	.953
1931	NYG-N	78	303	38	91	12	6	5	36	26	—	12	0	0	—	5	—	.300	.356	.429	.960
1932	NYG-N	144	595	83	161	26	5	15	92	27	—	28	1	3	—	6	—	.271	.303	.407	.973
1933	Pit-N	138	538	70	167	39	10	5	55	33	—	22	0	25	—	1	—	.310	.350	.448	.988
1934	Pit-N	97	383	59	111	24	4	4	49	23	—	21	2	6	—	1	—	.290	.333	.405	.990
1935	**ChC-N**	**90**	**342**	**49**	**94**	**22**	**4**	**3**	**62**	**10**	**—**	**13**	**1**	**10**	**—**	**1**	**—**	**.275**	**.297**	**.389**	**.967**
1936	Bro-N	26	106	12	28	4	0	0	10	5	—	7	0	3	—	1	—	.264	.297	.302	.982
Career average		111	432	69	134	23	6	8	60	26	—	21	1	11	—	6	1	.311	.351	.449	.965
Cubs average		**90**	**342**	**49**	**94**	**22**	**4**	**3**	**62**	**10**	**—**	**13**	**1**	**10**	**—**	**1**	**0**	**.275**	**.297**	**.389**	**.967**
Career total		1438	5611	895	1747	301	81	103	779	334	—	276	13	146	—	84	10	.311	.351	.449	.965
Cubs total		**90**	**342**	**49**	**94**	**22**	**4**	**3**	**62**	**10**	**—**	**13**	**1**	**10**	**—**	**1**	**0**	**.275**	**.297**	**.389**	**.967**

Liniak, Cole Edward
HEIGHT: 6'1" THROWS: RIGHT BATS: RIGHT BORN: 8/23/1976 ENCINITAS, CALIFORNIA POSITIONS PLAYED: 3B

YEAR	TEAM	GAMES	AB	RUNS	HITS	2B	3B	HR	RBI	BB	IBB	SO	HBP	SH	SF	SB	CS	BA	OBA	SA	FA
1999	ChC-N	12	29	3	7	2	0	0	2	1	0	4	0	0	0	0	1	.241	.267	.310	1.000
2000	ChC-N	3	3	0	0	0	0	0	0	0	0	2	0	0	0	0	0	.000	.000	.000	—
Career average		8	16	2	4	1	0	0	1	1	0	3	0	0	0	0	1	.219	.242	.281	1.000
Cubs average		8	16	2	4	1	0	0	1	1	0	3	0	0	0	0	1	.219	.242	.281	1.000
Career total		15	32	3	7	2	0	0	2	1	0	6	0	0	0	0	1	.219	.242	.281	1.000
Cubs total		15	32	3	7	2	0	0	2	1	0	6	0	0	0	0	1	.219	.242	.281	1.000

Littrell, Jack Napier
HEIGHT: 6'0" THROWS: RIGHT BATS: RIGHT BORN: 1/22/1929 LOUISVILLE, KENTUCKY POSITIONS PLAYED: 1B, 2B, 3B, SS

YEAR	TEAM	GAMES	AB	RUNS	HITS	2B	3B	HR	RBI	BB	IBB	SO	HBP	SH	SF	SB	CS	BA	OBA	SA	FA
1952	Phi-A	4	2	0	0	0	0	0	0	1	—	2	0	0	—	0	0	.000	.333	.000	1.000
1954	Phi-A	9	30	7	9	2	0	1	3	6	—	3	0	0	0	1	0	.300	.417	.467	.976
1955	KCA-A	37	70	7	14	0	1	0	1	4	0	12	0	2	0	0	0	.200	.243	.229	.946
1957	**ChC-N**	**61**	**153**	**8**	**29**	**4**	**2**	**1**	**13**	**9**	**1**	**43**	**0**	**1**	**1**	**0**	**0**	**.190**	**.233**	**.261**	**.947**
Career average		28	64	6	13	2	1	1	4	5	0	15	0	1	0	0	0	.204	.261	.275	.950
Cubs average		**61**	**153**	**8**	**29**	**4**	**2**	**1**	**13**	**9**	**1**	**43**	**0**	**1**	**1**	**0**	**0**	**.190**	**.233**	**.261**	**.947**
Career total		111	255	22	52	6	3	2	17	20	1	60	0	3	1	1	0	.204	.261	.275	.950
Cubs total		**61**	**153**	**8**	**29**	**4**	**2**	**1**	**13**	**9**	**1**	**43**	**0**	**1**	**1**	**0**	**0**	**.190**	**.233**	**.261**	**.947**

Livingston, Thompson Orville (Mickey)

HEIGHT: 6'1" THROWS: RIGHT BATS: RIGHT BORN: 11/15/1914 NEWBERRY, SOUTH CAROLINA DIED: 4/3/1983 NEWBERRY, SOUTH CAROLINA
POSITIONS PLAYED: C, 1B

YEAR	TEAM	GAMES	AB	RUNS	HITS	2B	3B	HR	RBI	BB	IBB	SO	HBP	SH	SF	SB	CS	BA	OBA	SA	FA
1938	Was-A	2	4	0	3	2	0	0	1	0	—	1	0	0	—	0	0	.750	.750	1.250	.667
1941	Phi-N	95	207	16	42	6	1	0	18	20	—	38	1	0	—	2	—	.203	.276	.242	.974
1942	Phi-N	89	239	20	49	6	1	2	22	25	—	20	1	3	—	0	—	.205	.283	.264	.987
1943	Phi-N	84	265	25	66	9	2	3	18	19	—	18	1	1	—	1	—	.249	.304	.332	.988
1943	**ChC-N**	**36**	**111**	**11**	**29**	**5**	**1**	**4**	**16**	**12**	**—**	**8**	**0**	**1**	**—**	**1**	**—**	**.261**	**.333**	**.432**	**1.000**
1945	**ChC-N**	**71**	**224**	**19**	**57**	**4**	**2**	**2**	**23**	**19**	**—**	**6**	**0**	**1**	**—**	**1**	**—**	**.254**	**.324**	**.317**	**.990**
1946	**ChC-N**	**66**	**176**	**14**	**45**	**14**	**0**	**2**	**20**	**20**	**—**	**19**	**4**	**6**	**—**	**2**	**—**	**.256**	**.338**	**.369**	**.981**
1947	**ChC-N**	**19**	**33**	**2**	**7**	**2**	**0**	**0**	**3**	**1**	**—**	**5**	**2**	**3**	**—**	**0**	**—**	**.212**	**.235**	**.273**	**1.000**
1947	NYG-N	5	6	0	1	0	0	0	0	1	—	2	0	1	—	0	—	.167	.286	.167	.800
1948	NYG-N	45	99	9	21	4	1	2	12	21	—	11	0	2	—	1	—	.212	.350	.333	.980
1949	NYG-N	19	57	6	17	2	0	4	12	2	—	8	1	0	—	0	0	.298	.333	.544	.985
1949	Bos-N	28	64	6	15	2	1	0	6	3	—	5	2	0	—	0	0	.234	.290	.297	.977
1951	Bro-N	2	5	0	2	0	0	0	2	1	—	0	0	1	—	0	0	.400	.500	.400	1.000
Career average		56	149	13	35	6	1	2	15	14	—	14	1	2	—	1	0	.238	.310	.326	.984
Cubs average		**48**	**136**	**12**	**35**	**6**	**1**	**2**	**16**	**13**	**—**	**10**	**2**	**3**	**—**	**1**	**0**	**.254**	**.326**	**.355**	**.989**
Career total		561	1490	128	354	56	9	19	153	144	—	141	13	18	—	7	0	.238	.310	.326	.984
Cubs total		**192**	**544**	**46**	**138**	**25**	**3**	**8**	**62**	**52**	**—**	**38**	**6**	**11**	**—**	**3**	**0**	**.254**	**.326**	**.355**	**.989**

Lobert, John Bernard (Hans or Honus)

HEIGHT: 5'9" THROWS: RIGHT BATS: RIGHT BORN: 10/18/1881 WILMINGTON, DELAWARE DIED: 9/14/1968 PHILADELPHIA, PENNSYLVANIA
POSITIONS PLAYED: 2B, 3B, SS, OF

YEAR	TEAM	GAMES	AB	RUNS	HITS	2B	3B	HR	RBI	BB	IBB	SO	HBP	SH	SF	SB	CS	BA	OBA	SA	FA
1903	Pit-N	5	13	1	1	1	0	0	0	1	—	—	0	1	—	1	—	.077	.143	.154	.824
1905	**ChC-N**	**14**	**46**	**7**	**9**	**2**	**0**	**0**	**1**	**3**	**—**	**—**	**1**	**6**	**—**	**4**	**—**	**.196**	**.260**	**.239**	**.918**
1906	Cin-N	79	268	39	83	5	5	0	19	19	—	—	5	13	—	20	—	.310	.366	.366	.937
1907	Cin-N	148	537	61	132	9	12	1	41	37	—	—	4	27	—	30	—	.246	.299	.313	.939
1908	Cin-N	155	570	71	167	17	18	4	63	46	—	—	2	32	—	47	—	.293	.348	.407	.921
1909	Cin-N	122	425	50	90	13	5	4	52	48	—	—	8	14	—	30	—	.212	.304	.294	.931
1910	Cin-N	93	314	43	97	6	6	3	40	30	—	9	0	20	—	41	—	.309	.369	.395	.932
1911	Phi-N	147	541	94	154	20	9	9	72	66	—	31	5	38	—	40	—	.285	.368	.405	.954
1912	Phi-N	65	257	37	84	12	5	2	33	19	—	13	0	10	—	13	—	.327	.373	.436	.976
1913	Phi-N	150	573	98	172	28	11	7	55	42	—	34	5	26	—	41	—	.300	.353	.424	.974
1914	Phi-N	135	505	83	139	24	5	1	52	49	—	32	3	24	—	31	—	.275	.343	.349	.944
1915	NYG-N	106	386	46	97	18	4	0	38	25	—	24	4	15	—	14	15	.251	.304	.319	.950
1916	NYG-N	48	76	6	17	3	2	0	11	5	—	8	0	4	—	2	—	.224	.272	.316	.961
1917	NYG-N	50	52	4	10	1	0	1	5	5	—	5	1	1	—	2	—	.192	.276	.269	.906
Career average		94	326	46	89	11	6	2	34	28	—	11	3	17	—	23	1	.274	.337	.366	.942
Cubs average		**14**	**46**	**7**	**9**	**2**	**0**	**0**	**1**	**3**	**—**	**—**	**1**	**6**	**—**	**4**	**—**	**.196**	**.260**	**.239**	**.918**
Career total		1317	4563	640	1252	159	82	32	482	395	—	156	38	231	—	316	15	.274	.337	.366	.942
Cubs total		**14**	**46**	**7**	**9**	**2**	**0**	**0**	**1**	**3**	**—**	**—**	**1**	**6**	**—**	**4**	**—**	**.196**	**.260**	**.239**	**.918**

Long, Richard Dale (Dale)

HEIGHT: 6'4" THROWS: LEFT BATS: LEFT BORN: 2/6/1926 SPRINGFIELD, MISSOURI DIED: 1/27/1991 PALM COAST, FLORIDA POSITIONS PLAYED: C, 1B, OF

YEAR	TEAM	GAMES	AB	RUNS	HITS	2B	3B	HR	RBI	BB	IBB	SO	HBP	SH	SF	SB	CS	BA	OBA	SA	FA
1951	Pit-N	10	12	1	2	0	0	1	1	0	—	3	0	0	—	0	0	.167	.167	.417	1.000
1951	StL-A	34	105	11	25	5	1	2	11	10	—	22	1	0	—	0	0	.238	.310	.362	.988
1955	Pit-N	131	419	59	122	19	13	16	79	48	6	72	1	6	4	0	1	.291	.362	.513	.988
1956	Pit-N	148	517	64	136	20	7	27	91	54	11	85	1	0	11	1	0	.263	.326	.485	.982
1957	Pit-N	7	22	0	4	1	0	0	5	4	1	10	0	0	1	0	0	.182	.296	.227	1.000
1957	**ChC-N**	**123**	**397**	**55**	**121**	**19**	**0**	**21**	**62**	**52**	**4**	**63**	**1**	**1**	**4**	**1**	**1**	**.305**	**.383**	**.511**	**.995**
1958	**ChC-N**	**142**	**480**	**68**	**130**	**26**	**4**	**20**	**75**	**66**	**9**	**64**	**2**	**0**	**6**	**2**	**0**	**.271**	**.357**	**.467**	**.992**
1959	**ChC-N**	**110**	**296**	**34**	**70**	**10**	**3**	**14**	**37**	**31**	**2**	**53**	**0**	**0**	**3**	**0**	**0**	**.236**	**.306**	**.432**	**.985**
1960	SF-N	37	54	4	9	0	0	3	6	7	1	7	0	0	0	0	0	.167	.262	.333	1.000
1960	NYY-A	26	41	6	15	3	1	3	10	5	0	6	0	0	0	0	0	.366	.435	.707	.988
1961	Was-A	123	377	52	94	20	4	17	49	39	5	41	1	0	6	0	0	.249	.317	.459	.983
1962	Was-A	67	191	17	46	8	0	4	24	18	0	22	1	0	2	5	1	.241	.307	.346	.996
1962	NYY-A	41	94	12	28	4	0	4	17	18	0	9	0	0	2	1	0	.298	.404	.468	.992
1963	NYY-A	14	15	1	3	0	0	0	0	1	0	3	0	0	0	0	0	.200	.250	.200	.917
Career average		101	302	38	81	14	3	13	47	35	4	46	1	1	4	1	0	.267	.341	.464	.988
Cubs average		**125**	**391**	**52**	**107**	**18**	**2**	**18**	**58**	**50**	**5**	**60**	**1**	**0**	**4**	**1**	**0**	**.267**	**.341**	**.464**	**.988**
Career total		1013	3020	384	805	135	33	132	467	353	40	460	7	7	39	10	3	.274	.354	.473	.991
Cubs total		**375**	**1173**	**157**	**321**	**55**	**7**	**55**	**174**	**149**	**15**	**180**	**3**	**1**	**13**	**3**	**1**	**.274**	**.354**	**.473**	**.991**

Lopes, David Earl (Davey)

HEIGHT: 5'9" THROWS: RIGHT BATS: RIGHT BORN: 5/3/1945 EAST PROVIDENCE, RHODE ISLAND POSITIONS PLAYED: 2B, 3B, SS, OF

YEAR	TEAM	GAMES	AB	RUNS	HITS	2B	3B	HR	RBI	BB	IBB	SO	HBP	SH	SF	SB	CS	BA	OBA	SA	FA
1972	LA-N	11	42	6	9	4	0	0	1	7	0	6	0	0	0	4	0	.214	.327	.310	.964
1973	LA-N	142	535	77	147	13	5	6	37	62	6	77	5	7	6	36	16	.275	.352	.351	.985
1974	LA-N	145	530	95	141	26	3	10	35	66	3	71	4	10	3	59	18	.266	.350	.383	.965
1975	LA-N	155	618	108	162	24	6	8	41	91	3	93	2	13	2	77	12	.262	.358	.359	.979
1976	LA-N	117	427	72	103	17	7	4	20	56	1	49	4	2	2	63	10	.241	.333	.342	.965
1977	LA-N	134	502	85	142	19	5	11	53	73	3	69	2	6	6	47	12	.283	.372	.406	.979
1978	LA-N	151	587	93	163	25	4	17	58	71	3	70	0	6	1	45	4	.278	.355	.421	.974
1979	LA-N	153	582	109	154	20	6	28	73	97	4	88	4	6	3	44	4	.265	.372	.464	.981
1980	LA-N	141	553	79	139	15	3	10	49	58	2	71	1	9	4	23	7	.251	.321	.344	.980
1981	LA-N	58	214	35	44	2	0	5	17	22	1	35	3	4	0	20	2	.206	.289	.285	.993
1982	Oak-A	128	450	58	109	19	3	11	42	40	1	51	1	2	3	28	12	.242	.304	.371	.977
1983	Oak-A	147	494	64	137	13	4	17	67	51	7	61	2	4	10	22	4	.277	.341	.423	.984
1984	Oak-A	72	230	32	59	11	1	9	36	31	1	36	1	2	3	12	0	.257	.343	.430	.961
1984	**ChC-N**	**16**	**17**	**5**	**4**	**1**	**0**	**0**	**0**	**6**	**0**	**5**	**0**	**0**	**0**	**3**	**0**	**.235**	**.435**	**.294**	**1.000**
1985	**ChC-N**	**99**	**275**	**52**	**78**	**11**	**0**	**11**	**44**	**46**	**1**	**37**	**0**	**1**	**3**	**47**	**4**	**.284**	**.383**	**.444**	**.992**
1986	**ChC-N**	**59**	**157**	**38**	**47**	**8**	**2**	**6**	**22**	**31**	**0**	**16**	**2**	**0**	**1**	**17**	**6**	**.299**	**.419**	**.490**	**.929**
1986	Hou-N	37	98	11	23	2	1	1	13	12	0	9	0	2	1	8	2	.235	.315	.306	1.000
1987	Hou-N	47	43	4	10	2	0	1	6	13	2	8	0	0	0	2	1	.233	.411	.349	.857
Career average		113	397	64	104	15	3	10	38	52	2	53	2	5	3	35	7	.287	.398	.454	.977
Cubs average		**58**	**150**	**32**	**43**	**7**	**1**	**6**	**22**	**28**	**0**	**19**	**1**	**0**	**1**	**22**	**3**	**.287**	**.398**	**.454**	**.963**
Career total		1812	6354	1023	1671	232	50	155	614	833	38	852	31	74	48	557	114	.287	.398	.454	.963
Cubs total		**174**	**449**	**95**	**129**	**20**	**2**	**17**	**66**	**83**	**1**	**58**	**2**	**1**	**4**	**67**	**10**	**.263**	**.349**	**.388**	**.977**

Loviglio, John Paul (Jay)

HEIGHT: 5'9" THROWS: RIGHT BATS: RIGHT BORN: 5/30/1956 FREEPORT, NEW YORK POSITIONS PLAYED: 2B, 3B

YEAR	TEAM	GAMES	AB	RUNS	HITS	2B	3B	HR	RBI	BB	IBB	SO	HBP	SH	SF	SB	CS	BA	OBA	SA	FA
1980	Phi-N	16	5	7	0	0	0	0	0	1	0	0	0	0	0	1	2	.000	.167	.000	1.000
1981	CWS-A	14	15	5	4	0	0	0	2	1	0	1	0	0	0	2	2	.267	.313	.267	.864
1982	CWS-A	15	31	5	6	0	0	0	2	1	0	4	0	1	0	2	1	.194	.219	.194	.964
1983	**ChC-N**	**1**	**1**	**0**	**0**	**0**	**0**	**0**	**0**	**0**	**0**	**1**	**0**	**0**	**0**	**0**	**0**	**.000**	**.000**	**.000**	**—**
Career average		12	13	4	3	0	0	0	1	1	0	2	0	0	0	1	1	.192	.236	.192	.940
Cubs average		**1**	**1**	**0**	**0**	**0**	**0**	**0**	**0**	**0**	**0**	**1**	**0**	**0**	**0**	**0**	**0**	**.000**	**.000**	**.000**	**—**
Career total		46	52	17	10	0	0	0	4	3	0	6	0	1	0	5	5	.192	.236	.192	.940
Cubs total		**1**	**1**	**0**	**0**	**0**	**0**	**0**	**0**	**0**	**0**	**1**	**0**	**0**	**0**	**0**	**0**	**.000**	**.000**	**.000**	**—**

Lowe, Robert Lincoln (Bobby or Link)

HEIGHT: 5'10" THROWS: RIGHT BATS: RIGHT BORN: 7/10/1868 PITTSBURGH, PENNSYLVANIA DIED: 12/8/1951 DETROIT, MICHIGAN
POSITIONS PLAYED: P, 1B, 2B, 3B, SS, OF

YEAR	TEAM	GAMES	AB	RUNS	HITS	2B	3B	HR	RBI	BB	IBB	SO	HBP	SH	SF	SB	CS	BA	OBA	SA	FA
1890	Bos-N	52	207	35	58	13	2	2	21	26	—	32	2	—	—	15	—	.280	.366	.391	.944
1891	Bos-N	125	497	92	129	19	5	6	74	53	—	54	9	—	—	43	—	.260	.342	.354	.922
1892	Bos-N	124	475	79	115	16	7	3	57	37	—	47	8	—	—	36	—	.242	.308	.324	.912
1893	Bos-N	126	526	130	157	19	5	14	89	55	—	29	4	—	—	22	—	.298	.369	.433	.935
1894	Bos-N	133	613	158	212	34	11	17	115	50	—	25	6	9	—	23	—	.346	.401	.520	.928
1895	Bos-N	99	412	101	122	12	7	7	62	40	—	16	8	16	—	24	—	.296	.370	.410	.954
1896	Bos-N	73	305	59	98	11	4	2	48	20	—	11	4	6	—	15	—	.321	.371	.403	.965
1897	Bos-N	123	499	87	154	24	8	5	106	32	—	—	3	13	—	16	—	.309	.355	.419	.952
1898	Bos-N	147	559	65	152	11	7	5	94	29	—	—	3	20	—	12	—	.272	.311	.338	.958
1899	Bos-N	152	559	81	152	5	9	4	88	35	—	—	1	19	—	17	—	.272	.316	.335	.951
1900	Bos-N	127	474	65	132	11	5	3	71	26	—	—	5	9	—	15	—	.278	.323	.342	.921
1901	Bos-N	129	491	47	125	11	1	3	47	17	—	—	3	8	—	22	—	.255	.284	.299	.921
1902	**ChC-N**	**119**	**472**	**41**	**116**	**13**	**3**	**0**	**31**	**11**	**—**	**—**	**5**	**9**	**—**	**16**	**—**	**.246**	**.270**	**.286**	**.957**
1903	**ChC-N**	**32**	**105**	**14**	**28**	**5**	**3**	**0**	**15**	**4**	**—**	**—**	**4**	**3**	**—**	**5**	**—**	**.267**	**.319**	**.371**	**.940**
1904	Pit-N	1	1	0	0	0	0	0	0	0	—	—	0	0	—	0	—	.208	.236	.259	—
1904	Det-A	140	506	47	105	14	6	0	40	17	—	—	2	15	—	15	—	.208	.236	.259	.964
1905	Det-A	60	181	17	35	7	2	0	9	13	—	—	2	10	—	3	—	.193	.255	.254	.974
1906	Det-A	41	145	11	30	3	0	1	12	4	—	—	1	3	—	3	—	.207	.233	.248	.936
1907	Det-A	17	37	2	9	2	0	0	5	4	—	—	0	3	—	0	—	.243	.317	.297	.889
Career average		101	392	63	107	13	5	4	55	26	—	12	4	8	—	17	—	.250	.280	.302	.954
Cubs average		**76**	**289**	**28**	**72**	**9**	**3**	**0**	**23**	**8**	**—**	**0**	**5**	**6**	**—**	**11**	**—**	**.273**	**.325**	**.360**	**.946**
Career total		1820	7064	1131	1929	230	85	71	984	473	—	214	71	143	—	302	—	.250	.280	.302	.954
Cubs total		**151**	**577**	**55**	**144**	**18**	**6**	**0**	**46**	**15**	**—**	**0**	**9**	**12**	**—**	**21**	**—**	**.273**	**.325**	**.360**	**.946**

Lowery, Quenton Terrell (Terrell)

HEIGHT: 6'3" THROWS: RIGHT BATS: RIGHT BORN: 10/25/1970 OAKLAND, CALIFORNIA POSITIONS PLAYED: OF

YEAR	TEAM	GAMES	AB	RUNS	HITS	2B	3B	HR	RBI	BB	IBB	SO	HBP	SH	SF	SB	CS	BA	OBA	SA	FA
1997	**ChC-N**	**9**	**14**	**2**	**4**	**0**	**0**	**0**	**0**	**3**	**0**	**3**	**0**	**0**	**0**	**1**	**0**	**.286**	**.412**	**.286**	**1.000**
1998	**ChC-N**	**24**	**15**	**2**	**3**	**1**	**0**	**0**	**1**	**3**	**0**	**7**	**0**	**0**	**0**	**0**	**0**	**.200**	**.333**	**.267**	**.929**
1999	TB-A	66	185	25	48	15	1	2	17	19	0	53	1	0	1	0	2	.259	.330	.384	.971
2000	SF-N	24	34	13	15	4	0	1	5	7	0	8	1	0	0	1	0	.441	.548	.647	.917
Career average		31	62	11	18	5	0	1	6	8	0	18	1	0	0	1	1	.282	.367	.407	.964
Cubs average		**17**	**15**	**2**	**4**	**1**	**0**	**0**	**1**	**3**	**0**	**5**	**0**	**0**	**0**	**1**	**1**	**.241**	**.371**	**.276**	**.957**
Career total		123	248	42	70	20	1	3	23	32	0	71	2	0	1	2	2	.282	.367	.407	.964
Cubs total		**33**	**29**	**4**	**7**	**1**	**0**	**0**	**1**	**6**	**0**	**10**	**0**	**0**	**0**	**1**	**0**	**.241**	**.371**	**.276**	**.957**

Lowrey, Harry Lee (Peanuts)

HEIGHT: 5'8" THROWS: RIGHT BATS: RIGHT BORN: 8/27/1917 CULVER CITY, CALIFORNIA DIED: 7/2/1986 INGLEWOOD, CALIFORNIA
POSITIONS PLAYED: 1B, 2B, 3B, SS, OF

YEAR	TEAM	GAMES	AB	RUNS	HITS	2B	3B	HR	RBI	BB	IBB	SO	HBP	SH	SF	SB	CS	BA	OBA	SA	FA
1942	ChC-N	27	58	4	11	0	0	1	4	4	—	4	0	2	—	0	—	.190	.242	.241	.978
1943	ChC-N	130	480	59	140	25	12	1	63	35	—	24	0	11	—	13	—	.292	.340	.400	.976
1945	ChC-N	143	523	72	148	22	7	7	89	48	—	27	0	21	—	11	—	.283	.343	.392	.984
1946	ChC-N	144	540	75	139	24	5	4	54	56	—	22	1	17	—	10	—	.257	.328	.343	.969
1947	ChC-N	115	448	56	126	17	5	5	37	38	—	26	1	6	—	2	—	.281	.339	.375	.952
1948	ChC-N	129	435	47	128	12	3	2	54	34	—	31	1	7	—	2	—	.294	.347	.349	.982
1949	ChC-N	38	111	18	30	5	0	2	10	9	—	8	0	2	—	3	—	.270	.325	.369	.952
1949	Cin-N	89	309	48	85	16	2	2	25	37	—	11	1	7	—	1	—	.275	.354	.359	.995
1950	Cin-N	91	264	34	60	14	0	1	11	36	—	7	0	6	—	0	—	.227	.320	.292	.988
1950	StL-N	17	56	10	15	0	0	1	4	6	—	1	1	0	—	0	—	.268	.349	.321	.969
1951	StL-N	114	370	52	112	19	5	5	40	35	—	12	2	12	—	0	1	.303	.366	.422	.966
1952	StL-N	132	374	48	107	18	2	1	48	34	—	13	4	5	—	3	2	.286	.352	.353	.966
1953	StL-N	104	182	26	49	9	2	5	27	15	—	21	0	1	—	1	0	.269	.325	.423	.966
1954	StL-N	74	61	6	7	1	2	0	5	9	—	9	0	0	2	0	0	.115	.222	.197	1.000
1955	Phi-N	54	106	9	20	4	0	0	8	7	0	10	0	0	1	2	0	.189	.237	.226	.980
Career average		108	332	43	91	14	3	3	37	31	0	17	1	7	0	4	0	.273	.336	.362	.973
Cubs average		**104**	**371**	**47**	**103**	**15**	**5**	**3**	**44**	**32**	**—**	**20**	**0**	**9**	**—**	**6**	**—**	**.278**	**.336**	**.369**	**.971**
Career total		1401	4317	564	1177	186	45	37	479	403	0	226	11	97	3	48	3	.273	.336	.362	.973
Cubs total		**726**	**2595**	**331**	**722**	**105**	**32**	**22**	**311**	**224**	**—**	**142**	**3**	**66**	**—**	**41**	**—**	**.278**	**.336**	**.369**	**.971**

Luderus, Frederick William (Fred)

HEIGHT: 5'11" THROWS: RIGHT BATS: LEFT BORN: 9/12/1885 MILWAUKEE, WISCONSIN DIED: 1/5/1961 THREE LAKES, WISCONSIN POSITIONS PLAYED: 1B

YEAR	TEAM	GAMES	AB	RUNS	HITS	2B	3B	HR	RBI	BB	IBB	SO	HBP	SH	SF	SB	CS	BA	OBA	SA	FA
1909	**ChC-N**	**11**	**37**	**8**	**11**	**1**	**1**	**1**	**9**	**3**	**—**	**—**	**1**	**0**	**—**	**0**	**—**	**.297**	**.366**	**.459**	**.950**
1910	**ChC-N**	**24**	**54**	**5**	**11**	**1**	**1**	**0**	**3**	**4**	**—**	**3**	**0**	**1**	**—**	**0**	**—**	**.204**	**.259**	**.259**	**.975**
1910	Phi-N	21	68	10	20	5	2	0	14	9	—	5	1	0	—	2	—	.294	.385	.426	.985
1911	Phi-N	146	551	69	166	24	11	16	99	40	—	76	4	14	—	6	—	.301	.353	.472	.985
1912	Phi-N	148	572	77	147	31	5	10	69	44	—	65	7	5	—	8	—	.257	.318	.381	.990
1913	Phi-N	155	588	67	154	32	7	18	86	34	—	51	2	9	—	5	—	.262	.304	.432	.984
1914	Phi-N	121	443	55	110	16	5	12	55	33	—	31	5	7	—	2	—	.248	.308	.388	.975
1915	Phi-N	141	499	55	157	36	7	7	62	42	—	36	7	12	—	9	7	.315	.376	.457	.993
1916	Phi-N	146	508	52	143	26	3	5	53	41	—	32	5	13	—	8	—	.281	.341	.374	.982
1917	Phi-N	154	522	57	136	24	4	5	72	65	—	35	6	14	—	5	—	.261	.349	.351	.991
1918	Phi-N	125	468	54	135	23	2	5	67	42	—	33	3	9	—	4	—	.288	.351	.378	.988
1919	Phi-N	138	509	60	149	30	6	5	49	54	—	48	4	9	—	6	—	.293	.365	.405	.985
1920	Phi-N	16	32	1	5	2	0	0	4	3	—	6	0	1	—	0	1	.156	.229	.219	.983
Career average		112	404	48	112	21	5	7	54	35	—	35	4	8	—	5	1	.277	.340	.403	.986
Cubs average		**18**	**46**	**7**	**11**	**1**	**1**	**1**	**6**	**4**	**—**	**2**	**1**	**1**	**—**	**0**	**—**	**.242**	**.303**	**.341**	**.965**
Career total		1346	4851	570	1344	251	54	84	642	414	—	421	45	94	—	55	8	.277	.340	.403	.986
Cubs total		**35**	**91**	**13**	**22**	**2**	**2**	**1**	**12**	**7**	**—**	**3**	**1**	**1**	**—**	**0**	**—**	**.242**	**.303**	**.341**	**.965**

Lum, Michael Ken-Wai (Mike)
HEIGHT: 6'0"　THROWS: LEFT　BATS: LEFT　BORN: 10/27/1945 HONOLULU, HAWAII　POSITIONS PLAYED: 1B, OF

YEAR	TEAM	GAMES	AB	RUNS	HITS	2B	3B	HR	RBI	BB	IBB	SO	HBP	SH	SF	SB	CS	BA	OBA	SA	FA
1967	Atl-N	9	26	1	6	0	0	0	1	1	0	4	0	0	0	0	1	.231	.259	.231	.944
1968	Atl-N	122	232	22	52	7	3	3	21	14	2	35	4	3	3	3	5	.224	.277	.319	.976
1969	Atl-N	121	168	20	45	8	0	1	22	16	4	18	0	0	3	0	0	.268	.326	.333	.992
1970	Atl-N	123	291	25	74	17	2	7	28	17	0	43	5	2	1	3	2	.254	.306	.399	.988
1971	Atl-N	145	454	56	122	14	1	13	55	47	5	43	5	0	6	0	3	.269	.340	.390	.990
1972	Atl-N	123	369	40	84	14	2	9	38	50	4	52	3	0	2	1	4	.228	.323	.350	.977
1973	Atl-N	138	513	74	151	26	6	16	82	41	7	89	6	4	4	2	5	.294	.351	.462	.990
1974	Atl-N	106	361	50	84	11	2	11	50	45	12	49	2	0	3	0	5	.233	.319	.366	.993
1975	Atl-N	124	364	32	83	8	2	8	36	39	7	38	0	2	1	2	4	.228	.302	.327	.993
1976	Cin-N	84	136	15	31	5	1	3	20	22	1	24	1	1	4	0	1	.228	.331	.346	1.000
1977	Cin-N	81	125	14	20	1	0	5	16	9	1	33	1	0	1	2	0	.160	.221	.288	.988
1978	Cin-N	86	146	15	39	7	1	6	23	22	4	18	0	0	1	0	0	.267	.361	.452	.982
1979	Atl-N	111	217	27	54	6	0	6	27	18	1	34	0	5	2	0	2	.249	.304	.359	.998
1980	Atl-N	93	83	7	17	3	0	0	5	18	3	19	0	1	1	0	0	.205	.343	.241	1.000
1981	Atl-N	10	11	1	1	0	0	0	0	2	1	2	0	0	0	0	0	.091	.231	.091	1.000
1981	**ChC-N**	**41**	**58**	**5**	**14**	**1**	**0**	**2**	**7**	**5**	**2**	**5**	**1**	**0**	**1**	**0**	**0**	**.241**	**.308**	**.362**	**.929**
Career average		101	237	27	58	9	1	6	29	24	4	34	2	1	2	1	2	.241	.308	.362	.929
Cubs average		**41**	**58**	**5**	**14**	**1**	**0**	**2**	**7**	**5**	**2**	**5**	**1**	**0**	**1**	**0**	**0**	**.241**	**.308**	**.362**	**.929**
Career total		1517	3554	404	877	128	20	90	431	366	54	506	28	18	33	13	29	.247	.319	.370	.990
Cubs total		**41**	**58**	**5**	**14**	**1**	**0**	**2**	**7**	**5**	**2**	**5**	**1**	**0**	**1**	**0**	**0**	**.241**	**.308**	**.362**	**.929**

Lundstedt, Thomas Robert (Tom)
HEIGHT: 6'4"　THROWS: RIGHT　BATS: BOTH　BORN: 4/10/1949 DAVENPORT, IOWA　POSITIONS PLAYED: C

YEAR	TEAM	GAMES	AB	RUNS	HITS	2B	3B	HR	RBI	BB	IBB	SO	HBP	SH	SF	SB	CS	BA	OBA	SA	FA
1973	**ChC-N**	**4**	**5**	**0**	**0**	**0**	**0**	**0**	**0**	**0**	**0**	**1**	**0**	**0**	**0**	**0**	**0**	**.000**	**.000**	**.000**	**1.000**
1974	**ChC-N**	**22**	**32**	**1**	**3**	**0**	**0**	**0**	**0**	**5**	**0**	**7**	**0**	**0**	**0**	**0**	**0**	**.094**	**.216**	**.094**	**.987**
1975	Min-A	18	28	2	3	0	0	0	1	4	1	5	0	0	0	0	0	.107	.219	.107	1.000
Career average		15	22	1	2	0	0	0	0	3	0	4	0	0	0	0	0	.092	.203	.092	.993
Cubs average		**13**	**19**	**1**	**2**	**0**	**0**	**0**	**0**	**3**	**0**	**4**	**0**	**0**	**0**	**0**	**0**	**.081**	**.190**	**.081**	**.988**
Career total		44	65	3	6	0	0	0	1	9	1	13	0	0	0	0	0	.092	.203	.092	.993
Cubs total		**26**	**37**	**1**	**3**	**0**	**0**	**0**	**0**	**5**	**0**	**8**	**0**	**0**	**0**	**0**	**0**	**.081**	**.190**	**.081**	**.988**

Lynch, Henry W.
HEIGHT: 5'7"　THROWS: —　BATS: BOTH　BORN: 4/8/1866 WORCESTER, MASSACHUSETTS　DIED: 11/23/1925 WORCESTER, MASSACHUSETTS
POSITIONS PLAYED: OF

YEAR	TEAM	GAMES	AB	RUNS	HITS	2B	3B	HR	RBI	BB	IBB	SO	HBP	SH	SF	SB	CS	BA	OBA	SA	FA
1893	**ChN-N**	**4**	**14**	**0**	**3**	**2**	**0**	**0**	**2**	**1**	**—**	**1**	**0**	**—**	**—**	**0**	**—**	**.214**	**.267**	**.357**	**.833**
Career average		4	14	0	3	2	0	0	2	1	—	1	0	—	—	0	—	.214	.267	.357	.833
Cubs average		**4**	**14**	**0**	**3**	**2**	**0**	**0**	**2**	**1**	**—**	**1**	**0**	**—**	**—**	**0**	**—**	**.214**	**.267**	**.357**	**.833**
Career total		4	14	0	3	2	0	0	2	1	—	1	0	—	—	0	—	.214	.267	.357	.833
Cubs total		**4**	**14**	**0**	**3**	**2**	**0**	**0**	**2**	**1**	**—**	**1**	**0**	**—**	**—**	**0**	**—**	**.214**	**.267**	**.357**	**.833**

Lynch, Matthew Daniel (Danny *or* Dummy)
HEIGHT: 5'11"　THROWS: RIGHT　BATS: RIGHT　BORN: 2/7/1926 DALLAS, TEXAS　DIED: 6/30/1978 PLANO, TEXAS　POSITIONS PLAYED: 2B

YEAR	TEAM	GAMES	AB	RUNS	HITS	2B	3B	HR	RBI	BB	IBB	SO	HBP	SH	SF	SB	CS	BA	OBA	SA	FA
1948	**ChC-N**	**7**	**7**	**3**	**2**	**0**	**0**	**1**	**1**	**1**	**—**	**1**	**0**	**0**	**—**	**0**	**—**	**.286**	**.375**	**.714**	**1.000**
Career average		7	7	3	2	0	0	1	1	1	—	1	0	0	—	0	—	.286	.375	.714	1.000
Cubs average		**7**	**7**	**3**	**2**	**0**	**0**	**1**	**1**	**1**	**—**	**1**	**0**	**0**	**—**	**0**	**—**	**.286**	**.375**	**.714**	**1.000**
Career total		7	7	3	2	0	0	1	1	1	—	1	0	0	—	0	—	.286	.375	.714	1.000
Cubs total		**7**	**7**	**3**	**2**	**0**	**0**	**1**	**1**	**1**	**—**	**1**	**0**	**0**	**—**	**0**	**—**	**.286**	**.375**	**.714**	**1.000**

Lynch, Michael Joseph (Mike)

HEIGHT: 5'10" THROWS: RIGHT BATS: — BORN: 9/10/1875 ST. PAUL, MINNESOTA DIED: 4/1/1947 JENNINGS LODGE, OREGON POSITIONS PLAYED: OF

YEAR	TEAM	GAMES	AB	RUNS	HITS	2B	3B	HR	RBI	BB	IBB	SO	HBP	SH	SF	SB	CS	BA	OBA	SA	FA
1902	ChC-N	7	28	4	4	0	0	0	0	2	—	—	0	1	—	0	—	.143	.200	.143	.929
Career average		7	28	4	4	0	0	0	0	2	—	—	0	1	—	0	—	.143	.200	.143	.929
Cubs average		7	28	4	4	0	0	0	0	2	—	—	0	1	—	0	—	.143	.200	.143	.929
Career total		7	28	4	4	0	0	0	0	2	—	—	0	1	—	0	—	.143	.200	.143	.929
Cubs total		7	28	4	4	0	0	0	0	2	—	—	0	1	—	0	—	.143	.200	.143	.929

Lytle, Edward Benson (Dad *or* Pop)

HEIGHT: 5'11" THROWS: RIGHT BATS: RIGHT BORN: 3/10/1862 RACINE, WISCONSIN DIED: 12/21/1950 LONG BEACH, CALIFORNIA
POSITIONS PLAYED: 2B, OF

YEAR	TEAM	GAMES	AB	RUNS	HITS	2B	3B	HR	RBI	BB	IBB	SO	HBP	SH	SF	SB	CS	BA	OBA	SA	FA
1890	ChN-N	1	4	1	0	0	0	0	0	0	—	1	0	—	—	0	—	.000	.000	.000	1.000
1890	Pit-N	15	55	2	8	1	0	0	0	8	—	9	0	—	—	0	—	.145	.254	.164	.821
Career average		16	59	3	8	1	0	0	0	8	—	10	0	—	—	0	—	.136	.239	.153	.833
Cubs average		1	4	1	0	0	0	0	0	0	—	1	0	—	—	0	—	.000	.000	.000	1.000
Career total		16	59	3	8	1	0	0	0	8	—	10	0	—	—	0	—	.136	.239	.153	.833
Cubs total		1	4	1	0	0	0	0	0	0	—	1	0	—	—	0	—	.000	.000	.000	1.000

Machado, Robert Alexis

HEIGHT: 6'1" THROWS: RIGHT BATS: RIGHT BORN: 6/3/1973 CARACAS, VENEZUELA POSITIONS PLAYED: C

YEAR	TEAM	GAMES	AB	RUNS	HITS	2B	3B	HR	RBI	BB	IBB	SO	HBP	SH	SF	SB	CS	BA	OBA	SA	FA
1996	CWS-A	4	6	1	4	1	0	0	2	0	0	0	0	0	0	0	0	.667	.667	.833	1.000
1997	CWS-A	10	15	1	3	0	1	0	2	1	0	6	0	1	0	0	0	.200	.250	.333	1.000
1998	CWS-A	34	111	14	23	6	0	3	15	7	0	22	0	3	0	0	0	.207	.254	.342	.981
1999	Mon-N	17	22	3	4	1	0	0	0	2	0	6	0	0	0	0	0	.182	.250	.227	1.000
2000	Sea-A	8	14	2	3	0	0	1	1	1	0	4	0	0	0	0	0	.214	.267	.429	1.000
2001	ChC-N	52	135	13	30	10	0	2	13	7	3	26	1	3	0	0	0	.222	.266	.341	.997
Career average		21	51	6	11	3	0	1	6	3	1	11	0	1	0	0	0	.221	.267	.347	.992
Cubs average		52	135	13	30	10	0	2	13	7	3	26	1	3	0	0	0	.222	.266	.341	.997
Career total		125	303	34	67	18	1	6	33	18	3	64	1	7	0	0	0	.221	.267	.347	.992
Cubs total		52	135	13	30	10	0	2	13	7	3	26	1	3	0	0	0	.222	.266	.341	.997

Mack, Raymond James (Ray)

HEIGHT: 6'0" THROWS: RIGHT BATS: RIGHT BORN: 8/31/1916 CLEVELAND, OHIO DIED: 5/7/1969 BUCYRUS, OHIO POSITIONS PLAYED: 2B, 3B

YEAR	TEAM	GAMES	AB	RUNS	HITS	2B	3B	HR	RBI	BB	IBB	SO	HBP	SH	SF	SB	CS	BA	OBA	SA	FA
1938	Cle-A	2	6	2	2	0	1	0	2	0	—	1	0	0	—	0	0	.333	.333	.667	1.000
1939	Cle-A	36	112	12	17	4	1	1	6	12	—	19	1	1	—	0	2	.152	.240	.232	.977
1940	Cle-A	146	530	60	150	21	5	12	69	51	—	77	0	2	—	4	2	.283	.346	.409	.965
1941	Cle-A	145	501	54	114	22	4	9	44	54	—	69	0	11	—	8	4	.228	.303	.341	.970
1942	Cle-A	143	481	43	108	14	6	2	45	41	—	51	2	7	—	9	3	.225	.288	.291	.969
1943	Cle-A	153	545	56	120	25	2	7	62	47	—	61	2	14	—	8	3	.220	.285	.312	.967
1944	Cle-A	83	284	24	66	15	3	0	29	28	—	45	0	7	—	4	1	.232	.301	.306	.951
1946	Cle-A	61	171	13	35	6	2	1	9	23	—	27	0	0	—	2	2	.205	.299	.281	.970
1947	NYY-A	1	0	0	0	0	0	0	0	0	—	0	0	0	—	0	0	—	—	—	—
1947	ChC-N	21	78	9	17	6	0	2	12	5	—	15	1	0	—	0	—	.218	.274	.372	.965
Career average		88	301	30	70	13	3	4	31	29	—	41	1	5	—	4	2	.232	.301	.329	.966
Cubs average		21	78	9	17	6	0	2	12	5	—	15	1	0	—	0	0	.218	.274	.372	.965
Career total		791	2708	273	629	113	24	34	278	261	—	365	6	42	—	35	17	.232	.301	.329	.966
Cubs total		21	78	9	17	6	0	2	12	5	—	15	1	0	—	0	0	.218	.274	.372	.965

Macko, Steven Joseph (Steve)
HEIGHT: 5'10" THROWS: RIGHT BATS: LEFT BORN: 9/6/1954 BURLINGTON, IOWA DIED: 11/15/1981 ARLINGTON, TEXAS POSITIONS PLAYED: 2B, 3B, SS

YEAR	TEAM	GAMES	AB	RUNS	HITS	2B	3B	HR	RBI	BB	IBB	SO	HBP	SH	SF	SB	CS	BA	OBA	SA	FA
1979	ChC-N	19	40	2	9	1	0	0	3	4	0	8	0	0	0	0	0	.225	.295	.250	1.000
1980	ChC-N	6	20	2	6	2	0	0	2	0	0	3	0	0	0	0	0	.300	.300	.400	1.000
Career average		13	30	2	8	2	0	0	3	2	0	6	0	0	0	0	0	.250	.297	.300	1.000
Cubs average		13	30	2	8	2	0	0	3	2	0	6	0	0	0	0	0	.250	.297	.300	1.000
Career total		25	60	4	15	3	0	0	5	4	0	11	0	0	0	0	0	.250	.297	.300	1.000
Cubs total		25	60	4	15	3	0	0	5	4	0	11	0	0	0	0	0	.250	.297	.300	1.000

Maddern, Clarence James
HEIGHT: 6'1" THROWS: RIGHT BATS: RIGHT BORN: 9/26/1921 BISBEE, ARIZONA DIED: 8/9/1986 TUCSON, ARIZONA POSITIONS PLAYED: 1B, OF

YEAR	TEAM	GAMES	AB	RUNS	HITS	2B	3B	HR	RBI	BB	IBB	SO	HBP	SH	SF	SB	CS	BA	OBA	SA	FA
1946	ChC-N	3	3	0	0	0	0	0	0	0	—	0	1	0	—	0	—	.000	.250	.000	1.000
1948	ChC-N	80	214	16	54	12	1	4	27	10	—	25	5	2	—	0	—	.252	.301	.374	.981
1949	ChC-N	10	9	1	3	0	0	1	2	2	—	0	0	0	—	0	—	.333	.455	.667	1.000
1951	Cle-A	11	12	0	2	0	0	0	0	0	—	1	0	0	—	0	0	.167	.167	.167	.667
Career average		26	60	4	15	3	0	1	7	3	—	7	2	1	—	0	0	.248	.301	.370	.974
Cubs average		31	75	6	19	4	0	2	10	4	—	8	2	1	—	0	—	.252	.307	.381	.982
Career total		104	238	17	59	12	1	5	29	12	—	26	6	2	—	0	0	.252	.307	.381	.982
Cubs total		93	226	17	57	12	1	5	29	12	—	25	6	2	—	0	—	.252	.307	.381	.982

Madlock, Bill (Mad Dog)
HEIGHT: 5'11" THROWS: RIGHT BATS: RIGHT BORN: 1/2/1951 MEMPHIS, TENNESSEE POSITIONS PLAYED: 1B, 2B, 3B

YEAR	TEAM	GAMES	AB	RUNS	HITS	2B	3B	HR	RBI	BB	IBB	SO	HBP	SH	SF	SB	CS	BA	OBA	SA	FA
1973	Tex-A	21	77	16	27	5	3	1	5	7	0	9	1	0	0	3	2	.351	.412	.532	.918
1974	ChC-N	128	453	65	142	21	5	9	54	42	8	39	5	3	6	11	7	.313	.374	.442	.946
1975	ChC-N	130	514	77	182	29	7	7	64	42	5	34	3	1	5	9	7	.354	.402	.479	.943
1976	ChC-N	142	514	68	174	36	1	15	84	56	15	27	11	3	4	15	11	.339	.412	.500	.961
1977	SF-N	140	533	70	161	28	1	12	46	43	14	33	6	1	2	13	10	.302	.360	.426	.949
1978	SF-N	122	447	76	138	26	3	15	44	48	11	39	3	9	2	16	5	.309	.378	.481	.974
1979	SF-N	69	249	37	65	9	2	7	41	18	3	19	0	1	2	11	3	.261	.309	.398	.976
1979	Pit-N	85	311	48	102	17	3	7	44	34	8	22	1	2	5	21	8	.328	.390	.469	.969
1980	Pit-N	137	494	62	137	22	4	10	53	45	12	33	4	0	3	16	10	.277	.341	.399	.957
1981	Pit-N	82	279	35	95	23	1	6	45	34	7	17	3	0	4	18	6	.341	.413	.495	.956
1982	Pit-N	154	568	92	181	33	3	19	95	48	16	39	4	1	13	18	6	.319	.368	.488	.955
1983	Pit-N	130	473	68	153	21	0	12	68	49	10	24	2	1	5	3	4	.323	.386	.444	.958
1984	Pit-N	103	403	38	102	16	0	4	44	26	5	29	1	1	4	3	1	.253	.297	.323	.944
1985	Pit-N	110	399	49	100	23	1	10	41	39	2	42	5	3	3	7	1	.251	.323	.388	.956
1985	LA-N	34	114	20	41	4	0	2	15	10	0	11	3	0	1	6	3	.360	.422	.447	.906
1986	LA-N	111	379	38	106	17	0	10	60	30	4	43	5	1	6	3	0	.280	.336	.404	.912
1987	LA-N	21	61	5	11	1	0	3	7	6	0	5	1	1	0	0	0	.180	.265	.344	.989
1987	Det-A	87	326	56	91	17	0	14	50	28	1	45	10	8	4	4	3	.279	.351	.460	.989
Career average		120	440	61	134	23	2	11	57	40	8	34	5	2	5	12	6	.305	.365	.442	.955
Cubs average		133	494	70	166	29	4	10	67	47	9	33	6	2	5	12	8	.336	.397	.475	.950
Career total		1806	6594	920	2008	348	34	163	860	605	121	510	68	36	69	174	90	.305	.365	.442	.955
Cubs total		400	1481	210	498	86	13	31	202	140	28	100	19	7	15	35	25	.336	.397	.475	.950

Madrid, Salvator (Sal)
HEIGHT: 5'9" THROWS: RIGHT BATS: RIGHT BORN: 6/9/1920 EL PASO, TEXAS DIED: 2/24/1977 FORT WAYNE, INDIANA POSITIONS PLAYED: SS

YEAR	TEAM	GAMES	AB	RUNS	HITS	2B	3B	HR	RBI	BB	IBB	SO	HBP	SH	SF	SB	CS	BA	OBA	SA	FA
1947	ChC-N	8	24	0	3	1	0	0	1	1	—	6	0	0	—	0	—	.125	.160	.167	.956
Career average		8	24	0	3	1	0	0	1	1	—	6	0	0	—	0	—	.125	.160	.167	.956
Cubs average		8	24	0	3	1	0	0	1	1	—	6	0	0	—	0	—	.125	.160	.167	.956
Career total		8	24	0	3	1	0	0	1	1	—	6	0	0	—	0	—	.125	.160	.167	.956
Cubs total		8	24	0	3	1	0	0	1	1	—	6	0	0	—	0	—	.125	.160	.167	.956

Bill "Mad Dog" Madlock, 1b-2b-3b, 1973–87

Batting Bill Madlock only spent three of his 15 years with the Cubs, but they were three of his most productive seasons.

Madlock was born on January 2, 1951, in Memphis, Tennessee. He was initially signed by Texas, but after an outstanding rookie season in 1973, he was traded to the Cubs in 1974 along with Vic Harris for Ferguson (Fergie) Jenkins.

This was actually a pretty good deal for Chicago. Madlock hit .313 with 142 hits and 54 RBIs in 1974. But he picked things up the next two years, winning the batting title for Chicago in 1975 and 1976.

Madlock had a tight, compact swing that sprayed hits to all fields, particularly in Wrigley Field. In 1975 Madlock made 182 hits and 29 doubles for a .354 average that was the eighth-best single season mark in Cubs history, and the best average for a Cub since Phil Cavarretta's .355 in 1945.

In the All-Star Game that year, Madlock's two run single off Rich Gossage in the ninth inning was the game winner, and Madlock was named co-MVP. That made Madlock the first Cub to be named MVP of the All-Star Game.

The next year, Madlock wasn't quite as overpowering, hitting .339, with 36 doubles and 84 RBIs. He did, however, become the first and only Cub to win back-to-back batting titles and the only other Cub besides Adrian "Cap" Anson to win more than one such title.

The moody Madlock had a reputation for sitting down against the tougher pitchers in the league, but what hastened his departure from Chicago was his contract demands, deemed exorbitant by owner Phil Wrigley.

The Cubs dealt Madlock to the Giants in 1977. From there, Madlock spent time in Pittsburgh, Los Angeles and Detroit. He helped the Pirates to the 1979 world championship and won batting titles in Pittsburgh in 1981 and 1983. That made Madlock the first player to win batting championships with two separate teams. After his stay in Pittsburgh, Madlock played for the Dodgers and Tigers, and he finished up his career with a year in Japan in 1988.

Magadan, David Joseph (Dave)

HEIGHT: 6'4" THROWS: RIGHT BATS: LEFT BORN: 9/30/1962 TAMPA, FLORIDA POSITIONS PLAYED: 1B, 2B, 3B, SS

YEAR	TEAM	GAMES	AB	RUNS	HITS	2B	3B	HR	RBI	BB	IBB	SO	HBP	SH	SF	SB	CS	BA	OBA	SA	FA
1986	NYM-N	10	18	3	8	0	0	0	3	3	0	1	0	0	0	0	0	.444	.524	.444	1.000
1987	NYM-N	85	192	21	61	13	1	3	24	22	2	22	0	1	1	0	0	.318	.386	.443	.978
1988	NYM-N	112	314	39	87	15	0	1	35	60	4	39	2	1	3	0	1	.277	.393	.334	.982
1989	NYM-N	127	374	47	107	22	3	4	41	49	6	37	1	1	4	1	0	.286	.367	.393	.990
1990	NYM-N	144	451	74	148	28	6	6	72	74	4	55	2	4	10	2	1	.328	.417	.457	.997
1991	NYM-N	124	418	58	108	23	0	4	51	83	3	50	2	7	7	1	1	.258	.378	.342	.996
1992	NYM-N	99	321	33	91	9	1	3	28	56	3	44	0	2	0	1	0	.283	.390	.346	.945
1993	Fla-N	66	227	22	65	12	0	4	29	44	4	30	1	0	3	0	1	.286	.400	.392	.962
1993	Sea-A	71	228	27	59	11	0	1	21	36	3	33	0	2	3	2	0	.259	.356	.320	.988
1994	Fla-N	74	211	30	58	7	0	1	17	39	0	25	1	0	3	0	0	.275	.386	.322	.981
1995	Hou-N	127	348	44	109	24	0	2	51	71	9	56	0	1	2	2	1	.313	.428	.399	.940
1996	**ChC-N**	**78**	**169**	**23**	**43**	**10**	**0**	**3**	**17**	**29**	**3**	**23**	**0**	**1**	**2**	**0**	**2**	**.254**	**.360**	**.367**	**.979**
1997	Oak-A	128	271	38	82	10	1	4	30	50	1	40	2	4	1	1	0	.303	.414	.391	.977
1998	Oak-A	35	109	12	35	8	0	1	13	13	1	12	0	0	1	0	1	.321	.390	.422	.945
1999	SD-N	116	248	20	68	12	1	2	30	45	2	36	0	0	7	1	3	.274	.377	.355	.980
2000	SD-N	95	132	13	36	7	0	2	21	32	1	23	0	0	2	0	0	.273	.410	.371	.980
2001	SD-N	91	128	12	32	7	0	1	12	12	0	20	1	0	1	0	0	.250	.317	.328	.955
Career average		99	260	32	75	14	1	3	31	45	3	34	1	2	3	1	1	.288	.390	.377	.983
Cubs average		**78**	**169**	**23**	**43**	**10**	**0**	**3**	**17**	**29**	**3**	**23**	**0**	**1**	**2**	**0**	**2**	**.254**	**.360**	**.367**	**.979**
Career total		1582	4159	516	1197	218	13	42	495	718	46	546	12	24	50	11	11	.288	.390	.377	.983
Cubs total		**78**	**169**	**23**	**43**	**10**	**0**	**3**	**17**	**29**	**3**	**23**	**0**	**1**	**2**	**0**	**2**	**.254**	**.360**	**.367**	**.979**

Magee, Leo Christopher (Lee)
HEIGHT: 5'11" THROWS: RIGHT BATS: BOTH BORN: 6/4/1889 CINCINNATI, OHIO DIED: 3/14/1966 COLUMBUS, OHIO POSITIONS PLAYED: 1B, 2B, 3B, SS, OF

YEAR	TEAM	GAMES	AB	RUNS	HITS	2B	3B	HR	RBI	BB	IBB	SO	HBP	SH	SF	SB	CS	BA	OBA	SA	FA
1911	StL-N	26	69	9	18	1	1	0	8	8	—	8	0	0	—	4	—	.261	.338	.304	.947
1912	StL-N	128	458	60	133	13	8	0	40	39	—	29	1	25	—	16	33	.290	.347	.354	.952
1913	StL-N	137	531	54	142	13	7	2	31	34	—	30	2	22	—	23	—	.267	.314	.330	.981
1914	StL-N	142	529	59	150	23	4	2	40	42	—	24	1	35	—	36	—	.284	.337	.353	.988
1915	Bro-F	121	452	87	146	19	10	4	49	22	—	19	1	19	—	34	—	.323	.356	.436	.937
1916	NYY-A	131	510	57	131	18	4	3	45	50	—	31	1	20	—	29	25	.257	.324	.325	.976
1917	NYY-A	51	173	17	38	4	1	0	8	13	—	18	1	13	—	3	—	.220	.278	.254	.938
1917	StL-A	36	112	11	19	1	0	0	4	6	—	6	0	7	—	3	—	.170	.212	.179	1.000
1918	Cin-N	119	459	61	133	22	13	0	28	28	—	19	0	27	—	19	—	.290	.331	.394	.957
1919	Bro-N	45	181	16	43	7	2	0	7	5	—	8	1	13	—	5	—	.238	.262	.298	.940
1919	**ChC-N**	**79**	**267**	**36**	**78**	**12**	**4**	**1**	**17**	**18**	**—**	**16**	**1**	**13**	**—**	**14**	**—**	**.292**	**.339**	**.378**	**.944**
Career average		113	416	52	115	15	6	1	31	29	—	23	1	22	—	21	6	.276	.325	.350	.962
Cubs average		**79**	**267**	**36**	**78**	**12**	**4**	**1**	**17**	**18**	**—**	**16**	**1**	**13**	**—**	**14**	**0**	**.292**	**.339**	**.378**	**.944**
Career total		1015	3741	467	1031	133	54	12	277	265	—	208	9	194	—	186	58	.276	.325	.350	.962
Cubs total		**79**	**267**	**36**	**78**	**12**	**4**	**1**	**17**	**18**	**—**	**16**	**1**	**13**	**—**	**14**	**0**	**.292**	**.339**	**.378**	**.944**

Magoon, George Henry (Maggie *or* Topsie)
HEIGHT: 5'10" THROWS: RIGHT BATS: RIGHT BORN: 3/27/1875 ST. ALBANS, MAINE DIED: 12/6/1943 ROCHESTER, NEW HAMPSHIRE
POSITIONS PLAYED: 2B, 3B, SS

YEAR	TEAM	GAMES	AB	RUNS	HITS	2B	3B	HR	RBI	BB	IBB	SO	HBP	SH	SF	SB	CS	BA	OBA	SA	FA
1898	Bro-N	93	343	35	77	7	0	1	39	30	—	—	3	1	—	7	—	.224	.293	.254	.925
1899	Bal-N	62	207	26	53	8	3	0	31	26	—	—	5	5	—	7	—	.256	.353	.324	.923
1899	**ChN-N**	**59**	**189**	**24**	**43**	**5**	**1**	**0**	**21**	**24**	**—**	**—**	**6**	**13**	**—**	**5**	**—**	**.228**	**.333**	**.265**	**.896**
1901	Cin-N	127	460	47	116	16	7	1	53	52	—	—	2	8	—	7	—	.252	.331	.324	.921
1902	Cin-N	45	162	29	44	9	2	0	23	13	—	—	5	9	—	7	—	.272	.344	.352	.924
1903	Cin-N	42	139	6	30	6	0	0	9	19	—	—	1	5	—	2	—	.216	.314	.259	.957
1903	CWS-A	94	334	32	76	11	3	0	25	30	—	—	6	7	—	4	—	.228	.303	.278	.936
Career average		104	367	40	88	12	3	0	40	39	—	—	6	10	—	9	—	.239	.321	.294	.924
Cubs average		**59**	**189**	**24**	**43**	**5**	**1**	**0**	**21**	**24**	**—**	**—**	**6**	**13**	**—**	**5**	**—**	**.228**	**.333**	**.265**	**.896**
Career total		522	1834	199	439	62	16	2	201	194	—	—	28	48	—	47	—	.239	.321	.294	.924
Cubs total		**59**	**189**	**24**	**43**	**5**	**1**	**0**	**21**	**24**	**—**	**—**	**6**	**13**	**—**	**5**	**—**	**.228**	**.333**	**.265**	**.896**

Maguire, Frederick Edward (Freddie)
HEIGHT: 5'11" THROWS: RIGHT BATS: RIGHT BORN: 5/10/1899 ROXBURY, MASSACHUSETTS DIED: 11/3/1961 BOSTON, MASSACHUSETTS
POSITIONS PLAYED: 2B, 3B

YEAR	TEAM	GAMES	AB	RUNS	HITS	2B	3B	HR	RBI	BB	IBB	SO	HBP	SH	SF	SB	CS	BA	OBA	SA	FA
1922	NYG-N	5	12	4	4	0	0	0	1	0	—	1	0	0	—	1	0	.333	.333	.333	.944
1923	NYG-N	41	30	11	6	1	0	0	2	2	—	4	0	2	—	1	0	.200	.250	.233	.881
1928	**ChC-N**	**140**	**574**	**67**	**160**	**24**	**7**	**1**	**41**	**25**	**—**	**38**	**3**	**37**	**—**	**6**	**—**	**.279**	**.312**	**.350**	**.976**
1929	Bos-N	138	496	54	125	26	8	0	41	19	—	40	3	26	—	8	—	.252	.284	.337	.971
1930	Bos-N	146	516	54	138	21	5	0	52	20	—	22	2	19	—	4	—	.267	.297	.328	.969
1931	Bos-N	148	492	36	112	18	2	0	26	16	—	26	5	31	—	3	—	.228	.259	.272	.976
Career average		103	353	38	91	15	4	0	27	14	—	22	2	19	—	4	0	.257	.289	.322	.971
Cubs average		**140**	**574**	**67**	**160**	**24**	**7**	**1**	**41**	**25**	**—**	**38**	**3**	**37**	**—**	**6**	**0**	**.279**	**.312**	**.350**	**.976**
Career total		618	2120	226	545	90	22	1	163	82	—	131	13	115	—	23	0	.257	.289	.322	.971
Cubs total		**140**	**574**	**67**	**160**	**24**	**7**	**1**	**41**	**25**	**—**	**38**	**3**	**37**	**—**	**6**	**0**	**.279**	**.312**	**.350**	**.976**

Mahoney, Michael John (Mike)
HEIGHT: 6'1" THROWS: RIGHT BATS: RIGHT BORN: 12/5/1972 DES MOINES, IOWA POSITIONS PLAYED: C

YEAR	TEAM	GAMES	AB	RUNS	HITS	2B	3B	HR	RBI	BB	IBB	SO	HBP	SH	SF	SB	CS	BA	OBA	SA	FA
2000	**ChC-N**	**4**	**7**	**1**	**2**	**1**	**0**	**0**	**1**	**1**	**0**	**0**	**1**	**0**	**0**	**0**	**0**	**.286**	**.444**	**.429**	**1.000**
Career average		4	7	1	2	1	0	0	1	1	0	0	1	0	0	0	0	.286	.444	.429	1.000
Cubs average		**4**	**7**	**1**	**2**	**1**	**0**	**0**	**1**	**1**	**0**	**0**	**1**	**0**	**0**	**0**	**0**	**.286**	**.444**	**.429**	**1.000**
Career total		4	7	1	2	1	0	0	1	1	0	0	1	0	0	0	0	.286	.444	.429	1.000
Cubs total		**4**	**7**	**1**	**2**	**1**	**0**	**0**	**1**	**1**	**0**	**0**	**1**	**0**	**0**	**0**	**0**	**.286**	**.444**	**.429**	**1.000**

Maisel, George John
HEIGHT: 5'10"   THROWS: RIGHT   BATS: RIGHT   BORN: 3/12/1892 CATONSVILLE, MARYLAND   DIED: 11/20/1968 BALTIMORE, MARYLAND
POSITIONS PLAYED: 3B, OF

YEAR	TEAM	GAMES	AB	RUNS	HITS	2B	3B	HR	RBI	BB	IBB	SO	HBP	SH	SF	SB	CS	BA	OBA	SA	FA
1913	StL-A	11	18	2	3	2	0	0	1	1	—	7	0	0	—	0	—	.167	.211	.278	.833
1916	Det-A	8	5	2	0	0	0	0	0	0	—	2	0	0	—	0	—	.000	.000	.000	.857
1921	**ChC-N**	111	393	54	122	7	2	0	43	11	—	13	3	20	—	17	7	**.310**	**.334**	**.338**	**.978**
1922	**ChC-N**	38	84	9	16	1	1	0	6	8	—	2	0	6	—	1	3	**.190**	**.261**	**.226**	**1.000**
Career average		42	125	17	35	3	1	0	13	5	—	6	1	7	—	5	3	.282	.314	.314	.977
Cubs average		75	239	32	69	4	2	0	25	10	—	8	2	13	—	9	5	**.289**	**.321**	**.319**	**.982**
Career total		168	500	67	141	10	3	0	50	20	—	24	3	26	—	18	10	.282	.314	.314	.977
Cubs total		149	477	63	138	8	3	0	49	19	—	15	3	26	—	18	10	**.289**	**.321**	**.319**	**.982**

Maksudian, Michael Bryant (Mike)
HEIGHT: 5'11"   THROWS: RIGHT   BATS: LEFT   BORN: 5/28/1966 BELLEVILLE, ILLINOIS   POSITIONS PLAYED: C, 1B, 3B

YEAR	TEAM	GAMES	AB	RUNS	HITS	2B	3B	HR	RBI	BB	IBB	SO	HBP	SH	SF	SB	CS	BA	OBA	SA	FA
1992	Tor-A	3	3	0	0	0	0	0	0	0	0	0	0	0	0	0	0	.000	.000	.000	—
1993	Min-A	5	12	2	2	1	0	0	2	4	0	2	0	0	0	0	0	.167	.353	.250	1.000
1994	**ChC-N**	26	26	6	7	2	0	0	4	10	0	4	0	0	1	0	1	**.269**	**.472**	**.346**	**1.000**
Career average		11	14	3	3	1	0	0	2	5	0	2	0	0	0	0	1	.220	.411	.293	1.000
Cubs average		26	26	6	7	2	0	0	4	10	0	4	0	0	0	0	1	**.269**	**.472**	**.346**	**1.000**
Career total		34	41	8	9	3	0	0	6	14	0	6	0	0	1	0	1	.220	.411	.293	1.000
Cubs total		26	26	6	7	2	0	0	4	10	0	4	0	0	1	0	1	**.269**	**.472**	**.346**	**1.000**

Maldonado, Candido (Candy)
HEIGHT: 6'0"   THROWS: RIGHT   BATS: RIGHT   BORN: 9/5/1960 HUMACAO, PUERTO RICO   POSITIONS PLAYED: 3B, OF

YEAR	TEAM	GAMES	AB	RUNS	HITS	2B	3B	HR	RBI	BB	IBB	SO	HBP	SH	SF	SB	CS	BA	OBA	SA	FA
1981	LA-N	11	12	0	1	0	0	0	0	0	0	5	0	0	0	0	0	.083	.083	.083	1.000
1982	LA-N	6	4	0	0	0	0	0	0	1	1	2	0	0	0	0	0	.000	.200	.000	1.000
1983	LA-N	42	62	5	12	1	1	1	6	5	0	14	0	1	0	0	0	.194	.254	.290	1.000
1984	LA-N	116	254	25	68	14	0	5	28	19	0	29	1	1	3	0	3	.268	.318	.382	.942
1985	LA-N	121	213	20	48	7	1	5	19	19	4	40	0	2	1	1	1	.225	.288	.338	.984
1986	SF-N	133	405	49	102	31	3	18	85	20	4	77	3	0	4	4	4	.252	.289	.477	.983
1987	SF-N	118	442	69	129	28	4	20	85	34	4	78	6	0	7	8	8	.292	.346	.509	.973
1988	SF-N	142	499	53	127	23	1	12	68	37	1	89	7	3	6	6	5	.255	.311	.377	.962
1989	SF-N	129	345	39	75	23	0	9	41	37	4	69	3	1	3	4	1	.217	.296	.362	.974
1990	Cle-A	155	590	76	161	32	2	22	95	49	4	134	5	0	7	3	5	.273	.330	.446	.993
1991	Mil-A	34	111	11	23	6	0	5	20	13	0	23	0	0	1	1	0	.207	.288	.396	.976
1991	Tor-A	52	177	26	49	9	0	7	28	23	4	53	6	0	2	3	0	.277	.375	.446	.990
1992	Tor-A	137	489	64	133	25	4	20	66	59	3	112	7	2	3	2	2	.272	.357	.462	.978
1993	**ChC-N**	70	140	8	26	5	0	3	15	13	0	40	1	0	0	0	0	**.186**	**.260**	**.286**	**.914**
1993	Cle-A	28	81	11	20	2	0	5	20	11	2	18	0	1	1	0	0	.247	.333	.457	.976
1994	Cle-A	42	92	14	18	5	1	5	12	19	1	31	0	0	0	1	1	.196	.333	.435	1.000
1995	Tor-A	61	160	22	43	13	0	7	25	25	1	45	2	0	3	1	1	.269	.368	.481	.988
1995	Tex-A	13	30	6	7	3	0	2	5	7	0	5	0	0	1	1	1	.233	.378	.533	1.000
Career average		94	274	33	69	15	1	10	41	26	2	58	3	1	3	2	2	.254	.322	.424	.976
Cubs average		70	140	8	26	5	0	3	15	13	0	40	1	0	0	0	0	**.186**	**.260**	**.286**	**.914**
Career total		1410	4106	498	1042	227	17	146	618	391	32	864	41	11	41	34	33	.254	.322	.424	.976
Cubs total		70	140	8	26	5	0	3	15	13	0	40	1	0	0	0	0	**.186**	**.260**	**.286**	**.914**

Maloney, William Alphonse (Billy)
HEIGHT: 5'10"   THROWS: RIGHT   BATS: LEFT   BORN: 6/5/1878 LEWISTON, MAINE   DIED: 9/2/1960 BRECKINRIDGE, TEXAS   POSITIONS PLAYED: C, OF

YEAR	TEAM	GAMES	AB	RUNS	HITS	2B	3B	HR	RBI	BB	IBB	SO	HBP	SH	SF	SB	CS	BA	OBA	SA	FA
1901	Mil-A	86	290	42	85	3	4	0	22	7	—	—	8	9	—	11	—	.293	.328	.331	.947
1902	StL-A	30	112	8	23	3	0	0	11	6	—	—	2	1	—	0	—	.205	.258	.232	.919
1902	Cin-N	27	89	13	22	4	0	1	7	2	—	—	1	3	—	8	—	.247	.272	.326	.890
1905	**ChC-N**	145	558	78	145	17	14	2	56	43	—	—	11	15	—	59	—	**.260**	**.325**	**.351**	**.954**

(continued)

(Maloney, continued)

YEAR	TEAM	GAMES	AB	RUNS	HITS	2B	3B	HR	RBI	BB	IBB	SO	HBP	SH	SF	SB	CS	BA	OBA	SA	FA
1906	Bro-N	151	566	71	125	15	7	0	32	49	—	—	3	17	—	38	—	.221	.286	.272	.966
1907	Bro-N	144	502	51	115	7	10	0	32	31	—	—	10	25	—	25	—	.229	.287	.283	.967
1908	Bro-N	113	359	31	70	5	7	3	17	24	—	—	5	14	—	14	—	.195	.255	.273	.951
Career average		116	413	49	98	9	7	1	30	27	—	—	7	14	—	26	—	.236	.294	.299	.954
Cubs average		**145**	**558**	**78**	**145**	**17**	**14**	**2**	**56**	**43**	—	—	**11**	**15**	—	**59**	—	**.260**	**.325**	**.351**	**.954**
Career total		696	2476	294	585	54	42	6	177	162	—	—	40	84	—	155	—	.236	.294	.299	.954
Cubs total		**145**	**558**	**78**	**145**	**17**	**14**	**2**	**56**	**43**	—	—	**11**	**15**	—	**59**	—	**.260**	**.325**	**.351**	**.954**

Mancuso, August Rodney (Gus *or* Blackie)
HEIGHT: 5'10"   THROWS: RIGHT   BATS: RIGHT   BORN: 12/5/1905 GALVESTON, TEXAS   DIED: 10/26/1984 HOUSTON, TEXAS   POSITIONS PLAYED: C

YEAR	TEAM	GAMES	AB	RUNS	HITS	2B	3B	HR	RBI	BB	IBB	SO	HBP	SH	SF	SB	CS	BA	OBA	SA	FA
1928	StL-N	11	38	2	7	0	1	0	3	0	—	5	0	2	—	0	—	.184	.184	.237	.984
1930	StL-N	76	227	39	83	17	2	7	59	18	—	16	1	8	—	1	—	.366	.415	.551	.969
1931	StL-N	67	187	13	49	16	1	1	23	18	—	13	0	3	—	2	—	.262	.327	.374	.972
1932	StL-N	103	310	25	88	23	1	5	43	30	—	15	0	4	—	0	—	.284	.347	.413	.972
1933	NYG-N	144	481	39	127	17	2	6	56	48	—	21	0	11	—	0	—	.264	.331	.345	.972
1934	NYG-N	122	383	32	94	14	0	7	46	27	—	19	0	12	—	0	—	.245	.295	.337	.977
1935	NYG-N	128	447	33	133	18	2	5	56	30	—	16	0	12	—	1	—	.298	.342	.380	.972
1936	NYG-N	139	519	55	156	21	3	9	63	39	—	28	1	5	—	1	—	.301	.351	.405	.982
1937	NYG-N	86	287	30	80	17	1	4	39	17	—	20	0	3	—	0	—	.279	.319	.387	.977
1938	NYG-N	52	158	19	55	8	0	2	15	17	—	13	0	3	—	0	—	.348	.411	.437	.977
1939	**ChC-N**	**80**	**251**	**17**	**58**	**10**	**0**	**2**	**17**	**24**	—	**19**	**0**	**6**	—	**0**	—	**.231**	**.298**	**.295**	**.981**
1940	Bro-N	60	144	16	33	8	0	0	16	13	—	7	0	0	—	0	—	.229	.293	.285	.982
1941	StL-N	106	328	25	75	13	1	2	37	37	—	19	1	9	—	0	—	.229	.309	.293	.989
1942	StL-N	5	13	0	1	0	0	0	1	0	—	0	0	0	—	0	—	.077	.077	.077	.917
1942	NYG-N	39	109	4	21	1	1	0	8	14	—	7	0	3	—	1	—	.193	.285	.220	.982
1943	NYG-N	94	252	11	50	5	0	2	20	28	—	16	2	8	—	0	0	.198	.284	.242	.974
1944	NYG-N	78	195	15	49	4	1	1	25	30	—	20	0	6	—	0	0	.251	.351	.297	.976
1945	Phi-N	70	176	11	35	5	0	0	16	28	—	10	0	2	—	2	—	.199	.309	.227	.988
Career average		86	265	23	70	12	1	3	32	25	—	16	0	6	—	0	0	.265	.328	.351	.977
Cubs average		**80**	**251**	**17**	**58**	**10**	**0**	**2**	**17**	**24**	—	**19**	**0**	**6**	—	**0**	—	**.231**	**.298**	**.295**	**.981**
Career total		1460	4505	386	1194	197	16	53	543	418	—	264	5	97	—	8	0	.265	.328	.351	.977
Cubs total		**80**	**251**	**17**	**58**	**10**	**0**	**2**	**17**	**24**	—	**19**	**0**	**6**	—	**0**	—	**.231**	**.298**	**.295**	**.981**

Mann, Ben Garth (Garth)
HEIGHT: 6'0"   THROWS: RIGHT   BATS: RIGHT   BORN: 11/16/1915 BRANDON, TEXAS   DIED: 9/11/1980 ITALY, TEXAS

YEAR	TEAM	GAMES	AB	RUNS	HITS	2B	3B	HR	RBI	BB	IBB	SO	HBP	SH	SF	SB	CS	BA	OBA	SA	FA
1944	**ChC-N**	**1**	**0**	**1**	**0**	**0**	**0**	**0**	**0**	**0**	—	**0**	**0**	**0**	—	**0**	—	—	—	—	—
Career average		1	0	1	0	0	0	0	0	0	—	0	0	0	—	0	—	—	—	—	—
Cubs average		**1**	**0**	**1**	**0**	**0**	**0**	**0**	**0**	**0**	—	**0**	**0**	**0**	—	**0**	—	—	—	—	—
Career total		1	0	1	0	0	0	0	0	0	—	0	0	0	—	0	—	—	—	—	—
Cubs total		**1**	**0**	**1**	**0**	**0**	**0**	**0**	**0**	**0**	—	**0**	**0**	**0**	—	**0**	—	—	—	—	—

Mann, Leslie (Les *or* Major)
HEIGHT: 5'9"   THROWS: RIGHT   BATS: RIGHT   BORN: 11/18/1893 LINCOLN, NEBRASKA   DIED: 1/14/1962 PASADENA, CALIFORNIA   POSITIONS PLAYED: SS, OF

YEAR	TEAM	GAMES	AB	RUNS	HITS	2B	3B	HR	RBI	BB	IBB	SO	HBP	SH	SF	SB	CS	BA	OBA	SA	FA
1913	Bos-N	120	407	54	103	24	7	3	51	18	—	73	4	6	—	7	—	.253	.291	.369	.960
1914	Bos-N	126	389	44	96	16	11	4	40	24	—	50	1	11	—	9	—	.247	.292	.375	.952
1915	Chi-F	135	470	74	144	12	19	4	58	36	—	40	1	9	—	18	—	.306	.357	.438	.969
1916	**ChC-N**	**127**	**415**	**46**	**113**	**13**	**9**	**2**	**29**	**19**	—	**31**	**2**	**8**	—	**11**	**7**	**.272**	**.307**	**.361**	**.972**
1917	**ChC-N**	**117**	**444**	**63**	**121**	**19**	**10**	**1**	**44**	**27**	—	**46**	**1**	**13**	—	**14**	—	**.273**	**.316**	**.367**	**.953**
1918	**ChC-N**	**129**	**489**	**69**	**141**	**27**	**7**	**2**	**55**	**38**	—	**45**	**2**	**26**	—	**21**	—	**.288**	**.342**	**.384**	**.961**
1919	**ChC-N**	**80**	**299**	**31**	**68**	**8**	**8**	**1**	**22**	**11**	—	**29**	**1**	**11**	—	**12**	—	**.227**	**.257**	**.318**	**.982**
1919	Bos-N	40	145	15	41	6	4	3	20	9	—	14	1	5	—	7	—	.283	.329	.441	.929
1920	Bos-N	115	424	48	117	7	8	3	32	38	—	42	4	11	—	7	7	.276	.341	.351	.980
1921	StL-N	97	256	57	84	12	7	7	30	23	—	28	3	7	—	5	5	.328	.390	.512	.969
1922	StL-N	84	147	42	51	14	1	2	20	16	—	12	1	3	—	0	1	.347	.415	.497	.978
1923	StL-N	38	89	20	33	5	2	5	11	9	—	5	1	0	—	0	0	.371	.434	.640	.979
1923	Cin-N	8	1	1	0	0	0	0	0	0	—	0	0	0	—	0	0	.000	.000	.000	—
1924	Bos-N	32	102	13	28	7	4	0	10	8	—	10	1	1	—	1	0	.275	.333	.422	1.000

(continued)

(continued)

YEAR	TEAM	GAMES	AB	RUNS	HITS	2B	3B	HR	RBI	BB	IBB	SO	HBP	SH	SF	SB	CS	BA	OBA	SA	FA
1925	Bos-N	60	184	27	63	11	4	2	20	5	—	11	4	6	—	6	1	.342	.373	.478	.992
1926	Bos-N	50	129	23	39	8	2	1	20	9	—	9	0	3	—	5	—	.302	.348	.419	.966
1927	Bos-N	29	66	8	17	3	1	0	6	8	—	3	0	1	—	2	—	.258	.338	.333	.955
1927	NYG-N	29	67	13	22	4	1	2	10	8	—	7	0	0	—	2	—	.328	.400	.507	1.000
1928	NYG-N	82	193	29	51	7	1	2	25	18	—	9	1	12	—	2	—	.264	.330	.342	.952
Career average		94	295	42	83	13	7	3	31	20	—	29	2	8	—	8	1	.282	.332	.398	.966
Cubs average		**113**	**412**	**52**	**111**	**17**	**9**	**2**	**38**	**24**	**—**	**38**	**2**	**15**	**—**	**15**	**2**	**.269**	**.311**	**.362**	**.966**
Career total		1498	4716	677	1332	203	106	44	503	324	—	464	28	133	—	129	21	.282	.332	.398	.966
Cubs total		**453**	**1647**	**209**	**443**	**67**	**34**	**6**	**150**	**95**	**—**	**151**	**6**	**58**	**—**	**58**	**7**	**.269**	**.311**	**.362**	**.966**

Maranville, Walter James Vincent (Rabbit)

HEIGHT: 5'5"   THROWS: RIGHT   BATS: RIGHT   BORN: 11/11/1891 SPRINGFIELD, MASSACHUSETTS   DIED: 1/5/1954 NEW YORK, NEW YORK
POSITIONS PLAYED: 2B, 3B, SS

YEAR	TEAM	GAMES	AB	RUNS	HITS	2B	3B	HR	RBI	BB	IBB	SO	HBP	SH	SF	SB	CS	BA	OBA	SA	FA
1912	Bos-N	26	86	8	18	2	0	0	8	9	—	14	1	5	—	1	—	.209	.292	.233	.929
1913	Bos-N	143	571	68	141	13	8	2	48	68	—	62	3	17	—	25	—	.247	.330	.308	.949
1914	Bos-N	156	586	74	144	23	6	4	78	45	—	56	6	27	—	28	—	.246	.306	.326	.938
1915	Bos-N	149	509	51	124	23	6	2	43	45	—	65	2	23	—	18	12	.244	.308	.324	.941
1916	Bos-N	155	604	79	142	16	13	4	38	50	—	69	2	24	—	32	15	.235	.296	.325	.947
1917	Bos-N	142	561	69	146	19	13	3	43	40	—	47	2	10	—	27	—	.260	.312	.357	.947
1918	Bos-N	11	38	3	12	0	1	0	3	4	—	0	0	0	—	0	—	.316	.381	.368	.932
1919	Bos-N	131	480	44	128	18	10	5	43	36	—	23	1	12	—	12	—	.267	.319	.377	.941
1920	Bos-N	134	493	48	131	19	15	1	43	28	—	24	0	13	—	14	11	.266	.305	.371	.948
1921	Pit-N	153	612	90	180	25	12	1	70	47	—	38	3	23	—	25	12	.294	.347	.379	.962
1922	Pit-N	155	672	115	198	26	15	0	63	61	—	43	2	12	—	24	13	.295	.355	.378	.963
1923	Pit-N	141	581	78	161	19	9	1	41	42	—	34	1	9	—	14	11	.277	.327	.346	.965
1924	Pit-N	152	594	62	158	33	20	2	71	35	—	53	0	11	—	18	14	.266	.307	.399	.973
1925	**ChC-N**	**75**	**266**	**37**	**62**	**10**	**3**	**0**	**23**	**29**	**—**	**20**	**0**	**10**	**—**	**6**	**5**	**.233**	**.308**	**.293**	**.955**
1926	Bro-N	78	234	32	55	8	5	0	24	26	—	24	0	6	—	7	—	.235	.312	.312	.955
1927	StL-N	9	29	0	7	1	0	0	0	2	—	2	0	0	—	0	—	.241	.290	.276	.962
1928	StL-N	112	366	40	88	14	10	1	34	36	—	27	1	9	—	3	—	.240	.310	.342	.970
1929	Bos-N	146	560	87	159	26	10	0	55	47	—	33	4	23	—	13	—	.284	.344	.366	.961
1930	Bos-N	142	558	85	157	26	8	2	43	48	—	23	5	17	—	9	—	.281	.344	.367	.965
1931	Bos-N	145	562	69	146	22	5	0	33	56	—	34	2	16	—	9	—	.260	.329	.317	.948
1932	Bos-N	149	571	67	134	20	4	0	37	46	—	28	3	15	—	4	—	.235	.295	.284	.975
1933	Bos-N	143	478	46	104	15	4	0	38	36	—	34	1	17	—	2	—	.218	.274	.266	.971
1935	Bos-N	23	67	3	10	2	0	0	5	3	—	3	0	1	—	0	—	.149	.186	.179	.963
Career average		116	438	55	113	17	8	1	38	36	—	33	2	13	—	13	4	.258	.318	.340	.956
Cubs average		**75**	**266**	**37**	**62**	**10**	**3**	**0**	**23**	**29**	**—**	**20**	**0**	**10**	**—**	**6**	**5**	**.233**	**.308**	**.293**	**.955**
Career total		2670	10078	1255	2605	380	177	28	884	839	—	756	39	300	—	291	93	.258	.318	.340	.956
Cubs total		**75**	**266**	**37**	**62**	**10**	**3**	**0**	**23**	**29**	**—**	**20**	**0**	**10**	**—**	**6**	**5**	**.233**	**.308**	**.293**	**.955**

Marquez, Gonzalo Enrique

HEIGHT: 5'11"   THROWS: LEFT   BATS: LEFT   BORN: 3/31/1946 CAUPANO, VENEZUELA   DIED: 12/20/1984 VALENCIA, VENEZUELA
POSITIONS PLAYED: 1B, 2B, OF

YEAR	TEAM	GAMES	AB	RUNS	HITS	2B	3B	HR	RBI	BB	IBB	SO	HBP	SH	SF	SB	CS	BA	OBA	SA	FA
1972	Oak-A	23	21	2	8	0	0	0	4	3	0	4	1	0	1	1	1	.381	.462	.381	.929
1973	Oak-A	23	25	1	6	1	0	0	2	0	0	4	0	0	0	0	0	.240	.240	.280	1.000
1973	**ChC-N**	**19**	**58**	**5**	**13**	**2**	**0**	**1**	**4**	**3**	**1**	**4**	**1**	**2**	**1**	**0**	**0**	**.224**	**.270**	**.310**	**.994**
1974	**ChC-N**	**11**	**11**	**1**	**0**	**0**	**0**	**0**	**0**	**1**	**1**	**2**	**0**	**0**	**0**	**0**	**0**	**.000**	**.083**	**.000**	**1.000**
Career average		25	38	3	9	1	0	0	3	2	1	5	1	1	1	0	0	.235	.286	.287	.989
Cubs average		**15**	**35**	**3**	**7**	**1**	**0**	**1**	**2**	**2**	**1**	**3**	**1**	**1**	**1**	**0**	**0**	**.188**	**.240**	**.261**	**.994**
Career total		76	115	9	27	3	0	1	10	7	2	14	2	2	2	1	1	.235	.286	.287	.989
Cubs total		**30**	**69**	**6**	**13**	**2**	**0**	**1**	**4**	**4**	**2**	**6**	**1**	**2**	**1**	**0**	**1**	**.188**	**.240**	**.261**	**.994**

Marquez, Luis Angel
HEIGHT: 5'10" THROWS: RIGHT BATS: RIGHT   BORN: 10/28/1925 AGUADILLA, PUERTO RICO   DIED: 3/1/1988 AGUADILLA, PUERTO RICO
POSITIONS PLAYED: OF

YEAR	TEAM	GAMES	AB	RUNS	HITS	2B	3B	HR	RBI	BB	IBB	SO	HBP	SH	SF	SB	CS	BA	OBA	SA	FA
1951	Bos-N	68	122	19	24	5	1	0	11	10	—	20	3	3	—	4	4	.197	.274	.254	1.000
1954	**ChC-N**	**17**	**12**	**2**	**1**	**0**	**0**	**0**	**0**	**2**	**—**	**4**	**0**	**1**	**0**	**3**	**0**	**.083**	**.214**	**.083**	**1.000**
1954	Pit-N	14	9	3	1	0	0	0	0	4	—	0	0	1	0	0	0	.111	.385	.111	1.000
Career average		50	72	12	13	3	1	0	6	8	—	12	2	3	0	4	2	.182	.278	.231	1.000
Cubs average		**17**	**12**	**2**	**1**	**0**	**0**	**0**	**0**	**2**	**—**	**4**	**0**	**1**	**0**	**3**	**0**	**.083**	**.214**	**.083**	**1.000**
Career total		99	143	24	26	5	1	0	11	16	—	24	3	5	0	7	4	.182	.278	.231	1.000
Cubs total		**17**	**12**	**2**	**1**	**0**	**0**	**0**	**0**	**2**	**—**	**4**	**0**	**1**	**0**	**3**	**0**	**.083**	**.214**	**.083**	**1.000**

Marriott, William Earl
HEIGHT: 6'0" THROWS: RIGHT BATS: LEFT   BORN: 8/18/1893 PRATT, KANSAS   DIED: 8/11/1969 BERKELEY, CALIFORNIA   POSITIONS PLAYED: 2B, 3B, SS, OF

YEAR	TEAM	GAMES	AB	RUNS	HITS	2B	3B	HR	RBI	BB	IBB	SO	HBP	SH	SF	SB	CS	BA	OBA	SA	FA
1917	**ChC-N**	**3**	**6**	**0**	**0**	**0**	**0**	**0**	**0**	**0**	**—**	**1**	**0**	**0**	**—**	**0**	**—**	**.000**	**.000**	**.000**	**.667**
1920	**ChC-N**	**14**	**43**	**7**	**12**	**4**	**2**	**0**	**5**	**6**	**—**	**5**	**0**	**1**	**—**	**1**	**1**	**.279**	**.367**	**.465**	**.892**
1921	**ChC-N**	**30**	**38**	**3**	**12**	**1**	**1**	**0**	**7**	**4**	**—**	**1**	**0**	**2**	**—**	**0**	**1**	**.316**	**.381**	**.395**	**.828**
1925	Bos-N	103	370	37	99	9	1	1	40	28	—	26	2	11	—	3	8	.268	.323	.305	.929
1926	Bro-N	109	360	39	96	13	9	3	42	17	—	20	2	10	—	12	—	.267	.303	.378	.927
1927	Bro-N	6	9	0	1	0	1	0	1	2	—	2	0	0	—	0	—	.111	.273	.333	.889
Career average		44	138	14	37	5	2	1	16	10	—	9	1	4	—	3	2	.266	.317	.347	.918
Cubs average		**16**	**29**	**3**	**8**	**2**	**1**	**0**	**4**	**3**	**—**	**2**	**0**	**1**	**—**	**0**	**1**	**.276**	**.351**	**.402**	**.868**
Career total		265	826	86	220	27	14	4	95	57	—	55	4	24	—	16	10	.266	.317	.347	.918
Cubs total		**47**	**87**	**10**	**24**	**5**	**3**	**0**	**12**	**10**	**—**	**7**	**0**	**3**	**—**	**1**	**2**	**.276**	**.351**	**.402**	**.868**

Marshall, Rufus James (Jim)
HEIGHT: 6'1" THROWS: LEFT BATS: LEFT   BORN: 5/25/1931 DANVILLE, ILLINOIS   POSITIONS PLAYED: 1B, OF

YEAR	TEAM	GAMES	AB	RUNS	HITS	2B	3B	HR	RBI	BB	IBB	SO	HBP	SH	SF	SB	CS	BA	OBA	SA	FA
1958	Bal-A	85	191	17	41	4	3	5	19	18	1	30	0	0	2	3	2	.215	.280	.346	1.000
1958	**ChC-N**	**26**	**81**	**12**	**22**	**2**	**0**	**5**	**11**	**12**	**0**	**13**	**1**	**0**	**0**	**1**	**0**	**.272**	**.372**	**.481**	**.992**
1959	**ChC-N**	**108**	**294**	**39**	**74**	**10**	**2**	**11**	**40**	**33**	**1**	**39**	**0**	**1**	**3**	**0**	**1**	**.252**	**.324**	**.405**	**.997**
1960	SF-N	75	118	19	28	2	2	2	13	17	1	24	0	0	1	0	1	.237	.331	.339	.969
1961	SF-N	44	36	5	8	0	0	1	7	3	0	8	0	0	1	0	0	.222	.275	.306	1.000
1962	NYM-N	17	32	6	11	1	0	3	4	3	0	6	0	0	0	0	0	.344	.400	.656	1.000
1962	Pit-N	55	100	13	22	5	1	2	12	15	0	19	0	0	1	1	0	.220	.319	.350	1.000
Career average		82	170	22	41	5	1	6	21	20	1	28	0	0	2	1	1	.242	.320	.388	.994
Cubs average		**67**	**188**	**26**	**48**	**6**	**1**	**8**	**26**	**23**	**1**	**26**	**1**	**1**	**2**	**1**	**1**	**.256**	**.335**	**.421**	**.996**
Career total		410	852	111	206	24	7	29	106	101	3	139	1	1	8	5	4	.242	.320	.388	.994
Cubs total		**134**	**375**	**51**	**96**	**12**	**1**	**16**	**51**	**45**	**1**	**52**	**1**	**1**	**3**	**1**	**1**	**.256**	**.335**	**.421**	**.996**

Marshall, William Riddle (Doc)
HEIGHT: 6'0" THROWS: RIGHT BATS: RIGHT   BORN: 9/22/1875 BUTLER, PENNSYLVANIA   DIED: 12/11/1959 CLINTON, ILLINOIS
POSITIONS PLAYED: C, 1B, 2B, OF

YEAR	TEAM	GAMES	AB	RUNS	HITS	2B	3B	HR	RBI	BB	IBB	SO	HBP	SH	SF	SB	CS	BA	OBA	SA	FA
1904	Phi-N	8	20	1	2	0	0	0	1	0	—	—	0	0	—	0	—	.100	.100	.100	.944
1904	NYG-N	11	17	3	6	1	0	0	2	1	—	—	0	0	—	0	—	.353	.389	.412	.871
1904	Bos-N	13	43	3	9	0	1	0	2	2	—	—	0	0	—	2	—	.209	.244	.256	.955
1906	NYG-N	38	102	8	17	3	2	0	7	7	—	—	2	2	—	7	—	.167	.234	.235	1.000
1906	StL-N	39	123	6	34	4	1	0	10	6	—	—	1	3	—	1	—	.276	.315	.325	.961
1907	StL-N	84	268	19	54	8	2	2	18	12	—	—	4	4	—	2	—	.201	.246	.269	.952
1908	StL-N	6	14	0	1	0	0	0	1	0	—	—	0	1	—	0	—	.071	.071	.071	1.000
1908	**ChC-N**	**12**	**20**	**4**	**6**	**0**	**1**	**0**	**3**	**0**	**—**	**—**	**0**	**0**	**—**	**0**	**—**	**.300**	**.300**	**.400**	**.963**
1909	Bro-N	50	149	7	30	7	1	0	10	6	—	—	0	1	—	3	—	.201	.232	.262	.968
Career average		52	151	10	32	5	2	0	11	7	—	—	1	2	—	3	—	.210	.251	.270	.960
Cubs average		**12**	**20**	**4**	**6**	**0**	**1**	**0**	**3**	**0**	**—**	**—**	**0**	**0**	**—**	**0**	**—**	**.300**	**.300**	**.400**	**.963**
Career total		261	756	51	159	23	8	2	54	34	—	—	7	11	—	15	—	.210	.251	.270	.960
Cubs total		**12**	**20**	**4**	**6**	**0**	**1**	**0**	**3**	**0**	**—**	**—**	**0**	**0**	**—**	**0**	**—**	**.300**	**.300**	**.400**	**.963**

Martin, Frank
HEIGHT: —   THROWS: —   BATS: —   BORN: 2/28/1879 CHICAGO, ILLINOIS   DIED: 9/30/1924 CHICAGO, ILLINOIS   POSITIONS PLAYED: 2B, 3B

YEAR	TEAM	GAMES	AB	RUNS	HITS	2B	3B	HR	RBI	BB	IBB	SO	HBP	SH	SF	SB	CS	BA	OBA	SA	FA
1897	Lou-N	2	8	1	2	0	0	0	0	0	—	—	0	0	—	0	—	.250	.250	.250	.813
1898	**ChN-N**	**1**	**4**	**0**	**0**	**0**	**0**	**0**	**0**	**0**	**—**	**—**	**0**	**0**	**—**	**0**	**—**	**.000**	**.000**	**.000**	**1.000**
1899	NYG-N	17	54	5	14	2	0	0	1	2	—	—	1	0	—	0	—	.259	.298	.296	.824
Career average		7	22	2	5	1	0	0	0	1	—	—	0	0	—	0	—	.242	.275	.273	.835
Cubs average		**1**	**4**	**0**	**0**	**0**	**0**	**0**	**0**	**0**	**—**	**—**	**0**	**0**	**—**	**0**	**—**	**.000**	**.000**	**.000**	**1.000**
Career total		20	66	6	16	2	0	0	1	2	—	—	1	0	—	0	—	.242	.275	.273	.835
Cubs total		**1**	**4**	**0**	**0**	**0**	**0**	**0**	**0**	**0**	**—**	**—**	**0**	**0**	**—**	**0**	**—**	**.000**	**.000**	**.000**	**1.000**

Martin, Joseph Clifton (J.C.)
HEIGHT: 6'2"   THROWS: RIGHT   BATS: LEFT   BORN: 12/13/1936 AXTON, VIRGINIA   POSITIONS PLAYED: C, 1B, 3B, OF

YEAR	TEAM	GAMES	AB	RUNS	HITS	2B	3B	HR	RBI	BB	IBB	SO	HBP	SH	SF	SB	CS	BA	OBA	SA	FA
1959	CWS-A	3	4	0	1	0	0	0	1	0	0	1	0	0	0	0	0	.250	.250	.250	.667
1960	CWS-A	7	20	0	2	1	0	0	2	0	0	6	0	0	0	0	0	.100	.100	.150	1.000
1961	CWS-A	110	274	26	63	8	3	5	32	21	2	31	2	3	0	1	2	.230	.290	.336	.979
1962	CWS-A	18	26	0	2	0	0	0	2	0	0	3	0	0	0	0	0	.077	.077	.077	1.000
1963	CWS-A	105	259	25	53	11	1	5	28	26	6	35	1	2	2	0	0	.205	.278	.313	.983
1964	CWS-A	122	294	23	58	10	1	4	22	16	7	30	2	3	3	0	0	.197	.241	.279	.986
1965	CWS-A	119	230	21	60	12	0	2	21	24	10	29	2	3	2	2	1	.261	.333	.339	.984
1966	CWS-A	67	157	13	40	5	3	2	20	14	6	24	1	1	2	0	0	.255	.316	.363	.982
1967	CWS-A	101	252	22	59	12	1	4	22	30	4	41	1	2	1	0	0	.234	.317	.337	.987
1968	NYM-N	78	244	20	55	9	2	3	31	21	3	31	5	3	2	4	4	.225	.298	.316	.988
1969	NYM-N	66	177	12	37	5	1	4	21	12	1	32	0	1	2	0	0	.209	.257	.316	.997
1970	**ChC-N**	**40**	**77**	**11**	**12**	**1**	**0**	**1**	**4**	**20**	**7**	**11**	**1**	**1**	**1**	**0**	**0**	**.156**	**.333**	**.208**	**.973**
1971	**ChC-N**	**47**	**125**	**13**	**33**	**5**	**0**	**2**	**17**	**12**	**6**	**16**	**2**	**2**	**1**	**1**	**1**	**.264**	**.336**	**.352**	**.996**
1972	**ChC-N**	**25**	**50**	**3**	**12**	**3**	**0**	**0**	**7**	**5**	**1**	**9**	**0**	**1**	**1**	**1**	**0**	**.240**	**.304**	**.300**	**.970**
Career average		65	156	14	35	6	1	2	16	14	4	21	1	2	1	1	1	.222	.291	.315	.985
Cubs average		**37**	**84**	**9**	**19**	**3**	**0**	**1**	**9**	**12**	**5**	**12**	**1**	**1**	**1**	**1**	**0**	**.226**	**.329**	**.298**	**.984**
Career total		908	2189	189	487	82	12	32	230	201	53	299	17	22	17	9	8	.222	.291	.315	.985
Cubs total		**112**	**252**	**27**	**57**	**9**	**0**	**3**	**28**	**37**	**14**	**36**	**3**	**4**	**3**	**2**	**1**	**.226**	**.329**	**.298**	**.984**

Martin, Jerry Lindsey
HEIGHT: 6'1"   THROWS: RIGHT   BATS: RIGHT   BORN: 5/11/1949 COLUMBIA, SOUTH CAROLINA   POSITIONS PLAYED: 1B, OF

YEAR	TEAM	GAMES	AB	RUNS	HITS	2B	3B	HR	RBI	BB	IBB	SO	HBP	SH	SF	SB	CS	BA	OBA	SA	FA
1974	Phi-N	13	14	2	3	1	0	0	1	1	0	5	0	0	0	0	0	.214	.267	.286	1.000
1975	Phi-N	57	113	15	24	7	1	2	11	11	4	16	1	3	0	2	2	.212	.288	.345	.979
1976	Phi-N	130	121	30	30	7	0	2	15	7	0	28	0	0	1	3	2	.248	.287	.355	.977
1977	Phi-N	116	215	34	56	16	3	6	28	18	2	42	4	0	1	6	4	.260	.328	.447	.984
1978	Phi-N	128	266	40	72	13	4	9	36	28	3	65	1	0	3	9	5	.271	.339	.451	.987
1979	**ChC-N**	**150**	**534**	**74**	**145**	**34**	**3**	**19**	**73**	**38**	**3**	**85**	**3**	**0**	**4**	**2**	**4**	**.272**	**.321**	**.453**	**.981**
1980	**ChC-N**	**141**	**494**	**57**	**112**	**22**	**2**	**23**	**73**	**38**	**6**	**107**	**2**	**0**	**6**	**8**	**3**	**.227**	**.281**	**.419**	**.978**
1981	SF-N	72	241	23	58	5	3	4	25	21	2	52	3	1	1	6	2	.241	.308	.336	.993
1982	KC-A	147	519	52	138	22	1	15	65	38	0	138	2	2	4	1	1	.266	.316	.399	.980
1983	KC-A	13	44	4	14	2	0	2	13	1	0	7	0	0	3	1	0	.318	.313	.500	.957
1984	NYM-N	51	91	6	14	1	0	3	5	6	0	29	0	0	0	0	0	.154	.206	.264	1.000
Career average		93	241	31	61	12	2	8	31	19	2	52	1	1	2	3	2	.251	.307	.409	.982
Cubs average		**146**	**514**	**66**	**129**	**28**	**3**	**21**	**73**	**38**	**5**	**96**	**3**	**0**	**5**	**5**	**4**	**.250**	**.302**	**.437**	**.980**
Career total		1018	2652	337	666	130	17	85	345	207	20	574	16	6	23	38	23	.251	.307	.409	.982
Cubs total		**291**	**1028**	**131**	**257**	**56**	**5**	**42**	**146**	**76**	**9**	**192**	**5**	**0**	**10**	**10**	**7**	**.250**	**.302**	**.437**	**.980**

Martin, Joseph Michael (Mike)
HEIGHT: 6'2" THROWS: RIGHT BATS: LEFT BORN: 12/3/1958 PORTLAND, OREGON POSITIONS PLAYED: C

YEAR	TEAM	GAMES	AB	RUNS	HITS	2B	3B	HR	RBI	BB	IBB	SO	HBP	SH	SF	SB	CS	BA	OBA	SA	FA
1986	ChC-N	8	13	1	1	1	0	0	0	2	1	4	0	0	0	0	0	.077	.200	.154	1.000
Career average		8	13	1	1	1	0	0	0	2	1	4	0	0	0	0	0	.077	.200	.154	1.000
Cubs average		**8**	**13**	**1**	**1**	**1**	**0**	**0**	**0**	**2**	**1**	**4**	**0**	**0**	**0**	**0**	**0**	**.077**	**.200**	**.154**	**1.000**
Career total		8	13	1	1	1	0	0	0	2	1	4	0	0	0	0	0	.077	.200	.154	1.000
Cubs total		**8**	**13**	**1**	**1**	**1**	**0**	**0**	**0**	**2**	**1**	**4**	**0**	**0**	**0**	**0**	**0**	**.077**	**.200**	**.154**	**1.000**

Martin, Stuart McGuire (Stu)
HEIGHT: 6'0" THROWS: RIGHT BATS: LEFT BORN: 11/17/1913 RICH SQUARE, NORTH CAROLINA DIED: 1/11/1997 SEVERN, NORTH CAROLINA
POSITIONS PLAYED: 1B, 2B, 3B, SS

YEAR	TEAM	GAMES	AB	RUNS	HITS	2B	3B	HR	RBI	BB	IBB	SO	HBP	SH	SF	SB	CS	BA	OBA	SA	FA
1936	StL-N	92	332	63	99	21	4	6	41	29	—	27	1	4	—	17	—	.298	.356	.440	.951
1937	StL-N	90	223	34	58	6	1	1	17	32	—	18	0	5	—	3	—	.260	.353	.309	.956
1938	StL-N	114	417	54	116	26	2	1	27	30	—	28	1	12	—	4	—	.278	.328	.357	.967
1939	StL-N	120	425	60	114	26	7	3	30	33	—	40	3	11	—	4	—	.268	.325	.384	.977
1940	StL-N	112	369	45	88	12	6	4	32	33	—	35	0	5	—	4	—	.238	.301	.336	.974
1941	Pit-N	88	233	37	71	13	2	0	19	10	—	17	3	5	—	2	—	.305	.341	.378	.970
1942	Pit-N	42	120	16	27	4	2	1	12	8	—	10	0	2	—	1	—	.225	.273	.317	.979
1943	**ChC-N**	**64**	**118**	**13**	**26**	**4**	**0**	**0**	**5**	**15**	**—**	**10**	**0**	**2**	**—**	**1**	**—**	**.220**	**.308**	**.254**	**.985**
Career average		90	280	40	75	14	3	2	23	24	—	23	1	6	—	5	—	.268	.327	.361	.968
Cubs average		**64**	**118**	**13**	**26**	**4**	**0**	**0**	**5**	**15**	**—**	**10**	**0**	**2**	**—**	**1**	**—**	**.220**	**.308**	**.254**	**.985**
Career total		722	2237	322	599	112	24	16	183	190	—	185	8	46	—	36	—	.268	.327	.361	.968
Cubs total		**64**	**118**	**13**	**26**	**4**	**0**	**0**	**5**	**15**	**—**	**10**	**0**	**2**	**—**	**1**	**—**	**.220**	**.308**	**.254**	**.985**

Martinez, Angel Sandy (Sandy)
HEIGHT: 6'2" THROWS: RIGHT BATS: LEFT BORN: 10/3/1972 VILLA MELLA, DOMINICAN REPUBLIC POSITIONS PLAYED: C

YEAR	TEAM	GAMES	AB	RUNS	HITS	2B	3B	HR	RBI	BB	IBB	SO	HBP	SH	SF	SB	CS	BA	OBA	SA	FA
1995	Tor-A	62	191	12	46	12	0	2	25	7	0	45	1	0	1	0	0	.241	.270	.335	.986
1996	Tor-A	76	229	17	52	9	3	3	18	16	0	58	4	1	1	0	0	.227	.288	.332	.993
1997	Tor-A	3	2	1	0	0	0	0	0	1	0	1	0	0	0	0	0	.000	.333	.000	.933
1998	**ChC-N**	**45**	**87**	**7**	**23**	**9**	**1**	**0**	**7**	**13**	**0**	**21**	**1**	**0**	**1**	**1**	**0**	**.264**	**.363**	**.391**	**.985**
1999	**ChC-N**	**17**	**30**	**1**	**5**	**0**	**0**	**1**	**1**	**0**	**0**	**11**	**0**	**0**	**0**	**0**	**0**	**.167**	**.167**	**.267**	**.959**
2000	Fla-N	10	18	1	4	2	0	0	0	0	0	8	0	0	0	0	0	.222	.222	.333	1.000
2001	Mon-N	1	1	0	0	0	0	0	0	0	0	0	0	0	0	0	0	.000	.000	.000	1.000
Career average		31	80	6	19	5	1	1	7	5	0	21	1	0	0	0	0	.233	.286	.337	.987
Cubs average		**31**	**59**	**4**	**14**	**5**	**1**	**1**	**4**	**7**	**0**	**16**	**1**	**0**	**1**	**1**	**0**	**.239**	**.318**	**.359**	**.980**
Career total		214	558	39	130	32	4	6	51	37	0	144	6	1	3	1	0	.233	.286	.337	.987
Cubs total		**62**	**117**	**8**	**28**	**9**	**1**	**1**	**8**	**13**	**0**	**32**	**1**	**0**	**1**	**1**	**0**	**.239**	**.318**	**.359**	**.980**

Martinez, Carmelo (Bitu)
HEIGHT: 6'2" THROWS: RIGHT BATS: RIGHT BORN: 7/28/1960 DORADO, PUERTO RICO POSITIONS PLAYED: 1B, 3B, OF

YEAR	TEAM	GAMES	AB	RUNS	HITS	2B	3B	HR	RBI	BB	IBB	SO	HBP	SH	SF	SB	CS	BA	OBA	SA	FA
1983	**ChC-N**	**29**	**89**	**8**	**23**	**3**	**0**	**6**	**16**	**4**	**0**	**19**	**0**	**0**	**1**	**0**	**0**	**.258**	**.287**	**.494**	**.992**
1984	SD-N	149	488	64	122	28	2	13	66	68	4	82	4	0	10	1	3	.250	.340	.395	.976
1985	SD-N	150	514	64	130	28	1	21	72	87	4	82	3	2	4	0	4	.253	.362	.434	.978
1986	SD-N	113	244	28	58	10	0	9	25	35	2	46	1	1	2	1	1	.238	.333	.389	.987
1987	SD-N	139	447	59	122	21	2	15	70	70	5	82	3	1	4	5	5	.273	.372	.430	.986
1988	SD-N	121	365	48	86	12	0	18	65	35	3	57	0	3	2	1	1	.236	.301	.416	.991
1989	SD-N	111	267	23	59	12	2	6	39	32	3	54	0	0	2	0	0	.221	.302	.348	.992
1990	Phi-N	71	198	23	48	8	0	8	31	29	0	37	0	0	0	2	1	.242	.339	.404	.995
1990	Pit-N	12	19	3	4	1	0	2	4	1	0	5	0	0	0	0	0	.211	.250	.579	1.000
1991	Pit-N	11	16	1	4	0	0	0	0	1	0	2	0	0	0	0	0	.250	.294	.250	.945
1991	KC-A	44	121	17	25	6	0	4	17	27	3	25	0	0	3	0	1	.207	.351	.355	.991
1991	Cin-N	53	138	12	32	5	0	6	19	15	1	37	0	0	3	0	0	.232	.301	.399	.987

(continued)

(continued)

YEAR	TEAM	GAMES	AB	RUNS	HITS	2B	3B	HR	RBI	BB	IBB	SO	HBP	SH	SF	SB	CS	BA	OBA	SA	FA
Career average		111	323	39	79	15	1	12	47	45	3	59	1	1	3	1	2	.245	.337	.408	.987
Cubs average		**29**	**89**	**8**	**23**	**3**	**0**	**6**	**16**	**4**	**0**	**19**	**0**	**0**	**1**	**0**	**0**	**.258**	**.287**	**.494**	**.992**
Career total		1003	2906	350	713	134	7	108	424	404	25	528	11	7	28	10	16	.245	.337	.408	.987
Cubs total		**29**	**89**	**8**	**23**	**3**	**0**	**6**	**16**	**4**	**0**	**19**	**0**	**0**	**1**	**0**	**0**	**.258**	**.287**	**.494**	**.992**

Martinez, David (Dave)

HEIGHT: 5'10"   THROWS: LEFT   BATS: LEFT   BORN: 9/26/1964 NEW YORK, NEW YORK   POSITIONS PLAYED: P, 1B, OF

YEAR	TEAM	GAMES	AB	RUNS	HITS	2B	3B	HR	RBI	BB	IBB	SO	HBP	SH	SF	SB	CS	BA	OBA	SA	FA
1986	**ChC-N**	**53**	**108**	**13**	**15**	**1**	**1**	**1**	**7**	**6**	**0**	**22**	**1**	**0**	**1**	**4**	**2**	**.139**	**.190**	**.194**	**.988**
1987	**ChC-N**	**142**	**459**	**70**	**134**	**18**	**8**	**8**	**36**	**57**	**4**	**96**	**2**	**1**	**1**	**16**	**8**	**.292**	**.372**	**.418**	**.980**
1988	**ChC-N**	**75**	**256**	**27**	**65**	**10**	**1**	**4**	**34**	**21**	**5**	**46**	**2**	**0**	**4**	**7**	**3**	**.254**	**.311**	**.348**	**.970**
1988	Mon-N	63	191	24	49	3	5	2	12	17	3	48	0	2	1	16	6	.257	.316	.356	.992
1989	Mon-N	126	361	41	99	16	7	3	27	27	2	57	0	7	1	23	4	.274	.324	.382	.967
1990	Mon-N	118	391	60	109	13	5	11	39	24	2	48	1	3	2	13	11	.279	.321	.422	.989
1991	Mon-N	124	396	47	117	18	5	7	42	20	3	54	3	5	3	16	7	.295	.332	.419	.982
1992	Cin-N	135	393	47	100	20	5	3	31	42	4	54	0	6	4	12	8	.254	.323	.354	.985
1993	SF-N	91	241	28	58	12	1	5	27	27	3	39	0	0	0	6	3	.241	.317	.361	.993
1994	SF-N	97	235	23	58	9	3	4	27	21	1	22	2	2	0	3	4	.247	.314	.362	.989
1995	CWS-A	119	303	49	93	16	4	5	37	32	2	41	1	9	4	8	2	.307	.371	.436	.993
1996	CWS-A	146	440	85	140	20	8	10	53	52	1	52	3	2	1	15	7	.318	.393	.468	.985
1997	CWS-A	145	504	78	144	16	6	12	55	55	7	69	3	5	6	12	6	.286	.356	.413	.987
1998	TB-A	90	309	31	79	11	0	3	20	35	4	52	2	0	1	8	7	.256	.334	.320	.994
1999	TB-A	143	514	79	146	25	5	6	66	60	3	76	5	10	5	13	6	.284	.361	.387	.985
2000	TB-A	29	104	12	27	4	2	1	12	10	1	17	0	1	2	1	4	.260	.319	.365	1.000
2000	**ChC-N**	**18**	**54**	**5**	**10**	**1**	**1**	**0**	**1**	**2**	**0**	**8**	**0**	**0**	**0**	**1**	**0**	**.185**	**.214**	**.241**	**.988**
2000	Tex-A	38	119	14	32	4	1	2	12	14	2	20	1	0	0	2	1	.269	.351	.370	1.000
2000	Tor-A	47	180	29	56	10	1	2	22	24	2	28	1	0	1	4	2	.311	.393	.411	.982
2001	Atl-N	120	237	33	68	11	3	2	20	21	0	44	1	0	0	3	3	.287	.347	.384	1.000
Career average		120	362	50	100	15	5	6	36	35	3	56	2	3	2	11	6	.276	.341	.389	.986
Cubs average		**72**	**219**	**29**	**56**	**8**	**3**	**3**	**20**	**22**	**2**	**43**	**1**	**0**	**2**	**7**	**3**	**.255**	**.323**	**.359**	**.979**
Career total		1919	5795	795	1599	238	72	91	580	567	47	893	28	53	37	183	94	.276	.341	.389	.986
Cubs total		**288**	**877**	**115**	**224**	**30**	**11**	**13**	**78**	**86**	**9**	**172**	**5**	**1**	**6**	**28**	**13**	**.255**	**.323**	**.359**	**.979**

Marty, Joseph Anton (Joe)

HEIGHT: 6'0"   THROWS: RIGHT   BATS: RIGHT   BORN: 9/1/1913 SACRAMENTO, CALIFORNIA   DIED: 10/4/1984 SACRAMENTO, CALIFORNIA
POSITIONS PLAYED: P, OF

YEAR	TEAM	GAMES	AB	RUNS	HITS	2B	3B	HR	RBI	BB	IBB	SO	HBP	SH	SF	SB	CS	BA	OBA	SA	FA
1937	**ChC-N**	**88**	**290**	**41**	**84**	**17**	**2**	**5**	**44**	**28**	**—**	**30**	**2**	**4**	**—**	**3**	**—**	**.290**	**.356**	**.414**	**.976**
1938	**ChC-N**	**76**	**235**	**32**	**57**	**8**	**3**	**7**	**35**	**18**	**—**	**26**	**3**	**5**	**—**	**0**	**—**	**.243**	**.305**	**.391**	**.987**
1939	**ChC-N**	**23**	**76**	**6**	**10**	**1**	**0**	**2**	**10**	**4**	**—**	**13**	**0**	**0**	**—**	**2**	**—**	**.132**	**.175**	**.224**	**.933**
1939	Phi-N	91	299	32	76	12	6	9	44	24	—	27	0	5	—	1	—	.254	.310	.425	.974
1940	Phi-N	123	455	52	123	21	8	13	50	17	—	50	1	9	—	2	—	.270	.298	.437	.974
1941	Phi-N	137	477	60	128	19	3	8	39	51	—	41	4	16	—	6	—	.268	.344	.371	.964
Career average		108	366	45	96	16	4	9	44	28	—	37	2	8	—	3	—	.261	.318	.400	.972
Cubs average		**62**	**200**	**26**	**50**	**9**	**2**	**5**	**30**	**17**	**—**	**23**	**2**	**3**	**—**	**2**	**—**	**.251**	**.314**	**.381**	**.977**
Career total		538	1832	223	478	78	22	44	222	142	—	187	10	39	—	14	—	.261	.318	.400	.972
Cubs total		**187**	**601**	**79**	**151**	**26**	**5**	**14**	**89**	**50**	**—**	**69**	**5**	**9**	**—**	**5**	**—**	**.251**	**.314**	**.381**	**.977**

Massa, Gordon Richard (Moose *or* Duke)

HEIGHT: 6'3"   THROWS: RIGHT   BATS: LEFT   BORN: 9/2/1935 CINCINNATI, OHIO   POSITIONS PLAYED: C

YEAR	TEAM	GAMES	AB	RUNS	HITS	2B	3B	HR	RBI	BB	IBB	SO	HBP	SH	SF	SB	CS	BA	OBA	SA	FA
1957	**ChC-N**	**6**	**15**	**2**	**7**	**1**	**0**	**0**	**3**	**4**	**0**	**3**	**0**	**0**	**0**	**0**	**0**	**.467**	**.579**	**.533**	**1.000**
1958	**ChC-N**	**2**	**2**	**0**	**0**	**0**	**0**	**0**	**0**	**0**	**0**	**2**	**0**	**0**	**0**	**0**	**0**	**.000**	**.000**	**.000**	**—**
Career average		4	9	1	4	1	0	0	2	2	0	3	0	0	0	0	0	.412	.524	.471	1.000
Cubs average		**4**	**9**	**1**	**4**	**1**	**0**	**0**	**2**	**2**	**0**	**3**	**0**	**0**	**0**	**0**	**0**	**.412**	**.524**	**.471**	**1.000**
Career total		8	17	2	7	1	0	0	3	4	0	5	0	0	0	0	0	.412	.524	.471	1.000
Cubs total		**8**	**17**	**2**	**7**	**1**	**0**	**0**	**3**	**4**	**0**	**5**	**0**	**0**	**0**	**0**	**0**	**.412**	**.524**	**.471**	**1.000**

Mathews, Nelson Elmer
HEIGHT: 6'4" THROWS: RIGHT BATS: RIGHT BORN: 7/21/1941 COLUMBIA, ILLINOIS POSITIONS PLAYED: OF

YEAR	TEAM	GAMES	AB	RUNS	HITS	2B	3B	HR	RBI	BB	IBB	SO	HBP	SH	SF	SB	CS	BA	OBA	SA	FA
1960	ChC-N	3	8	1	2	0	0	0	0	0	0	2	0	0	0	0	0	.250	.250	.250	1.000
1961	ChC-N	3	9	0	1	0	0	0	0	0	0	2	0	0	0	0	0	.111	.111	.111	1.000
1962	ChC-N	15	49	5	15	2	0	2	13	5	0	4	2	0	1	3	3	.306	.393	.469	.962
1963	ChC-N	61	155	12	24	3	2	4	10	16	2	48	0	0	0	3	4	.155	.234	.277	.979
1964	KCA-A	157	573	58	137	27	5	14	60	43	7	143	1	2	1	2	3	.239	.293	.377	.968
1965	KCA-A	67	184	17	39	7	7	2	15	24	4	49	0	1	2	0	2	.212	.300	.359	.981
Career average		51	163	16	36	7	2	4	16	15	2	41	1	1	1	1	2	.223	.288	.359	.972
Cubs average		21	55	5	11	1	1	2	6	5	1	14	1	0	0	2	2	.190	.266	.312	.977
Career total		306	978	93	218	39	14	22	98	88	13	248	3	4	3	8	12	.223	.288	.359	.972
Cubs total		82	221	18	42	5	2	6	23	21	2	56	2	1	0	6	7	.190	.266	.312	.977

Matthews, Gary Nathaniel (Sarge)
HEIGHT: 6'2" THROWS: RIGHT BATS: RIGHT BORN: 7/5/1950 SAN FERNANDO, CALIFORNIA POSITIONS PLAYED: OF

YEAR	TEAM	GAMES	AB	RUNS	HITS	2B	3B	HR	RBI	BB	IBB	SO	HBP	SH	SF	SB	CS	BA	OBA	SA	FA
1972	SF-N	20	62	11	18	1	1	4	14	7	2	13	0	1	1	0	1	.290	.357	.532	.971
1973	SF-N	148	540	74	162	22	10	12	58	58	7	83	1	3	3	17	5	.300	.367	.444	.983
1974	SF-N	154	561	87	161	27	6	16	82	70	5	69	3	2	2	11	9	.287	.368	.442	.970
1975	SF-N	116	425	67	119	22	3	12	58	65	5	53	2	0	2	13	4	.280	.377	.431	.967
1976	SF-N	156	587	79	164	28	4	20	84	75	3	94	1	2	6	12	5	.279	.359	.443	.975
1977	Atl-N	148	555	89	157	25	5	17	64	67	3	90	2	2	1	22	8	.283	.362	.438	.965
1978	Atl-N	129	474	75	135	20	5	18	62	61	2	92	2	1	4	8	7	.285	.366	.462	.969
1979	Atl-N	156	631	97	192	34	5	27	90	60	5	75	0	1	3	18	6	.304	.363	.502	.974
1980	Atl-N	155	571	79	159	17	3	19	75	42	2	93	0	1	5	11	3	.278	.325	.419	.960
1981	Phi-N	101	359	62	108	21	3	9	67	59	2	42	3	1	6	15	2	.301	.398	.451	.963
1982	Phi-N	162	616	89	173	31	1	19	83	66	1	87	2	0	6	21	4	.281	.349	.427	.966
1983	Phi-N	132	446	66	115	18	2	10	50	69	3	81	0	4	7	13	9	.258	.352	.374	.974
1984	ChC-N	147	491	101	143	21	2	14	82	103	2	97	3	1	10	17	8	.291	.410	.428	.955
1985	ChC-N	97	298	45	70	12	0	13	40	59	2	64	2	0	3	2	0	.235	.362	.406	.977
1986	ChC-N	123	370	49	96	16	1	21	46	60	1	59	0	0	2	3	2	.259	.361	.478	.940
1987	ChC-N	44	42	3	11	3	0	0	8	4	1	11	0	0	0	0	0	.262	.326	.333	1.000
1987	Sea-A	45	119	10	28	1	0	3	15	15	0	22	0	0	1	0	1	.235	.319	.319	—
Career average		127	447	68	126	20	3	15	61	59	3	70	1	1	4	11	5	.281	.364	.439	.968
Cubs average		103	300	50	80	13	1	12	44	57	2	58	1	0	4	6	3	.266	.381	.435	.956
Career total		2033	7147	1083	2011	319	51	234	978	940	46	1125	21	19	62	183	74	.281	.364	.439	.968
Cubs total		411	1201	198	320	52	3	48	176	226	6	231	5	1	15	22	10	.266	.381	.435	.956

Matthews Jr., Gary Nathaniel
HEIGHT: 6'3" THROWS: RIGHT BATS: BOTH BORN: 8/25/1974 SAN FRANCISCO, CALIFORNIA POSITIONS PLAYED: OF

YEAR	TEAM	GAMES	AB	RUNS	HITS	2B	3B	HR	RBI	BB	IBB	SO	HBP	SH	SF	SB	CS	BA	OBA	SA	FA
1999	SD-N	23	36	4	8	0	0	0	7	9	0	9	0	0	0	2	0	.222	.378	.222	1.000
2000	ChC-N	80	158	24	30	1	2	4	14	15	1	28	1	1	0	3	0	.190	.264	.297	.978
2001	ChC-N	106	258	41	56	9	1	9	30	38	2	55	1	5	0	5	3	.217	.320	.364	.976
2001	Pit-N	46	147	22	36	6	1	5	14	22	0	45	0	0	1	3	2	.245	.341	.401	.971
Career average		85	200	30	43	5	1	6	22	28	1	46	1	2	0	4	2	.217	.315	.347	.976
Cubs average		93	208	33	43	5	2	7	22	27	2	42	1	3	0	4	2	.207	.299	.339	.976
Career total		255	599	91	130	16	4	18	65	84	3	137	2	6	1	13	5	.217	.315	.347	.976
Cubs total		186	416	65	86	10	3	13	44	53	3	83	2	6	0	8	3	.207	.299	.339	.976

Gary Nathaniel "Sarge" Matthews, of-dh, 1972–87

Tough, aggressive, hardworking Gary Matthews was picked up by the Cubs in 1984 and helped Chicago to a National League Eastern Division championship.

Matthews was born on July 5, 1950, in San Fernando, California. After a cup of coffee with the San Francisco Giants in 1972, Matthews hit the ground running the next year, hitting .300 and winning the National League's Rookie of the Year award.

Matthews was traded to the Atlanta Braves in 1977 and made the All-Star team for Atlanta in 1979. He signed with the Phillies in 1981 and helped Philadelphia to the postseason twice in three years there.

Chicago general manager Dallas Green, in the process of remaking the Cubs, picked up a number of veteran performers in 1984, including Matthews. Green traded for Matthews to take advantage of Matthews's hustle and leadership, and it paid off. Chicago won the NL East title that year.

Matthews hit .291 for Chicago in 1984 and led the league in walks with 103. Those two stats also helped him have the highest on-base percentage in the league, with a .410 percentage.

But statistics tell only part of Matthews's story for the Cubs. He was an aggressive base runner, known around the league for his punishing slides, as well as a hustling outfielder, known for his diving catches. He was nicknamed "Sarge" for his take-charge attitude.

Matthews, according to Ryne Sandberg, was a very positive force in the clubhouse. Prior to a game, Matthews would sit in front of his locker, talking about the pitcher the Cubs had to face. Before long, there would be a dozen players around Matthews, all talking baseball.

His next two years with the Cubs were not as striking, statistically, although he led the team in home runs in 1986 with 21. Matthews remained a favorite of the fans for his all-out style.

In 1987 Matthews was released by the Cubs early in the season after getting off to a slow start. He was signed by Seattle and played the rest of the year for the Mariners before retiring.

Mattick, Robert James (Bobby)

HEIGHT: 5'11"   THROWS: RIGHT   BATS: RIGHT   BORN: 12/5/1915 SIOUX CITY, IOWA   POSITIONS PLAYED: 2B, 3B, SS

YEAR	TEAM	GAMES	AB	RUNS	HITS	2B	3B	HR	RBI	BB	IBB	SO	HBP	SH	SF	SB	CS	BA	OBA	SA	FA
1938	ChC-N	1	1	0	1	0	0	0	1	0	—	0	0	0	—	0	—	1.000	1.000	1.000	—
1939	ChC-N	51	178	16	51	12	1	0	23	6	—	19	1	4	—	1	—	.287	.314	.365	.927
1940	ChC-N	128	441	30	96	15	0	0	33	19	—	33	0	4	—	5	—	.218	.250	.252	.946
1941	Cin-N	20	60	8	11	3	0	0	7	8	—	7	0	1	—	1	—	.183	.279	.233	.986
1942	Cin-N	6	10	0	2	1	0	0	0	0	—	1	0	0	—	0	—	.200	.200	.300	1.000
Career average		41	138	11	32	6	0	0	13	7	—	12	0	2	—	1	—	.233	.269	.281	.944
Cubs average		**60**	**207**	**15**	**49**	**9**	**0**	**0**	**19**	**8**	**—**	**17**	**0**	**3**	**—**	**2**	**—**	**.239**	**.269**	**.285**	**.944**
Career total		206	690	54	161	31	1	0	64	33	—	60	1	9	—	7	—	.233	.269	.281	.944
Cubs total		**180**	**620**	**46**	**148**	**27**	**1**	**0**	**57**	**25**	**—**	**52**	**1**	**8**	**—**	**6**	**—**	**.239**	**.269**	**.285**	**.940**

Mauch, Gene William (Skip)
HEIGHT: 5'10"   THROWS: RIGHT   BATS: RIGHT   BORN: 11/18/1925 SALINA, KANSAS   POSITIONS PLAYED: 2B, 3B, SS

YEAR	TEAM	GAMES	AB	RUNS	HITS	2B	3B	HR	RBI	BB	IBB	SO	HBP	SH	SF	SB	CS	BA	OBA	SA	FA
1944	Bro-N	5	15	2	2	1	0	0	2	2	—	3	0	0	—	0	0	.133	.235	.200	1.000
1947	Pit-N	16	30	8	9	0	0	0	1	7	—	6	0	0	—	0	—	.300	.432	.300	.927
1948	Bro-N	12	13	1	2	0	0	0	0	1	—	4	0	1	—	0	—	.154	.214	.154	.952
1948	**ChC-N**	53	138	18	28	3	2	1	7	26	—	10	0	2	—	1	—	.203	.329	.275	.941
1949	**ChC-N**	72	150	15	37	6	2	1	7	21	—	15	0	0	—	3	—	.247	.339	.333	.961
1950	Bos-N	48	121	17	28	5	0	1	15	14	—	9	1	1	—	1	—	.231	.316	.298	.960
1951	Bos-N	19	20	5	2	0	0	0	1	7	—	4	0	1	—	0	0	.100	.333	.100	.970
1952	StL-N	7	3	0	0	0	0	0	0	1	—	2	0	0	—	0	0	.000	.250	.000	.500
1956	Bos-A	7	25	4	8	0	0	0	1	3	0	3	0	0	0	0	0	.320	.393	.320	.935
1957	Bos-A	65	222	23	60	10	3	2	28	22	0	26	1	2	3	1	0	.270	.335	.369	.962
Career average		34	82	10	20	3	1	1	7	12	0	9	0	1	0	1	0	.239	.333	.312	.955
Cubs average		**63**	**144**	**17**	**33**	**5**	**2**	**1**	**7**	**24**	—	**13**	**0**	**1**	—	**2**	**0**	**.226**	**.334**	**.306**	**.952**
Career total		304	737	93	176	25	7	5	62	104	0	82	2	7	3	6	0	.239	.333	.312	.955
Cubs total		**125**	**288**	**33**	**65**	**9**	**4**	**2**	**14**	**47**	—	**25**	**0**	**2**	—	**4**	**0**	**.226**	**.334**	**.306**	**.952**

Mauro, Carmen Louis
HEIGHT: 6'0"   THROWS: RIGHT   BATS: LEFT   BORN: 11/10/1926 ST. PAUL, MINNESOTA   POSITIONS PLAYED: 3B, OF

YEAR	TEAM	GAMES	AB	RUNS	HITS	2B	3B	HR	RBI	BB	IBB	SO	HBP	SH	SF	SB	CS	BA	OBA	SA	FA
1948	**ChC-N**	3	5	2	1	0	0	1	1	2	—	0	0	0	—	0	—	.200	.429	.800	1.000
1950	**ChC-N**	62	185	19	42	4	3	1	10	13	—	31	2	0	—	3	—	.227	.285	.297	.946
1951	**ChC-N**	13	29	3	5	1	0	0	3	2	—	6	1	0	—	0	0	.172	.250	.207	.900
1953	Bro-N	8	9	1	0	0	0	0	0	0	—	4	0	0	—	0	0	.000	.000	.000	1.000
1953	Was-A	17	23	1	4	0	1	0	2	1	—	3	0	0	—	0	0	.174	.208	.261	1.000
1953	Phi-A	64	165	14	44	4	4	0	17	19	—	21	0	0	—	3	4	.267	.342	.339	.969
Career average		42	104	10	24	2	2	1	8	9	—	16	1	0	—	2	1	.231	.298	.305	.958
Cubs average		**26**	**73**	**8**	**16**	**2**	**1**	**1**	**5**	**6**	—	**12**	**1**	**0**	—	**1**	**0**	**.219**	**.285**	**.297**	**.942**
Career total		167	416	40	96	9	8	2	33	37	—	65	3	0	—	6	4	.231	.298	.305	.958
Cubs total		**78**	**219**	**24**	**48**	**5**	**3**	**2**	**14**	**17**	—	**37**	**3**	**0**	—	**3**	**0**	**.219**	**.285**	**.297**	**.942**

Maxwell, Jason Ramond
HEIGHT: 6'1"   THROWS: RIGHT   BATS: RIGHT   BORN: 3/26/1972 LEWISBURG, TENNESSEE   POSITIONS PLAYED: 2B, 3B, SS, OF

YEAR	TEAM	GAMES	AB	RUNS	HITS	2B	3B	HR	RBI	BB	IBB	SO	HBP	SH	SF	SB	CS	BA	OBA	SA	FA
1998	**ChC-N**	7	3	2	1	0	0	1	2	0	0	2	0	1	0	0	0	.333	.333	1.333	1.000
2000	Min-A	64	111	14	27	6	0	1	11	9	0	32	1	0	3	2	1	.243	.298	.324	.957
2001	Min-A	39	68	4	13	4	0	1	10	9	2	23	0	1	0	2	0	.191	.286	.294	.959
Career average		37	61	7	14	3	0	1	8	6	1	19	0	1	1	1	0	.225	.294	.330	.958
Cubs average		**7**	**3**	**2**	**1**	**0**	**0**	**1**	**2**	**0**	**0**	**2**	**0**	**1**	**0**	**0**	**0**	**.333**	**.333**	**1.333**	**1.000**
Career total		110	182	20	41	10	0	3	23	18	2	57	1	2	3	4	1	.225	.294	.330	.958
Cubs total		**7**	**3**	**2**	**1**	**0**	**0**	**1**	**2**	**0**	**0**	**2**	**0**	**1**	**0**	**0**	**0**	**.333**	**.333**	**1.333**	**1.000**

May, Derrick Brant
HEIGHT: 6'4"   THROWS: RIGHT   BATS: LEFT   BORN: 7/14/1968 ROCHESTER, NEW YORK   POSITIONS PLAYED: 1B, OF

YEAR	TEAM	GAMES	AB	RUNS	HITS	2B	3B	HR	RBI	BB	IBB	SO	HBP	SH	SF	SB	CS	BA	OBA	SA	FA
1990	**ChC-N**	17	61	8	15	3	0	1	11	2	0	7	0	0	0	1	0	.246	.270	.344	.972
1991	**ChC-N**	15	22	4	5	2	0	1	3	2	0	1	0	0	1	0	0	.227	.280	.455	1.000
1992	**ChC-N**	124	351	33	96	11	0	8	45	14	4	40	3	2	1	5	3	.274	.306	.373	.969
1993	**ChC-N**	128	465	62	137	25	2	10	77	31	6	41	1	0	6	10	3	.295	.336	.422	.970
1994	**ChC-N**	100	345	43	98	19	2	8	51	30	4	34	0	1	2	3	2	.284	.340	.420	.994
1995	Mil-A	32	113	15	28	3	1	1	9	5	0	18	1	0	0	0	1	.248	.286	.319	.971
1995	Hou-N	78	206	29	62	15	1	8	41	19	0	24	1	0	3	5	0	.301	.358	.500	.974
1996	Hou-N	109	259	24	65	12	3	5	33	30	8	33	2	0	3	2	2	.251	.330	.378	.970
1997	Phi-N	83	149	8	34	5	1	1	13	8	3	26	0	0	1	4	1	.228	.266	.295	.961
1998	Mon-N	85	180	13	43	8	0	5	15	11	1	24	0	0	1	0	0	.239	.281	.367	.984
1999	Bal-A	26	49	5	13	0	0	4	12	4	0	6	0	0	1	0	0	.265	.315	.510	1.000

(continued)

(continued)

	GAMES	AB	RUNS	HITS	2B	3B	HR	RBI	BB	IBB	SO	HBP	SH	SF	SB	CS	BA	OBA	SA	FA
Career average	80	220	24	60	10	1	5	31	16	3	25	1	0	2	3	1	.271	.319	.398	.975
Cubs average	**77**	**249**	**30**	**70**	**12**	**1**	**6**	**37**	**16**	**3**	**25**	**1**	**1**	**2**	**4**	**2**	**.282**	**.325**	**.404**	**.977**
Career total	797	2200	244	596	103	10	52	310	156	26	254	8	3	19	30	12	.271	.319	.398	.975
Cubs total	**384**	**1244**	**150**	**351**	**60**	**4**	**28**	**187**	**79**	**14**	**123**	**4**	**3**	**10**	**19**	**8**	**.282**	**.325**	**.404**	**.977**

McAnany, James (Jim)
HEIGHT: 5'10" THROWS: RIGHT BATS: RIGHT BORN: 9/4/1936 LOS ANGELES, CALIFORNIA POSITIONS PLAYED: OF

YEAR	TEAM	GAMES	AB	RUNS	HITS	2B	3B	HR	RBI	BB	IBB	SO	HBP	SH	SF	SB	CS	BA	OBA	SA	FA
1958	CWS-A	5	13	0	0	0	0	0	0	0	0	5	0	0	0	0	0	.000	.000	.000	1.000
1959	CWS-A	67	210	22	58	9	3	0	27	19	4	26	1	1	0	2	1	.276	.339	.348	.966
1960	CWS-A	3	2	0	0	0	0	0	0	0	0	2	0	0	0	0	0	.000	.000	.000	—
1961	**ChC-N**	**11**	**10**	**1**	**3**	**1**	**0**	**0**	**0**	**1**	**0**	**3**	**0**	**0**	**0**	**0**	**0**	**.300**	**.364**	**.400**	**—**
1962	**ChC-N**	**7**	**6**	**0**	**0**	**0**	**0**	**0**	**0**	**1**	**0**	**2**	**0**	**0**	**0**	**0**	**0**	**.000**	**.143**	**.000**	**—**
Career average		19	48	5	12	2	1	0	5	4	1	8	0	0	0	0	0	.253	.316	.320	.968
Cubs average		**9**	**8**	**1**	**2**	**1**	**0**	**0**	**0**	**1**	**0**	**3**	**0**	**0**	**0**	**0**	**0**	**.188**	**.278**	**.250**	**—**
Career total		93	241	23	61	10	3	0	27	21	4	38	1	1	0	2	1	.253	.316	.320	.968
Cubs total		**18**	**16**	**1**	**3**	**1**	**0**	**0**	**0**	**2**	**0**	**5**	**0**	**0**	**0**	**0**	**0**	**.188**	**.278**	**.250**	**—**

McAuley, James Earl (Ike)
HEIGHT: 5'9" THROWS: RIGHT BATS: RIGHT BORN: 8/19/1891 WICHITA, KANSAS DIED: 4/6/1928 DES MOINES, IOWA POSITIONS PLAYED: 2B, 3B, SS

YEAR	TEAM	GAMES	AB	RUNS	HITS	2B	3B	HR	RBI	BB	IBB	SO	HBP	SH	SF	SB	CS	BA	OBA	SA	FA
1914	Pit-N	15	24	3	3	0	0	0	0	0	—	8	0	2	—	0	0	.125	.125	.125	.875
1915	Pit-N	5	15	0	2	1	0	0	0	0	—	6	0	0	—	0	0	.133	.133	.200	.917
1916	Pit-N	4	8	1	2	0	0	0	1	0	—	1	0	1	—	0	—	.250	.250	.250	.938
1917	StL-N	3	7	0	2	0	0	0	1	0	—	1	0	2	—	0	—	.286	.286	.286	.833
1925	**ChC-N**	**37**	**125**	**10**	**35**	**7**	**2**	**0**	**11**	**11**	**—**	**12**	**1**	**8**	**—**	**1**	**0**	**.280**	**.343**	**.368**	**.949**
Career average		13	36	3	9	2	0	0	3	2	—	6	0	3	—	0	0	.246	.293	.313	.935
Cubs average		**37**	**125**	**10**	**35**	**7**	**2**	**0**	**11**	**11**	**—**	**12**	**1**	**8**	**—**	**1**	**0**	**.280**	**.343**	**.368**	**.949**
Career total		64	179	14	44	8	2	0	13	11	—	28	1	13	—	1	0	.246	.293	.313	.935
Cubs total		**37**	**125**	**10**	**35**	**7**	**2**	**0**	**11**	**11**	**—**	**12**	**1**	**8**	**—**	**1**	**0**	**.280**	**.343**	**.368**	**.949**

McBride, Algernon Griggs (Algie)
HEIGHT: 5'9" THROWS: LEFT BATS: LEFT BORN: 5/23/1869 WASHINGTON, DISTRICT OF COLUMBIA DIED: 1/10/1956 GEORGETOWN, OHIO
POSITIONS PLAYED: OF

YEAR	TEAM	GAMES	AB	RUNS	HITS	2B	3B	HR	RBI	BB	IBB	SO	HBP	SH	SF	SB	CS	BA	OBA	SA	FA
1896	**ChN-N**	**9**	**29**	**2**	**7**	**1**	**1**	**1**	**7**	**7**	**—**	**3**	**0**	**0**	**—**	**0**	**—**	**.241**	**.389**	**.448**	**.917**
1898	Cin-N	120	486	94	147	14	12	2	43	51	—		12	8	—	16	—	.302	.383	.393	.959
1899	Cin-N	64	251	57	87	12	5	1	23	30	—		7	4	—	5	—	.347	.431	.446	.950
1900	Cin-N	112	436	59	120	15	8	4	59	25	—		4	5	—	12	—	.275	.320	.374	.915
1901	Cin-N	30	123	19	29	7	0	2	18	7	—		1	1	—	0	—	.236	.282	.341	.968
1901	NYG-N	68	264	27	74	11	0	2	29	12	—		2	5	—	3	—	.280	.317	.345	.948
Career average		81	318	52	93	12	5	2	36	26	—	1	5	5	—	7	—	.292	.356	.385	.946
Cubs average		**9**	**29**	**2**	**7**	**1**	**1**	**1**	**7**	**7**	**—**	**3**	**0**	**0**	**—**	**0**	**—**	**.241**	**.389**	**.448**	**.917**
Career total		403	1589	258	464	60	26	12	179	132	—	3	26	23	—	36	—	.292	.356	.385	.946
Cubs total		**9**	**29**	**2**	**7**	**1**	**1**	**1**	**7**	**7**	**—**	**3**	**0**	**0**	**—**	**0**	**—**	**.241**	**.389**	**.448**	**.917**

McCabe, William Francis (Bill)
HEIGHT: 5'9" THROWS: RIGHT BATS: BOTH BORN: 10/28/1892 CHICAGO, ILLINOIS DIED: 9/2/1966 CHICAGO, ILLINOIS POSITIONS PLAYED: 2B, 3B, SS, OF

YEAR	TEAM	GAMES	AB	RUNS	HITS	2B	3B	HR	RBI	BB	IBB	SO	HBP	SH	SF	SB	CS	BA	OBA	SA	FA
1918	**ChC-N**	**29**	**45**	**9**	**8**	**0**	**1**	**0**	**5**	**4**	**—**	**7**	**0**	**1**	**—**	**2**	**1**	**.178**	**.245**	**.222**	**.942**
1919	**ChC-N**	**33**	**84**	**8**	**13**	**3**	**1**	**0**	**5**	**9**	**—**	**15**	**2**	**1**	**—**	**3**	**—**	**.155**	**.253**	**.214**	**.930**
1920	**ChC-N**	**3**	**2**	**1**	**1**	**0**	**0**	**0**	**0**	**0**	**—**	**0**	**0**	**0**	**—**	**0**	**0**	**.500**	**.500**	**.500**	**—**
1920	Bro-N	41	68	10	10	0	0	0	3	2	—	6	0	1	—	1	2	.147	.171	.147	.884
Career average		35	66	9	11	1	1	0	4	5	—	9	1	1	—	2	1	.161	.227	.196	.914
Cubs average		**22**	**44**	**6**	**7**	**1**	**1**	**0**	**3**	**4**	**—**	**7**	**1**	**1**	**—**	**2**	**0**	**.168**	**.253**	**.221**	**.937**
Career total		106	199	28	32	3	2	0	13	15	—	28	2	3	—	6	2	.161	.227	.196	.914
Cubs total		**65**	**131**	**18**	**22**	**3**	**2**	**0**	**10**	**13**	**—**	**22**	**2**	**2**	**—**	**5**	**0**	**.168**	**.253**	**.221**	**.937**

McCarthy, Alexander George (Alex)

HEIGHT: 5'9"   THROWS: RIGHT   BATS: RIGHT   BORN: 5/12/1888 CHICAGO, ILLINOIS   DIED: 3/12/1978 SALISBURY, MARYLAND
POSITIONS PLAYED: 1B, 2B, 3B, SS, OF

YEAR	TEAM	GAMES	AB	RUNS	HITS	2B	3B	HR	RBI	BB	IBB	SO	HBP	SH	SF	SB	CS	BA	OBA	SA	FA
1910	Pit-N	3	12	1	1	0	1	0	0	0	—	2	0	0	—	0	—	.083	.083	.250	.875
1911	Pit-N	50	150	18	36	5	1	2	31	14	—	24	0	8	—	4	—	.240	.305	.327	.978
1912	Pit-N	111	401	53	111	12	4	1	41	30	—	26	3	16	—	8	—	.277	.332	.334	.963
1913	Pit-N	31	74	7	15	5	0	0	10	7	—	7	3	6	—	1	—	.203	.298	.270	.946
1914	Pit-N	57	173	14	26	0	1	1	14	6	—	17	3	7	—	2	2	.150	.192	.179	.948
1915	Pit-N	21	49	3	10	0	1	0	3	5	—	10	1	2	—	1	2	.204	.291	.245	.963
1915	**ChC-N**	**23**	**72**	**4**	**19**	**3**	**0**	**1**	**6**	**5**	**—**	**7**	**2**	**4**	**—**	**2**	**3**	**.264**	**.329**	**.347**	**.983**
1916	**ChC-N**	**37**	**107**	**10**	**26**	**2**	**3**	**0**	**6**	**11**	**—**	**7**	**5**	**3**	**—**	**1**	**—**	**.243**	**.341**	**.318**	**.927**
1916	Pit-N	50	146	11	29	3	0	0	3	15	—	10	2	9	—	3	—	.199	.282	.219	.956
1917	Pit-N	49	151	15	33	4	0	0	8	11	—	13	1	5	—	1	—	.219	.276	.245	.971
Career average		54	167	17	38	4	1	1	15	13	—	15	3	8	—	3	1	.229	.295	.282	.960
Cubs average		**30**	**90**	**7**	**23**	**3**	**2**	**1**	**6**	**8**	**—**	**7**	**4**	**4**	**—**	**2**	**2**	**.251**	**.337**	**.330**	**.950**
Career total		432	1335	136	306	34	11	5	122	104	—	123	20	60	—	23	7	.229	.295	.282	.960
Cubs total		**60**	**179**	**14**	**45**	**5**	**3**	**1**	**12**	**16**	**—**	**14**	**7**	**7**	**—**	**3**	**3**	**.251**	**.337**	**.330**	**.950**

McCarthy, John Arthur (Jack)

HEIGHT: 5'9"   THROWS: LEFT   BATS: LEFT   BORN: 3/26/1869 GILBERTVILLE, MASSACHUSETTS   DIED: 9/11/1931 CHICAGO, ILLINOIS
POSITIONS PLAYED: 1B, OF

YEAR	TEAM	GAMES	AB	RUNS	HITS	2B	3B	HR	RBI	BB	IBB	SO	HBP	SH	SF	SB	CS	BA	OBA	SA	FA
1893	Cin-N	49	195	28	55	8	3	0	22	22	—	7	0	—	—	6	—	.282	.355	.354	.902
1894	Cin-N	40	167	29	45	9	1	0	21	17	—	6	3	4	—	3	—	.269	.348	.335	.942
1898	Pit-N	137	537	75	155	13	12	4	78	34	—	—	4	21	—	7	—	.289	.336	.380	.935
1899	Pit-N	138	560	108	171	22	17	3	67	39	—	—	4	27	—	28	—	.305	.355	.421	.961
1900	**ChN-N**	**124**	**503**	**68**	**148**	**16**	**7**	**0**	**48**	**24**	**—**	**—**	**2**	**11**	**—**	**22**	**—**	**.294**	**.329**	**.354**	**.944**
1901	Cle-A	86	343	60	110	14	7	0	32	30	—	—	4	19	—	9	—	.321	.382	.402	.949
1902	Cle-A	95	359	45	102	31	5	0	41	24	—	—	0	18	—	12	—	.284	.329	.398	.944
1903	Cle-A	108	415	47	110	20	8	0	43	19	—	—	1	21	—	15	—	.265	.299	.352	.964
1903	**ChC-N**	**24**	**101**	**11**	**28**	**5**	**0**	**0**	**14**	**4**	**—**	**—**	**0**	**2**	**—**	**8**	**—**	**.277**	**.305**	**.327**	**.947**
1904	**ChC-N**	**115**	**432**	**36**	**114**	**14**	**2**	**0**	**51**	**23**	**—**	**—**	**4**	**17**	**—**	**14**	**—**	**.264**	**.307**	**.306**	**.961**
1905	**ChC-N**	**59**	**170**	**16**	**47**	**4**	**3**	**0**	**14**	**10**	**—**	**—**	**1**	**5**	**—**	**8**	**—**	**.276**	**.320**	**.335**	**.967**
1906	Bro-N	91	322	23	98	13	1	0	35	20	—	—	1	10	—	9	—	.304	.347	.351	.924
1907	Bro-N	25	91	4	20	2	0	0	8	2	—	—	0	2	—	4	—	.220	.237	.242	1.000
Career average		91	350	46	100	14	6	1	40	22	—	1	2	13	—	12	—	.287	.333	.364	.947
Cubs average		**81**	**302**	**33**	**84**	**10**	**3**	**0**	**32**	**15**	**—**	**0**	**2**	**9**	**—**	**13**	**—**	**.279**	**.318**	**.332**	**.954**
Career total		1091	4195	550	1203	171	66	7	474	268	—	13	24	157	—	145	—	.287	.333	.364	.947
Cubs total		**322**	**1206**	**131**	**337**	**39**	**12**	**0**	**127**	**61**	**—**	**0**	**7**	**35**	**—**	**52**	**—**	**.279**	**.318**	**.332**	**.954**

McCauley, James Adelbert (Jim)

HEIGHT: 6'0"   THROWS: RIGHT   BATS: LEFT   BORN: 3/24/1863 STANLEY, NEW YORK   DIED: 9/14/1930 CANADAIGUA, NEW YORK   POSITIONS PLAYED: C, OF

YEAR	TEAM	GAMES	AB	RUNS	HITS	2B	3B	HR	RBI	BB	IBB	SO	HBP	SH	SF	SB	CS	BA	OBA	SA	FA
1884	StL-AA	1	2	0	0	0	0	0	—	0	—	—	0	—	—	—	—	.000	.000	.000	.818
1885	Buf-N	24	84	4	15	2	1	0	7	11	—	12	—	—	—	—	—	.179	.274	.226	.938
1885	**ChN-N**	**3**	**6**	**1**	**1**	**0**	**0**	**0**	**0**	**2**	**—**	**3**	**—**	**—**	**—**	**—**	**—**	**.167**	**.375**	**.167**	**.800**
1886	Bro-AA	11	30	5	7	1	0	0	3	11	—	—	0	—	—	2	—	.233	.439	.267	.846
Career average		13	41	3	8	1	0	0	3	8	—	5	0	—	—	1	—	.189	.322	.230	.895
Cubs average		**3**	**6**	**1**	**1**	**0**	**0**	**0**	**0**	**2**	**—**	**3**	**0**	**—**	**—**	**—**	**—**	**.167**	**.375**	**.167**	**.800**
Career total		39	122	10	23	3	1	0	10	24	—	15	0	—	—	2	—	.189	.322	.230	.895
Cubs total		**3**	**6**	**1**	**1**	**0**	**0**	**0**	**0**	**2**	**—**	**3**	**0**	**—**	**—**	**—**	**—**	**.167**	**.375**	**.167**	**.800**

McChesney, Harry Vincent (Pud)

HEIGHT: 5'9" THROWS: RIGHT BATS: RIGHT BORN: 6/1/1880 PITTSBURGH, PENNSYLVANIA DIED: 8/11/1960 PITTSBURGH, PENNSYLVANIA
POSITIONS PLAYED: OF

YEAR	TEAM	GAMES	AB	RUNS	HITS	2B	3B	HR	RBI	BB	IBB	SO	HBP	SH	SF	SB	CS	BA	OBA	SA	FA
1904	ChC-N	22	88	9	23	6	2	0	11	4	—	—	0	0	—	2	—	.261	.293	.375	.967
Career average		22	88	9	23	6	2	0	11	4	—	—	0	0	—	2	—	.261	.293	.375	.967
Cubs average		**22**	**88**	**9**	**23**	**6**	**2**	**0**	**11**	**4**	**—**	**—**	**0**	**0**	**—**	**2**	**—**	**.261**	**.293**	**.375**	**.967**
Career total		22	88	9	23	6	2	0	11	4	—	—	0	0	—	2	—	.261	.293	.375	.967
Cubs total		**22**	**88**	**9**	**23**	**6**	**2**	**0**	**11**	**4**	**—**	**—**	**0**	**0**	**—**	**2**	**—**	**.261**	**.293**	**.375**	**.967**

McClellan, William Henry (Bill)

HEIGHT: 5'6" THROWS: LEFT BATS: LEFT BORN: 3/22/1856 CHICAGO, ILLINOIS DIED: 7/3/1929 CHICAGO, ILLINOIS POSITIONS PLAYED: 2B, 3B, SS, OF

YEAR	TEAM	GAMES	AB	RUNS	HITS	2B	3B	HR	RBI	BB	IBB	SO	HBP	SH	SF	SB	CS	BA	OBA	SA	FA
1878	ChN-N	48	205	26	46	6	1	0	29	2	—	13	—	—	—	—	—	.224	.232	.263	.861
1881	Prv-N	68	259	30	43	3	1	0	16	15	—	21	—	—	—	—	—	.166	.212	.185	.858
1883	Phi-N	80	326	42	75	21	4	1	33	19	—	18	—	—	—	—	—	.230	.272	.328	.846
1884	Phi-N	111	450	71	116	13	2	3	33	28	—	43	—	—	—	—	—	.258	.301	.316	.851
1885	Bro-AA	112	464	85	124	22	7	0	46	28	—	—	6	—	—	—	—	.267	.317	.345	.881
1886	Bro-AA	141	595	131	152	33	9	1	68	56	—	—	2	—	—	43	—	.255	.322	.346	.907
1887	Bro-AA	136	628	109	224	24	6	1	53	80	—	—	6	—	—	70	—	.357	.434	.419	.879
1888	Bro-AA	74	278	33	57	7	3	0	21	40	—	—	1	—	—	13	—	.205	.307	.252	.913
1888	Cle-AA	22	72	6	16	0	0	0	5	6	—	—	0	—	—	6	—	.222	.282	.222	.782
Career average		99	410	67	107	16	4	1	38	34	—	12	2	—	—	17	—	.260	.320	.325	.877
Cubs average		**48**	**205**	**26**	**46**	**6**	**1**	**0**	**29**	**2**	**—**	**13**	**—**	**—**	**—**	**—**	**—**	**.224**	**.232**	**.263**	**.861**
Career total		792	3277	533	853	129	33	6	304	274	—	95	15	—	—	132	—	.260	.320	.325	.877
Cubs total		**48**	**205**	**26**	**46**	**6**	**1**	**0**	**29**	**2**	**—**	**13**	**—**	**—**	**—**	**—**	**—**	**.224**	**.232**	**.263**	**.861**

McClendon, Lloyd Glenn

HEIGHT: 6'0" THROWS: RIGHT BATS: RIGHT BORN: 1/11/1959 GARY, INDIANA POSITIONS PLAYED: C, 1B, 3B, OF

YEAR	TEAM	GAMES	AB	RUNS	HITS	2B	3B	HR	RBI	BB	IBB	SO	HBP	SH	SF	SB	CS	BA	OBA	SA	FA
1987	Cin-N	45	72	8	15	5	0	2	13	4	0	15	0	0	1	1	0	.208	.247	.361	.977
1988	Cin-N	72	137	9	30	4	0	3	14	15	1	22	2	1	2	4	0	.219	.301	.314	.981
1989	**ChC-N**	92	259	47	74	12	1	12	40	37	3	31	1	1	7	6	4	.286	.368	.479	.982
1990	**ChC-N**	49	107	5	17	3	0	1	10	14	2	21	1	0	1	1	0	.159	.254	.215	.992
1990	Pit-N	4	3	1	1	0	0	1	2	0	0	1	0	0	1	0	0	.333	.333	1.333	—
1991	Pit-N	85	163	24	47	7	0	7	24	18	0	23	2	0	0	0	1	.288	.366	.460	.983
1992	Pit-N	84	190	26	48	8	1	3	20	28	0	24	2	1	3	1	3	.253	.350	.353	.980
1993	Pit-N	88	181	21	40	11	1	2	19	23	1	17	0	1	2	0	3	.221	.306	.326	.972
1994	Pit-N	51	92	9	22	4	0	4	12	4	0	11	1	0	0	0	1	.239	.278	.413	.980
Career average		71	151	19	37	7	0	4	19	18	1	21	1	1	2	2	2	.244	.325	.381	.982
Cubs average		**71**	**183**	**26**	**46**	**8**	**1**	**7**	**25**	**26**	**3**	**26**	**1**	**1**	**4**	**4**	**2**	**.249**	**.336**	**.402**	**.985**
Career total		570	1204	150	294	54	3	35	154	143	7	165	8	4	16	15	12	.244	.325	.381	.982
Cubs total		**141**	**366**	**52**	**91**	**15**	**1**	**13**	**50**	**51**	**5**	**52**	**1**	**1**	**8**	**7**	**4**	**.249**	**.336**	**.402**	**.985**

McCormick, William J. (Barry)

HEIGHT: 5'9" THROWS: RIGHT BATS: — BORN: 12/25/1874 MAYSVILLE, KENTUCKY DIED: 1/28/1956 CINCINNATI, OHIO POSITIONS PLAYED: 2B, 3B, SS, OF

YEAR	TEAM	GAMES	AB	RUNS	HITS	2B	3B	HR	RBI	BB	IBB	SO	HBP	SH	SF	SB	CS	BA	OBA	SA	FA
1895	Lou-N	3	12	2	3	0	1	0	0	0	—	0	0	1	—	1	—	.250	.250	.417	.917
1896	**ChN-N**	45	168	22	37	3	1	1	23	14	—	30	0	3	—	9	—	.220	.280	.268	.828
1897	**ChN-N**	101	419	87	112	8	10	2	55	33	—	—	2	4	—	44	—	.267	.324	.348	.882
1898	**ChN-N**	137	530	76	131	15	9	2	78	47	—	—	5	12	—	15	—	.247	.314	.321	.884
1899	**ChN-N**	102	376	48	97	15	2	2	52	25	—	—	4	10	—	14	—	.258	.311	.324	.938
1900	**ChN-N**	110	379	35	83	13	5	3	48	38	—	—	1	18	—	8	—	.219	.292	.303	.900
1901	**ChN-N**	115	427	45	100	15	6	1	32	31	—	—	1	4	—	12	—	.234	.288	.304	.911
1902	StL-A	139	504	55	124	14	4	3	51	37	—	—	5	16	—	10	—	.246	.304	.308	.910
1903	StL-A	61	207	13	45	6	1	1	16	18	—	—	1	2	—	5	—	.217	.283	.271	.954
1903	Was-A	63	219	14	47	10	2	0	23	10	—	—	2	0	—	3	—	.215	.255	.279	.960
1904	Was-A	113	404	36	88	11	1	0	39	27	—	—	4	9	—	9	—	.218	.274	.250	.938

(continued)

(McCormick, continued)

	GAMES	AB	RUNS	HITS	2B	3B	HR	RBI	BB	IBB	SO	HBP	SH	SF	SB	CS	BA	OBA	SA	FA
Career average	99	365	43	87	11	4	2	42	28	—	3	3	8	—	13	—	.238	.297	.303	.913
Cubs average	**102**	**383**	**52**	**93**	**12**	**6**	**2**	**48**	**31**	**—**	**5**	**2**	**9**	**—**	**17**	**—**	**.244**	**.304**	**.317**	**.900**
Career total	989	3645	433	867	110	42	15	417	280	—	30	25	79	—	130	—	.238	.297	.303	.913
Cubs total	**610**	**2299**	**313**	**560**	**69**	**33**	**11**	**288**	**188**	**—**	**30**	**13**	**51**	**—**	**102**	**—**	**.244**	**.304**	**.317**	**.900**

McCullough, Clyde Edward

HEIGHT: 5'11"   THROWS: RIGHT   BATS: RIGHT   BORN: 3/4/1917 NASHVILLE, TENNESSEE   DIED: 9/18/1982 SAN FRANCISCO, CALIFORNIA
POSITIONS PLAYED: C, 1B, 3B

YEAR	TEAM	GAMES	AB	RUNS	HITS	2B	3B	HR	RBI	BB	IBB	SO	HBP	SH	SF	SB	CS	BA	OBA	SA	FA
1940	ChC-N	9	26	4	4	1	0	0	1	5	—	5	0	0	—	0	—	.154	.290	.192	1.000
1941	ChC-N	125	418	41	95	9	2	9	53	34	—	67	2	8	—	5	—	.227	.289	.323	.982
1942	ChC-N	109	337	39	95	22	1	5	31	25	—	47	0	10	—	7	—	.282	.331	.398	.980
1943	ChC-N	87	266	20	63	5	2	2	23	24	—	33	1	3	—	6	—	.237	.302	.293	.977
1946	ChC-N	95	307	38	88	18	5	4	34	22	—	39	2	5	—	2	—	.287	.338	.417	.991
1947	ChC-N	86	234	25	59	12	4	3	30	20	—	20	1	2	—	1	—	.252	.314	.376	.984
1948	ChC-N	69	172	10	36	4	2	1	7	15	—	25	0	1	—	0	—	.209	.273	.273	.973
1949	Pit-N	91	241	30	57	9	3	4	21	24	—	30	4	2	—	1	—	.237	.316	.349	.985
1950	Pit-N	103	279	28	71	16	4	6	34	31	—	35	5	4	—	3	—	.254	.340	.405	.985
1951	Pit-N	92	259	26	77	9	2	8	39	27	—	31	1	3	—	2	0	.297	.366	.440	.988
1952	Pit-N	66	172	10	40	5	1	1	15	10	—	18	2	5	—	0	1	.233	.283	.291	.981
1953	ChC-N	77	229	21	59	3	2	6	23	15	—	23	0	3	—	0	0	.258	.303	.367	.987
1954	ChC-N	31	81	9	21	7	0	3	17	5	—	5	1	0	0	0	0	.259	.310	.457	.982
1955	ChC-N	44	81	7	16	0	0	0	10	8	3	15	1	2	2	0	0	.198	.272	.198	.989
1956	ChC-N	14	19	0	4	1	0	0	1	0	0	5	0	2	1	0	0	.211	.200	.263	1.000
Career average		73	208	21	52	8	2	3	23	18	0	27	1	3	0	2	0	.252	.314	.358	.984
Cubs average		**68**	**197**	**19**	**49**	**7**	**2**	**3**	**21**	**16**	**0**	**26**	**1**	**3**	**0**	**2**	**0**	**.249**	**.306**	**.349**	**.983**
Career total		1098	3121	308	785	121	28	52	339	265	3	398	20	50	3	27	1	.252	.314	.358	.984
Cubs total		**746**	**2170**	**214**	**540**	**82**	**18**	**33**	**230**	**173**	**3**	**284**	**8**	**36**	**3**	**21**	**0**	**.249**	**.306**	**.349**	**.983**

McDonald, Edward C. (Ed)

HEIGHT: 6'0"   THROWS: RIGHT   BATS: RIGHT   BORN: 10/28/1886 ALBANY, NEW YORK   DIED: 3/11/1946 ALBANY, NEW YORK   POSITIONS PLAYED: 3B

YEAR	TEAM	GAMES	AB	RUNS	HITS	2B	3B	HR	RBI	BB	IBB	SO	HBP	SH	SF	SB	CS	BA	OBA	SA	FA
1911	Bos-N	54	175	28	36	7	3	1	21	40	—	39	2	3	—	11	—	.206	.359	.297	.955
1912	Bos-N	121	459	70	119	23	6	2	34	70	—	91	5	6	—	22	—	.259	.363	.349	.940
1913	**ChC-N**	**1**	**0**	**0**	**0**	**0**	**0**	**0**	**0**	**0**	**—**	**0**	**0**	**0**	**—**	**0**	**—**	**—**	**—**	**—**	**—**
Career average		59	211	33	52	10	3	1	18	37	—	43	2	3	—	11	—	.244	.362	.334	.945
Cubs average		**1**	**0**	**0**	**0**	**0**	**0**	**0**	**0**	**0**	**—**	**0**	**0**	**0**	**—**	**0**	**—**	**—**	**—**	**—**	**—**
Career total		176	634	98	155	30	9	3	55	110	—	130	7	9	—	33	—	.244	.362	.334	.945
Cubs total		**1**	**0**	**0**	**0**	**0**	**0**	**0**	**0**	**0**	**—**	**0**	**0**	**0**	**—**	**0**	**—**	**—**	**—**	**—**	**—**

McGriff, Frederick Stanley (Fred *or* Crime Dog)

HEIGHT: 6'3"   THROWS: LEFT   BATS: LEFT   BORN: 10/31/1963 TAMPA, FLORIDA   POSITIONS PLAYED: 1B

YEAR	TEAM	GAMES	AB	RUNS	HITS	2B	3B	HR	RBI	BB	IBB	SO	HBP	SH	SF	SB	CS	BA	OBA	SA	FA
1986	Tor-A	3	5	1	1	0	0	0	0	0	0	2	0	0	0	0	0	.200	.200	.200	1.000
1987	Tor-A	107	295	58	73	16	0	20	43	60	4	104	1	0	0	3	2	.247	.376	.505	.983
1988	Tor-A	154	536	100	151	35	4	34	82	79	3	149	4	0	4	6	1	.282	.376	.552	.997
1989	Tor-A	161	551	98	148	27	3	36	92	119	12	132	4	1	5	7	4	.269	.399	.525	.989
1990	Tor-A	153	557	91	167	21	1	35	88	94	12	108	2	1	4	5	3	.300	.400	.530	.996
1991	SD-N	153	528	84	147	19	1	31	106	105	26	135	2	0	7	4	1	.278	.396	.494	.990
1992	SD-N	152	531	79	152	30	4	35	104	96	23	108	1	0	4	8	6	.286	.394	.556	.991
1993	SD-N	83	302	52	83	11	1	18	46	42	4	55	1	0	4	4	3	.275	.361	.497	.983
1993	Atl-N	68	255	59	79	18	1	19	55	34	2	51	1	0	1	1	0	.310	.392	.612	.992
1994	Atl-N	113	424	81	135	25	1	34	94	50	8	76	1	0	3	7	3	.318	.389	.623	.994
1995	Atl-N	144	528	85	148	27	1	27	93	65	6	99	5	0	6	3	6	.280	.361	.489	.996
1996	Atl-N	159	617	81	182	37	1	28	107	68	12	116	2	0	4	7	3	.295	.365	.494	.992
1997	Atl-N	152	564	77	156	25	1	22	97	68	4	112	4	0	5	5	0	.277	.356	.441	.990
1998	TB-A	151	564	73	160	33	0	19	81	79	9	118	2	0	4	7	2	.284	.371	.443	.995
1999	TB-A	144	529	75	164	30	1	32	104	86	11	107	1	0	4	1	0	.310	.405	.552	.989
2000	TB-A	158	566	82	157	18	0	27	106	91	10	120	0	0	7	2	0	.277	.373	.452	.993

(continued)

(continued)

YEAR	TEAM	GAMES	AB	RUNS	HITS	2B	3B	HR	RBI	BB	IBB	SO	HBP	SH	SF	SB	CS	BA	OBA	SA	FA
2001	TB-A	97	343	40	109	18	0	19	61	40	9	69	0	0	2	1	1	.318	.387	.536	.986
2001	**ChC-N**	**49**	**170**	**27**	**48**	**7**	**2**	**12**	**41**	**26**	**4**	**37**	**3**	**0**	**2**	**0**	**1**	**.282**	**.383**	**.559**	**.990**
Career average		138	492	78	141	25	1	28	88	75	10	106	2	0	4	4	2	.287	.381	.514	.992
Cubs average		**49**	**170**	**27**	**48**	**7**	**2**	**12**	**41**	**26**	**4**	**37**	**3**	**0**	**2**	**0**	**1**	**.282**	**.383**	**.559**	**.990**
Career total		2201	7865	1243	2260	397	22	448	1400	1202	159	1698	34	2	66	71	36	.287	.381	.514	.992
Cubs total		**49**	**170**	**27**	**48**	**7**	**2**	**12**	**41**	**26**	**4**	**37**	**3**	**0**	**2**	**0**	**1**	**.282**	**.383**	**.559**	**.990**

McKnight, James Arthur (Jim)

HEIGHT: 6'1" THROWS: RIGHT BATS: RIGHT BORN: 6/1/1936 BEE BRANCH, ARKANSAS DIED: 1/24/1994 VAN BUREN COUNTY, ARKANSAS POSITIONS PLAYED: 2B, 3B, OF

YEAR	TEAM	GAMES	AB	RUNS	HITS	2B	3B	HR	RBI	BB	IBB	SO	HBP	SH	SF	SB	CS	BA	OBA	SA	FA
1960	ChC-N	3	6	0	2	0	0	0	1	0	0	1	0	0	0	0	0	.333	.333	.333	.667
1962	ChC-N	60	85	6	19	0	1	0	5	2	0	13	0	0	0	0	0	.224	.241	.247	.949
Career average		32	46	3	11	0	1	0	3	1	0	7	0	0	0	0	0	.231	.247	.253	.929
Cubs average		**32**	**46**	**3**	**11**	**0**	**1**	**0**	**3**	**1**	**0**	**7**	**0**	**0**	**0**	**0**	**0**	**.231**	**.247**	**.253**	**.929**
Career total		63	91	6	21	0	1	0	6	2	0	14	0	0	0	0	0	.231	.247	.253	.929
Cubs total		**63**	**91**	**6**	**21**	**0**	**1**	**0**	**6**	**2**	**0**	**14**	**0**	**0**	**0**	**0**	**0**	**.231**	**.247**	**.253**	**.929**

McLarry, Howard Zell (Polly)

HEIGHT: 6'0" THROWS: RIGHT BATS: LEFT BORN: 3/25/1891 LEONARD, TEXAS DIED: 11/4/1971 BONHAM, TEXAS POSITIONS PLAYED: 1B, 2B

YEAR	TEAM	GAMES	AB	RUNS	HITS	2B	3B	HR	RBI	BB	IBB	SO	HBP	SH	SF	SB	CS	BA	OBA	SA	FA
1912	CWS-A	2	2	0	0	0	0	0	0	0	—	—	0	0	—	0	—	.000	.000	.000	
1915	ChC-N	68	127	16	25	3	0	1	12	14	—	20	0	5	—	2	2	.197	.277	.244	.970
Career average		35	65	8	13	2	0	1	6	7	—	10	0	3	—	1	1	.194	.273	.240	.970
Cubs average		**68**	**127**	**16**	**25**	**3**	**0**	**1**	**12**	**14**	**—**	**20**	**0**	**5**	**—**	**2**	**2**	**.197**	**.277**	**.244**	**.970**
Career total		70	129	16	25	3	0	1	12	14	—	20	0	5	—	2	2	.194	.273	.240	.970
Cubs total		**68**	**127**	**16**	**25**	**3**	**0**	**1**	**12**	**14**	**—**	**20**	**0**	**5**	**—**	**2**	**2**	**.197**	**.277**	**.244**	**.970**

McLean, John Bannerman (Larry)

HEIGHT: 6'5" THROWS: RIGHT BATS: RIGHT BORN: 7/18/1881 FREDERICTON, NEW BRUNSWICK, CANADA DIED: 3/24/1921 BOSTON, MASSACHUSETTS POSITIONS PLAYED: C, 1B

YEAR	TEAM	GAMES	AB	RUNS	HITS	2B	3B	HR	RBI	BB	IBB	SO	HBP	SH	SF	SB	CS	BA	OBA	SA	FA
1901	Bos-A	9	19	4	4	1	0	0	2	0	—	—	0	0	—	1	—	.211	.211	.263	1.000
1903	**ChC-N**	**1**	**4**	**0**	**0**	**0**	**0**	**0**	**1**	**1**	**—**	**—**	**0**	**0**	**—**	**1**	**—**	**.000**	**.200**	**.000**	**.889**
1904	StL-N	27	84	5	14	2	1	0	4	4	—	—	0	0	—	0	—	.167	.205	.214	.889
1906	Cin-N	12	35	3	7	2	0	0	2	4	—	—	0	2	—	0	—	.200	.282	.257	.954
1907	Cin-N	113	374	35	108	9	9	0	54	13	—	—	0	4	—	4	—	.289	.313	.361	.954
1908	Cin-N	99	309	24	67	9	4	1	28	15	—	—	2	8	—	2	—	.217	.258	.282	.975
1909	Cin-N	95	324	26	83	12	2	2	36	21	—	—	3	10	—	1	—	.256	.307	.324	.960
1910	Cin-N	127	423	27	126	14	7	2	71	26	—	23	1	5	—	4	—	.298	.340	.378	.983
1911	Cin-N	107	328	24	94	7	2	2	34	20	—	18	1	5	—	1	—	.287	.330	.320	.968
1912	Cin-N	102	333	17	81	15	1	1	27	18	—	15	1	6	—	1	—	.243	.284	.303	.973
1913	StL-N	48	152	7	41	9	0	0	12	6	—	9	1	0	—	0	—	.270	.297	.329	.981
1913	NYG-N	30	75	3	24	4	0	0	9	4	—	4	0	0	—	1	—	.320	.354	.373	.953
1914	NYG-N	79	154	8	40	6	0	0	14	4	—	9	1	2	—	4	—	.260	.283	.299	.973
1915	NYG-N	13	33	0	5	0	0	0	4	0	—	1	0	1	—	0	0	.152	.152	.152	.985
Career average		66	204	14	53	7	2	0	23	10	—	6	1	3	—	2	0	.262	.301	.323	.972
Cubs average		**1**	**4**	**0**	**0**	**0**	**0**	**0**	**1**	**1**	**—**	**—**	**0**	**0**	**—**	**0**	**—**	**.000**	**.200**	**.000**	**.889**
Career total		862	2647	183	694	90	26	6	298	136	—	79	9	43	—	20	0	.262	.301	.323	.972
Cubs total		**1**	**4**	**0**	**0**	**0**	**0**	**0**	**1**	**1**	**—**	**—**	**0**	**0**	**—**	**0**	**—**	**.000**	**.200**	**.000**	**.889**

McMath, Jimmy Lee
HEIGHT: 6'1" THROWS: LEFT BATS: LEFT BORN: 8/10/1949 TUSCALOOSA, ALABAMA POSITIONS PLAYED: OF

YEAR	TEAM	GAMES	AB	RUNS	HITS	2B	3B	HR	RBI	BB	IBB	SO	HBP	SH	SF	SB	CS	BA	OBA	SA	FA
1968	ChC-N	6	14	0	2	0	0	0	2	0	0	6	0	0	0	0	0	.143	.143	.143	1.000
Career average		6	14	0	2	0	0	0	2	0	0	6	0	0	0	0	0	.143	.143	.143	1.000
Cubs average		**6**	**14**	**0**	**2**	**0**	**0**	**0**	**2**	**0**	**0**	**6**	**0**	**0**	**0**	**0**	**0**	**.143**	**.143**	**.143**	**1.000**
Career total		6	14	0	2	0	0	0	2	0	0	6	0	0	0	0	0	.143	.143	.143	1.000
Cubs total		**6**	**14**	**0**	**2**	**0**	**0**	**0**	**2**	**0**	**0**	**6**	**0**	**0**	**0**	**0**	**0**	**.143**	**.143**	**.143**	**1.000**

McMillan, Norman Alexis (Norm *or* Bub)
HEIGHT: 6'0" THROWS: RIGHT BATS: RIGHT BORN: 10/5/1895 LATTA, SOUTH CAROLINA DIED: 9/28/1969 MARION, SOUTH CAROLINA
POSITIONS PLAYED: 2B, 3B, SS, OF

YEAR	TEAM	GAMES	AB	RUNS	HITS	2B	3B	HR	RBI	BB	IBB	SO	HBP	SH	SF	SB	CS	BA	OBA	SA	FA
1922	NYY-A	33	78	7	20	1	2	0	11	6	—	10	0	5	—	4	1	.256	.310	.321	.927
1923	Bos-A	131	459	37	116	24	5	0	42	28	—	44	2	10	—	13	5	.253	.299	.327	.962
1924	StL-A	76	201	25	56	12	2	0	27	12	—	17	4	9	—	6	4	.279	.332	.358	.965
1928	**ChC-N**	**49**	**123**	**11**	**27**	**2**	**2**	**1**	**12**	**13**	**—**	**19**	**1**	**6**	**—**	**0**	**—**	**.220**	**.299**	**.293**	**.962**
1929	**ChC-N**	**124**	**495**	**77**	**134**	**35**	**5**	**5**	**55**	**36**	**—**	**43**	**3**	**7**	**—**	**13**	**—**	**.271**	**.324**	**.392**	**.944**
Career average		83	271	31	71	15	3	1	29	19	—	27	2	7	—	7	2	.260	.313	.352	.957
Cubs average		**87**	**309**	**44**	**81**	**19**	**4**	**3**	**34**	**25**	**—**	**31**	**2**	**7**	**—**	**7**	**0**	**.261**	**.319**	**.372**	**.949**
Career total		413	1356	157	353	74	16	6	147	95	—	133	10	37	—	36	10	.260	.313	.352	.957
Cubs total		**173**	**618**	**88**	**161**	**37**	**7**	**6**	**67**	**49**	**—**	**62**	**4**	**13**	**—**	**13**	**0**	**.261**	**.319**	**.372**	**.949**

McRae, Brian Wesley
HEIGHT: 6'0" THROWS: RIGHT BATS: BOTH BORN: 8/27/1967 BRADENTON, FLORIDA POSITIONS PLAYED: OF

YEAR	TEAM	GAMES	AB	RUNS	HITS	2B	3B	HR	RBI	BB	IBB	SO	HBP	SH	SF	SB	CS	BA	OBA	SA	FA
1990	KC-A	46	168	21	48	8	3	2	23	9	0	29	0	3	2	4	3	.286	.318	.405	1.000
1991	KC-A	152	629	86	164	28	9	8	64	24	1	99	2	3	5	20	11	.261	.288	.372	.993
1992	KC-A	149	533	63	119	23	5	4	52	42	1	88	6	7	4	18	5	.223	.285	.308	.993
1993	KC-A	153	627	78	177	28	9	12	69	37	1	105	4	14	3	23	14	.282	.325	.413	.983
1994	KC-A	114	436	71	119	22	6	4	40	54	3	67	6	6	3	28	8	.273	.359	.378	.988
1995	**ChC-N**	**137**	**580**	**92**	**167**	**38**	**7**	**12**	**48**	**47**	**1**	**92**	**7**	**3**	**1**	**27**	**8**	**.288**	**.348**	**.440**	**.991**
1996	**ChC-N**	**157**	**624**	**111**	**172**	**32**	**5**	**17**	**66**	**73**	**6**	**84**	**12**	**2**	**5**	**37**	**9**	**.276**	**.360**	**.425**	**.986**
1997	**ChC-N**	**108**	**417**	**63**	**100**	**27**	**5**	**6**	**28**	**52**	**2**	**62**	**4**	**3**	**1**	**14**	**6**	**.240**	**.329**	**.372**	**.996**
1997	NYM-N	45	145	23	36	5	2	5	15	13	0	22	2	1	1	3	4	.248	.317	.414	.957
1998	NYM-N	159	552	79	146	36	5	21	79	80	3	90	5	3	5	20	11	.264	.360	.462	.987
1999	NYM-N	96	298	35	66	12	1	8	36	39	1	57	5	0	2	2	6	.221	.320	.349	.994
1999	Col-N	7	23	1	6	2	0	1	1	2	0	7	2	0	0	0	0	.261	.370	.478	1.000
1999	Tor-A	31	82	11	16	3	1	3	11	16	1	22	2	1	0	0	1	.195	.340	.366	1.000
Career average		135	511	73	134	26	6	10	53	49	2	82	6	5	3	20	9	.261	.331	.396	.990
Cubs average		**134**	**540**	**89**	**146**	**32**	**6**	**12**	**47**	**57**	**3**	**79**	**8**	**3**	**2**	**26**	**8**	**.271**	**.348**	**.416**	**.991**
Career total		1354	5114	734	1336	264	58	103	532	488	20	824	57	46	32	196	86	.261	.331	.396	.990
Cubs total		**402**	**1621**	**266**	**439**	**97**	**17**	**35**	**142**	**172**	**9**	**238**	**23**	**8**	**7**	**78**	**23**	**.271**	**.348**	**.416**	**.991**

McVey, Calvin Alexander (Cal)
HEIGHT: 5'9" THROWS: RIGHT BATS: RIGHT BORN: 8/30/1850 MONTROSE, IOWA DIED: 8/20/1926 SAN FRANCISCO, CALIFORNIA
POSITIONS PLAYED: P, C, 1B, 2B, 3B, OF

YEAR	TEAM	GAMES	AB	RUNS	HITS	2B	3B	HR	RBI	BB	IBB	SO	HBP	SH	SF	SB	CS	BA	OBA	SA	FA
1876	**ChN-N**	**63**	**310**	**62**	**107**	**15**	**0**	**1**	**53**	**2**	**—**	**4**	**—**	**—**	**—**	**—**	**—**	**.345**	**.349**	**.403**	**.952**
1877	**ChN-N**	**60**	**266**	**58**	**98**	**9**	**7**	**0**	**36**	**8**	**—**	**11**	**—**	**—**	**—**	**—**	**—**	**.368**	**.387**	**.455**	**.858**
1878	Cin-N	61	271	43	83	10	4	2	28	5	—	10	—	—	—	—	—	.306	.319	.395	.819
1879	Cin-N	81	354	64	105	18	6	0	55	8	—	13	—	—	—	—	—	.297	.312	.381	.945
Career average		66	300	57	98	13	4	1	43	6	—	10	—	—	—	—	—	.327	.340	.406	.918
Cubs average		**62**	**288**	**60**	**103**	**12**	**4**	**1**	**45**	**5**	**—**	**8**	**—**	**—**	**—**	**—**	**—**	**.356**	**.367**	**.427**	**.920**
Career total		265	1201	227	393	52	17	3	172	23	—	38	—	—	—	—	—	.327	.340	.406	.918
Cubs total		**123**	**576**	**120**	**205**	**24**	**7**	**1**	**89**	**10**	**—**	**15**	**—**	**—**	**—**	**—**	**—**	**.356**	**.367**	**.427**	**.920**

Meier, David Keith (Dave)
HEIGHT: 6'0"   THROWS: RIGHT   BATS: RIGHT   BORN: 8/8/1959 HELENA, MONTANA   POSITIONS PLAYED: 3B, OF

YEAR	TEAM	GAMES	AB	RUNS	HITS	2B	3B	HR	RBI	BB	IBB	SO	HBP	SH	SF	SB	CS	BA	OBA	SA	FA
1984	Min-A	59	147	18	35	8	1	0	13	6	0	9	1	3	1	0	1	.238	.271	.306	.978
1985	Min-A	71	104	15	27	6	0	1	8	18	0	12	1	3	0	0	6	.260	.374	.346	.987
1987	Tex-A	13	21	4	6	1	0	0	0	0	0	4	0	0	0	0	0	.286	.286	.333	.917
1988	**ChC-N**	**2**	**5**	**0**	**2**	**0**	**0**	**0**	**1**	**0**	**0**	**1**	**0**	**0**	**0**	**0**	**0**	**.400**	**.400**	**.400**	**1.000**
Career average		36	69	9	18	4	0	0	6	6	0	7	1	2	0	0	2	.253	.316	.325	.978
Cubs average		**2**	**5**	**0**	**2**	**0**	**0**	**0**	**1**	**0**	**0**	**1**	**0**	**0**	**0**	**0**	**0**	**.400**	**.400**	**.400**	**.978**
Career total		145	277	37	70	15	1	1	22	24	0	26	2	6	1	0	7	.253	.316	.325	.978
Cubs total		**2**	**5**	**0**	**2**	**0**	**0**	**0**	**1**	**0**	**0**	**1**	**0**	**0**	**0**	**0**	**0**	**.400**	**.400**	**.400**	**1.000**

Mejias, Samuel Elias (Sam)
HEIGHT: 6'0"   THROWS: RIGHT   BATS: RIGHT   BORN: 5/9/1952 SANTIAGO, DOMINICAN REPUBLIC   POSITIONS PLAYED: P, OF

YEAR	TEAM	GAMES	AB	RUNS	HITS	2B	3B	HR	RBI	BB	IBB	SO	HBP	SH	SF	SB	CS	BA	OBA	SA	FA
1976	StL-N	18	21	1	3	1	0	0	0	2	1	2	0	0	0	2	0	.143	.217	.190	1.000
1977	Mon-N	74	101	14	23	4	1	3	8	2	0	17	0	1	0	1	0	.228	.243	.376	.966
1978	Mon-N	67	56	9	13	1	0	0	6	2	1	5	0	1	0	0	0	.232	.259	.250	.949
1979	**ChC-N**	**31**	**11**	**4**	**2**	**0**	**0**	**0**	**0**	**2**	**0**	**5**	**0**	**1**	**0**	**0**	**0**	**.182**	**.308**	**.182**	**.875**
1979	Cin-N	7	2	1	1	0	0	0	0	0	0	0	0	0	0	0	0	.500	.500	.500	1.000
1980	Cin-N	71	108	16	30	5	1	1	10	6	0	13	1	2	0	4	2	.278	.322	.370	.989
1981	Cin-N	66	49	6	14	2	0	0	7	2	1	9	0	3	2	1	0	.286	.302	.327	.972
Career average		56	58	9	14	2	0	1	5	3	1	9	0	1	0	1	0	.247	.281	.330	.973
Cubs average		**31**	**11**	**4**	**2**	**0**	**0**	**0**	**0**	**2**	**0**	**5**	**0**	**1**	**0**	**0**	**0**	**.182**	**.308**	**.182**	**.875**
Career total		334	348	51	86	13	2	4	31	16	3	51	1	8	2	8	2	.247	.281	.330	.973
Cubs total		**31**	**11**	**4**	**2**	**0**	**0**	**0**	**0**	**2**	**0**	**5**	**0**	**1**	**0**	**0**	**0**	**.182**	**.308**	**.182**	**.875**

Meoli, Rudolph Bartholomew (Rudy)
HEIGHT: 5'9"   THROWS: RIGHT   BATS: LEFT   BORN: 5/1/1951 TROY, NEW YORK   POSITIONS PLAYED: 1B, 2B, 3B, SS

YEAR	TEAM	GAMES	AB	RUNS	HITS	2B	3B	HR	RBI	BB	IBB	SO	HBP	SH	SF	SB	CS	BA	OBA	SA	FA
1971	Cal-A	7	3	0	0	0	0	0	0	0	0	1	0	0	0	0	0	.000	.000	.000	—
1973	Cal-A	120	305	36	68	12	1	2	23	31	1	38	0	3	5	2	4	.223	.290	.289	.934
1974	Cal-A	36	90	9	22	2	0	0	3	8	0	10	0	2	0	2	4	.244	.306	.267	.943
1975	Cal-A	70	126	12	27	2	1	0	6	15	0	20	0	2	0	3	4	.214	.298	.246	.932
1978	**ChC-N**	**47**	**29**	**10**	**3**	**0**	**1**	**0**	**2**	**6**	**0**	**4**	**0**	**0**	**0**	**1**	**0**	**.103**	**.257**	**.172**	**.952**
1979	Phi-N	30	73	2	13	4	1	0	6	9	1	15	0	2	0	2	0	.178	.268	.260	.982
Career average		52	104	12	22	3	1	0	7	12	0	15	0	2	1	2	1	.212	.289	.267	.942
Cubs average		**47**	**29**	**10**	**3**	**0**	**1**	**0**	**2**	**6**	**0**	**4**	**0**	**0**	**0**	**1**	**0**	**.103**	**.257**	**.172**	**.952**
Career total		310	626	69	133	20	4	2	40	69	2	88	0	9	5	10	8	.212	.289	.267	.942
Cubs total		**47**	**29**	**10**	**3**	**0**	**1**	**0**	**2**	**6**	**0**	**4**	**0**	**0**	**0**	**1**	**0**	**.103**	**.257**	**.172**	**.952**

Merced, Orlando Luis
HEIGHT: 6'1"   THROWS: RIGHT   BATS: LEFT   BORN: 11/2/1966 SAN JUAN, PUERTO RICO   POSITIONS PLAYED: C, 1B, 3B, OF

YEAR	TEAM	GAMES	AB	RUNS	HITS	2B	3B	HR	RBI	BB	IBB	SO	HBP	SH	SF	SB	CS	BA	OBA	SA	FA
1990	Pit-N	25	24	3	5	1	0	0	0	1	0	9	0	0	0	0	0	.208	.240	.250	—
1991	Pit-N	120	411	83	113	17	2	10	50	64	4	81	1	1	1	8	4	.275	.373	.399	.988
1992	Pit-N	134	405	50	100	28	5	6	60	52	8	63	2	1	5	5	4	.247	.332	.385	.995
1993	Pit-N	137	447	68	140	26	4	8	70	77	10	64	1	0	5	3	3	.313	.414	.443	.981
1994	Pit-N	108	386	48	105	21	3	9	51	42	5	58	1	0	2	4	1	.272	.343	.412	.991
1995	Pit-N	132	487	75	146	29	4	15	83	52	9	74	1	0	5	7	2	.300	.365	.468	.985
1996	Pit-N	120	453	69	130	24	1	17	80	51	5	74	0	0	3	8	4	.287	.357	.457	.988
1997	Tor-A	98	368	45	98	23	2	9	40	47	1	62	3	0	2	7	3	.266	.352	.413	.985
1998	Min-A	63	204	22	59	12	0	5	33	17	3	29	1	0	1	0	4	.289	.345	.422	.983
1998	Bos-A	9	9	0	0	0	0	0	2	2	0	3	0	0	1	0	0	.000	.167	.000	1.000
1998	**ChC-N**	**12**	**10**	**2**	**3**	**0**	**0**	**1**	**5**	**1**	**0**	**2**	**0**	**0**	**1**	**0**	**0**	**.300**	**.333**	**.600**	**1.000**
1999	Mon-N	93	194	25	52	12	1	8	26	26	0	27	0	0	1	2	1	.268	.353	.464	.952
2001	Hou-N	94	137	19	36	6	1	6	29	14	1	32	1	0	1	5	1	.263	.333	.453	.976
Career average		104	321	46	90	18	2	9	48	41	4	53	1	0	2	5	2	.279	.359	.428	.987
Cubs average		**12**	**10**	**2**	**3**	**0**	**0**	**1**	**5**	**1**	**0**	**2**	**0**	**0**	**1**	**0**	**0**	**.300**	**.333**	**.428**	**.987**
Career total		1145	3535	509	987	199	23	94	529	446	46	578	11	2	25	50	27	.279	.359	.600	1.000
Cubs total		**12**	**10**	**2**	**3**	**0**	**0**	**1**	**5**	**1**	**0**	**2**	**0**	**0**	**1**	**0**	**0**	**.300**	**.333**	**.600**	**1.000**

Merkle, Carl Frederick Rudolf (Fred)
HEIGHT: 6'1" THROWS: RIGHT BATS: RIGHT BORN: 12/20/1888 WATERTOWN, WISCONSIN DIED: 3/2/1956 DAYTONA BEACH, FLORIDA
POSITIONS PLAYED: 1B, 2B, 3B, OF

YEAR	TEAM	GAMES	AB	RUNS	HITS	2B	3B	HR	RBI	BB	IBB	SO	HBP	SH	SF	SB	CS	BA	OBA	SA	FA
1907	NYG-N	15	47	0	12	1	0	0	5	1	—	—	0	1	—	0	—	.255	.271	.277	.949
1908	NYG-N	38	41	6	11	2	1	1	7	4	—	—	0	2	—	0	—	.268	.333	.439	1.000
1909	NYG-N	79	236	15	45	9	1	0	20	16	—	—	1	4	—	8	—	.191	.245	.237	.976
1910	NYG-N	144	506	75	148	35	14	4	70	44	—	59	3	19	—	23	—	.292	.353	.441	.981
1911	NYG-N	149	541	80	153	24	10	12	84	43	—	60	6	14	—	49	—	.283	.342	.431	.985
1912	NYG-N	129	479	82	148	22	6	11	84	42	—	70	8	8	—	37	—	.309	.374	.449	.980
1913	NYG-N	153	563	78	147	30	13	2	69	41	—	60	3	10	—	35	—	.261	.315	.371	.986
1914	NYG-N	146	512	71	132	25	7	7	63	52	—	80	1	7	—	23	—	.258	.327	.375	.990
1915	NYG-N	140	505	52	151	25	3	4	62	36	—	39	2	14	—	20	15	.299	.348	.384	.988
1916	NYG-N	112	401	45	95	19	3	7	44	33	—	46	8	7	—	17	—	.237	.308	.352	.984
1916	Bro-N	23	69	6	16	1	0	0	2	7	—	4	1	1	—	2	—	.232	.312	.246	.993
1917	Bro-N	2	8	1	1	1	0	0	0	0	—	1	0	0	—	0	—	.125	.125	.250	1.000
1917	**ChC-N**	**146**	**549**	**65**	**146**	**30**	**9**	**3**	**57**	**42**	**—**	**60**	**4**	**13**	**—**	**13**	**—**	**.266**	**.323**	**.370**	**.983**
1918	**ChC-N**	**129**	**482**	**55**	**143**	**25**	**5**	**3**	**65**	**35**	**—**	**36**	**4**	**20**	**—**	**21**	**—**	**.297**	**.349**	**.388**	**.990**
1919	**ChC-N**	**133**	**498**	**52**	**133**	**20**	**6**	**3**	**62**	**33**	**—**	**35**	**2**	**12**	**—**	**20**	**—**	**.267**	**.315**	**.349**	**.985**
1920	**ChC-N**	**92**	**330**	**33**	**94**	**20**	**4**	**3**	**38**	**24**	**—**	**32**	**1**	**12**	**—**	**3**	**5**	**.285**	**.335**	**.397**	**.985**
1925	NYY-A	7	13	4	5	1	0	0	1	1	—	1	0	2	—	1	0	.385	.429	.462	1.000
1926	NYY-A	1	2	0	0	0	0	0	0	0	—	0	0	0	—	0	0	.000	.000	.000	1.000
Career average		102	361	45	99	18	5	4	46	28	—	36	3	9	—	17	1	.273	.331	.383	.985
Cubs average		**125**	**465**	**51**	**129**	**24**	**6**	**3**	**56**	**34**	**—**	**41**	**3**	**14**	**—**	**14**	**1**	**.278**	**.330**	**.374**	**.986**
Career total		1638	5782	720	1580	290	82	60	733	454	—	583	44	146	—	272	20	.273	.331	.383	.985
Cubs total		**500**	**1859**	**205**	**516**	**95**	**24**	**12**	**222**	**134**	**—**	**163**	**11**	**57**	**—**	**57**	**5**	**.278**	**.330**	**.374**	**.986**

Merriman, Lloyd Archer (Citation)
HEIGHT: 6'0" THROWS: LEFT BATS: LEFT BORN: 8/2/1924 CLOVIS, CALIFORNIA POSITIONS PLAYED: OF

YEAR	TEAM	GAMES	AB	RUNS	HITS	2B	3B	HR	RBI	BB	IBB	SO	HBP	SH	SF	SB	CS	BA	OBA	SA	FA
1949	Cin-N	103	287	35	66	12	5	4	26	21	—	36	1	1	—	2	—	.230	.285	.348	.969
1950	Cin-N	92	298	44	77	15	3	2	31	30	—	23	2	5	—	6	—	.258	.330	.349	.989
1951	Cin-N	114	359	34	87	23	2	5	36	31	—	34	0	2	—	8	4	.242	.303	.359	.997
1954	Cin-N	73	112	12	30	8	1	0	16	23	—	10	3	0	3	3	0	.268	.397	.357	.981
1955	CWS-A	1	1	0	0	0	0	0	0	0	0	0	0	0	0	0	0	.000	.000	.000	—
1955	**ChC-N**	**72**	**145**	**15**	**31**	**6**	**1**	**1**	**8**	**21**	**0**	**21**	**0**	**0**	**1**	**1**	**0**	**.214**	**.311**	**.290**	**.977**
Career average		91	240	28	58	13	2	2	23	25	0	25	1	2	1	4	1	.242	.316	.345	.985
Cubs average		**72**	**145**	**15**	**31**	**6**	**1**	**1**	**8**	**21**	**0**	**21**	**0**	**0**	**1**	**1**	**0**	**.214**	**.311**	**.290**	**.977**
Career total		455	1202	140	291	64	12	12	117	126	0	124	6	8	4	20	4	.242	.316	.345	.985
Cubs total		**72**	**145**	**15**	**31**	**6**	**1**	**1**	**8**	**21**	**0**	**21**	**0**	**0**	**1**	**1**	**0**	**.214**	**.311**	**.290**	**.977**

Merritt, William Henry (Bill)
HEIGHT: 5'7" THROWS: RIGHT BATS: RIGHT BORN: 7/30/1870 LOWELL, MASSACHUSETTS DIED: 11/17/1937 LOWELL, MASSACHUSETTS
POSITIONS PLAYED: C, 1B, 2B, 3B, SS, OF

YEAR	TEAM	GAMES	AB	RUNS	HITS	2B	3B	HR	RBI	BB	IBB	SO	HBP	SH	SF	SB	CS	BA	OBA	SA	FA
1891	**ChN-N**	**11**	**42**	**4**	**9**	**1**	**0**	**0**	**4**	**2**	**—**	**2**	**0**	**—**	**—**	**0**	**—**	**.214**	**.250**	**.238**	**.945**
1892	Lou-N	46	168	22	33	4	2	1	13	11	—	15	0	—	—	3	—	.196	.246	.262	.940
1893	Bos-N	39	141	30	49	6	3	3	26	13	—	13	0	—	—	3	—	.348	.403	.496	.945
1894	Bos-N	10	26	3	6	1	0	0	6	8	—	0	0	2	—	0	—	.231	.412	.269	.889
1894	Pit-N	36	109	18	30	1	2	1	18	15	—	7	0	0	—	2	—	.275	.363	.349	.959
1894	Cin-N	29	113	17	37	6	1	1	21	9	—	3	2	0	—	4	—	.177	.235	.203	.947
1895	Cin-N	22	79	9	14	2	0	0	12	6	—	5	0	3	—	2	—	.285	.340	.314	.938
1895	Pit-N	67	239	32	68	5	1	0	27	18	—	16	2	4	—	2	—	.291	.336	.344	.938
1896	Pit-N	77	282	26	82	8	2	1	42	18	—	10	1	10	—	3	—	.263	.297	.316	.955
1897	Pit-N	62	209	21	55	6	1	1	26	9	—	—	1	6	—	2	—	.263	.297	.316	—
1899	Bos-N	1	2	0	0	0	0	0	0	0	—	—	1	0	—	0	—	.000	.333	.000	1.000
Career average		50	176	23	48	5	2	1	24	14	—	9	1	3	—	3	—	.272	.327	.334	.943
Cubs average		**11**	**42**	**4**	**9**	**1**	**0**	**0**	**4**	**2**	**—**	**2**	**0**	**—**	**—**	**0**	**—**	**.214**	**.250**	**.238**	**.945**
Career total		400	1410	182	383	40	12	8	195	109	—	71	7	25	—	21	—	.272	.327	.334	.943
Cubs total		**11**	**42**	**4**	**9**	**1**	**0**	**0**	**4**	**2**	**—**	**2**	**0**	**—**	**—**	**0**	**—**	**.214**	**.250**	**.238**	**.945**

Mertes, Samuel Blair (Sam *or* Sandow)
HEIGHT: 5'10" THROWS: RIGHT BATS: RIGHT BORN: 8/6/1872 SAN FRANCISCO, CALIFORNIA DIED: 3/11/1945 SAN FRANCISCO, CALIFORNIA
POSITIONS PLAYED: P, C, 1B, 2B, 3B, SS, OF

YEAR	TEAM	GAMES	AB	RUNS	HITS	2B	3B	HR	RBI	BB	IBB	SO	HBP	SH	SF	SB	CS	BA	OBA	SA	FA
1896	Phi-N	37	143	20	34	4	4	0	14	8	—	10	2	4	—	19	—	.238	.288	.322	.910
1898	**ChN-N**	**83**	**269**	**45**	**80**	**4**	**8**	**1**	**47**	**34**	**—**		**6**	**7**	**—**	**27**	**—**	**.297**	**.388**	**.383**	**.870**
1899	ChN-N	117	426	83	127	13	16	9	81	33	—		0	15	—	45	—	.298	.349	.467	.923
1900	**ChN-N**	**127**	**481**	**72**	**142**	**25**	**4**	**7**	**60**	**42**	**—**		**3**	**22**	**—**	**38**	**—**	**.295**	**.356**	**.407**	**.954**
1901	CWS-A	137	545	94	151	16	17	5	98	52	—		6	20	—	46	—	.277	.347	.396	.941
1902	CWS-A	129	497	60	140	23	7	1	79	37	—		2	8	—	46	—	.282	.334	.362	.931
1903	NYG-N	138	517	100	145	32	14	7	104	61	—		3	11	—	45	—	.280	.360	.437	.971
1904	NYG-N	148	532	83	147	28	11	4	78	54	—		3	22	—	47	—	.276	.346	.393	.957
1905	NYG-N	150	551	81	154	27	17	5	108	56	—		5	15	—	52	—	.279	.351	.417	.960
1906	NYG-N	71	253	37	60	9	6	1	33	29	—		3	6	—	21	—	.237	.323	.332	.970
1906	StL-N	53	191	20	47	7	4	0	19	16	—		0	9	—	10	—	.246	.304	.325	.890
Career average		119	441	70	123	19	11	4	72	42	—	1	3	14	—	40	—	.279	.346	.398	.941
Cubs average		**109**	**392**	**67**	**116**	**14**	**9**	**6**	**63**	**36**	**—**	**0**	**3**	**15**	**—**	**37**	**—**	**.297**	**.361**	**.423**	**.930**
Career total		1190	4405	695	1227	188	108	40	721	422	—	10	33	139	—	396	—	.279	.346	.398	.941
Cubs total		**327**	**1176**	**200**	**349**	**42**	**28**	**17**	**188**	**109**	**—**	**0**	**9**	**44**	**—**	**110**	**—**	**.297**	**.361**	**.423**	**.930**

Merullo, Leonard Richard (Lennie)
HEIGHT: 5'11" THROWS: RIGHT BATS: RIGHT BORN: 5/5/1917 BOSTON, MASSACHUSETTS POSITIONS PLAYED: 1B, SS

YEAR	TEAM	GAMES	AB	RUNS	HITS	2B	3B	HR	RBI	BB	IBB	SO	HBP	SH	SF	SB	CS	BA	OBA	SA	FA
1941	**ChC-N**	**7**	**17**	**3**	**6**	**1**	**0**	**0**	**1**	**2**	**—**	**0**	**0**	**0**	**—**	**1**	**—**	**.353**	**.421**	**.412**	**.968**
1942	ChC-N	143	515	53	132	23	3	2	37	35	—	45	5	22	—	14	—	.256	.310	.324	.946
1943	ChC-N	129	453	37	115	18	3	1	25	26	—	42	2	6	—	7	—	.254	.297	.313	.940
1944	ChC-N	66	193	20	41	8	1	1	16	16	—	18	1	7	—	3	—	.212	.276	.280	.937
1945	ChC-N	121	394	40	94	18	0	2	37	31	—	30	2	6	—	7	—	.239	.297	.299	.948
1946	ChC-N	65	126	14	19	4	0	0	7	11	—	13	0	1	—	2	—	.151	.219	.214	.946
1947	ChC-N	108	373	24	90	16	1	0	29	15	—	26	2	3	—	4	—	.241	.274	.290	.949
Career average		91	296	27	71	13	1	1	22	19	—	25	2	6	—	5	—	.240	.291	.301	.945
Cubs average		**91**	**296**	**27**	**71**	**13**	**1**	**1**	**22**	**19**	**—**	**25**	**2**	**6**	**—**	**5**	**—**	**.240**	**.291**	**.301**	**.945**
Career total		639	2071	191	497	92	8	6	152	136	—	174	12	45	—	38	—	.240	.291	.301	.945
Cubs total		**639**	**2071**	**191**	**497**	**92**	**8**	**6**	**152**	**136**	**—**	**174**	**12**	**45**	**—**	**38**	**—**	**.240**	**.291**	**.301**	**.945**

Mesner, Stephen Mathias (Steve)
HEIGHT: 5'9" THROWS: RIGHT BATS: RIGHT BORN: 1/13/1918 LOS ANGELES, CALIFORNIA DIED: 4/6/1981 SAN DIEGO, CALIFORNIA
POSITIONS PLAYED: 2B, 3B, SS

YEAR	TEAM	GAMES	AB	RUNS	HITS	2B	3B	HR	RBI	BB	IBB	SO	HBP	SH	SF	SB	CS	BA	OBA	SA	FA
1938	**ChC-N**	**2**	**4**	**2**	**1**	**0**	**0**	**0**	**0**	**1**	**—**	**1**	**0**	**0**	**—**	**0**	**—**	**.250**	**.400**	**.250**	**.667**
1939	**ChC-N**	**17**	**43**	**7**	**12**	**4**	**0**	**0**	**6**	**3**	**—**	**4**	**1**	**1**	**—**	**0**	**—**	**.279**	**.340**	**.372**	**.937**
1941	StL-N	24	69	8	10	1	0	0	10	5	—	6	0	2	—	0	—	.145	.203	.159	.958
1943	Cin-N	137	504	53	137	26	1	0	52	26	—	20	1	17	—	6	—	.272	.309	.327	.944
1944	Cin-N	121	414	31	100	17	4	1	47	34	—	20	1	5	—	1	—	.242	.301	.309	.951
1945	Cin-N	150	540	52	137	19	1	1	52	52	—	18	2	17	—	4	—	.254	.322	.298	.971
Career average		75	262	26	66	11	1	0	28	20	—	12	1	7	—	2	—	.252	.308	.306	.955
Cubs average		**10**	**24**	**5**	**7**	**2**	**0**	**0**	**3**	**2**	**—**	**3**	**1**	**1**	**—**	**0**	**—**	**.277**	**.346**	**.362**	**.924**
Career total		451	1574	153	397	67	6	2	167	121	—	69	5	42	—	11	—	.252	.308	.306	.955
Cubs total		**19**	**47**	**9**	**13**	**4**	**0**	**0**	**6**	**4**	**—**	**5**	**1**	**1**	**—**	**0**	**—**	**.277**	**.346**	**.362**	**.924**

Metkovich, George Michael (Catfish)
HEIGHT: 6'1" THROWS: LEFT BATS: LEFT BORN: 10/8/1920 ANGEL'S CAMP, CALIFORNIA DIED: 5/17/1995 COSTA MESA, CALIFORNIA
POSITIONS PLAYED: 1B, OF

YEAR	TEAM	GAMES	AB	RUNS	HITS	2B	3B	HR	RBI	BB	IBB	SO	HBP	SH	SF	SB	CS	BA	OBA	SA	FA
1943	Bos-A	78	321	34	79	14	4	5	27	19	—	38	3	9	—	1	3	.246	.294	.361	.960
1944	Bos-A	134	549	94	152	28	8	9	59	31	—	57	3	4	—	13	4	.277	.319	.406	.978
1945	Bos-A	138	539	65	140	26	3	5	62	51	—	70	6	2	—	19	6	.260	.331	.347	.986

(continued)

(Metkovich, continued)

YEAR	TEAM	GAMES	AB	RUNS	HITS	2B	3B	HR	RBI	BB	IBB	SO	HBP	SH	SF	SB	CS	BA	OBA	SA	FA
1946	Bos-A	86	281	42	69	15	2	4	25	36	—	39	1	2	—	8	3	.246	.333	.356	.948
1947	Cle-A	126	473	68	120	22	7	5	40	32	—	51	1	9	—	5	3	.254	.302	.362	.989
1949	CWS-A	93	338	50	80	9	4	5	45	41	—	24	1	1	—	5	4	.237	.321	.331	.968
1951	Pit-N	120	423	51	124	21	3	3	40	28	—	23	1	3	—	3	2	.293	.338	.378	.992
1952	Pit-N	125	373	41	101	18	3	7	41	32	—	29	4	5	—	5	2	.271	.335	.391	.989
1953	Pit-N	26	41	5	6	0	1	1	7	6	—	3	0	0	—	0	0	.146	.255	.268	1.000
1953	**ChC-N**	**61**	**124**	**19**	**29**	**9**	**0**	**2**	**12**	**16**	**—**	**10**	**1**	**3**	**—**	**2**	**1**	**.234**	**.326**	**.355**	**.981**
1954	Mil-N	68	123	7	34	5	1	1	15	15	—	15	1	0	3	0	0	.276	.352	.358	1.000
Career average		106	359	48	93	17	4	5	37	31	—	36	2	4	0	6	3	.261	.322	.367	.983
Cubs average		**61**	**124**	**19**	**29**	**9**	**0**	**2**	**12**	**16**	**—**	**10**	**1**	**3**	**—**	**2**	**1**	**.234**	**.326**	**.355**	**.981**
Career total		1055	3585	476	934	167	36	47	373	307	—	359	22	38	3	61	28	.261	.322	.367	.983
Cubs total		**61**	**124**	**19**	**29**	**9**	**0**	**2**	**12**	**16**	**—**	**10**	**1**	**3**	**—**	**2**	**1**	**.234**	**.326**	**.355**	**.981**

Metzger, Roger Henry

HEIGHT: 6'0" THROWS: RIGHT BATS: BOTH BORN: 10/10/1947 FREDERICKSBURG, TEXAS POSITIONS PLAYED: 2B, 3B, SS

YEAR	TEAM	GAMES	AB	RUNS	HITS	2B	3B	HR	RBI	BB	IBB	SO	HBP	SH	SF	SB	CS	BA	OBA	SA	FA
1970	**ChC-N**	**1**	**2**	**0**	**0**	**0**	**0**	**0**	**0**	**0**	**0**	**0**	**0**	**0**	**0**	**0**	**0**	**.000**	**.000**	**.000**	**.833**
1971	Hou-N	150	562	64	132	14	11	0	26	44	4	50	4	5	2	15	6	.235	.294	.299	.977
1972	Hou-N	153	641	84	142	12	3	2	38	60	1	71	1	9	4	23	9	.222	.288	.259	.971
1973	Hou-N	154	580	67	145	11	14	1	35	39	0	70	3	12	3	10	4	.250	.299	.322	.982
1974	Hou-N	143	572	66	145	18	10	0	30	37	1	73	0	21	3	9	7	.253	.297	.320	.976
1975	Hou-N	127	450	54	102	7	9	2	26	41	10	39	0	15	4	4	5	.227	.289	.270	.977
1976	Hou-N	152	481	37	101	13	8	0	29	52	10	63	0	8	2	1	1	.210	.286	.264	.986
1977	Hou-N	97	269	24	50	9	6	0	16	32	3	24	0	5	1	2	0	.186	.272	.264	.973
1978	Hou-N	45	123	11	27	4	1	0	6	12	3	9	0	2	1	0	0	.220	.287	.268	.965
1978	SF-N	75	235	17	61	6	1	0	17	12	0	17	0	7	1	8	1	.260	.294	.294	.974
1979	SF-N	94	259	24	65	7	8	0	31	23	2	31	0	5	1	11	3	.251	.311	.340	.960
1980	SF-N	28	27	5	2	0	0	0	0	3	0	2	0	1	0	0	0	.074	.167	.074	.971
Career average		111	382	41	88	9	6	0	23	32	3	41	1	8	2	8	3	.231	.291	.293	.976
Cubs average		**1**	**2**	**0**	**0**	**0**	**0**	**0**	**0**	**0**	**0**	**0**	**0**	**0**	**0**	**0**	**0**	**.000**	**.000**	**.000**	**.833**
Career total		1219	4201	453	972	101	71	5	254	355	34	449	8	90	22	83	36	.231	.291	.293	.976
Cubs total		**1**	**2**	**0**	**0**	**0**	**0**	**0**	**0**	**0**	**0**	**0**	**0**	**0**	**0**	**0**	**0**	**.000**	**.000**	**.000**	**.833**

Metzler, Alexander (Alex)

HEIGHT: 5'9" THROWS: RIGHT BATS: LEFT BORN: 1/4/1903 FRESNO, CALIFORNIA DIED: 11/30/1973 FRESNO, CALIFORNIA POSITIONS PLAYED: OF

YEAR	TEAM	GAMES	AB	RUNS	HITS	2B	3B	HR	RBI	BB	IBB	SO	HBP	SH	SF	SB	CS	BA	OBA	SA	FA
1925	**ChC-N**	**9**	**38**	**2**	**7**	**2**	**0**	**0**	**2**	**3**	**—**	**7**	**0**	**1**	**—**	**0**	**0**	**.184**	**.244**	**.237**	**1.000**
1926	Phi-A	20	67	8	16	3	0	0	12	7	—	5	0	1	—	1	0	.239	.311	.284	1.000
1927	CWS-A	134	543	87	173	29	11	3	61	61	—	39	9	11	—	15	11	.319	.396	.429	.965
1928	CWS-A	139	464	71	141	18	14	3	55	77	—	30	6	20	—	16	8	.304	.410	.422	.968
1929	CWS-A	146	568	80	156	23	13	2	49	80	—	45	3	7	—	9	5	.275	.367	.371	.960
1930	CWS-A	56	79	12	14	4	0	0	5	11	—	6	0	2	—	0	2	.177	.278	.228	.969
1930	StL-A	56	209	30	54	6	3	1	23	21	—	12	0	10	—	5	1	.258	.326	.330	.951
Career average		93	328	48	94	14	7	2	35	43	—	24	3	9	—	8	5	.285	.374	.384	.965
Cubs average		**9**	**38**	**2**	**7**	**2**	**0**	**0**	**2**	**3**	**—**	**7**	**0**	**1**	**—**	**0**	**0**	**.184**	**.244**	**.237**	**1.000**
Career total		560	1968	290	561	85	41	9	207	260	—	144	18	52	—	46	27	.285	.374	.384	.965
Cubs total		**9**	**38**	**2**	**7**	**2**	**0**	**0**	**2**	**3**	**—**	**7**	**0**	**1**	**—**	**0**	**0**	**.184**	**.244**	**.237**	**1.000**

Meyer, Lambert Dalton (Dutch)

HEIGHT: 5'10" THROWS: RIGHT BATS: RIGHT BORN: 10/6/1915 WACO, TEXAS POSITIONS PLAYED: 2B

YEAR	TEAM	GAMES	AB	RUNS	HITS	2B	3B	HR	RBI	BB	IBB	SO	HBP	SH	SF	SB	CS	BA	OBA	SA	FA
1937	**ChC-N**	**1**	**0**	**0**	**0**	**0**	**0**	**0**	**0**	**0**	**—**	**0**	**0**	**0**	**—**	**0**		**—**	**—**	**—**	**—**
1940	Det-A	23	58	12	15	3	0	0	6	4	—	10	1	2	—	2	0	.259	.317	.310	.960
1941	Det-A	46	153	12	29	9	1	1	14	8	—	13	0	0	—	1	1	.190	.230	.281	.972
1942	Det-A	14	52	5	17	3	0	2	9	4	—	4	1	0	—	0	1	.327	.386	.500	.989
1945	Cle-A	130	524	71	153	29	8	7	48	40	—	32	0	3	—	2	4	.292	.342	.418	.978
1946	Cle-A	72	207	13	48	5	3	0	16	26	—	16	1	1	—	0	1	.232	.321	.285	.977
Career average		48	166	19	44	8	2	2	16	14	—	13	1	1	—	1	1	.264	.322	.367	.977
Cubs average		**1**	**0**	**0**	**0**	**0**	**0**	**0**	**0**	**0**	**—**	**0**	**0**	**0**	**—**	**0**		**—**	**—**	**—**	**—**
Career total		286	994	113	262	49	12	10	93	82	—	75	3	6	—	5	7	.264	.322	.367	.977
Cubs total		**1**	**0**	**0**	**0**	**0**	**0**	**0**	**0**	**0**	**—**	**0**	**0**	**0**	**—**	**0**		**—**	**—**	**—**	**—**

Meyers, Chad William

HEIGHT: 5'11" THROWS: RIGHT BATS: RIGHT BORN: 8/8/1975 OMAHA, NEBRASKA POSITIONS PLAYED: 2B, 3B, OF

YEAR	TEAM	GAMES	AB	RUNS	HITS	2B	3B	HR	RBI	BB	IBB	SO	HBP	SH	SF	SB	CS	BA	OBA	SA	FA
1999	ChC-N	43	142	17	33	9	0	0	4	9	1	27	3	2	0	4	2	.232	.292	.296	.986
2000	ChC-N	36	52	8	9	2	0	0	5	3	0	11	1	0	1	1	0	.173	.228	.212	.938
2001	ChC-N	18	17	1	2	0	0	0	0	2	0	5	4	0	0	0	1	.118	.348	.118	1.000
Career average		32	70	9	15	4	0	0	3	5	0	14	3	1	0	2	1	.209	.282	.261	.979
Cubs average		32	70	9	15	4	0	0	3	5	0	14	3	1	0	2	1	.209	.282	.261	.979
Career total		97	211	26	44	11	0	0	9	14	1	43	8	2	1	5	3	.209	.282	.261	.979
Cubs total		97	211	26	44	11	0	0	9	14	1	43	8	2	1	5	3	.209	.282	.261	.979

Michaels, Ralph Joseph

HEIGHT: 5'10" THROWS: RIGHT BATS: RIGHT BORN: 5/3/1902 ETNA, PENNSYLVANIA DIED: 8/5/1988 MONROEVILLE, PENNSYLVANIA
POSITIONS PLAYED: 1B, 2B, 3B, SS

YEAR	TEAM	GAMES	AB	RUNS	HITS	2B	3B	HR	RBI	BB	IBB	SO	HBP	SH	SF	SB	CS	BA	OBA	SA	FA
1924	ChC-N	8	11	0	4	0	0	0	2	0	—	1	0	1	—	0	0	.364	.364	.364	.929
1925	ChC-N	22	50	10	14	1	0	0	6	6	—	9	0	0	—	1	0	.280	.357	.300	.981
1926	ChC-N	2	0	1	0	0	0	0	0	0	—	0	0	0	—	0	—	—	—	—	—
Career average		11	20	4	6	0	0	0	3	2	—	3	0	0	—	0	0	.295	.358	.311	.970
Cubs average		11	20	4	6	0	0	0	3	2	—	3	0	0	—	0	0	.295	.358	.311	.970
Career total		32	61	11	18	1	0	0	8	6	—	10	0	1	—	1	0	.295	.358	.311	.970
Cubs total		32	61	11	18	1	0	0	8	6	—	10	0	1	—	1	0	.295	.358	.311	.970

Mickelson, Edward Allen (Ed)

HEIGHT: 6'3" THROWS: RIGHT BATS: RIGHT BORN: 9/9/1926 OTTAWA, ILLINOIS POSITIONS PLAYED: 1B

YEAR	TEAM	GAMES	AB	RUNS	HITS	2B	3B	HR	RBI	BB	IBB	SO	HBP	SH	SF	SB	CS	BA	OBA	SA	FA
1950	StL-N	5	10	1	1	0	0	0	0	2	—	3	0	0	—	0	—	.100	.250	.100	1.000
1953	StL-A	7	15	1	2	1	0	0	2	2	—	6	0	0	—	0	—	.133	.235	.200	1.000
1957	ChC-N	6	12	0	0	0	0	0	1	0	0	4	0	0	0	0	0	.000	.000	.000	1.000
Career average		6	12	1	1	0	0	0	1	1	0	4	0	0	0	0	0	.081	.171	.108	1.000
Cubs average		6	12	0	0	0	0	0	1	0	0	4	0	0	0	0	0	.000	.000	.000	1.000
Career total		18	37	2	3	1	0	0	3	4	0	13	0	0	0	0	0	.081	.171	.108	1.000
Cubs total		6	12	0	0	0	0	0	1	0	0	4	0	0	0	0	0	.000	.000	.000	1.000

Mieske, Matthew Todd (Matt)

HEIGHT: 6'0" THROWS: RIGHT BATS: RIGHT BORN: 2/13/1968 MIDLAND, MICHIGAN POSITIONS PLAYED: OF

YEAR	TEAM	GAMES	AB	RUNS	HITS	2B	3B	HR	RBI	BB	IBB	SO	HBP	SH	SF	SB	CS	BA	OBA	SA	FA
1993	Mil-A	23	58	9	14	0	0	3	7	4	0	14	0	1	0	0	2	.241	.290	.397	.936
1994	Mil-A	84	259	39	67	13	1	10	38	21	0	62	3	2	1	3	5	.259	.320	.432	.976
1995	Mil-A	117	267	42	67	13	1	12	48	27	0	45	4	0	5	2	4	.251	.323	.442	.979
1996	Mil-A	127	374	46	104	24	3	14	64	26	2	76	2	1	6	1	5	.278	.324	.471	.996
1997	Mil-A	84	253	39	63	15	3	5	21	19	2	50	0	0	1	1	5	.249	.300	.391	.996
1998	ChC-N	77	97	16	29	7	0	1	12	11	1	17	1	1	1	0	0	.299	.373	.402	.974
1999	Sea-A	24	41	11	15	0	0	4	7	2	1	9	1	0	0	0	0	.366	.395	.659	1.000
1999	Hou-N	54	109	13	31	5	0	5	22	6	1	22	0	1	2	0	0	.284	.316	.468	1.000
2000	Hou-N	62	81	7	14	1	2	1	5	7	0	17	1	0	0	0	0	.173	.247	.272	.933
2000	Ari-N	11	8	3	2	0	0	1	2	1	0	1	0	0	1	0	0	.250	.300	.625	1.000
Career average		83	193	28	51	10	1	7	28	16	1	39	1	1	2	1	2	.262	.318	.434	.979
Cubs average		77	97	16	29	7	0	1	12	11	1	17	1	1	1	0	0	.299	.373	.402	.974
Career total		663	1547	225	406	78	10	56	226	124	7	313	11	6	17	7	16	.262	.318	.434	.979
Cubs total		77	97	16	29	7	0	1	12	11	1	17	1	1	1	0	0	.299	.373	.402	.974

Miksis, Edward Thomas (Eddie)
HEIGHT: 6'0" THROWS: RIGHT BATS: RIGHT BORN: 9/11/1926 BURLINGTON, NEW JERSEY POSITIONS PLAYED: 1B, 2B, 3B, SS, OF

YEAR	TEAM	GAMES	AB	RUNS	HITS	2B	3B	HR	RBI	BB	IBB	SO	HBP	SH	SF	SB	CS	BA	OBA	SA	FA
1944	Bro-N	26	91	12	20	2	0	0	11	6	—	11	0	1	—	4	1	.220	.268	.242	.914
1946	Bro-N	23	48	3	7	0	0	0	5	3	—	3	1	1	—	0	0	.146	.212	.146	.971
1947	Bro-N	45	86	18	23	1	0	4	10	9	—	8	0	0	—	5	1	.267	.337	.419	.968
1948	Bro-N	86	221	28	47	7	1	2	16	19	—	27	1	3	—	5	2	.213	.278	.281	.980
1949	Bro-N	50	113	17	25	5	0	1	6	7	—	8	0	7	—	3	—	.221	.267	.292	.949
1950	Bro-N	51	76	13	19	2	1	2	10	5	—	10	1	0	—	0	0	.250	.305	.382	1.000
1951	Bro-N	19	10	6	2	1	0	0	0	1	—	2	0	0	—	0	0	.200	.273	.300	.969
1951	**ChC-N**	**102**	**421**	**48**	**112**	**13**	**3**	**4**	**35**	**33**	**—**	**36**	**0**	**7**	**—**	**11**	**5**	**.266**	**.319**	**.340**	**.962**
1952	**ChC-N**	**93**	**383**	**44**	**89**	**20**	**1**	**2**	**19**	**20**	**—**	**32**	**1**	**3**	**—**	**4**	**4**	**.232**	**.272**	**.305**	**.954**
1953	**ChC-N**	**142**	**577**	**61**	**145**	**17**	**6**	**8**	**39**	**33**	**—**	**59**	**1**	**13**	**—**	**13**	**4**	**.251**	**.293**	**.343**	**.962**
1954	**ChC-N**	**38**	**99**	**9**	**20**	**3**	**0**	**2**	**3**	**3**	**—**	**9**	**0**	**2**	**0**	**1**	**0**	**.202**	**.225**	**.293**	**.983**
1955	**ChC-N**	**131**	**481**	**52**	**113**	**14**	**2**	**9**	**41**	**32**	**3**	**55**	**0**	**10**	**1**	**3**	**6**	**.235**	**.282**	**.328**	**.977**
1956	**ChC-N**	**114**	**356**	**54**	**85**	**10**	**3**	**9**	**27**	**32**	**2**	**40**	**1**	**5**	**1**	**4**	**2**	**.239**	**.303**	**.360**	**1.000**
1957	StL-N	49	38	3	8	0	0	1	2	7	1	7	0	0	0	0	0	.211	.333	.289	—
1957	Bal-A	1	1	0	0	0	0	0	0	0	0	0	0	0	0	0	0	.000	.000	.000	—
1958	Bal-A	3	2	0	0	0	0	0	0	0	0	1	0	0	0	0	0	.000	.000	.000	.948
1958	Cin-N	69	50	15	7	0	0	0	4	5	0	5	0	4	0	1	1	.140	.218	.140	.948
Career average		74	218	27	52	7	1	3	16	15	0	22	0	4	0	4	2	.236	.288	.322	.965
Cubs average		**103**	**386**	**45**	**94**	**13**	**3**	**6**	**27**	**26**	**1**	**39**	**1**	**7**	**0**	**6**	**4**	**.243**	**.291**	**.334**	**.966**
Career total		1042	3053	383	722	95	17	44	228	215	6	313	6	62	2	52	26	.236	.288	.322	.965
Cubs total		**620**	**2317**	**268**	**564**	**77**	**15**	**34**	**164**	**153**	**5**	**231**	**3**	**40**	**2**	**36**	**21**	**.243**	**.291**	**.334**	**.966**

Miller, Dakin Evans (Dusty)
HEIGHT: 5'10" THROWS: RIGHT BATS: LEFT BORN: 9/3/1876 MALVERN, IOWA DIED: 4/19/1950 STOCKTON, CALIFORNIA POSITIONS PLAYED: OF

YEAR	TEAM	GAMES	AB	RUNS	HITS	2B	3B	HR	RBI	BB	IBB	SO	HBP	SH	SF	SB	CS	BA	OBA	SA	FA
1902	**ChC-N**	**51**	**187**	**17**	**46**	**4**	**1**	**0**	**13**	**7**	**—**	**—**	**7**	**6**	**—**	**10**	**—**	**.246**	**.299**	**.278**	**.955**
Career average		51	187	17	46	4	1	0	13	7	—	—	7	6	—	10	—	.246	.299	.278	.955
Cubs average		**51**	**187**	**17**	**46**	**4**	**1**	**0**	**13**	**7**	**—**	**—**	**7**	**6**	**—**	**10**	**—**	**.246**	**.299**	**.278**	**.955**
Career total		51	187	17	46	4	1	0	13	7	—	—	7	6	—	10	—	.246	.299	.278	.955
Cubs total		**51**	**187**	**17**	**46**	**4**	**1**	**0**	**13**	**7**	**—**	**—**	**7**	**6**	**—**	**10**	**—**	**.246**	**.299**	**.278**	**.955**

Miller, Laurence H. (Hack)
HEIGHT: 5'9" THROWS: RIGHT BATS: RIGHT BORN: 1/1/1894 NEW YORK, NEW YORK DIED: 9/16/1971 OAKLAND, CALIFORNIA POSITIONS PLAYED: OF

YEAR	TEAM	GAMES	AB	RUNS	HITS	2B	3B	HR	RBI	BB	IBB	SO	HBP	SH	SF	SB	CS	BA	OBA	SA	FA
1916	Bro-N	3	3	0	1	0	1	0	1	1	—	1	0	0	—	0	—	.333	.500	1.000	1.000
1918	Bos-A	12	29	2	8	2	0	0	4	0	—	4	0	0	—	0	—	.276	.276	.345	1.000
1922	**ChC-N**	**122**	**466**	**61**	**164**	**28**	**5**	**12**	**78**	**26**	**—**	**39**	**2**	**6**	**—**	**3**	**3**	**.352**	**.389**	**.511**	**.959**
1923	**ChC-N**	**135**	**485**	**74**	**146**	**24**	**2**	**20**	**88**	**27**	**—**	**39**	**4**	**8**	**—**	**6**	**5**	**.301**	**.343**	**.482**	**.978**
1924	**ChC-N**	**53**	**131**	**17**	**44**	**8**	**1**	**4**	**25**	**8**	**—**	**11**	**1**	**3**	**—**	**1**	**0**	**.336**	**.379**	**.504**	**.948**
1925	**ChC-N**	**24**	**86**	**10**	**24**	**3**	**2**	**2**	**9**	**2**	**—**	**9**	**1**	**0**	**—**	**0**	**1**	**.279**	**.303**	**.430**	**.878**
Career average		58	200	27	65	11	2	6	34	11	—	17	1	3	—	2	2	.323	.361	.490	.962
Cubs average		**84**	**292**	**41**	**95**	**16**	**3**	**10**	**50**	**16**	**—**	**25**	**2**	**4**	**—**	**3**	**2**	**.324**	**.362**	**.492**	**.961**
Career total		349	1200	164	387	65	11	38	205	64	—	103	8	17	—	10	9	.323	.361	.490	.962
Cubs total		**334**	**1168**	**162**	**378**	**63**	**10**	**38**	**200**	**63**	**—**	**98**	**8**	**17**	**—**	**10**	**9**	**.324**	**.362**	**.492**	**.961**

Miller, Roy Oscar (Doc)
HEIGHT: 5'10" THROWS: LEFT BATS: LEFT BORN: 2/4/1883 CHATHAM, ONTARIO, CANADA DIED: 7/31/1938 JERSEY CITY, NEW JERSEY
POSITIONS PLAYED: OF

YEAR	TEAM	GAMES	AB	RUNS	HITS	2B	3B	HR	RBI	BB	IBB	SO	HBP	SH	SF	SB	CS	BA	OBA	SA	FA
1910	**ChC-N**	**1**	**1**	**0**	**0**	**0**	**0**	**0**	**0**	**0**	**—**	**0**	**0**	**0**	**—**	**0**	**—**	**.000**	**.000**	**.000**	**—**
1910	Bos-N	130	482	48	138	27	4	3	55	33	—	52	1	18	—	17	—	.286	.333	.442	.951
1911	Bos-N	146	577	69	192	36	3	7	91	43	—	43	0	12	—	32	—	.333	.379	.442	.961
1912	Bos-N	51	201	26	47	8	1	2	24	14	—	17	1	8	—	6	—	.234	.287	.313	.948
1912	Phi-N	67	177	24	51	12	5	0	21	9	—	13	0	5	—	3	—	.288	.323	.412	.986

(continued)

(continued) YEAR	TEAM	GAMES	AB	RUNS	HITS	2B	3B	HR	RBI	BB	IBB	SO	HBP	SH	SF	SB	CS	BA	OBA	SA	FA
1913	Phi-N	69	87	9	30	6	0	0	11	6	—	6	2	0	—	2	—	.345	.400	.414	.800
1914	Cin-N	93	192	8	49	7	2	0	33	16	—	18	0	4	—	4	—	.255	.313	.313	.976
Career average		111	343	37	101	19	3	2	47	24	—	30	1	9	—	13	—	.295	.343	.390	.958
Cubs average		**1**	**1**	**0**	**0**	**0**	**0**	**0**	**0**	**0**	**—**	**0**	**0**	**0**	**—**	**0**	**—**	**.000**	**.000**	**.000**	**—**
Career total		557	1717	184	507	96	15	12	235	121	—	149	4	47	—	64	—	.295	.343	.390	.958
Cubs total		**1**	**1**	**0**	**0**	**0**	**0**	**0**	**0**	**0**	**—**	**0**	**0**	**0**	**—**	**0**	**—**	**.000**	**.000**	**.000**	**.958**

Miller, Ward Taylor (Windy or Grump)

HEIGHT: 5'11" THROWS: RIGHT BATS: LEFT BORN: 7/5/1884 MOUNT CARROLL, ILLINOIS DIED: 9/4/1958 DIXON, ILLINOIS POSITIONS PLAYED: 2B, OF

YEAR	TEAM	GAMES	AB	RUNS	HITS	2B	3B	HR	RBI	BB	IBB	SO	HBP	SH	SF	SB	CS	BA	OBA	SA	FA
1909	Pit-N	15	56	2	8	0	1	0	4	4	—	—	1	1	—	2	—	.143	.213	.179	.967
1909	Cin-N	43	113	17	35	3	1	0	4	6	—	—	0	3	—	9	—	.310	.345	.354	.981
1910	Cin-N	81	126	21	30	6	0	0	10	22	—	13	1	7	—	10	—	.238	.356	.286	.944
1912	**ChC-N**	**86**	**241**	**45**	**74**	**11**	**4**	**0**	**22**	**26**	**—**	**18**	**1**	**8**	**—**	**11**	**—**	**.307**	**.377**	**.386**	**.943**
1913	**ChC-N**	**80**	**203**	**23**	**48**	**5**	**7**	**1**	**16**	**34**	**—**	**33**	**1**	**3**	**—**	**13**	**—**	**.236**	**.349**	**.345**	**.980**
1914	StL-F	121	402	49	118	17	7	4	50	59	—	36	10	11	—	18	—	.294	.397	.400	.953
1915	StL-F	154	536	80	164	19	9	1	63	79	—	39	5	26	—	33	—	.306	.400	.381	.963
1916	StL-A	146	485	72	129	17	5	1	50	72	—	76	9	28	—	25	21	.266	.371	.328	.943
1917	StL-A	43	82	13	17	1	1	1	2	16	—	15	2	2	—	7	—	.207	.350	.280	.966
Career average		96	281	40	78	10	4	1	28	40	—	29	4	11	—	16	3	.278	.375	.355	.957
Cubs average		**83**	**222**	**34**	**61**	**8**	**6**	**1**	**19**	**30**	**—**	**26**	**1**	**6**	**—**	**12**	**—**	**.275**	**.364**	**.367**	**.963**
Career total		769	2244	322	623	79	35	8	221	318	—	230	30	89	—	128	21	.278	.375	.355	.957
Cubs total		**166**	**444**	**68**	**122**	**16**	**11**	**1**	**38**	**60**	**—**	**51**	**2**	**11**	**—**	**24**	**—**	**.275**	**.364**	**.367**	**.963**

Mitchell, Michael Francis (Mike)

HEIGHT: 6'1" THROWS: RIGHT BATS: RIGHT BORN: 12/12/1879 SPRINGFIELD, OHIO DIED: 7/16/1961 PHOENIX, ARIZONA POSITIONS PLAYED: 1B, OF

YEAR	TEAM	GAMES	AB	RUNS	HITS	2B	3B	HR	RBI	BB	IBB	SO	HBP	SH	SF	SB	CS	BA	OBA	SA	FA
1907	Cin-N	148	558	64	163	17	12	3	47	37	—	—	3	15	—	17	—	.292	.339	.382	.958
1908	Cin-N	119	406	41	90	9	6	1	37	46	—	—	2	14	—	18	—	.222	.304	.281	.960
1909	Cin-N	145	523	83	162	17	17	4	86	57	—	—	0	15	—	37	—	.310	.378	.430	.962
1910	Cin-N	156	583	79	167	16	18	5	88	59	—	56	4	22	—	35	—	.286	.356	.401	.963
1911	Cin-N	142	529	74	154	22	22	2	84	44	—	34	2	19	—	35	—	.291	.348	.427	.971
1912	Cin-N	147	552	60	156	14	13	4	78	41	—	43	1	18	—	23	—	.283	.333	.377	.947
1913	**ChC-N**	**82**	**279**	**37**	**73**	**11**	**6**	**4**	**35**	**32**	**—**	**33**	**1**	**12**	**—**	**15**	**—**	**.262**	**.340**	**.387**	**.941**
1913	Pit-N	54	199	25	54	8	2	1	16	14	—	15	0	1	—	8	—	.271	.319	.347	.946
1914	Pit-N	76	273	31	64	11	5	2	23	16	—	16	1	7	—	5	4	.234	.279	.333	.984
1914	Was-A	55	193	20	55	5	3	1	20	22	—	19	1	10	—	9	7	.285	.361	.358	.957
Career average		141	512	64	142	16	13	3	64	46	—	27	2	17	—	25	1	.278	.340	.380	.960
Cubs average		**82**	**279**	**37**	**73**	**11**	**6**	**4**	**35**	**32**	**—**	**33**	**1**	**12**	**—**	**15**	**—**	**.262**	**.340**	**.387**	**.941**
Career total		1124	4095	514	1138	130	104	27	514	368	—	216	15	133	—	202	11	.278	.340	.380	.960
Cubs total		**82**	**279**	**37**	**73**	**11**	**6**	**4**	**35**	**32**	**—**	**33**	**1**	**12**	**—**	**15**	**—**	**.262**	**.340**	**.387**	**.941**

Mitterwald, George Eugene

HEIGHT: 6'2" THROWS: RIGHT BATS: RIGHT BORN: 6/7/1945 BERKELEY, CALIFORNIA POSITIONS PLAYED: C, 1B, OF

YEAR	TEAM	GAMES	AB	RUNS	HITS	2B	3B	HR	RBI	BB	IBB	SO	HBP	SH	SF	SB	CS	BA	OBA	SA	FA
1966	Min-A	3	5	1	1	0	0	0	0	0	0	0	0	0	0	0	0	.200	.200	.200	1.000
1968	Min-A	11	34	1	7	1	0	0	1	3	0	8	0	1	0	0	0	.206	.270	.235	.961
1969	Min-A	69	187	18	48	8	0	5	13	17	1	47	3	2	1	0	1	.257	.327	.380	.987
1970	Min-A	117	369	36	82	12	2	15	46	34	6	84	2	4	0	3	5	.222	.291	.388	.996
1971	Min-A	125	388	38	97	13	1	13	44	39	9	104	0	3	4	3	3	.250	.316	.389	.986
1972	Min-A	64	163	12	30	4	1	1	8	9	2	37	0	0	1	0	1	.184	.225	.239	.984
1973	Min-A	125	432	50	112	15	0	16	64	39	0	111	5	2	3	3	1	.259	.326	.405	.992
1974	**ChC-N**	**78**	**215**	**17**	**54**	**7**	**0**	**7**	**28**	**18**	**4**	**42**	**2**	**1**	**4**	**1**	**3**	**.251**	**.310**	**.381**	**.974**
1975	**ChC-N**	**84**	**200**	**19**	**44**	**4**	**3**	**5**	**26**	**19**	**7**	**42**	**0**	**1**	**2**	**0**	**0**	**.220**	**.285**	**.345**	**.978**
1976	**ChC-N**	**101**	**303**	**19**	**65**	**7**	**0**	**5**	**28**	**16**	**2**	**63**	**0**	**0**	**6**	**1**	**2**	**.215**	**.249**	**.287**	**.986**
1977	**ChC-N**	**110**	**349**	**40**	**83**	**22**	**0**	**9**	**43**	**28**	**7**	**69**	**1**	**2**	**2**	**1**	**3**	**.238**	**.295**	**.378**	**.989**
Career average		81	240	23	57	8	1	7	27	20	3	55	1	1	2	1	2	.236	.296	.362	.987
Cubs average		**93**	**267**	**24**	**62**	**10**	**1**	**7**	**31**	**20**	**5**	**54**	**1**	**1**	**4**	**1**	**2**	**.231**	**.283**	**.347**	**.983**
Career total		887	2645	251	623	93	7	76	301	222	38	607	13	16	23	14	17	.236	.296	.362	.987
Cubs total		**373**	**1067**	**95**	**246**	**40**	**3**	**26**	**125**	**81**	**20**	**216**	**3**	**4**	**14**	**5**	**6**	**.231**	**.283**	**.347**	**.983**

Molina, Jose Benjamin

HEIGHT: 6'2" THROWS: RIGHT BATS: RIGHT BORN: 6/3/1975 BAYAMON, PUERTO RICO POSITIONS PLAYED: C

YEAR	TEAM	GAMES	AB	RUNS	HITS	2B	3B	HR	RBI	BB	IBB	SO	HBP	SH	SF	SB	CS	BA	OBA	SA	FA
1999	ChC-N	10	19	3	5	1	0	0	1	2	1	4	0	0	0	0	0	.263	.333	.316	1.000
2001	Ana-A	15	37	8	10	3	0	2	4	3	0	8	0	2	0	0	0	.270	.325	.514	1.000
Career average		13	28	6	8	2	0	1	3	3	1	6	0	1	0	0	0	.268	.328	.446	1.000
Cubs average		10	19	3	5	1	0	0	1	2	1	4	0	0	0	0	0	.263	.333	.316	1.000
Career total		25	56	11	15	4	0	2	5	5	1	12	0	2	0	0	0	.268	.328	.446	1.000
Cubs total		10	19	3	5	1	0	0	1	2	1	4	0	0	0	0	0	.263	.333	.316	1.000

Molinaro, Robert Joseph (Bob *or* Molly)

HEIGHT: 6'0" THROWS: RIGHT BATS: LEFT BORN: 5/21/1950 NEWARK, NEW JERSEY POSITIONS PLAYED: OF

YEAR	TEAM	GAMES	AB	RUNS	HITS	2B	3B	HR	RBI	BB	IBB	SO	HBP	SH	SF	SB	CS	BA	OBA	SA	FA
1975	Det-A	6	19	2	5	0	1	0	1	1	0	0	0	1	0	0	0	.263	.300	.368	1.000
1977	Det-A	4	4	0	1	1	0	0	0	0	0	2	0	0	0	0	0	.250	.250	.500	—
1977	CWS-A	1	2	0	1	0	0	0	0	0	0	1	0	0	0	1	0	.500	.500	.500	1.000
1978	CWS-A	105	286	39	75	5	5	6	27	19	2	12	3	2	1	22	6	.262	.314	.378	1.000
1979	Bal-A	8	6	0	0	0	0	0	0	1	0	3	0	0	0	1	0	.000	.143	.000	1.000
1980	CWS-A	119	344	48	100	16	4	5	36	26	7	29	7	2	5	18	7	.291	.348	.404	.957
1981	CWS-A	47	42	7	11	1	1	1	9	8	1	1	1	0	2	1	0	.262	.377	.405	1.000
1982	ChC-N	65	66	6	13	1	0	1	12	6	1	5	0	0	0	1	1	.197	.264	.258	1.000
1982	Phi-N	19	14	0	4	0	0	0	2	3	1	1	0	0	0	1	0	.286	.412	.286	—
1983	Phi-N	19	18	1	2	1	0	1	3	0	0	2	0	0	1	0	0	.111	.105	.333	—
1983	Det-A	8	2	3	0	0	0	0	0	1	0	1	0	0	0	1	1	.000	.333	.000	—
Career average		50	100	13	27	3	1	2	11	8	2	7	1	1	1	6	2	.264	.324	.375	.980
Cubs average		65	66	6	13	1	0	1	12	6	1	5	0	0	0	1	1	.197	.264	.258	1.000
Career total		401	803	106	212	25	11	14	90	65	12	57	11	5	9	46	15	.264	.324	.375	.980
Cubs total		65	66	6	13	1	0	1	12	6	1	5	0	0	0	1	1	.197	.264	.258	1.000

Mollwitz, Frederick August (Fritz)

HEIGHT: 6'2" THROWS: RIGHT BATS: RIGHT BORN: 6/16/1890 KOBURG, GERMANY DIED: 10/3/1967 BRADENTON, FLORIDA POSITIONS PLAYED: 1B, 2B, OF

YEAR	TEAM	GAMES	AB	RUNS	HITS	2B	3B	HR	RBI	BB	IBB	SO	HBP	SH	SF	SB	CS	BA	OBA	SA	FA
1913	ChC-N	2	7	1	3	0	0	0	0	0	—	0	0	1	—	0	—	.429	.429	.429	1.000
1914	ChC-N	13	20	0	3	0	0	0	1	0	—	3	0	0	—	1	—	.150	.150	.150	.962
1914	Cin-N	32	111	12	18	2	0	0	5	3	—	9	2	2	—	2	—	.162	.198	.180	.991
1915	Cin-N	153	525	36	136	21	3	1	51	15	—	49	1	18	—	19	11	.259	.281	.316	.996
1916	Cin-N	65	183	12	41	4	4	0	16	5	—	12	0	9	—	6	—	.224	.245	.290	.981
1916	ChC-N	33	71	1	19	2	0	0	11	7	—	6	0	2	—	4	—	.268	.333	.296	.970
1917	Pit-N	36	140	15	36	4	1	0	12	8	—	8	0	8	—	4	—	.257	.297	.300	.994
1918	Pit-N	119	432	43	116	12	7	0	45	23	—	24	0	30	—	23	—	.269	.305	.329	.990
1919	Pit-N	56	168	11	29	2	4	0	12	15	—	18	2	3	—	9	—	.173	.249	.232	.994
1919	StL-N	25	83	7	19	3	0	0	5	7	—	3	0	3	—	2	—	.229	.289	.265	.994
Career average		76	249	20	60	7	3	0	23	12	—	19	1	11	—	10	2	.241	.278	.294	.991
Cubs average		16	33	1	8	1	0	0	4	2	—	3	0	1	—	2	0	.255	.305	.276	.972
Career total		534	1740	138	420	50	19	1	158	83	—	132	5	76	—	70	11	.241	.278	.294	.991
Cubs total		48	98	2	25	2	0	0	12	7	—	9	0	3	—	5	0	.255	.305	.276	.972

Monday, Robert James (Rick)

HEIGHT: 6'3" THROWS: LEFT BATS: LEFT BORN: 11/20/1945 BATESVILLE, ARKANSAS POSITIONS PLAYED: 1B, OF

YEAR	TEAM	GAMES	AB	RUNS	HITS	2B	3B	HR	RBI	BB	IBB	SO	HBP	SH	SF	SB	CS	BA	OBA	SA	FA
1966	KCA-A	17	41	4	4	1	1	0	2	6	0	16	0	0	0	1	1	.098	.213	.171	.964
1967	KCA-A	124	406	52	102	14	6	14	58	42	2	107	2	5	4	3	6	.251	.322	.419	.972
1968	Oak-A	148	482	56	132	24	7	8	49	72	7	143	4	2	3	14	6	.274	.371	.402	.978
1969	Oak-A	122	399	57	108	17	4	12	54	72	11	100	5	4	1	12	3	.271	.388	.424	.964
1970	Oak-A	112	376	63	109	19	7	10	37	58	0	99	2	5	1	17	11	.290	.387	.457	.981
1971	Oak-A	116	355	53	87	9	3	18	56	49	5	93	0	3	2	6	9	.245	.335	.439	.984
1972	ChC-N	138	434	68	108	22	5	11	42	78	8	102	1	3	4	12	9	.249	.362	.399	.996
1973	ChC-N	149	554	93	148	24	5	26	56	92	7	124	1	3	1	5	12	.267	.372	.469	.973
1974	ChC-N	142	538	84	158	19	7	20	58	70	6	94	2	4	3	7	9	.294	.375	.467	.984
1975	ChC-N	136	491	89	131	29	4	17	60	83	12	95	1	7	1	8	3	.267	.373	.446	.973

(continued)

Robert James "Rick" Monday, of-1b, 1966–84

Rick Monday spent the middle years of his 19-season career in Chicago, where he stabilized the center-field position like no one since the Andy Pafko days.

Monday was born in Batesville, Arkansas, on November 20, 1945. He began his career with the Kansas City and, later, the Oakland Athletics, where he played from 1966 to 1971. After helping the A's to their 1971 world championship, Monday was traded to Chicago even-up for Ken Holtzman.

Monday cracked 108 hits with 22 doubles for the Cubs in 1972. It was the first of five consecutive seasons Monday would reach the 100-plus mark in hits for Chicago. He also led all National League center fielders in fielding percentage with a .996 mark that year.

The free-swinging Monday wasn't the perfect candidate to lead off for the Cubs, as he struck out 100 or more times three of the five years he played in the Windy City. But he had some power, stroking 17 leadoff home runs in his five years in Chicago, including a club record eight in 1976. He was also an excellent fielder with an accurate arm and a better base runner than is popularly thought: he hit into only 71 double plays in his career.

His best season as a Cub was 1976. Monday hit .272 with a career-high 32 home runs and scored a career-high 107 runs. After that season, Monday was traded to the Dodgers.

Monday was a clean-cut guy, everyone's vision of the all-American boy. In April 1976 at Dodger Stadium, Monday grabbed a flag from a fan who was about to set it on fire. He ripped the flag out of the fan's hand, to a tremendous ovation from the crowd. Monday probably gleaned more notoriety from that act than he did from anything else in his career.

Monday spent his last eight years in Los Angeles, retiring in 1984.

(continued)

YEAR	TEAM	G	AB	R	H	2B	3B	HR	RBI	BB	IBB	SO	HBP	SH	SF	SB	CS	BA	OBA	SA	FA
1976	ChC-N	137	534	107	145	20	5	32	77	60	8	125	2	2	3	5	9	.272	.346	.507	.992
1977	LA-N	118	392	47	90	13	1	15	48	60	6	109	0	2	2	1	4	.230	.330	.383	.991
1978	LA-N	119	342	54	87	14	1	19	57	49	11	100	1	3	2	2	4	.254	.348	.468	.995
1979	LA-N	12	33	2	10	0	0	0	2	5	0	6	0	0	0	0	0	.303	.395	.303	.964
1980	LA-N	96	194	35	52	7	1	10	25	28	3	49	1	0	0	2	2	.268	.363	.469	.969
1981	LA-N	66	130	24	41	1	2	11	25	24	3	42	1	0	1	1	2	.315	.423	.608	.962
1982	LA-N	104	210	37	54	6	4	11	42	39	6	51	1	1	3	2	1	.257	.372	.481	.959
1983	LA-N	99	178	21	44	7	1	6	20	29	9	42	0	0	1	0	0	.247	.351	.399	.965
1984	LA-N	31	47	4	9	2	0	1	7	8	3	16	0	2	0	0	0	.191	.309	.298	.987
Career average		105	323	50	85	13	3	13	41	49	6	80	1	2	2	5	5	.264	.361	.443	.981
Cubs average		**140**	**510**	**88**	**138**	**23**	**5**	**21**	**59**	**77**	**8**	**108**	**1**	**4**	**2**	**7**	**8**	**.264**	**.366**	**.460**	**.985**
Career total		1986	6136	950	1619	248	64	241	775	924	107	1513	24	46	32	98	91	.264	.361	.443	.981
Cubs total		**702**	**2551**	**441**	**690**	**114**	**26**	**106**	**293**	**383**	**41**	**540**	**7**	**19**	**12**	**37**	**42**	**.270**	**.366**	**.460**	**.985**

Montreuil, Allan Arthur (Al)

HEIGHT: 5'5"   THROWS: RIGHT   BATS: RIGHT   BORN: 8/23/1943 NEW ORLEANS, LOUISIANA   POSITIONS PLAYED: 2B

YEAR	TEAM	GAMES	AB	RUNS	HITS	2B	3B	HR	RBI	BB	IBB	SO	HBP	SH	SF	SB	CS	BA	OBA	SA	FA
1972	ChC-N	5	11	0	1	0	0	0	0	1	0	4	0	0	0	0	0	.091	.167	.091	1.000
Career average		5	11	0	1	0	0	0	0	1	0	4	0	0	0	0	0	.091	.167	.091	1.000
Cubs average		**5**	**11**	**0**	**1**	**0**	**0**	**0**	**0**	**1**	**0**	**4**	**0**	**0**	**0**	**0**	**0**	**.091**	**.167**	**.091**	**1.000**
Career total		5	11	0	1	0	0	0	0	1	0	4	0	0	0	0	0	.091	.167	.091	1.000
Cubs total		**5**	**11**	**0**	**1**	**0**	**0**	**0**	**0**	**1**	**0**	**4**	**0**	**0**	**0**	**0**	**0**	**.091**	**.167**	**.091**	**1.000**

Moolic, George Henry (Prunes)
HEIGHT: 5'7" THROWS: RIGHT BATS: RIGHT BORN: 3/12/1867 LAWRENCE, MASSACHUSETTS DIED: 2/19/1915 METHUEN, MASSACHUSETTS
POSITIONS PLAYED: C, OF

YEAR	TEAM	GAMES	AB	RUNS	HITS	2B	3B	HR	RBI	BB	IBB	SO	HBP	SH	SF	SB	CS	BA	OBA	SA	FA
1886	ChN-N	16	56	9	8	3	0	0	2	2	—	17	—	—	—	0	—	.143	.172	.196	.945
Career average		16	56	9	8	3	0	0	2	2	—	17	—	—	—	0	—	.143	.172	.196	.945
Cubs average		16	56	9	8	3	0	0	2	2	—	17	—	—	—	0	—	.143	.172	.196	.945
Career total		16	56	9	8	3	0	0	2	2	—	17	—	—	—	0	—	.143	.172	.196	.945
Cubs total		16	56	9	8	3	0	0	2	2	—	17	—	—	—	0	—	.143	.172	.196	.945

Moore, Charles Wesley (Charley)
HEIGHT: 5'10" THROWS: RIGHT BATS: RIGHT BORN: 12/1/1884 JACKSON COUNTY, INDIANA DIED: 7/29/1970 PORTLAND, OREGON
POSITIONS PLAYED: 2B, 3B, SS

YEAR	TEAM	GAMES	AB	RUNS	HITS	2B	3B	HR	RBI	BB	IBB	SO	HBP	SH	SF	SB	CS	BA	OBA	SA	FA
1912	ChC-N	5	9	2	2	0	1	0	2	0	—	1	0	0	—	0	—	.222	.222	.444	.900
Career average		5	9	2	2	0	1	0	2	0	—	1	0	0	—	0	—	.222	.222	.444	.900
Cubs average		5	9	2	2	0	1	0	2	0	—	1	0	0	—	0	—	.222	.222	.444	.900
Career total		5	9	2	2	0	1	0	2	0	—	1	0	0	—	0	—	.222	.222	.444	.900
Cubs total		5	9	2	2	0	1	0	2	0	—	1	0	0	—	0	—	.222	.222	.444	.900

Moore, John Francis (Johnny)
HEIGHT: 5'10" THROWS: RIGHT BATS: LEFT BORN: 3/23/1902 WATERVILLE, CONNECTICUT DIED: 4/4/1991 BRADENTON, FLORIDA POSITIONS PLAYED: OF

YEAR	TEAM	GAMES	AB	RUNS	HITS	2B	3B	HR	RBI	BB	IBB	SO	HBP	SH	SF	SB	CS	BA	OBA	SA	FA
1928	ChC-N	4	4	0	0	0	0	0	0	0	—	0	0	0	—	0	—	.000	.000	.000	—
1929	ChC-N	37	63	13	18	1	0	2	8	4	—	6	1	1	—	0	—	.286	.338	.397	.971
1931	ChC-N	39	104	19	25	3	1	2	16	7	—	5	0	4	—	1	—	.240	.288	.346	.964
1932	ChC-N	119	443	59	135	24	5	13	64	22	—	38	3	7	—	4	—	.305	.342	.470	.983
1933	Cin-N	133	514	60	135	19	5	1	44	29	—	16	3	16	—	4	—	.263	.306	.325	.974
1934	Cin-N	16	42	5	8	1	1	0	5	3	—	2	0	0	—	0	—	.190	.244	.262	1.000
1934	Phi-N	116	458	68	157	34	6	11	93	40	—	18	1	4	—	7	—	.343	.397	.515	.981
1935	Phi-N	153	600	84	194	33	3	19	93	45	—	50	5	4	—	4	—	.323	.375	.483	.973
1936	Phi-N	124	472	85	155	24	3	16	68	26	—	22	1	6	—	1	—	.328	.365	.494	.948
1937	Phi-N	96	307	46	98	16	2	9	59	18	—	18	0	5	—	2	—	.319	.357	.472	.943
1945	ChC-N	7	6	0	1	0	0	0	2	1	—	1	0	0	—	0	—	.167	.286	.167	—
Career average		84	301	44	93	16	3	7	45	20	—	18	1	5	—	2	—	.307	.352	.449	.970
Cubs average		41	124	18	36	6	1	3	18	7	—	10	1	2	—	1	—	.289	.330	.435	.979
Career total		844	3013	439	926	155	26	73	452	195	—	176	14	47	—	23	—	.307	.352	.449	.970
Cubs total		206	620	91	179	28	6	17	90	34	—	50	4	12	—	5	—	.289	.330	.435	.979

Morales, Julio Ruben (Jerry)
HEIGHT: 5'10" THROWS: RIGHT BATS: RIGHT BORN: 2/18/1949 YABUCOA, PUERTO RICO POSITIONS PLAYED: 3B, OF

YEAR	TEAM	GAMES	AB	RUNS	HITS	2B	3B	HR	RBI	BB	IBB	SO	HBP	SH	SF	SB	CS	BA	OBA	SA	FA
1969	SD-N	19	41	5	8	2	0	1	6	5	0	7	0	0	0	0	2	.195	.283	.317	1.000
1970	SD-N	28	58	6	9	0	1	1	4	3	0	11	0	0	0	0	0	.155	.197	.241	.926
1971	SD-N	12	17	1	2	0	0	0	1	2	0	2	0	0	0	1	0	.118	.211	.118	1.000
1972	SD-N	115	347	38	83	15	7	4	18	35	3	54	0	9	2	4	6	.239	.307	.357	.982
1973	SD-N	122	388	47	109	23	2	9	34	27	3	55	0	1	4	6	5	.281	.325	.420	.991
1974	ChC-N	151	534	70	146	21	7	15	82	46	3	63	2	3	5	2	12	.273	.330	.369	.975
1975	ChC-N	153	578	62	156	21	0	12	91	50	9	65	5	0	11	3	7	.270	.328	.369	.979
1976	ChC-N	140	537	66	147	17	0	16	67	41	7	49	0	1	4	3	8	.274	.323	.395	.983
1977	ChC-N	136	490	56	142	34	5	11	69	43	4	75	2	0	3	0	3	.290	.348	.447	.985
1978	StL-N	130	457	44	109	19	4	8	46	33	1	44	1	2	6	4	4	.239	.288	.341	.977
1979	Det-A	129	440	50	93	23	1	14	56	30	0	56	2	2	8	10	4	.211	.260	.364	.986
1980	NYM-N	94	193	19	49	7	1	3	30	13	2	31	1	1	8	2	3	.254	.293	.347	.986
1981	ChC-N	84	245	27	70	6	2	1	25	22	0	29	1	1	3	1	1	.286	.343	.339	.986
1982	ChC-N	65	116	14	33	2	2	4	30	9	1	7	0	0	1	1	2	.284	.333	.440	1.000
1983	ChC-N	63	87	11	17	9	0	0	11	7	0	19	0	0	1	0	0	.195	.253	.299	1.000

(continued)

(continued)

	GAMES	AB	RUNS	HITS	2B	3B	HR	RBI	BB	IBB	SO	HBP	SH	SF	SB	CS	BA	OBA	SA	FA
Career average	96	302	34	78	13	2	6	38	24	2	38	1	1	4	2	4	.259	.313	.382	.982
Cubs average	**113**	**370**	**44**	**102**	**16**	**2**	**8**	**54**	**31**	**3**	**44**	**1**	**1**	**4**	**1**	**5**	**.275**	**.330**	**.398**	**.982**
Career total	1441	4528	516	1173	199	36	95	570	366	33	567	14	20	56	37	57	.259	.313	.382	.982
Cubs total	**792**	**2587**	**306**	**711**	**110**	**16**	**59**	**375**	**218**	**24**	**307**	**10**	**5**	**28**	**10**	**33**	**.275**	**.330**	**.398**	**.982**

Moran, Patrick Joseph (Pat)

HEIGHT: 5'10"   THROWS: RIGHT   BATS: RIGHT   BORN: 2/7/1876 FITCHBURG, MASSACHUSETTS   DIED: 3/7/1924 ORLANDO, FLORIDA
POSITIONS PLAYED: C, 1B, 2B, 3B, SS, OF

YEAR	TEAM	GAMES	AB	RUNS	HITS	2B	3B	HR	RBI	BB	IBB	SO	HBP	SH	SF	SB	CS	BA	OBA	SA	FA
1901	Bos-N	52	180	12	38	5	1	2	18	3	—	—	1	7	—	3	—	.211	.228	.283	.960
1902	Bos-N	80	251	22	60	5	5	1	24	17	—	—	6	4	—	6	—	.239	.303	.311	.982
1903	Bos-N	109	389	40	102	25	5	7	54	29	—	—	11	7	—	8	—	.262	.331	.406	.968
1904	Bos-N	113	398	26	90	11	3	4	34	18	—	—	4	3	—	10	—	.226	.267	.299	.941
1905	Bos-N	85	267	22	64	11	5	2	22	8	—	—	3	1	—	3	—	.240	.270	.341	.986
1906	**ChC-N**	**70**	**226**	**22**	**57**	**13**	**1**	**0**	**35**	**7**	**—**	**—**	**2**	**8**	**—**	**6**	**—**	**.252**	**.281**	**.319**	**.979**
1907	**ChC-N**	**65**	**198**	**8**	**45**	**5**	**1**	**1**	**19**	**10**	**—**	**—**	**2**	**4**	**—**	**6**	**—**	**.227**	**.271**	**.278**	**.973**
1908	**ChC-N**	**50**	**150**	**12**	**39**	**5**	**1**	**0**	**12**	**13**	**—**	**—**	**1**	**8**	**—**	**5**	**—**	**.260**	**.323**	**.307**	**.968**
1909	**ChC-N**	**77**	**246**	**18**	**54**	**11**	**1**	**1**	**23**	**16**	**—**	**—**	**4**	**3**	**—**	**2**	**—**	**.220**	**.278**	**.285**	**.984**
1910	Phi-N	68	199	13	47	7	1	0	11	17	—	16	3	3	—	6	—	.236	.306	.281	.989
1911	Phi-N	34	103	2	19	3	0	0	8	3	—	13	0	3	—	0	—	.184	.208	.214	.984
1912	Phi-N	13	26	1	3	1	0	0	1	1	—	7	0	0	—	0	—	.115	.148	.154	.955
1913	Phi-N	1	1	0	0	0	0	0	0	0	—	0	0	0	—	0	—	.000	.000	.000	
1914	Phi-N	1	0	0	0	0	0	0	1	0	—	0	0	0	—	0	—				
Career average		58	188	14	44	7	2	1	19	10	—	3	3	4	—	4	—	.235	.283	.312	.972
Cubs average		**66**	**205**	**15**	**49**	**9**	**1**	**1**	**22**	**12**	**—**	**—**	**2**	**6**	**—**	**5**	**—**	**.238**	**.286**	**.296**	**.977**
Career total		818	2634	198	618	102	24	18	262	142	—	36	37	51	—	55	—	.235	.283	.312	.972
Cubs total		**262**	**820**	**60**	**195**	**34**	**4**	**2**	**89**	**46**	**—**	**—**	**9**	**23**	**—**	**19**	**—**	**.238**	**.286**	**.296**	**.977**

Moran, William L. (Bill)

HEIGHT: 5'11"   THROWS: —   BATS: —   BORN: 10/10/1869 JOLIET, ILLINOIS   DIED: 4/8/1916 JOLIET, ILLINOIS   POSITIONS PLAYED: C, OF

YEAR	TEAM	GAMES	AB	RUNS	HITS	2B	3B	HR	RBI	BB	IBB	SO	HBP	SH	SF	SB	CS	BA	OBA	SA	FA
1892	StL-N	24	81	2	11	1	0	0	5	2	—	12	0	—	—	0	—	.136	.157	.148	.901
1895	**ChN-N**	**15**	**55**	**8**	**9**	**2**	**1**	**1**	**9**	**3**	**—**	**2**	**1**	**0**	**—**	**2**	**—**	**.164**	**.220**	**.291**	**.827**
Career average		20	68	5	10	2	1	1	7	3	—	7	1	0	—	1	—	.147	.183	.206	.873
Cubs average		**15**	**55**	**8**	**9**	**2**	**1**	**1**	**9**	**3**	**—**	**2**	**1**	**0**	**—**	**2**	**—**	**.164**	**.220**	**.291**	**.827**
Career total		39	136	10	20	3	1	1	14	5	—	14	1	0	—	2	—	.147	.183	.206	.873
Cubs total		**15**	**55**	**8**	**9**	**2**	**1**	**1**	**9**	**3**	**—**	**2**	**1**	**0**	**—**	**2**	**—**	**.164**	**.220**	**.291**	**.827**

Morandini, Michael Robert (Mickey)

HEIGHT: 5'11"   THROWS: RIGHT   BATS: LEFT   BORN: 4/22/1966 LEECHBURG, PENNSYLVANIA   POSITIONS PLAYED: 2B, SS

YEAR	TEAM	GAMES	AB	RUNS	HITS	2B	3B	HR	RBI	BB	IBB	SO	HBP	SH	SF	SB	CS	BA	OBA	SA	FA
1990	Phi-N	25	79	9	19	4	0	1	3	6	0	19	0	2	0	3	0	.241	.294	.329	.990
1991	Phi-N	98	325	38	81	11	4	1	20	29	0	45	2	6	2	13	2	.249	.313	.317	.986
1992	Phi-N	127	422	47	112	8	8	3	30	25	2	64	0	6	2	8	3	.265	.305	.344	.990
1993	Phi-N	120	425	57	105	19	9	3	33	34	2	73	5	4	2	13	2	.247	.309	.355	.990
1994	Phi-N	87	274	40	80	16	5	2	26	34	5	33	4	4	0	10	5	.292	.378	.409	.985
1995	Phi-N	127	494	65	140	34	7	6	49	42	3	80	9	4	1	9	6	.283	.350	.417	.989
1996	Phi-N	140	539	64	135	24	6	3	32	49	0	87	9	5	4	26	5	.250	.321	.334	.982
1997	Phi-N	150	553	83	163	40	2	1	39	62	0	91	8	12	5	16	13	.295	.371	.380	.990
1998	**ChC-N**	**154**	**582**	**93**	**172**	**20**	**4**	**8**	**53**	**72**	**4**	**84**	**9**	**4**	**2**	**13**	**1**	**.296**	**.380**	**.385**	**.990**
1999	**ChC-N**	**144**	**456**	**60**	**110**	**18**	**5**	**4**	**37**	**48**	**2**	**61**	**6**	**7**	**4**	**6**	**6**	**.241**	**.319**	**.329**	**.993**
2000	Phi-N	91	302	31	76	13	3	0	22	29	1	54	4	5	1	5	2	.252	.324	.315	.991
2000	Tor-A	35	107	10	29	2	1	0	7	7	0	23	0	2	0	1	0	.271	.316	.308	.987
Career average		118	414	54	111	19	5	3	32	40	2	65	5	6	2	11	4	.268	.338	.359	.993
Cubs average		**149**	**519**	**77**	**141**	**19**	**5**	**6**	**45**	**60**	**3**	**73**	**8**	**6**	**3**	**10**	**4**	**.272**	**.354**	**.360**	**.989**
Career total		1298	4558	597	1222	209	54	32	351	437	19	714	56	61	23	123	45	.268	.338	.359	.992
Cubs total		**298**	**1038**	**153**	**282**	**38**	**9**	**12**	**90**	**120**	**6**	**145**	**15**	**11**	**6**	**19**	**7**	**.272**	**.354**	**.360**	**.989**

Bobby Keith "Zonk" Moreland, of-3b-c-1b-dh, 1978–89

In the six years he wore a Cubs uniform, Keith Moreland was a key contributor to the Chicago effort, filling in just about everywhere and always playing pretty well.

Moreland was born on May 2, 1954, in Dallas, Texas. He was originally brought up to the big leagues by the Philadelphia Phillies and was primarily a catcher in that organization. The Cubs acquired him in 1982 and moved him into the outfield, although the versatile Moreland still caught 44 games and even played a couple games at third base. The 1982 season was Moreland's first year as a full-time player, and he responded with 124 hits, 17 doubles and 15 home runs.

For the duration of his career with the Cubs, Moreland would make 120 hits each year. Twice he hit better than .300 with Chicago, in 1983 (.302) and 1985 (.307).

The 1985 season was his best as a Cub; Moreland had 106 RBIs, 30 doubles and 14 homers in addition to the aforementioned .307 mark, a career high. But beyond Moreland's production, his versatility was vital to the Cubs. He was primarily an outfielder, but in 1987, when Ron Cey was shipped to Oakland, Moreland was moved to third base and did a good job under tough circumstances.

In 1988 the 34-year-old Moreland was traded to San Diego. In 1989 Moreland spent time with the Orioles and Tigers before retiring for good.

Moreland, Bobby Keith (Keith *or* Zonk)
HEIGHT: 6'0" THROWS: RIGHT BATS: RIGHT BORN: 5/2/1954 DALLAS, TEXAS POSITIONS PLAYED: C, 1B, 3B, OF

YEAR	TEAM	GAMES	AB	RUNS	HITS	2B	3B	HR	RBI	BB	IBB	SO	HBP	SH	SF	SB	CS	BA	OBA	SA	FA
1978	Phi-N	1	2	0	0	0	0	0	0	0	0	0	0	0	0	0	0	.000	.000	.000	1.000
1979	Phi-N	14	48	3	18	3	2	0	8	3	0	5	0	0	0	0	0	.375	.412	.521	1.000
1980	Phi-N	62	159	13	50	8	0	4	29	8	2	14	0	1	3	3	1	.314	.341	.440	.964
1981	Phi-N	61	196	16	50	7	0	6	37	15	1	13	1	0	3	1	2	.255	.307	.383	.971
1982	**ChC-N**	**138**	**476**	**50**	**124**	**17**	**2**	**15**	**68**	**46**	**8**	**71**	**3**	**1**	**6**	**0**	**6**	**.261**	**.326**	**.399**	**.981**
1983	**ChC-N**	**154**	**533**	**76**	**161**	**30**	**3**	**16**	**70**	**68**	**8**	**73**	**3**	**5**	**10**	**0**	**3**	**.302**	**.378**	**.460**	**.977**
1984	**ChC-N**	**140**	**495**	**59**	**138**	**17**	**3**	**16**	**80**	**34**	**5**	**71**	**3**	**2**	**5**	**1**	**4**	**.279**	**.326**	**.422**	**.977**
1985	**ChC-N**	**161**	**587**	**74**	**180**	**30**	**3**	**14**	**106**	**68**	**7**	**58**	**1**	**2**	**9**	**12**	**3**	**.307**	**.374**	**.440**	**.963**
1986	**ChC-N**	**156**	**586**	**72**	**159**	**30**	**0**	**12**	**79**	**53**	**10**	**48**	**0**	**2**	**11**	**3**	**6**	**.271**	**.326**	**.384**	**.978**
1987	**ChC-N**	**153**	**563**	**63**	**150**	**29**	**1**	**27**	**88**	**39**	**4**	**66**	**0**	**3**	**9**	**3**	**3**	**.266**	**.309**	**.465**	**.934**
1988	SD-N	143	511	40	131	23	0	5	64	40	6	51	0	2	9	2	3	.256	.305	.331	.991
1989	Det-A	90	318	34	95	16	0	5	35	27	5	33	2	0	3	2	.299	.357	.396	.986
1989	Bal-A	33	107	11	23	4	0	1	10	4	0	12	0	0	0	0	0	.215	.243	.280	—
Career average		109	382	43	107	18	1	10	56	34	5	43	1	2	5	2	3	.279	.335	.411	.975
Cubs average		**150**	**540**	**66**	**152**	**26**	**2**	**17**	**82**	**51**	**7**	**65**	**2**	**3**	**8**	**3**	**4**	**.281**	**.341**	**.429**	**.968**
Career total		1306	4581	511	1279	214	14	121	674	405	56	515	13	18	65	28	33	.279	.335	.411	.975
Cubs total		**902**	**3240**	**394**	**912**	**153**	**12**	**100**	**491**	**308**	**42**	**387**	**10**	**15**	**50**	**19**	**25**	**.281**	**.341**	**.429**	**.968**

Morgan, Robert Morris (Bobby)
HEIGHT: 5'9" THROWS: RIGHT BATS: RIGHT BORN: 6/29/1926 OKLAHOMA CITY, OKLAHOMA POSITIONS PLAYED: 1B, 2B, 3B, SS

YEAR	TEAM	GAMES	AB	RUNS	HITS	2B	3B	HR	RBI	BB	IBB	SO	HBP	SH	SF	SB	CS	BA	OBA	SA	FA
1950	Bro-N	67	199	38	45	10	3	7	21	32	—	43	3	2	—	0	—	.226	.342	.412	.959
1952	Bro-N	67	191	36	45	8	0	7	16	46	—	35	3	2	—	2	2	.236	.392	.387	.962
1953	Bro-N	69	196	35	51	6	2	7	33	33	—	47	1	2	—	2	2	.260	.370	.418	.946
1954	Phi-N	135	455	58	119	25	2	14	50	70	—	68	0	8	4	3	1	.262	.357	.418	.955

(continued)

(continued)

YEAR	TEAM	GAMES	AB	RUNS	HITS	2B	3B	HR	RBI	BB	IBB	SO	HBP	SH	SF	SB	CS	BA	OBA	SA	FA
1955	Phi-N	136	483	61	112	20	2	10	49	73	0	72	0	6	3	6	4	.232	.331	.344	.972
1956	Phi-N	8	25	1	5	0	0	0	1	6	0	4	0	0	0	0	0	.200	.355	.200	.914
1956	StL-N	61	113	14	22	7	0	3	20	15	0	24	0	1	1	0	2	.195	.287	.336	.942
1957	Phi-N	2	0	0	0	0	0	0	0	0	0	0	0	0	0	0	0	—	—	—	1.000
1957	**ChC-N**	**125**	**425**	**43**	**88**	**20**	**2**	**5**	**27**	**52**	**1**	**87**	**1**	**5**	**2**	**5**	**0**	**.207**	**.294**	**.299**	**.975**
1958	**ChC-N**	**1**	**1**	**0**	**0**	**0**	**0**	**0**	**0**	**0**	**0**	**1**	**0**	**0**	**0**	**0**	**0**	**.000**	**.000**	**.000**	**—**
Career average		84	261	36	61	12	1	7	27	41	0	48	1	3	1	2	1	.233	.338	.366	.963
Cubs average		**63**	**213**	**22**	**44**	**10**	**1**	**3**	**14**	**26**	**1**	**44**	**1**	**3**	**1**	**3**	**0**	**.207**	**.293**	**.298**	**.975**
Career total		671	2088	286	487	96	11	53	217	327	1	381	8	26	10	18	11	.233	.338	.366	.963
Cubs total		**126**	**426**	**43**	**88**	**20**	**2**	**5**	**27**	**52**	**1**	**88**	**1**	**5**	**2**	**5**	**0**	**.207**	**.293**	**.298**	**.975**

Morgan, Vernon Thomas (Vern)
HEIGHT: 6'1" THROWS: RIGHT BATS: LEFT BORN: 8/8/1928 EMPORIA, VIRGINIA DIED: 11/8/1975 MINNEAPOLIS, MINNESOTA POSITIONS PLAYED: 3B

YEAR	TEAM	GAMES	AB	RUNS	HITS	2B	3B	HR	RBI	BB	IBB	SO	HBP	SH	SF	SB	CS	BA	OBA	SA	FA
1954	**ChC-N**	**24**	**64**	**3**	**15**	**2**	**0**	**0**	**2**	**1**	**—**	**10**	**0**	**1**	**1**	**0**	**0**	**.234**	**.242**	**.266**	**.895**
1955	**ChC-N**	**7**	**7**	**1**	**1**	**0**	**0**	**0**	**1**	**3**	**0**	**4**	**0**	**0**	**0**	**0**	**0**	**.143**	**.400**	**.143**	**.667**
Career average		16	36	2	8	1	0	0	2	2	0	7	0	1	1	0	0	.225	.263	.254	.864
Cubs average		**16**	**36**	**2**	**8**	**1**	**0**	**0**	**2**	**2**	**0**	**7**	**0**	**1**	**1**	**0**	**0**	**.225**	**.263**	**.254**	**.864**
Career total		31	71	4	16	2	0	0	3	4	0	14	0	1	1	0	0	.225	.263	.254	.864
Cubs total		**31**	**71**	**4**	**16**	**2**	**0**	**0**	**3**	**4**	**0**	**14**	**0**	**1**	**1**	**0**	**0**	**.225**	**.263**	**.254**	**.864**

Morhardt, Meredith Goodwin (Moe)
HEIGHT: 6'1" THROWS: LEFT BATS: LEFT BORN: 1/16/1937 MANCHESTER, CONNECTICUT POSITIONS PLAYED: 1B

YEAR	TEAM	GAMES	AB	RUNS	HITS	2B	3B	HR	RBI	BB	IBB	SO	HBP	SH	SF	SB	CS	BA	OBA	SA	FA
1961	**ChC-N**	**7**	**18**	**3**	**5**	**0**	**0**	**0**	**1**	**3**	**0**	**5**	**0**	**0**	**0**	**0**	**0**	**.278**	**.381**	**.278**	**.962**
1962	**ChC-N**	**18**	**16**	**1**	**2**	**0**	**0**	**0**	**2**	**2**	**0**	**8**	**0**	**0**	**0**	**0**	**0**	**.125**	**.222**	**.125**	**—**
Career average		13	17	2	4	0	0	0	2	3	0	7	0	0	0	0	0	.206	.308	.206	.962
Cubs average		**13**	**17**	**2**	**4**	**0**	**0**	**0**	**2**	**3**	**0**	**7**	**0**	**0**	**0**	**0**	**0**	**.206**	**.308**	**.206**	**.962**
Career total		25	34	4	7	0	0	0	3	5	0	13	0	0	0	0	0	.206	.308	.206	.962
Cubs total		**25**	**34**	**4**	**7**	**0**	**0**	**0**	**3**	**5**	**0**	**13**	**0**	**0**	**0**	**0**	**0**	**.206**	**.308**	**.206**	**.962**

Moriarty, George Joseph
HEIGHT: 6'0" THROWS: RIGHT BATS: RIGHT BORN: 6/7/1884 CHICAGO, ILLINOIS DIED: 4/8/1964 MIAMI, FLORIDA POSITIONS PLAYED: 1B, 2B, 3B, SS, OF

YEAR	TEAM	GAMES	AB	RUNS	HITS	2B	3B	HR	RBI	BB	IBB	SO	HBP	SH	SF	SB	CS	BA	OBA	SA	FA
1903	**ChC-N**	**1**	**5**	**1**	**0**	**0**	**0**	**0**	**0**	**0**	**—**	**—**	**0**	**0**	**—**	**0**	**—**	**.000**	**.000**	**.000**	**1.000**
1904	**ChC-N**	**4**	**13**	**0**	**0**	**0**	**0**	**0**	**0**	**1**	**—**	**—**	**0**	**0**	**—**	**0**	**—**	**.000**	**.071**	**.000**	**.786**
1906	NYA-A	65	197	22	46	7	7	0	23	17	—	—	1	14	—	8	—	.234	.298	.340	.926
1907	NYA-A	126	437	51	121	16	5	0	43	25	—	—	3	9	—	28	—	.277	.320	.336	.928
1908	NYA-A	101	348	25	82	12	1	0	27	11	—	—	5	8	—	22	—	.236	.269	.276	.968
1909	Det-A	133	473	43	129	20	4	1	39	24	—	—	1	17	—	34	—	.273	.309	.338	.961
1910	Det-A	136	490	53	123	24	3	2	60	33	—	—	7	14	—	33	—	.251	.308	.324	.927
1911	Det-A	130	478	51	116	20	4	1	60	27	—	—	3	28	—	28	—	.243	.287	.308	.930
1912	Det-A	105	375	38	93	23	1	0	54	26	—	—	11	20	—	27	—	.248	.316	.315	.980
1913	Det-A	102	347	29	83	5	2	0	30	24	—	25	7	15	—	33	—	.239	.302	.265	.938
1914	Det-A	132	465	56	118	19	5	1	40	39	—	27	5	25	—	34	15	.254	.318	.323	.959
1915	Det-A	31	38	2	8	1	0	0	0	5	—	7	1	2	—	1	1	.211	.318	.237	.893
1916	CWS-A	7	5	1	1	0	0	0	0	2	—	0	0	0	—	0	—	.200	.429	.200	1.000
Career average		83	282	29	71	12	2	0	29	18	—	5	3	12	—	19	1	.251	.303	.312	.951
Cubs average		**3**	**9**	**1**	**0**	**0**	**0**	**0**	**0**	**1**	**—**	**—**	**0**	**0**	**—**	**0**	**—**	**.000**	**.053**	**.000**	**.833**
Career total		1073	3671	372	920	147	32	5	376	234	—	59	44	152	—	248	16	.251	.303	.312	.951
Cubs total		**5**	**18**	**1**	**0**	**0**	**0**	**0**	**0**	**1**	**—**	**—**	**0**	**0**	**—**	**0**	**—**	**.000**	**.053**	**.000**	**.833**

Moryn, Walter Joseph (Walt or Moose)
HEIGHT: 6'2" THROWS: RIGHT BATS: LEFT BORN: 4/12/1926 ST. PAUL, MINNESOTA DIED: 7/21/1996 WINFIELD, ILLINOIS POSITIONS PLAYED: OF

YEAR	TEAM	GAMES	AB	RUNS	HITS	2B	3B	HR	RBI	BB	IBB	SO	HBP	SH	SF	SB	CS	BA	OBA	SA	FA
1954	Bro-N	48	91	16	25	4	2	2	14	7	—	11	1	2	1	0	0	.275	.330	.429	.881
1955	Bro-N	11	19	3	5	1	0	1	3	5	1	4	0	0	0	0	0	.263	.417	.474	.833
1956	**ChC-N**	**147**	**529**	**69**	**151**	**27**	**3**	**23**	**67**	**50**	**2**	**67**	**3**	**1**	**5**	**4**	**2**	**.285**	**.348**	**.478**	**.983**
1957	**ChC-N**	**149**	**568**	**76**	**164**	**33**	**0**	**19**	**88**	**50**	**6**	**90**	**3**	**1**	**2**	**0**	**2**	**.289**	**.348**	**.447**	**.960**
1958	**ChC-N**	**143**	**512**	**77**	**135**	**26**	**7**	**26**	**77**	**62**	**7**	**83**	**8**	**2**	**3**	**1**	**2**	**.264**	**.350**	**.494**	**.978**
1959	**ChC-N**	**117**	**381**	**41**	**89**	**14**	**1**	**14**	**48**	**44**	**2**	**66**	**3**	**2**	**2**	**0**	**0**	**.234**	**.316**	**.386**	**.989**
1960	**ChC-N**	**38**	**109**	**12**	**32**	**4**	**0**	**2**	**11**	**13**	**0**	**19**	**0**	**0**	**1**	**2**	**1**	**.294**	**.366**	**.385**	**.964**
1960	StL-N	75	200	24	49	4	3	11	35	17	4	38	0	0	4	0	0	.245	.299	.460	.990
1961	StL-N	17	32	0	4	2	0	0	2	1	0	5	0	0	0	0	0	.125	.152	.188	.889
1961	Pit-N	40	65	6	13	1	0	3	9	2	0	10	1	0	0	0	0	.200	.235	.354	.950
Career average		98	313	41	83	15	2	13	44	31	3	49	2	1	2	1	1	.266	.335	.446	.972
Cubs average		**119**	**420**	**55**	**114**	**21**	**2**	**17**	**58**	**44**	**3**	**65**	**3**	**1**	**3**	**1**	**1**	**.272**	**.344**	**.452**	**.976**
Career total		785	2506	324	667	116	16	101	354	251	22	393	19	8	18	7	7	.266	.335	.446	.972
Cubs total		**594**	**2099**	**275**	**571**	**104**	**11**	**84**	**291**	**219**	**17**	**325**	**17**	**6**	**13**	**7**	**7**	**.272**	**.344**	**.452**	**.976**

Mosolf, James Frederick (Jim)
HEIGHT: 5'10" THROWS: RIGHT BATS: LEFT BORN: 8/21/1905 PUYALLUP, WASHINGTON DIED: 12/28/1979 DALLAS, OREGON POSITIONS PLAYED: P, OF

YEAR	TEAM	GAMES	AB	RUNS	HITS	2B	3B	HR	RBI	BB	IBB	SO	HBP	SH	SF	SB	CS	BA	OBA	SA	FA
1929	Pit-N	8	13	3	6	1	1	0	2	1	—	1	0	0	—	0	—	.462	.500	.692	1.000
1930	Pit-N	40	51	16	17	2	1	0	9	8	—	7	0	1	—	0	—	.333	.424	.412	.765
1931	Pit-N	39	44	7	11	1	0	1	8	8	—	5	0	1	—	0	—	.250	.365	.341	1.000
1933	**ChC-N**	**31**	**82**	**13**	**22**	**5**	**1**	**1**	**9**	**5**	**—**	**8**	**2**	**3**	**—**	**0**	**—**	**.268**	**.326**	**.390**	**.964**
Career average		30	48	10	14	2	1	1	7	6	—	5	1	1	—	0	—	.295	.374	.405	.929
Cubs average		**31**	**82**	**13**	**22**	**5**	**1**	**1**	**9**	**5**	**—**	**8**	**2**	**3**	**—**	**0**	**—**	**.268**	**.326**	**.390**	**.964**
Career total		118	190	39	56	9	3	2	28	22	—	21	2	5	—	0	—	.295	.374	.405	.929
Cubs total		**31**	**82**	**13**	**22**	**5**	**1**	**1**	**9**	**5**	**—**	**8**	**2**	**3**	**—**	**0**	**—**	**.268**	**.326**	**.390**	**.964**

Mueller, William Richard (Bill or Ferris or Muley)
HEIGHT: 5'10" THROWS: RIGHT BATS: BOTH BORN: 3/17/1971 MARYLAND HEIGHTS, MISSOURI POSITIONS PLAYED: 2B, 3B

YEAR	TEAM	GAMES	AB	RUNS	HITS	2B	3B	HR	RBI	BB	IBB	SO	HBP	SH	SF	SB	CS	BA	OBA	SA	FA
1996	SF-N	55	200	31	66	15	1	0	19	24	0	26	1	1	2	0	0	.330	.401	.415	.962
1997	SF-N	128	390	51	114	26	3	7	44	48	1	71	3	6	6	4	3	.292	.369	.428	.956
1998	SF-N	145	534	93	157	27	0	9	59	79	1	83	1	3	5	3	3	.294	.383	.395	.953
1999	SF-N	116	414	61	120	24	0	2	36	65	1	52	3	8	2	4	2	.290	.388	.362	.959
2000	SF-N	153	560	97	150	29	4	10	55	52	0	62	6	7	6	4	2	.268	.333	.388	.975
2001	**ChC-N**	**70**	**210**	**38**	**62**	**12**	**1**	**6**	**23**	**37**	**3**	**19**	**3**	**4**	**3**	**1**	**1**	**.295**	**.403**	**.448**	**.942**
Career average		111	385	62	112	22	2	6	39	51	1	52	3	5	4	3	2	.290	.373	.399	.959
Cubs average		**70**	**210**	**38**	**62**	**12**	**1**	**6**	**23**	**37**	**3**	**19**	**3**	**4**	**3**	**1**	**1**	**.295**	**.403**	**.448**	**.942**
Career total		667	2308	371	669	133	9	34	236	305	6	313	17	29	24	16	11	.290	.373	.399	.959
Cubs total		**70**	**210**	**38**	**62**	**12**	**1**	**6**	**23**	**37**	**3**	**19**	**3**	**4**	**3**	**1**	**1**	**.295**	**.403**	**.448**	**.942**

Mulligan, Edward Joseph (Joe or Big Joe)
HEIGHT: 5'9" THROWS: RIGHT BATS: RIGHT BORN: 8/27/1894 ST. LOUIS, MISSOURI DIED: 3/15/1982 SAN RAFAEL, CALIFORNIA
POSITIONS PLAYED: 2B, 3B, SS

YEAR	TEAM	GAMES	AB	RUNS	HITS	2B	3B	HR	RBI	BB	IBB	SO	HBP	SH	SF	SB	CS	BA	OBA	SA	FA
1915	**ChC-N**	**11**	**22**	**5**	**8**	**1**	**0**	**0**	**2**	**5**	**—**	**1**	**0**	**3**	**—**	**2**	**2**	**.364**	**.481**	**.409**	**.907**
1916	**ChC-N**	**58**	**189**	**13**	**29**	**3**	**4**	**0**	**9**	**8**	**—**	**30**	**3**	**7**	**—**	**1**	**—**	**.153**	**.200**	**.212**	**.888**
1921	CWS-A	152	609	82	153	21	12	1	45	32	—	53	4	34	—	13	18	.251	.293	.330	.955
1922	CWS-A	103	372	39	87	14	8	0	31	22	—	32	1	28	—	7	7	.234	.278	.315	.967
1928	Pit-N	27	43	4	10	2	0	0	1	3	—	4	0	4	—	0	—	.233	.283	.279	.947
Career average		70	247	29	57	8	5	0	18	14	—	24	2	15	—	5	5	.232	.278	.307	.937
Cubs average		**35**	**106**	**9**	**19**	**2**	**2**	**0**	**6**	**7**	**—**	**16**	**2**	**5**	**—**	**2**	**1**	**.175**	**.233**	**.232**	**.890**
Career total		351	1235	143	287	41	24	1	88	70	—	120	8	76	—	23	27	.232	.278	.307	.937
Cubs total		**69**	**211**	**18**	**37**	**4**	**4**	**0**	**11**	**13**	**—**	**31**	**3**	**10**	**—**	**3**	**2**	**.175**	**.233**	**.232**	**.890**

Mumphrey, Jerry Wayne

HEIGHT: 6'2"   THROWS: RIGHT   BATS: BOTH   BORN: 9/9/1952 TYLER, TEXAS   POSITIONS PLAYED: OF

YEAR	TEAM	GAMES	AB	RUNS	HITS	2B	3B	HR	RBI	BB	IBB	SO	HBP	SH	SF	SB	CS	BA	OBA	SA	FA
1974	StL-N	5	2	2	0	0	0	0	0	0	0	0	0	0	0	0	0	.000	.000	.000	—
1975	StL-N	11	16	2	6	2	0	0	1	4	0	3	0	0	0	0	0	.375	.500	.500	1.000
1976	StL-N	112	384	51	99	15	5	1	26	37	0	53	1	2	3	22	6	.258	.322	.331	.993
1977	StL-N	145	463	73	133	20	10	2	38	47	6	70	1	1	0	22	15	.287	.354	.387	.971
1978	StL-N	125	367	41	96	13	4	2	37	30	0	40	1	2	3	14	10	.262	.317	.335	.995
1979	StL-N	124	339	53	100	10	3	3	32	26	2	39	1	2	3	0	3	.295	.341	.369	.984
1980	SD-N	160	564	61	168	24	3	4	59	49	4	90	0	4	4	52	15	.298	.352	.372	.974
1981	NYY-A	80	319	44	98	11	5	6	32	24	1	27	0	5	4	14	5	.307	.354	.429	.966
1982	NYY-A	123	477	76	143	24	10	9	68	50	4	66	0	5	2	14	9	.300	.364	.449	.986
1983	NYY-A	83	267	41	70	11	4	7	36	28	2	33	0	3	5	11	3	.262	.327	.412	.983
1983	Hou-N	44	143	17	48	10	2	1	17	22	3	23	1	2	1	2	3	.336	.425	.455	.990
1984	Hou-N	151	524	66	152	20	3	9	83	56	7	79	1	0	6	5	0	.290	.355	.391	.988
1985	Hou-N	130	444	52	123	25	2	8	61	37	8	57	0	1	6	15	7	.277	.329	.396	.969
1986	**ChC-N**	**111**	**309**	**37**	**94**	**11**	**2**	**5**	**32**	**26**	**4**	**45**	**0**	**1**	**3**	**2**	**3**	**.304**	**.355**	**.401**	**.982**
1987	**ChC-N**	**118**	**309**	**41**	**103**	**19**	**2**	**13**	**44**	**35**	**6**	**47**	**0**	**1**	**1**	**1**	**1**	**.333**	**.400**	**.534**	**.992**
1988	**ChC-N**	**63**	**66**	**3**	**9**	**2**	**0**	**0**	**9**	**7**	**2**	**16**	**0**	**0**	**0**	**0**	**0**	**.136**	**.219**	**.167**	**1.000**
Career average		106	333	44	96	14	4	5	38	32	3	46	0	2	3	12	5	.289	.349	.396	.981
Cubs average		**97**	**228**	**27**	**69**	**11**	**1**	**6**	**28**	**23**	**4**	**36**	**0**	**1**	**1**	**1**	**1**	**.301**	**.362**	**.439**	**.987**
Career total		1585	4993	660	1442	217	55	70	575	478	49	688	4	29	41	174	80	.289	.349	.396	.981
Cubs total		**292**	**684**	**81**	**206**	**32**	**4**	**18**	**85**	**68**	**12**	**108**	**0**	**2**	**4**	**3**	**4**	**.301**	**.362**	**.439**	**.987**

Munson, Joseph Martin Napoleon (Joe)

HEIGHT: 5'9"   THROWS: RIGHT   BATS: LEFT   BORN: 11/6/1899 RENOVO, PENNSYLVANIA   DIED: 2/24/1991 DREXEL HILL, PENNSYLVANIA
POSITIONS PLAYED: OF

YEAR	TEAM	GAMES	AB	RUNS	HITS	2B	3B	HR	RBI	BB	IBB	SO	HBP	SH	SF	SB	CS	BA	OBA	SA	FA
1925	**ChC-N**	**9**	**35**	**5**	**13**	**3**	**1**	**0**	**3**	**3**	**—**	**1**	**1**	**1**	**—**	**1**	**1**	**.371**	**.436**	**.514**	**1.000**
1926	**ChC-N**	**33**	**101**	**17**	**26**	**2**	**2**	**3**	**15**	**8**	**—**	**4**	**1**	**6**	**—**	**0**	**—**	**.257**	**.318**	**.406**	**.898**
Career average		21	68	11	20	3	2	2	9	6	—	3	1	4	—	1	1	.287	.349	.434	.922
Cubs average		**21**	**68**	**11**	**20**	**3**	**2**	**2**	**9**	**6**	**—**	**3**	**1**	**4**	**—**	**1**	**1**	**.287**	**.349**	**.434**	**.922**
Career total		42	136	22	39	5	3	3	18	11	—	5	2	7	—	1	1	.287	.349	.434	.922
Cubs total		**42**	**136**	**22**	**39**	**5**	**3**	**3**	**18**	**11**	**—**	**5**	**2**	**7**	**—**	**1**	**1**	**.287**	**.349**	**.434**	**.922**

Murcer, Bobby Ray

HEIGHT: 5'11"   THROWS: RIGHT   BATS: LEFT   BORN: 5/20/1946 OKLAHOMA CITY, OKLAHOMA   POSITIONS PLAYED: 2B, 3B, SS, OF

YEAR	TEAM	GAMES	AB	RUNS	HITS	2B	3B	HR	RBI	BB	IBB	SO	HBP	SH	SF	SB	CS	BA	OBA	SA	FA
1965	NYY-A	11	37	2	9	0	1	1	4	5	0	12	0	0	0	0	0	.243	.333	.378	.932
1966	NYY-A	21	69	3	12	1	1	0	5	4	0	5	0	0	0	2	0	.174	.219	.217	.931
1969	NYY-A	152	564	82	146	24	4	26	82	50	2	103	3	2	6	7	5	.259	.319	.454	.935
1970	NYY-A	159	581	95	146	23	3	23	78	87	5	100	2	4	6	15	10	.251	.348	.420	.992
1971	NYY-A	146	529	94	175	25	6	25	94	91	13	60	0	1	3	14	8	.331	.427	.543	.985
1972	NYY-A	153	585	102	171	30	7	33	96	63	7	67	2	0	4	11	9	.292	.361	.537	.992
1973	NYY-A	160	616	83	187	29	2	22	95	50	6	67	3	0	3	6	7	.304	.357	.464	.985
1974	NYY-A	156	606	69	166	25	4	10	88	57	10	59	2	2	12	14	7	.274	.332	.378	.978
1975	SF-N	147	526	80	157	29	4	11	91	91	6	45	2	1	12	9	5	.298	.396	.432	.981
1976	SF-N	147	533	73	138	20	2	23	90	84	10	78	4	0	3	9	5	.259	.362	.433	.961
1977	**ChC-N**	**154**	**554**	**90**	**147**	**18**	**3**	**27**	**89**	**80**	**13**	**77**	**3**	**2**	**10**	**16**	**7**	**.265**	**.355**	**.455**	**.980**
1978	**ChC-N**	**146**	**499**	**66**	**140**	**22**	**6**	**9**	**64**	**80**	**15**	**57**	**0**	**0**	**6**	**14**	**5**	**.281**	**.376**	**.403**	**.979**
1979	**ChC-N**	**58**	**190**	**22**	**49**	**4**	**1**	**7**	**22**	**36**	**2**	**20**	**1**	**1**	**3**	**2**	**3**	**.258**	**.374**	**.400**	**1.000**
1979	NYY-A	74	264	42	72	12	0	8	33	25	2	32	2	2	1	1	0	.273	.339	.409	.983
1980	NYY-A	100	297	41	80	9	1	13	57	34	2	28	2	3	9	2	0	.269	.339	.438	.955
1981	NYY-A	50	117	14	31	6	0	6	24	12	1	15	0	0	1	0	0	.265	.331	.470	—
1982	NYY-A	65	141	12	32	6	0	7	30	12	2	15	1	0	2	2	1	.227	.288	.418	—
1983	NYY-A	9	22	2	4	2	0	1	1	1	0	1	0	0	0	0	0	.182	.217	.409	—
Career average		112	396	57	110	17	3	15	61	51	6	49	2	1	5	7	4	.277	.357	.445	.976
Cubs average		**119**	**414**	**59**	**112**	**15**	**3**	**14**	**58**	**65**	**10**	**51**	**1**	**1**	**6**	**11**	**5**	**.270**	**.367**	**.426**	**.983**
Career total		1908	6730	972	1862	285	45	252	1043	862	96	841	27	18	81	127	75	.277	.357	.445	.976
Cubs total		**358**	**1243**	**178**	**336**	**44**	**10**	**43**	**175**	**196**	**30**	**154**	**4**	**3**	**19**	**32**	**15**	**.270**	**.367**	**.426**	**.983**

Murphy, Daniel Francis (Danny)
HEIGHT: 5'11" THROWS: RIGHT BATS: LEFT BORN: 8/23/1942 BEVERLY, MASSACHUSETTS POSITIONS PLAYED: P, OF

YEAR	TEAM	GAMES	AB	RUNS	HITS	2B	3B	HR	RBI	BB	IBB	SO	HBP	SH	SF	SB	CS	BA	OBA	SA	FA
1960	ChC-N	31	75	7	9	2	0	1	6	4	0	13	1	1	0	0	0	.120	.175	.187	.976
1961	ChC-N	4	13	3	5	0	0	2	3	1	0	5	0	0	0	0	0	.385	.429	.846	1.000
1962	ChC-N	14	35	5	7	3	1	0	3	2	0	9	0	0	0	0	0	.200	.243	.343	1.000
1969	CWS-A	17	1	0	0	0	0	0	0	2	0	0	0	0	0	0	0	.000	.667	.000	1.000
1970	CWS-A	51	6	3	2	0	0	1	1	2	0	2	0	0	0	0	0	.333	.500	.833	.933
Career average		23	26	4	5	1	0	1	3	2	0	6	0	0	·0	0	0	.177	.246	.323	.972
Cubs average		**16**	**41**	**5**	**7**	**2**	**0**	**1**	**4**	**2**	**0**	**9**	**0**	**0**	**0**	**0**	**0**	**.171**	**.221**	**.301**	**.981**
Career total		117	130	18	23	5	1	4	13	11	0	29	1	1	0	0	0	.177	.246	.323	.972
Cubs total		**49**	**123**	**15**	**21**	**5**	**1**	**3**	**12**	**7**	**0**	**27**	**1**	**1**	**0**	**0**	**0**	**.171**	**.221**	**.301**	**.981**

Murray, Anthony Joseph (Tony)
HEIGHT: 5'10" THROWS: RIGHT BATS: RIGHT BORN: 4/30/1904 CHICAGO, ILLINOIS DIED: 3/19/1974 CHICAGO, ILLINOIS POSITIONS PLAYED: OF

YEAR	TEAM	GAMES	AB	RUNS	HITS	2B	3B	HR	RBI	BB	IBB	SO	HBP	SH	SF	SB	CS	BA	OBA	SA	FA
1923	ChC-N	2	4	0	1	0	0	0	0	0	—	0	1	0	—	0	0	.250	.400	.250	1.000
Career average		2	4	0	1	0	0	0	0	0	—	0	1	0	—	0	0	.250	.400	.250	1.000
Cubs average		**2**	**4**	**0**	**1**	**0**	**0**	**0**	**0**	**0**	**—**	**0**	**1**	**0**	**—**	**0**	**0**	**.250**	**.400**	**.250**	**1.000**
Career total		2	4	0	1	0	0	0	0	0	—	0	1	0	—	0	0	.250	.400	.250	1.000
Cubs total		**2**	**4**	**0**	**1**	**0**	**0**	**0**	**0**	**0**	**—**	**0**	**1**	**0**	**—**	**0**	**0**	**.250**	**.400**	**.250**	**1.000**

Murray, James Oscar (Jim)
HEIGHT: 5'10" THROWS: LEFT BATS: RIGHT BORN: 1/16/1878 GALVESTON, TEXAS DIED: 4/25/1945 GALVESTON, TEXAS POSITIONS PLAYED: OF

YEAR	TEAM	GAMES	AB	RUNS	HITS	2B	3B	HR	RBI	BB	IBB	SO	HBP	SH	SF	SB	CS	BA	OBA	SA	FA
1902	ChC-N	12	47	3	8	0	0	0	1	2	—	—	0	1	—	0	—	.170	.204	.170	1.000
1911	StL-A	31	102	8	19	5	0	3	11	5	—	—	0	2	—	0	—	.186	.224	.324	.935
1914	Bos-N	39	112	10	26	4	2	0	12	6	—	24	1	2	—	2	—	.232	.277	.304	.941
Career average		27	87	7	18	3	1	1	8	4	—	8	0	2	—	1	—	.203	.244	.287	.949
Cubs average		**12**	**47**	**3**	**8**	**0**	**0**	**0**	**1**	**2**	**—**	**—**	**0**	**1**	**—**	**0**	**—**	**.170**	**.204**	**.170**	**1.000**
Career total		82	261	21	53	9	2	3	24	13	—	24	1	5	—	2	—	.203	.244	.287	.949
Cubs total		**12**	**47**	**3**	**8**	**0**	**0**	**0**	**1**	**2**	**—**	**—**	**0**	**1**	**—**	**0**	**—**	**.170**	**.204**	**.170**	**1.000**

Murray, John Joseph (Red)
HEIGHT: 5'10" THROWS: RIGHT BATS: RIGHT BORN: 3/4/1884 ARNOT, PENNSYLVANIA DIED: 12/4/1958 SAYRE, PENNSYLVANIA
POSITIONS PLAYED: C, 2B, OF

YEAR	TEAM	GAMES	AB	RUNS	HITS	2B	3B	HR	RBI	BB	IBB	SO	HBP	SH	SF	SB	CS	BA	OBA	SA	FA
1906	StL-N	46	144	18	37	9	7	1	16	9	—	—	1	0	—	5	—	.257	.305	.438	.947
1907	StL-N	132	485	46	127	10	10	7	46	24	—	—	3	8	—	23	—	.262	.301	.367	.935
1908	StL-N	154	593	64	167	19	15	7	62	37	—	—	8	4	—	48	—	.282	.332	.400	.914
1909	NYG-N	149	570	74	150	15	12	7	91	45	—	—	6	2	—	48	—	.263	.319	.368	.947
1910	NYG-N	149	553	78	153	27	8	4	87	52	—	51	6	23	—	57	—	.277	.345	.376	.948
1911	NYG-N	140	488	70	142	27	15	3	78	43	—	37	5	11	—	48	—	.291	.354	.426	.954
1912	NYG-N	143	549	83	152	26	20	3	92	27	—	45	8	19	—	38	—	.277	.320	.413	.968
1913	NYG-N	147	520	70	139	21	3	2	59	34	—	28	6	18	—	35	—	.267	.320	.331	.965
1914	NYG-N	86	139	19	31	6	3	0	23	9	—	7	0	7	—	11	—	.223	.270	.309	.959
1915	NYG-N	45	127	12	28	1	2	3	11	7	—	15	0	0	—	2	3	.220	.261	.331	1.000
1915	**ChC-N**	**51**	**144**	**20**	**43**	**6**	**1**	**0**	**11**	**8**	**—**	**8**	**1**	**6**	**—**	**6**	**5**	**.299**	**.340**	**.354**	**.968**
1917	NYG-N	22	22	1	1	1	0	0	3	4	—	3	0	1	—	0	—	.045	.192	.091	1.000
Career average		115	394	50	106	15	9	3	53	27	—	18	4	10	—	29	1	.270	.323	.379	.950
Cubs average		**51**	**144**	**20**	**43**	**6**	**1**	**0**	**11**	**8**	**—**	**8**	**1**	**6**	**—**	**6**	**5**	**.299**	**.340**	**.354**	**.968**
Career total		1264	4334	555	1170	168	96	37	579	299	—	194	40	113	—	321	8	.270	.323	.379	.950
Cubs total		**51**	**144**	**20**	**43**	**6**	**1**	**0**	**11**	**8**	**—**	**8**	**1**	**6**	**—**	**6**	**5**	**.299**	**.340**	**.354**	**.968**

Myers, Richard (Richie)

HEIGHT: 5'6"   THROWS: RIGHT   BATS: RIGHT   BORN: 4/7/1930 SACRAMENTO, CALIFORNIA

YEAR	TEAM	GAMES	AB	RUNS	HITS	2B	3B	HR	RBI	BB	IBB	SO	HBP	SH	SF	SB	CS	BA	OBA	SA	FA
1956	ChC-N	4	1	1	0	0	0	0	0	0	0	0	0	0	0	0	0	.000	.000	.000	—
Career average		4	1	1	0	0	0	0	0	0	0	0	0	0	0	0	0	.000	.000	.000	—
Cubs average		**4**	**1**	**1**	**0**	**0**	**0**	**0**	**0**	**0**	**0**	**0**	**0**	**0**	**0**	**0**	**0**	**.000**	**.000**	**.000**	**—**
Career total		4	1	1	0	0	0	0	0	0	0	0	0	0	0	0	0	.000	.000	.000	—
Cubs total		**4**	**1**	**1**	**0**	**0**	**0**	**0**	**0**	**0**	**0**	**0**	**0**	**0**	**0**	**0**	**0**	**.000**	**.000**	**.000**	**—**

Myers, William Harrison (Billy)

HEIGHT: 5'8"   THROWS: RIGHT   BATS: RIGHT   BORN: 8/14/1910 ENOLA, PENNSYLVANIA   DIED: 4/10/1995 CARLISLE, PENNSYLVANIA
POSITIONS PLAYED: 2B, SS

YEAR	TEAM	GAMES	AB	RUNS	HITS	2B	3B	HR	RBI	BB	IBB	SO	HBP	SH	SF	SB	CS	BA	OBA	SA	FA
1935	Cin-N	117	445	60	119	15	10	5	36	29	—	81	2	10	—	10	—	.267	.315	.380	.939
1936	Cin-N	98	323	45	87	9	6	6	27	28	—	56	0	8	—	6	—	.269	.328	.390	.938
1937	Cin-N	124	335	35	84	13	3	7	43	44	—	57	1	8	—	0	—	.251	.339	.370	.951
1938	Cin-N	134	442	57	112	18	6	12	47	41	—	80	0	10	—	2	—	.253	.317	.403	.937
1939	Cin-N	151	509	79	143	18	6	9	56	71	—	90	0	22	—	4	—	.281	.369	.393	.951
1940	Cin-N	90	282	33	57	14	2	5	30	30	—	56	2	9	—	0	—	.202	.283	.319	.961
1941	ChC-N	24	63	10	14	1	0	1	4	7	—	25	1	3	—	1	—	.222	.310	.286	.945
Career average		105	343	46	88	13	5	6	35	36	—	64	1	10	—	3	—	.257	.328	.377	.946
Cubs average		**24**	**63**	**10**	**14**	**1**	**0**	**1**	**4**	**7**	**—**	**25**	**1**	**3**	**—**	**1**	**—**	**.222**	**.310**	**.286**	**.945**
Career total		738	2399	319	616	88	33	45	243	250	—	445	6	70	—	23	—	.257	.328	.377	.946
Cubs total		**24**	**63**	**10**	**14**	**1**	**0**	**1**	**4**	**7**	**—**	**25**	**1**	**3**	**—**	**1**	**—**	**.222**	**.310**	**.286**	**.945**

Nagle, Thomas Edward (Tom)

HEIGHT: 5'10"   THROWS: RIGHT   BATS: RIGHT   BORN: 10/30/1865 MILWAUKEE, WISCONSIN   DIED: 3/9/1946 MILWAUKEE, WISCONSIN
POSITIONS PLAYED: C, OF

YEAR	TEAM	GAMES	AB	RUNS	HITS	2B	3B	HR	RBI	BB	IBB	SO	HBP	SH	SF	SB	CS	BA	OBA	SA	FA
1890	ChN-N	38	144	21	39	5	1	1	11	7	—	24	3	—	—	4	—	.271	.318	.340	.937
1891	ChN-N	8	25	3	3	0	0	0	1	1	—	3	0	—	—	0	—	.120	.154	.120	.906
Career average		23	85	12	21	3	1	1	6	4	—	14	2	—	—	2	—	.249	.294	.308	.932
Cubs average		**23**	**85**	**12**	**21**	**3**	**1**	**1**	**6**	**4**	**—**	**14**	**2**	**—**	**—**	**2**	**—**	**.249**	**.294**	**.308**	**.932**
Career total		46	169	24	42	5	1	1	12	8	—	27	3	—	—	4	—	.249	.294	.308	.932
Cubs total		**46**	**169**	**24**	**42**	**5**	**1**	**1**	**12**	**8**	**—**	**27**	**3**	**—**	**—**	**4**	**—**	**.249**	**.294**	**.308**	**.932**

Needham, Thomas Joseph (Tom *or* Deerfoot)

HEIGHT: 5'10"   THROWS: RIGHT   BATS: RIGHT   BORN: 5/17/1879 STEUBENVILLE, OHIO   DIED: 12/14/1926 STEUBENVILLE, OHIO
POSITIONS PLAYED: C, 1B, 2B, 3B, OF

YEAR	TEAM	GAMES	AB	RUNS	HITS	2B	3B	HR	RBI	BB	IBB	SO	HBP	SH	SF	SB	CS	BA	OBA	SA	FA
1904	Bos-N	84	269	18	70	12	3	4	19	11	—	—	1	1	—	3	—	.260	.292	.372	.945
1905	Bos-N	83	271	21	59	6	1	2	17	24	—	—	5	1	—	3	—	.218	.293	.269	.949
1906	Bos-N	83	285	11	54	8	2	1	12	13	—	—	2	2	—	3	—	.189	.230	.242	.957
1907	Bos-N	86	260	19	51	6	2	1	19	18	—	—	6	5	—	4	—	.196	.264	.246	.968
1908	NYG-N	54	91	8	19	3	0	0	11	12	—	—	6	6	—	0	—	.209	.339	.242	.975
1909	ChC-N	13	28	3	4	0	0	0	0	0	—	—	0	0	—	0	—	.143	.143	.143	.980
1910	ChC-N	31	76	9	14	3	1	0	10	10	—	10	1	5	—	1	—	.184	.287	.250	.982
1911	ChC-N	27	62	4	12	2	0	0	5	9	—	14	2	0	—	2	—	.194	.315	.226	.984
1912	ChC-N	33	90	12	16	5	0	0	10	7	—	13	3	4	—	3	—	.178	.260	.233	.994
1913	ChC-N	20	42	5	10	4	1	0	11	4	—	8	0	1	—	0	—	.238	.304	.381	.963
1914	ChC-N	9	17	3	2	1	0	0	3	1	—	4	0	0	—	1	—	.118	.167	.176	.943
Career average		48	136	10	28	5	1	1	11	10	—	4	2	2	—	2	—	.209	.274	.272	.962
Cubs average		**22**	**53**	**6**	**10**	**3**	**0**	**0**	**7**	**5**	**—**	**8**	**1**	**2**	**—**	**1**	**—**	**.184**	**.270**	**.244**	**.981**
Career total		523	1491	113	311	50	10	8	117	109	—	49	26	25	—	20	—	.209	.274	.272	.962
Cubs total		**133**	**315**	**36**	**58**	**15**	**2**	**0**	**39**	**31**	**—**	**49**	**6**	**10**	**—**	**7**	**—**	**.184**	**.270**	**.244**	**.981**

Neeman, Calvin Amandus (Cal)
HEIGHT: 6'1" THROWS: RIGHT BATS: RIGHT BORN: 2/18/1929 VALMEYER, ILLINOIS POSITIONS PLAYED: C

YEAR	TEAM	GAMES	AB	RUNS	HITS	2B	3B	HR	RBI	BB	IBB	SO	HBP	SH	SF	SB	CS	BA	OBA	SA	FA
1957	ChC-N	122	415	37	107	17	1	10	39	22	5	87	3	2	3	0	0	.258	.298	.376	.990
1958	ChC-N	76	201	30	52	7	0	12	29	21	2	41	3	0	1	0	0	.259	.336	.473	.992
1959	ChC-N	44	105	7	17	2	0	3	9	11	2	23	0	1	0	0	0	.162	.241	.267	.994
1960	ChC-N	9	13	0	2	1	0	0	0	0	0	5	0	0	0	0	0	.154	.154	.231	1.000
1960	Phi-N	59	160	13	29	6	2	4	13	16	2	42	2	2	1	1	0	.181	.264	.319	.979
1961	Phi-N	19	31	0	7	1	0	0	2	4	1	8	0	0	0	0	0	.226	.306	.258	.986
1962	Pit-N	24	50	5	9	1	1	1	5	3	0	10	0	0	0	0	0	.180	.226	.300	.983
1963	Cle-A	9	9	0	0	0	0	0	0	1	0	5	0	1	0	0	0	.000	.100	.000	1.000
1963	Was-A	14	18	1	1	0	0	0	0	1	0	0	0	0	0	0	0	.056	.105	.056	.970
Career average		54	143	13	32	5	1	4	14	11	2	32	1	1	1	0	0	.224	.284	.356	.988
Cubs average		**63**	**184**	**19**	**45**	**7**	**0**	**6**	**19**	**14**	**2**	**39**	**2**	**1**	**1**	**0**	**0**	**.243**	**.298**	**.384**	**.991**
Career total		376	1002	93	224	35	4	30	97	79	12	221	8	6	5	1	0	.224	.284	.356	.988
Cubs total		**251**	**734**	**74**	**178**	**27**	**1**	**25**	**77**	**54**	**9**	**156**	**6**	**3**	**4**	**0**	**0**	**.243**	**.298**	**.384**	**.991**

Nen, Richard Leroy (Dick)
HEIGHT: 6'2" THROWS: LEFT BATS: LEFT BORN: 9/24/1939 SOUTH GATE, CALIFORNIA POSITIONS PLAYED: 1B, OF

YEAR	TEAM	GAMES	AB	RUNS	HITS	2B	3B	HR	RBI	BB	IBB	SO	HBP	SH	SF	SB	CS	BA	OBA	SA	FA
1963	LA-N	7	8	2	1	0	0	1	1	3	1	3	0	0	0	0	0	.125	.364	.500	1.000
1965	Was-A	69	246	18	64	7	1	6	31	19	1	47	1	2	3	1	2	.260	.312	.370	.993
1966	Was-A	94	235	20	50	8	0	6	30	28	2	46	0	1	2	0	2	.213	.294	.323	.990
1967	Was-A	110	238	21	52	7	1	6	29	21	4	39	0	1	2	0	1	.218	.280	.332	.995
1968	ChC-N	81	94	8	17	1	1	2	16	6	2	17	0	1	2	0	0	.181	.225	.277	.987
1970	Was-A	6	5	1	1	0	0	0	0	0	0	0	0	0	0	0	0	.200	.200	.200	1.000
Career average		61	138	12	31	4	1	4	18	13	2	25	0	1	2	0	1	.224	.288	.335	.992
Cubs average		**81**	**94**	**8**	**17**	**1**	**1**	**2**	**16**	**6**	**2**	**17**	**0**	**1**	**2**	**0**	**0**	**.181**	**.225**	**.277**	**.987**
Career total		367	826	70	185	23	3	21	107	77	10	152	1	5	9	1	5	.224	.288	.335	.992
Cubs total		**81**	**94**	**8**	**17**	**1**	**1**	**2**	**16**	**6**	**2**	**17**	**0**	**1**	**2**	**0**	**0**	**.181**	**.225**	**.277**	**.987**

Newman, Charles (Charlie *or* Decker)
HEIGHT: 5'11" THROWS: RIGHT BATS: RIGHT BORN: 11/5/1868 JUDA, WISCONSIN DIED: 11/23/1947 SAN DIEGO, CALIFORNIA POSITIONS PLAYED: OF

YEAR	TEAM	GAMES	AB	RUNS	HITS	2B	3B	HR	RBI	BB	IBB	SO	HBP	SH	SF	SB	CS	BA	OBA	SA	FA
1892	NYG-N	3	12	1	4	0	0	0	1	2	—	0	0	—	—	3	—	.333	.429	.333	.750
1892	**ChN-N**	16	61	4	10	0	0	0	2	1	—	6	0	—	—	2	—	.164	.177	.164	.950
Career average		19	73	5	14	0	0	0	3	3	—	6	0	—	—	5	—	.192	.224	.192	.917
Cubs average		**16**	**61**	**4**	**10**	**0**	**0**	**0**	**2**	**1**	**—**	**6**	**0**	**—**	**—**	**2**	**—**	**.164**	**.177**	**.164**	**.950**
Career total		19	73	5	14	0	0	0	3	3	—	6	0	—	—	5	—	.192	.224	.192	.917
Cubs total		**16**	**61**	**4**	**10**	**0**	**0**	**0**	**2**	**1**	**—**	**6**	**0**	**—**	**—**	**2**	**—**	**.164**	**.177**	**.164**	**.950**

Nichols, Arthur Francis (Art)
HEIGHT: 5'10" THROWS: RIGHT BATS: RIGHT BORN: 7/14/1871 MANCHESTER, NEW HAMPSHIRE DIED: 8/9/1945 WILLIMANTIC, CONNECTICUT
POSITIONS PLAYED: C, 1B, OF

YEAR	TEAM	GAMES	AB	RUNS	HITS	2B	3B	HR	RBI	BB	IBB	SO	HBP	SH	SF	SB	CS	BA	OBA	SA	FA
1898	**ChN-N**	14	42	7	12	1	0	0	6	4	—	—	3	1	—	6	—	.286	.388	.310	.968
1899	**ChN-N**	17	47	5	12	2	0	1	11	0	—	—	2	1	—	3	—	.255	.286	.362	.931
1900	**ChN-N**	8	25	1	5	0	0	0	0	3	—	—	0	0	—	1	—	.200	.286	.200	.938
1901	StL-N	93	308	50	75	11	3	1	33	10	—	—	10	10	—	14	—	.244	.290	.308	.960
1902	StL-N	73	251	36	67	12	0	1	31	21	—	—	4	9	—	18	—	.267	.333	.327	.980
1903	StL-N	36	120	13	23	2	0	0	9	12	—	—	3	9	—	9	—	.192	.281	.208	.968
Career average		40	132	19	32	5	1	1	15	8	—	—	4	5	—	9	—	.245	.308	.299	.970
Cubs average		**13**	**38**	**4**	**10**	**1**	**0**	**0**	**6**	**2**	**—**	**—**	**2**	**1**	**—**	**3**	**—**	**.254**	**.325**	**.307**	**.947**
Career total		241	793	112	194	28	3	3	90	50	—	—	22	30	—	51	—	.245	.308	.299	.970
Cubs total		**39**	**114**	**13**	**29**	**3**	**0**	**1**	**17**	**7**	**—**	**—**	**5**	**2**	**—**	**10**	**—**	**.254**	**.325**	**.307**	**.947**

William (Bill) Beck "Swish" Nicholson, of, 1936, 1939–53

When the lean-muscled Bill Nicholson took his cuts at the plate, fans in the stands would yell "Swish!" it was a term of respect, as his powerful swing often produced home runs or extra-base hits.

Nicholson was born on December 11, 1914, in Chestertown, Maryland. The Philadelphia Athletics signed Nicholson out of college and sent him to the minor leagues. Nicholson was assigned to Chattanooga of the Southern League, where his coach was former Cubs standout Hazen "Kiki" Cuyler.

Cuyler got Nicholson to stop lunging after the pitch, and Bill's hitting improved dramatically. In 1939 the Cubs purchased his contract and brought him up. Nicholson hit .295 in limited duty that year.

By 1940 Nicholson was the team's starting right fielder. He hit .297, with 98 RBIs and 25 home runs.

The 6' 205-pound Nicholson was built like a weight lifter. His powerful swing sometimes cut through the air with a huge *whoosh!* He was a frightening presence at the plate. One year, in the early 1940s, Boston Braves' manager Charles Dillon "Casey" Stengel offered to allow Cubs manager Jimmie Wilson to play two men

in right field if he would take Nicholson out of the game. Wilson understandably declined.

In a 1944 game against the Giants, after he had hit four consecutive home runs, Nicholson was walked with the bases loaded on orders from New York manager Mel Ott. The strategy worked, as the Giants won, 12-10.

Nicholson was a four-time All-Star for Chicago who led the league in home runs in 1943 with 29 and in 1944 with 33. He also had a league-leading 128 and 122 RBIs in those two seasons, respectively.

He was also an excellent fielder. In 1947 Nicholson led all outfielders in fielding percentage with a .990 mark. He was fundamentally solid, always hitting the cutoff man and always making the right throw to the right base.

Nicholson's production began dropping off during the Cubs' pennant year of 1945 when his eyesight began to fail. He bounced back with strong years in 1947 and 1948 but was traded to the Phillies in 1949. In 1950 he revealed he had diabetes, which had led to the deterioration of his eyesight. Nicholson remained in the majors as a part-time player until 1953.

Nicholson's four consecutive home runs in 1944 is still a team record, while he is second all-time on the Cubs list of most career grand slams with eight. He died in his homeown, in 1996.

Nicholson, William Beck (Bill *or* Swish)

HEIGHT: 6'0" THROWS: RIGHT BATS: LEFT BORN: 12/11/1914 CHESTERTOWN, MARYLAND DIED: 3/8/1996 CHESTERTOWN, MARYLAND POSITIONS PLAYED: OF

YEAR	TEAM	GAMES	AB	RUNS	HITS	2B	3B	HR	RBI	BB	IBB	SO	HBP	SH	SF	SB	CS	BA	OBA	SA	FA
1936	Phi-A	11	12	2	0	0	0	0	0	0	—	5	0	0	—	0	0	.000	.000	.000	1.000
1939	ChC-N	58	220	37	65	12	5	5	38	20	—	29	0	3	—	0	—	.295	.354	.464	.955
1940	ChC-N	135	491	78	146	27	7	25	98	50	—	67	3	1	—	2	—	.297	.366	.534	.950
1941	ChC-N	147	532	74	135	26	1	26	98	82	—	91	3	0	—	1	—	.254	.357	.453	.971
1942	ChC-N	152	588	83	173	22	11	21	78	76	—	80	8	1	—	1	—	.294	.382	.476	.986
1943	ChC-N	154	608	95	188	30	9	29	128	71	—	86	5	0	—	8	—	.309	.386	.531	.978
1944	ChC-N	156	582	116	167	35	8	33	122	93	—	71	6	5	—	4	—	.287	.391	.545	.979
1945	ChC-N	151	559	82	136	28	4	13	88	92	—	73	6	3	—	3	—	.243	.356	.377	.990
1946	ChC-N	105	296	36	65	13	2	8	41	44	—	44	2	3	—	4	—	.220	.325	.358	.973
1947	ChC-N	148	487	69	119	28	1	26	75	87	—	83	5	1	—	1	—	.244	.348	.445	.990
1948	ChC-N	143	494	68	129	24	5	19	67	81	—	60	5	1	—	1	—	.261	.371	.445	.980
1949	Phi-N	98	299	42	70	8	3	11	40	45	—	53	5	1	—	1	—	.234	.344	.391	.995
1950	Phi-N	41	58	3	13	2	1	3	10	8	—	16	0	0	—	0	—	.224	.318	.448	.952
1951	Phi-N	85	170	23	41	9	2	8	30	25	—	24	1	0	—	0	—	.241	.342	.459	.987
1952	Phi-N	55	88	17	24	3	0	6	19	14	—	26	3	1	—	0	1	.273	.390	.511	1.000
1953	Phi-N	38	62	12	13	5	1	2	16	12	—	20	0	0	—	0	0	.210	.338	.419	1.000
Career average		105	347	52	93	17	4	15	59	50	—	52	3	1	—	2	0	.268	.365	.465	.979
Cubs average		**135**	**486**	**74**	**132**	**25**	**5**	**21**	**83**	**70**	**—**	**68**	**4**	**2**	**—**	**3**	**0**	**.272**	**.368**	**.471**	**.977**
Career total		1677	5546	837	1484	272	60	235	948	800	—	828	52	20	—	27	1	.268	.365	.465	.979
Cubs total		**1349**	**4857**	**738**	**1323**	**245**	**53**	**205**	**833**	**696**	**—**	**684**	**43**	**18**	**—**	**26**	**0**	**.272**	**.368**	**.471**	**.977**

Nicol, George Edward
HEIGHT: 5'7" THROWS: LEFT BATS: — BORN: 10/17/1870 BARRY, ILLINOIS DIED: 8/10/1924 MILWAUKEE, WISCONSIN POSITIONS PLAYED: P, OF

YEAR	TEAM	GAMES	AB	RUNS	HITS	2B	3B	HR	RBI	BB	IBB	SO	HBP	SH	SF	SB	CS	BA	OBA	SA	FA
1890	StL-AA	3	7	4	2	1	0	0	1	4	—	—	0	—	—	0	—	.286	.545	.429	1.000
1891	**ChN-N**	3	6	0	2	0	1	0	3	0	—	1	0	—	—	0	—	.333	.333	.667	.000
1894	Pit-N	9	20	8	9	1	0	0	3	0	—	1	0	2	—	0	—	.450	.450	.500	.800
1894	Lou-N	27	108	12	38	6	4	0	19	2	—	3	2	1	—	4	—	.352	.375	.481	.804
Career average		14	47	8	17	3	2	0	9	2	—	2	1	1	—	1	—	.362	.396	.489	.768
Cubs average		3	6	0	2	0	1	0	3	0	—	1	0	—	—	0	—	.333	.333	.667	.000
Career total		42	141	24	51	8	5	0	26	6	—	5	2	3	—	4	—	.362	.396	.489	.768
Cubs total		3	6	0	2	0	1	0	3	0	—	1	0	—	—	0	—	.333	.333	.667	.000

Nicol, Hugh N.
HEIGHT: 5'4" THROWS: RIGHT BATS: RIGHT BORN: 1/1/1858 CAMPSIE, SCOTLAND DIED: 6/27/1921 LAFAYETTE, INDIANA
POSITIONS PLAYED: 2B, 3B, SS, OF

YEAR	TEAM	GAMES	AB	RUNS	HITS	2B	3B	HR	RBI	BB	IBB	SO	HBP	SH	SF	SB	CS	BA	OBA	SA	FA
1881	**ChN-N**	26	108	13	22	2	0	0	7	4	—	12	—	—	—	—	—	.204	.232	.222	.919
1882	**ChN-N**	47	186	19	37	9	1	1	16	7	—	29	—	—	—	—	—	.199	.228	.274	.866
1883	StL-AA	94	368	73	105	13	3	0	39	18	—	—	—	—	—	—	—	.285	.319	.337	.893
1884	StL-AA	110	442	79	116	14	5	0	—	22	—	—	3	—	—	—	—	.262	.302	.317	.879
1885	StL-AA	112	425	59	88	11	1	0	45	34	—	—	3	—	—	—	—	.207	.271	.238	.889
1886	StL-AA	67	253	44	52	6	3	0	19	26	—	—	0	—	—	38	—	.206	.280	.253	.883
1887	Cin-AA	125	561	122	188	18	2	1	34	86	—	—	5	—	—	138	—	.335	.428	.380	.918
1888	Cin-AA	135	548	112	131	10	2	1	35	67	—	—	7	—	—	103	—	.239	.330	.270	.956
1889	Cin-AA	122	474	82	121	7	8	2	58	54	—	35	5	—	—	80	—	.255	.338	.316	.924
1890	Cin-N	50	186	28	39	1	4	0	19	19	—	12	0	—	—	24	—	.210	.283	.258	.862
Career average		89	355	63	90	9	3	1	27	34	—	9	2	—	—	38	—	.253	.322	.299	.902
Cubs average		37	147	16	30	6	1	1	12	6	—	21	—	—	—	—	—	.201	.230	.255	.885
Career total		888	3551	631	899	91	29	5	272	337	—	88	23	—	—	383	—	.253	.322	.299	.902
Cubs total		73	294	32	59	11	1	1	23	11	—	41	—	—	—	—	—	.201	.230	.255	.885

Nieves, Jose Miguel
HEIGHT: 6'1" THROWS: RIGHT BATS: RIGHT BORN: 6/16/1975 GUACARA, VENEZUELA POSITIONS PLAYED: 1B, 2B, 3B, SS

YEAR	TEAM	GAMES	AB	RUNS	HITS	2B	3B	HR	RBI	BB	IBB	SO	HBP	SH	SF	SB	CS	BA	OBA	SA	FA
1998	**ChC-N**	2	1	0	0	0	0	0	0	0	0	0	0	1	0	0	0	.000	.000	.000	—
1999	**ChC-N**	54	181	16	45	9	1	2	18	8	0	25	4	3	3	0	2	.249	.291	.343	.935
2000	**ChC-N**	82	198	17	42	9	3	5	24	11	1	43	0	2	2	1	1	.212	.251	.348	.968
2001	Ana-A	29	53	5	13	3	1	2	3	2	0	20	2	2	0	0	1	.245	.298	.453	.988
Career average		42	108	10	25	5	1	2	11	5	0	22	2	2	1	0	1	.231	.273	.358	.954
Cubs average		46	127	11	29	5	1	2	14	6	0	23	1	2	2	0	1	.229	.270	.345	.947
Career total		167	433	38	100	18	5	9	45	21	1	88	6	8	5	1	4	.231	.273	.358	.954
Cubs total		138	380	33	87	15	4	7	42	19	1	68	4	6	5	1	3	.229	.270	.345	.947

Noce, Paul David
HEIGHT: 5'11" THROWS: RIGHT BATS: RIGHT BORN: 12/16/1959 SAN FRANCISCO, CALIFORNIA POSITIONS PLAYED: 2B, 3B, SS

YEAR	TEAM	GAMES	AB	RUNS	HITS	2B	3B	HR	RBI	BB	IBB	SO	HBP	SH	SF	SB	CS	BA	OBA	SA	FA
1987	**ChC-N**	70	180	17	41	9	2	3	14	6	1	49	2	4	0	5	3	.228	.261	.350	.982
1990	Cin-N	1	1	0	1	0	0	0	0	0	0	0	0	0	0	0	0	1.000	1.000	1.000	—
Career average		36	91	9	21	5	1	2	7	3	1	25	1	2	0	3	2	.232	.265	.354	.982
Cubs average		70	180	17	41	9	2	3	14	6	1	49	2	4	0	5	3	.232	.265	.354	.982
Career total		71	181	17	42	9	2	3	14	6	1	49	2	4	0	5	3	.228	.261	.350	.982
Cubs total		70	180	17	41	9	2	3	14	6	1	49	2	4	0	5	3	.228	.261	.350	.982

Noonan, Peter John (Pete)
HEIGHT: 6'0" THROWS: RIGHT BATS: RIGHT BORN: 11/24/1881 WEST STOCKBRIDGE, MASSACHUSETTS DIED: 2/11/1965 GREAT BARRINGTON, MASSACHUSETTS POSITIONS PLAYED: C, 1B

YEAR	TEAM	GAMES	AB	RUNS	HITS	2B	3B	HR	RBI	BB	IBB	SO	HBP	SH	SF	SB	CS	BA	OBA	SA	FA
1904	Phi-A	39	114	13	23	3	1	2	13	1	—	—	0	2	—	1	—	.202	.209	.298	.979
1906	**ChC-N**	**5**	**3**	**0**	**1**	**0**	**0**	**0**	**0**	**0**	**—**	**—**	**0**	**6**	**—**	**0**	**—**	**.333**	**.333**	**.333**	**1.000**
1906	StL-N	44	125	8	21	1	3	1	9	11	—	—	0	0	—	1	—	.168	.235	.248	.958
1907	StL-N	74	237	19	53	7	3	1	16	9	—	—	0	6	—	3	—	.224	.252	.291	.951
Career average		54	160	13	33	4	2	1	13	7	—	—	0	5	—	2	—	.205	.238	.282	.959
Cubs average		**5**	**3**	**0**	**1**	**0**	**0**	**0**	**0**	**0**	**—**	**—**	**0**	**6**	**—**	**0**	**—**	**.333**	**.333**	**.333**	**1.000**
Career total		162	479	40	98	11	7	4	38	21	—	—	0	14	—	5	—	.205	.238	.282	.959
Cubs total		**5**	**3**	**0**	**1**	**0**	**0**	**0**	**0**	**0**	**—**	**—**	**0**	**6**	**—**	**0**	**—**	**.333**	**.333**	**.333**	**1.000**

Nordhagen, Wayne Oren
HEIGHT: 6'2" THROWS: RIGHT BATS: RIGHT BORN: 7/4/1948 THIEF RIVER FALLS, MINNESOTA POSITIONS PLAYED: P, C, OF

YEAR	TEAM	GAMES	AB	RUNS	HITS	2B	3B	HR	RBI	BB	IBB	SO	HBP	SH	SF	SB	CS	BA	OBA	SA	FA
1976	CWS-A	22	53	6	10	2	0	0	5	4	0	12	0	1	3	0	0	.189	.233	.226	.974
1977	CWS-A	52	124	16	39	7	3	4	22	2	0	12	0	1	1	1	0	.315	.323	.516	.914
1978	CWS-A	68	206	28	62	16	0	5	35	5	0	18	0	0	5	0	1	.301	.310	.451	.943
1979	CWS-A	78	193	20	54	15	0	7	25	13	2	22	0	0	1	0	0	.280	.324	.466	.914
1980	CWS-A	123	415	45	115	22	4	15	59	10	3	45	1	0	2	0	1	.277	.294	.458	.969
1981	CWS-A	65	208	19	64	8	1	6	33	10	0	25	1	0	3	0	1	.308	.338	.442	.947
1982	Tor-A	72	185	12	50	6	0	1	20	10	1	22	0	0	2	0	2	.270	.305	.319	1.000
1982	Pit-N	1	4	0	2	0	0	0	2	0	0	1	0	0	0	0	2	.270	.305	.319	1.000
1983	**ChC-N**	**21**	**35**	**1**	**5**	**1**	**0**	**1**	**4**	**0**	**0**	**5**	**1**	**0**	**1**	**0**	**0**	**.500**	**.500**	**.500**	**1.000**
Career average		63	178	18	50	10	1	5	26	7	1	20	0	0	2	0	1	.282	.306	.429	.951
Cubs average		**21**	**35**	**1**	**5**	**1**	**0**	**1**	**4**	**0**	**0**	**5**	**1**	**0**	**1**	**0**	**0**	**.143**	**.162**	**.257**	**1.000**
Career total		502	1423	147	401	77	8	39	205	54	6	162	3	2	18	1	5	.282	.306	.429	.951
Cubs total		**21**	**35**	**1**	**5**	**1**	**0**	**1**	**4**	**0**	**0**	**5**	**1**	**0**	**1**	**0**	**0**	**.143**	**.162**	**.257**	**1.000**

Noren, Irving Arnold (Irv)
HEIGHT: 6'0" THROWS: LEFT BATS: LEFT BORN: 11/29/1924 JAMESTOWN, NEW YORK POSITIONS PLAYED: 1B, OF

YEAR	TEAM	GAMES	AB	RUNS	HITS	2B	3B	HR	RBI	BB	IBB	SO	HBP	SH	SF	SB	CS	BA	OBA	SA	FA
1950	Was-A	138	542	80	160	27	10	14	98	67	—	77	2	4	—	5	2	.295	.375	.459	.976
1951	Was-A	129	509	82	142	33	5	8	86	51	—	35	0	4	—	10	7	.279	.345	.411	.978
1952	Was-A	12	49	4	12	3	1	0	2	6	—	3	0	1	—	1	0	.245	.327	.347	1.000
1952	NYY-A	93	272	36	64	13	2	5	21	26	—	34	6	2	—	4	2	.235	.316	.353	.992
1953	NYY-A	109	345	55	92	12	6	6	46	42	—	39	2	2	—	3	3	.267	.350	.388	.991
1954	NYY-A	125	426	70	136	21	6	12	66	43	—	38	1	3	7	4	6	.319	.377	.481	.991
1955	NYY-A	132	371	49	94	19	1	8	59	43	5	33	3	0	6	5	2	.253	.331	.375	.980
1956	NYY-A	29	37	4	8	1	0	0	6	12	2	7	0	0	0	0	0	.216	.408	.243	.923
1957	KCA-A	81	160	8	34	8	0	2	16	11	2	19	1	0	0	0	0	.213	.267	.300	.991
1957	StL-N	17	30	3	11	4	1	1	10	4	2	6	0	0	1	0	1	.367	.429	.667	1.000
1958	StL-N	117	178	24	47	9	1	4	22	13	2	21	4	0	1	0	1	.264	.327	.393	.974
1959	StL-N	8	8	0	1	1	0	0	0	0	0	2	0	0	0	0	0	.125	.125	.250	1.000
1959	**ChC-N**	**65**	**156**	**27**	**50**	**6**	**2**	**4**	**19**	**13**	**1**	**24**	**3**	**0**	**0**	**0**	**0**	**.321**	**.384**	**.462**	**1.000**
1960	**ChC-N**	**12**	**11**	**0**	**1**	**0**	**0**	**0**	**1**	**3**	**0**	**4**	**0**	**0**	**0**	**2**	**0**	**.091**	**.286**	**.091**	**.857**
1960	LA-N	26	25	1	5	0	1	1	1	1	0	8	1	0	0	0	0	.200	.259	.320	—
Career average		99	284	40	78	14	3	6	41	30	1	32	2	1	1	3	2	.275	.348	.410	.982
Cubs average		**39**	**84**	**14**	**26**	**3**	**1**	**2**	**10**	**8**	**1**	**14**	**2**	**0**	**0**	**1**	**0**	**.305**	**.376**	**.437**	**.989**
Career total		1093	3119	443	857	157	35	65	453	335	14	350	23	16	15	34	24	.275	.348	.410	.982
Cubs total		**77**	**167**	**27**	**51**	**6**	**2**	**4**	**20**	**16**	**1**	**28**	**3**	**0**	**0**	**2**	**0**	**.305**	**.376**	**.437**	**.989**

North, William Alex (Bill)

HEIGHT: 5'11" THROWS: RIGHT BATS: BOTH BORN: 5/15/1948 SEATTLE, WASHINGTON POSITIONS PLAYED: OF

YEAR	TEAM	GAMES	AB	RUNS	HITS	2B	3B	HR	RBI	BB	IBB	SO	HBP	SH	SF	SB	CS	BA	OBA	SA	FA
1971	**ChC-N**	**8**	**16**	**3**	**6**	**0**	**0**	**0**	**0**	**4**	**1**	**6**	**1**	**0**	**0**	**1**	**1**	**.375**	**.524**	**.375**	**1.000**
1972	**ChC-N**	**66**	**127**	**22**	**23**	**2**	**3**	**0**	**4**	**13**	**1**	**33**	**1**	**1**	**0**	**6**	**0**	**.181**	**.262**	**.244**	**.955**
1973	Oak-A	146	554	98	158	10	5	5	34	78	5	89	3	7	0	53	20	.285	.376	.348	.980
1974	Oak-A	149	543	79	141	20	5	4	33	69	1	86	5	11	2	54	26	.260	.347	.337	.991
1975	Oak-A	140	524	74	143	17	5	1	43	81	3	80	4	13	2	30	12	.273	.373	.330	.975
1976	Oak-A	154	590	91	163	20	5	2	31	73	3	95	2	6	4	75	29	.276	.356	.337	.978
1977	Oak-A	56	184	32	48	3	3	1	9	32	2	25	2	5	0	17	13	.261	.376	.326	.983
1978	Oak-A	24	52	5	11	4	0	0	5	9	2	13	2	1	1	3	2	.212	.344	.288	1.000
1978	LA-N	110	304	54	71	10	0	0	10	65	2	48	2	5	1	27	8	.234	.371	.266	.975
1979	SF-N	142	460	87	119	15	4	5	30	96	3	84	1	1	3	58	24	.259	.386	.341	.987
1980	SF-N	128	415	73	104	12	1	1	19	81	5	78	1	2	1	45	19	.251	.373	.292	.982
1981	SF-N	46	131	22	29	7	0	1	12	26	0	28	1	3	0	26	8	.221	.354	.298	.966
Career average		106	355	58	92	11	3	2	21	57	3	60	2	5	1	36	15	.261	.365	.323	.981
Cubs average		**37**	**72**	**13**	**15**	**1**	**2**	**0**	**2**	**9**	**1**	**20**	**1**	**1**	**0**	**4**	**1**	**.203**	**.296**	**.259**	**.958**
Career total		1169	3900	640	1016	120	31	20	230	627	28	665	25	55	14	395	162	.261	.365	.323	.981
Cubs total		**74**	**143**	**25**	**29**	**2**	**3**	**0**	**4**	**17**	**2**	**39**	**2**	**1**	**0**	**7**	**1**	**.203**	**.296**	**.259**	**.958**

Northey, Ronald James (Ron *or* The Round Man)

HEIGHT: 5'10" THROWS: RIGHT BATS: LEFT BORN: 4/26/1920 MAHANOY CITY, PENNSYLVANIA DIED: 4/16/1971 PITTSBURGH, PENNSYLVANIA
POSITIONS PLAYED: 3B, OF

YEAR	TEAM	GAMES	AB	RUNS	HITS	2B	3B	HR	RBI	BB	IBB	SO	HBP	SH	SF	SB	CS	BA	OBA	SA	FA
1942	Phi-N	127	402	31	101	13	2	5	31	28	—	33	0	3	—	2	—	.251	.300	.331	.952
1943	Phi-N	147	586	72	163	31	5	16	68	51	—	52	3	4	—	2	—	.278	.339	.430	.978
1944	Phi-N	152	570	72	164	35	9	22	104	67	—	51	4	4	—	1	—	.288	.367	.496	.981
1946	Phi-N	128	438	55	109	24	6	16	62	39	—	59	2	1	—	1	—	.249	.313	.441	.971
1947	Phi-N	13	47	7	12	3	0	0	3	6	—	3	0	0	—	1	—	.255	.340	.319	1.000
1947	StL-N	110	311	52	91	19	3	15	63	48	—	29	2	0	—	0	—	.293	.391	.518	.946
1948	StL-N	96	246	40	79	10	1	13	64	38	—	25	4	0	—	0	—	.321	.420	.528	.989
1949	StL-N	90	265	28	69	18	2	7	50	31	—	15	0	1	—	0	—	.260	.338	.423	.980
1950	Cin-N	27	77	11	20	5	0	5	9	15	—	6	0	0	—	0	—	.260	.380	.519	.955
1950	**ChC-N**	**53**	**114**	**11**	**32**	**9**	**0**	**4**	**20**	**10**	**—**	**9**	**0**	**1**	**—**	**0**	**—**	**.281**	**.339**	**.465**	**.976**
1952	**ChC-N**	**1**	**1**	**0**	**0**	**0**	**0**	**0**	**0**	**0**	**—**	**0**	**0**	**0**	**—**	**0**	**0**	**.000**	**.000**	**.000**	**—**
1955	CWS-A	14	14	1	5	2	0	1	4	3	0	3	0	0	0	0	0	.357	.471	.714	1.000
1956	CWS-A	53	48	4	17	2	0	3	23	8	2	1	0	0	4	0	0	.354	.417	.583	1.000
1957	CWS-A	40	27	0	5	1	0	0	7	11	1	5	0	0	1	0	0	.185	.410	.222	—
1957	Phi-N	33	26	1	7	0	0	1	5	6	1	6	0	0	0	0	0	.269	.406	.385	—
Career average		90	264	32	73	14	2	9	43	30	0	25	1	1	0	1	0	.276	.352	.450	.971
Cubs average		**27**	**58**	**6**	**16**	**5**	**0**	**2**	**10**	**5**	**—**	**5**	**0**	**1**	**—**	**0**	**0**	**.278**	**.336**	**.461**	**.976**
Career total		1084	3172	385	874	172	28	108	513	361	4	297	15	14	5	7	0	.276	.352	.450	.971
Cubs total		**54**	**115**	**11**	**32**	**9**	**0**	**4**	**20**	**10**	**—**	**9**	**0**	**1**	**—**	**0**	**0**	**.278**	**.336**	**.461**	**.976**

Novikoff, Louis Alexander (Lou *or* The Mad Russian)

HEIGHT: 5'10" THROWS: RIGHT BATS: RIGHT BORN: 10/12/1915 GLENDALE, ARIZONA DIED: 9/30/1970 SOUTH GATE, CALIFORNIA POSITIONS PLAYED: OF

YEAR	TEAM	GAMES	AB	RUNS	HITS	2B	3B	HR	RBI	BB	IBB	SO	HBP	SH	SF	SB	CS	BA	OBA	SA	FA
1941	**ChC-N**	**62**	**203**	**22**	**49**	**8**	**0**	**5**	**24**	**11**	**—**	**15**	**1**	**1**	**—**	**0**	**—**	**.241**	**.284**	**.355**	**1.000**
1942	**ChC-N**	**128**	**483**	**48**	**145**	**25**	**5**	**7**	**64**	**24**	**—**	**28**	**3**	**4**	**—**	**3**	**—**	**.300**	**.337**	**.416**	**.964**
1943	**ChC-N**	**78**	**233**	**22**	**65**	**7**	**3**	**0**	**28**	**18**	**—**	**15**	**1**	**2**	**—**	**0**	**—**	**.279**	**.333**	**.335**	**.980**
1944	**ChC-N**	**71**	**139**	**15**	**39**	**4**	**2**	**3**	**19**	**10**	**—**	**11**	**0**	**2**	**—**	**1**	**—**	**.281**	**.329**	**.403**	**.976**
1946	Phi-N	17	23	0	7	1	0	0	3	1	—	2	0	0	—	0	—	.304	.333	.348	1.000
Career average		71	216	21	61	9	2	3	28	13	—	14	1	2	—	1	—	.282	.325	.384	.976
Cubs average		**85**	**265**	**27**	**75**	**11**	**3**	**4**	**34**	**16**	**—**	**17**	**1**	**2**	**—**	**1**	**—**	**.282**	**.325**	**.385**	**.975**
Career total		356	1081	107	305	45	10	15	138	64	—	71	5	9	—	4	—	.282	.325	.384	.976
Cubs total		**339**	**1058**	**107**	**298**	**44**	**10**	**15**	**135**	**63**	**—**	**69**	**5**	**9**	**—**	**4**	**—**	**.282**	**.325**	**.385**	**.975**

Novotney, Ralph Joseph (Rube)
HEIGHT: 6'0"   THROWS: RIGHT   BATS: RIGHT   BORN: 8/5/1924 STREATOR, ILLINOIS   DIED: 7/16/1987 REDONDO BEACH, CALIFORNIA   POSITIONS PLAYED: C

YEAR	TEAM	GAMES	AB	RUNS	HITS	2B	3B	HR	RBI	BB	IBB	SO	HBP	SH	SF	SB	CS	BA	OBA	SA	FA
1949	ChC-N	22	67	4	18	2	1	0	6	3	—	11	0	0	—	0	—	.269	.300	.328	.958
Career average		22	67	4	18	2	1	0	6	3	—	11	0	0	—	0	—	.269	.300	.328	.958
Cubs average		**22**	**67**	**4**	**18**	**2**	**1**	**0**	**6**	**3**	**—**	**11**	**0**	**0**	**—**	**0**	**—**	**.269**	**.300**	**.328**	**.958**
Career total		22	67	4	18	2	1	0	6	3	—	11	0	0	—	0	—	.269	.300	.328	.958
Cubs total		**22**	**67**	**4**	**18**	**2**	**1**	**0**	**6**	**3**	**—**	**11**	**0**	**0**	**—**	**0**	**—**	**.269**	**.300**	**.328**	**.958**

O'Berry, Preston Michael (Mike)
HEIGHT: 6'2"   THROWS: RIGHT   BATS: RIGHT   BORN: 4/20/1954 BIRMINGHAM, ALABAMA   POSITIONS PLAYED: C, 3B

YEAR	TEAM	GAMES	AB	RUNS	HITS	2B	3B	HR	RBI	BB	IBB	SO	HBP	SH	SF	SB	CS	BA	OBA	SA	FA
1979	Bos-A	43	59	8	10	1	0	1	4	5	0	16	1	2	1	0	0	.169	.242	.237	.957
1980	**ChC-N**	19	48	7	10	1	0	0	5	5	0	13	0	2	2	0	0	.208	.273	.229	.982
1981	Cin-N	55	111	6	20	3	1	1	5	14	0	19	0	3	0	0	0	.180	.272	.252	.983
1982	Cin-N	21	45	5	10	2	0	0	5	10	0	13	0	0	0	0	0	.222	.364	.267	.990
1983	Cal-A	26	60	7	10	1	0	1	5	3	0	11	0	2	0	0	0	.167	.206	.233	1.000
1984	NYY-A	13	32	3	8	2	0	0	5	2	0	2	0	0	0	0	0	.250	.294	.313	1.000
1985	Mon-N	20	21	2	4	0	0	0	0	4	0	3	0	1	0	1	0	.190	.320	.190	1.000
Career average		28	54	5	10	1	0	0	4	6	0	11	0	1	0	0	0	.191	.274	.247	.984
Cubs average		**19**	**48**	**7**	**10**	**1**	**0**	**0**	**5**	**5**	**0**	**13**	**0**	**2**	**2**	**0**	**0**	**.208**	**.273**	**.229**	**.982**
Career total		197	376	38	72	10	1	3	27	43	0	77	1	10	3	1	0	.191	.274	.247	.984
Cubs total		**19**	**48**	**7**	**10**	**1**	**0**	**0**	**5**	**5**	**0**	**13**	**0**	**2**	**2**	**0**	**0**	**.208**	**.273**	**.229**	**.982**

O'Brien, John J. (Chewing Gum)
HEIGHT: 5'9"   THROWS: RIGHT   BATS: LEFT   BORN: 7/14/1870 ST. JOHN, NEW BRUNSWICK, CANADA   DIED: 5/13/1913 LEWISTON, MAINE
POSITIONS PLAYED: 1B, 2B

YEAR	TEAM	GAMES	AB	RUNS	HITS	2B	3B	HR	RBI	BB	IBB	SO	HBP	SH	SF	SB	CS	BA	OBA	SA	FA
1891	Bro-N	43	167	22	41	4	2	0	26	12	—	17	3	—	—	4	—	.246	.308	.293	.854
1893	**ChN-N**	4	14	3	5	0	1	0	1	2	—	2	1	—	—	0	—	.357	.471	.500	.854
1895	Lou-N	128	539	82	138	10	4	1	50	45	—	20	10	18	—	15	—	.256	.325	.295	.900
1896	Lou-N	49	186	24	63	9	1	2	24	13	—	7	1	1	—	4	—	.339	.385	.430	.940
1896	Was-N	73	270	38	72	6	3	4	33	27	—	12	5	7	—	4	—	.267	.344	.356	.919
1897	Was-N	86	320	37	78	12	2	3	45	19	—		11	3	—	4	—	.244	.309	.322	.952
1899	Bal-N	39	135	14	26	4	0	1	17	15	—		2	3	—	6	—	.193	.283	.244	.942
1899	Pit-N	79	279	26	63	2	4	1	33	21	—		2	10	—	8	—	.226	.285	.272	.966
Career average		84	318	41	81	8	3	2	38	26	—	10	6	7	—	8	—	.254	.322	.316	.946
Cubs average		**4**	**14**	**3**	**5**	**0**	**1**	**0**	**1**	**2**	**—**	**2**	**1**	**—**	**—**	**0**	**—**	**.357**	**.471**	**.500**	**.936**
Career total		501	1910	246	486	47	17	12	229	154	—	58	35	42	—	45	—	.254	.322	.316	.900
Cubs total		**4**	**14**	**3**	**5**	**0**	**1**	**0**	**1**	**2**	**—**	**2**	**1**	**—**	**—**	**0**	**—**	**.357**	**.471**	**.500**	**.936**

O'Brien, Peter James (Pete)
HEIGHT: 5'9"   THROWS: RIGHT   BATS: RIGHT   BORN: 6/16/1867 CHICAGO, ILLINOIS   DIED: 6/30/1937 YORK, ILLINOIS   POSITIONS PLAYED: 2B

YEAR	TEAM	GAMES	AB	RUNS	HITS	2B	3B	HR	RBI	BB	IBB	SO	HBP	SH	SF	SB	CS	BA	OBA	SA	FA
1890	ChN-N	27	106	15	30	7	0	3	16	5	—	10	0	—	—	4	—	.283	.315	.434	.929
Career average		27	106	15	30	7	0	3	16	5	—	10	0	—	—	4	—	.283	.315	.434	.929
Cubs average		**27**	**106**	**15**	**30**	**7**	**0**	**3**	**16**	**5**	**—**	**10**	**0**	**—**	**—**	**4**	**—**	**.283**	**.315**	**.434**	**.929**
Career total		27	106	15	30	7	0	3	16	5	—	10	0	—	—	4	—	.283	.315	.434	.929
Cubs total		**27**	**106**	**15**	**30**	**7**	**0**	**3**	**16**	**5**	**—**	**10**	**0**	**—**	**—**	**4**	**—**	**.283**	**.315**	**.434**	**.929**

O'Connor, John Charles (Johnny *or* Bucky)
HEIGHT: 5'9" THROWS: RIGHT BATS: RIGHT BORN: 12/1/1891 CAHIRCIVEEN, IRELAND DIED: 5/30/1982 BONNER SPRINGS, KANSAS POSITIONS PLAYED: C

YEAR	TEAM	GAMES	AB	RUNS	HITS	2B	3B	HR	RBI	BB	IBB	SO	HBP	SH	SF	SB	CS	BA	OBA	SA	FA
1916	ChC-N	1	0	0	0	0	0	0	0	0	—	0	0	0	—	0	—	—	—	—	—
Career average		1	0	0	0	0	0	0	0	0	—	0	0	0	—	0	—	—	—	—	—
Cubs average		**1**	**0**	**0**	**0**	**0**	**0**	**0**	**0**	**0**	**—**	**0**	**0**	**0**	**—**	**0**	**—**	**—**	**—**	**—**	**—**
Career total		1	0	0	0	0	0	0	0	0	—	0	0	0	—	0	—	—	—	—	—
Cubs total		**1**	**0**	**0**	**0**	**0**	**0**	**0**	**0**	**0**	**—**	**0**	**0**	**0**	**—**	**0**	**—**	**—**	**—**	**—**	**—**

O'Dea, James Kenneth (Ken)
HEIGHT: 6'0" THROWS: RIGHT BATS: LEFT BORN: 3/16/1913 LIMA, NEW YORK DIED: 12/17/1985 LIMA, NEW YORK POSITIONS PLAYED: C

YEAR	TEAM	GAMES	AB	RUNS	HITS	2B	3B	HR	RBI	BB	IBB	SO	HBP	SH	SF	SB	CS	BA	OBA	SA	FA
1935	ChC-N	76	202	30	52	13	2	6	38	26	—	18	1	2	—	0	—	.257	.345	.431	.964
1936	ChC-N	80	189	36	58	10	3	2	38	38	—	18	0	3	—	0	—	.307	.423	.423	.979
1937	ChC-N	83	219	31	66	7	5	4	32	24	—	26	0	4	—	1	—	.301	.370	.434	.985
1938	ChC-N	86	247	22	65	12	1	3	33	12	—	18	0	3	—	1	—	.263	.297	.356	.970
1939	NYG-N	52	97	7	17	1	0	3	11	10	—	16	0	2	—	0	—	.175	.252	.278	.947
1940	NYG-N	48	96	9	23	4	1	0	12	16	—	15	0	2	—	0	—	.240	.348	.302	.992
1941	NYG-N	59	89	13	19	5	1	3	17	8	—	20	0	1	—	0	—	.213	.278	.393	1.000
1942	StL-N	58	192	22	45	7	1	5	32	17	—	23	0	2	—	0	—	.234	.297	.359	.979
1943	StL-N	71	203	15	57	11	2	3	25	19	—	25	1	4	—	0	—	.281	.345	.399	.989
1944	StL-N	85	265	35	66	11	2	6	37	37	—	29	1	7	—	1	—	.249	.343	.374	.994
1945	StL-N	100	307	36	78	18	2	4	43	50	—	31	0	5	—	0	—	.254	.359	.365	.995
1946	StL-N	22	57	2	7	2	0	1	3	8	—	8	0	3	—	0	—	.123	.231	.211	.991
1946	Bos-N	12	32	4	7	0	0	0	2	8	—	4	0	1	—	0	—	.219	.375	.219	1.000
Career average		69	183	22	47	8	2	3	27	23	—	21	0	3	—	0	—	.255	.338	.374	.983
Cubs average		**81**	**214**	**30**	**60**	**11**	**3**	**4**	**35**	**25**	**—**	**20**	**0**	**3**	**—**	**1**	**—**	**.281**	**.357**	**.408**	**.974**
Career total		832	2195	262	560	101	20	40	323	273	—	251	3	39	—	3	—	.255	.338	.374	.983
Cubs total		**325**	**857**	**119**	**241**	**42**	**11**	**15**	**141**	**100**	**—**	**80**	**1**	**12**	**—**	**2**	**—**	**.281**	**.357**	**.408**	**.974**

O'Farrell, Robert Arthur (Bob)
HEIGHT: 5'9" THROWS: RIGHT BATS: RIGHT BORN: 10/19/1896 WAUKEGAN, ILLINOIS DIED: 2/20/1988 WAUKEGAN, ILLINOIS POSITIONS PLAYED: C

YEAR	TEAM	GAMES	AB	RUNS	HITS	2B	3B	HR	RBI	BB	IBB	SO	HBP	SH	SF	SB	CS	BA	OBA	SA	FA
1915	ChC-N	2	3	0	1	0	0	0	0	0	—	0	0	0	—	0	0	.333	.333	.333	.667
1916	ChC-N	1	0	0	0	0	0	0	0	0	—	0	0	0	—	0	—	—	—	—	—
1917	ChC-N	3	8	1	3	2	0	0	1	1	—	0	0	0	—	1	—	.375	.444	.625	1.000
1918	ChC-N	52	113	9	32	7	3	1	14	10	—	15	1	1	—	0	—	.283	.347	.425	.974
1919	ChC-N	49	125	11	27	4	2	0	9	7	—	10	0	3	—	2	—	.216	.258	.280	.965
1920	ChC-N	94	270	29	67	11	4	3	19	34	—	23	0	8	—	1	0	.248	.332	.352	.956
1921	ChC-N	96	260	32	65	12	7	4	32	18	—	14	0	3	—	2	0	.250	.299	.396	.967
1922	ChC-N	128	392	68	127	18	8	4	60	79	—	34	1	9	—	5	3	.324	.439	.441	.977
1923	ChC-N	131	452	73	144	25	4	12	84	67	—	38	1	6	—	10	3	.319	.408	.471	.976
1924	ChC-N	71	183	25	44	6	2	3	28	30	—	13	0	8	—	2	0	.240	.347	.344	.984
1925	ChC-N	17	22	2	4	0	1	0	3	2	—	5	0	0	—	0	0	.182	.250	.273	1.000
1925	StL-N	94	317	37	88	13	2	3	32	46	—	26	2	2	—	0	1	.278	.373	.360	.975
1926	StL-N	147	492	63	144	30	9	7	68	61	—	44	0	14	—	1	—	.293	.371	.433	.983
1927	StL-N	61	178	19	47	10	1	0	18	23	—	22	0	2	—	3	—	.264	.348	.331	.979
1928	StL-N	16	52	6	11	1	0	0	4	13	—	9	0	0	—	2	—	.212	.369	.231	.985
1928	NYG-N	75	133	23	26	6	0	2	20	34	—	16	0	8	—	0	—	.195	.359	.286	.988
1929	NYG-N	91	248	35	76	14	3	4	42	28	—	30	3	3	—	3	—	.306	.384	.435	.979
1930	NYG-N	94	249	37	75	16	4	4	54	31	—	21	1	7	—	1	—	.301	.381	.446	.973
1931	NYG-N	85	174	11	39	8	3	1	19	21	—	23	1	1	—	0	—	.224	.311	.322	.980
1932	NYG-N	50	67	7	16	3	0	0	8	11	—	10	1	1	—	0	—	.239	.354	.284	.969
1933	StL-N	55	163	16	39	4	2	2	20	15	—	25	0	1	—	0	—	.239	.303	.325	.970
1934	Cin-N	44	123	10	30	8	3	1	9	11	—	19	0	5	—	0	—	.244	.306	.382	.993
1934	**ChC-N**	**22**	**67**	**3**	**15**	**3**	**0**	**0**	**5**	**3**	**—**	**11**	**0**	**1**	**—**	**0**	**—**	**.224**	**.257**	**.269**	**1.000**
1935	StL-N	14	10	0	0	0	0	0	0	2	—	0	0	0	—	0	—	.000	.167	.000	1.000
Career average		71	195	25	53	10	3	2	26	26	—	19	1	4	—	2	0	.273	.360	.388	.976
Cubs average		**56**	**158**	**21**	**44**	**7**	**3**	**2**	**21**	**21**	**—**	**14**	**0**	**3**	**—**	**2**	**1**	**.279**	**.364**	**.401**	**.972**
Career total		1492	4101	517	1120	201	58	51	549	547	—	408	11	83	—	35	7	.273	.360	.388	.976
Cubs total		**666**	**1895**	**253**	**529**	**88**	**31**	**27**	**255**	**251**	**—**	**163**	**3**	**39**	**—**	**23**	**6**	**.279**	**.364**	**.401**	**.972**

O'Hagen, Harry P. (Hal)

HEIGHT: 6'0" THROWS: — BATS: — BORN: 9/30/1873 WASHINGTON, DISTRICT OF COLUMBIA DIED: 1/14/1913 NEWARK, NEW JERSEY
POSITIONS PLAYED: C, 1B, OF

YEAR	TEAM	GAMES	AB	RUNS	HITS	2B	3B	HR	RBI	BB	IBB	SO	HBP	SH	SF	SB	CS	BA	OBA	SA	FA
1892	Was-N	1	4	1	1	0	0	0	0	0	—	—	2	0	—	0	—	.250	.250	.250	1.000
1902	**ChC-N**	**31**	**108**	**10**	**21**	**1**	**3**	**0**	**10**	**11**	—	—	**0**	**4**	—	**8**	—	**.194**	**.269**	**.259**	**.982**
1902	NYG-N	26	84	5	12	2	1	0	8	2	—	—	0	0	—	3	—	.143	.182	.190	.970
1902	Cle-A	3	13	2	5	2	0	0	1	0	—	—	0	3	—	2	—	.385	.385	.538	1.000
Career average		31	105	9	20	3	2	0	10	7	—	—	1	2	—	7	—	.187	.241	.249	.980
Cubs average		**31**	**108**	**10**	**21**	**1**	**3**	**0**	**10**	**11**	—	—	**0**	**4**	—	**8**	—	**.194**	**.269**	**.259**	**.982**
Career total		61	209	18	39	5	4	0	19	13	—	—	2	7	—	13	—	.187	.241	.249	.980
Cubs total		**31**	**108**	**10**	**21**	**1**	**3**	**0**	**10**	**11**	—	—	**0**	**4**	—	**8**	—	**.194**	**.269**	**.259**	**.982**

O'Neill, John Joseph (Jack)

HEIGHT: 5'10" THROWS: RIGHT BATS: RIGHT BORN: 1/10/1873 GALWAY, IRELAND DIED: 6/25/1935 SCRANTON, PENNSYLVANIA
POSITIONS PLAYED: C, 1B, OF

YEAR	TEAM	GAMES	AB	RUNS	HITS	2B	3B	HR	RBI	BB	IBB	SO	HBP	SH	SF	SB	CS	BA	OBA	SA	FA
1902	StL-N	63	192	13	27	1	1	0	12	13	—	—	5	1	—	2	—	.141	.214	.156	.973
1903	StL-N	75	246	23	58	9	1	0	27	13	—	—	5	5	—	2	—	.236	.288	.280	.972
1904	**ChC-N**	**51**	**168**	**8**	**36**	**5**	**0**	**1**	**19**	**6**	—	—	**4**	**4**	—	**11**	—	**.214**	**.258**	**.262**	**.981**
1905	**ChC-N**	**53**	**172**	**16**	**34**	**4**	**2**	**0**	**12**	**8**	—	—	**11**	**6**	—	**1**	—	**.198**	**.277**	**.244**	**.974**
1906	Bos-N	61	167	14	30	5	1	0	4	12	—	—	2	5	—	6	—	.180	.243	.222	.970
Career average		61	189	15	37	5	1	0	15	10	—	—	5	4	—	4	—	.196	.258	.235	.974
Cubs average		**52**	**170**	**12**	**35**	**5**	**1**	**1**	**16**	**7**	—	—	**8**	**5**	—	**4**	—	**.206**	**.268**	**.253**	**.978**
Career total		303	945	74	185	24	5	1	74	52	—	—	27	21	—	20	—	.196	.258	.235	.974
Cubs total		**104**	**340**	**24**	**70**	**9**	**2**	**1**	**31**	**14**	—	—	**15**	**10**	—	**7**	—	**.206**	**.268**	**.253**	**.978**

Ojeda, Octavio Augie (Augie)

HEIGHT: 5'8" THROWS: RIGHT BATS: BOTH BORN: 12/20/1974 LOS ANGELES, CALIFORNIA POSITIONS PLAYED: 2B, 3B, SS

YEAR	TEAM	GAMES	AB	RUNS	HITS	2B	3B	HR	RBI	BB	IBB	SO	HBP	SH	SF	SB	CS	BA	OBA	SA	FA
2000	**ChC-N**	**28**	**77**	**10**	**17**	**3**	**1**	**2**	**8**	**10**	**1**	**9**	**0**	**1**	**1**	**0**	**1**	**.221**	**.307**	**.364**	**.990**
2001	**ChC-N**	**78**	**144**	**16**	**29**	**5**	**1**	**1**	**12**	**12**	**1**	**20**	**2**	**2**	**2**	**1**	**0**	**.201**	**.269**	**.271**	**.962**
Career average		53	111	13	23	4	1	2	10	11	1	15	1	2	2	1	1	.208	.282	.303	.973
Cubs average		**53**	**111**	**13**	**23**	**4**	**1**	**2**	**10**	**11**	**1**	**15**	**1**	**2**	**2**	**1**	**1**	**.208**	**.282**	**.303**	**.973**
Career total		106	221	26	46	8	2	3	20	22	2	29	2	3	3	1	1	.208	.282	.303	.973
Cubs total		**106**	**221**	**26**	**46**	**8**	**2**	**3**	**20**	**22**	**2**	**29**	**2**	**3**	**3**	**1**	**1**	**.208**	**.282**	**.303**	**.973**

Oliver, Eugene George (Gene)

HEIGHT: 6'2" THROWS: RIGHT BATS: RIGHT BORN: 3/22/1935 MOLINE, ILLINOIS POSITIONS PLAYED: C, 1B, OF

YEAR	TEAM	GAMES	AB	RUNS	HITS	2B	3B	HR	RBI	BB	IBB	SO	HBP	SH	SF	SB	CS	BA	OBA	SA	FA
1959	StL-N	68	172	14	42	9	0	6	28	7	0	41	0	0	2	3	2	.244	.271	.401	.970
1961	StL-N	22	52	8	14	2	0	4	9	6	1	10	2	1	0	0	0	.269	.367	.538	.988
1962	StL-N	122	345	42	89	19	1	14	45	50	4	59	1	1	2	0	2	.258	.352	.441	.991
1963	StL-N	39	102	10	23	4	0	6	18	13	3	19	0	1	2	5	2	.225	.308	.441	.981
1963	Mil-N	95	296	34	74	12	2	11	47	27	1	59	5	0	3	4	4	.250	.320	.416	.982
1964	Mil-N	93	279	45	77	15	1	13	49	27	1	41	1	0	1	3	7	.276	.319	.477	.982
1965	Mil-N	122	392	56	106	20	0	21	58	36	5	61	3	0	1	5	4	.276	.336	.482	.980
1966	Atl-N	76	191	19	37	9	1	8	24	16	3	43	0	1	1	5	4	.194	.255	.377	.991
1967	Atl-N	17	51	8	10	2	0	3	6	6	1	8	0	0	0	2	0	.196	.281	.412	.968
1967	Phi-N	85	263	29	59	16	0	7	34	29	3	56	1	1	4	0	2	.224	.281	.412	.987
1968	Bos-A	16	35	2	5	0	0	0	1	4	1	12	1	0	0	0	0	.143	.250	.143	.984
1968	**ChC-N**	**8**	**11**	**1**	**4**	**0**	**0**	**0**	**1**	**3**	**0**	**2**	**0**	**0**	**0**	**0**	**0**	**.364**	**.500**	**.364**	**1.000**
1969	**ChC-N**	**23**	**27**	**0**	**6**	**3**	**0**	**0**	**0**	**1**	**1**	**9**	**1**	**0**	**0**	**0**	**0**	**.222**	**.276**	**.333**	**1.000**
Career average		79	222	27	55	11	1	9	32	22	2	42	2	1	2	2	2	.246	.315	.427	.984
Cubs average		**16**	**19**	**1**	**5**	**2**	**0**	**0**	**1**	**2**	**1**	**6**	**1**	**0**	**0**	**0**	**0**	**.263**	**.349**	**.342**	**1.000**
Career total		786	2216	268	546	111	5	93	320	215	22	420	15	5	16	24	21	.246	.315	.427	.984
Cubs total		**31**	**38**	**1**	**10**	**3**	**0**	**0**	**1**	**4**	**1**	**11**	**1**	**0**	**0**	**0**	**0**	**.263**	**.349**	**.342**	**1.000**

Oliver, Nathaniel (Nate *or* Pee Wee)
HEIGHT: 5'10" THROWS: RIGHT BATS: RIGHT BORN: 12/13/1940 ST. PETERSBURG, FLORIDA POSITIONS PLAYED: 2B, 3B, SS, OF

YEAR	TEAM	GAMES	AB	RUNS	HITS	2B	3B	HR	RBI	BB	IBB	SO	HBP	SH	SF	SB	CS	BA	OBA	SA	FA
1963	LA-N	65	163	23	39	2	3	1	9	13	0	25	1	0	1	3	4	.239	.298	.307	.962
1964	LA-N	99	321	28	78	9	0	0	21	31	6	57	0	4	1	7	4	.243	.309	.271	.967
1965	LA-N	8	1	3	1	0	0	0	0	0	0	0	0	1	0	0	0	1.000	1.000	1.000	1.000
1966	LA-N	80	119	17	23	2	0	0	3	13	2	17	1	4	1	3	3	.193	.276	.210	.973
1967	LA-N	77	232	18	55	6	2	0	7	13	0	50	2	2	0	3	2	.237	.283	.280	.959
1968	SF-N	36	73	3	13	2	0	0	1	1	0	13	0	2	0	0	1	.178	.189	.205	.892
1969	NYY-A	1	1	0	0	0	0	0	0	0	0	0	0	0	0	0	0	.000	.000	.000	—
1969	**ChC-N**	**44**	**44**	**15**	**7**	**3**	**0**	**1**	**4**	**1**	**0**	**10**	**1**	**3**	**0**	**0**	**1**	**.159**	**.196**	**.295**	**1.000**
Career average		59	136	15	31	3	1	0	6	10	1	25	1	2	0	2	2	.226	.283	.268	.962
Cubs average		**44**	**44**	**15**	**7**	**3**	**0**	**1**	**4**	**1**	**0**	**10**	**1**	**3**	**0**	**0**	**1**	**.159**	**.196**	**.295**	**1.000**
Career total		410	954	107	216	24	5	2	45	72	8	172	5	16	3	17	15	.226	.283	.268	.962
Cubs total		**44**	**44**	**15**	**7**	**3**	**0**	**1**	**4**	**1**	**0**	**10**	**1**	**3**	**0**	**0**	**1**	**.159**	**.196**	**.295**	**1.000**

Olsen, Bernard Charles (Barney)
HEIGHT: 5'11" THROWS: RIGHT BATS: RIGHT BORN: 9/11/1919 EVERETT, MASSACHUSETTS DIED: 3/30/1977 EVERETT, MASSACHUSETTS
POSITIONS PLAYED: OF

YEAR	TEAM	GAMES	AB	RUNS	HITS	2B	3B	HR	RBI	BB	IBB	SO	HBP	SH	SF	SB	CS	BA	OBA	SA	FA
1941	**ChC-N**	**24**	**73**	**13**	**21**	**6**	**1**	**1**	**4**	**4**	**—**	**11**	**0**	**1**	**—**	**0**	**—**	**.288**	**.325**	**.438**	**.947**
Career average		24	73	13	21	6	1	1	4	4	—	11	0	1	—	0	—	.288	.325	.438	.947
Cubs average		**24**	**73**	**13**	**21**	**6**	**1**	**1**	**4**	**4**	**—**	**11**	**0**	**1**	**—**	**0**	**—**	**.288**	**.325**	**.438**	**.947**
Career total		24	73	13	21	6	1	1	4	4	—	11	0	1	—	0	—	.288	.325	.438	.947
Cubs total		**24**	**73**	**13**	**21**	**6**	**1**	**1**	**4**	**4**	**—**	**11**	**0**	**1**	**—**	**0**	**—**	**.288**	**.325**	**.438**	**.947**

Ontiveros, Steven Robert (Steve)
HEIGHT: 6'0" THROWS: RIGHT BATS: BOTH BORN: 10/26/1951 BAKERSFIELD, CALIFORNIA POSITIONS PLAYED: 1B, 3B, OF

YEAR	TEAM	GAMES	AB	RUNS	HITS	2B	3B	HR	RBI	BB	IBB	SO	HBP	SH	SF	SB	CS	BA	OBA	SA	FA
1973	SF-N	24	33	3	8	0	0	1	5	4	0	7	0	0	0	0	0	.242	.324	.333	1.000
1974	SF-N	120	343	45	91	15	1	4	33	57	4	41	3	0	0	0	0	.265	.375	.350	.953
1975	SF-N	108	325	21	94	16	0	3	31	55	4	44	2	2	4	2	0	.289	.391	.366	.928
1976	SF-N	59	74	8	13	3	0	0	5	6	0	11	1	0	1	0	0	.176	.244	.216	.929
1977	**ChC-N**	**156**	**546**	**54**	**163**	**32**	**3**	**10**	**68**	**81**	**4**	**69**	**3**	**2**	**4**	**3**	**3**	**.299**	**.390**	**.423**	**.955**
1978	**ChC-N**	**82**	**276**	**34**	**67**	**14**	**4**	**1**	**22**	**34**	**3**	**33**	**0**	**1**	**5**	**0**	**2**	**.243**	**.321**	**.333**	**.966**
1979	**ChC-N**	**152**	**519**	**58**	**148**	**28**	**2**	**4**	**57**	**58**	**7**	**68**	**7**	**1**	**5**	**0**	**1**	**.285**	**.362**	**.370**	**.942**
1980	**ChC-N**	**31**	**77**	**7**	**16**	**3**	**0**	**1**	**3**	**14**	**1**	**17**	**0**	**0**	**0**	**0**	**0**	**.208**	**.330**	**.286**	**.929**
Career average		92	274	29	75	14	1	3	28	39	3	36	2	1	2	1	1	.274	.365	.366	.949
Cubs average		**105**	**355**	**38**	**99**	**19**	**2**	**4**	**38**	**47**	**4**	**47**	**3**	**1**	**4**	**1**	**2**	**.278**	**.363**	**.379**	**.952**
Career total		732	2193	230	600	111	10	24	224	309	23	290	16	6	19	5	6	.274	.365	.366	.949
Cubs total		**421**	**1418**	**153**	**394**	**77**	**9**	**16**	**150**	**187**	**15**	**187**	**10**	**4**	**14**	**3**	**6**	**.278**	**.363**	**.379**	**.952**

Orie, Kevin Leonardo
HEIGHT: 6'4" THROWS: RIGHT BATS: RIGHT BORN: 9/1/1972 WEST CHESTER, PENNSYLVANIA POSITIONS PLAYED: 1B, 3B, SS

YEAR	TEAM	GAMES	AB	RUNS	HITS	2B	3B	HR	RBI	BB	IBB	SO	HBP	SH	SF	SB	CS	BA	OBA	SA	FA
1997	**ChC-N**	**114**	**364**	**40**	**100**	**23**	**5**	**8**	**44**	**39**	**3**	**57**	**5**	**3**	**4**	**2**	**2**	**.275**	**.350**	**.431**	**.971**
1998	**ChC-N**	**64**	**204**	**24**	**37**	**14**	**0**	**2**	**21**	**18**	**0**	**35**	**3**	**1**	**4**	**1**	**1**	**.181**	**.253**	**.279**	**.966**
1998	Fla-N	48	175	23	46	8	1	6	17	14	2	24	5	1	0	1	0	.263	.335	.423	.939
1999	Fla-N	77	240	26	61	16	0	6	29	22	1	43	3	0	2	1	0	.254	.322	.396	.961
Career average		101	328	38	81	20	2	7	37	31	2	53	5	2	3	2	1	.248	.320	.390	.961
Cubs average		**89**	**284**	**32**	**69**	**19**	**3**	**5**	**33**	**29**	**2**	**46**	**4**	**2**	**4**	**2**	**2**	**.241**	**.315**	**.377**	**.969**
Career total		303	983	113	244	61	6	22	111	93	6	159	16	5	10	5	3	.248	.320	.390	.961
Cubs total		**178**	**568**	**64**	**137**	**37**	**5**	**10**	**65**	**57**	**3**	**92**	**8**	**4**	**8**	**3**	**3**	**.241**	**.315**	**.377**	**.969**

Ortiz, Jose Luis
HEIGHT: 5'9" THROWS: RIGHT BATS: RIGHT BORN: 6/25/1947 PONCE, PUERTO RICO POSITIONS PLAYED: OF

YEAR	TEAM	GAMES	AB	RUNS	HITS	2B	3B	HR	RBI	BB	IBB	SO	HBP	SH	SF	SB	CS	BA	OBA	SA	FA
1969	CWS-A	16	11	0	3	1	0	0	2	1	1	0	0	0	0	0	0	.273	.333	.364	1.000
1970	CWS-A	15	24	4	8	1	0	0	1	2	0	2	1	1	0	1	0	.333	.407	.375	1.000
1971	**ChC-N**	**36**	**88**	**10**	**26**	**7**	**1**	**0**	**3**	**4**	**0**	**10**	**3**	**1**	**0**	**2**	**2**	**.295**	**.347**	**.398**	**1.000**
Career average		22	41	5	12	3	0	0	2	2	0	4	1	1	0	1	1	.301	.358	.390	1.000
Cubs average		**36**	**88**	**10**	**26**	**7**	**1**	**0**	**3**	**4**	**0**	**10**	**3**	**1**	**0**	**2**	**2**	**.295**	**.347**	**.398**	**1.000**
Career total		67	123	14	37	9	1	0	6	7	1	12	4	2	0	3	2	.301	.358	.390	1.000
Cubs total		**36**	**88**	**10**	**26**	**7**	**1**	**0**	**3**	**4**	**0**	**10**	**3**	**1**	**0**	**2**	**2**	**.295**	**.347**	**.398**	**1.000**

Ostrowski, John Thaddeus (Johnny)
HEIGHT: 5'10" THROWS: RIGHT BATS: RIGHT BORN: 10/17/1917 CHICAGO, ILLINOIS DIED: 11/13/1992 CHICAGO, ILLINOIS POSITIONS PLAYED: 2B, 3B, OF

YEAR	TEAM	GAMES	AB	RUNS	HITS	2B	3B	HR	RBI	BB	IBB	SO	HBP	SH	SF	SB	CS	BA	OBA	SA	FA
1943	ChC-N	10	29	2	6	0	1	0	3	3	—	8	1	0	—	0	—	.207	.303	.276	.889
1944	ChC-N	8	13	2	2	1	0	0	2	1	—	4	0	0	—	0	—	.154	.214	.231	.500
1945	ChC-N	7	10	4	3	2	0	0	1	0	—	0	0	0	—	0	—	.300	.300	.500	.750
1946	ChC-N	64	160	20	34	4	2	3	12	20	—	31	0	1	—	0	—	.213	.300	.319	.936
1948	Bos-A	1	1	0	0	0	0	0	0	0	—	1	0	0	—	1	0	.000	.000	.000	—
1949	CWS-A	49	158	19	42	9	4	5	31	15	—	41	1	1	—	4	3	.266	.333	.468	.942
1950	CWS-A	22	49	10	12	2	1	2	2	9	—	8	1	1	—	0	0	.245	.373	.449	1.000
1950	Was-A	55	141	16	32	2	1	4	23	20	—	31	1	1	—	2	0	.227	.327	.340	.947
Career average		31	80	10	19	3	1	2	11	10	—	18	1	1	—	1	0	.234	.321	.376	.939
Cubs average		**22**	**53**	**7**	**11**	**2**	**1**	**1**	**5**	**6**	**—**	**11**	**0**	**0**	**—**	**0**	**—**	**.212**	**.295**	**.316**	**.919**
Career total		216	561	73	131	20	9	14	74	68	—	124	4	4	—	7	3	.234	.321	.376	.939
Cubs total		**89**	**212**	**28**	**45**	**7**	**3**	**3**	**18**	**24**	**—**	**43**	**1**	**1**	**—**	**1**	**—**	**.212**	**.295**	**.316**	**.919**

Otero, Regino Jose (Reggie)
HEIGHT: 6'0" THROWS: RIGHT BATS: LEFT BORN: 9/7/1915 HAVANA, CUBA DIED: 10/21/1988 HIALEAH, FLORIDA POSITIONS PLAYED: 1B

YEAR	TEAM	GAMES	AB	RUNS	HITS	2B	3B	HR	RBI	BB	IBB	SO	HBP	SH	SF	SB	CS	BA	OBA	SA	FA
1945	ChC-N	14	23	1	9	0	0	0	5	2	—	2	0	1	—	0	—	.391	.440	.391	.967
Career average		14	23	1	9	0	0	0	5	2	—	2	0	1	—	0	—	.391	.440	.391	.967
Cubs average		**14**	**23**	**1**	**9**	**0**	**0**	**0**	**5**	**2**	**—**	**2**	**0**	**1**	**—**	**0**	**—**	**.391**	**.440**	**.391**	**.967**
Career total		14	23	1	9	0	0	0	5	2	—	2	0	1	—	0	—	.391	.440	.391	.967
Cubs total		**14**	**23**	**1**	**9**	**0**	**0**	**0**	**5**	**2**	**—**	**2**	**0**	**1**	**—**	**0**	**—**	**.391**	**.440**	**.391**	**.967**

Ott, William Joseph (Billy)
HEIGHT: 6'1" THROWS: RIGHT BATS: BOTH BORN: 11/23/1940 NEW YORK, NEW YORK POSITIONS PLAYED: OF

YEAR	TEAM	GAMES	AB	RUNS	HITS	2B	3B	HR	RBI	BB	IBB	SO	HBP	SH	SF	SB	CS	BA	OBA	SA	FA
1962	ChC-N	12	28	3	4	0	0	1	2	2	0	10	0	0	0	0	0	.143	.200	.250	1.000
1964	ChC-N	20	39	4	7	3	0	0	1	3	0	10	0	1	0	0	1	.179	.238	.256	1.000
Career average		16	34	4	6	2	0	1	2	3	0	10	0	1	0	0	1	.164	.222	.254	1.000
Cubs average		**16**	**34**	**4**	**6**	**2**	**0**	**1**	**2**	**3**	**0**	**10**	**0**	**1**	**0**	**0**	**1**	**.164**	**.222**	**.254**	**1.000**
Career total		32	67	7	11	3	0	1	3	5	0	20	0	1	0	0	1	.164	.222	.254	1.000
Cubs total		**32**	**67**	**7**	**11**	**3**	**0**	**1**	**3**	**5**	**0**	**20**	**0**	**1**	**0**	**0**	**1**	**.164**	**.222**	**.254**	**1.000**

Owen, Dave
HEIGHT: 6'2" THROWS: RIGHT BATS: BOTH BORN: 4/25/1958 CLEBURNE, TEXAS POSITIONS PLAYED: 2B, 3B, SS

YEAR	TEAM	GAMES	AB	RUNS	HITS	2B	3B	HR	RBI	BB	IBB	SO	HBP	SH	SF	SB	CS	BA	OBA	SA	FA
1983	ChC-N	16	22	1	2	0	1	0	2	2	0	7	0	1	1	1	0	.091	.160	.182	1.000
1984	ChC-N	47	93	8	18	2	2	1	10	8	1	15	2	0	1	1	2	.194	.269	.290	.949
1985	ChC-N	22	19	6	7	0	0	0	4	1	0	5	0	0	0	1	1	.368	.400	.368	.909
1988	KC-A	7	5	0	0	0	0	0	0	0	0	3	0	0	0	0	0	.000	.000	.000	.941
Career average		23	35	4	7	1	1	0	4	3	0	8	1	0	1	1	1	.194	.260	.273	.954
Cubs average		28	45	5	9	1	1	0	5	4	0	9	1	0	1	1	1	.201	.268	.284	.955
Career total		92	139	15	27	2	3	1	16	11	1	30	2	1	2	3	3	.194	.260	.273	.954
Cubs total		85	134	15	27	2	3	1	16	11	1	27	2	1	2	3	3	.201	.268	.284	.955

Owen, Arnold Malcolm (Mickey)
HEIGHT: 5'10" THROWS: RIGHT BATS: RIGHT BORN: 4/4/1916 NIXA, MISSOURI POSITIONS PLAYED: C, 2B, 3B, SS

YEAR	TEAM	GAMES	AB	RUNS	HITS	2B	3B	HR	RBI	BB	IBB	SO	HBP	SH	SF	SB	CS	BA	OBA	SA	FA
1937	StL-N	80	234	17	54	4	2	0	20	15	—	13	0	4	—	1	—	.231	.277	.265	.974
1938	StL-N	122	397	45	106	25	2	4	36	32	—	14	2	2	—	2	—	.267	.325	.370	.980
1939	StL-N	131	344	32	89	18	2	3	35	43	—	28	2	13	—	6	—	.259	.344	.349	.982
1940	StL-N	117	307	27	81	16	2	0	27	34	—	13	2	6	—	4	—	.264	.341	.329	.980
1941	Bro-N	128	386	32	89	15	2	1	44	34	—	14	2	15	—	1	—	.231	.296	.288	.995
1942	Bro-N	133	421	53	109	16	3	0	44	44	—	17	1	18	—	10	—	.259	.330	.311	.987
1943	Bro-N	106	365	31	95	11	2	0	54	25	—	15	1	4	—	4	2	.260	.309	.301	.986
1944	Bro-N	130	461	43	126	20	3	1	42	36	—	17	0	6	—	4	0	.273	.326	.336	.979
1945	Bro-N	24	84	5	24	9	0	0	11	10	—	2	1	3	—	0	—	.286	.368	.393	.963
1949	**ChC-N**	**62**	**198**	**15**	**54**	**9**	**3**	**2**	**18**	**12**	—	**13**	**1**	**3**	—	**1**	—	**.243**	**.282**	**.309**	**.978**
1950	**ChC-N**	**86**	**259**	**22**	**63**	**11**	**0**	**2**	**21**	**13**	—	**16**	**1**	**4**	—	**2**	—	**.184**	**.292**	**.232**	**.969**
1951	**ChC-N**	**58**	**125**	**10**	**23**	**6**	**0**	**0**	**15**	**19**	—	**13**	**0**	**2**	—	**1**	**0**	**.235**	**.309**	**.324**	**.989**
1954	Bos-A	32	68	6	16	3	0	1	11	9	—	6	0	0	4	0	1	.255	.318	.322	.981
Career average		93	281	26	71	13	2	1	29	25	—	14	1	6	0	3	0	.255	.318	.322	.981
Cubs average		69	194	16	47	9	1	1	18	15	—	14	1	3	—	1	0	.241	.296	.316	.973
Career total		1209	3649	338	929	163	21	14	378	326	—	181	13	80	4	36	3	.255	.318	.322	.981
Cubs total		206	582	47	140	26	3	4	54	44	—	42	2	9	—	4	0	.241	.296	.316	.973

Pafko, Andrew (Andy *or* Handy Andy *or* Pruschka)
HEIGHT: 6'0" THROWS: RIGHT BATS: RIGHT BORN: 2/25/1921 BOYCEVILLE, WISCONSIN POSITIONS PLAYED: 3B, OF

YEAR	TEAM	GAMES	AB	RUNS	HITS	2B	3B	HR	RBI	BB	IBB	SO	HBP	SH	SF	SB	CS	BA	OBA	SA	FA
1943	**ChC-N**	**13**	**58**	**7**	**22**	**3**	**0**	**0**	**10**	**2**	—	**5**	**0**	**0**	—	**1**	—	**.379**	**.400**	**.431**	**1.000**
1944	**ChC-N**	**128**	**469**	**47**	**126**	**16**	**2**	**6**	**62**	**28**	—	**23**	**4**	**11**	—	**2**	—	**.269**	**.315**	**.350**	**.983**
1945	**ChC-N**	**144**	**534**	**64**	**159**	**24**	**12**	**12**	**110**	**45**	—	**36**	**8**	**21**	—	**5**	—	**.298**	**.366**	**.380**	**.978**
1946	**ChC-N**	**65**	**234**	**18**	**66**	**6**	**4**	**3**	**39**	**27**	—	**15**	**4**	**8**	—	**4**	—	**.282**	**.366**	**.454**	**.985**
1947	**ChC-N**	**129**	**513**	**68**	**155**	**25**	**7**	**13**	**66**	**31**	—	**39**	**3**	**3**	—	**4**	—	**.302**	**.346**	**.516**	**.938**
1948	**ChC-N**	**142**	**548**	**82**	**171**	**30**	**2**	**26**	**101**	**50**	—	**50**	**5**	**3**	—	**3**	—	**.312**	**.375**	**.591**	**.966**
1949	**ChC-N**	**144**	**519**	**79**	**146**	**29**	**2**	**18**	**69**	**63**	—	**33**	**9**	**1**	—	**4**	—	**.281**	**.369**	**.449**	**.978**
1950	**ChC-N**	**146**	**514**	**95**	**156**	**24**	**8**	**36**	**92**	**69**	—	**32**	**11**	**1**	—	**4**	—	**.304**	**.397**	**.528**	**.992**
1951	**ChC-N**	**49**	**178**	**26**	**47**	**5**	**3**	**12**	**35**	**17**	—	**10**	**4**	**0**	—	**1**	**1**	**.264**	**.350**	**.484**	**.993**
1951	Bro-N	84	277	42	69	11	0	18	58	35	—	27	8	0	—	4	3	.249	.366	.439	.979
1952	Bro-N	150	551	76	158	17	5	19	85	64	—	48	5	4	—	2	1	.287	.347	.455	.976
1953	Mil-N	140	516	70	153	23	4	17	72	37	—	33	3	12	—	1	2	.297	.335	.427	.969
1954	Mil-N	138	510	61	146	22	4	14	69	37	—	36	4	12	7	1	2	.286	.293	.377	.978
1955	Mil-N	86	252	29	67	3	5	5	34	10	1	23	4	1	3	0	0	.266	.330	.376	.978
1956	Mil-N	45	93	15	24	5	0	2	9	10	0	13	0	1	3	0	0	.258	.308	.423	.982
1957	Mil-N	83	220	31	61	6	1	8	27	10	2	22	1	1	2	0	0	.277	.306	.348	1.000
1958	Mil-N	95	164	17	39	7	1	3	23	15	3	17	2	1	0	0	0	.238	.293	.324	.978
1959	Mil-N	71	142	17	31	8	2	1	15	14	1	15	1	1	0	0	0	.218	.293	.324	.978
Career average		109	370	50	106	16	4	13	57	33	0	28	4	5	1	2	1	.285	.350	.449	.976
Cubs average		107	396	54	116	18	4	14	65	37	—	27	5	5	—	3	0	.294	.362	.468	.974
Career total		1852	6292	844	1796	264	62	213	976	561	7	477	76	82	15	38	13	.285	.350	.449	.976
Cubs total		960	3567	486	1048	162	40	126	584	332	—	243	48	48	—	28	1	.294	.362	.468	.974

Andrew (Andy) "Handy Andy," "Pruschka" Pafko, of-3b, 1943–59

This Cubs four-time All-Star was perhaps the best defensive center fielder in Cubs history. He could also hit for power.

Pafko was born on February 25, 1921, in Boyceville, Wisconsin. Pafko made the big team in 1943, playing 13 games in September and hitting a more-than-respectable .379. The next season, Pafko was the starting center fielder on Opening Day.

He was a solid hitter that year, with a .269 average and 16 doubles, but the Cubs loved Pafko's arm in center field. In 1944 Pafko led the National League with an outstanding 24 assists, second only to another Cub only one other time—Arnold "Jigger" Statz, who accomplished 26 in 1923.

More impressive, Pafko handled an average of 3.0 chances per game, the mark of an outfielder with exceptional range. (Joe DiMaggio only did it three times in his career, and Tris Speaker, considered one of the best defensive outfielders ever, did it five times.)

In 1945 Pafko put it all together, leading the league in fielding percentage with a .995 mark,

batting .298 and making 110 RBIs as the Cubs won the pennant.

Pafko was limited by injuries to only 65 games in 1946, but in 1947 he began a run as one of the Cubs' most consistent players. He hit over .300 three of the next four years, hit 26 homers in 1948 and a career-high 36 dingers in 1950.

He made the All-Star team four consecutive years. Three of those seasons, he was an All-Star outfielder. But in 1948 he made the team as a third baseman, a position he also played with the Cubs. Then-manager Charlie Grimm called Pafko "Handy Andy" for his versatility.

Despite this, the Cubs opted to trade the extremely popular Pafko to the Dodgers midway through the 1951 season. In return, Chicago got, well, not much. Pafko went on to help the Dodgers to the 1951 and 1952 pennants. Later, he was traded to Milwaukee, where he was platooned on the Braves' world champions of 1957 and National League champions of 1958.

Pafko retired in 1959. He coached for three years in the Braves organization, from 1960 to 1962.

Pagel, Karl Douglas

HEIGHT: 6'2"   THROWS: LEFT   BATS: LEFT   BORN: 3/29/1955 MADISON, WISCONSIN   POSITIONS PLAYED: 1B, OF

YEAR	TEAM	GAMES	AB	RUNS	HITS	2B	3B	HR	RBI	BB	IBB	SO	HBP	SH	SF	SB	CS	BA	OBA	SA	FA
1978	ChC-N	2	2	0	0	0	0	0	0	0	0	2	0	0	0	0	0	.000	.000	.000	—
1979	ChC-N	1	1	0	0	0	0	0	0	0	0	1	0	0	0	0	0	.000	.000	.000	—
1981	Cle-A	14	15	3	4	0	2	1	4	4	1	1	0	0	0	0	0	.267	.421	.733	1.000
1982	Cle-A	23	18	3	3	0	0	0	2	7	1	11	0	0	0	0	0	.167	.400	.167	.970
1983	Cle-A	8	20	1	6	0	0	0	1	0	0	5	0	0	0	0	0	.300	.300	.300	.000
Career average		10	11	1	3	0	0	0	1	2	0	4	0	0	0	0	0	.232	.358	.357	.971
Cubs average		2	2	0	0	0	0	0	0	0	0	2	0	0	0	0	0	.000	.000	.000	—
Career total		48	56	7	13	0	2	1	7	11	2	20	0	0	0	0	0	.232	.358	.357	.971
Cubs total		3	3	0	0	0	0	0	0	0	0	3	0	0	0	0	0	.000	.000	.000	—

Palmeiro, Rafael (Raffy)
HEIGHT: 6'0"   THROWS: LEFT   BATS: LEFT   BORN: 9/24/1964 HAVANA, CUBA   POSITIONS PLAYED: 1B, OF

YEAR	TEAM	GAMES	AB	RUNS	HITS	2B	3B	HR	RBI	BB	IBB	SO	HBP	SH	SF	SB	CS	BA	OBA	SA	FA
1986	ChC-N	22	73	9	18	4	0	3	12	4	0	6	1	0	0	1	1	.247	.295	.425	.900
1987	ChC-N	84	221	32	61	15	1	14	30	20	1	26	1	0	2	2	2	.276	.336	.543	.995
1988	ChC-N	152	580	75	178	41	5	8	53	38	6	34	3	2	6	12	2	.307	.349	.436	.985
1989	Tex-A	156	559	76	154	23	4	8	64	63	3	48	6	2	2	4	3	.275	.354	.374	.991
1990	Tex-A	154	598	72	191	35	6	14	89	40	6	59	3	2	8	3	3	.319	.361	.468	.995
1991	Tex-A	159	631	115	203	49	3	26	88	68	10	72	6	2	7	4	3	.322	.389	.532	.992
1992	Tex-A	159	608	84	163	27	4	22	85	72	8	83	10	5	6	2	3	.268	.352	.434	.995
1993	Tex-A	160	597	124	176	40	2	37	105	73	22	85	5	2	9	22	3	.295	.371	.554	.997
1994	Bal-A	111	436	82	139	32	0	23	76	54	1	63	2	0	6	7	3	.319	.392	.550	.996
1995	Bal-A	143	554	89	172	30	2	39	104	62	5	65	3	0	5	3	1	.310	.380	.583	.997
1996	Bal-A	162	626	110	181	40	2	39	142	95	12	96	3	0	8	8	0	.289	.381	.546	.995
1997	Bal-A	158	614	95	156	24	2	38	110	67	7	109	5	0	6	5	2	.254	.329	.485	.993
1998	Bal-A	162	619	98	183	36	1	43	121	79	8	91	7	0	4	11	7	.296	.379	.565	.994
1999	Tex-A	158	565	96	183	30	1	47	148	97	14	69	3	0	9	2	4	.324	.420	.630	.996
2000	Tex-A	158	565	102	163	29	3	39	120	103	17	77	3	0	7	2	1	.288	.397	.558	.995
2001	Tex-A	160	600	98	164	33	0	47	123	101	8	90	7	0	6	1	1	.273	.381	.563	.992
Career average		141	528	85	155	31	2	28	92	65	8	67	4	1	6	6	2	.294	.372	.519	.994
Cubs average		**86**	**291**	**39**	**86**	**20**	**2**	**8**	**32**	**21**	**2**	**22**	**2**	**1**	**3**	**5**	**2**	**.294**	**.341**	**.462**	**.982**
Career total		2258	8446	1357	2485	488	36	447	1470	1036	128	1073	68	15	91	89	39	.294	.372	.519	.994
Cubs total		**258**	**874**	**116**	**257**	**60**	**6**	**25**	**95**	**62**	**7**	**66**	**5**	**2**	**8**	**15**	**5**	**.294**	**.341**	**.462**	**.982**

Pappas, Erik Daniel
HEIGHT: 6'0"   THROWS: RIGHT   BATS: RIGHT   BORN: 4/25/1966 CHICAGO, ILLINOIS   POSITIONS PLAYED: C, 1B, OF

YEAR	TEAM	GAMES	AB	RUNS	HITS	2B	3B	HR	RBI	BB	IBB	SO	HBP	SH	SF	SB	CS	BA	OBA	SA	FA
1991	ChC-N	7	17	1	3	0	0	0	2	1	0	5	0	0	0	0	0	.176	.222	.176	1.000
1993	StL-N	82	228	25	63	12	0	1	28	35	2	35	0	0	3	1	3	.276	.368	.342	.984
1994	StL-N	15	44	8	4	1	0	0	5	10	0	13	1	0	3	0	0	.091	.259	.114	.955
Career average		35	96	11	23	4	0	0	12	15	1	18	0	0	2	0	1	.242	.342	.298	.980
Cubs average		**7**	**17**	**1**	**3**	**0**	**0**	**0**	**2**	**1**	**0**	**5**	**0**	**0**	**0**	**0**	**0**	**.176**	**.222**	**.176**	**1.000**
Career total		104	289	34	70	13	0	1	35	46	2	53	1	0	6	1	3	.242	.342	.298	.980
Cubs total		**7**	**17**	**1**	**3**	**0**	**0**	**0**	**2**	**1**	**0**	**5**	**0**	**0**	**0**	**0**	**0**	**.176**	**.222**	**.176**	**1.000**

Parent, Mark Alan
HEIGHT: 6'5"   THROWS: RIGHT   BATS: RIGHT   BORN: 9/16/1961 ASHLAND, OREGON   POSITIONS PLAYED: C, 1B

YEAR	TEAM	GAMES	AB	RUNS	HITS	2B	3B	HR	RBI	BB	IBB	SO	HBP	SH	SF	SB	CS	BA	OBA	SA	FA
1986	SD-N	8	14	1	2	0	0	0	0	1	0	3	0	0	0	0	0	.143	.200	.143	.889
1987	SD-N	12	25	0	2	0	0	0	2	0	0	9	0	0	0	0	0	.080	.080	.080	1.000
1988	SD-N	41	118	9	23	3	0	6	15	6	0	23	0	0	1	0	0	.195	.232	.373	.986
1989	SD-N	52	141	12	27	4	0	7	21	8	2	34	0	1	4	1	0	.191	.229	.369	1.000
1990	SD-N	65	189	13	42	11	0	3	16	16	3	29	0	3	0	1	0	.222	.283	.328	.992
1991	Tex-A	3	1	0	0	0	0	0	0	0	0	1	0	0	0	0	0	.000	.000	.000	1.000
1992	Bal-A	17	34	4	8	1	0	2	4	3	0	7	1	2	0	0	0	.235	.316	.441	.988
1993	Bal-A	22	54	7	14	2	0	4	12	3	0	14	0	3	1	0	0	.259	.293	.519	.989
1994	**ChC-N**	**44**	**99**	**8**	**26**	**4**	**0**	**3**	**16**	**13**	**1**	**24**	**1**	**1**	**2**	**0**	**1**	**.263**	**.348**	**.394**	**.976**
1995	Pit-N	69	233	25	54	9	0	15	33	23	2	62	0	1	0	0	0	.232	.301	.464	.990
1995	**ChC-N**	**12**	**32**	**5**	**8**	**2**	**0**	**3**	**5**	**3**	**0**	**7**	**0**	**0**	**0**	**0**	**0**	**.250**	**.314**	**.594**	**1.000**
1996	Det-A	38	104	13	25	6	0	7	17	3	0	27	0	0	1	0	0	.240	.259	.500	.994
1996	Bal-A	18	33	4	6	1	0	2	6	2	0	10	0	1	0	0	0	.182	.229	.394	.987
1997	Phi-N	39	113	4	17	3	0	0	8	7	0	39	0	0	1	0	1	.150	.198	.177	.996
1998	Phi-N	34	113	7	25	4	0	1	13	10	0	30	0	0	3	1	1	.221	.278	.283	.987
Career average		36	100	9	21	4	0	4	13	8	1	25	0	1	1	0	0	.214	.268	.375	.990
Cubs average		**28**	**66**	**7**	**17**	**3**	**0**	**3**	**11**	**8**	**1**	**16**	**1**	**1**	**1**	**0**	**1**	**.260**	**.340**	**.443**	**.982**
Career total		474	1303	112	279	50	0	53	168	98	8	319	2	12	13	3	3	.214	.268	.375	.990
Cubs total		**56**	**131**	**13**	**34**	**6**	**0**	**6**	**21**	**16**	**1**	**31**	**1**	**1**	**2**	**0**	**1**	**.260**	**.340**	**.443**	**.982**

Parrott, Thomas William (Tom or Tacky Tom)
HEIGHT: 5'10"   THROWS: RIGHT   BATS: RIGHT   BORN: 4/10/1868 PORTLAND, OREGON   DIED: 1/1/1932 DUNDEE, OREGON
POSITIONS PLAYED: P, 1B, 2B, 3B, SS, OF

YEAR	TEAM	GAMES	AB	RUNS	HITS	2B	3B	HR	RBI	BB	IBB	SO	HBP	SH	SF	SB	CS	BA	OBA	SA	FA
1893	ChN-N	7	27	4	7	1	0	0	3	1	—	2	0	—	—	0	—	.259	.286	.296	.929
1893	Cin-N	24	68	5	13	1	1	1	9	1	—	9	0	—	—	0	—	.191	.203	.279	.915
1894	Cin-N	68	229	51	74	12	6	4	40	17	—	10	1	1	—	4	—	.323	.372	.480	.913
1895	Cin-N	64	201	35	69	13	7	3	41	11	—	8	0	6	—	10	—	.343	.377	.522	.944
1896	StL-N	118	474	62	138	13	12	7	70	11	—	24	0	14	—	12	—	.291	.307	.414	.953
Career average		70	250	39	75	10	7	4	41	10	—	13	0	5	—	7	—	.301	.329	.438	.937
Cubs average		**7**	**27**	**4**	**7**	**1**	**0**	**0**	**3**	**1**	**—**	**2**	**0**	**—**	**—**	**0**	**—**	**.259**	**.286**	**.296**	**.929**
Career total		281	999	157	301	40	26	15	163	41	—	53	1	21	—	26	—	.301	.329	.438	.937
Cubs total		**7**	**27**	**4**	**7**	**1**	**0**	**0**	**3**	**1**	**—**	**2**	**0**	**—**	**—**	**0**	**—**	**.259**	**.286**	**.296**	**.929**

Parrott, Walter Edward (Jiggs)
HEIGHT: 5'11"   THROWS: —   BATS: —   BORN: 7/14/1871 PORTLAND, OREGON   DIED: 4/16/1898 PHOENIX, ARIZONA   POSITIONS PLAYED: 1B, 2B, 3B, SS, OF

YEAR	TEAM	GAMES	AB	RUNS	HITS	2B	3B	HR	RBI	BB	IBB	SO	HBP	SH	SF	SB	CS	BA	OBA	SA	FA
1892	ChN-N	78	333	38	67	8	5	2	22	8	—	30	1	—	—	7	—	.201	.222	.273	.891
1893	ChN-N	110	455	54	111	10	9	1	65	13	—	25	1	—	—	25	—	.244	.267	.312	.907
1894	ChN-N	124	517	82	128	17	9	3	64	16	—	35	3	9	—	30	—	.248	.274	.333	.932
1895	ChN-N	3	4	0	1	0	0	0	0	0	—	0	0	1	—	0	—	.250	.250	.250	1.000
Career average		79	327	44	77	9	6	2	38	9	—	23	1	3	—	16	—	.235	.258	.310	.915
Cubs average		**79**	**327**	**44**	**77**	**9**	**6**	**2**	**38**	**9**	**—**	**23**	**1**	**3**	**—**	**16**	**—**	**.235**	**.258**	**.310**	**.915**
Career total		315	1309	174	307	35	23	6	151	37	—	90	5	10	—	62	—	.235	.258	.310	.915
Cubs total		**315**	**1309**	**174**	**307**	**35**	**23**	**6**	**151**	**37**	**—**	**90**	**5**	**10**	**—**	**62**	**—**	**.235**	**.258**	**.310**	**.915**

Paskert, George Henry (Dode)
HEIGHT: 5'11"   THROWS: RIGHT   BATS: RIGHT   BORN: 8/28/1881 CLEVELAND, OHIO   DIED: 2/12/1959 CLEVELAND, OHIO
POSITIONS PLAYED: 1B, 2B, 3B, SS, OF

YEAR	TEAM	GAMES	AB	RUNS	HITS	2B	3B	HR	RBI	BB	IBB	SO	HBP	SH	SF	SB	CS	BA	OBA	SA	FA
1907	Cin-N	16	50	10	14	4	0	1	8	2	—	—	2	0	—	2	—	.280	.333	.420	.973
1908	Cin-N	118	395	40	96	14	4	1	36	27	—	—	4	16	—	25	—	.243	.298	.306	.953
1909	Cin-N	104	322	49	81	7	4	0	33	34	—	—	2	11	—	23	—	.252	.327	.298	.973
1910	Cin-N	144	506	63	152	21	5	2	46	70	—	60	3	16	—	51	—	.300	.389	.374	.954
1911	Phi-N	153	560	96	153	18	5	4	47	70	—	70	4	30	—	28	—	.273	.358	.345	.979
1912	Phi-N	145	540	102	170	37	5	2	43	91	—	67	7	11	—	36	—	.315	.420	.413	.966
1913	Phi-N	124	454	83	119	21	9	4	29	65	—	69	3	19	—	12	—	.262	.358	.374	.972
1914	Phi-N	132	451	59	119	25	6	3	44	56	—	68	3	19	—	23	—	.264	.349	.366	.949
1915	Phi-N	109	328	51	80	17	4	3	39	35	—	38	1	28	—	9	6	.244	.319	.348	.972
1916	Phi-N	149	555	82	155	30	7	8	46	54	—	76	3	12	—	22	21	.279	.346	.402	.983
1917	Phi-N	141	546	78	137	27	11	4	43	62	—	63	3	9	—	19	—	.251	.331	.363	.984
1918	ChC-N	127	461	69	132	24	3	3	59	53	—	49	2	23	—	20	—	.286	.362	.371	.972
1919	ChC-N	88	270	21	53	11	3	2	29	28	—	33	1	10	—	7	—	.196	.274	.281	.969
1920	ChC-N	139	487	57	136	22	10	5	71	64	—	58	3	18	—	16	14	.279	.366	.396	.956
1921	Cin-N	27	92	8	16	1	1	0	4	4	—	8	0	2	—	0	2	.174	.208	.207	.984
Career average		114	401	58	108	19	5	3	38	48	—	44	3	15	—	20	3	.268	.350	.361	.968
Cubs average		**118**	**406**	**49**	**107**	**19**	**5**	**3**	**53**	**48**	**—**	**47**	**2**	**17**	**—**	**14**	**5**	**.264**	**.345**	**.361**	**.965**
Career total		1716	6017	868	1613	279	77	42	577	715	—	659	41	224	—	293	43	.268	.350	.361	.968
Cubs total		**354**	**1218**	**147**	**321**	**57**	**16**	**10**	**159**	**145**	**—**	**140**	**6**	**51**	**—**	**43**	**14**	**.264**	**.345**	**.361**	**.965**

Patterson, Donald Corey (Corey)
HEIGHT: 5'9"   THROWS: RIGHT   BATS: LEFT   BORN: 8/13/1979 ATLANTA, GEORGIA   POSITIONS PLAYED: OF

YEAR	TEAM	GAMES	AB	RUNS	HITS	2B	3B	HR	RBI	BB	IBB	SO	HBP	SH	SF	SB	CS	BA	OBA	SA	FA
2000	ChC-N	11	42	9	7	1	0	2	2	3	0	14	1	1	0	1	1	.167	.239	.333	.963
2001	ChC-N	59	131	26	29	3	0	4	14	6	0	33	3	2	3	4	0	.221	.266	.336	.976
Career average		35	87	18	18	2	0	3	8	5	0	24	2	2	2	3	1	.208	.259	.335	.973
Cubs average		**35**	**87**	**18**	**18**	**2**	**0**	**3**	**8**	**5**	**0**	**24**	**2**	**2**	**2**	**3**	**1**	**.208**	**.259**	**.335**	**.973**
Career total		70	173	35	36	4	0	6	16	9	0	47	4	3	3	5	1	.208	.259	.335	.973
Cubs total		**70**	**173**	**35**	**36**	**4**	**0**	**6**	**16**	**9**	**0**	**47**	**4**	**3**	**3**	**5**	**1**	**.208**	**.259**	**.335**	**.973**

Pawelek, Theodore John (Ted *or* Porky)
HEIGHT: 5'10" THROWS: RIGHT BATS: LEFT BORN: 8/15/1919 CHICAGO HEIGHTS, ILLINOIS DIED: 2/12/1964 CHICAGO HEIGHTS, ILLINOIS
POSITIONS PLAYED: C

YEAR	TEAM	GAMES	AB	RUNS	HITS	2B	3B	HR	RBI	BB	IBB	SO	HBP	SH	SF	SB	CS	BA	OBA	SA	FA
1946	ChC-N	4	4	0	1	1	0	0	0	0	—	0	0	0	—	0	—	.250	.250	.500	—
Career average		4	4	0	1	1	0	0	0	0	—	0	0	0	—	0	—	.250	.250	.500	—
Cubs average		**4**	**4**	**0**	**1**	**1**	**0**	**0**	**0**	**0**	**—**	**0**	**0**	**0**	**—**	**0**	**—**	**.250**	**.250**	**.500**	**—**
Career total		4	4	0	1	1	0	0	0	0	—	0	0	0	—	0	—	.250	.250	.500	—
Cubs total		**4**	**4**	**0**	**1**	**1**	**0**	**0**	**0**	**0**	**—**	**0**	**0**	**0**	**—**	**0**	**—**	**.250**	**.250**	**.500**	**—**

Pechous, Charles Edward (Charlie)
HEIGHT: 6'0" THROWS: RIGHT BATS: RIGHT BORN: 10/5/1896 CHICAGO, ILLINOIS DIED: 9/13/1980 KENOSHA, WISCONSIN POSITIONS PLAYED: 3B, SS

YEAR	TEAM	GAMES	AB	RUNS	HITS	2B	3B	HR	RBI	BB	IBB	SO	HBP	SH	SF	SB	CS	BA	OBA	SA	FA
1915	Chi-F	18	51	4	9	3	0	0	4	4	—	15	0	5	—	1	—	.176	.236	.235	.938
1916	ChC-N	22	69	5	10	1	1	0	4	3	—	21	0	2	—	1	—	.145	.181	.188	.940
1917	ChC-N	13	41	2	10	0	0	0	1	2	—	9	1	0	—	1	—	.244	.295	.244	.913
Career average		18	54	4	10	1	0	0	3	3	—	15	0	2	—	1	—	.180	.228	.217	.932
Cubs average		**18**	**55**	**4**	**10**	**1**	**1**	**0**	**3**	**3**	**—**	**15**	**1**	**1**	**—**	**1**	**—**	**.182**	**.224**	**.209**	**.930**
Career total		53	161	11	29	4	1	0	9	9	—	45	1	7	—	3	—	.180	.228	.217	.932
Cubs total		**35**	**110**	**7**	**20**	**1**	**1**	**0**	**5**	**5**	**—**	**30**	**1**	**2**	**—**	**2**	**—**	**.182**	**.224**	**.209**	**.930**

Pedre, Jorge Enrique
HEIGHT: 5'11" THROWS: RIGHT BATS: RIGHT BORN: 10/12/1966 CULVER CITY, CALIFORNIA POSITIONS PLAYED: C, 1B

YEAR	TEAM	GAMES	AB	RUNS	HITS	2B	3B	HR	RBI	BB	IBB	SO	HBP	SH	SF	SB	CS	BA	OBA	SA	FA
1991	KC-A	10	19	2	5	1	1	0	3	3	0	5	0	0	0	0	0	.263	.364	.421	.975
1992	ChC-N	4	4	0	0	0	0	0	0	0	0	1	0	0	0	0	0	.000	.000	.000	1.000
Career average		7	12	1	3	1	1	0	2	2	0	3	0	0	0	0	0	.217	.308	.348	.977
Cubs average		**4**	**4**	**0**	**0**	**0**	**0**	**0**	**0**	**0**	**0**	**1**	**0**	**0**	**0**	**0**	**0**	**.000**	**.000**	**.000**	**1.000**
Career total		14	23	2	5	1	1	0	3	3	0	6	0	0	0	0	0	.217	.308	.348	.977
Cubs total		**4**	**4**	**0**	**0**	**0**	**0**	**0**	**0**	**0**	**0**	**1**	**0**	**0**	**0**	**0**	**0**	**.000**	**.000**	**.000**	**1.000**

Pedroes, Charles P. (Chick)
HEIGHT: — THROWS: — BATS: — BORN: 10/27/1869 CHICAGO, ILLINOIS DIED: 8/6/1927 CHICAGO, ILLINOIS POSITIONS PLAYED: OF

YEAR	TEAM	GAMES	AB	RUNS	HITS	2B	3B	HR	RBI	BB	IBB	SO	HBP	SH	SF	SB	CS	BA	OBA	SA	FA
1902	ChC-N	2	6	0	0	0	0	0	0	0	—	—	0	0	—	0	—	.000	.000	.000	1.000
Career average		2	6	0	0	0	0	0	0	0	—	—	0	0	—	0	—	.000	.000	.000	1.000
Cubs average		**2**	**6**	**0**	**0**	**0**	**0**	**0**	**0**	**0**	**—**	**—**	**0**	**0**	**—**	**0**	**—**	**.000**	**.000**	**.000**	**1.000**
Career total		2	6	0	0	0	0	0	0	0	—	—	0	0	—	0	—	.000	.000	.000	1.000
Cubs total		**2**	**6**	**0**	**0**	**0**	**0**	**0**	**0**	**0**	**—**	**—**	**0**	**0**	**—**	**0**	**—**	**.000**	**.000**	**.000**	**1.000**

Pena, Roberto Cesar (Baby)
HEIGHT: 5'8" THROWS: RIGHT BATS: RIGHT BORN: 4/17/1937 SANTO DOMINGO, DOMINICAN REPUBLIC DIED: 7/23/1982 SANTIAGO, DOMINICAN REPUBLIC
POSITIONS PLAYED: 1B, 2B, 3B, SS

YEAR	TEAM	GAMES	AB	RUNS	HITS	2B	3B	HR	RBI	BB	IBB	SO	HBP	SH	SF	SB	CS	BA	OBA	SA	FA
1965	**ChC-N**	**51**	**170**	**17**	**37**	**5**	**1**	**2**	**12**	**16**	**4**	**19**	**2**	**3**	**1**	**1**	**2**	**.218**	**.291**	**.294**	**.930**
1966	**ChC-N**	**6**	**17**	**0**	**3**	**2**	**0**	**0**	**1**	**0**	**0**	**4**	**0**	**0**	**0**	**0**	**0**	**.176**	**.176**	**.294**	**.957**
1968	Phi-N	138	500	56	130	13	2	1	38	34	2	63	2	6	4	3	5	.260	.307	.300	.954
1969	SD-N	139	472	44	118	16	3	4	30	21	0	63	3	4	1	0	3	.250	.286	.322	.978
1970	Oak-A	19	58	4	15	1	0	0	3	3	0	4	0	1	0	1	1	.259	.295	.276	.922
1970	Mil-A	121	416	36	99	19	1	3	42	25	4	45	2	6	4	3	5	.238	.282	.310	.982
1971	Mil-A	113	274	17	65	9	3	3	28	15	3	37	1	3	0	2	1	.237	.279	.325	.990

(continued)

(continued)

	GAMES	AB	RUNS	HITS	2B	3B	HR	RBI	BB	IBB	SO	HBP	SH	SF	SB	CS	BA	OBA	SA	FA
Career average	98	318	29	78	11	2	2	26	19	2	39	2	4	2	2	3	.245	.290	.310	.968
Cubs average	**29**	**94**	**9**	**20**	**4**	**1**	**1**	**7**	**8**	**2**	**12**	**1**	**2**	**1**	**1**	**1**	**.214**	**.282**	**.294**	**.932**
Career total	587	1907	174	467	65	10	13	154	114	13	235	10	23	10	10	17	.245	.290	.310	.968
Cubs total	**57**	**187**	**17**	**40**	**7**	**1**	**2**	**13**	**16**	**4**	**23**	**2**	**3**	**1**	**1**	**2**	**.214**	**.282**	**.294**	**.932**

Pepitone, Joseph Anthony (Joe or Pepi)

HEIGHT: 6'2"   THROWS: LEFT   BATS: LEFT   BORN: 10/9/1940 BROOKLYN, NEW YORK   POSITIONS PLAYED: 1B, OF

YEAR	TEAM	GAMES	AB	RUNS	HITS	2B	3B	HR	RBI	BB	IBB	SO	HBP	SH	SF	SB	CS	BA	OBA	SA	FA
1962	NYY-A	63	138	14	33	3	2	7	17	3	0	21	0	0	0	1	1	.239	.255	.442	.986
1963	NYY-A	157	580	79	157	16	3	27	89	23	2	63	7	0	5	3	5	.271	.304	.448	.994
1964	NYY-A	160	613	71	154	12	3	28	100	24	7	63	3	2	5	2	1	.251	.281	.418	.988
1965	NYY-A	143	531	51	131	18	3	18	62	43	11	59	2	3	1	4	2	.247	.305	.394	.997
1966	NYY-A	152	585	85	149	21	4	31	83	29	6	58	2	0	5	4	3	.255	.290	.463	.993
1967	NYY-A	133	501	45	126	18	3	13	64	34	4	62	3	3	4	1	3	.251	.301	.377	.977
1968	NYY-A	108	380	41	93	9	3	15	56	37	9	45	1	0	3	8	2	.245	.311	.403	.988
1969	NYY-A	135	513	49	124	16	3	27	70	30	11	42	1	0	2	8	6	.242	.284	.442	.995
1970	Hou-N	75	279	44	70	9	5	14	35	18	9	28	1	0	1	5	2	.251	.298	.470	.993
1970	**ChC-N**	**56**	**213**	**38**	**57**	**9**	**2**	**12**	**44**	**15**	**2**	**15**	**0**	**4**	**2**	**0**	**2**	**.268**	**.313**	**.498**	**.993**
1971	**ChC-N**	**115**	**427**	**50**	**131**	**19**	**4**	**16**	**61**	**24**	**8**	**41**	**4**	**2**	**3**	**1**	**2**	**.307**	**.347**	**.482**	**.990**
1972	**ChC-N**	**66**	**214**	**23**	**56**	**5**	**0**	**8**	**21**	**13**	**4**	**22**	**3**	**0**	**3**	**1**	**2**	**.262**	**.309**	**.397**	**.997**
1973	**ChC-N**	**31**	**112**	**16**	**30**	**3**	**0**	**3**	**18**	**8**	**0**	**6**	**1**	**0**	**1**	**3**	**1**	**.268**	**.320**	**.375**	**.985**
1973	Atl-N	3	11	0	4	0	0	0	1	1	0	1	0	0	0	0	0	.364	.417	.364	.963
Career average	116	425	51	110	13	3	18	60	25	6	44	2	1	3	3	3	.258	.301	.432	.992
Cubs average	**67**	**242**	**32**	**69**	**9**	**2**	**10**	**36**	**15**	**4**	**21**	**2**	**2**	**2**	**1**	**2**	**.284**	**.328**	**.454**	**.991**
Career total	1397	5097	606	1315	158	35	219	721	302	73	526	28	14	35	41	32	.258	.301	.432	.992
Cubs total	**268**	**966**	**127**	**274**	**36**	**6**	**39**	**144**	**60**	**14**	**84**	**8**	**6**	**9**	**5**	**7**	**.284**	**.328**	**.454**	**.991**

Peters, John Paul

HEIGHT: 5'7"   THROWS: RIGHT   BATS: RIGHT   BORN: 4/8/1850 LOUISIANA, MISSOURI   DIED: 1/4/1924 ST. LOUIS, MISSOURI   POSITIONS PLAYED: P, 2B, SS, OF

YEAR	TEAM	GAMES	AB	RUNS	HITS	2B	3B	HR	RBI	BB	IBB	SO	HBP	SH	SF	SB	CS	BA	OBA	SA	FA
1876	**ChN-N**	**66**	**319**	**70**	**111**	**14**	**2**	**1**	**47**	**3**	**—**	**2**	**—**	**—**	**—**	**—**	**—**	**.348**	**.354**	**.414**	**.932**
1877	**ChN-N**	**60**	**265**	**45**	**84**	**10**	**3**	**0**	**41**	**1**	**—**	**7**	**—**	**—**	**—**	**—**	**—**	**.317**	**.320**	**.377**	**.883**
1878	Mil-N	55	246	33	76	6	1	0	22	5	—	8	—	—	—	—	—	.309	.323	.341	.863
1879	**ChN-N**	**83**	**379**	**45**	**93**	**13**	**2**	**1**	**31**	**1**	**—**	**19**	**—**	**—**	**—**	**—**	**—**	**.245**	**.247**	**.298**	**.837**
1880	Prv-N	86	359	30	82	5	0	0	24	5	—	15	—	—	—	—	—	.228	.239	.242	.900
1881	Buf-N	54	229	21	49	8	1	0	25	3	—	12	—	—	—	—	—	.214	.224	.258	.861
1882	Pit-AA	78	333	46	96	10	1	0	—	4	—	—	—	—	—	—	—	.288	.297	.324	.880
1883	Pit-AA	8	28	3	3	0	0	0	—	0	—	—	0	—	—	—	—	.107	.107	.107	.818
1884	Pit-AA	1	4	0	0	0	0	0	—	0	—	—	—	—	—	—	—	.000	.000	.000	.667
Career average	55	240	33	66	7	1	0	21	2	—	7	0	—	—	—	—	.275	.282	.317	.877
Cubs average	**70**	**321**	**53**	**96**	**12**	**2**	**1**	**40**	**2**	**—**	**9**	**—**	**—**	**—**	**—**	**—**	**.299**	**.303**	**.358**	**.879**
Career total	491	2162	293	594	66	10	2	190	22	—	63	0	—	—	—	—	.275	.282	.317	.877
Cubs total	**209**	**963**	**160**	**288**	**37**	**7**	**2**	**119**	**5**	**—**	**28**	**—**	**—**	**—**	**—**	**—**	**.299**	**.303**	**.358**	**.879**

Pettit, Robert Henry (Bob)

HEIGHT: 5'9"   THROWS: RIGHT   BATS: LEFT   BORN: 7/19/1861 WILLIAMSTOWN, MASSACHUSETTS   DIED: 11/1/1910 DERBY, CONNECTICUT
POSITIONS PLAYED: P, C, 2B, 3B, OF

YEAR	TEAM	GAMES	AB	RUNS	HITS	2B	3B	HR	RBI	BB	IBB	SO	HBP	SH	SF	SB	CS	BA	OBA	SA	FA
1887	**ChN-N**	**32**	**146**	**29**	**44**	**3**	**3**	**2**	**12**	**8**	**—**	**15**	**0**	**—**	**—**	**16**	**—**	**.301**	**.338**	**.404**	**.878**
1888	**ChN-N**	**43**	**169**	**23**	**43**	**1**	**4**	**4**	**23**	**7**	**—**	**9**	**1**	**—**	**—**	**7**	**—**	**.254**	**.288**	**.379**	**.931**
1891	Mil-AA	21	80	10	14	4	0	1	5	7	—	7	3	—	—	2	—	.175	.267	.263	.905
Career average	32	132	21	34	3	2	2	13	7	—	10	1	—	—	8	—	.256	.302	.365	.906
Cubs average	**38**	**158**	**26**	**44**	**2**	**4**	**3**	**18**	**8**	**—**	**12**	**1**	**—**	**—**	**12**	**—**	**.276**	**.311**	**.390**	**.907**
Career total	96	395	62	101	8	7	7	40	22	—	31	4	—	—	25	—	.256	.302	.365	.906
Cubs total	**75**	**315**	**52**	**87**	**4**	**7**	**6**	**35**	**15**	**—**	**24**	**1**	**—**	**—**	**23**	**—**	**.276**	**.311**	**.390**	**.907**

Pfeffer, Nathaniel Frederick (Fred *or* Fritz *or* Dandelion)
HEIGHT: 5'10"   THROWS: RIGHT   BATS: RIGHT   BORN: 3/17/1860 LOUISVILLE, KENTUCKY   DIED: 4/10/1932 CHICAGO, ILLINOIS
POSITIONS PLAYED: P, 1B, 2B, 3B, SS, OF

YEAR	TEAM	GAMES	AB	RUNS	HITS	2B	3B	HR	RBI	BB	IBB	SO	HBP	SH	SF	SB	CS	BA	OBA	SA	FA
1882	Try-N	85	330	26	72	7	4	1	43	1	—	24	—	—	—	—	—	.218	.221	.273	.856
1883	ChN-N	96	371	41	87	22	7	1	45	8	—	50	—	—	—	—	—	.235	.251	.340	.876
1884	ChN-N	112	467	105	135	10	10	25	101	25	—	47	—	—	—	—	—	.289	.325	.514	.903
1885	ChN-N	112	469	90	113	12	7	5	73	26	—	47	—	—	—	—	—	.241	.281	.328	.894
1886	ChN-N	118	474	88	125	17	8	7	95	36	—	46	—	—	—	30	—	.264	.316	.378	.904
1887	ChN-N	123	513	95	167	21	6	16	89	34	—	20	1	—	—	57	—	.326	.369	.483	.917
1888	ChN-N	135	517	90	129	22	10	8	57	32	—	38	3	—	—	64	—	.250	.297	.377	.931
1889	ChN-N	134	531	85	121	15	7	7	77	53	—	51	3	—	—	45	—	.228	.302	.322	.943
1890	Chi-P	124	499	86	128	21	8	5	80	44	—	23	2	—	—	27	—	.257	.319	.361	.916
1891	ChN-N	137	498	93	123	12	9	7	77	79	—	60	3	—	—	40	—	.247	.353	.349	.921
1892	Lou-N	124	470	78	121	14	9	2	76	67	—	36	2	—	—	27	—	.257	.353	.338	.933
1893	Lou-N	125	508	85	129	29	12	3	75	51	—	18	0	—	—	32	—	.254	.322	.376	.939
1894	Lou-N	104	409	68	126	12	14	5	59	30	—	14	1	15	—	31	—	.308	.357	.443	.928
1895	Lou-N	11	45	8	13	1	0	0	5	5	—	3	0	0	—	2	—	.289	.360	.311	.862
1896	NYG-N	4	14	1	2	0	0	0	4	1	—	1	1	0	—	0	—	.143	.250	.143	.760
1896	ChN-N	94	360	45	88	16	7	2	52	23	—	20	2	3	—	22	—	.244	.294	.344	.947
1897	ChN-N	32	114	10	26	0	1	0	11	12	—	—	3	2	—	5	—	.228	.318	.246	.883
Career average		104	412	68	107	14	7	6	64	33	—	31	1	1	—	24	—	.259	.316	.373	.915
Cubs average		109	431	74	111	15	7	8	68	33	—	38	2	1	—	26	—	.258	.313	.380	.915
Career total		1670	6589	1094	1705	231	119	94	1019	527	—	498	21	20	—	382	—	.259	.316	.373	.915
Cubs total		1093	4314	742	1114	147	72	78	677	328	—	379	15	5	—	263	—	.258	.313	.380	.915

Phelan, Arthur Thomas (Art *or* Dugan)
HEIGHT: 5'8"   THROWS: RIGHT   BATS: RIGHT   BORN: 8/14/1887 NIANTIC, ILLINOIS   DIED: 12/27/1964 FORT WORTH, TEXAS   POSITIONS PLAYED: 2B, 3B, SS, OF

YEAR	TEAM	GAMES	AB	RUNS	HITS	2B	3B	HR	RBI	BB	IBB	SO	HBP	SH	SF	SB	CS	BA	OBA	SA	FA
1910	Cin-N	23	42	7	9	0	0	0	4	7	—	6	0	1	—	5	—	.214	.327	.214	1.000
1912	Cin-N	130	461	56	112	9	11	3	54	46	—	37	2	17	—	25	—	.243	.314	.330	.926
1913	ChC-N	91	261	41	65	11	6	2	35	29	—	26	3	7	—	8	—	.249	.331	.360	.930
1914	ChC-N	25	46	5	13	2	1	0	3	4	—	3	0	2	—	0	—	.283	.340	.370	.917
1915	ChC-N	133	448	41	98	16	7	3	35	55	—	42	2	18	—	12	9	.219	.307	.306	.943
Career average		80	252	30	59	8	5	2	26	28	—	23	1	9	—	10	2	.236	.317	.325	.935
Cubs average		83	252	29	59	10	5	2	24	29	—	24	2	9	—	7	3	.233	.317	.328	.937
Career total		402	1258	150	297	38	25	8	131	141	—	114	7	45	—	50	9	.236	.317	.325	.935
Cubs total		249	755	87	176	29	14	5	73	88	—	71	5	27	—	20	9	.233	.317	.328	.937

Phelps, Ernest Gordon (Babe *or* Blimp)
HEIGHT: 6'2"   THROWS: RIGHT   BATS: LEFT   BORN: 4/16/1908 ODENTON, MARYLAND   DIED: 12/10/1992 ODENTON, MARYLAND   POSITIONS PLAYED: C, OF

YEAR	TEAM	GAMES	AB	RUNS	HITS	2B	3B	HR	RBI	BB	IBB	SO	HBP	SH	SF	SB	CS	BA	OBA	SA	FA
1931	Was-A	3	3	0	1	0	0	0	0	0	—	0	0	0	—	0	0	.333	.333	.333	—
1933	ChC-N	3	7	0	2	0	0	0	2	0	—	1	0	0	—	0	—	.286	.286	.286	1.000
1934	ChC-N	44	70	7	20	5	2	2	12	1	—	8	0	0	—	0	—	.286	.296	.500	.981
1935	Bro-N	47	121	17	44	7	2	5	22	9	—	10	0	0	—	0	—	.364	.408	.579	.957
1936	Bro-N	115	319	36	117	23	2	5	57	27	—	18	3	0	—	1	—	.367	.421	.498	.977
1937	Bro-N	121	409	42	128	37	3	7	58	25	—	28	3	5	—	2	—	.313	.357	.469	.971
1938	Bro-N	66	208	33	64	12	2	5	46	23	—	15	1	0	—	2	—	.308	.379	.457	.980
1939	Bro-N	98	323	33	92	21	2	6	42	24	—	24	1	8	—	0	—	.285	.336	.418	.980
1940	Bro-N	118	370	47	109	24	5	13	61	30	—	27	1	3	—	2	—	.295	.349	.492	.977
1941	Bro-N	16	30	3	7	3	0	2	4	1	—	2	0	0	—	0	—	.233	.258	.533	.971
1942	Pit-N	95	257	21	73	11	1	9	41	20	—	24	4	0	—	2	—	.284	.345	.440	.959
Career average		66	192	22	60	13	2	5	31	15	—	14	1	1	—	1	0	.310	.362	.472	.974
Cubs average		24	39	4	11	3	1	1	7	1	—	5	0	0	—	0	0	.286	.295	.481	.983
Career total		726	2117	239	657	143	19	54	345	160	—	157	13	16	—	9	0	.310	.362	.472	.974
Cubs total		47	77	7	22	5	2	2	14	1	—	9	0	0	—	0	0	.286	.295	.481	.983

Nathaniel Frederick (Fred) "Dandelion," "Fritz" Pfeffer, 2b-ss-1b-p-of-3b, 1882–97

Known as "Dandelion" because he could really "pick it," Fred Pfeffer's defensive skills were all the more remarkable because he played most of his career without a glove.

Pfeffer was born on March 17, 1860, in Louisville, Kentucky. He made his major league debut with Troy, New York, in 1882. When that franchise folded after that season, Pfeffer signed with Chicago.

As did many of his contemporaries in major league baseball at the time, Pfeffer played a variety of positions in his big-league career. But second base was his strength. He wound up playing 1,073 games for Chicago at the position, fifth best in team history.

Like many fielders of his day, Pfeffer declined to wear a glove. This was not the disadvantage it would be even a few decades later; most players who wore a glove in the 19th century generally donned a hand covering only a little more protective than a golf glove. But even after players began using gloves, Pfeffer resisted the practice for many years.

Pfeffer had outstanding range. He led the National League in most chances per game by a second baseman a total of six times while he was in Chicago. Chicago catcher Mike Kelly considered him the greatest second baseman he had ever seen. Kelly and Pfeffer are believed to have pioneered the play whereby a second baseman cuts off the throw from his catcher and throws the ball back to nail the lead runner on a double steal.

Many old-time Chicago fans and players believe that Pfeffer should be in the Hall of Fame.

Pfeffer was part of Chicago's famous "stone wall infield," along with third baseman Ned Williamson, shortstop Tom Burns and first baseman-manager Adrian "Cap" Anson. Anson, in his autobiography, declared that the 1885 and 1886 Chicago teams were the best in the history of baseball, in large part because of its infield.

Pfeffer was also a deadly clutch hitter. He only topped the .300 mark once in his career, with Louisville in 1894, but Chicago player-manager Cap Anson once remarked that Pfeffer was one of the most dangerous hitters in the league with the game on the line.

A canny base runner, Pfeffer twice led the Cubs in stolen bases, with 57 in 1887 and 64 in 1888. He also led the team in triples in 1884 with 10.

In 1890 Pfeffer, along with a host of other ballplayers, jumped to the Players' League, which flourished for a year before folding. Anson allowed Pfeffer to come back to Chicago in 1891 before trading him to Louisville. After four strong years there, Pfeffer was sold to the Giants in 1896 and, later that year, returned to Chicago for his third stint with the team. Pfeffer played 1½ years before retiring in 1897. He died in 1932.

Pfeffer remains ninth on the Cubs' all-time stolen base leaders with 263, a number that should certainly be higher, but stolen bases were not tabulated until 1886, his fourth year with the team.

Phillips, Adolfo Emilio
HEIGHT: 6'1"   THROWS: RIGHT   BATS: RIGHT   BORN: 12/16/1941 BETHANIA, PANAMA   POSITIONS PLAYED: OF

YEAR	TEAM	GAMES	AB	RUNS	HITS	2B	3B	HR	RBI	BB	IBB	SO	HBP	SH	SF	SB	CS	BA	OBA	SA	FA
1964	Phi-N	13	13	4	3	0	0	0	0	3	0	3	0	1	0	0	0	.231	.375	.231	1.000
1965	Phi-N	41	87	14	20	4	0	3	5	5	0	34	0	1	0	3	3	.230	.272	.379	1.000
1966	Phi-N	2	3	1	0	0	0	0	0	0	0	0	0	0	0	0	0	.000	.000	.000	1.000
1966	**ChC-N**	**116**	**416**	**68**	**109**	**29**	**1**	**16**	**36**	**43**	**3**	**135**	**12**	**2**	**0**	**32**	**15**	**.262**	**.348**	**.452**	**.978**
1967	**ChC-N**	**144**	**448**	**66**	**120**	**20**	**7**	**17**	**70**	**80**	**29**	**93**	**6**	**5**	**2**	**24**	**10**	**.268**	**.384**	**.458**	**.981**
1968	**ChC-N**	**143**	**439**	**49**	**106**	**20**	**5**	**13**	**33**	**47**	**20**	**90**	**5**	**4**	**2**	**9**	**7**	**.241**	**.320**	**.399**	**.979**
1969	**ChC-N**	**28**	**49**	**5**	**11**	**3**	**1**	**0**	**1**	**16**	**3**	**15**	**1**	**0**	**0**	**1**	**3**	**.224**	**.424**	**.327**	**.956**
1969	Mon-N	58	199	25	43	4	4	4	7	19	1	62	1	0	1	6	5	.216	.286	.337	.981
1970	Mon-N	92	214	36	51	6	3	6	21	36	1	51	2	1	1	7	1	.238	.352	.379	.985
1972	Cle-A	12	7	2	0	0	0	0	0	2	0	2	0	0	0	0	0	.000	.222	.000	1.000

(continued)

(Phillips, continued)

	GAMES	AB	RUNS	HITS	2B	3B	HR	RBI	BB	IBB	SO	HBP	SH	SF	SB	CS	BA	OBA	SA	FA
Career average	81	234	34	58	11	3	7	22	31	7	61	3	2	1	10	6	.247	.343	.410	.980
Cubs average	**108**	**338**	**47**	**87**	**18**	**4**	**12**	**35**	**47**	**14**	**83**	**6**	**3**	**1**	**17**	**9**	**.256**	**.355**	**.432**	**.978**
Career total	649	1875	270	463	86	21	59	173	251	57	485	27	14	6	82	44	.247	.343	.410	.980
Cubs total	**431**	**1352**	**188**	**346**	**72**	**14**	**46**	**140**	**186**	**55**	**333**	**24**	**11**	**4**	**66**	**35**	**.256**	**.355**	**.432**	**.978**

Pick, Charles Thomas (Charlie)
HEIGHT: 5'10" THROWS: RIGHT BATS: LEFT BORN: 4/10/1888 BROOKNEAL, VIRGINIA DIED: 6/26/1954 LYNCHBURG, VIRGINIA
POSITIONS PLAYED: 1B, 2B, 3B, OF

YEAR	TEAM	GAMES	AB	RUNS	HITS	2B	3B	HR	RBI	BB	IBB	SO	HBP	SH	SF	SB	CS	BA	OBA	SA	FA
1914	Was-A	10	23	0	9	0	0	0	1	4	—	4	0	1	—	1	2	.391	.481	.391	.833
1915	Was-A	3	2	0	0	0	0	0	0	0	—	0	0	0	—	0	0	.000	.000	.000	.898
1916	Phi-A	121	398	29	96	10	3	0	20	40	—	24	3	11	—	25	16	.241	.315	.281	.898
1918	**ChC-N**	**29**	**89**	**13**	**29**	**4**	**1**	**0**	**12**	**14**	**—**	**4**	**0**	**5**	**—**	**7**	**—**	**.326**	**.417**	**.393**	**.946**
1919	**ChC-N**	**75**	**269**	**27**	**65**	**8**	**6**	**0**	**18**	**14**	**—**	**12**	**5**	**12**	**—**	**17**	**—**	**.242**	**.292**	**.316**	**.945**
1919	Bos-N	34	114	12	29	1	1	1	7	7	—	5	5	2	—	4	—	.254	.325	.307	.932
1920	Bos-N	95	383	34	105	16	6	2	28	23	—	11	3	18	—	10	16	.274	.320	.363	.952
Career average	61	213	19	56	7	3	1	14	17	—	10	3	8	—	11	6	.261	.323	.325	.934
Cubs average	**52**	**179**	**20**	**47**	**6**	**4**	**0**	**15**	**14**	**—**	**8**	**3**	**9**	**—**	**12**	**0**	**.263**	**.325**	**.335**	**.945**
Career total	367	1278	115	333	39	17	3	86	102	—	60	16	49	—	64	34	.261	.323	.325	.934
Cubs total	**104**	**358**	**40**	**94**	**12**	**7**	**0**	**30**	**28**	**—**	**16**	**5**	**17**	**—**	**24**	**0**	**.263**	**.325**	**.335**	**.945**

Pick, Edgar Everett (Eddie)
HEIGHT: 6'0" THROWS: RIGHT BATS: BOTH BORN: 5/7/1899 ATTLEBORO, MASSACHUSETTS DIED: 5/13/1967 SANTA MONICA, CALIFORNIA
POSITIONS PLAYED: 2B, 3B, OF

YEAR	TEAM	GAMES	AB	RUNS	HITS	2B	3B	HR	RBI	BB	IBB	SO	HBP	SH	SF	SB	CS	BA	OBA	SA	FA
1923	Cin-N	9	8	2	3	0	0	0	2	3	—	3	0	1	—	0	0	.375	.545	.375	1.000
1924	Cin-N	3	2	0	0	0	0	0	0	0	—	1	0	0	—	0	0	.000	.000	.000	1.000
1927	**ChC-N**	**54**	**181**	**23**	**31**	**5**	**2**	**2**	**15**	**20**	**—**	**26**	**0**	**9**	**—**	**0**	**—**	**.171**	**.254**	**.254**	**.912**
Career average	22	64	8	11	2	1	1	6	8	—	10	0	3	—	0	0	.178	.266	.257	.913
Cubs average	**54**	**181**	**23**	**31**	**5**	**2**	**2**	**15**	**20**	**—**	**26**	**0**	**9**	**—**	**0**	**0**	**.171**	**.254**	**.254**	**.912**
Career total	66	191	25	34	5	2	2	17	23	—	30	0	10	—	0	0	.178	.266	.257	.913
Cubs total	**54**	**181**	**23**	**31**	**5**	**2**	**2**	**15**	**20**	**—**	**26**	**0**	**9**	**—**	**0**	**0**	**.171**	**.254**	**.254**	**.912**

Piercy, Andrew J. (Andy)
HEIGHT: - THROWS: RIGHT BATS: — BORN: 8/1856 SAN JOSE, CALIFORNIA DIED: 12/27/1932 SAN JOSE, CALIFORNIA POSITIONS PLAYED: 2B, 3B

YEAR	TEAM	GAMES	AB	RUNS	HITS	2B	3B	HR	RBI	BB	IBB	SO	HBP	SH	SF	SB	CS	BA	OBA	SA	FA
1881	**ChN-N**	**2**	**8**	**1**	**2**	**0**	**0**	**0**	**0**	**0**	**—**	**1**	**—**	**—**	**—**	**—**	**—**	**.250**	**.250**	**.250**	**.750**
Career average	2	8	1	2	0	0	0	0	0	—	1	—	—	—	—	—	.250	.250	.250	.750
Cubs average	**2**	**8**	**1**	**2**	**0**	**0**	**0**	**0**	**0**	**—**	**1**	**—**	**—**	**—**	**—**	**—**	**.250**	**.250**	**.250**	**.750**
Career total	2	8	1	2	0	0	0	0	0	—	1	—	—	—	—	—	.250	.250	.250	.750
Cubs total	**2**	**8**	**1**	**2**	**0**	**0**	**0**	**0**	**0**	**—**	**1**	**—**	**—**	**—**	**—**	**—**	**.250**	**.250**	**.250**	**.750**

Pittenger, Clarke Alonzo (Pinky)
HEIGHT: 5'10" THROWS: RIGHT BATS: RIGHT BORN: 2/24/1899 HUDSON, MICHIGAN DIED: 11/4/1977 FORT LAUDERDALE, FLORIDA
POSITIONS PLAYED: 2B, 3B, SS, OF

YEAR	TEAM	GAMES	AB	RUNS	HITS	2B	3B	HR	RBI	BB	IBB	SO	HBP	SH	SF	SB	CS	BA	OBA	SA	FA
1921	Bos-A	40	91	6	18	1	0	0	5	4	—	13	0	3	—	3	2	.198	.232	.209	.988
1922	Bos-A	66	186	16	48	3	0	0	7	9	—	10	2	6	—	2	5	.258	.299	.274	.915
1923	Bos-A	60	177	15	38	5	0	0	15	5	—	10	0	2	—	3	1	.215	.236	.243	.963
1925	**ChC-N**	**59**	**173**	**21**	**54**	**7**	**2**	**0**	**15**	**12**	**—**	**7**	**2**	**8**	**—**	**5**	**4**	**.312**	**.364**	**.376**	**.947**
1927	Cin-N	31	84	17	23	5	0	1	10	2	—	5	0	4	—	4	—	.274	.291	.369	.945
1928	Cin-N	40	38	12	9	0	1	0	4	0	—	1	0	0	—	2	—	.237	.237	.289	.923
1929	Cin-N	77	210	31	62	11	0	0	27	5	—	4	2	10	—	8	—	.295	.318	.348	.955
Career average	53	137	17	36	5	0	0	12	5	—	7	1	5	—	4	2	.263	.294	.306	.947
Cubs average	**59**	**173**	**21**	**54**	**7**	**2**	**0**	**15**	**12**	**—**	**7**	**2**	**8**	**—**	**5**	**4**	**.312**	**.364**	**.376**	**.947**
Career total	373	959	118	252	32	3	1	83	37	—	50	6	33	—	27	12	.263	.294	.306	.947
Cubs total	**59**	**173**	**21**	**54**	**7**	**2**	**0**	**15**	**12**	**—**	**7**	**2**	**8**	**—**	**5**	**4**	**.312**	**.364**	**.376**	**.947**

Platt, Mizell George (Whitey)
HEIGHT: 6'1" THROWS: RIGHT BATS: RIGHT BORN: 8/21/1920 WEST PALM BEACH, FLORIDA DIED: 7/27/1970 WEST PALM BEACH, FLORIDA
POSITIONS PLAYED: 1B, OF

YEAR	TEAM	GAMES	AB	RUNS	HITS	2B	3B	HR	RBI	BB	IBB	SO	HBP	SH	SF	SB	CS	BA	OBA	SA	FA
1942	ChC-N	4	16	1	1	0	0	0	2	0	—	3	0	0	—	0	—	.063	.063	.063	1.000
1943	ChC-N	20	41	2	7	3	0	0	2	1	—	7	0	0	—	0	—	.171	.190	.244	.952
1946	CWS-A	84	247	28	62	8	5	3	32	17	—	34	3	1	—	1	7	.251	.307	.360	.971
1948	StL-A	123	454	57	123	22	10	7	82	39	—	51	2	4	—	1	4	.271	.331	.410	.948
1949	StL-A	102	244	29	63	8	2	3	29	24	—	27	0	1	—	0	1	.258	.325	.344	.982
Career average		67	200	23	51	8	3	3	29	16	—	24	1	1	—	0	2	.255	.314	.369	.964
Cubs average		**12**	**29**	**2**	**4**	**2**	**0**	**0**	**2**	**1**	—	**5**	**0**	**0**	—	**0**	—	**.140**	**.155**	**.193**	**.966**
Career total		333	1002	117	256	41	17	13	147	81	—	122	5	6	—	2	12	.255	.314	.369	.964
Cubs total		**24**	**57**	**3**	**8**	**3**	**0**	**0**	**4**	**1**	—	**10**	**0**	**0**	—	**0**	—	**.140**	**.155**	**.193**	**.966**

Plummer, William Francis (Bill)
HEIGHT: 6'1" THROWS: RIGHT BATS: RIGHT BORN: 3/21/1947 OAKLAND, CALIFORNIA POSITIONS PLAYED: C, 1B, 3B

YEAR	TEAM	GAMES	AB	RUNS	HITS	2B	3B	HR	RBI	BB	IBB	SO	HBP	SH	SF	SB	CS	BA	OBA	SA	FA
1968	ChC-N	2	2	0	0	0	0	0	0	0	0	1	0	0	0	0	0	.000	.000	.000	1.000
1970	Cin-N	4	8	0	1	0	0	0	0	0	0	2	1	0	0	0	0	.125	.222	.125	.857
1971	Cin-N	10	19	0	0	0	0	0	0	0	0	4	0	0	0	0	0	.000	.000	.000	1.000
1972	Cin-N	38	102	8	19	4	0	2	9	4	2	20	0	2	3	0	0	.186	.211	.284	.994
1973	Cin-N	50	119	8	18	3	0	2	11	18	5	26	1	1	0	1	0	.151	.268	.227	.989
1974	Cin-N	50	120	7	27	7	0	2	10	6	0	21	0	1	2	1	0	.225	.258	.333	.974
1975	Cin-N	65	159	17	29	7	0	1	19	24	2	28	2	0	4	1	0	.182	.291	.245	.990
1976	Cin-N	56	153	16	38	6	1	4	19	14	0	36	0	1	0	0	2	.248	.311	.379	.977
1977	Cin-N	51	117	10	16	5	0	1	7	17	1	34	0	0	1	1	1	.137	.244	.205	.986
1978	Sea-A	41	93	6	20	5	0	2	7	12	0	19	0	1	1	0	0	.215	.305	.333	.978
Career average		37	89	7	17	4	0	1	8	10	1	19	0	1	1	0	0	.188	.267	.279	.983
Cubs average		**2**	**2**	**0**	**0**	**0**	**0**	**0**	**0**	**0**	**0**	**1**	**0**	**0**	**0**	**0**	**0**	**.000**	**.000**	**.000**	**1.000**
Career total		367	892	72	168	37	1	14	82	95	10	191	4	6	10	4	3	.188	.267	.279	.983
Cubs total		**2**	**2**	**0**	**0**	**0**	**0**	**0**	**0**	**0**	**0**	**1**	**0**	**0**	**0**	**0**	**0**	**.000**	**.000**	**.000**	**1.000**

Poorman, Thomas Iverson (Tom)
HEIGHT: 5'7" THROWS: RIGHT BATS: LEFT BORN: 10/14/1857 LOCK HAVEN, PENNSYLVANIA DIED: 2/18/1905 LOCK HAVEN, PENNSYLVANIA
POSITIONS PLAYED: P, 2B, OF

YEAR	TEAM	GAMES	AB	RUNS	HITS	2B	3B	HR	RBI	BB	IBB	SO	HBP	SH	SF	SB	CS	BA	OBA	SA	FA
1880	Buf-N	19	70	5	11	1	0	0	1	0	—	13	—	—	—	—	—	.157	.157	.171	.841
1880	**ChN-N**	**7**	**25**	**3**	**5**	**1**	**2**	**0**	**0**	**0**	—	**2**	—	—	—	—	—	**.200**	**.200**	**.400**	**.778**
1884	Tol-AA	94	382	56	89	8	7	0	—	10	—	—	1	—	—	—	—	.233	.254	.291	.778
1885	Bos-N	56	227	44	54	5	3	3	25	7	—	32	—	—	—	—	—	.238	.261	.326	.843
1886	Bos-N	88	371	72	97	16	6	3	41	19	—	52	—	—	—	31	—	.261	.297	.361	.867
1887	Phi-AA	135	620	140	190	18	19	4	61	35	—	—	10	—	—	88	—	.306	.353	.416	.902
1888	Phi-AA	97	383	76	87	16	6	2	44	31	—	—	5	—	—	46	—	.227	.294	.316	.911
Career average		83	346	66	89	11	7	2	29	17	—	17	3	—	—	28	—	.256	.296	.346	.884
Cubs average		**7**	**25**	**3**	**5**	**1**	**2**	**0**	**0**	**0**	—	**2**	—	—	—	—	—	**.200**	**.200**	**.400**	**.778**
Career total		496	2078	396	533	65	43	12	172	102	—	99	16	—	—	165	—	.256	.296	.346	.884
Cubs total		**7**	**25**	**3**	**5**	**1**	**2**	**0**	**0**	**0**	—	**2**	—	—	—	—	—	**.200**	**.200**	**.400**	**.778**

Popovich, Paul Edward
HEIGHT: 6'0" THROWS: RIGHT BATS: BOTH BORN: 8/18/1940 FLEMINGTON, WEST VIRGINIA POSITIONS PLAYED: 2B, 3B, SS, OF

YEAR	TEAM	GAMES	AB	RUNS	HITS	2B	3B	HR	RBI	BB	IBB	SO	HBP	SH	SF	SB	CS	BA	OBA	SA	FA
1964	ChC-N	1	1	0	1	0	0	0	0	0	0	0	0	0	0	0	0	1.000	1.000	1.000	—
1966	ChC-N	2	6	0	0	0	0	0	0	0	0	2	0	0	0	0	0	.000	.000	.000	.889
1967	ChC-N	49	159	18	34	4	0	0	2	9	0	12	2	3	0	0	1	.214	.265	.239	.973
1968	LA-N	134	418	35	97	8	1	2	25	29	2	37	1	9	5	1	3	.232	.280	.270	.981
1969	LA-N	28	50	5	10	0	0	0	4	1	0	4	0	2	1	0	0	.200	.212	.200	.971
1969	ChC-N	60	154	26	48	6	0	1	14	18	0	14	1	4	0	0	1	.312	.387	.370	.976

(continued)

(Popovich, continued)

YEAR	TEAM	GAMES	AB	RUNS	HITS	2B	3B	HR	RBI	BB	IBB	SO	HBP	SH	SF	SB	CS	BA	OBA	SA	FA
1970	ChC-N	78	186	22	47	5	1	4	20	18	4	18	2	2	1	0	1	.253	.324	.355	.977
1971	ChC-N	89	226	24	49	7	1	4	28	14	0	17	0	1	2	0	1	.217	.260	.310	.982
1972	ChC-N	58	129	8	25	3	2	1	11	12	2	8	0	0	1	0	1	.194	.261	.271	.981
1973	ChC-N	99	280	24	66	6	3	2	24	18	5	27	1	4	5	3	2	.236	.280	.300	.982
1974	Pit-N	59	83	9	18	2	1	0	5	5	1	10	0	0	2	0	0	.217	.256	.265	.969
1975	Pit-N	25	40	5	8	1	0	0	1	3	0	2	1	0	0	0	0	.200	.273	.225	.974
Career average		62	157	16	37	4	1	1	12	12	1	14	1	2	2	0	1	.233	.286	.292	.979
Cubs average		55	143	15	34	4	1	2	12	11	1	12	1	2	1	0	1	.237	.293	.308	.979
Career total		682	1732	176	403	42	9	14	134	127	14	151	8	25	17	4	10	.233	.286	.292	.979
Cubs total		436	1141	122	270	31	7	12	99	89	11	98	6	14	9	3	7	.237	.293	.308	.979

Porter, Marquis Donnell (Bo)

HEIGHT: 6'2"   THROWS: RIGHT   BATS: RIGHT   BORN: 7/5/1972 NEWARK, NEW JERSEY   POSITIONS PLAYED: OF

YEAR	TEAM	GAMES	AB	RUNS	HITS	2B	3B	HR	RBI	BB	IBB	SO	HBP	SH	SF	SB	CS	BA	OBA	SA	FA
1999	ChC-N	24	26	2	5	1	0	0	0	2	0	13	0	1	0	0	0	.192	.250	.231	.941
2000	Oak-A	17	13	3	2	0	0	1	2	2	0	5	0	0	0	0	0	.154	.267	.385	1.000
2001	Tex-A	48	87	18	20	4	2	1	6	9	0	34	0	0	2	3	2	.230	.296	.356	.969
Career average		30	42	8	9	2	1	1	3	4	0	17	0	0	1	1	1	.214	.284	.333	.968
Cubs average		24	26	2	5	1	0	0	0	2	0	13	0	1	0	0	0	.192	.250	.231	.941
Career total		89	126	23	27	5	2	2	8	13	0	52	0	1	2	3	2	.214	.284	.333	.968
Cubs total		24	26	2	5	1	0	0	0	2	0	13	0	1	0	0	0	.192	.250	.231	.941

Powers, Philip B. (Phil *or* Grandmother)

HEIGHT: 5'7"   THROWS: RIGHT   BATS: RIGHT   BORN: 7/26/1854 NEW YORK, NEW YORK   DIED: 12/22/1914 NEW YORK, NEW YORK
POSITIONS PLAYED: C, 1B, 3B, OF

YEAR	TEAM	GAMES	AB	RUNS	HITS	2B	3B	HR	RBI	BB	IBB	SO	HBP	SH	SF	SB	CS	BA	OBA	SA	FA
1878	ChN-N	8	31	2	5	1	1	0	2	1	—	5	—	—	—	—	—	.161	.188	.258	.930
1880	Bos-N	37	126	11	18	5	0	0	10	5	—	15	—	—	—	—	—	.143	.176	.183	.851
1881	Cle-N	5	15	1	1	0	0	0	0	1	—	2	—	—	—	—	—	.067	.125	.067	.957
1882	Cin-AA	16	60	4	13	1	1	0	5	3	—	—	—	—	—	—	—	.217	.254	.267	.936
1883	Cin-AA	30	114	16	28	1	4	0	8	3	—	—	—	—	—	—	—	.246	.265	.325	.887
1884	Cin-AA	34	130	10	18	1	0	0	8	5	—	—	0	—	—	—	—	.138	.170	.146	.893
1885	Cin-AA	15	60	6	16	2	0	0	7	0	—	—	0	—	—	—	—	.267	.267	.300	.833
1885	Bal-AA	9	34	6	4	1	0	0	2	1	—	—	0	—	—	—	—	.118	.143	.147	.854
Career average		22	81	8	15	2	1	0	6	3	—	3	0	—	—	—	—	.181	.207	.223	.882
Cubs average		8	31	2	5	1	1	0	2	1	—	5	—	—	—	—	—	.161	.188	.258	.930
Career total		154	570	56	103	12	6	0	42	19	—	22	0	—	—	—	—	.181	.207	.223	.882
Cubs total		8	31	2	5	1	1	0	2	1	—	5	—	—	—	—	—	.161	.188	.258	.930

Pramesa, John Steven (Johnny)

HEIGHT: 6'2"   THROWS: RIGHT   BATS: RIGHT   BORN: 8/28/1925 BARTON, OHIO   DIED: 9/9/1996 LOS ANGELES, CALIFORNIA   POSITIONS PLAYED: C

YEAR	TEAM	GAMES	AB	RUNS	HITS	2B	3B	HR	RBI	BB	IBB	SO	HBP	SH	SF	SB	CS	BA	OBA	SA	FA
1949	Cin-N	17	25	2	6	1	0	1	2	3	—	5	0	0	—	0	—	.240	.321	.400	.966
1950	Cin-N	74	228	14	70	10	1	5	30	19	—	15	1	3	—	0	—	.307	.363	.425	.981
1951	Cin-N	72	227	12	52	5	2	6	22	5	—	17	0	2	—	0	0	.229	.246	.348	.968
1952	ChC-N	22	46	1	13	1	0	1	5	4	—	4	0	0	—	0	0	.283	.340	.370	.958
Career average		46	132	7	35	4	1	3	15	8	—	10	0	1	—	0	0	.268	.310	.386	.973
Cubs average		22	46	1	13	1	0	1	5	4	—	4	0	0	—	0	0	.283	.340	.370	.958
Career total		185	526	29	141	17	3	13	59	31	—	41	1	5	—	0	0	.268	.310	.386	.973
Cubs total		22	46	1	13	1	0	1	5	4	—	4	0	0	—	0	0	.283	.340	.370	.958

Pratt, Todd Alan

HEIGHT: 6'3" THROWS: RIGHT BATS: RIGHT BORN: 2/9/1967 BELLEVUE, NEBRASKA POSITIONS PLAYED: C, 1B, OF

YEAR	TEAM	GAMES	AB	RUNS	HITS	2B	3B	HR	RBI	BB	IBB	SO	HBP	SH	SF	SB	CS	BA	OBA	SA	FA
1992	Phi-N	16	46	6	13	1	0	2	10	4	0	12	0	0	0	0	0	.283	.340	.435	.972
1993	Phi-N	33	87	8	25	6	0	5	13	5	0	19	1	1	1	0	0	.287	.330	.529	.989
1994	Phi-N	28	102	10	20	6	1	2	9	12	0	29	0	0	0	0	1	.196	.281	.333	1.000
1995	**ChC-N**	**25**	**60**	**3**	**8**	**2**	**0**	**0**	**4**	**6**	**1**	**21**	**0**	**0**	**1**	**0**	**0**	**.133**	**.209**	**.167**	**.981**
1997	NYM-N	39	106	12	30	6	0	2	19	13	0	32	2	0	0	0	1	.283	.372	.396	.990
1998	NYM-N	41	69	9	19	9	1	2	18	2	0	20	0	0	0	0	0	.275	.296	.522	.976
1999	NYM-N	71	140	18	41	4	0	3	21	15	0	32	3	0	2	2	0	.293	.369	.386	.996
2000	NYM-N	80	160	33	44	6	0	8	25	22	1	31	5	2	1	0	0	.275	.378	.463	.997
2001	NYM-N	45	80	6	13	5	0	2	4	15	1	36	2	0	1	1	0	.163	.306	.300	.994
2001	Phi-N	35	93	12	19	3	0	2	7	19	2	25	1	1	0	0	0	.204	.345	.301	.986
Career average		46	105	13	26	5	0	3	14	13	1	29	2	0	1	0	0	.246	.334	.390	.991
Cubs average		**25**	**60**	**3**	**8**	**2**	**0**	**0**	**4**	**6**	**1**	**21**	**0**	**0**	**1**	**0**	**0**	**.133**	**.209**	**.167**	**.981**
Career total		413	943	117	232	48	2	28	130	113	5	257	14	4	6	3	2	.246	.334	.390	.991
Cubs total		**25**	**60**	**3**	**8**	**2**	**0**	**0**	**4**	**6**	**1**	**21**	**0**	**0**	**1**	**0**	**0**	**.133**	**.209**	**.167**	**.981**

Putman, Eddy William (Ed)

HEIGHT: 6'1" THROWS: RIGHT BATS: RIGHT BORN: 9/25/1953 LOS ANGELES, CALIFORNIA POSITIONS PLAYED: C, 1B, 3B

YEAR	TEAM	GAMES	AB	RUNS	HITS	2B	3B	HR	RBI	BB	IBB	SO	HBP	SH	SF	SB	CS	BA	OBA	SA	FA
1976	ChC-N	5	7	0	3	0	0	0	0	0	0	0	0	0	0	0	0	.429	.429	.429	1.000
1978	ChC-N	17	25	2	5	0	0	0	3	4	0	6	0	0	0	0	0	.200	.310	.200	.933
1979	Det-A	21	39	4	9	3	0	2	4	4	0	12	0	0	0	0	1	.231	.302	.462	.988
Career average		14	24	2	6	1	0	1	2	3	0	6	0	0	0	0	0	.239	.316	.366	.977
Cubs average		**11**	**16**	**1**	**4**	**0**	**0**	**0**	**2**	**2**	**0**	**3**	**0**	**0**	**0**	**0**	**0**	**.250**	**.333**	**.250**	**.957**
Career total		43	71	6	17	3	0	2	7	8	0	18	0	0	0	0	1	.239	.316	.366	.977
Cubs total		**22**	**32**	**2**	**8**	**0**	**0**	**0**	**3**	**4**	**0**	**6**	**0**	**0**	**0**	**0**	**0**	**.250**	**.333**	**.250**	**.957**

Qualls, James Robert (Jim)

HEIGHT: 5'10" THROWS: RIGHT BATS: BOTH BORN: 10/9/1946 EXETER, CALIFORNIA POSITIONS PLAYED: 2B, OF

YEAR	TEAM	GAMES	AB	RUNS	HITS	2B	3B	HR	RBI	BB	IBB	SO	HBP	SH	SF	SB	CS	BA	OBA	SA	FA
1969	ChC-N	43	120	12	30	5	3	0	9	2	0	14	1	0	1	2	1	.250	.266	.342	1.000
1970	Mon-N	9	9	1	1	0	0	0	1	0	0	0	0	0	0	0	0	.111	.111	.111	1.000
1972	CWS-A	11	10	0	0	0	0	0	0	0	0	2	0	1	0	0	0	.000	.000	.000	1.000
Career average		21	46	4	10	2	1	0	3	1	0	5	0	0	0	1	0	.223	.238	.302	1.000
Cubs average		**43**	**120**	**12**	**30**	**5**	**3**	**0**	**9**	**2**	**0**	**14**	**1**	**0**	**1**	**2**	**1**	**.250**	**.266**	**.342**	**1.000**
Career total		63	139	13	31	5	3	0	10	2	0	16	1	1	1	2	1	.223	.238	.302	1.000
Cubs total		**43**	**120**	**12**	**30**	**5**	**3**	**0**	**9**	**2**	**0**	**14**	**1**	**0**	**1**	**2**	**1**	**.250**	**.266**	**.342**	**1.000**

Quest, Joseph L. (Joe)

HEIGHT: 5'6" THROWS: RIGHT BATS: RIGHT BORN: 11/16/1852 NEW CASTLE, PENNSYLVANIA DIED: 4/7/1923 CLEVELAND, OHIO
POSITIONS PLAYED: 2B, 3B, SS, OF

YEAR	TEAM	GAMES	AB	RUNS	HITS	2B	3B	HR	RBI	BB	IBB	SO	HBP	SH	SF	SB	CS	BA	OBA	SA	FA
1878	Ind-N	62	278	45	57	3	2	0	13	12	—	24	—	—	—	—	—	.205	.238	.230	.876
1879	**ChN-N**	**83**	**334**	**38**	**69**	**16**	**1**	**0**	**22**	**9**	**—**	**33**	**—**	**—**	**—**	**—**	**—**	**.207**	**.227**	**.260**	**.925**
1880	**ChN-N**	**82**	**300**	**37**	**71**	**12**	**1**	**0**	**27**	**8**	**—**	**16**	**—**	**—**	**—**	**—**	**—**	**.237**	**.256**	**.283**	**.894**
1881	**ChN-N**	**78**	**293**	**35**	**72**	**6**	**0**	**1**	**26**	**2**	**—**	**29**	**—**	**—**	**—**	**—**	**—**	**.246**	**.251**	**.276**	**.930**
1882	**ChN-N**	**42**	**159**	**24**	**32**	**5**	**2**	**0**	**15**	**8**	**—**	**16**	**—**	**—**	**—**	**—**	**—**	**.201**	**.240**	**.258**	**.873**
1883	Det-N	37	137	22	32	8	2	0	15	10	—	18	—	—	—	—	—	.234	.286	.321	.897
1883	StL-AA	19	78	12	20	3	1	0	10	1	—	—	—	—	—	—	—	.256	.266	.321	.890
1884	StL-AA	81	310	46	64	9	5	0	—	19	—	—	2	—	—	—	—	.206	.257	.268	.893
1884	Pit-AA	12	43	2	9	3	0	0	—	0	—	—	1	—	—	—	—	.209	.227	.279	.908
1885	Det-N	55	200	24	39	8	2	0	21	14	—	25	—	—	—	—	—	.195	.248	.255	.885
1886	Phi-AA	42	150	14	31	4	1	0	10	20	—	—	0	—	—	—	5	.207	.300	.247	.843
Career average		66	254	33	55	9	2	0	18	11	—	18	0	—	—	1	—	.217	.252	.267	.897
Cubs average		**71**	**272**	**34**	**61**	**10**	**1**	**0**	**23**	**7**	**—**	**24**	**—**	**—**	**—**	**—**	**—**	**.225**	**.243**	**.271**	**.911**
Career total		593	2282	299	496	77	17	1	159	103	—	161	3	—	—	5	—	.217	.252	.267	.897
Cubs total		**285**	**1086**	**134**	**244**	**39**	**4**	**1**	**90**	**27**	**—**	**94**	**—**	**—**	**—**	**—**	**—**	**.225**	**.243**	**.271**	**.911**

Quinn, Frank J.

HEIGHT: 5'8"   THROWS: —   BATS: —   BORN: 1876 GRAND RAPIDS, MICHIGAN   DIED: 2/17/1920 CAMDEN, INDIANA   POSITIONS PLAYED: 2B, OF

YEAR	TEAM	GAMES	AB	RUNS	HITS	2B	3B	HR	RBI	BB	IBB	SO	HBP	SH	SF	SB	CS	BA	OBA	SA	FA
1899	ChN-N	12	34	6	6	0	1	0	1	6	—	—	0	2	—	1	—	.176	.300	.235	.917
Career average		12	34	6	6	0	1	0	1	6	—	—	0	2	—	1	—	.176	.300	.235	.917
Cubs average		**12**	**34**	**6**	**6**	**0**	**1**	**0**	**1**	**6**	**—**	**—**	**0**	**2**	**—**	**1**	**—**	**.176**	**.300**	**.235**	**.917**
Career total		12	34	6	6	0	1	0	1	6	—	—	0	2	—	1	—	.176	.300	.235	.917
Cubs total		**12**	**34**	**6**	**6**	**0**	**1**	**0**	**1**	**6**	**—**	**—**	**0**	**2**	**—**	**1**	**—**	**.176**	**.300**	**.235**	**.917**

Quinn, Joseph C. (Joe)

HEIGHT: 5'8"   THROWS: —   BATS: —   BORN: 8/1849 CHICAGO, ILLINOIS   DIED: 1/2/1909 CHICAGO, ILLINOIS   POSITIONS PLAYED: OF

YEAR	TEAM	GAMES	AB	RUNS	HITS	2B	3B	HR	RBI	BB	IBB	SO	HBP	SH	SF	SB	CS	BA	OBA	SA	FA
1877	ChN-N	4	14	1	1	0	0	0	0	1	—	0	—	—	—	—	—	.071	.133	.071	.667
Career average		4	14	1	1	0	0	0	0	1	—	0	—	—	—	—	—	.071	.133	.071	.667
Cubs average		**4**	**14**	**1**	**1**	**0**	**0**	**0**	**0**	**1**	**—**	**0**	**—**	**—**	**—**	**—**	**—**	**.071**	**.133**	**.071**	**.667**
Career total		4	14	1	1	0	0	0	0	1	—	0	—	—	—	—	—	.071	.133	.071	.667
Cubs total		**4**	**14**	**1**	**1**	**0**	**0**	**0**	**0**	**1**	**—**	**0**	**—**	**—**	**—**	**—**	**—**	**.071**	**.133**	**.071**	**.667**

Quinones, Luis Raul

HEIGHT: 5'11"   THROWS: RIGHT   BATS: BOTH   BORN: 4/28/1962 PONCE, PUERTO RICO   POSITIONS PLAYED: 1B, 2B, 3B, SS, OF

YEAR	TEAM	GAMES	AB	RUNS	HITS	2B	3B	HR	RBI	BB	IBB	SO	HBP	SH	SF	SB	CS	BA	OBA	SA	FA
1983	Oak-A	19	42	5	8	2	1	0	4	1	0	4	0	1	1	1	1	.190	.205	.286	.979
1986	SF-N	71	106	13	19	1	3	0	11	3	1	17	1	4	1	3	1	.179	.207	.245	.922
1987	**ChC-N**	**49**	**101**	**12**	**22**	**6**	**0**	**0**	**8**	**10**	**0**	**16**	**0**	**0**	**0**	**0**	**0**	**.218**	**.288**	**.277**	**.969**
1988	Cin-N	23	52	4	12	3	0	1	11	2	1	11	0	2	1	0	1	.231	.255	.346	.963
1989	Cin-N	97	340	43	83	13	4	12	34	25	0	46	3	8	2	2	4	.244	.300	.412	.970
1990	Cin-N	83	145	10	35	7	2	2	17	13	3	29	1	1	4	1	0	.241	.301	.331	.956
1991	Cin-N	97	212	15	47	4	3	4	20	21	3	31	2	1	1	1	2	.222	.297	.325	.961
1992	Min-A	3	5	0	1	0	0	0	1	0	0	0	0	0	1	0	0	.200	.167	.200	.714
Career average		55	125	13	28	5	1	2	13	9	1	19	1	2	1	1	1	.226	.282	.341	.959
Cubs average		**49**	**101**	**12**	**22**	**6**	**0**	**0**	**8**	**10**	**0**	**16**	**0**	**0**	**0**	**0**	**0**	**.218**	**.288**	**.277**	**.969**
Career total		442	1003	102	227	36	11	19	106	75	8	154	7	17	11	9	9	.226	.282	.341	.959
Cubs total		**49**	**101**	**12**	**22**	**6**	**0**	**0**	**8**	**10**	**0**	**16**	**0**	**0**	**0**	**0**	**0**	**.218**	**.288**	**.277**	**.969**

Rader, David Martin (Dave)

HEIGHT: 5'11"   THROWS: RIGHT   BATS: LEFT   BORN: 12/26/1948 CLAREMORE, OKLAHOMA   POSITIONS PLAYED: C

YEAR	TEAM	GAMES	AB	RUNS	HITS	2B	3B	HR	RBI	BB	IBB	SO	HBP	SH	SF	SB	CS	BA	OBA	SA	FA
1971	SF-N	3	4	0	0	0	0	0	0	0	0	0	0	0	0	0	0	.000	.000	.000	1.000
1972	SF-N	133	459	44	119	14	1	6	41	29	4	31	3	1	2	1	2	.259	.306	.333	.985
1973	SF-N	148	462	59	106	15	4	9	41	63	23	22	6	4	5	0	0	.229	.326	.338	.991
1974	SF-N	113	323	26	94	16	2	1	26	31	9	21	0	5	2	1	0	.291	.351	.362	.984
1975	SF-N	98	292	39	85	15	0	5	31	32	12	30	1	0	3	1	0	.291	.360	.394	.984
1976	SF-N	88	255	25	67	15	0	1	22	27	8	21	0	1	1	2	0	.263	.332	.333	.984
1977	StL-N	66	114	15	30	7	1	1	16	9	0	10	0	3	3	1	0	.263	.310	.368	.976
1978	**ChC-N**	**116**	**305**	**29**	**62**	**13**	**3**	**3**	**36**	**34**	**7**	**26**	**1**	**3**	**5**	**1**	**1**	**.203**	**.281**	**.295**	**.977**
1979	Phi-N	31	54	3	11	1	1	1	5	6	0	7	0	2	0	0	1	.204	.283	.315	.932
1980	Bos-A	50	137	14	45	11	0	3	17	14	1	12	0	0	1	1	1	.328	.388	.474	.981
Career average		85	241	25	62	11	1	3	24	25	6	18	1	2	2	1	0	.257	.326	.349	.983
Cubs average		**116**	**305**	**29**	**62**	**13**	**3**	**3**	**36**	**34**	**7**	**26**	**1**	**3**	**5**	**1**	**1**	**.203**	**.281**	**.295**	**.977**
Career total		846	2405	254	619	107	12	30	235	245	64	180	11	19	22	8	4	.257	.326	.349	.983
Cubs total		**116**	**305**	**29**	**62**	**13**	**3**	**3**	**36**	**34**	**7**	**26**	**1**	**3**	**5**	**1**	**1**	**.203**	**.281**	**.295**	**.977**

Ramazzotti, Robert Louis (Bob)

HEIGHT: 5'8" THROWS: RIGHT BATS: RIGHT BORN: 1/16/1917 ELANORA, PENNSYLVANIA DIED: 2/15/2000 ALTOONA, PENNSYLVANIA
POSITIONS PLAYED: 2B, 3B, SS

YEAR	TEAM	GAMES	AB	RUNS	HITS	2B	3B	HR	RBI	BB	IBB	SO	HBP	SH	SF	SB	CS	BA	OBA	SA	FA
1946	Bro-N	62	120	10	25	4	0	0	7	9	—	13	0	4	—	0	1	.208	.264	.242	.967
1948	Bro-N	4	3	0	0	0	0	0	0	0	—	1	0	0	—	0	—	.000	.000	.000	1.000
1949	Bro-N	5	13	1	2	0	0	1	3	0	—	3	0	0	—	0	0	.154	.154	.385	.833
1949	ChC-N	65	190	14	34	3	1	0	6	5	—	33	0	6	—	9	—	.179	.200	.205	.969
1950	ChC-N	61	145	19	38	3	3	1	6	4	—	16	1	1	—	3	—	.262	.287	.345	.948
1951	ChC-N	73	158	13	39	5	2	1	15	10	—	23	0	2	—	0	0	.247	.292	.323	.955
1952	ChC-N	50	183	26	52	5	3	1	12	14	—	14	1	0	—	3	1	.284	.338	.361	.979
1953	ChC-N	26	39	3	6	2	0	0	4	3	—	4	0	1	—	0	0	.154	.214	.205	.911
Career average		49	122	12	28	3	1	1	8	6	—	15	0	2	—	2	0	.230	.271	.291	.960
Cubs average		**55**	**143**	**15**	**34**	**4**	**2**	**1**	**9**	**7**	**—**	**18**	**0**	**2**	**—**	**3**	**0**	**.236**	**.275**	**.299**	**.960**
Career total		346	851	86	196	22	9	4	53	45	—	107	2	14	—	15	2	.230	.271	.291	.960
Cubs total		**275**	**715**	**75**	**169**	**18**	**9**	**3**	**43**	**36**	**—**	**90**	**2**	**10**	**—**	**15**	**1**	**.236**	**.275**	**.299**	**.960**

Ramos, Domingo Antonio

HEIGHT: 5'10" THROWS: RIGHT BATS: RIGHT BORN: 3/29/1958 SANTIAGO, DOMINICAN REPUBLIC POSITIONS PLAYED: 1B, 2B, 3B, SS, OF

YEAR	TEAM	GAMES	AB	RUNS	HITS	2B	3B	HR	RBI	BB	IBB	SO	HBP	SH	SF	SB	CS	BA	OBA	SA	FA
1978	NYY-A	1	0	0	0	0	0	0	0	0	0	0	0	0	0	0	0	—	—	—	—
1980	Tor-A	5	16	0	2	0	0	0	0	2	0	5	0	0	0	0	0	.125	.222	.125	1.000
1982	Sea-A	8	26	3	4	2	0	0	1	3	0	2	0	1	0	0	0	.154	.241	.231	.920
1983	Sea-A	53	127	14	36	4	0	2	10	7	0	12	1	1	0	3	1	.283	.326	.362	.952
1984	Sea-A	59	81	6	15	2	0	0	2	5	0	12	0	1	0	2	2	.185	.233	.210	.952
1985	Sea-A	75	168	19	33	6	0	1	15	17	0	23	0	3	2	0	1	.196	.267	.250	.954
1986	Sea-A	49	99	8	18	2	0	0	5	8	0	13	1	2	0	0	1	.182	.250	.202	.961
1987	Sea-A	42	103	9	32	6	0	2	11	3	0	12	1	2	0	1	1	.311	.336	.427	.964
1988	Cle-A	22	46	7	12	1	0	0	5	3	0	7	1	0	2	0	0	.261	.308	.283	.986
1988	Cal-A	10	15	3	2	0	0	0	0	0	0	0	0	0	0	0	0	.133	.133	.133	1.000
1989	ChC-N	85	179	18	47	6	2	1	19	17	4	23	2	6	0	1	1	.263	.333	.335	.946
1990	ChC-N	98	226	22	60	5	0	2	17	27	1	29	1	2	3	0	2	.265	.342	.314	.942
Career average		46	99	10	24	3	0	1	8	8	0	13	1	2	1	1	1	.240	.302	.297	.955
Cubs average		**92**	**203**	**20**	**54**	**6**	**1**	**2**	**18**	**22**	**3**	**26**	**2**	**4**	**2**	**1**	**2**	**.264**	**.338**	**.323**	**.944**
Career total		507	1086	109	261	34	2	8	85	92	5	138	7	18	7	6	9	.240	.302	.297	.955
Cubs total		**183**	**405**	**40**	**107**	**11**	**2**	**3**	**36**	**44**	**5**	**52**	**3**	**8**	**3**	**1**	**3**	**.264**	**.338**	**.323**	**.944**

Ramsey, Fernando David

HEIGHT: 6'1" THROWS: RIGHT BATS: RIGHT BORN: 12/20/1965 RAINBOW, PANAMA POSITIONS PLAYED: OF

YEAR	TEAM	GAMES	AB	RUNS	HITS	2B	3B	HR	RBI	BB	IBB	SO	HBP	SH	SF	SB	CS	BA	OBA	SA	FA
1992	ChC-N	18	25	0	3	0	0	0	2	0	0	6	0	0	0	0	0	.120	.120	.120	1.000
Career average		18	25	0	3	0	0	0	2	0	0	6	0	0	0	0	0	.120	.120	.120	1.000
Cubs average		**18**	**25**	**0**	**3**	**0**	**0**	**0**	**2**	**0**	**0**	**6**	**0**	**0**	**0**	**0**	**0**	**.120**	**.120**	**.120**	**1.000**
Career total		18	25	0	3	0	0	0	2	0	0	6	0	0	0	0	0	.120	.120	.120	1.000
Cubs total		**18**	**25**	**0**	**3**	**0**	**0**	**0**	**2**	**0**	**0**	**6**	**0**	**0**	**0**	**0**	**0**	**.120**	**.120**	**.120**	**1.000**

Randall, Newton J. (Newt)

HEIGHT: 5'10" THROWS: RIGHT BATS: RIGHT BORN: 2/3/1880 NEW LOWELL, ONTARIO, CANADA DIED: 5/3/1955 DULUTH, MINNESOTA
POSITIONS PLAYED: OF

YEAR	TEAM	GAMES	AB	RUNS	HITS	2B	3B	HR	RBI	BB	IBB	SO	HBP	SH	SF	SB	CS	BA	OBA	SA	FA
1907	ChC-N	22	78	6	16	4	2	0	4	8	—	—	0	2	—	2	—	.205	.279	.308	.904
1907	Bos-N	75	258	16	55	6	3	0	15	19	—	—	7	6	—	4	—	.213	.285	.260	.920
Career average		97	336	22	71	10	5	0	19	27	—	—	7	8	—	6	—	.211	.284	.271	.915
Cubs average		**22**	**78**	**6**	**16**	**4**	**2**	**0**	**4**	**8**	**—**	**—**	**0**	**2**	**—**	**2**	**—**	**.205**	**.279**	**.308**	**.904**
Career total		97	336	22	71	10	5	0	19	27	—	—	7	8	—	6	—	.211	.284	.271	.915
Cubs total		**22**	**78**	**6**	**16**	**4**	**2**	**0**	**4**	**8**	**—**	**—**	**0**	**2**	**—**	**2**	**—**	**.205**	**.279**	**.308**	**.904**

Randle, Leonard Shenoff (Lenny)

HEIGHT: 5'10" THROWS: RIGHT BATS: BOTH BORN: 2/12/1949 LONG BEACH, CALIFORNIA POSITIONS PLAYED: C, 2B, 3B, SS, OF

YEAR	TEAM	GAMES	AB	RUNS	HITS	2B	3B	HR	RBI	BB	IBB	SO	HBP	SH	SF	SB	CS	BA	OBA	SA	FA
1971	Was-A	75	215	27	47	11	0	2	13	24	2	56	1	7	2	1	1	.219	.298	.298	.967
1972	Tex-A	74	249	23	48	13	0	2	21	13	2	51	1	3	1	4	5	.193	.235	.269	.944
1973	Tex-A	10	29	3	6	1	1	1	1	0	0	2	0	1	0	0	2	.207	.207	.414	.933
1974	Tex-A	151	520	65	157	17	4	1	49	29	2	43	2	16	6	26	17	.302	.338	.356	.956
1975	Tex-A	156	601	85	166	24	7	4	57	57	3	80	4	10	4	16	19	.276	.341	.359	.976
1976	Tex-A	142	539	53	121	11	6	1	51	46	2	63	2	6	4	30	15	.224	.286	.273	.971
1977	NYM-N	136	513	78	156	22	7	5	27	65	3	70	2	3	2	33	21	.304	.383	.404	.965
1978	NYM-N	132	437	53	102	16	8	2	35	64	7	57	1	2	4	14	11	.233	.330	.320	.967
1979	NYY-A	20	39	2	7	0	0	0	3	3	0	2	0	0	0	0	0	.179	.238	.179	1.000
1980	**ChC-N**	**130**	**489**	**67**	**135**	**19**	**6**	**5**	**39**	**50**	**2**	**55**	**1**	**7**	**2**	**19**	**13**	**.276**	**.343**	**.370**	**.940**
1981	Sea-A	82	273	22	63	9	1	4	25	17	4	22	1	6	3	11	6	.231	.276	.315	.982
1982	Sea-A	30	46	10	8	2	0	0	1	4	0	4	0	1	0	2	2	.174	.240	.217	.925
Career average		95	329	41	85	12	3	2	27	31	2	42	1	5	2	13	9	.257	.321	.335	.963
Cubs average		**130**	**489**	**67**	**135**	**19**	**6**	**5**	**39**	**50**	**2**	**55**	**1**	**7**	**2**	**19**	**13**	**.276**	**.343**	**.370**	**.940**
Career total		1138	3950	488	1016	145	40	27	322	372	27	505	15	62	28	156	112	.257	.321	.335	.963
Cubs total		**130**	**489**	**67**	**135**	**19**	**6**	**5**	**39**	**50**	**2**	**55**	**1**	**7**	**2**	**19**	**13**	**.276**	**.343**	**.370**	**.940**

Ranew, Merritt Thomas

HEIGHT: 5'11" THROWS: RIGHT BATS: LEFT BORN: 5/10/1938 ALBANY, GEORGIA POSITIONS PLAYED: C, 1B, 3B, OF

YEAR	TEAM	GAMES	AB	RUNS	HITS	2B	3B	HR	RBI	BB	IBB	SO	HBP	SH	SF	SB	CS	BA	OBA	SA	FA
1962	Hou-N	71	218	26	51	6	8	4	24	14	5	43	3	2	2	2	2	.234	.287	.390	.980
1963	**ChC-N**	**78**	**154**	**18**	**52**	**8**	**1**	**3**	**15**	**9**	**1**	**32**	**2**	**0**	**1**	**1**	**0**	**.338**	**.380**	**.461**	**.987**
1964	**ChC-N**	**16**	**33**	**0**	**3**	**0**	**0**	**0**	**1**	**2**	**0**	**6**	**1**	**0**	**0**	**0**	**0**	**.091**	**.167**	**.091**	**1.000**
1964	Mil-N	9	17	1	2	0	0	0	0	0	0	3	0	0	0	0	1	.118	.118	.118	1.000
1965	Cal-A	41	91	12	19	4	0	1	10	7	0	22	0	2	2	0	0	.209	.260	.286	.988
1969	Sea-A	54	81	11	20	2	0	0	4	10	3	14	0	1	0	0	0	.247	.330	.272	.971
Career average		54	119	14	29	4	2	2	11	8	2	24	1	1	1	1	1	.247	.301	.352	.984
Cubs average		**47**	**94**	**9**	**28**	**4**	**1**	**2**	**8**	**6**	**1**	**19**	**2**	**0**	**1**	**1**	**0**	**.294**	**.342**	**.396**	**.989**
Career total		269	594	68	147	20	9	8	54	42	9	120	6	5	5	3	3	.247	.301	.352	.984
Cubs total		**94**	**187**	**18**	**55**	**8**	**1**	**3**	**16**	**11**	**1**	**38**	**3**	**0**	**1**	**1**	**0**	**.294**	**.342**	**.396**	**.989**

Raub, Thomas Jefferson (Tommy)

HEIGHT: 5'10" THROWS: RIGHT BATS: RIGHT BORN: 12/1/1870 RAUBSVILLE, PENNSYLVANIA DIED: 2/15/1949 PHILLIPSBURG, NEW JERSEY
POSITIONS PLAYED: C, 1B, 3B, OF

YEAR	TEAM	GAMES	AB	RUNS	HITS	2B	3B	HR	RBI	BB	IBB	SO	HBP	SH	SF	SB	CS	BA	OBA	SA	FA
1903	**ChC-N**	**36**	**84**	**6**	**19**	**3**	**2**	**0**	**7**	**5**	**—**	**—**	**1**	**2**	**—**	**3**	**—**	**.226**	**.278**	**.310**	**.880**
1906	StL-N	24	78	9	22	2	4	0	2	4	—	—	1	0	—	2	—	.282	.325	.410	.957
Career average		30	81	8	21	3	3	0	5	5	—	—	1	1	—	3	—	.253	.301	.358	.917
Cubs average		**36**	**84**	**6**	**19**	**3**	**2**	**0**	**7**	**5**	**—**	**—**	**1**	**2**	**—**	**3**	**—**	**.226**	**.278**	**.310**	**.880**
Career total		60	162	15	41	5	6	0	9	9	—	—	2	2	—	5	—	.253	.301	.358	.917
Cubs total		**36**	**84**	**6**	**19**	**3**	**2**	**0**	**7**	**5**	**—**	**—**	**1**	**2**	**—**	**3**	**—**	**.226**	**.278**	**.310**	**.880**

Raudman, Robert Joyce (Bob *or* Shorty)

HEIGHT: 5'9" THROWS: LEFT BATS: LEFT BORN: 3/14/1942 ERIE, PENNSYLVANIA POSITIONS PLAYED: OF

YEAR	TEAM	GAMES	AB	RUNS	HITS	2B	3B	HR	RBI	BB	IBB	SO	HBP	SH	SF	SB	CS	BA	OBA	SA	FA
1966	**ChC-N**	**8**	**29**	**1**	**7**	**2**	**0**	**0**	**2**	**1**	**0**	**4**	**0**	**0**	**0**	**0**	**0**	**.241**	**.267**	**.310**	**.909**
1967	**ChC-N**	**8**	**26**	**0**	**4**	**0**	**0**	**0**	**1**	**1**	**1**	**4**	**0**	**0**	**0**	**0**	**0**	**.154**	**.185**	**.154**	**.875**
Career average		8	28	1	6	1	0	0	2	1	1	4	0	0	0	0	0	.200	.228	.236	.889
Cubs average		**8**	**28**	**1**	**6**	**1**	**0**	**0**	**2**	**1**	**1**	**4**	**0**	**0**	**0**	**0**	**0**	**.200**	**.228**	**.236**	**.889**
Career total		16	55	1	11	2	0	0	3	2	1	8	0	0	0	0	0	.200	.228	.236	.889
Cubs total		**16**	**55**	**1**	**11**	**2**	**0**	**0**	**3**	**2**	**1**	**8**	**0**	**0**	**0**	**0**	**0**	**.200**	**.228**	**.236**	**.889**

Raymer, Frederick Charles (Fred)

HEIGHT: 5'11" THROWS: RIGHT BATS: RIGHT BORN: 11/12/1875 LEAVENWORTH, KANSAS DIED: 6/11/1957 LOS ANGELES, CALIFORNIA
POSITIONS PLAYED: 1B, 2B, 3B, SS, OF

YEAR	TEAM	GAMES	AB	RUNS	HITS	2B	3B	HR	RBI	BB	IBB	SO	HBP	SH	SF	SB	CS	BA	OBA	SA	FA
1901	ChN-N	120	463	41	108	14	2	0	43	11	—	—	4	9	—	18	—	.233	.257	.272	.909
1904	Bos-N	114	419	28	88	12	3	1	27	13	—	—	1	20	—	17	—	.210	.236	.260	.958
1905	Bos-N	137	498	26	105	14	2	0	31	8	—	—	6	10	—	15	—	.211	.232	.247	.950
Career average		124	460	32	100	13	2	0	34	11	—	—	4	13	—	17	—	.218	.242	.259	.943
Cubs average		**120**	**463**	**41**	**108**	**14**	**2**	**0**	**43**	**11**	—	—	**4**	**9**	—	**18**	—	**.233**	**.257**	**.272**	**.909**
Career total		371	1380	95	301	40	7	1	101	32	—	—	11	39	—	50	—	.218	.242	.259	.943
Cubs total		**120**	**463**	**41**	**108**	**14**	**2**	**0**	**43**	**11**	—	—	**4**	**9**	—	**18**	—	**.233**	**.257**	**.272**	**.909**

Reed, Jeffrey Scott (Jeff)

HEIGHT: 6'2" THROWS: RIGHT BATS: LEFT BORN: 11/12/1962 JOLIET, ILLINOIS POSITIONS PLAYED: C, 3B

YEAR	TEAM	GAMES	AB	RUNS	HITS	2B	3B	HR	RBI	BB	IBB	SO	HBP	SH	SF	SB	CS	BA	OBA	SA	FA
1984	Min-A	18	21	3	3	3	0	0	1	2	0	6	0	1	0	0	0	.143	.217	.286	.977
1985	Min-A	7	10	2	2	0	0	0	0	0	0	3	0	0	0	0	0	.200	.200	.200	1.000
1986	Min-A	68	165	13	39	6	1	2	9	16	0	19	1	3	0	1	0	.236	.308	.321	.994
1987	Mon-N	75	207	15	44	11	0	1	21	12	1	20	1	4	4	0	1	.213	.254	.280	.970
1988	Mon-N	43	123	10	27	3	2	0	9	13	1	22	0	1	1	1	0	.220	.292	.276	.995
1988	Cin-N	49	142	10	33	6	0	1	7	15	0	19	0	0	0	0	0	.232	.306	.296	.993
1989	Cin-N	102	287	16	64	11	0	3	23	34	5	46	2	3	4	0	0	.223	.306	.293	.988
1990	Cin-N	72	175	12	44	8	1	3	16	24	5	26	0	5	1	0	0	.251	.340	.360	.987
1991	Cin-N	91	270	20	72	15	2	3	31	23	3	38	1	1	5	0	1	.267	.321	.370	.991
1992	Cin-N	15	25	2	4	0	0	0	2	1	1	4	0	0	0	0	0	.160	.192	.160	1.000
1993	SF-N	66	119	10	31	3	0	6	12	16	4	22	0	0	1	0	1	.261	.346	.437	1.000
1994	SF-N	50	103	11	18	3	0	1	7	11	4	21	0	0	0	0	0	.175	.254	.233	.993
1995	SF-N	66	113	12	30	2	0	0	9	20	3	17	0	1	0	0	0	.265	.376	.283	.995
1996	Col-N	116	341	34	97	20	1	8	37	43	8	65	2	6	3	2	2	.284	.365	.419	.982
1997	Col-N	90	256	43	76	10	0	17	47	35	1	55	2	5	0	2	1	.297	.386	.535	.987
1998	Col-N	113	259	43	75	17	1	9	39	37	4	57	1	3	3	0	0	.290	.377	.467	.986
1999	Col-N	46	106	11	27	5	0	2	11	17	1	24	1	0	1	0	1	.255	.360	.358	.983
1999	**ChC-N**	**57**	**150**	**18**	**39**	**11**	**2**	**1**	**17**	**28**	**0**	**34**	**2**	**0**	**1**	**1**	**1**	**.260**	**.381**	**.380**	**.987**
2000	**ChC-N**	**90**	**229**	**26**	**49**	**10**	**0**	**4**	**25**	**44**	**2**	**68**	**1**	**2**	**1**	**0**	**1**	**.214**	**.342**	**.310**	**.990**
Career average		73	182	18	46	8	1	4	19	23	3	33	1	2	1	0	1	.250	.334	.361	.988
Cubs average		**74**	**190**	**22**	**44**	**11**	**1**	**3**	**21**	**36**	**1**	**51**	**2**	**1**	**1**	**1**	**1**	**.232**	**.357**	**.338**	**.989**
Career total		1234	3101	311	774	144	10	61	323	391	43	566	14	35	25	7	9	.250	.334	.361	.988
Cubs total		**147**	**379**	**44**	**88**	**21**	**2**	**5**	**42**	**72**	**2**	**102**	**3**	**2**	**2**	**1**	**2**	**.232**	**.357**	**.338**	**.989**

Reich, Herman Charles

HEIGHT: 6'2" THROWS: LEFT BATS: RIGHT BORN: 11/23/1917 BELL, CALIFORNIA POSITIONS PLAYED: 1B, OF

YEAR	TEAM	GAMES	AB	RUNS	HITS	2B	3B	HR	RBI	BB	IBB	SO	HBP	SH	SF	SB	CS	BA	OBA	SA	FA
1949	Was-A	2	2	0	0	0	0	0	0	0	—	1	0	0	—	0	0	.000	.000	.000	—
1949	Cle-A	1	2	0	1	0	0	0	0	1	—	0	0	0	—	0	0	.500	.667	.500	—
1949	**ChC-N**	**108**	**386**	**43**	**108**	**18**	**2**	**3**	**34**	**13**	—	**32**	**1**	**7**	—	**4**	—	**.280**	**.305**	**.360**	**.989**
Career average		111	390	43	109	18	2	3	34	14	—	33	1	7	—	4	0	.279	.306	.359	.989
Cubs average		**108**	**386**	**43**	**108**	**18**	**2**	**3**	**34**	**13**	—	**32**	**1**	**7**	—	**4**	**0**	**.280**	**.305**	**.360**	**.989**
Career total		111	390	43	109	18	2	3	34	14	—	33	1	7	—	4	0	.279	.306	.359	.989
Cubs total		**108**	**386**	**43**	**108**	**18**	**2**	**3**	**34**	**13**	—	**32**	**1**	**7**	—	**4**	**0**	**.280**	**.305**	**.360**	**.989**

Reilly, Harold John (Hal)

HEIGHT: 6'0" THROWS: LEFT BATS: LEFT BORN: 4/1/1894 OSHKOSH, WISCONSIN DIED: 12/24/1957 CHICAGO, ILLINOIS POSITIONS PLAYED: OF

YEAR	TEAM	GAMES	AB	RUNS	HITS	2B	3B	HR	RBI	BB	IBB	SO	HBP	SH	SF	SB	CS	BA	OBA	SA	FA
1919	ChC-N	1	3	0	0	0	0	0	0	0	—	1	0	0	—	0	—	.000	.000	.000	—
Career average		1	3	0	0	0	0	0	0	0	—	1	0	0	—	0	—	.000	.000	.000	—
Cubs average		**1**	**3**	**0**	**0**	**0**	**0**	**0**	**0**	**0**	—	**1**	**0**	**0**	—	**0**	—	**.000**	**.000**	**.000**	—
Career total		1	3	0	0	0	0	0	0	0	—	1	0	0	—	0	—	.000	.000	.000	—
Cubs total		**1**	**3**	**0**	**0**	**0**	**0**	**0**	**0**	**0**	—	**1**	**0**	**0**	—	**0**	—	**.000**	**.000**	**.000**	—

Reilly, William H. (Josh)
HEIGHT: 5'8" THROWS: — BATS: — BORN: 5/9/1868 SAN FRANCISCO, CALIFORNIA DIED: 6/12/1938 SAN FRANCISCO, CALIFORNIA
POSITIONS PLAYED: 2B, SS

YEAR	TEAM	GAMES	AB	RUNS	HITS	2B	3B	HR	RBI	BB	IBB	SO	HBP	SH	SF	SB	CS	BA	OBA	SA	FA
1896	ChN-N	9	42	6	9	1	0	0	2	1	—	1	0	0	—	2	—	.214	.233	.238	.828
Career average		9	42	6	9	1	0	0	2	1	—	1	0	0	—	2	—	.214	.233	.238	.828
Cubs average		**9**	**42**	**6**	**9**	**1**	**0**	**0**	**2**	**1**	**—**	**1**	**0**	**0**	**—**	**2**	**—**	**.214**	**.233**	**.238**	**.828**
Career total		9	42	6	9	1	0	0	2	1	—	1	0	0	—	2	—	.214	.233	.238	.828
Cubs total		**9**	**42**	**6**	**9**	**1**	**0**	**0**	**2**	**1**	**—**	**1**	**0**	**0**	**—**	**2**	**—**	**.214**	**.233**	**.238**	**.828**

Reitz, Kenneth John (Ken *or* The Zamboni Machine)
HEIGHT: 6'0" THROWS: RIGHT BATS: RIGHT BORN: 6/24/1951 SAN FRANCISCO, CALIFORNIA POSITIONS PLAYED: 2B, 3B, SS

YEAR	TEAM	GAMES	AB	RUNS	HITS	2B	3B	HR	RBI	BB	IBB	SO	HBP	SH	SF	SB	CS	BA	OBA	SA	FA
1972	StL-N	21	78	5	28	4	0	0	10	2	0	4	0	0	1	0	1	.359	.370	.410	.956
1973	StL-N	147	426	40	100	20	2	6	42	9	2	25	4	4	3	0	1	.235	.256	.333	.974
1974	StL-N	154	579	48	157	28	2	7	54	23	7	63	2	3	5	0	0	.271	.299	.363	.972
1975	StL-N	161	592	43	159	25	1	5	63	22	9	54	5	2	6	1	1	.269	.298	.340	.946
1976	SF-N	155	577	40	154	21	1	5	66	24	5	48	1	3	9	5	4	.267	.293	.333	.959
1977	StL-N	157	587	58	153	36	1	17	79	19	4	74	7	5	2	2	6	.261	.291	.412	.980
1978	StL-N	150	540	41	133	26	2	10	75	23	5	61	5	3	7	1	0	.246	.280	.357	.973
1979	StL-N	159	605	42	162	41	2	8	73	25	7	85	4	4	5	1	0	.268	.299	.382	.972
1980	StL-N	151	523	39	141	33	0	8	58	22	5	44	3	8	5	0	1	.270	.300	.379	.979
1981	ChC-N	82	260	10	56	9	1	2	28	15	3	56	3	2	6	0	0	.215	.261	.281	.977
1982	Pit-N	7	10	0	0	0	0	0	0	0	0	4	1	0	0	0	0	.000	.091	.000	1.000
Career average		122	434	33	113	22	1	6	50	17	4	47	3	3	4	1	1	.260	.290	.359	.969
Cubs average		**82**	**260**	**10**	**56**	**9**	**1**	**2**	**28**	**15**	**3**	**56**	**3**	**2**	**6**	**0**	**0**	**.215**	**.261**	**.281**	**.977**
Career total		1344	4777	366	1243	243	12	68	548	184	47	518	35	34	49	10	14	.260	.290	.359	.969
Cubs total		**82**	**260**	**10**	**56**	**9**	**1**	**2**	**28**	**15**	**3**	**56**	**3**	**2**	**6**	**0**	**0**	**.215**	**.261**	**.281**	**.977**

Remsen, John Jay (Jack)
HEIGHT: 5'11" THROWS: RIGHT BATS: RIGHT BORN: 4/1850 BROOKLYN, NEW YORK POSITIONS PLAYED: 1B, OF

YEAR	TEAM	GAMES	AB	RUNS	HITS	2B	3B	HR	RBI	BB	IBB	SO	HBP	SH	SF	SB	CS	BA	OBA	SA	FA
1876	Har-N	69	325	62	89	12	5	1	30	1	—	15	—	—	—	—	—	.274	.276	.351	.887
1877	StL-N	33	123	14	32	3	4	0	13	4	—	3	—	—	—	—	—	.260	.283	.350	.906
1878	ChN-N	56	224	32	52	11	1	1	19	17	—	33	—	—	—	—	—	.232	.286	.304	.944
1879	ChN-N	42	152	14	33	4	2	0	8	2	—	23	—	—	—	—	—	.217	.227	.270	.899
1881	Cle-N	48	172	14	30	4	3	0	13	9	—	31	—	—	—	—	—	.174	.215	.233	.873
1884	Phi-N	12	43	9	9	2	0	0	3	6	—	9	—	—	—	—	—	.209	.306	.256	.952
1884	Bro-AA	81	301	45	67	6	6	3	—	23	—	—	0	—	—	—	—	.223	.278	.312	.914
Career average		57	223	32	52	7	4	1	14	10	—	19	0	—	—	—	—	.233	.267	.307	.903
Cubs average		**49**	**188**	**23**	**43**	**8**	**2**	**1**	**14**	**10**	**—**	**28**	**—**	**—**	**—**	**—**	**—**	**.226**	**.263**	**.290**	**.915**
Career total		341	1340	190	312	42	21	5	86	62	—	114	0	—	—	—	—	.233	.267	.307	.903
Cubs total		**98**	**376**	**46**	**85**	**15**	**3**	**1**	**27**	**19**	**—**	**56**	**—**	**—**	**—**	**—**	**—**	**.226**	**.263**	**.290**	**.915**

Reynolds, Carl Nettles
HEIGHT: 6'0" THROWS: RIGHT BATS: RIGHT BORN: 2/1/1903 LARUE, TEXAS DIED: 5/29/1978 HOUSTON, TEXAS POSITIONS PLAYED: OF

YEAR	TEAM	GAMES	AB	RUNS	HITS	2B	3B	HR	RBI	BB	IBB	SO	HBP	SH	SF	SB	CS	BA	OBA	SA	FA
1927	CWS-A	14	42	5	9	3	0	1	7	5	—	7	1	1	—	1	2	.214	.313	.357	1.000
1928	CWS-A	84	291	51	94	21	11	2	36	17	—	13	5	6	—	15	3	.323	.371	.491	.979
1929	CWS-A	131	517	81	164	24	12	11	67	20	—	37	4	18	—	19	9	.317	.348	.474	.949
1930	CWS-A	138	563	103	202	25	18	22	104	20	—	39	7	12	—	16	4	.359	.388	.584	.975
1931	CWS-A	118	462	71	134	24	14	6	77	24	—	26	6	3	—	17	6	.290	.333	.442	.949
1932	Was-A	102	406	53	124	28	7	9	63	13	—	19	2	2	—	8	4	.305	.330	.475	.983
1933	StL-A	135	475	81	136	26	14	8	71	49	—	25	2	11	—	5	4	.286	.356	.451	.965
1934	Bos-A	113	413	61	125	26	9	4	86	27	—	28	3	3	—	5	3	.303	.350	.438	.975
1935	Bos-A	78	244	33	66	13	4	6	35	24	—	20	0	5	—	4	1	.270	.336	.430	.975
1936	Was-A	89	293	41	81	18	2	4	41	21	—	22	2	2	—	8	4	.276	.329	.392	.968
1937	ChC-N	7	11	0	3	1	0	0	1	2	—	2	0	0	—	0	—	.273	.385	.364	.800

(continued)

(continued)

YEAR	TEAM	GAMES	AB	RUNS	HITS	2B	3B	HR	RBI	BB	IBB	SO	HBP	SH	SF	SB	CS	BA	OBA	SA	FA
1938	ChC-N	125	497	59	150	28	10	3	67	22	—	32	3	8	—	9	—	.302	.335	.416	.983
1939	ChC-N	88	281	33	69	10	6	4	44	16	—	38	5	11	—	5	—	.246	.298	.367	.972
Career average		94	346	52	104	19	8	6	54	20	—	24	3	6	—	9	3	.302	.346	.458	.970
Cubs average		73	263	31	74	13	5	2	37	13	—	24	3	6	—	5	0	.281	.323	.398	.977
Career total		1222	4495	672	1357	247	107	80	699	260	—	308	40	82	—	112	40	.302	.346	.458	.970
Cubs total		220	789	92	222	39	16	7	112	40	—	72	8	19	—	14	0	.281	.323	.398	.977

Rhodes, Karl Derrick (Tuffy)

HEIGHT: 6'0"   THROWS: LEFT   BATS: LEFT   BORN: 8/21/1968 CINCINNATI, OHIO   POSITIONS PLAYED: OF

YEAR	TEAM	GAMES	AB	RUNS	HITS	2B	3B	HR	RBI	BB	IBB	SO	HBP	SH	SF	SB	CS	BA	OBA	SA	FA
1990	Hou-N	38	86	12	21	6	1	1	3	13	3	12	0	1	1	4	1	.244	.340	.372	.955
1991	Hou-N	44	136	7	29	3	1	1	12	14	3	26	1	0	1	2	2	.213	.289	.272	.958
1992	Hou-N	5	4	0	0	0	0	0	0	0	0	2	0	0	0	0	0	.000	.000	.000	—
1993	Hou-N	5	2	0	0	0	0	0	0	0	0	0	0	0	0	0	0	.000	.000	.000	1.000
1993	ChC-N	15	52	12	15	2	1	3	7	11	0	9	0	0	0	0	0	.288	.413	.538	.970
1994	ChC-N	95	269	39	63	17	0	8	19	33	1	64	1	3	2	6	4	.234	.318	.387	.967
1995	ChC-N	13	16	2	2	0	0	0	2	0	0	4	0	0	1	0	0	.125	.118	.125	.889
1995	Bos-A	10	25	2	2	1	0	0	1	3	0	4	0	0	0	0	0	.080	.179	.120	.947
Career average		38	98	12	22	5	1	2	7	12	1	20	0	1	1	2	1	.224	.310	.349	.960
Cubs average		41	112	18	27	6	0	4	9	15	0	26	0	1	1	3	1	.237	.325	.398	.964
Career total		225	590	74	132	29	3	13	44	74	7	121	2	4	5	14	7	.224	.310	.349	.960
Cubs total		123	337	53	80	19	1	11	28	44	1	77	1	3	3	8	4	.237	.325	.398	.964

Rice, Delbert W. (Del)

HEIGHT: 6'2"   THROWS: RIGHT   BATS: RIGHT   BORN: 10/27/1922 PORTSMOUTH, OHIO   DIED: 1/26/1983 BUENA PARK, CALIFORNIA   POSITIONS PLAYED: C

YEAR	TEAM	GAMES	AB	RUNS	HITS	2B	3B	HR	RBI	BB	IBB	SO	HBP	SH	SF	SB	CS	BA	OBA	SA	FA
1945	StL-N	83	253	27	66	17	3	1	28	16	—	33	3	5	—	0	—	.261	.313	.364	.994
1946	StL-N	55	139	10	38	8	1	1	12	8	—	16	0	3	—	0	—	.273	.313	.367	.977
1947	StL-N	97	261	28	57	7	3	12	44	36	—	40	1	3	—	1	—	.218	.315	.406	.981
1948	StL-N	100	290	24	57	10	1	4	34	37	—	46	5	6	—	1	—	.197	.298	.279	.996
1949	StL-N	92	284	25	67	16	1	4	29	30	—	40	5	6	—	0	—	.236	.320	.342	.992
1950	StL-N	130	414	39	101	20	3	9	54	43	—	65	5	9	—	0	—	.244	.323	.372	.984
1951	StL-N	122	374	34	94	13	1	9	47	34	—	26	3	8	—	0	0	.251	.319	.364	.985
1952	StL-N	147	495	43	128	27	2	11	65	33	—	38	6	3	—	0	1	.259	.313	.388	.992
1953	StL-N	135	419	32	99	22	1	6	37	48	—	49	6	7	—	0	0	.236	.323	.337	.988
1954	StL-N	56	147	13	37	10	1	2	16	16	—	21	0	2	2	0	1	.252	.321	.374	.985
1955	StL-N	20	59	6	12	3	0	1	7	7	0	6	0	1	1	0	0	.203	.284	.305	.964
1955	Mil-N	27	71	5	14	0	1	2	7	6	2	12	0	1	0	0	0	.197	.260	.310	.981
1956	Mil-N	71	188	15	40	9	1	3	17	18	7	34	0	2	0	0	0	.213	.282	.319	.983
1957	Mil-N	54	144	15	33	1	1	9	20	17	7	37	0	0	1	0	0	.229	.309	.438	.992
1958	Mil-N	43	121	10	27	7	0	1	8	8	1	30	0	3	0	0	0	.223	.271	.306	.995
1959	Mil-N	13	29	3	6	0	0	0	1	2	0	3	0	0	0	0	0	.207	.250	.207	.956
1960	ChC-N	18	52	2	12	3	0	0	4	2	1	7	0	0	1	0	0	.231	.255	.288	.968
1960	StL-N	1	2	0	0	0	0	0	0	1	0	0	0	0	0	0	0	.000	.333	.000	1.000
1960	Bal-A	1	1	0	0	0	0	0	0	0	0	0	0	0	0	0	0	.000	.000	.000	1.000
1961	LAA-A	44	83	11	20	4	0	4	11	20	5	19	0	3	1	0	1	.241	.385	.434	.994
Career average		77	225	20	53	10	1	5	26	22	1	31	2	4	0	0	0	.237	.312	.356	.987
Cubs average		18	52	2	12	3	0	0	4	2	1	7	0	0	1	0	0	.231	.255	.288	.968
Career total		1309	3826	342	908	177	20	79	441	382	23	522	34	63	7	2	3	.237	.312	.356	.987
Cubs total		18	52	2	12	3	0	0	4	2	1	7	0	0	1	0	0	.231	.255	.288	.968

Rice, Harold Housten (Hal or Hoot)

HEIGHT: 6'1"   THROWS: RIGHT   BATS: LEFT   BORN: 2/11/1924 MORGANETTE, WEST VIRGINIA   DIED: 12/22/1997 BLOOMINGTON, INDIANA
POSITIONS PLAYED: OF

YEAR	TEAM	GAMES	AB	RUNS	HITS	2B	3B	HR	RBI	BB	IBB	SO	HBP	SH	SF	SB	CS	BA	OBA	SA	FA
1948	StL-N	8	31	3	10	1	2	0	3	2	—	4	0	0	—	0	—	.323	.364	.484	1.000
1949	StL-N	40	46	3	9	2	1	1	9	3	—	7	0	0	—	0	—	.196	.245	.348	1.000
1950	StL-N	44	128	12	27	3	1	2	11	10	—	10	0	1	—	0	—	.211	.268	.297	.972
1951	StL-N	69	236	20	60	12	1	4	38	24	—	22	0	0	—	0	1	.254	.323	.364	.953
1952	StL-N	98	295	37	85	14	5	7	45	16	—	26	0	1	—	1	3	.288	.325	.441	.972
1953	StL-N	8	8	0	2	0	0	0	0	0	—	3	0	0	—	0	0	.250	.250	.250	—
1953	Pit-N	78	286	39	89	16	1	4	42	17	—	22	0	2	—	0	1	.311	.350	.416	.973
1954	Pit-N	28	81	10	14	4	1	1	9	14	—	24	0	1	—	0	2	.173	.295	.284	1.000
1954	ChC-N	51	72	5	11	0	0	0	5	8	—	15	0	0	1	0	0	.153	.235	.153	.897

(continued)

(Rice, H.H., continued)

	GAMES	AB	RUNS	HITS	2B	3B	HR	RBI	BB	IBB	SO	HBP	SH	SF	SB	CS	BA	OBA	SA	FA
Career average	61	169	18	44	7	2	3	23	13	—	19	0	1	0	0	1	.260	.314	.372	.969
Cubs average	**51**	**72**	**5**	**11**	**0**	**0**	**0**	**5**	**8**	**—**	**15**	**0**	**0**	**1**	**0**	**0**	**.153**	**.235**	**.153**	**.897**
Career total	424	1183	129	307	52	12	19	162	94	—	133	0	5	1	1	7	.260	.314	.372	.969
Cubs total	**51**	**72**	**5**	**11**	**0**	**0**	**0**	**5**	**8**	**—**	**15**	**0**	**0**	**1**	**0**	**0**	**.153**	**.235**	**.153**	**.897**

Rice, Leonard Oliver (Len)
HEIGHT: 6'0" THROWS: RIGHT BATS: RIGHT BORN: 9/2/1918 LEAD, SOUTH DAKOTA DIED: 6/13/1992 SONORA, CALIFORNIA POSITIONS PLAYED: C

YEAR	TEAM	GAMES	AB	RUNS	HITS	2B	3B	HR	RBI	BB	IBB	SO	HBP	SH	SF	SB	CS	BA	OBA	SA	FA
1944	Cin-N	10	4	1	0	0	0	0	0	0	—	0	0	0	—	0	—	.000	.000	.000	1.000
1945	**ChC-N**	**32**	**99**	**10**	**23**	**3**	**0**	**0**	**7**	**5**	**—**	**8**	**0**	**3**	**—**	**2**	**—**	**.232**	**.269**	**.263**	**.976**
Career average		21	52	6	12	2	0	0	4	3	—	4	0	2	—	1	—	.223	.259	.252	.977
Cubs average		**32**	**99**	**10**	**23**	**3**	**0**	**0**	**7**	**5**	**—**	**8**	**0**	**3**	**—**	**2**	**—**	**.232**	**.269**	**.263**	**.976**
Career total		42	103	11	23	3	0	0	7	5	—	8	0	3	—	2	—	.223	.259	.252	.977
Cubs total		**32**	**99**	**10**	**23**	**3**	**0**	**0**	**7**	**5**	**—**	**8**	**0**	**3**	**—**	**2**	**—**	**.232**	**.269**	**.263**	**.976**

Richards, Fred Charles (Fuzzy)
HEIGHT: 6'1" THROWS: LEFT BATS: LEFT BORN: 11/3/1927 WARREN, OHIO POSITIONS PLAYED: 1B

YEAR	TEAM	GAMES	AB	RUNS	HITS	2B	3B	HR	RBI	BB	IBB	SO	HBP	SH	SF	SB	CS	BA	OBA	SA	FA
1951	**ChC-N**	**10**	**27**	**1**	**8**	**2**	**0**	**0**	**4**	**2**	**—**	**3**	**0**	**1**	**—**	**0**	**0**	**.296**	**.345**	**.370**	**1.000**
Career average		10	27	1	8	2	0	0	4	2	—	3	0	1	—	0	0	.296	.345	.370	1.000
Cubs average		**10**	**27**	**1**	**8**	**2**	**0**	**0**	**4**	**2**	**—**	**3**	**0**	**1**	**—**	**0**	**0**	**.296**	**.345**	**.370**	**1.000**
Career total		10	27	1	8	2	0	0	4	2	—	3	0	1	—	0	0	.296	.345	.370	1.000
Cubs total		**10**	**27**	**1**	**8**	**2**	**0**	**0**	**4**	**2**	**—**	**3**	**0**	**1**	**—**	**0**	**0**	**.296**	**.345**	**.370**	**1.000**

Richbourg, Lance Clayton
HEIGHT: 5'10" THROWS: RIGHT BATS: LEFT BORN: 12/18/1897 DEFUNIAK SPRINGS, FLORIDA DIED: 9/10/1975 CRESTVIEW, FLORIDA
POSITIONS PLAYED: 2B, OF

YEAR	TEAM	GAMES	AB	RUNS	HITS	2B	3B	HR	RBI	BB	IBB	SO	HBP	SH	SF	SB	CS	BA	OBA	SA	FA
1921	Phi-N	10	5	2	1	1	0	0	0	0	—	3	0	0	—	1	1	.200	.200	.400	1.000
1924	Was-A	15	32	3	9	2	1	0	1	2	—	0	0	1	—	0	0	.281	.324	.406	1.000
1927	Bos-N	115	450	57	139	12	9	2	34	22	—	30	1	18	—	24	—	.309	.342	.389	.951
1928	Bos-N	148	612	105	206	26	12	2	52	62	—	39	2	9	—	11	—	.337	.399	.428	.972
1929	Bos-N	139	557	76	170	24	13	3	56	42	—	26	1	16	—	7	—	.305	.355	.411	.971
1930	Bos-N	130	529	81	161	23	8	3	54	19	—	31	2	7	—	13	—	.304	.331	.395	.971
1931	Bos-N	97	286	32	82	11	6	2	29	19	—	14	0	6	—	9	—	.287	.331	.388	.981
1932	**ChC-N**	**44**	**148**	**22**	**38**	**2**	**2**	**1**	**21**	**8**	**—**	**4**	**0**	**3**	**—**	**0**	**—**	**.257**	**.295**	**.318**	**.986**
Career average		87	327	47	101	13	6	2	31	22	—	18	1	8	—	8	0	.308	.352	.400	.970
Cubs average		**44**	**148**	**22**	**38**	**2**	**2**	**1**	**21**	**8**	**—**	**4**	**0**	**3**	**—**	**0**	**0**	**.257**	**.295**	**.318**	**.986**
Career total		698	2619	378	806	101	51	13	247	174	—	147	6	60	—	65	1	.308	.352	.400	.970
Cubs total		**44**	**148**	**22**	**38**	**2**	**2**	**1**	**21**	**8**	**—**	**4**	**0**	**3**	**—**	**0**	**0**	**.257**	**.295**	**.318**	**.986**

Rickert, Marvin August (Marv or Twitch)
HEIGHT: 6'2" THROWS: RIGHT BATS: LEFT BORN: 1/8/1921 LONGBRANCH, WASHINGTON DIED: 6/3/1978 OAKVILLE, WASHINGTON
POSITIONS PLAYED: 1B, OF

YEAR	TEAM	GAMES	AB	RUNS	HITS	2B	3B	HR	RBI	BB	IBB	SO	HBP	SH	SF	SB	CS	BA	OBA	SA	FA
1942	**ChC-N**	**8**	**26**	**5**	**7**	**0**	**0**	**0**	**1**	**1**	**—**	**5**	**0**	**0**	**—**	**0**	**—**	**.269**	**.296**	**.269**	**1.000**
1946	**ChC-N**	**111**	**392**	**44**	**103**	**18**	**3**	**7**	**47**	**28**	**—**	**54**	**1**	**4**	**—**	**3**	**—**	**.263**	**.314**	**.378**	**.972**
1947	**ChC-N**	**71**	**137**	**7**	**20**	**0**	**0**	**2**	**15**	**15**	**—**	**17**	**0**	**2**	**—**	**0**	**—**	**.146**	**.230**	**.190**	**.992**
1948	Cin-N	8	6	0	1	0	0	0	0	0	—	0	0	0	—	0	—	.167	.167	.167	
1948	Bos-N	3	13	1	3	0	1	0	2	0	—	1	1	0	—	0	—	.231	.286	.385	1.000
1949	Bos-N	100	277	44	81	18	3	6	49	23	—	38	0	1	—	1	—	.292	.347	.444	.975
1950	Pit-N	17	20	0	3	0	0	0	4	0	—	4	0	0	—	0	—	.150	.150	.150	
1950	CWS-A	84	278	38	66	9	2	4	27	21	—	42	0	2	—	0	1	.237	.291	.327	.969
Career average		67	192	23	47	8	2	3	24	15	—	27	0	2	—	1	0	.247	.302	.352	.977
Cubs average		**63**	**185**	**19**	**43**	**6**	**1**	**3**	**21**	**15**	**—**	**25**	**0**	**2**	**—**	**1**	**—**	**.234**	**.292**	**.326**	**.981**
Career total		402	1149	139	284	45	9	19	145	88	—	161	2	9	—	4	1	.247	.302	.352	.977
Cubs total		**190**	**555**	**56**	**130**	**18**	**3**	**9**	**63**	**44**	**—**	**76**	**1**	**6**	**—**	**3**	**—**	**.234**	**.292**	**.326**	**.981**

Roach, Melvin Earl (Mel)
HEIGHT: 6'1"   THROWS: RIGHT   BATS: RIGHT   BORN: 1/25/1933 RICHMOND, VIRGINIA   POSITIONS PLAYED: 1B, 2B, 3B, OF

YEAR	TEAM	GAMES	AB	RUNS	HITS	2B	3B	HR	RBI	BB	IBB	SO	HBP	SH	SF	SB	CS	BA	OBA	SA	FA
1953	Mil-N	5	2	1	0	0	0	0	0	0	—	1	0	0	—	0	0	.000	.000	.000	—
1954	Mil-N	3	4	0	0	0	0	0	0	0	—	1	0	0	0	0	0	.000	.000	.000	1.000
1957	Mil-N	7	6	1	1	0	0	0	0	0	0	3	0	1	0	0	0	.167	.167	.167	1.000
1958	Mil-N	44	136	14	42	7	0	3	10	6	0	15	0	4	1	0	0	.309	.336	.426	.980
1959	Mil-N	19	31	1	3	0	0	0	0	2	0	4	0	0	0	0	0	.097	.152	.097	.848
1960	Mil-N	48	140	12	42	12	0	3	18	6	1	19	1	3	2	0	0	.300	.329	.450	.961
1961	Mil-N	13	36	3	6	0	0	1	6	2	0	4	2	1	1	0	0	.167	.244	.250	1.000
1961	**ChC-N**	**23**	**39**	**1**	**5**	**2**	**0**	**0**	**1**	**3**	**0**	**9**	**0**	**0**	**0**	**1**	**0**	**.128**	**.190**	**.179**	**.968**
1962	Phi-N	65	105	9	20	4	0	0	8	5	0	19	0	0	1	0	0	.190	.225	.229	.963
Career average		28	62	5	15	3	0	1	5	3	0	9	0	1	1	0	0	.238	.275	.331	.964
Cubs average		**23**	**39**	**1**	**5**	**2**	**0**	**0**	**1**	**3**	**0**	**9**	**0**	**0**	**0**	**1**	**0**	**.128**	**.190**	**.179**	**.968**
Career total		227	499	42	119	25	0	7	43	24	1	75	3	9	5	1	0	.238	.275	.331	.964
Cubs total		**23**	**39**	**1**	**5**	**2**	**0**	**0**	**1**	**3**	**0**	**9**	**0**	**0**	**0**	**1**	**0**	**.128**	**.190**	**.179**	**.968**

Roat, Frederick R. (Fred)
HEIGHT: —   THROWS: RIGHT   BATS: —   BORN: 11/10/1867 OREGON, ILLINOIS   DIED: 9/24/1913 OREGON, ILLINOIS   POSITIONS PLAYED: 1B, 2B, 3B, OF

YEAR	TEAM	GAMES	AB	RUNS	HITS	2B	3B	HR	RBI	BB	IBB	SO	HBP	SH	SF	SB	CS	BA	OBA	SA	FA
1890	Pit-N	57	215	18	48	2	0	2	17	16	—	22	3	—	—	7	—	.223	.286	.260	.880
1892	**ChN-N**	**8**	**31**	**4**	**6**	**0**	**1**	**0**	**2**	**2**	**—**	**3**	**0**	**—**	**—**	**2**	**—**	**.194**	**.242**	**.258**	**.897**
Career average		33	123	11	27	1	1	1	10	9	—	13	2	—	—	5	—	.220	.281	.260	.882
Cubs average		**8**	**31**	**4**	**6**	**0**	**1**	**0**	**2**	**2**	**—**	**3**	**0**	**—**	**—**	**2**	**—**	**.194**	**.242**	**.258**	**.897**
Career total		65	246	22	54	2	1	2	19	18	—	25	3	—	—	9	—	.220	.281	.260	.882
Cubs total		**8**	**31**	**4**	**6**	**0**	**1**	**0**	**2**	**2**	**—**	**3**	**0**	**—**	**—**	**2**	**—**	**.194**	**.242**	**.258**	**.897**

Roberson, Kevin Lynn
HEIGHT: 6'4"   THROWS: RIGHT   BATS: BOTH   BORN: 1/29/1968 DECATUR, ILLINOIS   POSITIONS PLAYED: OF

YEAR	TEAM	GAMES	AB	RUNS	HITS	2B	3B	HR	RBI	BB	IBB	SO	HBP	SH	SF	SB	CS	BA	OBA	SA	FA
1993	ChC-N	62	180	23	34	4	1	9	27	12	0	48	3	0	0	0	1	.189	.251	.372	.963
1994	ChC-N	44	55	8	12	4	0	4	9	2	0	14	2	0	0	0	0	.218	.271	.509	.800
1995	ChC-N	32	38	5	7	1	0	4	6	6	0	14	1	0	0	0	1	.184	.311	.526	1.000
1996	NYM-N	27	36	8	8	1	0	3	9	7	0	17	1	0	2	0	0	.222	.348	.500	1.000
Career average		41	77	11	15	3	0	5	13	7	0	23	2	0	1	0	1	.197	.275	.430	.955
Cubs average		**46**	**91**	**12**	**18**	**3**	**0**	**6**	**14**	**7**	**0**	**25**	**2**	**0**	**0**	**0**	**1**	**.194**	**.264**	**.421**	**.950**
Career total		165	309	44	61	10	1	20	51	27	0	93	7	0	2	0	2	.197	.275	.430	.955
Cubs total		**138**	**273**	**36**	**53**	**9**	**1**	**17**	**42**	**20**	**0**	**76**	**6**	**0**	**0**	**0**	**2**	**.194**	**.264**	**.421**	**.950**

Robertson, Daryl Berdene
HEIGHT: 6'0"   THROWS: RIGHT   BATS: RIGHT   BORN: 1/5/1936 CRIPPLE CREEK, COLORADO   POSITIONS PLAYED: 3B, SS

YEAR	TEAM	GAMES	AB	RUNS	HITS	2B	3B	HR	RBI	BB	IBB	SO	HBP	SH	SF	SB	CS	BA	OBA	SA	FA
1962	ChC-N	9	19	0	2	0	0	0	2	2	0	10	0	0	1	0	0	.105	.182	.105	1.000
Career average		9	19	0	2	0	0	0	2	2	0	10	0	0	1	0	0	.105	.182	.105	1.000
Cubs average		**9**	**19**	**0**	**2**	**0**	**0**	**0**	**2**	**2**	**0**	**10**	**0**	**0**	**1**	**0**	**0**	**.105**	**.182**	**.105**	**1.000**
Career total		9	19	0	2	0	0	0	2	2	0	10	0	0	1	0	0	.105	.182	.105	1.000
Cubs total		**9**	**19**	**0**	**2**	**0**	**0**	**0**	**2**	**2**	**0**	**10**	**0**	**0**	**1**	**0**	**0**	**.105**	**.182**	**.105**	**1.000**

Robertson, Davis Aydelotte (Dave)

HEIGHT: 6'0" THROWS: LEFT BATS: LEFT BORN: 9/25/1889 PORTSMOUTH, VIRGINIA DIED: 11/5/1970 VIRGINIA BEACH, VIRGINIA
POSITIONS PLAYED: 1B, OF

YEAR	TEAM	GAMES	AB	RUNS	HITS	2B	3B	HR	RBI	BB	IBB	SO	HBP	SH	SF	SB	CS	BA	OBA	SA	FA
1912	NYG-N	3	2	0	1	0	0	0	1	0	—	1	0	0	—	1	—	.500	.500	.500	—
1914	NYG-N	82	256	25	68	12	3	2	32	10	—	26	2	7	—	9	—	.266	.299	.359	.950
1915	NYG-N	141	544	72	160	17	10	3	58	22	—	52	4	14	—	22	10	.294	.326	.379	.956
1916	NYG-N	150	587	88	180	18	8	12	69	14	—	56	3	16	—	21	17	.307	.326	.426	.960
1917	NYG-N	142	532	64	138	16	9	12	54	10	—	47	2	16	—	17	—	.259	.276	.391	.942
1919	NYG-N	1	0	0	0	0	0	0	0	0	—	0	0	0	—	0	—	—	—	—	—
1919	**ChC-N**	**27**	**96**	**8**	**20**	**2**	**0**	**1**	**10**	**1**	**—**	**10**	**1**	**0**	**—**	**3**	**—**	**.208**	**.224**	**.260**	**.932**
1920	**ChC-N**	**134**	**500**	**68**	**150**	**29**	**11**	**10**	**75**	**40**	**—**	**44**	**1**	**14**	**—**	**17**	**23**	**.300**	**.353**	**.462**	**.968**
1921	**ChC-N**	**22**	**36**	**7**	**8**	**3**	**0**	**0**	**14**	**1**	**—**	**3**	**0**	**1**	**—**	**0**	**2**	**.222**	**.243**	**.306**	**1.000**
1921	Pit-N	60	230	29	74	18	3	6	48	12	—	16	2	8	—	4	5	.322	.361	.504	.960
1922	NYG-N	42	47	5	13	2	0	1	3	3	—	7	0	0	—	0	0	.277	.320	.383	.909
Career average		89	314	41	90	13	5	5	40	13	—	29	2	8	—	10	6	.287	.318	.409	.955
Cubs average		**61**	**211**	**28**	**59**	**11**	**4**	**4**	**33**	**14**	**—**	**19**	**1**	**5**	**—**	**7**	**8**	**.282**	**.328**	**.422**	**.962**
Career total		804	2830	366	812	117	44	47	364	113	—	262	15	76	—	94	57	.287	.318	.409	.955
Cubs total		**183**	**632**	**83**	**178**	**34**	**11**	**11**	**99**	**42**	**—**	**57**	**2**	**15**	**—**	**20**	**25**	**.282**	**.328**	**.422**	**.962**

Robertson, Donald Alexander (Don)

HEIGHT: 5'10" THROWS: LEFT BATS: LEFT BORN: 10/15/1930 HARVEY, ILLINOIS POSITIONS PLAYED: OF

YEAR	TEAM	GAMES	AB	RUNS	HITS	2B	3B	HR	RBI	BB	IBB	SO	HBP	SH	SF	SB	CS	BA	OBA	SA	FA
1954	**ChC-N**	**14**	**6**	**2**	**0**	**0**	**0**	**0**	**0**	**0**	**—**	**2**	**0**	**0**	**0**	**0**	**0**	**.000**	**.000**	**.000**	**1.000**
Career average		14	6	2	0	0	0	0	0	0	—	2	0	0	0	0	0	.000	.000	.000	1.000
Cubs average		**14**	**6**	**2**	**0**	**0**	**0**	**0**	**0**	**0**	**—**	**2**	**0**	**0**	**0**	**0**	**0**	**.000**	**.000**	**.000**	**1.000**
Career total		14	6	2	0	0	0	0	0	0	—	2	0	0	0	0	0	.000	.000	.000	1.000
Cubs total		**14**	**6**	**2**	**0**	**0**	**0**	**0**	**0**	**0**	**—**	**2**	**0**	**0**	**0**	**0**	**0**	**.000**	**.000**	**.000**	**1.000**

Rodgers, Kenneth Andre Ian (Andre *or* Andy)

HEIGHT: 6'3" THROWS: RIGHT BATS: RIGHT BORN: 12/2/1934 NASSAU, BAHAMAS POSITIONS PLAYED: 1B, 2B, 3B, SS, OF

YEAR	TEAM	GAMES	AB	RUNS	HITS	2B	3B	HR	RBI	BB	IBB	SO	HBP	SH	SF	SB	CS	BA	OBA	SA	FA
1957	NYG-N	32	86	8	21	2	1	3	9	9	0	21	1	0	1	0	0	.244	.320	.395	.937
1958	SF-N	22	63	7	13	3	1	2	11	4	0	14	0	0	3	0	0	.206	.243	.381	.972
1959	SF-N	71	228	32	57	12	1	6	24	32	1	50	1	3	2	2	1	.250	.342	.390	.933
1960	SF-N	81	217	22	53	8	5	2	22	24	4	44	3	0	2	1	1	.244	.325	.355	.953
1961	**ChC-N**	**73**	**214**	**27**	**57**	**17**	**0**	**6**	**23**	**25**	**1**	**54**	**1**	**1**	**2**	**1**	**1**	**.266**	**.343**	**.430**	**.982**
1962	**ChC-N**	**138**	**461**	**40**	**128**	**20**	**8**	**5**	**44**	**44**	**4**	**93**	**3**	**2**	**2**	**5**	**6**	**.278**	**.343**	**.388**	**.961**
1963	**ChC-N**	**150**	**516**	**51**	**118**	**17**	**4**	**5**	**33**	**65**	**6**	**90**	**9**	**8**	**3**	**5**	**7**	**.229**	**.324**	**.306**	**.954**
1964	**ChC-N**	**129**	**448**	**50**	**107**	**17**	**3**	**12**	**46**	**53**	**5**	**88**	**0**	**4**	**3**	**5**	**1**	**.239**	**.324**	**.371**	**.965**
1965	Pit-N	75	178	17	51	12	0	2	25	18	3	28	0	2	1	2	1	.287	.350	.388	.961
1966	Pit-N	36	49	6	9	1	0	0	4	8	0	7	0	1	1	0	1	.184	.293	.204	.943
1967	Pit-N	47	61	8	14	3	0	2	4	8	2	18	0	0	1	1	1	.230	.314	.377	.973
Career average		78	229	24	57	10	2	4	22	26	2	46	2	2	2	2	2	.249	.328	.365	.959
Cubs average		**123**	**410**	**42**	**103**	**18**	**4**	**7**	**37**	**47**	**4**	**81**	**3**	**4**	**3**	**4**	**4**	**.250**	**.330**	**.363**	**.964**
Career total		854	2521	268	628	112	23	45	245	290	26	507	18	21	21	22	20	.249	.328	.365	.959
Cubs total		**490**	**1639**	**168**	**410**	**71**	**15**	**28**	**146**	**187**	**16**	**325**	**13**	**15**	**10**	**16**	**15**	**.250**	**.330**	**.363**	**.964**

Rodriguez, Henry Anderson

HEIGHT: 6'2" THROWS: LEFT BATS: LEFT BORN: 11/8/1967 SANTO DOMINGO, DOMINICAN REPUBLIC POSITIONS PLAYED: 1B, OF

YEAR	TEAM	GAMES	AB	RUNS	HITS	2B	3B	HR	RBI	BB	IBB	SO	HBP	SH	SF	SB	CS	BA	OBA	SA	FA
1992	LA-N	53	146	11	32	7	0	3	14	8	0	30	0	1	1	0	0	.219	.258	.329	.962
1993	LA-N	76	176	20	39	10	0	8	23	11	2	39	0	0	1	1	0	.222	.266	.415	.993
1994	LA-N	104	306	33	82	14	2	8	49	17	2	58	2	1	4	0	1	.268	.307	.405	.990
1995	LA-N	21	80	6	21	4	1	1	10	5	2	17	0	0	0	0	1	.263	.306	.375	1.000
1995	Mon-N	24	58	7	12	0	0	1	5	6	0	11	0	1	0	0	0	.207	.277	.259	.990
1996	Mon-N	145	532	81	147	42	1	36	103	37	7	160	3	0	4	2	0	.276	.325	.562	.981

(continued)

(continued)

YEAR	TEAM	GAMES	AB	RUNS	HITS	2B	3B	HR	RBI	BB	IBB	SO	HBP	SH	SF	SB	CS	BA	OBA	SA	FA
1997	Mon-N	132	476	55	116	28	3	26	83	42	5	149	2	0	3	3	3	.244	.306	.479	.987
1998	**ChC-N**	**128**	**415**	**56**	**104**	**21**	**1**	**31**	**85**	**54**	**7**	**113**	**0**	**0**	**4**	**1**	**3**	**.251**	**.334**	**.530**	**.996**
1999	**ChC-N**	**130**	**447**	**72**	**136**	**29**	**0**	**26**	**87**	**56**	**6**	**113**	**0**	**0**	**1**	**2**	**4**	**.304**	**.381**	**.544**	**.974**
2000	**ChC-N**	**76**	**259**	**37**	**65**	**15**	**1**	**18**	**51**	**22**	**2**	**76**	**3**	**0**	**3**	**1**	**2**	**.251**	**.314**	**.525**	**.983**
2000	Fla-N	36	108	10	29	6	0	2	10	14	0	23	1	0	0	0	0	.269	.358	.380	1.000
2001	NYY-A	5	8	0	0	0	0	0	0	0	0	6	0	0	0	0	0	.000	.000	.000	—
Career average		93	301	39	78	18	1	16	52	27	3	80	1	0	2	1	1	.260	.321	.484	.985
Cubs average		**111**	**374**	**55**	**102**	**22**	**1**	**25**	**74**	**44**	**5**	**101**	**1**	**0**	**3**	**1**	**3**	**.272**	**.348**	**.534**	**.984**
Career total		930	3011	388	783	176	9	160	520	272	33	795	11	2	22	10	14	.260	.321	.484	.985
Cubs total		**334**	**1121**	**165**	**305**	**65**	**2**	**75**	**223**	**132**	**15**	**302**	**3**	**0**	**8**	**4**	**9**	**.272**	**.348**	**.534**	**.984**

Rogell, William George (Billy)
HEIGHT: 5'10" THROWS: RIGHT BATS: BOTH BORN: 11/24/1904 SPRINGFIELD, ILLINOIS POSITIONS PLAYED: 2B, 3B, SS, OF

YEAR	TEAM	GAMES	AB	RUNS	HITS	2B	3B	HR	RBI	BB	IBB	SO	HBP	SH	SF	SB	CS	BA	OBA	SA	FA
1925	Bos-A	58	169	12	33	5	1	0	17	11	—	17	0	8	—	0	3	.195	.244	.237	.934
1927	Bos-A	82	207	35	55	14	6	2	28	24	—	28	0	5	—	3	1	.266	.342	.420	.968
1928	Bos-A	102	296	33	69	10	4	0	29	22	—	47	4	17	—	2	6	.233	.295	.294	.944
1930	Det-A	54	144	20	24	4	2	0	9	15	—	23	1	5	—	1	2	.167	.250	.222	.946
1931	Det-A	48	185	21	56	12	3	2	24	24	—	17	0	2	—	8	8	.303	.383	.432	.958
1932	Det-A	144	554	88	150	29	6	9	61	50	—	38	1	8	—	14	6	.271	.332	.394	.944
1933	Det-A	155	587	67	173	42	11	0	57	79	—	33	3	6	—	6	9	.295	.381	.404	.944
1934	Det-A	154	592	114	175	32	8	3	100	74	—	36	0	13	—	13	3	.296	.374	.392	.962
1935	Det-A	150	560	88	154	23	11	6	71	80	—	29	1	7	—	3	6	.275	.367	.388	.971
1936	Det-A	146	585	85	160	27	5	6	68	73	—	41	3	6	—	14	10	.274	.357	.368	.965
1937	Det-A	146	536	85	148	30	7	8	64	83	—	48	3	10	—	5	5	.276	.376	.403	.968
1938	Det-A	136	501	76	130	22	8	3	55	86	—	37	4	5	—	9	2	.259	.372	.353	.959
1939	Det-A	74	174	24	40	6	3	2	23	26	—	14	0	6	—	3	1	.230	.330	.333	.932
1940	**ChC-N**	**33**	**59**	**7**	**8**	**0**	**0**	**1**	**3**	**2**	**—**	**8**	**0**	**2**	**—**	**1**	**—**	**.136**	**.164**	**.186**	**.878**
Career average		106	368	54	98	18	5	3	44	46	—	30	1	7	—	6	4	.267	.351	.370	.955
Cubs average		**33**	**59**	**7**	**8**	**0**	**0**	**1**	**3**	**2**	**—**	**8**	**0**	**2**	**—**	**1**	**0**	**.136**	**.164**	**.186**	**.878**
Career total		1482	5149	755	1375	256	75	42	609	649	—	416	20	100	—	82	62	.267	.351	.370	.955
Cubs total		**33**	**59**	**7**	**8**	**0**	**0**	**1**	**3**	**2**	**—**	**8**	**0**	**2**	**—**	**1**	**0**	**.136**	**.164**	**.186**	**.878**

Rohn, Daniel Jay (Dan)
HEIGHT: 5'8" THROWS: RIGHT BATS: LEFT BORN: 1/10/1956 ALPENA, MICHIGAN POSITIONS PLAYED: 2B, 3B, SS

YEAR	TEAM	GAMES	AB	RUNS	HITS	2B	3B	HR	RBI	BB	IBB	SO	HBP	SH	SF	SB	CS	BA	OBA	SA	FA
1983	**ChC-N**	**23**	**31**	**3**	**12**	**3**	**2**	**0**	**6**	**2**	**0**	**2**	**0**	**1**	**0**	**1**	**0**	**.387**	**.424**	**.613**	**.923**
1984	**ChC-N**	**25**	**31**	**1**	**4**	**0**	**0**	**1**	**3**	**1**	**0**	**6**	**0**	**0**	**1**	**0**	**0**	**.129**	**.152**	**.226**	**1.000**
1986	Cle-A	6	10	1	2	0	0	0	2	1	0	1	0	0	0	0	0	.200	.273	.200	.875
Career average		18	24	2	6	1	1	0	4	1	0	3	0	0	0	0	0	.250	.286	.389	.935
Cubs average		**24**	**31**	**2**	**8**	**2**	**1**	**1**	**5**	**2**	**0**	**4**	**0**	**1**	**1**	**1**	**0**	**.258**	**.288**	**.419**	**.957**
Career total		54	72	5	18	3	2	1	11	4	0	9	0	1	1	1	0	.250	.286	.389	.935
Cubs total		**48**	**62**	**4**	**16**	**3**	**2**	**1**	**9**	**3**	**0**	**8**	**0**	**1**	**1**	**1**	**0**	**.258**	**.288**	**.419**	**.957**

Roomes, Rolando Audley
HEIGHT: 6'3" THROWS: RIGHT BATS: RIGHT BORN: 2/15/1962 KINGSTON, JAMAICA POSITIONS PLAYED: OF

YEAR	TEAM	GAMES	AB	RUNS	HITS	2B	3B	HR	RBI	BB	IBB	SO	HBP	SH	SF	SB	CS	BA	OBA	SA	FA
1988	**ChC-N**	**17**	**16**	**3**	**3**	**0**	**0**	**0**	**0**	**0**	**0**	**4**	**0**	**0**	**0**	**0**	**1**	**.188**	**.188**	**.188**	**.833**
1989	Cin-N	107	315	36	83	18	5	7	34	13	0	100	3	0	3	12	8	.263	.296	.419	.981
1990	Cin-N	30	61	5	13	0	0	2	7	0	0	20	0	0	0	0	0	.213	.213	.311	1.000
1990	Mon-N	16	14	1	4	0	1	0	1	1	1	6	0	0	0	0	2	.286	.333	.429	1.000
Career average		57	135	15	34	6	2	3	14	5	0	43	1	0	1	4	4	.254	.282	.394	.980
Cubs average		**17**	**16**	**3**	**3**	**0**	**0**	**0**	**0**	**0**	**0**	**4**	**0**	**0**	**0**	**0**	**1**	**.188**	**.188**	**.188**	**.833**
Career total		170	406	45	103	18	6	9	42	14	1	130	3	0	3	12	11	.254	.282	.394	.980
Cubs total		**17**	**16**	**3**	**3**	**0**	**0**	**0**	**0**	**0**	**0**	**4**	**0**	**0**	**0**	**0**	**1**	**.188**	**.188**	**.188**	**.833**

Rosello, David (Dave)

HEIGHT: 5'11" THROWS: RIGHT BATS: RIGHT BORN: 6/26/1950 MAYAGUEZ, PUERTO RICO POSITIONS PLAYED: 2B, 3B, SS

YEAR	TEAM	GAMES	AB	RUNS	HITS	2B	3B	HR	RBI	BB	IBB	SO	HBP	SH	SF	SB	CS	BA	OBA	SA	FA
1972	ChC-N	5	12	2	3	0	0	1	3	3	0	2	0	0	0	0	0	.250	.400	.500	.846
1973	ChC-N	16	38	4	10	2	0	0	2	2	0	4	0	0	0	2	2	.263	.300	.316	.952
1974	ChC-N	62	148	9	30	7	0	0	10	10	1	28	0	2	1	1	1	.203	.252	.250	.963
1975	ChC-N	19	58	7	15	2	0	1	8	9	2	8	0	2	2	0	1	.259	.348	.345	.952
1976	ChC-N	91	227	27	55	5	1	1	11	41	8	33	1	1	1	1	2	.242	.359	.286	.966
1977	ChC-N	56	82	18	18	2	1	1	9	12	1	12	0	1	0	0	0	.220	.319	.305	.893
1979	Cle-A	59	107	20	26	6	1	3	14	15	0	27	0	9	3	1	0	.243	.328	.402	.966
1980	Cle-A	71	117	16	29	3	0	2	12	9	0	19	0	2	3	0	0	.248	.295	.325	.977
1981	Cle-A	43	84	11	20	4	0	1	7	7	0	12	0	5	0	0	1	.238	.297	.321	.975
Career average		47	97	13	23	3	0	1	8	12	1	16	0	2	1	1	1	.236	.318	.313	.961
Cubs average		**42**	**94**	**11**	**22**	**3**	**0**	**1**	**7**	**13**	**2**	**15**	**0**	**1**	**1**	**1**	**1**	**.232**	**.323**	**.292**	**.954**
Career total		422	873	114	206	31	3	10	76	108	12	145	1	22	10	5	7	.236	.318	.313	.961
Cubs total		**249**	**565**	**67**	**131**	**18**	**2**	**4**	**43**	**77**	**12**	**87**	**1**	**6**	**4**	**4**	**6**	**.232**	**.323**	**.292**	**.954**

Rowdon, Wade Lee

HEIGHT: 6'2" THROWS: RIGHT BATS: RIGHT BORN: 9/7/1960 RIVERHEAD, NEW YORK POSITIONS PLAYED: 2B, 3B, SS, OF

YEAR	TEAM	GAMES	AB	RUNS	HITS	2B	3B	HR	RBI	BB	IBB	SO	HBP	SH	SF	SB	CS	BA	OBA	SA	FA
1984	Cin-N	4	7	0	2	0	0	0	0	0	0	1	0	0	0	0	0	.286	.286	.286	1.000
1985	Cin-N	5	9	2	2	0	0	0	2	2	0	1	0	0	0	0	0	.222	.364	.222	.667
1986	Cin-N	38	80	9	20	5	1	0	10	9	0	17	1	1	1	2	0	.250	.330	.338	.903
1987	**ChC-N**	**11**	**31**	**2**	**7**	**1**	**1**	**1**	**4**	**3**	**0**	**10**	**0**	**0**	**0**	**0**	**2**	**.226**	**.294**	**.419**	**.818**
1988	Bal-A	20	30	1	3	0	0	0	0	0	0	6	0	0	0	1	1	.100	.100	.100	.955
Career average		16	31	3	7	1	0	0	3	3	0	7	0	0	0	1	1	.217	.283	.299	.892
Cubs average		**11**	**31**	**2**	**7**	**1**	**1**	**1**	**4**	**3**	**0**	**10**	**0**	**0**	**0**	**0**	**2**	**.226**	**.294**	**.419**	**.818**
Career total		78	157	14	34	6	2	1	16	14	0	35	1	1	1	3	3	.217	.283	.299	.892
Cubs total		**11**	**31**	**2**	**7**	**1**	**1**	**1**	**4**	**3**	**0**	**10**	**0**	**0**	**0**	**0**	**2**	**.226**	**.294**	**.419**	**.818**

Rowe, David Elwood (Dave)

HEIGHT: 5'9" THROWS: RIGHT BATS: RIGHT BORN: 10/9/1854 HARRISBURG, PENNSYLVANIA DIED: 12/9/1930 GLENDALE, CALIFORNIA
POSITIONS PLAYED: P, 1B, 2B, SS, OF

YEAR	TEAM	GAMES	AB	RUNS	HITS	2B	3B	HR	RBI	BB	IBB	SO	HBP	SH	SF	SB	CS	BA	OBA	SA	FA
1877	**ChN-N**	**2**	**7**	**0**	**2**	**0**	**0**	**0**	**0**	**0**	**—**	**3**	**—**	**—**	**—**	**—**	**—**	**.286**	**.286**	**.286**	**.667**
1882	Cle-N	24	97	13	25	4	3	1	17	4	—	9	—	—	—	—	—	.258	.287	.392	.841
1883	Bal-AA	59	256	40	80	11	6	0	—	2	—	—	—	—	—	—	—	.313	.318	.402	.838
1884	STL-U	109	485	95	142	32	11	4	—	10	—	—	—	—	—	—	—	.293	.307	.429	.887
1885	StL-N	16	62	8	10	3	0	0	3	5	—	8	—	—	—	—	—	.161	.224	.210	.906
1886	KCN-N	105	429	53	103	24	8	3	57	15	—	43	—	—	—	2	—	.240	.266	.354	.849
1888	KC-AA	32	122	14	21	3	4	0	13	6	—	—	1	—	—	2	—	.172	.217	.262	.914
Career average		50	208	32	55	11	5	1	13	6	—	9	0	—	—	1	—	.263	.284	.376	.866
Cubs average		**2**	**7**	**0**	**2**	**0**	**0**	**0**	**0**	**0**	**—**	**3**	**—**	**—**	**—**	**—**	**—**	**.286**	**.286**	**.286**	**.667**
Career total		347	1458	223	383	77	32	8	90	42	—	63	1	—	—	4	—	.263	.284	.376	.866
Cubs total		**2**	**7**	**0**	**2**	**0**	**0**	**0**	**0**	**0**	**—**	**3**	**—**	**—**	**—**	**—**	**—**	**.286**	**.286**	**.286**	**.667**

Roznovsky, Victor Joseph (Vic)

HEIGHT: 6'0" THROWS: RIGHT BATS: LEFT BORN: 10/19/1938 SHINER, TEXAS POSITIONS PLAYED: C

YEAR	TEAM	GAMES	AB	RUNS	HITS	2B	3B	HR	RBI	BB	IBB	SO	HBP	SH	SF	SB	CS	BA	OBA	SA	FA
1964	ChC-N	35	76	2	15	1	0	0	2	5	0	18	0	2	1	0	1	.197	.244	.211	.976
1965	ChC-N	71	172	9	38	4	1	3	15	16	1	30	3	0	2	1	0	.221	.295	.308	.984
1966	Bal-A	41	97	4	23	5	0	1	10	9	4	11	1	4	0	0	0	.237	.308	.320	.995
1967	Bal-A	45	97	7	20	5	0	0	10	1	0	20	0	0	1	0	0	.206	.212	.258	.993
1969	Phi-N	13	13	0	3	0	0	0	1	1	0	4	0	0	0	0	0	.231	.286	.231	1.000
Career average		41	91	4	20	3	0	1	8	6	1	17	1	1	1	0	0	.218	.273	.281	.988
Cubs average		**53**	**124**	**6**	**27**	**3**	**1**	**2**	**9**	**11**	**1**	**24**	**2**	**1**	**2**	**1**	**1**	**.214**	**.280**	**.278**	**.982**
Career total		205	455	22	99	15	1	4	38	32	5	83	4	6	4	1	1	.218	.273	.281	.988
Cubs total		**106**	**248**	**11**	**53**	**5**	**1**	**3**	**17**	**21**	**1**	**48**	**3**	**2**	**3**	**1**	**1**	**.214**	**.280**	**.278**	**.982**

Rudolph, John Herman (Dutch)

HEIGHT: 5'10" THROWS: LEFT BATS: LEFT BORN: 7/10/1882 NATRONA, PENNSYLVANIA DIED: 4/17/1967 NATRONA, PENNSYLVANIA POSITIONS PLAYED: OF

YEAR	TEAM	GAMES	AB	RUNS	HITS	2B	3B	HR	RBI	BB	IBB	SO	HBP	SH	SF	SB	CS	BA	OBA	SA	FA
1903	Phi-N	1	1	0	0	0	0	0	0	0	—	—	0	0	—	0	—	.000	.000	.000	—
1904	ChC-N	2	3	0	1	0	0	0	0	0	—	—	0	0	—	0	—	.333	.333	.333	1.000
Career average		2	2	0	1	0	0	0	0	0	—	—	0	0	—	0	—	.250	.250	.250	1.000
Cubs average		2	3	0	1	0	0	0	0	0	—	—	0	0	—	0	—	.333	.333	.333	1.000
Career total		3	4	0	1	0	0	0	0	0	—	—	0	0	—	0	—	.250	.250	.250	1.000
Cubs total		2	3	0	1	0	0	0	0	0	—	—	0	0	—	0	—	.333	.333	.333	1.000

Rudolph, Kenneth Victor (Ken)

HEIGHT: 6'1" THROWS: RIGHT BATS: RIGHT BORN: 12/29/1946 ROCKFORD, ILLINOIS POSITIONS PLAYED: C, OF

YEAR	TEAM	GAMES	AB	RUNS	HITS	2B	3B	HR	RBI	BB	IBB	SO	HBP	SH	SF	SB	CS	BA	OBA	SA	FA
1969	ChC-N	27	34	7	7	1	0	1	6	6	0	11	0	0	0	0	0	.206	.325	.324	.978
1970	ChC-N	20	40	1	4	1	0	0	2	1	1	12	0	2	0	0	0	.100	.122	.125	1.000
1971	ChC-N	25	76	5	15	3	0	0	7	6	0	20	1	3	0	0	0	.197	.265	.237	1.000
1972	ChC-N	42	106	10	25	1	1	2	9	6	0	14	1	3	0	1	2	.236	.283	.321	.966
1973	ChC-N	64	170	12	35	8	1	2	17	7	0	25	1	2	2	1	4	.206	.239	.300	.970
1974	SF-N	57	158	11	41	3	0	0	10	21	5	15	1	1	0	0	0	.259	.350	.278	.996
1975	StL-N	44	80	5	16	2	0	1	6	3	0	10	0	0	0	0	0	.200	.229	.263	.972
1976	StL-N	27	50	1	8	3	0	0	5	1	0	7	0	0	0	0	0	.160	.176	.220	.940
1977	SF-N	11	15	1	3	0	0	0	0	1	1	3	0	0	0	0	0	.200	.250	.200	.946
1977	Bal-A	11	14	2	4	1	0	0	2	0	0	4	0	0	0	0	0	.286	.286	.357	1.000
Career average		36	83	6	18	3	0	1	7	6	1	13	0	1	0	0	1	.213	.267	.273	.980
Cubs average		36	85	7	17	3	0	1	8	5	0	16	1	2	0	0	1	.202	.252	.279	.979
Career total		328	743	55	158	23	2	6	64	52	7	121	4	11	2	2	6	.213	.267	.273	.980
Cubs total		178	426	35	86	14	2	5	41	26	1	82	3	10	2	2	6	.202	.252	.279	.979

Russell, Glen David (Rip)

HEIGHT: 6'1" THROWS: RIGHT BATS: RIGHT BORN: 1/26/1915 LOS ANGELES, CALIFORNIA DIED: 9/26/1976 LOS ALAMITOS, CALIFORNIA
POSITIONS PLAYED: 1B, 2B, 3B, OF

YEAR	TEAM	GAMES	AB	RUNS	HITS	2B	3B	HR	RBI	BB	IBB	SO	HBP	SH	SF	SB	CS	BA	OBA	SA	FA
1939	ChC-N	143	542	55	148	24	5	9	79	36	—	56	0	16	—	2	—	.273	.318	.386	.988
1940	ChC-N	68	215	15	53	7	2	5	33	8	—	23	1	3	—	1	—	.247	.277	.367	.982
1941	ChC-N	6	17	1	5	1	0	0	1	1	—	5	0	1	—	0	—	.294	.333	.353	.975
1942	ChC-N	102	302	32	73	9	0	8	41	17	—	21	0	6	—	0	—	.242	.282	.351	.972
1946	Bos-A	80	274	22	57	10	1	6	35	13	—	30	1	7	—	1	1	.208	.247	.318	.944
1947	Bos-A	26	52	8	8	1	0	1	3	8	—	7	0	2	—	0	0	.154	.267	.231	.923
Career average		71	234	22	57	9	1	5	32	14	—	24	0	6	—	1	0	.245	.289	.356	.979
Cubs average		80	269	26	70	10	2	6	39	16	—	26	0	7	—	1	—	.259	.300	.372	.979
Career total		425	1402	133	344	52	8	29	192	83	—	142	2	35	—	4	1	.245	.289	.356	.979
Cubs total		319	1076	103	279	41	7	22	154	62	—	105	1	26	—	3	—	.259	.300	.372	.983

Ryan, James Edward (Jimmy *or* Pony)

HEIGHT: 5'9" THROWS: LEFT BATS: RIGHT BORN: 2/11/1863 CLINTON, MASSACHUSETTS DIED: 10/26/1923 CHICAGO, ILLINOIS
POSITIONS PLAYED: P, 2B, 3B, SS, OF

YEAR	TEAM	GAMES	AB	RUNS	HITS	2B	3B	HR	RBI	BB	IBB	SO	HBP	SH	SF	SB	CS	BA	OBA	SA	FA
1885	ChN-N	3	13	2	6	1	0	0	2	1	—	1	—	—	—	—	—	.462	.500	.538	.680
1886	ChN-N	84	327	58	100	17	6	4	53	12	—	28	—	—	—	10	—	.306	.330	.431	.850
1887	ChN-N	126	561	117	198	23	10	11	74	53	—	19	6	—	—	50	—	.353	.415	.488	.853
1888	ChN-N	129	549	115	182	33	10	16	64	35	—	50	5	—	—	60	—	.332	.377	.515	.873
1889	ChN-N	135	576	140	177	31	14	17	72	70	—	62	6	—	—	45	—	.307	.388	.498	.880
1890	Chi-P	118	486	99	165	32	5	6	89	60	—	36	4	—	—	30	—	.340	.416	.463	.919
1891	ChN-N	118	505	110	140	22	15	9	66	53	—	38	8	—	—	27	—	.277	.355	.434	.904
1892	ChN-N	128	505	105	148	21	11	10	65	61	—	41	5	—	—	27	—	.293	.375	.438	.911
1893	ChN-N	83	341	82	102	21	7	3	30	59	—	25	3	—	—	8	—	.299	.407	.428	.899
1894	ChN-N	108	474	132	171	37	7	3	62	50	—	23	3	8	—	11	—	.361	.425	.487	.910
1895	ChN-N	108	438	83	139	22	8	6	49	48	—	22	6	4	—	18	—	.317	.392	.445	.937
1896	ChN-N	128	489	83	149	24	10	3	86	46	—	16	4	10	—	29	—	.305	.369	.413	.912
1897	ChN-N	136	520	103	156	33	17	5	85	50	—	—	7	10	—	27	—	.300	.369	.458	.945

(continued)

James (Jimmy) Edward "Pony" Ryan, of-ss-3b-p, 1885–1903

Hell-raising Jimmy Ryan was one of the best players of the 19th century, but 100 years after he roamed the outfield for Chicago, he is all but forgotten.

Born on February 11, 1863, in Clinton, Massachusetts, Ryan broke in with Adrian "Cap" Anson's powerhouse squad of 1885, hitting .462 in a handful of games.

The 1887 season was Ryan's first as a regular, and he hit .285 with 23 doubles and 11 home runs. The next year, 1888, Ryan led the National League with 182 hits, 33 doubles and 16 home runs. His slugging percentage of .515 was also tops in the circuit.

Ryan, a lefthander, was also a pretty hard thrower, and manager Cap Anson wasn't afraid to use him on the mound. The same year he led the league in home runs, Ryan also led the league with three relief wins. He was 6-1 with two saves in his pitching career for Chicago.

But like many of his Chicago teammates, Ryan enjoyed a drink or three—and wasn't above playing an all-night card game. One thing that set Ryan apart from his teammates, somewhat anyway, was that he preferred not to try to show up the stern Anson by staying out late. Ryan much preferred buying a keg of beer and drinking in his room.

Ryan was one of a long list of players who jumped to the Players' League in 1890. He had one of his best years in that league, hitting .340 with 89 RBIs.

But when the Players' League folded, Ryan was one of many players who sheepishly returned to the National League in 1891.

He was a heck of a hitter, one of the early power hitters in baseball. He is the only Cubs to hit for the cycle twice, in 1888 and 1891. Ryan was also an aggressive base runner. He has 12 inside-the-park home runs for the Cubs, second best of all-time.

Ryan was no slouch defensively, either. He remains the career leader in outfield assists in the National League with 375, although assists were tabulated far more loosely in the 19th century. He led the league once in that category, in 1888, and was runner-up three other times. But whether all his assists were legitimate, Ryan clearly got the ball where it was supposed to be.

Ryan is one of a handful of players with 2,500 hits or more (2,502) and a .300-plus career average (.306) who is not in the Hall of Fame. It is difficult to see how he has been overlooked, given his versatility, his outfield skills and his output at the plate. In 17 of his 18 seasons, Ryan had more than 100 hits; in 9 of those seasons, he scored more than 100 runs. He had 20 or more doubles 16 seasons in a row, 10 or more triples in 9 of his 18 years and hit over .300 in 12 of those years.

Ryan played with Chicago until the 1900 season and then spent two years with the Washington franchise of the American League before retiring. He died in 1923.

Ryan is second behind Anson on the Cubs career list for runs scored with 1,409. He is number one on the career Cubs list in triples with 142; seventh all-time in singles with 1,470, eighth in doubles with 362; eighth in extra-base hits with 606; ninth in RBIs with 914 and third in stolen bases with 369.

(Ryan, continued)

Year	Team																				
1898	ChN-N	144	572	122	185	32	13	4	79	73	—	—	5	7	—	29	—	.323	.405	.446	.914
1899	ChN-N	125	525	91	158	20	10	3	68	43	—	—	3	4	—	9	—	.301	.357	.394	.956
1900	ChN-N	105	415	66	115	25	4	5	59	29	—	—	3	3	—	19	—	.277	.329	.393	.913
1902	Was-A	120	484	92	155	32	6	6	44	43	—	—	7	6	—	10	—	.320	.384	.448	.949
1903	Was-A	114	437	42	109	25	4	7	46	17	—	—	8	12	—	9	—	.249	.290	.373	.970
Career average		112	457	91	142	25	9	7	61	45	—	20	5	4	—	23	—	.311	.378	.447	.910
Cubs average		**111**	**454**	**94**	**142**	**24**	**9**	**7**	**61**	**46**	**—**	**22**	**4**	**3**	**—**	**25**	**—**	**.312**	**.380**	**.451**	**.902**
Career total		2012	8217	1642	2555	451	157	118	1093	803	—	361	83	64	—	418	—	.311	.378	.447	.910
Cubs total		**1660**	**6810**	**1409**	**2126**	**362**	**142**	**99**	**914**	**683**	**—**	**325**	**64**	**46**	**—**	**369**	**—**	**.312**	**.380**	**.451**	**.902**

Victor (Vic) Sylvester Saier, 1b, 1911–17, 1919

Saddled with the unenviable task of following all-time all-star Frank Chance at first base, Vic Saier nonetheless turned in several solid seasons for Chicago before an injury curtailed his career.

Saier was born on May 4, 1891, in Lansing, Michigan. He was signed by the Cubs in 1911 and Chance inserted him at first base for a good part of the season. Saier hit .259 that year as the Cubs finished second.

In 1912 Saier was second among the league's first basemen in fielding percentage and tied for first for fewest errors with Brooklyn's Jake Daubert. His .288 batting average was third among Cubs regulars.

Saier was clearly not going to replace Chance, but by the 1913 season, he was firmly established as the Cubs' regular first baseman. That year, he led the National League in triples with 21 and led the Cubs in hits with 150, doubles with 15 and stolen bases with 26. He also drove in a career-high 92 runs.

In 1914 and again in 1915, Saier led Chicago in runs scored with 87 and 74, respectively. In 1915 Saier also led or was tied for the team lead in doubles with 35, triples with 11, RBIs with 64 and stolen bases with 29. Saier's 21 triples in 1913 remains a Cubs team record.

In 1917 Saier suffered a back injury in a game and was sidelined for the season. After taking a year off, he attempted to make a comeback with the Pirates and played in 58 games that year before retiring for good. Saier died in East Lansing in 1967.

Saier, Victor Sylvester (Vic)
HEIGHT: 5'11"   THROWS: RIGHT   BATS: LEFT   BORN: 5/4/1891 LANSING, MICHIGAN   DIED: 5/14/1967 EAST LANSING, MICHIGAN   POSITIONS PLAYED: 1B

YEAR	TEAM	GAMES	AB	RUNS	HITS	2B	3B	HR	RBI	BB	IBB	SO	HBP	SH	SF	SB	CS	BA	OBA	SA	FA
1911	ChC-N	86	259	42	67	15	1	1	37	25	—	37	7	11	—	11	—	.259	.340	.336	.980
1912	ChC-N	122	451	74	130	25	14	2	61	34	—	65	1	14	—	11	—	.288	.340	.419	.992
1913	ChC-N	149	519	94	150	15	21	14	92	62	—	62	5	14	—	26	—	.289	.370	.480	.983
1914	ChC-N	153	537	87	129	24	8	18	72	94	—	61	4	23	—	19	—	.240	.357	.415	.986
1915	ChC-N	144	497	74	131	35	11	11	64	64	—	62	2	5	—	29	9	.264	.350	.445	.985
1916	ChC-N	147	498	60	126	25	3	7	50	79	—	68	1	12	—	20	17	.253	.356	.357	.984
1917	ChC-N	6	21	5	5	1	0	0	2	2	—	1	0	0	—	0	—	.238	.304	.286	1.000
1919	Pit-N	58	166	19	37	3	3	2	17	18	—	13	2	4	—	5	—	.223	.306	.313	.985
Career average		108	369	57	97	18	8	7	49	47	—	46	3	10	—	15	3	.263	.351	.409	.986
Cubs average		**115**	**397**	**62**	**105**	**20**	**8**	**8**	**54**	**51**	**—**	**51**	**3**	**11**	**—**	**17**	**4**	**.265**	**.354**	**.414**	**.986**
Career total		865	2948	455	775	143	61	55	395	378	—	369	22	83	—	121	26	.263	.351	.409	.986
Cubs total		**807**	**2782**	**436**	**738**	**140**	**58**	**53**	**378**	**360**	**—**	**356**	**20**	**79**	**—**	**116**	**26**	**.265**	**.354**	**.414**	**.986**

Salazar, Argenis Antonio (Angel)
HEIGHT: 6'0"   THROWS: RIGHT   BATS: RIGHT   BORN: 11/4/1961 ANACO, VENEZUELA   POSITIONS PLAYED: 2B, 3B, SS

YEAR	TEAM	GAMES	AB	RUNS	HITS	2B	3B	HR	RBI	BB	IBB	SO	HBP	SH	SF	SB	CS	BA	OBA	SA	FA
1983	Mon-N	36	37	5	8	1	1	0	1	1	0	8	0	1	1	0	0	.216	.231	.297	.966
1984	Mon-N	80	174	12	27	4	2	0	12	4	0	38	1	4	1	1	1	.155	.178	.201	.960
1986	KC-A	117	298	24	73	20	2	0	24	7	0	47	2	5	1	1	1	.245	.266	.326	.978
1987	KC-A	116	317	24	65	7	0	2	21	6	0	46	0	8	1	4	4	.205	.219	.246	.981
1988	**ChC-N**	**34**	**60**	**4**	**15**	**1**	**1**	**0**	**1**	**1**	**1**	**11**	**0**	**2**	**0**	**0**	**0**	**.250**	**.262**	**.300**	**.968**
Career average		77	177	14	38	7	1	0	12	4	0	30	1	4	1	1	1	.212	.230	.270	.974
Cubs average		**34**	**60**	**4**	**15**	**1**	**1**	**0**	**1**	**1**	**1**	**11**	**0**	**2**	**0**	**0**	**0**	**.250**	**.262**	**.300**	**.968**
Career total		383	886	69	188	33	6	2	59	19	1	150	3	20	4	6	6	.212	.230	.270	.974
Cubs total		**34**	**60**	**4**	**15**	**1**	**1**	**0**	**1**	**1**	**1**	**11**	**0**	**2**	**0**	**0**	**0**	**.250**	**.262**	**.300**	**.968**

Salazar, Luis Ernesto
HEIGHT: 5'9" THROWS: RIGHT BATS: RIGHT BORN: 5/19/1956 BARCELONA, VENEZUELA POSITIONS PLAYED: P, 1B, 2B, 3B, SS, OF

YEAR	TEAM	GAMES	AB	RUNS	HITS	2B	3B	HR	RBI	BB	IBB	SO	HBP	SH	SF	SB	CS	BA	OBA	SA	FA
1980	SD-N	44	169	28	57	4	7	1	25	9	1	25	1	3	1	11	2	.337	.372	.462	.948
1981	SD-N	109	400	37	121	19	6	3	38	16	2	72	1	5	2	11	8	.303	.329	.403	.955
1982	SD-N	145	524	55	127	15	5	8	62	23	10	80	2	5	5	32	9	.242	.274	.336	.941
1983	SD-N	134	481	52	124	16	2	14	45	17	8	80	2	8	2	24	9	.258	.285	.387	.950
1984	SD-N	93	228	20	55	7	2	3	17	6	1	38	0	2	0	11	7	.241	.261	.329	.968
1985	CWS-A	122	327	39	80	18	2	10	45	12	2	60	0	9	5	14	4	.245	.267	.404	.960
1986	CWS-A	4	7	1	1	0	0	0	0	1	0	3	0	0	0	0	0	.143	.250	.143	—
1987	SD-N	84	189	13	48	5	0	3	17	14	2	30	0	1	2	3	3	.254	.302	.328	.944
1988	Det-A	130	452	61	122	14	1	12	62	21	2	70	3	10	3	6	0	.270	.305	.385	.972
1989	SD-N	95	246	27	66	7	2	8	22	11	3	44	1	7	0	1	3	.268	.302	.411	.966
1989	**ChC-N**	**26**	**80**	**7**	**26**	**5**	**0**	**1**	**12**	**4**	**0**	**13**	**0**	**0**	**0**	**0**	**1**	**.325**	**.357**	**.425**	**.925**
1990	**ChC-N**	**115**	**410**	**44**	**104**	**13**	**3**	**12**	**47**	**19**	**3**	**59**	**4**	**0**	**1**	**3**	**1**	**.254**	**.293**	**.388**	**.951**
1991	**ChC-N**	**103**	**333**	**34**	**86**	**14**	**1**	**14**	**38**	**15**	**1**	**45**	**1**	**2**	**0**	**0**	**3**	**.258**	**.292**	**.432**	**.958**
1992	**ChC-N**	**98**	**255**	**20**	**53**	**7**	**2**	**5**	**25**	**11**	**2**	**34**	**0**	**3**	**4**	**1**	**1**	**.208**	**.237**	**.310**	**.972**
Career average		100	315	34	82	11	3	7	35	14	3	50	1	4	2	9	4	.261	.293	.381	.956
Cubs average		**86**	**270**	**26**	**67**	**10**	**2**	**8**	**31**	**12**	**2**	**38**	**1**	**1**	**1**	**1**	**2**	**.250**	**.284**	**.386**	**.958**
Career total		1302	4101	438	1070	144	33	94	455	179	37	653	15	55	25	117	51	.261	.293	.381	.956
Cubs total		**342**	**1078**	**105**	**269**	**39**	**6**	**32**	**122**	**49**	**6**	**151**	**5**	**5**	**5**	**4**	**6**	**.250**	**.284**	**.386**	**.958**

Sanchez, Rey Francisco
HEIGHT: 5'9" THROWS: RIGHT BATS: RIGHT BORN: 10/5/1967 RIO PIEDRAS, PUERTO RICO POSITIONS PLAYED: 2B, 3B, SS

YEAR	TEAM	GAMES	AB	RUNS	HITS	2B	3B	HR	RBI	BB	IBB	SO	HBP	SH	SF	SB	CS	BA	OBA	SA	FA
1991	**ChC-N**	**13**	**23**	**1**	**6**	**0**	**0**	**0**	**2**	**4**	**0**	**3**	**0**	**0**	**0**	**0**	**0**	**.261**	**.370**	**.261**	**1.000**
1992	**ChC-N**	**74**	**255**	**24**	**64**	**14**	**3**	**1**	**19**	**10**	**1**	**17**	**3**	**5**	**2**	**2**	**1**	**.251**	**.285**	**.341**	**.975**
1993	**ChC-N**	**105**	**344**	**35**	**97**	**11**	**2**	**0**	**28**	**15**	**7**	**22**	**3**	**9**	**2**	**1**	**1**	**.282**	**.316**	**.326**	**.969**
1994	**ChC-N**	**96**	**291**	**26**	**83**	**13**	**1**	**0**	**24**	**20**	**4**	**29**	**7**	**4**	**1**	**2**	**5**	**.285**	**.345**	**.337**	**.979**
1995	**ChC-N**	**114**	**428**	**57**	**119**	**22**	**2**	**3**	**27**	**14**	**2**	**48**	**1**	**8**	**2**	**6**	**4**	**.278**	**.301**	**.360**	**.987**
1996	**ChC-N**	**95**	**289**	**28**	**61**	**9**	**0**	**1**	**12**	**22**	**6**	**42**	**3**	**8**	**2**	**7**	**1**	**.211**	**.272**	**.253**	**.977**
1997	**ChC-N**	**97**	**205**	**14**	**51**	**9**	**0**	**1**	**12**	**11**	**2**	**26**	**0**	**4**	**0**	**4**	**2**	**.249**	**.287**	**.307**	**.977**
1997	NYY-A	38	138	21	43	12	0	1	15	5	0	21	1	5	1	0	4	.312	.338	.420	.978
1998	SF-N	109	316	44	90	14	2	2	30	16	0	47	4	1	2	0	0	.285	.325	.361	.981
1999	KC-A	134	479	66	141	18	6	2	56	22	2	48	4	10	3	11	5	.294	.329	.370	.982
2000	KC-A	143	509	68	139	18	2	1	38	28	0	55	4	11	3	7	3	.273	.314	.322	.994
2001	KC-A	100	390	46	118	14	5	0	28	11	0	34	2	9	4	9	1	.303	.322	.364	.994
2001	Atl-N	49	154	10	35	4	1	0	9	4	1	15	0	4	1	2	0	.227	.245	.266	.986
Career average		106	347	40	95	14	2	1	27	17	2	37	3	7	2	5	2	.274	.311	.337	.983
Cubs average		**85**	**262**	**26**	**69**	**11**	**1**	**1**	**18**	**14**	**3**	**27**	**2**	**5**	**1**	**3**	**2**	**.262**	**.304**	**.323**	**.978**
Career total		1167	3821	440	1047	158	24	12	300	182	25	407	32	78	23	51	27	.274	.311	.337	.983
Cubs total		**594**	**1835**	**185**	**481**	**78**	**8**	**6**	**124**	**96**	**22**	**187**	**17**	**38**	**9**	**22**	**14**	**.262**	**.304**	**.323**	**.978**

Sandberg, Ryne Dee (Ryno)
HEIGHT: 6'2" THROWS: RIGHT BATS: RIGHT BORN: 9/18/1959 SPOKANE, WASHINGTON POSITIONS PLAYED: 2B, 3B, SS

YEAR	TEAM	GAMES	AB	RUNS	HITS	2B	3B	HR	RBI	BB	IBB	SO	HBP	SH	SF	SB	CS	BA	OBA	SA	FA
1981	Phi-N	13	6	2	1	0	0	0	0	0	0	1	0	0	0	0	0	.167	.167	.167	1.000
1982	**ChC-N**	**156**	**635**	**103**	**172**	**33**	**5**	**7**	**54**	**36**	**3**	**90**	**4**	**7**	**5**	**32**	**12**	**.271**	**.312**	**.372**	**.977**
1983	**ChC-N**	**158**	**633**	**94**	**165**	**25**	**4**	**8**	**48**	**51**	**3**	**79**	**3**	**7**	**5**	**37**	**11**	**.261**	**.316**	**.351**	**.986**
1984	**ChC-N**	**156**	**636**	**114**	**200**	**36**	**19**	**19**	**84**	**52**	**3**	**101**	**3**	**5**	**4**	**32**	**7**	**.314**	**.367**	**.520**	**.993**
1985	**ChC-N**	**153**	**609**	**113**	**186**	**31**	**6**	**26**	**83**	**57**	**5**	**97**	**1**	**2**	**4**	**54**	**11**	**.305**	**.364**	**.504**	**.986**
1986	**ChC-N**	**154**	**627**	**68**	**178**	**28**	**5**	**14**	**76**	**46**	**6**	**79**	**0**	**3**	**6**	**34**	**11**	**.284**	**.330**	**.411**	**.994**
1987	**ChC-N**	**132**	**523**	**81**	**154**	**25**	**2**	**16**	**59**	**59**	**4**	**79**	**2**	**1**	**5**	**21**	**2**	**.294**	**.367**	**.442**	**.985**
1988	**ChC-N**	**155**	**618**	**77**	**163**	**23**	**8**	**19**	**69**	**54**	**3**	**91**	**1**	**1**	**5**	**25**	**10**	**.264**	**.322**	**.419**	**.987**
1989	**ChC-N**	**157**	**606**	**104**	**176**	**25**	**5**	**30**	**76**	**59**	**8**	**85**	**4**	**1**	**2**	**15**	**5**	**.290**	**.356**	**.497**	**.992**
1990	**ChC-N**	**155**	**615**	**116**	**188**	**30**	**3**	**40**	**100**	**50**	**8**	**84**	**1**	**0**	**9**	**25**	**7**	**.306**	**.354**	**.559**	**.989**
1991	**ChC-N**	**158**	**585**	**104**	**170**	**32**	**2**	**26**	**100**	**87**	**4**	**89**	**2**	**1**	**9**	**22**	**8**	**.291**	**.379**	**.485**	**.995**
1992	**ChC-N**	**158**	**612**	**100**	**186**	**32**	**8**	**26**	**87**	**68**	**4**	**73**	**1**	**0**	**6**	**17**	**6**	**.304**	**.371**	**.510**	**.990**
1993	**ChC-N**	**117**	**456**	**67**	**141**	**20**	**0**	**9**	**45**	**37**	**1**	**62**	**2**	**2**	**6**	**9**	**2**	**.309**	**.359**	**.412**	**.988**
1994	**ChC-N**	**57**	**223**	**36**	**53**	**9**	**5**	**5**	**24**	**23**	**0**	**40**	**1**	**0**	**0**	**2**	**3**	**.238**	**.312**	**.390**	**.987**
1996	**ChC-N**	**150**	**554**	**85**	**135**	**28**	**4**	**25**	**92**	**54**	**4**	**116**	**7**	**1**	**5**	**12**	**8**	**.244**	**.316**	**.444**	**.991**
1997	**ChC-N**	**135**	**447**	**54**	**118**	**26**	**0**	**12**	**64**	**28**	**3**	**94**	**1**	**3**	**4**	**7**	**4**	**.264**	**.308**	**.403**	**.984**
Career average		135	524	82	149	25	5	18	66	48	4	79	2	2	4	22	7	.285	.344	.452	.989
Cubs average		**143**	**559**	**88**	**159**	**27**	**5**	**19**	**71**	**51**	**4**	**84**	**2**	**2**	**5**	**23**	**7**	**.285**	**.344**	**.452**	**.989**
Career total		2164	8385	1318	2386	403	76	282	1061	761	59	1260	34	31	71	344	107	.285	.344	.452	.989
Cubs total		**2151**	**8379**	**1316**	**2385**	**403**	**76**	**282**	**1061**	**761**	**59**	**1259**	**34**	**31**	**71**	**344**	**107**	**.285**	**.344**	**.452**	**.989**

Ryne Dee "Ryno" Sandberg, 2b-3b-ss-dh, 1981—97

In the eyes of Cubs fans, "Ryno" was great from just about day one. But it took a game on June 23, 1984, to showcase his talents before a national television audience.

Sandberg was born on September 18, 1959, in Spokane, Washington. He was named after former Yankee relief ace Rinold (Ryne) Duren. According to Sandberg, his parents weren't big baseball fans; they heard the name on television and liked the sound of it.

Sandberg was the original "Can't Miss Kid": a three-sport athlete in high school who was recruited by a number of colleges to play either football, basketball or baseball, or a combination of some or all of the above.

He was also drafted by the Philadelphia Phillies and eventually opted for professional baseball over college. He spent three years in the minor leagues and was moved up to the Phillies in late 1981.

In 1982 he was a throw-in on the deal that sent Ivan DeJesus to Philadelphia for Larry Bowa. But what a throw-in! In 1982, his first full season, Sandberg played third base, hit .271, set a Cubs record for stolen bases by a third baseman (32) and scored 103 runs, which was a record for a Cubs rookie.

Sandberg was moved over to second base in 1983 and won the first of his nine consecutive Gold Glove awards for fielding excellence. He also scored a team-high 94 runs and stole a team-high 37 bases.

In 1984 Sandberg had gotten off to a good start, but the Cubs were struggling. At one point, they had lost six of eight games when the St. Louis Cardinals came to town on June 23. St. Louis took a 7-0 lead in the nationally televised tilt, but Chicago battled back to trail only 9-8 in the bottom of the ninth.

The NBC broadcasters had already named Cardinals outfielder Willie McGee as the Player of the Game when Sandberg sent a Bruce Sutter sinker into the seats to tie the game. In the bottom of the 11th, NBC was rolling the credits when Sandberg came to bat again. No one had hit two home runs off the dominating Sutter in one game all year.

Sandberg became the first, ripping a two-run shot to tie the game again, this time at 11-11. The Cubs won the game in the 12th inning and, forever after, the contest became known as "the Sandberg Game." Sandberg had gone five for six with seven RBIs. The NBC broadcasters also named him Player of the Game.

"I don't know how Bruce Sutter felt about it," said Sanberg in his autobiography, "but the game changed my life forever and took my career to a whole different level."

More important, it sparked the Cubs to the National League East title, the team's first in 39 seasons. Sandberg easily won the MVP award, hitting .314, with 32 stolen bases, a league-leading 19 triples, 19 home runs, 84 RBIs and a league-leading 114 runs scored.

Baseball statisticians point out that Sandberg came within a home run and triple of being the first player to top 100 runs scored and make more than 20 doubles, triples, homers and stolen bases in one season. That kind of performance has a certain symmetry, but Sandberg himself, who called the feat "the 20-20-whatever thing," emphasized that the important thing for him was helping the Cubs become winners again.

Sandberg's consistency, year in and year out, was Hall of Fame–like. In addition to the nine Gold Gloves, Sandberg was named to 10 All-Star Games, and at one point, he played a major league record 123 games without an error.

Six times, he hit 25 or more home runs, a record for second basemen that even the great Rogers Hornsby did not match. Seven times, he scored 100 runs or more, a mark topped only by Charlie Gehringer and Joe Morgan among second sackers. His career .986 fielding mark is the best ever for second basemen.

(continued)

(continued)

In 1994, after struggling with injuries, Sandberg retired, but he loved the game too much. In 1996 he unretired and played two more fairly productive seasons. But they were not really up to Sanberg's standards, and in 1997 he retired for good. He remains first in the hearts of Cubs fans, and pretty close to first in the pantheon of great second basemen.

Sandberg is sprinkled throughout the Cubs record book. Among his most prominent accomplishments, he is third all-time in Chicago in runs scored, fourth in singles with 1,624, fourth in hits with 2,835, fourth in total bases with 3,786, fourth in doubles with 403, fourth in stolen bases with 344 and fifth all-time in home runs with 282.

Santiago, Benito

HEIGHT: 6'1" THROWS: RIGHT BATS: RIGHT BORN: 3/9/1965 PONCE, PUERTO RICO POSITIONS PLAYED: C, 1B, OF

YEAR	TEAM	GAMES	AB	RUNS	HITS	2B	3B	HR	RBI	BB	IBB	SO	HBP	SH	SF	SB	CS	BA	OBA	SA	FA
1986	SD-N	17	62	10	18	2	0	3	6	2	0	12	0	0	1	0	1	.290	.308	.468	.946
1987	SD-N	146	546	64	164	33	2	18	79	16	2	112	5	1	4	21	12	.300	.324	.467	.976
1988	SD-N	139	492	49	122	22	2	10	46	24	2	82	1	5	5	15	7	.248	.282	.362	.985
1989	SD-N	129	462	50	109	16	3	16	62	26	6	89	1	3	2	11	6	.270	.323	.419	.980
1990	SD-N	100	344	42	93	8	5	11	53	27	2	55	3	1	7	5	5	.267	.296	.403	.985
1991	SD-N	152	580	60	155	22	3	17	87	23	5	114	4	0	7	8	10	.251	.287	.383	.982
1992	SD-N	106	386	37	97	21	2	10	42	21	1	52	0	0	4	2	5	.230	.291	.380	.987
1993	Fla-N	139	469	49	108	19	6	13	50	37	2	88	5	0	4	10	7	.273	.322	.424	.991
1994	Fla-N	101	337	35	92	14	2	11	41	25	1	57	1	2	4	1	2	.286	.351	.485	.996
1995	Cin-N	81	266	40	76	20	0	11	44	24	1	48	4	0	2	2	2	.264	.332	.503	.988
1996	Phi-N	136	481	71	127	21	2	30	85	49	7	104	1	0	2	2	0	.243	.279	.387	.997
1997	Tor-A	97	341	31	83	10	0	13	42	17	1	80	2	1	5	1	0	.310	.333	.483	1.000
1998	Tor-A	15	29	3	9	5	0	0	4	1	0	6	0	0	0	0	0	.249	.313	.377	.990
1999	**ChC-N**	**109**	**350**	**28**	**87**	**18**	**3**	**7**	**36**	**32**	**6**	**71**	**2**	**0**	**2**	**1**	**1**	**.262**	**.310**	**.409**	**.994**
2000	Cin-N	89	252	22	66	11	1	8	45	19	8	45	1	0	5	2	2	.262	.295	.369	.994
2001	SF-N	133	477	39	125	25	4	6	45	23	0	78	2	7	6	5	4	.261	.305	.411	.986
Career average		106	367	39	96	17	2	12	48	23	3	68	2	1	4	5	4	.261	.305	.411	.986
Cubs average		**109**	**350**	**28**	**87**	**18**	**3**	**7**	**36**	**32**	**6**	**71**	**2**	**0**	**2**	**1**	**1**	**.249**	**.313**	**.377**	**.990**
Career total		1689	5874	630	1531	267	33	184	767	366	44	1093	32	20	60	86	64	.261	.305	.411	.986
Cubs total		**109**	**350**	**28**	**87**	**18**	**3**	**7**	**36**	**32**	**6**	**71**	**2**	**0**	**2**	**1**	**1**	**.249**	**.313**	**.377**	**.990**

Santo, Ronald Edward (Ron)

HEIGHT: 6'0" THROWS: RIGHT BATS: RIGHT BORN: 2/25/1940 SEATTLE, WASHINGTON POSITIONS PLAYED: 1B, 2B, 3B, SS, OF

YEAR	TEAM	GAMES	AB	RUNS	HITS	2B	3B	HR	RBI	BB	IBB	SO	HBP	SH	SF	SB	CS	BA	OBA	SA	FA
1960	ChC-N	95	347	44	87	24	2	9	44	31	5	44	0	2	2	0	3	.251	.311	.409	.945
1961	ChC-N	154	578	84	164	32	6	23	83	73	7	77	0	1	3	2	3	.284	.362	.479	.937
1962	ChC-N	162	604	44	137	20	4	17	83	65	5	94	2	3	5	4	1	.227	.302	.358	.955
1963	ChC-N	162	630	79	187	29	6	25	99	42	7	92	4	0	11	6	4	.297	.339	.481	.951
1964	ChC-N	161	592	94	185	33	13	30	114	86	5	96	2	0	6	3	4	.313	.398	.564	.963
1965	ChC-N	164	608	88	173	30	4	33	101	88	7	109	5	0	3	3	1	.285	.378	.510	.957
1966	ChC-N	155	561	93	175	21	8	30	94	95	7	78	6	2	8	4	5	.312	.412	.538	.956
1967	ChC-N	161	586	107	176	23	4	31	98	96	9	103	3	0	12	1	5	.300	.395	.512	.957
1968	ChC-N	162	577	86	142	17	3	26	98	96	7	106	3	1	5	3	4	.246	.354	.421	.971
1969	ChC-N	160	575	97	166	18	4	29	123	96	7	97	2	0	14	1	3	.289	.384	.485	.947
1970	ChC-N	154	555	83	148	30	4	26	114	92	6	108	1	1	6	2	0	.267	.369	.476	.945
1971	ChC-N	154	555	77	148	22	1	21	88	79	8	95	0	1	7	4	0	.267	.354	.423	.948
1972	ChC-N	133	464	68	140	25	5	17	74	69	8	75	4	2	8	1	4	.302	.391	.487	.950
1973	ChC-N	149	536	65	143	29	2	20	77	63	8	97	4	0	1	1	2	.267	.348	.440	.950
1974	CWS-A	117	375	29	83	12	1	5	41	37	1	72	2	0	3	0	2	.221	.293	.299	.973
Career average		150	543	76	150	24	4	23	89	74	6	90	3	1	6	2	3	.277	.362	.464	.954
Cubs average		**152**	**555**	**79**	**155**	**25**	**5**	**24**	**92**	**77**	**7**	**91**	**3**	**1**	**7**	**3**	**3**	**.279**	**.366**	**.472**	**.953**
Career total		2243	8143	1138	2254	365	67	342	1331	1108	94	1343	38	13	94	35	41	.277	.362	.464	.954
Cubs total		**2126**	**7768**	**1109**	**2171**	**353**	**66**	**337**	**1290**	**1071**	**93**	**1271**	**36**	**13**	**91**	**35**	**39**	**.279**	**.366**	**.472**	**.953**

Ronald (Ron) Edward Santo, 1b-2b-3b-dh, 1960–74

This is the story according to Ron Santo in his autobiography.

It was 1959, and Santo and outfielder Billy Williams were sitting in the bleachers with 18 other prospects following a Cubs tryout. The immortal Rogers Hornsby, a former Cub himself, was working as a hitting instructor and evaluating the talent. Hornsby walked up to the 20 ballplayers.

"Kid," he said, pointing at Williams, "you can hit in the major leagues."

Then he turned to Santo.

"Kid," he told Santo, "you can hit in the major leagues. Today."

"The rest of you guys," Hornsby said, "aren't going to make it."

"He was 20 for 20," admitted Santo ruefully years later. "The rest of the guys didn't make it."

What Hornsby saw in Santo that day, certainly, was a sweet swing, excellent instincts on defense and a deep desire to excel.

Santo was born on February 25, 1940, in Seattle, Washington. He was a fresh-faced 20-year-old when the Cubs brought him up to the big leagues. He played 94 games at third base that year, hitting .251 with 44 RBIs and 24 doubles.

The next season, Santo was the Cubs' regular third baseman, hitting .284 with 23 home runs, a total that was second among National League third basemen to the Braves' Eddie Mathews's 32.

Santo was a fiery leader on and off the field, a player whose determination to win was almost palpable. But he was greatly frustrated by his team, which never finished higher than seventh in his first seven seasons. Still, Santo played hard every game. He was a nine-time All-Star for the Cubs and won five consecutive Gold Glove awards from 1964 to 1968. He was a very consistent performer in the field, leading National

League third basemen in putouts a record-tying seven times, in assists seven times and in double plays four times.

On offense, Santo was a tough out. A powerful man with great upper-body strength, he also had very quick reflexes, enabling him to wait almost until the last fraction of a second for the ball to come to him at the plate before he had to make a decision to hit it or not.

Santo had 20 or more home runs 11 times in his 15-year career, and 30 or more dingers 4 times. He led the National League in walks four times and in on-base percentage twice. Seven times, Santo had 98 RBIs or more.

His best season was 1964 when he hit .313, with 30 home runs, 114 RBIs and a league-leading 13 triples. And he did it all while battling juvenile diabetes, a disease that in the 1960s and 1970s was a potentially debilitating illness. Santo not only never complained, he kept his disability from the general public for most of his career.

In 1966 Santo hit safely in 28 consecutive games, fourth best all-time in Cubs history.

By 1967 the Cubs, with a stronger pitching staff and better everyday players, began to crack the upper echelon of the league standings, finishing third three times and second three times between 1967 and 1972. Santo, a four-time All Star in that span, was a key element on those clubs.

Chicago, however, could never get over the hump to a division championship. By 1973 the Cubs were sliding back in the standings. Santo turned in another All-Star year, hitting .267 with 77 RBIs, but it was his last year in a Cubs uniform. The next season, he was traded across town to the White Sox.

Santo played several positions and also saw action as a designated hitter as a "Pale Hoser" before retiring for good in 1974. He is now a member of the Cubs radio broadcast team at WGN radio. More important to Santo, he is also a member of the board of directors of the National Juvenile Diabetes Foundation

(continued)

(continued)

and has helped raise millions of dollars for research of the disease.

Cubs fans admit to being frustrated that Santo is not yet a member of the Hall of Fame. Certainly, he was the best defensive third baseman in the National League in the 1960s, setting a major league record (since broken) for assists in one season at third base with 393. He is the Cubs career leader at the position in assists with 4,523, total chances with 6,777, double plays with 389 and errors with 315.

Offensively, he is the Cubs leader in the less-than-glamorous category of strikeouts with 1,271. However, he is also among the career leaders in Chicago in games, at-bats, runs scored, hits, total bases, singles, doubles, home runs, RBIs and walks. Among third basemen, Santo is the fourth highest home run hitter of all time, behind Mike Schmidt, Eddie Mathews and Graig Nettles.

Sauer, Edward (Eddie *or* Horn)

HEIGHT: 6'1" THROWS: RIGHT BATS: RIGHT BORN: 1/3/1919 PITTSBURGH, PENNSYLVANIA DIED: 7/1/1988 THOUSAND OAKS, CALIFORNIA
POSITIONS PLAYED: OF

YEAR	TEAM	GAMES	AB	RUNS	HITS	2B	3B	HR	RBI	BB	IBB	SO	HBP	SH	SF	SB	CS	BA	OBA	SA	FA
1943	ChC-N	14	55	3	15	3	0	0	9	3	—	6	1	1	—	1	—	.273	.322	.327	1.000
1944	ChC-N	23	50	3	11	4	0	0	5	2	—	6	0	1	—	0	—	.220	.250	.300	.960
1945	ChC-N	49	93	8	24	4	1	2	11	8	—	23	0	3	—	2	—	.258	.317	.387	1.000
1949	StL-N	24	45	5	10	2	1	0	1	3	—	8	0	1	—	0	—	.222	.271	.311	1.000
1949	Bos-N	79	214	26	57	12	0	3	31	17	—	34	1	2	—	0	—	.266	.323	.364	.972
Career average		47	114	11	29	6	1	1	14	8	—	19	1	2	—	1	—	.256	.309	.352	.981
Cubs average		**29**	**66**	**5**	**17**	**4**	**0**	**1**	**8**	**4**	**—**	**12**	**0**	**2**	**—**	**1**	**—**	**.253**	**.302**	**.348**	**.991**
Career total		189	457	45	117	25	2	5	57	33	—	77	2	8	—	3	—	.256	.309	.352	.981
Cubs total		**86**	**198**	**14**	**50**	**11**	**1**	**2**	**25**	**13**	**—**	**35**	**1**	**5**	**—**	**3**	**—**	**.253**	**.302**	**.348**	**.991**

Sauer, Henry John (Hank *or* The Honker)

HEIGHT: 6'3" THROWS: RIGHT BATS: RIGHT BORN: 3/17/1917 PITTSBURGH, PENNSYLVANIA DIED: 8/24/2001 BURLINGAME, CALIFORNIA
POSITIONS PLAYED: 1B, OF

YEAR	TEAM	GAMES	AB	RUNS	HITS	2B	3B	HR	RBI	BB	IBB	SO	HBP	SH	SF	SB	CS	BA	OBA	SA	FA
1941	Cin-N	9	33	4	10	4	0	0	5	1	—	4	0	0	—	0	—	.303	.324	.424	.957
1942	Cin-N	7	20	4	5	0	0	2	4	2	—	2	0	0	—	0	—	.250	.318	.550	.976
1945	Cin-N	31	116	18	34	1	0	5	20	6	—	16	0	0	—	2	—	.293	.328	.431	.972
1948	Cin-N	145	530	78	138	22	1	35	97	60	—	85	4	4	—	2	—	.260	.340	.504	.977
1949	Cin-N	42	152	22	36	6	0	4	16	18	—	19	0	0	—	0	—	.237	.318	.355	.956
1949	ChC-N	96	357	59	104	17	1	27	83	37	—	47	3	1	—	0	—	.291	.363	.571	.981
1950	ChC-N	145	540	85	148	32	2	32	103	60	—	67	3	0	—	1	—	.274	.350	.519	.969
1951	ChC-N	141	525	77	138	19	4	30	89	45	—	77	3	1	—	2	1	.263	.325	.486	.981
1952	ChC-N	151	567	89	153	31	3	37	121	77	—	92	4	1	—	1	2	.270	.361	.531	.983
1953	ChC-N	108	395	61	104	16	5	19	60	50	—	56	2	0	—	0	0	.288	.349	.473	.970
1954	ChC-N	142	520	98	150	18	1	41	103	70	0	68	6	2	7	0	1	.211	.286	.387	.984
1955	ChC-N	79	261	29	55	8	1	12	28	26	0	47	2	0	1	0	0	.298	.403	.424	1.000
1956	StL-N	75	151	11	45	4	0	5	24	25	3	31	3	0	2	0	0	.259	.343	.508	.992
1957	NYG-N	127	378	46	98	14	1	26	76	49	2	59	0	0	2	1	0	.259	.354	.436	.950
1958	SF-N	88	236	27	59	8	0	12	46	35	2	37	4	0	2	0	0	.250	.348	.436	.950
1959	SF-N	13	15	1	1	0	0	1	1	0	0	7	0	0	0	0	0	.067	.067	.267	—
Career average		93	320	47	85	13	1	19	58	37	0	48	2	1	1	1	0	.266	.347	.496	.975
Cubs average		**123**	**452**	**71**	**122**	**20**	**2**	**28**	**84**	**52**	**0**	**65**	**3**	**1**	**1**	**1**	**1**	**.269**	**.348**	**.512**	**.975**
Career total		1399	4796	709	1278	200	19	288	876	561	7	714	34	9	14	11	4	.266	.347	.496	.975
Cubs total		**862**	**3165**	**498**	**852**	**141**	**17**	**198**	**587**	**365**	**0**	**454**	**23**	**5**	**8**	**6**	**4**	**.269**	**.348**	**.512**	**.975**

Henry (Hank) John "the Honker" Sauer, of-1b, 1941—59

A big, hard-hitting outfielder who enjoyed several productive years in Chicago, it wasn't long before Hank Sauer became a darling of the ever-loyal Cubs fans.

Sauer was born on March 17, 1917, in Pittsburgh, Pennsylvania. He began his career with Cincinnati in 1941. World War II lopped almost four years off his career and he didn't really make the major leagues until 1948, when he was 31 years old.

That season, he socked 35 homers and had 97 RBIs for the Reds, but when he got off to a slow start in 1949, he was traded to the Cubs along with fellow outfielder Frankie Baumholtz.

It was a steal for Chicago; Sauer hit .291, with 27 homers and 83 RBIs for Chicago in 96 games. In 1950 Sauer was an All-Star for the Cubs, swatting 32 homers with 103 RBIs.

Sauer wasn't the fastest player in the league, but he always hustled, much to the delight of the crowd. Cubs fans called him "the mayor of Wrigley Field." Sauer chewed tobacco, and Cubs fans in the outfield were always tossing him packs of chew. What Sauer couldn't stuff in his pockets, he stuffed into the ivy growing on the outfield wall.

His defense was not nearly as poor as some critics lead people to believe. In 1951 and 1952, Sauer led all National League left fielders in putouts and assists. To parapharase Casey Stengel, you could look it up.

In 1952 Sauer started like a house on fire, belting 18 home runs in his first 51 games. Sportswriters quickly pointed out that this accomplishment put Sauer on a pace similar to when former Yankee slugger Babe Ruth blasted 60 home runs in 1927.

Sauer cooled off somewhat, but he still ended up tying Ralph Kiner for the league lead in home runs with 37 and making a league-high 121 RBIs. At the age of 35, Sauer was the National League MVP. He also won the All-Star Game, belting a pitch off the Indians' Bob Lemon for a home run to give the National League a 3-2 win. Teammate Bob Rush was the winning pitcher.

Still, the Cubs had struggled that year, going only 77-77 (still the best record in Sauer's years with the team). Sauer was thus the first player from a nonwinning team to win an MVP.

A broken finger in 1953 slowed Sauer all season, but he bounced back with another strong season in 1954: 41 homers, 103 RBIs and a .288 average.

Sauer was the first player to hit three home runs off the same pitcher in two separate games. The victim was the Phillies' Curt Simmons. Sauer popped three homers off Simmons in 1950 and again in his MVP year of 1952.

Sauer was traded to St. Louis in 1956 and finished his career as a part-time player with the Giants from 1957 to 1959 He also worked as a coach for the Giants in 1959.

Sauer's 198 home runs with the Cubs leave him eighth on the team's all-time list.

Savage, Theodore Edmund (Ted)

HEIGHT: 6'1" THROWS: RIGHT BATS: RIGHT BORN: 2/21/1937 VENICE, ILLINOIS POSITIONS PLAYED: 1B, 2B, 3B, OF

YEAR	TEAM	GAMES	AB	RUNS	HITS	2B	3B	HR	RBI	BB	IBB	SO	HBP	SH	SF	SB	CS	BA	OBA	SA	FA
1962	Phi-N	127	335	54	89	11	2	7	39	40	0	66	2	7	3	16	5	.266	.345	.373	.974
1963	Pit-N	85	149	22	29	2	1	5	14	14	1	31	1	2	0	4	3	.195	.268	.322	.943
1965	StL-N	30	63	7	10	3	0	1	4	6	1	9	0	0	0	4	0	.159	.232	.254	.938
1966	StL-N	16	29	4	5	2	1	0	3	4	0	7	0	0	0	0	0	.172	.273	.310	1.000
1967	StL-N	9	8	1	1	0	0	0	0	1	0	3	0	0	0	0	0	.125	.222	.125	—
1967	**ChC-N**	**96**	**225**	**40**	**49**	**10**	**1**	**5**	**33**	**40**	**6**	**54**	**5**	**3**	**2**	**7**	**6**	**.218**	**.346**	**.338**	**.979**
1968	**ChC-N**	**3**	**8**	**0**	**2**	**0**	**0**	**0**	**0**	**0**	**0**	**1**	**0**	**0**	**0**	**0**	**1**	**.250**	**.250**	**.250**	**1.000**
1968	LA-N	61	126	7	26	6	1	2	7	10	0	20	1	0	0	1	2	.206	.270	.317	.985
1969	Cin-N	68	110	20	25	7	0	2	11	20	0	27	0	1	1	3	0	.227	.344	.345	.983
1970	Mil-A	114	276	43	77	10	5	12	50	57	1	44	2	5	3	10	6	.279	.402	.482	.955
1971	Mil-A	14	17	2	3	0	0	0	1	5	0	4	0	0	0	1	0	.176	.364	.176	1.000
1971	KC-A	19	29	2	5	0	0	0	1	3	0	6	0	0	0	2	0	.172	.250	.172	1.000
Career average		71	153	22	36	6	1	4	18	22	1	30	1	2	1	5	3	.233	.334	.361	.970
Cubs average		**50**	**117**	**20**	**26**	**5**	**1**	**3**	**17**	**20**	**3**	**28**	**3**	**2**	**1**	**4**	**4**	**.219**	**.343**	**.335**	**.979**
Career total		642	1375	202	321	51	11	34	163	200	9	272	11	18	9	49	24	.233	.334	.361	.970
Cubs total		**99**	**233**	**40**	**51**	**10**	**1**	**5**	**33**	**40**	**6**	**55**	**5**	**3**	**2**	**7**	**7**	**.219**	**.343**	**.335**	**.979**

Sawatski, Carl Ernest (Swats or Swish)

HEIGHT: 5'10" THROWS: RIGHT BATS: LEFT BORN: 11/4/1927 SHICKSHINNY, PENNSYLVANIA DIED: 11/24/1991 LITTLE ROCK, ARKANSAS
POSITIONS PLAYED: C, OF

YEAR	TEAM	GAMES	AB	RUNS	HITS	2B	3B	HR	RBI	BB	IBB	SO	HBP	SH	SF	SB	CS	BA	OBA	SA	FA
1948	**ChC-N**	**2**	**2**	**0**	**0**	**0**	**0**	**0**	**0**	**0**	**—**	**0**	**0**	**0**	**—**	**0**	**—**	**.000**	**.000**	**.000**	**—**
1950	**ChC-N**	**38**	**103**	**4**	**18**	**1**	**0**	**1**	**7**	**11**	**—**	**19**	**0**	**0**	**—**	**0**	**—**	**.175**	**.254**	**.214**	**.983**
1953	**ChC-N**	**43**	**59**	**5**	**13**	**3**	**0**	**1**	**5**	**7**	**—**	**7**	**0**	**0**	**—**	**0**	**0**	**.220**	**.303**	**.322**	**.943**
1954	CWS-A	43	109	6	20	3	3	1	12	15	—	20	0	0	3	0	0	.183	.276	.294	.987
1957	Mil-N	58	105	13	25	4	0	6	17	10	2	15	2	1	0	0	0	.238	.316	.448	.986
1958	Mil-N	10	10	1	1	0	0	0	1	2	0	5	0	0	1	0	0	.100	.231	.100	1.000
1958	Phi-N	60	183	12	42	4	1	5	12	16	4	42	3	0	1	0	0	.230	.300	.344	.986
1959	Phi-N	74	198	15	58	10	1	9	43	32	11	36	1	1	1	0	0	.293	.392	.480	.979
1960	StL-N	78	179	16	41	4	0	6	27	22	2	24	0	0	2	0	0	.229	.310	.352	.993
1961	StL-N	86	174	23	52	8	0	10	33	25	7	17	0	0	1	0	0	.299	.385	.517	.996
1962	StL-N	85	222	26	56	9	1	13	42	36	5	38	0	0	4	0	0	.252	.351	.477	.997
1963	StL-N	56	105	12	25	0	0	6	14	15	7	28	0	0	0	2	0	.238	.333	.410	.986
Career average		58	132	12	32	4	0	5	19	17	3	23	1	0	1	0	0	.242	.330	.401	.988
Cubs average		**28**	**55**	**3**	**10**	**1**	**0**	**1**	**4**	**6**	**—**	**9**	**0**	**0**	**—**	**0**	**0**	**.189**	**.269**	**.250**	**.971**
Career total		633	1449	133	351	46	5	58	213	191	38	251	6	2	13	2	0	.242	.330	.401	.988
Cubs total		**83**	**164**	**9**	**31**	**4**	**0**	**2**	**12**	**18**	**—**	**26**	**0**	**0**	**—**	**0**	**0**	**.189**	**.269**	**.250**	**.971**

Schaefer, Herman A. (Germany)

HEIGHT: 5'9" THROWS: RIGHT BATS: RIGHT BORN: 2/4/1877 CHICAGO, ILLINOIS DIED: 5/16/1919 SARANAC LAKE, NEW YORK
POSITIONS PLAYED: P, 1B, 2B, 3B, SS, OF

YEAR	TEAM	GAMES	AB	RUNS	HITS	2B	3B	HR	RBI	BB	IBB	SO	HBP	SH	SF	SB	CS	BA	OBA	SA	FA
1901	**ChN-N**	**2**	**5**	**0**	**3**	**1**	**0**	**0**	**0**	**2**	**—**	**—**	**0**	**0**	**—**	**0**	**—**	**.600**	**.714**	**.800**	**1.000**
1902	**ChC-N**	**81**	**291**	**32**	**57**	**2**	**3**	**0**	**14**	**19**	**—**	**—**	**0**	**2**	**—**	**12**	**—**	**.196**	**.250**	**.223**	**.874**
1905	Det-A	153	554	64	135	17	9	2	47	45	—	—	1	29	—	31	—	.244	.302	.318	.956
1906	Det-A	124	446	48	106	14	3	2	42	32	—	—	0	19	—	21	—	.238	.290	.296	.944
1907	Det-A	109	372	45	96	12	3	1	32	30	—	—	0	17	—	40	—	.258	.313	.315	.958
1908	Det-A	153	584	96	151	20	10	3	52	37	—	—	1	43	—	12	—	.259	.304	.342	.933
1909	Det-A	87	280	26	70	12	0	0	22	14	—	—	0	14	—	12	—	.250	.286	.293	.966
1909	Was-A	37	128	13	31	5	1	1	4	6	—	—	1	5	—	2	—	.242	.281	.320	.936
1910	Was-A	74	229	27	63	6	5	0	14	25	—	—	2	9	—	17	—	.275	.352	.345	.949
1911	Was-A	125	440	74	147	14	7	0	45	57	—	—	1	18	—	22	—	.334	.412	.398	.980
1912	Was-A	60	166	21	41	7	3	0	19	23	—	12	2	3	—	11	—	.247	.342	.325	.961
1913	Was-A	52	100	17	32	1	1	0	7	15	—	5	0	1	—	4	1	.320	.419	.350	.948
1914	Was-A	25	29	6	7	1	0	0	2	3	—	—	0	1	—	4	1	.241	.313	.276	1.000
1915	New-F	59	154	26	33	5	3	0	8	25	—	11	1	3	—	3	—	.214	.328	.286	.962
1916	NYY-A	1	1	0	0	0	0	0	0	0	—	—	0	0	—	0	—	.000	.000	.000	—
1918	Cle-A	1	5	2	0	0	0	0	0	0	—	—	0	1	—	1	—	.000	.000	.000	1.000
Career average		76	252	33	65	8	3	1	21	22	—	2	1	12	—	13	0	.257	.319	.320	.952
Cubs average		**42**	**148**	**16**	**30**	**2**	**2**	**0**	**7**	**11**	**—**	**1**	**6**	**—**	**6**	**—**		**.203**	**.260**	**.233**	**.878**
Career total		1143	3784	497	972	117	48	9	308	333	—	28	13	177	—	201	1	.257	.319	.320	.952
Cubs total		**83**	**296**	**32**	**60**	**3**	**3**	**0**	**14**	**21**	**—**	**2**	**11**	**—**	**12**	**—**		**.203**	**.260**	**.233**	**.878**

Schaffer, Jimmie Ronald
HEIGHT: 5'9"   THROWS: RIGHT   BATS: RIGHT   BORN: 4/5/1936 LIMEPORT, PENNSYLVANIA   POSITIONS PLAYED: C

YEAR	TEAM	GAMES	AB	RUNS	HITS	2B	3B	HR	RBI	BB	IBB	SO	HBP	SH	SF	SB	CS	BA	OBA	SA	FA
1961	StL-N	68	153	15	39	7	0	1	16	9	1	29	1	4	0	0	0	.255	.301	.320	.996
1962	StL-N	70	66	7	16	2	1	0	6	6	0	16	0	1	1	1	0	.242	.301	.303	.968
1963	**ChC-N**	**57**	**142**	**17**	**34**	**7**	**0**	**7**	**19**	**11**	**2**	**35**	**0**	**0**	**0**	**0**	**0**	**.239**	**.294**	**.437**	**.996**
1964	**ChC-N**	**54**	**122**	**9**	**25**	**6**	**1**	**2**	**9**	**17**	**4**	**17**	**1**	**0**	**0**	**2**	**4**	**.205**	**.307**	**.320**	**.970**
1965	CWS-A	17	31	2	6	3	1	0	1	3	0	4	0	0	0	0	0	.194	.265	.355	1.000
1965	NYM-N	24	37	0	5	2	0	0	0	1	0	15	0	0	0	0	0	.135	.158	.189	.968
1966	Phi-N	8	15	2	2	1	0	1	4	1	0	7	0	0	0	0	0	.133	.188	.400	.952
1967	Phi-N	2	2	1	0	0	0	0	0	1	1	1	0	0	0	0	0	.000	.333	.000	1.000
1968	Cin-N	4	6	0	1	0	0	0	1	0	0	3	0	0	0	0	0	.167	.167	.167	1.000
Career average		38	72	7	16	4	0	1	7	6	1	16	0	1	0	0	1	.223	.286	.340	.989
Cubs average		**56**	**132**	**13**	**30**	**7**	**1**	**5**	**14**	**14**	**3**	**26**	**1**	**0**	**0**	**1**	**2**	**.223**	**.300**	**.383**	**.986**
Career total		304	574	53	128	28	3	11	56	49	8	127	2	5	1	3	4	.223	.286	.340	.989
Cubs total		**111**	**264**	**26**	**59**	**13**	**1**	**9**	**28**	**28**	**6**	**52**	**1**	**0**	**0**	**2**	**4**	**.223**	**.300**	**.383**	**.986**

Scheffing, Robert Boden (Bob *or* Grump)
HEIGHT: 6'2"   THROWS: RIGHT   BATS: RIGHT   BORN: 8/11/1913 OVERLAND, MISSOURI   DIED: 10/26/1985 PHOENIX, ARIZONA   POSITIONS PLAYED: C

YEAR	TEAM	GAMES	AB	RUNS	HITS	2B	3B	HR	RBI	BB	IBB	SO	HBP	SH	SF	SB	CS	BA	OBA	SA	FA
1941	**ChC-N**	**51**	**132**	**9**	**32**	**8**	**0**	**1**	**20**	**5**	**—**	**19**	**0**	**1**	**—**	**2**	**—**	**.242**	**.270**	**.326**	**.966**
1942	**ChC-N**	**44**	**102**	**7**	**20**	**3**	**0**	**2**	**12**	**7**	**—**	**11**	**0**	**0**	**—**	**2**	**—**	**.196**	**.248**	**.284**	**.986**
1946	**ChC-N**	**63**	**115**	**8**	**32**	**4**	**1**	**0**	**18**	**12**	**—**	**18**	**0**	**1**	**—**	**0**	**—**	**.278**	**.346**	**.330**	**1.000**
1947	**ChC-N**	**110**	**363**	**33**	**96**	**11**	**5**	**5**	**50**	**25**	**—**	**25**	**0**	**4**	**—**	**2**	**—**	**.264**	**.312**	**.364**	**.984**
1948	**ChC-N**	**102**	**293**	**23**	**88**	**18**	**2**	**5**	**45**	**22**	**—**	**27**	**1**	**1**	**—**	**0**	**—**	**.300**	**.351**	**.427**	**.989**
1949	**ChC-N**	**55**	**149**	**12**	**40**	**6**	**1**	**3**	**19**	**9**	**—**	**9**	**1**	**3**	**—**	**0**	**—**	**.268**	**.314**	**.383**	**.977**
1950	**ChC-N**	**12**	**16**	**0**	**3**	**1**	**0**	**0**	**1**	**0**	**—**	**2**	**0**	**0**	**—**	**0**	**—**	**.188**	**.188**	**.250**	**.917**
1950	Cin-N	21	47	4	13	0	0	2	6	4	—	2	0	0	—	0	—	.277	.333	.404	1.000
1951	Cin-N	47	122	9	31	2	0	2	14	16	—	9	1	0	—	0	0	.254	.345	.320	.976
1951	StL-N	12	18	0	2	0	0	0	2	3	—	5	0	1	—	0	0	.111	.238	.111	1.000
Career average		65	170	13	45	7	1	3	23	13	—	16	0	1	—	1	0	.263	.316	.360	.984
Cubs average		**62**	**167**	**13**	**44**	**7**	**1**	**2**	**24**	**11**	**—**	**16**	**0**	**1**	**—**	**1**	**—**	**.266**	**.314**	**.366**	**.983**
Career total		517	1357	105	357	53	9	20	187	103	—	127	3	11	—	6	0	.263	.316	.360	.984
Cubs total		**437**	**1170**	**92**	**311**	**51**	**9**	**16**	**165**	**80**	**—**	**111**	**2**	**10**	**—**	**6**	**—**	**.266**	**.314**	**.366**	**.983**

Schenz, Henry Leonard (Hank)
HEIGHT: 5'9"   THROWS: RIGHT   BATS: RIGHT   BORN: 4/11/1919 NEW RICHMOND, OHIO   DIED: 5/12/1988 CINCINNATI, OHIO   POSITIONS PLAYED: 2B, 3B, SS

YEAR	TEAM	GAMES	AB	RUNS	HITS	2B	3B	HR	RBI	BB	IBB	SO	HBP	SH	SF	SB	CS	BA	OBA	SA	FA
1946	**ChC-N**	**6**	**11**	**0**	**2**	**0**	**0**	**0**	**1**	**0**	**—**	**0**	**0**	**0**	**—**	**1**	**—**	**.182**	**.182**	**.182**	**1.000**
1947	**ChC-N**	**7**	**14**	**2**	**1**	**0**	**0**	**0**	**0**	**2**	**—**	**1**	**1**	**1**	**—**	**0**	**—**	**.071**	**.235**	**.071**	**.917**
1948	**ChC-N**	**96**	**337**	**43**	**88**	**17**	**1**	**1**	**14**	**18**	**—**	**15**	**4**	**2**	**—**	**3**	**—**	**.261**	**.306**	**.326**	**.975**
1949	**ChC-N**	**7**	**14**	**2**	**6**	**0**	**0**	**0**	**1**	**1**	**—**	**0**	**0**	**0**	**—**	**2**	**—**	**.429**	**.467**	**.429**	**1.000**
1950	Pit-N	58	101	17	23	4	2	1	5	6	—	7	0	0	—	0	—	.228	.271	.337	.991
1951	Pit-N	25	61	5	13	1	0	0	3	0	—	2	1	1	—	0	2	.213	.226	.230	.962
1951	NYG-N	8	0	1	0	0	0	0	0	0	—	0	0	0	—	0	0				
Career average		35	90	12	22	4	1	0	4	5	—	4	1	1	—	1	0	.247	.291	.310	.975
Cubs average		**29**	**94**	**12**	**24**	**4**	**0**	**0**	**4**	**5**	**—**	**4**	**1**	**1**	**—**	**2**	**—**	**.258**	**.306**	**.316**	**.974**
Career total		207	538	70	133	22	3	2	24	27	—	25	6	4	—	6	2	.247	.291	.310	.975
Cubs total		**116**	**376**	**47**	**97**	**17**	**1**	**1**	**16**	**21**	**—**	**16**	**5**	**3**	**—**	**6**	**—**	**.258**	**.306**	**.316**	**.974**

Schick, Maurice Francis (Morrie)
HEIGHT: 5'11"   THROWS: RIGHT   BATS: RIGHT   BORN: 4/17/1892 CHICAGO, ILLINOIS   DIED: 10/25/1979 HAZEL CREST, ILLINOIS   POSITIONS PLAYED: OF

YEAR	TEAM	GAMES	AB	RUNS	HITS	2B	3B	HR	RBI	BB	IBB	SO	HBP	SH	SF	SB	CS	BA	OBA	SA	FA
1917	**ChC-N**	**14**	**34**	**3**	**5**	**0**	**0**	**0**	**3**	**3**	**—**	**10**	**0**	**2**	**—**	**0**	**—**	**.147**	**.216**	**.147**	**.960**
Career average		14	34	3	5	0	0	0	3	3	—	10	0	2	—	0	—	.147	.216	.147	.960
Cubs average		**14**	**34**	**3**	**5**	**0**	**0**	**0**	**3**	**3**	**—**	**10**	**0**	**2**	**—**	**0**	**—**	**.147**	**.216**	**.147**	**.960**
Career total		14	34	3	5	0	0	0	3	3	—	10	0	2	—	0	—	.147	.216	.147	.960
Cubs total		**14**	**34**	**3**	**5**	**0**	**0**	**0**	**3**	**3**	**—**	**10**	**0**	**2**	**—**	**0**	**—**	**.147**	**.216**	**.147**	**.960**

Schlafly, Harry Linton

HEIGHT: 5'11" THROWS: RIGHT BATS: RIGHT BORN: 9/20/1878 PORT WASHINGTON, OHIO DIED: 6/27/1919 CANTON, OHIO
POSITIONS PLAYED: C, 1B, 2B, 3B, OF

YEAR	TEAM	GAMES	AB	RUNS	HITS	2B	3B	HR	RBI	BB	IBB	SO	HBP	SH	SF	SB	CS	BA	OBA	SA	FA
1902	ChC-N	10	31	5	10	0	3	0	5	6	—	—	0	0	—	2	—	.323	.432	.516	.906
1906	Was-A	123	426	60	105	13	8	2	30	50	—	—	14	21	—	29	—	.246	.345	.329	.961
1907	Was-A	24	74	10	10	0	0	1	4	22	—	—	2	4	—	7	—	.135	.347	.176	.928
1914	Buf-F	51	127	16	33	7	1	2	19	12	—	22	3	1	—	3	—	.260	.338	.378	.969
Career average		52	165	23	40	5	3	1	15	23	—	6	5	7	—	10	—	.240	.348	.330	.957
Cubs average		**10**	**31**	**5**	**10**	**0**	**3**	**0**	**5**	**6**	**—**	**—**	**0**	**0**	**—**	**2**	**—**	**.323**	**.432**	**.516**	**.906**
Career total		208	658	91	158	20	12	5	58	90	—	22	19	26	—	41	—	.240	.348	.330	.957
Cubs total		**10**	**31**	**5**	**10**	**0**	**3**	**0**	**5**	**6**	**—**	**—**	**0**	**0**	**—**	**2**	**—**	**.323**	**.432**	**.516**	**.906**

Schramka, Paul Edward

HEIGHT: 6'0" THROWS: LEFT BATS: LEFT BORN: 3/22/1928 MILWAUKEE, WISCONSIN POSITIONS PLAYED: OF

YEAR	TEAM	GAMES	AB	RUNS	HITS	2B	3B	HR	RBI	BB	IBB	SO	HBP	SH	SF	SB	CS	BA	OBA	SA	FA
1953	ChC-N	2	0	0	0	0	0	0	0	0	—	0	0	0	—	0	0	—	—	—	—
Career average		2	0	0	0	0	0	0	0	0	—	0	0	0	—	0	0	—	—	—	—
Cubs average		**2**	**0**	**0**	**0**	**0**	**0**	**0**	**0**	**0**	**—**	**0**	**0**	**0**	**—**	**0**	**0**	**—**	**—**	**—**	**—**
Career total		2	0	0	0	0	0	0	0	0	—	0	0	0	—	0	0	—	—	—	—
Cubs total		**2**	**0**	**0**	**0**	**0**	**0**	**0**	**0**	**0**	**—**	**0**	**0**	**0**	**—**	**0**	**0**	**—**	**—**	**—**	**—**

Schreiber, Henry Walter (Hank)

HEIGHT: 5'11" THROWS: RIGHT BATS: RIGHT BORN: 7/12/1891 CLEVELAND, OHIO DIED: 2/23/1968 INDIANAPOLIS, INDIANA
POSITIONS PLAYED: 2B, 3B, SS, OF

YEAR	TEAM	GAMES	AB	RUNS	HITS	2B	3B	HR	RBI	BB	IBB	SO	HBP	SH	SF	SB	CS	BA	OBA	SA	FA
1914	CWS-A	1	2	0	0	0	0	0	0	0	—	1	0	0	—	0	0	.000	.000	.000	—
1917	Bos-N	2	7	1	2	0	0	0	0	0	—	1	0	0	—	0	—	.286	.286	.286	1.000
1919	Cin-N	19	58	5	13	4	0	0	4	0	—	12	0	2	—	0	—	.224	.224	.293	.985
1921	NYG-N	4	6	2	2	0	0	0	2	1	—	1	0	0	—	0	0	.333	.429	.333	.846
1926	**ChC-N**	**10**	**18**	**2**	**1**	**1**	**0**	**0**	**0**	**0**	**—**	**1**	**0**	**2**	**—**	**0**	**—**	**.056**	**.056**	**.111**	**1.000**
Career average		7	18	2	4	1	0	0	1	0	—	3	0	1	—	0	0	.198	.207	.253	.970
Cubs average		**10**	**18**	**2**	**1**	**1**	**0**	**0**	**0**	**0**	**—**	**1**	**0**	**2**	**—**	**0**	**0**	**.056**	**.056**	**.111**	**1.000**
Career total		36	91	10	18	5	0	0	6	1	—	16	0	4	—	0	0	.198	.207	.253	.970
Cubs total		**10**	**18**	**2**	**1**	**1**	**0**	**0**	**0**	**0**	**—**	**1**	**0**	**2**	**—**	**0**	**0**	**.056**	**.056**	**.111**	**1.000**

Schriver, William Frederick (Pop)

HEIGHT: 5'9" THROWS: RIGHT BATS: RIGHT BORN: 7/11/1865 BROOKLYN, NEW YORK DIED: 12/27/1932 BROOKLYN, NEW YORK
POSITIONS PLAYED: C, 1B, 2B, 3B, SS, OF

YEAR	TEAM	GAMES	AB	RUNS	HITS	2B	3B	HR	RBI	BB	IBB	SO	HBP	SH	SF	SB	CS	BA	OBA	SA	FA
1886	Bro-AA	8	21	2	1	0	0	0	0	2	—	—	0	—	—	0	—	.048	.130	.048	.857
1888	Phi-N	40	134	15	26	5	2	1	23	7	—	21	3	—	—	2	—	.194	.250	.284	.858
1889	Phi-N	55	211	24	56	10	1	1	19	16	—	8	2	—	—	5	—	.265	.323	.327	.904
1890	Phi-N	57	223	37	61	9	6	0	35	22	—	15	0	—	—	9	—	.274	.339	.368	.910
1891	**ChN-N**	**27**	**90**	**15**	**30**	**1**	**4**	**1**	**21**	**10**	**—**	**9**	**2**	**—**	**—**	**1**	**—**	**.333**	**.412**	**.467**	**.964**
1892	**ChN-N**	**92**	**326**	**40**	**73**	**10**	**6**	**1**	**34**	**27**	**—**	**25**	**7**	**—**	**—**	**4**	**—**	**.224**	**.297**	**.301**	**.929**
1893	**ChN-N**	**64**	**229**	**49**	**65**	**8**	**3**	**4**	**34**	**14**	**—**	**9**	**4**	**—**	**—**	**4**	**—**	**.284**	**.336**	**.397**	**.926**
1894	**ChN-N**	**96**	**349**	**55**	**96**	**12**	**3**	**3**	**47**	**29**	**—**	**21**	**6**	**5**	**—**	**9**	**—**	**.275**	**.341**	**.352**	**.920**
1895	NYG-N	24	92	16	29	2	1	1	16	9	—	10	1	1	—	3	—	.315	.382	.391	.904
1897	Cin-N	61	178	29	54	12	4	1	30	19	—	—	1	4	—	3	—	.303	.374	.433	.959
1898	Pit-N	95	315	25	72	15	3	0	32	23	—	—	3	10	—	0	—	.229	.287	.295	.957
1899	Pit-N	91	301	31	85	19	5	1	49	23	—	—	5	11	—	4	—	.282	.343	.389	.966
1900	Pit-N	37	92	12	27	7	0	1	12	10	—	—	3	0	—	0	—	.293	.381	.402	.959
1901	StL-N	53	166	17	45	7	3	1	23	12	—	—	4	7	—	2	—	.271	.335	.367	.971
Career average		57	195	26	51	8	3	1	27	16	—	8	3	3	—	3	—	.264	.329	.354	.932
Cubs average		**70**	**249**	**40**	**66**	**8**	**4**	**2**	**34**	**20**	**—**	**16**	**5**	**1**	**—**	**5**	**—**	**.266**	**.332**	**.356**	**.930**
Career total		800	2727	367	720	117	40	16	375	223	—	118	41	38	—	46	—	.264	.329	.354	.932
Cubs total		**279**	**994**	**159**	**264**	**31**	**16**	**9**	**136**	**80**	**—**	**64**	**19**	**5**	**—**	**18**	**—**	**.266**	**.332**	**.356**	**.930**

Schult, Arthur William (Art *or* Dutch)
HEIGHT: 6'3"   THROWS: RIGHT   BATS: RIGHT   BORN: 6/20/1928 BROOKLYN, NEW YORK   POSITIONS PLAYED: 1B, OF

YEAR	TEAM	GAMES	AB	RUNS	HITS	2B	3B	HR	RBI	BB	IBB	SO	HBP	SH	SF	SB	CS	BA	OBA	SA	FA
1953	NYY-A	7	0	3	0	0	0	0	0	0	—	0	0	0	—	0	0	—	—	—	—
1956	Cin-N	5	7	3	3	0	0	0	2	1	0	1	0	0	0	0	0	.429	.500	.429	—
1957	Cin-N	21	34	4	9	2	0	0	4	0	0	2	1	0	0	0	0	.265	.286	.324	1.000
1957	Was-A	77	247	30	65	14	0	4	35	14	0	30	1	1	2	0	1	.263	.303	.368	.984
1959	**ChC-N**	**42**	**118**	**17**	**32**	**7**	**0**	**2**	**14**	**7**	**0**	**14**	**2**	**2**	**1**	**0**	**0**	**.271**	**.320**	**.381**	**.988**
1960	**ChC-N**	**12**	**15**	**1**	**2**	**1**	**0**	**0**	**1**	**1**	**1**	**3**	**0**	**0**	**0**	**0**	**0**	**.133**	**.188**	**.200**	**1.000**
Career average		33	84	12	22	5	0	1	11	5	0	10	1	1	1	0	0	.264	.306	.363	.986
Cubs average		**27**	**67**	**9**	**17**	**4**	**0**	**1**	**8**	**4**	**1**	**9**	**1**	**1**	**1**	**0**	**0**	**.256**	**.306**	**.361**	**.988**
Career total		164	421	58	111	24	0	6	56	23	1	50	4	3	3	0	1	.264	.306	.363	.986
Cubs total		**54**	**133**	**18**	**34**	**8**	**0**	**2**	**15**	**8**	**1**	**17**	**2**	**2**	**1**	**0**	**0**	**.256**	**.306**	**.361**	**.988**

Schulte, Frank M. (Wildfire)
HEIGHT: 5'11"   THROWS: RIGHT   BATS: LEFT   BORN: 9/17/1882 COHOCTON, NEW YORK   DIED: 10/2/1949 OAKLAND, CALIFORNIA   POSITIONS PLAYED: OF

YEAR	TEAM	GAMES	AB	RUNS	HITS	2B	3B	HR	RBI	BB	IBB	SO	HBP	SH	SF	SB	CS	BA	OBA	SA	FA
1904	ChC-N	20	84	16	24	4	3	2	13	2	—	—	1	0	—	1	—	.286	.310	.476	.949
1905	ChC-N	123	493	67	135	15	14	1	47	32	—	—	6	18	—	16	—	.274	.326	.367	.981
1906	ChC-N	146	563	77	158	18	13	7	60	31	—	—	5	31	—	25	—	.281	.324	.396	.975
1907	ChC-N	97	342	44	98	14	7	2	32	22	—	—	5	20	—	7	—	.287	.339	.386	.972
1908	ChC-N	102	386	42	91	20	2	1	43	29	—	—	3	25	—	15	—	.236	.294	.306	.994
1909	ChC-N	140	538	57	142	16	11	4	60	24	—	—	2	27	—	23	—	.264	.298	.357	.968
1910	ChC-N	151	559	93	168	29	15	10	68	39	—	57	3	27	—	22	—	.301	.349	.460	.968
1911	ChC-N	154	577	105	173	30	21	21	107	76	—	68	3	31	—	23	—	.300	.384	.534	.971
1912	ChC-N	139	553	90	146	27	11	12	64	53	—	70	7	19	—	17	—	.264	.336	.418	.952
1913	ChC-N	132	497	85	138	28	6	9	68	39	—	68	5	17	—	21	—	.278	.336	.412	.956
1914	ChC-N	137	465	54	112	22	7	5	61	39	—	55	5	18	—	16	—	.241	.306	.351	.954
1915	ChC-N	151	550	66	137	20	6	12	62	49	—	68	2	27	—	19	17	.249	.313	.373	.962
1916	ChC-N	72	230	31	68	11	1	5	27	20	—	35	0	3	—	9	—	.296	.352	.417	.951
1916	Pit-N	55	177	12	45	5	3	0	14	17	—	19	1	2	—	5	—	.254	.323	.316	.968
1917	Pit-N	30	103	11	22	5	1	0	7	10	—	14	0	1	—	5	—	.214	.283	.282	.963
1917	Phi-N	64	149	21	32	10	0	1	15	16	—	22	2	4	—	4	—	.215	.299	.302	.923
1918	Was-A	93	267	35	77	14	3	0	44	47	—	36	6	9	—	5	—	.288	.406	.363	.969
Career average		120	436	60	118	19	8	6	53	36	—	34	4	19	—	16	1	.270	.332	.395	.966
Cubs average		**120**	**449**	**64**	**122**	**20**	**9**	**7**	**55**	**35**	**—**	**32**	**4**	**20**	**—**	**16**	**1**	**.272**	**.330**	**.403**	**.966**
Career total		1806	6533	906	1766	288	124	92	792	545	—	512	56	279	—	233	17	.270	.332	.395	.966
Cubs total		**1564**	**5837**	**827**	**1590**	**254**	**117**	**91**	**712**	**455**	**—**	**421**	**47**	**263**	**—**	**214**	**17**	**.272**	**.330**	**.403**	**.966**

Schulte, John Clement (Johnny *or* Eagle Eye)
HEIGHT: 5'11"   THROWS: RIGHT   BATS: LEFT   BORN: 9/8/1896 FREDERICKTOWN, MARYLAND   DIED: 6/28/1978 ST. LOUIS, MISSOURI
POSITIONS PLAYED: C, 1B

YEAR	TEAM	GAMES	AB	RUNS	HITS	2B	3B	HR	RBI	BB	IBB	SO	HBP	SH	SF	SB	CS	BA	OBA	SA	FA
1923	StL-A	7	3	1	0	0	0	0	1	4	—	0	0	0	—	0	0	.000	.571	.000	1.000
1927	StL-N	64	156	35	45	8	2	9	32	47	—	19	1	4	—	1	—	.288	.456	.538	.956
1928	Phi-N	65	113	14	28	2	2	4	17	15	—	12	0	3	—	0	—	.248	.336	.407	.949
1929	**ChC-N**	**31**	**69**	**6**	**18**	**3**	**0**	**0**	**9**	**7**	**—**	**11**	**0**	**2**	**—**	**0**	**—**	**.261**	**.329**	**.304**	**.978**
1932	StL-A	15	24	2	5	2	0	0	3	1	—	6	0	0	—	0	0	.208	.240	.292	.864
1932	Bos-N	10	9	1	2	0	0	1	2	2	—	1	0	1	—	0	—	.222	.364	.556	1.000
Career average		38	75	12	20	3	1	3	13	15	—	10	0	2	—	0	0	.262	.388	.436	.957
Cubs average		**31**	**69**	**6**	**18**	**3**	**0**	**0**	**9**	**7**	**—**	**11**	**0**	**2**	**—**	**0**	**0**	**.261**	**.329**	**.304**	**.978**
Career total		192	374	59	98	15	4	14	64	76	—	49	1	10	—	1	0	.262	.388	.436	.957
Cubs total		**31**	**69**	**6**	**18**	**3**	**0**	**0**	**9**	**7**	**—**	**11**	**0**	**2**	**—**	**0**	**0**	**.261**	**.329**	**.304**	**.978**

Frank M. "Wildfire" Schulte, of, 1904–18

With a nickname like "Wildfire," one might picture Frank Schulte as a fiery competitor, excitable and aggressive. In reality, Schulte was a cool customer, a great clutch player who could hit, play defense and run the bases.

The nickname? That was also the name of his favorite horse, on which Schulte doted.

Wildfire, the player, was born on September 17, 1882, in Cohocton, New York. Signed by Frank Chance after a brief minor league career, Schulte was a part-time player for the Cubs in 1904, playing in 20 games and hitting .286.

In 1905, though, Schulte was installed as the Cubs' regular left fielder. He hit .274 and led the team in triples with 14. The next year, when the Cubs acquired outfielder Jimmy Sheckard, Chance moved Schulte to right, where he spent much of his Chicago career.

Solid and unspectacular, Schulte got the job done. By the 1906 championship season, he was an excellent defensive outfielder, leading the league in double plays and third among right fielders in both putouts and assists. He led the team in home runs with seven and was the league leader in triples with 13 that year.

In the humiliating 1906 World Series against the White Sox, Schulte was one of the few Cubs who hit the ball well, leading the team with seven hits, including three doubles and three RBIs.

In 1911 Schulte had a career year, hitting a league-leading 21 home runs, to go with 21 triples, 30 doubles, 23 stolen bases and and a league-leading 107 RBIs. He became the first player in major league history to have more than 20 doubles, triples, home runs and stolen bases and more than 100 RBIs in one season. That feat won him the Chalmers Award, which was what the MVP award was known as in that era. Schulte also hit four grand slams that year, the major league record until Ernie Banks hit five in 1955.

Schulte was clearly one of the canniest base runners to ever don a Cubs uniform. Schulte holds the team record for inside-the-park home runs in a career with 18. He also holds the Cubs career record for most steals of home: 22.

He is one of the Cubs' best clutch players. Schulte leads Chicago in career World Series hits with 25, career RBIs with 9 and is second in runs scored with 11. His career World Series average is .309, a total of 39 points higher than his career batting average in the regular season.

Schulte was a Cub until 1916, when he was traded to Pittsburgh. He later played for the Phillies and Senators before retiring in 1918. He died in 1949 in Oakland, California.

Schulte is third on the Cubs career triples list with 117. He is also the team's all-time leader in outfield assists with 178.

Schultz, Joseph Charles (Joe *or* Germany)

HEIGHT: 5'11" THROWS: RIGHT BATS: RIGHT BORN: 7/24/1893 PITTSBURGH, PENNSYLVANIA DIED: 4/13/1941 COLUMBIA, SOUTH CAROLINA
POSITIONS PLAYED: 1B, 2B, 3B, SS, OF

YEAR	TEAM	GAMES	AB	RUNS	HITS	2B	3B	HR	RBI	BB	IBB	SO	HBP	SH	SF	SB	CS	BA	OBA	SA	FA
1912	Bos-N	4	12	1	3	1	0	0	4	0	—	2	0	0	—	0	—	.250	.250	.333	.824
1913	Bos-N	9	18	2	4	0	0	0	1	2	—	7	1	2	—	0	—	.222	.333	.222	1.000
1915	Bro-N	56	120	13	35	3	2	0	4	10	—	18	0	2	—	3	4	.292	.346	.350	.896
1915	**ChC-N**	**7**	**8**	**1**	**2**	**0**	**0**	**0**	**3**	**0**	—	**2**	**0**	**0**	—	**0**	**0**	**.250**	**.250**	**.250**	**.857**
1916	Pit-N	77	204	18	53	8	2	0	22	7	—	14	4	6	—	6	—	.260	.298	.319	.880

(continued)

(continued)

YEAR	TEAM	GAMES	AB	RUNS	HITS	2B	3B	HR	RBI	BB	IBB	SO	HBP	SH	SF	SB	CS	BA	OBA	SA	FA
1919	StL-N	88	229	24	58	9	1	2	21	11	—	7	0	5	—	4	—	.253	.288	.328	.962
1920	StL-N	99	320	38	84	5	5	2	32	21	—	11	0	12	—	5	4	.263	.308	.309	.945
1921	StL-N	92	275	37	85	20	3	6	45	15	—	11	1	13	—	4	3	.309	.347	.469	.962
1922	StL-N	112	344	50	108	13	4	2	64	19	—	10	0	10	—	3	1	.314	.350	.392	.976
1923	StL-N	2	7	0	2	0	0	0	1	1	—	0	0	1	—	0	0	.286	.375	.286	1.000
1924	StL-N	12	12	0	2	0	0	0	2	3	—	0	0	1	—	0	0	.167	.333	.167	1.000
1924	Phi-N	88	284	35	80	15	0	5	29	20	—	18	0	7	—	6	2	.282	.329	.394	.960
1925	Phi-N	24	64	10	22	6	0	0	8	4	—	1	0	0	—	1	1	.344	.382	.438	.923
1925	Cin-N	33	62	6	20	3	1	0	13	3	—	1	0	1	—	3	1	.323	.354	.403	.950
Career average		64	178	21	51	8	2	1	23	11	—	9	1	5	—	3	1	.285	.327	.370	.940
Cubs average		**7**	**8**	**1**	**2**	**0**	**0**	**0**	**3**	**0**	—	**2**	**0**	**0**	—	**0**	**0**	**.250**	**.250**	**.250**	**.857**
Career total		703	1959	235	558	83	19	15	249	116	—	102	6	60	—	35	16	.285	.327	.370	.940
Cubs total		**7**	**8**	**1**	**2**	**0**	**0**	**0**	**3**	**0**	—	**2**	**0**	**0**	—	**0**	**0**	**.250**	**.250**	**.250**	**.857**

Schuster, William Charles (Bill *or* Broadway Bill)

HEIGHT: 5'9"   THROWS: RIGHT   BATS: RIGHT   BORN: 8/4/1912 BUFFALO, NEW YORK   DIED: 6/28/1987 EL MONTE, CALIFORNIA   POSITIONS PLAYED: 2B, 3B, SS

YEAR	TEAM	GAMES	AB	RUNS	HITS	2B	3B	HR	RBI	BB	IBB	SO	HBP	SH	SF	SB	CS	BA	OBA	SA	FA
1937	Pit-N	3	6	2	3	0	0	0	1	1	—	0	0	0	—	0	—	.500	.571	.500	1.000
1939	Bos-N	2	3	0	0	0	0	0	0	0	—	1	0	0	—	0	—	.000	.000	.000	.833
1943	**ChC-N**	**13**	**51**	**3**	**15**	**2**	**1**	**0**	**0**	**3**	—	**2**	**0**	**0**	—	**0**	—	**.294**	**.333**	**.373**	**.977**
1944	**ChC-N**	**60**	**154**	**14**	**34**	**7**	**1**	**1**	**14**	**12**	—	**16**	**0**	**1**	—	**4**	—	**.221**	**.277**	**.299**	**.952**
1945	**ChC-N**	**45**	**47**	**8**	**9**	**2**	**1**	**0**	**2**	**7**	—	**4**	**0**	**2**	—	**2**	—	**.191**	**.296**	**.277**	**.951**
Career average		25	52	5	12	2	1	0	3	5	—	5	0	1	—	1	—	.234	.296	.310	.957
Cubs average		**39**	**84**	**8**	**19**	**4**	**1**	**0**	**5**	**7**	—	**7**	**0**	**1**	—	**2**	—	**.230**	**.292**	**.310**	**.958**
Career total		123	261	27	61	11	3	1	17	23	—	23	0	3	—	6	—	.234	.296	.310	.957
Cubs total		**118**	**252**	**25**	**58**	**11**	**3**	**1**	**16**	**22**	—	**22**	**0**	**3**	—	**6**	—	**.230**	**.292**	**.310**	**.958**

Scott, Floyd John (Pete)

HEIGHT: 5'11"   THROWS: RIGHT   BATS: RIGHT   BORN: 12/21/1898 WOODLAND, CALIFORNIA   DIED: 5/3/1953 DALY CITY, CALIFORNIA
POSITIONS PLAYED: 1B, 3B, OF

YEAR	TEAM	GAMES	AB	RUNS	HITS	2B	3B	HR	RBI	BB	IBB	SO	HBP	SH	SF	SB	CS	BA	OBA	SA	FA
1926	**ChC-N**	**77**	**189**	**34**	**54**	**13**	**1**	**3**	**34**	**22**	—	**31**	**1**	**12**	—	**3**	—	**.286**	**.363**	**.413**	**.962**
1927	**ChC-N**	**71**	**156**	**28**	**49**	**18**	**1**	**0**	**21**	**19**	—	**18**	**1**	**4**	—	**1**	—	**.314**	**.392**	**.442**	**.986**
1928	Pit-N	60	177	33	55	10	4	5	33	18	—	14	1	7	—	1	—	.311	.378	.497	.980
Career average		69	174	32	53	14	2	3	29	20	—	21	1	8	—	2	—	.303	.377	.450	.975
Cubs average		**74**	**173**	**31**	**52**	**16**	**1**	**2**	**28**	**21**	—	**25**	**1**	**8**	—	**2**	—	**.299**	**.376**	**.426**	**.971**
Career total		208	522	95	158	41	6	8	88	59	—	63	3	23	—	5	—	.303	.377	.450	.975
Cubs total		**148**	**345**	**62**	**103**	**31**	**2**	**3**	**55**	**41**	—	**49**	**2**	**16**	—	**4**	—	**.299**	**.376**	**.426**	**.971**

Scott, Gary Thomas

HEIGHT: 6'0"   THROWS: RIGHT   BATS: RIGHT   BORN: 8/22/1968 NEW ROCHELLE, NEW YORK   POSITIONS PLAYED: 3B, SS

YEAR	TEAM	GAMES	AB	RUNS	HITS	2B	3B	HR	RBI	BB	IBB	SO	HBP	SH	SF	SB	CS	BA	OBA	SA	FA
1991	**ChC-N**	**31**	**79**	**8**	**13**	**3**	**0**	**1**	**5**	**13**	**4**	**14**	**3**	**1**	**0**	**0**	**1**	**.165**	**.305**	**.241**	**.969**
1992	**ChC-N**	**36**	**96**	**8**	**15**	**2**	**0**	**2**	**11**	**5**	**1**	**14**	**0**	**1**	**0**	**0**	**1**	**.156**	**.198**	**.240**	**.924**
Career average		34	88	8	14	3	0	2	8	9	3	14	2	1	0	0	1	.160	.250	.240	.947
Cubs average		**34**	**88**	**8**	**14**	**3**	**0**	**2**	**8**	**9**	**3**	**14**	**2**	**1**	**0**	**0**	**1**	**.160**	**.250**	**.240**	**.947**
Career total		67	175	16	28	5	0	3	16	18	5	28	3	2	0	0	2	.160	.250	.240	.947
Cubs total		**67**	**175**	**16**	**28**	**5**	**0**	**3**	**16**	**18**	**5**	**28**	**3**	**2**	**0**	**0**	**2**	**.160**	**.250**	**.240**	**.947**

Scott, Milton Parker (Milt *or* Mikado Milt)
HEIGHT: 5'9" THROWS: — BATS: RIGHT BORN: 1/17/1866 CHICAGO, ILLINOIS DIED: 11/3/1938 BALTIMORE, MARYLAND POSITIONS PLAYED: P, 1B

YEAR	TEAM	GAMES	AB	RUNS	HITS	2B	3B	HR	RBI	BB	IBB	SO	HBP	SH	SF	SB	CS	BA	OBA	SA	FA
1882	ChN-N	1	5	1	2	0	0	0	0	0	—	0	—	—	—	—	—	.400	.400	.400	1.000
1884	Det-N	110	438	29	108	17	5	3	50	9	—	62	—	—	—	—	—	.247	.262	.329	.968
1885	Det-N	38	148	14	39	7	0	0	12	4	—	16	—	—	—	—	—	.264	.283	.311	.967
1885	Pit-AA	55	210	15	52	7	1	0	18	5	—	—	2	—	—	—	—	.248	.272	.290	.986
1886	Bal-AA	137	484	48	92	11	4	2	52	22	—	—	9	—	—	11	—	.190	.239	.242	.974
Career average		85	321	27	73	11	3	1	33	10	—	20	3	—	—	3	—	.228	.257	.288	.973
Cubs average		**1**	**5**	**1**	**2**	**0**	**0**	**0**	**0**	**0**	**—**	**0**	**—**	**—**	**—**	**—**	**—**	**.400**	**.400**	**.400**	**1.000**
Career total		341	1285	107	293	42	10	5	132	40	—	78	11	—	—	11	—	.228	.257	.288	.973
Cubs total		**1**	**5**	**1**	**2**	**0**	**0**	**0**	**0**	**0**	**—**	**0**	**—**	**—**	**—**	**—**	**—**	**.400**	**.400**	**.400**	**1.000**

Scott, Rodney Darrell (Cool Breeze)
HEIGHT: 6'0" THROWS: RIGHT BATS: BOTH BORN: 10/16/1953 INDIANAPOLIS, INDIANA POSITIONS PLAYED: 2B, 3B, SS, OF

YEAR	TEAM	GAMES	AB	RUNS	HITS	2B	3B	HR	RBI	BB	IBB	SO	HBP	SH	SF	SB	CS	BA	OBA	SA	FA
1975	KC-A	48	15	13	1	0	0	0	0	1	0	3	0	2	0	4	2	.067	.125	.067	.909
1976	Mon-N	7	10	3	4	0	0	0	0	1	0	1	0	0	0	2	0	.400	.455	.400	1.000
1977	Oak-A	133	364	56	95	4	4	0	20	43	0	50	3	5	2	33	18	.261	.342	.294	.957
1978	ChC-N	78	227	41	64	5	1	0	15	43	0	41	3	7	0	27	10	.282	.403	.313	.933
1979	Mon-N	151	562	69	134	12	5	3	42	66	2	82	2	12	3	39	12	.238	.319	.294	.974
1980	Mon-N	154	567	84	127	13	13	0	46	70	0	75	1	11	6	63	13	.224	.307	.293	.977
1981	Mon-N	95	336	43	69	9	3	0	26	50	0	35	1	13	2	30	7	.205	.308	.250	.983
1982	Mon-N	14	25	2	5	0	0	0	1	3	0	2	0	0	0	5	0	.200	.286	.200	.971
1982	NYY-A	10	26	5	5	0	0	0	0	4	0	2	0	1	0	2	0	.192	.300	.192	.975
Career average		86	267	40	63	5	3	0	19	35	0	36	1	6	2	26	8	.236	.326	.285	.970
Cubs average		**78**	**227**	**41**	**64**	**5**	**1**	**0**	**15**	**43**	**0**	**41**	**3**	**7**	**0**	**27**	**10**	**.282**	**.403**	**.313**	**.933**
Career total		690	2132	316	504	43	26	3	150	281	2	291	10	51	13	205	62	.236	.326	.285	.970
Cubs total		**78**	**227**	**41**	**64**	**5**	**1**	**0**	**15**	**43**	**0**	**41**	**3**	**7**	**0**	**27**	**10**	**.282**	**.403**	**.313**	**.933**

Secory, Frank Edward
HEIGHT: 6'1" THROWS: RIGHT BATS: RIGHT BORN: 8/24/1912 MASON CITY, IOWA DIED: 4/7/1995 PORT HURON, MICHIGAN POSITIONS PLAYED: OF

YEAR	TEAM	GAMES	AB	RUNS	HITS	2B	3B	HR	RBI	BB	IBB	SO	HBP	SH	SF	SB	CS	BA	OBA	SA	FA
1940	Det-A	1	1	0	0	0	0	0	0	0	—	1	0	0	—	0	0	.000	.000	.000	—
1942	Cin-N	2	5	1	0	0	0	0	1	3	—	2	0	0	—	0	—	.000	.375	.000	.857
1944	ChC-N	22	56	10	18	1	0	4	17	6	—	8	0	4	—	1	—	.321	.387	.554	1.000
1945	ChC-N	35	57	4	9	1	0	0	6	2	—	7	0	3	—	0	—	.158	.186	.175	1.000
1946	ChC-N	33	43	6	10	3	0	3	12	6	—	6	0	0	—	0	—	.233	.327	.512	.833
Career average		19	32	4	7	1	0	1	7	3	—	5	0	1	—	0	0	.228	.302	.389	.964
Cubs average		**30**	**52**	**7**	**12**	**2**	**0**	**2**	**12**	**5**	**—**	**7**	**0**	**2**	**—**	**0**	**0**	**.237**	**.300**	**.404**	**.974**
Career total		93	162	21	37	5	0	7	36	17	—	24	0	7	—	1	0	.228	.302	.389	.964
Cubs total		**90**	**156**	**20**	**37**	**5**	**0**	**7**	**35**	**14**	**—**	**21**	**0**	**7**	**—**	**0**	**0**	**.237**	**.300**	**.404**	**.974**

Seibert, Kurt Elliott
HEIGHT: 6'0" THROWS: RIGHT BATS: BOTH BORN: 10/16/1955 CHEVERLY, MARYLAND POSITIONS PLAYED: 2B

YEAR	TEAM	GAMES	AB	RUNS	HITS	2B	3B	HR	RBI	BB	IBB	SO	HBP	SH	SF	SB	CS	BA	OBA	SA	FA
1979	ChC-N	7	2	2	0	0	0	0	0	0	0	1	0	0	0	0	0	.000	.000	.000	1.000
Career average		7	2	2	0	0	0	0	0	0	0	1	0	0	0	0	0	.000	.000	.000	1.000
Cubs average		**7**	**2**	**2**	**0**	**0**	**0**	**0**	**0**	**0**	**0**	**1**	**0**	**0**	**0**	**0**	**0**	**.000**	**.000**	**.000**	**1.000**
Career total		7	2	2	0	0	0	0	0	0	0	1	0	0	0	0	0	.000	.000	.000	1.000
Cubs total		**7**	**2**	**2**	**0**	**0**	**0**	**0**	**0**	**0**	**0**	**1**	**0**	**0**	**0**	**0**	**0**	**.000**	**.000**	**.000**	**1.000**

Sember, Michael David (Mike)
HEIGHT: 6'0" THROWS: RIGHT BATS: RIGHT BORN: 2/24/1953 HAMMOND, INDIANA POSITIONS PLAYED: 2B, 3B, SS

YEAR	TEAM	GAMES	AB	RUNS	HITS	2B	3B	HR	RBI	BB	IBB	SO	HBP	SH	SF	SB	CS	BA	OBA	SA	FA
1977	ChC-N	3	4	0	1	0	0	0	0	0	0	2	0	0	0	0	0	.250	.250	.250	1.000
1978	ChC-N	9	3	2	1	0	0	0	0	1	0	1	0	0	0	0	0	.333	.500	.333	.800
Career average		6	4	1	1	0	0	0	0	1	0	2	0	0	0	0	0	.286	.375	.286	.889
Cubs average		**6**	**4**	**1**	**1**	**0**	**0**	**0**	**0**	**1**	**0**	**2**	**0**	**0**	**0**	**0**	**0**	**.286**	**.375**	**.286**	**.889**
Career total		12	7	2	2	0	0	0	0	1	0	3	0	0	0	0	0	.286	.375	.286	.889
Cubs total		**12**	**7**	**2**	**2**	**0**	**0**	**0**	**0**	**1**	**0**	**3**	**0**	**0**	**0**	**0**	**0**	**.286**	**.375**	**.286**	**.889**

Serena, William Robert (Bill)
HEIGHT: 5'9" THROWS: RIGHT BATS: RIGHT BORN: 10/2/1924 ALAMEDA, CALIFORNIA DIED: 4/17/1996 HAYWARD, CALIFORNIA POSITIONS PLAYED: 2B, 3B

YEAR	TEAM	GAMES	AB	RUNS	HITS	2B	3B	HR	RBI	BB	IBB	SO	HBP	SH	SF	SB	CS	BA	OBA	SA	FA
1949	ChC-N	12	37	3	8	3	0	1	7	7	—	9	0	0	—	0	—	.216	.341	.378	.923
1950	ChC-N	127	435	56	104	20	4	17	61	65	—	75	1	2	—	1	—	.239	.339	.421	.945
1951	ChC-N	13	39	8	13	3	1	1	4	11	—	4	1	0	—	0	2	.333	.490	.538	.941
1952	ChC-N	122	390	49	107	21	5	15	61	39	—	83	3	3	—	1	0	.274	.345	.469	.982
1953	ChC-N	93	275	30	69	10	5	10	52	41	—	46	1	2	—	0	0	.251	.350	.433	.977
1954	ChC-N	41	63	8	10	0	1	4	13	14	—	18	1	0	1	0	0	.159	.316	.381	.939
Career average		68	207	26	52	10	3	8	33	30	—	39	1	1	0	0	0	.251	.348	.439	.965
Cubs average		**68**	**207**	**26**	**52**	**10**	**3**	**8**	**33**	**30**	**—**	**39**	**1**	**1**	**0**	**0**	**0**	**.251**	**.348**	**.439**	**.965**
Career total		408	1239	154	311	57	16	48	198	177	—	235	7	7	1	2	2	.251	.348	.439	.965
Cubs total		**408**	**1239**	**154**	**311**	**57**	**16**	**48**	**198**	**177**	**—**	**235**	**7**	**7**	**1**	**2**	**2**	**.251**	**.348**	**.439**	**.965**

Servais, Scott Daniel
HEIGHT: 6'2" THROWS: RIGHT BATS: RIGHT BORN: 6/4/1967 LACROSSE, WISCONSIN POSITIONS PLAYED: C, 1B

YEAR	TEAM	GAMES	AB	RUNS	HITS	2B	3B	HR	RBI	BB	IBB	SO	HBP	SH	SF	SB	CS	BA	OBA	SA	FA
1991	Hou-N	16	37	0	6	3	0	0	6	4	0	8	0	1	0	0	0	.162	.244	.243	.988
1992	Hou-N	77	205	12	49	9	0	0	15	11	2	25	5	6	0	0	0	.239	.294	.283	.995
1993	Hou-N	85	258	24	63	11	0	11	32	22	2	45	5	3	3	0	0	.244	.313	.415	.996
1994	Hou-N	78	251	27	49	15	1	9	41	10	0	44	4	7	3	0	0	.195	.313	.415	.996
1995	Hou-N	28	89	7	20	10	0	1	12	9	2	15	1	1	1	0	1	.225	.235	.371	.996
1995	**ChC-N**	**52**	**175**	**31**	**50**	**12**	**0**	**12**	**35**	**23**	**6**	**37**	**2**	**1**	**2**	**2**	**1**	**.286**	**.300**	**.371**	**.977**
1996	**ChC-N**	**129**	**445**	**42**	**118**	**20**	**0**	**11**	**63**	**30**	**1**	**75**	**14**	**3**	**7**	**0**	**2**	**.265**	**.371**	**.560**	**.981**
1997	**ChC-N**	**122**	**385**	**36**	**100**	**21**	**0**	**6**	**45**	**24**	**7**	**56**	**6**	**7**	**3**	**0**	**1**	**.260**	**.327**	**.384**	**.988**
1998	**ChC-N**	**113**	**325**	**35**	**72**	**15**	**1**	**7**	**36**	**26**	**6**	**51**	**5**	**3**	**1**	**1**	**0**	**.222**	**.311**	**.361**	**.990**
1999	SF-N	69	198	21	54	10	0	5	21	13	2	31	3	3	0	1	0	.273	.289	.338	.994
2000	Col-N	33	101	6	22	4	0	1	13	7	2	16	1	0	1	0	1	.218	.327	.399	.992
2000	SF-N	7	8	1	2	0	0	0	0	2	1	1	0	0	0	0	0	.250	.273	.287	.987
2001	Hou-N	11	16	1	6	0	0	0	0	2	0	3	0	0	0	0	0	.375	.400	.250	1.000
Career average		75	227	22	56	12	0	6	29	17	3	37	4	3	2	0	1	.245	.306	.375	.991
Cubs average		**104**	**333**	**36**	**85**	**17**	**0**	**9**	**45**	**26**	**5**	**55**	**7**	**4**	**3**	**1**	**1**	**.256**	**.319**	**.389**	**.989**
Career total		820	2493	243	611	130	2	63	319	183	31	407	46	35	21	3	6	.245	.306	.375	.991
Cubs total		**416**	**1330**	**144**	**340**	**68**	**1**	**36**	**179**	**103**	**20**	**219**	**27**	**14**	**13**	**3**	**4**	**.256**	**.319**	**.389**	**.989**

Sewell, Thomas Wesley (Tommy)
HEIGHT: 5'7" THROWS: RIGHT BATS: LEFT BORN: 4/16/1906 TITUS, ALABAMA DIED: 7/30/1956 MONTGOMERY, ALABAMA

YEAR	TEAM	GAMES	AB	RUNS	HITS	2B	3B	HR	RBI	BB	IBB	SO	HBP	SH	SF	SB	CS	BA	OBA	SA	FA
1927	ChC-N	1	1	0	0	0	0	0	0	0	—	0	0	0	—	0	—	.000	.000	.000	—
Career average		1	1	0	0	0	0	0	0	0	—	0	0	0	—	0	—	.000	.000	.000	—
Cubs average		**1**	**1**	**0**	**0**	**0**	**0**	**0**	**0**	**0**	**—**	**0**	**0**	**0**	**—**	**0**	**—**	**.000**	**.000**	**.000**	**—**
Career total		1	1	0	0	0	0	0	0	0	—	0	0	0	—	0	—	.000	.000	.000	—
Cubs total		**1**	**1**	**0**	**0**	**0**	**0**	**0**	**0**	**0**	**—**	**0**	**0**	**0**	**—**	**0**	**—**	**.000**	**.000**	**.000**	**—**

Shaffer, George (Orator)

HEIGHT: 5'9" THROWS: RIGHT BATS: LEFT BORN: 1852 PHILADELPHIA, PENNSYLVANIA POSITIONS PLAYED: 1B, 2B, 3B, OF

YEAR	TEAM	GAMES	AB	RUNS	HITS	2B	3B	HR	RBI	BB	IBB	SO	HBP	SH	SF	SB	CS	BA	OBA	SA	FA
1877	Lou-N	61	260	38	74	9	5	3	34	9	—	17	—	—	—	—	—	.285	.309	.392	.846
1878	Ind-N	63	266	48	90	19	6	0	30	13	—	20	—	—	—	—	—	.338	.369	.455	.842
1879	**ChN-N**	**73**	**316**	**53**	**96**	**13**	**0**	**0**	**35**	**6**	—	**28**	—	—	—	—	—	**.304**	**.317**	**.345**	**.798**
1880	Cle-N	83	338	62	90	14	9	0	21	17	—	36	—	—	—	—	—	.266	.301	.361	.901
1881	Cle-N	85	343	48	88	13	6	1	34	23	—	20	—	—	—	—	—	.257	.303	.338	.880
1882	Cle-N	84	313	37	67	14	2	3	28	27	—	27	—	—	—	—	—	.214	.276	.300	.805
1883	Buf-N	95	401	67	117	11	3	0	41	27	—	39	—	—	—	—	—	.292	.336	.334	.861
1884	STL-U	106	467	130	168	40	10	2	—	30	—	—	—	—	—	—	—	.360	.398	.501	.869
1885	StL-N	69	257	30	50	11	2	0	18	19	—	31	—	—	—	—	—	.195	.250	.253	.918
1885	Phi-AA	2	9	1	2	0	1	0	1	1	—	—	0	—	—	—	—	.222	.300	.444	1.000
1886	Phi-AA	21	82	15	22	3	3	0	8	8	—	—	0	—	—	3	—	.268	.333	.378	.815
1890	Phi-AA	100	390	55	110	15	5	1	58	47	—	—	5	—	—	29	—	.282	.367	.354	.959
Career average		77	313	53	89	15	5	1	28	21	—	20	0	—	—	3	—	.283	.328	.369	.867
Cubs average		**73**	**316**	**53**	**96**	**13**	**0**	**0**	**35**	**6**	—	**28**	—	—	—	—	—	**.304**	**.317**	**.345**	**.798**
Career total		842	3442	584	974	162	52	10	308	227	—	218	5	—	—	32	—	.283	.328	.369	.867
Cubs total		**73**	**316**	**53**	**96**	**13**	**0**	**0**	**35**	**6**	—	**28**	—	—	—	—	—	**.304**	**.317**	**.345**	**.798**

Shamsky, Arthur Louis (Art)

HEIGHT: 6'1" THROWS: LEFT BATS: LEFT BORN: 10/14/1941 ST. LOUIS, MISSOURI POSITIONS PLAYED: 1B, OF

YEAR	TEAM	GAMES	AB	RUNS	HITS	2B	3B	HR	RBI	BB	IBB	SO	HBP	SH	SF	SB	CS	BA	OBA	SA	FA
1965	Cin-N	64	96	13	25	4	3	2	10	10	0	29	0	0	0	1	0	.260	.330	.427	.971
1966	Cin-N	96	234	41	54	5	0	21	47	32	1	45	0	3	2	0	2	.231	.321	.521	.973
1967	Cin-N	76	147	6	29	3	1	3	13	15	5	34	1	0	4	1	1	.197	.274	.293	.984
1968	NYM-N	116	345	30	82	14	4	12	48	21	6	58	7	4	5	1	2	.238	.292	.406	.988
1969	NYM-N	100	303	42	91	9	3	14	47	36	2	32	3	2	4	1	1	.300	.375	.488	.990
1970	NYM-N	122	403	48	118	19	2	11	49	49	13	33	3	0	0	1	1	.293	.371	.432	.996
1971	NYM-N	68	135	13	25	6	2	5	18	21	2	18	1	0	0	0	0	.185	.299	.370	.985
1972	**ChC-N**	**15**	**16**	**1**	**2**	**0**	**0**	**0**	**1**	**3**	**0**	**3**	**0**	**0**	**0**	**0**	**0**	**.125**	**.263**	**.125**	**1.000**
1972	Oak-A	8	7	0	0	0	0	0	0	1	0	2	0	0	0	0	0	.000	.125	.000	—
Career average		83	211	24	53	8	2	9	29	24	4	32	2	1	2	0	1	.253	.330	.427	.990
Cubs average		**15**	**16**	**1**	**2**	**0**	**0**	**0**	**1**	**3**	**0**	**3**	**0**	**0**	**0**	**0**	**0**	**.125**	**.263**	**.125**	**1.000**
Career total		665	1686	194	426	60	15	68	233	188	29	254	15	9	15	5	7	.253	.330	.427	.990
Cubs total		**15**	**16**	**1**	**2**	**0**	**0**	**0**	**1**	**3**	**0**	**3**	**0**	**0**	**0**	**0**	**0**	**.125**	**.263**	**.125**	**1.000**

Shannon, Maurice Joseph (Red)

HEIGHT: 5'11" THROWS: RIGHT BATS: BOTH BORN: 2/11/1897 JERSEY CITY, NEW JERSEY DIED: 4/12/1970 JERSEY CITY, NEW JERSEY
POSITIONS PLAYED: 2B, 3B, SS

YEAR	TEAM	GAMES	AB	RUNS	HITS	2B	3B	HR	RBI	BB	IBB	SO	HBP	SH	SF	SB	CS	BA	OBA	SA	FA
1915	Bos-N	1	3	0	0	0	0	0	0	0	—	0	0	0	—	0	0	.000	.000	.000	.857
1917	Phi-A	11	35	8	10	0	0	0	7	6	—	9	0	0	—	2	—	.286	.390	.286	.875
1918	Phi-A	72	225	23	54	6	5	0	16	42	—	52	3	8	—	5	—	.240	.367	.311	.906
1919	Phi-A	39	155	14	42	7	2	0	14	12	—	28	2	2	—	4	—	.271	.331	.342	.948
1919	Bos-A	80	290	36	75	11	7	0	17	17	—	42	6	7	—	7	—	.259	.313	.345	.973
1920	Was-A	62	222	30	64	8	7	0	30	22	—	32	0	6	—	2	5	.288	.352	.387	.929
1920	Phi-A	25	88	4	15	1	1	0	3	4	—	12	0	3	—	1	1	.170	.207	.205	.945
1921	Phi-A	1	1	0	0	0	0	0	0	0	—	0	0	0	—	0	0	.000	.000	.000	—
1926	**ChC-N**	**19**	**51**	**9**	**17**	**5**	**0**	**0**	**4**	**6**	—	**3**	**1**	**3**	—	**0**	—	**.333**	**.414**	**.431**	**.957**
Career average		44	153	18	40	5	3	0	13	16	—	25	2	4	—	3	1	.259	.334	.336	.937
Cubs average		**19**	**51**	**9**	**17**	**5**	**0**	**0**	**4**	**6**	—	**3**	**1**	**3**	—	**0**	—	**.333**	**.414**	**.431**	**.957**
Career total		310	1070	124	277	38	22	0	91	109	—	178	12	29	—	21	6	.259	.334	.336	.937
Cubs total		**19**	**51**	**9**	**17**	**5**	**0**	**0**	**4**	**6**	—	**3**	**1**	**3**	—	**0**	—	**.333**	**.414**	**.431**	**.957**

Shay, Arthur Joseph (Marty)
HEIGHT: 5'7" THROWS: RIGHT BATS: RIGHT BORN: 4/25/1896 BOSTON, MASSACHUSETTS DIED: 2/20/1951 WORCESTER, MASSACHUSETTS
POSITIONS PLAYED: 2B, SS

YEAR	TEAM	GAMES	AB	RUNS	HITS	2B	3B	HR	RBI	BB	IBB	SO	HBP	SH	SF	SB	CS	BA	OBA	SA	FA
1916	ChC-N	2	7	0	2	0	0	0	0	0	—	1	0	0	—	0	—	.286	.286	.286	.917
1924	Bos-N	19	68	4	16	3	1	0	2	5	—	5	1	0	—	2	1	.235	.297	.309	.951
Career average		11	38	2	9	2	1	0	1	3	—	3	1	0	—	1	1	.240	.296	.307	.947
Cubs average		**2**	**7**	**0**	**2**	**0**	**0**	**0**	**0**	**0**	**—**	**1**	**0**	**0**	**—**	**0**	**—**	**.286**	**.286**	**.286**	**.917**
Career total		21	75	4	18	3	1	0	2	5	—	6	1	0	—	2	1	.240	.296	.307	.947
Cubs total		**2**	**7**	**0**	**2**	**0**	**0**	**0**	**0**	**0**	**—**	**1**	**0**	**0**	**—**	**0**	**—**	**.286**	**.286**	**.286**	**.917**

Shean, David William (Dave)
HEIGHT: 5'11" THROWS: RIGHT BATS: RIGHT BORN: 7/9/1883 ARLINGTON, MASSACHUSETTS DIED: 5/22/1963 BOSTON, MASSACHUSETTS
POSITIONS PLAYED: 1B, 2B, 3B, SS, OF

YEAR	TEAM	GAMES	AB	RUNS	HITS	2B	3B	HR	RBI	BB	IBB	SO	HBP	SH	SF	SB	CS	BA	OBA	SA	FA
1906	Phi-A	22	75	7	16	3	2	0	3	5	—	—	2	2	—	6	—	.213	.280	.307	.980
1908	Phi-N	14	48	4	7	2	0	0	2	1	—	—	1	3	—	1	—	.146	.180	.188	.871
1909	Phi-N	36	112	14	26	2	2	0	4	14	—	—	1	17	—	3	—	.232	.323	.286	.988
1909	Bos-N	75	267	32	66	11	4	1	29	17	—	—	2	17	—	14	—	.247	.297	.330	.956
1910	Bos-N	150	543	52	130	12	7	3	36	42	—	45	0	17	—	16	—	.239	.294	.304	.953
1911	**ChC-N**	**54**	**145**	**17**	**28**	**4**	**0**	**0**	**15**	**8**	**—**	**15**	**1**	**7**	**—**	**4**	**—**	**.193**	**.240**	**.221**	**.940**
1912	Bos-N	4	10	1	3	0	0	0	0	1	—	2	1	0	—	0	—	.300	.417	.300	.917
1917	Cin-N	131	442	36	93	9	5	2	35	22	—	39	1	17	—	10	—	.210	.249	.267	.961
1918	Bos-A	115	425	58	112	16	3	0	34	40	—	25	3	36	—	11	—	.264	.331	.315	.967
1919	Bos-A	29	100	4	14	0	0	0	8	5	—	7	1	4	—	1	—	.140	.189	.140	.981
Career average		70	241	25	55	7	3	1	18	17	—	15	1	13	—	7	—	.228	.284	.285	.959
Cubs average		**54**	**145**	**17**	**28**	**4**	**0**	**0**	**15**	**8**	**—**	**15**	**1**	**7**	**—**	**4**	**—**	**.193**	**.240**	**.221**	**.940**
Career total		630	2167	225	495	59	23	6	166	155	—	133	13	120	—	66	—	.228	.284	.285	.959
Cubs total		**54**	**145**	**17**	**28**	**4**	**0**	**0**	**15**	**8**	**—**	**15**	**1**	**7**	**—**	**4**	**—**	**.193**	**.240**	**.221**	**.940**

Sheckard, Samuel James Tilden (Jimmy)
HEIGHT: 5'9" THROWS: RIGHT BATS: LEFT BORN: 11/23/1878 UPPER CHANCEFORD, PENNSYLVANIA DIED: 1/15/1947 LANCASTER, PENNSYLVANIA
POSITIONS PLAYED: 1B, 2B, 3B, SS, OF

YEAR	TEAM	GAMES	AB	RUNS	HITS	2B	3B	HR	RBI	BB	IBB	SO	HBP	SH	SF	SB	CS	BA	OBA	SA	FA
1897	Bro-N	13	49	12	14	3	2	3	14	6	—	—	0	0	—	5	—	.286	.364	.612	.756
1898	Bro-N	105	408	51	113	17	9	4	64	37	—	—	8	6	—	8	—	.277	.349	.392	.922
1899	Bal-N	147	536	104	158	18	10	3	75	56	—	—	18	6	—	77	—	.295	.380	.382	.944
1900	Bro-N	85	273	74	82	19	10	1	39	42	—	—	12	4	—	30	—	.300	.416	.454	.925
1901	Bro-N	133	554	116	196	29	19	11	104	47	—	—	3	3	—	35	—	.354	.407	.534	.917
1902	Bal-A	4	15	3	4	1	0	0	0	1	—	—	0	1	—	2	—	.267	.313	.333	1.000
1902	Bro-N	123	486	86	129	20	10	4	37	57	—	—	5	7	—	23	—	.265	.349	.372	.964
1903	Bro-N	139	515	99	171	29	9	9	75	75	—	—	6	20	—	67	—	.332	.423	.476	.951
1904	Bro-N	143	507	70	121	23	6	1	46	56	—	—	2	18	—	21	—	.239	.317	.314	.954
1905	**Bro-N**	**130**	**480**	**58**	**140**	**20**	**11**	**3**	**41**	**61**	**—**	**—**	**7**	**15**	**—**	**23**	**—**	**.292**	**.380**	**.398**	**.967**
1906	**ChC-N**	**149**	**549**	**90**	**144**	**27**	**10**	**1**	**45**	**67**	**—**	**—**	**6**	**40**	**—**	**30**	**—**	**.262**	**.349**	**.353**	**.986**
1907	**ChC-N**	**143**	**484**	**76**	**129**	**23**	**1**	**1**	**36**	**76**	**—**	**—**	**6**	**35**	**—**	**31**	**—**	**.267**	**.349**	**.324**	**.975**
1908	**ChC-N**	**115**	**403**	**54**	**93**	**18**	**3**	**2**	**22**	**62**	**—**	**—**	**2**	**21**	**—**	**18**	**—**	**.231**	**.336**	**.305**	**.955**
1909	**ChC-N**	**148**	**525**	**81**	**134**	**29**	**5**	**1**	**43**	**72**	**—**	**—**	**1**	**46**	**—**	**15**	**—**	**.255**	**.346**	**.335**	**.967**
1910	**ChC-N**	**144**	**507**	**82**	**130**	**27**	**6**	**5**	**51**	**83**	**—**	**53**	**5**	**31**	**—**	**22**	**—**	**.256**	**.366**	**.363**	**.976**
1911	**ChC-N**	**156**	**539**	**121**	**149**	**26**	**11**	**4**	**50**	**147**	**—**	**58**	**3**	**15**	**—**	**32**	**—**	**.276**	**.434**	**.388**	**.963**
1912	**ChC-N**	**146**	**523**	**85**	**128**	**22**	**10**	**3**	**47**	**122**	**—**	**81**	**5**	**10**	**—**	**15**	**—**	**.245**	**.392**	**.342**	**.962**
1913	StL-N	52	136	18	27	2	1	0	17	41	—	25	1	3	—	5	—	.199	.388	.228	.953
1913	Cin-N	47	116	16	22	1	3	0	7	27	—	16	0	6	—	6	—	.190	.343	.250	.969
Career average		125	447	76	123	21	8	3	48	67	—	14	5	17	—	27	—	.274	.375	.378	.953
Cubs average		**143**	**504**	**84**	**130**	**25**	**7**	**2**	**42**	**90**	**—**	**27**	**4**	**28**	**—**	**23**	**—**	**.274**	**.375**	**.378**	**.953**
Career total		2122	7605	1296	2084	354	136	56	813	1135	—	233	90	287	—	465	—	.274	.375	.378	.953
Cubs total		**1001**	**3530**	**589**	**907**	**172**	**46**	**17**	**294**	**629**	**—**	**192**	**28**	**198**	**—**	**163**	**—**	**.257**	**.374**	**.346**	**.969**

Samuel James (Jimmy) Tilden Sheckard, of-3b-ss, 1897–1913

Jimmy Sheckard was one of the unsung heroes who excelled for the Cubs during their glory years.

Sheckard was born on November 23, 1878, in Upper Chanceford, Pennsylvania. He was one of the few Pennsylvania Dutch in baseball. He broke in with the Dodgers in 1897 and became a regular for them in 1898.

Sheckard was brash and didn't bother to hide his dissatisfaction with his contract while with Brooklyn. In 1902, the year after he led the National League in triples (19) and slugging percentage (.534), he jumped to the Baltimore franchise of the American League for a few games until he was lured back to Brooklyn by the promise of a better contract. But his stock was dropping in Brooklyn, and prior to the 1906 season, he was sent to Chicago, where he became the team's starting left fielder.

Sheckard hit .262, with 30 stolen bases, 90 runs scored, and 27 doubles that year. He was also second among left fielders in putouts with 264. His four errors were the fewest among National League left fielders.

But the outspoken Sheckard put his foot in his pie hole prior to the 1906 World Series, boasting that he would hit .400 against the American League champion White Sox.

It's safe to say that most of the Cubs expected to handle the White Sox easily, but Sheckard was the only one to woof about it. The Sox beat the Cubs in the World Series and

Sheckard went a very embarrassing zero for 21. He did manage to redeem himself somewhat in the next two World Series for Chicago, collecting five hits in each as the Cubs bounced back to win both years.

In 1908 Sheckard was almost out of baseball. He was taunting rookie outfielder Henry "Heinie" Zimmerman in June of that season, and Zimmerman retaliated by throwing a bottle of ammonia at him. The bottle broke just above Sheckard's eyes, partially burning them. Sheckard was rushed to a local hospital, where he spent several weeks recovering. Sheckard eventually returned that season, but his eyesight was not the same that year, and he ended up hitting only .231.

Sheckard had begun his career as a power hitter, finishing second, third and first, respectively, in home runs while he was with Brooklyn from 1901 to 1903. By 1911 he had evolved into a more patient batter and set a team record for most walks with a league-leading 147, as well as leading the National League in runs scored with 121. He would again lead the league in walks in 1912 with 122.

But that was his last year with the Cubs, as the 34-year-old Sheckard was traded to the Cardinals in 1913. He was sent to the Reds later that year, before retiring at the end of the season. Sheckard died in 1947.

Sheckard still holds several Cubs records, including most assists by an outfielder in a season (32), most total chances by a left fielder in a season (378) and most double plays by an outfielder in a season (12). All three of those records were set in 1911.

Shields, Thomas Charles (Tommy)

HEIGHT: 6'0"   THROWS: RIGHT   BATS: LEFT   BORN: 8/14/1964 FAIRFAX, VIRGINIA   POSITIONS PLAYED: 1B, 2B, 3B, OF

YEAR	TEAM	GAMES	AB	RUNS	HITS	2B	3B	HR	RBI	BB	IBB	SO	HBP	SH	SF	SB	CS	BA	OBA	SA	FA
1992	Bal-A	2	0	0	0	0	0	0	0	0	0	0	0	0	0	0	0	—	—	—	—
1993	ChC-N	20	34	4	6	1	0	0	1	2	0	10	0	0	0	0	0	.176	.222	.206	1.000
Career average		11	17	2	3	1	0	0	1	1	0	5	0	0	0	0	0	.176	.222	.206	1.000
Cubs average		20	34	4	6	1	0	0	1	2	0	10	0	0	0	0	0	.176	.222	.206	1.000
Career total		22	34	4	6	1	0	0	1	2	0	10	0	0	0	0	0	.176	.222	.206	1.000
Cubs total		20	34	4	6	1	0	0	1	2	0	10	0	0	0	0	0	.176	.222	.206	1.000

Shumpert, Terrance Darnell (Terry)

HEIGHT: 6'0"   THROWS: RIGHT   BATS: RIGHT   BORN: 8/16/1966 PADUCAH, KENTUCKY   POSITIONS PLAYED: 1B, 2B, 3B, SS, OF

YEAR	TEAM	GAMES	AB	RUNS	HITS	2B	3B	HR	RBI	BB	IBB	SO	HBP	SH	SF	SB	CS	BA	OBA	SA	FA
1990	KC-A	32	91	7	25	6	1	0	8	2	0	17	1	0	2	3	3	.275	.292	.363	.977
1991	KC-A	144	369	45	80	16	4	5	34	30	0	75	5	10	3	17	11	.217	.283	.322	.975
1992	KC-A	36	94	6	14	5	1	1	11	3	0	17	0	2	0	2	2	.149	.175	.255	.969
1993	KC-A	8	10	0	1	0	0	0	0	2	0	2	0	0	0	1	0	.100	.250	.100	1.000
1994	KC-A	64	183	28	44	6	2	8	24	13	0	39	0	5	1	18	3	.240	.289	.426	.961
1995	Bos-A	21	47	6	11	3	0	0	3	4	0	13	0	0	0	3	1	.234	.294	.298	.966
1996	ChC-N	27	31	5	7	1	0	2	6	2	0	11	1	0	1	0	1	.226	.286	.452	.952
1997	SD-N	13	33	4	9	3	0	1	6	3	0	4	0	0	1	0	0	.273	.324	.455	.952
1998	Col-N	23	26	3	6	1	0	1	2	2	0	8	0	0	0	0	0	.231	.286	.385	1.000
1999	Col-N	92	262	58	91	26	3	10	37	31	2	41	2	4	5	14	0	.347	.413	.584	.983
2000	Col-N	115	263	52	68	11	7	9	40	28	1	40	6	0	3	8	4	.259	.340	.456	.977
2001	Col-N	114	242	37	70	14	5	4	24	15	2	44	3	4	1	14	3	.289	.337	.438	.959
Career average		57	138	21	36	8	2	3	16	11	0	26	2	2	1	7	2	.258	.318	.416	.973
Cubs average		27	31	5	7	1	0	2	6	2	0	11	1	0	1	0	1	.226	.286	.452	.952
Career total		689	1651	251	426	92	23	41	195	135	5	311	18	25	17	80	28	.258	.318	.416	.973
Cubs total		27	31	5	7	1	0	2	6	2	0	11	1	0	1	0	1	.226	.286	.452	.952

Sicking, Edward Joseph (Ed)

HEIGHT: 5'9"   THROWS: RIGHT   BATS: RIGHT   BORN: 3/30/1897 ST. BERNARD, OHIO   DIED: 8/30/1978 MADEIRA, OHIO   POSITIONS PLAYED: 2B, 3B, SS

YEAR	TEAM	GAMES	AB	RUNS	HITS	2B	3B	HR	RBI	BB	IBB	SO	HBP	SH	SF	SB	CS	BA	OBA	SA	FA
1916	ChC-N	1	1	0	0	0	0	0	0	0	—	0	0	0	—	0	—	.000	.000	.000	—
1918	NYG-N	46	132	9	33	4	0	0	12	6	—	11	0	2	—	2	—	.250	.283	.280	.939
1919	NYG-N	6	15	2	5	0	0	0	3	1	—	0	1	1	—	0	—	.333	.412	.333	.971
1919	Phi-N	61	185	16	40	2	1	0	15	8	—	17	1	7	—	4	—	.216	.253	.238	.950
1920	NYG-N	46	134	11	23	3	1	0	9	10	—	10	1	4	—	6	2	.172	.234	.209	.925
1920	Cin-N	37	123	12	33	3	0	0	17	13	—	5	0	1	—	2	3	.268	.338	.293	.948
1927	Pit-N	6	7	1	1	1	0	0	3	1	—	0	0	0	—	0	—	.143	.250	.286	1.000
Career average		41	119	10	27	3	0	0	12	8	—	9	1	3	—	3	1	.226	.277	.255	.945
Cubs average		1	1	0	0	0	0	0	0	0	—	0	0	0	—	0	—	.000	.000	.000	—
Career total		203	597	51	135	13	2	0	59	39	—	43	3	15	—	14	5	.226	.277	.255	.945
Cubs total		1	1	0	0	0	0	0	0	0	—	0	0	0	—	0	—	.000	.000	.000	—

Silvera, Charles Anthony Ryan (Charlie or Swede)

HEIGHT: 5'10"   THROWS: RIGHT   BATS: RIGHT   BORN: 10/13/1924 SAN FRANCISCO, CALIFORNIA   POSITIONS PLAYED: C, 3B

YEAR	TEAM	GAMES	AB	RUNS	HITS	2B	3B	HR	RBI	BB	IBB	SO	HBP	SH	SF	SB	CS	BA	OBA	SA	FA
1948	NYY-A	4	14	1	8	0	1	0	1	0	—	1	0	0	—	0	0	.571	.571	.714	1.000
1949	NYY-A	58	130	8	41	2	0	0	13	18	—	5	1	0	—	2	1	.315	.403	.331	.985
1950	NYY-A	18	25	2	4	0	0	0	1	1	—	2	0	0	—	0	0	.160	.192	.160	.959
1951	NYY-A	18	51	5	14	3	0	1	7	5	—	3	0	0	—	0	0	.275	.339	.392	1.000
1952	NYY-A	20	55	4	18	3	0	0	11	5	—	2	0	0	—	0	0	.327	.383	.382	1.000
1953	NYY-A	42	82	11	23	3	1	0	12	9	—	5	0	3	—	0	3	.280	.352	.341	.992
1954	NYY-A	20	37	1	10	1	0	0	4	3	—	2	1	1	0	0	1	.270	.341	.297	.963
1955	NYY-A	14	26	1	5	0	0	0	1	6	0	4	0	0	0	0	1	.192	.344	.192	1.000
1956	NYY-A	7	9	0	2	0	0	0	0	2	0	3	0	0	0	0	0	.222	.364	.222	.909
1957	ChC-N	26	53	1	11	3	0	0	2	4	0	5	0	0	0	0	0	.208	.263	.264	.982
Career average		23	48	3	14	2	0	0	5	5	0	3	0	0	0	0	1	.282	.356	.328	.985
Cubs average		26	53	1	11	3	0	0	2	4	0	5	0	0	0	0	0	.208	.263	.264	.982
Career total		227	482	34	136	15	2	1	52	53	0	32	2	4	0	2	6	.282	.356	.328	.985
Cubs total		26	53	1	11	3	0	0	2	4	0	5	0	0	0	0	0	.208	.263	.264	.982

Sizemore, Theodore Crawford (Ted)

HEIGHT: 5'10" THROWS: RIGHT BATS: RIGHT BORN: 4/15/1945 GADSDEN, ALABAMA POSITIONS PLAYED: C, 2B, 3B, SS, OF

YEAR	TEAM	GAMES	AB	RUNS	HITS	2B	3B	HR	RBI	BB	IBB	SO	HBP	SH	SF	SB	CS	BA	OBA	SA	FA
1969	LA-N	159	590	69	160	20	5	4	46	45	7	40	5	9	1	5	5	.271	.328	.342	.971
1970	LA-N	96	340	40	104	10	1	1	34	34	6	19	0	0	2	5	1	.306	.367	.350	.980
1971	StL-N	135	478	53	126	14	5	3	42	42	5	26	1	7	4	4	6	.264	.322	.333	.973
1972	StL-N	120	439	53	116	17	4	2	38	37	1	36	4	4	5	8	3	.264	.324	.335	.976
1973	StL-N	142	521	69	147	22	1	1	54	68	0	34	2	25	4	6	4	.282	.365	.334	.981
1974	StL-N	129	504	68	126	17	0	2	47	70	2	37	0	18	5	8	4	.250	.339	.296	.979
1975	StL-N	153	562	56	135	23	1	3	49	45	2	37	2	21	5	1	5	.240	.296	.301	.972
1976	LA-N	84	266	18	64	8	1	0	18	15	1	22	0	10	1	2	3	.241	.280	.278	.981
1977	Phi-N	152	519	64	146	20	3	4	47	52	21	40	1	5	4	8	11	.281	.345	.355	.986
1978	Phi-N	108	351	38	77	12	0	0	25	25	8	29	1	4	5	8	1	.219	.270	.254	.978
1979	**ChC-N**	**98**	**330**	**36**	**82**	**17**	**0**	**2**	**24**	**32**	**7**	**25**	**3**	**7**	**2**	**3**	**3**	**.248**	**.319**	**.318**	**.973**
1979	Bos-A	26	88	12	23	7	0	1	6	4	0	5	1	0	0	1	0	.261	.301	.375	.993
1980	Bos-A	9	23	1	5	1	0	0	0	0	0	0	0	0	0	0	0	.217	.217	.261	.927
Career average		118	418	48	109	16	2	2	36	39	5	29	2	9	3	5	4	.262	.325	.321	.977
Cubs average		**98**	**330**	**36**	**82**	**17**	**0**	**2**	**24**	**32**	**7**	**25**	**3**	**7**	**2**	**3**	**3**	**.248**	**.319**	**.318**	**.973**
Career total		1411	5011	577	1311	188	21	23	430	469	60	350	20	110	38	59	46	.262	.325	.321	.977
Cubs total		**98**	**330**	**36**	**82**	**17**	**0**	**2**	**24**	**32**	**7**	**25**	**3**	**7**	**2**	**3**	**3**	**.248**	**.319**	**.318**	**.973**

Skidmore, Robert Roe (Roe)

HEIGHT: 6'3" THROWS: RIGHT BATS: RIGHT BORN: 10/30/1945 DECATUR, ILLINOIS

YEAR	TEAM	GAMES	AB	RUNS	HITS	2B	3B	HR	RBI	BB	IBB	SO	HBP	SH	SF	SB	CS	BA	OBA	SA	FA
1970	ChC-N	1	1	0	1	0	0	0	0	0	0	0	0	0	0	0	0	1.000	1.000	1.000	—
Career average		1	1	0	1	0	0	0	0	0	0	0	0	0	0	0	0	1.000	1.000	1.000	—
Cubs average		**1**	**1**	**0**	**1**	**0**	**0**	**0**	**0**	**0**	**0**	**0**	**0**	**0**	**0**	**0**	**0**	**1.000**	**1.000**	**1.000**	**—**
Career total		1	1	0	1	0	0	0	0	0	0	0	0	0	0	0	0	1.000	1.000	1.000	—
Cubs total		**1**	**1**	**0**	**1**	**0**	**0**	**0**	**0**	**0**	**0**	**0**	**0**	**0**	**0**	**0**	**0**	**1.000**	**1.000**	**1.000**	**—**

Slagle, James Franklin (Jimmy *or* Rabbit *or* Shorty)

HEIGHT: 5'7" THROWS: RIGHT BATS: LEFT BORN: 7/11/1873 WORTHVILLE, PENNSYLVANIA DIED: 5/10/1956 CHICAGO, ILLINOIS POSITIONS PLAYED: OF

YEAR	TEAM	GAMES	AB	RUNS	HITS	2B	3B	HR	RBI	BB	IBB	SO	HBP	SH	SF	SB	CS	BA	OBA	SA	FA
1899	Was-N	147	599	92	163	15	8	0	41	55	—	—	5	9	—	22	—	.272	.338	.324	.953
1900	Phi-N	141	574	115	165	16	9	0	45	60	—	—	3	27	—	34	—	.287	.358	.347	.922
1901	Phi-N	48	183	20	37	6	2	1	20	16	—	—	3	7	—	5	—	.202	.277	.273	.930
1901	Bos-N	66	255	35	69	7	0	0	7	34	—	—	1	6	—	14	—	.271	.359	.298	.935
1902	**ChC-N**	**115**	**454**	**64**	**143**	**11**	**4**	**0**	**28**	**53**	**—**	**—**	**0**	**7**	**—**	**40**	**—**	**.315**	**.387**	**.357**	**.965**
1903	**ChC-N**	**139**	**543**	**104**	**162**	**20**	**6**	**0**	**44**	**81**	**—**	**—**	**4**	**15**	**—**	**33**	**—**	**.298**	**.393**	**.357**	**.936**
1904	**ChC-N**	**120**	**481**	**73**	**125**	**12**	**10**	**1**	**31**	**41**	**—**	**—**	**3**	**7**	**—**	**28**	**—**	**.260**	**.322**	**.333**	**.921**
1905	**ChC-N**	**155**	**568**	**96**	**153**	**19**	**4**	**0**	**37**	**97**	**—**	**—**	**3**	**13**	**—**	**27**	**—**	**.269**	**.379**	**.317**	**.962**
1906	**ChC-N**	**127**	**498**	**71**	**119**	**8**	**6**	**0**	**33**	**63**	**—**	**—**	**0**	**10**	**—**	**25**	**—**	**.239**	**.324**	**.279**	**.976**
1907	**ChC-N**	**136**	**489**	**71**	**126**	**6**	**6**	**0**	**32**	**76**	**—**	**—**	**1**	**9**	**—**	**28**	**—**	**.258**	**.359**	**.294**	**.962**
1908	**ChC-N**	**104**	**352**	**38**	**78**	**4**	**1**	**0**	**26**	**43**	**—**	**—**	**0**	**22**	**—**	**17**	**—**	**.222**	**.306**	**.239**	**.976**
Career average		130	500	78	134	12	6	0	34	62	—	—	2	13	—	27	—	.268	.352	.317	.950
Cubs average		**128**	**484**	**74**	**129**	**11**	**5**	**0**	**33**	**65**	**—**	**—**	**2**	**12**	**—**	**28**	**—**	**.268**	**.356**	**.314**	**.957**
Career total		1298	4996	779	1340	124	56	2	344	619	—	—	23	132	—	273	—	.268	.352	.317	.950
Cubs total		**896**	**3385**	**517**	**906**	**80**	**37**	**1**	**231**	**454**	**—**	**—**	**11**	**83**	**—**	**198**	**—**	**.268**	**.356**	**.314**	**.957**

Smalley, Roy Frederick

HEIGHT: 6'3" THROWS: RIGHT BATS: RIGHT BORN: 6/9/1926 SPRINGFIELD, MISSOURI POSITIONS PLAYED: 1B, 2B, 3B, SS

YEAR	TEAM	GAMES	AB	RUNS	HITS	2B	3B	HR	RBI	BB	IBB	SO	HBP	SH	SF	SB	CS	BA	OBA	SA	FA
1948	**ChC-N**	**124**	**361**	**25**	**78**	**11**	**4**	**4**	**36**	**23**	**—**	**76**	**1**	**2**	**—**	**0**	**—**	**.216**	**.265**	**.302**	**.941**
1949	**ChC-N**	**135**	**477**	**57**	**117**	**21**	**10**	**8**	**35**	**36**	**—**	**77**	**4**	**2**	**—**	**2**	**—**	**.245**	**.304**	**.382**	**.947**
1950	**ChC-N**	**154**	**557**	**58**	**128**	**21**	**9**	**21**	**85**	**49**	**—**	**114**	**4**	**6**	**—**	**2**	**—**	**.230**	**.297**	**.413**	**.945**
1951	**ChC-N**	**79**	**238**	**24**	**55**	**7**	**4**	**8**	**31**	**25**	**—**	**53**	**0**	**3**	**—**	**0**	**0**	**.231**	**.304**	**.395**	**.953**
1952	**ChC-N**	**87**	**261**	**36**	**58**	**14**	**1**	**5**	**30**	**29**	**—**	**58**	**2**	**1**	**—**	**0**	**0**	**.222**	**.305**	**.341**	**.952**

(continued)

(continued)

YEAR	TEAM	GAMES	AB	RUNS	HITS	2B	3B	HR	RBI	BB	IBB	SO	HBP	SH	SF	SB	CS	BA	OBA	SA	FA
1953	ChC-N	82	253	20	63	9	0	6	25	28	—	57	2	5	—	0	0	.249	.329	.356	.932
1954	Mil-N	25	36	5	8	0	0	1	7	4	—	9	1	0	1	0	0	.222	.310	.306	.985
1955	Phi-N	92	260	33	51	11	1	7	39	39	2	58	2	5	2	0	0	.196	.304	.327	.975
1956	Phi-N	65	168	14	38	9	3	0	16	23	4	29	1	2	0	0	0	.226	.323	.315	.949
1957	Phi-N	28	31	5	5	0	1	1	1	1	0	9	1	0	0	0	0	.161	.212	.323	.941
1958	Phi-N	1	2	0	0	0	0	0	0	0	0	1	0	0	0	0	0	.000	.000	.000	.714
Career average		79	240	25	55	9	3	6	28	23	1	49	2	2	0	0	0	.227	.300	.360	.948
Cubs average		**110**	**358**	**37**	**83**	**14**	**5**	**9**	**40**	**32**	**—**	**73**	**2**	**3**	**—**	**1**	**0**	**.232**	**.299**	**.370**	**.945**
Career total		872	2644	277	601	103	33	61	305	257	—	541	18	26	3	4	0	.227	.300	.360	.948
Cubs total		**661**	**2147**	**220**	**499**	**83**	**28**	**52**	**242**	**190**	**6**	**435**	**13**	**19**	**—**	**4**	**0**	**.232**	**.299**	**.370**	**.945**

Smith, Alexander Benjamin (Aleck *or* Broadway Aleck)

HEIGHT: —   THROWS: RIGHT   BATS: —   BORN: 1871 NEW YORK, NEW YORK   DIED: 7/9/1919 NEW YORK, NEW YORK   POSITIONS PLAYED: C, 1B, 2B, 3B, OF

YEAR	TEAM	GAMES	AB	RUNS	HITS	2B	3B	HR	RBI	BB	IBB	SO	HBP	SH	SF	SB	CS	BA	OBA	SA	FA
1897	Bro-N	66	237	36	71	13	1	1	39	4	—	—	2	6	—	12	—	.300	.317	.376	.924
1898	Bro-N	52	199	25	52	6	5	0	23	3	—	—	1	7	—	7	—	.261	.276	.342	.885
1899	Bro-N	17	61	6	11	0	1	0	6	2	—	—	0	1	—	0	—	.180	.206	.213	.917
1899	Bal-N	41	120	17	46	6	4	0	25	4	—	—	3	3	—	7	—	.383	.417	.500	.952
1900	Bro-N	7	25	2	6	0	0	0	3	1	—	—	0	1	—	2	—	.240	.269	.240	.864
1901	NYG-N	26	78	5	11	0	0	0	6	0	—	—	0	1	—	2	—	.141	.141	.141	.962
1902	Bal-A	41	145	10	34	3	0	0	21	8	—	—	0	4	—	5	—	.234	.275	.255	.960
1903	Bos-A	11	33	4	10	1	0	0	4	0	—	—	0	0	—	0	—	.303	.303	.333	.932
1904	ChC-N	10	29	2	6	1	0	0	1	3	—	—	0	0	—	1	—	.207	.281	.241	.846
1906	NYG-N	16	28	0	5	0	0	0	2	1	—	—	0	0	—	1	—	.179	.207	.179	1.000
Career average		32	106	12	28	3	1	0	14	3	—	—	1	3	—	4	—	.264	.288	.321	.934
Cubs average		**10**	**29**	**2**	**6**	**1**	**0**	**0**	**1**	**3**	**—**	**—**	**0**	**0**	**—**	**1**	**—**	**.207**	**.281**	**.241**	**.846**
Career total		287	955	107	252	30	11	1	130	26	—	—	6	23	—	37	—	.264	.288	.321	.934
Cubs total		**10**	**29**	**2**	**6**	**1**	**0**	**0**	**1**	**3**	**—**	**—**	**0**	**0**	**—**	**1**	**—**	**.207**	**.281**	**.241**	**.846**

Smith, Bobby Gene

HEIGHT: 5'11"   THROWS: RIGHT   BATS: RIGHT   BORN: 5/28/1934 HOOD RIVER, OREGON   POSITIONS PLAYED: 3B, OF

YEAR	TEAM	GAMES	AB	RUNS	HITS	2B	3B	HR	RBI	BB	IBB	SO	HBP	SH	SF	SB	CS	BA	OBA	SA	FA
1957	StL-N	93	185	24	39	7	1	3	18	13	3	35	0	1	2	1	1	.211	.260	.308	.973
1958	StL-N	28	88	8	25	3	0	2	5	2	0	18	1	0	1	1	0	.284	.304	.386	1.000
1959	StL-N	43	60	11	13	1	1	1	7	1	0	9	0	0	0	1	0	.217	.230	.317	.971
1960	Phi-N	98	217	24	62	5	2	4	27	10	1	28	0	3	0	2	3	.286	.317	.382	1.000
1961	Phi-N	79	174	16	44	7	0	2	18	15	2	32	1	0	2	0	1	.253	.313	.328	.971
1962	NYM-N	8	22	1	3	0	1	0	2	3	0	2	0	0	0	0	1	.136	.240	.227	1.000
1962	**ChC-N**	**13**	**29**	**3**	**5**	**0**	**0**	**1**	**2**	**2**	**0**	**6**	**0**	**0**	**1**	**0**	**1**	**.172**	**.219**	**.276**	**1.000**
1962	StL-N	91	130	13	30	9	0	0	12	7	0	14	0	2	0	0	1	.231	.270	.300	1.000
1965	Cal-A	23	57	1	13	3	0	0	5	2	0	10	1	1	1	0	1	.228	.262	.281	1.000
Career average		68	137	14	33	5	1	2	14	8	1	22	0	1	1	1	1	.243	.284	.331	.986
Cubs average		**13**	**29**	**3**	**5**	**0**	**0**	**1**	**2**	**2**	**0**	**6**	**0**	**0**	**1**	**0**	**1**	**.172**	**.219**	**.276**	**1.000**
Career total		476	962	101	234	35	5	13	96	55	6	154	3	7	7	5	9	.243	.284	.331	.986
Cubs total		**13**	**29**	**3**	**5**	**0**	**0**	**1**	**2**	**2**	**0**	**6**	**0**	**0**	**1**	**0**	**1**	**.172**	**.219**	**.276**	**1.000**

Smith, Charles William (Charley)

HEIGHT: 6'1"   THROWS: RIGHT   BATS: RIGHT   BORN: 9/15/1937 CHARLESTON, SOUTH CAROLINA   DIED: 11/29/1994 RENO, NEVADA
POSITIONS PLAYED: 2B, 3B, SS, OF

YEAR	TEAM	GAMES	AB	RUNS	HITS	2B	3B	HR	RBI	BB	IBB	SO	HBP	SH	SF	SB	CS	BA	OBA	SA	FA
1960	LA-N	18	60	2	10	1	1	0	5	1	0	15	0	2	3	0	0	.167	.172	.217	.953
1961	LA-N	9	24	4	6	1	0	2	3	1	0	6	0	0	0	0	0	.250	.280	.542	.947
1961	Phi-N	112	411	43	102	13	4	9	47	23	3	76	5	10	3	3	4	.248	.294	.365	.923
1962	CWS-A	65	145	11	30	4	0	2	17	9	3	32	1	3	3	0	1	.207	.256	.276	.944
1963	CWS-A	4	7	0	2	0	1	0	1	0	0	2	0	0	0	0	1	.286	.286	.571	1.000
1964	CWS-A	2	7	1	1	0	0	0	0	1	0	2	0	0	0	0	0	.143	.250	.143	1.000
1964	NYM-N	127	443	44	106	12	0	20	58	19	1	101	3	5	1	2	0	.239	.275	.402	.924
1965	NYM-N	135	499	49	122	20	3	16	62	17	3	123	4	7	4	2	2	.244	.273	.393	.958
1966	StL-N	116	391	34	104	13	4	10	43	22	4	81	0	5	5	0	2	.266	.301	.396	.965

(continued)

(Smith, C.W., continued)

YEAR	TEAM	GAMES	AB	RUNS	HITS	2B	3B	HR	RBI	BB	IBB	SO	HBP	SH	SF	SB	CS	BA	OBA	SA	FA
1967	NYY-A	135	425	38	95	15	3	9	38	32	6	110	1	4	3	0	2	.224	.278	.336	.947
1968	NYY-A	46	70	2	16	4	1	1	7	5	2	18	0	2	0	0	0	.229	.280	.357	.961
1969	**ChC-N**	**2**	**2**	**0**	**0**	**0**	**0**	**0**	**0**	**0**	**0**	**0**	**0**	**0**	**0**	**0**	**0**	**.000**	**.000**	**.000**	**—**
Career average		77	248	23	59	8	2	7	28	13	2	57	1	4	2	1	1	.239	.279	.370	.944
Cubs average		**2**	**2**	**0**	**0**	**0**	**0**	**0**	**0**	**0**	**0**	**0**	**0**	**0**	**0**	**0**	**0**	**.000**	**.000**	**.000**	**—**
Career total		771	2484	228	594	83	18	69	281	130	19	565	14	38	20	7	12	.239	.279	.370	.944
Cubs total		**2**	**2**	**0**	**0**	**0**	**0**	**0**	**0**	**0**	**0**	**0**	**0**	**0**	**0**	**0**	**0**	**.000**	**.000**	**.000**	**—**

Smith, Earl Leonard (Sheriff)

HEIGHT: 5'11" THROWS: RIGHT BATS: BOTH BORN: 1/20/1891 OAK HILL, OHIO DIED: 3/14/1943 PORTSMOUTH, OHIO POSITIONS PLAYED: 3B, OF

YEAR	TEAM	GAMES	AB	RUNS	HITS	2B	3B	HR	RBI	BB	IBB	SO	HBP	SH	SF	SB	CS	BA	OBA	SA	FA
1916	**ChC-N**	**14**	**27**	**2**	**7**	**1**	**1**	**0**	**4**	**2**	**—**	**5**	**0**	**1**	**—**	**1**	**—**	**.259**	**.310**	**.370**	**.800**
1917	StL-A	52	199	31	56	7	7	0	10	15	—	21	0	8	—	5	—	.281	.332	.387	.977
1918	StL-A	89	286	28	77	10	5	0	32	13	—	16	1	19	—	13	—	.269	.303	.339	.952
1919	StL-A	88	252	21	63	12	5	1	36	18	—	27	0	15	—	1	—	.250	.300	.349	.971
1920	StL-A	103	353	45	108	21	8	3	55	13	—	18	3	8	—	11	4	.306	.336	.436	.918
1921	StL-A	25	78	7	26	4	2	2	14	3	—	4	1	1	—	0	0	.333	.366	.513	.879
1921	Was-A	59	180	20	39	5	2	2	12	10	—	19	2	4	—	1	0	.217	.266	.300	.941
1922	Was-A	65	205	22	53	12	2	1	23	8	—	17	2	6	—	4	4	.259	.293	.351	.923
Career average		71	226	25	61	10	5	1	27	12	—	18	1	9	—	5	1	.272	.311	.375	.940
Cubs average		**14**	**27**	**2**	**7**	**1**	**1**	**0**	**4**	**2**	**—**	**5**	**0**	**1**	**—**	**1**	**—**	**.259**	**.310**	**.370**	**.800**
Career total		495	1580	176	429	72	32	9	186	82	—	127	9	62	—	36	8	.272	.311	.375	.940
Cubs total		**14**	**27**	**2**	**7**	**1**	**1**	**0**	**4**	**2**	**—**	**5**	**0**	**1**	**—**	**1**	**—**	**.259**	**.310**	**.370**	**.800**

Smith, Gregory Alan (Greg)

HEIGHT: 5'11" THROWS: RIGHT BATS: BOTH BORN: 4/5/1967 BALTIMORE, MARYLAND POSITIONS PLAYED: 2B, SS

YEAR	TEAM	GAMES	AB	RUNS	HITS	2B	3B	HR	RBI	BB	IBB	SO	HBP	SH	SF	SB	CS	BA	OBA	SA	FA
1989	**ChC-N**	**4**	**5**	**1**	**2**	**0**	**0**	**0**	**2**	**0**	**0**	**0**	**1**	**0**	**0**	**0**	**0**	**.400**	**.500**	**.400**	**.778**
1990	**ChC-N**	**18**	**44**	**4**	**9**	**2**	**1**	**0**	**5**	**2**	**0**	**5**	**0**	**1**	**1**	**1**	**0**	**.205**	**.234**	**.295**	**.951**
1991	LA-N	5	3	1	0	0	0	0	0	0	0	2	0	1	0	0	0	.000	.000	.000	—
Career average		9	17	2	4	1	0	0	2	1	0	2	0	1	0	0	0	.212	.250	.288	.929
Cubs average		**11**	**25**	**3**	**6**	**1**	**1**	**0**	**4**	**1**	**0**	**3**	**1**	**1**	**1**	**1**	**0**	**.224**	**.264**	**.306**	**.929**
Career total		27	52	6	11	2	1	0	7	2	0	7	1	2	1	1	0	.212	.250	.288	.929
Cubs total		**22**	**49**	**5**	**11**	**2**	**1**	**0**	**7**	**2**	**0**	**5**	**1**	**1**	**1**	**1**	**0**	**.224**	**.264**	**.306**	**.929**

Smith, Harry W.

HEIGHT: 6'0" THROWS: RIGHT BATS: RIGHT BORN: 2/5/1856 NORTH VERNON, INDIANA DIED: 6/4/1898 QUEENSVILLE, INDIANA
POSITIONS PLAYED: C, 2B, OF

YEAR	TEAM	GAMES	AB	RUNS	HITS	2B	3B	HR	RBI	BB	IBB	SO	HBP	SH	SF	SB	CS	BA	OBA	SA	FA
1877	**ChN-N**	**24**	**94**	**7**	**19**	**1**	**0**	**0**	**3**	**4**	**—**	**6**	**—**	**—**	**—**	**—**	**—**	**.202**	**.235**	**.213**	**.814**
1877	Cin-N	10	36	4	9	2	1	0	3	1	—	5	—	—	—	—	—	.250	.270	.361	.863
1889	Lou-AA	1	2	0	1	0	0	0	1	0	—	1	0	—	—	0	—	.500	.500	.500	.667
Career average		18	66	6	15	2	1	0	4	3	—	6	0	—	—	0	—	.220	.248	.258	.833
Cubs average		**24**	**94**	**7**	**19**	**1**	**0**	**0**	**3**	**4**	**—**	**6**	**—**	**—**	**—**	**—**	**—**	**.202**	**.235**	**.213**	**.814**
Career total		35	132	11	29	3	1	0	7	5	—	12	0	—	—	0	—	.220	.248	.258	.833
Cubs total		**24**	**94**	**7**	**19**	**1**	**0**	**0**	**3**	**4**	**—**	**6**	**—**	**—**	**—**	**—**	**—**	**.202**	**.235**	**.213**	**.814**

Smith, Jason William

HEIGHT: 6'3" THROWS: RIGHT BATS: LEFT BORN: 7/24/1977 MERIDIAN, MISSISSIPPI POSITIONS PLAYED: SS

YEAR	TEAM	GAMES	AB	RUNS	HITS	2B	3B	HR	RBI	BB	IBB	SO	HBP	SH	SF	SB	CS	BA	OBA	SA	FA
2001	**ChC-N**	**2**	**1**	**0**	**0**	**0**	**0**	**0**	**0**	**0**	**0**	**1**	**0**	**0**	**0**	**0**	**0**	**.000**	**.000**	**.000**	**1.000**
Career average		2	1	0	0	0	0	0	0	0	0	1	0	0	0	0	0	.000	.000	.000	1.000
Cubs average		**2**	**1**	**0**	**0**	**0**	**0**	**0**	**0**	**0**	**0**	**1**	**0**	**0**	**0**	**0**	**0**	**.000**	**.000**	**.000**	**1.000**
Career total		2	1	0	0	0	0	0	0	0	0	1	0	0	0	0	0	.000	.000	.000	1.000
Cubs total		**2**	**1**	**0**	**0**	**0**	**0**	**0**	**0**	**0**	**0**	**1**	**0**	**0**	**0**	**0**	**0**	**.000**	**.000**	**.000**	**1.000**

Smith, John Dwight (Dwight)
HEIGHT: 5'11" THROWS: RIGHT BATS: LEFT BORN: 11/8/1963 TALLAHASSEE, FLORIDA POSITIONS PLAYED: OF

YEAR	TEAM	GAMES	AB	RUNS	HITS	2B	3B	HR	RBI	BB	IBB	SO	HBP	SH	SF	SB	CS	BA	OBA	SA	FA
1989	ChC-N	109	343	52	111	19	6	9	52	31	0	51	2	4	1	9	4	.324	.382	.493	.975
1990	ChC-N	117	290	34	76	15	0	6	27	28	2	46	2	0	2	11	6	.262	.329	.376	.986
1991	ChC-N	90	167	16	38	7	2	3	21	11	2	32	1	1	0	2	3	.228	.279	.347	.962
1992	ChC-N	109	217	28	60	10	3	3	24	13	0	40	1	0	2	9	8	.276	.318	.392	.979
1993	ChC-N	111	310	51	93	17	5	11	35	25	1	51	1	1	3	8	6	.300	.355	.494	.955
1994	Cal-A	45	122	19	32	5	1	5	18	7	0	20	0	0	1	2	3	.262	.300	.443	.912
1994	Bal-A	28	74	12	23	2	1	3	12	5	1	17	1	0	0	0	1	.311	.363	.486	.939
1995	Atl-N	103	131	16	33	8	2	3	21	13	1	35	2	0	1	0	3	.252	.327	.412	.923
1996	Atl-N	101	153	16	31	5	0	3	16	17	1	42	1	0	1	1	3	.203	.285	.294	.962
Career average		102	226	31	62	11	3	6	28	19	1	42	2	1	1	5	5	.275	.333	.422	.964
Cubs average		**107**	**265**	**36**	**76**	**14**	**3**	**6**	**32**	**22**	**1**	**44**	**2**	**1**	**2**	**8**	**5**	**.285**	**.341**	**.433**	**.964**
Career total		813	1807	244	497	88	20	46	226	150	8	334	13	6	11	42	37	.275	.333	.422	.964
Cubs total		**536**	**1327**	**181**	**378**	**68**	**16**	**32**	**159**	**108**	**5**	**220**	**9**	**6**	**8**	**39**	**27**	**.285**	**.341**	**.433**	**.971**

Smith, Lewis Oscar (Bull)
HEIGHT: 6'0" THROWS: RIGHT BATS: RIGHT BORN: 8/20/1880 PLUM, WEST VIRGINIA DIED: 5/1/1928 CHARLESTON, WEST VIRGINIA POSITIONS PLAYED: OF

YEAR	TEAM	GAMES	AB	RUNS	HITS	2B	3B	HR	RBI	BB	IBB	SO	HBP	SH	SF	SB	CS	BA	OBA	SA	FA
1904	Pit-N	13	42	2	6	0	1	0	0	1	—	—	0	0	—	0	—	.143	.163	.190	.857
1906	ChC-N	1	1	0	0	0	0	0	0	0	—	—	0	0	—	0	—	.000	.000	.000	—
1911	Was-A	1	0	0	0	0	0	0	0	0	—	0	0	0	—	0	—	.000	.000	.000	—
Career average		5	14	1	2	0	0	0	0	0	—	0	0	0	—	0	—	.140	.159	.186	.857
Cubs average		**1**	**1**	**0**	**0**	**0**	**0**	**0**	**0**	**0**	**—**	**0**	**0**	**0**	**—**	**0**	**—**	**.140**	**.159**	**.186**	**.857**
Career total		15	43	2	6	0	1	0	0	1	—	0	0	0	—	0	—	.140	.159	.186	—
Cubs total		**1**	**1**	**0**	**0**	**0**	**0**	**0**	**0**	**0**	**—**	**0**	**0**	**0**	**—**	**0**	**—**	**.000**	**.000**	**.000**	**.857**

Smith, Paul Leslie
HEIGHT: 5'8" THROWS: LEFT BATS: LEFT BORN: 3/19/1931 NEW CASTLE, PENNSYLVANIA POSITIONS PLAYED: 1B, OF

YEAR	TEAM	GAMES	AB	RUNS	HITS	2B	3B	HR	RBI	BB	IBB	SO	HBP	SH	SF	SB	CS	BA	OBA	SA	FA
1953	Pit-N	118	389	41	110	12	7	4	44	24	—	23	3	11	—	3	0	.283	.329	.380	.985
1957	Pit-N	81	150	12	38	4	0	3	11	12	1	17	1	4	0	0	2	.253	.313	.340	1.000
1958	Pit-N	6	3	0	1	0	0	0	0	3	0	0	0	0	0	0	0	.333	.667	.333	—
1958	**ChC-N**	**18**	**20**	**1**	**3**	**0**	**0**	**0**	**1**	**3**	**0**	**4**	**0**	**0**	**0**	**0**	**0**	**.150**	**.261**	**.150**	**.941**
Career average		74	187	18	51	5	2	2	19	14	0	15	1	5	0	1	1	.270	.326	.361	.985
Cubs average		**18**	**20**	**1**	**3**	**0**	**0**	**0**	**1**	**3**	**0**	**4**	**0**	**0**	**0**	**0**	**0**	**.150**	**.261**	**.150**	**.941**
Career total		223	562	54	152	16	7	7	56	42	1	44	4	15	0	3	2	.270	.326	.361	.985
Cubs total		**18**	**20**	**1**	**3**	**0**	**0**	**0**	**1**	**3**	**0**	**4**	**0**	**0**	**0**	**0**	**0**	**.150**	**.261**	**.150**	**.941**

Smith, Willie
HEIGHT: 6'0" THROWS: LEFT BATS: LEFT BORN: 2/11/1939 ANNISTON, ALABAMA POSITIONS PLAYED: P, 1B, OF

YEAR	TEAM	GAMES	AB	RUNS	HITS	2B	3B	HR	RBI	BB	IBB	SO	HBP	SH	SF	SB	CS	BA	OBA	SA	FA
1963	Det-A	17	8	2	1	0	0	0	0	0	0	1	0	0	0	0	0	.125	.125	.125	1.000
1964	LAA-A	118	359	46	108	14	6	11	51	8	1	39	2	1	3	7	5	.301	.317	.465	.979
1965	Cal-A	136	459	52	120	14	9	14	57	32	10	60	1	1	5	9	8	.261	.308	.423	.977
1966	Cal-A	90	195	18	36	3	2	1	20	12	2	37	3	2	5	1	0	.185	.239	.236	.974
1967	Cle-A	21	32	0	7	2	0	0	2	1	0	10	0	0	3	1	0	.219	.242	.281	.923
1968	Cle-A	33	42	1	6	2	0	0	3	3	2	14	1	0	1	0	2	.143	.213	.190	1.000
1968	**ChC-N**	**55**	**142**	**13**	**39**	**8**	**2**	**5**	**25**	**12**	**2**	**33**	**1**	**1**	**1**	**0**	**0**	**.275**	**.333**	**.465**	**1.000**
1969	**ChC-N**	**103**	**195**	**21**	**48**	**9**	**1**	**9**	**25**	**25**	**3**	**49**	**0**	**2**	**1**	**1**	**0**	**.246**	**.330**	**.441**	**.985**
1970	**ChC-N**	**87**	**167**	**15**	**36**	**9**	**1**	**5**	**24**	**11**	**0**	**32**	**1**	**2**	**1**	**2**	**1**	**.216**	**.267**	**.371**	**.994**
1971	Cin-N	31	55	3	9	2	0	1	4	3	0	9	0	0	0	0	0	.164	.207	.255	1.000
Career average		77	184	19	46	7	2	5	23	12	2	32	1	1	2	2	2	.248	.295	.395	.986
Cubs average		**82**	**168**	**16**	**41**	**9**	**1**	**6**	**25**	**16**	**2**	**38**	**1**	**2**	**1**	**1**	**0**	**.244**	**.311**	**.425**	**.992**
Career total		691	1654	171	410	63	21	46	211	107	20	284	9	9	15	20	16	.248	.295	.395	.986
Cubs total		**245**	**504**	**49**	**123**	**26**	**4**	**19**	**74**	**48**	**5**	**114**	**2**	**5**	**3**	**3**	**1**	**.244**	**.311**	**.425**	**.992**

Sommers, Joseph Andrews (Pete)

HEIGHT: 5'11"   THROWS: RIGHT   BATS: RIGHT   BORN: 10/26/1866 CLEVELAND, OHIO   DIED: 7/22/1908 CLEVELAND, OHIO   POSITIONS PLAYED: C, 1B, OF

YEAR	TEAM	GAMES	AB	RUNS	HITS	2B	3B	HR	RBI	BB	IBB	SO	HBP	SH	SF	SB	CS	BA	OBA	SA	FA
1887	NY-AA	33	123	9	28	3	0	1	12	7	—	—	1	—	—	6	—	.228	.275	.276	.840
1888	Bos-N	4	13	1	3	1	0	0	0	0	—	3	0	—	—	0	—	.231	.231	.308	.880
1889	**ChN-N**	**12**	**45**	**5**	**10**	**5**	**0**	**0**	**8**	**2**	**—**	**8**	**1**	**—**	**—**	**0**	**—**	**.222**	**.271**	**.333**	**.836**
1889	Ind-N	23	84	12	21	2	2	2	14	1	—	16	1	—	—	2	—	.250	.267	.393	.900
1890	NYG-N	17	47	4	5	1	1	0	1	4	—	13	1	—	—	0	—	.106	.192	.170	.885
1890	Cle-N	9	34	4	7	1	1	0	1	2	—	3	0	—	—	0	—	.206	.250	.294	.907
Career average		25	87	9	19	3	1	1	9	4	—	11	1	—	—	2	—	.214	.257	.301	.870
Cubs average		**12**	**45**	**5**	**10**	**5**	**0**	**0**	**8**	**2**	**—**	**8**	**1**	**—**	**—**	**0**	**—**	**.222**	**.271**	**.333**	**.836**
Career total		98	346	35	74	13	4	3	36	16	—	43	4	—	—	8	—	.214	.257	.301	.870
Cubs total		**12**	**45**	**5**	**10**	**5**	**0**	**0**	**8**	**2**	**—**	**8**	**1**	**—**	**—**	**0**	**—**	**.222**	**.271**	**.333**	**.836**

Sosa, Samuel Peralta (Sammy)

HEIGHT: 6'0"   THROWS: RIGHT   BATS: RIGHT   BORN: 11/12/1968 SAN PEDRO DE MACORIS, DOMINICAN REPUBLIC   POSITIONS PLAYED: OF

YEAR	TEAM	GAMES	AB	RUNS	HITS	2B	3B	HR	RBI	BB	IBB	SO	HBP	SH	SF	SB	CS	BA	OBA	SA	FA
1989	Tex-A	25	84	8	20	3	0	1	3	0	0	20	0	4	0	0	2	.238	.238	.310	.944
1989	CWS-A	33	99	19	27	5	0	3	10	11	2	27	2	1	2	7	3	.273	.351	.414	.969
1990	CWS-A	153	532	72	124	26	10	15	70	33	4	150	6	2	6	32	16	.233	.282	.404	.962
1991	CWS-A	116	316	39	64	10	1	10	33	14	2	98	2	5	1	13	6	.203	.240	.335	.973
1992	**ChC-N**	**67**	**262**	**41**	**68**	**7**	**2**	**8**	**25**	**19**	**1**	**63**	**4**	**4**	**2**	**15**	**7**	**.260**	**.317**	**.393**	**.961**
1993	**ChC-N**	**159**	**598**	**92**	**156**	**25**	**5**	**33**	**93**	**38**	**6**	**135**	**4**	**0**	**1**	**36**	**11**	**.261**	**.309**	**.485**	**.976**
1994	**ChC-N**	**105**	**426**	**59**	**128**	**17**	**6**	**25**	**70**	**25**	**1**	**92**	**2**	**1**	**4**	**22**	**13**	**.300**	**.339**	**.545**	**.973**
1995	**ChC-N**	**144**	**564**	**89**	**151**	**17**	**3**	**36**	**119**	**58**	**11**	**134**	**5**	**0**	**2**	**34**	**7**	**.268**	**.340**	**.500**	**.962**
1996	**ChC-N**	**124**	**498**	**84**	**136**	**21**	**2**	**40**	**100**	**34**	**6**	**134**	**5**	**0**	**4**	**18**	**5**	**.273**	**.323**	**.564**	**.964**
1997	**ChC-N**	**162**	**642**	**90**	**161**	**31**	**4**	**36**	**119**	**45**	**9**	**174**	**2**	**0**	**5**	**22**	**12**	**.251**	**.300**	**.480**	**.977**
1998	**ChC-N**	**159**	**643**	**134**	**198**	**20**	**0**	**66**	**158**	**73**	**14**	**171**	**1**	**0**	**5**	**18**	**9**	**.308**	**.377**	**.647**	**.975**
1999	**ChC-N**	**162**	**625**	**114**	**180**	**24**	**2**	**63**	**141**	**78**	**8**	**171**	**3**	**0**	**6**	**7**	**8**	**.288**	**.367**	**.635**	**.978**
2000	**ChC-N**	**156**	**604**	**106**	**193**	**38**	**1**	**50**	**138**	**91**	**19**	**168**	**2**	**0**	**8**	**7**	**4**	**.320**	**.406**	**.634**	**.970**
2001	**ChC-N**	**160**	**577**	**146**	**189**	**34**	**5**	**64**	**160**	**116**	**37**	**153**	**6**	**0**	**12**	**0**	**2**	**.328**	**.437**	**.737**	**.982**
Career average		133	498	84	138	21	3	35	95	49	9	130	3	1	4	18	8	.277	.343	.542	.972
Cubs average		**140**	**544**	**96**	**156**	**23**	**3**	**42**	**112**	**58**	**11**	**140**	**3**	**1**	**5**	**18**	**8**	**.287**	**.356**	**.573**	**.973**
Career total		1725	6470	1093	1795	278	41	450	1239	635	120	1690	44	17	58	231	105	.277	.343	.542	.972
Cubs total		**1398**	**5439**	**955**	**1560**	**234**	**30**	**421**	**1123**	**577**	**112**	**1395**	**34**	**5**	**49**	**179**	**78**	**.287**	**.356**	**.573**	**.973**

Spangler, Albert Donald (Al)

HEIGHT: 6'0"   THROWS: LEFT   BATS: LEFT   BORN: 7/8/1933 PHILADELPHIA, PENNSYLVANIA   POSITIONS PLAYED: OF

YEAR	TEAM	GAMES	AB	RUNS	HITS	2B	3B	HR	RBI	BB	IBB	SO	HBP	SH	SF	SB	CS	BA	OBA	SA	FA
1959	Mil-N	6	12	3	5	0	1	0	0	1	0	1	0	1	0	1	0	.417	.462	.583	1.000
1960	Mil-N	101	105	26	28	5	2	0	6	14	1	17	1	1	1	6	2	.267	.355	.352	.989
1961	Mil-N	68	97	23	26	2	0	0	6	28	2	9	0	0	0	4	2	.268	.432	.289	1.000
1962	Hou-N	129	418	51	119	10	9	5	35	70	6	46	3	6	2	7	6	.285	.389	.388	.960
1963	Hou-N	120	430	52	121	25	4	4	27	50	5	38	1	5	4	5	8	.281	.355	.386	.987
1964	Hou-N	135	449	51	110	18	5	4	38	41	1	43	4	6	5	7	8	.245	.311	.334	.964
1965	Hou-N	38	112	18	24	1	1	1	7	14	2	8	0	0	1	1	1	.214	.299	.268	.956
1965	Cal-A	51	96	17	25	1	0	0	1	8	0	9	0	0	0	4	0	.260	.317	.271	.973
1966	Cal-A	6	9	2	6	0	0	0	0	2	0	2	0	0	0	0	0	.667	.727	.667	1.000
1967	**ChC-N**	**62**	**130**	**18**	**33**	**7**	**0**	**0**	**13**	**23**	**4**	**17**	**0**	**0**	**2**	**2**	**2**	**.254**	**.361**	**.308**	**.986**
1968	**ChC-N**	**88**	**177**	**21**	**48**	**9**	**3**	**2**	**18**	**20**	**2**	**24**	**1**	**2**	**3**	**0**	**1**	**.271**	**.343**	**.390**	**.973**
1969	**ChC-N**	**82**	**213**	**23**	**45**	**8**	**1**	**4**	**23**	**21**	**0**	**16**	**1**	**2**	**1**	**0**	**2**	**.211**	**.284**	**.315**	**.950**
1970	**ChC-N**	**21**	**14**	**2**	**2**	**1**	**0**	**1**	**1**	**3**	**0**	**3**	**0**	**0**	**0**	**0**	**0**	**.143**	**.294**	**.429**	**1.000**
1971	**ChC-N**	**5**	**5**	**0**	**2**	**0**	**0**	**0**	**0**	**0**	**0**	**1**	**0**	**0**	**0**	**0**	**0**	**.400**	**.400**	**.400**	**—**
Career average		70	174	24	46	7	2	2	13	23	2	18	1	2	1	3	2	.262	.347	.351	.973
Cubs average		**52**	**108**	**13**	**26**	**5**	**1**	**1**	**11**	**13**	**1**	**12**	**0**	**1**	**1**	**0**	**1**	**.241**	**.324**	**.341**	**.970**
Career total		912	2267	307	594	87	26	21	175	295	23	234	11	23	19	37	32	.262	.347	.351	.973
Cubs total		**258**	**539**	**64**	**130**	**25**	**4**	**7**	**55**	**67**	**6**	**61**	**2**	**4**	**6**	**2**	**5**	**.241**	**.324**	**.341**	**.970**

Samuel (Sammy) Peralta Sosa, of-dh, 1989–present

It may be time to understand that Sammy Sosa, in the autumn of his career, has become much more than a home-run-hitting machine for the Chicago Cubs. Certainly, anyone who has hit 60-plus home runs three of the past four years cannot duck that label, but the 2001 season showed Sosa to be so much more.

Sosa, born on November 12, 1968, in San Pedro de Macoris, in the Dominican Republic, was initially signed by the Texas Rangers in 1985. He moved up through the Rangers farm system for four years before finally making the big team in 1989.

He was traded to the Chicago White Sox later that year, and spent 2½ years in that organization. Sosa was no great shakes with the Sox. He struck out way too much and seemed to be trying to hit everything out of the ballpark.

Just prior to the 1992 season, the Sox traded Sosa, along with Ken Patterson, to the Cubs for George Bell. At first it looked like the Cubs had been rooked. Bell was a solid performer with the Sox in 1992, with 25 home runs and 112 RBIs. Sosa played in only 67 games and had eight homers.

But two years later, Bell was out of baseball, and Sosa had his first .300 season, with 25 home runs and 70 RBIs. The next season, 1995, Sammy was named to the National League All-Star team for the first time in his career. He hit 36 home runs and stole 34 bases, making him only the second Cub in the 20th century to lead the team in both categories in three seasons. Ryne Sandberg had also accomplished this.

In 1998 Sosa had a magic year, with 66 home runs, a league-leading 158 RBIs and a league-leading 134 runs scored. The year was kick-started by a phenomenal June, for Sosa cracked 20 homers, had 40 RBIs and had a stunning .860 slugging percentage.

Although the focus of 1998 was primarily on the quest of Sosa and the Cardinals' Mark McGwire to break the home run record set by the Yankees' Roger Maris in 1961, there was a more urgent quest for Cubs fans: to make the playoffs for the first time in nine years.

This they did, beating the San Francisco Giants, 5-3, in a one-game playoff at Wrigley Field, a tidy 90 years after their forefathers accomplished a similar feat on the Polo Grounds against the New York version of the Giants.

Sosa was a big part of the stretch drive, belting several clutch home runs to initiate or prolong Cubs rallies. While McGwire, his team well out of contention, could concentrate on records, Sosa had to play to win the entire season.

As a result, Sosa did not set the new home run record—McGwire did, hitting 70 (since broken in 2001 by the Giants' Barry Bonds). Sosa, though, was the player who led his team into the playoffs. The Cubs were beaten by Atlanta in the first round, but all the games were fairly close.

Sosa was rewarded for his stellar season with the MVP award, an accolade few could contest, even die-hard St. Louis fans.

Sosa had not yet hit his peak. He and McGwire staged another home run derby in 1999, with Mark winning out again, 65 homers to Sammy's 63. The 2000 season represented a relative downswing for Sosa, if 50 home runs and a .320 batting average could be considered a slump.

But Sosa's 2001 campaign was perhaps his best all-around year yet. With the security of a new long-term contract in his possession, Sosa produced 64 home runs, 160 RBIs, 116 walks, 34 doubles, 146 runs scored, a .328 batting average and a .737 slugging percentage. Sosa is now one of the best players in either league, and the challenge for him is to continue that level of play.

Speake, Robert Charles (Bob *or* Spook)
HEIGHT: 6'1" THROWS: LEFT BATS: LEFT BORN: 8/22/1930 SPRINGFIELD, MISSOURI POSITIONS PLAYED: 1B, OF

YEAR	TEAM	GAMES	AB	RUNS	HITS	2B	3B	HR	RBI	BB	IBB	SO	HBP	SH	SF	SB	CS	BA	OBA	SA	FA
1955	ChC-N	95	261	36	57	9	5	12	43	28	4	71	3	0	1	3	4	.218	.300	.429	.966
1957	ChC-N	129	418	65	97	14	5	16	50	38	1	68	3	1	3	5	6	.232	.299	.404	.987
1958	SF-N	66	71	9	15	3	0	3	10	13	1	15	0	0	0	0	1	.211	.333	.380	.938
1959	SF-N	15	11	0	1	0	0	0	1	1	0	4	0	1	0	0	0	.091	.167	.091	—
Career average		76	190	28	43	7	3	8	26	20	2	40	2	1	1	2	3	.223	.301	.406	.981
Cubs average		**112**	**340**	**51**	**77**	**12**	**5**	**14**	**47**	**33**	**3**	**70**	**3**	**1**	**2**	**4**	**5**	**.227**	**.299**	**.414**	**.982**
Career total		305	761	110	170	26	10	31	104	80	6	158	6	2	4	8	11	.223	.301	.406	.981
Cubs total		**224**	**679**	**101**	**154**	**23**	**10**	**28**	**93**	**66**	**5**	**139**	**6**	**1**	**4**	**8**	**10**	**.227**	**.299**	**.414**	**.982**

Speier, Chris Edward
HEIGHT: 6'1" THROWS: RIGHT BATS: RIGHT BORN: 6/28/1950 ALAMEDA, CALIFORNIA POSITIONS PLAYED: 1B, 2B, 3B, SS

YEAR	TEAM	GAMES	AB	RUNS	HITS	2B	3B	HR	RBI	BB	IBB	SO	HBP	SH	SF	SB	CS	BA	OBA	SA	FA
1971	SF-N	157	601	74	141	17	6	8	46	56	6	90	7	5	1	4	7	.235	.307	.323	.958
1972	SF-N	150	562	74	151	25	2	15	71	82	2	92	3	4	7	9	4	.269	.361	.400	.974
1973	SF-N	153	542	58	135	17	4	11	71	66	4	69	2	5	2	4	5	.249	.332	.356	.957
1974	SF-N	141	501	55	125	19	5	9	53	62	8	64	4	8	2	3	2	.250	.336	.361	.970
1975	SF-N	141	487	60	132	30	5	10	69	70	7	50	1	3	3	4	5	.271	.362	.415	.982
1976	SF-N	145	495	51	112	18	4	3	40	60	1	52	4	6	7	2	2	.226	.311	.297	.974
1977	SF-N	6	17	1	3	1	0	0	0	0	0	3	0	0	0	0	0	.176	.176	.235	.920
1977	Mon-N	139	531	58	125	30	6	5	38	67	3	78	1	3	2	1	2	.235	.321	.343	.970
1978	Mon-N	150	501	47	126	18	3	5	51	60	10	75	1	2	6	1	0	.251	.329	.329	.975
1979	Mon-N	113	344	31	78	13	1	7	26	43	10	45	3	0	1	0	0	.227	.317	.331	.970
1980	Mon-N	128	388	35	103	14	4	1	32	52	18	38	0	6	1	0	3	.265	.351	.330	.965
1981	Mon-N	96	307	33	69	10	2	2	25	38	10	29	0	6	0	1	2	.225	.310	.290	.964
1982	Mon-N	156	530	41	136	26	4	7	60	47	12	67	1	3	4	1	6	.257	.316	.360	.982
1983	Mon-N	88	261	31	67	12	2	2	22	29	4	37	2	3	3	2	1	.257	.332	.341	.958
1984	Mon-N	25	40	1	6	0	0	0	1	1	0	8	0	2	0	0	0	.150	.171	.150	.971
1984	StL-N	38	118	9	21	7	1	3	8	9	1	19	1	1	0	0	0	.178	.242	.331	.983
1984	Min-A	12	33	2	7	0	0	0	1	3	0	7	0	1	0	0	0	.212	.278	.212	.977
1985	ChC-N	106	218	16	53	11	0	4	24	17	0	34	0	3	2	1	3	.243	.295	.349	.960
1986	ChC-N	95	155	21	44	8	0	6	23	15	3	32	1	4	1	2	2	.284	.349	.452	.982
1987	SF-N	111	317	39	79	13	0	11	39	42	5	51	3	1	1	4	7	.249	.342	.394	.989
1988	SF-N	82	171	26	37	9	1	3	18	23	2	39	1	5	1	3	3	.216	.311	.333	.986
1989	SF-N	28	37	7	9	4	0	0	2	5	0	9	0	2	0	0	0	.243	.333	.351	.975
Career average		119	377	41	93	16	3	6	38	45	6	52	2	4	2	2	3	.246	.327	.349	.971
Cubs average		**101**	**187**	**19**	**49**	**10**	**0**	**5**	**24**	**16**	**2**	**33**	**1**	**4**	**2**	**2**	**3**	**.260**	**.318**	**.391**	**.969**
Career total		2260	7156	770	1759	302	50	112	720	847	106	988	35	73	44	42	54	.246	.327	.349	.971
Cubs total		**201**	**373**	**37**	**97**	**19**	**0**	**10**	**47**	**32**	**3**	**66**	**1**	**7**	**3**	**3**	**5**	**.260**	**.318**	**.391**	**.969**

Sperring, Robert Walter (Rob)
HEIGHT: 6'1" THROWS: RIGHT BATS: RIGHT BORN: 10/10/1949 SAN FRANCISCO, CALIFORNIA POSITIONS PLAYED: 2B, 3B, SS, OF

YEAR	TEAM	GAMES	AB	RUNS	HITS	2B	3B	HR	RBI	BB	IBB	SO	HBP	SH	SF	SB	CS	BA	OBA	SA	FA
1974	ChC-N	42	107	9	22	3	0	1	5	9	1	28	0	1	0	1	2	.206	.267	.262	.943
1975	ChC-N	65	144	25	30	4	1	1	9	16	3	31	1	3	2	0	2	.208	.288	.271	.939
1976	ChC-N	43	93	8	24	3	0	0	7	9	0	25	0	4	1	0	2	.258	.320	.290	.987
1977	Hou-N	58	129	6	24	3	0	1	9	12	2	23	0	1	1	0	0	.186	.254	.233	.963
Career average		52	118	12	25	3	0	1	8	12	2	27	0	2	1	0	2	.211	.281	.262	.952
Cubs average		**50**	**115**	**14**	**25**	**3**	**0**	**1**	**7**	**11**	**1**	**28**	**0**	**3**	**1**	**0**	**2**	**.221**	**.291**	**.273**	**.949**
Career total		208	473	48	100	13	1	3	30	46	6	107	1	9	4	1	6	.211	.281	.262	.952
Cubs total		**150**	**344**	**42**	**76**	**10**	**1**	**2**	**21**	**34**	**4**	**84**	**1**	**8**	**3**	**1**	**6**	**.221**	**.291**	**.273**	**.949**

Sprague, Charles Wellington (Charlie)
HEIGHT: 5'11"   THROWS: LEFT   BATS: LEFT   BORN: 10/10/1864 CLEVELAND, OHIO   DIED: 12/31/1912 DES MOINES, IOWA   POSITIONS PLAYED: P, OF

YEAR	TEAM	GAMES	AB	RUNS	HITS	2B	3B	HR	RBI	BB	IBB	SO	HBP	SH	SF	SB	CS	BA	OBA	SA	FA
1887	**ChN-N**	**3**	**13**	**0**	**2**	**0**	**0**	**0**	**0**	**0**	—	**2**	**0**	—	—	**0**	—	**.154**	**.154**	**.154**	**.667**
1889	Cle-N	2	7	2	1	0	0	0	1	1	—	0	0	—	—	1	—	.143	.250	.143	.857
1890	Tol-AA	55	199	25	47	5	6	1	19	16	—	—	3	—	—	10	—	.236	.303	.337	.907
Career average		20	73	9	17	2	2	0	7	6	—	1	1	—	—	4	—	.228	.293	.320	.896
Cubs average		**3**	**13**	**0**	**2**	**0**	**0**	**0**	**0**	**0**	—	**2**	**0**	—	—	**0**	—	**.154**	**.154**	**.154**	**.667**
Career total		60	219	27	50	5	6	1	20	17	—	2	3	—	—	11	—	.228	.293	.320	.896
Cubs total		**3**	**13**	**0**	**2**	**0**	**0**	**0**	**0**	**0**	—	**2**	**0**	—	—	**0**	—	**.154**	**.154**	**.154**	**.667**

Stainback, George Tucker (Tuck or Goldilocks)
HEIGHT: 5'11"   THROWS: RIGHT   BATS: RIGHT   BORN: 8/4/1911 LOS ANGELES, CALIFORNIA   DIED: 11/29/1992 CAMARILLO, CALIFORNIA
POSITIONS PLAYED: 3B, OF

YEAR	TEAM	GAMES	AB	RUNS	HITS	2B	3B	HR	RBI	BB	IBB	SO	HBP	SH	SF	SB	CS	BA	OBA	SA	FA
1934	**ChC-N**	**104**	**359**	**47**	**110**	**14**	**3**	**2**	**46**	**8**	—	**42**	**3**	**7**	—	**7**	—	**.306**	**.327**	**.379**	**.955**
1935	**ChC-N**	**47**	**94**	**16**	**24**	**4**	**0**	**3**	**11**	**0**	—	**13**	**2**	**1**	—	**1**	—	**.255**	**.271**	**.394**	**.932**
1936	**ChC-N**	**44**	**75**	**13**	**13**	**3**	**0**	**1**	**5**	**6**	—	**14**	**0**	**1**	—	**1**	—	**.173**	**.235**	**.253**	**1.000**
1937	**ChC-N**	**72**	**160**	**18**	**37**	**7**	**1**	**0**	**14**	**7**	—	**16**	**1**	**3**	—	**3**	—	**.231**	**.268**	**.288**	**.981**
1938	StL-N	6	10	2	0	0	0	0	0	0	—	3	0	1	—	0	—	.000	.000	.000	1.000
1938	Phi-N	30	81	9	21	3	0	1	11	3	—	3	1	0	—	1	—	.259	.294	.333	.980
1938	Bro-N	35	104	15	34	6	3	0	20	2	—	4	1	2	—	1	—	.327	.346	.442	.981
1939	Bro-N	68	201	22	54	7	0	3	19	4	—	23	2	2	—	0	—	.269	.290	.348	.938
1940	Det-A	15	40	4	9	2	0	0	1	1	—	9	0	2	—	0	0	.225	.244	.275	.968
1941	Det-A	94	200	19	49	8	1	2	10	3	—	21	1	7	—	6	3	.245	.260	.325	.948
1942	NYY-A	15	10	0	2	0	0	0	0	0	—	2	0	0	—	0	0	.200	.200	.200	1.000
1943	NYY-A	71	231	31	60	11	2	0	10	7	—	16	1	4	—	3	3	.260	.285	.325	.993
1944	NYY-A	30	78	13	17	3	0	0	5	3	—	7	0	4	—	1	0	.218	.247	.256	.957
1945	NYY-A	95	327	40	84	12	2	5	32	13	—	20	2	7	—	0	4	.257	.289	.352	.968
1946	Phi-A	91	291	35	71	10	2	0	20	7	—	20	1	1	—	3	2	.244	.264	.292	.963
Career average		63	174	22	45	7	1	1	16	5	—	16	1	3	—	2	1	.259	.284	.333	.965
Cubs average		**67**	**172**	**24**	**46**	**7**	**1**	**2**	**19**	**5**	—	**21**	**2**	**3**	—	**3**	—	**.267**	**.295**	**.346**	**.964**
Career total		817	2261	284	585	90	14	17	204	64	—	213	15	42	—	27	12	.259	.284	.333	.965
Cubs total		**267**	**688**	**94**	**184**	**28**	**4**	**6**	**76**	**21**	—	**85**	**6**	**12**	—	**12**	—	**.267**	**.295**	**.346**	**.964**

Stairs, Matthew Wade (Matt)
HEIGHT: 5'9"   THROWS: RIGHT   BATS: LEFT   BORN: 2/27/1968 SAINT JOHN, NEW BRUNSWICK, CANADA   POSITIONS PLAYED: 1B, 2B, OF

YEAR	TEAM	GAMES	AB	RUNS	HITS	2B	3B	HR	RBI	BB	IBB	SO	HBP	SH	SF	SB	CS	BA	OBA	SA	FA
1992	Mon-N	13	30	2	5	2	0	0	5	7	0	7	0	0	1	0	0	.167	.316	.233	.933
1993	Mon-N	6	8	1	3	1	0	0	2	0	0	1	0	0	0	0	0	.375	.375	.500	1.000
1995	Bos-A	39	88	8	23	7	1	1	17	4	0	14	1	1	1	0	1	.261	.298	.398	.913
1996	Oak-A	61	137	21	38	5	1	10	23	19	2	23	1	0	1	1	1	.277	.367	.547	.987
1997	Oak-A	133	352	62	105	19	0	27	73	50	1	60	3	1	4	3	2	.298	.386	.582	.974
1998	Oak-A	149	523	88	154	33	4	26	106	59	4	93	6	1	4	8	3	.294	.370	.511	1.000
1999	Oak-A	146	531	94	137	26	3	38	102	89	6	124	2	0	1	2	7	.258	.366	.533	.981
2000	Oak-A	143	476	74	108	26	0	21	81	78	4	122	1	1	6	5	2	.227	.333	.414	.980
2001	**ChC-N**	**128**	**340**	**48**	**85**	**21**	**0**	**17**	**61**	**52**	**7**	**76**	**7**	**1**	**3**	**2**	**3**	**.250**	**.358**	**.462**	**.993**
Career average		91	276	44	73	16	1	16	52	40	3	58	2	1	2	2	2	.265	.359	.495	.985
Cubs average		**128**	**340**	**48**	**85**	**21**	**0**	**17**	**61**	**52**	**7**	**76**	**7**	**1**	**3**	**2**	**3**	**.250**	**.358**	**.462**	**.993**
Career total		818	2485	398	658	140	6	140	470	358	24	520	21	5	21	21	19	.265	.359	.495	.985
Cubs total		**128**	**340**	**48**	**85**	**21**	**0**	**17**	**61**	**52**	**7**	**76**	**7**	**1**	**3**	**2**	**3**	**.250**	**.358**	**.462**	**.993**

Staley, George Gaylord (Gale)
HEIGHT: 5'8"   THROWS: RIGHT   BATS: LEFT   BORN: 5/2/1899 DEPERE, WISCONSIN   DIED: 4/19/1989 WALNUT CREEK, CALIFORNIA   POSITIONS PLAYED: 2B

YEAR	TEAM	GAMES	AB	RUNS	HITS	2B	3B	HR	RBI	BB	IBB	SO	HBP	SH	SF	SB	CS	BA	OBA	SA	FA
1925	ChC-N	7	26	2	11	2	0	0	3	2	—	1	0	0	—	0	1	.423	.464	.500	.979
Career average		7	26	2	11	2	0	0	3	2	—	1	0	0	—	0	1	.423	.464	.500	.979
Cubs average		**7**	**26**	**2**	**11**	**2**	**0**	**0**	**3**	**2**	**—**	**1**	**0**	**0**	**—**	**0**	**1**	**.423**	**.464**	**.500**	**.979**
Career total		7	26	2	11	2	0	0	3	2	—	1	0	0	—	0	1	.423	.464	.500	.979
Cubs total		**7**	**26**	**2**	**11**	**2**	**0**	**0**	**3**	**2**	**—**	**1**	**0**	**0**	**—**	**0**	**1**	**.423**	**.464**	**.500**	**.979**

Stanky, Edward Raymond (Eddie *or* The Brat *or* Muggsy)
HEIGHT: 5'8"   THROWS: RIGHT   BATS: RIGHT   BORN: 9/3/1916 PHILADELPHIA, PENNSYLVANIA   DIED: 6/6/1999 FAIRHOPE, ALABAMA
POSITIONS PLAYED: 2B, 3B, SS

YEAR	TEAM	GAMES	AB	RUNS	HITS	2B	3B	HR	RBI	BB	IBB	SO	HBP	SH	SF	SB	CS	BA	OBA	SA	FA
1943	ChC-N	142	510	92	125	15	1	0	47	92	—	42	2	12	—	4	—	.245	.363	.278	.964
1944	ChC-N	13	25	4	6	0	1	0	0	2	—	2	0	1	—	1	—	.240	.296	.320	.885
1944	Bro-N	89	261	32	72	9	2	0	16	44	—	13	1	9	—	3	0	.276	.382	.326	.958
1945	Bro-N	153	555	128	143	29	5	1	39	148	—	42	4	19	—	6	—	.258	.417	.333	.962
1946	Bro-N	144	483	98	132	24	7	0	36	137	—	56	2	20	—	8	2	.273	.436	.352	.977
1947	Bro-N	146	559	97	141	24	5	3	53	103	—	39	5	12	—	3	3	.252	.373	.329	.985
1948	Bos-N	67	247	49	79	14	2	2	29	61	—	13	0	4	—	3	—	.320	.455	.417	.981
1949	Bos-N	138	506	90	144	24	5	1	42	113	—	41	2	7	—	3	—	.285	.417	.358	.979
1950	NYG-N	152	527	115	158	25	5	8	51	144	—	50	12	8	—	9	—	.300	.460	.412	.976
1951	NYG-N	145	515	88	127	17	2	14	43	127	—	63	6	5	—	8	5	.247	.401	.369	.977
1952	StL-N	53	83	13	19	4	0	0	7	19	—	9	0	3	—	0	0	.229	.373	.277	1.000
1953	StL-N	17	30	5	8	0	0	0	1	6	—	4	1	3	—	0	0	.267	.405	.267	1.000
Career average		114	391	74	105	17	3	3	33	91	—	34	3	9	—	4	1	.268	.410	.348	.974
Cubs average		**78**	**268**	**48**	**66**	**8**	**1**	**0**	**24**	**47**	**—**	**22**	**1**	**7**	**—**	**3**	**—**	**.245**	**.360**	**.280**	**.961**
Career total		1259	4301	811	1154	185	35	29	364	996	—	374	35	103	—	48	10	.268	.410	.348	.974
Cubs total		**155**	**535**	**96**	**131**	**15**	**2**	**0**	**47**	**94**	**—**	**44**	**2**	**13**	**—**	**5**	**—**	**.245**	**.360**	**.280**	**.961**

Stanley, Joseph Bernard (Joe)
HEIGHT: 5'9"   THROWS: RIGHT   BATS: BOTH   BORN: 4/2/1881 WASHINGTON, DISTRICT OF COLUMBIA   DIED: 9/13/1967 DETROIT, MICHIGAN
POSITIONS PLAYED: P, SS, OF

YEAR	TEAM	GAMES	AB	RUNS	HITS	2B	3B	HR	RBI	BB	IBB	SO	HBP	SH	SF	SB	CS	BA	OBA	SA	FA
1897	Was-N	1	1	0	0	0	0	0	0	0	—	—	0	0	—	0	—	.000	.000	.000	—
1902	Was-A	3	12	2	4	0	0	0	1	0	—	—	0	0	—	0	—	.333	.333	.333	.833
1903	Bos-N	86	308	40	77	12	5	1	47	18	—	—	7	4	—	10	—	.250	.306	.331	.882
1904	Bos-N	3	8	0	0	0	0	0	0	0	—	—	0	0	—	0	—	.000	.000	.000	.800
1905	Was-A	28	92	13	24	2	1	1	17	7	—	—	0	3	—	4	—	.261	.313	.337	.944
1906	Was-A	73	221	18	36	0	4	0	9	20	—	—	1	16	—	6	—	.163	.236	.199	.934
1909	ChC-N	22	52	4	7	1	0	0	2	6	—	—	0	2	—	0	—	.135	.224	.154	.947
Career average		31	99	11	21	2	1	0	11	7	—	—	1	4	—	3	—	.213	.275	.272	.908
Cubs average		**22**	**52**	**4**	**7**	**1**	**0**	**0**	**2**	**6**	**—**	**—**	**0**	**2**	**—**	**0**	**—**	**.135**	**.224**	**.154**	**.947**
Career total		216	694	77	148	15	10	2	76	51	—	—	8	25	—	20	—	.213	.275	.272	.908
Cubs total		**22**	**52**	**4**	**7**	**1**	**0**	**0**	**2**	**6**	**—**	**—**	**0**	**2**	**—**	**0**	**—**	**.135**	**.224**	**.154**	**.947**

Stanton, Thomas Patrick (Tom)
HEIGHT: 5'10"   THROWS: RIGHT   BATS: BOTH   BORN: 10/25/1874 ST. LOUIS, MISSOURI   DIED: 1/17/1957 ST. LOUIS, MISSOURI   POSITIONS PLAYED: C

YEAR	TEAM	GAMES	AB	RUNS	HITS	2B	3B	HR	RBI	BB	IBB	SO	HBP	SH	SF	SB	CS	BA	OBA	SA	FA
1904	ChC-N	1	3	0	0	0	0	0	0	0	—	—	0	0	—	0	—	.000	.000	.000	1.000
Career average		1	3	0	0	0	0	0	0	0	—	—	0	0	—	0	—	.000	.000	.000	1.000
Cubs average		**1**	**3**	**0**	**0**	**0**	**0**	**0**	**0**	**0**	**—**	**—**	**0**	**0**	**—**	**0**	**—**	**.000**	**.000**	**.000**	**1.000**
Career total		1	3	0	0	0	0	0	0	0	—	—	0	0	—	0	—	.000	.000	.000	1.000
Cubs total		**1**	**3**	**0**	**0**	**0**	**0**	**0**	**0**	**0**	**—**	**—**	**0**	**0**	**—**	**0**	**—**	**.000**	**.000**	**.000**	**1.000**

Start, Joseph (Joe *or* Old Reliable *or* Rocks)

HEIGHT: 5'9"   THROWS: LEFT   BATS: LEFT   BORN: 10/14/1842 NEW YORK, NEW YORK   DIED: 3/27/1927 PROVIDENCE, RHODE ISLAND
POSITIONS PLAYED: 1B, OF

YEAR	TEAM	GAMES	AB	RUNS	HITS	2B	3B	HR	RBI	BB	IBB	SO	HBP	SH	SF	SB	CS	BA	OBA	SA	FA
1876	NYM-N	56	265	40	73	6	0	0	21	1	—	2	—	—	—	—	—	.275	.278	.298	.964
1877	Har-N	60	271	55	90	3	6	1	21	6	—	2	—	—	—	—	—	.332	.347	.399	.964
1878	**ChN-N**	**61**	**285**	**58**	**100**	**12**	**5**	**1**	**27**	**2**	**—**	**3**	**—**	**—**	**—**	**—**	**—**	**.351**	**.355**	**.439**	**.957**
1879	Prv-N	66	317	70	101	11	5	2	37	7	—	4	—	—	—	—	—	.319	.333	.404	.973
1880	Prv-N	82	345	53	96	14	6	0	27	13	—	20	—	—	—	—	—	.278	.304	.354	.971
1881	Prv-N	79	348	56	114	12	6	0	29	9	—	7	—	—	—	—	—	.328	.345	.397	.963
1882	Prv-N	82	356	58	117	8	10	0	48	11	—	7	—	—	—	—	—	.329	.349	.407	.974
1883	Prv-N	87	370	63	105	16	7	1	57	22	—	16	—	—	—	—	—	.284	.324	.373	.957
1884	Prv-N	93	381	80	105	10	5	2	32	35	—	25	—	—	—	—	—	.276	.337	.344	.980
1885	Prv-N	101	374	47	103	11	4	0	41	39	—	10	—	—	—	—	—	.275	.344	.326	.972
1886	WaN-N	31	122	10	27	4	1	0	17	5	—	13	—	—	—	4	—	.221	.252	.270	.973
Career average		73	312	54	94	10	5	1	32	14	—	10	—	—	—	—	0	—	.300	.330	.370	.968
Cubs average		**61**	**285**	**58**	**100**	**12**	**5**	**1**	**27**	**2**	**—**	**3**	**—**	**—**	**—**	**—**	**—**	**.351**	**.355**	**.439**	**.957**
Career total		798	3434	590	1031	107	55	7	357	150	—	109	—	—	—	4	—	.300	.330	.370	.968
Cubs total		**61**	**285**	**58**	**100**	**12**	**5**	**1**	**27**	**2**	**—**	**3**	**—**	**—**	**—**	**—**	**—**	**.351**	**.355**	**.439**	**.957**

Statz, Arnold John (Jigger)

HEIGHT: 5'7"   THROWS: RIGHT   BATS: RIGHT   BORN: 10/20/1897 WAUKEGAN, ILLINOIS   DIED: 3/16/1988 CORONA DEL MAR, CALIFORNIA
POSITIONS PLAYED: 2B, OF

YEAR	TEAM	GAMES	AB	RUNS	HITS	2B	3B	HR	RBI	BB	IBB	SO	HBP	SH	SF	SB	CS	BA	OBA	SA	FA
1919	NYG-N	21	60	7	18	2	1	0	6	3	—	8	0	0	—	2	—	.300	.333	.367	.978
1920	NYG-N	16	30	0	4	0	1	0	5	2	—	9	0	1	—	0	1	.133	.188	.200	.944
1920	Bos-A	2	3	0	0	0	0	0	0	0	—	0	0	0	—	0	0	.000	.000	.000	1.000
1922	**ChC-N**	**110**	**462**	**77**	**137**	**19**	**5**	**1**	**34**	**41**	**—**	**31**	**1**	**4**	**—**	**16**	**13**	**.297**	**.355**	**.366**	**.959**
1923	**ChC-N**	**154**	**655**	**110**	**209**	**33**	**8**	**10**	**70**	**56**	**—**	**42**	**3**	**8**	**—**	**29**	**23**	**.319**	**.375**	**.440**	**.975**
1924	**ChC-N**	**135**	**549**	**69**	**152**	**22**	**5**	**3**	**49**	**37**	**—**	**50**	**2**	**13**	**—**	**13**	**9**	**.277**	**.325**	**.352**	**.955**
1925	**ChC-N**	**38**	**148**	**21**	**38**	**6**	**3**	**2**	**14**	**11**	**—**	**16**	**2**	**6**	**—**	**4**	**0**	**.257**	**.317**	**.378**	**.943**
1927	Bro-N	130	507	64	139	24	7	1	21	26	—	43	0	14	—	10	—	.274	.310	.355	.990
1928	Bro-N	77	171	28	40	8	1	0	16	18	—	12	1	9	—	3	—	.234	.311	.292	.966
Career average		85	323	47	92	14	4	2	27	24	—	26	1	7	—	10	6	.285	.337	.373	.968
Cubs average		**109**	**454**	**69**	**134**	**20**	**5**	**4**	**42**	**36**	**—**	**35**	**2**	**8**	**—**	**16**	**11**	**.295**	**.350**	**.389**	**.962**
Career total		683	2585	376	737	114	31	17	215	194	—	211	9	55	—	77	46	.285	.337	.373	.968
Cubs total		**437**	**1814**	**277**	**536**	**80**	**21**	**16**	**167**	**145**	**—**	**139**	**8**	**31**	**—**	**62**	**45**	**.295**	**.350**	**.389**	**.962**

Stedronsky, John

HEIGHT: —   THROWS: —   BATS: —   BORN: — CLEVELAND, OHIO   POSITIONS PLAYED: 3B

YEAR	TEAM	GAMES	AB	RUNS	HITS	2B	3B	HR	RBI	BB	IBB	SO	HBP	SH	SF	SB	CS	BA	OBA	SA	FA
1879	ChN-N	4	12	0	1	0	0	0	0	0	—	3	—	—	—	—	—	.083	.083	.083	.789
Career average		4	12	0	1	0	0	0	0	0	—	3	—	—	—	—	—	.083	.083	.083	.789
Cubs average		**4**	**12**	**0**	**1**	**0**	**0**	**0**	**0**	**0**	**—**	**3**	**—**	**—**	**—**	**—**	**—**	**.083**	**.083**	**.083**	**.789**
Career total		4	12	0	1	0	0	0	0	0	—	3	—	—	—	—	—	.083	.083	.083	.789
Cubs total		**4**	**12**	**0**	**1**	**0**	**0**	**0**	**0**	**0**	**—**	**3**	**—**	**—**	**—**	**—**	**—**	**.083**	**.083**	**.083**	**.789**

Steinfeldt, Harry M.

HEIGHT: 5'9"   THROWS: RIGHT   BATS: RIGHT   BORN: 9/29/1877 ST. LOUIS, MISSOURI   DIED: 8/17/1914 BELLEVUE, KENTUCKY
POSITIONS PLAYED: 1B, 2B, 3B, SS, OF

YEAR	TEAM	GAMES	AB	RUNS	HITS	2B	3B	HR	RBI	BB	IBB	SO	HBP	SH	SF	SB	CS	BA	OBA	SA	FA
1898	Cin-N	88	308	47	91	18	6	0	43	27	—		1	19	—	9	—	.295	.354	.393	.898
1899	Cin-N	107	386	62	94	16	8	0	43	40	—		6	8	—	19	—	.244	.324	.326	.909
1900	Cin-N	134	510	57	125	29	7	2	66	27	—		7	19	—	14	—	.245	.292	.341	.937
1901	Cin-N	105	382	40	95	18	7	6	47	28	—		2	10	—	10	—	.249	.303	.380	.917
1902	Cin-N	129	479	53	133	20	7	1	49	24	—		3	9	—	12	—	.278	.316	.355	.910
1903	Cin-N	118	439	71	137	32	12	6	83	47	—		6	6	—	13	—	.312	.386	.481	.930

Harry M. Steinfeldt, 3b-2b-of-1b-ss, 1898-1911

Well, he didn't make the poem, but third baseman Harry Steinfeldt played on four pennant winners and was, in 1906, the best hitter on the greatest team, recordwise, in the history of the game.

Born on September 29, 1877, in St. Louis, Missouri, Steinfeldt aspired to the stage as a youngster. But while on the road in Texas, he deserted his musical troupe to play for a local baseball team—he never returned to the troupe.

Steinfeldt broke into the National League with the Cincinnati Reds in 1898, hitting .295 in part-time duty. For the next three years, Steinfeldt was used at all four infield positions and in the outfield. He had, by far, the strongest and surest arm on the team, but he never really hit very well in that span.

Steinfeldt hated not knowing where, or if, he would be playing on a specific day, so in 1902 he asked Red manager John Alexander "Bid" McPhee to play him regularly at one position. McPhee agreed, putting Steinfeldt at third base all year. Steinfeldt hit .278 that year and .312 the next season.

But the Reds were going nowhere, and the competitive Steinfeldt wanted out. He communicated that to Cubs player-manager Frank Chance, who had played with Steinfeldt in the California Winter League a few years earlier. By the end of the 1905 season, Chance went after Steinfeldt.

It paid off handsomely. Steinfeldt led the league in hits in 1906 with 176, as well as RBIs with 83. His .327 batting average topped Cubs regulars and, of course, Chicago won a league-record 116 games.

But Steinfeldt was worth even more defensively. In 1906 and 1907, he led National League third basemen in fielding average, was second in 1908 and 1909 and third in 1910. He had a rocket arm and was also a bit of a cutie on the base paths. Steinfeldt, for example, was the master of the art of subtly "bumping" a base runner as he rounded the bases, a trick that often slowed them up just enough to get them thrown out at home plate. It drove opposing managers nuts.

He was also, of course, the third baseman in the "Tinker to Evers to Chance" infield. Steinfeldt isn't mentioned in the poem, but he might have been the best defensive player in those infields.

The 1910 season was Steinfeldt's last as a Cub. He was traded to the Boston Braves in 1911 and played 19 games before retiring.

He did not live long after leaving baseball. In 1914, probably suffering from one or more blood clots in his brain, he died of a cerebral hemorrhage at the age of 36.

1904	Cin-N	99	349	35	85	11	6	1	52	29	—	—	6	14	—	16	—	.244	.313	.318	.887
1905	Cin-N	114	384	49	104	16	9	1	39	30	—	—	3	12	—	15	—	.271	.329	.367	.920
1906	ChC-N	151	539	81	176	27	10	3	83	47	—	—	14	25	—	29	—	.327	.395	.430	.954
1907	ChC-N	152	542	52	144	25	5	1	70	37	—	—	9	25	—	19	—	.266	.323	.336	.967
1908	ChC-N	150	539	63	130	20	6	1	62	36	—	—	4	32	—	12	—	.241	.294	.306	.940
1909	ChC-N	151	528	73	133	27	6	2	59	57	—	—	5	31	—	22	—	.252	.331	.337	.940
1910	ChC-N	129	448	70	113	21	1	2	58	36	—	29	11	31	—	10	—	.252	.323	.317	.946
1911	Bos-N	19	63	5	16	4	0	1	8	6	—	3	2	0	—	1	—	.254	.338	.365	.810
Career average		118	421	54	113	20	6	2	54	34	—	2	6	17	—	14	—	.267	.330	.360	.927
Cubs average		**147**	**519**	**68**	**139**	**24**	**6**	**2**	**66**	**43**	**—**	**6**	**9**	**29**	**—**	**18**	**—**	**.268**	**.334**	**.346**	**.949**
Career total		1646	5896	758	1576	284	90	27	762	471	—	32	79	241	—	201	—	.267	.330	.360	.927
Cubs total		**733**	**2596**	**339**	**696**	**120**	**28**	**9**	**332**	**213**	**—**	**29**	**43**	**144**	**—**	**92**	**—**	**.268**	**.334**	**.346**	**.949**

Stelmaszek, Richard Francis (Rick)
HEIGHT: 6'1" THROWS: RIGHT BATS: LEFT BORN: 10/8/1948 CHICAGO, ILLINOIS POSITIONS PLAYED: C

YEAR	TEAM	GAMES	AB	RUNS	HITS	2B	3B	HR	RBI	BB	IBB	SO	HBP	SH	SF	SB	CS	BA	OBA	SA	FA
1971	Was-A	6	9	0	0	0	0	0	0	0	0	3	0	0	0	0	0	.000	.000	.000	1.000
1973	Tex-A	7	9	0	1	0	0	0	0	1	0	2	0	0	0	0	0	.111	.200	.111	1.000
1973	Cal-A	22	26	2	4	1	0	0	3	6	0	7	0	1	0	0	0	.154	.313	.192	1.000
1974	**ChC-N**	**25**	**44**	**2**	**10**	**2**	**0**	**1**	**7**	**10**	**0**	**6**	**0**	**1**	**1**	**0**	**0**	**.227**	**.364**	**.341**	**.983**
Career average		20	29	1	5	1	0	0	3	6	0	6	0	1	0	0	0	.170	.302	.239	.993
Cubs average		**25**	**44**	**2**	**10**	**2**	**0**	**1**	**7**	**10**	**0**	**6**	**0**	**1**	**1**	**0**	**0**	**.227**	**.364**	**.341**	**.983**
Career total		60	88	4	15	3	0	1	10	17	0	18	0	2	1	0	0	.170	.302	.239	.993
Cubs total		**25**	**44**	**2**	**10**	**2**	**0**	**1**	**7**	**10**	**0**	**6**	**0**	**1**	**1**	**0**	**0**	**.227**	**.364**	**.341**	**.983**

Stenzel, Jacob Charles (Jake)
HEIGHT: 5'10" THROWS: RIGHT BATS: RIGHT BORN: 6/24/1867 CINCINNATI, OHIO DIED: 1/6/1919 CINCINNATI, OHIO POSITIONS PLAYED: C, 1B, 2B, SS, OF

YEAR	TEAM	GAMES	AB	RUNS	HITS	2B	3B	HR	RBI	BB	IBB	SO	HBP	SH	SF	SB	CS	BA	OBA	SA	FA
1890	ChN-N	11	41	3	11	1	0	0	3	1	—	0	0	—	—	0	—	.268	.286	.293	.949
1892	Pit-N	3	9	0	0	0	0	0	0	1	—	3	0	—	—	1	—	.000	.100	.000	1.000
1893	Pit-N	60	224	57	81	13	4	4	37	24	—	17	0	—	—	16	—	.362	.423	.509	.864
1894	Pit-N	131	522	148	185	39	20	13	121	75	—	13	6	5	—	61	—	.354	.441	.580	.925
1895	Pit-N	129	514	114	192	38	13	7	97	57	—	25	11	6	—	53	—	.374	.447	.539	.912
1896	Pit-N	114	479	104	173	26	14	2	82	32	—	13	7	6	—	57	—	.361	.409	.486	.920
1897	Bal-N	131	536	113	189	43	7	4	116	36	—	—	10	3	—	69	—	.353	.404	.481	.932
1898	Bal-N	35	138	33	35	5	2	0	22	12	—	—	6	0	—	4	—	.254	.340	.319	.926
1898	StL-N	108	404	64	114	15	11	1	33	41	—	—	13	11	—	21	—	.282	.367	.381	.943
1899	StL-N	35	128	21	35	9	0	1	19	16	—	—	3	5	—	8	—	.273	.367	.367	.949
1899	Cin-N	9	29	5	9	1	0	0	3	4	—	—	1	0	—	2	—	.310	.412	.345	1.000
Career average		85	336	74	114	21	8	4	59	33	—	8	6	4	—	32	—	.339	.408	.480	.923
Cubs average		**11**	**41**	**3**	**11**	**1**	**0**	**0**	**3**	**1**	**—**	**0**	**0**	**—**	**—**	**0**	**—**	**.268**	**.286**	**.293**	**.949**
Career total		766	3024	662	1024	190	71	32	533	299	—	71	57	36	—	292	—	.339	.408	.480	.923
Cubs total		**11**	**41**	**3**	**11**	**1**	**0**	**0**	**3**	**1**	**—**	**0**	**0**	**—**	**—**	**0**	**—**	**.268**	**.286**	**.293**	**.949**

Stephenson, Jackson Riggs (Riggs *or* Old Hoss)
HEIGHT: 5'10" THROWS: RIGHT BATS: RIGHT BORN: 1/5/1898 AKRON, ALABAMA DIED: 11/15/1985 TUSCALOOSA, ALABAMA POSITIONS PLAYED: 2B, 3B, OF

YEAR	TEAM	GAMES	AB	RUNS	HITS	2B	3B	HR	RBI	BB	IBB	SO	HBP	SH	SF	SB	CS	BA	OBA	SA	FA
1921	Cle-A	65	206	45	68	17	2	2	34	23	—	15	4	7	—	4	1	.330	.408	.461	.942
1922	Cle-A	86	233	47	79	24	5	2	32	27	—	18	6	1	—	3	0	.339	.421	.511	.951
1923	Cle-A	91	301	48	96	20	6	5	65	15	—	25	3	1	—	5	0	.319	.357	.475	.970
1924	Cle-A	71	240	33	89	20	0	4	44	27	—	10	2	3	—	1	2	.371	.439	.504	.962
1925	Cle-A	19	54	8	16	3	1	1	9	7	—	3	1	2	—	1	1	.296	.387	.444	.946
1926	**ChC-N**	**82**	**281**	**40**	**95**	**18**	**3**	**3**	**44**	**31**	**—**	**16**	**0**	**12**	**—**	**2**	**—**	**.338**	**.404**	**.456**	**.950**
1927	**ChC-N**	**152**	**579**	**101**	**199**	**46**	**9**	**7**	**82**	**65**	**—**	**28**	**6**	**18**	**—**	**8**	**—**	**.338**	**.404**	**.456**	**.950**
1928	**ChC-N**	**137**	**512**	**75**	**166**	**36**	**9**	**8**	**90**	**68**	**—**	**29**	**3**	**8**	**—**	**8**	**—**	**.344**	**.415**	**.491**	**.971**
1929	**ChC-N**	**136**	**495**	**91**	**179**	**36**	**6**	**17**	**110**	**67**	**—**	**21**	**7**	**13**	**—**	**10**	**—**	**.324**	**.407**	**.477**	**.982**
1930	**ChC-N**	**109**	**341**	**56**	**125**	**21**	**1**	**5**	**68**	**32**	**—**	**20**	**0**	**9**	**—**	**2**	**—**	**.362**	**.445**	**.562**	**.984**
1931	**ChC-N**	**80**	**263**	**34**	**84**	**14**	**4**	**1**	**52**	**37**	**—**	**14**	**1**	**1**	**—**	**1**	**—**	**.367**	**.421**	**.478**	**.958**
1932	**ChC-N**	**147**	**583**	**86**	**189**	**49**	**4**	**4**	**85**	**54**	**—**	**27**	**2**	**5**	**—**	**3**	**—**	**.319**	**.405**	**.414**	**.985**
1933	**ChC-N**	**97**	**346**	**45**	**114**	**17**	**4**	**4**	**51**	**34**	**—**	**16**	**5**	**3**	**—**	**5**	**—**	**.324**	**.383**	**.443**	**.984**
1934	**ChC-N**	**38**	**74**	**5**	**16**	**0**	**0**	**0**	**7**	**7**	**—**	**5**	**1**	**1**	**—**	**0**	**—**	**.329**	**.397**	**.436**	**.985**
Career average		94	322	51	108	23	4	5	55	35	—	18	3	7	—	4	1	.216	.293	.216	1.000
Cubs average		**109**	**386**	**59**	**130**	**26**	**4**	**5**	**65**	**44**	**—**	**20**	**3**	**8**	**—**	**4**	**0**	**.336**	**.407**	**.473**	**.969**
Career total		1310	4508	714	1515	321	54	63	773	494	—	247	41	91	—	53	9	.336	.408	.469	.977
Cubs total		**978**	**3474**	**533**	**1167**	**237**	**40**	**49**	**589**	**395**	**—**	**176**	**25**	**70**	**—**	**39**	**0**	**.336**	**.407**	**.473**	**.969**

Jackson Riggs "Old Hoss" Stephenson, of-2b-3b, 1921–34

Throughout his career, in Chicago and elsewhere, Riggs Stephenson earned his paycheck at the plate.

Born on January 5, 1898, in Akron, Alabama, Stephenson was a three-sport star in high school. His best sport may have been football, and he was a star for the University of Alabama before opting for a baseball career.

Stephenson was a great hitter and a not-so-great defensive player. He was mainly an infielder in his early baseball days, but a shoulder injury sustained while playing football hindered his throwing motion.

Stephenson played five years in Cleveland, hitting the heck out of the ball as a part-timer. His batting average in those years was .330, .339, .319, .371 and .296. Cleveland manager Tris Speaker was wary of Stephenson's arm problems and was reluctant to use him in the field regularly.

Chicago was not. Stephenson was back in the minor leagues in the latter part of 1925, and the Cubs drafted him. In 1926 Cubs manager Joe McCarthy installed Stephenson in left field.

The "Old Hoss" as he was called—for his powerful build and Southern drawl—hit .344, with a league-leading 46 doubles in 1927.

Stephenson hit .317 or better for eight consecutive years in Chicago. In 1929 he combined with fellow outfielders Lewis Robert "Hack" Wilson and Hazen "Kiki" Cuyler to become the only outfield in major league history to have all three members crack the 100 RBIs mark. Wilson had 159, Stephenson 110 and Cuyler 102.

Stephenson was relatively slow afoot, but he was not the plodding Clydesdale he was made out to be. He was second in putouts by National League left fielders in 1927 and 1928, although his totals began to drop after those years.

His shoulder troubles didn't really inhibit his hitting but did limit his throwing. He was always near the bottom of the league in outfield assists. In 1931 he recorded only one assist; he had been sidelined with arm and leg injuries and had only played about half the year.

He played in two World Series with Chicago, in 1929 and 1932. While the Cubs lost both, Stephenson played well both times. His lifetime .378 World Series average is tops all-time for the Cubs.

Stephenson, a quiet, modest man, was very popular with his teammates, many of whom believed he should have been named to the Hall of Fame.

By 1934 Stephenson's various injuries began to take a toll, and he hit only .216 in very limited action. He retired after the season but worked as a minor league manager until 1939. He died on November 15, 1985 in Tuscaloosa, Alabama.

Stephenson's lifetime .336 batting average is second all-time with the Cubs, while his .362 average in 1929 is still a single-season record for Cubs left fielders.

Stephenson, John Herman

HEIGHT: 5'11" **THROWS:** RIGHT **BATS:** LEFT **BORN:** 4/13/1941 SOUTH PORTSMOUTH, KENTUCKY **POSITIONS PLAYED:** C, 3B, OF

YEAR	TEAM	GAMES	AB	RUNS	HITS	2B	3B	HR	RBI	BB	IBB	SO	HBP	SH	SF	SB	CS	BA	OBA	SA	FA
1964	NYM-N	37	57	2	9	0	0	1	2	4	0	18	1	0	0	0	0	.158	.226	.211	.824
1965	NYM-N	62	121	9	26	5	0	4	15	8	2	19	0	2	0	0	1	.215	.264	.355	.982
1966	NYM-N	63	143	17	28	1	1	1	11	8	0	28	2	0	0	0	0	.196	.248	.238	.973
1967	**ChC-N**	**18**	**49**	**3**	**11**	**3**	**1**	**0**	**5**	**1**	**1**	**6**	**1**	**1**	**0**	**0**	**0**	**.224**	**.255**	**.327**	**1.000**
1968	**ChC-N**	**2**	**2**	**0**	**0**	**0**	**0**	**0**	**0**	**0**	**0**	**0**	**0**	**0**	**0**	**0**	**0**	**.000**	**.000**	**.000**	**—**
1969	SF-N	22	27	2	6	2	0	0	3	0	0	4	0	1	1	0	0	.222	.214	.296	.842
1970	SF-N	23	43	3	3	1	0	0	6	2	0	7	0	0	1	0	0	.070	.109	.093	1.000
1971	Cal-A	98	279	24	61	17	0	3	25	22	6	21	3	2	2	0	0	.219	.281	.312	.992
1972	Cal-A	66	146	14	40	3	1	2	17	11	5	8	4	0	0	0	0	.274	.342	.349	.993
1973	Cal-A	60	122	9	30	5	0	1	9	7	1	7	1	2	0	0	0	.246	.292	.311	.980
Career average		45	99	8	21	4	0	1	9	6	2	12	1	1	0	0	0	.216	.271	.296	.982
Cubs average		**10**	**26**	**2**	**6**	**2**	**1**	**0**	**3**	**1**	**1**	**3**	**1**	**1**	**0**	**0**	**0**	**.216**	**.245**	**.314**	**1.000**
Career total		451	989	83	214	37	3	12	93	63	15	118	12	8	4	0	1	.216	.271	.296	.982
Cubs total		**20**	**51**	**3**	**11**	**3**	**1**	**0**	**5**	**1**	**1**	**6**	**1**	**1**	**0**	**0**	**0**	**.216**	**.245**	**.314**	**1.000**

Stephenson, Joseph Chester (Joe)
HEIGHT: 6'2" THROWS: RIGHT BATS: RIGHT BORN: 6/30/1921 DETROIT, MICHIGAN DIED: 9/20/2001 FULLERTON, CALIFORNIA POSITIONS PLAYED: C

YEAR	TEAM	GAMES	AB	RUNS	HITS	2B	3B	HR	RBI	BB	IBB	SO	HBP	SH	SF	SB	CS	BA	OBA	SA	FA
1943	NYG-N	9	24	4	6	1	0	0	1	0	—	5	0	0	—	0	0	.250	.250	.292	.973
1944	**ChC-N**	**4**	**8**	**1**	**1**	**0**	**0**	**0**	**0**	**1**	**—**	**3**	**0**	**0**	**—**	**1**	**—**	**.125**	**.222**	**.125**	**1.000**
1947	CWS-A	16	35	3	5	0	0	0	3	1	—	7	2	0	—	0	0	.143	.211	.143	.959
Career average		10	22	3	4	0	0	0	1	1	—	5	1	0	—	0	0	.179	.225	.194	.970
Cubs average		**4**	**8**	**1**	**1**	**0**	**0**	**0**	**0**	**1**	**—**	**3**	**0**	**0**	**—**	**1**	**0**	**.125**	**.222**	**.125**	**1.000**
Career total		29	67	8	12	1	0	0	4	2	—	15	2	0	—	1	0	.179	.225	.194	.970
Cubs total		**4**	**8**	**1**	**1**	**0**	**0**	**0**	**0**	**1**	**—**	**3**	**0**	**0**	**—**	**1**	**0**	**.125**	**.222**	**.125**	**1.000**

Stephenson, Phillip Raymond (Phil)
HEIGHT: 6'1" THROWS: LEFT BATS: LEFT BORN: 9/19/1960 GUTHRIE, OKLAHOMA POSITIONS PLAYED: 1B, OF

YEAR	TEAM	GAMES	AB	RUNS	HITS	2B	3B	HR	RBI	BB	IBB	SO	HBP	SH	SF	SB	CS	BA	OBA	SA	FA
1989	**ChC-N**	**17**	**21**	**0**	**3**	**0**	**0**	**0**	**0**	**2**	**0**	**3**	**0**	**0**	**0**	**1**	**0**	**.143**	**.217**	**.143**	**1.000**
1989	SD-N	10	17	4	6	0	0	2	2	3	0	2	0	2	0	0	0	.353	.450	.706	.977
1990	SD-N	103	182	26	38	9	1	4	19	30	1	43	0	0	1	2	1	.209	.319	.335	.997
1991	SD-N	11	7	0	2	0	0	0	0	2	0	3	0	0	0	0	0	.286	.444	.286	—
1992	SD-N	53	71	5	11	2	1	0	8	10	0	11	0	3	0	0	0	.155	.259	.211	.981
Career average		49	75	9	15	3	1	2	7	12	0	16	0	1	0	1	0	.201	.309	.312	.994
Cubs average		**17**	**21**	**0**	**3**	**0**	**0**	**0**	**0**	**2**	**0**	**3**	**0**	**0**	**0**	**1**	**0**	**.143**	**.217**	**.143**	**1.000**
Career total		194	298	35	60	11	2	6	29	47	1	62	0	5	1	3	1	.201	.309	.312	.994
Cubs total		**17**	**21**	**0**	**3**	**0**	**0**	**0**	**0**	**2**	**0**	**3**	**0**	**0**	**0**	**1**	**0**	**.143**	**.217**	**.143**	**1.000**

Stephenson, Walter McQueen (Tarzan)
HEIGHT: 6'0" THROWS: RIGHT BATS: RIGHT BORN: 3/27/1911 SALUDA, NORTH CAROLINA DIED: 7/4/1993 SHREVEPORT, LOUISIANA POSITIONS PLAYED: C

YEAR	TEAM	GAMES	AB	RUNS	HITS	2B	3B	HR	RBI	BB	IBB	SO	HBP	SH	SF	SB	CS	BA	OBA	SA	FA
1935	**ChC-N**	**16**	**26**	**2**	**10**	**1**	**1**	**0**	**2**	**1**	**—**	**5**	**0**	**0**	**—**	**0**	**—**	**.385**	**.407**	**.500**	**1.000**
1936	**ChC-N**	**6**	**12**	**0**	**1**	**0**	**0**	**0**	**1**	**0**	**—**	**5**	**0**	**0**	**—**	**0**	**—**	**.083**	**.083**	**.083**	**1.000**
1937	Phi-N	10	23	1	6	0	0	0	2	2	—	3	0	0	—	0	—	.261	.320	.261	.967
Career average		11	20	1	6	0	0	0	2	1	—	4	0	0	—	0	—	.279	.313	.328	.984
Cubs average		**11**	**19**	**1**	**6**	**1**	**1**	**0**	**2**	**1**	**—**	**5**	**0**	**0**	**—**	**0**	**—**	**.289**	**.308**	**.368**	**1.000**
Career total		32	61	3	17	1	1	0	5	3	—	13	0	0	—	0	—	.279	.313	.328	.984
Cubs total		**22**	**38**	**2**	**11**	**1**	**1**	**0**	**3**	**1**	**—**	**10**	**0**	**0**	**—**	**0**	**—**	**.289**	**.308**	**.368**	**1.000**

Stewart, Asa (Ace)
HEIGHT: 5'10" THROWS: RIGHT BATS: RIGHT BORN: 2/14/1869 TERRE HAUTE, INDIANA DIED: 4/17/1912 TERRE HAUTE, INDIANA POSITIONS PLAYED: 2B, OF

YEAR	TEAM	GAMES	AB	RUNS	HITS	2B	3B	HR	RBI	BB	IBB	SO	HBP	SH	SF	SB	CS	BA	OBA	SA	FA
1895	**ChN-N**	**97**	**365**	**52**	**88**	**8**	**10**	**8**	**76**	**39**	**—**	**40**	**0**	**4**	**—**	**14**	**—**	**.241**	**.314**	**.384**	**.911**
Career average		97	365	52	88	8	10	8	76	39	—	40	0	4	—	14	—	.241	.314	.384	.911
Cubs average		**97**	**365**	**52**	**88**	**8**	**10**	**8**	**76**	**39**	**—**	**40**	**0**	**4**	**—**	**14**	**—**	**.241**	**.314**	**.384**	**.911**
Career total		97	365	52	88	8	10	8	76	39	—	40	0	4	—	14	—	.241	.314	.384	.911
Cubs total		**97**	**365**	**52**	**88**	**8**	**10**	**8**	**76**	**39**	**—**	**40**	**0**	**4**	**—**	**14**	**—**	**.241**	**.314**	**.384**	**.911**

Stewart, Charles Eugene (Tuffy)
HEIGHT: 5'10" THROWS: LEFT BATS: LEFT BORN: 7/31/1883 CHICAGO, ILLINOIS DIED: 11/18/1934 CHICAGO, ILLINOIS POSITIONS PLAYED: OF

YEAR	TEAM	GAMES	AB	RUNS	HITS	2B	3B	HR	RBI	BB	IBB	SO	HBP	SH	SF	SB	CS	BA	OBA	SA	FA
1913	**ChC-N**	**9**	**8**	**1**	**1**	**1**	**0**	**0**	**2**	**2**	**—**	**5**	**0**	**0**	**—**	**1**	**—**	**.125**	**.300**	**.250**	**1.000**
1914	**ChC-N**	**2**	**1**	**0**	**0**	**0**	**0**	**0**	**0**	**0**	**—**	**0**	**0**	**0**	**—**	**0**	**—**	**.000**	**.000**	**.000**	**—**
Career average		6	5	1	1	1	0	0	1	1	—	3	0	0	—	1	—	.111	.273	.222	1.000
Cubs average		**6**	**5**	**1**	**1**	**1**	**0**	**0**	**1**	**1**	**—**	**3**	**0**	**0**	**—**	**1**	**—**	**.111**	**.273**	**.222**	**1.000**
Career total		11	9	1	1	1	0	0	2	2	—	5	0	0	—	1	—	.111	.273	.222	1.000
Cubs total		**11**	**9**	**1**	**1**	**1**	**0**	**0**	**2**	**2**	**—**	**5**	**0**	**0**	**—**	**1**	**—**	**.111**	**.273**	**.222**	**1.000**

Stewart, James Franklin (Jimmy)
HEIGHT: 6'0" THROWS: RIGHT BATS: BOTH BORN: 6/11/1939 OPELIKA, ALABAMA POSITIONS PLAYED: C, 1B, 2B, 3B, SS, OF

YEAR	TEAM	GAMES	AB	RUNS	HITS	2B	3B	HR	RBI	BB	IBB	SO	HBP	SH	SF	SB	CS	BA	OBA	SA	FA
1963	ChC-N	13	37	1	11	2	0	0	1	1	0	7	0	1	0	1	1	.297	.316	.351	.977
1964	ChC-N	132	415	59	105	17	0	3	33	49	0	61	2	9	6	10	8	.253	.331	.316	.976
1965	ChC-N	116	282	26	63	9	4	0	19	30	1	53	2	1	2	13	3	.223	.301	.284	.956
1966	ChC-N	57	90	4	16	4	1	0	4	7	0	12	2	1	0	1	1	.178	.253	.244	1.000
1967	ChC-N	6	6	1	1	0	0	0	1	0	0	0	0	0	0	0	0	.167	.167	.167	—
1967	CWS-A	24	18	5	3	0	0	0	1	1	0	6	0	1	0	1	0	.167	.211	.167	.850
1969	Cin-N	119	221	26	56	3	4	4	24	19	3	33	0	4	1	4	2	.253	.311	.357	.970
1970	Cin-N	101	105	15	28	3	1	1	8	8	1	13	1	1	1	5	3	.267	.322	.343	.965
1971	Cin-N	80	82	7	19	2	2	0	9	9	1	12	0	1	0	3	1	.232	.308	.305	.946
1972	Hou-N	68	96	14	21	5	2	0	9	6	2	9	0	3	3	0	1	.219	.257	.313	1.000
1973	Hou-N	61	68	6	13	0	0	0	3	9	1	12	1	3	0	0	0	.191	.295	.191	1.000
Career average		78	142	16	34	5	1	1	11	14	1	22	1	2	1	4	2	.237	.306	.305	.972
Cubs average		65	166	18	39	6	1	1	12	17	0	27	1	2	2	5	3	.236	.310	.298	.973
Career total		777	1420	164	336	45	14	8	112	139	9	218	8	22	13	38	20	.237	.306	.305	.972
Cubs total		324	830	91	196	32	5	3	58	87	1	133	6	12	8	25	13	.236	.310	.298	.973

Strain, Joseph Allan (Joe)
HEIGHT: 5'10" THROWS: RIGHT BATS: RIGHT BORN: 4/30/1954 DENVER, COLORADO POSITIONS PLAYED: 2B, 3B, SS

YEAR	TEAM	GAMES	AB	RUNS	HITS	2B	3B	HR	RBI	BB	IBB	SO	HBP	SH	SF	SB	CS	BA	OBA	SA	FA
1979	SF-N	67	257	27	62	8	1	1	12	13	0	21	3	11	1	8	4	.241	.285	.292	.982
1980	SF-N	77	189	26	54	6	0	0	16	10	0	10	0	7	1	1	2	.286	.320	.317	.980
1981	ChC-N	25	74	7	14	1	0	0	1	5	0	7	1	0	0	0	0	.189	.250	.203	.975
Career average		56	173	20	43	5	0	0	10	9	0	13	1	6	1	3	2	.250	.292	.288	.981
Cubs average		25	74	7	14	1	0	0	1	5	0	7	1	0	0	0	0	.189	.250	.203	.975
Career total		169	520	60	130	15	1	1	29	28	0	38	4	18	2	9	6	.250	.292	.288	.981
Cubs total		25	74	7	14	1	0	0	1	5	0	7	1	0	0	0	0	.189	.250	.203	.975

Strang, Samuel Nicklin (Sammy or The Dixie Thrush)
HEIGHT: 5'8" THROWS: RIGHT BATS: BOTH BORN: 12/16/1876 CHATTANOOGA, TENNESSEE DIED: 3/13/1932 CHATTANOOGA, TENNESSEE
POSITIONS PLAYED: 1B, 2B, 3B, SS, OF

YEAR	TEAM	GAMES	AB	RUNS	HITS	2B	3B	HR	RBI	BB	IBB	SO	HBP	SH	SF	SB	CS	BA	OBA	SA	FA
1896	Lou-N	14	46	6	12	0	0	0	7	6	—	6	0	0	—	4	—	.261	.346	.261	.803
1900	ChN-N	27	102	15	29	3	0	0	9	8	—		2	4	—	1	—	.284	.348	.314	.852
1901	NYG-N	135	493	55	139	14	6	1	34	59	—		5	20	—	40	—	.282	.364	.341	.892
1902	CWS-A	137	536	108	158	18	5	3	46	76	—		5	11	—	38	—	.295	.387	.364	.890
1902	ChC-N	3	11	1	4	0	0	0	0	0	—		0	0	—	1	—	.364	.364	.364	.900
1903	Bro-N	135	508	101	138	21	5	0	38	75	—		10	8	—	46	—	.272	.376	.333	.916
1904	Bro-N	77	271	28	52	11	0	1	9	45	—		4	4	—	16	—	.192	.316	.244	.885
1905	NYG-N	111	294	51	76	9	4	3	29	58	—		5	12	—	23	—	.259	.389	.347	.914
1906	NYG-N	113	313	50	100	16	4	4	49	54	—		2	7	—	21	—	.252	.388	.382	.951
1907	NYG-N	123	306	56	77	20	4	4	30	60	—		8	4	—	21	—	.319	.423	.435	.938
1908	NYG-N	28	53	8	5	0	0	0	2	23	—		2	2	—	5	—	.094	.385	.094	.864
Career average		90	293	48	79	11	3	2	25	46	—	1	4	7	—	22	—	.269	.377	.343	.903
Cubs average		15	57	8	17	2	0	0	5	4	—	0	1	2	—	1	—	.292	.350	.319	.856
Career total		903	2933	479	790	112	28	16	253	464	—	6	43	72	—	216	—	.269	.377	.343	.903
Cubs total		30	113	16	33	3	0	0	9	8	—	0	2	4	—	2	—	.292	.350	.319	.856

Strange, Joseph Douglas (Doug)
HEIGHT: 6'1" THROWS: RIGHT BATS: BOTH BORN: 4/13/1964 GREENVILLE, SOUTH CAROLINA POSITIONS PLAYED: 1B, 2B, 3B, SS, OF

YEAR	TEAM	GAMES	AB	RUNS	HITS	2B	3B	HR	RBI	BB	IBB	SO	HBP	SH	SF	SB	CS	BA	OBA	SA	FA
1989	Det-A	64	196	16	42	4	1	1	14	17	0	36	1	3	0	3	3	.214	.280	.260	.900
1991	ChC-N	3	9	0	4	1	0	0	1	0	0	1	1	0	1	1	0	.444	.455	.556	.800
1992	ChC-N	52	94	7	15	1	0	1	5	10	2	15	0	2	0	1	0	.160	.240	.202	.926
1993	Tex-A	145	484	58	124	29	0	7	60	43	3	69	3	8	4	6	4	.256	.318	.360	.960
1994	Tex-A	73	226	26	48	12	1	5	26	15	0	38	3	4	2	1	3	.212	.268	.341	.960
1995	Sea-A	74	155	19	42	9	2	2	21	10	0	25	2	1	0	3	0	.271	.323	.394	.970
1996	Sea-A	88	183	19	43	7	1	3	23	14	0	31	1	0	2	0	2	.235	.290	.333	.970
1997	Mon-N	118	327	40	84	16	2	12	47	36	9	76	2	5	2	1	0	.257	.332	.428	.950
1998	Pit-N	90	185	9	32	8	0	0	14	10	1	39	1	3	2	1	0	.173	.217	.216	.959

(continued)

(continued)

	GAMES	AB	RUNS	HITS	2B	3B	HR	RBI	BB	IBB	SO	HBP	SH	SF	SB	CS	BA	OBA	SA	FA
Career average	79	207	22	48	10	1	3	23	17	2	37	2	3	1	2	2	.233	.295	.338	.958
Cubs average	**28**	**52**	**4**	**10**	**1**	**0**	**1**	**3**	**5**	**1**	**8**	**1**	**1**	**1**	**1**	**0**	**.184**	**.261**	**.233**	**.919**
Career total	707	1859	194	434	87	7	31	211	155	15	330	14	26	13	14	15	.233	.295	.338	.958
Cubs total	**55**	**103**	**7**	**19**	**2**	**0**	**1**	**6**	**10**	**2**	**16**	**1**	**2**	**1**	**2**	**0**	**.184**	**.261**	**.233**	**.919**

Stringer, Louis Bernard (Lou)
HEIGHT: 5'11"   THROWS: RIGHT   BATS: RIGHT   BORN: 5/13/1917 GRAND RAPIDS, MICHIGAN   POSITIONS PLAYED: 2B, 3B, SS

YEAR	TEAM	GAMES	AB	RUNS	HITS	2B	3B	HR	RBI	BB	IBB	SO	HBP	SH	SF	SB	CS	BA	OBA	SA	FA
1941	ChC-N	145	512	59	126	31	4	5	53	59	—	86	0	10	—	3	—	.246	.324	.352	.956
1942	ChC-N	121	406	45	96	10	5	9	41	31	—	55	1	10	—	3	—	.236	.292	.352	.955
1946	ChC-N	80	209	26	51	3	1	3	19	26	—	34	0	8	—	0	—	.244	.328	.311	.957
1948	Bos-A	4	11	1	1	0	0	1	1	0	—	3	0	0	—	0	0	.091	.091	.364	.947
1949	Bos-A	35	41	10	11	4	0	1	6	5	—	10	0	0	—	0	0	.268	.348	.439	.978
1950	Bos-A	24	17	7	5	1	0	0	2	0	—	4	0	0	—	1	0	.294	.294	.353	.846
Career average		68	199	25	48	8	2	3	20	20	—	32	0	5	—	1	0	.242	.313	.348	.955
Cubs average		**115**	**376**	**43**	**91**	**15**	**3**	**6**	**38**	**39**	**—**	**58**	**0**	**9**	**—**	**2**	**—**	**.242**	**.314**	**.344**	**.956**
Career total		409	1196	148	290	49	10	19	122	121	—	192	1	28	—	7	0	.242	.313	.348	.955
Cubs total		**346**	**1127**	**130**	**273**	**44**	**10**	**17**	**113**	**116**	**—**	**175**	**1**	**28**	**—**	**6**	**—**	**.242**	**.314**	**.344**	**.956**

Sturgeon, Robert Howard (Bobby)
HEIGHT: 6'0"   THROWS: RIGHT   BATS: RIGHT   BORN: 8/6/1919 CLINTON, INDIANA   POSITIONS PLAYED: 2B, 3B, SS

YEAR	TEAM	GAMES	AB	RUNS	HITS	2B	3B	HR	RBI	BB	IBB	SO	HBP	SH	SF	SB	CS	BA	OBA	SA	FA
1940	ChC-N	7	21	1	4	1	0	0	2	0	—	1	0	0	—	0	—	.190	.190	.238	.848
1941	ChC-N	129	433	45	106	15	3	0	25	9	—	30	0	11	—	5	—	.245	.260	.293	.956
1942	ChC-N	63	162	8	40	7	1	0	7	4	—	13	1	2	—	2	—	.247	.269	.302	.986
1946	ChC-N	100	294	26	87	12	2	1	21	10	—	18	0	7	—	0	—	.296	.319	.361	.944
1947	ChC-N	87	232	16	59	10	5	0	21	7	—	12	0	4	—	0	—	.254	.276	.341	.983
1948	Bos-N	34	78	10	17	3	1	0	4	4	—	5	0	0	—	0	—	.218	.256	.282	.927
Career average		70	203	18	52	8	2	0	13	6	—	13	0	4	—	1	—	.257	.277	.318	.959
Cubs average		**77**	**228**	**19**	**59**	**9**	**2**	**0**	**15**	**6**	**—**	**15**	**0**	**5**	**—**	**1**	**—**	**.259**	**.279**	**.320**	**.960**
Career total		420	1220	106	313	48	12	1	80	34	—	79	1	24	—	7	—	.257	.277	.318	.959
Cubs total		**386**	**1142**	**96**	**296**	**45**	**11**	**1**	**76**	**30**	**—**	**74**	**1**	**24**	**—**	**7**	**—**	**.259**	**.279**	**.320**	**.960**

Sullivan, John Lawrence
HEIGHT: 5'11"   THROWS: RIGHT   BATS: RIGHT   BORN: 3/21/1890 WILLIAMSPORT, PENNSYLVANIA   DIED: 4/1/1966 MILTON, PENNSYLVANIA
POSITIONS PLAYED: 1B, OF

YEAR	TEAM	GAMES	AB	RUNS	HITS	2B	3B	HR	RBI	BB	IBB	SO	HBP	SH	SF	SB	CS	BA	OBA	SA	FA
1920	Bos-N	81	250	36	74	14	4	1	28	29	—	29	2	9	—	3	2	.296	.374	.396	.978
1921	Bos-N	5	5	0	0	0	0	0	0	0	—	0	0	0	—	0	0	.000	.000	.000	—
1921	ChC-N	76	240	28	79	14	4	4	41	19	—	26	1	9	—	3	5	.329	.381	.471	.962
Career average		81	248	32	77	14	4	3	35	24	—	28	2	9	—	3	4	.309	.374	.428	.971
Cubs average		**76**	**240**	**28**	**79**	**14**	**4**	**4**	**41**	**19**	**—**	**26**	**1**	**9**	**—**	**3**	**5**	**.329**	**.381**	**.471**	**.962**
Career total		162	495	64	153	28	8	5	69	48	—	55	3	18	—	6	7	.309	.374	.428	.971
Cubs total		**76**	**240**	**28**	**79**	**14**	**4**	**4**	**41**	**19**	**—**	**26**	**1**	**9**	**—**	**3**	**5**	**.329**	**.381**	**.471**	**.962**

Sullivan, Martin C. (Marty)
HEIGHT: —   THROWS: RIGHT   BATS: RIGHT   BORN: 10/20/1862 LOWELL, MASSACHUSETTS   DIED: 1/6/1894 LOWELL, MASSACHUSETTS
POSITIONS PLAYED: P, 1B, 3B, OF

YEAR	TEAM	GAMES	AB	RUNS	HITS	2B	3B	HR	RBI	BB	IBB	SO	HBP	SH	SF	SB	CS	BA	OBA	SA	FA
1887	ChN-N	115	508	98	170	13	16	6	77	36	—	53	4	—	—	35	—	.335	.383	.459	.847
1888	ChN-N	75	314	40	74	12	6	7	39	15	—	32	1	—	—	9	—	.236	.273	.379	.927
1889	Ind-N	69	256	45	73	11	3	4	35	50	—	31	1	—	—	15	—	.285	.404	.398	.930
1890	Bos-N	121	505	82	144	19	7	6	61	56	—	48	0	—	—	33	—	.285	.357	.386	.952
1891	Bos-N	17	67	15	15	1	0	2	7	5	—	3	1	—	—	7	—	.224	.288	.328	.926
1891	Cle-N	1	4	0	1	0	0	0	1	0	—	1	0	—	—	0	—	.250	.250	.250	—
Career average		80	331	56	95	11	6	5	44	32	—	34	1	—	—	20	—	.288	.354	.406	.914
Cubs average		**95**	**411**	**69**	**122**	**13**	**11**	**7**	**58**	**26**	**—**	**43**	**3**	**—**	**—**	**22**	**—**	**.297**	**.342**	**.428**	**.876**
Career total		398	1654	280	477	56	32	25	220	162	—	168	7	—	—	99	—	.288	.354	.406	.914
Cubs total		**190**	**822**	**138**	**244**	**25**	**22**	**13**	**116**	**51**	**—**	**85**	**5**	**—**	**—**	**44**	**—**	**.297**	**.342**	**.428**	**.876**

Sullivan, William (Bill)

HEIGHT: — THROWS: — BATS: — BORN: 7/4/1853 HOLYOKE, MASSACHUSETTS DIED: 11/13/1884 HOLYOKE, MASSACHUSETTS POSITIONS PLAYED: OF

YEAR	TEAM	GAMES	AB	RUNS	HITS	2B	3B	HR	RBI	BB	IBB	SO	HBP	SH	SF	SB	CS	BA	OBA	SA	FA
1878	ChN-N	2	6	1	1	0	0	0	0	0	—	0	—	—	—	—	—	.167	.167	.167	1.000
Career average		2	6	1	1	0	0	0	0	0	—	0	—	—	—	—	—	.167	.167	.167	1.000
Cubs average		**2**	**6**	**1**	**1**	**0**	**0**	**0**	**0**	**0**	**—**	**0**	**—**	**—**	**—**	**—**	**—**	**.167**	**.167**	**.167**	**1.000**
Career total		2	6	1	1	0	0	0	0	0	—	0	—	—	—	—	—	.167	.167	.167	1.000
Cubs total		**2**	**6**	**1**	**1**	**0**	**0**	**0**	**0**	**0**	**—**	**0**	**—**	**—**	**—**	**—**	**—**	**.167**	**.167**	**.167**	**1.000**

Summers, John Junior (Champ)

HEIGHT: 6'2" THROWS: RIGHT BATS: LEFT BORN: 6/15/1946 BREMERTON, WASHINGTON POSITIONS PLAYED: C, 1B, 3B, OF

YEAR	TEAM	GAMES	AB	RUNS	HITS	2B	3B	HR	RBI	BB	IBB	SO	HBP	SH	SF	SB	CS	BA	OBA	SA	FA
1974	Oak-A	20	24	2	3	1	0	0	3	1	0	5	0	0	0	0	0	.125	.160	.167	1.000
1975	ChC-N	76	91	14	21	5	1	1	16	10	0	13	1	0	1	0	0	.231	.311	.341	.889
1976	ChC-N	83	126	11	26	2	0	3	13	13	1	31	1	1	1	1	0	.206	.284	.294	.990
1977	Cin-N	59	76	11	13	4	0	3	6	6	1	16	1	0	1	0	0	.171	.238	.342	1.000
1978	Cin-N	13	35	4	9	2	0	1	3	7	1	4	0	0	0	2	1	.257	.381	.400	.933
1979	Cin-N	27	60	10	12	2	1	1	11	13	0	15	1	0	0	0	1	.200	.351	.317	.969
1979	Det-A	90	246	47	77	12	1	20	51	40	4	33	3	0	1	7	6	.313	.414	.614	.991
1980	Det-A	120	347	61	103	19	1	17	60	52	6	52	5	1	3	4	3	.297	.393	.504	.953
1981	Det-A	64	165	16	42	8	0	3	21	19	3	35	3	0	2	1	1	.255	.339	.358	.964
1982	SF-N	70	125	15	31	5	0	4	19	16	0	17	3	1	2	0	1	.248	.342	.384	.925
1983	SF-N	29	22	3	3	0	0	0	3	7	0	8	0	0	1	0	0	.136	.333	.136	1.000
1984	SD-N	47	54	5	10	3	0	1	12	4	1	15	1	0	0	0	0	.185	.254	.296	1.000
Career average		63	125	18	32	6	0	5	20	17	2	22	2	0	1	1	1	.255	.350	.425	.973
Cubs average		**80**	**109**	**13**	**24**	**4**	**1**	**2**	**15**	**12**	**1**	**22**	**1**	**1**	**1**	**1**	**0**	**.217**	**.295**	**.313**	**.975**
Career total		698	1371	199	350	63	4	54	218	188	17	244	19	3	12	15	13	.255	.350	.425	.973
Cubs total		**159**	**217**	**25**	**47**	**7**	**1**	**4**	**29**	**23**	**1**	**44**	**2**	**1**	**2**	**1**	**0**	**.217**	**.295**	**.313**	**.975**

Sunday, William Ashley (Billy *or* Parson *or* The Evangelist)

HEIGHT: 5'10" THROWS: RIGHT BATS: LEFT BORN: 11/9/1862 AMES, IOWA DIED: 11/6/1935 CHICAGO, ILLINOIS POSITIONS PLAYED: P, OF

YEAR	TEAM	GAMES	AB	RUNS	HITS	2B	3B	HR	RBI	BB	IBB	SO	HBP	SH	SF	SB	CS	BA	OBA	SA	FA
1883	ChN-N	14	54	6	13	4	0	0	5	1	—	18	—	—	—	—	—	.241	.255	.315	.647
1884	ChN-N	43	176	25	39	4	1	4	28	4	—	36	—	—	—	—	—	.222	.239	.324	.663
1885	ChN-N	46	172	36	44	3	3	2	20	12	—	33	—	—	—	—	—	.256	.304	.343	.825
1886	ChN-N	28	103	16	25	2	2	0	6	7	—	26	—	—	—	10	—	.243	.291	.301	.914
1887	ChN-N	50	220	41	79	6	6	3	32	21	—	20	1	—	—	34	—	.359	.417	.482	.766
1888	Pit-N	120	505	69	119	14	3	0	15	12	—	36	2	—	—	71	—	.236	.256	.275	.939
1889	Pit-N	81	321	62	77	10	6	2	25	27	—	33	4	—	—	47	—	.240	.307	.327	.946
1890	Pit-N	86	358	58	92	9	2	1	33	32	—	20	5	—	—	56	—	.257	.327	.302	.883
1890	Phi-N	31	119	26	31	3	1	0	6	18	—	7	2	—	—	28	—	.261	.367	.303	.950
Career average		62	254	42	65	7	3	2	21	17	—	29	2	—	—	31	—	.256	.307	.324	.883
Cubs average		**36**	**145**	**25**	**40**	**4**	**2**	**2**	**18**	**9**	**—**	**27**	**0**	**—**	**—**	**9**	**—**	**.276**	**.319**	**.372**	**.772**
Career total		499	2028	339	519	55	24	12	170	134	—	229	14	—	—	246	—	.256	.307	.324	.883
Cubs total		**181**	**725**	**124**	**200**	**19**	**12**	**9**	**91**	**45**	**—**	**133**	**1**	**—**	**—**	**44**	**—**	**.276**	**.319**	**.372**	**.772**

Sundberg, James Howard (Jim)

HEIGHT: 6'0" THROWS: RIGHT BATS: RIGHT BORN: 5/18/1951 GALESBURG, ILLINOIS POSITIONS PLAYED: C, OF

YEAR	TEAM	GAMES	AB	RUNS	HITS	2B	3B	HR	RBI	BB	IBB	SO	HBP	SH	SF	SB	CS	BA	OBA	SA	FA
1974	Tex-A	132	368	45	91	13	3	3	36	62	0	61	0	17	2	2	4	.247	.354	.323	.990
1975	Tex-A	155	472	45	94	9	0	6	36	51	0	77	4	13	0	3	1	.199	.283	.256	.981
1976	Tex-A	140	448	33	102	24	2	3	34	37	0	61	0	9	2	0	0	.228	.285	.310	.991
1977	Tex-A	149	453	61	132	20	3	6	65	53	0	77	2	20	5	2	3	.291	.365	.389	.994
1978	Tex-A	149	518	54	144	23	6	6	58	64	6	70	3	3	4	2	5	.278	.358	.380	.997
1979	Tex-A	150	495	50	136	23	4	5	64	51	5	51	5	5	5	3	3	.275	.345	.368	.995
1980	Tex-A	151	505	59	138	24	1	10	63	64	3	67	1	6	5	2	2	.273	.353	.384	.993
1981	Tex-A	102	339	42	94	17	2	3	28	50	6	48	1	3	3	2	5	.277	.369	.366	.996
1982	Tex-A	139	470	37	118	22	5	10	47	49	2	57	1	9	1	2	6	.251	.322	.383	.991
1983	Tex-A	131	378	30	76	14	0	2	28	35	0	64	2	7	1	0	4	.201	.272	.254	.993
1984	Mil-A	110	348	43	91	19	4	7	43	38	2	63	0	6	3	1	1	.261	.332	.399	.995

(continued)

(continued)

YEAR	TEAM	GAMES	AB	RUNS	HITS	2B	3B	HR	RBI	BB	IBB	SO	HBP	SH	SF	SB	CS	BA	OBA	SA	FA
1985	KC-A	115	367	38	90	12	4	10	35	33	3	67	1	4	2	0	2	.245	.308	.381	.992
1986	KC-A	140	429	41	91	9	1	12	42	57	1	91	0	2	3	1	1	.212	.303	.322	.995
1987	**ChC-N**	**61**	**139**	**9**	**28**	**2**	**0**	**4**	**15**	**19**	**3**	**40**	**2**	**1**	**0**	**0**	**1**	**.201**	**.306**	**.302**	**.994**
1988	**ChC-N**	**24**	**54**	**8**	**13**	**1**	**0**	**2**	**9**	**8**	**0**	**15**	**2**	**3**	**1**	**0**	**0**	**.241**	**.333**	**.370**	**1.000**
1988	Tex-A	38	91	13	26	4	0	4	13	5	0	17	0	3	1	0	0	.286	.323	.462	1.000
1989	Tex-A	76	147	13	29	7	1	2	8	23	0	37	0	7	1	0	0	.197	.304	.299	.992
Career average		123	376	39	93	15	2	6	39	44	2	60	1	7	2	1	2	.248	.327	.348	.993
Cubs average		**43**	**97**	**9**	**21**	**2**	**0**	**3**	**12**	**14**	**2**	**28**	**1**	**2**	**1**	**0**	**0**	**.212**	**.314**	**.321**	**.993**
Career total		1962	6021	621	1493	243	36	95	624	699	31	963	22	118	38	20	37	.248	.327	.348	.993
Cubs total		**85**	**193**	**17**	**41**	**3**	**0**	**6**	**24**	**27**	**3**	**55**	**2**	**4**	**1**	**0**	**0**	**.212**	**.314**	**.321**	**.995**

Sutcliffe, Elmer Ellsworth (Sy)

HEIGHT: 6'2" THROWS: LEFT BATS: LEFT BORN: 4/15/1862 WHEATON, ILLINOIS DIED: 2/13/1893 WHEATON, ILLINOIS
POSITIONS PLAYED: C, 1B, 2B, 3B, SS, OF

YEAR	TEAM	GAMES	AB	RUNS	HITS	2B	3B	HR	RBI	BB	IBB	SO	HBP	SH	SF	SB	CS	BA	OBA	SA	FA
1884	**ChN-N**	**4**	**15**	**4**	**3**	**1**	**0**	**0**	**2**	**2**	—	**4**	—	—	—	—	—	**.200**	**.294**	**.267**	**.976**
1885	**ChN-N**	**11**	**43**	**5**	**8**	**1**	**1**	**0**	**4**	**2**	—	**5**	—	—	—	—	—	**.186**	**.222**	**.256**	**.829**
1885	StL-N	16	49	2	6	1	0	0	4	5	—	10	—	—	—	—	—	.122	.204	.143	.856
1888	Det-N	49	191	17	49	5	3	0	23	5	—	14	0	—	—	—	6	.257	.276	.314	.885
1889	Cle-N	46	161	17	40	3	2	1	21	14	—	6	0	—	—	—	5	.248	.309	.311	.913
1890	Cle-P	99	386	62	127	14	8	2	60	33	—	16	0	—	—	—	10	.329	.382	.422	.877
1891	Was-AA	53	201	29	71	8	3	2	33	17	—	17	2	—	—	—	8	.353	.409	.453	.883
1892	Bal-N	66	276	41	77	10	7	1	27	14	—	15	1	—	—	—	12	.279	.316	.377	.958
Career average		49	189	25	54	6	3	1	25	13	—	12	0	—	—	—	6	.288	.336	.371	.910
Cubs average		**8**	**29**	**5**	**6**	**1**	**1**	**0**	**3**	**2**	—	**5**	—	—	—	—	6	**.190**	**.242**	**.259**	**.883**
Career total		344	1322	177	381	43	24	6	174	92	—	87	3	—	—	—	41	.288	.336	.371	.910
Cubs total		**15**	**58**	**9**	**11**	**2**	**1**	**0**	**6**	**4**	—	**9**	—	—	—	—	—	**.190**	**.242**	**.259**	**.883**

Sweeney, William John (Bill)

HEIGHT: 5'11" THROWS: RIGHT BATS: RIGHT BORN: 3/6/1886 COVINGTON, KENTUCKY DIED: 5/26/1948 CAMBRIDGE, MASSACHUSETTS
POSITIONS PLAYED: 1B, 2B, 3B, SS, OF

YEAR	TEAM	GAMES	AB	RUNS	HITS	2B	3B	HR	RBI	BB	IBB	SO	HBP	SH	SF	SB	CS	BA	OBA	SA	FA
1907	**ChC-N**	**3**	**10**	**1**	**1**	**0**	**0**	**0**	**1**	**1**	—	—	**0**	**1**	—	**1**	—	**.100**	**.182**	**.100**	**.571**
1907	Bos-N	58	191	24	50	2	0	0	18	15	—	—	0	9	—	8	—	.262	.316	.272	.889
1908	Bos-N	127	418	44	102	15	3	0	40	45	—	—	0	18	—	17	—	.244	.317	.294	.929
1909	Bos-N	138	493	44	120	19	3	1	36	37	—	—	0	9	—	25	—	.243	.296	.300	.913
1910	Bos-N	150	499	43	133	22	4	5	46	61	—	28	2	17	—	25	—	.267	.349	.357	.924
1911	Bos-N	137	523	92	164	33	6	3	63	77	—	26	2	11	—	33	—	.314	.404	.417	.944
1912	Bos-N	153	593	84	204	31	13	1	100	68	—	34	5	33	—	27	—	.344	.416	.445	.959
1913	Bos-N	139	502	65	129	17	6	0	47	66	—	50	3	13	—	18	—	.257	.347	.315	.939
1914	**ChC-N**	**134**	**463**	**45**	**101**	**14**	**5**	**1**	**38**	**53**	—	**15**	**0**	**24**	—	**18**	—	**.218**	**.298**	**.276**	**.954**
Career average		130	462	55	126	19	5	1	49	53	—	19	2	17	—	22	—	.272	.349	.344	.937
Cubs average		**69**	**237**	**23**	**51**	**7**	**3**	**1**	**20**	**27**	—	**8**	**0**	**13**	—	**10**	—	**.216**	**.296**	**.273**	**.947**
Career total		1039	3692	442	1004	153	40	11	389	423	—	153	12	135	—	172	—	.272	.349	.344	.937
Cubs total		**137**	**473**	**46**	**102**	**14**	**5**	**1**	**39**	**54**	—	**15**	**0**	**25**	—	**19**	—	**.216**	**.296**	**.273**	**.947**

Swisher, Steven Eugene (Steve)

HEIGHT: 6'2" THROWS: RIGHT BATS: RIGHT BORN: 8/9/1951 PARKERSBURG, WEST VIRGINIA POSITIONS PLAYED: C

YEAR	TEAM	GAMES	AB	RUNS	HITS	2B	3B	HR	RBI	BB	IBB	SO	HBP	SH	SF	SB	CS	BA	OBA	SA	FA
1974	**ChC-N**	**90**	**280**	**21**	**60**	**5**	**0**	**5**	**27**	**37**	**1**	**63**	**2**	**3**	**3**	**0**	**3**	**.214**	**.307**	**.286**	**.987**
1975	**ChC-N**	**93**	**254**	**20**	**54**	**16**	**2**	**1**	**22**	**30**	**7**	**57**	**4**	**6**	**4**	**1**	**0**	**.213**	**.301**	**.303**	**.979**
1976	**ChC-N**	**109**	**377**	**25**	**89**	**13**	**3**	**5**	**42**	**20**	**3**	**82**	**2**	**7**	**5**	**2**	**1**	**.236**	**.275**	**.326**	**.983**
1977	**ChC-N**	**74**	**205**	**21**	**39**	**7**	**0**	**5**	**15**	**9**	**5**	**47**	**2**	**2**	**5**	**2**	**1**	**.190**	**.229**	**.298**	**.976**
1978	StL-N	45	115	11	32	5	1	1	10	8	0	14	1	0	0	1	0	.278	.331	.365	.991
1979	StL-N	38	73	4	11	1	1	1	3	6	0	17	0	0	1	0	0	.151	.213	.233	.974
1980	StL-N	18	24	2	6	1	0	0	2	1	0	7	0	0	1	0	0	.250	.280	.292	.957
1981	SD-N	16	28	2	4	0	0	0	0	2	0	11	0	0	0	0	0	.143	.200	.143	.971
1982	SD-N	26	58	2	10	1	0	2	3	5	0	24	0	1	0	0	0	.172	.238	.293	.981
Career average		57	157	12	34	5	1	2	14	13	2	36	1	2	2	0	0	.216	.279	.303	.982
Cubs average		**92**	**279**	**22**	**61**	**10**	**1**	**4**	**27**	**24**	**4**	**62**	**3**	**5**	**4**	**1**	**1**	**.217**	**.282**	**.306**	**.982**
Career total		509	1414	108	305	49	7	20	124	118	16	322	11	19	15	4	4	.216	.279	.303	.982
Cubs total		**366**	**1116**	**87**	**242**	**41**	**5**	**16**	**106**	**96**	**16**	**249**	**10**	**18**	**14**	**3**	**4**	**.217**	**.282**	**.306**	**.982**

Tabb, Jerry Lynn
HEIGHT: 6'2" THROWS: RIGHT BATS: LEFT BORN: 3/17/1952 ALTUS, OKLAHOMA POSITIONS PLAYED: 1B

YEAR	TEAM	GAMES	AB	RUNS	HITS	2B	3B	HR	RBI	BB	IBB	SO	HBP	SH	SF	SB	CS	BA	OBA	SA	FA
1976	**ChC-N**	**11**	**24**	**2**	**7**	**0**	**0**	**0**	**0**	**3**	**0**	**2**	**0**	**0**	**0**	**0**	**0**	**.292**	**.370**	**.292**	**1.000**
1977	Oak-A	51	144	8	32	3	0	6	19	10	2	26	0	1	2	0	1	.222	.269	.368	.993
1978	Oak-A	12	9	0	1	0	0	0	1	2	1	5	0	0	0	0	0	.111	.273	.111	1.000
Career average		25	59	3	13	1	0	2	7	5	1	11	0	0	1	0	0	.226	.284	.345	.994
Cubs average		**11**	**24**	**2**	**7**	**0**	**0**	**0**	**0**	**3**	**0**	**2**	**0**	**0**	**0**	**0**	**0**	**.292**	**.370**	**.292**	**1.000**
Career total		74	177	10	40	3	0	6	20	15	3	33	0	1	2	0	1	.226	.284	.345	.994
Cubs total		**11**	**24**	**2**	**7**	**0**	**0**	**0**	**0**	**3**	**0**	**2**	**0**	**0**	**0**	**0**	**0**	**.292**	**.370**	**.292**	**1.000**

Tabler, Patrick Sean (Pat)
HEIGHT: 6'3" THROWS: RIGHT BATS: RIGHT BORN: 2/2/1958 HAMILTON, OHIO POSITIONS PLAYED: 1B, 2B, 3B, OF

YEAR	TEAM	GAMES	AB	RUNS	HITS	2B	3B	HR	RBI	BB	IBB	SO	HBP	SH	SF	SB	CS	BA	OBA	SA	FA
1981	**ChC-N**	**35**	**101**	**11**	**19**	**3**	**1**	**1**	**5**	**13**	**0**	**26**	**0**	**3**	**0**	**0**	**1**	**.188**	**.281**	**.267**	**.982**
1982	**ChC-N**	**25**	**85**	**9**	**20**	**4**	**2**	**1**	**7**	**6**	**0**	**20**	**1**	**0**	**2**	**0**	**0**	**.235**	**.287**	**.365**	**.949**
1983	Cle-A	124	430	56	125	23	5	6	65	56	1	63	1	0	5	2	4	.291	.370	.409	.958
1984	Cle-A	144	473	66	137	21	3	10	68	47	2	62	3	0	5	3	1	.290	.354	.410	.989
1985	Cle-A	117	404	47	111	18	3	5	59	27	2	55	2	2	3	0	6	.275	.321	.371	.983
1986	Cle-A	130	473	61	154	29	2	6	48	29	3	75	3	2	1	3	1	.326	.368	.433	.990
1987	Cle-A	151	553	66	170	34	3	11	86	51	6	84	6	3	5	5	2	.307	.369	.439	.984
1988	Cle-A	41	143	16	32	5	1	1	17	23	1	27	1	0	1	1	0	.224	.333	.294	1.000
1988	KC-A	89	301	37	93	17	2	1	49	23	0	41	2	0	4	2	3	.309	.358	.389	.958
1989	KC-A	123	390	36	101	11	1	2	42	37	0	42	2	3	2	0	0	.259	.325	.308	.984
1990	KC-A	75	195	12	53	14	0	1	19	20	2	21	1	0	3	0	2	.272	.338	.359	.982
1990	NYM-N	17	43	6	12	1	1	1	10	3	0	8	1	0	0	0	0	.279	.340	.419	1.000
1991	Tor-A	82	185	20	40	5	1	1	21	29	5	21	1	2	5	0	0	.216	.318	.270	.985
1992	Tor-A	49	135	11	34	5	0	0	16	11	0	14	0	0	1	0	0	.252	.306	.289	1.000
Career average		100	326	38	92	16	2	4	43	31	2	47	2	1	3	1	2	.282	.345	.379	.985
Cubs average		**30**	**93**	**10**	**20**	**4**	**2**	**1**	**6**	**10**	**0**	**23**	**1**	**2**	**1**	**0**	**1**	**.210**	**.284**	**.312**	**.973**
Career total		1202	3911	454	1101	190	25	47	512	375	22	559	24	15	37	16	20	.282	.345	.379	.985
Cubs total		**60**	**186**	**20**	**39**	**7**	**3**	**2**	**12**	**19**	**0**	**46**	**1**	**3**	**2**	**0**	**1**	**.210**	**.284**	**.312**	**.973**

Talbot, Robert Dale (Dale)
HEIGHT: 6'0" THROWS: RIGHT BATS: RIGHT BORN: 6/6/1927 VISALIA, CALIFORNIA POSITIONS PLAYED: OF

YEAR	TEAM	GAMES	AB	RUNS	HITS	2B	3B	HR	RBI	BB	IBB	SO	HBP	SH	SF	SB	CS	BA	OBA	SA	FA
1953	**ChC-N**	**8**	**30**	**5**	**10**	**0**	**1**	**0**	**0**	**0**	**—**	**4**	**0**	**2**	**—**	**1**	**0**	**.333**	**.333**	**.400**	**1.000**
1954	**ChC-N**	**114**	**403**	**45**	**97**	**15**	**4**	**1**	**19**	**16**	**—**	**25**	**3**	**5**	**1**	**3**	**6**	**.241**	**.274**	**.305**	**.985**
Career average		61	217	25	54	8	3	1	10	8	—	15	2	4	1	2	3	.247	.278	.312	.986
Cubs average		**61**	**217**	**25**	**54**	**8**	**3**	**1**	**10**	**8**	**—**	**15**	**2**	**4**	**1**	**2**	**3**	**.247**	**.278**	**.312**	**.986**
Career total		122	433	50	107	15	5	1	19	16	—	29	3	7	1	4	6	.247	.278	.312	.986
Cubs total		**122**	**433**	**50**	**107**	**15**	**5**	**1**	**19**	**16**	**—**	**29**	**3**	**7**	**1**	**4**	**6**	**.247**	**.278**	**.312**	**.986**

Tanner, Charles William (Chuck)
HEIGHT: 6'0" THROWS: LEFT BATS: LEFT BORN: 7/4/1929 NEW CASTLE, PENNSYLVANIA POSITIONS PLAYED: OF

YEAR	TEAM	GAMES	AB	RUNS	HITS	2B	3B	HR	RBI	BB	IBB	SO	HBP	SH	SF	SB	CS	BA	OBA	SA	FA
1955	Mil-N	97	243	27	60	9	3	6	27	27	3	32	0	2	3	0	0	.247	.319	.383	.981
1956	Mil-N	60	63	6	15	2	0	1	4	10	2	10	0	0	0	0	0	.238	.342	.317	.800
1957	Mil-N	22	69	5	17	3	0	2	6	5	0	4	0	0	0	0	0	.246	.297	.377	1.000
1957	**ChC-N**	**95**	**318**	**42**	**91**	**16**	**2**	**7**	**42**	**23**	**2**	**20**	**2**	**5**	**2**	**0**	**2**	**.286**	**.336**	**.415**	**.988**
1958	**ChC-N**	**73**	**103**	**10**	**27**	**6**	**0**	**4**	**17**	**9**	**2**	**10**	**0**	**0**	**0**	**1**	**0**	**.262**	**.321**	**.437**	**.955**
1959	Cle-A	14	48	6	12	2	0	1	5	2	0	9	0	0	0	0	0	.250	.280	.354	1.000
1960	Cle-A	21	25	2	7	1	0	0	4	4	0	6	0	0	1	1	0	.280	.367	.320	1.000
1961	LAA-A	7	8	0	1	0	0	0	0	2	0	2	0	0	0	0	0	.125	.300	.125	—
1962	LAA-A	7	8	0	1	0	0	0	0	0	0	0	0	0	0	0	0	.125	.125	.125	—
Career average		50	111	12	29	5	1	3	13	10	1	12	0	1	1	0	0	.261	.323	.388	.983
Cubs average		**84**	**211**	**26**	**59**	**11**	**1**	**6**	**30**	**16**	**2**	**15**	**1**	**3**	**1**	**1**	**1**	**.280**	**.333**	**.420**	**.984**
Career total		396	885	98	231	39	5	21	105	82	9	93	2	7	6	2	2	.261	.323	.388	.983
Cubs total		**168**	**421**	**52**	**118**	**22**	**2**	**11**	**59**	**32**	**4**	**30**	**2**	**5**	**2**	**1**	**2**	**.280**	**.333**	**.420**	**.984**

Tappe, Elvin Walter (El)

HEIGHT: 5'11"   THROWS: RIGHT   BATS: RIGHT   BORN: 5/21/1927 QUINCY, ILLINOIS   DIED: 10/10/1998 QUINCY, ILLINOIS   POSITIONS PLAYED: C

YEAR	TEAM	GAMES	AB	RUNS	HITS	2B	3B	HR	RBI	BB	IBB	SO	HBP	SH	SF	SB	CS	BA	OBA	SA	FA
1954	ChC-N	46	119	5	22	3	0	0	4	10	—	9	0	2	1	0	0	.185	.246	.210	.986
1955	ChC-N	2	0	0	0	0	0	0	0	0	0	0	0	0	0	0	0	—	—	—	1.000
1956	ChC-N	3	1	0	0	0	0	0	0	0	0	0	0	0	0	0	0	.000	.000	.000	1.000
1958	ChC-N	17	28	2	6	0	0	0	4	3	2	1	0	1	0	0	0	.214	.290	.214	.962
1960	ChC-N	51	103	11	24	7	0	0	3	11	1	12	1	6	0	0	1	.233	.313	.301	.992
1962	ChC-N	26	53	3	11	0	0	0	6	4	0	3	2	1	0	0	0	.208	.288	.208	1.000
Career average		24	51	4	11	2	0	0	3	5	1	4	1	2	0	0	0	.207	.282	.240	.989
Cubs average		**24**	**51**	**4**	**11**	**2**	**0**	**0**	**3**	**5**	**1**	**4**	**1**	**2**	**0**	**0**	**0**	**.207**	**.282**	**.240**	**.989**
Career total		145	304	21	63	10	0	0	17	29	3	25	3	10	1	0	1	.207	.282	.240	.989
Cubs total		**145**	**304**	**21**	**63**	**10**	**0**	**0**	**17**	**29**	**3**	**25**	**3**	**10**	**1**	**0**	**1**	**.207**	**.282**	**.240**	**.989**

Tappe, Theodore Nash (Ted)

HEIGHT: 6'3"   THROWS: RIGHT   BATS: LEFT   BORN: 2/2/1931 SEATTLE, WASHINGTON   POSITIONS PLAYED: OF

YEAR	TEAM	GAMES	AB	RUNS	HITS	2B	3B	HR	RBI	BB	IBB	SO	HBP	SH	SF	SB	CS	BA	OBA	SA	FA
1950	Cin-N	7	5	1	1	0	0	1	1	1	—	1	0	0	—	0	—	.200	.333	.800	—
1951	Cin-N	4	3	0	1	0	0	0	0	0	—	0	0	0	—	0	—	.333	.333	.333	—
1955	**ChC-N**	**23**	**50**	**12**	**13**	**2**	**0**	**4**	**10**	**11**	**3**	**11**	**2**	**0**	**0**	**0**	**0**	**.260**	**.413**	**.540**	**1.000**
Career average		11	19	4	5	1	0	2	4	4	1	4	1	0	0	0	0	.259	.403	.552	1.000
Cubs average		**23**	**50**	**12**	**13**	**2**	**0**	**4**	**10**	**11**	**3**	**11**	**2**	**0**	**0**	**0**	**0**	**.260**	**.413**	**.540**	**1.000**
Career total		34	58	13	15	2	0	5	11	12	3	12	2	0	0	0	0	.259	.403	.552	1.000
Cubs total		**23**	**50**	**12**	**13**	**2**	**0**	**4**	**10**	**11**	**3**	**11**	**2**	**0**	**0**	**0**	**0**	**.260**	**.413**	**.540**	**1.000**

Tate, Henry Bennett (Bennie)

HEIGHT: 5'8"   THROWS: RIGHT   BATS: LEFT   BORN: 12/3/1901 WHITWELL, TENNESSEE   DIED: 10/27/1973 WEST FRANKFORT, ILLINOIS   POSITIONS PLAYED: C

YEAR	TEAM	GAMES	AB	RUNS	HITS	2B	3B	HR	RBI	BB	IBB	SO	HBP	SH	SF	SB	CS	BA	OBA	SA	FA
1924	Was-A	21	43	2	13	2	0	0	7	1	—	2	0	1	—	0	0	.302	.318	.349	.841
1925	Was-A	16	27	0	13	3	0	0	7	2	—	2	0	1	—	0	0	.481	.517	.593	.955
1926	Was-A	59	142	17	38	5	2	1	13	15	—	1	0	2	—	0	0	.268	.338	.352	.960
1927	Was-A	61	131	12	41	5	1	1	24	8	—	4	1	5	—	0	3	.313	.357	.389	.977
1928	Was-A	57	122	10	30	6	0	0	15	10	—	4	0	3	—	0	4	.246	.303	.295	.985
1929	Was-A	81	265	26	78	12	3	0	30	16	—	8	0	8	—	2	5	.294	.335	.362	.971
1930	Was-A	14	20	1	5	0	0	0	2	0	—	1	0	0	—	0	0	.250	.250	.250	.933
1930	CWS-A	72	230	26	73	11	2	0	27	18	—	10	0	5	—	2	1	.317	.367	.383	.981
1931	CWS-A	89	273	27	73	12	3	0	22	26	—	10	0	6	—	1	1	.267	.331	.333	.987
1932	CWS-A	4	10	1	1	0	0	0	0	1	—	0	0	0	—	0	0	.100	.182	.100	1.000
1932	Bos-A	81	273	21	67	12	5	2	26	20	—	6	0	3	—	0	1	.245	.297	.348	.974
1934	**ChC-N**	**11**	**24**	**1**	**3**	**0**	**0**	**0**	**0**	**1**	**—**	**3**	**0**	**0**	**—**	**0**	**—**	**.125**	**.160**	**.125**	**1.000**
Career average		57	156	14	44	7	2	0	17	12	—	5	0	3	—	1	2	.279	.330	.351	.974
Cubs average		**11**	**24**	**1**	**3**	**0**	**0**	**0**	**0**	**1**	**—**	**3**	**0**	**0**	**—**	**0**	**0**	**.125**	**.160**	**.125**	**1.000**
Career total		566	1560	144	435	68	16	4	173	118	—	51	1	34	—	5	15	.279	.330	.351	.974
Cubs total		**11**	**24**	**1**	**3**	**0**	**0**	**0**	**0**	**1**	**—**	**3**	**0**	**0**	**—**	**0**	**0**	**.125**	**.160**	**.125**	**1.000**

Taylor, Antonio Nemesio (Tony)

HEIGHT: 5'9"   THROWS: RIGHT   BATS: RIGHT   BORN: 12/19/1935 CENTRAL ALARA, CUBA   POSITIONS PLAYED: 1B, 2B, 3B, SS, OF

YEAR	TEAM	GAMES	AB	RUNS	HITS	2B	3B	HR	RBI	BB	IBB	SO	HBP	SH	SF	SB	CS	BA	OBA	SA	FA
1958	**ChC-N**	**140**	**497**	**63**	**117**	**15**	**3**	**6**	**27**	**40**	**0**	**93**	**7**	**7**	**4**	**21**	**6**	**.235**	**.299**	**.314**	**.968**
1959	**ChC-N**	**150**	**624**	**96**	**175**	**30**	**8**	**8**	**38**	**45**	**0**	**86**	**6**	**6**	**7**	**23**	**9**	**.280**	**.331**	**.393**	**.970**
1960	**ChC-N**	**19**	**76**	**14**	**20**	**3**	**3**	**1**	**9**	**8**	**0**	**12**	**1**	**3**	**1**	**2**	**0**	**.263**	**.337**	**.421**	**.977**
1960	Phi-N	127	505	66	145	22	4	4	35	33	2	86	2	6	5	24	11	.287	.330	.370	.969
1961	Phi-N	106	400	47	100	17	3	2	26	29	4	59	2	6	0	11	5	.250	.304	.323	.981
1962	Phi-N	152	625	87	162	21	5	7	43	68	4	82	5	3	1	20	5	.259	.336	.342	.972
1963	Phi-N	157	640	102	180	20	10	5	49	42	1	99	7	7	4	23	9	.281	.330	.367	.987
1964	Phi-N	154	570	62	143	13	6	4	46	46	8	74	13	5	2	13	7	.251	.320	.316	.977
1965	Phi-N	106	323	41	74	14	3	3	27	22	0	58	12	5	1	5	4	.229	.302	.319	.958
1966	Phi-N	125	434	47	105	14	8	5	40	31	0	56	1	7	0	8	4	.242	.294	.346	.981

(continued)

(Taylor, A.N., continued)

YEAR	TEAM	GAMES	AB	RUNS	HITS	2B	3B	HR	RBI	BB	IBB	SO	HBP	SH	SF	SB	CS	BA	OBA	SA	FA
1967	Phi-N	132	462	55	110	16	6	2	34	42	8	74	5	11	0	10	9	.238	.308	.312	.987
1968	Phi-N	145	547	59	137	20	2	3	38	39	7	60	3	6	3	22	5	.250	.302	.311	.965
1969	Phi-N	138	557	68	146	24	5	3	30	42	1	62	4	3	2	19	10	.262	.317	.339	.974
1970	Phi-N	124	439	74	132	26	9	9	55	50	9	67	3	1	2	9	11	.301	.374	.462	.989
1971	Phi-N	36	107	9	25	2	1	1	5	9	2	10	0	1	1	2	2	.234	.291	.299	.992
1971	Det-A	55	181	27	52	10	2	3	19	12	1	11	1	2	0	5	1	.287	.335	.414	.996
1972	Det-A	78	228	33	69	12	4	1	20	14	0	34	2	1	2	5	1	.303	.346	.404	.969
1973	Det-A	84	275	35	63	9	3	5	24	17	0	29	1	8	1	9	5	.229	.276	.338	.988
1974	Phi-N	62	64	5	21	4	0	2	13	6	0	6	1	1	1	0	0	.328	.389	.484	1.000
1975	Phi-N	79	103	13	25	5	1	1	17	17	2	18	1	1	2	3	3	.243	.350	.340	.932
1976	Phi-N	26	23	2	6	1	0	0	3	1	0	7	1	1	0	0	0	.261	.320	.304	1.000
Career average		116	404	53	106	16	5	4	31	32	3	57	4	5	2	12	6	.261	.321	.352	.976
Cubs average		**103**	**399**	**58**	**104**	**16**	**5**	**5**	**25**	**31**	**0**	**64**	**5**	**5**	**4**	**15**	**5**	**.261**	**.318**	**.362**	**.969**
Career total		2195	7680	1005	2007	298	86	75	598	613	49	1083	78	91	39	234	111	.261	.321	.352	.976
Cubs total		**309**	**1197**	**173**	**312**	**48**	**14**	**15**	**74**	**93**	**0**	**191**	**14**	**16**	**12**	**46**	**15**	**.261**	**.318**	**.362**	**.969**

Taylor, C.L. (Chink)
HEIGHT: 5'9" THROWS: RIGHT BATS: RIGHT BORN: 2/9/1898 BURNET, TEXAS DIED: 7/7/1980 TEMPLE, TEXAS POSITIONS PLAYED: OF

YEAR	TEAM	GAMES	AB	RUNS	HITS	2B	3B	HR	RBI	BB	IBB	SO	HBP	SH	SF	SB	CS	BA	OBA	SA	FA
1925	ChC-N	8	6	2	0	0	0	0	0	0	—	0	0	0	—	0	0	.000	.000	.000	1.000
Career average		8	6	2	0	0	0	0	0	0	—	0	0	0	—	0	0	.000	.000	.000	1.000
Cubs average		**8**	**6**	**2**	**0**	**0**	**0**	**0**	**0**	**0**	**—**	**0**	**0**	**0**	**—**	**0**	**0**	**.000**	**.000**	**.000**	**1.000**
Career total		8	6	2	0	0	0	0	0	0	—	0	0	0	—	0	0	.000	.000	.000	1.000
Cubs total		**8**	**6**	**2**	**0**	**0**	**0**	**0**	**0**	**0**	**—**	**0**	**0**	**0**	**—**	**0**	**0**	**.000**	**.000**	**.000**	**1.000**

Taylor, Daniel Turney (Danny)
HEIGHT: 5'10" THROWS: RIGHT BATS: RIGHT BORN: 12/23/1900 LASH, PENNSYLVANIA DIED: 10/11/1972 LATROBE, PENNSYLVANIA POSITIONS PLAYED: OF

YEAR	TEAM	GAMES	AB	RUNS	HITS	2B	3B	HR	RBI	BB	IBB	SO	HBP	SH	SF	SB	CS	BA	OBA	SA	FA
1926	Was-A	21	50	10	15	0	1	1	5	5	—	7	0	0	—	1	2	.300	.364	.400	1.000
1929	**ChC-N**	**2**	**3**	**0**	**0**	**0**	**0**	**0**	**0**	**1**	**—**	**1**	**0**	**0**	**—**	**0**	**—**	**.000**	**.250**	**.000**	**1.000**
1930	**ChC-N**	**74**	**219**	**43**	**62**	**14**	**3**	**2**	**37**	**27**	**—**	**34**	**1**	**7**	**—**	**6**	**—**	**.283**	**.364**	**.402**	**.971**
1931	**ChC-N**	**88**	**270**	**48**	**81**	**13**	**6**	**5**	**41**	**31**	**—**	**46**	**0**	**2**	**—**	**4**	**—**	**.300**	**.372**	**.448**	**.989**
1932	**ChC-N**	**6**	**22**	**3**	**5**	**2**	**0**	**0**	**3**	**3**	**—**	**1**	**0**	**0**	**—**	**1**	**—**	**.227**	**.320**	**.318**	**.900**
1932	Bro-N	105	395	84	128	22	7	11	48	33	—	41	1	6	—	13	—	.324	.378	.499	.989
1933	Bro-N	103	358	75	102	21	9	9	40	47	—	45	0	5	—	11	—	.285	.368	.469	.977
1934	Bro-N	120	405	62	121	24	6	7	57	63	—	47	2	6	—	12	—	.299	.396	.440	.975
1935	Bro-N	112	352	51	102	19	5	7	59	46	—	32	0	6	—	6	—	.290	.372	.432	.970
1936	Bro-N	43	116	12	34	6	0	2	15	11	—	14	1	0	—	2	—	.293	.359	.397	.981
Career average		75	243	43	72	13	4	5	34	30	—	30	1	4	—	6	0	.297	.374	.446	.979
Cubs average		**43**	**129**	**24**	**37**	**7**	**2**	**2**	**20**	**16**	**—**	**21**	**0**	**2**	**—**	**3**	**0**	**.288**	**.366**	**.420**	**.977**
Career total		674	2190	388	650	121	37	44	305	267	—	268	5	32	—	56	2	.297	.374	.446	.979
Cubs total		**170**	**514**	**94**	**148**	**29**	**9**	**7**	**81**	**62**	**—**	**82**	**1**	**9**	**—**	**11**	**0**	**.288**	**.366**	**.420**	**.977**

Taylor, Harry Warren
HEIGHT: 6'1" THROWS: LEFT BATS: LEFT BORN: 12/26/1907 MCKEESPORT, PENNSYLVANIA DIED: 4/27/1969 TOLEDO, OHIO POSITIONS PLAYED: 1B

YEAR	TEAM	GAMES	AB	RUNS	HITS	2B	3B	HR	RBI	BB	IBB	SO	HBP	SH	SF	SB	CS	BA	OBA	SA	FA
1932	ChC-N	10	8	1	1	0	0	0	0	1	—	1	0	0	—	0	—	.125	.222	.125	1.000
Career average		10	8	1	1	0	0	0	0	1	—	1	0	0	—	0	—	.125	.222	.125	1.000
Cubs average		**10**	**8**	**1**	**1**	**0**	**0**	**0**	**0**	**1**	**—**	**1**	**0**	**0**	**—**	**0**	**—**	**.125**	**.222**	**.125**	**1.000**
Career total		10	8	1	1	0	0	0	0	1	—	1	0	0	—	0	—	.125	.222	.125	1.000
Cubs total		**10**	**8**	**1**	**1**	**0**	**0**	**0**	**0**	**1**	**—**	**1**	**0**	**0**	**—**	**0**	**—**	**.125**	**.222**	**.125**	**1.000**

Taylor, James Wren (Zack)

HEIGHT: 5'11"   THROWS: RIGHT   BATS: RIGHT   BORN: 7/27/1898 YULEE, FLORIDA   DIED: 9/19/1974 ORLANDO, FLORIDA   POSITIONS PLAYED: C

YEAR	TEAM	GAMES	AB	RUNS	HITS	2B	3B	HR	RBI	BB	IBB	SO	HBP	SH	SF	SB	CS	BA	OBA	SA	FA
1920	Bro-N	9	13	3	5	2	0	0	5	0	—	2	0	0	—	0	1	.385	.385	.538	.882
1921	Bro-N	30	102	6	20	0	2	0	8	1	—	8	1	4	—	2	0	.196	.212	.235	.965
1922	Bro-N	7	14	0	3	0	0	0	2	1	—	1	0	1	—	0	0	.214	.267	.214	.950
1923	Bro-N	96	337	29	97	11	6	0	46	9	—	13	3	4	—	2	5	.288	.312	.356	.967
1924	Bro-N	99	345	36	100	9	4	1	39	14	—	14	1	8	—	0	1	.290	.319	.348	.988
1925	Bro-N	109	352	33	109	16	4	3	44	17	—	19	1	4	—	0	0	.310	.343	.403	.959
1926	Bos-N	125	432	36	110	22	3	0	42	28	—	27	2	8	—	1	—	.255	.303	.319	.985
1927	Bos-N	30	96	8	23	2	1	1	14	8	—	5	0	1	—	0	—	.240	.298	.313	.988
1927	NYG-N	83	258	18	60	7	3	0	21	17	—	20	1	7	—	2	—	.233	.283	.283	.972
1928	Bos-N	125	399	36	100	15	1	2	30	33	—	29	3	7	—	2	—	.251	.313	.308	.985
1929	Bos-N	34	101	8	25	7	0	0	10	7	—	9	1	5	—	0	—	.248	.303	.317	.965
1929	**ChC-N**	**64**	**215**	**29**	**59**	**16**	**3**	**1**	**31**	**19**	**—**	**18**	**1**	**3**	**—**	**0**	**—**	**.274**	**.336**	**.391**	**.979**
1930	**ChC-N**	**32**	**95**	**12**	**22**	**2**	**1**	**1**	**11**	**2**	**—**	**12**	**1**	**4**	**—**	**0**	**—**	**.232**	**.255**	**.305**	**1.000**
1931	**ChC-N**	**8**	**4**	**0**	**1**	**0**	**0**	**0**	**0**	**2**	**—**	**1**	**0**	**2**	**—**	**0**	**—**	**.250**	**.500**	**.250**	**1.000**
1932	**ChC-N**	**21**	**30**	**2**	**6**	**1**	**0**	**0**	**3**	**1**	**—**	**4**	**0**	**1**	**—**	**0**	**—**	**.200**	**.226**	**.233**	**1.000**
1933	**ChC-N**	**16**	**11**	**0**	**0**	**0**	**0**	**0**	**0**	**0**	**—**	**1**	**0**	**0**	**—**	**0**	**—**	**.000**	**.000**	**.000**	**1.000**
1934	NYY-A	4	7	0	1	0	0	0	0	0	—	1	0	0	—	0	0	.143	.143	.143	1.000
1935	Bro-N	26	54	2	7	3	0	0	5	2	—	8	1	0	—	0	—	.130	.175	.185	.970
Career average		57	179	16	47	7	2	1	19	10	—	12	1	4	—	1	0	.261	.304	.329	.977
Cubs average		**28**	**71**	**9**	**18**	**4**	**1**	**0**	**9**	**5**	**—**	**7**	**0**	**2**	**—**	**0**	**0**	**.248**	**.299**	**.341**	**.987**
Career total		918	2865	258	748	113	28	9	311	161	—	192	16	59	—	9	7	.261	.304	.329	.977
Cubs total		**141**	**355**	**43**	**88**	**19**	**4**	**2**	**45**	**24**	**—**	**36**	**2**	**10**	**—**	**0**	**0**	**.248**	**.299**	**.341**	**.987**

Taylor, Samuel Douglas (Sammy)

HEIGHT: 6'2"   THROWS: RIGHT   BATS: LEFT   BORN: 2/27/1933 WOODRUFF, SOUTH CAROLINA   POSITIONS PLAYED: C

YEAR	TEAM	GAMES	AB	RUNS	HITS	2B	3B	HR	RBI	BB	IBB	SO	HBP	SH	SF	SB	CS	BA	OBA	SA	FA
1958	**ChC-N**	**96**	**301**	**30**	**78**	**12**	**2**	**6**	**36**	**27**	**4**	**46**	**0**	**0**	**1**	**2**	**1**	**.259**	**.319**	**.372**	**.988**
1959	**ChC-N**	**110**	**353**	**41**	**95**	**13**	**2**	**13**	**43**	**35**	**13**	**47**	**1**	**0**	**1**	**1**	**0**	**.269**	**.336**	**.428**	**.982**
1960	**ChC-N**	**74**	**150**	**14**	**31**	**9**	**0**	**3**	**17**	**6**	**0**	**18**	**1**	**1**	**1**	**0**	**1**	**.207**	**.241**	**.327**	**.978**
1961	**ChC-N**	**89**	**235**	**26**	**56**	**8**	**2**	**8**	**23**	**23**	**7**	**39**	**4**	**1**	**1**	**0**	**0**	**.238**	**.316**	**.391**	**.989**
1962	**ChC-N**	**7**	**15**	**0**	**2**	**1**	**0**	**0**	**1**	**3**	**1**	**3**	**0**	**0**	**0**	**0**	**0**	**.133**	**.278**	**.200**	**1.000**
1962	NYM-N	68	158	12	35	4	2	3	20	23	1	17	2	0	3	0	0	.222	.323	.329	.991
1963	NYM-N	22	35	3	9	0	1	0	6	5	1	7	0	0	1	0	0	.257	.341	.314	1.000
1963	Cin-N	3	6	0	0	0	0	0	0	0	0	2	0	0	0	0	0	.000	.000	.000	.833
1963	Cle-A	4	10	1	3	0	0	0	1	0	0	2	0	0	0	0	0	.300	.300	.300	1.000
Career average		79	211	21	52	8	2	6	25	20	5	30	1	0	1	1	0	.245	.313	.375	.986
Cubs average		**75**	**211**	**22**	**52**	**9**	**1**	**6**	**24**	**19**	**5**	**31**	**1**	**0**	**1**	**1**	**0**	**.249**	**.313**	**.386**	**.985**
Career total		473	1263	127	309	47	9	33	147	122	27	181	8	2	8	3	2	.245	.313	.375	.986
Cubs total		**376**	**1054**	**111**	**262**	**43**	**6**	**30**	**120**	**94**	**25**	**153**	**6**	**2**	**4**	**3**	**2**	**.249**	**.313**	**.386**	**.985**

Tebeau, Oliver Wendell (Patsy)

HEIGHT: 5'8"   THROWS: RIGHT   BATS: RIGHT   BORN: 12/5/1864 ST. LOUIS, MISSOURI   DIED: 5/15/1918 ST. LOUIS, MISSOURI
POSITIONS PLAYED: P, 1B, 2B, 3B, SS, OF

YEAR	TEAM	GAMES	AB	RUNS	HITS	2B	3B	HR	RBI	BB	IBB	SO	HBP	SH	SF	SB	CS	BA	OBA	SA	FA
1887	**ChN-N**	**20**	**72**	**8**	**15**	**3**	**0**	**0**	**10**	**4**	**—**	**4**	**0**	**—**	**—**	**8**	**—**	**.208**	**.250**	**.250**	**.855**
1889	Cle-N	136	521	72	147	20	6	8	76	37	—	41	2	—	—	26	—	.282	.332	.390	.897
1890	Cle-P	110	450	86	134	26	6	5	74	34	—	20	3	—	—	14	—	.298	.351	.416	.872
1891	Cle-N	61	249	38	65	8	3	1	41	16	—	13	3	—	—	12	—	.261	.313	.329	.884
1892	Cle-N	86	340	47	83	13	3	2	49	23	—	34	8	—	—	6	—	.244	.307	.318	.913
1893	Cle-N	116	486	90	160	32	8	2	102	32	—	11	4	—	—	19	—	.329	.375	.440	.951
1894	Cle-N	125	523	82	158	23	7	3	89	35	—	35	1	9	—	30	—	.302	.347	.390	.974
1895	Cle-N	63	264	50	84	13	2	2	52	16	—	18	2	4	—	8	—	.318	.362	.405	.987
1896	Cle-N	132	543	56	146	22	6	2	94	21	—	22	3	14	—	20	—	.269	.300	.343	.982
1897	Cle-N	109	412	62	110	15	9	0	59	30	—	—	4	9	—	11	—	.267	.323	.347	.989
1898	Cle-N	131	477	53	123	11	4	1	63	53	—	—	7	9	—	5	—	.258	.341	.304	.976
1899	StL-N	77	281	27	69	10	3	1	26	18	—	—	5	1	—	5	—	.246	.303	.313	.971
1900	StL-N	1	4	0	0	0	0	0	0	0	—	—	0	0	—	0	—	.000	.000	.000	.700
Career average		90	356	52	100	15	4	2	57	25	—	15	3	4	—	13	—	.280	.332	.365	.959
Cubs average		**20**	**72**	**8**	**15**	**3**	**0**	**0**	**10**	**4**	**—**	**4**	**0**	**—**	**—**	**8**	**—**	**.208**	**.250**	**.250**	**.855**
Career total		1167	4622	671	1294	196	57	27	735	319	—	198	42	46	—	164	—	.280	.332	.365	.959
Cubs total		**20**	**72**	**8**	**15**	**3**	**0**	**0**	**10**	**4**	**—**	**4**	**0**	**—**	**—**	**8**	**—**	**.208**	**.250**	**.250**	**.855**

Terry, Zebulon Alexander (Zeb)
HEIGHT: 5'8"   THROWS: RIGHT   BATS: RIGHT   BORN: 6/17/1891 DENISON, TEXAS   DIED: 3/14/1988 LOS ANGELES, CALIFORNIA
POSITIONS PLAYED: 2B, 3B, SS

YEAR	TEAM	GAMES	AB	RUNS	HITS	2B	3B	HR	RBI	BB	IBB	SO	HBP	SH	SF	SB	CS	BA	OBA	SA	FA
1916	CWS-A	94	269	20	51	8	4	0	17	33	—	36	6	16	—	4	—	.190	.292	.249	.935
1917	CWS-A	2	1	0	0	0	0	0	0	2	—	0	0	0	—	0	—	.000	.667	.000	1.000
1918	Bos-N	28	105	17	32	2	2	0	8	8	—	14	1	4	—	1	—	.305	.360	.362	.977
1919	Pit-N	129	472	46	107	12	6	0	27	31	—	26	4	15	—	12	—	.227	.280	.278	.960
1920	**ChC-N**	**133**	**496**	**56**	**139**	**26**	**9**	**0**	**52**	**44**	—	**22**	**2**	**33**	—	**12**	**16**	**.280**	**.341**	**.369**	**.968**
1921	**ChC-N**	**123**	**488**	**59**	**134**	**18**	**1**	**2**	**45**	**27**	—	**19**	**4**	**34**	—	**1**	**13**	**.275**	**.318**	**.328**	**.972**
1922	**ChC-N**	**131**	**496**	**56**	**142**	**24**	**2**	**0**	**67**	**34**	—	**16**	**2**	**39**	—	**2**	**11**	**.286**	**.335**	**.343**	**.964**
Career average		91	332	36	86	13	3	0	31	26	—	19	3	20	—	5	6	.260	.318	.322	.963
Cubs average		**129**	**493**	**57**	**138**	**23**	**4**	**1**	**55**	**35**	—	**19**	**3**	**35**	—	**5**	**13**	**.280**	**.331**	**.347**	**.968**
Career total		640	2327	254	605	90	24	2	216	179	—	133	19	141	—	32	40	.260	.318	.322	.963
Cubs total		**387**	**1480**	**171**	**415**	**68**	**12**	**2**	**164**	**105**	—	**57**	**8**	**106**	—	**15**	**40**	**.280**	**.331**	**.347**	**.968**

Terwilliger, Willard Wayne (Wayne *or* Twig)
HEIGHT: 5'11"   THROWS: RIGHT   BATS: RIGHT   BORN: 6/27/1925 CLARE, MICHIGAN   POSITIONS PLAYED: 1B, 2B, 3B, SS, OF

YEAR	TEAM	GAMES	AB	RUNS	HITS	2B	3B	HR	RBI	BB	IBB	SO	HBP	SH	SF	SB	CS	BA	OBA	SA	FA
1949	**ChC-N**	**36**	**112**	**11**	**25**	**2**	**1**	**2**	**10**	**16**	—	**22**	**1**	**1**	—	**0**	—	**.223**	**.326**	**.313**	**.978**
1950	**ChC-N**	**133**	**480**	**63**	**116**	**22**	**3**	**10**	**32**	**43**	—	**63**	**5**	**9**	—	**13**	—	**.242**	**.311**	**.363**	**.967**
1951	**ChC-N**	**50**	**192**	**26**	**41**	**6**	**0**	**0**	**10**	**29**	—	**21**	**0**	**2**	—	**3**	**1**	**.214**	**.317**	**.245**	**.969**
1951	Bro-N	37	50	11	14	1	0	0	4	8	—	7	1	0	—	1	0	.280	.390	.300	.950
1953	Was-A	134	464	62	117	24	4	4	46	64	—	65	0	13	—	7	4	.252	.343	.347	.982
1954	Was-A	106	337	42	70	10	1	3	24	32	—	40	3	9	1	3	3	.208	.282	.270	.969
1955	NYG-N	80	257	29	66	16	1	1	18	36	1	42	1	5	2	2	4	.257	.348	.339	.985
1956	NYG-N	14	18	0	4	1	0	0	0	0	0	5	0	0	0	0	0	.222	.222	.278	.958
1959	KCA-A	74	180	27	48	11	0	2	18	19	0	31	0	4	1	2	2	.267	.335	.361	.972
1960	KCA-A	2	1	0	0	0	0	0	0	0	0	0	0	0	0	0	0	.000	.000	.000	1.000
Career average		74	232	30	56	10	1	2	18	27	0	33	1	5	0	3	2	.240	.323	.325	.974
Cubs average		**73**	**261**	**33**	**61**	**10**	**1**	**4**	**17**	**29**	—	**35**	**2**	**4**	—	**5**	**0**	**.232**	**.314**	**.327**	**.969**
Career total		666	2091	271	501	93	10	22	162	247	1	296	11	43	4	31	14	.240	.323	.325	.974
Cubs total		**219**	**784**	**100**	**182**	**30**	**4**	**12**	**52**	**88**	—	**106**	**6**	**12**	—	**16**	**1**	**.232**	**.314**	**.327**	**.969**

Thacker, Morris Benton (Moe)
HEIGHT: 6'3"   THROWS: RIGHT   BATS: RIGHT   BORN: 5/21/1934 LOUISVILLE, KENTUCKY   DIED: 11/13/1997 LOUISVILLE, KENTUCKY   POSITIONS PLAYED: C

YEAR	TEAM	GAMES	AB	RUNS	HITS	2B	3B	HR	RBI	BB	IBB	SO	HBP	SH	SF	SB	CS	BA	OBA	SA	FA
1958	ChC-N	11	24	4	6	1	0	2	3	1	1	7	0	0	1	0	0	.250	.269	.542	.952
1960	ChC-N	54	90	5	14	1	0	0	6	14	5	20	0	0	0	1	1	.156	.269	.167	.980
1961	ChC-N	25	35	3	6	0	0	0	2	11	1	11	1	0	0	0	0	.171	.383	.171	.973
1962	ChC-N	65	107	8	20	5	0	0	9	14	1	40	1	0	0	0	1	.187	.287	.234	.996
1963	StL-N	3	4	0	0	0	0	0	0	0	0	3	0	0	0	0	0	.000	.000	.000	1.000
Career average		32	52	4	9	1	0	0	4	8	2	16	0	0	0	0	0	.177	.290	.227	.984
Cubs average		**39**	**64**	**5**	**12**	**2**	**0**	**1**	**5**	**10**	**2**	**20**	**1**	**0**	**0**	**0**	**1**	**.180**	**.294**	**.230**	**.984**
Career total		158	260	20	46	7	0	2	20	40	8	81	2	0	1	1	2	.177	.290	.227	.984
Cubs total		**155**	**256**	**20**	**46**	**7**	**0**	**2**	**20**	**40**	**8**	**78**	**2**	**0**	**1**	**1**	**2**	**.180**	**.294**	**.230**	**.984**

Thomas, Frank Joseph
HEIGHT: 6'3"   THROWS: RIGHT   BATS: RIGHT   BORN: 6/11/1929 PITTSBURGH, PENNSYLVANIA   POSITIONS PLAYED: 1B, 2B, 3B, OF

YEAR	TEAM	GAMES	AB	RUNS	HITS	2B	3B	HR	RBI	BB	IBB	SO	HBP	SH	SF	SB	CS	BA	OBA	SA	FA
1951	Pit-N	39	148	21	39	9	2	2	16	9	—	15	0	0	—	0	2	.264	.306	.392	1.000
1952	Pit-N	6	21	1	2	0	0	0	0	1	—	1	0	0	—	0	0	.095	.136	.095	1.000
1953	Pit-N	128	455	68	116	22	1	30	102	50	—	93	2	3	—	1	2	.255	.331	.505	.976
1954	Pit-N	153	577	81	172	32	7	23	94	51	—	74	10	4	11	3	2	.298	.359	.497	.989
1955	Pit-N	142	510	72	125	16	2	25	72	60	10	76	2	3	6	2	0	.245	.324	.431	.984
1956	Pit-N	157	588	69	166	24	3	25	80	36	5	61	5	2	6	0	5	.282	.326	.461	.956
1957	Pit-N	151	594	72	172	30	1	23	89	44	9	66	3	5	12	3	1	.290	.335	.460	.971
1958	Pit-N	149	562	89	158	26	4	35	109	42	2	79	7	1	8	0	1	.281	.334	.528	.931
1959	Cin-N	108	374	41	84	18	2	12	47	27	6	56	3	2	6	0	2	.225	.278	.380	.946
1960	**ChC-N**	**135**	**479**	**54**	**114**	**12**	**1**	**21**	**64**	**28**	**4**	**74**	**0**	**1**	**1**	**1**	**0**	**.238**	**.280**	**.399**	**.973**

(continued)

YEAR	TEAM	GAMES	AB	RUNS	HITS	2B	3B	HR	RBI	BB	IBB	SO	HBP	SH	SF	SB	CS	BA	OBA	SA	FA
1961	ChC-N	15	50	7	13	2	0	2	6	2	0	8	0	0	0	0	0	.260	.288	.420	1.000
1961	Mil-N	124	423	58	120	13	3	25	67	29	7	70	6	2	4	2	4	.284	.335	.506	.963
1962	NYM-N	156	571	69	152	23	3	34	94	48	4	95	8	0	6	2	1	.266	.329	.496	.961
1963	NYM-N	126	420	34	109	9	1	15	60	33	5	48	3	0	2	0	0	.260	.317	.393	.988
1964	NYM-N	60	197	19	50	6	1	3	19	10	1	29	2	0	1	1	1	.254	.295	.340	.995
1964	Phi-N	39	143	20	42	11	0	7	26	5	2	12	0	0	1	1	1	.294	.311	.517	.976
1965	Phi-N	35	77	7	20	4	0	1	7	4	0	10	0	3	3	0	1	.260	.289	.351	.981
1965	Hou-N	23	58	7	10	2	0	3	9	3	0	15	0	0	2	0	0	.172	.210	.362	.984
1965	Mil-N	15	33	3	7	3	0	0	1	2	0	11	0	0	1	0	0	.212	.250	.303	.980
1966	ChC-N	5	5	0	0	0	0	0	0	0	0	1	0	0	0	0	0	.000	.000	.000	—
Career average		110	393	50	104	16	2	18	60	30	3	56	3	2	4	1	1	.266	.320	.454	.971
Cubs average		52	178	20	42	5	0	8	23	10	1	28	0	0	0	0	0	.238	.278	.397	.975
Career total		1766	6285	792	1671	262	31	286	962	484	55	894	51	26	70	15	22	.266	.320	.454	.971
Cubs total		155	534	61	127	14	1	23	70	30	4	83	0	1	1	1	0	.238	.278	.397	.975

Thomas, James Leroy (Lee or Mad Dog)

HEIGHT: 6'2" THROWS: LEFT BATS: LEFT BORN: 2/5/1936 PEORIA, ILLINOIS POSITIONS PLAYED: 1B, OF

YEAR	TEAM	GAMES	AB	RUNS	HITS	2B	3B	HR	RBI	BB	IBB	SO	HBP	SH	SF	SB	CS	BA	OBA	SA	FA
1961	NYY-A	2	2	0	1	0	0	0	0	0	0	0	0	0	0	0	0	.500	.500	.500	—
1961	LAA-A	130	450	77	128	11	5	24	70	47	2	74	2	2	3	0	5	.284	.353	.491	.976
1962	LAA-A	160	583	88	169	21	2	26	104	55	3	74	6	4	4	6	1	.290	.355	.467	.981
1963	LAA-A	149	528	52	116	12	6	9	55	53	6	82	9	2	2	6	1	.220	.301	.316	.996
1964	LAA-A	47	172	14	47	8	1	2	24	18	1	22	0	3	1	1	0	.273	.340	.366	.951
1964	Bos-A	107	401	44	103	19	2	13	42	34	4	29	4	0	3	2	1	.257	.319	.411	.995
1965	Bos-A	151	521	74	141	27	4	22	75	72	8	42	3	5	2	6	2	.271	.361	.464	.984
1966	Atl-N	39	126	11	25	1	1	6	15	10	1	15	1	1	1	1	1	.198	.261	.365	.987
1966	**ChC-N**	**75**	**149**	**15**	**36**	**4**	**0**	**1**	**9**	**14**	**1**	**15**	**3**	**1**	**0**	**0**	**0**	**.242**	**.319**	**.289**	**.994**
1967	**ChC-N**	**77**	**191**	**16**	**42**	**4**	**1**	**2**	**23**	**15**	**5**	**22**	**3**	**1**	**2**	**1**	**0**	**.220**	**.284**	**.289**	**.986**
1968	Hou-N	90	201	14	39	4	0	1	11	14	4	22	1	4	1	2	1	.194	.249	.229	.986
Career average		128	416	51	106	14	3	13	54	42	4	50	4	3	2	3	1	.255	.327	.397	.986
Cubs average		76	170	16	39	4	1	2	16	15	3	19	3	1	1	1	0	.229	.300	.285	.990
Career total		1027	3324	405	847	111	22	106	428	332	35	397	32	23	19	25	11	.255	.327	.397	.986
Cubs total		152	340	31	78	8	1	3	32	29	6	37	6	2	2	1	0	.229	.300	.285	.990

Thomas, Robert William (Red)

HEIGHT: 5'11" THROWS: RIGHT BATS: RIGHT BORN: 4/25/1898 HARGROVE, ALABAMA DIED: 3/29/1962 FREMONT, OHIO POSITIONS PLAYED: OF

YEAR	TEAM	GAMES	AB	RUNS	HITS	2B	3B	HR	RBI	BB	IBB	SO	HBP	SH	SF	SB	CS	BA	OBA	SA	FA
1921	ChC-N	8	30	5	8	3	0	1	5	4	—	5	1	1	—	0	1	.267	.371	.467	.962
Career average		8	30	5	8	3	0	1	5	4	—	5	1	1	—	0	1	.267	.371	.467	.962
Cubs average		8	30	5	8	3	0	1	5	4	—	5	1	1	—	0	1	.267	.371	.467	.962
Career total		8	30	5	8	3	0	1	5	4	—	5	1	1	—	0	1	.267	.371	.467	.962
Cubs total		8	30	5	8	3	0	1	5	4	—	5	1	1	—	0	1	.267	.371	.467	.962

Thompson, Vernon Scot (Scot)

HEIGHT: 6'3" THROWS: LEFT BATS: LEFT BORN: 12/7/1955 GROVE CITY, PENNSYLVANIA POSITIONS PLAYED: 1B, OF

YEAR	TEAM	GAMES	AB	RUNS	HITS	2B	3B	HR	RBI	BB	IBB	SO	HBP	SH	SF	SB	CS	BA	OBA	SA	FA
1978	ChC-N	19	36	7	15	3	0	0	2	2	0	4	0	1	0	0	0	.417	.447	.500	1.000
1979	ChC-N	128	346	36	100	13	5	2	29	17	1	37	1	1	3	4	3	.289	.322	.373	.971
1980	ChC-N	102	226	26	48	10	1	2	13	28	3	31	1	1	1	6	6	.212	.301	.292	.975
1981	ChC-N	57	115	8	19	5	0	0	8	7	1	8	0	2	3	2	0	.165	.208	.209	.966
1982	ChC-N	49	74	11	27	5	1	0	7	5	0	4	0	0	0	0	1	.365	.405	.459	1.000
1983	ChC-N	53	88	4	17	3	1	0	10	3	0	14	0	0	0	0	0	.193	.220	.250	1.000
1984	SF-N	120	245	30	75	7	1	1	31	30	5	26	0	1	4	5	3	.306	.376	.355	.997
1985	SF-N	64	111	8	23	5	0	0	6	2	0	10	0	0	0	0	0	.207	.221	.252	.995
1985	Mon-N	34	32	2	9	1	0	0	4	3	0	7	0	0	1	0	0	.281	.333	.313	1.000
Career average		78	159	17	42	7	1	1	14	12	1	18	0	1	2	2	2	.262	.312	.328	.989
Cubs average		68	148	15	38	7	1	1	12	10	1	16	0	1	1	2	2	.255	.303	.331	.977
Career total		626	1273	132	333	52	9	5	110	97	10	141	2	7	12	17	13	.262	.312	.328	.989
Cubs total		408	885	92	226	39	8	4	69	62	5	98	2	5	7	12	10	.255	.303	.331	.977

Thomson, Robert Brown (Bobby *or* The Staten Island Scot)

HEIGHT: 6'2" THROWS: RIGHT BATS: RIGHT BORN: 10/25/1923 GLASGOW, SCOTLAND POSITIONS PLAYED: 1B, 2B, 3B, OF

YEAR	TEAM	GAMES	AB	RUNS	HITS	2B	3B	HR	RBI	BB	IBB	SO	HBP	SH	SF	SB	CS	BA	OBA	SA	FA
1946	NYG-N	18	54	8	17	4	1	2	9	4	—	5	0	0	—	0	0	.315	.362	.537	.935
1947	NYG-N	138	545	105	154	26	5	29	85	40	—	78	4	2	—	1	0	.283	.336	.508	.970
1948	NYG-N	138	471	75	117	20	2	16	63	30	—	77	2	3	—	2	—	.248	.296	.401	.970
1949	NYG-N	156	641	99	198	35	9	27	109	44	—	45	2	2	—	10	2	.309	.355	.518	.982
1950	NYG-N	149	563	79	142	22	7	25	85	55	—	45	5	2	—	3	—	.252	.324	.449	.978
1951	NYG-N	148	518	89	152	27	8	32	101	73	—	57	4	7	—	5	5	.293	.385	.562	.952
1952	NYG-N	153	608	89	164	29	14	24	108	52	—	74	4	2	—	5	2	.270	.331	.482	.959
1953	NYG-N	154	608	80	175	22	6	26	106	43	—	57	3	2	—	4	2	.288	.338	.472	.983
1954	Mil-N	43	99	7	23	3	0	2	15	12	—	29	0	2	0	0	0	.232	.315	.323	.980
1955	Mil-N	101	343	40	88	12	3	12	56	34	4	52	0	1	5	2	1	.257	.319	.414	.969
1956	Mil-N	142	451	59	106	10	4	20	74	43	4	75	2	5	4	2	4	.235	.302	.408	.965
1957	Mil-N	41	148	15	35	5	3	4	23	8	0	27	2	2	0	2	1	.236	.285	.392	.988
1957	NYG-N	81	215	24	52	7	4	8	38	19	2	39	0	2	1	1	2	.242	.302	.423	.992
1958	**ChC-N**	**152**	**547**	**67**	**155**	**27**	**5**	**21**	**82**	**56**	**7**	**76**	**4**	**2**	**6**	**0**	**2**	**.283**	**.351**	**.466**	**.987**
1959	**ChC-N**	**122**	**374**	**55**	**97**	**15**	**2**	**11**	**52**	**35**	**6**	**50**	**2**	**2**	**5**	**1**	**0**	**.259**	**.322**	**.398**	**.987**
1960	Bos-A	40	114	12	30	3	1	5	20	11	0	15	0	0	2	0	1	.263	.323	.439	.950
1960	Bal-A	3	6	0	0	0	0	0	0	0	0	3	0	0	0	0	0	.000	.000	.000	—
Career average		119	420	60	114	18	5	18	68	37	2	54	2	2	2	3	1	.270	.332	.462	.973
Cubs average		**137**	**461**	**61**	**126**	**21**	**4**	**16**	**67**	**46**	**7**	**63**	**3**	**2**	**6**	**1**	**1**	**.274**	**.339**	**.439**	**.987**
Career total		1779	6305	903	1705	267	74	264	1026	559	23	804	34	36	23	38	22	.270	.332	.462	.973
Cubs total		**274**	**921**	**122**	**252**	**42**	**7**	**32**	**134**	**91**	**13**	**126**	**6**	**4**	**11**	**1**	**2**	**.274**	**.339**	**.439**	**.987**

Thornton, Andre

HEIGHT: 6'3" THROWS: RIGHT BATS: RIGHT BORN: 8/13/1949 TUSKEGEE, ALABAMA POSITIONS PLAYED: 1B, 3B, OF

YEAR	TEAM	GAMES	AB	RUNS	HITS	2B	3B	HR	RBI	BB	IBB	SO	HBP	SH	SF	SB	CS	BA	OBA	SA	FA
1973	**ChC-N**	**17**	**35**	**3**	**7**	**3**	**0**	**0**	**2**	**7**	**0**	**9**	**0**	**0**	**0**	**0**	**0**	**.200**	**.333**	**.286**	**.989**
1974	**ChC-N**	**107**	**303**	**41**	**79**	**16**	**4**	**10**	**46**	**48**	**4**	**50**	**4**	**1**	**1**	**2**	**1**	**.261**	**.368**	**.439**	**.992**
1975	**ChC-N**	**120**	**372**	**70**	**109**	**21**	**4**	**18**	**60**	**88**	**12**	**63**	**4**	**3**	**6**	**3**	**2**	**.293**	**.428**	**.516**	**.988**
1976	**ChC-N**	**27**	**85**	**8**	**17**	**6**	**0**	**2**	**14**	**20**	**1**	**14**	**2**	**0**	**1**	**2**	**0**	**.200**	**.361**	**.341**	**.987**
1976	Mon-N	69	183	20	35	5	2	9	24	28	0	32	3	1	3	2	1	.191	.304	.388	.992
1977	Cle-A	131	433	77	114	20	5	28	70	70	1	82	11	1	2	3	4	.263	.378	.527	.995
1978	Cle-A	145	508	97	133	22	4	33	105	93	4	72	6	2	8	4	7	.262	.377	.516	.995
1979	Cle-A	143	515	89	120	31	1	26	93	90	2	93	4	1	7	5	4	.233	.347	.449	.994
1981	Cle-A	69	226	22	54	12	0	6	30	23	1	37	0	2	5	3	1	.239	.303	.372	.986
1982	Cle-A	161	589	90	161	26	1	32	116	109	18	81	2	3	5	6	7	.273	.386	.484	1.000
1983	Cle-A	141	508	78	143	27	1	17	77	87	14	72	2	0	8	4	2	.281	.383	.439	.991
1984	Cle-A	155	587	91	159	26	0	33	99	91	11	79	2	0	9	6	5	.271	.366	.484	.979
1985	Cle-A	124	461	49	109	13	0	22	88	47	1	75	0	0	6	3	2	.236	.304	.408	—
1986	Cle-A	120	401	49	92	14	0	17	66	65	0	67	1	0	8	4	1	.229	.333	.392	—
1987	Cle-A	36	85	8	10	2	0	0	5	10	0	25	0	0	2	1	0	.118	.206	.141	—
Career average		112	378	57	96	17	2	18	64	63	5	61	3	1	5	3	3	.254	.360	.452	.992
Cubs average		**68**	**199**	**31**	**53**	**12**	**2**	**8**	**31**	**41**	**4**	**34**	**3**	**1**	**2**	**2**	**1**	**.267**	**.394**	**.458**	**.989**
Career total		1565	5291	792	1342	244	22	253	895	876	69	851	41	14	71	48	37	.254	.360	.452	.992
Cubs total		**271**	**795**	**122**	**212**	**46**	**8**	**30**	**122**	**163**	**17**	**136**	**10**	**4**	**8**	**7**	**3**	**.267**	**.394**	**.458**	**.989**

Thornton, Walter Miller

HEIGHT: 6'1" THROWS: LEFT BATS: LEFT BORN: 2/18/1875 LEWISTON, MAINE DIED: 7/14/1960 LOS ANGELES, CALIFORNIA POSITIONS PLAYED: P, 1B, OF

YEAR	TEAM	GAMES	AB	RUNS	HITS	2B	3B	HR	RBI	BB	IBB	SO	HBP	SH	SF	SB	CS	BA	OBA	SA	FA
1895	ChN-N	8	22	4	7	1	0	1	7	3	—	1	0	0	—	0	—	.318	.400	.500	.923
1896	ChN-N	9	22	6	8	0	1	0	1	5	—	2	0	0	—	2	—	.364	.481	.455	.786
1897	ChN-N	75	265	39	85	9	6	0	55	30	—	—	6	4	—	13	—	.321	.402	.400	.831
1898	ChN-N	62	210	34	62	5	2	0	14	22	—	—	0	3	—	8	—	.295	.362	.338	.882
Career average		39	130	21	41	4	2	0	19	15	—	1	2	2	—	6	—	.312	.390	.382	.856
Cubs average		**39**	**130**	**21**	**41**	**4**	**2**	**0**	**19**	**15**	**—**	**1**	**2**	**2**	**—**	**6**	**—**	**.312**	**.390**	**.382**	**.856**
Career total		154	519	83	162	15	9	1	77	60	—	3	6	7	—	23	—	.312	.390	.382	.856
Cubs total		**154**	**519**	**83**	**162**	**15**	**9**	**1**	**77**	**60**	**—**	**3**	**6**	**7**	**—**	**23**	**—**	**.312**	**.390**	**.382**	**.856**

Timmons, Osborne Llewellyn (Ozzie)
HEIGHT: 6'2"   THROWS: RIGHT   BATS: RIGHT   BORN: 9/18/1970 TAMPA, FLORIDA   POSITIONS PLAYED: 1B, OF

YEAR	TEAM	GAMES	AB	RUNS	HITS	2B	3B	HR	RBI	BB	IBB	SO	HBP	SH	SF	SB	CS	BA	OBA	SA	FA
1995	ChC-N	77	171	30	45	10	1	8	28	13	2	32	0	0	1	3	0	.263	.314	.474	.970
1996	ChC-N	65	140	18	28	4	0	7	16	15	0	30	1	1	0	1	0	.200	.282	.379	1.000
1997	Cin-N	6	9	1	3	1	0	0	0	0	0	1	0	0	0	0	0	.333	.333	.444	1.000
1999	Sea-A	26	44	4	5	2	0	1	3	4	0	12	0	0	0	0	0	.114	.188	.227	1.000
2000	TB-A	12	41	9	14	3	0	4	13	1	0	7	0	0	0	0	1	.341	.357	.707	1.000
Career average		37	81	12	19	4	0	4	12	7	0	16	0	0	0	1	0	.235	.293	.437	.981
Cubs average		**71**	**156**	**24**	**37**	**7**	**1**	**8**	**22**	**14**	**1**	**31**	**0**	**0**	**0**	**1**	**0**	**.235**	**.293**	**.437**	**.981**
Career total		186	405	62	95	20	1	20	60	33	2	82	1	1	1	4	1	.235	.293	.437	.981
Cubs total		**142**	**311**	**48**	**73**	**14**	**1**	**15**	**44**	**28**	**2**	**62**	**1**	**1**	**1**	**4**	**0**	**.235**	**.299**	**.431**	**.985**

Tinker, Joseph Bert (Joe)
HEIGHT: 5'9"   THROWS: RIGHT   BATS: RIGHT   BORN: 7/27/1880 MUSCOTAH, KANSAS   DIED: 7/27/1948 ORLANDO, FLORIDA
POSITIONS PLAYED: 2B, 3B, SS, OF

YEAR	TEAM	GAMES	AB	RUNS	HITS	2B	3B	HR	RBI	BB	IBB	SO	HBP	SH	SF	SB	CS	BA	OBA	SA	FA
1902	ChC-N	131	494	55	129	19	5	2	54	26	—	—	0	18	—	27	—	.261	.298	.332	.907
1903	ChC-N	124	460	67	134	21	7	2	70	37	—	—	1	13	—	27	—	.291	.345	.380	.906
1904	ChC-N	141	488	55	108	12	13	3	41	29	—	—	2	12	—	41	—	.221	.268	.318	.926
1905	ChC-N	149	547	70	135	18	8	2	66	34	—	—	1	29	—	31	—	.247	.292	.320	.940
1906	ChC-N	148	523	75	122	18	4	1	64	43	—	—	1	36	—	30	—	.233	.293	.289	.943
1907	ChC-N	117	402	36	89	11	3	1	36	25	—	—	1	16	—	20	—	.221	.269	.271	.939
1908	ChC-N	157	548	67	146	22	14	6	68	32	—	—	0	29	—	30	—	.266	.307	.391	.958
1909	ChC-N	143	516	56	132	26	11	4	57	17	—	—	0	22	—	23	—	.256	.280	.372	.940
1910	ChC-N	133	473	48	136	25	9	3	69	24	—	35	0	18	—	20	—	.288	.322	.397	.942
1911	ChC-N	144	536	61	149	24	12	4	69	39	—	31	0	18	—	30	—	.278	.327	.390	.937
1912	ChC-N	142	550	80	155	24	7	0	75	38	—	21	2	34	—	25	—	.282	.331	.351	.943
1913	Cin-N	110	382	47	121	20	13	1	57	20	—	26	1	15	—	10	—	.317	.352	.445	.968
1914	Chi-F	126	438	50	112	21	7	2	46	38	—	30	1	23	—	19	—	.256	.317	.349	.947
1915	Chi-F	31	67	7	18	2	1	0	9	13	—	5	0	1	—	3	—	.269	.388	.328	.914
1916	ChC-N	7	10	0	1	0	0	0	1	1	—	1	0	1	—	0	—	.100	.182	.100	.929
Career average		120	429	52	112	18	8	2	52	28	—	10	1	19	—	22	—	.262	.308	.353	.938
Cubs average		**128**	**462**	**56**	**120**	**18**	**8**	**2**	**56**	**29**	**—**	**7**	**1**	**21**	**—**	**25**	**—**	**.259**	**.303**	**.347**	**.938**
Career total		1803	6434	774	1687	263	114	31	782	416	—	149	10	285	—	336	—	.262	.308	.353	.938
Cubs total		**1536**	**5547**	**670**	**1436**	**220**	**93**	**28**	**670**	**345**	**—**	**88**	**8**	**246**	**—**	**304**	**—**	**.259**	**.303**	**.347**	**.935**

Todd, Alfred Chester (Al)
HEIGHT: 6'1"   THROWS: RIGHT   BATS: RIGHT   BORN: 1/7/1902 TROY, NEW YORK   DIED: 3/8/1985 ELMIRA, NEW YORK   POSITIONS PLAYED: C, OF

YEAR	TEAM	GAMES	AB	RUNS	HITS	2B	3B	HR	RBI	BB	IBB	SO	HBP	SH	SF	SB	CS	BA	OBA	SA	FA
1932	Phi-N	33	70	8	16	5	0	0	9	1	—	9	2	2	—	1	—	.229	.260	.300	.899
1933	Phi-N	73	136	13	28	4	0	0	10	4	—	18	2	2	—	1	—	.206	.239	.235	.983
1934	Phi-N	91	302	33	96	22	2	4	41	10	—	39	2	0	—	3	—	.318	.344	.444	.976
1935	Phi-N	107	328	40	95	18	3	3	42	19	—	35	3	3	—	3	—	.290	.334	.390	.968
1936	Pit-N	76	267	28	73	10	5	2	28	11	—	24	2	0	—	4	—	.273	.307	.371	.976
1937	Pit-N	133	514	51	158	18	10	8	86	16	—	36	1	3	—	2	—	.307	.330	.428	.972
1938	Pit-N	133	491	52	130	19	7	7	75	18	—	31	4	3	—	2	—	.265	.296	.375	.985
1939	Bro-N	86	245	28	68	10	0	5	32	13	—	16	1	6	—	1	—	.278	.317	.380	.985
1940	ChC-N	104	381	31	97	13	2	6	42	11	—	29	4	5	—	1	—	.255	.283	.346	.985
1941	ChC-N	6	6	1	1	0	0	0	0	0	—	1	0	0	—	0	—	.167	.167	.167	.984
1943	ChC-N	21	45	1	6	0	0	0	1	1	—	5	0	0	—	0	—	.133	.152	.133	.986
Career average		78	253	26	70	11	3	3	33	9	—	22	2	3	—	2	—	.276	.307	.377	.977
Cubs average		**44**	**144**	**11**	**35**	**4**	**1**	**2**	**14**	**4**	**—**	**12**	**1**	**2**	**—**	**0**	**—**	**.241**	**.268**	**.322**	**.984**
Career total		863	2785	286	768	119	29	35	366	104	—	243	21	29	—	18	—	.276	.307	.377	.977
Cubs total		**131**	**432**	**33**	**104**	**13**	**2**	**6**	**43**	**12**	**—**	**35**	**4**	**5**	**—**	**1**	**—**	**.241**	**.268**	**.322**	**.984**

Tolson, Charles Julius (Chick *or* Toby *or* Slug)
HEIGHT: 6'0"   THROWS: RIGHT   BATS: RIGHT   BORN: 5/3/1895 WASHINGTON, DISTRICT OF COLUMBIA   DIED: 4/16/1965 WASHINGTON, DISTRICT OF COLUMBIA
POSITIONS PLAYED: 1B

YEAR	TEAM	GAMES	AB	RUNS	HITS	2B	3B	HR	RBI	BB	IBB	SO	HBP	SH	SF	SB	CS	BA	OBA	SA	FA
1925	Cle-A	3	12	0	3	0	0	0	0	2	—	1	0	0	—	0	0	.250	.357	.250	1.000
1926	**ChC-N**	57	80	4	25	6	1	1	8	5	—	8	0	3	—	0	—	.313	.353	.450	.991
1927	ChC-N	39	54	6	16	4	0	2	17	4	—	9	0	3	—	0	—	.296	.345	.481	1.000
1929	ChC-N	32	109	13	28	5	0	1	19	9	—	16	2	3	—	0	—	.257	.325	.330	.978
1930	ChC-N	13	20	0	6	1	0	0	1	6	—	5	0	0	—	1	—	.300	.462	.350	.979
Career average		29	55	5	16	3	0	1	9	5	—	8	0	2	—	0	0	.284	.350	.393	.985
Cubs average		**35**	**66**	**6**	**19**	**4**	**0**	**1**	**11**	**6**	**—**	**10**	**1**	**2**	**—**	**0**	**0**	**.285**	**.349**	**.399**	**.984**
Career total		144	275	23	78	16	1	4	45	26	—	39	2	9	—	1	0	.284	.350	.393	.985
Cubs total		**141**	**263**	**23**	**75**	**16**	**1**	**4**	**45**	**24**	**—**	**38**	**2**	**9**	**—**	**1**	**0**	**.285**	**.349**	**.399**	**.984**

Torres, Hector Epitacio
HEIGHT: 6'0"   THROWS: RIGHT   BATS: RIGHT   BORN: 9/16/1945 MONTERREY, MEXICO   POSITIONS PLAYED: P, 2B, 3B, SS, OF

YEAR	TEAM	GAMES	AB	RUNS	HITS	2B	3B	HR	RBI	BB	IBB	SO	HBP	SH	SF	SB	CS	BA	OBA	SA	FA
1968	Hou-N	128	466	44	104	11	1	1	24	18	2	64	0	12	0	2	3	.223	.252	.258	.958
1969	Hou-N	34	69	5	11	1	0	1	8	2	0	12	0	1	0	0	0	.159	.183	.217	.944
1970	Hou-N	31	65	6	16	1	2	0	5	6	0	8	0	0	0	0	0	.246	.310	.323	.955
1971	**ChC-N**	**31**	**58**	**4**	**13**	**3**	**0**	**0**	**2**	**4**	**0**	**10**	**0**	**0**	**0**	**0**	**0**	**.224**	**.274**	**.276**	**.950**
1972	Mon-N	83	181	14	28	4	1	2	7	13	1	26	1	2	0	0	2	.155	.215	.221	.969
1973	Hou-N	38	66	3	6	1	0	0	2	7	0	13	1	3	0	0	1	.091	.189	.106	.955
1975	SD-N	112	352	31	91	12	0	5	26	22	3	32	0	7	6	2	3	.259	.297	.335	.973
1976	SD-N	74	215	8	42	6	0	4	15	16	3	31	1	3	0	2	1	.195	.254	.279	.952
1977	Tor-A	91	266	33	64	7	3	5	26	16	1	33	1	5	4	1	1	.241	.282	.346	.975
Career average		69	193	16	42	5	1	2	13	12	1	25	0	4	1	1	1	.216	.260	.281	.964
Cubs average		**31**	**58**	**4**	**13**	**3**	**0**	**0**	**2**	**4**	**0**	**10**	**0**	**0**	**0**	**0**	**0**	**.224**	**.274**	**.276**	**.950**
Career total		622	1738	148	375	46	7	18	115	104	10	229	4	33	10	7	11	.216	.260	.281	.964
Cubs total		**31**	**58**	**4**	**13**	**3**	**0**	**0**	**2**	**4**	**0**	**10**	**0**	**0**	**0**	**0**	**0**	**.224**	**.274**	**.276**	**.950**

Tracy, James Edwin (Jim)
HEIGHT: 6'0"   THROWS: RIGHT   BATS: LEFT   BORN: 12/31/1955 HAMILTON, OHIO   POSITIONS PLAYED: 1B, OF

YEAR	TEAM	GAMES	AB	RUNS	HITS	2B	3B	HR	RBI	BB	IBB	SO	HBP	SH	SF	SB	CS	BA	OBA	SA	FA
1980	**ChC-N**	**42**	**122**	**12**	**31**	**3**	**3**	**3**	**9**	**13**	**1**	**37**	**0**	**2**	**0**	**2**	**2**	**.254**	**.326**	**.402**	**.957**
1981	**ChC-N**	**45**	**63**	**6**	**15**	**2**	**1**	**0**	**5**	**12**	**0**	**14**	**0**	**0**	**1**	**1**	**0**	**.238**	**.355**	**.302**	**1.000**
Career average		44	93	9	23	3	2	2	7	13	1	26	0	1	1	2	1	.249	.336	.368	.968
Cubs average		**44**	**93**	**9**	**23**	**3**	**2**	**2**	**7**	**13**	**1**	**26**	**0**	**1**	**1**	**2**	**1**	**.249**	**.336**	**.368**	**.968**
Career total		87	185	18	46	5	4	3	14	25	1	51	0	2	1	3	2	.249	.336	.368	.968
Cubs total		**87**	**185**	**18**	**46**	**5**	**4**	**3**	**14**	**25**	**1**	**51**	**0**	**2**	**1**	**3**	**2**	**.249**	**.336**	**.368**	**.968**

Traffley, William Franklin (Bill)
HEIGHT: 5'11"   THROWS: RIGHT   BATS: RIGHT   BORN: 12/21/1859 STATEN ISLAND, NEW YORK   DIED: 6/23/1908 DESMOINES, IOWA
POSITIONS PLAYED: C, 1B, 2B, SS, OF

YEAR	TEAM	GAMES	AB	RUNS	HITS	2B	3B	HR	RBI	BB	IBB	SO	HBP	SH	SF	SB	CS	BA	OBA	SA	FA
1878	**ChN-N**	**2**	**9**	**1**	**1**	**0**	**0**	**0**	**1**	**0**	**—**	**1**	**—**	**—**	**—**	**—**	**—**	**.111**	**.111**	**.111**	**1.000**
1883	Cin-AA	30	105	17	21	5	0	0	8	4	—	—	—	—	—	—	—	.200	.229	.248	.847
1884	Bal-AA	53	210	25	37	4	6	0	—	—	—	—	1	—	—	—	—	.176	.192	.252	.929
1885	Bal-AA	69	254	27	39	4	5	1	20	17	—	—	3	—	—	—	—	.154	.215	.220	.937
1886	Bal-AA	25	85	15	18	0	1	0	7	10	—	—	0	—	—	8	—	.212	.295	.235	.952
Career average		36	133	17	23	3	2	0	7	7	—	0	1	—	—	2	—	.175	.220	.235	.925
Cubs average		**2**	**9**	**1**	**1**	**0**	**0**	**0**	**1**	**0**	**—**	**1**	**—**	**—**	**—**	**—**	**—**	**.111**	**.111**	**.111**	**1.000**
Career total		179	663	85	116	13	12	1	36	34	—	1	4	—	—	8	—	.175	.220	.235	.925
Cubs total		**2**	**9**	**1**	**1**	**0**	**0**	**0**	**1**	**0**	**—**	**1**	**—**	**—**	**—**	**—**	**—**	**.111**	**.111**	**.111**	**1.000**

Trillo, Jesus Manuel (Manny *or* Indio)
HEIGHT: 6'1"   THROWS: RIGHT   BATS: RIGHT   BORN: 12/25/1950 CARIPITO, VENEZUELA   POSITIONS PLAYED: 1B, 2B, 3B, SS

YEAR	TEAM	GAMES	AB	RUNS	HITS	2B	3B	HR	RBI	BB	IBB	SO	HBP	SH	SF	SB	CS	BA	OBA	SA	FA
1973	Oak-A	17	12	0	3	2	0	0	3	0	0	4	0	0	0	0	0	.250	.250	.417	.941
1974	Oak-A	21	33	3	5	0	0	0	2	2	0	8	1	1	0	0	0	.152	.222	.152	.949
1975	**ChC-N**	**154**	**545**	**55**	**135**	**12**	**2**	**7**	**70**	**45**	**3**	**78**	**3**	**15**	**5**	**1**	**7**	**.248**	**.306**	**.316**	**.967**
1976	**ChC-N**	**158**	**582**	**42**	**139**	**24**	**3**	**4**	**59**	**53**	**4**	**70**	**3**	**7**	**4**	**17**	**6**	**.239**	**.304**	**.311**	**.981**
1977	**ChC-N**	**152**	**504**	**51**	**141**	**18**	**5**	**7**	**57**	**44**	**6**	**58**	**5**	**4**	**8**	**3**	**5**	**.280**	**.339**	**.377**	**.970**
1978	**ChC-N**	**152**	**552**	**53**	**144**	**17**	**5**	**4**	**55**	**50**	**3**	**67**	**2**	**3**	**8**	**0**	**7**	**.261**	**.320**	**.332**	**.978**
1979	Phi-N	118	431	40	112	22	1	6	42	20	3	59	4	8	4	4	7	.260	.296	.357	.985
1980	Phi-N	141	531	68	155	25	9	7	43	32	8	46	3	4	3	8	3	.292	.334	.412	.987
1981	Phi-N	94	349	37	100	14	3	6	36	26	3	37	3	5	4	10	4	.287	.338	.395	.987
1982	Phi-N	149	549	52	149	24	1	0	39	33	3	53	3	9	1	8	10	.271	.316	.319	.994
1983	Cle-A	88	320	33	87	13	1	1	29	21	2	46	0	4	2	1	3	.272	.315	.328	.989
1983	Mon-N	31	121	16	32	8	0	2	16	10	0	18	2	3	0	0	0	.264	.331	.380	.979
1984	SF-N	98	401	45	102	21	1	4	36	25	0	55	3	4	4	0	0	.254	.300	.342	.988
1985	SF-N	125	451	36	101	16	2	3	25	40	0	44	1	11	2	2	0	.224	.287	.288	.980
1986	**ChC-N**	**81**	**152**	**22**	**45**	**10**	**0**	**1**	**19**	**16**	**0**	**21**	**0**	**2**	**2**	**0**	**2**	**.296**	**.359**	**.382**	**.973**
1987	**ChC-N**	**108**	**214**	**27**	**63**	**8**	**0**	**8**	**26**	**25**	**0**	**37**	**0**	**4**	**1**	**0**	**3**	**.294**	**.367**	**.444**	**.989**
1988	**ChC-N**	**76**	**164**	**15**	**41**	**5**	**0**	**1**	**14**	**8**	**0**	**32**	**0**	**4**	**1**	**2**	**0**	**.250**	**.283**	**.299**	**.989**
1989	Cin-N	17	39	3	8	0	0	0	0	2	0	9	1	0	0	0	0	.205	.262	.205	.978
Career average		105	350	35	92	14	2	4	34	27	2	44	2	5	3	3	3	.263	.316	.345	.981
Cubs average		**126**	**388**	**38**	**101**	**13**	**2**	**5**	**43**	**34**	**2**	**52**	**2**	**6**	**4**	**3**	**4**	**.261**	**.321**	**.342**	**.976**
Career total		1780	5950	598	1562	239	33	61	571	452	35	742	34	88	49	56	57	.263	.316	.345	.981
Cubs total		**881**	**2713**	**265**	**708**	**94**	**15**	**32**	**300**	**241**	**16**	**363**	**13**	**39**	**29**	**23**	**30**	**.261**	**.321**	**.342**	**.976**

Triplett, Herman Coaker (Coaker)
HEIGHT: 5'11"   THROWS: RIGHT   BATS: RIGHT   BORN: 12/18/1911 BOONE, NORTH CAROLINA   DIED: 1/30/1992 BOONE, NORTH CAROLINA
POSITIONS PLAYED: OF

YEAR	TEAM	GAMES	AB	RUNS	HITS	2B	3B	HR	RBI	BB	IBB	SO	HBP	SH	SF	SB	CS	BA	OBA	SA	FA
1938	**ChC-N**	**12**	**36**	**4**	**9**	**2**	**1**	**0**	**2**	**0**	**—**	**1**	**0**	**0**	**—**	**0**	**—**	**.250**	**.250**	**.361**	**1.000**
1941	StL-N	76	185	29	53	6	3	3	21	18	—	27	0	3	—	0	—	.286	.350	.400	.965
1942	StL-N	64	154	18	42	7	4	1	23	17	—	15	0	0	—	1	—	.273	.345	.390	.966
1943	StL-N	9	25	1	2	0	0	1	4	1	—	6	0	0	—	0	—	.080	.115	.200	.684
1943	Phi-N	105	360	45	98	16	4	14	52	28	—	28	0	1	—	2	—	.272	.325	.456	.970
1944	Phi-N	84	184	15	43	5	1	1	25	19	—	10	0	0	—	1	—	.234	.288	.288	.989
1945	Phi-N	120	363	36	87	11	1	7	46	40	—	27	0	0	—	6	—	.240	.315	.333	.945
Career average		78	218	25	56	8	2	5	29	21	—	19	0	1	—	2	—	.256	.320	.375	.957
Cubs average		**12**	**36**	**4**	**9**	**2**	**1**	**0**	**2**	**0**	**—**	**1**	**0**	**0**	**—**	**0**	**—**	**.250**	**.250**	**.361**	**1.000**
Career total		470	1307	148	334	47	14	27	173	123	—	114	0	4	—	10	—	.256	.320	.375	.957
Cubs total		**12**	**36**	**4**	**9**	**2**	**1**	**0**	**2**	**0**	**—**	**1**	**0**	**0**	**—**	**0**	**—**	**.250**	**.250**	**.361**	**1.000**

Truby, Harry Garvin (Bird Eye)
HEIGHT: 5'11"   THROWS: RIGHT   BATS: —   BORN: 5/12/1870 IRONTON, OHIO   DIED: 3/21/1953 IRONTON, OHIO   POSITIONS PLAYED: 2B

YEAR	TEAM	GAMES	AB	RUNS	HITS	2B	3B	HR	RBI	BB	IBB	SO	HBP	SH	SF	SB	CS	BA	OBA	SA	FA
1895	**ChN-N**	**33**	**119**	**17**	**40**	**3**	**0**	**0**	**16**	**10**	**—**	**7**	**3**	**3**	**—**	**7**	**—**	**.336**	**.402**	**.361**	**.950**
1896	**ChN-N**	**29**	**109**	**13**	**28**	**2**	**2**	**2**	**31**	**6**	**—**	**5**	**3**	**0**	**—**	**4**	**—**	**.257**	**.314**	**.367**	**.935**
1896	Pit-N	8	32	1	5	0	0	0	3	2	—	4	0	1	—	1	—	.156	.206	.156	.949
Career average		35	130	16	37	3	1	1	25	9	—	8	3	2	—	6	—	.281	.342	.338	.944
Cubs average		**31**	**114**	**15**	**34**	**3**	**1**	**1**	**24**	**8**	**—**	**6**	**3**	**2**	**—**	**6**	**—**	**.298**	**.360**	**.364**	**.943**
Career total		70	260	31	73	5	2	2	50	18	—	16	6	4	—	12	—	.281	.342	.338	.944
Cubs total		**62**	**228**	**30**	**68**	**5**	**2**	**2**	**47**	**16**	**—**	**12**	**6**	**3**	**—**	**11**	**—**	**.298**	**.360**	**.364**	**.943**

Tucker, Michael Anthony
HEIGHT: 6'2" THROWS: RIGHT BATS: LEFT BORN: 6/25/1971 SOUTH BOSTON, VIRGINIA POSITIONS PLAYED: 1B, 2B, OF

YEAR	TEAM	GAMES	AB	RUNS	HITS	2B	3B	HR	RBI	BB	IBB	SO	HBP	SH	SF	SB	CS	BA	OBA	SA	FA
1995	KC-A	62	177	23	46	10	0	4	17	18	2	51	1	2	0	2	3	.260	.332	.384	.986
1996	KC-A	108	339	55	88	18	4	12	53	40	1	69	7	3	4	10	4	.260	.346	.442	.992
1997	Atl-N	138	499	80	141	25	7	14	56	44	0	116	6	4	1	12	7	.283	.347	.445	.980
1998	Atl-N	130	414	54	101	27	3	13	46	49	10	112	3	1	2	8	3	.244	.327	.418	.995
1999	Cin-N	133	296	55	75	8	5	11	44	37	3	81	3	0	4	11	4	.253	.338	.426	.990
2000	Cin-N	148	270	55	72	13	4	15	36	44	1	64	7	0	2	13	6	.267	.381	.511	.969
2001	Cin-N	86	231	31	56	10	1	7	30	23	1	55	1	5	5	12	5	.242	.308	.385	.978
2001	**ChC-N**	**63**	**205**	**31**	**54**	**9**	**7**	**5**	**31**	**23**	**3**	**47**	**1**	**5**	**1**	**4**	**3**	**.263**	**.339**	**.449**	**.978**
Career average		124	347	55	90	17	4	12	45	40	3	85	4	3	3	10	5	.260	.341	.435	.984
Cubs average		**63**	**205**	**31**	**54**	**9**	**7**	**5**	**31**	**23**	**3**	**47**	**1**	**5**	**1**	**4**	**3**	**.263**	**.339**	**.449**	**.978**
Career total		868	2431	384	633	120	31	81	313	278	21	595	29	20	19	72	35	.260	.341	.435	.984
Cubs total		**63**	**205**	**31**	**54**	**9**	**7**	**5**	**31**	**23**	**3**	**47**	**1**	**5**	**1**	**4**	**3**	**.263**	**.339**	**.449**	**.978**

Turgeon, Eugene Joseph (Pete)
HEIGHT: 5'6" THROWS: RIGHT BATS: RIGHT BORN: 1/3/1897 MINNEAPOLIS, MINNESOTA DIED: 1/24/1977 WICHITA FALLS, TEXAS POSITIONS PLAYED: SS

YEAR	TEAM	GAMES	AB	RUNS	HITS	2B	3B	HR	RBI	BB	IBB	SO	HBP	SH	SF	SB	CS	BA	OBA	SA	FA
1923	ChC-N	3	6	1	1	0	0	0	0	0	—	0	0	0	—	0	0	.167	.167	.167	.875
Career average		3	6	1	1	0	0	0	0	0	—	0	0	0	—	0	0	.167	.167	.167	.875
Cubs average		**3**	**6**	**1**	**1**	**0**	**0**	**0**	**0**	**0**	**—**	**0**	**0**	**0**	**—**	**0**	**0**	**.167**	**.167**	**.167**	**.875**
Career total		3	6	1	1	0	0	0	0	0	—	0	0	0	—	0	0	.167	.167	.167	.875
Cubs total		**3**	**6**	**1**	**1**	**0**	**0**	**0**	**0**	**0**	**—**	**0**	**0**	**0**	**—**	**0**	**0**	**.167**	**.167**	**.167**	**.875**

Twombly, Clarence Edward (Babe)
HEIGHT: 5'10" THROWS: RIGHT BATS: LEFT BORN: 1/18/1896 JAMAICA PLAIN, MASSACHUSETTS DIED: 11/23/1974 SAN CLEMENTE, CALIFORNIA
POSITIONS PLAYED: 2B, OF

YEAR	TEAM	GAMES	AB	RUNS	HITS	2B	3B	HR	RBI	BB	IBB	SO	HBP	SH	SF	SB	CS	BA	OBA	SA	FA
1920	ChC-N	78	183	25	43	1	1	2	14	17	—	20	1	4	—	5	9	.235	.303	.284	.970
1921	ChC-N	87	175	22	66	8	1	1	18	11	—	10	0	4	—	4	6	.377	.414	.451	.968
Career average		83	179	24	55	5	1	2	16	14	—	15	1	4	—	5	8	.304	.357	.366	.969
Cubs average		**83**	**179**	**24**	**55**	**5**	**1**	**2**	**16**	**14**	**—**	**15**	**1**	**4**	**—**	**5**	**8**	**.304**	**.357**	**.366**	**.969**
Career total		165	358	47	109	9	2	3	32	28	—	30	1	8	—	9	15	.304	.357	.366	.969
Cubs total		**165**	**358**	**47**	**109**	**9**	**2**	**3**	**32**	**28**	**—**	**30**	**1**	**8**	**—**	**9**	**15**	**.304**	**.357**	**.366**	**.969**

Tyree, Earl Carlton (Ty)
HEIGHT: 5'8" THROWS: RIGHT BATS: RIGHT BORN: 3/4/1890 HUNTSVILLE, ILLINOIS DIED: 5/17/1954 RUSHVILLE, ILLINOIS POSITIONS PLAYED: C

YEAR	TEAM	GAMES	AB	RUNS	HITS	2B	3B	HR	RBI	BB	IBB	SO	HBP	SH	SF	SB	CS	BA	OBA	SA	FA
1914	ChC-N	1	4	1	0	0	0	0	0	0	—	0	0	0	—	0	—	.000	.000	.000	1.000
Career average		1	4	1	0	0	0	0	0	0	—	0	0	0	—	0	—	.000	.000	.000	1.000
Cubs average		**1**	**4**	**1**	**0**	**0**	**0**	**0**	**0**	**0**	**—**	**0**	**0**	**0**	**—**	**0**	**—**	**.000**	**.000**	**.000**	**1.000**
Career total		1	4	1	0	0	0	0	0	0	—	0	0	0	—	0	—	.000	.000	.000	1.000
Cubs total		**1**	**4**	**1**	**0**	**0**	**0**	**0**	**0**	**0**	**—**	**0**	**0**	**0**	**—**	**0**	**—**	**.000**	**.000**	**.000**	**1.000**

Tyrone, James Vernon (Jim)
HEIGHT: 6'1" THROWS: RIGHT BATS: RIGHT BORN: 1/29/1949 ALICE, TEXAS POSITIONS PLAYED: 1B, 3B, SS, OF

YEAR	TEAM	GAMES	AB	RUNS	HITS	2B	3B	HR	RBI	BB	IBB	SO	HBP	SH	SF	SB	CS	BA	OBA	SA	FA
1972	ChC-N	13	8	1	0	0	0	0	0	0	0	3	0	0	0	1	0	.000	.000	.000	1.000
1974	ChC-N	57	81	19	15	0	1	3	3	6	0	8	0	0	0	1	1	.185	.241	.321	.966
1975	ChC-N	11	22	0	5	0	1	0	3	1	0	4	0	0	1	1	1	.227	.250	.318	1.000
1977	Oak-A	96	294	32	72	11	1	5	26	25	2	62	0	5	4	3	1	.245	.300	.340	.951

(continued)

(continued)

	GAMES	AB	RUNS	HITS	2B	3B	HR	RBI	BB	IBB	SO	HBP	SH	SF	SB	CS	BA	OBA	SA	FA
Career average	44	101	13	23	3	1	2	8	8	1	19	0	1	1	2	1	.227	.281	.328	.956
Cubs average	27	37	7	7	0	1	1	2	2	0	5	0	0	0	1	1	.180	.227	.297	.977
Career total	177	405	52	92	11	3	8	32	32	2	77	0	5	5	6	3	.227	.281	.328	.956
Cubs total	81	111	20	20	0	2	3	6	7	0	15	0	0	1	3	2	.180	.227	.297	.977

Tyrone, Oscar Wayne (Wayne)
HEIGHT: 6'1" THROWS: RIGHT BATS: RIGHT BORN: 8/1/1950 ALICE, TEXAS POSITIONS PLAYED: 1B, 3B, OF

YEAR	TEAM	GAMES	AB	RUNS	HITS	2B	3B	HR	RBI	BB	IBB	SO	HBP	SH	SF	SB	CS	BA	OBA	SA	FA
1976	ChC-N	30	57	3	13	1	0	1	8	3	2	21	0	1	1	0	0	.228	.262	.298	1.000
Career average		30	57	3	13	1	0	1	8	3	2	21	0	1	1	0	0	.228	.262	.298	1.000
Cubs average		30	57	3	13	1	0	1	8	3	2	21	0	1	1	0	0	.228	.262	.298	1.000
Career total		30	57	3	13	1	0	1	8	3	2	21	0	1	1	0	0	.228	.262	.298	1.000
Cubs total		30	57	3	13	1	0	1	8	3	2	21	0	1	1	0	0	.228	.262	.298	1.000

Tyson, Michael Ray (Mike)
HEIGHT: 5'9" THROWS: RIGHT BATS: RIGHT BORN: 1/13/1950 ROCKY MOUNT, NORTH CAROLINA POSITIONS PLAYED: 2B, 3B, SS

YEAR	TEAM	GAMES	AB	RUNS	HITS	2B	3B	HR	RBI	BB	IBB	SO	HBP	SH	SF	SB	CS	BA	OBA	SA	FA
1972	StL-N	13	37	1	7	1	0	0	0	1	0	9	0	0	0	0	1	.189	.211	.216	.954
1973	StL-N	144	469	48	114	15	4	1	33	23	10	66	2	7	5	2	5	.243	.279	.299	.951
1974	StL-N	151	422	35	94	14	5	1	37	22	9	70	3	4	4	4	2	.223	.264	.287	.956
1975	StL-N	122	368	45	98	16	3	2	37	24	4	39	3	6	1	5	2	.266	.316	.342	.970
1976	StL-N	76	245	26	70	12	9	3	28	16	5	34	0	0	3	3	1	.286	.326	.445	.971
1977	StL-N	138	418	42	103	15	2	7	57	30	11	48	2	5	2	3	4	.246	.299	.342	.979
1978	StL-N	125	377	26	88	16	0	3	26	24	7	41	0	1	3	2	0	.233	.277	.300	.977
1979	StL-N	75	190	18	42	8	2	5	20	13	6	28	1	1	2	2	1	.221	.272	.363	.975
1980	**ChC-N**	**123**	**341**	**34**	**81**	**19**	**3**	**3**	**23**	**15**	**3**	**61**	**2**	**4**	**1**	**1**	**2**	**.238**	**.273**	**.337**	**.968**
1981	**ChC-N**	**50**	**92**	**6**	**17**	**2**	**0**	**2**	**8**	**7**	**1**	**15**	**1**	**2**	**1**	**1**	**0**	**.185**	**.248**	**.272**	**.940**
Career average		102	296	28	71	12	3	3	27	18	6	41	1	3	2	2	2	.241	.285	.327	.966
Cubs average		87	217	20	49	11	2	3	16	11	2	38	2	3	1	1	1	.226	.267	.323	.963
Career total		1017	2959	281	714	118	28	27	269	175	56	411	14	30	22	23	18	.241	.285	.327	.966
Cubs total		173	433	40	98	21	3	5	31	22	4	76	3	6	2	2	2	.226	.267	.323	.963

Upham, John Leslie
HEIGHT: 6'0" THROWS: LEFT BATS: LEFT BORN: 12/29/1941 WINDSOR, ONTARIO, CANADA POSITIONS PLAYED: P, OF

YEAR	TEAM	GAMES	AB	RUNS	HITS	2B	3B	HR	RBI	BB	IBB	SO	HBP	SH	SF	SB	CS	BA	OBA	SA	FA
1967	ChC-N	8	3	1	2	0	0	0	0	0	0	0	0	0	0	0	0	.667	.667	.667	—
1968	ChC-N	13	10	0	2	0	0	0	0	0	0	3	0	0	0	0	0	.200	.200	.200	1.000
Career average		11	7	1	2	0	0	0	0	0	0	2	0	0	0	0	0	.308	.308	.308	1.000
Cubs average		11	7	1	2	0	0	0	0	0	0	2	0	0	0	0	0	.308	.308	.308	1.000
Career total		21	13	1	4	0	0	0	0	0	0	3	0	0	0	0	0	.308	.308	.308	1.000
Cubs total		21	13	1	4	0	0	0	0	0	0	3	0	0	0	0	0	.308	.308	.308	1.000

Usher, Robert Royce (Bob)
HEIGHT: 6'1" THROWS: RIGHT BATS: RIGHT BORN: 3/1/1925 SAN DIEGO, CALIFORNIA POSITIONS PLAYED: 3B, OF

YEAR	TEAM	GAMES	AB	RUNS	HITS	2B	3B	HR	RBI	BB	IBB	SO	HBP	SH	SF	SB	CS	BA	OBA	SA	FA
1946	Cin-N	92	152	16	31	5	1	1	14	13	—	27	1	1	—	2	—	.204	.271	.270	.983
1947	Cin-N	9	22	2	4	0	0	1	1	2	—	2	0	0	—	0	—	.182	.250	.318	1.000
1950	Cin-N	106	321	51	83	17	0	6	35	27	—	38	0	5	—	3	—	.259	.316	.368	.985
1951	Cin-N	114	303	27	63	12	2	5	25	19	—	36	1	10	—	4	5	.208	.257	.310	.974
1952	**ChC-N**	**1**	**0**	**0**	**0**	**0**	**0**	**0**	**0**	**1**	**—**	**0**	**0**	**0**	**—**	**0**	**0**	**—**	**1.000**	**—**	**—**
1957	Cle-A	10	8	1	1	0	0	0	0	1	0	3	0	1	0	0	0	.125	.222	.125	1.000
1957	Was-A	96	295	36	77	7	1	5	27	27	2	30	2	3	3	0	0	.261	.324	.342	.979
Career average		71	184	22	43	7	1	3	17	15	0	23	1	3	1	2	1	.235	.295	.329	.980
Cubs average		1	0	0	0	0	0	0	0	1	—	0	0	0	—	0	0	—	1.000	—	—
Career total		428	1101	133	259	41	4	18	102	90	2	136	4	20	3	9	5	.235	.295	.329	.980
Cubs total		1	0	0	0	0	0	0	0	1	—	0	0	0	—	0	0	—	1.000	—	—

Vail, Michael Lewis (Mike)

HEIGHT: 6'1"   THROWS: RIGHT   BATS: RIGHT   BORN: 11/10/1951 SAN FRANCISCO, CALIFORNIA   POSITIONS PLAYED: 1B, 3B, OF

YEAR	TEAM	GAMES	AB	RUNS	HITS	2B	3B	HR	RBI	BB	IBB	SO	HBP	SH	SF	SB	CS	BA	OBA	SA	FA
1975	NYM-N	38	162	17	49	8	1	3	17	9	1	37	0	0	0	0	0	.302	.339	.420	.971
1976	NYM-N	53	143	8	31	5	1	0	9	6	0	19	0	0	3	0	1	.217	.243	.266	.941
1977	NYM-N	108	279	29	73	12	1	8	35	19	0	58	2	0	3	0	7	.262	.310	.398	.965
1978	Cle-A	14	34	2	8	2	1	0	2	1	1	9	0	1	1	1	1	.235	.250	.353	1.000
1978	**ChC-N**	**74**	**180**	**15**	**60**	**6**	**2**	**4**	**33**	**3**	**0**	**24**	**0**	**0**	**2**	**0**	**1**	**.333**	**.341**	**.456**	**.981**
1979	**ChC-N**	**87**	**179**	**28**	**60**	**8**	**2**	**7**	**35**	**14**	**1**	**27**	**0**	**0**	**2**	**0**	**2**	**.335**	**.379**	**.520**	**.965**
1980	**ChC-N**	**114**	**312**	**30**	**93**	**17**	**2**	**6**	**47**	**14**	**1**	**77**	**1**	**1**	**0**	**2**	**5**	**.298**	**.330**	**.423**	**.963**
1981	Cin-N	31	31	1	5	0	0	0	3	0	0	9	0	0	0	0	0	.161	.161	.161	1.000
1982	Cin-N	78	189	9	48	10	1	4	29	6	1	33	0	2	0	0	0	.254	.274	.381	.988
1983	SF-N	18	26	1	4	1	0	0	3	0	0	7	1	0	0	0	0	.154	.185	.192	1.000
1983	Mon-N	34	53	5	15	2	0	2	4	8	0	10	1	0	0	0	0	.283	.387	.434	.968
1984	LA-N	16	16	1	1	0	0	0	2	1	0	7	1	0	0	0	0	.063	.118	.063	—
Career average		67	160	15	45	7	1	3	22	8	1	32	1	0	1	0	2	.279	.313	.400	.969
Cubs average		92	224	24	71	10	2	6	38	10	1	43	0	0	1	1	3	.317	.347	.458	.967
Career total		665	1604	146	447	71	11	34	219	81	5	317	5	2	13	3	17	.279	.313	.400	.969
Cubs total		275	671	73	213	31	6	17	115	31	2	128	1	1	4	2	8	.317	.347	.458	.967

Valdes, Pedro Jose

HEIGHT: 6'1"   THROWS: LEFT   BATS: LEFT   BORN: 6/29/1973 FAJARDO, PUERTO RICO   POSITIONS PLAYED: OF

YEAR	TEAM	GAMES	AB	RUNS	HITS	2B	3B	HR	RBI	BB	IBB	SO	HBP	SH	SF	SB	CS	BA	OBA	SA	FA
1996	**ChC-N**	**9**	**8**	**2**	**1**	**1**	**0**	**0**	**1**	**1**	**0**	**5**	**0**	**0**	**0**	**0**	**0**	**.125**	**.222**	**.250**	**1.000**
1998	**ChC-N**	**14**	**23**	**1**	**5**	**1**	**1**	**0**	**2**	**1**	**0**	**3**	**0**	**0**	**0**	**0**	**1**	**.217**	**.250**	**.348**	**1.000**
2000	Tex-A	30	54	4	15	5	0	1	5	6	0	7	0	0	0	0	0	.278	.350	.426	1.000
Career average		18	28	2	7	2	0	0	3	3	0	5	0	0	0	0	0	.247	.312	.388	1.000
Cubs average		12	16	2	3	1	1	0	2	1	0	4	0	0	0	0	1	.194	.242	.323	1.000
Career total		53	85	7	21	7	1	1	8	8	0	15	0	0	0	0	1	.247	.312	.388	1.000
Cubs total		23	31	3	6	2	1	0	3	2	0	8	0	0	0	0	1	.194	.242	.323	1.000

Van Haltren, George Edward Martin (Rip)

HEIGHT: 5'11"   THROWS: LEFT   BATS: LEFT   BORN: 3/30/1866 ST. LOUIS, MISSOURI   DIED: 9/29/1945 OAKLAND, CALIFORNIA
POSITIONS PLAYED: P, 1B, 2B, 3B, SS, OF

YEAR	TEAM	GAMES	AB	RUNS	HITS	2B	3B	HR	RBI	BB	IBB	SO	HBP	SH	SF	SB	CS	BA	OBA	SA	FA
1887	**ChN-N**	**45**	**187**	**30**	**50**	**4**	**0**	**3**	**17**	**15**	**—**	**15**	**1**	**—**	**—**	**12**	**—**	**.267**	**.325**	**.337**	**.901**
1888	**ChN-N**	**81**	**318**	**46**	**90**	**9**	**14**	**4**	**34**	**22**	**—**	**34**	**0**	**—**	**—**	**21**	**—**	**.283**	**.329**	**.437**	**.904**
1889	**ChN-N**	**134**	**543**	**126**	**168**	**20**	**10**	**9**	**81**	**82**	**—**	**41**	**5**	**—**	**—**	**28**	**—**	**.309**	**.405**	**.433**	**.914**
1890	Bro-P	92	376	84	126	8	9	5	54	41	—	23	3	—	—	35	—	.335	.405	.443	.850
1891	Bal-AA	139	566	136	180	14	15	9	83	71	—	46	4	—	—	75	—	.318	.398	.443	.856
1892	Bal-N	135	556	105	168	20	12	7	57	70	—	34	2	—	—	6	—	.302	.382	.419	.905
1892	Pit-N	13	55	10	11	2	2	0	5	6	—	0	0	—	—	37	—	.200	.279	.309	.865
1893	Pit-N	124	529	129	179	14	11	3	79	75	—	25	2	13	—	43	—	.338	.422	.423	.914
1894	NYG-N	137	519	109	172	22	4	7	104	55	—	22	4	6	—	32	—	.331	.400	.430	.912
1895	NYG-N	131	521	113	177	23	19	8	103	57	—	29	3	4	—	39	—	.340	.408	.503	.952
1896	NYG-N	133	562	136	197	18	21	5	74	55	—	36	2	6	—	50	—	.351	.410	.484	.937
1897	NYG-N	129	564	117	186	22	9	3	64	40	—	—	1	5	—	36	—	.330	.375	.417	.917
1898	NYG-N	156	654	129	204	28	16	2	68	59	—	—	4	4	—	31	—	.312	.372	.413	.932
1899	NYG-N	151	604	117	182	21	3	2	58	74	—	—	1	13	—	45	—	.301	.378	.356	.939
1900	NYG-N	141	571	114	180	30	7	1	51	50	—	—	4	7	—	24	—	.315	.374	.398	.942
1901	NYG-N	135	543	82	182	23	6	1	47	51	—	—	0	0	—	6	—	.335	.392	.405	.925
1902	NYG-N	24	88	14	23	1	2	0	7	17	—	—	0	7	—	14	—	.261	.381	.318	.959
1903	NYG-N	84	280	42	72	6	1	0	28	28	—	—	1	7	—	49	—	.257	.327	.286	.908
Career average		117	473	96	150	17	9	4	60	51	—	18	2	4	—	34	—	.317	.386	.418	.908
Cubs average		87	349	67	103	11	8	5	44	40	—	30	2	—	—	20	—	.294	.369	.417	.897
Career total		1984	8036	1639	2547	285	161	69	1014	868	—	305	38	65	—	583	—	.317	.386	.418	.908
Cubs total		260	1048	202	308	33	24	16	132	119	—	90	6	—	—	61	—	.294	.369	.417	.897

Van Zandt, Charles Isaac (Ike)
HEIGHT: — THROWS: — BATS: LEFT BORN: 2/1876 BROOKLYN, NEW YORK DIED: 9/14/1908 NASHUA, NEW HAMPSHIRE POSITIONS PLAYED: P, 1B, OF

YEAR	TEAM	GAMES	AB	RUNS	HITS	2B	3B	HR	RBI	BB	IBB	SO	HBP	SH	SF	SB	CS	BA	OBA	SA	FA
1901	NYG-N	3	6	1	1	0	0	0	0	0	—	—	0	0	—	0	—	.167	.167	.167	.250
1904	**ChC-N**	**3**	**11**	**0**	**0**	**0**	**0**	**0**	**0**	**0**	—	—	**0**	**1**	—	**0**	—	**.000**	**.000**	**.000**	**1.000**
1905	StL-A	94	322	31	75	15	1	1	20	7	—	—	1	9	—	7	—	.233	.252	.295	.885
Career average		33	113	11	25	5	0	0	7	2	—	—	0	3	—	2	—	.224	.242	.283	.864
Cubs average		**3**	**11**	**0**	**0**	**0**	**0**	**0**	**0**	**0**	—	—	**0**	**1**	—	**0**	—	**.000**	**.000**	**.000**	**1.000**
Career total		100	339	32	76	15	1	1	20	7	—	—	1	10	—	7	—	.224	.242	.283	.864
Cubs total		**3**	**11**	**0**	**0**	**0**	**0**	**0**	**0**	**0**	—	—	**0**	**1**	—	**0**	—	**.000**	**.000**	**.000**	**1.000**

Varsho, Gary Andrew
HEIGHT: 5'11" THROWS: RIGHT BATS: LEFT BORN: 6/20/1961 MARSHFIELD, WISCONSIN POSITIONS PLAYED: 1B, OF

YEAR	TEAM	GAMES	AB	RUNS	HITS	2B	3B	HR	RBI	BB	IBB	SO	HBP	SH	SF	SB	CS	BA	OBA	SA	FA
1988	**ChC-N**	**46**	**73**	**6**	**20**	**3**	**0**	**0**	**5**	**1**	**0**	**6**	**0**	**0**	**1**	**5**	**0**	**.274**	**.280**	**.315**	**.906**
1989	**ChC-N**	**61**	**87**	**10**	**16**	**4**	**2**	**0**	**6**	**4**	**1**	**13**	**0**	**0**	**0**	**3**	**0**	**.184**	**.220**	**.276**	**.929**
1990	**ChC-N**	**46**	**48**	**10**	**12**	**4**	**0**	**0**	**1**	**1**	**1**	**6**	**0**	**0**	**0**	**2**	**0**	**.250**	**.265**	**.333**	**1.000**
1991	Pit-N	99	187	23	51	11	2	4	23	19	2	34	2	1	1	9	2	.273	.344	.417	.990
1992	Pit-N	103	162	22	36	6	3	4	22	10	1	32	0	0	1	5	2	.222	.266	.370	.984
1993	Cin-N	77	95	8	22	6	0	2	11	9	0	19	1	3	1	1	0	.232	.302	.358	1.000
1994	Pit-N	67	82	15	21	6	3	0	5	4	1	19	2	2	0	0	1	.256	.307	.402	.926
1995	Phi-N	72	103	7	26	1	1	0	11	7	1	17	2	0	2	2	0	.252	.310	.282	.939
Career average		71	105	13	26	5	1	1	11	7	1	18	1	1	1	3	1	.244	.294	.355	.965
Cubs average		**51**	**69**	**9**	**16**	**4**	**1**	**0**	**4**	**2**	**1**	**8**	**0**	**0**	**0**	**3**	**0**	**.231**	**.251**	**.303**	**.919**
Career total		571	837	101	204	41	11	10	84	55	7	146	7	6	5	27	5	.244	.294	.355	.965
Cubs total		**153**	**208**	**26**	**48**	**11**	**2**	**0**	**12**	**6**	**2**	**25**	**0**	**0**	**1**	**10**	**0**	**.231**	**.251**	**.303**	**.919**

Verban, Emil Matthew (Dutch *or* Antelope)
HEIGHT: 5'11" THROWS: RIGHT BATS: RIGHT BORN: 8/27/1915 LINCOLN, ILLINOIS DIED: 6/8/1989 QUINCY, ILLINOIS POSITIONS PLAYED: 2B, 3B, SS, OF

YEAR	TEAM	GAMES	AB	RUNS	HITS	2B	3B	HR	RBI	BB	IBB	SO	HBP	SH	SF	SB	CS	BA	OBA	SA	FA
1944	StL-N	146	498	51	128	14	2	0	43	19	—	14	2	19	—	0	—	.257	.287	.293	.968
1945	StL-N	155	597	59	166	22	8	0	72	19	—	15	3	16	—	4	—	.278	.304	.342	.978
1946	StL-N	1	1	0	0	0	0	0	0	0	—	0	0	0	—	0	—	.000	.000	.000	—
1946	Phi-N	138	473	44	130	17	5	0	34	21	—	18	0	13	—	5	—	.275	.306	.332	.963
1947	Phi-N	155	540	50	154	14	8	0	42	23	—	8	1	9	—	5	—	.285	.316	.341	.982
1948	Phi-N	55	169	14	39	5	1	0	11	11	—	5	1	11	—	0	—	.231	.282	.272	.975
1948	**ChC-N**	**56**	**248**	**37**	**73**	**15**	**1**	**1**	**16**	**4**	—	**7**	**1**	**0**	—	**4**	—	**.294**	**.308**	**.375**	**.964**
1949	**ChC-N**	**98**	**343**	**38**	**99**	**11**	**1**	**0**	**22**	**8**	—	**2**	**2**	**10**	—	**3**	—	**.289**	**.309**	**.327**	**.965**
1950	**ChC-N**	**45**	**37**	**7**	**4**	**1**	**0**	**0**	**1**	**3**	—	**5**	**0**	**3**	—	**0**	—	**.108**	**.175**	**.135**	**.939**
1950	Bos-N	4	5	1	0	0	0	0	0	0	—	0	0	0	—	0	—	.000	.000	.000	.833
Career average		122	416	43	113	14	4	0	34	15	—	11	1	12	—	3	—	.272	.301	.325	.971
Cubs average		**66**	**209**	**27**	**59**	**9**	**1**	**0**	**13**	**5**	—	**5**	**1**	**4**	—	**2**	—	**.280**	**.300**	**.334**	**.964**
Career total		853	2911	301	793	99	26	1	241	108	—	74	10	81	—	21	—	.272	.301	.325	.971
Cubs total		**199**	**628**	**82**	**176**	**27**	**2**	**1**	**39**	**15**	—	**14**	**3**	**13**	—	**7**	—	**.280**	**.300**	**.334**	**.964**

Veryzer, Thomas Martin (Tom)
HEIGHT: 6'1" THROWS: RIGHT BATS: RIGHT BORN: 2/11/1953 PORT JEFFERSON, NEW YORK POSITIONS PLAYED: 2B, 3B, SS

YEAR	TEAM	GAMES	AB	RUNS	HITS	2B	3B	HR	RBI	BB	IBB	SO	HBP	SH	SF	SB	CS	BA	OBA	SA	FA
1973	Det-A	18	20	1	6	0	1	0	2	2	0	4	0	0	0	0	0	.300	.364	.400	.857
1974	Det-A	22	55	4	13	2	0	2	9	5	0	8	0	0	0	1	0	.236	.300	.382	.927
1975	Det-A	128	404	37	102	13	1	5	48	23	1	76	5	2	5	2	6	.252	.297	.327	.960
1976	Det-A	97	354	31	83	8	2	1	25	21	1	44	6	6	3	1	4	.234	.286	.277	.966
1977	Det-A	125	350	31	69	12	1	2	28	16	0	44	0	4	3	0	1	.197	.230	.254	.969
1978	Cle-A	130	421	48	114	18	4	1	32	13	0	36	5	15	4	1	2	.271	.298	.340	.963
1979	Cle-A	149	449	41	99	9	3	0	34	34	0	54	4	10	4	2	5	.220	.279	.254	.974
1980	Cle-A	109	358	28	97	12	0	2	28	10	1	25	8	4	3	0	5	.271	.303	.321	.971
1981	Cle-A	75	221	13	54	12	0	0	14	10	1	10	1	5	2	1	0	.244	.278	.262	.970

(continued)

(Veryzer, continued)

YEAR	TEAM																	BA	OBA	SA	FA
1982	NYM-N	40	54	6	18	2	0	0	4	3	2	4	0	0	1	1	0	.333	.362	.370	.923
1983	ChC-N	59	88	5	18	3	0	1	3	3	1	13	0	1	0	0	0	.205	.231	.273	.980
1984	ChC-N	44	74	5	14	1	0	0	4	3	1	11	4	2	0	0	0	.189	.259	.203	.955
Career average		83	237	21	57	7	1	1	19	12	1	27	3	4	2	1	2	.241	.283	.294	.966
Cubs average		52	81	5	16	2	0	1	4	3	1	12	2	2	0	0	0	.198	.244	.241	.967
Career total		996	2848	250	687	84	12	14	231	143	8	329	33	49	25	9	23	.241	.283	.294	.966
Cubs total		103	162	10	32	4	0	1	7	6	2	24	4	3	0	0	0	.198	.244	.241	.967

Villanueva, Hector
HEIGHT: 6'1" THROWS: RIGHT BATS: RIGHT BORN: 10/2/1964 RIO PIEDRAS, PUERTO RICO POSITIONS PLAYED: C, 1B

YEAR	TEAM	GAMES	AB	RUNS	HITS	2B	3B	HR	RBI	BB	IBB	SO	HBP	SH	SF	SB	CS	BA	OBA	SA	FA
1990	ChC-N	52	114	14	31	4	1	7	18	4	2	27	2	0	0	1	0	.272	.308	.509	.989
1991	ChC-N	71	192	23	53	10	1	13	32	21	1	30	0	0	1	0	0	.276	.346	.542	.981
1992	ChC-N	51	112	9	17	6	0	2	13	11	2	24	0	0	0	0	0	.152	.228	.259	.981
1993	StL-N	17	55	7	8	1	0	3	9	4	1	17	0	0	0	0	0	.145	.203	.327	1.000
Career average		48	118	13	27	5	1	6	18	10	2	25	1	0	0	0	0	.230	.293	.442	.985
Cubs average		58	139	15	34	7	1	7	21	12	2	27	1	0	0	0	0	.242	.304	.457	.983
Career total		191	473	53	109	21	2	25	72	40	6	98	2	0	1	1	0	.230	.293	.442	.985
Cubs total		174	418	46	101	20	2	22	63	36	5	81	2	0	1	1	0	.242	.304	.457	.983

Vizcaino, Jose Luis
HEIGHT: 6'1" THROWS: RIGHT BATS: BOTH BORN: 3/26/1968 SAN CRISTOBAL, DOMINICAN REPUBLIC POSITIONS PLAYED: 1B, 2B, 3B, SS, OF

YEAR	TEAM	GAMES	AB	RUNS	HITS	2B	3B	HR	RBI	BB	IBB	SO	HBP	SH	SF	SB	CS	BA	OBA	SA	FA
1989	LA-N	7	10	2	2	0	0	0	0	0	0	1	0	1	0	0	0	.200	.200	.200	.882
1990	LA-N	37	51	3	14	1	1	0	2	4	1	8	0	0	0	1	1	.275	.327	.333	.962
1991	ChC-N	93	145	7	38	5	0	0	10	5	0	18	0	2	2	2	1	.262	.283	.297	.960
1992	ChC-N	86	285	25	64	10	4	1	17	14	2	35	0	5	1	3	0	.225	.260	.298	.970
1993	ChC-N	151	551	74	158	19	4	4	54	46	2	71	3	8	9	12	9	.287	.340	.358	.974
1994	NYM-N	103	410	47	105	13	3	3	33	33	3	62	2	5	6	1	11	.256	.310	.324	.970
1995	NYM-N	135	509	66	146	21	5	3	56	35	4	76	1	13	3	8	3	.287	.332	.365	.984
1996	NYM-N	96	363	47	110	12	6	1	32	28	0	58	3	6	2	9	5	.303	.356	.377	.986
1996	Cle-A	48	179	23	51	5	2	0	13	7	0	24	0	4	1	6	2	.285	.310	.335	.982
1997	SF-N	151	568	77	151	19	7	5	50	48	1	87	1	13	1	8	8	.266	.323	.350	.976
1998	LA-N	67	237	30	62	9	0	3	29	17	0	35	1	10	2	7	3	.262	.311	.338	.985
1999	LA-N	94	266	27	67	9	0	1	29	20	0	23	1	9	2	2	1	.252	.304	.297	.976
2000	LA-N	40	93	9	19	2	1	0	4	10	3	15	1	2	0	1	0	.204	.288	.247	.978
2000	NYY-A	73	174	23	48	8	1	0	10	12	0	28	0	3	2	5	7	.276	.319	.333	.991
2001	Hou-N	107	256	38	71	8	3	1	14	15	0	33	2	9	0	3	2	.277	.322	.344	.939
Career average		99	315	38	85	11	3	2	27	23	1	44	1	7	2	5	4	.270	.319	.339	.975
Cubs average		110	327	35	87	11	3	2	27	22	1	41	1	5	4	6	3	.265	.309	.331	.970
Career total		1288	4097	498	1106	141	37	22	353	294	16	574	14	90	31	68	53	.270	.319	.339	.975
Cubs total		330	981	106	260	34	8	5	81	65	4	124	3	15	12	17	10	.265	.309	.331	.970

Vogel, Otto Henry
HEIGHT: 6'0" THROWS: RIGHT BATS: RIGHT BORN: 10/26/1899 MENDOTA, ILLINOIS DIED: 7/19/1969 IOWA CITY, IOWA POSITIONS PLAYED: 3B, OF

YEAR	TEAM	GAMES	AB	RUNS	HITS	2B	3B	HR	RBI	BB	IBB	SO	HBP	SH	SF	SB	CS	BA	OBA	SA	FA
1923	ChC-N	41	81	10	17	0	1	1	6	7	—	11	3	1	—	2	3	.210	.297	.272	.932
1924	ChC-N	70	172	28	46	11	2	1	24	10	—	26	3	7	—	4	4	.267	.319	.372	.957
Career average		56	127	19	32	6	2	1	15	9	—	19	3	4	—	3	4	.249	.312	.340	.950
Cubs average		56	127	19	32	6	2	1	15	9	—	19	3	4	—	3	4	.249	.312	.340	.950
Career total		111	253	38	63	11	3	2	30	17	—	37	6	8	—	6	7	.249	.312	.340	.950
Cubs total		111	253	38	63	11	3	2	30	17	—	37	6	8	—	6	7	.249	.312	.340	.950

Wade, Galeard Lee (Gale)
HEIGHT: 6'1"   THROWS: RIGHT   BATS: LEFT   BORN: 1/20/1929 HOLLISTER, MISSOURI   POSITIONS PLAYED: OF

YEAR	TEAM	GAMES	AB	RUNS	HITS	2B	3B	HR	RBI	BB	IBB	SO	HBP	SH	SF	SB	CS	BA	OBA	SA	FA
1955	ChC-N	9	33	5	6	1	0	1	1	4	0	3	0	1	0	0	0	.182	.270	.303	.867
1956	ChC-N	10	12	0	0	0	0	0	0	1	0	0	0	0	0	0	0	.000	.077	.000	.875
Career average		10	23	3	3	1	0	1	1	3	0	2	0	1	0	0	0	.133	.220	.222	.870
Cubs average		**10**	**23**	**3**	**3**	**1**	**0**	**1**	**1**	**3**	**0**	**2**	**0**	**1**	**0**	**0**	**0**	**.133**	**.220**	**.222**	**.870**
Career total		19	45	5	6	1	0	1	1	5	0	3	0	1	0	0	0	.133	.220	.222	.870
Cubs total		**19**	**45**	**5**	**6**	**1**	**0**	**1**	**1**	**5**	**0**	**3**	**0**	**1**	**0**	**0**	**0**	**.133**	**.220**	**.222**	**.870**

Waitkus, Edward Stephen (Eddie)
HEIGHT: 6'0"   THROWS: LEFT   BATS: LEFT   BORN: 9/4/1919 CAMBRIDGE, MASSACHUSETTS   DIED: 9/15/1972 JAMAICA PLAIN, MASSACHUSETTS
POSITIONS PLAYED: 1B, OF

YEAR	TEAM	GAMES	AB	RUNS	HITS	2B	3B	HR	RBI	BB	IBB	SO	HBP	SH	SF	SB	CS	BA	OBA	SA	FA
1941	ChC-N	12	28	1	5	0	0	0	0	0	—	3	1	0	—	0	—	.179	.207	.179	.949
1946	ChC-N	113	441	50	134	24	5	4	55	23	—	14	1	7	—	3	—	.304	.340	.408	.996
1947	ChC-N	130	514	60	150	28	6	2	35	32	—	17	2	6	—	3	—	.292	.336	.381	.994
1948	ChC-N	139	562	87	166	27	10	7	44	43	—	19	2	7	—	11	—	.295	.348	.416	.992
1949	Phi-N	54	209	41	64	16	3	1	28	33	—	12	1	3	—	3	—	.306	.403	.426	.994
1950	Phi-N	154	641	102	182	32	5	2	44	55	—	29	1	5	—	3	—	.284	.341	.359	.993
1951	Phi-N	145	610	65	157	27	4	1	46	53	—	22	0	1	—	0	3	.257	.317	.320	.992
1952	Phi-N	146	499	51	144	29	4	2	49	64	—	23	1	4	—	2	2	.289	.371	.375	.991
1953	Phi-N	81	247	24	72	9	2	1	16	13	—	23	1	1	—	1	1	.291	.330	.356	.989
1954	Bal-A	95	311	35	88	17	4	2	33	28	—	25	1	6	3	0	1	.283	.341	.383	1.000
1955	Bal-A	38	85	2	22	1	1	0	9	11	3	10	0	0	0	2	0	.259	.344	.294	.974
1955	Phi-N	33	107	10	30	5	0	2	14	17	1	7	0	0	0	0	1	.280	.379	.383	.996
Career average		104	387	48	110	20	4	2	34	34	0	19	1	4	0	3	1	.285	.344	.374	.993
Cubs average		**99**	**386**	**50**	**114**	**20**	**5**	**3**	**34**	**25**	**—**	**13**	**2**	**5**	**—**	**4**	**—**	**.294**	**.339**	**.398**	**.993**
Career total		1140	4254	528	1214	215	44	24	373	372	4	204	11	40	3	28	8	.285	.344	.374	.993
Cubs total		**394**	**1545**	**198**	**455**	**79**	**21**	**13**	**134**	**98**	**—**	**53**	**6**	**20**	**—**	**17**	**—**	**.294**	**.339**	**.398**	**.993**

Waitt, Charles C. (Charlie)
HEIGHT: 5'11"   THROWS: RIGHT   BATS: —   BORN: 10/14/1853 HALLOWELL, MAINE   DIED: 10/21/1912 SAN FRANCISCO, CALIFORNIA   POSITIONS PLAYED: OF

YEAR	TEAM	GAMES	AB	RUNS	HITS	2B	3B	HR	RBI	BB	IBB	SO	HBP	SH	SF	SB	CS	BA	OBA	SA	FA
1877	ChN-N	10	41	2	4	0	0	0	2	0	—	3	—	—	—	—	—	.098	.098	.098	.793
1882	Bal-AA	72	250	19	39	4	0	0	—	13	—	—	—	—	—	—	—	.156	.198	.172	.874
1883	Phi-N	1	3	0	1	0	0	0	0	0	—	1	—	—	—	—	—	.333	.333	.333	.333
Career average		28	98	7	15	1	0	0	1	4	—	1	—	—	—	—	—	.150	.186	.163	.855
Cubs average		**10**	**41**	**2**	**4**	**0**	**0**	**0**	**2**	**0**	**—**	**3**	**—**	**—**	**—**	**—**	**—**	**.098**	**.098**	**.098**	**.793**
Career total		83	294	21	44	4	0	0	2	13	—	4	—	—	—	—	—	.150	.186	.163	.855
Cubs total		**10**	**41**	**2**	**4**	**0**	**0**	**0**	**2**	**0**	**—**	**3**	**—**	**—**	**—**	**—**	**—**	**.098**	**.098**	**.098**	**.793**

Walbeck, Matthew Lovick (Matt)
HEIGHT: 5'11"   THROWS: RIGHT   BATS: BOTH   BORN: 10/2/1969 SACRAMENTO, CALIFORNIA   POSITIONS PLAYED: C, 1B

YEAR	TEAM	GAMES	AB	RUNS	HITS	2B	3B	HR	RBI	BB	IBB	SO	HBP	SH	SF	SB	CS	BA	OBA	SA	FA
1993	ChC-N	11	30	2	6	2	0	1	6	1	0	6	0	0	0	0	0	.200	.226	.367	1.000
1994	Min-A	97	338	31	69	12	0	5	35	17	1	37	2	1	1	0	1	.204	.246	.284	.993
1995	Min-A	115	393	40	101	18	1	1	44	25	2	71	1	1	1	1	1	.257	.302	.316	.991
1996	Min-A	63	215	25	48	10	0	2	24	9	0	34	0	1	2	3	1	.223	.252	.298	.994
1997	Det-A	47	137	18	38	3	0	3	10	12	0	19	0	0	2	3	3	.277	.331	.365	.988
1998	Ana-A	108	338	41	87	15	2	6	46	30	0	68	2	5	5	1	3	.257	.317	.367	.990
1999	Ana-A	107	288	26	69	8	1	3	22	26	1	46	3	3	1	2	3	.240	.308	.306	.989
2000	Ana-A	47	146	17	29	5	0	6	12	7	0	22	1	1	0	0	1	.199	.240	.356	.991
2001	Phi-N	1	1	0	1	0	0	0	0	0	0	0	0	0	0	0	0	1.000	1.000	1.000	—
Career average		66	210	22	50	8	0	3	22	14	0	34	1	1	1	1	1	.238	.287	.323	.991
Cubs average		**11**	**30**	**2**	**6**	**2**	**0**	**1**	**6**	**1**	**0**	**6**	**0**	**0**	**0**	**0**	**0**	**.238**	**.287**	**.323**	**.991**
Career total		596	1886	200	448	73	4	27	199	127	4	303	9	12	13	13	11	.238	.287	.323	.991
Cubs total		**11**	**30**	**2**	**6**	**2**	**0**	**1**	**6**	**1**	**0**	**6**	**0**	**0**	**0**	**0**	**0**	**.200**	**.226**	**.367**	**1.000**

Walker, Albert Bluford (Rube)

HEIGHT: 6'0" THROWS: RIGHT BATS: LEFT BORN: 5/16/1926 LENOIR, NORTH CAROLINA DIED: 12/12/1992 MORGANTOWN, NORTH CAROLINA
POSITIONS PLAYED: C

YEAR	TEAM	GAMES	AB	RUNS	HITS	2B	3B	HR	RBI	BB	IBB	SO	HBP	SH	SF	SB	CS	BA	OBA	SA	FA
1948	ChC-N	79	171	17	47	8	0	5	26	24	—	17	2	0	—	0	—	.275	.371	.409	.980
1949	ChC-N	56	172	11	42	4	1	3	22	9	—	18	0	0	—	0	—	.244	.282	.331	.964
1950	ChC-N	74	213	19	49	7	1	6	16	18	—	34	0	0	—	0	—	.230	.290	.357	.975
1951	ChC-N	37	107	9	25	4	0	2	5	12	—	13	0	0	—	0	0	.234	.311	.327	.969
1951	Bro-N	36	74	6	18	4	0	2	9	6	—	14	0	1	—	0	0	.243	.300	.378	.972
1952	Bro-N	46	139	9	36	8	0	1	19	8	—	17	1	2	—	0	0	.259	.304	.338	.987
1953	Bro-N	43	95	5	23	6	0	3	9	7	—	11	1	0	—	0	0	.242	.301	.400	.978
1954	Bro-N	50	155	12	28	7	0	5	23	24	—	17	1	1	2	0	0	.181	.291	.323	.996
1955	Bro-N	48	103	6	26	5	0	2	13	15	4	11	0	0	2	1	0	.252	.342	.359	.987
1956	Bro-N	54	146	5	31	6	1	3	20	7	2	18	0	1	2	0	1	.212	.245	.329	.986
1957	Bro-N	60	166	12	30	8	0	2	23	15	4	33	0	2	4	2	0	.181	.243	.265	.992
1958	LA-N	25	44	3	5	2	0	1	7	5	2	10	0	0	1	0	0	.114	.200	.227	.985
Career average		55	144	10	33	6	0	3	17	14	1	19	0	1	1	0	0	.227	.294	.341	.982
Cubs average		**62**	**166**	**14**	**41**	**6**	**1**	**4**	**17**	**16**	**—**	**21**	**1**	**0**	**—**	**0**	**0**	**.246**	**.313**	**.359**	**.973**
Career total		608	1585	114	360	69	3	35	192	150	12	213	5	7	11	3	1	.227	.294	.341	.982
Cubs total		**246**	**663**	**56**	**163**	**23**	**2**	**16**	**69**	**63**	**—**	**82**	**2**	**0**	**—**	**0**	**0**	**.246**	**.313**	**.359**	**.973**

Walker, Cleotha (Chico)

HEIGHT: 5'9" THROWS: RIGHT BATS: BOTH BORN: 11/25/1958 JACKSON, MISSISSIPPI POSITIONS PLAYED: 2B, 3B, OF

YEAR	TEAM	GAMES	AB	RUNS	HITS	2B	3B	HR	RBI	BB	IBB	SO	HBP	SH	SF	SB	CS	BA	OBA	SA	FA
1980	Bos-A	19	57	3	12	0	0	1	5	6	1	10	1	1	1	3	2	.211	.292	.263	.958
1981	Bos-A	6	17	3	6	0	0	0	2	1	0	2	0	0	0	0	2	.353	.389	.353	1.000
1983	Bos-A	4	5	2	2	0	2	0	1	0	0	0	0	0	0	0	0	.400	.400	1.200	1.000
1984	Bos-A	3	2	0	0	0	0	0	1	0	0	1	0	0	1	0	0	.000	.000	.000	1.000
1985	ChC-N	21	12	3	1	0	0	0	0	0	0	5	0	0	0	1	0	.083	.083	.083	1.000
1986	ChC-N	28	101	21	28	3	2	1	7	10	0	20	0	0	1	15	4	.277	.339	.376	.956
1987	ChC-N	47	105	15	21	4	0	0	7	12	1	23	0	2	2	11	4	.200	.277	.238	.974
1988	Cal-A	33	78	8	12	1	0	0	2	6	0	15	0	2	0	2	1	.154	.214	.167	.964
1991	ChC-N	124	374	51	96	10	1	6	34	33	2	57	0	1	3	13	5	.257	.315	.337	.961
1992	ChC-N	19	26	2	3	0	0	0	2	3	0	4	0	1	1	1	0	.115	.200	.115	.947
1992	NYM-N	107	227	24	70	12	1	4	36	24	3	46	0	0	4	14	1	.308	.369	.423	.945
1993	NYM-N	115	213	18	48	7	1	5	19	14	0	29	0	0	2	7	0	.225	.271	.338	.949
Career average		48	111	14	27	3	1	2	11	10	1	19	0	1	1	6	2	.246	.305	.329	.957
Cubs average		**48**	**124**	**18**	**30**	**3**	**1**	**1**	**10**	**12**	**1**	**22**	**0**	**1**	**1**	**8**	**3**	**.241**	**.303**	**.312**	**.961**
Career total		526	1217	150	299	37	7	17	116	109	7	212	1	6	15	67	19	.246	.305	.329	.957
Cubs total		**239**	**618**	**92**	**149**	**17**	**3**	**7**	**50**	**58**	**3**	**109**	**0**	**3**	**7**	**41**	**13**	**.241**	**.303**	**.312**	**.961**

Walker, Harry William (Harry the Hat)

HEIGHT: 6'2" THROWS: RIGHT BATS: LEFT BORN: 10/22/1916 PASCAGOULA, MISSISSIPPI DIED: 8/8/1999 BIRMINGHAM, ALABAMA
POSITIONS PLAYED: 1B, 2B, 3B, OF

YEAR	TEAM	GAMES	AB	RUNS	HITS	2B	3B	HR	RBI	BB	IBB	SO	HBP	SH	SF	SB	CS	BA	OBA	SA	FA
1940	StL-N	7	27	2	5	2	0	0	6	0	—	2	0	1	—	0	—	.185	.185	.259	1.000
1941	StL-N	7	15	3	4	1	0	0	1	2	—	1	0	0	—	0	—	.267	.353	.333	.875
1942	StL-N	74	191	38	60	12	2	0	16	11	—	14	1	6	—	2	—	.314	.355	.398	.968
1943	StL-N	148	564	76	166	28	6	2	53	40	—	24	0	36	—	5	—	.294	.341	.376	.963
1946	StL-N	112	346	53	82	14	6	3	27	30	—	29	1	8	—	12	—	.237	.300	.338	.976
1947	StL-N	10	25	2	5	1	0	0	0	4	—	2	0	0	—	0	—	.200	.310	.240	.938
1947	Phi-N	130	488	79	181	28	16	1	41	59	—	37	4	18	—	13	—	.371	.443	.500	.967
1948	Phi-N	112	332	34	97	11	2	2	23	33	—	30	1	2	—	4	—	.292	.358	.355	.983
1949	ChC-N	42	159	20	42	6	3	1	14	11	—	6	0	2	—	2	—	.264	.312	.358	.947
1949	Cin-N	86	314	53	100	15	2	1	23	34	—	17	0	5	—	4	—	.318	.385	.389	.963
1950	StL-N	60	150	17	31	5	0	0	7	18	—	12	0	0	—	0	—	.207	.292	.240	.972
1951	StL-N	8	26	6	8	1	0	0	2	2	—	1	0	0	—	0	0	.308	.357	.346	1.000
1955	StL-N	11	14	2	5	2	0	0	1	1	0	0	0	0	0	0	0	.357	.400	.500	1.000
Career average		73	241	35	71	11	3	1	19	22	0	16	1	7	0	4	0	.296	.358	.383	.969
Cubs average		**42**	**159**	**20**	**42**	**6**	**3**	**1**	**14**	**11**	**—**	**6**	**0**	**2**	**—**	**2**	**—**	**.264**	**.312**	**.358**	**.947**
Career total		807	2651	385	786	126	37	10	214	245	0	175	7	78	0	42	0	.296	.358	.383	.969
Cubs total		**42**	**159**	**20**	**42**	**6**	**3**	**1**	**14**	**11**	**—**	**6**	**0**	**2**	**—**	**2**	**—**	**.264**	**.312**	**.358**	**.947**

Wallace, Clarence Eugene (Jack)
HEIGHT: 5'10" THROWS: RIGHT BATS: RIGHT BORN: 8/6/1890 WINNFIELD, LOUISIANA DIED: 10/15/1960 WINNFIELD, LOUISIANA POSITIONS PLAYED: C

YEAR	TEAM	GAMES	AB	RUNS	HITS	2B	3B	HR	RBI	BB	IBB	SO	HBP	SH	SF	SB	CS	BA	OBA	SA	FA
1915	ChC-N	2	7	1	2	0	0	0	1	0	—	2	1	0	—	0	0	.286	.375	.286	1.000
Career average		2	7	1	2	0	0	0	1	0	—	2	1	0	—	0	0	.286	.375	.286	1.000
Cubs average		**2**	**7**	**1**	**2**	**0**	**0**	**0**	**1**	**0**	**—**	**2**	**1**	**0**	**—**	**0**	**0**	**.286**	**.375**	**.286**	**1.000**
Career total		2	7	1	2	0	0	0	1	0	—	2	1	0	—	0	0	.286	.375	.286	1.000
Cubs total		**2**	**7**	**1**	**2**	**0**	**0**	**0**	**1**	**0**	**—**	**2**	**1**	**0**	**—**	**0**	**0**	**.286**	**.375**	**.286**	**1.000**

Waller, Elliott Tyrone (Ty)
HEIGHT: 6'0" THROWS: RIGHT BATS: RIGHT BORN: 3/14/1957 FRESNO, CALIFORNIA POSITIONS PLAYED: 2B, 3B, OF

YEAR	TEAM	GAMES	AB	RUNS	HITS	2B	3B	HR	RBI	BB	IBB	SO	HBP	SH	SF	SB	CS	BA	OBA	SA	FA
1980	StL-N	5	12	3	1	0	0	0	0	1	0	5	0	0	0	0	0	.083	.154	.083	1.000
1981	ChC-N	30	71	10	19	2	1	3	13	4	1	18	0	1	1	2	0	.268	.303	.451	.981
1982	ChC-N	17	21	4	5	0	0	0	1	2	0	5	0	1	0	0	0	.238	.304	.238	.917
1987	Hou-N	11	6	1	1	1	0	0	0	0	0	3	0	0	0	0	0	.167	.167	.333	1.000
Career average		16	28	5	7	1	0	1	4	2	0	8	0	1	0	1	0	.236	.280	.364	.972
Cubs average		**24**	**46**	**7**	**12**	**1**	**1**	**2**	**7**	**3**	**1**	**12**	**0**	**1**	**1**	**1**	**0**	**.261**	**.303**	**.402**	**.970**
Career total		63	110	18	26	3	1	3	14	7	1	31	0	2	1	2	0	.236	.280	.364	.972
Cubs total		**47**	**92**	**14**	**24**	**2**	**1**	**3**	**14**	**6**	**1**	**23**	**0**	**2**	**1**	**2**	**0**	**.261**	**.303**	**.402**	**.970**

Wallis, Harold Joseph (Joe *or* Tarzan)
HEIGHT: 5'11" THROWS: RIGHT BATS: BOTH BORN: 1/9/1952 EAST ST. LOUIS, ILLINOIS POSITIONS PLAYED: OF

YEAR	TEAM	GAMES	AB	RUNS	HITS	2B	3B	HR	RBI	BB	IBB	SO	HBP	SH	SF	SB	CS	BA	OBA	SA	FA
1975	**ChC-N**	**16**	**56**	**9**	**16**	**2**	**2**	**1**	**4**	**5**	**0**	**14**	**0**	**0**	**0**	**2**	**0**	**.286**	**.344**	**.446**	**1.000**
1976	**ChC-N**	**121**	**338**	**51**	**86**	**11**	**5**	**5**	**21**	**33**	**3**	**62**	**1**	**4**	**1**	**3**	**9**	**.254**	**.322**	**.361**	**.976**
1977	**ChC-N**	**56**	**80**	**14**	**20**	**3**	**0**	**2**	**8**	**16**	**1**	**25**	**0**	**0**	**0**	**0**	**1**	**.250**	**.375**	**.363**	**.974**
1978	**ChC-N**	**28**	**55**	**7**	**17**	**2**	**1**	**1**	**6**	**5**	**1**	**13**	**0**	**0**	**0**	**0**	**2**	**.309**	**.367**	**.436**	**1.000**
1978	Oak-A	85	279	28	66	16	1	6	26	26	1	42	0	4	2	1	4	.237	.300	.366	.980
1979	Oak-A	23	78	6	11	2	0	1	3	10	1	18	1	2	0	1	0	.141	.247	.205	1.000
Career average		66	177	23	43	7	2	3	14	19	1	35	0	2	1	1	3	.244	.317	.359	.982
Cubs average		**55**	**132**	**20**	**35**	**5**	**2**	**2**	**10**	**15**	**1**	**29**	**0**	**1**	**0**	**1**	**3**	**.263**	**.337**	**.378**	**.981**
Career total		329	886	115	216	36	9	16	68	95	7	174	2	10	3	7	16	.244	.317	.359	.982
Cubs total		**221**	**529**	**81**	**139**	**18**	**8**	**9**	**39**	**59**	**5**	**114**	**1**	**4**	**1**	**5**	**12**	**.263**	**.337**	**.378**	**.981**

Walls, Ray Lee (Lee *or* Captain Midnight)
HEIGHT: 6'3" THROWS: RIGHT BATS: RIGHT BORN: 1/6/1933 SAN DIEGO, CALIFORNIA DIED: 10/11/1993 LOS ANGELES, CALIFORNIA
POSITIONS PLAYED: C, 1B, 3B, OF

YEAR	TEAM	GAMES	AB	RUNS	HITS	2B	3B	HR	RBI	BB	IBB	SO	HBP	SH	SF	SB	CS	BA	OBA	SA	FA
1952	Pit-N	32	80	6	15	0	1	2	5	8	—	22	0	0	—	0	0	.188	.261	.288	1.000
1956	Pit-N	143	474	72	130	20	11	11	54	50	0	83	2	9	2	3	0	.274	.345	.432	.964
1957	Pit-N	8	22	3	4	1	0	0	0	2	0	5	0	0	0	1	0	.182	.250	.227	1.000
1957	**ChC-N**	**117**	**366**	**42**	**88**	**10**	**5**	**6**	**33**	**27**	**1**	**67**	**1**	**5**	**3**	**5**	**3**	**.240**	**.292**	**.344**	**.984**
1958	**ChC-N**	**136**	**513**	**80**	**156**	**19**	**3**	**24**	**72**	**47**	**0**	**62**	**8**	**6**	**2**	**4**	**4**	**.304**	**.370**	**.493**	**.992**
1959	**ChC-N**	**120**	**354**	**43**	**91**	**18**	**3**	**8**	**33**	**42**	**1**	**73**	**5**	**5**	**3**	**0**	**2**	**.257**	**.342**	**.393**	**.967**
1960	Cin-N	29	84	12	23	3	2	1	7	17	1	20	0	1	1	2	0	.274	.392	.393	.966
1960	Phi-N	65	181	19	36	6	1	3	19	14	1	32	0	1	3	3	0	.199	.253	.293	.954
1961	Phi-N	91	261	32	73	6	4	8	30	19	1	48	0	5	0	2	2	.280	.329	.425	.975
1962	LA-N	60	109	9	29	3	1	0	17	10	0	21	0	1	1	1	0	.266	.325	.312	.982
1963	LA-N	64	86	12	20	1	0	3	11	7	1	25	0	1	0	0	0	.233	.290	.349	.985
1964	LA-N	37	28	1	5	1	0	0	3	2	0	12	0	0	0	0	0	.179	.233	.214	1.000
Career average		90	256	33	67	9	3	7	28	25	1	47	2	3	2	2	2	.262	.329	.398	.975
Cubs average		**124**	**411**	**55**	**112**	**16**	**4**	**13**	**46**	**39**	**1**	**67**	**5**	**5**	**2**	**2**	**2**	**.272**	**.339**	**.420**	**.981**
Career total		902	2558	331	670	88	31	66	284	245	6	470	16	34	15	21	18	.262	.329	.398	.975
Cubs total		**373**	**1233**	**165**	**335**	**47**	**11**	**38**	**138**	**116**	**2**	**202**	**14**	**16**	**8**	**9**	**9**	**.272**	**.339**	**.420**	**.981**

Walsh, Thomas Joseph (Tom)
HEIGHT: 5'11" THROWS: RIGHT BATS: RIGHT BORN: 2/28/1885 DAVENPORT, IOWA DIED: 3/16/1963 NAPLES, FLORIDA POSITIONS PLAYED: C

YEAR	TEAM	GAMES	AB	RUNS	HITS	2B	3B	HR	RBI	BB	IBB	SO	HBP	SH	SF	SB	CS	BA	OBA	SA	FA
1906	ChC-N	2	1	0	0	0	0	0	0	0	—	—	0	0	—	0	—	.000	.000	.000	1.000
Career average		2	1	0	0	0	0	0	0	0	—	—	0	0	—	0	—	.000	.000	.000	1.000
Cubs average		2	1	0	0	0	0	0	0	0	—	—	0	0	—	0	—	.000	.000	.000	1.000
Career total		2	1	0	0	0	0	0	0	0	—	—	0	0	—	0	—	.000	.000	.000	1.000
Cubs total		2	1	0	0	0	0	0	0	0	—	—	0	0	—	0	—	.000	.000	.000	1.000

Walton, Jerome O'Terrell
HEIGHT: 6'1" THROWS: RIGHT BATS: RIGHT BORN: 7/8/1965 COWETA CO., GEORGIA POSITIONS PLAYED: 1B, OF

YEAR	TEAM	GAMES	AB	RUNS	HITS	2B	3B	HR	RBI	BB	IBB	SO	HBP	SH	SF	SB	CS	BA	OBA	SA	FA
1989	ChC-N	116	475	64	139	23	3	5	46	27	1	77	6	2	5	24	7	.293	.335	.385	.990
1990	ChC-N	101	392	63	103	16	2	2	21	50	1	70	4	1	2	14	7	.263	.350	.329	.977
1991	ChC-N	123	270	42	59	13	1	5	17	19	0	55	3	3	3	7	3	.219	.275	.330	.983
1992	ChC-N	30	55	7	7	0	1	0	1	9	0	13	2	3	0	1	2	.127	.273	.164	.944
1993	Cal-A	5	2	2	0	0	0	0	0	1	0	2	0	0	0	1	0	.000	.333	.000	1.000
1994	Cin-N	46	68	10	21	4	0	1	9	4	0	12	0	1	0	1	3	.309	.347	.412	.983
1995	Cin-N	102	162	32	47	12	1	8	22	17	0	25	4	3	2	10	7	.290	.368	.525	.982
1996	Atl-N	37	47	9	16	5	0	1	4	5	0	10	0	1	2	0	0	.340	.389	.511	1.000
1997	Bal-A	26	68	8	20	1	0	3	9	4	0	10	0	2	0	0	0	.294	.333	.441	1.000
1998	TB-A	12	34	4	11	3	0	0	3	2	0	6	0	0	0	0	0	.324	.361	.412	1.000
Career average		60	157	24	42	8	1	3	13	14	0	28	2	2	1	6	3	.269	.333	.376	.984
Cubs average		93	298	44	77	13	2	3	21	26	1	54	4	2	3	12	5	.258	.324	.344	.982
Career total		598	1573	241	423	77	8	25	132	138	2	280	19	16	14	58	29	.269	.333	.376	.984
Cubs total		370	1192	176	308	52	7	12	85	105	2	215	15	9	10	46	19	.258	.324	.344	.982

Ward, Chris Gilbert
HEIGHT: 6'0" THROWS: LEFT BATS: LEFT BORN: 5/18/1949 OAKLAND, CALIFORNIA POSITIONS PLAYED: 1B, OF

YEAR	TEAM	GAMES	AB	RUNS	HITS	2B	3B	HR	RBI	BB	IBB	SO	HBP	SH	SF	SB	CS	BA	OBA	SA	FA
1972	ChC-N	1	1	0	0	0	0	0	0	0	0	0	0	0	0	0	0	.000	.000	.000	—
1974	ChC-N	92	137	8	28	4	0	1	15	18	3	13	0	1	2	0	2	.204	.293	.255	.990
Career average		47	69	4	14	2	0	1	8	9	2	7	0	1	1	0	1	.203	.291	.254	.990
Cubs average		47	69	4	14	2	0	1	8	9	2	7	0	1	1	0	1	.203	.291	.254	.990
Career total		93	138	8	28	4	0	1	15	18	3	13	0	1	2	0	2	.203	.291	.254	.990
Cubs total		93	138	8	28	4	0	1	15	18	3	13	0	1	2	0	2	.203	.291	.254	.990

Ward, Preston Meyer
HEIGHT: 6'4" THROWS: RIGHT BATS: LEFT BORN: 7/24/1927 COLUMBIA, MISSOURI POSITIONS PLAYED: 1B, 3B, OF

YEAR	TEAM	GAMES	AB	RUNS	HITS	2B	3B	HR	RBI	BB	IBB	SO	HBP	SH	SF	SB	CS	BA	OBA	SA	FA
1948	Bro-N	42	146	9	38	9	2	1	21	15	—	23	0	1	—	0	—	.260	.329	.370	.990
1950	ChC-N	80	285	31	72	11	2	6	33	27	—	42	0	7	—	3	—	.253	.317	.368	.995
1953	ChC-N	33	100	10	23	5	0	4	12	18	—	21	0	1	—	3	1	.230	.347	.400	.917
1953	Pit-N	88	281	35	59	7	1	8	27	44	—	39	1	5	—	1	3	.210	.319	.327	.991
1954	Pit-N	117	360	37	97	16	2	7	48	39	—	61	0	3	4	0	0	.269	.337	.383	.970
1955	Pit-N	84	179	16	38	7	4	5	25	22	4	28	0	5	2	0	0	.212	.296	.380	.998
1956	Pit-N	16	30	3	10	0	1	1	11	6	0	4	0	0	1	0	0	.333	.432	.500	1.000
1956	Cle-A	87	150	18	38	10	0	6	21	16	0	20	0	4	0	0	0	.253	.325	.440	.989
1957	Cle-A	10	11	2	2	1	0	0	0	0	0	2	0	0	0	0	0	.182	.182	.273	1.000
1958	Cle-A	48	148	22	50	3	1	4	21	10	1	27	1	1	2	0	1	.338	.379	.453	.990
1958	KCA-A	81	268	28	68	10	1	6	24	27	2	36	0	4	3	0	0	.254	.319	.366	.974
1959	KCA-A	58	109	8	27	4	1	2	19	7	1	12	0	3	3	0	0	.248	.286	.358	.977
Career average		83	230	24	58	9	2	6	29	26	1	35	0	3	2	1	1	.253	.326	.380	.985
Cubs average		57	193	21	48	8	1	5	23	23	—	32	0	4	—	3	1	.247	.326	.377	.986
Career total		744	2067	219	522	83	15	50	262	231	8	315	2	31	15	7	6	.253	.326	.380	.985
Cubs total		113	385	41	95	16	2	10	45	45	—	63	0	8	—	6	1	.247	.326	.377	.986

Warner, Hoke Hayden (Hooks)
HEIGHT: 5'10" THROWS: RIGHT BATS: LEFT BORN: 5/22/1894 DEL RIO, TEXAS DIED: 2/19/1947 SAN FRANCISCO, CALIFORNIA POSITIONS PLAYED: 2B, 3B

YEAR	TEAM	GAMES	AB	RUNS	HITS	2B	3B	HR	RBI	BB	IBB	SO	HBP	SH	SF	SB	CS	BA	OBA	SA	FA
1916	Pit-N	44	168	12	40	1	1	2	14	6	—	19	0	3	—	6	—	.238	.264	.292	.903
1917	Pit-N	3	5	0	1	0	0	0	0	0	—	1	0	0	—	0	—	.200	.200	.200	1.000
1919	Pit-N	6	8	0	1	0	0	0	2	3	—	1	0	0	—	0	—	.125	.364	.125	.818
1921	**ChC-N**	**14**	**38**	**4**	**8**	**1**	**0**	**0**	**3**	**2**	**—**	**1**	**1**	**0**	**—**	**1**	**1**	**.211**	**.268**	**.237**	**.957**
Career average		17	55	4	13	1	0	1	5	3	—	6	0	1	—	2	0	.228	.268	.274	.909
Cubs average		**14**	**38**	**4**	**8**	**1**	**0**	**0**	**3**	**2**	**—**	**1**	**1**	**0**	**—**	**1**	**1**	**.211**	**.268**	**.237**	**.957**
Career total		67	219	16	50	2	1	2	19	11	—	22	1	3	—	7	1	.228	.268	.274	.909
Cubs total		**14**	**38**	**4**	**8**	**1**	**0**	**0**	**3**	**2**	**—**	**1**	**1**	**0**	**—**	**1**	**1**	**.211**	**.268**	**.237**	**.957**

Warstler, Harold Burton (Rabbit)
HEIGHT: 5'7" THROWS: RIGHT BATS: RIGHT BORN: 9/13/1903 NORTH CANTON, OHIO DIED: 5/31/1964 NORTH CANTON, OHIO POSITIONS PLAYED: 2B, 3B, SS

YEAR	TEAM	GAMES	AB	RUNS	HITS	2B	3B	HR	RBI	BB	IBB	SO	HBP	SH	SF	SB	CS	BA	OBA	SA	FA
1930	Bos-A	54	162	16	30	2	3	1	13	20	—	21	0	5	—	0	2	.185	.275	.253	.947
1931	Bos-A	66	181	20	44	5	3	0	10	15	—	27	2	3	—	2	3	.243	.308	.304	.935
1932	Bos-A	115	388	26	82	15	5	0	34	22	—	43	3	9	—	9	6	.211	.259	.276	.939
1933	Bos-A	92	322	44	70	13	1	1	17	42	—	36	0	6	—	2	4	.217	.308	.273	.951
1934	Phi-A	117	419	56	99	19	3	1	36	51	—	30	1	15	—	9	3	.236	.321	.303	.966
1935	Phi-A	138	496	62	124	20	7	3	59	56	—	53	0	17	—	8	4	.250	.326	.337	.959
1936	Phi-A	66	236	27	59	8	6	1	24	36	—	16	2	17	—	0	0	.250	.354	.347	.973
1936	Bos-N	74	304	27	64	6	0	0	17	22	—	33	1	2	—	2	—	.211	.266	.230	.948
1937	Bos-N	149	555	57	124	20	0	3	36	51	—	62	2	22	—	4	—	.223	.291	.276	.942
1938	Bos-N	142	467	37	108	10	4	0	40	48	—	38	0	5	—	3	—	.231	.303	.270	.938
1939	Bos-N	114	342	34	83	11	3	0	24	24	—	31	0	4	—	2	—	.243	.292	.292	.961
1940	Bos-N	33	57	6	12	0	0	0	4	10	—	5	0	1	—	0	—	.211	.328	.211	.974
1940	**ChC-N**	**45**	**159**	**19**	**36**	**4**	**1**	**1**	**18**	**8**	**—**	**19**	**0**	**1**	**—**	**1**	**—**	**.226**	**.263**	**.283**	**.943**
Career average		110	372	39	85	12	3	1	30	37	—	38	1	10	—	4	2	.229	.300	.287	.951
Cubs average		**45**	**159**	**19**	**36**	**4**	**1**	**1**	**18**	**8**	**—**	**19**	**0**	**1**	**—**	**1**	**0**	**.226**	**.263**	**.283**	**.943**
Career total		1205	4088	431	935	133	36	11	332	405	—	414	11	107	—	42	22	.229	.300	.287	.951
Cubs total		**45**	**159**	**19**	**36**	**4**	**1**	**1**	**18**	**8**	**—**	**19**	**0**	**1**	**—**	**1**	**0**	**.226**	**.263**	**.283**	**.943**

Warwick, Carl Wayne
HEIGHT: 5'10" THROWS: LEFT BATS: RIGHT BORN: 2/27/1937 DALLAS, TEXAS POSITIONS PLAYED: 1B, OF

YEAR	TEAM	GAMES	AB	RUNS	HITS	2B	3B	HR	RBI	BB	IBB	SO	HBP	SH	SF	SB	CS	BA	OBA	SA	FA
1961	LA-N	19	11	2	1	0	0	0	1	2	0	3	0	0	0	0	0	.091	.231	.091	1.000
1961	StL-N	55	152	27	38	6	2	4	16	18	0	33	0	4	3	3	0	.250	.324	.395	.970
1962	StL-N	13	23	4	8	0	0	1	4	2	0	2	0	0	1	2	0	.348	.385	.478	1.000
1962	Hou-N	130	477	63	124	17	1	16	60	38	1	77	0	5	5	2	3	.260	.312	.400	.986
1963	Hou-N	150	528	49	134	19	5	7	47	49	4	70	2	3	1	3	3	.254	.319	.348	.989
1964	StL-N	88	158	14	41	7	1	3	15	11	1	30	0	2	1	2	0	.259	.306	.373	.933
1965	StL-N	50	77	3	12	2	1	0	6	4	0	18	0	0	0	1	0	.156	.198	.208	.979
1965	Bal-A	9	14	3	0	0	0	0	0	3	0	2	0	0	0	0	0	.000	.176	.000	1.000
1966	**ChC-N**	**16**	**22**	**3**	**5**	**0**	**0**	**0**	**0**	**0**	**0**	**6**	**0**	**0**	**0**	**0**	**0**	**.227**	**.227**	**.227**	**1.000**
Career average		88	244	28	61	9	2	5	25	21	1	40	0	2	2	2	1	.248	.307	.360	.981
Cubs average		**16**	**22**	**3**	**5**	**0**	**0**	**0**	**0**	**0**	**0**	**6**	**0**	**0**	**0**	**0**	**0**	**.227**	**.307**	**.227**	**1.000**
Career total		530	1462	168	363	51	10	31	149	127	6	241	2	14	11	13	6	.248	.307	.360	.981
Cubs total		**16**	**22**	**3**	**5**	**0**	**0**	**0**	**0**	**0**	**0**	**6**	**0**	**0**	**0**	**0**	**0**	**.227**	**.227**	**.227**	**1.000**

Webb, William Earl (Earl)
HEIGHT: 6'1" THROWS: RIGHT BATS: LEFT BORN: 9/17/1897 BON AIR, TENNESSEE DIED: 5/23/1965 JAMESTOWN, TENNESSEE POSITIONS PLAYED: 1B, OF

YEAR	TEAM	GAMES	AB	RUNS	HITS	2B	3B	HR	RBI	BB	IBB	SO	HBP	SH	SF	SB	CS	BA	OBA	SA	FA
1925	NYG-N	4	3	0	0	0	0	0	0	1	—	1	0	0	—	0	0	.000	.250	.000	—
1927	**ChC-N**	**102**	**332**	**58**	**100**	**18**	**4**	**14**	**52**	**48**	**—**	**31**	**1**	**14**	**—**	**0**	**—**	**.301**	**.391**	**.506**	**.959**
1928	**ChC-N**	**62**	**140**	**22**	**35**	**7**	**3**	**3**	**23**	**14**	**—**	**17**	**0**	**5**	**—**	**3**	**—**	**.250**	**.318**	**.407**	**.986**
1930	Bos-A	127	449	61	145	30	6	16	66	44	—	56	1	12	—	2	1	.323	.385	.523	.959
1931	Bos-A	151	589	96	196	67	3	14	103	70	—	51	0	1	—	2	2	.333	.404	.528	.948

(continued)

(Webb, continued)

YEAR	TEAM	GAMES	AB	RUNS	HITS	2B	3B	HR	RBI	BB	IBB	SO	HBP	SH	SF	SB	CS	BA	OBA	SA	FA
1932	Bos-A	52	192	23	54	9	1	5	27	25	—	15	0	2	—	0	0	.281	.364	.417	.960
1932	Det-A	88	338	49	97	19	8	3	51	39	—	18	0	1	—	1	1	.287	.361	.417	.955
1933	Det-A	6	11	1	3	0	0	0	3	3	—	0	0	0	—	0	0	.273	.429	.273	1.000
1933	CWS-A	58	107	16	31	5	0	1	8	16	—	13	0	2	—	0	0	.290	.382	.364	.950
Career average		93	309	47	94	22	4	8	48	37	—	29	0	5	—	1	1	.306	.381	.478	.956
Cubs average		**82**	**236**	**40**	**68**	**13**	**4**	**9**	**38**	**31**	**—**	**24**	**1**	**10**	**—**	**2**	**0**	**.286**	**.370**	**.477**	**.966**
Career total		650	2161	326	661	155	25	56	333	260	—	202	2	37	—	8	4	.306	.381	.478	.956
Cubs total		**164**	**472**	**80**	**135**	**25**	**7**	**17**	**75**	**62**	**—**	**48**	**1**	**19**	**—**	**3**	**0**	**.286**	**.370**	**.477**	**.966**

Webster, Mitchell Dean (Mitch)

HEIGHT: 6'1" THROWS: LEFT BATS: BOTH BORN: 5/16/1959 LARNED, KANSAS POSITIONS PLAYED: 1B, OF

YEAR	TEAM	GAMES	AB	RUNS	HITS	2B	3B	HR	RBI	BB	IBB	SO	HBP	SH	SF	SB	CS	BA	OBA	SA	FA
1983	Tor-A	11	11	2	2	0	0	0	0	1	0	1	0	0	0	0	0	.182	.250	.182	1.000
1984	Tor-A	26	22	9	5	2	1	0	4	1	0	7	0	0	0	0	0	.227	.261	.409	.889
1985	Tor-A	4	1	0	0	0	0	0	0	0	0	0	0	0	0	0	1	.000	.000	.000	—
1985	Mon-N	74	212	32	58	8	2	11	30	20	3	33	0	1	1	15	9	.274	.335	.486	.993
1986	Mon-N	151	576	89	167	31	13	8	49	57	4	78	4	3	5	36	15	.290	.355	.431	.977
1987	Mon-N	156	588	101	165	30	15	15	63	70	5	95	6	8	4	33	10	.281	.361	.435	.982
1988	Mon-N	81	259	33	66	5	2	2	13	36	2	37	5	4	2	12	10	.255	.354	.313	.994
1988	**ChC-N**	**70**	**264**	**36**	**70**	**11**	**6**	**4**	**26**	**19**	**0**	**50**	**3**	**1**	**2**	**10**	**4**	**.265**	**.319**	**.398**	**.971**
1989	**ChC-N**	**98**	**272**	**40**	**70**	**12**	**4**	**3**	**19**	**30**	**5**	**55**	**1**	**3**	**2**	**14**	**2**	**.257**	**.331**	**.364**	**.965**
1990	Cle-A	128	437	58	110	20	6	12	55	20	1	61	3	11	6	22	6	.252	.285	.407	.986
1991	Cle-A	13	32	2	4	0	0	0	0	3	0	9	0	1	0	2	2	.125	.200	.125	1.000
1991	Pit-N	36	97	9	17	3	4	1	9	9	1	31	0	0	0	0	0	.175	.245	.320	.963
1991	LA-N	58	74	12	21	5	1	1	10	9	0	21	0	1	0	0	1	.284	.361	.419	1.000
1992	LA-N	135	262	33	70	12	5	6	35	27	3	49	2	8	5	11	5	.267	.334	.420	.977
1993	LA-N	88	172	26	42	6	2	2	14	11	2	24	2	4	3	4	6	.244	.293	.337	.950
1994	LA-N	82	84	16	23	4	0	4	12	8	1	13	1	0	0	1	2	.274	.344	.464	1.000
1995	LA-N	54	56	6	10	1	1	1	3	4	1	14	1	2	0	0	0	.179	.246	.286	1.000
Career average		97	263	39	69	12	4	5	26	25	2	44	2	4	2	12	6	.263	.330	.401	.979
Cubs average		**84**	**268**	**38**	**70**	**12**	**5**	**4**	**23**	**25**	**3**	**53**	**2**	**2**	**2**	**12**	**3**	**.261**	**.325**	**.381**	**.968**
Career total		1265	3419	504	900	150	55	70	342	325	28	578	28	47	30	160	73	.263	.330	.401	.979
Cubs total		**168**	**536**	**76**	**140**	**23**	**10**	**7**	**45**	**49**	**5**	**105**	**4**	**4**	**4**	**24**	**6**	**.261**	**.325**	**.381**	**.968**

Webster, Ramon Alberto (Ray)

HEIGHT: 6'0" THROWS: LEFT BATS: LEFT BORN: 8/31/1942 COLON, PANAMA POSITIONS PLAYED: 1B, OF

YEAR	TEAM	GAMES	AB	RUNS	HITS	2B	3B	HR	RBI	BB	IBB	SO	HBP	SH	SF	SB	CS	BA	OBA	SA	FA
1967	KCA-A	122	360	41	92	15	4	11	51	32	1	44	2	1	0	5	3	.256	.320	.411	.988
1968	Oak-A	66	196	17	42	11	1	3	23	12	6	24	0	2	1	3	0	.214	.258	.327	.988
1969	Oak-A	64	77	5	20	0	1	1	13	12	5	8	1	0	2	0	0	.260	.359	.325	1.000
1970	SD-N	95	116	12	30	3	0	2	11	11	0	12	0	0	0	1	1	.259	.323	.336	.981
1971	SD-N	10	8	0	1	0	0	0	0	2	0	1	0	0	0	0	0	.125	.300	.125	—
1971	**ChC-N**	**16**	**16**	**1**	**5**	**2**	**0**	**0**	**0**	**1**	**0**	**3**	**0**	**0**	**0**	**0**	**0**	**.313**	**.353**	**.438**	**1.000**
1971	Oak-A	7	5	0	0	0	0	0	0	0	0	2	0	0	0	0	0	.000	.000	.000	1.000
Career average		76	156	15	38	6	1	3	20	14	2	19	1	1	1	2	1	.244	.308	.365	.988
Cubs average		**16**	**16**	**1**	**5**	**2**	**0**	**0**	**0**	**1**	**0**	**3**	**0**	**0**	**0**	**0**	**0**	**.313**	**.353**	**.438**	**1.000**
Career total		380	778	76	190	31	6	17	98	70	12	94	3	3	3	9	4	.244	.308	.365	.988
Cubs total		**16**	**16**	**1**	**5**	**2**	**0**	**0**	**0**	**1**	**0**	**3**	**0**	**0**	**0**	**0**	**0**	**.313**	**.353**	**.438**	**1.000**

Weis, Arthur John (Butch)

HEIGHT: 5'11" THROWS: LEFT BATS: LEFT BORN: 3/2/1901 ST. LOUIS, MISSOURI DIED: 5/4/1997 ST. LOUIS, MISSOURI POSITIONS PLAYED: OF

YEAR	TEAM	GAMES	AB	RUNS	HITS	2B	3B	HR	RBI	BB	IBB	SO	HBP	SH	SF	SB	CS	BA	OBA	SA	FA
1922	**ChC-N**	**2**	**2**	**2**	**1**	**0**	**0**	**0**	**0**	**0**	**—**	**0**	**0**	**0**	**—**	**0**	**0**	**.500**	**.500**	**.500**	**—**
1923	**ChC-N**	**22**	**26**	**2**	**6**	**1**	**0**	**0**	**2**	**5**	**—**	**8**	**0**	**0**	**—**	**0**	**1**	**.231**	**.355**	**.269**	**1.000**
1924	**ChC-N**	**37**	**133**	**19**	**37**	**8**	**1**	**0**	**23**	**15**	**—**	**14**	**1**	**4**	**—**	**4**	**5**	**.278**	**.356**	**.353**	**.978**
1925	**ChC-N**	**67**	**180**	**16**	**48**	**5**	**3**	**2**	**25**	**23**	**—**	**22**	**0**	**3**	**—**	**2**	**4**	**.267**	**.350**	**.361**	**.964**
Career average		32	85	10	23	4	1	1	13	11	—	11	0	2	—	2	3	.270	.353	.352	.973
Cubs average		**32**	**85**	**10**	**23**	**4**	**1**	**1**	**13**	**11**	**—**	**11**	**0**	**2**	**—**	**2**	**3**	**.270**	**.353**	**.352**	**.973**
Career total		128	341	39	92	14	4	2	50	43	—	44	1	7	—	6	10	.270	.353	.352	.973
Cubs total		**128**	**341**	**39**	**92**	**14**	**4**	**2**	**50**	**43**	**—**	**44**	**1**	**7**	**—**	**6**	**10**	**.270**	**.353**	**.352**	**.973**

Whisenant, Thomas Peter (Pete)

HEIGHT: 6'2"   THROWS: RIGHT   BATS: RIGHT   BORN: 12/14/1929 ASHEVILLE, NORTH CAROLINA   DIED: 3/22/1996 PORT CHARLOTTE, FLORIDA
POSITIONS PLAYED: C, 2B, 3B, OF

YEAR	TEAM	GAMES	AB	RUNS	HITS	2B	3B	HR	RBI	BB	IBB	SO	HBP	SH	SF	SB	CS	BA	OBA	SA	FA
1952	Bos-N	24	52	3	10	2	0	0	7	4	—	13	0	0	—	1	1	.192	.250	.231	.973
1955	StL-N	58	115	10	22	5	1	2	9	5	0	29	0	1	1	2	0	.191	.223	.304	.964
1956	**ChC-N**	**103**	**314**	**37**	**75**	**16**	**3**	**11**	**46**	**24**	**1**	**53**	**0**	**1**	**1**	**2**	**0**	**.239**	**.292**	**.304**	**.964**
1957	Cin-N	67	90	18	19	3	2	5	11	5	0	24	1	5	3	8	2	.239	.292	.414	.992
1958	Cin-N	85	203	33	48	9	2	11	40	18	0	37	0	2	1	0	1	.211	.250	.456	.982
1959	Cin-N	36	71	13	17	2	0	5	11	8	0	18	0	3	5	3	0	.236	.292	.463	1.000
1960	Cin-N	1	1	0	0	0	0	0	0	0	0	0	0	0	0	0	0	.000	.000	.000	—
1960	Cle-A	7	6	0	1	0	0	0	0	0	0	2	0	0	0	0	0	.167	.167	.167	1.000
1960	Was-A	58	115	19	26	9	0	3	9	19	0	14	0	0	0	0	0	.226	.336	.383	1.000
1961	Min-A	10	6	1	0	0	0	0	0	1	0	2	0	0	0	2	1	.000	.143	.000	1.000
1961	Cin-N	26	15	6	3	0	0	0	1	2	0	4	0	0	0	1	0	.200	.294	.200	.857
Career average		59	124	18	28	6	1	5	17	11	0	25	0	1	1	2	1	.224	.284	.399	.986
Cubs average		**103**	**314**	**37**	**75**	**16**	**3**	**11**	**46**	**24**	**1**	**53**	**1**	**5**	**3**	**8**	**2**	**.239**	**.292**	**.414**	**.992**
Career total		475	988	140	221	46	8	37	134	86	1	196	1	11	10	17	5	.224	.284	.399	.986
Cubs total		**103**	**314**	**37**	**75**	**16**	**3**	**11**	**46**	**24**	**1**	**53**	**1**	**5**	**3**	**8**	**2**	**.239**	**.292**	**.414**	**.992**

White, Derrick Ramon

HEIGHT: 6'1"   THROWS: RIGHT   BATS: RIGHT   BORN: 10/12/1969 SAN RAFAEL, CALIFORNIA   POSITIONS PLAYED: 1B, OF

YEAR	TEAM	GAMES	AB	RUNS	HITS	2B	3B	HR	RBI	BB	IBB	SO	HBP	SH	SF	SB	CS	BA	OBA	SA	FA
1993	Mon-N	17	49	6	11	3	0	2	4	2	1	12	1	0	0	2	0	.224	.269	.408	.993
1995	Det-A	39	48	3	9	2	0	0	2	2	0	7	0	0	0	1	0	.188	.188	.229	.968
1998	**ChC-N**	**11**	**10**	**1**	**1**	**0**	**0**	**1**	**2**	**0**	**0**	**5**	**0**	**0**	**0**	**0**	**0**	**.100**	**.100**	**.400**	—
1998	Col-N	9	9	0	0	0	0	0	0	0	0	4	0	0	0	0	0	.000	.000	.000	1.000
Career average		25	39	3	7	2	0	1	3	1	0	9	0	0	0	1	0	.181	.202	.302	.985
Cubs average		**11**	**10**	**1**	**1**	**0**	**0**	**1**	**2**	**0**	**0**	**5**	**0**	**0**	**0**	**0**	**0**	**.100**	**.100**	**.400**	—
Career total		76	116	10	21	5	0	3	8	2	1	28	1	0	0	3	0	.181	.202	.302	.985
Cubs total		**11**	**10**	**1**	**1**	**0**	**0**	**1**	**2**	**0**	**0**	**5**	**0**	**0**	**0**	**0**	**0**	**.100**	**.100**	**.400**	—

White, Elder Lafayette

HEIGHT: 5'11"   THROWS: RIGHT   BATS: RIGHT   BORN: 12/23/1934 COLERAIN, NORTH CAROLINA   POSITIONS PLAYED: 3B, SS

YEAR	TEAM	GAMES	AB	RUNS	HITS	2B	3B	HR	RBI	BB	IBB	SO	HBP	SH	SF	SB	CS	BA	OBA	SA	FA
1962	**ChC-N**	**23**	**53**	**4**	**8**	**2**	**0**	**0**	**1**	**8**	**0**	**11**	**1**	**2**	**0**	**3**	**0**	**.151**	**.274**	**.189**	**.986**
Career average		23	53	4	8	2	0	0	1	8	0	11	1	2	0	3	0	.151	.274	.189	.986
Cubs average		**23**	**53**	**4**	**8**	**2**	**0**	**0**	**1**	**8**	**0**	**11**	**1**	**2**	**0**	**3**	**0**	**.151**	**.274**	**.189**	**.986**
Career total		23	53	4	8	2	0	0	1	8	0	11	1	2	0	3	0	.151	.274	.189	.986
Cubs total		**23**	**53**	**4**	**8**	**2**	**0**	**0**	**1**	**8**	**0**	**11**	**1**	**2**	**0**	**3**	**0**	**.151**	**.274**	**.189**	**.986**

White, James Laurie (Deacon)

HEIGHT: 5'11"   THROWS: RIGHT   BATS: LEFT   BORN: 12/7/1847 CATON, NEW YORK   DIED: 7/7/1939 AURORA, ILLINOIS   POSITIONS PLAYED: P, C, 1B, 2B, 3B, SS, OF

YEAR	TEAM	GAMES	AB	RUNS	HITS	2B	3B	HR	RBI	BB	IBB	SO	HBP	SH	SF	SB	CS	BA	OBA	SA	FA
1876	**ChN-N**	**66**	**310**	**66**	**104**	**18**	**1**	**1**	**60**	**7**	—	**3**	—	—	—	—	—	**.335**	**.350**	**.410**	**.842**
1877	Bos-N	59	266	51	103	14	11	2	49	8	—	3	—	—	—	—	—	.387	.405	.545	.944
1878	Cin-N	61	258	41	81	4	1	0	29	10	—	5	—	—	—	—	—	.314	.340	.337	.899
1879	Cin-N	78	333	55	110	16	6	1	52	6	—	9	—	—	—	—	—	.330	.342	.423	.890
1880	Cin-N	35	141	21	42	4	2	0	7	9	—	7	—	—	—	—	—	.298	.340	.355	.800
1881	Buf-N	78	319	58	99	24	4	0	53	9	—	8	—	—	—	—	—	.310	.329	.411	.875
1882	Buf-N	83	337	51	95	17	0	1	33	15	—	16	—	—	—	—	—	.282	.313	.341	.854
1883	Buf-N	94	391	62	114	14	5	0	47	23	—	18	—	—	—	—	—	.292	.331	.353	.839
1884	Buf-N	110	452	82	147	16	11	5	74	32	—	13	—	—	—	—	—	.325	.370	.442	.835
1885	Buf-N	98	404	54	118	6	6	0	57	12	—	11	—	—	—	—	—	.292	.313	.337	.888
1886	Det-N	124	491	65	142	19	5	1	76	31	—	35	—	—	—	9	—	.289	.331	.354	.847
1887	Det-N	111	475	71	162	20	11	3	75	26	—	15	9	—	—	20	—	.341	.386	.448	.854
1888	Det-N	125	527	75	157	22	5	4	71	21	—	24	9	—	—	12	—	.298	.336	.381	.857
1889	Pit-N	55	225	35	57	10	1	0	26	16	—	18	4	—	—	2	—	.253	.314	.307	.882
1890	Buf-P	122	439	62	114	13	4	0	47	67	—	30	19	—	—	3	—	.260	.381	.308	.949
Career average		87	358	57	110	14	5	1	50	19	—	14	3	—	—	3	—	.306	.347	.384	.880
Cubs average		**66**	**310**	**66**	**104**	**18**	**1**	**1**	**60**	**7**	—	**3**	—	—	—	—	—	**.335**	**.350**	**.410**	**.842**
Career total		1299	5368	849	1645	217	73	18	756	292	—	215	41	—	—	46	—	.306	.347	.384	.880
Cubs total		**66**	**310**	**66**	**104**	**18**	**1**	**1**	**60**	**7**	—	**3**	—	—	—	—	—	**.335**	**.350**	**.410**	**.842**

White, Jerome Cardell (Jerry)
HEIGHT: 5'10" THROWS: RIGHT BATS: BOTH BORN: 8/23/1952 SHIRLEY, MASSACHUSETTS POSITIONS PLAYED: OF

YEAR	TEAM	GAMES	AB	RUNS	HITS	2B	3B	HR	RBI	BB	IBB	SO	HBP	SH	SF	SB	CS	BA	OBA	SA	FA
1974	Mon-N	9	10	0	4	1	1	0	2	0	0	0	0	0	0	3	0	.400	.400	.700	1.000
1975	Mon-N	39	97	14	29	4	1	2	7	10	1	7	0	0	0	5	2	.299	.364	.423	.976
1976	Mon-N	114	278	32	68	11	1	2	21	27	2	31	2	2	0	15	7	.245	.316	.313	.982
1977	Mon-N	16	21	4	4	0	0	0	1	1	0	3	0	0	0	1	0	.190	.227	.190	1.000
1978	Mon-N	18	10	2	2	0	0	0	0	1	0	3	0	0	0	1	0	.200	.273	.200	—
1978	**ChC-N**	**59**	**136**	**22**	**37**	**6**	**0**	**1**	**10**	**23**	**1**	**16**	**0**	**1**	**2**	**4**	**3**	**.272**	**.373**	**.338**	**.981**
1979	Mon-N	88	138	30	41	7	1	3	18	21	2	23	1	0	1	8	4	.297	.391	.428	.983
1980	Mon-N	110	214	22	56	9	3	7	23	30	0	37	1	1	3	8	7	.262	.351	.430	.946
1981	Mon-N	59	119	11	26	5	1	3	11	13	0	17	0	2	1	5	2	.218	.293	.353	.952
1982	Mon-N	69	115	13	28	6	1	2	13	8	1	26	2	0	0	3	3	.243	.304	.365	1.000
1983	Mon-N	40	34	4	5	1	0	0	0	12	0	8	1	0	0	4	0	.147	.383	.176	1.000
1986	StL-N	25	24	1	3	0	0	1	3	2	0	3	0	1	2	0	0	.125	.179	.250	1.000
Career average		59	109	14	28	5	1	2	10	13	1	16	1	1	1	5	3	.253	.337	.363	.974
Cubs average		**59**	**136**	**22**	**37**	**6**	**0**	**1**	**10**	**23**	**1**	**16**	**0**	**1**	**2**	**4**	**3**	**.272**	**.373**	**.338**	**.981**
Career total		646	1196	155	303	50	9	21	109	148	7	174	7	7	9	57	28	.253	.373	.338	.974
Cubs total		**59**	**136**	**22**	**37**	**6**	**0**	**1**	**10**	**23**	**1**	**16**	**0**	**1**	**2**	**4**	**3**	**.272**	**.373**	**.338**	**.981**

White, Rondell Bernard
HEIGHT: 6'1" THROWS: RIGHT BATS: RIGHT BORN: 2/23/1972 MILLEDGEVILLE, GEORGIA POSITIONS PLAYED: OF

YEAR	TEAM	GAMES	AB	RUNS	HITS	2B	3B	HR	RBI	BB	IBB	SO	HBP	SH	SF	SB	CS	BA	OBA	SA	FA
1993	Mon-N	23	73	9	19	3	1	2	15	7	0	16	0	2	1	1	2	.260	.321	.411	1.000
1994	Mon-N	40	97	16	27	10	1	2	13	9	0	18	3	0	0	1	1	.278	.358	.464	.946
1995	Mon-N	130	474	87	140	33	4	13	57	41	1	87	6	0	4	25	5	.295	.356	.464	.986
1996	Mon-N	88	334	35	98	19	4	6	41	22	0	53	2	0	1	14	6	.293	.340	.428	.990
1997	Mon-N	151	592	84	160	29	5	28	82	31	3	111	10	1	4	16	8	.300	.363	.513	.996
1998	Mon-N	97	357	54	107	21	2	17	58	30	2	57	7	0	3	16	7	.312	.359	.505	.964
1999	Mon-N	138	539	83	168	26	6	22	64	32	2	85	11	0	6	10	6	.307	.370	.503	.994
2000	Mon-N	75	290	52	89	24	0	11	54	28	0	67	2	0	2	5	1	.307	.370	.503	.994
2000	**ChC-N**	**19**	**67**	**7**	**22**	**2**	**0**	**2**	**7**	**5**	**0**	**12**	**2**	**0**	**0**	**0**	**2**	**.328**	**.392**	**.448**	**1.000**
2001	**ChC-N**	**95**	**323**	**43**	**99**	**19**	**1**	**17**	**50**	**26**	**4**	**56**	**7**	**1**	**1**	**1**	**0**	**.307**	**.371**	**.529**	**.979**
Career average		95	350	52	103	21	3	13	49	26	1	62	6	0	2	10	4	.295	.351	.484	.985
Cubs average		**57**	**195**	**25**	**61**	**11**	**1**	**10**	**29**	**16**	**2**	**34**	**5**	**1**	**0**	**1**	**1**	**.310**	**.374**	**.515**	**.983**
Career total		856	3146	470	929	186	24	120	441	231	12	562	50	4	21	89	38	.295	.351	.484	.985
Cubs total		**114**	**390**	**50**	**121**	**21**	**1**	**19**	**57**	**31**	**4**	**68**	**9**	**1**	**0**	**1**	**2**	**.310**	**.374**	**.515**	**.983**

Wilke, Henry Joseph (Harry)
HEIGHT: 5'10" THROWS: RIGHT BATS: RIGHT BORN: 12/14/1900 CINCINNATI, OHIO DIED: 6/21/1991 HAMILTON, OHIO POSITIONS PLAYED: 3B

YEAR	TEAM	GAMES	AB	RUNS	HITS	2B	3B	HR	RBI	BB	IBB	SO	HBP	SH	SF	SB	CS	BA	OBA	SA	FA
1927	**ChC-N**	**3**	**9**	**0**	**0**	**0**	**0**	**0**	**0**	**0**	**—**	**1**	**0**	**0**	**—**	**0**	**—**	**.000**	**.000**	**.000**	**1.000**
Career average		3	9	0	0	0	0	0	0	0	—	1	0	0	—	0	—	.000	.000	.000	1.000
Cubs average		**3**	**9**	**0**	**0**	**0**	**0**	**0**	**0**	**0**	**—**	**1**	**0**	**0**	**—**	**0**	**—**	**.000**	**.000**	**.000**	**1.000**
Career total		3	9	0	0	0	0	0	0	0	—	1	0	0	—	0	—	.000	.000	.000	1.000
Cubs total		**3**	**9**	**0**	**0**	**0**	**0**	**0**	**0**	**0**	**—**	**1**	**0**	**0**	**—**	**0**	**—**	**.000**	**.000**	**.000**	**1.000**

Wilkerson, Curtis Vernon (Curt)
HEIGHT: 5'9" THROWS: RIGHT BATS: BOTH BORN: 4/26/1961 PETERSBURG, VIRGINIA POSITIONS PLAYED: 2B, 3B, SS, OF

YEAR	TEAM	GAMES	AB	RUNS	HITS	2B	3B	HR	RBI	BB	IBB	SO	HBP	SH	SF	SB	CS	BA	OBA	SA	FA
1983	Tex-A	16	35	7	6	0	1	0	1	2	0	5	0	0	0	3	0	.171	.216	.229	.980
1984	Tex-A	153	484	47	120	12	0	1	26	22	0	72	2	12	2	12	10	.248	.282	.279	.954
1985	Tex-A	129	360	35	88	11	6	0	22	22	0	63	4	6	3	14	7	.244	.293	.308	.959
1986	Tex-A	110	236	27	56	10	3	0	15	11	0	42	1	0	1	9	7	.237	.273	.305	.961
1987	Tex-A	85	138	28	37	5	3	2	14	6	0	16	2	0	0	6	3	.268	.308	.391	.967
1988	Tex-A	117	338	41	99	12	5	0	28	26	3	43	2	3	2	9	4	.293	.345	.358	.970
1989	**ChC-N**	**77**	**160**	**18**	**39**	**4**	**2**	**1**	**10**	**8**	**0**	**33**	**0**	**1**	**1**	**4**	**2**	**.244**	**.278**	**.313**	**.943**

(continued)

(continued)

YEAR	TEAM	GAMES	AB	RUNS	HITS	2B	3B	HR	RBI	BB	IBB	SO	HBP	SH	SF	SB	CS	BA	OBA	SA	FA
1990	ChC-N	77	186	21	41	5	1	0	16	7	2	36	0	3	0	2	2	.220	.249	.258	.910
1991	Pit-N	85	191	20	36	9	1	2	18	15	0	40	0	0	4	2	1	.188	.243	.277	.990
1992	KC-A	111	296	27	74	10	1	2	29	18	3	47	1	7	4	18	7	.250	.292	.311	.976
1993	KC-A	12	28	1	4	0	0	0	0	1	0	6	0	0	0	2	0	.143	.172	.143	1.000
Career average		88	223	25	55	7	2	1	16	13	1	37	1	3	2	7	4	.245	.286	.305	.962
Cubs average		**77**	**173**	**20**	**40**	**5**	**2**	**1**	**13**	**8**	**1**	**35**	**0**	**2**	**1**	**3**	**2**	**.231**	**.262**	**.283**	**.926**
Career total		972	2452	272	600	78	23	8	179	138	8	403	12	32	17	81	43	.245	.286	.305	.962
Cubs total		**154**	**346**	**39**	**80**	**9**	**3**	**1**	**26**	**15**	**2**	**69**	**0**	**4**	**1**	**6**	**4**	**.231**	**.262**	**.283**	**.926**

Wilkins, Richard David (Rick)

HEIGHT: 6'2"   THROWS: RIGHT   BATS: LEFT   BORN: 6/4/1967 JACKSONVILLE, FLORIDA   POSITIONS PLAYED: C, 1B

YEAR	TEAM	GAMES	AB	RUNS	HITS	2B	3B	HR	RBI	BB	IBB	SO	HBP	SH	SF	SB	CS	BA	OBA	SA	FA
1991	ChC-N	86	203	21	45	9	0	6	22	19	2	56	6	7	0	3	3	.222	.307	.355	.993
1992	ChC-N	83	244	20	66	9	1	8	22	28	7	53	0	1	1	0	2	.270	.344	.414	.993
1993	ChC-N	136	446	78	135	23	1	30	73	50	13	99	3	0	1	2	1	.303	.376	.561	.996
1994	ChC-N	100	313	44	71	25	2	7	39	40	5	86	2	1	2	4	3	.227	.317	.387	.993
1995	ChC-N	50	162	24	31	2	0	6	14	36	1	51	1	0	1	0	0	.191	.340	.315	.988
1995	Hou-N	15	40	6	10	1	0	1	5	10	1	10	0	0	1	0	0	.250	.392	.350	1.000
1996	Hou-N	84	254	34	54	8	2	6	23	46	10	81	1	0	5	0	1	.213	.330	.331	.990
1996	SF-N	52	157	19	46	10	0	8	36	21	3	40	0	0	5	0	2	.293	.366	.510	.993
1997	SF-N	66	190	18	37	5	0	6	23	17	0	65	0	0	3	0	0	.195	.257	.316	.986
1997	Sea-A	5	12	2	3	1	0	1	4	1	0	2	0	0	1	0	0	.250	.286	.583	1.000
1998	Sea-A	19	41	5	8	1	1	1	4	4	0	14	0	0	1	0	0	.195	.261	.341	1.000
1998	NYM-N	5	15	3	2	0	0	0	1	2	0	2	0	0	1	0	0	.133	.235	.133	.957
1999	LA-N	3	4	0	0	0	0	0	0	2	0	2	0	0	0	0	0	.000	.000	.000	1.000
2000	StL-N	4	11	3	3	0	0	0	1	2	0	2	0	0	0	0	0	.273	.385	.273	1.000
2001	SD-N	12	22	3	4	1	0	1	8	2	0	8	0	0	0	0	0	.182	.250	.364	1.000
Career average		65	192	25	47	9	1	7	25	25	4	52	1	1	2	1	1	.244	.332	.410	.992
Cubs average		**91**	**274**	**37**	**70**	**14**	**1**	**11**	**34**	**35**	**6**	**69**	**2**	**2**	**1**	**2**	**2**	**.254**	**.342**	**.435**	**.994**
Career total		720	2114	280	515	95	7	81	275	278	42	571	13	9	21	9	12	.244	.332	.410	.992
Cubs total		**455**	**1368**	**187**	**348**	**68**	**4**	**57**	**170**	**173**	**28**	**345**	**12**	**9**	**5**	**9**	**9**	**.254**	**.342**	**.435**	**.994**

Will, Robert Lee (Bob *or* Butch)

HEIGHT: 5'10"   THROWS: LEFT   BATS: LEFT   BORN: 7/15/1931 BERWYN, ILLINOIS   POSITIONS PLAYED: 1B, OF

YEAR	TEAM	GAMES	AB	RUNS	HITS	2B	3B	HR	RBI	BB	IBB	SO	HBP	SH	SF	SB	CS	BA	OBA	SA	FA
1957	ChC-N	70	112	13	25	3	0	1	10	5	0	21	0	5	1	1	0	.223	.254	.277	.963
1958	ChC-N	6	4	1	1	0	0	0	0	2	0	0	0	0	0	0	0	.250	.500	.250	—
1960	ChC-N	138	475	58	121	20	9	6	53	47	3	54	1	8	3	1	5	.255	.321	.373	.992
1961	ChC-N	86	113	9	29	9	0	0	8	15	0	19	0	1	1	0	1	.257	.341	.336	.973
1962	ChC-N	87	92	6	22	3	0	2	15	13	2	22	0	1	2	0	0	.239	.327	.337	1.000
1963	ChC-N	23	23	0	4	0	0	0	1	1	0	3	0	0	0	0	0	.174	.208	.174	1.000
Career average		68	137	15	34	6	2	2	15	14	1	20	0	3	1	0	1	.247	.314	.344	.986
Cubs average		**68**	**137**	**15**	**34**	**6**	**2**	**2**	**15**	**14**	**1**	**20**	**0**	**3**	**1**	**0**	**1**	**.247**	**.314**	**.344**	**.986**
Career total		410	819	87	202	35	9	9	87	83	5	119	1	15	7	2	6	.247	.314	.344	.986
Cubs total		**410**	**819**	**87**	**202**	**35**	**9**	**9**	**87**	**83**	**5**	**119**	**1**	**15**	**7**	**2**	**6**	**.247**	**.314**	**.344**	**.986**

Williams, Arthur Franklin (Art)

HEIGHT: —   THROWS: RIGHT   BATS: —   BORN: 8/26/1877 SOMERVILLE, MASSACHUSETTS   DIED: 5/16/1941 ARLINGTON, VIRGINIA   POSITIONS PLAYED: 1B, OF

YEAR	TEAM	GAMES	AB	RUNS	HITS	2B	3B	HR	RBI	BB	IBB	SO	HBP	SH	SF	SB	CS	BA	OBA	SA	FA
1902	ChC-N	47	160	17	37	3	0	0	14	15	—	—	3	4	—	9	—	.231	.309	.250	.956
Career average		47	160	17	37	3	0	0	14	15	—	—	3	4	—	9	—	.231	.309	.250	.956
Cubs average		**47**	**160**	**17**	**37**	**3**	**0**	**0**	**14**	**15**	**—**	**—**	**3**	**4**	**—**	**9**	**—**	**.231**	**.309**	**.250**	**.956**
Career total		47	160	17	37	3	0	0	14	15	—	—	3	4	—	9	—	.231	.309	.250	.956
Cubs total		**47**	**160**	**17**	**37**	**3**	**0**	**0**	**14**	**15**	**—**	**—**	**3**	**4**	**—**	**9**	**—**	**.231**	**.309**	**.250**	**.956**

Billy Leo Williams, of-1b-dh, 1959–76

Consistent, durable, immensely talented, Billy Williams was one of the best players of his generation, and the best lefthanded hitter to ever don a Cubs uniform.

Williams was born on June 15, 1938, in Whistler, Alabama. He was a terrific athlete and a much sought-after baseball player as a young man. He signed with the Cubs and admitted years later that while other players were commanding several thousand dollars in bonus money in those days, all he got was "a cigar and a bus ticket."

If so, then he was the steal of steals for the Cubs. Williams spent three years in the minor leagues, tearing up pitching at various levels, before getting the call to play for the Cubs in 1959. He played in 18 games that year and in 12 more the next, both September call-ups.

The times were not always fun in the minor leagues. In 1959, in San Antonio, Texas, the Cubs AA affiliate, Williams was one of several black players who endured racial taunts and had to stay in separate facilities from the white players. For a while, Williams considered quitting.

In 1960 Rogers Hornsby, then a Cubs hitting instructor, took one look at Williams's elegant swing and told him he would be playing in the majors very soon. And indeed, fairly soon after, Hornsby contacted the Cubs front office and told the big brass that the kid from Alabama was ready to play in the big leagues. So it was that in 1961, Williams was in Chicago to stay.

He put together a terrific rookie season: 25 home runs, 20 doubles, 86 RBIs and a .278 batting average. Those numbers won him the National League Rookie of the Year award.

His rookie year, 1961, marked the first of 13 consecutive years that Williams would hit 20 or more home runs (14 of 16 seasons overall); the first of 15 consecutive years that he would hit more than 20 doubles; the first of 15 consecutive years he would make more than 140 hits; the first of 13 consecutive years in which Williams would collect more than 84 RBIs; the first of 15 consecutive years that Williams's on-base percentage would be .340 or better.

But Williams's superb year was overshadowed by the scintillating home run race in the American League between New York Yankees teammates Roger Maris and Mickey Mantle. That seemed to be the story of Williams's life. For much of his career, he was overshadowed by "Mr. Cub," Ernie Banks. When the Cubs began to turn things around in the late 1960s, it was flamboyant manager Leo Durocher who got most of the ink, along with fiery third baseman Ron Santo and younger phenoms like Fergie Jenkins.

Through all his major league years, Williams pulled on his uniform, laced up his baseball shoes, went out and produced. He hit .298, with 22 homers and 22 doubles, in 1962, and made the All-Star team for the first time. If sportswriters seemed to ignore Williams for long stretches, Cubs fans, teammates and opposing players did not.

"Put him in the lineup and watch him swing the bat," said teammate Glenn Beckert, who usually batted behind Williams in the lineup.

"I can't imagine where the Chicago Cubs would have been in the 1960s, particularly in

Williams, Billy Leo

HEIGHT: 6'1"   THROWS: RIGHT   BATS: LEFT   BORN: 6/15/1938 WHISTLER, ALABAMA   POSITIONS PLAYED: 1B, OF

YEAR	TEAM	GAMES	AB	RUNS	HITS	2B	3B	HR	RBI	BB	IBB	SO	HBP	SH	SF	SB	CS	BA	OBA	SA	FA
1959	ChC-N	18	33	0	5	0	1	0	2	1	0	7	0	0	0	0	0	.152	.176	.212	1.000
1960	ChC-N	12	47	4	13	0	2	2	7	5	0	12	0	0	0	0	0	.277	.346	.489	.962
1961	ChC-N	146	529	75	147	20	7	25	86	45	11	70	5	1	4	6	0	.278	.338	.484	.954
1962	ChC-N	159	618	94	184	22	8	22	91	70	3	72	4	0	7	9	9	.298	.369	.466	.967
1963	ChC-N	161	612	87	175	36	9	25	95	68	9	78	2	2	3	7	6	.286	.358	.497	.987
1964	ChC-N	162	645	100	201	39	2	33	98	59	8	84	2	0	3	10	7	.312	.370	.532	.950
1965	ChC-N	164	645	115	203	39	6	34	108	65	7	76	3	1	5	10	1	.315	.377	.552	.968
1966	ChC-N	162	648	100	179	23	5	29	91	69	16	61	4	0	6	6	3	.276	.347	.461	.976
1967	ChC-N	162	634	92	176	21	12	28	84	68	8	67	2	2	6	6	3	.278	.346	.481	.989

(continued)

1969, without Billy Williams," said Santo in his autobiography.

"He is one of the greatest hitters of all time and one of the most underrated players ever," Banks said in 1969.

Williams had tremendous strength in his wrists and arms. During the 1960s and early 1970s, weight training was not a regimen in which baseball players usually participated. But even without lifting weights, Williams was a powerfully muscled man.

He was never one to blow his own horn, and teammates respected that. Fergie Jenkins, who often fished with Williams and socialized with him, recalled that Williams "kept to himself. He was a proud man."

In 1968, as the Cubs were inching toward respectability, Williams had two of his most memorable games. On July 17, against the Cardinals, he became the ninth Cub to hit for the cycle. On September 10, Williams hit three home runs.

By 1969, with Durocher at the helm, the Cubs appeared to be moving toward their first National League championship since 1945. But in September, the team began slumping. Hitters weren't hitting as well and pitchers weren't pitching as well; the New York Mets charged past the Cubs.

Excuses were flying through the latter part of the season as the Mets caught and passed Chicago. Williams just played. The team had been slumping, but Williams hit .304 in September of that year.

The 1969 season also saw Williams break Stan Musial's National League consecutive game streak at 896. That day was designated Billy Williams Day by Cubs management. Williams went five for nine as the Cubs swept a doubleheader from the Cardinals.

Williams went on to play 1,117 games in a row, still a National League record.

In 1970 Williams led the National League in hits with 205 and in runs scored with 137. He finished second to the Reds' Johnny Bench in home runs and RBIs. In 1972 he had another great year, winning the batting championship with a .333 average. He finished second to Bench in the MVP voting that year, although the *Sporting News* named him Player of the Year in that publication.

Williams played for the Cubs through 1974; then he was traded to the Oakland Athletics in 1975. He hit .244 with 23 home runs for the A's, primarily as a designated hitter. He finally got into the postseason, although Oakland was swept by the Red Sox in the American League Championship Series.

Williams retired the next season and returned to the Cubs as a hitting coach and batting instructor. He went over to work for the A's as a coach before returning to the Cubs and presently works as a first-base coach for the team. He holds the Cubs record for most years playing and coaching with the Cubs (31). In 1987 Williams was elected to the Hall of Fame. His number (26) was retired by the Cubs that year.

Williams's name pops up often in the Cubs record book. He holds team records for lefthanded hitters for most hits in a season (205), most home runs (42), most RBIs (129), extra base hits (80), most total bases (373) and highest slugging percentage (.606).

Williams also holds several career records for the Cubs for a lefthanded hitter, including most at-bats (8,479), hits (2,510), home runs (392), grand slams (8, along with Bill Nicholson), RBIs (1,353), extra-base hits (881), total bases (4,362) and slugging percentage (.503).

(continued)																				
1968	ChC-N	163	642	91	185	30	8	30	98	48	10	53	2	0	7	4	1	.288	.336	.500	.967
1969	ChC-N	163	642	103	188	33	10	21	95	59	15	70	4	0	3	3	2	.293	.355	.474	.957
1970	ChC-N	161	636	137	205	34	4	42	129	72	9	65	2	0	4	7	1	.322	.391	.586	.989
1971	ChC-N	157	594	86	179	27	5	28	93	77	18	44	3	0	3	7	5	.301	.383	.505	.977
1972	ChC-N	150	574	95	191	34	6	37	122	62	20	59	6	0	8	3	1	.333	.398	.606	.986
1973	ChC-N	156	576	72	166	22	2	20	86	76	14	72	1	0	6	4	3	.288	.369	.438	.987
1974	ChC-N	117	404	55	113	22	0	16	68	67	12	44	1	0	2	4	5	.280	.382	.453	.984
1975	Oak-A	155	520	68	127	20	1	23	81	76	7	68	2	1	3	0	0	.244	.341	.419	.971
1976	Oak-A	120	351	36	74	12	0	11	41	58	15	44	0	1	3	4	2	.211	.320	.339	—
Career average		138	519	78	151	24	5	24	82	58	10	58	2	0	4	5	3	.290	.361	.492	.976
Cubs average		**138**	**530**	**82**	**157**	**25**	**5**	**25**	**85**	**57**	**10**	**58**	**3**	**0**	**4**	**5**	**3**	**.296**	**.364**	**.503**	**.976**
Career total		2488	9350	1410	2711	434	88	426	1475	1045	182	1046	43	8	73	90	49	.290	.361	.492	.976
Cubs total		**2213**	**8479**	**1306**	**2510**	**402**	**87**	**392**	**1353**	**911**	**160**	**934**	**41**	**6**	**67**	**86**	**47**	**.296**	**.364**	**.503**	**.976**

Williams, Dewey Edgar (Dee)

HEIGHT: 6'0" THROWS: RIGHT BATS: RIGHT BORN: 2/5/1916 DURHAM, NORTH CAROLINA DIED: 3/19/2000 WILLISTON, NORTH DAKOTA
POSITIONS PLAYED: C

YEAR	TEAM	GAMES	AB	RUNS	HITS	2B	3B	HR	RBI	BB	IBB	SO	HBP	SH	SF	SB	CS	BA	OBA	SA	FA
1944	ChC-N	79	262	23	63	7	2	0	27	23	—	18	0	3	—	2	—	.240	.302	.282	.981
1945	ChC-N	59	100	16	28	2	2	2	5	13	—	13	0	2	—	0	—	.280	.363	.400	.978
1946	ChC-N	4	5	0	1	0	0	0	0	0	—	2	0	0	—	0	—	.200	.200	.200	1.000
1947	ChC-N	3	2	0	0	0	0	0	0	0	—	1	0	0	—	0	—	.000	.000	.000	—
1948	Cin-N	48	95	9	16	2	0	1	5	10	—	18	0	3	—	0	—	.168	.248	.221	.961
Career average		39	93	10	22	2	1	1	7	9	—	10	0	2	—	0	—	.233	.302	.293	.976
Cubs average		**36**	**92**	**10**	**23**	**2**	**1**	**1**	**8**	**9**	**—**	**9**	**0**	**1**	**—**	**1**	**—**	**.249**	**.316**	**.312**	**.981**
Career total		193	464	48	108	11	4	3	37	46	—	52	0	8	—	2	—	.233	.302	.293	.976
Cubs total		**145**	**369**	**39**	**92**	**9**	**4**	**2**	**32**	**36**	**—**	**34**	**0**	**5**	**—**	**2**	**—**	**.249**	**.316**	**.312**	**.981**

Williams, Fred (Cy)

HEIGHT: 6'2" THROWS: LEFT BATS: LEFT BORN: 12/21/1887 WADENA, INDIANA DIED: 4/23/1974 EAGLE RIVER, WISCONSIN POSITIONS PLAYED: OF

YEAR	TEAM	GAMES	AB	RUNS	HITS	2B	3B	HR	RBI	BB	IBB	SO	HBP	SH	SF	SB	CS	BA	OBA	SA	FA
1912	ChC-N	28	62	3	15	1	1	0	1	6	—	14	0	2	—	2	—	.242	.309	.290	1.000
1913	ChC-N	49	156	17	35	3	3	4	32	5	—	26	3	3	—	5	—	.224	.262	.359	.976
1914	ChC-N	55	94	12	19	2	2	0	5	13	—	13	2	2	—	2	—	.202	.312	.266	.941
1915	ChC-N	151	518	59	133	22	6	13	64	26	—	49	10	12	—	15	10	.257	.305	.398	.968
1916	ChC-N	118	405	55	113	19	9	12	66	51	—	64	9	19	—	6	—	.279	.372	.459	.989
1917	ChC-N	138	468	53	113	22	4	5	42	38	—	78	7	26	—	8	—	.241	.308	.338	.960
1918	Phi-N	94	351	49	97	14	1	6	39	27	—	30	5	15	—	10	—	.276	.337	.373	.968
1919	Phi-N	109	435	54	121	21	1	9	39	30	—	43	7	9	—	9	—	.278	.335	.393	.970
1920	Phi-N	148	590	88	192	36	10	15	72	32	—	45	4	17	—	18	12	.325	.364	.497	.972
1921	Phi-N	146	562	67	180	28	6	18	75	30	—	32	2	9	—	5	15	.320	.357	.488	.979
1922	Phi-N	151	584	98	180	30	6	26	92	74	—	49	6	12	—	11	14	.308	.392	.514	.973
1923	Phi-N	136	535	98	157	22	3	41	114	59	—	57	7	3	—	11	10	.293	.371	.576	.981
1924	Phi-N	148	558	101	183	31	11	24	93	67	—	49	3	8	—	7	12	.328	.403	.552	.962
1925	Phi-N	107	314	78	104	11	5	13	60	53	—	34	5	3	—	4	9	.331	.435	.522	.989
1926	Phi-N	107	336	63	116	13	4	18	53	38	—	35	4	6	—	2	—	.345	.418	.568	.963
1927	Phi-N	131	492	86	135	18	2	30	98	61	—	57	9	8	—	0	—	.274	.365	.502	.970
1928	Phi-N	99	238	31	61	9	0	12	37	54	—	34	3	8	—	0	—	.256	.400	.445	1.000
1929	Phi-N	66	65	11	19	2	0	5	21	22	—	9	0	2	—	0	—	.292	.471	.554	.966
1930	Phi-N	21	17	1	8	2	0	0	2	4	—	3	0	0	—	0	—	.471	.571	.588	1.000
Career average		105	357	54	104	16	4	13	53	36	—	38	5	9	—	6	4	.292	.365	.470	.973
Cubs average		**90**	**284**	**33**	**71**	**12**	**4**	**6**	**35**	**23**	**—**	**41**	**5**	**11**	**—**	**6**	**2**	**.251**	**.319**	**.381**	**.971**
Career total		2002	6780	1024	1981	306	74	251	1005	690	—	721	86	164	—	115	82	.292	.365	.470	.973
Cubs total		**539**	**1703**	**199**	**428**	**69**	**25**	**34**	**210**	**139**	**—**	**244**	**31**	**64**	**—**	**38**	**10**	**.251**	**.319**	**.381**	**.971**

Williams, Otto George

HEIGHT: 5'8" THROWS: RIGHT BATS: RIGHT BORN: 11/2/1877 NEWARK, NEW JERSEY DIED: 3/19/1937 OMAHA, NEBRASKA
POSITIONS PLAYED: 1B, 2B, 3B, SS, OF

YEAR	TEAM	GAMES	AB	RUNS	HITS	2B	3B	HR	RBI	BB	IBB	SO	HBP	SH	SF	SB	CS	BA	OBA	SA	FA
1902	StL-N	2	5	0	2	0	0	0	2	1	—	—	0	0	—	1	—	.400	.500	.400	.813
1903	StL-N	53	187	10	38	4	2	0	9	9	—	—	0	5	—	6	—	.203	.240	.246	.887
1903	**ChC-N**	**38**	**130**	**14**	**29**	**5**	**0**	**0**	**13**	**4**	**—**	**—**	**0**	**2**	**—**	**8**	**—**	**.223**	**.246**	**.262**	**.932**
1904	**ChC-N**	**57**	**185**	**21**	**37**	**4**	**1**	**0**	**8**	**13**	**—**	**—**	**1**	**7**	**—**	**9**	**—**	**.200**	**.256**	**.232**	**.962**
1906	Was-A	20	51	3	7	0	0	0	2	2	—	—	1	2	—	0	—	.137	.185	.137	.928
Career average		43	140	12	28	3	1	0	9	7	—	—	1	4	—	6	—	.203	.244	.237	.922
Cubs average		**48**	**158**	**18**	**33**	**5**	**1**	**0**	**11**	**9**	**—**	**—**	**1**	**5**	**—**	**9**	**—**	**.210**	**.252**	**.244**	**.948**
Career total		170	558	48	113	13	3	0	34	29	—	—	2	16	—	24	—	.203	.244	.237	.922
Cubs total		**95**	**315**	**35**	**66**	**9**	**1**	**0**	**21**	**17**	**—**	**—**	**1**	**9**	**—**	**17**	**—**	**.210**	**.252**	**.244**	**.948**

Fred "Cy" Williams, of, 1912–30

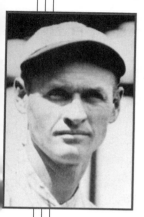

Cy Williams was a player who would probably have more of a kinship with today's players than he did with those of his era. He was a slugger before Babe Ruth made it fashionable, a player who preferred to win games by swinging for the fences rather than bunting a runner over to second base.

Williams was born on December 21, 1887, in Wadena, Indiana. He was a three-sport star in high school and matriculated to Notre Dame, where he was a sprinter on the track team and played football for Knute Rockne. He was also a power-hitting center fielder for the Notre Dame baseball team, and he was signed by the Cubs a few days after graduation.

The Cubs didn't waste any time with Williams; a few weeks after he was signed, he was playing in Chicago. He was a part-time player for the Cubs in his first three years, but in 1915, playing for his fourth manager in as many years, he was elevated to the starting center fielder's job.

He led the team in home runs that year with 13, which was second in the league. Williams was second on the Cubs in RBIs with 64. He was also second among National League center fielders in putouts with 347.

The next year, Williams won the home run crown with 12 round-trippers, and he was also the league leader among center fielders in fielding average with a .989 mark. A quick word about home runs and the early 20th century. The Dead Ball Era, as it was known, was so designated because the balls that were manufactured in those days were simply not as tightly constructed as they would be in the 1920s and thereafter. Thus, they didn't carry as far when struck by a bat; it was tough to hit them out of a park.

Back then, the home run was not a premier weapon as it is now. Teams played for one run at a time, bunting runners over, hitting balls through the infield, stealing bases. Williams did not exactly eschew this strategy, but he did like to hit balls a long way. In this philosophy, he was somewhat unique.

Williams was a dead-pull, lefthanded hitter, and so consistent that teams began playing three outfielders in center and right field, knowing that Williams rarely stroked the ball into left field. In effect, he was a victim of the original "Williams shift" long before celebrated Red Sox Hall of Famer Ted Williams had to endure it.

Nagging injuries cut into Williams's production in 1916, although he was still eighth in the league in homers and also in the top 10 in RBIs. But the Cubs seemed to feel that Williams, at 30, was nearing retirement, so they shipped him to the Phillies after the 1917 season.

Williams, unfortunately for the Cubs, disproved that notion, playing another 13 seasons, all in Philadelphia. In that span, he led the league in home runs three more times and finished second or third six other times.

Williams retired in 1930 and put his Notre Dame degree to good use, becoming an architect in Eagle River, Wisconsin. He died there in 1974.

Williams, Washington J. (Wash)

HEIGHT: 5'11"   THROWS: —   BATS: —   BORN: — PHILADELPHIA, PENNSYLVANIA   DIED: 8/9/1892 PHILADELPHIA, PENNSYLVANIA   POSITIONS PLAYED: P, OF

YEAR	TEAM	GAMES	AB	RUNS	HITS	2B	3B	HR	RBI	BB	IBB	SO	HBP	SH	SF	SB	CS	BA	OBA	SA	FA
1884	Ric-AA	2	8	0	2	0	0	0	—	0	—	—	0	—	—	—	—	.250	.250	.250	.500
1885	**ChN-N**	**1**	**4**	**0**	**1**	**0**	**0**	**0**	**0**	**0**	**—**	**0**	**—**	**—**	**—**	**—**	**—**	**.250**	**.250**	**.250**	**.667**
Career average		2	6	0	2	0	0	0	0	0	—	0	0	—	—	—	—	.250	.250	.250	.600
Cubs average		**1**	**4**	**0**	**1**	**0**	**0**	**0**	**0**	**0**	**—**	**0**	**0**	**—**	**—**	**—**	**—**	**.250**	**.250**	**.250**	**.667**
Career total		3	12	0	3	0	0	0	0	0	—	0	0	—	—	—	—	.250	.250	.250	.600
Cubs total		**1**	**4**	**0**	**1**	**0**	**0**	**0**	**0**	**0**	**—**	**0**	**0**	**—**	**—**	**—**	**—**	**.250**	**.250**	**.250**	**.667**

Williamson, Edward Nagle (Ned)

HEIGHT: 5'11" THROWS: RIGHT BATS: RIGHT BORN: 10/24/1857 PHILADELPHIA, PENNSYLVANIA DIED: 3/3/1894 MOUNTAIN VALLEY SPRINGS, ARKANSAS
POSITIONS PLAYED: P, C, 1B, 2B, 3B, SS

YEAR	TEAM	GAMES	AB	RUNS	HITS	2B	3B	HR	RBI	BB	IBB	SO	HBP	SH	SF	SB	CS	BA	OBA	SA	FA
1878	Ind-N	63	250	31	58	10	2	1	19	5	—	15	—	—	—	—	—	.232	.247	.300	.867
1879	ChN-N	80	320	66	94	20	13	1	36	24	—	31	—	—	—	—	—	.294	.343	.447	.886
1880	ChN-N	75	311	65	78	20	2	0	31	15	—	26	—	—	—	—	—	.251	.285	.328	.905
1881	ChN-N	82	343	56	92	12	6	1	48	19	—	19	—	—	—	—	—	.268	.307	.347	.908
1882	ChN-N	83	348	66	98	27	4	3	60	27	—	21	—	—	—	—	—	.282	.333	.408	.881
1883	ChN-N	98	402	83	111	49	5	2	59	22	—	48	—	—	—	—	—	.276	.314	.438	.809
1884	ChN-N	107	417	84	116	18	8	27	84	42	—	56	—	—	—	—	—	.278	.344	.554	.864
1885	ChN-N	113	407	87	97	16	5	3	65	75	—	60	—	—	—	—	—	.238	.357	.324	.894
1886	ChN-N	121	430	69	93	17	8	6	58	80	—	71	—	—	—	13	—	.216	.339	.335	.868
1887	ChN-N	127	512	77	190	20	14	9	78	73	—	57	5	—	—	45	—	.371	.454	.518	.890
1888	ChN-N	132	452	75	113	9	14	8	73	65	—	71	6	—	—	25	—	.250	.352	.385	.884
1889	ChN-N	47	173	16	41	3	1	1	30	23	—	22	4	—	—	2	—	.237	.340	.283	.844
1890	Chi-P	73	261	34	51	7	3	2	26	36	—	35	8	—	—	3	—	.195	.311	.268	.815
Career average		92	356	62	95	18	7	5	51	39	—	41	2	—	—	7	—	.266	.342	.394	.873
Cubs average		97	374	68	102	19	7	6	57	42	—	44	1	—	—	8	—	.273	.349	.408	.876
Career total		1201	4626	809	1232	228	85	64	667	506	—	532	23	—	—	88	—	.266	.342	.394	.873
Cubs total		1065	4115	744	1123	211	80	61	622	465	—	482	15	—	—	85	—	.273	.349	.408	.876

Wills, Elliott Taylor (Bump)

HEIGHT: 5'9" THROWS: RIGHT BATS: BOTH BORN: 7/27/1952 WASHINGTON, DISTRICT OF COLUMBIA POSITIONS PLAYED: 1B, 2B, SS

YEAR	TEAM	GAMES	AB	RUNS	HITS	2B	3B	HR	RBI	BB	IBB	SO	HBP	SH	SF	SB	CS	BA	OBA	SA	FA
1977	Tex-A	152	541	87	155	28	6	9	62	65	7	96	0	7	4	28	12	.287	.361	.410	.982
1978	Tex-A	157	539	78	135	17	4	9	57	63	3	91	4	9	4	52	14	.250	.331	.347	.981
1979	Tex-A	146	543	90	148	21	3	5	46	53	4	58	4	14	3	35	11	.273	.340	.350	.976
1980	Tex-A	146	578	102	152	31	5	5	58	51	1	71	3	15	8	34	9	.263	.322	.360	.984
1981	Tex-A	102	410	51	103	13	2	2	41	32	2	49	1	6	5	12	9	.251	.304	.307	.983
1982	ChC-N	128	419	64	114	18	4	6	38	46	3	76	5	2	5	35	10	.272	.347	.377	.963
Career average		139	505	79	135	21	4	6	50	52	3	74	3	9	5	33	11	.266	.335	.360	.979
Cubs average		128	419	64	114	18	4	6	38	46	3	76	5	2	5	35	10	.272	.347	.377	.963
Career total		831	3030	472	807	128	24	36	302	310	20	441	17	53	29	196	65	.266	.335	.360	.979
Cubs total		128	419	64	114	18	4	6	38	46	3	76	5	2	5	35	10	.272	.347	.377	.963

Wilmot, Walter Robert (Walt)

HEIGHT: — THROWS: RIGHT BATS: BOTH BORN: 10/18/1863 PLOVER, WISCONSIN DIED: 2/1/1929 CHICAGO, ILLINOIS POSITIONS PLAYED: OF

YEAR	TEAM	GAMES	AB	RUNS	HITS	2B	3B	HR	RBI	BB	IBB	SO	HBP	SH	SF	SB	CS	BA	OBA	SA	FA
1888	WaN-N	119	473	61	106	16	9	4	43	23	—	55	2	—	—	46	—	.224	.263	.321	.872
1889	WaN-N	108	432	88	125	19	19	9	57	51	—	32	2	—	—	40	—	.289	.367	.484	.927
1890	ChN-N	139	571	114	159	15	13	13	99	64	—	44	2	—	—	76	—	.278	.353	.419	.938
1891	ChN-N	121	498	102	137	14	10	11	71	55	—	21	5	—	—	42	—	.275	.353	.410	.922
1892	ChN-N	92	380	47	82	7	7	2	35	40	—	20	4	—	—	31	—	.216	.297	.287	.903
1893	ChN-N	94	392	69	118	14	14	3	61	40	—	8	1	—	—	39	—	.301	.367	.431	.873
1894	ChN-N	133	597	134	197	45	12	5	130	35	—	23	1	14	—	74	—	.330	.368	.471	.872
1895	ChN-N	108	466	86	132	16	6	8	72	30	—	19	0	10	—	28	—	.283	.327	.395	.914
1897	NYG-N	11	34	8	9	2	0	1	4	2	—	—	0	1	—	1	—	.265	.306	.412	.938
1898	NYG-N	35	138	16	33	4	2	2	22	9	—	—	0	2	—	4	—	.239	.286	.341	.886
Career average		96	398	73	110	15	9	6	59	35	—	22	2	3	—	38	—	.276	.337	.404	.903
Cubs average		115	484	92	138	19	10	7	78	44	—	23	2	4	—	48	—	.284	.346	.408	.905
Career total		960	3981	725	1098	152	92	58	594	349	—	222	17	27	—	381	—	.276	.337	.404	.903
Cubs total		687	2904	552	825	111	62	42	468	264	—	135	13	24	—	290	—	.284	.346	.408	.905

Edward (Ned) Nagle Williamson, 3b-ss-c-p-2b-1b, 1878–90

Ned Williamson was the greatest third baseman of the 1880s, and his all-around brilliance helped Chicago to five National League pennants.

Williamson was born on October 24, 1857, in Philadelphia, Pennsylvania. A semipro star in Pennsylvania, he broke into the National League in 1878 with the Indianapolis franchise. When Indianapolis folded, Williamson signed with Adrian "Cap" Anson's Chicago White Stockings.

Anson loved Ned's athletic ability. Williamson, primarily a third baseman, led the National League third sackers in putouts, assists, double plays and fielding percentage that year. He also hit .294 and was second in the league in triples with 13 and walks with 24. Anson also used Williamson at first base and catcher that year; in subsequent seasons, he used Williamson at every infield position and even on the mound. In 1885 Williamson's two saves led the league.

This was an era when there were no relief pitchers, so relief appearances in general were extremely rare. But Williamson had a pretty good fastball and also enjoyed staying after practice with teammate and friend Mike Kelly and working on his curveball. Rather than use one of his starters, Anson preferred to use Williamson when the occasion arose.

Williamson was a big man (5'11", 170 pounds) for his day, but he moved with athletic grace. He covered probably more territory than any other third baseman in the league in that era. He regularly led the league in assists, putouts and double plays.

Williamson was also a great hitter. In 1883 he set a major league record with 49 doubles in Lake Front Park. At the time, balls hit over the short left- and right-field fences (185 feet) were two-base hits.

In 1884, however, that rule was changed. Those same hits were now home runs. Williamson belted 27 home runs that year (24 at home), nearly doubling the previous record of 14. The rule change at Lake Front Park enabled the White Stockings to hit 142 home runs, with Chicago's Fred Pfeffer socking 25 homers, Abner Dalrymple 22 and Cap Anson 21.

Williamson's record wasn't broken until Babe Ruth of the Red Sox hit 29 in 1919. When the White Stockings moved, in 1885, into a new park with deeper outfield walls, their home run totals returned to normal.

The 1885 season was also the year the White Stockings acquired Tom Burns. Burns was a good shortstop, but Anson wanted to move him to third base to take advantage of his rifle arm. Anson moved Williamson over to shortstop. The switch seemed to help both men, and Chicago won the National League championship.

All was well with Williamson until the 1888 season. Williamson was part of a group of National League players who toured the world, playing exhibitions. Early in 1889, and late in the tour, Williamson tore up his knee sliding into second base in Paris. Williamson's knee was treated in a London hospital, but it was set incorrectly. Williamson had to stay in London for several months until it finally healed properly.

Anson, one of the promoters of the tour, was considerably annoyed that Williamson had the gall to be injured. He refused to pay some of Williamson's medical bills and also refused to pay his fare back to the United States.

Williamson played in only 47 games in 1889 and was a shadow of his former self. In 1890 Williamson jumped to the newly formed Players' League but played only 73 games. He retired after that season.

Williamson opened a saloon in Chicago. For many years, he was bitter about his treatment at the end of his career by Anson. He often ended the evening in a drunken stupor. Four years after his retirement, Williamson drank himself to death.

Williamson still holds the Cubs season record for inside-the-park home runs, set in 1915, with six. Williamson was also the first Chicago player to hit three home runs in a game, doing it twice in the home-run-happy 1884 season. He is also the team's record holder for most hits in an inning with three.

Wilson, Arthur Earl (Art *or* Dutch)
HEIGHT: 5'8" THROWS: RIGHT BATS: RIGHT BORN: 12/11/1885 MACON, ILLINOIS DIED: 6/12/1960 CHICAGO, ILLINOIS POSITIONS PLAYED: C, 1B, 3B

YEAR	TEAM	GAMES	AB	RUNS	HITS	2B	3B	HR	RBI	BB	IBB	SO	HBP	SH	SF	SB	CS	BA	OBA	SA	FA
1908	NYG-N	1	0	0	0	0	0	0	0	0	—	0	0	0	—	0	—	—	—	—	—
1909	NYG-N	19	42	4	10	2	1	0	5	4	—	—	0	0	—	0	—	.238	.304	.333	.985
1910	NYG-N	26	52	10	14	4	1	0	5	9	—	6	1	3	—	2	—	.269	.387	.385	.975
1911	NYG-N	66	109	17	33	9	1	1	17	19	—	12	1	5	—	6	—	.303	.411	.431	.963
1912	NYG-N	65	121	17	35	6	0	3	19	13	—	14	0	6	—	2	—	.289	.358	.413	.960
1913	NYG-N	54	79	5	15	0	1	0	8	11	—	11	0	1	—	1	—	.190	.289	.215	.968
1914	Chi-F	137	440	78	128	31	8	10	64	70	—	80	5	15	—	13	—	.291	.394	.466	.974
1915	Chi-F	96	269	44	82	11	2	7	31	65	—	38	1	16	—	8	—	.305	.442	.439	.980
1916	Pit-N	53	128	11	33	5	2	1	12	13	—	27	1	7	—	4	—	.258	.331	.352	.981
1916	**ChC-N**	**36**	**114**	**5**	**22**	**3**	**1**	**0**	**5**	**6**	**—**	**14**	**0**	**3**	**—**	**1**	**—**	**.193**	**.233**	**.237**	**.953**
1917	**ChC-N**	**81**	**211**	**17**	**45**	**9**	**2**	**2**	**25**	**32**	**—**	**36**	**2**	**7**	**—**	**6**	**—**	**.213**	**.322**	**.303**	**.968**
1918	Bos-N	89	280	15	69	8	2	0	19	24	—	31	2	5	—	5	—	.246	.310	.289	.977
1919	Bos-N	71	191	14	49	8	1	0	16	25	—	19	1	9	—	2	—	.257	.346	.309	.977
1920	Bos-N	16	19	0	1	0	0	0	0	1	—	1	1	0	—	0	—	.053	.143	.053	.900
1921	Cle-A	2	1	0	0	0	0	0	0	0	—	0	0	0	—	0	0	.000	.000	.000	1.000
Career average		58	147	17	38	7	2	2	16	21	—	21	1	6	—	4	0	.261	.357	.364	.972
Cubs average		**59**	**163**	**11**	**34**	**6**	**2**	**1**	**15**	**19**	**—**	**25**	**1**	**5**	**—**	**4**	**—**	**.206**	**.293**	**.280**	**.964**
Career total		812	2056	237	536	96	22	24	226	292	—	289	15	77	—	50	0	.261	.357	.364	.972
Cubs total		**117**	**325**	**22**	**67**	**12**	**3**	**2**	**30**	**38**	**—**	**50**	**2**	**10**	**—**	**7**	**—**	**.206**	**.293**	**.280**	**.964**

Lewis Robert "Hack" Wilson, of-2b, 1923–34

He wore a size-18 collar and a size-6 shoe. He was as short as Phil Rizzuto and almost as heavy as Bill "Moose" Skowron. In short, "Hack" Wilson looked a lot more like a cartoon character than a ballplayer.

But, goodness, could he hit!

Lewis Wilson was born on April 26, 1900, in Ellwood City, Pennsylvania. He was the illegitimate son of a factory worker and a 16-year-old girl. After his mother died in 1908, Wilson was raised by the owner of the boarding-house where he and his father lived.

In 1916 Wilson dropped out of school to work in a factory, not the same one as his dad. His horizons extended to the end of the week—when he would get his paycheck and go out drinking with the other workers.

He began playing in semiprofessional leagues, and startled himself because he was so good. His prowess came to the attention of the New York Giants' John McGraw, who signed him to a professional contract. In 1923 he played a handful of games for the Giants. By 1924 he was a regular, hitting .295 for the National League champions.

McGraw, however, had a glut of outfielders. He sent Wilson down to the minor leagues the next year, ostensibly to better learn to hit the curveball, in reality to hide Wilson for a year until McGraw could decide what to do with him. Wilson was no longer under contract with the Giants, so he could be drafted by any team. McGraw didn't believe anyone knew how good Wilson was.

Cubs manager Joe McCarthy did. He drafted Wilson and signed him for $5,000. It was a steal, and McGraw fumed about it for years.

Wilson batted fourth in an already potent Cubs lineup. Hack hit the heck out of the ball in 1926, leading the league in home runs with 21. He was also the league leader in walks with 69. Wilson was the National League's home run king for three years, from 1926 to 1928. His overdeveloped upper body, honed by a decade of factory work, generated tremendous power. As blocky as Wilson looked, his bat was very quick. He was, for most of his tenure with the Cubs, one of the toughest men to get out in the major leagues.

His nickname was as odd as he. He was said to resemble former Cubs outfielder Lawrence Miller, who, in turn, resembled a famous wrestler at the time, George Hackenschmidt. "Hack" Miller had been with the Cubs from 1922 to 1925. Wilson

Wilson, Lewis Robert (Hack)

HEIGHT: 5'6" THROWS: RIGHT BATS: RIGHT BORN: 4/26/1900 ELLWOOD CITY, PENNSYLVANIA DIED: 11/23/1948 BALTIMORE, MARYLAND
POSITIONS PLAYED: 2B, OF

YEAR	TEAM	GAMES	AB	RUNS	HITS	2B	3B	HR	RBI	BB	IBB	SO	HBP	SH	SF	SB	CS	BA	OBA	SA	FA
1923	NYG-N	3	10	0	2	0	0	0	0	0	—	1	0	0	—	0	0	.200	.200	.200	.857
1924	NYG-N	107	383	62	113	19	12	10	57	44	—	46	1	6	—	4	3	.295	.369	.486	.967
1925	NYG-N	62	180	28	43	7	4	6	30	21	—	33	1	4	—	5	2	.239	.322	.422	.975
1926	**ChC-N**	**142**	**529**	**97**	**170**	**36**	**8**	**21**	**109**	**69**	**—**	**61**	**6**	**9**	**—**	**10**	**—**	**.321**	**.406**	**.539**	**.973**
1927	**ChC-N**	**146**	**551**	**119**	**175**	**30**	**12**	**30**	**129**	**71**	**—**	**70**	**6**	**18**	**—**	**13**	**—**	**.318**	**.401**	**.579**	**.967**
1928	**ChC-N**	**145**	**520**	**89**	**163**	**32**	**9**	**31**	**120**	**77**	**—**	**94**	**2**	**24**	**—**	**4**	**—**	**.313**	**.404**	**.588**	**.960**
1929	**ChC-N**	**150**	**574**	**135**	**198**	**30**	**5**	**39**	**159**	**78**	**—**	**83**	**2**	**16**	**—**	**3**	**—**	**.345**	**.425**	**.618**	**.970**
1930	**ChC-N**	**155**	**585**	**146**	**208**	**35**	**6**	**56**	**191**	**105**	**—**	**84**	**1**	**18**	**—**	**3**	**—**	**.356**	**.454**	**.723**	**.951**
1931	**ChC-N**	**112**	**395**	**66**	**103**	**22**	**4**	**13**	**61**	**63**	**—**	**69**	**0**	**0**	**—**	**1**	**—**	**.261**	**.362**	**.435**	**.978**
1932	Bro-N	135	481	77	143	37	5	23	123	51	—	85	1	6	—	2	—	.297	.366	.538	.955
1933	Bro-N	117	360	41	96	13	2	9	54	52	—	50	0	1	—	7	—	.267	.359	.389	.955
1934	Bro-N	67	172	24	45	5	0	6	27	40	—	33	0	0	—	0	—	.262	.401	.395	.974
1934	Phi-N	7	20	0	2	0	0	0	3	3	—	4	0	0	—	0	—	.100	.217	.100	1.000
Career average		112	397	74	122	22	6	20	89	56	—	59	2	9	—	4	0	.307	.395	.545	.965
Cubs average		**142**	**526**	**109**	**170**	**31**	**7**	**32**	**128**	**77**	**—**	**77**	**3**	**14**	**—**	**6**	**0**	**.322**	**.412**	**.590**	**.966**
Career total		1348	4760	884	1461	266	67	244	1063	674	—	713	20	102	—	52	5	.307	.395	.545	.965
Cubs total		**850**	**3154**	**652**	**1017**	**185**	**44**	**190**	**769**	**463**	**—**	**461**	**17**	**85**	**—**	**34**	**0**	**.322**	**.412**	**.590**	**.966**

came along in 1926. Early in the season, Wilson's entry into the clubhouse was greeted by shouts of "Here comes the new Hackenschmidt!" That was eventually reduced to "Here's Hack!"

In 1930 Wilson had one of the greatest seasons a baseball player ever enjoyed. He hit a National League record 56 home runs, a record not broken until 1998 when both Mark McGwire of St. Louis (72 homers) and Sammy Sosa of the Cubs (66) passed it. Wilson led the league in walks with 105 and he had an amazing 191 RBIs, a mark that still stands today and is rarely even approached.

"We didn't lose a game all year," recalled McCarthy, "when Wilson came to bat in the late innings."

The puritanical McCarthy frowned on drinkers, but he had a soft spot for Wilson and his drinking buddy, pitcher Perce Leigh "Pat" Malone, because both men respected McCarthy and tried to be good boys. They often failed, but they often still produced.

Wilson was a terror for the Cubs in the 1929 World Series, hitting .471 to lead the team against the Athletics. This was the notorious Series in which the Athletics rallied for 10 runs in the seventh inning of Game 4 to take a 10-8 win in Chicago. At one point in the inning, Wilson lost a ball in the sun that went for a three-run, inside-the-park home run. Although it was a key miscue, no one blamed Wilson for it and he was not charged with an error. Still, the mistake weighed heavily on Wilson. After the series, he was seen sobbing as he exited the train from Philadelphia.

Through it all, though, Wilson never stopped drinking. Although this was during the depth of Prohibition, Wilson had great connections to bootleggers. The booze never seemed to stop flowing. In August 1931, a drunken Malone got into a brawl at a train station. Wilson was just as potted, but witnesses affirmed that he had not taken part in the altercation. The Cubs new manager, Rogers Hornsby, wasn't as tolerant as McCarthy. Malone and Wilson, the latter guilty by association, were suspended for the rest of the season. The next year, Wilson was traded to Brooklyn. He enjoyed two more successful seasons with the Dodgers, but the bottle was now beginning to swallow him up. By 1934 he was out of baseball.

The rest of his life was bad. He drifted from job to job, divorced his wife and remarried, but the boozing never stopped. In 1948 he died of acute alcoholism. He was elected to the Hall of Fame in 1979.

He remains the Cubs record holder with the aforementioned 191 RBIs. His 97 extra-base hits, 423 total bases, .723 slugging percentage and one-month total of 53 RBIs, all set in 1930, are still team records. Wilson also had a 27-game hitting streak that is fourth best all-time for Chicago.

Wilson, Willie James
HEIGHT: 6'2" THROWS: RIGHT BATS: BOTH BORN: 7/9/1955 MONTGOMERY, ALABAMA POSITIONS PLAYED: OF

YEAR	TEAM	GAMES	AB	RUNS	HITS	2B	3B	HR	RBI	BB	IBB	SO	HBP	SH	SF	SB	CS	BA	OBA	SA	FA
1976	KC-A	12	6	0	1	0	0	0	0	0	0	2	0	0	0	2	1	.167	.167	.167	.875
1977	KC-A	13	34	10	11	2	0	0	1	1	0	8	0	2	0	6	3	.324	.343	.382	.960
1978	KC-A	127	198	43	43	8	2	0	16	16	0	33	2	5	2	46	12	.217	.280	.278	.978
1979	KC-A	154	588	113	185	18	13	6	49	28	3	92	7	13	4	83	12	.315	.351	.420	.985
1980	KC-A	161	705	133	230	28	15	3	49	28	3	81	6	5	1	79	10	.326	.357	.421	.988
1981	KC-A	102	439	54	133	10	7	1	32	18	3	42	4	3	1	34	8	.303	.335	.364	.987
1982	KC-A	136	585	87	194	19	15	3	46	26	2	81	6	2	2	37	11	.332	.365	.431	.987
1983	KC-A	137	576	90	159	22	8	2	33	33	2	75	1	1	0	59	8	.276	.316	.352	.975
1984	KC-A	128	541	81	163	24	9	2	44	39	2	56	3	2	3	47	5	.301	.350	.390	.990
1985	KC-A	141	605	87	168	25	21	4	43	29	3	94	5	2	1	43	11	.278	.316	.408	.995
1986	KC-A	156	631	77	170	20	7	9	44	31	1	97	9	3	1	34	8	.269	.313	.366	.993
1987	KC-A	146	610	97	170	18	15	4	30	32	2	88	6	4	1	59	11	.279	.320	.377	.997
1988	KC-A	147	591	81	155	17	11	1	37	22	1	106	2	8	5	35	7	.262	.289	.333	.989
1989	KC-A	112	383	58	97	17	7	3	43	27	0	78	1	6	6	24	6	.253	.300	.358	.977
1990	KC-A	115	307	49	89	13	3	2	42	30	1	57	2	3	3	24	6	.290	.354	.371	1.000
1991	Oak-A	113	294	38	70	14	4	0	28	18	1	43	4	1	1	20	5	.238	.290	.313	.983
1992	Oak-A	132	396	38	107	15	5	0	37	35	2	65	1	2	3	28	8	.270	.329	.333	.981
1993	**ChC-N**	**105**	**221**	**29**	**57**	**11**	**3**	**1**	**11**	**11**	**1**	**40**	**3**	**1**	**1**	**7**	**2**	**.258**	**.301**	**.348**	**.991**
1994	**ChC-N**	**17**	**21**	**4**	**5**	**0**	**2**	**0**	**0**	**1**	**0**	**6**	**0**	**1**	**0**	**1**	**0**	**.238**	**.273**	**.429**	**1.000**
Career average		113	407	62	116	15	8	2	31	22	1	60	3	3	2	35	7	.285	.326	.376	.987
Cubs average		**61**	**121**	**17**	**31**	**6**	**3**	**1**	**6**	**6**	**1**	**23**	**2**	**1**	**1**	**4**	**1**	**.256**	**.298**	**.355**	**.992**
Career total		2154	7731	1169	2207	281	147	41	585	425	27	1144	62	64	35	668	134	.285	.326	.376	.987
Cubs total		**122**	**242**	**33**	**62**	**11**	**5**	**1**	**11**	**12**	**1**	**46**	**3**	**2**	**1**	**8**	**2**	**.256**	**.298**	**.355**	**.992**

Winceniak, Edward Joseph (Ed)
HEIGHT: 5'9" THROWS: RIGHT BATS: RIGHT BORN: 4/16/1929 CHICAGO, ILLINOIS POSITIONS PLAYED: 2B, 3B, SS

YEAR	TEAM	GAMES	AB	RUNS	HITS	2B	3B	HR	RBI	BB	IBB	SO	HBP	SH	SF	SB	CS	BA	OBA	SA	FA
1956	**ChC-N**	**15**	**17**	**1**	**2**	**0**	**0**	**0**	**0**	**1**	**0**	**3**	**0**	**0**	**0**	**0**	**0**	**.118**	**.167**	**.118**	**.900**
1957	**ChC-N**	**17**	**50**	**5**	**12**	**3**	**0**	**1**	**8**	**2**	**0**	**9**	**0**	**1**	**0**	**0**	**0**	**.240**	**.269**	**.360**	**.952**
Career average		16	34	3	7	2	0	1	4	2	0	6	0	1	0	0	0	.209	.243	.299	.942
Cubs average		**16**	**34**	**3**	**7**	**2**	**0**	**1**	**4**	**2**	**0**	**6**	**0**	**1**	**0**	**0**	**0**	**.209**	**.243**	**.299**	**.942**
Career total		32	67	6	14	3	0	1	8	3	0	12	0	1	0	0	0	.209	.243	.299	.942
Cubs total		**32**	**67**	**6**	**14**	**3**	**0**	**1**	**8**	**3**	**0**	**12**	**0**	**1**	**0**	**0**	**0**	**.209**	**.243**	**.299**	**.942**

Wirts, Elwood Vernon (Kettle)
HEIGHT: 5'11" THROWS: RIGHT BATS: RIGHT BORN: 10/31/1897 CONSUMNES, CALIFORNIA DIED: 7/12/1968 SACRAMENTO, CALIFORNIA POSITIONS PLAYED: C

YEAR	TEAM	GAMES	AB	RUNS	HITS	2B	3B	HR	RBI	BB	IBB	SO	HBP	SH	SF	SB	CS	BA	OBA	SA	FA
1921	**ChC-N**	**7**	**11**	**0**	**2**	**0**	**0**	**0**	**1**	**0**	**—**	**3**	**0**	**0**	**—**	**0**	**0**	**.182**	**.182**	**.182**	**1.000**
1922	**ChC-N**	**31**	**58**	**7**	**10**	**2**	**0**	**1**	**6**	**12**	**—**	**15**	**0**	**0**	**—**	**0**	**0**	**.172**	**.314**	**.259**	**.968**
1923	**ChC-N**	**5**	**5**	**2**	**1**	**0**	**0**	**0**	**1**	**2**	**—**	**0**	**0**	**0**	**—**	**0**	**0**	**.200**	**.429**	**.200**	**1.000**
1924	CWS-A	6	12	0	1	0	0	0	0	2	—	2	0	0	—	1	0	.083	.214	.083	1.000
Career average		12	22	2	4	1	0	0	2	4	—	5	0	0	—	0	0	.163	.294	.221	.981
Cubs average		**14**	**25**	**3**	**4**	**1**	**0**	**0**	**3**	**5**	**—**	**6**	**0**	**0**	**—**	**0**	**0**	**.176**	**.307**	**.243**	**.978**
Career total		49	86	9	14	2	0	1	8	16	—	20	0	0	—	1	0	.163	.294	.221	.981
Cubs total		**43**	**74**	**9**	**13**	**2**	**0**	**1**	**8**	**14**	**—**	**18**	**0**	**0**	**—**	**0**	**0**	**.176**	**.307**	**.243**	**.978**

Wise, Kendall Cole (Casey)
HEIGHT: 6'0" THROWS: RIGHT BATS: BOTH BORN: 9/8/1932 LAFAYETTE, INDIANA POSITIONS PLAYED: 2B, 3B, SS

YEAR	TEAM	GAMES	AB	RUNS	HITS	2B	3B	HR	RBI	BB	IBB	SO	HBP	SH	SF	SB	CS	BA	OBA	SA	FA
1957	**ChC-N**	**43**	**106**	**12**	**19**	**3**	**1**	**0**	**7**	**11**	**0**	**14**	**0**	**1**	**0**	**0**	**0**	**.179**	**.256**	**.226**	**.939**
1958	Mil-N	31	71	8	14	1	0	0	0	4	0	8	0	1	0	1	1	.197	.240	.211	.987
1959	Mil-N	22	76	11	13	2	0	1	5	10	0	5	0	0	0	0	0	.171	.267	.237	.968
1960	Det-A	30	68	6	10	0	2	2	5	4	0	9	0	0	0	1	0	.147	.194	.294	.989
Career average		32	80	9	14	2	1	1	4	7	0	9	0	1	0	1	0	.174	.243	.240	.965
Cubs average		**43**	**106**	**12**	**19**	**3**	**1**	**0**	**7**	**11**	**0**	**14**	**0**	**1**	**0**	**0**	**0**	**.179**	**.256**	**.226**	**.939**
Career total		126	321	37	56	6	3	3	17	29	0	36	0	2	0	2	1	.174	.243	.240	.965
Cubs total		**43**	**106**	**12**	**19**	**3**	**1**	**0**	**7**	**11**	**0**	**14**	**0**	**1**	**0**	**0**	**0**	**.179**	**.256**	**.226**	**.939**

Wolfe, Harold (Harry *or* Whitey)

HEIGHT: 5'8"   THROWS: RIGHT   BATS: RIGHT   BORN: 11/24/1890 WORCESTER, MASSACHUSETTS   DIED: 7/28/1971 FORT WAYNE, INDIANA
POSITIONS PLAYED: 2B, SS, OF

YEAR	TEAM	GAMES	AB	RUNS	HITS	2B	3B	HR	RBI	BB	IBB	SO	HBP	SH	SF	SB	CS	BA	OBA	SA	FA
1917	ChC-N	9	5	1	2	0	0	0	1	1	—	1	0	0	—	0	—	.400	.500	.400	1.000
1917	Pit-N	3	5	0	0	0	0	0	0	1	—	4	0	0	—	0	—	.000	.167	.000	.900
Career average		12	10	1	2	0	0	0	1	2	—	5	0	0	—	0	—	.200	.333	.200	.929
Cubs average		**9**	**5**	**1**	**2**	**0**	**0**	**0**	**1**	**1**	**—**	**1**	**0**	**0**	**—**	**0**	**—**	**.400**	**.500**	**.400**	**1.000**
Career total		12	10	1	2	0	0	0	1	2	—	5	0	0	—	0	—	.200	.333	.200	.929
Cubs total		**9**	**5**	**1**	**2**	**0**	**0**	**0**	**1**	**1**	**—**	**1**	**0**	**0**	**—**	**0**	**—**	**.400**	**.500**	**.400**	**1.000**

Wolter, Harry Meigs

HEIGHT: 5'10"   THROWS: RIGHT   BATS: LEFT   BORN: 7/11/1884 MONTEREY, CALIFORNIA   DIED: 7/6/1970 PALO ALTO, CALIFORNIA
POSITIONS PLAYED: P, 1B, OF

YEAR	TEAM	GAMES	AB	RUNS	HITS	2B	3B	HR	RBI	BB	IBB	SO	HBP	SH	SF	SB	CS	BA	OBA	SA	FA
1907	Cin-N	4	15	1	2	0	0	0	1	0	—	—	0	0	—	0	—	.133	.133	.133	1.000
1907	Pit-N	1	1	0	0	0	0	0	0	0	—	—	0	0	—	0	—	.000	.000	.000	—
1907	StL-N	16	47	4	16	0	0	0	6	3	—	—	0	0	—	1	—	.340	.380	.340	.935
1909	Bos-A	54	121	14	29	2	4	2	10	9	—	—	0	5	—	2	—	.240	.292	.372	.960
1910	NYA-A	135	479	84	128	15	9	4	42	66	—	—	7	20	—	39	—	.267	.364	.361	.940
1911	NYA-A	122	434	78	132	17	15	4	36	62	—	—	4	10	—	28	—	.304	.396	.440	.946
1912	NYA-A	12	32	8	11	2	1	0	1	10	—	—	1	0	—	5	—	.344	.512	.469	.923
1913	NYY-A	126	425	53	108	18	6	2	43	80	—	50	4	12	—	13	—	.254	.377	.339	.946
1917	ChC-N	117	353	44	88	15	7	0	28	38	—	40	1	9	—	7	—	.249	.324	.331	.943
Career average		84	272	41	73	10	6	2	24	38	—	13	2	8	—	14	—	.270	.365	.369	.947
Cubs average		**117**	**353**	**44**	**88**	**15**	**7**	**0**	**28**	**38**	**—**	**40**	**1**	**9**	**—**	**7**	**—**	**.249**	**.324**	**.331**	**.943**
Career total		587	1907	286	514	69	42	12	167	268	—	90	17	56	—	95	—	.270	.365	.369	.947
Cubs total		**117**	**353**	**44**	**88**	**15**	**7**	**0**	**28**	**38**	**—**	**40**	**1**	**9**	**—**	**7**	**—**	**.249**	**.324**	**.331**	**.943**

Wolverton, Harry Sterling (Fighting Harry)

HEIGHT: 5'11"   THROWS: RIGHT   BATS: LEFT   BORN: 12/6/1873 MOUNT VERNON, OHIO   DIED: 2/4/1937 OAKLAND, CALIFORNIA   POSITIONS PLAYED: 3B, SS

YEAR	TEAM	GAMES	AB	RUNS	HITS	2B	3B	HR	RBI	BB	IBB	SO	HBP	SH	SF	SB	CS	BA	OBA	SA	FA
1898	ChN-N	13	49	4	16	1	0	0	2	1	—	—	1	3	—	1	—	.327	.353	.347	.848
1899	ChN-N	99	389	50	111	14	11	1	49	30	—	—	9	14	—	14	—	.285	.350	.386	.859
1900	ChN-N	3	11	2	2	0	0	0	0	2	—	—	0	0	—	1	—	.182	.308	.182	.875
1900	Phi-N	101	383	42	108	10	8	3	58	20	—	—	3	8	—	4	—	.282	.323	.373	.881
1901	Phi-N	93	379	42	117	15	4	0	43	22	—	—	6	6	—	13	—	.309	.356	.369	.921
1902	Was-A	59	249	35	62	8	3	1	23	13	—	—	2	2	—	8	—	.249	.292	.317	.904
1902	Phi-N	34	136	12	40	3	2	0	16	9	—	—	2	5	—	3	—	.294	.347	.346	.931
1903	Phi-N	123	494	72	152	13	12	0	53	18	—	—	8	23	—	10	—	.308	.342	.383	.941
1904	Phi-N	102	398	43	106	15	5	0	49	26	—	—	6	10	—	18	—	.266	.321	.329	.925
1905	Bos-N	122	463	38	104	15	7	2	55	23	—	—	10	9	—	10	—	.225	.276	.300	.934
1912	NYA-A	33	50	6	15	1	1	0	4	2	—	—	1	1	—	1	—	.300	.340	.360	.821
Career average		87	333	38	93	11	6	1	39	18	—	—	5	9	—	9	—	.278	.326	.352	.908
Cubs average		**38**	**150**	**19**	**43**	**5**	**4**	**0**	**17**	**11**	**—**	**—**	**3**	**6**	**—**	**5**	**—**	**.287**	**.350**	**.376**	**.857**
Career total		782	3001	346	833	95	53	7	352	166	—	—	48	81	—	83	—	.278	.326	.352	.908
Cubs total		**115**	**449**	**56**	**129**	**15**	**11**	**1**	**51**	**33**	**—**	**—**	**10**	**17**	**—**	**16**	**—**	**.287**	**.350**	**.376**	**.857**

Woods, Gary Lee

HEIGHT: 6'2"   THROWS: RIGHT   BATS: RIGHT   BORN: 7/20/1954 SANTA BARBARA, CALIFORNIA   POSITIONS PLAYED: 2B, OF

YEAR	TEAM	GAMES	AB	RUNS	HITS	2B	3B	HR	RBI	BB	IBB	SO	HBP	SH	SF	SB	CS	BA	OBA	SA	FA
1976	Oak-A	6	8	0	1	0	0	0	0	0	0	3	0	0	0	0	0	.125	.125	.125	1.000
1977	Tor-A	60	227	21	49	9	1	0	17	7	0	38	2	3	0	5	4	.216	.246	.264	.994
1978	Tor-A	8	19	1	3	1	0	0	0	1	0	1	0	0	0	1	0	.158	.200	.211	1.000
1980	Hou-N	19	53	8	20	5	0	2	15	2	0	9	0	0	0	1	0	.377	.400	.585	1.000
1981	Hou-N	54	110	10	23	4	1	0	12	11	4	22	0	3	2	2	1	.209	.276	.264	.984
1982	ChC-N	117	245	28	66	15	1	4	30	21	2	48	0	4	0	3	3	.269	.327	.388	1.000

(continued)

(Woods, G.L., continued)

YEAR	TEAM	GAMES	AB	RUNS	HITS	2B	3B	HR	RBI	BB	IBB	SO	HBP	SH	SF	SB	CS	BA	OBA	SA	FA
1983	ChC-N	93	190	25	46	9	0	4	22	15	2	27	0	1	1	5	3	.242	.296	.353	.971
1984	ChC-N	87	98	13	23	4	1	3	10	15	0	21	0	2	1	2	1	.235	.333	.388	1.000
1985	ChC-N	81	82	11	20	3	0	0	4	14	0	18	0	1	0	0	1	.244	.354	.280	1.000
Career average		58	115	13	28	6	0	1	12	10	1	21	0	2	0	2	1	.243	.302	.337	.992
Cubs average		**95**	**154**	**19**	**39**	**8**	**1**	**3**	**17**	**16**	**1**	**29**	**0**	**2**	**1**	**3**	**2**	**.252**	**.323**	**.363**	**.992**
Career total		525	1032	117	251	50	4	13	110	86	8	187	2	14	4	19	13	.243	.302	.337	.992
Cubs total		**378**	**615**	**77**	**155**	**31**	**2**	**11**	**66**	**65**	**4**	**114**	**0**	**8**	**2**	**10**	**8**	**.252**	**.323**	**.363**	**.992**

Woods, James Jerome (Jim *or* Woody)
HEIGHT: 6'0"   THROWS: RIGHT   BATS: RIGHT   BORN: 9/17/1939 CHICAGO, ILLINOIS   POSITIONS PLAYED: 3B

YEAR	TEAM	GAMES	AB	RUNS	HITS	2B	3B	HR	RBI	BB	IBB	SO	HBP	SH	SF	SB	CS	BA	OBA	SA	FA
1957	ChC-N	2	0	1	0	0	0	0	0	0	0	0	0	0	0	0	0	—	—	—	—
1960	Phi-N	11	34	4	6	0	0	1	3	3	1	13	0	0	0	0	0	.176	.243	.265	.939
1961	Phi-N	23	48	6	11	3	0	2	9	4	2	15	1	1	1	0	0	.229	.296	.417	.968
Career average		12	27	4	6	1	0	1	4	2	1	9	0	0	0	0	0	.207	.275	.354	.953
Cubs average		**2**	**0**	**1**	**0**	**0**	**0**	**0**	**0**	**0**	**0**	**0**	**0**	**0**	**0**	**0**	**0**	**—**	**—**	**—**	**—**
Career total		36	82	11	17	3	0	3	12	7	3	28	1	1	1	0	0	.207	.275	.354	.953
Cubs total		**2**	**0**	**1**	**0**	**0**	**0**	**0**	**0**	**0**	**0**	**0**	**0**	**0**	**0**	**0**	**0**	**—**	**—**	**—**	**—**

Wortman, William Lewis (Chuck)
HEIGHT: 5'7"   THROWS: RIGHT   BATS: RIGHT   BORN: 1/5/1892 BALTIMORE, MARYLAND   DIED: 8/19/1977 LAS VEGAS, NEVADA   POSITIONS PLAYED: 2B, 3B, SS

YEAR	TEAM	GAMES	AB	RUNS	HITS	2B	3B	HR	RBI	BB	IBB	SO	HBP	SH	SF	SB	CS	BA	OBA	SA	FA
1916	ChC-N	69	234	17	47	4	2	2	16	18	—	22	0	4	—	4	—	.201	.258	.261	.908
1917	ChC-N	75	190	24	33	4	1	0	9	18	—	23	0	12	—	6	—	.174	.245	.205	.919
1918	ChC-N	17	17	4	2	0	0	1	3	1	—	2	0	0	—	3	—	.118	.167	.294	.897
Career average		54	147	15	27	3	1	1	9	12	—	16	0	5	—	4	—	.186	.249	.238	.912
Cubs average		**54**	**147**	**15**	**27**	**3**	**1**	**1**	**9**	**12**	**—**	**16**	**0**	**5**	**—**	**4**	**—**	**.186**	**.249**	**.238**	**.912**
Career total		161	441	45	82	8	3	3	28	37	—	47	0	16	—	13	—	.186	.249	.238	.912
Cubs total		**161**	**441**	**45**	**82**	**8**	**3**	**3**	**28**	**37**	**—**	**47**	**0**	**16**	**—**	**13**	**—**	**.186**	**.249**	**.238**	**.912**

Wright, Patrick W. (Pat)
HEIGHT: 6'2"   THROWS: RIGHT   BATS: BOTH   BORN: 7/5/1868 POTTSVILLE, PENNSYLVANIA   DIED: 5/29/1943 SPRINGFIELD, ILLINOIS   POSITIONS PLAYED: 2B

YEAR	TEAM	GAMES	AB	RUNS	HITS	2B	3B	HR	RBI	BB	IBB	SO	HBP	SH	SF	SB	CS	BA	OBA	SA	FA
1890	ChN-N	1	2	0	0	0	0	0	0	1	—	0	0	—	—	0	—	.000	.333	.000	1.000
Career average		1	2	0	0	0	0	0	0	1	—	0	0	—	—	0	—	.000	.333	.000	1.000
Cubs average		**1**	**2**	**0**	**0**	**0**	**0**	**0**	**0**	**1**	**—**	**0**	**0**	**—**	**—**	**0**	**—**	**.000**	**.333**	**.000**	**1.000**
Career total		1	2	0	0	0	0	0	0	1	—	0	0	—	—	0	—	.000	.333	.000	1.000
Cubs total		**1**	**2**	**0**	**0**	**0**	**0**	**0**	**0**	**1**	**—**	**0**	**0**	**—**	**—**	**0**	**—**	**.000**	**.333**	**.000**	**1.000**

Wrona, Richard James (Rick)
HEIGHT: 6'1"   THROWS: RIGHT   BATS: RIGHT   BORN: 12/10/1963 TULSA, OKLAHOMA   POSITIONS PLAYED: C, 1B

YEAR	TEAM	GAMES	AB	RUNS	HITS	2B	3B	HR	RBI	BB	IBB	SO	HBP	SH	SF	SB	CS	BA	OBA	SA	FA
1988	ChC-N	4	6	0	0	0	0	0	0	0	0	1	0	0	0	0	0	.000	.000	.000	1.000
1989	ChC-N	38	92	11	26	2	1	2	14	2	1	21	1	0	2	0	0	.283	.299	.391	.983
1990	ChC-N	16	29	3	5	0	0	0	0	2	1	11	0	1	0	1	0	.172	.226	.172	.970
1992	Cin-N	11	23	0	4	0	0	0	0	0	0	3	0	0	0	0	0	.174	.174	.174	.966
1993	CWS-A	4	8	0	1	0	0	0	1	0	0	4	0	0	0	0	0	.125	.125	.125	1.000
1994	Mil-A	6	10	2	5	4	0	1	3	1	0	1	0	1	0	0	0	.500	.545	1.200	.923
Career average		13	28	3	7	1	0	1	3	1	0	7	0	0	0	0	0	.244	.267	.345	.976
Cubs average		**19**	**42**	**5**	**10**	**1**	**0**	**1**	**5**	**1**	**1**	**11**	**0**	**0**	**1**	**0**	**0**	**.244**	**.269**	**.323**	**.980**
Career total		79	168	16	41	6	1	3	18	5	2	41	1	2	2	1	0	.244	.267	.345	.976
Cubs total		**58**	**127**	**14**	**31**	**2**	**1**	**2**	**14**	**4**	**2**	**33**	**1**	**1**	**2**	**1**	**0**	**.244**	**.269**	**.323**	**.980**

Wynne, Marvell
HEIGHT: 5'11" THROWS: LEFT   BATS: LEFT   BORN: 12/17/1959 CHICAGO, ILLINOIS   POSITIONS PLAYED: OF

YEAR	TEAM	GAMES	AB	RUNS	HITS	2B	3B	HR	RBI	BB	IBB	SO	HBP	SH	SF	SB	CS	BA	OBA	SA	FA
1983	Pit-N	103	366	66	89	16	2	7	26	38	0	52	3	7	1	12	10	.243	.319	.355	.983
1984	Pit-N	154	653	77	174	24	11	0	39	42	0	81	0	5	2	24	19	.266	.310	.337	.990
1985	Pit-N	103	337	21	69	6	3	2	18	18	2	48	1	7	0	10	5	.205	.247	.258	.987
1986	SD-N	137	288	34	76	19	2	7	37	15	2	45	1	1	3	11	11	.264	.300	.417	.986
1987	SD-N	98	188	17	47	8	2	2	24	20	1	37	0	4	1	11	6	.250	.321	.346	.981
1988	SD-N	128	333	37	88	13	4	11	42	31	2	62	0	3	2	3	4	.264	.325	.426	.987
1989	SD-N	105	294	19	74	11	1	6	35	12	1	41	1	6	1	4	1	.252	.282	.357	.971
1989	**ChC-N**	**20**	**48**	**8**	**9**	**2**	**1**	**1**	**4**	**1**	**1**	**7**	**1**	**1**	**0**	**2**	**0**	**.188**	**.220**	**.333**	**.944**
1990	**ChC-N**	**92**	**186**	**21**	**38**	**8**	**2**	**4**	**19**	**14**	**3**	**25**	**1**	**1**	**0**	**3**	**2**	**.204**	**.264**	**.333**	**.991**
Career average		118	337	38	83	13	4	5	31	24	2	50	1	4	1	10	7	.247	.297	.352	.985
Cubs average		**56**	**117**	**15**	**24**	**5**	**2**	**3**	**12**	**8**	**2**	**16**	**1**	**1**	**0**	**3**	**1**	**.201**	**.255**	**.333**	**.985**
Career total		940	2693	300	664	107	28	40	244	191	12	398	8	35	10	80	58	.247	.297	.352	.985
Cubs total		**112**	**234**	**29**	**47**	**10**	**3**	**5**	**23**	**15**	**4**	**32**	**2**	**2**	**0**	**5**	**2**	**.201**	**.255**	**.333**	**.985**

Yantz, George Webb
HEIGHT: 5'6" THROWS: RIGHT   BATS: RIGHT   BORN: 7/27/1886 LOUISVILLE, KENTUCKY   DIED: 2/26/1967 LOUISVILLE, KENTUCKY   POSITIONS PLAYED: C

YEAR	TEAM	GAMES	AB	RUNS	HITS	2B	3B	HR	RBI	BB	IBB	SO	HBP	SH	SF	SB	CS	BA	OBA	SA	FA
1912	**ChC-N**	**1**	**1**	**0**	**1**	**0**	**0**	**0**	**0**	**0**	—	**0**	**0**	**0**	—	**0**	—	**1.000**	**1.000**	**1.000**	—
Career average		1	1	0	1	0	0	0	0	0	—	0	0	0	—	0	—	1.000	1.000	1.000	—
Cubs average		**1**	**1**	**0**	**1**	**0**	**0**	**0**	**0**	**0**	—	**0**	**0**	**0**	—	**0**	—	**1.000**	**1.000**	**1.000**	—
Career total		1	1	0	1	0	0	0	0	0	—	0	0	0	—	0	—	1.000	1.000	1.000	—
Cubs total		**1**	**1**	**0**	**1**	**0**	**0**	**0**	**0**	**0**	—	**0**	**0**	**0**	—	**0**	—	**1.000**	**1.000**	**1.000**	—

Yelding, Eric Girard
HEIGHT: 5'11" THROWS: RIGHT   BATS: RIGHT   BORN: 2/22/1965 MONTROSE, ALABAMA   POSITIONS PLAYED: 2B, 3B, SS, OF

YEAR	TEAM	GAMES	AB	RUNS	HITS	2B	3B	HR	RBI	BB	IBB	SO	HBP	SH	SF	SB	CS	BA	OBA	SA	FA
1989	Hou-N	70	90	19	21	2	0	0	9	7	0	19	1	2	2	11	5	.233	.290	.256	.969
1990	Hou-N	142	511	69	130	9	5	1	28	39	1	87	0	4	5	64	25	.254	.305	.297	.963
1991	Hou-N	78	276	19	67	11	1	1	20	13	3	46	0	3	1	11	9	.243	.276	.301	.933
1992	Hou-N	9	8	1	2	0	0	0	0	0	0	3	0	0	0	0	0	.250	.250	.250	1.000
1993	**ChC-N**	**69**	**108**	**14**	**22**	**5**	**1**	**1**	**10**	**11**	**2**	**22**	**0**	**4**	**0**	**3**	**2**	**.204**	**.277**	**.296**	**.972**
Career average		74	199	24	48	5	1	1	13	14	1	35	0	3	2	18	8	.244	.292	.294	.956
Cubs average		**69**	**108**	**14**	**22**	**5**	**1**	**1**	**10**	**11**	**2**	**22**	**0**	**4**	**0**	**3**	**2**	**.204**	**.277**	**.296**	**.972**
Career total		368	993	122	242	27	7	3	67	70	6	177	1	13	8	89	41	.244	.292	.294	.956
Cubs total		**69**	**108**	**14**	**22**	**5**	**1**	**1**	**10**	**11**	**2**	**22**	**0**	**4**	**0**	**3**	**2**	**.204**	**.277**	**.296**	**.972**

Yerkes, Stephen Douglas (Steve)
HEIGHT: 5'9" THROWS: RIGHT   BATS: RIGHT   BORN: 5/15/1888 HATBORO, PENNSYLVANIA   DIED: 1/31/1971 LANSDALE, PENNSYLVANIA
POSITIONS PLAYED: 2B, 3B, SS

YEAR	TEAM	GAMES	AB	RUNS	HITS	2B	3B	HR	RBI	BB	IBB	SO	HBP	SH	SF	SB	CS	BA	OBA	SA	FA
1909	Bos-A	5	7	0	2	0	0	0	0	0	—	—	0	0	—	0	—	.286	.286	.286	1.000
1911	Bos-A	142	502	70	140	24	3	1	57	52	—	—	6	31	—	14	—	.279	.354	.345	.929
1912	Bos-A	131	523	73	132	22	6	0	42	41	—	—	4	25	—	4	—	.252	.312	.317	.943
1913	Bos-A	137	483	67	129	29	6	1	48	50	—	32	2	25	—	11	—	.267	.338	.358	.957
1914	Bos-A	92	293	23	64	17	2	1	23	14	—	23	2	12	—	5	6	.218	.259	.300	.972
1914	Pit-F	39	142	18	48	9	5	1	25	11	—	13	0	5	—	2	—	.338	.386	.493	.974
1915	Pit-F	121	434	44	125	17	8	1	49	30	—	27	2	14	—	17	—	.288	.337	.371	.961
1916	**ChC-N**	**44**	**137**	**12**	**36**	**6**	**2**	**1**	**10**	**9**	—	**7**	**0**	**3**	—	**1**	—	**.263**	**.308**	**.358**	**.919**
Career average		102	360	44	97	18	5	1	36	30	—	15	2	16	—	8	1	.268	.328	.350	.950
Cubs average		**44**	**137**	**12**	**36**	**6**	**2**	**1**	**10**	**9**	—	**7**	**0**	**3**	—	**1**	**0**	**.263**	**.308**	**.358**	**.919**
Career total		711	2521	307	676	124	32	6	254	207	—	102	16	115	—	54	6	.268	.328	.350	.950
Cubs total		**44**	**137**	**12**	**36**	**6**	**2**	**1**	**10**	**9**	—	**7**	**0**	**3**	—	**1**	**0**	**.263**	**.308**	**.358**	**.919**

York, Tony Batton
HEIGHT: 5'10" THROWS: RIGHT BATS: RIGHT BORN: 11/27/1912 IRENE, TEXAS DIED: 4/18/1970 HILLSBORO, TEXAS POSITIONS PLAYED: 3B, SS

YEAR	TEAM	GAMES	AB	RUNS	HITS	2B	3B	HR	RBI	BB	IBB	SO	HBP	SH	SF	SB	CS	BA	OBA	SA	FA
1944	ChC-N	28	85	4	20	1	0	0	7	4	—	11	0	1	—	0	—	.235	.270	.247	.960
Career average		28	85	4	20	1	0	0	7	4	—	11	0	1	—	0	—	.235	.270	.247	.960
Cubs average		28	85	4	20	1	0	0	7	4	—	11	0	1	—	0	—	.235	.270	.247	.960
Career total		28	85	4	20	1	0	0	7	4	—	11	0	1	—	0	—	.235	.270	.247	.960
Cubs total		28	85	4	20	1	0	0	7	4	—	11	0	1	—	0	—	.235	.270	.247	.960

Yoter, Elmer Ellsworth
HEIGHT: 5'7" THROWS: RIGHT BATS: RIGHT BORN: 6/26/1900 PLAINFIELD, PENNSYLVANIA DIED: 7/26/1966 CAMP HILL, PENNSYLVANIA
POSITIONS PLAYED: 3B

YEAR	TEAM	GAMES	AB	RUNS	HITS	2B	3B	HR	RBI	BB	IBB	SO	HBP	SH	SF	SB	CS	BA	OBA	SA	FA
1921	Phi-A	3	3	0	0	0	0	0	0	0	—	0	0	0	—	0	0	.000	.000	.000	—
1924	Cle-A	19	66	3	18	1	1	0	7	5	—	8	0	3	—	0	—	.273	.324	.318	.905
1927	ChC-N	13	27	2	6	1	1	0	5	4	—	4	0	0	—	0	—	.222	.323	.333	.947
1928	ChC-N	1	0	0	0	0	0	0	0	0	—	0	0	0	—	0	—	—	—	—	—
Career average		9	24	1	6	1	1	0	3	2	—	3	0	1	—	0	0	.250	.314	.313	.915
Cubs average		7	14	1	3	1	1	0	3	2	—	2	0	0	—	0	0	.222	.323	.333	.947
Career total		36	96	5	24	2	2	0	12	9	—	12	0	3	—	0	0	.250	.314	.313	.915
Cubs total		14	27	2	6	1	1	0	5	4	—	4	0	0	—	0	0	.222	.323	.333	.947

Young, Donald Wayne (Don)
HEIGHT: 6'2" THROWS: RIGHT BATS: RIGHT BORN: 10/18/1945 HOUSTON, TEXAS POSITIONS PLAYED: OF

YEAR	TEAM	GAMES	AB	RUNS	HITS	2B	3B	HR	RBI	BB	IBB	SO	HBP	SH	SF	SB	CS	BA	OBA	SA	FA
1965	ChC-N	11	35	1	2	0	0	1	2	0	0	11	0	0	1	0	0	.057	.056	.143	.933
1969	ChC-N	101	272	36	65	12	3	6	27	38	5	74	5	8	0	1	5	.239	.343	.371	.975
Career average		56	154	19	34	6	2	4	15	19	3	43	3	4	1	1	3	.218	.313	.345	.972
Cubs average		56	154	19	34	6	2	4	15	19	3	43	3	4	1	1	3	.218	.313	.345	.972
Career total		112	307	37	67	12	3	7	29	38	5	85	5	8	1	1	5	.218	.313	.345	.972
Cubs total		112	307	37	67	12	3	7	29	38	5	85	5	8	1	1	5	.218	.313	.345	.972

Young, Eric Orlando (E.Y.)
HEIGHT: 5'8" THROWS: RIGHT BATS: RIGHT BORN: 5/18/1967 NEW BRUNSWICK, NEW JERSEY POSITIONS PLAYED: 2B, OF

YEAR	TEAM	GAMES	AB	RUNS	HITS	2B	3B	HR	RBI	BB	IBB	SO	HBP	SH	SF	SB	CS	BA	OBA	SA	FA
1992	LA-N	49	132	9	34	1	0	1	11	8	0	9	0	4	0	6	1	.258	.300	.288	.957
1993	Col-N	144	490	82	132	16	8	3	42	63	3	41	4	4	4	42	19	.269	.355	.353	.964
1994	Col-N	90	228	37	62	13	1	7	30	38	1	17	2	5	2	18	7	.272	.378	.430	.974
1995	Col-N	120	366	68	116	21	9	6	36	49	3	29	5	3	1	35	12	.317	.404	.473	.974
1996	Col-N	141	568	113	184	23	4	8	74	47	1	31	21	2	5	53	19	.324	.393	.421	.985
1997	Col-N	118	468	78	132	29	6	6	45	57	0	37	5	8	5	32	12	.282	.363	.408	.978
1997	LA-N	37	154	28	42	4	2	2	16	14	1	17	4	2	1	13	2	.273	.347	.364	.979
1998	LA-N	117	452	78	129	24	1	8	43	45	0	32	5	9	2	42	13	.285	.355	.396	.976
1999	LA-N	119	456	73	128	24	2	2	41	63	0	26	5	6	4	51	22	.281	.371	.355	.984
2000	ChC-N	153	607	98	180	40	2	6	47	63	1	39	8	7	5	54	7	.297	.367	.399	.979
2001	ChC-N	149	603	98	168	43	4	6	42	42	1	45	9	15	3	31	14	.279	.333	.393	.981
Career average		124	452	76	131	24	4	6	43	49	1	32	7	7	3	38	13	.289	.365	.395	.978
Cubs average		151	605	98	174	42	3	6	45	53	1	42	9	11	4	43	11	.288	.351	.396	.980
Career total		1237	4524	762	1307	238	39	55	427	489	11	323	68	65	32	377	128	.289	.365	.395	.978
Cubs total		302	1210	196	348	83	6	12	89	105	2	84	17	22	8	85	21	.288	.351	.396	.980

Zambrano, Eduardo Jose (Eddie)

HEIGHT: 6'3" THROWS: RIGHT BATS: RIGHT BORN: 2/1/1966 MARACAIBO, VENEZUELA POSITIONS PLAYED: 1B, 3B, OF

YEAR	TEAM	GAMES	AB	RUNS	HITS	2B	3B	HR	RBI	BB	IBB	SO	HBP	SH	SF	SB	CS	BA	OBA	SA	FA
1993	ChC-N	8	17	1	5	0	0	0	2	1	0	3	0	0	0	0	0	.294	.333	.294	.933
1994	ChC-N	67	116	17	30	7	0	6	18	16	0	29	1	0	0	2	1	.259	.353	.474	.978
Career average		38	67	9	18	4	0	3	10	9	0	16	1	0	0	1	1	.263	.351	.451	.972
Cubs average		**38**	**67**	**9**	**18**	**4**	**0**	**3**	**10**	**9**	**0**	**16**	**1**	**0**	**0**	**1**	**1**	**.263**	**.351**	**.451**	**.972**
Career total		75	133	18	35	7	0	6	20	17	0	32	1	0	0	2	1	.263	.351	.451	.972
Cubs total		**75**	**133**	**18**	**35**	**7**	**0**	**6**	**20**	**17**	**0**	**32**	**1**	**0**	**0**	**2**	**1**	**.263**	**.351**	**.451**	**.972**

Zeider, Rollie Hubert (Bunions)

HEIGHT: 5'10" THROWS: RIGHT BATS: RIGHT BORN: 11/16/1883 AUBURN, INDIANA DIED: 9/12/1967 GARRETT, INDIANA
POSITIONS PLAYED: 1B, 2B, 3B, SS, OF

YEAR	TEAM	GAMES	AB	RUNS	HITS	2B	3B	HR	RBI	BB	IBB	SO	HBP	SH	SF	SB	CS	BA	OBA	SA	FA
1910	CWS-A	136	498	57	108	9	2	0	31	62	—	—	1	20	—	49	—	.217	.305	.243	.919
1911	CWS-A	73	217	39	55	3	0	2	21	29	—	—	2	12	—	28	—	.253	.347	.295	.964
1912	CWS-A	129	420	57	103	12	10	1	42	50	—	—	3	24	—	47	—	.245	.330	.329	.970
1913	CWS-A	13	20	4	7	0	0	0	2	4	—	1	0	1	—	3	—	.350	.458	.350	1.000
1913	NYY-A	49	159	15	37	2	0	0	12	25	—	9	1	4	—	3	—	.233	.341	.245	.934
1914	Chi-F	119	452	60	124	13	2	1	36	44	—	28	4	18	—	3	—	.274	.344	.319	.934
1915	Chi-F	129	494	65	112	22	2	2	34	43	—	24	6	15	—	35	—	.227	.297	.279	.945
1916	**ChC-N**	**98**	**345**	**29**	**81**	**11**	**2**	**1**	**22**	**26**	**—**	**26**	**3**	**5**	**—**	**9**	**—**	**.235**	**.294**	**.287**	**.941**
1917	**ChC-N**	**108**	**354**	**36**	**86**	**14**	**2**	**0**	**27**	**28**	**—**	**30**	**2**	**9**	**—**	**17**	**—**	**.243**	**.302**	**.294**	**.931**
1918	**ChC-N**	**82**	**251**	**31**	**56**	**3**	**2**	**0**	**26**	**23**	**—**	**20**	**0**	**14**	**—**	**16**	**—**	**.223**	**.288**	**.251**	**.957**
Career average		104	357	44	85	10	2	1	28	37	—	15	2	14	—	25	—	.240	.315	.286	.946
Cubs average		**96**	**317**	**32**	**74**	**9**	**2**	**0**	**25**	**26**	**—**	**25**	**2**	**9**	**—**	**14**	**—**	**.235**	**.296**	**.280**	**.942**
Career total		936	3210	393	769	89	22	5	253	334	—	138	22	122	—	223	—	.240	.315	.286	.946
Cubs total		**288**	**950**	**96**	**223**	**28**	**6**	**1**	**75**	**77**	**—**	**76**	**5**	**28**	**—**	**42**	**—**	**.235**	**.296**	**.280**	**.942**

Zeile, Todd Edward

HEIGHT: 6'1" THROWS: RIGHT BATS: RIGHT BORN: 9/9/1965 VAN NUYS, CALIFORNIA POSITIONS PLAYED: C, 1B, 3B, OF

YEAR	TEAM	GAMES	AB	RUNS	HITS	2B	3B	HR	RBI	BB	IBB	SO	HBP	SH	SF	SB	CS	BA	OBA	SA	FA
1989	StL-N	28	82	7	21	3	1	1	8	9	1	14	0	1	1	0	0	.256	.326	.354	.971
1990	StL-N	144	495	62	121	25	3	15	57	67	3	77	2	0	6	2	4	.244	.333	.398	.980
1991	StL-N	155	565	76	158	36	3	11	81	62	3	94	5	0	6	17	11	.280	.353	.412	.943
1992	StL-N	126	439	51	113	18	4	7	48	68	4	70	0	0	7	7	10	.257	.352	.364	.960
1993	StL-N	157	571	82	158	36	1	17	103	70	5	76	0	0	6	5	4	.277	.352	.433	.923
1994	StL-N	113	415	62	111	25	1	19	75	52	3	56	3	0	6	5	4	.267	.352	.433	.923
1995	StL-N	34	127	16	37	6	0	5	22	18	1	23	1	0	2	1	3	.267	.348	.470	.960
1995	**ChC-N**	**79**	**299**	**34**	**68**	**16**	**0**	**9**	**30**	**16**	**0**	**53**	**3**	**4**	**3**	**0**	**0**	**.227**	**.271**	**.457**	**.980**
1996	Phi-N	134	500	61	134	24	0	20	80	67	4	88	1	0	4	1	1	.268	.353	.436	.972
1996	Bal-A	29	117	17	28	8	0	5	19	15	0	16	0	0	0	0	0	.239	.326	.436	.964
1997	LA-N	160	575	89	154	17	0	31	90	85	7	112	6	0	6	8	7	.268	.365	.459	.931
1998	LA-N	40	158	22	40	6	1	7	27	10	0	24	1	0	1	1	1	.253	.300	.437	.930
1998	Fla-N	66	234	37	68	12	1	6	39	31	2	34	2	0	3	2	3	.291	.374	.427	.971
1998	Tex-A	52	180	26	47	14	1	6	28	28	0	32	1	1	3	1	0	.261	.358	.450	.915
1999	Tex-A	156	588	80	172	41	1	24	98	56	3	94	4	1	7	1	0	.293	.354	.488	.941
2000	NYM-N	153	544	67	146	36	3	22	79	74	4	85	2	0	3	3	2	.268	.356	.467	.992
2001	NYM-N	151	531	66	141	25	1	10	62	73	3	102	6	0	2	1	0	.266	.359	.373	.992
Career average		137	494	66	132	27	2	17	73	62	3	81	3	1	5	4	4	.267	.349	.429	.968
Cubs average		**79**	**299**	**34**	**68**	**16**	**0**	**9**	**30**	**16**	**0**	**53**	**3**	**4**	**3**	**0**	**0**	**.227**	**.271**	**.371**	**.939**
Career total		1777	6420	855	1717	348	21	215	946	801	43	1050	37	7	67	51	50	.267	.349	.429	.968
Cubs total		**79**	**299**	**34**	**68**	**16**	**0**	**9**	**30**	**16**	**0**	**53**	**3**	**4**	**3**	**0**	**0**	**.227**	**.271**	**.371**	**.939**

Zimmer, Donald William (Don *or* Popeye)

HEIGHT: 5'9" THROWS: RIGHT BATS: RIGHT BORN: 1/17/1931 CINCINNATI, OHIO POSITIONS PLAYED: C, 2B, 3B, SS, OF

YEAR	TEAM	GAMES	AB	RUNS	HITS	2B	3B	HR	RBI	BB	IBB	SO	HBP	SH	SF	SB	CS	BA	OBA	SA	FA
1954	Bro-N	24	33	3	6	0	1	0	0	3	—	8	1	0	0	2	0	.182	.270	.242	.939
1955	Bro-N	88	280	38	67	10	1	15	50	19	5	66	2	4	4	5	3	.239	.289	.443	.970
1956	Bro-N	17	20	4	6	1	0	0	2	0	0	7	1	0	0	0	1	.300	.333	.350	.955
1957	Bro-N	84	269	23	59	9	1	6	19	16	5	63	0	3	1	1	3	.219	.262	.327	.952
1958	LA-N	127	455	52	119	15	2	17	60	28	1	92	1	9	2	14	2	.262	.305	.415	.963
1959	LA-N	97	249	21	41	7	1	4	28	37	7	56	1	4	1	3	1	.165	.274	.249	.973
1960	**ChC-N**	**132**	**368**	**37**	**95**	**16**	**7**	**6**	**35**	**27**	**4**	**56**	**0**	**5**	**2**	**8**	**6**	**.258**	**.307**	**.389**	**.968**
1961	**ChC-N**	**128**	**477**	**57**	**120**	**25**	**4**	**13**	**40**	**25**	**1**	**70**	**2**	**7**	**1**	**5**	**1**	**.252**	**.291**	**.403**	**.969**
1962	NYM-N	14	52	3	4	1	0	0	1	3	0	10	0	0	0	0	2	.077	.127	.096	.961
1962	Cin-N	63	192	16	48	11	2	2	16	14	1	30	1	0	0	0	0	.250	.304	.359	.946
1963	LA-N	22	23	4	5	1	0	1	2	3	0	10	0	0	0	0	0	.217	.308	.391	.895
1963	Was-A	83	298	37	74	12	1	13	44	18	2	57	2	2	0	3	2	.248	.296	.426	.937
1964	Was-A	121	341	38	84	16	2	12	38	27	0	94	0	2	0	1	3	.246	.302	.411	.956
1965	Was-A	95	226	20	45	6	0	2	17	26	1	59	2	1	3	2	0	.199	.284	.252	.956
Career average		91	274	29	64	11	2	8	29	21	2	57	1	3	1	4	2	.235	.290	.372	.961
Cubs average		**130**	**423**	**47**	**108**	**21**	**6**	**10**	**38**	**26**	**3**	**63**	**1**	**6**	**2**	**7**	**4**	**.254**	**.298**	**.396**	**.968**
Career total		1095	3283	353	773	130	22	91	352	246	27	678	13	37	14	45	25	.235	.290	.372	.961
Cubs total		**260**	**845**	**94**	**215**	**41**	**11**	**19**	**75**	**52**	**5**	**126**	**2**	**12**	**3**	**13**	**7**	**.254**	**.298**	**.396**	**.968**

Zimmerman, Henry (Heinie)

HEIGHT: 5'11" THROWS: RIGHT BATS: RIGHT BORN: 2/9/1887 NEW YORK, NEW YORK DIED: 3/14/1969 NEW YORK, NEW YORK
POSITIONS PLAYED: 1B, 2B, 3B, SS, OF

YEAR	TEAM	GAMES	AB	RUNS	HITS	2B	3B	HR	RBI	BB	IBB	SO	HBP	SH	SF	SB	CS	BA	OBA	SA	FA
1907	**ChC-N**	**5**	**9**	**0**	**2**	**1**	**0**	**0**	**1**	**0**	**—**	**—**	**0**	**0**	**—**	**0**	**—**	**.222**	**.222**	**.333**	**.818**
1908	**ChC-N**	**46**	**113**	**17**	**33**	**4**	**1**	**0**	**9**	**1**	**—**	**—**	**0**	**4**	**—**	**2**	**—**	**.292**	**.298**	**.345**	**.914**
1909	**ChC-N**	**65**	**183**	**23**	**50**	**9**	**2**	**0**	**21**	**3**	**—**	**—**	**0**	**4**	**—**	**7**	**—**	**.273**	**.285**	**.344**	**.913**
1910	**ChC-N**	**99**	**335**	**35**	**95**	**16**	**6**	**3**	**38**	**20**	**—**	**36**	**1**	**7**	**—**	**7**	**—**	**.284**	**.326**	**.394**	**.913**
1911	**ChC-N**	**143**	**535**	**80**	**164**	**22**	**17**	**9**	**85**	**25**	**—**	**50**	**5**	**18**	**—**	**23**	**—**	**.307**	**.343**	**.462**	**.946**
1912	**ChC-N**	**145**	**557**	**95**	**207**	**41**	**14**	**14**	**99**	**38**	**—**	**60**	**6**	**18**	**—**	**23**	**—**	**.372**	**.418**	**.571**	**.940**
1913	**ChC-N**	**127**	**447**	**69**	**140**	**28**	**12**	**9**	**95**	**41**	**—**	**40**	**6**	**16**	**—**	**18**	**—**	**.313**	**.379**	**.490**	**.912**
1914	**ChC-N**	**146**	**564**	**75**	**167**	**36**	**12**	**4**	**87**	**20**	**—**	**46**	**5**	**12**	**—**	**17**	**—**	**.296**	**.326**	**.424**	**.896**
1915	**ChC-N**	**139**	**520**	**65**	**138**	**28**	**11**	**3**	**62**	**21**	**—**	**33**	**5**	**15**	**—**	**19**	**13**	**.265**	**.300**	**.379**	**.937**
1916	**ChC-N**	**107**	**398**	**54**	**116**	**25**	**5**	**6**	**64**	**16**	**—**	**33**	**3**	**10**	**—**	**15**	**—**	**.291**	**.324**	**.425**	**.932**
1916	NYG-N	40	151	22	41	4	0	0	19	7	—	10	0	3	—	9	—	.272	.304	.298	.943
1917	NYG-N	150	585	61	174	22	9	5	102	16	—	43	1	18	—	13	—	.297	.317	.391	.946
1918	NYG-N	121	463	43	126	19	10	1	56	13	—	23	1	11	—	14	—	.272	.294	.363	.969
1919	NYG-N	123	444	56	113	20	6	4	58	21	—	30	5	20	—	8	—	.255	.296	.354	.940
Career average		112	408	53	120	21	8	4	61	19	—	31	3	12	—	13	1	.295	.331	.419	.933
Cubs average		**102**	**366**	**51**	**111**	**21**	**8**	**5**	**56**	**19**	**—**	**30**	**3**	**10**	**—**	**13**	**1**	**.304**	**.343**	**.444**	**.926**
Career total		1456	5304	695	1566	275	105	58	796	242	—	404	38	156	—	175	13	.295	.331	.419	.933
Cubs total		**1022**	**3661**	**513**	**1112**	**210**	**80**	**48**	**561**	**185**	**—**	**298**	**31**	**104**	**—**	**131**	**13**	**.304**	**.343**	**.444**	**.926**

Zuleta, Julio Ernesto

HEIGHT: 6'5" THROWS: RIGHT BATS: RIGHT BORN: 3/28/1975 PANAMA CITY, PANAMA POSITIONS PLAYED: 1B, OF

YEAR	TEAM	GAMES	AB	RUNS	HITS	2B	3B	HR	RBI	BB	IBB	SO	HBP	SH	SF	SB	CS	BA	OBA	SA	FA
2000	**ChC-N**	**30**	**68**	**13**	**20**	**8**	**0**	**3**	**12**	**2**	**0**	**19**	**3**	**0**	**0**	**0**	**1**	**.294**	**.342**	**.544**	**.968**
2001	**ChC-N**	**49**	**106**	**11**	**23**	**3**	**0**	**6**	**24**	**8**	**1**	**32**	**3**	**0**	**1**	**0**	**1**	**.217**	**.288**	**.415**	**.991**
Career average		40	87	12	22	6	0	5	18	5	1	26	3	0	1	0	1	.247	.309	.466	.984
Cubs average		**40**	**87**	**12**	**22**	**6**	**0**	**5**	**18**	**5**	**1**	**26**	**3**	**0**	**1**	**0**	**1**	**.247**	**.309**	**.466**	**.984**
Career total		79	174	24	43	11	0	9	36	10	1	51	6	0	1	0	2	.247	.309	.466	.984
Cubs total		**79**	**174**	**24**	**43**	**11**	**0**	**9**	**36**	**10**	**1**	**51**	**6**	**0**	**1**	**0**	**2**	**.247**	**.309**	**.466**	**.984**

Henry "Heinie" Zimmerman, 3b-2b-ss-1b-of, 1907–19

Cocky, outspoken and possibly a little too smart for his own good, Heinie Zimmerman was a key member of the post-dynasty Cubs of the 1910s, as well as a part of the scandal-ridden 1919 season while with his hometown New York Giants.

Born on February 9, 1887, in New York, New York, Zimmerman was signed by the Cubs as a 20-year-old. He spent the 1907 to 1910 seasons as a utilityman for the perennial National League contenders.

There were no complaints about Zimmerman on the diamond. He hit .292 in 1908 and .284 in 1910, but he was a wiseacre. He referred to himself in the third person, calling himself "the Great Zim," a habit that did not endear himself to his teammates.

Zimmerman got into a name-calling match with outfielder Jimmy Sheckard during the 1908 season, and he ended up tossing a bottle of ammonia at Sheckard and almost blinding the man. Both Sheckard and Zimmerman went to the hospital, though, because several of Sheckard's friends beat the heck out of Zimmerman.

A few years later, Zimmerman was outspoken in criticizing manager Frank Chance and his strategy. After reading the comments in the newspaper, Chance challenged Zimmerman in the clubhouse, a challenge Zimmerman accepted. It was a bad idea, as Chance, a former amateur boxer, beat the heck out of Zimmerman again.

In Zimmerman's first year as a regular in the outfield, 1911, he played very well, leading the team with a .307 batting average. He was even better in 1912, hitting .372, with 207 hits, 99 RBIs, 41 doubles, 14 home runs and a .571 slugging percentage, all nearly tops in the league. But his work at third base was shaky. He led the league in errors four years in a row, from 1911 to 1914.

New Cubs manager Roger Bresnahan moved Zimmerman to second base in 1915, and his errors declined.

Zimmerman was traded to the Giants late in the 1916 season, and he hit .272 in his hometown. He seemed a little more comfortable in New York, and in 1917 was a key member of the Giants National League champions, with a league-leading 102 RBIs and a .297 batting average.

He could not escape controversy, however. Following the 1919 season, Zimmerman and Giants first baseman Harold "Prince Hal" Chase were suspended indefinitely by New York manager John McGraw. The official reason was not divulged until a long time later: Chase and Zimmerman were alleged to have tried to fix baseball games. Both were banned from organized baseball for life. Zimmerman died in New York City, in 1969.

Zimmerman's .372 batting average in 1912 remains a Cubs record for third basemen, as do his 207 hits, 41 doubles and 14 triples that year.

Zwilling, Edward Harrison (Dutch)

HEIGHT: 5'6" THROWS: LEFT BATS: LEFT BORN: 11/2/1888 ST. LOUIS, MISSOURI DIED: 3/27/1978 LA CRESCENTA, CALIFORNIA POSITIONS PLAYED: 1B, OF

YEAR	TEAM	GAMES	AB	RUNS	HITS	2B	3B	HR	RBI	BB	IBB	SO	HBP	SH	SF	SB	CS	BA	OBA	SA	FA
1910	CWS-A	27	87	7	16	5	0	0	5	11	—	—	1	1	—	1	—	.184	.283	.241	.940
1914	Chi-F	154	592	91	185	38	8	16	95	46	—	68	1	10	—	21	—	.313	.363	.485	.962
1915	Chi-F	150	548	65	157	32	7	13	94	67	—	65	2	18	—	24	—	.286	.366	.442	.979
1916	**ChC-N**	**35**	**53**	**4**	**6**	**1**	**0**	**1**	**8**	**4**	**—**	**6**	**0**	**2**	**—**	**0**	**—**	**.113**	**.175**	**.189**	**1.000**
Career average		92	320	42	91	19	4	8	51	32	—	35	1	8	—	12	—	.284	.351	.438	.969
Cubs average		**35**	**53**	**4**	**6**	**1**	**0**	**1**	**8**	**4**	**—**	**6**	**0**	**2**	**—**	**0**	**—**	**.113**	**.175**	**.189**	**1.000**
Career total		366	1280	167	364	76	15	30	202	128	—	139	4	31	—	46	—	.284	.351	.438	.969
Cubs total		**35**	**53**	**4**	**6**	**1**	**0**	**1**	**8**	**4**	**—**	**6**	**0**	**2**	**—**	**0**	**—**	**.113**	**.175**	**.189**	**1.000**

Brown, Mordecai Peter Centennial (Three Finger *or* Miner)

HEIGHT: 5'10"   RIGHTHANDER   BORN: 10/19/1876 NYESVILLE, INDIANA   DIED: 2/14/1948 TERRE HAUTE, INDIANA

YEAR	TEAM	STARTS	GAMES	WON	LOST	PCT	ER	ERA	INNINGS PITCHED	STRIKE-OUTS	WALKS	HITS ALLOWED	HRS ALLOWED	COMP. GAMES	SHUT-OUTS	SAVES
1903	StL-N	24	26	9	13	.409	58	2.60	201	83	59	231	7	19	1	0
1904	ChC-N	23	26	15	10	.600	44	1.86	212 ⅓	81	50	155	1	21	4	1
1905	ChC-N	24	30	18	12	.600	60	2.17	249	89	44	219	3	24	4	0
1906	ChC-N	32	36	26	6	.813	32	1.04	277 ⅓	144	61	198	1	27	9	3
1907	ChC-N	27	34	20	6	.769	36	1.39	233	107	40	180	2	20	6	3
1908	ChC-N	31	44	29	9	.763	51	1.47	312 ⅓	123	49	214	1	27	9	5
1909	ChC-N	34	50	27	9	.750	50	1.31	342 ⅔	172	53	246	1	32	8	7
1910	ChC-N	31	46	25	13	.658	61	1.86	295 ⅓	143	64	256	3	27	6	7
1911	ChC-N	27	53	21	11	.656	84	2.80	270	129	55	267	5	21	0	13
1912	ChC-N	8	15	5	6	.455	26	2.64	88 ⅔	34	20	92	2	5	2	0
1913	Cin-N	16	39	11	12	.478	56	2.91	173 ⅓	41	44	174	7	11	1	6
1914	STL-F	18	26	12	6	.667	64	3.29	175	81	43	172	7	13	2	0
1914	Bro-F	8	9	2	5	.286	27	4.21	57 ⅔	32	18	63	1	5	0	0
1915	Chi-F	25	35	17	8	.680	55	2.09	236 ⅓	95	64	189	2	17	3	4
1916	ChC-N	4	12	2	3	.400	21	3.91	48 ⅓	21	9	52	0	2	0	0
Career average		24	34	17	9	.649	52	2.06	226 ⅔	98	48	193	3	19	4	4
Cubs average		24	35	19	9	.689	47	1.80	233	104	45	188	2	21	5	4
Career total		332	481	239	129	.649	725	2.06	3172 ⅓	1375	673	2708	43	271	55	49
Cubs total		241	346	188	85	.689	465	1.80	2329	1043	445	1879	19	206	48	39

Sample pitcher entry

STATISTICAL ABBREVIATIONS (PITCHERS)

YEAR — Year

TEAM — Team

STARTS — Games started by a pitcher

GAMES — Pitching appearances

WON — Games won by a pitcher

LOST — Games lost by a pitcher

PCT — Pitcher's winning percentage (Wins / (Wins + Losses))

ER — Earned Runs

ERA — Earned Run Average ((Earned Runs/Innings Pitched) x 9)

INNINGS PITCHED — Innings Pitched

STRIKEOUTS — Strikeouts

WALKS — Total Bases-on-Balls

HITS ALLOWED — Hits Allowed

HRS ALLOWED — Homeruns Allowed

COMP. GAMES — Complete Games

SHUTOUTS — Shutouts

SAVES — Saves

TEAM ABBREVIATIONS

Atl — Atlanta
Ari — Arizona
Bal — Baltimore
Bos — Boston
Bro — Brooklyn
Buf — Buffalo
Cal — California
Chi — Chicago
Cin — Cincinnati
Cle — Cleveland
Col — Colorado
Clm — Columbus
Det — Detroit
Fla — Florida

Hou — Houston
Ind — Indianapolis
KC — Kansas City
LA — Los Angeles
Lou — Louisville
Mil — Milwaukee
Min — Minnesota
Mon — Montreal
NY — New York
Oak — Oakland
Phi — Philadelphia
Pit — Pittsburgh
Roc — Rochester
SD — San Diego
Sea — Seattle

SF — San Francisco
StL — St. Louis
Tex — Texas
Tor — Toronto
Was — Washington

LEAGUE ABBREVIATIONS

N — National League
A — American League
F — Federal League (1914-15)
AA — American Association (1882–91)

Abbey, Bert Wood
HEIGHT: 5'11"   RIGHTHANDER   BORN: 11/11/1869 ESSEX, VERMONT   DIED: 6/11/1962 ESSEX JUNCTION, VERMONT

YEAR	TEAM	STARTS	GAMES	WON	LOST	PCT	ER	ERA	INNINGS PITCHED	STRIKE-OUTS	WALKS	HITS ALLOWED	HRS ALLOWED	COMP. GAMES	SHUT-OUTS	SAVES
1892	Was-N	22	27	5	18	.217	75	3.45	195⅔	77	76	207	7	19	0	1
1893	**ChN-N**	**7**	**7**	**2**	**5**	**.286**	**34**	**5.46**	**56**	**6**	**20**	**74**	**1**	**5**	**0**	**0**
1894	**ChN-N**	**11**	**11**	**2**	**8**	**.200**	**53**	**5.18**	**92**	**24**	**37**	**119**	**3**	**10**	**0**	**0**
1895	**ChN-N**	**1**	**1**	**0**	**1**	**.000**	**4**	**4.50**	**8**	**3**	**2**	**10**	**0**	**1**	**0**	**0**
1895	Bro-N	6	8	4	2	.667	25	4.33	52	14	9	66	0	5	0	0
1896	Bro-N	18	25	7	8	.467	94	5.15	164⅓	37	48	210	7	12	0	1
Career average		13	16	4	8	.323	57	4.52	113⅔	32	38	137	4	10	0	0
Cubs average		**6**	**6**	**1**	**5**	**.222**	**30**	**5.25**	**52**	**11**	**20**	**68**	**1**	**5**	**0**	**0**
Career total		65	79	20	42	.323	285	4.52	568	161	192	686	18	52	0	2
Cubs total		**19**	**19**	**4**	**14**	**.222**	**91**	**5.25**	**156**	**33**	**59**	**203**	**4**	**16**	**0**	**0**

Abernathy, Theodore Wade (Ted *or* Angleworm)
HEIGHT: 6'4"   RIGHTHANDER   BORN: 3/6/1933 STANLEY, NORTH CAROLINA

YEAR	TEAM	STARTS	GAMES	WON	LOST	PCT	ER	ERA	INNINGS PITCHED	STRIKE-OUTS	WALKS	HITS ALLOWED	HRS ALLOWED	COMP. GAMES	SHUT-OUTS	SAVES
1955	Was-A	14	40	5	9	.357	79	5.96	119⅓	79	67	136	9	3	2	0
1956	Was-A	4	5	1	3	.250	14	4.15	30⅓	18	10	35	2	2	0	0
1957	Was-A	16	26	2	10	.167	64	6.78	85	50	65	100	9	2	0	0
1960	Was-A	0	2	0	0	—	4	12.00	3	1	4	4	0	0	0	0
1963	Cle-A	0	43	7	2	.778	19	2.88	59⅓	47	29	54	3	0	0	12
1964	Cle-A	0	53	2	6	.250	35	4.33	72⅔	57	46	66	5	0	0	11
1965	**ChC-N**	**0**	**84**	**4**	**6**	**.400**	**39**	**2.57**	**136⅓**	**104**	**56**	**113**	**7**	**0**	**0**	**31**
1966	**ChC-N**	**0**	**20**	**1**	**3**	**.250**	**19**	**6.18**	**27⅔**	**18**	**17**	**26**	**4**	**0**	**0**	**4**
1966	Atl-N	0	38	4	4	.500	28	3.86	65⅓	42	36	58	5	0	0	4
1967	Cin-N	0	70	6	3	.667	15	1.27	106⅓	88	41	63	1	0	0	28
1968	Cin-N	0	78	10	7	.588	37	2.47	134⅔	64	55	111	9	0	0	13
1969	**ChC-N**	**0**	**56**	**4**	**3**	**.571**	**30**	**3.16**	**85⅓**	**55**	**42**	**75**	**8**	**0**	**0**	**3**
1970	**ChC-N**	**0**	**11**	**0**	**0**	**—**	**2**	**2.00**	**9**	**2**	**5**	**9**	**0**	**0**	**0**	**1**
1970	StL-N	0	11	1	0	1.000	6	2.95	18⅓	8	12	15	0	0	0	1
1970	KC-A	0	36	9	3	.750	16	2.59	55⅔	49	38	41	3	0	0	12
1971	KC-A	0	63	4	6	.400	23	2.56	81	55	50	60	3	0	0	23
1972	KC-A	0	45	3	4	.429	11	1.70	58⅓	28	19	44	2	0	0	5
Career average		2	49	5	5	.477	32	3.46	82	55	42	72	5	1	0	11
Cubs average		**0**	**43**	**2**	**3**	**.429**	**23**	**3.14**	**64⅔**	**45**	**30**	**56**	**5**	**0**	**0**	**10**
Career total		34	681	63	69	.477	441	3.46	1147⅔	765	592	1010	70	7	2	148
Cubs total		**0**	**171**	**9**	**12**	**.429**	**90**	**3.14**	**258⅓**	**179**	**120**	**223**	**19**	**0**	**0**	**39**

Abrego, Johnny Ray
HEIGHT: 6'0"   RIGHTHANDER   BORN: 7/4/1962 CORPUS CHRISTI, TEXAS

YEAR	TEAM	STARTS	GAMES	WON	LOST	PCT	ER	ERA	INNINGS PITCHED	STRIKE-OUTS	WALKS	HITS ALLOWED	HRS ALLOWED	COMP. GAMES	SHUT-OUTS	SAVES
1985	ChC-N	5	6	1	1	.500	17	6.38	24	13	12	32	3	0	0	0
Career average		5	6	1	1	.500	17	6.38	24	13	12	32	3	0	0	0
Cubs average		5	6	1	1	.500	17	6.38	24	13	12	32	3	0	0	0
Career total		5	6	1	1	.500	17	6.38	24	13	12	32	3	0	0	0
Cubs total		5	6	1	1	.500	17	6.38	24	13	12	32	3	0	0	0

Adams, Charles Dwight (Red)
HEIGHT: 6'0"   RIGHTHANDER   BORN: 10/7/1921 PARLIER, CALIFORNIA

YEAR	TEAM	STARTS	GAMES	WON	LOST	PCT	ER	ERA	INNINGS PITCHED	STRIKE-OUTS	WALKS	HITS ALLOWED	HRS ALLOWED	COMP. GAMES	SHUT-OUTS	SAVES
1946	ChC-N	0	8	0	1	.000	11	8.25	12	8	7	18	1	0	0	0
Career average		0	8	0	1	.000	11	8.25	12	8	7	18	1	0	0	0
Cubs average		0	8	0	1	.000	11	8.25	12	8	7	18	1	0	0	0
Career total		0	8	0	1	.000	11	8.25	12	8	7	18	1	0	0	0
Cubs total		0	8	0	1	.000	11	8.25	12	8	7	18	1	0	0	0

Adams, Karl Tutwiler (Rebel)
HEIGHT: 6'2"   RIGHTHANDER   BORN: 8/11/1891 COLUMBUS, GEORGIA   DIED: 9/17/1967 EVERETT, WASHINGTON

YEAR	TEAM	STARTS	GAMES	WON	LOST	PCT	ER	ERA	INNINGS PITCHED	STRIKE-OUTS	WALKS	HITS ALLOWED	HRS ALLOWED	COMP. GAMES	SHUT-OUTS	SAVES
1914	Cin-N	0	4	0	0	—	8	9.00	8	5	5	14	1	0	0	0
1915	ChC-N	12	26	1	9	.100	56	4.71	107	57	43	105	5	3	0	0
Career average		6	15	1	5	.100	32	5.01	57 2/3	31	24	60	3	2	0	0
Cubs average		12	26	1	9	.100	56	4.71	107	57	43	105	5	3	0	0
Career total		12	30	1	9	.100	64	5.01	115	62	48	119	6	3	0	0
Cubs total		12	26	1	9	.100	56	4.71	107	57	43	105	5	3	0	0

Adams, Terry Wayne
HEIGHT: 6'3"   RIGHTHANDER   BORN: 3/6/1973 MOBILE, ALABAMA

YEAR	TEAM	STARTS	GAMES	WON	LOST	PCT	ER	ERA	INNINGS PITCHED	STRIKE-OUTS	WALKS	HITS ALLOWED	HRS ALLOWED	COMP. GAMES	SHUT-OUTS	SAVES
1995	ChC-N	0	18	1	1	.500	13	6.50	18	15	10	22	0	0	0	1
1996	ChC-N	0	69	3	6	.333	33	2.94	101	78	49	84	6	0	0	4
1997	ChC-N	0	74	2	9	.182	38	4.62	74	64	40	91	3	0	0	18
1998	ChC-N	0	63	7	7	.500	35	4.33	72 2/3	73	41	72	7	0	0	1
1999	ChC-N	0	52	6	3	.667	29	4.02	65	57	28	60	9	0	0	13
2000	LA-N	0	66	6	9	.400	33	3.52	84 1/3	56	39	80	6	0	0	2
2001	LA-N	22	43	12	8	.600	80	4.33	166 1/3	141	54	172	9	0	0	0
Career average		3	55	5	6	.463	37	4.04	83	69	37	83	6	0	0	6
Cubs average		0	55	4	5	.422	30	4.03	66	57	34	66	5	0	0	7
Career total		22	385	37	43	.463	261	4.04	581 1/3	484	261	581	40	0	0	39
Cubs total		0	276	19	26	.422	148	4.03	330 2/3	287	168	329	25	0	0	37

Adkins, John Dewey (Dewey)
HEIGHT: 6'2"   RIGHTHANDER   BORN: 5/11/1918 NORCATUR, KANSAS   DIED: 12/26/1998 SANTA MONICA, CALIFORNIA

YEAR	TEAM	STARTS	GAMES	WON	LOST	PCT	ER	ERA	INNINGS PITCHED	STRIKE-OUTS	WALKS	HITS ALLOWED	HRS ALLOWED	COMP. GAMES	SHUT-OUTS	SAVES
1942	Was-A	1	1	0	0	—	7	9.95	6 1/3	3	6	7	0	0	0	0
1943	Was-A	0	7	0	0	—	3	2.61	10 1/3	1	5	9	0	0	0	0
1949	ChC-N	5	30	2	4	.333	52	5.68	82 1/3	43	39	98	10	1	0	0

(continued)

(continued)

	STARTS	GAMES	WON	LOST	PCT	ER	ERA	INNINGS PITCHED	STRIKE-OUTS	WALKS	HITS ALLOWED	HRS ALLOWED	COMP. GAMES	SHUT-OUTS	SAVES
Career average	2	13	1	1	.333	21	5.64	33	16	17	38	3	0	0	0
Cubs average	**5**	**30**	**2**	**4**	**.333**	**52**	**5.68**	**82⅓**	**43**	**39**	**98**	**3**	**0**	**0**	**0**
Career total	6	38	2	4	.333	62	5.64	99	47	50	114	10	1	0	0
Cubs total	**5**	**30**	**2**	**4**	**.333**	**52**	**5.68**	**82⅓**	**43**	**39**	**98**	**10**	**1**	**0**	**0**

Aguilera, Richard Warren (Rick *or* Aggie)
HEIGHT: 6'5" RIGHTHANDER BORN: 12/31/1961 SAN GABRIEL, CALIFORNIA

YEAR	TEAM	STARTS	GAMES	WON	LOST	PCT	ER	ERA	INNINGS PITCHED	STRIKE-OUTS	WALKS	HITS ALLOWED	HRS ALLOWED	COMP. GAMES	SHUT-OUTS	SAVES
1985	NYM-N	19	21	10	7	.588	44	3.24	122⅓	74	37	118	8	2	0	0
1986	NYM-N	20	28	10	7	.588	61	3.88	141⅔	104	36	145	15	2	0	0
1987	NYM-N	17	18	11	3	.786	46	3.60	115	77	33	124	12	1	0	0
1988	NYM-N	3	11	0	4	.000	19	6.93	24⅔	16	10	29	2	0	0	0
1989	NYM-N	0	36	6	6	.500	18	2.34	69⅓	80	21	59	2	0	0	7
1989	Min-A	11	11	3	5	.375	27	3.21	75⅔	57	17	71	3	0	0	0
1990	Min-A	0	56	5	3	.625	20	2.76	65⅓	61	19	55	5	3	0	32
1991	Min-A	0	63	4	5	.444	18	2.35	69	61	30	44	3	0	0	42
1992	Min-A	0	64	2	6	.250	21	2.84	66⅔	52	17	60	7	0	0	41
1993	Min-A	0	65	4	3	.571	25	3.11	72⅓	59	14	60	9	0	0	34
1994	Min-A	0	44	1	4	.200	18	3.63	44⅔	46	10	57	7	0	0	23
1995	Min-A	0	22	1	1	.500	7	2.52	25	29	6	20	2	0	0	12
1995	Bos-A	0	30	2	2	.500	9	2.67	30⅓	23	7	26	4	0	0	20
1996	Min-A	19	19	8	6	.571	67	5.42	111⅓	83	27	124	20	2	0	0
1997	Min-A	0	61	5	4	.556	29	3.82	68⅓	68	22	65	9	0	0	26
1998	Min-A	0	68	4	9	.308	35	4.24	74⅓	57	15	75	8	0	0	38
1999	Min-A	0	17	3	1	.750	3	1.27	21⅓	13	2	10	2	0	0	6
1999	**ChC-N**	**0**	**44**	**6**	**3**	**.667**	**19**	**3.69**	**46⅓**	**32**	**10**	**44**	**6**	**0**	**0**	**8**
2000	**ChC-N**	**0**	**54**	**1**	**2**	**.333**	**26**	**4.91**	**47⅔**	**38**	**18**	**47**	**11**	**0**	**0**	**29**
Career average		6	46	5	5	.515	32	3.57	80⅔	64	22	77	9	1	0	20
Cubs average		**0**	**49**	**4**	**3**	**.583**	**23**	**4.31**	**47**	**35**	**14**	**46**	**9**	**0**	**0**	**19**
Career total		89	732	86	81	.515	512	3.57	1291⅓	1030	351	1233	138	10	0	318
Cubs total		**0**	**98**	**7**	**5**	**.583**	**45**	**4.31**	**94**	**70**	**28**	**91**	**17**	**0**	**0**	**37**

Aguirre, Henry John (Hank)
HEIGHT: 6'4" LEFTHANDER BORN: 1/31/1931 AZUSA, CALIFORNIA DIED: 9/5/1994 BLOOMFIELD, MICHIGAN

YEAR	TEAM	STARTS	GAMES	WON	LOST	PCT	ER	ERA	INNINGS PITCHED	STRIKE-OUTS	WALKS	HITS ALLOWED	HRS ALLOWED	COMP. GAMES	SHUT-OUTS	SAVES
1955	Cle-A	1	4	2	0	1.000	2	1.42	12⅔	6	12	6	0	1	1	0
1956	Cle-A	9	16	3	5	.375	27	3.72	65⅓	31	27	63	7	2	1	1
1957	Cle-A	1	10	1	1	.500	13	5.75	20⅓	9	13	26	7	0	0	0
1958	Det-A	3	44	3	4	.429	29	3.75	69⅔	38	27	67	5	0	0	5
1959	Det-A	0	3	0	0	—	1	3.38	2⅔	3	3	4	0	0	0	0
1960	Det-A	6	37	5	3	.625	30	2.85	94⅔	80	30	75	7	0	0	10
1961	Det-A	0	45	4	4	.500	20	3.25	55⅓	32	38	44	5	0	0	8
1962	Det-A	22	42	16	8	.667	53	2.21	216	156	65	162	14	11	2	3
1963	Det-A	33	38	14	15	.483	92	3.67	225⅔	134	68	222	25	14	3	0
1964	Det-A	27	32	5	10	.333	68	3.79	161⅔	88	59	134	15	3	0	1
1965	Det-A	32	32	14	10	.583	83	3.59	208⅓	141	60	185	24	10	2	0
1966	Det-A	14	30	3	9	.250	44	3.82	103⅔	50	26	104	14	2	0	0
1967	Det-A	1	31	0	1	.000	11	2.40	41⅓	33	17	34	2	0	0	0
1968	LA-N	0	25	1	2	.333	3	0.69	39⅓	25	13	32	0	0	0	3
1969	**ChC-N**	**0**	**41**	**1**	**0**	**1.000**	**13**	**2.60**	**45**	**19**	**12**	**45**	**2**	**0**	**0**	**1**
1970	**ChC-N**	**0**	**17**	**3**	**0**	**1.000**	**7**	**4.50**	**14**	**11**	**9**	**13**	**3**	**0**	**0**	**1**
Career average		9	28	5	5	.510	31	3.24	86	54	30	76	8	3	1	2
Cubs average		**0**	**29**	**2**	**0**	**1.000**	**10**	**3.05**	**29⅔**	**15**	**11**	**29**	**3**	**0**	**0**	**1**
Career total		149	447	75	72	.510	496	3.24	1375⅔	856	479	1216	123	44	9	33
Cubs total		**0**	**58**	**4**	**0**	**1.000**	**20**	**3.05**	**59**	**30**	**21**	**58**	**5**	**0**	**0**	**2**

Aker, Jackie Delane (Jack *or* Chief)
HEIGHT: 6'2"   RIGHTHANDER   BORN: 7/13/1940 TULARE, CALIFORNIA

YEAR	TEAM	STARTS	GAMES	WON	LOST	PCT	ER	ERA	INNINGS PITCHED	STRIKE-OUTS	WALKS	HITS ALLOWED	HRS ALLOWED	COMP. GAMES	SHUT-OUTS	SAVES
1964	KCA-A	0	9	0	1	.000	16	8.82	16 1/3	7	10	17	6	0	0	0
1965	KCA-A	0	34	4	3	.571	18	3.16	51 1/3	26	18	45	3	0	0	3
1966	KCA-A	0	66	8	4	.667	25	1.99	113	68	28	81	7	0	0	32
1967	KCA-A	0	57	3	8	.273	42	4.30	88	65	32	87	9	0	0	12
1968	Oak-A	0	54	4	4	.500	34	4.10	74 2/3	44	33	72	6	0	0	11
1969	Sea-A	0	15	0	2	.000	14	7.56	16 2/3	13	13	25	4	0	0	3
1969	NYY-A	0	38	8	4	.667	15	2.06	65 2/3	40	22	51	4	0	0	11
1970	NYY-A	0	41	4	2	.667	16	2.06	70	36	20	57	3	0	0	16
1971	NYY-A	0	41	4	4	.500	16	2.59	55 2/3	24	26	48	3	0	0	4
1972	NYY-A	0	4	0	0	—	2	3.00	6	1	3	5	0	0	0	0
1972	**ChC-N**	**0**	**48**	**6**	**6**	**.500**	**22**	**2.96**	**67**	**36**	**23**	**65**	**4**	**0**	**0**	**17**
1973	**ChC-N**	**0**	**47**	**4**	**5**	**.444**	**29**	**4.10**	**63 2/3**	**25**	**23**	**76**	**8**	**0**	**0**	**12**
1974	Atl-N	0	17	0	1	.000	7	3.78	16 2/3	7	9	17	3	0	0	0
1974	NYM-N	0	24	2	1	.667	16	3.48	41 1/3	18	14	33	4	0	0	2
Career average	0	45	4	4	.511	25	3.28	67 2/3	37	25	62	6	0	0	11
Cubs average	**0**	**48**	**5**	**6**	**.476**	**26**	**3.51**	**65 1/3**	**31**	**23**	**71**	**6**	**0**	**0**	**15**
Career total	0	495	47	45	.511	272	3.28	746	404	274	679	64	0	0	123
Cubs total	**0**	**95**	**10**	**11**	**.476**	**51**	**3.51**	**130 2/3**	**61**	**46**	**141**	**12**	**0**	**0**	**29**

Alderson, Dale Leonard
HEIGHT: 5'10"   RIGHTHANDER   BORN: 3/9/1918 BELDEN, NEBRASKA   DIED: 2/12/1982 GARDEN GROVE, CALIFORNIA

YEAR	TEAM	STARTS	GAMES	WON	LOST	PCT	ER	ERA	INNINGS PITCHED	STRIKE-OUTS	WALKS	HITS ALLOWED	HRS ALLOWED	COMP. GAMES	SHUT-OUTS	SAVES
1943	ChC-N	2	4	0	1	.000	10	6.43	14	4	3	21	2	0	0	0
1944	ChC-N	1	12	0	0	—	16	6.65	21 2/3	7	9	31	2	0	0	0
Career average	2	8	0	1	.000	13	6.56	18	6	6	26	2	0	0	0
Cubs average	**2**	**8**	**0**	**1**	**.000**	**13**	**6.56**	**18**	**6**	**6**	**26**	**2**	**0**	**0**	**0**
Career total	3	16	0	1	.000	26	6.56	35 2/3	11	12	52	4	0	0	0
Cubs total	**3**	**16**	**0**	**1**	**.000**	**26**	**6.56**	**35 2/3**	**11**	**12**	**52**	**4**	**0**	**0**	**0**

Aldridge, Victor Eddington (Vic *or* Hoosier Schoolmaster)
HEIGHT: 5'9"   RIGHTHANDER   BORN: 10/25/1893 INDIAN SPRINGS, INDIANA   DIED: 4/17/1973 TERRE HAUTE, INDIANA

YEAR	TEAM	STARTS	GAMES	WON	LOST	PCT	ER	ERA	INNINGS PITCHED	STRIKE-OUTS	WALKS	HITS ALLOWED	HRS ALLOWED	COMP. GAMES	SHUT-OUTS	SAVES
1917	**ChC-N**	**6**	**30**	**6**	**6**	**.500**	**37**	**3.12**	**106 2/3**	**44**	**37**	**100**	**1**	**1**	**1**	**2**
1918	**ChC-N**	**0**	**3**	**0**	**1**	**.000**	**2**	**1.46**	**12 1/3**	**10**	**6**	**11**	**0**	**0**	**0**	**0**
1922	**ChC-N**	**34**	**36**	**16**	**15**	**.516**	**101**	**3.52**	**258 1/3**	**66**	**56**	**287**	**14**	**20**	**2**	**0**
1923	**ChC-N**	**30**	**30**	**16**	**9**	**.640**	**84**	**3.48**	**217**	**64**	**67**	**209**	**17**	**15**	**2**	**0**
1924	**ChC-N**	**32**	**32**	**15**	**12**	**.556**	**95**	**3.50**	**244 1/3**	**74**	**80**	**261**	**10**	**20**	**0**	**0**
1925	Pit-N	26	30	15	7	.682	86	3.63	213 1/3	88	74	218	15	14	1	0
1926	Pit-N	26	30	10	13	.435	86	4.07	190	61	73	204	7	12	1	1
1927	Pit-N	34	35	15	10	.600	113	4.25	239 1/3	86	74	248	16	17	1	1
1928	NYG-N	17	22	4	7	.364	64	4.83	119 1/3	33	45	133	7	3	0	2
Career average	23	28	11	9	.548	74	3.76	178	58	57	186	10	11	1	1
Cubs average	**20**	**26**	**11**	**9**	**.552**	**64**	**3.42**	**167 2/3**	**52**	**49**	**174**	**8**	**11**	**1**	**0**
Career total	205	248	97	80	.548	668	3.76	1600 2/3	526	512	1671	87	102	8	6
Cubs total	**102**	**131**	**53**	**43**	**.552**	**319**	**3.42**	**838 2/3**	**258**	**246**	**868**	**42**	**56**	**5**	**2**

Alexander, Grover Cleveland (Pete)
HEIGHT: 6'1"   RIGHTHANDER   BORN: 2/26/1887 ELBA, NEBRASKA   DIED: 11/4/1950 ST. PAUL, NEBRASKA

YEAR	TEAM	STARTS	GAMES	WON	LOST	PCT	ER	ERA	INNINGS PITCHED	STRIKE-OUTS	WALKS	HITS ALLOWED	HRS ALLOWED	COMP. GAMES	SHUT-OUTS	SAVES
1911	Phi-N	37	48	28	13	.683	105	2.57	367	227	129	285	5	31	7	3
1912	Phi-N	34	46	19	17	.528	97	2.81	310 1/3	195	105	289	11	25	3	3
1913	Phi-N	36	47	22	8	.733	95	2.79	306 1/3	159	75	288	9	23	9	2
1914	Phi-N	39	46	27	15	.643	94	2.38	355	214	76	327	8	32	6	1
1915	Phi-N	42	49	31	10	.756	51	1.22	376 1/3	241	64	253	3	36	12	3
1916	Phi-N	45	48	33	12	.733	67	1.55	389	167	50	323	6	38	16	3
1917	Phi-N	44	45	30	13	.698	79	1.83	388	200	56	336	4	34	8	0
1918	ChC-N	3	3	2	1	.667	5	1.73	26	15	3	19	0	3	0	0
1919	ChC-N	27	30	16	11	.593	45	1.72	235	121	38	180	3	20	9	1
1920	ChC-N	40	46	27	14	.659	77	1.91	363 1/3	173	69	335	8	33	7	5
1921	ChC-N	30	31	15	13	.536	95	3.39	252	77	33	286	10	21	3	1
1922	ChC-N	31	33	16	13	.552	99	3.63	245 2/3	48	34	283	8	20	1	1
1923	ChC-N	36	39	22	12	.647	108	3.19	305	72	30	308	17	26	3	2
1924	ChC-N	20	21	12	5	.706	57	3.03	169 1/3	33	25	183	9	12	0	0
1925	ChC-N	30	32	15	11	.577	89	3.39	236	63	29	270	14	20	1	0
1926	ChC-N	7	7	3	3	.500	20	3.46	52	12	7	55	0	4	0	0

(continued)

Grover Cleveland "Pete" Alexander, rhp, 1911–30

It is, alas, a case of myth over-coming reality. Grover Cleveland "Pete" Alexander was one of the great pitchers of the 1910s and 1920s, but he is of course known almost exclusively for one strikeout in the twilight of his career.

Alexander was born on February 26, 1887, in Elba, Nebraska. He was a minor league star before he made it to the bigs in 1911, winning 29 games for the Syracuse Chiefs in 1910. That total included 15 shutouts.

He was purchased from the Chiefs by the Philadelphia Phillies for $750. It turned out to be a stunning bargain: Alexander had one of the more dominating rookie careers in major league history. He led the National League in wins (28), complete games (31), shutouts (7) and innings pitched (367). His 227 strikeouts set a rookie record not broken until the Mets' Dwight Gooden topped him in 1984, and the 28 wins are still a standard for first-year pitchers—and four of those were consecutive shutouts. The last was a 1-0 victory over Cy

Young, who was winding up his career that year in Boston.

From 1911 to 1914, Alexander and the Giants' Christy Mathewson were the dominant righthanders in the league, but by 1915 Alexander was in a class of his own. He led the Phillies to the National League pennant, winning 31 games, including 12 shutouts, and striking out 241 batters, all tops in the league. Most Valuable Player awards weren't passed out in those days, but had they been, Alexander would have won in a walk.

The Phillies were defeated in the World Series that year by the Boston Red Sox, although Alexander pitched well.

In 1917 Alexander had completed his third consecutive 30-plus win season for the Phillies when he went into the service at the onset of World War I. In the service, a shell burst near his ear, which Alexander later believed may have worsened his epilepsy, which was relatively dormant at that point.

He was traded in 1918 to the Cubs, along with his batterymate and friend, "Reindeer Bill" Killefer. Alexander wasn't quite as dominant with the Cubs as he was in Philadelphia, but he still won 128 games for Chicago in eight

(continued)

(continued)

years. He also pitched 159 complete games for the Cubs, still fourth all-time for the club. Alexander was frightened, however, by the escalating number of epileptic fits he was enduring and began to drink more. Still, he won 27 games for the Cubs in 1920, and 22 more in 1923.

Alexander was a power pitcher in his days with Philadelphia and early on in Chicago, augmenting a live fastball with a nasty curve. But after 1920, his strikeout totals dropped sharply, and Alexander began relying more on changing speeds than trying to blow pitches by opposing batters. He was still successful, but perhaps not as dramatic.

The Cubs never finished higher than fourth during Alexander's tenure, and in 1926, when Chicago hired Joe McCarthy, the writing was on the wall. McCarthy could not put up with Alexander's drinking and shipped him to the Cardinals in midseason.

But Alexander was a key pickup for the National League champion Redbirds. Alexander won nine games down the stretch for manager Rogers Hornsby, which helped the team win the pennant.

In the World Series, Alexander won Game 2 in New York with a masterful four-hitter over the Yankees. He also won Game 6, scattering eight hits in a 10-2 St. Louis rout.

Alexander, figuring that was it for him in the Series, went out and celebrated hard, probably in Billy LaHiff's Tavern in downtown Manhattan. He got back to the Cardinals' hotel the next morning and didn't show up for Game 7 until the third inning.

But in the seventh, with the bases loaded and two outs, and the Cardinals up only 3-2, Hornsby summoned Alexander from the bull pen. In subsequent years, Hornsby was adamant that Alexander was not drunk at that point, and in fact, Alexander was not. But he was sure hungover. Still, he punched out Yankees second baseman Tony Lazzeri on knee-high fastballs to end the inning. He allowed no more hits the next two innings, and the Cards were champs.

The Lazzeri strikeout, which has grown in stature over the years, is often believed to have been the final out of that game.

Alexander held on for four more years after that, retiring in 1930. He was named to the Hall of Fame in 1938.

His later years were tough. His alcoholism worsened, and for several years, he made a living reenacting in bars across New York the famous strikeout. He died in a small rented room, in St. Paul, Nebraska, in 1950.

Alexander is seventh overall on the Cubs all-time list with 24 shutouts. His 27 wins in 1920 is the third-best one-season mark, and his 363⅓ innings pitched that year is still a team record, as is his 33 complete games.

(Alexander, continued)

1926	StL-N	16	23	9	7	.563	48	2.91	148 ⅓	35	24	136	8	11	2	2
1927	StL-N	30	37	21	10	.677	75	2.52	268	48	38	261	11	22	2	3
1928	StL-N	31	34	16	9	.640	91	3.36	243 ⅔	59	37	262	15	18	1	2
1929	StL-N	19	22	9	8	.529	57	3.89	132	33	23	149	10	8	0	0
1930	Phi-N	3	9	0	3	.000	22	9.14	21 ⅔	6	6	40	5	0	0	0
Career average		30	35	19	10	.642	74	2.56	259 ⅔	110	48	243	8	22	5	2
Cubs average		**25**	**27**	**14**	**9**	**.607**	**66**	**2.84**	**209 ⅓**	**68**	**30**	**213**	**8**	**18**	**3**	**1**
Career total		600	696	373	208	.642	1476	2.56	5190	2198	951	4868	164	437	90	32
Cubs total		**224**	**242**	**128**	**83**	**.607**	**595**	**2.84**	**1884 ⅓**	**614**	**268**	**1919**	**69**	**159**	**24**	**10**

Altamirano, Porfirio (Porfi)
HEIGHT: 6'0"   RIGHTHANDER   BORN: 5/17/1952 DARILLO, NICARAGUA

YEAR	TEAM	STARTS	GAMES	WON	LOST	PCT	ER	ERA	INNINGS PITCHED	STRIKE-OUTS	WALKS	HITS ALLOWED	HRS ALLOWED	COMP. GAMES	SHUT-OUTS	SAVES
1982	Phi-N	0	29	5	1	.833	18	4.15	39	26	14	41	2	0	0	2
1983	Phi-N	0	31	2	3	.400	17	3.70	41 1/3	24	15	38	9	0	0	0
1984	**ChC-N**	**0**	**5**	**0**	**0**	**—**	**6**	**4.76**	**11 1/3**	**7**	**1**	**8**	**2**	**0**	**0**	**0**
Career average		0	22	2	1	.636	14	4.03	30 2/3	19	10	29	4	0	0	1
Cubs average		**0**	**5**	**0**	**0**	**—**	**6**	**4.76**	**11 1/3**	**7**	**1**	**8**	**2**	**0**	**0**	**0**
Career total		0	65	7	4	.636	41	4.03	91 2/3	57	30	87	13	0	0	2
Cubs total		**0**	**5**	**0**	**0**	**—**	**6**	**4.76**	**11 1/3**	**7**	**1**	**8**	**2**	**0**	**0**	**0**

Amor, Vincente
HEIGHT: 6'3"   RIGHTHANDER   BORN: 8/8/1932 HAVANA, CUBA

YEAR	TEAM	STARTS	GAMES	WON	LOST	PCT	ER	ERA	INNINGS PITCHED	STRIKE-OUTS	WALKS	HITS ALLOWED	HRS ALLOWED	COMP. GAMES	SHUT-OUTS	SAVES
1955	ChC-N	0	4	0	1	.000	3	4.50	6	3	3	11	0	0	0	0
1957	Cin-N	4	9	1	2	.333	18	5.93	27 1/3	9	10	39	2	1	0	0
Career average		2	7	1	2	.250	11	5.67	16 2/3	6	7	25	1	1	0	0
Cubs average		**0**	**4**	**0**	**1**	**.000**	**3**	**4.50**	**6**	**3**	**3**	**11**	**0**	**0**	**0**	**0**
Career total		4	13	1	3	.250	21	5.67	33 1/3	12	13	50	2	1	0	0
Cubs total		**0**	**4**	**0**	**1**	**.000**	**3**	**4.50**	**6**	**3**	**3**	**11**	**0**	**0**	**0**	**0**

Anderson, Robert Carl (Bob *or* Hammond Hummer)
HEIGHT: 6'4"   RIGHTHANDER   BORN: 9/29/1935 EAST CHICAGO, INDIANA

YEAR	TEAM	STARTS	GAMES	WON	LOST	PCT	ER	ERA	INNINGS PITCHED	STRIKE-OUTS	WALKS	HITS ALLOWED	HRS ALLOWED	COMP. GAMES	SHUT-OUTS	SAVES
1957	ChC-N	0	8	0	1	.000	14	7.71	16 1/3	7	8	20	2	0	0	0
1958	ChC-N	8	17	3	3	.500	29	3.97	65 2/3	51	29	61	3	2	0	0
1959	ChC-N	36	37	12	13	.480	108	4.13	235 1/3	113	77	245	21	7	1	0
1960	ChC-N	30	38	9	11	.450	93	4.11	203 2/3	115	68	201	26	5	0	1
1961	ChC-N	12	57	7	10	.412	72	4.26	152	96	56	162	14	1	0	8
1962	ChC-N	4	57	2	7	.222	60	5.02	107 2/3	82	60	111	9	0	0	4
1963	Det-A	3	32	3	1	.750	22	3.30	60	38	21	58	5	0	0	0
Career average		13	35	5	7	.439	57	4.26	120	72	46	123	11	2	0	2
Cubs average		**15**	**36**	**6**	**8**	**.423**	**63**	**4.33**	**130**	**77**	**50**	**133**	**13**	**3**	**0**	**2**
Career total		93	246	36	46	.439	398	4.26	840 2/3	502	319	858	80	15	1	13
Cubs total		**90**	**214**	**33**	**45**	**.423**	**376**	**4.33**	**780 2/3**	**464**	**298**	**800**	**75**	**15**	**1**	**13**

Andre, John Edward (Long John)
HEIGHT: 6'4"   RIGHTHANDER   BORN: 1/3/1923 BROCKTON, MASSACHUSETTS   DIED: 11/25/1976 BARNSTABLE, MASSACHUSETTS

YEAR	TEAM	STARTS	GAMES	WON	LOST	PCT	ER	ERA	INNINGS PITCHED	STRIKE-OUTS	WALKS	HITS ALLOWED	HRS ALLOWED	COMP. GAMES	SHUT-OUTS	SAVES
1955	ChC-N	3	22	0	1	.000	29	5.80	45	19	28	45	7	0	0	1
Career average		3	22	0	1	.000	29	5.80	45	19	28	45	7	0	0	1
Cubs average		**3**	**22**	**0**	**1**	**.000**	**29**	**5.80**	**45**	**19**	**28**	**45**	**7**	**0**	**0**	**1**
Career total		3	22	0	1	.000	29	5.80	45	19	28	45	7	0	0	1
Cubs total		**3**	**22**	**0**	**1**	**.000**	**29**	**5.80**	**45**	**19**	**28**	**45**	**7**	**0**	**0**	**1**

Andrus, Frederick Hotham (Fred)
HEIGHT: 6'2" RIGHTHANDER BORN: 8/23/1850 WASHINGTON, MICHIGAN DIED: 11/10/1937 DETROIT, MICHIGAN

YEAR	TEAM	STARTS	GAMES	WON	LOST	PCT	ER	ERA	INNINGS PITCHED	STRIKE-OUTS	WALKS	HITS ALLOWED	HRS ALLOWED	COMP. GAMES	SHUT-OUTS	SAVES
1884	ChN-N	1	1	1	0	1.000	2	2.00	9	2	2	11	1	1	0	0
Career average		1	1	1	0	1.000	2	2.00	9	2	2	11	1	1	0	0
Cubs average		**1**	**1**	**1**	**0**	**1.000**	**2**	**2.00**	**9**	**2**	**2**	**11**	**1**	**1**	**0**	**0**
Career total		1	1	1	0	1.000	2	2.00	9	2	2	11	1	1	0	0
Cubs total		**1**	**1**	**1**	**0**	**1.000**	**2**	**2.00**	**9**	**2**	**2**	**11**	**1**	**1**	**0**	**0**

Anson, Adrian Constantine (Cap *or* Pop)
HEIGHT: 6'0" RIGHTHANDER BORN: 4/11/1852 MARSHALLTOWN, IOWA DIED: 4/14/1922 CHICAGO, ILLINOIS

YEAR	TEAM	STARTS	GAMES	WON	LOST	PCT	ER	ERA	INNINGS PITCHED	STRIKE-OUTS	WALKS	HITS ALLOWED	HRS ALLOWED	COMP. GAMES	SHUT-OUTS	SAVES
1883	ChN-N	0	2	0	0	—	0	0.00	3	0	1	1	0	0	0	1
1884	ChN-N	0	1	0	1	.000	2	18.00	1	1	1	3	2	0	0	0
Career average		0	2	0	1	.000	1	4.50	2	1	1	2	1	0	0	1
Cubs average		**0**	**2**	**0**	**1**	**.000**	**1**	**4.50**	**2**	**1**	**1**	**2**	**1**	**0**	**0**	**1**
Career total		0	3	0	1	.000	2	4.50	4	1	2	4	2	0	0	1
Cubs total		**0**	**3**	**0**	**1**	**.000**	**2**	**4.50**	**4**	**1**	**2**	**4**	**2**	**0**	**0**	**1**

Arnold, James Lee (Jamie)
HEIGHT: 6'2" RIGHTHANDER BORN: 3/24/1974 DEARBORN, MICHIGAN

YEAR	TEAM	STARTS	GAMES	WON	LOST	PCT	ER	ERA	INNINGS PITCHED	STRIKE-OUTS	WALKS	HITS ALLOWED	HRS ALLOWED	COMP. GAMES	SHUT-OUTS	SAVES
1999	LA-N	3	36	2	4	.333	42	5.48	69	26	34	81	6	0	0	1
2000	LA-N	0	2	0	0	—	3	4.05	6 2/3	3	5	4	0	0	0	0
2000	**ChC-N**	**4**	**12**	**0**	**3**	**.000**	**24**	**6.61**	**32 2/3**	**13**	**19**	**34**	**1**	**0**	**0**	**1**
Career average		4	25	1	4	.222	35	5.73	54 1/3	21	29	60	4	0	0	1
Cubs average		**4**	**12**	**0**	**3**	**.000**	**24**	**6.61**	**32 2/3**	**13**	**19**	**34**	**1**	**0**	**0**	**1**
Career total		7	50	2	7	.222	69	5.73	108 1/3	42	58	119	7	0	0	2
Cubs total		**4**	**12**	**0**	**3**	**.000**	**24**	**6.61**	**32 2/3**	**13**	**19**	**34**	**1**	**0**	**0**	**1**

Assenmacher, Paul Andre
HEIGHT: 6'3" LEFTHANDER BORN: 12/10/1960 ALLEN PARK, MICHIGAN

YEAR	TEAM	STARTS	GAMES	WON	LOST	PCT	ER	ERA	INNINGS PITCHED	STRIKE-OUTS	WALKS	HITS ALLOWED	HRS ALLOWED	COMP. GAMES	SHUT-OUTS	SAVES
1986	Atl-N	0	61	7	3	.700	19	2.50	68 1/3	56	26	61	5	0	0	7
1987	Atl-N	0	52	1	1	.500	31	5.10	54 2/3	39	24	58	8	0	0	2
1988	Atl-N	0	64	8	7	.533	27	3.06	79 1/3	71	32	72	4	0	0	5
1989	Atl-N	0	49	1	3	.250	23	3.59	57 2/3	64	16	55	2	0	0	0
1989	**ChC-N**	**0**	**14**	**2**	**1**	**.667**	**11**	**5.21**	**19**	**15**	**12**	**19**	**1**	**0**	**0**	**0**
1990	**ChC-N**	**1**	**74**	**7**	**2**	**.778**	**32**	**2.80**	**103**	**95**	**36**	**90**	**10**	**0**	**0**	**10**
1991	**ChC-N**	**0**	**75**	**7**	**8**	**.467**	**37**	**3.24**	**102 2/3**	**117**	**31**	**85**	**10**	**0**	**0**	**15**
1992	**ChC-N**	**0**	**70**	**4**	**4**	**.500**	**31**	**4.10**	**68**	**67**	**26**	**72**	**6**	**0**	**0**	**8**
1993	**ChC-N**	**0**	**46**	**2**	**1**	**.667**	**15**	**3.49**	**38 2/3**	**34**	**13**	**44**	**5**	**0**	**0**	**0**
1993	NYY-A	0	26	2	2	.500	6	3.12	17 1/3	11	9	10	0	0	0	0
1994	CWS-A	0	44	1	2	.333	13	3.55	33	29	13	26	2	0	0	1
1995	Cle-A	0	47	6	2	.750	12	2.82	38 1/3	40	12	32	3	0	0	0
1996	Cle-A	0	63	4	2	.667	16	3.09	46 2/3	44	14	46	1	0	0	1
1997	Cle-A	0	75	5	0	1.000	16	2.94	49	53	15	43	5	0	0	4
1998	Cle-A	0	69	2	5	.286	17	3.26	47	43	19	54	5	0	0	3
1999	Cle-A	0	55	2	1	.667	30	8.18	33	29	17	50	6	0	0	0
Career average		0	63	4	3	.581	24	3.53	61	58	23	58	5	0	0	4
Cubs average		**0**	**56**	**4**	**3**	**.579**	**25**	**3.42**	**66 1/3**	**66**	**24**	**62**	**6**	**0**	**0**	**7**
Career total		1	884	61	44	.581	336	3.53	855 2/3	807	315	817	73	0	0	56
Cubs total		**1**	**279**	**22**	**16**	**.579**	**126**	**3.42**	**331 1/3**	**328**	**118**	**310**	**32**	**0**	**0**	**33**

Ayala, Robert Joseph (Bobby)
HEIGHT: 6'3" RIGHTHANDER BORN: 7/8/1969 VENTURA, CALIFORNIA

YEAR	TEAM	STARTS	GAMES	WON	LOST	PCT	ER	ERA	INNINGS PITCHED	STRIKE-OUTS	WALKS	HITS ALLOWED	HRS ALLOWED	COMP. GAMES	SHUT-OUTS	SAVES
1992	Cin-N	5	5	2	1	.667	14	4.34	29	23	13	33	1	0	0	0
1993	Cin-N	9	43	7	10	.412	61	5.60	98	65	45	106	16	0	0	0
1994	Sea-A	0	46	4	3	.571	18	2.86	56 2/3	76	26	42	2	0	0	3
1995	Sea-A	0	63	6	5	.545	35	4.44	71	77	30	73	9	0	0	18
1996	Sea-A	0	50	6	3	.667	44	5.88	67 1/3	61	25	65	10	0	0	19
1997	Sea-A	0	71	10	5	.667	41	3.82	96 2/3	92	41	91	14	0	0	3
1998	Sea-A	0	62	1	10	.091	61	7.29	75 1/3	68	26	100	9	0	0	8
1999	Mon-N	0	53	1	6	.143	27	3.68	66	64	34	60	6	0	0	8
1999	**ChC-N**	**0**	**13**	**0**	**1**	**.000**	**5**	**2.81**	**16**	**15**	**5**	**11**	**4**	**0**	**0**	**0**
Career average		2	51	5	6	.457	38	4.78	72	68	31	73	9	0	0	7
Cubs average		**0**	**13**	**0**	**1**	**.000**	**5**	**2.81**	**16**	**15**	**5**	**11**	**4**	**0**	**0**	**0**
Career total		14	406	37	44	.457	306	4.78	576	541	245	581	71	0	0	59
Cubs total		**0**	**13**	**0**	**1**	**.000**	**5**	**2.81**	**16**	**15**	**5**	**11**	**4**	**0**	**0**	**0**

Aybar, Manuel Antonio (Manny)
HEIGHT: 6'1" RIGHTHANDER BORN: 10/5/1974 BANI, DOMINICAN REPUBLIC

YEAR	TEAM	STARTS	GAMES	WON	LOST	PCT	ER	ERA	INNINGS PITCHED	STRIKE-OUTS	WALKS	HITS ALLOWED	HRS ALLOWED	COMP. GAMES	SHUT-OUTS	SAVES
1997	StL-N	12	12	2	4	.333	32	4.24	68	41	29	66	8	0	0	0
1998	StL-N	14	20	6	6	.500	54	5.98	81 1/3	57	42	90	6	0	0	0
1999	StL-N	1	65	4	5	.444	59	5.47	97	74	36	104	13	0	0	3
2000	Col-N	0	1	0	1	.000	3	16.20	1 2/3	0	0	5	1	0	0	0
2000	Cin-N	0	32	1	1	.500	27	4.83	50 1/3	31	22	51	7	0	0	0
2000	Fla-N	0	21	1	0	1.000	8	2.63	27 1/3	14	13	18	3	0	0	0
2001	**ChC-N**	**1**	**17**	**2**	**1**	**.667**	**16**	**6.35**	**22 2/3**	**16**	**17**	**28**	**5**	**0**	**0**	**0**
Career average		6	34	3	4	.471	40	5.14	69 2/3	47	32	72	9	0	0	1
Cubs average		**1**	**17**	**2**	**1**	**.667**	**16**	**6.35**	**22 2/3**	**16**	**17**	**28**	**5**	**0**	**0**	**0**
Career total		28	168	16	18	.471	199	5.14	348 1/3	233	159	362	43	0	0	3
Cubs total		**1**	**17**	**2**	**1**	**.667**	**16**	**6.35**	**22 2/3**	**16**	**17**	**28**	**5**	**0**	**0**	**0**

Baczewski, Frederic John (Fred or Lefty)
HEIGHT: 6'2" LEFTHANDER BORN: 5/15/1926 ST. PAUL, MINNESOTA DIED: 11/14/1976 CULVER CITY, CALIFORNIA

YEAR	TEAM	STARTS	GAMES	WON	LOST	PCT	ER	ERA	INNINGS PITCHED	STRIKE-OUTS	WALKS	HITS ALLOWED	HRS ALLOWED	COMP. GAMES	SHUT-OUTS	SAVES
1953	**ChC-N**	**0**	**9**	**0**	**0**	**—**	**7**	**6.30**	**10**	**3**	**6**	**20**	**1**	**0**	**0**	**0**
1953	Cin-N	18	24	11	4	.733	53	3.45	138 1/3	58	52	125	13	10	1	1
1954	Cin-N	22	29	6	6	.500	76	5.26	130	43	53	159	22	4	1	0
1955	Cin-N	0	1	0	0	—	2	18.00	1	0	0	2	2	0	0	0
Career average		13	21	6	3	.630	46	4.45	93	35	37	102	13	5	1	0
Cubs average		**0**	**9**	**0**	**0**	**—**	**7**	**6.30**	**10**	**3**	**6**	**20**	**1**	**0**	**0**	**0**
Career total		40	63	17	10	.630	138	4.45	279 1/3	104	111	306	38	14	2	1
Cubs total		**0**	**9**	**0**	**0**	**—**	**7**	**6.30**	**10**	**3**	**6**	**20**	**1**	**0**	**0**	**0**

Baecht, Edward Joseph (Ed)
HEIGHT: 6'3" RIGHTHANDER BORN: 5/15/1907 PADEN, OKLAHOMA DIED: 8/15/1957 GRAFTON, ILLINOIS

YEAR	TEAM	STARTS	GAMES	WON	LOST	PCT	ER	ERA	INNINGS PITCHED	STRIKE-OUTS	WALKS	HITS ALLOWED	HRS ALLOWED	COMP. GAMES	SHUT-OUTS	SAVES
1926	Phi-N	1	28	2	0	1.000	38	6.11	56	14	28	73	4	1	0	0
1927	Phi-N	1	1	0	1	.000	8	12.00	6	0	2	12	0	0	0	0
1928	Phi-N	1	9	1	1	.500	16	6.00	24	10	9	37	1	0	0	0
1931	**ChC-N**	**6**	**22**	**2**	**4**	**.333**	**28**	**3.76**	**67**	**34**	**32**	**64**	**1**	**2**	**0**	**0**
1932	**ChC-N**	**0**	**1**	**0**	**0**	**—**	**0**	**0.00**	**1**	**0**	**1**	**1**	**0**	**0**	**0**	**0**
1937	StL-A	0	3	0	0	—	9	12.79	6 1/3	3	6	13	3	0	0	0
Career average		2	11	1	1	.455	17	5.56	26 2/3	10	13	33	2	1	0	0
Cubs average		**3**	**12**	**1**	**2**	**.333**	**14**	**3.71**	**34**	**17**	**17**	**33**	**1**	**1**	**0**	**0**
Career total		9	64	5	6	.455	99	5.56	160 1/3	61	78	200	9	3	0	0
Cubs total		**6**	**23**	**2**	**4**	**.333**	**28**	**3.71**	**68**	**34**	**33**	**65**	**1**	**2**	**0**	**0**

Bailey, Abraham Lincoln (Sweetbreads)
HEIGHT: 6'0"   RIGHTHANDER   BORN: 2/12/1895 JOLIET, ILLINOIS   DIED: 9/27/1939 JOLIET, ILLINOIS

YEAR	TEAM	STARTS	GAMES	WON	LOST	PCT	ER	ERA	INNINGS PITCHED	STRIKE-OUTS	WALKS	HITS ALLOWED	HRS ALLOWED	COMP. GAMES	SHUT-OUTS	SAVES
1919	ChC-N	5	21	3	5	.375	25	3.15	71⅓	19	20	75	2	0	0	0
1920	ChC-N	1	21	1	2	.333	29	7.12	36⅔	8	11	55	1	0	0	0
1921	ChC-N	0	3	0	0	—	2	3.60	5	2	2	6	0	0	0	0
1921	Bro-N	0	7	0	0		14	5.18	24⅓	6	7	35	1	0	0	0
Career average		2	17	1	2	.364	23	4.59	45⅔	12	13	57	1	0	0	0
Cubs average		**2**	**15**	**1**	**2**	**.364**	**19**	**4.46**	**37⅔**	**10**	**11**	**45**	**1**	**0**	**0**	**0**
Career total		6	52	4	7	.364	70	4.59	137⅓	35	40	171	4	0	0	0
Cubs total		**6**	**45**	**4**	**7**	**.364**	**56**	**4.46**	**113**	**29**	**33**	**136**	**3**	**0**	**0**	**0**

Baker, Thomas Henry (Tom)
HEIGHT: 6'0"   LEFTHANDER   BORN: 5/6/1934 PORT TOWNSEND, WASHINGTON   DIED: 3/9/1980 PORT TOWNSEND, WASHINGTON

YEAR	TEAM	STARTS	GAMES	WON	LOST	PCT	ER	ERA	INNINGS PITCHED	STRIKE-OUTS	WALKS	HITS ALLOWED	HRS ALLOWED	COMP. GAMES	SHUT-OUTS	SAVES
1963	ChC-N	1	10	0	1	.000	6	3.00	18	14	7	20	2	0	0	0
Career average		1	10	0	1	.000	6	3.00	18	14	7	20	2	0	0	0
Cubs average		**1**	**10**	**0**	**1**	**.000**	**6**	**3.00**	**18**	**14**	**7**	**20**	**2**	**0**	**0**	**0**
Career total		1	10	0	1	.000	6	3.00	18	14	7	20	2	0	0	0
Cubs total		**1**	**10**	**0**	**1**	**.000**	**6**	**3.00**	**18**	**14**	**7**	**20**	**2**	**0**	**0**	**0**

Baldwin, Marcus Elmore (Mark or Fido)
HEIGHT: 6'0"   RIGHTHANDER   BORN: 10/29/1863 PITTSBURGH, PENNSYLVANIA   DIED: 11/10/1929 PITTSBURGH, PENNSYLVANIA

YEAR	TEAM	STARTS	GAMES	WON	LOST	PCT	ER	ERA	INNINGS PITCHED	STRIKE-OUTS	WALKS	HITS ALLOWED	HRS ALLOWED	COMP. GAMES	SHUT-OUTS	SAVES
1887	**ChN-N**	**39**	**40**	**18**	**17**	**.514**	**126**	**3.40**	**334**	**164**	**122**	**451**	**23**	**35**	**1**	**1**
1888	**ChN-N**	**30**	**30**	**13**	**15**	**.464**	**77**	**2.76**	**251**	**157**	**99**	**241**	**13**	**27**	**2**	**0**
1889	CoC-AA	59	63	27	34	.443	206	3.61	513⅔	368	274	458	9	54	6	1
1890	Chi-P	57	59	34	24	.586	184	3.31	501	211	249	498	10	54	1	0
1891	Pit-N	51	53	21	29	.420	134	2.76	437⅔	197	227	385	10	48	2	1
1892	Pit-N	53	56	25	25	.500	170	3.47	440⅓	157	194	447	11	45	0	1
1893	Pit-N	1	1	0	0	—	3	11.57	2⅓	0	1	6	0	0	0	0
1893	NYG-N	39	45	16	20	.444	151	4.10	331⅓	100	141	335	6	33	2	3
Career average		47	50	22	23	.484	150	3.36	401⅔	193	187	403	12	42	2	1
Cubs average		**35**	**35**	**16**	**16**	**.492**	**102**	**3.12**	**292⅔**	**161**	**111**	**346**	**18**	**31**	**2**	**1**
Career total		329	347	154	164	.484	1051	3.36	2811⅓	1354	1307	2821	82	296	14	7
Cubs total		**69**	**70**	**31**	**32**	**.492**	**203**	**3.12**	**585**	**321**	**221**	**692**	**36**	**62**	**3**	**1**

Baller, Jay Scott
HEIGHT: 6'6"   RIGHTHANDER   BORN: 10/6/1960 STAYTON, OREGON

YEAR	TEAM	STARTS	GAMES	WON	LOST	PCT	ER	ERA	INNINGS PITCHED	STRIKE-OUTS	WALKS	HITS ALLOWED	HRS ALLOWED	COMP. GAMES	SHUT-OUTS	SAVES
1982	Phi-N	1	4	0	0	—	3	3.38	8	7	2	7	1	0	0	0
1985	**ChC-N**	**4**	**20**	**2**	**3**	**.400**	**20**	**3.46**	**52**	**31**	**17**	**52**	**8**	**0**	**0**	**1**
1986	**ChC-N**	**0**	**36**	**2**	**4**	**.333**	**32**	**5.37**	**53⅔**	**42**	**28**	**58**	**7**	**0**	**0**	**5**
1987	**ChC-N**	**0**	**23**	**0**	**1**	**.000**	**22**	**6.75**	**29⅓**	**27**	**20**	**38**	**4**	**0**	**0**	**0**
1990	KC-A	0	3	0	1	.000	4	15.43	2⅓	1	2	4	1	0	0	0
1992	Phi-N	0	8	0	0	—	10	8.18	11	9	10	10	5	0	0	0
Career average		1	16	1	2	.308	15	5.24	26	20	13	28	4	0	0	1
Cubs average		**1**	**26**	**1**	**3**	**.333**	**25**	**4.93**	**45**	**33**	**22**	**49**	**6**	**0**	**0**	**2**
Career total		5	94	4	9	.308	91	5.24	156⅓	117	79	169	26	0	0	6
Cubs total		**4**	**79**	**4**	**8**	**.333**	**74**	**4.93**	**135**	**100**	**65**	**148**	**19**	**0**	**0**	**6**

Balsamo, Anthony Fred (Tony)

HEIGHT: 6'2" RIGHTHANDER BORN: 11/21/1937 BROOKLYN, NEW YORK

YEAR	TEAM	STARTS	GAMES	WON	LOST	PCT	ER	ERA	INNINGS PITCHED	STRIKE-OUTS	WALKS	HITS ALLOWED	HRS ALLOWED	COMP. GAMES	SHUT-OUTS	SAVES
1962	ChC-N	0	18	0	1	.000	21	6.44	29 1/3	27	20	34	1	0	0	0
Career average		0	18	0	1	.000	21	6.44	29 1/3	27	20	34	1	0	0	0
Cubs average		**0**	**18**	**0**	**1**	**.000**	**21**	**6.44**	**29 1/3**	**27**	**20**	**34**	**1**	**0**	**0**	**0**
Career total		0	18	0	1	.000	21	6.44	29 1/3	27	20	34	1	0	0	0
Cubs total		**0**	**18**	**0**	**1**	**.000**	**21**	**6.44**	**29 1/3**	**27**	**20**	**34**	**1**	**0**	**0**	**0**

Banks, Willie Anthony

HEIGHT: 6'1" RIGHTHANDER BORN: 2/27/1969 JERSEY CITY, NEW JERSEY

YEAR	TEAM	STARTS	GAMES	WON	LOST	PCT	ER	ERA	INNINGS PITCHED	STRIKE-OUTS	WALKS	HITS ALLOWED	HRS ALLOWED	COMP. GAMES	SHUT-OUTS	SAVES
1991	Min-A	3	5	1	1	.500	11	5.71	17 1/3	16	12	21	1	0	0	0
1992	Min-A	12	16	4	4	.500	45	5.70	71	37	37	80	6	0	0	0
1993	Min-A	30	31	11	12	.478	77	4.04	171 1/3	138	78	186	17	0	0	0
1994	**ChC-N**	**23**	**23**	**8**	**12**	**.400**	**83**	**5.40**	**138 1/3**	**91**	**56**	**139**	**16**	**0**	**0**	**0**
1995	**ChC-N**	**0**	**10**	**0**	**1**	**.000**	**20**	**15.43**	**11 2/3**	**9**	**12**	**27**	**5**	**0**	**0**	**0**
1995	LA-N	6	6	0	2	.000	13	4.03	29	23	16	36	2	0	0	0
1995	Fla-N	9	9	2	3	.400	24	4.32	50	30	30	43	7	0	0	0
1997	NYY-A	1	5	3	0	1.000	3	1.93	14	8	6	9	0	0	0	0
1998	NYY-A	0	9	1	1	.500	16	10.05	14 1/3	8	12	20	4	0	0	0
1998	Ari-N	0	33	1	2	.333	15	3.09	43 2/3	32	25	34	2	0	0	1
2001	Bos-A	0	5	0	0	—	1	0.84	10 2/3	10	4	5	0	0	0	0
Career average		11	19	4	5	.449	39	4.85	71 1/3	50	36	75	8	0	0	0
Cubs average		**12**	**17**	**4**	**7**	**.381**	**52**	**6.18**	**75**	**50**	**34**	**83**	**11**	**0**	**0**	**0**
Career total		84	152	31	38	.449	308	4.85	571 1/3	402	288	600	60	1	1	1
Cubs total		**23**	**33**	**8**	**13**	**.381**	**103**	**6.18**	**150**	**100**	**68**	**166**	**21**	**1**	**1**	**0**

Barber, Stephen David (Steve)

HEIGHT: 6'0" LEFTHANDER BORN: 2/22/1939 TAKOMA PARK, MARYLAND

YEAR	TEAM	STARTS	GAMES	WON	LOST	PCT	ER	ERA	INNINGS PITCHED	STRIKE-OUTS	WALKS	HITS ALLOWED	HRS ALLOWED	COMP. GAMES	SHUT-OUTS	SAVES
1960	Bal-A	27	36	10	7	.588	65	3.22	181 2/3	112	113	148	10	6	1	2
1961	Bal-A	34	37	18	12	.600	92	3.33	248 1/3	150	130	194	13	14	8	1
1962	Bal-A	19	28	9	6	.600	54	3.46	140 1/3	89	61	145	9	5	2	0
1963	Bal-A	36	39	20	13	.606	79	2.75	258 2/3	180	92	253	12	11	2	0
1964	Bal-A	26	36	9	13	.409	67	3.84	157	118	81	144	15	4	0	1
1965	Bal-A	32	37	15	10	.600	66	2.69	220 2/3	130	81	177	16	7	2	0
1966	Bal-A	22	25	10	5	.667	34	2.30	133 1/3	91	49	104	6	5	3	0
1967	Bal-A	15	15	4	9	.308	34	4.10	74 2/3	48	61	47	6	1	1	0
1967	NYY-A	17	17	6	9	.400	44	4.05	97 2/3	70	54	103	4	3	1	0
1968	NYY-A	19	20	6	5	.545	46	3.23	128 1/3	87	54	127	7	3	1	0
1969	Sea-A	16	25	4	7	.364	46	4.80	86 1/3	69	48	99	9	0	0	0
1970	**ChC-N**	**0**	**5**	**0**	**1**	**.000**	**6**	**9.53**	**5 2/3**	**3**	**6**	**10**	**0**	**0**	**0**	**0**
1970	Atl-N	2	5	0	1	.000	8	4.91	14 2/3	11	5	17	3	0	0	0
1971	Atl-N	3	39	3	1	.750	40	4.80	75	40	25	92	6	0	0	2
1972	Atl-N	0	5	0	0	—	10	5.74	15 2/3	6	6	18	1	0	0	0
1972	Cal-A	3	34	4	4	.500	13	2.02	58	34	30	37	4	0	0	2
1973	Cal-A	1	50	3	2	.600	35	3.53	89 1/3	58	32	90	5	0	0	4
1974	SF-N	0	13	0	1	.000	8	5.27	13 2/3	13	12	13	0	0	0	1
Career average		18	31	8	7	.533	50	3.36	133 1/3	87	63	121	8	4	1	1
Cubs average		**0**	**5**	**0**	**1**	**.000**	**6**	**9.53**	**5 2/3**	**3**	**6**	**10**	**0**	**0**	**0**	**0**
Career total		272	466	121	106	.533	747	3.36	1999	1309	950	1818	125	59	21	13
Cubs total		**0**	**5**	**0**	**1**	**.000**	**6**	**9.53**	**5 2/3**	**3**	**6**	**10**	**0**	**0**	**0**	**0**

Barker, Richard Frank (Richie)
HEIGHT: 6'2"   RIGHTHANDER   BORN: 10/29/1972 REVERE, MASSACHUSETTS

YEAR	TEAM	STARTS	GAMES	WON	LOST	PCT	ER	ERA	INNINGS PITCHED	STRIKE-OUTS	WALKS	HITS ALLOWED	HRS ALLOWED	COMP. GAMES	SHUT-OUTS	SAVES
1999	ChC-N	0	5	0	0	—	4	7.20	5	3	4	6	0	0	0	0
Career average		0	5	0	0	—	4	7.20	5	3	4	6	0	0	0	0
Cubs average		0	5	0	0	—	4	7.20	5	3	4	6	0	0	0	0
Career total		0	5	0	0	—	4	7.20	5	3	4	6	0	0	0	0
Cubs total		0	5	0	0	—	4	7.20	5	3	4	6	0	0	0	0

Barnes, Roscoe Charles (Ross)
HEIGHT: 5'8"   RIGHTHANDER   BORN: 5/8/1850 MOUNT MORRIS, ILLINOIS   DIED: 2/5/1915 CHICAGO, ILLINOIS

YEAR	TEAM	STARTS	GAMES	WON	LOST	PCT	ER	ERA	INNINGS PITCHED	STRIKE-OUTS	WALKS	HITS ALLOWED	HRS ALLOWED	COMP. GAMES	SHUT-OUTS	SAVES
1876	ChN-N	0	1	0	0	—	3	20.25	1 1/3	0	0	7	0	0	0	0
Career average		0	1	0	0	—	3	20.25	1 1/3	0	0	7	0	0	0	0
Cubs average		0	1	0	0	—	3	20.25	1 1/3	0	0	7	0	0	0	0
Career total		0	1	0	0	—	3	20.25	1 1/3	0	0	7	0	0	0	0
Cubs total		0	1	0	0	—	3	20.25	1 1/3	0	0	7	0	0	0	0

Barrett, Tracy Souter (Dick *or* Kewpie Dick)
HEIGHT: 5'9"   RIGHTHANDER   BORN: 9/28/1906 MONTOURSVILLE, PENNSYLVANIA   DIED: 10/30/1966 SEATTLE, WASHINGTON

YEAR	TEAM	STARTS	GAMES	WON	LOST	PCT	ER	ERA	INNINGS PITCHED	STRIKE-OUTS	WALKS	HITS ALLOWED	HRS ALLOWED	COMP. GAMES	SHUT-OUTS	SAVES
1933	Phi-A	7	15	4	4	.500	45	5.76	70 1/3	26	49	74	2	3	0	0
1934	Bos-N	3	15	1	3	.250	24	6.68	32 1/3	14	12	50	2	0	0	0
1943	ChC-N	4	15	0	4	.000	24	4.80	45	20	28	52	2	0	0	1
1943	Phi-N	20	23	10	9	.526	45	2.39	169 1/3	65	51	137	5	10	2	1
1944	Phi-N	27	37	12	18	.400	95	3.86	221 1/3	74	88	223	7	11	1	0
1945	Phi-N	30	36	8	20	.286	115	5.43	190 2/3	72	92	217	11	8	0	1
Career average		18	28	7	12	.376	70	4.30	145 2/3	54	64	151	6	6	1	0
Cubs average		4	15	0	4	.000	24	4.80	45	20	28	52	2	0	0	0
Career total		91	141	35	58	.376	348	4.30	729	271	320	753	29	32	3	2
Cubs total		4	15	0	4	.000	24	4.80	45	20	28	52	2	0	0	0

Batista, Miguel Jerez
HEIGHT: 6'2"   RIGHTHANDER   BORN: 2/19/1971 SANTO DOMINGO, DOMINICAN REPUBLIC

YEAR	TEAM	STARTS	GAMES	WON	LOST	PCT	ER	ERA	INNINGS PITCHED	STRIKE-OUTS	WALKS	HITS ALLOWED	HRS ALLOWED	COMP. GAMES	SHUT-OUTS	SAVES
1992	Pit-N	0	1	0	0	—	2	9.00	2	1	3	4	1	0	0	0
1996	Fla-N	0	9	0	0	—	7	5.56	11 1/3	6	7	9	0	0	0	0
1997	ChC-N	6	11	0	5	.000	23	5.70	36 1/3	27	24	36	4	0	0	0
1998	Mon-N	13	56	3	5	.375	57	3.80	135	92	65	141	12	0	0	1
1999	Mon-N	17	39	8	7	.533	73	4.88	134 2/3	95	58	146	10	2	1	0
2000	Mon-N	0	4	0	1	.000	13	14.04	8 1/3	7	3	19	2	0	0	0
2000	KC-A	9	14	2	6	.250	49	7.74	57	30	34	66	17	0	0	0
2001	Ari-N	18	48	11	8	.579	52	3.36	139 1/3	90	60	113	13	0	0	0
Career average		9	26	3	5	.429	39	4.74	75	50	36	76	8	0	0	0
Cubs average		6	11	0	5	.000	23	5.70	36 1/3	27	24	36	4	0	0	0
Career total		63	182	24	32	.429	276	4.74	524	348	254	534	59	2	1	1
Cubs total		6	11	0	5	.000	23	5.70	36 1/3	27	24	36	4	0	0	0

Bauers, Russell Lee (Russ)
HEIGHT: 6'3" RIGHTHANDER BORN: 5/10/1914 TOWNSEND, WISCONSIN DIED: 1/21/1995 HINES, ILLINOIS

YEAR	TEAM	STARTS	GAMES	WON	LOST	PCT	ER	ERA	INNINGS PITCHED	STRIKE-OUTS	WALKS	HITS ALLOWED	HRS ALLOWED	COMP. GAMES	SHUT-OUTS	SAVES
1936	Pit-N	1	1	0	0	—	5	33.75	1 1/3	0	4	2	0	0	0	0
1937	Pit-N	19	34	13	6	.684	60	2.88	187 2/3	118	80	174	0	11	2	1
1938	Pit-N	34	40	13	14	.481	83	3.07	243	117	99	207	7	12	3	3
1939	Pit-N	8	15	2	4	.333	20	3.35	53 2/3	12	25	46	4	1	0	0
1940	Pit-N	2	15	0	2	.000	26	7.63	30 2/3	11	18	42	2	0	0	0
1941	Pit-N	5	8	1	3	.250	23	5.54	37 1/3	20	25	40	1	1	0	0
1946	**ChC-N**	**2**	**15**	**2**	**1**	**.667**	**17**	**3.53**	**43 1/3**	**22**	**19**	**45**	**1**	**2**	**0**	**1**
1950	StL-A	0	1	0	0	—	1	4.50	2	0	1	6	0	0	0	0
Career average		9	16	4	4	.508	29	3.53	75	38	34	70	2	3	1	1
Cubs average		**2**	**15**	**2**	**1**	**.667**	**17**	**3.53**	**43 1/3**	**22**	**19**	**45**	**1**	**2**	**0**	**1**
Career total		71	129	31	30	.508	235	3.53	599	300	271	562	17	27	5	5
Cubs total		**2**	**15**	**2**	**1**	**.667**	**17**	**3.53**	**43 1/3**	**22**	**19**	**45**	**1**	**2**	**0**	**1**

Baumann, Frank Matt (The Beau)
HEIGHT: 6'0" LEFTHANDER BORN: 7/1/1933 ST. LOUIS, MISSOURI

YEAR	TEAM	STARTS	GAMES	WON	LOST	PCT	ER	ERA	INNINGS PITCHED	STRIKE-OUTS	WALKS	HITS ALLOWED	HRS ALLOWED	COMP. GAMES	SHUT-OUTS	SAVES
1955	Bos-A	5	7	2	1	.667	22	5.82	34	27	17	38	2	0	0	0
1956	Bos-A	1	7	2	1	.667	9	3.28	24 2/3	18	14	22	3	0	0	0
1957	Bos-A	1	4	1	0	1.000	5	3.75	12	7	3	13	1	0	0	0
1958	Bos-A	7	10	2	2	.500	26	4.47	52 1/3	31	27	56	4	2	0	0
1959	Bos-A	10	26	6	4	.600	43	4.05	95 2/3	48	55	96	11	2	0	0
1960	CWS-A	20	47	13	6	.684	55	2.67	185 1/3	71	53	169	11	7	2	1
1961	CWS-A	23	53	10	13	.435	117	5.61	187 2/3	75	59	249	22	5	1	3
1962	CWS-A	10	40	7	6	.538	45	3.38	119 2/3	55	36	117	10	3	1	3
1963	CWS-A	1	24	2	1	.667	17	3.04	50 1/3	31	17	52	2	0	0	4
1964	CWS-A	0	22	0	3	.000	22	6.19	32	19	17	40	4	0	0	1
1965	**ChC-N**	**0**	**4**	**0**	**1**	**.000**	**3**	**7.36**	**3 2/3**	**2**	**3**	**4**	**0**	**0**	**0**	**0**
Career average		7	22	4	3	.542	33	4.11	72 1/3	35	27	78	6	2	0	1
Cubs average		**0**	**4**	**0**	**1**	**.000**	**3**	**7.36**	**3 2/3**	**2**	**3**	**4**	**0**	**0**	**0**	**0**
Career total		78	244	45	38	.542	364	4.11	797 1/3	384	300	856	70	19	4	13
Cubs total		**0**	**4**	**0**	**1**	**.542**	**3**	**7.36**	**3 2/3**	**2**	**3**	**4**	**0**	**0**	**0**	**0**

Bautista, Jose Joaquin
HEIGHT: 6'2" RIGHTHANDER BORN: 7/25/1964 BANI, DOMINICAN REPUBLIC

YEAR	TEAM	STARTS	GAMES	WON	LOST	PCT	ER	ERA	INNINGS PITCHED	STRIKE-OUTS	WALKS	HITS ALLOWED	HRS ALLOWED	COMP. GAMES	SHUT-OUTS	SAVES
1988	Bal-A	25	33	6	15	.286	82	4.30	171 2/3	76	45	171	21	3	0	0
1989	Bal-A	10	15	3	4	.429	46	5.31	78	30	15	84	17	0	0	0
1990	Bal-A	0	22	1	0	1.000	12	4.05	26 2/3	15	7	28	4	0	0	0
1991	Bal-A	0	5	0	1	.000	10	16.88	5 1/3	3	5	13	1	0	0	0
1993	**ChC-N**	**7**	**58**	**10**	**3**	**.769**	**35**	**2.82**	**111 2/3**	**63**	**27**	**105**	**11**	**1**	**0**	**2**
1994	**ChC-N**	**0**	**58**	**4**	**5**	**.444**	**30**	**3.89**	**69 1/3**	**45**	**17**	**75**	**10**	**0**	**0**	**1**
1995	SF-N	6	52	3	8	.273	72	6.44	100 2/3	45	26	120	24	0	0	0
1996	SF-N	1	37	3	4	.429	26	3.36	69 2/3	28	15	66	10	0	0	0
1997	Det-A	0	21	2	2	.500	30	6.69	40 1/3	19	12	55	6	0	0	0
1997	StL-N	0	11	0	0	—	9	6.57	12 1/3	4	2	15	2	0	0	0
Career average		5	35	4	5	.432	39	4.62	76 1/3	36	19	81	12	0	0	0
Cubs average		**4**	**58**	**7**	**4**	**.636**	**33**	**3.23**	**90 2/3**	**54**	**22**	**90**	**11**	**1**	**0**	**2**
Career total		49	312	32	42	.432	352	4.62	685 2/3	328	171	732	106	4	0	3
Cubs total		**7**	**116**	**14**	**8**	**.636**	**65**	**3.23**	**181**	**108**	**44**	**180**	**21**	**1**	**0**	**3**

Beard, Charles David (Dave)
HEIGHT: 6'5" RIGHTHANDER BORN: 10/2/1959 ATLANTA, GEORGIA

YEAR	TEAM	STARTS	GAMES	WON	LOST	PCT	ER	ERA	INNINGS PITCHED	STRIKE-OUTS	WALKS	HITS ALLOWED	HRS ALLOWED	COMP. GAMES	SHUT-OUTS	SAVES
1980	Oak-A	0	13	0	1	.000	6	3.38	16	12	7	12	0	0	0	1
1981	Oak-A	0	8	1	1	.500	4	2.77	13	15	4	9	1	0	0	3
1982	Oak-A	2	54	10	9	.526	35	3.44	91 2/3	73	35	85	9	0	0	11
1983	Oak-A	0	43	5	5	.500	38	5.61	61	40	36	55	8	0	0	10
1984	Sea-A	0	43	3	2	.600	49	5.80	76	76	33	88	15	0	0	5
1985	**ChC-N**	0	9	0	0	—	9	6.39	12 2/3	4	7	16	2	0	0	0
1989	Det-A	1	2	0	2	.000	3	5.06	5 1/3	1	2	9	2	0	0	0
Career average		0	25	3	3	.487	21	4.70	39 1/3	26	18	39	5	0	0	4
Cubs average		**0**	**9**	**0**	**0**	**—**	**9**	**6.39**	**12 2/3**	**4**	**7**	**16**	**2**	**0**	**0**	**0**
Career total		3	172	19	20	.487	144	4.70	275 2/3	185	124	274	37	0	0	30
Cubs total		**0**	**9**	**0**	**0**	**—**	**9**	**6.39**	**12 2/3**	**4**	**7**	**16**	**2**	**0**	**0**	**0**

Beck, Rodney Roy (Rod *or* Shooter)
HEIGHT: 6'1" RIGHTHANDER BORN: 8/3/1968 BURBANK, CALIFORNIA

YEAR	TEAM	STARTS	GAMES	WON	LOST	PCT	ER	ERA	INNINGS PITCHED	STRIKE-OUTS	WALKS	HITS ALLOWED	HRS ALLOWED	COMP. GAMES	SHUT-OUTS	SAVES
1991	SF-N	0	31	1	1	.500	22	3.78	52 1/3	38	13	53	4	0	0	1
1992	SF-N	0	65	3	3	.500	18	1.76	92	87	15	62	4	0	0	17
1993	SF-N	0	76	3	1	.750	19	2.16	79 1/3	86	13	57	11	0	0	48
1994	SF-N	0	48	2	4	.333	15	2.77	48 2/3	39	13	49	10	0	0	28
1995	SF-N	0	60	5	6	.455	29	4.45	58 2/3	42	21	60	7	0	0	33
1996	SF-N	0	63	0	9	.000	23	3.34	62	48	10	56	9	0	0	35
1997	SF-N	0	73	7	4	.636	27	3.47	70	53	8	67	7	0	0	37
1998	**ChC-N**	0	81	3	4	.429	27	3.02	80 1/3	81	20	86	11	0	0	51
1999	**ChC-N**	0	31	2	4	.333	26	7.80	30	13	13	41	5	0	0	7
1999	Bos-A	0	12	0	1	.000	3	1.93	14	12	5	9	0	0	0	3
2000	Bos-A	0	34	3	0	1.000	14	3.10	40 2/3	35	12	34	2	0	0	0
2001	Bos-A	0	68	6	4	.600	35	3.90	80 2/3	63	28	77	15	0	0	6
Career average		0	58	3	4	.461	23	3.28	64 1/3	54	16	59	8	0	0	24
Cubs average		**0**	**56**	**3**	**4**	**.385**	**27**	**4.32**	**55 1/3**	**47**	**17**	**64**	**8**	**0**	**0**	**29**
Career total		0	642	35	41	.461	258	3.28	708 2/3	597	171	651	85	0	0	266
Cubs total		**0**	**112**	**5**	**8**	**.385**	**53**	**4.32**	**110 1/3**	**94**	**33**	**127**	**16**	**0**	**0**	**58**

Beebe, Frederick Leonard (Fred)
HEIGHT: 6'1" RIGHTHANDER BORN: 12/31/1880 LINCOLN, NEBRASKA DIED: 10/30/1957 ELGIN, ILLINOIS

YEAR	TEAM	STARTS	GAMES	WON	LOST	PCT	ER	ERA	INNINGS PITCHED	STRIKE-OUTS	WALKS	HITS ALLOWED	HRS ALLOWED	COMP. GAMES	SHUT-OUTS	SAVES
1906	**ChC-N**	6	14	7	1	.875	21	2.70	70	55	32	56	1	4	0	1
1906	StL-N	19	20	9	9	.500	54	3.02	160 2/3	116	68	115	1	16	1	0
1907	StL-N	29	31	7	19	.269	72	2.72	238 1/3	141	109	192	1	24	4	0
1908	StL-N	19	29	5	13	.278	51	2.63	174 1/3	72	66	134	3	12	0	0
1909	StL-N	34	44	15	21	.417	90	2.82	287 2/3	105	104	256	5	18	1	1
1910	Cin-N	26	35	12	14	.462	73	3.07	214 1/3	93	94	193	3	11	2	0
1911	Phi-N	8	9	3	3	.500	24	4.47	48 1/3	20	24	52	2	3	0	0
1916	Cle-A	12	20	5	3	.625	27	2.41	100 2/3	32	37	92	1	5	1	2
Career average		22	29	9	12	.432	59	2.86	185	91	76	156	2	13	1	1
Cubs average		**6**	**14**	**7**	**1**	**.875**	**21**	**2.70**	**70**	**55**	**32**	**56**	**1**	**4**	**0**	**1**
Career total		153	202	63	83	.432	412	2.86	1294 1/3	634	534	1090	17	93	9	4
Cubs total		**6**	**14**	**7**	**1**	**.875**	**21**	**2.70**	**70**	**55**	**32**	**56**	**1**	**4**	**0**	**1**

Bere, Jason Phillip
HEIGHT: 6'3"   RIGHTHANDER   BORN: 5/26/1971 CAMBRIDGE, MASSACHUSETTS

YEAR	TEAM	STARTS	GAMES	WON	LOST	PCT	ER	ERA	INNINGS PITCHED	STRIKE-OUTS	WALKS	HITS ALLOWED	HRS ALLOWED	COMP. GAMES	SHUT-OUTS	SAVES
1993	CWS-A	24	24	12	5	.706	55	3.47	142 ⅔	129	81	109	12	1	0	0
1994	CWS-A	24	24	12	2	.857	60	3.81	141 ⅔	127	80	119	17	0	0	0
1995	CWS-A	27	27	8	15	.348	110	7.19	137 ⅔	110	106	151	21	1	0	0
1996	CWS-A	5	5	0	1	.000	19	10.26	16 ⅔	19	18	26	3	0	0	0
1997	CWS-A	6	6	4	2	.667	15	4.71	28 ⅔	21	17	20	4	0	0	0
1998	CWS-A	15	18	3	7	.300	60	6.45	83 ⅔	53	58	98	14	0	0	0
1998	Cin-N	7	9	3	2	.600	20	4.12	43 ⅔	31	20	39	3	0	0	0
1999	Cin-N	10	12	3	0	1.000	33	6.85	43 ⅓	28	40	56	6	0	0	0
1999	Mil-N	4	5	2	0	1.000	12	4.63	23 ⅓	19	10	23	3	0	0	0
2000	Mil-N	20	20	6	7	.462	63	4.93	115	98	63	115	19	0	0	0
2000	Cle-A	11	11	6	3	.667	40	6.63	54 ⅓	44	26	65	6	0	0	0
2001	**ChC-N**	**32**	**32**	**11**	**11**	**.500**	**90**	**4.31**	**188**	**175**	**77**	**171**	**24**	**2**	**0**	**0**
Career average		21	21	8	6	.560	64	5.10	113 ⅓	95	66	110	15	0	0	0
Cubs average		**32**	**32**	**11**	**11**	**.500**	**90**	**4.31**	**188**	**175**	**77**	**171**	**24**	**2**	**0**	**0**
Career total		185	193	70	55	.560	577	5.10	1018 ⅔	854	596	992	132	4	0	0
Cubs total		**32**	**32**	**11**	**11**	**.500**	**90**	**4.31**	**188**	**175**	**77**	**171**	**24**	**2**	**0**	**0**

Berry, Jonas Arthur (Joe *or* Jittery Joe)
HEIGHT: 5'10"   RIGHTHANDER   BORN: 12/16/1904 HUNTSVILLE, ARKANSAS   DIED: 9/27/1958 ANAHEIM, CALIFORNIA

YEAR	TEAM	STARTS	GAMES	WON	LOST	PCT	ER	ERA	INNINGS PITCHED	STRIKE-OUTS	WALKS	HITS ALLOWED	HRS ALLOWED	COMP. GAMES	SHUT-OUTS	SAVES
1942	**ChC-N**	**0**	**2**	**0**	**0**	**—**	**4**	**18.00**	**2**	**1**	**2**	**7**	**0**	**0**	**0**	**0**
1944	Phi-A	0	53	10	8	.556	24	1.94	111 ⅓	44	23	78	4	0	0	12
1945	Phi-A	0	52	8	7	.533	34	2.35	130 ⅓	51	38	114	5	0	0	5
1946	Phi-A	0	5	0	1	.000	4	2.77	13	5	3	15	1	0	0	0
1946	Cle-A	0	21	3	6	.333	14	3.38	37 ⅓	16	21	32	4	0	0	1
Career average		0	33	5	6	.488	20	2.45	73 ⅔	29	22	62	4	0	0	5
Cubs average		**0**	**2**	**0**	**0**	**—**	**4**	**18.00**	**2**	**1**	**2**	**7**	**0**	**0**	**0**	**0**
Career total		0	133	21	22	.488	80	2.45	294	117	87	246	14	0	0	18
Cubs total		**0**	**2**	**0**	**0**	**—**	**4**	**18.00**	**2**	**1**	**2**	**7**	**0**	**0**	**0**	**0**

Bielecki, Michael Joseph (Mike)
HEIGHT: 6'3"   RIGHTHANDER   BORN: 7/31/1959 BALTIMORE, MARYLAND

YEAR	TEAM	STARTS	GAMES	WON	LOST	PCT	ER	ERA	INNINGS PITCHED	STRIKE-OUTS	WALKS	HITS ALLOWED	HRS ALLOWED	COMP. GAMES	SHUT-OUTS	SAVES
1984	Pit-N	0	4	0	0	—	0	0.00	4 ⅓	1	0	4	0	0	0	0
1985	Pit-N	7	12	2	3	.400	23	4.53	45 ⅔	22	31	45	5	0	0	0
1986	Pit-N	27	31	6	11	.353	77	4.66	148 ⅔	83	83	149	10	0	0	0
1987	Pit-N	8	8	2	3	.400	24	4.73	45 ⅔	25	12	43	6	2	0	0
1988	**ChC-N**	**5**	**19**	**2**	**2**	**.500**	**18**	**3.35**	**48 ⅓**	**33**	**16**	**55**	**4**	**0**	**0**	**0**
1989	**ChC-N**	**33**	**33**	**18**	**7**	**.720**	**74**	**3.14**	**212 ⅓**	**147**	**81**	**187**	**16**	**4**	**3**	**0**
1990	**ChC-N**	**29**	**36**	**8**	**11**	**.421**	**92**	**4.93**	**168**	**103**	**70**	**188**	**13**	**0**	**0**	**1**
1991	**ChC-N**	**25**	**39**	**13**	**11**	**.542**	**86**	**4.50**	**172**	**72**	**54**	**169**	**18**	**0**	**0**	**0**
1991	Atl-N	0	2	0	0	—	0	0.00	1 ⅔	3	2	2	0	0	0	0
1992	Atl-N	14	19	2	4	.333	23	2.57	80 ⅔	62	27	77	2	1	1	0
1993	Cle-A	13	13	4	5	.444	45	5.90	68 ⅔	38	23	90	8	0	0	0
1994	Atl-N	1	19	2	0	1.000	12	4.00	27	18	12	28	2	0	0	0
1995	Cal-A	11	22	4	6	.400	50	5.97	75 ⅓	45	31	80	15	0	0	2
1996	Atl-N	5	40	4	3	.571	22	2.63	75 ⅓	71	33	63	8	0	0	2
1997	Atl-N	0	50	3	7	.300	26	4.08	57 ⅓	60	21	56	9	0	0	2
Career average		13	25	5	5	.490	41	4.18	88	56	35	88	8	1	0	0
Cubs average		**23**	**32**	**10**	**8**	**.569**	**68**	**4.05**	**150 ⅓**	**89**	**55**	**150**	**13**	**1**	**1**	**0**
Career total		178	347	70	73	.490	572	4.18	1231	783	496	1236	116	7	4	5
Cubs total		**92**	**127**	**41**	**31**	**.569**	**270**	**4.05**	**600 ⅔**	**355**	**221**	**599**	**51**	**4**	**3**	**1**

Biittner, Lawrence David (Larry)
HEIGHT: 6'2"   LEFTHANDER   BORN: 7/27/1945 POCAHONTAS, IOWA

YEAR	TEAM	STARTS	GAMES	WON	LOST	PCT	ER	ERA	INNINGS PITCHED	STRIKE-OUTS	WALKS	HITS ALLOWED	HRS ALLOWED	COMP. GAMES	SHUT-OUTS	SAVES
1977	ChC-N	0	1	0	0	—	6	40.50	1⅓	3	1	5	3	0	0	0
Career average		0	1	0	0	—	6	40.50	1⅓	3	1	5	3	0	0	0
Cubs average		**0**	**1**	**0**	**0**	**—**	**6**	**40.50**	**1⅓**	**3**	**1**	**5**	**3**	**0**	**0**	**0**
Career total		0	1	0	0	—	6	40.50	1⅓	3	1	5	3	0	0	0
Cubs total		**0**	**1**	**0**	**0**	**—**	**6**	**40.50**	**1⅓**	**3**	**1**	**5**	**3**	**0**	**0**	**0**

Bird, James Douglas (Doug)
HEIGHT: 6'4"   RIGHTHANDER   BORN: 3/5/1950 CORONA, CALIFORNIA

YEAR	TEAM	STARTS	GAMES	WON	LOST	PCT	ER	ERA	INNINGS PITCHED	STRIKE-OUTS	WALKS	HITS ALLOWED	HRS ALLOWED	COMP. GAMES	SHUT-OUTS	SAVES
1973	KC-A	0	54	4	4	.500	34	2.99	102⅓	83	30	81	10	0	0	20
1974	KC-A	1	55	7	6	.538	28	2.73	92⅓	62	27	100	6	1	0	10
1975	KC-A	4	51	9	6	.600	38	3.25	105⅓	81	40	100	7	0	0	11
1976	KC-A	27	39	12	10	.545	74	3.37	197⅔	107	31	191	17	2	1	2
1977	KC-A	5	53	11	4	.733	51	3.88	118⅓	83	29	120	14	0	0	14
1978	KC-A	6	40	6	6	.500	58	5.29	98⅔	48	31	110	8	0	0	1
1979	Phi-N	1	32	2	0	1.000	35	5.16	61	33	16	73	7	1	0	0
1980	NYY-A	1	22	3	0	1.000	15	2.66	50⅔	17	14	47	3	0	0	1
1981	NYY-A	4	17	5	1	.833	16	2.70	53⅓	28	16	58	5	0	0	0
1981	**ChC-N**	**12**	**12**	**4**	**5**	**.444**	**30**	**3.58**	**75⅓**	**34**	**16**	**72**	**5**	**2**	**1**	**0**
1982	**ChC-N**	**33**	**35**	**9**	**14**	**.391**	**109**	**5.14**	**191**	**71**	**30**	**230**	**26**	**2**	**1**	**0**
1983	Bos-A	6	22	1	4	.200	50	6.65	67⅔	33	16	91	14	0	0	1
Career average		9	39	7	5	.549	49	3.99	110⅓	62	27	116	11	1	0	5
Cubs average		**23**	**24**	**7**	**10**	**.406**	**70**	**4.70**	**133⅓**	**53**	**23**	**151**	**16**	**2**	**1**	**0**
Career total		100	432	73	60	.549	538	3.99	1213⅔	680	296	1273	122	8	3	60
Cubs total		**45**	**47**	**13**	**19**	**.406**	**139**	**4.70**	**266⅓**	**105**	**46**	**302**	**31**	**4**	**2**	**0**

Bishop, William Robinson (Bill)
HEIGHT: 5'8"   RIGHTHANDER   BORN: 12/27/1869 ADAMSBURG, PENNSYLVANIA   DIED: 12/15/1932 PITTSBURGH, PENNSYLVANIA

YEAR	TEAM	STARTS	GAMES	WON	LOST	PCT	ER	ERA	INNINGS PITCHED	STRIKE-OUTS	WALKS	HITS ALLOWED	HRS ALLOWED	COMP. GAMES	SHUT-OUTS	SAVES
1886	Pit-AA	2	2	0	1	.000	6	3.18	17	4	11	17	0	2	0	0
1887	Pit-N	3	3	0	3	.000	40	13.33	27	4	22	67	2	3	0	0
1889	**ChN-N**	**0**	**2**	**0**	**0**	**—**	**6**	**18.00**	**3**	**1**	**6**	**6**	**0**	**0**	**0**	**2**
Career average		2	2	0	1	.000	17	9.96	15⅔	3	13	30	1	2	0	1
Cubs average		**0**	**2**	**0**	**0**	**—**	**6**	**18.00**	**3**	**1**	**6**	**6**	**0**	**0**	**0**	**2**
Career total		5	7	0	4	.000	52	9.96	47	9	39	90	2	5	0	2
Cubs total		**0**	**2**	**0**	**0**	**—**	**6**	**18.00**	**3**	**1**	**6**	**6**	**0**	**0**	**0**	**2**

Bithorn, Hiram Gabriel (Hi)
HEIGHT: 6'1"   RIGHTHANDER   BORN: 3/18/1916 SANTURCE, PUERTO RICO   DIED: 1/1/1952 EL MANTE, MEXICO

YEAR	TEAM	STARTS	GAMES	WON	LOST	PCT	ER	ERA	INNINGS PITCHED	STRIKE-OUTS	WALKS	HITS ALLOWED	HRS ALLOWED	COMP. GAMES	SHUT-OUTS	SAVES
1942	**ChC-N**	**16**	**38**	**9**	**14**	**.391**	**70**	**3.68**	**171⅓**	**65**	**81**	**191**	**8**	**9**	**0**	**2**
1943	**ChC-N**	**30**	**39**	**18**	**12**	**.600**	**72**	**2.60**	**249⅔**	**86**	**65**	**227**	**8**	**19**	**7**	**2**
1946	**ChC-N**	**7**	**26**	**6**	**5**	**.545**	**37**	**3.84**	**86⅔**	**34**	**25**	**97**	**5**	**2**	**1**	**1**
1947	CWS-A	0	2	1	0	1.000	0	0.00	2	0	0	2	0	0	0	0
Career average		13	26	9	8	.523	45	3.16	127⅓	46	43	129	5	8	2	1
Cubs average		**18**	**34**	**11**	**10**	**.516**	**60**	**3.17**	**169⅓**	**62**	**57**	**172**	**7**	**10**	**3**	**2**
Career total		53	105	34	31	.523	179	3.16	509⅔	185	171	517	21	30	8	5
Cubs total		**53**	**103**	**33**	**31**	**.516**	**179**	**3.17**	**507⅔**	**185**	**171**	**515**	**21**	**30**	**8**	**5**

Blake, John Frederick (Sheriff)
HEIGHT: 6'0"   RIGHTHANDER   BORN: 9/17/1899 ANSTED, WEST VIRGINIA   DIED: 10/31/1982 BECKLEY, WEST VIRGINIA

YEAR	TEAM	STARTS	GAMES	WON	LOST	PCT	ER	ERA	INNINGS PITCHED	STRIKE-OUTS	WALKS	HITS ALLOWED	HRS ALLOWED	COMP. GAMES	SHUT-OUTS	SAVES
1920	Pit-N	0	6	0	0	—	12	8.10	13 1/3	7	6	21	0	0	0	0
1924	ChC-N	11	29	6	6	.500	54	4.57	106 1/3	42	44	123	3	4	0	1
1925	ChC-N	31	36	10	18	.357	125	4.86	231 1/3	93	114	260	17	14	0	2
1926	ChC-N	27	39	11	12	.478	79	3.60	197 2/3	95	92	204	7	11	4	1
1927	ChC-N	27	32	13	14	.481	82	3.29	224 1/3	64	82	238	3	13	2	0
1928	ChC-N	29	34	17	11	.607	66	2.47	240 2/3	78	101	209	4	16	4	1
1929	ChC-N	29	35	14	13	.519	104	4.29	218 1/3	70	103	244	8	13	1	1
1930	ChC-N	24	34	10	14	.417	100	4.82	186 2/3	80	99	213	14	7	0	0
1931	ChC-N	5	16	0	4	.000	29	5.22	50	29	26	64	4	0	0	0
1931	Phi-N	9	14	4	5	.444	44	5.58	71	31	35	90	2	1	0	1
1937	StL-A	1	15	2	2	.500	31	7.61	36 2/3	12	20	55	5	0	0	1
1937	StL-N	2	14	0	3	.000	18	3.71	43 2/3	20	18	45	1	2	0	0
Career average		20	30	9	10	.460	74	4.13	162	62	74	177	7	8	1	1
Cubs average		23	32	10	12	.468	80	3.95	182	69	83	194	8	10	1	1
Career total		195	304	87	102	.460	744	4.13	1620	621	740	1766	68	81	11	8
Cubs total		183	255	81	92	.468	639	3.95	1455 1/3	551	661	1555	60	78	11	6

Blankenship, Kevin DeWayne
HEIGHT: 6'0"   RIGHTHANDER   BORN: 1/26/1963 ANAHEIM, CALIFORNIA

YEAR	TEAM	STARTS	GAMES	WON	LOST	PCT	ER	ERA	INNINGS PITCHED	STRIKE-OUTS	WALKS	HITS ALLOWED	HRS ALLOWED	COMP. GAMES	SHUT-OUTS	SAVES
1988	Atl-N	2	2	0	1	.000	4	3.38	10 2/3	5	7	7	0	0	0	0
1988	ChC-N	1	1	1	0	1.000	4	7.20	5	4	1	7	2	0	0	0
1989	ChC-N	0	2	0	0	—	1	1.69	5 1/3	2	2	4	0	0	0	0
1990	ChC-N	2	3	0	2	.000	8	5.84	12 1/3	5	6	13	1	0	0	0
Career average		2	3	0	1	.250	6	4.59	11	5	5	10	1	0	0	0
Cubs average		1	2	0	1	.333	4	5.16	7 2/3	4	3	8	1	0	0	0
Career total		5	8	1	3	.250	17	4.59	33 1/3	16	16	31	3	0	0	0
Cubs total		3	6	1	2	.333	13	5.16	22 2/3	11	9	24	3	0	0	0

Bonetti, Julio Giacomo
HEIGHT: 6'0"   RIGHTHANDER   BORN: 7/14/1911 GENOA, ITALY   DIED: 6/17/1952 BELMONT, CALIFORNIA

YEAR	TEAM	STARTS	GAMES	WON	LOST	PCT	ER	ERA	INNINGS PITCHED	STRIKE-OUTS	WALKS	HITS ALLOWED	HRS ALLOWED	COMP. GAMES	SHUT-OUTS	SAVES
1937	StL-A	16	28	4	11	.267	93	5.84	143 1/3	43	60	190	13	7	0	1
1938	StL-A	0	17	2	3	.400	20	6.35	28 1/3	7	13	41	1	0	0	0
1940	ChC-N	0	1	0	0	—	3	20.25	1 1/3	0	4	3	0	0	0	0
Career average		5	15	2	5	.300	39	6.03	57 2/3	17	26	78	5	2	0	0
Cubs average		0	1	0	0	—	3	20.25	1 1/3	0	4	3	0	0	0	0
Career total		16	46	6	14	.300	116	6.03	173	50	77	234	14	7	0	1
Cubs total		0	1	0	0	—	3	20.25	1 1/3	0	4	3	0	0	0	0

Bonham, William Gordon (Bill)
HEIGHT: 6'3"   RIGHTHANDER   BORN: 10/1/1948 GLENDALE, CALIFORNIA

YEAR	TEAM	STARTS	GAMES	WON	LOST	PCT	ER	ERA	INNINGS PITCHED	STRIKE-OUTS	WALKS	HITS ALLOWED	HRS ALLOWED	COMP. GAMES	SHUT-OUTS	SAVES
1971	ChC-N	2	33	2	1	.667	31	4.65	60	41	36	63	6	0	0	0
1972	ChC-N	4	19	1	1	.500	20	3.12	57 2/3	49	25	56	4	0	0	4
1973	ChC-N	15	44	7	5	.583	51	3.02	152	121	64	126	10	3	0	6
1974	ChC-N	36	44	11	22	.333	104	3.86	242 2/3	191	109	246	13	10	0	1
1975	ChC-N	36	38	13	15	.464	120	4.71	229 1/3	165	109	254	15	7	2	0
1976	ChC-N	31	32	9	13	.409	93	4.27	196	110	96	215	11	3	0	0
1977	ChC-N	34	34	10	13	.435	104	4.36	214 2/3	134	82	207	15	1	0	0
1978	Cin-N	23	23	11	5	.688	55	3.53	140 1/3	83	50	151	9	1	0	0

(continued)

(Bonham, continued)

YEAR	TEAM	STARTS	GAMES	WON	LOST	PCT	ER	ERA	INNINGS PITCHED	STRIKE-OUTS	WALKS	HITS ALLOWED	HRS ALLOWED	COMP. GAMES	SHUT-OUTS	SAVES
1979	Cin-N	29	29	9	7	.563	74	3.79	175⅔	78	60	173	14	2	0	0
1980	Cin-N	4	4	2	1	.667	10	4.74	19	13	5	21	1	0	0	0
Career average		21	30	8	8	.475	66	4.01	148⅔	99	64	151	10	3	0	1
Cubs average		23	35	8	10	.431	75	4.08	164⅔	116	74	167	11	3	1	2
Career total		214	300	75	83	.475	662	4.01	1487⅓	985	636	1512	98	27	4	11
Cubs total		158	244	53	70	.431	523	4.08	1152⅓	811	521	1167	74	24	4	11

Borchers, George Bernard (Chief)
HEIGHT: 5'10"   RIGHTHANDER   BORN: 4/18/1869 SACRAMENTO, CALIFORNIA   DIED: 10/24/1938 SACRAMENTO, CALIFORNIA

YEAR	TEAM	STARTS	GAMES	WON	LOST	PCT	ER	ERA	INNINGS PITCHED	STRIKE-OUTS	WALKS	HITS ALLOWED	HRS ALLOWED	COMP. GAMES	SHUT-OUTS	SAVES
1888	ChN-N	10	10	4	4	.500	26	3.49	67	26	29	67	2	7	1	0
1895	Lou-N	1	1	0	1	.000	2	27.00	0⅔	0	3	1	0	0	0	0
Career average		6	6	2	3	.444	14	3.72	34	13	16	34	1	4	1	0
Cubs average		10	10	4	4	.500	26	3.49	67	26	29	67	2	7	1	0
Career total		11	11	4	5	.444	28	3.72	67⅔	26	32	68	2	7	1	0
Cubs total		10	10	4	4	.500	26	3.49	67	26	29	67	2	7	1	0

Bordi, Richard Albert (Rich)
HEIGHT: 6'7"   RIGHTHANDER   BORN: 4/18/1959 SAN FRANCISCO, CALIFORNIA

YEAR	TEAM	STARTS	GAMES	WON	LOST	PCT	ER	ERA	INNINGS PITCHED	STRIKE-OUTS	WALKS	HITS ALLOWED	HRS ALLOWED	COMP. GAMES	SHUT-OUTS	SAVES
1980	Oak-A	0	1	0	0	—	1	4.50	2	0	0	4	0	0	0	0
1981	Oak-A	0	2	0	0	—	0	0.00	2	0	1	1	0	0	0	0
1982	Sea-A	2	7	0	2	.000	12	8.31	13	10	1	18	4	0	0	1
1983	ChC-N	1	11	0	2	.000	14	4.97	25⅓	20	12	34	2	0	0	4
1984	ChC-N	7	31	5	2	.714	32	3.46	83⅓	41	20	78	11	0	0	2
1985	NYY-A	3	51	6	8	.429	35	3.21	98	64	29	95	5	0	0	3
1986	Bal-A	1	52	6	4	.600	53	4.46	107	83	41	105	13	0	0	0
1987	NYY-A	1	16	3	1	.750	28	7.64	33	23	12	42	7	0	0	0
1988	Oak-A	2	2	0	1	.000	4	4.70	7⅔	6	5	6	0	0	0	0
Career average		2	19	2	2	.500	20	4.34	41⅓	27	13	43	5	0	0	1
Cubs average		4	21	3	2	.556	23	3.81	54⅓	31	16	56	7	0	0	3
Career total		17	173	20	20	.500	179	4.34	371⅓	247	121	383	42	0	0	10
Cubs total		8	42	5	4	.556	46	3.81	108⅔	61	32	112	13	0	0	5

Borowski, Joseph Thomas (Joe)
HEIGHT: 6'2"   RIGHTHANDER   BORN: 5/4/1971 BAYONNE, NEW JERSEY

YEAR	TEAM	STARTS	GAMES	WON	LOST	PCT	ER	ERA	INNINGS PITCHED	STRIKE-OUTS	WALKS	HITS ALLOWED	HRS ALLOWED	COMP. GAMES	SHUT-OUTS	SAVES
1995	Bal-A	0	6	0	0	—	1	1.23	7⅓	3	4	5	0	0	0	0
1996	Atl-N	0	22	2	4	.333	14	4.85	26	15	13	33	4	0	0	0
1997	Atl-N	0	20	2	2	.500	10	3.75	24	6	16	27	2	0	0	0
1997	NYY-A	0	1	0	1	.000	2	9.00	2	2	4	2	0	0	0	0
1998	NYY-A	0	8	1	0	1.000	7	6.52	9⅔	7	4	11	0	0	0	0
2001	ChC-N	1	1	0	1	.000	6	32.40	1⅔	1	3	6	1	0	0	0
Career average		0	12	1	2	.385	8	5.09	14	7	9	17	1	0	0	0
Cubs average		1	1	0	1	.000	6	32.40	1⅔	1	3	6	1	0	0	0
Career total		1	58	5	8	.385	40	5.09	70⅔	34	44	84	7	0	0	0
Cubs total		1	1	0	1	.000	6	32.40	1⅔	1	3	6	1	0	0	0

Borowy, Henry Ludwig (Hank)
HEIGHT: 6'0" RIGHTHANDER BORN: 5/12/1916 BLOOMFIELD, NEW JERSEY

YEAR	TEAM	STARTS	GAMES	WON	LOST	PCT	ER	ERA	INNINGS PITCHED	STRIKE-OUTS	WALKS	HITS ALLOWED	HRS ALLOWED	COMP. GAMES	SHUT-OUTS	SAVES
1942	NYY-A	21	25	15	4	.789	50	2.52	178 1/3	85	66	157	6	13	4	1
1943	NYY-A	27	29	14	9	.609	68	2.82	217 1/3	113	72	195	11	14	3	0
1944	NYY-A	30	35	17	12	.586	74	2.64	252 2/3	107	88	224	15	19	3	2
1945	NYY-A	18	18	10	5	.667	46	3.13	132 1/3	35	58	107	6	7	1	0
1945	**ChC-N**	**14**	**15**	**11**	**2**	**.846**	**29**	**2.13**	**122 1/3**	**47**	**47**	**105**	**6**	**7**	**1**	**0**
1946	**ChC-N**	**28**	**32**	**12**	**10**	**.545**	**84**	**3.76**	**201**	**95**	**61**	**220**	**2**	**11**	**1**	**1**
1947	**ChC-N**	**25**	**40**	**8**	**12**	**.400**	**89**	**4.38**	**183**	**95**	**63**	**190**	**9**	**8**	**1**	**0**
1948	**ChC-N**	**17**	**39**	**5**	**10**	**.333**	**69**	**4.89**	**127**	**50**	**49**	**156**	**19**	**7**	**1**	**2**
1949	Phi-N	28	28	12	12	.500	90	4.19	193 1/3	43	63	188	19	2	1	1
1950	Phi-N	0	3	0	0	—	4	5.68	6 1/3	3	4	5	0	0	0	0
1950	Pit-N	3	11	1	3	.250	18	6.39	25 1/3	9	9	32	6	0	0	0
1950	Det-A	2	13	1	1	.500	12	3.31	32 2/3	12	16	23	3	1	0	0
1951	Det-A	1	26	2	2	.500	35	6.95	45 1/3	16	27	58	3	0	0	0
Career average		21	31	11	8	.568	67	3.50	171 2/3	69	62	166	11	9	2	1
Cubs average		**21**	**32**	**9**	**9**	**.514**	**68**	**3.85**	**158 1/3**	**67**	**55**	**168**	**10**	**7**	**1**	**1**
Career total		214	314	108	82	.568	668	3.50	1717	690	623	1660	108	94	17	7
Cubs total		**84**	**126**	**36**	**34**	**.514**	**271**	**3.85**	**633 1/3**	**267**	**220**	**671**	**39**	**28**	**4**	**4**

Boskie, Shawn Kealoha
HEIGHT: 6'3" RIGHTHANDER BORN: 3/28/1967 HAWTHORNE, NEVADA

YEAR	TEAM	STARTS	GAMES	WON	LOST	PCT	ER	ERA	INNINGS PITCHED	STRIKE-OUTS	WALKS	HITS ALLOWED	HRS ALLOWED	COMP. GAMES	SHUT-OUTS	SAVES
1990	**ChC-N**	**15**	**15**	**5**	**6**	**.455**	**40**	**3.69**	**97 2/3**	**49**	**31**	**99**	**8**	**1**	**0**	**0**
1991	**ChC-N**	**20**	**28**	**4**	**9**	**.308**	**75**	**5.23**	**129**	**62**	**52**	**150**	**14**	**0**	**0**	**0**
1992	**ChC-N**	**18**	**23**	**5**	**11**	**.313**	**51**	**5.01**	**91 2/3**	**39**	**36**	**96**	**14**	**0**	**0**	**0**
1993	**ChC-N**	**2**	**39**	**5**	**3**	**.625**	**25**	**3.43**	**65 2/3**	**39**	**21**	**63**	**7**	**0**	**0**	**0**
1994	**ChC-N**	**0**	**2**	**0**	**0**	**—**	**0**	**0.00**	**3 2/3**	**2**	**0**	**3**	**0**	**0**	**0**	**0**
1994	Phi-N	14	18	4	6	.400	49	5.23	84 1/3	59	29	85	14	1	0	0
1994	Sea-A	1	2	0	1	.000	2	6.75	2 2/3	0	1	4	1	0	0	0
1995	Cal-A	20	20	7	7	.500	70	5.64	111 2/3	51	25	127	16	0	0	0
1996	Cal-A	28	37	12	11	.522	112	5.32	189 1/3	133	67	226	40	1	0	0
1997	Bal-A	9	28	6	6	.500	55	6.43	77	50	26	95	14	0	0	1
1998	Mon-N	5	5	1	3	.250	18	9.17	17 2/3	10	4	34	5	0	0	0
Career average		15	24	5	7	.438	55	5.14	96 2/3	55	32	109	15	0	0	0
Cubs average		**11**	**21**	**4**	**6**	**.396**	**38**	**4.43**	**77 2/3**	**38**	**28**	**82**	**9**	**0**	**0**	**0**
Career total		132	217	49	63	.438	497	5.14	870 1/3	494	292	982	133	4	0	1
Cubs total		**55**	**107**	**19**	**29**	**.396**	**191**	**4.43**	**387 2/3**	**191**	**140**	**411**	**43**	**1**	**0**	**0**

Botelho, Derek Wayne
HEIGHT: 6'2" RIGHTHANDER BORN: 8/2/1956 LONG BEACH, CALIFORNIA

YEAR	TEAM	STARTS	GAMES	WON	LOST	PCT	ER	ERA	INNINGS PITCHED	STRIKE-OUTS	WALKS	HITS ALLOWED	HRS ALLOWED	COMP. GAMES	SHUT-OUTS	SAVES
1982	KC-A	4	8	2	1	.667	11	4.13	24	12	8	25	4	0	0	0
1985	**ChC-N**	**7**	**11**	**1**	**3**	**.250**	**26**	**5.32**	**44**	**23**	**23**	**52**	**8**	**1**	**0**	**0**
Career average		6	10	2	2	.429	19	4.90	34	18	16	39	6	1	0	0
Cubs average		**7**	**11**	**1**	**3**	**.250**	**26**	**5.32**	**44**	**23**	**23**	**52**	**8**	**1**	**0**	**0**
Career total		11	19	3	4	.429	37	4.90	68	35	31	77	12	1	0	0
Cubs total		**7**	**11**	**1**	**3**	**.250**	**26**	**5.32**	**44**	**23**	**23**	**52**	**8**	**1**	**0**	**0**

Bottenfield, Kent Dennis
HEIGHT: 6'3"   RIGHTHANDER   BORN: 11/14/1968 PORTLAND, OREGON

YEAR	TEAM	STARTS	GAMES	WON	LOST	PCT	ER	ERA	INNINGS PITCHED	STRIKE-OUTS	WALKS	HITS ALLOWED	HRS ALLOWED	COMP. GAMES	SHUT-OUTS	SAVES
1992	Mon-N	4	10	1	2	.333	8	2.23	32 1/3	14	11	26	1	0	0	1
1993	Mon-N	11	23	2	5	.286	38	4.12	83	33	33	93	11	0	0	0
1993	Col-N	14	14	3	5	.375	52	6.10	76 2/3	30	38	86	13	1	0	0
1994	Col-N	1	15	3	1	.750	16	5.84	24 2/3	15	10	28	1	0	0	1
1994	SF-N	0	1	0	0	—	2	10.80	1 2/3	0	0	5	1	0	0	0
1996	**ChC-N**	**0**	**48**	**3**	**5**	**.375**	**18**	**2.63**	**61 2/3**	**33**	**19**	**59**	**3**	**0**	**0**	**1**
1997	**ChC-N**	**0**	**64**	**2**	**3**	**.400**	**36**	**3.86**	**84**	**74**	**35**	**82**	**13**	**0**	**0**	**2**
1998	StL-N	17	44	4	6	.400	66	4.44	133 2/3	98	57	128	13	0	0	4
1999	StL-N	31	31	18	7	.720	84	3.97	190 1/3	124	89	197	21	0	0	0
2000	Ana-A	21	21	7	8	.467	81	5.71	127 2/3	75	56	144	25	0	1	0
2000	Phi-N	8	8	1	2	.333	22	4.50	44	31	21	41	5	1	0	1
2001	Hou-N	9	13	2	5	.286	37	6.40	52	39	16	61	16	0	0	0
Career average		13	32	5	5	.484	51	4.54	101 1/3	63	43	106	14	0	0	2
Cubs average		**0**	**56**	**3**	**4**	**.385**	**27**	**3.34**	**73**	**54**	**27**	**71**	**8**	**0**	**0**	
Career total		116	292	46	49	.484	460	4.54	911 2/3	566	385	950	123	2	1	10
Cubs total		**0**	**112**	**5**	**8**	**.385**	**54**	**3.34**	**145 2/3**	**107**	**54**	**141**	**16**	**0**	**0**	**3**

Bowie, Micah Andrew
HEIGHT: 6'4"   LEFTHANDER   BORN: 11/10/1974 WEBSTER, TEXAS

YEAR	TEAM	STARTS	GAMES	WON	LOST	PCT	ER	ERA	INNINGS PITCHED	STRIKE-OUTS	WALKS	HITS ALLOWED	HRS ALLOWED	COMP. GAMES	SHUT-OUTS	SAVES
1999	Atl-N	0	3	0	1	.000	6	13.50	4	2	4	8	1	0	0	0
1999	**ChC-N**	**11**	**11**	**2**	**6**	**.250**	**52**	**9.96**	**47**	**39**	**30**	**73**	**8**	**0**	**0**	**0**
Career average		11	14	2	7	.222	58	10.24	51	41	34	81	9	0	0	0
Cubs average		**11**	**11**	**2**	**6**	**.250**	**52**	**9.96**	**47**	**39**	**30**	**73**	**8**	**0**	**0**	**0**
Career total		11	14	2	7	.222	58	10.24	51	41	34	81	9	0	0	0
Cubs total		**11**	**11**	**2**	**6**	**.250**	**52**	**9.96**	**47**	**39**	**30**	**73**	**8**	**0**	**0**	**0**

Bowman, Robert James (Bob)
HEIGHT: 5'10"   RIGHTHANDER   BORN: 10/3/1910 KEYSTONE, WEST VIRGINIA   DIED: 9/4/1972 BLUEFIELD, WEST VIRGINIA

YEAR	TEAM	STARTS	GAMES	WON	LOST	PCT	ER	ERA	INNINGS PITCHED	STRIKE-OUTS	WALKS	HITS ALLOWED	HRS ALLOWED	COMP. GAMES	SHUT-OUTS	SAVES
1939	StL-N	15	51	13	5	.722	49	2.60	169 1/3	78	60	141	8	4	2	9
1940	StL-N	17	28	7	5	.583	55	4.33	114 1/3	43	43	118	9	7	0	0
1941	NYG-N	6	29	6	7	.462	51	5.71	80 1/3	25	36	100	10	2	0	1
1942	**ChC-N**	**0**	**1**	**0**	**0**	**—**	**0**	**0.00**	**1**	**0**	**0**	**1**	**0**	**0**	**0**	**0**
Career average		10	27	7	4	.605	39	3.82	91 1/3	37	35	90	7	3	1	3
Cubs average		**0**	**1**	**0**	**0**	**—**	**0**	**0.00**	**1**	**0**	**0**	**1**	**0**	**0**	**0**	**0**
Career total		38	109	26	17	.605	155	3.82	365	146	139	360	27	13	2	10
Cubs total		**0**	**1**	**0**	**0**	**—**	**0**	**0.00**	**1**	**0**	**0**	**1**	**0**	**0**	**0**	**0**

Bradley, George Washington (Grin)
HEIGHT: 5'10"   RIGHTHANDER   BORN: 7/13/1852 READING, PENNSYLVANIA   DIED: 10/2/1931 PHILADELPHIA, PENNSYLVANIA

YEAR	TEAM	STARTS	GAMES	WON	LOST	PCT	ER	ERA	INNINGS PITCHED	STRIKE-OUTS	WALKS	HITS ALLOWED	HRS ALLOWED	COMP. GAMES	SHUT-OUTS	SAVES
1876	StL-N	64	64	45	19	.703	78	1.23	573	103	38	470	3	63	16	0
1877	**ChN-N**	**44**	**50**	**18**	**23**	**.439**	**145**	**3.31**	**394**	**59**	**39**	**452**	**4**	**35**	**2**	**0**
1879	Try-N	54	54	13	40	.245	154	2.85	487	133	26	590	12	53	3	0
1880	Prv-N	20	28	13	8	.619	30	1.38	196	54	6	158	2	16	4	1
1881	Cle-N	6	6	2	4	.333	22	3.88	51	6	3	70	2	5	0	0
1882	Cle-N	16	18	6	9	.400	61	3.73	147	32	22	164	5	15	0	0
1883	Phi-AA	23	26	16	7	.696	75	3.15	214 1/3	56	22	215	7	22	0	0
1884	Cin-U	38	41	25	15	.625	103	2.71	342	168	23	350	7	36	3	0
Career average		33	36	17	16	.525	84	2.50	300 2/3	76	22	309	5	31	4	0
Cubs average		**44**	**50**	**18**	**23**	**.439**	**145**	**3.31**	**394**	**59**	**39**	**452**	**4**	**35**	**2**	**0**
Career total		265	287	138	125	.525	668	2.50	2404 1/3	611	179	2469	42	245	28	1
Cubs total		**44**	**50**	**18**	**23**	**.439**	**145**	**3.31**	**394**	**59**	**39**	**452**	**4**	**35**	**2**	**0**

Brennan, William Raymond (Bill)
HEIGHT: 6'3" RIGHTHANDER BORN: 1/15/1963 TAMPA, FLORIDA

YEAR	TEAM	STARTS	GAMES	WON	LOST	PCT	ER	ERA	INNINGS PITCHED	STRIKE-OUTS	WALKS	HITS ALLOWED	HRS ALLOWED	COMP. GAMES	SHUT-OUTS	SAVES
1988	LA-N	2	4	0	1	.000	7	6.75	9 1/3	7	6	13	0	0	0	0
1993	ChC-N	1	8	2	1	.667	7	4.20	15	11	8	16	2	0	0	0
Career average		2	6	1	1	.500	7	5.18	12 1/3	9	7	15	1	0	0	0
Cubs average		**1**	**8**	**2**	**1**	**.667**	**7**	**4.20**	**15**	**11**	**8**	**16**	**2**	**0**	**0**	**0**
Career total		3	12	2	2	.500	14	5.18	24 1/3	18	14	29	2	0	0	0
Cubs total		**1**	**8**	**2**	**1**	**.667**	**7**	**4.20**	**15**	**11**	**8**	**16**	**2**	**0**	**0**	**0**

Brett, Herbert James (Herb *or* Duke)
HEIGHT: 6'0" RIGHTHANDER BORN: 5/23/1900 LAWRENCEVILLE, VIRGINIA DIED: 11/25/1974 ST. PETERSBURG, FLORIDA

YEAR	TEAM	STARTS	GAMES	WON	LOST	PCT	ER	ERA	INNINGS PITCHED	STRIKE-OUTS	WALKS	HITS ALLOWED	HRS ALLOWED	COMP. GAMES	SHUT-OUTS	SAVES
1924	ChC-N	1	1	0	0	—	3	5.06	5 1/3	1	7	6	0	0	0	0
1925	ChC-N	1	10	1	1	.500	7	3.63	17 1/3	6	3	12	0	0	0	0
Career average		1	6	1	1	.500	5	3.97	11 1/3	4	5	9	0	0	0	0
Cubs average		**1**	**6**	**1**	**1**	**.500**	**5**	**3.97**	**11 1/3**	**4**	**5**	**9**	**0**	**0**	**0**	**0**
Career total		2	11	1	1	.500	10	3.97	22 2/3	7	10	18	0	0	0	0
Cubs total		**2**	**11**	**1**	**1**	**.500**	**10**	**3.97**	**22 2/3**	**7**	**10**	**18**	**0**	**0**	**0**	**0**

Brewer, James Thomas (Jim)
HEIGHT: 6'1" LEFTHANDER BORN: 11/14/1937 MERCED, CALIFORNIA DIED: 11/16/1987 TYLER, TEXAS

YEAR	TEAM	STARTS	GAMES	WON	LOST	PCT	ER	ERA	INNINGS PITCHED	STRIKE-OUTS	WALKS	HITS ALLOWED	HRS ALLOWED	COMP. GAMES	SHUT-OUTS	SAVES
1960	ChC-N	4	5	0	3	.000	14	5.82	21 2/3	7	6	25	2	0	0	0
1961	ChC-N	11	36	1	7	.125	56	5.82	86 2/3	57	21	116	17	0	0	0
1962	ChC-N	1	6	0	1	.000	6	9.53	5 2/3	1	3	10	2	0	0	0
1963	ChC-N	1	29	3	2	.600	27	4.89	49 2/3	35	15	59	10	0	0	0
1964	LA-N	5	34	4	3	.571	31	3.00	93	63	25	79	5	1	1	1
1965	LA-N	2	19	3	2	.600	10	1.82	49 1/3	31	28	33	1	0	0	2
1966	LA-N	0	13	0	2	.000	9	3.68	22	8	11	17	0	0	0	2
1967	LA-N	11	30	5	4	.556	30	2.68	100 2/3	74	31	78	8	0	0	1
1968	LA-N	0	54	8	3	.727	21	2.48	76 1/3	75	33	59	5	0	0	14
1969	LA-N	0	59	7	6	.538	25	2.55	88 1/3	92	41	71	5	0	0	20
1970	LA-N	0	58	7	6	.538	31	3.13	89	91	33	66	10	0	0	24
1971	LA-N	0	55	6	5	.545	17	1.88	81 1/3	66	24	55	4	0	0	22
1972	LA-N	0	51	8	7	.533	11	1.26	78 1/3	69	25	41	6	0	0	17
1973	LA-N	0	56	6	8	.429	24	3.01	71 2/3	56	25	58	8	0	0	20
1974	LA-N	0	24	4	4	.500	11	2.52	39 1/3	26	10	29	5	0	0	0
1975	LA-N	0	21	3	1	.750	19	5.18	33	21	12	44	2	0	0	2
1975	Cal-A	0	21	1	0	1.000	7	1.82	34 2/3	22	11	38	2	0	0	5
1976	Cal-A	0	13	3	1	.750	6	2.70	20	16	6	20	0	0	0	2
Career average		2	34	4	4	.515	21	3.07	61 1/3	48	21	53	5	0	0	8
Cubs average		**4**	**19**	**1**	**3**	**.235**	**26**	**5.66**	**41**	**25**	**11**	**53**	**8**	**0**	**0**	**0**
Career total		35	584	69	65	.515	355	3.07	1040 2/3	810	360	898	92	1	1	132
Cubs total		**17**	**76**	**4**	**13**	**.235**	**103**	**5.66**	**163 2/3**	**100**	**45**	**210**	**31**	**0**	**0**	**0**

Briggs, Herbert Theodore (Buttons)
HEIGHT: 6'1" RIGHTHANDER BORN: 7/8/1875 POUGHKEEPSIE, NEW YORK DIED: 2/18/1911 CLEVELAND, OHIO

YEAR	TEAM	STARTS	GAMES	WON	LOST	PCT	ER	ERA	INNINGS PITCHED	STRIKE-OUTS	WALKS	HITS ALLOWED	HRS ALLOWED	COMP. GAMES	SHUT-OUTS	SAVES
1896	ChN-N	21	26	12	9	.571	93	4.31	194	84	108	202	6	19	0	1
1897	ChN-N	22	22	4	16	.200	109	5.26	186 2/3	60	85	246	6	21	0	0
1898	ChN-N	4	4	1	3	.250	19	5.70	30	14	10	38	0	3	0	0
1904	ChC-N	30	34	19	11	.633	63	2.05	277	112	77	252	3	28	3	3
1905	ChC-N	20	20	8	8	.500	40	2.14	168	68	52	141	1	13	5	0

(continued)

(Briggs, H.T., continued)

Career average	19	21	9	9	.484	65	3.41	171	68	66	176	3	17	2	1
Cubs average	**19**	**21**	**9**	**9**	**.484**	**65**	**3.41**	**171**	**68**	**66**	**176**	**3**	**17**	**2**	**1**
Career total	97	106	44	47	.484	324	3.41	855 ⅔	338	332	879	16	84	8	4
Cubs total	**97**	**106**	**44**	**47**	**.484**	**324**	**3.41**	**855 ⅔**	**338**	**332**	**879**	**16**	**84**	**8**	**4**

Briggs, Jonathan Tift (John)
HEIGHT: 5'10"   RIGHTHANDER   BORN: 1/24/1934 NATOMA, CALIFORNIA

YEAR	TEAM	STARTS	GAMES	WON	LOST	PCT	ER	ERA	INNINGS PITCHED	STRIKE-OUTS	WALKS	HITS ALLOWED	HRS ALLOWED	COMP. GAMES	SHUT-OUTS	SAVES
1956	**ChC-N**	**0**	**3**	**0**	**0**	**—**	**1**	**1.69**	**5 ⅓**	**1**	**4**	**5**	**1**	**0**	**0**	**0**
1957	**ChC-N**	**0**	**3**	**0**	**1**	**.000**	**6**	**12.46**	**4 ⅓**	**1**	**3**	**7**	**2**	**0**	**0**	**0**
1958	**ChC-N**	**17**	**20**	**5**	**5**	**.500**	**48**	**4.52**	**95 ⅔**	**46**	**45**	**99**	**12**	**3**	**1**	**0**
1959	Cle-A	1	4	0	1	.000	3	2.13	12 ⅔	5	3	12	1	0	0	0
1960	Cle-A	2	21	4	2	.667	18	4.46	36 ⅓	19	15	32	4	0	0	1
1960	KCA-A	1	8	0	2	.000	16	12.71	11 ⅓	8	12	19	3	0	0	0
Career average	4	12	2	2	.450	18	5.00	33	16	16	35	5	1	0	0
Cubs average	**6**	**9**	**2**	**2**	**.455**	**18**	**4.70**	**35**	**16**	**17**	**37**	**5**	**1**	**0**	**0**
Career total	21	59	9	11	.450	92	5.00	165 ⅔	80	82	174	23	3	1	1
Cubs total	**17**	**26**	**5**	**6**	**.455**	**55**	**4.70**	**105 ⅓**	**48**	**52**	**111**	**15**	**3**	**1**	**0**

Brillheart, James Benson (Jim)
HEIGHT: 5'11"   LEFTHANDER   BORN: 9/28/1903 DUBLIN, VIRGINIA   DIED: 9/2/1972 RADFORD, VIRGINIA

YEAR	TEAM	STARTS	GAMES	WON	LOST	PCT	ER	ERA	INNINGS PITCHED	STRIKE-OUTS	WALKS	HITS ALLOWED	HRS ALLOWED	COMP. GAMES	SHUT-OUTS	SAVES
1922	Was-A	10	31	4	6	.400	48	3.61	119 ⅔	47	72	120	3	3	0	1
1923	Was-A	0	12	0	1	.000	14	7.00	18	8	12	27	1	0	0	0
1927	**ChC-N**	**12**	**32**	**4**	**2**	**.667**	**59**	**4.13**	**128 ⅔**	**36**	**38**	**140**	**4**	**4**	**0**	**0**
1931	Bos-A	1	11	0	0	—	12	5.49	19 ⅔	7	15	27	2	0	0	0
Career average	6	22	2	2	.471	33	4.19	71 ⅔	25	34	79	3	2	0	0
Cubs average	**12**	**32**	**4**	**2**	**.667**	**59**	**4.13**	**128 ⅔**	**36**	**38**	**140**	**4**	**4**	**0**	**0**
Career total	23	86	8	9	.471	133	4.19	286	98	137	314	10	7	0	1
Cubs total	**12**	**32**	**4**	**2**	**.667**	**59**	**4.13**	**128 ⅔**	**36**	**38**	**140**	**4**	**4**	**0**	**0**

Broberg, Peter Sven (Pete)
HEIGHT: 6'3"   RIGHTHANDER   BORN: 3/2/1950 WEST PALM BEACH, FLORIDA

YEAR	TEAM	STARTS	GAMES	WON	LOST	PCT	ER	ERA	INNINGS PITCHED	STRIKE-OUTS	WALKS	HITS ALLOWED	HRS ALLOWED	COMP. GAMES	SHUT-OUTS	SAVES
1971	Was-A	18	18	5	9	.357	48	3.47	124 ⅔	89	53	104	10	7	1	0
1972	Tex-A	25	39	5	12	.294	84	4.29	176 ⅓	133	85	153	14	3	2	1
1973	Tex-A	20	22	5	9	.357	74	5.61	118 ⅔	57	66	130	8	6	1	0
1974	Tex-A	2	12	0	4	.000	26	8.07	29	15	13	29	7	0	0	0
1975	Mil-A	32	38	14	16	.467	101	4.13	220 ⅓	100	106	219	17	7	2	0
1976	Mil-A	11	20	1	7	.125	51	4.97	92 ⅓	28	72	99	5	1	0	0
1977	**ChC-N**	**0**	**22**	**1**	**2**	**.333**	**19**	**4.75**	**36**	**20**	**18**	**34**	**8**	**0**	**0**	**0**
1978	Oak-A	26	35	10	12	.455	85	4.62	165 ⅔	94	65	174	16	2	0	0
Career average	17	26	5	9	.366	61	4.56	120 ⅓	67	60	118	11	3	1	0
Cubs average	**0**	**22**	**1**	**2**	**.333**	**19**	**4.75**	**36**	**20**	**18**	**34**	**8**	**0**	**0**	**0**
Career total	134	206	41	71	.366	488	4.56	963	536	478	942	85	26	6	1
Cubs total	**0**	**22**	**1**	**2**	**.333**	**19**	**4.75**	**36**	**20**	**18**	**34**	**8**	**0**	**0**	**0**

Broglio, Ernest Gilbert (Ernie)
HEIGHT: 6'2"   RIGHTHANDER   BORN: 8/27/1935 BERKELEY, CALIFORNIA

YEAR	TEAM	STARTS	GAMES	WON	LOST	PCT	ER	ERA	INNINGS PITCHED	STRIKE-OUTS	WALKS	HITS ALLOWED	HRS ALLOWED	COMP. GAMES	SHUT-OUTS	SAVES
1959	StL-N	25	35	7	12	.368	95	4.72	181 ⅓	133	89	174	20	6	3	0
1960	StL-N	24	52	21	9	.700	69	2.74	226 ⅓	188	100	172	18	9	3	0
1961	StL-N	26	29	9	12	.429	80	4.12	174 ⅔	113	75	166	19	7	2	0
1962	StL-N	30	34	12	9	.571	74	3.00	222 ⅓	132	93	193	22	11	4	0

(continued)

(continued)

YEAR	TEAM	STARTS	GAMES	WON	LOST	PCT	ER	ERA	INNINGS PITCHED	STRIKE-OUTS	WALKS	HITS ALLOWED	HRS ALLOWED	COMP. GAMES	SHUT-OUTS	SAVES
1963	StL-N	35	39	18	8	.692	83	2.99	250	145	90	202	24	11	5	0
1964	StL-N	11	11	3	5	.375	27	3.50	69⅓	36	26	65	7	3	1	0
1964	**ChC-N**	**16**	**18**	**4**	**7**	**.364**	**45**	**4.04**	**100⅓**	**46**	**30**	**111**	**12**	**3**	**0**	**1**
1965	**ChC-N**	**6**	**26**	**1**	**6**	**.143**	**39**	**6.93**	**50⅔**	**22**	**46**	**63**	**7**	**0**	**0**	**0**
1966	**ChC-N**	**11**	**15**	**2**	**6**	**.250**	**44**	**6.35**	**62⅓**	**34**	**38**	**70**	**14**	**2**	**0**	**1**
Career average		23	32	10	9	.510	70	3.74	167⅓	106	73	152	18	7	2	0
Cubs average		**11**	**20**	**2**	**6**	**.269**	**43**	**5.40**	**71**	**34**	**38**	**81**	**11**	**2**	**0**	**1**
Career total		184	259	77	74	.510	556	3.74	1337⅓	849	587	1216	143	52	18	2
Cubs total		**33**	**59**	**7**	**19**	**.269**	**128**	**5.40**	**213⅓**	**102**	**114**	**244**	**33**	**5**	**0**	**2**

Brosnan, James Patrick (Jim *or* Professor)
HEIGHT: 6'4"   RIGHTHANDER   BORN: 10/24/1929 CINCINNATI, OHIO

YEAR	TEAM	STARTS	GAMES	WON	LOST	PCT	ER	ERA	INNINGS PITCHED	STRIKE-OUTS	WALKS	HITS ALLOWED	HRS ALLOWED	COMP. GAMES	SHUT-OUTS	SAVES
1954	**ChC-N**	**0**	**18**	**1**	**0**	**1.000**	**35**	**9.45**	**33⅓**	**17**	**18**	**44**	**9**	**0**	**0**	**0**
1956	**ChC-N**	**10**	**30**	**5**	**9**	**.357**	**40**	**3.79**	**95**	**51**	**45**	**95**	**9**	**1**	**1**	**1**
1957	**ChC-N**	**5**	**41**	**5**	**5**	**.500**	**37**	**3.38**	**98⅔**	**73**	**46**	**79**	**11**	**1**	**0**	**0**
1958	**ChC-N**	**8**	**8**	**3**	**4**	**.429**	**18**	**3.14**	**51⅔**	**24**	**29**	**41**	**3**	**2**	**0**	**0**
1958	StL-N	12	33	8	4	.667	44	3.44	115	65	50	107	10	2	0	7
1959	StL-N	1	20	1	3	.250	18	4.91	33	18	15	34	5	0	0	2
1959	Cin-N	9	26	8	3	.727	31	3.35	83⅓	56	26	79	7	1	1	2
1960	Cin-N	2	57	7	2	.778	26	2.36	99	62	22	79	4	0	0	12
1961	Cin-N	0	53	10	4	.714	27	3.04	80	40	18	77	7	0	0	16
1962	Cin-N	0	48	4	4	.500	24	3.34	64⅔	51	18	76	6	0	0	13
1963	Cin-N	0	6	0	1	.000	4	7.71	4⅔	4	3	8	2	0	0	0
1963	CWS-A	0	45	3	8	.273	23	2.84	73	46	22	71	7	0	0	14
Career average		5	43	6	5	.539	36	3.54	92⅓	56	35	88	9	1	0	7
Cubs average		**6**	**24**	**4**	**5**	**.438**	**33**	**4.20**	**69⅔**	**41**	**35**	**65**	**8**	**1**	**0**	**0**
Career total		47	385	55	47	.539	327	3.54	831⅓	507	312	790	80	7	2	67
Cubs total		**23**	**97**	**14**	**18**	**.438**	**130**	**4.20**	**278⅔**	**165**	**138**	**259**	**32**	**4**	**1**	**1**

Brown, Jophrey Clifford
HEIGHT: 6'2"   RIGHTHANDER   BORN: 1/22/1945 GRAMBLING, LOUISIANA

YEAR	TEAM	STARTS	GAMES	WON	LOST	PCT	ER	ERA	INNINGS PITCHED	STRIKE-OUTS	WALKS	HITS ALLOWED	HRS ALLOWED	COMP. GAMES	SHUT-OUTS	SAVES
1968	**ChC-N**	**0**	**1**	**0**	**0**	**—**	**1**	**4.50**	**2**	**0**	**1**	**2**	**0**	**0**	**0**	**0**
Career average		0	1	0	0	—	1	4.50	2	0	1	2	0	0	0	0
Cubs average		**0**	**1**	**0**	**0**	**—**	**1**	**4.50**	**2**	**0**	**1**	**2**	**0**	**0**	**0**	**0**
Career total		0	1	0	0	—	1	4.50	2	0	1	2	0	0	0	0
Cubs total		**0**	**1**	**0**	**0**	**—**	**1**	**4.50**	**2**	**0**	**1**	**2**	**0**	**0**	**0**	**0**

Brown, Joseph E. (Joe)
HEIGHT: 5'10"   BORN: 4/4/1859 WARREN, PENNSYLVANIA   DIED: 6/28/1888 WARREN, PENNSYLVANIA

YEAR	TEAM	STARTS	GAMES	WON	LOST	PCT	ER	ERA	INNINGS PITCHED	STRIKE-OUTS	WALKS	HITS ALLOWED	HRS ALLOWED	COMP. GAMES	SHUT-OUTS	SAVES
1884	**ChN-N**	**6**	**7**	**4**	**2**	**.667**	**26**	**4.68**	**50**	**27**	**7**	**56**	**4**	**5**	**0**	**0**
1885	Bal-AA	4	4	0	4	.000	24	5.68	38	9	4	52	0	4	0	0
Career average		5	6	2	3	.400	25	5.11	44	18	6	54	2	5	0	0
Cubs average		**6**	**7**	**4**	**2**	**.667**	**26**	**4.68**	**50**	**27**	**7**	**56**	**4**	**5**	**0**	**0**
Career total		10	11	4	6	.400	50	5.11	88	36	11	108	4	9	0	0
Cubs total		**6**	**7**	**4**	**2**	**.667**	**26**	**4.68**	**50**	**27**	**7**	**56**	**4**	**5**	**0**	**0**

Mordecai Peter Centennial "Three-Finger," "Miner" Brown, rhp, 1903–16

Mordecai Brown is perhaps the ultimate big-league story of turning a lemon into big-league lemonade.

Born on October 19, 1876 (hence one of his middle names), in Nyesville, Indiana, Brown caught his right hand in his uncle's grain grinder when he was seven. The hand was badly injured, and it was necessary to amputate the forefinger. The middle finger was mangled, and the little finger of that hand was stubbed. Worse, a few weeks later, while chasing down a pig, Brown broke the third and fourth fingers of the hand, leaving the entire hand a busted mess.

Brown could still pitch, though. After several years in the minor leagues, he was signed by the Cardinals in 1903. Brown's record with St. Louis was 9-13, but Cubs manager Frank Chance liked Brown's control and lobbied Cubs owner Jim Hart to trade for Brown in 1904.

It was a huge steal for Chicago. Brown went 15-10 in 1904 and 18-12 in 1905, and then proceeded to reel off six consecutive 20-win seasons. He won a league-leading 27 games in 1909 and in 1906 he had a stunning 1.04 ERA, with nine shutouts, both league bests.

Newspapers of the day made much of the way Brown turned a handicap into an advantage. Teammate Johnny Evers believed, as did many players of the day, that the stumpy forefinger on Brown's pitching hand enabled him to put more and different kinds of spin on the ball as he released it. But Brown's catcher in those days, Jimmy Archer, marveled more at Brown's amazing control. Indeed, Brown walked a little less than two batters per start during his time with the Cubs. During that nine-year span, his ERA broke above 2.00 only twice.

Brown was 5'10" and about 175 pounds throughout his playing days. He was a fitness fanatic, developing his own regimen. This kept him durable and effective throughout his career. He was very proud of the way he could relieve in between starts. In fact, he led the National League in saves from 1908 to 1911. In both 1909 and 1910, Brown also led the league in complete games, an impressive feat in any era.

He was respected by teammates and opponents alike, as much for his gamesmanship as his

Brown, Mordecai Peter Centennial (Three Finger *or* Miner)

HEIGHT: 5'10"   RIGHTHANDER   BORN: 10/19/1876 NYESVILLE, INDIANA   DIED: 2/14/1948 TERRE HAUTE, INDIANA

YEAR	TEAM	STARTS	GAMES	WON	LOST	PCT	ER	ERA	INNINGS PITCHED	STRIKE-OUTS	WALKS	HITS ALLOWED	HRS ALLOWED	COMP. GAMES	SHUT-OUTS	SAVES
1903	StL-N	24	26	9	13	.409	58	2.60	201	83	59	231	7	19	1	0
1904	ChC-N	23	26	15	10	.600	44	1.86	212⅓	81	50	155	1	21	4	1
1905	ChC-N	24	30	18	12	.600	60	2.17	249	89	44	219	3	24	4	0
1906	ChC-N	32	36	26	6	.813	32	1.04	277⅓	144	61	198	1	27	9	3
1907	ChC-N	27	34	20	6	.769	36	1.39	233	107	40	180	2	20	6	3
1908	ChC-N	31	44	29	9	.763	51	1.47	312⅓	123	49	214	1	27	9	5
1909	ChC-N	34	50	27	9	.750	50	1.31	342⅔	172	53	246	1	32	8	7
1910	ChC-N	31	46	25	13	.658	61	1.86	295⅓	143	64	256	3	27	6	7
1911	ChC-N	27	53	21	11	.656	84	2.80	270	129	55	267	5	21	0	13
1912	ChC-N	8	15	5	6	.455	26	2.64	88⅔	34	20	92	2	5	2	0
1913	Cin-N	16	39	11	12	.478	56	2.91	173⅓	41	44	174	7	11	1	6
1914	StL-F	18	26	12	6	.667	64	3.29	175	81	43	172	7	13	2	0
1914	Bro-F	8	9	2	5	.286	27	4.21	57⅔	32	18	63	1	5	0	0

(continued)

efforts in overcoming his handicap. In fact, his teammates disdained the ugly-sounding "Three Finger" nickname hung on him by sportswriters of the day and rarely even called him "Miner" (a nickname he picked up after working the Pennsylvania mines). Mostly, they called him "Brownie."

By whatever name, Brown loved pitching in big games, against big-name opponents. His battles against the Giants' Christy Mathewson were almost always epic. At one point, Brown had beaten Mathewson nine consecutive times.

In 1908 he won his most famous game against Mathewson, coming in to relieve in the first inning of the playoff game with the Giants at the Polo Grounds. Brown had only had two days' rest, so manager Frank Chance was reluctant to use him. That was somewhat confusing to Brown, who pointed out that he had either started or relieved in 14 of the Cubs' final 19 games that year.

Nonetheless, after Cubs starter Jack Pfiester ran into trouble, Chance had no compunction about calling in Brown, who allowed only one run the rest of the way in the 4-2 win. In the ninth, he needed only four pitches to finish off the Giants.

Brown was 5-4 in World Series play for the Cubs. In the 1907 and 1908 Series, he made 3 starts, threw 2 shutouts, allowed a total of 13 hits, 2 walks and 0 earned runs. In Game 4 of the 1907 Fall Classic, several sportswriters speculated that the Tigers, down 0-3 at that point, might have a chance in this game because the Cubs would probably prefer to win the World Series in front of their home fans in Game 5.

"To blazes with that," said Brown. "I'll finish 'em off today."

Which he did, firing a tidy seven-hit shutout.

Brown was traded to the Reds in 1913, and in 1914 he jumped to the St. Louis team of the new Federal League. In 1915 he was signed by the Chicago Federal League representative and helped pitch them to the league title.

But the Federal League folded after that year, and Brown found himself back with the Cubs for one final season. He ended up 2-3 in 1916.

Brown's 239-130 career record, not to mention his career 2.06 ERA, helped get him elected to the Hall of Fame in 1949, a year after his death in 1948.

Brown is second all-time with the Cubs in victories with 188 and tops all-time in ERA with 1.80, as well as the overall leader in complete games since 1900 with 206. Brown is also far and away the shutout leader of the Cubs with 48, 13 better than James "Hippo" Vaughn's 35. He is also fifth best all-time in innings pitched for the Cubs with 2,329, eighth in strikeouts with 1,043 and ninth in appearances with 346.

(continued)

YEAR	TEAM	STARTS	GAMES	WON	LOST	PCT	ER	ERA	INNINGS PITCHED	STRIKE-OUTS	WALKS	HITS ALLOWED	HRS ALLOWED	COMP. GAMES	SHUT-OUTS	SAVES
1915	Chi-F	25	35	17	8	.680	55	2.09	236⅓	95	64	189	2	17	3	4
1916	**ChC-N**	**4**	**12**	**2**	**3**	**.400**	**21**	**3.91**	**48⅓**	**21**	**9**	**52**	**0**	**2**	**0**	**0**
Career average		24	34	17	9	.649	52	2.06	226⅔	98	48	193	3	19	4	4
Cubs average		**24**	**35**	**19**	**9**	**.689**	**47**	**1.80**	**233**	**104**	**45**	**188**	**2**	**21**	**5**	**4**
Career total		332	481	239	129	.649	725	2.06	3172⅓	1375	673	2708	43	271	55	49
Cubs total		**241**	**346**	**188**	**85**	**.689**	**465**	**1.80**	**2329**	**1043**	**445**	**1879**	**19**	**206**	**48**	**39**

Brown, Paul Percival (Ray)

HEIGHT: 6'1"   RIGHTHANDER   BORN: 1/31/1889 CHICAGO, ILLINOIS   DIED: 5/29/1955 LOS ANGELES, CALIFORNIA

YEAR	TEAM	STARTS	GAMES	WON	LOST	PCT	ER	ERA	INNINGS PITCHED	STRIKE-OUTS	WALKS	HITS ALLOWED	HRS ALLOWED	COMP. GAMES	SHUT-OUTS	SAVES
1909	ChC-N	1	1	1	0	1.000	2	2.00	9	2	4	5	0	1	0	0
Career average		1	1	1	0	1.000	2	2.00	9	2	4	5	0	*(continued)*		0
Cubs average		**1**	**1**	**1**	**0**	**1.000**	**2**	**2.00**	**9**	**2**	**4**	**5**	**0**	**1**	**0**	**0**
Career total		1	1	1	0	1.000	2	2.00	9	2	4	5	0	1	0	0
Cubs total		**1**	**1**	**1**	**0**	**1.000**	**2**	**2.00**	**9**	**2**	**4**	**5**	**0**	**1**	**0**	**0**

Brown, Walter George (Jumbo)
HEIGHT: 6'4"   RIGHTHANDER   BORN: 4/30/1907 GREENE, RHODE ISLAND   DIED: 10/2/1966 FREEPORT, NEW YORK

YEAR	TEAM	STARTS	GAMES	WON	LOST	PCT	ER	ERA	INNINGS PITCHED	STRIKE-OUTS	WALKS	HITS ALLOWED	HRS ALLOWED	COMP. GAMES	SHUT-OUTS	SAVES
1925	ChC-N	0	2	0	0	—	2	3.00	6	0	4	5	0	0	0	0
1927	Cle-A	0	8	0	2	.000	13	6.27	18 2/3	8	26	19	3	0	0	0
1928	Cle-A	0	5	0	1	.000	11	6.75	14 2/3	12	15	19	0	0	0	0
1932	NYY-A	3	19	5	2	.714	28	4.53	55 2/3	31	30	58	1	3	1	1
1933	NYY-A	8	21	7	5	.583	43	5.23	74	55	52	78	3	1	0	0
1935	NYY-A	8	20	6	5	.545	35	3.61	87 1/3	41	37	94	2	3	1	1
1936	NYY-A	3	20	1	4	.200	42	5.91	64	19	29	93	4	0	0	0
1937	Cin-N	1	4	1	0	1.000	9	8.38	9 2/3	4	3	16	0	0	0	0
1937	NYG-N	0	4	1	0	1.000	1	1.04	8 2/3	4	5	5	0	0	0	0
1938	NYG-N	0	43	5	3	.625	18	1.80	90	42	28	65	5	0	0	5
1939	NYG-N	0	31	4	0	1.000	26	4.15	56 1/3	24	25	69	1	0	0	7
1940	NYG-N	0	41	2	4	.333	21	3.42	55 1/3	31	25	49	5	0	0	7
1941	NYG-N	0	31	1	5	.167	21	3.32	57	30	21	49	2	0	0	8
Career average		2	21	3	3	.516	23	4.07	49 2/3	25	25	52	2	1	0	2
Cubs average		0	2	0	0	—	2	3.00	6	0	4	5	0	0	0	0
Career total		23	249	33	31	.516	270	4.07	597 1/3	301	300	619	26	7	2	29
Cubs total		0	2	0	0	—	2	3.00	6	0	4	5	0	0	0	0

Brusstar, Warren Scott
HEIGHT: 6'3"   RIGHTHANDER   BORN: 2/2/1952 OAKLAND, CALIFORNIA

YEAR	TEAM	STARTS	GAMES	WON	LOST	PCT	ER	ERA	INNINGS PITCHED	STRIKE-OUTS	WALKS	HITS ALLOWED	HRS ALLOWED	COMP. GAMES	SHUT-OUTS	SAVES
1977	Phi-N	0	46	7	2	.778	21	2.65	71 1/3	46	24	64	7	0	0	3
1978	Phi-N	0	58	6	3	.667	23	2.33	88 2/3	60	30	74	0	0	0	0
1979	Phi-N	0	13	1	0	1.000	11	6.91	14 1/3	3	4	23	1	0	0	1
1980	Phi-N	0	26	2	2	.500	16	3.72	38 2/3	21	13	42	3	0	0	0
1981	Phi-N	0	14	0	1	.000	6	4.38	12 1/3	8	10	12	0	0	0	2
1982	Phi-N	0	22	2	3	.400	12	4.76	22 2/3	11	5	31	2	0	0	0
1982	CWS-A	0	10	2	0	1.000	7	3.44	18 1/3	8	3	19	2	0	0	1
1983	ChC-N	0	59	3	1	.750	21	2.35	80 1/3	46	37	67	1	0	0	3
1984	ChC-N	0	41	1	1	.500	22	3.11	63 2/3	36	21	57	4	0	0	4
1985	ChC-N	0	51	4	3	.571	50	6.05	74 1/3	34	36	87	8	0	0	1
Career average		0	38	3	2	.636	21	3.51	54	30	20	53	3	0	0	2
Cubs average		0	50	3	2	.615	31	3.83	72 2/3	39	31	70	4	0	0	3
Career total		0	340	28	16	.636	189	3.51	484 2/3	273	183	476	28	0	0	14
Cubs total		0	151	8	5	.615	93	3.83	218 1/3	116	94	211	13	0	0	8

Bryant, Claiborne Henry (Clay)
HEIGHT: 6'2"   RIGHTHANDER   BORN: 11/26/1911 MADISON HEIGHTS, VIRGINIA   DIED: 4/9/1999 BOCA RATON, FLORIDA

YEAR	TEAM	STARTS	GAMES	WON	LOST	PCT	ER	ERA	INNINGS PITCHED	STRIKE-OUTS	WALKS	HITS ALLOWED	HRS ALLOWED	COMP. GAMES	SHUT-OUTS	SAVES
1935	ChC-N	1	9	1	2	.333	13	5.16	22 2/3	13	7	34	1	0	0	2
1936	ChC-N	0	26	1	2	.333	21	3.30	57 1/3	35	24	57	0	0	0	0
1937	ChC-N	9	38	9	3	.750	64	4.26	135 1/3	75	78	117	1	4	1	3
1938	ChC-N	30	44	19	11	.633	93	3.10	270 1/3	135	125	235	6	17	3	2
1939	ChC-N	4	4	2	1	.667	20	5.74	31 1/3	9	14	42	3	2	0	0
1940	ChC-N	0	8	0	1	.000	14	4.78	26 1/3	5	14	26	2	0	0	0
Career average		7	22	5	3	.615	38	3.73	90 2/3	45	44	85	2	4	1	1
Cubs average		7	22	5	3	.615	38	3.73	90 2/3	45	44	85	2	4	1	1
Career total		44	129	32	20	.615	225	3.73	543 1/3	272	262	511	13	23	4	7
Cubs total		44	129	32	20	.615	225	3.73	543 1/3	272	262	511	13	23	4	7

Brynan, Charles Ruley (Tod)
HEIGHT: —   RIGHTHANDER   BORN: 7/1863 PHILADELPHIA, PENNSYLVANIA   DIED: 5/10/1925 PHILADELPHIA, PENNSYLVANIA

YEAR	TEAM	STARTS	GAMES	WON	LOST	PCT	ER	ERA	INNINGS PITCHED	STRIKE-OUTS	WALKS	HITS ALLOWED	HRS ALLOWED	COMP. GAMES	SHUT-OUTS	SAVES
1888	ChN-N	3	3	2	1	.667	18	6.48	25	11	7	29	2	2	0	0
1891	Bos-N	1	1	0	1	.000	6	54.00	1	0	3	4	0	0	0	0

(continued)

(continued)

	STARTS	GAMES	WON	LOST	PCT	ER	ERA	INNINGS PITCHED	STRIKE-OUTS	WALKS	HITS ALLOWED	HRS ALLOWED	COMP. GAMES	SHUT-OUTS	SAVES
Career average	2	2	1	1	.500	12	8.31	13	6	5	17	1	1	0	0
Cubs average	**3**	**3**	**2**	**1**	**.667**	**18**	**6.48**	**25**	**11**	**7**	**29**	**2**	**2**	**0**	**0**
Career total	4	4	2	2	.500	24	8.31	26	11	10	33	2	2	0	0
Cubs total	**3**	**3**	**2**	**1**	**.667**	**18**	**6.48**	**25**	**11**	**7**	**29**	**2**	**2**	**0**	**0**

Buhl, Robert Ray (Bob)

HEIGHT: 6'2"   RIGHTHANDER   BORN: 8/12/1928 SAGINAW, MICHIGAN   DIED: 2/16/2001 TITUSVILLE, FLORIDA

YEAR	TEAM	STARTS	GAMES	WON	LOST	PCT	ER	ERA	INNINGS PITCHED	STRIKE-OUTS	WALKS	HITS ALLOWED	HRS ALLOWED	COMP. GAMES	SHUT-OUTS	SAVES
1953	Mil-N	18	30	13	8	.619	51	2.97	154 1/3	83	73	133	9	8	3	0
1954	Mil-N	14	31	2	7	.222	49	4.00	110 1/3	57	65	117	5	2	1	3
1955	Mil-N	27	38	13	11	.542	72	3.21	201 2/3	117	109	168	13	11	1	1
1956	Mil-N	33	38	18	8	.692	80	3.32	216 2/3	86	105	190	18	13	2	0
1957	Mil-N	31	34	18	7	.720	66	2.74	216 2/3	117	121	191	15	14	2	0
1958	Mil-N	10	11	5	2	.714	28	3.45	73	27	30	74	5	3	0	1
1959	Mil-N	25	31	15	9	.625	63	2.86	198	105	74	181	19	12	4	0
1960	Mil-N	33	36	16	9	.640	82	3.09	238 2/3	121	103	202	23	11	2	0
1961	Mil-N	28	32	9	10	.474	86	4.11	188 1/3	77	98	180	23	9	1	0
1962	Mil-N	1	1	0	1	.000	5	22.50	2	1	4	6	0	0	0	0
1962	**ChC-N**	**30**	**34**	**12**	**13**	**.480**	**87**	**3.69**	**212**	**109**	**94**	**204**	**23**	**8**	**1**	**0**
1963	**ChC-N**	**34**	**37**	**11**	**14**	**.440**	**85**	**3.38**	**226**	**108**	**62**	**219**	**24**	**6**	**0**	**0**
1964	**ChC-N**	**35**	**36**	**15**	**14**	**.517**	**97**	**3.83**	**227 2/3**	**107**	**68**	**208**	**22**	**11**	**3**	**0**
1965	**ChC-N**	**31**	**32**	**13**	**11**	**.542**	**90**	**4.39**	**184 1/3**	**92**	**57**	**207**	**26**	**2**	**0**	**0**
1966	**ChC-N**	**1**	**1**	**0**	**0**	**—**	**4**	**15.43**	**2 1/3**	**1**	**1**	**4**	**1**	**0**	**0**	**0**
1966	Phi-N	18	32	6	8	.429	70	4.77	132	59	39	156	10	1	0	1
1967	Phi-N	0	3	0	0	—	4	12.00	3	1	2	6	2	0	0	0
Career average	25	30	11	9	.557	68	3.55	172 1/3	85	74	163	16	7	1	0
Cubs average	**26**	**28**	**10**	**10**	**.495**	**73**	**3.83**	**170 1/3**	**83**	**56**	**168**	**19**	**5**	**1**	**0**
Career total	369	457	166	132	.557	1019	3.55	2587	1268	1105	2446	238	111	20	6
Cubs total	**131**	**140**	**51**	**52**	**.495**	**363**	**3.83**	**852 1/3**	**417**	**282**	**842**	**96**	**27**	**4**	**0**

Bullinger, James Eric (Jim)

HEIGHT: 6'2"   RIGHTHANDER   BORN: 8/21/1965 NEW ORLEANS, LOUISIANA

YEAR	TEAM	STARTS	GAMES	WON	LOST	PCT	ER	ERA	INNINGS PITCHED	STRIKE-OUTS	WALKS	HITS ALLOWED	HRS ALLOWED	COMP. GAMES	SHUT-OUTS	SAVES
1992	**ChC-N**	**9**	**39**	**2**	**8**	**.200**	**44**	**4.66**	**85**	**36**	**54**	**72**	**9**	**1**	**0**	**7**
1993	**ChC-N**	**0**	**15**	**1**	**0**	**1.000**	**8**	**4.32**	**16 2/3**	**10**	**9**	**18**	**1**	**0**	**0**	**1**
1994	**ChC-N**	**10**	**33**	**6**	**2**	**.750**	**40**	**3.60**	**100**	**72**	**34**	**87**	**6**	**0**	**0**	**1**
1995	**ChC-N**	**24**	**24**	**12**	**8**	**.600**	**69**	**4.14**	**150**	**93**	**65**	**152**	**14**	**1**	**1**	**0**
1996	**ChC-N**	**20**	**37**	**6**	**10**	**.375**	**94**	**6.54**	**129 1/3**	**90**	**68**	**144**	**15**	**1**	**1**	**1**
1997	Mon-N	25	36	7	12	.368	96	5.56	155 1/3	87	74	165	17	2	2	1
1998	Sea-A	1	2	0	1	.000	10	15.88	5 2/3	4	2	13	3	0	0	0
Career average	13	27	5	6	.453	52	5.06	91 2/3	56	44	93	9	1	1	2
Cubs average	**13**	**30**	**5**	**6**	**.491**	**51**	**4.77**	**96 1/3**	**60**	**46**	**95**	**9**	**1**	**0**	**2**
Career total	89	186	34	41	.453	361	5.06	642	392	306	651	65	6	4	11
Cubs total	**63**	**148**	**27**	**28**	**.491**	**255**	**4.77**	**481**	**301**	**230**	**473**	**45**	**4**	**2**	**11**

Burdette, Freddie Thomason

HEIGHT: 6'1"   RIGHTHANDER   BORN: 9/15/1936 MOULTRIE, GEORGIA

YEAR	TEAM	STARTS	GAMES	WON	LOST	PCT	ER	ERA	INNINGS PITCHED	STRIKE-OUTS	WALKS	HITS ALLOWED	HRS ALLOWED	COMP. GAMES	SHUT-OUTS	SAVES
1962	**ChC-N**	**0**	**8**	**0**	**0**	**—**	**4**	**3.72**	**9 2/3**	**5**	**8**	**5**	**2**	**0**	**0**	**1**
1963	**ChC-N**	**0**	**4**	**0**	**0**	**—**	**2**	**3.86**	**4 2/3**	**1**	**2**	**5**	**1**	**0**	**0**	**0**
1964	**ChC-N**	**0**	**18**	**1**	**0**	**1.000**	**7**	**3.15**	**20**	**4**	**10**	**17**	**2**	**0**	**0**	**0**
Career average	0	10	0	0	1.000	4	3.41	11 1/3	3	7	9	2	0	0	0
Cubs average	**0**	**10**	**0**	**0**	**1.000**	**4**	**3.41**	**11 1/3**	**3**	**7**	**9**	**2**	**0**	**0**	**0**
Career total	0	30	1	0	1.000	13	3.41	34 1/3	10	20	27	5	0	0	1
Cubs total	**0**	**30**	**1**	**0**	**1.000**	**13**	**3.41**	**34 1/3**	**10**	**20**	**27**	**5**	**0**	**0**	**1**

Burdette, Selva Lewis (Lew)
HEIGHT: 6'2" RIGHTHANDER BORN: 11/22/1926 NITRO, WEST VIRGINIA

YEAR	TEAM	STARTS	GAMES	WON	LOST	PCT	ER	ERA	INNINGS PITCHED	STRIKE-OUTS	WALKS	HITS ALLOWED	HRS ALLOWED	COMP. GAMES	SHUT-OUTS	SAVES
1950	NYY-A	0	2	0	0	—	1	6.75	1 ⅓	0	0	3	0	0	0	0
1951	Bos-N	0	3	0	0	—	3	6.23	4 ⅓	1	5	6	0	0	0	0
1952	Bos-N	9	45	6	11	.353	55	3.61	137	47	47	138	8	5	0	7
1953	Mil-N	13	46	15	5	.750	63	3.24	175	58	56	177	7	6	1	8
1954	Mil-N	32	38	15	14	.517	73	2.76	238	79	62	224	17	13	4	0
1955	Mil-N	33	42	13	8	.619	103	4.03	230	70	73	253	25	11	2	0
1956	Mil-N	35	39	19	10	.655	77	2.70	256 ⅓	110	52	234	22	16	6	1
1957	Mil-N	33	37	17	9	.654	106	3.72	256 ⅔	78	59	260	25	14	1	0
1958	Mil-N	36	40	20	10	.667	89	2.91	275 ⅓	113	50	279	18	19	3	0
1959	Mil-N	39	41	21	15	.583	131	4.07	289 ⅔	105	38	312	38	20	4	1
1960	Mil-N	32	45	19	13	.594	103	3.36	275 ⅔	83	35	277	19	18	4	4
1961	Mil-N	36	40	18	11	.621	121	4.00	272 ⅓	92	33	295	31	14	3	0
1962	Mil-N	19	37	10	9	.526	78	4.89	143 ⅔	59	23	172	26	6	1	2
1963	Mil-N	13	15	6	5	.545	34	3.64	84	28	24	71	15	4	1	0
1963	StL-N	14	21	3	8	.273	41	3.77	98	45	16	106	6	3	0	2
1964	StL-N	0	8	1	0	1.000	2	1.80	10	3	3	10	1	0	0	0
1964	**ChC-N**	**17**	**28**	**9**	**9**	**.500**	**71**	**4.88**	**131**	**40**	**19**	**152**	**15**	**8**	**2**	**0**
1965	**ChC-N**	**3**	**7**	**0**	**2**	**.000**	**12**	**5.31**	**20 ⅓**	**5**	**4**	**26**	**3**	**0**	**0**	**0**
1965	Phi-N	9	19	3	3	.500	43	5.48	70 ⅔	23	17	95	5	1	1	0
1966	Cal-A	0	54	7	2	.778	30	3.39	79 ⅔	27	12	80	4	0	0	5
1967	Cal-A	0	19	1	0	1.000	10	4.91	18 ⅓	8	0	16	4	0	.0	1
Career average		21	35	11	8	.585	69	3.66	170 ⅓	60	35	177	16	9	2	2
Cubs average		**10**	**18**	**5**	**6**	**.450**	**42**	**4.94**	**75 ⅔**	**23**	**12**	**89**	**9**	**4**	**1**	**0**
Career total		373	626	203	144	.585	1246	3.66	3067 ⅓	1074	628	3186	289	158	33	31
Cubs total		**20**	**35**	**9**	**11**	**.450**	**83**	**4.94**	**151 ⅓**	**45**	**23**	**178**	**18**	**8**	**2**	**0**

Burns, Thomas Everett (Tom)
HEIGHT: 5'7" RIGHTHANDER BORN: 3/30/1857 HONESDALE, PENNSYLVANIA DIED: 3/19/1902 JERSEY CITY, NEW JERSEY

YEAR	TEAM	STARTS	GAMES	WON	LOST	PCT	ER	ERA	INNINGS PITCHED	STRIKE-OUTS	WALKS	HITS ALLOWED	HRS ALLOWED	COMP. GAMES	SHUT-OUTS	SAVES
1880	**ChN-N**	**0**	**1**	**0**	**0**	**—**	**0**	**0.00**	**1 ⅓**	**1**	**2**	**2**	**0**	**0**	**0**	**0**
Career average		0	1	0	0	—	0	0.00	1 ⅓	1	2	2	0	0	0	0
Cubs average		**0**	**1**	**0**	**0**	**—**	**0**	**0.00**	**1 ⅓**	**1**	**2**	**2**	**0**	**0**	**0**	**0**
Career total		0	1	0	0	—	0	0.00	1 ⅓	1	2	2	0	0	0	0
Cubs total		**0**	**1**	**0**	**0**	**—**	**0**	**0.00**	**1 ⅓**	**1**	**2**	**2**	**0**	**0**	**0**	**0**

Burris, Bertram Ray (Ray)
HEIGHT: 6'5" RIGHTHANDER BORN: 8/22/1950 IDABEL, OKLAHOMA

YEAR	TEAM	STARTS	GAMES	WON	LOST	PCT	ER	ERA	INNINGS PITCHED	STRIKE-OUTS	WALKS	HITS ALLOWED	HRS ALLOWED	COMP. GAMES	SHUT-OUTS	SAVES
1973	**ChC-N**	**1**	**31**	**1**	**1**	**.500**	**21**	**2.92**	**64 ⅔**	**57**	**27**	**65**	**2**	**0**	**0**	**0**
1974	**ChC-N**	**5**	**40**	**3**	**5**	**.375**	**55**	**6.60**	**75**	**40**	**26**	**91**	**8**	**0**	**0**	**1**
1975	**ChC-N**	**35**	**36**	**15**	**10**	**.600**	**109**	**4.12**	**238 ⅓**	**108**	**73**	**259**	**25**	**8**	**2**	**0**
1976	**ChC-N**	**36**	**37**	**15**	**13**	**.536**	**86**	**3.11**	**249**	**112**	**70**	**251**	**22**	**10**	**4**	**0**
1977	**ChC-N**	**39**	**39**	**14**	**16**	**.467**	**116**	**4.72**	**221**	**105**	**67**	**270**	**29**	**5**	**1**	**1**
1978	**ChC-N**	**32**	**40**	**7**	**13**	**.350**	**105**	**4.76**	**198 ⅔**	**94**	**79**	**210**	**15**	**0**	**0**	**0**
1979	**ChC-N**	**0**	**14**	**0**	**0**	**—**	**15**	**6.23**	**21 ⅔**	**14**	**15**	**23**	**0**	**0**	**0**	**0**
1979	NYY-A	0	15	1	3	.250	19	6.18	27 ⅔	19	10	40	5	0	0	0
1979	NYM-N	4	4	0	2	.000	8	3.32	21 ⅔	10	6	21	2	1	0	0
1980	NYM-N	29	29	7	13	.350	76	4.02	170 ⅓	83	54	181	20	4	0	0
1981	Mon-N	21	22	9	7	.563	46	3.05	135 ⅔	52	41	117	9	2	0	2
1982	Mon-N	15	37	4	14	.222	65	4.73	123 ⅔	55	53	143	14	2	0	0
1983	Mon-N	17	40	4	7	.364	63	3.68	154	100	56	139	13	2	1	0
1984	Oak-A	28	34	13	10	.565	74	3.15	211 ⅔	93	90	193	15	5	1	0
1985	Mil-A	28	29	9	13	.409	91	4.81	170 ⅓	81	53	182	25	6	0	0
1986	StL-N	10	23	4	5	.444	51	5.60	82	34	32	92	13	0	0	0
1987	Mil-A	2	10	2	2	.500	15	5.87	23	8	12	33	4	0	0	0

(continued)

(continued)

Career average	20	32	7	9	.446	68	4.17	146	71	51	154	15	3	1	0
Cubs average	21	34	8	8	.487	72	4.27	152 2/3	76	51	167	14	4	1	0
Career total	302	480	108	134	.446	1015	4.17	2188 1/3	1065	764	2310	221	47	10	4
Cubs total	148	237	55	58	.487	507	4.27	1068 1/3	530	357	1169	101	27	8	2

Burrows, John
HEIGHT: 5'10"   LEFTHANDER   BORN: 10/30/1913 WINFIELD, LOUISIANA   DIED: 4/27/1987 COAL RUN, OHIO

YEAR	TEAM	STARTS	GAMES	WON	LOST	PCT	ER	ERA	INNINGS PITCHED	STRIKE-OUTS	WALKS	HITS ALLOWED	HRS ALLOWED	COMP. GAMES	SHUT-OUTS	SAVES
1943	Phi-A	1	4	0	1	.000	7	8.22	7 2/3	3	9	8	0	0	0	0
1943	ChC-N	1	23	0	2	.000	14	3.86	32 2/3	18	16	25	0	0	0	2
1944	ChC-N	0	3	0	0	—	6	18.00	3	1	3	7	0	0	0	0
Career average		1	15	0	2	.000	14	5.61	21 2/3	11	14	20	0	0	0	1
Cubs average		1	13	0	1	.000	10	5.05	18	10	10	16	0	0	0	1
Career total		2	30	0	3	.000	27	5.61	43 1/3	22	28	40	0	0	0	2
Cubs total		1	26	0	2	.000	20	5.05	35 2/3	19	19	32	0	0	0	2

Burwell, Richard Matthew (Dick)
HEIGHT: 6'1"   RIGHTHANDER   BORN: 1/23/1940 ALTON, ILLINOIS

YEAR	TEAM	STARTS	GAMES	WON	LOST	PCT	ER	ERA	INNINGS PITCHED	STRIKE-OUTS	WALKS	HITS ALLOWED	HRS ALLOWED	COMP. GAMES	SHUT-OUTS	SAVES
1960	ChC-N	1	3	0	0	—	6	5.59	9 2/3	1	7	11	2	0	0	0
1961	ChC-N	0	2	0	0	—	4	9.00	4	0	4	6	0	0	0	0
Career average		1	3	0	0	—	5	6.59	7	1	6	9	1	0	0	0
Cubs average		1	3	0	0	—	5	6.59	7	1	6	9	1	0	0	0
Career total		1	5	0	0	—	10	6.59	13 2/3	1	11	17	2	0	0	0
Cubs total		1	5	0	0	—	10	6.59	13 2/3	1	11	17	2	0	0	0

Bush, Guy Terrell (The Mississippi Mudcat)
HEIGHT: 6'0"   RIGHTHANDER   BORN: 8/23/1901 ABERDEEN, MISSISSIPPI   DIED: 7/2/1985 SHANNON, MISSISSIPPI

YEAR	TEAM	STARTS	GAMES	WON	LOST	PCT	ER	ERA	INNINGS PITCHED	STRIKE-OUTS	WALKS	HITS ALLOWED	HRS ALLOWED	COMP. GAMES	SHUT-OUTS	SAVES
1923	ChC-N	0	1	0	0	—	0	0.00	1	2	0	1	0	0	0	0
1924	ChC-N	8	16	2	5	.286	36	4.02	80 2/3	36	24	91	7	4	0	0
1925	ChC-N	15	42	6	13	.316	87	4.30	182	76	52	213	15	5	0	4
1926	ChC-N	15	35	13	9	.591	50	2.86	157 1/3	32	42	149	3	7	2	2
1927	ChC-N	22	36	10	10	.500	65	3.03	193 1/3	62	79	177	3	9	1	2
1928	ChC-N	24	42	15	6	.714	87	3.83	204 1/3	61	86	229	10	9	2	2
1929	ChC-N	30	50	18	7	.720	110	3.66	270 2/3	82	107	277	16	18	2	8
1930	ChC-N	25	46	15	10	.600	155	6.20	225	75	86	291	22	11	0	3
1931	ChC-N	24	39	16	8	.667	90	4.49	180 1/3	54	66	190	9	14	1	2
1932	ChC-N	30	40	19	11	.633	85	3.21	238 2/3	73	70	262	13	15	1	0
1933	ChC-N	32	41	20	12	.625	79	2.75	259	84	68	261	9	20	4	2
1934	ChC-N	27	40	18	10	.643	89	3.83	209 1/3	75	54	213	15	15	1	2
1935	Pit-N	25	41	11	11	.500	98	4.32	204 1/3	42	40	237	16	8	1	2
1936	Pit-N	0	16	1	3	.250	23	5.97	34 2/3	10	11	49	3	0	0	2
1936	Bos-N	11	15	4	5	.444	34	3.39	90 1/3	28	20	98	2	5	0	1
1937	Bos-N	20	32	8	15	.348	71	3.54	180 2/3	56	48	201	8	11	1	1
1938	StL-N	0	6	0	1	.000	3	4.50	6	1	3	6	1	0	0	1
1945	Cin-N	0	4	0	0	—	4	8.31	4 1/3	1	3	5	0	0	0	1
Career average		18	32	10	8	.564	69	3.86	160	50	51	174	9	9	1	2
Cubs average		21	36	13	8	.601	78	3.81	183 1/3	59	61	196	10	11	1	2
Career total		308	542	176	136	.564	1166	3.86	2722	850	859	2950	152	151	16	34
Cubs total		252	428	152	101	.601	933	3.81	2201 2/3	712	734	2354	122	127	14	27

Guy Terrell "the Mississippi Mudcat" Bush, rhp, 1923–38, 1945

Guy Bush was one of the mainstays of the staff of several pennant-winning Cubs squads in the late 1920s and early 1930s.

Bush was born on August 23, 1901, in Aberdeen, Mississippi, which explained his exotic nickname. He made a brief one-inning appearance for the Cubs in September 1923. By 1924 he was starting and relieving, dual roles he accepted willingly.

In fact, Bush quickly became the iron man of the Cubs staff. In 1925 he started 15 games and appeared in 27 others to lead the team. He also led the National League in saves that year with four.

From 1928 to 1933, he led the Cubs in appearances, usually averaging about 24-25 starts and 14-16 relief stints.

Bush was not a strikeout king, never striking out more than 84 batters in a season, and often a good deal fewer than that. Instead, he relied on keeping the ball down and generating plenty of ground balls.

Bush participated in two World Series, with mixed results. He pitched a superb Game 3 in the 1929 World Series against the powerful Athletics, scattering 12 hits and striking out four in a 3-1 victory, the only win Chicago would post in that matchup.

In 1932 Bush struggled in two appearances against the red-hot Yankees, allowing nine earned runs in 5⅔ innings as the Yankees swept that Series.

Bush won 19, 20 and 18 games from 1932 to 1934, but Cubs management feared he was growing old. He was traded to Pittsburgh in 1935, where he went 11-11. More memorable than that record was that on May 25 Bush relieved in a game against the Boston Braves at Forbes Field and gave up the last two home runs of Babe Ruth's career.

Bush retired in 1938, except for a brief stint in 1945 with the Reds. He is 6th all-time on the Cubs list of victories with 152, 10th all-time in appearances with 339, 9th in starts with 252, 10th in complete games with 127, 9th in innings pitched with 2,201⅔ and 2nd in terms of years of service as a pitcher with 12 years.

Bush died in Shannon, Mississippi, on July 2, 1985.

Buzhardt, John William

HEIGHT: 6'2"   RIGHTHANDER   BORN: 8/17/1936 PROSPERITY, SOUTH CAROLINA

YEAR	TEAM	STARTS	GAMES	WON	LOST	PCT	ER	ERA	INNINGS PITCHED	STRIKE-OUTS	WALKS	HITS ALLOWED	HRS ALLOWED	COMP. GAMES	SHUT-OUTS	SAVES
1958	**ChC-N**	**2**	**6**	**3**	**0**	**1.000**	**5**	**1.85**	**24⅓**	**9**	**7**	**16**	**2**	**1**	**0**	**0**
1959	**ChC-N**	**10**	**31**	**4**	**5**	**.444**	**56**	**4.97**	**101⅓**	**33**	**29**	**107**	**12**	**1**	**1**	**0**
1960	Phi-N	29	30	5	16	.238	86	3.86	200⅓	73	68	198	14	5	0	0
1961	Phi-N	27	41	6	18	.250	101	4.49	202⅓	92	65	200	28	6	1	0
1962	CWS-A	25	28	8	12	.400	71	4.19	152⅓	64	59	156	16	8	2	0
1963	CWS-A	18	19	9	4	.692	34	2.42	126⅓	59	31	100	8	6	3	0
1964	CWS-A	25	31	10	8	.556	53	2.98	160	97	35	150	13	8	3	0
1965	CWS-A	30	32	13	8	.619	63	3.01	188⅔	108	56	167	12	4	1	1
1966	CWS-A	22	33	6	11	.353	64	3.83	150⅓	66	30	144	13	5	4	1
1967	CWS-A	7	28	3	9	.250	39	3.96	88⅔	33	37	100	11	0	0	0
1967	Bal-A	1	7	0	1	.000	6	4.63	11⅔	7	5	14	1	0	0	0
1967	Hou-N	0	1	0	0	—	0	0.00	0⅔	0	0	0	0	0	0	0
1968	Hou-N	4	39	4	4	.500	29	3.12	83⅔	37	35	73	0	0	0	5
Career average		18	30	6	9	.425	55	3.66	135⅔	62	42	130	12	4	1	1
Cubs average		**6**	**19**	**4**	**3**	**.583**	**31**	**4.37**	**63**	**21**	**18**	**62**	**7**	**1**	**1**	**0**
Career total		200	326	71	96	.425	607	3.66	1490⅔	678	457	1425	130	44	15	7
Cubs total		**12**	**37**	**7**	**5**	**.583**	**61**	**4.37**	**125⅔**	**42**	**36**	**123**	**14**	**2**	**1**	**0**

Callahan, James Joseph (Nixey)
HEIGHT: 5'10"   RIGHTHANDER   BORN: 3/18/1874 FITCHBURG, MASSACHUSETTS   DIED: 10/4/1934 BOSTON, MASSACHUSETTS

YEAR	TEAM	STARTS	GAMES	WON	LOST	PCT	ER	ERA	INNINGS PITCHED	STRIKE-OUTS	WALKS	HITS ALLOWED	HRS ALLOWED	COMP. GAMES	SHUT-OUTS	SAVES
1894	Phi-N	2	9	1	3	.250	37	9.89	33 ⅔	9	17	64	3	1	0	2
1897	**ChN-N**	**22**	**23**	**12**	**9**	**.571**	**85**	**4.03**	**189 ⅔**	**52**	**55**	**221**	**6**	**21**	**1**	**0**
1898	**ChN-N**	**31**	**31**	**20**	**11**	**.645**	**75**	**2.46**	**274 ⅓**	**73**	**71**	**267**	**2**	**30**	**2**	**0**
1899	**ChN-N**	**34**	**35**	**21**	**12**	**.636**	**100**	**3.06**	**294 ⅓**	**77**	**76**	**327**	**5**	**33**	**3**	**0**
1900	**ChN-N**	**32**	**32**	**13**	**16**	**.448**	**121**	**3.82**	**285 ⅓**	**77**	**74**	**347**	**5**	**32**	**3**	**0**
1901	CWS-A	22	27	15	8	.652	58	2.42	215 ⅓	70	50	195	4	20	1	0
1902	CWS-A	31	35	16	14	.533	113	3.60	282 ⅓	75	89	287	8	29	2	0
1903	CWS-A	3	3	1	2	.333	14	4.50	28	12	5	40	0	3	0	0
Career average		22	24	12	9	.569	75	3.39	200 ⅓	56	55	219	4	21	1	0
Cubs average		**30**	**30**	**17**	**12**	**.579**	**95**	**3.29**	**261**	**70**	**69**	**291**	**5**	**29**	**2**	**0**
Career total		177	195	99	75	.569	603	3.39	1603	445	437	1748	33	169	11	2
Cubs total		**119**	**121**	**66**	**48**	**.579**	**381**	**3.29**	**1043 ⅔**	**279**	**276**	**1162**	**18**	**116**	**8**	**0**

Calmus, Richard Lee (Dick)
HEIGHT: 6'4"   RIGHTHANDER   BORN: 1/7/1944 LOS ANGELES, CALIFORNIA

YEAR	TEAM	STARTS	GAMES	WON	LOST	PCT	ER	ERA	INNINGS PITCHED	STRIKE-OUTS	WALKS	HITS ALLOWED	HRS ALLOWED	COMP. GAMES	SHUT-OUTS	SAVES
1963	LA-N	1	21	3	1	.750	13	2.66	44	25	16	32	3	0	0	0
1967	**ChC-N**	**1**	**1**	**0**	**0**	**—**	**4**	**8.31**	**4 ⅓**	**1**	**0**	**5**	**2**	**0**	**0**	**0**
Career average		1	11	2	1	.750	9	3.17	24 ⅓	13	8	19	3	0	0	0
Cubs average		**1**	**1**	**0**	**0**	**—**	**4**	**8.31**	**4 ⅓**	**1**	**0**	**5**	**2**	**0**	**0**	**0**
Career total		2	22	3	1	.750	17	3.17	48 ⅓	26	16	37	5	0	0	0
Cubs total		**1**	**1**	**0**	**0**	**—**	**4**	**8.31**	**4 ⅓**	**1**	**0**	**5**	**2**	**0**	**0**	**0**

Camp, Winfield Scott (Kid)
HEIGHT: 6'0"   RIGHTHANDER   BORN: 8/8/1869 NEW ALBANY, OHIO   DIED: 3/2/1895 OMAHA, NEBRASKA

YEAR	TEAM	STARTS	GAMES	WON	LOST	PCT	ER	ERA	INNINGS PITCHED	STRIKE-OUTS	WALKS	HITS ALLOWED	HRS ALLOWED	COMP. GAMES	SHUT-OUTS	SAVES
1892	Pit-N	1	4	0	2	.000	16	6.26	23	6	9	31	4	1	0	0
1894	**ChN-N**	**2**	**3**	**0**	**1**	**.000**	**16**	**6.55**	**22**	**6**	**12**	**34**	**0**	**2**	**0**	**0**
Career average		2	4	0	2	.000	16	6.40	22 ⅔	6	11	33	2	2	0	0
Cubs average		**2**	**3**	**0**	**1**	**.000**	**16**	**6.55**	**22**	**6**	**12**	**34**	**0**	**2**	**0**	**0**
Career total		3	7	0	3	.000	32	6.40	45	12	21	65	4	3	0	0
Cubs total		**2**	**3**	**0**	**1**	**.000**	**16**	**6.55**	**22**	**6**	**12**	**34**	**0**	**2**	**0**	**0**

Campbell, Michael Thomas (Mike)
HEIGHT: 6'3"   RIGHTHANDER   BORN: 2/17/1964 SEATTLE, WASHINGTON

YEAR	TEAM	STARTS	GAMES	WON	LOST	PCT	ER	ERA	INNINGS PITCHED	STRIKE-OUTS	WALKS	HITS ALLOWED	HRS ALLOWED	COMP. GAMES	SHUT-OUTS	SAVES
1987	Sea-A	9	9	1	4	.200	26	4.74	49 ⅓	35	25	41	9	1	0	0
1988	Sea-A	20	20	6	10	.375	75	5.89	114 ⅔	63	43	128	18	2	0	0
1989	Sea-A	5	5	1	2	.333	17	7.29	21	6	10	28	4	0	0	0
1992	Tex-A	0	1	0	1	.000	4	9.82	3 ⅔	2	2	3	1	0	0	0
1994	SD-N	2	3	1	1	.500	12	12.96	8 ⅓	10	5	13	5	0	0	0
1996	**ChC-N**	**5**	**13**	**3**	**1**	**.750**	**18**	**4.46**	**36 ⅓**	**19**	**10**	**29**	**7**	**0**	**0**	**0**
Career average		7	9	2	3	.387	25	5.86	39	23	16	40	7	1	0	0
Cubs average		**5**	**13**	**3**	**1**	**.750**	**18**	**4.46**	**36 ⅓**	**19**	**10**	**29**	**7**	**0**	**0**	**0**
Career total		41	51	12	19	.387	152	5.86	233 ⅓	135	95	242	44	3	0	0
Cubs total		**5**	**13**	**3**	**1**	**.750**	**18**	**4.46**	**36 ⅓**	**19**	**10**	**29**	**7**	**0**	**0**	**0**

Campbell, William Richard (Bill)
HEIGHT: 6'3"   RIGHTHANDER   BORN: 8/9/1948 HIGHLAND PARK, MICHIGAN

YEAR	TEAM	STARTS	GAMES	WON	LOST	PCT	ER	ERA	INNINGS PITCHED	STRIKE-OUTS	WALKS	HITS ALLOWED	HRS ALLOWED	COMP. GAMES	SHUT-OUTS	SAVES
1973	Min-A	2	28	3	3	.500	18	3.14	51 2/3	42	20	44	5	0	0	7
1974	Min-A	0	63	8	7	.533	35	2.62	120 1/3	89	55	109	4	0	0	19
1975	Min-A	7	47	4	6	.400	51	3.79	121	76	46	119	13	2	1	5
1976	Min-A	0	78	17	5	.773	56	3.01	167 2/3	115	62	145	9	0	0	20
1977	Bos-A	0	69	13	9	.591	46	2.96	140	114	60	112	13	0	0	31
1978	Bos-A	0	29	7	5	.583	22	3.91	50 2/3	47	17	62	3	0	0	4
1979	Bos-A	0	41	3	4	.429	26	4.28	54 2/3	25	23	55	5	0	0	9
1980	Bos-A	0	23	4	0	1.000	22	4.79	41 1/3	17	22	44	1	0	0	0
1981	Bos-A	0	30	1	1	.500	17	3.17	48 1/3	37	20	45	5	0	0	7
1982	**ChC-N**	**0**	**62**	**3**	**6**	**.333**	**41**	**3.69**	**100**	**71**	**40**	**89**	**6**	**0**	**0**	**8**
1983	**ChC-N**	**0**	**82**	**6**	**8**	**.429**	**61**	**4.49**	**122 1/3**	**97**	**49**	**128**	**4**	**0**	**0**	**8**
1984	Phi-N	0	57	6	5	.545	31	3.43	81 1/3	52	35	68	2	0	0	1
1985	StL-N	0	50	5	3	.625	25	3.50	64 1/3	41	21	55	5	0	0	4
1986	Det-A	0	34	3	6	.333	24	3.88	55 2/3	37	21	46	5	0	0	3
1987	Mon-N	0	7	0	0	—	9	8.10	10	4	4	18	2	0	0	0
Career average		1	47	6	5	.550	32	3.54	82	58	33	76	5	0	0	8
Cubs average		**0**	**72**	**5**	**7**	**.391**	**51**	**4.13**	**111 1/3**	**84**	**45**	**109**	**5**	**0**	**0**	**8**
Career total		9	700	83	68	.550	484	3.54	1229 1/3	864	495	1139	82	2	1	126
Cubs total		**0**	**144**	**9**	**14**	**.391**	**102**	**4.13**	**222 1/3**	**168**	**89**	**217**	**10**	**0**	**0**	**16**

Capel, Michael Lee (Mike)
HEIGHT: 6'2"   RIGHTHANDER   BORN: 10/13/1961 MARSHALL, TEXAS

YEAR	TEAM	STARTS	GAMES	WON	LOST	PCT	ER	ERA	INNINGS PITCHED	STRIKE-OUTS	WALKS	HITS ALLOWED	HRS ALLOWED	COMP. GAMES	SHUT-OUTS	SAVES
1988	**ChC-N**	**0**	**22**	**2**	**1**	**.667**	**16**	**4.91**	**29 1/3**	**19**	**13**	**34**	**5**	**0**	**0**	**0**
1990	Mil-A	0	2	0	0	—	5	135.00	0 1/3	1	1	6	0	0	0	0
1991	Hou-N	0	25	1	3	.250	11	3.03	32 2/3	23	15	33	3	0	0	3
Career average		0	16	1	1	.429	11	4.62	20 2/3	14	10	24	3	0	0	1
Cubs average		**0**	**22**	**2**	**1**	**.667**	**16**	**4.91**	**29 1/3**	**19**	**13**	**34**	**5**	**0**	**0**	**0**
Career total		0	49	3	4	.429	32	4.62	62 1/3	43	29	73	8	0	0	3
Cubs total		**0**	**22**	**2**	**1**	**.667**	**16**	**4.91**	**29 1/3**	**19**	**13**	**34**	**5**	**0**	**0**	**0**

Capilla, Douglas Edmund (Doug)
HEIGHT: 5'11"   LEFTHANDER   BORN: 1/7/1952 HONOLULU, HAWAII

YEAR	TEAM	STARTS	GAMES	WON	LOST	PCT	ER	ERA	INNINGS PITCHED	STRIKE-OUTS	WALKS	HITS ALLOWED	HRS ALLOWED	COMP. GAMES	SHUT-OUTS	SAVES
1976	StL-N	0	7	1	0	1.000	5	5.40	8 1/3	5	4	8	0	0	0	0
1977	StL-N	0	2	0	0	—	4	15.43	2 1/3	1	2	2	0	0	0	0
1977	Cin-N	16	22	7	8	.467	50	4.23	106 1/3	74	59	94	10	1	0	0
1978	Cin-N	3	6	0	1	.000	12	9.82	11	9	11	14	1	0	0	0
1979	Cin-N	0	5	1	0	1.000	6	8.53	6 1/3	0	5	7	1	0	0	0
1979	**ChC-N**	**1**	**13**	**0**	**1**	**.000**	**5**	**2.60**	**17 1/3**	**10**	**7**	**14**	**1**	**0**	**0**	**0**
1980	**ChC-N**	**11**	**39**	**2**	**8**	**.200**	**41**	**4.12**	**89 2/3**	**51**	**51**	**82**	**7**	**0**	**0**	**0**
1981	**ChC-N**	**0**	**42**	**1**	**0**	**1.000**	**18**	**3.18**	**51**	**28**	**34**	**52**	**1**	**0**	**0**	**0**
Career average		5	23	2	3	.400	24	4.34	48 2/3	30	29	46	4	0	0	0
Cubs average		**4**	**31**	**1**	**3**	**.250**	**21**	**3.65**	**52 2/3**	**30**	**31**	**49**	**3**	**0**	**0**	**0**
Career total		31	136	12	18	.400	141	4.34	292 1/3	178	173	273	21	1	0	0
Cubs total		**12**	**94**	**3**	**9**	**.250**	**64**	**3.65**	**158**	**89**	**92**	**148**	**9**	**0**	**0**	**0**

Cardwell, Donald Eugene (Don)
HEIGHT: 6'4"   RIGHTHANDER   BORN: 12/7/1935 WINSTON-SALEM, NORTH CAROLINA

YEAR	TEAM	STARTS	GAMES	WON	LOST	PCT	ER	ERA	INNINGS PITCHED	STRIKE-OUTS	WALKS	HITS ALLOWED	HRS ALLOWED	COMP. GAMES	SHUT-OUTS	SAVES
1957	Phi-N	19	30	4	8	.333	70	4.91	128 1/3	92	42	122	17	5	1	1
1958	Phi-N	14	16	3	6	.333	54	4.51	107 2/3	77	37	99	16	3	0	0
1959	Phi-N	22	25	9	10	.474	69	4.06	153	106	65	135	22	5	1	0

(continued)

(continued)

YEAR	TEAM	STARTS	GAMES	WON	LOST	PCT	ER	ERA	INNINGS PITCHED	STRIKE-OUTS	WALKS	HITS ALLOWED	HRS ALLOWED	COMP. GAMES	SHUT-OUTS	SAVES
1960	Phi-N	4	5	1	2	.333	14	4.45	28 1/3	21	11	28	4	0	0	0
1960	**ChC-N**	**26**	**31**	**8**	**14**	**.364**	**86**	**4.37**	**177**	**129**	**68**	**166**	**19**	**6**	**1**	**0**
1961	**ChC-N**	**38**	**39**	**15**	**14**	**.517**	**110**	**3.82**	**259 1/3**	**156**	**88**	**243**	**22**	**13**	**3**	**0**
1962	**ChC-N**	**29**	**41**	**7**	**16**	**.304**	**107**	**4.92**	**195 2/3**	**104**	**60**	**205**	**27**	**6**	**1**	**4**
1963	Pit-N	32	33	13	15	.464	73	3.07	213 2/3	112	52	195	21	7	2	0
1964	Pit-N	4	4	1	2	.333	6	2.79	19 1/3	10	7	15	1	1	1	0
1965	Pit-N	34	37	13	10	.565	85	3.18	240 1/3	107	59	214	21	12	2	0
1966	Pit-N	14	32	6	6	.500	52	4.60	101 2/3	60	27	112	15	1	0	1
1967	NYM-N	16	26	5	9	.357	47	3.57	118 1/3	71	39	112	8	3	3	0
1968	NYM-N	25	29	7	13	.350	59	2.96	179 2/3	82	50	156	9	5	1	1
1969	NYM-N	21	30	8	10	.444	51	3.01	152 1/3	60	47	145	15	4	0	0
1970	NYM-N	1	16	0	2	.000	18	6.48	25	8	6	31	3	0	0	0
1970	Atl-N	2	16	2	1	.667	23	9.00	23	16	13	31	5	1	1	0
Career average		22	29	7	10	.425	66	3.92	87	87	48	144	16	5	1	1
Cubs average		**31**	**37**	**10**	**15**	**.405**	**101**	**4.31**	**210 2/3**	**130**	**72**	**205**	**23**	**8**	**2**	**1**
Career total		301	410	102	138	.425	924	3.92	2122 2/3	1211	671	2009	225	72	17	7
Cubs total		**93**	**111**	**30**	**44**	**.405**	**303**	**4.31**	**632**	**389**	**216**	**614**	**68**	**25**	**5**	**4**

Carleton, James Otto (Tex)

HEIGHT: 6'1" RIGHTHANDER BORN: 8/19/1906 COMANCHE, TEXAS DIED: 1/11/1977 FORT WORTH, TEXAS

YEAR	TEAM	STARTS	GAMES	WON	LOST	PCT	ER	ERA	INNINGS PITCHED	STRIKE-OUTS	WALKS	HITS ALLOWED	HRS ALLOWED	COMP. GAMES	SHUT-OUTS	SAVES
1932	StL-N	22	44	10	13	.435	89	4.08	196 1/3	113	70	198	12	9	3	0
1933	StL-N	33	44	17	11	.607	104	3.38	277	147	97	263	15	15	4	3
1934	StL-N	31	40	16	11	.593	114	4.26	240 2/3	103	52	260	14	16	0	2
1935	**ChC-N**	**22**	**31**	**11**	**8**	**.579**	**74**	**3.89**	**171**	**84**	**60**	**169**	**17**	**8**	**0**	**1**
1936	**ChC-N**	**26**	**35**	**14**	**10**	**.583**	**80**	**3.65**	**197 1/3**	**88**	**67**	**204**	**14**	**12**	**4**	**1**
1937	**ChC-N**	**27**	**32**	**16**	**8**	**.667**	**73**	**3.15**	**208 1/3**	**105**	**94**	**183**	**10**	**18**	**4**	**0**
1938	**ChC-N**	**24**	**33**	**10**	**9**	**.526**	**101**	**5.42**	**167 2/3**	**80**	**74**	**213**	**11**	**9**	**0**	**0**
1940	Bro-N	17	34	6	6	.500	63	3.81	149	88	47	140	12	4	1	2
Career average		25	37	13	10	.568	87	3.91	201	101	70	204	13	11	2	1
Cubs average		**25**	**33**	**13**	**9**	**.593**	**82**	**3.97**	**186**	**89**	**74**	**192**	**13**	**11**	**2**	**1**
Career total		202	293	100	76	.568	698	3.91	1607 1/3	808	561	1630	105	91	16	9
Cubs total		**99**	**131**	**51**	**35**	**.593**	**328**	**3.97**	**744 1/3**	**357**	**295**	**769**	**52**	**47**	**8**	**2**

Carlsen, Donald Herbert (Don)

HEIGHT: 6'1" RIGHTHANDER BORN: 10/15/1926 CHICAGO, ILLINOIS

YEAR	TEAM	STARTS	GAMES	WON	LOST	PCT	ER	ERA	INNINGS PITCHED	STRIKE-OUTS	WALKS	HITS ALLOWED	HRS ALLOWED	COMP. GAMES	SHUT-OUTS	SAVES
1948	**ChC-N**	**0**	**1**	**0**	**0**	**—**	**4**	**36.00**	**1**	**1**	**2**	**5**	**0**	**0**	**0**	**0**
1951	Pit-N	6	7	2	3	.400	20	4.19	43	20	14	50	4	2	0	0
1952	Pit-N	1	5	0	1	.000	12	10.80	10	2	5	20	1	0	0	0
Career average		2	4	1	1	.333	12	6.00	18	8	7	25	2	1	0	0
Cubs average		**0**	**1**	**0**	**0**	**—**	**4**	**36.00**	**1**	**1**	**2**	**5**	**0**	**0**	**0**	**0**
Career total		7	13	2	4	.333	36	6.00	54	23	21	75	5	2	0	0
Cubs total		**0**	**1**	**0**	**0**	**—**	**4**	**36.00**	**1**	**1**	**2**	**5**	**0**	**0**	**0**	**0**

Carlson, Harold Gust (Hal)

HEIGHT: 6'0" RIGHTHANDER BORN: 5/17/1892 ROCKFORD, ILLINOIS DIED: 5/28/1930 CHICAGO, ILLINOIS

YEAR	TEAM	STARTS	GAMES	WON	LOST	PCT	ER	ERA	INNINGS PITCHED	STRIKE-OUTS	WALKS	HITS ALLOWED	HRS ALLOWED	COMP. GAMES	SHUT-OUTS	SAVES
1917	Pit-N	17	34	7	11	.389	52	2.90	161 1/3	68	49	140	0	9	1	1
1918	Pit-N	2	3	0	1	.000	5	3.75	12	5	5	12	1	0	0	0
1919	Pit-N	14	22	8	10	.444	35	2.23	141	49	39	114	0	7	1	0
1920	Pit-N	31	39	14	13	.519	92	3.36	246 2/3	62	63	262	5	16	3	3
1921	Pit-N	10	31	4	8	.333	52	4.27	109 2/3	37	23	121	6	3	0	4
1922	Pit-N	18	39	9	12	.429	92	5.70	145 1/3	64	58	193	10	6	0	2
1923	Pit-N	0	4	0	0	—	7	4.73	13 1/3	4	2	19	2	0	0	2
1924	Phi-N	24	38	8	17	.320	110	4.86	203 2/3	66	55	267	9	12	1	0
1925	Phi-N	32	35	13	14	.481	110	4.23	234	80	52	281	19	18	4	0

(continued)

(Carlson, continued)		STARTS	GAMES	WON	LOST	PCT	ER	ERA	INNINGS PITCHED	STRIKEOUTS	WALKS	HITS ALLOWED	HRS ALLOWED	COMP. GAMES	SHUTOUTS	SAVES
1926	Phi-N	34	35	17	12	.586	96	3.23	267⅓	55	47	293	9	20	3	0
1927	Phi-N	9	11	4	5	.444	37	5.23	63⅔	13	18	80	7	4	0	1
1927	ChC-N	22	27	12	8	.600	65	3.17	184⅓	27	27	201	9	15	2	0
1928	ChC-N	4	20	3	2	.600	37	5.91	56⅓	11	15	74	4	2	0	4
1929	ChC-N	13	31	11	5	.688	64	5.16	111⅔	35	31	131	8	6	2	2
1930	ChC-N	6	8	4	2	.667	29	5.05	51⅔	14	14	68	5	3	0	0
Career average		17	27	8	9	.487	63	3.97	143	42	36	161	7	9	1	1
Cubs average		11	22	8	4	.638	49	4.34	101	22	22	119	7	7	1	2
Career total		236	377	114	120	.487	883	3.97	2002	590	498	2256	94	121	17	19
Cubs total		45	86	30	17	.638	195	4.34	404	87	87	474	26	26	4	6

Carpenter, Robert Louis (Bob)
HEIGHT: 6'3"   RIGHTHANDER   BORN: 12/12/1917 CHICAGO, ILLINOIS

YEAR	TEAM	STARTS	GAMES	WON	LOST	PCT	ER	ERA	INNINGS PITCHED	STRIKEOUTS	WALKS	HITS ALLOWED	HRS ALLOWED	COMP. GAMES	SHUTOUTS	SAVES
1940	NYG-N	3	5	2	0	1.000	10	2.73	33	25	14	29	2	2	0	0
1941	NYG-N	19	29	11	6	.647	56	3.83	131⅔	42	42	138	15	8	1	2
1942	NYG-N	25	28	11	10	.524	65	3.15	185⅔	53	51	192	13	12	2	0
1946	NYG-N	6	12	1	3	.250	21	4.85	39	13	18	37	7	1	0	0
1947	NYG-N	0	2	0	0	—	4	12.00	3	0	3	5	0	0	0	0
1947	ChC-N	1	4	0	1	.000	4	4.91	7⅓	1	4	10	1	0	0	0
Career average		11	16	5	4	.556	32	3.60	80	27	26	82	8	5	1	0
Cubs average		1	4	0	1	.000	4	4.91	7⅓	1	4	10	1	0	0	0
Career total		54	80	25	20	.556	160	3.60	399⅔	134	132	411	38	23	4	2
Cubs total		1	4	0	1	.000	4	4.91	7⅓	1	4	10	1	0	0	0

Carson, Albert James (Al *or* Soldier)
HEIGHT: —   RIGHTHANDER   BORN: 8/22/1882 CHICAGO, ILLINOIS   DIED: 11/26/1962 SAN DIEGO, CALIFORNIA

YEAR	TEAM	STARTS	GAMES	WON	LOST	PCT	ER	ERA	INNINGS PITCHED	STRIKEOUTS	WALKS	HITS ALLOWED	HRS ALLOWED	COMP. GAMES	SHUTOUTS	SAVES
1910	ChC-N	0	2	0	0	—	3	4.05	6⅔	2	1	6	0	0	0	0
Career average		0	2	0	0	—	3	4.05	6⅔	2	1	6	0	0	0	0
Cubs average		0	2	0	0	—	3	4.05	6⅔	2	1	6	0	0	0	0
Career total		0	2	0	0	—	3	4.05	6⅔	2	1	6	0	0	0	0
Cubs total		0	2	0	0	—	3	4.05	6⅔	2	1	6	0	0	0	0

Carter, Paul Warren (Nick)
HEIGHT: 6'3"   RIGHTHANDER   BORN: 5/1/1894 LAKE PARK, GEORGIA   DIED: 9/11/1984 LAKE PARK, GEORGIA

YEAR	TEAM	STARTS	GAMES	WON	LOST	PCT	ER	ERA	INNINGS PITCHED	STRIKEOUTS	WALKS	HITS ALLOWED	HRS ALLOWED	COMP. GAMES	SHUTOUTS	SAVES
1914	Cle-A	4	5	1	3	.250	8	2.92	24⅔	9	5	35	0	1	0	0
1915	Cle-A	2	11	1	1	.500	15	3.21	42	14	18	44	1	2	0	0
1916	ChC-N	5	8	2	2	.500	11	2.75	36	14	17	26	1	2	0	2
1917	ChC-N	13	23	5	8	.385	41	3.26	113⅓	34	19	115	2	6	0	2
1918	ChC-N	4	21	3	2	.600	22	2.71	73	13	19	78	2	1	0	2
1919	ChC-N	7	28	5	4	.556	25	2.65	85	17	28	81	1	2	0	1
1920	ChC-N	8	31	3	6	.333	55	4.67	106	14	36	131	3	2	0	2
Career average		6	18	3	4	.435	25	3.32	68⅔	16	20	73	1	2	0	1
Cubs average		7	22	4	4	.450	31	3.35	82⅔	18	24	86	2	3	0	1
Career total		43	127	20	26	.435	177	3.32	480	115	142	510	10	16	0	7
Cubs total		37	111	18	22	.450	154	3.35	413⅓	92	119	431	9	13	0	7

Casey, Hugh Thomas
HEIGHT: 6'1" RIGHTHANDER BORN: 10/14/1913 ATLANTA, GEORGIA   DIED: 7/3/1951 ATLANTA, GEORGIA

YEAR	TEAM	STARTS	GAMES	WON	LOST	PCT	ER	ERA	INNINGS PITCHED	STRIKE-OUTS	WALKS	HITS ALLOWED	HRS ALLOWED	COMP. GAMES	SHUT-OUTS	SAVES
1935	ChC-N	0	13	0	0	—	11	3.86	25 2/3	10	14	29	2	0	0	0
1939	Bro-N	25	40	15	10	.600	74	2.93	227 1/3	79	54	228	13	15	0	1
1940	Bro-N	10	44	11	8	.579	62	3.62	154	53	51	136	13	5	2	2
1941	Bro-N	18	45	14	11	.560	70	3.89	162	61	57	155	8	4	1	7
1942	Bro-N	2	50	6	3	.667	28	2.25	112	54	44	91	3	0	0	13
1946	Bro-N	1	46	11	5	.688	22	1.99	99 2/3	31	33	101	2	0	0	5
1947	Bro-N	0	46	10	4	.714	34	3.99	76 2/3	40	29	75	7	0	0	18
1948	Bro-N	0	22	3	0	1.000	32	8.00	36	7	17	59	6	0	0	4
1949	Pit-N	0	33	4	1	.800	20	4.66	38 2/3	9	14	50	4	0	0	5
1949	NYY-A	0	4	1	0	1.000	7	8.22	7 2/3	5	8	11	0	0	0	0
Career average		6	38	8	5	.641	40	3.45	104 1/3	39	36	104	6	3	0	6
Cubs average		0	13	0	0	—	11	3.86	25 2/3	10	14	29	2	0	0	0
Career total		56	343	75	42	.641	360	3.45	939 2/3	349	321	935	58	24	3	55
Cubs total		0	13	0	0	—	11	3.86	25 2/3	10	14	29	2	0	0	0

Casian, Lawrence Paul (Larry)
HEIGHT: 6'0" LEFTHANDER BORN: 10/28/1965 LYNWOOD, CALIFORNIA

YEAR	TEAM	STARTS	GAMES	WON	LOST	PCT	ER	ERA	INNINGS PITCHED	STRIKE-OUTS	WALKS	HITS ALLOWED	HRS ALLOWED	COMP. GAMES	SHUT-OUTS	SAVES
1990	Min-A	3	5	2	1	.667	8	3.22	22 1/3	11	4	26	2	0	0	0
1991	Min-A	0	15	0	0		15	7.36	18 1/3	6	7	28	4	0	0	0
1992	Min-A	0	6	1	0	1.000	2	2.70	6 2/3	2	1	7	0	0	0	0
1993	Min-A	0	54	5	3	.625	19	3.02	56 2/3	31	14	59	1	0	0	1
1994	Min-A	0	33	1	3	.250	32	7.08	40 2/3	18	12	57	11	0	0	1
1994	Cle-A	0	7	0	2	.000	8	8.64	8 1/3	2	4	16	1	0	0	0
1995	ChC-N	0	42	1	0	1.000	5	1.93	23 1/3	11	15	23	1	0	0	0
1996	ChC-N	0	35	1	1	.500	5	1.88	24	15	11	14	2	0	0	0
1997	ChC-N	0	12	0	1	.000	8	7.45	9 2/3	7	2	16	3	0	0	0
1997	KC-A	0	32	0	2	.000	15	5.06	26 2/3	16	6	32	5	0	0	0
1998	CWS-A	0	4	0	0	—	5	11.25	4	6	1	8	0	0	0	0
Career average		0	27	1	1	.458	14	4.56	26 2/3	14	9	32	3	0	0	0
Cubs average		0	30	1	1	.500	6	2.84	19	11	9	18	2	0	0	0
Career total		3	245	11	13	.458	122	4.56	240 2/3	125	77	286	30	0	0	2
Cubs total		0	89	2	2	.500	18	2.84	57	33	28	53	6	0	0	0

Castillo, Frank Anthony
HEIGHT: 6'1" RIGHTHANDER BORN: 4/1/1969 EL PASO, TEXAS

YEAR	TEAM	STARTS	GAMES	WON	LOST	PCT	ER	ERA	INNINGS PITCHED	STRIKE-OUTS	WALKS	HITS ALLOWED	HRS ALLOWED	COMP. GAMES	SHUT-OUTS	SAVES
1991	ChC-N	18	18	6	7	.462	54	4.35	111 2/3	73	33	107	5	4	0	0
1992	ChC-N	33	33	10	11	.476	79	3.46	205 1/3	135	63	179	19	0	0	0
1993	ChC-N	25	29	5	8	.385	76	4.84	141 1/3	84	39	162	20	2	0	0
1994	ChC-N	4	4	2	1	.667	11	4.30	23	19	5	25	3	1	0	0
1995	ChC-N	29	29	11	10	.524	67	3.21	188	135	52	179	22	2	2	0
1996	ChC-N	33	33	7	16	.304	107	5.28	182 1/3	139	46	209	28	1	1	0
1997	ChC-N	19	20	6	9	.400	59	5.42	98	67	44	113	9	0	0	0
1997	Col-N	14	14	6	3	.667	52	5.42	86 1/3	59	25	107	16	0	0	0
1998	Det-A	19	27	3	9	.250	88	6.83	116	81	44	150	17	0	0	1
2000	Tor-A	24	25	10	5	.667	55	3.59	138	104	56	112	18	0	0	0
2001	Bos-A	26	26	10	9	.526	64	4.21	136 2/3	89	35	138	14	0	0	0
Career average		24	26	8	9	.463	71	4.49	142 2/3	99	44	148	17	1	0	0
Cubs average		23	24	7	9	.431	65	4.29	135 2/3	93	40	139	15	1	0	0
Career total		244	258	76	88	.463	712	4.49	1426 2/3	985	442	1481	171	10	3	1
Cubs total		161	166	47	62	.431	453	4.29	949 2/3	652	282	974	106	10	3	0

Caudill, William Holland (Bill *or* Cuffs *or* Inspector)
HEIGHT: 6'1"   RIGHTHANDER   BORN: 7/13/1956 SANTA MONICA, CALIFORNIA

YEAR	TEAM	STARTS	GAMES	WON	LOST	PCT	ER	ERA	INNINGS PITCHED	STRIKE-OUTS	WALKS	HITS ALLOWED	HRS ALLOWED	COMP. GAMES	SHUT-OUTS	SAVES
1979	ChC-N	12	29	1	7	.125	48	4.80	90	104	41	89	16	0	0	0
1980	ChC-N	2	72	4	6	.400	31	2.19	127 2/3	112	59	100	10	0	0	1
1981	ChC-N	10	30	1	5	.167	46	5.83	71	111	31	87	9	0	0	0
1982	Sea-A	0	70	12	9	.571	25	2.35	95 2/3	111	35	65	9	0	0	26
1983	Sea-A	0	63	2	8	.200	38	4.71	72 2/3	73	38	70	10	0	0	26
1984	Oak-A	0	68	9	7	.563	29	2.71	96 1/3	89	31	77	9	0	0	36
1985	Tor-A	0	67	4	6	.400	23	2.99	69 1/3	46	35	53	9	0	0	14
1986	Tor-A	0	40	2	4	.333	25	6.19	36 1/3	32	17	36	6	0	0	2
1987	Oak-A	0	6	0	0	—	8	9.00	8	8	1	10	3	0	0	1
Career average		3	49	4	6	.402	30	3.68	74	69	32	65	9	0	0	12
Cubs average		**8**	**44**	**2**	**6**	**.250**	**42**	**3.90**	**96 1/3**	**87**	**44**	**92**	**12**	**0**	**0**	**0**
Career total		24	445	35	52	.402	273	3.68	667	620	288	587	81	0	0	106
Cubs total		**24**	**131**	**6**	**18**	**.250**	**125**	**3.90**	**288 2/3**	**261**	**131**	**276**	**35**	**0**	**0**	**1**

Ceccarelli, Arthur Edward (Art *or* Chic)
HEIGHT: 6'0"   LEFTHANDER   BORN: 4/2/1930 NEW HAVEN, CONNECTICUT

YEAR	TEAM	STARTS	GAMES	WON	LOST	PCT	ER	ERA	INNINGS PITCHED	STRIKE-OUTS	WALKS	HITS ALLOWED	HRS ALLOWED	COMP. GAMES	SHUT-OUTS	SAVES
1955	KCA-A	16	31	4	7	.364	73	5.31	123 2/3	68	71	123	20	3	1	0
1956	KCA-A	2	3	0	1	.000	8	7.20	10	2	4	13	3	0	0	0
1957	Bal-A	8	20	0	5	.000	29	4.50	58	30	31	62	3	1	0	0
1959	ChC-N	15	18	5	5	.500	54	4.76	102	56	37	95	19	4	2	0
1960	ChC-N	1	7	0	0	—	8	5.54	13	10	4	16	1	0	0	0
Career average		8	16	2	4	.333	34	5.05	61 1/3	33	29	62	9	2	1	0
Cubs average		**8**	**13**	**3**	**3**	**.500**	**31**	**4.85**	**57 2/3**	**33**	**21**	**56**	**10**	**2**	**1**	**0**
Career total		42	79	9	18	.333	172	5.05	306 2/3	166	147	309	46	8	3	0
Cubs total		**16**	**25**	**5**	**5**	**.500**	**62**	**4.85**	**115**	**66**	**41**	**111**	**20**	**4**	**2**	**0**

Chambers, Clifford Day (Cliff *or* Lefty)
HEIGHT: 6'3"   LEFTHANDER   BORN: 1/10/1922 PORTLAND, OREGON

YEAR	TEAM	STARTS	GAMES	WON	LOST	PCT	ER	ERA	INNINGS PITCHED	STRIKE-OUTS	WALKS	HITS ALLOWED	HRS ALLOWED	COMP. GAMES	SHUT-OUTS	SAVES
1948	ChC-N	12	29	2	9	.182	51	4.43	103 2/3	51	48	100	4	3	1	0
1949	Pit-N	21	34	13	7	.650	78	3.96	177 1/3	93	58	186	15	10	1	0
1950	Pit-N	33	37	12	15	.444	119	4.30	249 1/3	93	92	262	18	11	2	0
1951	Pit-N	10	10	3	6	.333	37	5.58	59 2/3	19	31	64	5	2	1	0
1951	StL-N	16	21	11	6	.647	55	3.83	129 1/3	45	56	120	13	9	1	1
1952	StL-N	13	26	4	4	.500	45	4.12	98 1/3	47	33	110	8	2	1	0
1953	StL-N	8	32	3	6	.333	43	4.86	79 2/3	26	43	82	7	0	0	0
Career average		19	32	8	9	.475	71	4.29	149 2/3	62	60	154	12	6	1	0
Cubs average		**12**	**29**	**2**	**9**	**.182**	**51**	**4.43**	**103 2/3**	**51**	**48**	**100**	**4**	**3**	**1**	**0**
Career total		113	189	48	53	.475	428	4.29	897 1/3	374	361	924	70	37	7	1
Cubs total		**12**	**29**	**2**	**9**	**.182**	**51**	**4.43**	**103 2/3**	**51**	**48**	**100**	**4**	**3**	**1**	**0**

Cheeves, Virgil Earl (Chief)
HEIGHT: 6'0"   RIGHTHANDER   BORN: 2/12/1901 OKLAHOMA CITY, OKLAHOMA   DIED: 5/5/1979 DALLAS, TEXAS

YEAR	TEAM	STARTS	GAMES	WON	LOST	PCT	ER	ERA	INNINGS PITCHED	STRIKE-OUTS	WALKS	HITS ALLOWED	HRS ALLOWED	COMP. GAMES	SHUT-OUTS	SAVES
1920	ChC-N	2	5	0	0	—	7	3.50	18	3	7	16	0	0	0	0
1921	ChC-N	22	37	11	12	.478	84	4.64	163	39	47	192	8	9	1	0
1922	ChC-N	22	39	12	11	.522	83	4.09	182 2/3	40	76	195	9	9	1	2
1923	ChC-N	8	19	3	4	.429	49	6.18	71 1/3	13	37	89	8	0	0	0
1924	Cle-A	1	8	0	0	—	15	7.79	17 1/3	2	17	26	2	0	0	0
1927	NYG-N	0	3	0	0	—	3	4.26	6 1/3	1	4	8	1	0	0	0

(continued)

(continued)

	STARTS	GAMES	WON	LOST	PCT	ER	ERA	INNINGS PITCHED	STRIKE-OUTS	WALKS	HITS ALLOWED	HRS ALLOWED	COMP. GAMES	SHUT-OUTS	SAVES
Career average	9	19	4	5	.491	40	4.73	76 ⅓	16	31	88	5	3	0	0
Cubs average	**14**	**25**	**7**	**7**	**.491**	**56**	**4.61**	**108 ⅔**	**24**	**42**	**123**	**6**	**5**	**1**	**1**
Career total	55	111	26	27	.491	241	4.73	458 ⅔	98	188	526	28	18	2	2
Cubs total	**54**	**100**	**26**	**27**	**.491**	**223**	**4.61**	**435**	**95**	**167**	**492**	**25**	**18**	**2**	**2**

Cheney, Laurence Russell (Larry)

HEIGHT: 6'1"   RIGHTHANDER   BORN: 5/2/1886 BELLEVILLE, KANSAS   DIED: 1/6/1969 DAYTONA BEACH, FLORIDA

YEAR	TEAM	STARTS	GAMES	WON	LOST	PCT	ER	ERA	INNINGS PITCHED	STRIKE-OUTS	WALKS	HITS ALLOWED	HRS ALLOWED	COMP. GAMES	SHUT-OUTS	SAVES
1911	ChC-N	1	3	1	0	1.000	0	0.00	10	11	3	8	0	0	0	0
1912	ChC-N	37	42	26	10	.722	96	2.85	303 ⅓	140	111	262	5	28	4	0
1913	ChC-N	36	54	21	14	.600	87	2.57	305	136	98	271	7	25	2	11
1914	ChC-N	40	50	20	18	.526	88	2.54	311 ⅓	157	140	239	9	21	6	5
1915	ChC-N	18	25	8	9	.471	52	3.56	131 ⅓	68	55	120	1	6	2	0
1915	Bro-N	4	5	0	2	.000	5	1.67	27	11	17	16	0	1	0	0
1916	Bro-N	32	41	18	12	.600	54	1.92	253	166	105	178	5	15	5	0
1917	Bro-N	24	35	8	12	.400	55	2.35	210 ⅓	102	73	185	4	14	1	2
1918	Bro-N	21	32	11	13	.458	67	3.00	200 ⅔	83	74	177	2	15	0	1
1919	Bro-N	4	9	1	3	.250	18	4.15	39	14	14	45	1	2	0	0
1919	Bos-N	2	8	0	2	.000	13	3.55	33	13	15	35	0	0	0	0
1919	Phi-N	6	9	2	5	.286	29	4.55	57 ⅓	25	28	69	2	5	0	0
Career average	25	35	13	11	.537	63	2.70	209	103	81	178	4	15	2	2
Cubs average	**26**	**35**	**15**	**10**	**.598**	**65**	**2.74**	**212 ⅓**	**102**	**81**	**180**	**4**	**16**	**3**	**3**
Career total	225	313	116	100	.537	564	2.70	1881 ⅓	926	733	1605	36	132	20	19
Cubs total	**132**	**174**	**76**	**51**	**.598**	**323**	**2.74**	**1061**	**512**	**407**	**900**	**22**	**80**	**14**	**16**

Laurence (Larry) Russell Cheney, rhp, 1911–19

A fluke accident at the end of 1911 turned Larry Cheney into an effective pitcher for the Cubs over the next three years.

Cheney, born on May 2, 1886, in Belleville, Kansas, had been called up at the tail end of the 1911 season to pitch for Frank Chance's Cubs. But a line drive back to the box late in his first game against Brooklyn injured his pitching hand, forcing him to grip the ball differently the next spring.

It was a happy accident, as Cheney's new grip, which was something like a knuckleball grip, gave him better control, and he won 26 games and completed 28 for Chicago in 1912, both league highs.

The next two years, Cheney became the Cubs workhorse, leading the league in appearances both seasons, winning 21 and 20 games, respectively, and finishing first and second in the league in saves as well.

In addition to the knuckleball, Cheney had developed, in 1913, a very good spitball, which helped in his success against batters. But although he struck out 100 or more batters five times in his career, he also walked 100 or more three times in that span.

Bothered by nagging injuries in 1915, Cheney was traded by the Cubs late in the year to the Dodgers. Cheney's 18 wins in 1916 helped Brooklyn win the National League pennant. But Cheney's effectiveness waned after that year, and he never had a winning season after that. He retired in 1919 and died in 1969 in Daytona Beach, Florida.

Cheney still holds the Cubs rookie record for most wins with 26, most consecutive games won with 9 and most starts with 37. The 26 wins are the third most in one season since 1900 by a Cub. Cheney also holds the record for most wild pitches in a season with 26 in 1914.

Chiasson, Scott
HEIGHT: 6'3" RIGHTHANDER BORN: 8/14/1977 NORWICH, CONNECTICUT

YEAR	TEAM	STARTS	GAMES	WON	LOST	PCT	ER	ERA	INNINGS PITCHED	STRIKE-OUTS	WALKS	HITS ALLOWED	HRS ALLOWED	COMP. GAMES	SHUT-OUTS	SAVES
2001	ChC-N	0	6	1	1	.500	2	2.70	6 2/3	6	2	5	2	0	0	0
Career average		0	6	1	1	.500	2	2.70	6 2/3	6	2	5	2	0	0	0
Cubs average		**0**	**6**	**1**	**1**	**.500**	**2**	**2.70**	**6 2/3**	**6**	**2**	**5**	**2**	**0**	**0**	**0**
Career total		0	6	1	1	.500	2	2.70	6 2/3	6	2	5	2	0	0	0
Cubs total		**0**	**6**	**1**	**1**	**.500**	**2**	**2.70**	**6 2/3**	**6**	**2**	**5**	**2**	**0**	**0**	**0**

Chipman, Robert Howard (Bob *or* Mr. Chips)
HEIGHT: 6'2" LEFTHANDER BORN: 10/11/1918 BROOKLYN, NEW YORK DIED: 11/8/1973 HUNTINGTON, NEW YORK

YEAR	TEAM	STARTS	GAMES	WON	LOST	PCT	ER	ERA	INNINGS PITCHED	STRIKE-OUTS	WALKS	HITS ALLOWED	HRS ALLOWED	COMP. GAMES	SHUT-OUTS	SAVES
1941	Bro-N	0	1	1	0	1.000	0	0.00	5	3	1	3	0	0	0	0
1942	Bro-N	0	2	0	0	—	0	0.00	1 1/3	1	2	1	0	0	0	0
1943	Bro-N	0	1	0	0	—	0	0.00	1 2/3	0	2	2	0	0	0	0
1944	Bro-N	3	11	3	1	.750	17	4.21	36 1/3	20	24	38	1	1	0	2
1944	**ChC-N**	21	26	9	9	.500	50	3.49	129	41	40	147	9	8	1	0
1945	**ChC-N**	10	25	4	5	.444	28	3.50	72	29	34	63	4	3	1	2
1946	**ChC-N**	10	34	6	5	.545	38	3.13	109 1/3	42	54	103	8	5	3	2
1947	**ChC-N**	17	32	7	6	.538	55	3.68	134 2/3	51	66	135	6	5	1	0
1948	**ChC-N**	3	34	2	1	.667	24	3.58	60 1/3	16	24	73	5	0	0	4
1949	**ChC-N**	11	38	7	8	.467	50	3.97	113 1/3	46	63	110	7	3	1	1
1950	Bos-N	12	27	7	7	.500	61	4.43	124	40	37	127	10	4	0	4
1951	Bos-N	0	33	4	3	.571	28	4.85	52	17	19	59	5	0	0	0
1952	Bos-N	0	29	1	1	.500	13	2.81	41 2/3	16	20	28	5	0	0	1
Career average		7	24	4	4	.526	30	3.72	73 1/3	27	32	74	5	2	1	1
Cubs average		**12**	**32**	**6**	**6**	**.507**	**41**	**3.56**	**103**	**38**	**47**	**105**	**7**	**4**	**1**	**2**
Career total		87	293	51	46	.526	364	3.72	880 2/3	322	386	889	60	29	7	14
Cubs total		**72**	**189**	**35**	**34**	**.507**	**245**	**3.56**	**618 2/3**	**225**	**281**	**631**	**39**	**24**	**7**	**9**

Church, Emory Nicholas (Bubba)
HEIGHT: 6'0" RIGHTHANDER BORN: 9/12/1924 BIRMINGHAM, ALABAMA DIED: 9/17/2001 BIRMINGHAM, ALABAMA

YEAR	TEAM	STARTS	GAMES	WON	LOST	PCT	ER	ERA	INNINGS PITCHED	STRIKE-OUTS	WALKS	HITS ALLOWED	HRS ALLOWED	COMP. GAMES	SHUT-OUTS	SAVES
1950	Phi-N	18	31	8	6	.571	43	2.73	142	50	56	113	12	8	2	1
1951	Phi-N	33	38	15	11	.577	97	3.53	247	104	90	246	17	15	4	1
1952	Phi-N	1	2	0	0	—	6	10.80	5	3	1	11	0	0	0	0
1952	Cin-N	22	29	5	9	.357	74	4.34	153 1/3	47	48	173	21	5	1	0
1953	Cin-N	7	11	3	3	.500	29	5.98	43 2/3	12	19	55	9	2	0	0
1953	**ChC-N**	12	27	4	5	.444	58	5.00	104 1/3	47	49	115	16	1	0	1
1954	**ChC-N**	3	7	1	3	.250	16	9.82	14 2/3	8	13	21	8	1	0	0
1955	**ChC-N**	0	2	0	0	—	2	5.40	3 1/3	3	1	4	1	0	0	1
Career average		16	25	6	6	.493	54	4.10	119	46	46	123	14	5	1	1
Cubs average		**5**	**12**	**2**	**3**	**.385**	**25**	**5.59**	**40 2/3**	**19**	**21**	**47**	**8**	**1**	**0**	**1**
Career total		96	147	36	37	.493	325	4.10	713 1/3	274	277	738	84	32	7	4
Cubs total		**15**	**36**	**5**	**8**	**.385**	**76**	**5.59**	**122 1/3**	**58**	**63**	**140**	**25**	**2**	**0**	**2**

Church, Leonard (Len)
HEIGHT: 6'0" RIGHTHANDER BORN: 3/21/1942 CHICAGO, ILLINOIS DIED: 4/22/1988 RICHARDSON, TEXAS

YEAR	TEAM	STARTS	GAMES	WON	LOST	PCT	ER	ERA	INNINGS PITCHED	STRIKE-OUTS	WALKS	HITS ALLOWED	HRS ALLOWED	COMP. GAMES	SHUT-OUTS	SAVES
1966	ChC-N	0	4	0	1	.000	5	7.50	6	3	7	10	1	0	0	0
Career average		0	4	0	1	.000	5	7.50	6	3	7	10	1	0	0	0
Cubs average		**0**	**4**	**0**	**1**	**.000**	**5**	**7.50**	**6**	**3**	**7**	**10**	**1**	**0**	**0**	**0**
Career total		0	4	0	1	.000	5	7.50	6	3	7	10	1	0	0	0
Cubs total		**0**	**4**	**0**	**1**	**.000**	**5**	**7.50**	**6**	**3**	**7**	**10**	**1**	**0**	**0**	**0**

Clark, Mark Willard

HEIGHT: 6'5" RIGHTHANDER BORN: 5/12/1968 BATH, ILLINOIS

YEAR	TEAM	STARTS	GAMES	WON	LOST	PCT	ER	ERA	INNINGS PITCHED	STRIKE-OUTS	WALKS	HITS ALLOWED	HRS ALLOWED	COMP. GAMES	SHUT-OUTS	SAVES
1991	StL-N	2	7	1	1	.500	10	4.03	22⅓	13	11	17	3	0	0	0
1992	StL-N	20	20	3	10	.231	56	4.45	113⅓	44	36	117	12	1	0	0
1993	Cle-A	15	26	7	5	.583	52	4.28	109⅓	57	25	119	18	1	1	0
1994	Cle-A	20	20	11	3	.786	54	3.82	127⅓	60	40	133	14	4	1	0
1995	Cle-A	21	22	9	7	.563	73	5.27	124⅔	68	42	143	13	2	0	0
1996	NYM-N	32	32	14	11	.560	81	3.43	212⅓	142	48	217	20	2	0	0
1997	NYM-N	22	23	8	7	.533	67	4.25	142	72	47	158	18	1	0	0
1997	**ChC-N**	**9**	**9**	**6**	**1**	**.857**	**20**	**2.86**	**63**	**51**	**12**	**55**	**6**	**1**	**0**	**0**
1998	**ChC-N**	**33**	**33**	**9**	**14**	**.391**	**115**	**4.84**	**213⅔**	**161**	**48**	**236**	**23**	**2**	**0**	**0**
1999	Tex-A	15	15	3	7	.300	71	8.60	74⅓	44	34	103	17	0	1	0
2000	Tex-A	8	12	3	5	.375	39	7.98	44	16	24	66	10	0	0	0
Career average		20	22	7	7	.510	64	4.61	124⅔	73	37	136	15	2	0	0
Cubs average		**21**	**21**	**8**	**8**	**.500**	**68**	**4.39**	**138⅓**	**106**	**30**	**146**	**15**	**2**	**0**	**0**
Career total		197	219	74	71	.510	638	4.61	1246⅓	728	367	1364	154	15	3	0
Cubs total		**42**	**42**	**15**	**15**	**.500**	**135**	**4.39**	**276⅔**	**212**	**60**	**291**	**29**	**4**	**1**	**0**

Clarke, Henry Tefft

HEIGHT: — RIGHTHANDER BORN: 8/28/1875 BELLEVUE, NEBRASKA DIED: 3/28/1950 COLORADO SPRINGS, COLORADO

YEAR	TEAM	STARTS	GAMES	WON	LOST	PCT	ER	ERA	INNINGS PITCHED	STRIKE-OUTS	WALKS	HITS ALLOWED	HRS ALLOWED	COMP. GAMES	SHUT-OUTS	SAVES
1897	Cle-N	4	5	0	4	.000	20	5.87	30⅔	3	12	32	4	3	0	0
1898	**ChN-N**	**1**	**1**	**1**	**0**	**1.000**	**2**	**2.00**	**9**	**1**	**5**	**8**	**0**	**1**	**0**	**0**
Career average		3	3	1	2	.200	11	4.99	20	2	9	20	2	2	0	0
Cubs average		**1**	**1**	**1**	**0**	**1.000**	**2**	**2.00**	**9**	**1**	**5**	**8**	**0**	**1**	**0**	**0**
Career total		5	6	1	4	.200	22	4.99	39⅔	4	17	40	4	4	0	0
Cubs total		**1**	**1**	**1**	**0**	**1.000**	**2**	**2.00**	**9**	**1**	**5**	**8**	**0**	**1**	**0**	**0**

Clarke, William H. (Dad)

HEIGHT: 5'7" RIGHTHANDER BORN: 1/7/1865 OSWEGO, NEW YORK DIED: 6/3/1911 LORIAN, OHIO

YEAR	TEAM	STARTS	GAMES	WON	LOST	PCT	ER	ERA	INNINGS PITCHED	STRIKE-OUTS	WALKS	HITS ALLOWED	HRS ALLOWED	COMP. GAMES	SHUT-OUTS	SAVES
1888	**ChN-N**	**2**	**2**	**1**	**0**	**1.000**	**9**	**5.06**	**16**	**6**	**6**	**23**	**2**	**1**	**0**	**0**
1891	CoC-AA	3	4	1	2	.333	16	6.86	21	2	16	30	0	2	0	0
1894	NYG-N	6	15	3	3	.500	46	4.93	84	15	26	114	0	5	0	1
1895	NYG-N	30	37	17	15	.531	106	3.39	281⅔	67	60	336	3	28	1	2
1896	NYG-N	40	48	17	23	.425	166	4.26	351	66	60	431	9	33	1	1
1897	NYG-N	4	6	1	1	.500	21	6.10	31	10	11	43	1	2	0	0
1897	Lou-N	6	7	2	4	.333	24	3.95	54⅔	7	10	74	3	6	0	0
1898	Lou-N	1	1	0	1	.000	5	5.00	9	1	2	10	1	1	0	0
Career average		13	17	6	7	.462	56	4.17	121⅓	25	27	152	3	11	0	1
Cubs average		**2**	**2**	**1**	**0**	**1.000**	**9**	**5.06**	**16**	**6**	**6**	**23**	**2**	**1**	**0**	**0**
Career total		92	120	42	49	.462	393	4.17	848⅓	174	191	1061	24	78	2	4
Cubs total		**2**	**2**	**1**	**0**	**1.000**	**9**	**5.06**	**16**	**6**	**6**	**23**	**2**	**1**	**0**	**0**

Clarkson, John Gibson

HEIGHT: 5'10" RIGHTHANDER BORN: 7/1/1861 CAMBRIDGE, MASSACHUSETTS DIED: 2/4/1909 BELMONT, MASSACHUSETTS

YEAR	TEAM	STARTS	GAMES	WON	LOST	PCT	ER	ERA	INNINGS PITCHED	STRIKE-OUTS	WALKS	HITS ALLOWED	HRS ALLOWED	COMP. GAMES	SHUT-OUTS	SAVES
1882	Wor-N	3	3	1	2	.333	12	4.50	24	3	2	49	0	2	0	0
1884	**ChN-N**	**13**	**14**	**10**	**3**	**.769**	**28**	**2.14**	**118**	**102**	**25**	**94**	**0**	**2**	**0**	**0**
1885	**ChN-N**	**70**	**70**	**53**	**16**	**.768**	**128**	**1.85**	**623**	**308**	**97**	**497**	**10**	**12**	**0**	**0**
1886	**ChN-N**	**55**	**55**	**36**	**17**	**.679**	**125**	**2.41**	**466⅔**	**313**	**86**	**419**	**21**	**68**	**10**	**0**
1887	**ChN-N**	**59**	**60**	**38**	**21**	**.644**	**179**	**3.08**	**523**	**237**	**92**	**605**	**19**	**50**	**3**	**0**
1888	Bos-N	54	54	33	20	.623	148	2.76	483⅓	223	119	448	20	56	2	0
1889	Bos-N	72	73	49	19	.721	188	2.73	620	284	203	589	17	68	3	1

(continued)

John Gibson "Handsome" Clarkson, rhp, 1882–94

John Clarkson was the James "Catfish" Hunter of the 19th century: a cool, calculating pitcher who enjoyed pitching big games.

Clarkson was born on July 1, 1861, in Cambridge, Massachusetts. His father, Arthur "Dad" Clarkson, and younger brother Walter also pitched in the major leagues, but neither with the success of John.

At 21, he was already well known in the northeast minor leagues, and Chicago signed him to replace fading stars Larry Corcoran and Fred Goldsmith in 1884.

Clarkson obliged, dominating the league with a National League–best 53 wins, 68 complete games, 10 shutouts, 623 innings pitched and 308 strikeouts. The Chicago team won the National League pennant that year with 87 wins, meaning Clarkson won almost two-thirds of those contests.

That year, Charles "Old Hoss" Radbourn of the Providence team was billed as one of the top hurlers in the league. Clarkson asked for the ball every time Radbourn faced Chicago, and he ended up beating him 10 of 12 times, which included a no-hitter in Providence on July 27.

In 1886 manager Adrian "Cap" Anson rotated Clarkson more often with fellow pitcher Jim McCormick, and Clarkson's win total "dropped" to 36. But with McCormick winning 31 games, Chicago again won the National League championship.

Clarkson was not an overpowering thrower, but he had a wicked curveball. Teammates report he could make a cue ball spin up and back on a pool table. He also threw a hellacious change-up.

Clarkson studied hitters carefully and would record their strengths and weaknesses. He had a very slow, deliberate windup but delivered the ball explosively.

He was also something of a prima donna, by 19th-century baseball standards anyway.

Anson knew that if he scolded Clarkson too harshly, the pitcher would pout. Clarkson was also a stubborn man when it came to arguing with umpires.

Once, after an umpire had not heeded his (and Anson's) opinion that a game should be called due to darkness, Clarkson pocketed a lemon between innings, took the mound and threw the fruit instead of a ball to the first batter. When the umpire called a strike, Clarkson stepped off the mound and pointed out what he had done. The unnamed ump called the game.

Clarkson won a league-leading 38 games in 1887, easily making him the best pitcher in the league, but the Detroit Wolverines won the pennant by 3⅓ games over Philadelphia and 6½ over Chicago.

Clarkson believed he was not being paid enough money by Chicago, given his success on the mound. He demanded his $3,000 salary be doubled, and Chicago owner Albert Spalding refused. Instead, he sold Clarkson to Boston in 1888, in a blockbuster deal that stunned Chicago fans. This was just a year after Chicago had sent star Mike "King" Kelly to Beantown. Spalding and Anson believed both men could be replaced—particularly Clarkson, who, Anson opined, was losing his pitching touch.

That turned out to be a bad assessment. Clarkson won 33 games in 1888, and three years after that, the Boston Beaneaters were NL champions, with Clarkson leading the way.

Clarkson pitched one more year for Boston, before being traded to Cleveland in 1892. He wound up his career in Cleveland in 1894.

Following his career, Clarkson returned to Cambridge and opened a cigar store, which he ran until his death in 1909. In 1963 he was voted into the Hall of Fame.

Clarkson is still 10th all-time in wins in the major leagues with 328, and 8th all-time in complete games with 485 and 20th all-time in innings pitched with 4,536⅓. As a Chicago player, he is 10th in victories with 137, 8th in ERA with a mark of 2.39 and 10th in strikeouts with 960.

(Clarkson, continued)

YEAR	TEAM	STARTS	GAMES	WON	LOST	PCT	ER	ERA	INNINGS PITCHED	STRIKEOUTS	WALKS	HITS ALLOWED	HRS ALLOWED	COMP. GAMES	SHUTOUTS	SAVES
1890	Bos-N	44	44	26	18	.591	139	3.27	383	138	140	370	14	43	2	0
1891	Bos-N	51	55	34	18	.654	143	2.79	460⅔	141	154	435	18	47	3	2
1892	Bos-N	16	16	8	7	.533	38	2.35	145⅔	48	60	115	4	15	4	0
1892	Cle-N	28	29	17	10	.630	69	2.55	243⅓	91	72	235	4	27	1	1
1893	Cle-N	35	36	16	18	.471	146	4.45	295	62	95	358	11	31	0	1
1894	Cle-N	18	22	8	8	.500	74	4.42	150⅔	28	46	173	6	13	1	0
Career average		43	44	27	15	.650	118	2.81	378	165	99	366	13	40	3	0
Cubs average		**49**	**50**	**34**	**14**	**.706**	**115**	**2.39**	**432⅔**	**240**	**75**	**404**	**18**	**47**	**4**	**0**
Career total		518	531	329	177	.650	1417	2.81	4536⅓	1978	1191	4387	160	485	37	4
Cubs total		**197**	**199**	**137**	**57**	**.706**	**460**	**2.39**	**1730⅔**	**960**	**300**	**1615**	**70**	**186**	**15**	**0**

Clausen, Frederick William (Fritz)

HEIGHT: 5'11" LEFTHANDER BORN: 4/26/1869 NEW YORK, NEW YORK DIED: 2/11/1960 MEMPHIS, TENNESSEE

YEAR	TEAM	STARTS	GAMES	WON	LOST	PCT	ER	ERA	INNINGS PITCHED	STRIKEOUTS	WALKS	HITS ALLOWED	HRS ALLOWED	COMP. GAMES	SHUTOUTS	SAVES
1892	Lou-N	24	24	9	13	.409	68	3.06	200	94	87	181	3	24	2	0
1893	Lou-N	5	5	1	3	.250	22	6.00	33	4	22	41	2	3	0	0
1893	**ChN-N**	**9**	**10**	**6**	**2**	**.750**	**26**	**3.08**	**76**	**31**	**39**	**71**	**1**	**8**	**0**	**0**
1894	**ChN-N**	**2**	**2**	**0**	**1**	**.000**	**5**	**10.38**	**4⅓**	**1**	**3**	**5**	**0**	**0**	**0**	**1**
1896	Lou-N	2	2	0	2	.000	8	6.55	11	4	6	17	1	1	0	0
Career average		11	11	4	5	.432	32	3.58	81	34	39	79	2	9	1	0
Cubs average		**6**	**6**	**3**	**2**	**.667**	**16**	**3.47**	**40⅓**	**16**	**21**	**38**	**1**	**4**	**0**	**1**
Career total		42	43	16	21	.432	129	3.58	324⅓	134	157	315	7	36	2	1
Cubs total		**11**	**12**	**6**	**3**	**.667**	**31**	**3.47**	**80⅓**	**32**	**42**	**76**	**1**	**8**	**0**	**1**

Coakley, Andrew James (Andy)

HEIGHT: 6'0" RIGHTHANDER BORN: 11/20/1882 PROVIDENCE, RHODE ISLAND DIED: 9/27/1963 NEW YORK, NEW YORK

YEAR	TEAM	STARTS	GAMES	WON	LOST	PCT	ER	ERA	INNINGS PITCHED	STRIKEOUTS	WALKS	HITS ALLOWED	HRS ALLOWED	COMP. GAMES	SHUTOUTS	SAVES
1902	Phi-A	3	3	2	1	.667	8	2.67	27	9	9	25	0	3	0	0
1903	Phi-A	3	6	0	3	.000	23	5.50	37⅔	20	11	48	2	2	0	0
1904	Phi-A	8	8	4	3	.571	13	1.89	62	33	23	48	1	7	2	0
1905	Phi-A	31	35	18	8	.692	52	1.84	255	145	73	227	2	21	3	0
1906	Phi-A	16	22	7	8	.467	52	3.14	149	59	44	144	0	10	0	0
1907	Cin-N	30	37	17	16	.515	69	2.34	265⅓	89	79	269	1	21	1	1
1908	Cin-N	28	32	8	18	.308	50	1.86	242⅓	61	64	219	3	20	4	2
1908	**ChC-N**	**3**	**4**	**2**	**0**	**1.000**	**2**	**0.89**	**20⅓**	**7**	**6**	**14**	**0**	**2**	**1**	**0**
1909	**ChC-N**	**1**	**1**	**0**	**1**	**.000**	**4**	**18.00**	**2**	**1**	**3**	**7**	**0**	**0**	**0**	**0**
1911	NYA-A	1	2	0	1	.000	7	5.40	11⅔	4	2	20	0	1	0	0
Career average		14	17	6	7	.496	31	2.35	119	48	35	113	1	10	1	0
Cubs average		**2**	**3**	**1**	**1**	**.667**	**3**	**2.42**	**11⅓**	**4**	**5**	**11**	**0**	**1**	**1**	**0**
Career total		124	150	58	59	.496	280	2.35	1072⅓	428	314	1021	9	87	11	3
Cubs total		**4**	**5**	**2**	**1**	**.667**	**6**	**2.42**	**22⅓**	**8**	**9**	**21**	**0**	**2**	**1**	**0**

Coffman, Kevin Reese

HEIGHT: 6'3" RIGHTHANDER BORN: 1/19/1965 AUSTIN, TEXAS

YEAR	TEAM	STARTS	GAMES	WON	LOST	PCT	ER	ERA	INNINGS PITCHED	STRIKEOUTS	WALKS	HITS ALLOWED	HRS ALLOWED	COMP. GAMES	SHUTOUTS	SAVES
1987	Atl-N	5	5	2	3	.400	13	4.62	25⅓	14	22	31	2	0	0	0
1988	Atl-N	11	18	2	6	.250	43	5.78	67	24	54	62	3	0	0	0
1990	**ChC-N**	**2**	**8**	**0**	**2**	**.000**	**23**	**11.29**	**18⅓**	**9**	**19**	**26**	**0**	**0**	**0**	**0**
Career average		6	10	1	4	.267	26	6.42	37	16	32	40	2	0	0	0
Cubs average		**2**	**8**	**0**	**2**	**.000**	**23**	**11.29**	**18⅓**	**9**	**19**	**26**	**0**	**0**	**0**	**0**
Career total		18	31	4	11	.267	79	6.42	110⅔	47	95	119	5	0	0	0
Cubs total		**2**	**8**	**0**	**2**	**.000**	**23**	**11.29**	**18⅓**	**9**	**19**	**26**	**0**	**0**	**0**	**0**

Cogan, Richard Henry (Dick)

HEIGHT: 5'7"   RIGHTHANDER   BORN: 12/5/1871 PATERSON, NEW JERSEY   DIED: 5/2/1948 PATERSON, NEW JERSEY

YEAR	TEAM	STARTS	GAMES	WON	LOST	PCT	ER	ERA	INNINGS PITCHED	STRIKE-OUTS	WALKS	HITS ALLOWED	HRS ALLOWED	COMP. GAMES	SHUT-OUTS	SAVES
1897	Bal-N	0	1	0	0	—	3	13.50	2	0	2	4	0	0	0	0
1899	ChN-N	5	5	2	3	.400	21	4.30	44	9	24	54	1	5	0	0
1900	NYG-N	0	2	0	0	—	6	6.75	8	1	6	10	0	0	0	0
Career average		2	3	1	1	.400	10	5.00	18	3	11	23	0	2	0	0
Cubs average		5	5	2	3	.400	21	4.30	44	9	24	54	1	5	0	0
Career total		5	8	2	3	.400	30	5.00	54	10	32	68	1	5	0	0
Cubs total		5	5	2	3	.400	21	4.30	44	9	24	54	1	5	0	0

Cohen, Hyman (Hy)

HEIGHT: 6'5"   RIGHTHANDER   BORN: 1/29/1931 BROOKLYN, NEW YORK

YEAR	TEAM	STARTS	GAMES	WON	LOST	PCT	ER	ERA	INNINGS PITCHED	STRIKE-OUTS	WALKS	HITS ALLOWED	HRS ALLOWED	COMP. GAMES	SHUT-OUTS	SAVES
1955	ChC-N	1	7	0	0	—	15	7.94	17	4	10	28	2	0	0	0
Career average		1	7	0	0	—	15	7.94	17	4	10	28	2	0	0	0
Cubs average		1	7	0	0	—	15	7.94	17	4	10	28	2	0	0	0
Career total		1	7	0	0	—	15	7.94	17	4	10	28	2	0	0	0
Cubs total		1	7	0	0	—	15	7.94	17	4	10	28	2	0	0	0

Colborn, James William (Jim)

HEIGHT: 6'0"   RIGHTHANDER   BORN: 5/22/1946 SANTA PAULA, CALIFORNIA

YEAR	TEAM	STARTS	GAMES	WON	LOST	PCT	ER	ERA	INNINGS PITCHED	STRIKE-OUTS	WALKS	HITS ALLOWED	HRS ALLOWED	COMP. GAMES	SHUT-OUTS	SAVES
1969	ChC-N	2	6	1	0	1.000	5	3.07	14 2/3	4	9	15	2	0	0	0
1970	ChC-N	5	34	3	1	.750	29	3.59	72 2/3	50	23	88	3	0	0	4
1971	ChC-N	0	14	0	1	.000	8	6.97	10 1/3	2	3	18	1	0	0	0
1972	Mil-A	12	39	7	7	.500	51	3.11	147 2/3	97	43	135	14	4	1	1
1973	Mil-A	36	43	20	12	.625	111	3.18	314 1/3	135	87	297	21	22	4	1
1974	Mil-A	31	33	10	13	.435	101	4.06	224	83	60	230	27	10	1	2
1975	Mil-A	29	36	11	13	.458	98	4.27	206 1/3	79	65	215	18	7	0	0
1976	Mil-A	32	32	9	15	.375	93	3.71	225 2/3	101	54	232	20	7	0	0
1977	KC-A	35	36	18	14	.563	96	3.62	239	103	81	233	22	6	1	0
1978	KC-A	3	8	1	2	.333	15	4.76	28 1/3	8	12	31	4	0	0	0
1978	Sea-A	19	20	3	10	.231	68	5.35	114 1/3	26	38	125	21	3	0	0
Career average		20	30	8	9	.485	68	3.80	159 2/3	69	48	162	15	6	1	1
Cubs average		2	18	1	1	.667	14	3.87	32 2/3	19	12	40	2	0	0	1
Career total		204	301	83	88	.485	675	3.80	1597 1/3	688	475	1619	153	60	8	7
Cubs total		7	54	4	2	.667	42	3.87	97 2/3	56	35	121	6	0	0	4

Cole, David Bruce (Dave)

HEIGHT: 6'2"   RIGHTHANDER   BORN: 8/29/1930 WILLIAMSPORT, MARYLAND

YEAR	TEAM	STARTS	GAMES	WON	LOST	PCT	ER	ERA	INNINGS PITCHED	STRIKE-OUTS	WALKS	HITS ALLOWED	HRS ALLOWED	COMP. GAMES	SHUT-OUTS	SAVES
1950	Bos-N	0	4	0	1	.000	1	1.13	8	8	3	7	0	0	0	0
1951	Bos-N	7	23	2	4	.333	32	4.26	67 2/3	33	64	64	3	1	0	0
1952	Bos-N	3	22	1	1	.500	20	4.03	44 2/3	22	42	38	2	0	0	0
1953	Mil-N	0	10	0	1	.000	14	8.59	14 2/3	13	14	17	1	0	0	0
1954	ChC-N	14	18	3	8	.273	50	5.36	84	37	62	74	7	2	1	0
1955	Phi-N	3	7	0	3	.000	13	6.38	18 1/3	6	14	21	3	0	0	0
Career average		5	14	1	3	.250	22	4.93	39 2/3	20	33	37	3	1	0	0
Cubs average		14	18	3	8	.273	50	5.36	84	37	62	74	7	2	1	0
Career total		27	84	6	18	.250	130	4.93	237 1/3	119	199	221	16	3	1	0
Cubs total		14	18	3	8	.273	50	5.36	84	37	62	74	7	2	1	0

Cole, Leonard Leslie (King)

HEIGHT: 6'1"   RIGHTHANDER   BORN: 4/15/1886 TOLEDO, IOWA   DIED: 1/6/1916 BAY CITY, MICHIGAN

YEAR	TEAM	STARTS	GAMES	WON	LOST	PCT	ER	ERA	INNINGS PITCHED	STRIKE-OUTS	WALKS	HITS ALLOWED	HRS ALLOWED	COMP. GAMES	SHUT-OUTS	SAVES
1909	ChC-N	1	1	1	0	1.000	0	0.00	9	1	3	6	0	1	1	0
1910	ChC-N	29	33	20	4	.833	48	1.80	239 2/3	114	130	174	2	21	4	1
1911	ChC-N	27	32	18	7	.720	77	3.13	221 1/3	101	99	188	3	13	2	0
1912	ChC-N	3	8	1	2	.333	23	10.89	19	9	8	36	2	0	0	0
1912	Pit-N	4	12	2	2	.500	35	6.43	49	11	18	61	1	2	0	0
1914	NYY-A	15	33	11	9	.550	52	3.30	141 2/3	43	51	151	3	8	2	0
1915	NYY-A	6	10	3	3	.500	18	3.18	51	19	22	41	2	2	0	1
Career average		14	22	9	5	.675	42	3.12	121 2/3	50	55	110	2	8	2	0
Cubs average		**15**	**19**	**10**	**3**	**.755**	**37**	**2.72**	**122 1/3**	**56**	**60**	**101**	**2**	**9**	**2**	**0**
Career total		85	129	56	27	.675	253	3.12	730 2/3	298	331	657	13	47	9	2
Cubs total		**60**	**74**	**40**	**13**	**.755**	**148**	**2.72**	**489**	**225**	**240**	**404**	**7**	**35**	**7**	**1**

Coleman, Joseph Howard (Joe)

HEIGHT: 6'3"   RIGHTHANDER   BORN: 2/3/1947 BOSTON, MASSACHUSETTS

YEAR	TEAM	STARTS	GAMES	WON	LOST	PCT	ER	ERA	INNINGS PITCHED	STRIKE-OUTS	WALKS	HITS ALLOWED	HRS ALLOWED	COMP. GAMES	SHUT-OUTS	SAVES
1965	Was-A	2	2	2	0	1.000	3	1.50	18	7	8	9	0	2	0	0
1966	Was-A	1	1	1	0	1.000	2	2.00	9	4	2	6	0	1	0	0
1967	Was-A	22	28	8	9	.471	69	4.63	134	77	47	154	6	3	0	0
1968	Was-A	33	33	12	16	.429	81	3.27	223	139	51	212	19	12	2	0
1969	Was-A	36	40	12	13	.480	90	3.27	247 2/3	182	100	222	26	12	4	0
1970	Was-A	29	39	8	12	.400	87	3.58	218 2/3	152	89	190	25	6	1	1
1971	Det-A	38	39	20	9	.690	100	3.15	286	236	96	241	17	16	3	0
1972	Det-A	39	40	19	14	.576	87	2.80	280	222	110	216	23	9	3	0
1973	Det-A	40	40	23	15	.605	113	3.53	288 1/3	202	93	283	32	13	2	0
1974	Det-A	41	41	14	12	.538	137	4.32	285 2/3	177	158	272	30	11	2	0
1975	Det-A	31	31	10	18	.357	124	5.55	201	125	85	234	27	6	1	0
1976	Det-A	12	12	2	5	.286	36	4.86	66 2/3	38	34	80	1	1	0	0
1976	ChC-N	4	39	2	8	.200	36	4.10	79	66	35	72	9	0	0	4
1977	Oak-A	12	43	4	4	.500	42	2.96	127 2/3	55	49	114	11	2	0	2
1978	Oak-A	0	10	3	0	1.000	3	1.37	19 2/3	4	5	12	1	0	0	0
1978	Tor-A	0	31	2	0	1.000	31	4.60	60 2/3	28	30	67	6	0	0	0
1979	SF-N	0	5	0	0	—	0	0.00	3 2/3	0	2	3	0	0	0	0
1979	Pit-N	0	10	0	0	—	14	6.10	20 2/3	14	9	29	1	0	0	0
Career average		23	32	9	9	.513	70	3.70	171 1/3	115	67	161	16	6	1	0
Cubs average		**4**	**39**	**2**	**8**	**.200**	**36**	**4.10**	**79**	**66**	**35**	**72**	**9**	**0**	**0**	**4**
Career total		340	484	142	135	.513	1055	3.70	2569 1/3	1728	1003	2416	234	94	18	7
Cubs total		**4**	**39**	**2**	**8**	**.200**	**36**	**4.10**	**79**	**66**	**35**	**72**	**9**	**0**	**0**	**4**

Collins, Philip Eugene (Phil or Fidgety Phil)

HEIGHT: 5'11"   RIGHTHANDER   BORN: 8/27/1901 CHICAGO, ILLINOIS   DIED: 8/14/1948 CHICAGO, ILLINOIS

YEAR	TEAM	STARTS	GAMES	WON	LOST	PCT	ER	ERA	INNINGS PITCHED	STRIKE-OUTS	WALKS	HITS ALLOWED	HRS ALLOWED	COMP. GAMES	SHUT-OUTS	SAVES
1923	ChC-N	1	1	1	0	1.000	2	3.60	5	2	1	8	0	0	0	0
1929	Phi-N	11	43	9	7	.563	98	5.75	153 1/3	61	83	172	18	3	0	5
1930	Phi-N	25	47	16	11	.593	127	4.78	239	87	86	287	22	17	1	3
1931	Phi-N	27	42	12	16	.429	103	3.86	240 1/3	73	83	268	14	16	2	4
1932	Phi-N	21	43	14	12	.538	108	5.27	184 1/3	66	65	231	21	6	0	3
1933	Phi-N	13	42	8	13	.381	69	4.11	151	40	57	178	9	5	0	6
1934	Phi-N	32	45	13	18	.419	118	4.18	254	72	87	277	30	5	1	6
1935	Phi-N	3	3	0	2	.000	19	11.66	14 2/3	4	9	24	5	0	0	1
1935	StL-N	8	26	7	6	.538	42	4.57	82 2/3	18	26	96	6	2	0	2
Career average		18	37	10	11	.485	86	4.66	165 2/3	53	62	193	16	8	1	3
Cubs average		**1**	**1**	**1**	**0**	**1.000**	**2**	**3.60**	**5**	**2**	**1**	**8**	**0**	**0**	**0**	**0**
Career total		141	292	80	85	.485	686	4.66	1324 1/3	423	497	1541	125	64	4	24
Cubs total		**1**	**1**	**1**	**0**	**1.000**	**2**	**3.60**	**5**	**2**	**1**	**8**	**0**	**0**	**0**	**0**

Collum, Jack Dean (Jackie)
HEIGHT: 5'7"   LEFTHANDER   BORN: 6/21/1927 VICTOR, IOWA

YEAR	TEAM	STARTS	GAMES	WON	LOST	PCT	ER	ERA	INNINGS PITCHED	STRIKE-OUTS	WALKS	HITS ALLOWED	HRS ALLOWED	COMP. GAMES	SHUT-OUTS	SAVES
1951	StL-N	2	3	2	1	.667	3	1.59	17	5	10	11	0	1	1	0
1952	StL-N	0	2	0	0	—	0	0.00	3	0	1	2	0	0	0	0
1953	StL-N	0	7	0	0	—	8	6.35	11 1/3	5	4	15	1	0	0	0
1953	Cin-N	12	30	7	11	.389	52	3.75	124 2/3	51	39	123	8	4	1	3
1954	Cin-N	2	36	7	3	.700	33	3.76	79	28	32	86	8	1	0	0
1955	Cin-N	17	32	9	8	.529	54	3.63	134	49	37	128	17	5	0	1
1956	StL-N	1	38	6	2	.750	28	4.20	60	17	27	63	6	0	0	7
1957	**ChC-N**	**0**	**9**	**1**	**1**	**.500**	**8**	**6.75**	**10 2/3**	**7**	**9**	**8**	**0**	**0**	**0**	**1**
1957	Bro-N	0	3	0	0	—	4	8.31	4 1/3	3	1	7	1	0	0	0
1958	LA-A	0	2	0	0	—	3	8.10	3 1/3	0	2	4	2	0	0	0
1962	Min-A	3	8	0	2	.000	19	11.15	15 1/3	5	11	29	1	0	0	0
1962	Cle-A	0	1	0	0	—	2	13.50	1 1/3	1	0	4	0	0	0	0
Career average		4	19	4	3	.533	24	4.15	51 2/3	19	19	53	5	1	0	1
Cubs average		**0**	**9**	**1**	**1**	**.500**	**8**	**6.75**	**10 2/3**	**7**	**9**	**8**	**0**	**0**	**0**	**1**
Career total		37	171	32	28	.533	214	4.15	464	171	173	480	44	11	2	12
Cubs total		**0**	**9**	**1**	**1**	**.500**	**8**	**6.75**	**10 2/3**	**7**	**9**	**8**	**0**	**0**	**0**	**1**

Comellas, Jorge (Pancho)
HEIGHT: 6'0"   RIGHTHANDER   BORN: 12/7/1916 HAVANA, CUBA

YEAR	TEAM	STARTS	GAMES	WON	LOST	PCT	ER	ERA	INNINGS PITCHED	STRIKE-OUTS	WALKS	HITS ALLOWED	HRS ALLOWED	COMP. GAMES	SHUT-OUTS	SAVES
1945	**ChC-N**	**1**	**7**	**0**	**2**	**.000**	**6**	**4.50**	**12**	**6**	**6**	**11**	**1**	**0**	**0**	**0**
Career average		1	7	0	2	.000	6	4.50	12	6	6	11	1	0	0	0
Cubs average		**1**	**7**	**0**	**2**	**.000**	**6**	**4.50**	**12**	**6**	**6**	**11**	**1**	**0**	**0**	**0**
Career total		1	7	0	2	.000	6	4.50	12	6	6	11	1	0	0	0
Cubs total		**1**	**7**	**0**	**2**	**.000**	**6**	**4.50**	**12**	**6**	**6**	**11**	**1**	**0**	**0**	**0**

Compton, Robert Clinton (Clint)
HEIGHT: 5'11"   LEFTHANDER   BORN: 11/1/1950 MONTGOMERY, ALABAMA

YEAR	TEAM	STARTS	GAMES	WON	LOST	PCT	ER	ERA	INNINGS PITCHED	STRIKE-OUTS	WALKS	HITS ALLOWED	HRS ALLOWED	COMP. GAMES	SHUT-OUTS	SAVES
1972	**ChC-N**	**0**	**1**	**0**	**0**	**—**	**2**	**9.00**	**2**	**0**	**2**	**2**	**0**	**0**	**0**	**0**
Career average		0	1	0	0	—	2	9.00	2	0	2	2	0	0	0	0
Cubs average		**0**	**1**	**0**	**0**	**—**	**2**	**9.00**	**2**	**0**	**2**	**2**	**0**	**0**	**0**	**0**
Career total		0	1	0	0	—	2	9.00	2	0	2	2	0	0	0	0
Cubs total		**0**	**1**	**0**	**0**	**—**	**2**	**9.00**	**2**	**0**	**2**	**2**	**0**	**0**	**0**	**0**

Connors, William Joseph (Billy)
HEIGHT: 6'1"   RIGHTHANDER   BORN: 11/2/1941 SCHENECTADY, NEW YORK

YEAR	TEAM	STARTS	GAMES	WON	LOST	PCT	ER	ERA	INNINGS PITCHED	STRIKE-OUTS	WALKS	HITS ALLOWED	HRS ALLOWED	COMP. GAMES	SHUT-OUTS	SAVES
1966	**ChC-N**	**0**	**11**	**0**	**1**	**.000**	**13**	**7.31**	**16**	**3**	**7**	**20**	**4**	**0**	**0**	**0**
1967	NYM-N	1	6	0	0	—	9	6.23	13	13	5	8	3	0	0	0
1968	NYM-N	0	9	0	1	.000	14	9.00	14	8	7	21	0	0	0	0
Career average		0	9	0	1	.000	12	7.53	14 1/3	8	6	16	2	0	0	0
Cubs average		**0**	**11**	**0**	**1**	**.000**	**13**	**7.31**	**16**	**3**	**7**	**20**	**4**	**0**	**0**	**0**
Career total		1	26	0	2	.000	36	7.53	43	24	19	49	7	0	0	0
Cubs total		**0**	**11**	**0**	**1**	**.000**	**13**	**7.31**	**16**	**3**	**7**	**20**	**4**	**0**	**0**	**0**

Cooper, Arley Wilbur (Wilbur)
HEIGHT: 5'11"   LEFTHANDER   BORN: 2/24/1892 BEARSVILLE, WEST VIRGINIA   DIED: 8/7/1973 ENCINO, CALIFORNIA

YEAR	TEAM	STARTS	GAMES	WON	LOST	PCT	ER	ERA	INNINGS PITCHED	STRIKE-OUTS	WALKS	HITS ALLOWED	HRS ALLOWED	COMP. GAMES	SHUT-OUTS	SAVES
1912	Pit-N	4	6	3	0	1.000	7	1.66	38	30	15	32	1	3	2	0
1913	Pit-N	9	30	5	3	.625	34	3.29	93	39	45	98	0	3	1	0
1914	Pit-N	34	40	16	15	.516	63	2.13	266 2/3	102	79	246	4	19	0	0
1915	Pit-N	19	38	5	16	.238	68	3.30	185 2/3	71	52	180	4	11	1	4
1916	Pit-N	23	42	12	11	.522	51	1.87	246	111	74	189	4	16	2	2
1917	Pit-N	34	40	17	11	.607	78	2.36	297 2/3	99	54	276	4	23	7	1
1918	Pit-N	29	38	19	14	.576	64	2.11	273 1/3	117	65	219	2	26	2	3
1919	Pit-N	32	35	19	13	.594	85	2.67	286 2/3	106	74	229	10	27	4	1
1920	Pit-N	37	44	24	15	.615	87	2.39	327	114	52	307	4	28	3	2
1921	Pit-N	38	38	22	14	.611	118	3.25	327	134	80	341	9	29	2	0
1922	Pit-N	36	41	23	14	.622	104	3.18	294 2/3	129	61	330	13	27	4	0
1923	Pit-N	38	39	17	19	.472	117	3.57	294 2/3	77	71	331	11	27	1	0
1924	Pit-N	35	38	20	14	.588	98	3.28	268 2/3	62	40	296	13	25	4	1
1925	**ChC-N**	**26**	**32**	**12**	**14**	**.462**	**101**	**4.28**	**212 1/3**	**41**	**61**	**249**	**18**	**13**	**0**	**0**
1926	**ChC-N**	**8**	**8**	**2**	**1**	**.667**	**27**	**4.42**	**55**	**18**	**21**	**65**	**6**	**3**	**0**	**0**
1926	Det-A	3	8	0	4	.000	17	11.20	13 2/3	2	9	27	0	0	0	0
Career average		27	34	14	12	.548	75	2.89	232	83	57	228	7	19	2	1
Cubs average		**17**	**20**	**7**	**8**	**.483**	**64**	**4.31**	**133 2/3**	**30**	**41**	**157**	**12**	**8**	**1**	**0**
Career total		405	517	216	178	.548	1119	2.89	3480	1252	853	3415	103	279	35	14
Cubs total		**34**	**40**	**14**	**15**	**.483**	**128**	**4.31**	**267 1/3**	**59**	**82**	**314**	**24**	**16**	**2**	**0**

Cooper, Morton Cecil (Mort)
HEIGHT: 6'2"   RIGHTHANDER   BORN: 3/2/1913 ATHERTON, MISSOURI   DIED: 11/17/1958 LITTLE ROCK, ARKANSAS

YEAR	TEAM	STARTS	GAMES	WON	LOST	PCT	ER	ERA	INNINGS PITCHED	STRIKE-OUTS	WALKS	HITS ALLOWED	HRS ALLOWED	COMP. GAMES	SHUT-OUTS	SAVES
1938	StL-N	3	4	2	1	.667	8	3.04	23 2/3	11	12	17	1	1	0	1
1939	StL-N	26	45	12	6	.667	76	3.25	210 2/3	130	97	208	6	7	2	4
1940	StL-N	29	38	11	12	.478	93	3.63	230 2/3	95	86	225	12	16	3	3
1941	StL-N	25	29	13	9	.591	81	3.91	186 2/3	118	69	175	15	12	0	0
1942	StL-N	35	37	22	7	.759	55	1.78	278 2/3	152	68	207	9	22	10	0
1943	StL-N	32	37	21	8	.724	70	2.30	274	141	79	228	5	24	6	3
1944	StL-N	33	34	22	7	.759	69	2.46	252 1/3	97	60	227	6	22	7	1
1945	StL-N	3	4	2	0	1.000	4	1.52	23 2/3	14	7	20	1	1	0	0
1945	Bos-N	11	20	7	4	.636	29	3.35	78	45	27	77	4	4	1	0
1946	Bos-N	27	28	13	11	.542	69	3.12	199	83	39	181	16	15	4	1
1947	Bos-N	7	10	2	5	.286	21	4.05	46 2/3	15	13	48	2	2	0	0
1947	NYG-N	8	8	1	5	.167	29	7.12	36 2/3	12	13	51	7	2	0	0
1949	**ChC-N**	**0**	**1**	**0**	**0**	**—**	**3**	**—**	**0**	**0**	**1**	**2**	**1**	**0**	**0**	**0**
Career average		22	27	12	7	.631	55	2.97	167 1/3	83	52	151	8	12	3	1
Cubs average		**0**	**1**	**0**	**0**	**—**	**3**	**—**	**0**	**0**	**1**	**2**	**1**	**0**	**0**	**0**
Career total		239	295	128	75	.631	607	2.97	1840 2/3	913	571	1666	85	128	33	14
Cubs total		**0**	**1**	**0**	**0**	**—**	**3**	**—**	**0**	**0**	**1**	**2**	**1**	**0**	**0**	**0**

Corcoran, Lawrence J. (Larry)
HEIGHT: —   RIGHTHANDER   BORN: 8/10/1859 BROOKLYN, NEW YORK   DIED: 10/14/1891 NEWARK, NEW JERSEY

YEAR	TEAM	STARTS	GAMES	WON	LOST	PCT	ER	ERA	INNINGS PITCHED	STRIKE-OUTS	WALKS	HITS ALLOWED	HRS ALLOWED	COMP. GAMES	SHUT-OUTS	SAVES
1880	**ChN-N**	**60**	**63**	**43**	**14**	**.754**	**116**	**1.95**	**536 1/3**	**268**	**99**	**404**	**6**	**57**	**4**	**2**
1881	**ChN-N**	**44**	**45**	**31**	**14**	**.689**	**102**	**2.31**	**396 2/3**	**150**	**78**	**380**	**10**	**43**	**4**	**0**
1882	**ChN-N**	**39**	**39**	**27**	**12**	**.692**	**77**	**1.95**	**355 2/3**	**170**	**63**	**281**	**5**	**38**	**3**	**0**
1883	**ChN-N**	**53**	**56**	**34**	**20**	**.630**	**131**	**2.49**	**473 2/3**	**216**	**82**	**483**	**7**	**51**	**3**	**0**
1884	**ChN-N**	**59**	**60**	**35**	**23**	**.603**	**138**	**2.40**	**516 2/3**	**272**	**116**	**473**	**35**	**57**	**7**	**0**
1885	**ChN-N**	**7**	**7**	**5**	**2**	**.714**	**24**	**3.64**	**59 1/3**	**10**	**24**	**63**	**2**	**6**	**1**	**0**
1885	NYG-N	3	3	2	1	.667	8	2.88	25	10	11	24	1	2	0	0
1886	WaN-N	1	2	0	1	.000	9	5.79	14	3	4	16	0	1	0	0
1887	Ind-N	2	2	0	2	.000	21	12.60	15	4	19	42	3	1	0	0
Career average		34	35	22	11	.665	78	2.36	299	138	62	271	9	32	3	0
Cubs average		**44**	**45**	**29**	**14**	**.673**	**98**	**2.26**	**389 2/3**	**181**	**77**	**347**	**11**	**42**	**4**	**0**
Career total		268	277	177	89	.665	626	2.36	2392 1/3	1103	496	2166	69	256	22	2
Cubs total		**262**	**270**	**175**	**85**	**.673**	**588**	**2.26**	**2338 1/3**	**1086**	**462**	**2084**	**65**	**252**	**22**	**2**

Lawrence "Larry" J. Corcoran, rhp, 1880–87

Larry Corcoran, in his brief career, was one of the best pitchers of the 1880s, helping Chicago to several National League pennants.

Corcoran was born in Brooklyn, New York, on August 10, 1859. He was a small man, just 5'5", and weighed a mere 120 pounds during his major league career. But according to Adrian "Cap" Anson, he was possibly the fastest pitcher in the league.

Corcoran was an excellent athlete who was one of the best fielding pitchers in the National League in his time. He was also handy with his fists, which was probably a necessity for a player of his stature in the rough-and-tumble world of pro baseball in the 19th century. More than one opposing player found himself badly overmatched when seeking a tussle with Corcoran.

Corcoran came into the league in 1880, winning 43 games and leading the Chicago team to the National League championship. Anson alternated him with pitcher Fred Goldsmith, giving Chicago the first true pitching "rotation" in professional baseball.

Corcoran won a league-leading 31 games in 1881 and was 27-12 in 1882, with a league-leading 1.96 ERA, as Chicago won champi-

onships each year. His success continued in 1883 and 1884 as he won 34 and 35 games, respectively.

Corcoran was one of the first pitchers, if not *the* first, to develop a series of signs with his catcher to indicate what type of pitch was coming. At first he would rotate his chaw of chewing tobacco to one side or the other of his cheek to tip off his catcher that he was throwing a curveball. Eventually, he developed a series of subtle hand signals.

Corcoran is the only Cubs pitcher in history to throw three no-hitters. They came in 1880, a 6-0 win over the Boston Braves on August 19; in 1882, a 5-0 win over Worcester on September 20; and in 1884, a 6-0 win over Providence on June 27. He is also the first Cubs pitcher to hit a grand slam, doing that in 1882 against Worcester on June 20.

Corcoran's arm was dead by 1885, and by 1887 he was out of the league. He suffered from Bright's disease, a degenerative liver malady, and in 1891, at the age of 32, he died.

Corcoran, despite a relatively brief career in Chicago, is fourth all-time in victories with Chicago with 175; he's fifth all-time in ERA at 2.26, fourth in innings pitched with 2,338⅓ and sixth in strikeouts with 1,086.

Corcoran, Michael (Mike)
HEIGHT: —   BORN: — BROOKLYN, NEW YORK

YEAR	TEAM	STARTS	GAMES	WON	LOST	PCT	ER	ERA	INNINGS PITCHED	STRIKE-OUTS	WALKS	HITS ALLOWED	HRS ALLOWED	COMP. GAMES	SHUT-OUTS	SAVES
1884	ChN-N	1	1	0	1	.000	4	4.00	9	2	7	16	1	1	0	0
Career average		1	1	0	1	.000	4	4.00	9	2	7	16	1	1	0	0
Cubs average		**1**	**1**	**0**	**1**	**.000**	**4**	**4.00**	**9**	**2**	**7**	**16**	**1**	**1**	**0**	**0**
Career total		1	1	0	1	.000	4	4.00	9	2	7	16	1	1	0	0
Cubs total		**1**	**1**	**0**	**1**	**.000**	**4**	**4.00**	**9**	**2**	**7**	**16**	**1**	**1**	**0**	**0**

Corridon, Frank J. (Fiddler)
HEIGHT: 6'0"   RIGHTHANDER   BORN: 11/25/1880 NEWPORT, RHODE ISLAND   DIED: 2/21/1941 SYRACUSE, NEW YORK

YEAR	TEAM	STARTS	GAMES	WON	LOST	PCT	ER	ERA	INNINGS PITCHED	STRIKE-OUTS	WALKS	HITS ALLOWED	HRS ALLOWED	COMP. GAMES	SHUT-OUTS	SAVES
1904	ChC-N	10	12	5	5	.500	34	3.05	100⅓	34	37	88	2	9	0	0
1904	Phi-N	11	12	6	5	.545	23	2.19	94⅓	44	28	88	2	11	1	0
1905	Phi-N	26	35	10	13	.435	82	3.48	212	79	57	203	2	18	1	1
1907	Phi-N	32	37	18	14	.563	75	2.46	274	131	89	228	0	23	3	2

(continued)

(continued)

YEAR	TEAM	STARTS	GAMES	WON	LOST	PCT	ER	ERA	INNINGS PITCHED	STRIKE-OUTS	WALKS	HITS ALLOWED	HRS ALLOWED	COMP. GAMES	SHUT-OUTS	SAVES
1908	Phi-N	24	27	14	10	.583	58	2.51	208 1/3	50	48	178	0	18	2	1
1909	Phi-N	19	27	11	7	.611	40	2.11	171	69	61	147	0	11	3	0
1910	StL-N	18	30	6	14	.300	66	3.81	156	51	55	168	1	9	0	3
Career average		23	30	12	11	.507	63	2.80	202 2/3	76	63	183	1	17	2	1
Cubs average		**10**	**12**	**5**	**5**	**.500**	**34**	**3.05**	**100 1/3**	**34**	**37**	**88**	**2**	**9**	**0**	**0**
Career total		140	180	70	68	.507	378	2.80	1216	458	375	1100	7	99	10	7
Cubs total		**10**	**12**	**5**	**5**	**.500**	**34**	**3.05**	**100 1/3**	**34**	**37**	**88**	**2**	**9**	**0**	**0**

Cosman, James Henry (Jim)
HEIGHT: 6'4" RIGHTHANDER BORN: 2/19/1943 BROCKPORT, NEW YORK

YEAR	TEAM	STARTS	GAMES	WON	LOST	PCT	ER	ERA	INNINGS PITCHED	STRIKE-OUTS	WALKS	HITS ALLOWED	HRS ALLOWED	COMP. GAMES	SHUT-OUTS	SAVES
1966	StL-N	1	1	1	0	1.000	0	0.00	9	5	2	2	0	1	1	0
1967	StL-N	5	10	1	0	1.000	11	3.16	31 1/3	11	24	21	2	0	0	0
1970	**ChC-N**	**0**	**1**	**0**	**0**	**—**	**3**	**27.00**	**1**	**0**	**1**	**3**	**1**	**0**	**0**	**0**
Career average		2	4	1	0	1.000	5	3.05	13 2/3	5	9	9	1	0	0	0
Cubs average		**0**	**1**	**0**	**0**	**—**	**3**	**27.00**	**1**	**0**	**1**	**3**	**1**	**0**	**0**	**0**
Career total		6	12	2	0	1.000	14	3.05	41 1/3	16	27	26	3	1	1	0
Cubs total		**0**	**1**	**0**	**0**	**—**	**3**	**27.00**	**1**	**0**	**1**	**3**	**1**	**0**	**0**	**0**

Cottrell, Ensign Stover
HEIGHT: 5'9" LEFTHANDER BORN: 8/29/1888 HOOSICK FALLS, NEW YORK DIED: 2/27/1947 SYRACUSE, NEW YORK

YEAR	TEAM	STARTS	GAMES	WON	LOST	PCT	ER	ERA	INNINGS PITCHED	STRIKE-OUTS	WALKS	HITS ALLOWED	HRS ALLOWED	COMP. GAMES	SHUT-OUTS	SAVES
1911	Pit-N	0	1	0	0	—	1	9.00	1	0	1	4	0	0	0	0
1912	**ChC-N**	**0**	**1**	**0**	**0**	**—**	**4**	**9.00**	**4**	**1**	**1**	**8**	**0**	**0**	**0**	**0**
1913	Phi-A	1	2	1	0	1.000	6	5.40	10	3	2	15	0	1	0	0
1914	Bos-N	1	1	0	1	.000	1	9.00	1	1	3	2	0	0	0	0
1915	NYY-A	0	7	0	1	.000	8	3.38	21 1/3	7	7	29	2	0	0	0
Career average		0	2	0	0	.333	4	4.82	7 1/3	2	3	12	0	0	0	0
Cubs average		**0**	**1**	**0**	**0**	**—**	**4**	**9.00**	**4**	**1**	**1**	**8**	**0**	**0**	**0**	**0**
Career total		2	12	1	2	.333	20	4.82	37 1/3	12	14	58	2	1	0	0
Cubs total		**0**	**1**	**0**	**0**	**—**	**4**	**9.00**	**4**	**1**	**1**	**8**	**0**	**0**	**0**	**0**

Coughlin, William Edward (Roscoe)
HEIGHT: 5'10" RIGHTHANDER BORN: 3/15/1868 WALPOLE, MASSACHUSETTS DIED: 3/20/1951 CHELSEA, MASSACHUSETTS

YEAR	TEAM	STARTS	GAMES	WON	LOST	PCT	ER	ERA	INNINGS PITCHED	STRIKE-OUTS	WALKS	HITS ALLOWED	HRS ALLOWED	COMP. GAMES	SHUT-OUTS	SAVES
1890	**ChN-N**	**10**	**11**	**4**	**7**	**.364**	**45**	**4.26**	**95**	**29**	**40**	**102**	**3**	**10**	**0**	**0**
1891	NYG-N	7	8	3	4	.429	26	3.84	61	22	23	74	5	6	0	0
Career average		9	10	4	6	.389	36	4.10	78	26	32	88	4	8	0	0
Cubs average		**10**	**11**	**4**	**7**	**.364**	**45**	**4.26**	**95**	**29**	**40**	**102**	**3**	**10**	**0**	**0**
Career total		17	19	7	11	.389	71	4.10	156	51	63	176	8	16	0	0
Cubs total		**10**	**11**	**4**	**7**	**.364**	**45**	**4.26**	**95**	**29**	**40**	**102**	**3**	**10**	**0**	**0**

Creek, Paul Douglas (Doug)
HEIGHT: 6'0" LEFTHANDER BORN: 3/1/1969 WINCHESTER, VIRGINIA

YEAR	TEAM	STARTS	GAMES	WON	LOST	PCT	ER	ERA	INNINGS PITCHED	STRIKE-OUTS	WALKS	HITS ALLOWED	HRS ALLOWED	COMP. GAMES	SHUT-OUTS	SAVES
1995	StL-N	0	6	0	0	—	0	0.00	6 2/3	10	3	2	0	0	0	0
1996	SF-N	0	63	0	2	.000	35	6.52	48 1/3	38	32	45	11	0	0	0
1997	SF-N	3	3	1	2	.333	10	6.75	13 1/3	14	14	12	1	0	0	0
1999	**ChC-N**	**0**	**3**	**0**	**0**	**—**	**7**	**10.50**	**6**	**6**	**8**	**6**	**1**	**0**	**0**	**0**
2000	TB-A	0	45	1	3	.250	31	4.60	60 2/3	73	39	49	10	0	0	1
2001	TB-A	0	66	2	5	.286	30	4.31	62 2/3	66	49	51	7	0	0	0

(continued)

(Creek, continued)

Career average	1	31	1	2	.250	19	5.15	33	35	24	28	5	0	0	0
Cubs average	**0**	**3**	**0**	**0**	**—**	**7**	**10.50**	**6**	**6**	**8**	**6**	**1**	**0**	**0**	**0**
Career total	3	186	4	12	.250	113	5.15	197 ⅔	207	145	165	30	0	0	1
Cubs total	**0**	**3**	**0**	**0**	**—**	**7**	**10.50**	**6**	**6**	**8**	**6**	**1**	**0**	**0**	**0**

Crim, Charles Robert (Chuck)
HEIGHT: 6'0"   RIGHTHANDER   BORN: 7/23/1961 VAN NUYS, CALIFORNIA

YEAR	TEAM	STARTS	GAMES	WON	LOST	PCT	ER	ERA	INNINGS PITCHED	STRIKE-OUTS	WALKS	HITS ALLOWED	HRS ALLOWED	COMP. GAMES	SHUT-OUTS	SAVES
1987	Mil-A	5	53	6	8	.429	53	3.67	130	56	39	133	15	0	0	12
1988	Mil-A	0	70	7	6	.538	34	2.91	105	58	28	95	11	0	0	9
1989	Mil-A	0	76	9	7	.563	37	2.83	117 ⅔	59	36	114	7	0	0	7
1990	Mil-A	0	67	3	5	.375	33	3.47	85 ⅔	39	23	88	7	0	0	11
1991	Mil-A	0	66	8	5	.615	47	4.63	91 ⅓	39	25	115	9	0	0	3
1992	Cal-A	0	57	7	6	.538	50	5.17	87	30	29	100	11	0	0	1
1993	Cal-A	0	11	2	2	.500	10	5.87	15 ⅓	10	5	17	2	0	0	0
1994	**ChC-N**	**1**	**49**	**5**	**4**	**.556**	**32**	**4.48**	**64 ⅓**	**43**	**24**	**69**	**9**	**0**	**0**	**2**
Career average	1	56	6	5	.522	37	3.83	87	42	26	91	9	0	0	6
Cubs average	**1**	**49**	**5**	**4**	**.556**	**32**	**4.48**	**64 ⅓**	**43**	**24**	**69**	**9**	**0**	**0**	**2**
Career total	6	449	47	43	.522	296	3.83	696 ⅓	334	209	731	71	0	0	45
Cubs total	**1**	**49**	**5**	**4**	**.556**	**32**	**4.48**	**64 ⅓**	**43**	**24**	**69**	**9**	**0**	**0**	**2**

Crosby, George Washington
HEIGHT: —   BORN: 1860 CHICAGO, ILLINOIS   DIED: 1/9/1913 SAN FRANCISCO, CALIFORNIA

YEAR	TEAM	STARTS	GAMES	WON	LOST	PCT	ER	ERA	INNINGS PITCHED	STRIKE-OUTS	WALKS	HITS ALLOWED	HRS ALLOWED	COMP. GAMES	SHUT-OUTS	SAVES
1884	ChN-N	3	3	1	2	.333	11	3.54	28	11	12	27	3	3	0	0
Career average	3	3	1	2	.333	11	3.54	28	11	12	27	3	3	0	0
Cubs average	**3**	**3**	**1**	**2**	**.333**	**11**	**3.54**	**28**	**11**	**12**	**27**	**3**	**3**	**0**	**0**
Career total	3	3	1	2	.333	11	3.54	28	11	12	27	3	3	0	0
Cubs total	**3**	**3**	**1**	**2**	**.333**	**11**	**3.54**	**28**	**11**	**12**	**27**	**3**	**3**	**0**	**0**

Crosby, Kenneth Stewart (Ken)
HEIGHT: 6'2"   RIGHTHANDER   BORN: 12/15/1947 NEW DENVER, BRITISH COLUMBIA, CANADA

YEAR	TEAM	STARTS	GAMES	WON	LOST	PCT	ER	ERA	INNINGS PITCHED	STRIKE-OUTS	WALKS	HITS ALLOWED	HRS ALLOWED	COMP. GAMES	SHUT-OUTS	SAVES
1975	ChC-N	0	9	1	0	1.000	3	3.24	8 ⅓	6	7	10	0	0	0	0
1976	ChC-N	1	7	0	0	—	16	12.00	12	5	8	20	3	0	0	0
Career average	1	8	1	0	1.000	10	8.41	10 ⅓	6	8	15	2	0	0	0
Cubs average	**1**	**8**	**1**	**0**	**1.000**	**10**	**8.41**	**10 ⅓**	**6**	**8**	**15**	**2**	**0**	**0**	**0**
Career total	1	16	1	0	1.000	19	8.41	20 ⅓	11	15	30	3	0	0	0
Cubs total	**1**	**16**	**1**	**0**	**1.000**	**19**	**8.41**	**20 ⅓**	**11**	**15**	**30**	**3**	**0**	**0**	**0**

Cruz, Juan Carlos
HEIGHT: 6'2"   RIGHTHANDER   BORN: 10/15/1980 BANAO, DOMINICAN REPUBLIC

YEAR	TEAM	STARTS	GAMES	WON	LOST	PCT	ER	ERA	INNINGS PITCHED	STRIKE-OUTS	WALKS	HITS ALLOWED	HRS ALLOWED	COMP. GAMES	SHUT-OUTS	SAVES
2001	ChC-N	8	8	3	1	.750	16	3.22	44 ⅔	39	17	40	4	0	0	0
Career average	8	8	3	1	.750	16	3.22	44 ⅔	39	17	40	4	0	0	0
Cubs average	**8**	**8**	**3**	**1**	**.750**	**16**	**3.22**	**44 ⅔**	**39**	**17**	**40**	**4**	**0**	**0**	**0**
Career total	8	8	3	1	.750	16	3.22	44 ⅔	39	17	40	4	0	0	0
Cubs total	**8**	**8**	**3**	**1**	**.750**	**16**	**3.22**	**44 ⅔**	**39**	**17**	**40**	**4**	**0**	**0**	**0**

Culp, Raymond Leonard (Ray)
HEIGHT: 6'0" RIGHTHANDER BORN: 8/6/1941 ELGIN, TEXAS

YEAR	TEAM	STARTS	GAMES	WON	LOST	PCT	ER	ERA	INNINGS PITCHED	STRIKE-OUTS	WALKS	HITS ALLOWED	HRS ALLOWED	COMP. GAMES	SHUT-OUTS	SAVES
1963	Phi-N	30	34	14	11	.560	67	2.97	203⅓	176	102	148	15	10	5	0
1964	Phi-N	19	30	8	7	.533	62	4.13	135	96	56	139	15	3	1	0
1965	Phi-N	30	33	14	10	.583	73	3.22	204⅓	134	78	188	14	11	1	0
1966	Phi-N	12	34	7	4	.636	62	5.04	110⅔	100	53	106	19	1	0	1
1967	**ChC-N**	**22**	**30**	**8**	**11**	**.421**	**66**	**3.89**	**152⅔**	**111**	**59**	**138**	**22**	**4**	**1**	0
1968	Bos-A	30	35	16	6	.727	70	2.91	216⅓	190	82	166	18	11	6	0
1969	Bos-A	32	32	17	8	.680	96	3.81	227	172	79	195	25	9	2	0
1970	Bos-A	33	33	17	14	.548	85	3.04	251⅓	197	91	211	22	15	1	0
1971	Bos-A	35	35	14	16	.467	97	3.60	242⅓	151	67	236	21	12	3	0
1972	Bos-A	16	16	5	8	.385	52	4.46	105	52	53	104	8	4	1	0
1973	Bos-A	9	10	2	6	.250	25	4.47	50⅓	32	32	46	9	0	0	0
Career average		24	29	11	9	.547	69	3.58	172⅔	128	68	152	17	7	2	0
Cubs average		**22**	**30**	**8**	**11**	**.421**	**66**	**3.89**	**152⅔**	**111**	**59**	**138**	**17**	**7**	**2**	**0**
Career total		268	322	122	101	.547	755	3.58	1898⅓	1411	752	1677	188	80	22	1
Cubs total		**22**	**30**	**8**	**11**	**.421**	**66**	**3.89**	**152⅔**	**111**	**59**	**138**	**22**	**4**	**1**	**0**

Cunningham, Ellsworth Elmer (Bert)
HEIGHT: 5'6" RIGHTHANDER BORN: 11/25/1865 WILMINGTON, DELAWARE DIED: 5/14/1952 CRAGMERE, DELAWARE

YEAR	TEAM	STARTS	GAMES	WON	LOST	PCT	ER	ERA	INNINGS PITCHED	STRIKE-OUTS	WALKS	HITS ALLOWED	HRS ALLOWED	COMP. GAMES	SHUT-OUTS	SAVES
1887	Bro-AA	3	3	0	2	.000	13	5.09	23	8	13	39	0	3	0	0
1888	Bal-AA	51	51	22	29	.431	171	3.39	453⅓	186	157	412	8	50	0	0
1889	Bal-AA	33	39	16	19	.457	151	4.87	279⅓	140	141	306	11	29	0	0
1890	Phi-P	11	14	3	9	.250	63	5.22	108⅔	33	67	133	0	11	0	1
1890	Buf-P	25	25	9	15	.375	137	5.84	211	78	134	251	8	24	2	0
1891	Bal-AA	25	30	11	14	.440	106	4.01	237⅔	59	138	241	8	21	0	0
1895	Lou-N	28	31	11	17	.393	122	4.75	231	49	104	299	6	24	1	0
1896	Lou-N	20	27	7	14	.333	107	5.09	189⅓	37	74	242	6	17	0	1
1897	Lou-N	28	30	14	14	.500	108	4.14	234⅔	49	72	286	2	26	0	0
1898	Lou-N	42	44	28	14	.667	127	3.16	362	34	65	387	8	41	0	0
1899	Lou-N	37	39	17	19	.472	138	3.84	323⅔	36	75	385	4	33	1	0
1900	**ChN-N**	**7**	**8**	**4**	**3**	**.571**	**31**	**4.36**	**64**	**7**	**21**	**84**	**0**	**7**	**0**	**0**
1901	**ChN-N**	**1**	**1**	**0**	**1**	**.000**	**5**	**5.00**	**9**	**2**	**3**	**11**	**0**	**1**	**0**	**0**
Career average		26	29	12	14	.455	107	4.22	227⅓	60	89	256	5	24	0	0
Cubs average		**4**	**5**	**2**	**2**	**.500**	**18**	**4.44**	**36⅔**	**5**	**12**	**48**	**0**	**4**	**0**	**0**
Career total		311	342	142	170	.455	1279	4.22	2726⅔	718	1064	3076	61	287	4	2
Cubs total		**8**	**9**	**4**	**4**	**.500**	**36**	**4.44**	**73**	**9**	**24**	**95**	**0**	**8**	**0**	**0**

Currie, Clarence Franklin
HEIGHT: — RIGHTHANDER BORN: 12/30/1878 GLENCOE, ONTARIO, CANADA DIED: 7/15/1941 LITTLE CHUTE, WISCONSIN

YEAR	TEAM	STARTS	GAMES	WON	LOST	PCT	ER	ERA	INNINGS PITCHED	STRIKE-OUTS	WALKS	HITS ALLOWED	HRS ALLOWED	COMP. GAMES	SHUT-OUTS	SAVES
1902	Cin-N	7	10	3	4	.429	27	3.72	65⅓	20	17	70	1	6	1	0
1902	StL-N	12	15	7	5	.583	36	2.60	124⅔	30	35	125	0	10	2	0
1903	StL-N	16	22	4	12	.250	66	4.01	148	52	60	155	7	13	1	1
1903	**ChC-N**	**3**	**6**	**1**	**2**	**.333**	**11**	**2.97**	**33⅓**	**9**	**9**	**35**	**1**	**2**	**0**	**1**
Career average		19	27	8	12	.395	70	3.39	185⅔	56	61	193	5	16	2	1
Cubs average		**3**	**6**	**1**	**2**	**.333**	**11**	**2.97**	**33⅓**	**9**	**9**	**35**	**1**	**2**	**0**	**1**
Career total		38	53	15	23	.395	140	3.39	371⅓	111	121	385	9	31	4	2
Cubs total		**3**	**6**	**1**	**2**	**.333**	**11**	**2.97**	**33⅓**	**9**	**9**	**35**	**1**	**2**	**0**	**1**

Curtis, Clifton Garfield (Cliff)
HEIGHT: 6'2"   RIGHTHANDER   BORN: 7/3/1881 DELAWARE, OHIO   DIED: 4/23/1943 UTICA, OHIO

YEAR	TEAM	STARTS	GAMES	WON	LOST	PCT	ER	ERA	INNINGS PITCHED	STRIKE-OUTS	WALKS	HITS ALLOWED	HRS ALLOWED	COMP. GAMES	SHUT-OUTS	SAVES
1909	Bos-N	9	10	4	5	.444	13	1.41	83	22	30	53	1	8	2	0
1910	Bos-N	37	43	6	24	.200	99	3.55	251	75	124	251	9	12	2	2
1911	Bos-N	9	12	1	8	.111	38	4.44	77	23	34	79	4	5	0	1
1911	**ChC-N**	1	4	1	2	.333	3	3.86	7	4	5	7	0	0	0	0
1911	Phi-N	5	8	2	1	.667	13	2.60	45	13	15	45	0	3	1	0
1912	Phi-N	8	10	2	5	.286	18	3.24	50	20	17	55	3	2	0	0
1912	Bro-N	9	19	4	7	.364	35	3.94	80	22	37	72	4	3	0	1
1913	Bro-N	16	30	8	9	.471	55	3.26	151 2/3	57	55	145	1	6	0	2
Career average		19	27	6	12	.315	55	3.31	149	47	63	141	4	8	1	1
Cubs average		**1**	**4**	**1**	**2**	**.333**	**3**	**3.86**	**7**	**4**	**5**	**7**	**0**	**0**	**0**	**0**
Career total		94	136	28	61	.315	274	3.31	744 2/3	236	317	707	22	39	5	6
Cubs total		**1**	**4**	**1**	**2**	**.333**	**3**	**3.86**	**7**	**4**	**5**	**7**	**0**	**0**	**0**	**0**

Curtis, Jack Patrick
HEIGHT: 5'10"   LEFTHANDER   BORN: 1/11/1937 RHODHISS, NORTH CAROLINA

YEAR	TEAM	STARTS	GAMES	WON	LOST	PCT	ER	ERA	INNINGS PITCHED	STRIKE-OUTS	WALKS	HITS ALLOWED	HRS ALLOWED	COMP. GAMES	SHUT-OUTS	SAVES
1961	**ChC-N**	27	31	10	13	.435	98	4.89	180 1/3	57	51	220	23	6	0	0
1962	**ChC-N**	3	4	0	2	.000	7	3.50	18	8	6	18	2	0	0	0
1962	Mil-N	5	30	4	4	.500	35	4.16	75 2/3	40	27	82	8	0	0	1
1963	Cle-A	0	4	0	0	—	10	18.00	5	3	5	8	0	0	0	0
Career average		12	23	5	6	.424	50	4.84	93	36	30	109	11	2	0	0
Cubs average		**15**	**18**	**5**	**8**	**.400**	**53**	**4.76**	**99 1/3**	**33**	**29**	**119**	**13**	**3**	**0**	**0**
Career total		35	69	14	19	.424	150	4.84	279	108	89	328	33	6	0	1
Cubs total		**30**	**35**	**10**	**15**	**.400**	**105**	**4.76**	**198 1/3**	**65**	**57**	**238**	**25**	**6**	**0**	**0**

Cvengros, Michael John (Mike)
HEIGHT: 5'8"   LEFTHANDER   BORN: 12/1/1901 PANA, ILLINOIS   DIED: 8/2/1970 HOT SPRINGS, ARKANSAS

YEAR	TEAM	STARTS	GAMES	WON	LOST	PCT	ER	ERA	INNINGS PITCHED	STRIKE-OUTS	WALKS	HITS ALLOWED	HRS ALLOWED	COMP. GAMES	SHUT-OUTS	SAVES
1922	NYG-N	1	1	0	1	.000	4	4.00	9	3	3	6	1	1	0	0
1923	CWS-A	26	40	12	13	.480	105	4.41	214 1/3	86	107	216	6	14	0	3
1924	CWS-A	15	26	3	12	.200	69	5.88	105 2/3	36	67	119	5	2	0	0
1925	CWS-A	11	22	3	9	.250	50	4.30	104 2/3	32	55	109	7	4	0	1
1927	Pit-N	4	23	2	1	.667	20	3.35	53 2/3	21	24	55	3	0	0	2
1929	**ChC-N**	4	32	5	4	.556	33	4.64	64	23	29	82	2	0	0	2
Career average		10	24	4	7	.385	47	4.59	92	34	48	98	4	4	0	1
Cubs average		**4**	**32**	**5**	**4**	**.556**	**33**	**4.64**	**64**	**23**	**29**	**82**	**2**	**0**	**0**	**2**
Career total		61	144	25	40	.385	281	4.59	551 1/3	201	285	587	24	21	0	6
Cubs total		**4**	**32**	**5**	**4**	**.556**	**33**	**4.64**	**64**	**23**	**29**	**82**	**2**	**0**	**0**	**2**

Dascenzo, Douglas Craig (Doug)
HEIGHT: 5'8"   LEFTHANDER   BORN: 6/30/1964 CLEVELAND, OHIO

YEAR	TEAM	STARTS	GAMES	WON	LOST	PCT	ER	ERA	INNINGS PITCHED	STRIKE-OUTS	WALKS	HITS ALLOWED	HRS ALLOWED	COMP. GAMES	SHUT-OUTS	SAVES
1990	ChC-N	0	1	0	0	—	0	0.00	1	0	0	1	0	0	0	0
1991	ChC-N	0	3	0	0	—	0	0.00	4	2	2	2	0	0	0	0
Career average		0	2	0	0	—	0	0.00	2 2/3	1	1	2	0	0	0	0
Cubs average		**0**	**2**	**0**	**0**	**—**	**0**	**0.00**	**2 2/3**	**1**	**1**	**2**	**0**	**0**	**0**	**0**
Career total		0	4	0	0	—	0	0.00	5	2	2	3	0	0	0	0
Cubs total		**0**	**4**	**0**	**0**	**—**	**0**	**0.00**	**5**	**2**	**2**	**3**	**0**	**0**	**0**	**0**

Davis, Curtis Benton (Curt or Coonskin)

HEIGHT: 6'2" RIGHTHANDER BORN: 9/7/1903 GREENFIELD, MISSOURI DIED: 10/13/1965 COVINA, CALIFORNIA

YEAR	TEAM	STARTS	GAMES	WON	LOST	PCT	ER	ERA	INNINGS PITCHED	STRIKE-OUTS	WALKS	HITS ALLOWED	HRS ALLOWED	COMP. GAMES	SHUT-OUTS	SAVES
1934	Phi-N	31	51	19	17	.528	90	2.95	274 1/3	99	60	283	14	18	3	5
1935	Phi-N	27	44	16	14	.533	94	3.66	231	74	47	264	14	19	3	2
1936	Phi-N	8	10	2	4	.333	31	4.62	60 1/3	18	19	71	6	3	0	0
1936	**ChC-N**	**19**	**24**	**11**	**9**	**.550**	**51**	**3.00**	**153**	**52**	**31**	**146**	**11**	**10**	**0**	**1**
1937	**ChC-N**	**14**	**28**	**10**	**5**	**.667**	**56**	**4.08**	**123 2/3**	**32**	**30**	**138**	**7**	**8**	**0**	**1**
1938	StL-N	21	40	12	8	.600	70	3.63	173 1/3	36	27	187	9	8	2	3
1939	StL-N	31	49	22	16	.579	100	3.63	248	70	48	279	18	13	3	7
1940	StL-N	7	14	0	4	.000	31	5.17	54	12	19	73	4	0	0	1
1940	Bro-N	18	22	8	7	.533	58	3.81	137	46	19	135	13	9	0	2
1941	Bro-N	16	28	13	7	.650	51	2.97	154 1/3	50	27	141	7	10	5	2
1942	Bro-N	26	32	15	6	.714	54	2.36	206	60	51	179	10	13	5	2
1943	Bro-N	21	31	10	13	.435	69	3.78	164 1/3	47	39	182	8	8	2	3
1944	Bro-N	23	31	10	11	.476	72	3.34	194	49	39	207	12	12	1	4
1945	Bro-N	18	24	10	10	.500	54	3.25	149 2/3	39	21	171	9	10	0	0
1946	Bro-N	0	1	0	0	—	3	13.50	2	0	2	3	1	0	0	0
Career average		22	33	12	10	.547	68	3.42	179	53	37	189	11	11	2	3
Cubs average		**17**	**26**	**11**	**7**	**.600**	**54**	**3.48**	**138 1/3**	**42**	**31**	**142**	**9**	**9**	**0**	**1**
Career total		280	429	158	131	.547	884	3.42	2325	684	479	2459	143	141	24	33
Cubs total		**33**	**52**	**21**	**14**	**.600**	**107**	**3.48**	**276 2/3**	**84**	**61**	**284**	**18**	**18**	**0**	**2**

Davis, James Bennett (Jim)

HEIGHT: 6'0" LEFTHANDER BORN: 9/15/1924 RED BLUFF, CALIFORNIA DIED: 11/30/1995 SAN MATEO, CALIFORNIA

YEAR	TEAM	STARTS	GAMES	WON	LOST	PCT	ER	ERA	INNINGS PITCHED	STRIKE-OUTS	WALKS	HITS ALLOWED	HRS ALLOWED	COMP. GAMES	SHUT-OUTS	SAVES
1954	**ChC-N**	**12**	**46**	**11**	**7**	**.611**	**50**	**3.52**	**127 2/3**	**58**	**51**	**114**	**12**	**2**	**0**	**4**
1955	**ChC-N**	**16**	**42**	**7**	**11**	**.389**	**66**	**4.44**	**133 2/3**	**62**	**58**	**122**	**16**	**0**	**0**	**3**
1956	**ChC-N**	**11**	**46**	**5**	**7**	**.417**	**49**	**3.66**	**120 1/3**	**66**	**59**	**116**	**11**	**2**	**1**	**2**
1957	StL-N	0	10	0	1	.000	8	5.27	13 2/3	5	6	18	1	0	0	1
1957	NYG-N	0	10	1	0	1.000	8	6.55	11	6	5	13	2	0	0	0
Career average		10	39	6	7	.480	45	4.01	101 2/3	49	45	96	11	1	0	3
Cubs average		**13**	**45**	**8**	**8**	**.479**	**55**	**3.89**	**127 1/3**	**62**	**56**	**117**	**13**	**1**	**0**	**3**
Career total		39	154	24	26	.480	181	4.01	406 1/3	197	179	383	42	4	1	10
Cubs total		**39**	**134**	**23**	**25**	**.479**	**165**	**3.89**	**381 2/3**	**186**	**168**	**352**	**39**	**4**	**1**	**9**

Davis, Ronald Gene (Ron)

HEIGHT: 6'4" RIGHTHANDER BORN: 8/6/1955 HOUSTON, TEXAS

YEAR	TEAM	STARTS	GAMES	WON	LOST	PCT	ER	ERA	INNINGS PITCHED	STRIKE-OUTS	WALKS	HITS ALLOWED	HRS ALLOWED	COMP. GAMES	SHUT-OUTS	SAVES
1978	NYY-A	0	4	0	0	—	3	11.57	2 1/3	0	3	3	0	0	0	0
1979	NYY-A	0	44	14	2	.875	27	2.85	85 1/3	43	28	84	5	0	0	9
1980	NYY-A	0	53	9	3	.750	43	2.95	131	65	32	121	9	0	0	7
1981	NYY-A	0	43	4	5	.444	22	2.71	73	83	25	47	6	0	0	6
1982	Min-A	0	63	3	9	.250	52	4.42	106	89	47	106	16	0	0	22
1983	Min-A	0	66	5	8	.385	33	3.34	89	84	33	89	6	0	0	30
1984	Min-A	0	64	7	11	.389	42	4.55	83	74	41	79	11	0	0	29
1985	Min-A	0	57	2	6	.250	25	3.48	64 2/3	72	35	55	7	0	0	25
1986	Min-A	0	36	2	6	.250	39	9.08	38 2/3	30	29	55	7	0	0	2
1986	**ChC-N**	**0**	**17**	**0**	**2**	**.000**	**17**	**7.65**	**20**	**10**	**3**	**31**	**3**	**0**	**0**	**0**
1987	**ChC-N**	**0**	**21**	**0**	**0**	**—**	**21**	**5.85**	**32 1/3**	**31**	**12**	**43**	**8**	**0**	**0**	**0**
1987	LA-N	0	4	0	0	—	3	6.75	4	1	6	7	0	0	0	0
1988	SF-N	0	9	1	1	.500	9	4.67	17 1/3	15	6	15	4	0	0	0
Career average		0	44	4	5	.470	31	4.05	68	54	27	67	7	0	0	12
Cubs average		**0**	**19**	**0**	**1**	**.000**	**19**	**6.54**	**26 1/3**	**21**	**8**	**37**	**6**	**0**	**0**	**0**
Career total		0	481	47	53	.470	336	4.05	746 2/3	597	300	735	82	0	0	130
Cubs total		**0**	**38**	**0**	**2**	**.000**	**38**	**6.54**	**52 1/3**	**41**	**15**	**74**	**11**	**0**	**0**	**0**

Dean, Jay Hanna (Dizzy)
HEIGHT: 6'2" RIGHTHANDER BORN: 1/16/1910 LUCAS, ARKANSAS DIED: 7/17/1974 RENO, NEVADA

YEAR	TEAM	STARTS	GAMES	WON	LOST	PCT	ER	ERA	INNINGS PITCHED	STRIKE-OUTS	WALKS	HITS ALLOWED	HRS ALLOWED	COMP. GAMES	SHUT-OUTS	SAVES
1930	StL-N	1	1	1	0	1.000	1	1.00	9	5	3	3	0	1	0	0
1932	StL-N	33	46	18	15	.545	105	3.30	286	191	102	280	14	16	4	2
1933	StL-N	34	48	20	18	.526	99	3.04	293	199	64	279	11	26	3	4
1934	StL-N	33	50	30	7	.811	92	2.66	311⅔	195	75	288	14	24	7	7
1935	StL-N	36	50	28	12	.700	110	3.04	325⅓	190	77	324	16	29	3	5
1936	StL-N	34	51	24	13	.649	111	3.17	315	195	53	310	21	28	2	11
1937	StL-N	25	27	13	10	.565	59	2.69	197⅓	120	33	200	9	17	4	1
1938	**ChC-N**	**10**	**13**	**7**	**1**	**.875**	**15**	**1.81**	**74⅔**	**22**	**8**	**63**	**2**	**3**	**1**	**0**
1939	**ChC-N**	**13**	**19**	**6**	**4**	**.600**	**36**	**3.36**	**96⅓**	**27**	**17**	**98**	**4**	**7**	**2**	**0**
1940	**ChC-N**	**9**	**10**	**3**	**3**	**.500**	**31**	**5.17**	**54**	**18**	**20**	**68**	**4**	**3**	**0**	**0**
1941	**ChC-N**	**1**	**1**	**0**	**0**	**—**	**2**	**18.00**	**1**	**1**	**0**	**3**	**0**	**0**	**0**	**0**
1947	StL-A	1	1	0	0	—	0	0.00	4	0	1	3	0	0	0	0
Career average		19	26	13	7	.644	55	3.02	164	97	38	160	8	13	2	3
Cubs average		**8**	**11**	**4**	**2**	**.667**	**21**	**3.35**	**56⅔**	**17**	**11**	**58**	**3**	**3**	**1**	**0**
Career total		230	317	150	83	.644	661	3.02	1967⅓	1163	453	1919	95	154	26	30
Cubs total		**33**	**43**	**16**	**8**	**.667**	**84**	**3.35**	**226**	**68**	**45**	**232**	**10**	**13**	**3**	**0**

Dean, Wayland Ogden
HEIGHT: 6'1" RIGHTHANDER BORN: 6/20/1902 RICHWOOD, WEST VIRGINIA DIED: 4/10/1930 HUNTINGTON, WEST VIRGINIA

YEAR	TEAM	STARTS	GAMES	WON	LOST	PCT	ER	ERA	INNINGS PITCHED	STRIKE-OUTS	WALKS	HITS ALLOWED	HRS ALLOWED	COMP. GAMES	SHUT-OUTS	SAVES
1924	NYG-N	20	26	6	12	.333	70	5.01	125⅔	39	45	139	9	6	0	0
1925	NYG-N	14	33	10	7	.588	78	4.64	151⅓	53	50	169	13	6	1	1
1926	Phi-N	26	33	8	16	.333	111	4.91	203⅔	52	89	245	9	15	1	0
1927	Phi-N	0	2	0	1	.000	4	12.00	3	1	2	6	0	0	0	0
1927	**ChC-N**	**0**	**2**	**0**	**0**	**—**	**0**	**0.00**	**2**	**2**	**2**	**0**	**0**	**0**	**0**	**0**
Career average		15	24	6	9	.400	66	4.87	121⅓	37	47	140	8	7	1	0
Cubs average		**0**	**2**	**0**	**0**	**—**	**0**	**0.00**	**2**	**2**	**2**	**0**	**0**	**0**	**0**	**0**
Career total		60	96	24	36	.400	263	4.87	485⅔	147	188	559	31	27	2	1
Cubs total		**0**	**2**	**0**	**0**	**—**	**0**	**0.00**	**2**	**2**	**2**	**0**	**0**	**0**	**0**	**0**

Decker, George Henry (Joe)
HEIGHT: 6'0" RIGHTHANDER BORN: 6/16/1947 STORM LAKE, IOWA

YEAR	TEAM	STARTS	GAMES	WON	LOST	PCT	ER	ERA	INNINGS PITCHED	STRIKE-OUTS	WALKS	HITS ALLOWED	HRS ALLOWED	COMP. GAMES	SHUT-OUTS	SAVES
1969	**ChC-N**	**1**	**4**	**1**	**0**	**1.000**	**4**	**2.92**	**12⅓**	**13**	**6**	**10**	**0**	**0**	**0**	**0**
1970	**ChC-N**	**17**	**24**	**2**	**7**	**.222**	**56**	**4.64**	**108⅔**	**79**	**56**	**108**	**12**	**1**	**0**	**0**
1971	**ChC-N**	**4**	**21**	**3**	**2**	**.600**	**24**	**4.73**	**45⅔**	**37**	**25**	**62**	**2**	**0**	**0**	**0**
1972	**ChC-N**	**1**	**5**	**1**	**0**	**1.000**	**3**	**2.13**	**12⅔**	**7**	**4**	**9**	**1**	**0**	**0**	**0**
1973	Min-A	24	29	10	10	.500	79	4.17	170⅓	109	88	167	12	6	3	0
1974	Min-A	37	37	16	14	.533	91	3.29	248⅔	158	97	234	24	11	1	0
1975	Min-A	7	10	1	3	.250	25	8.54	26⅓	8	36	25	2	1	0	0
1976	Min-A	12	13	2	7	.222	34	5.28	58	35	51	60	3	0	0	0
1979	Sea-A	2	9	0	1	.000	13	4.28	27⅓	12	14	27	2	0	0	0
Career average		12	17	4	5	.450	37	4.17	79	51	42	78	6	2	0	0
Cubs average		**6**	**14**	**2**	**2**	**.438**	**22**	**4.37**	**45**	**34**	**23**	**47**	**4**	**0**	**0**	**0**
Career total		105	152	36	44	.450	329	4.17	710	458	377	702	58	19	4	0
Cubs total		**23**	**54**	**7**	**9**	**.438**	**87**	**4.37**	**179⅓**	**136**	**91**	**189**	**15**	**1**	**0**	**0**

Demarais, Frederick (Fred)
HEIGHT: 5'9" RIGHTHANDER BORN: 11/1/1866 QUEBEC, CANADA DIED: 3/6/1919 STAMFORD, CONNECTICUT

YEAR	TEAM	STARTS	GAMES	WON	LOST	PCT	ER	ERA	INNINGS PITCHED	STRIKE-OUTS	WALKS	HITS ALLOWED	HRS ALLOWED	COMP. GAMES	SHUT-OUTS	SAVES
1890	ChN-N	0	1	0	0	—	0	0.00	2	1	1	1	0	0	0	0
Career average		0	1	0	0	—	0	0.00	2	1	1	1	0	0	0	0
Cubs average		**0**	**1**	**0**	**0**	**—**	**0**	**0.00**	**2**	**1**	**1**	**1**	**0**	**0**	**0**	**0**
Career total		0	1	0	0	—	0	0.00	2	1	1	1	0	0	0	0
Cubs total		**0**	**1**	**0**	**0**	**—**	**0**	**0.00**	**2**	**1**	**1**	**1**	**0**	**0**	**0**	**0**

Demaree, Albert Wentworth (Al)
HEIGHT: 6'0" RIGHTHANDER BORN: 9/8/1884 QUINCY, ILLINOIS DIED: 4/30/1962 LOS ANGELES, CALIFORNIA

YEAR	TEAM	STARTS	GAMES	WON	LOST	PCT	ER	ERA	INNINGS PITCHED	STRIKE-OUTS	WALKS	HITS ALLOWED	HRS ALLOWED	COMP. GAMES	SHUT-OUTS	SAVES
1912	NYG-N	2	2	1	0	1.000	3	1.69	16	11	2	17	0	1	1	0
1913	NYG-N	24	31	13	4	.765	49	2.21	199 2/3	76	38	176	4	11	2	2
1914	NYG-N	29	38	10	17	.370	77	3.09	224	89	77	219	3	13	2	0
1915	Phi-N	26	32	14	11	.560	71	3.05	209 2/3	69	58	201	4	13	3	1
1916	Phi-N	35	39	19	14	.576	83	2.62	285	130	48	252	4	25	4	1
1917	**ChC-N**	**18**	**24**	**5**	**9**	**.357**	**40**	**2.55**	**141 1/3**	**43**	**37**	**125**	**5**	**6**	**1**	**1**
1917	NYG-N	11	15	4	5	.444	23	2.64	78 1/3	23	17	70	1	1	0	0
1918	NYG-N	14	26	8	6	.571	39	2.47	142	39	25	143	5	8	2	1
1919	Bos-N	13	25	6	6	.500	54	3.80	128	34	35	147	8	6	0	3
Career average		22	29	10	9	.526	55	2.77	178	64	42	169	4	11	2	1
Cubs average		**18**	**24**	**5**	**9**	**.357**	**40**	**2.55**	**141 1/3**	**43**	**37**	**125**	**5**	**6**	**1**	**1**
Career total		172	232	80	72	.526	439	2.77	1424	514	337	1350	34	84	15	9
Cubs total		**18**	**24**	**5**	**9**	**.357**	**40**	**2.55**	**141 1/3**	**43**	**37**	**125**	**5**	**6**	**1**	**1**

DeMiller, Harry
HEIGHT: — LEFTHANDER BORN: 11/12/1867 WOOSTER, OHIO DIED: 10/19/1928 SANTA ANA, CALIFORNIA

YEAR	TEAM	STARTS	GAMES	WON	LOST	PCT	ER	ERA	INNINGS PITCHED	STRIKE-OUTS	WALKS	HITS ALLOWED	HRS ALLOWED	COMP. GAMES	SHUT-OUTS	SAVES
1892	ChN-N	2	4	1	1	.500	17	6.38	24	15	16	29	1	2	0	0
Career average		2	4	1	1	.500	17	6.38	24	15	16	29	1	2	0	0
Cubs average		**2**	**4**	**1**	**1**	**.500**	**17**	**6.38**	**24**	**15**	**16**	**29**	**1**	**2**	**0**	**0**
Career total		2	4	1	1	.500	17	6.38	24	15	16	29	1	2	0	0
Cubs total		**2**	**4**	**1**	**1**	**.500**	**17**	**6.38**	**24**	**15**	**16**	**29**	**1**	**2**	**0**	**0**

Denzer, Roger (Peaceful Valley)
HEIGHT: 6'0" RIGHTHANDER BORN: 10/5/1871 LE SUEUR, MINNESOTA DIED: 9/18/1949 LE SUEUR, MINNESOTA

YEAR	TEAM	STARTS	GAMES	WON	LOST	PCT	ER	ERA	INNINGS PITCHED	STRIKE-OUTS	WALKS	HITS ALLOWED	HRS ALLOWED	COMP. GAMES	SHUT-OUTS	SAVES
1897	**ChN-N**	**10**	**12**	**2**	**7**	**.222**	**54**	**5.13**	**94 2/3**	**17**	**34**	**125**	**4**	**8**	**0**	**0**
1901	NYG-N	9	11	2	6	.250	23	3.36	61 2/3	22	5	69	2	3	1	0
Career average		10	12	2	7	.235	39	4.43	78 1/3	20	20	97	3	6	1	0
Cubs average		**10**	**12**	**2**	**7**	**.222**	**54**	**5.13**	**94 2/3**	**17**	**34**	**125**	**4**	**8**	**0**	**0**
Career total		19	23	4	13	.235	77	4.43	156 1/3	39	39	194	6	11	1	0
Cubs total		**10**	**12**	**2**	**7**	**.222**	**54**	**5.13**	**94 2/3**	**17**	**34**	**125**	**4**	**8**	**0**	**0**

Derringer, Samuel Paul (Paul *or* Duke *or* 'Oom Paul)
HEIGHT: 6'3" RIGHTHANDER BORN: 10/17/1906 SPRINGFIELD, KENTUCKY DIED: 11/17/1987 SARASOTA, FLORIDA

YEAR	TEAM	STARTS	GAMES	WON	LOST	PCT	ER	ERA	INNINGS PITCHED	STRIKE-OUTS	WALKS	HITS ALLOWED	HRS ALLOWED	COMP. GAMES	SHUT-OUTS	SAVES
1931	StL-N	23	35	18	8	.692	79	3.36	211 2/3	134	65	225	9	15	4	2
1932	StL-N	30	39	11	14	.440	105	4.05	233 1/3	78	67	296	6	14	1	0
1933	StL-N	2	3	0	2	.000	8	4.24	17	3	9	24	0	1	0	0
1933	Cin-N	31	33	7	25	.219	83	3.23	231	86	51	240	4	16	2	1
1934	Cin-N	31	47	15	21	.417	104	3.59	261	122	59	297	8	18	1	4
1935	Cin-N	33	45	22	13	.629	108	3.51	276 2/3	120	49	295	13	20	3	2
1936	Cin-N	37	51	19	19	.500	126	4.02	282 1/3	121	42	331	11	13	2	5
1937	Cin-N	26	43	10	14	.417	100	4.04	222 2/3	94	55	240	7	12	1	1
1938	Cin-N	37	41	21	14	.600	100	2.93	307	132	49	315	20	26	4	3
1939	Cin-N	35	38	25	7	.781	98	2.93	301	128	35	321	15	28	5	0
1940	Cin-N	37	37	20	12	.625	101	3.06	296 2/3	115	48	280	17	26	3	0
1941	Cin-N	28	29	12	14	.462	84	3.31	228 1/3	76	54	233	16	17	2	1
1942	Cin-N	27	29	10	11	.476	71	3.06	208 2/3	68	49	203	4	13	1	0
1943	**ChC-N**	**22**	**32**	**10**	**14**	**.417**	**69**	**3.57**	**174**	**75**	**39**	**184**	**7**	**10**	**2**	**3**
1944	**ChC-N**	**16**	**42**	**7**	**13**	**.350**	**83**	**4.15**	**180**	**69**	**39**	**205**	**13**	**7**	**0**	**3**
1945	**ChC-N**	**30**	**35**	**16**	**11**	**.593**	**82**	**3.45**	**213 2/3**	**86**	**51**	**223**	**8**	**15**	**1**	**4**

(continued)

(Derringer, continued)

Career average	30	39	15	14	.513	93	3.46	243	100	51	261	11	17	2	2
Cubs average	**23**	**36**	**11**	**13**	**.465**	**78**	**3.71**	**189 1/3**	**77**	**43**	**204**	**9**	**11**	**1**	**3**
Career total	445	579	223	212	.513	1401	3.46	3645	1507	761	3912	158	251	32	29
Cubs total	**68**	**109**	**33**	**38**	**.465**	**234**	**3.71**	**567 2/3**	**230**	**129**	**612**	**28**	**32**	**3**	**10**

Dettore, Thomas Anthony (Tom)

HEIGHT: 6'4"   RIGHTHANDER   BORN: 11/17/1947 CANONSBURG, PENNSYLVANIA

YEAR	TEAM	STARTS	GAMES	WON	LOST	PCT	ER	ERA	INNINGS PITCHED	STRIKE-OUTS	WALKS	HITS ALLOWED	HRS ALLOWED	COMP. GAMES	SHUT-OUTS	SAVES
1973	Pit-N	1	12	0	1	.000	15	5.96	22 2/3	13	14	33	1	0	0	0
1974	ChC-N	9	16	3	5	.375	30	4.18	64 2/3	43	31	64	4	0	0	0
1975	ChC-N	5	36	5	4	.556	51	5.38	85 1/3	46	31	88	8	0	0	0
1976	ChC-N	0	4	0	1	.000	8	10.29	7	4	2	11	3	0	0	0
Career average		4	17	2	3	.421	26	5.21	45	27	20	49	4	0	0	0
Cubs average		**5**	**19**	**3**	**3**	**.444**	**30**	**5.10**	**52 1/3**	**31**	**21**	**54**	**5**	**0**	**0**	**0**
Career total		15	68	8	11	.421	104	5.21	179 2/3	106	78	196	16	0	0	0
Cubs total		**14**	**56**	**8**	**10**	**.444**	**89**	**5.10**	**157**	**93**	**64**	**163**	**15**	**0**	**0**	**0**

Dickson, Lance Michael

HEIGHT: 6'0"   LEFTHANDER   BORN: 10/19/1969 FULLERTON, CALIFORNIA

YEAR	TEAM	STARTS	GAMES	WON	LOST	PCT	ER	ERA	INNINGS PITCHED	STRIKE-OUTS	WALKS	HITS ALLOWED	HRS ALLOWED	COMP. GAMES	SHUT-OUTS	SAVES
1990	ChC-N	3	3	0	3	.000	11	7.24	13 2/3	4	4	20	2	0	0	0
Career average		3	3	0	3	.000	11	7.24	13 2/3	4	4	20	2	0	0	0
Cubs average		**3**	**3**	**0**	**3**	**.000**	**11**	**7.24**	**13 2/3**	**4**	**4**	**20**	**2**	**0**	**0**	**0**
Career total		3	3	0	3	.000	11	7.24	13 2/3	4	4	20	2	0	0	0
Cubs total		**3**	**3**	**0**	**3**	**.000**	**11**	**7.24**	**13 2/3**	**4**	**4**	**20**	**2**	**0**	**0**	**0**

DiPino, Frank Michael

HEIGHT: 5'10"   LEFTHANDER   BORN: 10/22/1956 SYRACUSE, NEW YORK

YEAR	TEAM	STARTS	GAMES	WON	LOST	PCT	ER	ERA	INNINGS PITCHED	STRIKE-OUTS	WALKS	HITS ALLOWED	HRS ALLOWED	COMP. GAMES	SHUT-OUTS	SAVES
1981	Mil-A	0	2	0	0	—	0	0.00	2 1/3	3	3	0	0	0	0	0
1982	Hou-N	6	6	2	2	.500	19	6.04	28 1/3	25	11	32	1	0	0	0
1983	Hou-N	0	53	3	4	.429	21	2.65	71 1/3	67	20	52	2	0	0	20
1984	Hou-N	0	57	4	9	.308	28	3.35	75 1/3	65	36	74	3	0	0	14
1985	Hou-N	0	54	3	7	.300	34	4.03	76	49	43	69	7	0	0	6
1986	Hou-N	0	31	1	3	.250	16	3.57	40 1/3	27	16	27	5	0	0	3
1986	**ChC-N**	**0**	**30**	**2**	**4**	**.333**	**23**	**5.18**	**40**	**43**	**14**	**47**	**6**	**0**	**0**	**0**
1987	**ChC-N**	**0**	**69**	**3**	**3**	**.500**	**28**	**3.15**	**80**	**61**	**34**	**75**	**7**	**0**	**0**	**4**
1988	**ChC-N**	**0**	**63**	**2**	**3**	**.400**	**50**	**4.98**	**90 1/3**	**69**	**32**	**102**	**6**	**0**	**0**	**6**
1989	StL-N	0	67	9	0	1.000	24	2.45	88 1/3	44	20	73	6	0	0	0
1990	StL-N	0	62	5	2	.714	41	4.56	81	49	31	92	8	0	0	3
1992	StL-N	0	9	0	0	—	2	1.64	11	8	3	9	0	0	0	0
1993	KC-A	0	11	1	1	.500	12	6.89	15 2/3	5	6	21	2	0	0	0
Career average		1	43	3	3	.479	25	3.83	58 1/3	43	22	56	4	0	0	5
Cubs average		**0**	**54**	**2**	**3**	**.412**	**34**	**4.32**	**70**	**58**	**27**	**75**	**6**	**0**	**0**	**3**
Career total		6	514	35	38	.479	298	3.83	700	515	269	673	53	0	0	56
Cubs total		**0**	**162**	**7**	**10**	**.412**	**101**	**4.32**	**210 1/3**	**173**	**80**	**224**	**19**	**0**	**0**	**10**

Distaso, Alec John
HEIGHT: 6'2" RIGHTHANDER BORN: 12/23/1948 LOS ANGELES, CALIFORNIA

YEAR	TEAM	STARTS	GAMES	WON	LOST	PCT	ER	ERA	INNINGS PITCHED	STRIKE-OUTS	WALKS	HITS ALLOWED	HRS ALLOWED	COMP. GAMES	SHUT-OUTS	SAVES
1969	ChC-N	0	2	0	0	—	2	3.86	4 2/3	1	1	6	0	0	0	0
Career average		0	2	0	0	—	2	3.86	4 2/3	1	1	6	0	0	0	0
Cubs average		**0**	**2**	**0**	**0**	**—**	**2**	**3.86**	**4 2/3**	**1**	**1**	**6**	**0**	**0**	**0**	**0**
Career total		0	2	0	0	—	2	3.86	4 2/3	1	1	6	0	0	0	0
Cubs total		**0**	**2**	**0**	**0**	**—**	**2**	**3.86**	**4 2/3**	**1**	**1**	**6**	**0**	**0**	**0**	**0**

Dobernic, Andrew Joseph (Jess)
HEIGHT: 5'10" RIGHTHANDER BORN: 11/20/1917 MOUNT OLIVE, ILLINOIS DIED: 7/16/1998 ST. LOUIS, MISSOURI

YEAR	TEAM	STARTS	GAMES	WON	LOST	PCT	ER	ERA	INNINGS PITCHED	STRIKE-OUTS	WALKS	HITS ALLOWED	HRS ALLOWED	COMP. GAMES	SHUT-OUTS	SAVES
1939	CWS-A	0	4	0	1	.000	5	13.50	3 1/3	1	6	3	0	0	0	0
1948	ChC-N	0	54	7	2	.778	30	3.15	85 2/3	48	40	67	8	0	0	1
1949	ChC-N	0	4	0	0	—	9	20.25	4	0	4	9	2	0	0	0
1949	Cin-N	0	14	0	0	—	21	9.78	19 1/3	6	16	28	7	0	0	0
Career average		0	25	2	1	.700	22	5.21	37 1/3	18	22	36	6	0	0	0
Cubs average		**0**	**29**	**4**	**1**	**.778**	**20**	**3.91**	**45**	**24**	**22**	**38**	**5**	**0**	**0**	**1**
Career total		0	76	7	3	.700	65	5.21	112 1/3	55	66	107	17	0	0	1
Cubs total		**0**	**58**	**7**	**2**	**.778**	**39**	**3.91**	**89 2/3**	**48**	**44**	**76**	**10**	**0**	**0**	**1**

Dolan, John
HEIGHT: 5'10" RIGHTHANDER BORN: 9/12/1867 NEWPORT, KENTUCKY DIED: 5/8/1948 SPRINGFIELD, OHIO

YEAR	TEAM	STARTS	GAMES	WON	LOST	PCT	ER	ERA	INNINGS PITCHED	STRIKE-OUTS	WALKS	HITS ALLOWED	HRS ALLOWED	COMP. GAMES	SHUT-OUTS	SAVES
1890	Cin-N	2	2	1	1	.500	9	4.50	18	9	10	17	3	2	0	0
1891	CoC-AA	24	27	12	11	.522	94	4.16	203 1/3	68	84	216	8	19	0	0
1893	StL-N	1	3	0	2	.000	8	4.15	17 1/3	1	7	26	1	1	0	1
1895	**ChN-N**	2	2	0	0	—	8	6.55	11	1	6	16	0	1	0	0
Career average		7	9	3	4	.481	30	4.29	62 1/3	20	27	69	3	6	0	0
Cubs average		**2**	**2**	**0**	**0**	**—**	**8**	**6.55**	**11**	**1**	**6**	**16**	**0**	**1**	**0**	**0**
Career total		29	34	13	14	.481	119	4.29	249 2/3	79	107	275	12	23	0	1
Cubs total		**2**	**2**	**0**	**0**	**—**	**8**	**6.55**	**11**	**1**	**6**	**16**	**0**	**1**	**0**	**0**

Donnelly, Edward Vincent (Ed)
HEIGHT: 6'0" RIGHTHANDER BORN: 12/10/1932 ALLEN, MICHIGAN DIED: 12/25/1992 HOUSTON, TEXAS

YEAR	TEAM	STARTS	GAMES	WON	LOST	PCT	ER	ERA	INNINGS PITCHED	STRIKE-OUTS	WALKS	HITS ALLOWED	HRS ALLOWED	COMP. GAMES	SHUT-OUTS	SAVES
1959	ChC-N	0	9	1	1	.500	5	3.14	14 1/3	6	9	18	1	0	0	0
Career average		0	9	1	1	.500	5	3.14	14 1/3	6	9	18	1	0	0	0
Cubs average		**0**	**9**	**1**	**1**	**.500**	**5**	**3.14**	**14 1/3**	**6**	**9**	**18**	**1**	**0**	**0**	**0**
Career total		0	9	1	1	.500	5	3.14	14 1/3	6	9	18	1	0	0	0
Cubs total		**0**	**9**	**1**	**1**	**.500**	**5**	**3.14**	**14 1/3**	**6**	**9**	**18**	**1**	**0**	**0**	**0**

Donnelly, Franklin Marion (Frank)
HEIGHT: 5'6" BORN: 10/7/1869 TAMAROA, ILLINOIS DIED: 2/3/1953 CANTON, ILLINOIS

YEAR	TEAM	STARTS	GAMES	WON	LOST	PCT	ER	ERA	INNINGS PITCHED	STRIKE-OUTS	WALKS	HITS ALLOWED	HRS ALLOWED	COMP. GAMES	SHUT-OUTS	SAVES
1893	ChN-N	5	7	3	1	.750	25	5.36	42	6	17	51	1	3	0	2
Career average		5	7	3	1	.750	25	5.36	42	6	17	51	1	3	0	2
Cubs average		5	7	3	1	.750	25	5.36	42	6	17	51	1	3	0	2
Career total		5	7	3	1	.750	25	5.36	42	6	17	51	1	3	0	2
Cubs total		5	7	3	1	.750	25	5.36	42	6	17	51	1	3	0	2

Doscher, John Henry (Jack)
HEIGHT: 6'1" LEFTHANDER BORN: 7/27/1880 TROY, NEW YORK DIED: 5/27/1971 PARK RIDGE, NEW JERSEY

YEAR	TEAM	STARTS	GAMES	WON	LOST	PCT	ER	ERA	INNINGS PITCHED	STRIKE-OUTS	WALKS	HITS ALLOWED	HRS ALLOWED	COMP. GAMES	SHUT-OUTS	SAVES
1903	ChC-N	1	1	0	1	.000	4	12.00	3	5	2	6	0	0	0	0
1903	Bro-N	0	3	0	0	—	6	7.71	7	4	9	8	1	0	0	0
1904	Bro-N	0	2	0	0	—	0	0.00	6 1/3	2	1	1	0	0	0	0
1905	Bro-N	7	12	1	5	.167	25	3.17	71	33	30	60	1	6	0	0
1906	Bro-N	1	2	0	1	.000	2	1.29	14	10	4	12	0	1	0	0
1908	Cin-N	4	7	1	3	.250	9	1.83	44 1/3	7	22	31	1	3	0	0
Career average		3	5	0	2	.167	9	2.84	29	12	14	24	1	2	0	0
Cubs average		1	1	0	1	.000	4	12.00	3	5	2	6	0	0	0	0
Career total		13	27	2	10	.167	46	2.84	145 2/3	61	68	118	3	10	0	0
Cubs total		1	1	0	1	.000	4	12.00	3	5	2	6	0	0	0	0

Douglas, Phillip Brooks (Phil *or* Shufflin' Phil)
HEIGHT: 6'3" RIGHTHANDER BORN: 6/17/1890 CEDARTOWN, GEORGIA DIED: 8/2/1952 SEQUATCHIE VALLEY, TENNESSEE

YEAR	TEAM	STARTS	GAMES	WON	LOST	PCT	ER	ERA	INNINGS PITCHED	STRIKE-OUTS	WALKS	HITS ALLOWED	HRS ALLOWED	COMP. GAMES	SHUT-OUTS	SAVES
1912	CWS-A	1	3	0	1	.000	10	7.30	12 1/3	7	6	21	0	0	0	0
1914	Cin-N	25	45	11	18	.379	68	2.56	239 1/3	121	92	186	7	13	0	1
1915	Cin-N	7	8	1	5	.167	28	5.40	46 2/3	29	23	53	0	0	0	0
1915	Bro-N	13	20	5	5	.500	34	2.62	116 2/3	63	17	104	1	5	1	0
1915	ChC-N	4	4	1	1	.500	6	2.16	25	18	7	17	0	2	1	0
1917	ChC-N	37	51	14	20	.412	83	2.55	293 1/3	151	50	269	13	20	5	1
1918	ChC-N	19	25	10	9	.526	37	2.13	156 2/3	51	31	145	2	11	2	2
1919	ChC-N	19	25	10	6	.625	36	2.00	161 3/4	63	34	133	0	8	4	0
1919	NYG-N	6	8	2	4	.333	12	2.10	51 1/3	21	6	53	0	4	0	0
1920	NYG-N	21	46	14	10	.583	68	2.71	226	71	55	225	6	10	3	2
1921	NYG-N	27	40	15	10	.600	104	4.22	221 2/3	55	55	266	17	13	3	2
1922	NYG-N	21	24	11	4	.733	46	2.63	157 2/3	33	35	154	6	9	1	0
Career average		22	33	10	10	.503	59	2.80	189 2/3	76	46	181	6	11	2	1
Cubs average		20	26	9	9	.493	41	2.29	159 1/3	71	31	141	4	10	3	1
Career total		200	299	94	93	.503	532	2.80	1708 1/3	683	411	1626	52	95	20	8
Cubs total		79	105	35	36	.493	162	2.29	636 2/3	283	122	564	15	41	12	3

Dowling, David Barclay (Dave)
HEIGHT: 6'2" LEFTHANDER BORN: 8/23/1942 BATON ROUGE, LOUISIANA

YEAR	TEAM	STARTS	GAMES	WON	LOST	PCT	ER	ERA	INNINGS PITCHED	STRIKE-OUTS	WALKS	HITS ALLOWED	HRS ALLOWED	COMP. GAMES	SHUT-OUTS	SAVES
1964	StL-N	0	1	0	0	—	0	0.00	1	0	0	2	0	0	0	0
1966	ChC-N	1	1	1	0	1.000	2	2.00	9	3	0	10	0	1	0	0
Career average		1	1	1	0	1.000	1	1.80	5	2	0	6	0	1	0	0
Cubs average		1	1	1	0	1.000	2	2.00	9	3	0	10	0	1	0	0
Career total		1	2	1	0	1.000	2	1.80	10	3	0	12	0	1	0	0
Cubs total		1	1	1	0	1.000	2	2.00	9	3	0	10	0	1	0	0

Downs, Scott Jeremy
HEIGHT: 6'2" LEFTHANDER BORN: 3/17/1976 LOUISVILLE, KENTUCKY

YEAR	TEAM	STARTS	GAMES	WON	LOST	PCT	ER	ERA	INNINGS PITCHED	STRIKE-OUTS	WALKS	HITS ALLOWED	HRS ALLOWED	COMP. GAMES	SHUT-OUTS	SAVES
2000	ChC-N	18	18	4	3	.571	54	5.17	94	63	37	117	13	0	0	0
2000	Mon-N	1	1	0	0	—	3	9.00	3	0	3	5	0	0	0	0
Career average		19	19	4	3	.571	57	5.29	97	63	40	122	13	0	0	0
Cubs average		18	18	4	3	.571	54	5.17	94	63	37	117	13	0	0	0
Career total		19	19	4	3	.571	57	5.29	97	63	40	122	13	0	0	0
Cubs total		18	18	4	3	.571	54	5.17	94	63	37	117	13	0	0	0

Drabowsky, Myron Walter (Moe *or* The Snakeman)
HEIGHT: 6'3" RIGHTHANDER BORN: 7/21/1935 OZANNA, POLAND

YEAR	TEAM	STARTS	GAMES	WON	LOST	PCT	ER	ERA	INNINGS PITCHED	STRIKE-OUTS	WALKS	HITS ALLOWED	HRS ALLOWED	COMP. GAMES	SHUT-OUTS	SAVES
1956	ChC-N	7	9	2	4	.333	14	2.47	51	36	39	37	1	3	0	0
1957	ChC-N	33	36	13	15	.464	94	3.53	239 2/3	170	94	214	22	12	2	0
1958	ChC-N	20	22	9	11	.450	63	4.51	125 2/3	77	73	118	19	4	1	0
1959	ChC-N	23	31	5	10	.333	65	4.13	141 2/3	70	75	138	21	3	1	0
1960	ChC-N	7	32	3	1	.750	36	6.44	50 1/3	26	23	71	3	0	0	1
1961	Mil-N	0	16	0	2	.000	13	4.62	25 1/3	5	18	26	4	0	0	2
1962	Cin-N	10	23	2	6	.250	46	4.99	83	56	31	84	13	1	0	1
1962	KCA-A	3	10	1	1	.500	16	5.14	28	19	10	29	8	0	0	0
1963	KCA-A	22	26	7	13	.350	59	3.05	174 1/3	109	64	135	16	9	2	0
1964	KCA-A	21	53	5	13	.278	99	5.29	168 1/3	119	72	176	24	1	0	1
1965	KCA-A	5	14	1	5	.167	19	4.42	38 2/3	25	18	44	5	0	0	0
1966	Bal-A	3	44	6	0	1.000	30	2.81	96	98	29	62	10	0	0	7
1967	Bal-A	0	43	7	5	.583	17	1.60	95 1/3	96	25	66	7	0	0	12
1968	Bal-A	0	45	4	4	.500	13	1.91	61 1/3	46	25	35	3	0	0	7
1969	KC-A	0	52	11	9	.550	32	2.94	98	76	30	68	10	0	0	11
1970	KC-A	0	24	1	2	.333	13	3.28	35 2/3	38	12	28	3	0	0	2
1970	Bal-A	0	21	4	2	.667	14	3.78	33 1/3	21	15	30	7	0	0	1
1971	StL-N	0	51	6	1	.857	23	3.43	60 1/3	49	33	45	2	0	0	8
1972	StL-N	0	30	1	1	.500	8	2.60	27 2/3	22	14	29	4	0	0	2
1972	CWS-A	0	7	0	0	—	2	2.45	7 1/3	4	2	6	0	0	0	0
Career average		9	35	5	6	.456	40	3.71	96 2/3	68	41	85	11	2	0	3
Cubs average		18	26	6	8	.438	54	4.02	121 2/3	76	61	116	13	4	1	0
Career total		154	589	88	105	.456	676	3.71	1641	1162	702	1441	182	33	6	55
Cubs total		90	130	32	41	.438	272	4.02	608 1/3	379	304	578	66	22	4	1

Drott, Richard Fred (Dick *or* Hummer)
HEIGHT: 6'0" RIGHTHANDER BORN: 7/1/1936 CINCINNATI, OHIO   DIED: 8/16/1985 GLENDALE HEIGHTS, ILLINOIS

YEAR	TEAM	STARTS	GAMES	WON	LOST	PCT	ER	ERA	INNINGS PITCHED	STRIKE-OUTS	WALKS	HITS ALLOWED	HRS ALLOWED	COMP. GAMES	SHUT-OUTS	SAVES
1957	ChC-N	32	38	15	11	.577	91	3.58	229	170	129	200	22	7	3	0
1958	ChC-N	31	39	7	11	.389	101	5.43	167 1/3	127	99	156	23	4	0	0
1959	ChC-N	6	8	1	2	.333	18	5.93	27 1/3	15	26	25	5	1	0	0
1960	ChC-N	9	23	0	6	.000	44	7.16	55 1/3	32	42	63	7	0	1	0
1961	ChC-N	8	35	1	4	.200	46	4.22	98	48	51	75	13	0	0	0
1962	Hou-N	1	6	1	0	1.000	11	7.62	13	10	9	12	1	0	0	0
1963	Hou-N	14	27	2	12	.143	54	4.98	97 2/3	58	49	95	13	2	1	0
Career average		14	25	4	7	.370	52	4.78	98 1/3	66	58	89	12	2	1	0
Cubs average		17	29	5	7	.414	60	4.68	115 1/3	78	69	104	14	2	1	0
Career total		101	176	27	46	.370	365	4.78	687 2/3	460	405	626	84	14	5	0
Cubs total		86	143	24	34	.414	300	4.68	577	392	347	519	70	12	4	0

Dubiel, Walter John (Monk)

HEIGHT: 6'0"   RIGHTHANDER   BORN: 2/12/1918 HARTFORD, CONNECTICUT   DIED: 10/23/1969 HARTFORD, CONNECTICUT

YEAR	TEAM	STARTS	GAMES	WON	LOST	PCT	ER	ERA	INNINGS PITCHED	STRIKE-OUTS	WALKS	HITS ALLOWED	HRS ALLOWED	COMP. GAMES	SHUT-OUTS	SAVES
1944	NYY-A	28	30	13	13	.500	87	3.38	232	79	86	217	12	19	3	0
1945	NYY-A	20	26	10	9	.526	78	4.64	151 1/3	45	62	157	9	9	1	0
1948	Phi-N	17	37	8	10	.444	65	3.89	150 1/3	42	58	139	13	6	2	4
1949	**ChC-N**	**20**	**32**	**6**	**9**	**.400**	**68**	**4.14**	**147 2/3**	**52**	**54**	**142**	**16**	**3**	**1**	**4**
1950	**ChC-N**	**12**	**39**	**6**	**10**	**.375**	**66**	**4.16**	**142 2/3**	**51**	**67**	**152**	**12**	**4**	**2**	**2**
1951	**ChC-N**	**0**	**22**	**2**	**2**	**.500**	**14**	**2.30**	**54 2/3**	**19**	**22**	**46**	**3**	**0**	**0**	**1**
1952	**ChC-N**	**0**	**1**	**0**	**0**	**—**	**0**	**0.00**	**0 2/3**	**1**	**0**	**1**	**0**	**0**	**0**	**0**
Career average		14	27	6	8	.459	54	3.87	125 2/3	41	50	122	9	6	1	2
Cubs average		**8**	**24**	**4**	**5**	**.400**	**37**	**3.85**	**86 1/3**	**31**	**36**	**85**	**8**	**2**	**1**	**2**
Career total		97	187	45	53	.459	378	3.87	879 1/3	289	349	854	65	41	9	11
Cubs total		**32**	**94**	**14**	**21**	**.400**	**148**	**3.85**	**345 2/3**	**123**	**143**	**341**	**31**	**7**	**3**	**7**

Dumovich, Nicholas (Nick)

HEIGHT: 6'0"   LEFTHANDER   BORN: 1/2/1902 SACRAMENTO, CALIFORNIA   DIED: 12/12/1979 LAGUNA HILLS, CALIFORNIA

YEAR	TEAM	STARTS	GAMES	WON	LOST	PCT	ER	ERA	INNINGS PITCHED	STRIKE-OUTS	WALKS	HITS ALLOWED	HRS ALLOWED	COMP. GAMES	SHUT-OUTS	SAVES
1923	ChC-N	8	28	3	5	.375	48	4.60	94	23	45	118	4	1	0	1
Career average		8	28	3	5	.375	48	4.60	94	23	45	118	4	1	0	1
Cubs average		**8**	**28**	**3**	**5**	**.375**	**48**	**4.60**	**94**	**23**	**45**	**118**	**4**	**1**	**0**	**1**
Career total		8	28	3	5	.375	48	4.60	94	23	45	118	4	1	0	1
Cubs total		**8**	**28**	**3**	**5**	**.375**	**48**	**4.60**	**94**	**23**	**45**	**118**	**4**	**1**	**0**	**1**

Duncan, Courtney

HEIGHT: 6'0"   RIGHTHANDER   BORN: 10/9/1974 MOBILE, ALABAMA

YEAR	TEAM	STARTS	GAMES	WON	LOST	PCT	ER	ERA	INNINGS PITCHED	STRIKE-OUTS	WALKS	HITS ALLOWED	HRS ALLOWED	COMP. GAMES	SHUT-OUTS	SAVES
2001	ChC-N	0	36	3	3	.500	24	5.06	42 2/3	49	25	42	5	0	0	0
Career average		0	36	3	3	.500	24	5.06	42 2/3	49	25	42	5	0	0	0
Cubs average		**0**	**36**	**3**	**3**	**.500**	**24**	**5.06**	**42 2/3**	**49**	**25**	**42**	**5**	**0**	**0**	**0**
Career total		0	36	3	3	.500	24	5.06	42 2/3	49	25	42	5	0	0	0
Cubs total		**0**	**36**	**3**	**3**	**.500**	**24**	**5.06**	**42 2/3**	**49**	**25**	**42**	**5**	**0**	**0**	**0**

Dunegan, James William (Jim)

HEIGHT: 6'1"   RIGHTHANDER   BORN: 8/6/1947 BURLINGTON, IOWA

YEAR	TEAM	STARTS	GAMES	WON	LOST	PCT	ER	ERA	INNINGS PITCHED	STRIKE-OUTS	WALKS	HITS ALLOWED	HRS ALLOWED	COMP. GAMES	SHUT-OUTS	SAVES
1970	ChC-N	0	7	0	2	.000	7	4.73	13 1/3	3	12	13	2	0	0	0
Career average		0	7	0	2	.000	7	4.73	13 1/3	3	12	13	2	0	0	0
Cubs average		**0**	**7**	**0**	**2**	**.000**	**7**	**4.73**	**13 1/3**	**3**	**12**	**13**	**2**	**0**	**0**	**0**
Career total		0	7	0	2	.000	7	4.73	13 1/3	3	12	13	2	0	0	0
Cubs total		**0**	**7**	**0**	**2**	**.000**	**7**	**4.73**	**13 1/3**	**3**	**12**	**13**	**2**	**0**	**0**	**0**

Durbin, Blaine Alphonsus (Kid)

HEIGHT: 5'8"   LEFTHANDER   BORN: 9/10/1886 LAMAR, MISSOURI   DIED: 9/11/1943 KIRKWOOD, MISSOURI

YEAR	TEAM	STARTS	GAMES	WON	LOST	PCT	ER	ERA	INNINGS PITCHED	STRIKE-OUTS	WALKS	HITS ALLOWED	HRS ALLOWED	COMP. GAMES	SHUT-OUTS	SAVES
1907	ChC-N	1	5	0	1	.000	10	5.40	16 2/3	5	10	14	0	1	0	1
Career average		1	5	0	1	.000	10	5.40	16 2/3	5	10	14	0	1	0	1
Cubs average		**1**	**5**	**0**	**1**	**.000**	**10**	**5.40**	**16 2/3**	**5**	**10**	**14**	**0**	**1**	**0**	**1**
Career total		1	5	0	1	.000	10	5.40	16 2/3	5	10	14	0	1	0	1
Cubs total		**1**	**5**	**0**	**1**	**.000**	**10**	**5.40**	**16 2/3**	**5**	**10**	**14**	**0**	**1**	**0**	**1**

Dwyer, John Francis (Frank)

HEIGHT: 5'8"   RIGHTHANDER   BORN: 3/25/1868 LEE, MASSACHUSETTS   DIED: 2/4/1943 PITTSFIELD, MASSACHUSETTS

YEAR	TEAM	STARTS	GAMES	WON	LOST	PCT	ER	ERA	INNINGS PITCHED	STRIKE-OUTS	WALKS	HITS ALLOWED	HRS ALLOWED	COMP. GAMES	SHUT-OUTS	SAVES
1888	ChN-N	5	5	4	1	.800	5	1.07	42	17	9	32	1	5	1	0
1889	ChN-N	30	32	16	13	.552	110	3.59	276	63	72	307	14	27	0	0
1890	Chi-P	6	12	3	6	.333	48	6.23	69 1/3	17	25	98	4	6	0	1
1891	Cin-AA	31	35	13	19	.406	145	4.52	289	101	124	332	10	29	1	0
1891	Mil-AA	10	10	6	4	.600	21	2.20	86	27	21	92	2	10	0	0
1892	StL-N	10	10	2	6	.250	40	5.63	64	16	24	90	1	6	0	0
1892	Cin-N	28	34	20	9	.690	69	2.31	268 1/3	47	49	262	6	25	3	1
1893	Cin-N	30	37	17	13	.567	132	4.13	287 1/3	53	93	332	17	28	1	2
1894	Cin-N	39	45	19	19	.500	196	5.07	348	49	106	471	27	35	1	1
1895	Cin-N	31	37	18	15	.545	132	4.24	280 1/3	46	74	355	10	23	2	0
1896	Cin-N	34	36	24	9	.727	101	3.15	288 2/3	57	60	321	8	30	3	1
1897	Cin-N	31	37	18	14	.563	104	3.78	247 1/3	41	56	315	5	22	0	0
1898	Cin-N	28	31	17	9	.654	81	3.04	240	29	42	257	3	24	0	0
1899	Cin-N	5	5	0	4	.000	20	5.51	32 2/3	2	9	48	1	2	0	0
Career average		27	31	15	12	.557	100	3.84	235	47	64	276	9	23	1	1
Cubs average		**18**	**19**	**10**	**7**	**.588**	**58**	**3.25**	**159**	**40**	**41**	**170**	**8**	**16**	**1**	**0**
Career total		318	366	177	141	.557	1204	3.84	2819	565	764	3312	109	272	12	6
Cubs total		**35**	**37**	**20**	**14**	**.588**	**115**	**3.25**	**318**	**80**	**81**	**339**	**15**	**32**	**1**	**0**

Earley, Arnold Carl

HEIGHT: 6'1"   LEFTHANDER   BORN: 6/4/1933 LINCOLN PARK, MICHIGAN   DIED: 9/29/1999 FLINT, MICHIGAN

YEAR	TEAM	STARTS	GAMES	WON	LOST	PCT	ER	ERA	INNINGS PITCHED	STRIKE-OUTS	WALKS	HITS ALLOWED	HRS ALLOWED	COMP. GAMES	SHUT-OUTS	SAVES
1960	Bos-A	0	2	0	1	.000	7	15.75	4	5	4	9	1	0	0	0
1961	Bos-A	0	33	2	4	.333	22	3.99	49 2/3	44	34	42	3	0	0	7
1962	Bos-A	3	38	4	5	.444	44	5.80	68 1/3	59	46	76	8	0	0	5
1963	Bos-A	4	53	3	7	.300	61	4.75	115 2/3	97	43	124	13	0	0	1
1964	Bos-A	3	25	1	1	.500	15	2.68	50 1/3	45	18	51	3	1	0	1
1965	Bos-A	0	57	0	1	.000	30	3.63	74 1/3	47	29	79	5	0	0	0
1966	ChC-N	0	13	2	1	.667	7	3.57	17 2/3	12	9	14	1	0	0	0
1967	Hou-N	0	2	0	0	—	4	27.00	1 1/3	1	1	5	1	0	0	0
Career average		1	28	2	3	.375	24	4.48	47 2/3	39	23	50	4	0	0	2
Cubs average		**0**	**13**	**2**	**1**	**.667**	**7**	**3.57**	**17 2/3**	**12**	**9**	**14**	**1**	**0**	**0**	**0**
Career total		10	223	12	20	.375	190	4.48	381 1/3	310	184	400	35	1	0	14
Cubs total		**0**	**13**	**2**	**1**	**.667**	**7**	**3.57**	**17 2/3**	**12**	**9**	**14**	**1**	**0**	**0**	**0**

Eason, Malcolm Wayne (Mal *or* Kid)

HEIGHT: 6'0"   RIGHTHANDER   BORN: 3/13/1879 BROOKVILLE, PENNSYLVANIA   DIED: 4/16/1970 DOUGLAS, ARIZONA

YEAR	TEAM	STARTS	GAMES	WON	LOST	PCT	ER	ERA	INNINGS PITCHED	STRIKE-OUTS	WALKS	HITS ALLOWED	HRS ALLOWED	COMP. GAMES	SHUT-OUTS	SAVES
1900	ChN-N	1	1	1	0	1.000	1	1.00	9	2	3	9	0	1	0	0
1901	ChN-N	25	27	8	17	.320	88	3.59	220 2/3	68	60	246	9	23	1	0
1902	ChC-N	2	2	1	1	.500	2	1.00	18	4	2	21	0	2	0	0
1902	Bos-N	26	27	9	12	.429	63	2.66	213 1/3	50	59	237	4	20	2	0
1903	Det-A	6	7	2	5	.286	21	3.36	56 1/3	21	19	60	1	6	1	0
1905	Bro-N	27	27	5	21	.192	99	4.30	207	64	72	230	5	20	3	0
1906	Bro-N	26	34	10	17	.370	82	3.25	227	64	74	212	1	18	3	1
Career average		19	21	6	12	.330	59	3.37	158 2/3	46	48	169	3	15	2	0
Cubs average		**9**	**10**	**3**	**6**	**.357**	**30**	**3.31**	**82 2/3**	**25**	**22**	**92**	**3**	**9**	**0**	**0**
Career total		113	125	36	73	.330	356	3.37	951 1/3	273	289	1015	20	90	10	1
Cubs total		**28**	**30**	**10**	**18**	**.357**	**91**	**3.31**	**247 2/3**	**74**	**65**	**276**	**9**	**26**	**1**	**0**

Eastwick, Rawlins Jackson (Rawly)
HEIGHT: 6'3"   RIGHTHANDER   BORN: 10/24/1950 CAMDEN, NEW JERSEY

YEAR	TEAM	STARTS	GAMES	WON	LOST	PCT	ER	ERA	INNINGS PITCHED	STRIKE-OUTS	WALKS	HITS ALLOWED	HRS ALLOWED	COMP. GAMES	SHUT-OUTS	SAVES
1974	Cin-N	0	8	0	0	—	4	2.04	17 2/3	14	5	12	1	0	0	2
1975	Cin-N	0	58	5	3	.625	26	2.60	90	61	25	77	6	0	0	22
1976	Cin-N	0	71	11	5	.688	25	2.09	107 2/3	70	27	93	3	0	0	26
1977	Cin-N	0	23	2	2	.500	14	2.91	43 1/3	17	8	40	3	0	0	7
1977	StL-N	1	41	3	7	.300	28	4.70	53 2/3	30	21	74	6	0	0	4
1978	NYY-A	0	8	2	1	.667	9	3.28	24 2/3	13	4	22	2	0	0	0
1978	Phi-N	0	22	2	1	.667	18	4.02	40 1/3	14	18	31	5	0	0	6
1979	Phi-N	0	51	3	6	.333	45	4.90	82 2/3	47	25	90	8	0	0	6
1980	KC-A	0	14	0	1	.000	13	5.32	22	5	8	37	2	0	0	1
1981	**ChC-N**	0	**30**	0	1	**.000**	11	**2.28**	43 1/3	**24**	**15**	**43**	**2**	0	0	1
Career average		0	41	4	3	.509	24	3.31	65 2/3	37	20	65	5	0	0	9
Cubs average		**0**	**30**	**0**	**1**	**.000**	**11**	**2.28**	**43 1/3**	**24**	**15**	**43**	**2**	**0**	**0**	**1**
Career total		1	326	28	27	.509	193	3.31	525 1/3	295	156	519	38	0	0	68
Cubs total		**0**	**30**	**0**	**1**	**.000**	**11**	**2.28**	**43 1/3**	**24**	**15**	**43**	**2**	**0**	**0**	**1**

Eaves, Vallie Ennis (Chief or Tom)
HEIGHT: 6'2"   RIGHTHANDER   BORN: 9/6/1911 ALLEN, OKLAHOMA   DIED: 4/19/1960 NORMAN, OKLAHOMA

YEAR	TEAM	STARTS	GAMES	WON	LOST	PCT	ER	ERA	INNINGS PITCHED	STRIKE-OUTS	WALKS	HITS ALLOWED	HRS ALLOWED	COMP. GAMES	SHUT-OUTS	SAVES
1935	Phi-A	3	3	1	2	.333	8	5.14	14	6	15	12	0	1	0	0
1939	CWS-A	1	2	0	1	.000	6	4.63	11 2/3	5	8	11	1	1	0	0
1940	CWS-A	3	5	0	2	.000	14	6.75	18 2/3	11	24	22	2	0	0	0
1941	**ChC-N**	**7**	**12**	**3**	**3**	**.500**	**23**	**3.53**	**58 2/3**	**24**	**21**	**56**	**4**	**4**	**0**	**0**
1942	**ChC-N**	**0**	**2**	**0**	**0**	**—**	**3**	**9.00**	**3**	**0**	**2**	**4**	**0**	**0**	**0**	**0**
Career average		3	5	1	2	.333	11	4.58	21 1/3	9	14	21	1	1	0	0
Cubs average		**4**	**7**	**2**	**2**	**.500**	**13**	**3.79**	**31**	**12**	**12**	**30**	**2**	**2**	**0**	**0**
Career total		14	24	4	8	.333	54	4.58	106	46	70	105	7	6	0	0
Cubs total		**7**	**14**	**3**	**3**	**.500**	**26**	**3.79**	**61 2/3**	**24**	**23**	**60**	**4**	**4**	**0**	**0**

Eckersley, Dennis Lee (The Eck)
HEIGHT: 6'2"   RIGHTHANDER   BORN: 10/3/1954 OAKLAND, CALIFORNIA

YEAR	TEAM	STARTS	GAMES	WON	LOST	PCT	ER	ERA	INNINGS PITCHED	STRIKE-OUTS	WALKS	HITS ALLOWED	HRS ALLOWED	COMP. GAMES	SHUT-OUTS	SAVES
1975	Cle-A	24	34	13	7	.650	54	2.60	186 2/3	152	90	147	16	6	2	2
1976	Cle-A	30	36	13	12	.520	76	3.43	199 1/3	200	78	155	13	9	3	1
1977	Cle-A	33	33	14	13	.519	97	3.53	247 1/3	191	54	214	31	12	3	0
1978	Bos-A	35	35	20	8	.714	89	2.99	268 1/3	162	71	258	30	16	2	0
1979	Bos-A	33	33	17	10	.630	82	2.99	246 2/3	150	59	234	29	17	2	0
1980	Bos-A	30	30	12	14	.462	94	4.28	197 2/3	121	44	188	25	8	2	0
1981	Bos-A	23	23	9	8	.529	73	4.27	154	79	35	160	9	8	2	0
1982	Bos-A	33	33	13	13	.500	93	3.73	224 1/3	127	43	228	31	11	3	0
1983	Bos-A	28	28	9	13	.409	110	5.61	176 1/3	77	39	223	27	2	0	0
1984	Bos-A	9	9	4	4	.500	36	5.01	64 2/3	33	13	71	10	2	0	0
1984	**ChC-N**	**24**	**24**	**10**	**8**	**.556**	**54**	**3.03**	**160 1/3**	**81**	**36**	**152**	**11**	**2**	**0**	**0**
1985	**ChC-N**	**25**	**25**	**11**	**7**	**.611**	**58**	**3.08**	**169 1/3**	**117**	**19**	**145**	**15**	**6**	**2**	**0**
1986	**ChC-N**	**32**	**33**	**6**	**11**	**.353**	**102**	**4.57**	**201**	**137**	**43**	**226**	**21**	**1**	**0**	**0**
1987	Oak-A	2	54	6	8	.429	39	3.03	115 2/3	113	17	99	11	0	0	16
1988	Oak-A	0	60	4	2	.667	19	2.35	72 2/3	70	11	52	5	0	0	45
1989	Oak-A	0	51	4	0	1.000	10	1.56	57 2/3	55	3	32	5	0	0	33
1990	Oak-A	0	63	4	2	.667	5	0.61	73 1/3	73	4	41	2	0	0	48
1991	Oak-A	0	67	5	4	.556	25	2.96	76	87	9	60	11	0	0	43
1992	Oak-A	0	69	7	1	.875	17	1.91	80	93	11	62	5	0	0	51
1993	Oak-A	0	64	2	4	.333	31	4.16	67	80	13	67	7	0	0	36
1994	Oak-A	0	45	5	4	.556	21	4.26	44 1/3	47	13	49	5	0	0	19
1995	Oak-A	0	52	4	6	.400	27	4.83	50 1/3	40	11	53	5	0	0	29
1996	StL-N	0	63	0	6	.000	22	3.30	60	49	6	65	8	0	0	30
1997	StL-N	0	57	1	5	.167	23	3.91	53	45	8	49	9	0	0	36
1998	Bos-A	0	50	4	1	.800	21	4.76	39 2/3	22	8	46	6	0	0	1
Career average		15	45	8	7	.535	53	3.50	137	100	31	128	14	4	1	16
Cubs average		**27**	**27**	**9**	**9**	**.509**	**71**	**3.63**	**177**	**112**	**33**	**174**	**16**	**3**	**1**	**0**
Career total		361	1071	197	171	.535	1278	3.50	3285 2/3	2401	738	3076	347	100	20	390
Cubs total		**81**	**82**	**27**	**26**	**.509**	**214**	**3.63**	**530 2/3**	**335**	**98**	**523**	**47**	**9**	**2**	**0**

Edens, Thomas Patrick (Tom)
HEIGHT: 6'2" RIGHTHANDER BORN: 6/9/1961 ONTARIO, OREGON

YEAR	TEAM	STARTS	GAMES	WON	LOST	PCT	ER	ERA	INNINGS PITCHED	STRIKE-OUTS	WALKS	HITS ALLOWED	HRS ALLOWED	COMP. GAMES	SHUT-OUTS	SAVES
1987	NYM-N	2	2	0	0	—	6	6.75	8	4	4	15	2	0	0	0
1990	Mil-A	6	35	4	5	.444	44	4.45	89	40	33	89	8	0	0	2
1991	Min-A	6	8	2	2	.500	15	4.09	33	19	10	34	2	0	0	0
1992	Min-A	0	52	6	3	.667	24	2.83	76⅓	57	36	65	1	0	0	3
1993	Hou-N	0	38	1	1	.500	17	3.12	49	21	19	47	4	0	0	0
1994	Hou-N	0	39	4	1	.800	25	4.50	50	38	17	55	3	0	0	1
1994	Phi-N	0	3	1	0	1.000	1	2.25	4	1	1	4	0	0	0	0
1995	**ChC-N**	**0**	**5**	**1**	**0**	**1.000**	**2**	**6.00**	**3**	**2**	**3**	**6**	**0**	**0**	**0**	**0**
Career average		2	26	3	2	.613	19	3.86	44⅔	26	18	45	3	0	0	1
Cubs average		**0**	**5**	**1**	**0**	**1.000**	**2**	**6.00**	**3**	**2**	**3**	**6**	**0**	**0**	**0**	**0**
Career total		14	182	19	12	.613	134	3.86	312⅓	182	123	315	20	0	0	6
Cubs total		**0**	**5**	**1**	**0**	**1.000**	**2**	**6.00**	**3**	**2**	**3**	**6**	**0**	**0**	**0**	**0**

Eiteljorge, Edward Henry (Ed)
HEIGHT: 6'2" RIGHTHANDER BORN: 10/14/1871 BERLIN, GERMANY DIED: 12/5/1942 GREENCASTLE, INDIANA

YEAR	TEAM	STARTS	GAMES	WON	LOST	PCT	ER	ERA	INNINGS PITCHED	STRIKE-OUTS	WALKS	HITS ALLOWED	HRS ALLOWED	COMP. GAMES	SHUT-OUTS	SAVES
1890	**ChN-N**	**1**	**1**	**0**	**0**	—	**5**	**22.50**	**2**	**1**	**1**	**5**	**0**	**0**	**0**	**0**
1891	Was-AA	7	8	1	5	.167	42	6.16	61⅓	23	41	79	3	6	0	0
Career average		4	5	1	3	.167	24	6.68	31⅔	12	21	42	2	3	0	0
Cubs average		**1**	**1**	**0**	**0**	—	**5**	**22.50**	**2**	**1**	**1**	**5**	**0**	**0**	**0**	**0**
Career total		8	9	1	5	.167	47	6.68	63⅓	24	42	84	3	6	0	0
Cubs total		**1**	**1**	**0**	**0**	—	**5**	**22.50**	**2**	**1**	**1**	**5**	**0**	**0**	**0**	**0**

Ellis, James Russell (Jim)
HEIGHT: 6'2" LEFTHANDER BORN: 3/25/1945 TULARE, CALIFORNIA

YEAR	TEAM	STARTS	GAMES	WON	LOST	PCT	ER	ERA	INNINGS PITCHED	STRIKE-OUTS	WALKS	HITS ALLOWED	HRS ALLOWED	COMP. GAMES	SHUT-OUTS	SAVES
1967	**ChC-N**	**1**	**8**	**1**	**1**	**.500**	**6**	**3.24**	**16⅔**	**8**	**9**	**20**	**1**	**0**	**0**	**0**
1969	StL-N	1	2	0	0	—	1	1.69	5⅓	0	3	7	0	0	0	0
Career average		1	5	1	1	.500	4	2.86	11	4	6	14	1	0	0	0
Cubs average		**1**	**8**	**1**	**1**	**.500**	**6**	**3.24**	**16⅔**	**8**	**9**	**20**	**1**	**0**	**0**	**0**
Career total		2	10	1	1	.500	7	2.86	22	8	12	27	1	0	0	0
Cubs total		**1**	**8**	**1**	**1**	**.500**	**6**	**3.24**	**16⅔**	**8**	**9**	**20**	**1**	**0**	**0**	**0**

Ellsworth, Richard Clark (Dick)
HEIGHT: 6'3" LEFTHANDER BORN: 3/22/1940 LUSK, WYOMING

YEAR	TEAM	STARTS	GAMES	WON	LOST	PCT	ER	ERA	INNINGS PITCHED	STRIKE-OUTS	WALKS	HITS ALLOWED	HRS ALLOWED	COMP. GAMES	SHUT-OUTS	SAVES
1958	**ChC-N**	**1**	**1**	**0**	**1**	**.000**	**4**	**15.43**	**2⅓**	**0**	**3**	**4**	**0**	**0**	**0**	**0**
1960	**ChC-N**	**27**	**31**	**7**	**13**	**.350**	**73**	**3.72**	**176⅔**	**94**	**72**	**170**	**12**	**6**	**0**	**0**
1961	**ChC-N**	**31**	**37**	**10**	**11**	**.476**	**80**	**3.86**	**186⅔**	**91**	**48**	**213**	**23**	**7**	**1**	**0**
1962	**ChC-N**	**33**	**37**	**9**	**20**	**.310**	**118**	**5.09**	**208⅔**	**113**	**77**	**241**	**23**	**6**	**0**	**1**
1963	**ChC-N**	**37**	**37**	**22**	**10**	**.688**	**68**	**2.11**	**290⅔**	**185**	**75**	**223**	**14**	**19**	**4**	**0**
1964	**ChC-N**	**36**	**37**	**14**	**18**	**.438**	**107**	**3.75**	**256⅔**	**148**	**71**	**267**	**34**	**16**	**1**	**0**
1965	**ChC-N**	**34**	**36**	**14**	**15**	**.483**	**94**	**3.81**	**222⅓**	**130**	**57**	**227**	**22**	**8**	**0**	**1**
1966	**ChC-N**	**37**	**38**	**8**	**22**	**.267**	**119**	**3.98**	**269⅓**	**144**	**51**	**321**	**28**	**9**	**0**	**0**
1967	Phi-N	21	32	6	7	.462	61	4.38	125⅓	45	36	152	6	3	1	0
1968	Bos-A	28	31	16	7	.696	66	3.03	196	106	37	196	16	10	1	0
1969	Bos-A	2	2	0	0	—	5	3.75	12	4	4	16	1	0	0	0
1969	Cle-A	22	34	6	9	.400	62	4.13	135	48	40	162	10	3	1	0
1970	Cle-A	1	29	3	3	.500	22	4.53	43⅔	13	14	49	4	0	0	2
1970	Mil-A	0	14	0	0	—	3	1.72	15⅔	9	3	11	0	0	0	1
1971	Mil-A	0	11	0	1	.000	8	4.91	14⅔	10	7	22	1	0	0	0
Career average		24	31	9	11	.456	68	3.72	165⅔	88	46	175	15	7	1	0
Cubs average		**30**	**32**	**11**	**14**	**.433**	**83**	**3.70**	**201⅔**	**113**	**57**	**208**	**20**	**9**	**1**	**0**
Career total		310	407	115	137	.456	890	3.72	2155⅔	1140	595	2274	194	87	9	5
Cubs total		**236**	**254**	**84**	**110**	**.433**	**663**	**3.70**	**1613⅓**	**905**	**454**	**1666**	**156**	**71**	**6**	**2**

Richard (Dick) Clark Ellsworth, lhp, 1958–71

Dick Ellsworth was a valiant toiler for a number of dismal Cubs teams from the early to mid-1960s.

Ellsworth was born on March 22, 1940, in Lusk, Wyoming. He came to Chicago as a big (6'3"), power-pitching, promising lefthander. And after a cup of coffee with the Cubs in 1958, Ellsworth was called up for good in 1960.

The problem was, Ellsworth was a good pitcher on a very bad team. He remains, for example, the only lefthander to win more than 20 games in a season for the Cubs since James "Hippo" Vaughn in 1919. Ellsworth accomplished that feat in 1963 when he went a stunning 22-10, winning 27 percent of the Cubs' 82 wins. (This was, by far, the most successful Cubs team of Ellsworth's eight-year Cubs career. Chicago's average record was 69-92 in this span.)

More typically, Ellsworth would win 45 to 47 percent of his games. In 1962 and again in 1966, the Cubs were exceptionally bad, winning only 59 games each time. In 1962 Chicago was 43½ games out of first; in 1966 they were 36 games out.

Ellsworth still took the ball every start and ended up losing 20 and 22 games in those two seasons.

Ellsworth ended up 84-110 with Chicago in those eight years, but he was still the winningest Cub of the 1960s; he also led the team in starts for the decade with 235, complete games with 71 and innings pitched with 1,611. He also led the Cubs in strikeouts three years in a row, with a high of 185 in 1963.

Ellsworth's strikeout to walk ratio was 2-1, and when he got any kind of run support, he was successful. But he didn't often get that support.

Ellsworth was traded to Philadelphia in 1967, and from there he went to Boston in 1968. With a more potent lineup in Boston, he went 16-7, was fourth in the league in winning percentage and third in fewest walks per game. He finished up his career in Cleveland and Milwaukee.

Not surprisingly, Ellsworth is seventh all-time with the Cubs with 110 losses.

Elston, Donald Ray (Don *or* Everyday)

HEIGHT: 6'0"   RIGHTHANDER   BORN: 4/6/1929 CAMPBELLSTOWN, OHIO   DIED: 1/2/1995 EVANSTON, ILLINOIS

YEAR	TEAM	STARTS	GAMES	WON	LOST	PCT	ER	ERA	INNINGS PITCHED	STRIKE-OUTS	WALKS	HITS ALLOWED	HRS ALLOWED	COMP. GAMES	SHUT-OUTS	SAVES
1953	ChC-N	1	2	0	1	.000	8	14.40	5	2	0	11	1	0	0	0
1957	Bro-N	0	1	0	0	—	0	0.00	1	1	0	1	0	0	0	0
1957	ChC-N	14	39	6	7	.462	57	3.56	144	102	55	139	15	2	0	8
1958	ChC-N	0	69	9	8	.529	31	2.88	97	84	39	75	9	0	0	10
1959	ChC-N	0	65	10	8	.556	36	3.32	97 ⅔	82	46	77	11	0	0	13
1960	ChC-N	0	60	8	9	.471	48	3.40	127	85	55	109	17	0	0	11
1961	ChC-N	0	58	6	7	.462	58	5.59	93 ⅓	59	45	108	11	0	0	8
1962	ChC-N	0	57	4	8	.333	18	2.44	66 ⅓	37	32	57	6	0	0	8
1963	ChC-N	0	51	4	1	.800	22	2.83	70	41	21	57	6	0	0	4
1964	ChC-N	0	48	2	5	.286	32	5.30	54 ⅓	26	34	68	4	0	0	1
Career average		2	50	5	6	.476	34	3.69	84	58	36	78	9	0	0	7
Cubs average		**2**	**50**	**5**	**6**	**.476**	**34**	**3.70**	**84**	**58**	**36**	**78**	**9**	**0**	**0**	**7**
Career total		15	450	49	54	.476	310	3.69	755 ⅔	519	327	702	80	2	0	63
Cubs total		**15**	**449**	**49**	**54**	**.476**	**310**	**3.70**	**754 ⅔**	**518**	**327**	**701**	**80**	**2**	**0**	**63**

Engel, Steven Michael (Steve)
HEIGHT: 6'3"   LEFTHANDER   BORN: 12/31/1961 CINCINNATI, OHIO

YEAR	TEAM	STARTS	GAMES	WON	LOST	PCT	ER	ERA	INNINGS PITCHED	STRIKE-OUTS	WALKS	HITS ALLOWED	HRS ALLOWED	COMP. GAMES	SHUT-OUTS	SAVES
1985	ChC-N	8	11	1	5	.167	32	5.57	51 2/3	29	26	61	10	1	0	1
Career average		8	11	1	5	.167	32	5.57	51 2/3	29	26	61	10	1	0	1
Cubs average		**8**	**11**	**1**	**5**	**.167**	**32**	**5.57**	**51 2/3**	**29**	**26**	**61**	**10**	**1**	**0**	**1**
Career total		8	11	1	5	.167	32	5.57	51 2/3	29	26	61	10	1	0	1
Cubs total		**8**	**11**	**1**	**5**	**.167**	**32**	**5.57**	**51 2/3**	**29**	**26**	**61**	**10**	**1**	**0**	**1**

Epperly, Albert Paul (Al *or* Tub *or* Pard)
HEIGHT: 6'2"   RIGHTHANDER   BORN: 5/7/1918 GLIDDEN, IOWA

YEAR	TEAM	STARTS	GAMES	WON	LOST	PCT	ER	ERA	INNINGS PITCHED	STRIKE-OUTS	WALKS	HITS ALLOWED	HRS ALLOWED	COMP. GAMES	SHUT-OUTS	SAVES
1938	ChC-N	4	9	2	0	1.000	11	3.67	27	10	15	28	1	1	0	0
1950	Bro-N	0	5	0	0	—	5	5.00	9	3	5	14	1	0	0	0
Career average		2	7	1	0	1.000	8	4.00	18	7	10	21	1	1	0	0
Cubs average		**4**	**9**	**2**	**0**	**1.000**	**11**	**3.67**	**27**	**10**	**15**	**28**	**1**	**1**	**0**	**0**
Career total		4	14	2	0	1.000	16	4.00	36	13	20	42	2	1	0	0
Cubs total		**4**	**9**	**2**	**0**	**1.000**	**11**	**3.67**	**27**	**10**	**15**	**28**	**1**	**1**	**0**	**0**

Erickson, Paul Walford (Li'l Abner *or* Swede)
HEIGHT: 6'2"   RIGHTHANDER   BORN: 12/14/1915 ZION, ILLINOIS

YEAR	TEAM	STARTS	GAMES	WON	LOST	PCT	ER	ERA	INNINGS PITCHED	STRIKE-OUTS	WALKS	HITS ALLOWED	HRS ALLOWED	COMP. GAMES	SHUT-OUTS	SAVES
1941	ChC-N	15	32	5	7	.417	58	3.70	141	85	64	126	2	7	1	1
1942	ChC-N	7	18	1	6	.143	38	5.43	63	26	41	70	4	1	0	0
1943	ChC-N	4	15	1	3	.250	29	6.12	42 2/3	24	22	47	4	0	0	0
1944	ChC-N	15	33	5	9	.357	49	3.55	124 1/3	82	67	113	5	5	3	1
1945	ChC-N	9	28	7	4	.636	40	3.32	108 1/3	53	48	94	5	3	0	3
1946	ChC-N	14	32	9	7	.563	37	2.43	137	70	65	119	2	5	1	0
1947	ChC-N	20	40	7	12	.368	84	4.34	174	82	93	179	17	6	0	1
1948	ChC-N	0	3	0	0	—	4	6.35	5 2/3	4	6	7	0	0	0	0
1948	Phi-N	2	4	2	0	1.000	10	5.19	17 1/3	5	17	19	2	0	0	0
1948	NYG-N	0	2	0	0	—	0	0.00	1	1	2	0	0	0	0	0
Career average		11	26	5	6	.435	44	3.86	101 2/3	54	53	97	5	3	1	1
Cubs average		**11**	**25**	**4**	**6**	**.422**	**42**	**3.83**	**99 2/3**	**53**	**51**	**94**	**5**	**3**	**1**	**1**
Career total		86	207	37	48	.435	349	3.86	814 1/3	432	425	774	41	27	5	6
Cubs total		**84**	**201**	**35**	**48**	**.422**	**339**	**3.83**	**796**	**426**	**406**	**755**	**39**	**27**	**5**	**6**

Errickson, Richard Merriwell (Dick *or* Lief)
HEIGHT: 6'1"   RIGHTHANDER   BORN: 3/5/1912 VINELAND, NEW JERSEY   DIED: 11/28/1999 VINELAND, NEW JERSEY

YEAR	TEAM	STARTS	GAMES	WON	LOST	PCT	ER	ERA	INNINGS PITCHED	STRIKE-OUTS	WALKS	HITS ALLOWED	HRS ALLOWED	COMP. GAMES	SHUT-OUTS	SAVES
1938	Bos-N	10	34	9	7	.563	43	3.15	122 2/3	40	56	113	1	6	1	6
1939	Bos-N	11	28	6	9	.400	57	4.00	128 1/3	33	54	143	6	3	0	1
1940	Bos-N	29	34	12	13	.480	83	3.16	236 1/3	34	90	241	8	17	3	4
1941	Bos-N	23	38	6	12	.333	88	4.78	165 2/3	45	62	192	12	5	2	1
1942	Bos-N	4	21	2	5	.286	33	5.01	59 1/3	15	20	76	8	0	0	1
1942	ChC-N	0	13	1	1	.500	11	4.13	24	9	8	39	1	0	0	0
Career average		15	34	7	9	.434	63	3.85	147 1/3	35	58	161	7	6	1	3
Cubs average		**0**	**13**	**1**	**1**	**.500**	**11**	**4.13**	**24**	**9**	**8**	**39**	**1**	**0**	**0**	**0**
Career total		77	168	36	47	.434	315	3.85	736 1/3	176	290	804	36	31	6	13
Cubs total		**0**	**13**	**1**	**1**	**.500**	**11**	**4.13**	**24**	**9**	**8**	**39**	**1**	**0**	**0**	**0**

Estrada, Charles Leonard (Chuck *or* Droopy)
HEIGHT: 6'1" RIGHTHANDER BORN: 2/15/1938 SAN LUIS OBISPO, CALIFORNIA

YEAR	TEAM	STARTS	GAMES	WON	LOST	PCT	ER	ERA	INNINGS PITCHED	STRIKE-OUTS	WALKS	HITS ALLOWED	HRS ALLOWED	COMP. GAMES	SHUT-OUTS	SAVES
1960	Bal-A	25	36	18	11	.621	83	3.58	208 ⅔	144	101	162	18	12	1	2
1961	Bal-A	31	33	15	9	.625	87	3.69	212	160	132	159	19	6	1	0
1962	Bal-A	33	34	9	17	.346	95	3.83	223 ⅓	165	121	199	24	6	0	0
1963	Bal-A	7	8	3	2	.600	16	4.60	31 ⅓	16	19	26	2	0	0	0
1964	Bal-A	6	17	3	2	.600	32	5.27	54 ⅔	32	21	62	8	0	0	0
1966	**ChC-N**	**1**	**9**	**1**	**1**	**.500**	**10**	**7.30**	**12 ⅓**	**3**	**5**	**16**	**2**	**0**	**0**	**0**
1967	NYM-N	2	9	1	2	.333	23	9.41	22	15	17	28	5	0	0	0
Career average		15	21	7	6	.532	49	4.07	109 ⅓	76	59	93	11	3	0	0
Cubs average		**1**	**9**	**1**	**1**	**.500**	**10**	**7.30**	**12 ⅓**	**3**	**5**	**16**	**2**	**0**	**0**	**0**
Career total		105	146	50	44	.532	346	4.07	764 ⅓	535	416	652	78	24	2	2
Cubs total		**1**	**9**	**1**	**1**	**.500**	**10**	**7.30**	**12 ⅓**	**3**	**5**	**16**	**2**	**0**	**0**	**0**

Eubanks, Uel Melvin (Poss)
HEIGHT: 6'3" RIGHTHANDER BORN: 2/14/1903 QUINLAN, TEXAS DIED: 11/21/1954 DALLAS, TEXAS

YEAR	TEAM	STARTS	GAMES	WON	LOST	PCT	ER	ERA	INNINGS PITCHED	STRIKE-OUTS	WALKS	HITS ALLOWED	HRS ALLOWED	COMP. GAMES	SHUT-OUTS	SAVES
1922	**ChC-N**	**0**	**2**	**0**	**0**	**—**	**5**	**27.00**	**1 ⅔**	**1**	**4**	**5**	**0**	**0**	**0**	**0**
Career average		0	2	0	0	—	5	27.00	1 ⅔	1	4	5	0	0	0	0
Cubs average		**0**	**2**	**0**	**0**	**—**	**5**	**27.00**	**1 ⅔**	**1**	**4**	**5**	**0**	**0**	**0**	**0**
Career total		0	2	0	0	—	5	27.00	1 ⅔	1	4	5	0	0	0	0
Cubs total		**0**	**2**	**0**	**0**	**—**	**5**	**27.00**	**1 ⅔**	**1**	**4**	**5**	**0**	**0**	**0**	**0**

Farnsworth, Kyle Lynn
HEIGHT: 6'4" RIGHTHANDER BORN: 4/14/1976 WICHITA, KANSAS

YEAR	TEAM	STARTS	GAMES	WON	LOST	PCT	ER	ERA	INNINGS PITCHED	STRIKE-OUTS	WALKS	HITS ALLOWED	HRS ALLOWED	COMP. GAMES	SHUT-OUTS	SAVES
1999	**ChC-N**	**21**	**27**	**5**	**9**	**.357**	**73**	**5.05**	**130**	**70**	**52**	**140**	**28**	**1**	**1**	**0**
2000	**ChC-N**	**5**	**46**	**2**	**9**	**.182**	**55**	**6.43**	**77**	**74**	**50**	**90**	**14**	**0**	**0**	**1**
2001	**ChC-N**	**0**	**76**	**4**	**6**	**.400**	**25**	**2.74**	**82**	**107**	**29**	**65**	**8**	**0**	**0**	**2**
Career average		9	50	4	8	.314	51	4.76	96 ⅓	84	44	98	17	0	0	1
Cubs average		**9**	**50**	**4**	**8**	**.314**	**51**	**4.76**	**96 ⅓**	**84**	**44**	**98**	**17**	**0**	**0**	**1**
Career total		26	149	11	24	.314	153	4.76	289	251	131	295	50	1	1	3
Cubs total		**26**	**149**	**11**	**24**	**.314**	**153**	**4.76**	**289**	**251**	**131**	**295**	**50**	**1**	**1**	**3**

Fassero, Jeffrey Joseph (Jeff)
HEIGHT: 6'1" LEFTHANDER BORN: 1/5/1963 SPRINGFIELD, ILLINOIS

YEAR	TEAM	STARTS	GAMES	WON	LOST	PCT	ER	ERA	INNINGS PITCHED	STRIKE-OUTS	WALKS	HITS ALLOWED	HRS ALLOWED	COMP. GAMES	SHUT-OUTS	SAVES
1991	Mon-N	0	51	2	5	.286	15	2.44	55 ⅓	42	17	39	1	0	0	8
1992	Mon-N	0	70	8	7	.533	27	2.84	85 ⅔	63	34	81	1	0	0	1
1993	Mon-N	15	56	12	5	.706	38	2.29	149 ⅔	140	54	119	7	1	0	1
1994	Mon-N	21	21	8	6	.571	46	2.99	138 ⅔	119	40	119	13	1	0	0
1995	Mon-N	30	30	13	14	.481	91	4.33	189	164	74	207	15	1	0	0
1996	Mon-N	34	34	15	11	.577	85	3.30	231 ⅔	222	55	226	21	5	1	0
1997	Sea-A	35	35	16	9	.640	94	3.61	234 ⅓	189	84	217	20	2	1	0
1998	Sea-A	32	32	13	12	.520	99	3.97	224 ⅔	176	66	223	33	7	0	0
1999	Sea-A	24	30	4	14	.222	114	7.38	139	101	73	188	34	0	0	0
1999	Tex-A	3	7	1	0	1.000	11	5.71	17 ⅓	13	10	20	1	0	0	0
2000	Bos-A	23	38	8	8	.500	69	4.78	130	97	50	153	16	0	0	12
2001	**ChC-N**	**0**	**82**	**4**	**4**	**.500**	**28**	**3.42**	**73 ⅔**	**79**	**23**	**66**	**6**	**0**	**0**	**12**
Career average		20	44	9	9	.523	65	3.87	151 ⅔	128	53	151	15	2	0	2
Cubs average		**0**	**82**	**4**	**4**	**.500**	**28**	**3.42**	**73 ⅔**	**79**	**23**	**66**	**6**	**0**	**0**	**12**
Career total		217	486	104	95	.523	717	3.87	1669	1405	580	1658	168	17	2	22
Cubs total		**0**	**82**	**4**	**4**	**.500**	**28**	**3.42**	**73 ⅔**	**79**	**23**	**66**	**6**	**0**	**0**	**12**

Fast, Darcy Rae

HEIGHT: 6'3"   LEFTHANDER   BORN: 3/10/1947 DALLAS, OREGON

YEAR	TEAM	STARTS	GAMES	WON	LOST	PCT	ER	ERA	INNINGS PITCHED	STRIKE-OUTS	WALKS	HITS ALLOWED	HRS ALLOWED	COMP. GAMES	SHUT-OUTS	SAVES
1968	ChC-N	1	8	0	1	.000	6	5.40	10	10	8	8	1	0	0	0
Career average		1	8	0	1	.000	6	5.40	10	10	8	8	1	0	0	0
Cubs average		**1**	**8**	**0**	**1**	**.000**	**6**	**5.40**	**10**	**10**	**8**	**8**	**1**	**0**	**0**	**0**
Career total		1	8	0	1	.000	6	5.40	10	10	8	8	1	0	0	0
Cubs total		**1**	**8**	**0**	**1**	**.000**	**6**	**5.40**	**10**	**10**	**8**	**8**	**1**	**0**	**0**	**0**

Faul, William Alvan (Bill)

HEIGHT: 5'10"   RIGHTHANDER   BORN: 4/21/1940 CINCINNATI, OHIO

YEAR	TEAM	STARTS	GAMES	WON	LOST	PCT	ER	ERA	INNINGS PITCHED	STRIKE-OUTS	WALKS	HITS ALLOWED	HRS ALLOWED	COMP. GAMES	SHUT-OUTS	SAVES
1962	Det-A	0	1	0	0	—	6	32.40	1 2/3	2	3	4	1	0	0	0
1963	Det-A	10	28	5	6	.455	50	4.64	97	64	48	93	14	2	0	1
1964	Det-A	1	1	0	0	—	6	10.80	5	1	2	5	2	0	0	0
1965	**ChC-N**	**16**	**17**	**6**	**6**	**.500**	**38**	**3.54**	**96 2/3**	**59**	**18**	**83**	**12**	**5**	**3**	**0**
1966	**ChC-N**	**6**	**17**	**1**	**4**	**.200**	**29**	**5.08**	**51 1/3**	**32**	**18**	**47**	**12**	**1**	**0**	**0**
1970	SF-N	0	7	0	0	—	8	7.45	9 2/3	6	6	15	1	0	0	1
Career average		6	12	2	3	.429	23	4.72	43 2/3	27	16	41	7	1	1	0
Cubs average		**11**	**17**	**4**	**5**	**.412**	**34**	**4.07**	**74**	**46**	**18**	**65**	**12**	**3**	**2**	**0**
Career total		33	71	12	16	.429	137	4.72	261 1/3	164	95	247	42	8	3	2
Cubs total		**22**	**34**	**7**	**10**	**.412**	**67**	**4.07**	**148**	**91**	**36**	**130**	**24**	**6**	**3**	**0**

Fear, Luvern Carl (Vern)

HEIGHT: 6'0"   RIGHTHANDER   BORN: 8/21/1924 EVERLY, IOWA   DIED: 9/6/1976 SPENCER, IOWA

YEAR	TEAM	STARTS	GAMES	WON	LOST	PCT	ER	ERA	INNINGS PITCHED	STRIKE-OUTS	WALKS	HITS ALLOWED	HRS ALLOWED	COMP. GAMES	SHUT-OUTS	SAVES
1952	ChC-N	0	4	0	0	—	7	7.88	8	4	3	9	1	0	0	0
Career average		0	4	0	0	—	7	7.88	8	4	3	9	1	0	0	0
Cubs average		**0**	**4**	**0**	**0**	**—**	**7**	**7.88**	**8**	**4**	**3**	**9**	**1**	**0**	**0**	**0**
Career total		0	4	0	0	—	7	7.88	8	4	3	9	1	0	0	0
Cubs total		**0**	**4**	**0**	**0**	**—**	**7**	**7.88**	**8**	**4**	**3**	**9**	**1**	**0**	**0**	**0**

Ferguson, Charles Augustus (Charlie)

HEIGHT: 5'11"   RIGHTHANDER   BORN: 5/10/1875 OKEMOS, MICHIGAN   DIED: 5/17/1931 SAULT STE. MARIE, MICHIGAN

YEAR	TEAM	STARTS	GAMES	WON	LOST	PCT	ER	ERA	INNINGS PITCHED	STRIKE-OUTS	WALKS	HITS ALLOWED	HRS ALLOWED	COMP. GAMES	SHUT-OUTS	SAVES
1901	ChN-N	0	1	0	0	—	0	0.00	2	0	2	1	0	0	0	0
Career average		0	1	0	0	—	0	0.00	2	0	2	1	0	0	0	0
Cubs average		**0**	**1**	**0**	**0**	**—**	**0**	**0.00**	**2**	**0**	**2**	**1**	**0**	**0**	**0**	**0**
Career total		0	1	0	0	—	0	0.00	2	0	2	1	0	0	0	0
Cubs total		**0**	**1**	**0**	**0**	**—**	**0**	**0.00**	**2**	**0**	**2**	**1**	**0**	**0**	**0**	**0**

Filer, Thomas Carson (Tom)

HEIGHT: 6'1"   RIGHTHANDER   BORN: 12/1/1956 PHILADELPHIA, PENNSYLVANIA

YEAR	TEAM	STARTS	GAMES	WON	LOST	PCT	ER	ERA	INNINGS PITCHED	STRIKE-OUTS	WALKS	HITS ALLOWED	HRS ALLOWED	COMP. GAMES	SHUT-OUTS	SAVES
1982	**ChC-N**	**8**	**8**	**1**	**2**	**.333**	**25**	**5.53**	**40 2/3**	**15**	**18**	**50**	**5**	**0**	**0**	**0**
1985	Tor-A	9	11	7	0	1.000	21	3.88	48 2/3	24	18	38	6	0	0	0
1988	Mil-A	16	19	5	8	.385	50	4.43	101 2/3	39	33	108	8	2	1	0
1989	Mil-A	13	13	7	3	.700	29	3.61	72 1/3	20	23	74	6	0	0	0
1990	Mil-A	4	7	2	3	.400	15	6.14	22	8	9	26	2	0	0	0
1992	NYM-N	1	9	0	1	.000	5	2.05	22	9	6	18	2	0	0	0

(continued)

(Filer, continued)

Career average	9	11	4	3	.564	24	4.25	51⅓	19	18	52	5	0	0	0
Cubs average	**8**	**8**	**1**	**2**	**.333**	**25**	**5.53**	**40⅔**	**15**	**18**	**50**	**5**	**0**	**0**	**0**
Career total	51	67	22	17	.564	145	4.25	307⅓	115	107	314	29	2	1	0
Cubs total	**8**	**8**	**1**	**2**	**.333**	**25**	**5.53**	**40⅔**	**15**	**18**	**50**	**5**	**0**	**0**	**0**

Flavin, John Thomas
HEIGHT: 6'2"   LEFTHANDER   BORN: 5/7/1942 ALBANY, CALIFORNIA

YEAR	TEAM	STARTS	GAMES	WON	LOST	PCT	ER	ERA	INNINGS PITCHED	STRIKE-OUTS	WALKS	HITS ALLOWED	HRS ALLOWED	COMP. GAMES	SHUT-OUTS	SAVES
1964	ChC-N	1	5	0	1	.000	7	13.50	4⅔	5	3	11	0	0	0	0
Career average		1	5	0	1	.000	7	13.50	4⅔	5	3	11	0	0	0	0
Cubs average		**1**	**5**	**0**	**1**	**.000**	**7**	**13.50**	**4⅔**	**5**	**3**	**11**	**0**	**0**	**0**	**0**
Career total		1	5	0	1	.000	7	13.50	4⅔	5	3	11	0	0	0	0
Cubs total		**1**	**5**	**0**	**1**	**.000**	**7**	**13.50**	**4⅔**	**5**	**3**	**11**	**0**	**0**	**0**	**0**

Fleming, Leslie Fletchard (Bill)
HEIGHT: 6'0"   RIGHTHANDER   BORN: 7/31/1913 ROWLAND, CALIFORNIA

YEAR	TEAM	STARTS	GAMES	WON	LOST	PCT	ER	ERA	INNINGS PITCHED	STRIKE-OUTS	WALKS	HITS ALLOWED	HRS ALLOWED	COMP. GAMES	SHUT-OUTS	SAVES
1940	Bos-A	6	10	1	2	.333	25	4.86	46⅓	24	20	53	4	1	0	0
1941	Bos-A	1	16	1	1	.500	18	3.92	41⅓	20	24	32	4	0	0	1
1942	ChC-N	14	33	5	6	.455	45	3.01	134⅓	59	63	117	9	4	2	2
1943	ChC-N	0	11	0	1	.000	23	6.40	32⅓	12	12	41	2	0	0	0
1944	ChC-N	18	39	9	10	.474	55	3.13	158⅓	42	62	163	6	9	1	0
1946	ChC-N	1	14	0	1	.000	20	6.14	29⅓	10	12	37	2	0	0	0
Career average		7	21	3	4	.432	31	3.79	73⅔	28	32	74	5	2	1	1
Cubs average		**8**	**24**	**4**	**5**	**.438**	**36**	**3.63**	**88⅔**	**31**	**37**	**90**	**5**	**3**	**1**	**1**
Career total		40	123	16	21	.432	186	3.79	442	167	193	443	27	14	3	3
Cubs total		**33**	**97**	**14**	**18**	**.438**	**143**	**3.63**	**354⅓**	**123**	**149**	**358**	**19**	**13**	**3**	**2**

Flores, Jesse
HEIGHT: 5'10"   RIGHTHANDER   BORN: 11/2/1914 GUADALAJARA, MEXICO   DIED: 12/17/1991 ORANGE, CALIFORNIA

YEAR	TEAM	STARTS	GAMES	WON	LOST	PCT	ER	ERA	INNINGS PITCHED	STRIKE-OUTS	WALKS	HITS ALLOWED	HRS ALLOWED	COMP. GAMES	SHUT-OUTS	SAVES
1942	ChC-N	0	4	0	1	.000	2	3.38	5⅓	6	2	5	1	0	0	0
1943	Phi-A	27	31	12	14	.462	80	3.11	231⅓	113	70	208	13	13	0	0
1944	Phi-A	25	27	9	11	.450	70	3.39	185⅔	65	49	172	8	11	2	0
1945	Phi-A	24	29	7	10	.412	73	3.43	191⅓	52	63	180	6	9	4	1
1946	Phi-A	15	29	9	7	.563	40	2.32	155	48	38	147	8	8	4	1
1947	Phi-A	20	28	4	13	.235	57	3.39	151⅓	41	59	139	10	4	0	4
1950	Cle-A	2	28	3	3	.500	22	3.74	53	27	25	53	3	1	1	0
Career average		16	25	6	8	.427	49	3.18	139	50	44	129	7	7	2	1
Cubs average		**0**	**4**	**0**	**1**	**.000**	**2**	**3.38**	**5⅓**	**6**	**2**	**5**	**1**	**0**	**0**	**0**
Career total		113	176	44	59	.427	344	3.18	973	352	306	904	49	46	11	6
Cubs total		**0**	**4**	**0**	**1**	**.000**	**2**	**3.38**	**5⅓**	**6**	**2**	**5**	**1**	**0**	**0**	**0**

Flynn, John A. (Jocko)
HEIGHT: 5'6"   RIGHTHANDER   BORN: 6/30/1864 LAWRENCE, MASSACHUSETTS   DIED: 12/30/1907 LAWRENCE, MASSACHUSETTS

YEAR	TEAM	STARTS	GAMES	WON	LOST	PCT	ER	ERA	INNINGS PITCHED	STRIKE-OUTS	WALKS	HITS ALLOWED	HRS ALLOWED	COMP. GAMES	SHUT-OUTS	SAVES
1886	ChN-N	29	32	23	6	.793	64	2.24	257	146	63	207	9	28	2	1
Career average		29	32	23	6	.793	64	2.24	257	146	63	207	9	28	2	1
Cubs average		**29**	**32**	**23**	**6**	**.793**	**64**	**2.24**	**257**	**146**	**63**	**207**	**9**	**28**	**2**	**1**
Career total		29	32	23	6	.793	64	2.24	257	146	63	207	9	28	2	1
Cubs total		**29**	**32**	**23**	**6**	**.793**	**64**	**2.24**	**257**	**146**	**63**	**207**	**9**	**28**	**2**	**1**

Fodge, Gene Arlan (Suds)
HEIGHT: 6'0"   RIGHTHANDER   BORN: 7/9/1931 SOUTH BEND, INDIANA

YEAR	TEAM	STARTS	GAMES	WON	LOST	PCT	ER	ERA	INNINGS PITCHED	STRIKE-OUTS	WALKS	HITS ALLOWED	HRS ALLOWED	COMP. GAMES	SHUT-OUTS	SAVES
1958	ChC-N	4	16	1	1	.500	21	4.76	39 2/3	15	11	47	5	1	0	0
Career average		4	16	1	1	.500	21	4.76	39 2/3	15	11	47	5	1	0	0
Cubs average		**4**	**16**	**1**	**1**	**.500**	**21**	**4.76**	**39 2/3**	**15**	**11**	**47**	**5**	**1**	**0**	**0**
Career total		4	16	1	1	.500	21	4.76	39 2/3	15	11	47	5	1	0	0
Cubs total		**4**	**16**	**1**	**1**	**.500**	**21**	**4.76**	**39 2/3**	**15**	**11**	**47**	**5**	**1**	**0**	**0**

Fontenot, Silton Ray (Ray)
HEIGHT: 6'0"   LEFTHANDER   BORN: 8/8/1957 LAKE CHARLES, LOUISIANA

YEAR	TEAM	STARTS	GAMES	WON	LOST	PCT	ER	ERA	INNINGS PITCHED	STRIKE-OUTS	WALKS	HITS ALLOWED	HRS ALLOWED	COMP. GAMES	SHUT-OUTS	SAVES
1983	NYY-A	15	15	8	2	.800	36	3.33	97 1/3	27	25	101	3	3	1	0
1984	NYY-A	24	35	8	9	.471	68	3.61	169 1/3	85	58	189	8	0	0	0
1985	**ChC-N**	**23**	**38**	**6**	**10**	**.375**	**75**	**4.36**	**154 2/3**	**70**	**45**	**177**	**23**	**0**	**0**	**0**
1986	**ChC-N**	**0**	**42**	**3**	**5**	**.375**	**24**	**3.86**	**56**	**24**	**21**	**57**	**5**	**0**	**0**	**2**
1986	Min-A	0	15	0	0	—	18	9.92	16 1/3	10	4	27	3	0	0	0
Career average		16	36	6	7	.490	55	4.03	123 1/3	54	38	138	11	1	0	1
Cubs average		**12**	**40**	**5**	**8**	**.375**	**50**	**4.23**	**105 1/3**	**47**	**33**	**117**	**14**	**0**	**0**	**1**
Career total		62	145	25	26	.490	221	4.03	493 2/3	216	153	551	42	3	1	2
Cubs total		**23**	**80**	**9**	**15**	**.375**	**99**	**4.23**	**210 2/3**	**94**	**66**	**234**	**28**	**0**	**0**	**2**

Fossas, Emilio Antonio (Tony)
HEIGHT: 6'0"   LEFTHANDER   BORN: 9/23/1957 HAVANA, CUBA

YEAR	TEAM	STARTS	GAMES	WON	LOST	PCT	ER	ERA	INNINGS PITCHED	STRIKE-OUTS	WALKS	HITS ALLOWED	HRS ALLOWED	COMP. GAMES	SHUT-OUTS	SAVES
1988	Tex-A	0	5	0	0	—	3	4.76	5 2/3	0	2	11	0	0	0	0
1989	Mil-A	0	51	2	2	.500	24	3.54	61	42	22	57	3	0	0	1
1990	Mil-A	0	32	2	3	.400	21	6.44	29 1/3	24	10	44	5	0	0	0
1991	Bos-A	0	64	3	2	.600	22	3.47	57	29	28	49	3	0	0	1
1992	Bos-A	0	60	1	2	.333	8	2.43	29 2/3	19	14	31	1	0	0	2
1993	Bos-A	0	71	1	1	.500	23	5.18	40	39	15	38	4	0	0	0
1994	Bos-A	0	44	2	0	1.000	18	4.76	34	31	15	35	6	0	0	1
1995	StL-N	0	58	3	0	1.000	6	1.47	36 2/3	40	10	28	1	0	0	0
1996	StL-N	0	65	0	4	.000	14	2.68	47	36	21	43	7	0	0	2
1997	StL-N	0	71	2	7	.222	22	3.83	51 2/3	41	26	62	7	0	0	0
1998	Sea-A	0	23	0	3	.000	11	8.74	11 1/3	10	6	19	1	0	0	0
1998	**ChC-N**	**0**	**8**	**0**	**0**	**—**	**4**	**9.00**	**4**	**6**	**6**	**8**	**0**	**0**	**0**	**0**
1998	Tex-A	0	10	1	0	1.000	0	0.00	7 1/3	7	4	3	0	0	0	0
1999	NYY-A	0	5	0	0	—	4	36.00	1	0	1	6	1	0	0	0
Career average		0	47	1	2	.415	15	3.90	34 2/3	27	15	36	3	0	0	1
Cubs average		**0**	**8**	**0**	**0**	**—**	**4**	**9.00**	**4**	**6**	**6**	**8**	**0**	**0**	**0**
Career total		0	567	17	24	.415	180	3.90	415 2/3	324	180	434	39	0	0	7
Cubs total		**0**	**8**	**0**	**0**	**—**	**4**	**9.00**	**4**	**6**	**6**	**8**	**0**	**0**	**0**

Foster, Kevin Chris
HEIGHT: 6'1"   RIGHTHANDER   BORN: 1/13/1969 EVANSTON, ILLINOIS

YEAR	TEAM	STARTS	GAMES	WON	LOST	PCT	ER	ERA	INNINGS PITCHED	STRIKE-OUTS	WALKS	HITS ALLOWED	HRS ALLOWED	COMP. GAMES	SHUT-OUTS	SAVES
1993	Phi-N	1	2	0	1	.000	11	14.85	6 2/3	6	7	13	3	0	0	0
1994	**ChC-N**	**13**	**13**	**3**	**4**	**.429**	**26**	**2.89**	**81**	**75**	**35**	**70**	**7**	**0**	**0**	**0**
1995	**ChC-N**	**28**	**30**	**12**	**11**	**.522**	**84**	**4.51**	**167 2/3**	**146**	**65**	**149**	**32**	**0**	**0**	**0**
1996	**ChC-N**	**16**	**17**	**7**	**6**	**.538**	**60**	**6.21**	**87**	**53**	**35**	**98**	**16**	**1**	**0**	**0**
1997	**ChC-N**	**25**	**26**	**10**	**7**	**.588**	**75**	**4.61**	**146 1/3**	**118**	**66**	**141**	**27**	**1**	**0**	**0**
1998	**ChC-N**	**0**	**3**	**0**	**0**	**—**	**6**	**16.20**	**3 1/3**	**3**	**2**	**8**	**1**	**0**	**0**	**0**
2001	Tex-A	0	9	0	1	.000	13	6.62	17 2/3	16	10	21	2	0	0	0

(continued)

(Foster, continued)

Career average	12	14	5	4	.516	39	4.86	72 ⅔	60	31	71	13	0	0	0
Cubs average	**16**	**18**	**6**	**6**	**.533**	**50**	**4.65**	**97**	**79**	**41**	**93**	**17**	**0**	**0**	**0**
Career total	83	100	32	30	.516	275	4.86	509 ⅔	417	220	500	88	2	0	0
Cubs total	**82**	**89**	**32**	**28**	**.533**	**251**	**4.65**	**485 ⅓**	**395**	**203**	**466**	**83**	**2**	**0**	**0**

Foxen, William Aloysius (Bill)
HEIGHT: 5'11"   LEFTHANDER   BORN: 5/31/1884 TENAFLY, NEW JERSEY   DIED: 4/17/1937 BROOKLYN, NEW YORK

YEAR	TEAM	STARTS	GAMES	WON	LOST	PCT	ER	ERA	INNINGS PITCHED	STRIKE-OUTS	WALKS	HITS ALLOWED	HRS ALLOWED	COMP. GAMES	SHUT-OUTS	SAVES
1908	Phi-N	16	22	7	7	.500	32	1.95	147 ⅓	52	53	126	2	10	2	0
1909	Phi-N	7	18	3	7	.300	31	3.35	83 ⅓	37	32	65	0	5	1	0
1910	Phi-N	9	16	5	5	.500	22	2.55	77 ⅔	33	40	73	2	5	0	0
1910	**ChC-N**	**0**	**2**	**0**	**0**	**—**	**5**	**9.00**	**5**	**2**	**3**	**7**	**0**	**0**	**0**	**0**
1911	**ChC-N**	**1**	**3**	**1**	**1**	**.500**	**3**	**2.08**	**13**	**6**	**12**	**12**	**0**	**0**	**0**	**0**
Career average	8	15	4	5	.444	23	2.56	81 ⅔	33	35	71	1	5	1	0
Cubs average	**1**	**3**	**1**	**1**	**.500**	**4**	**4.00**	**9**	**4**	**8**	**10**	**0**	**0**	**0**	**0**
Career total	33	61	16	20	.444	93	2.56	326 ⅓	130	140	283	4	20	3	0
Cubs total	**1**	**5**	**1**	**1**	**.500**	**8**	**4.00**	**18**	**8**	**15**	**19**	**0**	**0**	**0**	**0**

Frailing, Kenneth Douglas (Ken)
HEIGHT: 6'0"   LEFTHANDER   BORN: 1/19/1948 MADISON, WISCONSIN

YEAR	TEAM	STARTS	GAMES	WON	LOST	PCT	ER	ERA	INNINGS PITCHED	STRIKE-OUTS	WALKS	HITS ALLOWED	HRS ALLOWED	COMP. GAMES	SHUT-OUTS	SAVES
1972	CWS-A	0	4	1	0	1.000	1	3.00	3	1	1	3	1	0	0	0
1973	CWS-A	0	10	0	0	—	4	1.96	18 ⅓	15	7	18	1	0	0	0
1974	ChC-N	16	55	6	9	.400	54	3.88	125 ⅓	71	43	150	11	1	0	1
1975	ChC-N	0	41	2	5	.286	32	5.43	53	39	26	61	6	0	0	1
1976	ChC-N	3	6	1	2	.333	5	2.41	18 ⅔	10	5	20	0	0	0	0
Career average	4	23	2	3	.385	19	3.96	43 ⅔	27	16	50	4	0	0	0
Cubs average	**6**	**34**	**3**	**5**	**.360**	**30**	**4.16**	**65 ⅔**	**40**	**25**	**77**	**6**	**0**	**0**	**1**
Career total	19	116	10	16	.385	96	3.96	218 ⅓	136	82	252	19	1	0	2
Cubs total	**19**	**102**	**9**	**16**	**.360**	**91**	**4.16**	**197**	**120**	**74**	**231**	**17**	**1**	**0**	**2**

France, Osman Beverly (Ossie *or* O.B.)
HEIGHT: 5'8"   LEFTHANDER   BORN: 10/4/1858 GREENSBURG, OHIO   DIED: 5/2/1947 AKRON, OHIO

YEAR	TEAM	STARTS	GAMES	WON	LOST	PCT	ER	ERA	INNINGS PITCHED	STRIKE-OUTS	WALKS	HITS ALLOWED	HRS ALLOWED	COMP. GAMES	SHUT-OUTS	SAVES
1890	ChN-N	0	1	0	1	.000	3	13.50	2	0	2	3	0	0	0	0
Career average	0	1	0	1	.000	3	13.50	2	0	2	3	0	0	0	0
Cubs average	**0**	**1**	**0**	**1**	**.000**	**3**	**13.50**	**2**	**0**	**2**	**3**	**0**	**0**	**0**	**0**
Career total	0	1	0	1	.000	3	13.50	2	0	2	3	0	0	0	0
Cubs total	**0**	**1**	**0**	**1**	**.000**	**3**	**13.50**	**2**	**0**	**2**	**3**	**0**	**0**	**0**	**0**

Fraser, Charles Carrolton (Chick)
HEIGHT: 5'10"   RIGHTHANDER   BORN: 3/17/1871 CHICAGO, ILLINOIS   DIED: 5/8/1940 WENDELL, IDAHO

YEAR	TEAM	STARTS	GAMES	WON	LOST	PCT	ER	ERA	INNINGS PITCHED	STRIKE-OUTS	WALKS	HITS ALLOWED	HRS ALLOWED	COMP. GAMES	SHUT-OUTS	SAVES
1896	Lou-N	38	43	12	27	.308	189	4.87	349 ⅓	91	166	396	9	37	0	1
1897	Lou-N	34	35	15	19	.441	130	4.09	286 ⅓	70	133	332	11	32	0	0
1898	Lou-N	26	26	7	19	.269	120	5.32	203	58	100	230	4	20	1	0
1898	Cle-N	6	6	2	3	.400	26	5.57	42	19	12	49	2	6	0	0
1899	Phi-N	33	35	21	13	.618	101	3.36	270 ⅔	68	85	278	1	29	4	0
1900	Phi-N	26	29	15	9	.625	78	3.14	223 ⅓	58	93	250	7	22	1	0
1901	Phi-A	37	40	22	16	.579	140	3.81	331	110	132	344	6	35	2	0
1902	Phi-N	26	27	13	14	.481	85	3.42	224	97	74	238	2	24	3	0
1903	Phi-N	29	31	12	17	.414	125	4.50	250	104	97	260	8	26	1	1

(continued)

(continued)

YEAR	TEAM				PCT		ERA								
1904	Phi-N	36	42	14	24	.368	109	3.25	302	127	100	287	5	32	2	1
1905	Bos-N	37	39	14	21	.400	122	3.28	334⅓	130	149	320	8	35	2	0
1906	Cin-N	28	31	10	20	.333	70	2.67	236	58	80	221	1	25	2	0
1907	**ChC-N**	**15**	**22**	**8**	**5**	**.615**	**35**	**2.28**	**138⅓**	**41**	**46**	**112**	**1**	**9**	**2**	**1**
1908	**ChC-N**	**17**	**26**	**11**	**9**	**.550**	**41**	**2.27**	**162⅔**	**66**	**61**	**141**	**4**	**11**	**2**	**2**
1909	**ChC-N**	**0**	**1**	**0**	**0**	**—**	**0**	**0.00**	**3**	**1**	**4**	**2**	**0**	**0**	**0**	**0**
Career average		28	31	13	15	.449	98	3.68	239⅔	78	95	247	5	25	2	0
Cubs average		**11**	**16**	**6**	**5**	**.576**	**25**	**2.25**	**101⅓**	**36**	**37**	**85**	**2**	**7**	**1**	**1**
Career total		388	433	176	216	.449	1371	3.68	3356	1098	1332	3460	69	343	22	6
Cubs total		**32**	**49**	**19**	**14**	**.576**	**76**	**2.25**	**304**	**108**	**111**	**255**	**5**	**20**	**4**	**3**

Frazier, George Allen
HEIGHT: 6'5"   RIGHTHANDER   BORN: 10/13/1954 OKLAHOMA CITY, OKLAHOMA

YEAR	TEAM	STARTS	GAMES	WON	LOST	PCT	ER	ERA	INNINGS PITCHED	STRIKE-OUTS	WALKS	HITS ALLOWED	HRS ALLOWED	COMP. GAMES	SHUT-OUTS	SAVES
1978	StL-N	0	14	0	3	.000	10	4.09	22	8	6	22	2	0	0	0
1979	StL-N	0	25	2	4	.333	16	4.45	32⅓	14	12	35	3	0	0	0
1980	StL-N	0	22	1	4	.200	7	2.74	23	11	7	24	2	0	0	3
1981	NYY-A	0	16	0	1	.000	5	1.63	27⅔	17	11	26	1	0	0	3
1982	NYY-A	0	63	4	4	.500	43	3.47	111⅔	69	39	103	7	0	0	1
1983	NYY-A	0	61	4	4	.500	44	3.43	115⅓	78	45	94	5	0	0	8
1984	Cle-A	0	22	3	2	.600	18	3.65	44⅓	24	14	45	3	0	0	1
1984	**ChC-N**	**0**	**37**	**6**	**3**	**.667**	**29**	**4.10**	**63⅔**	**58**	**26**	**53**	**4**	**0**	**0**	**3**
1985	**ChC-N**	**0**	**51**	**7**	**8**	**.467**	**54**	**6.39**	**76**	**46**	**52**	**88**	**11**	**0**	**0**	**2**
1986	**ChC-N**	**0**	**35**	**2**	**4**	**.333**	**31**	**5.40**	**51⅔**	**41**	**34**	**63**	**5**	**0**	**0**	**0**
1986	Min-A	0	15	1	1	.500	13	4.39	26⅔	25	16	23	2	0	0	6
1987	Min-A	0	54	5	5	.500	45	4.98	81⅓	58	51	77	9	0	0	2
Career average		0	42	4	4	.449	32	4.20	67⅔	45	31	65	5	0	0	3
Cubs average		**0**	**41**	**5**	**5**	**.500**	**38**	**5.36**	**63⅔**	**48**	**37**	**68**	**7**	**0**	**0**	**2**
Career total		0	415	35	43	.449	315	4.20	675⅔	449	313	653	54	0	0	29
Cubs total		**0**	**123**	**15**	**15**	**.500**	**114**	**5.36**	**191⅓**	**145**	**112**	**204**	**20**	**0**	**0**	**5**

Freeman, Alexander Vernon (Buck)
HEIGHT: 5'10"   RIGHTHANDER   BORN: 7/5/1896 MART, TEXAS   DIED: 2/21/1953 FORT SAM HOUSTON, TEXAS

YEAR	TEAM	STARTS	GAMES	WON	LOST	PCT	ER	ERA	INNINGS PITCHED	STRIKE-OUTS	WALKS	HITS ALLOWED	HRS ALLOWED	COMP. GAMES	SHUT-OUTS	SAVES
1921	ChC-N	20	38	9	10	.474	81	4.11	177⅓	42	70	189	12	6	0	3
1922	ChC-N	1	11	0	1	.000	25	8.77	25⅔	10	10	47	0	0	0	1
Career average		11	25	5	6	.450	53	4.70	101⅔	26	40	118	6	3	0	2
Cubs average		**11**	**25**	**5**	**6**	**.450**	**53**	**4.70**	**101⅔**	**26**	**40**	**118**	**6**	**3**	**0**	**2**
Career total		21	49	9	11	.450	106	4.70	203	52	80	236	12	6	0	4
Cubs total		**21**	**49**	**9**	**11**	**.450**	**106**	**4.70**	**203**	**52**	**80**	**236**	**12**	**6**	**0**	**4**

Freeman, Hershell Baskin (Hersh *or* Buster)
HEIGHT: 6'3"   RIGHTHANDER   BORN: 7/1/1928 GADSDEN, ALABAMA

YEAR	TEAM	STARTS	GAMES	WON	LOST	PCT	ER	ERA	INNINGS PITCHED	STRIKE-OUTS	WALKS	HITS ALLOWED	HRS ALLOWED	COMP. GAMES	SHUT-OUTS	SAVES
1952	Bos-A	1	4	1	0	1.000	5	3.29	13⅔	5	5	13	1	1	0	0
1953	Bos-A	2	18	1	4	.200	24	5.54	39	15	17	50	2	0	0	0
1955	Bos-A	0	2	0	0	—	0	0.00	1⅔	1	1	1	0	0	0	0
1955	Cin-N	0	52	7	4	.636	22	2.16	91⅔	37	30	94	3	0	0	11
1956	Cin-N	0	64	14	5	.737	41	3.40	108⅔	50	34	112	2	0	0	18
1957	Cin-N	0	52	7	2	.778	42	4.52	83⅔	36	14	90	14	0	0	8
1958	Cin-N	0	3	0	0	—	3	3.52	7⅔	7	5	4	0	0	0	0
1958	**ChC-N**	**0**	**9**	**0**	**1**	**.000**	**12**	**8.31**	**13**	**7**	**3**	**23**	**3**	**0**	**0**	**0**
Career average		1	34	5	3	.652	25	3.74	60	26	18	65	4	0	0	6
Cubs average		**0**	**9**	**0**	**1**	**.000**	**12**	**8.31**	**13**	**7**	**3**	**23**	**3**	**0**	**0**	**0**
Career total		3	204	30	16	.652	149	3.74	359	158	109	387	25	1	0	37
Cubs total		**0**	**9**	**0**	**1**	**.000**	**12**	**8.31**	**13**	**7**	**3**	**23**	**3**	**0**	**0**	**0**

Freeman, Mark Price (Stretch)
HEIGHT: 6'4" RIGHTHANDER BORN: 12/7/1930 MEMPHIS, TENNESSEE

YEAR	TEAM	STARTS	GAMES	WON	LOST	PCT	ER	ERA	INNINGS PITCHED	STRIKE-OUTS	WALKS	HITS ALLOWED	HRS ALLOWED	COMP. GAMES	SHUT-OUTS	SAVES
1959	NYY-A	1	1	0	0	—	2	2.57	7	4	2	6	0	0	0	0
1959	KCA-A	0	3	0	0	—	4	9.82	3⅔	1	3	6	0	0	0	0
1960	**ChC-N**	**8**	**30**	**3**	**3**	**.500**	**48**	**5.63**	**76⅔**	**50**	**33**	**70**	**10**	**1**	**0**	**1**
Career average		5	17	2	2	.500	27	5.56	43⅔	28	19	41	5	1	0	1
Cubs average		**8**	**30**	**3**	**3**	**.500**	**48**	**5.63**	**76⅔**	**50**	**33**	**70**	**10**	**1**	**0**	**1**
Career total		9	34	3	3	.500	54	5.56	87⅓	55	38	82	10	1	0	1
Cubs total		**8**	**30**	**3**	**3**	**.500**	**48**	**5.63**	**76⅔**	**50**	**33**	**70**	**10**	**1**	**0**	**1**

French, Lawrence Herbert (Larry)
HEIGHT: 6'1" LEFTHANDER BORN: 11/1/1907 VISALIA, CALIFORNIA DIED: 2/9/1987 SAN DIEGO, CALIFORNIA

YEAR	TEAM	STARTS	GAMES	WON	LOST	PCT	ER	ERA	INNINGS PITCHED	STRIKE-OUTS	WALKS	HITS ALLOWED	HRS ALLOWED	COMP. GAMES	SHUT-OUTS	SAVES
1929	Pit-N	13	30	7	5	.583	67	4.90	123	49	62	130	10	6	0	1
1930	Pit-N	35	42	17	18	.486	133	4.36	274⅔	90	89	325	20	21	3	1
1931	Pit-N	33	39	15	13	.536	100	3.26	275⅔	73	70	301	9	20	1	1
1932	Pit-N	33	47	18	16	.529	92	3.02	274⅓	72	62	301	17	19	3	4
1933	Pit-N	35	47	18	13	.581	88	2.72	291⅓	88	55	290	9	21	5	1
1934	Pit-N	34	49	12	18	.400	105	3.58	263⅔	103	59	299	8	16	3	1
1935	**ChC-N**	**30**	**42**	**17**	**10**	**.630**	**81**	**2.96**	**246⅓**	**90**	**44**	**279**	**10**	**16**	**4**	**2**
1936	**ChC-N**	**28**	**43**	**18**	**9**	**.667**	**95**	**3.39**	**252⅓**	**104**	**54**	**262**	**16**	**16**	**4**	**3**
1937	**ChC-N**	**28**	**42**	**16**	**10**	**.615**	**92**	**3.98**	**208**	**100**	**65**	**229**	**17**	**11**	**4**	**0**
1938	**ChC-N**	**27**	**43**	**10**	**19**	**.345**	**85**	**3.80**	**201⅓**	**83**	**62**	**210**	**17**	**10**	**3**	**0**
1939	**ChC-N**	**21**	**36**	**15**	**8**	**.652**	**71**	**3.29**	**194**	**98**	**50**	**205**	**7**	**10**	**2**	**1**
1940	**ChC-N**	**33**	**40**	**14**	**14**	**.500**	**90**	**3.29**	**246**	**107**	**64**	**240**	**12**	**18**	**3**	**2**
1941	**ChC-N**	**18**	**26**	**5**	**14**	**.263**	**71**	**4.63**	**138**	**60**	**43**	**161**	**10**	**6**	**1**	**0**
1941	Bro-N	1	6	0	0	—	6	3.45	15⅔	8	4	16	1	0	0	0
1942	Bro-N	14	38	15	4	.789	30	1.83	147⅔	62	36	127	1	8	4	0
Career average		27	41	14	12	.535	86	3.44	225	85	59	241	12	14	3	1
Cubs average		**26**	**39**	**14**	**12**	**.531**	**84**	**3.54**	**212⅓**	**92**	**55**	**227**	**13**	**12**	**3**	**1**
Career total		383	570	197	171	.535	1206	3.44	3152	1187	819	3375	164	198	40	17
Cubs total		**185**	**272**	**95**	**84**	**.531**	**585**	**3.54**	**1486**	**642**	**382**	**1586**	**89**	**87**	**21**	**8**

Friend, Daniel Sebastian (Danny)
HEIGHT: 5'9" LEFTHANDER BORN: 4/18/1873 CINCINNATI, OHIO DIED: 6/1/1942 CHILLICOTHE, OHIO

YEAR	TEAM	STARTS	GAMES	WON	LOST	PCT	ER	ERA	INNINGS PITCHED	STRIKE-OUTS	WALKS	HITS ALLOWED	HRS ALLOWED	COMP. GAMES	SHUT-OUTS	SAVES
1895	**ChN-N**	**5**	**5**	**2**	**2**	**.500**	**24**	**5.27**	**41**	**10**	**14**	**50**	**5**	**5**	**0**	**0**
1896	**ChN-N**	**33**	**36**	**19**	**12**	**.613**	**153**	**4.74**	**290⅔**	**86**	**139**	**298**	**11**	**28**	**1**	**0**
1897	**ChN-N**	**24**	**24**	**12**	**10**	**.545**	**102**	**4.52**	**203**	**58**	**86**	**244**	**5**	**23**	**0**	**0**
1898	**ChN-N**	**2**	**2**	**0**	**2**	**.000**	**10**	**5.29**	**17**	**4**	**10**	**20**	**1**	**2**	**0**	**0**
Career average		16	17	8	7	.559	72	4.71	138	40	62	153	6	15	0	0
Cubs average		**16**	**17**	**8**	**7**	**.559**	**72**	**4.71**	**138**	**40**	**62**	**153**	**6**	**15**	**0**	**0**
Career total		64	67	33	26	.559	289	4.71	551⅔	158	249	612	22	58	1	0
Cubs total		**64**	**67**	**33**	**26**	**.559**	**289**	**4.71**	**551⅔**	**158**	**249**	**612**	**22**	**58**	**1**	**0**

Fryman, Woodrow Thompson (Woodie)
HEIGHT: 6'3" LEFTHANDER BORN: 4/15/1940 EWING, KENTUCKY

YEAR	TEAM	STARTS	GAMES	WON	LOST	PCT	ER	ERA	INNINGS PITCHED	STRIKE-OUTS	WALKS	HITS ALLOWED	HRS ALLOWED	COMP. GAMES	SHUT-OUTS	SAVES
1966	Pit-N	28	36	12	9	.571	77	3.81	181⅔	105	47	182	13	9	3	1
1967	Pit-N	18	28	3	8	.273	51	4.05	113⅓	74	44	121	12	3	1	1
1968	Phi-N	32	34	12	14	.462	66	2.78	213⅔	151	64	198	12	10	5	0
1969	Phi-N	35	36	12	15	.444	112	4.41	228⅓	150	89	243	15	10	1	0
1970	Phi-N	20	27	8	6	.571	58	4.09	127⅔	97	43	122	11	4	3	0
1971	Phi-N	17	37	10	7	.588	56	3.38	149⅓	104	46	133	7	3	2	2
1972	Phi-N	17	23	4	10	.286	58	4.36	119⅔	69	39	131	15	3	2	1
1972	Det-A	14	16	10	3	.769	26	2.06	113⅔	72	31	93	6	6	1	0
1973	Det-A	29	34	6	13	.316	101	5.36	169⅔	119	64	200	23	1	0	0

(continued)

Lawrence (Larry) Herbert French, lhp, 1929–42

Larry French was the most consistent and durable lefthand pitcher for Chicago during the prewar years.

French was born on November 1, 1907, in Visalia, California. He came to the major leagues through the Pittsburgh organization and debuted with the Pirates in 1929, winning seven games. By the next season, French was in the Pirates' regular rotation.

And he almost never dropped out of it. In the 1930s, only Giants star Carl Hubbell pitched more innings than French's 2,481. And while Hubbell had five seasons in his career in which he started 40 or more games, French had nine, almost twice as many, in his career.

The key to French's success was similar to Hubbell's: both men threw a wicked screwball that broke inside sharply to right-hand batters. The French screwball might not have been quite as effective as the Hubbell version, but it was a tough pitch to hit nonetheless.

French toiled for the Pirates for six years, winning 15 or more games from 1930 to 1933. But in 1934, he went 12-18. This was more a function of bad luck than anything else: French struck out 103 batters, his career high to that point, and allowed only eight home runs and 299 hits on the year, both the lowest totals since he became a full-time pitcher.

But the Pirates thought he was on the downside of his career and made him available to Chicago. The Cubs snapped French up, and he started 40 or more games five of the next six years, led the league in shutouts in 1935 and 1936 and struck out 90 or more hitters every season from 1935 to 1940 but 1938.

He was a clubhouse leader and a great practical joker. One of his specialties was the hotfoot, which he gave to most of his teammates at one time or another. In 1935 French was one of the architects of the greatest stretch drive in National League history, winning five of five starts as the Cubs won 21 games in a row to come from behind and win the pennant.

French pitched well in World Series play, but he ended up with an 0-2 record in the Fall Classic. He was handed the ball in Game 6 of the 1935 Series against the Tigers and battled the Detroit hitters for 8⅔ innings, scattering 12 hits on the day. He was undone by a bloop single by Leon Allen "Goose" Goslin that scored Gordon Stanley "Mickey" Cochrane with two outs in the bottom of the ninth inning. French's other loss was in relief in Game 3 of the same Series.

In 1940 French struck out a career-high 107 batters and was selected to the All-Star team, but it was his last hurrah for Chicago. He won five games before being shipped to Brooklyn. His final year was a solid one, however, as he went 15-4 for the Dodgers before enlisting in the U.S. Navy.

French remained in the navy until retiring in 1969. He died in 1987, in San Diego, California. He is still 9th in ERA for Cubs postseason pitchers with a 3.21 mark and 10th in World Series strikeouts for the Cubs with 10.

(continued)

1974	Det-A	22	27	6	9	.400	68	4.32	141⅔	92	67	120	16	4	1	0
1975	Mon-N	20	38	9	12	.429	58	3.32	157	118	68	141	10	7	3	3
1976	Mon-N	32	34	13	13	.500	81	3.37	216⅓	123	76	218	14	4	2	2
1977	Cin-N	12	17	5	5	.500	45	5.38	75⅓	57	45	83	13	0	0	1
1978	**ChC-N**	**9**	**13**	**2**	**4**	**.333**	**32**	**5.17**	**55⅔**	**28**	**37**	**64**	**6**	**0**	**0**	**0**
1978	Mon-N	17	19	5	7	.417	38	3.61	94⅔	53	37	93	4	4	3	1
1979	Mon-N	0	44	3	6	.333	18	2.79	58	44	22	52	4	0	0	10
1980	Mon-N	0	61	7	4	.636	20	2.25	80	59	30	61	1	0	0	17
1981	Mon-N	0	35	5	3	.625	9	1.88	43	25	14	38	1	0	0	7
1982	Mon-N	0	60	9	4	.692	29	3.75	69⅔	46	26	66	1	0	0	12
1983	Mon-N	0	6	0	3	.000	7	21.00	3	1	1	8	1	0	0	0
Career average		18	35	8	9	.476	56	3.77	134	88	49	132	10	4	2	3
Cubs average		**9**	**13**	**2**	**4**	**.333**	**32**	**5.17**	**55⅔**	**28**	**37**	**64**	**6**	**0**	**0**	**0**
Career total		322	625	141	155	.476	1010	3.77	2411⅓	1587	890	2367	187	68	27	58
Cubs total		**9**	**13**	**2**	**4**	**.333**	**32**	**5.17**	**55⅔**	**28**	**37**	**64**	**6**	**0**	**0**	**0**

Fuhr, Oscar Lawrence
HEIGHT: 6'0"   LEFTHANDER   BORN: 8/22/1893 DEFIANCE, MISSOURI   DIED: 3/27/1975 DALLAS, TEXAS

YEAR	TEAM	STARTS	GAMES	WON	LOST	PCT	ER	ERA	INNINGS PITCHED	STRIKE-OUTS	WALKS	HITS ALLOWED	HRS ALLOWED	COMP. GAMES	SHUT-OUTS	SAVES
1921	ChC-N	0	1	0	0	—	4	9.00	4	2	0	11	1	0	0	0
1924	Bos-A	10	23	3	6	.333	53	5.94	80 1/3	30	39	100	1	4	1	0
1925	Bos-A	5	39	0	6	.000	67	6.60	91 1/3	27	30	138	7	0	0	0
Career average		5	21	1	4	.200	41	6.35	58 2/3	20	23	83	3	1	0	0
Cubs average		0	1	0	0	—	4	9.00	4	2	0	11	1	0	0	0
Career total		15	63	3	12	.200	124	6.35	175 2/3	59	69	249	9	4	1	0
Cubs total		0	1	0	0	—	4	9.00	4	2	0	11	1	0	0	0

Fussell, Frederick Morris (Fred *or* Moonlight Ace)
HEIGHT: 5'10"   LEFTHANDER   BORN: 10/7/1895 SHERIDAN, MISSOURI   DIED: 10/23/1966 SYRACUSE, NEW YORK

YEAR	TEAM	STARTS	GAMES	WON	LOST	PCT	ER	ERA	INNINGS PITCHED	STRIKE-OUTS	WALKS	HITS ALLOWED	HRS ALLOWED	COMP. GAMES	SHUT-OUTS	SAVES
1922	ChC-N	2	3	1	1	.500	10	4.74	19	4	8	24	0	1	0	0
1923	ChC-N	2	28	3	5	.375	47	5.54	76 1/3	38	31	90	2	1	0	3
1928	Pit-N	20	28	8	9	.471	64	3.61	159 2/3	43	41	183	6	9	2	1
1929	Pit-N	3	21	2	2	.500	38	8.62	39 2/3	18	8	68	8	0	0	1
Career average		7	20	4	4	.452	40	4.86	73 2/3	26	22	91	4	3	1	1
Cubs average		2	16	2	3	.400	29	5.38	47 2/3	21	20	57	1	1	0	2
Career total		27	80	14	17	.452	159	4.86	294 2/3	103	88	365	16	11	2	5
Cubs total		4	31	4	6	.400	57	5.38	95 1/3	42	39	114	2	2	0	3

Fyhrie, Michael Edwin (Mike)
HEIGHT: 6'2"   RIGHTHANDER   BORN: 12/9/1969 LONG BEACH, CALIFORNIA

YEAR	TEAM	STARTS	GAMES	WON	LOST	PCT	ER	ERA	INNINGS PITCHED	STRIKE-OUTS	WALKS	HITS ALLOWED	HRS ALLOWED	COMP. GAMES	SHUT-OUTS	SAVES
1996	NYM-N	0	2	0	1	.000	4	15.43	2 1/3	0	3	4	0	0	0	0
1999	Ana-A	7	16	0	4	.000	29	5.05	51 2/3	26	21	61	8	0	0	0
2000	Ana-A	0	32	0	0	—	14	2.39	52 2/3	43	15	54	4	0	0	0
2001	ChC-N	0	15	0	2	.000	7	4.20	15	6	7	16	1	0	0	0
2001	Oak-A	0	3	0	0	—	0	0.00	5	5	1	2	0	0	0	0
Career average		2	17	0	2	.000	14	3.84	31 2/3	20	12	34	3	0	0	0
Cubs average		0	15	0	2	.000	7	4.20	15	6	7	16	1	0	0	0
Career total		7	68	0	7	.000	54	3.84	126 2/3	80	47	137	13	0	0	0
Cubs total		0	15	0	2	.000	7	4.20	15	6	7	16	1	0	0	0

Gaetti, Gary Joseph
HEIGHT: 6'0"   RIGHTHANDER   BORN: 8/19/1958 CENTRALIA, ILLINOIS

YEAR	TEAM	STARTS	GAMES	WON	LOST	PCT	ER	ERA	INNINGS PITCHED	STRIKE-OUTS	WALKS	HITS ALLOWED	HRS ALLOWED	COMP. GAMES	SHUT-OUTS	SAVES
1997	StL-N	0	1	0	0	—	0	0.00	0 1/3	0	0	1	0	0	0	0
1998	StL-N	0	1	0	0	—	0	0.00	1	0	0	2	0	0	0	0
1999	ChC-N	0	1	0	0	—	2	18.00	1	1	1	2	1	0	0	0
Career average		0	1	0	0	—	1	7.71	0 2/3	0	0	2	0	0	0	0
Cubs average		0	1	0	0	—	2	18.00	1	1	1	2	1	0	0	0
Career total		0	3	0	0	—	2	7.71	2 1/3	1	1	5	1	0	0	0
Cubs total		0	1	0	0	—	2	18.00	1	1	1	2	1	0	0	0

Garces, Richard Aron (Rich *or* El Guapo)
HEIGHT: 6'0" RIGHTHANDER BORN: 5/18/1971 MARACAY, VENEZUELA

YEAR	TEAM	STARTS	GAMES	WON	LOST	PCT	ER	ERA	INNINGS PITCHED	STRIKE-OUTS	WALKS	HITS ALLOWED	HRS ALLOWED	COMP. GAMES	SHUT-OUTS	SAVES
1990	Min-A	0	5	0	0	—	1	1.59	5 2/3	1	4	4	0	0	0	2
1993	Min-A	0	3	0	0	—	0	0.00	4	3	2	4	0	0	0	0
1995	**ChC-N**	**0**	**7**	**0**	**0**	**—**	**4**	**3.27**	**11**	**6**	**3**	**11**	**0**	**0**	**0**	**0**
1995	Fla-N	0	11	0	2	.000	8	5.40	13 1/3	16	8	14	1	0	0	0
1996	Bos-A	0	37	3	2	.600	24	4.91	44	55	33	42	5	0	0	0
1997	Bos-A	0	12	0	1	.000	7	4.61	13 2/3	12	9	14	2	0	0	0
1998	Bos-A	0	30	1	1	.500	17	3.33	46	34	27	36	6	0	0	1
1999	Bos-A	0	30	5	1	.833	7	1.55	40 2/3	33	18	25	1	0	0	2
2000	Bos-A	0	64	8	1	.889	27	3.25	74 2/3	69	23	64	7	0	0	1
2001	Bos-A	0	62	6	1	.857	29	3.90	67	51	25	55	6	0	0	1
Career average		0	29	3	1	.719	14	3.49	35 2/3	31	17	30	3	0	0	1
Cubs average		**0**	**7**	**0**	**0**	**—**	**4**	**3.27**	**11**	**6**	**3**	**11**	**0**	**0**	**0**	**0**
Career total		0	261	23	9	.719	124	3.49	320	280	152	269	28	0	0	7
Cubs total		**0**	**7**	**0**	**0**	**—**	**4**	**3.27**	**11**	**6**	**3**	**11**	**0**	**0**	**0**	**0**

Gardner, James Anderson (Jim)
HEIGHT: — RIGHTHANDER BORN: 10/4/1874 PITTSBURGH, PENNSYLVANIA DIED: 4/24/1905 PITTSBURGH, PENNSYLVANIA

YEAR	TEAM	STARTS	GAMES	WON	LOST	PCT	ER	ERA	INNINGS PITCHED	STRIKE-OUTS	WALKS	HITS ALLOWED	HRS ALLOWED	COMP. GAMES	SHUT-OUTS	SAVES
1895	Pit-N	10	11	6	2	.750	25	2.64	85 1/3	31	27	99	1	8	0	0
1897	Pit-N	11	14	5	6	.455	55	5.19	95 1/3	35	32	115	4	8	0	0
1898	Pit-N	22	25	10	12	.455	66	3.21	185 1/3	41	48	179	3	19	1	0
1899	Pit-N	3	6	1	0	1.000	27	7.52	32 1/3	2	13	52	1	0	0	0
1902	**ChC-N**	**3**	**3**	**1**	**2**	**.333**	**8**	**2.88**	**25**	**6**	**10**	**23**	**0**	**2**	**0**	**0**
Career average		10	12	5	4	.511	36	3.85	84 2/3	23	26	94	2	7	0	0
Cubs average		**3**	**3**	**1**	**2**	**.333**	**8**	**2.88**	**25**	**6**	**10**	**23**	**0**	**2**	**0**	**0**
Career total		49	59	23	22	.511	181	3.85	423 1/3	115	130	468	9	37	1	0
Cubs total		**3**	**3**	**1**	**2**	**.333**	**8**	**2.88**	**25**	**6**	**10**	**23**	**0**	**2**	**0**	**0**

Gardner, Richard Frank (Rob)
HEIGHT: 6'1" LEFTHANDER BORN: 12/19/1944 BINGHAMTON, NEW YORK

YEAR	TEAM	STARTS	GAMES	WON	LOST	PCT	ER	ERA	INNINGS PITCHED	STRIKE-OUTS	WALKS	HITS ALLOWED	HRS ALLOWED	COMP. GAMES	SHUT-OUTS	SAVES
1965	NYM-N	4	5	0	2	.000	10	3.21	28	19	7	23	4	0	0	0
1966	NYM-N	17	41	4	8	.333	76	5.12	133 2/3	74	64	147	15	3	0	1
1967	**ChC-N**	**5**	**18**	**0**	**2**	**.000**	**14**	**3.98**	**31 2/3**	**16**	**6**	**33**	**2**	**0**	**0**	**0**
1968	Cle-A	0	5	0	0	—	2	6.75	2 2/3	6	2	5	0	0	0	0
1970	NYY-A	1	1	1	0	1.000	4	4.91	7 1/3	6	4	8	2	0	0	0
1971	Oak-A	1	4	0	0	—	2	2.35	7 2/3	5	3	8	1	0	0	0
1971	NYY-A	0	2	0	0	—	1	3.00	3	2	2	3	0	0	0	0
1972	NYY-A	14	20	8	5	.615	33	3.06	97	58	28	91	9	1	0	0
1973	Mil-A	0	10	1	1	.500	14	9.95	12 2/3	5	13	17	0	0	0	1
1973	Oak-A	0	3	0	0	—	4	4.91	7 1/3	2	4	10	2	0	0	0
Career average		5	14	2	2	.438	20	4.35	41 1/3	24	17	43	4	1	0	0
Cubs average		**5**	**18**	**0**	**2**	**.000**	**14**	**3.98**	**31 2/3**	**16**	**6**	**33**	**2**	**0**	**0**	**0**
Career total		42	109	14	18	.438	160	4.35	331	193	133	345	35	4	0	2
Cubs total		**5**	**18**	**0**	**2**	**.000**	**14**	**3.98**	**31 2/3**	**16**	**6**	**33**	**2**	**0**	**0**	**0**

Garibay, Daniel
HEIGHT: 5'11" LEFTHANDER BORN: 2/14/1973 MANEADERO, MEXICO

YEAR	TEAM	STARTS	GAMES	WON	LOST	PCT	ER	ERA	INNINGS PITCHED	STRIKE-OUTS	WALKS	HITS ALLOWED	HRS ALLOWED	COMP. GAMES	SHUT-OUTS	SAVES
2000	**ChC-N**	**8**	**30**	**2**	**8**	**.200**	**50**	**6.03**	**74 2/3**	**46**	**39**	**88**	**9**	**0**	**0**	**0**
Career average		8	30	2	8	.200	50	6.03	74 2/3	46	39	88	9	0	0	0
Cubs average		**8**	**30**	**2**	**8**	**.200**	**50**	**6.03**	**74 2/3**	**46**	**39**	**88**	**9**	**0**	**0**	**0**
Career total		8	30	2	8	.200	50	6.03	74 2/3	46	39	88	9	0	0	0
Cubs total		**8**	**30**	**2**	**8**	**.200**	**50**	**6.03**	**74 2/3**	**46**	**39**	**88**	**9**	**0**	**0**	**0**

Garman, Michael Douglas (Mike)
HEIGHT: 6'3"   RIGHTHANDER   BORN: 9/16/1949 CALDWELL, IDAHO

YEAR	TEAM	STARTS	GAMES	WON	LOST	PCT	ER	ERA	INNINGS PITCHED	STRIKE-OUTS	WALKS	HITS ALLOWED	HRS ALLOWED	COMP. GAMES	SHUT-OUTS	SAVES
1969	Bos-A	2	2	1	0	1.000	6	4.38	12 ⅓	10	10	13	0	0	0	0
1971	Bos-A	3	3	1	1	.500	8	3.86	18 ⅔	6	9	15	3	0	0	0
1972	Bos-A	1	3	0	1	.000	4	10.80	3 ⅓	1	2	4	1	0	0	0
1973	Bos-A	0	12	0	0	—	13	5.32	22	9	15	32	1	0	0	6
1974	StL-N	0	64	7	2	.778	24	2.64	81 ⅔	45	27	66	4	0	0	10
1975	StL-N	0	66	3	8	.273	21	2.39	79	48	48	73	3	0	0	1
1976	**ChC-N**	2	47	2	4	.333	42	4.95	76 ⅓	37	35	79	7	0	0	12
1977	LA-N	0	49	4	4	.500	19	2.73	62 ⅔	29	22	60	7	0	0	0
1978	LA-N	0	10	0	1	.000	8	4.41	16 ⅓	5	3	15	3	0	0	13
1978	Mon-N	0	47	4	6	.400	30	4.40	61 ⅓	23	31	54	5	0	0	
Career average		1	34	2	3	.449	19	3.63	48 ⅓	24	22	46	4	0	0	5
Cubs average		**2**	**47**	**2**	**4**	**.333**	**42**	**4.95**	**76 ⅓**	**37**	**35**	**79**	**7**	**0**	**0**	**1**
Career total		8	303	22	27	.449	175	3.63	433 ⅔	213	202	411	34	0	0	42
Cubs total		**2**	**47**	**2**	**4**	**.333**	**42**	**4.95**	**76 ⅓**	**37**	**35**	**79**	**7**	**0**	**0**	**1**

Garvin, Virgil Lee (Ned)
HEIGHT: 6'3"   RIGHTHANDER   BORN: 1/1/1874 NAVASOTA, TEXAS   DIED: 6/16/1908 FRESNO, CALIFORNIA

YEAR	TEAM	STARTS	GAMES	WON	LOST	PCT	ER	ERA	INNINGS PITCHED	STRIKE-OUTS	WALKS	HITS ALLOWED	HRS ALLOWED	COMP. GAMES	SHUT-OUTS	SAVES
1896	Phi-N	1	2	0	2	.000	11	7.62	13	4	7	19	0	1	0	0
1899	**ChN-N**	23	24	9	13	.409	63	2.85	199	69	42	202	1	22	4	0
1900	**ChN-N**	28	30	10	18	.357	66	2.41	246 ⅓	107	63	225	4	25	1	0
1901	Mil-A	27	37	7	20	.259	99	3.46	257 ⅓	122	90	258	4	22	1	2
1902	CWS-A	19	23	10	10	.500	43	2.21	175 ⅓	55	43	169	3	16	2	0
1902	Bro-N	2	2	1	1	.500	2	1.00	18	7	4	15	0	2	1	0
1903	Bro-N	34	38	15	18	.455	102	3.08	298	154	84	277	2	30	2	2
1904	Bro-N	22	23	5	15	.250	34	1.68	181 ⅔	86	78	141	6	16	2	0
1904	NYA-A	2	2	0	1	.000	3	2.25	12	8	2	14	0	0	0	0
Career average		23	26	8	14	.368	60	2.72	200	87	59	189	3	19	2	1
Cubs average		**26**	**27**	**10**	**16**	**.380**	**65**	**2.61**	**222 ⅔**	**88**	**53**	**214**	**3**	**24**	**3**	**0**
Career total		158	181	57	98	.368	423	2.72	1400 ⅔	612	413	1320	20	134	13	4
Cubs total		**51**	**54**	**19**	**31**	**.380**	**129**	**2.61**	**445 ⅓**	**176**	**105**	**427**	**5**	**47**	**5**	**0**

Gassaway, Charles Cason (Charlie or Sheriff)
HEIGHT: 6'2"   LEFTHANDER   BORN: 8/12/1918 GASSAWAY, TENNESSEE   DIED: 1/15/1992 MIAMI, FLORIDA

YEAR	TEAM	STARTS	GAMES	WON	LOST	PCT	ER	ERA	INNINGS PITCHED	STRIKE-OUTS	WALKS	HITS ALLOWED	HRS ALLOWED	COMP. GAMES	SHUT-OUTS	SAVES
1944	**ChC-N**	2	2	0	1	.000	10	7.71	11 ⅔	7	10	20	3	0	0	0
1945	Phi-A	11	24	4	7	.364	49	3.74	118	50	55	114	4	4	0	0
1946	Cle-A	6	13	1	1	.500	22	3.91	50 ⅔	23	26	54	2	0	0	0
Career average		6	13	2	3	.357	27	4.04	60	27	30	63	3	1	0	0
Cubs average		**2**	**2**	**0**	**1**	**.000**	**10**	**7.71**	**11 ⅔**	**7**	**10**	**20**	**3**	**0**	**0**	**0**
Career total		19	39	5	9	.357	81	4.04	180 ⅓	80	91	188	9	4	0	0
Cubs total		**2**	**2**	**0**	**1**	**.000**	**10**	**7.71**	**11 ⅔**	**7**	**10**	**20**	**3**	**0**	**0**	**0**

Gaw, George Joseph (Chippy)
HEIGHT: 5'11"   RIGHTHANDER   BORN: 3/13/1892 WEST NEWTON, MASSACHUSETTS   DIED: 5/26/1968 BOSTON, MASSACHUSETTS

YEAR	TEAM	STARTS	GAMES	WON	LOST	PCT	ER	ERA	INNINGS PITCHED	STRIKE-OUTS	WALKS	HITS ALLOWED	HRS ALLOWED	COMP. GAMES	SHUT-OUTS	SAVES
1920	**ChC-N**	1	6	1	1	.500	7	4.85	13	4	3	16	1	0	0	0
Career average		1	6	1	1	.500	7	4.85	13	4	3	16	1	0	0	0
Cubs average		**1**	**6**	**1**	**1**	**.500**	**7**	**4.85**	**13**	**4**	**3**	**16**	**1**	**0**	**0**	**0**
Career total		1	6	1	1	.500	7	4.85	13	4	3	16	1	0	0	0
Cubs total		**1**	**6**	**1**	**1**	**.500**	**7**	**4.85**	**13**	**4**	**3**	**16**	**1**	**0**	**0**	**0**

Geisel, John David (Dave)

HEIGHT: 6'3" LEFTHANDER BORN: 1/18/1955 WINDBER, PENNSYLVANIA

YEAR	TEAM	STARTS	GAMES	WON	LOST	PCT	ER	ERA	INNINGS PITCHED	STRIKE-OUTS	WALKS	HITS ALLOWED	HRS ALLOWED	COMP. GAMES	SHUT-OUTS	SAVES
1978	ChC-N	1	18	1	0	1.000	11	4.24	23 1/3	15	11	27	0	0	0	0
1979	ChC-N	0	7	0	0	—	1	0.60	15	5	4	10	0	0	0	0
1981	ChC-N	2	11	2	0	1.000	1	0.56	16	7	10	11	0	0	0	0
1982	Tor-A	2	16	1	1	.500	14	3.98	31 2/3	22	17	32	6	0	0	0
1983	Tor-A	0	47	0	3	.000	27	4.64	52 1/3	50	31	47	4	0	0	5
1984	Sea-A	3	20	1	1	.500	20	4.15	43 1/3	28	9	47	2	0	0	3
1985	Sea-A	0	12	0	0	—	19	6.33	27	17	15	35	3	0	0	0
Career average		1	19	1	1	.500	13	4.01	29 2/3	21	14	30	2	0	0	1
Cubs average		1	12	1	0	1.000	4	2.15	18	9	8	16	0	0	0	0
Career total		8	131	5	5	.500	93	4.01	208 2/3	144	97	209	15	0	0	8
Cubs total		3	36	3	0	1.000	13	2.15	54 1/3	27	25	48	0	0	0	0

Geiss, Emil August

HEIGHT: 5'11" RIGHTHANDER BORN: 3/20/1867 CHICAGO, ILLINOIS DIED: 10/4/1911 CHICAGO, ILLINOIS

YEAR	TEAM	STARTS	GAMES	WON	LOST	PCT	ER	ERA	INNINGS PITCHED	STRIKE-OUTS	WALKS	HITS ALLOWED	HRS ALLOWED	COMP. GAMES	SHUT-OUTS	SAVES
1887	ChN-N	1	1	0	1	.000	8	8.00	9	4	3	20	0	1	0	0
Career average		1	1	0	1	.000	8	8.00	9	4	3	20	0	1	0	0
Cubs average		1	1	0	1	.000	8	8.00	9	4	3	20	0	1	0	0
Career total		1	1	0	1	.000	8	8.00	9	4	3	20	0	1	0	0
Cubs total		1	1	0	1	.000	8	8.00	9	4	3	20	0	1	0	0

Gerard, David Frederick (Dave)

HEIGHT: 6'2" RIGHTHANDER BORN: 8/6/1936 NEW YORK, NEW YORK

YEAR	TEAM	STARTS	GAMES	WON	LOST	PCT	ER	ERA	INNINGS PITCHED	STRIKE-OUTS	WALKS	HITS ALLOWED	HRS ALLOWED	COMP. GAMES	SHUT-OUTS	SAVES
1962	ChC-N	0	39	2	3	.400	32	4.91	58 2/3	30	28	67	10	0	0	3
Career average		0	39	2	3	.400	32	4.91	58 2/3	30	28	67	10	0	0	3
Cubs average		0	39	2	3	.400	32	4.91	58 2/3	30	28	67	10	0	0	3
Career total		0	39	2	3	.400	32	4.91	58 2/3	30	28	67	10	0	0	3
Cubs total		0	39	2	3	.400	32	4.91	58 2/3	30	28	67	10	0	0	3

Gerberman, George Alois

HEIGHT: 6'0" RIGHTHANDER BORN: 3/8/1942 EL CAMPO, TEXAS

YEAR	TEAM	STARTS	GAMES	WON	LOST	PCT	ER	ERA	INNINGS PITCHED	STRIKE-OUTS	WALKS	HITS ALLOWED	HRS ALLOWED	COMP. GAMES	SHUT-OUTS	SAVES
1962	ChC-N	1	1	0	0	—	1	1.69	5 1/3	1	5	3	1	0	0	0
Career average		1	1	0	0	—	1	1.69	5 1/3	1	5	3	1	0	0	0
Cubs average		1	1	0	0	—	1	1.69	5 1/3	1	5	3	1	0	0	0
Career total		1	1	0	0	—	1	1.69	5 1/3	1	5	3	1	0	0	0
Cubs total		1	1	0	0	—	1	1.69	5 1/3	1	5	3	1	0	0	0

Gibson, Robert Murray

HEIGHT: 6'3" RIGHTHANDER BORN: 8/20/1869 DUNCANSVILLE, PENNSYLVANIA DIED: 12/19/1949 PITTSBURGH, PENNSYLVANIA

YEAR	TEAM	STARTS	GAMES	WON	LOST	PCT	ER	ERA	INNINGS PITCHED	STRIKE-OUTS	WALKS	HITS ALLOWED	HRS ALLOWED	COMP. GAMES	SHUT-OUTS	SAVES
1890	ChN-N	1	1	1	0	1.000	0	0.00	9	1	2	6	0	1	0	0
1890	Pit-N	3	3	0	3	.000	23	17.25	12	3	23	24	0	1	0	0
Career average		4	4	1	3	.250	23	9.86	21	4	25	30	0	2	0	0
Cubs average		1	1	1	0	1.000	0	0.00	9	1	2	6	0	1	0	0
Career total		4	4	1	3	.250	23	9.86	21	4	25	30	0	2	0	0
Cubs total		1	1	1	0	1.000	0	0.00	9	1	2	6	0	1	0	0

Giusti, David John (Dave)
HEIGHT: 5'11" RIGHTHANDER BORN: 11/27/1939 SENECA FALLS, NEW YORK

YEAR	TEAM	STARTS	GAMES	WON	LOST	PCT	ER	ERA	INNINGS PITCHED	STRIKE-OUTS	WALKS	HITS ALLOWED	HRS ALLOWED	COMP. GAMES	SHUT-OUTS	SAVES
1962	Hou-N	5	22	2	3	.400	46	5.62	73 2/3	43	30	82	7	0	0	0
1964	Hou-N	0	8	0	0	—	9	3.16	25 2/3	16	8	24	1	0	0	0
1965	Hou-N	13	38	8	7	.533	63	4.32	131 1/3	92	46	132	13	4	1	3
1966	Hou-N	33	34	15	14	.517	98	4.20	210	131	54	215	23	9	4	0
1967	Hou-N	33	37	11	15	.423	103	4.18	221 2/3	157	58	231	20	8	1	1
1968	Hou-N	34	37	11	14	.440	89	3.19	251	186	67	226	15	12	2	1
1969	StL-N	12	22	3	7	.300	40	3.61	99 2/3	62	37	96	7	2	1	0
1970	Pit-N	1	66	9	3	.750	35	3.06	103	85	39	98	7	0	0	26
1971	Pit-N	0	58	5	6	.455	28	2.93	86	55	31	79	5	0	0	30
1972	Pit-N	0	54	7	4	.636	16	1.93	74 2/3	54	20	59	3	0	0	22
1973	Pit-N	0	67	9	2	.818	26	2.37	98 2/3	64	37	89	9	0	0	20
1974	Pit-N	2	64	7	5	.583	39	3.32	105 2/3	53	40	101	2	0	0	12
1975	Pit-N	0	61	5	4	.556	30	2.95	91 2/3	38	42	79	3	0	0	17
1976	Pit-N	0	40	5	4	.556	28	4.32	58 1/3	24	27	59	5	0	0	6
1977	Oak-A	0	40	3	3	.500	20	2.98	60 1/3	28	20	54	4	0	0	6
1977	**ChC-N**	**0**	**20**	**0**	**2**	**.000**	**17**	**6.04**	**25 1/3**	**15**	**14**	**30**	**2**	**0**	**0**	**1**
Career average	9	45	7	6	.518	46	3.60	114 1/3	74	38	110	8	2	1	10
Cubs average	**0**	**20**	**0**	**2**	**.000**	**17**	**6.04**	**25 1/3**	**15**	**14**	**30**	**2**	**0**	**0**	**1**
Career total	133	668	100	93	.518	687	3.60	1716 2/3	1103	570	1654	126	35	9	145
Cubs total	**0**	**20**	**0**	**2**	**.000**	**17**	**6.04**	**25 1/3**	**15**	**14**	**30**	**2**	**0**	**0**	**1**

Glade, Frederick Monroe (Fred *or* Lucky)
HEIGHT: 5'10" RIGHTHANDER BORN: 1/25/1876 DUBUQUE, IOWA DIED: 11/21/1934 GRAND ISLAND, NEBRASKA

YEAR	TEAM	STARTS	GAMES	WON	LOST	PCT	ER	ERA	INNINGS PITCHED	STRIKE-OUTS	WALKS	HITS ALLOWED	HRS ALLOWED	COMP. GAMES	SHUT-OUTS	SAVES
1902	**ChC-N**	**1**	**1**	**0**	**1**	**.000**	**8**	**9.00**	**8**	**3**	**3**	**13**	**0**	**1**	**0**	**0**
1904	StL-A	34	35	18	15	.545	73	2.27	289	156	58	248	2	30	6	1
1905	StL-A	32	32	6	25	.194	86	2.81	275	127	58	257	3	28	2	0
1906	StL-A	32	35	15	14	.517	70	2.36	266 2/3	96	59	215	4	28	4	1
1907	StL-A	22	24	13	9	.591	60	2.67	202	71	45	187	2	18	2	0
1908	NYA-A	5	5	0	4	.000	15	4.22	32	11	14	30	0	2	0	0
Career average	21	22	9	11	.433	52	2.62	178 2/3	77	40	158	2	18	2	0
Cubs average	**1**	**1**	**0**	**1**	**.000**	**8**	**9.00**	**8**	**3**	**3**	**13**	**0**	**1**	**0**	**0**
Career total	126	132	52	68	.433	312	2.62	1072 2/3	464	237	950	11	107	14	2
Cubs total	**1**	**1**	**0**	**1**	**.000**	**8**	**9.00**	**8**	**3**	**3**	**13**	**0**	**1**	**0**	**0**

Goetz, John Hardy
HEIGHT: 6'0" RIGHTHANDER BORN: 10/24/1937 GOETZVILLE, MICHIGAN

YEAR	TEAM	STARTS	GAMES	WON	LOST	PCT	ER	ERA	INNINGS PITCHED	STRIKE-OUTS	WALKS	HITS ALLOWED	HRS ALLOWED	COMP. GAMES	SHUT-OUTS	SAVES
1960	**ChC-N**	**0**	**4**	**0**	**0**	**—**	**9**	**12.79**	**6 1/3**	**6**	**4**	**10**	**2**	**0**	**0**	**0**
Career average	0	4	0	0	—	9	12.79	6 1/3	6	4	10	2	0	0	0
Cubs average	**0**	**4**	**0**	**0**	**—**	**9**	**12.79**	**6 1/3**	**6**	**4**	**10**	**2**	**0**	**0**	**0**
Career total	0	4	0	0	—	9	12.79	6 1/3	6	4	10	2	0	0	0
Cubs total	**0**	**4**	**0**	**0**	**—**	**9**	**12.79**	**6 1/3**	**6**	**4**	**10**	**2**	**0**	**0**	**0**

Goldsmith, Fredrick Ernest (Fred)
HEIGHT: 6'1" RIGHTHANDER BORN: 5/15/1852 NEW HAVEN, CONNECTICUT DIED: 3/28/1939 BERKLEY, MICHIGAN

YEAR	TEAM	STARTS	GAMES	WON	LOST	PCT	ER	ERA	INNINGS PITCHED	STRIKE-OUTS	WALKS	HITS ALLOWED	HRS ALLOWED	COMP. GAMES	SHUT-OUTS	SAVES
1879	Try-N	7	8	2	4	.333	11	1.57	63	31	1	61	0	7	0	0
1880	ChN-N	24	26	21	3	.875	41	1.75	210 1/3	90	18	189	2	22	4	1
1881	ChN-N	39	39	24	13	.649	95	2.59	330	76	44	328	4	37	5	0
1882	ChN-N	45	45	28	17	.622	109	2.42	405	109	38	377	7	45	4	0

(continued)

(continued)

1883	ChN-N	45	46	25	19	.568	134	3.15	383⅓	82	39	456	14	40	2	0
1884	ChN-N	21	21	9	11	.450	89	4.26	188	34	29	245	11	20	1	0
1884	Bal-AA	4	4	3	1	.750	9	2.70	30	11	2	29	0	3	0	0
Career average		31	32	19	11	.622	81	2.73	268⅓	72	29	281	6	29	3	0
Cubs average		**35**	**35**	**21**	**13**	**.629**	**94**	**2.78**	**303⅓**	**78**	**34**	**319**	**8**	**33**	**3**	**0**
Career total		185	189	112	68	.622	488	2.73	1609⅔	433	171	1685	38	174	16	1
Cubs total		**174**	**177**	**107**	**63**	**.629**	**468**	**2.78**	**1516⅔**	**391**	**168**	**1595**	**38**	**164**	**16**	**1**

Fredrick (Fred) Ernest Goldsmith, rhp, 1879–84

Was Fred Goldsmith the man who invented the curveball? No one knows for sure, but Goldsmith was certainly one of its first practitioners.

In fact, Fred Goldsmith was a pitching pioneer in a number of aspects. Born in New Haven, Connecticut, on May 15, 1852, Goldsmith claimed to discover how to "curve" a thrown baseball in his early teens.

Certainly, there is documented evidence of this as several newspapers reported that Goldsmith, then a lad of 18, gave a demonstration of his new pitch on August 17, 1870, in his hometown.

Goldsmith's claim was always disputed by William Arthur "Candy" Cummings of Ware, Massachusetts. Cummings claimed to have discovered the pitch while skimming seashells on a beach in 1863, when he was 14.

Goldsmith was pitching in the Canadian minor leagues before he became a major leaguer. He pitched eight games for Troy, New York, in 1879, going 2-4 on the year.

But Chicago was interested in him. Chicago manager Adrian "Cap" Anson liked Goldsmith's control and appreciated his new curveball pitch. Goldsmith was signed by Anson prior to the beginning of the 1880 season.

Anson already had a great pitcher in Larry Corcoran, but one thing Anson noticed was that many pitchers of the era tended to burn out after a few years. What Anson proposed to do was sign Goldsmith and use him almost as much as Corcoran. Such an arrangement,

Anson felt, would have the double advantage of resting the fireballing Corcoran and alternating him with the curveballing Goldsmith.

It worked perfectly for several years. In 1880 Goldsmith went 21-3 and led the league in winning percentage, was second in the league in average strikeouts per game with 3.85 and fourth in the league in ERA with a 1.75 mark. Chicago easily won the National League crown by 15 games over second-place Providence.

For the next four years, Goldsmith would win 21 or more games and be among the league leaders in winning percentage.

As good a pitcher as Goldsmith was, he was also a person who would be called an "airhead" these days. In those days, Anson wouldn't repeat what he called Goldsmith when Fred forgot to back up a base on a hit by the other team. Yet, he was a cool customer on the mound and a competitor.

Chicago won championships in 1881 and 1882 with the two-man rotation a key factor. The team fell to second in 1883, and Goldsmith began developing arm trouble. His drop-off was precipitous, and he was 9-11 for Chicago in 1884, before being traded to Baltimore, where he pitched in four games before retiring after that year.

In 1886 Goldsmith umpired for a year before settling down in the Midwest, tending bar in several towns and finally becoming a businessman. In 1909, the invention of the curveball was officially credited to Cummings, and that infuriated Goldsmith. At his death in 1939, he was reportedly holding the news clipping of his 1870 curveball demonstration.

Gonzalez, Geremis Segundo (Jeremi)
HEIGHT: 6'0"   RIGHTHANDER   BORN: 1/8/1975 MARACAIBO, VENEZUELA

YEAR	TEAM	STARTS	GAMES	WON	LOST	PCT	ER	ERA	INNINGS PITCHED	STRIKE-OUTS	WALKS	HITS ALLOWED	HRS ALLOWED	COMP. GAMES	SHUT-OUTS	SAVES
1997	ChC-N	23	23	11	9	.550	68	4.25	144	93	69	126	16	1	1	0
1998	ChC-N	20	20	7	7	.500	65	5.32	110	70	41	124	13	1	1	0
Career average		22	22	9	8	.529	67	4.71	127	82	55	125	15	1	1	0
Cubs average		22	22	9	8	.529	67	4.71	127	82	55	125	15	1	1	0
Career total		43	43	18	16	.529	133	4.71	254	163	110	250	29	2	2	0
Cubs total		43	43	18	16	.529	133	4.71	254	163	110	250	29	2	2	0

Gordon, Thomas (Flash)
HEIGHT: 5'10"   RIGHTHANDER   BORN: 11/18/1967 SEBRING, FLORIDA

YEAR	TEAM	STARTS	GAMES	WON	LOST	PCT	ER	ERA	INNINGS PITCHED	STRIKE-OUTS	WALKS	HITS ALLOWED	HRS ALLOWED	COMP. GAMES	SHUT-OUTS	SAVES
1988	KC-A	2	5	0	2	.000	9	5.17	15 2/3	18	7	16	1	0	0	0
1989	KC-A	16	49	17	9	.654	66	3.64	163	153	86	122	10	1	1	1
1990	KC-A	32	32	12	11	.522	81	3.73	195 1/3	175	99	192	17	6	1	0
1991	KC-A	14	45	9	14	.391	68	3.87	158	167	87	129	16	1	0	1
1992	KC-A	11	40	6	10	.375	60	4.59	117 2/3	98	55	116	9	0	0	0
1993	KC-A	14	48	12	6	.667	62	3.58	155 2/3	143	77	125	11	2	0	1
1994	KC-A	24	24	11	7	.611	75	4.35	155 1/3	126	87	136	15	0	0	0
1995	KC-A	31	31	12	12	.500	93	4.43	189	119	89	204	12	2	0	0
1996	Bos-A	34	34	12	9	.571	134	5.59	215 2/3	171	105	249	28	4	1	0
1997	Bos-A	25	42	6	10	.375	76	3.74	182 2/3	159	78	155	10	2	1	11
1998	Bos-A	0	73	7	4	.636	24	2.72	79 1/3	78	25	55	2	0	0	46
1999	Bos-A	0	21	0	2	.000	11	5.60	17 2/3	24	12	17	2	0	0	11
2001	ChC-N	0	47	1	2	.333	17	3.38	45 1/3	67	16	32	4	0	0	27
Career average		16	38	8	8	.517	60	4.13	130	115	63	119	11	1	0	8
Cubs average		0	47	1	2	.333	17	3.38	45 1/3	67	16	32	4	0	0	27
Career total		203	491	105	98	.517	776	4.13	1690 1/3	1498	823	1548	137	18	4	98
Cubs total		0	47	1	2	.333	17	3.38	45 1/3	67	16	32	4	0	0	27

Gornicki, Henry Frank (Hank)
HEIGHT: 6'1"   RIGHTHANDER   BORN: 1/14/1911 NIAGARA FALLS, NEW YORK   DIED: 2/16/1996 RIVIERA BEACH, FLORIDA

YEAR	TEAM	STARTS	GAMES	WON	LOST	PCT	ER	ERA	INNINGS PITCHED	STRIKE-OUTS	WALKS	HITS ALLOWED	HRS ALLOWED	COMP. GAMES	SHUT-OUTS	SAVES
1941	StL-N	1	4	1	0	1.000	4	3.18	11 1/3	6	9	6	0	1	1	0
1941	ChC-N	0	1	0	0	—	1	4.50	2	2	0	3	0	0	0	0
1942	Pit-N	14	25	5	6	.455	32	2.57	112	48	40	89	2	7	2	2
1943	Pit-N	18	42	9	13	.409	65	3.98	147	63	47	165	10	4	1	4
1946	Pit-N	0	7	0	0	—	5	3.55	12 2/3	4	11	12	0	0	0	0
Career average		8	20	4	5	.441	27	3.38	71 1/3	31	27	69	3	3	1	2
Cubs average		0	1	0	0	—	1	4.50	2	2	0	3	0	0	0	0
Career total		33	79	15	19	.441	107	3.38	285	123	107	275	12	12	4	6
Cubs total		0	1	0	0	—	1	4.50	2	2	0	3	0	0	0	0

Gossage, Richard Michael (Goose)
HEIGHT: 6'3"   RIGHTHANDER   BORN: 7/5/1951 COLORADO SPRINGS, COLORADO

YEAR	TEAM	STARTS	GAMES	WON	LOST	PCT	ER	ERA	INNINGS PITCHED	STRIKE-OUTS	WALKS	HITS ALLOWED	HRS ALLOWED	COMP. GAMES	SHUT-OUTS	SAVES
1972	CWS-A	1	36	7	1	.875	38	4.28	80	57	44	72	2	0	0	2
1973	CWS-A	4	20	0	4	.000	41	7.43	49 2/3	33	37	57	9	1	0	0
1974	CWS-A	3	39	4	6	.400	41	4.13	89 1/3	64	47	92	4	0	0	1
1975	CWS-A	0	62	9	8	.529	29	1.84	141 2/3	130	70	99	3	0	0	26
1976	CWS-A	29	31	9	17	.346	98	3.94	224	135	90	214	16	15	0	1
1977	Pit-N	0	72	11	9	.550	24	1.62	133	151	49	78	9	0	0	26
1978	NYY-A	0	63	10	11	.476	30	2.01	134 1/3	122	59	87	9	0	0	27

(continued)

(continued)

YEAR	TEAM	STARTS	GAMES	WON	LOST	PCT	ER	ERA	INNINGS PITCHED	STRIKE-OUTS	WALKS	HITS ALLOWED	HRS ALLOWED	COMP. GAMES	SHUT-OUTS	SAVES
1979	NYY-A	0	36	5	3	.625	17	2.62	58⅓	41	19	48	5	0	0	18
1980	NYY-A	0	64	6	2	.750	25	2.27	99	103	37	74	5	0	0	33
1981	NYY-A	0	32	3	2	.600	4	0.77	46⅔	48	14	22	2	0	0	20
1982	NYY-A	0	56	4	5	.444	23	2.23	93	102	28	63	5	0	0	30
1983	NYY-A	0	57	13	5	.722	22	2.27	87⅓	90	25	82	5	0	0	22
1984	SD-N	0	62	10	6	.625	33	2.90	102⅓	84	36	75	6	0	0	25
1985	SD-N	0	50	5	3	.625	16	1.82	79	52	17	64	1	0	0	26
1986	SD-N	0	45	5	7	.417	32	4.45	64⅔	63	20	69	8	0	0	21
1987	SD-N	0	40	5	4	.556	18	3.12	52	44	19	47	4	0	0	11
1988	**ChC-N**	**0**	**46**	**4**	**4**	**.500**	**21**	**4.33**	**43⅔**	**30**	**15**	**50**	**3**	**0**	**0**	**13**
1989	SF-N	0	31	2	1	.667	13	2.68	43⅔	24	27	32	2	0	0	4
1989	NYY-A	0	11	1	0	1.000	6	3.77	14⅓	6	3	14	0	0	0	1
1991	Tex-A	0	44	4	2	.667	16	3.57	40⅓	28	16	33	4	0	0	1
1992	Oak-A	0	30	0	2	.000	12	2.84	38	26	19	32	5	0	0	0
1993	Oak-A	0	39	4	5	.444	24	4.53	47⅔	40	26	49	6	0	0	1
1994	Sea-A	0	36	3	0	1.000	22	4.18	47⅓	29	15	44	6	0	0	1
Career average		2	46	6	5	.537	28	3.01	82⅓	68	33	68	5	1	0	14
Cubs average		**0**	**46**	**4**	**4**	**.500**	**21**	**4.33**	**43⅔**	**30**	**15**	**50**	**3**	**0**	**0**	**13**
Career total		37	1002	124	107	.537	605	3.01	1809⅓	1502	732	1497	119	16	0	310
Cubs total		**0**	**46**	**4**	**4**	**.500**	**21**	**4.33**	**43⅔**	**30**	**15**	**50**	**3**	**0**	**0**	**13**

Graham, George Frederick (Peaches)
HEIGHT: 5'9"   RIGHTHANDER   BORN: 3/23/1877 ALEDO, ILLINOIS   DIED: 7/25/1939 LONG BEACH, CALIFORNIA

YEAR	TEAM	STARTS	GAMES	WON	LOST	PCT	ER	ERA	INNINGS PITCHED	STRIKE-OUTS	WALKS	HITS ALLOWED	HRS ALLOWED	COMP. GAMES	SHUT-OUTS	SAVES
1903	ChC-N	1	1	0	1	.000	3	5.40	5	4	3	9	0	0	0	0
Career average		1	1	0	1	.000	3	5.40	5	4	3	9	0	0	0	0
Cubs average		**1**	**1**	**0**	**1**	**.000**	**3**	**5.40**	**5**	**4**	**3**	**9**	**0**	**0**	**0**	**0**
Career total		1	1	0	1	.000	3	5.40	5	4	3	9	0	0	0	0
Cubs total		**1**	**1**	**0**	**1**	**.000**	**3**	**5.40**	**5**	**4**	**3**	**9**	**0**	**0**	**0**	**0**

Grampp, Henry Erchardt (Hank)
HEIGHT: 6'1"   RIGHTHANDER   BORN: 9/28/1903 NEW YORK, NEW YORK   DIED: 3/24/1986 NEW YORK, NEW YORK

YEAR	TEAM	STARTS	GAMES	WON	LOST	PCT	ER	ERA	INNINGS PITCHED	STRIKE-OUTS	WALKS	HITS ALLOWED	HRS ALLOWED	COMP. GAMES	SHUT-OUTS	SAVES
1927	ChC-N	0	2	0	0	—	3	9.00	3	3	1	4	0	0	0	0
1929	ChC-N	1	1	0	1	.000	6	27.00	2	0	3	4	0	0	0	0
Career average		1	2	0	1	.000	5	16.20	2⅔	2	2	4	0	0	0	0
Cubs average		**1**	**2**	**0**	**1**	**.000**	**5**	**16.20**	**2⅔**	**2**	**2**	**4**	**0**	**0**	**0**	**0**
Career total		1	3	0	1	.000	9	16.20	5	3	4	8	0	0	0	0
Cubs total		**1**	**3**	**0**	**1**	**.000**	**9**	**16.20**	**5**	**3**	**4**	**8**	**0**	**0**	**0**	**0**

Gregory, Grover LeRoy (Lee)
HEIGHT: 6'1"   LEFTHANDER   BORN: 6/2/1938 BAKERSFIELD, CALIFORNIA

YEAR	TEAM	STARTS	GAMES	WON	LOST	PCT	ER	ERA	INNINGS PITCHED	STRIKE-OUTS	WALKS	HITS ALLOWED	HRS ALLOWED	COMP. GAMES	SHUT-OUTS	SAVES
1964	ChC-N	0	11	0	0	—	7	3.50	18	8	5	23	3	0	0	0
Career average		0	11	0	0	—	7	3.50	18	8	5	23	3	0	0	0
Cubs average		**0**	**11**	**0**	**0**	**—**	**7**	**3.50**	**18**	**8**	**5**	**23**	**3**	**0**	**0**	**0**
Career total		0	11	0	0	—	7	3.50	18	8	5	23	3	0	0	0
Cubs total		**0**	**11**	**0**	**0**	**—**	**7**	**3.50**	**18**	**8**	**5**	**23**	**3**	**0**	**0**	**0**

Griffin, James Linton (Hank *or* Pepper)
HEIGHT: 6'0"   RIGHTHANDER   BORN: 7/11/1886 WHITEHOUSE, TEXAS   DIED: 2/11/1950 TERRELL, TEXAS

YEAR	TEAM	STARTS	GAMES	WON	LOST	PCT	ER	ERA	INNINGS PITCHED	STRIKE-OUTS	WALKS	HITS ALLOWED	HRS ALLOWED	COMP. GAMES	SHUT-OUTS	SAVES
1911	**ChC-N**	**1**	**1**	**0**	**0**	**—**	**2**	**18.00**	**1**	**1**	**3**	**1**	**1**	**0**	**0**	**0**
1911	Bos-N	6	15	0	6	.000	48	5.23	82 ⅔	30	34	96	3	1	0	0
1912	Bos-N	0	3	0	0	—	5	27.00	1 ⅔	0	3	3	0	0	0	0
Career average		4	10	0	3	.000	28	5.80	42 ⅔	16	20	50	2	1	0	0
Cubs average		**1**	**1**	**0**	**0**	**—**	**2**	**18.00**	**1**	**1**	**3**	**1**	**1**	**0**	**0**	**0**
Career total		7	19	0	6	.000	55	5.80	85 ⅓	31	40	100	4	1	0	0
Cubs total		**1**	**1**	**0**	**0**		**2**	**18.00**	**1**	**1**	**3**	**1**	**1**	**0**	**0**	**0**

Griffin, Michael Leroy (Mike)
HEIGHT: 6'4"   RIGHTHANDER   BORN: 6/26/1957 COLUSA, CALIFORNIA

YEAR	TEAM	STARTS	GAMES	WON	LOST	PCT	ER	ERA	INNINGS PITCHED	STRIKE-OUTS	WALKS	HITS ALLOWED	HRS ALLOWED	COMP. GAMES	SHUT-OUTS	SAVES
1979	NYY-A	0	3	0	0	—	2	4.15	4 ⅓	5	2	5	0	0	0	1
1980	NYY-A	9	13	2	4	.333	29	4.83	54	25	23	64	6	0	0	0
1981	NYY-A	0	2	0	0	—	1	2.08	4 ⅓	4	0	5	0	0	0	0
1981	**ChC-N**	**9**	**16**	**2**	**5**	**.286**	**26**	**4.50**	**52**	**20**	**9**	**64**	**4**	**0**	**0**	**1**
1982	SD-N	0	7	0	1	.000	4	3.48	10 ⅓	4	3	9	0	0	0	0
1987	Bal-A	6	23	3	5	.375	36	4.36	74 ⅓	42	33	78	9	1	0	1
1989	Cin-N	0	3	0	0	—	6	12.46	4 ⅓	1	3	10	0	0	0	0
Career average		4	11	1	3	.318	17	4.60	34	17	12	39	3	0	0	1
Cubs average		**9**	**16**	**2**	**5**	**.286**	**26**	**4.50**	**52**	**20**	**9**	**64**	**4**	**0**	**0**	**1**
Career total		24	67	7	15	.318	104	4.60	203 ⅔	101	73	235	19	1	0	3
Cubs total		**9**	**16**	**2**	**5**	**.286**	**26**	**4.50**	**52**	**20**	**9**	**64**	**4**	**0**	**0**	**1**

Griffith, Clark Calvin (The Old Fox)
HEIGHT: 5'6"   RIGHTHANDER   BORN: 11/20/1869 CLEAR CREEK, MISSOURI   DIED: 10/27/1955 WASHINGTON, DISTRICT OF COLUMBIA

YEAR	TEAM	STARTS	GAMES	WON	LOST	PCT	ER	ERA	INNINGS PITCHED	STRIKE-OUTS	WALKS	HITS ALLOWED	HRS ALLOWED	COMP. GAMES	SHUT-OUTS	SAVES
1891	StL-AA	17	27	11	8	.579	69	3.33	186 ⅓	68	58	195	8	12	0	0
1891	Bos-AA	4	7	3	1	.750	25	5.63	40	20	15	47	3	3	0	0
1893	**ChN-N**	**2**	**4**	**1**	**2**	**.333**	**11**	**5.03**	**19 ⅔**	**9**	**5**	**24**	**1**	**2**	**0**	**0**
1894	**ChN-N**	**30**	**36**	**21**	**11**	**.656**	**143**	**4.92**	**261 ⅓**	**71**	**85**	**328**	**12**	**29**	**0**	**0**
1895	**ChN-N**	**41**	**42**	**25**	**13**	**.658**	**154**	**3.93**	**353**	**79**	**91**	**434**	**11**	**39**	**0**	**1**
1896	**ChN-N**	**35**	**36**	**23**	**12**	**.657**	**125**	**3.54**	**317 ⅔**	**81**	**70**	**370**	**3**	**35**	**0**	**0**
1897	**ChN-N**	**38**	**41**	**21**	**19**	**.525**	**142**	**3.72**	**343 ⅔**	**102**	**86**	**410**	**3**	**38**	**1**	**1**
1898	**ChN-N**	**37**	**37**	**24**	**10**	**.706**	**68**	**1.88**	**325 ⅓**	**97**	**64**	**305**	**1**	**35**	**4**	**0**
1899	**ChN-N**	**38**	**38**	**22**	**13**	**.629**	**99**	**2.79**	**319 ⅔**	**73**	**65**	**329**	**5**	**35**	**0**	**0**
1900	**ChN-N**	**30**	**30**	**14**	**13**	**.519**	**84**	**3.05**	**248**	**61**	**51**	**245**	**6**	**27**	**4**	**0**
1901	CWS-A	30	35	24	7	.774	79	2.67	266 ⅔	67	50	275	4	26	5	1
1902	CWS-A	24	28	15	9	.625	99	4.18	213	51	47	247	11	20	3	0
1903	NYA-A	24	25	14	11	.560	64	2.70	213	69	33	201	3	22	2	0
1904	NYA-A	11	16	7	5	.583	32	2.87	100 ⅓	36	16	91	3	8	1	0
1905	NYA-A	7	25	9	6	.600	19	1.68	101 ⅔	46	15	82	1	4	2	1
1906	NYA-A	2	17	2	2	.500	20	3.02	59 ⅔	16	15	58	0	1	0	2
1907	NYA-A	0	4	0	0	—	8	8.64	8 ⅓	5	6	15	0	0	0	0
1909	Cin-N	1	1	0	1	.000	4	6.00	6	3	2	11	0	1	0	0
1912	Was-A	0	1	0	0	—	1	—	0	0	0	1	1	0	0	0
1913	Was-A	0	1	0	0	—	0	0.00	1	0	0	1	0	0	0	0
1914	Was-A	0	1	0	0	—	0	0.00	1	1	0	1	0	0	0	1
Career average		19	23	12	7	.623	62	3.31	169 ⅓	48	39	184	4	17	1	0
Cubs average		**31**	**33**	**19**	**12**	**.619**	**103**	**3.40**	**273 ⅔**	**72**	**65**	**306**	**5**	**30**	**1**	**0**
Career total		371	452	236	143	.623	1246	3.31	3385 ⅔	955	774	3670	76	337	22	7
Cubs total		**251**	**264**	**151**	**93**	**.619**	**826**	**3.40**	**2188 ⅔**	**573**	**517**	**2445**	**42**	**240**	**9**	**2**

Clark Calvin "the Old Fox" Griffith, rhp, 1891–1914

As a manager, Clark Griffith was one of baseball's innovators of the early–20th century; as a player, his most productive years came as a pitcher for the Chicago franchise of the National League.

Griffith was born on November 20, 1869, in Clear Creek, Missouri. For a time, it seemed as though Griffith might have followed in the footsteps of his father and become a hunter and trapper in the Old West. But the family moved to Bloomington, Illinois, and Griffith almost immediately became involved with professional baseball.

In 1888 the 19-year-old Griffith signed with Milwaukee of the Western League. He was already consumed by the sport, playing scheduled games with his Milwaukee team and playing for "hat money" with any number of semipro teams around Milwaukee on off days. (Hat money was the practice of players passing a hat around the ballpark for donations from fans during the game.)

In 1891 Griffith was signed by St. Louis of the American Association. Later that year, he jumped to the Boston team in that league, but the American Association was on its last legs and collapsed after the season.

Griffith played in Oakland for most of 1893 before being signed by Adrian "Cap" Anson for his Chicago team. By this time, Griffith was one of the best professional pitchers around. He had mastered a number of pitches, including the screwball, which he later claimed he invented.

Griffith could also change speeds at will, threw a devastating "quick pitch," which was then legal, and also tossed spitballs, emery balls and scuff balls, also legal. (A quick pitch is a pitch thrown by a hurler before a batter is completely set in the batter's box.)

In 1894, his first full year with Chicago, Griffith led the team in wins (21), ERA (4.92),

strikeouts (71), and in complete games with 29.

He was, as sportswriters pointed out, "the lone bright spot" on an otherwise mediocre team. Griffith's 21 wins were more than a third of Chicago's 57 victories that year as Anson's squad finished 8th out of 12 teams.

But as well as he pitched, Griffith's odd superstitions had Anson and his teammates rolling their collective eyes. He believed that shutouts were bad luck and often, if his team was well ahead, he would allow the other team a run or two as Anson stood on first base howling invectives at him.

He was also involved in one of the odder games ever played.

He was pitching against the Reds in Chicago (and was ahead, 8-1) when a fire broke out in the bleachers. Panicked fans bolted for the exits and also tried escaping by knocking down a wire fence erected to keep them off the field. As the fire began to rage out of control, the umpire called the game.

The 1894 season was the first of six that would see Griffith win 20 or more games on the mound for Chicago. In 1897 he would lead the league in complete games with 38, and in 1898 Griffith led the National League in ERA with a 1.88 mark.

In 1900 he led National League players in the first universal strike as he tried to increase salaries to a minimum wage of $3,000 a year. He was also trying to help old friend Bancroft (Ban) Johnson form the American League.

In return for helping several dozen National Leaguers jump to the American League, Johnson awarded him the managerial reins of the new Chicago franchise in 1901. Of course, Johnson's ulterior motive was to place Griffith, a star pitcher with the National League's Chicago franchise in 1900, as the head of the American League's Chicago franchise.

Griffith led the new league in wins with 24 and shutouts with five in 1901 and managed them to the first-ever American League flag.

(continued)

(continued)

He played one more season in Chicago before moving to the New York Highlanders in 1903.

By now, Griffith was managing more and pitching less. He was a part-time thrower in New York for five years before moving back to the National League to handle the Reds. He pitched in scattered games for Cincinnati and later for Washington when he took the managerial seat for the Senators.

As a manager, Griffith was among those who developed the relief pitcher. In 1904, while managing the Highlanders, he was forced to use his two aces, Jack Chesbro and Jack Powell, day after day during the heat of the pennant race that year. The two were markedly less effective the next year. Griffith began to think about the possibilities of developing a pitcher who could come in during the later innings of a game to pitch when a starter tired or did not have control of his pitches.

The concept did not develop overnight, but Griffith was one of the managers who began experimenting with it over the first decades of the 20th century. In Washington he eventually developed two of the better bull-pen aces of the early 20th century, Fred "Firpo" Marberry and Allan Russell.

In 1920 Griffith purchased controlling interest in the Senators and took the team over. The team won a world championship in 1924 and pennants in 1925 and 1933, but Griffith was always strapped for cash. In fact, his financial problems almost certainly led him to explore signing minority players, mostly Latins, who were bypassed by other clubs who could afford to continue to sign whites.

He also popularized night games and the use of entertainers and other gimmicks, all in an effort to increase his gate.

Griffith is 7th all-time on the Cubs win list with 152, 10th all-time in losses with 96, 9th all-time with 252 starts, 10th in innings pitched with 2,188⅔ and 3rd overall in hits allowed with 2,445.

Griffith was elected to the Hall of Fame in 1946. He died in Washington, D.C., in 1955.

Griffith, Frank Wesley
HEIGHT: —   LEFTHANDER   BORN: 11/18/1872 GILMAN, ILLINOIS   DIED: 12/8/1908 WATERMAN, ILLINOIS

YEAR	TEAM	STARTS	GAMES	WON	LOST	PCT	ER	ERA	INNINGS PITCHED	STRIKE-OUTS	WALKS	HITS ALLOWED	HRS ALLOWED	COMP. GAMES	SHUT-OUTS	SAVES
1892	ChN-N	1	1	0	1	.000	5	11.25	4	3	6	3	1	0	0	0
1894	Cle-N	6	7	3	2	.600	47	9.99	42 ⅓	15	37	64	5	3	0	0
Career average		4	4	2	2	.500	26	10.10	23 ⅓	9	22	34	3	2	0	0
Cubs average		**1**	**1**	**0**	**1**	**.000**	**5**	**11.25**	**4**	**3**	**6**	**3**	**1**	**0**	**0**	**0**
Career total		7	8	3	3	.500	52	10.10	46 ⅓	18	43	67	6	3	0	0
Cubs total		**1**	**1**	**0**	**1**	**.000**	**5**	**11.25**	**4**	**3**	**6**	**3**	**1**	**0**	**0**	**0**

Grimes, Burleigh Arland (Ol' Stubblebeard)
HEIGHT: 5'10"   RIGHTHANDER   BORN: 8/18/1893 EMERALD, WISCONSIN   DIED: 12/6/1985 CLEAR LAKE, WISCONSIN

YEAR	TEAM	STARTS	GAMES	WON	LOST	PCT	ER	ERA	INNINGS PITCHED	STRIKE-OUTS	WALKS	HITS ALLOWED	HRS ALLOWED	COMP. GAMES	SHUT-OUTS	SAVES
1916	Pit-N	5	6	2	3	.400	12	2.36	45 ⅔	20	10	40	1	4	0	0
1917	Pit-N	17	37	3	16	.158	76	3.53	194	72	70	186	5	8	1	0
1918	Bro-N	28	40	19	9	.679	64	2.14	269 ⅔	113	76	210	3	19	7	1
1919	Bro-N	21	25	10	11	.476	70	3.47	181 ⅓	82	60	179	2	13	1	0
1920	Bro-N	33	40	23	11	.676	75	2.22	303 ⅔	131	67	271	5	25	5	2
1921	Bro-N	35	37	22	13	.629	95	2.83	302 ⅓	136	76	313	6	30	2	1
1922	Bro-N	34	36	17	14	.548	137	4.76	259	99	84	324	17	18	1	1
1923	Bro-N	38	39	21	18	.538	130	3.58	327	119	100	356	9	33	2	0

(continued)

(continued)

YEAR	TEAM	STARTS	GAMES	WON	LOST	PCT	ER	ERA	INNINGS PITCHED	STRIKEOUTS	WALKS	HITS ALLOWED	HRS ALLOWED	COMP. GAMES	SHUTOUTS	SAVES
1924	Bro-N	36	38	22	13	.629	132	3.82	310⅔	135	91	351	15	30	1	1
1925	Bro-N	31	33	12	19	.387	138	5.04	246⅔	73	102	305	15	19	0	0
1926	Bro-N	29	30	12	13	.480	93	3.71	225⅓	64	88	238	4	18	1	0
1927	NYG-N	34	39	19	8	.704	102	3.54	259⅔	102	87	274	12	15	2	2
1928	Pit-N	37	48	25	14	.641	110	2.99	330⅔	97	77	311	11	28	4	3
1929	Pit-N	29	33	17	7	.708	81	3.13	232⅔	62	70	245	11	18	2	2
1930	Bos-N	9	11	3	5	.375	40	7.35	49	15	22	72	4	1	0	0
1930	StL-N	19	22	13	6	.684	51	3.01	152⅓	58	43	174	5	10	1	0
1931	StL-N	28	29	17	9	.654	86	3.65	212⅓	67	59	240	11	17	3	0
1932	**ChC-N**	**18**	**30**	**6**	**11**	**.353**	**75**	**4.78**	**141⅓**	**36**	**50**	**240**	**11**	**17**	**3**	**0**
1933	**ChC-N**	**7**	**17**	**3**	**6**	**.333**	**27**	**3.49**	**69⅔**	**12**	**29**	**174**	**8**	**5**	**1**	**1**
1933	StL-N	3	4	0	1	.000	8	5.27	13⅔	4	8	71	2	3	1	3
1934	StL-N	0	4	2	1	.667	3	3.52	7⅔	1	2	15	1	0	0	1
1934	Pit-N	4	8	1	2	.333	22	7.24	27⅓	9	10	5	1	0	0	0
1934	NYY-A	0	10	1	2	.333	11	5.50	18	5	14	36	0	0	0	0
												22	0	0	0	1
Career average		26	32	14	11	.560	86	3.53	220	80	68	232	8	17	2	1
Cubs average		**13**	**24**	**5**	**9**	**.346**	**51**	**4.35**	**105⅔**	**24**	**40**	**123**	**5**	**4**	**1**	**2**
Career total		495	616	270	212	.560	1638	3.53	4179⅔	1512	1295	4412	148	314	35	18
Cubs total		**25**	**47**	**9**	**17**	**.346**	**102**	**4.35**	**211**	**48**	**79**	**245**	**10**	**8**	**2**	**4**

Groth, Ernest John (Ernie *or* Dango)
HEIGHT: 5'11"   RIGHTHANDER   BORN: 12/24/1884 CEDARSBURG, WISCONSIN   DIED: 5/23/1950 MILWAUKEE, WISCONSIN

YEAR	TEAM	STARTS	GAMES	WON	LOST	PCT	ER	ERA	INNINGS PITCHED	STRIKEOUTS	WALKS	HITS ALLOWED	HRS ALLOWED	COMP. GAMES	SHUTOUTS	SAVES
1904	ChC-N	2	3	0	2	.000	10	5.63	16	9	6	22	1	2	0	1
Career average		2	3	0	2	.000	10	5.63	16	9	6	22	1	2	0	1
Cubs average		**2**	**3**	**0**	**2**	**.000**	**10**	**5.63**	**16**	**9**	**6**	**22**	**1**	**2**	**0**	**1**
Career total		2	3	0	2	.000	10	5.63	16	9	6	22	1	2	0	1
Cubs total		**2**	**3**	**0**	**2**	**.000**	**10**	**5.63**	**16**	**9**	**6**	**22**	**1**	**2**	**0**	**1**

Gudat, Marvin John (Marv)
HEIGHT: 5'11"   LEFTHANDER   BORN: 8/27/1905 GOLIAD, TEXAS   DIED: 3/1/1954 LOS ANGELES, CALIFORNIA

YEAR	TEAM	STARTS	GAMES	WON	LOST	PCT	ER	ERA	INNINGS PITCHED	STRIKEOUTS	WALKS	HITS ALLOWED	HRS ALLOWED	COMP. GAMES	SHUTOUTS	SAVES
1929	Cin-N	2	7	1	1	.500	10	3.38	26⅔	0	4	29	0	2	0	0
1932	**ChC-N**	**0**	**1**	**0**	**0**	**—**	**0**	**0.00**	**1**	**2**	**0**	**1**	**0**	**0**	**0**	**0**
Career average		1	4	1	1	.500	5	3.25	14	1	2	15	0	1	0	0
Cubs average		**0**	**1**	**0**	**0**	**—**	**0**	**0.00**	**1**	**2**	**0**	**1**	**0**	**0**	**0**	**0**
Career total		2	8	1	1	.500	10	3.25	27⅔	2	4	30	0	2	0	0
Cubs total		**0**	**1**	**0**	**0**	**—**	**0**	**0.00**	**1**	**2**	**0**	**1**	**0**	**0**	**0**	**0**

Gumbert, Addison Courtney (Ad)
HEIGHT: 5'10"   RIGHTHANDER   BORN: 10/10/1868 PITTSBURGH, PENNSYLVANIA   DIED: 4/23/1925 PITTSBURGH, PENNSYLVANIA

YEAR	TEAM	STARTS	GAMES	WON	LOST	PCT	ER	ERA	INNINGS PITCHED	STRIKEOUTS	WALKS	HITS ALLOWED	HRS ALLOWED	COMP. GAMES	SHUTOUTS	SAVES
1888	**ChN-N**	**6**	**6**	**3**	**3**	**.500**	**17**	**3.14**	**48⅔**	**16**	**10**	**44**	**0**	**5**	**0**	**0**
1889	**ChN-N**	**28**	**31**	**16**	**13**	**.552**	**99**	**3.62**	**246⅓**	**91**	**76**	**258**	**16**	**25**	**2**	**0**
1890	Bos-P	33	39	23	12	.657	122	3.96	277⅓	81	86	338	18	27	1	0
1891	**ChN-N**	**31**	**32**	**17**	**11**	**.607**	**102**	**3.58**	**256⅓**	**73**	**90**	**282**	**5**	**24**	**1**	**0**
1892	**ChN-N**	**45**	**46**	**22**	**20**	**.524**	**145**	**3.41**	**382⅔**	**118**	**107**	**399**	**11**	**39**	**0**	**0**
1893	Pit-N	20	22	12	6	.667	93	5.15	162⅔	40	78	207	5	16	2	0
1894	Pit-N	32	38	18	12	.600	180	6.02	269	65	84	372	14	26	0	0
1895	Bro-N	26	33	12	14	.462	132	5.08	234	45	69	288	11	20	0	1
1896	Bro-N	4	5	0	4	.000	13	3.77	31	3	11	34	2	2	0	0
1896	Phi-N	10	11	5	4	.556	39	4.54	77⅓	14	23	99	0	7	1	0
Career average		26	29	14	11	.564	105	4.27	220⅔	61	70	258	9	21	1	0
Cubs average		**28**	**29**	**15**	**12**	**.552**	**91**	**3.50**	**233⅔**	**75**	**71**	**246**	**8**	**23**	**1**	**0**
Career total		235	263	128	99	.564	942	4.27	1985⅓	546	634	2321	82	191	7	1
Cubs total		**110**	**115**	**58**	**47**	**.552**	**363**	**3.50**	**934**	**298**	**283**	**983**	**32**	**93**	**3**	**0**

Gumpert, David Lawrence (Dave)
HEIGHT: 6'1" RIGHTHANDER BORN: 5/5/1958 SOUTH HAVEN, MICHIGAN

YEAR	TEAM	STARTS	GAMES	WON	LOST	PCT	ER	ERA	INNINGS PITCHED	STRIKE-OUTS	WALKS	HITS ALLOWED	HRS ALLOWED	COMP. GAMES	SHUT-OUTS	SAVES
1982	Det-A	1	5	0	0	—	6	27.00	2	0	2	7	1	0	0	1
1983	Det-A	0	26	0	2	.000	13	2.64	44 1/3	14	7	43	1	0	0	2
1985	**ChC-N**	**0**	**9**	**1**	**0**	**1.000**	**4**	**3.48**	**10 1/3**	**4**	**7**	**12**	**0**	**0**	**0**	**0**
1986	**ChC-N**	**0**	**38**	**2**	**0**	**1.000**	**29**	**4.37**	**59 2/3**	**45**	**28**	**60**	**4**	**0**	**0**	**2**
1987	KC-A	0	8	0	0	—	13	6.05	19 1/3	13	6	27	3	0	0	0
Career average		0	17	1	0	.600	13	4.31	27	15	10	30	2	0	0	1
Cubs average		**0**	**24**	**2**	**0**	**1.000**	**17**	**4.24**	**35**	**25**	**18**	**36**	**2**	**0**	**0**	**1**
Career total		1	86	3	2	.600	65	4.31	135 2/3	76	50	149	9	0	0	5
Cubs total		**0**	**47**	**3**	**0**	**1.000**	**33**	**4.24**	**70**	**49**	**35**	**72**	**4**	**0**	**0**	**2**

Gura, Lawrence Cyril (Larry)
HEIGHT: 6'0" LEFTHANDER BORN: 11/26/1947 JOLIET, ILLINOIS

YEAR	TEAM	STARTS	GAMES	WON	LOST	PCT	ER	ERA	INNINGS PITCHED	STRIKE-OUTS	WALKS	HITS ALLOWED	HRS ALLOWED	COMP. GAMES	SHUT-OUTS	SAVES
1970	**ChC-N**	**3**	**20**	**1**	**3**	**.250**	**16**	**3.79**	**38**	**21**	**23**	**35**	**6**	**1**	**0**	**1**
1971	**ChC-N**	**0**	**6**	**0**	**0**	**—**	**2**	**6.00**	**3**	**2**	**1**	**6**	**0**	**0**	**0**	**1**
1972	**ChC-N**	**0**	**7**	**0**	**0**	**—**	**5**	**3.65**	**12 1/3**	**13**	**3**	**11**	**3**	**0**	**0**	**0**
1973	**ChC-N**	**7**	**21**	**2**	**4**	**.333**	**35**	**4.87**	**64 2/3**	**43**	**11**	**79**	**10**	**0**	**0**	**0**
1974	NYY-A	8	8	5	1	.833	15	2.41	56	17	12	54	2	4	2	0
1975	NYY-A	20	26	7	8	.467	59	3.51	151 1/3	65	41	173	13	5	0	0
1976	KC-A	2	20	4	0	1.000	16	2.30	62 2/3	22	20	47	4	1	1	1
1977	KC-A	6	52	8	5	.615	37	3.13	106 1/3	46	28	108	8	1	1	10
1978	KC-A	26	35	16	4	.800	67	2.72	221 2/3	81	60	183	13	8	2	0
1979	KC-A	33	39	13	12	.520	116	4.47	233 2/3	85	73	226	29	7	1	0
1980	KC-A	36	36	18	10	.643	93	2.95	283 1/3	113	76	272	20	16	4	0
1981	KC-A	23	23	11	8	.579	52	2.72	172 1/3	61	35	139	11	12	2	0
1982	KC-A	37	37	18	12	.600	111	4.03	248	98	64	251	31	8	3	0
1983	KC-A	31	34	11	18	.379	109	4.90	200 1/3	57	76	220	23	5	0	0
1984	KC-A	25	31	12	9	.571	97	5.18	168 2/3	68	67	175	26	3	0	0
1985	KC-A	0	3	0	0	—	6	12.46	4 1/3	2	4	7	1	0	0	1
1985	**ChC-N**	**4**	**5**	**0**	**3**	**.000**	**19**	**8.41**	**20 1/3**	**7**	**6**	**34**	**4**	**0**	**0**	**0**
Career average		16	25	8	6	.565	53	3.76	128	50	38	126	13	4	1	1
Cubs average		**3**	**12**	**1**	**2**	**.231**	**15**	**5.01**	**27 2/3**	**17**	**9**	**33**	**5**	**0**	**0**	**0**
Career total		261	403	126	97	.565	855	3.76	2047	801	600	2020	204	71	16	14
Cubs total		**14**	**59**	**3**	**10**	**.231**	**77**	**5.01**	**138 1/3**	**86**	**44**	**165**	**23**	**1**	**0**	**2**

Guth, Charles J. (Charlie)
HEIGHT: — BORN: 1856 CHICAGO, ILLINOIS DIED: 7/5/1883 CAMBRIDGE, MASSACHUSETTS

YEAR	TEAM	STARTS	GAMES	WON	LOST	PCT	ER	ERA	INNINGS PITCHED	STRIKE-OUTS	WALKS	HITS ALLOWED	HRS ALLOWED	COMP. GAMES	SHUT-OUTS	SAVES
1880	**ChN-N**	**1**	**1**	**1**	**0**	**1.000**	**5**	**5.00**	**9**	**7**	**1**	**12**	**0**	**1**	**0**	**0**
Career average		1	1	1	0	1.000	5	5.00	9	7	1	12	0	1	0	0
Cubs average		**1**	**1**	**1**	**0**	**1.000**	**5**	**5.00**	**9**	**7**	**1**	**12**	**0**	**1**	**0**	**0**
Career total		1	1	1	0	1.000	5	5.00	9	7	1	12	0	1	0	0
Cubs total		**1**	**1**	**1**	**0**	**1.000**	**5**	**5.00**	**9**	**7**	**1**	**12**	**0**	**1**	**0**	**0**

Guthrie, Mark Andrew
HEIGHT: 6'4" LEFTHANDER BORN: 9/22/1965 BUFFALO, NEW YORK

YEAR	TEAM	STARTS	GAMES	WON	LOST	PCT	ER	ERA	INNINGS PITCHED	STRIKE-OUTS	WALKS	HITS ALLOWED	HRS ALLOWED	COMP. GAMES	SHUT-OUTS	SAVES
1989	Min-A	8	13	2	4	.333	29	4.55	57 1/3	38	21	66	7	0	0	0
1990	Min-A	21	24	7	9	.438	61	3.79	144 2/3	101	39	154	8	3	1	0
1991	Min-A	12	41	7	5	.583	47	4.32	98	72	41	116	11	0	0	2
1992	Min-A	0	54	2	3	.400	24	2.88	75	76	23	59	7	0	0	5
1993	Min-A	0	22	2	1	.667	11	4.71	21	15	16	20	2	0	0	0

(continued)

(continued)

YEAR	TEAM	STARTS	GAMES	WON	LOST	PCT	ER	ERA	INNINGS PITCHED	STRIKE-OUTS	WALKS	HITS ALLOWED	HRS ALLOWED	COMP. GAMES	SHUT-OUTS	SAVES
1994	Min-A	2	50	4	2	.667	35	6.14	51 1/3	38	18	65	8	0	0	1
1995	Min-A	0	36	5	3	.625	21	4.46	42 1/3	48	16	47	5	0	0	0
1995	LA-N	0	24	0	2	.000	8	3.66	19 2/3	19	9	19	1	0	0	0
1996	LA-N	0	66	2	3	.400	18	2.22	73	56	22	65	3	0	0	1
1997	LA-N	0	62	1	4	.200	41	5.32	69 1/3	42	30	71	12	0	0	1
1998	LA-N	0	53	2	1	.667	21	3.50	54	45	24	56	3	0	0	0
1999	Bos-A	0	46	1	1	.500	30	5.83	46 1/3	36	20	50	9	0	0	2
1999	**ChC-N**	**0**	**11**	**0**	**2**	**.000**	**5**	**3.65**	**12 1/3**	**9**	**4**	**7**	**1**	**0**	**0**	**0**
2000	**ChC-N**	**0**	**19**	**2**	**3**	**.400**	**10**	**4.82**	**18 2/3**	**17**	**10**	**17**	**1**	**0**	**0**	**0**
2000	TB-A	0	34	1	1	.500	16	4.50	32	26	18	33	4	0	0	0
2000	Tor-A	0	23	0	2	.000	11	4.79	20 2/3	20	9	20	3	0	0	0
2001	Oak-A	0	54	6	2	.750	26	4.47	52 1/3	52	20	49	7	0	0	1
Career average		3	49	3	4	.478	32	4.20	68 1/3	55	26	70	7	0	0	1
Cubs average		**0**	**15**	**1**	**3**	**.286**	**8**	**4.35**	**15 2/3**	**13**	**7**	**12**	**1**	**0**	**0**	**0**
Career total		43	632	44	48	.478	414	4.20	888	710	340	914	92	3	1	13
Cubs total		**0**	**30**	**2**	**5**	**.286**	**15**	**4.35**	**31**	**26**	**14**	**24**	**2**	**0**	**0**	**0**

Guzman, Jose Alberto
HEIGHT: 6'3"   RIGHTHANDER   BORN: 4/9/1963 SANTA ISABEL, PUERTO RICO

YEAR	TEAM	STARTS	GAMES	WON	LOST	PCT	ER	ERA	INNINGS PITCHED	STRIKE-OUTS	WALKS	HITS ALLOWED	HRS ALLOWED	COMP. GAMES	SHUT-OUTS	SAVES
1985	Tex-A	5	5	3	2	.600	10	2.76	32 2/3	24	14	27	3	0	0	0
1986	Tex-A	29	29	9	15	.375	87	4.54	172 1/3	87	60	199	23	2	0	0
1987	Tex-A	30	37	14	14	.500	108	4.67	208 1/3	143	82	196	30	6	0	0
1988	Tex-A	30	30	11	13	.458	85	3.70	206 2/3	157	82	180	20	6	2	0
1991	Tex-A	25	25	13	7	.650	58	3.08	169 2/3	125	84	152	10	5	1	0
1992	Tex-A	33	33	16	11	.593	91	3.66	224	179	73	229	17	5	0	0
1993	**ChC-N**	**30**	**30**	**12**	**10**	**.545**	**92**	**4.34**	**191**	**163**	**74**	**188**	**25**	**5**	**0**	**0**
1994	**ChC-N**	**4**	**4**	**2**	**2**	**.500**	**20**	**9.15**	**19 2/3**	**11**	**13**	**22**	**1**	**0**	**0**	**0**
Career average		23	24	10	9	.519	69	4.05	153	111	60	149	16	3	1	0
Cubs average		**17**	**17**	**7**	**6**	**.538**	**56**	**4.78**	**105 1/3**	**87**	**44**	**105**	**13**	**1**	**1**	**0**
Career total		186	193	80	74	.519	551	4.05	1224 1/3	889	482	1193	129	26	4	0
Cubs total		**34**	**34**	**14**	**12**	**.538**	**112**	**4.78**	**210 2/3**	**174**	**87**	**210**	**26**	**2**	**1**	**0**

Hacker, Warren Louis
HEIGHT: 6'1"   RIGHTHANDER   BORN: 11/21/1924 MARISSA, ILLINOIS

YEAR	TEAM	STARTS	GAMES	WON	LOST	PCT	ER	ERA	INNINGS PITCHED	STRIKE-OUTS	WALKS	HITS ALLOWED	HRS ALLOWED	COMP. GAMES	SHUT-OUTS	SAVES
1948	**ChC-N**	**1**	**3**	**0**	**1**	**.000**	**7**	**21.00**	**3**	**0**	**3**	**7**	**0**	**0**	**0**	**0**
1949	**ChC-N**	**12**	**30**	**5**	**8**	**.385**	**59**	**4.23**	**125 2/3**	**40**	**53**	**141**	**7**	**3**	**0**	**0**
1950	**ChC-N**	**3**	**5**	**0**	**1**	**.000**	**9**	**5.28**	**15 1/3**	**5**	**8**	**20**	**3**	**1**	**0**	**1**
1951	**ChC-N**	**0**	**2**	**0**	**0**	**—**	**2**	**13.50**	**1 1/3**	**2**	**0**	**3**	**0**	**0**	**0**	**0**
1952	**ChC-N**	**20**	**33**	**15**	**9**	**.625**	**53**	**2.58**	**185**	**84**	**31**	**144**	**17**	**12**	**5**	**1**
1953	**ChC-N**	**32**	**39**	**12**	**19**	**.387**	**108**	**4.38**	**221 2/3**	**106**	**54**	**225**	**35**	**9**	**0**	**2**
1954	**ChC-N**	**18**	**39**	**6**	**13**	**.316**	**75**	**4.25**	**158 2/3**	**80**	**37**	**157**	**28**	**4**	**1**	**2**
1955	**ChC-N**	**30**	**35**	**11**	**15**	**.423**	**101**	**4.27**	**213**	**80**	**43**	**202**	**38**	**13**	**0**	**3**
1956	**ChC-N**	**24**	**34**	**3**	**13**	**.188**	**87**	**4.66**	**168**	**65**	**44**	**190**	**28**	**4**	**0**	**0**
1957	Cin-N	6	15	3	2	.600	25	5.19	43 1/3	18	13	50	5	0	0	0
1957	Phi-N	10	20	4	4	.500	37	4.50	74	33	18	72	10	1	0	0
1958	Phi-N	1	9	0	1	.000	14	7.41	17	4	8	24	2	0	0	0
1961	CWS-A	0	42	3	3	.500	24	3.77	57 1/3	40	8	62	8	0	0	8
Career average		13	26	5	7	.411	50	4.21	107	46	27	108	15	4	1	1
Cubs average		**16**	**24**	**6**	**9**	**.397**	**56**	**4.13**	**121 1/3**	**51**	**30**	**121**	**17**	**5**	**1**	**1**
Career total		157	306	62	89	.411	601	4.21	1283 1/3	557	320	1297	181	47	6	17
Cubs total		**140**	**220**	**52**	**79**	**.397**	**501**	**4.13**	**1091 2/3**	**462**	**273**	**1089**	**156**	**46**	**6**	**9**

Hageman, Kurt Moritz (Casey)
HEIGHT: 5'10"   RIGHTHANDER   BORN: 5/12/1887 MOUNT OLIVER, PENNSYLVANIA   DIED: 4/1/1964 NEW BEDFORD, PENNSYLVANIA

YEAR	TEAM	STARTS	GAMES	WON	LOST	PCT	ER	ERA	INNINGS PITCHED	STRIKE-OUTS	WALKS	HITS ALLOWED	HRS ALLOWED	COMP. GAMES	SHUT-OUTS	SAVES
1911	Bos-A	2	2	0	2	.000	4	2.12	17	8	5	16	2	2	0	0
1912	Bos-A	1	2	0	0	—	4	27.00	1 1/3	1	3	5	0	0	0	0
1914	StL-N	7	12	1	4	.200	15	2.44	55 1/3	21	20	43	0	2	0	1
1914	**ChC-N**	**1**	**16**	**2**	**1**	**.667**	**18**	**3.47**	**46 2/3**	**17**	**12**	**44**	**0**	**0**	**0**	**1**
Career average		4	11	1	2	.300	14	3.07	40	16	13	36	1	1	0	0
Cubs average		**1**	**16**	**2**	**1**	**.667**	**18**	**3.47**	**46 2/3**	**17**	**12**	**44**	**0**	**0**	**0**	**1**
Career total		11	32	3	7	.300	41	3.07	120 1/3	47	40	108	2	4	0	1
Cubs total		**1**	**16**	**2**	**1**	**.667**	**18**	**3.47**	**46 2/3**	**17**	**12**	**44**	**0**	**0**	**0**	**1**

Hagerman, Zerah Zequiel (Rip)
HEIGHT: 6'2"   RIGHTHANDER   BORN: 6/20/1888 LYNDON, KANSAS   DIED: 1/30/1930 ALBUQUERQUE, NEW MEXICO

YEAR	TEAM	STARTS	GAMES	WON	LOST	PCT	ER	ERA	INNINGS PITCHED	STRIKE-OUTS	WALKS	HITS ALLOWED	HRS ALLOWED	COMP. GAMES	SHUT-OUTS	SAVES
1909	**ChC-N**	**7**	**13**	**4**	**4**	**.500**	**16**	**1.82**	**79**	**32**	**28**	**64**	**0**	**4**	**1**	**0**
1914	Cle-A	26	37	9	15	.375	68	3.09	198	112	118	189	3	12	3	0
1915	Cle-A	22	29	6	14	.300	59	3.52	151	69	77	156	4	7	0	0
1916	Cle-A	0	2	0	0	—	5	12.27	3 2/3	1	2	5	1	0	0	0
Career average		14	20	5	8	.365	37	3.09	108	54	56	104	2	6	1	0
Cubs average		**7**	**13**	**4**	**4**	**.500**	**16**	**1.82**	**79**	**32**	**28**	**64**	**0**	**4**	**1**	**0**
Career total		55	81	19	33	.365	148	3.09	431 2/3	214	225	414	8	23	4	0
Cubs total		**7**	**13**	**4**	**4**	**.500**	**16**	**1.82**	**79**	**32**	**28**	**64**	**0**	**4**	**1**	**0**

Hall, Andrew Clark (Drew)
HEIGHT: 6'4"   LEFTHANDER   BORN: 3/27/1963 LOUISVILLE, KENTUCKY

YEAR	TEAM	STARTS	GAMES	WON	LOST	PCT	ER	ERA	INNINGS PITCHED	STRIKE-OUTS	WALKS	HITS ALLOWED	HRS ALLOWED	COMP. GAMES	SHUT-OUTS	SAVES
1986	**ChC-N**	**4**	**5**	**1**	**2**	**.333**	**12**	**4.56**	**23 2/3**	**21**	**10**	**24**	**3**	**1**	**0**	**1**
1987	**ChC-N**	**0**	**21**	**1**	**1**	**.500**	**25**	**6.89**	**32 2/3**	**20**	**14**	**40**	**4**	**0**	**0**	**0**
1988	**ChC-N**	**0**	**19**	**1**	**1**	**.500**	**19**	**7.66**	**22 1/3**	**22**	**9**	**26**	**4**	**0**	**0**	**1**
1989	Tex-A	0	38	2	1	.667	24	3.70	58 1/3	45	33	42	3	0	0	3
1990	Mon-N	0	42	4	7	.364	33	5.09	58 1/3	40	29	52	6	0	0	1
Career average		1	25	2	2	.429	23	5.21	39	30	19	37	4	0	0	1
Cubs average		**1**	**15**	**1**	**1**	**.429**	**19**	**6.41**	**26 1/3**	**21**	**11**	**30**	**4**	**0**	**0**	**1**
Career total		4	125	9	12	.429	113	5.21	195 1/3	148	95	184	20	1	0	5
Cubs total		**4**	**45**	**3**	**4**	**.429**	**56**	**6.41**	**78 2/3**	**63**	**33**	**90**	**11**	**1**	**0**	**2**

Hamilton, Steven Absher (Steve)
HEIGHT: 6'6"   LEFTHANDER   BORN: 11/30/1935 COLUMBIA, KENTUCKY   DIED: 12/2/1997 MOREHEAD, KENTUCKY

YEAR	TEAM	STARTS	GAMES	WON	LOST	PCT	ER	ERA	INNINGS PITCHED	STRIKE-OUTS	WALKS	HITS ALLOWED	HRS ALLOWED	COMP. GAMES	SHUT-OUTS	SAVES
1961	Cle-A	0	2	0	0	—	1	3.00	3	4	3	2	0	0	0	0
1962	Was-A	10	41	3	8	.273	45	3.77	107 1/3	83	39	103	10	1	0	2
1963	Was-A	0	3	0	1	.000	3	13.50	2	1	2	5	0	0	0	0
1963	NYY-A	0	34	5	1	.833	18	2.60	62 1/3	63	24	49	3	0	0	5
1964	NYY-A	3	30	7	2	.778	22	3.28	60 1/3	49	15	55	6	1	0	3
1965	NYY-A	1	46	3	1	.750	9	1.39	58 1/3	51	16	47	2	0	1	5
1966	NYY-A	3	44	8	3	.727	30	3.00	90	57	22	69	8	1	1	3
1967	NYY-A	0	44	2	4	.333	24	3.48	62	55	23	57	7	0	0	11
1968	NYY-A	0	40	2	2	.500	12	2.13	50 2/3	42	13	37	0	0	0	2
1969	NYY-A	0	38	3	4	.429	21	3.32	57	39	21	39	7	0	0	3
1970	NYY-A	0	35	4	3	.571	14	2.78	45 1/3	33	16	36	3	0	0	0
1970	CWS-A	0	3	0	0	—	2	6.00	3	3	1	4	0	0	0	4
1971	SF-N	0	39	2	2	.500	15	3.02	44 2/3	38	11	29	4	0	0	0
1972	**ChC-N**	**0**	**22**	**1**	**0**	**1.000**	**9**	**4.76**	**17**	**13**	**8**	**24**	**1**	**0**	**0**	**0**
Career average		1	35	3	3	.563	19	3.05	55 1/3	44	18	46	4	0	0	4
Cubs average		**0**	**22**	**1**	**0**	**1.000**	**9**	**4.76**	**17**	**13**	**8**	**24**	**1**	**0**	**0**	**0**
Career total		17	421	40	31	.563	225	3.05	663	531	214	556	51	3	1	42
Cubs total		**0**	**22**	**1**	**0**	**1.000**	**9**	**4.76**	**17**	**13**	**8**	**24**	**1**	**0**	**0**	**0**

Hamner, Ralph Conant (Bruz)

HEIGHT: 6'3" RIGHTHANDER BORN: 9/12/1916 GIBSLAND, LOUISIANA DIED: 5/22/2001 LITTLE ROCK, ARKANSAS

YEAR	TEAM	STARTS	GAMES	WON	LOST	PCT	ER	ERA	INNINGS PITCHED	STRIKE-OUTS	WALKS	HITS ALLOWED	HRS ALLOWED	COMP. GAMES	SHUT-OUTS	SAVES
1946	CWS-A	7	25	2	7	.222	35	4.42	71 ⅓	29	39	80	2	1	0	1
1947	ChC-N	3	3	1	2	.333	7	2.52	25	14	16	24	0	2	0	0
1948	ChC-N	17	27	5	9	.357	58	4.69	111 ⅓	53	69	110	12	5	0	0
1949	ChC-N	1	6	0	2	.000	12	8.76	12 ⅓	3	8	22	1	0	0	0
Career average		7	15	2	5	.286	28	4.58	55	25	33	59	4	2	0	0
Cubs average		**7**	**12**	**2**	**4**	**.316**	**26**	**4.66**	**49 ⅔**	**23**	**31**	**52**	**4**	**2**	**0**	**0**
Career total		28	61	8	20	.286	112	4.58	220	99	132	236	15	8	0	1
Cubs total		**21**	**36**	**6**	**13**	**.316**	**77**	**4.66**	**148 ⅔**	**70**	**93**	**156**	**13**	**7**	**0**	**0**

Hands, William Alfred (Bill)

HEIGHT: 6'2" RIGHTHANDER BORN: 5/6/1940 HACKENSACK, NEW JERSEY

YEAR	TEAM	STARTS	GAMES	WON	LOST	PCT	ER	ERA	INNINGS PITCHED	STRIKE-OUTS	WALKS	HITS ALLOWED	HRS ALLOWED	COMP. GAMES	SHUT-OUTS	SAVES
1965	SF-N	2	4	0	2	.000	11	16.50	6	5	6	13	0	0	0	0
1966	ChC-N	26	41	8	13	.381	81	4.58	159	93	59	168	17	0	0	2
1967	ChC-N	11	49	7	8	.467	41	2.46	150	84	48	134	9	3	1	6
1968	ChC-N	34	38	16	10	.615	83	2.89	258 ⅔	148	36	221	26	11	4	0
1969	ChC-N	41	41	20	14	.588	83	2.49	300	181	73	268	21	18	3	0
1970	ChC-N	38	39	18	15	.545	109	3.70	265	170	76	278	20	12	2	1
1971	ChC-N	35	36	12	18	.400	92	3.42	242 ⅓	128	50	248	27	14	1	0
1972	ChC-N	28	32	11	8	.579	63	3.00	189	96	47	168	12	6	3	0
1973	Min-A	15	39	7	10	.412	55	3.49	142	78	41	138	14	3	1	2

(continued)

William (Bill) Alfred Hands, rhp, 1965–75

Bill Hands is something of a forgotten man to many Cubs fans these days, but the hard-nosed righthander put together several solid years for the Cubs in the late 1960s and early 1970s.

Hands was born in Hackensack, New Jersey, on May 6, 1940. He pitched briefly for San Francisco in 1965 but was traded to the Cubs the next year. Hands (and the Cubs) struggled the next two years, but Chicago was slowly rebuilding.

In 1968 Hands was 16-10 with four shutouts. In 1969 he was 20-14, with 18 complete games and a career-best 2.49 ERA. He teamed with Fergie Jenkins and Ken Holtzman in this span to provide Chicago with a formidable pitching staff.

Hands, at 6'2" and 185 pounds, was also the Cubs' intimidator. He never hesitated to pitch inside or knock opponents down when the situation called for it. He was one of the Cubs' most consistent pitchers in the nightmare 1969 season, stopping several losing streaks with gutty performances.

Hands went 18-15 in 1970, but injuries to his back and pitching arm limited his effectiveness over the next few years. He had only one winning season after 1970, going 11-8 in 1972.

As tough a pitcher as Hands was, he was not a batsman. His career average was .078 and he set a major league record in 1968 by striking out in 14 consecutive official at-bats. Hands was 92-86 with Chicago, with 14 career shutouts and an ERA of 3.18.

(Hands, continued)

YEAR	TEAM				PCT	ER	ERA	IP						
1974	Min-A	10	35	4	5	.444	57	4.45	115 1/3	74	25	130	9	0	0	3
1974	Tex-A	2	2	2	0	1.000	3	1.93	14	4	3	11	0	1	1	0
1975	Tex-A	18	18	6	7	.462	49	4.02	109 2/3	67	28	118	12	4	1	0

Career average	24	34	10	10	.502	66	3.35	177 1/3	103	45	172	15	7	2	1
Cubs average	**30**	**39**	**13**	**12**	**.517**	**79**	**3.18**	**223 1/3**	**129**	**56**	**212**	**19**	**9**	**2**	**1**

Career total	260	374	111	110	.502	727	3.35	1951	1128	492	1895	167	72	17	14
Cubs total	**213**	**276**	**92**	**86**	**.517**	**552**	**3.18**	**1564**	**900**	**389**	**1485**	**132**	**64**	**14**	**9**

Haney, Christopher Deane (Chris)
HEIGHT: 6'3" LEFTHANDER BORN: 11/16/1968 BALTIMORE, MARYLAND

YEAR	TEAM	STARTS	GAMES	WON	LOST	PCT	ER	ERA	INNINGS PITCHED	STRIKE-OUTS	WALKS	HITS ALLOWED	HRS ALLOWED	COMP. GAMES	SHUT-OUTS	SAVES
1991	Mon-N	16	16	3	7	.300	38	4.04	84 2/3	51	43	94	6	0	0	0
1992	Mon-N	6	9	2	3	.400	23	5.45	38	27	10	40	6	1	1	0
1992	KC-A	7	7	2	3	.400	18	3.86	42	27	16	35	5	1	1	0
1993	KC-A	23	23	9	9	.500	83	6.02	124	65	53	141	13	1	1	0
1994	KC-A	6	6	2	2	.500	23	7.31	28 1/3	18	11	36	2	0	0	0
1995	KC-A	13	16	3	4	.429	33	3.65	81 1/3	31	33	78	7	1	0	0
1996	KC-A	35	35	10	14	.417	119	4.70	228	115	51	267	29	4	1	0
1997	KC-A	3	8	1	2	.333	12	4.38	24 2/3	16	5	29	1	0	0	0
1998	KC-A	12	33	6	6	.500	76	7.03	97 1/3	51	36	125	18	0	0	0
1998	**ChC-N**	**0**	**5**	**0**	**0**	**—**	**4**	**7.20**	**5**	**4**	**1**	**3**	**2**	**0**	**0**	**0**
1999	Cle-A	4	13	0	2	.000	21	4.69	40 1/3	22	16	43	3	0	0	0
2000	Cle-A	0	1	0	0	—	1	9.00	1	0	1	1	0	0	0	0

Career average	13	17	4	5	.422	45	5.11	79 1/3	43	28	89	9	1	0	0
Cubs average	**0**	**5**	**0**	**0**	**—**	**4**	**7.20**	**5**	**4**	**1**	**3**	**2**	**0**	**0**	**0**

Career total	125	172	38	52	.422	451	5.11	794 2/3	427	276	892	92	8	4	0
Cubs total	**0**	**5**	**0**	**0**	**—**	**4**	**7.20**	**5**	**4**	**1**	**3**	**2**	**0**	**0**	**0**

Hankinson, Frank Edward
HEIGHT: 5'11" RIGHTHANDER BORN: 4/29/1856 NEW YORK, NEW YORK DIED: 4/5/1911 PALISADES PARK, NEW JERSEY

YEAR	TEAM	STARTS	GAMES	WON	LOST	PCT	ER	ERA	INNINGS PITCHED	STRIKE-OUTS	WALKS	HITS ALLOWED	HRS ALLOWED	COMP. GAMES	SHUT-OUTS	SAVES
1878	**ChN-N**	**1**	**1**	**0**	**1**	**.000**	**6**	**6.00**	**9**	**4**	**0**	**11**	**0**	**1**	**0**	**0**
1879	**ChN-N**	**25**	**26**	**15**	**10**	**.600**	**64**	**2.50**	**230 2/3**	**69**	**27**	**248**	**0**	**25**	**2**	**0**
1880	Cle-N	2	4	1	1	.500	3	1.08	25	8	3	20	0	2	0	1
1885	NY-AA	0	1	0	0	—	1	4.50	2	0	1	2	1	0	0	0

Career average	7	8	4	3	.571	19	2.50	66 2/3	20	8	70	0	7	1	0
Cubs average	**13**	**14**	**8**	**6**	**.577**	**35**	**2.63**	**120**	**37**	**14**	**130**	**0**	**13**	**1**	**0**

Career total	28	32	16	12	.571	74	2.50	266 2/3	81	31	281	1	28	2	1
Cubs total	**26**	**27**	**15**	**11**	**.577**	**70**	**2.63**	**239 2/3**	**73**	**27**	**259**	**0**	**26**	**2**	**0**

Hanson, Earl Sylvester (Ollie)
HEIGHT: 5'11" RIGHTHANDER BORN: 1/19/1896 HOLBROOK, MASSACHUSETTS DIED: 8/19/1951 CLIFTON, NEW JERSEY

YEAR	TEAM	STARTS	GAMES	WON	LOST	PCT	ER	ERA	INNINGS PITCHED	STRIKE-OUTS	WALKS	HITS ALLOWED	HRS ALLOWED	COMP. GAMES	SHUT-OUTS	SAVES
1921	ChC-N	2	2	0	2	.000	7	7.00	9	2	6	9	0	1	0	0

Career average	2	2	0	2	.000	7	7.00	9	2	6	9	0	1	0	0
Cubs average	**2**	**2**	**0**	**2**	**.000**	**7**	**7.00**	**9**	**2**	**6**	**9**	**0**	**1**	**0**	**0**

Career total	2	2	0	2	.000	7	7.00	9	2	6	9	0	1	0	0
Cubs total	**2**	**2**	**0**	**2**	**.000**	**7**	**7.00**	**9**	**2**	**6**	**9**	**0**	**1**	**0**	**0**

Hanyzewski, Edward Michael (Ed)
HEIGHT: 6'1"   RIGHTHANDER   BORN: 9/18/1920 UNION MILLS, INDIANA   DIED: 10/8/1991 FARGO, NORTH DAKOTA

YEAR	TEAM	STARTS	GAMES	WON	LOST	PCT	ER	ERA	INNINGS PITCHED	STRIKE-OUTS	WALKS	HITS ALLOWED	HRS ALLOWED	COMP. GAMES	SHUT-OUTS	SAVES
1942	ChC-N	1	6	1	1	.500	8	3.79	19	6	8	17	2	0	0	0
1943	ChC-N	16	33	8	7	.533	37	2.56	130	55	45	120	2	3	0	0
1944	ChC-N	7	14	2	5	.286	29	4.47	58 ⅓	19	20	61	6	3	0	0
1945	ChC-N	1	2	0	0	—	3	5.79	4 ⅔	0	1	7	1	0	0	0
1946	ChC-N	0	3	1	0	1.000	3	4.50	6	1	5	8	0	0	0	0
Career average		5	12	2	3	.480	16	3.30	43 ⅔	16	16	43	2	1	0	0
Cubs average		**5**	**12**	**2**	**3**	**.480**	**16**	**3.30**	**43 ⅔**	**16**	**16**	**43**	**2**	**1**	**0**	**0**
Career total		25	58	12	13	.480	80	3.30	218	81	79	213	11	6	0	0
Cubs total		**25**	**58**	**12**	**13**	**.480**	**80**	**3.30**	**218**	**81**	**79**	**213**	**11**	**6**	**0**	**0**

Hardy, David Alexander (Alex *or* Dooney)
HEIGHT: —   LEFTHANDER   BORN: 9/29/1877 TORONTO, ONTARIO, CANADA   DIED: 4/22/1940 TORONTO, ONTARIO, CANADA

YEAR	TEAM	STARTS	GAMES	WON	LOST	PCT	ER	ERA	INNINGS PITCHED	STRIKE-OUTS	WALKS	HITS ALLOWED	HRS ALLOWED	COMP. GAMES	SHUT-OUTS	SAVES
1902	ChC-N	4	4	2	2	.500	14	3.60	35	12	12	29	0	4	1	0
1903	ChC-N	3	3	1	1	.500	9	6.39	12 ⅔	4	7	21	0	1	0	0
Career average		4	4	2	2	.500	12	4.34	24	8	10	25	0	3	1	0
Cubs average		**4**	**4**	**2**	**2**	**.500**	**12**	**4.34**	**24**	**8**	**10**	**25**	**0**	**3**	**1**	**0**
Career total		7	7	3	3	.500	23	4.34	47 ⅔	16	19	50	0	5	1	0
Cubs total		**7**	**7**	**3**	**3**	**.500**	**23**	**4.34**	**47 ⅔**	**16**	**19**	**50**	**0**	**5**	**1**	**0**

Hargesheimer, Alan Robert
HEIGHT: 6'3"   RIGHTHANDER   BORN: 11/21/1954 CHICAGO, ILLINOIS

YEAR	TEAM	STARTS	GAMES	WON	LOST	PCT	ER	ERA	INNINGS PITCHED	STRIKE-OUTS	WALKS	HITS ALLOWED	HRS ALLOWED	COMP. GAMES	SHUT-OUTS	SAVES
1980	SF-N	13	15	4	6	.400	36	4.32	75	40	32	82	3	0	0	0
1981	SF-N	3	6	1	2	.333	9	4.34	18 ⅔	6	9	20	1	0	0	0
1983	ChC-N	0	5	0	0	—	4	9.00	4	5	2	6	0	0	0	0
1986	KC-A	1	5	0	1	.000	9	6.23	13	4	7	18	1	0	0	0
Career average		4	8	1	2	.357	15	4.72	27 ⅔	14	13	32	1	0	0	0
Cubs average		**0**	**5**	**0**	**0**	**—**	**4**	**9.00**	**4**	**5**	**2**	**6**	**0**	**0**	**0**	**0**
Career total		17	31	5	9	.357	58	4.72	110 ⅔	55	50	126	5	0	0	0
Cubs total		**0**	**5**	**0**	**0**	**—**	**4**	**9.00**	**4**	**5**	**2**	**6**	**0**	**0**	**0**	**0**

Harkey, Michael Anthony (Mike)
HEIGHT: 6'5"   RIGHTHANDER   BORN: 10/25/1966 SAN DIEGO, CALIFORNIA

YEAR	TEAM	STARTS	GAMES	WON	LOST	PCT	ER	ERA	INNINGS PITCHED	STRIKE-OUTS	WALKS	HITS ALLOWED	HRS ALLOWED	COMP. GAMES	SHUT-OUTS	SAVES
1988	ChC-N	5	5	0	3	.000	10	2.60	34 ⅔	18	15	33	0	0	0	0
1990	ChC-N	27	27	12	6	.667	63	3.26	173 ⅔	94	59	153	14	2	1	0
1991	ChC-N	4	4	0	2	.000	11	5.30	18 ⅔	15	6	21	3	0	0	0
1992	ChC-N	7	7	4	0	1.000	8	1.89	38	21	15	34	4	0	0	0
1993	ChC-N	28	28	10	10	.500	92	5.26	157 ⅓	67	43	187	17	1	0	0
1994	Col-N	13	24	1	6	.143	59	5.79	91 ⅔	39	35	125	10	0	0	0
1995	Oak-A	12	14	4	6	.400	46	6.27	66	28	31	75	12	0	0	0
1995	Cal-A	8	12	4	3	.571	31	4.55	61 ⅓	28	16	80	12	1	0	0
1997	LA-N	0	10	1	0	1.000	7	4.30	14 ⅔	6	5	12	3	0	0	0
Career average		13	16	5	5	.500	41	4.49	82	40	28	90	9	1	0	0
Cubs average		**14**	**14**	**5**	**4**	**.553**	**37**	**3.92**	**84 ⅓**	**43**	**28**	**86**	**8**	**1**	**0**	**0**
Career total		104	131	36	36	.500	327	4.49	656	316	225	720	75	4	1	0
Cubs total		**71**	**71**	**26**	**21**	**.553**	**184**	**3.92**	**422 ⅓**	**215**	**138**	**428**	**38**	**3**	**1**	**0**

Harper, Charles William (Jack)
HEIGHT: 6'0" RIGHTHANDER BORN: 4/2/1878 GALLOWAY, PENNSYLVANIA   DIED: 9/30/1950 JAMESTOWN, NEW YORK

YEAR	TEAM	STARTS	GAMES	WON	LOST	PCT	ER	ERA	INNINGS PITCHED	STRIKE-OUTS	WALKS	HITS ALLOWED	HRS ALLOWED	COMP. GAMES	SHUT-OUTS	SAVES
1899	Cle-N	5	5	1	4	.200	16	3.89	37	14	12	44	3	5	0	0
1900	StL-N	1	1	0	1	.000	4	12.00	3	0	2	4	0	0	0	0
1901	StL-N	37	39	23	12	.657	124	3.62	308 2/3	128	99	294	7	28	1	0
1902	StL-A	26	29	15	11	.577	102	4.13	222 1/3	74	81	224	8	20	2	0
1903	Cin-N	15	17	8	9	.471	65	4.34	134 2/3	45	70	143	2	13	0	0
1904	Cin-N	35	35	23	9	.719	75	2.30	293 2/3	125	85	262	2	31	6	0
1905	Cin-N	23	26	9	13	.409	77	3.86	179 1/3	70	69	189	2	15	1	1
1906	Cin-N	5	5	1	4	.200	17	4.17	36 2/3	10	20	38	1	3	0	0
1906	**ChC-N**	1	1	0	0	—	0	0.00	1	0	0	0	0	0	0	0
Career average		19	20	10	8	.559	60	3.55	152	58	55	150	3	14	1	0
Cubs average		1	1	0	0	—	0	0.00	1	0	0	0	0	0	0	0
Career total		148	158	80	63	.559	480	3.55	1216 1/3	466	438	1198	25	115	10	1
Cubs total		1	1	0	0	—	0	0.00	1	0	0	0	0	0	0	0

Harrell, Raymond James (Ray)
HEIGHT: 6'1" RIGHTHANDER BORN: 2/16/1912 PETROLIA, TEXAS   DIED: 1/28/1984 ALEXANDRIA, LOUISIANA

YEAR	TEAM	STARTS	GAMES	WON	LOST	PCT	ER	ERA	INNINGS PITCHED	STRIKE-OUTS	WALKS	HITS ALLOWED	HRS ALLOWED	COMP. GAMES	SHUT-OUTS	SAVES
1935	StL-N	1	11	1	1	.500	22	6.67	29 2/3	13	11	39	4	0	0	0
1937	StL-N	15	35	3	7	.300	63	5.87	96 2/3	41	59	99	7	1	1	1
1938	StL-N	3	32	2	3	.400	34	4.86	63	32	29	78	6	1	0	2
1939	**ChC-N**	2	4	0	2	.000	16	8.31	17 1/3	5	6	29	2	0	0	0
1939	Phi-N	10	22	3	7	.300	57	5.42	94 2/3	35	56	101	6	4	0	0
1940	Pit-N	0	3	0	0	—	3	8.10	3 1/3	3	2	5	0	0	0	0
1945	NYG-N	0	12	0	0	—	14	4.97	25 1/3	7	14	34	1	0	0	0
Career average		5	20	2	3	.310	35	5.70	55	23	30	64	4	1	0	1
Cubs average		2	4	0	2	.000	16	8.31	17 1/3	5	6	29	2	0	0	0
Career total		31	119	9	20	.310	209	5.70	330	136	177	385	26	6	1	3
Cubs total		2	4	0	2	.000	16	8.31	17 1/3	5	6	29	2	0	0	0

Hartenstein, Charles Oscar (Chuck *or* Twiggy)
HEIGHT: 5'11" RIGHTHANDER BORN: 5/26/1942 SEGUIN, TEXAS

YEAR	TEAM	STARTS	GAMES	WON	LOST	PCT	ER	ERA	INNINGS PITCHED	STRIKE-OUTS	WALKS	HITS ALLOWED	HRS ALLOWED	COMP. GAMES	SHUT-OUTS	SAVES
1966	**ChC-N**	0	5	0	0	—	2	1.93	9 1/3	4	3	8	0	0	0	0
1967	**ChC-N**	0	45	9	5	.643	25	3.08	73	20	17	74	4	0	0	10
1968	**ChC-N**	0	28	2	4	.333	18	4.54	35 2/3	17	11	41	3	0	0	1
1969	Pit-N	0	56	5	4	.556	42	3.95	95 2/3	44	27	84	9	0	0	10
1970	Pit-N	0	17	1	1	.500	12	4.56	23 2/3	14	8	25	3	0	0	1
1970	StL-N	0	6	0	0	—	13	8.78	13 1/3	9	5	24	1	0	0	1
1970	Bos-A	0	17	0	3	.000	17	8.05	19	12	12	21	6	0	0	0
1977	Tor-A	0	13	0	2	.000	20	6.59	27 1/3	15	6	40	8	0	0	4
Career average		0	31	3	3	.472	25	4.52	49 2/3	23	15	53	6	0	0	4
Cubs average		0	26	4	3	.550	15	3.43	39 1/3	14	10	41	2	0	0	4
Career total		0	187	17	19	.472	149	4.52	297	135	89	317	34	0	0	23
Cubs total		0	78	11	9	.550	45	3.43	118	41	31	123	7	0	0	11

Hartsock, Jeffrey Roger (Jeff)
HEIGHT: 6'0" RIGHTHANDER BORN: 11/19/1966 FAIRFIELD, OHIO

YEAR	TEAM	STARTS	GAMES	WON	LOST	PCT	ER	ERA	INNINGS PITCHED	STRIKE-OUTS	WALKS	HITS ALLOWED	HRS ALLOWED	COMP. GAMES	SHUT-OUTS	SAVES
1992	ChC-N	0	4	0	0	—	7	6.75	9 1/3	6	4	15	2	0	0	0
Career average		0	4	0	0	—	7	6.75	9 1/3	6	4	15	2	0	0	0
Cubs average		0	4	0	0	—	7	6.75	9 1/3	6	4	15	2	0	0	0
Career total		0	4	0	0	—	7	6.75	9 1/3	6	4	15	2	0	0	0
Cubs total		0	4	0	0	—	7	6.75	9 1/3	6	4	15	2	0	0	0

Harvey, Ervin King (Erwin *or* ZaZa)
HEIGHT: 6'0"   LEFTHANDER   BORN: 1/5/1879 SARATOGA, CALIFORNIA   DIED: 6/3/1954 SANTA MONICA, CALIFORNIA

YEAR	TEAM	STARTS	GAMES	WON	LOST	PCT	ER	ERA	INNINGS PITCHED	STRIKE-OUTS	WALKS	HITS ALLOWED	HRS ALLOWED	COMP. GAMES	SHUT-OUTS	SAVES
1900	ChN-N	0	1	0	0	—	0	0.00	4	0	1	3	0	0	0	0
1901	CWS-A	9	16	3	6	.333	37	3.62	92	27	34	91	2	5	0	1
Career average		5	9	2	3	.333	19	3.47	48	14	18	47	1	3	0	1
Cubs average		**0**	**1**	**0**	**0**	**—**	**0**	**0.00**	**4**	**0**	**1**	**3**	**0**	**0**	**0**	**0**
Career total		9	17	3	6	.333	37	3.47	96	27	35	94	2	5	0	1
Cubs total		**0**	**1**	**0**	**0**	**—**	**0**	**0.00**	**4**	**0**	**1**	**3**	**0**	**0**	**0**	**0**

Hatten, Joseph Hilarian (Joe)
HEIGHT: 6'0"   LEFTHANDER   BORN: 11/17/1916 BANCROFT, IOWA   DIED: 12/16/1988 REDDING, CALIFORNIA

YEAR	TEAM	STARTS	GAMES	WON	LOST	PCT	ER	ERA	INNINGS PITCHED	STRIKE-OUTS	WALKS	HITS ALLOWED	HRS ALLOWED	COMP. GAMES	SHUT-OUTS	SAVES
1946	Bro-N	30	42	14	11	.560	70	2.84	222	85	110	207	10	13	1	2
1947	Bro-N	32	42	17	8	.680	91	3.63	225 1/3	76	105	211	9	11	3	0
1948	Bro-N	30	42	13	10	.565	83	3.58	208 2/3	73	94	228	9	11	1	0
1949	Bro-N	29	37	12	8	.600	87	4.18	187 1/3	58	69	194	15	11	2	2
1950	Bro-N	8	23	2	2	.500	35	4.59	68 2/3	29	31	82	10	2	1	0
1951	Bro-N	6	11	1	0	1.000	25	4.56	49 1/3	22	21	55	3	0	0	0
1951	**ChN-N**	**6**	**23**	**2**	**6**	**.250**	**43**	**5.14**	**75 1/3**	**23**	**37**	**82**	**8**	**1**	**0**	**0**
1952	**ChN-N**	**8**	**13**	**4**	**4**	**.500**	**34**	**6.08**	**50 1/3**	**15**	**25**	**65**	**6**	**2**	**0**	**0**
Career average		21	33	9	7	.570	67	3.87	155 1/3	54	70	161	10	7	1	1
Cubs average		**7**	**18**	**3**	**5**	**.375**	**39**	**5.51**	**63**	**19**	**31**	**74**	**7**	**2**	**0**	**0**
Career total		149	233	65	49	.570	468	3.87	1087	381	492	1124	70	51	8	4
Cubs total		**14**	**36**	**6**	**10**	**.375**	**77**	**5.51**	**125 2/3**	**38**	**62**	**147**	**14**	**3**	**0**	**0**

Healy, John J. (Egyptian *or* Long John)
HEIGHT: 6'2"   RIGHTHANDER   BORN: 10/27/1866 CAIRO, ILLINOIS   DIED: 3/16/1899 ST. LOUIS, MISSOURI

YEAR	TEAM	STARTS	GAMES	WON	LOST	PCT	ER	ERA	INNINGS PITCHED	STRIKE-OUTS	WALKS	HITS ALLOWED	HRS ALLOWED	COMP. GAMES	SHUT-OUTS	SAVES
1885	StL-N	8	8	1	7	.125	22	3.00	66	32	20	54	0	8	0	0
1886	StL-N	41	43	17	23	.425	113	2.88	353 2/3	213	118	315	5	39	3	0
1887	Ind-N	41	41	12	29	.293	196	5.17	341	75	108	523	24	40	3	0
1888	Ind-N	37	37	12	24	.333	139	3.89	321 1/3	124	87	347	13	36	1	0
1889	WaN-N	12	13	1	11	.083	70	6.24	101	49	38	139	2	10	0	0
1889	**ChN-N**	**5**	**5**	**1**	**4**	**.200**	**23**	**4.50**	**46**	**22**	**18**	**48**	**4**	**5**	**0**	**0**
1890	Tol-AA	46	46	22	21	.512	125	2.89	389	225	127	326	5	44	2	0
1891	Bal-AA	22	23	8	10	.444	71	3.75	170 1/3	54	57	179	6	19	0	0
1892	Bal-N	8	9	3	6	.333	36	4.74	68 1/3	24	21	82	4	5	0	0
1892	Lou-N	2	2	1	1	.500	4	1.96	18 1/3	4	5	15	0	2	0	0
Career average		28	28	10	17	.364	100	3.84	234 1/3	103	75	254	8	26	1	0
Cubs average		**5**	**5**	**1**	**4**	**.200**	**23**	**4.50**	**46**	**22**	**18**	**48**	**4**	**5**	**0**	**0**
Career total		222	227	78	136	.364	799	3.84	1875	822	599	2028	63	208	9	0
Cubs total		**5**	**5**	**1**	**4**	**.200**	**23**	**4.50**	**46**	**22**	**18**	**48**	**4**	**5**	**0**	**0**

Hendley, Charles Robert (Bob)
HEIGHT: 6'2"   LEFTHANDER   BORN: 4/30/1939 MACON, GEORGIA

YEAR	TEAM	STARTS	GAMES	WON	LOST	PCT	ER	ERA	INNINGS PITCHED	STRIKE-OUTS	WALKS	HITS ALLOWED	HRS ALLOWED	COMP. GAMES	SHUT-OUTS	SAVES
1961	Mil-N	13	19	5	7	.417	42	3.90	97	44	39	96	8	3	0	0
1962	Mil-N	29	35	11	13	.458	80	3.60	200	112	59	188	17	7	2	1
1963	Mil-N	24	41	9	9	.500	74	3.93	169 1/3	105	64	153	16	7	3	3
1964	SF-N	29	30	10	11	.476	66	3.64	163 1/3	104	59	161	18	4	1	0
1965	SF-N	2	8	0	0	—	21	12.60	15	8	13	27	6	0	0	0
1965	**ChC-N**	**10**	**18**	**4**	**4**	**.500**	**30**	**4.35**	**62**	**38**	**25**	**59**	**9**	**2**	**0**	**0**
1966	**ChC-N**	**6**	**43**	**4**	**5**	**.444**	**39**	**3.91**	**89 2/3**	**65**	**39**	**98**	**10**	**0**	**0**	**7**

(continued)

	YEAR	TEAM	STARTS	GAMES	WON	LOST	PCT	ER	ERA	INNINGS PITCHED	STRIKE-OUTS	WALKS	HITS ALLOWED	HRS ALLOWED	COMP. GAMES	SHUT-OUTS	SAVES
(Hendley, continued)																	
	1967	ChC-N	0	7	2	0	1.000	9	6.57	12⅓	10	3	17	4	0	0	1
	1967	NYM-N	13	15	3	3	.500	27	3.44	70⅔	36	28	65	11	2	0	0
Career average			18	31	7	7	.480	55	3.97	125⅔	75	47	123	14	4	1	2
Cubs average			5	23	3	3	.526	26	4.28	54⅔	38	22	58	8	1	0	3
Career total			126	216	48	52	.480	388	3.97	879⅓	522	329	864	99	25	6	12
Cubs total			16	68	10	9	.526	78	4.28	164	113	67	174	23	2	0	8

Hendrix, Claude Raymond

HEIGHT: 6'0" RIGHTHANDER BORN: 4/13/1889 OLATHE, KANSAS DIED: 3/22/1944 ALLENTOWN, PENNSYLVANIA

YEAR	TEAM	STARTS	GAMES	WON	LOST	PCT	ER	ERA	INNINGS PITCHED	STRIKE-OUTS	WALKS	HITS ALLOWED	HRS ALLOWED	COMP. GAMES	SHUT-OUTS	SAVES
1911	Pit-N	12	22	4	6	.400	36	2.73	118⅔	57	53	85	1	6	1	1
1912	Pit-N	32	39	24	9	.727	83	2.59	288⅔	176	105	256	6	25	4	1
1913	Pit-N	25	42	14	15	.483	76	2.84	241	138	89	216	3	17	2	3
1914	Chi-F	37	49	29	11	.725	68	1.69	362	189	77	262	6	34	6	5
1915	Chi-F	31	40	16	15	.516	95	3.00	285	107	84	256	7	26	5	4
1916	ChC-N	24	36	8	16	.333	65	2.68	218	117	67	193	4	15	3	2
1917	ChC-N	21	40	10	12	.455	62	2.60	215	81	72	202	3	13	1	1
1918	ChC-N	27	32	20	7	.741	72	2.78	233	86	54	229	2	21	3	0
1919	ChC-N	25	33	10	14	.417	60	2.62	206⅓	69	42	208	3	15	2	0
1920	ChC-N	23	27	9	12	.429	81	3.58	203⅔	72	54	216	6	12	0	0
Career average		26	36	14	12	.552	70	2.65	237	109	70	212	4	18	3	2
Cubs average		24	34	11	12	.483	68	2.84	215⅓	85	58	210	4	15	2	1
Career total		257	360	144	117	.552	698	2.65	2371⅓	1092	697	2123	41	184	27	17
Cubs total		120	168	57	61	.483	340	2.84	1076	425	289	1048	18	76	9	3

Hennessey, George (Three Star)

HEIGHT: 5'10" RIGHTHANDER BORN: 10/28/1907 SLATINGTON, PENNSYLVANIA DIED: 1/15/1988 PRINCETON, NEW JERSEY

YEAR	TEAM	STARTS	GAMES	WON	LOST	PCT	ER	ERA	INNINGS PITCHED	STRIKE-OUTS	WALKS	HITS ALLOWED	HRS ALLOWED	COMP. GAMES	SHUT-OUTS	SAVES
1937	StL-A	0	5	0	1	.000	8	10.29	7	4	6	15	2	0	0	0
1942	Phi-N	1	5	1	1	.500	5	2.65	17	2	10	11	1	0	0	0
1945	ChC-N	0	2	0	0	—	3	7.36	3⅔	2	1	7	0	0	0	0
Career average		0	4	0	1	.333	5	5.20	9⅓	3	6	11	1	0	0	0
Cubs average		0	2	0	0	—	3	7.36	3⅔	2	1	7	0	0	0	0
Career total		1	12	1	2	.333	16	5.20	27⅔	8	17	33	3	0	0	0
Cubs total		0	2	0	0	—	3	7.36	3⅔	2	1	7	0	0	0	0

Henry, William Rodman (Bill *or* Gabby)

HEIGHT: 6'2" LEFTHANDER BORN: 10/15/1927 ALICE, TEXAS

YEAR	TEAM	STARTS	GAMES	WON	LOST	PCT	ER	ERA	INNINGS PITCHED	STRIKE-OUTS	WALKS	HITS ALLOWED	HRS ALLOWED	COMP. GAMES	SHUT-OUTS	SAVES
1952	Bos-A	10	13	5	4	.556	33	3.87	76⅔	23	36	75	7	5	0	0
1953	Bos-A	12	21	5	5	.500	31	3.26	85⅔	56	33	86	4	4	1	1
1954	Bos-A	13	24	3	7	.300	48	4.52	95⅔	38	49	104	9	3	1	0
1955	Bos-A	7	17	2	4	.333	22	3.32	59⅔	23	21	56	7	0	0	6
1958	ChC-N	0	44	5	4	.556	26	2.88	81⅓	58	17	63	8	0	0	12
1959	ChC-N	0	65	9	8	.529	40	2.68	134⅓	115	26	111	19	0	0	17
1960	Cin-N	0	51	1	5	.167	24	3.19	67⅔	58	20	62	8	0	0	16
1961	Cin-N	0	47	2	1	.667	13	2.19	53⅓	53	15	50	5	0	0	11
1962	Cin-N	0	40	4	2	.667	19	4.58	37⅓	35	20	40	4	0	0	14
1963	Cin-N	0	47	1	3	.250	24	4.15	52	45	11	55	2	0	0	6
1964	Cin-N	0	37	2	2	.500	5	0.87	52	28	12	31	0	0	0	0
1965	Cin-N	0	3	2	0	1.000	0	0.00	5	5	1	3	0	0	0	4
1965	SF-N	0	35	2	2	.500	17	3.64	42	35	8	40	3	0	0	1
1966	SF-N	0	35	1	1	.500	6	2.45	22	15	10	15	1	0	0	2
1967	SF-N	1	28	2	0	1.000	5	2.08	21⅔	23	9	16	0	0	0	0
1968	SF-N	1	7	0	2	.000	3	5.40	5	0	3	4	0	0	0	0
1968	Pit-N	0	10	0	0	—	15	8.10	16⅔	9	3	29	2	0	0	0
1969	Hou-N	0	3	0	0	—	0	0.00	5	2	2	2	0	0	0	0

(continued)

(continued)

Career average	3	33	3	3	.479	21	3.26	57	39	19	53	6	1	0	6
Cubs average	**0**	**55**	**7**	**6**	**.538**	**33**	**2.75**	**108**	**87**	**22**	**87**	**14**	**0**	**0**	**9**
Career total	44	527	46	50	.479	331	3.26	913	621	296	842	89	12	2	90
Cubs total	**0**	**109**	**14**	**12**	**.538**	**66**	**2.75**	**215 2/3**	**173**	**43**	**174**	**27**	**0**	**0**	**18**

Henshaw, Roy Kniklebine
HEIGHT: 5'8"   LEFTHANDER   BORN: 7/29/1911 CHICAGO, ILLINOIS   DIED: 6/8/1993 LA GRANGE, ILLINOIS

YEAR	TEAM	STARTS	GAMES	WON	LOST	PCT	ER	ERA	INNINGS PITCHED	STRIKE-OUTS	WALKS	HITS ALLOWED	HRS ALLOWED	COMP. GAMES	SHUT-OUTS	SAVES
1933	ChC-N	0	21	2	1	.667	18	4.19	38 2/3	16	20	32	0	0	0	0
1935	ChC-N	18	31	13	5	.722	52	3.28	142 2/3	53	68	135	6	7	3	1
1936	ChC-N	16	39	6	5	.545	57	3.97	129 1/3	69	56	152	8	6	2	1
1937	Bro-N	16	42	5	12	.294	88	5.07	156 1/3	98	69	176	14	5	0	2
1938	StL-N	15	27	5	11	.313	58	4.02	130	34	48	132	7	4	0	0
1942	Det-A	2	23	2	4	.333	28	4.09	61 2/3	24	27	63	3	0	0	1
1943	Det-A	3	26	0	2	.000	30	3.79	71 1/3	33	33	75	2	0	0	2
1944	Det-A	1	7	0	0	—	12	8.76	12 1/3	10	6	17	0	0	0	0
Career average	9	27	4	5	.452	43	4.16	92 2/3	42	41	98	5	3	1	1
Cubs average	**11**	**30**	**7**	**4**	**.656**	**42**	**3.68**	**103 2/3**	**46**	**48**	**106**	**5**	**4**	**2**	**1**
Career total	71	216	33	40	.452	343	4.16	742 1/3	337	327	782	40	22	5	7
Cubs total	**34**	**91**	**21**	**11**	**.656**	**127**	**3.68**	**310 2/3**	**138**	**144**	**319**	**14**	**13**	**5**	**2**

Heredia, Felix
HEIGHT: 6'0"   LEFTHANDER   BORN: 6/18/1976 BARAHONA, DOMINICAN REPUBLIC

YEAR	TEAM	STARTS	GAMES	WON	LOST	PCT	ER	ERA	INNINGS PITCHED	STRIKE-OUTS	WALKS	HITS ALLOWED	HRS ALLOWED	COMP. GAMES	SHUT-OUTS	SAVES
1996	Fla-N	0	21	1	1	.500	8	4.32	16 2/3	10	10	21	1	0	0	0
1997	Fla-N	0	56	5	3	.625	27	4.29	56 2/3	54	30	53	3	0	0	0
1998	Fla-N	2	41	0	3	.000	25	5.49	41	38	32	38	1	0	0	2
1998	ChC-N	0	30	3	0	1.000	8	4.08	17 2/3	16	6	19	1	0	0	0
1999	ChC-N	0	69	3	1	.750	28	4.85	52	50	25	56	7	0	0	1
2000	ChC-N	0	74	7	3	.700	31	4.76	58 2/3	52	33	46	6	0	0	2
2001	ChC-N	0	48	2	2	.500	24	6.17	35	28	16	45	6	0	0	0
Career average	0	57	4	2	.618	25	4.89	46 1/3	41	25	46	4	0	0	1
Cubs average	**0**	**55**	**4**	**2**	**.714**	**23**	**5.01**	**41**	**37**	**20**	**42**	**5**	**0**	**0**	**1**
Career total	2	339	21	13	.618	151	4.89	277 2/3	248	152	278	25	0	0	5
Cubs total	**0**	**221**	**15**	**6**	**.714**	**91**	**5.01**	**163 1/3**	**146**	**80**	**166**	**20**	**0**	**0**	**3**

Hernandez, Guillermo (Willie)
HEIGHT: 6'3"   LEFTHANDER   BORN: 11/14/1954 AGUADA, PUERTO RICO

YEAR	TEAM	STARTS	GAMES	WON	LOST	PCT	ER	ERA	INNINGS PITCHED	STRIKE-OUTS	WALKS	HITS ALLOWED	HRS ALLOWED	COMP. GAMES	SHUT-OUTS	SAVES
1977	ChC-N	1	67	8	7	.533	37	3.03	110	78	28	94	11	0	0	4
1978	ChC-N	0	54	8	2	.800	25	3.77	59 2/3	38	35	57	6	0	0	3
1979	ChC-N	2	51	4	4	.500	44	5.01	79	53	39	85	8	0	0	0
1980	ChC-N	7	53	1	9	.100	53	4.40	108 1/3	75	45	115	8	0	0	0
1981	ChC-N	0	12	0	0	—	6	3.95	13 2/3	13	8	14	1	0	0	2
1982	ChC-N	0	75	4	6	.400	25	3.00	75	54	24	74	3	0	0	10
1983	ChC-N	1	11	1	0	1.000	7	3.20	19 2/3	18	6	16	0	0	0	1
1983	Phi-N	0	63	8	4	.667	35	3.29	95 2/3	75	26	93	9	0	0	7
1984	Det-A	0	80	9	3	.750	30	1.92	140 1/3	112	36	96	6	0	0	32
1985	Det-A	0	74	8	10	.444	32	2.70	106 2/3	76	14	82	13	0	0	31
1986	Det-A	0	64	8	7	.533	35	3.55	88 2/3	77	21	87	13	0	0	24
1987	Det-A	0	45	3	4	.429	20	3.67	49	30	20	53	8	0	0	8
1988	Det-A	0	63	6	5	.545	23	3.06	67 2/3	59	31	50	8	0	0	10
1989	Det-A	0	32	2	2	.500	20	5.74	31 1/3	30	16	36	4	0	0	15
Career average	1	57	5	5	.526	30	3.38	80 1/3	61	27	73	7	0	0	11
Cubs average	**2**	**46**	**4**	**4**	**.481**	**28**	**3.81**	**66 1/3**	**47**	**26**	**65**	**5**	**0**	**0**	**3**
Career total	11	744	70	63	.526	392	3.38	1044 2/3	788	349	952	97	0	0	147
Cubs total	**11**	**323**	**26**	**28**	**.481**	**197**	**3.81**	**465 1/3**	**329**	**185**	**455**	**36**	**0**	**0**	**20**

Hernandez, Ramon
HEIGHT: 5'11"   LEFTHANDER   BORN: 8/31/1940 CAROLINA, PUERTO RICO

YEAR	TEAM	STARTS	GAMES	WON	LOST	PCT	ER	ERA	INNINGS PITCHED	STRIKE-OUTS	WALKS	HITS ALLOWED	HRS ALLOWED	COMP. GAMES	SHUT-OUTS	SAVES
1967	Atl-N	0	46	0	2	.000	24	4.18	51⅔	28	14	60	5	0	0	5
1968	ChC-N	0	8	0	0	—	9	9.00	9	3	0	14	1	0	0	0
1971	Pit-N	0	10	0	1	.000	1	0.73	12⅓	7	2	5	0	0	0	4
1972	Pit-N	0	53	5	0	1.000	13	1.67	70	47	22	50	3	0	0	11
1973	Pit-N	0	59	4	5	.444	24	2.41	89⅔	64	25	71	5	0	0	2
1974	Pit-N	0	58	5	2	.714	21	2.75	68⅔	33	18	68	3	0	0	5
1975	Pit-N	0	46	7	2	.778	21	2.95	64	43	28	62	0	0	0	3
1976	Pit-N	0	37	2	2	.500	17	3.56	43	17	16	42	3	0	0	0
1976	ChC-N	0	2	0	0	—	0	0.00	1⅔	1	0	2	0	0	0	1
1977	ChC-N	0	6	0	0	—	7	8.22	7⅔	4	3	11	1	0	0	1
1977	Bos-A	0	12	0	1	.000	8	5.68	12⅔	8	7	14	2	0	0	1
Career average		0	37	3	2	.605	16	3.03	47⅔	28	15	44	3	0	0	5
Cubs average		0	5	0	0	—	5	7.85	6	3	1	9	1	0	0	0
Career total		0	337	23	15	.605	145	3.03	430⅓	255	135	399	23	0	0	46
Cubs total		0	16	0	0	—	16	7.85	18⅓	8	3	27	2	0	0	1

Herrmann, Leroy George
HEIGHT: 5'10"   RIGHTHANDER   BORN: 2/27/1906 STEWARD, ILLINOIS   DIED: 7/3/1972 LIVERMORE, CALIFORNIA

YEAR	TEAM	STARTS	GAMES	WON	LOST	PCT	ER	ERA	INNINGS PITCHED	STRIKE-OUTS	WALKS	HITS ALLOWED	HRS ALLOWED	COMP. GAMES	SHUT-OUTS	SAVES
1932	ChC-N	0	7	2	1	.667	9	6.39	12⅔	5	9	18	0	0	0	1
1933	ChC-N	1	9	0	1	.000	13	5.57	21	4	8	26	3	0	0	0
1935	Cin-N	8	29	3	5	.375	43	3.58	108	30	31	124	9	2	0	0
Career average		3	15	2	2	.417	22	4.13	47⅓	13	16	56	4	1	0	1
Cubs average		1	8	1	1	.500	11	5.88	17	5	9	22	2	0	0	1
Career total		9	45	5	7	.417	65	4.13	141⅔	39	48	168	12	2	0	1
Cubs total		1	16	2	2	.500	22	5.88	33⅔	9	17	44	3	0	0	1

Hibbard, James Gregory (Greg *or* The Little Bulldog)
HEIGHT: 6'0"   LEFTHANDER   BORN: 9/13/1964 NEW ORLEANS, LOUISIANA

YEAR	TEAM	STARTS	GAMES	WON	LOST	PCT	ER	ERA	INNINGS PITCHED	STRIKE-OUTS	WALKS	HITS ALLOWED	HRS ALLOWED	COMP. GAMES	SHUT-OUTS	SAVES
1989	CWS-A	23	23	6	7	.462	49	3.21	137⅓	55	41	142	5	2	0	0
1990	CWS-A	33	33	14	9	.609	74	3.16	211	92	55	202	11	3	1	0
1991	CWS-A	29	32	11	11	.500	93	4.31	194	71	57	196	23	5	0	1
1992	CWS-A	28	31	10	7	.588	86	4.40	176	69	57	187	17	0	0	0
1993	ChC-N	31	31	15	11	.577	84	3.96	191	82	47	209	19	1	0	0
1994	Sea-A	14	15	1	5	.167	60	6.69	80⅔	39	31	115	11	0	0	0
Career average		26	28	10	8	.533	74	4.05	165	68	48	175	14	2	0	0
Cubs average		31	31	15	11	.577	84	3.96	191	82	47	209	19	1	0	0
Career total		158	165	57	50	.533	446	4.05	990	408	288	1051	86	11	1	1
Cubs total		31	31	15	11	.577	84	3.96	191	82	47	209	19	1	0	0

Hibbard, John Denison
HEIGHT: —   LEFTHANDER   BORN: 12/2/1864 CHICAGO, ILLINOIS   DIED: 11/17/1937 HOLLYWOOD, CALIFORNIA

YEAR	TEAM	STARTS	GAMES	WON	LOST	PCT	ER	ERA	INNINGS PITCHED	STRIKE-OUTS	WALKS	HITS ALLOWED	HRS ALLOWED	COMP. GAMES	SHUT-OUTS	SAVES
1884	ChN-N	2	2	1	1	.500	5	2.65	17	4	9	18	1	2	1	0
Career average		2	2	1	1	.500	5	2.65	17	4	9	18	1	2	1	0
Cubs average		2	2	1	1	.500	5	2.65	17	4	9	18	1	2	1	0
Career total		2	2	1	1	.500	5	2.65	17	4	9	18	1	2	1	0
Cubs total		2	2	1	1	.500	5	2.65	17	4	9	18	1	2	1	0

Hickerson, Bryan David
HEIGHT: 6'2"   LEFTHANDER   BORN: 10/13/1963 BEMIDJI, MINNESOTA

YEAR	TEAM	STARTS	GAMES	WON	LOST	PCT	ER	ERA	INNINGS PITCHED	STRIKE-OUTS	WALKS	HITS ALLOWED	HRS ALLOWED	COMP. GAMES	SHUT-OUTS	SAVES
1991	SF-N	6	17	2	2	.500	20	3.60	50	43	17	53	3	0	0	0
1992	SF-N	1	61	5	3	.625	30	3.09	87 1/3	68	21	74	7	0	0	0
1993	SF-N	15	47	7	5	.583	57	4.26	120 1/3	69	39	137	14	0	0	0
1994	SF-N	14	28	4	8	.333	59	5.40	98 1/3	59	38	118	20	0	0	1
1995	**ChC-N**	**0**	**38**	**2**	**3**	**.400**	**24**	**6.82**	**31 2/3**	**28**	**15**	**36**	**3**	**0**	**0**	**1**
1995	Col-N	0	18	1	0	1.000	22	11.88	16 2/3	12	13	33	5	0	0	0
Career average		7	42	4	4	.500	42	4.72	81	56	29	90	10	0	0	0
Cubs average		**0**	**38**	**2**	**3**	**.400**	**24**	**6.82**	**31 2/3**	**28**	**15**	**36**	**3**	**0**	**0**	**1**
Career total		36	209	21	21	.500	212	4.72	404 1/3	279	143	451	52	0	0	2
Cubs total		**0**	**38**	**2**	**3**	**.400**	**24**	**6.82**	**31 2/3**	**28**	**15**	**36**	**3**	**0**	**0**	**1**

Higbe, Walter Kirby (Kirby *or* Old Hig)
HEIGHT: 5'11"   RIGHTHANDER   BORN: 4/8/1915 COLUMBIA, SOUTH CAROLINA   DIED: 5/6/1985 COLUMBIA, SOUTH CAROLINA

YEAR	TEAM	STARTS	GAMES	WON	LOST	PCT	ER	ERA	INNINGS PITCHED	STRIKE-OUTS	WALKS	HITS ALLOWED	HRS ALLOWED	COMP. GAMES	SHUT-OUTS	SAVES
1937	**ChC-N**	**0**	**1**	**1**	**0**	**1.000**	**3**	**5.40**	**5**	**2**	**1**	**4**	**1**	**0**	**0**	**0**
1938	**ChC-N**	**2**	**2**	**0**	**0**	**—**	**6**	**5.40**	**10**	**4**	**6**	**10**	**1**	**0**	**0**	**0**
1939	**ChC-N**	**2**	**9**	**2**	**1**	**.667**	**8**	**3.18**	**22 2/3**	**16**	**22**	**12**	**0**	**0**	**0**	**0**
1939	Phi-N	26	34	10	14	.417	101	4.85	187 1/3	79	101	208	10	14	1	2
1940	Phi-N	36	41	14	19	.424	117	3.72	283	137	121	242	12	20	1	1
1941	Bro-N	39	48	22	9	.710	104	3.14	298	121	132	244	16	19	2	3
1942	Bro-N	32	38	16	11	.593	80	3.25	221 2/3	115	106	180	17	13	2	0
1943	Bro-N	27	35	13	10	.565	76	3.70	185	108	95	189	4	8	1	0
1946	Bro-N	29	42	17	8	.680	71	3.03	210 2/3	134	107	178	6	11	3	1
1947	Bro-N	3	4	2	0	1.000	9	5.17	15 2/3	10	12	18	0	0	0	0
1947	Pit-N	30	46	11	17	.393	93	3.72	225	99	110	204	22	10	1	5
1948	Pit-N	8	56	8	7	.533	59	3.36	158	86	83	140	11	3	0	10
1949	Pit-N	1	7	0	2	.000	23	13.50	15 1/3	5	12	25	2	0	0	0
1949	NYG-N	2	37	2	0	1.000	31	3.47	80 1/3	38	41	72	12	0	0	2
1950	NYG-N	1	18	0	3	.000	19	4.93	34 2/3	17	30	37	2	0	0	0
Career average		20	35	10	8	.539	67	3.69	162 2/3	81	82	147	10	8	1	2
Cubs average		**1**	**4**	**1**	**0**	**.750**	**6**	**4.06**	**12 2/3**	**7**	**10**	**9**	**1**	**0**	**0**	**0**
Career total		238	418	118	101	.539	800	3.69	1952 1/3	971	979	1763	116	98	11	24
Cubs total		**4**	**12**	**3**	**1**	**.750**	**17**	**4.06**	**37 2/3**	**22**	**29**	**26**	**2**	**0**	**0**	**0**

Higginbotham, Irving Clinton (Irv)
HEIGHT: 6'1"   RIGHTHANDER   BORN: 4/26/1882 HOMER, NEBRASKA   DIED: 6/12/1959 SEATTLE, WASHINGTON

YEAR	TEAM	STARTS	GAMES	WON	LOST	PCT	ER	ERA	INNINGS PITCHED	STRIKE-OUTS	WALKS	HITS ALLOWED	HRS ALLOWED	COMP. GAMES	SHUT-OUTS	SAVES
1906	StL-N	6	7	1	4	.200	17	3.23	47 1/3	14	11	50	1	4	0	0
1908	StL-N	11	19	3	8	.273	38	3.20	107	38	33	113	0	7	1	0
1909	StL-N	1	3	1	0	1.000	2	1.59	11 1/3	2	2	5	0	1	0	0
1909	**ChC-N**	**6**	**19**	**5**	**2**	**.714**	**19**	**2.19**	**78**	**32**	**20**	**64**	**0**	**4**	**0**	**1**
Career average		8	16	3	5	.417	25	2.81	81 1/3	29	22	77	0	5	0	0
Cubs average		**6**	**19**	**5**	**2**	**.714**	**19**	**2.19**	**78**	**32**	**20**	**64**	**0**	**4**	**0**	**1**
Career total		24	48	10	14	.417	76	2.81	243 2/3	86	66	232	1	16	1	1
Cubs total		**6**	**19**	**5**	**2**	**.714**	**19**	**2.19**	**78**	**32**	**20**	**64**	**0**	**4**	**0**	**1**

Hiller, Frank Walter (Dutch)
HEIGHT: 6'0"   RIGHTHANDER   BORN: 7/13/1920 IRVINGTON, NEW JERSEY   DIED: 1/10/1987 WEST CHESTER, PENNSYLVANIA

YEAR	TEAM	STARTS	GAMES	WON	LOST	PCT	ER	ERA	INNINGS PITCHED	STRIKE-OUTS	WALKS	HITS ALLOWED	HRS ALLOWED	COMP. GAMES	SHUT-OUTS	SAVES
1946	NYY-A	1	3	0	2	.000	6	4.76	11 1/3	4	6	13	2	0	0	0
1948	NYY-A	5	22	5	2	.714	28	4.04	62 1/3	25	30	59	8	1	0	0
1949	NYY-A	0	4	0	2	.000	5	5.87	7 2/3	3	7	9	0	0	0	1
1950	**ChC-N**	**17**	**38**	**12**	**5**	**.706**	**60**	**3.53**	**153**	**55**	**32**	**153**	**16**	**9**	**2**	**1**
1951	**ChC-N**	**21**	**24**	**6**	**12**	**.333**	**76**	**4.84**	**141 1/3**	**50**	**31**	**147**	**17**	**6**	**2**	**1**
1952	Cin-N	15	28	5	8	.385	64	4.63	124 1/3	50	37	129	7	6	1	1
1953	NYG-N	1	19	2	1	.667	23	6.15	33 2/3	10	15	43	6	0	0	0

(continued)

(Hiller, continued)

YEAR	TEAM	STARTS	GAMES	WON	LOST	PCT	ER	ERA	INNINGS PITCHED	STRIKE-OUTS	WALKS	HITS ALLOWED	HRS ALLOWED	COMP. GAMES	SHUT-OUTS	SAVES
Career average		9	20	4	5	.484	37	4.42	76⅓	28	23	79	8	3	1	1
Cubs average		**19**	**31**	**9**	**9**	**.514**	**68**	**4.16**	**147⅓**	**53**	**32**	**150**	**17**	**8**	**2**	**1**
Career total		60	138	30	32	.484	262	4.42	533⅔	197	158	553	56	22	5	4
Cubs total		**38**	**62**	**18**	**17**	**.514**	**136**	**4.16**	**294⅓**	**105**	**63**	**300**	**33**	**15**	**4**	**2**

Hillman, Darius Dutton (Dave)

HEIGHT: 5'11" RIGHTHANDER BORN: 9/14/1927 DUNGANNON, VIRGINIA

YEAR	TEAM	STARTS	GAMES	WON	LOST	PCT	ER	ERA	INNINGS PITCHED	STRIKE-OUTS	WALKS	HITS ALLOWED	HRS ALLOWED	COMP. GAMES	SHUT-OUTS	SAVES
1955	ChC-N	3	25	0	0	—	34	5.31	57⅔	23	25	63	10	0	0	0
1956	ChC-N	2	2	0	2	.000	3	2.19	12⅓	6	5	11	0	0	0	0
1957	ChC-N	14	32	6	11	.353	50	4.35	103⅓	53	37	115	13	1	0	1
1958	ChC-N	16	31	4	8	.333	44	3.15	125⅔	65	31	132	12	3	0	1
1959	ChC-N	24	39	8	11	.421	75	3.53	191	88	43	178	17	4	1	0
1960	Bos-A	3	16	0	3	.000	23	5.65	36⅔	14	12	41	6	0	0	0
1961	Bos-A	1	28	3	2	.600	24	2.77	78	39	23	70	8	0	0	0
1962	Cin-N	0	2	0	0	—	4	9.82	3⅔	0	1	8	0	0	0	1
1962	NYM-N	1	13	0	0	—	11	6.32	15⅔	8	8	21	5	0	0	0
Career average		8	24	3	5	.362	34	3.87	78	37	23	80	9	1	0	0
Cubs average		**12**	**26**	**4**	**6**	**.360**	**41**	**3.78**	**98**	**47**	**28**	**100**	**10**	**2**	**0**	**0**
Career total		64	188	21	37	.362	268	3.87	624	296	185	639	71	8	1	3
Cubs total		**59**	**129**	**18**	**32**	**.360**	**206**	**3.78**	**490**	**235**	**141**	**499**	**52**	**8**	**1**	**2**

Hobbie, Glen Frederick

HEIGHT: 6'2" RIGHTHANDER BORN: 4/24/1936 WITT, ILLINOIS

YEAR	TEAM	STARTS	GAMES	WON	LOST	PCT	ER	ERA	INNINGS PITCHED	STRIKE-OUTS	WALKS	HITS ALLOWED	HRS ALLOWED	COMP. GAMES	SHUT-OUTS	SAVES
1957	ChC-N	0	2	0	0	—	5	10.38	4⅓	3	5	6	0	0	0	0
1958	ChC-N	16	55	10	6	.625	70	3.74	168⅓	91	93	163	13	2	1	2
1959	ChC-N	33	46	16	13	.552	96	3.69	234	138	106	204	15	10	3	0
1960	ChC-N	36	46	16	20	.444	114	3.97	258⅔	134	101	253	27	16	4	1
1961	ChC-N	29	36	7	13	.350	94	4.26	198⅔	103	54	207	26	7	2	2
1962	ChC-N	23	42	5	14	.263	94	5.22	162	87	62	198	19	5	0	0
1963	ChC-N	24	36	7	10	.412	72	3.92	165⅓	94	49	172	17	4	1	0
1964	ChC-N	4	8	0	3	.000	24	7.90	27⅓	14	10	39	4	0	0	1
1964	StL-N	5	13	1	2	.333	21	4.26	44⅓	18	15	41	4	1	0	0
Career average		21	36	8	10	.434	74	4.20	158	85	62	160	16	6	1	1
Cubs average		**21**	**34**	**8**	**10**	**.436**	**71**	**4.20**	**152⅓**	**83**	**60**	**155**	**15**	**6**	**1**	**1**
Career total		170	284	62	81	.434	590	4.20	1263	682	495	1283	125	45	11	6
Cubs total		**165**	**271**	**61**	**79**	**.436**	**569**	**4.20**	**1218⅔**	**664**	**480**	**1242**	**121**	**44**	**11**	**5**

Hoeft, William Frederick (Billy)

HEIGHT: 6'3" LEFTHANDER BORN: 5/17/1932 OSHKOSH, WISCONSIN

YEAR	TEAM	STARTS	GAMES	WON	LOST	PCT	ER	ERA	INNINGS PITCHED	STRIKE-OUTS	WALKS	HITS ALLOWED	HRS ALLOWED	COMP. GAMES	SHUT-OUTS	SAVES
1952	Det-A	10	34	2	7	.222	60	4.32	125	67	63	123	14	1	0	4
1953	Det-A	27	29	9	14	.391	106	4.83	197⅔	90	58	223	24	9	4	2
1954	Det-A	25	34	7	15	.318	89	4.58	175	114	59	180	22	10	4	1
1955	Det-A	29	32	16	7	.696	73	2.99	220	133	75	187	17	17	7	0
1956	Det-A	34	38	20	14	.588	112	4.06	248	172	104	276	22	18	4	1
1957	Det-A	28	34	9	11	.450	80	3.48	207	111	69	188	15	6	0	3
1958	Det-A	21	36	10	9	.526	66	4.15	143	94	49	148	15	6	0	0
1959	Det-A	2	2	1	1	.500	5	5.00	9	2	4	6	0	0	0	0
1959	Bos-A	3	5	0	3	.000	11	5.60	17⅔	8	8	22	1	0	0	0
1959	Bal-A	3	16	1	1	.500	26	5.71	41	30	19	50	6	0	0	0
1960	Bal-A	0	19	2	1	.667	9	4.34	18⅔	14	14	18	2	0	0	3
1961	Bal-A	12	35	7	4	.636	31	2.02	138	100	55	106	7	3	1	7
1962	Bal-A	4	57	4	8	.333	58	4.59	113⅔	73	43	103	7	0	0	4
1963	SF-N	0	23	2	0	1.000	12	4.44	24⅓	8	10	26	5	0	0	4
1964	Mil-N	0	42	4	0	1.000	31	3.80	73⅓	47	18	76	9	0	0	4
1965	**ChC-N**	**2**	**29**	**2**	**2**	**.500**	**16**	**2.81**	**51⅓**	**44**	**20**	**43**	**4**	**0**	**0**	**3**
1966	**ChC-N**	**0**	**36**	**1**	**2**	**.333**	**21**	**4.61**	**41**	**30**	**14**	**43**	**4**	**0**	**0**	**0**
1966	SF-N	0	4	0	2	.000	3	7.36	3⅔	3	3	4	0	0	0	0

(continued)

Glen Frederick Hobbie, rhp, 1957–64

Glen Hobbie didn't really have a nickname during his career with the Cubs, but "Hard Luck" Hobbie would not have been a bad one.

Hobbie was born on April 24, 1936, in Witt, Illinois. He made his Cubs debut as a 21-year-old rookie in 1957, pitching 4.1 innings in two appearances in September.

The next year, Hobbie was in the Cubs rotation. From 1958 to 1960, he led the Cubs in wins and was either first or second on the team in strikeouts. He was also among the league leaders during that span in fewest hits allowed per nine innings.

Hobbie had to be that good because he didn't have much of a margin for error on the mound. The Cubs finished fifth, fifth and seventh in hitting during that three-year span.

After finishing third in batting in 1958, (aided by Ernie Banks's MVP season), the Cubs finished seventh in hitting the next two years.

Hobbie was not overpowering, but he always had good stuff and was a tough competitor. In 1959 he threw a one-hitter to beat the Cardinals, 1-0. His perfect game was spoiled by a Stan Musial double in the seventh.

He won a career-high 16 games in 1960, also losing a league-leading 20 contests. He began to have arm problems in 1961, specifically a strained shoulder that altered his pitching motion. Although he was second on the team that year in innings pitched, he won only 7 games as the Cubs went from bad to truly horrible, winning only 64 games and finishing 29 games out of first place. He would go 12-27 for the Cubs the next three years. Hobbie finished his career with the Cardinals in 1964.

(continued)

								INNINGS PITCHED	STRIKE-OUTS	WALKS	HITS ALLOWED	HRS ALLOWED	COMP. GAMES	SHUT-OUTS	SAVES
Career average	13	34	6	7	.490	54	3.94	123	76	46	121	12	5	1	2
Cubs average	**1**	**33**	**2**	**2**	**.429**	**19**	**3.61**	**46 1/3**	**37**	**17**	**42**	**4**	**1**	**0**	**2**
Career total	200	505	97	101	.490	809	3.94	1847 1/3	1140	685	1820	173	75	17	33
Cubs total	**2**	**65**	**3**	**4**	**.429**	**37**	**3.61**	**92 1/3**	**74**	**34**	**84**	**7**	**1**	**0**	**4**

Hoffman, Guy Alan
HEIGHT: 5'9"   LEFTHANDER   BORN: 7/9/1956 OTTAWA, ILLINOIS

YEAR	TEAM	STARTS	GAMES	WON	LOST	PCT	ER	ERA	INNINGS PITCHED	STRIKE-OUTS	WALKS	HITS ALLOWED	HRS ALLOWED	COMP. GAMES	SHUT-OUTS	SAVES
1979	CWS-A	0	24	0	5	.000	18	5.34	30 1/3	18	23	30	0	0	0	2
1980	CWS-A	1	23	1	0	1.000	11	2.63	37 2/3	24	17	38	1	0	0	1
1983	CWS-A	0	11	1	0	1.000	5	7.50	6	2	2	14	1	0	0	0
1986	**ChC-N**	**8**	**32**	**6**	**2**	**.750**	**36**	**3.86**	**84**	**47**	**29**	**92**	**6**	**1**	**0**	**0**
1987	Cin-N	22	36	9	10	.474	77	4.37	158 2/3	87	49	160	20	0	0	0
1988	Tex-A	0	11	0	0	—	13	5.24	22 1/3	9	8	22	5	0	0	0
Career average	5	23	3	3	.500	27	4.25	56 2/3	31	21	59	6	0	0	1
Cubs average	**8**	**32**	**6**	**2**	**.750**	**36**	**3.86**	**84**	**47**	**29**	**92**	**6**	**1**	**0**	**0**
Career total	31	137	17	17	.500	160	4.25	339	187	128	356	33	1	0	3
Cubs total	**8**	**32**	**6**	**2**	**.750**	**36**	**3.86**	**84**	**47**	**29**	**92**	**6**	**1**	**0**	**0**

Hogg, Carter Bradley (Brad)
HEIGHT: 6'0"   RIGHTHANDER   BORN: 3/26/1888 BUENA VISTA, GEORGIA   DIED: 4/2/1935 BUENA VISTA, GEORGIA

YEAR	TEAM	STARTS	GAMES	WON	LOST	PCT	ER	ERA	INNINGS PITCHED	STRIKE-OUTS	WALKS	HITS ALLOWED	HRS ALLOWED	COMP. GAMES	SHUT-OUTS	SAVES
1911	Bos-N	3	8	0	3	.000	19	6.66	25 2/3	8	14	33	0	2	0	1
1912	Bos-N	1	10	1	1	.500	24	6.97	31	12	16	37	2	0	0	1
1915	**ChC-N**	**2**	**2**	**1**	**0**	**1.000**	**3**	**2.08**	**13**	**0**	**6**	**12**	**1**	**1**	**1**	**0**
1918	Phi-N	25	29	13	13	.500	64	2.53	228	81	61	201	3	17	3	1
1919	Phi-N	19	22	5	12	.294	74	4.43	150 1/3	48	55	163	7	13	0	0
Career average	10	14	4	6	.408	37	3.70	89 2/3	30	30	89	3	7	1	1
Cubs average	**2**	**2**	**1**	**0**	**1.000**	**3**	**2.08**	**13**	**0**	**6**	**12**	**1**	**1**	**1**	**0**
Career total	50	71	20	29	.408	184	3.70	448	149	152	446	13	33	4	3
Cubs total	**2**	**2**	**1**	**0**	**1.000**	**3**	**2.08**	**13**	**0**	**6**	**12**	**1**	**1**	**1**	**0**

Holley, Edward Edgar (Ed)
HEIGHT: 6'1"   RIGHTHANDER   BORN: 7/23/1899 BENTON, KENTUCKY   DIED: 10/26/1986 PADUCAH, KENTUCKY

YEAR	TEAM	STARTS	GAMES	WON	LOST	PCT	ER	ERA	INNINGS PITCHED	STRIKE-OUTS	WALKS	HITS ALLOWED	HRS ALLOWED	COMP. GAMES	SHUT-OUTS	SAVES
1928	**ChC-N**	**1**	**13**	**0**	**0**	**—**	**13**	**3.77**	**31**	**10**	**16**	**31**	**1**	**0**	**0**	**0**
1932	Phi-N	30	34	11	14	.440	100	3.95	228	87	55	247	15	16	2	0
1933	Phi-N	28	30	13	15	.464	81	3.53	206 ⅔	56	62	219	18	12	3	0
1934	Phi-N	13	15	1	8	.111	58	7.18	72 ⅔	14	31	85	10	2	0	0
1934	Pit-N	4	5	0	3	.000	16	15.43	9 ⅓	2	6	20	1	0	0	0
Career average		19	24	6	10	.385	67	4.40	137	42	43	151	11	8	1	0
Cubs average		**1**	**13**	**0**	**0**	**—**	**13**	**3.77**	**31**	**10**	**16**	**31**	**1**	**0**	**0**	**0**
Career total		76	97	25	40	.385	268	4.40	547 ⅔	169	170	602	45	30	5	0
Cubs total		**1**	**13**	**0**	**0**	**—**	**13**	**3.77**	**31**	**10**	**16**	**31**	**1**	**0**	**0**	**0**

Hollins, Jessie Edward
HEIGHT: 6'3"   RIGHTHANDER   BORN: 1/27/1970 CONROE, TEXAS

YEAR	TEAM	STARTS	GAMES	WON	LOST	PCT	ER	ERA	INNINGS PITCHED	STRIKE-OUTS	WALKS	HITS ALLOWED	HRS ALLOWED	COMP. GAMES	SHUT-OUTS	SAVES
1992	**ChC-N**	**0**	**4**	**0**	**0**	**—**	**7**	**13.50**	**4 ⅔**	**0**	**5**	**8**	**1**	**0**	**0**	**0**
Career average		0	4	0	0	—	7	13.50	4 ⅔	0	5	8	1	0	0	0
Cubs average		**0**	**4**	**0**	**0**	**—**	**7**	**13.50**	**4 ⅔**	**0**	**5**	**8**	**1**	**0**	**0**	**0**
Career total		0	4	0	0	—	7	13.50	4 ⅔	0	5	8	1	0	0	0
Cubs total		**0**	**4**	**0**	**0**	**—**	**7**	**13.50**	**4 ⅔**	**0**	**5**	**8**	**1**	**0**	**0**	**0**

Hollison, John Henry (Swede)
HEIGHT: 5'8"   LEFTHANDER   BORN: 5/3/1870 CHICAGO, ILLINOIS   DIED: 8/19/1969 CHICAGO, ILLINOIS

YEAR	TEAM	STARTS	GAMES	WON	LOST	PCT	ER	ERA	INNINGS PITCHED	STRIKE-OUTS	WALKS	HITS ALLOWED	HRS ALLOWED	COMP. GAMES	SHUT-OUTS	SAVES
1892	**ChN-N**	**0**	**1**	**0**	**0**	**—**	**1**	**2.25**	**4**	**2**	**0**	**1**	**1**	**0**	**0**	**0**
Career average		0	1	0	0	—	1	2.25	4	2	0	1	1	0	0	0
Cubs average		**0**	**1**	**0**	**0**	**—**	**1**	**2.25**	**4**	**2**	**0**	**1**	**1**	**0**	**0**	**0**
Career total		0	1	0	0	—	1	2.25	4	2	0	1	1	0	0	0
Cubs total		**0**	**1**	**0**	**0**	**—**	**1**	**2.25**	**4**	**2**	**0**	**1**	**1**	**0**	**0**	**0**

Holtzman, Kenneth Dale (Ken)
HEIGHT: 6'2"   LEFTHANDER   BORN: 11/3/1945 ST. LOUIS, MISSOURI

YEAR	TEAM	STARTS	GAMES	WON	LOST	PCT	ER	ERA	INNINGS PITCHED	STRIKE-OUTS	WALKS	HITS ALLOWED	HRS ALLOWED	COMP. GAMES	SHUT-OUTS	SAVES
1965	**ChC-N**	**0**	**3**	**0**	**0**	**—**	**1**	**2.25**	**4**	**3**	**3**	**2**	**1**	**0**	**0**	**0**
1966	**ChC-N**	**33**	**34**	**11**	**16**	**.407**	**93**	**3.79**	**220 ⅔**	**171**	**68**	**194**	**27**	**9**	**0**	**0**
1967	**ChC-N**	**12**	**12**	**9**	**0**	**1.000**	**26**	**2.53**	**92 ⅔**	**62**	**44**	**76**	**11**	**3**	**0**	**0**
1968	**ChC-N**	**32**	**34**	**11**	**14**	**.440**	**80**	**3.35**	**215**	**151**	**76**	**201**	**17**	**6**	**3**	**1**
1969	**ChC-N**	**39**	**39**	**17**	**13**	**.567**	**104**	**3.58**	**261 ⅓**	**176**	**93**	**248**	**18**	**12**	**6**	**0**
1970	**ChC-N**	**38**	**39**	**17**	**11**	**.607**	**108**	**3.38**	**287 ⅔**	**202**	**94**	**271**	**30**	**15**	**1**	**0**
1971	**ChC-N**	**29**	**30**	**9**	**15**	**.375**	**97**	**4.48**	**195**	**143**	**64**	**213**	**18**	**9**	**3**	**0**
1972	Oak-A	37	39	19	11	.633	74	2.51	265 ⅓	134	52	232	23	16	4	0
1973	Oak-A	40	40	21	13	.618	98	2.97	297 ⅓	157	66	275	22	16	4	0
1974	Oak-A	38	39	19	17	.528	87	3.07	255 ⅓	117	51	273	14	9	3	0
1975	Oak-A	38	39	18	14	.563	93	3.14	266 ⅓	122	108	217	16	13	2	0
1976	Bal-A	13	13	5	4	.556	31	2.86	97 ⅔	25	35	100	4	6	1	0
1976	NYY-A	21	21	9	7	.563	69	4.17	149	41	35	165	14	10	2	0
1977	NYY-A	11	18	2	3	.400	46	5.78	71 ⅔	14	24	105	7	0	0	0
1978	NYY-A	3	5	1	0	1.000	8	4.08	17 ⅔	3	9	21	2	0	0	0
1978	**ChC-N**	**6**	**23**	**0**	**3**	**.000**	**36**	**6.11**	**53**	**36**	**35**	**61**	**10**	**0**	**0**	**2**
1979	**ChC-N**	**20**	**23**	**6**	**9**	**.400**	**60**	**4.59**	**117 ⅔**	**44**	**53**	**133**	**15**	**3**	**2**	**0**
Career average		27	30	12	10	.537	74	3.49	191	107	61	186	17	8	2	0
Cubs average		**23**	**26**	**9**	**9**	**.497**	**67**	**3.76**	**160 ⅔**	**110**	**59**	**155**	**16**	**6**	**2**	**0**
Career total		410	451	174	150	.537	1111	3.49	2867 ⅓	1601	910	2787	249	127	31	3
Cubs total		**209**	**237**	**80**	**81**	**.497**	**605**	**3.76**	**1447**	**988**	**530**	**1399**	**147**	**57**	**15**	**3**

Kenneth (Ken) Dale Holtzman, lhp, 1965–79

Lefty. Jewish. Great fastball. It was inevitable that Ken Holtzman, when he started out with the Cubs in the mid-1960s, should be dubbed "the new Sandy Koufax." He wasn't that good of course, but he did have a heck of a major league career.

Holtzman was born on November 3, 1945, in St. Louis, Missouri. He was a 19-year-old phenom when he made a brief debut with the Cubs, appearing in three games and pitching in a handful of innings.

The next year, Holtzman had a losing record (11-16), but that total still topped all Cubs pitchers and his ERA was second on the team to Fergie Jenkins.

And that year, the rookie squared off against the legend as Holtzman and Koufax faced each other on September 26 for the first and only time. (Koufax retired later that year.) Holtzman, to the delight of Cubs fans seeking a savior, took a no-hitter into the ninth inning, eking out a 2-1 win.

In 1967 Holtzman was 9-0, but he spent half the year in the military. He struggled in 1968 with an 11-14 mark, but he bounced back to have a great season the next year, with 17 wins and 13 losses. He tossed his first no-hitter that year, on August 19, 1969, shutting down the heavy-hitting Atlanta Braves, 3-0, at Wrigley Field. In 1971 he fired a second no-no, defeating the Reds, 1-0, in Cincinnati, on June 3.

Holtzman was a competitor. He had a great fastball, but he worked tirelessly on his control throughout his career. He could always get the big strikeout but preferred to induce batters into hitting bad pitches. It was a source of pride for Holtzman that he no-hit the Braves without the benefit of a single strikeout. He and 19th-century ace Larry Corcoran are the only two pitchers to ever throw more than one no-hitter for the Chicago franchise. (Corcoran has three.)

After back-to-back 17-win seasons, Holtzman slumped to 9-15 in 1971. He was also feuding with Cubs manager Leo Durocher. The two men had a love-hate relationship that usually worked itself out when the Cubs were winning and festered into animosity when things weren't going so well.

In 1971 things weren't going so well. The Cubs had finished second in 1969 and 1970, but they slumped to third in 1971. Durocher wasn't happy—he wasn't happy at all with Holtzman, whose ERA had ballooned up more than a full run to 4.48 that year from 3.38 in 1970.

Prior to the beginning of the 1972 season, Holtzman was traded to Oakland for outfielder Rick Monday. Monday played well for the Cubs, but Holtzman was outstanding for the Athletics, helping them to three consecutive world championships and being named to two All-Star teams.

After a brief stint with Baltimore, he moved on to New York, where his service with the 1977 world champs was limited by injury. Holtzman returned to the Cubs in 1978 and played one more year before retiring.

Holtzman still holds a number of Cubs records, including most games started by a lefthander (39 in 1969), most strikeouts by a lefty (202 in 1970) and most wins without a loss by a pitcher (9-0 in 1967).

Hooton, Burt Carlton (Happy)
HEIGHT: 6'1" RIGHTHANDER BORN: 2/7/1950 GREENVILLE, TEXAS

YEAR	TEAM	STARTS	GAMES	WON	LOST	PCT	ER	ERA	INNINGS PITCHED	STRIKE-OUTS	WALKS	HITS ALLOWED	HRS ALLOWED	COMP. GAMES	SHUT-OUTS	SAVES
1971	ChC-N	3	3	2	0	1.000	5	2.11	21⅓	22	10	8	2	2	1	0
1972	ChC-N	31	33	11	14	.440	68	2.80	218⅓	132	81	201	13	9	3	0
1973	ChC-N	34	42	14	17	.452	98	3.68	239⅔	134	73	248	12	9	2	0
1974	ChC-N	21	48	7	11	.389	94	4.80	176⅓	94	51	214	16	3	1	1
1975	ChC-N	3	3	0	2	.000	10	8.18	11	5	4	18	2	0	0	0
1975	LA-N	30	31	18	7	.720	70	2.82	223⅔	148	64	172	16	12	4	0
1976	LA-N	33	33	11	15	.423	82	3.26	226⅔	116	60	203	16	8	4	1
1977	LA-N	31	32	12	7	.632	65	2.62	223⅓	153	60	184	14	6	2	0
1978	LA-N	32	32	19	10	.655	71	2.71	236	104	61	196	17	10	3	0
1979	LA-N	29	29	11	10	.524	70	2.97	212	129	63	191	11	12	1	1
1980	LA-N	33	34	14	8	.636	84	3.66	206⅔	118	64	194	22	4	4	0
1981	LA-N	23	23	11	6	.647	36	2.28	142⅓	74	33	124	3	5	2	0
1982	LA-N	21	21	4	7	.364	54	4.03	120⅔	51	33	130	5	2	0	0
1983	LA-N	27	33	9	8	.529	75	4.22	160	87	59	156	21	2	0	4
1984	LA-N	6	54	3	6	.333	42	3.44	110	62	43	109	5	0	0	0
1985	Tex-A	20	29	5	8	.385	72	5.23	124	62	40	149	18	2	0	0
Career average		25	32	10	9	.526	66	3.38	176⅔	99	53	166	13	6	2	0
Cubs average		18	26	7	9	.436	55	3.71	133⅓	77	44	138	9	5	1	0
Career total		377	480	151	136	.526	996	3.38	2652	1491	799	2497	193	86	29	7
Cubs total		92	129	34	44	.436	275	3.71	666⅔	387	219	689	45	23	7	1

Horne, Berlyn Dale (Trader *or* Sonny)
HEIGHT: 5'9" RIGHTHANDER BORN: 4/12/1899 BACHMAN, OHIO DIED: 2/3/1983 FRANKLIN, OHIO

YEAR	TEAM	STARTS	GAMES	WON	LOST	PCT	ER	ERA	INNINGS PITCHED	STRIKE-OUTS	WALKS	HITS ALLOWED	HRS ALLOWED	COMP. GAMES	SHUT-OUTS	SAVES
1929	ChC-N	1	11	1	1	.500	13	5.09	23	6	21	24	3	0	0	0
Career average		1	11	1	1	.500	13	5.09	23	6	21	24	3	0	0	0
Cubs average		1	11	1	1	.500	13	5.09	23	6	21	24	3	0	0	0
Career total		1	11	1	1	.500	13	5.09	23	6	21	24	3	0	0	0
Cubs total		1	11	1	1	.500	13	5.09	23	6	21	24	3	0	0	0

Howe, Calvin Earl (Cal)
HEIGHT: 6'3" LEFTHANDER BORN: 11/27/1924 ROCK FALLS, ILLINOIS

YEAR	TEAM	STARTS	GAMES	WON	LOST	PCT	ER	ERA	INNINGS PITCHED	STRIKE-OUTS	WALKS	HITS ALLOWED	HRS ALLOWED	COMP. GAMES	SHUT-OUTS	SAVES
1952	ChC-N	0	1	0	0	—	0	0.00	2	2	1	0	0	0	0	0
Career average		0	1	0	0	—	0	0.00	2	2	1	0	0	0	0	0
Cubs average		0	1	0	0	—	0	0.00	2	2	1	0	0	0	0	0
Career total		0	1	0	0	—	0	0.00	2	2	1	0	0	0	0	0
Cubs total		0	1	0	0	—	0	0.00	2	2	1	0	0	0	0	0

Howell, Jay Canfield
HEIGHT: 6'3" RIGHTHANDER BORN: 11/26/1955 MIAMI, FLORIDA

YEAR	TEAM	STARTS	GAMES	WON	LOST	PCT	ER	ERA	INNINGS PITCHED	STRIKE-OUTS	WALKS	HITS ALLOWED	HRS ALLOWED	COMP. GAMES	SHUT-OUTS	SAVES
1980	Cin-N	0	5	0	0	—	5	13.50	3⅓	1	0	8	0	0	0	0
1981	ChC-N	2	10	2	0	1.000	12	4.84	22⅓	10	10	23	3	0	0	0
1982	NYY-A	6	6	2	3	.400	24	7.71	28	21	13	42	1	0	0	0
1983	NYY-A	12	19	1	5	.167	49	5.38	82	61	35	89	7	2	0	0
1984	NYY-A	1	61	9	4	.692	31	2.69	103⅔	109	34	86	5	0	0	7
1985	Oak-A	0	63	9	8	.529	31	2.85	98	68	31	98	5	0	0	29
1986	Oak-A	0	38	3	6	.333	20	3.38	53⅓	42	23	53	3	0	0	16
1987	Oak-A	0	36	3	4	.429	29	5.89	44⅓	35	21	48	6	0	0	16
1988	LA-N	0	50	5	3	.625	15	2.08	65	70	21	44	1	0	0	21

(continued)

(continued)

YEAR	TEAM	STARTS	GAMES	WON	LOST	PCT	ER	ERA	INNINGS PITCHED	STRIKE-OUTS	WALKS	HITS ALLOWED	HRS ALLOWED	COMP. GAMES	SHUT-OUTS	SAVES
1989	LA-N	0	56	5	3	.625	14	1.58	79 2/3	55	22	60	3	0	0	28
1990	LA-N	0	45	5	5	.500	16	2.18	66	59	20	59	5	0	0	16
1991	LA-N	0	44	6	5	.545	18	3.18	51	40	11	39	3	0	0	16
1992	LA-N	0	41	1	3	.250	8	1.54	46 2/3	36	18	41	2	0	0	4
1993	Atl-N	0	54	3	3	.500	15	2.31	58 1/3	37	16	48	3	0	0	0
1994	Tex-A	0	40	4	1	.800	26	5.44	43	22	16	44	10	0	0	2
Career average		1	38	4	4	.523	21	3.34	56 1/3	44	19	52	4	0	0	10
Cubs average		**2**	**10**	**2**	**0**	**1.000**	**12**	**4.84**	**22 1/3**	**10**	**10**	**23**	**3**	**0**	**0**	**0**
Career total		21	568	58	53	.523	313	3.34	844 2/3	666	291	782	57	2	0	155
Cubs total		**2**	**10**	**2**	**0**	**1.000**	**12**	**4.84**	**22 1/3**	**10**	**10**	**23**	**3**	**0**	**0**	**0**

Hughes, James Robert (Jim)

HEIGHT: 6'1"   RIGHTHANDER   BORN: 3/21/1923 CHICAGO, ILLINOIS   DIED: 8/13/2001 PALOS HEIGHTS, ILLINOIS

YEAR	TEAM	STARTS	GAMES	WON	LOST	PCT	ER	ERA	INNINGS PITCHED	STRIKE-OUTS	WALKS	HITS ALLOWED	HRS ALLOWED	COMP. GAMES	SHUT-OUTS	SAVES
1952	Bro-N	0	6	2	1	.667	3	1.45	18 2/3	8	11	16	0	0	0	0
1953	Bro-N	0	48	4	3	.571	33	3.47	85 2/3	49	41	80	6	0	0	9
1954	Bro-N	0	60	8	4	.667	31	3.22	86 2/3	58	44	76	7	0	0	24
1955	Bro-N	0	24	0	2	.000	20	4.22	42 2/3	20	19	41	10	0	0	6
1956	Bro-N	0	5	0	0	—	7	5.25	12	8	4	10	3	0	0	0
1956	**ChC-N**	**1**	**25**	**1**	**3**	**.250**	**26**	**5.16**	**45 1/3**	**20**	**30**	**43**	**4**	**0**	**0**	**0**
1957	CWS-A	0	4	0	0	—	6	10.80	5	2	3	12	0	0	0	0
Career average		0	29	3	2	.536	21	3.83	49 1/3	28	25	46	5	0	0	7
Cubs average		**1**	**25**	**1**	**3**	**.250**	**26**	**5.16**	**45 1/3**	**20**	**30**	**43**	**4**	**0**	**0**	**0**
Career total		1	172	15	13	.536	126	3.83	296	165	152	278	30	0	0	39
Cubs total		**1**	**25**	**1**	**3**	**.250**	**26**	**5.16**	**45 1/3**	**20**	**30**	**43**	**4**	**0**	**0**	**0**

Hughes, Thomas James (Long Tom)

HEIGHT: 6'1"   RIGHTHANDER   BORN: 11/29/1878 CHICAGO, ILLINOIS   DIED: 2/8/1956 CHICAGO, ILLINOIS

YEAR	TEAM	STARTS	GAMES	WON	LOST	PCT	ER	ERA	INNINGS PITCHED	STRIKE-OUTS	WALKS	HITS ALLOWED	HRS ALLOWED	COMP. GAMES	SHUT-OUTS	SAVES
1900	**ChN-N**	**3**	**3**	**1**	**1**	**.500**	**12**	**5.14**	**21**	**12**	**7**	**31**	**0**	**3**	**0**	**0**
1901	**ChN-N**	**35**	**37**	**10**	**23**	**.303**	**111**	**3.24**	**308 1/3**	**225**	**115**	**309**	**4**	**32**	**0**	**0**
1902	Bal-A	13	13	7	5	.583	47	3.90	108 1/3	45	32	120	2	12	1	0
1902	Bos-A	8	9	3	3	.500	18	3.28	49 1/3	15	24	51	0	4	0	0
1903	Bos-A	31	33	20	7	.741	70	2.57	244 2/3	112	60	232	5	25	5	0
1904	NYA-A	18	19	7	11	.389	56	3.70	136 1/3	75	48	141	3	12	1	0
1904	Was-A	14	16	2	13	.133	48	3.47	124 1/3	48	34	133	4	14	0	1
1905	Was-A	35	39	17	20	.459	76	2.35	291 1/3	149	79	239	3	26	6	0
1906	Was-A	24	30	7	17	.292	82	3.62	204	90	81	230	5	18	1	0
1907	Was-A	23	34	7	14	.333	73	3.11	211	102	47	206	1	18	2	4
1908	Was-A	31	43	18	15	.545	68	2.21	276 1/3	165	77	224	3	24	3	4
1909	Was-A	13	22	4	7	.364	36	2.69	120 1/3	77	33	113	1	7	2	1
1911	Was-A	27	34	11	17	.393	86	3.47	223	86	77	251	7	17	2	0
1912	Was-A	26	31	13	10	.565	64	2.94	196	108	78	201	8	11	1	1
1913	Was-A	13	36	4	12	.250	62	4.30	129 2/3	59	61	129	6	4	0	6
Career average		24	31	10	13	.428	70	3.09	203 1/3	105	66	201	4	17	2	1
Cubs average		**19**	**20**	**6**	**12**	**.314**	**62**	**3.36**	**164 2/3**	**119**	**61**	**170**	**2**	**18**	**1**	**0**
Career total		314	399	131	175	.428	909	3.09	2644	1368	853	2610	52	227	25	17
Cubs total		**38**	**40**	**11**	**24**	**.314**	**123**	**3.36**	**329 1/3**	**237**	**122**	**340**	**4**	**35**	**1**	**0**

Hughey, James Ulysses (Jim or Coldwater Jim)

HEIGHT: 6'0"   RIGHTHANDER   BORN: 3/8/1869 WAKASHMA, MICHIGAN   DIED: 3/29/1945 COLDWATER, MICHIGAN

YEAR	TEAM	STARTS	GAMES	WON	LOST	PCT	ER	ERA	INNINGS PITCHED	STRIKE-OUTS	WALKS	HITS ALLOWED	HRS ALLOWED	COMP. GAMES	SHUT-OUTS	SAVES
1891	Mil-AA	1	2	1	0	1.000	5	3.00	15	9	3	18	0	1	0	0
1893	**ChN-N**	**2**	**2**	**0**	**1**	**.000**	**11**	**11.00**	**9**	**4**	**3**	**14**	**0**	**1**	**0**	**0**
1896	Pit-N	14	25	5	11	.313	86	4.99	155	48	67	171	3	11	0	1
1897	Pit-N	17	25	6	11	.353	84	5.06	149 1/3	38	45	193	3	13	0	1
1898	StL-N	33	35	8	24	.250	124	3.93	283 2/3	74	71	325	2	31	0	0

(continued)

(Hughey, continued)																
1899	Cle-N	33	35	4	29	.121	170	5.41	283	54	88	403	9	31	0	0
1900	StL-N	12	20	5	7	.417	65	5.19	112 2/3	23	40	147	4	11	0	0
Career average		16	21	4	12	.259	78	4.87	144	36	45	182	3	14	0	0
Cubs average		**2**	**2**	**0**	**1**	**.000**	**11**	**11.00**	**9**	**4**	**3**	**14**	**0**	**1**	**0**	**0**
Career total		112	144	29	83	.259	545	4.87	1007 2/3	250	317	1271	21	99	0	2
Cubs total		**2**	**2**	**0**	**1**	**.000**	**11**	**11.00**	**9**	**4**	**3**	**14**	**0**	**1**	**0**	**0**

Humphreys, Robert William (Bob)
HEIGHT: 5'11"   RIGHTHANDER   BORN: 8/18/1935 COVINGTON, VIRGINIA

YEAR	TEAM	STARTS	GAMES	WON	LOST	PCT	ER	ERA	INNINGS PITCHED	STRIKE-OUTS	WALKS	HITS ALLOWED	HRS ALLOWED	COMP. GAMES	SHUT-OUTS	SAVES
1962	Det-A	0	4	0	1	.000	4	7.20	5	3	2	8	3	0	0	1
1963	StL-N	0	9	0	1	.000	6	5.06	10 2/3	8	7	11	4	0	0	0
1964	StL-N	0	28	2	0	1.000	12	2.53	42 2/3	36	15	32	3	0	0	2
1965	**ChC-N**	**0**	**41**	**2**	**0**	**1.000**	**23**	**3.15**	**65 2/3**	**38**	**27**	**59**	**6**	**0**	**0**	**0**
1966	Was-A	1	58	7	3	.700	35	2.82	111 2/3	88	28	91	6	0	0	3
1967	Was-A	2	48	6	2	.750	49	4.17	105 2/3	54	41	93	13	0	0	4
1968	Was-A	0	56	5	7	.417	38	3.69	92 2/3	56	30	78	13	0	0	2
1969	Was-A	0	47	3	3	.500	27	3.05	79 2/3	43	38	69	3	0	0	5
1970	Was-A	0	5	0	0	—	1	1.35	6 2/3	6	9	4	1	0	0	0
1970	Mil-A	1	23	2	4	.333	16	3.15	45 2/3	32	22	37	3	0	0	3
Career average		0	35	3	2	.563	23	3.36	63	40	24	54	6	0	0	2
Cubs average		**0**	**41**	**2**	**0**	**1.000**	**23**	**3.15**	**65 2/3**	**38**	**27**	**59**	**6**	**0**	**0**	**0**
Career total		4	319	27	21	.563	211	3.36	566	364	219	482	55	0	0	20
Cubs total		**0**	**41**	**2**	**0**	**1.000**	**23**	**3.15**	**65 2/3**	**38**	**27**	**59**	**6**	**0**	**0**	**0**

Humphries, Albert (Bert)
HEIGHT: 5'11"   RIGHTHANDER   BORN: 9/26/1880 CALIFORNIA, PENNSYLVANIA   DIED: 9/21/1945 ORLANDO, FLORIDA

YEAR	TEAM	STARTS	GAMES	WON	LOST	PCT	ER	ERA	INNINGS PITCHED	STRIKE-OUTS	WALKS	HITS ALLOWED	HRS ALLOWED	COMP. GAMES	SHUT-OUTS	SAVES
1910	Phi-N	0	5	0	0	—	5	4.66	9 2/3	3	3	13	0	0	0	2
1911	Phi-N	5	11	3	1	.750	19	4.17	41	13	10	56	1	2	0	1
1911	Cin-N	7	14	4	3	.571	17	2.35	65	16	18	62	3	3	0	0
1912	Cin-N	15	30	9	11	.450	57	3.23	158 2/3	58	36	162	6	9	1	2
1913	**ChC-N**	**20**	**28**	**16**	**4**	**.800**	**54**	**2.69**	**181**	**61**	**24**	**169**	**10**	**13**	**2**	**1**
1914	**ChC-N**	**21**	**34**	**10**	**11**	**.476**	**51**	**2.68**	**171**	**62**	**37**	**162**	**5**	**8**	**2**	**0**
1915	**ChC-N**	**22**	**31**	**8**	**13**	**.381**	**44**	**2.31**	**171 2/3**	**45**	**23**	**183**	**6**	**10**	**4**	**3**
Career average		15	26	8	7	.538	41	2.79	133	43	25	135	5	8	2	2
Cubs average		**21**	**31**	**11**	**9**	**.548**	**50**	**2.56**	**174 2/3**	**56**	**28**	**171**	**7**	**10**	**3**	**1**
Career total		90	153	50	43	.538	247	2.79	798	258	151	807	31	45	9	9
Cubs total		**63**	**93**	**34**	**28**	**.548**	**149**	**2.56**	**523 2/3**	**168**	**84**	**514**	**21**	**31**	**8**	**4**

Huntzinger, Walter Henry (Shakes)
HEIGHT: 6'0"   RIGHTHANDER   BORN: 2/6/1899 POTTSVILLE, PENNSYLVANIA   DIED: 8/11/1981 UPPER DARBY, PENNSYLVANIA

YEAR	TEAM	STARTS	GAMES	WON	LOST	PCT	ER	ERA	INNINGS PITCHED	STRIKE-OUTS	WALKS	HITS ALLOWED	HRS ALLOWED	COMP. GAMES	SHUT-OUTS	SAVES
1923	NYG-N	1	2	0	1	.000	7	7.88	8	2	1	9	0	0	0	0
1924	NYG-N	2	12	1	1	.500	16	4.45	32 1/3	6	9	41	3	0	0	1
1925	NYG-N	1	26	5	1	.833	25	3.50	64 1/3	19	17	68	3	0	0	0
1926	StL-N	4	9	0	4	.000	16	4.24	34	9	14	35	4	2	0	2
1926	**ChC-N**	**0**	**11**	**1**	**1**	**.500**	**3**	**0.94**	**28 2/3**	**4**	**8**	**26**	**0**	**0**	**0**	**2**
Career average		2	15	2	2	.467	17	3.60	42	10	12	45	3	1	0	1
Cubs average		**0**	**11**	**1**	**1**	**.500**	**3**	**0.94**	**28 2/3**	**4**	**8**	**26**	**0**	**0**	**0**	**2**
Career total		8	60	7	8	.467	67	3.60	167 1/3	40	49	179	10	2	0	3
Cubs total		**0**	**11**	**1**	**1**	**.500**	**3**	**0.94**	**28 2/3**	**4**	**8**	**26**	**0**	**0**	**0**	**2**

Hutchison, William Forrest (Bill *or* Wild Bill)

HEIGHT: 5'9"   RIGHTHANDER   BORN: 12/17/1859 NEW HAVEN, CONNECTICUT   DIED: 3/19/1926 KANSAS CITY, MISSOURI

YEAR	TEAM	STARTS	GAMES	WON	LOST	PCT	ER	ERA	INNINGS PITCHED	STRIKE-OUTS	WALKS	HITS ALLOWED	HRS ALLOWED	COMP. GAMES	SHUT-OUTS	SAVES
1884	KC-U	2	2	1	1	.500	5	2.65	17	5	1	14	0	2	0	0
1889	ChN-N	36	37	16	17	.485	125	3.54	318	136	117	306	11	33	3	0
1890	ChN-N	66	71	42	25	.627	181	2.70	603	289	199	505	20	65	5	0
1891	ChN-N	58	66	42	19	.689	175	2.81	561	261	178	508	26	56	4	2
1892	ChN-N	70	75	36	34	.514	191	2.76	622	312	190	571	11	67	5	1
1893	ChN-N	40	44	16	24	.400	184	4.75	348 1/3	80	156	420	9	38	2	0
1894	ChN-N	34	37	14	16	.467	187	6.06	277 2/3	59	140	373	9	28	0	0
1895	ChN-N	35	38	13	18	.419	153	4.73	291	85	129	371	13	30	2	0
1897	StL-N	5	6	1	4	.200	27	6.08	40	5	22	55	5	2	0	0
Career average		38	42	20	18	.534	136	3.59	342	137	126	347	12	36	2	0
Cubs average		**48**	**53**	**26**	**22**	**.539**	**171**	**3.56**	**431 2/3**	**175**	**158**	**436**	**14**	**45**	**3**	**0**
Career total		346	376	181	158	.534	1228	3.59	3078	1232	1132	3123	104	321	21	3
Cubs total		**339**	**368**	**179**	**153**	**.539**	**1196**	**3.56**	**3021**	**1222**	**1109**	**3054**	**99**	**317**	**21**	**3**

William Forrest "Wild Bill" Hutchison, rhp, 1884, 1889–97

Ivy Leaguer Bill Hutchison went from semipro ball to the bigs to win 179 games for Chicago in seven years.

Hutchison, also known as "Wild Bill" Hutchison, was born on December 17, 1859, in New Haven, Connecticut. He was a schoolboy star in New Haven and continued his career at Yale. Hutchison played in a semipro league before being signed in 1884 by Kansas City of the old Union Association. Hutchison was 1-1 for a truly awful Kansas City nine, which was only three wins shy of team leader Ernie Hickman that year.

When the Union League folded the next year, no team picked up Hutchison. He played ball on weekends for a few years before being signed by Chicago in 1889.

He led the team in ERA with a 3.54 mark that year and tied for the team lead in wins with 16. The next season, Chicago, Brooklyn and Philadelphia were locked in a tight pennant race and Chicago manager Adrian "Cap" Anson pitched Hutchison every other day. Chicago finished six games behind first place Brooklyn in 1890.

In 1891 Hutchison led the league in wins, games pitched, innings, complete games and tied for the league lead in saves (with two). That was part of a three-year stretch (1890–92) in which Hutchison won 42, 42 and 36 games for Chicago and became the best pitcher in baseball. That last season, 1892, Hutchison also lost 34 games. He also led the league in strikeouts with 312.

Hutchison was also a pretty good hitter. He set a Chicago record for most home runs by a pitcher with 9 in 1894. His nickname was a comical take on his Ivy League pipe-smoking persona.

In 1893 the pitcher's mound was moved back to the present 60'6" and Hutchison was not as overpowering as he was from 50' away. He was still the ace of the staff but went 16-24. His win totals dropped to 14 and 13 with Chicago the next two years. After a brief stint with St. Louis, he was out of baseball after the 1897 season.

Hutchison died in Kansas City, Missouri, in 1926. He is third all-time with the Cubs in victories (179) and second in losses with 153, third in games started with 339, second in innings pitched with 3,021, second in hits allowed with 3,054 and first in walks issued with 1,109.

Hutson, George Herbert (Herb)
HEIGHT: 6'2" RIGHTHANDER BORN: 7/17/1949 SAVANNAH, GEORGIA

YEAR	TEAM	STARTS	GAMES	WON	LOST	PCT	ER	ERA	INNINGS PITCHED	STRIKE-OUTS	WALKS	HITS ALLOWED	HRS ALLOWED	COMP. GAMES	SHUT-OUTS	SAVES
1974	ChC-N	2	20	0	2	.000	11	3.45	28 ⅔	22	15	24	3	0	0	0
Career average		2	20	0	2	.000	11	3.45	28 ⅔	22	15	24	3	0	0	0
Cubs average		2	20	0	2	.000	11	3.45	28 ⅔	22	15	24	3	0	0	0
Career total		2	20	0	2	.000	11	3.45	28 ⅔	22	15	24	3	0	0	0
Cubs total		2	20	0	2	.000	11	3.45	28 ⅔	22	15	24	3	0	0	0

Ilsley, Blaise Francis
HEIGHT: 6'1" LEFTHANDER BORN: 4/9/1964 ALPENA, MICHIGAN

YEAR	TEAM	STARTS	GAMES	WON	LOST	PCT	ER	ERA	INNINGS PITCHED	STRIKE-OUTS	WALKS	HITS ALLOWED	HRS ALLOWED	COMP. GAMES	SHUT-OUTS	SAVES
1994	ChC-N	0	10	0	0	—	13	7.80	15	9	9	25	2	0	0	0
Career average		0	10	0	0	—	13	7.80	15	9	9	25	2	0	0	0
Cubs average		0	10	0	0	—	13	7.80	15	9	9	25	2	0	0	0
Career total		0	10	0	0	—	13	7.80	15	9	9	25	2	0	0	0
Cubs total		0	10	0	0	—	13	7.80	15	9	9	25	2	0	0	0

Isbell, William Frank (Frank *or* Bald Eagle)
HEIGHT: 5'11" RIGHTHANDER BORN: 8/21/1875 DELEVAN, NEW YORK DIED: 7/15/1941 WICHITA, KANSAS

YEAR	TEAM	STARTS	GAMES	WON	LOST	PCT	ER	ERA	INNINGS PITCHED	STRIKE-OUTS	WALKS	HITS ALLOWED	HRS ALLOWED	COMP. GAMES	SHUT-OUTS	SAVES
1898	ChN-N	9	13	4	7	.364	32	3.56	81	16	42	86	0	7	0	0
1901	CWS-A	0	1	0	0	—	1	9.00	1	0	0	2	0	0	0	0
1902	CWS-A	1	1	0	0	—	1	9.00	1	1	1	3	0	0	0	0
1906	CWS-A	0	1	0	0	—	0	0.00	2	2	0	1	0	0	0	1
1907	CWS-A	0	1	0	0	—	0	0.00	0 ⅓	0	0	0	0	0	0	0
Career average		2	3	1	1	.364	7	3.59	17	4	9	18	0	1	0	0
Cubs average		9	13	4	7	.364	32	3.56	81	16	42	86	0	7	0	0
Career total		10	17	4	7	.364	34	3.59	85 ⅓	19	43	92	0	7	0	1
Cubs total		9	13	4	7	.364	32	3.56	81	16	42	86	0	7	0	0

Jackson, Danny Lynn
HEIGHT: 6'0" LEFTHANDER BORN: 1/5/1962 SAN ANTONIO, TEXAS

YEAR	TEAM	STARTS	GAMES	WON	LOST	PCT	ER	ERA	INNINGS PITCHED	STRIKE-OUTS	WALKS	HITS ALLOWED	HRS ALLOWED	COMP. GAMES	SHUT-OUTS	SAVES
1983	KC-A	3	4	1	1	.500	11	5.21	19	9	6	26	1	0	0	0
1984	KC-A	11	15	2	6	.250	36	4.26	76	40	35	84	4	1	0	0
1985	KC-A	32	32	14	12	.538	79	3.42	208	114	76	209	7	4	3	0
1986	KC-A	27	32	11	12	.478	66	3.20	185 ⅔	115	79	177	13	4	1	1
1987	KC-A	34	36	9	18	.333	100	4.02	224	152	109	219	11	11	2	0
1988	Cin-N	35	35	23	8	.742	79	2.73	260 ⅔	161	71	206	13	15	6	0
1989	Cin-N	20	20	6	11	.353	72	5.60	115 ⅔	70	57	122	10	1	0	0
1990	Cin-N	21	22	6	6	.500	47	3.61	117 ⅓	76	40	119	11	0	0	0
1991	ChC-N	14	17	1	5	.167	53	6.75	70 ⅔	31	48	89	8	0	0	0
1992	ChC-N	19	19	4	9	.308	53	4.22	113	51	48	117	5	0	0	0
1992	Pit-N	15	15	4	4	.500	33	3.36	88 ⅓	46	29	94	1	0	0	0
1993	Phi-N	32	32	12	11	.522	88	3.77	210 ⅓	120	80	214	12	2	1	0
1994	Phi-N	25	25	14	6	.700	65	3.26	179 ⅓	129	46	183	13	4	1	0
1995	StL-N	19	19	2	12	.143	66	5.90	100 ⅔	52	48	120	10	2	1	0
1996	StL-N	4	13	1	1	.500	18	4.46	36 ⅓	27	16	33	3	0	0	0
1997	StL-N	4	4	1	2	.333	16	7.71	18 ⅔	13	8	26	3	0	0	0
1997	SD-N	9	13	1	7	.125	41	7.53	49	19	20	72	8	0	0	0
Career average		22	24	7	9	.461	62	4.01	138 ⅓	82	54	141	9	3	1	0
Cubs average		17	18	3	7	.263	53	5.19	92	41	48	103	7	0	0	0
Career total		324	353	112	131	.461	923	4.01	2072 ⅔	1225	816	2110	133	44	15	1
Cubs total		33	36	5	14	.263	106	5.19	183 ⅔	82	96	206	13	0	0	0

Lawrence (Larry) Curtis Jackson, rhp, 1955–68

While the Chicago Cubs were staggering to near-cellar finishes every year in the mid-1960s, Larry Jackson was soldiering on.

Jackson, born on June 2, 1931, in Nampa, Idaho, made his major league debut with the St. Louis Cardinals in 1955, going 9-14. By 1957 the big righty was an All-Star for St. Louis, a feat he would repeat in 1958 and 1960.

In all, Jackson would spend eight years with the Cardinals and post six consecutive winning records. St. Louis often used him as a reliever, and Jackson's nine saves in 1956 were fourth in the league overall.

In 1963 Jackson and reliever Lindy McDaniel were traded to the Cubs. Chicago had hoped to bolster their sagging pitching staff with the trade, and they did: Chicago's team ERA dropped from 4.54 in 1962 to 3.08 in 1963, second in the National League.

Unfortunately, the Cubs still couldn't hit their way out of a paper bag, with the team's .238 batting average eighth in a 10-team league. This translated into a 14-18 record for Jackson and a seventh-place finish for Chicago. Three of Jackson's losses were by 1-0 scores, and he dropped a total of eight one-run decisions that year. Brutal.

Jackson made the All-Star team in 1963 and became the second Cub in history to earn an All Star Game win (Bob Rush being the first in 1952).

The next year, though, Jackson came close to winning the Cy Young award. He went 24-11,

winning almost a third of his team's 72 games. He led the league in wins with 24, was third in complete games with 19 and second in innings pitched with 297⅔. He was second (a distant second, admittedly) to the Los Angeles Angels' Dean Chance in the Cy Young voting. This was when the award was presented to only one pitcher—not one from each league.

He was a workhorse for Chicago, leading the team in starts for the three full years he toiled in Chicago, and topping the team in innings pitched and complete games in 1964 and 1965. His 24 wins in 1964 were the most by a Cub since Charlie Root's 26 in 1927.

The 1965 season was another struggle, though, with the Cubs at 72-90 and Jackson at 14-21. His 21 defeats after a 20-win season in 1964 has only been accomplished by a handful of pitchers in the 20th century.

Early into the 1966 season, Jackson was traded to the Phillies for, among other people, Ferguson (Fergie) Jenkins. Jackson, back on a winning team, showed he could pitch, leading the league in shutouts that year with five.

In 1969, rather than report to the expansion Montreal Expos, the 38-year-old Jackson retired. He returned to his native Idaho and worked as a state legislator for several years. Jackson died in Boise, Idaho, in 1990.

Jackson didn't play for the Cubs long enough to break into any of the team's all-time lists, but his 24 wins in 1964 were eighth best all-time for one season and his 21 losses in 1965 third worst all-time. His 39 starts in 1965 is sixth best all-time.

Jackson, Lawrence Curtis (Larry)

HEIGHT: 6'1"   RIGHTHANDER   BORN: 6/2/1931 NAMPA, IDAHO   DIED: 8/28/1990 BOISE, IDAHO

YEAR	TEAM	STARTS	GAMES	WON	LOST	PCT	ER	ERA	INNINGS PITCHED	STRIKE-OUTS	WALKS	HITS ALLOWED	HRS ALLOWED	COMP. GAMES	SHUT-OUTS	SAVES
1955	StL-N	25	37	9	14	.391	85	4.31	177⅓	88	72	189	25	4	1	2
1956	StL-N	1	51	2	2	.500	39	4.11	85⅓	50	45	75	5	0	0	9
1957	StL-N	22	41	15	9	.625	81	3.47	210⅓	96	57	196	21	6	2	1
1958	StL-N	23	49	13	13	.500	81	3.68	198	124	51	211	21	11	1	8
1959	StL-N	37	40	14	13	.519	94	3.30	256	145	64	271	13	12	3	0
1960	StL-N	38	43	18	13	.581	109	3.48	282	171	70	277	22	14	3	0
1961	StL-N	28	33	14	11	.560	88	3.75	211	113	56	203	20	12	3	0
1962	StL-N	35	36	16	11	.593	105	3.75	252⅓	112	64	267	25	11	2	0
1963	**ChC-N**	**37**	**37**	**14**	**18**	**.438**	**78**	**2.55**	**275**	**153**	**54**	**256**	**11**	**13**	**4**	**0**
1964	**ChC-N**	**38**	**40**	**24**	**11**	**.686**	**104**	**3.14**	**297⅔**	**148**	**58**	**265**	**17**	**19**	**3**	**0**
1965	**ChC-N**	**39**	**39**	**14**	**21**	**.400**	**110**	**3.85**	**257⅓**	**131**	**57**	**268**	**28**	**12**	**4**	**0**

(continued)

(L.C. Jackson, continued)

YEAR	TEAM	STARTS	GAMES	WON	LOST	PCT	ER	ERA	INNINGS PITCHED	STRIKE-OUTS	WALKS	HITS ALLOWED	HRS ALLOWED	COMP. GAMES	SHUT-OUTS	SAVES
1966	ChC-N	2	3	0	2	.000	12	13.50	8	5	4	14	3	0	0	0
1966	Phi-N	33	35	15	13	.536	82	2.99	247	107	58	243	22	12	5	0
1967	Phi-N	37	40	13	15	.464	90	3.10	261 ⅔	139	54	242	17	11	4	0
1968	Phi-N	34	34	13	17	.433	75	2.77	243 ⅔	127	60	229	9	12	2	0
Career average		31	40	14	13	.515	88	3.40	233	122	59	229	19	11	3	1
Cubs average		29	30	13	13	.500	76	3.26	209 ⅔	109	43	201	15	11	3	0
Career total		429	558	194	183	.515	1233	3.40	3262 ⅔	1709	824	3206	259	149	37	20
Cubs total		116	119	52	52	.500	304	3.26	838	437	173	803	59	44	11	0

Jacobs, Anthony Robert (Tony)

HEIGHT: 5'9" RIGHTHANDER BORN: 8/5/1925 DIXMOOR, ILLINOIS DIED: 12/21/1980 NASHVILLE, TENNESSEE

YEAR	TEAM	STARTS	GAMES	WON	LOST	PCT	ER	ERA	INNINGS PITCHED	STRIKE-OUTS	WALKS	HITS ALLOWED	HRS ALLOWED	COMP. GAMES	SHUT-OUTS	SAVES
1948	ChC-N	0	1	0	0	—	1	4.50	2	2	0	3	1	0	0	0
1955	StL-N	0	1	0	0	—	4	18.00	2	1	1	6	1	0	0	0
Career average		0	1	0	0	—	3	11.25	2	2	1	5	1	0	0	0
Cubs average		0	1	0	0	—	1	4.50	2	2	0	3	1	0	0	0
Career total		0	2	0	0	—	5	11.25	4	3	1	9	2	0	0	0
Cubs total		0	1	0	0	—	1	4.50	2	2	0	3	1	0	0	0

Jacobs, William Elmer (Elmer)

HEIGHT: 6'0" RIGHTHANDER BORN: 8/10/1892 SALEM, MISSOURI DIED: 2/10/1958 SALEM, MISSOURI

YEAR	TEAM	STARTS	GAMES	WON	LOST	PCT	ER	ERA	INNINGS PITCHED	STRIKE-OUTS	WALKS	HITS ALLOWED	HRS ALLOWED	COMP. GAMES	SHUT-OUTS	SAVES
1914	Phi-N	7	14	1	3	.250	27	4.80	50 ⅔	17	20	65	2	1	0	0
1916	Pit-N	17	34	6	10	.375	50	2.94	153	46	38	151	2	8	0	0
1917	Pit-N	25	38	6	19	.240	71	2.81	227 ⅓	58	76	214	3	10	1	2
1918	Pit-N	4	8	0	1	.000	15	5.79	23 ⅓	2	14	31	0	0	0	0
1918	Phi-N	14	18	9	5	.643	33	2.41	123	33	42	91	3	12	4	1
1919	Phi-N	15	17	6	10	.375	55	3.85	128 ⅔	37	44	150	5	13	0	0
1919	StL-N	8	17	3	6	.333	24	2.53	85 ⅓	31	25	81	2	4	1	1
1920	StL-N	9	23	4	8	.333	45	5.21	77 ⅔	21	33	91	2	1	0	1
1924	ChC-N	22	38	11	12	.478	79	3.74	190 ⅓	50	72	181	9	13	1	1
1925	ChC-N	4	18	2	3	.400	32	5.17	55 ⅔	19	22	63	9	1	1	1
1927	CWS-A	8	25	2	4	.333	38	4.60	74 ⅓	22	37	105	3	2	1	0
Career average		15	28	6	9	.382	52	3.55	132	37	47	136	4	7	1	1
Cubs average		13	28	7	8	.464	56	4.06	123	35	47	122	9	7	1	1
Career total		133	250	50	81	.382	469	3.55	1189 ⅓	336	423	1223	40	65	9	7
Cubs total		26	56	13	15	.464	111	4.06	246	69	94	244	18	14	2	2

Jaeckel, Paul Henry (Jake)

HEIGHT: 5'10" RIGHTHANDER BORN: 4/1/1942 EAST LOS ANGELES, CALIFORNIA

YEAR	TEAM	STARTS	GAMES	WON	LOST	PCT	ER	ERA	INNINGS PITCHED	STRIKE-OUTS	WALKS	HITS ALLOWED	HRS ALLOWED	COMP. GAMES	SHUT-OUTS	SAVES
1964	ChC-N	0	4	1	0	1.000	0	0.00	8	2	3	4	0	0	0	1
Career average		0	4	1	0	1.000	0	0.00	8	2	3	4	0	0	0	1
Cubs average		0	4	1	0	1.000	0	0.00	8	2	3	4	0	0	0	1
Career total		0	4	1	0	1.000	0	0.00	8	2	3	4	0	0	0	1
Cubs total		0	4	1	0	1.000	0	0.00	8	2	3	4	0	0	0	1

Jaeger, Joseph Peter (Joe *or* Zip)

HEIGHT: 6'1" RIGHTHANDER BORN: 3/3/1895 ST. CLOUD, MINNESOTA DIED: 12/13/1963 HAMPTON, IOWA

YEAR	TEAM	STARTS	GAMES	WON	LOST	PCT	ER	ERA	INNINGS PITCHED	STRIKE-OUTS	WALKS	HITS ALLOWED	HRS ALLOWED	COMP. GAMES	SHUT-OUTS	SAVES
1920	ChC-N	0	2	0	0	—	4	12.00	3	0	4	6	0	0	0	0

(continued)

(continued)

									INNINGS PITCHED	STRIKE-OUTS	WALKS	HITS ALLOWED	HRS ALLOWED	COMP. GAMES	SHUT-OUTS	SAVES
Career average	0	2	0	0	—	4	12.00	3		0	4	6	0	0	0	0
Cubs average	**0**	**2**	**0**	**0**	**—**	**4**	**12.00**	**3**		**0**	**4**	**6**	**0**	**0**	**0**	**0**
Career total	0	2	0	0	—	4	12.00	3		0	4	6	0	0	0	0
Cubs total	**0**	**2**	**0**	**0**	**—**	**4**	**12.00**	**3**		**0**	**4**	**6**	**0**	**0**	**0**	**0**

James, Richard Lee (Rick)
HEIGHT: 6'2"   RIGHTHANDER   BORN: 10/11/1947 SHEFFIELD, ALABAMA

YEAR	TEAM	STARTS	GAMES	WON	LOST	PCT	ER	ERA	INNINGS PITCHED	STRIKE-OUTS	WALKS	HITS ALLOWED	HRS ALLOWED	COMP. GAMES	SHUT-OUTS	SAVES
1967	ChC-N	1	3	0	1	.000	7	13.50	4 2/3	2	2	9	1	0	0	0
Career average	1	3	0	1	.000	7	13.50	4 2/3	2	2	9	1	0	0	0
Cubs average	**1**	**3**	**0**	**1**	**.000**	**7**	**13.50**	**4 2/3**	**2**	**2**	**9**	**1**	**0**	**0**	**0**
Career total	1	3	0	1	.000	7	13.50	4 2/3	2	2	9	1	0	0	0
Cubs total	**1**	**3**	**0**	**1**	**.000**	**7**	**13.50**	**4 2/3**	**2**	**2**	**9**	**1**	**0**	**0**	**0**

Jeffcoat, Harold Bentley (Hal)
HEIGHT: 5'10"   RIGHTHANDER   BORN: 9/6/1924 WEST COLUMBIA, SOUTH CAROLINA

YEAR	TEAM	STARTS	GAMES	WON	LOST	PCT	ER	ERA	INNINGS PITCHED	STRIKE-OUTS	WALKS	HITS ALLOWED	HRS ALLOWED	COMP. GAMES	SHUT-OUTS	SAVES
1954	ChC-N	3	43	5	6	.455	60	5.19	104	35	58	110	12	1	0	7
1955	ChC-N	1	50	8	6	.571	33	2.95	100 2/3	32	53	107	5	0	0	6
1956	Cin-N	16	38	8	2	.800	73	3.84	171	55	55	189	12	2	0	2
1957	Cin-N	31	37	12	13	.480	104	4.52	207	63	46	236	29	10	1	0
1958	Cin-N	0	49	6	8	.429	31	3.72	75	35	26	76	8	0	0	9
1959	Cin-N	0	17	0	1	.000	8	3.32	21 2/3	12	10	21	3	0	0	1
1959	StL-N	0	11	0	1	.000	18	9.17	17 2/3	7	9	33	4	0	0	0
Career average	9	41	7	6	.513	55	4.22	116 1/3	40	43	129	12	2	0	4
Cubs average	**2**	**47**	**7**	**6**	**.520**	**47**	**4.09**	**102 1/3**	**34**	**56**	**109**	**9**	**1**	**0**	**7**
Career total	51	245	39	37	.513	327	4.22	697	239	257	772	73	13	1	25
Cubs total	**4**	**93**	**13**	**12**	**.520**	**93**	**4.09**	**204 2/3**	**67**	**111**	**217**	**17**	**1**	**0**	**13**

Jenkins, Ferguson Arthur (Fergie)
HEIGHT: 6'5"   RIGHTHANDER   BORN: 12/13/1943 CHATHAM, ONTARIO, CANADA

YEAR	TEAM	STARTS	GAMES	WON	LOST	PCT	ER	ERA	INNINGS PITCHED	STRIKE-OUTS	WALKS	HITS ALLOWED	HRS ALLOWED	COMP. GAMES	SHUT-OUTS	SAVES
1965	Phi-N	0	7	2	1	.667	3	2.19	12 1/3	10	2	7	2	0	0	1
1966	Phi-N	0	1	0	0	—	1	3.86	2 1/3	2	1	3	0	0	0	0
1966	ChC-N	12	60	6	8	.429	67	3.31	182	148	51	147	24	2	1	5
1967	ChC-N	38	38	20	13	.606	90	2.80	289 1/3	236	83	230	30	20	3	0
1968	ChC-N	40	40	20	15	.571	90	2.63	308	260	65	255	26	20	3	0
1969	ChC-N	42	43	21	15	.583	111	3.21	311 1/3	273	71	284	27	23	7	1
1970	ChC-N	39	40	22	16	.579	118	3.39	313	274	60	265	30	24	3	0
1971	ChC-N	39	39	24	13	.649	100	2.77	325	263	37	304	29	30	3	0
1972	ChC-N	36	36	20	12	.625	103	3.20	289 1/3	184	62	253	32	23	5	0
1973	ChC-N	38	38	14	16	.467	117	3.89	271	170	57	267	35	7	2	0
1974	Tex-A	41	41	25	12	.676	103	2.82	328 1/3	225	45	286	27	29	6	0
1975	Tex-A	37	37	17	18	.486	118	3.93	270	157	56	261	37	22	4	0
1976	Bos-A	29	30	12	11	.522	76	3.27	209	142	43	201	20	12	2	0
1977	Bos-A	28	28	10	10	.500	79	3.68	193	105	36	190	30	11	1	0
1978	Tex-A	30	34	18	8	.692	84	3.04	249	157	41	228	21	16	4	0
1979	Tex-A	37	37	16	14	.533	117	4.07	259	164	81	252	40	10	3	0
1980	Tex-A	29	29	12	12	.500	83	3.77	198	129	52	190	22	12	0	0
1981	Tex-A	16	19	5	8	.385	53	4.50	106	63	40	122	14	1	0	0
1982	ChC-N	34	34	14	15	.483	76	3.15	217 1/3	134	68	221	19	4	1	0
1983	ChC-N	29	33	6	9	.400	80	4.30	167 1/3	96	46	176	19	1	1	0
Career average	31	35	15	12	.557	88	3.34	237	168	52	218	25	14	3	0
Cubs average	**35**	**40**	**17**	**13**	**.559**	**95**	**3.20**	**267 1/3**	**204**	**60**	**240**	**27**	**15**	**3**	**1**
Career total	594	664	284	226	.557	1669	3.34	4500 2/3	3192	997	4142	484	267	49	7
Cubs total	**347**	**401**	**167**	**132**	**.559**	**952**	**3.20**	**2673 2/3**	**2038**	**600**	**2402**	**271**	**154**	**29**	**6**

Ferguson (Fergie) Arthur Jenkins, rhp, 1965–83

One of the more popular pastimes for Cubs fans these days is to remember, with great pleasure, the eight-year reign of Ferguson Arthur Jenkins.

Born on December 13, 1943, in Chatham, Ontario, Canada, Jenkins was a four-sport athlete in high school, playing football, basketball, track and field and, of course, hockey. But his Canadian all-boys prep school didn't have a baseball team. Jenkins did, however, play on several club teams, which is how the Philadelphia Phillies signed him in 1963.

Jenkins played for Philadelphia's Little Rock, Arkansas, team in 1963 and 1964. Prior to that season, he had played for the Miami Marlins of the Florida State League.

It was during these early years that Jenkins recalled having his first brush with racism. He and other black teammates could not eat in the same restaurants and sleep in the same motels as white ballplayers.

Jenkins admitted years later that he was stung by the treatment he and other black players received at the hands of white business owners.

"But," he said, "I wasn't there as a crusader. I was there as an athlete."

Little Rock, in particular, was nasty, in large part because the Phillies organization had decided to integrate the team in 1963, the year Jenkins arrived. No one, however, had told Jenkins or any of his teammates.

The Phillies brought him up to the big club in 1965. Jenkins appeared as a reliever in seven games, and went 2-1 with one save. He showed excellent control, striking out 10 in 12⅓ innings and walking only two.

But the Phillies didn't have a lot of confidence in him. He didn't appear to have a major league fastball. His stamina was an issue for some Philadelphia scouts, so he was shipped to the Cubs early in the 1966 season.

Jenkins was 6-8 for Cubs manager Leo Durocher that season, pitching mostly in relief. At the end of the year, Durocher told Jenkins that he planned to use him solely as a starter for the 1967 season. But, Leo added, Jenkins would have to pitch well all year to stay in the rotation.

Jenkins pitched well all year. He won 20 games, led the National League in complete games with 20, and led the Cubs in wins, starts, innings pitched (289⅓), strikeouts (236) and ERA (2.80).

That began a streak of six consecutive 20-win seasons for Jenkins, tying a club record set by Mordecai Brown. But in addition to leading the club in wins from 1967 to 1972, Jenkins also led the

Johnson, Abraham (Abe)

HEIGHT: — BORN: — CHICAGO, ILLINOIS

YEAR	TEAM	STARTS	GAMES	WON	LOST	PCT	ER	ERA	INNINGS PITCHED	STRIKE-OUTS	WALKS	HITS ALLOWED	HRS ALLOWED	COMP. GAMES	SHUT-OUTS	SAVES
1893	ChN-N	0	1	0	0	—	4	36.00	1	0	2	2	0	0	0	1
Career average		0	1	0	0	—	4	36.00	1	0	2	2	0	0	0	1
Cubs average		0	1	0	0	—	4	36.00	1	0	2	2	0	0	0	1
Career total		0	1	0	0	—	4	36.00	1	0	2	2	0	0	0	1
Cubs total		0	1	0	0	—	4	36.00	1	0	2	2	0	0	0	1

club in that span in starts, complete games, innings pitched and strikeouts. He was also the Cubs leader in ERA four of those six years. No Cub, and few pitchers for any team, could claim such a period of statistical excellence.

And, of course, he was doing all this at least half the time in the confines of Wrigley Field, which is a hitter's park in anybody's book. Jenkins survived in Wrigley by learning to change speeds and pitch with control and confidence. He was a lot like his contemporary, James "Catfish" Hunter: excellent control, great durability and guts. Like Hunter, he sometimes cut things a little too close and could be touched for home runs, but rarely when it counted.

With Jenkins, and a host of young stars like Glenn Beckert, Ron Santo, Randy Hundley and Ken Holtzman, the Cubs began to make their move in 1968, finishing third, and in 1969, finishing second after leading the National League East for most of the year.

Jenkins was in his prime. He started seven consecutive Opening Day games for the Cubs, a team record. In 1967 Jenkins equaled Carl Hubbell's famous feat of striking out six batters in three innings. In 1971 he led the National League in wins while compiling a 24-13 record, also topping the league with 30 complete games and 325 innings pitched, which earned him the Cy Young.

That year, he also became the first pitcher in baseball history to strike out more than 250 batters and walk less than 40 (his numbers were 263

strikeouts and 37 walks), although the feat generated scant attention. Since then, Pedro Martinez of the Boston Red Sox has done it twice, in 1999 and 2000.

In 1973 Jenkins went 14-16 for the Cubs, and the thinking was that he was backsliding. He was traded to Texas for third baseman Bill Madlock the next year. Jenkins bounced back strongly, leading the National League in wins with a 25-12 record and topping the league in complete games with 29.

He was traded to Boston in 1976, where he recorded a 22-21 record in two years. It was back to Texas for four years starting with the 1978 season. He regained his form in 1978, going 18-8, but was 33-34 the next three years in Arlington. He returned to the Cubs for two more years in 1982 and 1983 before retiring.

Jenkins became a pitching coach for the Cubs in the mid-1990s for a few years. He is also a regular at Randy Hundley's Baseball Fantasy Camp.

He remains a fixture in the Cubs record book. He is tops all-time in Chicago in games started with 347, in strikeouts with 2,038 and in home runs allowed with 271.

Jenkins is also 5th all-time in victories with 167, 4th in losses with 132, 5th in games pitched with 401, 5th in complete games with 154, 4th in shutouts with 29, 3rd in innings pitched with 2,673⅔, 4th in hits allowed with 2,402 and 10th in walks issued with 600.

In 1991 Jenkins was elected to the Baseball Hall of Fame.

Johnson, Benjamin Franklin (Ben)

HEIGHT: 6'2"   RIGHTHANDER   BORN: 5/15/1931 GREENWOOD, SOUTH CAROLINA

YEAR	TEAM	STARTS	GAMES	WON	LOST	PCT	ER	ERA	INNINGS PITCHED	STRIKE-OUTS	WALKS	HITS ALLOWED	HRS ALLOWED	COMP. GAMES	SHUT-OUTS	SAVES
1959	ChC-N	2	4	0	0	—	4	2.16	16⅔	6	4	17	1	0	0	0
1960	ChC-N	0	17	2	1	.667	16	4.91	29⅓	9	11	39	3	0	0	1
Career average		1	11	1	1	.667	10	3.91	23	8	8	28	2	0	0	1
Cubs average		**1**	**11**	**1**	**1**	**.667**	**10**	**3.91**	**23**	**8**	**8**	**28**	**2**	**0**	**0**	**1**
Career total		2	21	2	1	.667	20	3.91	46	15	15	56	4	0	0	1
Cubs total		**2**	**21**	**2**	**1**	**.667**	**20**	**3.91**	**46**	**15**	**15**	**56**	**4**	**0**	**0**	**1**

Johnson, Kenneth Travis (Ken)

HEIGHT: 6'4"   RIGHTHANDER   BORN: 6/16/1933 WEST PALM BEACH, FLORIDA

YEAR	TEAM	STARTS	GAMES	WON	LOST	PCT	ER	ERA	INNINGS PITCHED	STRIKE-OUTS	WALKS	HITS ALLOWED	HRS ALLOWED	COMP. GAMES	SHUT-OUTS	SAVES
1958	KCA-A	0	2	0	0	—	7	27.00	2 ⅓	1	3	6	1	0	0	0
1959	KCA-A	2	2	1	1	.500	5	4.09	11	8	5	11	2	0	0	0
1960	KCA-A	6	42	5	10	.333	57	4.26	120 ⅓	83	45	120	16	2	0	3
1961	KCA-A	1	6	0	4	.000	11	10.61	9 ⅓	4	7	11	2	0	0	0
1961	Cin-N	11	15	6	2	.750	30	3.25	83	42	22	71	11	3	1	1
1962	Hou-N	31	33	7	16	.304	84	3.84	197	178	46	195	18	5	1	0
1963	Hou-N	32	37	11	17	.393	66	2.65	224	148	50	204	12	6	1	1
1964	Hou-N	35	35	11	16	.407	88	3.63	218	117	44	209	15	7	1	0
1965	Hou-N	8	8	3	2	.600	24	4.18	51 ⅔	28	11	52	4	1	0	0
1965	Mil-N	26	29	13	8	.619	64	3.21	179 ⅔	123	37	165	15	8	1	2
1966	Atl-N	31	32	14	8	.636	79	3.30	215 ⅔	105	46	213	24	11	2	0
1967	Atl-N	29	29	13	9	.591	64	2.74	210 ⅓	85	38	191	19	6	0	0
1968	Atl-N	16	31	5	8	.385	52	3.47	135	57	25	145	10	1	0	0
1969	Atl-N	2	9	0	1	.000	16	4.97	29	20	9	32	4	0	0	1
1969	NYY-A	0	12	1	2	.333	10	3.46	26	21	11	19	1	0	0	0
1969	**ChC-N**	**1**	**9**	**1**	**2**	**.333**	**6**	**2.84**	**19**	**18**	**13**	**17**	**2**	**0**	**0**	**1**
1970	Mon-N	0	3	0	0	—	5	7.50	6	4	1	9	1	0	0	0
Career average		18	26	7	8	.462	51	3.46	133 ⅔	80	32	128	12	4	1	1
Cubs average		**1**	**9**	**1**	**2**	**.333**	**6**	**2.84**	**19**	**18**	**13**	**17**	**2**	**0**	**0**	**1**
Career total		231	334	91	106	.462	668	3.46	1737 ⅓	1042	413	1670	157	50	7	9
Cubs total		**1**	**9**	**1**	**2**	**.333**	**6**	**2.84**	**19**	**18**	**13**	**17**	**2**	**0**	**0**	**1**

Johnson, William Charles (Bill)

HEIGHT: 6'5"   RIGHTHANDER   BORN: 10/6/1960 WILMINGTON, DELAWARE

YEAR	TEAM	STARTS	GAMES	WON	LOST	PCT	ER	ERA	INNINGS PITCHED	STRIKE-OUTS	WALKS	HITS ALLOWED	HRS ALLOWED	COMP. GAMES	SHUT-OUTS	SAVES
1983	**ChC-N**	**0**	**10**	**1**	**0**	**1.000**	**6**	**4.38**	**12 ⅓**	**4**	**3**	**17**	**0**	**0**	**0**	**0**
1984	**ChC-N**	**0**	**4**	**0**	**0**	**—**	**1**	**1.69**	**5 ⅓**	**3**	**1**	**4**	**0**	**0**	**0**	**0**
Career average		0	7	1	0	1.000	4	3.57	9	4	2	11	0	0	0	0
Cubs average		**0**	**7**	**1**	**0**	**1.000**	**4**	**3.57**	**9**	**4**	**2**	**11**	**0**	**0**	**0**	**0**
Career total		0	14	1	0	1.000	7	3.57	17 ⅔	7	4	21	0	0	0	0
Cubs total		**0**	**14**	**1**	**0**	**1.000**	**7**	**3.57**	**17 ⅔**	**7**	**4**	**21**	**0**	**0**	**0**	**0**

Joiner, Roy Merrill (Pop)

HEIGHT: 6'0"   LEFTHANDER   BORN: 10/30/1906 RED BLUFF, CALIFORNIA   DIED: 12/26/1989 RED BLUFF, CALIFORNIA

YEAR	TEAM	STARTS	GAMES	WON	LOST	PCT	ER	ERA	INNINGS PITCHED	STRIKE-OUTS	WALKS	HITS ALLOWED	HRS ALLOWED	COMP. GAMES	SHUT-OUTS	SAVES
1934	**ChC-N**	**2**	**20**	**0**	**1**	**.000**	**31**	**8.21**	**34**	**9**	**8**	**61**	**3**	**0**	**0**	**0**
1935	**ChC-N**	**0**	**2**	**0**	**0**	**—**	**2**	**5.40**	**3 ⅓**	**0**	**2**	**6**	**0**	**0**	**0**	**0**
1940	NYG-N	2	30	3	2	.600	20	3.40	53	25	17	66	8	0	0	1
Career average		1	17	1	1	.500	18	5.28	30	11	9	44	4	0	0	0
Cubs average		**1**	**11**	**0**	**1**	**.000**	**17**	**7.96**	**18 ⅔**	**5**	**5**	**34**	**2**	**0**	**0**	**0**
Career total		4	52	3	3	.500	53	5.28	90 ⅓	34	27	133	11	0	0	1
Cubs total		**2**	**22**	**0**	**1**	**.000**	**33**	**7.96**	**37 ⅓**	**9**	**10**	**67**	**3**	**0**	**0**	**0**

Jones, Douglas Reid (Doug)

HEIGHT: 6'2"   RIGHTHANDER   BORN: 6/24/1957 COVINA, CALIFORNIA

YEAR	TEAM	STARTS	GAMES	WON	LOST	PCT	ER	ERA	INNINGS PITCHED	STRIKE-OUTS	WALKS	HITS ALLOWED	HRS ALLOWED	COMP. GAMES	SHUT-OUTS	SAVES
1982	Mil-A	0	4	0	0	—	3	10.13	2 ⅔	1	1	5	1	0	0	0
1986	Cle-A	0	11	1	0	1.000	5	2.50	18	12	6	18	0	0	0	1
1987	Cle-A	0	49	6	5	.545	32	3.15	91 ⅓	87	24	101	4	0	0	8
1988	Cle-A	0	51	3	4	.429	21	2.27	83 ⅓	72	16	69	1	0	0	37
1989	Cle-A	0	59	7	10	.412	21	2.34	80 ⅔	65	13	76	4	0	0	32

(continued)

(continued)

YEAR	TEAM	STARTS	GAMES	WON	LOST	PCT	ER	ERA	INNINGS PITCHED	STRIKE-OUTS	WALKS	HITS ALLOWED	HRS ALLOWED	COMP. GAMES	SHUT-OUTS	SAVES
1990	Cle-A	0	66	5	5	.500	24	2.56	84⅓	55	22	66	5	0	0	43
1991	Cle-A	4	36	4	8	.333	39	5.54	63⅓	48	17	87	7	0	0	7
1992	Hou-N	0	80	11	8	.579	23	1.85	111⅔	93	17	96	5	0	0	36
1993	Hou-N	0	71	4	10	.286	43	4.54	85⅓	66	21	102	7	0	0	26
1994	Phi-N	0	47	2	4	.333	13	2.17	54	38	6	55	2	0	0	27
1995	Bal-A	0	52	0	4	.000	26	5.01	46⅔	42	16	55	6	0	0	22
1996	**ChC-N**	**0**	**28**	**2**	**2**	**.500**	**18**	**5.01**	**32⅓**	**26**	**7**	**41**	**6**	**0**	**0**	**2**
1996	Mil-A	0	24	5	0	1.000	12	3.41	31⅔	34	13	31	3	0	0	1
1997	Mil-A	0	75	6	6	.500	18	2.02	80⅓	82	9	62	4	0	0	36
1998	Mil-N	0	46	3	4	.429	31	5.17	54	43	11	65	15	0	0	12
1998	Cle-A	0	23	1	2	.333	12	3.45	31⅓	28	6	34	2	0	0	1
1999	Oak-A	0	70	5	5	.500	41	3.55	104	63	24	106	10	0	0	10
2000	Oak-A	0	54	4	2	.667	32	3.93	73⅓	54	18	86	6	0	0	2
Career average		0	53	4	5	.466	26	3.30	70⅔	57	15	72	5	0	0	19
Cubs average		**0**	**28**	**2**	**2**	**.500**	**18**	**5.01**	**32⅓**	**26**	**7**	**41**	**4**	**0**	**0**	**2**
Career total		4	846	69	79	.466	414	3.30	1128⅓	909	247	1155	86	0	0	303
Cubs total		**0**	**28**	**2**	**2**	**.500**	**18**	**5.01**	**32⅓**	**26**	**7**	**41**	**4**	**0**	**0**	**2**

Jones, Percy Lee

HEIGHT: 5'11"   LEFTHANDER   BORN: 10/28/1899 HARWOOD, TEXAS   DIED: 3/18/1979 DALLAS, TEXAS

YEAR	TEAM	STARTS	GAMES	WON	LOST	PCT	ER	ERA	INNINGS PITCHED	STRIKE-OUTS	WALKS	HITS ALLOWED	HRS ALLOWED	COMP. GAMES	SHUT-OUTS	SAVES
1920	ChC-N	0	4	0	0	—	9	11.57	7	0	3	15	1	0	0	0
1921	ChC-N	3	32	3	5	.375	50	4.56	98⅔	46	39	116	2	1	0	0
1922	ChC-N	24	44	8	9	.471	86	4.72	164	46	69	197	10	7	2	1
1925	ChC-N	13	28	6	6	.500	64	4.65	124	60	71	123	12	6	1	0
1926	ChC-N	20	30	12	7	.632	55	3.09	160⅓	80	90	151	3	10	2	2
1927	ChC-N	11	30	7	8	.467	51	4.07	112⅔	37	72	123	3	5	1	0
1928	ChC-N	19	39	10	6	.625	69	4.03	154	41	56	167	4	9	1	3
1929	Bos-N	22	35	7	15	.318	97	4.64	188⅓	69	84	219	15	11	1	0
1930	Pit-N	2	9	0	1	.000	14	6.63	19	3	11	26	3	0	0	0
Career average		13	28	6	6	.482	55	4.33	114⅓	42	55	126	6	5	1	1
Cubs average		**13**	**30**	**7**	**6**	**.529**	**55**	**4.21**	**117⅓**	**44**	**57**	**127**	**5**	**5**	**1**	**1**
Career total		114	251	53	57	.482	495	4.33	1028	382	495	1137	53	49	8	6
Cubs total		**90**	**207**	**46**	**41**	**.529**	**384**	**4.21**	**820⅔**	**310**	**400**	**892**	**35**	**38**	**7**	**6**

Jones, Samuel (Sam *or* Toothpick *or* Sad Sam)

HEIGHT: 6'4"   RIGHTHANDER   BORN: 12/14/1925 STEWARTSVILLE, OHIO   DIED: 11/5/1971 MORGANTOWN, WEST VIRGINIA

YEAR	TEAM	STARTS	GAMES	WON	LOST	PCT	ER	ERA	INNINGS PITCHED	STRIKE-OUTS	WALKS	HITS ALLOWED	HRS ALLOWED	COMP. GAMES	SHUT-OUTS	SAVES
1951	Cle-A	1	2	0	1	.000	2	2.08	8⅔	4	5	4	0	0	0	0
1952	Cle-A	4	14	2	3	.400	29	7.25	36	28	37	38	6	0	0	1
1955	**ChC-N**	**34**	**36**	**14**	**20**	**.412**	**110**	**4.10**	**241⅔**	**198**	**185**	**175**	**22**	**12**	**4**	**0**
1956	**ChC-N**	**28**	**33**	**9**	**14**	**.391**	**82**	**3.91**	**188⅔**	**176**	**115**	**155**	**21**	**8**	**2**	**0**
1957	StL-N	27	28	12	9	.571	73	3.60	182⅔	154	71	164	17	10	2	0
1958	StL-N	35	35	14	13	.519	80	2.88	250	225	107	204	23	14	2	0
1959	SF-N	35	50	21	15	.583	85	2.83	270⅔	209	109	232	18	16	4	4
1960	SF-N	35	39	18	14	.563	83	3.19	234	190	91	200	18	13	3	0
1961	SF-N	17	37	8	8	.500	64	4.49	128⅓	105	57	134	12	2	0	1
1962	Det-A	6	30	2	4	.333	33	3.65	81⅓	73	35	77	13	1	0	1
1963	StL-N	0	11	2	0	1.000	11	9.00	11	8	5	15	0	0	0	2
1964	Bal-A	0	7	0	0	—	3	2.61	10⅓	6	5	5	1	0	0	0
Career average		19	27	9	8	.502	55	3.59	137	115	69	117	13	6	1	1
Cubs average		**31**	**35**	**12**	**17**	**.404**	**96**	**4.02**	**215⅓**	**187**	**150**	**165**	**22**	**10**	**3**	**0**
Career total		222	322	102	101	.502	655	3.59	1643⅓	1376	822	1403	151	76	17	9
Cubs total		**62**	**69**	**23**	**34**	**.404**	**192**	**4.02**	**430⅓**	**374**	**300**	**330**	**43**	**20**	**6**	**0**

Jones, Sheldon Leslie (Available)
HEIGHT: 6'0" RIGHTHANDER BORN: 2/2/1922 TECUMSEH, NEBRASKA   DIED: 4/18/1991 GREENVILLE, NORTH CAROLINA

YEAR	TEAM	STARTS	GAMES	WON	LOST	PCT	ER	ERA	INNINGS PITCHED	STRIKE-OUTS	WALKS	HITS ALLOWED	HRS ALLOWED	COMP. GAMES	SHUT-OUTS	SAVES
1946	NYG-N	4	6	1	2	.333	10	3.21	28	24	17	21	4	1	0	0
1947	NYG-N	6	15	2	2	.500	24	3.88	55 2/3	24	29	51	2	0	0	0
1948	NYG-N	21	55	16	8	.667	75	3.35	201 1/3	82	90	204	16	8	2	5
1949	NYG-N	27	42	15	12	.556	77	3.34	207 1/3	79	88	198	19	11	1	0
1950	NYG-N	28	40	13	16	.448	102	4.61	199	97	90	188	26	11	2	2
1951	NYG-N	12	41	6	11	.353	57	4.26	120 1/3	58	52	119	12	0	0	4
1952	Bos-N	1	39	1	4	.200	37	4.76	70	40	31	81	8	0	0	1
1953	**ChC-N**	**2**	**22**	**0**	**2**	**.000**	**23**	**5.40**	**38 1/3**	**9**	**16**	**47**	**3**	**0**	**0**	**0**
Career average		13	33	7	7	.486	51	3.96	115	52	52	114	11	4	1	2
Cubs average		**2**	**22**	**0**	**2**	**.000**	**23**	**5.40**	**38 1/3**	**9**	**16**	**47**	**3**	**0**	**0**	**0**
Career total		101	260	54	57	.486	405	3.96	920	413	413	909	90	33	5	12
Cubs total		**2**	**22**	**0**	**2**	**.000**	**23**	**5.40**	**38 1/3**	**9**	**16**	**47**	**3**	**0**	**0**	**0**

Jonnard, Claude Alfred
HEIGHT: 6'1" RIGHTHANDER BORN: 11/23/1897 NASHVILLE, TENNESSEE   DIED: 8/27/1959 NASHVILLE, TENNESSEE

YEAR	TEAM	STARTS	GAMES	WON	LOST	PCT	ER	ERA	INNINGS PITCHED	STRIKE-OUTS	WALKS	HITS ALLOWED	HRS ALLOWED	COMP. GAMES	SHUT-OUTS	SAVES
1921	NYG-N	0	1	0	0	—	0	0.00	4	7	0	4	0	0	0	1
1922	NYG-N	0	33	6	1	.857	41	3.84	96	44	28	96	7	0	0	5
1923	NYG-N	1	45	4	3	.571	35	3.28	96	45	35	105	6	1	0	5
1924	NYG-N	3	34	4	5	.444	24	2.41	89 2/3	40	24	80	2	1	0	5
1926	StL-A	3	12	0	2	.000	24	6.00	36	13	24	46	1	0	0	1
1929	**ChC-N**	**2**	**12**	**0**	**1**	**.000**	**23**	**7.48**	**27 2/3**	**11**	**11**	**41**	**4**	**0**	**0**	**0**
Career average		2	23	2	2	.538	25	3.79	58 1/3	27	20	62	3	0	0	3
Cubs average		**2**	**12**	**0**	**1**	**.000**	**23**	**7.48**	**27 2/3**	**11**	**11**	**41**	**4**	**0**	**0**	**0**
Career total		9	137	14	12	.538	147	3.79	349 1/3	160	122	372	20	2	0	17
Cubs total		**2**	**12**	**0**	**1**	**.000**	**23**	**7.48**	**27 2/3**	**11**	**11**	**41**	**4**	**0**	**0**	**0**

Kaiser, Clyde Donald (Don *or* Tiger)
HEIGHT: 6'5" RIGHTHANDER BORN: 2/3/1935 BYNG, OKLAHOMA

YEAR	TEAM	STARTS	GAMES	WON	LOST	PCT	ER	ERA	INNINGS PITCHED	STRIKE-OUTS	WALKS	HITS ALLOWED	HRS ALLOWED	COMP. GAMES	SHUT-OUTS	SAVES
1955	**ChC-N**	**0**	**11**	**0**	**0**	**—**	**11**	**5.40**	**18 1/3**	**11**	**5**	**20**	**2**	**0**	**0**	**0**
1956	**ChC-N**	**22**	**27**	**4**	**9**	**.308**	**60**	**3.59**	**150 1/3**	**74**	**52**	**144**	**15**	**5**	**1**	**0**
1957	**ChC-N**	**13**	**20**	**2**	**6**	**.250**	**40**	**5.00**	**72**	**23**	**28**	**91**	**4**	**1**	**0**	**0**
Career average		12	19	2	5	.286	37	4.15	80 1/3	36	28	85	7	2	0	0
Cubs average		**12**	**19**	**2**	**5**	**.286**	**37**	**4.15**	**80 1/3**	**36**	**28**	**85**	**7**	**2**	**0**	**0**
Career total		35	58	6	15	.286	111	4.15	240 2/3	108	85	255	21	6	1	0
Cubs total		**35**	**58**	**6**	**15**	**.286**	**111**	**4.15**	**240 2/3**	**108**	**85**	**255**	**21**	**6**	**1**	**0**

Karchner, Matthew Dean (Matt)
HEIGHT: 6'4" RIGHTHANDER BORN: 6/28/1967 BERWICK, PENNSYLVANIA

YEAR	TEAM	STARTS	GAMES	WON	LOST	PCT	ER	ERA	INNINGS PITCHED	STRIKE-OUTS	WALKS	HITS ALLOWED	HRS ALLOWED	COMP. GAMES	SHUT-OUTS	SAVES
1995	CWS-A	0	31	4	2	.667	6	1.69	32	24	12	33	2	0	0	0
1996	CWS-A	0	50	7	4	.636	38	5.76	59 1/3	46	41	61	10	0	0	1
1997	CWS-A	0	52	3	1	.750	17	2.91	52 2/3	30	26	50	4	0	0	15
1998	CWS-A	0	32	2	4	.333	21	5.15	36 2/3	30	19	33	2	0	0	11
1998	**ChC-N**	**0**	**29**	**3**	**1**	**.750**	**16**	**5.14**	**28**	**22**	**14**	**30**	**6**	**0**	**0**	**0**
1999	**ChC-N**	**0**	**16**	**1**	**0**	**1.000**	**5**	**2.50**	**18**	**9**	**9**	**16**	**3**	**0**	**0**	**0**
2000	**ChC-N**	**0**	**13**	**1**	**1**	**.500**	**10**	**6.14**	**14 2/3**	**5**	**11**	**19**	**3**	**0**	**0**	**0**
Career average		0	37	4	2	.618	19	4.60	40 1/3	28	22	40	5	0	0	5
Cubs average		**0**	**19**	**2**	**1**	**.714**	**10**	**4.60**	**20 1/3**	**12**	**11**	**22**	**4**	**0**	**0**	**0**
Career total		0	223	21	13	.618	113	4.21	241 1/3	166	132	242	30	0	0	27
Cubs total		**0**	**58**	**5**	**2**	**.714**	**31**	**4.60**	**60 2/3**	**36**	**34**	**65**	**12**	**0**	**0**	**0**

Katoll, John (Katy)
HEIGHT: 5'11" RIGHTHANDER BORN: 6/24/1872 GERMANY DIED: 6/18/1955 HARTLAND, ILLINOIS

YEAR	TEAM	STARTS	GAMES	WON	LOST	PCT	ER	ERA	INNINGS PITCHED	STRIKE-OUTS	WALKS	HITS ALLOWED	HRS ALLOWED	COMP. GAMES	SHUT-OUTS	SAVES
1898	ChN-N	1	2	0	1	.000	1	0.82	11	3	1	8	0	1	0	0
1899	ChN-N	2	2	1	1	.500	12	6.00	18	1	4	17	0	2	0	0
1901	CWS-A	25	27	11	10	.524	65	2.81	208	59	53	231	3	19	0	0
1902	CWS-A	0	1	0	0	—	0	0.00	1	2	0	1	0	0	0	0
1902	Bal-A	13	15	5	10	.333	55	4.02	123	25	32	175	5	13	0	0
Career average		10	12	4	6	.436	33	3.32	90 1/3	23	23	108	2	9	0	0
Cubs average		**2**	**2**	**1**	**1**	**.333**	**7**	**4.03**	**14 2/3**	**2**	**3**	**13**	**0**	**2**	**0**	**0**
Career total		41	47	17	22	.436	133	3.32	361	90	90	432	8	35	0	0
Cubs total		**3**	**4**	**1**	**2**	**.333**	**13**	**4.03**	**29**	**4**	**5**	**25**	**0**	**3**	**0**	**0**

Kaufmann, Anthony Charles (Tony)
HEIGHT: 5'11" RIGHTHANDER BORN: 12/16/1900 CHICAGO, ILLINOIS DIED: 6/4/1982 ELGIN, ILLINOIS

YEAR	TEAM	STARTS	GAMES	WON	LOST	PCT	ER	ERA	INNINGS PITCHED	STRIKE-OUTS	WALKS	HITS ALLOWED	HRS ALLOWED	COMP. GAMES	SHUT-OUTS	SAVES
1921	ChC-N	1	2	1	0	1.000	6	4.15	13	6	3	12	0	1	0	1
1922	ChC-N	14	37	7	13	.350	69	4.06	153	45	57	161	15	4	1	3
1923	ChC-N	24	33	14	10	.583	71	3.10	206 1/3	72	67	209	14	18	2	3
1924	ChC-N	26	34	16	11	.593	93	4.02	208 1/3	79	66	218	21	16	3	0
1925	ChC-N	23	31	13	13	.500	98	4.50	196	49	77	221	9	14	2	2
1926	ChC-N	22	26	9	7	.563	57	3.02	169 2/3	52	44	169	6	14	1	2
1927	ChC-N	6	9	3	3	.500	38	6.41	53 1/3	21	19	75	8	3	0	0
1927	Phi-N	5	5	0	3	.000	22	10.61	18 2/3	4	8	37	2	1	0	0
1927	StL-N	0	1	0	0	—	3	81.00	0 1/3	0	1	4	0	0	0	0
1928	StL-N	1	4	0	0	—	5	9.64	4 2/3	2	4	8	1	0	0	0
1930	StL-N	1	2	0	1	.000	9	7.84	10 1/3	2	4	15	2	0	0	0
1931	StL-N	1	15	1	1	.500	33	6.06	49	13	17	65	3	0	0	1
1935	StL-N	0	3	0	0	—	1	2.45	3 2/3	0	1	4	0	0	0	0
Career average		11	18	6	6	.508	46	4.18	98 2/3	31	33	109	7	6	1	1
Cubs average		**17**	**25**	**9**	**8**	**.525**	**62**	**3.89**	**142 2/3**	**46**	**48**	**152**	**10**	**10**	**1**	**2**
Career total		124	202	64	62	.508	505	4.18	1086 1/3	345	368	1198	81	71	9	12
Cubs total		**116**	**172**	**63**	**57**	**.525**	**432**	**3.89**	**999 2/3**	**324**	**333**	**1065**	**73**	**70**	**9**	**11**

Keen, Howard Victor (Vic)
HEIGHT: 5'9" RIGHTHANDER BORN: 3/16/1899 BEL AIR, MARYLAND DIED: 12/10/1976 SALISBURY, MARYLAND

YEAR	TEAM	STARTS	GAMES	WON	LOST	PCT	ER	ERA	INNINGS PITCHED	STRIKE-OUTS	WALKS	HITS ALLOWED	HRS ALLOWED	COMP. GAMES	SHUT-OUTS	SAVES
1918	Phi-A	1	1	0	1	.000	3	3.38	8	1	1	9	1	0	0	0
1921	ChC-N	4	5	0	3	.000	13	4.68	25	9	9	29	0	1	0	0
1922	ChC-N	2	7	1	2	.333	15	3.89	34 2/3	11	10	36	4	2	0	1
1923	ChC-N	17	35	12	8	.600	59	3.00	177	46	57	169	8	10	0	1
1924	ChC-N	28	40	15	14	.517	99	3.80	234 2/3	75	80	242	17	15	0	3
1925	ChC-N	8	30	2	6	.250	58	6.26	83 1/3	19	41	125	8	1	0	1
1926	StL-N	21	26	10	9	.526	77	4.56	152	29	42	179	15	12	1	0
1927	StL-N	0	21	2	1	.667	18	4.81	33 2/3	12	8	39	3	0	0	0
Career average		10	21	5	6	.488	43	4.11	93 2/3	25	31	104	7	5	0	1
Cubs average		**12**	**23**	**6**	**7**	**.476**	**49**	**3.96**	**111**	**32**	**39**	**120**	**7**	**6**	**0**	**1**
Career total		81	165	42	44	.488	342	4.11	748 1/3	202	248	828	56	41	1	6
Cubs total		**59**	**117**	**30**	**33**	**.476**	**244**	**3.96**	**554 2/3**	**160**	**197**	**601**	**37**	**29**	**0**	**6**

Kelly, Michael Joseph (King)
HEIGHT: 5'10" RIGHTHANDER BORN: 12/31/1857 TROY, NEW YORK DIED: 11/8/1894 BOSTON, MASSACHUSETTS

YEAR	TEAM	STARTS	GAMES	WON	LOST	PCT	ER	ERA	INNINGS PITCHED	STRIKE-OUTS	WALKS	HITS ALLOWED	HRS ALLOWED	COMP. GAMES	SHUT-OUTS	SAVES
1880	ChN-N	0	1	0	0	—	0	0.00	3	1	1	3	0	0	0	0
1883	ChN-N	0	1	0	0	—	0	0.00	1	0	0	1	0	0	0	0
1884	ChN-N	0	2	0	1	.000	5	8.44	5 1/3	1	2	12	2	0	0	0
1887	Bos-N	0	3	1	0	1.000	5	3.46	13	0	14	31	1	0	0	0

(continued)

(continued)

YEAR	TEAM		WON	LOST	PCT	ER	ERA	INNINGS PITCHED	STRIKE-OUTS	WALKS	HITS ALLOWED	HRS ALLOWED	COMP. GAMES	SHUT-OUTS	SAVES
1890	Bos-P	0	1	1	0	1.000	1	4.50	2	2	2	1	0	0	0	0
1891	Cin-AA	0	3	0	1	.000	9	5.28	15 1/3	0	7	21	2	0	0	0
1892	Bos-N	0	1	0	0	—	1	1.50	6	0	4	8	0	0	0	0
Career average		0	2	0	0	.500	3	4.14	6 2/3	1	4	11	1	0	0	0
Cubs average		**0**	**1**	**0**	**0**	**.000**	**2**	**4.82**	**3**	**1**	**1**	**5**	**1**	**0**	**0**	**0**
Career total		0	12	2	2	.500	21	4.14	45 2/3	4	30	77	5	0	0	0
Cubs total		**0**	**4**	**0**	**1**	**.000**	**5**	**4.82**	**9 1/3**	**2**	**3**	**16**	**2**	**0**	**0**	**0**

Kelly, Robert Edward (Bob)
HEIGHT: 6'0"   RIGHTHANDER   BORN: 10/4/1927 CLEVELAND, OHIO

YEAR	TEAM	STARTS	GAMES	WON	LOST	PCT	ER	ERA	INNINGS PITCHED	STRIKE-OUTS	WALKS	HITS ALLOWED	HRS ALLOWED	COMP. GAMES	SHUT-OUTS	SAVES
1951	**ChC-N**	**11**	**35**	**7**	**4**	**.636**	**64**	**4.66**	**123 2/3**	**48**	**55**	**130**	**8**	**4**	**0**	**0**
1952	**ChC-N**	**15**	**31**	**4**	**9**	**.308**	**50**	**3.59**	**125 1/3**	**50**	**46**	**114**	**7**	**3**	**2**	**0**
1953	**ChC-N**	**0**	**14**	**0**	**1**	**.000**	**18**	**9.53**	**17**	**6**	**9**	**27**	**2**	**0**	**0**	**0**
1953	Cin-N	5	28	1	2	.333	32	4.34	66 1/3	29	26	71	7	0	0	2
1958	Cin-N	1	2	0	0	—	1	4.50	2	1	3	3	0	0	0	0
1958	Cle-A	3	13	0	2	.000	16	5.20	27 2/3	12	13	29	4	0	0	0
Career average		9	31	3	5	.400	45	4.50	90 2/3	37	38	94	7	2	1	1
Cubs average		**9**	**27**	**4**	**5**	**.440**	**44**	**4.47**	**88 2/3**	**35**	**37**	**90**	**6**	**2**	**1**	**0**
Career total		35	123	12	18	.400	181	4.50	362	146	152	374	28	7	2	2
Cubs total		**26**	**80**	**11**	**14**	**.440**	**132**	**4.47**	**266**	**104**	**110**	**271**	**17**	**7**	**2**	**0**

Kennedy, Theodore A. (Ted)
HEIGHT: 5'8"   RIGHTHANDER   BORN: 2/1865 HENRY, ILLINOIS   DIED: 10/31/1907 ST. LOUIS, MISSOURI

YEAR	TEAM	STARTS	GAMES	WON	LOST	PCT	ER	ERA	INNINGS PITCHED	STRIKE-OUTS	WALKS	HITS ALLOWED	HRS ALLOWED	COMP. GAMES	SHUT-OUTS	SAVES
1885	**ChN-N**	**9**	**9**	**7**	**2**	**.778**	**30**	**3.43**	**78 2/3**	**36**	**28**	**91**	**5**	**8**	**0**	**0**
1886	Phi-AA	19	20	5	15	.250	71	4.53	172 2/3	68	65	196	4	19	0	0
1886	Lou-AA	4	4	0	4	.000	19	5.34	32	14	16	53	1	4	0	0
Career average		16	17	6	11	.364	68	4.32	141 2/3	59	55	170	5	16	0	0
Cubs average		**9**	**9**	**7**	**2**	**.778**	**30**	**3.43**	**78 2/3**	**36**	**28**	**91**	**5**	**8**	**0**	**0**
Career total		32	33	12	21	.364	136	4.32	283 1/3	118	109	340	10	31	0	0
Cubs total		**9**	**9**	**7**	**2**	**.778**	**30**	**3.43**	**78 2/3**	**36**	**28**	**91**	**5**	**8**	**0**	**0**

Keough, Matthew Lon (Matt)
HEIGHT: 6'3"   RIGHTHANDER   BORN: 7/3/1955 POMONA, CALIFORNIA

YEAR	TEAM	STARTS	GAMES	WON	LOST	PCT	ER	ERA	INNINGS PITCHED	STRIKE-OUTS	WALKS	HITS ALLOWED	HRS ALLOWED	COMP. GAMES	SHUT-OUTS	SAVES
1977	Oak-A	6	7	1	3	.250	23	4.85	42 2/3	23	22	39	4	0	0	0
1978	Oak-A	32	32	8	15	.348	71	3.24	197 1/3	108	85	178	9	6	0	0
1979	Oak-A	28	30	2	17	.105	99	5.04	176 2/3	95	78	220	18	7	1	0
1980	Oak-A	32	34	16	13	.552	81	2.92	250	121	94	218	24	20	2	0
1981	Oak-A	19	19	10	6	.625	53	3.40	140 1/3	60	45	125	11	10	2	0
1982	Oak-A	34	34	11	18	.379	133	5.72	209 1/3	75	101	233	38	10	2	0
1983	Oak-A	4	14	2	3	.400	27	5.52	44	28	31	50	7	0	0	0
1983	NYY-A	12	12	3	4	.429	32	5.17	55 2/3	26	20	59	12	0	0	0
1985	StL-N	1	4	0	1	.000	5	4.50	10	10	4	10	0	0	0	0
1986	**ChC-N**	**2**	**19**	**2**	**2**	**.500**	**16**	**4.97**	**29**	**19**	**12**	**36**	**4**	**0**	**0**	**0**
1986	Hou-N	5	10	3	2	.600	12	3.09	35	25	18	22	5	0	0	0
Career average		19	24	6	9	.408	61	4.17	132 1/3	66	57	132	15	6	1	0
Cubs average		**2**	**19**	**2**	**2**	**.500**	**16**	**4.97**	**29**	**19**	**12**	**36**	**4**	**0**	**0**	**0**
Career total		175	215	58	84	.408	552	4.17	1190	590	510	1190	132	53	7	0
Cubs total		**2**	**19**	**2**	**2**	**.500**	**16**	**4.97**	**29**	**19**	**12**	**36**	**4**	**0**	**0**	**0**

Kilgus, Paul Nelson
HEIGHT: 6'1"   LEFTHANDER   BORN: 2/2/1962 BOWLING GREEN, KENTUCKY

YEAR	TEAM	STARTS	GAMES	WON	LOST	PCT	ER	ERA	INNINGS PITCHED	STRIKE-OUTS	WALKS	HITS ALLOWED	HRS ALLOWED	COMP. GAMES	SHUT-OUTS	SAVES
1987	Tex-A	12	25	2	7	.222	41	4.13	89 1/3	42	31	95	14	0	0	0
1988	Tex-A	32	32	12	15	.444	94	4.16	203 1/3	88	71	190	18	5	3	0
1989	**ChC-N**	**23**	**35**	**6**	**10**	**.375**	**71**	**4.39**	**145 2/3**	**61**	**49**	**164**	**9**	**0**	**0**	**2**
1990	Tor-A	0	11	0	0	—	11	6.06	16 1/3	7	7	19	2	0	0	0
1991	Bal-A	0	38	0	2	.000	35	5.08	62	32	24	60	8	0	0	1
1993	StL-N	1	22	1	0	1.000	2	0.63	28 2/3	21	8	18	1	0	0	1
Career average		11	27	4	6	.382	42	4.19	91	42	32	91	9	1	1	1
Cubs average		**23**	**35**	**6**	**10**	**.375**	**71**	**4.39**	**145 2/3**	**61**	**49**	**164**	**9**	**0**	**0**	**2**
Career total		68	163	21	34	.382	254	4.19	545 1/3	251	190	546	52	5	3	4
Cubs total		**23**	**35**	**6**	**10**	**.375**	**71**	**4.39**	**145 2/3**	**61**	**49**	**164**	**9**	**0**	**0**	**2**

Killen, Frank Bissell (Lefty)
HEIGHT: 6'1"   LEFTHANDER   BORN: 11/30/1870 PITTSBURGH, PENNSYLVANIA   DIED: 12/3/1939 PITTSBURGH, PENNSYLVANIA

YEAR	TEAM	STARTS	GAMES	WON	LOST	PCT	ER	ERA	INNINGS PITCHED	STRIKE-OUTS	WALKS	HITS ALLOWED	HRS ALLOWED	COMP. GAMES	SHUT-OUTS	SAVES
1891	Mil-AA	11	11	7	4	.636	18	1.68	96 2/3	38	51	73	1	11	2	0
1892	Was-N	52	60	28	26	.519	169	3.31	459 2/3	147	182	448	15	46	2	1
1893	Pit-N	48	55	34	10	.773	168	3.64	415	99	140	401	12	38	2	2
1894	Pit-N	28	28	14	10	.583	102	4.50	204	62	86	261	3	20	1	0
1895	Pit-N	11	13	7	6	.538	58	5.49	95	25	57	113	2	6	0	0
1896	Pit-N	50	52	30	17	.638	164	3.41	432 1/3	134	119	476	7	44	5	1
1897	Pit-N	41	42	17	21	.447	167	4.46	337 1/3	99	76	417	4	38	1	0
1898	Pit-N	23	23	10	11	.476	74	3.75	177 2/3	48	41	201	3	17	0	0
1898	Was-N	16	17	6	9	.400	51	3.58	128 1/3	43	29	149	4	15	0	0
1899	Was-N	2	2	0	2	.000	8	6.00	12	3	4	18	0	1	0	0
1899	Bos-N	12	12	7	5	.583	47	4.26	99 1/3	23	26	108	3	11	0	0
1900	**ChN-N**	**6**	**6**	**3**	**3**	**.500**	**28**	**4.67**	**54**	**4**	**11**	**65**	**1**	**6**	**0**	**0**
Career average		30	32	16	12	.568	105	3.78	251	73	82	273	6	25	1	0
Cubs average		**6**	**6**	**3**	**3**	**.500**	**28**	**4.67**	**54**	**4**	**11**	**65**	**1**	**6**	**0**	**0**
Career total		300	321	163	124	.568	1054	3.78	2511 1/3	725	822	2730	55	253	13	4
Cubs total		**6**	**6**	**3**	**3**	**.500**	**28**	**4.67**	**54**	**4**	**11**	**65**	**1**	**6**	**0**	**0**

Kilroy, Matthew Aloysius (Matt *or* Matches)
HEIGHT: 5'9"   LEFTHANDER   BORN: 6/21/1866 PHILADELPHIA, PENNSYLVANIA   DIED: 3/2/1940 PHILADELPHIA, PENNSYLVANIA

YEAR	TEAM	STARTS	GAMES	WON	LOST	PCT	ER	ERA	INNINGS PITCHED	STRIKE-OUTS	WALKS	HITS ALLOWED	HRS ALLOWED	COMP. GAMES	SHUT-OUTS	SAVES
1886	Bal-AA	68	68	29	34	.460	218	3.37	583	513	182	476	10	66	5	0
1887	Bal-AA	69	69	46	19	.708	201	3.07	589 1/3	217	157	742	9	66	6	0
1888	Bal-AA	40	40	17	21	.447	144	4.04	321	135	79	347	5	35	2	0
1889	Bal-AA	56	59	29	25	.537	152	2.85	480 2/3	217	142	476	8	55	5	0
1890	Bos-P	27	30	9	15	.375	103	4.26	217 2/3	48	87	268	14	18	0	1
1891	Cin-AA	6	7	1	4	.200	15	2.98	45 1/3	6	19	51	1	4	0	0
1892	Was-N	3	4	1	1	.500	7	2.39	26 1/3	1	15	20	0	2	0	0
1893	Lou-N	5	5	3	2	.600	35	9.00	35	4	23	57	2	5	1	0
1894	Lou-N	7	8	0	5	.000	16	3.89	37	11	20	46	2	3	0	0
1898	**ChN-N**	**11**	**13**	**6**	**6**	**.500**	**48**	**4.31**	**100 1/3**	**18**	**30**	**119**	**2**	**10**	**0**	**0**
Career average		29	30	14	13	.516	94	3.47	243 2/3	117	75	260	5	26	2	0
Cubs average		**11**	**13**	**6**	**6**	**.500**	**48**	**4.31**	**100 1/3**	**18**	**30**	**119**	**2**	**10**	**0**	**0**
Career total		292	303	141	132	.516	939	3.47	2435 2/3	1170	754	2602	53	264	19	1
Cubs total		**11**	**13**	**6**	**6**	**.500**	**48**	**4.31**	**100 1/3**	**18**	**30**	**119**	**2**	**10**	**0**	**0**

Kimball, Newell W. (Newt)
HEIGHT: 6'2"   RIGHTHANDER   BORN: 3/27/1915 LOGAN, UTAH   DIED: 3/22/2001 LAS VEGAS, NEVADA

YEAR	TEAM	STARTS	GAMES	WON	LOST	PCT	ER	ERA	INNINGS PITCHED	STRIKE-OUTS	WALKS	HITS ALLOWED	HRS ALLOWED	COMP. GAMES	SHUT-OUTS	SAVES
1937	**ChC-N**	**0**	**2**	**0**	**0**	**—**	**6**	**10.80**	**5**	**0**	**1**	**12**	**1**	**0**	**0**	**0**
1938	**ChC-N**	**0**	**1**	**0**	**0**	**—**	**1**	**9.00**	**1**	**1**	**0**	**3**	**0**	**0**	**0**	**0**
1940	Bro-N	0	21	3	1	.750	12	3.21	33 ⅔	21	15	29	2	0	0	1
1940	StL-N	1	2	1	0	1.000	4	2.57	14	6	6	11	1	1	0	0
1941	Bro-N	5	15	3	1	.750	21	3.63	52	17	29	43	0	1	0	1
1942	Bro-N	1	14	2	0	1.000	12	3.68	29 ⅓	8	19	27	0	0	0	0
1943	Bro-N	0	5	1	1	.500	2	1.64	11	2	5	9	0	0	0	1
1943	Phi-N	6	34	1	6	.143	41	4.12	89 ⅔	33	42	85	4	2	0	2
Career average	2	16	2	2	.550	17	3.78	39 ⅓	15	20	37	1	1	0	1
Cubs average	**0**	**2**	**0**	**0**	**—**	**4**	**10.50**	**3**	**1**	**1**	**8**	**1**	**0**	**0**	**0**
Career total	13	94	11	9	.550	99	3.78	235 ⅔	88	117	219	8	4	0	5
Cubs total	**0**	**3**	**0**	**0**	**—**	**7**	**10.50**	**6**	**1**	**1**	**15**	**1**	**0**	**0**	**0**

King, Raymond Keith (Ray)
HEIGHT: 6'1"   LEFTHANDER   BORN: 1/15/1974 CHICAGO, ILLINOIS

YEAR	TEAM	STARTS	GAMES	WON	LOST	PCT	ER	ERA	INNINGS PITCHED	STRIKE-OUTS	WALKS	HITS ALLOWED	HRS ALLOWED	COMP. GAMES	SHUT-OUTS	SAVES
1999	**ChC-N**	**0**	**10**	**0**	**0**	**—**	**7**	**5.91**	**10 ⅔**	**5**	**10**	**11**	**2**	**0**	**0**	**0**
2000	Mil-N	0	36	3	2	.600	4	1.26	28 ⅔	19	10	18	1	0	0	0
2001	Mil-N	0	82	0	4	.000	22	3.60	55	49	25	49	5	0	0	1
Career average	0	43	1	2	.333	11	3.15	31 ⅓	24	15	26	3	0	0	0
Cubs average	**0**	**10**	**0**	**0**	**—**	**7**	**5.91**	**10 ⅔**	**5**	**10**	**11**	**2**	**0**	**0**	**0**
Career total	0	128	3	6	.333	33	3.15	94 ⅓	73	45	78	8	0	0	1
Cubs total	**0**	**10**	**0**	**0**	**—**	**7**	**5.91**	**10 ⅔**	**5**	**10**	**11**	**2**	**0**	**0**	**0**

Kittridge, Malachi Jeddidah (Jedediah)
HEIGHT: 5'7"   RIGHTHANDER   BORN: 10/12/1869 CLINTON, MASSACHUSETTS   DIED: 6/23/1928 GARY, INDIANA

YEAR	TEAM	STARTS	GAMES	WON	LOST	PCT	ER	ERA	INNINGS PITCHED	STRIKE-OUTS	WALKS	HITS ALLOWED	HRS ALLOWED	COMP. GAMES	SHUT-OUTS	SAVES
1896	**ChN-N**	**0**	**1**	**0**	**0**	**—**	**1**	**5.40**	**1 ⅔**	**0**	**1**	**2**	**0**	**0**	**0**	**0**
Career average	0	1	0	0	—	1	5.40	1 ⅔	0	1	2	0	0	0	0
Cubs average	**0**	**1**	**0**	**0**	**—**	**1**	**5.40**	**1 ⅔**	**0**	**1**	**2**	**0**	**0**	**0**	**0**
Career total	0	1	0	0	—	1	5.40	1 ⅔	0	1	2	0	0	0	0
Cubs total	**0**	**1**	**0**	**0**	**—**	**1**	**5.40**	**1 ⅔**	**0**	**1**	**2**	**0**	**0**	**0**	**0**

Klippstein, John Calvin (Johnny)
HEIGHT: 6'1"   RIGHTHANDER   BORN: 10/17/1927 WASHINGTON, DISTRICT OF COLUMBIA

YEAR	TEAM	STARTS	GAMES	WON	LOST	PCT	ER	ERA	INNINGS PITCHED	STRIKE-OUTS	WALKS	HITS ALLOWED	HRS ALLOWED	COMP. GAMES	SHUT-OUTS	SAVES
1950	**ChC-N**	**11**	**33**	**2**	**9**	**.182**	**61**	**5.25**	**104 ⅔**	**51**	**64**	**112**	**9**	**3**	**0**	**1**
1951	**ChC-N**	**11**	**35**	**6**	**6**	**.500**	**59**	**4.29**	**123 ⅔**	**56**	**53**	**125**	**10**	**1**	**1**	**2**
1952	**ChC-N**	**25**	**41**	**9**	**14**	**.391**	**100**	**4.44**	**202 ⅔**	**110**	**89**	**208**	**17**	**7**	**2**	**3**
1953	**ChC-N**	**19**	**48**	**10**	**11**	**.476**	**90**	**4.83**	**167 ⅔**	**113**	**107**	**169**	**15**	**5**	**0**	**6**
1954	**ChC-N**	**21**	**36**	**4**	**11**	**.267**	**87**	**5.29**	**148**	**69**	**96**	**155**	**13**	**4**	**0**	**1**
1955	Cin-N	14	39	9	10	.474	52	3.39	138	68	60	120	13	3	2	0
1956	Cin-N	29	37	12	11	.522	96	4.09	211	86	82	219	26	11	0	1
1957	Cin-N	18	46	8	11	.421	82	5.05	146	99	68	146	17	3	0	3
1958	LA-N	4	12	3	2	.600	18	4.91	33	22	14	37	5	0	0	1
1958	LA-N	0	45	3	5	.375	38	3.80	90	73	44	81	12	0	0	9
1959	LA-N	0	28	4	0	1.000	30	5.91	45 ⅔	30	33	48	8	0	0	2
1960	Cle-A	0	49	5	5	.500	24	2.91	74 ⅓	46	35	53	8	0	0	14
1961	Was-A	1	42	2	2	.500	54	6.78	71 ⅔	41	43	83	13	0	0	0
1962	Cin-N	7	40	7	6	.538	54	4.47	108 ⅔	67	64	113	13	0	0	4
1963	Phi-N	1	49	5	6	.455	24	1.93	112	86	46	80	3	0	0	8

(continued)

(continued)

YEAR	TEAM	STARTS	GAMES	WON	LOST	PCT	ER	ERA	INNINGS PITCHED	STRIKE-OUTS	WALKS	HITS ALLOWED	HRS ALLOWED	COMP. GAMES	SHUT-OUTS	SAVES
1964	Phi-N	0	11	2	1	.667	10	4.03	22 ⅓	13	8	22	6	0	0	1
1964	Min-A	0	33	0	4	.000	10	1.97	45 ⅔	39	20	44	4	0	0	2
1965	Min-A	0	56	9	3	.750	19	2.24	76 ⅓	59	31	59	8	0	0	5
1966	Min-A	0	26	1	1	.500	15	3.40	39 ⅔	26	20	35	2	0	0	3
1967	Det-A	0	5	0	0	—	4	5.40	6 ⅔	4	1	6	1	0	0	0
Career average		9	40	6	7	.461	52	4.24	109 ⅓	64	54	106	11	2	0	4
Cubs average		**17**	**39**	**6**	**10**	**.378**	**79**	**4.79**	**149 ⅓**	**80**	**82**	**154**	**13**	**4**	**1**	**3**
Career total		161	711	101	118	.461	927	4.24	1967 ⅔	1158	978	1915	203	37	6	66
Cubs total		**87**	**193**	**31**	**51**	**.378**	**397**	**4.79**	**746 ⅔**	**399**	**409**	**769**	**64**	**20**	**3**	**13**

Knowles, Darold Duane

HEIGHT: 6'0" LEFTHANDER BORN: 12/9/1941 BRUNSWICK, MISSOURI

YEAR	TEAM	STARTS	GAMES	WON	LOST	PCT	ER	ERA	INNINGS PITCHED	STRIKE-OUTS	WALKS	HITS ALLOWED	HRS ALLOWED	COMP. GAMES	SHUT-OUTS	SAVES
1965	Bal-A	1	5	0	1	.000	15	9.20	14 ⅔	12	10	14	2	0	0	0
1966	Phi-N	0	69	6	5	.545	34	3.05	100 ⅓	88	46	98	4	0	0	13
1967	Was-A	1	61	6	8	.429	34	2.70	113 ⅓	85	52	91	5	0	0	14
1968	Was-A	0	32	1	1	.500	10	2.18	41 ⅓	37	12	38	0	0	0	4
1969	Was-A	0	53	9	2	.818	21	2.24	84 ⅓	59	31	73	8	0	0	13
1970	Was-A	0	71	2	14	.125	27	2.04	119 ⅓	71	58	100	4	0	0	27
1971	Was-A	0	12	2	2	.500	6	3.52	15 ⅓	16	6	17	2	0	0	2
1971	Oak-A	0	43	5	2	.714	21	3.59	52 ⅔	40	16	40	3	0	0	7
1972	Oak-A	0	54	5	1	.833	10	1.37	65 ⅔	36	37	49	1	0	0	11
1973	Oak-A	5	52	6	8	.429	34	3.09	99	46	49	87	7	1	1	9
1974	Oak-A	1	45	3	3	.500	25	4.22	53 ⅓	18	35	61	6	0	0	3
1975	**ChC-N**	**0**	**58**	**6**	**9**	**.400**	**57**	**5.81**	**88 ⅓**	**63**	**36**	**107**	**3**	**0**	**0**	**15**
1976	**ChC-N**	**0**	**58**	**5**	**7**	**.417**	**23**	**2.89**	**71 ⅔**	**39**	**22**	**61**	**6**	**0**	**0**	**9**
1977	Tex-A	0	42	5	2	.714	18	3.22	50 ⅓	14	23	50	3	0	0	4
1978	Mon-N	0	60	3	3	.500	19	2.38	72	34	30	63	5	0	0	6
1979	StL-N	0	48	2	5	.286	22	4.07	48 ⅔	22	17	54	5	0	0	6
1980	StL-N	0	2	0	1	.000	2	10.80	1 ⅔	1	0	3	1	0	0	0
Career average		1	48	4	5	.471	24	3.12	68 ⅓	43	30	63	4	0	0	9
Cubs average		**0**	**58**	**6**	**8**	**.407**	**40**	**4.50**	**80**	**51**	**29**	**84**	**5**	**0**	**0**	**12**
Career total		8	765	66	74	.471	378	3.12	1092	681	480	1006	65	1	1	143
Cubs total		**0**	**116**	**11**	**16**	**.407**	**80**	**4.50**	**160**	**102**	**58**	**168**	**9**	**0**	**0**	**24**

Koestner, Elmer Joseph (Bob)

HEIGHT: 6'1" RIGHTHANDER BORN: 11/30/1885 PIPER CITY, ILLINOIS DIED: 10/27/1959 FAIRBURY, ILLINOIS

YEAR	TEAM	STARTS	GAMES	WON	LOST	PCT	ER	ERA	INNINGS PITCHED	STRIKE-OUTS	WALKS	HITS ALLOWED	HRS ALLOWED	COMP. GAMES	SHUT-OUTS	SAVES
1910	Cle-A	13	27	5	10	.333	49	3.04	145	44	63	145	0	8	1	2
1914	**ChC-N**	**0**	**4**	**0**	**0**	**—**	**2**	**2.84**	**6 ⅓**	**6**	**4**	**6**	**0**	**0**	**0**	**0**
1914	Cin-N	1	5	0	0	—	9	4.42	18 ⅓	6	9	18	0	0	0	0
Career average		7	18	3	5	.333	30	3.18	85	28	38	85	0	4	1	1
Cubs average		**0**	**4**	**0**	**0**	**—**	**2**	**2.84**	**6 ⅓**	**6**	**4**	**6**	**0**	**0**	**0**	**0**
Career total		14	36	5	10	.333	60	3.18	169 ⅔	56	76	169	0	8	1	2
Cubs total		**0**	**4**	**0**	**0**	**—**	**2**	**2.84**	**6 ⅓**	**6**	**4**	**6**	**0**	**0**	**0**	**0**

Koonce, Calvin Lee (Cal)

HEIGHT: 6'1" RIGHTHANDER BORN: 11/18/1940 FAYETTEVILLE, NORTH CAROLINA DIED: 10/28/1993 WINSTON-SALEM, NORTH CAROLINA

YEAR	TEAM	STARTS	GAMES	WON	LOST	PCT	ER	ERA	INNINGS PITCHED	STRIKE-OUTS	WALKS	HITS ALLOWED	HRS ALLOWED	COMP. GAMES	SHUT-OUTS	SAVES
1962	**ChC-N**	**30**	**35**	**10**	**10**	**.500**	**84**	**3.97**	**190 ⅔**	**84**	**86**	**200**	**17**	**3**	**1**	**0**
1963	**ChC-N**	**13**	**21**	**2**	**6**	**.250**	**37**	**4.58**	**72 ⅔**	**44**	**32**	**75**	**9**	**0**	**0**	**0**
1964	**ChC-N**	**2**	**6**	**3**	**0**	**1.000**	**7**	**2.03**	**31**	**17**	**7**	**30**	**1**	**0**	**0**	**0**
1965	**ChC-N**	**23**	**38**	**7**	**9**	**.438**	**71**	**3.69**	**173**	**88**	**52**	**181**	**17**	**3**	**1**	**0**
1966	**ChC-N**	**5**	**45**	**5**	**5**	**.500**	**46**	**3.81**	**108 ⅔**	**65**	**35**	**113**	**13**	**0**	**0**	**2**
1967	**ChC-N**	**0**	**34**	**2**	**2**	**.500**	**26**	**4.59**	**51**	**28**	**21**	**52**	**2**	**0**	**0**	**2**
1967	NYM-N	6	11	3	3	.500	14	2.80	45	24	7	45	2	2	1	0
1968	NYM-N	2	55	6	4	.600	26	2.41	97	50	32	80	4	0	0	11

(continued)

(Koonce, continued)

YEAR	TEAM	STARTS	GAMES	WON	LOST	PCT	ER	ERA	INNINGS PITCHED	STRIKE-OUTS	WALKS	HITS ALLOWED	HRS ALLOWED	COMP. GAMES	SHUT-OUTS	SAVES
1969	NYM-N	0	40	6	3	.667	46	4.99	83	48	42	85	8	0	0	7
1970	NYM-N	0	13	0	2	.000	8	3.27	22	10	14	25	2	0	0	0
1970	Bos-A	8	23	3	4	.429	30	3.54	76⅓	37	29	64	7	1	0	2
1971	Bos-A	1	13	0	1	.000	13	5.57	21	9	11	22	3	0	0	0
Career average		9	33	5	5	.490	41	3.78	97	50	37	97	9	1	0	2
Cubs average		12	30	5	5	.475	45	3.89	104⅔	54	39	109	10	1	0	1
Career total		90	334	47	49	.490	408	3.78	971⅓	504	368	972	85	9	3	24
Cubs total		73	179	29	32	.475	271	3.89	627	326	233	651	59	6	2	4

Korwan, James (Jim *or* Long Jim)

HEIGHT: 6'1"   RIGHTHANDER   BORN: 3/4/1874 BROOKLYN, NEW YORK   DIED: 7/24/1899 BROOKLYN, NEW YORK

YEAR	TEAM	STARTS	GAMES	WON	LOST	PCT	ER	ERA	INNINGS PITCHED	STRIKE-OUTS	WALKS	HITS ALLOWED	HRS ALLOWED	COMP. GAMES	SHUT-OUTS	SAVES
1894	Bro-N	0	1	0	1	.000	8	14.40	5	2	5	9	1	0	0	0
1897	ChN-N	4	5	1	3	.250	22	5.82	34	12	28	47	1	3	0	0
Career average		2	3	1	2	.200	15	6.92	19⅔	7	17	28	1	2	0	0
Cubs average		4	5	1	3	.250	22	5.82	34	12	28	47	1	3	0	0
Career total		4	6	1	4	.200	30	6.92	39	14	33	56	2	3	0	0
Cubs total		4	5	1	3	.250	22	5.82	34	12	28	47	1	3	0	0

Kowalik, Fabian Lorenz

HEIGHT: 5'11"   RIGHTHANDER   BORN: 4/22/1908 FALLS CITY, TEXAS   DIED: 8/14/1954 KARNES CITY, TEXAS

YEAR	TEAM	STARTS	GAMES	WON	LOST	PCT	ER	ERA	INNINGS PITCHED	STRIKE-OUTS	WALKS	HITS ALLOWED	HRS ALLOWED	COMP. GAMES	SHUT-OUTS	SAVES
1932	CWS-A	1	2	0	1	.000	8	6.97	10⅓	2	4	16	2	0	0	1
1935	ChC-N	2	20	2	2	.500	27	4.42	55	20	19	60	2	1	0	1
1936	ChC-N	0	6	0	2	.000	12	6.75	16	1	7	24	1	0	0	0
1936	Phi-N	8	22	1	5	.167	46	5.38	77	19	31	100	5	2	0	0
1936	Bos-N	1	1	0	1	.000	8	8.00	9	0	2	18	0	1	0	0
Career average		4	17	1	4	.214	34	5.43	55⅔	14	21	73	3	1	0	1
Cubs average		1	13	1	2	.333	20	4.94	35⅔	11	13	42	2	1	0	1
Career total		12	51	3	11	.214	101	5.43	167⅓	42	63	218	10	1	0	2
Cubs total		2	26	2	4	.333	39	4.94	71	21	26	84	3	1	0	2

Kraemer, Joseph Wayne (Joe)

HEIGHT: 6'2"   LEFTHANDER   BORN: 9/10/1964 OLYMPIA, WASHINGTON

YEAR	TEAM	STARTS	GAMES	WON	LOST	PCT	ER	ERA	INNINGS PITCHED	STRIKE-OUTS	WALKS	HITS ALLOWED	HRS ALLOWED	COMP. GAMES	SHUT-OUTS	SAVES
1989	ChC-N	1	1	0	1	.000	2	4.91	3⅔	5	2	7	0	0	0	0
1990	ChC-N	0	18	0	0	—	20	7.20	25	16	14	31	2	0	0	0
Career average		1	10	0	1	.000	11	6.91	14⅓	11	8	19	1	0	0	0
Cubs average		1	10	0	1	.000	11	6.91	14⅓	11	8	19	1	0	0	0
Career total		1	19	0	1	.000	22	6.91	28⅔	21	16	38	2	0	0	0
Cubs total		1	19	0	1	.000	22	6.91	28⅔	21	16	38	2	0	0	0

Kramer, Randall John (Randy)

HEIGHT: 6'2"   RIGHTHANDER   BORN: 9/20/1960 PALO ALTO, CALIFORNIA

YEAR	TEAM	STARTS	GAMES	WON	LOST	PCT	ER	ERA	INNINGS PITCHED	STRIKE-OUTS	WALKS	HITS ALLOWED	HRS ALLOWED	COMP. GAMES	SHUT-OUTS	SAVES
1988	Pit-N	1	5	1	2	.333	6	5.40	10	7	1	12	1	0	0	0
1989	Pit-N	15	35	5	9	.357	49	3.96	111⅓	52	61	90	10	1	1	2
1990	Pit-N	2	12	0	1	.000	14	4.91	25⅔	15	9	27	3	0	0	0
1990	ChC-N	2	10	0	2	.000	9	3.98	20⅓	12	12	20	3	0	0	0
1992	Sea-A	4	4	0	1	.000	14	7.71	16⅓	6	7	30	2	0	0	0
Career average		6	17	2	4	.286	23	4.51	46	23	23	45	5	0	0	1
Cubs average		2	10	0	2	.000	9	3.98	20⅓	12	12	20	3	0	0	0
Career total		24	66	6	15	.286	92	4.51	183⅔	92	90	179	19	1	1	2
Cubs total		2	10	0	2	.000	9	3.98	20⅓	12	12	20	3	0	0	0

Kravec, Kenneth Peter (Ken)
HEIGHT: 6'2" LEFTHANDER BORN: 7/29/1951 CLEVELAND, OHIO

YEAR	TEAM	STARTS	GAMES	WON	LOST	PCT	ER	ERA	INNINGS PITCHED	STRIKE-OUTS	WALKS	HITS ALLOWED	HRS ALLOWED	COMP. GAMES	SHUT-OUTS	SAVES
1975	CWS-A	1	2	0	1	.000	3	6.23	4 1/3	1	8	1	0	0	0	0
1976	CWS-A	8	9	1	5	.167	27	4.89	49 2/3	38	32	49	3	1	0	0
1977	CWS-A	25	26	11	8	.579	76	4.10	166 2/3	125	57	161	12	6	1	0
1978	CWS-A	30	30	11	16	.407	92	4.08	203	154	95	188	22	7	2	0
1979	CWS-A	35	36	15	13	.536	104	3.74	250	132	111	208	20	10	3	1
1980	CWS-A	15	20	3	6	.333	63	6.94	81 2/3	37	44	100	13	0	0	0
1981	**ChC-N**	**12**	**24**	**1**	**6**	**.143**	**44**	**5.06**	**78 1/3**	**50**	**39**	**80**	**13**	**0**	**0**	**0**
1982	**ChC-N**	**2**	**13**	**1**	**1**	**.500**	**17**	**6.12**	**25**	**20**	**18**	**27**	**3**	**0**	**0**	**0**
Career average		16	20	5	7	.434	53	4.47	107 1/3	70	51	102	10	3	1	0
Cubs average		**7**	**19**	**1**	**4**	**.222**	**31**	**5.31**	**51 2/3**	**35**	**29**	**54**	**4**	**0**	**0**	**0**
Career total		128	160	43	56	.434	426	4.47	858 2/3	557	404	814	78	24	6	1
Cubs total		**14**	**37**	**2**	**7**	**.222**	**61**	**5.31**	**103 1/3**	**70**	**57**	**107**	**8**	**0**	**0**	**0**

Kremmel, James Louis (Jim)
HEIGHT: 6'0" LEFTHANDER BORN: 2/28/1948 BELLEVILLE, ILLINOIS

YEAR	TEAM	STARTS	GAMES	WON	LOST	PCT	ER	ERA	INNINGS PITCHED	STRIKE-OUTS	WALKS	HITS ALLOWED	HRS ALLOWED	COMP. GAMES	SHUT-OUTS	SAVES
1973	Tex-A	2	4	0	2	.000	9	9.00	9	6	6	15	1	0	0	0
1974	**ChC-N**	**2**	**23**	**0**	**2**	**.000**	**18**	**5.23**	**31**	**22**	**18**	**37**	**3**	**0**	**0**	**0**
Career average		2	14	0	2	.000	14	6.08	20	14	12	26	2	0	0	0
Cubs average		**2**	**23**	**0**	**2**	**.000**	**18**	**5.23**	**31**	**22**	**18**	**37**	**3**	**0**	**0**	**0**
Career total		4	27	0	4	.000	27	6.08	40	28	24	52	4	0	0	0
Cubs total		**2**	**23**	**0**	**2**	**.000**	**18**	**5.23**	**31**	**22**	**18**	**37**	**3**	**0**	**0**	**0**

Krock, August H. (Gus)
HEIGHT: 6'0" RIGHTHANDER BORN: 5/9/1866 MILWAUKEE, WISCONSIN DIED: 3/22/1905 PASADENA, CALIFORNIA

YEAR	TEAM	STARTS	GAMES	WON	LOST	PCT	ER	ERA	INNINGS PITCHED	STRIKE-OUTS	WALKS	HITS ALLOWED	HRS ALLOWED	COMP. GAMES	SHUT-OUTS	SAVES
1888	**ChN-N**	**39**	**39**	**25**	**14**	**.641**	**92**	**2.44**	**339 2/3**	**161**	**45**	**295**	**20**	**39**	**4**	**0**
1889	**ChN-N**	**7**	**7**	**3**	**3**	**.500**	**33**	**4.90**	**60 2/3**	**16**	**14**	**86**	**10**	**5**	**0**	**0**
1889	Ind-N	4	4	2	2	.500	26	7.31	32	10	14	48	2	3	0	0
1889	WaN-N	6	6	2	4	.333	28	5.25	48	17	22	65	1	6	0	0
1890	Buf-P	3	4	0	3	.000	17	6.12	25	5	15	43	1	3	0	0
Career average		20	20	11	9	.552	65	3.49	168 1/3	70	37	179	11	19	1	0
Cubs average		**23**	**23**	**14**	**9**	**.622**	**63**	**2.81**	**200 1/3**	**89**	**30**	**191**	**15**	**22**	**2**	**0**
Career total		59	60	32	26	.552	196	3.49	505 1/3	209	110	537	34	56	4	0
Cubs total		**46**	**46**	**28**	**17**	**.622**	**125**	**2.81**	**400 1/3**	**177**	**59**	**381**	**30**	**44**	**4**	**0**

Kroh, Floyd Myron (Rube)
HEIGHT: 6'2" LEFTHANDER BORN: 8/25/1886 FRIENDSHIP, NEW YORK DIED: 3/17/1944 NEW ORLEANS, LOUISIANA

YEAR	TEAM	STARTS	GAMES	WON	LOST	PCT	ER	ERA	INNINGS PITCHED	STRIKE-OUTS	WALKS	HITS ALLOWED	HRS ALLOWED	COMP. GAMES	SHUT-OUTS	SAVES
1906	Bos-A	1	1	1	0	1.000	0	0.00	9	5	4	2	0	1	1	0
1907	Bos-A	5	7	0	4	.000	10	2.62	34 1/3	8	8	33	0	1	0	0
1908	**ChC-N**	**1**	**2**	**0**	**0**	**—**	**2**	**1.50**	**12**	**11**	**4**	**9**	**0**	**1**	**0**	**0**
1909	**ChC-N**	**13**	**17**	**9**	**4**	**.692**	**22**	**1.65**	**120 1/3**	**51**	**30**	**97**	**2**	**10**	**2**	**0**
1910	**ChC-N**	**4**	**6**	**3**	**1**	**.750**	**17**	**4.46**	**34 1/3**	**16**	**15**	**33**	**1**	**2**	**0**	**0**
1912	Bos-N	1	3	0	0	—	4	5.68	6 1/3	1	6	8	0	0	0	0
Career average		4	6	2	2	.591	9	2.29	36	15	11	30	1	2	1	0
Cubs average		**6**	**8**	**4**	**2**	**.706**	**14**	**2.21**	**55 2/3**	**26**	**16**	**46**	**1**	**4**	**1**	**0**
Career total		25	36	13	9	.591	55	2.29	216 1/3	92	67	182	3	13	3	0
Cubs total		**18**	**25**	**12**	**5**	**.706**	**41**	**2.21**	**166 2/3**	**78**	**49**	**139**	**3**	**11**	**2**	**0**

Krukow, Michael Edward (Mike)
HEIGHT: 6'5" RIGHTHANDER BORN: 1/21/1952 LONG BEACH, CALIFORNIA

YEAR	TEAM	STARTS	GAMES	WON	LOST	PCT	ER	ERA	INNINGS PITCHED	STRIKE-OUTS	WALKS	HITS ALLOWED	HRS ALLOWED	COMP. GAMES	SHUT-OUTS	SAVES
1976	ChC-N	0	2	0	0	—	4	8.31	4 1/3	1	2	6	0	0	0	0
1977	ChC-N	33	34	8	14	.364	84	4.40	172	106	61	195	16	1	1	0
1978	ChC-N	20	27	9	3	.750	60	3.91	138	81	53	125	11	3	1	0
1979	ChC-N	28	28	9	9	.500	77	4.21	164 2/3	119	81	172	13	0	0	0
1980	ChC-N	34	34	10	15	.400	100	4.39	205	130	80	200	13	3	0	0
1981	ChC-N	25	25	9	9	.500	59	3.68	144 1/3	101	55	146	11	2	1	0
1982	Phi-N	33	33	13	11	.542	72	3.12	208	138	82	211	8	7	2	0
1983	SF-N	31	31	11	11	.500	81	3.95	184 1/3	136	76	189	17	2	1	0
1984	SF-N	33	35	11	12	.478	101	4.56	199 1/3	141	78	234	22	3	1	1
1985	SF-N	28	28	8	11	.421	73	3.38	194 2/3	150	49	176	19	6	1	0
1986	SF-N	34	34	20	9	.690	83	3.05	245	178	55	204	24	10	2	0
1987	SF-N	28	30	5	6	.455	87	4.80	163	104	46	182	24	3	0	0
1988	SF-N	20	20	7	4	.636	49	3.54	124 2/3	75	31	111	13	1	0	0
1989	SF-N	8	8	4	3	.571	19	3.98	43	18	18	37	5	0	0	0
Career average		25	26	9	8	.515	68	3.90	156 1/3	106	55	156	14	3	1	0
Cubs average		**23**	**25**	**8**	**8**	**.474**	**64**	**4.17**	**138**	**90**	**55**	**141**	**11**	**2**	**1**	**0**
Career total		355	369	124	117	.515	949	3.90	2190 1/3	1478	767	2188	196	41	10	1
Cubs total		**140**	**150**	**45**	**50**	**.474**	**384**	**4.17**	**828 1/3**	**538**	**332**	**844**	**64**	**9**	**3**	**0**

Kush, Emil Benedict (Kuputa)
HEIGHT: 5'11" RIGHTHANDER BORN: 11/4/1916 CHICAGO, ILLINOIS DIED: 11/26/1969 RIVER GROVE, ILLINOIS

YEAR	TEAM	STARTS	GAMES	WON	LOST	PCT	ER	ERA	INNINGS PITCHED	STRIKE-OUTS	WALKS	HITS ALLOWED	HRS ALLOWED	COMP. GAMES	SHUT-OUTS	SAVES
1941	ChC-N	0	2	0	0	—	1	2.25	4	2	0	2	0	0	0	0
1942	ChC-N	0	1	0	0	—	0	0.00	2	1	1	1	0	0	0	2
1946	ChC-N	6	40	9	2	.818	44	3.05	129 2/3	50	43	120	4	1	0	5
1947	ChC-N	1	47	8	3	.727	34	3.36	91	44	53	80	8	1	0	3
1948	ChC-N	1	34	1	4	.200	35	4.38	72	31	37	70	5	0	0	2
1949	ChC-N	0	26	3	3	.500	20	3.78	47 2/3	22	24	51	7	0	0	2
Career average		1	25	4	2	.636	22	3.48	57 2/3	25	26	54	4	0	0	2
Cubs average		**1**	**25**	**4**	**2**	**.636**	**22**	**3.48**	**57 2/3**	**25**	**26**	**54**	**4**	**0**	**0**	**2**
Career total		8	150	21	12	.636	134	3.48	346 1/3	150	158	324	24	2	1	12
Cubs total		**8**	**150**	**21**	**12**	**.636**	**134**	**3.48**	**346 1/3**	**150**	**158**	**324**	**24**	**2**	**1**	**12**

Lade, Doyle Marion (Porky)
HEIGHT: 5'10" RIGHTHANDER BORN: 2/17/1921 FAIRBURY, NEBRASKA DIED: 5/18/2000 LINCOLN, NEBRASKA

YEAR	TEAM	STARTS	GAMES	WON	LOST	PCT	ER	ERA	INNINGS PITCHED	STRIKE-OUTS	WALKS	HITS ALLOWED	HRS ALLOWED	COMP. GAMES	SHUT-OUTS	SAVES
1946	ChC-N	2	3	0	2	.000	7	4.11	15 1/3	8	3	15	0	0	0	0
1947	ChC-N	25	34	11	10	.524	82	3.94	187 1/3	62	79	202	15	7	1	0
1948	ChC-N	12	19	5	6	.455	39	4.02	87 1/3	29	31	99	4	6	0	0
1949	ChC-N	13	36	4	5	.444	72	5.00	129 2/3	43	58	141	14	5	1	1
1950	ChC-N	12	34	5	6	.455	62	4.74	117 2/3	36	50	126	14	2	0	2
Career average		13	25	5	6	.463	52	4.39	107 1/3	36	44	117	9	4	0	1
Cubs average		**13**	**25**	**5**	**6**	**.463**	**52**	**4.39**	**107 1/3**	**36**	**44**	**117**	**9**	**4**	**0**	**1**
Career total		64	126	25	29	.463	262	4.39	537 1/3	178	221	583	47	20	2	3
Cubs total		**64**	**126**	**25**	**29**	**.463**	**262**	**4.39**	**537 1/3**	**178**	**221**	**583**	**47**	**20**	**2**	**3**

Lamabe, John Alexander (Jack *or* Tomatoes)
HEIGHT: 6'1" RIGHTHANDER BORN: 10/3/1936 FARMINGDALE, NEW YORK

YEAR	TEAM	STARTS	GAMES	WON	LOST	PCT	ER	ERA	INNINGS PITCHED	STRIKE-OUTS	WALKS	HITS ALLOWED	HRS ALLOWED	COMP. GAMES	SHUT-OUTS	SAVES
1962	Pit-N	0	46	3	1	.750	25	2.88	78	56	40	70	4	0	0	2
1963	Bos-A	2	65	7	4	.636	53	3.15	151 1/3	93	46	139	8	0	0	6
1964	Bos-A	25	39	9	13	.409	116	5.89	177 1/3	109	57	235	25	3	0	1
1965	Bos-A	0	14	0	3	.000	23	8.17	25 1/3	17	14	34	5	0	0	0
1965	Hou-N	2	3	0	2	.000	6	4.26	12 2/3	6	3	17	3	0	0	0
1966	CWS-A	17	34	7	9	.438	53	3.93	121 1/3	67	35	116	9	3	2	0

(continued)

(continued)

YEAR	TEAM	STARTS	GAMES	WON	LOST	PCT	ER	ERA	INNINGS PITCHED	STRIKE-OUTS	WALKS	HITS ALLOWED	HRS ALLOWED	COMP. GAMES	SHUT-OUTS	SAVES
1967	CWS-A	0	3	1	0	1.000	1	1.80	5	3	1	7	0	0	0	0
1967	NYM-N	2	16	0	3	.000	14	3.98	31 2/3	23	8	24	4	0	0	1
1967	StL-N	1	23	3	4	.429	15	2.83	47 2/3	30	10	43	2	1	1	4
1968	**ChC-N**	**0**	**42**	**3**	**2**	**.600**	**29**	**4.26**	**61 1/3**	**30**	**24**	**68**	**7**	**0**	**0**	**1**
Career average		7	41	5	6	.446	48	4.24	101 2/3	62	34	108	10	1	0	2
Cubs average		**0**	**42**	**3**	**2**	**.600**	**29**	**4.26**	**61 1/3**	**30**	**24**	**68**	**7**	**0**	**0**	**1**
Career total		49	285	33	41	.446	335	4.24	711 2/3	434	238	753	67	7	3	15
Cubs total		**0**	**42**	**3**	**2**	**.600**	**29**	**4.26**	**61 1/3**	**30**	**24**	**68**	**7**	**0**	**0**	**1**

Lamp, Dennis Patrick

HEIGHT: 6'4" RIGHTHANDER BORN: 9/23/1952 LOS ANGELES, CALIFORNIA

YEAR	TEAM	STARTS	GAMES	WON	LOST	PCT	ER	ERA	INNINGS PITCHED	STRIKE-OUTS	WALKS	HITS ALLOWED	HRS ALLOWED	COMP. GAMES	SHUT-OUTS	SAVES
1977	ChC-N	3	11	0	2	.000	21	6.30	30	12	8	43	3	0	0	0
1978	ChC-N	36	37	7	15	.318	82	3.30	223 2/3	73	56	221	3	0	0	0
1979	ChC-N	32	38	11	10	.524	78	3.50	200 1/3	86	46	223	16	6	3	0
1980	ChC-N	37	41	10	14	.417	117	5.20	202 2/3	83	82	259	14	6	1	0
1981	CWS-A	10	27	7	6	.538	34	2.41	127	71	43	103	4	2	1	0
1982	CWS-A	27	44	11	8	.579	84	3.99	189 2/3	78	59	206	9	3	0	5
1983	CWS-A	5	49	7	7	.500	48	3.71	116 1/3	44	29	123	6	1	0	15
1984	Tor-A	4	56	8	8	.500	43	4.55	85	45	38	97	6	0	0	15
1985	Tor-A	1	53	11	0	1.000	39	3.32	105 2/3	68	27	96	9	0	0	9
1986	Tor-A	2	40	2	6	.250	41	5.05	73	30	23	93	7	0	0	2
1987	Oak-A	5	36	1	3	.250	32	5.08	56 2/3	36	22	76	5	0	0	2
1988	Bos-A	0	46	7	6	.538	32	3.48	82 2/3	49	19	92	3	0	0	0
1989	Bos-A	0	42	4	2	.667	29	2.32	112 1/3	61	27	96	4	0	0	2
1990	Bos-A	1	47	3	5	.375	55	4.68	105 2/3	49	30	114	10	0	0	0
1991	Bos-A	0	51	6	3	.667	48	4.70	92	57	31	100	8	0	0	0
1992	Pit-N	0	21	1	1	.500	16	5.14	28	15	9	33	3	0	0	0
Career average		10	40	6	6	.500	50	3.93	114 1/3	54	34	123	8	1	0	2
Cubs average		**27**	**32**	**7**	**10**	**.406**	**75**	**4.08**	**164 1/3**	**64**	**48**	**187**	**12**	**4**	**1**	**0**
Career total		163	639	96	96	.500	799	3.93	1830 2/3	857	549	1975	122	21	7	35
Cubs total		**108**	**127**	**28**	**41**	**.406**	**298**	**4.08**	**656 2/3**	**254**	**192**	**746**	**49**	**14**	**5**	**0**

Lancaster, Lester Wayne (Les)

HEIGHT: 6'2" RIGHTHANDER BORN: 4/21/1962 DALLAS, TEXAS

YEAR	TEAM	STARTS	GAMES	WON	LOST	PCT	ER	ERA	INNINGS PITCHED	STRIKE-OUTS	WALKS	HITS ALLOWED	HRS ALLOWED	COMP. GAMES	SHUT-OUTS	SAVES
1987	ChC-N	18	27	8	3	.727	72	4.90	132 1/3	78	51	138	14	0	0	0
1988	ChC-N	3	44	4	6	.400	36	3.78	85 2/3	36	34	89	4	1	0	5
1989	ChC-N	0	42	4	2	.667	11	1.36	72 2/3	56	15	60	2	0	0	8
1990	ChC-N	6	55	9	5	.643	56	4.62	109	65	40	121	11	1	1	6
1991	ChC-N	11	64	9	7	.563	61	3.52	156	102	49	150	13	1	0	3
1992	Det-A	1	41	3	4	.429	61	6.33	86 2/3	35	51	101	11	0	0	0
1993	StL-N	0	50	4	1	.800	20	2.93	61 1/3	36	21	56	5	0	0	0
Career average		6	46	6	4	.594	45	4.05	100 2/3	58	37	102	9	0	0	3
Cubs average		**8**	**46**	**7**	**5**	**.596**	**47**	**3.82**	**111**	**67**	**38**	**112**	**9**	**1**	**0**	**4**
Career total		39	323	41	28	.594	317	4.05	703 2/3	408	261	715	60	3	1	22
Cubs total		**38**	**232**	**34**	**23**	**.596**	**236**	**3.82**	**555 2/3**	**337**	**189**	**558**	**44**	**3**	**1**	**22**

Landrum, Thomas William (Bill)

HEIGHT: 6'2" RIGHTHANDER BORN: 8/17/1957 COLUMBIA, SOUTH CAROLINA

YEAR	TEAM	STARTS	GAMES	WON	LOST	PCT	ER	ERA	INNINGS PITCHED	STRIKE-OUTS	WALKS	HITS ALLOWED	HRS ALLOWED	COMP. GAMES	SHUT-OUTS	SAVES
1986	Cin-N	0	10	0	0	—	10	6.75	13 1/3	14	4	23	0	0	0	0
1987	Cin-N	2	44	3	2	.600	34	4.71	65	42	34	68	3	0	0	2
1988	**ChC-N**	**0**	**7**	**1**	**0**	**1.000**	**8**	**5.84**	**12 1/3**	**6**	**3**	**19**	**1**	**0**	**0**	**0**
1989	Pit-N	0	56	2	3	.400	15	1.67	81	51	28	60	2	0	0	26
1990	Pit-N	0	54	7	3	.700	17	2.13	71 2/3	39	21	69	4	0	0	13
1991	Pit-N	0	61	4	4	.500	27	3.18	76 1/3	45	19	76	4	0	0	17

(continued)

(Landrum, continued)

YEAR	TEAM		GAMES	WON	LOST	PCT	ER	ERA	INNINGS PITCHED	STRIKE-OUTS	WALKS	HITS ALLOWED	HRS ALLOWED	COMP. GAMES	SHUT-OUTS	SAVES
1992	Mon-N	0	18	1	1	.500	16	7.20	20	7	9	27	3	0	0	0
1993	Cin-N	0	18	0	2	.000	9	3.74	21 ⅔	14	6	18	1	0	0	0
Career average		0	34	2	2	.545	17	3.39	45 ⅓	27	16	45	2	0	0	7
Cubs average		**0**	**7**	**1**	**0**	**1.000**	**8**	**5.84**	**12 ⅓**	**6**	**3**	**19**	**1**	**0**	**0**	**0**
Career total		2	268	18	15	.545	136	3.39	361 ⅓	218	124	360	18	0	0	58
Cubs total		**0**	**7**	**1**	**0**	**1.000**	**8**	**5.84**	**12 ⅓**	**6**	**3**	**19**	**1**	**0**	**0**	**0**

Lanfranconi, Walter Oswald (Walt)

HEIGHT: 5'7"   RIGHTHANDER   BORN: 11/9/1916 BARRE, VERMONT   DIED: 8/18/1986 BARRE, VERMONT

YEAR	TEAM	STARTS	GAMES	WON	LOST	PCT	ER	ERA	INNINGS PITCHED	STRIKE-OUTS	WALKS	HITS ALLOWED	HRS ALLOWED	COMP. GAMES	SHUT-OUTS	SAVES
1941	**ChC-N**	1	2	0	1	.000	2	3.00	6	1	2	7	0	0	0	0
1947	Bos-N	4	36	4	4	.500	21	2.95	64	18	27	65	2	1	0	1
Career average		3	19	2	3	.444	12	2.96	35	10	15	36	1	1	0	1
Cubs average		**1**	**2**	**0**	**1**	**.000**	**2**	**3.00**	**6**	**1**	**2**	**7**	**0**	**0**	**0**	**0**
Career total		5	38	4	5	.444	23	2.96	70	19	29	72	2	1	0	1
Cubs total		**1**	**2**	**0**	**1**	**.000**	**2**	**3.00**	**6**	**1**	**2**	**7**	**0**	**0**	**0**	**0**

Larkin, Frank S. (Terry)

HEIGHT: —   RIGHTHANDER   BORN: — BROOKLYN, NEW YORK   DIED: 9/16/1894 BROOKLYN, NEW YORK

YEAR	TEAM	STARTS	GAMES	WON	LOST	PCT	ER	ERA	INNINGS PITCHED	STRIKE-OUTS	WALKS	HITS ALLOWED	HRS ALLOWED	COMP. GAMES	SHUT-OUTS	SAVES
1876	NYM-N	1	1	0	1	.000	3	3.00	9	0	0	9	0	1	0	0
1877	Har-N	56	56	29	25	.537	119	2.14	501	96	53	510	2	55	4	0
1878	**ChN-N**	**56**	**56**	**29**	**26**	**.527**	**126**	**2.24**	**506**	**163**	**31**	**511**	**4**	**56**	**1**	**0**
1879	**ChN-N**	**58**	**58**	**31**	**23**	**.574**	**139**	**2.44**	**513 ⅓**	**142**	**30**	**514**	**5**	**57**	**4**	**0**
1880	Try-N	5	5	0	5	.000	37	8.76	38	5	10	83	1	3	0	0
Career average		35	35	18	16	.527	85	2.43	313 ⅓	81	25	325	2	34	2	0
Cubs average		**57**	**57**	**30**	**25**	**.550**	**133**	**2.34**	**509 ⅔**	**153**	**31**	**513**	**5**	**57**	**3**	**0**
Career total		176	176	89	80	.527	424	2.43	1567 ⅓	406	124	1627	12	172	9	0
Cubs total		**114**	**114**	**60**	**49**	**.550**	**265**	**2.34**	**1019 ⅓**	**305**	**61**	**1025**	**9**	**113**	**5**	**0**

LaRoche, David Eugene (Dave)

HEIGHT: 6'2"   LEFTHANDER   BORN: 5/14/1948 COLORADO SPRINGS, COLORADO

YEAR	TEAM	STARTS	GAMES	WON	LOST	PCT	ER	ERA	INNINGS PITCHED	STRIKE-OUTS	WALKS	HITS ALLOWED	HRS ALLOWED	COMP. GAMES	SHUT-OUTS	SAVES
1970	Cal-A	0	38	4	1	.800	19	3.44	49 ⅔	44	21	41	6	0	0	4
1971	Cal-A	0	56	5	1	.833	20	2.50	72	63	27	55	3	0	0	9
1972	Min-A	0	62	5	7	.417	30	2.83	95 ⅓	79	39	72	9	0	0	10
1973	**ChC-N**	**0**	**45**	**4**	**1**	**.800**	**35**	**5.80**	**54 ⅓**	**34**	**29**	**55**	**7**	**0**	**0**	**4**
1974	**ChC-N**	**4**	**49**	**5**	**6**	**.455**	**49**	**4.79**	**92**	**49**	**47**	**103**	**9**	**0**	**0**	**5**
1975	Cle-A	0	61	5	3	.625	20	2.19	82 ⅓	94	57	61	5	0	0	17
1976	Cle-A	0	61	1	4	.200	24	2.24	96 ⅓	104	49	57	2	0	0	21
1977	Cle-A	0	13	2	2	.500	11	5.30	18 ⅔	18	7	15	3	0	0	4
1977	Cal-A	0	46	6	5	.545	28	3.10	81 ⅓	61	37	64	8	0	0	13
1978	Cal-A	0	59	10	9	.526	30	2.82	95 ⅔	70	48	73	7	0	0	25
1979	Cal-A	1	53	7	11	.389	53	5.57	85 ⅔	59	32	107	13	0	0	10
1980	Cal-A	9	52	3	5	.375	58	4.08	128	89	39	122	14	1	0	4
1981	NYY-A	1	26	4	1	.800	13	2.49	47	24	16	38	3	0	0	0
1982	NYY-A	0	25	4	2	.667	19	3.42	50	31	11	54	4	0	0	0
1983	NYY-A	0	1	0	0	—	2	18.00	1	0	0	2	1	0	0	0
Career average		1	46	5	4	.528	29	3.53	75	59	33	66	7	0	0	9
Cubs average		**2**	**47**	**5**	**4**	**.563**	**42**	**5.17**	**73 ⅓**	**42**	**38**	**79**	**8**	**0**	**0**	**5**
Career total		15	647	65	58	.528	411	3.53	1049 ⅓	819	459	919	94	1	0	126
Cubs total		**4**	**94**	**9**	**7**	**.563**	**84**	**5.17**	**146 ⅓**	**83**	**76**	**158**	**16**	**0**	**0**	**9**

Frank S. "Terry" Larkin, rhp, 1876-1880

The story of Terry Larkin is a strange one, even for the wild and wooly days of the National League in the 1870s.

Except for his records as a big-league pitcher, and a few confused newspaper articles in the 1880s, there isn't a lot known about Larkin, including exactly when and where he died.

He appears to have been born in 1857, according to a sportswriter who wrote a story about him when he pitched for Chicago. But that is unverifiable, and in subsequent years, it became clear Larkin wasn't exactly a stickler for the truth.

But the 1857 date sounds about right. After a brief stint in New York in 1876, Larkin jumped to the Hartford club and enjoyed success there, winning 29 games and finishing second in the league in innings pitched.

After the Hartford club folded, Larkin signed with Chicago in 1877 and became the ace of the staff. Player-manager Albert Spalding, who had heretofore handled the pitching duties, handed those chores to Larkin, who won 29 games and completed all of his 56 starts.

Larkin had exceptional control and was always among the league leaders in fewest walks allowed. He was also a perennial league leader in strikeouts with Chicago. He became the first Chicago pitcher to pitch more than 1,000 innings and he did it in just two years.

But Larkin was also a drinker. Spalding, who took over ownership of the team in 1877, was not comfortable with that, but his manager, Bob Ferguson, didn't appear to have a problem with it. Ferguson was also the team's shortstop.

The next year, 1878, Larkin was again among the leaders in wins, complete games, shutouts, innings pitched, strikeouts and fewest walks issued per game. But Spalding had elevated Adrian "Cap" Anson, to player-manager, and Anson didn't like Larkin's style much.

Anson and Spalding began looking for a replacement for Larkin, and after the 1878 season, they actually found two: Larry Corcoran and Fred Goldsmith. That made Larkin expendable, and he was released. He signed with Troy, New York, which at that time had a franchise in the league, but he pitched ineffectually and was soon out of the league.

His life after 1880 is difficult to follow. Records of the time show that he pitched for several years in the minor leagues, and in 1883 he shot his wife in the mouth in a domestic dispute at their Williamsburg, New York, home. Reports at the time indicate he was drunk. In his deposition, Larkin claimed that while he was arguing with his wife, he heard the police coming to the door. In a bit of logic that only a drunk could understand, Larkin found his gun and fired several shots, to scare the police off. One of the shots hit Mrs. Larkin, who later refused to press charges. Later that day, Larkin reportedly tried to commit suicide by slashing himself with a straight razor.

That story caused some confusion, as a later sports article reported that Larkin killed himself in 1897 by slitting his throat with a razor. But there is no record of his death in municipal files that year. Another report had Larkin dying of an alcohol-related illness in 1893. He also reportedly suffered from malaria, which, he told another writer, was the reason he began drinking in 1876. That, too, is unverifiable.

Larkin is still sixth overall in career ERA with Chicago with a 2.34 mark.

Larsen, Don James (Night Rider)
HEIGHT: 6'4"   RIGHTHANDER   BORN: 8/7/1929 MICHIGAN CITY, INDIANA

YEAR	TEAM	STARTS	GAMES	WON	LOST	PCT	ER	ERA	INNINGS PITCHED	STRIKE-OUTS	WALKS	HITS ALLOWED	HRS ALLOWED	COMP. GAMES	SHUT-OUTS	SAVES
1953	StL-A	22	38	7	12	.368	89	4.16	192 2/3	96	64	201	11	7	2	2
1954	Bal-A	28	29	3	21	.125	98	4.37	201 2/3	80	89	213	18	12	1	0
1955	NYY-A	13	19	9	2	.818	33	3.06	97	44	51	81	8	5	1	2
1956	NYY-A	20	38	11	5	.688	65	3.26	179 2/3	107	96	133	19	6	1	1
1957	NYY-A	20	27	10	4	.714	58	3.74	139 2/3	81	87	113	12	4	1	0
1958	NYY-A	19	19	9	6	.600	39	3.07	114 1/3	55	52	100	4	5	3	0
1959	NYY-A	18	25	6	7	.462	60	4.33	124 2/3	69	76	122	14	3	1	0
1960	KCA-A	15	22	1	10	.091	50	5.38	83 2/3	43	42	97	11	0	0	0
1961	KCA-A	1	8	1	0	1.000	7	4.20	15	13	11	21	2	0	0	0
1961	CWS-A	3	25	7	2	.778	34	4.12	74 1/3	53	29	64	5	0	0	2
1962	SF-N	0	49	5	4	.556	42	4.38	86 1/3	58	47	83	9	0	0	11
1963	SF-N	0	46	7	7	.500	21	3.05	62	44	30	46	8	0	0	3
1964	SF-N	0	6	0	1	.000	5	4.35	10 1/3	6	6	10	0	0	0	0
1964	Hou-N	10	30	4	8	.333	26	2.26	103 1/3	58	20	92	4	2	1	1
1965	Hou-N	1	1	0	0	—	3	5.06	5 1/3	1	3	8	0	0	0	0
1965	Bal-A	1	27	1	2	.333	16	2.67	54	40	20	53	4	0	0	1
1967	**ChC-N**	**0**	**3**	**0**	**0**	**—**	**4**	**9.00**	**4**	**1**	**2**	**5**	**1**	**0**	**0**	**0**
Career average		12	29	6	7	.471	46	3.78	110 2/3	61	52	103	9	3	1	2
Cubs average		**0**	**3**	**0**	**0**	**—**	**4**	**9.00**	**4**	**1**	**2**	**5**	**1**	**0**	**0**	**0**
Career total		171	412	81	91	.471	650	3.78	1548	849	725	1442	130	44	11	23
Cubs total		**0**	**3**	**0**	**0**	**—**	**4**	**9.00**	**4**	**1**	**2**	**5**	**1**	**0**	**0**	**0**

Larson, Daniel James (Dan)
HEIGHT: 6'0"   RIGHTHANDER   BORN: 7/4/1954 LOS ANGELES, CALIFORNIA

YEAR	TEAM	STARTS	GAMES	WON	LOST	PCT	ER	ERA	INNINGS PITCHED	STRIKE-OUTS	WALKS	HITS ALLOWED	HRS ALLOWED	COMP. GAMES	SHUT-OUTS	SAVES
1976	Hou-N	13	13	5	8	.385	31	3.02	92 1/3	42	28	81	3	5	0	0
1977	Hou-N	10	32	1	7	.125	63	5.81	97 2/3	44	45	108	13	1	0	1
1978	Phi-N	0	1	0	0	—	1	9.00	1	2	1	1	1	0	0	0
1979	Phi-N	3	3	1	1	.500	9	4.26	19	9	9	17	1	0	0	0
1980	Phi-N	7	12	0	5	.000	16	3.15	45 2/3	17	24	46	4	0	0	0
1981	Phi-N	4	5	3	0	1.000	13	4.18	28	15	15	27	4	1	0	0
1982	**ChC-N**	**6**	**12**	**0**	**4**	**.000**	**25**	**5.67**	**39 2/3**	**22**	**18**	**51**	**4**	**0**	**0**	**0**
Career average		6	11	1	4	.286	23	4.40	46 1/3	22	20	47	4	1	0	0
Cubs average		**6**	**12**	**0**	**4**	**.000**	**25**	**5.67**	**39 2/3**	**22**	**18**	**51**	**4**	**0**	**0**	**0**
Career total		43	78	10	25	.286	158	4.40	323 1/3	151	140	331	30	7	0	1
Cubs total		**6**	**12**	**0**	**4**	**.000**	**25**	**5.67**	**39 2/3**	**22**	**18**	**51**	**4**	**0**	**0**	**0**

Lary, Alfred Allen (Al)
HEIGHT: 6'3"   RIGHTHANDER   BORN: 9/26/1928 NORTHPORT, ALABAMA   DIED: 7/10/2001 NORTHPORT, ALABAMA

YEAR	TEAM	STARTS	GAMES	WON	LOST	PCT	ER	ERA	INNINGS PITCHED	STRIKE-OUTS	WALKS	HITS ALLOWED	HRS ALLOWED	COMP. GAMES	SHUT-OUTS	SAVES
1954	ChC-N	1	1	0	0	—	2	3.00	6	4	7	3	0	0	0	0
1962	ChC-N	3	15	0	1	.000	27	7.15	34	18	15	42	5	0	0	0
Career average		2	8	0	1	.000	15	6.53	20	11	11	23	3	0	0	0
Cubs average		**2**	**8**	**0**	**1**	**.000**	**15**	**6.53**	**20**	**11**	**11**	**23**	**3**	**0**	**0**	**0**
Career total		4	16	0	1	.000	29	6.53	40	22	22	45	5	0	0	0
Cubs total		**4**	**16**	**0**	**1**	**.000**	**29**	**6.53**	**40**	**22**	**22**	**45**	**5**	**0**	**0**	**0**

Lavender, James Sanford (Jimmy)
HEIGHT: 5'11"   RIGHTHANDER   BORN: 3/25/1884 BARNESVILLE, GEORGIA   DIED: 1/12/1960 CARTERSVILLE, GEORGIA

YEAR	TEAM	STARTS	GAMES	WON	LOST	PCT	ER	ERA	INNINGS PITCHED	STRIKE-OUTS	WALKS	HITS ALLOWED	HRS ALLOWED	COMP. GAMES	SHUT-OUTS	SAVES
1912	ChC-N	31	42	16	13	.552	85	3.04	251 2/3	109	89	240	8	15	3	3
1913	ChC-N	20	40	10	14	.417	83	3.66	204	91	98	206	6	10	0	2

(continued)

YEAR	TEAM	STARTS	GAMES	WON	LOST	PCT	ER	ERA	INNINGS PITCHED	STRIKE-OUTS	WALKS	HITS ALLOWED	HRS ALLOWED	COMP. GAMES	SHUT-OUTS	SAVES
(continued)																
1914	ChC-N	28	37	11	11	.500	73	3.07	214⅓	87	87	191	11	11	2	0
1915	ChC-N	24	41	10	16	.385	63	2.58	220	117	67	178	5	13	1	4
1916	ChC-N	25	36	10	14	.417	59	2.82	188	91	62	163	3	9	4	2
1917	Phi-N	14	28	6	8	.429	51	3.55	129⅓	52	44	119	5	7	0	1
Career average		24	37	11	13	.453	69	3.09	201⅓	91	75	183	6	11	2	2
Cubs average		**26**	**39**	**11**	**14**	**.456**	**73**	**3.03**	**215⅔**	**99**	**81**	**196**	**7**	**12**	**2**	**2**
Career total		142	224	63	76	.453	414	3.09	1207⅓	547	447	1097	38	65	10	12
Cubs total		**128**	**196**	**57**	**68**	**.456**	**363**	**3.03**	**1078**	**495**	**403**	**978**	**33**	**58**	**10**	**11**

Lee, Donald Edward (Don *or* Moose)
HEIGHT: 6'4"   RIGHTHANDER   BORN: 2/26/1934 GLOBE, ARIZONA

YEAR	TEAM	STARTS	GAMES	WON	LOST	PCT	ER	ERA	INNINGS PITCHED	STRIKE-OUTS	WALKS	HITS ALLOWED	HRS ALLOWED	COMP. GAMES	SHUT-OUTS	SAVES
1957	Det-A	6	11	1	3	.250	20	4.66	38⅔	19	18	48	6	0	0	0
1958	Det-A	0	1	0	0	—	2	9.00	2	0	1	1	1	0	0	0
1960	Was-A	20	44	8	7	.533	63	3.44	165	88	64	160	16	1	0	3
1961	Min-A	10	37	3	6	.333	45	3.52	115	65	35	93	12	4	0	3
1962	Min-A	9	9	3	3	.500	26	4.50	52	28	24	51	8	1	0	0
1962	LAA-A	22	27	8	8	.500	53	3.11	153⅓	74	39	153	12	4	2	2
1963	LAA-A	22	40	8	11	.421	63	3.68	154	89	51	148	12	4	2	2
1964	LAA-A	8	33	5	4	.556	27	2.72	89⅓	73	25	99	6	3	2	1
1965	Cal-A	0	10	0	1	.000	10	6.43	14	12	5	21	4	0	0	2
1965	Hou-N	0	7	0	0	—	3	3.38	8	3	3	8	0	0	0	0
1966	Hou-N	0	9	2	0	1.000	5	2.50	18	9	4	17	1	0	0	0
1966	**ChC-N**	**0**	**16**	**2**	**1**	**.667**	**15**	**7.11**	**19**	**7**	**12**	**28**	**3**	**0**	**0**	**0**
Career average		11	27	4	5	.476	37	3.61	92	52	31	92	9	1	0	1
Cubs average		**0**	**16**	**2**	**1**	**.667**	**15**	**7.11**	**19**	**7**	**12**	**28**	**3**	**0**	**0**	**0**
Career total		97	244	40	44	.476	332	3.61	828⅓	467	281	827	81	13	4	11
Cubs total		**0**	**16**	**2**	**1**	**.667**	**15**	**7.11**	**19**	**7**	**12**	**28**	**3**	**0**	**0**	**0**

Lee, Thomas Frank (Tom)
HEIGHT: —   BORN: 6/8/1862 MILWAUKEE, WISCONSIN   DIED: 3/4/1886 MILWAUKEE, WISCONSIN

YEAR	TEAM	STARTS	GAMES	WON	LOST	PCT	ER	ERA	INNINGS PITCHED	STRIKE-OUTS	WALKS	HITS ALLOWED	HRS ALLOWED	COMP. GAMES	SHUT-OUTS	SAVES
1884	**ChN-N**	**5**	**5**	**1**	**4**	**.200**	**19**	**3.77**	**45⅓**	**14**	**15**	**55**	**12**	**5**	**0**	**0**
1884	Bal-U	14	15	5	8	.385	46	3.39	122	81	29	121	1	12	0	0
Career average		19	20	6	12	.333	65	3.50	167⅓	95	44	176	13	17	0	0
Cubs average		**5**	**5**	**1**	**4**	**.200**	**19**	**3.77**	**45⅓**	**14**	**15**	**55**	**12**	**5**	**0**	**0**
Career total		19	20	6	12	.333	65	3.50	167⅓	95	44	176	13	17	0	0
Cubs total		**5**	**5**	**1**	**4**	**.200**	**19**	**3.77**	**45⅓**	**14**	**15**	**55**	**12**	**5**	**0**	**0**

Lee, William Crutcher (Bill *or* Big Bill)
HEIGHT: 6'3"   RIGHTHANDER   BORN: 10/21/1909 PLAQUEMINE, LOUISIANA   DIED: 6/15/1977 PLAQUEMINE, LOUISIANA

YEAR	TEAM	STARTS	GAMES	WON	LOST	PCT	ER	ERA	INNINGS PITCHED	STRIKE-OUTS	WALKS	HITS ALLOWED	HRS ALLOWED	COMP. GAMES	SHUT-OUTS	SAVES
1934	ChC-N	29	35	13	14	.481	81	3.40	214⅓	104	74	218	9	16	4	1
1935	ChC-N	32	39	20	6	.769	83	2.96	252	100	84	241	11	18	3	1
1936	ChC-N	33	43	18	11	.621	95	3.31	258⅔	102	93	238	14	20	4	1
1937	ChC-N	34	42	14	15	.483	107	3.54	272⅓	108	73	289	14	17	2	3
1938	ChC-N	37	44	22	9	.710	86	2.66	291	121	74	281	18	19	9	2
1939	ChC-N	36	37	19	15	.559	108	3.44	282⅓	105	85	295	18	20	1	0
1940	ChC-N	30	37	9	17	.346	118	5.03	211⅓	70	70	246	12	9	1	0
1941	ChC-N	22	28	8	14	.364	70	3.76	167⅓	62	43	179	6	12	0	1
1942	ChC-N	30	32	13	13	.500	94	3.85	219⅔	75	67	221	4	18	1	0
1943	ChC-N	12	13	3	7	.300	31	3.56	78⅓	18	27	83	4	4	0	0
1943	Phi-N	7	13	1	5	.167	31	4.60	60⅔	17	21	70	4	2	0	3
1944	Phi-N	28	31	10	11	.476	73	3.15	208⅓	50	57	199	9	11	3	1
1945	Phi-N	13	13	3	6	.333	40	4.66	77⅓	13	30	107	0	2	0	0
1945	Bos-N	13	16	6	3	.667	33	2.79	106⅓	12	36	112	6	6	1	0
1946	Bos-N	21	25	10	9	.526	65	4.18	140	32	45	148	7	8	0	0
1947	**ChC-N**	**2**	**14**	**0**	**2**	**.000**	**12**	**4.50**	**24**	**9**	**14**	**26**	**2**	**0**	**0**	**0**

(continued)

William Crutcher "Big Bill," "General" Lee, rhp, 1934—47

His career record in the major leagues was only a few games over .500, but in his first six seasons with the Cubs, "Big Bill" Lee was one of the best pitchers in the National League.

Lee was born in Plaquemine, Louisiana, on October 21, 1909. He was signed by the Cardinals and spent several years in their minor league system. Eventually, Lee was sold to the Cubs prior to the 1934 season.

Lee was 13-14 in 1934, with four shutouts that year. In his sophomore year, Lee was 20-6 and led the National League in winning percentage and was tied with Larry French for the team lead in ERA with a 2.96 mark. That was the year the Cubs won 21 games in a row in September to seize the National League championship. Lee was 5-0 in that stretch, including a victory in the pennant-clinching game.

Lee was a hard-throwing righty with a good fastball and an even better curve. He was not afraid to throw his curveball on a full count, and more often than not, he would throw it for a strike. By the 1938 season, he was an All-Star.

That year, Lee led the league in wins, with a 22-9 record, and he was also tops in shutouts with nine and in ERA with a 2.66 mark. At 6'3" and 195 pounds, Lee was an imposing presence on the mound. At one point, he pitched 37⅓ consecutive scoreless innings, which included four consecutive shutouts, a team record set by Mordecai "Three Finger" Brown.

Lee pitched well until he began having trouble with his eyes in 1940. He pitched for the Cubs until 1943 and then moved on to the Phillies and, later, the Boston Braves, but never won more than 10 games a season in that span.

He returned to the Cubs for the 1947 season before retiring. After retirement, Lee eventually underwent surgery for detached retinas in both eyes. The operations were marginally successful, but he eventually lost his sight. He died in his hometown in 1977.

Lee is among the Cubs leaders in several all-time categories, including ninth in victories with 139, sixth in losses with 123, seventh in games played with 364, fifth in starts with 296, sixth in complete games with 153, sixth in shutouts with 25, seventh in innings pitched with 2,271⅓, seventh in hits allowed with 2,317 and fifth in walks issued with 704.

(Lee, W.C., continued)

Career average	27	33	12	11	.518	81	3.54	204⅔	71	64	211	10	13	2	1
Cubs average	**27**	**33**	**13**	**11**	**.531**	**80**	**3.51**	**206⅓**	**79**	**64**	**211**	**10**	**14**	**2**	**1**
Career total	379	462	169	157	.518	1127	3.54	2864	998	893	2953	138	182	29	13
Cubs total	**297**	**364**	**139**	**123**	**.531**	**885**	**3.51**	**2271⅓**	**874**	**704**	**2317**	**112**	**153**	**25**	**9**

Lefferts, Craig Lindsay
HEIGHT: 6'1"   LEFTHANDER   BORN: 9/29/1957 MUNICH, WEST GERMANY

YEAR	TEAM	STARTS	GAMES	WON	LOST	PCT	ER	ERA	INNINGS PITCHED	STRIKE-OUTS	WALKS	HITS ALLOWED	HRS ALLOWED	COMP. GAMES	SHUT-OUTS	SAVES
1983	**ChC-N**	**5**	**56**	**3**	**4**	**.429**	**31**	**3.13**	**89**	**60**	**29**	**80**	**13**	**0**	**0**	**1**
1984	SD-N	0	62	3	4	.429	25	2.13	105⅔	56	24	88	4	0	0	10
1985	SD-N	0	60	7	6	.538	31	3.35	83⅓	48	30	75	7	0	0	2
1986	SD-N	0	83	9	8	.529	37	3.09	107⅔	72	44	98	7	0	0	4
1987	SD-N	0	33	2	2	.500	25	4.38	51⅓	39	15	56	9	0	0	2
1987	SF-N	0	44	3	3	.500	17	3.23	47⅓	18	18	36	4	0	0	4
1988	SF-N	0	64	3	8	.273	30	2.92	92⅓	58	23	74	7	0	0	11
1989	SF-N	0	70	2	4	.333	32	2.69	107	71	22	93	11	0	0	20

(continued)

(continued)

YEAR	TEAM	STARTS	GAMES	WON	LOST	PCT	ER	ERA	INNINGS PITCHED	STRIKEOUTS	WALKS	HITS ALLOWED	HRS ALLOWED	COMP. GAMES	SHUTOUTS	SAVES
1990	SD-N	0	56	7	5	.583	22	2.52	78⅔	60	22	68	10	0	0	23
1991	SD-N	0	54	1	6	.143	30	3.91	69	48	14	74	5	0	0	23
1992	SD-N	27	27	13	9	.591	67	3.69	163⅓	81	35	180	16	0	0	23
1992	Bal-A	5	5	1	3	.250	15	4.09	33	23	6	34	3	1	0	0
1993	Tex-A	8	52	3	9	.250	56	6.05	83⅓	58	28	102	17	0	0	0
1994	Cal-A	0	30	1	1	.500	18	4.67	34⅔	27	12	50	7	0	0	1
Career average		4	58	5	6	.446	36	3.43	95⅓	60	27	92	10	0	0	8
Cubs average		**5**	**56**	**3**	**4**	**.429**	**31**	**3.13**	**89**	**60**	**29**	**80**	**13**	**0**	**0**	**1**
Career total		45	696	58	72	.446	436	3.43	1145⅔	719	322	1108	120	1	0	101
Cubs total		**5**	**56**	**3**	**4**	**.429**	**31**	**3.13**	**89**	**60**	**29**	**80**	**13**	**0**	**0**	**1**

Leifield, Albert Peter (Lefty)
HEIGHT: 6'1" LEFTHANDER BORN: 9/5/1883 TRENTON, ILLINOIS DIED: 10/10/1970 ALEXANDRIA, VIRGINIA

YEAR	TEAM	STARTS	GAMES	WON	LOST	PCT	ER	ERA	INNINGS PITCHED	STRIKEOUTS	WALKS	HITS ALLOWED	HRS ALLOWED	COMP. GAMES	SHUTOUTS	SAVES
1905	Pit-N	7	8	5	2	.714	18	2.89	56	10	14	52	0	6	1	0
1906	Pit-N	31	37	18	13	.581	53	1.87	255⅔	111	68	214	3	24	8	1
1907	Pit-N	33	40	20	16	.556	74	2.33	286	112	100	270	1	24	6	1
1908	Pit-N	26	34	15	14	.517	51	2.10	218⅓	87	86	168	1	18	5	2
1909	Pit-N	27	32	19	8	.704	53	2.37	201⅔	43	54	172	4	13	3	0
1910	Pit-N	30	40	15	13	.536	64	2.64	218⅓	64	67	197	6	13	3	2
1911	Pit-N	37	42	16	16	.500	93	2.63	318	111	82	301	7	26	2	1
1912	Pit-N	1	6	1	2	.333	11	4.18	23⅔	8	10	29	0	1	1	0
1912	**ChC-N**	**9**	**13**	**7**	**2**	**.778**	**19**	**2.42**	**70⅔**	**23**	**21**	**68**	**0**	**4**	**1**	**0**
1913	**ChC-N**	**1**	**6**	**0**	**1**	**.000**	**13**	**5.48**	**21⅓**	**4**	**5**	**28**	**0**	**0**	**0**	**0**
1918	StL-A	6	15	2	6	.250	19	2.55	67	22	19	61	1	3	1	0
1919	StL-A	9	19	6	4	.600	30	2.93	92	18	25	96	4	6	2	0
1920	StL-A	0	4	0	0	—	7	7.00	9	3	3	17	0	0	0	0
Career average		18	25	10	8	.561	42	2.47	153⅓	51	46	139	2	12	3	1
Cubs average		**5**	**10**	**4**	**2**	**.700**	**16**	**3.13**	**46**	**14**	**13**	**48**	**0**	**2**	**1**	**0**
Career total		217	296	124	97	.561	505	2.47	1838	616	554	1673	27	138	33	7
Cubs total		**10**	**19**	**7**	**3**	**.700**	**32**	**3.13**	**92**	**27**	**26**	**96**	**0**	**4**	**1**	**0**

LeMay, Richard Paul (Dick)
HEIGHT: 6'3" LEFTHANDER BORN: 8/28/1938 CINCINNATI, OHIO

YEAR	TEAM	STARTS	GAMES	WON	LOST	PCT	ER	ERA	INNINGS PITCHED	STRIKEOUTS	WALKS	HITS ALLOWED	HRS ALLOWED	COMP. GAMES	SHUTOUTS	SAVES
1961	SF-N	5	27	3	6	.333	33	3.56	83⅓	54	36	65	11	1	0	3
1962	SF-N	0	9	0	1	.000	8	7.71	9⅓	5	9	9	2	0	0	1
1963	**ChC-N**	**1**	**9**	**0**	**1**	**.000**	**9**	**5.28**	**15⅓**	**10**	**4**	**26**	**1**	**0**	**0**	**0**
Career average		2	15	1	3	.273	17	4.17	36	23	16	33	5	0	0	1
Cubs average		**1**	**9**	**0**	**1**	**.000**	**9**	**5.28**	**15⅓**	**10**	**4**	**26**	**1**	**0**	**0**	**0**
Career total		6	45	3	8	.273	50	4.17	108	69	49	100	14	1	0	4
Cubs total		**1**	**9**	**0**	**1**	**.000**	**9**	**5.28**	**15⅓**	**10**	**4**	**26**	**1**	**0**	**0**	**0**

Lemonds, David Lee (Dave)
HEIGHT: 6'1" LEFTHANDER BORN: 7/5/1948 CHARLOTTE, NORTH CAROLINA

YEAR	TEAM	STARTS	GAMES	WON	LOST	PCT	ER	ERA	INNINGS PITCHED	STRIKEOUTS	WALKS	HITS ALLOWED	HRS ALLOWED	COMP. GAMES	SHUTOUTS	SAVES
1969	**ChC-N**	**1**	**2**	**0**	**1**	**.000**	**2**	**3.86**	**4⅔**	**0**	**5**	**5**	**0**	**0**	**0**	**0**
1972	CWS-A	18	31	4	7	.364	31	2.95	94⅔	69	38	87	6	0	0	0
Career average		10	17	2	4	.333	17	2.99	49⅔	35	22	46	3	0	0	0
Cubs average		**1**	**2**	**0**	**1**	**.000**	**2**	**3.86**	**4⅔**	**0**	**5**	**5**	**0**	**0**	**0**	**0**
Career total		19	33	4	8	.333	33	2.99	99⅓	69	43	92	6	0	0	0
Cubs total		**1**	**2**	**0**	**1**	**.000**	**2**	**3.86**	**4⅔**	**0**	**5**	**5**	**0**	**0**	**0**	**0**

Leonard, Emil John (Dutch)
HEIGHT: 6'0" RIGHTHANDER BORN: 3/25/1909 AUBURN, ILLINOIS DIED: 4/17/1983 SPRINGFIELD, ILLINOIS

YEAR	TEAM	STARTS	GAMES	WON	LOST	PCT	ER	ERA	INNINGS PITCHED	STRIKE-OUTS	WALKS	HITS ALLOWED	HRS ALLOWED	COMP. GAMES	SHUT-OUTS	SAVES
1933	Bro-N	3	10	2	3	.400	13	2.93	40	6	10	42	0	2	0	0
1934	Bro-N	21	44	14	11	.560	67	3.28	183 ⅔	58	33	210	12	11	2	5
1935	Bro-N	11	43	2	9	.182	60	3.92	137 ⅔	41	29	152	11	4	0	8
1936	Bro-N	0	16	0	0	—	13	3.66	32	8	5	34	2	0	0	1
1938	Was-A	31	33	12	15	.444	85	3.43	223 ⅓	68	53	221	11	15	3	0
1939	Was-A	34	34	20	8	.714	106	3.54	269 ⅓	88	59	273	16	21	2	0
1940	Was-A	35	35	14	19	.424	112	3.49	289	124	78	328	19	23	2	0
1941	Was-A	33	34	18	13	.581	98	3.45	256	91	54	271	6	19	4	0
1942	Was-A	5	6	2	2	.500	16	4.11	35	15	5	28	1	1	1	1
1943	Was-A	30	31	11	13	.458	80	3.28	219 ⅔	51	46	218	9	15	2	1
1944	Was-A	31	32	14	14	.500	78	3.06	229 ⅓	62	37	222	8	17	3	0
1945	Was-A	29	31	17	7	.708	51	2.13	216	96	35	208	5	12	4	1
1946	Was-A	23	26	10	10	.500	64	3.56	161 ⅔	62	36	182	9	7	2	0
1947	Phi-N	29	32	17	12	.586	70	2.68	235	103	57	224	14	19	3	0
1948	Phi-N	30	34	12	17	.414	63	2.51	225 ⅔	92	54	226	9	16	1	0
1949	**ChC-N**	**28**	**33**	**7**	**16**	**.304**	**83**	**4.15**	**180**	**83**	**43**	**198**	**4**	**10**	**1**	**0**
1950	**ChC-N**	**1**	**35**	**5**	**1**	**.833**	**31**	**3.77**	**74**	**28**	**27**	**70**	**7**	**0**	**0**	**6**
1951	**ChC-N**	**1**	**41**	**10**	**6**	**.625**	**24**	**2.64**	**81 ⅔**	**30**	**28**	**69**	**3**	**0**	**0**	**11**
1952	**ChC-N**	**0**	**45**	**2**	**2**	**.500**	**16**	**2.16**	**66 ⅔**	**37**	**24**	**56**	**3**	**0**	**0**	**8**
1953	**ChC-N**	**0**	**45**	**2**	**3**	**.400**	**32**	**4.60**	**62 ⅔**	**27**	**24**	**72**	**9**	**0**	**0**	**8**
Career average		19	32	10	9	.513	58	3.25	161	59	37	165	8	10	2	2
Cubs average		**6**	**40**	**5**	**6**	**.481**	**37**	**3.60**	**93**	**41**	**29**	**93**	**5**	**2**	**0**	**6**
Career total		375	640	191	181	.513	1162	3.25	3218 ⅓	1170	737	3304	158	192	30	44
Cubs total		**30**	**199**	**26**	**28**	**.481**	**186**	**3.60**	**465**	**205**	**146**	**465**	**26**	**10**	**1**	**28**

Lieber, Jonathan Ray (Jon)
HEIGHT: 6'2" RIGHTHANDER BORN: 4/2/1970 COUNCIL BLUFFS, IOWA

YEAR	TEAM	STARTS	GAMES	WON	LOST	PCT	ER	ERA	INNINGS PITCHED	STRIKE-OUTS	WALKS	HITS ALLOWED	HRS ALLOWED	COMP. GAMES	SHUT-OUTS	SAVES
1994	Pit-N	17	17	6	7	.462	45	3.73	108 ⅔	71	25	116	12	1	0	0
1995	Pit-N	12	21	4	7	.364	51	6.32	72 ⅔	45	14	103	7	0	0	0
1996	Pit-N	15	51	9	5	.643	63	3.99	142	94	28	156	19	0	0	1
1997	Pit-N	32	33	11	14	.440	94	4.49	188 ⅓	160	51	193	23	1	0	0
1998	Pit-N	28	29	8	14	.364	78	4.11	171	138	40	182	23	2	0	1
1999	**ChC-N**	**31**	**31**	**10**	**11**	**.476**	**92**	**4.07**	**203 ⅓**	**186**	**46**	**226**	**28**	**3**	**1**	**0**
2000	**ChC-N**	**35**	**35**	**12**	**11**	**.522**	**123**	**4.41**	**251**	**192**	**54**	**248**	**36**	**6**	**1**	**0**
2001	**ChC-N**	**34**	**34**	**20**	**6**	**.769**	**98**	**3.80**	**232 ⅓**	**148**	**41**	**226**	**25**	**5**	**1**	**0**
Career average		26	31	10	9	.516	81	4.23	171 ⅓	129	37	181	22	2	0	0
Cubs average		**33**	**33**	**14**	**9**	**.600**	**104**	**4.10**	**229**	**175**	**47**	**233**	**30**	**5**	**1**	**0**
Career total		204	251	80	75	.516	644	4.23	1369 ⅓	1034	299	1450	173	18	3	2
Cubs total		**100**	**100**	**42**	**28**	**.600**	**313**	**4.10**	**686 ⅔**	**526**	**141**	**700**	**89**	**14**	**3**	**0**

Lillard, Robert Eugene (Gene)
HEIGHT: 5'10" RIGHTHANDER BORN: 11/12/1913 SANTA BARBARA, CALIFORNIA DIED: 4/12/1991 GOLETA, CALIFORNIA

YEAR	TEAM	STARTS	GAMES	WON	LOST	PCT	ER	ERA	INNINGS PITCHED	STRIKE-OUTS	WALKS	HITS ALLOWED	HRS ALLOWED	COMP. GAMES	SHUT-OUTS	SAVES
1939	**ChC-N**	**7**	**20**	**3**	**5**	**.375**	**40**	**6.55**	**55**	**31**	**36**	**68**	**2**	**2**	**0**	**0**
1940	StL-N	1	2	0	1	.000	7	13.50	4 ⅔	2	4	8	1	0	0	0
Career average		4	11	2	3	.333	24	7.09	30	17	20	38	2	1	0	0
Cubs average		**7**	**20**	**3**	**5**	**.375**	**40**	**6.55**	**55**	**31**	**36**	**68**	**2**	**2**	**0**	**0**
Career total		8	22	3	6	.333	47	7.09	59 ⅔	33	40	76	3	2	0	0
Cubs total		**7**	**20**	**3**	**5**	**.375**	**40**	**6.55**	**55**	**31**	**36**	**68**	**2**	**2**	**0**	**0**

Littlefield, Richard Bernard (Dick)

HEIGHT: 6'0" LEFTHANDER BORN: 3/18/1926 DETROIT, MICHIGAN DIED: 11/20/1997 DETROIT, MICHIGAN

YEAR	TEAM	STARTS	GAMES	WON	LOST	PCT	ER	ERA	INNINGS PITCHED	STRIKE-OUTS	WALKS	HITS ALLOWED	HRS ALLOWED	COMP. GAMES	SHUT-OUTS	SAVES
1950	Bos-A	2	15	2	2	.500	24	9.26	23 1/3	13	24	27	6	0	0	1
1951	CWS-A	2	4	1	1	.500	9	8.38	9 2/3	7	17	9	1	0	0	0
1952	Det-A	1	28	0	3	.000	23	4.34	47 2/3	32	25	46	4	0	0	1
1952	StL-A	5	7	2	3	.400	14	2.72	46 1/3	34	17	35	4	3	0	0
1953	StL-A	22	36	7	12	.368	86	5.08	152 1/3	104	84	153	17	2	0	0
1954	Bal-A	0	3	0	0	—	7	10.50	6	5	6	8	0	0	0	0
1954	Pit-N	21	23	10	11	.476	62	3.60	155	92	85	140	10	7	1	0
1955	Pit-N	17	35	5	12	.294	74	5.12	130	70	68	148	15	4	1	0
1956	Pit-N	2	6	0	0	—	6	4.26	12 2/3	10	6	14	2	0	0	0
1956	StL-N	2	3	0	2	.000	8	7.45	9 2/3	5	4	9	2	0	0	0
1956	NYG-N	7	31	4	4	.500	44	4.08	97	65	39	78	16	0	0	2
1957	**ChC-N**	**2**	**48**	**2**	**3**	**.400**	**39**	**5.35**	**65 2/3**	**51**	**37**	**76**	**12**	**0**	**0**	**4**
1958	Mil-N	0	4	0	1	.000	3	4.26	6 1/3	7	1	7	2	0	0	1
Career average		9	27	4	6	.379	44	4.71	84 2/3	55	46	83	10	2	0	1
Cubs average		**2**	**48**	**2**	**3**	**.400**	**39**	**5.35**	**65 2/3**	**51**	**37**	**76**	**12**	**0**	**0**	**4**
Career total		83	243	33	54	.379	399	4.71	761 2/3	495	413	750	91	16	2	9
Cubs total		**2**	**48**	**2**	**3**	**.400**	**39**	**5.35**	**65 2/3**	**51**	**37**	**76**	**12**	**0**	**0**	**4**

Locker, Robert Awtry (Bob)

HEIGHT: 6'3" RIGHTHANDER BORN: 3/15/1938 GEORGE, IOWA

YEAR	TEAM	STARTS	GAMES	WON	LOST	PCT	ER	ERA	INNINGS PITCHED	STRIKE-OUTS	WALKS	HITS ALLOWED	HRS ALLOWED	COMP. GAMES	SHUT-OUTS	SAVES
1965	CWS-A	0	51	5	2	.714	32	3.15	91 1/3	69	30	71	6	0	0	2
1966	CWS-A	0	56	9	8	.529	26	2.46	95	70	23	73	2	0	0	12
1967	CWS-A	0	77	7	5	.583	29	2.09	124 2/3	80	23	102	5	0	0	20
1968	CWS-A	0	70	5	4	.556	23	2.29	90 1/3	62	27	78	4	0	0	10
1969	CWS-A	0	17	2	3	.400	16	6.55	22	15	6	26	6	0	0	4
1969	Sea-A	0	51	3	3	.500	19	2.18	78 1/3	46	26	69	3	0	0	6
1970	Mil-A	0	28	0	1	.000	12	3.41	31 2/3	19	10	37	1	0	0	3
1970	Oak-A	0	38	3	3	.500	18	2.88	56 1/3	33	19	49	1	0	0	4
1971	Oak-A	0	47	7	2	.778	23	2.86	72 1/3	46	19	68	3	0	0	6
1972	Oak-A	0	56	6	1	.857	23	2.65	78	47	16	69	1	0	0	10
1973	**ChC-N**	**0**	**63**	**10**	**6**	**.625**	**30**	**2.54**	**106 1/3**	**76**	**42**	**96**	**6**	**0**	**0**	**18**
1975	**ChC-N**	**0**	**22**	**0**	**1**	**.000**	**18**	**4.96**	**32 2/3**	**14**	**16**	**38**	**3**	**0**	**0**	**0**
Career average		0	58	6	4	.594	27	2.75	88	58	26	78	4	0	0	10
Cubs average		**0**	**43**	**5**	**4**	**.588**	**24**	**3.11**	**69 2/3**	**45**	**29**	**67**	**5**	**0**	**0**	**9**
Career total		0	576	57	39	.594	269	2.75	879	577	257	776	41	0	0	95
Cubs total		**0**	**85**	**10**	**7**	**.588**	**48**	**3.11**	**139**	**90**	**58**	**134**	**9**	**0**	**0**	**18**

Logan, Robert Dean (Bob)

HEIGHT: 5'10" LEFTHANDER BORN: 2/10/1910 THOMPSON, NEBRASKA DIED: 5/20/1978 INDIANAPOLIS, INDIANA

YEAR	TEAM	STARTS	GAMES	WON	LOST	PCT	ER	ERA	INNINGS PITCHED	STRIKE-OUTS	WALKS	HITS ALLOWED	HRS ALLOWED	COMP. GAMES	SHUT-OUTS	SAVES
1935	Bro-N	0	2	0	1	.000	1	3.38	2 2/3	1	1	2	0	0	0	0
1937	Det-A	0	1	0	0	—	0	0.00	0 2/3	1	1	1	0	0	0	0
1937	**ChC-N**	**0**	**4**	**0**	**0**	**—**	**1**	**1.42**	**6 1/3**	**2**	**4**	**6**	**0**	**0**	**0**	**1**
1938	**ChC-N**	**0**	**14**	**0**	**2**	**.000**	**7**	**2.78**	**22 2/3**	**10**	**17**	**18**	**0**	**0**	**0**	**2**
1941	Cin-N	0	2	0	1	.000	3	8.10	3 1/3	0	5	5	0	0	0	0
1945	Bos-N	25	34	7	11	.389	66	3.18	187	53	53	213	9	5	1	1
Career average		5	11	1	3	.318	16	3.15	44 2/3	13	16	49	2	1	0	1
Cubs average		**0**	**9**	**0**	**1**	**.000**	**4**	**2.48**	**14 2/3**	**6**	**11**	**12**	**0**	**0**	**0**	**2**
Career total		25	57	7	15	.318	78	3.15	222 2/3	67	81	245	9	5	1	4
Cubs total		**0**	**18**	**0**	**2**	**.000**	**8**	**2.48**	**29**	**12**	**21**	**24**	**0**	**0**	**0**	**3**

Long, William Douglas (Bill)
HEIGHT: 6'0" RIGHTHANDER BORN: 2/29/1960 CINCINNATI, OHIO

YEAR	TEAM	STARTS	GAMES	WON	LOST	PCT	ER	ERA	INNINGS PITCHED	STRIKE-OUTS	WALKS	HITS ALLOWED	HRS ALLOWED	COMP. GAMES	SHUT-OUTS	SAVES
1985	CWS-A	3	4	0	1	.000	16	10.29	14	13	5	25	4	0	0	0
1987	CWS-A	23	29	8	8	.500	82	4.37	169	72	28	179	20	5	2	1
1988	CWS-A	18	47	8	11	.421	78	4.03	174	77	43	187	21	3	0	2
1989	CWS-A	8	30	5	5	.500	43	3.92	98 2/3	51	37	101	8	0	0	1
1990	CWS-A	0	4	0	1	.000	4	6.35	5 2/3	2	2	6	2	0	0	0
1990	**ChC-N**	**0**	**42**	**6**	**1**	**.857**	**27**	**4.37**	**55 2/3**	**32**	**21**	**66**	**8**	**0**	**0**	**5**
1991	Mon-N	0	3	0	0	—	2	10.80	1 2/3	0	4	4	0	0	0	0
Career average		9	27	5	5	.500	42	4.37	86 1/3	41	23	95	11	1	0	2
Cubs average		**0**	**42**	**6**	**1**	**.857**	**27**	**4.37**	**55 2/3**	**32**	**21**	**66**	**8**	**0**	**0**	**5**
Career total		52	159	27	27	.500	252	4.37	518 2/3	247	140	568	63	8	2	9
Cubs total		**0**	**42**	**6**	**1**	**.857**	**27**	**4.37**	**55 2/3**	**32**	**21**	**66**	**8**	**0**	**0**	**5**

Lorraine, Andrew Jason
HEIGHT: 6'3" LEFTHANDER BORN: 8/11/1972 LOS ANGELES, CALIFORNIA

YEAR	TEAM	STARTS	GAMES	WON	LOST	PCT	ER	ERA	INNINGS PITCHED	STRIKE-OUTS	WALKS	HITS ALLOWED	HRS ALLOWED	COMP. GAMES	SHUT-OUTS	SAVES
1994	Cal-A	3	4	0	2	.000	22	10.61	18 2/3	10	11	30	7	0	0	0
1995	CWS-A	0	5	0	0	—	3	3.38	8	5	2	3	0	0	0	0
1997	Oak-A	6	12	3	1	.750	21	6.37	29 2/3	18	15	45	2	0	0	0
1998	Sea-A	0	4	0	0	—	1	2.45	3 2/3	0	4	3	0	0	1	0
1999	**ChC-N**	**11**	**11**	**2**	**5**	**.286**	**38**	**5.55**	**61 2/3**	**40**	**22**	**71**	**9**	**2**	**1**	**0**
2000	**ChC-N**	**5**	**8**	**1**	**2**	**.333**	**23**	**6.47**	**32**	**25**	**18**	**36**	**5**	**0**	**0**	**0**
2000	Cle-A	0	10	0	0	—	4	3.86	9 1/3	5	5	8	1	0	0	0
Career average		4	9	1	2	.375	19	6.18	27 1/3	17	13	33	4	0	0	0
Cubs average		**8**	**10**	**2**	**4**	**.300**	**31**	**5.86**	**47**	**33**	**20**	**54**	**7**	**1**	**1**	**0**
Career total		25	54	6	10	.375	112	6.18	163	103	77	196	24	2	1	0
Cubs total		**16**	**19**	**3**	**7**	**.300**	**61**	**5.86**	**93 2/3**	**65**	**40**	**107**	**14**	**2**	**1**	**0**

Lowdermilk, Grover Cleveland (Slim)
HEIGHT: 6'4" RIGHTHANDER BORN: 1/15/1885 SANDBORN, INDIANA DIED: 3/31/1968 ODIN, ILLINOIS

YEAR	TEAM	STARTS	GAMES	WON	LOST	PCT	ER	ERA	INNINGS PITCHED	STRIKE-OUTS	WALKS	HITS ALLOWED	HRS ALLOWED	COMP. GAMES	SHUT-OUTS	SAVES
1909	StL-N	3	7	0	2	.000	20	6.21	29	14	30	28	0	1	0	0
1911	StL-N	2	11	0	1	.000	27	7.29	33 1/3	15	33	37	1	1	1	0
1912	**ChC-N**	**1**	**2**	**0**	**1**	**.000**	**14**	**9.69**	**13**	**8**	**14**	**17**	**1**	**1**	**0**	**0**
1915	StL-A	29	38	9	17	.346	77	3.12	222 1/3	130	133	183	1	14	1	0
1915	Det-A	5	7	4	1	.800	13	4.18	28	18	24	17	0	0	0	0
1916	Det-A	0	1	0	0	—	0	0.00	0 1/3	0	3	0	0	0	0	0
1916	Cle-A	9	10	1	5	.167	18	3.16	51 1/3	28	45	52	0	2	1	0
1917	StL-A	2	3	2	1	.667	3	1.42	19	9	4	16	0	2	0	0
1918	StL-A	11	13	2	6	.250	28	3.15	80	25	38	74	1	4	0	0
1919	StL-A	0	7	0	0	—	1	0.75	12	6	4	6	0	5	0	0
1919	CWS-A	11	20	5	5	.500	30	2.79	96 2/3	43	43	95	0	0	0	0
1920	CWS-A	0	3	0	0	—	4	6.75	5 1/3	0	5	9	0	0	0	0
Career average		8	14	3	4	.371	26	3.58	65 2/3	33	42	59	0	1	0	0
Cubs average		**1**	**2**	**0**	**1**	**.000**	**14**	**9.69**	**13**	**8**	**14**	**17**	**1**	**1**	**0**	**0**
Career total		73	122	23	39	.371	235	3.58	590 1/3	296	376	534	4	30	3	0
Cubs total		**1**	**2**	**0**	**1**	**.000**	**14**	**9.69**	**13**	**8**	**14**	**17**	**1**	**1**	**0**	**0**

Lown, Omar Joseph (Turk)
HEIGHT: 6'0" RIGHTHANDER BORN: 5/30/1924 BROOKLYN, NEW YORK

YEAR	TEAM	STARTS	GAMES	WON	LOST	PCT	ER	ERA	INNINGS PITCHED	STRIKE-OUTS	WALKS	HITS ALLOWED	HRS ALLOWED	COMP. GAMES	SHUT-OUTS	SAVES
1951	ChC-N	18	31	4	9	.308	77	5.46	127	39	90	125	14	3	1	0
1952	ChC-N	19	33	4	11	.267	76	4.37	156⅔	73	93	154	13	5	0	0
1953	ChC-N	12	49	8	7	.533	85	5.16	148⅓	76	84	166	20	2	0	0
1954	ChC-N	0	15	0	2	.000	15	6.14	22	16	15	23	1	0	0	3
1956	ChC-N	0	61	9	8	.529	44	3.58	110⅔	74	78	95	10	0	0	13
1957	ChC-N	0	67	5	7	.417	39	3.77	93	51	51	74	10	0	0	12
1958	ChC-N	0	4	0	0	—	2	4.50	4	4	3	2	0	0	0	0
1958	Cin-N	0	11	0	2	.000	7	5.40	11⅔	9	12	12	2	0	0	0
1958	CWS-A	0	27	3	3	.500	18	3.98	40⅔	40	28	49	1	0	0	8
1959	CWS-A	0	60	9	2	.818	30	2.89	93⅓	63	42	73	12	0	0	15
1960	CWS-A	0	45	2	3	.400	29	3.88	67⅓	39	34	60	6	0	0	5
1961	CWS-A	0	59	7	5	.583	31	2.76	101	50	35	87	13	0	0	11
1962	CWS-A	0	42	4	2	.667	19	3.04	56⅓	40	25	58	3	0	0	6
Career average		4	46	5	6	.474	43	4.12	93⅔	52	54	89	10	1	0	7
Cubs average		**7**	**37**	**4**	**6**	**.405**	**48**	**4.60**	**94⅔**	**48**	**59**	**91**	**10**	**1**	**0**	**4**
Career total		49	504	55	61	.474	472	4.12	1032	574	590	978	105	10	1	73
Cubs total		**49**	**260**	**30**	**44**	**.405**	**338**	**4.60**	**661⅔**	**333**	**414**	**639**	**68**	**10**	**1**	**28**

Luby, John Perkins (Pat)
HEIGHT: 6'0" RIGHTHANDER BORN: 6/1869 CHARLESTON, SOUTH CAROLINA DIED: 4/24/1899 CHARLESTON, SOUTH CAROLINA

YEAR	TEAM	STARTS	GAMES	WON	LOST	PCT	ER	ERA	INNINGS PITCHED	STRIKE-OUTS	WALKS	HITS ALLOWED	HRS ALLOWED	COMP. GAMES	SHUT-OUTS	SAVES
1890	ChN-N	31	34	20	8	.714	95	3.19	267⅔	85	95	226	6	26	0	0
1891	ChN-N	24	30	10	12	.455	109	4.76	206	52	94	221	11	18	0	1
1892	ChN-N	27	31	11	17	.393	86	3.07	252⅓	68	103	248	10	24	0	0
1895	Lou-N	6	11	1	6	.143	54	6.81	71⅓	12	19	115	5	5	0	0
Career average		22	27	11	11	.494	86	3.88	199⅓	54	78	203	8	18	0	0
Cubs average		**27**	**32**	**14**	**12**	**.526**	**97**	**3.60**	**242**	**68**	**97**	**232**	**9**	**23**	**0**	**0**
Career total		88	106	42	43	.494	344	3.88	797⅓	217	311	810	32	73	1	1
Cubs total		**82**	**95**	**41**	**37**	**.526**	**290**	**3.60**	**726**	**205**	**292**	**695**	**27**	**68**	**1**	**1**

Lundgren, Carl Leonard (The Human Icicle)
HEIGHT: 5'11" RIGHTHANDER BORN: 2/16/1880 MARENGO, ILLINOIS DIED: 8/21/1934 MARENGO, ILLINOIS

YEAR	TEAM	STARTS	GAMES	WON	LOST	PCT	ER	ERA	INNINGS PITCHED	STRIKE-OUTS	WALKS	HITS ALLOWED	HRS ALLOWED	COMP. GAMES	SHUT-OUTS	SAVES
1902	ChC-N	18	18	9	9	.500	35	1.97	160	68	45	158	2	17	1	0
1903	ChC-N	20	27	11	9	.550	63	2.93	193⅓	67	60	191	1	16	0	3
1904	ChC-N	27	31	17	9	.654	70	2.60	242	106	77	203	2	25	2	1
1905	ChC-N	19	23	13	5	.722	42	2.23	169⅓	69	53	132	3	16	3	0
1906	ChC-N	24	27	17	6	.739	51	2.21	207⅔	103	89	160	3	21	5	2
1907	ChC-N	25	28	18	7	.720	27	1.17	207	84	92	130	0	21	7	0
1908	ChC-N	15	23	6	9	.400	65	4.22	138⅔	38	56	149	5	9	1	0
1909	ChC-N	1	2	0	1	.000	2	4.15	4⅓	0	4	6	0	0	0	0
Career average		19	22	11	7	.623	44	2.42	165⅓	67	60	141	2	16	2	1
Cubs average		**19**	**22**	**11**	**7**	**.623**	**44**	**2.42**	**165⅓**	**67**	**60**	**141**	**2**	**16**	**2**	**1**
Career total		149	179	91	55	.623	355	2.42	1322⅓	535	476	1129	16	125	19	6
Cubs total		**149**	**179**	**91**	**55**	**.623**	**355**	**2.42**	**1322⅓**	**535**	**476**	**1129**	**16**	**125**	**19**	**6**

Lynch, Edward Francis (Ed)
HEIGHT: 6'6" RIGHTHANDER BORN: 2/25/1956 BROOKLYN, NEW YORK

YEAR	TEAM	STARTS	GAMES	WON	LOST	PCT	ER	ERA	INNINGS PITCHED	STRIKE-OUTS	WALKS	HITS ALLOWED	HRS ALLOWED	COMP. GAMES	SHUT-OUTS	SAVES
1980	NYM-N	4	5	1	1	.500	11	5.12	19⅓	9	5	24	0	0	0	0
1981	NYM-N	13	17	4	5	.444	26	2.91	80⅓	27	21	79	6	0	0	0
1982	NYM-N	12	43	4	8	.333	55	3.55	139⅓	51	40	145	6	0	0	2
1983	NYM-N	27	30	10	10	.500	83	4.28	174⅔	44	41	208	17	1	0	0
1984	NYM-N	13	40	9	8	.529	62	4.50	124	62	24	169	14	0	0	2

(continued)

YEAR	TEAM	STARTS	GAMES	WON	LOST	PCT	ER	ERA	INNINGS PITCHED	STRIKE-OUTS	WALKS	HITS ALLOWED	HRS ALLOWED	COMP. GAMES	SHUT-OUTS	SAVES
(Lynch, E.F., continued)																
1985	NYM-N	29	31	10	8	.556	73	3.44	191	65	27	188	19	6	1	0
1986	NYM-N	0	1	0	0	—	0	0.00	1 2/3	1	0	2	0	0	0	0
1986	ChC-N	13	23	7	5	.583	42	3.79	99 2/3	57	23	105	10	1	1	0
1987	ChC-N	8	58	2	9	.182	66	5.38	110 1/3	80	48	130	17	0	0	4
Career average		15	31	6	7	.465	52	4.00	117 2/3	50	29	131	11	1	0	1
Cubs average		11	41	5	7	.391	54	4.63	105	69	36	118	14	1	1	2
Career total		119	248	47	54	.465	418	4.00	940 1/3	396	229	1050	89	8	2	8
Cubs total		21	81	9	14	.391	108	4.63	210	137	71	235	27	1	1	4

Lynch, Thomas S. (Dummy)

HEIGHT: 5'11"　BORN: 1863 PERU, ILLINOIS　DIED: 5/13/1903 PERU, ILLINOIS

YEAR	TEAM	STARTS	GAMES	WON	LOST	PCT	ER	ERA	INNINGS PITCHED	STRIKE-OUTS	WALKS	HITS ALLOWED	HRS ALLOWED	COMP. GAMES	SHUT-OUTS	SAVES
1884	ChN-N	1	1	0	0	—	2	2.57	7	2	3	7	1	0	0	0
Career average		1	1	0	0	—	2	2.57	7	2	3	7	1	0	0	0
Cubs average		1	1	0	0	—	2	2.57	7	2	3	7	1	0	0	0
Career total		1	1	0	0	—	2	2.57	7	2	3	7	1	0	0	0
Cubs total		1	1	0	0	—	2	2.57	7	2	3	7	1	0	0	0

Lynn, Japhet Monroe (Red)

HEIGHT: 6'0"　RIGHTHANDER　BORN: 12/27/1913 KENNEY, TEXAS　DIED: 10/27/1977 BELLVILLE, TEXAS

YEAR	TEAM	STARTS	GAMES	WON	LOST	PCT	ER	ERA	INNINGS PITCHED	STRIKE-OUTS	WALKS	HITS ALLOWED	HRS ALLOWED	COMP. GAMES	SHUT-OUTS	SAVES
1939	Det-A	0	4	0	1	.000	8	8.64	8 1/3	3	3	11	2	0	0	0
1939	NYG-N	0	26	1	0	1.000	17	3.08	49 2/3	22	21	44	3	0	0	1
1940	NYG-N	0	33	4	3	.571	18	3.83	42 1/3	25	24	40	3	0	0	3
1944	ChC-N	7	22	5	4	.556	38	4.06	84 1/3	35	37	80	4	4	1	1
Career average		2	28	3	3	.556	27	3.95	61 2/3	28	28	58	4	1	0	2
Cubs average		7	22	5	4	.556	38	4.06	84 1/3	35	37	80	4	4	1	1
Career total		7	85	10	8	.556	81	3.95	184 2/3	85	85	175	12	4	1	5
Cubs total		7	22	5	4	.556	38	4.06	84 1/3	35	37	80	4	4	1	1

Mack, William Francis (Bill)

HEIGHT: 6'1"　LEFTHANDER　BORN: 2/12/1885 ELMIRA, NEW YORK　DIED: 9/30/1971 ELMIRA, NEW YORK

YEAR	TEAM	STARTS	GAMES	WON	LOST	PCT	ER	ERA	INNINGS PITCHED	STRIKE-OUTS	WALKS	HITS ALLOWED	HRS ALLOWED	COMP. GAMES	SHUT-OUTS	SAVES
1908	ChC-N	0	2	0	0	—	2	3.00	6	2	1	5	1	0	0	0
Career average		0	2	0	0	—	2	3.00	6	2	1	5	1	0	0	0
Cubs average		0	2	0	0	—	2	3.00	6	2	1	5	1	0	0	0
Career total		0	2	0	0	—	2	3.00	6	2	1	5	1	0	0	0
Cubs total		0	2	0	0	—	2	3.00	6	2	1	5	1	0	0	0

Madden, Leonard Joseph (Len *or* Lefty)

HEIGHT: 6'2"　LEFTHANDER　BORN: 7/2/1890 TOLEDO, OHIO　DIED: 9/9/1949 TOLEDO, OHIO

YEAR	TEAM	STARTS	GAMES	WON	LOST	PCT	ER	ERA	INNINGS PITCHED	STRIKE-OUTS	WALKS	HITS ALLOWED	HRS ALLOWED	COMP. GAMES	SHUT-OUTS	SAVES
1912	ChC-N	2	6	0	1	.000	4	2.92	12 1/3	5	9	16	1	0	0	0
Career average		2	6	0	1	.000	4	2.92	12 1/3	5	9	16	1	0	0	0
Cubs average		2	6	0	1	.000	4	2.92	12 1/3	5	9	16	1	0	0	0
Career total		2	6	0	1	.000	4	2.92	12 1/3	5	9	16	1	0	0	0
Cubs total		2	6	0	1	.000	4	2.92	12 1/3	5	9	16	1	0	0	0

Gregory (Greg) Alan Maddux, rhp, 1986–present

Along with the Yankees' Roger Clemens, Greg Maddux has been the best pitcher of his generation—a talented, athletic righthander who has won four consecutive Cy Youngs.

Maddux was born on April 14, 1966, in San Angelo, Texas. After a brief stint in the minor leagues, he came to the Cubs as a skinny, baby-faced 20-year-old in 1986. He won eight games in his first two years in Chicago, but in 1988 he blossomed into a bona fide big leaguer, leading the team in wins (18), ERA (3.18), innings pitched (249) and games started (34).

From that season on, Maddux has been over-whelmingly consistent, starting 30 or more games 11 of the last 14 years, and always being among the league leaders in wins, ERA, innings pitched, complete games and shutouts.

He has done it with a cut fastball that he can throw for strikes no matter where he is in the count and an assortment of off-speed pitches that keep a batter off stride throughout his at-bat.

He is also one of the best fielding pitchers in either league. He has won three Gold Gloves as a pitcher and has long been known as "the fifth infielder" by teammates in Chicago and later Atlanta. Maddux has tied the National League record for putouts for a pitcher (39) three times in his career.

Maddux is also the ultimate teammate. In 1989 he was 19-12 with one start to go. The Cubs had already clinched the National League East flag, and Cubs manager Don Zimmer asked Maddux to forgo his final start to enable him to be rested for his first start in the National League Championship Series in a few days. Maddux didn't hesitate. (Unfortunately, it didn't help, as the Cubs lost the game.)

After two average seasons in 1990 and 1991 (30-26 in the two years), Maddux stepped up to the next level in 1992. His 20 wins led the league that year, as did his 268 innings pitched. That performance won him the first of his four Cy Young awards.

Maddux became a free agent at the end of the season, and the Cubs declined to match an offer extended to Maddux by the Atlanta Braves. The results were predictable: the Braves have made the postseason every season Maddux has been on the roster (except in 1994, when baseball cancelled the playoffs due to the strike). The Cubs have been a wild card once. Maddux led Atlanta into the play-offs again, in 2001, and he shows no signs of slowing down.

Maddux, Gregory Alan (Greg)

HEIGHT: 6'0"   RIGHTHANDER   BORN: 4/14/1966 SAN ANGELO, TEXAS

YEAR	TEAM	STARTS	GAMES	WON	LOST	PCT	ER	ERA	INNINGS PITCHED	STRIKE-OUTS	WALKS	HITS ALLOWED	HRS ALLOWED	COMP. GAMES	SHUT-OUTS	SAVES
1986	ChC-N	5	6	2	4	.333	19	5.52	31	20	11	44	3	1	0	0
1987	ChC-N	27	30	6	14	.300	97	5.61	155 ⅔	101	74	181	17	1	0	0
1988	ChC-N	34	34	18	8	.692	88	3.18	249	140	81	230	13	9	3	0
1989	ChC-N	35	35	19	12	.613	78	2.95	238 ⅓	135	82	222	13	7	1	0
1990	ChC-N	35	35	15	15	.500	91	3.46	237	144	71	242	11	8	2	0
1991	ChC-N	37	37	15	11	.577	98	3.35	263	198	66	232	18	7	2	0
1992	ChC-N	35	35	20	11	.645	65	2.18	268	199	70	201	7	9	4	0
1993	Atl-N	36	36	20	10	.667	70	2.36	267	197	52	228	14	8	1	0
1994	Atl-N	25	25	16	6	.727	35	1.56	202	156	31	150	4	10	3	0
1995	Atl-N	28	28	19	2	.905	38	1.63	209 ⅔	181	23	147	8	10	3	0
1996	Atl-N	35	35	15	11	.577	74	2.72	245	172	28	225	11	5	1	0
1997	Atl-N	33	33	19	4	.826	57	2.20	232 ⅔	177	20	200	9	5	2	0
1998	Atl-N	34	34	18	9	.667	62	2.22	251	204	45	201	13	9	5	0
1999	Atl-N	33	33	19	9	.679	87	3.57	219 ⅓	136	37	258	16	4	0	0
2000	Atl-N	35	35	19	9	.679	83	3.00	249 ⅓	190	42	225	19	6	3	0
2001	Atl-N	34	34	17	11	.607	79	3.05	233	173	27	220	20	3	3	0
Career average		31	32	16	9	.638	70	2.84	222	158	48	200	12	6	2	0
Cubs average		**30**	**30**	**14**	**11**	**.559**	**77**	**3.35**	**206**	**134**	**65**	**193**	**12**	**6**	**2**	**0**
Career total		501	505	257	146	.638	1121	2.84	3551	2523	760	3206	196	102	34	0
Cubs total		**208**	**212**	**95**	**75**	**.559**	**536**	**3.35**	**1442**	**937**	**455**	**1352**	**82**	**42**	**13**	**0**

Mahay, Ronald Matthew (Ron)
HEIGHT: 6'2" LEFTHANDER BORN: 6/28/1971 CRESTWOOD, ILLINOIS

YEAR	TEAM	STARTS	GAMES	WON	LOST	PCT	ER	ERA	INNINGS PITCHED	STRIKE-OUTS	WALKS	HITS ALLOWED	HRS ALLOWED	COMP. GAMES	SHUT-OUTS	SAVES
1997	Bos-A	0	28	3	0	1.000	7	2.52	25	22	11	19	3	0	0	0
1998	Bos-A	0	29	1	1	.500	10	3.46	26	14	15	26	2	0	0	1
1999	Oak-A	1	6	2	0	1.000	4	1.86	19⅓	15	3	8	2	0	0	1
2000	Oak-A	2	5	0	1	.000	16	9.00	16	5	9	26	4	0	0	0
2000	Fla-N	0	18	1	0	1.000	17	6.04	25⅓	27	16	31	6	0	0	0
2001	**ChC-N**	**0**	**17**	**0**	**0**	**—**	**6**	**2.61**	**20⅔**	**24**	**15**	**14**	**4**	**0**	**0**	**0**
Career average		1	21	1	0	.778	12	4.08	26⅓	21	14	25	4	0	0	0
Cubs average		**0**	**17**	**0**	**0**	**—**	**6**	**2.61**	**20⅔**	**24**	**15**	**14**	**4**	**0**	**0**	**0**
Career total		3	103	7	2	.778	60	4.08	132⅓	107	69	124	21	0	0	2
Cubs total		**0**	**17**	**0**	**0**	**—**	**6**	**2.61**	**20⅔**	**24**	**15**	**14**	**4**	**0**	**0**	**0**

Mains, Willard Eben (Grasshopper)
HEIGHT: 6'2" RIGHTHANDER BORN: 7/7/1868 NORTH WINDHAM, MAINE   DIED: 5/23/1923 BRIDGTON, MAINE

YEAR	TEAM	STARTS	GAMES	WON	LOST	PCT	ER	ERA	INNINGS PITCHED	STRIKE-OUTS	WALKS	HITS ALLOWED	HRS ALLOWED	COMP. GAMES	SHUT-OUTS	SAVES
1888	**ChN-N**	**2**	**2**	**1**	**1**	**.500**	**6**	**4.91**	**11**	**5**	**6**	**8**	**0**	**1**	**0**	**0**
1891	Cin-AA	23	30	12	12	.500	61	2.69	204	76	107	196	3	19	0	0
1891	Mil-AA	2	2	0	2	.000	12	10.80	10	2	10	14	1	1	0	1
1896	Bos-N	5	8	3	2	.600	26	5.48	42⅔	13	31	43	1	3	0	0
Career average		11	14	5	6	.485	35	3.53	89⅓	32	51	87	2	8	0	0
Cubs average		**2**	**2**	**1**	**1**	**.500**	**6**	**4.91**	**11**	**5**	**6**	**8**	**0**	**1**	**0**	**0**
Career total		32	42	16	17	.485	105	3.53	267⅔	96	154	261	5	24	0	1
Cubs total		**2**	**2**	**1**	**1**	**.500**	**6**	**4.91**	**11**	**5**	**6**	**8**	**0**	**1**	**0**	**0**

Mairena, Oswaldo Antonio
HEIGHT: 5'11" LEFTHANDER BORN: 7/30/1975 CHINANDEGA, NICARAGUA

YEAR	TEAM	STARTS	GAMES	WON	LOST	PCT	ER	ERA	INNINGS PITCHED	STRIKE-OUTS	WALKS	HITS ALLOWED	HRS ALLOWED	COMP. GAMES	SHUT-OUTS	SAVES
2000	**ChC-N**	**0**	**2**	**0**	**0**	**—**	**4**	**18.00**	**2**	**0**	**2**	**7**	**1**	**0**	**0**	**0**
Career average		0	2	0	0	—	4	18.00	2	0	2	7	1	0	0	0
Cubs average		**0**	**2**	**0**	**0**	**—**	**4**	**18.00**	**2**	**0**	**2**	**7**	**1**	**0**	**0**	**0**
Career total		0	2	0	0	—	4	18.00	2	0	2	7	1	0	0	0
Cubs total		**0**	**2**	**0**	**0**	**—**	**4**	**18.00**	**2**	**0**	**2**	**7**	**1**	**0**	**0**	**0**

Malarkey, John S.
HEIGHT: 5'11" RIGHTHANDER BORN: 5/4/1872 SPRINGFIELD, OHIO   DIED: 10/29/1949 CINCINNATI, OHIO

YEAR	TEAM	STARTS	GAMES	WON	LOST	PCT	ER	ERA	INNINGS PITCHED	STRIKE-OUTS	WALKS	HITS ALLOWED	HRS ALLOWED	COMP. GAMES	SHUT-OUTS	SAVES
1894	Was-N	3	3	2	1	.667	12	4.15	26	3	5	42	1	3	0	0
1895	Was-N	8	22	0	10	.000	67	5.99	100⅔	32	60	135	3	5	0	2
1896	Was-N	1	1	0	1	.000	1	1.29	7	0	3	9	1	0	0	0
1899	**ChN-N**	**1**	**1**	**0**	**1**	**.000**	**13**	**13.00**	**9**	**7**	**5**	**19**	**0**	**1**	**0**	**0**
1902	Bos-N	19	21	8	10	.444	49	2.59	170⅓	39	58	158	0	17	1	1
1903	Bos-N	27	32	11	16	.407	87	3.09	253	98	96	266	5	25	2	0
Career average		10	13	4	7	.350	38	3.64	94⅓	30	38	105	2	9	1	1
Cubs average		**1**	**1**	**0**	**1**	**.000**	**13**	**13.00**	**9**	**7**	**5**	**19**	**0**	**1**	**0**	**0**
Career total		59	80	21	39	.350	229	3.64	566	179	227	629	10	51	3	3
Cubs total		**1**	**1**	**0**	**1**	**.000**	**13**	**13.00**	**9**	**7**	**5**	**19**	**0**	**1**	**0**	**0**

Malone, Perce Leigh (Pat)

HEIGHT: 6'0"   RIGHTHANDER   BORN: 9/25/1902 ALTOONA, PENNSYLVANIA   DIED: 5/13/1943 ALTOONA, PENNSYLVANIA

YEAR	TEAM	STARTS	GAMES	WON	LOST	PCT	ER	ERA	INNINGS PITCHED	STRIKE-OUTS	WALKS	HITS ALLOWED	HRS ALLOWED	COMP. GAMES	SHUT-OUTS	SAVES
1928	ChC-N	25	42	18	13	.581	79	2.84	250 2/3	155	99	218	15	16	2	2
1929	ChC-N	30	40	22	10	.688	106	3.57	267	166	102	283	12	19	5	2
1930	ChC-N	35	45	20	9	.690	119	3.94	271 2/3	142	96	290	14	22	2	4
1931	ChC-N	30	36	16	9	.640	99	3.90	228 1/3	112	88	229	9	12	2	0
1932	ChC-N	32	37	15	17	.469	89	3.38	237	120	78	222	13	17	2	0
1933	ChC-N	26	31	10	14	.417	81	3.91	186 1/3	72	59	186	10	13	2	0
1934	ChC-N	21	34	14	7	.667	75	3.53	191	111	55	200	14	8	1	0
1935	NYY-A	2	29	3	5	.375	34	5.43	56 1/3	25	33	53	7	0	0	3
1936	NYY-A	9	35	12	4	.750	57	3.81	134 2/3	72	60	144	4	5	0	9
1937	NYY-A	9	28	4	4	.500	56	5.48	92	49	35	109	5	3	0	6
Career average		22	36	13	9	.593	80	3.74	191 2/3	102	71	193	10	12	2	3
Cubs average		28	38	16	11	.593	93	3.57	233	125	82	233	12	15	2	1
Career total		219	357	134	92	.593	795	3.74	1915	1024	705	1934	103	115	16	26
Cubs total		199	265	115	79	.593	648	3.57	1632	878	577	1628	87	107	16	8

Perce Leigh "Pat" Malone, rhp, 1928–37

"Pat" Malone was a Cubs mainstay in the late 1920s and the early 1930s, helping the "Baby Bears" to a pair of National League crowns.

Malone was born on September 25, 1902, in Altoona, Pennsylvania. In 1928, after knocking around the minors for a few years, he debuted with the Cubs in April. Malone was almost a New York Giant, as he was signed into the Giants organization. However, Giants manager John McGraw reportedly caught him partying and released him; the Cubs grabbed him.

It looked like a bad idea at first: Malone staggered to an 0-7 start. But he eventually righted his own ship and finished the year 18-13, meaning he went 18-6 the rest of that year.

In 1929 the hard-throwing Malone led the league in strikeouts with 166 and in wins with 22 as the Cubs annexed the National League crown. He stumbled in the World Series that year, losing a pair of games as the American League champion A's won the pennant.

Malone bounced back in 1930, going 20-9 and leading the league in complete games with 20, but after that season, his numbers began slowly dropping. His critics complained that the gregarious Malone was partaking of the nightlife too much, particularly on the road. Manager Joe McCarthy, who loved gamers (players who gave 110 percent on the field), had a soft spot for Malone even though McCarthy abhorred boozers.

Malone had a kindred spirit on the team in power-hitting outfielder Lewis Robert "Hack" Wilson. The two men were frequent drinking companions on the road (at home, their wives usually came to the park and got them before they could go out).

The 200-pound 6' Malone was also not averse to a fracas. More than once, he and Wilson would mix it up with a couple of strangers in a bar after some real or imagined slight.

Malone pitched in Chicago until 1934. After that year, he was sold to the Yankees for $15,000. His old manager, McCarthy, used him primarily in relief, and Malone led the American League in saves in 1936 as the Yankees won the World Series. Malone pitched briefly in 1937 before retiring. He died in Altoona, Pennsyvania, in 1943.

Manders, Harold Carl (Hal)
HEIGHT: 6'0"   RIGHTHANDER   BORN: 6/14/1917 WAUKEE, IOWA

YEAR	TEAM	STARTS	GAMES	WON	LOST	PCT	ER	ERA	INNINGS PITCHED	STRIKE-OUTS	WALKS	HITS ALLOWED	HRS ALLOWED	COMP. GAMES	SHUT-OUTS	SAVES
1941	Det-A	0	8	1	0	1.000	4	2.35	15 1/3	7	8	13	0	0	0	0
1942	Det-A	0	18	2	0	1.000	15	4.09	33	14	15	39	4	0	0	0
1946	Det-A	0	2	0	0	—	7	10.50	6	3	2	8	1	0	0	0
1946	**ChC-N**	**1**	**2**	**0**	**1**	**.000**	**6**	**9.00**	**6**	**4**	**3**	**11**	**1**	**0**	**0**	**0**
Career average		0	10	1	0	.750	11	4.77	20	9	9	24	2	0	0	0
Cubs average		**1**	**2**	**0**	**1**	**.000**	**6**	**9.00**	**6**	**4**	**3**	**11**	**1**	**0**	**0**	**0**
Career total		1	30	3	1	.750	32	4.77	60 1/3	28	28	71	6	0	0	0
Cubs total		**1**	**2**	**0**	**1**	**.000**	**6**	**9.00**	**6**	**4**	**3**	**11**	**1**	**0**	**0**	**0**

Manville, Richard Wesley (Dick)
HEIGHT: 6'4"   RIGHTHANDER   BORN: 12/25/1926 DES MOINES, IOWA

YEAR	TEAM	STARTS	GAMES	WON	LOST	PCT	ER	ERA	INNINGS PITCHED	STRIKE-OUTS	WALKS	HITS ALLOWED	HRS ALLOWED	COMP. GAMES	SHUT-OUTS	SAVES
1950	Bos-N	0	1	0	0	—	0	0.00	2	2	3	0	0	0	0	0
1952	**ChC-N**	**0**	**11**	**0**	**0**	**—**	**15**	**7.94**	**17**	**6**	**12**	**25**	**2**	**0**	**0**	**0**
Career average		0	6	0	0	—	8	7.11	9 2/3	4	8	13	1	0	0	0
Cubs average		**0**	**11**	**0**	**0**	**—**	**15**	**7.94**	**17**	**6**	**12**	**25**	**2**	**0**	**0**	**0**
Career total		0	12	0	0	—	15	7.11	19	8	15	25	2	0	0	0
Cubs total		**0**	**11**	**0**	**0**	**—**	**15**	**7.94**	**17**	**6**	**12**	**25**	**2**	**0**	**0**	**0**

Martin, Elwood Good (Speed)
HEIGHT: 6'0"   RIGHTHANDER   BORN: 9/15/1893 WAWAWAI, WASHINGTON   DIED: 6/14/1983 LEMON GROVE, CALIFORNIA

YEAR	TEAM	STARTS	GAMES	WON	LOST	PCT	ER	ERA	INNINGS PITCHED	STRIKE-OUTS	WALKS	HITS ALLOWED	HRS ALLOWED	COMP. GAMES	SHUT-OUTS	SAVES
1917	StL-A	2	9	0	2	.000	10	5.74	15 2/3	5	5	20	0	0	0	0
1918	**ChC-N**	**5**	**9**	**5**	**2**	**.714**	**11**	**1.84**	**53 2/3**	**16**	**14**	**47**	**0**	**4**	**1**	**1**
1919	**ChC-N**	**14**	**35**	**8**	**8**	**.500**	**45**	**2.47**	**163 2/3**	**54**	**52**	**158**	**2**	**7**	**2**	**2**
1920	**ChC-N**	**13**	**35**	**4**	**15**	**.211**	**73**	**4.83**	**136**	**44**	**50**	**165**	**2**	**6**	**0**	**2**
1921	**ChC-N**	**28**	**37**	**11**	**15**	**.423**	**105**	**4.35**	**217 1/3**	**86**	**68**	**245**	**12**	**13**	**1**	**1**
1922	**ChC-N**	**1**	**1**	**1**	**0**	**1.000**	**5**	**7.50**	**6**	**2**	**2**	**10**	**0**	**0**	**0**	**0**
Career average		11	21	5	7	.408	42	3.78	98 2/3	35	32	108	3	5	1	1
Cubs average		**12**	**23**	**6**	**8**	**.420**	**48**	**3.73**	**115 1/3**	**40**	**37**	**125**	**3**	**6**	**1**	**1**
Career total		63	126	29	42	.408	249	3.78	592 1/3	207	191	645	16	30	4	6
Cubs total		**61**	**117**	**29**	**40**	**.420**	**239**	**3.73**	**576 2/3**	**202**	**186**	**625**	**16**	**30**	**4**	**6**

Martin, Morris Webster (Morrie)
HEIGHT: 6'0"   LEFTHANDER   BORN: 9/3/1922 DIXON, MISSOURI

YEAR	TEAM	STARTS	GAMES	WON	LOST	PCT	ER	ERA	INNINGS PITCHED	STRIKE-OUTS	WALKS	HITS ALLOWED	HRS ALLOWED	COMP. GAMES	SHUT-OUTS	SAVES
1949	Bro-N	4	10	1	3	.250	24	7.04	30 2/3	15	15	39	5	0	0	0
1951	Phi-A	13	35	11	4	.733	58	3.78	138	35	63	139	13	3	1	0
1952	Phi-A	5	5	0	2	.000	18	6.39	25 1/3	13	15	32	1	0	0	0
1953	Phi-A	11	58	10	12	.455	77	4.43	156 1/3	64	59	158	12	2	0	7
1954	Phi-A	6	13	2	4	.333	32	5.47	52 2/3	24	19	57	9	2	0	0
1954	CWS-A	2	35	5	4	.556	16	2.06	70	31	24	52	5	1	0	5
1955	CWS-A	0	37	2	3	.400	21	3.63	52	22	20	50	4	0	0	5
1956	CWS-A	0	10	1	0	1.000	10	4.91	18 1/3	9	7	21	1	0	0	2
1956	Bal-A	0	9	1	1	.500	6	10.80	5	3	2	10	1	0	0	0
1957	StL-N	1	4	0	0	—	3	2.53	10 2/3	7	4	5	0	0	0	0
1958	StL-N	0	17	3	1	.750	13	4.74	24 2/3	16	12	19	3	0	0	0
1958	Cle-A	0	14	2	0	1.000	5	2.41	18 2/3	5	8	20	0	0	0	1
1959	**ChC-N**	**0**	**3**	**0**	**0**	**—**	**5**	**19.29**	**2 1/3**	**1**	**1**	**5**	**2**	**0**	**0**	**0**
Career average		4	25	4	3	.528	29	4.29	60 1/3	25	25	61	6	1	0	2
Cubs average		**0**	**3**	**0**	**0**	**—**	**5**	**19.29**	**2 1/3**	**1**	**1**	**5**	**2**	**0**	**0**	**0**
Career total		42	250	38	34	.528	288	4.29	604 2/3	245	249	607	56	8	1	15
Cubs total		**0**	**3**	**0**	**0**	**—**	**5**	**19.29**	**2 1/3**	**1**	**1**	**5**	**2**	**0**	**0**	**0**

Martz, Randy Carl
HEIGHT: 6'4" RIGHTHANDER BORN: 5/28/1956 HARRISBURG, PENNSYLVANIA

YEAR	TEAM	STARTS	GAMES	WON	LOST	PCT	ER	ERA	INNINGS PITCHED	STRIKE-OUTS	WALKS	HITS ALLOWED	HRS ALLOWED	COMP. GAMES	SHUT-OUTS	SAVES
1980	ChC-N	6	6	1	2	.333	7	2.08	30 1/3	5	11	28	1	0	0	0
1981	ChC-N	14	33	5	7	.417	44	3.68	107 2/3	32	49	103	6	1	0	6
1982	ChC-N	24	28	11	10	.524	69	4.21	147 2/3	40	36	157	17	1	0	0
1983	CWS-A	1	1	0	0	—	2	3.60	5	1	4	4	0	0	0	0
Career average		11	17	4	5	.472	31	3.78	72 2/3	20	25	73	6	1	0	2
Cubs average		**15**	**22**	**6**	**6**	**.472**	**40**	**3.78**	**95 1/3**	**26**	**32**	**96**	**8**	**1**	**0**	**2**
Career total		45	68	17	19	.472	122	3.78	290 2/3	78	100	292	24	2	0	7
Cubs total		**44**	**67**	**17**	**19**	**.472**	**120**	**3.78**	**285 2/3**	**77**	**96**	**288**	**24**	**2**	**0**	**7**

Mason, Michael Paul (Mike)
HEIGHT: 6'2" LEFTHANDER BORN: 11/21/1958 FAIRBAULT, MINNESOTA

YEAR	TEAM	STARTS	GAMES	WON	LOST	PCT	ER	ERA	INNINGS PITCHED	STRIKE-OUTS	WALKS	HITS ALLOWED	HRS ALLOWED	COMP. GAMES	SHUT-OUTS	SAVES
1982	Tex-A	4	4	1	2	.333	13	5.09	23	8	9	21	3	0	0	0
1983	Tex-A	0	5	0	2	.000	7	5.91	10 2/3	9	6	10	0	0	0	0
1984	Tex-A	24	36	9	13	.409	74	3.61	184 1/3	113	51	159	18	4	0	0
1985	Tex-A	30	38	8	15	.348	96	4.83	179	92	73	212	22	1	1	0
1986	Tex-A	22	27	7	3	.700	65	4.33	135	85	56	135	11	2	1	0
1987	Tex-A	6	8	0	2	.000	18	5.59	29	21	22	37	6	0	0	0
1987	ChC-N	4	17	4	1	.800	24	5.68	38	28	23	43	4	0	0	0
1988	Min-A	0	5	0	1	.000	8	10.80	6 2/3	7	9	8	1	0	0	0
Career average		13	20	4	6	.426	44	4.53	86 2/3	52	36	89	9	1	0	0
Cubs average		**4**	**17**	**4**	**1**	**.800**	**24**	**5.68**	**38**	**28**	**23**	**43**	**4**	**0**	**0**	**0**
Career total		90	140	29	39	.426	305	4.53	605 2/3	363	249	625	65	7	2	0
Cubs total		**4**	**17**	**4**	**1**	**.800**	**24**	**5.68**	**38**	**28**	**23**	**43**	**4**	**0**	**0**	**0**

Mauck, Alfred Maris (Hal)
HEIGHT: 5'11" RIGHTHANDER BORN: 3/6/1869 PRINCETON, INDIANA   DIED: 4/27/1921 PRINCETON, INDIANA

YEAR	TEAM	STARTS	GAMES	WON	LOST	PCT	ER	ERA	INNINGS PITCHED	STRIKE-OUTS	WALKS	HITS ALLOWED	HRS ALLOWED	COMP. GAMES	SHUT-OUTS	SAVES
1893	ChN-N	18	23	7	10	.412	70	4.41	143	23	60	168	2	12	1	1
Career average		18	23	7	10	.412	70	4.41	143	23	60	168	2	12	1	1
Cubs average		**18**	**23**	**7**	**10**	**.412**	**70**	**4.41**	**143**	**23**	**60**	**168**	**2**	**12**	**1**	**1**
Career total		18	23	7	10	.412	70	4.41	143	23	60	168	2	12	1	1
Cubs total		**18**	**23**	**7**	**10**	**.412**	**70**	**4.41**	**143**	**23**	**60**	**168**	**2**	**12**	**1**	**1**

May, Frank Spruiell (Jakie)
HEIGHT: 5'8" LEFTHANDER BORN: 11/25/1895 YOUNGSVILLE, NORTH CAROLINA   DIED: 6/3/1970 WENDELL, NORTH CAROLINA

YEAR	TEAM	STARTS	GAMES	WON	LOST	PCT	ER	ERA	INNINGS PITCHED	STRIKE-OUTS	WALKS	HITS ALLOWED	HRS ALLOWED	COMP. GAMES	SHUT-OUTS	SAVES
1917	StL-N	1	15	0	0	—	11	3.38	29 1/3	18	11	29	0	0	0	0
1918	StL-N	16	29	5	6	.455	65	3.83	152 2/3	61	69	149	2	6	0	0
1919	StL-N	19	28	3	12	.200	45	3.22	125 2/3	58	87	99	1	8	1	0
1920	StL-N	5	16	1	4	.200	24	3.06	70 2/3	33	37	65	0	3	0	0
1921	StL-N	5	5	1	3	.250	11	4.71	21	5	12	29	0	1	0	0
1924	Cin-N	3	38	3	3	.500	33	3.00	99	59	29	104	2	2	0	6
1925	Cin-N	12	36	8	9	.471	59	3.87	137 1/3	74	45	146	3	7	1	2
1926	Cin-N	15	45	13	9	.591	60	3.22	167 2/3	103	44	175	4	9	1	3
1927	Cin-N	28	44	15	12	.556	92	3.51	235 2/3	121	70	242	4	17	2	1
1928	Cin-N	11	21	3	5	.375	39	4.42	79 1/3	39	35	99	1	1	1	1
1929	Cin-N	24	41	10	14	.417	102	4.61	199	92	75	219	7	10	0	3
1930	Cin-N	18	26	3	11	.214	72	5.77	112 1/3	44	41	147	6	5	1	0
1931	ChC-N	4	31	5	5	.500	34	3.87	79	38	43	81	2	1	0	2
1932	ChC-N	0	35	2	2	.500	26	4.36	53 2/3	20	19	61	3	0	0	1
Career average		12	29	5	7	.431	48	3.88	111 2/3	55	44	118	3	5	1	1
Cubs average		**2**	**33**	**4**	**4**	**.500**	**30**	**4.07**	**66 1/3**	**29**	**31**	**71**	**3**	**1**	**0**	**2**
Career total		161	410	72	95	.431	673	3.88	1562 1/3	765	617	1645	35	70	7	19
Cubs total		**4**	**66**	**7**	**7**	**.500**	**60**	**4.07**	**132 2/3**	**58**	**62**	**142**	**5**	**1**	**0**	**3**

May, Scott Francis
HEIGHT: 6'1"   RIGHTHANDER   BORN: 11/11/1961 WEST BEND, WISCONSIN

YEAR	TEAM	STARTS	GAMES	WON	LOST	PCT	ER	ERA	INNINGS PITCHED	STRIKE-OUTS	WALKS	HITS ALLOWED	HRS ALLOWED	COMP. GAMES	SHUT-OUTS	SAVES
1988	Tex-A	1	3	0	0	—	7	8.59	7 1/3	4	4	8	3	0	0	0
1991	ChC-N	0	2	0	0	—	4	18.00	2	1	1	6	0	0	0	0
Career average		1	3	0	0	—	6	10.61	4 2/3	3	3	7	2	0	0	0
Cubs average		0	2	0	0	—	4	18.00	2	1	1	6	0	0	0	0
Career total		1	5	0	0	—	11	10.61	9 1/3	5	5	14	3	0	0	0
Cubs total		0	2	0	0	—	4	18.00	2	1	1	6	0	0	0	0

Mayer, Edwin David (Ed)
HEIGHT: 6'2"   LEFTHANDER   BORN: 11/30/1931 SAN FRANCISCO, CALIFORNIA

YEAR	TEAM	STARTS	GAMES	WON	LOST	PCT	ER	ERA	INNINGS PITCHED	STRIKE-OUTS	WALKS	HITS ALLOWED	HRS ALLOWED	COMP. GAMES	SHUT-OUTS	SAVES
1957	ChC-N	1	3	0	0	—	5	5.87	7 2/3	3	2	8	2	0	0	0
1958	ChC-N	0	19	2	2	.500	10	3.80	23 2/3	14	16	15	0	0	0	1
Career average		1	11	1	1	.500	8	4.31	15 2/3	9	9	12	1	0	0	1
Cubs average		1	11	1	1	.500	8	4.31	15 2/3	9	9	12	1	0	0	1
Career total		1	22	2	2	.500	15	4.31	31 1/3	17	18	23	2	0	0	1
Cubs total		1	22	2	2	.500	15	4.31	31 1/3	17	18	23	2	0	0	1

McAfee, William Fort (Bill)
HEIGHT: 6'2"   RIGHTHANDER   BORN: 9/7/1907 SMITHVILLE, GEORGIA   DIED: 7/8/1958 CULPEPPER, VIRGINIA

YEAR	TEAM	STARTS	GAMES	WON	LOST	PCT	ER	ERA	INNINGS PITCHED	STRIKE-OUTS	WALKS	HITS ALLOWED	HRS ALLOWED	COMP. GAMES	SHUT-OUTS	SAVES
1930	ChC-N	0	2	0	0	—	0	0.00	1	0	2	3	0	0	0	0
1931	Bos-N	1	18	0	1	.000	21	6.37	29 2/3	9	10	39	2	0	0	0
1932	Was-A	5	8	6	1	.857	18	3.92	41 1/3	10	22	47	3	2	0	5
1933	Was-A	1	27	3	2	.600	39	6.62	53	14	21	64	3	0	0	0
1934	StL-A	0	28	1	0	1.000	40	5.84	61 2/3	11	26	84	4	0	0	1
Career average		1	17	2	1	.714	24	5.69	37 1/3	9	16	47	2	0	0	0
Cubs average		0	2	0	0	—	0	0.00	1	0	2	3	0	0	0	0
Career total		7	83	10	4	.714	118	5.69	186 2/3	44	81	237	12	2	0	5
Cubs total		0	2	0	0	—	0	0.00	1	0	2	3	0	0	0	0

McCall, Robert Leonard (Dutch)
HEIGHT: 6'1"   LEFTHANDER   BORN: 12/27/1920 COLUMBIA, TENNESSEE   DIED: 1/7/1996 LITTLE ROCK, ARKANSAS

YEAR	TEAM	STARTS	GAMES	WON	LOST	PCT	ER	ERA	INNINGS PITCHED	STRIKE-OUTS	WALKS	HITS ALLOWED	HRS ALLOWED	COMP. GAMES	SHUT-OUTS	SAVES
1948	ChC-N	20	30	4	13	.235	81	4.82	151 1/3	89	85	158	14	5	0	0
Career average		20	30	4	13	.235	81	4.82	151 1/3	89	85	158	14	5	0	0
Cubs average		20	30	4	13	.235	81	4.82	151 1/3	89	85	158	14	5	0	0
Career total		20	30	4	13	.235	81	4.82	151 1/3	89	85	158	14	5	0	0
Cubs total		20	30	4	13	.235	81	4.82	151 1/3	89	85	158	14	5	0	0

McConnell, George Neely
HEIGHT: 6'3"   RIGHTHANDER   BORN: 9/16/1877 SHELBYVILLE, TENNESSEE   DIED: 5/10/1964 CHATTANOOGA, TENNESSEE

YEAR	TEAM	STARTS	GAMES	WON	LOST	PCT	ER	ERA	INNINGS PITCHED	STRIKE-OUTS	WALKS	HITS ALLOWED	HRS ALLOWED	COMP. GAMES	SHUT-OUTS	SAVES
1909	NYA-A	0	2	0	1	.000	1	2.25	4	4	3	3	0	0	0	0
1912	NYA-A	20	23	8	12	.400	54	2.75	176 2/3	91	52	172	3	19	0	3
1913	NYY-A	20	35	4	15	.211	64	3.20	180	72	60	162	2	8	0	3
1914	ChC-N	1	1	0	1	.000	1	1.29	7	3	3	3	0	0	0	0

(continued)

(continued)

YEAR	TEAM	STARTS	GAMES	WON	LOST	PCT	ER	ERA	INNINGS PITCHED	STRIKE-OUTS	WALKS	HITS ALLOWED	HRS ALLOWED	COMP. GAMES	SHUT-OUTS	SAVES
1915	Chi-F	35	44	25	10	.714	74	2.20	303	151	89	262	8	23	4	1
1916	**ChC-N**	**21**	**28**	**4**	**12**	**.250**	**49**	**2.57**	**$171\frac{1}{3}$**	**82**	**35**	**137**	**8**	**8**	**1**	**0**
Career average		16	22	7	9	.446	41	2.60	$140\frac{1}{3}$	67	40	123	4	10	1	1
Cubs average		**11**	**15**	**2**	**7**	**.235**	**25**	**2.52**	**$89\frac{1}{3}$**	**43**	**19**	**70**	**4**	**4**	**1**	**0**
Career total		98	133	41	51	.446	243	2.60	842	403	242	739	21	58	5	4
Cubs total		**22**	**29**	**4**	**13**	**.235**	**50**	**2.52**	**$178\frac{1}{3}$**	**85**	**38**	**140**	**8**	**8**	**1**	**0**

McCormick, James (Jim)

HEIGHT: 5'10"   RIGHTHANDER   BORN: 11/3/1856 GLASGOW, SCOTLAND   DIED: 3/10/1918 PATERSON, NEW JERSEY

YEAR	TEAM	STARTS	GAMES	WON	LOST	PCT	ER	ERA	INNINGS PITCHED	STRIKE-OUTS	WALKS	HITS ALLOWED	HRS ALLOWED	COMP. GAMES	SHUT-OUTS	SAVES
1878	Ind-N	14	14	5	8	.385	22	1.69	117	36	15	128	0	12	1	0
1879	Cle-N	60	62	20	40	.333	147	2.42	$546\frac{1}{3}$	197	74	582	3	59	3	0
1880	Cle-N	74	74	45	28	.616	135	1.85	$657\frac{2}{3}$	260	75	585	2	72	7	0
1881	Cle-N	58	59	26	30	.464	143	2.45	526	178	84	484	4	57	2	0
1882	Cle-N	67	68	36	30	.545	157	2.37	$595\frac{2}{3}$	200	103	550	14	65	4	0
1883	Cle-N	41	43	28	12	.700	70	1.84	342	145	65	316	1	36	1	1
1884	Cle-N	41	42	19	22	.463	114	2.86	359	182	75	357	17	39	3	0
1884	Cin-U	24	24	21	3	.875	36	1.54	210	161	14	151	3	24	7	0
1885	Prv-N	4	4	1	3	.250	10	2.43	37	8	20	34	1	4	0	0
1885	**ChN-N**	**24**	**24**	**20**	**4**	**.833**	**58**	**2.43**	**215**	**88**	**40**	**187**	**1**	**24**	**3**	**0**
1886	**ChN-N**	**42**	**42**	**31**	**11**	**.738**	**109**	**2.82**	**$347\frac{2}{3}$**	**172**	**100**	**341**	**8**	**38**	**2**	**0**
1887	Pit-N	36	36	13	23	.361	154	4.30	$322\frac{1}{3}$	77	84	461	12	36	0	0
Career average		49	49	27	21	.553	116	2.43	$427\frac{2}{3}$	170	75	418	8	47	3	0
Cubs average		**33**	**33**	**26**	**8**	**.773**	**84**	**2.67**	**$281\frac{1}{3}$**	**130**	**70**	**264**	**13**	**31**	**3**	**0**
Career total		485	492	265	214	.553	1155	2.43	$4275\frac{2}{3}$	1704	749	4176	83	466	33	1
Cubs total		**66**	**66**	**51**	**15**	**.773**	**167**	**2.67**	**$562\frac{2}{3}$**	**260**	**140**	**528**	**26**	**62**	**5**	**0**

McDaniel, Lyndall Dale (Lindy)

HEIGHT: 6'3"   RIGHTHANDER   BORN: 12/13/1935 HOLLIS, OKLAHOMA

YEAR	TEAM	STARTS	GAMES	WON	LOST	PCT	ER	ERA	INNINGS PITCHED	STRIKE-OUTS	WALKS	HITS ALLOWED	HRS ALLOWED	COMP. GAMES	SHUT-OUTS	SAVES
1955	StL-N	2	4	0	0	—	10	4.74	19	7	7	22	4	0	0	0
1956	StL-N	7	39	7	6	.538	44	3.40	$116\frac{1}{3}$	59	42	121	7	1	0	0
1957	StL-N	26	30	15	9	.625	74	3.49	191	75	53	196	13	10	1	0
1958	StL-N	17	26	5	7	.417	70	5.80	$108\frac{2}{3}$	47	31	139	17	10	1	0
1959	StL-N	7	62	14	12	.538	56	3.82	132	86	41	144	11	2	1	0
1960	StL-N	2	65	12	4	.750	27	2.09	$116\frac{1}{3}$	105	24	85	8	1	0	15
1961	StL-N	0	55	10	6	.625	51	4.87	$94\frac{1}{3}$	65	31	117	11	0	0	26
1962	StL-N	2	55	3	10	.231	49	4.12	107	79	29	96	12	0	0	9
1963	**ChC-N**	**0**	**57**	**13**	**7**	**.650**	**28**	**2.86**	**88**	**75**	**27**	**82**	**9**	**0**	**0**	**14**
1964	**ChC-N**	**0**	**63**	**1**	**7**	**.125**	**41**	**3.88**	**95**	**71**	**23**	**104**	**4**	**0**	**0**	**22**
1965	**ChC-N**	**0**	**71**	**5**	**6**	**.455**	**37**	**2.59**	**$128\frac{2}{3}$**	**92**	**47**	**115**	**12**	**0**	**0**	**15**
1966	SF-N	0	64	10	5	.667	36	2.66	$121\frac{2}{3}$	93	35	103	5	0	0	2
1967	SF-N	3	41	2	6	.250	30	3.72	$72\frac{2}{3}$	48	24	69	5	0	0	6
1968	SF-N	0	12	0	0	—	16	7.45	$19\frac{1}{3}$	9	5	30	2	0	0	3
1968	NYY-A	0	24	4	1	.800	10	1.75	$51\frac{1}{3}$	43	12	30	5	0	0	0
1969	NYY-A	0	51	5	6	.455	33	3.55	$83\frac{2}{3}$	60	23	84	4	0	0	10
1970	NYY-A	0	62	9	5	.643	25	2.01	$111\frac{2}{3}$	81	23	88	4	0	0	5
1971	NYY-A	0	44	5	10	.333	39	5.04	$69\frac{2}{3}$	39	24	82	7	0	0	29
1972	NYY-A	0	37	3	1	.750	17	2.25	68	47	25	54	4	0	0	4
1973	NYY-A	3	47	12	6	.667	51	2.86	$160\frac{1}{3}$	93	49	148	11	1	0	0
1974	KC-A	5	38	1	4	.200	41	3.46	$106\frac{2}{3}$	47	24	109	6	1	0	10
1975	KC-A	0	40	5	1	.833	36	4.15	78	40	24	81	3	2	0	1
Career average		4	47	7	6	.542	39	3.45	102	65	30	100	8	1	0	8
Cubs average		**0**	**64**	**6**	**7**	**.487**	**35**	**3.06**	**104**	**79**	**32**	**100**	**8**	**0**	**0**	**13**
Career total		74	987	141	119	.542	821	3.45	$2139\frac{1}{3}$	1361	623	2099	172	18	2	172
Cubs total		**0**	**191**	**19**	**20**	**.487**	**106**	**3.06**	**$311\frac{2}{3}$**	**238**	**97**	**301**	**25**	**0**	**0**	**39**

McElroy, Charles Dwayne (Chuck)
HEIGHT: 6'0"   LEFTHANDER   BORN: 10/1/1967 PORT ARTHUR, TEXAS

YEAR	TEAM	STARTS	GAMES	WON	LOST	PCT	ER	ERA	INNINGS PITCHED	STRIKE-OUTS	WALKS	HITS ALLOWED	HRS ALLOWED	COMP. GAMES	SHUT-OUTS	SAVES
1989	Phi-N	0	11	0	0	—	2	1.74	10⅓	8	4	12	1	0	0	0
1990	Phi-N	0	16	0	1	.000	12	7.71	14	16	10	24	0	0	0	3
1991	**ChC-N**	0	71	6	2	.750	22	1.95	101⅓	92	57	73	7	0	0	6
1992	**ChC-N**	0	72	4	7	.364	33	3.55	83⅔	83	51	73	5	0	0	0
1993	**ChC-N**	0	49	2	2	.500	24	4.56	47⅓	31	25	51	4	0	0	5
1994	Cin-N	0	52	1	2	.333	15	2.34	57⅔	38	15	52	3	0	0	0
1995	Cin-N	0	44	3	4	.429	27	6.02	40⅓	27	15	46	5	0	0	0
1996	Cin-N	0	12	2	0	1.000	9	6.57	12⅓	13	10	13	2	0	0	0
1996	Cal-A	0	40	5	1	.833	12	2.95	36⅔	32	13	32	2	0	0	0
1997	Ana-A	0	13	0	0	—	6	3.45	15⅔	18	3	17	2	0	0	1
1997	CWS-A	0	48	1	3	.250	26	3.94	59⅓	44	19	56	3	0	0	2
1998	Col-N	0	78	6	4	.600	22	2.90	68⅓	61	24	68	3	0	0	0
1999	Col-N	0	41	3	1	.750	28	6.20	40⅔	37	28	48	9	0	0	0
1999	NYM-N	0	15	0	0	—	5	3.38	13⅓	7	8	12	0	0	0	0
2000	Bal-A	2	43	3	0	1.000	33	4.69	63⅓	50	34	60	6	0	0	0
2001	Bal-A	5	18	1	2	.333	27	5.36	45⅓	22	28	49	8	0	0	0
2001	SD-N	0	31	1	1	.500	17	5.16	29⅔	25	18	38	6	0	0	0
Career average		1	50	3	2	.559	25	3.90	57	46	28	56	5	0	0	3
Cubs average		0	64	4	4	.522	26	3.06	77⅓	69	44	66	5	0	0	
Career total		7	654	38	30	.559	320	3.90	739⅓	604	362	724	16	0	0	17
Cubs total		0	192	12	11	.522	79	3.06	232⅓	206	133	197	16	0	0	9

McFarland, Lamont Amos (Monte)
HEIGHT: 5'10"   BORN: 11/7/1872 WHITE HALL, ILLINOIS   DIED: 11/15/1913 PEORIA, ILLINOIS

YEAR	TEAM	STARTS	GAMES	WON	LOST	PCT	ER	ERA	INNINGS PITCHED	STRIKE-OUTS	WALKS	HITS ALLOWED	HRS ALLOWED	COMP. GAMES	SHUT-OUTS	SAVES
1895	**ChN-N**	2	2	2	0	1.000	8	5.14	14	5	5	21	0	2	0	0
1896	**ChN-N**	3	4	0	4	.000	20	7.20	25	3	21	32	0	2	0	0
Career average		3	3	1	2	.333	14	6.46	19⅔	4	13	27	0	2	0	0
Cubs average		3	3	1	2	.333	14	6.46	19⅔	4	13	27	0	2	0	0
Career total		5	6	2	4	.333	28	6.46	39	8	26	53	0	4	0	0
Cubs total		5	6	2	4	.333	28	6.46	39	8	26	53	0	4	0	0

McGill, William Vaness (Willie *or* Kid)
HEIGHT: 5'6"   LEFTHANDER   BORN: 11/10/1873 ATLANTA, GEORGIA   DIED: 8/29/1944 INDIANAPOLIS, INDIANA

YEAR	TEAM	STARTS	GAMES	WON	LOST	PCT	ER	ERA	INNINGS PITCHED	STRIKE-OUTS	WALKS	HITS ALLOWED	HRS ALLOWED	COMP. GAMES	SHUT-OUTS	SAVES
1890	Cle-P	20	24	11	9	.550	84	4.12	183⅔	82	96	222	5	19	0	0
1891	Cin-AA	8	8	2	5	.286	36	4.98	65	19	37	69	1	6	0	0
1891	StL-AA	31	35	18	9	.667	81	2.93	249	154	131	225	10	22	1	1
1892	Cin-N	3	3	1	2	.333	10	5.29	17	7	5	18	0	1	0	0
1893	**ChN-N**	34	39	18	17	.514	155	4.61	302⅔	91	181	311	6	26	1	0
1894	**ChN-N**	23	27	7	17	.292	135	5.84	208	58	117	272	2	22	0	0
1895	Phi-N	20	20	10	6	.625	90	5.55	146	70	81	177	2	13	0	0
1896	Phi-N	11	12	4	5	.444	47	5.31	79⅔	29	53	87	0	7	0	0
Career average		21	24	10	10	.504	91	4.59	178⅔	73	100	197	4	17	0	0
Cubs average		29	33	13	17	.424	145	5.11	255⅓	75	149	292	4	24	1	0
Career total		150	168	71	70	.504	638	4.59	1251	510	701	1381	26	116	2	1
Cubs total		57	66	25	34	.424	290	5.11	510⅔	149	298	583	8	48	1	0

McGinn, Daniel Michael (Dan)
HEIGHT: 6'0"   LEFTHANDER   BORN: 11/29/1943 OMAHA, NEBRASKA

YEAR	TEAM	STARTS	GAMES	WON	LOST	PCT	ER	ERA	INNINGS PITCHED	STRIKE-OUTS	WALKS	HITS ALLOWED	HRS ALLOWED	COMP. GAMES	SHUT-OUTS	SAVES
1968	Cin-N	0	14	0	1	.000	7	5.25	12	16	11	13	1	0	0	6
1969	Mon-N	1	74	7	10	.412	58	3.94	132⅓	112	65	123	8	0	0	6
1970	Mon-N	19	52	7	10	.412	79	5.44	130⅔	83	78	154	13	3	2	0

(continued)

(continued)

YEAR	TEAM	STARTS	GAMES	WON	LOST	PCT	ER	ERA	INNINGS PITCHED	STRIKE-OUTS	WALKS	HITS ALLOWED	HRS ALLOWED	COMP. GAMES	SHUT-OUTS	SAVES
1971	Mon-N	6	28	1	4	.200	47	5.96	71	40	42	74	7	1	0	0
1972	**ChC-N**	**2**	**42**	**0**	**5**	**.000**	**41**	**5.89**	**62 2/3**	**42**	**29**	**78**	**5**	**0**	**0**	**4**
Career average		6	42	3	6	.333	46	5.11	81 2/3	59	45	88	7	1	0	2
Cubs average		**2**	**42**	**0**	**5**	**.000**	**41**	**5.89**	**62 2/3**	**42**	**29**	**78**	**5**	**0**	**0**	**4**
Career total		28	210	15	30	.333	232	5.11	408 2/3	293	225	442	34	4	2	10
Cubs total		**2**	**42**	**0**	**5**	**.000**	**41**	**5.89**	**62 2/3**	**42**	**29**	**78**	**5**	**0**	**0**	**4**

McGinnis, Albert (Gus)

HEIGHT: 5'11"   LEFTHANDER   BORN: 8/1870 BARNESVILLE, OHIO   DIED: 4/20/1904 BARESVILLE, OHIO

YEAR	TEAM	STARTS	GAMES	WON	LOST	PCT	ER	ERA	INNINGS PITCHED	STRIKE-OUTS	WALKS	HITS ALLOWED	HRS ALLOWED	COMP. GAMES	SHUT-OUTS	SAVES
1893	**ChN-N**	**5**	**13**	**2**	**6**	**.250**	**40**	**5.35**	**67 1/3**	**13**	**31**	**85**	**2**	**3**	**0**	**0**
1893	Phi-N	4	5	1	3	.250	18	4.34	37 1/3	12	17	39	0	4	1	0
Career average		9	18	3	9	.250	58	4.99	104 2/3	25	48	124	2	7	1	0
Cubs average		**5**	**13**	**2**	**6**	**.250**	**40**	**5.35**	**67 1/3**	**13**	**31**	**85**	**2**	**3**	**0**	**0**
Career total		9	18	3	9	.250	58	4.99	104 2/3	25	48	124	2	7	1	0
Cubs total		**5**	**13**	**2**	**6**	**.250**	**40**	**5.35**	**67 1/3**	**13**	**31**	**85**	**2**	**3**	**0**	**0**

McGlothen, Lynn Everett

HEIGHT: 6'2"   RIGHTHANDER   BORN: 3/27/1950 MONROE, LOUISIANA   DIED: 8/14/1984 DUBACH, LOUISIANA

YEAR	TEAM	STARTS	GAMES	WON	LOST	PCT	ER	ERA	INNINGS PITCHED	STRIKE-OUTS	WALKS	HITS ALLOWED	HRS ALLOWED	COMP. GAMES	SHUT-OUTS	SAVES
1972	Bos-A	22	22	8	7	.533	55	3.41	145	112	59	135	9	4	1	0
1973	Bos-A	3	6	1	2	.333	21	8.22	23	16	8	39	6	0	0	0
1974	StL-N	31	31	16	12	.571	71	2.69	237 1/3	142	89	212	12	8	3	0
1975	StL-N	34	35	15	13	.536	104	3.92	239	146	97	231	21	9	2	0
1976	StL-N	32	33	13	15	.464	89	3.91	205	106	68	209	10	10	4	0
1977	SF-N	15	21	2	9	.182	50	5.63	80	42	52	94	9	2	0	0
1978	SF-N	1	5	0	0	—	7	4.97	12 2/3	9	4	15	0	0	0	0
1978	**ChC-N**	**1**	**49**	**5**	**3**	**.625**	**27**	**3.04**	**80**	**60**	**39**	**77**	**7**	**0**	**0**	**0**
1979	**ChC-N**	**29**	**42**	**13**	**14**	**.481**	**97**	**4.12**	**212**	**147**	**55**	**236**	**27**	**6**	**1**	**2**
1980	**ChC-N**	**27**	**39**	**12**	**14**	**.462**	**97**	**4.79**	**182 1/3**	**119**	**64**	**211**	**24**	**2**	**2**	**0**
1981	**ChC-N**	**6**	**20**	**1**	**4**	**.200**	**29**	**4.77**	**54 2/3**	**26**	**28**	**71**	**1**	**0**	**0**	**0**
1981	CWS-A	0	11	0	0	—	10	4.15	21 2/3	12	7	14	0	0	0	0
1982	NYY-A	0	4	0	0	—	6	10.80	5	2	2	9	1	0	0	0
Career average		18	29	8	8	.480	60	3.98	136	85	52	141	12	4	1	0
Cubs average		**16**	**38**	**8**	**9**	**.470**	**63**	**4.25**	**132 1/3**	**88**	**47**	**149**	**15**	**2**	**1**	**1**
Career total		201	318	86	93	.480	663	3.98	1497 2/3	939	572	1553	127	41	13	2
Cubs total		**63**	**150**	**31**	**35**	**.470**	**250**	**4.25**	**529**	**352**	**186**	**595**	**59**	**8**	**3**	**2**

McIntire, John Reid (Harry *or* Rocks)

HEIGHT: 5'11"   RIGHTHANDER   BORN: 1/11/1879 DAYTON, OHIO   DIED: 1/9/1949 DAYTONA BEACH, FLORIDA

YEAR	TEAM	STARTS	GAMES	WON	LOST	PCT	ER	ERA	INNINGS PITCHED	STRIKE-OUTS	WALKS	HITS ALLOWED	HRS ALLOWED	COMP. GAMES	SHUT-OUTS	SAVES
1905	Bro-N	35	40	8	25	.242	127	3.70	308 2/3	135	101	340	6	29	1	1
1906	Bro-N	31	39	13	21	.382	91	2.97	276	121	89	254	2	25	4	3
1907	Bro-N	22	28	7	15	.318	53	2.39	199 2/3	49	79	178	6	19	3	0
1908	Bro-N	35	40	11	20	.355	86	2.69	288	108	90	259	5	26	4	2
1909	Bro-N	26	32	7	17	.292	92	3.63	228	84	91	200	5	20	2	1
1910	**ChC-N**	**19**	**28**	**13**	**9**	**.591**	**60**	**3.07**	**176**	**65**	**50**	**152**	**5**	**10**	**2**	**0**
1911	**ChC-N**	**17**	**25**	**11**	**7**	**.611**	**68**	**4.11**	**149**	**56**	**33**	**147**	**5**	**9**	**1**	**0**
1912	**ChC-N**	**3**	**4**	**1**	**2**	**.333**	**10**	**3.80**	**23 2/3**	**8**	**6**	**22**	**0**	**2**	**0**	**0**
1913	Cin-N	0	1	0	1	.000	3	27.00	1	0	0	3	0	0	0	0
Career average		21	26	8	13	.378	66	3.22	183 1/3	70	60	173	4	16	2	1
Cubs average		**13**	**19**	**8**	**6**	**.581**	**46**	**3.56**	**116 1/3**	**43**	**30**	**107**	**3**	**7**	**1**	**0**
Career total		188	237	71	117	.378	590	3.22	1650	626	539	1555	34	140	17	7
Cubs total		**39**	**57**	**25**	**18**	**.581**	**138**	**3.56**	**348 2/3**	**129**	**89**	**321**	**10**	**21**	**3**	**0**

McLish, Calvin Coolidge Julius Caesar Tusckahoma (Cal *or* Bus)
HEIGHT: 6'0" RIGHTHANDER BORN: 12/1/1925 ANADARKO, OKLAHOMA

YEAR	TEAM	STARTS	GAMES	WON	LOST	PCT	ER	ERA	INNINGS PITCHED	STRIKE-OUTS	WALKS	HITS ALLOWED	HRS ALLOWED	COMP. GAMES	SHUT-OUTS	SAVES
1944	Bro-N	13	23	3	10	.231	73	7.82	84	24	48	110	10	3	0	0
1946	Bro-N	0	1	0	0	—	2	—	0	0	0	1	0	0	0	0
1947	Pit-N	0	1	0	0	—	2	18.00	1	0	0	2	0	0	0	0
1948	Pit-N	1	2	0	0	—	5	9.00	5	1	2	8	0	0	0	0
1949	ChC-N	2	8	1	1	.500	15	5.87	23	6	12	31	5	0	0	0
1951	ChC-N	17	30	4	10	.286	72	4.45	145 2/3	46	52	159	16	5	1	1
1956	Cle-A	2	37	2	4	.333	34	4.96	61 2/3	27	32	67	5	0	0	1
1957	Cle-A	7	42	9	7	.563	44	2.74	144 1/3	88	67	118	11	2	0	1
1958	Cle-A	30	39	16	8	.667	75	2.99	225 2/3	97	70	214	25	13	0	1
1959	Cle-A	32	35	19	8	.704	95	3.63	235 1/3	113	72	253	26	13	0	0
1960	Cin-N	21	37	4	14	.222	70	4.16	151 1/3	56	48	170	16	2	1	0
1961	CWS-A	27	31	10	13	.435	79	4.38	162 1/3	80	47	178	21	4	0	1
1962	Phi-N	24	32	11	5	.688	73	4.25	154 2/3	71	45	184	15	5	1	1
1963	Phi-N	32	32	13	11	.542	76	3.26	209 2/3	98	56	184	14	10	2	0
1964	Phi-N	1	2	0	1	.000	2	3.38	5 1/3	6	1	6	0	0	0	0
Career average		14	23	6	6	.500	48	4.01	107 1/3	48	37	112	11	4	0	0
Cubs average		**10**	**19**	**3**	**6**	**.313**	**44**	**4.64**	**84 1/3**	**26**	**32**	**95**	**11**	**3**	**1**	**0**
Career total		209	352	92	92	.500	717	4.01	1609	713	552	1685	164	57	5	6
Cubs total		**19**	**38**	**5**	**11**	**.313**	**87**	**4.64**	**168 2/3**	**52**	**64**	**190**	**21**	**5**	**1**	**0**

McNichol, Brian David
HEIGHT: 6'5" LEFTHANDER BORN: 5/20/1974 FAIRFAX, VIRGINIA

YEAR	TEAM	STARTS	GAMES	WON	LOST	PCT	ER	ERA	INNINGS PITCHED	STRIKE-OUTS	WALKS	HITS ALLOWED	HRS ALLOWED	COMP. GAMES	SHUT-OUTS	SAVES
1999	ChC-N	2	4	0	2	.000	8	6.75	10 2/3	12	7	15	4	0	0	0
Career average		2	4	0	2	.000	8	6.75	10 2/3	12	7	15	4	0	0	0
Cubs average		**2**	**4**	**0**	**2**	**.000**	**8**	**6.75**	**10 2/3**	**12**	**7**	**15**	**4**	**0**	**0**	**0**
Career total		2	4	0	2	.000	8	6.75	10 2/3	12	7	15	4	0	0	0
Cubs total		**2**	**4**	**0**	**2**	**.000**	**8**	**6.75**	**10 2/3**	**12**	**7**	**15**	**4**	**0**	**0**	**0**

McVey, Calvin Alexander (Cal)
HEIGHT: 5'9" RIGHTHANDER BORN: 8/30/1850 MONTROSE, IOWA DIED: 8/20/1926 SAN FRANCISCO, CALIFORNIA

YEAR	TEAM	STARTS	GAMES	WON	LOST	PCT	ER	ERA	INNINGS PITCHED	STRIKE-OUTS	WALKS	HITS ALLOWED	HRS ALLOWED	COMP. GAMES	SHUT-OUTS	SAVES
1876	ChN-N	6	11	5	2	.714	10	1.52	59 1/3	9	2	57	0	5	0	2
1877	ChN-N	10	17	4	8	.333	46	4.50	92	20	11	129	2	6	0	2
1879	Cin-N	1	3	0	2	.000	13	8.36	14	7	2	34	1	1	0	0
Career average		6	10	3	4	.429	23	3.76	55	12	5	73	1	4	0	1
Cubs average		**8**	**14**	**5**	**5**	**.474**	**28**	**3.33**	**75 2/3**	**15**	**7**	**93**	**1**	**6**	**0**	**2**
Career total		17	31	9	12	.429	69	3.76	165 1/3	36	15	220	3	12	0	4
Cubs total		**16**	**28**	**9**	**10**	**.474**	**56**	**3.33**	**151 1/3**	**29**	**13**	**186**	**2**	**11**	**0**	**4**

Meakim, George Clinton
HEIGHT: 5'7" RIGHTHANDER BORN: 7/11/1865 BROOKLYN, NEW YORK DIED: 2/17/1923 QUEENS, NEW YORK

YEAR	TEAM	STARTS	GAMES	WON	LOST	PCT	ER	ERA	INNINGS PITCHED	STRIKE-OUTS	WALKS	HITS ALLOWED	HRS ALLOWED	COMP. GAMES	SHUT-OUTS	SAVES
1890	Lou-AA	21	28	12	7	.632	62	2.91	192	123	63	173	4	16	3	1
1891	Phi-AA	6	6	1	4	.200	27	6.94	35	13	22	51	1	4	0	0
1892	ChN-N	1	1	0	1	.000	11	11.00	9	0	2	18	0	1	0	0
1892	Cin-N	3	3	1	1	.500	13	8.56	13 2/3	4	9	19	1	1	0	0
1895	Lou-N	1	1	1	0	1.000	2	2.57	7	2	4	7	0	1	0	0
Career average		8	10	4	3	.536	29	4.03	64 1/3	36	25	67	2	6	1	0
Cubs average		**1**	**1**	**0**	**1**	**.000**	**11**	**11.00**	**9**	**0**	**2**	**18**	**0**	**1**	**0**	**0**
Career total		32	39	15	13	.536	115	4.03	256 2/3	142	100	268	6	23	3	1
Cubs total		**1**	**1**	**0**	**1**	**.000**	**11**	**11.00**	**9**	**0**	**2**	**18**	**0**	**1**	**0**	**0**

Meers, Russell Harlan (Russ *or* Babe)
HEIGHT: 5'10" LEFTHANDER BORN: 11/28/1918 TILTON, ILLINOIS DIED: 11/16/1994 LANCASTER, PENNSYLVANIA

YEAR	TEAM	STARTS	GAMES	WON	LOST	PCT	ER	ERA	INNINGS PITCHED	STRIKE-OUTS	WALKS	HITS ALLOWED	HRS ALLOWED	COMP. GAMES	SHUT-OUTS	SAVES
1941	ChC-N	1	1	0	1	.000	1	1.13	8	5	0	5	0	0	0	0
1946	ChC-N	2	7	1	2	.333	4	3.18	11 1/3	2	10	10	0	0	0	0
1947	ChC-N	1	35	2	0	1.000	32	4.48	64 1/3	28	38	61	5	0	0	0
Career average		1	14	1	1	.500	12	3.98	28	12	16	25	2	0	0	0
Cubs average		1	14	1	1	.500	12	3.98	28	12	16	25	2	0	0	0
Career total		4	43	3	3	.500	37	3.98	83 2/3	35	48	76	5	0	0	0
Cubs total		4	43	3	3	.500	37	3.98	83 2/3	35	48	76	5	0	0	0

Menefee, John (Jock)
HEIGHT: 6'0" RIGHTHANDER BORN: 1/15/1868 ROWLESBURG, WEST VIRGINIA DIED: 3/11/1953 BELLE VERNON, PENNSYLVANIA

YEAR	TEAM	STARTS	GAMES	WON	LOST	PCT	ER	ERA	INNINGS PITCHED	STRIKE-OUTS	WALKS	HITS ALLOWED	HRS ALLOWED	COMP. GAMES	SHUT-OUTS	SAVES
1892	Pit-N	0	1	0	0	—	5	11.25	4	0	2	10	0	0	0	0
1893	Lou-N	15	15	8	7	.533	61	4.24	129 1/3	30	40	150	0	0	0	0
1894	Lou-N	24	28	8	16	.333	101	4.29	211 2/3	43	50	258	3	14	1	0
1894	Pit-N	13	13	5	8	.385	67	5.40	111 2/3	33	39	159	3	20	1	0
1895	Pit-N	1	2	0	1	.000	3	16.20	1 2/3	0	7	2	0	0	0	0
1898	NYG-N	1	1	0	1	.000	5	4.82	9 1/3	3	2	11	0	1	0	0
1900	ChN-N	13	16	9	4	.692	50	3.85	117	30	35	140	1	11	0	0
1901	ChN-N	20	21	8	12	.400	77	3.80	182 1/3	55	34	201	4	19	0	0
1902	ChC-N	21	22	12	10	.545	53	2.42	197 1/3	60	26	202	1	20	4	0
1903	ChC-N	17	20	8	10	.444	49	3.01	146 2/3	39	38	157	3	13	1	0
Career average		14	15	6	8	.457	52	3.82	123 1/3	33	30	143	2	12	1	0
Cubs average		18	20	9	9	.507	57	3.20	161	46	33	175	2	16	1	0
Career total		125	139	58	69	.457	471	3.82	1111	293	273	1290	18	111	7	0
Cubs total		71	79	37	36	.507	229	3.20	643 1/3	184	133	700	9	63	5	0

Meridith, Ronald Knox (Ron)
HEIGHT: 6'0" LEFTHANDER BORN: 11/26/1956 SAN PEDRO, CALIFORNIA

YEAR	TEAM	STARTS	GAMES	WON	LOST	PCT	ER	ERA	INNINGS PITCHED	STRIKE-OUTS	WALKS	HITS ALLOWED	HRS ALLOWED	COMP. GAMES	SHUT-OUTS	SAVES
1984	ChC-N	0	3	0	0	—	2	3.38	5 1/3	4	2	6	1	0	0	0
1985	ChC-N	0	32	3	2	.600	23	4.47	46 1/3	23	24	53	3	0	0	1
1986	Tex-A	0	5	1	0	1.000	1	3.00	3	2	1	2	0	0	0	0
1987	Tex-A	0	11	1	0	1.000	14	6.10	20 2/3	17	12	25	7	0	0	0
Career average		0	13	1	1	.714	10	4.78	19	12	10	22	3	0	0	0
Cubs average		0	18	2	1	.600	13	4.35	26	14	13	30	2	0	0	1
Career total		0	51	5	2	.714	40	4.78	75 1/3	46	39	86	11	0	0	1
Cubs total		0	35	3	2	.600	25	4.35	51 2/3	27	26	59	4	0	0	1

Meyer, Russell Charles (Russ *or* The Mad Monk *or* Rowdy)
HEIGHT: 6'1" RIGHTHANDER BORN: 10/25/1923 PERU, ILLINOIS DIED: 11/16/1997 OGLESBY, ILLINOIS

YEAR	TEAM	STARTS	GAMES	WON	LOST	PCT	ER	ERA	INNINGS PITCHED	STRIKE-OUTS	WALKS	HITS ALLOWED	HRS ALLOWED	COMP. GAMES	SHUT-OUTS	SAVES
1946	ChC-N	1	4	0	0	—	6	3.18	17	10	10	21	2	0	0	1
1947	ChC-N	2	23	3	2	.600	17	3.40	45	22	14	43	4	1	0	0
1948	ChC-N	26	29	10	10	.500	67	3.66	164 2/3	89	77	157	8	8	3	0
1949	Phi-N	28	37	17	8	.680	73	3.08	213	78	70	199	14	14	2	1
1950	Phi-N	25	32	9	11	.450	94	5.30	159 2/3	74	67	193	21	3	0	1
1951	Phi-N	24	28	8	9	.471	65	3.48	168	65	55	172	13	7	2	0
1952	Phi-N	32	37	13	14	.481	81	3.14	232 1/3	92	65	235	10	14	1	1
1953	Bro-N	32	34	15	5	.750	97	4.56	191 1/3	106	63	201	25	10	2	0
1954	Bro-N	28	36	11	6	.647	80	3.99	180 1/3	70	49	193	17	6	2	0
1955	Bro-N	11	18	6	2	.750	44	5.42	73	26	31	86	8	2	1	0
1956	ChC-N	9	20	1	6	.143	40	6.32	57	28	26	71	11	0	0	0

(continued)

(Meyer, continued)

YEAR	TEAM	STARTS	GAMES	WON	LOST	PCT	ER	ERA	INNINGS PITCHED	STRIKE-OUTS	WALKS	HITS ALLOWED	HRS ALLOWED	COMP. GAMES	SHUT-OUTS	SAVES
1956	Cin-N	0	1	0	0	—	0	0.00	1	1	0	1	0	0	0	0
1957	Bos-A	1	2	0	0	—	3	5.40	5	1	3	10	0	0	0	0
1959	KCA-A	0	18	1	0	1.000	12	4.50	24	10	11	24	3	0	0	1
Career average		17	25	7	6	.563	52	3.99	117 2/3	52	42	124	10	5	1	0
Cubs average		**10**	**19**	**4**	**5**	**.438**	**33**	**4.12**	**71**	**37**	**32**	**73**	**6**	**2**	**1**	**0**
Career total		219	319	94	73	.563	679	3.99	1531 1/3	672	541	1606	136	65	13	5
Cubs total		**38**	**76**	**14**	**18**	**.438**	**130**	**4.12**	**283 2/3**	**149**	**127**	**292**	**25**	**9**	**3**	**1**

Mikkelsen, Peter James (Pete)
HEIGHT: 6'2"   RIGHTHANDER   BORN: 10/25/1939 STATEN ISLAND, NEW YORK

YEAR	TEAM	STARTS	GAMES	WON	LOST	PCT	ER	ERA	INNINGS PITCHED	STRIKE-OUTS	WALKS	HITS ALLOWED	HRS ALLOWED	COMP. GAMES	SHUT-OUTS	SAVES
1964	NYY-A	0	50	7	4	.636	34	3.56	86	63	41	79	3	0	0	12
1965	NYY-A	3	41	4	9	.308	30	3.28	82 1/3	69	36	78	10	0	0	1
1966	Pit-N	0	71	9	8	.529	43	3.07	126	76	51	106	8	0	0	14
1967	Pit-N	0	32	1	2	.333	27	4.31	56 1/3	30	19	50	7	0	0	2
1967	**ChC-N**	**0**	**7**	**0**	**0**	**—**	**5**	**6.43**	**7**	**0**	**5**	**9**	**1**	**0**	**0**	**0**
1968	**ChC-N**	**0**	**3**	**0**	**0**	**—**	**4**	**7.71**	**4 2/3**	**5**	**1**	**7**	**3**	**0**	**0**	**0**
1968	StL-N	0	5	0	0	—	2	1.13	16	8	7	10	0	0	0	0
1969	LA-N	0	48	7	5	.583	25	2.77	81 1/3	51	30	57	9	0	0	4
1970	LA-N	0	33	4	2	.667	19	2.76	62	47	20	48	5	0	0	6
1971	LA-N	0	41	8	5	.615	30	3.65	74	46	17	67	10	0	0	5
1972	LA-N	0	33	5	5	.500	26	4.06	57 2/3	41	23	65	3	0	0	5
Career average		0	40	5	4	.529	27	3.38	72 2/3	48	28	64	7	0	0	5
Cubs average		**0**	**5**	**0**	**0**	**—**	**5**	**6.94**	**6**	**3**	**3**	**8**	**2**	**0**	**0**	**0**
Career total		3	364	45	40	.529	245	3.38	653 1/3	436	250	576	59	0	0	49
Cubs total		**0**	**10**	**0**	**0**	**—**	**9**	**6.94**	**11 2/3**	**5**	**6**	**16**	**4**	**0**	**0**	**0**

Miklos, John Joseph (Hank)
HEIGHT: 5'11"   LEFTHANDER   BORN: 11/27/1910 CHICAGO, ILLINOIS   DIED: 3/29/2000 ADRIAN, MICHIGAN

YEAR	TEAM	STARTS	GAMES	WON	LOST	PCT	ER	ERA	INNINGS PITCHED	STRIKE-OUTS	WALKS	HITS ALLOWED	HRS ALLOWED	COMP. GAMES	SHUT-OUTS	SAVES
1944	**ChC-N**	**0**	**2**	**0**	**0**	**—**	**6**	**7.71**	**7**	**0**	**3**	**9**	**1**	**0**	**0**	**0**
Career average		0	2	0	0	—	6	7.71	7	0	3	9	1	0	0	0
Cubs average		**0**	**2**	**0**	**0**	**—**	**6**	**7.71**	**7**	**0**	**3**	**9**	**1**	**0**	**0**	**0**
Career total		0	2	0	0	—	6	7.71	7	0	3	9	1	0	0	0
Cubs total		**0**	**2**	**0**	**0**	**—**	**6**	**7.71**	**7**	**0**	**3**	**9**	**1**	**0**	**0**	**0**

Miller, Kurt Everett
HEIGHT: 6'5"   RIGHTHANDER   BORN: 8/24/1972 TUCSON, ARIZONA

YEAR	TEAM	STARTS	GAMES	WON	LOST	PCT	ER	ERA	INNINGS PITCHED	STRIKE-OUTS	WALKS	HITS ALLOWED	HRS ALLOWED	COMP. GAMES	SHUT-OUTS	SAVES
1994	Fla-N	4	4	1	3	.250	18	8.10	20	11	7	26	3	0	0	0
1996	Fla-N	5	26	1	3	.250	35	6.80	46 1/3	30	33	57	5	0	0	0
1997	Fla-N	0	7	0	1	.000	8	9.82	7 1/3	7	7	12	2	0	0	0
1998	**ChC-N**	**0**	**3**	**0**	**0**	**—**	**0**	**0.00**	**4**	**6**	**0**	**3**	**0**	**0**	**0**	**0**
1999	**ChC-N**	**0**	**4**	**0**	**0**	**—**	**6**	**18.00**	**3**	**1**	**3**	**6**	**1**	**0**	**0**	**0**
Career average		2	9	0	1	.222	13	7.48	16	11	10	21	2	0	0	0
Cubs average		**0**	**4**	**0**	**0**	**—**	**3**	**7.71**	**3 2/3**	**4**	**2**	**5**	**1**	**0**	**0**	**0**
Career total		9	44	2	7	.222	67	7.48	80 2/3	55	50	104	11	0	0	0
Cubs total		**0**	**7**	**0**	**0**	**—**	**6**	**7.71**	**7**	**7**	**3**	**9**	**1**	**0**	**0**	**0**

Miller, Robert Lane (Bob)
HEIGHT: 6'1" RIGHTHANDER BORN: 2/18/1939 ST. LOUIS, MISSOURI DIED: 8/6/1993 RANCHO BERNARDO, CALIFORNIA

YEAR	TEAM	STARTS	GAMES	WON	LOST	PCT	ER	ERA	INNINGS PITCHED	STRIKE-OUTS	WALKS	HITS ALLOWED	HRS ALLOWED	COMP. GAMES	SHUT-OUTS	SAVES
1957	StL-N	0	5	0	0	—	7	7.00	9	7	5	13	2	0	0	0
1959	StL-N	10	11	4	3	.571	26	3.31	70⅔	43	21	66	2	3	0	0
1960	StL-N	7	15	4	3	.571	20	3.42	52⅔	33	17	53	2	0	0	0
1961	StL-N	5	34	1	3	.250	35	4.24	74⅓	39	46	82	6	0	0	3
1962	NYM-N	21	33	1	12	.077	78	4.89	143⅔	91	62	146	20	1	0	0
1963	LA-N	23	42	10	8	.556	60	2.89	187	125	65	171	7	2	0	1
1964	LA-N	2	74	7	7	.500	40	2.62	137⅔	94	63	115	1	0	0	9
1965	LA-N	1	61	6	7	.462	34	2.97	103	77	26	82	9	0	0	9
1966	LA-N	0	46	4	2	.667	26	2.77	84⅓	58	29	70	5	0	0	5
1967	LA-N	4	52	2	9	.182	41	4.31	85⅔	32	27	88	9	0	0	0
1968	Min-A	0	45	0	3	.000	22	2.74	72⅓	41	24	65	1	0	0	2
1969	Min-A	11	48	5	5	.500	40	3.02	119⅓	57	32	118	9	1	0	3
1970	Cle-A	2	15	2	2	.500	13	4.18	28	15	15	35	1	0	0	1
1970	CWS-A	12	15	4	6	.400	39	5.01	70	36	33	88	11	0	0	0
1970	**ChC-N**	**1**	**7**	**0**	**0**	**—**	**5**	**5.00**	**9**	**4**	**6**	**6**	**3**	**0**	**0**	**2**
1971	**ChC-N**	**0**	**2**	**0**	**0**	**—**	**4**	**5.14**	**7**	**2**	**1**	**10**	**0**	**0**	**0**	**0**
1971	SD-N	0	38	7	3	.700	10	1.41	63⅔	36	26	53	0	0	0	7
1971	Pit-N	0	16	1	2	.333	4	1.29	28	13	13	20	1	0	0	3
1972	Pit-N	0	36	5	2	.714	16	2.65	54⅓	18	24	54	3	0	0	3
1973	Det-A	0	22	4	2	.667	16	3.43	42	23	22	54	3	0	0	1
1973	SD-N	0	18	0	0	—	14	4.11	30⅔	15	12	29	4	0	0	0
1973	NYM-N	0	1	0	0	—	0	0.00	1	1	0	0	0	0	0	0
1974	NYM-N	0	58	2	2	.500	31	3.58	78	35	39	89	2	0	0	2
Career average		6	41	4	5	.460	34	3.37	91⅓	53	36	87	6	0	0	3
Cubs average		**1**	**5**	**0**	**0**	**—**	**5**	**5.06**	**8**	**3**	**4**	**8**	**2**	**0**	**0**	**1**
Career total		99	694	69	81	.460	581	3.37	1551⅓	895	608	1487	101	7	0	51
Cubs total		**1**	**9**	**0**	**0**	**—**	**9**	**5.06**	**16**	**6**	**7**	**16**	**3**	**0**	**0**	**2**

Miller, John Anthony (Ox)
HEIGHT: 6'1" RIGHTHANDER BORN: 5/4/1915 GAUSE, TEXAS

YEAR	TEAM	STARTS	GAMES	WON	LOST	PCT	ER	ERA	INNINGS PITCHED	STRIKE-OUTS	WALKS	HITS ALLOWED	HRS ALLOWED	COMP. GAMES	SHUT-OUTS	SAVES
1943	Was-A	0	3	0	0	—	7	10.50	6	1	5	10	1	0	0	0
1943	StL-A	0	2	0	0	—	8	12.00	6	3	3	7	2	0	0	0
1945	StL-A	3	4	2	1	.667	5	1.59	28⅓	4	5	23	2	3	0	0
1946	StL-A	3	11	1	3	.250	27	6.88	35⅓	12	15	52	5	0	0	1
1947	**ChC-N**	**4**	**4**	**1**	**2**	**.333**	**18**	**10.13**	**16**	**7**	**5**	**31**	**2**	**1**	**0**	**0**
Career average		3	6	1	2	.400	16	6.38	23	7	8	31	3	1	0	0
Cubs average		**4**	**4**	**1**	**2**	**.333**	**18**	**10.13**	**16**	**7**	**5**	**31**	**2**	**1**	**0**	**0**
Career total		10	24	4	6	.400	65	6.38	91⅔	27	33	123	12	4	0	1
Cubs total		**4**	**4**	**1**	**2**	**.333**	**18**	**10.13**	**16**	**7**	**5**	**31**	**2**	**1**	**0**	**0**

Milstead, George Earl (Cowboy)
HEIGHT: 5'10" LEFTHANDER BORN: 6/26/1903 CLEBURNE, TEXAS DIED: 8/9/1977 CLEBURNE, TEXAS

YEAR	TEAM	STARTS	GAMES	WON	LOST	PCT	ER	ERA	INNINGS PITCHED	STRIKE-OUTS	WALKS	HITS ALLOWED	HRS ALLOWED	COMP. GAMES	SHUT-OUTS	SAVES
1924	ChC-N	2	13	1	1	.500	20	6.07	29⅔	6	13	41	3	1	0	0
1925	ChC-N	3	5	1	1	.500	7	3.00	21	7	8	26	0	1	0	0
1926	ChC-N	4	18	1	5	.167	22	3.58	55⅓	14	24	63	0	0	0	2
Career average		3	12	1	2	.300	16	4.16	35⅓	9	15	43	1	1	0	1
Cubs average		**3**	**12**	**1**	**2**	**.300**	**16**	**4.16**	**35⅓**	**9**	**15**	**43**	**1**	**1**	**0**	**1**
Career total		9	36	3	7	.300	49	4.16	106	27	45	130	3	2	0	2
Cubs total		**9**	**36**	**3**	**7**	**.300**	**49**	**4.16**	**106**	**27**	**45**	**130**	**3**	**2**	**0**	**2**

(continued)

Minner, Paul Edison (Lefty)
HEIGHT: 6'5"   LEFTHANDER   BORN: 7/30/1923 NEW WILMINGTON, PENNSYLVANIA

YEAR	TEAM	STARTS	GAMES	WON	LOST	PCT	ER	ERA	INNINGS PITCHED	STRIKE-OUTS	WALKS	HITS ALLOWED	HRS ALLOWED	COMP. GAMES	SHUT-OUTS	SAVES
1946	Bro-N	0	3	0	1	.000	3	6.75	4	3	3	6	1	0	0	0
1948	Bro-N	2	28	4	3	.571	17	2.44	62 ⅔	23	26	61	5	0	0	1
1949	Bro-N	1	27	3	1	.750	20	3.80	47 ⅓	17	18	49	7	0	0	2
1950	ChC-N	24	39	8	13	.381	87	4.11	190 ⅓	99	72	217	18	9	1	4
1951	ChC-N	28	33	6	17	.261	85	3.79	201 ⅔	68	64	219	20	14	3	1
1952	ChC-N	27	28	14	9	.609	75	3.74	180 ⅔	61	54	180	13	12	2	0
1953	ChC-N	27	31	12	15	.444	94	4.21	201	64	40	227	15	9	2	1
1954	ChC-N	29	32	11	11	.500	96	3.96	218	79	50	236	19	12	0	1
1955	ChC-N	22	22	9	9	.500	61	3.48	157 ⅔	53	47	173	15	7	1	0
1956	ChC-N	9	10	2	5	.286	36	6.89	47	14	19	60	9	1	0	0
Career average		17	25	7	8	.451	57	3.94	131	48	39	143	12	6	1	1
Cubs average		**24**	**28**	**9**	**11**	**.440**	**76**	**4.02**	**171**	**63**	**49**	**187**	**16**	**9**	**1**	**1**
Career total		169	253	69	84	.451	574	3.94	1310 ⅓	481	393	1428	122	64	9	10
Cubs total		**166**	**195**	**62**	**79**	**.440**	**534**	**4.02**	**1196 ⅓**	**438**	**346**	**1312**	**109**	**64**	**9**	**7**

Moisan, William Joseph (Bill)
HEIGHT: 6'1"   RIGHTHANDER   BORN: 7/30/1925 BRADFORD, MASSACHUSETTS

YEAR	TEAM	STARTS	GAMES	WON	LOST	PCT	ER	ERA	INNINGS PITCHED	STRIKE-OUTS	WALKS	HITS ALLOWED	HRS ALLOWED	COMP. GAMES	SHUT-OUTS	SAVES
1953	ChC-N	0	3	0	0	—	3	5.40	5	1	2	5	0	0	0	0
Career average		0	3	0	0	—	3	5.40	5	1	2	5	0	0	0	0
Cubs average		**0**	**3**	**0**	**0**	**—**	**3**	**5.40**	**5**	**1**	**2**	**5**	**0**	**0**	**0**	**0**
Career total		0	3	0	0	—	3	5.40	5	1	2	5	0	0	0	0
Cubs total		**0**	**3**	**0**	**0**	**—**	**3**	**5.40**	**5**	**1**	**2**	**5**	**0**	**0**	**0**	**0**

Moore, Donnie Ray
HEIGHT: 6'0"   RIGHTHANDER   BORN: 2/13/1954 LUBBOCK, TEXAS   DIED: 7/18/1989 ANAHEIM, CALIFORNIA

YEAR	TEAM	STARTS	GAMES	WON	LOST	PCT	ER	ERA	INNINGS PITCHED	STRIKE-OUTS	WALKS	HITS ALLOWED	HRS ALLOWED	COMP. GAMES	SHUT-OUTS	SAVES
1975	ChC-N	1	4	0	0	—	4	4.15	8 ⅔	8	4	12	1	0	0	0
1977	ChC-N	1	27	4	2	.667	22	4.07	48 ⅔	34	18	51	1	0	0	4
1978	ChC-N	1	71	9	7	.563	47	4.11	103	50	31	117	7	0	0	1
1979	ChC-N	1	39	1	4	.200	42	5.18	73	43	25	95	8	0	0	0
1980	StL-N	0	11	1	1	.500	15	6.23	21 ⅔	10	5	25	1	0	0	0
1981	Mil-A	0	3	0	0	—	3	6.75	4	2	4	4	0	0	0	1
1982	Atl-N	0	16	3	1	.750	13	4.23	27 ⅔	17	7	32	1	0	0	0
1983	Atl-N	0	43	2	3	.400	28	3.67	68 ⅔	41	10	72	6	0	0	6
1984	Atl-N	0	47	4	5	.444	21	2.94	64 ⅓	47	18	63	3	0	0	16
1985	Cal-A	0	65	8	8	.500	22	1.92	103	72	21	91	9	0	0	31
1986	Cal-A	0	49	4	5	.444	24	2.97	72 ⅔	53	22	60	10	0	0	21
1987	Cal-A	0	14	2	2	.500	8	2.70	26 ⅔	17	13	28	2	0	0	5
1988	Cal-A	0	27	5	2	.714	18	4.91	33	22	8	48	4	0	0	4
Career average		0	32	3	3	.518	21	3.67	50 ⅓	32	14	54	4	0	0	7
Cubs average		**1**	**35**	**4**	**3**	**.519**	**29**	**4.44**	**58 ⅓**	**34**	**20**	**69**	**4**	**0**	**0**	**1**
Career total		4	416	43	40	.518	267	3.67	655	416	186	698	53	0	0	89
Cubs total		**4**	**141**	**14**	**13**	**.519**	**115**	**4.44**	**233 ⅓**	**135**	**78**	**275**	**17**	**0**	**0**	**5**

Moore, Earl Alonzo (Steam Engine in Boots *or* Crossfire)
HEIGHT: 6'0"   RIGHTHANDER   BORN: 7/29/1879 PICKERINGTON, OHIO   DIED: 11/28/1961 COLUMBUS, OHIO

YEAR	TEAM	STARTS	GAMES	WON	LOST	PCT	ER	ERA	INNINGS PITCHED	STRIKE-OUTS	WALKS	HITS ALLOWED	HRS ALLOWED	COMP. GAMES	SHUT-OUTS	SAVES
1901	Cle-A	30	31	16	14	.533	81	2.90	251 ⅓	99	107	234	4	28	4	0
1902	Cle-A	34	36	17	17	.500	96	2.95	293	84	101	304	8	29	4	1
1903	Cle-A	27	29	19	9	.679	48	1.74	247 ⅔	148	62	196	0	27	3	1
1904	Cle-A	24	26	12	11	.522	57	2.25	227 ⅔	139	61	186	2	22	1	0

(continued)

(continued)

YEAR	TEAM	STARTS	GAMES	WON	LOST	PCT	ER	ERA	INNINGS PITCHED	STRIKE-OUTS	WALKS	HITS ALLOWED	HRS ALLOWED	COMP. GAMES	SHUT-OUTS	SAVES
1905	Cle-A	30	31	15	15	.500	79	2.64	269	131	92	232	6	28	3	0
1906	Cle-A	4	5	1	1	.500	13	3.94	29⅔	8	18	27	1	2	0	0
1907	Cle-A	2	3	1	1	.250	10	4.66	19⅓	7	8	18	0	1	0	0
1907	NYA-A	9	12	2	6	.250	28	3.94	64	28	30	72	0	3	0	1
1908	Phi-N	3	3	2	1	.667	0	0.00	26	16	8	20	1	3	0	1
1909	Phi-N	34	38	18	12	.600	70	2.10	299⅔	173	108	238	7	24	4	0
1910	Phi-N	35	46	22	15	.595	81	2.58	283	185	121	228	5	18	6	0
1911	Phi-N	36	42	15	19	.441	90	2.63	308⅓	174	164	265	11	21	5	1
1912	Phi-N	24	31	9	14	.391	67	3.31	182⅓	79	77	186	3	10	1	0
1913	Phi-N	5	12	1	3	.250	29	5.02	52	24	40	50	3	0	0	1
1913	**ChC-N**	**2**	**7**	**1**	**1**	**.500**	**14**	**4.45**	**28⅓**	**12**	**12**	**34**	**3**	**0**	**0**	**0**
1914	Buf-F	27	36	11	15	.423	93	4.30	194⅔	96	99	184	3	14	2	2
Career average		23	28	12	11	.513	61	2.78	198⅓	100	79	177	4	16	2	1
Cubs average		**2**	**7**	**1**	**1**	**.500**	**14**	**4.45**	**28⅓**	**12**	**12**	**34**	**3**	**0**	**0**	**0**
Career total		326	388	162	154	.513	856	2.78	2776	1403	1108	2474	57	230	34	7
Cubs total		**2**	**7**	**1**	**1**	**.500**	**14**	**4.45**	**28⅓**	**12**	**12**	**34**	**3**	**0**	**0**	**0**

Mooty, Jake T.
HEIGHT: 5'10" RIGHTHANDER BORN: 4/13/1912 BENNETT, TEXAS DIED: 4/20/1970 FORT WORTH, TEXAS

YEAR	TEAM	STARTS	GAMES	WON	LOST	PCT	ER	ERA	INNINGS PITCHED	STRIKE-OUTS	WALKS	HITS ALLOWED	HRS ALLOWED	COMP. GAMES	SHUT-OUTS	SAVES
1936	Cin-N	0	8	0	0	—	6	3.95	13⅔	11	4	10	0	0	0	1
1937	Cin-N	2	14	0	3	.000	36	8.31	39	11	22	54	2	0	0	1
1940	**ChC-N**	**12**	**20**	**6**	**6**	**.500**	**37**	**2.92**	**114**	**42**	**49**	**101**	**11**	**6**	**0**	**1**
1941	**ChC-N**	**14**	**33**	**8**	**9**	**.471**	**57**	**3.35**	**153⅓**	**45**	**56**	**143**	**9**	**7**	**1**	**4**
1942	**ChC-N**	**10**	**19**	**2**	**5**	**.286**	**44**	**4.70**	**84⅓**	**28**	**44**	**89**	**11**	**1**	**0**	**1**
1943	**ChC-N**	**0**	**2**	**0**	**0**	**—**	**0**	**0.00**	**1**	**1**	**1**	**2**	**0**	**0**	**0**	**0**
1944	Det-A	0	15	0	0	—	14	4.45	28⅓	7	18	35	0	0	0	0
Career average		5	16	2	3	.410	28	4.03	62	21	28	62	5	2	0	1
Cubs average		**9**	**19**	**4**	**5**	**.444**	**35**	**3.52**	**88⅓**	**29**	**38**	**84**	**8**	**4**	**0**	**2**
Career total		38	111	16	23	.410	194	4.03	433⅔	145	194	434	33	14	1	8
Cubs total		**36**	**74**	**16**	**20**	**.444**	**138**	**3.52**	**352⅔**	**116**	**150**	**335**	**31**	**14**	**1**	**6**

Morehead, Seth Marvin (Moe)
HEIGHT: 6'0" LEFTHANDER BORN: 8/15/1934 HOUSTON, TEXAS

YEAR	TEAM	STARTS	GAMES	WON	LOST	PCT	ER	ERA	INNINGS PITCHED	STRIKE-OUTS	WALKS	HITS ALLOWED	HRS ALLOWED	COMP. GAMES	SHUT-OUTS	SAVES
1957	Phi-N	1	34	1	1	.500	24	3.68	58⅔	36	20	57	1	1	0	1
1958	Phi-N	11	27	1	6	.143	60	5.85	92⅓	54	26	121	8	0	0	0
1959	Phi-N	3	3	0	2	.000	11	9.90	10	8	3	15	3	0	0	0
1959	**ChC-N**	**2**	**11**	**0**	**1**	**.000**	**10**	**4.82**	**18⅔**	**9**	**8**	**25**	**1**	**0**	**0**	**0**
1960	**ChC-N**	**7**	**45**	**2**	**9**	**.182**	**54**	**3.94**	**123⅓**	**64**	**46**	**123**	**17**	**2**	**0**	**4**
1961	Mil-N	0	12	1	0	1.000	11	6.46	15⅓	13	7	16	4	0	0	0
Career average		5	26	1	4	.208	34	4.81	63⅔	37	22	71	7	1	0	1
Cubs average		**5**	**28**	**1**	**5**	**.167**	**32**	**4.06**	**71**	**37**	**27**	**74**	**9**	**1**	**0**	**2**
Career total		24	132	5	19	.208	170	4.81	318⅓	184	110	357	34	3	0	5
Cubs total		**9**	**56**	**2**	**10**	**.167**	**64**	**4.06**	**142**	**73**	**54**	**148**	**18**	**2**	**0**	**4**

Morel, Ramon Rafael
HEIGHT: 6'2" RIGHTHANDER BORN: 8/15/1974 VILLA GONZALEZ, DOMINICAN REPUBLIC

YEAR	TEAM	STARTS	GAMES	WON	LOST	PCT	ER	ERA	INNINGS PITCHED	STRIKE-OUTS	WALKS	HITS ALLOWED	HRS ALLOWED	COMP. GAMES	SHUT-OUTS	SAVES
1995	Pit-N	0	5	0	1	.000	2	2.84	6⅓	3	2	6	0	0	0	0
1996	Pit-N	0	29	2	1	.667	25	5.36	42	22	19	57	4	0	0	0
1997	Pit-N	0	5	0	0	—	4	4.70	7⅔	4	4	11	2	0	0	0
1997	**ChC-N**	**0**	**3**	**0**	**0**	**—**	**2**	**4.91**	**3⅔**	**3**	**3**	**3**	**1**	**0**	**0**	**0**
Career average		0	14	1	1	.500	11	4.98	20	11	9	26	2	0	0	0
Cubs average		**0**	**3**	**0**	**0**	**—**	**2**	**4.91**	**3⅔**	**3**	**3**	**3**	**1**	**0**	**0**	**0**
Career total		0	42	2	2	.500	33	4.98	59⅔	32	28	77	7	0	0	0
Cubs total		**0**	**3**	**0**	**0**	**—**	**2**	**4.91**	**3⅔**	**3**	**3**	**3**	**1**	**0**	**0**	**0**

Morgan, Michael Thomas (Mike)
HEIGHT: 6'2"   RIGHTHANDER   BORN: 10/8/1959 TULARE, CALIFORNIA

YEAR	TEAM	STARTS	GAMES	WON	LOST	PCT	ER	ERA	INNINGS PITCHED	STRIKE-OUTS	WALKS	HITS ALLOWED	HRS ALLOWED	COMP. GAMES	SHUT-OUTS	SAVES
1978	Oak-A	3	3	0	3	.000	10	7.30	12 1/3	0	8	19	1	1	0	0
1979	Oak-A	13	13	2	10	.167	51	5.94	77 1/3	17	50	102	7	2	0	0
1982	NYY-A	23	30	7	11	.389	73	4.37	150 1/3	71	67	167	15	2	0	0
1983	Tor-A	4	16	0	3	.000	26	5.16	45 1/3	22	21	48	6	0	0	0
1985	Sea-A	2	2	1	1	.500	8	12.00	6	2	5	11	2	0	0	0
1986	Sea-A	33	37	11	17	.393	109	4.53	216 1/3	116	86	243	24	9	1	1
1987	Sea-A	31	34	12	17	.414	107	4.65	207	85	53	245	25	8	2	0
1988	Bal-A	10	22	1	6	.143	43	5.43	71 1/3	29	23	70	6	2	0	1
1989	LA-N	19	40	8	11	.421	43	2.53	152 2/3	72	33	130	6	0	0	0
1990	LA-N	33	33	11	15	.423	88	3.75	211	106	60	216	19	6	4	0
1991	LA-N	33	34	14	10	.583	73	2.78	236 1/3	140	61	197	12	5	1	1
1992	**ChC-N**	**34**	**34**	**16**	**8**	**.667**	**68**	**2.55**	**240**	**123**	**79**	**203**	**14**	**6**	**1**	**0**
1993	**ChC-N**	**32**	**32**	**10**	**15**	**.400**	**93**	**4.03**	**207 2/3**	**111**	**74**	**206**	**15**	**1**	**1**	**0**
1994	**ChC-N**	**15**	**15**	**2**	**10**	**.167**	**60**	**6.69**	**80 2/3**	**57**	**35**	**111**	**12**	**1**	**0**	**0**
1995	**ChC-N**	**4**	**4**	**2**	**1**	**.667**	**6**	**2.19**	**24 2/3**	**15**	**9**	**19**	**2**	**0**	**0**	**0**
1995	StL-N	17	17	5	6	.455	46	3.88	106 2/3	46	25	114	10	1	0	0
1996	StL-N	18	18	4	8	.333	60	5.24	103	55	40	118	14	0	0	0
1996	Cin-N	5	5	2	3	.400	7	2.30	27 1/3	19	7	28	2	0	0	0
1997	Cin-N	30	31	9	12	.429	86	4.78	162	103	49	165	13	1	0	0
1998	Min-A	17	18	4	2	.667	38	3.49	98	50	24	108	13	0	0	0
1998	**ChC-N**	**5**	**5**	**0**	**1**	**.000**	**18**	**7.15**	**22 2/3**	**10**	**15**	**30**	**8**	**0**	**0**	**0**
1999	Tex-A	25	34	13	10	.565	97	6.24	140	61	48	184	25	1	0	0
2000	Ari-N	4	60	5	5	.500	55	4.87	101 2/3	56	40	123	10	0	0	5
2001	Ari-N	1	31	1	0	1.000	18	4.26	38	24	17	45	2	0	0	0
Career average		20	27	7	9	.431	61	4.22	130 1/3	66	44	138	13	2	0	0
Cubs average		**18**	**18**	**6**	**7**	**.462**	**49**	**3.83**	**115**	**63**	**42**	**114**	**10**	**2**	**0**	**0**
Career total		411	568	140	185	.431	1283	4.22	2738 1/3	1390	929	2902	263	46	10	8
Cubs total		**90**	**90**	**30**	**35**	**.462**	**245**	**3.83**	**575 2/3**	**316**	**212**	**569**	**51**	**8**	**2**	**0**

Moroney, James Francis (Jim)
HEIGHT: 6'1"   LEFTHANDER   BORN: 12/4/1883 BOSTON, MASSACHUSETTS   DIED: 2/26/1929 PHILADELPHIA, PENNSYLVANIA

YEAR	TEAM	STARTS	GAMES	WON	LOST	PCT	ER	ERA	INNINGS PITCHED	STRIKE-OUTS	WALKS	HITS ALLOWED	HRS ALLOWED	COMP. GAMES	SHUT-OUTS	SAVES
1906	Bos-N	3	3	0	3	.000	16	5.33	27	11	12	28	1	3	0	0
1910	Phi-N	2	12	1	2	.333	10	2.14	42	13	11	43	1	1	0	1
1912	**ChC-N**	**3**	**10**	**1**	**1**	**.500**	**12**	**4.56**	**23 2/3**	**5**	**17**	**25**	**0**	**1**	**0**	**1**
Career average		3	8	1	2	.250	13	3.69	31	10	13	32	1	2	0	1
Cubs average		**3**	**10**	**1**	**1**	**.500**	**12**	**4.56**	**23 2/3**	**5**	**17**	**25**	**0**	**1**	**0**	**1**
Career total		8	25	2	6	.250	38	3.69	92 2/3	29	40	96	2	5	0	2
Cubs total		**3**	**10**	**1**	**1**	**.500**	**12**	**4.56**	**23 2/3**	**5**	**17**	**25**	**0**	**1**	**0**	**1**

Morris, Walter Edward (Ed *or* Big Ed)
HEIGHT: 6'2"   RIGHTHANDER   BORN: 12/7/1899 FOSHEE, ALABAMA   DIED: 3/3/1932 CENTURY, FLORIDA

YEAR	TEAM	STARTS	GAMES	WON	LOST	PCT	ER	ERA	INNINGS PITCHED	STRIKE-OUTS	WALKS	HITS ALLOWED	HRS ALLOWED	COMP. GAMES	SHUT-OUTS	SAVES
1922	**ChC-N**	**0**	**5**	**0**	**0**	**—**	**11**	**8.25**	**12**	**5**	**6**	**22**	**1**	**0**	**0**	**0**
1928	Bos-A	29	47	19	15	.559	101	3.53	257 2/3	104	80	255	7	20	0	5
1929	Bos-A	26	33	14	14	.500	103	4.45	208 1/3	73	95	227	7	17	2	1
1930	Bos-A	9	18	4	9	.308	30	4.13	65 1/3	28	38	67	1	3	0	0
1931	Bos-A	14	37	5	7	.417	69	4.75	130 2/3	46	74	131	4	3	0	0
Career average		16	28	8	9	.483	63	4.19	134 2/3	51	59	140	4	9	0	1
Cubs average		**0**	**5**	**0**	**0**	**—**	**11**	**8.25**	**12**	**5**	**6**	**22**	**1**	**0**	**0**	**0**
Career total		78	140	42	45	.483	314	4.19	674	256	293	702	20	43	2	6
Cubs total		**0**	**5**	**0**	**0**	**—**	**11**	**8.25**	**12**	**5**	**6**	**22**	**1**	**0**	**0**	**0**

Morrissey, Michael Joseph (Deacon)
HEIGHT: 5'4" RIGHTHANDER BORN: 5/3/1876 BALTIMORE, MARYLAND DIED: 2/22/1939 BALTIMORE, MARYLAND

YEAR	TEAM	STARTS	GAMES	WON	LOST	PCT	ER	ERA	INNINGS PITCHED	STRIKE-OUTS	WALKS	HITS ALLOWED	HRS ALLOWED	COMP. GAMES	SHUT-OUTS	SAVES
1901	Bos-A	0	1	0	0	—	1	2.08	4 ⅓	1	2	5	0	0	0	0
1902	**ChC-N**	**5**	**5**	**1**	**3**	**.250**	**10**	**2.25**	**40**	**13**	**8**	**40**	**0**	**5**	**0**	**0**
Career average		3	3	1	2	.250	6	2.23	22 ⅓	7	5	23	0	3	0	0
Cubs average		**5**	**5**	**1**	**3**	**.250**	**10**	**2.25**	**40**	**13**	**8**	**40**	**0**	**5**	**0**	**0**
Career total		5	6	1	3	.250	11	2.23	44 ⅓	14	10	45	0	5	0	0
Cubs total		**5**	**5**	**1**	**3**	**.250**	**10**	**2.25**	**40**	**13**	**8**	**40**	**0**	**5**	**0**	**0**

Moskau, Paul Richard
HEIGHT: 6'2" RIGHTHANDER BORN: 12/20/1953 ST. JOSEPH, MISSOURI

YEAR	TEAM	STARTS	GAMES	WON	LOST	PCT	ER	ERA	INNINGS PITCHED	STRIKE-OUTS	WALKS	HITS ALLOWED	HRS ALLOWED	COMP. GAMES	SHUT-OUTS	SAVES
1977	Cin-N	19	20	6	6	.500	48	4.00	108	71	40	116	10	2	2	0
1978	Cin-N	25	26	6	4	.600	64	3.97	145	88	57	139	17	2	1	1
1979	Cin-N	15	21	5	4	.556	46	3.89	106 ⅓	58	51	107	9	1	0	0
1980	Cin-N	19	33	9	7	.563	68	4.01	152 ⅔	94	41	147	13	2	0	2
1981	Cin-N	1	27	2	1	.667	30	4.94	54 ⅔	32	32	54	4	0	0	2
1982	Pit-N	5	13	1	3	.250	17	4.37	35	15	8	43	7	0	0	0
1983	**ChC-N**	**8**	**8**	**3**	**2**	**.600**	**24**	**6.75**	**32**	**16**	**14**	**44**	**7**	**0**	**0**	**0**
Career average		13	21	5	4	.542	42	4.22	90 ⅔	53	35	93	10	1	1	1
Cubs average		**8**	**8**	**3**	**2**	**.600**	**24**	**6.75**	**32**	**16**	**14**	**44**	**7**	**0**	**0**	**0**
Career total		92	148	32	27	.542	297	4.22	633 ⅔	374	243	650	67	7	4	5
Cubs total		**8**	**8**	**3**	**2**	**.600**	**24**	**6.75**	**32**	**16**	**14**	**44**	**7**	**0**	**0**	**0**

Moss, Charles Malcolm (Mal)
HEIGHT: 6'0" LEFTHANDER BORN: 4/18/1905 SULLIVAN, INDIANA DIED: 2/6/1983 SAVANNAH, GEORGIA

YEAR	TEAM	STARTS	GAMES	WON	LOST	PCT	ER	ERA	INNINGS PITCHED	STRIKE-OUTS	WALKS	HITS ALLOWED	HRS ALLOWED	COMP. GAMES	SHUT-OUTS	SAVES
1930	ChC-N	1	12	0	0	—	13	6.27	18 ⅔	4	14	18	0	0	0	1
Career average		1	12	0	0	—	13	6.27	18 ⅔	4	14	18	0	0	0	1
Cubs average		**1**	**12**	**0**	**0**	**—**	**13**	**6.27**	**18 ⅔**	**4**	**14**	**18**	**0**	**0**	**0**	**1**
Career total		1	12	0	0	—	13	6.27	18 ⅔	4	14	18	0	0	0	1
Cubs total		**1**	**12**	**0**	**0**	**—**	**13**	**6.27**	**18 ⅔**	**4**	**14**	**18**	**0**	**0**	**0**	**1**

Moyer, Jamie
HEIGHT: 6'0" LEFTHANDER BORN: 11/18/1962 SELLERSVILLE, PENNSYLVANIA

YEAR	TEAM	STARTS	GAMES	WON	LOST	PCT	ER	ERA	INNINGS PITCHED	STRIKE-OUTS	WALKS	HITS ALLOWED	HRS ALLOWED	COMP. GAMES	SHUT-OUTS	SAVES
1986	**ChC-N**	**16**	**16**	**7**	**4**	**.636**	**49**	**5.05**	**87 ⅓**	**45**	**42**	**107**	**10**	**1**	**1**	**0**
1987	**ChC-N**	**33**	**35**	**12**	**15**	**.444**	**114**	**5.10**	**201**	**147**	**97**	**210**	**28**	**1**	**0**	**0**
1988	**ChC-N**	**30**	**34**	**9**	**15**	**.375**	**78**	**3.48**	**202**	**121**	**55**	**212**	**20**	**3**	**1**	**0**
1989	Tex-A	15	15	4	9	.308	41	4.86	76	44	33	84	10	1	0	0
1990	Tex-A	10	33	2	6	.250	53	4.66	102 ⅓	58	39	115	6	1	0	0
1991	StL-N	7	8	0	5	.000	20	5.74	31 ⅓	20	16	38	5	0	0	0
1993	Bal-A	25	25	12	9	.571	58	3.43	152	90	38	154	11	3	1	0
1994	Bal-A	23	23	5	7	.417	79	4.77	149	87	38	158	23	0	0	0
1995	Bal-A	18	27	8	6	.571	67	5.21	115 ⅔	65	30	117	18	0	0	0
1996	Bos-A	10	23	7	1	.875	45	4.50	90	50	27	111	14	0	0	0
1996	Sea-A	11	11	6	2	.750	26	3.31	70 ⅔	29	19	66	9	0	0	0
1997	Sea-A	30	30	17	5	.773	81	3.86	188 ⅔	113	43	187	21	2	0	0
1998	Sea-A	34	34	15	9	.625	92	3.53	234 ⅓	158	42	234	23	4	0	0
1999	Sea-A	32	32	14	8	.636	98	3.87	228	137	48	235	23	4	3	0
2000	Sea-A	26	26	13	10	.565	94	5.49	154	98	53	173	22	0	0	0
2001	Sea-A	33	33	20	6	.769	80	3.43	209 ⅔	119	44	187	24	1	0	0
Career average		24	27	10	8	.563	72	4.22	152 ⅔	92	44	159	18	1	0	0
Cubs average		**26**	**28**	**9**	**11**	**.452**	**80**	**4.42**	**163 ⅓**	**104**	**65**	**176**	**19**	**2**	**1**	**0**
Career total		353	405	151	117	.563	1075	4.22	2292	1381	664	2388	267	21	6	0
Cubs total		**79**	**85**	**28**	**34**	**.452**	**241**	**4.42**	**490 ⅓**	**313**	**194**	**529**	**58**	**5**	**2**	**0**

Mudrock, Philip Ray (Phil)

HEIGHT: 6'1" RIGHTHANDER BORN: 1/12/1937 LOUISVILLE, COLORADO

YEAR	TEAM	STARTS	GAMES	WON	LOST	PCT	ER	ERA	INNINGS PITCHED	STRIKE-OUTS	WALKS	HITS ALLOWED	HRS ALLOWED	COMP. GAMES	SHUT-OUTS	SAVES
1963	ChC-N	0	1	0	0	—	1	9.00	1	0	0	2	0	0	0	0
Career average		0	1	0	0	—	1	9.00	1	0	0	2	0	0	0	0
Cubs average		**0**	**1**	**0**	**0**	**—**	**1**	**9.00**	**1**	**0**	**0**	**2**	**0**	**0**	**0**	**0**
Career total		0	1	0	0	—	1	9.00	1	0	0	2	0	0	0	0
Cubs total		**0**	**1**	**0**	**0**	**—**	**1**	**9.00**	**1**	**0**	**0**	**2**	**0**	**0**	**0**	**0**

Mulholland, Terence John (Terry)

HEIGHT: 6'3" LEFTHANDER BORN: 3/9/1963 UNIONTOWN, PENNSYLVANIA

YEAR	TEAM	STARTS	GAMES	WON	LOST	PCT	ER	ERA	INNINGS PITCHED	STRIKE-OUTS	WALKS	HITS ALLOWED	HRS ALLOWED	COMP. GAMES	SHUT-OUTS	SAVES
1986	SF-N	10	15	1	7	.125	30	4.94	54 2/3	27	35	51	3	0	0	0
1988	SF-N	6	9	2	1	.667	19	3.72	46	18	7	50	3	2	1	0
1989	SF-N	1	5	0	0	—	5	4.09	11	6	4	15	0	0	0	0
1989	Phi-N	17	20	4	7	.364	58	5.00	104 1/3	60	32	122	8	2	1	0
1990	Phi-N	26	33	9	10	.474	67	3.34	180 2/3	75	42	172	15	6	1	0
1991	Phi-N	34	34	16	13	.552	93	3.61	232	142	49	231	15	8	3	0
1992	Phi-N	32	32	13	11	.542	97	3.81	229	125	46	227	14	12	2	0
1993	Phi-N	28	29	12	9	.571	69	3.25	191	116	40	177	20	7	2	0
1994	NYY-A	19	24	6	7	.462	87	6.49	120 2/3	72	37	150	24	2	0	0
1995	SF-N	24	29	5	13	.278	96	5.80	149	65	38	190	25	2	0	0
1996	Phi-N	21	21	8	7	.533	69	4.66	133 1/3	52	21	157	17	3	0	0
1996	Sea-A	12	12	5	4	.556	36	4.67	69 1/3	34	28	75	5	0	0	0
1997	**ChC-N**	**25**	**25**	**6**	**12**	**.333**	**71**	**4.07**	**157**	**74**	**45**	**162**	**20**	**1**	**0**	**0**
1997	SF-N	2	15	0	1	.000	17	5.16	29 2/3	25	6	28	4	0	0	3
1998	**ChC-N**	**6**	**70**	**6**	**5**	**.545**	**36**	**2.89**	**112**	**72**	**39**	**100**	**7**	**0**	**0**	**0**
1999	**ChC-N**	**16**	**26**	**6**	**6**	**.500**	**63**	**5.15**	**110**	**44**	**32**	**137**	**16**	**0**	**0**	**1**
1999	Atl-N	8	16	4	2	.667	20	2.98	60 1/3	39	13	64	5	0	0	1
2000	Atl-N	20	54	9	9	.500	89	5.11	156 2/3	78	41	198	24	1	0	1
2001	Pit-N	1	22	0	0	—	15	3.72	36 1/3	17	10	38	5	0	0	0
2001	LA-N	3	19	1	1	.500	19	5.83	29 1/3	25	7	40	7	0	0	0
Career average		21	34	8	8	.475	70	4.30	147 1/3	78	38	159	16	3	1	0
Cubs average		**16**	**40**	**6**	**8**	**.439**	**57**	**4.04**	**126 1/3**	**63**	**39**	**133**	**14**	**0**	**0**	**1**
Career total		311	510	113	125	.475	1056	4.30	2212 1/3	1166	572	2384	237	46	10	5
Cubs total		**47**	**121**	**18**	**23**	**.439**	**170**	**4.04**	**379**	**190**	**116**	**399**	**43**	**1**	**0**	**3**

Muncrief, Robert Cleveland (Bob)

HEIGHT: 6'2" RIGHTHANDER BORN: 1/28/1916 MADILL, OKLAHOMA DIED: 2/6/1996 DUNCANVILLE, TEXAS

YEAR	TEAM	STARTS	GAMES	WON	LOST	PCT	ER	ERA	INNINGS PITCHED	STRIKE-OUTS	WALKS	HITS ALLOWED	HRS ALLOWED	COMP. GAMES	SHUT-OUTS	SAVES
1937	StL-A	1	1	0	0	—	1	4.50	2	0	2	3	1	0	0	0
1939	StL-A	0	2	0	0	—	5	15.00	3	1	3	7	1	0	0	0
1941	StL-A	24	36	13	9	.591	87	3.65	214 1/3	67	53	221	18	12	2	1
1942	StL-A	18	24	6	8	.429	58	3.89	134 1/3	39	31	149	11	7	1	0
1943	StL-A	27	35	13	12	.520	64	2.81	205	80	48	211	13	12	3	1
1944	StL-A	27	33	13	8	.619	75	3.08	219 1/3	88	50	216	11	12	3	1
1945	StL-A	15	27	13	4	.765	44	2.72	145 2/3	54	44	132	8	10	0	1
1946	StL-A	14	29	3	12	.200	64	4.99	115 1/3	49	31	149	6	4	1	0
1947	StL-A	23	31	8	14	.364	96	4.90	176 1/3	74	51	210	14	7	0	0
1948	Cle-A	9	21	5	4	.556	32	3.98	72 1/3	24	31	76	8	1	1	3
1949	Pit-N	4	13	1	5	.167	25	6.31	35 2/3	11	13	44	8	1	0	2
1949	**ChC-N**	**3**	**34**	**5**	**6**	**.455**	**38**	**4.56**	**75**	**36**	**31**	**80**	**9**	**1**	**0**	**2**
1951	NYY-A	0	2	0	0	—	3	9.00	3	2	4	5	0	0	0	0
Career average		14	24	7	7	.494	49	3.80	116 2/3	44	33	125	9	6	1	1
Cubs average		**3**	**34**	**5**	**6**	**.455**	**38**	**4.56**	**75**	**36**	**31**	**80**	**9**	**1**	**0**	**2**
Career total		165	288	80	82	.494	592	3.80	1401 1/3	525	392	1503	108	67	11	9
Cubs total		**3**	**34**	**5**	**6**	**.455**	**38**	**4.56**	**75**	**36**	**31**	**80**	**9**	**1**	**0**	**2**

Myers, Randall Kirk (Randy)

HEIGHT: 6'1"   LEFTHANDER   BORN: 9/19/1962 VANCOUVER, WASHINGTON

YEAR	TEAM	STARTS	GAMES	WON	LOST	PCT	ER	ERA	INNINGS PITCHED	STRIKE-OUTS	WALKS	HITS ALLOWED	HRS ALLOWED	COMP. GAMES	SHUT-OUTS	SAVES
1985	NYM-N	0	1	0	0	—	0	0.00	2	2	1	0	0	0	0	0
1986	NYM-N	0	10	0	0	—	5	4.22	10 2/3	13	9	11	1	0	0	0
1987	NYM-N	0	54	3	6	.333	33	3.96	75	92	30	61	6	0	0	6
1988	NYM-N	0	55	7	3	.700	13	1.72	68	69	17	45	5	0	0	26
1989	NYM-N	0	65	7	4	.636	22	2.35	84 1/3	88	40	62	4	0	0	24
1990	Cin-N	0	66	4	6	.400	20	2.08	86 2/3	98	38	59	6	0	0	31
1991	Cin-N	12	58	6	13	.316	52	3.55	132	108	80	116	8	1	0	6
1992	SD-N	0	66	3	6	.333	38	4.29	79 2/3	66	34	84	7	0	0	38
1993	**ChC-N**	**0**	**73**	**2**	**4**	**.333**	**26**	**3.11**	**75 1/3**	**86**	**26**	**65**	**7**	**0**	**0**	**53**
1994	**ChC-N**	**0**	**38**	**1**	**5**	**.167**	**17**	**3.79**	**40 1/3**	**32**	**16**	**40**	**3**	**0**	**0**	**21**
1995	**ChC-N**	**0**	**57**	**1**	**2**	**.333**	**24**	**3.88**	**55 2/3**	**59**	**28**	**49**	**7**	**0**	**0**	**38**
1996	Bal-A	0	62	4	4	.500	23	3.53	58 2/3	74	29	60	7	0	0	31
1997	Bal-A	0	61	2	3	.400	10	1.51	59 2/3	56	22	47	2	0	0	45
1998	Tor-A	0	41	3	4	.429	21	4.46	42 1/3	32	19	44	4	0	0	28
1998	SD-N	0	21	1	3	.250	10	6.28	14 1/3	9	7	15	2	0	0	0
Career average		1	52	3	5	.411	22	3.19	63 1/3	63	28	54	5	0	0	25
Cubs average		**0**	**56**	**1**	**4**	**.267**	**22**	**3.52**	**57**	**59**	**23**	**51**	**6**	**0**	**0**	**37**
Career total		12	728	44	63	.411	314	3.19	884 2/3	884	396	758	69	1	0	347
Cubs total		**0**	**168**	**4**	**11**	**.267**	**67**	**3.52**	**171 1/3**	**177**	**70**	**154**	**17**	**0**	**0**	**112**

Myers, Rodney Luther

HEIGHT: 6'1"   RIGHTHANDER   BORN: 6/26/1969 ROCKFORD, ILLINOIS

YEAR	TEAM	STARTS	GAMES	WON	LOST	PCT	ER	ERA	INNINGS PITCHED	STRIKE-OUTS	WALKS	HITS ALLOWED	HRS ALLOWED	COMP. GAMES	SHUT-OUTS	SAVES
1996	**ChC-N**	**0**	**45**	**2**	**1**	**.667**	**35**	**4.68**	**67 1/3**	**50**	**38**	**61**	**6**	**0**	**0**	**0**
1997	**ChC-N**	**1**	**5**	**0**	**0**	**—**	**6**	**6.00**	**9**	**6**	**7**	**12**	**1**	**0**	**0**	**0**
1998	**ChC-N**	**0**	**12**	**0**	**0**	**—**	**14**	**7.00**	**18**	**15**	**6**	**26**	**3**	**0**	**0**	**0**
1999	**ChC-N**	**0**	**46**	**3**	**1**	**.750**	**31**	**4.38**	**63 2/3**	**41**	**25**	**71**	**10**	**0**	**0**	**0**
2000	SD-N	0	3	0	0	—	1	4.50	2	3	0	2	0	0	0	0
2001	SD-N	0	37	1	2	.333	28	5.32	47 1/3	29	20	53	6	0	0	1
Career average		0	25	1	1	.600	19	4.99	34 2/3	24	16	38	4	0	0	0
Cubs average		**0**	**27**	**1**	**1**	**.714**	**22**	**4.90**	**39 2/3**	**28**	**19**	**43**	**5**	**0**	**0**	**0**
Career total		1	148	6	4	.600	115	4.99	207 1/3	144	96	225	26	0	0	1
Cubs total		**1**	**108**	**5**	**2**	**.714**	**86**	**4.90**	**158**	**112**	**76**	**170**	**20**	**0**	**0**	**0**

Nabholz, Christopher William (Chris)

HEIGHT: 6'5"   LEFTHANDER   BORN: 1/5/1967 HARRISBURG, PENNSYLVANIA

YEAR	TEAM	STARTS	GAMES	WON	LOST	PCT	ER	ERA	INNINGS PITCHED	STRIKE-OUTS	WALKS	HITS ALLOWED	HRS ALLOWED	COMP. GAMES	SHUT-OUTS	SAVES
1990	Mon-N	11	11	6	2	.750	22	2.83	70	53	32	43	6	1	1	0
1991	Mon-N	24	24	8	7	.533	62	3.63	153 2/3	99	57	134	5	1	0	0
1992	Mon-N	32	32	11	12	.478	72	3.32	195	130	74	176	11	1	1	0
1993	Mon-N	21	26	9	8	.529	53	4.09	116 2/3	74	63	100	9	1	0	0
1994	Cle-A	4	6	0	1	.000	14	11.45	11	5	9	23	1	0	0	0
1994	Bos-A	8	8	3	4	.429	31	6.64	42	23	29	44	5	0	0	0
1995	**ChC-N**	**0**	**34**	**0**	**1**	**.000**	**14**	**5.40**	**23 1/3**	**21**	**14**	**22**	**4**	**0**	**0**	**0**
Career average		17	24	6	6	.514	45	3.94	102	68	46	90	7	1	0	0
Cubs average		**0**	**34**	**0**	**1**	**.000**	**14**	**5.40**	**23 1/3**	**21**	**14**	**22**	**4**	**0**	**0**	**0**
Career total		100	141	37	35	.514	268	3.94	611 2/3	405	278	542	41	4	2	0
Cubs total		**0**	**34**	**0**	**1**	**.000**	**14**	**5.40**	**23 1/3**	**21**	**14**	**22**	**4**	**0**	**0**	**0**

Napier, Skelton Leroy (Buddy)
HEIGHT: 5'11" RIGHTHANDER BORN: 12/18/1889 BYROMVILLE, GEORGIA DIED: 3/29/1968 HUTCHINS, TEXAS

YEAR	TEAM	STARTS	GAMES	WON	LOST	PCT	ER	ERA	INNINGS PITCHED	STRIKE-OUTS	WALKS	HITS ALLOWED	HRS ALLOWED	COMP. GAMES	SHUT-OUTS	SAVES
1912	StL-A	2	7	1	2	.333	14	4.97	25 1/3	10	5	33	0	0	0	0
1918	**ChC-N**	**0**	**1**	**0**	**0**	**—**	**4**	**5.40**	**6 2/3**	**2**	**4**	**10**	**0**	**5**	**1**	**0**
1920	Cin-N	5	9	4	2	.667	7	1.29	49	17	7	47	0	5	1	0
1921	Cin-N	6	22	0	2	.000	35	5.56	56 2/3	14	13	72	2	1	0	1
Career average		3	10	1	2	.455	15	3.92	34 1/3	11	7	41	1	2	0	0
Cubs average		**0**	**1**	**0**	**0**	**—**	**4**	**5.40**	**6 2/3**	**2**	**4**	**10**	**0**	**0**	**0**	**0**
Career total		13	39	5	6	.455	60	3.92	137 2/3	43	29	162	2	6	1	1
Cubs total		**0**	**1**	**0**	**0**	**—**	**4**	**5.40**	**6 2/3**	**2**	**4**	**10**	**0**	**0**	**0**	**0**

Nation, Joseph Paul (Joey)
HEIGHT: 6'2" LEFTHANDER BORN: 9/28/1978 OKLAHOMA CITY, OKLAHOMA

YEAR	TEAM	STARTS	GAMES	WON	LOST	PCT	ER	ERA	INNINGS PITCHED	STRIKE-OUTS	WALKS	HITS ALLOWED	HRS ALLOWED	COMP. GAMES	SHUT-OUTS	SAVES
2000	ChC-N	2	2	0	2	.000	9	6.94	11 2/3	8	8	12	2	0	0	0
Career average		2	2	0	2	.000	9	6.94	11 2/3	8	8	12	2	0	0	0
Cubs average		**2**	**2**	**0**	**2**	**.000**	**9**	**6.94**	**11 2/3**	**8**	**8**	**12**	**2**	**0**	**0**	**0**
Career total		2	2	0	2	.000	9	6.94	11 2/3	8	8	12	2	0	0	0
Cubs total		**2**	**2**	**0**	**2**	**.000**	**9**	**6.94**	**11 2/3**	**8**	**8**	**12**	**2**	**0**	**0**	**0**

Navarro, Jaime
HEIGHT: 6'4" RIGHTHANDER BORN: 3/27/1968 BAYAMON, PUERTO RICO

YEAR	TEAM	STARTS	GAMES	WON	LOST	PCT	ER	ERA	INNINGS PITCHED	STRIKE-OUTS	WALKS	HITS ALLOWED	HRS ALLOWED	COMP. GAMES	SHUT-OUTS	SAVES
1989	Mil-A	17	19	7	8	.467	38	3.12	109 2/3	56	32	119	6	1	0	0
1990	Mil-A	22	32	8	7	.533	74	4.46	149 1/3	75	41	176	11	3	0	1
1991	Mil-A	34	34	15	12	.556	102	3.92	234	114	73	237	18	10	2	0
1992	Mil-A	34	34	17	11	.607	91	3.33	246	100	64	224	14	5	3	0
1993	Mil-A	34	35	11	12	.478	127	5.33	214 1/3	114	73	254	21	5	1	0
1994	Mil-A	10	29	4	9	.308	66	6.62	89 2/3	65	35	115	10	0	0	0
1995	**ChC-N**	**29**	**29**	**14**	**6**	**.700**	**73**	**3.28**	**200 1/3**	**128**	**56**	**194**	**19**	**1**	**1**	**0**
1996	**ChC-N**	**35**	**35**	**15**	**12**	**.556**	**103**	**3.92**	**236 2/3**	**158**	**72**	**244**	**25**	**4**	**1**	**0**
1997	CWS-A	33	33	9	14	.391	135	5.79	209 2/3	142	73	267	22	2	0	1
1998	CWS-A	27	37	8	16	.333	122	6.36	172 2/3	71	77	223	30	1	0	0
1999	CWS-A	27	32	8	13	.381	108	6.09	159 2/3	74	71	206	29	0	0	0
2000	Mil-N	5	5	0	5	.000	26	12.54	18 2/3	7	18	34	6	0	0	0
2000	Cle-A	2	7	0	1	.000	13	7.98	14 2/3	9	5	20	3	0	0	0
Career average		26	30	10	11	.479	90	4.72	171 1/3	93	58	193	18	3	1	0
Cubs average		**32**	**32**	**15**	**9**	**.617**	**88**	**3.62**	**218 2/3**	**143**	**64**	**219**	**22**	**3**	**1**	**0**
Career total		309	361	116	126	.479	1078	4.72	2055 1/3	1113	690	2313	214	32	8	2
Cubs total		**64**	**64**	**29**	**18**	**.617**	**176**	**3.62**	**437**	**286**	**128**	**438**	**44**	**5**	**2**	**0**

Nehf, Arthur Neukom (Art)
HEIGHT: 5'9" LEFTHANDER BORN: 7/31/1892 TERRE HAUTE, INDIANA DIED: 12/18/1960 PHOENIX, ARIZONA

YEAR	TEAM	STARTS	GAMES	WON	LOST	PCT	ER	ERA	INNINGS PITCHED	STRIKE-OUTS	WALKS	HITS ALLOWED	HRS ALLOWED	COMP. GAMES	SHUT-OUTS	SAVES
1915	Bos-N	10	12	5	4	.556	22	2.53	78 1/3	39	21	60	0	6	4	0
1916	Bos-N	13	22	7	5	.583	27	2.01	121	36	20	110	1	6	1	0
1917	Bos-N	23	38	17	8	.680	56	2.16	233 1/3	101	39	197	4	16	4	0
1918	Bos-N	31	32	15	15	.500	85	2.69	284 1/3	96	76	274	2	28	2	0
1919	Bos-N	19	22	8	9	.471	58	3.09	168 2/3	53	40	151	6	13	1	0
1919	NYG-N	12	13	9	2	.818	17	1.50	102	24	19	70	2	9	2	0
1920	NYG-N	32	40	21	12	.636	96	3.08	280 2/3	79	45	273	8	22	5	0
1921	NYG-N	34	41	20	10	.667	105	3.63	260 2/3	67	55	266	18	18	2	1
1922	NYG-N	35	37	19	13	.594	98	3.29	268 1/3	60	64	286	15	20	3	1
1923	NYG-N	27	34	13	10	.565	98	4.50	196	50	49	219	14	7	1	2

(continued)

(continued)

YEAR	TEAM	STARTS	GAMES	WON	LOST	PCT	ER	ERA	INNINGS PITCHED	STRIKE-OUTS	WALKS	HITS ALLOWED	HRS ALLOWED	COMP. GAMES	SHUT-OUTS	SAVES
1924	NYG-N	20	30	14	4	.778	69	3.62	171 2/3	72	42	167	14	11	0	2
1925	NYG-N	20	29	11	9	.550	65	3.77	155	63	50	193	7	8	1	1
1926	NYG-N	0	2	0	0	—	2	10.80	1 2/3	0	1	2	0	0	0	0
1926	Cin-N	1	7	0	1	.000	7	3.71	17	4	5	25	0	0	0	0
1927	Cin-N	5	21	3	5	.375	28	5.56	45 1/3	21	14	59	2	1	0	4
1927	**ChC-N**	**2**	**8**	**1**	**1**	**.500**	**4**	**1.37**	**26 1/3**	**12**	**9**	**25**	**0**	**2**	**1**	**1**
1928	**ChC-N**	**21**	**31**	**13**	**7**	**.650**	**52**	**2.65**	**176 2/3**	**40**	**52**	**190**	**3**	**10**	**2**	**0**
1929	**ChC-N**	**14**	**32**	**8**	**5**	**.615**	**75**	**5.59**	**120 2/3**	**27**	**39**	**148**	**11**	**4**	**0**	**1**
Career average		21	30	12	8	.605	64	3.20	180 2/3	56	43	181	7	12	2	1
Cubs average		**12**	**24**	**7**	**4**	**.629**	**44**	**3.64**	**108**	**26**	**33**	**121**	**5**	**5**	**1**	**1**
Career total		319	451	184	120	.605	964	3.20	2707 2/3	844	640	2715	107	181	29	13
Cubs total		**37**	**71**	**22**	**13**	**.629**	**131**	**3.64**	**323 2/3**	**79**	**100**	**363**	**14**	**16**	**3**	**2**

Nelson, Lynn Bernard (Line Drive)
HEIGHT: 5'10"   RIGHTHANDER   BORN: 2/24/1905 SHELDON, NORTH DAKOTA   DIED: 2/15/1955 KANSAS CITY, MISSOURI

YEAR	TEAM	STARTS	GAMES	WON	LOST	PCT	ER	ERA	INNINGS PITCHED	STRIKE-OUTS	WALKS	HITS ALLOWED	HRS ALLOWED	COMP. GAMES	SHUT-OUTS	SAVES
1930	**ChC-N**	**3**	**37**	**3**	**2**	**.600**	**46**	**5.09**	**81 1/3**	**29**	**28**	**97**	**10**	**0**	**0**	**0**
1933	**ChC-N**	**3**	**24**	**5**	**5**	**.500**	**27**	**3.21**	**75 2/3**	**20**	**30**	**65**	**2**	**3**	**0**	**1**
1934	**ChC-N**	**1**	**2**	**0**	**1**	**.000**	**4**	**36.00**	**1**	**0**	**1**	**4**	**1**	**0**	**0**	**0**
1937	Phi-A	4	30	4	9	.308	76	5.90	116	49	51	140	12	1	0	2
1938	Phi-A	23	32	10	11	.476	120	5.65	191	75	79	215	29	13	0	2
1939	Phi-A	24	35	10	13	.435	105	4.78	197 2/3	75	64	233	27	12	2	1
1940	Det-A	2	6	1	1	.500	17	10.93	14	7	9	23	5	0	0	0
Career average		9	24	5	6	.440	56	5.25	96 2/3	36	37	111	12	4	0	1
Cubs average		**2**	**21**	**3**	**3**	**.500**	**26**	**4.39**	**52 2/3**	**16**	**20**	**55**	**4**	**1**	**0**	**0**
Career total		60	166	33	42	.440	395	5.25	676 2/3	255	262	777	86	29	2	6
Cubs total		**7**	**63**	**8**	**8**	**.500**	**77**	**4.39**	**158**	**49**	**59**	**166**	**13**	**3**	**0**	**1**

Newkirk, Joel Ivan (Sailor)
HEIGHT: 6'0"   RIGHTHANDER   BORN: 6/1/1896 KYANA, INDIANA   DIED: 1/22/1966 ELDORADO, ILLINOIS

YEAR	TEAM	STARTS	GAMES	WON	LOST	PCT	ER	ERA	INNINGS PITCHED	STRIKE-OUTS	WALKS	HITS ALLOWED	HRS ALLOWED	COMP. GAMES	SHUT-OUTS	SAVES
1919	**ChC-N**	**0**	**1**	**0**	**0**	**—**	**3**	**13.50**	**2**	**1**	**3**	**2**	**0**	**0**	**0**	**0**
1920	**ChC-N**	**1**	**2**	**0**	**1**	**.000**	**4**	**5.40**	**6 2/3**	**2**	**6**	**8**	**1**	**0**	**0**	**0**
Career average		1	2	0	1	.000	4	7.27	4 1/3	2	5	5	1	0	0	0
Cubs average		**1**	**2**	**0**	**1**	**.000**	**4**	**7.27**	**4 1/3**	**2**	**5**	**5**	**1**	**0**	**0**	**0**
Career total		1	3	0	1	.000	7	7.27	8 2/3	3	9	10	1	0	0	0
Cubs total		**1**	**3**	**0**	**1**	**.000**	**7**	**7.27**	**8 2/3**	**3**	**9**	**10**	**1**	**0**	**0**	**0**

Newman, Raymond Francis (Ray)
HEIGHT: 6'5"   LEFTHANDER   BORN: 6/20/1945 EVANSVILLE, INDIANA

YEAR	TEAM	STARTS	GAMES	WON	LOST	PCT	ER	ERA	INNINGS PITCHED	STRIKE-OUTS	WALKS	HITS ALLOWED	HRS ALLOWED	COMP. GAMES	SHUT-OUTS	SAVES
1971	**ChC-N**	**0**	**30**	**1**	**2**	**.333**	**15**	**3.52**	**38 1/3**	**35**	**17**	**30**	**4**	**0**	**0**	**2**
1972	Mil-A	0	4	0	0	—	0	0.00	7	1	2	4	0	0	0	1
1973	Mil-A	0	11	2	1	.667	6	2.95	18 1/3	10	5	19	2	0	0	1
Career average		0	15	1	1	.500	7	2.97	21 1/3	15	8	18	2	0	0	2
Cubs average		**0**	**30**	**1**	**2**	**.333**	**15**	**3.52**	**38 1/3**	**35**	**17**	**30**	**4**	**0**	**0**	**2**
Career total		0	45	3	3	.500	21	2.97	63 2/3	46	24	53	6	0	0	4
Cubs total		**0**	**30**	**1**	**2**	**.333**	**15**	**3.52**	**38 1/3**	**35**	**17**	**30**	**4**	**0**	**0**	**2**

Newsom, Louis Norman (Bobo *or* Buck)
HEIGHT: 6'3" RIGHTHANDER BORN: 8/11/1907 HARTSVILLE, SOUTH CAROLINA DIED: 12/7/1962 ORLANDO, FLORIDA

YEAR	TEAM	STARTS	GAMES	WON	LOST	PCT	ER	ERA	INNINGS PITCHED	STRIKE-OUTS	WALKS	HITS ALLOWED	HRS ALLOWED	COMP. GAMES	SHUT-OUTS	SAVES
1929	Bro-N	2	3	0	3	.000	11	10.61	9⅓	6	5	15	0	0	0	0
1930	Bro-N	0	2	0	0	—	0	0.00	3	1	2	2	0	0	0	0
1932	**ChC-N**	**0**	**1**	**0**	**0**	**—**	**0**	**0.00**	**1**	**0**	**0**	**1**	**0**	**0**	**0**	**0**
1934	StL-A	32	47	16	20	.444	117	4.01	262⅓	135	149	259	15	15	2	5
1935	StL-A	6	7	0	6	.000	23	4.85	42⅔	22	13	54	2	1	0	1
1935	Was-A	23	28	11	12	.478	98	4.45	198⅓	65	84	222	9	17	2	2
1936	Was-A	38	43	17	15	.531	137	4.32	285⅔	156	146	294	13	24	4	2
1937	Was-A	10	11	3	4	.429	44	5.85	67⅔	39	48	76	4	3	0	0
1937	Bos-A	27	30	13	10	.565	103	4.46	207⅔	127	119	193	14	14	1	0
1938	StL-A	40	44	20	16	.556	186	5.08	329⅔	226	192	334	30	31	0	1
1939	StL-A	6	6	3	1	.750	24	4.73	45⅔	28	22	50	5	3	0	0
1939	Det-A	31	35	17	10	.630	92	3.37	246	164	104	222	14	21	3	2
1940	Det-A	34	36	21	5	.808	83	2.83	264	164	100	235	19	20	3	0
1941	Det-A	36	43	12	20	.375	128	4.60	250⅓	175	118	265	15	12	2	2
1942	Was-A	29	30	11	17	.393	117	4.93	213⅔	113	92	236	5	15	2	0
1942	Bro-N	5	6	2	2	.500	12	3.38	32	21	14	28	1	2	1	1
1943	Bro-N	12	22	9	4	.692	42	3.02	125	75	57	113	4	6	1	0
1943	StL-A	9	10	1	6	.143	43	7.39	52⅓	37	35	69	7	0	0	0
1943	Was-A	6	6	3	3	.500	17	3.83	40	11	21	38	1	2	0	1
1944	Phi-A	33	37	13	15	.464	83	2.82	265	142	82	243	11	18	2	0
1945	Phi-A	34	36	8	20	.286	94	3.29	257⅓	127	103	255	12	16	3	0
1946	Phi-A	9	10	3	5	.375	22	3.38	58⅔	32	30	61	2	3	1	1
1946	Was-A	22	24	11	8	.579	55	2.78	178	82	60	163	5	14	2	0
1947	Was-A	13	14	4	6	.400	38	4.09	83⅔	40	37	99	2	6	2	0
1947	NYY-A	15	17	7	5	.583	36	2.80	115⅔	42	30	109	1	0	0	0
1948	NYG-N	4	11	0	4	.000	12	4.21	25⅔	9	13	35	1	0	0	2
1952	Was-A	0	10	1	1	.500	7	4.97	12⅔	5	9	16	2	0	0	1
1952	Phi-A	5	14	3	3	.500	19	3.59	47⅔	22	23	38	2	1	0	0
1953	Phi-A	2	17	2	1	.667	21	4.89	38⅔	16	24	44	3	1	0	0
Career average		24	30	11	11	.487	83	3.98	188	104	87	188	10	12	2	1
Cubs average		**0**	**1**	**0**	**0**	**—**	**0**	**0.00**	**1**	**0**	**0**	**1**	**0**	**0**	**0**	**0**
Career total		483	600	211	222	.487	1664	3.98	3759⅓	2082	1732	3769	206	246	31	21
Cubs total		**0**	**1**	**0**	**0**	**—**	**0**	**0.00**	**1**	**0**	**0**	**1**	**0**	**0**	**0**	**0**

Nichols, Dolan Levon (Nick)
HEIGHT: 6'0" RIGHTHANDER BORN: 2/28/1930 TISHOMINGO, MISSISSIPPI DIED: 11/20/1989 TUPELO, MISSISSIPPI

YEAR	TEAM	STARTS	GAMES	WON	LOST	PCT	ER	ERA	INNINGS PITCHED	STRIKE-OUTS	WALKS	HITS ALLOWED	HRS ALLOWED	COMP. GAMES	SHUT-OUTS	SAVES
1958	ChC-N	0	24	0	4	.000	23	5.01	41⅓	9	16	46	1	0	0	1
Career average		0	24	0	4	.000	23	5.01	41⅓	9	16	46	1	0	0	1
Cubs average		**0**	**24**	**0**	**4**	**.000**	**23**	**5.01**	**41⅓**	**9**	**16**	**46**	**1**	**0**	**0**	**1**
Career total		0	24	0	4	.000	23	5.01	41⅓	9	16	46	1	0	0	1
Cubs total		**0**	**24**	**0**	**4**	**.000**	**23**	**5.01**	**41⅓**	**9**	**16**	**46**	**1**	**0**	**0**	**1**

Nicol, George Edward
HEIGHT: 5'7" LEFTHANDER BORN: 10/17/1870 BARRY, ILLINOIS DIED: 8/10/1924 MILWAUKEE, WISCONSIN

YEAR	TEAM	STARTS	GAMES	WON	LOST	PCT	ER	ERA	INNINGS PITCHED	STRIKE-OUTS	WALKS	HITS ALLOWED	HRS ALLOWED	COMP. GAMES	SHUT-OUTS	SAVES
1890	StL-AA	3	3	2	1	.667	9	4.76	17	16	19	11	1	2	0	0
1891	**ChN-N**	**2**	**3**	**0**	**1**	**.000**	**6**	**4.91**	**11**	**12**	**10**	**14**	**0**	**0**	**0**	**1**
1894	Pit-N	5	9	2	3	.400	32	6.50	44⅓	11	33	57	2	3	0	0
1894	Lou-N	2	2	0	1	.000	15	15.00	9	3	5	19	2	2	0	0
Career average		4	6	1	2	.400	21	6.86	27	14	22	34	2	2	0	0
Cubs average		**2**	**3**	**0**	**1**	**.000**	**6**	**4.91**	**11**	**12**	**10**	**14**	**0**	**0**	**0**	**0**
Career total		12	17	4	6	.400	62	6.86	81⅓	42	67	101	5	7	0	1
Cubs total		**2**	**3**	**0**	**1**	**.000**	**6**	**4.91**	**11**	**12**	**10**	**14**	**0**	**0**	**0**	**0**

Niekro, Joseph Franklin (Joe)
HEIGHT: 6'1"   RIGHTHANDER   BORN: 11/7/1944 MARTINS FERRY, OHIO

YEAR	TEAM	STARTS	GAMES	WON	LOST	PCT	ER	ERA	INNINGS PITCHED	STRIKE-OUTS	WALKS	HITS ALLOWED	HRS ALLOWED	COMP. GAMES	SHUT-OUTS	SAVES
1967	ChC-N	22	36	10	7	.588	63	3.34	169 ⅔	77	32	171	15	7	2	0
1968	ChC-N	29	34	14	10	.583	85	4.32	177	65	59	204	18	2	1	2
1969	ChC-N	3	4	0	1	.000	8	3.72	19 ⅓	7	6	24	3	0	0	0
1969	SD-N	31	37	8	17	.320	83	3.70	202	55	45	213	15	8	3	0
1970	Det-A	34	38	12	13	.480	96	4.06	213	101	72	221	28	6	2	0
1971	Det-A	15	31	6	7	.462	61	4.49	122 ⅓	43	49	136	13	0	0	1
1972	Det-A	7	18	3	2	.600	20	3.83	47	24	8	62	3	1	0	1
1973	Atl-N	0	20	2	4	.333	11	4.13	24	12	11	23	2	0	0	3
1974	Atl-N	2	27	3	2	.600	17	3.56	43	31	18	36	5	0	0	0
1975	Hou-N	4	40	6	4	.600	30	3.07	88	54	39	79	3	1	1	4
1976	Hou-N	13	36	4	8	.333	44	3.36	118	77	56	107	8	0	0	0
1977	Hou-N	14	44	13	8	.619	61	3.04	180 ⅔	101	64	155	14	9	2	5
1978	Hou-N	29	35	14	14	.500	87	3.86	202 ⅔	97	73	190	13	10	1	0
1979	Hou-N	38	38	21	11	.656	88	3.00	263 ⅔	119	107	221	17	11	5	0
1980	Hou-N	36	37	20	12	.625	101	3.55	256	127	79	268	12	11	2	0
1981	Hou-N	24	24	9	9	.500	52	2.82	166	77	47	150	8	5	2	0
1982	Hou-N	35	35	17	12	.586	74	2.47	270	130	64	224	12	16	5	0
1983	Hou-N	38	38	15	14	.517	102	3.48	263 ⅔	152	101	238	15	9	1	0
1984	Hou-N	38	38	16	12	.571	84	3.04	248 ⅓	127	89	223	16	6	1	0
1985	Hou-N	32	32	9	12	.429	88	3.72	213	117	99	197	21	4	1	0
1985	NYY-A	3	3	2	1	.667	8	5.84	12 ⅓	4	8	14	3	0	0	0
1986	NYY-A	25	25	9	10	.474	68	4.87	125 ⅔	59	63	139	15	0	0	0
1987	NYY-A	8	8	3	4	.429	20	3.55	50 ⅔	30	19	40	4	1	0	0
1987	Min-A	18	19	4	9	.308	67	6.26	96 ⅓	54	45	115	11	0	0	0
1988	Min-A	2	5	1	1	.500	13	10.03	11 ⅔	7	9	16	2	0	0	0
Career average		23	32	10	9	.520	65	3.59	163	79	57	158	13	5	1	1
Cubs average		**18**	**25**	**8**	**6**	**.571**	**52**	**3.84**	**122**	**50**	**32**	**133**	**12**	**3**	**1**	**1**
Career total		500	702	221	204	.520	1431	3.59	3584	1747	1262	3466	276	107	29	16
Cubs total		**54**	**74**	**24**	**18**	**.571**	**156**	**3.84**	**366**	**149**	**97**	**399**	**36**	**9**	**3**	**2**

Nipper, Albert Samuel (Al)
HEIGHT: 6'0"   RIGHTHANDER   BORN: 4/2/1959 SAN DIEGO, CALIFORNIA

YEAR	TEAM	STARTS	GAMES	WON	LOST	PCT	ER	ERA	INNINGS PITCHED	STRIKE-OUTS	WALKS	HITS ALLOWED	HRS ALLOWED	COMP. GAMES	SHUT-OUTS	SAVES
1983	Bos-A	2	3	1	1	.500	4	2.25	16	5	7	17	0	1	0	0
1984	Bos-A	24	29	11	6	.647	79	3.89	182 ⅔	84	52	183	18	6	0	0
1985	Bos-A	25	25	9	12	.429	73	4.06	162	85	82	157	14	5	0	0
1986	Bos-A	26	26	10	12	.455	95	5.38	159	79	47	186	24	3	0	0
1987	Bos-A	30	30	11	12	.478	105	5.43	174	89	62	196	30	6	0	0
1988	ChC-N	12	22	2	4	.333	27	3.04	80	27	34	72	9	0	0	0
1990	Cle-A	5	9	2	3	.400	18	6.75	24	12	19	35	2	0	0	1
Career average		18	21	7	7	.479	57	4.52	114	54	43	121	14	3	0	0
Cubs average		**12**	**22**	**2**	**4**	**.333**	**27**	**3.04**	**80**	**27**	**34**	**72**	**14**	**3**	**0**	**0**
Career total		124	144	46	50	.479	401	4.52	797 ⅔	381	303	846	97	21	0	1
Cubs total		**12**	**22**	**2**	**4**	**.333**	**27**	**3.04**	**80**	**27**	**34**	**72**	**9**	**0**	**0**	**1**

Noles, Dickie Ray
HEIGHT: 6'2"   RIGHTHANDER   BORN: 11/19/1956 CHARLOTTE, NORTH CAROLINA

YEAR	TEAM	STARTS	GAMES	WON	LOST	PCT	ER	ERA	INNINGS PITCHED	STRIKE-OUTS	WALKS	HITS ALLOWED	HRS ALLOWED	COMP. GAMES	SHUT-OUTS	SAVES
1979	Phi-N	14	14	3	4	.429	38	3.80	90	42	38	80	6	0	0	0
1980	Phi-N	3	48	1	4	.200	35	3.89	81	57	42	80	5	0	0	6
1981	Phi-N	8	13	2	2	.500	27	4.17	58 ⅓	34	23	57	2	0	0	0
1982	ChC-N	30	31	10	13	.435	84	4.42	171	85	61	180	11	2	2	0
1983	ChC-N	18	24	5	10	.333	61	4.72	116 ⅓	59	37	133	9	1	1	0
1984	ChC-N	1	21	2	2	.500	29	5.15	50 ⅔	14	16	60	4	0	0	0
1984	Tex-A	6	18	2	3	.400	33	5.15	57 ⅔	39	30	60	6	0	0	0
1985	Tex-A	13	28	4	8	.333	62	5.06	110 ⅓	59	33	129	11	0	0	1
1986	Cle-A	0	32	3	2	.600	31	5.10	54 ⅔	32	30	56	9	0	0	0
1987	ChC-N	1	41	4	2	.667	25	3.50	64 ⅓	33	27	59	1	0	0	2
1987	Det-A	0	4	0	0	—	1	4.50	2	0	1	2	0	0	0	2
1988	Bal-A	2	2	0	2	.000	9	24.30	3 ⅓	1	0	11	2	0	0	0
1990	Phi-N	0	1	0	1	.000	1	27.00	0 ⅓	0	0	2	0	0	0	0

(continued)

(Noles, continued)

Career average	9	25	3	5	.404	40	4.56	78 1/3	41	31	83	6	0	0	1
Cubs average	**13**	**29**	**5**	**7**	**.438**	**50**	**4.45**	**100 2/3**	**48**	**35**	**108**	**6**	**1**	**1**	**1**
Career total	96	277	36	53	.404	436	4.56	860	455	338	909	66	3	3	11
Cubs total	**50**	**117**	**21**	**27**	**.438**	**199**	**4.45**	**402 1/3**	**191**	**141**	**432**	**25**	**3**	**3**	**2**

Norman, Fredie Hubert (Fred)
HEIGHT: 5'8"   LEFTHANDER   BORN: 8/20/1942 SAN ANTONIO, TEXAS

YEAR	TEAM	STARTS	GAMES	WON	LOST	PCT	ER	ERA	INNINGS PITCHED	STRIKE-OUTS	WALKS	HITS ALLOWED	HRS ALLOWED	COMP. GAMES	SHUT-OUTS	SAVES
1962	KCA-A	0	2	0	0	—	1	2.25	4	2	1	4	0	0	0	0
1963	KCA-A	2	2	0	1	.000	8	11.37	6 1/3	6	7	9	1	0	0	0
1964	**ChC-N**	**5**	**8**	**0**	**4**	**.000**	**23**	**6.54**	**31 2/3**	**20**	**21**	**34**	**9**	**0**	**0**	**0**
1966	**ChC-N**	**0**	**2**	**0**	**0**	**—**	**2**	**4.50**	**4**	**6**	**2**	**5**	**0**	**0**	**0**	**0**
1967	**ChC-N**	**0**	**1**	**0**	**0**	**—**	**0**	**0.00**	**1**	**3**	**0**	**0**	**0**	**0**	**0**	**0**
1970	LA-N	0	30	2	0	1.000	36	5.23	62	47	33	65	8	0	0	1
1970	StL-N	0	1	0	0	—	0	0.00	1	0	0	1	0	0	0	0
1971	StL-N	0	4	0	0	—	5	12.27	3 2/3	4	7	7	1	0	0	0
1971	SD-N	18	20	3	12	.200	47	3.32	127 1/3	77	56	114	7	5	0	0
1972	SD-N	28	42	9	11	.450	81	3.44	211 2/3	167	88	195	18	10	6	2
1973	SD-N	11	12	1	7	.125	35	4.26	74	49	29	72	9	1	0	0
1973	Cin-N	24	24	12	6	.667	61	3.30	166 1/3	112	72	136	18	7	3	0
1974	Cin-N	26	35	13	12	.520	65	3.14	186 1/3	141	68	170	15	8	2	0
1975	Cin-N	26	34	12	4	.750	78	3.73	188	119	84	163	23	2	0	0
1976	Cin-N	24	33	12	7	.632	62	3.09	180 1/3	126	70	153	10	8	3	0
1977	Cin-N	34	35	14	13	.519	83	3.38	221 1/3	160	98	200	28	8	1	0
1978	Cin-N	31	36	11	9	.550	73	3.70	177 1/3	111	82	173	19	0	0	1
1979	Cin-N	31	34	11	13	.458	79	3.64	195 1/3	95	57	193	14	5	0	0
1980	Mon-N	8	48	4	4	.500	45	4.13	98	58	40	96	8	2	0	4
Career average	17	25	7	6	.502	49	3.64	121 1/3	81	51	112	12	4	1	1
Cubs average	**2**	**4**	**0**	**1**	**.000**	**8**	**6.14**	**12 1/3**	**10**	**8**	**13**	**3**	**0**	**0**	**0**
Career total	268	403	104	103	.502	784	3.64	1939 2/3	1303	815	1790	188	56	15	8
Cubs total	**5**	**11**	**0**	**4**	**.000**	**25**	**6.14**	**36 2/3**	**29**	**23**	**39**	**9**	**0**	**0**	**0**

Norton, Phillip Douglas (Phil)
HEIGHT: 6'1"   LEFTHANDER   BORN: 2/1/1976 TEXARKANA, TEXAS

YEAR	TEAM	STARTS	GAMES	WON	LOST	PCT	ER	ERA	INNINGS PITCHED	STRIKE-OUTS	WALKS	HITS ALLOWED	HRS ALLOWED	COMP. GAMES	SHUT-OUTS	SAVES
2000	**ChC-N**	**2**	**2**	**0**	**1**	**.000**	**9**	**9.35**	**8 2/3**	**6**	**7**	**14**	**5**	**0**	**0**	**0**
Career average	2	2	0	1	.000	9	9.35	8 2/3	6	7	14	5	0	0	0
Cubs average	**2**	**2**	**0**	**1**	**.000**	**9**	**9.35**	**8 2/3**	**6**	**7**	**14**	**5**	**0**	**0**	**0**
Career total	2	2	0	1	.000	9	9.35	8 2/3	6	7	14	5	0	0	0
Cubs total	**2**	**2**	**0**	**1**	**.000**	**9**	**9.35**	**8 2/3**	**6**	**7**	**14**	**5**	**0**	**0**	**0**

Nottebart, Donald Edward (Don)
HEIGHT: 6'1"   RIGHTHANDER   BORN: 1/23/1936 WEST NEWTON, MASSACHUSETTS

YEAR	TEAM	STARTS	GAMES	WON	LOST	PCT	ER	ERA	INNINGS PITCHED	STRIKE-OUTS	WALKS	HITS ALLOWED	HRS ALLOWED	COMP. GAMES	SHUT-OUTS	SAVES
1960	Mil-N	1	5	1	0	1.000	7	4.11	15 1/3	8	15	14	0	0	0	1
1961	Mil-N	11	38	6	7	.462	57	4.06	126 1/3	66	48	117	11	2	0	3
1962	Mil-N	0	39	2	2	.500	23	3.23	64	36	20	64	4	0	0	2
1963	Hou-N	27	31	11	8	.579	68	3.17	193	118	39	170	10	9	2	0
1964	Hou-N	24	28	6	11	.353	68	3.90	157	90	37	165	12	2	0	0
1965	Hou-N	25	29	4	15	.211	82	4.67	158	77	55	166	14	3	0	0
1966	Cin-N	1	59	5	4	.556	38	3.07	111 1/3	69	43	97	11	0	0	11
1967	Cin-N	0	47	0	3	.000	17	1.93	79 1/3	48	19	75	4	0	0	4
1969	NYY-A	0	4	0	0	—	3	4.50	6	5	0	6	1	0	0	0
1969	**ChC-N**	**0**	**16**	**1**	**1**	**.500**	**14**	**7.00**	**18**	**8**	**7**	**28**	**2**	**0**	**0**	**0**
Career average	10	33	4	6	.414	42	3.65	103	58	31	100	8	2	0	2
Cubs average	**0**	**16**	**1**	**1**	**.500**	**14**	**7.00**	**18**	**8**	**7**	**28**	**2**	**0**	**0**	**0**
Career total	89	296	36	51	.414	377	3.65	928 1/3	525	283	902	69	16	2	21
Cubs total	**0**	**16**	**1**	**1**	**.500**	**14**	**7.00**	**18**	**8**	**7**	**28**	**2**	**0**	**0**	**0**

Nunez, Jose
HEIGHT: 6'3"   RIGHTHANDER   BORN: 1/13/1964 JARABACOA, DOMINICAN REPUBLIC

YEAR	TEAM	STARTS	GAMES	WON	LOST	PCT	ER	ERA	INNINGS PITCHED	STRIKE-OUTS	WALKS	HITS ALLOWED	HRS ALLOWED	COMP. GAMES	SHUT-OUTS	SAVES
1987	Tor-A	9	37	5	2	.714	54	5.01	97	99	58	91	12	0	0	0
1988	Tor-A	2	13	0	1	.000	10	3.07	29 1/3	18	17	28	3	0	0	0
1989	Tor-A	1	6	0	0	—	3	2.53	10 2/3	14	2	8	0	0	0	0
1990	**ChC-N**	**10**	**21**	**4**	**7**	**.364**	**44**	**6.53**	**60 2/3**	**40**	**34**	**61**	**5**	**0**	**0**	**0**
Career average		6	19	2	3	.474	28	5.05	49 1/3	43	28	47	5	0	0	0
Cubs average		**10**	**21**	**4**	**7**	**.364**	**44**	**6.53**	**60 2/3**	**40**	**34**	**61**	**5**	**0**	**0**	**0**
Career total		22	77	9	10	.474	111	5.05	197 2/3	171	111	188	20	0	0	0
Cubs total		**10**	**21**	**4**	**7**	**.364**	**44**	**6.53**	**60 2/3**	**40**	**34**	**61**	**5**	**0**	**0**	**0**

Nye, Richard Raymond (Rich)
HEIGHT: 6'4"   LEFTHANDER   BORN: 8/4/1944 OAKLAND, CALIFORNIA

YEAR	TEAM	STARTS	GAMES	WON	LOST	PCT	ER	ERA	INNINGS PITCHED	STRIKE-OUTS	WALKS	HITS ALLOWED	HRS ALLOWED	COMP. GAMES	SHUT-OUTS	SAVES
1966	**ChC-N**	**2**	**3**	**0**	**2**	**.000**	**4**	**2.12**	**17**	**9**	**7**	**16**	**1**	**0**	**0**	**0**
1967	**ChC-N**	**30**	**35**	**13**	**10**	**.565**	**73**	**3.20**	**205**	**119**	**52**	**179**	**15**	**7**	**0**	**0**
1968	**ChC-N**	**20**	**27**	**7**	**12**	**.368**	**56**	**3.80**	**132 2/3**	**74**	**34**	**145**	**16**	**6**	**1**	**1**
1969	**ChC-N**	**5**	**34**	**3**	**5**	**.375**	**39**	**5.11**	**68 2/3**	**39**	**21**	**72**	**13**	**1**	**0**	**3**
1970	Mon-N	6	8	3	2	.600	21	4.08	46 1/3	21	20	47	3	2	0	0
1970	StL-N	0	6	0	0	—	4	4.50	8	5	6	13	2	0	0	0
Career average		13	23	5	6	.456	39	3.71	95 2/3	53	28	94	10	3	0	1
Cubs average		**14**	**25**	**6**	**7**	**.442**	**43**	**3.66**	**106**	**60**	**29**	**103**	**11**	**4**	**0**	**1**
Career total		63	113	26	31	.456	197	3.71	477 2/3	267	140	472	50	16	1	4
Cubs total		**57**	**99**	**23**	**29**	**.442**	**172**	**3.66**	**423 1/3**	**241**	**114**	**412**	**45**	**14**	**1**	**4**

O'Neill, Robert Emmett (Emmett *or* Pinkey)
HEIGHT: 6'3"   RIGHTHANDER   BORN: 1/13/1918 SAN MATEO, CALIFORNIA   DIED: 10/11/1993 SPARKS, NEVADA

YEAR	TEAM	STARTS	GAMES	WON	LOST	PCT	ER	ERA	INNINGS PITCHED	STRIKE-OUTS	WALKS	HITS ALLOWED	HRS ALLOWED	COMP. GAMES	SHUT-OUTS	SAVES
1943	Bos-A	5	11	1	4	.200	29	4.53	57 2/3	20	46	56	3	1	0	0
1944	Bos-A	22	28	6	11	.353	78	4.63	151 2/3	68	89	154	6	8	1	0
1945	Bos-A	22	24	8	11	.421	81	5.15	141 2/3	55	117	134	5	10	1	0
1946	**ChC-N**	**0**	**1**	**0**	**0**	**—**	**0**	**0.00**	**1**	**1**	**3**	**0**	**0**	**0**	**0**	**0**
1946	CWS-A	0	2	0	0	—	0	0.00	3 2/3	0	5	4	0	0	0	0
Career average		12	17	4	7	.366	47	4.76	89	36	65	87	4	5	1	0
Cubs average		**0**	**1**	**0**	**0**	**—**	**0**	**0.00**	**1**	**1**	**3**	**0**	**0**	**0**	**0**	**0**
Career total		49	66	15	26	.366	188	4.76	355 2/3	144	260	348	14	19	2	0
Cubs total		**0**	**1**	**0**	**0**	**—**	**0**	**0.00**	**1**	**1**	**3**	**0**	**0**	**0**	**0**	**0**

Ohman, William McDaniel (Will)
HEIGHT: 6'2"   LEFTHANDER   BORN: 8/13/1977 FRANKFURT, WEST GERMANY

YEAR	TEAM	STARTS	GAMES	WON	LOST	PCT	ER	ERA	INNINGS PITCHED	STRIKE-OUTS	WALKS	HITS ALLOWED	HRS ALLOWED	COMP. GAMES	SHUT-OUTS	SAVES
2000	**ChC-N**	**0**	**6**	**1**	**0**	**1.000**	**3**	**8.10**	**3 1/3**	**2**	**4**	**4**	**0**	**0**	**0**	**0**
2001	**ChC-N**	**0**	**11**	**0**	**1**	**.000**	**10**	**7.71**	**11 2/3**	**12**	**6**	**14**	**2**	**0**	**0**	**0**
Career average		0	9	1	1	.500	7	7.80	7 2/3	7	5	9	1	0	0	0
Cubs average		**0**	**9**	**1**	**1**	**.500**	**7**	**7.80**	**7 2/3**	**7**	**5**	**9**	**1**	**0**	**0**	**0**
Career total		0	17	1	1	.500	13	7.80	15	14	10	18	2	0	0	0
Cubs total		**0**	**17**	**1**	**1**	**.500**	**13**	**7.80**	**15**	**14**	**10**	**18**	**2**	**0**	**0**	**0**

Olsen, Vern Jarl

HEIGHT: 6'0" LEFTHANDER BORN: 3/16/1918 HILLSBORO, OREGON DIED: 7/13/1989 MAYWOOD, ILLINOIS

YEAR	TEAM	STARTS	GAMES	WON	LOST	PCT	ER	ERA	INNINGS PITCHED	STRIKE-OUTS	WALKS	HITS ALLOWED	HRS ALLOWED	COMP. GAMES	SHUT-OUTS	SAVES
1939	ChC-N	0	4	1	0	1.000	0	0.00	7 2/3	3	7	2	0	0	0	0
1940	ChC-N	20	34	13	9	.591	57	2.97	172 2/3	71	62	172	5	9	4	0
1941	ChC-N	23	37	10	8	.556	65	3.15	185 2/3	73	59	202	7	10	2	1
1942	ChC-N	17	32	6	9	.400	70	4.49	140 1/3	46	55	161	6	4	1	1
1946	ChC-N	0	5	0	0	—	3	2.79	9 2/3	8	9	10	0	0	0	0
Career average		12	22	6	5	.536	39	3.40	103 1/3	40	38	109	4	5	1	0
Cubs average		12	22	6	5	.536	39	3.40	103 1/3	40	38	109	4	5	1	0
Career total		60	112	30	26	.536	195	3.40	516	201	192	547	18	23	7	2
Cubs total		60	112	30	26	.536	195	3.40	516	201	192	547	18	23	7	2

Osborn, John Bode (Bob)

HEIGHT: 6'1" RIGHTHANDER BORN: 4/17/1903 SAN DIEGO, TEXAS DIED: 4/19/1960 PARIS, TEXAS

YEAR	TEAM	STARTS	GAMES	WON	LOST	PCT	ER	ERA	INNINGS PITCHED	STRIKE-OUTS	WALKS	HITS ALLOWED	HRS ALLOWED	COMP. GAMES	SHUT-OUTS	SAVES
1925	ChC-N	0	1	0	0	—	0	0.00	2	0	0	6	0	0	0	1
1926	ChC-N	15	31	6	5	.545	55	3.63	136 1/3	43	58	157	3	6	0	0
1927	ChC-N	12	24	5	5	.500	50	4.18	107 2/3	45	48	125	2	2	0	0
1929	ChC-N	1	3	0	0	—	3	3.00	9	1	2	8	0	0	0	1
1930	ChC-N	13	35	10	6	.625	70	4.97	126 2/3	42	53	147	9	3	0	0
1931	Pit-N	2	27	6	1	.857	36	5.01	64 2/3	9	20	85	3	0	0	0
Career average		7	20	5	3	.614	36	4.32	74 1/3	23	30	88	3	2	0	0
Cubs average		8	19	4	3	.568	36	4.20	76 1/3	26	32	89	3	2	0	0
Career total		43	121	27	17	.614	214	4.32	446 1/3	140	181	528	17	11	0	2
Cubs total		41	94	21	16	.568	178	4.20	381 2/3	131	161	443	14	11	0	2

Osborne, Earnest Preston (Tiny)

HEIGHT: 6'4" RIGHTHANDER BORN: 4/9/1893 PORTERDALE, GEORGIA DIED: 1/5/1969 ATLANTA, GEORGIA

YEAR	TEAM	STARTS	GAMES	WON	LOST	PCT	ER	ERA	INNINGS PITCHED	STRIKE-OUTS	WALKS	HITS ALLOWED	HRS ALLOWED	COMP. GAMES	SHUT-OUTS	SAVES
1922	ChC-N	14	41	9	5	.643	92	4.50	184	81	95	183	7	7	1	3
1923	ChC-N	25	37	8	15	.348	91	4.56	179 2/3	69	89	174	14	8	1	1
1924	ChC-N	0	2	0	0	—	1	3.00	3	2	2	3	0	0	0	1
1924	Bro-N	13	21	6	5	.545	60	5.18	104 1/3	52	54	123	1	6	0	0
1925	Bro-N	22	41	8	15	.348	96	4.94	175	59	75	210	9	10	0	1
Career average		19	36	8	10	.437	85	4.74	161 2/3	66	79	173	8	8	1	2
Cubs average		13	27	6	7	.459	61	4.52	122 1/3	51	62	120	7	5	1	2
Career total		74	142	31	40	.437	340	4.74	646	263	315	693	31	31	2	6
Cubs total		39	80	17	20	.459	184	4.52	366 2/3	152	186	360	21	15	2	5

Otto, David Alan (Dave)

HEIGHT: 6'7" LEFTHANDER BORN: 11/12/1964 CHICAGO, ILLINOIS

YEAR	TEAM	STARTS	GAMES	WON	LOST	PCT	ER	ERA	INNINGS PITCHED	STRIKE-OUTS	WALKS	HITS ALLOWED	HRS ALLOWED	COMP. GAMES	SHUT-OUTS	SAVES
1987	Oak-A	0	3	0	0	—	6	9.00	6	3	1	7	1	0	0	0
1988	Oak-A	2	3	0	0	—	2	1.80	10	7	6	9	0	0	0	0
1989	Oak-A	1	1	0	0	—	2	2.70	6 2/3	4	2	6	0	0	0	0
1990	Oak-A	0	2	0	0	—	2	7.71	2 1/3	2	3	3	0	0	0	0
1991	Cle-A	14	18	2	8	.200	47	4.23	100	47	27	108	7	1	0	0
1992	Cle-A	16	18	5	9	.357	63	7.06	80 1/3	32	33	110	12	0	0	0
1993	Pit-N	8	28	3	4	.429	38	5.03	68	30	28	85	9	0	0	0
1994	ChC-N	0	36	0	1	.000	19	3.80	45	19	22	49	4	0	0	0
Career average		5	14	1	3	.313	22	5.06	39 2/3	18	15	47	4	0	0	0
Cubs average		0	36	0	1	.000	19	3.80	45	19	22	49	4	0	0	0
Career total		41	109	10	22	.313	179	5.06	318 1/3	144	122	377	33	1	0	0
Cubs total		0	36	0	1	.000	19	3.80	45	19	22	49	4	0	0	0

Orval (Orvie) "Big Groundhog" Overall, rhp, 1905–10, 1913

One of the best big-game pitchers at the start of the 20th century, Orvie Overall was a member of the Cubs superb pitching staff.

Overall was born on February 2, 1881, in Farmersville, California. Overall was signed by the Reds but was coveted by Cubs manager Franck Chance, who had played with Overall in the minor leagues in California.

Overall struggled with the Reds, going 18-23 in his first major league season in 1905. When he began the 1906 season with a 4-5 record, Chance offered to take the big righthander. Chicago sent pitcher Bob Wicker and $2,000 to the Reds for Overall. In his book, Johnny Evers called the trade, "the joke of the season."

It may well have been. Wicker finished out 1906, then retired. Overall won 82 games for Chicago over the next five years.

Chance believed that Overall, a strapping 6'2", 214 pounds, was overworked in Cincinnati. "The Peerless Leader" reduced Overall's starts and wasn't afraid to pull him when he tired. The strategy worked; Overall won 23 games in 1907 and 20 in 1909. He also led the National League in shutouts with eight and nine, respectively those seasons.

Overall was one of the best pitchers in World Series play that the Cubs have ever had. His .750 winning percentage (a 3-1 record) is tops among Cubs hurlers with three or more decisions, and he is the team leader, with Mordecai "Three Finger" Brown, in strikeouts with 35. He is also second all-time for the Cubs in innings pitched in the Series with 51⅓ and third in club history in ERA with a 1.58 mark.

Overall is also the only World Series pitcher to strike out four batters in an inning, which he did in the first inning of the fifth game of the 1908 Fall Classic. Overall had struck out two Tigers and appeared to strike out Claude Rossman, but his pitch got by Cubs catcher Johnny Kling and Rossman reached on a passed ball. But Overall then fanned Herman "Germany" Schaefer to finally end the inning.

Overall retired in 1910 because of a contract dispute, and did not play in the major leagues for two years, although he did play in the Pacific League during part of that span. When he came back, in 1913, he struggled, earning only a 4-5 mark that year. He retired for good after that season.

Overall's nine shutouts in 1909 set a Cubs team record that has been tied several times but not yet broken. He is also tops on the all-time Cubs list in opponents' batting average, allowing only a .212 batting average in games he pitched.

Overall is also fifth in shutouts all-time with 28 and his 1.92 ERA is third all-time in Chicago.

Overall died on July 14, 1947, in Fresno, California.

Overall, Orval (Big Groundhog)

HEIGHT: 6'2"   RIGHTHANDER   BORN: 2/2/1881 FARMERSVILLE, CALIFORNIA   DIED: 7/14/1947 FRESNO, CALIFORNIA

YEAR	TEAM	STARTS	GAMES	WON	LOST	PCT	ER	ERA	INNINGS PITCHED	STRIKE-OUTS	WALKS	HITS ALLOWED	HRS ALLOWED	COMP. GAMES	SHUT-OUTS	SAVES
1905	Cin-N	39	42	18	23	.439	101	2.86	318	173	147	290	4	32	2	0
1906	Cin-N	10	13	4	5	.444	39	4.26	82⅓	33	46	77	1	6	0	0
1906	**ChC-N**	**14**	**18**	**12**	**3**	**.800**	**30**	**1.88**	**144**	**94**	**51**	**116**	**1**	**13**	**2**	**1**
1907	**ChC-N**	**30**	**36**	**23**	**8**	**.742**	**50**	**1.68**	**268⅓**	**141**	**69**	**201**	**1**	**26**	**8**	**3**
1908	**ChC-N**	**27**	**37**	**15**	**11**	**.577**	**48**	**1.92**	**225**	**167**	**78**	**165**	**3**	**16**	**4**	**4**
1909	**ChC-N**	**32**	**38**	**20**	**11**	**.645**	**45**	**1.42**	**285**	**205**	**80**	**204**	**1**	**23**	**9**	**3**
1910	**ChC-N**	**21**	**23**	**12**	**6**	**.667**	**43**	**2.68**	**144⅔**	**92**	**54**	**106**	**2**	**11**	**4**	**1**
1913	**ChC-N**	**9**	**11**	**4**	**5**	**.444**	**25**	**3.31**	**68**	**30**	**26**	**73**	**1**	**6**	**1**	**0**
Career average		26	31	15	10	.600	54	2.23	219⅓	134	79	176	2	19	4	2
Cubs average		**22**	**27**	**14**	**7**	**.662**	**40**	**1.91**	**189⅓**	**122**	**60**	**144**	**2**	**16**	**5**	**2**
Career total		182	218	108	72	.600	381	2.23	1535⅓	935	551	1232	16	133	30	12
Cubs total		**133**	**163**	**86**	**44**	**.662**	**241**	**1.91**	**1135**	**729**	**358**	**865**	**11**	**95**	**28**	**12**

Ovitz, Ernest Gayhart (Ernie)
HEIGHT: 5'8" RIGHTHANDER BORN: 10/7/1885 MINERAL POINT, WISCONSIN DIED: 9/11/1980 GREEN BAY, WISCONSIN

YEAR	TEAM	STARTS	GAMES	WON	LOST	PCT	ER	ERA	INNINGS PITCHED	STRIKE-OUTS	WALKS	HITS ALLOWED	HRS ALLOWED	COMP. GAMES	SHUT-OUTS	SAVES
1911	ChC-N	0	1	0	0	—	1	4.50	2	0	3	3	0	0	0	0
Career average		0	1	0	0	—	1	4.50	2	0	3	3	0	0	0	0
Cubs average		0	1	0	0	—	1	4.50	2	0	3	3	0	0	0	0
Career total		0	1	0	0	—	1	4.50	2	0	3	3	0	0	0	0
Cubs total		0	1	0	0	—	1	4.50	2	0	3	3	0	0	0	0

Packard, Eugene Milo (Gene)
HEIGHT: 5'10" LEFTHANDER BORN: 7/13/1887 COLORADO SPRINGS, COLORADO DIED: 5/19/1959 RIVERSIDE, CALIFORNIA

YEAR	TEAM	STARTS	GAMES	WON	LOST	PCT	ER	ERA	INNINGS PITCHED	STRIKE-OUTS	WALKS	HITS ALLOWED	HRS ALLOWED	COMP. GAMES	SHUT-OUTS	SAVES
1912	Cin-N	1	1	1	0	1.000	3	3.00	9	2	4	7	0	1	0	0
1913	Cin-N	21	39	7	11	.389	63	2.97	190⅔	73	64	208	2	9	2	0
1914	KC-F	34	42	21	13	.618	97	2.89	302	154	88	282	5	24	4	5
1915	KC-F	31	42	20	11	.645	84	2.68	281⅓	108	74	250	3	21	5	2
1916	**ChC-N**	**16**	**37**	**10**	**6**	**.625**	**48**	**2.78**	**155⅓**	**36**	**38**	**154**	**4**	**5**	**2**	**5**
1917	**ChC-N**	**0**	**2**	**0**	**0**	**—**	**2**	**10.80**	**1⅔**	**1**	**0**	**3**	**1**	**0**	**0**	**2**
1917	StL-N	11	34	9	6	.600	42	2.47	153⅓	44	25	138	4	6	0	2
1918	StL-N	23	30	12	12	.500	71	3.50	182⅓	46	33	184	6	10	1	2
1919	Phi-N	16	21	6	8	.429	62	4.15	134⅓	24	30	167	3	10	1	1
Career average		19	31	11	8	.562	59	3.01	176⅓	61	45	174	4	11	2	3
Cubs average		8	20	5	3	.625	25	2.87	78⅔	19	19	79	3	3	1	3
Career total		153	248	86	67	.562	472	3.01	1410⅓	488	356	1393	28	86	15	17
Cubs total		16	39	10	6	.625	50	2.87	157	37	38	157	5	5	2	5

Page, Vance Linwood
HEIGHT: 6'0" RIGHTHANDER BORN: 9/15/1905 ELM CITY, NORTH CAROLINA DIED: 7/14/1951 WILSON, NORTH CAROLINA

YEAR	TEAM	STARTS	GAMES	WON	LOST	PCT	ER	ERA	INNINGS PITCHED	STRIKE-OUTS	WALKS	HITS ALLOWED	HRS ALLOWED	COMP. GAMES	SHUT-OUTS	SAVES
1938	**ChC-N**	**9**	**13**	**5**	**4**	**.556**	**29**	**3.84**	**68**	**18**	**13**	**90**	**4**	**3**	**0**	**1**
1939	**ChC-N**	**17**	**27**	**7**	**7**	**.500**	**60**	**3.88**	**139⅓**	**43**	**37**	**169**	**8**	**8**	**1**	**1**
1940	**ChC-N**	**1**	**30**	**1**	**3**	**.250**	**29**	**4.42**	**59**	**22**	**26**	**65**	**1**	**0**	**0**	**2**
1941	**ChC-N**	**3**	**25**	**2**	**2**	**.500**	**23**	**4.28**	**48⅓**	**17**	**30**	**48**	**2**	**1**	**0**	**1**
Career average		8	24	4	4	.484	35	4.03	78⅔	25	27	93	4	3	0	1
Cubs average		8	24	4	4	.484	35	4.03	78⅔	25	27	93	4	3	0	1
Career total		30	95	15	16	.484	141	4.03	314⅔	100	106	372	15	12	1	5
Cubs total		30	95	15	16	.484	141	4.03	314⅔	100	106	372	15	12	1	5

Pall, Donn Steven (The Pope)
HEIGHT: 6'1" RIGHTHANDER BORN: 1/11/1962 CHICAGO, ILLINOIS

YEAR	TEAM	STARTS	GAMES	WON	LOST	PCT	ER	ERA	INNINGS PITCHED	STRIKE-OUTS	WALKS	HITS ALLOWED	HRS ALLOWED	COMP. GAMES	SHUT-OUTS	SAVES
1988	CWS-A	0	17	0	2	.000	11	3.45	28⅔	16	8	39	1	0	0	0
1989	CWS-A	0	53	4	5	.444	32	3.31	87	58	19	90	9	0	0	6
1990	CWS-A	0	56	3	5	.375	28	3.32	76	39	24	63	7	0	0	2
1991	CWS-A	0	51	7	2	.778	19	2.41	71	40	20	59	7	0	0	1
1992	CWS-A	0	39	5	2	.714	40	4.93	73	27	27	79	9	0	0	1
1993	CWS-A	0	39	2	3	.400	21	3.22	17⅔	29	11	62	5	0	0	0
1993	Phi-N	0	8	1	0	1.000	5	2.55	17⅔	11	3	15	1	0	0	0
1994	NYY-A	0	26	1	2	.333	14	3.60	35	21	9	43	3	0	0	0
1994	**ChC-N**	**0**	**2**	**0**	**0**	**—**	**2**	**4.50**	**4**	**2**	**1**	**8**	**1**	**0**	**0**	**0**
1996	Fla-N	0	12	1	1	.500	12	5.79	18⅔	9	9	16	3	0	0	0
1997	Fla-N	0	2	1	0	—	1	3.86	2⅓	0	1	3	1	0	0	0
1998	Fla-N	0	23	0	1	.000	19	5.13	33⅓	26	7	42	5	0	0	0
Career average		0	33	2	2	.511	20	3.63	50⅔	28	14	52	5	0	0	1
Cubs average		0	2	0	0	—	2	4.50	4	2	1	8	1	0	0	0
Career total		0	328	24	23	.511	204	3.63	505⅓	278	139	519	52	0	0	10
Cubs total		0	2	0	0	—	2	4.50	4	2	1	8	1	0	0	0

Milton (Milt) Stephen "Gimpy" Pappas, rhp, 1957–73

At the end of his 17-year career when he came to the Cubs, Milt Pappas nonetheless had a couple of seasons in which he established career bests.

Pappas was born on May 11, 1939, in Detroit, Michigan. The 6'3" righthander pitched only three games in the minor leagues before getting the call-up to the Baltimore Orioles in 1957.

With a lively fastball and better-than-average slider, Pappas had great things predicted for him in the late 1950s and early 1960s. But despite earning double-figures in victories for the Orioles eight consecutive years, as well as two All Star Game appearances in that span, the word on Pappas was that he wasn't living up to his potential.

Part of that, perhaps, was Pappas's colorful reputation. He was not shy about showing up home plate umpires with gestures and antics from the mound when he felt a call had gone against him.

Pappas was traded to the Reds in 1966, and after nearly three years there, he moved on to the Atlanta Braves in 1968. The Braves, in turn, sent him on to the Cubs in 1970.

Pappas went 10-8 for Chicago that year but blossomed in 1971 and 1972. He won 17 games back-to-back in those years, the best two-year span of his career.

In addition, Pappas led the National League in shutouts with five that year, and he also pitched a career-high 261⅓ innings that season.

In 1972 Pappas again won 17 games, and his 17-7 mark was his best winning percentage (.708) of his career.

Not coincidentally, Pappas was clearly a much more focused pitcher by this time, having left his antics on the mound far behind him. On September 2, 1972, he came within one out of a perfect game, blanking the San Diego Padres, 8-0, and settling instead for throwing the latest of the Cubs' 15 no-hitters in team history.

Pappas walked the Padres' Larry Stahl on a 3-2 pitch with two outs in the ninth inning. In his autobiography, Ron Santo related that he was sure Pappas had caught the outside corner.

"Milt should have had the first no-hitter in Cubs history," said Santo. "I couldn't believe Stahl took the pitch and I couldn't believe (umpire) Bruce Froemming called that pitch a ball."

Pappas retired in 1973 after going 7-12 for the Cubs. He won 99 games in the National League and 108 in the American League.

Pappas, Milton Stephen (Milt *or* Gimpy)
HEIGHT: 6'3"   RIGHTHANDER   BORN: 5/11/1939 DETROIT, MICHIGAN

YEAR	TEAM	STARTS	GAMES	WON	LOST	PCT	ER	ERA	INNINGS PITCHED	STRIKE-OUTS	WALKS	HITS ALLOWED	HRS ALLOWED	COMP. GAMES	SHUT-OUTS	SAVES
1957	Bal-A	0	4	0	0	—	1	1.00	9	3	3	6	0	0	0	0
1958	Bal-A	21	31	10	10	.500	61	4.06	135⅓	72	48	135	8	0	0	0
1959	Bal-A	27	33	15	9	.625	76	3.27	209⅓	120	75	175	8	3	0	0
1960	Bal-A	27	30	15	11	.577	77	3.37	205⅔	126	83	184	15	15	4	3
1961	Bal-A	23	26	13	9	.591	60	3.04	177⅔	89	78	134	16	11	3	0
1962	Bal-A	32	35	12	10	.545	92	4.03	205⅓	120	75	200	31	9	1	1
1963	Bal-A	32	34	16	9	.640	73	3.03	216⅔	120	69	186	21	11	4	0
1964	Bal-A	36	37	16	7	.696	83	2.97	251⅔	157	48	225	21	13	7	0
1965	Bal-A	34	34	13	9	.591	64	2.60	221⅓	127	52	192	22	9	3	0
1966	Cin-N	32	33	12	11	.522	100	4.29	209⅔	133	39	224	23	6	2	0
1967	Cin-N	32	34	16	13	.552	81	3.35	217⅔	129	38	218	19	5	3	0
1968	Cin-N	11	15	2	5	.286	39	5.60	62⅔	43	10	70	9	0	0	0
1968	Atl-N	19	22	10	8	.556	32	2.37	121⅓	75	22	111	8	3	1	0
1969	Atl-N	24	26	6	10	.375	58	3.63	144	72	44	149	14	1	0	0
1970	Atl-N	3	11	2	2	.500	24	6.06	35⅔	25	7	44	6	1	0	0
1970	**ChC-N**	**20**	**21**	**10**	**8**	**.556**	**43**	**2.68**	**144⅔**	**80**	**36**	**135**	**14**	**6**	**2**	**0**

(continued)

(Pappas, continued)

YEAR	TEAM	STARTS	GAMES	WON	LOST	PCT	ER	ERA	INNINGS PITCHED	STRIKE-OUTS	WALKS	HITS ALLOWED	HRS ALLOWED	COMP. GAMES	SHUT-OUTS	SAVES
1971	ChC-N	35	35	17	14	.548	102	3.51	261⅓	99	62	279	25	14	5	0
1972	ChC-N	28	29	17	7	.708	60	2.77	195	80	29	187	18	10	3	0
1973	ChC-N	29	30	7	12	.368	77	4.28	162	48	40	192	20	1	1	0
Career average		27	31	12	10	.560	71	3.40	187⅓	102	50	179	18	8	3	0
Cubs average		**28**	**29**	**13**	**10**	**.554**	**71**	**3.33**	**190⅔**	**77**	**42**	**198**	**19**	**8**	**3**	**0**
Career total		465	520	209	164	.560	1203	3.40	3186	1728	858	3046	298	129	43	4
Cubs total		**112**	**115**	**51**	**41**	**.554**	**282**	**3.33**	**763**	**307**	**167**	**793**	**77**	**31**	**11**	**0**

Parker, Harley Park (Doc)

HEIGHT: 6'2" RIGHTHANDER BORN: 6/14/1872 THERESA, NEW YORK DIED: 3/3/1941 CHICAGO, ILLINOIS

YEAR	TEAM	STARTS	GAMES	WON	LOST	PCT	ER	ERA	INNINGS PITCHED	STRIKE-OUTS	WALKS	HITS ALLOWED	HRS ALLOWED	COMP. GAMES	SHUT-OUTS	SAVES
1893	**ChN-N**	**0**	**1**	**0**	**0**	**—**	**3**	**13.50**	**2**	**0**	**1**	**5**	**0**	**0**	**0**	**1**
1895	**ChN-N**	**6**	**7**	**4**	**2**	**.667**	**21**	**3.68**	**51⅓**	**9**	**9**	**65**	**1**	**5**	**1**	**0**
1896	**ChN-N**	**7**	**9**	**1**	**5**	**.167**	**50**	**6.16**	**73**	**15**	**27**	**100**	**3**	**7**	**0**	**0**
1901	Cin-N	1	1	0	1	.000	14	15.75	8	0	2	26	1	1	0	0
Career average		4	5	1	2	.385	22	5.90	33⅔	6	10	49	1	3	0	0
Cubs average		**4**	**6**	**2**	**2**	**.417**	**25**	**5.27**	**42**	**8**	**12**	**57**	**1**	**4**	**0**	**0**
Career total		14	18	5	8	.385	88	5.90	134⅓	24	39	196	5	13	1	1
Cubs total		**13**	**17**	**5**	**7**	**.417**	**74**	**5.27**	**126⅓**	**24**	**37**	**170**	**4**	**12**	**1**	**1**

Parmelee, Leroy Earl (Roy *or* Bud *or* Tarzan)

HEIGHT: 6'1" RIGHTHANDER BORN: 4/25/1907 LAMBERTVILLE, MICHIGAN DIED: 8/31/1981 MONROE, MICHIGAN

YEAR	TEAM	STARTS	GAMES	WON	LOST	PCT	ER	ERA	INNINGS PITCHED	STRIKE-OUTS	WALKS	HITS ALLOWED	HRS ALLOWED	COMP. GAMES	SHUT-OUTS	SAVES
1929	NYG-N	1	2	1	0	1.000	7	9.00	7	1	3	13	1	0	0	0
1930	NYG-N	1	11	0	1	.000	22	9.43	21	19	26	18	3	0	0	0
1931	NYG-N	5	13	2	2	.500	24	3.68	58⅔	30	33	47	1	4	0	0
1932	NYG-N	3	8	0	3	.000	11	3.91	25⅓	23	14	25	0	0	0	0
1933	NYG-N	32	32	13	8	.619	77	3.17	218⅓	132	77	191	9	14	3	0
1934	NYG-N	21	22	10	6	.625	58	3.42	152⅔	83	60	134	6	7	2	0
1935	NYG-N	31	34	14	10	.583	106	4.22	226	79	97	214	20	13	0	0
1936	StL-N	28	37	11	11	.500	112	4.56	221	79	107	226	13	9	0	2
1937	**ChC-N**	**18**	**33**	**7**	**8**	**.467**	**83**	**5.13**	**145⅔**	**55**	**79**	**165**	**13**	**8**	**0**	**0**
1939	Phi-A	5	14	1	6	.143	32	6.45	44⅔	13	35	42	2	0	0	1
Career average		15	21	6	6	.518	53	4.27	112	51	53	108	7	6	1	0
Cubs average		**18**	**33**	**7**	**8**	**.467**	**83**	**5.13**	**145⅔**	**55**	**79**	**165**	**13**	**8**	**0**	**0**
Career total		145	206	59	55	.518	532	4.27	1120⅓	514	531	1075	68	55	5	3
Cubs total		**18**	**33**	**7**	**8**	**.467**	**83**	**5.13**	**145⅔**	**55**	**79**	**165**	**13**	**8**	**0**	**0**

Parrott, Thomas William (Tom *or* Tacky Tom)

HEIGHT: 5'10" RIGHTHANDER BORN: 4/10/1868 PORTLAND, OREGON DIED: 1/1/1932 DUNDEE, OREGON

YEAR	TEAM	STARTS	GAMES	WON	LOST	PCT	ER	ERA	INNINGS PITCHED	STRIKE-OUTS	WALKS	HITS ALLOWED	HRS ALLOWED	COMP. GAMES	SHUT-OUTS	SAVES
1893	**ChN-N**	**3**	**4**	**0**	**3**	**.000**	**20**	**6.67**	**27**	**7**	**17**	**35**	**1**	**2**	**0**	**0**
1893	Cin-N	17	22	10	7	.588	70	4.09	154	33	70	174	1	11	1	0
1894	Cin-N	36	41	17	20	.459	192	5.60	308⅔	61	126	402	19	31	1	1
1895	Cin-N	31	41	12	18	.400	160	5.47	263⅓	57	76	382	8	23	0	2
1896	StL-N	2	7	1	1	.500	29	6.21	42	8	18	62	4	2	0	0
Career average		22	29	10	12	.449	118	5.33	198⅔	42	77	264	8	17	1	1
Cubs average		**3**	**4**	**0**	**3**	**.000**	**20**	**6.67**	**27**	**7**	**17**	**35**	**1**	**2**	**0**	**0**
Career total		89	115	40	49	.449	471	5.33	795	166	307	1055	33	69	2	3
Cubs total		**3**	**4**	**0**	**3**	**.000**	**20**	**6.67**	**27**	**7**	**17**	**35**	**1**	**2**	**0**	**0**

Claude William Passeau, rhp, 1935–47

The lanky Passeau came to the Cubs in 1939 and became a five-time All Star in Chicago.

Passeau was born in Waynesboro, Mississippi, on April 9, 1909. He broke in with Pittsburgh in 1935, but in his four years there, he never managed a winning record. Early in the 1939 season, Passeau was traded to the Cubs. He went 13-9 the rest of the season, managing to lead the league in strikeouts with 137.

Passeau quickly established himself as one of the aces of the Cubs staff. In 1940 he led the team with a 20-13 mark and also led Chicago in ERA with a 2.50 mark, as well as in innings pitched (280⅔) and complete games (20).

That season began a three-year stretch in which Passeau would complete 20 or more games and pitch an average of 263⅓ innings a season. He was named to the All-Star team from 1941 to 1943.

Passeau was a junkballer who was one of the earliest practitioners of the slider, but he was so effective because he was unafraid to pitch inside. In fact, a majority of his teammates described him as downright mean on the mound.

In 1945 Passeau was 17-9 and led the league in shutouts with five as the Cubs won their final pennant of the 20th century. Chicago faced the Tigers in the World Series, and Passeau was easily their best pitcher, firing a one-hit shutout in Game 3 and holding Detroit to one run in six innings of work in Game 6.

But a line drive in that inning caught the index finger on Passeau's right hand, forcing him to leave the game. The Cubs went on to win, but manager Charlie Grimm was forced to use Game 7 starter Hank Borowy for four innings before Chicago won the contest in the 12th inning. Unfortunately, it took too much out of Borowy, and the Tigers hammered him in Game 7 the next day.

Passeau had another strong year in 1946 and was selected to start the 1946 All Star Game in Boston's Fenway Park. Passeau was the losing pitcher in a 12-0 American League rout, although he only allowed two runs and was far from the worst National League pitcher in that game.

But 1946 was the first time in 11 years that Passeau did not earn 10 or more wins. By 1947 he was losing his effectiveness and opted to retire.

Passeau is eighth all-time for the Cubs in shutouts with 22 and ninth all-time in complete games with 143. He also shares, with 1979's Rick Reuschel, the Cubs record for most double plays turned in a season by a pitcher (9); Passeau accomplished it in 1942.

Passeau, Claude William (Deacon)

HEIGHT: 6'3" RIGHTHANDER BORN: 4/9/1909 WAYNESBORO, MISSISSIPPI

YEAR	TEAM	STARTS	GAMES	WON	LOST	PCT	ER	ERA	INNINGS PITCHED	STRIKE-OUTS	WALKS	HITS ALLOWED	HRS ALLOWED	COMP. GAMES	SHUT-OUTS	SAVES
1935	Pit-N	1	1	0	1	.000	4	12.00	3	1	2	7	0	0	0	0
1936	Phi-N	21	49	11	15	.423	84	3.48	217⅓	85	55	247	7	8	2	3
1937	Phi-N	34	50	14	18	.438	141	4.34	292⅓	135	79	348	16	18	1	2
1938	Phi-N	33	44	11	18	.379	120	4.52	239	100	93	281	8	15	0	1
1939	Phi-N	8	8	2	4	.333	25	4.22	53⅓	29	25	54	1	4	1	0
1939	ChC-N	27	34	13	9	.591	75	3.05	221	108	48	215	8	13	1	3
1940	ChC-N	31	46	20	13	.606	78	2.50	280⅔	124	59	259	8	20	4	5
1941	ChC-N	30	34	14	14	.500	86	3.35	231	80	52	262	10	20	3	0
1942	ChC-N	34	35	19	14	.576	83	2.68	278⅓	89	74	284	13	24	3	0
1943	ChC-N	31	35	15	12	.556	83	2.91	257	93	66	245	10	18	1	1
1944	ChC-N	27	34	15	9	.625	73	2.89	227	89	50	234	8	18	2	3
1945	ChC-N	27	34	17	9	.654	62	2.46	227	98	59	205	4	19	5	1
1946	ChC-N	21	21	9	8	.529	45	3.13	129⅓	47	42	118	5	10	2	0
1947	ChC-N	6	19	2	6	.250	44	6.25	63⅓	26	24	97	7	1	1	2
Career average		25	34	12	12	.519	77	3.32	209⅓	85	56	220	8	14	2	2
Cubs average		**26**	**32**	**14**	**10**	**.569**	**70**	**2.96**	**212⅔**	**84**	**53**	**213**	**8**	**16**	**2**	**2**
Career total		331	444	162	150	.519	1003	3.32	2719⅔	1104	728	2856	105	188	26	21
Cubs total		**234**	**292**	**124**	**94**	**.569**	**629**	**2.96**	**1914⅔**	**754**	**474**	**1919**	**73**	**143**	**22**	**15**

Patterson, Kenneth Brian (Ken)

HEIGHT: 6'4"   LEFTHANDER   BORN: 7/8/1964 COSTA MESA, CALIFORNIA

YEAR	TEAM	STARTS	GAMES	WON	LOST	PCT	ER	ERA	INNINGS PITCHED	STRIKE-OUTS	WALKS	HITS ALLOWED	HRS ALLOWED	COMP. GAMES	SHUT-OUTS	SAVES
1988	CWS-A	2	9	0	2	.000	11	4.79	20 2/3	8	7	25	2	0	0	1
1989	CWS-A	1	50	6	1	.857	33	4.52	65 2/3	43	28	64	11	0	0	0
1990	CWS-A	0	43	2	1	.667	25	3.39	66 1/3	40	34	58	6	0	0	2
1991	CWS-A	0	43	3	0	1.000	20	2.83	63 2/3	32	35	48	5	0	0	1
1992	**ChC-N**	**1**	**32**	**2**	**3**	**.400**	**18**	**3.89**	**41 2/3**	**23**	**27**	**41**	**7**	**0**	**0**	**0**
1993	Cal-A	0	46	1	1	.500	30	4.58	59	36	35	54	7	0	0	1
1994	Cal-A	0	1	0	0	—	0	0.00	0 2/3	1	0	0	0	0	0	0
Career average		1	32	2	1	.636	20	3.88	45 1/3	26	24	41	5	0	0	1
Cubs average		**1**	**32**	**2**	**3**	**.400**	**18**	**3.89**	**41 2/3**	**23**	**27**	**41**	**7**	**0**	**0**	**0**
Career total		4	224	14	8	.636	137	3.88	317 2/3	183	166	290	38	0	0	5
Cubs total		**1**	**32**	**2**	**3**	**.400**	**18**	**3.89**	**41 2/3**	**23**	**27**	**41**	**7**	**0**	**0**	**0**

Patterson, Reginald Allen (Reggie)

HEIGHT: 6'4"   RIGHTHANDER   BORN: 11/7/1958 BIRMINGHAM, ALABAMA

YEAR	TEAM	STARTS	GAMES	WON	LOST	PCT	ER	ERA	INNINGS PITCHED	STRIKE-OUTS	WALKS	HITS ALLOWED	HRS ALLOWED	COMP. GAMES	SHUT-OUTS	SAVES
1981	CWS-A	1	6	0	1	.000	11	13.50	7 1/3	2	6	14	1	0	0	0
1983	**ChC-N**	**2**	**5**	**1**	**2**	**.333**	**10**	**4.82**	**18 2/3**	**10**	**6**	**17**	**3**	**0**	**0**	**0**
1984	**ChC-N**	**1**	**3**	**0**	**1**	**.000**	**7**	**10.50**	**6**	**5**	**2**	**10**	**1**	**0**	**0**	**0**
1985	**ChC-N**	**5**	**8**	**3**	**0**	**1.000**	**13**	**3.00**	**39**	**17**	**10**	**36**	**2**	**1**	**0**	**0**
Career average		2	6	1	1	.500	10	5.20	17 2/3	9	6	19	2	0	0	0
Cubs average		**3**	**5**	**1**	**1**	**.571**	**10**	**4.24**	**21 1/3**	**11**	**6**	**21**	**2**	**0**	**0**	**0**
Career total		9	22	4	4	.500	41	5.20	71	34	24	77	7	1	0	0
Cubs total		**8**	**16**	**4**	**3**	**.571**	**30**	**4.24**	**63 2/3**	**32**	**18**	**63**	**6**	**1**	**0**	**0**

Patterson, Robert Chandler (Bob)

HEIGHT: 6'1"   LEFTHANDER   BORN: 5/16/1959 JACKSONVILLE, FLORIDA

YEAR	TEAM	STARTS	GAMES	WON	LOST	PCT	ER	ERA	INNINGS PITCHED	STRIKE-OUTS	WALKS	HITS ALLOWED	HRS ALLOWED	COMP. GAMES	SHUT-OUTS	SAVES
1985	SD-N	0	3	0	0	—	11	24.75	4	1	3	13	2	0	0	0
1986	Pit-N	5	11	2	3	.400	20	4.95	36 1/3	20	5	49	0	0	0	0
1987	Pit-N	7	15	1	4	.200	32	6.70	43	27	22	49	5	0	0	0
1989	Pit-N	3	12	4	3	.571	12	4.05	26 2/3	20	8	23	3	0	0	1
1990	Pit-N	5	55	8	5	.615	31	2.95	94 2/3	70	21	88	9	0	0	5
1991	Pit-N	1	54	4	3	.571	30	4.11	65 2/3	57	15	67	7	0	0	2
1992	Pit-N	0	60	6	3	.667	21	2.92	64 2/3	43	23	59	7	0	0	9
1993	Tex-A	0	52	2	4	.333	28	4.78	52 2/3	46	11	59	8	0	0	1
1994	Cal-A	0	47	2	3	.400	19	4.07	42	30	15	35	6	0	0	1
1995	Cal-A	0	62	5	2	.714	18	3.04	53 1/3	41	13	48	6	0	0	0
1996	**ChC-N**	**0**	**79**	**3**	**3**	**.500**	**19**	**3.13**	**54 2/3**	**53**	**22**	**46**	**6**	**0**	**0**	**8**
1997	**ChC-N**	**0**	**76**	**1**	**6**	**.143**	**22**	**3.34**	**59 1/3**	**58**	**10**	**47**	**9**	**0**	**0**	**0**
1998	**ChC-N**	**0**	**33**	**1**	**1**	**.500**	**17**	**7.52**	**20 1/3**	**17**	**12**	**36**	**2**	**0**	**0**	**1**
Career average		2	43	3	3	.494	22	4.08	47 1/3	37	14	48	5	0	0	2
Cubs average		**0**	**63**	**2**	**3**	**.333**	**19**	**3.89**	**44 3/4**	**43**	**15**	**43**	**6**	**0**	**0**	**3**
Career total		21	559	39	40	.494	280	4.08	617 1/3	483	180	619	70	0	0	28
Cubs total		**0**	**188**	**5**	**10**	**.333**	**58**	**3.89**	**134 1/3**	**128**	**44**	**129**	**17**	**0**	**0**	**9**

Paul, Michael George (Mike)

HEIGHT: 6'0"   LEFTHANDER   BORN: 4/18/1945 DETROIT, MICHIGAN

YEAR	TEAM	STARTS	GAMES	WON	LOST	PCT	ER	ERA	INNINGS PITCHED	STRIKE-OUTS	WALKS	HITS ALLOWED	HRS ALLOWED	COMP. GAMES	SHUT-OUTS	SAVES
1968	Cle-A	7	36	5	8	.385	40	3.93	91 2/3	87	35	72	11	0	0	3
1969	Cle-A	12	47	5	10	.333	47	3.61	117 1/3	98	54	104	12	0	0	2
1970	Cle-A	15	30	2	8	.200	47	4.81	88	70	45	91	13	1	0	0
1971	Cle-A	12	17	2	7	.222	41	5.95	62	33	14	78	8	1	0	0

(continued)

(continued)

YEAR	TEAM	STARTS	GAMES	WON	LOST	PCT	ER	ERA	INNINGS PITCHED	STRIKE-OUTS	WALKS	HITS ALLOWED	HRS ALLOWED	COMP. GAMES	SHUT-OUTS	SAVES
1972	Tex-A	20	49	8	9	.471	39	2.17	161 2/3	108	52	149	4	2	1	1
1973	Tex-A	10	36	5	4	.556	48	4.95	87 1/3	49	36	104	9	1	0	2
1973	**ChC-N**	**1**	**11**	**0**	**1**	**.000**	**7**	**3.44**	**18 1/3**	**6**	**9**	**17**	**2**	**1**	**0**	**2**
1974	ChC-N	0	2	0	1	.000	4	27.00	1 1/3	1	1	4	1	0	0	0
Career average		11	33	4	7	.360	39	3.91	89 2/3	65	35	88	9	1	0	1
Cubs average		**1**	**7**	**0**	**1**	**.000**	**6**	**5.03**	**10**	**4**	**5**	**11**	**2**	**0**	**0**	**0**
Career total		77	228	27	48	.360	273	3.91	627 2/3	452	246	619	60	5	1	8
Cubs total		**1**	**13**	**0**	**2**	**.000**	**11**	**5.03**	**19 2/3**	**7**	**10**	**21**	**3**	**0**	**0**	**0**

Pavlas, David Lee (Dave)

HEIGHT: 6'7"   RIGHTHANDER   BORN: 8/12/1962 FRANKFURT, WEST GERMANY

YEAR	TEAM	STARTS	GAMES	WON	LOST	PCT	ER	ERA	INNINGS PITCHED	STRIKE-OUTS	WALKS	HITS ALLOWED	HRS ALLOWED	COMP. GAMES	SHUT-OUTS	SAVES
1990	ChC-N	0	13	2	0	1.000	5	2.11	21 1/3	12	6	23	2	0	0	0
1991	ChC-N	0	1	0	0	—	2	18.00	1	0	0	3	1	0	0	0
1995	NYY-A	0	4	0	0	—	2	3.18	5 2/3	3	0	8	0	0	0	0
1996	NYY-A	0	16	0	0	—	6	2.35	23	18	7	23	0	0	0	1
Career average		0	9	1	0	1.000	4	2.65	12 2/3	8	3	14	1	0	0	0
Cubs average		**0**	**7**	**1**	**0**	**1.000**	**4**	**2.82**	**11 1/3**	**6**	**3**	**13**	**2**	**0**	**0**	**0**
Career total		0	34	2	0	1.000	15	2.65	51	33	13	57	3	0	0	1
Cubs total		**0**	**14**	**2**	**0**	**1.000**	**7**	**2.82**	**22 1/3**	**12**	**6**	**26**	**3**	**0**	**0**	**0**

Pearce, George Thomas

HEIGHT: 5'10"   LEFTHANDER   BORN: 1/10/1888 AURORA, ILLINOIS   DIED: 10/11/1935 JOLIET, ILLINOIS

YEAR	TEAM	STARTS	GAMES	WON	LOST	PCT	ER	ERA	INNINGS PITCHED	STRIKE-OUTS	WALKS	HITS ALLOWED	HRS ALLOWED	COMP. GAMES	SHUT-OUTS	SAVES
1912	ChC-N	2	3	0	0	—	9	5.52	14 2/3	9	12	15	0	0	0	0
1913	ChC-N	21	25	13	5	.722	42	2.31	163 1/3	73	59	137	4	14	3	0
1914	ChC-N	17	30	8	12	.400	55	3.51	141	78	65	122	3	4	0	1
1915	ChC-N	20	36	13	9	.591	65	3.32	176	96	77	158	1	8	2	0
1916	ChC-N	1	4	0	0	—	1	2.08	4 1/3	0	1	6	0	0	0	0
1917	StL-N	0	5	1	1	.500	4	3.48	10 1/3	4	3	7	0	0	0	0
Career average		10	17	6	5	.565	29	3.11	85	43	36	74	1	4	1	0
Cubs average		**12**	**20**	**7**	**5**	**.567**	**34**	**3.10**	**100**	**51**	**43**	**88**	**2**	**5**	**1**	**0**
Career total		61	103	35	27	.565	176	3.11	509 2/3	260	217	445	8	26	5	1
Cubs total		**61**	**98**	**34**	**26**	**.567**	**172**	**3.10**	**499 1/3**	**256**	**214**	**438**	**8**	**26**	**5**	**1**

Penner, Kenneth William (Ken)

HEIGHT: 5'11"   RIGHTHANDER   BORN: 4/24/1896 BOONEVILLE, INDIANA   DIED: 5/28/1959 SACRAMENTO, CALIFORNIA

YEAR	TEAM	STARTS	GAMES	WON	LOST	PCT	ER	ERA	INNINGS PITCHED	STRIKE-OUTS	WALKS	HITS ALLOWED	HRS ALLOWED	COMP. GAMES	SHUT-OUTS	SAVES
1916	Cle-A	2	4	1	0	1.000	6	4.26	12 2/3	5	4	14	0	0	0	0
1929	**ChC-N**	**0**	**5**	**0**	**1**	**.000**	**4**	**2.84**	**12 2/3**	**3**	**6**	**14**	**1**	**0**	**0**	**0**
Career average		1	5	1	1	.500	5	3.55	12 2/3	4	5	14	1	0	0	0
Cubs average		**0**	**5**	**0**	**1**	**.000**	**4**	**2.84**	**12 2/3**	**3**	**6**	**14**	**1**	**0**	**0**	**0**
Career total		2	9	1	1	.500	10	3.55	25 1/3	8	10	28	1	0	0	0
Cubs total		**0**	**5**	**0**	**1**	**.000**	**4**	**2.84**	**12 2/3**	**3**	**6**	**14**	**1**	**0**	**0**	**0**

Perez, Michael Irvin (Mike)

HEIGHT: 6'0"   RIGHTHANDER   BORN: 10/19/1964 YAUCO, PUERTO RICO

YEAR	TEAM	STARTS	GAMES	WON	LOST	PCT	ER	ERA	INNINGS PITCHED	STRIKE-OUTS	WALKS	HITS ALLOWED	HRS ALLOWED	COMP. GAMES	SHUT-OUTS	SAVES
1990	StL-N	0	13	1	0	1.000	6	3.95	13 2/3	5	3	12	0	0	0	1
1991	StL-N	0	14	0	2	.000	11	5.82	17	7	7	19	1	0	0	0
1992	StL-N	0	77	9	3	.750	19	1.84	93	46	32	70	4	0	0	0

(continued)

(Perez, M.I., continued)

YEAR	TEAM	STARTS	GAMES	WON	LOST	PCT	ER	ERA	INNINGS PITCHED	STRIKE-OUTS	WALKS	HITS ALLOWED	HRS ALLOWED	COMP. GAMES	SHUT-OUTS	SAVES
1993	StL-N	0	65	7	2	.778	20	2.48	72⅔	58	20	65	4	0	0	7
1994	StL-N	0	36	2	3	.400	30	8.71	31	20	10	52	5	0	0	12
1995	**ChC-N**	0	**68**	**2**	**6**	**.250**	**29**	**3.66**	**71⅓**	**49**	**27**	**72**	**8**	0	0	**2**
1996	**ChC-N**	0	**24**	**1**	**0**	**1.000**	**14**	**4.67**	**27**	**22**	**13**	**29**	**2**	0	0	0
1997	KC-A	0	16	2	0	1.000	8	3.54	20⅓	17	8	15	2	0	0	0
Career average		0	39	3	2	.600	17	3.56	43⅓	28	15	42	3	0	0	3
Cubs average		**0**	**46**	**2**	**3**	**.333**	**22**	**3.94**	**49⅓**	**36**	**20**	**51**	**5**	**0**	**0**	**1**
Career total		0	313	24	16	.600	137	3.56	346	224	120	334	26	0	0	22
Cubs total		**0**	**92**	**3**	**6**	**.333**	**43**	**3.94**	**98⅓**	**71**	**40**	**101**	**10**	**0**	**0**	**2**

Perez, Yorkis Miguel

HEIGHT: 6'0"   LEFTHANDER   BORN: 9/30/1967 BAJOS DE HAINA, DOMINICAN REPUBLIC

YEAR	TEAM	STARTS	GAMES	WON	LOST	PCT	ER	ERA	INNINGS PITCHED	STRIKE-OUTS	WALKS	HITS ALLOWED	HRS ALLOWED	COMP. GAMES	SHUT-OUTS	SAVES
1991	**ChC-N**	0	**3**	**1**	**0**	**1.000**	**1**	**2.08**	**4⅓**	**3**	**2**	**2**	**0**	0	0	0
1994	Fla-N	0	44	3	0	1.000	16	3.54	40⅔	41	14	33	4	0	0	1
1995	Fla-N	0	69	2	6	.250	27	5.21	46⅔	47	28	35	6	0	0	0
1996	Fla-N	0	64	3	4	.429	28	5.29	47⅔	47	31	51	2	0	0	0
1997	NYM-N	0	9	0	1	.000	8	8.31	8⅔	7	4	15	2	0	0	0
1998	Phi-N	0	57	0	2	.000	22	3.81	52	42	25	40	3	0	0	0
1999	Phi-N	0	35	3	1	.750	14	3.94	32	26	15	29	4	0	0	0
2000	Hou-N	0	33	2	1	.667	13	5.16	22⅔	21	14	25	4	0	0	0
Career average		0	39	2	2	.483	16	4.56	32	29	17	29	3	0	0	0
Cubs average		**0**	**3**	**1**	**0**	**1.000**	**1**	**2.08**	**4⅓**	**3**	**2**	**2**	**0**	**0**	**0**	**0**
Career total		0	314	14	15	.483	129	4.56	254⅔	234	133	230	25	0	0	1
Cubs total		**0**	**3**	**1**	**0**	**1.000**	**1**	**2.08**	**4⅓**	**3**	**2**	**2**	**0**	**0**	**0**	**0**

Perkowski, Harry Walter

HEIGHT: 6'2"   LEFTHANDER   BORN: 9/6/1922 DANTE, VIRGINIA

YEAR	TEAM	STARTS	GAMES	WON	LOST	PCT	ER	ERA	INNINGS PITCHED	STRIKE-OUTS	WALKS	HITS ALLOWED	HRS ALLOWED	COMP. GAMES	SHUT-OUTS	SAVES
1947	Cin-N	1	3	0	0	—	3	3.68	7⅓	2	3	12	1	0	0	0
1949	Cin-N	3	5	1	1	.500	12	4.56	23⅔	3	14	21	2	2	0	0
1950	Cin-N	0	22	0	0	—	20	5.24	34⅓	19	23	36	6	0	0	1
1951	Cin-N	7	35	3	6	.333	32	2.82	102	56	46	96	2	1	0	0
1952	Cin-N	24	33	12	10	.545	82	3.80	194	86	89	197	9	11	1	2
1953	Cin-N	25	33	12	11	.522	97	4.52	193	70	62	204	26	7	2	2
1954	Cin-N	12	28	2	8	.200	65	6.11	95⅔	32	62	100	16	3	1	0
1955	**ChC-N**	**4**	**25**	**3**	**4**	**.429**	**28**	**5.29**	**47⅔**	**28**	**25**	**53**	**3**	**0**	**0**	**2**
Career average		10	23	4	5	.452	42	4.37	87⅓	37	41	90	8	3	1	1
Cubs average		**4**	**25**	**3**	**4**	**.429**	**28**	**5.29**	**47⅔**	**28**	**25**	**53**	**3**	**0**	**0**	**2**
Career total		76	184	33	40	.452	339	4.37	697⅔	296	324	719	65	24	4	5
Cubs total		**4**	**25**	**3**	**4**	**.429**	**28**	**5.29**	**47⅔**	**28**	**25**	**53**	**3**	**0**	**0**	**2**

Perlman, Jonathan Samuel (Jon)

HEIGHT: 6'3"   RIGHTHANDER   BORN: 12/13/1956 DALLAS, TEXAS

YEAR	TEAM	STARTS	GAMES	WON	LOST	PCT	ER	ERA	INNINGS PITCHED	STRIKE-OUTS	WALKS	HITS ALLOWED	HRS ALLOWED	COMP. GAMES	SHUT-OUTS	SAVES
1985	**ChC-N**	0	**6**	**1**	**0**	**1.000**	**11**	**11.42**	**8⅔**	**4**	**8**	**10**	**3**	0	0	0
1987	SF-N	0	10	0	0	—	5	3.97	11⅓	3	4	11	1	0	0	0
1988	Cle-A	0	10	0	2	.000	12	5.49	19⅔	10	11	25	0	0	0	0
Career average		0	9	0	1	.333	9	6.35	13⅓	6	8	15	1	0	0	0
Cubs average		**0**	**6**	**1**	**0**	**1.000**	**11**	**11.42**	**8⅔**	**4**	**8**	**10**	**3**	**0**	**0**	**0**
Career total		0	26	1	2	.333	28	6.35	39⅔	17	23	46	4	0	0	0
Cubs total		**0**	**6**	**1**	**0**	**1.000**	**11**	**11.42**	**8⅔**	**4**	**8**	**10**	**3**	**0**	**0**	**0**

Perry, Herbert Scott (Scott)
HEIGHT: 6'1" RIGHTHANDER BORN: 4/17/1891 DENISON, TEXAS DIED: 10/27/1959 KANSAS CITY, MISSOURI

YEAR	TEAM	STARTS	GAMES	WON	LOST	PCT	ER	ERA	INNINGS PITCHED	STRIKE-OUTS	WALKS	HITS ALLOWED	HRS ALLOWED	COMP. GAMES	SHUT-OUTS	SAVES
1915	StL-A	1	1	0	0	—	3	13.50	2	0	1	5	0	0	0	0
1916	**ChC-N**	**3**	**4**	**2**	**1**	**.667**	**8**	**2.54**	**28 1/3**	**10**	**3**	**30**	**0**	**2**	**1**	**0**
1917	Cin-N	1	4	0	0	—	10	6.75	13 1/3	4	8	17	0	0	0	0
1918	Phi-A	36	44	20	19	.513	73	1.98	332 1/3	81	111	295	1	30	3	2
1919	Phi-A	21	25	4	17	.190	73	3.58	183 2/3	38	72	193	4	12	0	1
1920	Phi-A	34	42	11	25	.306	106	3.62	263 2/3	79	65	310	14	20	1	1
1921	Phi-A	8	12	3	6	.333	32	4.11	70	19	24	77	4	5	0	1
Career average		15	19	6	10	.370	44	3.07	127 2/3	33	41	132	3	10	1	1
Cubs average		**3**	**4**	**2**	**1**	**.667**	**8**	**2.54**	**28 1/3**	**10**	**3**	**30**	**0**	**2**	**1**	**0**
Career total		104	132	40	68	.370	305	3.07	893 1/3	231	284	927	23	69	5	5
Cubs total		**3**	**4**	**2**	**1**	**.667**	**8**	**2.54**	**28 1/3**	**10**	**3**	**30**	**0**	**2**	**1**	**0**

Perry, William Patrick (Pat or Atlas)
HEIGHT: 6'1" LEFTHANDER BORN: 2/4/1959 TAYLORVILLE, ILLINOIS

YEAR	TEAM	STARTS	GAMES	WON	LOST	PCT	ER	ERA	INNINGS PITCHED	STRIKE-OUTS	WALKS	HITS ALLOWED	HRS ALLOWED	COMP. GAMES	SHUT-OUTS	SAVES
1985	StL-N	0	6	1	0	1.000	0	0.00	12 1/3	6	3	3	0	0	0	0
1986	StL-N	0	46	2	3	.400	29	3.80	68 2/3	29	34	59	5	0	0	2
1987	StL-N	0	45	4	2	.667	32	4.39	65 2/3	33	21	54	7	0	0	1
1987	Cin-N	0	12	1	0	1.000	0	0.00	15 1/3	6	4	6	0	0	0	1
1988	Cin-N	0	12	2	2	.500	13	5.66	20 2/3	11	9	21	4	0	0	0
1988	**ChC-N**	**0**	**35**	**2**	**2**	**.500**	**14**	**3.32**	**38**	**24**	**7**	**40**	**5**	**0**	**0**	**1**
1989	**ChC-N**	**0**	**19**	**0**	**1**	**.000**	**7**	**1.77**	**35 2/3**	**20**	**16**	**23**	**2**	**0**	**0**	**1**
1990	LA-N	0	7	0	0	—	6	8.10	6 2/3	2	5	9	0	0	0	0
Career average		0	30	2	2	.545	17	3.46	44	22	17	36	4	0	0	1
Cubs average		**0**	**27**	**1**	**2**	**.400**	**11**	**2.57**	**37**	**22**	**12**	**32**	**4**	**0**	**0**	**1**
Career total		0	182	12	10	.545	101	3.46	263	131	99	215	23	0	0	6
Cubs total		**0**	**54**	**2**	**3**	**.400**	**21**	**2.57**	**73 2/3**	**44**	**23**	**63**	**7**	**0**	**0**	**2**

Peters, John Paul
HEIGHT: 5'7" RIGHTHANDER BORN: 4/8/1850 LOUISIANA, MISSOURI DIED: 1/4/1924 ST. LOUIS, MISSOURI

YEAR	TEAM	STARTS	GAMES	WON	LOST	PCT	ER	ERA	INNINGS PITCHED	STRIKE-OUTS	WALKS	HITS ALLOWED	HRS ALLOWED	COMP. GAMES	SHUT-OUTS	SAVES
1876	**ChN-N**	**0**	**1**	**0**	**0**	**—**	**0**	**0.00**	**1**	**0**	**1**	**1**	**0**	**0**	**0**	**1**
Career average		0	1	0	0	—	0	0.00	1	0	1	1	0	0	0	1
Cubs average		**0**	**1**	**0**	**0**	**—**	**0**	**0.00**	**1**	**0**	**1**	**1**	**0**	**0**	**0**	**1**
Career total		0	1	0	0	—	0	0.00	1	0	1	1	0	0	0	1
Cubs total		**0**	**1**	**0**	**0**	**—**	**0**	**0.00**	**1**	**0**	**1**	**1**	**0**	**0**	**0**	**1**

Pettit, Robert Henry (Bob)
HEIGHT: 5'9" RIGHTHANDER BORN: 7/19/1861 WILLIAMSTOWN, MASSACHUSETTS DIED: 11/1/1910 DERBY, CONNECTICUT

YEAR	TEAM	STARTS	GAMES	WON	LOST	PCT	ER	ERA	INNINGS PITCHED	STRIKE-OUTS	WALKS	HITS ALLOWED	HRS ALLOWED	COMP. GAMES	SHUT-OUTS	SAVES
1887	**ChN-N**	**0**	**1**	**0**	**0**	**—**	**0**	**0.00**	**1**	**0**	**2**	**5**	**0**	**0**	**0**	**1**
Career average		0	1	0	0	—	0	0.00	1	0	2	5	0	0	0	1
Cubs average		**0**	**1**	**0**	**0**	**—**	**0**	**0.00**	**1**	**0**	**2**	**5**	**0**	**0**	**0**	**1**
Career total		0	1	0	0	—	0	0.00	1	0	2	5	0	0	0	1
Cubs total		**0**	**1**	**0**	**0**	**—**	**0**	**0.00**	**1**	**0**	**2**	**5**	**0**	**0**	**0**	**1**

Petty, Jesse Lee (The Silver Fox)
HEIGHT: 6'0"   LEFTHANDER   BORN: 11/23/1894 ORR, OKLAHOMA   DIED: 10/23/1971 ST. PAUL, MINNESOTA

YEAR	TEAM	STARTS	GAMES	WON	LOST	PCT	ER	ERA	INNINGS PITCHED	STRIKE-OUTS	WALKS	HITS ALLOWED	HRS ALLOWED	COMP. GAMES	SHUT-OUTS	SAVES
1921	Cle-A	0	4	0	0	—	2	2.00	9	0	0	10	0	0	0	0
1925	Bro-N	21	28	9	9	.500	83	4.88	153	39	47	188	15	7	0	0
1926	Bro-N	33	38	17	17	.500	87	2.84	275 2/3	101	79	246	9	23	1	1
1927	Bro-N	33	42	13	18	.419	90	2.98	271 2/3	101	53	263	13	19	2	1
1928	Bro-N	31	40	15	15	.500	105	4.04	234	74	56	264	18	15	2	1
1929	Pit-N	25	36	11	10	.524	76	3.71	184 1/3	58	42	197	12	12	1	0
1930	Pit-N	7	10	1	6	.143	38	8.27	41 1/3	16	13	67	8	0	0	1
1930	**ChC-N**	3	9	1	3	.250	13	2.97	39 1/3	18	6	51	2	0	0	0
Career average		22	30	10	11	.462	71	3.68	172 2/3	58	42	184	11	11	1	1
Cubs average		3	9	1	3	.250	13	2.97	39 1/3	18	6	51	2	0	0	0
Career total		153	207	67	78	.462	494	3.68	1208 1/3	407	296	1286	77	76	6	4
Cubs total		3	9	1	3	.250	13	2.97	39 1/3	18	6	51	2	0	0	0

Pfeffer, Francis Xavier (Big Jeff)
HEIGHT: 6'1"   RIGHTHANDER   BORN: 3/31/1882 CHAMPAIGN, ILLINOIS   DIED: 12/19/1954 KANKAKEE, ILLINOIS

YEAR	TEAM	STARTS	GAMES	WON	LOST	PCT	ER	ERA	INNINGS PITCHED	STRIKE-OUTS	WALKS	HITS ALLOWED	HRS ALLOWED	COMP. GAMES	SHUT-OUTS	SAVES
1905	**ChC-N**	11	15	4	4	.500	28	2.50	101	56	36	84	2	9	0	0
1906	Bos-N	36	36	13	22	.371	99	2.95	302 1/3	158	114	270	4	33	4	0
1907	Bos-N	16	19	6	8	.429	48	3.00	144	65	61	129	3	12	1	0
1908	Bos-N	0	4	0	0	—	14	12.60	10	3	8	18	1	0	0	0
1910	**ChC-N**	1	13	1	0	1.000	15	3.27	41 1/3	11	16	43	1	1	0	0
1911	Bos-N	6	26	7	5	.583	51	4.73	97	24	57	116	3	4	1	2
Career average		12	19	5	7	.443	43	3.30	116	53	49	110	2	10	1	0
Cubs average		6	14	3	2	.556	22	2.72	71 1/3	34	26	64	2	5	0	0
Career total		70	113	31	39	.443	255	3.30	695 2/3	317	292	660	14	59	6	2
Cubs total		12	28	5	4	.556	43	2.72	142 1/3	67	52	127	3	10	0	0

Pfeffer, Nathaniel Frederick (Fred or Fritz or Dandelion)
HEIGHT: 5'10"   RIGHTHANDER   BORN: 3/17/1860 LOUISVILLE, KENTUCKY   DIED: 4/10/1932 CHICAGO, ILLINOIS

YEAR	TEAM	STARTS	GAMES	WON	LOST	PCT	ER	ERA	INNINGS PITCHED	STRIKE-OUTS	WALKS	HITS ALLOWED	HRS ALLOWED	COMP. GAMES	SHUT-OUTS	SAVES
1884	**ChN-N**	0	1	0	0	—	1	9.00	1	0	1	3	0	0	0	0
1885	**ChN-N**	2	5	2	1	.667	9	2.56	31 2/3	13	8	26	1	2	0	2
1892	Lou-N	0	1	0	0	—	1	1.80	5	0	5	4	0	0	0	0
1894	Lou-N	0	1	0	0	—	2	2.57	7	0	6	8	0	0	0	0
Career average		1	2	1	0	.667	3	2.62	11 1/3	3	5	10	0	1	0	1
Cubs average		1	3	1	1	.667	5	2.76	16 1/3	7	5	15	1	1	0	1
Career total		2	8	2	1	.667	13	2.62	44 2/3	13	20	41	1	2	0	2
Cubs total		2	6	2	1	.667	10	2.76	32 2/3	13	9	29	1	2	0	2

Pfiester, John Albert (Jack or Jack the Giant Killer)
HEIGHT: 5'11"   LEFTHANDER   BORN: 5/24/1878 CINCINNATI, OHIO   DIED: 9/3/1953 LOVELAND, OHIO

YEAR	TEAM	STARTS	GAMES	WON	LOST	PCT	ER	ERA	INNINGS PITCHED	STRIKE-OUTS	WALKS	HITS ALLOWED	HRS ALLOWED	COMP. GAMES	SHUT-OUTS	SAVES
1903	Pit-N	3	3	0	3	.000	13	6.16	19	15	10	26	0	2	0	0
1904	Pit-N	2	3	1	1	.500	16	7.20	20	6	9	28	0	1	0	0
1906	**ChC-N**	29	31	20	8	.714	42	1.51	250 2/3	153	63	173	3	20	4	0
1907	**ChC-N**	22	30	14	9	.609	25	1.15	195	90	48	143	1	13	3	0
1908	**ChC-N**	29	33	12	10	.545	56	2.00	252	117	70	204	1	18	3	0
1909	**ChC-N**	25	29	17	6	.739	53	2.43	196 2/3	73	49	179	1	13	5	0
1910	**ChC-N**	13	14	6	3	.667	20	1.79	100 1/3	34	26	82	0	5	2	0
1911	**ChC-N**	5	6	0	4	.000	15	4.01	33 2/3	15	18	34	0	3	0	0
Career average		16	19	9	6	.614	30	2.02	133 1/3	63	37	109	1	9	2	0
Cubs average		21	24	12	7	.633	35	1.85	171 1/3	80	46	136	1	12	3	0
Career total		128	149	70	44	.614	240	2.02	1067 1/3	503	293	869	6	75	17	0
Cubs total		123	143	69	40	.633	211	1.85	1028 1/3	482	274	815	6	72	17	0

John (Jack) Albert "Jack the Giant Killer" Hagenbush Pfiester, lhp, 1903–04, 1906–11

Possessing one of the most colorful nicknames in major league history, lanky lefty Jack Pfiester was one of the team mainstays during Chicago's most illustrious era.

Born on May 24, 1878, in Cincinnati, Ohio,. Pfiester knocked around in the minor leagues for several years in the late 1890s and early 1900s before signing with Pittsburgh. He made only six appearances in two years and compiled a record of 1-4; he was released.

Pfiester was pitching for a minor league nine in Omaha, Nebraska, in 1905 when he was discovered by Cubs manager Frank Chance. Pfiester had worked out a nonreserve clause with Omaha, which enabled him to deal with any team in the majors. Chicago signed him for $2,500.

Pfiester began his career with Chicago the next year and compiled one of the most impressive inaugural campaigns in the history of the franchise, going 20-8, with a 1.51 ERA and a team-high 153 strikeouts.

This was the year the Cubs utterly dominated the National League, winning 116 games and losing just 36, still the highest winning percentage in the history of the majors. But neither the Cubs nor Pfiester did very well in the World Series that year as the Cubs succumbed to the White Sox in six games. Pfiester was 0-2,

which included a loss in relief in Game 5, with a 6.10 ERA.

Both bounced back in 1907—Chicago once again won the National League pennant with 107 wins. Pfiester was 14-9, with a league-leading 1.15 ERA. He followed that up with a win in the World Series against the Tigers as the Cubs swept to the championship.

Pfiester was a hard thrower, adept at holding base runners on. But his most prominent attribute, the one that completely endeared him to Cubs fans, was his dominance over the hated New York Giants. Pfiester was 15-5 against the Giants in his six-year Cubs career.

He was so successful against New York that Chance started him in the final game of 1908 against Giant ace Christy Mathewson. But Pfiester was shelled in the first inning of the game, moving Chance to replace him with Mordecai "Three Finger" Brown, who eventually won the tilt.

Pfiester was a tough man and he battled arm trouble in 1910 and 1911, which limited his starts those seasons. By the end of the 1911 season, he was forced to retire. Pfiester died on September 3, 1953, in Loveland, Ohio.

Pfiester's 1.15 ERA in 1907 remains a Cubs record for lefthanders, and it is the fifth best for lefties all-time. Pfiester's career .633 winning percentage (69-40) is also a team record for lefthanders. Pfiester is also second in opponents' career batting average, allowing a .218 mark.

Phillips, William Taylor (Taylor or T-Bone)
HEIGHT: 5'11"   LEFTHANDER   BORN: 6/18/1933 ATLANTA, GEORGIA

YEAR	TEAM	STARTS	GAMES	WON	LOST	PCT	ER	ERA	INNINGS PITCHED	STRIKE-OUTS	WALKS	HITS ALLOWED	HRS ALLOWED	COMP. GAMES	SHUT-OUTS	SAVES
1956	Mil-N	6	23	5	3	.625	22	2.26	87 ⅔	36	33	69	6	3	0	2
1957	Mil-N	6	27	3	2	.600	45	5.55	73	36	40	82	3	0	0	2
1958	**ChC-N**	**27**	**39**	**7**	**10**	**.412**	**90**	**4.76**	**170 ⅓**	**102**	**79**	**178**	**22**	**5**	**1**	**1**
1959	**ChC-N**	**2**	**7**	**0**	**2**	**.000**	**14**	**7.56**	**16 ⅔**	**5**	**11**	**22**	**3**	**0**	**0**	**0**
1959	Phi-N	3	32	1	4	.200	35	5.00	63	35	31	72	4	1	0	1
1960	Phi-N	1	10	0	1	.000	13	8.36	14	6	4	21	2	0	0	0
1963	CWS-A	0	9	0	0	—	16	10.29	14	13	13	16	2	0	0	0

(continued)

(Phillips, continued)

Career average	8	25	3	4	.421	39	4.82	73	39	35	77	7	2	0	1
Cubs average	**15**	**23**	**4**	**6**	**.368**	**52**	**5.01**	**93 ⅔**	**54**	**45**	**100**	**13**	**3**	**1**	**1**
Career total	45	147	16	22	.421	235	4.82	438 ⅔	233	211	460	42	9	1	6
Cubs total	**29**	**46**	**7**	**12**	**.368**	**104**	**5.01**	**187**	**107**	**90**	**200**	**25**	**5**	**1**	**1**

Phoebus, Thomas Harold (Tom)
HEIGHT: 5'8"   RIGHTHANDER   BORN: 4/7/1942 BALTIMORE, MARYLAND

YEAR	TEAM	STARTS	GAMES	WON	LOST	PCT	ER	ERA	INNINGS PITCHED	STRIKE-OUTS	WALKS	HITS ALLOWED	HRS ALLOWED	COMP. GAMES	SHUT-OUTS	SAVES
1966	Bal-A	3	3	2	1	.667	3	1.23	22	17	6	16	0	2	2	0
1967	Bal-A	33	33	14	9	.609	77	3.33	208	179	114	177	16	7	4	0
1968	Bal-A	36	36	15	15	.500	70	2.62	240 ⅔	193	105	186	10	9	3	0
1969	Bal-A	33	35	14	7	.667	79	3.52	202	117	87	180	23	6	2	0
1970	Bal-A	21	27	5	5	.500	46	3.07	135	72	62	106	11	3	0	0
1971	SD-N	21	29	3	11	.214	66	4.46	133 ⅓	80	64	144	14	2	0	0
1972	SD-N	1	1	0	1	.000	5	7.94	5 ⅔	8	6	3	2	0	0	0
1972	**ChC-N**	**1**	**37**	**3**	**3**	**.500**	**35**	**3.78**	**83 ⅓**	**59**	**45**	**76**	**9**	**0**	**0**	**6**
Career average	21	29	8	7	.519	54	3.33	147	104	70	127	12	4	2	1
Cubs average	**1**	**37**	**3**	**3**	**.500**	**35**	**3.78**	**83 ⅓**	**59**	**45**	**76**	**9**	**0**	**0**	**6**
Career total	149	201	56	52	.519	381	3.33	1030	725	489	888	85	29	11	6
Cubs total	**1**	**37**	**3**	**3**	**.500**	**35**	**3.78**	**83 ⅓**	**59**	**45**	**76**	**9**	**0**	**0**	**6**

Phyle, William Joseph (Bill)
HEIGHT: —   RIGHTHANDER   BORN: 6/25/1875 DULUTH, MINNESOTA   DIED: 8/6/1953 LOS ANGELES, CALIFORNIA

YEAR	TEAM	STARTS	GAMES	WON	LOST	PCT	ER	ERA	INNINGS PITCHED	STRIKE-OUTS	WALKS	HITS ALLOWED	HRS ALLOWED	COMP. GAMES	SHUT-OUTS	SAVES
1898	**ChN-N**	**3**	**3**	**2**	**1**	**.667**	**2**	**0.78**	**23**	**4**	**6**	**24**	**0**	**3**	**2**	**0**
1899	**ChN-N**	**9**	**10**	**1**	**8**	**.111**	**39**	**4.20**	**83 ⅔**	**10**	**29**	**92**	**2**	**9**	**0**	**1**
1901	NYG-N	19	24	7	10	.412	80	4.27	168 ⅔	62	54	208	2	16	0	1
Career average	10	12	3	6	.345	40	3.96	91 ⅔	25	30	108	1	9	1	1
Cubs average	**6**	**7**	**2**	**5**	**.250**	**21**	**3.46**	**53 ⅓**	**7**	**18**	**58**	**1**	**6**	**1**	**1**
Career total	31	37	10	19	.345	121	3.96	275 ⅓	76	89	324	4	28	2	2
Cubs total	**12**	**13**	**3**	**9**	**.250**	**41**	**3.46**	**106 ⅔**	**14**	**35**	**116**	**2**	**12**	**2**	**1**

Pico, Jeffrey Mark (Jeff)
HEIGHT: 6'2"   RIGHTHANDER   BORN: 2/12/1966 ANTIOCH, CALIFORNIA

YEAR	TEAM	STARTS	GAMES	WON	LOST	PCT	ER	ERA	INNINGS PITCHED	STRIKE-OUTS	WALKS	HITS ALLOWED	HRS ALLOWED	COMP. GAMES	SHUT-OUTS	SAVES
1988	ChC-N	13	29	6	7	.462	52	4.15	112 ⅔	57	37	108	6	3	2	1
1989	ChC-N	5	53	3	1	.750	38	3.77	90 ⅔	38	31	99	8	0	0	2
1990	ChC-N	8	31	4	4	.500	49	4.79	92	37	37	120	7	0	0	2
Career average	9	38	4	4	.520	46	4.24	98 ⅓	44	35	109	7	1	1	2
Cubs average	**9**	**38**	**4**	**4**	**.520**	**46**	**4.24**	**98 ⅓**	**44**	**35**	**109**	**7**	**1**	**1**	**2**
Career total	26	113	13	12	.520	139	4.24	295 ⅓	132	105	327	21	3	2	5
Cubs total	**26**	**113**	**13**	**12**	**.520**	**139**	**4.24**	**295 ⅓**	**132**	**105**	**327**	**21**	**3**	**2**	**5**

Pierce, Raymond Lester (Ray *or* Lefty)
HEIGHT: 5'7"   LEFTHANDER   BORN: 6/6/1897 EMPORIA, KANSAS   DIED: 5/4/1963 DENVER, COLORADO

YEAR	TEAM	STARTS	GAMES	WON	LOST	PCT	ER	ERA	INNINGS PITCHED	STRIKE-OUTS	WALKS	HITS ALLOWED	HRS ALLOWED	COMP. GAMES	SHUT-OUTS	SAVES
1924	**ChC-N**	**0**	**6**	**0**	**0**	**—**	**6**	**7.36**	**7 ⅓**	**2**	**4**	**7**	**2**	**0**	**0**	**0**
1925	Phi-N	8	23	5	4	.556	55	5.50	90	18	24	134	7	4	0	0
1926	Phi-N	7	37	2	7	.222	53	5.63	84 ⅔	18	35	128	3	1	0	0
Career average	5	22	2	4	.389	38	5.64	60 ⅔	13	21	90	4	2	0	0
Cubs average	**0**	**6**	**0**	**0**	**—**	**6**	**7.36**	**7 ⅓**	**2**	**4**	**7**	**2**	**0**	**0**	**0**
Career total	15	66	7	11	.389	114	5.64	182	38	63	269	12	5	0	0
Cubs total	**0**	**6**	**0**	**0**	**—**	**6**	**7.36**	**7 ⅓**	**2**	**4**	**7**	**2**	**0**	**0**	**0**

Piercy, William Benton (Bill *or* Wild Bill)
HEIGHT: 6'1" RIGHTHANDER BORN: 5/2/1896 EL MONTE, CALIFORNIA DIED: 8/28/1951 LONG BEACH, CALIFORNIA

YEAR	TEAM	STARTS	GAMES	WON	LOST	PCT	ER	ERA	INNINGS PITCHED	STRIKE-OUTS	WALKS	HITS ALLOWED	HRS ALLOWED	COMP. GAMES	SHUT-OUTS	SAVES
1917	NYY-A	1	1	0	1	.000	3	3.00	9	2	4	9	0	1	0	0
1921	NYY-A	10	14	5	4	.556	27	2.98	81 2/3	35	28	82	4	5	1	0
1922	Bos-A	12	29	3	9	.250	63	4.67	121 1/3	24	62	140	2	7	1	0
1923	Bos-A	24	30	8	17	.320	71	3.41	187 1/3	51	73	193	5	11	0	0
1924	Bos-A	18	22	5	7	.417	80	5.95	121	20	66	156	4	3	0	0
1926	**ChC-N**	**5**	**19**	**6**	**5**	**.545**	**45**	**4.48**	**90 1/3**	**31**	**37**	**96**	**1**	**1**	**0**	**0**
Career average		12	19	5	7	.386	48	4.26	101 2/3	28	45	113	3	5	0	0
Cubs average		**5**	**19**	**6**	**5**	**.545**	**45**	**4.48**	**90 1/3**	**31**	**37**	**96**	**1**	**1**	**0**	**0**
Career total		70	115	27	43	.386	289	4.26	610 2/3	165	268	676	16	28	2	0
Cubs total		**5**	**19**	**6**	**5**	**.545**	**45**	**4.48**	**90 1/3**	**31**	**37**	**96**	**1**	**1**	**0**	**0**

Piktuzis, George Richard (Dee)
HEIGHT: 6'2" LEFTHANDER BORN: 1/3/1932 CHICAGO, ILLINOIS DIED: 11/28/1993 LONG BEACH, CALIFORNIA

YEAR	TEAM	STARTS	GAMES	WON	LOST	PCT	ER	ERA	INNINGS PITCHED	STRIKE-OUTS	WALKS	HITS ALLOWED	HRS ALLOWED	COMP. GAMES	SHUT-OUTS	SAVES
1956	ChC-N	0	2	0	0	—	4	7.20	5	3	2	6	1	0	0	0
Career average		0	2	0	0	—	4	7.20	5	3	2	6	1	0	0	0
Cubs average		**0**	**2**	**0**	**0**	**—**	**4**	**7.20**	**5**	**3**	**2**	**6**	**1**	**0**	**0**	**0**
Career total		0	2	0	0	—	4	7.20	5	3	2	6	1	0	0	0
Cubs total		**0**	**2**	**0**	**0**	**—**	**4**	**7.20**	**5**	**3**	**2**	**6**	**1**	**0**	**0**	**0**

Pina, Horacio
HEIGHT: 6'2" RIGHTHANDER BORN: 3/12/1945 COAHUILA, MEXICO

YEAR	TEAM	STARTS	GAMES	WON	LOST	PCT	ER	ERA	INNINGS PITCHED	STRIKE-OUTS	WALKS	HITS ALLOWED	HRS ALLOWED	COMP. GAMES	SHUT-OUTS	SAVES
1968	Cle-A	3	12	1	1	.500	6	1.72	31 1/3	24	15	24	0	0	0	2
1969	Cle-A	4	31	4	2	.667	27	5.21	46 2/3	32	27	44	6	0	0	1
1970	Was-A	0	61	5	3	.625	22	2.79	71	41	35	66	4	0	0	6
1971	Was-A	0	56	1	1	.500	23	3.59	57 2/3	38	31	47	2	0	0	2
1972	Tex-A	0	60	2	7	.222	27	3.20	76	60	43	61	3	0	0	15
1973	Oak-A	0	47	6	3	.667	27	2.76	88	41	34	58	8	0	0	8
1974	**ChC-N**	**0**	**34**	**3**	**4**	**.429**	**21**	**3.99**	**47 1/3**	**32**	**28**	**49**	**4**	**0**	**0**	**4**
1974	Cal-A	0	11	1	2	.333	3	2.31	11 2/3	6	3	9	1	0	0	0
1978	Phi-N	0	2	0	0	—	0	0.00	2 1/3	4	0	0	0	0	0	0
Career average		1	39	3	3	.500	20	3.25	54	35	27	45	4	0	0	5
Cubs average		**0**	**34**	**3**	**4**	**.429**	**21**	**3.99**	**47 1/3**	**32**	**28**	**49**	**4**	**0**	**0**	**4**
Career total		7	314	23	23	.500	156	3.25	432	278	216	358	28	0	0	38
Cubs total		**0**	**34**	**3**	**4**	**.429**	**21**	**3.99**	**47 1/3**	**32**	**28**	**49**	**4**	**0**	**0**	**4**

Pisciotta, Marc George
HEIGHT: 6'5" RIGHTHANDER BORN: 8/7/1970 EDISON, NEW JERSEY

YEAR	TEAM	STARTS	GAMES	WON	LOST	PCT	ER	ERA	INNINGS PITCHED	STRIKE-OUTS	WALKS	HITS ALLOWED	HRS ALLOWED	COMP. GAMES	SHUT-OUTS	SAVES
1997	**ChC-N**	**0**	**24**	**3**	**1**	**.750**	**10**	**3.18**	**28 1/3**	**21**	**16**	**20**	**1**	**0**	**0**	**0**
1998	**ChC-N**	**0**	**43**	**1**	**2**	**.333**	**20**	**4.09**	**44**	**31**	**32**	**44**	**4**	**0**	**0**	**0**
1999	KC-A	0	8	0	2	.000	8	8.64	8 1/3	3	10	9	1	0	0	0
Career average		0	25	1	2	.444	13	4.24	27	18	19	24	2	0	0	0
Cubs average		**0**	**34**	**2**	**2**	**.571**	**15**	**3.73**	**36 1/3**	**26**	**24**	**32**	**3**	**0**	**0**	**0**
Career total		0	75	4	5	.444	38	4.24	80 2/3	55	58	73	6	0	0	0
Cubs total		**0**	**67**	**4**	**3**	**.571**	**30**	**3.73**	**72 1/3**	**52**	**48**	**64**	**5**	**0**	**0**	**0**

Pizarro, Juan Roman
HEIGHT: 5'11" LEFTHANDER BORN: 2/7/1937 SANTURCE, PUERTO RICO

YEAR	TEAM	STARTS	GAMES	WON	LOST	PCT	ER	ERA	INNINGS PITCHED	STRIKE-OUTS	WALKS	HITS ALLOWED	HRS ALLOWED	COMP. GAMES	SHUT-OUTS	SAVES
1957	Mil-N	10	24	5	6	.455	51	4.62	99 1/3	68	51	99	16	3	0	0
1958	Mil-N	10	16	6	4	.600	29	2.70	96 2/3	84	47	75	12	7	1	1
1959	Mil-N	14	29	6	2	.750	56	3.77	133 2/3	126	70	117	13	6	2	0
1960	Mil-N	17	21	6	7	.462	58	4.55	114 2/3	88	72	105	13	3	0	0
1961	CWS-A	25	39	14	7	.667	66	3.05	194 1/3	188	89	164	17	12	1	2
1962	CWS-A	32	36	12	14	.462	86	3.81	203 1/3	173	97	182	16	9	1	1
1963	CWS-A	28	32	16	8	.667	57	2.39	214 2/3	163	63	177	14	10	3	1
1964	CWS-A	33	33	19	9	.679	68	2.56	239	162	55	193	23	11	4	0
1965	CWS-A	18	18	6	3	.667	37	3.43	97	65	37	96	9	2	1	0
1966	CWS-A	9	34	8	6	.571	37	3.76	88 2/3	42	39	91	9	1	0	3
1967	Pit-N	9	50	8	10	.444	47	3.95	107	96	52	99	10	1	1	9
1968	Pit-N	0	12	1	1	.500	4	3.27	11	6	10	14	2	0	0	0
1968	Bos-A	12	19	6	8	.429	43	3.59	107 2/3	84	44	97	15	6	0	2
1969	Bos-A	0	6	0	1	.000	6	6.00	9	4	6	14	2	0	0	2
1969	Cle-A	4	48	3	3	.500	29	3.16	82 2/3	44	49	67	6	1	0	4
1969	Oak-A	0	3	1	1	.500	2	2.35	7 2/3	4	3	3	1	0	0	1
1970	**ChC-N**	**0**	**12**	**0**	**0**	**—**	**8**	**4.60**	**15 2/3**	**14**	**9**	**16**	**2**	**0**	**0**	**1**
1971	**ChC-N**	**14**	**16**	**7**	**6**	**.538**	**39**	**3.46**	**101 1/3**	**67**	**40**	**78**	**10**	**6**	**3**	**0**
1972	**ChC-N**	**7**	**16**	**4**	**5**	**.444**	**26**	**3.94**	**59 1/3**	**24**	**32**	**66**	**7**	**1**	**0**	**1**
1973	**ChC-N**	**0**	**2**	**0**	**1**	**.000**	**5**	**11.25**	**4**	**3**	**1**	**6**	**1**	**0**	**0**	**0**
1973	Hou-N	1	15	2	2	.500	17	6.56	23 1/3	10	11	28	1	0	0	0
1974	Pit-N	2	7	1	1	.500	5	1.88	24	7	11	20	2	0	0	0

Career average		14	27	7	6	.555	43	3.43	113	85	49	100	11	4	1	2
Cubs average		**5**	**12**	**3**	**3**	**.478**	**20**	**3.89**	**45**	**27**	**21**	**42**	**5**	**2**	**1**	**1**
Career total		245	488	131	105	.555	776	3.43	2034 1/3	1522	888	1807	201	79	17	28
Cubs total		**21**	**46**	**11**	**12**	**.478**	**78**	**3.89**	**180 1/3**	**108**	**82**	**166**	**20**	**7**	**3**	**2**

Plesac, Daniel Thomas (Dan *or* Sac *or* Sac-Man)
HEIGHT: 6'5" LEFTHANDER BORN: 2/4/1962 GARY, INDIANA

YEAR	TEAM	STARTS	GAMES	WON	LOST	PCT	ER	ERA	INNINGS PITCHED	STRIKE-OUTS	WALKS	HITS ALLOWED	HRS ALLOWED	COMP. GAMES	SHUT-OUTS	SAVES
1986	Mil-A	0	51	10	7	.588	30	2.97	91	75	29	81	5	0	0	14
1987	Mil-A	0	57	5	6	.455	23	2.61	79 1/3	89	23	63	8	0	0	23
1988	Mil-A	0	50	1	2	.333	14	2.41	52 1/3	52	12	46	2	0	0	30
1989	Mil-A	0	52	3	4	.429	16	2.35	61 1/3	52	17	47	6	0	0	33
1990	Mil-A	0	66	3	7	.300	34	4.43	69	65	31	67	5	0	0	24
1991	Mil-A	10	45	2	7	.222	44	4.29	92 1/3	61	39	92	12	0	0	8
1992	Mil-A	4	44	5	4	.556	26	2.96	79	54	35	64	5	0	0	1
1993	**ChC-N**	**0**	**57**	**2**	**1**	**.667**	**33**	**4.74**	**62 2/3**	**47**	**21**	**74**	**10**	**0**	**0**	**0**
1994	**ChC-N**	**0**	**54**	**2**	**3**	**.400**	**28**	**4.61**	**54 2/3**	**53**	**13**	**61**	**9**	**0**	**0**	**1**
1995	Pit-N	0	58	4	4	.500	24	3.58	60 1/3	57	27	53	3	0	0	3
1996	Pit-N	0	73	6	5	.545	32	4.09	70 1/3	76	24	67	4	0	0	11
1997	Tor-A	0	73	2	4	.333	20	3.58	50 1/3	61	19	47	8	0	0	1
1998	Tor-A	0	78	4	3	.571	21	3.78	50	55	16	41	4	0	0	4
1999	Tor-A	0	30	0	3	.000	21	8.34	22 2/3	26	9	28	4	0	0	0
1999	Ari-N	0	34	2	1	.667	8	3.32	21 2/3	27	8	22	3	0	0	1
2000	Ari-N	0	62	5	1	.833	14	3.15	40	45	26	34	4	0	0	0
2001	Tor-A	0	62	4	5	.444	18	3.57	45 1/3	68	24	34	4	0	0	1

Career average		1	59	4	4	.472	25	3.65	62 2/3	60	23	58	6	0	0	10
Cubs average		**0**	**56**	**2**	**2**	**.500**	**31**	**4.68**	**58 2/3**	**50**	**17**	**68**	**10**	**0**	**0**	**1**
Career total		14	946	60	67	.472	406	3.65	1002 1/3	963	373	921	96	0	0	155
Cubs total		**0**	**111**	**4**	**4**	**.500**	**61**	**4.68**	**117 1/3**	**100**	**34**	**135**	**19**	**0**	**0**	**1**

Poholsky, Thomas George (Tom)
HEIGHT: 6'3" RIGHTHANDER BORN: 8/26/1929 DETROIT, MICHIGAN DIED: 1/6/2001 KIRKWOOD, MISSOURI

YEAR	TEAM	STARTS	GAMES	WON	LOST	PCT	ER	ERA	INNINGS PITCHED	STRIKE-OUTS	WALKS	HITS ALLOWED	HRS ALLOWED	COMP. GAMES	SHUT-OUTS	SAVES
1950	StL-N	1	5	0	0	—	6	3.68	14 2/3	2	3	16	2	0	0	0
1951	StL-N	26	38	7	13	.350	96	4.43	195	70	68	204	15	10	1	1
1954	StL-N	13	25	5	7	.417	36	3.06	106	55	20	101	11	4	0	0

(continued)

(continued)

1955	StL-N	24	30	9	11	.450	64	3.81	151	66	35	143	26	8	2	0
1956	StL-N	29	33	9	14	.391	81	3.59	203	95	44	210	27	7	2	0
1957	**ChC-N**	**11**	**28**	**1**	**7**	**.125**	**46**	**4.93**	**84**	**28**	**22**	**117**	**9**	**1**	**0**	**0**
Career average		17	27	5	9	.373	55	3.93	125 ⅔	53	32	132	15	5	1	0
Cubs average		**11**	**28**	**1**	**7**	**.125**	**46**	**4.93**	**84**	**28**	**22**	**117**	**9**	**1**	**0**	**0**
Career total		104	159	31	52	.373	329	3.93	753 ⅔	316	192	791	90	30	5	1
Cubs total		**11**	**28**	**1**	**7**	**.125**	**46**	**4.93**	**84**	**28**	**22**	**117**	**9**	**1**	**0**	**0**

Pollet, Howard Joseph (Howie)
HEIGHT: 6'1"   LEFTHANDER   BORN: 6/26/1921 NEW ORLEANS, LOUISIANA   DIED: 8/8/1974 HOUSTON, TEXAS

YEAR	TEAM	STARTS	GAMES	WON	LOST	PCT	ER	ERA	INNINGS PITCHED	STRIKE-OUTS	WALKS	HITS ALLOWED	HRS ALLOWED	COMP. GAMES	SHUT-OUTS	SAVES
1941	StL-N	8	9	5	2	.714	15	1.93	70	37	27	55	1	6	2	0
1942	StL-N	13	27	7	5	.583	35	2.88	109 ⅓	42	39	102	7	5	2	0
1943	StL-N	14	16	8	4	.667	23	1.75	118 ⅓	61	32	83	2	12	5	0
1946	StL-N	32	40	21	10	.677	62	2.10	266	107	86	228	12	22	4	5
1947	StL-N	24	37	9	11	.450	85	4.34	176 ⅓	73	87	195	11	9	0	2
1948	StL-N	26	36	13	8	.619	94	4.54	186 ⅓	80	67	216	10	11	0	0
1949	StL-N	28	39	20	9	.690	71	2.77	230 ⅔	108	59	228	9	17	5	1
1950	StL-N	30	37	14	13	.519	85	3.29	232 ⅓	117	68	228	19	14	2	2
1951	StL-N	2	6	0	3	.000	6	4.38	12 ⅓	10	8	10	1	0	0	1
1951	Pit-N	21	21	6	10	.375	72	5.04	128 ⅔	47	51	149	24	4	1	0
1952	Pit-N	30	31	7	16	.304	98	4.12	214	90	71	217	22	9	1	0
1953	Pit-N	2	5	1	1	.500	15	10.66	12 ⅔	8	6	27	2	0	0	0
1953	**ChC-N**	**16**	**25**	**5**	**6**	**.455**	**51**	**4.12**	**111 ⅓**	**45**	**44**	**120**	**6**	**2**	**0**	**1**
1954	**ChC-N**	**20**	**20**	**8**	**10**	**.444**	**51**	**3.58**	**128 ⅓**	**58**	**54**	**131**	**4**	**4**	**2**	**0**
1955	**ChC-N**	**7**	**24**	**4**	**3**	**.571**	**38**	**5.61**	**61**	**27**	**27**	**62**	**11**	**1**	**1**	**5**
1956	CWS-A	4	11	3	1	.750	12	4.10	26 ⅓	14	11	27	2	0	0	0
1956	Pit-N	0	19	0	4	.000	8	3.09	23 ⅓	10	8	18	3	0	0	3
Career average		20	29	9	8	.530	59	3.51	150 ⅔	67	53	150	10	8	2	1
Cubs average		**14**	**23**	**6**	**6**	**.472**	**47**	**4.19**	**100 ⅓**	**43**	**42**	**104**	**7**	**2**	**1**	**2**
Career total		277	403	131	116	.530	821	3.51	2107 ⅓	934	745	2096	146	116	25	20
Cubs total		**43**	**69**	**17**	**19**	**.472**	**140**	**4.19**	**300 ⅔**	**130**	**125**	**313**	**21**	**7**	**3**	**6**

Ponder, Charles Elmer (Elmer)
HEIGHT: 6'0"   RIGHTHANDER   BORN: 6/26/1893 REED, OKLAHOMA   DIED: 4/20/1974 ALBUQUERQUE, NEW MEXICO

YEAR	TEAM	STARTS	GAMES	WON	LOST	PCT	ER	ERA	INNINGS PITCHED	STRIKE-OUTS	WALKS	HITS ALLOWED	HRS ALLOWED	COMP. GAMES	SHUT-OUTS	SAVES
1917	Pit-N	2	3	1	1	.500	4	1.69	21 ⅓	11	6	12	0	1	1	0
1919	Pit-N	5	9	0	5	.000	21	3.99	47 ⅓	6	6	55	0	0	0	0
1920	Pit-N	23	33	11	15	.423	57	2.62	196	62	40	182	3	13	2	0
1921	Pit-N	1	8	2	0	1.000	6	2.19	24 ⅔	3	3	29	1	1	0	0
1921	**ChC-N**	**11**	**16**	**3**	**6**	**.333**	**47**	**4.74**	**89 ⅓**	**31**	**17**	**117**	**7**	**5**	**0**	**0**
Career average		11	17	4	7	.386	34	3.21	94 ⅔	28	18	99	3	5	1	0
Cubs average		**11**	**16**	**3**	**6**	**.333**	**47**	**4.74**	**89 ⅓**	**31**	**17**	**117**	**7**	**5**	**0**	**0**
Career total		42	69	17	27	.386	135	3.21	378 ⅔	113	72	395	11	20	3	0
Cubs total		**11**	**16**	**3**	**6**	**.333**	**47**	**4.74**	**89 ⅓**	**31**	**17**	**117**	**7**	**5**	**0**	**0**

Poorman, Thomas Iverson (Tom)
HEIGHT: 5'7"   RIGHTHANDER   BORN: 10/14/1857 LOCK HAVEN, PENNSYLVANIA   DIED: 2/18/1905 LOCK HAVEN, PENNSYLVANIA

YEAR	TEAM	STARTS	GAMES	WON	LOST	PCT	ER	ERA	INNINGS PITCHED	STRIKE-OUTS	WALKS	HITS ALLOWED	HRS ALLOWED	COMP. GAMES	SHUT-OUTS	SAVES
1880	Buf-N	9	11	1	8	.111	39	4.13	85	13	19	117	3	9	0	1
1880	**ChN-N**	**1**	**2**	**2**	**0**	**1.000**	**4**	**2.40**	**15**	**0**	**8**	**12**	**0**	**0**	**0**	**0**
1884	Tol-AA	1	1	0	1	.000	3	3.00	9	0	2	13	1	1	0	0
1887	Phi-AA	0	1	0	0	—	3	40.50	0 ⅔	1	1	6	1	0	0	0
Career average		4	5	1	3	.250	16	4.02	36 ⅔	5	10	49	2	3	0	0
Cubs average		**1**	**2**	**2**	**0**	**1.000**	**4**	**2.40**	**15**	**0**	**8**	**12**	**0**	**0**	**0**	**0**
Career total		11	15	3	9	.250	49	4.02	109 ⅔	14	30	148	5	10	0	1
Cubs total		**1**	**2**	**2**	**0**	**1.000**	**4**	**2.40**	**15**	**0**	**8**	**12**	**0**	**0**	**0**	**0**

Porterfield, Erwin Cooledge (Bob)
HEIGHT: 6'0" RIGHTHANDER BORN: 8/10/1923 NEWPORT, VIRGINIA DIED: 4/28/1980 CHARLOTTE, NORTH CAROLINA

YEAR	TEAM	STARTS	GAMES	WON	LOST	PCT	ER	ERA	INNINGS PITCHED	STRIKE-OUTS	WALKS	HITS ALLOWED	HRS ALLOWED	COMP. GAMES	SHUT-OUTS	SAVES
1948	NYY-A	12	16	5	3	.625	39	4.50	78	30	34	85	5	2	1	0
1949	NYY-A	8	12	2	5	.286	26	4.06	57 2/3	25	29	53	3	3	0	0
1950	NYY-A	2	10	1	1	.500	19	8.69	19 2/3	9	8	28	2	0	0	1
1951	NYY-A	0	2	0	0	—	5	15.00	3	2	3	5	0	0	0	0
1951	Was-A	19	19	9	8	.529	48	3.24	133 1/3	53	54	109	8	10	3	0
1952	Was-A	29	31	13	14	.481	70	2.72	231 1/3	80	85	222	7	15	3	0
1953	Was-A	32	34	22	10	.688	95	3.35	255	77	73	243	19	24	9	0
1954	Was-A	31	32	13	15	.464	90	3.32	244	82	77	249	14	21	2	0
1955	Was-A	27	30	10	17	.370	88	4.45	178	74	54	197	14	8	2	0
1956	Bos-A	18	25	3	12	.200	72	5.14	126	53	64	127	21	4	1	1
1957	Bos-A	9	28	4	4	.500	46	4.05	102 1/3	28	30	107	8	3	1	1
1958	Bos-A	0	2	0	0		2	4.50	4	1	0	3	1	0	0	5
1958	Pit-N	6	37	4	6	.400	32	3.29	87 2/3	39	19	78	7	2	1	5
1959	Pit-N	0	36	1	2	.333	20	4.35	41 1/3	19	19	51	3	0	0	1
1959	**ChC-N**	**0**	**4**	**0**	**0**	**—**	**8**	**11.37**	**6 1/3**	**0**	**3**	**14**	**1**	**0**	**0**	**0**
Career average		16	27	7	8	.473	55	3.79	130 2/3	48	46	131	9	8	2	1
Cubs average		**0**	**4**	**0**	**0**	**—**	**8**	**11.37**	**6 1/3**	**0**	**3**	**14**	**1**	**0**	**0**	**0**
Career total		193	318	87	97	.473	660	3.79	1567 2/3	572	552	1571	113	92	23	8
Cubs total		**0**	**4**	**0**	**0**	**—**	**8**	**11.37**	**6 1/3**	**0**	**3**	**14**	**1**	**0**	**0**	**0**

Powell, William Burris (Bill)
HEIGHT: 6'2" RIGHTHANDER BORN: 5/8/1885 TAYLOR COUNTY, WEST VIRGINIA DIED: 9/28/1967 EAST LIVERPOOL, OHIO

YEAR	TEAM	STARTS	GAMES	WON	LOST	PCT	ER	ERA	INNINGS PITCHED	STRIKE-OUTS	WALKS	HITS ALLOWED	HRS ALLOWED	COMP. GAMES	SHUT-OUTS	SAVES
1909	Pit-N	1	3	0	1	.000	3	3.68	7 1/3	2	6	7	0	0	0	0
1910	Pit-N	9	12	4	6	.400	20	2.40	75	23	34	65	0	4	2	0
1912	**ChC-N**	**0**	**1**	**0**	**0**	**—**	**2**	**9.00**	**2**	**0**	**1**	**2**	**0**	**0**	**0**	**0**
1913	Cin-N	1	1	0	1	.000	2	54.00	0 1/3	0	2	2	0	0	0	0
Career average		3	4	1	2	.333	7	2.87	21 1/3	6	11	19	0	1	1	0
Cubs average		**0**	**1**	**0**	**0**	**—**	**2**	**9.00**	**2**	**0**	**1**	**2**	**0**	**0**	**0**	**0**
Career total		11	17	4	8	.333	27	2.87	84 2/3	25	43	76	0	4	2	0
Cubs total		**0**	**1**	**0**	**0**	**—**	**2**	**9.00**	**2**	**0**	**1**	**2**	**0**	**0**	**0**	**0**

Prall, Wilfred Anthony (Willie)
HEIGHT: 6'3" LEFTHANDER BORN: 4/20/1950 HACKENSACK, NEW JERSEY

YEAR	TEAM	STARTS	GAMES	WON	LOST	PCT	ER	ERA	INNINGS PITCHED	STRIKE-OUTS	WALKS	HITS ALLOWED	HRS ALLOWED	COMP. GAMES	SHUT-OUTS	SAVES
1975	**ChC-N**	**3**	**3**	**0**	**2**	**.000**	**14**	**8.59**	**14 2/3**	**7**	**8**	**21**	**1**	**0**	**0**	**0**
Career average		3	3	0	2	.000	14	8.59	14 2/3	7	8	21	1	0	0	0
Cubs average		**3**	**3**	**0**	**2**	**.000**	**14**	**8.59**	**14 2/3**	**7**	**8**	**21**	**1**	**0**	**0**	**0**
Career total		3	3	0	2	.000	14	8.59	14 2/3	7	8	21	1	0	0	0
Cubs total		**3**	**3**	**0**	**2**	**.000**	**14**	**8.59**	**14 2/3**	**7**	**8**	**21**	**1**	**0**	**0**	**0**

Prendergast, Michael Thomas (Mike *or* Iron Mike)
HEIGHT: 5'9" RIGHTHANDER BORN: 12/15/1888 ARLINGTON, ILLINOIS DIED: 11/18/1967 OMAHA, NEBRASKA

YEAR	TEAM	STARTS	GAMES	WON	LOST	PCT	ER	ERA	INNINGS PITCHED	STRIKE-OUTS	WALKS	HITS ALLOWED	HRS ALLOWED	COMP. GAMES	SHUT-OUTS	SAVES
1914	Chi-F	19	30	5	9	.357	36	2.38	136	71	40	131	5	7	1	0
1915	Chi-F	30	42	14	12	.538	70	2.48	253 2/3	95	67	220	6	16	3	0
1916	**ChC-N**	**10**	**35**	**6**	**11**	**.353**	**39**	**2.31**	**152**	**56**	**23**	**127**	**5**	**4**	**2**	**2**
1917	**ChC-N**	**8**	**35**	**3**	**6**	**.333**	**37**	**3.35**	**99 1/3**	**43**	**21**	**112**	**6**	**1**	**0**	**1**
1918	Phi-N	30	33	13	14	.481	81	2.89	252 1/3	41	46	257	6	20	0	1
1919	Phi-N	1	5	0	1	.000	14	8.40	15	5	10	20	0	0	0	0
Career average		16	30	7	9	.436	46	2.74	151 1/3	52	35	145	5	8	1	1
Cubs average		**9**	**35**	**5**	**9**	**.346**	**38**	**2.72**	**125 2/3**	**50**	**22**	**120**	**6**	**3**	**1**	**2**
Career total		98	180	41	53	.436	277	2.74	908 1/3	311	207	867	28	48	6	4
Cubs total		**18**	**70**	**9**	**17**	**.346**	**76**	**2.72**	**251 1/3**	**99**	**44**	**239**	**11**	**5**	**2**	**3**

Pressnell, Forest Charles (Tot)
HEIGHT: 5'10"   RIGHTHANDER   BORN: 8/8/1906 FINDLAY, OHIO   DIED: 1/6/2001 FINDLAY, OHIO

YEAR	TEAM	STARTS	GAMES	WON	LOST	PCT	ER	ERA	INNINGS PITCHED	STRIKE-OUTS	WALKS	HITS ALLOWED	HRS ALLOWED	COMP. GAMES	SHUT-OUTS	SAVES
1938	Bro-N	19	43	11	14	.440	76	3.56	192	57	56	209	11	6	1	3
1939	Bro-N	18	31	9	7	.563	70	4.02	156 2/3	43	33	171	8	10	2	2
1940	Bro-N	4	24	6	5	.545	28	3.69	68 1/3	21	17	58	4	1	1	2
1941	**ChC-N**	**1**	**29**	**5**	**3**	**.625**	**24**	**3.09**	**70**	**27**	**23**	**69**	**4**	**1**	**1**	**2**
1942	**ChC-N**	**0**	**27**	**1**	**1**	**.500**	**24**	**5.49**	**39 1/3**	**9**	**5**	**40**	**5**	**0**	**0**	**4**
Career average		8	31	6	6	.516	44	3.80	105 1/3	31	27	109	6	3	1	2
Cubs average		**1**	**28**	**3**	**2**	**.600**	**24**	**3.95**	**54 2/3**	**18**	**14**	**55**	**4**	**0**	**0**	**3**
Career total		42	154	32	30	.516	222	3.80	526 1/3	157	134	547	30	17	4	12
Cubs total		**1**	**56**	**6**	**4**	**.600**	**48**	**3.95**	**109 1/3**	**36**	**28**	**109**	**7**	**0**	**0**	**5**

Prim, Raymond Lee (Ray *or* Pop)
HEIGHT: 6'0"   LEFTHANDER   BORN: 12/30/1906 SALITPA, ALABAMA   DIED: 4/29/1995 MONTE RIO, CALIFORNIA

YEAR	TEAM	STARTS	GAMES	WON	LOST	PCT	ER	ERA	INNINGS PITCHED	STRIKE-OUTS	WALKS	HITS ALLOWED	HRS ALLOWED	COMP. GAMES	SHUT-OUTS	SAVES
1933	Was-A	1	2	0	1	.000	5	3.14	14 1/3	6	2	13	0	0	0	0
1934	Was-A	1	8	0	2	.000	11	6.75	14 2/3	3	8	19	1	0	0	0
1935	Phi-N	6	29	3	4	.429	47	5.77	73 1/3	27	15	110	4	1	0	0
1943	**ChC-N**	**5**	**29**	**4**	**3**	**.571**	**17**	**2.55**	**60**	**27**	**14**	**67**	**2**	**0**	**0**	**1**
1945	**ChC-N**	**19**	**34**	**13**	**8**	**.619**	**44**	**2.40**	**165 1/3**	**88**	**23**	**142**	**9**	**9**	**2**	**2**
1946	**ChC-N**	**2**	**14**	**2**	**3**	**.400**	**15**	**5.79**	**23 1/3**	**10**	**10**	**28**	**5**	**0**	**0**	**1**
Career average		6	19	4	4	.512	23	3.56	58 2/3	27	12	63	4	2	0	1
Cubs average		**9**	**26**	**6**	**5**	**.576**	**25**	**2.75**	**83**	**42**	**16**	**79**	**5**	**3**	**1**	**1**
Career total		34	116	22	21	.512	139	3.56	351	161	72	379	21	10	2	4
Cubs total		**26**	**77**	**19**	**14**	**.576**	**76**	**2.75**	**248 2/3**	**125**	**47**	**237**	**16**	**9**	**2**	**4**

Prince, Donald Mark (Don)
HEIGHT: 6'4"   RIGHTHANDER   BORN: 4/5/1938 CLARKTON, NORTH CAROLINA

YEAR	TEAM	STARTS	GAMES	WON	LOST	PCT	ER	ERA	INNINGS PITCHED	STRIKE-OUTS	WALKS	HITS ALLOWED	HRS ALLOWED	COMP. GAMES	SHUT-OUTS	SAVES
1962	ChC-N	0	1	0	0	—	0	0.00	1	0	1	0	0	0	0	0
Career average		0	1	0	0	—	0	0.00	1	0	1	0	0	0	0	0
Cubs average		**0**	**1**	**0**	**0**	**—**	**0**	**0.00**	**1**	**0**	**1**	**0**	**0**	**0**	**0**	**0**
Career total		0	1	0	0	—	0	0.00	1	0	1	0	0	0	0	0
Cubs total		**0**	**1**	**0**	**0**	**—**	**0**	**0.00**	**1**	**0**	**1**	**0**	**0**	**0**	**0**	**0**

Proly, Michael James (Mike)
HEIGHT: 6'0"   RIGHTHANDER   BORN: 12/15/1950 JAMAICA, NEW YORK

YEAR	TEAM	STARTS	GAMES	WON	LOST	PCT	ER	ERA	INNINGS PITCHED	STRIKE-OUTS	WALKS	HITS ALLOWED	HRS ALLOWED	COMP. GAMES	SHUT-OUTS	SAVES
1976	StL-N	0	14	1	0	1.000	7	3.71	17	4	6	21	0	0	0	0
1978	CWS-A	6	14	5	2	.714	20	2.74	65 2/3	19	12	63	4	2	0	1
1979	CWS-A	6	38	3	8	.273	38	3.87	88 1/3	32	40	89	6	0	0	9
1980	CWS-A	3	62	5	10	.333	50	3.07	146 2/3	56	58	136	7	0	0	8
1981	Phi-N	2	35	2	1	.667	27	3.86	63	19	19	66	6	0	0	2
1982	**ChC-N**	**1**	**44**	**5**	**3**	**.625**	**21**	**2.30**	**82**	**24**	**22**	**77**	**5**	**0**	**0**	**1**
1983	**ChC-N**	**0**	**60**	**1**	**5**	**.167**	**33**	**3.58**	**83**	**31**	**38**	**79**	**5**	**0**	**0**	**1**
Career average		3	38	3	4	.431	28	3.23	78	26	28	76	5	0	0	3
Cubs average		**1**	**52**	**3**	**4**	**.429**	**27**	**2.95**	**82 2/3**	**28**	**30**	**78**	**5**	**0**	**0**	**1**
Career total		18	267	22	29	.431	196	3.23	545 2/3	185	195	531	33	2	0	22
Cubs total		**1**	**104**	**6**	**8**	**.429**	**54**	**2.95**	**165**	**55**	**60**	**156**	**10**	**0**	**0**	**2**

Pyecha, John Nicholas
HEIGHT: 6'5"   RIGHTHANDER   BORN: 11/25/1931 ALIQUIPPA, PENNSYLVANIA

YEAR	TEAM	STARTS	GAMES	WON	LOST	PCT	ER	ERA	INNINGS PITCHED	STRIKE-OUTS	WALKS	HITS ALLOWED	HRS ALLOWED	COMP. GAMES	SHUT-OUTS	SAVES
1954	ChC-N	0	1	0	1	.000	3	10.13	2 2/3	2	2	4	1	0	0	0
Career average		0	1	0	1	.000	3	10.13	2 2/3	2	2	4	1	0	0	0
Cubs average		**0**	**1**	**0**	**1**	**.000**	**3**	**10.13**	**2 2/3**	**2**	**2**	**4**	**1**	**0**	**0**	**0**
Career total		0	1	0	1	.000	3	10.13	2 2/3	2	2	4	1	0	0	0
Cubs total		**0**	**1**	**0**	**1**	**.000**	**3**	**10.13**	**2 2/3**	**2**	**2**	**4**	**1**	**0**	**0**	**0**

Pyle, Harry Thomas (Shadow)
HEIGHT: 5'8"   LEFTHANDER   BORN: 11/29/1861 READING, PENNSYLVANIA   DIED: 12/26/1908 READING, PENNSYLVANIA

YEAR	TEAM	STARTS	GAMES	WON	LOST	PCT	ER	ERA	INNINGS PITCHED	STRIKE-OUTS	WALKS	HITS ALLOWED	HRS ALLOWED	COMP. GAMES	SHUT-OUTS	SAVES
1884	Phi-N	1	1	0	1	.000	4	4.00	9	4	6	9	0	1	0	0
1887	ChN-N	4	4	1	3	.250	14	4.73	26 2/3	5	21	53	1	3	0	0
Career average		3	3	1	2	.200	9	4.54	18	5	14	31	1	2	0	0
Cubs average		**4**	**4**	**1**	**3**	**.250**	**14**	**4.73**	**26 2/3**	**5**	**21**	**53**	**1**	**3**	**0**	**0**
Career total		5	5	1	4	.200	18	4.54	35 2/3	9	27	62	1	4	0	0
Cubs total		**4**	**4**	**1**	**3**	**.250**	**14**	**4.73**	**26 2/3**	**5**	**21**	**53**	**1**	**3**	**0**	**0**

Quevedo, Ruben Eduardo
HEIGHT: 6'1"   RIGHTHANDER   BORN: 1/5/1979 VALENCIA CARABOBO, VENEZUELA

YEAR	TEAM	STARTS	GAMES	WON	LOST	PCT	ER	ERA	INNINGS PITCHED	STRIKE-OUTS	WALKS	HITS ALLOWED	HRS ALLOWED	COMP. GAMES	SHUT-OUTS	SAVES
2000	ChC-N	15	21	3	10	.231	73	7.47	88	65	54	96	21	1	0	0
2001	Mil-N	10	10	4	5	.444	29	4.61	56 2/3	60	30	56	9	0	0	0
Career average		13	16	4	8	.318	51	6.35	72 1/3	63	42	76	15	1	0	0
Cubs average		**15**	**21**	**3**	**10**	**.231**	**73**	**7.47**	**88**	**65**	**54**	**96**	**21**	**1**	**0**	**0**
Career total		25	31	7	15	.318	102	6.35	144 2/3	125	84	152	30	1	0	0
Cubs total		**15**	**21**	**3**	**10**	**.231**	**73**	**7.47**	**88**	**65**	**54**	**96**	**21**	**1**	**0**	**0**

Quinn, Wellington Hunt (Wimpy)
HEIGHT: 6'2"   RIGHTHANDER   BORN: 5/12/1918 BIRMINGHAM, ALABAMA   DIED: 9/1/1954 SANTA MONICA, CALIFORNIA

YEAR	TEAM	STARTS	GAMES	WON	LOST	PCT	ER	ERA	INNINGS PITCHED	STRIKE-OUTS	WALKS	HITS ALLOWED	HRS ALLOWED	COMP. GAMES	SHUT-OUTS	SAVES
1941	ChC-N	0	3	0	0	—	4	7.20	5	2	3	3	0	0	0	0
Career average		0	3	0	0	—	4	7.20	5	2	3	3	0	0	0	0
Cubs average		**0**	**3**	**0**	**0**	**—**	**4**	**7.20**	**5**	**2**	**3**	**3**	**0**	**0**	**0**	**0**
Career total		0	3	0	0	—	4	7.20	5	2	3	3	0	0	0	0
Cubs total		**0**	**3**	**0**	**0**	**—**	**4**	**7.20**	**5**	**2**	**3**	**3**	**0**	**0**	**0**	**0**

Radatz, Richard Raymond (Dick *or* The Monster)
HEIGHT: 6'6"   RIGHTHANDER   BORN: 4/2/1937 DETROIT, MICHIGAN

YEAR	TEAM	STARTS	GAMES	WON	LOST	PCT	ER	ERA	INNINGS PITCHED	STRIKE-OUTS	WALKS	HITS ALLOWED	HRS ALLOWED	COMP. GAMES	SHUT-OUTS	SAVES
1962	Bos-A	0	62	9	6	.600	31	2.24	124 2/3	144	40	95	9	0	0	24
1963	Bos-A	0	66	15	6	.714	29	1.97	132 1/3	162	51	94	9	0	0	25
1964	Bos-A	0	79	16	9	.640	40	2.29	157	181	58	103	13	0	0	29
1965	Bos-A	0	63	9	11	.450	54	3.91	124 1/3	121	53	104	11	0	0	22
1966	Bos-A	0	16	0	2	.000	10	4.74	19	19	11	24	3	0	0	4
1966	Cle-A	0	39	0	3	.000	29	4.61	56 2/3	49	34	49	6	0	0	10
1967	Cle-A	0	3	0	0	—	2	6.00	3	1	2	5	1	0	0	0

(continued)

(continued)																
1967	**ChC-N**	0	20	1	0	1.000	17	6.56	23 1/3	18	24	12	4	0	0	5
1969	Det-A	0	11	2	2	.500	7	3.38	18 2/3	18	5	14	3	0	0	0
1969	Mon-N	0	22	0	4	.000	22	5.71	34 2/3	32	18	32	6	0	0	3
Career average		0	54	7	6	.547	34	3.13	99	106	42	76	9	0	0	17
Cubs average		**0**	**20**	**1**	**0**	**1.000**	**17**	**6.56**	**23 1/3**	**18**	**24**	**12**	**4**	**0**	**0**	**5**
Career total		0	381	52	43	.547	241	3.13	693 2/3	745	296	532	65	0	0	122
Cubs total		**0**	**20**	**1**	**0**	**1.000**	**17**	**6.56**	**23 1/3**	**18**	**24**	**12**	**4**	**0**	**0**	**5**

Raffensberger, Kenneth David (Ken)
HEIGHT: 6'2" LEFTHANDER BORN: 8/8/1917 YORK, PENNSYLVANIA

YEAR	TEAM	STARTS	GAMES	WON	LOST	PCT	ER	ERA	INNINGS PITCHED	STRIKE-OUTS	WALKS	HITS ALLOWED	HRS ALLOWED	COMP. GAMES	SHUT-OUTS	SAVES
1939	StL-N	0	1	0	0	—	0	0.00	1	1	0	2	0	0	0	0
1940	**ChC-N**	**10**	**43**	**7**	**9**	**.438**	**43**	**3.38**	**114 2/3**	**55**	**29**	**120**	**10**	**3**	**0**	**3**
1941	**ChC-N**	**1**	**10**	**0**	**1**	**.000**	**9**	**4.50**	**18**	**5**	**7**	**17**	**0**	**0**	**0**	**0**
1943	Phi-N	1	1	0	1	.000	1	1.13	8	3	2	7	0	1	0	0
1944	Phi-N	31	37	13	20	.394	88	3.06	258 2/3	136	45	257	9	18	3	0
1945	Phi-N	4	5	0	3	.000	12	4.44	24 1/3	6	14	28	3	1	0	0
1946	Phi-N	23	39	8	15	.348	79	3.63	196	73	39	203	10	14	2	6
1947	Phi-N	7	10	2	6	.250	25	5.49	41	16	8	50	4	3	1	0
1947	Cin-N	15	19	6	5	.545	49	4.13	106 2/3	38	29	132	11	7	0	1
1948	Cin-N	24	40	11	12	.478	77	3.84	180 1/3	57	37	187	15	7	4	0
1949	Cin-N	38	41	18	17	.514	107	3.39	284	103	80	289	23	20	5	0
1950	Cin-N	35	38	14	19	.424	113	4.26	239	87	40	271	34	18	4	0
1951	Cin-N	33	42	16	17	.485	95	3.44	248 2/3	81	38	232	29	14	5	5
1952	Cin-N	33	38	17	13	.567	77	2.81	247	93	45	247	18	18	6	1
1953	Cin-N	26	26	7	14	.333	76	3.93	174	47	33	200	23	9	1	0
1954	Cin-N	1	6	0	2	.000	9	7.84	10 1/3	5	3	15	2	0	0	0
Career average		19	26	8	10	.436	57	3.60	143 1/3	54	30	150	13	9	2	1
Cubs average		**6**	**27**	**4**	**5**	**.412**	**26**	**3.53**	**66 1/3**	**30**	**18**	**69**	**5**	**2**	**0**	**2**
Career total		282	396	119	154	.436	860	3.60	2151 2/3	806	449	2257	191	133	31	16
Cubs total		**11**	**53**	**7**	**10**	**.412**	**52**	**3.53**	**132 2/3**	**60**	**36**	**137**	**10**	**3**	**0**	**3**

Ragan, Don Carlos Patrick (Pat)
HEIGHT: 5'10" RIGHTHANDER BORN: 11/15/1888 BLANCHARD, IOWA DIED: 9/4/1956 LOS ANGELES, CALIFORNIA

YEAR	TEAM	STARTS	GAMES	WON	LOST	PCT	ER	ERA	INNINGS PITCHED	STRIKE-OUTS	WALKS	HITS ALLOWED	HRS ALLOWED	COMP. GAMES	SHUT-OUTS	SAVES
1909	Cin-N	0	2	0	1	.000	3	3.38	8	2	4	7	0	0	0	0
1909	**ChC-N**	**0**	**2**	**0**	**0**	**—**	**1**	**2.45**	**3 2/3**	**2**	**1**	**4**	**0**	**0**	**0**	**0**
1911	Bro-N	7	22	4	3	.571	22	2.11	93 2/3	39	31	81	0	5	1	1
1912	Bro-N	26	36	7	18	.280	84	3.63	208	101	65	211	7	12	1	1
1913	Bro-N	32	44	15	18	.455	111	3.77	264 2/3	109	64	284	10	14	0	0
1914	Bro-N	25	38	10	15	.400	69	2.98	208 1/3	106	85	214	5	14	1	3
1915	Bro-N	0	5	1	0	1.000	2	0.92	19 2/3	7	8	11	0	0	0	0
1915	Bos-N	26	33	16	12	.571	62	2.46	227	81	59	208	2	13	3	0
1916	Bos-N	23	28	9	9	.500	42	2.08	182	94	47	143	3	14	3	0
1917	Bos-N	13	30	6	9	.400	48	2.93	147 2/3	61	35	138	6	5	1	1
1918	Bos-N	25	30	8	17	.320	74	3.23	206 1/3	68	54	212	4	15	2	0
1919	Bos-N	3	4	0	2	.000	10	7.11	12 2/3	3	3	16	0	0	0	0
1919	NYG-N	1	7	1	0	1.000	4	1.59	22 2/3	7	14	19	0	1	0	0
1919	CWS-A	0	1	0	0	—	0	0.00	1	0	0	1	0	0	0	0
1923	Phi-N	0	1	0	0	—	2	6.00	3	0	0	6	1	0	0	0
Career arage			16	27	9	.425	49	2.99	146 1/3	62	43	141	3	8	1	1
Cubs average		**0**	**2**	**0**	**0**	**—**	**1**	**2.45**	**3 2/3**	**2**	**1**	**4**	**0**	**0**	**0**	**0**
Career total		181	283	77	104	.425	534	2.99	1608 1/3	680	470	1555	38	93	12	6
Cubs total		**0**	**2**	**0**	**0**	**—**	**1**	**2.45**	**3 2/3**	**2**	**1**	**4**	**0**	**0**	**0**	**0**

Rain, Steven Nicholas (Steve)
HEIGHT: 6'6" RIGHTHANDER BORN: 6/2/1975 LOS ANGELES, CALIFORNIA

YEAR	TEAM	STARTS	GAMES	WON	LOST	PCT	ER	ERA	INNINGS PITCHED	STRIKE-OUTS	WALKS	HITS ALLOWED	HRS ALLOWED	COMP. GAMES	SHUT-OUTS	SAVES
1999	ChC-N	0	16	0	1	.000	15	9.20	14 2/3	12	7	28	1	0	0	0
2000	ChC-N	0	37	3	4	.429	24	4.35	49 2/3	54	27	46	10	0	0	0
Career average		0	27	2	3	.375	20	5.46	32 1/3	33	17	37	6	0	0	0
Cubs average		**0**	**27**	**2**	**3**	**.375**	**20**	**5.46**	**32 1/3**	**33**	**17**	**37**	**6**	**0**	**0**	**0**
Career total		0	53	3	5	.375	39	5.46	64 1/3	66	34	74	11	0	0	0
Cubs total		**0**	**53**	**3**	**5**	**.375**	**39**	**5.46**	**64 1/3**	**66**	**34**	**74**	**11**	**0**	**0**	**0**

Rainey, Charles David (Chuck)
HEIGHT: 5'11" RIGHTHANDER BORN: 7/14/1954 SAN DIEGO, CALIFORNIA

YEAR	TEAM	STARTS	GAMES	WON	LOST	PCT	ER	ERA	INNINGS PITCHED	STRIKE-OUTS	WALKS	HITS ALLOWED	HRS ALLOWED	COMP. GAMES	SHUT-OUTS	SAVES
1979	Bos-A	16	20	8	5	.615	44	3.82	103 2/3	41	41	97	7	4	1	1
1980	Bos-A	13	16	8	3	.727	47	4.86	87	43	41	92	7	2	1	0
1981	Bos-A	2	11	0	1	.000	12	2.70	40	20	13	39	2	0	0	0
1982	Bos-A	25	27	7	5	.583	72	5.02	129	57	63	146	14	3	3	0
1983	**ChC-N**	**34**	**34**	**14**	**13**	**.519**	**95**	**4.48**	**191**	**84**	**74**	**219**	**17**	**1**	**1**	**0**
1984	**ChC-N**	**16**	**17**	**5**	**7**	**.417**	**42**	**4.28**	**88 1/3**	**45**	**38**	**102**	**4**	**0**	**0**	**0**
1984	Oak-A	0	16	1	1	.500	23	6.75	30 2/3	10	17	43	2	0	0	1
Career average		18	24	7	6	.551	56	4.50	111 2/3	50	48	123	9	2	1	0
Cubs average		**25**	**26**	**10**	**10**	**.487**	**69**	**4.41**	**139 2/3**	**65**	**56**	**161**	**11**	**1**	**1**	**0**
Career total		106	141	43	35	.551	335	4.50	669 2/3	300	287	738	53	10	6	2
Cubs total		**50**	**51**	**19**	**20**	**.487**	**137**	**4.41**	**279 1/3**	**129**	**112**	**321**	**21**	**1**	**1**	**0**

Ramsdell, James Willard (Willie *or* Willie the Knuck)
HEIGHT: 5'11" RIGHTHANDER BORN: 4/4/1916 WILLIAMSBURG, KANSAS DIED: 10/8/1969 WICHITA, KANSAS

YEAR	TEAM	STARTS	GAMES	WON	LOST	PCT	ER	ERA	INNINGS PITCHED	STRIKE-OUTS	WALKS	HITS ALLOWED	HRS ALLOWED	COMP. GAMES	SHUT-OUTS	SAVES
1947	Bro-N	0	2	1	1	.500	2	6.75	2 2/3	3	3	4	0	0	0	0
1948	Bro-N	1	27	4	4	.500	29	5.19	50 1/3	34	41	48	6	0	0	4
1950	Bro-N	0	5	1	2	.333	2	2.84	6 1/3	2	2	7	0	0	0	1
1950	Cin-N	22	27	7	12	.368	65	3.72	157 1/3	83	75	151	17	8	1	0
1951	Cin-N	31	31	9	17	.346	88	4.04	196	88	70	204	18	10	1	0
1952	**ChC-N**	**4**	**19**	**2**	**3**	**.400**	**18**	**2.42**	**67**	**30**	**24**	**41**	**5**	**0**	**0**	**0**
Career average		12	22	5	8	.381	41	3.83	96	48	43	91	9	4	0	1
Cubs average		**4**	**19**	**2**	**3**	**.400**	**18**	**2.42**	**67**	**30**	**24**	**41**	**5**	**0**	**0**	**0**
Career total		58	111	24	39	.381	204	3.83	479 2/3	240	215	455	46	18	2	5
Cubs total		**4**	**19**	**2**	**3**	**.400**	**18**	**2.42**	**67**	**30**	**24**	**41**	**5**	**0**	**0**	**0**

Rasmussen, Dennis Lee
HEIGHT: 6'7" LEFTHANDER BORN: 4/18/1959 LOS ANGELES, CALIFORNIA

YEAR	TEAM	STARTS	GAMES	WON	LOST	PCT	ER	ERA	INNINGS PITCHED	STRIKE-OUTS	WALKS	HITS ALLOWED	HRS ALLOWED	COMP. GAMES	SHUT-OUTS	SAVES
1983	SD-N	1	4	0	0	—	3	1.98	13 2/3	13	8	10	1	0	0	0
1984	NYY-A	24	24	9	6	.600	75	4.57	147 2/3	110	60	127	16	1	0	0
1985	NYY-A	16	22	3	5	.375	45	3.98	101 2/3	63	42	97	10	2	0	0
1986	NYY-A	31	31	18	6	.750	87	3.88	202	131	74	160	28	3	1	0
1987	NYY-A	25	26	9	7	.563	77	4.75	146	89	55	145	31	2	0	0
1987	Cin-N	7	7	4	1	.800	20	3.97	45 1/3	39	12	39	5	0	0	0
1988	Cin-N	11	11	2	6	.250	36	5.75	56 1/3	27	22	68	8	1	1	0
1988	SD-N	20	20	14	4	.778	42	2.55	148 1/3	85	36	131	9	6	0	0
1989	SD-N	33	33	10	10	.500	87	4.26	183 2/3	87	72	190	18	1	0	0
1990	SD-N	32	32	11	15	.423	94	4.51	187 2/3	86	62	217	28	3	1	0
1991	SD-N	24	24	6	13	.316	61	3.74	146 2/3	75	49	155	12	1	1	0
1992	**ChC-N**	**1**	**3**	**0**	**0**	**—**	**6**	**10.80**	**5**	**0**	**2**	**7**	**2**	**0**	**0**	**0**

(continued)

(continued)

YEAR	TEAM	STARTS	GAMES	WON	LOST	PCT	ER	ERA	INNINGS PITCHED	STRIKE-OUTS	WALKS	HITS ALLOWED	HRS ALLOWED	COMP. GAMES	SHUT-OUTS	SAVES
1992	KC-A	5	5	4	1	.800	6	1.43	37⅔	12	6	25	0	1	1	0
1993	KC-A	4	9	1	2	.333	24	7.45	29	12	14	40	4	0	0	0
1995	KC-A	1	5	0	1	.000	10	9.00	10	6	8	13	3	0	0	0
Career average		20	21	8	6	.542	56	4.15	121⅔	70	44	119	15	2	0	0
Cubs average		**1**	**3**	**0**	**0**	**—**	**6**	**10.80**	**5**	**0**	**2**	**7**	**2**	**0**	**0**	**0**
Career total		235	256	91	77	.542	673	4.15	1460⅔	835	522	1424	175	21	5	0
Cubs total		**1**	**3**	**0**	**0**	**—**	**6**	**10.80**	**5**	**0**	**2**	**7**	**2**	**0**	**0**	**0**

Reberger, Frank Beall (Crane)

HEIGHT: 6'5" RIGHTHANDER BORN: 6/7/1944 CALDWELL, IDAHO

YEAR	TEAM	STARTS	GAMES	WON	LOST	PCT	ER	ERA	INNINGS PITCHED	STRIKE-OUTS	WALKS	HITS ALLOWED	HRS ALLOWED	COMP. GAMES	SHUT-OUTS	SAVES
1968	**ChC-N**	**1**	**3**	**0**	**1**	**.000**	**3**	**4.50**	**6**	**3**	**2**	**9**	**1**	**0**	**0**	**0**
1969	SD-N	0	67	1	2	.333	35	3.59	87⅔	65	41	83	6	0	0	6
1970	SF-N	18	45	7	8	.467	94	5.57	152	117	98	178	13	3	0	2
1971	SF-N	7	13	3	0	1.000	19	3.92	43⅔	21	19	37	5	0	0	0
1972	SF-N	11	20	3	4	.429	44	3.99	99⅓	52	37	97	10	2	0	0
Career average		7	30	3	3	.483	39	4.52	77⅔	52	39	81	7	1	0	2
Cubs average		**1**	**3**	**0**	**1**	**.000**	**3**	**4.50**	**6**	**3**	**2**	**9**	**1**	**0**	**0**	**0**
Career total		37	148	14	15	.483	195	4.52	388⅔	258	197	404	35	5	0	8
Cubs total		**1**	**3**	**0**	**1**	**.000**	**3**	**4.50**	**6**	**3**	**2**	**9**	**1**	**0**	**0**	**0**

Regan, Philip Raymond (Phil *or* The Vulture)

HEIGHT: 6'3" RIGHTHANDER BORN: 4/6/1937 OTSEGO, MICHIGAN

YEAR	TEAM	STARTS	GAMES	WON	LOST	PCT	ER	ERA	INNINGS PITCHED	STRIKE-OUTS	WALKS	HITS ALLOWED	HRS ALLOWED	COMP. GAMES	SHUT-OUTS	SAVES
1960	Det-A	7	17	0	4	.000	34	4.50	68	38	25	70	11	0	0	1
1961	Det-A	16	32	10	7	.588	70	5.25	120	46	41	134	19	6	0	2
1962	Det-A	23	35	11	9	.550	77	4.04	171⅓	87	64	169	23	6	0	0
1963	Det-A	27	38	15	9	.625	81	3.86	189	115	59	179	33	5	1	1
1964	Det-A	21	32	5	10	.333	82	5.03	146⅔	91	49	162	21	2	0	1
1965	Det-A	7	16	1	5	.167	29	5.05	51⅓	37	20	57	6	1	0	0
1966	LA-N	0	65	14	1	.933	21	1.62	116⅔	88	24	85	6	0	0	21
1967	LA-N	3	55	6	9	.400	32	2.99	96⅓	53	32	108	2	0	0	6
1968	LA-N	0	5	2	0	1.000	3	3.52	7⅔	7	1	10	1	0	0	0
1968	**ChC-N**	**0**	**68**	**10**	**5**	**.667**	**31**	**2.20**	**127**	**60**	**24**	**109**	**9**	**0**	**0**	**25**
1969	**ChC-N**	**0**	**71**	**12**	**6**	**.667**	**46**	**3.70**	**112**	**56**	**35**	**120**	**6**	**0**	**0**	**17**
1970	**ChC-N**	**0**	**54**	**5**	**9**	**.357**	**40**	**4.76**	**75⅔**	**31**	**32**	**81**	**8**	**0**	**0**	**12**
1971	**ChC-N**	**1**	**48**	**5**	**5**	**.500**	**32**	**3.93**	**73⅓**	**28**	**33**	**84**	**4**	**0**	**0**	**6**
1972	**ChC-N**	**0**	**5**	**0**	**1**	**.000**	**1**	**2.25**	**4**	**2**	**2**	**6**	**0**	**0**	**0**	**0**
1972	CWS-A	0	10	0	1	.000	6	4.05	13⅓	4	6	18	1	0	0	0
Career average		8	42	7	6	.542	45	3.84	105⅔	57	34	107	12	2	0	7
Cubs average		**0**	**49**	**6**	**5**	**.552**	**30**	**3.44**	**78⅓**	**35**	**25**	**80**	**5**	**0**	**0**	**12**
Career total		105	551	96	81	.542	585	3.84	1372⅔	743	447	1392	150	20	1	92
Cubs total		**1**	**246**	**32**	**26**	**.552**	**150**	**3.44**	**392**	**177**	**126**	**400**	**27**	**0**	**0**	**60**

Reis, Lawrence P. (Laurie)

HEIGHT: — RIGHTHANDER BORN: 11/20/1858 CHICAGO, ILLINOIS DIED: 1/24/1921 CHICAGO, ILLINOIS

YEAR	TEAM	STARTS	GAMES	WON	LOST	PCT	ER	ERA	INNINGS PITCHED	STRIKE-OUTS	WALKS	HITS ALLOWED	HRS ALLOWED	COMP. GAMES	SHUT-OUTS	SAVES
1877	ChN-N	4	4	3	1	.750	3	0.75	36	11	6	29	1	4	1	0
1878	ChN-N	4	4	1	3	.250	13	3.25	36	8	4	55	0	4	0	0
Career average		4	4	2	2	.500	8	2.00	36	10	5	42	1	4	1	0
Cubs average		**4**	**4**	**2**	**2**	**.500**	**8**	**2.00**	**36**	**10**	**5**	**42**	**1**	**4**	**1**	**0**
Career total		8	8	4	4	.500	16	2.00	72	19	10	84	1	8	1	0
Cubs total		**8**	**8**	**4**	**4**	**.500**	**16**	**2.00**	**72**	**19**	**10**	**84**	**1**	**8**	**1**	**0**

Renfroe, Cohen Williams (Laddie)
HEIGHT: 5'11"   RIGHTHANDER   BORN: 5/9/1962 NATCHEZ, MISSISSIPPI

YEAR	TEAM	STARTS	GAMES	WON	LOST	PCT	ER	ERA	INNINGS PITCHED	STRIKE-OUTS	WALKS	HITS ALLOWED	HRS ALLOWED	COMP. GAMES	SHUT-OUTS	SAVES
1991	ChC-N	0	4	0	1	.000	7	13.50	4 ⅔	4	2	11	1	0	0	0
Career average		0	4	0	1	.000	7	13.50	4 ⅔	4	2	11	1	0	0	0
Cubs average		**0**	**4**	**0**	**1**	**.000**	**7**	**13.50**	**4 ⅔**	**4**	**2**	**11**	**1**	**0**	**0**	**0**
Career total		0	4	0	1	.000	7	13.50	4 ⅔	4	2	11	1	0	0	0
Cubs total		**0**	**4**	**0**	**1**	**.000**	**7**	**13.50**	**4 ⅔**	**4**	**2**	**11**	**1**	**0**	**0**	**0**

Renko, Steven (Steve *or* Lurch)
HEIGHT: 6'5"   RIGHTHANDER   BORN: 12/10/1944 KANSAS CITY, KANSAS

YEAR	TEAM	STARTS	GAMES	WON	LOST	PCT	ER	ERA	INNINGS PITCHED	STRIKE-OUTS	WALKS	HITS ALLOWED	HRS ALLOWED	COMP. GAMES	SHUT-OUTS	SAVES
1969	Mon-N	15	18	6	7	.462	46	4.01	103 ⅓	68	50	94	14	4	0	0
1970	Mon-N	33	41	13	11	.542	107	4.32	222 ⅔	142	104	203	27	7	1	1
1971	Mon-N	37	40	15	14	.517	115	3.75	275 ⅔	129	135	256	24	9	3	0
1972	Mon-N	12	30	1	10	.091	56	5.20	97	66	67	96	11	0	0	0
1973	Mon-N	34	36	15	11	.577	78	2.81	249 ⅔	164	108	201	26	9	0	1
1974	Mon-N	35	37	12	16	.429	102	4.03	227 ⅔	138	81	222	17	8	1	0
1975	Mon-N	25	31	6	12	.333	77	4.07	170 ⅓	99	76	175	20	3	1	1
1976	Mon-N	1	5	0	1	.000	8	5.54	13	4	3	15	2	0	0	0
1976	**ChC-N**	**27**	**28**	**8**	**11**	**.421**	**70**	**3.86**	**163 ⅓**	**112**	**43**	**164**	**12**	**4**	**1**	**0**
1977	**ChC-N**	**8**	**13**	**2**	**2**	**.500**	**26**	**4.56**	**51 ⅓**	**34**	**21**	**51**	**10**	**0**	**0**	**1**
1977	CWS-A	8	8	5	0	1.000	21	3.54	53 ⅓	36	17	55	3	0	0	0
1978	Oak-A	25	27	6	12	.333	72	4.29	151	89	67	152	10	3	1	0
1979	Bos-A	27	27	11	9	.550	78	4.11	171	99	53	174	22	4	1	0
1980	Bos-A	23	32	9	9	.500	77	4.19	165 ⅓	90	56	180	17	1	0	0
1981	Cal-A	15	22	8	4	.667	39	3.44	102	50	42	93	7	0	0	1
1982	Cal-A	23	31	11	6	.647	77	4.44	156	81	51	163	17	4	0	0
1983	KC-A	17	25	6	11	.353	58	4.30	121 ⅓	54	36	144	9	1	0	1
Career average		24	30	9	10	.479	74	3.99	166 ⅓	97	67	163	17	4	1	0
Cubs average		**18**	**21**	**5**	**7**	**.435**	**48**	**4.02**	**107 ⅓**	**73**	**32**	**108**	**11**	**2**	**1**	**1**
Career total		365	451	134	146	.479	1107	3.99	2494	1455	1010	2438	248	57	9	6
Cubs total		**35**	**41**	**10**	**13**	**.435**	**96**	**4.02**	**214 ⅔**	**146**	**64**	**215**	**22**	**4**	**1**	**1**

Reulbach, Edward Marvin (Ed *or* Big Ed)
HEIGHT: 6'1"   RIGHTHANDER   BORN: 12/1/1882 DETROIT, MICHIGAN   DIED: 7/17/1961 GLENS FALLS, NEW YORK

YEAR	TEAM	STARTS	GAMES	WON	LOST	PCT	ER	ERA	INNINGS PITCHED	STRIKE-OUTS	WALKS	HITS ALLOWED	HRS ALLOWED	COMP. GAMES	SHUT-OUTS	SAVES
1905	**ChC-N**	**29**	**34**	**18**	**14**	**.563**	**46**	**1.42**	**291 ⅔**	**152**	**73**	**208**	**1**	**28**	**5**	**1**
1906	**ChC-N**	**24**	**33**	**19**	**4**	**.826**	**40**	**1.65**	**218**	**94**	**92**	**129**	**2**	**20**	**6**	**3**
1907	**ChC-N**	**22**	**27**	**17**	**4**	**.810**	**36**	**1.69**	**192**	**96**	**64**	**147**	**1**	**16**	**4**	**0**
1908	**ChC-N**	**35**	**46**	**24**	**7**	**.774**	**67**	**2.03**	**297 ⅔**	**133**	**106**	**227**	**4**	**25**	**7**	**1**
1909	**ChC-N**	**32**	**35**	**19**	**10**	**.655**	**52**	**1.78**	**262 ⅔**	**105**	**82**	**194**	**1**	**23**	**6**	**0**
1910	**ChC-N**	**23**	**24**	**12**	**8**	**.600**	**60**	**3.12**	**173 ⅓**	**55**	**49**	**161**	**1**	**14**	**1**	**0**
1911	**ChC-N**	**29**	**33**	**16**	**9**	**.640**	**73**	**2.96**	**221 ⅔**	**79**	**103**	**191**	**3**	**15**	**2**	**0**
1912	**ChC-N**	**19**	**39**	**10**	**6**	**.625**	**71**	**3.78**	**169**	**75**	**60**	**161**	**7**	**8**	**0**	**4**
1913	**ChC-N**	**3**	**10**	**1**	**3**	**.250**	**19**	**4.42**	**38 ⅔**	**10**	**21**	**41**	**1**	**1**	**0**	**0**
1913	Bro-N	12	15	7	6	.538	25	2.05	110	46	34	77	3	8	2	0
1914	Bro-N	29	44	11	18	.379	75	2.64	256	119	83	228	5	14	3	3
1915	New-F	30	33	21	10	.677	67	2.23	270	117	69	233	3	23	4	1
1916	Bos-N	11	21	7	6	.538	30	2.47	109 ⅓	47	41	99	1	6	0	0
1917	Bos-N	2	5	0	1	.000	7	2.82	22 ⅓	9	15	21	0	0	0	0
Career average		23	31	14	8	.632	51	2.28	202 ⅓	87	69	163	3	15	3	1
Cubs average		**24**	**31**	**15**	**7**	**.677**	**52**	**2.24**	**207 ⅓**	**89**	**72**	**162**	**2**	**17**	**3**	**1**
Career total		300	399	182	106	.632	668	2.28	2632 ⅓	1137	892	2117	33	201	40	13
Cubs total		**216**	**281**	**136**	**65**	**.677**	**464**	**2.24**	**1864 ⅔**	**799**	**650**	**1459**	**21**	**150**	**31**	**9**

Edward Marvin "Big Ed" Reulbach, rhp, 1905–17

Although Mordecai "Three Finger" Brown was probably the best pitcher the Cubs had during the glory years of 1906 to 1910, Big Ed Reulbach remains the most legendary.

Reulbach was born on December 1, 1882, in Detroit, Michigan. A pitching star in high school, Reulbach matriculated to Notre Dame and was one of the best college pitchers in the country at the turn of the century.

In fact, Reulbach was so good that in addition to pitching for the Irish, he also pitched in the minor leagues under several assumed names. In his autobiography, Cubs second baseman Johnny Evers recalled that George Huff, athletic director at the University of Illinois and also a pal of Cubs manager Frank Chance's, was sent bouncing around the country one summer to look at several hot pitching prospects and discovered that two of them were actually Reulbach, who was pitching under aliases.

Reulbach was eventually signed by the Cubs and began his big-league career in 1905, going 18-14, with those 18 wins leading the team.

He was a big, powerful guy, (6'1", 190 pounds), with the physical dimensions of a Greek statue. In his rookie year, Reulbach pitched an 18-inning complete game and a 20-inning complete game, both victories. His 152 strikeouts led the team, and his 5.33 hits per nine innings that year is the third best all-time.

He had one weakness: bad eyesight, which forced him to wear glasses off the field. Chance ordered catcher Johnny Kling to wear white gloves while he was behind the plate so that Reulbach could see Kling's signs better.

From 1906 to 1908, Reulbach set a couple of records that haven't been broken since. His winning percentages in those three years were .826 (a 19-4 record), .810 (17-4) and .774 (24-7), each time leading the National League in that category.

In 1908 the Cubs were locked in a tight pennant race. On September 26, Reulbach pitched both ends of a doubleheader against Brooklyn. This was not a publicity stunt. The Cubs staff had been chewed up by several doubleheaders and extra-inning games, and Chance was down to the end of his bench.

After shutting down Brooklyn, 5-0 on five hits, in the morning game, Reulbach told Chance he could go in the afternoon tilt. This game he won, 3-0 on three hits.

"No pitcher," marveled a scribe in the *New York Herald,* "has ever shown such mastery over one team as Reulbach showed today in Brooklyn."

It is a feat no one has ever duplicated.

Reulbach was also the first pitcher in a World Series to throw a one-hitter, as he shut out the Chicago White Sox, 7-1, in the second game of the series. He was 2-0 in his World Series career for Chicago.

In 1913 he was traded to Brooklyn in a move that outraged Cubs fans. He jumped to the Federal League in 1915, winning 21 games. After the Federal League folded, he pitched for two more years for the Boston Braves before retiring. He died on July 17, 1961, in Glens Falls, New York.

Reulbach's name is still all over the Cubs record books. His 14-game winning streak in 1909 is third best all-time with the team, and his 44 consecutive shutout innings in 1908 are a team record. His 2.24 career ERA is fourth all-time on the Cubs list, and he is seventh all-time in complete games with 150, third all-time in shutouts with 31 and opponents batted only .220 against him as a Cub, the third best ever.

Reuschel, Paul Richard
HEIGHT: 6'4"   RIGHTHANDER   BORN: 1/12/1947 QUINCY, ILLINOIS

YEAR	TEAM	STARTS	GAMES	WON	LOST	PCT	ER	ERA	INNINGS PITCHED	STRIKE-OUTS	WALKS	HITS ALLOWED	HRS ALLOWED	COMP. GAMES	SHUT-OUTS	SAVES
1975	ChC-N	0	28	1	3	.250	14	3.50	36	12	13	44	1	0	0	5
1976	ChC-N	2	50	4	2	.667	44	4.55	87	55	33	94	12	0	0	3
1977	ChC-N	0	69	5	6	.455	52	4.37	107	62	40	105	9	0	0	4
1978	ChC-N	0	16	2	0	1.000	16	5.14	28	13	13	29	4	0	0	0
1978	Cle-A	6	18	2	4	.333	31	3.11	89 2/3	24	22	95	5	1	0	0
1979	Cle-A	1	17	2	1	.667	40	7.94	45 1/3	22	11	73	7	0	0	1
Career average		2	40	3	3	.500	39	4.51	78 2/3	38	26	88	8	0	0	3
Cubs average		**1**	**41**	**3**	**3**	**.522**	**32**	**4.40**	**64 2/3**	**36**	**25**	**68**	**7**	**0**	**0**	**3**
Career total		9	198	16	16	.500	197	4.51	393	188	132	440	38	1	0	13
Cubs total		**2**	**163**	**12**	**11**	**.522**	**126**	**4.40**	**258**	**142**	**99**	**272**	**26**	**0**	**0**	**12**

Reuschel, Rickey Eugene (Rick *or* Big Daddy)
HEIGHT: 6'3"   RIGHTHANDER   BORN: 5/16/1949 QUINCY, ILLINOIS

YEAR	TEAM	STARTS	GAMES	WON	LOST	PCT	ER	ERA	INNINGS PITCHED	STRIKE-OUTS	WALKS	HITS ALLOWED	HRS ALLOWED	COMP. GAMES	SHUT-OUTS	SAVES
1972	ChC-N	18	21	10	8	.556	42	2.93	129	87	29	127	3	5	4	0
1973	ChC-N	36	36	14	15	.483	79	3.00	237	168	62	244	15	7	3	0
1974	ChC-N	38	41	13	12	.520	115	4.30	240 2/3	160	83	262	18	8	2	0
1975	ChC-N	37	38	11	17	.393	97	3.73	234	155	67	244	17	6	0	1
1976	ChC-N	37	38	14	12	.538	100	3.46	260	146	64	260	17	9	2	1
1977	ChC-N	37	39	20	10	.667	78	2.79	252	166	74	233	13	8	4	1
1978	ChC-N	35	35	14	15	.483	92	3.41	242 2/3	115	54	235	16	9	1	0
1979	ChC-N	36	36	18	12	.600	96	3.62	239	125	75	251	16	5	1	0
1980	ChC-N	38	38	11	13	.458	97	3.40	257	140	76	281	13	6	0	0
1981	ChC-N	13	13	4	7	.364	33	3.47	85 2/3	53	23	87	4	1	0	0
1981	NYY-A	11	12	4	4	.500	21	2.67	70 2/3	22	10	75	4	3	0	0
1983	ChC-N	4	4	1	1	.500	9	3.92	20 2/3	9	10	18	1	0	0	0
1984	ChC-N	14	19	5	5	.500	53	5.17	92 1/3	43	23	123	7	1	0	0
1985	Pit-N	26	31	14	8	.636	49	2.27	194	138	52	153	7	9	1	1
1986	Pit-N	34	35	9	16	.360	95	3.96	215 2/3	125	57	232	20	4	2	0
1987	Pit-N	25	25	8	6	.571	54	2.75	177	80	35	163	12	9	3	0
1987	SF-N	8	9	5	3	.625	24	4.32	50	27	7	44	1	3	1	0
1988	SF-N	36	36	19	11	.633	85	3.12	245	92	42	242	11	7	2	0
1989	SF-N	32	32	17	8	.680	68	2.94	208 1/3	111	54	195	18	2	0	0
1990	SF-N	13	15	3	6	.333	38	3.93	87	49	31	102	8	0	0	1
1991	SF-N	1	4	0	2	.000	5	4.22	10 2/3	4	7	17	0	0	0	0
Career average		28	29	11	10	.528	70	3.37	186 2/3	106	49	189	12	5	1	0
Cubs average		**29**	**30**	**11**	**11**	**.515**	**74**	**3.50**	**191**	**114**	**53**	**197**	**12**	**5**	**1**	**0**
Career total		529	557	214	191	.528	1330	3.37	3548 1/3	2015	935	3588	221	102	26	5
Cubs total		**343**	**358**	**135**	**127**	**.515**	**891**	**3.50**	**2290**	**1367**	**640**	**2365**	**140**	**65**	**17**	**3**

Reynolds, Archie Edward
HEIGHT: 6'2"   RIGHTHANDER   BORN: 1/3/1946 GLENDALE, CALIFORNIA

YEAR	TEAM	STARTS	GAMES	WON	LOST	PCT	ER	ERA	INNINGS PITCHED	STRIKE-OUTS	WALKS	HITS ALLOWED	HRS ALLOWED	COMP. GAMES	SHUT-OUTS	SAVES
1968	ChC-N	1	7	0	1	.000	10	6.75	13 1/3	6	7	14	1	0	0	0
1969	ChC-N	2	2	0	1	.000	2	2.45	7 1/3	4	7	11	1	0	0	0
1970	ChC-N	1	7	0	2	.000	11	6.60	15	9	9	17	2	0	0	0
1971	Cal-A	1	15	0	3	.000	14	4.61	27 1/3	15	18	32	2	0	0	0
1972	Mil-A	2	5	0	1	.000	15	7.23	18 2/3	13	8	26	2	0	0	0
Career average		1	7	0	2	.000	10	5.73	16 1/3	9	10	20	2	0	0	0
Cubs average		**1**	**5**	**0**	**1**	**.000**	**8**	**5.80**	**12**	**6**	**8**	**14**	**1**	**0**	**0**	**0**
Career total		7	36	0	8	.000	52	5.73	81 2/3	47	49	100	8	0	0	0
Cubs total		**4**	**16**	**0**	**4**	**.000**	**23**	**5.80**	**35 2/3**	**19**	**23**	**42**	**4**	**0**	**0**	**0**

Rickey (Rick) Eugene "Big Daddy" Reuschel, rhp, 1972–81, 1983–91

Rick Reuschel was the most successful Cubs pitcher of the 1970s, a consistent, durable righthander who rarely missed a start.

Reuschel was born on May 16, 1949, in Quincy, Illinois. The Cubs brought him up as a wide-eyed 23-year-old rookie in 1972 and he delivered immediately. He won 10 games and lost 8, finishing with a 2.93 ERA, third best on the team.

That began a streak of nine consecutive years in which Reuschel would win 10 games or more with the Cubs. Five of those years, he would lead the team in wins. In 1977 Reuschel was 20-10, the only time in his 19-year career he would win 20 games. He also had 166 strikeouts and a 2.79 ERA. Reuschel made the All-Star team that year as well, his only All-Star appearance in a Chicago uniform.

He was a big man, at 6'3" and 235 pounds. His teammates tagged him with the nickname "Big Daddy." He was also a tough customer on the mound. Reuschel was unafraid to brush back a player or even hit one if he believed the player was taking up a batting stance too close to home plate.

At one point, in 1977, Reds star Pete Rose made several derogatory comments about the Cubs in a Chicago newspaper. A day later,

Reuschel was pitching and Rose was the first batter in the game. Reuschel drilled Rose with a pitch right in the ribs. Unwilling to mess with Big Daddy, Rose took first base without a word.

Teammates also loved Reuschel because in the clubhouse he was so even-keeled. Win or lose, his demeanor was the same.

Older brother Paul Reuschel joined the Cubs briefly, from 1975 to 1978, as a reliever and spot starter. On August 21, 1975, the two became the first brother combination to collaborate on a major league shutout, beating the Dodgers, 7-0.

In 1982 Reuschel missed the season with a torn rotator cuff which threatened to end his career. He played briefly for the Cubs in 1983, but bowed out of baseball during part of the 1984 season. He was signed by the Pirates in 1985 and began a new career. His 1985 season (a 14-8 record and a 2.27 ERA) in Pittsburgh won him Comeback Player of the Year.

Traded to the Giants midway through the 1987 season, he helped San Francisco make the playoffs in 1987 and in 1989, ironically helping to eliminate the Cubs from the National League Championship Series the latter year. Reuschel retired in 1991.

Reuschel is third all-time for the Cubs in strikeouts with 1,367, sixth in innings pitched with 2,290, second all-time in games started with 343 and eighth in appearances with 358.

Rhoads, Robert Barton (Bob or Dusty)

HEIGHT: 6'1"   RIGHTHANDER   BORN: 10/4/1879 WOOSTER, OHIO   DIED: 2/12/1967 SAN BERNARDINO, CALIFORNIA

YEAR	TEAM	STARTS	GAMES	WON	LOST	PCT	ER	ERA	INNINGS PITCHED	STRIKE-OUTS	WALKS	HITS ALLOWED	HRS ALLOWED	COMP. GAMES	SHUT-OUTS	SAVES
1902	ChC-N	12	16	4	8	.333	42	3.20	118	43	42	131	1	12	1	1
1903	StL-N	13	17	5	8	.385	66	4.60	129	52	47	154	3	12	1	0
1903	Cle-A	5	5	2	3	.400	24	5.27	41	21	3	55	2	5	0	0
1904	Cle-A	19	22	10	9	.526	56	2.87	175 1/3	72	48	175	1	18	0	0
1905	Cle-A	26	28	16	9	.640	74	2.83	235	61	55	219	4	24	4	0
1906	Cle-A	34	38	22	10	.688	63	1.80	315	89	92	259	5	31	7	0
1907	Cle-A	31	35	15	14	.517	70	2.29	275	76	84	258	0	23	5	1
1908	Cle-A	30	37	18	12	.600	53	1.77	270	62	73	229	2	20	1	0
1909	Cle-A	15	20	5	9	.357	43	2.90	133 1/3	46	50	124	1	9	2	0
Career average		23	27	12	10	.542	61	2.61	211 1/3	65	62	201	2	19	3	0
Cubs average		**12**	**16**	**4**	**8**	**.333**	**42**	**3.20**	**118**	**43**	**42**	**131**	**1**	**12**	**1**	**1**
Career total		185	218	97	82	.542	491	2.61	1691 2/3	522	494	1604	19	154	21	2
Cubs total		**12**	**16**	**4**	**8**	**.333**	**42**	**3.20**	**118**	**43**	**42**	**131**	**1**	**12**	**1**	**1**

Richie, Lewis A. (Lew)
HEIGHT: 5'8" RIGHTHANDER BORN: 8/23/1883 AMBLER, PENNSYLVANIA DIED: 8/15/1936 AMBLER, PENNSYLVANIA

YEAR	TEAM	STARTS	GAMES	WON	LOST	PCT	ER	ERA	INNINGS PITCHED	STRIKE-OUTS	WALKS	HITS ALLOWED	HRS ALLOWED	COMP. GAMES	SHUT-OUTS	SAVES
1906	Phi-N	22	33	9	11	.450	55	2.41	205 2/3	65	79	170	3	14	3	0
1907	Phi-N	12	25	6	6	.500	23	1.77	117	40	38	88	0	9	2	0
1908	Phi-N	15	25	7	10	.412	32	1.83	157 2/3	58	49	125	1	13	2	1
1909	Phi-N	1	11	1	1	.500	10	2.00	45	11	18	40	0	0	0	1
1909	Bos-N	13	22	7	7	.500	34	2.32	131 2/3	42	44	118	2	9	2	2
1910	Bos-N	2	4	0	3	.000	5	2.76	16 1/3	7	9	20	0	0	0	0
1910	ChC-N	11	30	11	4	.733	39	2.70	130	53	51	117	1	8	3	4
1911	ChC-N	28	36	15	11	.577	65	2.31	253	78	103	213	6	18	4	1
1912	ChC-N	27	39	16	8	.667	78	2.95	238	69	74	222	5	15	4	0
1913	ChC-N	5	16	2	4	.333	42	5.82	65	15	30	77	3	1	0	0
Career average		17	30	9	8	.532	48	2.54	170	55	62	149	3	11	3	1
Cubs average		18	30	11	7	.620	56	2.94	171 2/3	54	65	157	4	11	3	1
Career total		136	241	74	65	.532	383	2.54	1359 1/3	438	495	1190	21	87	20	9
Cubs total		71	121	44	27	.620	224	2.94	686	215	258	629	15	42	11	5

Richmond, Beryl Justice
HEIGHT: 6'1" LEFTHANDER BORN: 8/24/1907 GLEN EASTON, WEST VIRGINIA DIED: 4/24/1980 CAMERON, WEST VIRGINIA

YEAR	TEAM	STARTS	GAMES	WON	LOST	PCT	ER	ERA	INNINGS PITCHED	STRIKE-OUTS	WALKS	HITS ALLOWED	HRS ALLOWED	COMP. GAMES	SHUT-OUTS	SAVES
1933	ChC-N	0	4	0	0	—	1	1.93	4 2/3	2	2	10	0	0	0	0
1934	Cin-N	2	6	1	2	.333	8	3.72	19 1/3	9	10	23	0	1	0	0
Career average		1	5	1	1	.333	5	3.38	12	6	6	17	0	1	0	0
Cubs average		0	4	0	0	—	1	1.93	4 2/3	2	2	10	0	0	0	0
Career total		2	10	1	2	.333	9	3.38	24	11	12	33	0	1	0	0
Cubs total		0	4	0	0	—	1	1.93	4 2/3	2	2	10	0	0	0	0

Richter, Emil Henry (Reggie)
HEIGHT: 6'2" RIGHTHANDER BORN: 9/14/1888 DUSSELDORF, GERMANY DIED: 8/2/1934 WINFIELD, ILLINOIS

YEAR	TEAM	STARTS	GAMES	WON	LOST	PCT	ER	ERA	INNINGS PITCHED	STRIKE-OUTS	WALKS	HITS ALLOWED	HRS ALLOWED	COMP. GAMES	SHUT-OUTS	SAVES
1911	ChC-N	5	22	1	3	.250	19	3.13	54 2/3	34	20	62	1	0	0	2
Career average		5	22	1	3	.250	19	3.13	54 2/3	34	20	62	1	0	0	2
Cubs average		5	22	1	3	.250	19	3.13	54 2/3	34	20	62	1	0	0	2
Career total		5	22	1	3	.250	19	3.13	54 2/3	34	20	62	1	0	0	2
Cubs total		5	22	1	3	.250	19	3.13	54 2/3	34	20	62	1	0	0	2

Riley, George Michael
HEIGHT: 6'2" LEFTHANDER BORN: 10/6/1956 PHILADELPHIA, PENNSYLVANIA

YEAR	TEAM	STARTS	GAMES	WON	LOST	PCT	ER	ERA	INNINGS PITCHED	STRIKE-OUTS	WALKS	HITS ALLOWED	HRS ALLOWED	COMP. GAMES	SHUT-OUTS	SAVES
1979	ChC-N	1	4	0	1	.000	8	5.54	13	5	6	16	1	0	0	0
1980	ChC-N	0	22	0	4	.000	23	5.75	36	18	20	41	2	0	0	0
1984	SF-N	4	5	1	0	1.000	13	3.99	29 1/3	12	7	39	1	0	0	0
1986	Mon-N	0	10	0	0	—	4	4.15	8 2/3	5	8	7	0	0	0	0
Career average		1	10	0	1	.167	12	4.97	21 2/3	10	10	26	1	0	0	0
Cubs average		1	13	0	3	.000	16	5.69	24 2/3	12	13	29	2	0	0	0
Career total		5	41	1	5	.167	48	4.97	87	40	41	103	4	0	0	0
Cubs total		1	26	0	5	.000	31	5.69	49	23	26	57	3	0	0	0

Ripley, Allen Stevens
HEIGHT: 6'3"   RIGHTHANDER   BORN: 10/18/1952 NORWOOD, MASSACHUSETTS

YEAR	TEAM	STARTS	GAMES	WON	LOST	PCT	ER	ERA	INNINGS PITCHED	STRIKE-OUTS	WALKS	HITS ALLOWED	HRS ALLOWED	COMP. GAMES	SHUT-OUTS	SAVES
1978	Bos-A	11	15	2	5	.286	45	5.55	73	26	22	92	10	1	0	0
1979	Bos-A	3	16	3	1	.750	37	5.15	64⅔	34	25	77	9	0	0	1
1980	SF-N	20	23	9	10	.474	52	4.15	112⅔	65	36	119	10	0	0	0
1981	SF-N	14	19	4	4	.500	41	4.07	90⅔	47	27	103	5	1	0	0
1982	**ChC-N**	**19**	**28**	**5**	**7**	**.417**	**58**	**4.26**	**122⅔**	**57**	**38**	**130**	**12**	**0**	**0**	**0**
Career average		13	20	5	5	.460	47	4.52	92⅔	46	30	104	9	1	0	0
Cubs average		**19**	**28**	**5**	**7**	**.417**	**58**	**4.26**	**122⅔**	**57**	**38**	**130**	**12**	**0**	**0**	**0**
Career total		67	101	23	27	.460	233	4.52	463⅔	229	148	521	46	4	0	1
Cubs total		**19**	**28**	**5**	**7**	**.417**	**58**	**4.26**	**122⅔**	**57**	**38**	**130**	**12**	**0**	**0**	**0**

Rivera, Roberto
HEIGHT: 6'0"   LEFTHANDER   BORN: 1/1/1969 BAYAMON, PUERTO RICO

YEAR	TEAM	STARTS	GAMES	WON	LOST	PCT	ER	ERA	INNINGS PITCHED	STRIKE-OUTS	WALKS	HITS ALLOWED	HRS ALLOWED	COMP. GAMES	SHUT-OUTS	SAVES
1995	ChC-N	0	7	0	0	—	3	5.40	5	2	2	8	1	0	0	0
1999	SD-N	0	12	1	2	.333	3	3.86	7	3	3	6	1	0	0	0
Career average		0	10	1	1	.333	3	4.50	6	3	3	7	1	0	0	0
Cubs average		**0**	**7**	**0**	**0**	**—**	**3**	**5.40**	**5**	**2**	**2**	**8**	**1**	**0**	**0**	**0**
Career total		0	19	1	2	.333	6	4.50	12	5	5	14	2	0	0	0
Cubs total		**0**	**7**	**0**	**0**	**—**	**3**	**5.40**	**5**	**2**	**2**	**8**	**1**	**0**	**0**	**0**

Roach, Rudolph Charles (Skel)
HEIGHT: 6'2"   RIGHTHANDER   BORN: 10/20/1871 DANZIG, GERMANY   DIED: 3/9/1958 OAK PARK, ILLINOIS

YEAR	TEAM	STARTS	GAMES	WON	LOST	PCT	ER	ERA	INNINGS PITCHED	STRIKE-OUTS	WALKS	HITS ALLOWED	HRS ALLOWED	COMP. GAMES	SHUT-OUTS	SAVES
1899	ChN-N	1	1	1	0	1.000	3	3.00	9	0	1	13	0	1	0	0
Career average		1	1	1	0	1.000	3	3.00	9	0	1	13	0	1	0	0
Cubs average		**1**	**1**	**1**	**0**	**1.000**	**3**	**3.00**	**9**	**0**	**1**	**13**	**0**	**1**	**0**	**0**
Career total		1	1	1	0	1.000	3	3.00	9	0	1	13	0	1	0	0
Cubs total		**1**	**1**	**1**	**0**	**1.000**	**3**	**3.00**	**9**	**0**	**1**	**13**	**0**	**1**	**0**	**0**

Roberts, David Arthur (Dave)
HEIGHT: 6'3"   LEFTHANDER   BORN: 9/11/1944 GALLIPOLIS, OHIO

YEAR	TEAM	STARTS	GAMES	WON	LOST	PCT	ER	ERA	INNINGS PITCHED	STRIKE-OUTS	WALKS	HITS ALLOWED	HRS ALLOWED	COMP. GAMES	SHUT-OUTS	SAVES
1969	SD-N	5	22	0	3	.000	26	4.81	48⅔	19	19	65	5	0	0	1
1970	SD-N	21	43	8	14	.364	77	3.81	181⅔	102	43	182	16	3	2	1
1971	SD-N	34	37	14	17	.452	63	2.10	269⅔	135	61	238	9	14	2	0
1972	Hou-N	28	35	12	7	.632	96	4.50	192	111	57	227	18	7	3	2
1973	Hou-N	36	39	17	11	.607	79	2.85	249⅓	119	62	264	15	12	6	0
1974	Hou-N	30	34	10	12	.455	77	3.40	204	72	65	216	6	8	2	1
1975	Hou-N	27	32	8	14	.364	94	4.27	198⅓	101	73	182	16	7	0	1
1976	Det-A	36	36	16	17	.485	112	4.00	252	79	63	254	16	18	4	0
1977	Det-A	22	22	4	10	.286	74	5.15	129⅓	46	41	143	20	5	0	0
1977	**ChC-N**	**6**	**17**	**1**	**1**	**.500**	**19**	**3.23**	**53**	**23**	**12**	**55**	**1**	**1**	**0**	**1**
1978	**ChC-N**	**20**	**35**	**6**	**8**	**.429**	**51**	**5.25**	**142⅓**	**54**	**56**	**159**	**17**	**2**	**1**	**1**
1979	SF-N	1	26	0	2	.000	12	2.57	42	23	18	42	3	0	0	1
1979	Pit-N	3	21	5	2	.714	14	3.26	38⅔	15	12	47	1	0	0	3
1980	Pit-N	0	2	0	1	.000	1	3.86	2⅓	1	1	2	0	0	0	1
1980	Sea-A	4	37	2	3	.400	39	4.37	80⅓	47	27	86	7	0	0	0
1981	NYM-N	4	7	0	3	.000	16	9.39	15⅓	10	5	26	5	0	0	3
Career average		21	34	8	10	.452	68	3.78	161⅓	74	47	168	12	6	2	1
Cubs average		**13**	**26**	**4**	**5**	**.438**	**51**	**4.70**	**97⅔**	**39**	**34**	**107**	**9**	**2**	**1**	**1**
Career total		277	445	103	125	.452	882	3.78	2099	957	615	2188	155	77	20	15
Cubs total		**26**	**52**	**7**	**9**	**.438**	**102**	**4.70**	**195⅓**	**77**	**68**	**214**	**18**	**3**	**1**	**2**

Roberts, Robin Evan

HEIGHT: 6'0"   RIGHTHANDER   BORN: 9/30/1926 SPRINGFIELD, ILLINOIS

YEAR	TEAM	STARTS	GAMES	WON	LOST	PCT	ER	ERA	INNINGS PITCHED	STRIKE-OUTS	WALKS	HITS ALLOWED	HRS ALLOWED	COMP. GAMES	SHUT-OUTS	SAVES
1948	Phi-N	20	20	7	9	.438	52	3.19	146 2/3	84	61	148	10	9	0	0
1949	Phi-N	31	43	15	15	.500	93	3.69	226 2/3	95	75	229	15	11	3	4
1950	Phi-N	39	40	20	11	.645	102	3.02	304 1/3	146	77	282	29	21	5	1
1951	Phi-N	39	44	21	15	.583	106	3.03	315	127	64	284	20	22	6	2
1952	Phi-N	37	39	28	7	.800	95	2.59	330	148	45	292	22	30	3	2
1953	Phi-N	41	44	23	16	.590	106	2.75	346 2/3	198	61	324	30	33	5	2
1954	Phi-N	38	45	23	15	.605	111	2.97	336 2/3	185	56	289	35	29	4	4
1955	Phi-N	38	41	23	14	.622	111	3.28	305	160	53	292	41	26	1	3
1956	Phi-N	37	43	19	18	.514	147	4.45	297 1/3	157	40	328	46	22	1	3
1957	Phi-N	32	39	10	22	.313	113	4.07	249 2/3	128	43	246	40	14	2	2
1958	Phi-N	34	35	17	14	.548	97	3.24	269 2/3	130	51	270	30	21	1	0
1959	Phi-N	35	35	15	17	.469	122	4.27	257 1/3	137	35	267	34	19	2	0
1960	Phi-N	33	35	12	16	.429	106	4.02	237 1/3	122	34	256	31	13	2	1
1961	Phi-N	18	26	1	10	.091	76	5.85	117	54	23	154	19	2	0	0
1962	Bal-A	25	27	10	9	.526	59	2.78	191 1/3	102	41	176	17	6	2	0
1963	Bal-A	35	35	14	13	.519	93	3.33	251 1/3	124	40	230	35	9	2	0
1964	Bal-A	31	31	13	7	.650	66	2.91	204	109	52	203	18	8	4	0
1965	Bal-A	15	20	5	7	.417	43	3.38	114 2/3	63	20	110	17	5	1	0
1965	Hou-N	10	10	5	2	.714	16	1.89	76	34	10	61	1	3	2	1
1966	Hou-N	12	13	3	5	.375	27	3.82	63 2/3	26	10	79	7	1	1	0
1966	**ChC-N**	**9**	**11**	**2**	**3**	**.400**	**33**	**6.14**	**48 1/3**	**28**	**11**	**62**	**8**	**1**	**0**	**0**
Career average		32	36	15	13	.539	93	3.41	246 2/3	124	47	241	27	16	2	1
Cubs average		**9**	**11**	**2**	**3**	**.400**	**33**	**6.14**	**48 1/3**	**28**	**11**	**62**	**8**	**1**	**0**	**0**
Career total		609	676	286	245	.539	1774	3.41	4688 2/3	2357	902	4582	505	305	45	25
Cubs total		**9**	**11**	**2**	**3**	**.400**	**33**	**6.14**	**48 1/3**	**28**	**11**	**62**	**8**	**1**	**0**	**0**

Robinson, Jeffrey Daniel (Jeff)

HEIGHT: 6'4"   RIGHTHANDER   BORN: 12/13/1960 SANTA ANA, CALIFORNIA

YEAR	TEAM	STARTS	GAMES	WON	LOST	PCT	ER	ERA	INNINGS PITCHED	STRIKE-OUTS	WALKS	HITS ALLOWED	HRS ALLOWED	COMP. GAMES	SHUT-OUTS	SAVES
1984	SF-N	33	34	7	15	.318	87	4.56	171 2/3	102	52	195	12	1	1	0
1985	SF-N	0	8	0	0	—	7	5.11	12 1/3	8	10	16	2	0	0	8
1986	SF-N	1	64	6	3	.667	39	3.36	104 1/3	90	32	92	8	0	0	10
1987	SF-N	0	63	6	8	.429	30	2.79	96 2/3	82	48	69	10	0	0	4
1987	Pit-N	0	18	2	1	.667	9	3.04	26 2/3	19	6	20	1	0	0	9
1988	Pit-N	0	75	11	5	.688	42	3.03	124 2/3	87	39	113	6	0	0	4
1989	Pit-N	19	50	7	13	.350	72	4.58	141 1/3	95	59	161	14	1	0	0
1990	NYY-A	4	54	3	6	.333	34	3.45	88 2/3	43	34	82	8	0	0	3
1991	Cal-A	0	39	0	3	.000	34	5.37	57	57	29	56	9	0	0	1
1992	**ChC-N**	**5**	**49**	**4**	**3**	**.571**	**26**	**3.00**	**78**	**46**	**40**	**76**	**5**	**0**	**0**	**4**
Career average		7	50	5	6	.447	42	3.79	100	70	39	98	8	0	0	4
Cubs average		**5**	**49**	**4**	**3**	**.571**	**26**	**3.00**	**78**	**46**	**40**	**76**	**5**	**0**	**0**	**1**
Career total		62	454	46	57	.447	380	3.79	901 1/3	629	349	880	75	2	1	39
Cubs total		**5**	**49**	**4**	**3**	**.571**	**26**	**3.00**	**78**	**46**	**40**	**76**	**5**	**0**	**0**	**1**

Rodriguez, Fernando Pedro (Freddy)

HEIGHT: 6'0"   RIGHTHANDER   BORN: 4/29/1924 HAVANA, CUBA

YEAR	TEAM	STARTS	GAMES	WON	LOST	PCT	ER	ERA	INNINGS PITCHED	STRIKE-OUTS	WALKS	HITS ALLOWED	HRS ALLOWED	COMP. GAMES	SHUT-OUTS	SAVES
1958	**ChC-N**	**0**	**7**	**0**	**0**	**—**	**6**	**7.36**	**7 1/3**	**5**	**5**	**8**	**2**	**0**	**0**	**2**
1959	Phi-N	0	1	0	0	—	3	13.50	2	1	0	4	1	0	0	0
Career average		0	4	0	0	—	5	8.68	4 2/3	3	3	6	2	0	0	1
Cubs average		**0**	**7**	**0**	**0**	**—**	**6**	**7.36**	**7 1/3**	**5**	**5**	**8**	**2**	**0**	**0**	**2**
Career total		0	8	0	0	—	9	8.68	9 1/3	6	5	12	3	0	0	2
Cubs total		**0**	**7**	**0**	**0**	**—**	**6**	**7.36**	**7 1/3**	**5**	**5**	**8**	**2**	**0**	**0**	**2**

Rodriguez, Roberto (Bobby)
HEIGHT: 6'3" RIGHTHANDER BORN: 11/29/1941 CARACAS, VENEZUELA

YEAR	TEAM	STARTS	GAMES	WON	LOST	PCT	ER	ERA	INNINGS PITCHED	STRIKE-OUTS	WALKS	HITS ALLOWED	HRS ALLOWED	COMP. GAMES	SHUT-OUTS	SAVES
1967	KCA-A	5	15	1	1	.500	16	3.57	40 ⅓	29	14	42	4	0	0	2
1970	Oak-A	0	6	0	0	—	4	2.92	12 ⅓	8	3	10	2	0	0	0
1970	SD-N	0	10	0	0	—	12	6.61	16 ⅓	8	5	26	1	0	0	3
1970	**ChC-N**	**0**	**26**	**3**	**2**	**.600**	**28**	**5.82**	**43 ⅓**	**46**	**15**	**50**	**6**	**0**	**0**	**2**
Career average		3	29	2	2	.571	30	4.81	56 ⅓	46	19	64	7	0	0	4
Cubs average		**0**	**26**	**3**	**2**	**.600**	**28**	**5.82**	**43 ⅓**	**46**	**15**	**50**	**6**	**0**	**0**	**2**
Career total		5	57	4	3	.571	60	4.81	112 ⅓	91	37	128	13	0	0	7
Cubs total		**0**	**26**	**3**	**2**	**.600**	**28**	**5.82**	**43 ⅓**	**46**	**15**	**50**	**6**	**0**	**0**	**2**

Rojas, Melquiades (Mel)
HEIGHT: 5'11" RIGHTHANDER BORN: 12/10/1966 HAINA, DOMINICAN REPUBLIC

YEAR	TEAM	STARTS	GAMES	WON	LOST	PCT	ER	ERA	INNINGS PITCHED	STRIKE-OUTS	WALKS	HITS ALLOWED	HRS ALLOWED	COMP. GAMES	SHUT-OUTS	SAVES
1990	Mon-N	0	23	3	1	.750	16	3.60	40	26	24	34	5	0	0	1
1991	Mon-N	0	37	3	3	.500	20	3.75	48	37	13	42	4	0	0	6
1992	Mon-N	0	68	7	1	.875	16	1.43	100 ⅔	70	34	71	2	0	0	10
1993	Mon-N	0	66	5	8	.385	29	2.95	88 ⅓	48	30	80	6	0	0	10
1994	Mon-N	0	58	3	2	.600	31	3.32	84	84	21	71	11	0	0	16
1995	Mon-N	0	59	1	4	.200	31	4.12	67 ⅔	61	29	69	2	0	0	30
1996	Mon-N	0	74	7	4	.636	29	3.22	81	92	28	56	5	0	0	36
1997	**ChC-N**	**0**	**54**	**0**	**4**	**.000**	**29**	**4.42**	**59**	**61**	**30**	**54**	**11**	**0**	**0**	**13**
1997	NYM-N	0	23	0	2	.000	15	5.13	26 ⅓	32	6	24	4	0	0	2
1998	NYM-N	0	50	5	2	.714	39	6.05	58	41	30	68	9	0	0	2
1999	LA-N	0	5	0	0	—	7	12.60	5	3	3	5	3	0	0	0
1999	Det-A	0	5	0	0	—	16	22.74	6 ⅓	6	4	12	3	0	0	0
1999	Mon-N	0	3	0	0	—	5	16.88	2 ⅔	1	2	5	0	0	0	0
Career average		0	53	3	3	.523	28	3.82	66 ⅔	56	25	59	7	0	0	13
Cubs average		**0**	**54**	**0**	**4**	**.000**	**29**	**4.42**	**59**	**61**	**30**	**54**	**11**	**0**	**0**	**13**
Career total		0	525	34	31	.523	283	3.82	667	562	254	591	65	0	0	126
Cubs total		**0**	**54**	**0**	**4**	**.000**	**29**	**4.42**	**59**	**61**	**30**	**54**	**11**	**0**	**0**	**13**

Root, Charles Henry (Charlie *or* Chinski)
HEIGHT: 5'10" RIGHTHANDER BORN: 3/17/1899 MIDDLETOWN, OHIO DIED: 11/5/1970 HOLLISTER, CALIFORNIA

YEAR	TEAM	STARTS	GAMES	WON	LOST	PCT	ER	ERA	INNINGS PITCHED	STRIKE-OUTS	WALKS	HITS ALLOWED	HRS ALLOWED	COMP. GAMES	SHUT-OUTS	SAVES
1923	StL-A	2	27	0	4	.000	38	5.70	60	27	18	68	4	0	0	0
1926	ChC-N	31	42	18	17	.514	85	2.82	271 ⅓	127	62	267	10	21	2	2
1927	ChC-N	36	48	26	15	.634	129	3.76	309	145	117	296	16	21	4	2
1928	ChC-N	30	40	14	18	.438	94	3.57	237	122	73	214	15	13	1	2
1929	ChC-N	31	43	19	6	.760	105	3.47	272	124	83	286	12	19	4	5
1930	ChC-N	30	37	16	14	.533	106	4.33	220 ⅓	124	63	247	17	15	4	3
1931	ChC-N	31	39	17	14	.548	97	3.48	251	131	71	240	7	19	3	2
1932	ChC-N	24	39	15	10	.600	86	3.58	216 ⅓	96	55	211	10	11	0	3
1933	ChC-N	30	35	15	10	.600	70	2.60	242 ⅓	86	61	232	14	20	2	0
1934	ChC-N	9	34	4	7	.364	56	4.28	117 ⅔	46	53	141	8	2	0	0
1935	ChC-N	18	38	15	8	.652	69	3.08	201 ⅓	94	47	193	15	11	1	2
1936	ChC-N	3	33	3	6	.333	34	4.15	73 ⅔	32	20	81	3	0	0	1
1937	ChC-N	15	43	13	5	.722	67	3.38	178 ⅔	74	32	173	18	5	0	5
1938	ChC-N	11	44	8	7	.533	51	2.86	160 ⅔	70	30	163	10	5	0	8
1939	ChC-N	16	35	8	8	.500	75	4.03	167 ⅓	65	34	189	11	8	0	4
1940	ChC-N	8	36	2	4	.333	48	3.86	112	50	33	118	9	1	0	1
1941	ChC-N	15	19	8	7	.533	64	5.40	106 ⅔	46	37	133	8	6	0	0
Career average		20	37	12	9	.557	75	3.59	188	86	52	191	11	10	1	2
Cubs average		**21**	**38**	**13**	**10**	**.563**	**77**	**3.55**	**196**	**90**	**54**	**199**	**11**	**11**	**1**	**3**
Career total		340	632	201	160	.557	1274	3.59	3197 ⅓	1459	889	3252	187	177	21	40
Cubs total		**338**	**605**	**201**	**156**	**.563**	**1236**	**3.55**	**3137 ⅓**	**1432**	**871**	**3184**	**183**	**177**	**21**	**40**

Charles (Charlie) Henry "Chinski" Root, rhp, 1923–41

Only one Chicago Cubs pitcher has cracked the 200-win barrier in the Windy City, and that man was Charles Henry Root.

Root, born on March 17, 1899, in Middletown, Ohio, got his start with the old St. Louis Browns of the American League in 1923. But by his own admission years later, the powerfully built Root (5'10", 190 pounds) wasn't yet ready for the big leagues, going 0-4, with a 5.70 ERA that season.

He spent a couple of years in the minor leagues before the Cubs bought his contract and brought him up to Chicago for good in 1926. Root made his mark immediately, leading the team in wins (18), games started (32), complete games (21), innings pitched (271⅓) and strikeouts (127) that season.

Thus began a string of eight consecutive years in which Root would earn 14 or more victories for the Cubs. His best season was 1927—he went 26-15, led the National League in wins, appearances

(48) and innings pitched (309) and had a team-high 145 strikeouts.

Root was the backbone of the Cubs staff in 1929 and 1932, when Chicago won the National League championship. Throughout his career, the hard-throwing Root staked out the inside of the plate as his own by throwing "chin music" to stubborn batters. He was a tough, durable competitor.

That is why it is almost silly to believe that Yankees hitter George Herman "Babe" Ruth would have challenged Root in the 1932 World Series by "calling his shot" in the fifth inning of Game 3.

In fact, after reading the recollections of every Cub and Yankee who ever spoke about it—including Ruth—it's clear that at the time, very few people believed that Ruth had deliberately pointed to the center-field bleachers and announced he would hit a home run. As Cubs catcher Charles Leo "Gabby" Hartnett astutely pointed out years later, Ruth almost never hit home runs into center field; most of his shots landed in right field.

The Cubs were decided underdogs in the 1932 World Series, and they didn't disprove prognosti-

Ross, Gary Douglas

HEIGHT: 6'1"   RIGHTHANDER   BORN: 9/16/1947 MCKEESPORT, PENNSYLVANIA

YEAR	TEAM	STARTS	GAMES	WON	LOST	PCT	ER	ERA	INNINGS PITCHED	STRIKE-OUTS	WALKS	HITS ALLOWED	HRS ALLOWED	COMP. GAMES	SHUT-OUTS	SAVES
1968	ChC-N	5	13	1	1	.500	19	4.17	41	31	25	44	1	1	0	0
1969	ChC-N	1	2	0	0	—	3	13.50	2	2	2	1	0	0	0	0
1969	SD-N	7	46	3	12	.200	51	4.19	109⅔	58	56	104	5	0	0	3
1970	SD-N	2	33	2	3	.400	36	5.20	62⅓	39	36	72	8	0	0	1
1971	SD-N	0	13	1	3	.250	8	2.96	24⅓	13	11	27	0	0	0	0
1972	SD-N	0	60	4	3	.571	25	2.45	91⅔	46	49	87	2	0	0	3
1973	SD-N	0	58	4	4	.500	46	5.42	76⅓	44	33	93	8	0	0	0
1974	SD-N	0	9	0	0	—	9	4.50	18	11	6	23	1	0	0	0
1975	Cal-A	1	1	0	1	.000	3	5.40	5	4	1	6	1	0	0	0
1976	Cal-A	31	34	8	16	.333	75	3.00	225	100	58	224	12	7	2	0
1977	Cal-A	12	14	2	4	.333	36	5.55	58⅓	30	11	83	10	0	0	1
Career average	6	28	3	5	.347	31	3.92	71⅓	38	29	76	5	1	0	1
Cubs average	**3**	**8**	**1**	**1**	**.500**	**11**	**4.60**	**21⅔**	**17**	**14**	**23**	**1**	**1**	**0**	**0**
Career total	59	283	25	47	.347	311	3.92	713⅔	378	288	764	48	8	2	7
Cubs total	**6**	**15**	**1**	**1**	**.500**	**22**	**4.60**	**43**	**33**	**27**	**45**	**1**	**1**	**0**	**0**

cators in the first two games, falling 12-6 and 5-2. So when Ruth and the Yankees came to Chicago for the next two tilts, they endured a mountain of fan frustration.

Many of the Cubs players, like Root and pitchers Guy Bush and Perce Leigh "Pat" Malone, were not above razzing the opposition. The kindest epithet Ruth heard as Game 3 wore on was "Big Monkey." As nasty as things got, Ruth was well aware of Root's reputation as a knockdown pitcher. By the fifth inning, he was just hoping to make contact or, failing that, foul a ball into the Cubs dugout. The name-calling was getting to Ruth, though. So, with two strikes on him, Ruth pointed at Root and said, minus the expletives, "It only takes one to hit it, busher!"

Years later, Root explained that he thought Ruth would expect him to "waste" a pitch outside and decided to cross the Yankees slugger up by bringing one inside.

"It was gone," said Root ruefully, "as soon as I let it go."

"If I had pointed to the outfield that day," Ruth told a teammate years later, "Root would have knocked me on my ass."

After the 1933 season, Root's effectiveness waned. The man his teammates called "Chinski"— he had a penchant for throwing balls that grazed batters' chins—would have strong seasons, such as 1935,when he was 15-8, sandwiched between years of three and four wins. He became a spot starter and bull pen performer for the Cubs from 1937 to 1939, picking up 13 saves in that span. His final season, 1941, was pretty good; Root was 8-7 with six complete games.

Following his retirement, Root worked as a coach for the Cubs and in Chicago's minor league organization. Root died in 1970. In 1969 he had been named the franchise's greatest-ever righthander.

Root is at or near the top of most Cubs pitching categories. He is first in wins with 201, games played with 605, innings pitched with 3,137⅓, hits allowed with 3,184 and years of service (16) among pitchers.

He is also 2nd in losses with 156, complete games with 177, home runs allowed with 183, walks issued with 871 and strikeouts with 1,432. Root is also 4th in games started for the Cubs with 340, 10th in shutouts with 21 and 7th in relief appearances with 233.

Rowan, John Albert (Jack)

HEIGHT: 6'1"   RIGHTHANDER   BORN: 6/16/1887 NEW CASTLE, PENNSYLVANIA   DIED: 9/29/1966 DAYTON, OHIO

YEAR	TEAM	STARTS	GAMES	WON	LOST	PCT	ER	ERA	INNINGS PITCHED	STRIKE-OUTS	WALKS	HITS ALLOWED	HRS ALLOWED	COMP. GAMES	SHUT-OUTS	SAVES
1906	Det-A	1	1	0	1	.000	11	11.00	9	0	6	15	0	1	0	0
1908	Cin-N	7	8	3	3	.500	10	1.82	49⅓	24	16	46	0	4	1	0
1909	Cin-N	23	38	11	12	.478	70	2.79	225⅔	81	104	185	0	14	0	0
1910	Cin-N	30	42	14	13	.519	85	2.93	261	108	105	242	4	18	4	1
1911	Phi-N	6	12	2	4	.333	24	4.73	45⅔	17	20	59	3	2	0	0
1911	**ChC-N**	**0**	**1**	**0**	**0**	—	**1**	**4.50**	**2**	**0**	**2**	**1**	**0**	**0**	**0**	**0**
1913	Cin-N	5	5	0	4	.000	13	3.00	39	21	9	37	0	5	0	0
1914	Cin-N	2	12	1	3	.250	15	3.46	39	16	10	38	1	0	0	2
Career average		11	17	4	6	.437	33	3.07	95⅔	38	39	89	1	6	1	0
Cubs average		**0**	**1**	**0**	**0**	—	**1**	**4.50**	**2**	**0**	**2**	**1**	**0**	**0**	**0**	**0**
Career total		74	119	31	40	.437	229	3.07	670⅔	267	272	623	8	44	5	3
Cubs total		**0**	**1**	**0**	**0**	—	**1**	**4.50**	**2**	**0**	**2**	**1**	**0**	**0**	**0**	**0**

Rowe, David Elwood (Dave)
HEIGHT: 5'9"   RIGHTHANDER   BORN: 10/9/1854 HARRISBURG, PENNSYLVANIA   DIED: 12/9/1930 GLENDALE, CALIFORNIA

YEAR	TEAM	STARTS	GAMES	WON	LOST	PCT	ER	ERA	INNINGS PITCHED	STRIKE-OUTS	WALKS	HITS ALLOWED	HRS ALLOWED	COMP. GAMES	SHUT-OUTS	SAVES
1877	ChN-N	1	1	0	1	.000	2	18.00	1	0	2	3	0	0	0	0
1882	Cle-N	1	1	0	1	.000	12	12.00	9	0	7	29	3	1	0	0
1883	Bal-AA	0	1	0	0	—	9	20.25	4	1	2	12	1	0	0	0
1884	STL-U	1	1	1	0	1.000	2	2.00	9	2	0	10	0	1	0	0
Career average		1	1	0	1	.333	6	9.78	5 2/3	1	3	14	1	1	0	0
Cubs average		**1**	**1**	**0**	**1**	**.000**	**2**	**18.00**	**1**	**0**	**2**	**3**	**0**	**0**	**0**	**0**
Career total		3	4	1	2	.333	25	9.78	23	3	11	54	4	2	0	0
Cubs total		**1**	**1**	**0**	**1**	**.000**	**2**	**18.00**	**1**	**0**	**2**	**3**	**0**	**0**	**0**	**0**

Roy, Luther Franklin
HEIGHT: 5'10"   RIGHTHANDER   BORN: 7/29/1902 OOLETEWAH, TENNESSEE   DIED: 7/24/1963 GRAND RAPIDS, MICHIGAN

YEAR	TEAM	STARTS	GAMES	WON	LOST	PCT	ER	ERA	INNINGS PITCHED	STRIKE-OUTS	WALKS	HITS ALLOWED	HRS ALLOWED	COMP. GAMES	SHUT-OUTS	SAVES
1924	Cle-A	5	16	0	5	.000	42	7.77	48 2/3	14	31	62	3	2	0	0
1925	Cle-A	1	6	0	0	—	4	3.60	10	1	11	14	1	0	0	0
1927	ChC-N	0	11	3	1	.750	5	2.29	19 2/3	5	11	14	0	0	0	0
1929	Phi-N	11	21	3	6	.333	83	8.42	88 2/3	16	37	137	11	1	0	0
1929	Bro-N	0	2	0	0	—	2	4.91	3 2/3	0	2	4	0	0	0	0
Career average		4	14	2	3	.333	34	7.17	42 2/3	9	23	58	4	1	0	0
Cubs average		**0**	**11**	**3**	**1**	**.750**	**5**	**2.29**	**19 2/3**	**5**	**11**	**14**	**0**	**0**	**0**	**0**
Career total		17	56	6	12	.333	136	7.17	170 2/3	36	92	231	15	3	0	0
Cubs total		**0**	**11**	**3**	**1**	**.750**	**5**	**2.29**	**19 2/3**	**5**	**11**	**14**	**0**	**0**	**0**	**0**

Ruether, Walter Henry (Dutch)
HEIGHT: 6'1"   LEFTHANDER   BORN: 9/13/1893 ALAMEDA, CALIFORNIA   DIED: 5/16/1970 PHOENIX, ARIZONA

YEAR	TEAM	STARTS	GAMES	WON	LOST	PCT	ER	ERA	INNINGS PITCHED	STRIKE-OUTS	WALKS	HITS ALLOWED	HRS ALLOWED	COMP. GAMES	SHUT-OUTS	SAVES
1917	ChC-N	4	10	2	0	1.000	10	2.48	36 1/3	23	12	37	0	1	0	0
1917	Cin-N	4	7	1	2	.333	14	3.53	35 2/3	12	14	43	0	1	1	0
1918	Cin-N	2	2	0	1	.000	3	2.70	10	10	3	10	0	1	0	0
1919	Cin-N	29	33	19	6	.760	49	1.82	242 2/3	78	83	195	1	20	3	0
1920	Cin-N	33	37	16	12	.571	73	2.47	265 2/3	99	96	235	1	23	5	3
1921	Bro-N	27	36	10	13	.435	100	4.26	211 1/3	78	67	247	7	12	1	2
1922	Bro-N	35	35	21	12	.636	105	3.53	267 1/3	89	92	290	11	26	2	0
1923	Bro-N	34	34	15	14	.517	129	4.22	275	87	86	308	11	20	0	3
1924	Bro-N	21	30	8	13	.381	73	3.91	168	63	45	190	4	13	2	0
1925	Was-A	29	30	18	7	.720	96	3.87	223 1/3	68	105	241	5	16	1	0
1926	Was-A	23	23	12	6	.667	91	4.84	169 1/3	48	66	214	5	9	0	0
1926	NYY-A	5	5	2	3	.400	14	3.50	36	8	18	32	0	1	0	0
1927	NYY-A	26	27	13	6	.684	69	3.38	184	45	52	202	8	12	3	0
Career average		25	28	12	9	.591	75	3.50	193	64	67	204	5	14	2	1
Cubs average		**4**	**10**	**2**	**0**	**1.000**	**10**	**2.48**	**36 1/3**	**23**	**12**	**37**	**0**	**1**	**0**	**0**
Career total		272	309	137	95	.591	826	3.50	2124 2/3	708	739	2244	53	155	18	8
Cubs total		**4**	**10**	**2**	**0**	**1.000**	**10**	**2.48**	**36 1/3**	**23**	**12**	**37**	**0**	**1**	**0**	**0**

Rush, Robert Ransom (Bob)
HEIGHT: 6'4"   RIGHTHANDER   BORN: 12/21/1925 BATTLE CREEK, MICHIGAN

YEAR	TEAM	STARTS	GAMES	WON	LOST	PCT	ER	ERA	INNINGS PITCHED	STRIKE-OUTS	WALKS	HITS ALLOWED	HRS ALLOWED	COMP. GAMES	SHUT-OUTS	SAVES
1948	ChC-N	16	36	5	11	.313	58	3.92	133 1/3	72	37	153	8	4	0	0
1949	ChC-N	27	35	10	18	.357	91	4.07	201	80	79	197	10	9	1	4
1950	ChC-N	34	39	13	20	.394	105	3.71	254 2/3	93	93	261	11	19	1	1
1951	ChC-N	29	37	11	12	.478	90	3.83	211 1/3	129	68	212	16	12	2	2
1952	ChC-N	32	34	17	13	.567	75	2.70	250 1/3	157	81	205	14	17	4	0

(continued)

Robert (Bob) Ransom Rush, rhp, 1948–60

The Cubs' best pitcher of the 1950s, Bob Rush was a solid hurler who also had the distinction of being one of the few players developed by the anorexic Cubs farm system in the early- to mid-20th century.

Rush was born on December 21, 1925, in Battle Creek, Michigan. As a 22-year-old rookie, Rush struggled to a 5-11 record with the Cubs in 1948. He got better, winning at least 10 games for Chicago in seven of the next eight seasons, including a 17-13 mark in 1952, and a 13-10 mark with 13 complete games in 1956.

But the Cubs mostly got worse. In Rush's 10 seasons with Chicago, the Cubs never had a winning season and never finished higher than fifth in the National League. That Rush managed three winning seasons in that span is fairly impressive, since the team for which he played finished an average of 23 games under .500.

Rush's 1952 season was his high-water mark with Chicago. He had a seven-game winning streak that included three shutouts, and he was also the winning pitcher in the All-Star Game that year.

Rush won 95 games from 1950 to 1957, the most of any Cub in that decade. His 3.65 ERA was the Cubs' best in the 1950s, as was his 99 complete games, 924 strikeouts, 249 starts and 1,798⅓ innings pitched.

The baseball gods finally smiled on Rush in 1958—the Cubs traded him to the defending world champion Milwaukee Braves. Rush helped the Braves win the 1958 pennant and pitched Game 3 of the World Series against the Yankees. Rush threw a three-hitter over six strong innings, but the Yankees won the game, 4-0.

Rush pitched two more years before retiring in 1960. He is sixth all-time on the Cubs for most starts with 292, seventh in strikeouts with 1,076, tied for fifth in terms of years of service as a pitcher with Chicago with 10 and is third in most losses with 140.

(continued)

YEAR	TEAM	STARTS	GAMES	WON	LOST	PCT	ER	ERA	INNINGS PITCHED	STRIKE-OUTS	WALKS	HITS ALLOWED	HRS ALLOWED	COMP. GAMES	SHUT-OUTS	SAVES
1953	ChC-N	28	29	9	14	.391	84	4.54	166 ⅔	84	66	177	17	8	1	0
1954	ChC-N	32	33	13	15	.464	99	3.77	236 ⅓	124	103	213	12	11	0	0
1955	ChC-N	33	33	13	11	.542	91	3.50	234	130	73	204	19	14	3	0
1956	ChC-N	32	32	13	10	.565	85	3.19	239 ⅔	104	59	210	30	13	1	0
1957	ChC-N	29	31	6	16	.273	100	4.38	205 ⅓	103	66	211	16	5	0	0
1958	Mil-N	20	28	10	6	.625	56	3.42	147 ⅓	84	31	142	13	5	2	0
1959	Mil-N	9	31	5	6	.455	27	2.40	101 ⅓	64	23	102	5	1	1	0
1960	Mil-N	0	10	2	0	1.000	7	4.20	15	8	5	24	2	0	0	1
1960	CWS-A	0	9	0	0	—	9	5.65	14 ⅓	12	5	16	4	0	0	0
Career average		25	32	10	12	.455	75	3.65	185 ⅓	96	61	179	14	9	1	1
Cubs average		**29**	**34**	**11**	**14**	**.440**	**88**	**3.71**	**213 ⅓**	**108**	**73**	**204**	**15**	**11**	**1**	**1**
Career total		321	417	127	152	.455	977	3.65	2410 ⅔	1244	789	2327	177	118	16	8
Cubs total		**292**	**339**	**110**	**140**	**.440**	**878**	**3.71**	**2132 ⅔**	**1076**	**725**	**2043**	**153**	**112**	**13**	**7**

Russell, Jack Erwin

HEIGHT: 6'1" RIGHTHANDER BORN: 10/24/1905 PARIS, TEXAS DIED: 11/3/1990 CLEARWATER, FLORIDA

YEAR	TEAM	STARTS	GAMES	WON	LOST	PCT	ER	ERA	INNINGS PITCHED	STRIKE-OUTS	WALKS	HITS ALLOWED	HRS ALLOWED	COMP. GAMES	SHUT-OUTS	SAVES
1926	Bos-A	5	36	0	5	.000	39	3.58	98	17	24	94	2	1	0	0
1927	Bos-A	15	34	4	9	.308	67	4.10	147	25	40	172	5	4	1	0
1928	Bos-A	26	32	11	14	.440	86	3.84	201 ⅓	27	41	233	6	10	2	0
1929	Bos-A	32	35	6	18	.250	99	3.92	227 ⅓	37	40	263	12	13	0	0
1930	Bos-A	30	35	9	20	.310	139	5.45	229 ⅔	35	53	302	11	15	0	0
1931	Bos-A	31	36	10	18	.357	133	5.16	232	45	65	298	7	13	0	0

(continued)

(Russell, continued)

YEAR	TEAM	STARTS	GAMES	WON	LOST	PCT	ER	ERA	INNINGS PITCHED	STRIKE-OUTS	WALKS	HITS ALLOWED	HRS ALLOWED	COMP. GAMES	SHUT-OUTS	SAVES
1932	Bos-A	6	11	1	7	.125	30	6.81	39 2/3	7	15	61	2	1	0	0
1932	Cle-A	11	18	5	7	.417	59	4.70	113	27	27	146	5	6	0	1
1933	Was-A	3	50	12	6	.667	37	2.69	124	28	32	119	3	2	0	13
1934	Was-A	9	54	5	10	.333	73	4.17	157 2/3	38	56	179	6	3	0	7
1935	Was-A	7	43	4	9	.308	80	5.71	126	30	37	170	10	2	0	3
1936	Was-A	5	18	3	2	.600	35	6.34	49 2/3	6	25	66	3	1	0	3
1936	Bos-A	2	23	0	3	.000	25	5.63	40	9	16	57	2	0	0	0
1937	Det-A	0	25	2	5	.286	34	7.59	40 1/3	10	20	63	4	0	0	4
1938	**ChC-N**	**0**	**42**	**6**	**1**	**.857**	**38**	**3.34**	**102 1/3**	**29**	**30**	**100**	**1**	**0**	**0**	**3**
1939	**ChC-N**	**0**	**39**	**4**	**3**	**.571**	**28**	**3.67**	**68 2/3**	**32**	**24**	**78**	**3**	**0**	**0**	**3**
1940	StL-N	0	26	3	4	.429	15	2.50	54	16	26	53	1	0	0	1
Career average		12	37	6	9	.376	68	4.46	136 2/3	28	38	164	6	5	0	3
Cubs average		**0**	**41**	**5**	**2**	**.714**	**33**	**3.47**	**85 2/3**	**31**	**27**	**89**	**2**	**0**	**0**	**3**
Career total		182	557	85	141	.376	1017	4.46	2050 2/3	418	571	2454	83	71	3	38
Cubs total		**0**	**81**	**10**	**4**	**.714**	**66**	**3.47**	**171**	**61**	**54**	**178**	**4**	**0**	**0**	**6**

Ruthven, Richard David (Dick *or* Rufus)

HEIGHT: 6'3" RIGHTHANDER BORN: 3/27/1951 SACRAMENTO, CALIFORNIA

YEAR	TEAM	STARTS	GAMES	WON	LOST	PCT	ER	ERA	INNINGS PITCHED	STRIKE-OUTS	WALKS	HITS ALLOWED	HRS ALLOWED	COMP. GAMES	SHUT-OUTS	SAVES
1973	Phi-N	23	25	6	9	.400	60	4.21	128 1/3	98	75	125	10	3	1	1
1974	Phi-N	35	35	9	13	.409	95	4.02	212 1/3	153	116	182	11	6	0	0
1975	Phi-N	7	11	2	2	.500	19	4.20	40 2/3	26	22	37	2	0	0	0
1976	Atl-N	36	36	14	17	.452	112	4.19	240 1/3	142	90	255	14	8	4	0
1977	Atl-N	23	25	7	13	.350	71	4.23	151	84	62	158	14	6	2	0
1978	Atl-N	13	13	2	6	.250	37	4.11	81	45	28	78	8	2	1	0
1978	Phi-N	20	20	13	5	.722	50	2.99	150 2/3	75	28	136	13	9	2	0
1979	Phi-N	20	20	7	5	.583	58	4.27	122 1/3	58	37	121	10	3	2	0
1980	Phi-N	33	33	17	10	.630	88	3.55	223 1/3	86	74	241	9	6	1	0
1981	Phi-N	22	23	12	7	.632	84	5.15	146 2/3	80	54	162	10	5	0	0
1982	Phi-N	31	33	11	11	.500	86	3.79	204 1/3	115	59	189	18	8	2	0
1983	Phi-N	7	7	1	3	.250	21	5.61	33 2/3	26	10	46	5	0	0	0
1983	**ChC-N**	**25**	**25**	**12**	**9**	**.571**	**68**	**4.10**	**149 1/3**	**73**	**28**	**156**	**17**	**5**	**2**	**0**
1984	**ChC-N**	**22**	**23**	**6**	**10**	**.375**	**71**	**5.04**	**126 2/3**	**55**	**41**	**154**	**14**	**0**	**0**	**0**
1985	**ChC-N**	**15**	**20**	**4**	**7**	**.364**	**44**	**4.53**	**87 1/3**	**26**	**37**	**103**	**6**	**0**	**0**	**0**
1986	**ChC-N**	**0**	**6**	**0**	**0**	**—**	**6**	**5.06**	**10 2/3**	**3**	**6**	**12**	**4**	**0**	**0**	**0**
Career average		24	25	9	9	.492	69	4.14	150 1/3	82	55	154	12	4	1	0
Cubs average		**16**	**19**	**6**	**7**	**.458**	**47**	**4.55**	**93 2/3**	**39**	**28**	**106**	**10**	**1**	**1**	**0**
Career total		332	355	123	127	.492	970	4.14	2109	1145	767	2155	165	61	17	1
Cubs total		**62**	**74**	**22**	**26**	**.458**	**189**	**4.55**	**374**	**157**	**112**	**425**	**41**	**5**	**2**	**0**

Ryan, James Edward (Jimmy *or* Pony)

HEIGHT: 5'9" LEFTHANDER BORN: 2/11/1863 CLINTON, MASSACHUSETTS   DIED: 10/26/1923 CHICAGO, ILLINOIS

YEAR	TEAM	STARTS	GAMES	WON	LOST	PCT	ER	ERA	INNINGS PITCHED	STRIKE-OUTS	WALKS	HITS ALLOWED	HRS ALLOWED	COMP. GAMES	SHUT-OUTS	SAVES
1886	ChN-N	0	5	0	0	—	12	4.63	23 1/3	15	13	19	3	0	0	1
1887	ChN-N	3	8	2	1	.667	21	4.20	45	14	17	70	3	2	0	0
1888	ChN-N	2	8	4	0	1.000	13	3.05	38 1/3	11	12	47	2	1	0	0
1891	ChN-N	0	2	1	0	1.000	1	1.59	5 2/3	2	2	11	0	0	0	0
1893	ChN-N	0	1	0	0	—	0	0.00	4 2/3	1	0	3	0	0	0	0
Career average		1	5	1	0	.875	9	3.62	23 1/3	9	9	30	2	1	0	0
Cubs average		**1**	**5**	**1**	**0**	**.875**	**9**	**3.62**	**23 1/3**	**9**	**9**	**30**	**2**	**1**	**0**	**0**
Career total		5	24	7	1	.875	47	3.62	117	43	44	150	8	3	0	1
Cubs total		**5**	**24**	**7**	**1**	**.875**	**47**	**3.62**	**117**	**43**	**44**	**150**	**8**	**3**	**0**	**1**

Sanders, Scott Gerald
HEIGHT: 6'4"   RIGHTHANDER   BORN: 3/25/1969 HANNIBAL, MISSOURI

YEAR	TEAM	STARTS	GAMES	WON	LOST	PCT	ER	ERA	INNINGS PITCHED	STRIKE-OUTS	WALKS	HITS ALLOWED	HRS ALLOWED	COMP. GAMES	SHUT-OUTS	SAVES
1993	SD-N	9	9	3	3	.500	24	4.13	52 1/3	37	23	54	4	0	0	0
1994	SD-N	20	23	4	8	.333	59	4.78	111	109	48	103	10	0	0	1
1995	SD-N	15	17	5	5	.500	43	4.30	90	88	31	79	14	1	0	0
1996	SD-N	16	46	9	5	.643	54	3.38	144	157	48	117	10	0	0	2
1997	Sea-A	6	33	3	6	.333	47	6.47	65 1/3	62	38	73	16	0	0	2
1997	Det-A	14	14	3	8	.273	44	5.33	74 1/3	58	24	79	14	1	1	0
1998	Det-A	2	3	0	2	.000	19	17.69	9 2/3	6	6	24	1	0	0	0
1998	SD-N	0	23	3	1	.750	14	4.11	30 2/3	26	5	33	5	0	0	0
1999	**ChC-N**	**6**	**67**	**4**	**7**	**.364**	**64**	**5.52**	**104 1/3**	**89**	**53**	**112**	**19**	**0**	**0**	**2**
Career average		13	34	5	6	.430	53	4.86	97 1/3	90	39	96	13	0	0	1
Cubs average		**6**	**67**	**4**	**7**	**.364**	**64**	**5.52**	**104 1/3**	**89**	**53**	**112**	**19**	**0**	**0**	**2**
Career total		88	235	34	45	.430	368	4.86	681 2/3	632	276	674	93	2	1	5
Cubs total		**6**	**67**	**4**	**7**	**.364**	**64**	**5.52**	**104 1/3**	**89**	**53**	**112**	**19**	**0**	**0**	**2**

Sanderson, Scott Douglas
HEIGHT: 6'5"   RIGHTHANDER   BORN: 7/22/1956 DEARBORN, MICHIGAN

YEAR	TEAM	STARTS	GAMES	WON	LOST	PCT	ER	ERA	INNINGS PITCHED	STRIKE-OUTS	WALKS	HITS ALLOWED	HRS ALLOWED	COMP. GAMES	SHUT-OUTS	SAVES
1978	Mon-N	9	10	4	2	.667	17	2.51	61	50	21	52	3	1	1	0
1979	Mon-N	24	34	9	8	.529	64	3.43	168	138	54	148	16	5	3	1
1980	Mon-N	33	33	16	11	.593	73	3.11	211 1/3	125	56	206	18	7	3	0
1981	Mon-N	22	22	9	7	.563	45	2.95	137 1/3	77	31	122	10	4	1	0
1982	Mon-N	32	32	12	12	.500	86	3.46	224	158	58	212	24	7	0	0
1983	Mon-N	16	18	6	7	.462	42	4.65	81 1/3	55	20	98	12	0	0	0
1984	**ChC-N**	**24**	**24**	**8**	**5**	**.615**	**49**	**3.14**	**140 2/3**	**76**	**24**	**140**	**5**	**3**	**0**	**0**
1985	**ChC-N**	**19**	**19**	**5**	**6**	**.455**	**42**	**3.12**	**121**	**80**	**27**	**100**	**13**	**2**	**0**	**0**
1986	**ChC-N**	**28**	**37**	**9**	**11**	**.450**	**79**	**4.19**	**169 2/3**	**124**	**37**	**165**	**21**	**1**	**1**	**1**
1987	**ChC-N**	**22**	**32**	**8**	**9**	**.471**	**69**	**4.29**	**144 2/3**	**106**	**50**	**156**	**23**	**0**	**0**	**2**
1988	**ChC-N**	**0**	**11**	**1**	**2**	**.333**	**9**	**5.28**	**15 1/3**	**6**	**3**	**13**	**1**	**0**	**0**	**0**
1989	**ChC-N**	**23**	**37**	**11**	**9**	**.550**	**64**	**3.94**	**146 1/3**	**86**	**31**	**155**	**16**	**2**	**0**	**0**
1990	Oak-A	34	34	17	11	.607	89	3.88	206 1/3	128	66	205	27	2	1	0
1991	NYY-A	34	34	16	10	.615	88	3.81	208	130	29	200	22	2	2	0
1992	NYY-A	33	33	12	11	.522	106	4.93	193 1/3	104	64	220	28	2	1	0
1993	Cal-A	21	21	7	11	.389	67	4.46	135 1/3	66	27	153	15	4	1	0
1993	SF-N	8	11	4	2	.667	19	3.51	48 2/3	36	7	48	12	0	0	0
1994	CWS-A	14	18	8	4	.667	52	5.09	92	36	12	110	20	1	0	0
1995	Cal-A	7	7	1	3	.250	18	4.12	39 1/3	23	4	48	6	0	0	0
1996	Cal-A	4	5	0	2	.000	15	7.50	18	7	4	39	5	0	0	0
Career average		21	25	9	8	.533	58	3.84	134 2/3	85	33	136	16	2	1	0
Cubs average		**19**	**27**	**7**	**7**	**.500**	**52**	**3.81**	**123**	**80**	**29**	**122**	**13**	**1**	**0**	**1**
Career total		407	472	163	143	.533	1093	3.84	2561 2/3	1611	625	2590	297	43	14	5
Cubs total		**116**	**160**	**42**	**42**	**.500**	**312**	**3.81**	**737 2/3**	**478**	**172**	**729**	**79**	**8**	**1**	**3**

Scanlan, Robert Guy (Bob)
HEIGHT: 6'7"   RIGHTHANDER   BORN: 8/9/1966 BEVERLY HILLS, CALIFORNIA

YEAR	TEAM	STARTS	GAMES	WON	LOST	PCT	ER	ERA	INNINGS PITCHED	STRIKE-OUTS	WALKS	HITS ALLOWED	HRS ALLOWED	COMP. GAMES	SHUT-OUTS	SAVES
1991	**ChC-N**	**13**	**40**	**7**	**8**	**.467**	**48**	**3.89**	**111**	**44**	**40**	**114**	**5**	**0**	**0**	**1**
1992	**ChC-N**	**0**	**69**	**3**	**6**	**.333**	**28**	**2.89**	**87 1/3**	**42**	**30**	**76**	**4**	**0**	**0**	**14**
1993	**ChC-N**	**0**	**70**	**4**	**5**	**.444**	**38**	**4.54**	**75 1/3**	**44**	**28**	**79**	**6**	**0**	**0**	**0**
1994	Mil-A	12	30	2	6	.250	47	4.11	103	65	28	117	11	0	0	2
1995	Mil-A	14	17	4	7	.364	61	6.59	83 1/3	29	44	101	9	0	0	0
1996	Det-A	0	8	0	0	—	13	10.64	11	3	9	16	1	0	0	0
1996	KC-A	0	9	0	1	.000	4	3.18	11 1/3	3	3	13	1	0	0	0
1998	Hou-N	0	27	0	1	.000	9	3.08	26 1/3	9	13	24	4	0	0	0
2000	Mil-N	0	2	0	0	—	5	27.00	1 2/3	1	0	6	0	0	0	0
2001	Mon-N	0	18	0	0	—	23	7.86	26 1/3	5	14	37	0	0	0	0
Career average		4	32	2	4	.370	31	4.63	59 2/3	27	23	65	5	0	0	2
Cubs average		**4**	**60**	**5**	**6**	**.424**	**38**	**3.75**	**91 1/3**	**43**	**33**	**90**	**5**	**0**	**0**	**5**
Career total		39	290	20	34	.370	276	4.63	536 2/3	245	209	583	41	0	0	17
Cubs total		**13**	**179**	**14**	**19**	**.424**	**114**	**3.75**	**273 2/3**	**130**	**98**	**269**	**15**	**0**	**0**	**15**

Schaffernoth, Joseph Arthur (Joe *or* Soberdash)
HEIGHT: 6'4"   RIGHTHANDER   BORN: 8/6/1937 TRENTON, NEW JERSEY

YEAR	TEAM	STARTS	GAMES	WON	LOST	PCT	ER	ERA	INNINGS PITCHED	STRIKE-OUTS	WALKS	HITS ALLOWED	HRS ALLOWED	COMP. GAMES	SHUT-OUTS	SAVES
1959	ChC-N	1	5	1	0	1.000	7	8.22	7 2/3	3	4	11	1	0	0	0
1960	ChC-N	0	33	2	3	.400	17	2.78	55	33	17	46	2	0	0	3
1961	ChC-N	0	21	0	4	.000	27	6.34	38 1/3	23	18	43	7	0	0	0
1961	Cle-A	0	15	0	1	.000	9	4.76	17	9	14	16	2	0	0	0
Career average		0	25	1	3	.273	20	4.58	39 1/3	23	18	39	4	0	0	1
Cubs average		0	20	1	2	.300	17	4.54	33 2/3	20	13	33	3	0	0	1
Career total		1	74	3	8	.273	60	4.58	118	68	53	116	12	0	0	3
Cubs total		1	59	3	7	.300	51	4.54	101	59	39	100	10	0	0	3

Schiraldi, Calvin Drew
HEIGHT: 6'5"   RIGHTHANDER   BORN: 6/16/1962 HOUSTON, TEXAS

YEAR	TEAM	STARTS	GAMES	WON	LOST	PCT	ER	ERA	INNINGS PITCHED	STRIKE-OUTS	WALKS	HITS ALLOWED	HRS ALLOWED	COMP. GAMES	SHUT-OUTS	SAVES
1984	NYM-N	3	5	0	2	.000	11	5.71	17 1/3	16	10	20	3	0	0	0
1985	NYM-N	4	10	2	1	.667	26	8.89	26 1/3	21	11	43	4	0	0	0
1986	Bos-A	0	25	4	2	.667	8	1.41	51	55	15	36	5	0	0	9
1987	Bos-A	1	62	8	5	.615	41	4.41	83 2/3	93	40	75	15	0	0	6
1988	**ChC-N**	**27**	**29**	**9**	**13**	**.409**	**81**	**4.38**	**166 1/3**	**140**	**63**	**166**	**13**	**2**	**1**	**1**
1989	**ChC-N**	**0**	**54**	**3**	**6**	**.333**	**33**	**3.78**	**78 2/3**	**54**	**50**	**60**	**7**	**0**	**0**	**4**
1989	SD-N	4	5	3	1	.750	6	2.53	21 1/3	17	13	12	1	0	0	0
1990	SD-N	8	42	3	8	.273	51	4.41	104	74	60	105	11	0	0	1
1991	Tex-A	0	3	0	1	.000	6	11.57	4 2/3	1	5	5	3	0	0	0
Career average		6	29	4	5	.451	33	4.28	69 1/3	59	33	65	8	0	0	3
Cubs average		14	42	6	10	.387	57	4.19	122 2/3	97	57	113	10	1	1	3
Career total		47	235	32	39	.451	263	4.28	553 1/3	471	267	522	62	2	1	21
Cubs total		27	83	12	19	.387	114	4.19	245	194	113	226	20	2	1	5

Schmidt, Frederick Albert (Freddy)
HEIGHT: 6'1"   RIGHTHANDER   BORN: 2/9/1916 HARTFORD, CONNECTICUT

YEAR	TEAM	STARTS	GAMES	WON	LOST	PCT	ER	ERA	INNINGS PITCHED	STRIKE-OUTS	WALKS	HITS ALLOWED	HRS ALLOWED	COMP. GAMES	SHUT-OUTS	SAVES
1944	StL-N	9	37	7	3	.700	40	3.15	114 1/3	58	58	94	5	3	2	5
1946	StL-N	0	16	1	0	1.000	10	3.29	27 1/3	14	15	27	0	0	0	0
1947	StL-N	0	2	0	0	—	1	2.25	4	2	1	5	1	0	0	0
1947	Phi-N	5	29	5	8	.385	40	4.70	76 2/3	24	43	76	4	0	0	0
1947	**ChC-N**	**1**	**1**	**0**	**0**	**—**	**3**	**9.00**	**3**	**0**	**5**	**4**	**0**	**0**	**0**	**0**
Career average		5	28	4	4	.542	31	3.75	75	33	41	69	3	1	1	2
Cubs average		1	1	0	0	—	3	9.00	3	0	5	4	0	0	0	0
Career total		15	85	13	11	.542	94	3.75	225 1/3	98	122	206	10	3	2	5
Cubs total		1	1	0	0	—	3	9.00	3	0	5	4	0	0	0	0

Schmitz, John Albert (Johnny *or* Bear Tracks)
HEIGHT: 6'0"   LEFTHANDER   BORN: 11/27/1920 WAUSAU, WISCONSIN

YEAR	TEAM	STARTS	GAMES	WON	LOST	PCT	ER	ERA	INNINGS PITCHED	STRIKE-OUTS	WALKS	HITS ALLOWED	HRS ALLOWED	COMP. GAMES	SHUT-OUTS	SAVES
1941	ChC-N	3	5	2	0	1.000	3	1.31	20 2/3	11	9	12	0	1	0	0
1942	ChC-N	10	23	3	7	.300	33	3.43	86 2/3	51	45	70	3	1	0	2
1946	ChC-N	31	41	11	11	.500	65	2.61	224 1/3	135	94	184	6	14	2	2
1947	ChC-N	28	38	13	18	.419	74	3.22	207	97	80	209	8	10	3	4
1948	ChC-N	30	34	18	13	.581	71	2.64	242	100	97	186	11	18	2	1
1949	ChC-N	31	36	11	13	.458	100	4.35	207	75	92	227	11	9	3	3
1950	ChC-N	27	39	10	16	.385	107	4.99	193	75	91	217	23	8	3	0
1951	ChC-N	3	8	1	2	.333	16	8.00	18	6	15	22	1	0	0	0
1951	Bro-N	7	16	1	4	.200	33	5.34	55 2/3	20	28	55	4	0	0	0

(continued)

(continued)

YEAR	TEAM	STARTS	GAMES	WON	LOST	PCT	ER	ERA	INNINGS PITCHED	STRIKE-OUTS	WALKS	HITS ALLOWED	HRS ALLOWED	COMP. GAMES	SHUT-OUTS	SAVES
1952	Bro-N	3	10	1	1	.500	16	4.32	33⅓	11	18	29	3	1	0	0
1952	NYY-A	2	5	1	1	.500	6	3.60	15	3	9	15	0	1	0	1
1952	Cin-N	0	3	1	0	1.000	0	0.00	5	3	3	3	0	0	0	0
1953	NYY-A	0	3	0	0	—	1	2.08	4⅓	0	3	2	1	0	0	0
1953	Was-A	13	24	2	7	.222	44	3.68	107⅔	39	37	118	9	5	0	4
1954	Was-A	23	29	11	8	.579	60	2.91	185⅓	56	64	176	6	12	2	1
1955	Was-A	21	32	7	10	.412	68	3.71	165	49	54	187	8	6	1	1
1956	Bos-A	0	2	0	0	—	0	0.00	4⅓	0	4	5	0	0	0	0
1956	Bal-A	3	18	0	3	.000	17	3.99	38⅓	15	14	49	3	0	0	0
Career average		18	28	7	9	.449	55	3.55	139⅓	57	58	136	7	7	1	1
Cubs average		**20**	**28**	**9**	**10**	**.463**	**59**	**3.52**	**150**	**69**	**65**	**141**	**8**	**8**	**2**	**2**
Career total		235	366	93	114	.449	714	3.55	1812⅔	746	757	1766	97	86	16	19
Cubs total		**163**	**224**	**69**	**80**	**.463**	**469**	**3.52**	**1198⅔**	**550**	**523**	**1127**	**63**	**61**	**13**	**12**

Schorr, Edward Walter (Ed)
HEIGHT: 6'2" RIGHTHANDER BORN: 2/14/1891 BREMEN, OHIO DIED: 9/12/1969 ATLANTIC CITY, NEW JERSEY

YEAR	TEAM	STARTS	GAMES	WON	LOST	PCT	ER	ERA	INNINGS PITCHED	STRIKE-OUTS	WALKS	HITS ALLOWED	HRS ALLOWED	COMP. GAMES	SHUT-OUTS	SAVES
1915	ChC-N	0	2	0	0	—	5	7.50	6	3	5	9	0	0	0	0
Career average		0	2	0	0	—	5	7.50	6	3	5	9	0	0	0	0
Cubs average		**0**	**2**	**0**	**0**	**—**	**5**	**7.50**	**6**	**3**	**5**	**9**	**0**	**0**	**0**	**0**
Career total		0	2	0	0	—	5	7.50	6	3	5	9	0	0	0	0
Cubs total		**0**	**2**	**0**	**0**	**—**	**5**	**7.50**	**6**	**3**	**5**	**9**	**0**	**0**	**0**	**0**

Schroll, Albert Bringhurst (Al *or* Bull)
HEIGHT: 6'2" RIGHTHANDER BORN: 3/22/1932 NEW ORLEANS, LOUISIANA DIED: 11/30/1999 ALEXANDRIA, LOUISIANA

YEAR	TEAM	STARTS	GAMES	WON	LOST	PCT	ER	ERA	INNINGS PITCHED	STRIKE-OUTS	WALKS	HITS ALLOWED	HRS ALLOWED	COMP. GAMES	SHUT-OUTS	SAVES
1958	Bos-A	0	5	0	0	—	5	4.50	10	7	4	6	1	0	0	0
1959	Phi-N	0	3	1	1	.500	9	8.68	9⅓	4	6	12	1	0	0	0
1959	Bos-A	5	14	1	4	.200	24	4.70	46	26	22	47	3	1	0	0
1960	**ChC-N**	**0**	**2**	**0**	**0**	**—**	**3**	**10.13**	**2⅔**	**2**	**5**	**3**	**1**	**0**	**0**	**0**
1961	Min-A	8	11	4	4	.500	29	5.22	50	24	27	53	5	2	0	0
Career average		3	9	2	2	.400	18	5.34	29⅔	16	16	30	3	1	0	0
Cubs average		**0**	**2**	**0**	**0**	**—**	**3**	**10.13**	**2⅔**	**2**	**5**	**3**	**1**	**0**	**0**	**0**
Career total		13	35	6	9	.400	70	5.34	118	63	64	121	11	3	0	0
Cubs total		**0**	**2**	**0**	**0**	**—**	**3**	**10.13**	**2⅔**	**2**	**5**	**3**	**1**	**0**	**0**	**0**

Schultz, Charles Budd (Buddy)
HEIGHT: 6'0" LEFTHANDER BORN: 9/19/1950 CLEVELAND, OHIO

YEAR	TEAM	STARTS	GAMES	WON	LOST	PCT	ER	ERA	INNINGS PITCHED	STRIKE-OUTS	WALKS	HITS ALLOWED	HRS ALLOWED	COMP. GAMES	SHUT-OUTS	SAVES
1975	**ChC-N**	**0**	**6**	**2**	**0**	**1.000**	**4**	**6.35**	**5⅔**	**4**	**5**	**11**	**0**	**0**	**0**	**0**
1976	**ChC-N**	**0**	**29**	**1**	**1**	**.500**	**16**	**6.08**	**23⅔**	**15**	**9**	**37**	**3**	**0**	**0**	**2**
1977	StL-N	3	40	6	1	.857	22	2.32	85⅓	66	24	76	5	0	0	1
1978	StL-N	0	62	2	4	.333	35	3.80	83	70	36	68	6	0	0	6
1979	StL-N	0	31	4	3	.571	21	4.46	42⅓	38	14	40	7	0	0	3
Career average		1	34	3	2	.625	20	3.68	48	39	18	46	4	0	0	2
Cubs average		**0**	**18**	**2**	**1**	**.750**	**10**	**6.14**	**14⅔**	**10**	**7**	**24**	**2**	**0**	**0**	**1**
Career total		3	168	15	9	.625	98	3.68	240	193	88	232	21	0	0	12
Cubs total		**0**	**35**	**3**	**1**	**.750**	**20**	**6.14**	**29⅓**	**19**	**14**	**48**	**3**	**0**	**0**	**2**

Schultz, George Warren (Barney)
HEIGHT: 6'2" RIGHTHANDER BORN: 8/15/1926 BEVERLY, NEW JERSEY

YEAR	TEAM	STARTS	GAMES	WON	LOST	PCT	ER	ERA	INNINGS PITCHED	STRIKE-OUTS	WALKS	HITS ALLOWED	HRS ALLOWED	COMP. GAMES	SHUT-OUTS	SAVES
1955	StL-N	0	19	1	2	.333	26	7.89	29 2/3	19	15	28	5	0	0	4
1959	Det-A	0	13	1	2	.333	9	4.42	18 1/3	17	14	17	1	0	0	0
1961	**ChC-N**	0	41	7	6	.538	20	2.70	66 2/3	59	25	57	6	0	0	7
1962	**ChC-N**	0	51	5	5	.500	33	3.82	77 2/3	58	23	66	7	0	0	5
1963	**ChC-N**	0	15	1	0	1.000	11	3.62	27 1/3	18	9	25	5	0	0	2
1963	StL-N	0	24	2	0	1.000	14	3.57	35 1/3	26	8	36	5	0	0	14
1964	StL-N	0	30	1	3	.250	9	1.64	49 1/3	29	11	35	1	0	0	2
1965	StL-N	0	34	2	2	.500	18	3.83	42 1/3	38	11	39	8	0	0	2
Career average		0	32	3	3	.500	20	3.63	49 2/3	38	17	43	5	0	0	5
Cubs average		0	36	4	4	.542	21	3.36	57 1/3	45	19	49	6	0	0	5
Career total		0	227	20	20	.500	140	3.63	346 2/3	264	116	303	38	0	0	35
Cubs total		0	107	13	11	.542	64	3.36	171 2/3	135	57	148	18	0	0	14

Schultz, Robert Duffy (Bob *or* Bill)
HEIGHT: 6'3" LEFTHANDER BORN: 11/27/1923 LOUISVILLE, KENTUCKY   DIED: 3/31/1979 NASHVILLE, TENNESSEE

YEAR	TEAM	STARTS	GAMES	WON	LOST	PCT	ER	ERA	INNINGS PITCHED	STRIKE-OUTS	WALKS	HITS ALLOWED	HRS ALLOWED	COMP. GAMES	SHUT-OUTS	SAVES
1951	**ChC-N**	10	17	3	6	.333	45	5.24	77 1/3	27	51	75	9	2	0	0
1952	**ChC-N**	5	29	6	3	.667	33	4.01	74	31	51	63	3	1	0	0
1953	**ChC-N**	2	7	0	2	.000	7	5.40	11 2/3	4	11	13	2	0	0	0
1953	Pit-N	2	11	0	2	.000	17	8.20	18 2/3	5	10	26	3	0	0	0
1955	Det-A	0	1	0	0	—	3	20.25	1 1/3	0	2	2	0	0	0	0
Career average		5	16	2	3	.409	26	5.16	45 2/3	17	31	45	4	1	0	0
Cubs average		6	18	3	4	.450	28	4.69	54 1/3	21	38	50	5	1	0	0
Career total		19	65	9	13	.409	105	5.16	183	67	125	179	17	3	0	0
Cubs total		17	53	9	11	.450	85	4.69	163	62	113	151	14	3	0	0

Schulze, Donald Arthur (Don)
HEIGHT: 6'3" RIGHTHANDER BORN: 9/27/1962 ROSELLE, ILLINOIS

YEAR	TEAM	STARTS	GAMES	WON	LOST	PCT	ER	ERA	INNINGS PITCHED	STRIKE-OUTS	WALKS	HITS ALLOWED	HRS ALLOWED	COMP. GAMES	SHUT-OUTS	SAVES
1983	**ChC-N**	3	4	0	1	.000	11	7.07	14	8	7	19	1	0	0	0
1984	**ChC-N**	1	1	0	0	—	4	12.00	3	2	1	8	0	0	0	0
1984	Cle-A	14	19	3	6	.333	46	4.83	85 2/3	39	27	105	9	2	0	0
1985	Cle-A	18	19	4	10	.286	63	6.01	94 1/3	37	19	128	10	1	0	0
1986	Cle-A	13	19	4	4	.500	47	5.00	84 2/3	33	34	88	9	1	0	0
1987	NYM-N	4	5	1	2	.333	15	6.23	21 2/3	5	6	24	4	0	0	0
1989	NYY-A	2	2	1	1	.500	5	4.09	11	5	5	12	1	0	0	0
1989	SD-N	4	7	2	1	.667	15	5.55	24 1/3	15	6	38	6	0	0	0
Career average		10	13	3	4	.375	34	5.47	56 1/3	24	18	70	7	1	0	0
Cubs average		2	3	0	1	.000	8	7.94	8 2/3	5	4	14	1	0	0	0
Career total		59	76	15	25	.375	206	5.47	338 2/3	144	105	422	40	4	0	0
Cubs total		4	5	0	1	.000	15	7.94	17	10	8	27	1	0	0	0

Schurr, Wayne Allen
HEIGHT: 6'4" RIGHTHANDER BORN: 8/6/1937 GARRETT, INDIANA

YEAR	TEAM	STARTS	GAMES	WON	LOST	PCT	ER	ERA	INNINGS PITCHED	STRIKE-OUTS	WALKS	HITS ALLOWED	HRS ALLOWED	COMP. GAMES	SHUT-OUTS	SAVES
1964	**ChC-N**	0	26	0	0	—	20	3.72	48 1/3	29	11	57	3	0	0	0
Career average		0	26	0	0	—	20	3.72	48 1/3	29	11	57	3	0	0	0
Cubs average		0	26	0	0	—	20	3.72	48 1/3	29	11	57	3	0	0	0
Career total		0	26	0	0	—	20	3.72	48 1/3	29	11	57	3	0	0	0
Cubs total		0	26	0	0	—	20	3.72	48 1/3	29	11	57	3	0	0	0

Schwenck, Rudolph Christian (Rudy)
HEIGHT: 6'0"   LEFTHANDER   BORN: 4/6/1884 LOUISVILLE, KENTUCKY   DIED: 11/27/1941 ANCHORAGE, KENTUCKY

YEAR	TEAM	STARTS	GAMES	WON	LOST	PCT	ER	ERA	INNINGS PITCHED	STRIKE-OUTS	WALKS	HITS ALLOWED	HRS ALLOWED	COMP. GAMES	SHUT-OUTS	SAVES
1909	ChC-N	2	3	1	1	.500	6	13.50	4	3	3	16	0	0	0	0
Career average		2	3	1	1	.500	6	13.50	4	3	3	16	0	0	0	0
Cubs average		**2**	**3**	**1**	**1**	**.500**	**6**	**13.50**	**4**	**3**	**3**	**16**	**0**	**0**	**0**	**0**
Career total		2	3	1	1	.500	6	13.50	4	3	3	16	0	0	0	0
Cubs total		**2**	**3**	**1**	**1**	**.500**	**6**	**13.50**	**4**	**3**	**3**	**16**	**0**	**0**	**0**	**0**

Scott, Richard Lewis (Dick)
HEIGHT: 6'2"   LEFTHANDER   BORN: 3/15/1933 PORTSMOUTH, NEW HAMPSHIRE

YEAR	TEAM	STARTS	GAMES	WON	LOST	PCT	ER	ERA	INNINGS PITCHED	STRIKE-OUTS	WALKS	HITS ALLOWED	HRS ALLOWED	COMP. GAMES	SHUT-OUTS	SAVES
1963	LA-N	0	9	0	0	—	9	6.75	12	6	3	17	6	0	0	2
1964	ChC-N	0	3	0	0	—	6	12.46	4 1/3	1	1	10	2	0	0	0
Career average		0	6	0	0	—	8	8.27	8 1/3	4	2	14	4	0	0	1
Cubs average		**0**	**3**	**0**	**0**	**—**	**6**	**12.46**	**4 1/3**	**1**	**1**	**10**	**2**	**0**	**0**	**0**
Career total		0	12	0	0	—	15	8.27	16 1/3	7	4	27	8	0	0	2
Cubs total		**0**	**3**	**0**	**0**	**—**	**6**	**12.46**	**4 1/3**	**1**	**1**	**10**	**2**	**0**	**0**	**0**

Seaton, Thomas Gordon (Tom)
HEIGHT: 6'0"   RIGHTHANDER   BORN: 8/30/1887 BLAIR, NEBRASKA   DIED: 4/10/1940 EL PASO, TEXAS

YEAR	TEAM	STARTS	GAMES	WON	LOST	PCT	ER	ERA	INNINGS PITCHED	STRIKE-OUTS	WALKS	HITS ALLOWED	HRS ALLOWED	COMP. GAMES	SHUT-OUTS	SAVES
1912	Phi-N	27	44	16	12	.571	93	3.28	255	118	106	246	8	16	2	2
1913	Phi-N	35	52	27	12	.692	93	2.60	322 1/3	168	136	262	6	21	6	1
1914	Bro-F	38	44	25	14	.641	102	3.03	302 2/3	172	102	299	6	26	7	2
1915	Bro-F	23	32	12	11	.522	96	4.56	189 1/3	86	99	199	6	13	0	3
1915	New-F	10	12	2	6	.250	19	2.28	75	28	21	61	1	7	0	1
1916	ChC-N	12	31	6	6	.500	44	3.27	121	45	43	108	3	4	0	1
1917	ChC-N	9	16	5	4	.556	21	2.53	74 2/3	27	23	60	0	3	1	1
Career average		26	39	16	11	.589	78	3.14	223 1/3	107	88	206	5	15	3	2
Cubs average		**11**	**24**	**6**	**5**	**.524**	**33**	**2.99**	**98**	**36**	**33**	**84**	**2**	**4**	**1**	**1**
Career total		154	231	93	65	.589	468	3.14	1340	644	530	1235	30	90	16	11
Cubs total		**21**	**47**	**11**	**10**	**.524**	**65**	**2.99**	**195 2/3**	**72**	**66**	**168**	**3**	**7**	**1**	**2**

Segelke, Herman Neils
HEIGHT: 6'4"   RIGHTHANDER   BORN: 4/24/1958 SAN MATEO, CALIFORNIA

YEAR	TEAM	STARTS	GAMES	WON	LOST	PCT	ER	ERA	INNINGS PITCHED	STRIKE-OUTS	WALKS	HITS ALLOWED	HRS ALLOWED	COMP. GAMES	SHUT-OUTS	SAVES
1982	ChC-N	0	3	0	0	—	4	8.31	4 1/3	4	6	6	1	0	0	0
Career average		0	3	0	0	—	4	8.31	4 1/3	4	6	6	1	0	0	0
Cubs average		**0**	**3**	**0**	**0**	**—**	**4**	**8.31**	**4 1/3**	**4**	**6**	**6**	**1**	**0**	**0**	**0**
Career total		0	3	0	0	—	4	8.31	4 1/3	4	6	6	1	0	0	0
Cubs total		**0**	**3**	**0**	**0**	**—**	**4**	**8.31**	**4 1/3**	**4**	**6**	**6**	**1**	**0**	**0**	**0**

(continued)

Selma, Richard Jay (Dick *or* Mortimer Snerd)
HEIGHT: 5'11" RIGHTHANDER BORN: 11/4/1943 SANTA ANA, CALIFORNIA DIED: 8/29/2001 CLOVIS, CALIFORNIA

YEAR	TEAM	STARTS	GAMES	WON	LOST	PCT	ER	ERA	INNINGS PITCHED	STRIKE-OUTS	WALKS	HITS ALLOWED	HRS ALLOWED	COMP. GAMES	SHUT-OUTS	SAVES
1965	NYM-N	4	4	2	1	.667	11	3.71	26 2/3	26	9	22	2	1	1	0
1966	NYM-N	7	30	4	6	.400	38	4.24	80 2/3	58	39	84	11	0	0	1
1967	NYM-N	4	38	2	4	.333	25	2.77	81 1/3	52	36	71	3	0	0	2
1968	NYM-N	23	33	9	10	.474	52	2.76	169 2/3	117	54	148	11	4	3	0
1969	SD-N	3	4	2	2	.500	10	4.09	22	20	9	19	3	1	0	0
1969	**ChC-N**	**25**	**36**	**10**	**8**	**.556**	**68**	**3.63**	**168 2/3**	**161**	**72**	**137**	**13**	**4**	**2**	**1**
1970	Phi-N	0	73	8	9	.471	41	2.75	134 1/3	153	59	108	8	0	0	22
1971	Phi-N	0	17	0	2	.000	9	3.28	24 2/3	15	8	21	2	0	0	1
1972	Phi-N	10	46	2	9	.182	61	5.56	98 2/3	58	73	91	13	1	0	3
1973	Phi-N	0	6	1	1	.500	5	5.63	8	4	5	6	1	0	0	0
1974	Cal-A	0	18	2	2	.500	13	5.09	23	15	17	22	2	0	0	1
1974	Mil-A	0	2	0	0	—	5	19.29	2 1/3	2	0	5	0	0	0	0
Career average		8	31	4	5	.438	34	3.62	84	68	38	73	7	1	1	3
Cubs average		**25**	**36**	**10**	**8**	**.556**	**68**	**3.63**	**168 2/3**	**161**	**72**	**137**	**13**	**4**	**2**	**1**
Career total		76	307	42	54	.438	338	3.62	840	681	381	734	69	11	6	31
Cubs total		**25**	**36**	**10**	**8**	**.556**	**68**	**3.63**	**168 2/3**	**161**	**72**	**137**	**13**	**4**	**2**	**1**

Seoane, Manuel Modesto (Manny)
HEIGHT: 6'3" RIGHTHANDER BORN: 6/26/1955 TAMPA, FLORIDA

YEAR	TEAM	STARTS	GAMES	WON	LOST	PCT	ER	ERA	INNINGS PITCHED	STRIKE-OUTS	WALKS	HITS ALLOWED	HRS ALLOWED	COMP. GAMES	SHUT-OUTS	SAVES
1977	Phi-N	1	2	0	0	—	4	6.00	6	4	3	11	0	0	0	0
1978	**ChC-N**	**1**	**7**	**1**	**0**	**1.000**	**5**	**5.40**	**8 1/3**	**5**	**6**	**11**	**0**	**0**	**0**	**0**
Career average		1	5	1	0	1.000	5	5.65	7 1/3	5	5	11	0	0	0	0
Cubs average		**1**	**7**	**1**	**0**	**1.000**	**5**	**5.40**	**8 1/3**	**5**	**6**	**11**	**0**	**0**	**0**	**0**
Career total		2	9	1	0	1.000	9	5.65	14 1/3	9	9	22	0	0	0	0
Cubs total		**1**	**7**	**1**	**0**	**1.000**	**5**	**5.40**	**8 1/3**	**5**	**6**	**11**	**0**	**0**	**0**	**0**

Serafini, Daniel Joseph (Dan)
HEIGHT: 6'1" LEFTHANDER BORN: 1/25/1974 SAN FRANCISCO, CALIFORNIA

YEAR	TEAM	STARTS	GAMES	WON	LOST	PCT	ER	ERA	INNINGS PITCHED	STRIKE-OUTS	WALKS	HITS ALLOWED	HRS ALLOWED	COMP. GAMES	SHUT-OUTS	SAVES
1996	Min-A	1	1	0	1	.000	5	10.38	4 1/3	1	2	7	1	0	0	0
1997	Min-A	4	6	2	1	.667	10	3.42	26 1/3	15	11	27	1	1	0	0
1998	Min-A	9	28	7	4	.636	54	6.48	75	46	29	95	10	0	0	0
1999	**ChC-N**	**4**	**42**	**3**	**2**	**.600**	**48**	**6.93**	**62 1/3**	**17**	**32**	**86**	**9**	**0**	**0**	**1**
2000	SD-N	0	3	0	0	—	6	18.00	3	3	2	9	2	0	0	0
2000	Pit-N	11	11	2	5	.286	34	4.91	62 1/3	32	26	70	9	0	0	0
Career average		6	18	3	3	.519	31	6.06	46 2/3	23	20	59	6	0	0	0
Cubs average		**4**	**42**	**3**	**2**	**.600**	**48**	**6.93**	**62 1/3**	**17**	**32**	**86**	**9**	**0**	**0**	**1**
Career total		29	91	14	13	.519	157	6.06	233 1/3	114	102	294	32	1	0	1
Cubs total		**4**	**42**	**3**	**2**	**.600**	**48**	**6.93**	**62 1/3**	**17**	**32**	**86**	**9**	**0**	**0**	**1**

Shantz, Robert Clayton (Bobby)
HEIGHT: 5'6" LEFTHANDER BORN: 9/26/1925 POTTSTOWN, PENNSYLVANIA

YEAR	TEAM	STARTS	GAMES	WON	LOST	PCT	ER	ERA	INNINGS PITCHED	STRIKE-OUTS	WALKS	HITS ALLOWED	HRS ALLOWED	COMP. GAMES	SHUT-OUTS	SAVES
1949	Phi-A	7	33	6	8	.429	48	3.40	127	58	74	100	9	4	1	2
1950	Phi-A	23	36	8	14	.364	110	4.61	214 2/3	93	85	251	18	6	1	0
1951	Phi-A	25	32	18	10	.643	90	3.94	205 1/3	77	70	213	15	13	3	0
1952	Phi-A	33	33	24	7	.774	77	2.48	279 2/3	152	63	230	21	27	5	0
1953	Phi-A	16	16	5	9	.357	48	4.09	105 2/3	58	26	107	10	6	0	0
1954	Phi-A	1	2	1	0	1.000	7	7.88	8	3	3	12	2	0	0	0
1955	KCA-A	17	23	5	10	.333	63	4.54	125	58	66	124	8	4	1	0

(continued)

(continued)

YEAR	TEAM	STARTS	GAMES	WON	LOST	PCT	ER	ERA	INNINGS PITCHED	STRIKE-OUTS	WALKS	HITS ALLOWED	HRS ALLOWED	COMP. GAMES	SHUT-OUTS	SAVES
1956	KCA-A	2	45	2	7	.222	49	4.35	101⅓	67	37	95	12	1	0	9
1957	NYY-A	21	30	11	5	.688	47	2.45	173	72	40	157	15	9	1	5
1958	NYY-A	13	33	7	6	.538	47	3.36	126	80	35	127	8	3	0	0
1959	NYY-A	4	33	7	3	.700	25	2.38	94⅔	66	33	64	4	2	2	3
1960	NYY-A	0	42	5	4	.556	21	2.79	67⅔	54	24	57	5	0	0	11
1961	Pit-N	6	43	6	3	.667	33	3.32	89⅓	61	26	91	5	2	1	2
1962	Hou-N	3	3	1	1	.500	3	1.31	20⅔	14	5	15	1	1	0	0
1962	StL-N	0	28	5	3	.625	14	2.18	57⅔	47	20	45	7	0	0	4
1963	StL-N	0	55	6	4	.600	23	2.61	79⅓	70	17	55	6	0	0	11
1964	StL-N	0	16	1	3	.250	6	3.12	17⅓	12	7	14	2	0	0	0
1964	**ChC-N**	**0**	**20**	**0**	**1**	**.000**	**7**	**5.56**	**11⅓**	**12**	**6**	**15**	**2**	**0**	**0**	**1**
1964	Phi-N	0	14	1	1	.500	8	2.25	32	18	6	23	1	0	0	3
Career average		11	34	7	6	.546	45	3.38	121	67	40	112	9	5	1	3
Cubs average		**0**	**20**	**0**	**1**	**.000**	**7**	**5.56**	**11⅓**	**12**	**6**	**15**	**2**	**0**	**0**	**1**
Career total		171	537	119	99	.546	726	3.38	1935⅔	1072	643	1795	151	78	15	48
Cubs total		**0**	**20**	**0**	**1**	**.000**	**7**	**5.56**	**11⅓**	**12**	**6**	**15**	**2**	**0**	**0**	**1**

Shaw, Robert John (Bob *or* Buck)

HEIGHT: 6'2"   RIGHTHANDER   BORN: 6/29/1933 BRONX, NEW YORK

YEAR	TEAM	STARTS	GAMES	WON	LOST	PCT	ER	ERA	INNINGS PITCHED	STRIKE-OUTS	WALKS	HITS ALLOWED	HRS ALLOWED	COMP. GAMES	SHUT-OUTS	SAVES
1957	Det-A	0	7	0	1	.000	8	7.45	9⅔	4	7	11	2	0	0	0
1958	Det-A	2	11	1	2	.333	15	5.06	26⅔	17	13	32	2	0	0	0
1958	CWS-A	3	29	4	2	.667	33	4.64	64	18	28	67	8	0	0	1
1959	CWS-A	26	47	18	6	.750	69	2.69	230⅓	89	54	217	15	8	3	3
1960	CWS-A	32	36	13	13	.500	87	4.06	192⅔	46	62	221	16	7	1	0
1961	CWS-A	10	14	3	4	.429	30	3.79	71⅓	31	20	85	11	3	0	0
1961	KCA-A	24	26	9	10	.474	72	4.31	150⅓	60	58	165	13	6	0	0
1962	Mil-N	29	38	15	9	.625	70	2.80	225	124	44	223	20	12	3	2
1963	Mil-N	16	48	7	11	.389	47	2.66	159	105	55	144	10	3	3	13
1964	SF-N	1	61	7	6	.538	39	3.76	93⅓	57	31	105	5	0	0	11
1965	SF-N	33	42	16	9	.640	69	2.64	235	148	53	213	17	6	1	2
1966	SF-N	6	13	1	4	.200	22	6.25	31⅔	21	7	45	9	0	0	0
1966	NYM-N	25	26	11	10	.524	73	3.92	167⅔	104	42	171	12	7	2	0
1967	NYM-N	13	23	3	9	.250	47	4.29	98⅔	49	28	105	9	3	1	0
1967	**ChC-N**	**3**	**9**	**0**	**2**	**.000**	**15**	**6.04**	**22⅓**	**7**	**9**	**33**	**0**	**0**	**0**	**0**
Career average		20	39	10	9	.524	63	3.52	161⅔	80	46	167	14	5	1	3
Cubs average		**3**	**9**	**0**	**2**	**.000**	**15**	**6.04**	**22⅓**	**7**	**9**	**33**	**0**	**0**	**0**	**0**
Career total		223	430	108	98	.524	696	3.52	1778	880	511	1837	149	55	14	32
Cubs total		**3**	**9**	**0**	**2**	**.000**	**15**	**6.04**	**22⅓**	**7**	**9**	**33**	**0**	**0**	**0**	**0**

Shaw, Samuel E. (Sam)

HEIGHT: 5'5"   RIGHTHANDER   BORN: 5/1864 BALTIMORE, MARYLAND

YEAR	TEAM	STARTS	GAMES	WON	LOST	PCT	ER	ERA	INNINGS PITCHED	STRIKE-OUTS	WALKS	HITS ALLOWED	HRS ALLOWED	COMP. GAMES	SHUT-OUTS	SAVES
1888	Bal-AA	6	6	2	4	.333	20	3.40	53	22	15	65	2	6	0	0
1893	**ChN-N**	**2**	**2**	**1**	**0**	**1.000**	**10**	**5.63**	**16**	**1**	**13**	**12**	**2**	**1**	**0**	**0**
Career average		4	4	2	2	.429	15	3.91	34⅔	12	14	39	2	4	0	0
Cubs average		**2**	**2**	**1**	**0**	**1.000**	**10**	**5.63**	**16**	**1**	**13**	**12**	**2**	**1**	**0**	**0**
Career total		8	8	3	4	.429	30	3.91	69	23	28	77	4	7	0	0
Cubs total		**2**	**2**	**1**	**0**	**1.000**	**10**	**5.63**	**16**	**1**	**13**	**12**	**2**	**1**	**0**	**0**

Shealy, Albert Berly (Al)
HEIGHT: 5'11"   RIGHTHANDER   BORN: 3/20/1900 CHAPIN, SOUTH CAROLINA   DIED: 3/7/1967 HAGERSTOWN, MARYLAND

YEAR	TEAM	STARTS	GAMES	WON	LOST	PCT	ER	ERA	INNINGS PITCHED	STRIKE-OUTS	WALKS	HITS ALLOWED	HRS ALLOWED	COMP. GAMES	SHUT-OUTS	SAVES
1928	NYY-A	12	23	8	6	.571	54	5.06	96	39	42	124	4	3	0	2
1930	ChC-N	0	24	0	0	—	24	8.00	27	14	14	37	2	0	0	0
Career average		6	24	4	3	.571	39	5.71	61 ⅔	27	28	81	3	2	0	1
Cubs average		0	24	0	0	—	24	8.00	27	14	14	37	2	0	0	0
Career total		12	47	8	6	.571	78	5.71	123	53	56	161	6	3	0	2
Cubs total		0	24	0	0	—	24	8.00	27	14	14	37	2	0	0	0

Shoun, Clyde Mitchell (Hardrock)
HEIGHT: 6'1"   LEFTHANDER   BORN: 3/20/1912 MOUNTAIN CITY, TENNESSEE   DIED: 3/20/1968 MOUNTAIN HOME, TENNESSEE

YEAR	TEAM	STARTS	GAMES	WON	LOST	PCT	ER	ERA	INNINGS PITCHED	STRIKE-OUTS	WALKS	HITS ALLOWED	HRS ALLOWED	COMP. GAMES	SHUT-OUTS	SAVES
1935	ChC-N	1	5	1	0	1.000	4	2.84	12 ⅔	5	5	14	2	0	0	0
1936	ChC-N	0	4	0	0	—	6	12.46	4 ⅓	1	6	3	0	0	0	0
1937	ChC-N	9	37	7	7	.500	58	5.61	93	43	45	118	9	2	0	0
1938	StL-N	12	40	6	6	.500	54	4.14	117 ⅓	37	43	130	8	3	0	1
1939	StL-N	2	53	3	1	.750	43	3.76	103	50	42	98	4	0	0	9
1940	StL-N	19	54	13	11	.542	86	3.92	197 ⅓	82	46	193	13	13	1	5
1941	StL-N	6	26	3	5	.375	44	5.66	70	34	20	98	9	0	0	0
1942	StL-N	0	2	0	0	—	0	0.00	1 ⅔	0	0	1	0	0	0	0
1942	Cin-N	0	34	1	3	.250	18	2.23	72 ⅔	32	24	55	2	0	0	7
1943	Cin-N	5	45	14	5	.737	50	3.06	147	61	46	131	5	2	0	7
1944	Cin-N	21	38	13	10	.565	68	3.02	202 ⅔	55	42	193	10	12	1	2
1946	Cin-N	5	27	1	6	.143	36	4.10	79	20	26	87	3	0	0	0
1947	Cin-N	0	10	0	0	—	8	5.02	14 ⅓	7	5	16	2	0	0	0
1947	Bos-N	3	26	5	3	.625	36	4.40	73 ⅔	23	21	73	6	1	1	1
1948	Bos-N	2	36	5	1	.833	33	4.01	74	25	20	77	7	1	0	4
1949	Bos-N	0	1	0	0	—	0	0.00	1	0	0	1	0	0	0	0
1949	CWS-A	0	16	1	1	.500	15	5.79	23 ⅓	8	13	37	1	0	0	0
Career average		6	32	5	4	.553	40	3.91	92	35	29	95	6	2	0	2
Cubs average		3	15	3	2	.533	23	5.56	36 ⅔	16	19	45	4	1	0	0
Career total		85	454	73	59	.553	559	3.91	1287	483	404	1325	81	34	3	29
Cubs total		10	46	8	7	.533	68	5.56	110	49	56	135	11	2	0	0

Signer, Walter Donald Aloysius
HEIGHT: 6'0"   RIGHTHANDER   BORN: 10/12/1910 NEW YORK, NEW YORK   DIED: 7/23/1974 GREENWICH, CONNECTICUT

YEAR	TEAM	STARTS	GAMES	WON	LOST	PCT	ER	ERA	INNINGS PITCHED	STRIKE-OUTS	WALKS	HITS ALLOWED	HRS ALLOWED	COMP. GAMES	SHUT-OUTS	SAVES
1943	ChC-N	2	4	2	1	.667	8	2.88	25	5	4	24	3	1	0	0
1945	ChC-N	0	6	0	0	—	3	3.38	8	0	5	11	1	0	0	1
Career average		1	5	1	1	.667	6	3.00	16 ⅔	3	5	18	2	1	0	1
Cubs average		1	5	1	1	.667	6	3.00	16 ⅔	3	5	18	2	1	0	1
Career total		2	10	2	1	.667	11	3.00	33	5	9	35	4	1	0	1
Cubs total		2	10	2	1	.667	11	3.00	33	5	9	35	4	1	0	1

Simmons, Curtis Thomas (Curt)
HEIGHT: 5'11"   LEFTHANDER   BORN: 5/19/1929 EGYPT, PENNSYLVANIA

YEAR	TEAM	STARTS	GAMES	WON	LOST	PCT	ER	ERA	INNINGS PITCHED	STRIKE-OUTS	WALKS	HITS ALLOWED	HRS ALLOWED	COMP. GAMES	SHUT-OUTS	SAVES
1947	Phi-N	1	1	1	0	1.000	1	1.00	9	9	6	5	0	1	0	0
1948	Phi-N	23	31	7	13	.350	92	4.87	170	86	108	169	8	7	0	0
1949	Phi-N	14	38	4	10	.286	67	4.59	131 ⅓	83	55	133	7	2	0	1
1950	Phi-N	27	31	17	8	.680	81	3.40	214 ⅔	146	88	178	19	11	2	1
1952	Phi-N	28	28	14	8	.636	63	2.82	201 ⅓	141	70	170	11	15	6	0
1953	Phi-N	30	32	16	13	.552	85	3.21	238	138	82	211	17	19	4	0
1954	Phi-N	33	34	14	15	.483	79	2.81	253	125	98	226	14	21	3	1

(continued)

(continued)

YEAR	TEAM	STARTS	GAMES	WON	LOST	PCT	ER	ERA	INNINGS PITCHED	STRIKE-OUTS	WALKS	HITS ALLOWED	HRS ALLOWED	COMP. GAMES	SHUT-OUTS	SAVES
1955	Phi-N	22	25	8	8	.500	71	4.92	130	58	50	148	15	3	0	0
1956	Phi-N	27	33	15	10	.600	74	3.36	198	88	65	186	17	14	0	0
1957	Phi-N	29	32	12	11	.522	81	3.44	212	92	50	214	11	9	2	0
1958	Phi-N	27	29	7	14	.333	82	4.38	168 1/3	78	40	196	11	7	1	1
1959	Phi-N	0	7	0	0	—	5	4.50	10	4	0	16	2	0	0	0
1960	Phi-N	2	4	0	0	—	8	18.00	4	4	6	13	3	0	0	0
1960	StL-N	17	23	7	4	.636	45	2.66	152	63	31	149	11	3	1	0
1961	StL-N	29	30	9	10	.474	68	3.13	195 2/3	99	64	203	14	6	2	0
1962	StL-N	22	31	10	10	.500	60	3.51	154	74	32	167	18	9	4	0
1963	StL-N	32	32	15	9	.625	64	2.48	232 2/3	127	48	209	13	11	6	0
1964	StL-N	34	34	18	9	.667	93	3.43	244	104	49	233	24	12	3	0
1965	StL-N	32	34	9	15	.375	92	4.08	203	96	54	229	19	5	0	0
1966	StL-N	5	10	1	1	.500	17	4.59	33 1/3	14	14	35	3	1	0	0
1966	**ChC-N**	**10**	**19**	**4**	**7**	**.364**	**35**	**4.07**	**77 1/3**	**24**	**21**	**79**	**7**	**3**	**1**	**0**
1967	**ChC-N**	**14**	**17**	**3**	**7**	**.300**	**45**	**4.94**	**82**	**31**	**23**	**100**	**10**	**3**	**0**	**0**
1967	Cal-A	4	14	2	1	.667	10	2.60	34 2/3	13	9	44	1	1	1	1
Career average		23	28	10	9	.513	66	3.54	167 1/3	85	53	166	13	8	2	0
Cubs average		**12**	**18**	**4**	**7**	**.333**	**40**	**4.52**	**79 2/3**	**28**	**22**	**90**	**9**	**3**	**1**	**0**
Career total		462	569	193	183	.513	1318	3.54	3348 1/3	1697	1063	3313	255	163	36	5
Cubs total		**24**	**36**	**7**	**14**	**.333**	**80**	**4.52**	**159 1/3**	**55**	**44**	**179**	**17**	**6**	**1**	**0**

Simpson, Thomas Leo (Duke)
HEIGHT: 6'1"   RIGHTHANDER   BORN: 9/15/1927 COLUMBUS, OHIO

YEAR	TEAM	STARTS	GAMES	WON	LOST	PCT	ER	ERA	INNINGS PITCHED	STRIKE-OUTS	WALKS	HITS ALLOWED	HRS ALLOWED	COMP. GAMES	SHUT-OUTS	SAVES
1953	ChC-N	1	30	1	2	.333	40	8.00	45	21	25	60	8	0	0	0
Career average		1	30	1	2	.333	40	8.00	45	21	25	60	8	0	0	0
Cubs average		**1**	**30**	**1**	**2**	**.333**	**40**	**8.00**	**45**	**21**	**25**	**60**	**8**	**0**	**0**	**0**
Career total		1	30	1	2	.333	40	8.00	45	21	25	60	8	0	0	0
Cubs total		**1**	**30**	**1**	**2**	**.333**	**40**	**8.00**	**45**	**21**	**25**	**60**	**8**	**0**	**0**	**0**

Singleton, Bert Elmer (Elmer *or* Smokey)
HEIGHT: 6'2"   RIGHTHANDER   BORN: 6/26/1918 OGDEN, UTAH   DIED: 1/5/1996 OGDEN, UTAH

YEAR	TEAM	STARTS	GAMES	WON	LOST	PCT	ER	ERA	INNINGS PITCHED	STRIKE-OUTS	WALKS	HITS ALLOWED	HRS ALLOWED	COMP. GAMES	SHUT-OUTS	SAVES
1945	Bos-N	5	7	1	4	.200	20	4.82	37 1/3	14	14	35	1	1	0	0
1946	Bos-N	2	15	0	1	.000	14	3.74	33 2/3	17	21	27	3	0	0	1
1947	Pit-N	3	36	2	2	.500	47	6.31	67	24	39	70	9	0	0	1
1948	Pit-N	5	38	4	6	.400	51	4.97	92 1/3	53	40	90	11	1	0	2
1950	Was-A	1	21	1	2	.333	21	5.20	36 1/3	19	17	39	4	0	0	0
1957	**ChC-N**	**2**	**5**	**0**	**1**	**.000**	**10**	**6.75**	**13 1/3**	**6**	**2**	**20**	**3**	**0**	**0**	**0**
1958	**ChC-N**	**0**	**2**	**1**	**0**	**1.000**	**0**	**0.00**	**4 2/3**	**2**	**1**	**1**	**0**	**0**	**0**	**0**
1959	**ChC-N**	**1**	**21**	**2**	**1**	**.667**	**13**	**2.72**	**43**	**25**	**12**	**40**	**2**	**0**	**0**	**0**
Career average		2	18	1	2	.393	22	4.83	41	20	18	40	4	0	0	1
Cubs average		**1**	**9**	**1**	**1**	**.600**	**8**	**3.39**	**20 1/3**	**11**	**5**	**20**	**2**	**0**	**0**	**0**
Career total		19	145	11	17	.393	176	4.83	327 2/3	160	146	322	33	2	0	4
Cubs total		**3**	**28**	**3**	**2**	**.600**	**23**	**3.39**	**61**	**33**	**15**	**61**	**5**	**0**	**0**	**0**

Slapnicka, Cyril Charles (Cy)
HEIGHT: 5'10"   RIGHTHANDER   BORN: 3/23/1886 CEDAR RAPIDS, IOWA   DIED: 10/20/1979 CEDAR RAPIDS, IOWA

YEAR	TEAM	STARTS	GAMES	WON	LOST	PCT	ER	ERA	INNINGS PITCHED	STRIKE-OUTS	WALKS	HITS ALLOWED	HRS ALLOWED	COMP. GAMES	SHUT-OUTS	SAVES
1911	**ChC-N**	**2**	**3**	**0**	**2**	**.000**	**9**	**3.38**	**24**	**10**	**7**	**21**	**0**	**1**	**0**	**0**
1918	Pit-N	6	7	1	4	.200	26	4.74	49 1/3	3	22	50	2	4	0	1
Career average		4	5	1	3	.143	18	4.30	36 2/3	7	15	36	1	3	0	1
Cubs average		**2**	**3**	**0**	**2**	**.000**	**9**	**3.38**	**24**	**10**	**7**	**21**	**0**	**1**	**0**	**0**
Career total		8	10	1	6	.143	35	4.30	73 1/3	13	29	71	2	5	0	1
Cubs total		**2**	**3**	**0**	**2**	**.000**	**9**	**3.38**	**24**	**10**	**7**	**21**	**0**	**1**	**0**	**0**

Slaughter, Sterling Feore
HEIGHT: 5'11"   RIGHTHANDER   BORN: 11/18/1941 DANVILLE, ILLINOIS

YEAR	TEAM	STARTS	GAMES	WON	LOST	PCT	ER	ERA	INNINGS PITCHED	STRIKE-OUTS	WALKS	HITS ALLOWED	HRS ALLOWED	COMP. GAMES	SHUT-OUTS	SAVES
1964	ChC-N	6	20	2	4	.333	33	5.75	51 2/3	32	32	64	8	1	0	0
Career average		6	20	2	4	.333	33	5.75	51 2/3	32	32	64	8	1	0	0
Cubs average		**6**	**20**	**2**	**4**	**.333**	**33**	**5.75**	**51 2/3**	**32**	**32**	**64**	**8**	**1**	**0**	**0**
Career total		6	20	2	4	.333	33	5.75	51 2/3	32	32	64	8	1	0	0
Cubs total		**6**	**20**	**2**	**4**	**.333**	**33**	**5.75**	**51 2/3**	**32**	**32**	**64**	**8**	**1**	**0**	**0**

Sloat, Dwain Clifford (Lefty)
HEIGHT: 6'0"   LEFTHANDER   BORN: 12/1/1918 NOKOMIS, ILLINOIS

YEAR	TEAM	STARTS	GAMES	WON	LOST	PCT	ER	ERA	INNINGS PITCHED	STRIKE-OUTS	WALKS	HITS ALLOWED	HRS ALLOWED	COMP. GAMES	SHUT-OUTS	SAVES
1948	Bro-N	1	4	0	1	.000	5	6.14	7 1/3	1	8	7	0	0	0	0
1949	ChC-N	1	5	0	0	—	7	7.00	9	3	3	14	0	0	0	0
Career average		1	5	0	0	.000	6	6.61	8 1/3	2	6	11	0	0	0	0
Cubs average		**1**	**5**	**0**	**0**	**—**	**7**	**7.00**	**9**	**3**	**3**	**14**	**0**	**0**	**0**	**0**
Career total		2	9	0	1	.000	12	6.61	16 1/3	4	11	21	0	0	0	0
Cubs total		**1**	**5**	**0**	**0**	**—**	**7**	**7.00**	**9**	**3**	**3**	**14**	**0**	**0**	**0**	**0**

Slocumb, Heathcliff
HEIGHT: 6'3"   RIGHTHANDER   BORN: 6/7/1966 BROOKLYN, NEW YORK

YEAR	TEAM	STARTS	GAMES	WON	LOST	PCT	ER	ERA	INNINGS PITCHED	STRIKE-OUTS	WALKS	HITS ALLOWED	HRS ALLOWED	COMP. GAMES	SHUT-OUTS	SAVES
1991	ChC-N	0	52	2	1	.667	24	3.45	62 2/3	34	30	53	3	0	0	1
1992	ChC-N	0	30	0	3	.000	26	6.50	36	27	21	52	3	0	0	1
1993	ChC-N	0	10	1	0	1.000	4	3.38	10 2/3	4	4	7	0	0	0	0
1993	Cle-A	0	20	3	1	.750	13	4.28	27 1/3	18	16	28	3	0	0	0
1994	Phi-N	0	52	5	1	.833	23	2.86	72 1/3	58	28	75	0	0	0	0
1995	Phi-N	0	61	5	6	.455	21	2.89	65 1/3	63	35	64	2	0	0	32
1996	Bos-A	0	75	5	5	.500	28	3.02	83 1/3	88	55	68	2	0	0	31
1997	Bos-A	0	49	0	5	.000	30	5.79	46 2/3	36	34	58	4	0	0	17
1997	Sea-A	0	27	0	4	.000	13	4.13	28 1/3	28	15	26	2	0	0	10
1998	Sea-A	0	57	2	5	.286	40	5.32	67 2/3	51	44	72	5	0	0	3
1999	Bal-A	0	10	0	0	—	12	12.46	8 2/3	12	9	15	2	0	0	0
1999	StL-N	0	40	3	2	.600	14	2.36	53 1/3	48	30	49	3	0	0	2
2000	StL-N	0	43	2	3	.400	30	5.44	49 2/3	34	24	50	9	0	0	1
2000	SD-N	0	22	0	1	.000	8	3.79	19	12	13	19	0	0	0	0
Career average		0	55	3	4	.431	29	4.08	63	51	36	64	4	0	0	10
Cubs average		**0**	**31**	**1**	**1**	**.429**	**18**	**4.45**	**36 1/3**	**22**	**18**	**37**	**2**	**0**	**0**	**1**
Career total		0	548	28	37	.431	286	4.08	631	513	358	636	38	0	0	98
Cubs total		**0**	**92**	**3**	**4**	**.429**	**54**	**4.45**	**109 1/3**	**65**	**55**	**112**	**6**	**0**	**0**	**2**

Smith, Charles Edwin (Charlie)
HEIGHT: 6'1"   RIGHTHANDER   BORN: 4/20/1880 CLEVELAND, OHIO   DIED: 1/3/1929 WICKLIFFE, OHIO

YEAR	TEAM	STARTS	GAMES	WON	LOST	PCT	ER	ERA	INNINGS PITCHED	STRIKE-OUTS	WALKS	HITS ALLOWED	HRS ALLOWED	COMP. GAMES	SHUT-OUTS	SAVES
1902	Cle-A	3	3	2	1	.667	9	4.05	20	5	5	23	0	2	1	0
1906	Was-A	22	33	9	16	.360	76	2.91	235 1/3	105	75	250	2	17	2	0
1907	Was-A	31	36	10	20	.333	75	2.61	258 2/3	119	51	254	0	21	3	0
1908	Was-A	23	26	9	13	.409	49	2.40	184	83	60	166	2	14	1	1
1909	Was-A	15	23	3	12	.200	53	3.27	145 2/3	72	37	140	4	7	1	0
1909	Bos-A	3	3	3	0	1.000	6	2.16	25	11	2	23	2	2	0	0
1910	Bos-A	18	24	11	6	.647	40	2.30	156 1/3	53	35	141	4	11	0	1
1911	Bos-A	1	1	0	0	—	2	9.00	2	0	1	2	1	0	0	0
1911	ChC-N	5	7	3	2	.600	6	1.42	38	11	7	31	0	3	1	0
1912	ChC-N	5	21	7	4	.636	44	4.21	94	47	31	92	2	1	0	1

(continued)

(continued)

YEAR	TEAM	STARTS	GAMES	WON	LOST	PCT	ER	ERA	INNINGS PITCHED	STRIKE-OUTS	WALKS	HITS ALLOWED	HRS ALLOWED	COMP. GAMES	SHUT-OUTS	SAVES
1913	ChC-N	17	20	7	9	.438	39	2.55	137 2/3	47	34	138	2	8	1	0
1914	ChC-N	5	16	2	4	.333	23	3.86	53 2/3	17	15	49	3	1	0	0
Career average		15	21	7	9	.431	42	2.81	135	57	35	131	2	9	1	0
Cubs average		**8**	**16**	**5**	**5**	**.500**	**28**	**3.12**	**81**	**31**	**22**	**78**	**2**	**3**	**1**	**0**
Career total		148	213	66	87	.431	422	2.81	1350 1/3	570	353	1309	22	87	10	3
Cubs total		**32**	**64**	**19**	**19**	**.500**	**112**	**3.12**	**323 1/3**	**122**	**87**	**310**	**7**	**13**	**2**	**1**

Smith, David Stanley (Dave)
HEIGHT: 6'1"   RIGHTHANDER   BORN: 1/21/1955 RICHMOND, CALIFORNIA

YEAR	TEAM	STARTS	GAMES	WON	LOST	PCT	ER	ERA	INNINGS PITCHED	STRIKE-OUTS	WALKS	HITS ALLOWED	HRS ALLOWED	COMP. GAMES	SHUT-OUTS	SAVES
1980	Hou-N	0	57	7	5	.583	22	1.93	102 2/3	85	32	90	1	0	0	10
1981	Hou-N	0	42	5	3	.625	23	2.76	75	52	23	54	2	0	0	8
1982	Hou-N	1	49	5	4	.556	27	3.84	63 1/3	28	31	69	4	0	0	11
1983	Hou-N	0	42	3	1	.750	25	3.10	72 2/3	41	36	72	2	0	0	6
1984	Hou-N	0	53	5	4	.556	19	2.21	77 1/3	45	20	60	5	0	0	5
1985	Hou-N	0	64	9	5	.643	20	2.27	79 1/3	40	17	69	3	0	0	27
1986	Hou-N	0	54	4	7	.364	17	2.73	56	73	22	39	5	0	0	33
1987	Hou-N	0	50	2	3	.400	11	1.65	60	73	21	39	0	0	0	24
1988	Hou-N	0	51	4	5	.444	17	2.67	57 1/3	38	19	60	1	0	0	27
1989	Hou-N	0	52	3	4	.429	17	2.64	58	31	19	49	1	0	0	25
1990	Hou-N	0	49	6	6	.500	16	2.39	60 1/3	50	20	45	4	0	0	23
1991	**ChC-N**	**0**	**35**	**0**	**6**	**.000**	**22**	**6.00**	**33**	**16**	**19**	**39**	**6**	**0**	**0**	**17**
1992	**ChC-N**	**0**	**11**	**0**	**0**	**—**	**4**	**2.51**	**14 1/3**	**3**	**4**	**15**	**0**	**0**	**0**	**0**
Career average		0	47	4	4	.500	18	2.67	62 1/3	42	22	54	3	0	0	17
Cubs average		**0**	**23**	**0**	**3**	**.000**	**13**	**4.94**	**23 2/3**	**10**	**12**	**27**	**3**	**0**	**0**	**9**
Career total		1	609	53	53	.500	240	2.67	809 1/3	548	283	700	34	0	0	216
Cubs total		**0**	**46**	**0**	**6**	**.000**	**26**	**4.94**	**47 1/3**	**19**	**23**	**54**	**6**	**0**	**0**	**17**

Smith, Lee Arthur
HEIGHT: 6'6"   RIGHTHANDER   BORN: 12/4/1957 JAMESTOWN, LOUISIANA

YEAR	TEAM	STARTS	GAMES	WON	LOST	PCT	ER	ERA	INNINGS PITCHED	STRIKE-OUTS	WALKS	HITS ALLOWED	HRS ALLOWED	COMP. GAMES	SHUT-OUTS	SAVES
1980	**ChC-N**	**0**	**18**	**2**	**0**	**1.000**	**7**	**2.91**	**21 2/3**	**17**	**14**	**21**	**0**	**0**	**0**	**0**
1981	**ChC-N**	**1**	**40**	**3**	**6**	**.333**	**26**	**3.51**	**66 2/3**	**50**	**31**	**57**	**2**	**0**	**0**	**1**
1982	**ChC-N**	**5**	**72**	**2**	**5**	**.286**	**35**	**2.69**	**117**	**99**	**37**	**105**	**5**	**0**	**0**	**17**
1983	**ChC-N**	**0**	**66**	**4**	**10**	**.286**	**19**	**1.65**	**103 1/3**	**91**	**41**	**70**	**5**	**0**	**0**	**29**
1984	**ChC-N**	**0**	**69**	**9**	**7**	**.563**	**41**	**3.65**	**101**	**86**	**35**	**98**	**6**	**0**	**0**	**33**
1985	**ChC-N**	**0**	**65**	**7**	**4**	**.636**	**33**	**3.04**	**97 2/3**	**112**	**32**	**87**	**9**	**0**	**0**	**33**
1986	**ChC-N**	**0**	**66**	**9**	**9**	**.500**	**31**	**3.09**	**90 1/3**	**93**	**42**	**69**	**7**	**0**	**0**	**31**
1987	**ChC-N**	**0**	**62**	**4**	**10**	**.286**	**29**	**3.12**	**83 2/3**	**96**	**32**	**84**	**4**	**0**	**0**	**36**
1988	Bos-A	0	64	4	5	.444	26	2.80	83 2/3	96	37	72	7	0	0	29
1989	Bos-A	0	64	6	1	.857	28	3.57	70 2/3	96	33	53	6	0	0	25
1990	Bos-A	0	11	2	1	.667	3	1.88	14 1/3	17	9	13	0	0	0	4
1990	StL-N	0	53	3	4	.429	16	2.10	68 2/3	70	20	58	3	0	0	27
1991	StL-N	0	67	6	3	.667	19	2.34	73	67	13	70	5	0	0	47
1992	StL-N	0	70	4	9	.308	26	3.12	75	60	26	62	4	0	0	43
1993	StL-N	0	55	2	4	.333	25	4.50	50	49	9	49	11	0	0	43
1993	NYY-A	0	8	0	0	—	0	0.00	8	11	5	4	0	0	0	3
1994	Bal-A	0	41	1	4	.200	14	3.29	38 1/3	42	11	34	6	0	0	33
1995	Cal-A	0	52	0	5	.000	19	3.47	49 1/3	43	25	42	3	0	0	37
1996	Cal-A	0	11	0	0	—	3	2.45	11	6	3	8	0	0	0	0
1996	Cin-N	0	43	3	4	.429	20	4.06	44 1/3	35	23	49	4	0	0	2
1997	Mon-N	0	25	0	1	.000	14	5.82	21 2/3	15	8	28	2	0	0	5
Career average		0	57	4	5	.436	24	3.03	71 2/3	70	27	63	5	0	0	27
Cubs average		**1**	**57**	**5**	**6**	**.440**	**28**	**2.92**	**85 1/3**	**81**	**33**	**74**	**5**	**0**	**0**	**23**
Career total		6	1022	71	92	.436	434	3.03	1289 1/3	1251	486	1133	89	0	0	478
Cubs total		**6**	**458**	**40**	**51**	**.440**	**221**	**2.92**	**681 1/3**	**644**	**264**	**591**	**38**	**0**	**0**	**180**

(continued)

Lee Arthur Smith, rhp, 1980–97

The 6'6" 270-pound Smith was one of the hardest throwers in the game in the 1980s, and when he stared down from the mound with that baleful glare, many batters were licked before they got a chance to swing.

Lee Smith was born on December 4, 1957, in Jamestown, Louisiana. He was one of the few pitching prospects that came out of the Cubs farm system in the 1970s. Smith was 5-6 with exactly one save in 1980 and 1981, his first two years in Chicago.

But in 1982, Cubs manager Lee Elia gave Smith the ball more often, and he responded with a team-high 17 saves to go with 99 strikeouts and a team-best 2.69 ERA. In 1983 Smith led the National League with 29 saves and a 1.65 ERA, tops among relievers.

There was no artifice to big Lee. Catchers needed to memorize only one sign, because Smith's pitch of choice, thrown about 99.9 percent of the time, was a 95 to 98 mph fastball, delivered overhand and with great accuracy. In 1983 Smith struck out 91 batters in 103⅓ innings and walked 41.

In 1984 he was almost as dominating, with a 9-7 record and 33 saves. That save total was second in the league that year. His strikeout totals were down (86 in 101 innings) and his ERA was up to 3.65, but the bottom line was that Smith was still Smith, a pitcher who generally closed the door on the other team.

That year, the Cubs ascended to the postseason for the first time since 1945. They were favored against the National League West champion San Diego Padres. When Chicago won the first two games, with Smith picking up a save in Game 2, the way to the World Series seemed open.

But the Padres roared back to win three consecutive victories and claim the pennant. Included in that streak was a 7-5 Padre victory in Game 4. San Diego first baseman Steve Garvey belted a home run off Smith in the bottom of the ninth to give the Padres the win. It was probably the turning point in the series, as San Diego won the next game to clinch the best three-of-five matchup.

That 1984 season began a stretch of four consecutive years of recording 30 or more saves by Smith for the Cubs. And in 1987, Smith saved 36 regular season games and also came in and saved a win in the All-Star Game by pitching three scoreless innings.

Latest Cubs manager Jim Frey expressed concern about Smith's conditioning, and it was true. The big fellow was a little hefty, but he could still bring it on. Many Cubs players believed Frey was overreacting.

At the end of the 1987 season, Smith was shipped to Boston for reliever Calvin Schiraldi and righty Al Nipper. It was a hideous trade, one of the worst in Cubs history. Neither Schiraldi nor Nipper did much for the Cubs. Smith pitched for 10 more years with the Red Sox, Cardinals, Yankees, Orioles, Angels, Reds and Expos. He retired in 1997 at 39 with 478 saves, still the all-time mark. Smith was also the first pitcher to reach the 400-save milestone. He remains the Cubs save leader with 180.

Smith, Robert Eldridge (Bob)

HEIGHT: 5'10"   RIGHTHANDER   BORN: 4/22/1895 ROGERSVILLE, TENNESSEE   DIED: 7/19/1987 WAYCROSS, GEORGIA

YEAR	TEAM	STARTS	GAMES	WON	LOST	PCT	ER	ERA	INNINGS PITCHED	STRIKE-OUTS	WALKS	HITS ALLOWED	HRS ALLOWED	COMP. GAMES	SHUT-OUTS	SAVES
1925	Bos-N	10	13	5	3	.625	46	4.47	92⅔	19	36	110	6	6	0	0
1926	Bos-N	23	33	10	13	.435	84	3.75	201⅓	44	75	199	10	14	4	1
1927	Bos-N	31	41	10	18	.357	109	3.76	260⅔	81	75	297	9	16	1	3
1928	Bos-N	26	38	13	17	.433	105	3.87	244⅓	59	74	274	11	14	0	2
1929	Bos-N	29	34	11	17	.393	120	4.68	231	65	71	256	20	19	1	3
1930	Bos-N	24	38	10	14	.417	104	4.26	219⅔	84	85	247	25	14	2	5
1931	**ChC-N**	**29**	**36**	**15**	**12**	**.556**	**86**	**3.22**	**240⅓**	**63**	**62**	**239**	**10**	**18**	**2**	**2**
1932	**ChC-N**	**11**	**34**	**4**	**3**	**.571**	**61**	**4.61**	**119**	**35**	**36**	**148**	**4**	**4**	**1**	**2**
1933	Cin-N	6	16	4	4	.500	18	2.20	73⅔	18	11	75	3	4	0	0
1933	Bos-N	4	14	4	3	.571	21	3.22	58⅔	16	7	68	3	3	1	1

(continued)

(continued)

1934	Bos-N	5	39	6	9	.400	63	4.66	121 2/3	26	36	133	9	3	0	5
1935	Bos-N	20	46	8	18	.308	89	3.94	203 1/3	58	61	232	13	8	2	5
1936	Bos-N	11	35	6	7	.462	57	3.77	136	36	35	142	3	5	2	8
1937	Bos-N	0	18	0	1	.000	20	4.09	44	14	6	52	6	0	0	3
Career average		18	33	8	11	.433	76	3.94	172 2/3	48	52	190	10	10	1	3
Cubs average		**20**	**35**	**10**	**8**	**.559**	**74**	**3.68**	**179 2/3**	**49**	**49**	**194**	**7**	**11**	**2**	**2**
Career total		229	435	106	139	.433	983	3.94	2246 1/3	618	670	2472	132	128	16	40
Cubs total		**40**	**70**	**19**	**15**	**.559**	**147**	**3.68**	**359 1/3**	**98**	**98**	**387**	**14**	**22**	**3**	**4**

Smith, Robert Walkup (Riverboat)
HEIGHT: 6'0" LEFTHANDER BORN: 5/13/1928 CLARENCE, MISSOURI

YEAR	TEAM	STARTS	GAMES	WON	LOST	PCT	ER	ERA	INNINGS PITCHED	STRIKE-OUTS	WALKS	HITS ALLOWED	HRS ALLOWED	COMP. GAMES	SHUT-OUTS	SAVES
1958	Bos-A	7	17	4	3	.571	28	3.78	66 2/3	43	45	61	4	1	0	0
1959	**ChC-N**	0	1	0	0	—	6	81.00	0 2/3	0	2	5	0	0	0	0
1959	Cle-A	3	12	0	1	.000	17	5.22	29 1/3	17	12	31	2	0	0	0
Career average		5	15	2	2	.500	26	4.75	48 1/3	30	30	49	3	1	0	0
Cubs average		**0**	**1**	**0**	**0**	**—**	**6**	**81.00**	**0 2/3**	**0**	**2**	**5**	**0**	**0**	**0**	**0**
Career total		10	30	4	4	.500	51	4.75	96 2/3	60	59	97	6	1	0	0
Cubs total		**0**	**1**	**0**	**0**	**—**	**6**	**81.00**	**0 2/3**	**0**	**2**	**5**	**0**	**0**	**0**	**0**

Smith, Willie
HEIGHT: 6'0" LEFTHANDER BORN: 2/11/1939 ANNISTON, ALABAMA

YEAR	TEAM	STARTS	GAMES	WON	LOST	PCT	ER	ERA	INNINGS PITCHED	STRIKE-OUTS	WALKS	HITS ALLOWED	HRS ALLOWED	COMP. GAMES	SHUT-OUTS	SAVES
1963	Det-A	2	11	1	0	1.000	11	4.57	21 2/3	16	13	24	2	0	0	2
1964	LAA-A	1	15	1	4	.200	10	2.84	31 2/3	20	10	34	5	0	0	0
1968	Cle-A	0	2	0	0	—	0	0.00	5	1	1	2	0	0	0	0
1968	**ChC-N**	0	1	0	0	—	0	0.00	2 2/3	2	0	0	0	0	0	0
Career average		1	10	1	1	.333	7	3.10	20 1/3	13	8	20	2	0	0	1
Cubs average		**0**	**1**	**0**	**0**	**—**	**0**	**0.00**	**2 2/3**	**2**	**0**	**0**	**0**	**0**	**0**	**0**
Career total		3	29	2	4	.333	21	3.10	61	39	24	60	7	0	0	2
Cubs total		**0**	**1**	**0**	**0**	**—**	**0**	**3.10**	**2 2/3**	**2**	**0**	**0**	**0**	**0**	**0**	**0**

Solis, Marcelino
HEIGHT: 6'1" LEFTHANDER BORN: 7/19/1930 SAN LUIS POTOSI, MEXICO

YEAR	TEAM	STARTS	GAMES	WON	LOST	PCT	ER	ERA	INNINGS PITCHED	STRIKE-OUTS	WALKS	HITS ALLOWED	HRS ALLOWED	COMP. GAMES	SHUT-OUTS	SAVES
1958	ChC-N	4	15	3	3	.500	35	6.06	52	15	20	74	5	0	0	0
Career average		4	15	3	3	.500	35	6.06	52	15	20	74	5	0	0	0
Cubs average		**4**	**15**	**3**	**3**	**.500**	**35**	**6.06**	**52**	**15**	**20**	**74**	**5**	**0**	**0**	**0**
Career total		4	15	3	3	.500	35	6.06	52	15	20	74	5	0	0	0
Cubs total		**4**	**15**	**3**	**3**	**.500**	**35**	**6.06**	**52**	**15**	**20**	**74**	**5**	**0**	**0**	**0**

Solomon, Eddie (Buddy)
HEIGHT: 6'2" RIGHTHANDER BORN: 2/9/1951 PERRY, GEORGIA DIED: 1/12/1986 MACON, GEORGIA

YEAR	TEAM	STARTS	GAMES	WON	LOST	PCT	ER	ERA	INNINGS PITCHED	STRIKE-OUTS	WALKS	HITS ALLOWED	HRS ALLOWED	COMP. GAMES	SHUT-OUTS	SAVES
1973	LA-N	0	4	0	0	—	5	7.11	6 1/3	6	4	10	3	0	0	0
1974	LA-N	0	4	0	0	—	1	1.50	6	2	2	5	1	0	0	0
1975	**ChC-N**	0	6	0	0	—	1	1.35	6 2/3	3	6	7	1	0	0	0
1976	StL-N	2	26	1	1	.500	20	4.86	37	19	16	45	2	0	0	0
1977	Atl-N	16	18	6	6	.500	45	4.57	88 2/3	54	34	110	10	0	0	0
1978	Atl-N	8	37	4	6	.400	48	4.08	106	64	50	98	12	0	0	2
1979	Atl-N	30	31	7	14	.333	87	4.21	186	96	51	184	19	4	0	0
1980	Pit-N	12	26	7	3	.700	30	2.69	100 1/3	35	37	96	8	2	0	0
1981	Pit-N	17	22	8	6	.571	44	3.12	127	38	27	133	10	2	0	1
1982	Pit-N	10	11	2	6	.250	35	6.75	46 2/3	18	18	69	9	0	0	1
1982	CWS-A	0	6	1	0	1.000	3	3.68	7 1/3	2	2	7	1	0	0	0
Career average		10	19	4	4	.462	32	4.00	71 2/3	34	25	76	8	1	0	0
Cubs average		**0**	**6**	**0**	**0**	**—**	**1**	**1.35**	**6 2/3**	**3**	**6**	**7**	**1**	**0**	**0**	**0**
Career total		95	191	36	42	.462	319	4.00	718	337	247	764	76	8	0	4
Cubs total		**0**	**6**	**0**	**0**	**—**	**1**	**1.35**	**6 2/3**	**3**	**6**	**7**	**1**	**0**	**0**	**0**

Sommers, Rudolph (Rudy)
HEIGHT: 5'11"   LEFTHANDER   BORN: 10/30/1888 CINCINNATI, OHIO   DIED: 3/18/1949 LOUISVILLE, KENTUCKY

YEAR	TEAM	STARTS	GAMES	WON	LOST	PCT	ER	ERA	INNINGS PITCHED	STRIKE-OUTS	WALKS	HITS ALLOWED	HRS ALLOWED	COMP. GAMES	SHUT-OUTS	SAVES
1912	ChC-N	0	1	0	1	.000	1	3.00	3	2	2	4	0	0	0	0
1914	Bro-F	8	23	2	7	.222	37	4.06	82	40	34	88	2	2	0	2
1926	Bos-A	0	2	0	0	—	3	13.50	2	0	3	3	0	0	0	0
1927	Bos-A	0	7	0	0	—	13	8.36	14	2	14	18	2	0	0	0
Career average		2	8	1	2	.200	14	4.81	25 1/3	11	13	28	1	1	0	1
Cubs average		**0**	**1**	**0**	**1**	**.000**	**1**	**3.00**	**3**	**2**	**2**	**4**	**0**	**0**	**0**	**0**
Career total		8	33	2	8	.200	54	4.81	101	44	53	113	4	2	0	2
Cubs total		**0**	**1**	**0**	**1**	**.000**	**1**	**3.00**	**3**	**2**	**2**	**4**	**0**	**0**	**0**	**0**

Sorensen, Lary Alan
HEIGHT: 6'2"   RIGHTHANDER   BORN: 10/4/1955 DETROIT, MICHIGAN

YEAR	TEAM	STARTS	GAMES	WON	LOST	PCT	ER	ERA	INNINGS PITCHED	STRIKE-OUTS	WALKS	HITS ALLOWED	HRS ALLOWED	COMP. GAMES	SHUT-OUTS	SAVES
1977	Mil-A	20	23	7	10	.412	69	4.36	142 1/3	57	36	147	10	9	0	0
1978	Mil-A	36	37	18	12	.600	100	3.21	280 2/3	78	50	277	14	17	3	1
1979	Mil-A	34	34	15	14	.517	104	3.98	235 1/3	63	42	250	30	16	2	0
1980	Mil-A	29	35	12	10	.545	80	3.68	195 2/3	54	45	242	13	8	2	1
1981	StL-N	23	23	7	7	.500	51	3.27	140 1/3	52	26	149	3	3	1	0
1982	Cle-A	30	32	10	15	.400	118	5.61	189 1/3	62	55	251	19	6	1	0
1983	Cle-A	34	36	12	11	.522	105	4.24	222 2/3	76	65	238	21	8	1	0
1984	Oak-A	21	46	6	13	.316	100	4.91	183 1/3	63	44	240	21	2	0	1
1985	ChC-N	3	45	3	7	.300	39	4.26	82 1/3	34	24	86	8	0	0	1
1987	Mon-N	5	23	3	4	.429	25	4.72	47 2/3	21	12	56	7	0	0	2
1988	SF-N	0	12	0	0	—	9	4.86	16 2/3	9	3	24	1	0	0	0
Career average		21	31	8	9	.474	73	4.15	158	52	37	178	13	6	1	1
Cubs average		**3**	**45**	**3**	**7**	**.300**	**39**	**4.26**	**82 1/3**	**34**	**24**	**86**	**8**	**0**	**0**	**0**
Career total		235	346	93	103	.474	800	4.15	1736 1/3	569	402	1960	147	69	10	6
Cubs total		**3**	**45**	**3**	**7**	**.300**	**39**	**4.26**	**82 1/3**	**34**	**24**	**86**	**8**	**0**	**0**	**0**

Spalding, Albert Goodwill (Al)
HEIGHT: 6'1"   RIGHTHANDER   BORN: 9/2/1850 BYRON, ILLINOIS   DIED: 9/9/1915 SAN DIEGO, CALIFORNIA

YEAR	TEAM	STARTS	GAMES	WON	LOST	PCT	ER	ERA	INNINGS PITCHED	STRIKE-OUTS	WALKS	HITS ALLOWED	HRS ALLOWED	COMP. GAMES	SHUT-OUTS	SAVES
1876	ChN-N	60	61	47	12	.797	103	1.75	528 2/3	39	26	542	6	53	8	0
1877	ChN-N	1	4	1	0	1.000	4	3.27	11	2	0	17	0	0	0	1
Career average		31	33	24	6	.800	54	1.78	270	21	13	280	3	27	4	1
Cubs average		**31**	**33**	**24**	**6**	**.800**	**54**	**1.78**	**270**	**21**	**13**	**280**	**3**	**27**	**4**	**1**
Career total		61	65	48	12	.800	107	1.78	539 2/3	41	26	559	6	53	8	1
Cubs total		**61**	**65**	**48**	**12**	**.800**	**107**	**1.78**	**539 2/3**	**41**	**26**	**559**	**6**	**53**	**8**	**1**

Speier, Justin James
HEIGHT: 6'4"   RIGHTHANDER   BORN: 11/6/1973 WALNUT CREEK, CALIFORNIA

YEAR	TEAM	STARTS	GAMES	WON	LOST	PCT	ER	ERA	INNINGS PITCHED	STRIKE-OUTS	WALKS	HITS ALLOWED	HRS ALLOWED	COMP. GAMES	SHUT-OUTS	SAVES
1998	ChC-N	0	1	0	0	—	2	13.50	1 1/3	2	1	2	0	0	0	0
1998	Fla-N	0	18	0	3	.000	18	8.38	19 1/3	15	12	25	7	0	0	0
1999	Atl-N	0	19	0	0	—	18	5.65	28 2/3	22	13	28	8	0	0	0
2000	Cle-A	0	47	5	2	.714	25	3.29	68 1/3	69	28	57	9	0	0	0
2001	Cle-A	0	12	2	0	1.000	16	6.97	20 2/3	15	8	24	5	0	0	0
2001	Col-N	0	42	4	3	.571	23	3.70	56	47	12	47	8	0	0	0
Career average		0	35	3	2	.579	26	4.72	48 2/3	43	19	46	9	0	0	0
Cubs average		**0**	**1**	**0**	**0**	**—**	**2**	**13.50**	**1 1/3**	**2**	**1**	**2**	**0**	**0**	**0**	**0**
Career total		0	139	11	8	.579	102	4.72	194 1/3	170	74	183	37	0	0	0
Cubs total		**0**	**1**	**0**	**0**	**—**	**2**	**13.50**	**1 1/3**	**2**	**1**	**2**	**0**	**0**	**0**	**0**

Spongberg, Carl Gustav
HEIGHT: 6'2"   RIGHTHANDER   BORN: 5/21/1884 IDAHO FALLS, IDAHO   DIED: 7/21/1938 LOS ANGELES, CALIFORNIA

YEAR	TEAM	STARTS	GAMES	WON	LOST	PCT	ER	ERA	INNINGS PITCHED	STRIKE-OUTS	WALKS	HITS ALLOWED	HRS ALLOWED	COMP. GAMES	SHUT-OUTS	SAVES
1908	ChC-N	0	1	0	0	—	7	9.00	7	4	6	9	1	0	0	0
Career average		0	1	0	0	—	7	9.00	7	4	6	9	1	0	0	0
Cubs average		**0**	**1**	**0**	**0**	**—**	**7**	**9.00**	**7**	**4**	**6**	**9**	**1**	**0**	**0**	**0**
Career total		0	1	0	0	—	7	9.00	7	4	6	9	1	0	0	0
Cubs total		**0**	**1**	**0**	**0**	**—**	**7**	**9.00**	**7**	**4**	**6**	**9**	**1**	**0**	**0**	**0**

Spradlin, Jerry Carl
HEIGHT: 6'7"   RIGHTHANDER   BORN: 6/14/1967 FULLERTON, CALIFORNIA

YEAR	TEAM	STARTS	GAMES	WON	LOST	PCT	ER	ERA	INNINGS PITCHED	STRIKE-OUTS	WALKS	HITS ALLOWED	HRS ALLOWED	COMP. GAMES	SHUT-OUTS	SAVES
1993	Cin-N	0	37	2	1	.667	19	3.49	49	24	9	44	4	0	0	2
1994	Cin-N	0	6	0	0	—	9	10.13	8	4	2	12	2	0	0	0
1996	Cin-N	0	1	0	0	—	0	0.00	0 ⅓	0	0	0	0	0	0	0
1997	Phi-N	0	76	4	8	.333	43	4.74	81 ⅔	67	27	86	9	0	0	1
1998	Phi-N	0	69	4	4	.500	32	3.53	81 ⅔	76	20	63	9	0	0	1
1999	Cle-A	0	4	0	0	—	6	18.00	3	2	3	6	1	0	0	0
1999	SF-N	0	59	3	1	.750	27	4.19	58	52	29	59	4	0	0	0
2000	KC-A	0	50	4	4	.500	46	5.52	75	54	27	81	9	0	0	7
2000	**ChC-N**	**1**	**8**	**0**	**1**	**.000**	**14**	**8.40**	**15**	**13**	**5**	**20**	**2**	**0**	**0**	**0**
Career average		0	44	2	3	.472	28	4.75	53	42	17	53	6	0	0	2
Cubs average		**1**	**8**	**0**	**1**	**.000**	**14**	**8.40**	**15**	**13**	**5**	**20**	**2**	**0**	**0**	**0**
Career total		1	310	17	19	.472	196	4.75	371 ⅔	292	122	371	40	0	0	11
Cubs total		**1**	**8**	**0**	**1**	**.000**	**14**	**8.40**	**15**	**13**	**5**	**20**	**2**	**0**	**0**	**0**

Sprague, Charles Wellington (Charlie)
HEIGHT: 5'11"   LEFTHANDER   BORN: 10/10/1864 CLEVELAND, OHIO   DIED: 12/31/1912 DES MOINES, IOWA

YEAR	TEAM	STARTS	GAMES	WON	LOST	PCT	ER	ERA	INNINGS PITCHED	STRIKE-OUTS	WALKS	HITS ALLOWED	HRS ALLOWED	COMP. GAMES	SHUT-OUTS	SAVES
1887	**ChN-N**	**3**	**3**	**1**	**0**	**1.000**	**12**	**4.91**	**22**	**9**	**13**	**37**	**1**	**2**	**0**	**0**
1889	Cle-N	2	2	0	2	.000	16	8.47	17	8	10	27	0	2	0	0
1890	Tol-AA	12	19	9	5	.643	53	3.89	122 ⅔	59	78	111	0	9	0	0
Career average		6	8	3	2	.588	27	4.51	54	25	34	58	0	4	0	0
Cubs average		**3**	**3**	**1**	**0**	**1.000**	**12**	**4.91**	**22**	**9**	**13**	**37**	**1**	**2**	**0**	**0**
Career total		17	24	10	7	.588	81	4.51	161 ⅔	76	101	175	1	13	0	0
Cubs total		**3**	**3**	**1**	**0**	**1.000**	**12**	**4.91**	**22**	**9**	**13**	**37**	**1**	**2**	**0**	**0**

Spring, Jack Russell
HEIGHT: 6'1"   LEFTHANDER   BORN: 3/11/1933 SPOKANE, WASHINGTON

YEAR	TEAM	STARTS	GAMES	WON	LOST	PCT	ER	ERA	INNINGS PITCHED	STRIKE-OUTS	WALKS	HITS ALLOWED	HRS ALLOWED	COMP. GAMES	SHUT-OUTS	SAVES
1955	Phi-N	0	2	0	1	.000	2	6.75	2 ⅔	2	1	2	2	0	0	0
1957	Bos-A	0	1	0	0	—	0	0.00	1	2	0	0	0	0	0	0
1958	Was-A	1	3	0	0	—	11	14.14	7	1	7	16	1	0	0	0
1961	LAA-A	4	18	3	0	1.000	18	4.26	38	27	15	35	4	0	0	0
1962	LAA-A	0	57	4	2	.667	29	4.02	65	31	30	66	7	0	0	6
1963	LAA-A	0	45	3	0	1.000	13	3.05	38 ⅓	13	9	40	3	0	0	2
1964	LAA-A	0	6	1	0	1.000	1	2.70	3 ⅓	0	3	3	1	0	0	0
1964	**ChC-N**	**0**	**7**	**0**	**0**	**—**	**4**	**6.00**	**6**	**1**	**2**	**4**	**0**	**0**	**0**	**0**
1964	StL-N	0	2	0	0	—	1	3.00	3	0	1	8	1	0	0	0
1965	Cle-A	0	14	1	2	.333	9	3.74	21 ⅔	9	10	21	2	0	0	0
Career average		1	19	2	1	.706	11	4.26	23 ⅓	11	10	24	3	0	0	1
Cubs average		**0**	**7**	**0**	**0**	**—**	**4**	**6.00**	**6**	**1**	**2**	**4**	**0**	**0**	**0**	**0**
Career total		5	155	12	5	.706	88	4.26	186	86	78	195	21	0	0	8
Cubs total		**0**	**7**	**0**	**0**	**—**	**4**	**6.00**	**6**	**1**	**2**	**4**	**0**	**0**	**0**	**0**

St. Vrain, James Marcellin (Jim)
HEIGHT: 5'9" LEFTHANDER BORN: 6/6/1883 RALLS COUNTY, MISSOURI DIED: 6/12/1937 BUTTE, MONTANA

YEAR	TEAM	STARTS	GAMES	WON	LOST	PCT	ER	ERA	INNINGS PITCHED	STRIKE-OUTS	WALKS	HITS ALLOWED	HRS ALLOWED	COMP. GAMES	SHUT-OUTS	SAVES
1902	ChC-N	11	12	4	6	.400	22	2.08	95	51	25	88	0	10	1	0
Career average		11	12	4	6	.400	22	2.08	95	51	25	88	0	10	1	0
Cubs average		**11**	**12**	**4**	**6**	**.400**	**22**	**2.08**	**95**	**51**	**25**	**88**	**0**	**10**	**1**	**0**
Career total		11	12	4	6	.400	22	2.08	95	51	25	88	0	10	1	0
Cubs total		**11**	**12**	**4**	**6**	**.400**	**22**	**2.08**	**95**	**51**	**25**	**88**	**0**	**10**	**1**	**0**

Stack, William Edward (Eddie)
HEIGHT: 6'0" RIGHTHANDER BORN: 10/24/1887 CHICAGO, ILLINOIS DIED: 8/28/1958 CHICAGO, ILLINOIS

YEAR	TEAM	STARTS	GAMES	WON	LOST	PCT	ER	ERA	INNINGS PITCHED	STRIKE-OUTS	WALKS	HITS ALLOWED	HRS ALLOWED	COMP. GAMES	SHUT-OUTS	SAVES
1910	Phi-N	16	20	6	7	.462	52	4.00	117	48	34	115	7	8	1	0
1911	Phi-N	10	13	5	5	.500	31	3.59	77 2/3	36	41	67	3	5	0	0
1912	Bro-N	17	28	7	5	.583	53	3.36	142	45	55	139	3	4	0	1
1913	Bro-N	9	23	4	4	.500	23	2.38	87	34	32	79	0	4	1	0
1913	**ChC-N**	**7**	**11**	**4**	**2**	**.667**	**24**	**4.24**	**51**	**28**	**15**	**56**	**1**	**3**	**1**	**1**
1914	**ChC-N**	**1**	**7**	**0**	**1**	**.000**	**9**	**4.96**	**16 1/3**	**9**	**11**	**13**	**0**	**0**	**0**	**0**
Career average		12	20	5	5	.520	38	3.52	98 1/3	40	38	94	3	5	1	0
Cubs average		**4**	**9**	**2**	**2**	**.571**	**17**	**4.41**	**33 2/3**	**19**	**13**	**35**	**1**	**2**	**1**	**1**
Career total		60	102	26	24	.520	192	3.52	491	200	188	469	14	24	3	2
Cubs total		**8**	**18**	**4**	**3**	**.571**	**33**	**4.41**	**67 1/3**	**37**	**26**	**69**	**1**	**3**	**1**	**1**

Standridge, Alfred Peter (Pete)
HEIGHT: 5'10" RIGHTHANDER BORN: 4/25/1891 BLACK DIAMOND, WASHINGTON DIED: 8/2/1963 SAN FRANCISCO, CALIFORNIA

YEAR	TEAM	STARTS	GAMES	WON	LOST	PCT	ER	ERA	INNINGS PITCHED	STRIKE-OUTS	WALKS	HITS ALLOWED	HRS ALLOWED	COMP. GAMES	SHUT-OUTS	SAVES
1911	StL-N	0	2	0	0	—	5	9.64	4 2/3	3	4	10	0	0	0	0
1915	**ChC-N**	**3**	**29**	**4**	**1**	**.800**	**45**	**3.61**	**112 1/3**	**42**	**36**	**120**	**2**	**2**	**0**	**0**
Career average		2	16	2	1	.800	25	3.85	58 2/3	23	20	65	1	1	0	0
Cubs average		**3**	**29**	**4**	**1**	**.800**	**45**	**3.61**	**112 1/3**	**42**	**36**	**120**	**2**	**2**	**0**	**0**
Career total		3	31	4	1	.800	50	3.85	117	45	40	130	2	2	0	0
Cubs total		**3**	**29**	**4**	**1**	**.800**	**45**	**3.61**	**112 1/3**	**42**	**36**	**120**	**2**	**2**	**0**	**0**

Starr, Raymond Francis (Ray *or* Iron Man)
HEIGHT: 6'1" RIGHTHANDER BORN: 4/23/1906 NOWATA, OKLAHOMA DIED: 2/9/1963 BAYLIS, ILLINOIS

YEAR	TEAM	STARTS	GAMES	WON	LOST	PCT	ER	ERA	INNINGS PITCHED	STRIKE-OUTS	WALKS	HITS ALLOWED	HRS ALLOWED	COMP. GAMES	SHUT-OUTS	SAVES
1932	StL-N	2	3	1	1	.500	6	2.70	20	6	10	19	2	1	1	0
1933	NYG-N	2	6	0	1	.000	8	5.40	13 1/3	2	10	19	0	0	0	0
1933	Bos-N	1	9	0	1	.000	12	3.86	28	15	9	32	4	0	0	0
1941	Cin-N	4	7	3	2	.600	10	2.65	34	11	6	28	1	3	2	0
1942	Cin-N	33	37	15	13	.536	82	2.67	276 2/3	83	106	228	10	17	4	0
1943	Cin-N	33	36	11	10	.524	88	3.64	217 1/3	42	91	201	9	9	2	1
1944	Pit-N	12	27	6	5	.545	50	5.02	89 2/3	25	36	116	6	5	0	3
1945	Pit-N	0	4	0	2	.000	7	9.45	6 2/3	0	4	10	0	0	0	0
1945	**ChC-N**	**1**	**9**	**1**	**0**	**1.000**	**11**	**7.43**	**13 1/3**	**5**	**7**	**17**	**1**	**0**	**0**	**0**
Career average		13	20	5	5	.514	39	3.53	100	27	40	96	5	5	1	1
Cubs average		**1**	**9**	**1**	**0**	**1.000**	**11**	**7.43**	**13 1/3**	**5**	**7**	**17**	**1**	**0**	**0**	**0**
Career total		88	138	37	35	.514	274	3.53	699	189	279	670	33	35	9	4
Cubs total		**1**	**9**	**1**	**0**	**1.000**	**11**	**7.43**	**13 1/3**	**5**	**7**	**17**	**1**	**0**	**0**	**0**

Stauffer, Charles Edward (Ed)
HEIGHT: 5'11" RIGHTHANDER BORN: 1/10/1898 EMSWORTH, PENNSYLVANIA DIED: 7/2/1979 ST. PETERSBURG, FLORIDA

YEAR	TEAM	STARTS	GAMES	WON	LOST	PCT	ER	ERA	INNINGS PITCHED	STRIKE-OUTS	WALKS	HITS ALLOWED	HRS ALLOWED	COMP. GAMES	SHUT-OUTS	SAVES
1923	**ChC-N**	**0**	**1**	**0**	**0**	**—**	**3**	**13.50**	**2**	**0**	**1**	**5**	**0**	**0**	**0**	**0**
1925	StL-A	1	20	0	1	.000	18	5.34	30 1/3	13	21	34	1	0	0	0

(continued)

(continued)

					PCT	ER	ERA	INNINGS PITCHED	STRIKE-OUTS	WALKS	HITS ALLOWED	HRS ALLOWED	COMP. GAMES	SHUT-OUTS	SAVES
Career average	1	11	0	1	.000	11	5.85	16 1/3	7	11	20	1	0	0	0
Cubs average	**0**	**1**	**0**	**0**	**—**	**3**	**13.50**	**2**	**0**	**1**	**5**	**0**	**0**	**0**	**0**
Career total	1	21	0	1	.000	21	5.85	32 1/3	13	22	39	1	0	0	0
Cubs total	**0**	**1**	**0**	**0**	**—**	**3**	**13.50**	**2**	**0**	**1**	**5**	**0**	**0**	**0**	**0**

Steenstra, Kenneth Gregory (Kennie)
HEIGHT: 6'5"   RIGHTHANDER   BORN: 10/13/1970 SPRINGFIELD, MISSOURI

YEAR	TEAM	STARTS	GAMES	WON	LOST	PCT	ER	ERA	INNINGS PITCHED	STRIKE-OUTS	WALKS	HITS ALLOWED	HRS ALLOWED	COMP. GAMES	SHUT-OUTS	SAVES
1998	ChC-N	0	4	0	0	—	4	10.80	3 1/3	4	1	7	2	0	0	0
Career average	0	4	0	0	—	4	10.80	3 1/3	4	1	7	2	0	0	0
Cubs average	**0**	**4**	**0**	**0**	**—**	**4**	**10.80**	**3 1/3**	**4**	**1**	**7**	**2**	**0**	**0**	**0**
Career total	0	4	0	0	—	4	10.80	3 1/3	4	1	7	2	0	0	0
Cubs total	**0**	**4**	**0**	**0**	**—**	**4**	**10.80**	**3 1/3**	**4**	**1**	**7**	**2**	**0**	**0**	**0**

Steevens, Morris Dale (Morrie)
HEIGHT: 6'2"   LEFTHANDER   BORN: 10/7/1940 SALEM, ILLINOIS

YEAR	TEAM	STARTS	GAMES	WON	LOST	PCT	ER	ERA	INNINGS PITCHED	STRIKE-OUTS	WALKS	HITS ALLOWED	HRS ALLOWED	COMP. GAMES	SHUT-OUTS	SAVES
1962	ChC-N	1	12	0	1	.000	4	2.40	15	5	11	10	0	0	0	0
1964	Phi-N	0	4	0	0	—	1	3.38	2 2/3	3	1	5	0	0	0	0
1965	Phi-N	0	6	0	1	.000	5	16.88	2 2/3	3	4	5	1	0	0	0
Career average	0	7	0	1	.000	3	4.43	6 2/3	4	5	7	0	0	0	0
Cubs average	**1**	**12**	**0**	**1**	**.000**	**4**	**2.40**	**15**	**5**	**11**	**10**	**0**	**0**	**0**	**0**
Career total	1	22	0	2	.000	10	4.43	20 1/3	11	16	20	1	0	0	0
Cubs total	**1**	**12**	**0**	**1**	**.000**	**4**	**2.40**	**15**	**5**	**11**	**10**	**0**	**0**	**0**	**0**

Stein, Edward F. (Ed)
HEIGHT: 5'11"   RIGHTHANDER   BORN: 9/5/1869 DETROIT, MICHIGAN   DIED: 5/10/1928 DETROIT, MICHIGAN

YEAR	TEAM	STARTS	GAMES	WON	LOST	PCT	ER	ERA	INNINGS PITCHED	STRIKE-OUTS	WALKS	HITS ALLOWED	HRS ALLOWED	COMP. GAMES	SHUT-OUTS	SAVES
1890	ChN-N	18	20	11	6	.647	68	3.81	160 2/3	65	83	147	9	15	1	0
1891	ChN-N	10	14	6	6	.500	42	3.74	101	38	57	99	7	9	1	1
1892	Bro-N	42	48	25	16	.610	119	2.84	377 1/3	190	150	310	6	38	6	2
1893	Bro-N	34	37	19	14	.576	125	3.77	298 1/3	81	119	294	4	28	1	0
1894	Bro-N	40	44	26	14	.650	181	4.54	359	84	171	396	10	37	2	1
1895	Bro-N	27	32	15	13	.536	134	4.72	255 1/3	55	93	282	9	24	1	1
1896	Bro-N	10	17	3	7	.300	49	4.88	90 1/3	16	51	130	6	6	0	0
1898	Bro-N	2	3	0	2	.000	14	5.48	23	6	9	39	0	2	0	0
Career average	23	27	13	10	.574	92	3.96	208	67	92	212	6	20	2	1
Cubs average	**14**	**17**	**9**	**6**	**.586**	**55**	**3.78**	**131**	**52**	**70**	**123**	**8**	**12**	**1**	**1**
Career total	183	215	105	78	.574	732	3.96	1665	535	733	1697	51	159	12	5
Cubs total	**28**	**34**	**17**	**12**	**.586**	**110**	**3.78**	**261 2/3**	**103**	**140**	**246**	**16**	**24**	**2**	**1**

Stein, William Randolph (Randy)
HEIGHT: 6'4"   RIGHTHANDER   BORN: 3/7/1953 POMONA, CALIFORNIA

YEAR	TEAM	STARTS	GAMES	WON	LOST	PCT	ER	ERA	INNINGS PITCHED	STRIKE-OUTS	WALKS	HITS ALLOWED	HRS ALLOWED	COMP. GAMES	SHUT-OUTS	SAVES
1978	Mil-A	1	31	3	2	.600	43	5.33	72 2/3	42	39	78	5	0	0	1
1979	Sea-A	1	23	2	3	.400	27	5.88	41 1/3	39	27	48	7	0	0	0
1981	Sea-A	0	5	0	1	.000	11	10.61	9 1/3	6	8	18	1	0	0	0
1982	ChC-N	0	6	0	0	—	4	3.48	10 1/3	6	7	7	2	0	0	0
Career average	1	16	1	2	.455	21	5.72	33 1/3	23	20	38	4	0	0	0
Cubs average	**0**	**6**	**0**	**0**	**—**	**4**	**3.48**	**10 1/3**	**6**	**7**	**7**	**2**	**0**	**0**	**0**
Career total	2	65	5	6	.455	85	5.72	133 2/3	93	81	151	15	0	0	1
Cubs total	**0**	**6**	**0**	**0**	**—**	**4**	**3.48**	**10 1/3**	**6**	**7**	**7**	**2**	**0**	**0**	**0**

Stephenson, Chester Earl (Earl)
HEIGHT: 6'3"   LEFTHANDER   BORN: 7/31/1947 BENSON, NORTH CAROLINA

YEAR	TEAM	STARTS	GAMES	WON	LOST	PCT	ER	ERA	INNINGS PITCHED	STRIKE-OUTS	WALKS	HITS ALLOWED	HRS ALLOWED	COMP. GAMES	SHUT-OUTS	SAVES
1971	ChC-N	0	16	1	0	1.000	10	4.43	20 1/3	11	11	24	1	0	0	1
1972	Mil-A	8	35	3	5	.375	29	3.25	80 1/3	33	33	79	5	1	0	0
1977	Bal-A	0	1	0	0	—	3	9.00	3	2	0	5	1	0	0	0
1978	Bal-A	0	2	0	0	—	3	2.79	9 2/3	4	5	10	0	0	0	0
Career average		2	14	1	1	.444	11	3.57	28 1/3	13	12	30	2	0	0	0
Cubs average		0	16	1	0	1.000	10	4.43	20 1/3	11	11	24	1	0	0	1
Career total		8	54	4	5	.444	45	3.57	113 1/3	50	49	118	7	1	0	1
Cubs total		0	16	1	0	1.000	10	4.43	20 1/3	11	11	24	1	0	0	1

Stevens, David James (Dave)
HEIGHT: 6'3"   RIGHTHANDER   BORN: 3/4/1970 FULLERTON, CALIFORNIA

YEAR	TEAM	STARTS	GAMES	WON	LOST	PCT	ER	ERA	INNINGS PITCHED	STRIKE-OUTS	WALKS	HITS ALLOWED	HRS ALLOWED	COMP. GAMES	SHUT-OUTS	SAVES
1994	Min-A	0	24	5	2	.714	34	6.80	45	24	23	55	6	0	0	0
1995	Min-A	0	56	5	4	.556	37	5.07	65 2/3	47	32	74	14	0	0	10
1996	Min-A	0	49	3	3	.500	30	4.66	58	29	25	58	12	0	0	11
1997	Min-A	6	6	1	3	.250	23	9.00	23	16	17	41	8	0	0	0
1997	ChC-N	0	10	0	2	.000	10	9.64	9 1/3	13	9	13	0	0	0	0
1998	ChC-N	0	31	1	2	.333	20	4.74	38	31	17	42	6	0	0	0
1999	Cle-A	0	5	0	0	—	10	10.00	9	6	8	10	1	0	0	0
2000	Atl-N	0	2	0	0	—	4	12.00	3	4	1	5	2	0	0	0
Career average		1	26	2	2	.484	24	6.02	36	24	19	43	7	0	0	3
Cubs average		0	21	1	2	.200	15	5.70	23 2/3	22	13	28	3	0	0	0
Career total		6	183	15	16	.484	168	6.02	251	170	132	298	49	0	0	21
Cubs total		0	41	1	4	.200	30	5.70	47 1/3	44	26	55	6	0	0	0

Stewart, William Macklin (Mack)
HEIGHT: 6'0"   RIGHTHANDER   BORN: 9/23/1914 STEVENSON, ALABAMA   DIED: 3/21/1960 MACON, GEORGIA

YEAR	TEAM	STARTS	GAMES	WON	LOST	PCT	ER	ERA	INNINGS PITCHED	STRIKE-OUTS	WALKS	HITS ALLOWED	HRS ALLOWED	COMP. GAMES	SHUT-OUTS	SAVES
1944	ChC-N	0	8	0	0	—	2	1.46	12 1/3	3	4	11	1	0	0	0
1945	ChC-N	1	16	0	1	.000	15	4.76	28 1/3	9	14	37	0	0	0	0
Career average		1	12	0	1	.000	9	3.76	20 1/3	6	9	24	1	0	0	0
Cubs average		1	12	0	1	.000	9	3.76	20 1/3	6	9	24	1	0	0	0
Career total		1	24	0	1	.000	17	3.76	40 2/3	12	18	48	1	0	0	0
Cubs total		1	24	0	1	.000	17	3.76	40 2/3	12	18	48	1	0	0	0

Stoddard, Timothy Paul (Tim)
HEIGHT: 6'7"   RIGHTHANDER   BORN: 1/24/1953 EAST CHICAGO, INDIANA

YEAR	TEAM	STARTS	GAMES	WON	LOST	PCT	ER	ERA	INNINGS PITCHED	STRIKE-OUTS	WALKS	HITS ALLOWED	HRS ALLOWED	COMP. GAMES	SHUT-OUTS	SAVES
1975	CWS-A	0	1	0	0	—	1	9.00	1	0	0	2	1	0	0	0
1978	Bal-A	0	8	0	1	.000	12	6.00	18	14	8	22	3	0	0	0
1979	Bal-A	0	29	3	1	.750	11	1.71	58	47	19	44	3	0	0	3
1980	Bal-A	0	64	5	3	.625	24	2.51	86	64	38	72	2	0	0	26
1981	Bal-A	0	31	4	2	.667	16	3.86	37 1/3	32	18	38	6	0	0	7
1982	Bal-A	0	50	3	4	.429	25	4.02	56	42	29	53	4	0	0	12
1983	Bal-A	0	47	4	3	.571	39	6.09	57 2/3	50	29	65	10	0	0	9
1984	ChC-N	0	58	10	6	.625	39	3.82	92	87	57	77	9	0	0	7
1985	SD-N	0	44	1	6	.143	31	4.65	60	42	37	63	3	0	0	1
1986	SD-N	0	30	1	3	.250	19	3.77	45 1/3	47	34	33	6	0	0	0
1986	NYY-A	0	24	4	1	.800	21	3.83	49 1/3	34	23	41	6	0	0	8
1987	NYY-A	0	57	4	3	.571	36	3.50	92 2/3	78	30	83	13	0	0	3
1988	NYY-A	0	28	2	2	.500	39	6.38	55	33	27	62	5	0	0	3
1989	Cle-A	0	14	0	0	—	7	2.95	21 1/3	12	7	25	1	0	0	0

(continued)

(continued)

Career average	0	37	3	3	.539	25	3.95	56	45	27	52	6	0	0	6
Cubs average	**0**	**58**	**10**	**6**	**.625**	**39**	**3.82**	**92**	**87**	**57**	**77**	**9**	**0**	**0**	**7**
Career total	0	485	41	35	.539	320	3.95	729 2/3	582	356	680	72	0	0	76
Cubs total	**0**	**58**	**10**	**6**	**.625**	**39**	**3.82**	**92**	**87**	**57**	**77**	**9**	**0**	**0**	**7**

Stone, Steven Michael (Steve)
HEIGHT: 5'10"   RIGHTHANDER   BORN: 7/14/1947 EUCLID, OHIO

YEAR	TEAM	STARTS	GAMES	WON	LOST	PCT	ER	ERA	INNINGS PITCHED	STRIKE-OUTS	WALKS	HITS ALLOWED	HRS ALLOWED	COMP. GAMES	SHUT-OUTS	SAVES
1971	SF-N	19	24	5	9	.357	51	4.15	110 2/3	63	55	110	9	2	2	0
1972	SF-N	16	27	6	8	.429	41	2.98	123 2/3	85	49	97	11	4	1	0
1973	CWS-A	22	36	6	11	.353	83	4.24	176 1/3	138	82	163	11	3	0	1
1974	**ChC-N**	**23**	**38**	**8**	**6**	**.571**	**78**	**4.14**	**169 2/3**	**90**	**64**	**185**	**19**	**1**	**0**	**0**
1975	**ChC-N**	**32**	**33**	**12**	**8**	**.600**	**94**	**3.95**	**214 1/3**	**139**	**80**	**198**	**24**	**6**	**1**	**0**
1976	**ChC-N**	**15**	**17**	**3**	**6**	**.333**	**34**	**4.08**	**75**	**33**	**21**	**70**	**6**	**1**	**1**	**0**
1977	CWS-A	31	31	15	12	.556	104	4.51	207 1/3	124	80	228	25	8	0	0
1978	CWS-A	30	30	12	12	.500	103	4.37	212	118	84	196	19	6	1	0
1979	Bal-A	32	32	11	7	.611	78	3.77	186	96	73	173	31	3	0	0
1980	Bal-A	37	37	25	7	.781	90	3.23	250 2/3	149	101	224	22	9	1	0
1981	Bal-A	12	15	4	7	.364	32	4.60	62 2/3	30	27	63	7	0	0	0
Career average	24	29	10	8	.535	72	3.97	162 2/3	97	65	155	17	4	1	0
Cubs average	**23**	**29**	**8**	**7**	**.535**	**69**	**4.04**	**153**	**87**	**55**	**151**	**16**	**3**	**1**	**0**
Career total	269	320	107	93	.535	788	3.97	1788 1/3	1065	716	1707	184	43	7	1
Cubs total	**70**	**88**	**23**	**20**	**.535**	**206**	**4.04**	**459**	**262**	**165**	**453**	**49**	**8**	**2**	**0**

Stoneman, William Hambly (Bill)
HEIGHT: 5'10"   RIGHTHANDER   BORN: 4/7/1944 OAK PARK, ILLINOIS

YEAR	TEAM	STARTS	GAMES	WON	LOST	PCT	ER	ERA	INNINGS PITCHED	STRIKE-OUTS	WALKS	HITS ALLOWED	HRS ALLOWED	COMP. GAMES	SHUT-OUTS	SAVES
1967	**ChC-N**	**2**	**28**	**2**	**4**	**.333**	**23**	**3.29**	**52**	**52**	**22**	**51**	**7**	**0**	**0**	**4**
1968	**ChC-N**	**0**	**18**	**0**	**1**	**.000**	**18**	**5.52**	**29 1/3**	**18**	**14**	**35**	**6**	**0**	**0**	**0**
1969	Mon-N	36	42	11	19	.367	115	4.39	235 2/3	185	123	233	26	8	5	0
1970	Mon-N	30	40	7	15	.318	106	4.59	207 2/3	176	109	209	26	5	3	0
1971	Mon-N	39	39	17	16	.515	103	3.15	294 2/3	251	146	243	20	20	3	0
1972	Mon-N	35	36	12	14	.462	83	2.98	250 2/3	171	102	213	15	13	4	0
1973	Mon-N	17	29	4	8	.333	73	6.80	96 2/3	48	55	120	12	0	0	1
1974	Cal-A	11	13	1	8	.111	40	6.14	58 2/3	33	31	78	8	0	0	0
Career average	21	31	7	11	.388	70	4.08	154 2/3	117	75	148	15	6	2	1
Cubs average	**1**	**23**	**1**	**3**	**.286**	**21**	**4.00**	**46 1/3**	**35**	**18**	**43**	**7**	**0**	**0**	**2**
Career total	170	245	54	85	.388	561	4.08	1236 1/3	934	602	1182	120	46	15	5
Cubs total	**2**	**46**	**2**	**5**	**.286**	**41**	**4.00**	**92 1/3**	**70**	**36**	**86**	**13**	**0**	**0**	**4**

Stratton, C. Scott (Scott)
HEIGHT: 6'0"   RIGHTHANDER   BORN: 10/2/1869 CAMPBELLSBURG, KENTUCKY   DIED: 3/8/1939 LOUISVILLE, KENTUCKY

YEAR	TEAM	STARTS	GAMES	WON	LOST	PCT	ER	ERA	INNINGS PITCHED	STRIKE-OUTS	WALKS	HITS ALLOWED	HRS ALLOWED	COMP. GAMES	SHUT-OUTS	SAVES
1888	Lou-AA	28	33	10	17	.370	109	3.64	269 2/3	97	53	287	7	28	2	0
1889	Lou-AA	17	19	3	13	.188	48	3.23	133 2/3	42	42	157	6	13	0	1
1890	Lou-AA	49	50	34	14	.708	113	2.36	431	207	61	398	3	44	4	0
1891	Pit-N	2	2	0	2	.000	5	2.45	18 1/3	5	5	16	0	2	0	0
1891	Lou-AA	20	20	6	13	.316	78	4.08	172	52	34	204	10	20	1	0
1892	Lou-N	40	42	21	19	.525	114	2.92	351 2/3	93	70	342	1	39	2	0
1893	Lou-N	35	37	12	25	.324	190	5.43	314 2/3	43	100	451	8	35	1	0
1894	Lou-N	5	7	1	4	.200	40	8.37	43	3	13	72	3	4	0	0
1894	**ChN-N**	**13**	**16**	**8**	**7**	**.533**	**80**	**6.03**	**119 1/3**	**23**	**40**	**198**	**5**	**12**	**0**	**0**
1895	**ChN-N**	**5**	**5**	**2**	**3**	**.400**	**32**	**9.60**	**30**	**4**	**14**	**51**	**1**	**3**	**0**	**0**
Career average	27	29	12	15	.453	101	3.87	235 1/3	71	54	272	6	25	1	0
Cubs average	**9**	**11**	**5**	**5**	**.500**	**56**	**6.75**	**74 2/3**	**14**	**27**	**125**	**3**	**8**	**0**	**0**
Career total	214	231	97	117	.453	809	3.87	1883 1/3	569	432	2176	44	200	10	1
Cubs total	**18**	**21**	**10**	**10**	**.500**	**112**	**6.75**	**149 1/3**	**27**	**54**	**249**	**6**	**15**	**0**	**0**

Stueland, George Anton
HEIGHT: 6'1"   RIGHTHANDER   BORN: 3/2/1899 ALGONA, IOWA   DIED: 9/9/1964 ONAWA, IOWA

YEAR	TEAM	STARTS	GAMES	WON	LOST	PCT	ER	ERA	INNINGS PITCHED	STRIKE-OUTS	WALKS	HITS ALLOWED	HRS ALLOWED	COMP. GAMES	SHUT-OUTS	SAVES
1921	ChC-N	1	2	0	1	.000	7	5.73	11	4	7	11	0	0	0	0
1922	ChC-N	11	34	9	4	.692	73	5.92	111	43	48	129	9	4	0	0
1923	ChC-N	0	6	0	1	.000	5	5.63	8	2	5	11	0	0	0	0
1925	ChC-N	0	2	0	0	—	1	3.00	3	2	3	2	0	0	0	0
Career average		3	11	2	2	.600	22	5.82	33⅓	13	16	38	2	1	0	0
Cubs average		**3**	**11**	**2**	**2**	**.600**	**22**	**5.82**	**33⅓**	**13**	**16**	**38**	**2**	**1**	**0**	**0**
Career total		12	44	9	6	.600	86	5.82	133	51	63	153	9	4	0	0
Cubs total		**12**	**44**	**9**	**6**	**.600**	**86**	**5.82**	**133**	**51**	**63**	**153**	**9**	**4**	**0**	**0**

Sturtze, Tanyon James
HEIGHT: 6'5"   RIGHTHANDER   BORN: 10/12/1970 WORCESTER, MASSACHUSETTS

YEAR	TEAM	STARTS	GAMES	WON	LOST	PCT	ER	ERA	INNINGS PITCHED	STRIKE-OUTS	WALKS	HITS ALLOWED	HRS ALLOWED	COMP. GAMES	SHUT-OUTS	SAVES
1995	ChC-N	0	2	0	0	—	2	9.00	2	0	1	2	1	0	0	0
1996	ChC-N	0	6	1	0	1.000	11	9.00	11	7	5	16	3	0	0	0
1997	Tex-A	5	9	1	1	.500	30	8.27	32⅔	18	18	45	6	0	0	0
1999	CWS-A	1	1	0	0	—	0	0.00	6	2	2	4	0	0	0	0
2000	CWS-A	1	10	1	2	.333	21	12.06	15⅔	6	15	25	4	0	0	0
2000	TB-A	5	19	4	0	1.000	15	2.56	52⅔	38	14	47	4	0	0	1
2001	TB-A	27	39	11	12	.478	96	4.42	195⅓	110	79	200	23	0	0	1
Career average		7	14	3	3	.545	29	4.99	52⅔	30	22	57	7	0	0	0
Cubs average		**0**	**4**	**1**	**0**	**1.000**	**7**	**9.00**	**6⅔**	**4**	**3**	**9**	**2**	**0**	**0**	**0**
Career total		39	86	18	15	.545	175	4.99	315⅓	181	134	339	41	0	0	1
Cubs total		**0**	**8**	**1**	**0**	**1.000**	**13**	**9.00**	**13**	**7**	**6**	**18**	**4**	**0**	**0**	**0**

Sullivan, Martin C. (Marty)
HEIGHT: —   RIGHTHANDER   BORN: 10/20/1862 LOWELL, MASSACHUSETTS   DIED: 1/6/1894 LOWELL, MASSACHUSETTS

YEAR	TEAM	STARTS	GAMES	WON	LOST	PCT	ER	ERA	INNINGS PITCHED	STRIKE-OUTS	WALKS	HITS ALLOWED	HRS ALLOWED	COMP. GAMES	SHUT-OUTS	SAVES
1887	ChN-N	0	1	0	0	—	2	7.71	2⅓	1	1	7	0	0	0	0
Career average		0	1	0	0	—	2	7.71	2⅓	1	1	7	0	0	0	0
Cubs average		**0**	**1**	**0**	**0**	**—**	**2**	**7.71**	**2⅓**	**1**	**1**	**7**	**0**	**0**	**0**	**0**
Career total		0	1	0	0	—	2	7.71	2⅓	1	1	7	0	0	0	0
Cubs total		**0**	**1**	**0**	**0**	**—**	**2**	**7.71**	**2⅓**	**1**	**1**	**7**	**0**	**0**	**0**	**0**

Sullivan, Michael Joseph (Mike *or* Big Mike)
HEIGHT: 6'1"   BORN: 10/23/1866 BOSTON, MASSACHUSETTS   DIED: 6/14/1906 BOSTON, MASSACHUSETTS

YEAR	TEAM	STARTS	GAMES	WON	LOST	PCT	ER	ERA	INNINGS PITCHED	STRIKE-OUTS	WALKS	HITS ALLOWED	HRS ALLOWED	COMP. GAMES	SHUT-OUTS	SAVES
1889	WaN-N	3	9	0	3	.000	33	7.24	41	15	32	47	2	3	0	0
1890	ChN-N	12	12	5	6	.455	49	4.59	96	33	58	108	3	10	0	0
1891	Phi-AA	0	2	0	2	.000	7	3.50	18	7	10	17	2	2	0	0
1891	NYG-N	3	3	1	2	.333	9	3.38	24	11	8	24	0	3	0	0
1892	Cin-N	16	21	12	7	.632	57	3.08	166⅓	56	74	179	8	15	0	0
1893	Cin-N	18	27	8	13	.381	103	5.05	183⅔	40	103	200	5	14	0	1
1894	Was-N	12	20	2	10	.167	86	6.58	117⅔	21	74	166	10	11	0	1
1894	Cle-N	11	13	6	5	.545	64	6.35	90⅔	19	47	128	4	9	0	0
1895	Cle-N	3	4	1	3	.250	29	8.42	31	5	16	42	1	2	0	0
1896	NYG-N	22	25	8	13	.381	96	4.66	185⅓	42	71	188	3	18	0	2
1897	NYG-N	16	23	10	8	.556	84	5.09	148⅔	35	71	183	6	11	1	1
1898	Bos-N	2	3	0	0	—	16	12.00	12	1	9	19	1	0	0	0
1899	Bos-N	1	1	1	0	1.000	5	5.00	9	1	4	10	1	1	0	0
Career average		11	15	5	7	.429	58	5.11	102	26	52	119	4	9	0	0
Cubs average		**12**	**12**	**5**	**6**	**.455**	**49**	**4.59**	**96**	**33**	**58**	**108**	**3**	**10**	**0**	**0**
Career total		121	163	54	72	.429	638	5.11	1123⅓	286	577	1311	46	99	1	5
Cubs total		**12**	**12**	**5**	**6**	**.455**	**49**	**4.59**	**96**	**33**	**58**	**108**	**3**	**10**	**0**	**0**

Sutcliffe, Richard Lee (Rick)
HEIGHT: 6'7" RIGHTHANDER BORN: 6/21/1956 INDEPENDENCE, MISSOURI

YEAR	TEAM	STARTS	GAMES	WON	LOST	PCT	ER	ERA	INNINGS PITCHED	STRIKE-OUTS	WALKS	HITS ALLOWED	HRS ALLOWED	COMP. GAMES	SHUT-OUTS	SAVES
1976	LA-N	1	1	0	0	—	0	0.00	5	3	1	2	0	0	0	0
1978	LA-N	0	2	0	0	—	0	0.00	1 ⅔	0	1	2	0	0	0	0
1979	LA-N	30	39	17	10	.630	93	3.46	242	117	97	217	16	5	1	0
1980	LA-N	10	42	3	9	.250	68	5.56	110	59	55	122	10	1	1	5
1981	LA-N	6	14	2	2	.500	21	4.02	47	16	20	41	5	0	0	0
1982	Cle-A	27	34	14	8	.636	71	2.96	216	142	98	174	16	6	1	1
1983	Cle-A	35	36	17	11	.607	116	4.29	243 ⅓	160	102	251	23	10	2	0
1984	Cle-A	15	15	4	5	.444	54	5.15	94 ⅓	58	46	111	7	2	0	0
1984	**ChC-N**	**20**	**20**	**16**	**1**	**.941**	**45**	**2.69**	**150 ⅓**	**155**	**39**	**123**	**9**	**7**	**3**	**0**
1985	**ChC-N**	**20**	**20**	**8**	**8**	**.500**	**46**	**3.18**	**130**	**102**	**44**	**119**	**12**	**6**	**3**	**0**
1986	**ChC-N**	**27**	**28**	**5**	**14**	**.263**	**91**	**4.64**	**176 ⅔**	**122**	**96**	**166**	**18**	**4**	**1**	**0**
1987	**ChC-N**	**34**	**34**	**18**	**10**	**.643**	**97**	**3.68**	**237 ⅓**	**174**	**106**	**223**	**24**	**6**	**1**	**0**
1988	**ChC-N**	**32**	**32**	**13**	**14**	**.481**	**97**	**3.86**	**226**	**144**	**70**	**232**	**18**	**12**	**2**	**0**
1989	**ChC-N**	**34**	**35**	**16**	**11**	**.593**	**93**	**3.66**	**229**	**153**	**69**	**202**	**18**	**5**	**1**	**0**
1990	**ChC-N**	**5**	**5**	**0**	**2**	**.000**	**14**	**5.91**	**21 ⅓**	**7**	**12**	**25**	**2**	**0**	**0**	**0**
1991	**ChC-N**	**18**	**19**	**6**	**5**	**.545**	**44**	**4.10**	**96 ⅔**	**52**	**45**	**96**	**4**	**0**	**0**	**0**
1992	Bal-A	36	36	16	15	.516	118	4.47	237 ⅓	109	74	251	20	5	2	0
1993	Bal-A	28	29	10	10	.500	106	5.75	166	80	74	212	23	3	0	0
1994	StL-N	14	16	6	4	.600	49	6.52	67 ⅔	26	32	93	11	0	0	0
Career average		22	25	10	8	.552	68	4.08	150	93	60	148	13	4	1	0
Cubs average		**24**	**24**	**10**	**8**	**.558**	**66**	**3.74**	**158 ⅓**	**114**	**60**	**148**	**13**	**5**	**1**	**0**
Career total		392	457	171	139	.552	1223	4.08	2697 ⅔	1679	1081	2662	236	72	18	6
Cubs total		**190**	**193**	**82**	**65**	**.558**	**527**	**3.74**	**1267 ⅓**	**909**	**481**	**1186**	**105**	**40**	**11**	**0**

Richard (Rick) Lee Sutcliffe, rhp, 1976, 1978–94

What a difference a change of scenery makes. In 1984 Rick Sutcliffe went from the American to the National League and was transformed from being a sub-.500 righthander to being the Cy Young winner for a championship squad.

Sutcliffe, born on June 21, 1956, in Independence, Missouri, was a star rookie for the Los Angeles Dodgers in 1979, with a 17-10 record to go with 117 strikeouts. (Sutcliffe had made brief appearances in Los Angeles during the 1976 and 1978 seasons.) He was exiled, however, to the bull pen in 1980 and 1981, a move that produced mixed results for the Dodgers.

He was eventually traded to Cleveland prior to the 1982 season and had a strong year as a starter, earning a 14-8 record and leading the American League in ERA with a 2.96 mark. The next year, Sutcliffe won 17 games for the Indians.

But the ultracompetitive Sutcliffe had difficulty playing for a losing team, which the Indians were at the time. As 1984 opened, Sutcliffe was struggling with a 4-5 mark and he demanded a trade. Among the teams he vowed he would not be sent to was the Cubs, which were also losing more than they won.

But Cubs manager Dallas Green convinced Sutcliffe that he was rebuilding the Cubs and that Sutcliffe could help put the team over the top. Sutcliffe agreed to a one-year contract with the Windy City organization.

The trade was initially seen by skeptical Cubs fans and the press as a bad move for Chicago. The Cubs gave away super prospect Joe Carter and youngster Mel Hall for Sutcliffe and two lesser known veterans. Carter had already shown that he was going to be a great player.

Sutcliffe quieted the nay-sayers in emphatic fashion by going 16-1 for the Cubs and leading the team to the National League East crown.

"We got," said Ryne Sandberg in his autobiography, "a true leader in Sutcliffe. A gamer."

(continued)

(continued)

Sutcliffe's 1984 ERA with the Cubs was 2.69. He struck out 155 batters and walked a minuscule 39. Those numbers earned him the Cy Young, and he became the first player in major league history to win the award after pitching in both leagues in the same year.

The next year, however, Sutcliffe was slowed by a hamstring injury that forced him onto the disabled list three times that year. Worse, as Sutcliffe tried to pitch with the injury, he developed a compensatory injury to the shoulder on his pitching arm that precipitated control problems for Sutcliffe in 1985 and 1986.

Sutcliffe bounced back in 1987, leading the league in wins with 18 and striking out a career-high 174 batters. In 1989 he was 16-11 and helped the Cubs to their second National League East crown in the 1980s.

But Sutcliffe was pitching in pain. Teammates joked that he was stalling so much on the mound that he was becoming a "human rain delay." He confided to a teammate that at times he was in so much pain from either his arm or his leg or both that he simply had to step off the mound and give the pain time to subside.

Sutcliffe missed most of the 1990 and 1991 seasons with injuries. The Cubs opted not to sign him for the 1992 season. Sutcliffe eventually signed with the Orioles and started 36 games, winning 16 of them. After playing another year in Baltimore, he signed with St. Louis for the 1994 season before retiring.

Sutcliffe wasn't with the Cubs long enough to make any of the team's all-time lists, but his .941 winning percentage in 1984 is still a team record, as is the record for most games won in a row, 14, also set in 1984. He also won 16 consecutive games in the 1984 to 1985 season, another Cubs team record.

Sutter, Howard Bruce (Bruce)
HEIGHT: 6'2"   RIGHTHANDER   BORN: 1/8/1953 LANCASTER, PENNSYLVANIA

YEAR	TEAM	STARTS	GAMES	WON	LOST	PCT	ER	ERA	INNINGS PITCHED	STRIKE-OUTS	WALKS	HITS ALLOWED	HRS ALLOWED	COMP. GAMES	SHUT-OUTS	SAVES
1976	ChC-N	0	52	6	3	.667	25	2.70	83 1/3	73	26	63	4	0	0	10
1977	ChC-N	0	62	7	3	.700	16	1.34	107 1/3	129	23	69	5	0	0	31
1978	ChC-N	0	64	8	10	.444	35	3.18	99	106	34	82	10	0	0	27
1979	ChC-N	0	62	6	6	.500	25	2.22	101 1/3	110	32	67	3	0	0	37
1980	ChC-N	0	60	5	8	.385	30	2.64	102 1/3	76	34	90	5	0	0	28
1981	StL-N	0	48	3	5	.375	24	2.62	82 1/3	57	24	64	5	0	0	25
1982	StL-N	0	70	9	8	.529	33	2.90	102 1/3	61	34	88	8	0	0	36
1983	StL-N	0	60	9	10	.474	42	4.23	89 1/3	64	30	90	8	0	0	21
1984	StL-N	0	71	5	7	.417	21	1.54	122 2/3	77	23	109	9	0	0	45
1985	Atl-N	0	58	7	7	.500	44	4.48	88 1/3	52	29	91	13	0	0	23
1986	Atl-N	0	16	2	0	1.000	9	4.34	18 2/3	16	9	17	3	0	0	3
1988	Atl-N	0	38	1	4	.200	24	4.76	45 1/3	40	11	49	4	0	0	14
Career average		0	55	6	6	.489	27	2.83	87	72	26	73	6	0	0	25
Cubs average		**0**	**60**	**6**	**6**	**.516**	**26**	**2.39**	**98 2/3**	**99**	**30**	**74**	**5**	**0**	**0**	**27**
Career total		0	661	68	71	.489	328	2.83	1042 1/3	861	309	879	77	0	0	300
Cubs total		**0**	**300**	**32**	**30**	**.516**	**131**	**2.39**	**493 1/3**	**494**	**149**	**371**	**27**	**0**	**0**	**133**

Swartzbaugh, David Theodore (Dave)
HEIGHT: 6'2"   RIGHTHANDER   BORN: 2/11/1968 MIDDLETOWN, OHIO

YEAR	TEAM	STARTS	GAMES	WON	LOST	PCT	ER	ERA	INNINGS PITCHED	STRIKE-OUTS	WALKS	HITS ALLOWED	HRS ALLOWED	COMP. GAMES	SHUT-OUTS	SAVES
1995	ChC-N	0	7	0	0	—	0	0.00	7 1/3	5	3	5	0	0	0	0
1996	ChC-N	5	6	0	2	.000	17	6.38	24	13	14	26	3	0	0	0
1997	ChC-N	2	2	0	1	.000	8	9.00	8	4	7	12	1	0	0	0
Career average		2	5	0	1	.000	8	5.72	13	7	8	14	1	0	0	0
Cubs average		**2**	**5**	**0**	**1**	**.000**	**8**	**5.72**	**13**	**7**	**8**	**14**	**1**	**0**	**0**	**0**
Career total		7	15	0	3	.000	25	5.72	39 1/3	22	24	43	4	0	0	0
Cubs total		**7**	**15**	**0**	**3**	**.000**	**25**	**5.72**	**39 1/3**	**22**	**24**	**43**	**4**	**0**	**0**	**0**

Howard Bruce Sutter, rhp, 1976–86, 1988

Using what could be called a revolutionary pitch, Bruce Sutter became one of the most dominant closers in baseball history and a four-time All-Star with the Cubs in his brief five-year stint in the Windy City.

Born on January 8, 1953, in Lancaster, Pennsylvania, Sutter very nearly didn't make it to the major leagues at all. As an 18-year-old rookie in the Cubs farm system, Sutter injured his right elbow while pitching in a rookie league game. Rest and surgery helped only marginally, and Sutter began working with Fred Martin, a roving pitching coach with the Cubs.

Actually, Martin was *the* roving pitching coach for the Cubs, as the organization had only one such coach in their entire minor league system. Martin taught Sutter how to hold the baseball in a forkball grip (that is, basically clutching the baseball between one's forked index and middle fingers and using the thumb and other two fingers to "guide" the ball).

The technique, when mastered, caused the baseball to dip sharply just before it reached the plate. The pitch came in like a fastball and dropped like a curveball, an extremely difficult pitch to track and hit. Sutter had a major genetic advantage here: exceptionally large hands with long fingers, which enabled him to grip the ball very firmly and fire to the plate with tremendous velocity.

Early on, Sutter recalled that some of his splitters ended up bouncing in front of the plate, "but guys were swinging anyway" because the pitch looked so good as it came closer to the batter.

He was called up to the major leagues in 1976, and he finished with a 6-3 mark with 10 saves. By 1977 Sutter had mastered the split-fingered fastball, ending up with a 7-3 record and 31 saves despite missing six weeks of the season with injured ribs. What was the most telling about Sutter's season that year was his minuscule 1.34 ERA. Nobody could hit him, it seemed.

The 1978 season saw Sutter earn 27 saves. During the midseason All-Star Game, he picked up the win in a 7-3 National League victory. In 1979 Sutter saved a league-leading 37 games and was once again the winner in the All-Star Game, this time the score was 7-6, National League. Sutter became the only pitcher besides Don Drysdale, who did it in 1967 and 1968, to win two consecutive All-Star Games. Sutter's numbers in 1979 easily earned him the Cy Young award.

Nothing changed the next two years: Sutter saved a league-best 28 contests in 1980 and a league-leading 25 contests for the Cubs in 1981. It was basically Bruce Sutter's world: National League batters were just living in it.

But after the 1980 season, Sutter was understandably looking for a better contract—specifically, a pact with deferred money. After he won an arbitration hearing, the Cubs balked at the $700,000 contract and traded him to St. Louis. A key cog had left the team, and the Cubs would struggle in the standings for several years.

Sutter helped the Cardinals to the world championship in 1982. He was traded to the Braves for the 1985 season and pitched there until his retirement in 1988. Sutter is second all-time on the Cubs save list and fourth in appearances with an even 300.

Sweetland, Leo (Sugar)

HEIGHT: 5'11" LEFTHANDER BORN: 8/15/1901 ST. IGNACE, MICHIGAN DIED: 3/4/1974 MELBOURNE, FLORIDA

YEAR	TEAM	STARTS	GAMES	WON	LOST	PCT	ER	ERA	INNINGS PITCHED	STRIKE-OUTS	WALKS	HITS ALLOWED	HRS ALLOWED	COMP. GAMES	SHUT-OUTS	SAVES
1927	Phi-N	13	21	2	10	.167	71	6.16	103 2/3	21	53	147	3	6	0	0
1928	Phi-N	18	37	3	15	.167	99	6.58	135 1/3	23	97	163	15	5	0	2
1929	Phi-N	26	43	13	11	.542	116	5.11	204 1/3	47	87	255	23	10	2	2
1930	Phi-N	25	34	7	15	.318	143	7.71	167	36	60	271	24	8	1	0
1931	**ChC-N**	**14**	**26**	**8**	**7**	**.533**	**73**	**5.04**	**130 1/3**	**32**	**61**	**156**	**3**	**9**	**0**	**0**

(continued)

(Sweetland, continued)

Career average	19	32	7	12	.363	100	6.10	148	32	72	198	14	8	1	1
Cubs average	**14**	**26**	**8**	**7**	**.533**	**73**	**5.04**	**130 ⅓**	**32**	**61**	**156**	**3**	**9**	**0**	**0**
Career total	96	161	33	58	.363	502	6.10	740 ⅔	159	358	992	68	38	3	4
Cubs total	**14**	**26**	**8**	**7**	**.533**	**73**	**5.04**	**130 ⅓**	**32**	**61**	**156**	**3**	**9**	**0**	**0**

Tapani, Kevin Ray (Tap)

HEIGHT: 6'0"   RIGHTHANDER   BORN: 2/18/1964 DES MOINES, IOWA

YEAR	TEAM	STARTS	GAMES	WON	LOST	PCT	ER	ERA	INNINGS PITCHED	STRIKE-OUTS	WALKS	HITS ALLOWED	HRS ALLOWED	COMP. GAMES	SHUT-OUTS	SAVES
1989	NYM-N	0	3	0	0	—	3	3.68	7 ⅓	2	4	5	1	0	0	0
1989	Min-A	5	5	2	2	.500	14	3.86	32 ⅔	21	8	34	2	0	0	0
1990	Min-A	28	28	12	8	.600	72	4.07	159 ⅓	101	29	164	12	1	1	0
1991	Min-A	34	34	16	9	.640	81	2.99	244	135	40	225	23	4	1	0
1992	Min-A	34	34	16	11	.593	97	3.97	220	138	48	226	17	4	1	0
1993	Min-A	35	36	12	15	.444	111	4.43	225 ⅔	150	57	243	21	3	1	0
1994	Min-A	24	24	11	7	.611	80	4.62	156	91	39	181	13	4	1	0
1995	Min-A	20	20	6	11	.353	73	4.92	133 ⅔	88	34	155	21	3	1	0
1995	LA-N	11	13	4	2	.667	32	5.05	57	43	14	72	8	0	0	0
1996	CWS-A	34	34	13	10	.565	115	4.59	225 ⅓	150	76	236	34	1	0	0
1997	**ChC-N**	**13**	**13**	**9**	**3**	**.750**	**32**	**3.39**	**85**	**55**	**23**	**77**	**7**	**1**	**1**	**0**
1998	**ChC-N**	**34**	**35**	**19**	**9**	**.679**	**118**	**4.85**	**219**	**136**	**62**	**244**	**30**	**2**	**2**	**0**
1999	**ChC-N**	**23**	**23**	**6**	**12**	**.333**	**73**	**4.83**	**136**	**73**	**33**	**151**	**12**	**1**	**0**	**0**
2000	**ChC-N**	**30**	**30**	**8**	**12**	**.400**	**109**	**5.01**	**195 ⅔**	**150**	**47**	**208**	**35**	**2**	**0**	**0**
2001	**ChC-N**	**29**	**29**	**9**	**14**	**.391**	**84**	**4.49**	**168 ⅓**	**149**	**40**	**186**	**24**	**0**	**0**	**0**
Career average	27	28	11	10	.534	84	4.35	174 ⅓	114	43	185	20	2	1	0
Cubs average	**26**	**26**	**10**	**10**	**.505**	**83**	**4.66**	**160 ⅔**	**113**	**41**	**173**	**22**	**1**	**1**	**0**
Career total	354	361	143	125	.534	1094	4.35	2265	1482	554	2407	260	26	9	0
Cubs total	**129**	**130**	**51**	**50**	**.505**	**416**	**4.66**	**804**	**563**	**205**	**866**	**108**	**6**	**3**	**0**

Tatis, Ramon Francisco

HEIGHT: 6'3"   LEFTHANDER   BORN: 5/2/1973 GUAYUBIN, DOMINICAN REPUBLIC

YEAR	TEAM	STARTS	GAMES	WON	LOST	PCT	ER	ERA	INNINGS PITCHED	STRIKE-OUTS	WALKS	HITS ALLOWED	HRS ALLOWED	COMP. GAMES	SHUT-OUTS	SAVES
1997	**ChC-N**	**0**	**56**	**1**	**1**	**.500**	**33**	**5.34**	**55 ⅔**	**33**	**29**	**66**	**13**	**0**	**0**	**0**
1998	TB-A	0	22	0	0	—	18	13.89	11 ⅔	5	16	23	2	0	0	0
Career average	0	39	1	1	.500	26	6.82	33 ⅔	19	23	45	8	0	0	0
Cubs average	**0**	**56**	**1**	**1**	**.500**	**33**	**5.34**	**55 ⅔**	**33**	**29**	**66**	**13**	**0**	**0**	**0**
Career total	0	78	1	1	.500	51	6.82	67 ⅓	38	45	89	15	0	0	0
Cubs total	**0**	**56**	**1**	**1**	**.500**	**33**	**5.34**	**55 ⅔**	**33**	**29**	**66**	**13**	**0**	**0**	**0**

Tavarez, Julian

HEIGHT: 6'2"   RIGHTHANDER   BORN: 5/22/1973 SANTIAGO, DOMINICAN REPUBLIC

YEAR	TEAM	STARTS	GAMES	WON	LOST	PCT	ER	ERA	INNINGS PITCHED	STRIKE-OUTS	WALKS	HITS ALLOWED	HRS ALLOWED	COMP. GAMES	SHUT-OUTS	SAVES
1993	Cle-A	7	8	2	2	.500	27	6.57	37	19	13	53	7	0	0	0
1994	Cle-A	1	1	0	1	.000	4	21.60	1 ⅔	0	1	6	1	0	0	0
1995	Cle-A	0	57	10	2	.833	23	2.44	85	68	21	76	7	0	0	0
1996	Cle-A	4	51	4	7	.364	48	5.36	80 ⅔	46	22	101	9	0	0	0
1997	SF-N	0	89	6	4	.600	38	3.87	88 ⅓	38	34	91	6	0	0	1
1998	SF-N	0	60	5	3	.625	36	3.80	85 ⅓	52	36	96	5	0	0	0
1999	SF-N	0	47	2	0	1.000	36	5.93	54 ⅔	33	25	65	7	0	0	1
2000	Col-N	12	51	11	5	.688	59	4.43	120	62	53	124	11	1	0	1
2001	**ChC-N**	**28**	**34**	**10**	**9**	**.526**	**81**	**4.52**	**161 ⅓**	**107**	**69**	**172**	**13**	**0**	**0**	**0**
Career average	6	44	6	4	.602	39	4.44	79 ⅓	47	30	87	7	0	0	0
Cubs average	**28**	**34**	**10**	**9**	**.526**	**81**	**4.52**	**161 ⅓**	**107**	**69**	**172**	**13**	**0**	**0**	**0**
Career total	52	398	50	33	.602	352	4.44	714	425	274	784	66	1	0	2
Cubs total	**28**	**34**	**10**	**9**	**.526**	**81**	**4.52**	**161 ⅓**	**107**	**69**	**172**	**13**	**0**	**0**	**0**

Taylor, John W. (Jack)
HEIGHT: 5'10"   RIGHTHANDER   BORN: 1/14/1874 NEW STRAIGHTSVILLE, OHIO   DIED: 3/4/1938 COLUMBUS, OHIO

YEAR	TEAM	STARTS	GAMES	WON	LOST	PCT	ER	ERA	INNINGS PITCHED	STRIKE-OUTS	WALKS	HITS ALLOWED	HRS ALLOWED	COMP. GAMES	SHUT-OUTS	SAVES
1898	ChN-N	5	5	5	0	1.000	10	2.20	41	11	10	32	0	5	0	0
1899	ChN-N	39	41	18	22	.450	148	3.76	354 ⅔	67	84	380	6	39	1	0
1900	ChN-N	26	28	10	17	.370	63	2.55	222 ⅓	57	58	226	4	25	2	1
1901	ChN-N	31	33	13	19	.406	103	3.36	275 ⅔	68	44	341	5	30	0	0
1902	ChC-N	33	36	23	11	.676	48	1.33	324 ⅔	83	43	271	2	33	7	1
1903	ChC-N	33	37	21	14	.600	85	2.45	312 ⅓	83	57	277	2	33	1	1
1904	StL-N	39	41	20	19	.513	87	2.22	352	103	82	297	5	39	2	1
1905	StL-N	34	37	15	21	.417	118	3.44	309	102	85	302	10	34	3	1
1906	StL-N	17	17	8	9	.471	37	2.15	155	27	47	133	3	17	1	0
1906	ChC-N	16	17	12	3	.800	30	1.83	147 ⅓	34	39	116	1	15	2	0
1907	ChC-N	13	18	7	5	.583	45	3.29	123	22	33	127	3	8	0	0
Career average		29	31	15	14	.521	77	2.66	261 ⅔	66	58	250	4	28	2	1
Cubs average		**25**	**27**	**14**	**11**	**.545**	**67**	**2.66**	**225**	**53**	**46**	**221**	**3**	**24**	**2**	**0**
Career total		286	310	152	140	.521	774	2.66	2617	657	582	2502	41	278	19	5
Cubs total		**196**	**215**	**109**	**91**	**.545**	**532**	**2.66**	**1801**	**425**	**368**	**1770**	**23**	**188**	**13**	**3**

John W. (Jack) "The Brakeman," "Old Iron Arm" Taylor, rhp, 1898 –1907

Jack Taylor was the ultimate inning-eater in his day, a man who, during his career in Chicago and else-where, almost never came out of a game until the last out was recorded.

Taylor was born on January 14, 1874, in New Straightsville, Ohio. He was signed by the Cubs (then called the Orphans) in 1898 and made his debut in September of that season. Taylor started five games that year and completed them all. He finished the cam-paign with a 5-0 record and a 2.20 ERA.

Taylor was a regular starter in 1899, with an 18-22 record and a 3.76 ERA. More interesting, Taylor started 39 games and finished every one of them. Even in an era when relief pitchers were not really a part of a team's strategy, 39 for 39 was impressive. Usually, somewhere during the season, a pitcher would have a bad game and be sent to the showers. Even the legendary Denton True "Cy" Young, who led the league that same year in complete games, started 42 and finished 40.

Taylor wasn't a particularly big man (5'10", 170 pounds), but he was a mean cuss. He had a great fastball that he threw with a long, easy

motion and a good curveball. He rarely com-plained of arm trouble, at least in his early days. He also made it very clear to his catcher that he did not like conferences on the mound. Managers knew they faced a long argument if they yanked Taylor, followed by a clubhouse tantrum.

From 1898 to 1903, Taylor completed all but two starts in which he was scheduled to pitch. From 1901 until 1906, "Old Iron Arm," as Taylor was known, completed 187 consecutive starts for Chicago and St. Louis. That is easily a major league record, and probably one that will never be broken.

During this span, he pitched a 19-inning compete game and an 18-inning contest. He also pitched both ends of a doubleheader and even pitched 15 games in relief.

His best year was 1902 in Chicago, when he won 22 games as a starter and another game in relief, completing all 33 games he started and allowing a minuscule 1.33 ERA, nearly a half run lower than the number two pitcher, Frank "Noodles" Hahn of Cincinnati and his 1.77 ERA.

Like ballplayers at the turn of the 20th century, Taylor believed he was being under-

(continued)

(continued)

paid. His combative nature led him to complain long and loudly about this financial inequity. Chicago owner Jim Hart didn't really enjoy hearing it or reading about it in the newspapers.

Following the 1903 season, the Cubs and White Sox played their annual intercity series. Taylor was of the opinion that he should be paid extra to pitch in these games. Hart disagreed. Taylor pitched poorly in the series, and the White Sox defeated the Orphans three of four games.

Hart was sure Taylor had thrown the contests, and Taylor would probably have been

the first man to concede that he didn't play his best. Hart shipped Taylor to St. Louis for pitcher Mordecai "Three Finger" Brown and backup catcher Jack O'Neill.

Taylor pitched nearly three years for the Cardinals before being traded back to the Cubs, for whom he pitched in 1906 and 1907. Taylor retired after that season, his arm completely worn out. He died on March 4, 1938, in Columbus, Ohio.

Taylor's 33 complete games in 1902 is still a Cubs record. He was also the first 20-game winner for Chicago in the 20th century.

Teachout, Arthur John (Bud)

HEIGHT: 6'2"   LEFTHANDER   BORN: 2/27/1904 LOS ANGELES, CALIFORNIA   DIED: 5/11/1985 LAGUNA BEACH, CALIFORNIA

YEAR	TEAM	STARTS	GAMES	WON	LOST	PCT	ER	ERA	INNINGS PITCHED	STRIKE-OUTS	WALKS	HITS ALLOWED	HRS ALLOWED	COMP. GAMES	SHUT-OUTS	SAVES
1930	ChC-N	16	40	11	4	.733	69	4.06	153	59	48	178	16	6	0	0
1931	ChC-N	3	27	1	2	.333	39	5.72	61 1/3	14	28	79	6	1	0	0
1932	StL-N	0	1	0	0	—	0	0.00	1	0	0	2	0	0	0	0
Career average		6	23	4	2	.667	36	4.51	71 2/3	24	25	86	7	2	0	0
Cubs average		**10**	**34**	**6**	**3**	**.667**	**54**	**4.53**	**107 1/3**	**37**	**38**	**129**	**11**	**4**	**0**	**0**
Career total		19	68	12	6	.667	108	4.51	215 1/3	73	76	259	22	7	0	0
Cubs total		**19**	**67**	**12**	**6**	**.667**	**108**	**4.53**	**214 1/3**	**73**	**76**	**257**	**22**	**7**	**0**	**0**

Telemaco, Amaury

HEIGHT: 6'3"   RIGHTHANDER   BORN: 1/19/1974 HIGUEY, DOMINICAN REPUBLIC

YEAR	TEAM	STARTS	GAMES	WON	LOST	PCT	ER	ERA	INNINGS PITCHED	STRIKE-OUTS	WALKS	HITS ALLOWED	HRS ALLOWED	COMP. GAMES	SHUT-OUTS	SAVES
1996	ChC-N	17	25	5	7	.417	59	5.46	97 1/3	64	31	108	20	0	0	0
1997	ChC-N	5	10	0	3	.000	26	6.16	38	29	11	47	4	0	0	0
1998	ChC-N	0	14	1	1	.500	12	3.90	27 2/3	18	13	23	5	0	0	0
1998	Ari-N	18	27	6	9	.400	53	3.94	121	60	33	127	13	0	0	0
1999	Ari-N	0	5	1	0	1.000	5	7.50	6	2	6	7	2	0	0	0
1999	Phi-N	0	44	3	0	1.000	29	5.55	47	41	20	45	8	0	0	0
2000	Phi-N	2	13	1	3	.250	18	6.66	24 1/3	22	14	25	6	0	0	0
2001	Phi-N	14	24	5	5	.500	55	5.54	89 1/3	59	32	93	15	1	0	0
Career average		9	27	4	5	.440	43	5.13	75	49	27	79	12	0	0	0
Cubs average		**7**	**16**	**2**	**4**	**.353**	**32**	**5.36**	**54 1/3**	**37**	**18**	**59**	**10**	**0**	**0**	**0**
Career total		56	162	22	28	.440	257	5.13	450 2/3	295	160	475	73	1	0	0
Cubs total		**22**	**49**	**6**	**11**	**.353**	**97**	**5.36**	**163**	**111**	**55**	**178**	**29**	**0**	**0**	**0**

Tener, John Kinley
HEIGHT: 6'4"   RIGHTHANDER   BORN: 7/25/1863 COUNTY TYRONE, IRELAND   DIED: 5/19/1946 PITTSBURGH, PENNSYLVANIA

YEAR	TEAM	STARTS	GAMES	WON	LOST	PCT	ER	ERA	INNINGS PITCHED	STRIKE-OUTS	WALKS	HITS ALLOWED	HRS ALLOWED	COMP. GAMES	SHUT-OUTS	SAVES
1888	ChN-N	12	12	7	5	.583	31	2.74	102	39	25	90	6	11	1	0
1889	ChN-N	30	35	15	15	.500	116	3.64	287	105	105	302	16	28	1	0
1890	Pit-P	14	14	3	11	.214	95	7.31	117	30	70	160	6	13	0	0
Career average		19	20	8	10	.446	81	4.30	168 2/3	58	67	184	9	17	1	0
Cubs average		**21**	**24**	**11**	**10**	**.524**	**74**	**3.40**	**194 2/3**	**72**	**65**	**196**	**11**	**20**	**1**	**0**
Career total		56	61	25	31	.446	242	4.30	506	174	200	552	28	52	2	0
Cubs total		**42**	**47**	**22**	**20**	**.524**	**147**	**3.40**	**389**	**144**	**130**	**392**	**22**	**39**	**2**	**0**

Terry, William H. (Adonis)
HEIGHT: 5'11"   RIGHTHANDER   BORN: 8/7/1864 WESTFIELD, MASSACHUSETTS   DIED: 2/24/1915 MILWAUKEE, WISCONSIN

YEAR	TEAM	STARTS	GAMES	WON	LOST	PCT	ER	ERA	INNINGS PITCHED	STRIKE-OUTS	WALKS	HITS ALLOWED	HRS ALLOWED	COMP. GAMES	SHUT-OUTS	SAVES
1884	Bro-AA	56	57	20	35	.364	188	3.49	485	233	75	487	10	55	3	0
1885	Bro-AA	23	25	6	17	.261	99	4.26	209	96	42	213	9	23	0	1
1886	Bro-AA	34	34	18	16	.529	99	3.09	288 1/3	162	115	263	1	32	5	0
1887	Bro-AA	35	40	16	16	.500	142	4.02	318	138	99	430	10	35	1	3
1888	Bro-AA	23	23	13	8	.619	44	2.03	195	138	67	145	2	20	2	0
1889	Bro-AA	39	41	22	15	.595	119	3.29	326	186	126	285	6	35	2	0
1890	Bro-N	44	46	27	17	.614	121	2.94	370	185	133	362	3	38	1	0
1891	Bro-N	22	25	6	15	.286	91	4.22	194	65	80	207	5	18	1	1
1892	Bal-N	1	1	0	1	.000	4	4.00	9	3	7	7	0	1	0	0
1892	Pit-N	26	30	18	10	.643	67	2.51	240	95	106	185	3	25	2	1
1893	Pit-N	19	26	13	6	.684	84	4.45	170	52	99	177	5	14	0	0
1894	Pit-N	1	1	0	1	.000	5	67.50	0 2/3	0	4	2	0	0	0	0
1894	**ChN-N**	**21**	**23**	**5**	**13**	**.278**	**106**	**5.84**	**163 1/3**	**39**	**123**	**232**	**12**	**16**	**0**	**0**
1895	**ChN-N**	**34**	**38**	**21**	**16**	**.568**	**166**	**4.80**	**311 1/3**	**88**	**131**	**346**	**4**	**31**	**0**	**0**
1896	**ChN-N**	**28**	**30**	**14**	**15**	**.483**	**112**	**4.28**	**235 1/3**	**74**	**88**	**268**	**6**	**25**	**1**	**1**
1897	**ChN-N**	**1**	**1**	**0**	**1**	**.000**	**9**	**10.13**	**8**	**1**	**6**	**11**	**0**	**1**	**0**	**0**
Career average		29	32	14	14	.496	104	3.72	251 2/3	111	93	259	5	26	1	1
Cubs average		**21**	**23**	**10**	**11**	**.471**	**98**	**4.93**	**179 2/3**	**51**	**87**	**214**	**6**	**18**	**0**	**0**
Career total		407	441	199	202	.496	1456	3.72	3523	1555	1301	3620	76	369	18	7
Cubs total		**84**	**92**	**40**	**45**	**.471**	**393**	**4.93**	**718**	**202**	**348**	**857**	**22**	**73**	**1**	**1**

Tewksbury, Robert Alan (Bob)
HEIGHT: 6'4"   RIGHTHANDER   BORN: 11/30/1960 CONCORD, NEW HAMPSHIRE

YEAR	TEAM	STARTS	GAMES	WON	LOST	PCT	ER	ERA	INNINGS PITCHED	STRIKE-OUTS	WALKS	HITS ALLOWED	HRS ALLOWED	COMP. GAMES	SHUT-OUTS	SAVES
1986	NYY-A	20	23	9	5	.643	48	3.31	130 1/3	49	31	144	8	2	0	0
1987	NYY-A	6	8	1	4	.200	25	6.75	33 1/3	12	7	47	5	0	0	0
1987	**ChC-N**	**3**	**7**	**0**	**4**	**.000**	**13**	**6.50**	**18**	**10**	**13**	**32**	**1**	**0**	**0**	**0**
1988	**ChC-N**	**1**	**1**	**0**	**0**	**—**	**3**	**8.10**	**3 1/3**	**1**	**2**	**6**	**1**	**0**	**0**	**0**
1989	StL-N	4	7	1	0	1.000	11	3.30	30	17	10	25	2	1	1	0
1990	StL-N	20	28	10	9	.526	56	3.47	145 1/3	50	15	151	7	3	2	1
1991	StL-N	30	30	11	12	.478	69	3.25	191	75	38	206	13	3	0	0
1992	StL-N	32	33	16	5	.762	56	2.16	233	91	20	217	15	5	0	0
1993	StL-N	32	32	17	10	.630	91	3.83	213 2/3	97	20	258	15	2	0	0
1994	StL-N	24	24	12	10	.545	92	5.32	155 2/3	79	22	190	19	4	1	0
1995	Tex-A	21	21	8	7	.533	66	4.58	129 2/3	53	20	169	8	4	1	0
1996	SD-N	33	36	10	10	.500	99	4.31	206 2/3	126	43	224	17	1	0	0
1997	Min-A	26	26	8	13	.381	79	4.22	168 2/3	92	31	200	12	5	2	0
1998	Min-A	25	26	7	13	.350	79	4.79	148 1/3	60	20	174	19	1	0	0
Career average		21	23	8	8	.519	61	3.92	139	62	22	157	11	2	1	0
Cubs average		**2**	**4**	**0**	**2**	**.000**	**8**	**6.75**	**10 2/3**	**6**	**8**	**19**	**1**	**0**	**0**	**0**
Career total		277	302	110	102	.519	787	3.92	1807	812	292	2043	142	31	7	1
Cubs total		**4**	**8**	**0**	**4**	**.000**	**16**	**6.75**	**21 1/3**	**11**	**15**	**38**	**2**	**0**	**0**	**0**

Thornton, Walter Miller
HEIGHT: 6'1" LEFTHANDER BORN: 2/18/1875 LEWISTON, MAINE DIED: 7/14/1960 LOS ANGELES, CALIFORNIA

YEAR	TEAM	STARTS	GAMES	WON	LOST	PCT	ER	ERA	INNINGS PITCHED	STRIKE-OUTS	WALKS	HITS ALLOWED	HRS ALLOWED	COMP. GAMES	SHUT-OUTS	SAVES
1895	ChN-N	2	7	3	3	.500	27	6.08	40	13	31	58	3	2	0	0
1896	ChN-N	5	5	2	0	1.000	15	5.70	23 2/3	10	13	30	1	2	0	0
1897	ChN-N	16	16	6	8	.429	68	4.70	130 1/3	55	51	164	4	15	0	0
1898	ChN-N	25	28	13	10	.565	80	3.34	215 1/3	56	56	226	4	21	2	0
Career average		12	14	6	5	.533	48	4.18	102 1/3	34	38	120	3	10	1	0
Cubs average		**12**	**14**	**6**	**5**	**.533**	**48**	**4.18**	**102 1/3**	**34**	**38**	**120**	**3**	**10**	**1**	**0**
Career total		48	56	24	21	.533	190	4.18	409 1/3	134	151	478	12	40	2	0
Cubs total		**48**	**56**	**24**	**21**	**.533**	**190**	**4.18**	**409 1/3**	**134**	**151**	**478**	**12**	**40**	**2**	**0**

Thorpe, Robert Joseph (Bob)
HEIGHT: 6'1" RIGHTHANDER BORN: 6/12/1935 SAN DIEGO, CALIFORNIA DIED: 3/17/1960 SAN DIEGO, CALIFORNIA

YEAR	TEAM	STARTS	GAMES	WON	LOST	PCT	ER	ERA	INNINGS PITCHED	STRIKE-OUTS	WALKS	HITS ALLOWED	HRS ALLOWED	COMP. GAMES	SHUT-OUTS	SAVES
1955	ChC-N	0	2	0	0	—	1	3.00	3	0	0	4	0	0	0	0
Career average		0	2	0	0	—	1	3.00	3	0	0	4	0	0	0	0
Cubs average		**0**	**2**	**0**	**0**	**—**	**1**	**3.00**	**3**	**0**	**0**	**4**	**0**	**0**	**0**	**0**
Career total		0	2	0	0	—	1	3.00	3	0	0	4	0	0	0	0
Cubs total		**0**	**2**	**0**	**0**	**—**	**1**	**3.00**	**3**	**0**	**0**	**4**	**0**	**0**	**0**	**0**

Tidrow, Richard William (Dick *or* Dirt)
HEIGHT: 6'4" RIGHTHANDER BORN: 5/14/1947 SAN FRANCISCO, CALIFORNIA

YEAR	TEAM	STARTS	GAMES	WON	LOST	PCT	ER	ERA	INNINGS PITCHED	STRIKE-OUTS	WALKS	HITS ALLOWED	HRS ALLOWED	COMP. GAMES	SHUT-OUTS	SAVES
1972	Cle-A	34	39	14	15	.483	73	2.77	237 1/3	123	70	200	21	10	3	0
1973	Cle-A	40	42	14	16	.467	135	4.42	274 2/3	138	95	289	31	13	2	0
1974	Cle-A	4	4	1	3	.250	15	7.11	19	8	13	21	4	0	0	0
1974	NYY-A	25	33	11	9	.550	82	3.87	190 2/3	100	53	205	14	5	0	1
1975	NYY-A	0	37	6	3	.667	24	3.12	69 1/3	38	31	65	5	0	0	5
1976	NYY-A	2	47	4	5	.444	27	2.63	92 1/3	65	24	80	5	0	0	10
1977	NYY-A	7	49	11	4	.733	53	3.16	151	83	41	143	20	0	0	5
1978	NYY-A	25	31	7	11	.389	79	3.84	185 1/3	73	53	191	13	4	0	0
1979	NYY-A	0	14	2	1	.667	20	7.94	22 2/3	7	4	38	5	0	0	2
1979	**ChC-N**	**0**	**63**	**11**	**5**	**.688**	**31**	**2.72**	**102 2/3**	**68**	**42**	**86**	**5**	**0**	**0**	**4**
1980	**ChC-N**	**0**	**84**	**6**	**5**	**.545**	**36**	**2.79**	**116**	**97**	**53**	**97**	**10**	**0**	**0**	**6**
1981	**ChC-N**	**0**	**51**	**3**	**10**	**.231**	**42**	**5.06**	**74 2/3**	**39**	**30**	**73**	**6**	**0**	**0**	**9**
1982	**ChC-N**	**0**	**65**	**8**	**3**	**.727**	**39**	**3.39**	**103 2/3**	**62**	**29**	**106**	**6**	**0**	**0**	**6**
1983	CWS-A	1	50	2	4	.333	43	4.22	91 2/3	66	34	86	13	0	0	7
1984	NYM-N	0	11	0	0	—	16	9.19	15 2/3	8	7	25	5	0	0	0
Career average		11	48	8	7	.515	55	3.68	134 1/3	75	45	131	13	2	0	4
Cubs average		**0**	**66**	**7**	**6**	**.549**	**37**	**3.36**	**99 1/3**	**67**	**39**	**91**	**7**	**0**	**0**	**6**
Career total		138	620	100	94	.515	715	3.68	1746 2/3	975	579	1705	163	32	5	55
Cubs total		**0**	**263**	**28**	**23**	**.549**	**148**	**3.36**	**397**	**266**	**154**	**362**	**27**	**0**	**0**	**25**

Tiefenauer, Bobby Gene
HEIGHT: 6'2" RIGHTHANDER BORN: 10/10/1929 DESLOGE, MISSOURI DIED: 6/13/2000 DESLOGE, MISSOURI

YEAR	TEAM	STARTS	GAMES	WON	LOST	PCT	ER	ERA	INNINGS PITCHED	STRIKE-OUTS	WALKS	HITS ALLOWED	HRS ALLOWED	COMP. GAMES	SHUT-OUTS	SAVES
1952	StL-N	0	6	0	0	—	7	7.88	8	3	7	12	1	0	0	0
1955	StL-N	0	18	1	4	.200	16	4.41	32 2/3	16	10	31	6	0	0	0
1960	Cle-A	0	6	0	1	.000	2	2.00	9	2	3	8	0	0	0	0
1961	StL-N	0	3	0	0	—	3	6.23	4 1/3	3	4	9	0	0	0	0
1962	Hou-N	0	43	2	4	.333	41	4.34	85	60	21	91	6	0	0	1
1963	Mil-N	0	12	1	1	.500	4	1.21	29 2/3	22	4	20	1	0	0	2
1964	Mil-N	0	46	4	6	.400	26	3.21	73	48	15	61	6	0	0	13
1965	Mil-N	0	6	0	1	.000	6	7.71	7	7	3	8	1	0	0	0
1965	NYY-A	0	10	1	1	.500	8	3.54	20 1/3	15	5	19	3	0	0	2
1965	Cle-A	0	15	0	5	.000	12	4.84	22 1/3	13	10	24	3	0	0	4
1967	Cle-A	0	5	0	1	.000	1	0.79	11 1/3	6	3	9	0	0	0	0
1968	**ChC-N**	**0**	**9**	**0**	**1**	**.000**	**9**	**6.08**	**13 1/3**	**9**	**2**	**20**	**2**	**0**	**0**	**1**

(continued)

(continued)

Career average	0	18	1	3	.265	14	3.84	31 2/3	20	9	31	3	0	0	2
Cubs average	**0**	**9**	**0**	**1**	**.000**	**9**	**6.08**	**13 1/3**	**9**	**2**	**20**	**2**	**0**	**0**	**1**
Career total	0	179	9	25	.265	135	3.84	316	204	87	312	29	0	0	23
Cubs total	**0**	**9**	**0**	**1**	**.000**	**9**	**6.08**	**13 1/3**	**9**	**2**	**20**	**2**	**0**	**0**	**1**

Tincup, Austin Ben (Ben)

HEIGHT: 6'1" RIGHTHANDER BORN: 12/14/1890 ADAIR, OKLAHOMA DIED: 7/5/1980 CLAREMORE, OKLAHOMA

YEAR	TEAM	STARTS	GAMES	WON	LOST	PCT	ER	ERA	INNINGS PITCHED	STRIKE-OUTS	WALKS	HITS ALLOWED	HRS ALLOWED	COMP. GAMES	SHUT-OUTS	SAVES
1914	Phi-N	17	28	8	10	.444	45	2.61	155	108	62	165	0	9	3	2
1915	Phi-N	0	10	0	0	—	7	2.03	31	10	9	26	1	0	0	0
1918	Phi-N	1	8	0	1	.000	14	7.56	16 2/3	6	6	24	0	0	0	0
1928	**ChC-N**	**0**	**2**	**0**	**0**	**—**	**7**	**7.00**	**9**	**3**	**1**	**14**	**0**	**0**	**0**	**0**
Career average	5	12	2	3	.421	18	3.10	53	32	20	57	0	2	1	1	
Cubs average	**0**	**2**	**0**	**0**		**7**	**7.00**	**9**	**3**	**1**	**14**	**0**	**0**	**0**	**0**	
Career total	18	48	8	11	.421	73	3.10	211 2/3	127	78	229	1	9	3	2	
Cubs total	**0**	**2**	**0**	**0**		**7**	**7.00**	**9**	**3**	**1**	**14**	**0**	**0**	**0**	**0**	

Tinning, Lyle Forest (Bud)

HEIGHT: 5'11" RIGHTHANDER BORN: 3/12/1906 PILGER, NEBRASKA DIED: 1/17/1961 EVANSVILLE, INDIANA

YEAR	TEAM	STARTS	GAMES	WON	LOST	PCT	ER	ERA	INNINGS PITCHED	STRIKE-OUTS	WALKS	HITS ALLOWED	HRS ALLOWED	COMP. GAMES	SHUT-OUTS	SAVES
1932	**ChC-N**	**7**	**24**	**5**	**3**	**.625**	**29**	**2.80**	**93 1/3**	**30**	**24**	**93**	**3**	**2**	**0**	**0**
1933	**ChC-N**	**21**	**32**	**13**	**6**	**.684**	**62**	**3.18**	**175 1/3**	**59**	**60**	**169**	**3**	**10**	**3**	**1**
1934	**ChC-N**	**7**	**39**	**4**	**6**	**.400**	**48**	**3.34**	**129 1/3**	**44**	**46**	**134**	**9**	**1**	**1**	**3**
1935	StL-N	0	4	0	0	—	5	5.87	7 2/3	2	5	9	1	0	0	0
Career average	9	25	6	4	.595	36	3.19	101 1/3	34	34	101	4	3	1	1	
Cubs average	**12**	**32**	**7**	**5**	**.595**	**46**	**3.14**	**132 2/3**	**44**	**43**	**132**	**5**	**4**	**1**	**1**	
Career total	35	99	22	15	.595	144	3.19	405 2/3	135	135	405	16	13	4	4	
Cubs total	**35**	**95**	**22**	**15**	**.595**	**139**	**3.14**	**398**	**133**	**130**	**396**	**15**	**13**	**4**	**4**	

Todd, James Richard (Jim)

HEIGHT: 6'2" RIGHTHANDER BORN: 9/21/1947 LANCASTER, PENNSYLVANIA

YEAR	TEAM	STARTS	GAMES	WON	LOST	PCT	ER	ERA	INNINGS PITCHED	STRIKE-OUTS	WALKS	HITS ALLOWED	HRS ALLOWED	COMP. GAMES	SHUT-OUTS	SAVES
1974	**ChC-N**	**6**	**43**	**4**	**2**	**.667**	**38**	**3.89**	**88**	**42**	**41**	**82**	**7**	**0**	**0**	**3**
1975	Oak-A	0	58	8	3	.727	31	2.29	122	50	33	104	4	0	0	12
1976	Oak-A	0	49	7	8	.467	35	3.81	82 2/3	22	34	87	6	0	0	4
1977	**ChC-N**	**0**	**20**	**1**	**1**	**.500**	**31**	**9.10**	**30 2/3**	**17**	**19**	**47**	**1**	**0**	**0**	**0**
1978	Sea-A	2	49	3	4	.429	46	3.88	106 2/3	37	61	113	4	0	0	3
1979	Oak-A	0	51	2	5	.286	59	6.56	81	26	51	108	12	0	0	2
Career average	1	45	4	4	.521	40	4.23	85 1/3	32	40	90	6	0	0	4	
Cubs average	**3**	**32**	**3**	**2**	**.625**	**35**	**5.23**	**59 1/3**	**30**	**30**	**65**	**4**	**0**	**0**	**2**	
Career total	8	270	25	23	.521	240	4.23	511	194	239	541	34	0	0	24	
Cubs total	**6**	**63**	**5**	**3**	**.625**	**69**	**5.23**	**118 2/3**	**59**	**60**	**129**	**8**	**0**	**0**	**3**	

Tompkins, Ronald Everett (Ron *or* Stretch)

HEIGHT: 6'4" RIGHTHANDER BORN: 11/27/1944 SAN DIEGO, CALIFORNIA

YEAR	TEAM	STARTS	GAMES	WON	LOST	PCT	ER	ERA	INNINGS PITCHED	STRIKE-OUTS	WALKS	HITS ALLOWED	HRS ALLOWED	COMP. GAMES	SHUT-OUTS	SAVES
1965	KCA-A	1	5	0	0	—	4	3.48	10 1/3	4	3	9	0	0	0	0
1971	**ChC-N**	**0**	**35**	**0**	**2**	**.000**	**18**	**4.08**	**39 2/3**	**20**	**21**	**31**	**3**	**0**	**0**	**3**
Career average	1	20	0	1	.000	11	3.96	25	12	12	20	2	0	0	2	
Cubs average	**0**	**35**	**0**	**2**	**.000**	**18**	**4.08**	**39 2/3**	**20**	**21**	**31**	**3**	**0**	**0**	**3**	
Career total	1	40	0	2	.000	22	3.96	50	24	24	40	3	0	0	3	
Cubs total	**0**	**35**	**0**	**2**	**.000**	**18**	**4.08**	**39 2/3**	**20**	**21**	**31**	**3**	**0**	**0**	**3**	

Toney, Fred Alexandra

HEIGHT: 6'6"   RIGHTHANDER   BORN: 12/11/1888 NASHVILLE, TENNESSEE   DIED: 3/11/1953 NASHVILLE, TENNESSEE

YEAR	TEAM	STARTS	GAMES	WON	LOST	PCT	ER	ERA	INNINGS PITCHED	STRIKE-OUTS	WALKS	HITS ALLOWED	HRS ALLOWED	COMP. GAMES	SHUT-OUTS	SAVES
1911	ChC-N	4	18	1	1	.500	18	2.42	67	27	35	55	2	1	0	0
1912	ChC-N	2	9	1	2	.333	14	5.25	24	9	11	21	0	0	0	0
1913	ChC-N	5	7	2	2	.500	26	6.00	39	12	22	52	1	2	0	0
1915	Cin-N	23	36	15	6	.714	39	1.58	222 2/3	108	73	160	1	18	6	2
1916	Cin-N	38	41	14	17	.452	76	2.28	300	146	78	247	7	21	3	1
1917	Cin-N	42	43	24	16	.600	83	2.20	339 2/3	123	77	300	4	31	7	1
1918	Cin-N	19	21	6	10	.375	44	2.90	136 2/3	32	31	148	2	9	1	2
1918	NYG-N	9	11	6	2	.750	16	1.69	85 1/3	19	7	55	1	7	1	1
1919	NYG-N	20	24	13	6	.684	37	1.84	181	40	35	157	6	14	4	1
1920	NYG-N	37	42	21	11	.656	82	2.65	278 1/3	81	57	266	8	17	4	1
1921	NYG-N	32	42	18	11	.621	100	3.61	249 1/3	63	65	274	14	16	1	3
1922	NYG-N	12	13	5	6	.455	40	4.17	86 1/3	10	31	91	5	6	0	0
1923	StL-N	28	29	11	12	.478	84	3.84	196 2/3	48	61	211	8	16	1	0
Career average		23	28	11	9	.573	55	2.69	184	60	49	170	5	13	2	1
Cubs average		**4**	**11**	**1**	**2**	**.444**	**19**	**4.02**	**43 1/3**	**16**	**23**	**43**	**1**	**1**	**0**	**0**
Career total		271	336	137	102	.573	659	2.69	2206	718	583	2037	59	158	28	12
Cubs total		**11**	**34**	**4**	**5**	**.444**	**58**	**4.02**	**130**	**48**	**68**	**128**	**3**	**3**	**0**	**0**

Toth, Paul Louis

HEIGHT: 6'1"   RIGHTHANDER   BORN: 6/30/1935 MCROBERTS, KENTUCKY   DIED: 3/20/1999 ANAHEIM, CALIFORNIA

YEAR	TEAM	STARTS	GAMES	WON	LOST	PCT	ER	ERA	INNINGS PITCHED	STRIKE-OUTS	WALKS	HITS ALLOWED	HRS ALLOWED	COMP. GAMES	SHUT-OUTS	SAVES
1962	StL-N	1	6	1	0	1.000	10	5.40	16 2/3	5	4	18	1	1	0	0
1962	ChC-N	4	6	3	1	.750	16	4.24	34	11	10	29	2	1	0	0
1963	ChC-N	14	27	5	9	.357	45	3.10	130 2/3	66	35	115	9	3	2	0
1964	ChC-N	2	4	0	2	.000	10	8.44	10 2/3	0	5	15	2	0	0	0
Career average		7	14	3	4	.429	27	3.80	64	27	18	59	5	2	1	0
Cubs average		**7**	**12**	**3**	**4**	**.400**	**24**	**3.64**	**58 1/3**	**26**	**17**	**53**	**4**	**1**	**1**	**0**
Career total		21	43	9	12	.429	81	3.80	192	82	54	177	14	5	2	0
Cubs total		**20**	**37**	**8**	**12**	**.400**	**71**	**3.64**	**175 1/3**	**77**	**50**	**159**	**13**	**4**	**2**	**0**

Trachsel, Stephen Christopher (Steve)

HEIGHT: 6'4"   RIGHTHANDER   BORN: 10/31/1970 OXNARD, CALIFORNIA

YEAR	TEAM	STARTS	GAMES	WON	LOST	PCT	ER	ERA	INNINGS PITCHED	STRIKE-OUTS	WALKS	HITS ALLOWED	HRS ALLOWED	COMP. GAMES	SHUT-OUTS	SAVES
1993	ChC-N	3	3	0	2	.000	10	4.58	19 2/3	14	3	16	4	0	0	0
1994	ChC-N	22	22	9	7	.563	52	3.21	146	108	54	133	19	1	0	0
1995	ChC-N	29	30	7	13	.350	92	5.15	160 2/3	117	76	174	25	2	0	0
1996	ChC-N	31	31	13	9	.591	69	3.03	205	132	62	181	30	3	2	0
1997	ChC-N	34	34	8	12	.400	101	4.51	201 1/3	160	69	225	32	0	0	0
1998	ChC-N	33	33	15	8	.652	103	4.46	208	149	84	204	27	1	0	0
1999	ChC-N	34	34	8	18	.308	127	5.56	205 2/3	149	64	226	32	4	0	0
2000	TB-A	23	23	6	10	.375	70	4.58	137 2/3	78	49	160	16	3	1	0
2000	Tor-A	11	11	2	5	.286	37	5.29	63	32	25	72	10	0	0	0
2001	NYM-N	28	28	11	13	.458	86	4.46	173 2/3	144	47	168	28	1	1	0
Career average		28	28	9	11	.449	83	4.42	169	120	59	173	25	2	0	0
Cubs average		**27**	**27**	**9**	**10**	**.465**	**79**	**4.35**	**163 2/3**	**118**	**59**	**166**	**24**	**2**	**0**	**0**
Career total		248	249	79	97	.449	747	4.42	1520 2/3	1083	533	1559	223	15	4	0
Cubs total		**186**	**187**	**60**	**69**	**.465**	**554**	**4.35**	**1146 1/3**	**829**	**412**	**1159**	**169**	**11**	**2**	**0**

Tremel, William Leonard (Bill *or* Mumbles)
HEIGHT: 5'11"   RIGHTHANDER   BORN: 7/4/1929 LILLY, PENNSYLVANIA

YEAR	TEAM	STARTS	GAMES	WON	LOST	PCT	ER	ERA	INNINGS PITCHED	STRIKE-OUTS	WALKS	HITS ALLOWED	HRS ALLOWED	COMP. GAMES	SHUT-OUTS	SAVES
1954	ChC-N	0	33	1	2	.333	24	4.21	51 1/3	21	28	45	3	0	0	4
1955	ChC-N	0	23	3	0	1.000	16	3.72	38 2/3	13	18	33	2	0	0	2
1956	ChC-N	0	1	0	0	—	1	9.00	1	0	0	3	0	0	0	0
Career average	0	19	1	1	.667	14	4.05	30 1/3	11	15	27	2	0	0	2
Cubs average	0	19	1	1	.667	14	4.05	30 1/3	11	15	27	2	0	0	2
Career total	0	57	4	2	.667	41	4.05	91	34	46	81	5	0	0	6
Cubs total	0	57	4	2	.667	41	4.05	91	34	46	81	5	0	0	6

Trout, Steven Russell (Steve *or* Rainbow)
HEIGHT: 6'4"   LEFTHANDER   BORN: 7/30/1957 DETROIT, MICHIGAN

YEAR	TEAM	STARTS	GAMES	WON	LOST	PCT	ER	ERA	INNINGS PITCHED	STRIKE-OUTS	WALKS	HITS ALLOWED	HRS ALLOWED	COMP. GAMES	SHUT-OUTS	SAVES
1978	CWS-A	3	4	3	0	1.000	10	4.03	22 1/3	11	11	19	0	1	0	0
1979	CWS-A	18	34	11	8	.579	67	3.89	155	76	59	165	10	6	2	4
1980	CWS-A	30	32	9	16	.360	82	3.70	199 2/3	89	49	229	14	7	2	0
1981	CWS-A	18	20	8	7	.533	48	3.47	124 2/3	54	38	122	7	3	0	0
1982	CWS-A	19	25	6	9	.400	57	4.26	120 1/3	62	50	130	9	2	0	0
1983	ChC-N	32	34	10	14	.417	93	4.65	180	80	59	217	13	1	0	0
1984	ChC-N	31	32	13	7	.650	72	3.41	190	81	59	205	7	6	2	0
1985	ChC-N	24	24	9	7	.563	53	3.39	140 2/3	44	63	142	8	3	1	0
1986	ChC-N	25	37	5	7	.417	85	4.75	161	69	78	184	6	0	0	0
1987	ChC-N	11	11	6	3	.667	25	3.00	75	32	27	72	3	3	2	0
1987	NYY-A	9	14	0	4	.000	34	6.60	46 1/3	27	37	51	4	0	0	0
1988	Sea-A	13	15	4	7	.364	49	7.83	56 1/3	14	31	86	6	0	0	0
1989	Sea-A	3	19	4	3	.571	22	6.60	30	17	17	43	3	0	0	0
Career average	20	25	7	8	.489	58	4.18	125	55	48	139	8	3	1	0
Cubs average	25	28	9	8	.531	66	3.95	149 1/3	61	57	164	7	3	1	0
Career total	236	301	88	92	.489	697	4.18	1501 1/3	656	578	1665	90	32	9	4
Cubs total	123	138	43	38	.531	328	3.95	746 2/3	306	286	820	37	13	5	0

Turner, Theodore Holhot (Ted)
HEIGHT: 6'0"   RIGHTHANDER   BORN: 5/4/1892 LAWRENCEBURG, KENTUCKY   DIED: 2/4/1958 LEXINGTON, KENTUCKY

YEAR	TEAM	STARTS	GAMES	WON	LOST	PCT	ER	ERA	INNINGS PITCHED	STRIKE-OUTS	WALKS	HITS ALLOWED	HRS ALLOWED	COMP. GAMES	SHUT-OUTS	SAVES
1920	ChC-N	0	1	0	0	—	2	13.50	1 1/3	0	1	2	0	0	0	0
Career average	0	1	0	0	—	2	13.50	1 1/3	0	1	2	0	0	0	0
Cubs average	0	1	0	0	—	2	13.50	1 1/3	0	1	2	0	0	0	0
Career total	0	1	0	0	—	2	13.50	1 1/3	0	1	2	0	0	0	0
Cubs total	0	1	0	0	—	2	13.50	1 1/3	0	1	2	0	0	0	0

Tyler, George Albert (Lefty)
HEIGHT: 6'0"   LEFTHANDER   BORN: 12/14/1889 DERRY, NEW HAMPSHIRE   DIED: 9/29/1953 LOWELL, MASSACHUSETTS

YEAR	TEAM	STARTS	GAMES	WON	LOST	PCT	ER	ERA	INNINGS PITCHED	STRIKE-OUTS	WALKS	HITS ALLOWED	HRS ALLOWED	COMP. GAMES	SHUT-OUTS	SAVES
1910	Bos-N	0	2	0	0	—	3	2.38	11 1/3	6	6	11	1	0	0	0
1911	Bos-N	20	28	7	10	.412	93	5.06	165 1/3	90	109	150	11	10	1	0
1912	Bos-N	31	42	12	22	.353	119	4.18	256 1/3	144	126	262	8	15	1	0
1913	Bos-N	34	39	16	17	.485	90	2.79	290 1/3	143	108	245	2	28	4	2
1914	Bos-N	34	38	16	13	.552	81	2.69	271 1/3	140	101	247	7	21	5	2
1915	Bos-N	24	32	10	9	.526	65	2.86	204 2/3	89	84	182	6	15	1	0
1916	Bos-N	28	34	17	9	.654	56	2.02	249 1/3	117	58	200	6	21	6	1
1917	Bos-N	28	32	14	12	.538	67	2.52	239	98	86	203	1	22	4	1
1918	ChC-N	30	33	19	8	.704	60	2.00	269 1/3	102	67	218	1	22	8	1
1919	ChC-N	5	6	2	2	.500	7	2.10	30	9	13	20	0	3	0	0
1920	ChC-N	27	27	11	12	.478	71	3.31	193	57	57	193	6	18	2	0
1921	ChC-N	6	10	3	2	.600	18	3.24	50	8	14	59	2	4	0	0

(continued)

(Tyler, continued)

Career average	22	27	11	10	.523	61	2.95	186	84	69	166	4	15	3	1
Cubs average	**17**	**19**	**9**	**6**	**.593**	**39**	**2.59**	**135 ⅔**	**44**	**38**	**123**	**2**	**12**	**3**	**0**
Career total	267	323	127	116	.523	730	2.95	2230	1003	829	1990	51	179	32	7
Cubs total	**68**	**76**	**35**	**24**	**.593**	**156**	**2.59**	**542 ⅓**	**176**	**151**	**490**	**9**	**47**	**10**	**1**

Upham, John Leslie
HEIGHT: 6'0"   LEFTHANDER   BORN: 12/29/1941 WINDSOR, ONTARIO, CANADA

YEAR	TEAM	STARTS	GAMES	WON	LOST	PCT	ER	ERA	INNINGS PITCHED	STRIKE-OUTS	WALKS	HITS ALLOWED	HRS ALLOWED	COMP. GAMES	SHUT-OUTS	SAVES
1967	ChC-N	0	5	0	1	.000	5	33.75	1 ⅓	2	2	4	1	0	0	0
1968	ChC-N	0	2	0	0	—	0	0.00	7	2	3	2	0	0	0	0
Career average		0	4	0	1	.000	3	5.40	4 ⅓	2	3	3	1	0	0	0
Cubs average		**0**	**4**	**0**	**1**	**.000**	**3**	**5.40**	**4 ⅓**	**2**	**3**	**3**	**1**	**0**	**0**	**0**
Career total		0	7	0	1	.000	5	5.40	8 ⅓	4	5	6	1	0	0	0
Cubs total		**0**	**7**	**0**	**1**	**.000**	**5**	**5.40**	**8 ⅓**	**4**	**5**	**6**	**1**	**0**	**0**	**0**

Valdes, Ismael (Rocket)
HEIGHT: 6'4"   RIGHTHANDER   BORN: 8/21/1973 CIUDAD VICTORIA, MEXICO

YEAR	TEAM	STARTS	GAMES	WON	LOST	PCT	ER	ERA	INNINGS PITCHED	STRIKE-OUTS	WALKS	HITS ALLOWED	HRS ALLOWED	COMP. GAMES	SHUT-OUTS	SAVES
1994	LA-N	1	21	3	1	.750	10	3.18	28 ⅓	28	10	21	2	0	0	0
1995	LA-N	27	33	13	11	.542	67	3.05	197 ⅔	150	51	168	17	6	2	1
1996	LA-N	33	33	15	7	.682	83	3.32	225	173	54	219	20	0	0	0
1997	LA-N	30	30	10	11	.476	58	2.65	196 ⅔	140	47	171	16	0	0	0
1998	LA-N	27	27	11	10	.524	77	3.98	174	122	66	171	17	2	2	0
1999	LA-N	32	32	9	14	.391	90	3.98	203 ⅓	143	58	213	32	2	1	0
2000	**ChC-N**	**12**	**12**	**2**	**4**	**.333**	**40**	**5.37**	**67**	**45**	**27**	**71**	**17**	**0**	**0**	**0**
2000	LA-N	8	9	0	3	.000	27	6.08	40	29	13	53	5	0	0	0
2001	Ana-A	27	27	9	13	.409	81	4.45	163 ⅔	100	50	177	20	1	0	0
Career average		25	28	9	9	.493	67	3.70	162	116	47	158	18	1	1	0
Cubs average		**12**	**12**	**2**	**4**	**.333**	**40**	**5.37**	**67**	**45**	**27**	**71**	**17**	**0**	**0**	**0**
Career total		197	224	72	74	.493	533	3.70	1295 ⅔	930	376	1264	146	11	5	1
Cubs total		**12**	**12**	**2**	**4**	**.333**	**40**	**5.37**	**67**	**45**	**27**	**71**	**17**	**0**	**0**	**0**

Valentinetti, Vito John
HEIGHT: 6'0"   RIGHTHANDER   BORN: 9/16/1928 WEST NEW YORK, NEW JERSEY

YEAR	TEAM	STARTS	GAMES	WON	LOST	PCT	ER	ERA	INNINGS PITCHED	STRIKE-OUTS	WALKS	HITS ALLOWED	HRS ALLOWED	COMP. GAMES	SHUT-OUTS	SAVES
1954	CWS-A	0	1	0	0	—	6	54.00	1	1	2	4	1	0	0	0
1956	**ChC-N**	**2**	**42**	**6**	**4**	**.600**	**40**	**3.78**	**95 ⅓**	**26**	**36**	**84**	**10**	**0**	**0**	**1**
1957	**ChC-N**	**0**	**9**	**0**	**0**	**—**	**3**	**2.25**	**12**	**8**	**7**	**12**	**1**	**0**	**0**	**0**
1957	Cle-A	2	11	2	2	.500	13	4.94	23 ⅔	9	13	26	3	1	0	0
1958	Det-A	0	15	1	0	1.000	7	3.38	18 ⅔	10	5	18	4	0	0	2
1958	Was-A	10	23	4	6	.400	54	5.08	95 ⅔	33	49	106	16	2	0	0
1959	Was-A	1	7	0	2	.000	12	10.13	10 ⅔	7	10	16	0	0	0	0
Career average		3	22	3	3	.481	27	4.73	51 ⅓	19	24	53	7	1	0	1
Cubs average		**1**	**26**	**3**	**2**	**.600**	**22**	**3.61**	**53 ⅔**	**17**	**22**	**48**	**6**	**0**	**0**	**1**
Career total		15	108	13	14	.481	135	4.73	257	94	122	266	35	3	0	3
Cubs total		**2**	**51**	**6**	**4**	**.600**	**43**	**3.61**	**107 ⅓**	**34**	**43**	**96**	**11**	**0**	**0**	**1**

Van Haltren, George Edward Martin (Rip)
HEIGHT: 5'11"   LEFTHANDER   BORN: 3/30/1866 ST. LOUIS, MISSOURI   DIED: 9/29/1945 OAKLAND, CALIFORNIA

YEAR	TEAM	STARTS	GAMES	WON	LOST	PCT	ER	ERA	INNINGS PITCHED	STRIKE-OUTS	WALKS	HITS ALLOWED	HRS ALLOWED	COMP. GAMES	SHUT-OUTS	SAVES
1887	**ChN-N**	**18**	**20**	**11**	**7**	**.611**	**69**	**3.86**	**161**	**76**	**66**	**243**	**7**	**18**	**1**	**1**
1888	**ChN-N**	**24**	**30**	**13**	**13**	**.500**	**96**	**3.52**	**245 ⅔**	**139**	**60**	**263**	**15**	**24**	**4**	**1**
1890	Bro-P	25	28	15	10	.600	106	4.28	223	48	89	272	8	23	0	2
1891	Bal-AA	1	6	0	1	.000	13	5.09	23	7	10	38	1	0	0	0

(continued)

(continued)

YEAR	TEAM	STARTS	GAMES	WON	LOST	PCT	ER	ERA	INNINGS PITCHED	STRIKE-OUTS	WALKS	HITS ALLOWED	HRS ALLOWED	COMP. GAMES	SHUT-OUTS	SAVES
1892	Bal-N	0	4	0	0	—	15	9.20	14 2/3	5	7	28	1	0	0	0
1895	NYG-N	0	1	0	0	—	7	12.60	5	1	2	13	0	0	0	0
1896	NYG-N	0	2	1	0	1.000	2	2.25	8	3	1	5	0	0	0	0
1900	NYG-N	0	1	0	0	—	0	0.00	3	0	3	1	0	0	0	0
1901	NYG-N	0	1	0	0	—	2	3.00	6	2	6	12	0	0	0	0
Career average		8	10	4	3	.563	34	4.05	76 2/3	31	27	97	4	7	1	0
Cubs average		**21**	**25**	**12**	**10**	**.545**	**83**	**3.65**	**203 1/3**	**108**	**63**	**253**	**11**	**21**	**3**	**1**
Career total		68	93	40	31	.563	310	4.05	689 1/3	281	244	875	33	65	5	4
Cubs total		**42**	**50**	**24**	**20**	**.545**	**165**	**3.65**	**406 2/3**	**215**	**126**	**506**	**22**	**42**	**5**	**2**

Van Poppel, Todd Matthew
HEIGHT: 6'5" RIGHTHANDER BORN: 12/9/1971 HINSDALE, ILLINOIS

YEAR	TEAM	STARTS	GAMES	WON	LOST	PCT	ER	ERA	INNINGS PITCHED	STRIKE-OUTS	WALKS	HITS ALLOWED	HRS ALLOWED	COMP. GAMES	SHUT-OUTS	SAVES
1991	Oak-A	1	1	0	0	—	5	9.64	4 2/3	6	2	7	1	0	0	0
1993	Oak-A	16	16	6	6	.500	47	5.04	84	47	62	76	10	0	0	0
1994	Oak-A	23	23	7	10	.412	79	6.09	116 2/3	83	89	108	20	0	0	0
1995	Oak-A	14	36	4	8	.333	75	4.88	138 1/3	122	56	125	16	1	0	0
1996	Oak-A	6	28	1	5	.167	54	7.71	63	37	33	86	13	0	0	1
1996	Det-A	9	9	2	4	.333	46	11.39	36 1/3	16	29	53	11	1	1	0
1998	Tex-A	4	4	1	2	.333	19	8.84	19 1/3	10	10	26	5	0	0	0
1998	Pit-N	7	18	1	2	.333	28	5.36	47	32	18	53	4	0	0	0
2000	**ChC-N**	**2**	**51**	**4**	**5**	**.444**	**36**	**3.75**	**86 1/3**	**77**	**48**	**80**	**10**	**0**	**0**	**2**
2001	**ChC-N**	**0**	**59**	**4**	**1**	**.800**	**21**	**2.52**	**75**	**90**	**38**	**63**	**9**	**0**	**0**	**0**
Career average		10	31	4	5	.411	51	5.50	84	65	48	85	12	0	0	0
Cubs average		**1**	**55**	**4**	**3**	**.571**	**29**	**3.18**	**80 2/3**	**84**	**43**	**72**	**10**	**0**	**0**	**1**
Career total		82	245	30	43	.411	410	5.50	670 2/3	520	385	677	99	2	1	3
Cubs total		**2**	**110**	**8**	**6**	**.571**	**57**	**3.18**	**161 1/3**	**167**	**86**	**143**	**19**	**0**	**0**	**2**

Vandenberg, Harold Harris (Hy)
HEIGHT: 6'4" RIGHTHANDER BORN: 3/17/1907 ABILENE, KANSAS DIED: 7/31/1994 BLOOMINGTON, MINNESOTA

YEAR	TEAM	STARTS	GAMES	WON	LOST	PCT	ER	ERA	INNINGS PITCHED	STRIKE-OUTS	WALKS	HITS ALLOWED	HRS ALLOWED	COMP. GAMES	SHUT-OUTS	SAVES
1935	Bos-A	0	3	0	0	—	12	20.25	5 1/3	2	4	15	1	0	0	0
1937	NYG-N	1	1	0	1	.000	7	7.88	8	2	6	10	0	1	0	0
1938	NYG-N	1	6	0	1	.000	15	7.50	18	7	12	28	2	0	0	0
1939	NYG-N	1	2	0	0	—	4	5.68	6 1/3	3	6	10	0	0	0	0
1940	NYG-N	3	13	1	1	.500	14	3.90	32 1/3	17	16	27	2	1	0	1
1944	**ChC-N**	**9**	**35**	**7**	**4**	**.636**	**51**	**3.63**	**126 1/3**	**54**	**51**	**123**	**8**	**2**	**0**	**2**
1945	**ChC-N**	**7**	**30**	**7**	**3**	**.700**	**37**	**3.49**	**95 1/3**	**35**	**33**	**91**	**4**	**3**	**1**	**2**
Career average		3	13	2	1	.600	20	4.32	41 2/3	17	18	43	2	1	0	1
Cubs average		**8**	**33**	**7**	**4**	**.667**	**44**	**3.57**	**111**	**45**	**42**	**107**	**6**	**3**	**1**	**2**
Career total		22	90	15	10	.600	140	4.32	291 2/3	120	128	304	17	7	1	5
Cubs total		**16**	**65**	**14**	**7**	**.667**	**88**	**3.57**	**221 2/3**	**89**	**84**	**214**	**12**	**5**	**1**	**4**

Vander Meer, John Samuel (Johnny *or* The Dutch Master)
HEIGHT: 6'1" LEFTHANDER BORN: 11/2/1914 PROSPECT PARK, NEW JERSEY DIED: 10/6/1997 TAMPA, FLORIDA

YEAR	TEAM	STARTS	GAMES	WON	LOST	PCT	ER	ERA	INNINGS PITCHED	STRIKE-OUTS	WALKS	HITS ALLOWED	HRS ALLOWED	COMP. GAMES	SHUT-OUTS	SAVES
1937	Cin-N	10	19	3	5	.375	36	3.84	84 1/3	52	69	63	0	4	0	0
1938	Cin-N	29	32	15	10	.600	78	3.12	225 1/3	125	103	177	12	16	3	0
1939	Cin-N	21	30	5	9	.357	67	4.67	129	102	95	128	7	8	0	0
1940	Cin-N	7	10	3	1	.750	20	3.75	48	41	41	38	3	2	0	1
1941	Cin-N	32	33	16	13	.552	71	2.82	226 1/3	202	126	172	8	18	6	0
1942	Cin-N	33	33	18	12	.600	66	2.43	244	186	102	188	6	21	4	0
1943	Cin-N	36	36	15	16	.484	92	2.87	289	174	162	228	5	21	3	0
1946	Cin-N	25	29	10	12	.455	72	3.17	204 1/3	94	78	175	11	11	5	0
1947	Cin-N	29	30	9	14	.391	91	4.40	186	79	87	186	11	9	3	0
1948	Cin-N	33	33	17	14	.548	88	3.41	232	120	124	204	15	14	3	0
1949	Cin-N	24	28	5	10	.333	87	4.90	159 2/3	76	85	172	12	7	3	0
1950	**ChC-N**	**6**	**32**	**3**	**4**	**.429**	**31**	**3.79**	**73 2/3**	**41**	**59**	**60**	**10**	**0**	**0**	**1**
1951	Cle-A	1	1	0	1	.000	6	18.00	3	2	1	8	0	0	0	0

(continued)

(Vander Meer, continued)

Career average	22	27	9	9	.496	62	3.44	162	100	87	138	8	10	2	0
Cubs average	**6**	**32**	**3**	**4**	**.429**	**31**	**3.79**	**73 2/3**	**41**	**59**	**60**	**10**	**0**	**0**	**1**
Career total	286	346	119	121	.496	805	3.44	2104 2/3	1294	1132	1799	100	131	30	2
Cubs total	**6**	**32**	**3**	**4**	**.429**	**31**	**3.79**	**73 2/3**	**41**	**59**	**60**	**10**	**0**	**0**	**1**

VanRyn, Benjamin Ashley (Ben)
HEIGHT: 6'5" LEFTHANDER BORN: 8/9/1971 FORT WAYNE, INDIANA

YEAR	TEAM	STARTS	GAMES	WON	LOST	PCT	ER	ERA	INNINGS PITCHED	STRIKE-OUTS	WALKS	HITS ALLOWED	HRS ALLOWED	COMP. GAMES	SHUT-OUTS	SAVES
1996	Cal-A	0	1	0	0	—	0	0.00	1	0	1	1	0	0	0	0
1998	**ChC-N**	**0**	**9**	**0**	**0**	**—**	**3**	**3.38**	**8**	**6**	**6**	**9**	**0**	**0**	**0**	**0**
1998	SD-N	0	6	0	1	.000	3	10.13	2 2/3	1	4	3	0	0	0	0
1998	Tor-A	0	10	0	1	.000	4	9.00	4	3	2	6	0	0	0	0
Career average	0	13	0	1	.000	5	5.74	8	5	7	10	0	0	0	0
Cubs average	**0**	**9**	**0**	**0**	**—**	**3**	**3.38**	**8**	**6**	**6**	**9**	**0**	**0**	**0**	**0**
Career total	0	26	0	2	.000	10	5.74	15 2/3	10	13	19	0	0	0	0
Cubs total	**0**	**9**	**0**	**0**	**—**	**3**	**3.38**	**8**	**6**	**6**	**9**	**0**	**0**	**0**	**0**

Varga, Andrew William (Andy)
HEIGHT: 6'4" LEFTHANDER BORN: 12/11/1930 CHICAGO, ILLINOIS   DIED: 11/4/1992 ORLANDO, FLORIDA

YEAR	TEAM	STARTS	GAMES	WON	LOST	PCT	ER	ERA	INNINGS PITCHED	STRIKE-OUTS	WALKS	HITS ALLOWED	HRS ALLOWED	COMP. GAMES	SHUT-OUTS	SAVES
1950	ChC-N	0	1	0	0	—	0	0.00	1	0	1	0	0	0	0	0
1951	ChC-N	0	2	0	0	—	1	3.00	3	1	6	2	0	0	0	0
Career average	0	2	0	0	—	1	2.25	2	1	4	1	0	0	0	0
Cubs average	**0**	**2**	**0**	**0**	**—**	**1**	**2.25**	**2**	**1**	**4**	**1**	**0**	**0**	**0**	**0**
Career total	0	3	0	0	—	1	2.25	4	1	7	2	0	0	0	0
Cubs total	**0**	**3**	**0**	**0**	**—**	**1**	**2.25**	**4**	**1**	**7**	**2**	**0**	**0**	**0**	**0**

Vaughn, James Leslie (Hippo)
HEIGHT: 6'4" LEFTHANDER BORN: 4/9/1888 WEATHERFORD, TEXAS   DIED: 5/29/1966 CHICAGO, ILLINOIS

YEAR	TEAM	STARTS	GAMES	WON	LOST	PCT	ER	ERA	INNINGS PITCHED	STRIKE-OUTS	WALKS	HITS ALLOWED	HRS ALLOWED	COMP. GAMES	SHUT-OUTS	SAVES
1908	NYA-A	0	2	0	0	—	1	3.86	2 1/3	2	4	1	0	0	0	0
1910	NYA-A	25	30	13	11	.542	45	1.83	221 2/3	107	58	190	1	18	5	1
1911	NYA-A	18	26	8	10	.444	71	4.39	145 2/3	74	54	158	2	10	0	0
1912	NYA-A	10	15	2	8	.200	36	5.14	63	46	37	66	1	5	1	0
1912	Was-A	8	12	4	3	.571	26	2.89	81	49	43	75	0	4	0	0
1913	**ChC-N**	**6**	**7**	**5**	**1**	**.833**	**9**	**1.45**	**56**	**36**	**27**	**37**	**0**	**5**	**2**	**0**
1914	**ChC-N**	**35**	**42**	**21**	**13**	**.618**	**67**	**2.05**	**293 2/3**	**165**	**109**	**236**	**1**	**23**	**4**	**1**
1915	**ChC-N**	**34**	**41**	**20**	**12**	**.625**	**86**	**2.87**	**269 2/3**	**148**	**77**	**240**	**4**	**18**	**4**	**1**
1916	**ChC-N**	**35**	**44**	**17**	**15**	**.531**	**72**	**2.20**	**294**	**144**	**67**	**269**	**4**	**21**	**4**	**1**
1917	**ChC-N**	**38**	**41**	**23**	**13**	**.639**	**66**	**2.01**	**295 2/3**	**195**	**91**	**255**	**3**	**27**	**5**	**0**
1918	**ChC-N**	**33**	**35**	**22**	**10**	**.688**	**56**	**1.74**	**290 1/3**	**148**	**76**	**216**	**4**	**27**	**8**	**0**
1919	**ChC-N**	**37**	**38**	**21**	**14**	**.600**	**61**	**1.79**	**306 2/3**	**141**	**62**	**264**	**3**	**25**	**4**	**1**
1920	**ChC-N**	**38**	**40**	**19**	**16**	**.543**	**85**	**2.54**	**301**	**131**	**81**	**301**	**8**	**24**	**4**	**0**
1921	**ChC-N**	**14**	**17**	**3**	**11**	**.214**	**73**	**6.01**	**109 1/3**	**30**	**31**	**153**	**8**	**7**	**0**	**0**
Career average	25	30	14	11	.565	58	2.49	210	109	63	189	3	16	3	0
Cubs average	**30**	**34**	**17**	**12**	**.590**	**64**	**2.33**	**246 1/3**	**126**	**69**	**219**	**4**	**20**	**4**	**0**
Career total	331	390	178	137	.565	754	2.49	2730	1416	817	2461	39	214	41	5
Cubs total	**270**	**305**	**151**	**105**	**.590**	**575**	**2.33**	**2216 1/3**	**1138**	**621**	**1971**	**35**	**177**	**35**	**4**

James Leslie "Hippo" Vaughn, lhp, 1908, 1910–21

A big (6'4", 215 pounds) guy with a funny nickname, Vaughn was also the greatest lefthander in Cubs history, winning 20 or more games five times in his Cubs career.

Vaughn was born on April 9, 1888, in Weatherford, Texas. As a baby-faced 20-year-old, Vaughn had a cup of coffee with the New York Yankees, then known as the Highlanders, in 1908. After a spell in the minor leagues in 1909, Vaughn returned to New York for good in 1910.

His stay in New York was frustrating—he was 23-29 in that span. A short stay with Washington followed before Vaughn was traded to Chicago prior to the 1913 season. He won five of six decisions in that year and established himself as a true star the next season, going 21-13, with a 2.05 ERA and 165 strikeouts.

Vaughn was known as "Hippo" because of the way his hips swayed when he walked, not because of his large frame. He was a canny pitcher on the mound, a master of the curveball and change of pace. He also threw a deceptively quick fastball.

His one weakness was that he was an awkward fielder. He committed 74 errors in his 13 seasons, a relatively high number for pitchers. He led the league in errors five times in the span. Only Warren Spahn, who played eight more years, has led his league in errors five times. But as a gamer, Vaugh twice led the league in innings pitched and strikeouts while with the Cubs.

His most famous game was on May 2, 1917, when he and Reds pitcher Fred Toney each threw nine innings of no-hit ball, a "double no-hitter" that has never happened since. Unfortunately, in the 10th inning, Toney did allow a Cubs hit, but Vaughn allowed a clean single by Larry Kopf. Reds first baseman Hal Chase reached first on an error and Jim Thorpe (yes, *that* Jim Thorpe) hit a slow roller to Vaughn. Hippo threw the ball to catcher Art Wilson to try to get Kopf at the plate, but Wilson froze, bobbled the ball and Kopf scored.

Hippo is also one of the Cubs' best World Series pitchers ever, shutting down the Boston Red Sox in the 1919 Fall Classic and allowing only three earned runs in three complete games. But the Red Sox staff, including George Herman "Babe" Ruth (yes, *that* Babe Ruth), was even better. Ruth shut out the Cubs, 1-0, in Game 1, while Sox teammate Carl Mays beat Vaughn and the Cubs, 2-1, in Game 3. Vaughn won Game 5, 3-0, but the Red Sox clinched the Series the next day with a win over Chicago's Lefty Tyler.

Thus, Vaughn's World Series line was a 1-2 record with three complete games, 17 strikeouts and 1.00 ERA, the latter figure tops all-time for Chicago World Series pitchers.

Vaughn won 21 games in 1919 and 19 contests in 1920, but in 1921 his production dropped sharply, going 3-11. He retired after that season. Vaughn died on May 29, 1966, in Chicago, a Cubs fan to the end. He was often seen at Wrigley Field in his later years.

Vaughn holds a host of pitching records for Chicago, including most post-1900 wins (23 in 1917) for a lefthanded pitcher, most shutouts for a lefty (eight in 1918) and most walks issued by a lefthander (109 in 1914). Vaughn is also 8th on the Cubs all-time win list overall for pitchers with 151, 8th in losses with 105, 6th in ERA with a 2.33 mark, 7th in games started with 270, 8th in innings pitched with 2,126⅓, 5th in strikeouts with 1,138 and 10th in opponents' batting average at .241.

Veres, Randolph Ruhland (Randy)
HEIGHT: 6'3" RIGHTHANDER BORN: 11/25/1965 SAN FRANCISCO, CALIFORNIA

YEAR	TEAM	STARTS	GAMES	WON	LOST	PCT	ER	ERA	INNINGS PITCHED	STRIKE-OUTS	WALKS	HITS ALLOWED	HRS ALLOWED	COMP. GAMES	SHUT-OUTS	SAVES
1989	Mil-A	1	3	0	1	.000	4	4.32	8 1/3	8	4	9	0	0	0	0
1990	Mil-A	0	26	0	3	.000	17	3.67	41 2/3	16	16	38	5	0	0	1
1994	**ChC-N**	**0**	**10**	**1**	**1**	**.500**	**6**	**5.59**	**9 2/3**	**5**	**2**	**12**	**3**	**0**	**0**	**0**
1995	Fla-N	0	47	4	4	.500	21	3.88	48 2/3	31	22	46	6	0	0	1
1996	Det-A	0	25	0	4	.000	28	8.31	30 1/3	28	23	38	6	0	0	0
1997	KC-A	0	24	4	0	1.000	13	3.31	35 1/3	28	7	36	4	0	0	1
Career average		0	23	2	2	.409	15	4.60	29	19	12	30	4	0	0	1
Cubs average		**0**	**10**	**1**	**1**	**.500**	**6**	**5.59**	**9 2/3**	**5**	**2**	**12**	**3**	**0**	**0**	**0**
Career total		1	135	9	13	.409	89	4.60	174	116	74	179	24	0	0	3
Cubs total		**0**	**10**	**1**	**1**	**.500**	**6**	**5.59**	**9 2/3**	**5**	**2**	**12**	**3**	**0**	**0**	**0**

Vernon, Joseph Henry (Joe)
HEIGHT: 5'11" RIGHTHANDER BORN: 11/25/1889 MANSFIELD, MASSACHUSETTS   DIED: 3/13/1955 PHILADELPHIA, PENNSYLVANIA

YEAR	TEAM	STARTS	GAMES	WON	LOST	PCT	ER	ERA	INNINGS PITCHED	STRIKE-OUTS	WALKS	HITS ALLOWED	HRS ALLOWED	COMP. GAMES	SHUT-OUTS	SAVES
1912	**ChC-N**	**0**	**1**	**0**	**0**	**—**	**5**	**11.25**	**4**	**1**	**6**	**4**	**0**	**0**	**0**	**0**
1914	Bro-F	1	1	0	0	—	4	10.80	3 1/3	0	5	4	0	0	0	0
Career average		1	1	0	0	—	5	11.05	3 2/3	1	6	4	0	0	0	0
Cubs average		**0**	**1**	**0**	**0**	**—**	**5**	**11.25**	**4**	**1**	**6**	**4**	**0**	**0**	**0**	**0**
Career total		1	2	0	0	—	9	11.05	7 1/3	1	11	8	0	0	0	0
Cubs total		**0**	**1**	**0**	**0**	**—**	**5**	**11.25**	**4**	**1**	**6**	**4**	**0**	**0**	**0**	**0**

Vickery, Thomas Gill (Tom)
HEIGHT: 6'0" RIGHTHANDER BORN: 5/5/1867 MILFORD, MASSACHUSETTS   DIED: 3/21/1921 BURLINGTON, NEW JERSEY

YEAR	TEAM	STARTS	GAMES	WON	LOST	PCT	ER	ERA	INNINGS PITCHED	STRIKE-OUTS	WALKS	HITS ALLOWED	HRS ALLOWED	COMP. GAMES	SHUT-OUTS	SAVES
1890	Phi-N	46	46	24	18	.571	146	3.44	382	162	184	405	8	41	2	0
1891	**ChN-N**	**12**	**14**	**6**	**4**	**.600**	**36**	**4.07**	**79 2/3**	**39**	**44**	**72**	**4**	**7**	**0**	**0**
1892	Bal-N	21	24	8	11	.421	69	3.53	176	49	87	189	3	17	0	0
1893	Phi-N	11	13	4	4	.500	48	5.40	80	15	37	100	1	7	0	0
Career average		23	24	11	9	.532	75	3.75	179 1/3	66	88	192	4	18	1	0
Cubs average		**12**	**14**	**6**	**4**	**.600**	**36**	**4.07**	**79 2/3**	**39**	**44**	**72**	**4**	**7**	**0**	**0**
Career total		90	97	42	37	.532	299	3.75	717 2/3	265	352	766	16	72	2	0
Cubs total		**12**	**14**	**6**	**4**	**.600**	**36**	**4.07**	**79 2/3**	**39**	**44**	**72**	**4**	**7**	**0**	**0**

Voiselle, William Symmes (Bill *or* Ninety-Six *or* Big Bill)
HEIGHT: 6'4" RIGHTHANDER BORN: 1/29/1919 GREENWOOD, SOUTH CAROLINA

YEAR	TEAM	STARTS	GAMES	WON	LOST	PCT	ER	ERA	INNINGS PITCHED	STRIKE-OUTS	WALKS	HITS ALLOWED	HRS ALLOWED	COMP. GAMES	SHUT-OUTS	SAVES
1942	NYG-N	1	2	0	1	.000	2	2.00	9	5	4	6	1	0	0	0
1943	NYG-N	4	4	1	2	.333	7	2.03	31	19	14	18	1	3	0	0
1944	NYG-N	41	43	21	16	.568	105	3.02	312 2/3	161	118	276	31	25	1	0
1945	NYG-N	35	41	14	14	.500	116	4.49	232 1/3	115	97	249	15	14	4	0
1946	NYG-N	25	36	9	15	.375	74	3.74	178	89	85	171	14	10	2	0
1947	NYG-N	5	11	1	4	.200	22	4.64	42 2/3	20	22	44	4	1	0	0
1947	Bos-N	20	22	8	7	.533	63	4.32	131 1/3	59	51	146	10	7	0	0
1948	Bos-N	30	37	13	13	.500	87	3.63	215 2/3	89	90	226	18	9	2	2
1949	Bos-N	22	30	7	8	.467	76	4.04	169 1/3	63	78	170	14	5	4	1
1950	**ChC-N**	**7**	**19**	**0**	**4**	**.000**	**33**	**5.79**	**51 1/3**	**25**	**29**	**64**	**7**	**0**	**0**	**0**
Career average		21	27	8	9	.468	65	3.83	152 2/3	72	65	152	13	8	1	0
Cubs average		**7**	**19**	**0**	**4**	**.000**	**33**	**5.79**	**51 1/3**	**25**	**29**	**64**	**7**	**0**	**0**	**0**
Career total		190	245	74	84	.468	585	3.83	1373 1/3	645	588	1370	115	74	13	3
Cubs total		**7**	**19**	**0**	**4**	**.000**	**33**	**5.79**	**51 1/3**	**25**	**29**	**64**	**7**	**0**	**0**	**0**

Waddell, George Edward (Rube)
HEIGHT: 6'1"   LEFTHANDER   BORN: 10/13/1876 BRADFORD, PENNSYLVANIA   DIED: 4/1/1914 SAN ANTONIO, TEXAS

YEAR	TEAM	STARTS	GAMES	WON	LOST	PCT	ER	ERA	INNINGS PITCHED	STRIKE-OUTS	WALKS	HITS ALLOWED	HRS ALLOWED	COMP. GAMES	SHUT-OUTS	SAVES
1897	Lou-N	1	2	0	1	.000	5	3.21	14	5	6	17	0	1	0	0
1899	Lou-N	9	10	7	2	.778	27	3.08	79	44	14	69	4	9	1	1
1900	Pit-N	22	29	8	13	.381	55	2.37	208 ⅔	130	55	176	3	16	2	0
1901	Pit-N	2	2	0	2	.000	8	9.39	7 ⅔	4	9	10	0	0	0	0
1901	**ChN-N**	**28**	**29**	**14**	**14**	**.500**	**76**	**2.81**	**243 ⅔**	**168**	**66**	**239**	**5**	**26**	**0**	**0**
1902	Phi-A	27	33	24	7	.774	63	2.05	276 ⅓	210	64	224	7	26	3	0
1903	Phi-A	38	39	21	16	.568	88	2.44	324	302	85	274	3	34	4	0
1904	Phi-A	46	46	25	19	.568	69	1.62	383	349	91	307	5	39	8	0
1905	Phi-A	34	46	27	10	.730	54	1.48	328 ⅔	287	90	231	5	27	7	0
1906	Phi-A	34	43	15	17	.469	67	2.21	272 ⅔	196	92	221	1	22	8	0
1907	Phi-A	33	44	19	13	.594	68	2.15	284 ⅔	232	73	234	2	20	7	0
1908	StL-A	36	43	19	14	.576	60	1.89	285 ⅔	232	90	223	0	25	5	3
1909	StL-A	28	31	11	14	.440	58	2.37	220 ⅓	141	57	204	1	16	5	0
1910	StL-A	2	10	3	1	.750	13	3.55	33	16	11	31	1	0	0	1
Career average		26	31	15	11	.574	55	2.16	227 ⅔	178	62	189	3	20	4	0
Cubs average		**28**	**29**	**14**	**14**	**.500**	**76**	**2.81**	**243 ⅔**	**168**	**66**	**239**	**5**	**26**	**0**	**0**
Career total		340	407	193	143	.574	711	2.16	2961 ⅓	2316	803	2460	37	261	50	5
Cubs total		**28**	**29**	**14**	**14**	**.500**	**76**	**2.81**	**243 ⅔**	**168**	**66**	**239**	**5**	**26**	**0**	**0**

Wade, Benjamin Styron (Ben)
HEIGHT: 6'3"   RIGHTHANDER   BORN: 11/26/1922 MOREHEAD CITY, NORTH CAROLINA

YEAR	TEAM	STARTS	GAMES	WON	LOST	PCT	ER	ERA	INNINGS PITCHED	STRIKE-OUTS	WALKS	HITS ALLOWED	HRS ALLOWED	COMP. GAMES	SHUT-OUTS	SAVES
1948	**ChC-N**	**0**	**2**	**0**	**1**	**.000**	**4**	**7.20**	**5**	**1**	**4**	**4**	**0**	**0**	**0**	**0**
1952	Bro-N	24	37	11	9	.550	72	3.60	180	118	94	166	19	5	1	3
1953	Bro-N	0	32	7	5	.583	38	3.79	90 ⅓	65	33	79	15	0	0	3
1954	Bro-N	0	23	1	1	.500	41	8.20	45	25	21	62	9	0	0	3
1954	StL-N	0	13	0	0	—	14	5.48	23	19	15	27	3	0	0	0
1955	Pit-N	1	11	0	1	.000	10	3.21	28	7	14	26	3	0	0	1
Career average		5	24	4	3	.528	36	4.34	74 ⅓	47	36	73	10	1	0	2
Cubs average		**0**	**2**	**0**	**1**	**.000**	**4**	**7.20**	**5**	**1**	**4**	**4**	**0**	**0**	**0**	**0**
Career total		25	118	19	17	.528	179	4.34	371 ⅓	235	181	364	49	5	1	10
Cubs total		**0**	**2**	**0**	**1**	**.000**	**4**	**7.20**	**5**	**1**	**4**	**4**	**0**	**0**	**0**	**0**

Walker, James Roy (Roy)
HEIGHT: 6'1"   RIGHTHANDER   BORN: 4/13/1893 LAWRENCEBURG, TENNESSEE   DIED: 2/10/1962 NEW ORLEANS, LOUISIANA

YEAR	TEAM	STARTS	GAMES	WON	LOST	PCT	ER	ERA	INNINGS PITCHED	STRIKE-OUTS	WALKS	HITS ALLOWED	HRS ALLOWED	COMP. GAMES	SHUT-OUTS	SAVES
1912	Cle-A	0	1	0	0	—	0	0.00	2	1	2	0	0	0	0	0
1915	Cle-A	15	25	4	9	.308	58	3.98	131	57	65	122	1	4	0	1
1917	**ChC-N**	**1**	**2**	**0**	**1**	**.000**	**3**	**3.86**	**7**	**4**	**5**	**8**	**0**	**0**	**0**	**0**
1918	**ChC-N**	**7**	**13**	**1**	**3**	**.250**	**13**	**2.70**	**43 ⅓**	**20**	**15**	**50**	**1**	**2**	**0**	**1**
1921	StL-N	23	38	11	12	.478	80	4.22	170 ⅔	52	53	194	10	11	0	3
1922	StL-N	2	12	1	2	.333	17	4.78	32	14	15	34	1	0	0	0
Career average		8	15	3	5	.386	29	3.99	64 ⅓	25	26	68	2	3	0	1
Cubs average		**4**	**8**	**1**	**2**	**.200**	**8**	**2.86**	**25 ⅓**	**12**	**10**	**29**	**1**	**1**	**0**	**1**
Career total		48	91	17	27	.386	171	3.99	386	148	155	408	13	17	0	5
Cubs total		**8**	**15**	**1**	**4**	**.200**	**16**	**2.86**	**50 ⅓**	**24**	**20**	**58**	**1**	**2**	**0**	**1**

Walker, Michael Charles (Mike)
HEIGHT: 6'1"   RIGHTHANDER   BORN: 10/4/1966 CHICAGO, ILLINOIS

YEAR	TEAM	STARTS	GAMES	WON	LOST	PCT	ER	ERA	INNINGS PITCHED	STRIKE-OUTS	WALKS	HITS ALLOWED	HRS ALLOWED	COMP. GAMES	SHUT-OUTS	SAVES
1988	Cle-A	1	3	0	1	.000	7	7.27	8 2/3	7	10	8	0	0	0	0
1990	Cle-A	11	18	2	6	.250	41	4.88	75 2/3	34	42	82	6	0	0	0
1991	Cle-A	0	5	0	1	.000	1	2.08	4 1/3	2	2	6	0	0	0	0
1995	**ChC-N**	**0**	**42**	**1**	**3**	**.250**	**16**	**3.22**	**44 2/3**	**20**	**24**	**45**	**2**	**0**	**0**	**1**
1996	Det-A	0	20	0	0	—	26	8.46	27 2/3	13	17	40	10	0	0	1
Career average		2	18	1	2	.214	18	5.09	32 1/3	15	19	36	4	0	0	0
Cubs average		**0**	**42**	**1**	**3**	**.250**	**16**	**3.22**	**44 2/3**	**20**	**24**	**45**	**2**	**0**	**0**	**1**
Career total		12	88	3	11	.214	91	5.09	161	76	95	181	18	0	0	2
Cubs total		**0**	**42**	**1**	**3**	**.250**	**16**	**3.22**	**44 2/3**	**20**	**24**	**45**	**2**	**0**	**0**	**1**

Ward, Richard O. (Dick *or* Ole)
HEIGHT: 6'1"   RIGHTHANDER   BORN: 5/21/1909 HERRICK, SOUTH DAKOTA   DIED: 5/30/1966 FREELAND, WASHINGTON

YEAR	TEAM	STARTS	GAMES	WON	LOST	PCT	ER	ERA	INNINGS PITCHED	STRIKE-OUTS	WALKS	HITS ALLOWED	HRS ALLOWED	COMP. GAMES	SHUT-OUTS	SAVES
1934	**ChC-N**	**0**	**3**	**0**	**0**	**—**	**2**	**3.00**	**6**	**1**	**2**	**9**	**0**	**0**	**0**	**0**
1935	StL-N	0	1	0	0	—	0	—	0	0	1	0	0	0	0	0
Career average		0	2	0	0	—	1	3.00	3	1	2	5	0	0	0	0
Cubs average		**0**	**3**	**0**	**0**	**—**	**2**	**3.00**	**6**	**1**	**2**	**9**	**0**	**0**	**0**	**0**
Career total		0	4	0	0	—	2	3.00	6	1	3	9	0	0	0	0
Cubs total		**0**	**3**	**0**	**0**	**—**	**2**	**3.00**	**6**	**1**	**2**	**9**	**0**	**0**	**0**	**0**

Warneke, Lonnie (Lon *or* The Arkansas Hummingbird)
HEIGHT: 6'2"   RIGHTHANDER   BORN: 3/28/1909 MOUNT IDA, ARKANSAS   DIED: 6/23/1976 HOT SPRINGS, ARKANSAS

YEAR	TEAM	STARTS	GAMES	WON	LOST	PCT	ER	ERA	INNINGS PITCHED	STRIKE-OUTS	WALKS	HITS ALLOWED	HRS ALLOWED	COMP. GAMES	SHUT-OUTS	SAVES
1930	**ChC-N**	**0**	**1**	**0**	**0**	**—**	**5**	**33.75**	**1 1/3**	**0**	**5**	**2**	**0**	**0**	**0**	**0**
1931	**ChC-N**	**7**	**20**	**2**	**4**	**.333**	**23**	**3.22**	**64 1/3**	**27**	**37**	**67**	**1**	**3**	**0**	**0**
1932	**ChC-N**	**32**	**35**	**22**	**6**	**.786**	**73**	**2.37**	**277**	**106**	**64**	**247**	**12**	**25**	**4**	**0**
1933	**ChC-N**	**34**	**36**	**18**	**13**	**.581**	**64**	**2.00**	**287 1/3**	**133**	**75**	**262**	**8**	**26**	**4**	**1**
1934	**ChC-N**	**35**	**43**	**22**	**10**	**.688**	**104**	**3.21**	**291 1/3**	**143**	**66**	**273**	**16**	**23**	**3**	**3**
1935	**ChC-N**	**30**	**42**	**20**	**13**	**.606**	**89**	**3.06**	**261 3/3**	**120**	**50**	**257**	**19**	**20**	**1**	**4**
1936	**ChC-N**	**29**	**40**	**16**	**13**	**.552**	**92**	**3.45**	**240 1/3**	**113**	**76**	**246**	**10**	**13**	**4**	**1**
1937	StL-N	33	36	18	11	.621	120	4.53	238 2/3	87	69	280	32	18	2	0
1938	StL-N	26	31	13	8	.619	87	3.97	197	89	64	199	14	12	4	0
1939	StL-N	21	34	13	7	.650	68	3.78	162	59	49	160	14	6	3	2
1940	StL-N	31	33	16	10	.615	81	3.14	232	85	47	235	17	17	1	0
1941	StL-N	30	37	17	9	.654	86	3.15	246	83	82	227	19	12	4	0
1942	StL-N	12	12	6	4	.600	30	3.29	82	31	15	76	8	5	0	0
1942	**ChC-N**	**12**	**15**	**5**	**7**	**.417**	**25**	**2.27**	**99**	**28**	**21**	**97**	**2**	**8**	**1**	**2**
1943	**ChC-N**	**10**	**21**	**4**	**5**	**.444**	**31**	**3.16**	**88 1/3**	**30**	**18**	**82**	**3**	**4**	**0**	**0**
1945	**ChC-N**	**1**	**9**	**0**	**1**	**.000**	**6**	**3.86**	**14**	**6**	**1**	**16**	**0**	**0**	**0**	**0**
Career average		23	30	13	8	.613	66	3.18	185 1/3	76	49	182	12	13	2	1
Cubs average		**19**	**26**	**11**	**7**	**.602**	**51**	**2.84**	**162 1/3**	**71**	**41**	**155**	**7**	**12**	**2**	**1**
Career total		343	445	192	121	.613	984	3.18	2782 1/3	1140	739	2726	175	192	31	13
Cubs total		**190**	**262**	**109**	**72**	**.602**	**512**	**2.84**	**1624 2/3**	**706**	**413**	**1549**	**71**	**122**	**17**	**11**

Lonnie (Lon) "the Arkansas Hummingbird" Warneke, rhp, 1930–43, 1945

Lon Warneke, the best ukulele player in the majors in the 1930s (well, maybe the *only* ukulele player) was also one of the best pitchers in the big leagues from 1932 to 1936 while with the Cubs.

Born on March 28, 1909, in Mount Ida, Arkansas, Warneke made one appearance for the Cubs in 1930, pitching 1⅓ innings and issuing five walks. He was a spot starter in 1931 and worked his way into the Cubs pitching rotation by 1932.

Warneke was perhaps the team MVP as the Cubs annexed the 1932 National League crown, with 22 wins, 4 shutouts and a 2.37 ERA, all tops in the league that year.

The 1932 season saw Warneke as a mature veteran pitcher. He had mastered a very sharp overhand curve and a very "live" fastball that had a lot of movement as it came to the plate.

Warneke won 82 games for Chicago from 1932 to 1935, which included three seasons of 20 or more victories. He also topped 100 strikeouts for each of those seasons.

In 1935 Warneke was again a key to the success of the Cubs, winning 20 games and striking out 120 as they won another National League crown. He was also the team's most

successful postseason pitcher, picking up the only two Cubs wins against the Tigers in that Series, and allowing only a 0.54 ERA.

Warneke played in three All-Star Games for the Cubs, in 1933, 1934 and 1936.

Now, about that ukulele. Warneke was not really much of a musician, but he did like to bring a ukulele into the Cubs locker room and hum tunes while strumming the uke, a practice that produced his nickname.

In 1936 Warneke experienced some arm trouble, and his usually dependable win total dropped, although only to 16-13. Still, in 1937, the Cubs shipped him to St. Louis. Warneke performed well for the Cardinals, twice making the All-Star Game.

In 1942 the Cubs paid the Cardinals $75,000 to get Warneke back, but they soon lost him to the military as World War II escalated. After getting out of the army, Warneke pitched a handful of games in 1945 before retiring.

After his retirement, Warneke went to umpiring school and worked as a National League umpire until 1955. He died on June 23, 1976, in Hot Springs, Arkansas.

Warneke didn't stick around Chicago long enough to crack any all-time lists, but he had the lowest ERA (2.85) of any Cub in the 1930s, and he also pitched the most complete games (110) in that decade.

Warner, Jack Dyer

HEIGHT: 5'11"   RIGHTHANDER   BORN: 7/12/1940 BRANDYWINE, WEST VIRGINIA

YEAR	TEAM	STARTS	GAMES	WON	LOST	PCT	ER	ERA	INNINGS PITCHED	STRIKE-OUTS	WALKS	HITS ALLOWED	HRS ALLOWED	COMP. GAMES	SHUT-OUTS	SAVES
1962	ChC-N	0	7	0	0	—	6	7.71	7	3	0	9	3	0	0	0
1963	ChC-N	0	8	0	1	.000	7	2.78	22⅔	7	8	21	1	0	0	0
1964	ChC-N	0	7	0	0	—	3	2.89	9⅓	6	4	12	0	0	0	0
1965	ChC-N	0	11	0	1	.000	15	8.62	15⅔	7	9	22	1	0	0	0
Career average		0	8	0	1	.000	8	5.10	13⅔	6	5	16	1	0	0	0
Cubs average		**0**	**8**	**0**	**1**	**.000**	**8**	**5.10**	**13⅔**	**6**	**5**	**16**	**1**	**0**	**0**	**0**
Career total		0	33	0	2	.000	31	5.10	54⅔	23	21	64	5	0	0	0
Cubs total		**0**	**33**	**0**	**2**	**.000**	**31**	**5.10**	**54⅔**	**23**	**21**	**64**	**5**	**0**	**0**	**0**

Watson, Charles John (Doc)

HEIGHT: 6'0"   LEFTHANDER   BORN: 1/30/1885 CARROLL COUNTY, OHIO   DIED: 12/30/1949 SAN DIEGO, CALIFORNIA

YEAR	TEAM	STARTS	GAMES	WON	LOST	PCT	ER	ERA	INNINGS PITCHED	STRIKE-OUTS	WALKS	HITS ALLOWED	HRS ALLOWED	COMP. GAMES	SHUT-OUTS	SAVES
1913	**ChC-N**	1	1	1	0	1.000	1	1.00	9	1	6	8	0	1	0	0
1914	Chi-F	18	26	9	11	.450	39	2.04	172	69	49	145	2	10	3	1
1914	STL-F	7	9	3	4	.429	12	1.93	56	18	24	41	1	4	2	0
1915	STL-F	20	33	9	9	.500	60	3.98	135 ⅔	45	58	132	1	6	0	0
Career average		15	23	7	8	.478	37	2.70	124 ⅓	44	46	109	1	7	2	0
Cubs average		**1**	**1**	**1**	**0**	**1.000**	**1**	**1.00**	**9**	**1**	**6**	**8**	**0**	**1**	**0**	**0**
Career total		46	69	22	24	.478	112	2.70	372 ⅔	133	137	326	4	21	5	1
Cubs total		**1**	**1**	**1**	**0**	**1.000**	**1**	**1.00**	**9**	**1**	**6**	**8**	**0**	**1**	**0**	**0**

Watt, Edward Dean (Eddie)

HEIGHT: 5'10"   RIGHTHANDER   BORN: 4/4/1941 LAMONIE, IOWA

YEAR	TEAM	STARTS	GAMES	WON	LOST	PCT	ER	ERA	INNINGS PITCHED	STRIKE-OUTS	WALKS	HITS ALLOWED	HRS ALLOWED	COMP. GAMES	SHUT-OUTS	SAVES
1966	Bal-A	13	43	9	7	.563	62	3.83	145 ⅔	102	44	123	11	1	0	4
1967	Bal-A	0	49	3	5	.375	26	2.26	103 ⅔	93	37	67	5	0	0	8
1968	Bal-A	0	59	5	5	.500	21	2.27	83 ⅓	72	35	63	1	0	0	11
1969	Bal-A	0	56	5	2	.714	13	1.65	71	46	26	49	3	0	0	16
1970	Bal-A	0	53	7	7	.500	20	3.25	55 ⅓	33	29	44	3	0	0	12
1971	Bal-A	0	35	3	1	.750	8	1.82	39 ⅔	26	8	39	1	0	0	11
1972	Bal-A	0	38	2	3	.400	11	2.17	45 ⅔	23	20	30	2	0	0	7
1973	Bal-A	0	30	3	4	.429	26	3.30	71	38	21	62	8	0	0	5
1974	Phi-N	0	42	1	1	.500	17	3.99	38 ⅓	23	26	39	3	0	0	6
1975	**ChC-N**	**0**	**6**	**0**	**1**	**.000**	**9**	**13.50**	**6**	**6**	**8**	**14**	**0**	**0**	**0**	**0**
Career average		1	41	4	4	.514	21	2.91	66	46	25	53	4	0	0	8
Cubs average		**0**	**6**	**0**	**1**	**.000**	**9**	**13.50**	**6**	**6**	**8**	**14**	**0**	**0**	**0**	**0**
Career total		13	411	38	36	.514	213	2.91	659 ⅔	462	254	530	37	1	0	80
Cubs total		**0**	**6**	**0**	**1**	**.000**	**9**	**13.50**	**6**	**6**	**8**	**14**	**0**	**0**	**0**	**0**

Weathers, John David (Dave)

HEIGHT: 6'3"   RIGHTHANDER   BORN: 9/25/1969 LAWRENCEBURG, TENNESSEE

YEAR	TEAM	STARTS	GAMES	WON	LOST	PCT	ER	ERA	INNINGS PITCHED	STRIKE-OUTS	WALKS	HITS ALLOWED	HRS ALLOWED	COMP. GAMES	SHUT-OUTS	SAVES
1991	Tor-A	0	15	1	0	1.000	8	4.91	14 ⅔	13	17	15	1	0	0	0
1992	Tor-A	0	2	0	0	—	3	8.10	3 ⅓	3	2	5	1	0	0	0
1993	Fla-N	6	14	2	3	.400	26	5.12	45 ⅔	34	13	57	3	0	0	0
1994	Fla-N	24	24	8	12	.400	79	5.27	135	72	59	166	13	0	0	0
1995	Fla-N	15	28	4	5	.444	60	5.98	90 ⅓	60	52	104	8	0	0	0
1996	Fla-N	8	31	2	2	.500	36	4.54	71 ⅓	40	28	85	7	0	0	0
1996	NYY-A	4	11	0	2	.000	18	9.35	17 ⅓	13	14	23	1	0	0	0
1997	NYY-A	0	10	0	1	.000	10	10.00	9	4	7	15	1	0	0	0
1997	Cle-A	1	9	1	2	.333	14	7.56	16 ⅔	14	8	23	2	0	0	0
1998	Cin-N	9	16	2	4	.333	43	6.21	62 ⅓	51	27	86	3	0	0	0
1998	Mil-N	0	28	4	1	.800	17	3.21	47 ⅔	43	14	44	3	0	0	0
1999	Mil-N	0	63	7	4	.636	48	4.65	93	74	38	102	14	0	0	2
2000	Mil-N	0	69	3	5	.375	26	3.07	76 ⅓	50	32	73	7	0	0	1
2001	Mil-N	0	52	3	4	.429	13	2.03	57 ⅔	46	25	37	3	0	0	4
2001	**ChC-N**	**0**	**28**	**1**	**1**	**.500**	**10**	**3.18**	**28 ⅓**	**20**	**9**	**28**	**3**	**0**	**0**	**0**
Career average		6	36	3	4	.452	37	4.81	70	49	31	78	6	0	0	1
Cubs average		**0**	**28**	**1**	**1**	**.500**	**10**	**3.18**	**28 ⅓**	**20**	**9**	**28**	**3**	**0**	**0**	**0**
Career total		67	400	38	46	.452	411	4.81	768 ⅔	537	345	863	70	0	0	7
Cubs total		**0**	**28**	**1**	**1**	**.500**	**10**	**3.18**	**28 ⅓**	**20**	**9**	**28**	**3**	**0**	**0**	**0**

Weaver, Harry Abraham

HEIGHT: 5'11" RIGHTHANDER BORN: 2/26/1892 CLARENDON, PENNSYLVANIA DIED: 5/30/1983 ROCHESTER, NEW YORK

YEAR	TEAM	STARTS	GAMES	WON	LOST	PCT	ER	ERA	INNINGS PITCHED	STRIKE-OUTS	WALKS	HITS ALLOWED	HRS ALLOWED	COMP. GAMES	SHUT-OUTS	SAVES
1915	Phi-A	2	2	0	2	.000	6	3.00	18	1	10	18	1	2	0	0
1916	Phi-A	0	3	0	0	—	9	10.13	8	2	5	14	0	0	0	0
1917	**ChC-N**	**2**	**4**	**1**	**1**	**.500**	**6**	**2.75**	**19 2/3**	**8**	**7**	**17**	**0**	**1**	**1**	**0**
1918	ChC-N	3	8	2	2	.500	8	2.20	32 2/3	9	7	27	1	1	1	1
1919	ChC-N	1	2	0	1	.000	4	10.80	3 1/3	1	2	6	0	0	0	0
Career average		2	4	1	1	.333	7	3.64	16 1/3	4	6	16	0	1	0	0
Cubs average		**2**	**5**	**1**	**1**	**.429**	**6**	**2.91**	**18 2/3**	**6**	**5**	**17**	**0**	**1**	**1**	**0**
Career total		8	19	3	6	.333	33	3.64	81 2/3	21	31	82	2	4	2	1
Cubs total		**6**	**14**	**3**	**4**	**.429**	**18**	**2.91**	**55 2/3**	**18**	**16**	**50**	**1**	**2**	**2**	**1**

Weaver, James Dement (Jim *or* Big Jim)

HEIGHT: 6'6" RIGHTHANDER BORN: 11/25/1903 OBION COUNTY, TENNESSEE DIED: 12/12/1983 LAKELAND, FLORIDA

YEAR	TEAM	STARTS	GAMES	WON	LOST	PCT	ER	ERA	INNINGS PITCHED	STRIKE-OUTS	WALKS	HITS ALLOWED	HRS ALLOWED	COMP. GAMES	SHUT-OUTS	SAVES
1928	Was-A	0	3	0	0	—	1	1.50	6	2	6	2	0	0	0	0
1931	NYY-A	5	17	2	1	.667	34	5.31	57 2/3	28	29	66	1	2	0	0
1934	StL-A	5	5	2	0	1.000	14	6.41	19 2/3	11	20	17	3	2	0	0
1934	**ChC-N**	**20**	**27**	**11**	**9**	**.550**	**69**	**3.91**	**159**	**98**	**54**	**163**	**5**	**8**	**1**	**0**
1935	Pit-N	22	33	14	8	.636	67	3.42	176 1/3	87	58	177	9	11	4	0
1936	Pit-N	31	38	14	8	.636	108	4.31	225 2/3	108	74	239	12	11	1	0
1937	Pit-N	9	32	8	5	.615	39	3.20	109 2/3	44	31	106	2	2	1	0
1938	StL-A	1	1	0	1	.000	7	9.00	7	4	9	9	0	0	0	0
1938	Cin-N	15	30	6	4	.600	45	3.13	129 1/3	64	54	109	6	2	0	3
1939	Cin-N	0	3	0	0	—	1	3.00	3	3	1	3	0	0	0	0
Career average		14	24	7	5	.613	48	3.88	111 2/3	56	42	111	5	5	1	0
Cubs average		**20**	**27**	**11**	**9**	**.550**	**69**	**3.91**	**159**	**98**	**54**	**163**	**5**	**8**	**1**	**0**
Career total		108	189	57	36	.613	385	3.88	893 1/3	449	336	891	38	38	7	3
Cubs total		**20**	**27**	**11**	**9**	**.550**	**69**	**3.91**	**159**	**98**	**54**	**163**	**5**	**8**	**1**	**0**

Weaver, Orville Forest (Orlie)

HEIGHT: 6'0" RIGHTHANDER BORN: 6/4/1886 NEWPORT, KENTUCKY DIED: 11/28/1970 NEW ORLEANS, LOUISIANA

YEAR	TEAM	STARTS	GAMES	WON	LOST	PCT	ER	ERA	INNINGS PITCHED	STRIKE-OUTS	WALKS	HITS ALLOWED	HRS ALLOWED	COMP. GAMES	SHUT-OUTS	SAVES
1910	**ChC-N**	**2**	**7**	**1**	**2**	**.333**	**13**	**3.66**	**32**	**22**	**15**	**34**	**2**	**2**	**0**	**0**
1911	**ChC-N**	**4**	**6**	**3**	**2**	**.600**	**10**	**2.06**	**43 2/3**	**20**	**17**	**29**	**0**	**1**	**1**	**0**
1911	Bos-N	17	27	3	12	.200	87	6.47	121	50	84	140	9	4	0	0
Career average		12	20	4	8	.304	55	5.03	98 1/3	46	58	102	6	4	1	0
Cubs average		**3**	**7**	**2**	**2**	**.500**	**12**	**2.74**	**38**	**21**	**16**	**32**	**1**	**2**	**1**	**0**
Career total		23	40	7	16	.304	110	5.03	196 2/3	92	116	203	11	7	1	0
Cubs total		**6**	**13**	**4**	**4**	**.500**	**23**	**2.74**	**75 2/3**	**42**	**32**	**63**	**2**	**3**	**1**	**0**

Weimer, Jacob (Jake *or* Tornado Jake)

HEIGHT: 5'11" LEFTHANDER BORN: 11/29/1873 OTTUMWA, IOWA DIED: 6/19/1928 CHICAGO, ILLINOIS

YEAR	TEAM	STARTS	GAMES	WON	LOST	PCT	ER	ERA	INNINGS PITCHED	STRIKE-OUTS	WALKS	HITS ALLOWED	HRS ALLOWED	COMP. GAMES	SHUT-OUTS	SAVES
1903	**ChC-N**	**33**	**35**	**20**	**8**	**.714**	**72**	**2.30**	**282**	**128**	**104**	**241**	**4**	**27**	**3**	**0**
1904	**ChC-N**	**37**	**37**	**20**	**14**	**.588**	**65**	**1.91**	**307**	**177**	**97**	**229**	**1**	**31**	**5**	**0**
1905	**ChC-N**	**30**	**33**	**18**	**12**	**.600**	**63**	**2.26**	**250 1/3**	**107**	**80**	**212**	**1**	**26**	**2**	**1**
1906	Cin-N	39	41	20	14	.588	75	2.22	304 2/3	141	99	263	0	31	6	1
1907	Cin-N	26	29	11	14	.440	56	2.41	209	67	63	165	6	19	3	0
1908	Cin-N	15	15	8	7	.533	31	2.39	116 2/3	36	50	110	2	9	2	0
1909	NYG-N	0	1	0	0	—	3	9.00	3	1	0	7	0	0	0	0
Career average		26	27	14	10	.584	52	2.23	210 1/3	94	70	175	2	20	3	0
Cubs average		**33**	**35**	**19**	**11**	**.630**	**67**	**2.14**	**279 2/3**	**137**	**94**	**227**	**2**	**28**	**3**	**0**
Career total		180	191	97	69	.584	365	2.23	1472 2/3	657	493	1227	14	143	21	2
Cubs total		**100**	**105**	**58**	**34**	**.630**	**200**	**2.14**	**839 1/3**	**412**	**281**	**682**	**6**	**84**	**10**	**1**

Weinert, Philip Walter (Lefty)
HEIGHT: 6'1" LEFTHANDER BORN: 4/21/1902 PHILADELPHIA, PENNSYLVANIA DIED: 4/17/1973 ROCKLEDGE, FLORIDA

YEAR	TEAM	STARTS	GAMES	WON	LOST	PCT	ER	ERA	INNINGS PITCHED	STRIKE-OUTS	WALKS	HITS ALLOWED	HRS ALLOWED	COMP. GAMES	SHUT-OUTS	SAVES
1919	Phi-N	0	1	0	0	—	8	18.00	4	0	2	11	0	0	0	0
1920	Phi-N	2	10	1	1	.500	15	6.14	22	10	19	27	1	0	0	0
1921	Phi-N	0	8	1	0	1.000	2	1.46	12 1/3	2	5	8	1	0	0	0
1922	Phi-N	22	34	8	11	.421	63	3.40	166 2/3	58	70	189	10	10	0	1
1923	Phi-N	20	38	4	17	.190	94	5.42	156	46	81	207	10	8	0	1
1924	Phi-N	1	8	0	1	.000	4	2.45	14 2/3	7	11	10	0	0	0	0
1927	ChC-N	3	5	1	1	.500	10	4.58	19 2/3	5	6	21	2	1	0	0
1928	ChC-N	1	10	1	0	1.000	10	5.29	17	8	9	24	0	0	0	0
1931	NYY-A	0	17	2	2	.500	17	6.20	24 2/3	24	19	31	2	0	0	0
Career average		5	15	2	4	.353	25	4.59	48 2/3	18	25	59	3	2	0	0
Cubs average		2	8	1	1	.667	10	4.91	18 1/3	7	8	23	1	1	0	0
Career total		49	131	18	33	.353	223	4.59	437	160	222	528	26	19	0	2
Cubs total		4	15	2	1	.667	20	4.91	36 2/3	13	15	45	2	1	0	0

Welch, John Vernon (Johnny)
HEIGHT: 6'3" RIGHTHANDER BORN: 12/2/1906 WASHINGTON, DISTRICT OF COLUMBIA DIED: 9/2/1940 ST. LOUIS, MISSOURI

YEAR	TEAM	STARTS	GAMES	WON	LOST	PCT	ER	ERA	INNINGS PITCHED	STRIKE-OUTS	WALKS	HITS ALLOWED	HRS ALLOWED	COMP. GAMES	SHUT-OUTS	SAVES
1926	ChC-N	0	3	0	0	—	1	2.08	4 1/3	0	1	5	0	0	0	0
1927	ChC-N	0	1	0	0	—	1	9.00	1	1	3	0	0	0	0	0
1928	ChC-N	0	3	0	0	—	7	15.75	4	2	0	13	0	0	0	0
1931	ChC-N	3	8	2	1	.667	14	3.74	33 2/3	7	10	39	2	1	0	0
1932	Bos-A	8	20	4	6	.400	42	5.23	72 1/3	26	38	93	3	3	1	0
1933	Bos-A	7	47	4	9	.308	66	4.60	129	68	67	142	6	1	0	3
1934	Bos-A	22	41	13	15	.464	103	4.49	206 1/3	91	76	223	14	8	1	0
1935	Bos-A	19	31	10	9	.526	71	4.47	143	48	53	155	4	10	1	2
1936	Bos-A	3	9	2	1	.667	20	5.51	32 2/3	9	8	43	4	1	0	0
1936	Pit-N	1	9	0	0	—	11	4.50	22	5	6	22	3	0	0	1
Career average		7	19	4	5	.461	37	4.66	72	29	29	82	4	3	0	1
Cubs average		1	4	1	0	.667	6	4.81	10 2/3	3	4	14	1	0	0	0
Career total		63	172	35	41	.461	336	4.66	648 1/3	257	262	735	36	24	3	6
Cubs total		3	15	2	1	.667	23	4.81	43	10	14	57	2	1	0	0

Wendell, Steven John (Turk)
HEIGHT: 6'2" RIGHTHANDER BORN: 5/19/1967 PITTSFIELD, MASSACHUSETTS

YEAR	TEAM	STARTS	GAMES	WON	LOST	PCT	ER	ERA	INNINGS PITCHED	STRIKE-OUTS	WALKS	HITS ALLOWED	HRS ALLOWED	COMP. GAMES	SHUT-OUTS	SAVES
1993	ChC-N	4	7	1	2	.333	11	4.37	22 2/3	15	8	24	0	0	0	0
1994	ChC-N	2	6	0	1	.000	19	11.93	14 1/3	9	10	22	3	0	0	0
1995	ChC-N	0	43	3	1	.750	33	4.92	60 1/3	50	24	71	11	0	0	0
1996	ChC-N	0	70	4	5	.444	25	2.84	79 1/3	75	44	58	8	0	0	18
1997	ChC-N	0	52	3	5	.375	28	4.20	60	54	39	53	4	0	0	4
1997	NYM-N	0	13	0	0	—	9	4.96	16 1/3	10	14	15	3	0	0	1
1998	NYM-N	0	66	5	1	.833	25	2.93	76 2/3	58	33	62	4	0	0	4
1999	NYM-N	0	80	5	4	.556	29	3.05	85 2/3	77	37	80	9	0	0	3
2000	NYM-N	0	77	8	6	.571	33	3.59	82 2/3	73	41	60	9	0	0	1
2001	NYM-N	0	49	4	3	.571	20	3.51	51 1/3	41	22	42	8	0	0	0
2001	Phi-N	0	21	0	2	.000	13	7.47	15 2/3	15	12	21	4	0	0	0
Career average		1	54	4	3	.524	27	3.90	62 2/3	53	32	56	7	0	0	4
Cubs average		1	36	2	3	.440	23	4.41	47 1/3	41	25	46	5	0	0	4
Career total		6	484	33	30	.524	245	3.90	565	477	284	508	63	0	0	32
Cubs total		6	178	11	14	.440	116	4.41	236 2/3	203	125	228	26	0	0	22

Wengert, Donald Paul (Don)
HEIGHT: 6'3" RIGHTHANDER BORN: 11/6/1969 SIOUX CITY, IOWA

YEAR	TEAM	STARTS	GAMES	WON	LOST	PCT	ER	ERA	INNINGS PITCHED	STRIKE-OUTS	WALKS	HITS ALLOWED	HRS ALLOWED	COMP. GAMES	SHUT-OUTS	SAVES
1995	Oak-A	0	19	1	1	.500	11	3.34	29 2/3	16	12	30	3	0	0	0
1996	Oak-A	25	36	7	11	.389	100	5.58	161 1/3	75	60	200	29	1	1	0
1997	Oak-A	12	49	5	11	.313	90	6.04	134	68	41	177	21	1	0	2
1998	SD-N	0	10	0	0	—	9	5.93	13 2/3	5	5	21	2	0	0	1
1998	**ChC-N**	**6**	**21**	**1**	**5**	**.167**	**28**	**5.07**	**49 2/3**	**41**	**23**	**55**	**8**	**0**	**0**	**0**
1999	KC-A	1	11	0	1	.000	25	9.25	24 1/3	10	5	41	6	0	0	0
2000	Atl-N	0	10	0	1	.000	8	7.20	10	7	5	12	2	0	0	0
2001	Pit-N	4	4	0	2	.000	22	12.38	16	4	6	33	2	0	0	0
Career average		7	23	2	5	.304	42	6.01	62 2/3	32	22	81	10	0	0	0
Cubs average		**6**	**21**	**1**	**5**	**.167**	**28**	**5.07**	**49 2/3**	**41**	**23**	**55**	**8**	**0**	**0**	**0**
Career total		48	160	14	32	.304	293	6.01	438 2/3	226	157	569	73	2	1	3
Cubs total		**6**	**21**	**1**	**5**	**.167**	**28**	**5.07**	**49 2/3**	**41**	**23**	**55**	**8**	**0**	**0**	**0**

Wheeler, Floyd Clark (Rip)
HEIGHT: 6'0" RIGHTHANDER BORN: 3/2/1898 MARION, KENTUCKY DIED: 9/18/1968 MARION, KENTUCKY

YEAR	TEAM	STARTS	GAMES	WON	LOST	PCT	ER	ERA	INNINGS PITCHED	STRIKE-OUTS	WALKS	HITS ALLOWED	HRS ALLOWED	COMP. GAMES	SHUT-OUTS	SAVES
1921	Pit-N	0	1	0	0	—	3	9.00	3	0	1	6	0	0	0	0
1922	Pit-N	0	1	0	0	—	0	0.00	1	0	2	1	0	0	0	0
1923	**ChC-N**	**3**	**3**	**1**	**2**	**.333**	**13**	**4.88**	**24**	**5**	**5**	**28**	**2**	**1**	**0**	**0**
1924	**ChC-N**	**4**	**29**	**3**	**6**	**.333**	**44**	**3.91**	**101 1/3**	**16**	**21**	**103**	**8**	**0**	**0**	**0**
Career average		2	9	1	2	.333	15	4.18	32 1/3	5	7	35	3	0	0	0
Cubs average		**4**	**16**	**2**	**4**	**.333**	**29**	**4.09**	**62 2/3**	**11**	**13**	**66**	**5**	**0**	**0**	**0**
Career total		7	34	4	8	.333	60	4.18	129 1/3	21	29	138	10	1	0	0
Cubs total		**7**	**32**	**4**	**8**	**.333**	**57**	**4.09**	**125 1/3**	**21**	**26**	**131**	**10**	**1**	**0**	**0**

White, James Laurie (Deacon)
HEIGHT: 5'11" RIGHTHANDER BORN: 12/7/1847 CATON, NEW YORK DIED: 7/7/1939 AURORA, ILLINOIS

YEAR	TEAM	STARTS	GAMES	WON	LOST	PCT	ER	ERA	INNINGS PITCHED	STRIKE-OUTS	WALKS	HITS ALLOWED	HRS ALLOWED	COMP. GAMES	SHUT-OUTS	SAVES
1876	**ChN-N**	**0**	**1**	**0**	**0**	**—**	**0**	**0.00**	**2**	**3**	**0**	**1**	**0**	**0**	**0**	**1**
1890	Buf-P	0	1	0	0	—	8	9.00	8	0	2	18	0	0	0	0
Career average		0	1	0	0	—	4	7.20	5	2	1	10	0	0	0	1
Cubs average		**0**	**1**	**0**	**0**	**—**	**0**	**0.00**	**2**	**3**	**0**	**1**	**0**	**0**	**0**	**1**
Career total		0	2	0	0	—	8	7.20	10	3	2	19	0	0	0	1
Cubs total		**0**	**1**	**0**	**0**	**—**	**0**	**0.00**	**2**	**3**	**0**	**1**	**0**	**0**	**0**	**1**

Whitehill, Earl Oliver
HEIGHT: 5'9" LEFTHANDER BORN: 2/7/1900 CEDAR RAPIDS, IOWA DIED: 10/22/1954 OMAHA, NEBRASKA

YEAR	TEAM	STARTS	GAMES	WON	LOST	PCT	ER	ERA	INNINGS PITCHED	STRIKE-OUTS	WALKS	HITS ALLOWED	HRS ALLOWED	COMP. GAMES	SHUT-OUTS	SAVES
1923	Det-A	3	8	2	0	1.000	10	2.73	33	19	15	22	2	2	1	0
1924	Det-A	32	35	17	9	.654	100	3.86	233	65	79	260	8	16	2	0
1925	Det-A	33	35	11	11	.500	124	4.66	239 1/3	83	88	267	13	15	1	2
1926	Det-A	34	36	16	13	.552	112	3.99	252 1/3	109	79	271	7	13	0	0
1927	Det-A	31	41	16	14	.533	88	3.36	236	95	105	238	4	17	3	3
1928	Det-A	30	31	11	16	.407	94	4.31	196 1/3	93	78	214	8	12	1	0
1929	Det-A	28	38	14	15	.483	126	4.62	245 1/3	103	96	267	16	18	1	1
1930	Det-A	31	34	17	13	.567	104	4.24	220 2/3	109	80	248	8	16	0	1
1931	Det-A	34	34	13	16	.448	123	4.08	271 1/3	81	118	287	22	22	0	0
1932	Det-A	31	33	16	12	.571	123	4.54	244	81	93	255	17	17	3	0
1933	Was-A	37	39	22	8	.733	100	3.33	270	96	100	271	9	19	2	1
1934	Was-A	31	32	14	11	.560	118	4.52	235	96	94	269	10	15	0	0
1935	Was-A	34	34	14	13	.519	133	4.29	279 1/3	102	104	318	16	19	1	0

(continued)

(Whitehill, continued)

YEAR	TEAM	STARTS	GAMES	WON	LOST	PCT	ER	ERA	INNINGS PITCHED	STRIKE-OUTS	WALKS	HITS ALLOWED	HRS ALLOWED	COMP. GAMES	SHUT-OUTS	SAVES
1936	Was-A	28	28	14	11	.560	115	4.87	212 1/3	63	89	252	17	14	0	0
1937	Cle-A	22	33	8	8	.500	106	6.49	147	53	80	189	9	6	1	2
1938	Cle-A	23	26	9	8	.529	99	5.56	160 1/3	60	83	187	18	4	0	0
1939	**ChC-N**	**11**	**24**	**4**	**7**	**.364**	**51**	**5.14**	**89 1/3**	**42**	**50**	**102**	**8**	**2**	**1**	**1**
Career average		28	32	13	11	.541	102	4.36	209 2/3	79	84	230	11	13	1	1
Cubs average		**11**	**24**	**4**	**7**	**.364**	**51**	**5.14**	**89 1/3**	**42**	**50**	**102**	**8**	**2**	**1**	**1**
Career total		473	541	218	185	.541	1726	4.36	3564 2/3	1350	1431	3917	192	227	17	11
Cubs total		**11**	**24**	**4**	**7**	**.364**	**51**	**5.14**	**89 1/3**	**42**	**50**	**102**	**8**	**2**	**1**	**1**

Wicker, Robert Kitridge (Bob)
HEIGHT: 6'2" RIGHTHANDER BORN: 5/24/1878 BEDFORD, INDIANA   DIED: 1/22/1955 EVANSTON, ILLINOIS

YEAR	TEAM	STARTS	GAMES	WON	LOST	PCT	ER	ERA	INNINGS PITCHED	STRIKE-OUTS	WALKS	HITS ALLOWED	HRS ALLOWED	COMP. GAMES	SHUT-OUTS	SAVES
1901	StL-N	0	1	0	0	—	0	0.00	3	2	1	4	0	0	0	0
1902	StL-N	16	22	5	12	.294	54	3.19	152 1/3	78	45	159	1	14	1	0
1903	StL-N	0	1	0	0	—	0	0.00	5	3	3	4	0	0	0	0
1903	**ChC-N**	**27**	**32**	**20**	**9**	**.690**	**83**	**3.02**	**247**	**110**	**74**	**236**	**3**	**24**	**1**	**1**
1904	**ChC-N**	**27**	**30**	**17**	**9**	**.654**	**68**	**2.67**	**229**	**99**	**58**	**201**	**6**	**23**	**4**	**0**
1905	**ChC-N**	**22**	**22**	**13**	**6**	**.684**	**40**	**2.02**	**178**	**86**	**47**	**139**	**3**	**17**	**4**	**0**
1906	**ChC-N**	**8**	**10**	**3**	**5**	**.375**	**24**	**2.99**	**72 1/3**	**25**	**19**	**70**	**0**	**5**	**0**	**0**
1906	Cin-N	17	20	6	11	.353	45	2.70	150	69	46	150	3	14	0	0
Career average		20	23	11	9	.552	52	2.73	172 2/3	79	49	161	3	16	2	0
Cubs average		**21**	**24**	**13**	**7**	**.646**	**54**	**2.66**	**181 2/3**	**80**	**50**	**162**	**3**	**17**	**2**	**0**
Career total		117	138	64	52	.552	314	2.73	1036 2/3	472	293	963	16	97	10	1
Cubs total		**84**	**94**	**53**	**29**	**.646**	**215**	**2.66**	**726 1/3**	**320**	**198**	**646**	**12**	**69**	**9**	**1**

Wiedemeyer, Charles John (Charlie)
HEIGHT: 6'3" LEFTHANDER BORN: 1/31/1914 CHICAGO, ILLINOIS   DIED: 10/27/1979 LAKE GENEVA, FLORIDA

YEAR	TEAM	STARTS	GAMES	WON	LOST	PCT	ER	ERA	INNINGS PITCHED	STRIKE-OUTS	WALKS	HITS ALLOWED	HRS ALLOWED	COMP. GAMES	SHUT-OUTS	SAVES
1934	**ChC-N**	**1**	**4**	**0**	**0**	**—**	**9**	**9.72**	**8 1/3**	**2**	**4**	**16**	**0**	**0**	**0**	**0**
Career average		1	4	0	0	—	9	9.72	8 1/3	2	4	16	0	0	0	0
Cubs average		**1**	**4**	**0**	**0**	**—**	**9**	**9.72**	**8 1/3**	**2**	**4**	**16**	**0**	**0**	**0**	**0**
Career total		1	4	0	0	—	9	9.72	8 1/3	2	4	16	0	0	0	0
Cubs total		**1**	**4**	**0**	**0**	**—**	**9**	**9.72**	**8 1/3**	**2**	**4**	**16**	**0**	**0**	**0**	**0**

Wilcox, Milton Edward (Milt)
HEIGHT: 6'2" RIGHTHANDER BORN: 4/20/1950 HONOLULU, HAWAII

YEAR	TEAM	STARTS	GAMES	WON	LOST	PCT	ER	ERA	INNINGS PITCHED	STRIKE-OUTS	WALKS	HITS ALLOWED	HRS ALLOWED	COMP. GAMES	SHUT-OUTS	SAVES
1970	Cin-N	2	5	3	1	.750	6	2.42	22 1/3	13	7	19	2	1	1	1
1971	Cin-N	3	18	2	2	.500	16	3.32	43 1/3	21	17	43	2	0	0	1
1972	Cle-A	27	32	7	14	.333	59	3.40	156	90	72	145	18	4	2	0
1973	Cle-A	19	26	8	10	.444	87	5.83	134 1/3	82	68	143	14	4	0	0
1974	Cle-A	2	41	2	2	.500	37	4.67	71 1/3	33	24	74	10	1	0	4
1975	**ChC-N**	**0**	**25**	**0**	**1**	**.000**	**24**	**5.63**	**38 1/3**	**21**	**17**	**50**	**4**	**0**	**0**	**0**
1977	Det-A	13	20	6	2	.750	43	3.64	106 1/3	82	37	96	13	1	0	0
1978	Det-A	27	29	13	12	.520	90	3.76	215 1/3	132	68	208	22	16	2	0
1979	Det-A	29	33	12	10	.545	95	4.35	196 1/3	109	73	201	18	7	0	0
1980	Det-A	31	32	13	11	.542	99	4.48	198 2/3	97	68	201	24	13	1	0
1981	Det-A	24	24	12	9	.571	56	3.03	166 1/3	79	52	152	10	8	1	0
1982	Det-A	29	29	12	10	.545	78	3.62	193 2/3	112	85	187	18	9	1	0
1983	Det-A	26	26	11	10	.524	82	3.97	186	101	74	164	19	9	2	0
1984	Det-A	33	33	17	8	.680	86	4.00	193 2/3	119	66	183	13	0	0	0
1985	Det-A	8	8	1	3	.250	21	4.85	39	20	14	51	6	0	0	0
1986	Sea-A	10	13	0	8	.000	34	5.50	55 2/3	26	28	74	11	0	0	0
Career average		18	25	7	7	.513	57	4.07	126	71	48	124	13	5	1	0
Cubs average		**0**	**25**	**0**	**1**	**.000**	**24**	**5.63**	**38 1/3**	**21**	**17**	**50**	**4**	**0**	**0**	**0**
Career total		283	394	119	113	.513	913	4.07	2016 2/3	1137	770	1991	204	73	10	6
Cubs total		**0**	**25**	**0**	**1**	**.000**	**24**	**5.63**	**38 1/3**	**21**	**17**	**50**	**4**	**0**	**0**	**0**

Wilhelm, James Hoyt (Hoyt *or* Old Tilt)

HEIGHT: 6'0" RIGHTHANDER BORN: 7/26/1923 HUNTERSVILLE, NORTH CAROLINA

YEAR	TEAM	STARTS	GAMES	WON	LOST	PCT	ER	ERA	INNINGS PITCHED	STRIKE-OUTS	WALKS	HITS ALLOWED	HRS ALLOWED	COMP. GAMES	SHUT-OUTS	SAVES
1952	NYG-N	0	71	15	3	.833	43	2.43	159⅓	108	57	127	12	0	0	11
1953	NYG-N	0	68	7	8	.467	49	3.04	145	71	77	127	13	0	0	15
1954	NYG-N	0	57	12	4	.750	26	2.10	111⅓	64	52	77	5	0	0	7
1955	NYG-N	0	59	4	1	.800	45	3.93	103	71	40	104	10	0	0	0
1956	NYG-N	0	64	4	9	.308	38	3.83	89⅓	71	43	97	7	0	0	8
1957	StL-N	0	40	1	4	.200	26	4.25	55	29	21	52	7	0	0	11
1957	Cle-A	0	2	1	0	1.000	1	2.45	3⅔	0	1	2	1	0	0	1
1958	Cle-A	6	30	2	7	.222	25	2.49	90⅓	57	35	70	4	1	0	5
1958	Bal-A	4	9	1	3	.250	9	1.99	40⅔	35	10	25	2	3	1	0
1959	Bal-A	27	32	15	11	.577	55	2.19	226	139	77	178	13	13	3	0
1960	Bal-A	11	41	11	8	.579	54	3.31	147	107	39	125	13	3	1	7
1961	Bal-A	1	51	9	7	.563	28	2.30	109⅔	87	41	89	5	0	0	18
1962	Bal-A	0	52	7	10	.412	20	1.94	93	90	34	64	5	0	0	15
1963	CWS-A	3	55	5	8	.385	40	2.64	136⅓	111	30	106	8	0	0	21
1964	CWS-A	0	73	12	9	.571	29	1.99	131⅓	95	30	94	7	0	0	27
1965	CWS-A	0	66	7	7	.500	29	1.81	144	106	32	88	11	0	0	20
1966	CWS-A	0	46	5	2	.714	15	1.66	81⅓	61	17	50	6	0	0	6
1967	CWS-A	0	49	8	3	.727	13	1.31	89	76	34	58	2	0	0	12
1968	CWS-A	0	72	4	4	.500	18	1.73	93⅔	72	24	69	4	0	0	12
1969	Cal-A	0	44	5	7	.417	18	2.47	65⅔	53	18	45	4	0	0	10
1969	Atl-N	0	8	2	0	1.000	1	0.73	12⅓	14	4	5	0	0	0	4
1970	Atl-N	0	50	6	4	.600	27	3.10	78⅓	67	39	69	7	0	0	13
1970	**ChC-N**	**0**	**3**	**0**	**1**	**.000**	**4**	**9.82**	**3⅔**	**1**	**3**	**4**	**1**	**0**	**0**	**0**
1971	Atl-N	0	3	0	0	—	4	15.43	2⅓	1	1	6	2	0	0	0
1971	LA-N	0	9	0	1	.000	2	1.02	17⅔	15	4	6	1	0	0	3
1972	LA-N	0	16	0	1	.000	13	4.62	25⅓	9	15	20	0	0	0	1
Career average		2	51	7	6	.540	30	2.52	107⅓	77	37	84	7	1	0	11
Cubs average		**0**	**3**	**0**	**1**	**.000**	**4**	**9.82**	**3⅔**	**1**	**3**	**4**	**1**	**0**	**0**	**0**
Career total		52	1070	143	122	.540	632	2.52	2254⅓	1610	778	1757	150	20	5	227
Cubs total		**0**	**3**	**0**	**1**	**.000**	**4**	**9.82**	**3⅔**	**1**	**3**	**4**	**1**	**0**	**0**	**0**

Wilkins, Dean Allan

HEIGHT: 6'1" RIGHTHANDER BORN: 8/24/1966 BLUE ISLAND, ILLINOIS

YEAR	TEAM	STARTS	GAMES	WON	LOST	PCT	ER	ERA	INNINGS PITCHED	STRIKE-OUTS	WALKS	HITS ALLOWED	HRS ALLOWED	COMP. GAMES	SHUT-OUTS	SAVES
1989	**ChC-N**	**0**	**11**	**1**	**0**	**1.000**	**9**	**5.17**	**15⅔**	**14**	**9**	**13**	**2**	**0**	**0**	**0**
1990	**ChC-N**	**0**	**7**	**0**	**0**	**—**	**8**	**9.82**	**7⅓**	**3**	**7**	**11**	**1**	**0**	**0**	**1**
1991	Hou-N	0	7	2	1	.667	10	11.25	8	4	10	16	0	0	0	1
Career average		0	8	1	0	.750	9	7.84	10⅓	7	9	13	1	0	0	1
Cubs average		**0**	**9**	**1**	**0**	**1.000**	**9**	**6.65**	**11⅔**	**9**	**8**	**12**	**2**	**0**	**0**	**1**
Career total		0	25	3	1	.750	27	7.84	31	21	26	40	3	0	0	2
Cubs total		**0**	**18**	**1**	**0**	**1.000**	**17**	**6.65**	**23**	**17**	**16**	**24**	**3**	**0**	**0**	**1**

Williams, Brian O'Neal

HEIGHT: 6'3" RIGHTHANDER BORN: 2/15/1969 FORT LAWN, SOUTH CAROLINA

YEAR	TEAM	STARTS	GAMES	WON	LOST	PCT	ER	ERA	INNINGS PITCHED	STRIKE-OUTS	WALKS	HITS ALLOWED	HRS ALLOWED	COMP. GAMES	SHUT-OUTS	SAVES
1991	Hou-N	2	2	0	1	.000	5	3.75	12	4	4	11	2	0	0	0
1992	Hou-N	16	16	7	6	.538	42	3.92	96⅓	54	42	92	10	0	0	0
1993	Hou-N	5	42	4	4	.500	44	4.83	82	56	38	76	7	0	0	3
1994	Hou-N	13	20	6	5	.545	50	5.74	78⅓	49	41	112	9	0	0	0
1995	SD-N	6	44	3	10	.231	48	6.00	72	75	38	79	3	0	0	0
1996	Det-A	17	40	3	10	.231	91	6.77	121	72	85	145	21	2	1	2
1997	Bal-A	0	13	0	0	—	8	3.00	24	14	18	20	0	0	0	0
1999	Hou-N	0	50	2	1	.667	33	4.41	67⅓	53	35	69	4	0	0	0
2000	**ChC-N**	**0**	**22**	**1**	**1**	**.500**	**26**	**9.62**	**24⅓**	**14**	**23**	**28**	**4**	**0**	**0**	**1**
2000	Cle-A	0	7	0	0	—	8	4.00	18	6	8	23	2	0	0	0
Career average		7	28	3	4	.406	39	5.37	66	44	37	73	7	0	0	1
Cubs average		**0**	**22**	**1**	**1**	**.500**	**26**	**9.62**	**24⅓**	**14**	**23**	**28**	**4**	**0**	**0**	**1**
Career total		59	256	26	38	.406	355	5.37	595⅓	397	332	655	62	2	1	6
Cubs total		**0**	**22**	**1**	**1**	**.500**	**26**	**9.62**	**24⅓**	**14**	**23**	**28**	**4**	**0**	**0**	**1**

Williams, Mitchell Steven (Mitch *or* Wild Thing)

HEIGHT: 6'4"   LEFTHANDER   BORN: 11/17/1964 SANTA ANA, CALIFORNIA

YEAR	TEAM	STARTS	GAMES	WON	LOST	PCT	ER	ERA	INNINGS PITCHED	STRIKE-OUTS	WALKS	HITS ALLOWED	HRS ALLOWED	COMP. GAMES	SHUT-OUTS	SAVES
1986	Tex-A	0	80	8	6	.571	39	3.58	98	90	79	69	8	0	0	8
1987	Tex-A	1	85	8	6	.571	39	3.23	108 ⅔	129	94	63	9	0	0	6
1988	Tex-A	0	67	2	7	.222	35	4.63	68	61	47	48	4	0	0	18
1989	**ChC-N**	0	**76**	4	4	**.500**	24	**2.64**	**81 ⅔**	67	52	71	6	0	0	**36**
1990	**ChC-N**	2	**59**	1	8	**.111**	29	**3.93**	**66 ⅓**	55	50	60	4	0	0	**16**
1991	Phi-N	0	69	12	5	.706	23	2.34	88 ⅓	84	62	56	4	0	0	30
1992	Phi-N	0	66	5	8	.385	34	3.78	81	74	64	69	4	0	0	29
1993	Phi-N	0	65	3	7	.300	23	3.34	62	60	44	56	3	0	0	43
1994	Hou-N	0	25	1	4	.200	17	7.65	20	21	24	21	4	0	0	6
1995	Cal-A	0	20	1	2	.333	8	6.75	10 ⅔	9	21	13	1	0	0	0
1997	KC-A	0	7	0	1	.000	8	10.80	6 ⅔	10	7	11	2	0	0	0
Career average		0	56	4	5	.437	25	3.63	63	60	49	49	4	0	0	17
Cubs average		**1**	**68**	**3**	**6**	**.294**	**27**	**3.22**	**74**	**61**	**51**	**66**	**5**	**0**	**0**	**26**
Career total		3	619	45	58	.437	279	3.63	691 ⅓	660	544	537	49	0	0	192
Cubs total		**2**	**135**	**5**	**12**	**.294**	**53**	**3.22**	**148**	**122**	**102**	**131**	**10**	**0**	**0**	**52**

Williams, Walter Merrill (Pop)

HEIGHT: 5'11"   LEFTHANDER   BORN: 5/19/1874 BOWDOINHAM, MAINE   DIED: 8/4/1959 TOPSHAM, MAINE

YEAR	TEAM	STARTS	GAMES	WON	LOST	PCT	ER	ERA	INNINGS PITCHED	STRIKE-OUTS	WALKS	HITS ALLOWED	HRS ALLOWED	COMP. GAMES	SHUT-OUTS	SAVES
1898	Was-N	2	2	0	2	.000	16	8.47	17	3	7	32	0	2	0	0
1902	**ChC-N**	31	31	11	16	.407	71	2.51	254 ⅓	94	63	259	1	26	1	0
1903	**ChC-N**	1	1	0	1	.000	3	5.40	5	2	0	9	0	1	0	0
1903	Phi-N	2	2	1	1	.500	6	3.00	18	8	6	21	0	2	0	0
1903	Bos-N	10	10	4	5	.444	38	4.12	83	20	37	97	3	9	1	0
Career average		15	15	5	8	.390	45	3.20	125 ⅔	42	38	139	1	13	1	0
Cubs average		**16**	**16**	**6**	**9**	**.393**	**37**	**2.57**	**129 ⅔**	**48**	**32**	**134**	**1**	**14**	**1**	**0**
Career total		46	46	16	25	.390	134	3.20	377 ⅓	127	113	418	4	40	2	0
Cubs total		**32**	**32**	**11**	**17**	**.393**	**74**	**2.57**	**259 ⅓**	**96**	**63**	**268**	**1**	**27**	**1**	**0**

Williams, Washington J. (Wash)

HEIGHT: 5'11"   BORN: — PHILADELPHIA, PENNSYLVANIA   DIED: 8/9/1892 PHILADELPHIA, PENNSYLVANIA

YEAR	TEAM	STARTS	GAMES	WON	LOST	PCT	ER	ERA	INNINGS PITCHED	STRIKE-OUTS	WALKS	HITS ALLOWED	HRS ALLOWED	COMP. GAMES	SHUT-OUTS	SAVES
1885	ChN-N	1	1	0	0	—	3	13.50	2	0	5	2	0	0	0	0
Career average		1	1	0	0	—	3	13.50	2	0	5	2	0	0	0	0
Cubs average		**1**	**1**	**0**	**0**	**—**	**3**	**13.50**	**2**	**0**	**5**	**2**	**0**	**0**	**0**	**0**
Career total		1	1	0	0	—	3	13.50	2	0	5	2	0	0	0	0
Cubs total		**1**	**1**	**0**	**0**	**—**	**3**	**13.50**	**2**	**0**	**5**	**2**	**0**	**0**	**0**	**0**

Williamson, Edward Nagle (Ned)

HEIGHT: 5'11"   RIGHTHANDER   BORN: 10/24/1857 PHILADELPHIA, PENNSYLVANIA   DIED: 3/3/1894 MOUNTAIN VALLEY SPRINGS, ARKANSAS

YEAR	TEAM	STARTS	GAMES	WON	LOST	PCT	ER	ERA	INNINGS PITCHED	STRIKE-OUTS	WALKS	HITS ALLOWED	HRS ALLOWED	COMP. GAMES	SHUT-OUTS	SAVES
1881	ChN-N	1	3	1	1	.500	4	2.00	18	2	0	14	0	1	0	0
1882	ChN-N	0	1	0	0	—	2	6.00	3	0	1	9	1	0	0	0
1883	ChN-N	0	1	0	0	—	1	9.00	1	1	1	1	0	0	0	0
1884	ChN-N	0	2	0	0	—	4	18.00	2	0	2	8	0	0	0	0
1885	ChN-N	0	2	0	0	—	0	0.00	6	3	0	2	0	0	0	2
1886	ChN-N	0	2	0	0	—	0	0.00	3	1	0	2	0	0	0	1
1887	ChN-N	0	1	0	0	—	2	9.00	2	0	1	3	0	0	0	0
Career average		0	2	0	0	.500	2	3.34	5	1	1	6	0	0	0	0
Cubs average		**0**	**2**	**0**	**0**	**.500**	**2**	**3.34**	**5**	**1**	**1**	**6**	**0**	**0**	**0**	**0**
Career total		1	12	1	1	.500	13	3.34	35	7	5	39	1	1	0	3
Cubs total		**1**	**12**	**1**	**1**	**.500**	**13**	**3.34**	**35**	**7**	**5**	**39**	**1**	**1**	**0**	**3**

Willis, James Gladden (Jim)
HEIGHT: 6'3"   RIGHTHANDER   BORN: 3/20/1927 DOYLINE, ALABAMA

YEAR	TEAM	STARTS	GAMES	WON	LOST	PCT	ER	ERA	INNINGS PITCHED	STRIKE-OUTS	WALKS	HITS ALLOWED	HRS ALLOWED	COMP. GAMES	SHUT-OUTS	SAVES
1953	ChC-N	3	13	2	1	.667	15	3.12	43⅓	15	17	37	1	2	0	0
1954	ChC-N	1	14	0	1	.000	10	3.91	23	5	18	22	1	0	0	0
Career average		2	14	1	1	.500	13	3.39	33⅓	10	18	30	1	1	0	0
Cubs average		**2**	**14**	**1**	**1**	**.500**	**13**	**3.39**	**33⅓**	**10**	**18**	**30**	**1**	**1**	**0**	**0**
Career total		4	27	2	2	.500	25	3.39	66⅓	20	35	59	2	2	0	0
Cubs total		**4**	**27**	**2**	**2**	**.500**	**25**	**3.39**	**66⅓**	**20**	**35**	**59**	**2**	**2**	**0**	**0**

Wilson, Stephen Douglas (Steve)
HEIGHT: 6'4"   LEFTHANDER   BORN: 12/13/1964 VICTORIA, BRITISH COLUMBIA, CANADA

YEAR	TEAM	STARTS	GAMES	WON	LOST	PCT	ER	ERA	INNINGS PITCHED	STRIKE-OUTS	WALKS	HITS ALLOWED	HRS ALLOWED	COMP. GAMES	SHUT-OUTS	SAVES
1988	Tex-A	0	3	0	0	—	5	5.87	7⅔	1	4	7	1	0	0	0
1989	ChC-N	8	53	6	4	.600	40	4.20	85⅔	65	31	83	6	0	0	2
1990	ChC-N	15	45	4	9	.308	74	4.79	139	95	43	140	17	1	0	1
1991	ChC-N	0	8	0	0	—	6	4.38	12⅓	9	5	13	1	0	0	0
1991	LA-N	0	11	0	0	—	0	0.00	8⅓	5	4	1	0	0	0	2
1992	LA-N	0	60	2	5	.286	31	4.19	66⅔	54	29	74	6	0	0	0
1993	LA-N	0	25	1	0	1.000	13	4.56	25⅔	23	14	30	2	0	0	1
Career average		4	34	2	3	.419	28	4.40	57⅔	42	22	58	6	0	0	1
Cubs average		**8**	**35**	**3**	**4**	**.435**	**40**	**4.56**	**79**	**56**	**26**	**79**	**8**	**0**	**0**	**1**
Career total		23	205	13	18	.419	169	4.40	345⅓	252	130	348	33	1	0	6
Cubs total		**23**	**106**	**10**	**13**	**.435**	**120**	**4.56**	**237**	**169**	**79**	**236**	**24**	**1**	**0**	**3**

Wood, Kerry Lee
HEIGHT: 6'5"   RIGHTHANDER   BORN: 6/16/1977 IRVING, TEXAS

YEAR	TEAM	STARTS	GAMES	WON	LOST	PCT	ER	ERA	INNINGS PITCHED	STRIKE-OUTS	WALKS	HITS ALLOWED	HRS ALLOWED	COMP. GAMES	SHUT-OUTS	SAVES
1998	ChC-N	26	26	13	6	.684	63	3.40	166⅔	233	85	117	14	1	1	0
2000	ChC-N	23	23	8	7	.533	73	4.80	137	132	87	112	17	1	0	0
2001	ChC-N	28	28	12	6	.667	65	3.36	174⅓	217	92	127	16	1	1	0
Career average		26	26	11	6	.635	67	3.78	159⅓	194	88	119	16	1	1	0
Cubs average		**26**	**26**	**11**	**6**	**.635**	**67**	**3.78**	**159⅓**	**194**	**88**	**119**	**16**	**1**	**1**	**0**
Career total		77	77	33	19	.635	201	3.78	478	582	264	356	47	3	2	0
Cubs total		**77**	**77**	**33**	**19**	**.635**	**201**	**3.78**	**478**	**582**	**264**	**356**	**47**	**3**	**2**	**0**

Woodall, David Bradley (Brad)
HEIGHT: 6'0"   LEFTHANDER   BORN: 6/25/1969 ATLANTA, GEORGIA

YEAR	TEAM	STARTS	GAMES	WON	LOST	PCT	ER	ERA	INNINGS PITCHED	STRIKE-OUTS	WALKS	HITS ALLOWED	HRS ALLOWED	COMP. GAMES	SHUT-OUTS	SAVES
1994	Atl-N	1	1	0	1	.000	3	4.50	6	2	2	5	2	0	0	0
1995	Atl-N	0	9	1	1	.500	7	6.10	10⅓	5	8	13	1	0	0	0
1996	Atl-N	3	8	2	2	.500	16	7.32	19⅔	20	4	28	4	0	0	0
1998	Mil-N	20	31	7	9	.438	76	4.96	138	85	47	145	25	0	0	0
1999	ChC-N	3	6	0	1	.000	10	5.63	16	7	6	17	5	0	0	0
Career average		5	11	2	3	.417	22	5.31	38	24	13	42	7	0	0	0
Cubs average		**3**	**6**	**0**	**1**	**.000**	**10**	**5.63**	**16**	**7**	**6**	**17**	**5**	**0**	**0**	**0**
Career total		27	55	10	14	.417	112	5.31	190	119	67	208	37	0	0	0
Cubs total		**3**	**6**	**0**	**1**	**.000**	**10**	**5.63**	**16**	**7**	**6**	**17**	**5**	**0**	**0**	**0**

Woods, Walter Sydney (Walt)
HEIGHT: 5'9" RIGHTHANDER BORN: 4/28/1875 RYE, NEW HAMPSHIRE DIED: 10/30/1951 PORTSMOUTH, NEW HAMPSHIRE

YEAR	TEAM	STARTS	GAMES	WON	LOST	PCT	ER	ERA	INNINGS PITCHED	STRIKE-OUTS	WALKS	HITS ALLOWED	HRS ALLOWED	COMP. GAMES	SHUT-OUTS	SAVES
1898	**ChN-N**	**22**	**27**	**9**	**13**	**.409**	**75**	**3.14**	**215**	**26**	**59**	**224**	**7**	**18**	**3**	**0**
1899	Lou-N	21	26	9	12	.429	68	3.28	186 1/3	21	37	216	9	17	0	0
1900	Pit-N	0	1	0	0	—	7	21.00	3	1	1	9	0	0	0	0
Career average		14	18	6	8	.419	50	3.34	134 2/3	16	32	150	5	12	1	0
Cubs average		**22**	**27**	**9**	**13**	**.409**	**75**	**3.14**	**215**	**26**	**59**	**224**	**7**	**18**	**3**	**0**
Career total		43	54	18	25	.419	150	3.34	404 1/3	48	97	449	16	35	3	0
Cubs total		**22**	**27**	**9**	**13**	**.409**	**75**	**3.14**	**215**	**26**	**59**	**224**	**7**	**18**	**3**	**0**

Worrell, Timothy Howard (Tim)
HEIGHT: 6'4" RIGHTHANDER BORN: 7/5/1967 PASADENA, CALIFORNIA

YEAR	TEAM	STARTS	GAMES	WON	LOST	PCT	ER	ERA	INNINGS PITCHED	STRIKE-OUTS	WALKS	HITS ALLOWED	HRS ALLOWED	COMP. GAMES	SHUT-OUTS	SAVES
1993	SD-N	16	21	2	7	.222	55	4.92	100 2/3	52	43	104	11	0	0	0
1994	SD-N	3	3	0	1	.000	6	3.68	14 2/3	14	5	9	0	0	0	0
1995	SD-N	0	9	1	0	1.000	7	4.73	13 1/3	13	6	16	2	0	0	0
1996	SD-N	11	50	9	7	.563	41	3.05	121	99	39	109	9	0	0	1
1997	SD-N	10	60	4	8	.333	61	5.16	106 1/3	81	50	116	14	0	0	3
1998	Det-A	9	15	2	6	.250	41	5.98	61 2/3	47	19	66	11	0	0	0
1998	Cle-A	0	3	0	0	—	3	5.06	5 1/3	2	2	6	0	0	0	0
1998	Oak-A	0	25	0	1	.000	16	4.00	36	33	8	34	5	0	0	0
1999	Oak-A	0	53	2	2	.500	32	4.15	69 1/3	62	34	69	6	0	0	0
2000	Bal-A	0	5	2	2	.500	6	7.36	7 1/3	5	5	12	3	0	0	0
2000	**ChC-N**	**0**	**54**	**3**	**4**	**.429**	**17**	**2.47**	**62**	**52**	**24**	**60**	**7**	**0**	**0**	**3**
2001	SF-N	0	73	2	5	.286	30	3.45	78 1/3	63	33	71	4	0	0	0
Career average		5	41	3	5	.386	35	4.19	75	58	30	75	8	0	0	1
Cubs average		**0**	**54**	**3**	**4**	**.429**	**17**	**2.47**	**62**	**52**	**24**	**60**	**7**	**0**	**0**	**3**
Career total		49	371	27	43	.386	315	4.19	676	523	268	672	72	0	0	7
Cubs total		**0**	**54**	**3**	**4**	**.429**	**17**	**2.47**	**62**	**52**	**24**	**60**	**7**	**0**	**0**	**3**

Wright, David William (Dave)
HEIGHT: 6'0" RIGHTHANDER BORN: 8/27/1875 DENNISON, OHIO DIED: 1/18/1946 DENNISON, OHIO

YEAR	TEAM	STARTS	GAMES	WON	LOST	PCT	ER	ERA	INNINGS PITCHED	STRIKE-OUTS	WALKS	HITS ALLOWED	HRS ALLOWED	COMP. GAMES	SHUT-OUTS	SAVES
1895	Pit-N	0	1	0	0	—	6	27.00	2	0	1	6	0	0	0	0
1897	**ChN-N**	**1**	**1**	**1**	**0**	**1.000**	**12**	**15.43**	**7**	**4**	**2**	**17**	**1**	**1**	**0**	**0**
Career average		1	1	1	0	1.000	9	18.00	4 2/3	2	2	12	1	1	0	0
Cubs average		**1**	**1**	**1**	**0**	**1.000**	**12**	**15.43**	**7**	**4**	**2**	**17**	**1**	**1**	**0**	**0**
Career total		1	2	1	0	1.000	18	18.00	9	4	3	23	1	1	0	0
Cubs total		**1**	**1**	**1**	**0**	**1.000**	**12**	**15.43**	**7**	**4**	**2**	**17**	**1**	**1**	**0**	**0**

Wright, Melvin James (Mel)
HEIGHT: 6'3" RIGHTHANDER BORN: 5/11/1928 MANILA, ARKANSAS DIED: 5/16/1983 HOUSTON, TEXAS

YEAR	TEAM	STARTS	GAMES	WON	LOST	PCT	ER	ERA	INNINGS PITCHED	STRIKE-OUTS	WALKS	HITS ALLOWED	HRS ALLOWED	COMP. GAMES	SHUT-OUTS	SAVES
1954	StL-N	0	9	0	0	—	12	10.45	10 1/3	4	11	16	2	0	0	0
1955	StL-N	0	29	2	2	.500	25	6.19	36 1/3	18	9	44	4	0	0	1
1960	**ChC-N**	**0**	**9**	**0**	**1**	**.000**	**9**	**4.96**	**16 1/3**	**8**	**3**	**17**	**1**	**0**	**0**	**2**
1961	**ChC-N**	**0**	**11**	**0**	**1**	**.000**	**25**	**10.71**	**21**	**6**	**4**	**42**	**3**	**0**	**0**	**0**
Career average		0	15	1	1	.333	18	7.61	21	9	7	30	3	0	0	1
Cubs average		**0**	**10**	**0**	**1**	**.000**	**17**	**8.20**	**18 2/3**	**7**	**4**	**30**	**2**	**0**	**0**	**1**
Career total		0	58	2	4	.333	71	7.61	84	36	27	119	10	0	0	3
Cubs total		**0**	**20**	**0**	**2**	**.000**	**34**	**8.20**	**37 1/3**	**14**	**7**	**59**	**4**	**0**	**0**	**2**

Wright, Robert Cassius (Bob)
HEIGHT: 6'1" RIGHTHANDER BORN: 12/13/1891 DECATUR COUNTY, INDIANA DIED: 7/30/1993 CARMICHAEL, CALIFORNIA

YEAR	TEAM	STARTS	GAMES	WON	LOST	PCT	ER	ERA	INNINGS PITCHED	STRIKE-OUTS	WALKS	HITS ALLOWED	HRS ALLOWED	COMP. GAMES	SHUT-OUTS	SAVES
1915	ChC-N	0	2	0	0	—	1	2.25	4	3	0	6	0	0	0	0
Career average		0	2	0	0	—	1	2.25	4	3	0	6	0	0	0	0
Cubs average		**0**	**2**	**0**	**0**	**—**	**1**	**2.25**	**4**	**3**	**0**	**6**	**0**	**0**	**0**	**0**
Career total		0	2	0	0	—	1	2.25	4	3	0	6	0	0	0	0
Cubs total		**0**	**2**	**0**	**0**	**—**	**1**	**2.25**	**4**	**3**	**0**	**6**	**0**	**0**	**0**	**0**

Wyse, Henry Washington (Hank *or* Hooks)
HEIGHT: 5'11" RIGHTHANDER BORN: 3/1/1918 LUNSFORD, ARKANSAS DIED: 10/22/2000 PRYOR, OKLAHOMA

YEAR	TEAM	STARTS	GAMES	WON	LOST	PCT	ER	ERA	INNINGS PITCHED	STRIKE-OUTS	WALKS	HITS ALLOWED	HRS ALLOWED	COMP. GAMES	SHUT-OUTS	SAVES
1942	ChC-N	4	4	2	1	.667	6	1.93	28	8	6	33	1	1	1	0
1943	ChC-N	15	38	9	7	.563	51	2.94	156	45	34	159	4	8	2	5
1944	ChC-N	34	41	16	15	.516	90	3.15	257 1/3	86	57	277	9	14	3	1
1945	ChC-N	34	38	22	10	.688	83	2.68	278 1/3	77	55	272	17	23	2	0
1946	ChC-N	27	40	14	12	.538	60	2.68	201 1/3	52	52	206	7	12	2	1
1947	ChC-N	19	37	6	9	.400	68	4.31	142	53	64	158	12	5	1	1
1950	Phi-A	23	41	9	14	.391	111	5.85	170 2/3	33	87	192	16	4	0	0
1951	Phi-A	1	9	1	2	.333	13	7.98	14 2/3	5	8	24	0	0	0	0
1951	Was-A	2	3	0	0	—	10	9.64	9 1/3	3	10	17	0	0	0	0
Career average		20	31	10	9	.530	62	3.52	157 1/3	45	47	167	8	8	1	1
Cubs average		**22**	**33**	**12**	**9**	**.561**	**60**	**3.03**	**177 1/3**	**54**	**45**	**184**	**8**	**11**	**2**	**1**
Career total		159	251	79	70	.530	492	3.52	1257 2/3	362	373	1338	66	67	11	8
Cubs total		**133**	**198**	**69**	**54**	**.561**	**358**	**3.03**	**1063**	**321**	**268**	**1105**	**50**	**63**	**11**	**8**

Yerkes, Charles Carroll (Carroll *or* Lefty)
HEIGHT: 5'11" LEFTHANDER BORN: 6/13/1903 MCSHERRYSTOWN, PENNSYLVANIA DIED: 12/20/1950 OAKLAND, CALIFORNIA

YEAR	TEAM	STARTS	GAMES	WON	LOST	PCT	ER	ERA	INNINGS PITCHED	STRIKE-OUTS	WALKS	HITS ALLOWED	HRS ALLOWED	COMP. GAMES	SHUT-OUTS	SAVES
1927	Phi-A	0	1	0	0	—	0	0.00	1	0	1	0	0	0	0	0
1928	Phi-A	1	2	0	1	.000	2	2.08	8 2/3	1	2	7	0	1	0	0
1929	Phi-A	2	19	1	0	1.000	19	4.58	37 1/3	11	13	47	0	0	0	1
1932	**ChC-N**	**0**	**2**	**0**	**0**	**—**	**3**	**3.00**	**9**	**4**	**3**	**5**	**2**	**0**	**0**	**0**
1933	**ChC-N**	**0**	**1**	**0**	**0**	**—**	**1**	**4.50**	**2**	**0**	**1**	**2**	**0**	**0**	**0**	**0**
Career average		1	5	0	0	.500	5	3.88	11 2/3	3	4	12	0	0	0	0
Cubs average		**0**	**2**	**0**	**0**	**—**	**2**	**3.27**	**5 2/3**	**2**	**2**	**4**	**1**	**0**	**0**	**0**
Career total		3	25	1	1	.500	25	3.88	58	16	20	61	2	1	0	1
Cubs total		**0**	**3**	**0**	**0**	**—**	**4**	**3.27**	**11**	**4**	**4**	**7**	**2**	**0**	**0**	**0**

York, James Edward (Lefty)
HEIGHT: 5'10" LEFTHANDER BORN: 11/1/1892 WEST FORK, ARKANSAS DIED: 4/9/1961 YORK, PENNSYLVANIA

YEAR	TEAM	STARTS	GAMES	WON	LOST	PCT	ER	ERA	INNINGS PITCHED	STRIKE-OUTS	WALKS	HITS ALLOWED	HRS ALLOWED	COMP. GAMES	SHUT-OUTS	SAVES
1919	Phi-A	2	2	0	2	.000	12	24.92	4 1/3	2	5	13	0	0	0	0
1921	**ChC-N**	**11**	**40**	**5**	**9**	**.357**	**73**	**4.73**	**139**	**57**	**63**	**170**	**5**	**4**	**1**	**1**
Career average		7	21	3	6	.313	43	5.34	71 2/3	30	34	92	3	2	1	1
Cubs average		**11**	**40**	**5**	**9**	**.357**	**73**	**4.73**	**139**	**57**	**63**	**170**	**5**	**4**	**1**	**1**
Career total		13	42	5	11	.313	85	5.34	143 1/3	59	68	183	5	4	1	1
Cubs total		**11**	**40**	**5**	**9**	**.357**	**73**	**4.73**	**139**	**57**	**63**	**170**	**5**	**4**	**1**	**1**

Yost, August (Gus)
HEIGHT: 6'5" BORN: —

YEAR	TEAM	STARTS	GAMES	WON	LOST	PCT	ER	ERA	INNINGS PITCHED	STRIKE-OUTS	WALKS	HITS ALLOWED	HRS ALLOWED	COMP. GAMES	SHUT-OUTS	SAVES
1893	ChN-N	1	1	0	0	—	4	13.50	2 ⅔	1	8	3	0	0	0	0
Career average		1	1	0	0	—	4	13.50	2 ⅔	1	8	3	0	0	0	0
Cubs average		1	1	0	0	—	4	13.50	2 ⅔	1	8	3	0	0	0	0
Career total		1	1	0	0	—	4	13.50	2 ⅔	1	8	3	0	0	0	0
Cubs total		1	1	0	0	—	4	13.50	2 ⅔	1	8	3	0	0	0	0

Young, Anthony Wayne (A.Y.)
HEIGHT: 6'2" RIGHTHANDER BORN: 1/19/1966 HOUSTON, TEXAS

YEAR	TEAM	STARTS	GAMES	WON	LOST	PCT	ER	ERA	INNINGS PITCHED	STRIKE-OUTS	WALKS	HITS ALLOWED	HRS ALLOWED	COMP. GAMES	SHUT-OUTS	SAVES
1991	NYM-N	8	10	2	5	.286	17	3.10	49 ⅓	20	12	48	4	0	0	0
1992	NYM-N	13	52	2	14	.125	56	4.17	121	64	31	134	8	1	0	15
1993	NYM-N	10	39	1	16	.059	42	3.77	100 ⅓	62	42	103	8	1	0	3
1994	ChC-N	19	20	4	6	.400	50	3.92	114 ⅔	65	46	103	12	0	0	2
1995	ChC-N	1	32	3	4	.429	17	3.70	41 ⅓	15	14	47	5	0	0	2
1996	Hou-N	0	28	3	3	.500	17	4.59	33 ⅓	19	22	36	4	0	0	0
Career average		9	30	3	8	.238	33	3.89	76 ⅔	41	28	79	7	0	0	3
Cubs average		10	26	4	5	.412	34	3.87	78	40	30	75	9	0	0	1
Career total		51	181	15	48	.238	199	3.89	460	245	167	471	41	2	0	20
Cubs total		20	52	7	10	.412	67	3.87	156	80	60	150	17	0	0	2

Young, Daniel Bracey (Danny)
HEIGHT: 6'4" LEFTHANDER BORN: 11/3/1971 SMYRNA, TENNESSEE

YEAR	TEAM	STARTS	GAMES	WON	LOST	PCT	ER	ERA	INNINGS PITCHED	STRIKE-OUTS	WALKS	HITS ALLOWED	HRS ALLOWED	COMP. GAMES	SHUT-OUTS	SAVES
2000	ChC-N	0	4	0	1	.000	7	21.00	3	0	6	5	1	0	0	0
Career average		0	4	0	1	.000	7	21.00	3	0	6	5	1	0	0	0
Cubs average		0	4	0	1	.000	7	21.00	3	0	6	5	1	0	0	0
Career total		0	4	0	1	.000	7	21.00	3	0	6	5	1	0	0	0
Cubs total		0	4	0	1	.000	7	21.00	3	0	6	5	1	0	0	0

Zabel, George Washington (Zip)
HEIGHT: 6'1" RIGHTHANDER BORN: 2/18/1891 WETMORE, KANSAS DIED: 5/31/1970 BELOIT, WISCONSIN

YEAR	TEAM	STARTS	GAMES	WON	LOST	PCT	ER	ERA	INNINGS PITCHED	STRIKE-OUTS	WALKS	HITS ALLOWED	HRS ALLOWED	COMP. GAMES	SHUT-OUTS	SAVES
1913	ChC-N	1	1	1	0	1.000	0	0.00	5	0	1	3	0	0	0	0
1914	ChC-N	7	29	4	4	.500	31	2.18	128	50	45	104	5	2	0	3
1915	ChC-N	17	36	7	10	.412	58	3.20	163	60	84	124	3	8	3	0
Career average		8	22	4	5	.462	30	2.71	98 ⅔	37	43	77	3	3	1	1
Cubs average		8	22	4	5	.462	30	2.71	98 ⅔	37	43	77	3	3	1	1
Career total		25	66	12	14	.462	89	2.71	296	110	130	231	8	10	3	3
Cubs total		25	66	12	14	.462	89	2.71	296	110	130	231	8	10	3	3

Zahn, Geoffrey Clayton (Geoff)
HEIGHT: 6'1" LEFTHANDER BORN: 12/19/1945 BALTIMORE, MARYLAND

YEAR	TEAM	STARTS	GAMES	WON	LOST	PCT	ER	ERA	INNINGS PITCHED	STRIKE-OUTS	WALKS	HITS ALLOWED	HRS ALLOWED	COMP. GAMES	SHUT-OUTS	SAVES
1973	LA-N	1	6	1	0	1.000	2	1.35	13 ⅓	9	2	5	2	0	0	0
1974	LA-N	10	21	3	5	.375	18	2.03	79 ⅔	33	16	78	3	1	0	0
1975	LA-N	0	2	0	1	.000	3	9.00	3	1	5	2	0	0	0	0

(continued)

(continued)

YEAR	TEAM				PCT	ER	ERA	IP	SO	BB	HITS	HRS	COMP	SHUT	SAVES
1975	**ChC-N**	**10**	**16**	**2**	**7**	**.222**	**31**	**4.45**	**62 ⅔**	**21**	**26**	**67**	**2**	**0**	**0**	**1**
1976	**ChC-N**	**2**	**3**	**0**	**1**	**.000**	**10**	**10.80**	**8 ⅓**	**4**	**2**	**16**	**0**	**0**	**0**	**0**
1977	Min-A	32	34	12	14	.462	103	4.68	198	88	66	234	20	7	1	0
1978	Min-A	35	35	14	14	.500	85	3.03	252 ⅓	106	81	260	18	12	1	0
1979	Min-A	24	26	13	7	.650	67	3.57	169	58	41	181	13	4	0	0
1980	Min-A	35	38	14	18	.438	114	4.41	232 ⅔	96	66	273	17	13	5	0
1981	Cal-A	25	25	10	11	.476	79	4.41	161 ⅓	52	43	181	18	9	0	0
1982	Cal-A	34	34	18	8	.692	95	3.73	229 ⅓	81	65	225	18	12	4	0
1983	Cal-A	28	29	9	11	.450	75	3.33	203	81	51	212	22	11	3	0
1984	Cal-A	27	28	13	10	.565	69	3.12	199 ⅓	61	48	200	11	9	5	0
1985	Cal-A	7	7	2	2	.500	18	4.38	37	14	14	44	5	1	1	0
Career average		21	23	9	8	.505	59	3.74	142 ⅓	54	40	152	11	6	2	0
Cubs average		**6**	**10**	**1**	**4**	**.200**	**21**	**5.20**	**35 ⅔**	**13**	**14**	**42**	**1**	**0**	**0**	**1**
Career total		270	304	111	109	.505	769	3.74	1849	705	526	1978	149	79	20	1
Cubs total		**12**	**19**	**2**	**8**	**.200**	**41**	**5.20**	**71**	**25**	**28**	**83**	**2**	**0**	**0**	**1**

Zambrano, Carlos Alberto
HEIGHT: 6'4"   RIGHTHANDER   BORN: 6/1/1981 CARABOBO, VENEZUELA

YEAR	TEAM	STARTS	GAMES	WON	LOST	PCT	ER	ERA	INNINGS PITCHED	STRIKE-OUTS	WALKS	HITS ALLOWED	HRS ALLOWED	COMP. GAMES	SHUT-OUTS	SAVES
2001	**ChC-N**	**1**	**6**	**1**	**2**	**.333**	**13**	**15.26**	**7 ⅔**	**4**	**8**	**11**	**2**	**0**	**0**	**0**
Career average		1	6	1	2	.333	13	15.26	7 ⅔	4	8	11	2	0	0	0
Cubs average		**1**	**6**	**1**	**2**	**.333**	**13**	**15.26**	**7 ⅔**	**4**	**8**	**11**	**2**	**0**	**0**	**0**
Career total		1	6	1	2	.333	13	15.26	7 ⅔	4	8	11	2	0	0	0
Cubs total		**1**	**6**	**1**	**2**	**.333**	**13**	**15.26**	**7 ⅔**	**4**	**8**	**11**	**2**	**0**	**0**	**0**

Zamora, Oscar Jose
HEIGHT: 5'10"   RIGHTHANDER   BORN: 9/23/1944 CAMAGUEY, CUBA

YEAR	TEAM	STARTS	GAMES	WON	LOST	PCT	ER	ERA	INNINGS PITCHED	STRIKE-OUTS	WALKS	HITS ALLOWED	HRS ALLOWED	COMP. GAMES	SHUT-OUTS	SAVES
1974	**ChC-N**	**0**	**56**	**3**	**9**	**.250**	**29**	**3.12**	**83 ⅔**	**38**	**19**	**82**	**6**	**0**	**0**	**10**
1975	**ChC-N**	**0**	**52**	**5**	**2**	**.714**	**40**	**5.07**	**71**	**28**	**15**	**84**	**17**	**0**	**0**	**10**
1976	**ChC-N**	**2**	**40**	**5**	**3**	**.625**	**32**	**5.24**	**55**	**27**	**17**	**70**	**8**	**0**	**0**	**3**
1978	Hou-N	0	10	0	0	—	12	7.20	15	6	7	20	2	0	0	0
Career average		1	40	3	4	.481	28	4.53	56 ⅓	25	15	64	8	0	0	6
Cubs average		**1**	**49**	**4**	**5**	**.481**	**34**	**4.34**	**70**	**31**	**17**	**79**	**10**	**0**	**0**	**8**
Career total		2	158	13	14	.481	113	4.53	224 ⅔	99	58	256	33	0	0	23
Cubs total		**2**	**148**	**13**	**14**	**.481**	**101**	**4.34**	**209 ⅔**	**93**	**51**	**236**	**31**	**0**	**0**	**23**

Zick, Robert George (Bob)
HEIGHT: 6'0"   RIGHTHANDER   BORN: 4/26/1927 CHICAGO, ILLINOIS

YEAR	TEAM	STARTS	GAMES	WON	LOST	PCT	ER	ERA	INNINGS PITCHED	STRIKE-OUTS	WALKS	HITS ALLOWED	HRS ALLOWED	COMP. GAMES	SHUT-OUTS	SAVES
1954	**ChC-N**	**0**	**8**	**0**	**0**	**—**	**15**	**8.27**	**16 ⅓**	**9**	**7**	**23**	**1**	**0**	**0**	**0**
Career average		0	8	0	0	—	15	8.27	16 ⅓	9	7	23	1	0	0	0
Cubs average		**0**	**8**	**0**	**0**	**—**	**15**	**8.27**	**16 ⅓**	**9**	**7**	**23**	**1**	**0**	**0**	**0**
Career total		0	8	0	0	—	15	8.27	16 ⅓	9	7	23	1	0	0	0
Cubs total		**0**	**8**	**0**	**0**	**—**	**15**	**8.27**	**16 ⅓**	**9**	**7**	**23**	**1**	**0**	**0**	**0**

APPENDIX A: Postseason Play

1906 World Series

CHICAGO WHITE SOX (4) VS. CHICAGO CUBS (2)

GAME 1
Tuesday, October 9

	1	2	3	4	5	6	7	8	9	R	H	E
Chicago White Sox	0	0	0	0	1	1	0	0	0	2	4	1
Chicago Cubs	0	0	0	0	0	1	0	0	0	1	4	2

WP - Nick Altrock; LP - Three Finger Brown

GAME 2
Wednesday, October 10

	1	2	3	4	5	6	7	8	9	R	H	E
Chicago Cubs	0	3	1	0	0	1	0	2	0	7	10	2
Chicago White Sox	0	0	0	0	1	0	0	0	0	1	1	3

WP - Ed Reulbach; LP - Doc White

GAME 3
Thursday, October 11

	1	2	3	4	5	6	7	8	9	R	H	E
Chicago White Sox	0	0	0	0	0	3	0	0	0	3	4	1
Chicago Cubs	0	0	0	0	0	0	0	0	0	0	2	2

WP - Ed Walsh; LP - Jack Pfiester

GAME 4
Friday, October 12

	1	2	3	4	5	6	7	8	9	R	H	E
Chicago Cubs	0	0	0	0	0	0	1	0	0	1	7	1
Chicago White Sox	0	0	0	0	0	0	0	0	0	0	2	1

WP - Three Finger Brown; LP - Nick Altrock

GAME 5
Saturday, October 13

	1	2	3	4	5	6	7	8	9	R	H	E
Chicago White Sox	1	0	2	4	0	1	0	0	0	8	12	6
Chicago Cubs	3	0	0	1	0	2	0	0	0	6	6	0

WP - Ed Walsh; LP - Jack Pfiester; Sv - Doc White

GAME 6
Sunday, October 14

	1	2	3	4	5	6	7	8	9	R	H	E
Chicago Cubs	1	0	0	0	1	0	0	0	1	3	7	0
Chicago White Sox	3	4	0	0	0	0	0	1	x	8	14	3

WP - Doc White; LP - Three Finger Brown

BATTING STATISTICS

Chicago White Sox	G	AB	R	H	2B	3B	HR	RBI	BB	SO	SB	CS	BA
Nick Altrock	2	4	0	1	0	0	0	0	1	1	0	0	.250
George Davis	3	13	4	4	3	0	0	6	0	1	1	1	.308
Jiggs Donahue	6	18	0	5	2	1	0	4	3	4	0	2	.278
Patsy Dougherty	6	20	1	2	0	0	0	1	3	3	2	0	.100
Ed Hahn	6	22	4	6	0	0	0	0	1	1	0	2	.273
Frank Isbell	6	26	4	8	4	0	0	4	0	6	1	0	.308
Fielder Jones	6	21	4	3	0	0	0	0	3	3	0	1	.143
Ed McFarland	1	1	0	0	0	0	0	0	0	0	0	0	.000
Bill O'Neill	1	1	1	0	0	0	0	0	0	0	0	0	.000
Frank Owen	1	2	0	0	0	0	0	0	0	1	0	0	.000
George Rohe	6	21	2	7	1	2	0	4	3	1	2	0	.333
Billy Sullivan	6	21	0	0	0	0	0	0	0	9	0	0	.000
Lee Tannehill	3	9	1	1	0	0	0	0	0	2	0	0	.111
Babe Towne	1	1	0	0	0	0	0	0	0	0	0	0	.000
Ed Walsh	2	4	1	0	0	0	0	0	0	3	0	0	.000
Doc White	3	3	0	0	0	0	0	0	1	0	0	0	.000
Totals	6	187	22	37	10	3	0	19	18	35	6	6	.198

Chicago Cubs	G	AB	R	H	2B	3B	HR	RBI	BB	SO	SB	CS	BA
Three Finger Brown	3	6	0	2	0	0	0	0	0	4	0	0	.333
Frank Chance	6	21	3	5	1	0	0	0	2	1	2	1	.238
Johnny Evers	6	20	2	3	1	0	0	1	1	3	2	1	.150
Doc Gessler	2	1	0	0	0	0	0	0	1	0	0	0	.000
Solly Hofman	6	23	3	7	1	0	0	2	3	5	1	1	.304
Johnny Kling	6	17	2	3	1	0	0	0	4	3	0	0	.176
Pat Moran	2	2	0	0	0	0	0	0	0	0	0	0	.000
Orval Overall	2	4	1	1	1	0	0	0	1	1	0	0	.250
Jack Pfiester	2	2	0	0	0	0	0	0	0	1	0	0	.000
Ed Reulbach	2	3	0	0	0	0	0	1	0	1	0	0	.000
Wildfire Schulte	6	26	1	7	3	0	0	3	1	3	0	3	.269
Jimmy Sheckard	6	21	0	0	0	0	0	1	2	4	1	0	.000
Harry Steinfeldt	6	20	2	5	1	0	0	2	1	0	0	1	.250
Joe Tinker	6	18	4	3	0	0	0	1	2	2	3	0	.167
Totals	6	184	18	36	9	0	0	11	18	28	9	7	.196

PITCHING STATISTICS

Chicago White Sox	G	GS	CG	IP	H	ER	BB	SO	W-L	Sv	ERA
Nick Altrock	2	2	2	18	11	2	2	5	1-1	0	1.00
Frank Owen	1	0	0	6	6	2	3	2	0-0	0	3.00
Ed Walsh	2	2	1	15	7	2	6	17	2-0	0	1.20
Doc White	3	2	1	15	12	3	7	4	1-1	1	1.80
Totals	6	6	4	54	36	9	18	28	4-2	1	1.50

Chicago Cubs	G	GS	CG	IP	H	ER	BB	SO	W-L	Sv	ERA
Three Finger Brown	3	3	2	19 2/3	14	8	4	12	1-2	0	3.66
Orval Overall	2	0	0	12	10	2	3	8	0-0	0	1.50
Jack Pfiester	2	1	1	10 1/3	7	7	3	11	0-2	0	6.10
Ed Reulbach	2	2	1	11	6	3	8	4	1-0	0	2.45
Totals	6	6	4	53	37	20	18	35	2-4	0	3.40

1907 World Series

CHICAGO CUBS (4) VS. DETROIT TIGERS (0)

GAME 1
Tuesday, October 8

	1	2	3	4	5	6	7	8	9	10	11	12	R	H	E
Detroit Tigers	0	0	0	0	0	0	0	3	0	0	0	0	3	9	3
Chicago Cubs	0	0	0	1	0	0	0	0	2	0	0	0	3	10	5

GAME 2
Wednesday, October 9

	1	2	3	4	5	6	7	8	9	R	H	E
Detroit Tigers	0	1	0	0	0	0	0	0	0	1	9	1
Chicago Cubs	0	1	0	2	0	0	0	0	x	3	9	1

WP - Jack Pfiester; LP - George Mullin

GAME 3
Thursday, October 10

	1	2	3	4	5	6	7	8	9	R	H	E
Detroit Tigers	0	0	0	0	0	1	0	0	0	1	6	1
Chicago Cubs	0	1	0	3	1	0	0	0	x	5	10	1

WP - Ed Reulbach; LP - Ed Siever

GAME 4
Friday, October 11

	1	2	3	4	5	6	7	8	9	R	H	E
Chicago Cubs	0	0	0	0	2	0	3	0	1	6	7	2
Detroit Tigers	0	0	0	1	0	0	0	0	0	1	5	2

WP - Orval Overall; LP - Wild Bill Donovan

GAME 5
Saturday, October 12

	1	2	3	4	5	6	7	8	9	R	H	E
Chicago Cubs	1	1	0	0	0	0	0	0	0	2	7	1
Detroit Tigers	0	0	0	0	0	0	0	0	0	0	7	2

WP - Three Finger Brown; LP - George Mullin

BATTING STATISTICS

Chicago Cubs	G	AB	R	H	2B	3B	HR	RBI	BB	SO	SB	CS	BA
Three Finger Brown	1	3	0	0	0	0	0	0	1	0	0	0	.000
Frank Chance	4	14	3	3	1	0	0	0	3	2	3	1	.214
Johnny Evers	5	20	2	7	2	0	0	1	0	1	3	1	.350
Del Howard	2	5	0	1	0	0	0	0	0	2	1	0	.200
Johnny Kling	5	19	2	4	0	0	0	1	1	4	0	0	.211
Pat Moran	1	0	0	0	0	0	0	0	0	0	0	0	—
Orval Overall	2	5	0	1	0	0	0	2	0	1	0	0	.200
Jack Pfiester	1	2	0	0	0	0	0	0	0	1	0	0	.000
Ed Reulbach	2	5	0	1	0	0	0	1	0	0	0	0	.200
Wildfire Schulte	5	20	3	5	0	0	0	2	1	2	0	0	.250
Jimmy Sheckard	5	21	0	5	2	0	0	2	0	4	1	2	.238
Jimmy Slagle	5	22	3	6	0	0	0	4	2	3	6	2	.273
Harry Steinfeldt	5	17	2	8	1	1	0	2	1	2	1	0	.471
Joe Tinker	5	13	4	2	0	0	0	1	3	3	1	0	.154
Heinie Zimmerman	1	1	0	0	0	0	0	0	0	1	0	0	.000
Totals	5	167	19	43	6	1	0	16	12	26	16	6	.257

Detroit Tigers	G	AB	R	H	2B	3B	HR	RBI	BB	SO	SB	CS	BA
Jimmy Archer	1	3	0	0	0	0	0	0	0	1	0	0	.000
Ty Cobb	5	20	1	4	0	1	0	0	0	3	0	1	.200
Bill Coughlin	5	20	0	5	0	0	0	0	1	4	1	0	.250
Sam Crawford	5	21	1	5	1	0	0	3	0	3	0	0	.238
Wild Bill Donovan	2	8	0	0	0	0	0	0	0	3	0	0	.000
Davy Jones	5	17	1	6	0	0	0	0	4	0	3	1	.353
Ed Killian	1	2	1	1	0	0	0	0	0	0	0	0	.500
George Mullin	2	6	0	0	0	0	0	0	0	1	0	0	.000
Charley O'Leary	5	17	0	1	0	0	0	0	1	3	0	1	.059
Fred Payne	2	4	0	1	0	0	0	1	0	0	1	0	.250
Claude Rossman	5	20	1	8	0	1	0	2	1	0	1	0	.400
Germany Schaefer	5	21	1	3	0	0	0	0	0	3	0	2	.143
Boss Schmidt	4	12	0	2	0	0	0	0	2	1	0	0	.167
Ed Siever	1	1	0	0	0	0	0	0	0	0	0	0	.000
Totals	5	172	6	36	1	2	0	6	9	22	6	5	.209

PITCHING STATISTICS

Chicago Cubs	G	GS	CG	IP	H	ER	BB	SO	W-L	Sv	ERA
Three Finger Brown	1	1	1	9	7	0	1	4	1-0	0	0.00
Orval Overall	2	2	1	18	14	2	4	11	1-0	0	1.00
Jack Pfiester	1	1	1	9	9	1	1	3	1-0	0	1.00
Ed Reulbach	2	1	1	12	6	1	3	4	1-0	0	0.75
Totals	5	5	4	48	36	4	9	22	4-0	0	0.75

Detroit Tigers	G	GS	CG	IP	H	ER	BB	SO	W-L	Sv	ERA
Wild Bill Donovan	2	2	2	21	17	4	5	16	0-1	0	1.71
Ed Killian	1	0	0	4	3	1	1	1	0-0	0	2.25
George Mullin	2	2	2	17	16	4	6	8	0-2	0	2.12
Ed Siever	1	1	0	4	7	2	0	1	0-1	0	4.50
Totals	5	5	4	46	43	11	12	26	0-4	0	2.15

1908 World Series

CHICAGO CUBS (4) VS. DETROIT TIGERS (1)

GAME 1
Saturday, October 10

	1	2	3	4	5	6	7	8	9	R	H	E
Chicago Cubs	0	0	4	0	0	0	1	0	5	10	14	2
Detroit Tigers	1	0	0	0	0	0	3	2	0	6	10	3

WP - Three Finger Brown; LP - Ed Summers

GAME 2
Sunday, October 11

	1	2	3	4	5	6	7	8	9	R	H	E
Detroit Tigers	0	0	0	0	0	0	0	0	1	1	4	1
Chicago Cubs	0	0	0	0	0	0	0	6	x	6	7	0

HR - ChC Joe Tinker

WP - Orval Overall; LP - Wild Bill Donovan

GAME 3
Monday, October 12

	1	2	3	4	5	6	7	8	9	R	H	E
Detroit Tigers	1	0	0	0	0	5	0	2	0	8	11	4
Chicago Cubs	0	0	0	3	0	0	0	0	0	3	7	1

WP - George Mullin; LP - Jack Pfiester

GAME 4
Tuesday, October 13

	1	2	3	4	5	6	7	8	9	R	H	E
Chicago Cubs	0	0	2	0	0	0	0	0	1	3	10	0
Detroit Tigers	0	0	0	0	0	0	0	0	0	0	4	1

WP - Three Finger Brown; LP - Ed Summers

GAME 5
Wednesday, October 14

	1	2	3	4	5	6	7	8	9	R	H	E
Chicago Cubs	1	0	0	0	1	0	0	0	0	2	10	0
Detroit Tigers	0	0	0	0	0	0	0	0	0	0	3	0

WP - Orval Overall; LP - Wild Bill Donovan

BATTING STATISTICS

Chicago Cubs	G	AB	R	H	2B	3B	HR	RBI	BB	SO	SB	CS	BA
Three Finger Brown	2	4	0	0	0	0	0	0	0	2	0	0	.000
Frank Chance	5	19	4	8	0	0	0	2	3	1	5	0	.421
Johnny Evers	5	20	5	7	1	0	0	2	1	2	2	2	.350
Solly Hofman	5	19	2	6	0	1	0	4	1	4	2	0	.316
Del Howard	1	1	0	0	0	0	0	0	0	0	0	0	.000
Johnny Kling	5	16	2	4	1	0	0	2	2	2	0	2	.250
Orval Overall	3	6	0	2	0	0	0	0	0	1	0	0	.333
Jack Pfiester	1	2	0	0	0	0	0	0	0	2	0	0	.000
Ed Reulbach	2	3	0	0	0	0	0	0	0	1	0	0	.000
Wildfire Schulte	5	18	4	7	0	1	0	2	2	1	2	2	.389
Jimmy Sheckard	5	21	2	5	2	0	0	1	2	3	1	1	.238
Harry Steinfeldt	5	16	3	4	0	0	0	3	2	5	1	1	.250
Joe Tinker	5	19	2	5	0	0	1	4	0	2	2	1	.263
Totals	5	164	24	48	4	2	1	20	13	26	15	9	.293

Detroit Tigers	G	AB	R	H	2B	3B	HR	RBI	BB	SO	SB	CS	BA
Ty Cobb	5	19	3	7	1	0	0	4	1	2	2	1	.368
Bill Coughlin	3	8	0	1	0	0	0	1	0	1	0	0	.125
Sam Crawford	5	20	2	4	1	0	0	1	1	2	0	0	.200
Wild Bill Donovan	2	4	0	0	0	0	0	0	1	1	1	0	.000
Red Downs	2	6	1	1	1	0	0	1	1	2	0	0	.167
Davy Jones	3	2	1	0	0	0	0	0	1	1	0	0	.000
Ed Killian	1	0	0	0	0	0	0	0	0	0	0	0	—
Matty McIntyre	5	18	2	4	1	0	0	0	3	2	1	0	.222
George Mullin	1	3	1	1	0	0	0	1	1	0	0	0	.333
Charley O'Leary	5	20	2	4	0	0	0	0	0	3	0	0	.200
Claude Rossman	5	19	3	4	0	0	0	3	1	4	1	0	.211
Germany Schaefer	5	16	0	2	0	0	0	0	1	4	1	1	.125
Boss Schmidt	4	14	0	1	0	0	0	1	0	2	0	0	.071
Ed Summers	2	5	0	1	0	0	0	0	1	2	0	0	.200
Ira Thomas	2	4	0	2	1	0	0	1	1	0	0	0	.500
George Winter	2	0	0	0	0	0	0	0	0	0	0	0	—
Totals	5	158	15	32	5	0	0	14	12	26	6	2	.203

PITCHING STATISTICS

Chicago Cubs	G	GS	CG	IP	H	ER	BB	SO	W-L	Sv	ERA
Three Finger Brown	2	1	1	11	6	0	1	5	2-0	0	0.00
Orval Overall	3	2	2	18⅓	7	2	7	15	2-0	0	0.98
Jack Pfiester	1	1	0	8	10	7	3	1	0-1	0	7.88
Ed Reulbach	2	1	0	7 2⁄3	9	4	1	5	0-0	0	4.70
Totals	5	5	3	45	32	13	12	26	4-1	0	2.60

Detroit Tigers	G	GS	CG	IP	H	ER	BB	SO	W-L	Sv	ERA
Wild Bill Donovan	2	2	2	17	17	8	4	10	0-2	0	4.24
Ed Killian	1	1	0	2⅓	5	3	3	1	0-0	0	11.57
George Mullin	1	1	1	9	7	0	1	8	1-0	0	0.00
Ed Summers	2	1	0	14 2⁄3	18	7	4	7	0-2	0	4.30
George Winter	1	0	0	1	1	0	1	0	0-0	0	0.00
Totals	5	5	3	44	48	18	13	26	1-4	0	3.68

1910 World Series

PHILADELPHIA ATHLETICS (4) VS. CHICAGO CUBS (1)

GAME 1
Monday, October 17

	1	2	3	4	5	6	7	8	9	R	H	E
Chicago Cubs	0	0	0	0	0	0	0	0	1	1	3	1
Philadelphia Athletics	0	2	1	0	0	0	0	1	x	4	7	2

WP - Chief Bender; LP - Orval Overall

GAME 2
Tuesday, October 18

	1	2	3	4	5	6	7	8	9	R	H	E
Chicago Cubs	1	0	0	0	0	0	1	0	1	3	8	3
Philadelphia Athletics	0	0	2	0	1	0	6	0	x	9	14	4

WP - Jack Coombs; LP - Three Finger Brown

GAME 3
Thursday, October 20

	1	2	3	4	5	6	7	8	9	R	H	E
Philadelphia Athletics	1	2	5	0	0	0	4	0	0	12	15	1
Chicago Cubs	1	2	0	0	0	0	0	2	0	5	6	5

HR - Phi Danny Murphy

WP - Jack Coombs; LP - Harry McIntire

GAME 4
Saturday, October 22

	1	2	3	4	5	6	7	8	9	10	R	H	E
Philadelphia Athletics	0	0	1	2	0	0	0	0	0	0	3	11	3
Chicago Cubs	1	0	0	1	0	0	0	0	1	1	4	9	1

WP - Three Finger Brown; LP - Chief Bender

GAME 5
Sunday, October 23

	1	2	3	4	5	6	7	8	9	R	H	E
Philadelphia Athletics	1	0	0	0	1	0	0	5	0	7	9	1
Chicago Cubs	0	1	0	0	0	0	0	1	0	2	9	2

WP - Jack Coombs; LP - Three Finger Brown

BATTING STATISTICS

Philadelphia Athletics	G	AB	R	H	2B	3B	HR	RBI	BB	SO	SB	CS	BA
Home Run Baker	5	22	6	9	3	0	0	4	2	1	0	3	.409
Jack Barry	5	17	3	4	2	0	0	3	1	3	0	0	.235
Chief Bender	2	6	1	2	0	0	0	1	1	1	0	0	.333
Eddie Collins	5	21	5	9	4	0	0	3	2	0	4	2	.429
Jack Coombs	3	13	0	5	1	0	0	3	0	3	0	0	.385
Harry Davis	5	17	5	6	3	0	0	2	3	4	0	0	.353
Topsy Hartsel	1	5	2	1	0	0	0	0	0	1	2	0	.200
Jack Lapp	1	4	0	1	0	0	0	1	0	2	0	0	.250
Bris Lord	5	22	3	4	2	0	0	1	1	3	0	1	.182
Danny Murphy	5	20	6	7	3	0	1	9	1	0	1	0	.350
Amos Strunk	4	18	2	5	1	1	0	2	2	5	0	1	.278
Ira Thomas	4	12	2	3	0	0	0	1	4	1	0	0	.250
Totals	5	177	35	56	19	1	1	30	17	24	7	7	.316

Chicago Cubs	G	AB	R	H	2B	3B	HR	RBI	BB	SO	SB	CS	BA
Jimmy Archer	3	11	1	2	1	0	0	0	0	4	0	0	.182
Ginger Beaumont	3	2	1	0	0	0	0	0	1	1	0	0	.000
Three Finger Brown	3	7	0	0	0	0	0	0	0	1	0	0	.000
Frank Chance	5	17	1	6	1	1	0	4	0	2	0	0	.353
King Cole	1	2	0	0	0	0	0	0	0	2	0	0	.000
Solly Hofman	5	15	2	4	0	0	0	2	4	3	0	0	.267
John Kane	2	0	0	0	0	0	0	0	0	0	0	0	—
Johnny Kling	5	13	0	1	0	0	0	1	1	2	0	0	.077
Harry McIntire	2	1	0	0	0	0	0	0	0	1	0	0	.000
Tom Needham	1	1	0	0	0	0	0	0	0	0	0	0	.000
Orval Overall	1	1	0	0	0	0	0	0	0	0	0	0	.000
Jack Pfiester	1	2	0	0	0	0	0	0	0	1	0	0	.000
Ed Reulbach	1	0	0	0	0	0	0	0	0	0	0	0	—
Lew Richie	1	0	0	0	0	0	0	0	0	0	0	0	—
Wildfire Schulte	5	17	3	6	3	0	0	2	2	3	0	5	.353
Jimmy Sheckard	5	14	5	4	2	0	0	1	7	2	1	0	.286
Harry Steinfeldt	5	20	0	2	1	0	0	1	0	4	0	0	.100
Joe Tinker	5	18	2	6	2	0	0	0	2	2	1	2	.333
Heinie Zimmerman	5	17	0	4	1	0	0	2	1	3	1	1	.235
Totals	5	158	15	35	11	1	0	13	18	31	3	8	.222

PITCHING STATISTICS

Philadelphia Athletics	G	GS	CG	IP	H	ER	BB	SO	W-L	Sv	ERA
Chief Bender	2	2	2	18⅔	12	4	4	14	1-1	0	1.93
Jack Coombs	3	3	3	27	23	10	14	17	3-0	0	3.33
Totals	5	5	5	45⅔	35	14	18	31	4-1	0	2.76

Chicago Cubs	G	GS	CG	IP	H	ER	BB	SO	W-L	Sv	ERA
Three Finger Brown	3	2	1	18	23	10	7	14	1-2	0	5.00
King Cole	1	1	0	8	10	3	3	5	0-0	0	3.38
Harry McIntire	2	0	0	5⅓	4	4	3	3	0-1	0	6.75
Orval Overall	1	1	0	3	6	3	1	1	0-1	0	9.00
Jack Pfiester	1	0	0	6⅔	9	0	1	1	0-0	0	0.00
Ed Reulbach	1	1	0	2	3	3	2	0	0-0	0	13.50
Lew Richie	1	0	0	1	1	0	0	0	0-0	0	0.00
Totals	5	5	1	44	56	23	17	24	1-4	0	4.70

1918 World Series

BOSTON RED SOX (4) VS. CHICAGO CUBS (2)

GAME 1

Thursday, September 5

	1	2	3	4	5	6	7	8	9	R	H	E
Boston Red Sox	0	0	0	1	0	0	0	0	0	1	5	0
Chicago Cubs	0	0	0	0	0	0	0	0	0	0	6	0

WP - Babe Ruth; LP - Hippo Vaughn

GAME 2

Friday, September 6

	1	2	3	4	5	6	7	8	9	R	H	E
Boston Red Sox	0	0	0	0	0	0	0	0	1	1	6	1
Chicago Cubs	0	3	0	0	0	0	0	0	x	3	7	1

WP - Lefty Tyler; LP - Joe Bush

GAME 3

Saturday, September 7

	1	2	3	4	5	6	7	8	9	R	H	E
Boston Red Sox	0	0	0	2	0	0	0	0	0	2	7	0
Chicago Cubs	0	0	0	0	1	0	0	0	0	1	7	1

WP - Carl Mays; LP - Hippo Vaughn

GAME 4

Monday, September 9

	1	2	3	4	5	6	7	8	9	R	H	E
Chicago Cubs	0	0	0	0	0	0	0	2	0	2	7	1
Boston Red Sox	0	0	0	2	0	0	0	1	x	3	4	0

WP - Babe Ruth; LP - Phil Douglas; Sv - Joe Bush

GAME 5

Tuesday, September 10

	1	2	3	4	5	6	7	8	9	R	H	E
Chicago Cubs	0	0	1	0	0	0	0	2	0	3	7	0
Boston Red Sox	0	0	0	0	0	0	0	0	0	0	5	0

WP - Hippo Vaughn; LP - Sad Sam Jones

GAME 6

Wednesday, September 11

	1	2	3	4	5	6	7	8	9	R	H	E
Chicago Cubs	0	0	0	1	0	0	0	0	0	1	3	2
Boston Red Sox	0	0	2	0	0	0	0	0	x	2	5	0

WP - Carl Mays; LP - Lefty Tyler

BATTING STATISTICS

Boston Red Sox	G	AB	R	H	2B	3B	HR	RBI	BB	SO	SB	CS	BA
Sam Agnew	4	9	0	0	0	0	0	0	0	0	0	0	.000
Joe Bush	2	2	0	0	0	0	0	0	1	0	0	0	.000
Jean Dubuc	1	1	0	0	0	0	0	0	0	1	0	0	.000
Harry Hooper	6	20	0	4	0	0	0	0	2	2	0	2	.200
Sad Sam Jones	1	1	0	0	0	0	0	0	1	0	0	0	.000
Carl Mays	2	5	1	1	0	0	0	0	1	1	0	0	.200
Stuffy McInnis	6	20	2	5	0	0	0	1	1	1	0	0	.250
Hack Miller	1	1	0	0	0	0	0	0	0	0	0	0	.000
Babe Ruth	3	5	0	1	0	1	0	2	0	2	0	0	.200
Wally Schang	5	9	1	4	0	0	0	1	2	3	1	1	.444
Everett Scott	6	20	0	2	0	0	0	1	1	1	0	0	.100
Dave Shean	6	19	2	4	1	0	0	0	4	3	1	0	.211
Amos Strunk	6	23	1	4	1	1	0	0	0	5	0	1	.174
Fred Thomas	6	17	0	2	0	0	0	1	2	0	0	0	.118
George Whiteman	6	20	2	5	0	1	0	1	2	1	1	0	.250
Totals	6	172	9	32	2	3	0	6	16	21	3	4	.186

Chicago Cubs	G	AB	R	H	2B	3B	HR	RBI	BB	SO	SB	CS	BA
Turner Barber	3	2	0	0	0	0	0	0	0	0	0	0	.000
Charlie Deal	6	17	0	3	0	0	0	0	0	1	0	0	.176
Phil Douglas	1	0	0	0	0	0	0	0	0	0	0	0	—
Max Flack	6	19	2	5	0	0	0	0	4	1	1	1	.263
Claude Hendrix	2	1	0	1	0	0	0	0	0	0	0	0	1.000
Charlie Hollocher	6	21	2	4	0	1	0	1	1	1	1	0	.190
Bill Killefer	6	17	2	2	1	0	0	2	2	0	0	1	.118
Les Mann	6	22	0	5	2	0	0	2	0	0	0	1	.227
Bill McCabe	3	1	1	0	0	0	0	0	0	0	0	0	.000
Fred Merkle	6	18	1	5	0	0	0	1	4	3	0	1	.278
Bob O'Farrell	3	3	0	0	0	0	0	0	0	0	0	0	.000
Dode Paskert	6	21	0	4	1	0	0	2	2	2	0	0	.190
Charlie Pick	6	18	2	7	1	0	0	0	1	1	1	1	.389
Lefty Tyler	3	5	0	1	0	0	0	2	2	0	0	0	.200
Hippo Vaughn	3	10	0	0	0	0	0	0	0	5	0	0	.000
Chuck Wortman	1	1	0	0	0	0	0	0	0	0	0	0	.000
Rollie Zeider	2	0	0	0	0	0	0	0	2	0	0	0	—
Totals	6	176	10	37	5	1	0	10	18	14	3	5	.210

PITCHING STATISTICS

Boston Red Sox	G	GS	CG	IP	H	ER	BB	SO	W-L	Sv	ERA
Joe Bush	2	1	1	9	7	3	3	0	0-1	1	3.00
Sad Sam Jones	1	1	1	9	7	3	5	5	0-1	0	3.00
Carl Mays	2	2	2	18	10	2	3	5	2-0	0	1.00
Babe Ruth	2	2	1	17	13	2	7	4	2-0	0	1.06
Totals	6	6	5	53	37	10	18	14	4-2	1	1.70

Chicago Cubs	G	GS	CG	IP	H	ER	BB	SO	W-L	Sv	ERA
Phil Douglas	1	0	0	1	1	0	0	0	0-1	0	0.00
Claude Hendrix	1	0	0	1	0	0	0	0	0-0	0	0.00
Lefty Tyler	3	3	1	23	14	3	11	4	1-1	0	1.17
Hippo Vaughn	3	3	3	27	17	3	5	17	1-2	0	1.00
Totals	6	6	4	52	32	6	16	21	2-4	0	1.04

1929 World Series

PHILADELPHIA ATHLETICS (4) VS. CHICAGO CUBS (1)

GAME 1
Monday, October 7

	1	2	3	4	5	6	7	8	9	R	H	E
Philadelphia Athletics	0	0	0	0	0	0	1	0	2	3	6	1
Chicago Cubs	0	0	0	0	0	0	0	0	1	1	8	2

HR - Phi Jimmie Foxx

WP - Howard Ehmke; LP - Charlie Root

GAME 2
Wednesday, October 9

	1	2	3	4	5	6	7	8	9	R	H	E
Philadelphia Athletics	0	0	3	3	0	0	1	2	0	9	12	0
Chicago Cubs	0	0	0	0	3	0	0	0	0	3	11	1

HR - Phi Al Simmons, Jimmie Foxx

WP - Lefty Grove; LP - Pat Malone

GAME 3
Friday, October 11

	1	2	3	4	5	6	7	8	9	R	H	E
Chicago Cubs	0	0	0	0	0	3	0	0	0	3	6	1
Philadelphia Athletics	0	0	0	0	1	0	0	0	0	1	9	1

WP - Guy Bush; LP - George Earnshaw

GAME 4
Saturday, October 12

	1	2	3	4	5	6	7	8	9	R	H	E
Chicago Cubs	0	0	0	2	0	5	1	0	0	8	10	2
Philadelphia Athletics	0	0	0	0	0	0	10	0	x	10	15	2

HR - ChC Charlie Grimm; Phi Mule Haas, Al Simmons

WP - Eddie Rommel; LP - Sheriff Blake; Sv - Lefty Grove

GAME 5
Monday, October 14

	1	2	3	4	5	6	7	8	9	R	H	E
Chicago Cubs	0	0	0	2	0	0	0	0	0	2	8	1
Philadelphia Athletics	0	0	0	0	0	0	0	0	3	3	6	0

HR - Phi Mule Haas

WP - Rube Walberg; LP - Pat Malone

BATTING STATISTICS

Philadelphia Athletics	G	AB	R	H	2B	3B	HR	RBI	BB	SO	SB	CS	BA
Max Bishop	5	21	2	4	0	0	0	1	2	3	0	0	.190
Joe Boley	5	17	1	4	0	0	0	1	0	3	0	0	.235
George Burns	1	2	0	0	0	0	0	0	0	1	0	0	.000
Mickey Cochrane	5	15	5	6	1	0	0	0	7	0	0	0	.400
Jimmy Dykes	5	19	2	8	1	0	0	4	1	1	0	0	.421
George Earnshaw	2	5	1	0	0	0	0	0	0	4	0	0	.000
Howard Ehmke	2	5	0	1	0	0	0	0	0	0	0	0	.200
Jimmie Foxx	5	20	5	7	1	0	2	5	1	1	0	0	.350
Walt French	1	1	0	0	0	0	0	0	0	1	0	0	.000
Lefty Grove	2	2	0	0	0	0	0	0	0	1	0	0	.000
Mule Haas	5	21	3	5	0	0	2	6	1	3	0	0	.238
Bing Miller	5	19	1	7	1	0	0	4	0	2	0	2	.368
Jack Quinn	1	2	0	0	0	0	0	0	0	2	0	0	.000
Eddie Rommel	1	0	0	0	0	0	0	0	0	0	0	0	—
Al Simmons	5	20	6	6	1	0	2	5	1	4	0	0	.300
Homer Summa	1	1	0	0	0	0	0	0	0	1	0	0	.000
Rube Walberg	2	1	0	0	0	0	0	0	0	0	0	0	.000
Totals	5	171	26	48	5	0	6	26	13	27	0	2	.281

Chicago Cubs	G	AB	R	H	2B	3B	HR	RBI	BB	SO	SB	CS	BA
Footsie Blair	1	1	0	0	0	0	0	0	0	0	0	0	.000
Sheriff Blake	2	1	0	1	0	0	0	0	0	0	0	0	1.000
Guy Bush	2	3	1	0	0	0	0	0	1	3	0	0	.000
Hal Carlson	2	0	0	0	0	0	0	0	0	0	0	0	—
Kiki Cuyler	5	20	4	6	1	0	0	4	1	7	0	1	.300
Woody English	5	21	1	4	2	0	0	0	1	6	0	1	.190
Mike Gonzalez	2	1	0	0	0	0	0	0	0	1	0	0	.000
Charlie Grimm	5	18	2	7	0	0	1	4	1	2	0	1	.389
Gabby Hartnett	3	3	0	0	0	0	0	0	0	3	0	0	.000
Cliff Heathcote	2	1	0	0	0	0	0	0	0	0	0	0	.000
Rogers Hornsby	5	21	4	5	1	1	0	1	1	8	0	0	.238
Pat Malone	3	4	0	1	1	0	0	0	0	2	0	0	.250
Norm McMillan	5	20	0	2	0	0	0	0	2	6	1	0	.100
Art Nehf	2	0	0	0	0	0	0	0	0	0	0	0	—
Charlie Root	2	5	0	0	0	0	0	0	0	3	0	0	.000
Riggs Stephenson	5	19	3	6	1	0	0	3	2	2	0	0	.316
Zack Taylor	5	17	0	3	0	0	0	3	0	3	0	0	.176
Chick Tolson	1	1	0	0	0	0	0	0	0	1	0	0	.000
Hack Wilson	5	17	2	8	0	1	0	0	4	3	0	0	.471
Totals	5	173	17	43	6	2	1	15	13	50	1	3	.249

PITCHING STATISTICS

Philadelphia Athletics	G	GS	CG	IP	H	ER	BB	SO	W-L	Sv	ERA
George Earnshaw	2	2	1	13 2/3	14	4	6	17	0-1	0	2.63
Howard Ehmke	2	2	1	12 2/3	14	2	3	13	1-0	0	1.42
Lefty Grove	2	0	0	6 1/3	3	0	1	10	1-0	1	0.00
Jack Quinn	1	1	0	5	7	5	2	2	0-0	0	9.00
Eddie Rommel	1	0	0	1	2	1	1	0	1-0	0	9.00
Rube Walberg	2	0	0	6 1/3	3	0	0	8	1-0	0	0.00
Totals	5	5	2	45	43	12	13	50	4-1	1	2.40

Chicago Cubs	G	GS	CG	IP	H	ER	BB	SO	W-L	Sv	ERA
Sheriff Blake	2	0	0	1 1/3	4	2	0	1	0-1	0	13.50
Guy Bush	2	1	1	11	12	1	2	4	1-0	0	0.82
Hal Carlson	2	0	0	4	7	3	1	3	0-0	0	6.75
Pat Malone	3	2	1	13	12	6	7	11	0-2	0	4.15
Art Nehf	2	0	0	1	1	2	1	0	0-0	0	18.00
Charlie Root	2	2	0	13 1/3	12	7	2	8	0-1	0	4.73
Totals	5	5	2	43 2/3	48	21	13	27	1-4	0	4.33

1932 World Series

NEW YORK YANKEES (4) VS. CHICAGO CUBS (0)

GAME 1
Wednesday, September 28

	1	2	3	4	5	6	7	8	9	R	H	E
Chicago Cubs	2	0	0	0	0	0	2	2	0	6	10	1
New York Yankees	0	0	0	3	0	5	3	1	x	12	8	2

HR - NYY Lou Gehrig

WP - Red Ruffing; LP - Guy Bush

GAME 2
Thursday, September 29

	1	2	3	4	5	6	7	8	9	R	H	E
Chicago Cubs	1	0	1	0	0	0	0	0	0	2	9	0
New York Yankees	2	0	2	0	1	0	0	0	x	5	10	1

WP - Lefty Gomez; LP - Lon Warneke

GAME 3
Saturday, October 1

	1	2	3	4	5	6	7	8	9	R	H	E
New York Yankees	3	0	1	0	2	0	0	0	1	7	8	1
Chicago Cubs	1	0	2	1	0	0	0	0	1	5	9	4

HR - NYY Babe Ruth 2, Lou Gehrig 2; ChC Kiki Cuyler, Gabby Hartnett

WP - George Pipgras; LP - Charlie Root; Sv - Herb Pennock

GAME 4
Sunday, October 2

	1	2	3	4	5	6	7	8	9	R	H	E
New York Yankees	1	0	2	0	0	2	4	0	4	13	19	4
Chicago Cubs	4	0	0	0	0	1	0	0	1	6	9	1

HR - NYY Earle Combs, Tony Lazzeri 2; ChC Frank Demaree

WP - Wilcy Moore; LP - Jakie May; Sv - Herb Pennock

BATTING STATISTICS

New York Yankees	G	AB	R	H	2B	3B	HR	RBI	BB	SO	SB	CS	BA
Johnny Allen	1	0	0	0	0	0	0	0	0	0	0	0	—
Sammy Byrd	1	0	0	0	0	0	0	0	0	0	0	0	—
Ben Chapman	4	17	1	5	2	0	0	6	2	4	0	1	.294
Earle Combs	4	16	8	6	1	0	1	4	4	3	0	0	.375
Frankie Crosetti	4	15	2	2	1	0	0	0	2	3	0	0	.133
Bill Dickey	4	16	2	7	0	0	0	4	2	1	0	1	.438
Lou Gehrig	4	17	9	9	1	0	3	8	2	1	0	0	.529
Lefty Gomez	1	3	0	0	0	0	0	0	0	2	0	0	.000
Myril Hoag	1	0	1	0	0	0	0	0	0	0	0	0	—
Tony Lazzeri	4	17	4	5	0	0	2	5	2	1	0	0	.294
Wilcy Moore	1	3	0	1	0	0	0	0	0	2	0	0	.333
Herb Pennock	2	1	0	0	0	0	0	0	0	0	0	0	.000
George Pipgras	1	5	0	0	0	0	0	0	0	5	0	0	.000
Red Ruffing	2	4	0	0	0	0	0	0	1	1	0	0	.000
Babe Ruth	4	15	6	5	0	0	2	6	4	3	0	0	.333
Joe Sewell	4	15	4	5	1	0	0	3	4	0	0	0	.333
Totals	4	144	37	45	6	0	8	36	23	26	0	2	.313

Chicago Cubs	G	AB	R	H	2B	3B	HR	RBI	BB	SO	SB	CS	BA
Guy Bush	2	1	0	0	0	0	0	0	1	0	0	0	.000
Kiki Cuyler	4	18	2	5	1	1	1	2	0	3	1	0	.278
Frank Demaree	2	7	1	2	0	0	1	4	1	0	0	0	.286
Woody English	4	17	2	3	0	0	0	1	2	2	0	1	.176
Burleigh Grimes	2	1	0	0	0	0	0	0	0	1	0	0	.000
Charlie Grimm	4	15	2	5	2	0	0	1	2	2	0	0	.333
Marv Gudat	2	2	0	0	0	0	0	0	0	1	0	0	.000
Stan Hack	1	0	0	0	0	0	0	0	0	0	0	0	—
Gabby Hartnett	4	16	2	5	2	0	1	1	1	3	0	0	.313
Rollie Hemsley	3	3	0	0	0	0	0	0	0	0	0	0	.000
Billy Herman	4	18	5	4	1	0	0	1	1	3	0	0	.222
Billy Jurges	3	11	1	4	1	0	0	1	0	1	2	0	.364
Mark Koenig	2	4	1	1	0	1	0	1	1	0	0	0	.250
Pat Malone	1	0	0	0	0	0	0	0	0	0	0	0	—
Jakie May	2	2	0	0	0	0	0	0	0	0	0	0	.000
Johnny Moore	2	7	1	0	0	0	0	0	2	1	0	0	.000
Charlie Root	1	2	0	0	0	0	0	0	0	1	0	0	.000
Bob Smith	1	0	0	0	0	0	0	0	0	0	0	0	—
Riggs Stephenson	4	18	2	8	1	0	0	4	0	0	0	0	.444
Bud Tinning	2	0	0	0	0	0	0	0	0	0	0	0	—
Lon Warneke	2	4	0	0	0	0	0	0	0	3	0	0	.000
Totals	4	146	19	37	8	2	3	16	11	24	3	1	.253

PITCHING STATISTICS

New York Yankees	G	GS	CG	IP	H	ER	BB	SO	W-L	Sv	ERA
Johnny Allen	1	1	0	0⅔	5	3	0	0	0-0	0	40.50
Lefty Gomez	1	1	1	9	9	1	1	8	1-0	0	1.00
Wilcy Moore	1	0	0	5⅓	2	0	0	1	1-0	0	0.00
Herb Pennock	2	0	0	4	2	1	1	4	0-0	2	2.25
George Pipgras	1	1	0	8	9	4	3	1	1-0	0	4.50
Red Ruffing	1	1	1	9	10	3	6	10	1-0	0	3.00
Totals	4	4	2	36	37	12	11	24	4-0	2	3.00

Chicago Cubs	G	GS	CG	IP	H	ER	BB	SO	W-L	Sv	ERA
Guy Bush	2	2	0	5⅔	5	9	6	2	0-1	0	14.29
Burleigh Grimes	2	0	0	2⅔	7	7	2	0	0-0	0	23.63
Pat Malone	1	0	0	2⅔	1	0	4	4	0-0	0	0.00
Jakie May	2	0	0	4⅔	9	6	3	4	0-1	0	11.57
Charlie Root	1	1	0	4⅓	6	5	3	4	0-1	0	10.38
Bob Smith	1	0	0	1	2	1	0	1	0-0	0	9.00
Bud Tinning	2	0	0	2⅓	0	0	3	0	0-0	0	0.00
Lon Warneke	2	1	1	10⅔	15	7	5	8	0-1	0	5.91
Totals	4	4	1	34	45	35	23	26	0-4	0	9.26

1935 World Series

DETROIT TIGERS (4) VS. CHICAGO CUBS (2)

GAME 1
Wednesday, October 2

	1	2	3	4	5	6	7	8	9	R	H	E
Chicago Cubs	2	0	0	0	0	0	0	0	1	3	7	0
Detroit Tigers	0	0	0	0	0	0	0	0	0	0	4	3

HR - ChC Frank Demaree

WP - Lon Warneke; LP - Schoolboy Rowe

GAME 2
Thursday, October 3

	1	2	3	4	5	6	7	8	9	R	H	E
Chicago Cubs	0	0	0	0	1	0	2	0	0	3	6	1
Detroit Tigers	4	0	0	3	0	0	1	0	x	8	9	2

HR - Det Hank Greenberg

WP - Tommy Bridges; LP - Charlie Root

GAME 3
Friday, October 4

	1	2	3	4	5	6	7	8	9	10	11	R	H	E
Detroit Tigers	0	0	0	0	0	1	0	4	0	0	1	6	12	2
Chicago Cubs	0	2	0	0	1	0	0	0	2	0	0	5	10	3

HR - ChC Frank Demaree

WP - Schoolboy Rowe; LP - Larry French

GAME 4
Saturday, October 5

	1	2	3	4	5	6	7	8	9	R	H	E
Detroit Tigers	0	0	1	0	0	1	0	0	0	2	7	0
Chicago Cubs	0	1	0	0	0	0	0	0	0	1	5	2

HR - ChC Gabby Hartnett

WP - General Crowder; LP - Tex Carleton

GAME 5
Sunday, October 6

	1	2	3	4	5	6	7	8	9	R	H	E
Detroit Tigers	0	0	0	0	0	0	0	0	1	1	7	1
Chicago Cubs	0	0	2	0	0	0	1	0	x	3	8	0

HR - ChC Chuck Klein

WP - Lon Warneke; LP - Schoolboy Rowe; Sv - Bill Lee

GAME 6
Monday, October 7

	1	2	3	4	5	6	7	8	9	R	H	E
Chicago Cubs	0	0	1	0	2	0	0	0	0	3	12	0
Detroit Tigers	1	0	0	1	0	1	0	0	1	4	12	1

HR - ChC Billy Herman

WP - Tommy Bridges; LP - Larry French

BATTING STATISTICS

Detroit Tigers	G	AB	R	H	2B	3B	HR	RBI	BB	SO	SB	CS	BA
Eldon Auker	1	2	0	0	0	0	0	0	0	1	0	0	.000
Tommy Bridges	2	8	1	1	0	0	0	1	0	3	0	0	.125
Flea Clifton	4	16	1	0	0	0	0	0	2	4	0	0	.000
Mickey Cochrane	6	24	3	7	1	0	0	1	4	1	0	0	.292
General Crowder	1	3	1	1	0	0	0	0	1	0	0	0	.333
Pete Fox	6	26	1	10	3	1	0	4	0	1	0	0	.385
Charlie Gehringer	6	24	4	9	3	0	0	4	2	1	1	0	.375
Goose Goslin	6	22	2	6	1	0	0	3	5	0	0	0	.273
Hank Greenberg	2	6	1	1	0	0	1	2	1	0	0	0	.167
Chief Hogsett	1	0	0	0	0	0	0	0	0	0	0	0	—
Marv Owen	6	20	2	1	0	0	0	1	2	3	0	0	.050
Billy Rogell	6	24	1	7	2	0	0	1	2	5	0	1	.292
Schoolboy Rowe	3	8	0	2	1	0	0	0	0	1	0	0	.250
Gee Walker	3	4	0	1	0	0	0	0	1	0	0	0	.250
Jo-Jo White	5	19	3	5	0	0	0	1	5	7	0	0	.263
Totals	6	206	21	51	11	1	1	18	25	27	1	1	.248

Chicago Cubs	G	AB	R	H	2B	3B	HR	RBI	BB	SO	SB	CS	BA
Tex Carleton	1	1	0	0	0	0	0	0	1	1	0	0	.000
Phil Cavarretta	6	24	1	3	0	0	0	0	0	5	0	1	.125
Frank Demaree	6	24	2	6	1	0	2	2	1	4	0	0	.250
Larry French	2	4	1	1	0	0	0	0	0	2	0	0	.250
Augie Galan	6	25	2	4	1	0	0	2	2	2	0	0	.160
Stan Hack	6	22	2	5	1	1	0	0	2	1	1	0	.227
Gabby Hartnett	6	24	1	7	0	0	1	2	0	3	0	0	.292
Roy Henshaw	1	1	0	0	0	0	0	0	0	0	0	0	.000
Billy Herman	6	24	3	8	2	1	1	6	0	2	0	0	.333
Billy Jurges	6	16	3	4	0	0	0	1	4	4	0	0	.250
Chuck Klein	5	12	2	4	0	0	1	2	0	2	0	0	.333
Fabian Kowalik	1	2	1	1	0	0	0	0	0	0	0	0	.500
Bill Lee	2	1	0	0	0	0	0	1	0	0	0	0	.000
Freddy Lindstrom	4	15	0	3	1	0	0	0	1	1	0	1	.200
Ken O'Dea	1	1	0	1	0	0	0	1	0	0	0	0	1.000
Charlie Root	2	0	0	0	0	0	0	0	0	0	0	0	—
Walter Stephenson	1	1	0	0	0	0	0	0	0	1	0	0	.000
Lon Warneke	3	5	0	1	0	0	0	0	0	0	0	0	.200
Totals	6	202	18	48	6	2	5	17	11	29	1	2	.238

PITCHING STATISTICS

Detroit Tigers	G	GS	CG	IP	H	ER	BB	SO	W-L	Sv	ERA
Eldon Auker	1	1	0	6	6	2	2	1	0-0	0	3.00
Tommy Bridges	2	2	2	18	18	5	4	9	2-0	0	2.50
General Crowder	1	1	1	9	5	1	3	5	1-0	0	1.00
Chief Hogsett	1	0	0	1	0	0	1	0	0-0	0	0.00
Schoolboy Rowe	3	2	2	21	19	6	1	14	1-2	0	2.57
Totals	6	6	5	55	48	14	11	29	4-2	0	2.29

Chicago Cubs	G	GS	CG	IP	H	ER	BB	SO	W-L	Sv	ERA
Tex Carleton	1	1	0	7	6	1	7	4	0-1	0	1.29
Larry French	2	1	1	10⅔	15	4	2	8	0-2	0	3.38
Roy Henshaw	1	0	0	3⅔	2	3	5	2	0-0	0	7.36
Fabian Kowalik	1	0	0	4⅓	3	1	1	1	0-0	0	2.08
Bill Lee	2	1	0	10⅓	11	5	5	5	0-0	1	4.35
Charlie Root	2	1	0	2	5	4	1	2	0-1	0	18.00
Lon Warneke	3	2	1	16⅔	9	1	4	5	2-0	0	0.54
Totals	6	6	2	54⅔	51	19	25	27	2-4	1	3.13

1938 World Series

NEW YORK YANKEES (4) VS. CHICAGO CUBS (0)

GAME 1
Wednesday, October 5

	1	2	3	4	5	6	7	8	9	R	H	E
New York Yankees	0	2	0	0	0	1	0	0	0	3	12	1
Chicago Cubs	0	0	1	0	0	0	0	0	0	1	9	1

WP - Red Ruffing; LP - Bill Lee

GAME 2
Thursday, October 6

	1	2	3	4	5	6	7	8	9	R	H	E
New York Yankees	0	2	0	0	0	0	0	2	2	6	7	2
Chicago Cubs	1	0	2	0	0	0	0	0	0	3	11	0

HR - NYY Frankie Crosetti, Joe DiMaggio

WP - Lefty Gomez; LP - Dizzy Dean; Sv - Johnny Murphy

GAME 3
Saturday, October 8

	1	2	3	4	5	6	7	8	9	R	H	E
Chicago Cubs	0	0	0	0	1	0	0	1	0	2	5	1
New York Yankees	0	0	0	0	2	2	0	1	x	5	7	2

HR - ChC Joe Marty; NYY Bill Dickey, Joe Gordon

WP - Monte Pearson; LP - Clay Bryant

GAME 4
Sunday, October 9

	1	2	3	4	5	6	7	8	9	R	H	E
Chicago Cubs	0	0	0	1	0	0	0	2	0	3	8	1
New York Yankees	0	3	0	0	0	1	0	4	x	8	11	1

HR - ChC Ken O'Dea; NYY Tommy Henrich

WP - Red Ruffing; LP - Bill Lee

BATTING STATISTICS

New York Yankees	G	AB	R	H	2B	3B	HR	RBI	BB	SO	SB	CS	BA
Frankie Crosetti	4	16	1	4	2	1	1	6	2	4	0	1	.250
Bill Dickey	4	15	2	6	0	0	1	2	1	0	1	0	.400
Joe DiMaggio	4	15	4	4	0	0	1	2	1	1	0	0	.267
Lou Gehrig	4	14	4	4	0	0	0	0	2	3	0	0	.286
Lefty Gomez	1	2	0	0	0	0	0	0	0	0	0	0	.000
Joe Gordon	4	15	3	6	2	0	1	6	1	3	1	0	.400
Tommy Henrich	4	16	3	4	1	0	1	1	0	1	0	1	.250
Myril Hoag	2	5	3	2	1	0	0	1	0	0	0	0	.400
Johnny Murphy	1	0	0	0	0	0	0	0	0	0	0	0	—
Monte Pearson	1	3	1	1	0	0	0	0	1	0	0	0	.333
Jake Powell	1	0	0	0	0	0	0	0	0	0	0	0	—
Red Rolfe	4	18	0	3	0	0	0	1	0	3	1	0	.167
Red Ruffing	2	6	1	1	0	0	0	1	1	0	0	0	.167
George Selkirk	3	10	0	2	0	0	0	1	2	1	0	0	.200
Totals	4	135	22	37	6	1	5	21	11	16	3	2	.274

Chicago Cubs	G	AB	R	H	2B	3B	HR	RBI	BB	SO	SB	CS	BA
Clay Bryant	1	2	0	0	0	0	0	0	0	1	0	0	.000
Tex Carleton	1	0	0	0	0	0	0	0	0	0	0	0	—
Phil Cavarretta	4	13	1	6	1	0	0	0	0	1	0	0	.462
Ripper Collins	4	15	1	2	0	0	0	0	0	3	0	0	.133
Dizzy Dean	2	3	0	2	0	0	0	0	0	0	0	1	.667
Frank Demaree	3	10	1	1	0	0	0	0	1	2	0	0	.100
Larry French	3	0	0	0	0	0	0	0	0	0	0	0	—
Augie Galan	2	2	0	0	0	0	0	0	0	1	0	0	.000
Stan Hack	4	17	3	8	1	0	0	1	1	2	0	1	.471
Gabby Hartnett	3	11	0	1	0	1	0	0	0	3	0	0	.091
Billy Herman	4	16	1	3	0	0	0	0	1	4	0	0	.188
Billy Jurges	4	13	0	3	1	0	0	0	1	3	0	0	.231
Tony Lazzeri	2	2	0	0	0	0	0	0	0	1	0	0	.000
Bill Lee	2	3	0	0	0	0	0	0	0	1	0	0	.000
Joe Marty	3	12	1	6	1	0	1	5	0	2	0	1	.500
Ken O'Dea	3	5	1	1	0	0	1	2	1	0	0	0	.200
Vance Page	1	0	0	0	0	0	0	0	0	0	0	0	—
Carl Reynolds	4	12	0	0	0	0	0	0	1	3	0	0	.000
Charlie Root	1	0	0	0	0	0	0	0	0	0	0	0	—
Jack Russell	2	0	0	0	0	0	0	0	0	0	0	0	—
Totals	4	136	9	33	4	1	2	8	6	26	0	3	.243

PITCHING STATISTICS

New York Yankees	G	GS	CG	IP	H	ER	BB	SO	W-L	Sv	ERA
Lefty Gomez	1	1	0	7	9	3	1	5	1-0	0	3.86
Johnny Murphy	1	0	0	2	2	0	1	1	0-0	1	0.00
Monte Pearson	1	1	1	9	5	1	2	9	1-0	0	1.00
Red Ruffing	2	2	2	18	17	3	2	11	2-0	0	1.50
Totals	4	4	3	36	33	7	6	26	4-0	1	1.75

Chicago Cubs	G	GS	CG	IP	H	ER	BB	SO	W-L	Sv	ERA
Clay Bryant	1	1	0	5⅓	6	4	5	3	0-1	0	6.75
Tex Carleton	1	0	0	0	1	2	2	0	0-0	0	—
Dizzy Dean	2	1	0	8⅓	8	6	1	2	0-1	0	6.48
Larry French	3	0	0	3⅓	1	1	1	2	0-0	0	2.70
Bill Lee	2	2	0	11	15	3	1	8	0-2	0	2.45
Vance Page	1	0	0	1⅓	2	2	0	0	0-0	0	13.50
Charlie Root	1	0	0	3	3	1	0	1	0-0	0	3.00
Jack Russell	2	0	0	1⅔	1	0	1	0	0-0	0	0.00
Totals	4	4	0	34	37	19	11	16	0-4	0	5.03

1945 World Series

DETROIT TIGERS (4) VS. CHICAGO CUBS (3)

GAME 1

Wednesday, October 3

	1	2	3	4	5	6	7	8	9	R	H	E
Chicago Cubs	4	0	3	0	0	0	2	0	0	9	13	0
Detroit Tigers	0	0	0	0	0	0	0	0	0	0	6	0

HR - ChC Phil Cavarretta

WP - Hank Borowy; LP - Hal Newhouser

GAME 2

Thursday, October 4

	1	2	3	4	5	6	7	8	9	R	H	E
Chicago Cubs	0	0	0	1	0	0	0	0	0	1	7	0
Detroit Tigers	0	0	0	0	4	0	0	0	x	4	7	0

HR - Det Hank Greenberg

WP - Virgil Trucks; LP - Hank Wyse

GAME 3

Friday, October 5

	1	2	3	4	5	6	7	8	9	R	H	E
Chicago Cubs	0	0	0	2	0	0	1	0	0	3	8	0
Detroit Tigers	0	0	0	0	0	0	0	0	0	0	1	2

WP - Claude Passeau; LP - Stubby Overmire

GAME 4

Saturday, October 6

	1	2	3	4	5	6	7	8	9	R	H	E
Detroit Tigers	0	0	0	4	0	0	0	0	0	4	7	1
Chicago Cubs	0	0	0	0	0	1	0	0	0	1	5	1

WP - Dizzy Trout; LP - Ray Prim

GAME 5

Sunday, October 7

	1	2	3	4	5	6	7	8	9	R	H	E
Detroit Tigers	0	0	1	0	0	4	1	0	2	8	11	0
Chicago Cubs	0	0	1	0	0	0	2	0	1	4	7	2

WP - Hal Newhouser; LP - Hank Borowy

GAME 6

Monday, October 8

	1	2	3	4	5	6	7	8	9	10	11	12	R	H	E
Detroit Tigers	0	1	0	0	0	0	2	4	0	0	0	0	7	13	1
Chicago Cubs	0	0	0	0	4	1	2	0	0	0	0	1	8	15	3

HR - Det Hank Greenberg

WP - Hank Borowy; LP - Dizzy Trout

GAME 7

Wednesday, October 10

	1	2	3	4	5	6	7	8	9	R	H	E
Detroit Tigers	5	1	0	0	0	0	1	2	0	9	9	1
Chicago Cubs	1	0	0	1	0	0	0	1	0	3	10	0

WP - Hal Newhouser; LP - Hank Borowy

BATTING STATISTICS

Detroit Tigers	G	AB	R	H	2B	3B	HR	RBI	BB	SO	SB	CS	BA
Al Benton	3	0	0	0	0	0	0	0	0	0	0	0	—
Red Borom	2	1	0	0	0	0	0	0	0	0	0	0	.000
Tommy Bridges	1	0	0	0	0	0	0	0	0	0	0	0	—
George Caster	1	0	0	0	0	0	0	0	0	0	0	0	—
Doc Cramer	7	29	7	11	0	0	0	4	1	0	1	0	.379
Roy Cullenbine	7	22	5	5	2	0	0	4	8	2	1	0	.227
Zeb Eaton	1	1	0	0	0	0	0	0	0	1	0	0	.000
Hank Greenberg	7	23	7	7	3	0	2	7	6	5	0	0	.304
Joe Hoover	1	3	1	1	0	0	0	1	0	0	0	1	.333
Chuck Hostetler	3	3	0	0	0	0	0	0	0	0	0	0	.000
Bob Maier	1	1	0	1	0	0	0	0	0	0	0	0	1.000
Eddie Mayo	7	28	4	7	1	0	0	2	3	2	0	0	.250
John McHale	3	3	0	0	0	0	0	0	0	1	0	0	.000
Ed Mierkowicz	1	0	0	0	0	0	0	0	0	0	0	0	—
Les Mueller	1	0	0	0	0	0	0	0	0	0	0	0	—
Hal Newhouser	3	8	0	0	0	0	0	1	1	1	0	0	.000
Jimmy Outlaw	7	28	1	5	0	0	0	3	2	1	1	0	.179
Stubby Overmire	1	1	0	0	0	0	0	0	0	0	0	0	.000
Paul Richards	7	19	0	4	2	0	0	6	4	3	0	0	.211
Bob Swift	3	4	1	1	0	0	0	0	2	0	0	0	.250
Jim Tobin	1	1	0	0	0	0	0	0	0	0	0	0	.000
Dizzy Trout	2	6	0	1	0	0	0	0	0	0	0	0	.167
Virgil Trucks	2	4	0	0	0	0	0	0	1	1	0	0	.000
Hub Walker	2	2	1	1	0	0	0	0	0	0	0	0	.500
Skeeter Webb	7	27	4	5	0	0	0	1	2	1	0	0	.185
Rudy York	7	28	1	5	1	0	0	3	3	4	0	0	.179
Totals	7	242	32	54	10	0	2	32	33	22	3	1	.223

Chicago Cubs	G	AB	R	H	2B	3B	HR	RBI	BB	SO	SB	CS	BA
Heinz Becker	3	2	0	1	0	0	0	0	1	1	0	0	.500
Cy Block	1	0	0	0	0	0	0	0	0	0	0	0	—
Hank Borowy	4	6	1	1	1	0	0	0	3	3	0	0	.167
Phil Cavarretta	7	26	7	11	2	0	1	5	4	3	0	0	.423
Bob Chipman	1	0	0	0	0	0	0	0	0	0	0	0	—
Paul Derringer	3	0	0	0	0	0	0	0	0	0	0	0	—
Paul Erickson	4	0	0	0	0	0	0	0	0	0	0	0	—
Paul Gillespie	3	6	0	0	0	0	0	0	0	0	0	0	.000
Stan Hack	7	30	1	11	3	0	0	4	4	2	0	2	.367
Roy Hughes	6	17	1	5	1	0	0	3	4	5	0	1	.294
Don Johnson	7	29	4	5	2	1	0	0	0	8	1	0	.172
Mickey Livingston	6	22	3	8	3	0	0	4	1	1	0	2	.364
Peanuts Lowrey	7	29	4	9	1	0	0	0	1	2	0	0	.310
Clyde McCullough	1	1	0	0	0	0	0	0	0	1	0	0	.000
Lennie Merullo	3	2	0	0	0	0	0	0	0	1	0	0	.000
Bill Nicholson	7	28	1	6	1	1	0	8	2	5	0	0	.214
Andy Pafko	7	28	5	6	2	1	0	2	2	5	1	0	.214
Claude Passeau	3	7	1	0	0	0	0	1	0	4	0	0	.000
Ray Prim	2	0	0	0	0	0	0	0	0	0	0	0	—
Eddie Sauer	2	2	0	0	0	0	0	0	0	2	0	0	.000
Bill Schuster	2	1	1	0	0	0	0	0	0	0	0	0	.000
Frank Secory	5	5	0	2	0	0	0	0	0	2	0	0	.400
Hy Vandenberg	3	1	0	0	0	0	0	0	0	0	0	0	.000
Dewey Williams	2	2	0	0	0	0	0	0	0	1	0	0	.000
Hank Wyse	3	3	0	0	0	0	0	0	0	2	0	0	.000
Totals	7	247	29	65	16	3	1	27	19	48	2	5	.263

PITCHING STATISTICS

Detroit Tigers	G	GS	CG	IP	H	ER	BB	SO	W-L	Sv	ERA
Al Benton	3	0	0	4²/₃	6	1	0	5	0-0	0	1.93
Tommy Bridges	1	0	0	1²/₃	3	3	3	1	0-0	0	16.20
George Caster	1	0	0	0²/₃	0	0	0	1	0-0	0	0.00
Les Mueller	1	0	0	2	0	0	1	1	0-0	0	0.00
Hal Newhouser	3	3	2	20²/₃	25	14	4	22	2-1	0	6.10
Stubby Overmire	1	1	0	6	4	2	2	2	0-1	0	3.00
Jim Tobin	1	0	0	3	4	2	1	0	0-0	0	6.00
Dizzy Trout	2	1	1	13²/₃	9	1	3	9	1-1	0	0.66
Virgil Trucks	2	2	1	13¹/₃	14	5	5	7	1-0	0	3.38
Totals	7	7	4	65²/₃	65	28	19	48	4-3	0	3.84

Chicago Cubs	G	GS	CG	IP	H	ER	BB	SO	W-L	Sv	ERA
Hank Borowy	4	3	1	18	21	8	6	8	2-2	0	4.00
Bob Chipman	1	0	0	0¹/₃	0	0	1	0	0-0	0	0.00
Paul Derringer	3	0	0	5¹/₃	5	4	7	1	0-0	0	6.75
Paul Erickson	4	0	0	7	8	3	3	5	0-0	0	3.86
Claude Passeau	3	2	1	16²/₃	7	5	8	3	1-0	0	2.70
Ray Prim	2	1	0	4	4	5	1	1	0-1	0	11.25
Hy Vandenberg	3	0	0	6	1	0	3	3	0-0	0	0.00
Hank Wyse	3	1	0	7²/₃	8	6	4	1	0-1	0	7.04
Totals	7	7	2	65	54	31	33	22	3-4	0	4.29

1984 League Championship Series

SAN DIEGO PADRES (3) VS. CHICAGO CUBS (2)

GAME 1

Tuesday, October 2

	1	2	3	4	5	6	7	8	9	R	H	E
San Diego Padres	0	0	0	0	0	0	0	0	0	0	6	1
Chicago Cubs	2	0	3	0	6	2	0	0	x	13	16	0

HR - ChC Bob Dernier, Gary Matthews 2, Ron Cey, Rick Sutcliffe

WP - Rick Sutcliffe; LP - Eric Show

GAME 2

Wednesday, October 3

	1	2	3	4	5	6	7	8	9	R	H	E
San Diego Padres	0	0	0	1	0	1	0	0	0	2	5	0
Chicago Cubs	1	0	2	1	0	0	0	0	x	4	8	1

WP - Steve Trout; LP - Mark Thurmond; Sv - Lee Smith

GAME 3

Thursday, October 4

	1	2	3	4	5	6	7	8	9	R	H	E
Chicago Cubs	0	1	0	0	0	0	0	0	0	1	5	0
San Diego Padres	0	0	0	0	3	4	0	0	x	7	11	0

HR - SD Kevin McReynolds

WP - Ed Whitson; LP - Dennis Eckersley

GAME 4

Saturday, October 6

	1	2	3	4	5	6	7	8	9	R	H	E
Chicago Cubs	0	0	0	3	0	0	0	2	0	5	8	1
San Diego Padres	0	0	2	0	1	0	2	0	2	7	11	0

HR - ChC Jody Davis, Leon Durham; SD Steve Garvey

WP - Craig Lefferts; LP - Lee Smith

GAME 5

Sunday, October 7

	1	2	3	4	5	6	7	8	9	R	H	E
Chicago Cubs	2	1	0	0	0	0	0	0	0	3	5	1
San Diego Padres	0	0	0	0	0	2	4	0	x	6	8	0

HR - ChC Leon Durham, Jody Davis

WP - Craig Lefferts; LP - Rick Sutcliffe; Sv - Goose Gossage

BATTING STATISTICS

San Diego Padres	G	AB	R	H	2B	3B	HR	RBI	BB	SO	SB	CS	BA
Kurt Bevacqua	2	2	0	0	0	0	0	0	0	0	0	0	.000
Greg Booker	1	0	0	0	0	0	0	0	0	0	0	0	—
Bobby Brown	3	4	1	0	0	0	0	0	1	2	1	0	.000
Dave Dravecky	3	0	0	0	0	0	0	0	0	0	0	0	—
Tim Flannery	3	2	2	1	0	0	0	0	0	0	0	0	.500
Steve Garvey	5	20	1	8	1	0	1	7	1	2	0	0	.400
Goose Gossage	3	0	0	0	0	0	0	0	0	0	0	0	—
Tony Gwynn	5	19	6	7	3	0	0	3	1	2	0	0	.368
Greg Harris	1	0	0	0	0	0	0	0	0	0	0	0	—
Andy Hawkins	3	0	0	0	0	0	0	0	0	0	0	0	—
Terry Kennedy	5	18	2	4	0	0	0	1	1	3	0	0	.222
Craig Lefferts	3	0	0	0	0	0	0	0	0	0	0	0	—
Tim Lollar	1	1	0	0	0	0	0	0	0	1	0	0	.000
Carmelo Martinez	5	17	1	3	0	0	0	0	2	4	0	0	.176
Kevin McReynolds	4	10	2	3	0	0	1	4	3	1	0	0	.300
Graig Nettles	4	14	1	2	0	0	0	2	1	1	0	0	.143
Mario Ramirez	2	2	0	0	0	0	0	0	0	0	0	0	.000
Luis Salazar	3	5	0	1	0	1	0	0	0	1	0	1	.200
Eric Show	2	1	0	0	0	0	0	0	0	1	0	0	.000
Champ Summers	2	2	0	0	0	0	0	0	0	1	0	0	.000
Garry Templeton	5	15	2	5	1	0	0	2	2	0	1	0	.333
Mark Thurmond	1	1	0	1	0	0	0	0	0	0	0	0	1.000
Ed Whitson	1	3	0	0	0	0	0	0	0	1	0	0	.000
Alan Wiggins	5	19	4	6	0	0	0	1	2	2	0	1	.316
Totals	5	155	22	41	5	1	2	20	14	22	2	2	.265

Chicago Cubs	G	AB	R	H	2B	3B	HR	RBI	BB	SO	SB	CS	BA
Thad Bosley	2	2	0	0	0	0	0	0	0	0	0	0	.000
Larry Bowa	5	15	1	3	1	0	0	1	1	0	0	0	.200
Warren Brusstar	3	1	0	0	0	0	0	0	0	0	0	0	.000
Ron Cey	5	19	3	3	1	0	1	3	3	3	0	0	.158
Henry Cotto	3	1	1	1	0	0	0	0	0	0	0	1	1.000
Jody Davis	5	18	3	7	2	0	2	6	0	3	0	0	.389
Bob Dernier	5	17	5	4	2	0	1	1	5	4	2	1	.235
Leon Durham	5	20	2	3	0	0	2	4	1	4	0	0	.150
Dennis Eckersley	1	2	0	0	0	0	0	0	0	1	0	0	.000
George Frazier	1	0	0	0	0	0	0	0	0	0	0	0	—
Richie Hebner	2	1	0	0	0	0	0	0	0	0	0	0	.000
Steve Lake	1	1	0	1	1	0	0	0	0	0	0	0	1.000
Davey Lopes	2	1	0	0	0	0	0	0	0	0	0	0	.000
Gary Matthews	5	15	4	3	0	0	2	5	6	4	1	1	.200
Keith Moreland	5	18	3	6	2	0	0	2	1	1	0	0	.333
Ryne Sandberg	5	19	3	7	2	0	0	2	3	2	3	1	.368
Scott Sanderson	1	2	0	0	0	0	0	0	0	1	0	0	.000
Lee Smith	2	0	0	0	0	0	0	0	0	0	0	0	—
Tim Stoddard	2	0	0	0	0	0	0	0	0	0	0	0	—
Rick Sutcliffe	2	6	1	3	0	0	1	1	0	2	0	0	.500
Steve Trout	2	2	0	1	0	0	0	0	0	0	0	0	.500
Tom Veryzer	3	1	0	0	0	0	0	0	0	0	0	0	.000
Gary Woods	1	1	0	0	0	0	0	0	0	1	0	0	.000
Totals	5	162	26	42	11	0	9	25	20	28	6	3	.259

PITCHING STATISTICS

San Diego Padres	G	GS	CG	IP	H	ER	BB	SO	W-L	Sv	ERA
Greg Booker	1	0	0	2	2	0	1	2	0-0	0	0.00
Dave Dravecky	3	0	0	6	2	0	0	5	0-0	0	0.00
Goose Gossage	3	0	0	4	5	2	1	5	0-0	1	4.50
Greg Harris	1	0	0	2	9	7	3	2	0-0	0	31.50
Andy Hawkins	3	0	0	3⅔	0	0	2	1	0-0	0	0.00
Craig Lefferts	3	0	0	4	1	0	1	1	2-0	0	0.00
Tim Lollar	1	1	0	4⅓	3	3	4	3	0-0	0	6.23
Eric Show	2	2	0	5⅓	8	8	4	2	0-1	0	13.50
Mark Thurmond	1	1	0	3⅔	7	4	2	1	0-1	0	9.82
Ed Whitson	1	1	0	8	5	1	2	6	1-0	0	1.13
Totals	5	5	0	43	42	25	20	28	3-2	1	5.23

Chicago Cubs	G	GS	CG	IP	H	ER	BB	SO	W-L	Sv	ERA
Warren Brusstar	3	0	0	4⅓	6	0	0	1	0-0	0	0.00
Dennis Eckersley	1	1	0	5⅓	9	5	0	0	0-1	0	8.44
George Frazier	1	0	0	1⅔	2	2	0	1	0-0	0	10.80
Scott Sanderson	1	1	0	4⅔	6	3	1	2	0-0	0	5.79
Lee Smith	2	0	0	2	3	2	0	3	0-1	1	9.00
Tim Stoddard	2	0	0	2	1	1	2	2	0-0	0	4.50
Rick Sutcliffe	2	2	0	13⅓	9	5	8	10	1-1	0	3.38
Steve Trout	2	1	0	9	5	2	3	3	1-0	0	2.00
Totals	5	5	0	42⅓	41	20	14	22	2-3	1	4.25

1989 League Championship Series
SAN FRANCISCO GIANTS (4) VS. CHICAGO CUBS (1)

GAME 1
Wednesday, October 4

	1	2	3	4	5	6	7	8	9	R	H	E
San Francisco Giants	3	0	1	4	0	0	0	3	0	11	13	0
Chicago Cubs	2	0	1	0	0	0	0	3	1	0	1	

HR - SF Will Clark 2, Kevin Mitchell; ChC Ryne Sandberg, Mark Grace

WP - Scott Garrelts; LP - Greg Maddux

GAME 2
Thursday, October 5

	1	2	3	4	5	6	7	8	9	R	H	E
San Francisco Giants	0	0	0	2	0	0	0	2	1	5	10	0
Chicago Cubs	6	0	0	0	0	3	0	0	x	9	11	0

HR - SF Robby Thompson, Kevin Mitchell, Matt Williams

WP - Les Lancaster; LP - Rick Reuschel

GAME 3
Saturday, October 7

	1	2	3	4	5	6	7	8	9	R	H	E
Chicago Cubs	2	0	0	1	0	0	1	0	0	4	10	0
San Francisco Giants	3	0	0	0	0	0	2	0	x	5	8	3

HR - SF Robby Thompson

WP - Don Robinson; LP - Les Lancaster; Sv - Steve Bedrosian

GAME 4
Sunday, October 8

	1	2	3	4	5	6	7	8	9	R	H	E
Chicago Cubs	1	1	0	0	2	0	0	0	0	4	12	1
San Francisco Giants	1	0	2	1	2	0	0	0	x	6	9	1

HR - ChC Luis Salazar; SF Matt Williams

WP - Kelly Downs; LP - Steve Wilson; Sv - Steve Bedrosian

GAME 5
Monday, October 9

	1	2	3	4	5	6	7	8	9	R	H	E
Chicago Cubs	0	0	1	0	0	0	0	0	1	2	10	1
San Francisco Giants	0	0	0	0	0	0	1	2	x	3	4	1

WP - Rick Reuschel; LP - Mike Bielecki; Sv - Steve Bedrosian

BATTING STATISTICS

San Francisco Giants	G	AB	R	H	2B	3B	HR	RBI	BB	SO	SB	CS	BA
Bill Bathe	2	1	0	0	0	0	0	0	0	1	0	0	.000
Steve Bedrosian	4	0	0	0	0	0	0	0	0	0	0	0	—
Jeff Brantley	3	0	0	0	0	0	0	0	1	0	0	0	—
Brett Butler	5	19	6	4	0	0	0	0	3	3	0	1	.211
Will Clark	5	20	8	13	3	1	2	8	2	2	0	0	.650
Kelly Downs	2	3	0	0	0	0	0	0	0	1	0	0	.000
Scott Garrelts	2	4	0	0	0	0	0	0	1	1	0	0	.000
Atlee Hammaker	1	0	0	0	0	0	0	0	0	0	0	0	—
Terry Kennedy	5	16	0	3	1	0	0	1	1	4	0	0	.188
Mike LaCoss	1	1	0	0	0	0	0	0	0	0	0	0	.000
Craig Lefferts	2	0	0	0	0	0	0	0	0	0	0	0	—
Greg Litton	1	1	0	1	0	0	0	0	0	0	0	0	1.000
Candy Maldonado	3	3	1	0	0	0	0	1	2	0	0	0	.000
Kirt Manwaring	3	2	0	0	0	0	0	0	0	0	0	0	.000
Kevin Mitchell	5	17	5	6	0	0	2	7	3	3	0	0	.353
Donell Nixon	3	3	0	0	0	0	0	0	0	1	1	0	.000
Ken Oberkfell	3	4	0	0	0	0	0	0	0	0	0	0	.000
Rick Reuschel	2	2	0	0	0	0	0	0	0	0	0	0	.000
Ernest Riles	1	1	0	0	0	0	0	0	0	0	0	0	.000
Don Robinson	1	0	0	0	0	0	0	0	0	0	0	0	—
Pat Sheridan	5	13	1	2	0	1	0	0	0	4	0	1	.154
Robby Thompson	5	18	5	5	0	0	2	3	3	2	0	0	.278
Jose Uribe	5	17	2	4	1	0	0	1	1	5	1	0	.235
Matt Williams	5	20	2	6	1	0	2	9	0	2	0	0	.300
Totals	5	165	30	44	6	2	8	29	17	29	2	2	.267

Chicago Cubs	G	AB	R	H	2B	3B	HR	RBI	BB	SO	SB	CS	BA
Paul Assenmacher	2	0	0	0	0	0	0	0	0	0	0	0	—
Mike Bielecki	2	5	0	1	0	0	0	2	0	2	0	0	.200
Andre Dawson	5	19	0	2	1	0	0	3	2	6	0	0	.105
Shawon Dunston	5	19	2	6	0	0	0	0	1	1	1	0	.316
Joe Girardi	4	10	1	1	0	0	0	0	1	2	0	0	.100
Mark Grace	5	17	3	11	3	1	1	8	4	1	1	0	.647
Paul Kilgus	1	0	0	0	0	0	0	0	0	0	0	0	—
Les Lancaster	3	1	0	0	0	0	0	0	0	1	0	0	.000
Vance Law	2	3	0	0	0	0	0	0	0	3	0	0	.000
Greg Maddux	3	3	1	0	0	0	0	0	0	0	0	0	.000
Lloyd McClendon	3	3	0	2	0	0	0	1	1	0	0	0	.667
Domingo Ramos	1	1	0	0	0	0	0	0	0	0	0	0	.000
Luis Salazar	5	19	2	7	0	1	1	2	0	0	0	0	.368
Ryne Sandberg	5	20	6	8	3	1	1	4	3	4	0	0	.400
Scott Sanderson	1	0	0	0	0	0	0	0	0	0	0	0	—
Dwight Smith	4	15	2	3	1	0	0	0	2	2	1	0	.200
Rick Sutcliffe	1	2	0	1	1	0	0	0	0	0	0	0	.500
Jerome Walton	5	22	4	8	0	0	0	2	2	2	0	0	.364
Mitch Webster	3	3	0	1	0	0	0	0	0	0	0	0	.333
Curt Wilkerson	3	2	1	1	0	0	0	0	0	0	0	0	.500
Mitch Williams	2	0	0	0	0	0	0	0	0	0	0	0	—
Steve Wilson	2	0	0	0	0	0	0	0	0	0	0	0	—
Rick Wrona	2	5	0	0	0	0	0	0	0	3	0	0	.000
Marvell Wynne	4	6	0	1	0	0	0	0	0	0	0	0	.167
Totals	5	175	22	53	9	3	3	21	16	27	3	0	.303

PITCHING STATISTICS

San Francisco Giants	G	GS	CG	IP	H	ER	BB	SO	W-L	Sv	ERA
Steve Bedrosian	4	0	0	3⅓	4	1	2	2	0-0	3	2.70
Jeff Brantley	3	0	0	5	1	0	2	3	0-0	0	0.00
Kelly Downs	2	0	0	8⅔	8	3	6	6	1-0	0	3.12
Scott Garrelts	2	2	0	11⅔	16	7	2	8	1-0	0	5.40
Atlee Hammaker	1	0	0	1	1	0	0	0	0-0	0	0.00
Mike LaCoss	1	1	0	3	7	3	0	2	0-0	0	9.00
Craig Lefferts	2	0	0	1	1	1	2	1	0-0	0	9.00
Rick Reuschel	2	2	0	8⅔	12	5	2	5	1-1	0	5.19
Don Robinson	1	0	0	1⅔	3	0	0	0	1-0	0	0.00
Totals	5	5	0	44	53	20	16	27	4-1	3	4.09

Chicago Cubs	G	GS	CG	IP	H	ER	BB	SO	W-L	Sv	ERA
Paul Assenmacher	2	0	0	0⅔	3	1	0	0	0-0	0	13.50
Mike Bielecki	2	2	0	12⅓	7	5	6	11	0-1	0	3.65
Paul Kilgus	1	0	0	3	4	0	1	1	0-0	0	0.00
Les Lancaster	3	0	0	6	6	4	1	3	1-1	0	6.00
Greg Maddux	2	2	0	7⅓	13	11	4	5	0-1	0	13.50
Scott Sanderson	1	0	0	2	2	0	0	1	0-0	0	0.00
Rick Sutcliffe	1	1	0	6	5	3	4	2	0-0	0	4.50
Mitch Williams	2	0	0	1	1	0	0	2	0-0	0	0.00
Steve Wilson	2	0	0	3⅔	3	2	1	4	0-1	0	4.91
Totals	5	5	0	42	44	26	17	29	1-4	0	5.57

1998 League Division Series
ATLANTA BRAVES (3) VS. CHICAGO CUBS (0)

GAME 1
Wednesday, September 30

	1	2	3	4	5	6	7	8	9	R	H	E
Chicago Cubs	0	0	0	0	0	0	0	1	0	1	5	1
Atlanta Braves	0	2	0	0	0	1	4	0	x	7	8	0

HR - ChC Tyler Houston; Atl Ryan Klesko, Michael Tucker

WP - John Smoltz; LP - Mark Clark

GAME 2
Thursday, October 1

	1	2	3	4	5	6	7	8	9	10	R	H	E
Chicago Cubs	0	0	0	0	0	1	0	0	0	0	1	4	1
Atlanta Braves	0	0	0	0	0	0	0	0	1	1	2	6	0

HR - Atl Javy Lopez

WP - Odalis Perez; LP - Terry Mulholland

GAME 3
Saturday, October 3

	1	2	3	4	5	6	7	8	9	R	H	E
Atlanta Braves	0	0	1	0	0	0	0	5	0	6	9	0
Chicago Cubs	0	0	0	0	0	0	0	2	0	2	8	2

HR - Atl Eddie Perez

WP - Greg Maddux; LP - Kerry Wood

BATTING STATISTICS

Atlanta Braves	G	AB	R	H	2B	3B	HR	RBI	BB	SO	SB	CS	BA
Danny Bautista	2	2	0	1	1	0	0	0	0	0	0	0	.500
Greg Colbrunn	2	2	0	0	0	0	0	0	0	0	0	0	.000
Andres Galarraga	3	12	1	3	0	0	0	1	1	3	0	0	.250
Tom Glavine	1	1	0	0	0	0	0	0	0	0	0	0	.000
Tony Graffanino	1	0	0	0	0	0	0	0	0	0	0	0	—
Ozzie Guillen	1	1	0	0	0	0	0	0	0	0	0	0	.000
Andruw Jones	3	9	2	0	0	0	1	3	2	2	0	0	.000
Chipper Jones	3	10	2	2	0	0	0	1	4	3	0	0	.200
Ryan Klesko	3	11	1	3	0	0	1	4	0	3	0	0	.273
Kerry Ligtenberg	3	0	0	0	0	0	0	0	0	0	0	0	—
Keith Lockhart	3	12	2	4	0	0	0	0	1	0	0	0	.333
Javy Lopez	2	7	1	2	0	0	1	1	1	1	0	0	.286
Greg Maddux	1	4	1	1	1	0	0	0	0	1	0	0	.250
Eddie Perez	1	5	1	1	0	0	1	4	0	2	0	0	.200
Odalis Perez	1	0	0	0	0	0	0	0	0	0	0	0	—
John Rocker	2	0	0	0	0	0	0	0	0	0	0	0	—
Rudy Seanez	1	0	0	0	0	0	0	0	0	0	0	0	—
John Smoltz	1	2	0	1	0	0	0	0	1	1	0	0	.500
Michael Tucker	3	8	1	2	0	0	1	2	2	0	1	0	.250
Walt Weiss	3	13	2	2	0	0	0	0	1	3	0	0	.154
Gerald Williams	2	2	1	1	0	0	0	1	0	1	0	0	.500
Totals	3	101	15	23	2	0	4	14	14	20	3	0	.228

Chicago Cubs	G	AB	R	H	2B	3B	HR	RBI	BB	SO	SB	CS	BA
Manny Alexander	2	5	0	0	0	0	0	0	0	1	0	0	.000
Rod Beck	1	0	0	0	0	0	0	0	0	0	0	0	—
Jeff Blauser	2	2	0	0	0	0	0	0	0	1	0	0	.000
Brant Brown	1	1	0	0	0	0	0	0	0	0	0	0	.000
Mark Clark	1	2	0	1	0	0	0	0	0	0	0	0	.500
Gary Gaetti	3	11	0	1	0	0	0	0	0	4	0	0	.091
Mark Grace	3	12	0	1	0	0	0	1	0	2	0	0	.083
Felix Heredia	1	0	0	0	0	0	0	0	0	0	0	0	—
Jose Hernandez	2	7	1	2	0	0	0	0	0	2	0	0	.286
Glenallen Hill	1	3	0	1	0	0	0	0	1	2	1	0	.333
Tyler Houston	3	6	1	1	0	0	1	1	0	3	0	0	.167
Lance Johnson	3	12	0	2	0	0	0	1	0	1	0	0	.167
Matt Karchner	1	0	0	0	0	0	0	0	0	0	0	0	—
Sandy Martinez	1	1	1	1	0	0	0	0	0	0	0	0	1.000
Mickey Morandini	3	9	1	2	0	0	0	1	2	2	0	1	.222
Mike Morgan	2	0	0	0	0	0	0	0	0	0	0	0	—
Terry Mulholland	2	0	0	0	0	0	0	0	0	0	0	0	—
Henry Rodriguez	3	7	0	1	1	0	0	0	1	2	0	0	.143
Scott Servais	1	3	0	2	0	0	0	0	0	0	0	0	.667
Sammy Sosa	3	11	0	2	1	0	0	0	1	4	0	2	.182
Kevin Tapani	1	1	0	0	0	0	0	0	0	0	0	0	.000
Kerry Wood	1	1	0	0	0	0	0	0	0	0	0	0	.000
Totals	3	94	4	17	2	0	1	4	5	24	1	3	.181

PITCHING STATISTICS

Atlanta Braves	G	GS	CG	IP	H	ER	BB	SO	W-L	Sv	ERA
Tom Glavine	1	1	0	7	3	1	1	8	0-0	0	1.29
Kerry Ligtenberg	3	0	0	3 1/3	1	0	4	3	0-0	0	0.00
Greg Maddux	1	1	0	7	7	2	0	4	1-0	0	2.57
Odalis Perez	1	0	0	0 2/3	0	0	0	1	1-0	0	0.00
John Rocker	2	0	0	1 1/3	1	0	0	2	0-0	0	0.00
Rudy Seanez	1	0	0	1	0	0	0	0	0-0	0	0.00
John Smoltz	1	1	0	7 2/3	5	1	0	6	1-0	0	1.17
Totals	3	3	0	28	17	4	5	24	3-0	0	1.29

Chicago Cubs	G	GS	CG	IP	H	ER	BB	SO	W-L	Sv	ERA
Rod Beck	1	0	0	1 2/3	5	3	2	1	0-0	0	16.20
Mark Clark	1	1	0	6	7	2	1	4	0-1	0	3.00
Felix Heredia	1	0	0	0 1/3	0	2	2	0	0-0	0	54.00
Matt Karchner	1	0	0	0 2/3	1	1	0	1	0-0	0	13.50
Mike Morgan	2	0	0	1 1/3	0	0	0	1	0-0	0	0.00
Terry Mulholland	2	0	0	2 1/3	2	3	2	2	0-1	0	11.57
Kevin Tapani	1	1	0	9	5	1	3	6	0-0	0	1.00
Kerry Wood	1	1	0	5	3	1	4	5	0-1	0	1.80
Totals	3	3	0	26 1/3	23	13	14	20	0-3	0	4.44

APPENDIX B:

Chicago Cubs Record Holders

Hitting categories

GAMES PLAYED

1 E. Banks 2,528
2 Anson 2,276
3 B. Williams 2,213
4 Sandberg 2,151
5 Santo 2,126
6 Cavarretta 1,953
7 Hack 1,938
8 Hartnett 1,926
9 M. Grace 1,910
10 Ryan 1,660
11 Kessinger 1,648
12 F. Schulte 1,564
13 Tinker 1,536
14 Evers 1,409
15 Sosa 1,398
16 Nicholson 1,349
17 W. Herman 1,344
18 Grimm 1,334
19 Chance 1,274
20 Dunston 1,254

AT-BATS

1 E. Banks 9,421
2 Anson 9,173
3 B. Williams 8,479
4 Sandberg 8,379
5 Santo 7,768
6 Hack 7,278
7 M. Grace 7,156
8 Ryan 6,810
9 Cavarretta 6,592
10 Kessinger 6,355
11 Hartnett 6,282
12 F. Schulte 5,837
13 Tinker 5,547
14 W. Herman 5,532
15 Sosa 5,439
16 Beckert 5,020
17 Grimm 4,917
18 Burns 4,915
19 Evers 4,858
20 Nicholson 4,857

RUNS

1 Anson 1,719
2 Ryan 1,409
3 Sandberg 1,316
4 B. Williams 1,306
5 E. Banks 1,305
6 Hack 1,239
7 Santo 1,109
8 M. Grace 1,057
9 Cavarretta 968
10 Sosa 955
11 Dahlen 896
12 W. Herman 875
13 Hartnett 847
14 F. Schulte 827
15 Chance 794
16 Gore 772
17 Kessinger 769
18 English 747
19 Williamson 744
20 Evers 742
20 Pfeffer 742

HITS

1 Anson 3,055
2 E. Banks 2,583
3 B. Williams 2,510
4 Sandberg 2,385
5 M. Grace 2,201
6 Hack 2,193
7 Santo 2,171
8 Ryan 2,126
9 Cavarretta 1,927
10 Hartnett 1,867
11 W. Herman 1,710
12 Kessinger 1,619
13 F. Schulte 1,590
14 Sosa 1,560
15 Grimm 1,454
16 Tinker 1,436
17 Beckert 1,423
18 Evers 1,340
19 Burns 1,325
20 Nicholson 1,323

DOUBLES

1 Anson 528
2 M. Grace 456
3 E. Banks 407
4 Sandberg 403
5 B. Williams 402
6 Hartnett 391

7 Hack 363
8 Ryan 362
9 Santo 353
10 W. Herman 346
11 Cavarretta 341
12 Grimm 270
13 F. Schulte 254
14 Nicholson 245
15 J.R. Stephenson 237
16 Burns 236
17 Buckner 235
18 Sosa 234
19 Dunston 226
20 Cuyler 220
20 Tinker 220

TRIPLES

1 Ryan 142
2 Anson 124
3 F. Schulte 117
4 Dahlen 106
5 Cavarretta 99
6 Tinker 93
7 E. Banks 90
8 B. Williams 87
9 Hack 81
10 Lange 80
10 Williamson 80
10 Zimmerman 80
13 Chance 79
14 Sandberg 76
15 Pfeffer 72
16 Kessinger 71
17 W. Herman 69
17 Burns 69
19 Cuyler 66
19 Santo 66

HOME RUNS

1 E. Banks 512
2 Sosa 421
3 B. Williams 392
4 Santo 337
5 Sandberg 282
6 Hartnett 231
7 Nicholson 205
8 H. Sauer 198
9 L. Wilson 190
10 Dawson 174
11 M. Grace 148
12 Durham 138
13 Pafko 126

14 J.R. Davis 122
15 Dunston 107
16 Monday 106
17 Moreland 100
18 Ryan 99
19 Hickman 97
20 Anson 96

RBI

1 Anson 1,879
2 E. Banks 1,636
3 B. Williams 1,353
4 Santo 1,290
5 Hartnett 1,153
6 Sosa 1,123
7 Sandberg 1,061
8 M. Grace 1,004
9 Ryan 914
10 Cavarretta 896
11 Nicholson 833
12 L. Wilson 769
13 F. Schulte 712
14 Grimm 696
15 Burns 679
16 Pfeffer 677
17 Tinker 670
18 Hack 642
19 Williamson 622
20 Cuyler 602

STOLEN BASES

1 Chance 400
2 Lange 399
3 Ryan 369
4 Sandberg 344
5 Tinker 304
6 Evers 291
7 Wilmot 290
8 Dahlen 285
9 Pfeffer 263
10 Anson 247
11 F. Schulte 214
12 Slagle 198
13 Everitt 179
13 Sosa 179
15 Dunston 175
16 Hack 165
17 Sheckard 163
18 Burns 161
18 Cuyler 161
20 Hofman 158

BATTING AVERAGE
(500 games or more)

1 J.R. Stephenson .336
2 Anson .333
3 Lange .330
4 Cuyler .325
5 Everitt .323
6 L. Wilson .322
7 M. Kelly .316
8 Gore .315
9 Ryan .312
10 Demaree .309
11 W. Herman .309
12 M. Grace .308
13 Hollocher .304
14 Zimmerman .304
15 Hack .301
16 Buckner .300
17 Dahlen .299
18 Hartnett .297
19 Chance .297
20 Cardenal .296

INTENTIONAL WALKS

1 E. Banks 198
2 B. Williams 160
3 Sosa 112
4 M. Grace 100
5 Durham 94
6 Santo 93
7 Dawson 64
8 Kessinger 59
8 Sandberg 59
10 Phillips 55

SLUGGING PERCENTAGE
(500 games or more)

1 L. Wilson .590
2 Sosa .573
3 H. Sauer .512
4 Dawson .507
5 B. Williams .503
6 E. Banks .500
7 Hartnett .490
8 Cuyler .485
9 Durham .484
10 Santo .472

TOTAL BASES

1 E. Banks 4,706
2 B. Williams 4,262
3 Anson 4,119
4 Sandberg 3,786
5 Santo 3,667
6 M. Grace 3,187
7 Sosa 3,117
8 Hartnett 3,079
9 Ryan 3,069
10 Hack 2,889

ON-BASE PERCENTAGE
(500 games or more)

1 L. Wilson .412
2 J.R. Stephenson .408
3 Lange .401
4 Anson .398
5 Hack .394
6 Chance .394
7 Cuyler .391
8 M. Grace .386
9 Gore .386
10 Dahlen .384

HIT BY PITCH

1 Chance 137
2 E. Banks 70
3 Dahlen 68
4 Ryan 64
5 Pafko 48
6 F. Schulte 47
7 Cuyler 44
8 Nicholson 43
8 Steinfeldt 43
10 B. Williams 41

SACRIFICE FLIES

1 E. Banks 96
2 Santo 91
3 M. Grace 88
4 Sandberg 71
5 B. Williams 67
6 Moreland 50
7 Sosa 49
8 Buckner 43
9 Dunston 38
9 J.R. Davis 38

Cubs Single Season Leaders (by position):

HOME RUNS

Pitcher: Gumbert 7 (1889)
Catcher: Hartnett 37 (1930)
1st base: E. Banks 37 (1962)
2nd base: Sandberg 40 (1990)
3rd base: Santo 33 (1965)
Shortstop: E. Banks 47 (1958)
Outfield: Sosa 66 (1998)

RBI

Pitcher: Spalding 44 (1876)
Catcher: Hartnett 122 (1930)
1st base: Anson 147 (1886)
2nd base: Hornsby 149 (1929)
3rd base: Santo 123 (1969)
Shortstop: E. Banks 143 (1959)
Outfield: L. Wilson 191 (1930)

BATTING AVERAGE

Pitcher: Stratton .375 (1894)
Catcher: Hartnett .339 (1930)
1st base: Anson .421 (1887)
2nd base: Hornsby .380 (1929)
3rd base: Zimmerman .372 (1912)
Shortstop: Williamson .371 (1887)
Outfield: Lange .389 (1895)

FIELDING PERCENTAGE

Pitcher: L.C. Jackson 1.000 (1964)
  (109 chances)
Catcher: R. Wilkins .996 (1993)
1st base: M. Grace .998 (1992)
2nd base: Sandberg .995 (1991)
3rd base: Hack .975 (1945)
Shortstop: Gutierrez .986 (2000)
Outfield: Monday .996 (1972)

Pitching Leaders

GAMES PITCHED

1 Root 605
2 L. Smith 458
3 Elston 449
4 Bush 428
5 Jenkins 401
6 Hutchison 368
7 W. Lee 364
8 R. Reuschel 358
9 M. Brown 346
10 Rush 339
11 G. Hernandez 323
12 Vaughn 305
13 Sutter 300
14 Passeau 292
15 Reulbach 281
16 Assenmacher 279
17 Hands 276
17 T. Adams 276
19 French 272
20 Hobbie 271

INNINGS

1 Root 3,137$\frac{1}{3}$
2 Hutchison 3,021
3 Jenkins 2,673$\frac{2}{3}$
4 L. Corcoran 2,338$\frac{1}{3}$
5 M. Brown 2,329
6 R. Reuschel 2,290
7 W. Lee 2,271$\frac{1}{3}$
8 Vaughn 2,216$\frac{1}{3}$
9 Bush 2,201$\frac{2}{3}$
10 C. Griffith 2,188$\frac{2}{3}$
11 Rush 2,132$\frac{2}{3}$
12 Passeau 1,914$\frac{2}{3}$
13 Alexander 1,884$\frac{1}{3}$
14 Reulbach 1,864$\frac{2}{3}$
15 J. Taylor 1,801
16 Clarkson 1,730$\frac{2}{3}$
17 Malone 1,632
18 Warneke 1,624$\frac{2}{3}$
19 Ellsworth 1,613$\frac{1}{3}$
20 Hands 1,564

WINS

1 Root 201
2 M. Brown 188
3 Hutchison 179
4 L. Corcoran 175
5 Jenkins 167
6 Bush 152
7 C. Griffith 151
7 Vaughn 151
9 W. Lee 139
10 Clarkson 137
11 Reulbach 136
12 R. Reuschel 135
13 Alexander 128
14 Passeau 124
15 Malone 115
16 Rush 110
17 J. Taylor 109
17 Warneke 109
19 Goldsmith 107
20 French 95
20 Maddux 95

PERCENTAGE
(100 decisions or more)

1 Clarkson .706
2 M. Brown .689
3 Reulbach .677
4 L. Corcoran .673
5 Overall .662
6 Pfiester .633
7 Goldsmith .629
8 Lundgren .623
9 C. Griffith .619
10 Alexander .607
11 Warneke .602
12 Bush .601
13 Cheney .598
14 Malone .593
15 Vaughn .590
16 Callahan .579
17 Passeau .569
18 Root .563
19 Wyse .561
20 Maddux .559

STRIKEOUTS

1 Jenkins 2,038
2 Root 1,432
3 R. Reuschel 1,367
4 Hutchison 1,222
5 Vaughn 1,138
6 L. Corcoran 1,086
7 Rush 1,076
8 M. Brown 1,043
9 Holtzman 988
10 Clarkson 960
11 Maddux 937
12 Sutcliffe 909
13 Ellsworth 905
14 Hands 900
15 Malone 878
16 W. Lee 874
17 Trachsel 829
18 Bonham 811
19 Reulbach 799
20 Passeau 754

SHUTOUTS

1 M. Brown 48
2 Vaughn 35
3 Reulbach 31
4 Jenkins 29
5 Overall 28
6 W. Lee 25
7 Alexander 24
8 L. Corcoran 22
8 Passeau 22
10 French 21
10 Hutchison 21
10 Root 21
13 Lundgren 19
14 Pfiester 17
14 R. Reuschel 17
14 Warneke 17
17 Goldsmith 16
17 Malone 16
19 Clarkson 15
19 Holtzman 15

COMPLETE GAMES

1 Hutchison 317
2 L. Corcoran 252
3 C. Griffith 240
4 M. Brown 206
5 J. Taylor 188
6 Clarkson 186
7 Root 177
7 Vaughn 177
9 Goldsmith 164
10 Alexander 159
11 Jenkins 154
12 W. Lee 153
13 Reulbach 150
14 Passeau 143
15 Bush 127
16 Lundgren 125
17 Warneke 122
18 Callahan 116
19 Larkin 113
20 Rush 112

ERA

(800 innings or more)

1 M. Brown 1.80
2 Pfiester 1.85
3 Overall 1.91
4 Weimer 2.14
5 Reulbach 2.24
6 L. Corcoran 2.26
7 Vaughn 2.33
8 Larkin 2.34
9 Clarkson 2.39
10 Lundgren 2.42
11 J. Taylor 2.66
12 Cheney 2.74
13 Goldsmith 2.78
14 Warneke 2.84
15 Alexander 2.84
16 Hendrix 2.84
17 Passeau 2.96
18 Lavender 3.03
19 Wyse 3.03
20 Hands 3.18

SAVES

1 L. Smith 180
2 Sutter 133
3 R.K. Myers 112
4 Elston 63
5 Regan 60
6 Beck 58
7 M. Williams 52
8 Root 40
9 Abernathy 39
9 McDaniel 39
9 M. Brown 39
12 Aguilera 37
12 T. Adams 37
14 Assenmacher 33
15 Aker 29
16 Leonard 28
16 Lown 28
18 Bush 27
18 Gordon 27
20 Tidrow 25

RELIEF APPEARANCES

1 L. Smith 452
2 Elston 434
3 G. Hernandez 312
4 Sutter 300
5 Assenmacher 278
6 T. Adams 276
7 Root 267
8 Tidrow 263
9 Regan 245
10 Heredia 221

HIT BATTERS

1 Reulbach 85
2 Root 73
3 C. Griffith 67
4 Callahan 64
5 Vaughn 63
6 J. Taylor 61
7 R. Reuschel 59
8 Lavender 53
9 Jenkins 52
10 Maddux 44
10 M. Brown 44

Fielding Leaders

■ PITCHER

FIELDING PERCENTAGE
(800 innings or more)

1 Tapani .993
2 Warneke .990
3 Alexander .988
4 L.C. Jackson .985
5 Passeau .980

PUTOUTS

1 R. Reuschel 227
2 Maddux 188
3 Jenkins 187
4 L. Corcoran 180
5 M. Brown 149
6 Rush 148
7 Hutchison 137
8 C. Griffith 136
9 W. Lee 130
10 Bush 115
10 Hands 115

ERRORS

1 Hutchison 73
2 L. Corcoran 65
3 Vaughn 58
4 Clarkson 57
5 Goldsmith 55
6 W. Lee 50
7 C. Griffith 48
8 Reulbach 38
9 J. Taylor 33
10 Jenkins 30

■ CATCHER

FIELDING PERCENTAGE
(500 Games Played or more)

1 C.R. Hundley .992
2 J.R. Davis .987
3 Hartnett .984
4 McCullough .983
5 Kling .973

PUTOUTS

1 Hartnett 7,154
2 C.R. Hundley 5,346
3 J.R. Davis 5,124
4 Kling 4,585
5 Flint 3,235
6 Archer 3,104
7 Girardi 2,659
8 McCullough 2,637
9 Servais 2,512
10 Kittridge 2,452

ERRORS

1 Flint 397
2 Kittridge 170
3 Kling 161
4 Hartnett 138
5 M. Kelly 137
6 Donahue 127
7 Archer 120
8 Schriver 96
9 C.A. Farrell 78
10 J.R. Davis 75

■ 1ST BASE

FIELDING PERCENTAGE
(500 Games Played or more)

1 M. Grace .995
2 Durham .994
3 E. Banks .994
4 Grimm .992
5 Buckner .992

PUTOUTS

1 Anson 20,794
2 M. Grace 16,601
3 Grimm 12,668
4 E. Banks 12,005
5 Cavarretta 11,111
6 Chance 9,798
7 Buckner 8,100
8 Saier 7,899
9 Fondy 6,601
10 Merkle 5,203

■ ERRORS

1 Anson 583
2 Chance 135
3 Cavarretta 121
3 Saier 121
5 Grimm 103
6 M. Grace 96
7 Everitt 95
8 Fondy 82
9 E. Banks 80
10 Merkle 79

■ 2ND BASE

FIELDING PERCENTAGE
(500 Games Played or more)

1 Sandberg .989
2 Trillo .974
3 Beckert .974
4 W. Herman .966
5 Evers .952

PUTOUTS

1 Sandberg 3,806
2 W. Herman 3,658
3 Pfeffer 3,322
4 Evers 3,072
5 Beckert 2,640
6 Trillo 1,412
7 D.S. Johnson 1,175
8 Baker 1,160
9 E.J. Adams 900
10 Quest 837

ERRORS

1 Pfeffer 636
2 Evers 366
3 W. Herman 285
4 Quest 176
5 Beckert 169
6 Sandberg 109
7 Grantham 99
8 Zimmerman 97
9 D.S. Johnson 94
10 Connor 93

■ 3RD BASE

FIELDING PERCENTAGE
(500 Games Played or more)

1 Deal .964
2 Hack .957
3 Cey .954
4 Santo .954
5 R. Jackson .951

PUTOUTS

1 Hack 1,944
2 Santo 1,930
3 Burns 1,033
4 Steinfeldt 807
5 Williamson 737
6 R. Jackson 719
7 Deal 705
8 Zimmerman 646
9 Casey 460
10 Everitt 441

ERRORS

1 Williamson 334
2 Burns 318
3 Santo 315
4 Hack 246
5 Everitt 161
6 Zimmerman 160
7 McCormick 126
8 Steinfeldt 117
9 R. Jackson 108
10 Casey 92

■ SHORTSTOP

FIELDING PERCENTAGE
(500 Games Played or more)

1 E. Banks .969
2 Dunston .968
3 Kessinger .964
4 DeJesus .963
5 Jurges .963

PUTOUTS

1 Tinker 3,248
2 Kessinger 2,642
3 Dunston 2,114
4 E. Banks 2,087
5 Jurges 1,995
6 Dahlen 1,796
7 Hollocher 1,587
8 English 1,472
9 Smalley 1,195
10 DeJesus 1,151

ERRORS

1 Tinker 574
2 Dahlen 443
3 Burns 355
4 Kessinger 296
5 Williamson 238
6 Hollocher 202
7 Jurges 195
8 Dunston 183
9 Smalley 181
10 E. Banks 174

■ OUTFIELD

FIELDING PERCENTAGE
(500 Games Played or more)

1 Dawson .987
2 Pafko .986
3 Monday .983
4 Morales .982
5 Lowrey .982

PUTOUTS

1 B. Williams 3,562
2 Sosa 3,012
3 Ryan 2,873
4 Nicholson 2,627
5 F. Schulte 2,360
6 Cuyler 2,055
7 L. Wilson 2,016
8 Sheckard 1,937
9 Pafko 1,899
10 Slagle 1,768

ERRORS

1 Ryan 315
2 Dalrymple 221
3 Gore 217
4 Wilmot 160
5 M. Kelly 151
6 Lange 116
7 B. Williams 101
8 F. Schulte 89
9 Sosa 87
10 Slagle 84

ASSISTS

1 Ryan 327
2 M. Kelly 206
3 F. Schulte 181
4 Gore 160
5 B. Williams 143
6 Lange 136
6 Sheckard 136
8 Flack 109
9 Nicholson 107
10 Dalrymple 106

Single Season Club Records:

MOST WINS

Season: 116 (1906)
Home: 58 (1898, 1910)
Road: 60 (1906)

FEWEST WINS

Season: 26 (1877)
Home: 17 (1877, 1878)
Road: 9 (1877)

MOST LOSSES

Season: 103 (1962, 1966)
Home: 49 (1962, 1966, 1974)
Road: 56 (1956)

FEWEST LOSSES

Season: 14 (1876)
Home: 5 (1880)
Road: 8 (1876)
Most total players used: 51 (2000)
Fewest total players used: 11 (1876, 1883)
Most pitchers used: 25 (1999)
Fewest pitchers used: 2 (1879)

SINGLE-SEASON
CLUB BATTING RECORDS

Most at-bats: 5,675 (1988)

Most runs: 1,041 (1894)

Most hits: 1,722 (1930)

Fewest hits: 633 (1877)

Highest batting average: .337 (1876)

Lowest batting average: .235 (1892)

Most singles: 1,226 (1921)

Most doubles: 340 (1931)

Most triples: 101 (1911)

Most home runs: 212 (1998)

Most grand slams: 10 (1929)

Most pinch-hit home runs: 10 (1998)

Most total bases: 2,684 (1930)

Most bases on balls: 650 (1975)

Most hit by pitch: 71 (1898)

Fewest hit by pitch: 13 (1956, 1981)

Most stolen bases: 382 (1887)

Fewest stolen bases: 22 (1947)

Most caught stealing: 149 (1924)

Most strikeouts: 1,223 (1998)

Fewest strikeouts: 45 (1876)

Highest slugging percentage: .481 (1930)

Lowest slugging percentage: .298 (1902)

Most grounded into double plays: 161 (1933)

Fewest grounded into double plays: 78 (1981)

Most .300 hitters: 5 (1887)

Most hitters with 10 or more home runs: 8 (1955, 1959, 2000)

SINGLE-SEASON
CLUB PITCHING RECORDS

Lowest ERA: 1.73 (1907)

Highest ERA: 5.68 (1894)

Most innings pitched: 1,479 (1980)

Most complete games: 147 (1899)

Fewest complete games: 5 (1994)

Most shutouts: 32 (1907, 1909)

Fewest shutouts: 0 (1894)

Most saves: 56 (1993, 1998)

Fewest hits allowed: 577 (1878)

Most hits allowed: 1,642 (1930)

Fewest home runs allowed: 4 (1878)

Most home runs allowed: 231 (2000)

Fewest runs allowed: 257 (1876)

Most runs allowed: 1,066 (1894)

Fewest bases on balls: 29 (1876)

Most bases on balls: 658 (2000)

Fewest strikeouts: 51 (1876)

Most strikeouts: 1,344 (2001)

SINGLE-SEASON
CLUB FIELDING RECORDS

Highest fielding percentage: .984 (1998)

Lowest fielding percentage: .879 (1883)

Fewest errors: 81 (1994)

Most errors: 595 (1884)

Most double plays: 176 (1928)

Fewest double plays: 33 (1876)

Most passed balls: 144 (1886)

Fewest passed balls: 4 (1967)

INDIVIDUAL SINGLE-SEASON
PITCHING RECORDS

Most wins, RHP: 53, John Clarkson (1885)

Most wins, LHP: 23, Hippo Vaughn (1917)

Most shutouts: 10, John Clarkson (1885)

Lowest ERA, RHP: 1.04, Three Finger Brown (1906)

Lowest ERA, LHP: 1.15, Jack Pfiester (1907)

Highest winning pct: .941, Rick Sutcliffe (1984)

Most losses, RHP: 34, Bill Hutchison (1892)

Most losses, LHP: 22, Dick Ellsworth (1966)

Most innings pitched, RHP: 623, John Clarkson (1885)

Most innings pitched, LHP: 307, Jake Weimer (1904)

Most saves, RHP: 51, Rod Beck (1998)

Most saves, LHP: 53, Randy Myers (1993)

Most games, RHP: 84, Ted Abernathy (1965), Dick Tidrow (1980)

Most games, LHP: 82, Jeff Fassero (2001)

Most games started: 70, John Clarkson (1885), Bill Hutchison (1892)

Most complete games: 68, John Clarkson (1885)

Most strikeouts, RHP: 313, John Clarkson (1886)

Most strikeouts, LHP: 202, Ken Holtzman (1970)

Most walks, RHP: 199, Bill Hutchison (1890)

Most walks, LHP: 181, Willie McGill (1893)

Most hits allowed: 605, John Clarkson (1887)

Most runs allowed: 316, Bill Hutchison (1892)

Most earned runs allowed: 191, Bill Hutchison (1892)

Most home runs allowed: 38, Warren Hacker (1955)

Most wild pitches: 41, Mark Baldwin (1887)

INDIVIDUAL SINGLE-SEASON
BATTING RECORDS

Most at-bats: 666, Billy Herman (1935)

Highest batting average: .421, Cap Anson (1887)

Most hits: 229, Rogers Hornsby (1929)

Most runs: 156, Rogers Hornsby (1929)

Most singles: 172, Cap Anson (1887)

Most doubles: 57, Billy Herman (1935), Billy Herman (1936)

Most triples: 21, Wildfire Schulte (1911), Vic Saier (1913)

Most home runs, lefthander: 42, Billy Williams (1970)

Most home runs, righthander: 66, Sammy Sosa (1998)

Most home runs, switch-hitter: 18, Augie Galan (1937)

Most home runs, home: 35, Sammy Sosa (1998)

Most home runs, road: 31, Sammy Sosa (1998)

Most grand slams: 5, Ernie Banks (1955)

Most RBI: 191, Hack Wilson (1930)

Most extra-base hits: 103, Sammy Sosa (2001)

Most total bases: 425, Sammy Sosa (2001)

Most strikeouts: 174, Sammy Sosa (1997)

Most walks: 147, Jimmy Sheckard (1911)

Most sacrifice hits: 46, Jimmy Sheckard (1909)

Most sacrifice flies: 14, Ron Santo (1969)

Most stolen bases: 84, Bill Lange (1896)

Most times caught stealing: 29, Charlie Hollocher (1922)

Most hit by pitch: 23, Bill Dahlen (1898)

Most grounded into double play: 27, Ron Santo (1973)

Fewest grounded into double play: 0, Augie Galan (1935)

CUBS 20-GAME WINNERS

1876 Al Spalding, 47-12

1878 Terry Larkin, 29-26

1879 Terry Larkin, 31-23

1880 Larry Corcoran, 43-14; Fred Goldsmith, 21-3

1881 Larry Corcoran, 31-14; Fred Goldsmith, 24-13

1882 Fred Goldsmith, 28-17; Larry Corcoran, 27-12

1883 Larry Corcoran, 34-20; Fred Goldsmith, 25-19

1884 Larry Corcoran, 35-23
1885 John Clarkson, 53-16;
Jim McCormick, 20-4
1886 John Clarkson, 36-17;
Jim McCormick, 31-11;
Jocko Flynn, 23-6
1887 John Clarkson, 38-21
1888 Gus Krock, 25-14
1890 Bill Hutchison, 42-25; Pat Luby, 20-8
1891 Bill Hutchison, 42-19
1892 Bill Hutchison, 36-34;
Ad Gumbert, 22-20
1894 Clark Griffith, 21-11
1895 Clark Griffith, 25-13;
Adonis Terry, 21-16
1896 Clark Griffith, 23-12
1897 Clark Griffith, 21-19
1898 Clark Griffith, 24-10;
Nixey Callahan, 20-11
1899 Clark Griffith, 22-13;
Nixey Callahan, 21-12
1902 Jack Taylor, 23-11
1903 Jack Taylor, 21-14;
Jake Weimer, 20-8;
Bob Wicker, 20-9
1904 Jake Weimer, 20-14
1906 Three Finger Brown, 26-6;
Jack Pfiester, 20-8
1907 Orval Overall, 23-8;
Three Finger Brown, 20-6
1908 Three Finger Brown, 29-9;
Ed Reulbach, 24-7
1909 Three Finger Brown, 27-9;
Orval Overall, 20-11
1910 Three Finger Brown, 25-13;
King Cole, 20-4
1911 Three Finger Brown, 21-11
1912 Larry Cheney, 26-10
1913 Larry Cheney, 21-14
1914 Hippo Vaughn, 21-13;
Larry Cheney, 20-18
1915 Hippo Vaughn, 20-12
1917 Hippo Vaughn, 23-13
1918 Hippo Vaughn, 22-10;
Claude Hendrix, 20-7
1919 Hippo Vaughn, 21-14
1920 Pete Alexander, 27-14
1923 Pete Alexander, 22-12
1927 Charlie Root, 26-15
1929 Pat Malone, 22-10
1930 Pat Malone, 20-9
1932 Lon Warneke, 22-6
1933 Guy Bush, 20-12

1934 Lon Warneke, 22-10
1935 Bill Lee, 20-6; Lon Warneke, 20-13
1938 Bill Lee, 22-9
1940 Claude Passeau, 20-13
1945 Hank Wyse, 22-10
1963 Dick Ellsworth, 22-10
1964 Larry Jackson, 24-11
1967 Fergie Jenkins, 20-13
1968 Fergie Jenkins, 20-15
1969 Fergie Jenkins, 21-15;
Bill Hands, 20-14
1970 Fergie Jenkins, 22-16
1971 Fergie Jenkins, 24-13
1972 Fergie Jenkins, 20-12
1977 Rick Reuschel, 20-10
1992 Greg Maddux, 20-11
2001 Jon Lieber, 20-6

Cubs Individual Champions

BATTING CHAMPIONS

1876 Ross Barnes, .429
1880 George Gore, .360
1881 Cap Anson, .399
1884 King Kelly, .354
1886 King Kelly, .388
1888 Cap Anson, .344
1912 Heinie Zimmerman, .372
1945 Phil Cavarretta, .355
1972 Billy Williams, .333
1975 Bill Madlock, .354
1976 Bill Madlock, .339
1980 Bill Buckner, .324

HOME RUN CHAMPIONS

1884 Ned Williamson, 27
1885 Abner Dalrymple, 11
1888 Jimmy Ryan, 16
1890 Walt Wilmot, 13
1910 Wildfire Schulte, 10
1911 Wildfire Schulte, 21
1912 Heinie Zimmerman, 14
1916 Cy Williams, 12
1926 Hack Wilson, 21
1927 Hack Wilson, 30
1928 Hack Wilson, 31
1930 Hack Wilson, 56

1943 Bill Nicholson, 29
1944 Bill Nicholson, 33
1952 Hank Sauer, 37
1958 Ernie Banks, 47
1960 Ernie Banks, 41
1979 Dave Kingman, 48
1987 Andre Dawson, 49
1990 Ryne Sandberg, 40
2000 Sammy Sosa, 50

HITTING FOR THE CYCLE
(single, double, triple, home run in one game)

1888 Jimmy Ryan (July 28)
1891 Jimmy Ryan (July 1)
1930 Hack Wilson, vs. Philadelphia
(June 23)
1933 Babe Herman, at St. Louis (Sept 30)
1950 Roy Smalley, vs. St. Louis (June 28)
1957 Lee Walls, vs. Cincinnati (July 2)
1966 Billy Williams, at St. Louis (July 17);
Randy Hundley, vs. Houston (Aug 11)
1980 Ivan DeJesus, vs. St. Louis (Apr 22)
1987 Andre Dawson, vs. San Francisco
(Apr 29)
1993 Mark Grace, vs. San Diego (May 9)

NO-HITTERS

1880 Larry Corcoran, vs. Boston
(Aug 19) 6-0
1882 Larry Corcoran, vs. Worcester
(Sept 20) 5-0
1884 Larry Corcoran, vs. Providence
(June 27) 6-0
1885 John Clarkson, at Providence
(July 27) 4-0
1898 Walter Thornton, vs. Brooklyn
(Aug 21) 2-0
1915 Jimmy Lavender, at New York
(Aug 31) 2-0
1955 Sam Jones, vs. Pittsburgh
(May 12) 4-0
1960 Don Cardwell, vs. St. Louis
(May 15) 4-0
1969 Ken Holtzman, vs. Atlanta
(Aug 19) 3-0
1971 Ken Holtzman, at Cincinnati
(June 3) 1-0
1972 Burt Hooton, vs. Philadelphia
(Apr 16) 4-0; Milt Pappas, vs.
San Diego (Sept 2) 8-0

MVPs (MOST VALUABLE PLAYERS)

1911 Wildfire Schulte
1929 Rogers Hornsby
1935 Gabby Hartnett
1945 Phil Cavarretta
1952 Hank Sauer
1958 Ernie Banks
1959 Ernie Banks
1984 Ryne Sandberg
1987 Andre Dawson
1998 Sammy Sosa

CY YOUNG AWARD WINNERS

1971 Fergie Jenkins
1979 Bruce Sutter
1984 Rick Sutcliffe
1992 Greg Maddux

ROOKIE OF THE YEAR

1961 Billy Williams
1962 Ken Hubbs
1989 Jerome Walton
1998 Kerry Wood

GOLD GLOVE AWARD WINNERS

1960 Ernie Banks, ss
1962 Ken Hubbs, 2b
1964 Bobby Shantz, p; Ron Santo, 3b
1965 Ron Santo, 3b
1966 Ron Santo, 3b
1967 Randy Hundley, c; Ron Santo, 3b
1968 Glenn Beckert, 2b; Ron Santo, 3b
1969 Don Kessinger, ss
1970 Don Kessinger, ss
1983 Ryne Sandberg, 2b
1984 Ryne Sandberg, 2b; Bob Dernier, of
1985 Ryne Sandberg, 2b
1986 Jody Davis, c; Ryne Sandberg, 2b
1987 Ryne Sandberg, 2b; Andre Dawson, of
1988 Ryne Sandberg, 2b; Andre Dawson, of
1989 Ryne Sandberg, 2b
1990 Greg Maddux, p; Ryne Sandberg, 2b
1991 Greg Maddux, p; Ryne Sandberg, 2b
1992 Greg Maddux, p; Mark Grace, 1b
1993 Mark Grace, 1b
1995 Mark Grace, 1b
1996 Mark Grace, 1b

ALL-STARS

1933 Lon Warneke; Woody English; Gabby Hartnett
1934 Billy Herman; Lon Warneke; Chuck Klein; Gabby Hartnett; Kiki Cuyler
1935 Billy Herman; Gabby Hartnett
1936 Augie Galan; Curt Davis; Frank Demaree; Billy Herman; Lon Warneke; Gabby Hartnett
1937 Frank Demaree; Billy Herman; Billy Jurges; Ripper Collins; Gabby Hartnett
1938 Bill Lee; Stan Hack; Billy Herman; Gabby Hartnett
1939 Bill Lee; Stan Hack; Billy Herman
1940 Bill Nicholson; Hank Leiber; Billy Herman; Larry French
1941 Bill Nicholson; Claude Passeau; Hank Leiber; Stan Hack
1942 Claude Passeau
1943 Bill Nicholson; Claude Passeau; Stan Hack
1944 Don Johnson; Bill Nicholson; Phil Cavarretta
1945 Don Johnson; Andy Pafko; Hank Wyse; Bill Nicholson; Claude Passeau; Phil Cavarretta; Stan Hack
1946 Peanuts Lowrey; Johnny Schmitz; Claude Passeau; Phil Cavarretta
1947 Andy Pafko; Phil Cavarretta
1948 Andy Pafko; Johnny Schmitz; Eddie Waitkus; Clyde McCullough
1949 Andy Pafko
1950 Bob Rush; Andy Pafko; Hank Sauer
1951 Bruce Edwards; Dutch Leonard
1952 Toby Atwell; Bob Rush; Hank Sauer
1953 Ralph Kiner; Clyde McCullough
1954 Randy Jackson
1955 Gene Baker; Ernie Banks; Sam Jones; Randy Jackson
1956 Ernie Banks
1957 Ernie Banks
1958 Walt Moryn; Ernie Banks; Lee Walls
1959 Don Elston; Ernie Banks
1960 Ernie Banks
1961 George Altman; Don Zimmer; Ernie Banks
1962 Billy Williams; George Altman; Ernie Banks
1963 Ron Santo; Larry Jackson
1964 Ron Santo; Billy Williams; Dick Ellsworth
1965 Ron Santo; Billy Williams; Ernie Banks

1966 Ron Santo
1967 Fergie Jenkins; Ernie Banks
1968 Don Kessinger; Ron Santo; Billy Williams
1969 Glenn Beckert; Randy Hundley; Don Kessinger; Ron Santo; Ernie Banks
1970 Glenn Beckert; Don Kessinger; Jim Hickman
1971 Fergie Jenkins; Glenn Beckert; Don Kessinger; Ron Santo
1972 Fergie Jenkins; Glenn Beckert; Don Kessinger; Ron Santo; Billy Williams
1973 Ron Santo; Billy Williams
1974 Don Kessinger
1975 Bill Madlock
1976 Steve Swisher
1977 Manny Trillo; Jerry Morales; Rick Reuschel; Bruce Sutter
1978 Bruce Sutter
1979 Dave Kingman; Bruce Sutter
1980 Dave Kingman; Bruce Sutter
1981 Bill Buckner
1982 Leon Durham
1983 Leon Durham; Lee Smith
1984 Jody Davis; Ryne Sandberg
1985 Ryne Sandberg
1986 Jody Davis; Ryne Sandberg
1987 Andre Dawson; Rick Sutcliffe; Lee Smith; Ryne Sandberg
1988 Andre Dawson; Vance Law; Ryne Sandberg; Shawon Dunston; Rafael Palmeiro; Greg Maddux
1989 Andre Dawson; Rick Sutcliffe; Ryne Sandberg; Mitch Williams
1990 Andre Dawson; Ryne Sandberg; Shawon Dunston
1991 Andre Dawson; George Bell; Ryne Sandberg
1992 Ryne Sandberg; Greg Maddux
1993 Ryne Sandberg; Mark Grace
1994 Randy Myers
1995 Randy Myers; Mark Grace; Sammy Sosa
1996 Steve Trachsel
1997 Mark Grace
1998 Sammy Sosa
1999 Sammy Sosa
2000 Joe Girardi; Sammy Sosa
2001 Sammy Sosa; Jon Lieber

PHOTO CREDITS

AP/Wide World Photos: pp. 47, 88, 146, 159, 191, 341, 363, 549, 629

Baseball Hall of Fame Library, Cooperstown, NY: pp. 93, 189, 208, 269, 279

Cycleback Vintage Collecting Services: p. 32

National Baseball League: p. 519

Topps Chewing Gum Co.: p.577

Transcendental Graphics: pp. 11, 12, 17, 22, 28, 38, 39, 41, 43, 48, 55, 61, 78, 83, 95, 110, 113, 118, 121, 122, 123, 137, 138, 141, 145, 148, 150, 161, 165, 166, 167, 173, 180, 195, 198, 204, 213, 217, 221, 222, 227, 231, 239, 243, 246, 249, 252, 259, 295, 298, 305, 315, 321, 338, 339, 343, 345, 350, 356, 368, 370, 400, 403, 405, 406, 415, 421, 440, 446, 453, 456, 462, 478, 487, 493, 497, 503, 513, 515, 521, 524, 539, 542, 551, 575, 579, 585, 597, 599, 604, 607, 620, 631, 633, 643, 647